STATS
Minor League Handbook
2002

STATS, Inc.
and
Howe Sportsdata

STATS INC. ™
PUBLISHING

HOWE SPORTSDATA
A SERVICE OF SPORTSTICKER

Published by STATS Publishing
A division of Sports Team Analysis & Tracking Systems, Inc.

Cover by Ryan Balock

Front Cover photo by Ken Babbitt
Back Cover photo by Larry Goren

First Edition: November, 2001

Printed in the United States of America

ISBN 1-884064-92-2

Acknowledgments

The process of putting together the 11th edition of the *STATS Minor League Handbook* requires a heavy dose of teamwork, and we'd like to thank those people who contribute to this effort.

The STATS team is successfully anchored by President Alan Leib. Senior Vice President Steve Byrd steers our consumer and TV divisions, while Vice President Robert Schur directs our commercial divisions.

Tony Nistler manages the publications unit that produces this book and all of our other sports titles. Tony oversaw editorial responsibilities, with help from Thom Henninger, Taylor Bechtold and Norm DeNosaquo. Getting the numbers programmed appropriately fell into the hands of Tim Coletta, with help from Jim Henzler. Marc Carl manipulated the many columns and tables that are key to the book's design. Getting the word out about and fulfulling orders for the *STATS Minor League Handbook* and other STATS publications require the hard work of Ryan Balock and Andy Degnan. Ryan designed this book's cover.

We couldn't publish this book without our Data Collection Department. Managing the collection of the numbers you'll find on these pages and in many of our other publications is Allan Spear. Special thanks go to Jeff Chernow, who oversees the accuracy of our major league baseball data.

Keeping STATS at the forefront of the sports information business on a daily basis are Jim Capuano, our Senior Vice President of Sales; Jeff Smith, who manages our technical operations; and Howard Lanin, who oversees our financial and administration areas.

Our Research Department for Fox Sports in Los Angeles is headed by Don Zminda, with help from Director of Operations Steve Vanderpool. Their team of sports researchers and technical staff provides many of the stats that are broadcast daily from the Fox Sports studios, as well as from remote pre- and postgame and live game telecasts on Fox and Fox Sports Net.

This book is dedicated to all Chicago baseball fans. A combined 177 years of losing does not damper the spirit and loyalty we have for our teams and the ferociousness of the intra-city rivalry. With top prospects on both sides, a Windy City Classic is right around the corner, and hopefully for us White Sox fans, it will bear the same result as the last one did in 1906.

—Marc Carl

Table of Contents

Introduction

It's been 44 years since the lights went out in Ebbets Field and the Brooklyn Dodgers moved to Los Angeles. When the Dodgers shut out the Pirates before 6,702 fans on September 24, 1957, the days of Duke Snider, Gil Hodges, Jackie Robinson, Pee Wee Reese and Don Newcombe playing before the Brooklyn faithful came to an end. Da Bums were no more.

Last spring, more than four decades after baseball left Brooklyn, the pro game returned with the arrival of the Class-A Brooklyn Cyclones. The 21st-century version of Brooklyn baseball, affiliated with the Mets in the short-season New York-Penn League, made its home debut on June 25 before a sellout crowd of more than 7,500 fans at KeySpan Park. The beautiful, new stadium resides in Coney Island, the amusement park at the southern tip of the borough where land meets the Atlantic Ocean. It stands beneath the shadow of the Parachute Jump, a now-dormant but landmark ride that majestically towers over everything down the right-field line. The team is named for the Cyclone, the roller coaster that has thrilled generations of young New Yorkers and still operates just beyond the left-field wall.

The Opening Night sellout was the first of 35 during the Cyclones' 37-game home schedule. By year's end, the Cyclones set a new high for attendance in the New York-Penn League with 289,381 fans passing through the turnstiles, and they were named the league's co-champions after the events of September 11 cut short their championship series with the Williamsport Crosscutters.

Just as pro ball is back in Brooklyn, STATS, Inc. is back with the newest edition of the *STATS Minor League Handbook*. This 2002 version is our 11th go-round. We begin our second decade of publishing the complete statistical recap of the just-completed minor league season. In addition to league and team stats for the 2001 campaign, you'll find the complete career numbers for every player who appeared in a Double-A and Triple-A game last season. The exceptions are players who reached the major leagues in 2001. Those players appear in our companion book, the *STATS Major League Handbook 2002*. For players in Class-A and Rookie leagues, we supply complete 2001 statistical lines in the section that follows the career register of Double-A and Triple-A players.

The *Handbook*, of course, is much more than just a prospect's yearly stats. It also includes page after page of hard-to-find numbers, such as the lefty-righty and home-road breakdowns for Double-A and Triple-A hitters and pitchers. The lefty-righty splits provide some insight into whether minor league hitters have a chance to succeed as major league regulars. The home-road numbers offer a more complete picture of both hitters and pitchers who worked in extremely hitting-friendly and pitching-friendly minor league parks.

This 11th edition also features Major League Equivalencies for the best Double-A and Triple-A hitters in each organization. The MLEs translate a hitter's minor league numbers into what they would have looked like in the majors. Adjustments are made for home park (major and minor league parks), league and level of competition.

Something else you'll find here and nowhere else is roughly 25 pages of minor league leader boards, covering both the usual and the unusual stat. If you're a fan of those co-champion Cyclones, you can bet you'll find Brooklyn represented in *this* section of the 2002 *Handbook*. If it's pertinent to the 2001 minor league season, it's in the book.

—Thom Henninger

Career Register

Any player who appeared in Double-A or Triple-A in 2001 gets a profile in this section, *unless* he also played in the major leagues, in which case his statistics are in our companion book, the *STATS Major League Handbook*. The exception to this rule is our player on the book cover, Josh Beckett, the young phenom who pitched with the Florida Marlins. You'll find his career record in this book, as well. Two additional players appear in the register despite not playing during the 2001 season, Ryan Anderson from the Seattle Mariners' system and Paul Phillips from the Kansas City Royals' system. Both players were out with injuries, but they have been added to the register because we anticipate a solid return in 2002.

The profiles have complete major and minor league records for all qualifying players. Most of the statistical abbreviations are common and will be used throughout the book. Here's a quick review:

For all players, **Pos** = games played by position in 2001; **Ht** = Height; **Wt** = Weight; **Age** = age as of June 30, 2002.

For hitters, **G** = games; **AB** = at-bats; **H** = hits; **2B** = doubles; **3B** = triples; **HR** = home runs; **TB** = total bases; **R** = runs; **RBI** = runs batted in; **TBB** = total bases on balls; **IBB** = intentional bases on balls; **SO** = strikeouts; **HBP** = times hit by pitches; **SH** = sacrifice hits; **SF** = sacrifice flies; **SB** = stolen bases; **CS** = times caught stealing; **SB%** = stolen base percentage; **GDP** = times grounded into double plays; **Avg** = batting average; **OBP** = on-base percentage; **SLG** = slugging percentage.

For pitchers, **G** = games pitched; **GS** = games started; **CG** = complete games; **GF** = games finished; **IP** = innings pitched; **BFP** = batters facing pitcher; **H** = hits allowed; **R** = runs allowed; **ER** = earned runs allowed; **HR** = home runs allowed; **SH** = sacrifice hits allowed; **SF** = sacrifice flies allowed; **HB** = hits batsmen; **TBB** = total bases on balls; **IBB** = intentional bases on balls; **SO** = strikeouts; **WP** = wild pitches; **Bk** = balks; **W** = wins; **L** = losses; **Pct.** = winning percentage; **ShO** = shutouts; **Sv** = saves; **ERA** = earned run average.

Class-A (A+, A, A-) and Rookie (R+, R) have separate classifications to distinguish the level of competition.

Chuck Abbott

Bats: Right **Throws:** Right **Pos:** 2B-15; SS-3; PH-3; 3B-2; 1B-1; PR-1   **Ht:** 6'1" **Wt:** 180 **Born:** 1/26/75 **Age:** 27

Year Team	Lg Org	G	AB	H	2B	3B	HR	TB	R	RBI	TBB	IBB	SO	HBP	SH	SF	SB	CS	SB%	GDP	Avg	OBP	SLG
1996 Boise	A- Ana	70	268	53	9	2	0	66	41	20	24	0	59	5	4	4	11	5	.69	8	.198	.272	.246
1997 Cedar Rapds	A Ana	133	520	120	21	5	7	172	86	54	62	0	170	3	6	2	31	12	.72	7	.231	.315	.331
1998 Midland	AA Ana	132	525	138	21	9	2	183	74	62	38	0	135	4	8	4	16	9	.64	18	.263	.315	.349
1999 Erie	AA Ana	125	444	106	13	1	6	139	70	46	47	1	138	2	6	2	9	10	.47	10	.239	.313	.313
2000 Edmonton	AAA Ana	5	15	3	1	0	0	4	0	4	0	0	5	0	0	0	0	0	—	0	.200	.200	.267
Erie	AA Ana	97	330	82	14	3	5	117	39	39	22	0	96	4	7	2	3	3	.50	11	.248	.302	.355
2001 Salt Lake	AAA Ana	4	9	0	0	0	0	0	1	0	2	0	4	0	0	0	0	0	—	0	.000	.182	.000
Akron	AA Cle	17	41	8	1	1	3	20	6	8	2	0	17	0	1	0	1	1	.50	0	.195	.233	.488
6 Min. YEARS		583	2152	510	80	21	23	701	317	233	197	1	624	18	32	14	71	40	.64	54	.237	.304	.326

Dennis Abreu

Bats: Right **Throws:** Right **Pos:** 2B-49; SS-38; PH-11; 3B-9; PR-4; OF-2; DH-2; 1B-1   **Ht:** 6'0" **Wt:** 180 **Born:** 4/22/78 **Age:** 24

Year Team	Lg Org	G	AB	H	2B	3B	HR	TB	R	RBI	TBB	IBB	SO	HBP	SH	SF	SB	CS	SB%	GDP	Avg	OBP	SLG
1996 Cubs	R ChC	56	192	60	5	0	0	65	32	15	21	0	20	2	7	1	35	9	.80	6	.313	.384	.339
1997 Rockford	A ChC	126	483	155	19	3	1	183	71	37	45	2	99	7	5	1	36	26	.58	8	.321	.386	.379
1998 Daytona	A+ ChC	127	535	139	21	5	2	176	87	58	31	0	133	3	8	0	23	14	.62	14	.260	.304	.329
1999 Daytona	A+ ChC	105	374	96	10	2	2	116	44	30	13	0	69	3	2	1	29	9	.76	10	.257	.286	.310
2000 Daytona	A+ ChC	39	118	38	4	0	2	48	18	10	4	1	24	3	2	0	8	5	.62	4	.322	.360	.407
West Tenn	AA ChC	52	166	40	8	1	2	56	24	13	9	0	36	3	3	0	7	5	.58	4	.241	.292	.337
2001 West Tenn	AA ChC	102	331	84	7	1	4	105	35	30	19	2	74	3	4	1	14	4	.78	5	.254	.299	.317
Iowa	AAA ChC	4	12	6	1	0	0	7	3	1	0	0	2	0	0	0	0	0	—	0	.500	.500	.583
6 Min. YEARS		611	2211	618	75	12	13	756	314	194	142	5	457	24	31	4	152	72	.68	51	.280	.329	.342

Winston Abreu

Pitches: Right **Bats:** Right **Pos:** RP-27; SP-7   **Ht:** 6'2" **Wt:** 155 **Born:** 4/5/77 **Age:** 25

Year Team	Lg Org	G	GS	CG	GF	IP	BFP	H	R	ER	HR	SH	SF	HB	TBB	IBB	SO	WP	Bk	W	L	Pct.	ShO	Sv	ERA
1994 Braves	R Atl	13	11	0	1	57.1	257	57	35	26	2	0	5	4	24	0	53	3	4	0	8	.000	0	0	4.08
1995 Danville	R+ Atl	13	13	1	0	74	277	54	29	19	5	0	4	1	13	0	90	2	0	6	3	.667	0	0	2.31
1996 Macon	A Atl	12	12	0	0	60	247	51	29	20	4	1	0	1	25	1	60	3	1	4	3	.571	0	0	3.00
1998 Eugene	A- Atl	17	10	0	3	45.1	206	39	36	32	6	0	2	5	31	0	52	6	0	0	4	.000	0	0	6.35
1999 Macon	A Atl	14	14	0	0	69.1	272	41	17	13	3	0	2	4	26	0	95	7	1	7	2	.778	0	0	1.69
Myrtle Bch	A+ Atl	13	12	0	0	68.2	290	53	26	25	7	2	4	0	41	0	76	3	1	3	2	.600	0	0	3.28
2000 Greenville	AA Atl	1	1	0	0	4	17	4	1	1	0	0	0	0	3	0	5	0	0	0	1	.000	0	0	2.25
Braves	R Atl	2	2	0	0	3	14	2	1	1	1	0	0	1	2	0	2	0	0	0	0	—	0	0	3.00
Macon	A Atl	11	1	0	8	28.2	103	11	6	6	2	0	0	0	6	0	48	1	0	2	1	.667	0	3	1.88
Richmond	AAA Atl	3	0	0	0	9	42	7	8	7	2	1	1	1	10	0	5	0	0	0	1	.000	0	0	7.00
2001 Greenville	AA Atl	34	7	0	4	73.2	319	56	40	38	9	5	2	5	45	2	93	2	1	3	5	.375	0	0	4.64
7 Min. YEARS		133	83	1	16	493	2044	375	228	188	41	9	20	22	226	3	579	27	8	25	30	.455	0	3	3.43

Jon Acevas

Bats: Right **Throws:** Right **Pos:** C-60; 1B-13; PH-7; DH-4; PR-1   **Ht:** 6'2" **Wt:** 187 **Born:** 3/7/78 **Age:** 24

Year Team	Lg Org	G	AB	H	2B	3B	HR	TB	R	RBI	TBB	IBB	SO	HBP	SH	SF	SB	CS	SB%	GDP	Avg	OBP	SLG
1997 White Sox	R CWS	30	76	14	4	0	0	18	9	4	9	0	18	2	0	0	0	0	—	5	.184	.287	.237
1998 Bristol	R+ CWS	43	135	40	12	3	4	70	29	30	29	0	38	2	3	1	1	3	.25	2	.296	.425	.519
1999 Burlington	A CWS	65	202	38	9	2	4	63	28	23	35	3	52	8	5	1	3	2	.60	9	.188	.329	.312
2000 Winston-Sal	A+ CWS	76	259	55	17	2	3	85	41	17	20	2	65	5	1	2	3	1	.75	9	.212	.280	.328
2001 Birmingham	AA CWS	12	36	8	1	0	2	15	5	6	2	0	13	1	1	0	0	0	—	0	.222	.275	.417
Winston-Sal	A+ CWS	70	220	47	8	2	6	77	33	27	24	1	65	5	4	3	2	0	1.00	6	.214	.302	.350
5 Min. YEARS		296	928	202	51	9	19	328	145	107	119	6	251	23	14	8	9	6	.60	31	.218	.319	.353

Matt Achilles

Pitches: Right **Bats:** Right **Pos:** SP-24; RP-1   **Ht:** 6'3" **Wt:** 180 **Born:** 8/18/76 **Age:** 25

Year Team	Lg Org	G	GS	CG	GF	IP	BFP	H	R	ER	HR	SH	SF	HB	TBB	IBB	SO	WP	Bk	W	L	Pct.	ShO	Sv	ERA
1996 Orioles	R Bal	5	5	0	0	20	84	16	6	5	2	1	2	2	10	0	12	2	0	0	1	.000	0	0	2.25
Bluefield	R+ Bal	13	0	0	6	23.2	113	20	16	10	0	1	0	2	19	1	22	1	0	3	2	.600	0	0	3.80
1997 Delmarva	A Bal	3	0	0	1	5.2	36	11	9	6	0	0	0	2	3	0	2	0	0	0	1	—	0	1	9.53
Bluefield	R+ Bal	14	13	0	0	73	301	60	37	32	9	1	2	2	33	0	68	7	2	7	2	.778	0	0	3.95
1998 Delmarva	A Bal	26	25	2	0	150	654	143	71	63	14	4	2	2	70	0	125	6	2	8	7	.533	1	0	3.78
1999 Frederick	A+ Bal	16	15	1	1	94	413	103	57	45	6	2	6	5	32	2	77	5	0	5	8	.385	0	0	4.31
2000 Frederick	A+ Bal	26	26	0	0	150	667	166	75	57	13	2	5	12	65	0	137	7	0	8	11	.421	0	0	3.42
2001 Daytona	A+ ChC	16	15	1	0	93.2	381	84	37	27	1	4	4	5	22	1	60	1	0	4	8	.333	1	0	2.59
West Tenn	AA ChC	9	9	0	0	52.2	223	56	26	24	2	3	0	2	22	1	39	2	1	3	4	.429	0	0	4.10
6 Min. YEARS		128	108	4	8	662.2	2872	659	334	269	47	18	22	34	276	5	542	31	5	38	43	.469	2	1	3.65

Jon Adkins

Pitches: Right **Bats:** Left **Pos:** SP-26; RP-1   **Ht:** 6'0" **Wt:** 200 **Born:** 8/30/77 **Age:** 24

Year Team	Lg Org	G	GS	CG	GF	IP	BFP	H	R	ER	HR	SH	SF	HB	TBB	IBB	SO	WP	Bk	W	L	Pct.	ShO	Sv	ERA
1999 Modesto	A+ Oak	26	16	0	2	102	460	113	66	54	6	4	6	9	30	1	93	8	0	9	5	.643	0	1	4.76
2000 Athletics	R Oak	4	2	0	1	15	68	15	6	5	1	0	0	1	3	0	17	0	0	1	1	.500	0	0	3.00
Sacramento	AAA Oak	1	1	0	0	4	19	6	4	4	2	0	0	0	1	0	2	0	0	0	1	.000	0	0	9.00
Modesto	A+ Oak	9	7	1	0	49.2	203	41	17	10	1	1	2	1	17	0	38	2	0	5	2	.714	0	0	1.81

3

Year Team	Lg Org	G	GS	CG	GF	IP	BFP	H	R	ER	HR	SH	SF	HB	TBB	IBB	SO	WP	Bk	W	L	Pct.	ShO	Sv	ERA
		HOW MUCH HE PITCHED						WHAT HE GAVE UP												THE RESULTS					
2001 Midland	AA Oak	24	24	1	0	137.1	590	147	71	68	9	5	2	9	36	1	74	0	0	8	8	.500	1	0	4.46
Sacramento	AAA Oak	3	2	0	0	12.2	60	17	9	6	1	1	0	0	8	0	7	0	0	1	0	1.000	0	0	4.26
3 Min. YEARS		67	51	2	3	320.2	1400	339	172	147	20	11	10	20	95	2	231	10	0	24	17	.585	1	1	4.13

Tim Adkins

Pitches: Left **Bats:** Left **Pos:** RP-36; SP-5 **Ht:** 6'0" **Wt:** 205 **Born:** 5/12/74 **Age:** 28

Year Team	Lg Org	G	GS	CG	GF	IP	BFP	H	R	ER	HR	SH	SF	HB	TBB	IBB	SO	WP	Bk	W	L	Pct.	ShO	Sv	ERA
		HOW MUCH HE PITCHED						WHAT HE GAVE UP												THE RESULTS					
1992 Blue Jays	R Tor	11	10	0	1	57.2	230	50	15	11	2	1	1	1	11	0	49	3	1	6	2	.750	0	0	1.72
1993 St.Cathrnes	A- Tor	16	15	1	0	96.2	404	80	43	38	5	2	3	2	45	0	91	5	1	5	6	.455	1	0	3.54
1994 Hagerstown	A Tor	35	0	0	7	70.2	299	64	37	29	2	6	4	2	33	1	75	4	0	3	3	.500	0	2	3.69
1995 Dunedin	A+ Tor	45	0	0	37	48	215	36	29	20	2	3	2	1	33	0	49	7	0	7	4	.636	0	17	3.75
1996 Dunedin	A+ Tor	39	11	0	14	103.1	475	88	68	45	4	3	1	8	73	1	91	2	2	7	9	.438	0	2	3.92
1997 Dunedin	A+ Tor	39	0	0	10	49.2	252	52	43	26	1	2	3	3	58	0	55	9	2	1	1	.500	0	3	4.71
1998 Dunedin	A+ Tor	19	0	0	10	24.1	114	32	18	16	2	0	1	3	10	0	18	3	0	0	1	.000	0	1	5.92
1999 Bridgeport	IND —	26	21	1	1	140.2	614	152	74	62	17	7	2	6	49	0	100	3	0	8	6	.571	1	0	3.97
2000 Bridgeport	IND —	19	19	3	0	133.2	543	127	55	51	10	5	1	4	25	0	74	3	2	10	5	.667	0	0	3.43
Norwich	AA NYY	9	0	0	1	7	33	9	3	3	0	1	0	0	3	0	8	0	0	1	0	1.000	0	0	3.86
2001 Columbus	AAA NYY	1	0	0	1	0.1	3	2	0	0	0	0	0	0	0	0	1	0	0	0	0	—	0	0	0.00
Norwich	AA NYY	40	5	0	13	80	344	70	36	30	7	1	2	5	30	1	83	4	0	3	1	.750	0	0	3.38
10 Min. YEARS		299	81	5	95	812	3526	762	421	331	52	31	20	35	370	3	694	43	8	51	38	.573	2	25	3.67

Jeremy Affeldt

Pitches: Left **Bats:** Left **Pos:** SP-25 **Ht:** 6'4" **Wt:** 185 **Born:** 6/6/79 **Age:** 23

Year Team	Lg Org	G	GS	CG	GF	IP	BFP	H	R	ER	HR	SH	SF	HB	TBB	IBB	SO	WP	Bk	W	L	Pct.	ShO	Sv	ERA
		HOW MUCH HE PITCHED						WHAT HE GAVE UP												THE RESULTS					
1997 Royals	R KC	10	9	0	0	40	171	34	24	20	3	2	3	5	21	0	36	4	2	2	0	1.000	0	0	4.50
1998 Royals	R KC	12	9	0	0	56	241	50	24	18	1	3	0	8	24	0	67	7	0	4	3	.571	0	0	2.89
Lansing	A KC	6	3	0	0	17	90	27	21	18	1	0	1	0	12	0	12	8	2	0	3	.000	0	0	9.53
1999 Chston-WV	A KC	27	24	2	1	143.1	637	140	78	61	4	9	4	8	80	0	111	14	4	7	7	.500	1	0	3.83
2000 Wilmington	A+ KC	27	26	0	0	147.1	656	158	87	67	7	8	5	10	59	0	92	17	1	5	15	.250	0	0	4.09
2001 Wichita	AA KC	25	25	0	0	145.1	621	153	74	63	9	6	5	10	46	0	128	3	1	10	6	.625	0	0	3.90
5 Min. YEARS		107	96	2	1	549	2416	562	308	247	25	28	18	41	242	0	442	47	8	28	34	.452	1	0	4.05

Brandon Agamennone

Pitches: Right **Bats:** Right **Pos:** RP-53 **Ht:** 6'2" **Wt:** 190 **Born:** 11/6/75 **Age:** 26

Year Team	Lg Org	G	GS	CG	GF	IP	BFP	H	R	ER	HR	SH	SF	HB	TBB	IBB	SO	WP	Bk	W	L	Pct.	ShO	Sv	ERA
		HOW MUCH HE PITCHED						WHAT HE GAVE UP												THE RESULTS					
1998 Vermont	A- Mon	9	3	0	0	31.2	124	19	6	5	1	0	1	1	11	0	30	0	0	3	1	.750	0	0	1.42
Cape Fear	A Mon	6	6	1	0	35.1	134	24	15	12	2	0	1	2	6	0	29	0	0	2	0	1.000	1	0	3.06
1999 Jupiter	A+ Mon	16	9	0	0	65.2	268	51	31	23	4	2	4	3	15	0	41	1	2	4	2	.667	0	0	3.15
Harrisburg	AA Mon	22	4	0	11	52.1	210	44	19	18	5	3	0	2	14	0	41	2	0	5	2	.714	0	5	3.10
2000 Harrisburg	AA Mon	30	15	0	8	96	411	102	58	44	10	4	8	3	26	2	55	6	0	8	7	.533	0	4	4.13
2001 Ottawa	AAA Mon	8	0	0	2	11.1	46	6	5	3	0	1	0	1	3	0	7	0	0	1	0	1.000	0	0	2.38
Harrisburg	AA Mon	45	0	0	16	61	262	59	31	28	10	2	3	3	23	2	51	2	0	4	0	1.000	0	3	4.13
4 Min. YEARS		136	37	1	37	353.1	1455	305	165	133	32	12	17	15	98	4	254	11	2	27	12	.692	1	12	3.39

Steve Agosto

Pitches: Left **Bats:** Left **Pos:** SP-18; RP-15 **Ht:** 5'11" **Wt:** 170 **Born:** 9/2/76 **Age:** 25

Year Team	Lg Org	G	GS	CG	GF	IP	BFP	H	R	ER	HR	SH	SF	HB	TBB	IBB	SO	WP	Bk	W	L	Pct.	ShO	Sv	ERA
		HOW MUCH HE PITCHED						WHAT HE GAVE UP												THE RESULTS					
1994 Angels	R Ana	13	1	0	7	26.1	125	27	18	13	1	3	1	3	14	0	26	6	1	0	2	.000	0	1	4.44
1995 Angels	R Ana	1	1	0	0	5	22	3	5	3	0	2	1	1	2	0	2	3	0	0	1	.000	0	0	5.40
Boise	A- Ana	13	11	0	1	52.1	224	39	20	17	1	0	3	5	30	2	34	12	0	6	2	.750	0	0	2.92
1996 Cedar Rapds	A Ana	28	28	1	0	156.2	680	143	91	77	12	7	6	7	86	2	121	8	7	8	10	.444	0	0	4.42
1997 Lk Elsinore	A+ Ana	24	21	1	0	137	603	155	91	81	23	2	2	3	50	0	91	11	3	5	8	.385	1	0	5.32
Rancho Cuca	A+ SD	3	3	1	0	22	89	18	7	7	2	3	0	0	6	0	18	1	0	2	0	1.000	1	0	2.86
1998 Rancho Cuca	A+ SD	23	23	0	0	108	505	132	83	73	14	4	6	3	68	0	91	15	4	5	8	.385	0	0	6.08
1999 Mobile	AA SD	40	1	0	5	81	371	81	61	53	13	2	7	1	59	1	59	10	1	3	3	.500	0	0	5.89
2000 St. Pete	A+ TB	13	0	0	1	16.2	90	22	17	10	0	0	2	1	16	0	18	2	0	0	1	.000	0	0	5.40
Orlando	AA TB	28	3	0	5	51	210	37	18	14	4	1	1	2	24	1	38	2	0	2	2	.500	0	1	2.47
Durham	AAA TB	1	0	0	0	4	12	0	0	0	0	0	0	0	1	0	3	0	0	0	0	—	0	0	0.00
2001 Durham	AAA TB	3	0	0	0	5.1	27	5	6	6	2	0	0	0	5	0	5	1	0	0	0	—	0	0	10.13
Orlando	AA TB	30	18	2	4	129.1	545	114	62	56	12	10	5	3	57	1	113	4	4	8	10	.444	2	0	3.90
8 Min. YEARS		220	110	5	23	794.2	3503	776	479	410	84	34	34	29	418	7	619	75	20	39	47	.453	4	2	4.64

Chris Aguila

Bats: Right **Throws:** Right **Pos:** OF-137 **Ht:** 5'11" **Wt:** 180 **Born:** 2/23/79 **Age:** 23

Year Team	Lg Org	G	AB	H	2B	3B	HR	TB	R	RBI	TBB	IBB	SO	HBP	SH	SF	SB	CS	SB%	GDP	Avg	OBP	SLG
		BATTING															BASERUNNING				PERCENTAGES		
1997 Marlins	R Fla	46	157	34	7	0	1	44	12	17	21	0	49	1	2	2	2	1	.67	3	.217	.309	.280
1998 Marlins	R Fla	51	171	46	12	3	4	76	29	29	19	1	49	2	1	0	6	2	.75	4	.269	.349	.444
1999 Kane County	A Fla	122	430	105	21	7	15	185	74	78	40	2	127	9	3	2	14	4	.78	9	.244	.320	.430
2000 Brevard Cty	A+ Fla	136	518	125	27	3	9	185	68	56	37	1	105	1	3	3	8	8	.50	11	.241	.292	.357
2001 Brevard Cty	A+ Fla	73	272	75	15	3	10	126	44	34	21	1	54	2	0	4	8	4	.67	7	.276	.328	.463
Portland	AA Fla	64	241	62	16	1	4	92	25	29	18	1	50	3	3	4	5	7	.42	4	.257	.312	.382
5 Min. YEARS		492	1789	447	98	17	43	708	252	243	156	6	434	18	12	15	43	26	.62	38	.250	.314	.396

Pat Ahearne

Pitches: Right **Bats:** Right **Pos:** SP-26; RP-2 **Ht:** 6'3" **Wt:** 195 **Born:** 12/10/69 **Age:** 32

Year Team	Lg Org	G	GS	CG	GF	IP	BFP	H	R	ER	HR	SH	SF	HB	TBB	IBB	SO	WP	Bk	W	L	Pct.	ShO	Sv	ERA
1992 Lakeland	A+ Det	1	1	0	0	4.2	17	4	2	1	0	0	0	0	0	0	4	0	0	0	0	—	0	0	1.93
1993 Lakeland	A+ Det	25	24	2	0	147.1	650	160	87	73	8	7	4	6	48	0	51	3	1	6	15	.286	0	0	4.46
1994 Trenton	AA Det	30	13	2	3	108.2	467	126	55	48	8	1	6	5	25	1	57	5	0	7	5	.583	0	0	3.98
1995 Toledo	AAA Det	25	23	1	0	139.2	599	165	83	73	11	2	5	5	37	3	54	2	0	7	9	.438	1	0	4.70
1996 Norfolk	AAA NYM	5	4	0	0	25.1	108	26	14	13	1	3	0	1	9	1	14	0	1	1	2	.333	0	0	4.62
Duluth-Sup	IND —	1	1	0	0	4.1	24	10	6	6	3	0	0	0	1	0	1	1	0	0	0	—	0	0	12.46
San Antonio	AA LA	8	8	0	0	45.1	208	59	34	29	3	2	2	1	18	0	21	4	0	2	4	.333	0	0	5.76
Vero Beach	A+ LA	6	6	1	0	47	179	38	16	11	1	2	1	1	5	0	26	2	0	3	2	.600	1	0	2.11
1997 Albuquerque	AAA LA	20	8	0	3	60.2	280	82	43	33	9	4	2	1	20	1	44	2	0	2	4	.333	0	0	4.90
San Antonio	AA LA	14	14	3	0	84	364	109	48	42	1	6	2	2	13	0	45	4	0	4	5	.444	0	0	4.50
1998 Bridgeport	IND —	5	5	0	0	28	123	29	12	8	3	1	1	1	5	0	16	1	0	2	2	.500	0	0	2.57
1999 Bridgeport	IND —	7	7	1	0	46.1	188	35	17	13	4	1	1	0	14	0	43	4	0	6	0	1.000	1	0	2.53
New Haven	AA Sea	17	17	4	0	124	493	114	41	36	6	3	1	3	27	0	80	2	0	8	3	.727	2	0	2.61
2000 Tacoma	AAA Sea	29	26	1	0	168	725	190	92	72	11	5	2	1	53	5	92	5	1	13	8	.619	0	0	3.86
2001 Calgary	AAA Fla	28	26	0	0	144.2	659	212	112	101	14	6	2	3	35	0	80	8	0	6	10	.375	0	0	6.28
1995 Detroit	AL	4	3	0	0	10	55	20	13	13	2	0	0	0	5	1	4	1	0	0	2	.000	0	0	11.70
10 Min. YEARS		221	183	15	6	1178	5084	1359	662	559	83	43	29	30	310	11	628	43	3	67	69	.493	5	0	4.27

Alex Ahumada

Bats: Right **Throws:** Right **Pos:** SS-54; 3B-53; PR-6; 2B-2; 1B-1; PH-1 **Ht:** 6'1" **Wt:** 171 **Born:** 1/20/79 **Age:** 23

Year Team	Lg Org	G	AB	H	2B	3B	HR	TB	R	RBI	TBB	IBB	SO	HBP	SH	SF	SB	CS	SB%	GDP	Avg	OBP	SLG
1996 Red Sox	R Bos	37	122	34	6	0	0	40	14	15	3	0	32	3	1	0	1	5	.17	0	.279	.313	.328
1997 Michigan	A Bos	3	12	3	1	1	0	6	1	1	0	0	3	0	0	0	0	0	—	0	.250	.250	.500
Lowell	A- Bos	57	203	45	4	1	1	54	25	13	15	0	49	4	1	2	5	1	.83	5	.222	.286	.266
1998 Michigan	A Bos	111	390	108	22	2	0	134	45	35	25	0	91	8	3	4	4	7	.36	9	.277	.330	.344
1999 Augusta	A Bos	125	455	118	24	4	10	180	72	57	41	0	107	16	5	4	9	7	.56	16	.259	.339	.396
2000 Sarasota	A+ Bos	125	457	121	18	3	6	163	55	47	16	0	80	8	1	3	9	7	.56	8	.265	.300	.357
2001 Sarasota	A+ Bos	112	379	92	23	0	6	133	48	42	34	2	73	11	6	4	22	9	.71	7	.243	.320	.351
Trenton	AA Bos	4	15	4	0	0	0	4	3	1	0	0	4	1	0	0	0	0	—	0	.267	.313	.267
6 Min. YEARS		574	2033	525	98	11	23	714	263	211	134	2	439	51	17	17	50	36	.58	45	.258	.318	.351

Paul Ah Yat

Pitches: Left **Bats:** Right **Pos:** SP-8; RP-5 **Ht:** 6'1" **Wt:** 192 **Born:** 10/13/74 **Age:** 27

Year Team	Lg Org	G	GS	CG	GF	IP	BFP	H	R	ER	HR	SH	SF	HB	TBB	IBB	SO	WP	Bk	W	L	Pct.	ShO	Sv	ERA
1996 Erie	A- Pit	26	0	0	4	27.2	114	24	15	10	1	1	0	0	6	0	34	0	0	1	1	.500	0	1	3.25
1997 Augusta	A Pit	29	9	0	5	90	366	82	34	29	7	3	0	3	16	1	119	4	0	5	1	.833	0	0	2.90
Lynchburg	A+ Pit	6	6	3	0	48	182	37	8	7	2	2	0	1	4	0	38	1	0	5	1	.833	1	0	1.31
1998 Lynchburg	A+ Pit	14	14	4	0	102.1	410	95	40	31	9	1	3	4	13	2	77	2	0	6	3	.667	3	0	2.73
Carolina	AA Pit	13	13	1	0	84.1	362	84	43	34	10	1	3	4	21	0	60	6	0	5	5	.500	0	0	3.63
1999 Altoona	AA Pit	16	15	0	0	95.1	398	86	41	32	6	4	4	3	30	0	90	4	1	8	4	.667	0	0	3.02
Nashville	AAA Pit	13	11	1	1	64.2	291	75	45	41	10	3	2	4	24	1	41	1	1	4	3	.571	0	0	5.71
2000 Nashville	AAA Pit	19	18	0	1	110.2	468	110	55	50	14	1	5	3	36	0	60	6	0	3	9	.250	0	0	4.07
2001 Nashville	AAA Pit	8	4	0	2	20.1	104	37	22	21	0	2	2	0	9	1	15	0	0	1	4	.200	0	0	9.30
San Jose	A+ SF	5	4	0	0	18	79	14	13	9	4	1	1	0	7	0	17	4	1	2	1	.667	0	0	4.50
6 Min. YEARS		149	94	9	13	661.1	2774	644	316	264	63	19	20	20	166	5	551	28	3	40	32	.556	4	1	3.59

Kurt Airoso

Bats: Right **Throws:** Right **Pos:** OF-87; DH-4; PH-4; PR-3 **Ht:** 6'2" **Wt:** 190 **Born:** 2/12/75 **Age:** 27

Year Team	Lg Org	G	AB	H	2B	3B	HR	TB	R	RBI	TBB	IBB	SO	HBP	SH	SF	SB	CS	SB%	GDP	Avg	OBP	SLG
1996 Jamestown	A- Det	27	78	22	5	2	2	37	12	12	10	0	31	2	0	2	3	1	.75	1	.282	.370	.474
1997 Lakeland	A+ Det	22	62	12	1	2	0	17	12	7	11	0	23	1	1	0	0	0	—	0	.194	.324	.274
Tigers	R Det	4	10	0	0	0	0	0	1	0	3	0	3	1	0	0	0	0	—	0	.000	.286	.000
W Michigan	A Det	14	37	11	5	0	0	16	6	2	6	0	15	0	0	1	0	0	—	0	.297	.386	.432
1998 Lakeland	A+ Det	109	386	112	24	0	15	181	69	61	67	0	106	5	1	1	7	3	.70	7	.290	.401	.469
1999 Jacksnville	AA Det	134	536	146	28	6	10	216	95	72	89	1	113	5	0	6	10	3	.77	8	.272	.377	.403
2000 Jacksnville	AA Det	98	326	78	14	1	4	106	43	41	49	0	69	5	2	3	6	1	.86	7	.239	.345	.325
2001 Toledo	AAA Det	10	30	6	0	2	1	13	2	1	4	0	7	0	0	0	0	1	.00	1	.200	.294	.433
Erie	AA Det	82	276	65	16	1	14	125	45	44	32	0	62	0	0	2	1	0	1.00	3	.236	.313	.453
6 Min. YEARS		500	1741	452	93	14	46	711	285	240	271	1	429	19	4	15	27	9	.75	29	.260	.363	.408

Chad Akers

Bats: Right **Throws:** Right **Pos:** OF-35; 3B-30; 2B-25; PH-3; PR-3; SS-1; P-1 **Ht:** 5'8" **Wt:** 170 **Born:** 5/30/72 **Age:** 30

Year Team	Lg Org	G	AB	H	2B	3B	HR	TB	R	RBI	TBB	IBB	SO	HBP	SH	SF	SB	CS	SB%	GDP	Avg	OBP	SLG
1993 Billings	R+ Cin	65	247	66	14	3	2	92	54	35	24	0	26	8	1	3	14	7	.67	4	.267	.348	.372
1994 Chston-WV	A Cin	133	490	135	23	1	4	172	65	35	52	1	49	2	2	3	41	16	.72	14	.276	.346	.351
1995 Winston-Sal	A+ Cin	103	361	94	14	1	2	116	41	29	27	1	49	1	7	3	25	8	.76	7	.260	.311	.321
1996 Fargo-Mh	IND —	83	330	90	11	0	5	116	84	41	57	2	32	10	2	4	13	12	.52	8	.273	.392	.352
1997 Fargo-Mh	IND —	84	368	117	14	6	4	155	75	43	25	0	41	4	2	5	27	4	.87	6	.318	.363	.421
1998 Fargo-Mh	IND —	83	358	111	30	5	8	175	79	44	29	0	39	2	0	1	12	5	.71	8	.310	.364	.489
1999 Atlantic Ct	IND —	59	243	66	18	3	5	105	42	32	22	1	30	4	3	3	16	4	.80	2	.272	.338	.432
New Haven	AA Sea	1	0	0	0	0	0	0	1	0	0	0	0	0	0	0	0	0	—	0			
Tacoma	AAA Sea	48	192	60	9	3	1	78	31	14	18	1	25	1	1	2	7	3	.70	3	.313	.371	.406
2000 Tacoma	AAA Sea	103	389	106	31	5	6	165	56	34	24	0	41	6	4	3	13	5	.72	7	.272	.322	.424
2001 Tacoma	AAA Sea	86	316	94	16	3	3	125	44	32	13	0	36	3	1	1	6	5	.55	7	.297	.330	.396
9 Min. YEARS		848	3294	939	180	30	40	1299	572	339	291	6	368	41	23	28	174	69	.72	66	.285	.348	.394

5

Scott Albin

Pitches: Right **Bats:** Right **Pos:** RP-41   **Ht:** 6'0" **Wt:** 185 **Born:** 9/27/75 **Age:** 26

Year Team	Lg Org	G	GS	CG	GF	IP	BFP	H	R	ER	HR	SH	SF	HB	TBB	IBB	SO	WP	Bk	W	L	Pct.	ShO	Sv	ERA
1999 Vermont	A- Mon	26	0	0	16	55	226	50	22	16	3	0	1	1	11	1	57	3	0	4	2	.667	0	6	2.62
Jupiter	A+ Mon	2	0	0	2	2	12	4	4	1	0	0	1	0	1	1	3	0	0	0	1	.000	0	1	4.50
2000 Jupiter	A+ Mon	49	0	0	25	67	290	66	31	22	2	7	3	2	23	3	51	1	0	4	3	.571	0	2	2.96
2001 Harrisburg	AA Mon	4	0	0	0	3.2	17	4	2	2	1	0	0	0	2	1	4	0	0	0	0	—	0	0	4.91
St. Paul	IND —	37	0	0	19	73.2	310	61	36	25	4	3	2	3	26	4	82	6	0	4	3	.571	0	3	3.05
3 Min. YEARS		118	0	0	62	201.1	855	185	95	66	10	10	7	6	63	10	197	10	0	12	9	.571	0	12	2.95

Scott Aldred

Pitches: Left **Bats:** Left **Pos:** SP-7; RP-4   **Ht:** 6'4" **Wt:** 220 **Born:** 6/12/68 **Age:** 34

Year Team	Lg Org	G	GS	CG	GF	IP	BFP	H	R	ER	HR	SH	SF	HB	TBB	IBB	SO	WP	Bk	W	L	Pct.	ShO	Sv	ERA
1987 Fayetteville	A Det	21	20	0	0	111	485	101	56	44	5	2	7	3	69	0	91	8	1	4	9	.308	0	0	3.57
1988 Lakeland	A+ Det	25	25	1	0	131.1	583	122	61	52	6	3	3	8	72	1	102	5	4	8	7	.533	1	0	3.56
1989 London	AA Det	20	20	3	0	122	513	98	55	52	11	3	3	5	59	0	97	9	2	10	6	.625	1	0	3.84
1990 Toledo	AAA Det	29	29	2	0	158	687	145	93	86	16	2	10	4	81	1	133	9	4	6	15	.286	0	0	4.90
1991 Toledo	AAA Det	22	20	2	2	135.1	581	127	65	59	7	8	3	4	72	1	95	4	0	8	8	.500	0	1	3.92
1992 Toledo	AAA Det	16	13	3	1	86	392	92	57	49	13	1	1	2	47	0	81	6	0	4	6	.400	0	0	5.13
1995 Lakeland	A+ Det	13	7	0	3	67.2	275	57	25	24	3	2	1	3	19	0	64	2	0	4	2	.667	0	2	3.19
Jacksnville	AA Det	2	2	0	0	12	42	9	0	0	0	0	0	1	1	0	11	0	0	1	0	1.000	0	0	0.00
1997 Salt Lake	AAA Min	7	7	0	0	39.2	187	56	39	31	4	1	2	1	16	1	23	7	0	3	3	.500	0	0	7.03
1998 Durham	AAA TB	7	7	0	0	35.1	161	44	26	21	3	0	2	4	14	0	19	4	0	2	4	.333	0	0	5.35
2001 Norwich	AA NYY	11	7	0	2	37	154	36	19	15	3	1	0	2	7	0	43	1	0	4	3	.571	0	0	3.65
1990 Detroit	AL	4	3	0	0	14.1	63	13	6	6	0	2	1	1	10	1	7	0	0	1	2	.333	0	0	3.77
1991 Detroit	AL	11	11	1	0	57.1	253	58	37	33	9	3	2	0	30	2	35	3	1	2	4	.333	0	0	5.18
1992 Detroit	AL	16	13	0	0	65	304	80	51	49	12	4	3	3	33	4	34	1	0	3	8	.273	0	0	6.78
1993 Colorado	NL	5	0	0	1	6.2	40	10	10	8	1	2	0	1	9	1	5	1	0	0	0	—	0	0	10.80
Montreal	NL	3	0	0	1	5.1	25	9	4	4	1	0	0	0	1	0	4	1	0	1	0	1.000	0	0	6.75
1996 Detroit	AL	11	8	0	0	43.1	217	60	52	45	9	3	2	3	26	3	36	6	1	0	4	.000	0	0	9.35
Minnesota	AL	25	17	0	0	122	531	134	73	69	20	4	5	3	42	1	75	4	0	6	5	.545	0	0	5.09
1997 Minnesota	AL	17	15	0	0	77.1	350	102	66	66	20	2	1	3	28	2	33	7	0	2	10	.167	0	0	7.68
1998 Tampa Bay	AL	48	0	0	8	31.1	135	33	13	13	1	3	0	2	12	3	21	2	0	0	0	—	0	0	3.73
1999 Tampa Bay	AL	37	0	0	9	24.1	114	26	15	14	1	2	1	2	14	0	22	1	0	3	2	.600	0	0	5.18
Philadelphia	NL	29	0	0	5	32.1	140	33	15	14	1	1	5	0	15	3	19	3	0	1	1	.500	0	1	3.90
2000 Philadelphia	NL	23	0	0	5	25	95	23	14	13	3	1	2	1	10	0	21	1	0	1	3	.250	0	0	5.75
10 Min. YEARS		173	157	11	8	935.1	4060	887	496	433	71	23	32	36	457	4	759	55	11	54	63	.462	2	3	4.17
9 Maj. YEARS		229	67	1	29	499.2	2267	581	356	334	78	27	22	19	230	20	312	30	2	20	39	.339	0	1	6.02

Chad Alexander

Bats: Right **Throws:** Right **Pos:** OF-130; DH-6; PH-1; PR-1   **Ht:** 6'1" **Wt:** 195 **Born:** 5/22/74 **Age:** 28

Year Team	Lg Org	G	AB	H	2B	3B	HR	TB	R	RBI	TBB	IBB	SO	HBP	SH	SF	SB	CS	SB%	GDP	Avg	OBP	SLG
1995 Auburn	A- Hou	71	278	81	15	5	5	121	45	43	25	1	37	7	1	5	7	1	.88	11	.291	.359	.435
Quad City	A Hou	7	7	2	0	0	0	2	2	1	0	0	0	0	0	0	0	0	—	0	.286	.286	.286
1996 Quad City	A Hou	118	435	115	25	4	13	187	68	69	57	4	108	2	0	3	16	11	.59	11	.264	.350	.430
1997 Kissimmee	A+ Hou	129	469	127	31	6	4	182	67	46	56	1	91	4	2	3	11	8	.58	15	.271	.352	.388
1998 Jackson	AA Hou	128	416	119	33	2	13	195	77	45	71	0	80	5	3	3	6	7	.46	8	.286	.394	.469
New Orleans	AAA Hou	2	5	2	0	0	0	2	1	2	0	0	2	0	0	0	0	0	—	0	.400	.400	.400
1999 New Orleans	AAA Hou	28	96	23	5	0	2	34	7	8	6	0	22	0	0	2	0	1	.00	3	.240	.279	.354
Jackson	AA Hou	84	317	98	27	3	9	158	42	44	34	1	58	3	0	3	9	5	.64	4	.309	.378	.498
2000 Tacoma	AAA Sea	120	440	119	27	2	12	186	58	55	39	1	70	2	1	6	6	3	.67	14	.270	.329	.423
2001 Tacoma	AAA Sea	137	527	153	45	0	14	240	76	77	53	2	92	3	1	5	1	1	.50	16	.290	.355	.455
7 Min. YEARS		819	2990	839	208	22	72	1307	443	390	341	10	560	26	8	30	56	37	.60	82	.281	.356	.437

Manny Alexander

Bats: Right **Throws:** Right **Pos:** 2B-59; SS-20; 3B-18; PH-5; OF-2; PR-2; DH-1   **Ht:** 5'10" **Wt:** 180 **Born:** 3/20/71 **Age:** 31

Year Team	Lg Org	G	AB	H	2B	3B	HR	TB	R	RBI	TBB	IBB	SO	HBP	SH	SF	SB	CS	SB%	GDP	Avg	OBP	SLG
1989 Bluefield	R+ Bal	65	274	85	13	2	2	108	49	34	20	1	49	3	0	2	19	8	.70	2	.310	.361	.394
1990 Wausau	A Bal	44	152	27	3	1	0	32	16	11	12	1	41	1	1	3	4	3	.73	2	.178	.238	.211
1991 Frederick	A+ Bal	134	548	143	17	3	3	175	81	42	44	0	68	2	3	1	47	14	.77	4	.261	.318	.319
Hagerstown	AA Bal	3	9	3	1	0	0	4	3	2	1	0	3	1	0	1	0	0	—	0	.333	.417	.444
1992 Hagerstown	AA Bal	127	499	129	23	8	2	174	69	41	25	0	62	6	4	4	43	12	.78	10	.259	.300	.349
Rochester	AAA Bal	6	24	7	1	0	0	8	3	3	1	0	3	0	1	0	2	2	.50	0	.292	.320	.333
1993 Rochester	AAA Bal	120	471	115	23	8	6	172	55	51	22	0	60	4	2	1	19	7	.73	11	.244	.283	.365
1994 Rochester	AAA Bal	111	426	106	23	6	6	159	63	39	16	0	67	3	4	5	30	8	.79	7	.249	.278	.373
1997 St. Lucie	A+ NYM	1	4	1	0	0	0	1	0	0	0	0	1	0	0	0	0	0	—	0	.250	.250	.250
2001 Tacoma	AAA Sea	97	344	97	26	2	8	151	46	51	14	0	55	2	3	3	5	5	.36	6	.282	.311	.439
1992 Baltimore	AL	4	5	1	0	0	0	1	1	0	0	0	3	0	0	0	0	0	—	0	.200	.200	.200
1993 Baltimore	AL	3	0	0	0	0	0	0	0	1	0	0	0	0	0	0	0	0	—	0	—	—	—
1995 Baltimore	AL	94	242	57	9	1	3	77	35	23	20	0	30	2	4	0	11	4	.73	2	.236	.299	.318
1996 Baltimore	AL	54	68	7	0	0	0	7	6	4	3	0	27	0	2	0	3	3	.50	2	.103	.141	.103
1997 New York	NL	54	149	37	9	3	2	58	26	15	9	1	38	1	1	0	11	0	1.00	3	.248	.294	.389
Chicago	NL	33	99	29	3	1	0	37	11	7	8	2	16	2	2	0	2	1	.67	3	.293	.358	.374
1998 Chicago	NL	108	264	60	10	1	5	87	34	25	18	1	66	1	5	1	4	1	.80	6	.227	.278	.330
1999 Chicago	NL	90	177	48	11	2	0	63	17	15	10	0	38	0	1	4	4	0	1.00	1	.271	.309	.356
2000 Boston	AL	101	144	30	6	3	1	45	30	19	13	0	41	0	2	2	0	1	.00	6	.211	.261	.313
8 Min. YEARS		708	2751	713	130	30	27	984	385	274	155	2	409	22	18	20	173	63	.73	42	.259	.302	.358
8 Maj. YEARS		541	1198	280	46	11	15	393	161	108	81	4	259	6	17	3	37	9	.80	17	.234	.285	.328

Jeff Alfano

Bats: Right **Throws:** Right **Pos:** C-49; P-9   **Ht:** 6'3" **Wt:** 195 **Born:** 8/16/76 **Age:** 25

					BATTING												BASERUNNING				PERCENTAGES		
Year Team	Lg Org	G	AB	H	2B	3B	HR	TB	R	RBI	TBB	IBB	SO	HBP	SH	SF	SB	CS	SB%	GDP	Avg	OBP	SLG
1996 Ogden	R+ Mil	45	159	45	9	0	4	66	29	29	12	0	30	4	2	2	2	2	.50	2	.283	.345	.415
1997 Beloit	A Mil	37	121	28	3	2	2	41	14	16	9	0	32	7	1	1	3	1	.75	4	.231	.319	.339
Ogden	R+ Mil	46	175	63	12	4	7	104	39	29	17	1	31	4	0	1	9	4	.69	4	.360	.426	.594
1998 Stockton	A+ Mil	113	389	94	21	1	4	129	39	40	37	1	93	6	0	1	7	4	.64	14	.242	.316	.332
1999 Huntsville	AA Mil	83	247	61	15	0	5	91	20	31	35	2	65	6	0	0	4	1	.80	10	.247	.354	.368
2000 Mudville	A+ Mil	22	69	16	4	1	1	25	9	10	5	0	18	1	0	0	1	0	1.00	3	.232	.293	.362
2001 San Jose	A+ SF	56	164	35	7	0	6	60	15	22	10	0	57	5	2	1	0	3	.00	2	.213	.278	.366
Shreveport	AA SF	1	0	0	0	0	0	0	0	0	0	0	0	0	0	0	0	0	—	0	—	—	—
6 Min. YEARS		403	1324	342	71	8	29	516	165	177	125	4	326	33	5	6	26	15	.63	39	.258	.336	.390

Jason Alfaro

Bats: Right **Throws:** Right **Pos:** 2B-28; OF-19; SS-16; 3B-14; PH-9; DH-5; PR-5; P-1   **Ht:** 5'10" **Wt:** 189 **Born:** 11/29/77 **Age:** 24

					BATTING												BASERUNNING				PERCENTAGES		
Year Team	Lg Org	G	AB	H	2B	3B	HR	TB	R	RBI	TBB	IBB	SO	HBP	SH	SF	SB	CS	SB%	GDP	Avg	OBP	SLG
1997 Astros	R Hou	34	102	27	5	0	2	38	8	13	8	0	14	1	2	0	6	0	1.00	2	.265	.324	.373
1998 Astros	R Hou	47	178	43	8	0	1	54	20	18	11	0	24	0	2	0	5	5	.50	5	.242	.286	.303
1999 Michigan	A Hou	118	473	128	25	4	5	176	74	50	23	0	62	1	5	7	5	5	.50	10	.271	.302	.372
2000 Kissimmee	A+ Hou	117	460	115	20	1	7	158	58	41	25	1	63	1	5	5	2	6	.25	15	.250	.287	.343
2001 Round Rock	AA Hou	87	284	69	16	2	2	95	26	29	7	1	40	2	3	2	2	1	.67	13	.243	.264	.335
5 Min. YEARS		403	1497	382	74	7	17	521	186	151	74	2	203	5	17	14	20	17	.54	45	.255	.290	.348

Dusty Allen

Bats: Right **Throws:** Right **Pos:** DH-22; 1B-3; PH-3; OF-1   **Ht:** 6'4" **Wt:** 235 **Born:** 8/9/72 **Age:** 29

					BATTING												BASERUNNING				PERCENTAGES		
Year Team	Lg Org	G	AB	H	2B	3B	HR	TB	R	RBI	TBB	IBB	SO	HBP	SH	SF	SB	CS	SB%	GDP	Avg	OBP	SLG
1995 Idaho Falls	R+ SD	29	104	34	7	0	4	53	21	24	21	0	19	0	0	2	1	2	.33	2	.327	.433	.510
Clinton	A SD	36	139	37	12	1	5	66	25	31	12	1	29	1	0	0	1	0	1.00	3	.266	.329	.475
1996 Clinton	A SD	77	243	65	10	3	10	111	46	46	67	1	59	4	0	3	7	.36	7	.267	.429	.457
Rancho Cuca	A+ SD	55	208	62	15	1	10	109	41	45	38	1	65	2	0	3	3	2	.60	3	.298	.406	.524
1997 Mobile	AA SD	131	475	120	28	4	17	207	85	75	81	0	116	0	0	4	1	4	.20	12	.253	.360	.436
1998 Mobile	AA SD	42	154	39	10	4	6	75	30	42	32	1	26	1	0	2	1	0	1.00	3	.253	.381	.487
Las Vegas	AAA SD	87	292	78	21	1	16	149	42	45	31	0	80	4	0	4	2	0	.00	5	.267	.341	.510
1999 Las Vegas	AAA SD	128	454	124	30	3	18	214	68	89	79	0	143	1	0	2	3	5	.38	5	.273	.381	.471
2000 Las Vegas	AAA SD	67	222	69	14	4	14	133	52	55	58	0	50	0	0	3	3	0	1.00	6	.311	.449	.599
Toledo	AAA Det	25	90	20	5	0	2	31	9	12	5	0	27	1	0	0	2	.00	2	.222	.271	.344
2001 Toledo	AAA Det	29	87	19	1	0	4	32	18	11	19	1	31	0	0	2	0	0	—	0	.218	.352	.368
2000 San Diego	NL	9	12	0	0	0	0	0	0	0	2	0	5	0	0	1	0	0	—	1	.000	.143	.000
Detroit	AL	18	16	7	2	0	2	15	5	2	2	0	7	0	0	0	0	0	—	0	.438	.500	.938
7 Min. YEARS		706	2468	667	153	21	106	1180	437	475	443	5	645	14	0	24	17	24	.41	48	.270	.381	.478

Jeff Allen

Bats: Right **Throws:** Right **Pos:** OF-107; DH-8; PH-5   **Ht:** 6'1" **Wt:** 190 **Born:** 6/8/76 **Age:** 26

					BATTING												BASERUNNING				PERCENTAGES		
Year Team	Lg Org	G	AB	H	2B	3B	HR	TB	R	RBI	TBB	IBB	SO	HBP	SH	SF	SB	CS	SB%	GDP	Avg	OBP	SLG
1998 Salem-Keizr	A- SF	60	215	63	10	5	11	116	47	47	33	3	64	5	1	2	10	5	.67	2	.293	.396	.540
1999 Bakersfield	A+ SF	130	480	127	32	3	10	195	80	65	47	0	130	10	0	4	24	5	.83	12	.265	.340	.406
2000 Shreveport	AA SF	128	447	106	23	2	7	154	40	52	26	0	97	4	3	5	8	10	.44	9	.237	.282	.345
2001 Shreveport	AA SF	20	60	13	2	0	0	15	5	8	10	0	16	0	0	1	0	1	.00	1	.217	.324	.250
San Jose	A+ SF	99	371	113	19	4	14	182	60	61	43	2	103	12	1	2	12	5	.71	7	.305	.393	.491
4 Min. YEARS		437	1573	422	86	14	42	662	232	233	159	5	410	31	5	14	54	26	.68	31	.268	.344	.421

Luke Allen

Bats: Left **Throws:** Right **Pos:** OF-122; DH-3; PH-1; PR-1   **Ht:** 6'2" **Wt:** 208 **Born:** 8/4/78 **Age:** 23

					BATTING												BASERUNNING				PERCENTAGES		
Year Team	Lg Org	G	AB	H	2B	3B	HR	TB	R	RBI	TBB	IBB	SO	HBP	SH	SF	SB	CS	SB%	GDP	Avg	OBP	SLG
1997 Great Falls	R+ LA	67	263	81	12	6	7	134	50	40	19	1	53	0	1	0	12	11	.52	3	.345	.390	.519
1998 San Berndno	A+ LA	105	399	119	25	6	4	168	51	46	30	0	93	3	7	4	18	11	.62	4	.298	.349	.421
San Antonio	AA LA	23	78	26	3	1	3	40	9	10	6	1	16	0	1	0	1	2	.33	0	.333	.381	.513
1999 San Antonio	AA LA	137	533	150	16	12	14	232	90	82	44	0	102	1	2	2	14	8	.64	8	.281	.336	.435
2000 San Antonio	AA LA	90	339	90	15	5	7	136	55	60	40	3	71	1	0	5	14	5	.74	10	.265	.340	.401
2001 Las Vegas	AAA LA	2	9	2	1	0	0	3	1	0	0	0	0	0	0	0	0	0	—	1	.222	.222	.333
Jacksnville	AA LA	125	486	141	32	6	16	233	74	73	42	3	111	1	1	5	13	3	.81	7	.290	.345	.479
5 Min. YEARS		549	2102	617	104	36	51	946	330	311	181	8	446	6	12	16	72	40	.64	33	.294	.349	.450

Jermaine Allensworth

Bats: Right **Throws:** Right **Pos:** OF-133; PH-1; PR-1   **Ht:** 6'0" **Wt:** 190 **Born:** 1/11/72 **Age:** 30

					BATTING												BASERUNNING				PERCENTAGES		
Year Team	Lg Org	G	AB	H	2B	3B	HR	TB	R	RBI	TBB	IBB	SO	HBP	SH	SF	SB	CS	SB%	GDP	Avg	OBP	SLG
1993 Welland	A- Pit	67	263	81	16	4	1	108	44	32	24	0	38	12	2	1	18	3	.86	2	.308	.390	.411
1994 Carolina	AA Pit	118	452	109	26	8	1	154	63	34	39	0	79	11	5	3	16	14	.53	2	.241	.315	.341
1995 Carolina	AA Pit	56	219	59	14	2	1	80	37	14	25	0	34	5	2	0	13	8	.62	4	.269	.357	.365
Calgary	AAA Pit	51	190	60	13	4	3	90	46	11	13	0	30	5	1	0	13	4	.76	3	.316	.375	.474
1996 Calgary	AAA Pit	95	352	116	23	6	8	175	77	43	39	6	61	7	1	1	25	5	.83	6	.330	.406	.497
1997 Calgary	AAA Pit	5	20	8	3	1	0	13	5	1	2	0	4	0	0	0	1	1	.50	0	.400	.455	.650
1999 Norfolk	AAA NYM	81	273	72	20	5	5	117	44	20	36	0	39	7	2	1	10	5	.67	3	.264	.363	.429

7

Year Team	Lg Org	G	AB	H	2B	3B	HR	TB	R	RBI	TBB	IBB	SO	HBP	SH	SF	SB	CS	SB%	GDP	Avg	OBP	SLG
								BATTING											**BASERUNNING**		**PERCENTAGES**		
2001 Toledo	AAA Det	133	485	132	22	7	10	198	57	52	49	3	74	8	21	3	13	9	.59	4	.272	.347	.408
1996 Pittsburgh	NL	61	229	60	9	3	4	87	32	31	23	0	50	4	2	2	11	6	.65	2	.262	.337	.380
1997 Pittsburgh	NL	108	369	94	18	2	3	125	55	43	44	1	79	7	9	6	14	7	.67	5	.255	.340	.339
1998 Pittsburgh	NL	69	233	72	13	3	3	100	30	24	17	0	43	7	3	1	8	4	.67	1	.309	.372	.429
Kansas City	AL	30	73	15	5	0	0	20	15	3	9	0	17	4	5	0	7	0	1.00	0	.205	.326	.274
New York	NL	34	54	11	2	0	2	19	9	4	2	0	16	1	0	0	0	2	.00	0	.204	.246	.352
1999 New York	NL	40	73	16	2	0	3	27	14	9	9	0	23	1	2	1	2	1	.67	1	.219	.310	.370
7 Min. YEARS		606	2254	637	137	37	29	935	373	207	227	9	359	55	34	9	109	49	.69	22	.283	.361	.415
4 Maj. YEARS		342	1031	268	49	8	15	378	155	114	104	1	228	24	21	10	42	20	.68	9	.260	.339	.367

Charles Alley

Bats: Both **Throws:** Right **Pos:** C-55; PH-4; DH-3   **Ht:** 6'2" **Wt:** 205 **Born:** 12/20/76 **Age:** 25

Year Team	Lg Org	G	AB	H	2B	3B	HR	TB	R	RBI	TBB	IBB	SO	HBP	SH	SF	SB	CS	SB%	GDP	Avg	OBP	SLG
								BATTING											**BASERUNNING**		**PERCENTAGES**		
1995 Orioles	R Bal	12	30	9	4	0	0	13	10	3	11	0	4	1	0	2	0	0	—	1	.300	.477	.433
1996 Bluefield	R+ Bal	24	67	13	4	0	0	17	7	4	15	0	16	1	0	1	0	2	.00	2	.194	.345	.254
1997 Frederick	A Bal	82	250	59	17	1	3	87	19	32	34	3	45	8	1	2	7	2	.78	5	.236	.344	.348
1998 Frederick	A+ Bal	112	340	89	23	1	9	141	42	47	60	2	60	4	5	1	0	2	.00	5	.262	.378	.415
1999 Bowie	AA Bal	5	9	1	1	0	0	2	4	0	1	0	3	0	0	0	0	0	—	0	.111	.200	.222
Orioles	R Bal	2	3	0	0	0	0	0	2	0	2	0	0	0	0	0	0	0	—	0	.000	.400	.000
Frederick	A+ Bal	41	132	30	6	0	1	39	21	12	23	1	27	1	1	0	0	1	.00	1	.227	.346	.295
2000 Frederick	A+ Bal	35	98	24	3	0	2	33	15	12	18	0	20	1	2	1	0	0	—	4	.245	.364	.337
Orioles	R Bal	6	15	5	2	0	0	7	3	3	4	1	4	1	0	1	0	1	.00	0	.333	.476	.467
Delmarva	A Bal	15	44	12	2	0	0	14	10	0	15	1	5	2	0	0	1	0	1.00	1	.273	.475	.318
2001 Frederick	A+ Bal	43	126	23	5	0	1	31	13	10	27	0	25	3	1	0	2	1	.67	6	.183	.340	.246
Bowie	AA Bal	19	51	11	0	1	0	13	5	4	7	0	3	1	2	1	0	1	1.00	1	.216	.317	.255
7 Min. YEARS		396	1165	276	67	4	16	397	151	127	217	8	212	23	12	9	12	9	.57	26	.237	.365	.341

Edwin Almonte

Pitches: Right **Bats:** Right **Pos:** RP-54   **Ht:** 6'3" **Wt:** 200 **Born:** 12/17/76 **Age:** 25

Year Team	Lg Org	G	GS	CG	GF	IP	BFP	H	R	ER	HR	SH	SF	HB	TBB	IBB	SO	WP	Bk	W	L	Pct.	ShO	Sv	ERA
			HOW MUCH HE PITCHED								**WHAT HE GAVE UP**											**THE RESULTS**			
1998 White Sox	R CWS	5	0	0	2	9.2	37	6	5	1	0	0	0	1	1	0	8	0	0	0	0	—	0	0	0.93
Bristol	R+ CWS	8	3	0	0	26.2	113	29	14	10	3	0	1	1	4	0	26	2	0	3	0	1.000	0	0	3.38
1999 Burlington	A CWS	37	5	2	16	115.2	480	107	48	39	5	2	1	2	28	4	85	6	1	9	12	.429	0	5	3.03
2000 Winston-Sal	A+ CWS	33	7	0	10	77	320	66	32	27	2	3	1	5	20	0	73	4	1	3	1	.750	0	2	3.16
Birmingham	AA CWS	7	6	0	0	39.2	159	45	22	20	5	0	1	1	9	0	21	2	0	1	3	.250	0	0	4.54
2001 Birmingham	AA CWS	54	0	0	48	66.1	272	58	16	11	4	2	0	0	16	4	62	2	0	1	4	.200	0	36	1.49
4 Min. YEARS		144	21	2	76	335	1381	311	137	108	19	7	4	10	78	8	275	16	2	17	20	.459	0	43	2.90

Hector Almonte

Pitches: Right **Bats:** Right **Pos:** RP-18   **Ht:** 6'2" **Wt:** 190 **Born:** 10/17/75 **Age:** 26

Year Team	Lg Org	G	GS	CG	GF	IP	BFP	H	R	ER	HR	SH	SF	HB	TBB	IBB	SO	WP	Bk	W	L	Pct.	ShO	Sv	ERA
			HOW MUCH HE PITCHED								**WHAT HE GAVE UP**											**THE RESULTS**			
1997 Marlins	R Fla	8	0	0	7	23.2	89	12	3	2	0	0	1	2	6	0	25	1	0	2	0	1.000	0	3	0.76
Kane County	A Fla	8	1	0	3	14	59	11	6	6	1	1	2	1	6	0	10	2	0	1	0	1.000	0	1	3.86
1998 Kane County	A Fla	43	0	0	41	43.1	200	51	22	19	5	1	1	1	19	0	51	3	2	1	5	.167	0	21	3.95
1999 Portland	AA Fla	47	0	0	41	44.1	202	42	14	14	1	8	1	2	26	3	42	4	0	1	4	.200	0	23	2.84
2000 Calgary	AAA Fla	18	0	0	13	19.1	98	36	24	24	7	1	0	0	9	0	16	2	1	0	4	.000	0	3	11.17
Marlins	R Fla	1	1	0	0	2	8	3	1	1	0	0	0	0	1	0	2	0	0	0	0	—	0	0	4.50
Brevard Cty	A+ Fla	8	2	0	3	15.1	61	11	6	4	2	1	0	2	5	0	16	1	0	1	1	.500	0	0	2.35
Portland	AA Fla	4	0	0	4	5	25	5	2	2	1	0	0	0	4	0	6	0	0	1	0	.000	0	3	3.60
2001 Calgary	AAA Fla	18	0	0	11	24.2	123	36	29	23	6	0	2	0	15	0	21	2	0	0	0	—	0	0	8.39
1999 Florida	NL	15	0	0	6	15	67	20	7	7	1	1	1	0	6	2	8	2	0	0	2	.000	0	0	4.20
5 Min. YEARS		155	4	0	123	191.2	865	207	107	95	23	12	7	8	91	3	189	15	3	5	16	.238	0	54	4.46

Wady Almonte

Bats: Right **Throws:** Right **Pos:** OF-80; DH-5; PH-2; PR-1   **Ht:** 6'0" **Wt:** 200 **Born:** 4/20/75 **Age:** 27

Year Team	Lg Org	G	AB	H	2B	3B	HR	TB	R	RBI	TBB	IBB	SO	HBP	SH	SF	SB	CS	SB%	GDP	Avg	OBP	SLG
								BATTING											**BASERUNNING**		**PERCENTAGES**		
1994 Orioles	R Bal	42	120	24	2	0	2	32	11	9	8	0	22	1	1	0	1	2	.33	0	.200	.256	.267
1995 Bluefield	R+ Bal	51	189	58	12	1	6	90	37	30	9	2	49	1	0	2	6	5	.55	4	.307	.338	.476
1996 Orioles	R Bal	1	3	1	0	0	0	1	2	1	1	0	0	0	0	0	1	0	1.00	0	.333	.500	.333
Frederick	A+ Bal	85	287	82	12	2	12	134	45	44	21	2	59	6	4	1	1	5	.17	12	.286	.346	.467
1997 Bowie	AA Bal	69	222	46	7	2	6	75	25	25	27	0	64	5	0	1	2	4	.33	6	.207	.306	.338
Frederick	A+ Bal	57	202	52	13	2	10	99	34	36	16	4	59	4	1	3	4	1	.80	8	.257	.320	.490
1998 Bowie	AA Bal	7	21	1	0	0	1	4	2	2	4	0	9	1	0	0	0	0	—	0	.048	.231	.190
1999 Bowie	AA Bal	124	482	141	27	4	17	227	68	83	31	1	72	7	0	5	10	10	.50	12	.293	.341	.471
2000 Rochester	AAA Bal	73	229	60	18	5	1	91	25	33	11	0	34	1	3	1	5	3	.38	7	.262	.298	.397
2001 Rochester	AAA Bal	87	316	68	8	4	3	93	25	31	16	1	54	4	0	2	7	3	.70	16	.215	.260	.408
8 Min. YEARS		596	2071	533	99	20	58	846	274	294	144	10	422	30	9	15	35	35	.50	67	.257	.313	.408

Felipe Alou

Bats: Right **Throws:** Right **Pos:** OF-29; PH-1   **Ht:** 5'11" **Wt:** 165 **Born:** 11/29/78 **Age:** 23

					BATTING												BASERUNNING				PERCENTAGES		
Year Team	Lg Org	G	AB	H	2B	3B	HR	TB	R	RBI	TBB	IBB	SO	HBP	SH	SF	SB	CS	SB%	GDP	Avg	OBP	SLG
1998 Royals	R KC	44	162	41	7	1	2	56	20	22	8	0	31	1	4	1	6	3	.67	4	.253	.291	.346
1999 Chston-WV	A KC	57	185	36	8	1	0	46	18	13	13	0	50	2	2	2	11	4	.73	1	.195	.252	.249
Spokane	A- KC	17	42	10	1	1	0	13	4	4	5	0	12	0	0	0	2	0	1.00	1	.238	.319	.310
2001 Royals	R KC	18	76	19	3	0	0	22	8	9	1	0	14	0	1	0	1	1	.50	1	.250	.260	.289
Omaha	AAA KC	11	32	7	1	0	0	8	1	2	1	0	15	1	0	1	1	0	1.00	0	.219	.257	.250
3 Min. YEARS		147	497	113	20	3	2	145	51	50	28	0	122	4	7	4	21	8	.72	7	.227	.272	.292

Carlos Alvarado

Pitches: Right **Bats:** Right **Pos:** RP-19; SP-11   **Ht:** 6'3" **Wt:** 213 **Born:** 1/24/78 **Age:** 24

		HOW MUCH HE PITCHED					WHAT HE GAVE UP											THE RESULTS				
Year Team	Lg Org	G	GS	CG	GF	IP	BFP	H	R	ER	HR	SH	SF	HB	TBB	IBB	SO	WP	Bk	W	L	Pct.	ShO	Sv	ERA
1995 Pirates	R Pit	2	0	0	0	3	15	1	2	2	0	1	0	0	5	0	2	3	0	0	0	—	0	0	6.00
1996 Pirates	R Pit	11	1	0	4	27.1	125	32	20	15	1	1	1	2	10	0	31	2	2	1	1	.500	0	0	4.94
1997 Augusta	A Pit	29	20	0	2	113	499	114	58	41	4	3	8	11	45	0	109	9	4	6	5	.545	0	0	3.27
1998 Augusta	A Pit	14	10	0	0	50	209	48	20	20	2	2	2	1	24	0	50	6	0	4	1	.800	0	0	3.60
Lynchburg	A+ Pit	13	10	0	1	59.1	274	69	48	37	10	4	2	3	24	0	52	6	0	3	5	.375	0	0	5.61
1999 Lynchburg	A+ Pit	20	18	0	0	90.2	400	89	52	46	4	0	1	2	46	0	75	8	4	4	6	.400	0	0	4.57
2000 Lynchburg	A+ Pit	15	7	0	2	49.1	216	50	30	23	2	2	2	1	25	0	37	5	0	0	5	.000	0	0	4.20
Altoona	AA Pit	16	1	0	4	30.2	140	31	16	14	2	2	2	1	18	1	27	2	0	3	0	1.000	0	1	4.11
2001 Lynchburg	A+ Pit	4	1	0	1	11	42	8	5	4	0	0	0	0	7	0	8	2	0	0	0	—	0	0	3.27
Altoona	AA Pit	26	10	0	0	83	354	74	46	31	6	1	2	5	29	1	73	4	1	5	7	.417	0	1	3.36
7 Min. YEARS		150	78	0	14	517.1	2274	516	297	233	31	15	21	26	233	2	464	47	11	26	30	.464	0	1	4.05

Gabe Alvarez

Bats: Right **Throws:** Right **Pos:** 3B-67; 1B-17; OF-16; DH-1; PH-1; PR-1   **Ht:** 6'1" **Wt:** 205 **Born:** 3/6/74 **Age:** 28

					BATTING												BASERUNNING				PERCENTAGES		
Year Team	Lg Org	G	AB	H	2B	3B	HR	TB	R	RBI	TBB	IBB	SO	HBP	SH	SF	SB	CS	SB%	GDP	Avg	OBP	SLG
1995 Rancho Cuca	A+ SD	59	212	73	17	2	6	112	41	36	29	0	30	5	0	2	1	0	1.00	3	.344	.431	.528
Memphis	AA SD	2	9	5	1	0	0	6	0	4	1	0	1	0	0	0	0	0	—	0	.556	.600	.667
1996 Memphis	AA SD	104	368	91	23	1	8	140	58	40	64	1	87	3	0	3	2	3	.40	10	.247	.361	.380
1997 Mobile	AA SD	114	427	128	28	2	14	202	71	78	51	2	64	5	0	6	1	1	.50	21	.300	.376	.473
1998 Toledo	AAA Det	67	249	68	15	1	20	145	37	58	30	0	60	1	0	3	3	1	.75	7	.273	.350	.582
1999 Toledo	AAA Det	110	410	117	24	0	21	204	70	67	57	0	80	6	0	9	1	3	.25	8	.285	.373	.498
2000 Toledo	AAA Det	69	241	50	11	2	8	89	37	35	47	0	53	1	0	3	0	1	.00	4	.207	.336	.369
Las Vegas	AAA SD	43	141	43	11	0	9	81	33	26	33	0	44	4	1	2	2	0	1.00	3	.305	.444	.574
2001 Chattanooga	AA Cin	99	336	85	23	1	16	158	59	50	61	1	82	8	1	4	4	4	.50	7	.253	.377	.470
1998 Detroit	AL	58	199	46	11	0	5	72	16	29	18	1	65	2	0	2	1	3	.25	2	.231	.299	.362
1999 Detroit	AL	22	53	11	3	0	2	20	5	4	3	0	9	0	0	0	0	1	.00	0	.208	.250	.377
2000 Detroit	AL	1	1	0	0	0	0	0	0	0	2	0	1	0	0	0	0	0	—	0	.000	.667	.000
San Diego	NL	11	13	2	1	0	0	3	1	0	1	0	1	0	0	0	0	0	—	0	.154	.214	.231
7 Min. YEARS		667	2393	660	153	9	102	1137	406	394	373	4	501	33	2	32	14	13	.52	63	.276	.377	.475
3 Maj. YEARS		92	266	59	15	0	7	95	22	33	24	1	76	2	0	2	1	4	.20	2	.222	.289	.357

Jimmy Alvarez

Bats: Both **Throws:** Right **Pos:** SS-114; 2B-16; PR-3   **Ht:** 5'10" **Wt:** 168 **Born:** 10/4/79 **Age:** 22

					BATTING												BASERUNNING				PERCENTAGES		
Year Team	Lg Org	G	AB	H	2B	3B	HR	TB	R	RBI	TBB	IBB	SO	HBP	SH	SF	SB	CS	SB%	GDP	Avg	OBP	SLG
1997 Twins	R Min	52	185	46	5	4	0	59	25	14	21	0	46	1	1	1	12	5	.71	4	.249	.327	.319
1998 Elizabethtn	R+ Min	46	155	34	8	4	0	50	32	14	33	0	37	3	2	2	6	2	.75	4	.219	.363	.323
1999 Quad City	A Min	121	435	110	20	1	6	150	69	48	81	3	112	6	7	5	15	10	.60	9	.253	.374	.345
2000 Quad City	A Min	43	134	30	7	2	4	53	14	21	19	1	38	2	3	0	3	1	.75	3	.224	.329	.396
Hagerstown	A Tor	50	155	36	5	1	3	52	19	15	25	0	44	2	1	0	12	5	.71	4	.232	.346	.335
2001 Dunedin	A+ Tor	123	467	132	19	4	8	183	88	56	49	0	87	2	7	4	29	7	.81	7	.283	.351	.392
Tennessee	AA Tor	8	22	5	0	1	0	7	4	1	4	0	6	0	4	0	1	0	1.00	0	.227	.346	.318
5 Min. YEARS		443	1553	393	64	17	21	554	251	169	232	4	370	16	25	12	78	30	.72	24	.253	.354	.357

Juan Alvarez

Pitches: Left **Bats:** Left **Pos:** RP-47; SP-1   **Ht:** 6'0" **Wt:** 184 **Born:** 8/9/73 **Age:** 28

		HOW MUCH HE PITCHED					WHAT HE GAVE UP											THE RESULTS				
Year Team	Lg Org	G	GS	CG	GF	IP	BFP	H	R	ER	HR	SH	SF	HB	TBB	IBB	SO	WP	Bk	W	L	Pct.	ShO	Sv	ERA
1995 Boise	A- Ana	9	0	0	2	11.2	47	12	1	1	0	0	0	1	2	0	11	0	0	0	0	—	0	0	0.77
1996 Cedar Rapds	A Ana	40	0	0	14	53	238	50	25	20	0	3	1	7	30	1	53	4	0	1	2	.333	0	3	3.40
1997 Lk Elsinore	A+ Ana	27	0	0	10	51.1	196	33	9	8	2	2	1	4	13	2	46	2	2	4	2	.667	0	3	1.40
Midland	AA Ana	24	0	0	6	37	199	63	42	34	5	0	1	3	22	1	27	0	3	4	1	.800	0	0	8.27
1998 Midland	AA Ana	40	0	0	31	46	197	40	26	22	5	2	1	2	21	3	41	2	1	3	4	.429	0	12	4.30
Vancouver	AAA Ana	18	0	0	5	14.1	65	14	9	8	2	0	0	4	8	0	12	0	1	1	1	.500	0	0	5.02
1999 Erie	AA Ana	23	0	0	12	30.2	121	20	14	7	4	1	2	2	6	0	22	1	1	1	2	.333	0	4	2.05
Edmonton	AAA Ana	27	0	0	13	28.1	123	30	13	11	2	1	1	1	8	0	25	0	1	0	3	.000	0	0	3.49
2000 Edmonton	AAA Ana	44	0	0	14	38.1	150	30	13	12	12	3	3	0	19	1	27	2	0	3	1	.750	0	0	2.82
2001 Salt Lake	AAA Ana	48	1	0	14	67.1	289	68	42	37	13	0	4	0	27	0	44	4	1	2	2	.500	0	0	4.95
1999 Anaheim	AL	8	0	0	1	3	14	1	1	1	0	1	0	0	4	0	4	1	0	0	1	.000	0	0	3.00
2000 Anaheim	AL	11	0	0	3	6	38	14	9	9	3	0	1	0	7	1	2	1	0	0	0	—	0	0	13.50
7 Min. YEARS		300	1	0	122	378	1633	360	193	160	36	12	11	25	156	8	308	15	10	19	18	.514	0	22	3.81
2 Maj. YEARS		19	0	0	4	9	52	15	10	10	3	1	1	0	11	1	6	2	0	0	1	.000	0	0	10.00

Tony Alvarez

Bats: Right **Throws:** Right **Pos:** OF-86; PH-6; DH-4; 2B-1 **Ht:** 6'1" **Wt:** 202 **Born:** 5/10/79 **Age:** 23

Year Team	Lg Org	G	AB	H	2B	3B	HR	TB	R	RBI	TBB	IBB	SO	HBP	SH	SF	SB	CS	SB%	GDP	Avg	OBP	SLG
1998 Pirates	R Pit	50	190	47	13	1	4	74	27	29	13	1	24	3	1	5	19	1	.95	4	.247	.299	.389
1999 Williamsprt	A- Pit	58	196	63	14	1	7	100	44	45	21	1	36	16	1	6	38	9	.81	2	.321	.418	.510
2000 Hickory	A Pit	118	442	126	25	4	15	204	75	77	39	2	93	15	0	8	52	21	.71	8	.285	.357	.462
2001 Lynchburg	A+ Pit	25	93	32	4	0	2	42	10	11	7	0	11	0	0	0	7	3	.70	2	.344	.390	.452
Altoona	AA Pit	67	254	81	16	1	6	117	34	25	9	0	30	7	2	0	17	11	.61	6	.319	.359	.461
4 Min. YEARS		318	1175	349	72	7	34	537	190	187	89	4	194	41	4	19	133	45	.75	22	.297	.362	.457

Victor Alvarez

Pitches: Left **Bats:** Left **Pos:** SP-28 **Ht:** 5'10" **Wt:** 150 **Born:** 11/8/76 **Age:** 25

Year Team	Lg Org	G	GS	CG	GF	IP	BFP	H	R	ER	HR	SH	SF	HB	TBB	IBB	SO	WP	Bk	W	L	Pct.	ShO	Sv	ERA
1997 Great Falls	R+ LA	12	8	0	3	48.1	212	49	30	18	0	0	4	3	17	0	50	2	3	4	1	.800	0	0	3.35
1999 Vero Beach	A+ LA	12	12	1	0	73	280	56	21	16	4	1	1	2	16	0	57	1	1	4	4	.500	0	0	1.97
San Antonio	AA LA	9	9	0	0	56.1	234	58	27	23	5	3	1	2	10	0	43	1	0	4	3	.571	0	0	3.67
2000 Vero Beach	A+ LA	4	4	0	0	22.2	94	17	14	13	6	0	0	0	11	0	20	1	0	1	1	.500	0	0	5.16
San Antonio	AA LA	11	8	0	0	48.1	218	44	27	21	3	5	3	7	30	1	43	0	0	0	3	.000	0	0	3.91
2001 Jacksnville	AA LA	8	8	0	0	45	163	27	6	6	1	1	0	1	7	0	40	2	0	0	3	.000	0	0	1.20
Las Vegas	AAA LA	20	20	0	0	118	502	115	63	56	12	4	2	6	41	0	94	4	5	7	4	.636	0	0	4.27
4 Min. YEARS		76	69	1	3	411.2	1703	366	188	153	31	14	11	21	132	1	347	11	9	22	16	.579	0	0	3.34

Wilson Alvarez

Pitches: Left **Bats:** Left **Pos:** SP-9 **Ht:** 6'1" **Wt:** 245 **Born:** 3/24/70 **Age:** 32

Year Team	Lg Org	G	GS	CG	GF	IP	BFP	H	R	ER	HR	SH	SF	HB	TBB	IBB	SO	WP	Bk	W	L	Pct.	ShO	Sv	ERA
1987 Gastonia	A Tex	8	6	0	1	32	153	39	24	23	5	0	1	4	23	0	19	0	0	1	5	.167	0	0	6.47
Rangers	R Tex	10	10	0	0	44.2	193	41	29	26	6	1	1	3	21	0	46	3	0	2	5	.286	0	0	5.24
1988 Gastonia	A Tex	23	23	1	0	127	552	113	63	42	5	4	6	7	49	1	134	5	10	4	11	.267	0	0	2.98
Okla City	AAA Tex	5	3	0	1	16.2	71	17	8	7	2	0	2	1	6	0	9	0	0	1	1	.500	0	0	3.78
1989 Charlotte	A+ Tex	13	13	3	0	81	331	68	29	19	2	3	3	4	21	0	51	4	0	7	4	.636	2	0	2.11
Tulsa	AA Tex	7	7	1	0	48	196	40	14	11	1	2	2	0	16	3	29	1	4	2	2	.500	1	0	2.06
Birmingham	AA CWS	6	6	0	0	35.2	149	32	12	12	2	2	0	1	16	0	18	1	1	2	1	.667	0	0	3.03
1990 Vancouver	AAA CWS	17	15	1	0	75	350	91	54	50	7	2	3	4	51	0	35	1	2	5	7	.500	0	0	6.00
Birmingham	AA CWS	7	7	1	0	46.1	204	44	24	22	5	0	0	0	25	0	36	2	2	5	1	.833	0	0	4.27
1991 Birmingham	AA CWS	23	23	3	0	152.1	634	109	46	31	6	7	3	3	74	0	165	9	3	10	6	.625	2	0	1.83
1993 Nashville	AAA CWS	1	1	0	0	6.1	31	7	7	2	0	0	0	0	2	0	8	0	0	0	1	.000	0	0	2.84
1998 Devil Rays	R TB	1	1	0	0	3	11	2	0	0	0	0	0	0	1	0	4	0	0	0	0	—	0	0	0.00
St. Pete	A+ TB	1	1	0	0	1.2	12	5	5	5	1	0	0	0	2	0	2	0	0	0	1	.000	0	0	27.00
Durham	AAA TB	1	1	0	0	4.2	19	4	2	2	0	0	0	0	2	0	6	0	0	0	0	—	0	0	3.86
2000 St. Pete	A+ TB	1	1	0	0	4	12	0	0	0	0	0	0	0	0	0	2	0	0	0	0	—	0	0	0.00
2001 Orlando	AA TB	5	5	0	0	20.1	92	24	10	10	2	0	1	1	6	0	18	1	0	1	3	.250	0	0	4.43
Durham	AAA TB	4	4	0	0	18	79	20	8	6	2	0	2	0	6	0	16	1	0	1	1	.500	0	0	3.00
1989 Texas	AL	1	1	0	0	0	5	3	3	3	2	0	0	0	2	0	0	0	0	0	1	.000	0	0	—
1991 Chicago	AL	10	9	2	0	56.1	237	47	26	22	9	3	1	0	29	0	32	2	0	3	2	.600	1	0	3.51
1992 Chicago	AL	34	9	0	4	100.1	455	103	64	58	12	3	4	4	65	2	66	2	0	5	3	.625	0	1	5.20
1993 Chicago	AL	31	31	1	0	207.2	877	168	78	68	14	13	6	7	122	8	155	2	1	15	8	.652	1	0	2.95
1994 Chicago	AL	24	24	2	0	161.2	682	147	72	62	16	6	3	0	62	1	108	3	0	12	8	.600	1	0	3.45
1995 Chicago	AL	29	29	3	0	175	769	171	96	84	21	6	5	2	93	4	118	1	2	8	11	.421	0	0	4.32
1996 Chicago	AL	35	35	0	0	217.1	946	216	106	102	21	5	2	4	97	3	181	2	0	15	10	.600	0	0	4.22
1997 Chicago	AL	22	22	2	0	145.2	613	126	61	49	9	6	5	3	55	1	110	4	0	9	8	.529	1	0	3.03
San Francisco	NL	11	11	0	0	66.1	283	54	36	33	9	4	1	0	36	3	69	1	1	4	3	.571	0	0	4.48
1998 Tampa Bay	AL	25	25	0	0	142.2	624	130	78	75	18	1	2	9	68	0	107	4	0	6	14	.300	0	0	4.73
1999 Tampa Bay	AL	28	28	1	0	160	703	159	92	75	22	3	3	6	79	1	128	3	0	9	9	.500	0	0	4.22
9 Min. YEARS		133	127	10	2	716.2	3089	656	335	268	46	21	24	28	321	4	598	28	22	43	49	.467	5	0	3.37
10 Maj. YEARS		250	224	11	4	1433	6194	1324	712	631	153	50	32	36	708	23	1074	24	4	86	77	.528	4	1	3.96

Jerome Alviso

Bats: Both **Throws:** Right **Pos:** 2B-46; 1B-20; SS-18; PH-16; OF-14; 3B-9; PR-7; P-1 **Ht:** 6'1" **Wt:** 180 **Born:** 9/4/75 **Age:** 26

Year Team	Lg Org	G	AB	H	2B	3B	HR	TB	R	RBI	TBB	IBB	SO	HBP	SH	SF	SB	CS	SB%	GDP	Avg	OBP	SLG
1997 Portland	A- Col	69	270	86	15	3	2	113	48	45	19	1	46	7	6	6	12	5	.71	3	.319	.371	.419
1998 Asheville	A Col	134	486	134	30	1	6	184	64	41	18	0	60	7	10	3	11	11	.50	6	.276	.309	.379
1999 Salem	A+ Col	128	491	123	16	3	2	151	49	43	28	0	67	3	12	4	5	6	.45	4	.251	.293	.308
2000 Salem	A+ Col	95	321	87	11	3	1	107	39	44	17	0	46	6	7	7	11	9	.55	8	.271	.313	.333
2001 Colo Sprngs	AAA Col	111	266	64	12	0	1	79	30	18	14	1	43	4	7	3	3	1	.75	5	.241	.286	.297
5 Min. YEARS		537	1834	494	84	10	12	634	229	191	96	2	262	27	42	23	42	32	.57	26	.269	.312	.346

John Ambrose

Pitches: Right **Bats:** Right **Pos:** RP-16; SP-1 **Ht:** 6'5" **Wt:** 180 **Born:** 11/1/74 **Age:** 27

Year Team	Lg Org	G	GS	CG	GF	IP	BFP	H	R	ER	HR	SH	SF	HB	TBB	IBB	SO	WP	Bk	W	L	Pct.	ShO	Sv	ERA
1994 White Sox	R CWS	11	10	1	0	46.2	195	34	21	19	4	1	2	6	24	0	43	4	3	1	2	.333	0	0	3.66
Hickory	A CWS	3	1	0	1	12.2	58	16	11	10	1	0	0	0	6	0	7	0	0	1	1	.500	0	1	7.11
1995 Hickory	A CWS	14	14	0	0	73	314	65	41	32	6	2	3	3	35	0	49	9	2	4	8	.333	0	0	3.95
South Bend	A CWS	3	3	1	0	16.2	77	18	13	10	2	1	0	0	10	0	15	2	1	1	1	.500	0	0	5.40
1997 Winston-Sal	A+ CWS	27	27	1	0	149.2	688	136	102	91	17	5	9	8	117	2	137	16	5	8	13	.381	1	0	5.47
1998 Birmingham	AA CWS	31	22	0	3	140.2	641	156	90	81	18	2	4	13	69	2	103	14	2	9	12	.429	0	0	5.18
1999 Arkansas	AA StL	34	16	0	17	106.2	483	108	65	56	11	6	6	5	68	0	78	10	0	4	12	.250	0	9	4.73

		HOW MUCH HE PITCHED						WHAT HE GAVE UP												THE RESULTS					
Year Team	Lg Org	G	GS	CG	GF	IP	BFP	H	R	ER	HR	SH	SF	HB	TBB	IBB	SO	WP	Bk	W	L	Pct.	ShO	Sv	ERA
2000 Arkansas	AA StL	45	0	0	28	49	226	48	31	23	3	2	1	3	32	3	49	8	0	3	4	.429	0	15	4.22
Memphis	AAA StL	13	0	0	3	19.2	97	24	12	12	1	0	3	0	20	0	8	4	0	1	1	.500	0	1	5.49
2001 Sarasota	A+ Bos	10	1	0	2	15.2	67	13	8	5	0	1	0	3	5	0	18	1	0	0	1	.000	0	0	2.87
Pawtucket	AAA Bos	2	0	0	0	3.1	21	7	6	4	0	0	0	0	3	0	0	1	0	0	0	—	0	0	10.80
Trenton	AA Bos	5	0	0	0	6.1	35	12	10	10	1	1	0	0	5	0	7	1	1	0	0	—	0	0	14.21
7 Min. YEARS		198	94	3	54	640	2902	637	410	353	64	21	28	41	394	7	514	70	13	32	55	.368	1	27	4.96

Jesus Ametller

Bats: Left Throws: Right Pos: 2B-4; PH-4   Ht: 5'8" Wt: 175 Born: 7/25/74 Age: 27

		BATTING														BASERUNNING				PERCENTAGES		
Year Team	Lg Org	G	AB	H	2B	3B	HR	TB	R	RBI	TBB	IBB	SO	HBP	SH	SF	SB	CS	SB%	GDP	Avg	OBP	SLG
1997 Pr William	A+ StL	60	215	58	10	2	3	81	26	26	15	1	12	0	4	0	3	1	.75	5	.270	.317	.377
1998 Pr William	A+ StL	101	358	112	29	0	1	144	52	38	2	0	29	3	6	5	4	6	.40	8	.313	.318	.402
1999 Arkansas	AA StL	116	397	122	26	2	10	182	53	53	5	0	21	4	1	5	2	1	.67	13	.307	.319	.458
Memphis	AAA StL	2	4	1	0	0	0	1	0	0	0	0	0	0	0	0	0	0	—	0	.250	.250	.250
2000 Memphis	AAA StL	10	28	6	2	0	0	8	2	2	0	0	3	0	0	1	0	1	.00	0	.214	.207	.286
Arkansas	AA StL	5	16	4	1	0	0	5	1	2	0	0	0	0	0	0	0	0	—	2	.250	.250	.313
2001 New Haven	AA StL	3	3	0	0	0	0	0	0	0	0	0	1	0	0	0	0	0	—	0	.000	.000	.000
Elmira	IND —	4	14	2	1	0	0	3	1	2	0	0	1	0	1	0	0	0	—	0	.143	.143	.214
5 Min. YEARS		301	1035	305	69	4	14	424	135	123	22	1	68	7	12	11	9	9	.50	28	.295	.311	.410

Alfredo Amezaga

Bats: Both Throws: Right Pos: SS-119   Ht: 5'10" Wt: 165 Born: 1/16/78 Age: 24

		BATTING														BASERUNNING				PERCENTAGES		
Year Team	Lg Org	G	AB	H	2B	3B	HR	TB	R	RBI	TBB	IBB	SO	HBP	SH	SF	SB	CS	SB%	GDP	Avg	OBP	SLG
1999 Butte	R+ Ana	8	34	10	2	0	0	12	11	5	5	0	5	1	0	0	6	2	.75	0	.294	.400	.353
Boise	A- Ana	48	205	66	6	4	2	86	52	29	23	2	29	5	3	1	14	3	.82	7	.322	.402	.420
2000 Lk Elsinore	A+ Ana	108	420	117	13	4	4	150	90	44	63	0	70	4	5	1	73	21	.78	4	.279	.374	.357
2001 Arkansas	AA Ana	70	285	89	10	5	4	121	50	21	22	1	55	4	3	0	24	15	.62	0	.312	.370	.425
Salt Lake	AAA Ana	49	200	50	5	4	1	66	28	16	14	1	45	3	2	1	9	6	.60	2	.250	.307	.330
3 Min. YEARS		283	1144	332	36	17	11	435	231	115	127	4	204	17	13	7	126	47	.73	13	.290	.368	.380

Adan Amezcua

Bats: Right Throws: Right Pos: C-27; DH-11   Ht: 6'1" Wt: 195 Born: 3/9/74 Age: 28

		BATTING														BASERUNNING				PERCENTAGES		
Year Team	Lg Org	G	AB	H	2B	3B	HR	TB	R	RBI	TBB	IBB	SO	HBP	SH	SF	SB	CS	SB%	GDP	Avg	OBP	SLG
1993 Astros	R Hou	48	145	43	13	3	0	62	14	24	12	0	19	1	0	1	1	0	1.00	4	.297	.352	.428
1994 Auburn	A- Hou	32	99	26	9	0	0	35	12	9	4	0	21	4	1	1	0	1	.00	2	.263	.315	.354
1995 Quad City	A Hou	46	142	35	8	2	4	59	13	12	5	0	28	1	1	1	2	3	.40	4	.246	.275	.415
1996 Kissimmee	A+ Hou	88	264	75	16	1	0	93	24	29	25	0	42	3	8	3	0	1	.00	2	.284	.349	.352
1997 Kissimmee	A+ Hou	9	20	8	3	0	0	11	3	5	3	1	3	0	0	0	1	1	.50	3	.400	.458	.550
1998 Jackson	AA Hou	23	73	15	2	0	2	23	6	6	3	0	11	0	0	0	1	0	1.00	0	.205	.237	.315
Kissimmee	A+ Hou	72	262	72	19	1	8	117	40	35	22	0	43	7	1	2	2	0	1.00	0	.275	.345	.447
2000 Bowie	AA Bal	17	51	16	4	0	1	23	4	6	3	0	9	0	0	0	1	0	1.00	0	.314	.352	.451
Rochester	AAA Bal	38	132	31	5	1	1	41	9	14	14	0	25	0	1	1	0	0	—	7	.235	.306	.311
2001 Bowie	AA Bal	38	135	29	7	2	4	52	19	21	9	1	25	4	0	1	0	0	—	6	.215	.282	.385
8 Min. YEARS		411	1323	350	86	10	20	516	144	161	100	2	226	20	12	11	7	6	.54	36	.265	.323	.390

Mike Amrhein

Bats: Right Throws: Right Pos: C-45; 1B-40; PH-8; DH-5; OF-2   Ht: 6'2" Wt: 215 Born: 6/14/75 Age: 27

		BATTING														BASERUNNING				PERCENTAGES		
Year Team	Lg Org	G	AB	H	2B	3B	HR	TB	R	RBI	TBB	IBB	SO	HBP	SH	SF	SB	CS	SB%	GDP	Avg	OBP	SLG
1997 Williamsprt	A- ChC	62	237	66	11	1	1	82	17	31	10	1	19	2	0	4	0	2	.00	11	.278	.308	.346
1998 Rockford	A ChC	121	457	145	34	1	9	208	61	87	30	1	47	8	3	3	7	4	.64	20	.317	.367	.455
1999 Daytona	A+ ChC	127	449	125	27	1	10	184	55	58	31	1	67	13	3	6	1	1	.50	14	.278	.339	.410
2000 West Tenn	AA ChC	104	352	100	18	0	9	145	45	49	35	2	40	14	2	2	0	3	.00	19	.284	.370	.412
2001 West Tenn	AA ChC	96	311	75	14	0	4	101	30	33	23	0	45	10	1	4	0	1	.00	11	.241	.310	.325
5 Min. YEARS		510	1806	511	104	3	33	720	208	258	129	5	218	47	9	19	8	11	.42	66	.283	.343	.399

Bryan Anderson

Bats: Right Throws: Right Pos: OF-39; 3B-27; SS-10; PR-7; 2B-6; PH-2; DH-1; P-1   Ht: 6'2" Wt: 170 Born: 7/10/78 Age: 23

		BATTING														BASERUNNING				PERCENTAGES		
Year Team	Lg Org	G	AB	H	2B	3B	HR	TB	R	RBI	TBB	IBB	SO	HBP	SH	SF	SB	CS	SB%	GDP	Avg	OBP	SLG
2000 Billings	R+ Cin	58	218	56	4	3	3	75	51	24	42	0	38	5	4	0	7	2	.78	5	.257	.389	.344
2001 Dayton	A Cin	80	270	61	14	4	1	86	33	26	13	0	66	3	4	1	9	2	.82	6	.226	.268	.319
Louisville	AAA Cin	6	21	7	0	0	0	7	3	0	1	0	6	0	0	0	1	0	1.00	0	.333	.364	.333
2 Min. YEARS		144	509	124	18	7	4	168	87	50	56	0	110	8	8	1	17	4	.81	11	.244	.328	.330

Ryan Anderson

Pitches: Left Bats: Left Pos: SP-0   Ht: 6'10" Wt: 215 Born: 7/12/79 Age: 22

		HOW MUCH HE PITCHED						WHAT HE GAVE UP												THE RESULTS					
Year Team	Lg Org	G	GS	CG	GF	IP	BFP	H	R	ER	HR	SH	SF	HB	TBB	IBB	SO	WP	Bk	W	L	Pct.	ShO	Sv	ERA
1998 Wisconsin	A Sea	22	22	0	0	111.1	474	86	47	40	4	3	3	10	67	0	152	4	3	6	5	.545	0	0	3.23
1999 New Haven	AA Sea	24	24	0	0	134	606	131	77	67	9	2	5	8	86	1	162	9	3	9	13	.409	0	0	4.50
2000 Tacoma	AAA Sea	20	20	1	0	104	439	83	51	46	8	0	1	3	55	0	146	7	3	5	8	.385	1	0	3.98
2001	Sea							DNP—Shoulder Injury																	
3 Min. YEARS		66	66	1	0	349.1	1519	300	175	153	21	5	9	21	208	1	460	20	9	20	26	.435	1	0	3.94

Jeff Andra

Pitches: Left **Bats:** Left **Pos:** SP-24; RP-3   **Ht:** 6'5" **Wt:** 210 **Born:** 9/9/75 **Age:** 26

			HOW MUCH HE PITCHED						WHAT HE GAVE UP								THE RESULTS					
Year Team	Lg Org	G	GS	CG	GF	IP	BFP	H	R	ER	HR	SH	SF	HB	TBB	IBB	SO	WP	Bk	W	L	Pct.	ShO	Sv	ERA
1997 Salem-Keizr	A- SF	8	8	0	0	44.1	185	39	21	10	3	1	1	1	10	0	58	4	0	3	1	.750	0	0	2.03
San Jose	A+ SF	6	6	0	0	29.2	142	36	25	23	2	3	0	4	11	0	29	2	2	1	4	.200	0	0	6.98
1998 San Jose	A+ SF	15	15	2	0	86.2	358	75	36	32	2	4	0	2	28	0	80	5	1	8	2	.800	1	0	3.32
1999 San Jose	A+ SF	13	7	0	0	50	217	54	28	25	3	2	2	0	19	1	54	3	1	4	2	.667	0	0	4.50
2000 Shreveport	AA SF	17	17	0	0	91.1	403	106	51	39	6	7	5	1	35	2	64	1	0	6	6	.500	0	0	3.84
Fresno	AAA SF	7	7	0	0	33	171	49	35	32	9	1	1	1	24	0	16	1	0	0	3	.000	0	0	8.73
2001 Shreveport	AA SF	18	18	0	0	98	437	116	59	51	11	4	3	1	32	0	57	5	0	3	9	.250	0	0	4.68
Fresno	AAA SF	9	6	0	0	36.2	169	50	32	26	8	2	3	1	14	0	22	4	0	1	3	.250	0	0	6.38
5 Min. YEARS		93	84	2	0	469.2	2082	525	287	238	44	24	15	11	173	3	380	25	4	26	30	.464	1	0	4.56

Alex Andreopoulos

Bats: Left **Throws:** Right **Pos:** C-34; DH-2; PH-2; PR-1   **Ht:** 5'10" **Wt:** 190 **Born:** 8/19/72 **Age:** 29

			BATTING													BASERUNNING				PERCENTAGES		
Year Team	Lg Org	G	AB	H	2B	3B	HR	TB	R	RBI	TBB	IBB	SO	HBP	SH	SF	SB	CS	SB%	GDP	Avg	OBP	SLG
1995 Helena	R+ Mil	3	9	5	0	0	2	11	3	7	4	0	0	0	0	0	0	0	—	0	.556	.692	1.222
Beloit	A Mil	60	163	49	0	0	1	61	32	20	35	1	16	3	3	1	5	3	.63	2	.301	.431	.374
1996 Stockton	A+ Mil	87	291	88	17	2	5	124	52	41	40	2	33	5	2	4	10	3	.77	5	.302	.391	.426
1997 El Paso	AA Mil	7	26	4	1	0	0	5	1	3	1	0	2	0	0	0	0	0	—	1	.154	.185	.192
Tucson	AAA Mil	10	15	6	1	0	0	7	3	1	0	0	1	0	0	0	0	0	—	0	.400	.400	.467
1998 El Paso	AA Mil	113	377	121	35	1	10	188	72	93	54	4	31	9	2	5	2	3	.40	9	.321	.413	.499
1999 Louisville	AAA Mil	71	201	53	8	0	5	76	19	31	25	4	21	2	3	1	1	0	1.00	5	.264	.349	.378
2000 Huntsville	AA Mil	5	10	2	1	0	0	3	1	2	1	0	2	0	0	1	0	0	—	0	.200	.250	.300
Aberdeen	IND —	100	350	95	20	1	10	147	51	52	50	3	34	5	0	2	8	2	.80	11	.271	.369	.420
2001 Buffalo	AAA Cle	37	102	22	5	0	3	36	14	9	13	0	16	1	2	0	1	0	1.00	3	.216	.310	.353
7 Min. YEARS		493	1544	445	97	4	36	658	248	259	223	14	156	25	12	14	27	11	.71	36	.288	.384	.426

Clayton Andrews

Pitches: Left **Bats:** Right **Pos:** SP-14   **Ht:** 6'0" **Wt:** 180 **Born:** 5/15/78 **Age:** 24

			HOW MUCH HE PITCHED						WHAT HE GAVE UP								THE RESULTS					
Year Team	Lg Org	G	GS	CG	GF	IP	BFP	H	R	ER	HR	SH	SF	HB	TBB	IBB	SO	WP	Bk	W	L	Pct.	ShO	Sv	ERA
1996 Medcine Hat	R+ Tor	8	4	0	1	25.2	120	37	23	21	4	0	3	1	10	0	14	1	0	2	4	.333	0	0	7.36
1997 Hagerstown	A Tor	28	15	0	7	114.2	512	120	70	58	8	4	4	5	47	1	112	4	2	7	7	.500	0	0	4.55
1998 Hagerstown	A Tor	27	26	2	0	162	635	112	59	41	7	4	5	6	46	0	193	7	2	10	7	.588	1	0	2.28
1999 Knoxville	AA Tor	25	25	0	0	132.2	593	143	85	58	13	8	3	4	69	0	93	4	2	10	8	.556	0	0	3.93
Syracuse	AAA Tor	3	3	0	0	15	65	10	14	13	5	0	1	0	13	0	9	1	0	0	1	.000	0	0	7.80
2000 Syracuse	AAA Tor	19	18	0	0	102.2	449	114	56	55	8	2	3	2	42	0	59	1	2	8	7	.533	0	0	4.82
2001 Louisville	AAA Cin	8	8	0	0	43	196	57	28	23	7	2	0	1	13	0	19	0	0	2	2	.500	0	0	4.81
Chattanooga	AA Cin	6	6	0	0	36	163	41	27	24	4	1	3	0	16	0	19	0	0	1	3	.250	0	0	6.00
2000 Toronto	AL	8	2	0	1	20.2	102	34	23	23	6	1	1	0	9	0	12	0	1	1	2	.333	0	0	10.02
6 Min. YEARS		124	105	2	8	631.2	2733	634	362	293	56	21	22	19	256	1	518	18	8	40	39	.506	1	0	4.17

Jeff Andrews

Pitches: Right **Bats:** Right **Pos:** RP-9   **Ht:** 6'3" **Wt:** 190 **Born:** 9/1/74 **Age:** 27

			HOW MUCH HE PITCHED						WHAT HE GAVE UP								THE RESULTS					
Year Team	Lg Org	G	GS	CG	GF	IP	BFP	H	R	ER	HR	SH	SF	HB	TBB	IBB	SO	WP	Bk	W	L	Pct.	ShO	Sv	ERA
1997 South Bend	A Ari	23	4	0	7	55	237	52	37	32	4	2	1	2	27	1	32	3	0	1	5	.167	0	0	5.24
Lethbridge	R+ Ari	9	9	1	0	49.2	219	55	27	18	3	1	0	3	10	0	50	3	0	3	3	.500	0	0	3.26
1998 South Bend	A Ari	20	17	0	2	123	524	130	62	39	4	4	3	2	28	2	68	7	1	3	8	.273	0	0	2.85
High Desert	A+ Ari	6	3	0	2	25	119	36	19	12	1	0	2	0	7	0	8	0	1	1	1	.500	0	0	4.32
1999 High Desert	A+ Ari	6	6	0	0	29.2	143	41	27	21	5	0	1	2	13	0	25	1	0	0	3	.000	0	0	6.37
El Paso	AA Ari	35	8	0	21	73	323	87	47	43	6	3	5	3	24	3	40	1	1	3	8	.273	0	7	5.30
2000 El Paso	AA Ari	21	8	0	4	60.2	292	88	54	51	12	2	4	3	30	0	35	3	1	3	4	.429	0	0	7.57
Tucson	AAA Ari	16	5	0	2	38	182	47	31	28	2	2	4	1	26	1	21	3	1	1	2	.333	0	0	6.63
2001 Harrisburg	AA Mon	9	0	0	2	11.1	53	15	7	7	3	0	0	1	4	0	13	0	0	1	0	1.000	0	0	5.56
5 Min. YEARS		145	60	1	40	465.1	2092	551	311	251	40	14	20	17	169	7	292	21	4	16	34	.320	0	7	4.85

Shane Andrews

Bats: Right **Throws:** Right **Pos:** 1B-46; 3B-16; PH-8   **Ht:** 6'1" **Wt:** 220 **Born:** 8/28/71 **Age:** 30

			BATTING													BASERUNNING				PERCENTAGES		
Year Team	Lg Org	G	AB	H	2B	3B	HR	TB	R	RBI	TBB	IBB	SO	HBP	SH	SF	SB	CS	SB%	GDP	Avg	OBP	SLG
1990 Expos	R Mon	56	190	45	7	1	3	63	31	24	29	0	46	3	1	1	10	4	.71	7	.237	.345	.332
1991 Sumter	A Mon	105	356	74	16	7	11	137	46	49	65	2	132	3	0	5	5	4	.56	8	.208	.335	.385
1992 Albany	A Mon	136	453	104	18	1	25	199	76	87	107	4	174	7	0	3	8	3	.73	4	.230	.382	.439
1993 Harrisburg	AA Mon	124	442	115	29	1	18	200	77	70	64	2	118	1	1	4	10	6	.63	8	.260	.352	.452
1994 Ottawa	AAA Mon	137	460	117	25	2	16	194	79	85	80	5	126	5	0	5	6	5	.55	11	.254	.367	.422
1997 Ottawa	AAA Mon	3	12	3	0	0	1	6	3	1	1	0	0	0	0	0	0	0	—	1	.250	.308	.500
Wst Plm Bch	A+ Mon	5	17	3	2	0	1	8	2	5	2	0	7	0	0	0	0	1	.00	0	.176	.250	.471
1999 Ottawa	AAA Mon	2	8	2	0	0	1	5	1	4	0	0	2	0	0	0	0	0	—	1	.250	.250	.625
2000 Iowa	AAA ChC	15	38	7	3	0	2	16	5	7	7	1	10	0	0	0	0	0	—	3	.184	.304	.421
2001 Memphis	AAA StL	62	193	42	9	1	9	80	30	31	33	2	63	3	0	1	2	0	1.00	3	.218	.339	.415
1995 Montreal	NL	84	220	47	10	1	8	83	27	31	17	2	68	1	1	2	1	1	.50	4	.214	.271	.377
1996 Montreal	NL	127	375	85	15	2	19	161	43	64	35	8	119	2	0	2	3	1	.75	2	.227	.295	.429
1997 Montreal	NL	18	64	13	3	0	4	28	10	9	3	0	20	0	0	0	0	0	—	1	.203	.232	.438
1998 Montreal	NL	150	492	117	30	1	25	224	48	69	58	3	137	0	0	2	0	6	.14	10	.238	.314	.455
1999 Montreal	NL	98	281	51	8	0	11	92	28	37	43	2	88	0	0	1	0	1	1.00	10	.181	.287	.327
Chicago	NL	19	67	17	4	0	5	36	13	14	7	1	21	1	0	0	1	0	1.00	0	.254	.329	.537
2000 Chicago	NL	66	192	44	5	0	14	91	25	39	27	1	59	2	0	1	1	1	.50	9	.229	.329	.474
9 Min. YEARS		645	2169	512	109	13	87	908	350	363	388	16	678	22	2	16	41	23	.64	45	.236	.355	.419
6 Maj. YEARS		562	1691	374	75	4	86	715	194	263	190	17	512	6	3	19	7	10	.41	35	.221	.299	.423

12

Ricardo Aramboles

Pitches: Right **Bats:** Right **Pos:** SP-20; RP-2   **Ht:** 6'2" **Wt:** 170 **Born:** 12/4/81 **Age:** 20

		HOW MUCH HE PITCHED						WHAT HE GAVE UP											THE RESULTS					
Year Team	Lg Org	G	GS	CG	GF	IP	BFP	H	R	ER	HR	SH	SF	HB	TBB	IBB	SO	WP	Bk	W	L	Pct.	ShO	Sv	ERA
1998 Yankees	R NYY	10	9	0	0	40	160	33	14	13	0	2	1	1	13	0	44	2	2	2	1	.667	0	0	2.93
Oneonta	A- NYY	1	1	0	0	6	23	4	2	1	1	0	0	1	1	0	8	0	0	1	0	1.000	0	0	1.50
1999 Yankees	R NYY	9	7	0	2	34.2	149	35	18	15	1	3	4	1	14	0	42	6	0	2	3	.400	0	0	3.89
Greensboro	A NYY	6	6	1	0	34.2	136	25	9	9	1	1	1	0	12	0	34	5	0	1	2	.333	0	0	2.34
2000 Greensboro	A NYY	25	25	2	0	137.2	603	150	81	66	12	3	1	5	47	0	150	9	0	5	13	.278	0	0	4.31
2001 Columbus	AAA NYY	4	4	0	0	23.2	102	26	11	8	2	3	3	0	4	0	14	0	0	1	3	.250	0	0	3.04
Tampa	A+ NYY	12	11	0	0	68.2	289	72	37	31	5	1	1	2	19	0	59	3	0	7	2	.778	0	0	4.06
Chattanooga	AA Cin	2	1	0	1	9	42	12	8	8	1	1	1	3	0	0	5	0	0	0	2	.000	0	0	8.00
Dayton	A Cin	4	4	0	0	19.2	81	23	8	8	2	0	0	0	4	0	9	1	0	1	2	.333	0	0	3.66
4 Min. YEARS		73	68	3	3	374	1585	380	188	159	25	14	12	13	114	0	365	26	2	20	28	.417	0	0	3.83

Danny Ardoin

Bats: Right **Throws:** Right **Pos:** C-81; DH-6; PH-2; OF-1   **Ht:** 6'0" **Wt:** 218 **Born:** 7/8/74 **Age:** 27

		BATTING															BASERUNNING				PERCENTAGES		
Year Team	Lg Org	G	AB	H	2B	3B	HR	TB	R	RBI	TBB	IBB	SO	HBP	SH	SF	SB	CS	SB%	GDP	Avg	OBP	SLG
1995 Sou Oregon	A- Oak	58	175	41	9	1	2	58	28	23	31	0	50	9	5	4	2	1	.67	2	.234	.370	.331
1996 Modesto	A+ Oak	91	317	83	13	3	6	120	55	34	47	0	81	9	3	2	5	7	.42	9	.262	.371	.379
1997 Huntsville	AA Oak	57	208	48	10	1	4	72	26	23	17	0	38	3	0	2	2	3	.40	7	.231	.296	.346
Visalia	A+ Oak	43	145	34	7	1	3	52	16	19	21	0	39	4	1	0	1	.00	3	.234	.347	.359
1998 Huntsville	AA Oak	109	363	90	21	0	16	159	67	62	62	0	87	7	6	1	8	4	.67	10	.248	.367	.438
1999 Vancouver	AAA Oak	109	336	85	13	2	8	126	53	46	50	0	78	9	9	1	3	3	.50	12	.253	.364	.375
2000 Modesto	A+ Oak	4	10	3	1	0	0	4	1	2	0	0	4	1	0	0	0	0	—	0	.300	.364	.400
Sacramento	AAA Oak	67	234	65	16	1	6	101	42	34	34	3	72	8	3	2	6	0	1.00	5	.278	.385	.432
Salt Lake	AAA Min	3	9	2	0	0	0	2	1	0	3	0	4	0	0	0	0	0	—	0	.222	.417	.222
2001 Edmonton	AAA Min	88	302	77	18	1	5	112	37	37	22	1	81	1	2	4	2	6	.25	8	.255	.304	.371
2000 Minnesota	AL	15	32	4	1	0	1	8	4	5	8	0	10	0	0	0	0	0	—	0	.125	.300	.250
7 Min. YEARS		629	2099	528	108	10	50	806	326	280	287	4	534	51	29	16	28	25	.53	56	.252	.353	.384

Pablo Arias

Pitches: Right **Bats:** Right **Pos:** SP-25; RP-4   **Ht:** 6'2" **Wt:** 160 **Born:** 1/9/79 **Age:** 23

		HOW MUCH HE PITCHED						WHAT HE GAVE UP											THE RESULTS					
Year Team	Lg Org	G	GS	CG	GF	IP	BFP	H	R	ER	HR	SH	SF	HB	TBB	IBB	SO	WP	Bk	W	L	Pct.	ShO	Sv	ERA
1999 Tigers	R Det	12	12	1	0	65.2	282	57	31	22	2	1	2	8	22	1	60	2	0	3	2	.600	0	0	3.02
2000 Lakeland	A+ Det	5	5	0	0	27.2	120	26	21	18	2	0	5	3	13	0	21	1	1	2	1	.667	0	0	5.86
W Michigan	A Det	15	13	0	0	84	336	61	26	23	8	1	3	4	30	1	54	2	0	6	3	.667	0	0	2.46
2001 W Michigan	A Det	20	17	0	0	108	450	100	44	38	5	1	1	5	33	2	81	6	3	9	4	.692	0	0	3.17
Toledo	AAA Det	1	1	0	0	4.1	20	4	5	4	1	0	2	0	2	0	1	0	0	0	0	—	0	0	8.31
Lakeland	A+ Det	8	7	0	0	42.1	188	48	26	23	5	0	1	1	16	0	28	3	1	3	1	.750	0	0	4.89
3 Min. YEARS		61	55	1	0	332	1396	296	153	128	23	3	14	21	116	4	245	14	5	23	11	.676	0	0	3.47

Jamie Arnold

Pitches: Right **Bats:** Right **Pos:** RP-41; SP-3   **Ht:** 6'2" **Wt:** 188 **Born:** 3/24/74 **Age:** 28

		HOW MUCH HE PITCHED						WHAT HE GAVE UP											THE RESULTS					
Year Team	Lg Org	G	GS	CG	GF	IP	BFP	H	R	ER	HR	SH	SF	HB	TBB	IBB	SO	WP	Bk	W	L	Pct.	ShO	Sv	ERA
1992 Braves	R Atl	7	5	0	2	20	85	16	12	9	0	0	2	4	6	0	22	0	2	0	1	.000	0	0	4.05
1993 Macon	A Atl	27	27	1	0	164.1	692	142	67	57	5	3	4	16	56	0	124	13	2	8	9	.471	0	0	3.12
1994 Durham	A+ Atl	25	25	0	0	145	656	144	96	75	26	3	1	14	79	4	91	8	4	7	7	.500	0	0	4.66
1995 Durham	A+ Atl	15	14	1	0	80	347	86	42	35	5	4	1	9	21	0	44	4	0	4	8	.333	0	0	3.94
Greenville	AA Atl	10	10	0	0	56.2	266	76	42	40	8	0	2	7	25	1	19	6	0	1	5	.167	0	0	6.35
1996 Greenville	AA Atl	23	23	2	0	128	573	149	79	70	17	0	5	10	44	1	64	6	1	7	7	.500	0	0	4.92
1997 Braves	R Atl	5	5	0	0	19	74	13	6	6	1	0	0	6	6	0	21	0	0	1	0	1.000	0	0	2.84
Durham	A+ Atl	5	5	0	0	24.1	115	25	21	16	2	2	0	1	13	0	21	2	0	2	2	.500	0	0	5.92
Greenville	AA Atl	1	1	0	0	4.2	27	10	6	6	3	0	0	1	2	0	3	1	0	0	1	.000	0	0	11.57
1998 Greenville	AA Atl	32	6	0	7	83.1	387	93	51	41	12	2	1	3	46	2	48	12	0	1	4	.200	0	1	4.43
Richmond	AAA Atl	9	2	0	2	20.2	102	30	22	22	1	1	3	1	17	1	10	3	0	1	0	1.000	0	0	9.58
1999 Albuquerque	AAA LA	7	2	0	1	19.1	91	28	14	12	1	1	0	2	7	0	13	3	0	0	2	.000	0	0	5.59
2000 Albuquerque	AAA LA	20	13	0	1	92.1	415	94	62	52	5	3	1	6	54	0	47	3	0	4	7	.364	0	0	5.07
Iowa	AAA ChC	3	3	0	0	17.2	83	22	10	9	2	1	0	2	10	0	10	1	0	2	1	.667	0	0	4.58
2001 Fresno	AAA SF	44	3	0	23	76	361	96	58	50	13	3	3	10	36	0	56	5	0	1	4	.200	0	9	5.92
1999 Los Angeles	NL	36	3	0	18	69	313	81	50	42	6	3	0	6	34	2	26	3	0	2	4	.333	0	1	5.48
2000 Los Angeles	NL	2	0	0	2	6.2	30	4	3	3	0	0	1	1	5	0	3	1	0	0	0	—	0	0	4.05
Chicago	NL	12	4	0	3	32.2	151	34	28	24	1	2	3	3	19	0	13	1	0	0	3	.000	0	1	6.61
10 Min. YEARS		233	144	4	36	951.1	4274	1024	588	500	101	23	23	86	422	9	593	67	9	39	58	.402	0	11	4.73
2 Maj. YEARS		50	7	0	23	108.1	494	119	81	69	7	5	4	10	58	2	42	5	0	2	7	.222	0	2	5.73

Luis Arroyo

Pitches: Left **Bats:** Left **Pos:** RP-47   **Ht:** 6'0" **Wt:** 174 **Born:** 9/29/73 **Age:** 28

		HOW MUCH HE PITCHED						WHAT HE GAVE UP											THE RESULTS					
Year Team	Lg Org	G	GS	CG	GF	IP	BFP	H	R	ER	HR	SH	SF	HB	TBB	IBB	SO	WP	Bk	W	L	Pct.	ShO	Sv	ERA
1992 Padres	R SD	17	9	0	3	57.2	259	65	45	27	0	1	6	2	21	0	55	4	12	4	4	.500	0	0	4.21
1993 Waterloo	A SD	17	16	1	1	95.2	424	99	59	48	11	7	6	6	46	1	59	5	3	5	7	.417	0	0	4.52
1994 Springfield	A SD	16	16	1	0	99.2	434	86	50	38	6	5	2	1	47	4	76	4	4	8	2	.800	0	0	3.43
Rancho Cuca	A+ SD	10	10	0	0	54.1	243	62	33	29	6	1	1	3	30	0	34	2	0	3	4	.429	0	0	4.80
1995 Rancho Cuca	A+ SD	26	24	0	0	128.2	599	158	97	75	9	8	6	12	62	6	102	7	3	7	10	.412	0	0	5.25
1996 St. Lucie	A+ NYM	22	0	0	4	42	170	36	17	14	1	0	3	1	15	1	28	3	0	1	0	1.000	0	2	3.00
1997 Binghamton	AA NYM	7	0	0	1	14.2	60	14	6	5	2	2	1	0	6	0	9	0	1	0	0	—	0	0	3.07
St. Lucie	A+ NYM	36	2	0	11	56	231	37	21	13	2	3	1	3	23	2	57	1	3	3	3	.500	0	2	2.09

13

Year Team	Lg Org	HOW MUCH HE PITCHED						WHAT HE GAVE UP												THE RESULTS					
		G	GS	CG	GF	IP	BFP	H	R	ER	HR	SH	SF	HB	TBB	IBB	SO	WP	Bk	W	L	Pct.	ShO	Sv	ERA
1998 Norfolk	AAA NYM	8	0	0	5	8	41	11	7	6	1	0	1	1	7	0	7	0	0	0	1	.000	0	0	6.75
Binghamton	AA NYM	57	0	0	16	66.1	280	59	30	19	1	5	2	1	26	3	78	4	1	1	5	.167	0	3	2.58
1999 Knoxville	AA Tor	5	0	0	2	6.2	22	2	1	1	0	0	0	1	0	0	7	0	0	0	0	—	0	1	1.35
Syracuse	AAA Tor	9	0	0	3	12.2	65	18	13	12	1	1	1	0	9	1	10	1	1	0	1	.000	0	0	8.53
Portland	AA Fla	9	0	0	1	13.2	61	14	11	5	2	2	0	0	8	4	10	0	0	0	1	.000	0	1	3.29
Calgary	AAA Fla	22	0	0	8	33.1	157	42	33	24	6	2	2	3	17	0	26	0	1	2	1	.667	0	0	6.48
2000 Calgary	AAA Fla	7	0	0	2	15.2	71	16	11	10	3	1	2	0	8	0	9	0	1	1	1	.500	0	0	5.74
Portland	AA Fla	31	0	0	14	57	249	50	26	24	2	6	0	2	33	1	47	1	1	3	2	.600	0	0	3.79
2001 Trenton	AA Bos	7	0	0	2	13.2	81	28	17	14	1	1	0	1	10	1	10	2	0	0	1	.000	0	0	9.22
Somerset	IND —	40	0	0	12	60.2	246	53	27	17	2	1	1	3	22	1	52	3	0	8	0	1.000	0	5	2.52
10 Min. YEARS		346	77	2	85	836.1	3693	850	504	381	58	46	35	40	390	25	676	37	31	46	43	.517	0	12	4.10

J.D. Arteaga

Pitches: Left   **Bats:** Left   **Pos:** SP-21; RP-11   **Ht:** 6'3"   **Wt:** 227   **Born:** 8/2/74   **Age:** 27

Year Team	Lg Org	HOW MUCH HE PITCHED						WHAT HE GAVE UP												THE RESULTS					
		G	GS	CG	GF	IP	BFP	H	R	ER	HR	SH	SF	HB	TBB	IBB	SO	WP	Bk	W	L	Pct.	ShO	Sv	ERA
1997 Pittsfield	A- NYM	12	3	0	2	30.1	129	32	15	9	0	1	0	1	4	0	29	1	0	4	2	.667	0	0	2.67
Capital Cty	A NYM	1	1	0	0	6	20	3	0	0	0	0	0	0	0	0	4	0	0	1	0	1.000	0	0	0.00
1998 St. Lucie	A+ NYM	15	2	0	1	37.1	154	37	15	12	1	4	0	0	7	0	28	1	1	2	0	1.000	0	0	2.89
Binghamton	AA NYM	21	18	0	0	119	495	122	48	37	8	6	5	5	25	1	97	0	0	8	7	.533	0	0	2.80
1999 St. Lucie	A+ NYM	1	1	0	0	5	19	3	2	2	1	0	1	0	2	0	0	0	0	0	1	.000	0	0	3.60
Mets	R NYM	2	1	0	0	4	15	4	3	3	1	0	0	0	0	0	3	0	0	0	0	—	0	0	6.75
Binghamton	AA NYM	11	3	0	1	28.1	133	32	21	18	3	0	2	2	14	0	24	0	0	3	1	.750	0	0	5.72
2000 Norfolk	AAA NYM	1	1	0	0	5.2	23	4	1	1	0	0	0	0	2	0	1	0	0	1	0	1.000	0	0	1.59
Binghamton	AA NYM	34	14	2	2	112.1	490	125	60	43	6	7	5	6	25	0	76	1	0	10	7	.588	1	1	3.45
2001 New Orleans	AAA Hou	32	21	1	4	138	578	143	60	47	11	5	1	9	27	2	90	4	0	8	6	.571	0	1	3.07
5 Min. YEARS		130	65	3	10	486	2056	505	225	172	31	23	14	23	106	3	352	9	1	37	24	.607	1	2	3.19

Shane Arthurs

Pitches: Right   **Bats:** Right   **Pos:** RP-30; SP-3   **Ht:** 6'5"   **Wt:** 185   **Born:** 8/30/79   **Age:** 22

Year Team	Lg Org	HOW MUCH HE PITCHED						WHAT HE GAVE UP												THE RESULTS					
		G	GS	CG	GF	IP	BFP	H	R	ER	HR	SH	SF	HB	TBB	IBB	SO	WP	Bk	W	L	Pct.	ShO	Sv	ERA
1997 Expos	R Mon	8	7	0	0	25.2	128	37	31	28	1	0	3	2	14	0	12	1	1	0	3	.000	0	0	9.82
1998 Vermont	A- Mon	16	13	1	0	76.1	334	81	41	32	4	5	2	7	27	0	43	10	0	4	4	.500	0	0	3.77
1999 Cape Fear	A Mon	25	21	2	2	136.1	596	144	77	63	8	7	5	7	52	1	87	10	0	7	8	.467	0	0	4.16
2000 Cape Fear	A Mon	14	14	0	0	70.1	321	88	40	33	5	1	2	6	26	0	40	6	0	4	3	.571	0	0	4.22
2001 Jupiter	A+ Mon	28	3	0	7	56	261	69	29	22	1	2	2	6	19	0	33	6	2	2	0	1.000	0	1	3.54
Harrisburg	AA Mon	5	0	0	1	5.1	27	7	3	1	0	0	1	2	2	0	5	0	0	0	0	—	0	0	1.69
5 Min. YEARS		96	58	3	10	370	1667	426	221	179	19	15	15	30	140	1	220	33	3	17	18	.486	0	1	4.35

Kirk Asche

Bats: Right   **Throws:** Right   **Pos:** OF-119; PH-2; DH-1   **Ht:** 6'2"   **Wt:** 195   **Born:** 7/10/77   **Age:** 24

Year Team	Lg Org	BATTING															BASERUNNING				PERCENTAGES		
		G	AB	H	2B	3B	HR	TB	R	RBI	TBB	IBB	SO	HBP	SH	SF	SB	CS	SB%	GDP	Avg	OBP	SLG
1999 Sou Oregon	A- Oak	66	260	75	14	3	17	146	53	67	34	3	56	6	0	2	10	0	1.00	7	.288	.349	.562
2000 Visalia	A+ Oak	118	421	104	30	4	18	196	65	63	66	3	128	4	1	2	17	8	.68	4	.247	.353	.466
2001 Visalia	A+ Oak	105	405	108	24	2	21	199	64	89	33	2	111	12	0	7	10	6	.63	8	.267	.335	.491
Midland	AA Oak	16	56	12	2	0	3	23	9	5	9	0	16	1	0	0	0	0	—	0	.214	.333	.411
3 Min. YEARS		305	1142	299	70	9	59	564	191	224	142	8	311	23	1	11	37	14	.73	19	.262	.352	.494

Chris Ashby

Bats: Right   **Throws:** Right   **Pos:** OF-85; DH-9; PH-3   **Ht:** 6'3"   **Wt:** 196   **Born:** 12/15/74   **Age:** 27

Year Team	Lg Org	BATTING															BASERUNNING				PERCENTAGES		
		G	AB	H	2B	3B	HR	TB	R	RBI	TBB	IBB	SO	HBP	SH	SF	SB	CS	SB%	GDP	Avg	OBP	SLG
1993 Yankees	R NYY	49	175	37	12	0	0	49	24	23	32	0	45	6	0	2	5	3	.63	6	.211	.349	.280
Greensboro	A NYY	1	4	3	0	0	0	3	2	0	0	0	0	1	0	0	0	0	—	0	.750	.800	.750
1994 Yankees	R NYY	45	163	55	8	1	5	80	28	38	21	0	20	1	1	3	2	0	1.00	4	.337	.410	.491
Greensboro	A NYY	6	16	2	1	0	0	3	0	2	2	0	6	0	0	0	0	0	—	1	.125	.222	.188
1995 Greensboro	A NYY	88	288	79	23	1	9	131	45	45	61	2	68	6	2	2	3	3	.50	9	.274	.409	.455
1996 Tampa	A+ NYY	100	325	80	28	0	6	126	55	46	71	1	78	5	1	1	16	4	.80	5	.246	.388	.388
1997 Norwich	AA NYY	136	457	114	20	1	24	208	92	82	80	2	95	6	0	3	10	7	.59	14	.249	.366	.455
1998 Columbus	AAA NYY	5	11	1	0	0	0	1	0	1	3	0	6	0	0	0	0	0	—	0	.091	.286	.091
Norwich	AA NYY	126	438	125	24	0	11	182	65	53	65	3	99	7	0	1	17	3	.85	12	.285	.383	.416
1999 Norwich	AA NYY	29	108	27	5	1	3	43	11	16	11	0	20	3	0	2	3	4	.43	3	.250	.331	.398
Columbus	AAA NYY	70	206	55	13	1	9	97	46	32	21	0	39	2	1	0	6	3	.67	5	.267	.341	.471
2000 Albuquerque	AAA LA	134	465	138	34	3	7	199	98	59	55	1	74	2	1	1	16	11	.59	10	.297	.373	.428
2001 Charlotte	AAA CWS	62	197	45	8	1	2	61	21	12	16	0	39	0	2	0	2	2	.50	8	.228	.286	.310
Oklahoma	AAA Tex	33	121	28	7	0	2	41	11	16	12	2	24	1	0	2	2	0	.00	4	.231	.301	.339
9 Min. YEARS		884	2974	789	183	9	78	1224	498	425	450	11	613	40	8	20	80	42	.66	81	.265	.367	.412

Scott Atchison

Pitches: Right   **Bats:** Right   **Pos:** SP-24   **Ht:** 6'2"   **Wt:** 180   **Born:** 3/29/76   **Age:** 26

Year Team	Lg Org	HOW MUCH HE PITCHED						WHAT HE GAVE UP												THE RESULTS					
		G	GS	CG	GF	IP	BFP	H	R	ER	HR	SH	SF	HB	TBB	IBB	SO	WP	Bk	W	L	Pct.	ShO	Sv	ERA
1999 Wisconsin	A Sea	15	13	0	0	81.2	326	67	34	31	4	2	2	3	25	1	85	4	1	4	5	.444	0	0	3.42
2000 Tacoma	AAA Sea	5	5	0	0	26	103	22	11	11	3	0	0	0	6	0	18	0	0	1	1	.500	0	0	3.81
Lancaster	A+ Sea	18	18	1	0	97.2	436	117	58	40	10	2	4	4	21	0	77	2	0	5	5	.500	0	0	3.69
2001 San Antonio	AA Sea	24	24	1	0	136	596	171	84	64	11	8	5	12	28	0	83	6	0	9	10	.474	0	0	4.24
3 Min. YEARS		62	60	2	0	341.1	1461	377	187	146	28	12	11	19	80	1	263	12	1	19	21	.475	0	0	3.85

Rob Averette

Pitches: Right **Bats:** Right **Pos:** SP-27   **Ht:** 6'2" **Wt:** 195 **Born:** 9/30/76 **Age:** 25

			HOW MUCH HE PITCHED						WHAT HE GAVE UP									THE RESULTS					
Year Team	Lg Org	G	GS	CG	GF	IP	BFP	H	R	ER	HR	SH	SF	HB	TBB	IBB	SO	WP	Bk	W	L	Pct.	ShO	Sv	ERA
1997 Billings	R+ Cin	2	1	0	1	2.2	11	3	0	0	0	0	0	0	1	1	3	0	0	0	0	—	0	0	0.00
Chston-WV	A Cin	11	3	0	2	26.1	131	42	28	23	3	3	1	0	12	0	20	2	0	2	2	.500	0	1	7.86
1998 Chston-WV	A Cin	14	14	3	0	84	355	84	38	26	2	6	3	2	26	0	68	4	1	5	4	.556	0	0	2.79
Chattanooga	AA Cin	14	14	0	0	81	355	97	54	46	6	2	3	3	36	2	32	2	0	5	8	.385	0	0	5.11
1999 Rockford	A Cin	19	19	2	0	125.2	521	117	54	36	2	4	3	4	40	3	98	9	0	9	5	.643	2	0	2.58
Chattanooga	AA Cin	6	6	1	0	36.1	164	42	22	21	1	0	1	2	19	0	15	0	0	2	1	.667	0	0	5.20
2000 Louisville	AAA Cin	2	2	0	0	9.2	49	9	10	9	1	1	1	0	10	0	4	0	0	0	1	.000	0	0	8.38
Chattanooga	AA Cin	19	19	5	0	136.1	555	126	51	37	6	2	1	4	28	3	87	7	1	12	6	.667	2	0	2.44
Carolina	AA Col	5	5	0	0	31	131	25	12	11	3	1	0	1	10	0	29	2	0	1	3	.250	0	0	3.19
2001 Colo Sprngs	AAA Col	27	27	0	0	166.1	741	204	131	113	29	4	2	5	48	2	125	11	1	6	14	.300	0	0	6.11
5 Min. YEARS		119	110	11	3	699.1	3013	749	397	322	53	23	15	21	230	11	481	37	3	42	44	.488	4	1	4.14

Julio Ayala

Pitches: Left **Bats:** Left **Pos:** RP-4   **Ht:** 6'2" **Wt:** 203 **Born:** 4/20/75 **Age:** 27

			HOW MUCH HE PITCHED						WHAT HE GAVE UP									THE RESULTS					
Year Team	Lg Org	G	GS	CG	GF	IP	BFP	H	R	ER	HR	SH	SF	HB	TBB	IBB	SO	WP	Bk	W	L	Pct.	ShO	Sv	ERA
1996 Everett	A- Sea	12	6	0	2	44	185	43	20	17	2	2	1	4	10	0	28	2	2	1	3	.250	0	0	3.48
1997 Wisconsin	A Sea	36	9	0	13	103	443	114	47	42	4	2	1	4	30	4	81	7	2	11	3	.786	0	0	3.67
1998 Lancaster	A+ Sea	25	25	1	0	139.2	634	166	91	69	14	5	8	1	44	1	129	15	2	10	7	.588	1	0	4.45
2000 Lancaster	A+ Sea	14	3	0	1	26.1	124	34	19	15	4	0	0	4	5	0	20	2	0	4	1	.800	0	0	5.13
New Haven	AA Sea	11	11	1	0	63.1	259	55	21	19	4	2	3	0	23	0	41	3	0	7	1	.875	0	0	2.70
2001 Wisconsin	A Sea	1	0	0	1	2	7	1	1	1	1	0	0	0	0	0	0	0	0	0	0	—	0	0	4.50
San Antonio	AA Sea	3	0	0	2	5.2	29	7	4	4	2	0	0	1	2	0	4	0	0	0	0	—	0	0	6.35
5 Min. YEARS		102	54	2	19	384	1681	420	203	167	31	11	13	14	114	5	303	29	6	33	15	.688	1	0	3.91

Mike Ayers

Pitches: Left **Bats:** Left **Pos:** RP-12   **Ht:** 5'10" **Wt:** 206 **Born:** 12/23/73 **Age:** 28

			HOW MUCH HE PITCHED						WHAT HE GAVE UP									THE RESULTS					
Year Team	Lg Org	G	GS	CG	GF	IP	BFP	H	R	ER	HR	SH	SF	HB	TBB	IBB	SO	WP	Bk	W	L	Pct.	ShO	Sv	ERA
1996 Augusta	A Pit	27	0	0	7	30.1	134	33	21	14	1	2	2	0	8	0	31	4	0	3	0	1.000	0	0	4.15
1997 Lynchburg	A+ Pit	39	0	0	13	63	288	54	38	35	8	4	2	6	44	6	62	4	0	5	4	.556	0	4	5.00
1998 Augusta	A Pit	4	0	0	1	5.2	37	11	13	11	0	0	1	0	6	1	6	3	0	0	1	.000	0	0	17.47
Lynchburg	A+ Pit	34	0	0	15	40.1	188	53	36	34	5	1	2	5	17	0	31	2	1	3	3	.500	0	7	7.59
1999 Lynchburg	A+ Pit	27	0	0	14	36.2	153	34	13	11	1	2	2	1	16	0	28	4	0	1	2	.333	0	2	2.70
Altoona	AA Pit	11	0	0	3	17	70	10	4	3	1	1	1	0	11	0	16	5	0	0	0	—	0	0	1.59
2000 Altoona	AA Pit	38	0	0	12	58.1	250	47	30	21	2	5	1	1	29	2	49	4	0	3	2	.600	0	1	3.24
Nashville	AAA Pit	11	0	0	6	15.2	74	22	11	10	5	0	0	0	6	0	11	1	0	0	0	—	0	0	5.74
2001 Nashville	AAA Pit	5	0	0	4	4	20	5	4	4	0	1	1	0	5	1	3	0	0	1	1	.500	0	0	9.00
Altoona	AA Pit	7	0	0	4	8	33	8	2	2	0	0	0	0	3	0	6	0	0	1	1	.500	0	0	2.25
6 Min. YEARS		203	0	0	75	279	1247	277	172	145	23	16	12	13	145	10	243	27	1	16	13	.552	0	8	4.68

Shaun Babula

Pitches: Left **Bats:** Both **Pos:** RP-28   **Ht:** 6'0" **Wt:** 190 **Born:** 5/21/77 **Age:** 25

			HOW MUCH HE PITCHED						WHAT HE GAVE UP									THE RESULTS					
Year Team	Lg Org	G	GS	CG	GF	IP	BFP	H	R	ER	HR	SH	SF	HB	TBB	IBB	SO	WP	Bk	W	L	Pct.	ShO	Sv	ERA
1999 Bluefield	R+ Bal	4	0	0	0	8	33	4	2	1	0	0	0	0	5	0	10	0	0	1	0	1.000	0	0	1.13
Delmarva	A Bal	16	0	0	7	13.2	65	17	7	5	3	5	2	0	5	0	16	1	1	0	2	.000	0	2	3.29
2000 Delmarva	A Bal	9	0	0	4	14	60	13	2	1	0	1	0	2	4	0	11	0	0	1	0	1.000	0	0	0.64
Frederick	A+ Bal	37	0	0	17	46.1	206	40	25	17	4	3	2	3	25	2	47	1	0	3	2	.600	0	2	3.30
2001 Bowie	AA Bal	28	0	0	13	38.2	160	37	18	14	2	2	1	2	12	1	27	1	1	2	4	.333	0	2	3.26
3 Min. YEARS		94	0	0	41	120.2	524	111	54	38	9	11	5	7	51	3	111	3	2	7	8	.467	0	6	2.83

Brandon Backe

Pitches: Right **Bats:** Right **Pos:** RP-47   **Ht:** 6'0" **Wt:** 182 **Born:** 4/5/78 **Age:** 24

			HOW MUCH HE PITCHED						WHAT HE GAVE UP									THE RESULTS					
Year Team	Lg Org	G	GS	CG	GF	IP	BFP	H	R	ER	HR	SH	SF	HB	TBB	IBB	SO	WP	Bk	W	L	Pct.	ShO	Sv	ERA
1998 Princeton	R+ TB	1	0	0	1	2	9	0	0	0	0	0	0	0	2	0	3	0	0	0	0	—	0	0	0.00
2001 Chston-SC	A TB	16	0	0	15	24.2	98	17	8	8	2	2	0	4	7	1	20	2	0	2	1	.667	0	7	2.92
Bakersfield	A+ TB	17	0	0	12	24.2	97	13	7	3	1	0	2	0	8	0	33	2	0	1	0	1.000	0	3	1.09
Orlando	AA TB	14	0	0	1	22	94	20	14	14	1	0	0	4	11	0	20	2	0	1	0	1.000	0	0	5.73
2 Min. YEARS		48	0	0	29	73.1	298	50	29	25	4	2	2	8	28	1	76	6	0	4	1	.800	0	10	3.07

Brooks Badeaux

Bats: Both **Throws:** Right **Pos:** 2B-53; OF-47; 3B-31   **Ht:** 5'10" **Wt:** 175 **Born:** 10/20/76 **Age:** 25

			BATTING															BASERUNNING				PERCENTAGES		
Year Team	Lg Org	G	AB	H	2B	3B	HR	TB	R	RBI	TBB	IBB	SO	HBP	SH	SF	SB	CS	SB%	GDP	Avg	OBP	SLG		
1998 Hudson Val	A- TB	68	267	80	9	4	1	100	48	36	29	0	47	3	7	2	11	4	.73	4	.300	.372	.375		
1999 St. Pete	A+ TB	96	342	97	6	1	0	105	68	19	57	1	44	2	5	0	2	7	.22	4	.284	.389	.307		
Orlando	AA TB	3	2	1	0	0	0	1	4	1	1	0	0	0	0	0	0	0	—	0	.500	.500	2.000		
2000 Orlando	AA TB	73	260	68	8	6	1	91	37	27	34	1	29	5	5	1	2	2	.50	5	.262	.357	.350		
Durham	AAA TB	33	98	32	2	1	0	36	11	3	9	0	21	0	1	0	1	0	1.00	1	.327	.383	.367		
2001 Orlando	AA TB	127	470	117	11	6	1	143	48	27	33	2	50	5	11	2	14	7	.67	9	.249	.304	.304		
4 Min. YEARS		400	1439	395	36	18	4	479	213	113	162	4	191	15	29	5	30	20	.60	23	.274	.353	.333		

15

Ryan Baerlocher

Pitches: Right **Bats:** Right **Pos:** SP-28   **Ht:** 6'5" **Wt:** 220 **Born:** 8/6/77 **Age:** 24

Year Team	Lg Org	HOW MUCH HE PITCHED						WHAT HE GAVE UP										THE RESULTS					
		G	GS	CG	GF	IP	BFP	H	R	ER	HR	SH	SF	HB	TBB	IBB	SO	WP	Bk	W	L	Pct.	ShO	Sv	ERA
1999 Spokane	A- KC	15	15	0	0	74.2	326	78	43	39	7	2	0	6	32	0	68	0	0	7	2	.778	0	0	4.70
2000 Chston-WV	A KC	19	19	0	0	113.2	457	88	43	27	6	0	0	3	33	0	139	5	0	5	6	.455	0	0	2.14
Wilmington	A+ KC	8	8	0	0	51.1	206	35	18	17	3	3	1	2	17	0	54	0	1	5	1	.833	0	0	2.98
2001 Wichita	AA KC	28	28	2	0	180.2	777	180	94	80	26	2	6	12	55	2	124	6	2	13	8	.619	1	0	3.99
3 Min. YEARS		70	70	2	0	420.1	1766	381	198	163	42	7	7	23	137	2	385	11	3	30	17	.638	1	0	3.49

Kevin Baez

Bats: Right **Throws:** Right **Pos:** SS-54; 2B-28; 3B-18; PH-6; DH-3; P-2; PR-1   **Ht:** 5'11" **Wt:** 175 **Born:** 1/10/67 **Age:** 35

Year Team	Lg Org	BATTING															BASERUNNING				PERCENTAGES		
		G	AB	H	2B	3B	HR	TB	R	RBI	TBB	IBB	SO	HBP	SH	SF	SB	CS	SB%	GDP	Avg	OBP	SLG
1988 Little Fall	A- NYM	70	218	58	7	1	1	70	23	19	32	1	30	2	2	3	7	3	.70	3	.266	.361	.321
1989 Columbia	A NYM	123	426	108	25	1	5	150	59	44	58	3	53	6	9	3	11	9	.55	5	.254	.349	.352
1990 Jackson	AA NYM	106	327	76	11	0	2	93	29	29	37	4	44	2	11	2	3	4	.43	7	.232	.313	.284
1991 Tidewater	AAA NYM	65	210	36	8	0	0	44	18	13	12	1	32	4	5	4	0	1	.00	5	.171	.226	.210
1992 Tidewater	AAA NYM	109	352	83	16	1	2	107	30	33	13	1	57	4	5	5	1	1	.50	9	.236	.267	.304
1993 Norfolk	AAA NYM	63	209	54	11	1	2	73	23	21	20	1	29	1	2	1	0	2	.00	3	.258	.325	.349
1994 Rochester	AAA Bal	110	359	85	17	1	2	110	50	42	40	0	52	2	5	5	2	7	.22	13	.237	.313	.306
1995 Toledo	AAA Det	116	376	87	13	2	4	116	30	37	22	1	57	1	10	2	1	6	.14	13	.231	.274	.309
1996 Toledo	AAA Det	98	302	74	12	3	11	125	34	44	24	0	53	2	5	4	3	0	1.00	6	.245	.301	.414
1997 Salt Lake	AAA Min	112	383	105	25	3	5	151	38	54	29	0	74	4	3	6	3	4	.43	7	.274	.327	.394
1998 Chattanooga	AA Cin	49	180	46	10	0	0	56	30	22	26	1	27	1	1	2	0	1	.00	6	.256	.349	.311
Indianapols	AAA Cin	49	137	36	5	0	1	44	21	12	19	0	26	0	2	1	0	1	.00	6	.263	.350	.321
1999 Indianapols	AAA Cin	20	40	12	3	0	0	15	4	7	11	0	4	0	1	0	1	0	1.00	2	.300	.451	.375
Norfolk	AAA NYM	60	175	46	5	0	1	54	15	26	17	1	21	2	0	3	2	0	1.00	2	.263	.330	.309
2000 Norfolk	AAA NYM	122	407	113	27	0	5	155	52	50	51	1	50	6	4	8	4	11	.27	8	.278	.360	.381
2001 Norfolk	AAA NYM	100	311	68	16	0	4	96	35	28	33	1	62	6	9	4	0	3	.00	1	.219	.302	.309
1990 New York	NL	5	12	2	1	0	0	3	0	0	0	0	0	0	0	0	0	0	—	2	.167	.167	.250
1992 New York	NL	6	13	2	0	0	0	2	0	0	0	0	0	0	0	0	0	0	—	1	.154	.154	.154
1993 New York	NL	52	126	23	9	0	0	32	10	7	13	1	17	0	4	0	0	0	—	1	.183	.259	.254
14 Min. YEARS		1372	4412	1087	211	13	45	1459	491	481	444	16	671	43	74	53	38	53	.42	96	.246	.318	.331
3 Maj. YEARS		63	151	27	10	0	0	37	10	7	13	1	17	0	4	0	0	0	—	4	.179	.244	.245

Jeff Bailey

Bats: Right **Throws:** Right **Pos:** 1B-96; OF-15; DH-14; C-7; PH-5; PR-1   **Ht:** 6'2" **Wt:** 205 **Born:** 11/19/78 **Age:** 23

Year Team	Lg Org	BATTING															BASERUNNING				PERCENTAGES		
		G	AB	H	2B	3B	HR	TB	R	RBI	TBB	IBB	SO	HBP	SH	SF	SB	CS	SB%	GDP	Avg	OBP	SLG
1997 Marlins	R Fla	4	7	1	0	0	0	1	0	0	0	0	2	0	0	0	0	0	—	1	.143	.143	.143
1998 Marlins	R Fla	37	127	42	10	0	2	58	21	28	19	0	31	7	0	1	3	2	.60	3	.331	.442	.457
1999 Kane County	A Fla	76	277	77	19	1	10	128	49	53	34	2	77	6	0	5	1	1	.50	8	.278	.363	.462
2000 Brevard Cty	A+ Fla	125	458	113	19	3	14	180	56	66	50	2	116	7	1	4	3	3	.50	9	.247	.328	.393
2001 Portland	AA Fla	129	432	104	28	2	13	175	56	66	64	1	136	8	0	3	7	2	.78	4	.241	.347	.405
5 Min. YEARS		371	1301	337	76	6	39	542	182	213	167	5	362	28	1	13	14	8	.64	25	.259	.353	.417

Travis Bailey

Bats: Right **Throws:** Right **Pos:** 3B-31; DH-24; OF-23; 1B-20; PH-10; 2B-1; PR-1   **Ht:** 6'2" **Wt:** 198 **Born:** 1/26/77 **Age:** 25

Year Team	Lg Org	BATTING															BASERUNNING				PERCENTAGES		
		G	AB	H	2B	3B	HR	TB	R	RBI	TBB	IBB	SO	HBP	SH	SF	SB	CS	SB%	GDP	Avg	OBP	SLG
1999 New Jersey	A- StL	66	241	55	9	8	8	104	37	31	17	1	81	4	1	1	6	2	.75	2	.228	.289	.432
2000 Peoria	A StL	118	418	103	21	5	9	161	64	58	58	4	154	4	3	4	10	7	.59	4	.246	.341	.385
2001 Potomac	A+ StL	73	227	49	13	4	6	88	25	24	15	2	75	4	0	2	3	6	.33	1	.216	.274	.388
New Haven	AA StL	27	88	24	3	1	4	41	9	10	4	1	35	2	0	1	2	2	.50	2	.273	.316	.466
3 Min. YEARS		284	974	231	46	18	27	394	135	123	94	8	345	14	4	8	21	17	.55	9	.237	.311	.405

Matt Bailie

Pitches: Right **Bats:** Right **Pos:** RP-30; SP-6   **Ht:** 5'10" **Wt:** 195 **Born:** 10/1/75 **Age:** 26

Year Team	Lg Org	HOW MUCH HE PITCHED						WHAT HE GAVE UP										THE RESULTS					
		G	GS	CG	GF	IP	BFP	H	R	ER	HR	SH	SF	HB	TBB	IBB	SO	WP	Bk	W	L	Pct.	ShO	Sv	ERA
1998 Martinsvlle	R+ Phi	24	0	0	22	31.2	136	33	13	10	2	2	1	2	6	2	36	1	2	4	2	.667	0	9	2.84
Piedmont	A Phi	2	0	0	0	2.1	13	3	0	0	0	0	0	0	3	0	2	0	0	0	0	—	0	0	0.00
1999 Clearwater	A+ Phi	2	0	0	2	3	14	2	1	1	0	0	0	0	3	0	5	0	0	0	0	—	0	0	3.00
Batavia	A- Phi	10	0	0	8	17.1	72	15	8	8	1	1	0	2	4	1	23	4	0	2	2	.500	0	3	4.15
Piedmont	A Phi	6	1	0	4	18.1	75	13	5	3	0	0	0	0	7	0	24	1	0	0	0	—	0	1	1.47
Reading	AA Phi	1	1	0	0	6	20	3	0	0	0	0	0	0	1	0	6	0	0	1	0	1.000	0	0	0.00
2000 Piedmont	A Phi	44	0	0	17	71.1	285	50	15	11	2	4	6	2	24	0	82	1	0	7	0	1.000	0	6	1.39
2001 Scranton-WB	AAA Phi	1	0	0	1	1.1	4	0	0	0	0	0	0	0	0	0	0	0	0	0	0	—	0	0	0.00
Reading	AA Phi	35	6	0	7	67	303	76	52	51	13	3	7	2	30	1	72	3	0	1	6	.143	0	2	6.85
4 Min. YEARS		125	8	0	61	218.1	922	195	94	84	18	10	14	8	78	4	250	10	2	15	10	.600	0	21	3.46

Rod Bair

Bats: Right **Throws:** Right **Pos:** OF-51; DH-11; 3B-7; PH-4   **Ht:** 5'11" **Wt:** 195 **Born:** 10/29/74 **Age:** 27

Year Team	Lg Org	BATTING															BASERUNNING				PERCENTAGES		
		G	AB	H	2B	3B	HR	TB	R	RBI	TBB	IBB	SO	HBP	SH	SF	SB	CS	SB%	GDP	Avg	OBP	SLG
1996 Portland	A- Col	56	221	48	11	2	4	75	34	33	17	2	29	7	5	4	9	4	.69	2	.217	.289	.339
1997 Salem	A+ Col	16	44	12	3	0	0	15	5	6	0	0	6	2	3	1	2	0	1.00	1	.273	.298	.341
Asheville	A Col	91	356	100	20	1	8	146	50	51	13	1	51	11	3	1	9	6	.60	11	.281	.325	.410

16

Year Team	Lg Org	G	AB	H	2B	3B	HR	TB	R	RBI	TBB	IBB	SO	HBP	SH	SF	SB	CS	SB%	GDP	Avg	OBP	SLG
1998 Salem	A+ Col	114	425	127	42	5	8	203	62	60	24	3	64	13	0	5	12	6	.67	11	.299	.351	.478
1999 Carolina	AA Col	125	472	143	34	6	13	228	70	81	28	0	78	16	0	6	14	12	.54	11	.303	.358	.483
2000 Carolina	AA Col	27	89	15	6	0	1	24	13	6	12	1	16	5	0	1	1	2	.33	2	.169	.299	.270
2001 Carolina	AA Col	72	273	69	13	0	7	103	25	31	10	0	49	6	4	4	5	6	.45	5	.253	.290	.377
6 Min. YEARS		501	1880	514	129	14	41	794	259	268	104	7	293	60	15	22	52	36	.59	43	.273	.328	.422

Brad Baisley

Pitches: Right Bats: Right Pos: SP-19; RP-4 Ht: 6'9" Wt: 205 Born: 8/24/79 Age: 22

Year Team	Lg Org	G	GS	CG	GF	IP	BFP	H	R	ER	HR	SH	SF	HB	TBB	IBB	SO	WP	Bk	W	L	Pct.	ShO	Sv	ERA
1998 Martinsvlle	R+ Phi	7	7	0	0	27.2	113	27	12	11	2	0	1	2	4	0	14	2	0	3	2	.600	0	0	3.58
1999 Piedmont	A Phi	23	23	3	0	147.2	606	116	56	37	5	5	5	14	55	1	110	6	2	10	7	.588	2	0	2.26
2000 Clearwater	A+ Phi	16	15	2	1	89	391	95	47	37	9	0	2	3	34	0	60	4	0	3	9	.250	0	1	3.74
2001 Clearwater	A+ Phi	11	9	0	1	64.1	267	59	31	27	4	1	1	7	18	0	43	1	0	2	4	.333	0	0	3.78
Reading	AA Phi	12	10	0	0	62.1	285	82	50	45	14	1	3	6	14	0	37	5	0	5	4	.556	0	0	6.50
4 Min. YEARS		69	64	5	2	391	1662	379	196	157	34	7	12	32	125	1	264	18	2	23	26	.469	2	1	3.61

Jeff Bajenaru

Pitches: Right Bats: Right Pos: RP-37 Ht: 6'1" Wt: 190 Born: 3/21/78 Age: 24

Year Team	Lg Org	G	GS	CG	GF	IP	BFP	H	R	ER	HR	SH	SF	HB	TBB	IBB	SO	WP	Bk	W	L	Pct.	ShO	Sv	ERA
2000	R+ CWS	12	0	0	11	14.1	61	10	6	6	2	0	0	0	5	0	31	2	0	1	1	.500	0	5	3.77
Winston-Sal	A+ CWS	10	0	0	7	12.1	52	7	6	6	1	0	3	2	5	0	15	4	0	2	0	1.000	0	2	4.38
2001 Birmingham	AA CWS	2	0	0	0	4.1	21	4	0	0	0	0	0	0	3	0	5	1	0	0	0	—	0	0	0.00
Winston-Sal	A+ CWS	35	0	0	28	40.1	174	32	16	15	3	4	0	1	21	2	51	3	1	2	4	.333	0	10	3.35
2 Min. YEARS		59	0	0	46	71.1	308	53	28	27	6	4	3	3	34	2	102	10	1	5	5	.500	0	17	3.41

Chris Baker

Pitches: Right Bats: Right Pos: SP-26; RP-2 Ht: 6'1" Wt: 194 Born: 8/24/77 Age: 24

Year Team	Lg Org	G	GS	CG	GF	IP	BFP	H	R	ER	HR	SH	SF	HB	TBB	IBB	SO	WP	Bk	W	L	Pct.	ShO	Sv	ERA
1999 Medcine Hat	R+ Tor	3	1	0	1	8.2	37	8	4	3	0	0	0	1	2	0	9	1	1	0	1	.000	0	0	3.12
St.Cathrnes	A- Tor	12	10	0	0	49.1	221	61	37	34	6	1	1	0	14	1	55	7	2	4	4	.333	0	0	6.20
2000 Dunedin	A+ Tor	41	6	0	10	104	440	91	50	37	11	2	1	5	29	2	85	9	1	9	5	.643	0	5	3.20
2001 Tennessee	AA Tor	28	26	4	2	179	729	162	73	67	22	8	7	8	42	0	121	8	0	15	6	.714	1	1	3.37
3 Min. YEARS		84	43	4	13	341	1427	322	164	141	39	11	8	15	87	3	270	25	4	26	16	.619	1	6	3.72

Derek Baker

Bats: Left Throws: Right Pos: 1B-63; DH-14; PH-10; OF-1 Ht: 6'2" Wt: 220 Born: 10/5/75 Age: 26

Year Team	Lg Org	G	AB	H	2B	3B	HR	TB	R	RBI	TBB	IBB	SO	HBP	SH	SF	SB	CS	SB%	GDP	Avg	OBP	SLG
1996 Chston-SC	A Tex	46	160	39	8	1	5	64	21	31	19	0	37	3	0	3	1	1	.50	0	.244	.330	.400
1997 Rangers	R Tex	12	44	16	4	0	2	26	7	7	2	0	10	1	0	0	0	1	.00	1	.364	.404	.591
Charlotte	A+ Tex	8	32	11	1	0	1	15	2	5	1	0	7	0	0	0	0	0	—	0	.344	.364	.469
1999 Charlotte	A+ Tex	119	419	109	16	2	7	150	69	55	58	7	83	12	0	4	3	2	.60	9	.260	.363	.358
2000 Charlotte	A+ Tex	127	449	132	28	3	11	199	50	81	67	3	67	9	0	4	1	2	.33	8	.294	.395	.443
2001 Erie	AA Det	6	18	5	0	0	0	5	2	3	3	0	4	1	0	0	0	0	—	0	.278	.409	.278
Lakeland	A+ Det	77	213	57	16	0	0	73	31	34	60	5	43	3	1	2	1	2	.33	3	.268	.432	.343
5 Min. YEARS		395	1335	369	73	6	26	532	182	216	210	15	251	29	1	10	6	8	.43	22	.276	.384	.399

Ryan Balfe

Bats: Both Throws: Right Pos: OF-44; DH-26; 1B-24; 3B-23; PH-7 Ht: 6'1" Wt: 180 Born: 11/11/75 Age: 26

Year Team	Lg Org	G	AB	H	2B	3B	HR	TB	R	RBI	TBB	IBB	SO	HBP	SH	SF	SB	CS	SB%	GDP	Avg	OBP	SLG
1994 Bristol	R+ Det	43	121	26	3	0	1	32	12	11	23	0	38	1	1	1	2	4	.33	1	.215	.342	.264
1995 Fayettevlle	A Det	113	398	104	20	2	10	158	53	49	48	0	85	9	0	1	1	1	.50	11	.261	.353	.397
1996 Lakeland	A+ Det	92	347	97	21	1	11	153	48	66	24	2	66	5	0	3	3	0	1.00	13	.280	.332	.441
1997 Tigers	R Det	2	7	4	0	0	1	7	2	1	1	0	1	0	0	0	0	0	—	0	.571	.625	1.000
Lakeland	A+ Det	86	312	84	13	2	13	140	40	48	24	3	75	3	1	6	1	1	.50	7	.269	.322	.449
1998 Mobile	AA SD	23	69	16	5	1	2	29	9	11	8	0	10	0	0	0	1	0	1.00	3	.232	.312	.420
1999 Mobile	AA SD	111	400	112	31	3	11	182	69	70	50	4	95	4	0	3	0	1	.00	18	.280	.363	.455
2000 Mobile	AA SD	130	462	121	21	4	12	186	61	66	46	2	120	9	0	4	3	3	.50	12	.262	.338	.403
2001 Syracuse	AAA Tor	51	190	48	10	1	5	75	22	24	18	2	55	1	0	1	1	2	.33	3	.253	.319	.395
Memphis	AAA StL	67	232	74	20	2	8	122	35	37	23	0	59	2	0	1	1	1	.50	8	.319	.384	.526
8 Min. YEARS		718	2538	686	144	16	74	1084	351	383	265	13	604	34	2	20	13	13	.50	76	.270	.345	.427

Brian Banks

Bats: Both Throws: Right Pos: 1B-81; OF-20; C-9; PH-9; DH-6 Ht: 6'3" Wt: 210 Born: 9/28/70 Age: 31

Year Team	Lg Org	G	AB	H	2B	3B	HR	TB	R	RBI	TBB	IBB	SO	HBP	SH	SF	SB	CS	SB%	GDP	Avg	OBP	SLG
1993 Helena	R+ Mil	12	48	19	1	1	2	28	8	8	11	0	8	0	0	1	1	2	.33	1	.396	.500	.583
Beloit	A Mil	38	147	36	5	1	4	55	21	19	7	0	34	1	0	0	1	2	.33	1	.245	.284	.374
1994 Stockton	A+ Mil	67	246	58	9	1	4	81	29	28	38	2	46	2	3	2	3	8	.27	3	.236	.340	.329
Beloit	A Mil	65	237	71	13	1	9	113	41	47	29	5	40	2	1	4	11	1	.92	3	.300	.375	.477
1995 El Paso	AA Mil	128	441	136	39	10	12	231	81	78	81	6	113	3	3	8	9	9	.50	10	.308	.413	.524
1996 New Orleans	AAA Mil	137	487	132	29	7	16	223	71	64	66	3	105	2	2	7	17	8	.68	6	.271	.356	.458

Year Team	Lg Org	G	AB	H	2B	3B	HR	TB	R	RBI	TBB	IBB	SO	HBP	SH	SF	SB	CS	SB%	GDP	Avg	OBP	SLG
1997 Tucson	AAA Mil	98	378	112	26	3	10	174	53	63	35	2	83	1	2	5	7	3	.70	6	.296	.353	.460
1998 Louisville	AAA Mil	85	299	87	18	1	21	170	58	66	52	3	72	2	0	2	14	3	.82	5	.291	.397	.569
1999 Louisville	AAA Mil	6	24	5	2	1	1	12	3	6	2	1	5	0	0	1	0	0	—	0	.208	.259	.500
2001 Iowa	AAA ChC	17	39	7	2	0	1	12	2	4	4	0	11	0	0	0	0	0	—	2	.179	.256	.308
Calgary	AAA Fla	101	357	104	27	4	23	208	70	63	32	3	97	3	0	3	5	4	.56	5	.291	.352	.583
1996 Milwaukee	AL	4	7	4	2	0	1	9	2	2	1	0	2	0	0	0	0	0	—	0	.571	.625	1.286
1997 Milwaukee	AL	28	68	14	1	0	1	18	9	8	6	0	17	0	0	1	0	1	.00	1	.206	.267	.265
1998 Milwaukee	NL	24	24	7	2	0	1	12	3	5	4	0	7	0	0	0	0	0	—	0	.292	.393	.500
1999 Milwaukee	NL	105	219	53	7	1	5	77	34	22	25	5	59	0	3	2	6	1	.86	2	.242	.317	.352
8 Min. YEARS		754	2703	767	171	30	103	1307	437	446	357	25	614	16	11	33	68	40	.63	48	.284	.367	.484
4 Maj. YEARS		161	318	78	12	1	8	116	48	37	36	5	85	0	3	3	6	2	.75	3	.245	.319	.365

Travis Baptist

Pitches: Left   **Bats:** Left   **Pos:** RP-31; SP-12   **Ht:** 6'0"   **Wt:** 195   **Born:** 12/30/71   **Age:** 30

Year Team	Lg Org	G	GS	CG	GF	IP	BFP	H	R	ER	HR	SH	SF	HB	TBB	IBB	SO	WP	Bk	W	L	Pct.	ShO	Sv	ERA
1991 Medcine Hat	R+ Tor	14	14	1	0	85.1	379	100	52	39	2	5	2	1	21	0	48	4	1	4	4	.500	1	0	4.11
1992 Myrtle Bch	A Tor	19	19	2	0	118	455	81	24	19	2	6	2	4	22	0	97	5	4	11	2	.846	1	0	1.45
1993 Knoxville	AA Tor	7	7	0	0	33	139	37	17	15	2	2	3	2	7	0	24	3	0	1	3	.250	0	0	4.09
1994 Syracuse	AAA Tor	24	22	1	0	122.2	539	145	80	62	20	3	4	0	33	2	42	6	2	8	8	.500	0	0	4.55
1995 Syracuse	AAA Tor	15	13	0	0	79	356	83	56	38	12	2	3	2	32	2	52	4	1	3	4	.429	0	0	4.33
1996 Syracuse	AAA Tor	30	21	2	1	141	633	187	91	85	15	5	10	2	48	2	77	7	2	7	6	.538	0	0	5.43
1997 New Britain	AA Min	36	3	0	7	60.2	247	49	27	23	6	8	1	2	26	2	50	4	0	5	6	.455	0	0	3.41
Salt Lake	AAA Min	7	6	1	0	47.2	194	47	16	11	3	0	1	1	9	0	28	2	1	4	1	.800	1	0	2.08
1998 Salt Lake	AAA Min	21	21	1	0	135.2	559	128	53	47	12	3	0	4	41	1	98	7	1	8	5	.615	0	0	3.12
1999 Salt Lake	AAA Min	17	6	0	5	38.2	174	46	24	23	6	0	0	1	17	0	23	3	0	1	3	.250	0	1	5.35
Pawtucket	AAA Bos	17	3	0	2	42.1	195	49	27	25	5	1	1	0	19	0	30	2	0	4	2	.667	0	0	5.31
2000 Nashville	AAA Pit	34	16	3	6	133	578	146	85	83	17	8	4	7	51	3	93	11	2	4	10	.286	0	0	5.62
2001 Birmingham	AA CWS	10	3	0	5	37.1	156	37	16	8	0	4	0	4	9	3	42	3	0	1	4	.200	0	2	1.93
Charlotte	AAA CWS	33	9	0	5	61.1	279	74	38	35	8	1	1	2	19	2	43	2	4	2	5	.286	0	3	5.14
1998 Minnesota	AL	13	0	0	4	27	123	34	18	17	5	0	6	0	11	1	11	0	0	1	0	.000	0	0	5.67
11 Min. YEARS		284	163	11	31	1135.2	4883	1209	606	513	113	45	31	33	354	17	747	63	18	63	63	.500	3	6	4.07

Josh Bard

Bats: Both   **Throws:** Right   **Pos:** C-81; DH-17; PH-3   **Ht:** 6'3"   **Wt:** 205   **Born:** 3/30/78   **Age:** 24

Year Team	Lg Org	G	AB	H	2B	3B	HR	TB	R	RBI	TBB	IBB	SO	HBP	SH	SF	SB	CS	SB%	GDP	Avg	OBP	SLG
2000 Salem	A+ Col	93	309	88	17	0	2	111	40	25	32	1	33	1	1	2	3	1	.75	6	.285	.352	.359
Colo Sprngs	AAA Col	4	17	4	0	0	0	4	0	1	0	0	2	0	0	0	0	0	—	0	.235	.235	.235
2001 Carolina	AA Col	35	124	32	13	0	1	48	14	24	19	1	23	1	1	1	0	1	.00	1	.258	.359	.387
Mahoning Vy	A- Cle	13	44	12	4	0	2	22	7	8	6	0	2	1	0	0	0	1	.00	1	.273	.373	.500
Akron	AA Cle	51	194	54	11	0	4	77	26	25	16	1	27	2	1	1	0	0	—	4	.278	.338	.397
Buffalo	AAA Cle	1	4	0	0	0	0	0	0	0	0	0	1	0	0	0	0	0	—	0	.000	.000	.000
2 Min. YEARS		197	692	190	45	0	9	262	87	83	73	3	88	5	3	4	3	3	.50	12	.275	.346	.379

Kevin Barker

Bats: Left   **Throws:** Left   **Pos:** 1B-73; OF-37; PH-5; DH-1; PR-1   **Ht:** 6'3"   **Wt:** 205   **Born:** 7/26/75   **Age:** 26

Year Team	Lg Org	G	AB	H	2B	3B	HR	TB	R	RBI	TBB	IBB	SO	HBP	SH	SF	SB	CS	SB%	GDP	Avg	OBP	SLG
1996 Ogden	R+ Mil	71	281	89	19	4	9	143	61	56	46	4	54	3	0	5	0	2	.00	4	.317	.412	.509
1997 Stockton	A+ Mil	70	267	81	20	5	13	150	47	45	25	4	60	0	0	1	4	3	.57	6	.303	.362	.562
El Paso	AA Mil	65	238	66	15	6	10	123	37	63	28	0	40	2	0	5	3	3	.50	5	.277	.352	.517
1998 El Paso	AA Mil	20	85	26	6	0	5	47	14	14	3	0	21	2	0	2	2	1	.67	2	.306	.337	.553
Louisville	AAA Mil	124	463	128	26	4	23	231	59	96	36	1	97	3	0	4	2	5	.29	11	.276	.330	.499
1999 Louisville	AAA Mil	121	442	123	27	5	23	229	89	87	59	5	94	4	0	7	2	2	.50	13	.278	.363	.518
2000 Indianapols	AAA Mil	85	286	56	10	1	11	101	41	44	52	3	76	1	0	6	0	1	.00	6	.196	.316	.353
2001 Indianapols	AAA Mil	51	159	30	5	0	4	47	12	20	20	3	40	1	1	1	0	0	—	0	.189	.282	.296
Huntsville	AA Mil	66	232	75	16	1	8	117	42	38	35	4	51	1	1	3	0	2	.00	2	.323	.410	.504
1999 Milwaukee	NL	38	117	33	3	0	3	45	13	23	9	1	19	0	0	1	1	0	1.00	0	.282	.331	.385
2000 Milwaukee	NL	40	100	22	5	0	2	33	14	9	20	0	21	1	0	1	1	0	1.00	1	.220	.352	.330
6 Min. YEARS		673	2453	674	144	26	106	1188	402	463	304	24	533	17	2	34	13	19	.41	52	.275	.354	.484
2 Maj. YEARS		78	217	55	8	0	5	78	27	32	29	1	40	1	0	2	2	0	1.00	1	.253	.341	.359

B.J. Barns

Bats: Left   **Throws:** Left   **Pos:** OF-131; DH-2   **Ht:** 6'4"   **Wt:** 195   **Born:** 7/21/77   **Age:** 24

Year Team	Lg Org	G	AB	H	2B	3B	HR	TB	R	RBI	TBB	IBB	SO	HBP	SH	SF	SB	CS	SB%	GDP	Avg	OBP	SLG
1999 Williamsprt	A- Pit	14	50	20	4	0	1	27	10	11	12	0	11	3	0	0	0	2	.00	0	.400	.538	.540
Hickory	A Pit	52	174	40	8	4	6	74	16	25	25	0	47	2	1	0	5	3	.63	5	.230	.333	.425
2000 Lynchburg	A+ Pit	120	398	97	20	1	8	143	46	48	44	2	95	9	2	5	8	5	.62	8	.244	.329	.359
2001 Lynchburg	A+ Pit	103	386	95	18	4	6	139	60	57	31	0	87	13	0	3	5	2	.71	7	.246	.321	.360
Altoona	AA Pit	30	109	24	6	2	6	52	12	15	7	0	37	3	0	0	1	1	.75	1	.220	.286	.477
3 Min. YEARS		319	1117	276	56	11	27	435	144	156	119	2	277	30	3	8	21	13	.62	21	.247	.334	.389

Manny Barrios

Pitches: Right **Bats:** Right **Pos:** RP-4   **Ht:** 6'0" **Wt:** 185 **Born:** 9/21/74 **Age:** 27

Year Team	Lg Org	G	GS	CG	GF	IP	BFP	H	R	ER	HR	SH	SF	HB	TBB	IBB	SO	WP	Bk	W	L	Pct.	ShO	Sv	ERA
1994 Quad City	A Hou	43	0	0	11	65	295	73	44	43	4	5	2	7	23	4	63	8	2	0	6	.000	0	4	5.95
1995 Quad City	A Hou	50	0	0	48	52	219	44	16	13	1	2	1	4	17	1	55	1	0	1	5	.167	0	23	2.25
1996 Jackson	AA Hou	60	0	0	53	68.1	298	60	29	18	4	4	2	3	29	5	69	3	0	6	4	.600	0	23	2.37
1997 New Orleans	AAA Hou	57	0	0	17	82.2	350	70	32	30	5	10	4	1	34	9	77	2	0	4	8	.333	0	0	3.27
1998 Albuquerque	AAA LA	20	2	0	7	36	170	47	25	24	7	1	1	2	15	0	33	4	0	1	3	.250	0	0	6.00
Charlotte	AAA Fla	18	1	0	6	24.1	98	19	10	10	3	0	0	1	9	2	22	0	0	2	0	1.000	0	0	3.70
1999 Indianaplos	AAA Cin	49	8	0	9	90.1	399	94	60	53	8	3	2	7	35	0	73	9	2	2	7	.222	0	0	5.28
2000 Scranton-WB	AAA Phi	47	0	0	21	64	288	71	35	35	6	2	1	2	31	3	60	5	0	6	5	.545	0	4	4.92
2001 Binghamton	AA NYM	4	0	0	1	6	28	6	6	6	1	0	0	1	5	0	3	1	0	0	0	—	0	0	9.00
1997 Houston	NL	2	0	0	0	3	18	6	4	4	0	0	0	0	3	0	3	0	0	0	0	—	0	0	12.00
1998 Florida	NL	2	0	0	0	2.2	13	4	1	1	1	0	0	0	2	0	1	0	0	0	0	—	0	0	3.38
Los Angeles	NL	1	0	0	1	1	4	0	0	0	0	0	0	0	2	0	0	0	0	0	0	—	0	0	0.00
8 Min. YEARS		348	11	0	173	488.2	2145	484	257	232	39	27	13	28	198	24	455	33	4	22	38	.367	0	54	4.27
2 Maj. YEARS		5	0	0	1	6.2	35	10	5	5	1	0	0	0	7	0	4	0	0	0	0	—	0	0	6.75

Jeff Barry

Bats: Both **Throws:** Right **Pos:** OF-77; 1B-21; DH-5; PH-3   **Ht:** 6'1" **Wt:** 205 **Born:** 9/22/68 **Age:** 33

Year Team	Lg Org	G	AB	H	2B	3B	HR	TB	R	RBI	TBB	IBB	SO	HBP	SH	SF	SB	CS	SB%	GDP	Avg	OBP	SLG
1990 Jamestown	A- Mon	51	197	62	6	1	4	82	30	23	17	2	25	0	2	0	25	5	.83	1	.315	.369	.416
1991 Wst Plm Bch	A+ Mon	116	437	92	16	3	4	126	47	31	34	4	67	4	2	2	20	14	.59	7	.211	.273	.288
1992 St. Lucie	A+ NYM	3	9	3	2	0	0	5	0	1	0	0	0	0	0	0	0	0	—	0	.333	.333	.556
Mets	R NYM	8	23	4	1	0	0	5	5	2	6	1	2	0	0	0	2	0	1.00	1	.174	.345	.217
1993 St. Lucie	A+ NYM	114	420	108	17	5	4	147	68	50	49	4	37	5	2	6	17	14	.55	7	.257	.338	.350
1994 Binghamton	AA NYM	110	388	118	24	3	9	175	48	69	35	4	62	6	1	8	10	11	.48	10	.304	.364	.451
1995 Norfolk	AAA NYM	12	41	9	2	0	0	11	3	6	3	0	6	1	0	2	0	0	—	2	.220	.277	.268
Binghamton	AA NYM	80	290	78	17	6	11	140	49	53	31	6	61	9	0	9	4	1	.80	4	.269	.348	.483
1996 Las Vegas	AAA SD	4	12	1	0	0	0	1	1	0	3	0	0	0	0	0	0	0	—	0	.083	.267	.083
Memphis	AA SD	91	226	55	7	0	3	71	29	25	29	5	48	1	1	6	3	7	.30	6	.243	.324	.314
1997 New Haven	AA Col	40	146	32	4	0	5	51	21	12	4	0	34	3	1	1	3	2	.60	3	.219	.253	.349
Colo Sprngs	AAA Col	81	273	82	13	3	13	140	46	70	30	2	45	4	0	2	5	0	1.00	6	.300	.375	.513
1998 Colo Sprngs	AAA Col	100	349	91	19	6	8	146	55	55	46	3	52	7	0	2	5	1	.83	6	.261	.356	.418
1999 Colo Sprngs	AAA Col	64	185	63	15	0	10	108	36	27	19	2	31	0	0	0	6	3	.67	6	.341	.402	.584
2001 Las Vegas	AAA LA	89	314	91	20	2	12	151	49	42	33	0	66	3	0	3	11	5	.69	5	.290	.360	.481
Charlotte	AAA CWS	13	41	5	1	0	0	6	6	2	5	0	7	1	0	2	0	0	—	0	.122	.224	.146
1995 New York	NL	15	15	2	1	0	0	3	2	0	1	0	8	0	0	0	0	0	—	0	.133	.188	.200
1998 Colorado	NL	15	34	6	1	0	0	7	4	2	2	0	11	0	0	0	0	0	—	0	.176	.216	.206
1999 Colorado	NL	74	168	45	16	0	5	76	19	26	19	1	29	2	0	3	0	4	.00	4	.268	.344	.452
11 Min. YEARS		976	3351	894	164	29	83	1365	493	468	344	33	543	44	9	43	111	63	.64	65	.267	.339	.407
3 Maj. YEARS		104	217	53	18	0	5	86	25	28	22	1	48	2	0	4	0	4	.00	4	.244	.314	.396

Blake Barthol

Bats: Right **Throws:** Right **Pos:** C-77; PH-2; PR-1   **Ht:** 6'0" **Wt:** 200 **Born:** 4/7/73 **Age:** 29

Year Team	Lg Org	G	AB	H	2B	3B	HR	TB	R	RBI	TBB	IBB	SO	HBP	SH	SF	SB	CS	SB%	GDP	Avg	OBP	SLG
1995 Portland	A- Col	56	191	45	10	2	1	62	20	25	22	0	32	4	1	3	5	2	.71	5	.236	.323	.325
1996 Salem	A+ Col	109	375	107	17	2	13	167	58	67	36	0	48	12	6	1	12	5	.71	5	.285	.366	.445
1997 New Haven	AA Col	109	325	79	12	2	6	113	42	39	31	0	76	10	11	2	5	3	.63	6	.243	.326	.348
1998 Salem	A+ Col	122	441	128	37	2	11	202	56	68	46	5	94	7	4	5	5	3	.63	2	.290	.363	.458
1999 Carolina	AA Col	96	322	90	18	3	8	138	41	27	32	2	62	7	5	1	0	0	.00	8	.280	.356	.429
2000 New Haven	AA Sea	74	248	74	9	1	7	106	43	30	26	1	44	2	2	2	1	1	.50	13	.298	.367	.427
2001 Tacoma	AAA Sea	79	278	77	15	1	9	121	37	37	24	1	67	4	9	3	5	0	1.00	3	.277	.340	.435
7 Min. YEARS		645	2180	600	118	13	55	909	297	293	217	9	423	46	38	17	33	15	.69	42	.275	.351	.417

Cliff Bartosh

Pitches: Left **Bats:** Left **Pos:** RP-58   **Ht:** 6'2" **Wt:** 175 **Born:** 9/5/79 **Age:** 22

Year Team	Lg Org	G	GS	CG	GF	IP	BFP	H	R	ER	HR	SH	SF	HB	TBB	IBB	SO	WP	Bk	W	L	Pct.	ShO	Sv	ERA
1998 Padres	R SD	13	5	0	2	44	190	43	23	17	2	1	2	4	16	0	43	4	0	3	2	.600	0	4	3.48
1999 Fort Wayne	A SD	35	20	1	1	129.2	567	136	76	64	14	0	4	10	49	0	100	7	2	5	12	.294	1	0	4.44
2000 Fort Wayne	A SD	50	4	0	18	77	335	50	40	26	6	2	3	5	44	3	94	8	2	8	4	.667	0	1	3.04
2001 Lk Elsinore	A+ SD	38	0	0	25	45.2	194	42	17	8	2	2	1	2	12	5	66	7	2	6	2	.750	0	10	1.58
Mobile	AA SD	20	0	0	9	22.2	103	20	12	10	5	2	1	1	13	1	20	2	0	1	2	.333	0	2	3.97
4 Min. YEARS		156	29	1	53	319	1389	291	168	125	29	7	11	22	134	9	323	28	6	23	22	.511	1	13	3.53

Chris Basak

Bats: Right **Throws:** Right **Pos:** SS-131; DH-7; PH-2   **Ht:** 6'2" **Wt:** 185 **Born:** 12/6/78 **Age:** 23

Year Team	Lg Org	G	AB	H	2B	3B	HR	TB	R	RBI	TBB	IBB	SO	HBP	SH	SF	SB	CS	SB%	GDP	Avg	OBP	SLG
2000 Pittsfield	A- NYM	63	249	87	18	4	0	113	46	15	26	2	36	3	3	0	32	12	.73	1	.349	.417	.454
St. Lucie	A+ NYM	4	17	7	1	0	0	8	2	3	4	0	2	0	0	0	3	1	.75	1	.412	.524	.471
2001 St. Lucie	A+ NYM	126	472	110	19	4	4	149	71	46	47	0	125	5	4	8	30	9	.77	8	.233	.305	.316
Binghamton	AA NYM	13	43	16	6	1	1	27	11	7	3	0	10	2	0	1	2	0	1.00	1	.372	.429	.628
2 Min. YEARS		206	781	220	44	9	5	297	130	71	80	2	173	10	7	9	67	22	.75	11	.282	.352	.380

Jayson Bass

Bats: Left **Throws:** Left **Pos:** OF-93; PH-14; DH-11   **Ht:** 6'3" **Wt:** 225 **Born:** 6/22/74 **Age:** 28

Year Team	Lg Org	G	AB	H	2B	3B	HR	TB	R	RBI	TBB	IBB	SO	HBP	SH	SF	SB	CS	SB%	GDP	Avg	OBP	SLG
1993 Bristol	R+ Det	35	119	25	6	2	4	47	21	13	14	0	42	2	0	0	2	2	.50	0	.210	.304	.395
1994 Jamestown	A- Det	48	162	44	9	4	5	76	23	18	22	1	52	2	0	0	4	3	.57	2	.272	.366	.469
1995 Fayetteville	A Det	108	368	79	15	6	10	136	47	48	37	1	111	3	1	1	14	3	.82	3	.215	.291	.370
1996 Fayetteville	A Det	104	295	68	12	3	11	119	44	43	54	3	118	2	3	2	19	10	.66	2	.231	.351	.403
1997 Lakeland	A+ Det	108	376	97	18	4	13	162	58	53	41	5	130	2	0	4	17	7	.71	4	.258	.331	.431
1998 Lancaster	A+ Sea	110	392	113	26	6	21	214	80	84	40	2	102	4	0	2	31	12	.72	3	.288	.358	.546
1999 New Haven	AA Sea	123	431	114	23	5	21	210	79	67	72	1	160	3	0	5	34	14	.71	3	.265	.370	.487
2000 West Tenn	AA ChC	50	145	46	7	0	4	65	27	17	22	1	20	4	0	2	4	5	.44	4	.317	.416	.448
2001 West Tenn	AA ChC	48	162	50	5	1	6	75	17	24	14	0	42	2	0	0	6	3	.67	1	.309	.371	.463
Iowa	AAA ChC	70	226	74	17	1	8	117	34	42	26	1	65	2	2	0	7	6	.54	7	.327	.402	.518
9 Min. YEARS		804	2676	710	138	32	103	1221	430	409	342	15	842	26	6	16	138	65	.68	29	.265	.352	.456

Jayson Bass

Bats: Both **Throws:** Right **Pos:** OF-49; PH-10; DH-5; PR-3   **Ht:** 6'0" **Wt:** 180 **Born:** 6/2/76 **Age:** 26

Year Team	Lg Org	G	AB	H	2B	3B	HR	TB	R	RBI	TBB	IBB	SO	HBP	SH	SF	SB	CS	SB%	GDP	Avg	OBP	SLG
1994 Braves	R Atl	49	173	25	8	0	0	33	14	4	15	0	33	2	0	1	5	8	.38	2	.145	.220	.191
1995 Danville	R+ Atl	64	268	60	17	4	0	85	38	17	28	2	61	4	0	2	24	8	.75	2	.224	.305	.317
1996 Danville	R+ Atl	57	207	50	11	6	2	79	41	23	34	0	32	6	1	5	22	5	.81	1	.242	.357	.382
Macon	A Atl	5	22	8	0	0	1	11	2	1	0	0	5	1	0	0	3	1	.75	0	.364	.391	.500
1997 Durham	A+ Atl	75	277	71	20	4	4	111	48	34	29	1	57	2	2	0	8	4	.67	6	.256	.331	.401
1998 Danville	A+ Atl	10	38	6	1	1	0	9	3	1	0	0	12	1	0	0	2	1	.67	0	.158	.179	.237
Greenville	AA Atl	86	233	53	10	1	5	80	27	18	37	1	60	1	6	2	11	6	.65	2	.227	.333	.343
1999 Myrtle Bch	A+ Atl	44	164	36	7	3	2	55	20	19	15	1	45	2	1	1	8	3	.73	1	.220	.291	.335
Richmond	AAA Atl	59	153	32	4	1	1	41	20	10	19	0	46	2	2	2	9	2	.82	5	.209	.301	.268
2000 Greenville	AA Atl	31	65	9	0	1	1	14	9	4	8	1	18	2	0	1	5	2	.71	0	.138	.250	.215
Lehigh Val	IND —	56	212	63	5	4	8	100	39	27	31	0	48	0	1	0	11	10	.52	1	.297	.387	.472
Altoona	AA Pit	19	45	11	0	1	0	13	7	5	5	0	8	0	0	1	3	0	1.00	1	.244	.314	.289
2001 Altoona	AA Pit	67	170	40	14	3	1	63	18	13	10	1	47	2	2	1	9	5	.64	1	.235	.284	.371
8 Min. YEARS		622	2027	464	97	29	25	694	286	176	231	7	472	25	15	16	120	55	.69	22	.229	.313	.342

Fletcher Bates

Bats: Both **Throws:** Right **Pos:** OF-74; DH-23; 1B-4; PH-4; PR-1   **Ht:** 6'1" **Wt:** 193 **Born:** 3/24/74 **Age:** 28

Year Team	Lg Org	G	AB	H	2B	3B	HR	TB	R	RBI	TBB	IBB	SO	HBP	SH	SF	SB	CS	SB%	GDP	Avg	OBP	SLG
1994 Mets	R NYM	52	183	39	5	3	5	65	23	29	33	0	49	0	1	4	4	3	.57	1	.213	.327	.355
St. Lucie	A+ NYM	7	24	6	1	1	1	12	2	4	1	0	5	0	0	0	0	0	—	0	.250	.280	.500
1995 Pittsfield	A- NYM	75	276	90	14	9	6	140	52	37	41	0	72	4	1	3	17	9	.65	1	.326	.417	.507
Binghamton	AA NYM	2	8	0	0	0	0	0	1	0	1	0	6	0	0	0	0	0	—	0	.000	.111	.000
1996 Capital Cty	A NYM	132	491	127	21	13	15	219	84	72	64	4	162	3	4	3	16	6	.73	3	.259	.346	.446
1997 St. Lucie	A+ NYM	70	253	76	19	11	11	150	49	38	33	6	66	4	0	2	7	6	.54	4	.300	.387	.593
Binghamton	AA NYM	68	245	63	14	2	12	117	44	34	26	0	71	1	1	2	9	3	.75	2	.257	.328	.478
1998 Portland	AA Fla	140	537	147	23	5	11	213	67	60	46	2	118	2	1	1	19	6	.76	4	.274	.333	.397
1999 Portland	AA Fla	139	537	136	28	9	9	209	72	55	39	1	109	2	4	8	18	6	.75	10	.253	.302	.389
2000 El Paso	AA Ari	109	355	98	24	5	10	162	52	62	35	1	73	1	1	3	13	9	.59	4	.276	.340	.456
2001 Reading	AA Phi	15	37	5	2	0	1	10	5	4	7	0	5	0	1	0	0	2	.00	1	.135	.273	.270
Scranton-WB	AAA Phi	3	5	0	0	0	0	0	0	0	0	0	1	0	0	0	0	0	—	0	.000	.000	.000
St. Lucie	A+ NYM	82	300	74	18	2	11	129	45	46	27	2	48	0	0	2	13	5	.72	3	.247	.307	.430
8 Min. YEARS		894	3251	861	169	60	92	1426	496	441	353	16	785	17	14	28	116	55	.68	33	.265	.337	.439

Tom Batson

Bats: Right **Throws:** Right **Pos:** 3B-12; DH-4   **Ht:** 5'11" **Wt:** 180 **Born:** 2/9/77 **Age:** 25

Year Team	Lg Org	G	AB	H	2B	3B	HR	TB	R	RBI	TBB	IBB	SO	HBP	SH	SF	SB	CS	SB%	GDP	Avg	OBP	SLG
1999 Batavia	A- Phi	65	245	73	10	4	8	115	52	35	35	1	36	3	2	3	11	5	.69	3	.298	.388	.469
2000 Clearwater	A+ Phi	40	147	36	9	0	1	48	16	16	16	1	28	2	0	1	0	2	.00	4	.245	.325	.327
Piedmont	A Phi	52	191	55	15	1	3	81	26	35	18	0	27	2	1	3	7	4	.64	6	.288	.350	.424
2001 Reading	AA Phi	7	24	2	0	0	0	2	1	0	2	0	4	0	1	0	0	0	—	0	.083	.154	.083
Clearwater	A+ Phi	9	37	8	0	0	0	8	3	1	2	0	6	0	0	0	3	0	1.00	0	.216	.256	.216
3 Min. YEARS		173	644	174	34	5	12	254	98	85	73	2	101	7	4	7	21	11	.66	13	.270	.347	.394

Eric Battersby

Bats: Right **Throws:** Left **Pos:** 1B-133; PH-1   **Ht:** 6'1" **Wt:** 205 **Born:** 2/28/76 **Age:** 26

Year Team	Lg Org	G	AB	H	2B	3B	HR	TB	R	RBI	TBB	IBB	SO	HBP	SH	SF	SB	CS	SB%	GDP	Avg	OBP	SLG
1998 White Sox	R CWS	43	136	51	15	3	5	87	34	27	29	0	32	0	1	2	4	2	.67	0	.375	.479	.640
1999 Burlington	A CWS	132	472	137	27	2	18	222	78	93	83	1	90	4	0	9	13	2	.87	8	.290	.394	.470
2000 Birmingham	AA CWS	127	411	98	20	3	8	148	59	43	55	1	84	3	1	4	6	8	.43	8	.238	.330	.360
2001 Birmingham	AA CWS	133	438	111	19	1	14	174	69	67	80	1	87	3	4	9	6	4	.60	12	.253	.366	.397
4 Min. YEARS		435	1457	397	81	9	45	631	240	230	247	3	293	10	6	24	29	16	.64	28	.272	.376	.433

Howard Battle

Bats: Right **Throws:** Right **Pos:** 3B-114; DH-11; 1B-4; PH-3; SS-1   **Ht:** 6'0" **Wt:** 197 **Born:** 3/25/72 **Age:** 30

Year Team	Lg Org	G	AB	H	2B	3B	HR	TB	R	RBI	TBB	IBB	SO	HBP	SH	SF	SB	CS	SB%	GDP	Avg	OBP	SLG
1990 Medcine Hat	R+ Tor	61	233	62	17	1	5	96	25	32	15	2	38	2	0	0	5	2	.71	2	.266	.316	.412
1991 Myrtle Bch	A Tor	138	520	147	33	4	20	248	82	86	49	2	88	3	0	4	15	7	.68	1	.283	.345	.477
1992 Dunedin	A+ Tor	136	520	132	27	3	17	216	76	85	49	3	89	5	1	5	6	8	.43	5	.254	.321	.415
1993 Knoxville	AA Tor	141	521	145	21	5	7	197	66	70	45	3	94	7	1	3	12	9	.57	8	.278	.342	.378
1994 Syracuse	AAA Tor	139	517	143	26	8	14	227	72	75	40	4	82	3	1	7	26	2	.93	15	.277	.328	.439
1995 Syracuse	AAA Tor	118	443	111	17	4	8	160	43	48	39	2	73	3	1	2	10	11	.48	7	.251	.314	.361
1996 Scranton-WB	AAA Phi	115	391	89	24	1	8	139	37	44	21	0	53	2	2	6	3	8	.27	15	.228	.267	.355
1997 San Antonio	AA LA	16	33	8	1	0	0	9	2	1	0	0	7	2	1	0	0	0	—	0	.242	.286	.273
Albuquerque	AAA LA	50	139	33	3	2	3	49	14	16	6	0	23	0	0	2	1	2	.33	3	.237	.265	.353
1998 Birmingham	AA CWS	12	39	7	4	0	1	14	6	5	4	0	7	0	0	0	0	0	—	0	.179	.244	.359
Greenville	AA Atl	79	291	96	27	2	10	157	41	50	35	2	51	2	0	3	3	2	.60	12	.330	.402	.540
1999 Richmond	AAA Atl	121	454	129	29	1	24	232	80	74	33	2	66	3	0	5	2	3	.40	12	.284	.333	.511
2000 Louisville	AAA Cin	14	56	10	0	0	0	10	6	3	2	0	10	0	0	0	0	0	—	2	.179	.207	.179
2001 Richmond	AAA Atl	131	491	135	21	0	10	186	53	76	25	4	77	1	1	6	2	5	.29	9	.275	.308	.379
1995 Toronto	AL	9	15	3	0	0	0	3	3	0	4	0	8	0	0	0	1	0	1.00	0	.200	.368	.200
1996 Philadelphia	NL	5	5	0	0	0	0	0	0	0	0	0	2	0	0	0	0	0	—	0	.000	.000	.000
1999 Atlanta	NL	15	17	6	0	0	1	9	2	5	2	0	3	0	0	0	0	0	—	1	.353	.421	.529
12 Min. YEARS		1271	4648	1247	250	31	127	1940	603	665	363	24	758	33	8	45	85	59	.59	91	.268	.323	.417
3 Maj. YEARS		29	37	9	0	0	1	12	5	5	6	0	13	0	0	0	1	0	1.00	1	.243	.349	.324

Greg Bauer

Pitches: Right **Bats:** Right **Pos:** RP-43   **Ht:** 6'1" **Wt:** 195 **Born:** 11/30/77 **Age:** 24

Year Team	Lg Org	G	GS	CG	GF	IP	BFP	H	R	ER	HR	SH	SF	HB	TBB	IBB	SO	WP	Bk	W	L	Pct.	ShO	Sv	ERA
2000 Yakima	A- LA	21	0	0	16	33.2	148	26	17	13	2	1	2	1	19	4	50	5	2	2	1	.667	0	9	3.48
2001 Wilmington	A LA	25	0	0	22	30.1	115	22	6	6	3	1	1	0	8	0	32	1	0	1	1	.500	0	17	1.78
Vero Beach	A+ LA	12	0	0	5	23	112	28	13	10	3	3	0	1	13	2	15	1	0	2	3	.400	0	1	3.91
Jacksnville	AA LA	6	0	0	2	14.1	69	17	13	10	4	1	0	0	10	0	8	0	0	0	1	.000	0	0	6.28
2 Min. YEARS		64	0	0	45	101.1	444	93	49	39	12	6	2	3	50	6	105	7	2	5	6	.455	0	27	3.46

Pete Bauer

Pitches: Right **Bats:** Left **Pos:** SP-27   **Ht:** 6'7" **Wt:** 250 **Born:** 11/6/78 **Age:** 23

Year Team	Lg Org	G	GS	CG	GF	IP	BFP	H	R	ER	HR	SH	SF	HB	TBB	IBB	SO	WP	Bk	W	L	Pct.	ShO	Sv	ERA
2000 Hagerstown	A Tor	9	9	0	0	32	141	37	27	18	2	2	3	3	8	0	22	4	0	1	5	.167	0	0	5.06
2001 Chston-WV	A Tor	6	6	0	0	37.2	151	26	15	10	0	1	0	5	10	0	47	0	0	1	2	.333	0	0	2.39
Tennessee	AA Tor	21	21	0	0	128.2	574	147	84	73	12	5	3	10	37	1	71	8	1	6	8	.429	0	0	5.11
2 Min. YEARS		36	36	0	0	198.1	866	210	126	101	14	8	6	18	55	1	140	12	1	8	15	.348	0	0	4.58

Kenny Baugh

Pitches: Right **Bats:** Right **Pos:** SP-11   **Ht:** 6'4" **Wt:** 185 **Born:** 2/5/79 **Age:** 23

Year Team	Lg Org	G	GS	CG	GF	IP	BFP	H	R	ER	HR	SH	SF	HB	TBB	IBB	SO	WP	Bk	W	L	Pct.	ShO	Sv	ERA
2001 W Michigan	A Det	6	6	0	0	34	146	31	14	6	0	0	1	5	10	2	39	2	0	2	1	.667	0	0	1.59
Erie	AA Det	5	5	1	0	30.1	122	23	16	10	5	1	0	4	6	0	30	2	0	1	3	.250	0	0	2.97
1 Min. YEAR		11	11	1	0	64.1	268	54	30	16	5	1	1	9	16	2	69	4	0	3	4	.429	0	0	2.24

Justin Baughman

Bats: Right **Throws:** Right **Pos:** 2B-63; OF-13; SS-1; DH-1; PH-1; PR-1   **Ht:** 5'11" **Wt:** 175 **Born:** 8/1/74 **Age:** 27

Year Team	Lg Org	G	AB	H	2B	3B	HR	TB	R	RBI	TBB	IBB	SO	HBP	SH	SF	SB	CS	SB%	GDP	Avg	OBP	SLG
1995 Boise	A- Ana	58	215	50	4	3	1	63	26	20	18	0	38	2	4	1	19	4	.83	2	.233	.297	.293
1996 Cedar Rapds	A Ana	127	464	115	17	8	5	163	78	48	45	2	78	6	15	1	50	17	.75	13	.248	.322	.351
1997 Lk Elsinore	A+ Ana	134	478	131	14	3	2	157	71	48	40	3	79	13	11	5	68	15	.82	5	.274	.343	.328
1998 Vancouver	AAA Ana	54	222	66	10	4	0	84	35	15	13	0	28	4	5	2	26	8	.76	7	.297	.344	.378
2000 Erie	AA Ana	31	126	36	2	2	1	45	15	6	8	0	20	1	1	0	11	2	.85	1	.286	.333	.357
Edmonton	AAA Ana	80	303	71	7	2	1	85	44	35	30	1	41	7	4	6	28	5	.85	6	.234	.312	.281
2001 Salt Lake	AAA Ana	77	288	87	15	5	3	121	52	32	20	0	54	5	2	2	21	6	.78	7	.302	.356	.420
1998 Anaheim	AL	63	196	50	9	1	1	64	24	20	6	0	36	1	5	3	10	4	.71	4	.255	.277	.327
2000 Anaheim	AL	16	22	5	2	0	0	7	4	0	1	0	2	0	0	0	3	0	1.00	0	.227	.261	.318
6 Min. YEARS		561	2096	556	69	27	13	718	321	204	174	6	338	38	42	17	223	57	.80	41	.265	.330	.343
2 Maj. YEARS		79	218	55	11	1	1	71	28	20	7	0	38	1	5	3	13	4	.76	4	.252	.275	.326

Andy Bausher

Pitches: Left **Bats:** Right **Pos:** RP-39; SP-2   **Ht:** 6'2" **Wt:** 200 **Born:** 8/17/76 **Age:** 25

Year Team	Lg Org	G	GS	CG	GF	IP	BFP	H	R	ER	HR	SH	SF	HB	TBB	IBB	SO	WP	Bk	W	L	Pct.	ShO	Sv	ERA
1997 Erie	A- Pit	15	10	0	1	65	278	62	32	28	3	2	2	3	19	1	44	2	1	4	3	.571	0	1	3.88
1998 Augusta	A Pit	24	21	2	0	109.2	480	112	69	54	5	2	3	9	36	0	119	4	2	7	10	.412	0	0	4.43
1999 Lynchburg	A+ Pit	25	24	1	0	143.1	648	165	98	77	12	4	4	6	52	1	89	7	2	6	15	.286	0	0	4.83
2000 Lynchburg	A+ Pit	30	5	0	10	66.1	299	77	48	44	8	4	2	6	27	0	44	1	1	1	5	.167	0	0	5.97
Rancho Cuca	A+ SD	5	0	0	2	5.2	28	6	4	2	0	0	2	0	1	4	3	0	0	1	0	1.000	0	0	3.18
2001 Mobile	AA SD	4	0	0	1	6	36	9	8	8	1	1	0	0	9	0	4	1	0	0	1	.000	0	0	12.00
Lk Elsinore	A+ SD	37	2	0	12	65.1	269	55	28	20	3	2	0	1	16	2	53	1	1	2	2	.500	0	1	2.76
5 Min. YEARS		140	62	3	26	461.1	2038	486	287	233	32	17	11	25	163	5	356	16	7	21	36	.368	0	2	4.55

Shane Bazzell

Pitches: Right **Bats:** Left **Pos:** SP-22; RP-8   **Ht:** 6'2" **Wt:** 180 **Born:** 3/22/79 **Age:** 23

		HOW MUCH HE PITCHED						WHAT HE GAVE UP										THE RESULTS					
Year Team	Lg Org	G	GS	CG	GF	IP	BFP	H	R	ER	HR	SH	SF	HB	TBB	IBB	SO	WP	Bk	W	L	Pct.	ShO	Sv	ERA
1998 Athletics	R Oak	12	8	0	0	41.1	174	30	19	15	1	1	3	3	15	0	51	9	5	4	2	.667	0	0	3.27
1999 Sou Oregon	A- Oak	5	5	0	0	29	126	27	15	6	1	0	2	1	9	0	18	0	4	3	1	.750	0	0	1.86
Visalia	A+ Oak	8	8	0	0	40.1	182	50	27	23	4	1	1	0	19	0	29	0	1	2	4	.333	0	0	5.13
2000 Modesto	A+ Oak	32	5	0	10	72	331	91	57	46	6	1	4	1	30	4	71	7	1	3	4	.429	0	1	5.75
2001 Modesto	A+ Oak	28	20	0	1	135	549	116	51	41	9	1	4	3	38	1	129	6	3	10	4	.714	0	0	2.73
Midland	AA Oak	2	2	0	0	7.1	45	20	17	16	2	0	1	0	2	1	4	1	0	0	2	.000	0	0	19.64
4 Min. YEARS		87	48	0	11	325	1407	334	186	147	23	4	15	8	113	6	302	23	14	22	17	.564	0	1	4.07

Trey Beamon

Bats: Left **Throws:** Right **Pos:** OF-81; DH-19; PH-4; 1B-1; PR-1   **Ht:** 6'0" **Wt:** 192 **Born:** 2/11/74 **Age:** 28

		BATTING															BASERUNNING				PERCENTAGES		
Year Team	Lg Org	G	AB	H	2B	3B	HR	TB	R	RBI	TBB	IBB	SO	HBP	SH	SF	SB	CS	SB%	GDP	Avg	OBP	SLG
1992 Pirates	R Pit	13	39	12	1	0	1	16	9	6	4	1	0	0	0	0	1	1	.00	0	.308	.372	.410
Welland	A- Pit	19	69	20	5	0	3	34	15	9	8	0	9	0	0	0	4	3	.57	6	.290	.364	.493
1993 Augusta	A Pit	104	373	101	18	6	0	131	64	45	48	2	60	6	0	4	19	6	.76	12	.271	.360	.351
1994 Carolina	AA Pit	112	434	140	18	9	5	191	69	47	33	4	53	5	4	3	24	9	.73	8	.323	.375	.440
1995 Calgary	AAA Pit	118	452	151	29	5	5	205	74	62	39	4	55	2	2	3	18	8	.69	7	.334	.387	.454
1996 Calgary	AAA Pit	111	378	109	15	3	5	145	62	52	55	6	63	6	3	5	16	3	.84	12	.288	.383	.384
1997 Las Vegas	AAA SD	90	329	108	19	4	5	150	64	49	48	1	58	9	2	2	14	6	.70	11	.328	.425	.456
1998 Lakeland	A+ Det	2	6	3	0	0	0	3	2	0	3	0	0	0	0	0	0	0	—	0	.500	.667	.500
Toledo	AAA Det	56	207	49	6	0	3	64	31	18	28	0	38	2	0	3	16	2	.89	2	.237	.329	.309
1999 Charlotte	AAA CWS	18	54	14	5	0	1	22	11	6	3	0	10	0	0	0	4	0	1.00	2	.259	.298	.407
Binghamton	AA NYM	71	246	59	13	0	2	78	32	20	29	0	41	2	1	1	13	10	.57	12	.240	.324	.317
2000 Allentown	IND —	82	302	115	27	1	5	159	72	49	60	2	44	2	1	2	11	9	.55	5	.381	.484	.526
2001 San Antonio	AA Sea	64	238	61	14	2	1	82	33	19	18	0	32	2	1	1	7	3	.70	2	.256	.313	.345
New Jersey	IND —	38	138	48	7	1	2	63	33	23	25	4	22	1	0	2	9	1	.90	4	.348	.446	.457
1996 Pittsburgh	NL	24	51	11	2	0	0	13	7	6	4	0	6	0	1	0	1	1	.50	0	.216	.273	.255
1997 San Diego	NL	43	65	18	3	0	0	21	5	7	2	0	17	1	0	0	1	2	.33	1	.277	.309	.323
1998 Detroit	AL	28	42	11	4	0	0	15	4	2	5	0	13	0	1	0	1	0	1.00	3	.262	.340	.357
10 Min. YEARS		898	3265	990	177	31	38	1343	571	405	401	24	485	37	14	26	155	61	.72	83	.303	.383	.411
3 Maj. YEARS		95	158	40	9	0	0	49	16	15	11	0	36	1	2	0	3	3	.50	4	.253	.306	.310

Colter Bean

Pitches: Right **Bats:** Right **Pos:** RP-33   **Ht:** 6'6" **Wt:** 255 **Born:** 1/16/77 **Age:** 25

		HOW MUCH HE PITCHED						WHAT HE GAVE UP										THE RESULTS					
Year Team	Lg Org	G	GS	CG	GF	IP	BFP	H	R	ER	HR	SH	SF	HB	TBB	IBB	SO	WP	Bk	W	L	Pct.	ShO	Sv	ERA
2000 Staten IInd	A- NYY	3	0	0	2	2	14	3	3	1	0	0	0	0	3	1	2	0	0	0	0	—	0	0	4.50
Greensboro	A NYY	18	0	0	9	25.2	110	21	16	14	1	0	0	1	11	0	35	4	0	1	0	1.000	0	0	4.91
2001 Norwich	AA NYY	1	0	0	1	1	5	1	1	1	0	0	0	0	1	0	0	0	0	0	1	.000	0	0	9.00
Tampa	A+ NYY	32	0	0	10	49.1	195	27	9	8	0	0	0	3	18	2	77	2	0	7	1	.875	0	2	1.46
2 Min. YEARS		54	0	0	22	78	324	52	29	24	2	0	0	4	33	3	114	6	1	8	2	.800	0	2	2.77

Ray Beasley

Pitches: Left **Bats:** Right **Pos:** RP-65   **Ht:** 5'11" **Wt:** 168 **Born:** 10/26/76 **Age:** 25

		HOW MUCH HE PITCHED						WHAT HE GAVE UP										THE RESULTS					
Year Team	Lg Org	G	GS	CG	GF	IP	BFP	H	R	ER	HR	SH	SF	HB	TBB	IBB	SO	WP	Bk	W	L	Pct.	ShO	Sv	ERA
1996 Danville	R+ Atl	27	0	0	21	36.2	145	28	8	7	0	1	1	1	10	0	47	1	1	1	2	.333	0	12	1.72
Eugene	A- Atl	3	0	0	0	4	19	4	2	0	0	0	0	0	2	0	7	0	0	0	0	—	0	0	0.00
1997 Macon	A Atl	49	0	0	30	71.1	294	52	28	21	4	4	3	5	26	2	102	2	0	3	4	.429	0	8	2.65
1998 Danville	A+ Atl	54	0	0	20	55.2	241	54	26	22	3	3	2	3	24	4	55	2	1	6	8	.429	0	8	3.56
Richmond	AAA Atl	2	0	0	1	6	28	8	3	3	0	2	0	0	2	0	8	0	0	0	0	—	0	0	4.50
1999 Greenville	AA Atl	50	0	0	22	81.2	349	84	45	42	8	2	4	3	26	5	71	3	1	7	4	.636	0	4	4.63
2000 Richmond	AAA Atl	4	0	0	2	5	26	11	9	4	2	0	0	0	2	0	2	0	0	0	0	.000	0	0	7.20
Greenville	AA Atl	48	0	0	16	59	255	54	25	20	2	5	1	1	25	3	64	4	0	3	4	.429	0	3	3.05
2001 Richmond	AAA Atl	65	0	0	13	55	241	58	26	23	4	1	2	3	22	5	37	2	0	1	3	.250	0	0	3.76
6 Min. YEARS		302	0	0	125	374.1	1598	353	172	142	23	18	13	16	139	19	393	14	3	21	27	.438	0	34	3.41

Andy Beattie

Bats: Both **Throws:** Right **Pos:** 2B-41; OF-41; SS-14; 3B-11; PH-11; DH-2; PR-2   **Ht:** 5'10" **Wt:** 170 **Born:** 2/28/78 **Age:** 24

		BATTING															BASERUNNING				PERCENTAGES		
Year Team	Lg Org	G	AB	H	2B	3B	HR	TB	R	RBI	TBB	IBB	SO	HBP	SH	SF	SB	CS	SB%	GDP	Avg	OBP	SLG
1998 Billings	R+ Cin	43	128	32	8	2	4	56	36	25	34	0	33	3	1	2	3	0	1.00	0	.250	.413	.438
1999 Clinton	A Cin	108	335	77	11	3	6	112	58	41	60	1	75	3	8	5	18	4	.82	6	.230	.347	.334
2000 Dayton	A Cin	20	57	13	2	0	2	21	15	7	5	0	14	0	2	0	1	3	.25	2	.228	.290	.368
Clinton	A Cin	101	398	124	30	4	4	174	65	52	44	5	58	1	7	5	18	7	.72	5	.312	.377	.437
2001 Louisville	AAA Cin	7	9	2	0	0	0	2	0	0	0	0	5	0	0	0	0	0	—	0	.222	.222	.222
Mudville	A+ Cin	60	227	71	17	0	7	109	37	31	28	0	50	3	1	1	11	2	.85	3	.313	.394	.480
Chattanooga	AA Cin	51	169	45	12	0	3	66	32	24	21	0	30	1	1	1	4	2	.67	3	.266	.349	.391
4 Min. YEARS		390	1323	364	80	9	26	540	243	180	192	6	265	11	20	14	55	18	.75	19	.275	.368	.408

Matt Beaumont

Pitches: Left **Bats:** Left **Pos:** RP-4 **Ht:** 6'3" **Wt:** 210 **Born:** 4/22/73 **Age:** 29

Year Team	Lg Org	G	GS	CG	GF	IP	BFP	H	R	ER	HR	SH	SF	HB	TBB	IBB	SO	WP	Bk	W	L	Pct.	ShO	Sv	ERA
1994 Boise	A- Ana	12	10	0	0	64	268	52	27	25	2	4	2	7	22	1	77	3	0	3	3	.500	0	0	3.52
1995 Lk Elsinore	A+ Ana	27	26	0	0	175.1	724	162	80	64	15	1	6	7	57	1	149	1	1	16	9	.640	0	0	3.29
1996 Midland	AA Ana	28	28	2	0	161.2	746	198	124	105	20	4	6	12	71	0	132	5	0	7	16	.304	0	0	5.85
1997 Midland	AA Ana	4	3	0	0	9.2	62	24	27	27	5	0	0	0	10	0	11	1	0	0	2	.000	0	0	25.14
Lk Elsinore	A+ Ana	1	1	0	0	1.1	7	2	1	1	0	0	0	0	1	0	1	0	1	0	0	—	0	0	6.75
1998 Midland	AA Ana	34	18	1	6	128.2	583	124	81	60	10	5	4	10	67	1	107	3	3	9	12	.429	0	1	4.20
1999 Erie	AA Ana	32	12	0	6	106.2	474	97	64	56	13	5	3	7	59	0	76	3	3	5	6	.455	0	1	4.73
2000 Edmonton	AAA Ana	2	1	0	1	7.1	40	11	10	10	1	0	0	1	9	0	4	1	0	0	0	—	0	0	12.27
Erie	AA Ana	30	21	0	3	118.1	539	95	62	50	11	4	1	17	92	0	84	4	1	5	10	.333	0	0	3.80
2001 Birmingham	AA CWS	4	0	0	1	4	23	8	8	8	1	0	1	1	2	0	3	2	0	1	0	1.000	0	0	18.00
8 Min. YEARS		174	120	3	17	777	3466	773	484	406	78	23	23	62	390	3	644	23	9	46	58	.442	0	2	4.70

Steve Bechler

Pitches: Right **Bats:** Right **Pos:** SP-27 **Ht:** 6'2" **Wt:** 207 **Born:** 11/18/79 **Age:** 22

Year Team	Lg Org	G	GS	CG	GF	IP	BFP	H	R	ER	HR	SH	SF	HB	TBB	IBB	SO	WP	Bk	W	L	Pct.	ShO	Sv	ERA
1998 Orioles	R Bal	9	9	0	0	49.2	209	51	22	15	4	1	1	1	8	0	39	4	1	2	4	.333	0	0	2.72
1999 Delmarva	A Bal	26	26	1	0	152.1	642	137	69	60	12	5	2	4	58	0	139	9	0	8	12	.400	1	0	3.54
2000 Frederick	A+ Bal	27	27	2	0	162	712	179	98	87	19	3	1	6	57	1	137	6	0	8	12	.400	0	0	4.83
2001 Frederick	A+ Bal	13	13	1	0	83.1	330	73	24	21	3	3	4	2	22	0	71	3	0	5	2	.714	1	0	2.27
Rochester	AAA Bal	2	2	0	0	7.1	44	14	14	13	4	0	0	0	5	0	6	2	0	1	1	.500	0	0	15.95
Bowie	AA Bal	12	12	2	0	79	306	63	31	27	14	0	0	1	15	0	58	3	0	3	5	.375	0	0	3.08
4 Min. YEARS		89	89	6	0	533.2	2243	517	258	223	56	12	8	14	165	1	450	27	1	27	36	.429	2	0	3.76

Brian Becker

Bats: Right **Throws:** Right **Pos:** DH-64; 1B-51; PH-1 **Ht:** 6'7" **Wt:** 232 **Born:** 5/26/75 **Age:** 27

Year Team	Lg Org	G	AB	H	2B	3B	HR	TB	R	RBI	TBB	IBB	SO	HBP	SH	SF	SB	CS	SB%	GDP	Avg	OBP	SLG
1996 Devil Rays	R TB	52	199	54	12	0	2	72	31	27	13	0	28	3	0	4	3	1	.75	3	.271	.320	.362
1997 Chston-SC	A TB	135	494	116	31	2	11	184	55	70	53	3	120	4	0	9	12	1	.92	12	.235	.309	.372
1998 St. Pete	A+ TB	129	492	139	27	4	8	198	64	63	43	1	116	4	0	8	1	1	.50	14	.283	.340	.402
1999 Orlando	AA TB	129	480	121	24	1	18	201	67	74	42	2	89	4	0	3	0	0	—	16	.252	.316	.419
2000 Orlando	AA TB	132	503	140	27	2	9	198	45	58	40	1	88	5	0	3	1	3	.25	11	.278	.336	.394
2001 Orlando	AA TB	115	411	93	22	0	7	136	38	42	43	1	96	5	0	4	0	0	—	11	.226	.305	.331
6 Min. YEARS		692	2579	663	143	9	55	989	300	334	234	8	537	25	0	31	17	6	.74	67	.257	.321	.383

Rich Becker

Bats: Left **Throws:** Left **Pos:** OF-91; DH-16; PH-11 **Ht:** 5'10" **Wt:** 193 **Born:** 2/1/72 **Age:** 30

Year Team	Lg Org	G	AB	H	2B	3B	HR	TB	R	RBI	TBB	IBB	SO	HBP	SH	SF	SB	CS	SB%	GDP	Avg	OBP	SLG
1990 Elizabethtn	R+ Min	56	194	56	5	1	6	81	54	24	53	0	54	3	5	0	16	2	.89	3	.289	.448	.418
1991 Kenosha	A Min	130	494	132	38	3	13	215	100	53	72	3	108	2	1	4	19	4	.83	7	.267	.360	.435
1992 Visalia	A+ Min	136	506	160	37	2	15	246	118	82	114	2	122	4	1	6	29	13	.69	5	.316	.441	.486
1993 Nashville	AA Min	138	516	148	25	7	15	232	93	66	94	5	117	3	2	3	29	7	.81	10	.287	.398	.450
1994 Salt Lake	AAA Min	71	282	89	21	3	2	122	64	38	40	0	56	0	2	0	7	1	.88	9	.316	.401	.433
1995 Salt Lake	AAA Min	36	123	38	7	0	6	63	26	28	26	0	24	1	0	2	6	1	.86	1	.309	.428	.512
2001 Calgary	AAA Fla	50	163	43	9	0	8	76	35	28	28	0	40	0	0	2	3	1	.75	3	.264	.368	.466
Toledo	AAA Det	67	234	57	8	3	5	86	37	17	48	3	63	2	0	0	7	3	.70	1	.244	.377	.368
1993 Minnesota	AL	3	7	2	2	0	0	4	3	0	5	0	4	0	0	0	1	1	.50	0	.286	.583	.571
1994 Minnesota	AL	28	98	26	3	0	1	32	12	8	13	0	25	0	1	0	6	1	.86	2	.265	.351	.327
1995 Minnesota	AL	106	392	93	15	1	2	116	45	33	34	0	95	4	6	2	8	9	.47	1	.237	.303	.296
1996 Minnesota	AL	148	525	150	31	4	12	228	92	71	68	1	118	2	5	4	19	5	.79	14	.286	.372	.434
1997 Minnesota	AL	132	443	117	22	3	10	175	61	45	62	1	130	1	2	2	17	5	.77	4	.264	.354	.395
1998 New York	NL	49	100	19	4	2	3	36	15	10	21	2	42	0	0	0	3	1	.75	1	.190	.331	.360
Baltimore	AL	79	113	23	1	0	3	33	22	11	22	0	34	2	2	0	2	0	1.00	6	.204	.343	.292
1999 Milwaukee	NL	89	139	35	5	2	5	59	15	16	33	0	38	0	0	2	5	0	1.00	4	.252	.395	.424
Oakland	AL	40	125	33	3	0	1	39	21	10	25	0	43	2	1	0	3	2	.60	3	.264	.395	.312
2000 Oakland	AL	23	47	11	2	0	1	16	11	5	11	0	17	1	0	0	1	0	1.00	1	.234	.390	.340
Detroit	AL	92	238	58	12	0	7	91	48	34	56	0	70	0	0	4	1	2	.33	0	.244	.383	.382
7 Min. YEARS		684	2512	723	150	19	70	1121	527	336	475	13	584	15	11	17	116	32	.78	39	.288	.402	.446
8 Maj. YEARS		789	2227	570	100	12	45	829	345	243	350	4	616	12	19	12	66	26	.72	44	.256	.358	.372

Josh Beckett

Pitches: Right **Bats:** Right **Pos:** SP-25; RP-1 **Ht:** 6'4" **Wt:** 190 **Born:** 5/15/80 **Age:** 22

Year Team	Lg Org	G	GS	CG	GF	IP	BFP	H	R	ER	HR	SH	SF	HB	TBB	IBB	SO	WP	Bk	W	L	Pct.	ShO	Sv	ERA
2000 Kane County	A Fla	13	12	0	0	59.1	232	45	18	14	4	5	0	2	15	0	61	1	1	2	3	.400	0	0	2.12
2001 Brevard Cty	A+ Fla	13	12	0	0	65.2	238	32	13	9	0	2	1	0	15	0	101	1	1	6	0	1.000	0	0	1.23
Portland	AA Fla	13	13	0	0	74.1	286	50	16	15	8	0	1	4	19	0	102	1	1	8	1	.889	0	0	1.82
2001 Florida	NL	4	4	0	0	24	99	14	9	4	3	0	0	1	11	0	24	1	0	2	2	.500	0	0	1.50
2 Min. YEARS		39	37	0	0	199.1	756	127	47	38	12	7	2	6	49	0	264	3	3	16	4	.800	0	0	1.72

Matt Beech

Pitches: Left **Bats:** Left **Pos:** SP-18; RP-1   **Ht:** 6'2" **Wt:** 195 **Born:** 1/20/72 **Age:** 30

Year Team	Lg Org	G	GS	CG	GF	IP	BFP	H	R	ER	HR	SH	SF	HB	TBB	IBB	SO	WP	Bk	W	L	Pct.	ShO	Sv	ERA
1994 Batavia	A- Phi	4	3	0	1	18.2	80	9	4	4	0	1	0	0	12	0	27	0	0	2	1	.667	0	0	1.93
Spartanburg	A Phi	10	10	4	0	69.2	274	51	23	20	7	0	1	3	23	0	83	5	3	4	4	.500	1	0	2.58
1995 Clearwater	A+ Phi	15	15	0	0	86	363	87	45	40	5	3	2	3	30	0	85	6	0	9	4	.692	0	0	4.19
Reading	AA Phi	14	13	0	0	79	345	67	33	26	7	6	2	6	33	1	70	4	1	2	4	.333	0	0	2.96
1996 Reading	AA Phi	21	21	0	0	133.1	547	108	57	47	16	2	5	4	32	0	132	9	0	11	6	.647	0	0	3.17
Scranton-WB	AAA Phi	2	2	0	0	15	57	9	6	4	3	0	0	0	1	0	14	0	0	2	0	1.000	0	0	2.40
1997 Clearwater	A+ Phi	1	1	0	0	5.2	22	1	1	0	0	0	0	0	4	0	9	0	0	0	0	—	0	0	0.00
Scranton-WB	AAA Phi	5	5	1	0	30	127	24	20	19	5	0	1	0	10	0	38	2	0	3	1	.750	0	0	5.70
1999 Clearwater	A+ Phi	2	2	0	0	4.2	24	7	5	4	0	0	1	0	2	0	3	0	0	0	0	—	0	0	7.71
2001 Charlotte	A+ Tex	1	1	0	0	4.2	18	3	1	0	0	0	0	0	2	0	7	0	0	0	0	—	0	0	0.00
Tulsa	AA Tex	8	7	1	0	46	182	41	17	16	7	0	0	2	10	0	39	2	0	3	1	.750	1	0	3.13
Oklahoma	AAA Tex	10	10	0	0	59.2	284	83	49	39	10	2	1	4	24	0	44	2	0	1	6	.143	0	0	5.88
1996 Philadelphia	NL	8	8	0	0	41.1	182	49	32	32	8	2	6	3	11	0	33	0	0	1	4	.200	0	0	6.97
1997 Philadelphia	NL	24	24	0	0	136.2	602	147	81	77	25	7	6	5	57	9	120	6	2	4	9	.308	0	0	5.07
1998 Philadelphia	NL	21	21	0	0	117	531	126	78	67	19	4	2	4	63	2	113	8	0	3	9	.250	0	0	5.15
6 Min. YEARS		93	90	6	1	552.1	2323	490	261	219	60	14	13	26	183	1	551	30	4	37	27	.578	2	0	3.57
3 Maj. YEARS		53	53	0	0	295	1315	322	191	176	52	13	14	12	131	11	266	14	2	8	22	.267	0	0	5.37

Andrew Beinbrink

Bats: Right **Throws:** Right **Pos:** 3B-110; DH-23; 1B-1   **Ht:** 6'3" **Wt:** 207 **Born:** 9/24/76 **Age:** 25

Year Team	Lg Org	G	AB	H	2B	3B	HR	TB	R	RBI	TBB	IBB	SO	HBP	SH	SF	SB	CS	SB%	GDP	Avg	OBP	SLG
1999 Hudson Val	A- TB	76	292	99	24	2	11	160	46	51	39	2	49	8	0	4	13	4	.76	4	.339	.426	.548
2000 St. Pete	A+ TB	130	475	141	28	0	7	190	70	58	43	3	70	8	2	6	3	4	.43	10	.297	.361	.400
Orlando	AA TB	3	11	5	0	0	1	8	2	3	1	0	1	0	0	0	0	0	—	1	.455	.500	.727
2001 Bakersfield	A+ TB	7	24	6	2	0	0	8	4	3	0	0	4	0	1	0	0	0	—	3	.250	.250	.333
Orlando	AA TB	126	443	121	22	6	5	170	51	49	55	1	69	6	2	7	4	2	.67	16	.273	.356	.384
3 Min. YEARS		342	1245	372	76	8	24	536	173	164	138	6	193	22	5	17	20	10	.67	34	.299	.374	.431

Jay Belflower

Pitches: Right **Bats:** Right **Pos:** RP-28   **Ht:** 6'4" **Wt:** 215 **Born:** 11/12/79 **Age:** 22

Year Team	Lg Org	G	GS	CG	GF	IP	BFP	H	R	ER	HR	SH	SF	HB	TBB	IBB	SO	WP	Bk	W	L	Pct.	ShO	Sv	ERA
2001 Lancaster	A+ Ari	27	0	0	22	29	115	15	5	2	1	2	1	3	6	3	24	1	0	2	2	.500	0	11	0.62
Tucson	AAA Ari	1	0	0	0	1.2	8	2	0	0	0	0	0	0	1	0	2	1	0	0	0	—	0	0	0.00
1 Min. YEAR		28	0	0	22	30.2	123	17	5	2	1	2	1	3	7	3	26	2	0	2	2	.500	0	11	0.59

Heath Bell

Pitches: Right **Bats:** Right **Pos:** RP-43   **Ht:** 6'2" **Wt:** 237 **Born:** 9/29/77 **Age:** 24

Year Team	Lg Org	G	GS	CG	GF	IP	BFP	H	R	ER	HR	SH	SF	HB	TBB	IBB	SO	WP	Bk	W	L	Pct.	ShO	Sv	ERA
1998 Kingsport	R+ NYM	22	0	0	11	46	189	40	15	13	5	1	2	2	11	0	61	4	0	1	0	1.000	0	8	2.54
1999 Capital Cty	A NYM	55	0	0	48	62.1	251	47	23	18	2	0	1	0	17	0	68	3	1	1	7	.125	0	25	2.60
2000 St. Lucie	A+ NYM	48	0	0	37	60	241	43	19	17	4	2	2	2	21	2	75	1	0	5	1	.833	0	23	2.55
2001 Binghamton	AA NYM	43	0	0	22	61.1	285	82	44	41	14	3	1	4	19	3	55	4	0	3	1	.750	0	4	6.02
4 Min. YEARS		168	0	0	118	229.2	966	212	101	89	25	6	8	9	68	5	259	12	1	10	9	.526	0	60	3.49

Jason Bell

Pitches: Right **Bats:** Right **Pos:** RP-8   **Ht:** 6'3" **Wt:** 210 **Born:** 9/30/74 **Age:** 27

Year Team	Lg Org	G	GS	CG	GF	IP	BFP	H	R	ER	HR	SH	SF	HB	TBB	IBB	SO	WP	Bk	W	L	Pct.	ShO	Sv	ERA
1995 Fort Wayne	A Min	9	6	0	2	34.1	139	26	11	5	0	3	0	1	6	0	40	6	2	3	1	.750	0	0	1.31
1996 Fort Myers	A+ Min	13	13	0	0	90.1	350	61	20	17	1	4	2	6	22	0	83	3	0	6	3	.667	0	0	1.69
Hardware Cy	AA Min	16	16	2	0	94	410	93	54	46	13	5	2	5	38	1	94	6	1	2	6	.250	1	0	4.40
1997 New Britain	AA Min	28	28	3	0	164.2	700	163	71	62	19	3	2	5	64	0	142	13	2	11	9	.550	1	0	3.39
1998 New Britain	AA Min	29	29	2	0	169.2	694	148	90	88	21	3	2	5	61	1	166	4	2	8	11	.421	0	0	4.67
1999 Salt Lake	AAA Min	18	15	0	0	76.1	364	96	58	54	12	3	4	3	35	0	72	4	1	5	5	.500	0	0	6.37
New Britain	AA Min	7	7	0	0	47.1	198	46	21	18	4	2	1	2	11	0	34	0	1	3	3	.500	0	0	3.42
2000 Tennessee	AA Tor	12	2	0	3	35.2	151	30	19	14	2	6	4	2	10	1	32	0	0	4	3	.571	0	0	3.53
Syracuse	AAA Tor	22	3	0	7	41.2	175	41	25	23	3	3	4	1	16	1	28	2	0	3	4	.429	0	0	4.97
2001 Syracuse	AAA Tor	8	0	0	0	8.2	44	10	10	10	4	0	0	1	7	0	7	1	0	0	1	.000	0	0	10.38
7 Min. YEARS		162	119	7	13	762.2	3225	714	379	337	79	32	21	31	270	4	698	39	9	45	46	.495	2	0	3.98

Mike Bell

Bats: Right **Throws:** Right **Pos:** 3B-68; 2B-24; 1B-13; PH-3; C-1   **Ht:** 6'2" **Wt:** 210 **Born:** 12/7/74 **Age:** 27

Year Team	Lg Org	G	AB	H	2B	3B	HR	TB	R	RBI	TBB	IBB	SO	HBP	SH	SF	SB	CS	SB%	GDP	Avg	OBP	SLG
1993 Rangers	R Tex	60	230	73	13	6	3	107	48	34	27	0	23	4	1	2	9	2	.82	2	.317	.395	.465
1994 Chston-SC	A Tex	120	475	125	22	6	6	177	58	58	47	1	76	3	1	6	16	12	.57	14	.263	.330	.373
1995 Charlotte	A+ Tex	129	470	122	20	1	5	159	49	52	48	0	72	0	3	2	9	8	.53	11	.260	.327	.338
1996 Tulsa	AA Tex	128	484	129	31	3	16	214	62	59	42	1	75	3	4	0	3	1	.75	13	.267	.329	.442
1997 Okla City	AAA Tex	93	328	77	18	2	5	114	35	38	29	0	78	4	0	3	4	2	.67	10	.235	.302	.348
Tulsa	AA Tex	33	123	35	11	0	8	70	17	23	16	0	28	4	2	2	0	1	.00	2	.285	.375	.569
1998 Norfolk	AAA NYM	17	44	8	1	0	2	15	6	8	8	1	7	0	0	1	0	0	—	0	.182	.302	.341
St. Lucie	A+ NYM	18	63	22	5	2	1	34	11	14	8	2	10	2	2	5	2	1	.67	1	.349	.410	.540
Binghamton	AA NYM	78	275	73	14	1	14	131	47	56	35	1	50	2	0	6	5	5	.38	5	.265	.346	.476

Year Team	Lg Org	G	AB	H	2B	3B	HR	TB	R	RBI	TBB	IBB	SO	HBP	SH	SF	SB	CS	SB%	GDP	Avg	OBP	SLG
					BATTING												BASERUNNING				PERCENTAGES		
1999 Norfolk	AAA NYM	39	135	37	11	1	1	53	11	25	9	1	23	2	0	2	4	2	.67	5	.274	.324	.393
2000 Louisville	AAA Cin	115	429	115	29	2	22	214	70	78	45	6	76	7	0	7	0	0	—	10	.268	.342	.499
2001 Salem	A+ Col	4	13	5	1	0	0	6	1	0	5	0	1	0	0	0	1	0	1.00	0	.385	.556	.462
Colo Sprngs	AAA Col	84	320	90	21	1	13	152	43	53	16	1	80	3	3	0	0	4	.00	4	.281	.322	.475
2000 Cincinnati	NL	19	27	6	0	0	2	12	5	4	4	0	7	0	0	0	0	0	—	0	.222	.323	.444
9 Min. YEARS		918	3389	911	197	25	96	1446	458	498	334	14	599	34	16	36	51	38	.57	77	.269	.337	.427

Ricky Bell

Bats: Right Throws: Right Pos: 3B-58; PH-11; DH-1   Ht: 6'2" Wt: 180 Born: 4/5/79 Age: 23

Year Team	Lg Org	G	AB	H	2B	3B	HR	TB	R	RBI	TBB	IBB	SO	HBP	SH	SF	SB	CS	SB%	GDP	Avg	OBP	SLG
					BATTING												BASERUNNING				PERCENTAGES		
1997 Yakima	A- LA	66	264	68	15	1	2	91	42	24	15	0	52	4	3	3	9	0	1.00	7	.258	.304	.345
1998 San Berndno	A+ LA	133	483	112	18	3	5	151	38	50	16	0	99	6	3	3	6	9	.40	11	.232	.264	.313
1999 Vero Beach	A+ LA	100	376	88	26	1	5	131	37	46	27	0	81	4	4	4	1	3	.25	13	.234	.290	.348
2000 Vero Beach	A+ LA	127	481	122	18	0	5	155	59	45	37	2	75	3	1	6	7	3	.70	13	.254	.307	.322
2001 Vero Beach	A+ LA	6	24	6	0	0	0	6	3	0	0	0	3	1	0	0	1	0	1.00	0	.250	.280	.250
Jacksnville	AA LA	63	188	48	9	0	3	66	21	22	13	0	29	1	1	2	1	1	.50	3	.255	.304	.351
5 Min. YEARS		495	1816	444	86	5	20	600	200	187	108	2	339	19	12	18	24	17	.59	47	.244	.291	.330

Rigo Beltran

Pitches: Left Bats: Left Pos: RP-26; SP-11   Ht: 5'11" Wt: 200 Born: 11/13/69 Age: 32

Year Team	Lg Org	G	GS	CG	GF	IP	BFP	H	R	ER	HR	SH	SF	HB	TBB	IBB	SO	WP	Bk	W	L	Pct.	ShO	Sv	ERA
		HOW MUCH HE PITCHED						WHAT HE GAVE UP												THE RESULTS					
1991 Hamilton	A- StL	21	4	0	4	48	206	41	17	14	4	4	2	2	19	0	69	3	12	5	2	.714	0	0	2.63
1992 Savannah	A StL	13	13	2	0	83	316	38	20	20	4	1	0	4	40	0	106	8	6	6	1	.857	1	0	2.17
St. Pete	A+ StL	2	2	0	0	8	30	6	0	0	0	1	0	0	2	0	3	0	0	0	0	—	0	0	0.00
1993 Arkansas	AA StL	18	16	0	1	88.2	376	74	39	32	8	5	0	6	38	1	82	11	4	5	5	.500	0	0	3.25
1994 Arkansas	AA StL	4	4	1	0	28	95	12	3	2	2	1	0	0	3	0	21	0	0	4	0	1.000	1	0	0.64
Louisville	AAA StL	23	23	1	0	138.1	624	147	82	78	15	7	7	5	68	2	87	18	5	11	11	.500	0	0	5.07
1995 Louisville	AAA StL	24	24	0	0	129.2	575	156	81	75	12	2	8	5	34	0	92	4	2	8	9	.471	0	0	5.21
1996 Louisville	AAA StL	38	16	3	5	130.1	548	132	67	63	17	2	4	5	24	1	132	8	1	8	6	.571	1	0	4.35
1997 Louisville	AAA StL	9	8	1	1	54.1	227	45	17	14	7	0	1	1	21	0	46	0	0	5	2	.714	0	0	2.32
1998 Norfolk	AAA NYM	36	11	0	7	94.1	418	104	51	45	16	2	2	1	40	1	98	5	1	6	5	.545	0	1	4.29
1999 Norfolk	AAA NYM	21	0	0	4	22.1	93	16	5	4	1	1	0	1	12	1	27	1	0	2	1	.667	0	0	1.61
Colo Sprngs	AAA Col	6	0	0	2	8	41	12	3	2	1	0	0	1	5	1	12	1	0	1	0	1.000	0	0	2.25
2000 Colo Sprngs	AAA Col	25	21	1	1	125	563	132	85	82	15	5	3	7	63	0	95	8	2	6	10	.375	1	0	5.90
2001 Scranton-WB	AAA Phi	37	11	0	6	115.2	460	87	40	38	10	2	3	1	41	6	113	5	0	2	5	.286	0	2	2.96
1997 St. Louis	NL	35	4	0	16	54.1	224	47	25	21	3	6	3	0	17	0	50	1	0	1	2	.333	0	1	3.48
1998 New York	NL	7	0	0	0	8	33	6	3	3	1	0	1	0	4	0	5	0	0	0	0	—	0	0	3.38
1999 New York	NL	21	0	0	10	31	134	30	15	12	5	2	0	0	12	2	35	6	0	1	1	.500	0	0	3.48
Colorado	NL	12	0	0	2	11	61	20	9	9	2	1	0	1	7	1	15	1	0	0	0	—	0	0	7.36
2000 Colorado	NL	1	1	0	0	1.1	13	6	6	6	2	0	0	0	3	0	1	0	0	0	0	—	0	0	40.50
11 Min. YEARS		277	153	9	31	1073.2	4572	1002	510	469	112	33	30	39	410	13	983	72	33	69	57	.548	4	3	3.93
4 Maj. YEARS		76	5	0	28	105.2	465	109	58	51	13	9	4	1	43	3	106	8	0	2	3	.400	0	1	4.34

Brian Benefield

Bats: Right Throws: Right Pos: 2B-21; 3B-18; OF-18; DH-14; PR-14; SS-9; PH-7   Ht: 6'0" Wt: 181 Born: 8/12/76 Age: 25

Year Team	Lg Org	G	AB	H	2B	3B	HR	TB	R	RBI	TBB	IBB	SO	HBP	SH	SF	SB	CS	SB%	GDP	Avg	OBP	SLG
					BATTING												BASERUNNING				PERCENTAGES		
1997 Watertown	A- Cle	69	265	76	9	1	4	99	47	19	49	3	40	1	2	1	23	7	.77	3	.287	.399	.374
1998 Kinston	A+ Cle	71	259	57	9	2	5	85	44	34	31	1	50	4	4	2	8	4	.67	1	.220	.311	.328
1999 Columbus	A Cle	81	303	83	14	1	15	144	60	51	43	1	67	8	2	5	18	12	.60	4	.274	.373	.475
Akron	AA Cle	44	145	28	3	2	3	44	14	14	16	0	32	0	0	0	3	3	.50	1	.193	.273	.303
2000 Akron	AA Cle	1	2	0	0	0	0	0	0	0	1	0	2	0	0	0	0	0	—	0	.000	.333	.000
Kinston	A+ Cle	66	236	67	19	6	2	104	45	19	35	0	55	1	2	2	10	3	.77	9	.284	.376	.441
2001 Kinston	A+ Cle	17	57	19	5	1	1	29	14	8	8	1	9	5	1	1	5	0	1.00	1	.333	.451	.509
Akron	AA Cle	63	157	32	7	0	2	45	16	9	10	0	28	0	2	2	5	4	.56	3	.204	.249	.287
Wichita	AA KC	9	20	3	0	1	2	11	2	4	2	0	6	1	0	0	0	0	—	1	.150	.261	.550
5 Min. YEARS		421	1444	365	66	14	34	561	242	158	195	6	289	20	13	13	72	33	.69	24	.253	.347	.389

David Benham

Bats: Right Throws: Right Pos: C-27; DH-11; PH-7; PR-1; P-1   Ht: 6'2" Wt: 187 Born: 10/12/75 Age: 26

Year Team	Lg Org	G	AB	H	2B	3B	HR	TB	R	RBI	TBB	IBB	SO	HBP	SH	SF	SB	CS	SB%	GDP	Avg	OBP	SLG
					BATTING												BASERUNNING				PERCENTAGES		
1998 Red Sox	R Bos	6	22	8	3	0	1	14	3	3	2	0	1	1	0	0	0	0	—	0	.364	.440	.636
Lowell	A- Bos	41	131	36	12	0	2	54	17	6	7	0	23	3	1	0	1	0	1.00	4	.275	.326	.412
1999 Augusta	A Bos	3	9	0	0	0	0	0	0	0	0	0	7	0	0	0	0	0	—	0	.000	.000	.000
Sarasota	A+ Bos	33	105	25	5	0	3	39	10	11	5	0	18	3	0	1	0	0	—	3	.238	.289	.371
Potomac	A+ StL	9	26	4	1	0	0	5	2	1	1	0	7	2	1	0	0	0	—	2	.154	.241	.192
2000 Potomac	A+ StL	28	85	16	4	1	1	25	12	7	6	0	20	8	2	1	0	0	—	5	.188	.300	.294
Arkansas	AA StL	18	57	13	5	1	0	20	9	6	7	1	10	0	0	0	0	3	.00	0	.228	.313	.351
2001 New Haven	AA StL	46	132	32	5	0	1	40	8	15	4	1	31	2	2	1	2	0	1.00	2	.242	.273	.303
4 Min. YEARS		184	567	134	35	2	8	197	61	49	32	2	117	19	6	3	3	3	.50	16	.236	.298	.347

Al Benjamin

Bats: Right **Throws:** Right **Pos:** OF-113; PH-8; DH-4; PR-3   **Ht:** 6'1" **Wt:** 200 **Born:** 9/9/77 **Age:** 24

Year Team	Lg Org	G	AB	H	2B	3B	HR	TB	R	RBI	TBB	IBB	SO	HBP	SH	SF	SB	CS	SB%	GDP	Avg	OBP	SLG
1996 Pirates	R Pit	45	172	39	5	4	3	61	23	25	12	0	35	1	1	2	1	3	.25	7	.227	.278	.355
1997 Pirates	R Pit	39	152	49	14	2	2	73	18	21	4	0	26	1	1	2	7	1	.88	3	.322	.340	.480
Augusta	A Pit	5	14	2	0	0	0	2	2	1	0	0	3	0	1	0	1	0	1.00	6	.143	.143	.143
1998 Dubois Cty	IND —	57	215	64	11	3	7	102	31	40	8	1	32	2	2	3	14	3	.82	5	.298	.325	.474
1999 Cape Fear	A Mon	128	488	157	38	2	10	229	66	77	27	2	110	7	0	5	14	17	.45	9	.322	.362	.469
2000 Rancho Cuca	A+ SD	137	552	154	30	8	9	227	71	81	24	1	89	5	1	5	16	16	.50	14	.279	.312	.411
2001 Lk Elsinore	A+ SD	16	65	14	3	1	0	19	6	5	1	0	15	0	0	1	1	1	.50	1	.215	.224	.292
Mobile	AA SD	110	374	102	23	2	12	165	50	50	18	2	73	3	0	8	8	3	.73	9	.273	.305	.441
6 Min. YEARS		537	2032	581	124	22	43	878	267	300	94	6	383	19	6	26	62	44	.58	48	.286	.320	.432

Jeff Bennett

Pitches: Right **Bats:** Right **Pos:** SP-26   **Ht:** 6'1" **Wt:** 201 **Born:** 6/10/80 **Age:** 22

Year Team	Lg Org	G	GS	CG	GF	IP	BFP	H	R	ER	HR	SH	SF	HB	TBB	IBB	SO	WP	Bk	W	L	Pct.	ShO	Sv	ERA
1998 Pirates	R Pit	13	11	0	0	46.2	212	50	29	24	4	0	2	7	13	0	18	2	0	2	4	.333	0	0	4.63
1999 Pirates	R Pit	8	8	0	0	44.2	191	53	27	21	1	2	1	0	9	0	28	2	3	3	4	.429	0	0	4.23
Hickory	A Pit	8	6	0	2	35	161	48	25	23	5	2	0	1	9	0	16	2	0	2	2	.500	0	0	5.91
2000 Hickory	A Pit	27	27	1	0	171.2	761	189	106	84	14	5	7	16	47	1	126	11	2	10	13	.435	0	0	4.40
2001 Lynchburg	A+ Pit	25	25	2	0	166	691	171	78	63	14	6	2	13	30	1	98	2	0	11	10	.524	1	0	3.42
Altoona	AA Pit	1	1	0	0	7	34	9	3	3	0	0	0	2	2	0	6	0	0	0	1	.000	0	0	3.86
4 Min. YEARS		82	78	3	2	471	2050	520	278	218	38	15	12	39	110	2	292	19	5	28	34	.452	1	0	4.17

Ryan Bennett

Bats: Right **Throws:** Right **Pos:** C-38; PH-2   **Ht:** 6'0" **Wt:** 201 **Born:** 7/26/74 **Age:** 27

Year Team	Lg Org	G	AB	H	2B	3B	HR	TB	R	RBI	TBB	IBB	SO	HBP	SH	SF	SB	CS	SB%	GDP	Avg	OBP	SLG
1996 Pittsfield	A- NYM	27	79	19	2	1	0	23	11	14	13	1	21	0	0	2	0	0	—	1	.241	.340	.291
1997 St. Lucie	A+ NYM	2	2	0	0	0	0	0	0	0	0	0	2	0	0	0	0	0	—	0	.000	.000	.000
Capital Cty	A NYM	19	42	8	1	0	0	9	6	3	5	0	15	0	0	0	0	0	—	1	.190	.277	.214
1998 Capital Cty	A NYM	57	175	50	6	1	2	64	20	20	18	0	49	1	3	1	2	0	1.00	3	.286	.354	.366
1999 Binghamton	AA NYM	1	4	0	0	0	0	0	1	0	0	0	2	0	0	0	0	0	—	0	.000	.000	.000
St. Lucie	A+ NYM	56	165	37	4	0	0	41	19	12	19	0	32	1	3	3	2	1	.67	5	.224	.303	.248
2000 St. Lucie	A+ NYM	53	166	46	7	1	0	55	20	15	20	0	35	1	3	0	0	1	.00	4	.277	.358	.331
2001 St. Lucie	A+ NYM	26	82	24	2	0	1	29	12	5	12	0	13	2	0	1	1	0	1.00	1	.293	.392	.354
Norfolk	AAA NYM	12	21	3	0	0	0	3	2	1	4	0	7	0	1	0	0	0	—	1	.143	.280	.143
Binghamton	AA NYM	2	6	1	0	0	0	1	0	1	0	0	3	0	0	0	0	0	—	0	.167	.167	.167
6 Min. YEARS		255	742	188	22	3	3	225	91	71	91	1	179	5	10	7	5	2	.71	16	.253	.336	.303

Jeff Berblinger

Bats: Right **Throws:** Right **Pos:** 2B-37; DH-26; 3B-12; 1B-2; PH-2; PR-1   **Ht:** 6'0" **Wt:** 190 **Born:** 11/19/70 **Age:** 31

Year Team	Lg Org	G	AB	H	2B	3B	HR	TB	R	RBI	TBB	IBB	SO	HBP	SH	SF	SB	CS	SB%	GDP	Avg	OBP	SLG
1993 Glens Falls	A- StL	38	138	43	9	0	2	58	26	21	11	0	14	3	1	3	9	4	.69	2	.312	.368	.420
St. Pete	A+ StL	19	70	13	1	0	0	14	7	5	5	0	10	1	2	0	3	1	.75	1	.186	.250	.200
1994 Savannah	A StL	132	479	142	27	7	8	207	86	67	52	0	85	25	6	5	24	5	.83	8	.296	.390	.432
1995 Arkansas	AA StL	87	332	106	15	4	5	144	66	29	48	1	40	9	1	2	16	16	.50	2	.319	.417	.434
1996 Arkansas	AA StL	134	500	144	32	7	11	223	78	53	52	0	66	8	3	7	23	10	.70	9	.288	.360	.446
1997 Louisville	AAA StL	133	513	135	19	7	11	201	63	58	55	1	98	6	1	5	24	12	.67	15	.263	.339	.392
1998 Tacoma	AAA Sea	109	390	93	19	2	6	134	48	38	22	1	59	8	4	0	11	7	.61	5	.238	.293	.344
1999 Somerset	IND —	102	397	130	26	2	11	193	81	89	34	1	54	7	0	2	47	11	.81	6	.327	.389	.486
2000 Omaha	AAA KC	1	3	2	2	0	0	4	1	0	0	0	0	1	0	0	0	0	—	0	.667	.750	1.333
2001 Omaha	AAA KC	73	270	58	12	3	5	91	36	23	22	1	54	1	4	0	8	5	.62	6	.215	.276	.337
Nashville	AAA Pit	6	18	6	1	0	1	10	3	1	1	0	4	0	0	0	1	0	1.00	0	.333	.368	.556
1997 St. Louis	NL	7	5	0	0	0	0	0	1	0	0	0	1	0	1	0	0	0	—	0	.000	.000	.000
9 Min. YEARS		834	3110	872	163	32	60	1279	495	334	302	5	484	69	22	24	166	71	.70	54	.280	.355	.411

Dusty Bergman

Pitches: Left **Bats:** Left **Pos:** SP-25; RP-2   **Ht:** 6'4" **Wt:** 200 **Born:** 2/1/78 **Age:** 24

Year Team	Lg Org	G	GS	CG	GF	IP	BFP	H	R	ER	HR	SH	SF	HB	TBB	IBB	SO	WP	Bk	W	L	Pct.	ShO	Sv	ERA
1999 Boise	A- Ana	15	15	0	0	74.1	340	102	58	54	12	1	1	1	18	2	46	6	0	5	5	.500	0	0	6.54
2000 Cedar Rapds	A Ana	28	25	6	0	163.2	727	174	102	71	12	9	2	5	60	0	108	10	0	4	15	.211	1	0	3.90
Lk Elsinore	A+ Ana	1	1	0	0	4	18	3	4	1	0	0	0	0	1	0	3	0	0	1	0	1.000	0	0	2.25
2001 Arkansas	AA Ana	27	25	1	0	153.1	704	196	100	87	10	4	8	14	53	0	83	15	2	7	13	.350	0	0	5.11
3 Min. YEARS		71	66	7	0	395.1	1789	475	264	213	34	14	11	20	132	2	240	31	2	16	34	.320	1	0	4.85

Sean Bergman

Pitches: Right **Bats:** Right **Pos:** SP-2; RP-1   **Ht:** 6'4" **Wt:** 225 **Born:** 4/11/70 **Age:** 32

Year Team	Lg Org	G	GS	CG	GF	IP	BFP	H	R	ER	HR	SH	SF	HB	TBB	IBB	SO	WP	Bk	W	L	Pct.	ShO	Sv	ERA
1991 Niagara Fal	A- Det	15	15	0	0	84.2	384	88	57	42	1	4	2		42	0	77	5	7	5	7	.417	0	0	4.46
1992 Lakeland	A+ Det	13	13	0	0	83	320	61	28	23	2	3	0	2	14	0	67	2	2	5	2	.714	0	0	2.49
London	AA Det	14	14	1	0	88.1	390	85	52	42	2	6	1	6	45	2	59	4	0	7	4	.364	0	0	4.28
1993 Toledo	AAA Det	19	19	3	0	117	503	124	62	57	9	6	3	8	53	0	91	6	2	8	9	.471	0	0	4.38
1994 Toledo	AAA Det	25	25	2	0	154.2	656	147	77	64	15	2	3	5	53	1	145	7	0	11	8	.579	0	0	3.72

Year Team	Lg Org	G	GS	CG	GF	IP	BFP	H	R	ER	HR	SH	SF	HB	TBB	IBB	SO	WP	Bk	W	L	Pct.	ShO	Sv	ERA
1995 Toledo	AAA Det	1	1	0	0	3	13	4	2	2	1	0	0	1	0	0	4	0	0	0	1	.000	0	0	6.00
1999 New Orleans	AAA Hou	3	1	0	0	6.1	30	9	8	7	0	0	0	0	2	0	2	1	0	0	1	.000	0	0	9.95
2000 Calgary	AAA Fla	13	13	0	0	81.2	363	107	55	52	8	1	3	1	23	1	48	6	0	4	3	.571	0	0	5.73
2001 Colo Sprngs	AAA Col	3	2	0	0	17.2	71	15	7	4	1	0	0	1	4	0	12	0	0	2	1	.667	0	0	2.04
1993 Detroit	AL	9	6	1	1	39.2	189	47	29	25	6	3	2	1	23	3	19	3	1	1	4	.200	0	0	5.67
1994 Detroit	AL	3	3	0	0	17.2	82	22	11	11	2	0	1	1	7	0	12	1	0	2	1	.667	0	0	5.60
1995 Detroit	AL	28	28	1	0	135.1	630	169	95	77	19	5	3	4	67	8	86	13	0	7	10	.412	1	0	5.12
1996 San Diego	NL	41	14	0	11	113.1	482	119	63	55	14	8	4	2	33	3	85	7	2	6	8	.429	0	0	4.37
1997 San Diego	NL	44	9	0	13	99	451	126	72	67	11	7	4	3	38	4	74	6	0	2	4	.333	0	0	6.09
1998 Houston	NL	31	27	1	1	172	733	183	81	71	20	3	1	5	42	3	100	8	1	12	9	.571	0	0	3.72
1999 Houston	NL	19	16	2	1	99	428	130	60	59	9	3	4	3	26	1	38	3	0	4	6	.400	1	0	5.36
Atlanta	NL	6	0	0	1	6.1	27	5	2	2	0	1	0	0	3	0	6	0	0	1	0	1.000	0	0	2.84
2000 Minnesota	AL	15	4	0	0	68	337	111	76	73	18	2	3	2	33	1	35	2	0	4	5	.444	0	0	9.66
8 Min. YEARS		106	103	6	0	636.1	2730	640	348	293	39	19	14	26	236	4	505	31	11	39	39	.500	0	0	4.14
8 Maj. YEARS		196	117	5	28	750.1	3359	912	489	440	99	32	22	21	272	23	455	43	4	39	47	.453	2	0	5.28

Manny Bermudez

Pitches: Right **Bats:** Right **Pos:** RP-55   **Ht:** 6'1" **Wt:** 195 **Born:** 12/15/76 **Age:** 25

Year Team	Lg Org	G	GS	CG	GF	IP	BFP	H	R	ER	HR	SH	SF	HB	TBB	IBB	SO	WP	Bk	W	L	Pct.	ShO	Sv	ERA
1995 Bellingham	A- SF	13	13	0	0	56.2	244	51	28	24	3	2	2	2	25	0	39	4	1	1	2	.333	0	0	3.81
1996 Burlington	A SF	26	26	1	0	135.1	589	119	73	66	13	2	4	7	73	0	95	7	1	10	9	.526	1	0	4.39
1997 San Jose	A+ SF	9	9	2	0	44	208	61	35	33	4	1	3	1	22	1	27	5	2	2	6	.250	0	0	6.75
Bakersfield	A+ SF	19	18	1	0	112	482	121	69	61	12	2	2	4	41	1	71	6	8	8	8	.500	0	0	4.90
1998 San Jose	A+ SF	24	24	1	0	139.2	609	161	82	72	10	4	2	4	44	0	87	8	0	7	11	.389	0	0	4.64
Shreveport	AA SF	5	4	1	0	25	117	33	23	21	6	0	2	3	11	0	16	1	1	0	4	.000	0	0	7.56
1999 Bakersfield	A+ SF	32	22	1	1	145.2	687	183	121	97	8	7	5	18	66	1	65	7	1	5	14	.263	0	0	5.99
2000 Bakersfield	A+ SF	59	0	0	25	120.1	487	107	41	38	3	9	2	9	27	3	66	4	0	9	7	.563	0	7	2.84
2001 Shreveport	AA SF	12	0	0	3	26.2	115	25	11	11	0	3	1	7	7	2	13	1	0	2	3	.400	0	0	3.71
San Jose	A+ SF	43	0	0	11	81	346	87	36	32	3	6	1	8	23	0	40	2	0	8	2	.800	0	1	3.56
7 Min. YEARS		242	116	7	40	886.1	3884	948	519	455	62	36	24	63	339	8	519	45	14	52	66	.441	1	8	4.62

Harry Berrios

Bats: Right **Throws:** Right **Pos:** OF-54; DH-42; PH-3; 1B-1   **Ht:** 5'11" **Wt:** 205 **Born:** 12/2/71 **Age:** 30

Year Team	Lg Org	G	AB	H	2B	3B	HR	TB	R	RBI	TBB	IBB	SO	HBP	SH	SF	SB	CS	SB%	GDP	Avg	OBP	SLG
1993 Albany	A Bal	46	145	30	5	1	3	46	16	16	18	1	20	5	0	2	2	0	1.00	3	.207	.312	.317
1994 Albany	A Bal	42	162	54	12	2	6	88	42	35	18	1	23	9	0	1	14	0	1.00	4	.333	.426	.543
Frederick	A+ Bal	86	325	113	13	0	13	165	70	71	32	2	47	18	2	2	42	14	.75	6	.348	.432	.508
Bowie	AA Bal	1	4	1	1	0	0	2	1	0	0	0	1	0	0	0	0	0	—	0	.250	.250	.500
1995 Frederick	A+ Bal	71	240	50	5	2	10	89	33	28	32	3	66	4	0	2	10	6	.63	3	.208	.309	.371
Bowie	AA Bal	56	208	51	13	0	5	79	32	21	26	1	44	1	1	0	12	2	.86	6	.245	.332	.380
1996 Bowie	AA Bal	37	123	23	4	0	6	45	19	17	16	1	24	6	1	1	7	2	.78	5	.187	.308	.366
Frederick	A+ Bal	43	161	37	9	1	4	60	25	20	12	0	21	3	1	2	8	3	.73	5	.230	.292	.373
Kinston	A+ Cle	24	73	14	5	0	2	25	7	11	9	0	16	0	1	1	2	0	1.00	3	.192	.277	.342
1997 Sioux Falls	IND —	75	294	83	14	1	14	141	41	61	21	2	60	7	1	2	7	1	.88	6	.282	.343	.480
1998 Sioux Falls	IND —	25	94	30	8	0	5	53	20	16	14	0	19	4	0	1	2	0	1.00	5	.319	.425	.564
Thunder Bay	IND —	33	137	44	9	0	6	71	24	22	7	0	16	0	1	1	10	2	.83	6	.321	.352	.518
1999 Schaumburg	IND —	84	359	111	15	1	11	161	65	59	24	1	56	8	2	1	26	6	.81	8	.309	.365	.448
2000 Schaumburg	IND —	62	256	84	25	1	11	144	56	38	24	2	56	4	0	1	17	1	.94	5	.328	.393	.563
Tulsa	AA Tex	24	102	33	6	1	5	56	20	18	3	0	12	0	1	1	5	1	.83	3	.324	.340	.549
2001 Oklahoma	AAA Tex	61	231	59	8	4	7	96	33	33	14	0	47	3	0	2	3	0	1.00	7	.255	.304	.416
Tulsa	AA Tex	37	149	39	10	0	7	70	20	23	10	1	33	0	0	0	4	1	.80	2	.262	.308	.470
9 Min. YEARS		807	3063	856	162	14	115	1391	524	489	280	15	561	72	10	20	171	39	.81	74	.279	.352	.454

Cristian Berroa

Bats: Both **Throws:** Right **Pos:** SS-40; 2B-28; PH-8; PR-4; DH-3   **Ht:** 5'11" **Wt:** 150 **Born:** 4/27/79 **Age:** 23

Year Team	Lg Org	G	AB	H	2B	3B	HR	TB	R	RBI	TBB	IBB	SO	HBP	SH	SF	SB	CS	SB%	GDP	Avg	OBP	SLG
1998 Padres	R SD	53	207	66	22	2	1	95	33	33	4	1	38	4	0	3	8	4	.67	0	.319	.339	.459
1999 Fort Wayne	A SD	119	442	106	12	3	4	136	49	40	14	0	71	3	5	5	25	11	.69	9	.240	.265	.308
2000 Rancho Cuca	A+ SD	130	488	132	19	4	4	171	76	50	28	0	62	17	4	5	30	16	.65	25	.270	.329	.350
2001 Michigan	A Hou	36	123	40	4	0	2	50	19	23	7	0	13	5	1	1	5	7	.42	4	.325	.382	.407
New Orleans	AAA Hou	8	15	2	0	0	0	2	1	1	3	0	4	0	0	0	0	1	.00	0	.133	.278	.133
Round Rock	AA Hou	38	113	23	3	1	0	28	12	2	7	1	15	0	1	2	6	4	.60	1	.204	.246	.248
4 Min. YEARS		384	1388	369	60	10	11	482	190	149	63	2	203	29	11	16	74	43	.63	39	.266	.308	.347

Geronimo Berroa

Bats: Right **Throws:** Right **Pos:** DH-9; OF-4; 1B-3   **Ht:** 6'0" **Wt:** 210 **Born:** 3/18/65 **Age:** 37

Year Team	Lg Org	G	AB	H	2B	3B	HR	TB	R	RBI	TBB	IBB	SO	HBP	SH	SF	SB	CS	SB%	GDP	Avg	OBP	SLG
1984 Blue Jays	R Tor	62	235	59	16	1	3	86	31	34	12	2	34	2	0	2	2	3	.40	1	.251	.291	.366
1985 Kinston	A+ Tor	19	43	8	0	0	1	11	4	4	4	0	10	0	0	1	0	1	.00	0	.186	.256	.256
Medcine Hat	R+ Tor	54	201	69	22	2	6	113	39	45	18	0	40	3	0	1	7	2	.78	4	.343	.404	.562
Florence	A Tor	19	66	21	2	0	3	32	7	20	6	0	13	0	1	1	0	1	.00	0	.318	.370	.485
1986 Ventura	A+ Tor	128	459	137	22	5	21	232	76	73	38	2	92	5	1	8	12	9	.57	3	.298	.353	.505
Knoxville	AA Tor	1	4	0	0	0	0	0	0	0	0	0	1	0	0	0	0	0	—	0	.000	.000	.000
1987 Knoxville	AA Tor	134	523	150	33	3	36	297	87	108	46	1	104	5	0	7	2	1	.67	4	.287	.346	.568
1988 Syracuse	AAA Tor	131	470	122	29	1	8	177	55	64	38	5	88	10	0	8	7	5	.58	8	.260	.323	.377
1990 Richmond	AAA Atl	135	499	134	17	2	12	191	56	80	34	5	89	7	0	4	4	3	.57	17	.269	.322	.383

(Batting)

Year Team	Lg Org	G	AB	H	2B	3B	HR	TB	R	RBI	TBB	IBB	SO	HBP	SH	SF	SB	CS	SB%	GDP	Avg	OBP	SLG
1991 Colo Sprngs	AAA Cle	125	478	154	31	7	18	253	81	91	35	2	88	2	1	3	2	1	.67	10	.322	.369	.529
1992 Nashville	AAA Cin	112	461	151	33	2	22	254	73	88	32	1	69	8	0	4	8	9	.47	10	.328	.378	.551
1993 Edmonton	AAA Fla	90	327	107	33	4	16	196	64	68	36	3	71	4	0	3	1	2	.33	6	.327	.397	.599
1999 Syracuse	AAA Tor	10	33	9	0	0	3	18	7	8	8	1	5	0	0	0	0	0	—	2	.273	.415	.545
Dunedin	A+ Tor	4	5	1	1	0	0	2	1	2	2	0	1	1	0	0	0	0	—	0	.200	.500	.400
2001 Ottawa	AAA Mon	16	56	16	3	0	2	25	8	2	9	2	8	1	0	0	0	0	—	3	.286	.394	.446
1989 Atlanta	NL	81	136	36	4	0	2	46	7	9	7	1	32	0	0	0	0	1	.00	2	.265	.301	.338
1990 Atlanta	NL	7	4	0	0	0	0	0	0	0	1	1	1	0	0	0	0	0	—	0	.000	.200	.000
1992 Cincinnati	NL	13	15	4	1	0	0	5	2	0	2	0	1	1	0	0	0	0	.00	1	.267	.389	.333
1993 Florida	NL	14	34	4	1	0	0	5	3	0	2	0	7	0	0	0	0	0	—	2	.118	.167	.147
1994 Oakland	AL	96	340	104	18	2	13	165	55	65	41	0	62	3	0	7	7	2	.78	5	.306	.379	.485
1995 Oakland	AL	141	546	152	22	3	22	246	87	88	63	2	98	1	0	6	7	4	.64	12	.278	.351	.451
1996 Oakland	AL	153	586	170	32	1	36	312	101	106	47	0	122	4	0	6	0	3	.00	16	.290	.344	.532
1997 Oakland	AL	73	261	81	12	0	16	141	40	42	36	2	58	1	0	1	3	2	.60	12	.310	.395	.540
Baltimore	AL	83	300	78	13	0	10	121	48	48	40	2	62	3	0	6	1	2	.33	6	.260	.347	.403
1998 Cleveland	AL	20	65	13	3	1	0	18	6	3	7	0	17	0	0	0	1	0	1.00	2	.200	.278	.277
Detroit	AL	52	126	30	4	1	1	39	17	10	17	1	27	2	0	0	0	1	.00	3	.238	.338	.310
1999 Toronto	AL	22	62	12	3	0	1	18	11	6	9	0	15	2	0	0	0	0	—	5	.194	.315	.290
2000 Los Angeles	NL	24	31	8	0	1	0	10	2	5	4	1	8	0	0	0	0	0	—	0	.258	.343	.323
11 Min. YEARS		1040	3860	1138	242	27	151	1887	589	687	318	20	713	48	3	42	45	37	.55	68	.295	.352	.489
11 Maj. YEARS		779	2506	692	113	9	101	1126	379	382	276	10	510	17	0	26	19	16	.54	68	.276	.349	.449

Jon Berry

Pitches: Right **Bats:** Right **Pos:** RP-30; SP-6   **Ht:** 6'1" **Wt:** 185 **Born:** 11/17/77 **Age:** 24

Year Team	Lg Org	G	GS	CG	GF	IP	BFP	H	R	ER	HR	SH	SF	HB	TBB	IBB	SO	WP	Bk	W	L	Pct.	ShO	Sv	ERA
1999 Yakima	A- LA	16	10	0	1	58	299	81	68	56	3	1	4	3	46	0	31	15	0	1	6	.143	0	0	8.69
2000 San Berndno	A+ LA	40	0	0	24	68.2	310	57	33	24	3	6	2	5	47	2	68	6	0	7	4	.636	0	5	3.15
2001 Vero Beach	A+ LA	33	5	0	13	69	300	58	34	29	4	0	2	4	37	0	71	8	0	2	4	.333	0	8	3.78
Jacksnville	AA LA	3	1	0	0	9	35	6	3	3	0	1	0	0	4	0	5	0	0	0	1	.000	0	0	3.00
3 Min. YEARS		92	16	0	38	204.2	944	202	138	112	10	8	8	12	134	2	175	29	0	10	15	.400	0	13	4.93

Mike Bertotti

Pitches: Left **Bats:** Left **Pos:** RP-16; SP-15   **Ht:** 6'1" **Wt:** 185 **Born:** 1/18/70 **Age:** 32

Year Team	Lg Org	G	GS	CG	GF	IP	BFP	H	R	ER	HR	SH	SF	HB	TBB	IBB	SO	WP	Bk	W	L	Pct.	ShO	Sv	ERA
1991 Utica	A- CWS	14	5	0	3	37.1	186	38	33	24	2	1	3	2	36	0	33	9	0	3	4	.429	0	0	5.79
1992 South Bend	A CWS	11	0	0	5	19.1	86	12	8	8	1	1	1	1	22	0	17	1	1	0	3	.000	0	1	3.72
Utica	A- CWS	17	1	0	5	33.1	146	36	28	23	2	0	1	2	31	0	23	7	1	2	2	.500	0	1	6.21
1993 Hickory	A CWS	9	9	2	0	59.2	248	42	19	14	2	4	0	1	29	1	77	2	3	3	3	.500	0	1	2.11
South Bend	A CWS	17	16	2	0	111	466	93	51	43	5	6	6	6	44	2	108	7	1	5	7	.417	2	0	3.49
1994 Pr William	A+ CWS	16	15	2	0	104.2	435	90	48	41	13	2	1	3	43	0	103	8	1	7	6	.538	1	0	3.53
Birmingham	AA CWS	10	10	1	0	68.1	273	55	25	22	1	2	3	0	21	1	44	5	0	4	3	.571	0	0	2.90
1995 Birmingham	AA CWS	12	12	1	0	63	279	60	38	35	4	0	4	2	36	0	53	8	0	2	7	.222	0	0	5.00
Nashville	AAA CWS	7	6	0	1	32	164	41	34	31	8	0	1	3	17	0	35	0	0	2	3	.400	0	0	8.72
1996 Nashville	AAA CWS	28	9	1	5	82.1	365	80	43	40	10	5	4	2	42	3	73	3	0	5	3	.625	0	0	4.37
1997 Nashville	AAA CWS	21	20	1	0	107.2	505	91	70	64	17	1	7	2	105	0	87	15	0	5	9	.357	0	0	5.35
1998 Calgary	AAA CWS	43	6	0	16	80.1	383	90	56	53	10	3	6	4	50	0	64	8	0	3	2	.600	0	3	5.94
1999 Tacoma	AAA Sea	3	3	0	0	7	43	6	8	8	0	1	0	0	17	0	6	1	0	0	2	.000	0	0	10.29
Midland	AA Oak	20	0	0	6	25.2	141	30	26	24	0	0	1	1	37	0	25	7	0	2	3	.400	0	1	8.42
Waterbury	IND —	7	7	0	0	35.2	159	39	25	24	5	0	3	1	17	0	40	3	0	0	1	.000	0	0	6.06
2000 Waterbury	IND —	12	12	5	0	81.1	324	53	27	18	3	5	1	2	35	0	86	6	0	5	7	.417	1	0	1.99
Columbus	AAA NYY	7	3	0	2	24	104	23	16	12	2	0	0	0	8	0	23	2	0	1	1	.500	0	0	4.50
2001 Columbus	AAA NYY	19	4	0	6	41.1	189	37	21	17	4	4	1	1	28	0	43	2	0	1	2	.333	0	0	3.70
New Jersey	IND —	12	11	2	1	71	297	48	32	30	4	2	2	1	37	0	99	8	0	6	2	.750	0	0	3.80
1995 Chicago	AL	4	4	0	0	14.1	80	23	20	20	6	0	3	3	11	0	15	2	1	1	1	.500	0	0	12.56
1996 Chicago	AL	15	2	0	4	28	150	30	18	16	5	0	1	0	20	3	19	4	0	2	0	1.000	0	0	5.14
1997 Chicago	AL	9	0	0	2	3.2	23	9	3	3	0	0	1	0	2	0	4	0	1	0	0	—	0	0	7.36
11 Min. YEARS		285	149	17	50	1085	4801	964	608	531	93	37	45	34	655	7	1039	102	7	56	70	.444	5	7	4.40
3 Maj. YEARS		28	6	0	6	46	233	60	41	39	11	0	5	3	33	3	38	6	2	3	1	.750	0	0	7.63

Stephen Bess

Pitches: Right **Bats:** Right **Pos:** RP-42; SP-1   **Ht:** 6'4" **Wt:** 225 **Born:** 9/1/76 **Age:** 25

Year Team	Lg Org	G	GS	CG	GF	IP	BFP	H	R	ER	HR	SH	SF	HB	TBB	IBB	SO	WP	Bk	W	L	Pct.	ShO	Sv	ERA
1999 Oneonta	A- Det	7	1	0	2	17	67	9	2	2	1	0	0	0	7	2	23	1	0	0	0	—	0	2	1.06
W Michigan	A Det	12	0	0	7	19.1	76	12	2	2	0	0	0	0	7	0	23	1	0	1	1	.500	0	3	0.93
2000 Lakeland	A+ Det	26	0	0	11	36	178	40	26	22	2	2	2	1	27	0	23	6	0	1	3	.250	0	5	5.50
2001 Lakeland	A+ Det	33	0	0	29	37.1	151	25	12	11	1	1	2	4	12	1	39	2	0	2	3	.400	0	19	2.65
Erie	AA Det	10	1	0	2	18.2	73	15	6	6	1	0	1	2	4	0	8	0	0	0	2	.000	0	0	2.89
3 Min. YEARS		88	2	0	51	128.1	545	101	48	43	5	4	5	7	57	5	116	10	0	4	9	.308	0	29	3.02

Rafael Betancourt

Pitches: Right **Bats:** Right **Pos:** RP-16   **Ht:** 6'2" **Wt:** 176 **Born:** 4/29/75 **Age:** 27

Year Team	Lg Org	G	GS	CG	GF	IP	BFP	H	R	ER	HR	SH	SF	HB	TBB	IBB	SO	WP	Bk	W	L	Pct.	ShO	Sv	ERA
1997 Michigan	A Bos	27	0	0	22	32.1	125	26	9	7	2	1	0	0	2	0	52	3	1	0	3	.000	0	11	1.95
1998 Red Sox	R Bos	4	3	0	0	5	22	6	5	4	1	0	1	0	1	0	4	1	1	0	2	.000	0	0	7.20
Sarasota	A+ Bos	20	0	0	4	28	111	22	12	11	2	1	0	0	6	0	33	0	0	3	1	.750	0	2	3.54
Trenton	AA Bos	7	0	0	3	9.1	42	9	7	7	1	0	0	0	3	0	9	0	0	0	0	—	0	0	6.75

		HOW MUCH HE PITCHED				WHAT HE GAVE UP											THE RESULTS					
Year Team	Lg Org	G	GS	CG	GF	IP	BFP	H	R	ER	HR	SH	SF	HB	TBB	IBB	SO	WP	Bk	W	L	Pct.	ShO	Sv	ERA
1999 Sarasota	A+ Bos	6	0	0	5	7	25	5	0	0	0	0	0	0	1	0	6	0	0	0	0	—	0	4	0.00
Trenton	AA Bos	39	0	0	30	54.2	218	50	24	22	7	4	2	0	10	0	57	0	1	6	2	.750	0	13	3.62
2001 Trenton	AA Bos	16	0	0	10	24	100	28	16	15	0	0	0	2	3	0	27	1	0	0	1	.000	0	4	5.63
4 Min. YEARS		119	3	0	74	160.1	643	146	73	66	12	7	3	2	26	0	188	5	3	9	9	.500	0	34	3.70

Todd Betts

Bats: Left **Throws:** Right **Pos:** 1B-105; 3B-25; DH-9; PH-3   **Ht:** 6'0" **Wt:** 185 **Born:** 6/24/73 **Age:** 29

		BATTING														BASERUNNING				PERCENTAGES		
Year Team	Lg Org	G	AB	H	2B	3B	HR	TB	R	RBI	TBB	IBB	SO	HBP	SH	SF	SB	CS	SB%	GDP	Avg	OBP	SLG
1993 Burlington	R+ Cle	56	168	39	9	0	7	69	40	27	32	2	26	3	0	1	6	1	.86	4	.232	.363	.411
1994 Watertown	A- Cle	65	227	74	18	2	10	126	49	53	54	2	29	4	1	2	3	2	.60	1	.326	.460	.555
1995 Kinston	A+ Cle	109	331	90	15	3	9	138	52	44	88	2	56	6	1	4	2	3	.40	5	.272	.429	.417
1996 Canton-Akrn	AA Cle	77	238	60	13	0	1	76	35	26	38	2	51	5	0	4	0	1	.00	6	.252	.361	.319
1997 Akron	AA Cle	128	434	108	15	1	20	195	65	69	73	8	97	4	1	5	1	3	.25	6	.246	.355	.444
1998 Akron	AA Cle	91	318	86	18	3	17	161	55	46	64	5	71	4	0	2	1	0	1.00	7	.270	.397	.506
Buffalo	AAA Cle	14	35	8	3	0	2	17	5	6	8	0	7	0	0	1	0	0	—	0	.229	.364	.486
1999 Akron	AA Cle	104	375	105	24	1	19	188	60	67	61	2	65	7	0	3	2	1	.67	3	.280	.388	.501
2000 Calgary	AAA Fla	1	1	0	0	0	0	0	0	0	0	0	0	0	0	0	0	0	—	0	.000	.000	.000
Portland	AA Fla	119	434	135	26	2	9	192	74	71	64	3	57	8	0	5	4	3	.57	6	.321	.416	.456
2001 Tacoma	AAA Sea	135	506	156	40	5	14	248	87	65	51	4	55	3	1	4	3	4	.43	11	.308	.372	.490
9 Min. YEARS		899	3059	861	191	17	108	1410	522	474	533	30	514	44	4	31	22	18	.55	49	.281	.392	.461

Jim Betzsold

Bats: Right **Throws:** Right **Pos:** OF-42; DH-6; PR-1   **Ht:** 6'3" **Wt:** 210 **Born:** 8/7/72 **Age:** 29

		BATTING														BASERUNNING				PERCENTAGES		
Year Team	Lg Org	G	AB	H	2B	3B	HR	TB	R	RBI	TBB	IBB	SO	HBP	SH	SF	SB	CS	SB%	GDP	Avg	OBP	SLG
1994 Watertown	A- Cle	66	212	61	18	0	12	115	48	46	53	1	68	15	1	2	3	3	.50	2	.288	.457	.542
1995 Kinston	A+ Cle	126	455	122	22	2	25	223	77	71	55	3	137	10	0	4	3	5	.38	4	.268	.357	.490
1996 Canton-Akrn	AA Cle	84	268	64	11	5	3	94	35	35	30	1	74	6	1	1	4	1	.80	3	.239	.328	.351
1997 Akron	AA Cle	118	434	115	21	5	19	203	76	79	60	2	119	10	0	2	4	5	.44	12	.265	.366	.468
1998 Buffalo	AAA Cle	74	209	51	10	1	10	93	36	27	27	0	72	6	0	0	4	4	.50	3	.244	.347	.445
1999 Jackson	AA Hou	38	126	30	6	1	6	56	30	17	22	0	35	5	1	0	4	3	.57	2	.238	.373	.444
New Orleans	AAA Hou	63	198	43	15	0	7	79	29	27	14	0	64	3	0	2	3	2	.60	1	.217	.276	.399
2000 New Orleans	AAA Hou	93	314	89	17	1	8	132	47	49	29	1	101	4	0	1	16	7	.70	8	.283	.351	.420
2001 Tacoma	AAA Sea	48	157	25	4	2	8	57	20	25	21	0	71	3	0	0	0	0	—	3	.159	.271	.363
8 Min. YEARS		710	2373	600	124	17	98	1052	398	376	311	8	741	62	3	12	41	30	.58	38	.253	.353	.443

Bobby Bevel

Pitches: Left **Bats:** Left **Pos:** RP-55; SP-1   **Ht:** 5'10" **Wt:** 180 **Born:** 10/10/73 **Age:** 28

		HOW MUCH HE PITCHED						WHAT HE GAVE UP											THE RESULTS					
Year Team	Lg Org	G	GS	CG	GF	IP	BFP	H	R	ER	HR	SH	SF	HB	TBB	IBB	SO	WP	Bk	W	L	Pct.	ShO	Sv	ERA
1995 Portland	A- Col	25	0	0	8	28	128	24	13	11	0	3	2	1	18	4	25	5	0	2	3	.400	0	1	3.54
1996 Asheville	A Col	41	0	0	10	68	286	61	25	24	4	3	1	2	30	2	60	6	0	4	2	.667	0	0	3.18
1997 Salem	A+ Col	50	0	0	18	66	290	69	37	34	5	2	7	9	17	0	57	3	0	4	7	.364	0	3	4.64
1998 Salem	A+ Col	51	0	0	26	91.2	373	72	26	23	4	2	3	4	24	0	92	5	1	6	4	.600	0	3	2.26
1999 Carolina	AA Col	48	0	0	22	67	294	70	37	33	7	4	1	2	27	2	58	9	0	3	7	.300	0	7	4.43
2000 San Antonio	AA LA	47	1	0	19	78.1	365	86	52	49	8	8	0	6	44	5	75	7	0	4	5	.444	0	2	5.63
2001 Jacksnville	AA LA	31	0	0	16	46	189	42	14	10	3	2	2	2	11	0	33	1	0	2	2	.500	0	6	1.96
Las Vegas	AAA LA	25	1	0	3	35.1	153	36	19	18	5	2	4	1	16	3	29	1	0	0	2	.000	0	0	4.58
7 Min. YEARS		318	2	0	122	480.1	2078	460	223	202	36	26	20	27	187	16	429	37	1	25	32	.439	0	22	3.78

Jason Beverlin

Pitches: Right **Bats:** Left **Pos:** SP-18; RP-7   **Ht:** 6'5" **Wt:** 220 **Born:** 11/27/73 **Age:** 28

		HOW MUCH HE PITCHED						WHAT HE GAVE UP											THE RESULTS					
Year Team	Lg Org	G	GS	CG	GF	IP	BFP	H	R	ER	HR	SH	SF	HB	TBB	IBB	SO	WP	Bk	W	L	Pct.	ShO	Sv	ERA
1994 W Michigan	A Oak	17	1	0	5	41	168	32	12	8	0	1	0	2	14	0	48	3	4	3	2	.600	0	1	1.76
1995 W Michigan	A Oak	22	14	0	1	89	392	76	51	40	4	3	3	8	40	0	84	5	5	3	9	.250	0	0	4.04
Greensboro	A NYY	7	7	1	0	51	198	49	15	15	1	0	0	0	6	0	31	4	0	2	4	.333	1	0	2.65
1996 Norwich	AA NYY	8	4	0	1	16	81	25	21	15	2	0	2	0	6	1	17	0	0	3	.000	0	0	8.44
Tampa	A+ NYY	25	1	0	6	46.1	194	43	22	18	5	1	1	1	17	2	38	4	1	2	0	1.000	0	1	3.50
1997 Norwich	AA NYY	25	0	0	8	41.2	203	50	38	36	10	0	0	6	24	0	42	3	0	1	0	1.000	0	0	7.78
Tampa	A+ NYY	7	6	0	0	41.1	167	37	26	22	4	2	2	4	13	1	24	6	0	1	3	.250	0	0	4.79
1998 Norwich	AA NYY	25	9	0	8	81	343	68	34	33	5	2	4	3	38	0	86	6	1	3	5	.375	0	1	3.67
Tampa	A+ NYY	7	5	0	0	32	142	37	23	20	2	0	4	1	16	2	15	2	1	1	3	.250	0	0	5.63
1999 Norwich	AA NYY	28	27	1	0	173.1	743	153	91	71	16	6	7	6	81	0	147	10	1	15	9	.625	0	0	3.69
2000 Columbus	AAA NYY	3	3	0	0	6.2	45	19	14	14	1	0	0	0	14	0	6	1	0	0	3	.000	0	0	18.90
Norwich	AA NYY	24	24	1	0	143.2	618	110	61	45	7	3	4	10	87	2	100	6	0	8	9	.471	0	0	2.82
2001 Arkansas	AA Ana	6	6	0	0	39.1	164	36	15	12	4	0	1	3	11	0	30	4	0	4	2	.667	0	0	2.75
Salt Lake	AAA Ana	19	12	1	0	83	350	82	41	39	9	0	2	4	29	0	74	2	2	6	2	.750	0	0	4.23
8 Min. YEARS		223	119	4	29	885.1	3808	811	464	388	70	18	30	48	396	8	742	56	15	49	54	.476	1	3	3.94

29

Andy Bevins

Bats: Right **Throws:** Right **Pos:** OF-101; DH-21; 1B-17; PH-7   **Ht:** 6'3" **Wt:** 215 **Born:** 10/10/75 **Age:** 26

		BATTING																BASERUNNING				PERCENTAGES		
Year Team	Lg Org	G	AB	H	2B	3B	HR	TB	R	RBI	TBB	IBB	SO	HBP	SH	SF	SB	CS	SB%	GDP	Avg	OBP	SLG
1997 New Jersey	A- StL	65	235	64	9	5	9	110	35	44	18	1	66	3	0	3	2	1	.67	3	.272	.328	.468
1998 Peoria	A StL	130	508	124	30	3	18	214	68	98	34	1	145	10	1	3	6	4	.60	10	.244	.303	.421
1999 Potomac	A+ StL	138	513	142	30	2	25	251	92	97	44	2	128	11	3	4	6	2	.75	11	.277	.344	.489
2000 Arkansas	AA StL	125	430	138	27	4	25	248	84	88	34	0	87	11	0	3	0	4	.00	11	.321	.383	.577
Memphis	AAA StL	5	22	4	2	0	0	6	1	3	1	0	3	0	0	0	0	0	—	1	.182	.217	.273
2001 Memphis	AAA StL	43	146	37	8	0	7	66	24	20	12	1	47	4	0	1	0	2	.00	2	.253	.325	.452
New Haven	AA StL	99	348	69	14	1	13	124	43	40	36	2	65	9	0	0	5	7	.42	12	.198	.290	.356
5 Min. YEARS		605	2202	578	120	15	97	1019	347	390	179	7	541	48	4	14	19	20	.49	50	.262	.330	.463

P.J. Bevis

Pitches: Right **Bats:** Right **Pos:** RP-26   **Ht:** 6'3" **Wt:** 175 **Born:** 7/28/80 **Age:** 21

		HOW MUCH HE PITCHED						WHAT HE GAVE UP												THE RESULTS					
Year Team	Lg Org	G	GS	CG	GF	IP	BFP	H	R	ER	HR	SH	SF	HB	TBB	IBB	SO	WP	Bk	W	L	Pct.	ShO	Sv	ERA
1998 Diamondbcks	R Ari	14	9	0	1	45.1	205	55	39	30	6	0	0	5	10	0	48	3	3			.500	0	0	5.96
1999 Missoula	R+ Ari	15	15	0	0	85.2	357	83	51	44	11	1	0	7	30	0	69	6	2	6	2	.750	0	0	4.62
2000 Missoula	R+ Ari	14	14	0	0	83.2	354	92	50	31	4	1	2	2	22	1	63	8	1	3	6	.333	0	0	3.33
2001 Yakima	A- Ari	12	0	0	11	14	57	9	1	1	0	0	0	0	7	2	22	1	0	1	1	.500	0	8	0.64
El Paso	AA Ari	14	0	0	9	16.2	67	11	4	4	2	0	0	1	6	0	19	0	0	0	0	—	0	6	2.16
4 Min. YEARS		69	38	0	21	245.1	1040	250	145	110	23	2	2	15	75	3	221	22	3	13	12	.520	0	14	4.04

Kurt Bierek

Bats: Left **Throws:** Right **Pos:** OF-61; 1B-35; DH-12; PH-4; 3B-1   **Ht:** 6'4" **Wt:** 220 **Born:** 9/13/72 **Age:** 29

		BATTING																BASERUNNING				PERCENTAGES		
Year Team	Lg Org	G	AB	H	2B	3B	HR	TB	R	RBI	TBB	IBB	SO	HBP	SH	SF	SB	CS	SB%	GDP	Avg	OBP	SLG
1993 Oneonta	A- NYY	70	274	64	6	6	5	97	36	37	19	2	49	3	1	1	4	4	.50	4	.234	.290	.354
1994 Greensboro	A NYY	133	467	118	24	6	14	196	78	73	69	2	101	8	2	3	8	1	.89	10	.253	.356	.420
1995 Tampa	A+ NYY	126	447	111	16	2	4	143	60	53	61	3	73	4	2	2	3	4	.43	11	.248	.342	.320
1996 Tampa	A+ NYY	88	320	97	14	2	11	148	48	55	41	3	40	6	0	3	6	3	.67	5	.303	.389	.463
1997 Norwich	AA NYY	133	473	128	32	2	18	218	77	78	56	2	89	7	0	2	4	4	.50	8	.271	.355	.461
1998 Columbus	AAA NYY	14	50	15	5	1	1	25	8	8	5	0	8	0	0	0	0	0	—	2	.300	.364	.500
Norwich	AA NYY	95	344	81	13	2	13	137	44	61	50	1	61	3	0	2	0	1	.00	8	.235	.336	.398
1999 Columbus	AAA NYY	135	532	149	42	4	23	268	84	95	48	1	99	6	1	7	5	3	.63	14	.280	.342	.504
2000 Indianapols	AAA Mil	128	430	114	22	2	19	197	61	72	57	5	77	2	1	3	1	0	1.00	9	.265	.352	.458
2001 Toledo	AAA Det	105	394	107	27	1	16	184	64	53	32	1	76	3	0	6	2	2	.50	7	.272	.326	.467
9 Min. YEARS		1027	3731	984	201	28	124	1613	560	585	438	20	673	42	7	29	33	22	.60	78	.264	.345	.432

Steve Bieser

Bats: Left **Throws:** Right **Pos:** PH-6; OF-1   **Ht:** 5'10" **Wt:** 180 **Born:** 8/4/67 **Age:** 34

		BATTING																BASERUNNING				PERCENTAGES		
Year Team	Lg Org	G	AB	H	2B	3B	HR	TB	R	RBI	TBB	IBB	SO	HBP	SH	SF	SB	CS	SB%	GDP	Avg	OBP	SLG
1989 Batavia	A- Phi	25	75	18	3	1	1	26	13	13	12	0	20	2	2	2	2	1	.67	1	.240	.352	.347
1990 Batavia	A- Phi	54	160	37	11	1	0	50	36	12	26	1	27	1	2	2	13	2	.87	3	.231	.339	.313
1991 Spartanburg	A Phi	60	168	41	6	0	0	47	25	13	31	0	35	3	4	3	17	4	.81	4	.244	.366	.280
1992 Clearwater	A+ Phi	73	203	58	6	5	0	74	33	10	39	3	28	9	8	0	8	8	.50	2	.286	.422	.365
Reading	AA Phi	33	139	38	5	4	0	51	20	8	6	0	25	4	4	0	8	3	.73	3	.273	.322	.367
1993 Reading	AA Phi	53	170	53	6	3	1	68	21	19	15	1	24	2	1	0	9	5	.64	2	.312	.374	.400
Scranton-WB	AAA Phi	26	83	21	4	0	0	25	3	4	2	0	14	1	1	0	3	0	1.00	0	.253	.279	.301
1994 Scranton-WB	AAA Phi	93	228	61	13	1	0	76	42	15	17	1	40	5	4	2	12	8	.60	2	.268	.329	.333
1995 Scranton-WB	AAA Phi	95	245	66	12	6	1	93	37	33	22	1	56	10	6	2	14	5	.74	5	.269	.351	.380
1996 Ottawa	AAA Mon	123	382	123	24	4	1	158	63	32	35	4	55	6	23	2	27	7	.79	6	.322	.386	.414
1997 Norfolk	AAA NYM	41	122	20	5	0	0	25	6	4	9	0	20	5	2	0	4	3	.57	1	.164	.250	.205
1998 Nashville	AAA Pit	82	206	53	11	4	1	75	30	24	33	1	30	10	4	6	13	2	.87	4	.257	.376	.364
1999 Nashville	AAA Pit	6	13	3	1	0	0	4	3	3	2	0	4	1	0	0	0	0	—	0	.231	.375	.308
Altoona	AA Pit	40	148	31	5	2	4	52	24	23	21	0	32	4	0	1	3	4	.43	2	.209	.322	.351
Memphis	AAA StL	58	180	56	13	2	4	85	25	16	16	0	30	3	5	0	8	0	1.00	3	.311	.377	.472
2000 Memphis	AAA StL	94	262	67	11	3	0	84	41	14	35	2	29	7	4	1	10	3	.77	2	.256	.357	.321
2001 Memphis	AAA StL	7	8	0	0	0	0	0	1	0	1	0	5	1	0	1	0	0	—	1	.000	.200	.000
1997 New York	NL	47	69	17	3	0	0	20	16	4	7	1	20	4	0	1	2	3	.40	0	.246	.346	.290
1998 Pittsburgh	NL	13	11	3	1	0	0	4	2	1	2	0	2	0	0	0	0	0	—	1	.273	.385	.364
13 Min. YEARS		963	2792	746	136	36	13	993	423	243	322	14	474	74	70	21	151	55	.73	40	.267	.356	.356
2 Maj. YEARS		60	80	20	4	0	0	24	18	5	9	1	22	4	0	1	2	3	.40	1	.250	.351	.300

Brent Billingsley

Pitches: Left **Bats:** Left **Pos:** SP-20   **Ht:** 6'2" **Wt:** 200 **Born:** 4/19/75 **Age:** 27

		HOW MUCH HE PITCHED						WHAT HE GAVE UP												THE RESULTS					
Year Team	Lg Org	G	GS	CG	GF	IP	BFP	H	R	ER	HR	SH	SF	HB	TBB	IBB	SO	WP	Bk	W	L	Pct.	ShO	Sv	ERA
1996 Utica	A- Fla	15	15	0	0	89.2	373	83	46	40	6	0	4	3	28	0	82	5	1	4	5	.444	0	0	4.01
1997 Kane County	A Fla	26	26	3	0	170.2	697	146	67	57	9	7	1	11	50	0	175	13	1	14	7	.667	1	0	3.01
1998 Portland	AA Fla	28	28	0	0	171	741	172	90	71	24	5	6	6	70	2	183	17	1	6	13	.316	0	0	3.74
1999 Calgary	AAA Fla	21	21	0	0	116.2	522	133	81	72	15	9	3	1	48	0	79	8	0	2	9	.182	0	0	5.55
2000 Ottawa	AAA Mon	20	20	0	0	103.1	464	118	73	65	14	4	2	3	46	0	76	7	0	8	9	.471	0	0	5.66
2001 Ottawa	AAA Mon	1	1	0	0	3	16	6	5	5	0	0	0	0	2	0	2	0	0	0	0	—	0	0	15.00
Harrisburg	AA Mon	19	19	1	0	112.1	492	128	77	67	20	0	3	5	34	1	97	11	0	7	9	.438	0	0	5.37
1999 Florida	NL	8	0	0	3	7.2	35	11	14	14	3	0	1	2	10	0	3	1	0	0	0	—	0	0	16.43
6 Min. YEARS		130	130	4	0	766.2	3305	786	439	377	88	25	16	29	278	3	694	61	3	41	52	.441	1	0	4.43

Darren Blakely

Bats: Both **Throws:** Right **Pos:** OF-120; PH-4; PR-1   **Ht:** 6'0" **Wt:** 190 **Born:** 3/14/77 **Age:** 25

Year Team	Lg Org	G	AB	H	2B	3B	HR	TB	R	RBI	TBB	IBB	SO	HBP	SH	SF	SB	CS	SB%	GDP	Avg	OBP	SLG
1998 Boise	A- Ana	71	267	74	9	6	5	110	50	33	34	3	69	22	1	4	9	3	.75	2	.277	.398	.412
1999 Lk Elsinore	A+ Ana	124	510	128	38	10	12	222	88	63	36	1	159	20	1	4	23	13	.64	3	.251	.323	.435
2000 Erie	AA Ana	122	439	104	20	7	16	186	72	54	30	1	136	20	6	2	13	5	.72	11	.237	.314	.424
2001 Norwich	AA NYY	10	20	6	0	0	0	6	2	2	2	0	4	2	0	0	3	2	.60	0	.300	.417	.300
Tampa	A+ NYY	86	313	80	14	5	12	140	47	39	41	0	94	13	3	2	24	11	.69	3	.256	.363	.447
Mobile	AA SD	28	115	25	4	2	6	51	19	15	11	0	41	3	1	1	4	4	.50	0	.217	.300	.443
4 Min. YEARS		441	1664	417	85	30	51	715	278	206	154	5	503	80	12	13	76	38	.67	19	.251	.341	.430

Hank Blalock

Bats: Left **Throws:** Left **Pos:** 3B-129; DH-2   **Ht:** 6'1" **Wt:** 192 **Born:** 11/21/80 **Age:** 21

Year Team	Lg Org	G	AB	H	2B	3B	HR	TB	R	RBI	TBB	IBB	SO	HBP	SH	SF	SB	CS	SB%	GDP	Avg	OBP	SLG
1999 Rangers	R Tex	51	191	69	17	6	3	107	34	38	25	4	23	1	0	5	3	2	.60	7	.361	.428	.560
Savannah	A Tex	7	25	6	1	0	1	10	3	2	1	0	3	1	0	1	0	0	—	0	.240	.286	.400
2000 Savannah	A Tex	139	512	153	32	2	10	219	66	77	62	3	53	5	0	11	31	8	.79	14	.299	.373	.428
2001 Charlotte	A+ Tex	63	237	90	19	1	7	132	46	47	26	7	31	1	0	4	7	4	.64	6	.380	.437	.557
Tulsa	AA Tex	68	272	89	18	4	11	148	50	61	39	1	38	2	0	2	3	3	.50	5	.327	.413	.544
3 Min. YEARS		328	1237	407	87	13	32	616	199	225	153	15	148	10	0	23	44	17	.72	32	.329	.401	.498

Dave Bleazard

Pitches: Right **Bats:** Right **Pos:** SP-5; RP-3   **Ht:** 6'0" **Wt:** 175 **Born:** 3/7/74 **Age:** 28

Year Team	Lg Org	G	GS	CG	GF	IP	BFP	H	R	ER	HR	SH	SF	HB	TBB	IBB	SO	WP	Bk	W	L	Pct.	ShO	Sv	ERA
1996 Medcine Hat	R+ Tor	20	0	0	19	23.2	115	29	16	12	0	0	1	2	14	0	31	1	0	0	0	—	0	10	4.56
1997 Hagerstown	A Tor	10	10	0	0	59.2	250	52	25	22	1	1	2	5	20	0	58	5	4	5	0	1.000	0	0	3.32
1998 Dunedin	A+ Tor	14	0	0	4	19	88	20	14	9	1	1	0	2	11	0	20	4	1	1	0	1.000	0	0	4.26
1999 Dunedin	A+ Tor	14	13	1	1	90.2	374	73	36	23	1	2	1	2	30	1	58	5	1	6	6	.500	0	0	2.28
Knoxville	AA Tor	15	15	1	0	86.2	358	81	36	31	4	1	4	4	34	0	49	7	2	5	3	.625	1	0	3.22
2001 Tennessee	AA Tor	3	3	0	0	20	75	15	3	3	1	0	0	0	5	0	11	0	0	0	0	—	0	0	1.35
Syracuse	AAA Tor	5	2	0	2	13.2	66	15	15	15	2	0	0	1	11	0	7	0	0	0	2	.000	0	0	9.88
5 Min. YEARS		81	43	2	26	313.1	1326	285	145	115	10	5	8	16	125	1	234	22	8	17	11	.607	1	10	3.30

Jeremy Blevins

Pitches: Right **Bats:** Right **Pos:** RP-50   **Ht:** 6'3" **Wt:** 190 **Born:** 10/5/77 **Age:** 24

Year Team	Lg Org	G	GS	CG	GF	IP	BFP	H	R	ER	HR	SH	SF	HB	TBB	IBB	SO	WP	Bk	W	L	Pct.	ShO	Sv	ERA
1995 Angels	R Ana	11	9	0	0	51.1	224	39	20	14	0	2	0	4	32	0	48	4	1	5	1	.833	0	0	2.45
1996 Boise	A- Ana	14	13	0	0	58.2	283	54	49	43	4	1	6	5	58	2	39	13	1	2	3	.400	0	0	6.60
1997 Yankees	R NYY	11	9	0	0	55.2	235	50	27	15	1	0	0	4	23	1	46	4	0	5	3	.625	0	0	2.43
1998 Greensboro	A NYY	24	23	0	0	119.2	545	121	80	64	5	3	4	5	66	0	110	10	1	5	8	.385	0	0	4.81
1999 Tampa	A+ NYY	1	0	0	0	1.2	11	4	3	0	0	0	0	1	1	0	0	0	0	0	0	—	0	0	0.00
Greensboro	A NYY	19	19	0	0	106.2	449	105	56	48	7	1	3	3	30	0	81	8	0	10	5	.667	0	0	4.05
2000 Tampa	A+ NYY	42	12	0	26	95.1	417	96	50	47	5	2	2	3	49	2	104	6	1	3	7	.300	0	20	4.44
2001 Norwich	AA NYY	50	0	0	22	63.1	265	46	30	21	2	4	2	1	26	3	63	3	0	1	6	.143	0	6	2.98
7 Min. YEARS		172	85	0	48	552.1	2429	515	315	252	24	13	17	26	285	8	491	48	4	31	33	.484	0	26	4.11

Willie Bloomquist

Bats: Right **Throws:** Right **Pos:** SS-76; 2B-57; PR-2   **Ht:** 5'11" **Wt:** 180 **Born:** 11/27/77 **Age:** 24

Year Team	Lg Org	G	AB	H	2B	3B	HR	TB	R	RBI	TBB	IBB	SO	HBP	SH	SF	SB	CS	SB%	GDP	Avg	OBP	SLG
1999 Everett	A- Sea	42	178	51	10	3	2	73	35	27	22	0	25	1	0	1	17	5	.77	1	.287	.366	.410
2000 Lancaster	A+ Sea	64	256	97	19	6	2	134	63	51	37	2	27	0	1	1	22	12	.65	3	.379	.456	.523
Tacoma	AAA Sea	51	191	43	5	1	1	53	17	23	7	0	28	0	4	3	5	0	1.00	3	.225	.249	.277
2001 San Antonio	AA Sea	123	491	125	23	2	0	152	59	28	28	0	55	1	7	4	34	9	.79	11	.255	.294	.310
3 Min. YEARS		280	1116	316	57	12	5	412	174	129	94	2	135	2	12	9	78	26	.75	18	.283	.337	.369

Doug Bochtler

Pitches: Right **Bats:** Right **Pos:** RP-46; SP-3   **Ht:** 6'3" **Wt:** 200 **Born:** 7/5/70 **Age:** 31

Year Team	Lg Org	G	GS	CG	GF	IP	BFP	H	R	ER	HR	SH	SF	HB	TBB	IBB	SO	WP	Bk	W	L	Pct.	ShO	Sv	ERA
1989 Expos	R Mon	9	9	1	0	47.2	209	46	22	17	0	2	2	0	20	1	45	3	1	2	2	.500	0	0	3.21
1990 Rockford	A Mon	25	25	1	0	139	602	142	82	54	3	6	4	8	54	2	109	6	5	9	12	.429	1	0	3.50
1991 Wst Plm Bch	A+ Mon	26	24	7	1	160.1	647	148	63	52	6	6	2	6	54	2	109	7	0	12	9	.571	2	0	2.92
1992 Harrisburg	AA Mon	13	13	2	0	77.2	310	50	25	20	1	2	2	2	36	1	89	4	0	6	5	.545	1	0	2.32
1993 Central Val	A+ Col	8	8	0	0	47.2	205	40	23	18	2	1	0	1	28	0	43	2	0	3	1	.750	0	0	3.40
Colo Sprngs	AAA Col	12	11	0	0	50.2	239	71	41	39	3	2	2	1	26	1	38	2	0	1	4	.200	0	0	6.93
Las Vegas	AAA SD	7	7	1	0	39.2	177	52	26	23	2	1	1	0	11	1	30	1	0	0	5	.000	0	0	5.22
1994 Las Vegas	AAA SD	22	20	2	1	100.1	458	116	67	58	11	5	3	3	48	2	86	10	0	3	7	.300	1	0	5.20
1995 Las Vegas	AAA SD	18	2	0	7	36	161	31	18	17	5	1	1	2	26	6	32	2	0	2	3	.400	0	1	4.25
1999 Syracuse	AAA Tor	14	0	0	3	27.1	110	18	9	8	1	0	3	0	10	0	28	0	0	4	0	1.000	0	0	2.63
Albuquerque	AAA LA	18	0	0	9	22.2	93	16	9	8	3	0	0	0	11	1	25	5	0	3	4	.429	0	0	3.18
2000 Omaha	AAA KC	27	0	0	13	40.1	179	37	19	18	4	1	2	0	28	6	28	3	0	2	1	.667	0	2	4.02
2001 Wichita	AA KC	15	2	0	7	31	123	26	10	10	1	1	1	1	9	1	38	0	0	0	0	—	0	4	2.90
Edmonton	AAA Min	34	1	0	20	45.2	192	41	16	14	5	1	0	0	19	0	65	0	0	2	5	.286	0	3	2.76
1995 San Diego	NL	34	0	0	11	45.1	181	38	18	18	5	2	1	0	19	0	45	1	0	4	4	.500	0	3	3.57

Year Team	Lg Org	G	GS	CG	GF	IP	BFP	H	R	ER	HR	SH	SF	HB	TBB	IBB	SO	WP	Bk	W	L	Pct.	ShO	Sv	ERA
1996 San Diego	NL	63	0	0	17	65.2	278	45	25	22	6	5	2	1	39	8	68	8	2	2	4	.333	0	3	3.02
1997 San Diego	NL	54	0	0	13	60.1	281	51	35	32	3	4	3	1	50	4	46	5	0	3	6	.333	0	2	4.77
1998 Detroit	AL	51	0	0	11	67.1	312	73	48	46	17	2	3	3	42	6	45	6	0	0	2	.000	0	0	6.15
1999 Los Angeles	NL	12	0	0	4	13	58	11	8	8	3	1	1	1	6	1	7	1	0	0	2	—	0	0	5.54
2000 Kansas City	AL	6	0	0	2	8.1	46	13	6	6	2	1	0	0	10	4	4	1	0	0	2	.000	0	0	6.48
10 Min. YEARS		248	122	14	61	866	3705	834	430	356	47	29	24	21	380	24	765	45	6	49	58	.458	5	13	3.70
6 Maj. YEARS		220	0	0	58	260	1156	231	140	132	36	15	10	6	166	23	215	22	2	9	18	.333	0	6	4.57

Brad Bohannan

Pitches: Right **Bats:** Right **Pos:** RP-29 **Ht:** 6'3" **Wt:** 170 **Born:** 9/2/77 **Age:** 24

Year Team	Lg Org	G	GS	CG	GF	IP	BFP	H	R	ER	HR	SH	SF	HB	TBB	IBB	SO	WP	Bk	W	L	Pct.	ShO	Sv	ERA
2000 Bristol	R+ CWS	15	0	0	11	24.2	99	16	5	3	0	2	3	3	10	2	29	1	0	4	2	.667	0	4	1.09
Winston-Sal	A+ CWS	4	0	0	3	5.2	22	5	2	2	0	1	1	0	0	0	5	0	0	1	0	1.000	0	2	3.18
2001 Winston-Sal	A+ CWS	23	0	0	12	36.1	152	33	10	7	0	4	0	1	10	1	33	2	0	2	1	.667	0	5	1.73
Birmingham	AA CWS	29	0	0	12	51	234	61	36	32	9	4	5	3	21	2	25	2	0	3	5	.375	0	0	5.65
2 Min. YEARS		71	0	0	38	117.2	507	115	53	44	9	11	9	7	41	5	92	5	0	9	9	.500	0	11	2.83

Papo Bolivar

Bats: Right **Throws:** Right **Pos:** DH-61; OF-34; PH-7; PR-1 **Ht:** 5'9" **Wt:** 195 **Born:** 10/18/78 **Age:** 23

Year Team	Lg Org	G	AB	H	2B	3B	HR	TB	R	RBI	TBB	IBB	SO	HBP	SH	SF	SB	CS	SB%	GDP	Avg	OBP	SLG
1996 Twins	R Min	41	155	53	7	1	1	65	30	18	8	0	32	2	0	3	26	6	.81	2	.342	.375	.419
1997 Fort Wayne	A Min	91	324	85	12	6	7	130	30	42	11	0	82	3	2	3	18	9	.67	7	.262	.290	.401
1998 Fort Myers	A+ Min	126	489	129	15	2	5	163	59	45	29	1	104	1	3	1	14	11	.56	14	.264	.306	.333
1999 Fort Myers	A+ Min	114	433	132	21	3	3	168	54	37	27	1	56	4	3	1	8	9	.47	10	.305	.351	.388
2000 New Britain	AA Min	117	406	113	19	7	2	152	46	42	24	0	69	5	3	4	14	8	.64	14	.278	.323	.374
2001 Fort Myers	A+ Min	57	227	66	6	2	3	85	42	25	22	0	33	2	0	2	15	3	.83	6	.291	.356	.374
New Britain	AA Min	43	142	38	7	0	2	51	15	20	9	0	25	4	5	1	1	1	.50	2	.268	.327	.359
6 Min. YEARS		589	2176	616	87	21	23	814	276	229	130	2	401	21	16	15	96	47	.67	55	.283	.327	.374

Chris Booker

Pitches: Right **Bats:** Right **Pos:** RP-61 **Ht:** 6'3" **Wt:** 230 **Born:** 12/9/76 **Age:** 25

Year Team	Lg Org	G	GS	CG	GF	IP	BFP	H	R	ER	HR	SH	SF	HB	TBB	IBB	SO	WP	Bk	W	L	Pct.	ShO	Sv	ERA
1995 Cubs	R ChC	13	7	0	2	42.1	173	36	22	13	0	0	2	0	16	0	43	4	1	3	2	.600	0	1	2.76
1996 Daytona	A+ ChC	1	1	0	0	2.1	11	1	1	0	0	0	0	0	3	0	2	1	0	0	0	—	0	0	0.00
Williamsprt	A- ChC	14	14	0	0	61	292	57	51	36	2	0	6	3	51	1	52	7	2	4	6	.400	0	0	5.31
1997 Williamsprt	A- ChC	24	3	0	11	45.2	200	39	20	17	2	3	4	0	25	0	60	9	0	1	5	.167	0	1	3.35
1998 Rockford	A ChC	44	1	0	22	64.1	287	47	32	24	2	3	5	4	53	4	78	8	1	1	2	.333	0	4	3.36
1999 Daytona	A+ ChC	42	0	0	29	73	328	72	45	32	6	2	3	3	37	1	68	5	0	2	5	.286	0	5	3.95
2000 Daytona	A+ ChC	31	0	0	24	27.2	122	25	12	7	0	2	0	1	14	1	34	2	0	0	2	.000	0	10	2.28
West Tenn	AA ChC	12	0	0	3	14.2	65	10	8	6	1	0	0	0	12	0	21	0	0	1	0	1.000	0	1	3.68
2001 West Tenn	AA ChC	45	0	0	13	52	235	39	29	25	7	5	3	1	36	2	76	7	0	2	6	.250	0	1	4.33
Chattanooga	AA Cin	16	0	0	4	16	72	13	7	7	1	1	0	0	11	0	25	0	0	2	0	1.000	0	1	3.94
7 Min. YEARS		242	26	0	108	399	1785	339	227	167	21	16	23	12	258	9	459	43	4	16	28	.364	0	24	3.77

Chris Bootcheck

Pitches: Right **Bats:** Right **Pos:** SP-20; RP-1 **Ht:** 6'5" **Wt:** 205 **Born:** 10/24/78 **Age:** 23

Year Team	Lg Org	G	GS	CG	GF	IP	BFP	H	R	ER	HR	SH	SF	HB	TBB	IBB	SO	WP	Bk	W	L	Pct.	ShO	Sv	ERA
2001 Rancho Cuca	A+ Ana	15	14	1	0	87	359	84	45	38	11	0	1	0	23	0	86	4	0	8	4	.667	0	0	3.93
Arkansas	AA Ana	6	6	1	0	36.1	161	39	25	22	3	0	0	3	11	0	22	1	1	3	3	.500	0	0	5.45
1 Min. YEAR		21	20	2	0	123.1	520	123	70	60	14	0	1	3	34	0	108	5	1	11	7	.611	0	0	4.38

Joe Borchard

Bats: Both **Throws:** Right **Pos:** OF-133 **Ht:** 6'5" **Wt:** 220 **Born:** 11/25/78 **Age:** 23

Year Team	Lg Org	G	AB	H	2B	3B	HR	TB	R	RBI	TBB	IBB	SO	HBP	SH	SF	SB	CS	SB%	GDP	Avg	OBP	SLG
2000 White Sox	R CWS	7	29	12	4	0	0	16	3	8	4	0	4	0	0	0	0	0	—	0	.414	.485	.552
Winston-Sal	A+ CWS	14	52	15	3	0	2	24	7	7	6	0	9	2	0	1	0	0	—	0	.288	.377	.462
Birmingham	AA CWS	6	22	5	0	1	0	7	3	3	3	0	8	0	0	1	0	0	—	1	.227	.308	.318
2001 Birmingham	AA CWS	133	515	152	27	1	27	262	95	98	67	1	158	10	0	5	5	4	.56	13	.295	.384	.509
2 Min. YEARS		160	618	184	34	2	29	309	108	116	80	1	179	12	0	7	5	4	.56	14	.298	.385	.500

Ramon Borrego

Bats: Both **Throws:** Right **Pos:** 2B-26; SS-23; 3B-10; PH-6; PR-6 **Ht:** 5'6" **Wt:** 170 **Born:** 6/7/78 **Age:** 24

Year Team	Lg Org	G	AB	H	2B	3B	HR	TB	R	RBI	TBB	IBB	SO	HBP	SH	SF	SB	CS	SB%	GDP	Avg	OBP	SLG
1996 Twins	R Min	19	70	25	5	1	0	32	16	4	9	0	4	0	0	0	7	3	.70	1	.357	.430	.457
Fort Myers	A+ Min	16	56	11	2	1	0	15	10	5	4	0	13	2	1	0	1	4	.20	1	.196	.274	.268
1997 Elizabethtn	R+ Min	55	211	59	12	6	0	83	43	34	26	0	44	4	5	2	7	5	.58	3	.280	.366	.393
1998 Fort Wayne	A Min	119	422	110	18	3	5	149	60	55	59	0	75	2	11	4	17	10	.63	4	.261	.351	.353
1999 Fort Myers	A+ Min	27	86	19	3	0	0	22	9	6	7	0	15	1	0	0	4	0	1.00	1	.221	.287	.256
2000 Fort Myers	A+ Min	79	265	59	6	1	0	67	29	20	28	0	37	5	3	1	8	2	.80	6	.223	.308	.253
2001 New Britain	AA Min	60	136	25	6	2	1	38	17	3	14	0	30	1	8	0	5	0	1.00	2	.184	.265	.279
6 Min. YEARS		375	1246	308	52	8	10	406	184	127	147	0	218	15	28	7	49	24	.67	18	.247	.332	.326

Shawn Boskie

Pitches: Right **Bats:** Right **Pos:** SP-11; RP-1   **Ht:** 6'3" **Wt:** 210 **Born:** 3/28/67 **Age:** 35

		HOW MUCH HE PITCHED						WHAT HE GAVE UP												THE RESULTS					
Year Team	Lg Org	G	GS	CG	GF	IP	BFP	H	R	ER	HR	SH	SF	HB	TBB	IBB	SO	WP	Bk	W	L	Pct.	ShO	Sv	ERA
1986 Wytheville	R+ ChC	14	12	1	0	54	268	42	41	32	4	0	1	7	57	1	40	15	0	4	4	.500	0	0	5.33
1987 Peoria	A ChC	26	25	1	0	149	657	149	91	72	12	4	5	17	56	2	100	7	5	9	11	.450	0	0	4.35
1988 Winston-Sal	A+ ChC	27	27	4	0	186	825	176	83	70	9	4	7	17	89	1	164	14	4	12	7	.632	2	0	3.39
1989 Charlotte	AA ChC	28	28	5	0	181	813	196	105	88	10	3	8	19	84	3	164	11	1	11	8	.579	0	0	4.38
1990 Iowa	AAA ChC	8	8	1	0	51	217	46	22	18	1	2	1	2	21	1	51	1	0	4	2	.667	0	0	3.18
1991 Iowa	AAA ChC	7	6	2	0	45.1	186	43	19	18	1	5	1	2	11	0	29	1	1	2	2	.500	0	0	3.57
1992 Iowa	AAA ChC	2	2	0	0	7.1	32	8	4	3	0	0	0	0	3	0	3	0	0	0	0	—	0	0	3.68
1993 Iowa	AAA ChC	11	11	1	0	71.2	300	70	35	34	4	2	1	7	21	0	35	1	0	6	1	.857	0	0	4.27
1995 Lk Elsinore	A+ Ana	3	3	0	0	11	53	15	7	5	1	0	0	0	4	0	8	0	0	0	0	—	0	0	4.09
Vancouver	AAA Ana	1	1	0	0	6	25	4	2	2	1	0	0	0	4	0	1	0	0	1	0	1.000	0	0	3.00
1998 Ottawa	AAA Mon	13	13	0	0	87	375	100	48	44	7	0	2	5	21	1	51	5	0	5	7	.417	0	0	4.55
1999 Albuquerque	AAA LA	15	15	0	0	86.1	401	111	66	56	14	3	4	4	37	2	62	5	0	4	8	.333	0	0	5.84
2000 Erie	AA Ana	6	6	0	0	28	133	38	22	20	3	3	3	2	10	0	21	1	0	0	2	.000	0	0	6.43
Edmonton	AAA Ana	14	2	0	2	40	180	51	22	19	4	0	2	2	16	0	22	5	0	3	2	.600	0	0	4.28
Tucson	AAA Ari	6	5	0	1	32	147	37	26	18	4	2	4	3	6	0	16	1	0	2	4	.333	0	0	5.06
2001 Tucson	AAA Ari	12	11	1	0	62.1	297	95	55	48	8	4	0	3	17	2	31	3	0	6	4	.400	0	0	6.93
1990 Chicago	NL	15	15	1	0	97.2	415	99	42	40	8	8	2	1	31	3	49	3	2	5	6	.455	0	0	3.69
1991 Chicago	NL	28	20	0	2	129	582	150	78	75	14	8	6	5	52	4	62	1	1	4	9	.308	0	0	5.23
1992 Chicago	NL	23	18	0	2	91.2	393	96	55	51	14	9	6	4	36	3	39	5	1	5	11	.313	0	0	5.01
1993 Chicago	NL	39	2	0	10	65.2	277	63	30	25	7	4	1	7	21	2	39	5	0	5	3	.625	0	0	3.43
1994 Chicago	NL	2	0	0	0	3.2	14	3	0	0	0	0	0	0	0	0	2	1	0	0	0	—	0	0	0.00
Philadelphia	NL	18	14	1	1	84.1	367	85	56	49	14	2	3	3	29	2	59	6	0	4	6	.400	0	0	5.23
Seattle	AL	2	1	0	0	2.2	13	4	2	2	1	0	0	0	1	1	0	0	0	0	1	.000	0	0	6.75
1995 California	AL	20	20	1	0	111.2	494	127	73	70	16	4	6	7	25	0	51	4	0	7	7	.500	0	0	5.64
1996 California	AL	37	28	1	1	189.1	860	226	126	112	40	6	4	13	67	7	133	10	0	12	11	.522	0	0	5.32
1997 Baltimore	AL	28	9	0	8	77	349	95	57	55	14	2	7	2	26	1	50	1	0	6	6	.500	0	1	6.43
1998 Montreal	NL	5	5	0	0	17.2	90	34	21	18	5	1	1	2	4	1	10	0	0	1	3	.250	0	0	9.17
13 Min. YEARS		193	175	16	3	1098	4909	1181	648	547	83	32	39	90	457	13	798	70	11	67	64	.511	2	0	4.48
9 Maj. YEARS		217	132	4	24	870.1	3854	982	540	497	133	44	36	44	292	24	494	36	4	49	63	.438	0	1	5.14

Heath Bost

Pitches: Right **Bats:** Right **Pos:** RP-43; SP-2   **Ht:** 6'3" **Wt:** 195 **Born:** 10/13/74 **Age:** 27

		HOW MUCH HE PITCHED						WHAT HE GAVE UP												THE RESULTS					
Year Team	Lg Org	G	GS	CG	GF	IP	BFP	H	R	ER	HR	SH	SF	HB	TBB	IBB	SO	WP	Bk	W	L	Pct.	ShO	Sv	ERA
1995 Portland	A- Col	10	0	0	1	16	63	15	6	6	1	0	0	0	0	0	25	1	0	1	0	1.000	0	0	3.38
Asheville	A Col	9	2	0	4	23.2	90	20	6	4	1	0	0	1	3	0	17	1	2	4	1	.800	0	0	1.52
1996 New Haven	AA Col	4	0	0	2	6	24	5	1	1	0	0	0	0	2	0	7	0	0	1	0	1.000	0	0	1.50
Asheville	A Col	41	0	0	29	76	293	45	13	11	3	6	0	1	19	5	102	2	0	5	2	.714	0	15	1.30
1997 Salem	A+ Col	13	0	0	10	15	57	9	4	4	1	1	0	0	2	0	9	0	0	1	0	1.000	0	3	2.40
Colo Sprngs	AAA Col	2	0	0	0	3	21	10	8	7	1	0	1	0	1	0	3	0	0	0	1	.000	0	0	21.00
New Haven	AA Col	38	0	0	32	43	180	44	18	17	3	0	0	4	10	1	45	5	0	2	2	.500	0	20	3.56
1998 New Haven	AA Col	41	0	0	14	46.1	193	43	20	17	2	5	0	4	11	0	48	3	1	4	2	.667	0	2	3.30
1999 Colo Sprngs	AAA Col	38	6	0	8	86.1	378	120	59	53	10	2	1	4	12	2	67	0	0	5	4	.556	0	0	5.53
2000 Salem	A+ Col	7	1	0	2	14.2	69	24	10	10	2	0	0	0	1	0	14	1	0	2	1	.667	0	0	6.14
Carolina	AA Col	6	0	0	1	9	33	6	2	1	1	0	0	0	2	0	10	0	0	1	0	1.000	0	0	1.00
Colo Sprngs	AAA Col	7	0	0	1	11	46	8	8	6	1	0	1	0	4	0	7	0	0	0	0	—	0	0	4.91
2001 Colo Sprngs	AAA Col	45	2	0	13	75	326	82	37	36	13	1	0	4	23	2	64	2	0	2	2	.500	0	0	4.32
7 Min. YEARS		261	11	0	117	425	1773	431	192	173	39	15	3	14	90	10	418	15	3	28	15	.651	0	40	3.66

Tom Bost

Bats: Left **Throws:** Right **Pos:** OF-54; DH-17; PH-7; PR-3   **Ht:** 6'2" **Wt:** 220 **Born:** 10/5/75 **Age:** 26

		BATTING															BASERUNNING				PERCENTAGES		
Year Team	Lg Org	G	AB	H	2B	3B	HR	TB	R	RBI	TBB	IBB	SO	HBP	SH	SF	SB	CS	SB%	GDP	Avg	OBP	SLG
1999 Mahoning Vy	A- Cle	23	70	13	0	1	5	30	11	13	11	0	35	1	0	1	0	0	—	0	.186	.301	.429
2000 Columbus	A Cle	54	208	60	14	5	8	108	30	42	11	1	36	3	0	2	18	1	.95	4	.288	.330	.519
Kinston	A+ Cle	10	31	7	1	1	0	10	3	1	1	0	8	1	0	0	1	0	1.00	0	.226	.273	.323
2001 Akron	AA Cle	29	91	16	2	0	0	18	7	7	5	0	34	1	2	0	6	0	1.00	2	.176	.227	.198
Kinston	A+ Cle	50	130	33	7	1	6	60	18	21	16	0	31	5	0	1	3	1	.75	1	.254	.355	.462
3 Min. YEARS		166	530	129	24	8	19	226	69	84	44	1	144	11	3	4	27	3	.90	8	.243	.312	.426

Brandon Bowe

Pitches: Right **Bats:** Right **Pos:** RP-51   **Ht:** 6'3" **Wt:** 215 **Born:** 3/13/76 **Age:** 26

		HOW MUCH HE PITCHED						WHAT HE GAVE UP												THE RESULTS					
Year Team	Lg Org	G	GS	CG	GF	IP	BFP	H	R	ER	HR	SH	SF	HB	TBB	IBB	SO	WP	Bk	W	L	Pct.	ShO	Sv	ERA
1999 Brevard Cty	A+ Fla	9	0	0	3	20	86	18	7	7	4	0	0	0	10	0	21	3	1	2	0	1.000	0	1	3.15
Utica	A- Fla	6	0	0	1	12.1	54	14	6	4	0	0	0	0	2	0	24	1	0	2	0	1.000	0	0	2.92
2000 Kane County	A Fla	61	0	0	25	79.2	345	73	36	33	4	2	4	5	32	0	89	5	0	7	3	.700	0	6	3.73
2001 Brevard Cty	A+ Fla	42	0	0	27	58	237	52	21	10	1	7	3	2	11	1	45	2	0	6	4	.600	0	11	1.55
Portland	AA Fla	9	0	0	3	17.1	67	13	4	3	1	0	0	0	5	0	10	0	0	0	2	.000	0	0	1.56
3 Min. YEARS		127	0	0	59	187.1	789	170	74	57	10	9	7	7	60	1	189	11	1	17	9	.654	0	18	2.74

Cedrick Bowers

Pitches: Left **Bats:** Right **Pos:** RP-31; SP-11

Ht: 6'2" **Wt:** 223 **Born:** 2/10/78 **Age:** 24

			HOW MUCH HE PITCHED							WHAT HE GAVE UP										THE RESULTS					
Year Team	Lg Org	G	GS	CG	GF	IP	BFP	H	R	ER	HR	SH	SF	HB	TBB	IBB	SO	WP	Bk	W	L	Pct.	ShO	Sv	ERA
1996 Devil Rays	R TB	13	13	0	0	60.1	268	50	39	36	2	0	2	3	39	0	85	5	5	3	5	.375	0	0	5.37
1997 Chston-SC	A TB	28	28	0	0	157	657	119	74	56	11	4	3	3	78	0	164	15	1	8	10	.444	0	0	3.21
1998 St. Pete	A+ TB	28	26	0	1	150	655	144	89	73	14	6	4	1	80	1	156	6	2	5	9	.357	0	0	4.38
1999 Orlando	AA TB	27	27	1	0	125	567	125	94	83	18	3	5	4	76	0	138	12	1	6	9	.400	0	0	5.98
2000 Orlando	AA TB	20	19	1	0	106.2	443	85	45	33	8	4	2	3	44	0	92	3	1	5	8	.385	0	0	2.78
Durham	AAA TB	4	4	0	0	19.2	92	21	13	12	2	0	0	0	13	0	20	1	0	3	1	.750	0	0	5.49
2001 Durham	AAA TB	42	11	0	14	94	412	83	38	32	10	4	4	3	56	1	67	3	0	6	5	.545	0	0	3.06
6 Min. YEARS		162	128	2	15	712.2	3094	627	392	325	65	21	20	17	386	2	722	45	10	36	47	.434	0	0	4.10

Jason Bowers

Bats: Right **Throws:** Right **Pos:** SS-130; PH-6; 2B-1; DH-1; PR-1

Ht: 5'11" **Wt:** 170 **Born:** 1/27/78 **Age:** 24

					BATTING												BASERUNNING				PERCENTAGES		
Year Team	Lg Org	G	AB	H	2B	3B	HR	TB	R	RBI	TBB	IBB	SO	HBP	SH	SF	SB	CS	SB%	GDP	Avg	OBP	SLG
1998 Johnson Cty	R+ StL	60	213	62	10	5	3	91	31	38	13	0	43	5	1	4	10	8	.56	2	.291	.340	.427
1999 Peoria	A StL	112	414	109	14	8	2	145	53	49	32	1	78	9	5	1	10	9	.53	6	.263	.329	.350
2000 Potomac	A+ StL	91	342	93	16	6	1	124	53	35	48	0	72	6	3	0	10	5	.67	5	.272	.371	.363
2001 New Haven	AA StL	137	460	111	19	4	4	150	36	34	25	0	111	3	11	4	10	10	.50	10	.241	.283	.326
4 Min. YEARS		400	1429	375	59	23	10	510	173	156	118	1	304	23	20	9	40	32	.56	23	.262	.327	.357

Micah Bowie

Pitches: Left **Bats:** Left **Pos:** RP-28; SP-10

Ht: 6'4" **Wt:** 210 **Born:** 11/10/74 **Age:** 27

				HOW MUCH HE PITCHED							WHAT HE GAVE UP										THE RESULTS					
Year Team	Lg Org	G	GS	CG	GF	IP	BFP	H	R	ER	HR	SH	SF	HB	TBB	IBB	SO	WP	Bk	W	L	Pct.	ShO	Sv	ERA
1994 Braves	R Atl	6	5	0	1	29.2	124	27	14	10	1	0	2	1	5	0	35	1	0	0	3	.000	0	0	3.03
Danville	R+ Atl	7	5	0	0	32.2	141	28	16	13	4	2	3	3	13	1	38	2	0	3	1	.750	0	0	3.58
1995 Macon	A Atl	5	5	0	0	27.2	104	9	8	7	1	0	0	3	11	0	36	1	0	4	1	.800	0	0	2.28
Durham	A+ Atl	23	23	1	0	130.1	561	119	65	52	8	13	3	8	61	3	91	4	3	4	11	.267	0	0	3.59
1996 Durham	A+ Atl	14	13	0	0	66.1	283	55	29	27	4	6	3	7	33	0	65	2	0	3	6	.333	0	0	3.66
1997 Durham	A+ Atl	9	6	0	0	39.1	167	29	16	16	2	0	2	0	27	0	44	2	0	2	2	.500	0	0	3.66
Greenville	AA Atl	8	7	0	0	43.2	193	34	19	17	3	1	2	3	26	1	41	2	0	3	2	.600	0	0	3.50
1998 Greenville	AA Atl	30	29	1	0	163	676	132	73	63	12	7	2	6	64	0	160	7	3	11	6	.647	0	0	3.48
1999 Richmond	AAA Atl	13	13	0	0	73	288	65	24	24	4	2	2	0	14	0	82	2	0	4	4	.500	0	0	2.96
2000 Iowa	AAA ChC	9	9	0	0	45.1	220	59	44	40	9	3	1	1	31	3	35	2	0	1	7	.125	0	0	7.94
West Tenn	AA ChC	18	18	1	0	117.1	481	91	47	45	6	7	1	3	48	1	106	1	0	7	6	.538	1	0	3.45
2001 Sacramento	AAA Oak	38	10	1	9	116	506	123	68	65	13	2	2	5	44	1	102	1	0	6	8	.429	1	3	5.04
1999 Atlanta	NL	3	3	0	2	4	23	8	6	6	1	0	0	0	4	0	2	0	0	0	1	.000	0	0	13.50
Chicago	NL	11	11	0	0	47	242	73	54	52	8	3	3	2	30	2	39	4	2	2	6	.250	0	0	9.96
8 Min. YEARS		180	143	4	10	884.1	3744	771	423	379	67	43	23	40	377	10	835	27	6	48	57	.457	2	3	3.86

Jason Boyd

Pitches: Right **Bats:** Right **Pos:** RP-52

Ht: 6'3" **Wt:** 173 **Born:** 2/23/73 **Age:** 29

				HOW MUCH HE PITCHED							WHAT HE GAVE UP										THE RESULTS					
Year Team	Lg Org	G	GS	CG	GF	IP	BFP	H	R	ER	HR	SH	SF	HB	TBB	IBB	SO	WP	Bk	W	L	Pct.	ShO	Sv	ERA
1994 Martinsvlle	R+ Phi	14	13	1	0	69	306	65	46	32	6	0	1	4	32	0	45	7	6	3	7	.300	0	0	4.17
1995 Piedmont	A Phi	26	24	1	1	151	638	151	77	60	8	5	3	4	44	0	129	18	2	6	8	.429	0	0	3.58
1996 Clearwater	A+ Phi	26	26	2	0	161.2	674	160	75	70	12	3	6	3	49	1	120	7	1	11	8	.579	0	0	3.90
1997 Reading	AA Phi	48	7	0	9	115.2	509	113	65	62	16	2	3	3	64	7	98	1	2	10	6	.625	0	0	4.82
1998 Tucson	AAA Ari	15	0	0	3	21.2	109	28	22	15	4	0	0	1	14	1	13	0	1	2	2	.500	0	0	6.23
1999 Tucson	AAA Ari	44	0	0	17	75.2	325	76	42	38	6	2	4	3	27	2	60	6	2	6	5	.545	0	5	4.52
Nashville	AAA Pit	5	0	0	2	4.2	14	2	0	0	0	0	0	0	0	0	2	0	0	0	0	—	0	0	0.00
2000 Clearwater	A+ Phi	6	3	0	1	11.1	50	11	4	3	0	0	0	2	4	0	12	0	1	1	0	1.000	0	0	2.38
Scranton-WB	AAA Phi	11	2	0	1	15.2	66	8	3	3	0	1	0	0	14	0	10	1	0	1	0	1.000	0	0	1.72
2001 Scranton-WB	AAA Phi	52	0	0	35	59.1	243	44	17	13	4	2	2	2	22	1	66	1	0	2	7	.222	0	12	1.97
1999 Pittsburgh	NL	4	0	0	0	5.1	24	5	2	2	0	0	1	1	2	0	4	1	0	0	0	—	0	0	3.38
2000 Philadelphia	NL	30	0	0	11	34.1	161	39	28	25	2	3	0	1	24	4	32	1	0	0	1	.000	0	0	6.55
8 Min. YEARS		247	75	4	69	685.2	2934	658	351	296	56	15	19	22	270	12	555	41	15	42	43	.494	0	17	3.89
2 Maj. YEARS		34	0	0	11	39.2	185	44	30	27	2	3	1	2	26	4	36	2	0	0	1	.000	0	0	6.13

Ryan Bradley

Pitches: Right **Bats:** Right **Pos:** SP-19; RP-4

Ht: 6'4" **Wt:** 226 **Born:** 10/26/75 **Age:** 26

				HOW MUCH HE PITCHED							WHAT HE GAVE UP										THE RESULTS					
Year Team	Lg Org	G	GS	CG	GF	IP	BFP	H	R	ER	HR	SH	SF	HB	TBB	IBB	SO	WP	Bk	W	L	Pct.	ShO	Sv	ERA
1997 Oneonta	A- NYY	14	0	0	9	26.2	103	22	5	4	1	0	0	0	5	1	22	0	1	3	1	.750	0	1	1.35
1998 Tampa	A+ NYY	32	11	1	18	94.2	383	59	29	25	5	1	1	6	30	4	112	16	2	7	4	.636	1	7	2.38
Norwich	AA NYY	3	3	1	0	25	89	8	4	4	1	0	0	0	8	0	25	0	0	2	0	1.000	1	0	1.44
Columbus	AAA NYY	3	3	0	0	16	72	15	13	11	4	0	0	0	13	0	12	1	0	0	1	.000	0	0	6.19
1999 Columbus	AAA NYY	29	24	1	1	145	664	163	112	100	28	5	9	10	73	0	118	23	1	5	12	.294	0	0	6.21
2000 Columbus	AAA NYY	49	0	0	15	72.2	346	82	52	47	11	4	2	7	52	1	54	12	1	5	1	.833	0	0	5.82
2001 Norwich	AA NYY	16	12	0	3	58.1	275	47	51	43	7	2	1	12	48	0	53	10	1	4	5	.444	0	0	6.63
Tampa	A+ NYY	7	7	0	0	38	167	27	15	13	2	1	1	4	22	0	32	5	0	3	1	.750	0	0	3.08
1998 New York	AL	5	1	0	1	12.2	59	12	9	8	2	0	1	1	9	0	13	0	0	2	1	.667	0	0	5.68
5 Min. YEARS		153	60	3	46	476.1	2099	423	281	247	59	13	14	39	251	6	428	67	6	29	25	.537	2	8	4.67

34

Brian Brantley

Pitches: Right **Bats:** Right **Pos:** RP-41; SP-1 **Ht:** 6'4" **Wt:** 185 **Born:** 4/23/76 **Age:** 26

			HOW MUCH HE PITCHED						WHAT HE GAVE UP												THE RESULTS					
Year Team	Lg	Org	G	GS	CG	GF	IP	BFP	H	R	ER	HR	SH	SF	HB	TBB	IBB	SO	WP	Bk	W	L	Pct.	ShO	Sv	ERA
1998 Portland	A-	Col	10	10	0	0	49	218	43	27	22	1	2	2	7	26	0	39	7	0	3	4	.429	0	0	4.04
1999 Asheville	A	Col	34	3	0	13	90.1	406	89	65	59	6	7	2	11	44	0	100	13	1	6	6	.500	0	0	5.88
2000 Carolina	AA	Col	1	0	0	0	4	23	7	6	6	0	0	0	0	4	0	4	1	0	0	0	—	0	0	13.50
Salem	A+	Col	41	0	0	19	59	264	38	22	17	1	7	3	9	40	0	75	5	0	3	3	.500	0	4	2.59
2001 Carolina	AA	Col	14	0	0	11	22	108	31	19	18	1	2	2	0	16	2	23	3	0	0	2	.000	0	0	7.36
Salem	A+	Col	28	1	0	11	58.1	253	43	23	18	3	3	2	12	21	2	55	11	2	5	3	.625	0	2	2.78
4 Min. YEARS			128	14	0	54	282.2	1272	251	162	140	12	21	11	39	151	4	296	40	3	17	18	.486	0	9	4.46

Bryan Braswell

Pitches: Left **Bats:** Left **Pos:** SP-7; RP-7 **Ht:** 6'1" **Wt:** 200 **Born:** 6/30/75 **Age:** 27

			HOW MUCH HE PITCHED						WHAT HE GAVE UP												THE RESULTS					
Year Team	Lg	Org	G	GS	CG	GF	IP	BFP	H	R	ER	HR	SH	SF	HB	TBB	IBB	SO	WP	Bk	W	L	Pct.	ShO	Sv	ERA
1996 Auburn	A-	Hou	15	14	0	1	73	325	70	40	35	2	1	2	11	29	2	77	9	1	4	8	.333	0	0	4.32
1997 Quad City	A	Hou	19	19	1	0	116.1	495	107	70	49	10	0	4	2	32	0	118	2	5	6	6	.500	0	0	3.79
1998 Kissimmee	A+	Hou	27	26	2	0	159.2	698	176	92	70	22	3	3	4	48	0	118	7	2	11	9	.550	1	0	3.95
1999 Jackson	AA	Hou	28	28	1	0	171.1	741	180	104	86	27	4	6	4	54	0	131	10	0	9	10	.474	0	0	4.52
2000 Round Rock	AA	Hou	19	10	1	1	71.1	309	78	48	40	13	4	2	0	22	1	38	2	1	4	5	.444	0	0	5.05
2001 Brooklyn	A-	NYM	5	2	0	0	13	53	12	3	3	1	0	0	0	2	0	13	0	0	1	0	1.000	0	0	2.08
St. Lucie	A+	NYM	4	2	0	2	17.1	74	15	8	7	0	1	1	2	5	0	12	1	0	1	1	.500	0	0	3.63
Binghamton	AA	NYM	5	3	0	1	18.1	84	26	9	9	0	0	1	0	7	0	14	0	0	1	1	.500	0	0	4.42
6 Min. YEARS			122	104	5	5	640.1	2779	664	374	299	75	13	19	23	199	3	521	31	9	38	39	.494	1	0	4.20

Danny Bravo

Bats: Both **Throws:** Right **Pos:** SS-33; 2B-28; OF-12; PH-7; 3B-6; DH-1; PR-1 **Ht:** 5'11" **Wt:** 175 **Born:** 5/27/77 **Age:** 25

			BATTING															BASERUNNING				PERCENTAGES		
Year Team	Lg	Org	G	AB	H	2B	3B	HR	TB	R	RBI	TBB	IBB	SO	HBP	SH	SF	SB	CS	SB%	GDP	Avg	OBP	SLG
1996 Wst Plm Bch	A+	Mon	48	137	27	2	2	0	33	15	12	14	0	30	1	3	0	3	4	.43	0	.197	.276	.241
Delmarva	A	Mon	18	61	14	6	1	0	22	10	7	2	0	14	1	2	1	1	0	1.00	1	.230	.262	.361
1997 Wst Plm Bch	A+	Mon	15	37	6	1	1	0	9	3	0	2	0	5	0	0	0	0	0	—	0	.162	.205	.243
Cape Fear	A	Mon	73	253	68	9	1	3	88	28	34	9	0	31	4	3	3	3	4	.43	3	.269	.301	.348
1998 Cape Fear	A	Mon	101	343	95	12	4	4	127	48	44	32	2	65	8	14	1	7	10	.41	11	.277	.352	.370
Jupiter	A+	Mon	24	71	11	1	0	0	12	5	3	8	0	14	2	0	2	1	1	.50	0	.155	.253	.169
1999 Jupiter	A+	Mon	7	20	6	3	0	1	12	5	3	1	0	5	1	2	0	0	0	—	0	.300	.364	.600
Harrisburg	AA	Mon	12	28	4	1	0	0	5	0	2	1	0	6	0	1	0	0	0	—	0	.143	.172	.179
Birmingham	AA	CWS	76	270	76	12	1	2	96	49	38	41	1	39	2	3	3	6	5	.55	3	.281	.377	.356
2000 Birmingham	AA	CWS	96	340	79	12	0	3	100	48	29	42	0	56	2	2	3	11	9	.55	5	.232	.318	.294
2001 Charlotte	AAA	CWS	39	126	24	2	0	3	35	11	13	7	0	16	0	2	0	1	1	.50	4	.190	.233	.278
Birmingham	AA	CWS	42	168	49	12	2	2	71	22	22	17	0	17	1	1	0	3	2	.60	3	.292	.360	.423
6 Min. YEARS			551	1854	459	73	12	18	610	244	207	176	3	298	22	33	13	36	36	.50	38	.248	.318	.329

Yhency Brazoban

Bats: Right **Throws:** Right **Pos:** OF-123; DH-1; PH-1 **Ht:** 6'1" **Wt:** 170 **Born:** 6/11/80 **Age:** 22

			BATTING															BASERUNNING				PERCENTAGES		
Year Team	Lg	Org	G	AB	H	2B	3B	HR	TB	R	RBI	TBB	IBB	SO	HBP	SH	SF	SB	CS	SB%	GDP	Avg	OBP	SLG
1999 Yankees	R	NYY	56	200	64	14	5	1	91	33	26	12	0	47	4	1	2	7	3	.70	2	.320	.367	.455
2000 Greensboro	A	NYY	12	48	9	3	0	0	12	6	8	3	0	15	0	0	1	1	0	1.00	0	.188	.231	.250
Yankees	R	NYY	54	201	61	14	4	5	98	36	28	11	0	28	4	0	2	2	3	.40	7	.303	.349	.488
2001 Greensboro	A	NYY	124	469	128	23	3	6	175	51	52	19	4	98	9	2	5	6	3	.67	12	.273	.311	.373
Columbus	AAA	NYY	1	5	1	1	0	0	2	2	0	0	0	2	0	0	0	0	0	—	0	.200	.200	.400
3 Min. YEARS			247	923	263	55	12	12	378	128	114	45	4	190	17	3	10	16	9	.64	21	.285	.327	.410

Jamie Brewington

Pitches: Right **Bats:** Right **Pos:** RP-35; SP-4 **Ht:** 6'4" **Wt:** 190 **Born:** 9/28/71 **Age:** 30

			HOW MUCH HE PITCHED						WHAT HE GAVE UP												THE RESULTS					
Year Team	Lg	Org	G	GS	CG	GF	IP	BFP	H	R	ER	HR	SH	SF	HB	TBB	IBB	SO	WP	Bk	W	L	Pct.	ShO	Sv	ERA
1992 Everett	A-	SF	15	11	1	1	68.2	317	65	40	33	2	0	3	5	47	2	63	9	1	5	2	.714	1	0	4.33
1993 Clinton	A	SF	26	25	1	0	133.2	580	126	78	71	20	1	3	5	61	1	111	19	2	13	5	.722	0	0	4.78
1994 Clinton	A	SF	10	10	0	0	53	226	46	29	29	5	1	3	2	24	0	62	7	1	2	4	.333	0	0	4.92
San Jose	A+	SF	13	13	0	0	76	310	61	38	27	3	2	2	2	25	0	65	7	1	7	3	.700	0	0	3.20
1995 Shreveport	AA	SF	16	16	1	0	88.1	376	72	39	30	8	2	7	0	55	0	74	4	0	8	3	.727	1	0	3.06
1996 Phoenix	AAA	SF	35	17	0	7	110.1	526	130	93	86	14	5	3	6	72	1	75	15	0	6	9	.400	0	1	7.02
1997 Omaha	AAA	KC	7	4	0	0	21.2	98	21	21	20	10	0	1	1	13	0	20	1	1	2	2	.500	0	0	8.31
Wichita	AA	KC	10	10	0	0	51	245	68	43	38	12	0	1	4	28	0	31	2	0	2	5	.286	0	0	6.71
Tucson	AAA	Mil	6	5	0	0	20.1	112	33	26	23	2	0	1	2	17	0	13	0	0	1	3	.250	0	0	10.18
1999 Kinston	A+	Cle	36	5	0	15	81.1	353	74	42	35	6	2	4	2	37	0	81	8	1	1	10	.091	0	4	3.87
2000 Buffalo	AAA	Cle	17	0	0	6	23.2	99	19	8	8	3	0	1	0	12	0	25	1	0	1	0	1.000	0	0	3.04
2001 Twins	R	Min	4	0	0	0	6.2	25	4	0	0	0	0	0	0	1	0	8	0	0	0	0	—	0	0	0.00
Edmonton	AAA	Min	35	4	0	9	67	313	87	48	44	11	3	2	3	31	1	53	7	0	2	8	.200	0	0	5.91
1995 San Francisco	NL		13	13	0	0	75.1	334	68	38	38	8	4	4	4	45	6	45	3	0	6	4	.600	0	0	4.54
2000 Cleveland	AL		26	0	0	10	45.1	205	56	28	27	3	2	2	0	19	0	34	1	0	3	0	1.000	0	0	5.36
9 Min. YEARS			230	120	3	38	801.2	3580	806	505	444	96	16	31	32	423	5	681	80	7	50	54	.481	2	5	4.98
2 Maj. YEARS			39	13	0	10	120.2	539	124	66	65	11	6	6	6	64	6	79	4	0	9	4	.692	0	0	4.85

Donnie Bridges

Pitches: Right **Bats:** Right **Pos:** SP-19   **Ht:** 6'4" **Wt:** 195 **Born:** 12/10/78 **Age:** 23

Year Team	Lg Org	G	GS	CG	GF	IP	BFP	H	R	ER	HR	SH	SF	HB	TBB	IBB	SO	WP	Bk	W	L	Pct.	ShO	Sv	ERA
1997 Expos	R Mon	5	2	0	0	10	49	14	9	7	0	0	1	2	5	0	6	0	0	0	2	.000	0	0	6.30
1998 Vermont	A- Mon	13	13	0	0	68	311	71	42	37	2	2	2	8	37	0	43	8	0	5	6	.455	0	0	4.90
1999 Cape Fear	A Mon	8	8	1	0	47.1	189	37	12	12	2	2	0	5	17	0	44	5	0	6	1	.857	1	0	2.28
Jupiter	A+ Mon	18	18	1	0	99	429	116	53	45	5	3	4	6	36	0	63	7	0	4	6	.400	1	0	4.09
2000 Jupiter	A+ Mon	11	11	0	0	73.1	296	58	29	26	0	1	4	1	20	0	66	2	0	5	5	.500	0	0	3.19
Harrisburg	AA Mon	19	19	6	0	128	528	104	39	34	5	3	4	8	49	0	84	7	0	11	7	.611	4	0	2.39
2001 Expos	R Mon	2	2	0	0	5.1	25	2	6	5	0	0	0	1	5	0	9	3	0	0	1	.000	0	0	8.44
Jupiter	A+ Mon	1	1	0	0	4	23	7	6	3	0	0	0	1	3	0	2	0	0	0	1	.000	0	0	6.75
Harrisburg	AA Mon	3	3	0	0	16.2	76	14	10	6	2	0	1	2	13	0	14	2	0	1	2	.333	0	0	3.24
Ottawa	AAA Mon	13	13	0	0	55.1	269	60	50	46	11	2	2	9	43	0	49	8	0	3	5	.375	0	0	7.48
5 Min. YEARS		93	90	8	0	507	2195	483	256	221	27	13	22	39	228	0	380	42	0	35	36	.493	6	0	3.92

Kary Bridges

Bats: Left **Throws:** Right **Pos:** 2B-95; PH-5; DH-4; PR-4; SS-2; 3B-2   **Ht:** 5'10" **Wt:** 170 **Born:** 10/27/72 **Age:** 29

Year Team	Lg Org	G	AB	H	2B	3B	HR	TB	R	RBI	TBB	IBB	SO	HBP	SH	SF	SB	CS	SB%	GDP	Avg	OBP	SLG
1993 Quad City	A Hou	65	263	74	9	0	3	92	37	24	31	1	18	2	1	3	15	10	.60	7	.281	.358	.350
1994 Quad City	A Hou	117	447	135	20	4	1	166	66	53	38	3	29	3	8	4	14	11	.56	9	.302	.358	.371
1995 Jackson	AA Hou	118	418	126	22	4	3	165	56	43	49	3	17	0	6	4	10	12	.45	12	.301	.372	.395
1996 Jackson	AA Hou	87	338	110	12	2	4	138	51	33	32	1	14	1	7	3	4	5	.44	11	.325	.382	.408
Tucson	AAA Hou	42	140	44	9	1	1	58	24	21	9	1	8	1	2	3	1	3	.25	3	.314	.355	.414
1997 New Orleans	AAA Hou	23	64	11	1	2	0	16	6	3	5	0	9	1	0	1	1	0	1.00	1	.172	.239	.250
Carolina	AA Pit	66	283	95	17	1	3	123	43	29	9	0	10	0	3	2	9	5	.64	7	.336	.354	.435
Calgary	AAA Pit	33	95	25	4	0	0	29	9	6	7	1	6	0	1	0	1	0	1.00	3	.263	.314	.305
1998 West Tenn	AA ChC	48	196	60	7	1	0	69	30	21	18	1	9	0	1	1	6	4	.60	4	.306	.363	.352
Iowa	AAA ChC	64	181	39	10	1	0	51	25	14	11	0	12	1	0	2	0	2	.00	4	.215	.262	.282
1999 Iowa	AAA ChC	10	25	3	0	0	0	3	1	0	1	0	5	0	0	0	0	0	—	0	.120	.154	.120
Oklahoma	AAA Tex	75	239	82	14	0	7	117	38	39	21	2	14	1	4	3	6	3	.67	4	.343	.394	.490
2000 Ottawa	AAA Mon	61	210	71	12	3	2	95	35	27	27	0	7	1	5	2	10	3	.77	9	.338	.413	.452
2001 Columbus	AAA NYY	109	408	121	17	1	5	155	59	39	36	1	29	1	5	4	5	8	.38	11	.297	.352	.380
9 Min. YEARS		918	3307	996	154	20	29	1277	480	352	294	14	187	12	41	31	82	66	.55	88	.301	.357	.386

Stoney Briggs

Bats: Right **Throws:** Right **Pos:** OF-30; DH-21; PH-6; PR-1   **Ht:** 6'3" **Wt:** 215 **Born:** 12/26/71 **Age:** 30

Year Team	Lg Org	G	AB	H	2B	3B	HR	TB	R	RBI	TBB	IBB	SO	HBP	SH	SF	SB	CS	SB%	GDP	Avg	OBP	SLG
1991 Medcine Hat	R+ Tor	64	236	70	8	0	8	102	45	29	18	0	62	2	0	2	9	5	.64	2	.297	.349	.432
1992 Myrtle Bch	A Tor	136	514	123	18	5	11	184	75	41	43	0	156	8	6	2	33	14	.70	6	.239	.307	.358
1993 Waterloo	A SD	125	421	108	15	5	9	160	57	55	30	1	103	12	4	5	21	8	.72	3	.257	.321	.380
1994 Rancho Cuca	A+ SD	121	417	112	22	2	17	189	63	76	54	1	124	9	2	7	14	13	.52	7	.269	.359	.453
1995 Memphis	AA SD	118	385	95	14	7	8	147	60	46	40	5	133	10	1	3	17	8	.68	13	.247	.331	.382
1996 Memphis	AA SD	133	452	124	24	6	12	196	72	80	62	4	123	4	4	3	28	11	.72	18	.274	.365	.434
1997 Las Vegas	AAA SD	119	435	117	21	5	11	181	58	57	28	1	122	6	0	4	18	12	.60	10	.269	.319	.416
1998 Iowa	AAA ChC	2	4	1	0	0	0	1	1	1	0	0	0	0	0	0	0	0	—	0	.250	.250	.250
Newburgh	IND —	24	87	29	6	0	8	59	21	25	6	1	16	2	0	1	9	1	.90	2	.333	.385	.678
2000 Jacksnville	AA Det	134	496	126	39	2	17	220	65	65	60	1	145	6	2	4	17	6	.74	14	.254	.339	.444
2001 Bowie	AA Bal	55	164	40	5	1	8	71	25	22	24	0	40	3	1	1	2	2	.50	8	.244	.349	.433
10 Min. YEARS		1031	3611	945	172	33	109	1510	542	497	365	14	1024	62	20	32	168	80	.68	83	.262	.337	.418

Junior Brignac

Bats: Right **Throws:** Right **Pos:** OF-127; PH-2; PR-1   **Ht:** 6'3" **Wt:** 175 **Born:** 2/15/78 **Age:** 24

Year Team	Lg Org	G	AB	H	2B	3B	HR	TB	R	RBI	TBB	IBB	SO	HBP	SH	SF	SB	CS	SB%	GDP	Avg	OBP	SLG
1996 Braves	R Atl	53	191	37	7	0	0	44	15	8	9	0	60	4	1	1	3	7	.30	2	.194	.244	.230
1997 Danville	R+ Atl	59	225	55	10	0	4	77	47	25	29	0	70	7	1	0	12	4	.75	2	.244	.349	.342
1998 Eugene	A- Atl	70	270	63	13	1	3	87	36	29	23	0	74	6	0	3	15	7	.68	5	.233	.305	.322
1999 Macon	A Atl	69	268	80	18	3	7	125	35	38	11	0	68	2	0	2	17	5	.77	2	.299	.329	.466
Myrtle Bch	A+ Atl	64	254	58	7	2	7	90	32	35	24	3	84	4	2	4	11	10	.52	6	.228	.301	.354
2000 Myrtle Bch	A+ Atl	128	475	100	17	3	7	144	58	42	43	1	145	8	9	1	27	8	.77	5	.211	.287	.303
2001 Greenville	AA Atl	62	203	41	9	1	1	55	21	12	22	0	70	4	3	0	4	2	.67	3	.202	.293	.271
Myrtle Bch	A+ Atl	66	233	45	8	0	6	71	28	19	24	0	68	2	4	1	6	9	.40	6	.193	.273	.305
6 Min. YEARS		571	2119	479	89	10	35	693	272	208	185	4	639	37	20	12	95	52	.65	31	.226	.298	.327

Jim Brink

Pitches: Right **Bats:** Right **Pos:** RP-45   **Ht:** 6'0" **Wt:** 185 **Born:** 9/11/76 **Age:** 25

Year Team	Lg Org	G	GS	CG	GF	IP	BFP	H	R	ER	HR	SH	SF	HB	TBB	IBB	SO	WP	Bk	W	L	Pct.	ShO	Sv	ERA
1998 Sou Oregon	A- Oak	24	1	0	17	56.1	241	63	32	27	4	1	2	1	16	2	43	2	2	3	0	1.000	0	11	4.31
1999 Midland	AA Oak	5	0	0	2	8	35	10	7	7	4	0	0	1	1	0	4	0	0	1	1	.500	0	0	7.88
Modesto	A+ Oak	47	0	0	41	45.1	204	53	24	23	2	5	4	0	18	3	38	0	0	3	0	1.000	0	29	4.57
2000 Midland	AA Oak	6	0	0	3	9.1	44	13	8	8	2	0	1	0	5	1	5	1	0	0	0	—	0	0	7.71
Modesto	A+ Oak	42	0	0	33	47.1	209	49	21	18	2	3	2	2	17	5	41	3	0	3	2	.600	0	19	3.42
2001 Sacramento	AAA Oak	1	0	0	1	3	12	2	1	1	1	0	0	1	0	0	5	0	0	0	0	—	0	0	3.00
Modesto	A+ Oak	24	0	0	18	32.2	137	33	17	11	2	3	0	3	10	4	26	1	0	0	3	.000	0	4	3.03
Midland	AA Oak	20	0	0	11	31.1	144	34	15	14	5	3	2	2	20	1	24	2	0	0	1	.000	0	2	4.02
4 Min. YEARS		169	1	0	126	233.1	1026	257	125	109	22	15	11	10	87	16	186	9	2	10	7	.588	0	65	4.20

36

Darryl Brinkley

Bats: Right **Throws:** Right **Pos:** OF-7; DH-2   **Ht:** 5'11" **Wt:** 210 **Born:** 12/23/68 **Age:** 33

			BATTING														BASERUNNING				PERCENTAGES		
Year Team	Lg Org	G	AB	H	2B	3B	HR	TB	R	RBI	TBB	IBB	SO	HBP	SH	SF	SB	CS	SB%	GDP	Avg	OBP	SLG
1994 Winnipeg	IND —	72	294	86	18	3	8	134	48	44	21	0	31	6	3	1	32	13	.71	5	.293	.351	.456
1995 Winnipeg	IND —	30	131	44	2	1	4	60	22	19	8	1	13	3	1	2	6	4	.60	4	.336	.382	.458
1996 Rancho Cuca	A+ SD	65	259	94	28	2	9	153	52	59	23	2	37	2	0	6	18	10	.64	13	.363	.410	.591
Memphis	AA SD	60	203	60	9	0	9	96	36	29	22	2	33	3	1	1	13	5	.72	2	.296	.371	.473
1997 Mobile	AA SD	55	215	66	14	1	5	97	41	33	26	1	30	5	0	0	10	9	.53	6	.307	.394	.451
1998 Nashville	AAA Pit	114	372	132	23	3	9	188	57	51	27	2	53	13	0	1	10	8	.56	9	.355	.416	.505
1999 Nashville	AAA Pit	111	372	120	35	2	14	201	68	75	31	0	58	1	0	3	5	5	.50	11	.323	.373	.540
2000 Nashville	AAA Pit	38	113	34	5	1	2	47	19	16	13	1	27	1	0	1	3	3	.50	2	.301	.375	.416
Rochester	AAA Bal	31	120	43	5	1	0	50	16	20	9	1	14	1	0	2	6	0	1.00	1	.358	.402	.417
2001 Rochester	AAA Bal	9	36	11	3	0	2	20	4	7	0	0	3	1	0	2	1	1	.50	0	.306	.308	.556
8 Min. YEARS		585	2115	690	142	14	62	1046	363	353	180	10	299	36	5	19	104	58	.64	59	.326	.386	.495

Juan Brito

Bats: Right **Throws:** Right **Pos:** C-66; DH-4; OF-1   **Ht:** 5'11" **Wt:** 185 **Born:** 11/7/79 **Age:** 22

			BATTING														BASERUNNING				PERCENTAGES		
Year Team	Lg Org	G	AB	H	2B	3B	HR	TB	R	RBI	TBB	IBB	SO	HBP	SH	SF	SB	CS	SB%	GDP	Avg	OBP	SLG
1997 Royals	R KC	25	70	22	4	0	3	35	14	15	5	1	5	1	1	0	0	0	—	1	.314	.368	.500
1998 Lansing	A KC	63	212	52	7	0	0	59	16	22	17	0	41	2	1	2	2	2	.50	6	.245	.305	.278
1999 Wilmington	A+ KC	14	46	13	1	0	0	14	3	1	1	0	11	0	0	0	0	0	—	1	.283	.298	.304
Wichita	AA KC	4	11	1	0	0	0	1	0	0	2	0	3	0	0	0	0	0	—	2	.091	.231	.091
Chston-WV	A KC	61	208	50	6	0	0	56	14	19	11	0	37	1	3	0	1	2	.33	8	.240	.282	.269
Omaha	AAA KC	2	7	2	2	0	0	4	1	0	0	0	2	0	0	0	0	0	—	0	.286	.286	.571
2000 Wilmington	A+ KC	22	54	12	4	0	0	16	4	9	8	0	7	0	0	1	1	0	1.00	2	.222	.317	.296
Omaha	AAA KC	17	49	14	1	0	1	18	8	2	3	0	10	0	1	0	1	1	.50	0	.286	.327	.367
Wichita	AA KC	34	105	27	2	0	0	29	9	10	11	2	15	1	0	2	2	1	.67	4	.257	.328	.276
2001 Wichita	AA KC	70	236	63	10	0	4	85	22	28	17	0	29	0	7	1	3	3	.50	9	.267	.315	.360
5 Min. YEARS		312	998	256	37	0	8	317	91	106	75	3	160	5	13	6	10	9	.53	33	.257	.310	.318

Corey Brittan

Pitches: Right **Bats:** Right **Pos:** RP-58   **Ht:** 6'6" **Wt:** 209 **Born:** 2/23/75 **Age:** 27

		HOW MUCH HE PITCHED					WHAT HE GAVE UP											THE RESULTS				
Year Team	Lg Org	G	GS	CG	GF	IP	BFP	H	R	ER	HR	SH	SF	HB	TBB	IBB	SO	WP	Bk	W	L	Pct.	ShO	Sv	ERA
1996 Pittsfield	A- NYM	14	14	2	0	98	390	74	30	25	2	5	1	4	20	0	84	5	2	8	3	.727	0	0	2.30
1997 St. Lucie	A+ NYM	51	1	0	18	78	338	91	35	31	5	4	0	1	21	4	57	2	0	3	5	.375	0	3	3.58
1998 Binghamton	AA NYM	9	0	0	3	9.1	40	9	4	4	0	0	1	0	4	0	5	3	0	1	1	.500	0	0	3.86
St. Lucie	A+ NYM	34	0	0	17	67	290	74	35	29	1	2	2	2	14	0	40	5	1	4	2	.667	0	2	3.90
1999 Binghamton	AA NYM	54	0	0	27	90.2	375	84	36	28	6	3	2	1	23	0	60	3	2	4	4	.333	0	7	2.78
2000 Binghamton	AA NYM	55	0	0	27	74.1	305	67	28	19	1	2	1	2	28	1	48	2	0	7	1	.875	0	12	2.30
2001 Norfolk	AAA NYM	58	0	0	15	81.2	347	86	22	18	4	1	1	3	26	2	45	0	1	4	2	.667	0	4	1.98
6 Min. YEARS		275	15	2	107	499	2085	485	190	154	19	17	8	13	136	7	339	20	6	29	18	.617	0	28	2.78

Doug Brocail

Pitches: Right **Bats:** Left **Pos:** RP-2; SP-1   **Ht:** 6'5" **Wt:** 235 **Born:** 5/16/67 **Age:** 35

		HOW MUCH HE PITCHED					WHAT HE GAVE UP											THE RESULTS				
Year Team	Lg Org	G	GS	CG	GF	IP	BFP	H	R	ER	HR	SH	SF	HB	TBB	IBB	SO	WP	Bk	W	L	Pct.	ShO	Sv	ERA
1986 Spokane	A- SD	16	15	0	1	85	0	85	52	36	4	0	0	6	53	1	77	10	1	5	4	.556	0	0	3.81
1987 Chston-SC	A SD	19	18	0	0	92.1	393	94	51	42	6	3	3	1	28	0	68	4	0	2	6	.250	0	0	4.09
1988 Chston-SC	A SD	22	13	5	7	107	447	107	40	32	3	4	2	0	25	0	107	4	3	8	6	.571	0	2	2.69
1989 Wichita	AA SD	23	22	1	0	134.2	603	158	88	78	11	5	5	1	50	4	95	9	4	5	9	.357	1	0	5.21
1990 Wichita	AA SD	12	9	0	1	52	227	53	30	25	7	1	0	2	24	0	27	4	0	2	2	.500	0	0	4.33
1991 Wichita	AA SD	34	16	3	11	146.1	625	147	77	63	15	7	3	4	43	3	108	13	0	10	7	.588	3	6	3.87
1992 Las Vegas	AAA SD	29	25	4	2	172.1	733	187	82	76	7	6	1	6	63	5	103	6	0	10	10	.500	0	0	3.97
1993 Las Vegas	AAA SD	10	8	0	1	51.1	219	51	26	21	4	2	1	1	14	0	32	2	0	4	2	.667	0	1	3.68
1994 Wichita	AA SD	2	0	0	1	4	16	3	1	0	0	0	0	0	1	0	2	0	0	0	0	—	0	0	0.00
Las Vegas	AAA SD	7	3	0	1	12.2	59	21	12	10	1	0	0	1	2	0	8	0	0	1	0	1.000	0	0	7.11
1995 Tucson	AAA Hou	3	3	0	0	16.1	74	18	9	7	1	0	1	2	4	0	16	0	0	0	0	—	0	0	3.86
1996 Jackson	AA Hou	2	2	0	0	4	15	1	0	0	0	0	0	0	1	0	5	0	0	0	0	—	0	0	0.00
Tucson	AAA Hou	5	1	0	0	7.1	34	12	6	6	1	1	0	0	1	0	4	0	0	0	1	.000	0	0	7.36
2001 New Orleans	AAA Hou	2	0	0	0	2.1	10	2	0	0	0	0	0	0	1	0	2	0	0	0	0	—	0	0	0.00
Round Rock	AA Hou	1	1	0	0	1	3	0	0	0	0	0	0	0	0	0	1	0	0	0	0	—	0	0	0.00
1992 San Diego	NL	3	3	0	0	14	64	17	10	10	2	2	0	0	5	0	15	0	0	0	0	—	0	0	6.43
1993 San Diego	NL	24	24	0	0	128.1	571	143	75	65	16	10	8	4	42	4	70	4	1	4	13	.235	0	0	4.56
1994 San Diego	NL	12	0	0	4	17	78	21	13	11	1	1	1	2	5	3	11	1	1	0	0	—	0	0	5.82
1995 Houston	NL	36	7	0	12	77.1	339	87	40	36	10	1	1	4	22	2	39	1	1	6	4	.600	0	1	4.19
1996 Houston	NL	23	4	0	4	53	231	58	31	27	7	3	2	2	23	1	34	0	0	1	5	.167	0	0	4.58
1997 Detroit	AL	61	4	0	20	78	332	74	31	28	10	1	1	1	36	4	60	6	0	3	4	.429	0	2	3.23
1998 Detroit	AL	60	0	0	24	62.2	247	47	23	19	2	2	3	1	18	3	55	6	0	5	2	.714	0	0	2.73
1999 Detroit	AL	70	0	0	22	82	326	60	23	23	7	4	2	4	25	1	78	4	1	4	4	.500	0	2	2.52
2000 Detroit	AL	49	0	0	10	50.2	221	57	25	23	5	3	3	1	14	2	41	1	1	5	4	.556	0	0	4.09
12 Min. YEARS		187	136	13	24	888.2	3458	939	474	396	60	29	16	25	310	13	655	52	8	47	47	.500	4	9	4.01
9 Maj. YEARS		338	42	0	96	563	2409	564	271	242	60	27	23	21	190	20	403	23	5	28	36	.438	0	5	3.87

Antone Brooks

Pitches: Left **Bats:** Left **Pos:** RP-11   **Ht:** 6'0" **Wt:** 170 **Born:** 12/20/73 **Age:** 28

		HOW MUCH HE PITCHED					WHAT HE GAVE UP									THE RESULTS				
Year Team	Lg Org	G	GS	CG	GF	IP	BFP	H	R	ER	HR	SH	SF	HB	TBB	IBB	SO	WP	Bk	W	L	Pct.	ShO	Sv	ERA
1995 Eugene	A- Atl	15	0	0	5	17	67	9	5	1	1	0	0	0	8	1	26	0	0	2	0	1.000	0	0	0.53
1996 Macon	A Atl	43	0	0	26	80.1	334	57	24	20	5	2	2	5	36	4	101	8	0	9	4	.692	0	10	2.24
Durham	A+ Atl	2	0	0	1	3	10	1	0	0	0	0	0	0	0	0	6	0	0	0	0	—	0	0	0.00
1997 Greenville	AA Atl	14	0	0	3	20.2	93	21	14	11	3	0	2	2	8	1	10	1	0	1	0	1.000	0	0	4.79
1998 Greenville	AA Atl	26	0	0	7	38	168	42	16	15	1	3	4	1	19	0	37	2	0	6	3	.667	0	1	3.55
1999 Richmond	AAA Atl	43	0	0	18	56	241	57	28	24	2	5	5	0	21	0	39	3	0	3	5	.375	0	1	3.86
2001 Greenville	AA Atl	11	0	0	3	17.2	77	18	13	13	2	1	2	1	9	0	10	1	0	0	1	.000	0	0	6.62
6 Min. YEARS		154	0	0	63	232.2	990	205	100	84	14	11	15	9	101	6	229	15	0	21	13	.618	0	12	3.25

Ben Broussard

Bats: Left **Throws:** Left **Pos:** 1B-123; OF-3; PH-3; DH-2   **Ht:** 6'2" **Wt:** 220 **Born:** 9/24/76 **Age:** 25

		BATTING														BASERUNNING				PERCENTAGES		
Year Team	Lg Org	G	AB	H	2B	3B	HR	TB	R	RBI	TBB	IBB	SO	HBP	SH	SF	SB	CS	SB%	GDP	Avg	OBP	SLG
1999 Billings	R+ Cin	38	145	59	11	2	14	116	39	48	34	2	30	4	0	1	1	0	1.00	0	.407	.527	.800
Clinton	A Cin	5	20	11	4	1	2	23	8	6	3	0	4	0	0	0	0	0	—	1	.550	.609	1.150
Chattanooga	AA Cin	35	127	27	5	0	8	56	26	21	11	1	41	3	0	0	1	0	1.00	0	.213	.291	.441
2000 Chattanooga	AA Cin	87	286	73	8	4	14	131	64	51	72	3	78	6	0	2	15	2	.88	6	.255	.413	.458
2001 Mudville	A+ Cin	30	102	25	5	0	5	45	14	21	16	0	31	4	0	3	0	0	—	2	.245	.360	.441
Chattanooga	AA Cin	100	353	113	27	0	23	209	81	69	61	5	69	8	0	3	10	3	.77	5	.320	.428	.592
3 Min. YEARS		295	1033	308	60	7	66	580	232	216	197	11	253	25	0	9	27	5	.84	14	.298	.419	.561

Brant Brown

Bats: Left **Throws:** Left **Pos:** 1B-87; OF-8; PH-7   **Ht:** 6'3" **Wt:** 220 **Born:** 6/22/71 **Age:** 31

		BATTING														BASERUNNING				PERCENTAGES		
Year Team	Lg Org	G	AB	H	2B	3B	HR	TB	R	RBI	TBB	IBB	SO	HBP	SH	SF	SB	CS	SB%	GDP	Avg	OBP	SLG
1992 Peoria	A ChC	70	248	68	14	0	3	91	28	27	24	2	49	1	3	5	3	4	.43	4	.274	.335	.367
1993 Daytona	A+ ChC	75	266	91	8	7	3	122	26	33	11	0	38	1	1	4	8	7	.53	5	.342	.371	.459
Orlando	AA ChC	28	110	35	11	3	4	64	17	23	6	1	18	4	0	1	2	1	.67	2	.318	.372	.582
1994 Orlando	AA ChC	127	470	127	30	6	5	184	54	37	37	3	86	5	2	0	11	15	.42	10	.270	.330	.391
1995 Orlando	AA ChC	121	446	121	27	4	6	174	67	53	39	2	77	3	11	3	8	5	.62	6	.271	.332	.390
1996 Iowa	AAA ChC	94	342	104	25	3	10	165	48	43	19	1	65	3	0	0	6	6	.50	10	.304	.346	.482
1997 Iowa	AAA ChC	71	256	77	19	3	16	150	51	51	31	2	44	2	1	1	6	6	.50	5	.301	.379	.586
1998 Iowa	AAA ChC	3	11	4	0	0	0	4	1	0	0	0	6	0	0	0	0	0	—	0	.364	.364	.364
2001 Indianapolis	AAA Mil	50	154	31	8	1	5	56	22	13	12	1	47	3	3	0	1	2	.33	1	.201	.272	.364
Memphis	AAA StL	52	188	52	4	1	4	70	30	19	21	1	60	0	0	0	2	1	.67	0	.277	.349	.372
1996 Chicago	NL	29	69	21	1	0	5	37	11	9	2	1	17	1	0	1	3	3	.50	1	.304	.329	.536
1997 Chicago	NL	46	137	32	7	1	5	56	15	15	7	0	28	3	1	0	2	1	.67	2	.234	.286	.409
1998 Chicago	NL	124	347	101	17	7	14	174	56	48	30	2	95	1	1	1	4	5	.44	1	.291	.348	.501
1999 Pittsburgh	NL	130	341	79	20	3	16	153	49	58	22	3	114	4	0	4	3	4	.43	4	.232	.283	.449
2000 Florida	NL	41	73	14	6	0	2	26	4	6	3	0	33	0	0	1	1	0	1.00	1	.192	.224	.356
Chicago	NL	54	89	14	1	0	3	24	7	10	10	0	29	1	1	1	2	1	.67	2	.157	.248	.270
8 Min. YEARS		691	2491	710	146	28	56	1080	344	299	200	13	490	22	24	10	47	47	.50	43	.285	.342	.434
5 Maj. YEARS		424	1056	261	52	11	45	470	142	146	74	6	316	10	3	7	15	14	.52	11	.247	.301	.445

Derek Brown

Pitches: Right **Bats:** Right **Pos:** RP-40; SP-3   **Ht:** 6'1" **Wt:** 184 **Born:** 7/23/76 **Age:** 25

		HOW MUCH HE PITCHED						WHAT HE GAVE UP									THE RESULTS				
Year Team	Lg Org	G	GS	CG	GF	IP	BFP	H	R	ER	HR	SH	SF	HB	TBB	IBB	SO	WP	Bk	W	L	Pct.	ShO	Sv	ERA
1996 Orioles	R Bal	9	8	1	1	55	219	50	19	19	1	1	2	4	11	0	37	5	3	6	1	.857	1	0	3.11
Frederick	A+ Bal	1	1	0	0	4	18	6	4	4	0	0	0	0	3	0	1	0	0	0	1	.000	0	0	9.00
Bluefield	R+ Bal	2	2	0	0	5.1	29	12	10	10	5	0	0	0	2	0	3	0	0	0	1	.000	0	0	16.88
1997 Delmarva	A Bal	2	0	0	0	2	9	2	0	0	0	0	0	0	1	0	2	0	0	0	0	—	0	0	0.00
Bluefield	R+ Bal	17	5	1	2	41.1	180	44	26	23	3	1	1	0	13	0	48	3	1	2	5	.286	0	1	5.01
1998 Delmarva	A Bal	55	0	0	52	68	270	55	19	14	3	5	2	1	13	2	63	8	1	3	4	.429	0	33	1.85
1999 Frederick	A+ Bal	43	0	0	37	51.1	232	49	31	23	6	4	1	4	20	1	36	4	1	6	5	.545	0	14	4.03
2000 Frederick	A+ Bal	41	0	0	31	51.2	221	52	25	23	4	1	3	2	13	0	39	4	0	2	5	.286	0	8	4.01
2001 Rochester	AAA Bal	9	0	0	5	18.2	87	25	18	18	4	1	0	1	6	2	14	1	1	2	1	.667	0	1	8.68
Bowie	AA Bal	34	3	1	7	67	290	69	31	28	6	4	3	2	19	0	44	0	1	4	4	.500	0	1	3.76
6 Min. YEARS		213	19	3	135	364.1	1555	364	183	162	32	17	12	10	101	5	286	25	8	25	27	.481	1	59	4.00

Elliot Brown

Pitches: Right **Bats:** Both **Pos:** SP-22; RP-5   **Ht:** 6'2" **Wt:** 191 **Born:** 6/7/75 **Age:** 27

		HOW MUCH HE PITCHED						WHAT HE GAVE UP									THE RESULTS				
Year Team	Lg Org	G	GS	CG	GF	IP	BFP	H	R	ER	HR	SH	SF	HB	TBB	IBB	SO	WP	Bk	W	L	Pct.	ShO	Sv	ERA
1997 Chston-SC	A TB	33	16	0	6	118.2	525	117	73	57	11	4	2	8	45	0	86	12	0	5	8	.385	0	3	4.32
1998 Chston-SC	A TB	40	15	0	5	107	475	123	73	59	10	1	5	10	40	0	59	8	1	2	7	.222	0	0	4.96
1999 Orlando	AA TB	10	1	0	5	18.2	89	25	18	16	2	0	1	0	12	0	12	3	0	0	0	—	0	0	7.71
St. Pete	A+ TB	38	0	0	15	57.1	230	44	20	17	1	2	1	3	14	1	42	5	0	5	3	.625	0	3	2.67
2000 Orlando	AA TB	45	0	0	7	71.2	321	75	44	38	5	2	3	8	24	3	39	5	0	3	4	.429	0	1	4.77
Durham	AAA TB	1	0	0	1	1	6	1	1	1	1	0	0	0	2	0	1	0	0	0	1	.000	0	0	9.00
2001 San Jose	A+ SF	5	5	0	0	29	107	15	3	3	1	0	0	0	7	0	26	1	0	4	0	1.000	0	0	0.93
Shreveport	AA SF	14	10	0	0	62	280	77	50	31	6	5	2	2	17	2	28	2	1	0	8	.000	0	0	4.50
Fresno	AAA SF	8	7	0	0	34.1	180	61	32	30	4	3	3	4	18	0	21	1	0	2	2	.500	0	0	7.86
5 Min. YEARS		194	54	0	39	499.2	2213	538	313	252	41	17	17	35	179	6	313	38	2	21	35	.375	0	7	4.54

Jamie Brown

Pitches: Right **Bats:** Right **Pos:** SP-4 **Ht:** 6'2" **Wt:** 205 **Born:** 3/31/77 **Age:** 25

Year Team	Lg Org	G	GS	CG	GF	IP	BFP	H	R	ER	HR	SH	SF	HB	TBB	IBB	SO	WP	Bk	W	L	Pct.	ShO	Sv	ERA
1997 Watertown	A- Cle	13	13	1	0	73	303	66	35	25	6	1	2	4	15	0	57	1	1	10	2	.833	0	0	3.08
1998 Kinston	A+ Cle	27	27	2	0	172.2	717	162	91	73	12	10	3	11	44	1	148	4	2	11	9	.550	0	0	3.81
Akron	AA Cle	1	1	0	0	7	28	5	2	2	1	0	0	1	1	0	5	0	0	1	0	1.000	0	0	2.57
1999 Akron	AA Cle	23	23	1	0	138	586	140	72	70	11	7	10	13	39	1	98	2	3	5	9	.357	0	0	4.57
Buffalo	AAA Cle	1	0	0	0	5	23	8	4	3	0	1	1	0	1	0	2	0	0	1	0	1.000	0	0	5.40
2000 Akron	AA Cle	17	17	1	0	96.2	416	95	49	47	12	4	1	6	26	0	57	1	0	7	6	.538	0	0	4.38
2001 Akron	AA Cle	4	4	0	0	19.2	88	22	11	11	2	0	0	2	7	0	12	0	0	1	1	.500	0	0	5.03
5 Min. YEARS		86	85	5	0	512	2161	498	264	231	44	23	17	37	133	2	379	8	6	36	27	.571	0	0	4.06

Jason Brown

Bats: Right **Throws:** Right **Pos:** C-45; DH-16; OF-3; 1B-2; PH-2 **Ht:** 6'2" **Wt:** 208 **Born:** 5/22/74 **Age:** 28

Year Team	Lg Org	G	AB	H	2B	3B	HR	TB	R	RBI	TBB	IBB	SO	HBP	SH	SF	SB	CS	SB%	GDP	Avg	OBP	SLG
1997 Yakima	A- LA	18	59	12	0	0	1	15	6	5	6	0	13	4	1	0	0	0	—	0	.203	.319	.254
San Berndno	A+ LA	30	102	26	10	0	0	36	15	13	3	0	26	4	3	2	0	3	.00	2	.255	.297	.353
1998 Vero Beach	A+ LA	85	267	61	13	0	4	86	23	27	26	1	60	4	3	1	0	0	—	9	.228	.305	.322
1999 San Berndno	A+ LA	68	234	51	11	2	6	84	28	28	23	1	64	7	3	0	1	2	.33	9	.218	.307	.359
2000 Orlando	AA TB	69	230	60	12	1	8	98	21	29	14	0	53	7	1	4	1	0	1.00	8	.261	.318	.426
2001 Marlins	R Fla	1	3	1	0	0	0	1	0	1	0	0	2	0	0	0	0	0	—	0	.333	.333	.333
Orlando	AA TB	3	11	4	2	0	0	6	2	1	0	0	2	0	0	0	0	0	—	0	.364	.364	.545
Portland	AA Fla	17	51	17	3	0	1	23	6	10	5	1	12	0	0	0	0	0	—	0	.333	.393	.451
Brevard Cty	A+ Fla	34	127	35	6	1	2	49	14	20	10	0	29	7	2	0	0	0	—	4	.276	.361	.386
Calgary	AAA Fla	12	39	12	3	0	1	18	7	7	1	1	11	1	0	0	0	0	—	2	.308	.341	.462
5 Min. YEARS		337	1123	279	60	4	23	416	122	141	88	4	272	34	13	7	2	5	.29	34	.248	.320	.370

Rich Brown

Bats: Left **Throws:** Left **Pos:** DH-14 **Ht:** 6'1" **Wt:** 196 **Born:** 4/28/77 **Age:** 25

Year Team	Lg Org	G	AB	H	2B	3B	HR	TB	R	RBI	TBB	IBB	SO	HBP	SH	SF	SB	CS	SB%	GDP	Avg	OBP	SLG
1996 Yankees	R NYY	47	164	47	8	3	0	61	33	23	23	1	32	1	1	3	2	1	.67	2	.287	.372	.372
1997 Yankees	R NYY	10	30	11	3	0	0	14	7	3	5	0	6	0	0	1	0	0	—	2	.367	.444	.467
1998 Yankees	R NYY	6	14	6	0	0	2	6	2	1	0	0	3	1	0	0	2	0	1.00	0	.429	.500	.857
Tampa	A+ NYY	80	282	84	13	3	11	136	46	38	45	1	54	5	2	0	8	6	.57	3	.298	.404	.482
1999 Norwich	AA NYY	104	383	100	18	8	6	152	46	54	34	0	81	3	0	4	5	8	.38	6	.261	.323	.397
2000 Columbus	AAA NYY	10	37	8	2	0	0	10	1	2	1	0	7	0	0	0	0	0	—	1	.216	.237	.270
Norwich	AA NYY	82	319	76	15	3	4	109	52	30	25	0	34	1	1	0	15	7	.68	6	.238	.296	.342
2001 Norwich	AA NYY	11	43	15	2	0	3	26	7	7	5	1	9	0	0	1	1	1	.50	0	.349	.408	.605
Yankees	R NYY	2	6	1	1	0	0	2	1	2	2	0	4	0	0	0	0	0	—	0	.167	.375	.333
Tampa	A+ NYY	1	5	3	1	0	0	4	0	2	0	0	0	0	0	0	0	0	—	0	.600	.600	.800
6 Min. YEARS		353	1283	351	63	17	26	526	199	163	141	3	230	11	4	9	33	23	.59	20	.274	.348	.410

Tonayne Brown

Bats: Right **Throws:** Left **Pos:** OF-109; DH-2; PR-2; PH-1 **Ht:** 5'11" **Wt:** 190 **Born:** 8/24/77 **Age:** 24

Year Team	Lg Org	G	AB	H	2B	3B	HR	TB	R	RBI	TBB	IBB	SO	HBP	SH	SF	SB	CS	SB%	GDP	Avg	OBP	SLG
1998 Red Sox	R Bos	54	225	71	12	4	8	115	43	38	8	0	32	2	0	5	15	6	.71	4	.316	.338	.511
1999 Augusta	A Bos	135	541	141	24	7	4	191	82	45	46	0	89	8	8	4	25	22	.53	14	.261	.326	.353
2000 Sarasota	A+ Bos	127	507	138	16	5	2	170	83	40	33	1	79	9	11	2	33	13	.72	3	.272	.327	.335
2001 Trenton	AA Bos	111	396	115	21	1	4	150	41	31	16	0	76	8	3	1	4	12	.25	11	.290	.330	.379
4 Min. YEARS		427	1669	465	73	17	18	626	249	154	103	1	276	27	22	12	77	53	.59	32	.279	.329	.375

Mark Brownson

Pitches: Right **Bats:** Left **Pos:** SP-23; RP-1 **Ht:** 6'2" **Wt:** 185 **Born:** 6/17/75 **Age:** 27

Year Team	Lg Org	G	GS	CG	GF	IP	BFP	H	R	ER	HR	SH	SF	HB	TBB	IBB	SO	WP	Bk	W	L	Pct.	ShO	Sv	ERA
1994 Rockies	R Col	19	4	0	6	54.1	224	48	18	10	2	2	2	3	6	0	72	2	0	4	1	.800	0	3	1.66
1995 Asheville	A Col	23	12	0	4	98.2	422	106	52	44	12	2	2	4	29	0	94	4	2	6	7	.462	0	1	4.01
New Haven	AA Col	1	1	0	0	6	24	4	2	1	1	0	0	0	1	0	4	0	0	0	0	—	0	0	1.50
Salem	A+ Col	9	1	0	5	15.2	71	16	8	7	0	0	0	1	10	4	9	4	0	2	1	.667	0	1	4.02
1996 New Haven	AA Col	37	19	1	10	144	619	141	73	56	10	6	3	6	43	5	155	7	2	8	13	.381	0	3	3.50
1997 New Haven	AA Col	29	29	2	0	184.2	779	172	101	86	24	8	5	11	55	1	170	5	2	10	9	.526	0	0	4.19
1998 Colo Sprngs	AAA Col	21	21	3	0	124.2	542	131	85	74	22	5	8	14	37	0	82	2	3	6	8	.429	0	0	5.34
1999 Colo Sprngs	AAA Col	17	16	2	0	103	446	120	75	71	24	2	6	7	24	0	81	6	2	6	6	.500	0	0	6.20
2000 Scranton-WB	AAA Phi	31	20	4	1	132.2	556	134	70	67	15	4	4	6	36	1	104	2	3	10	8	.556	0	0	4.55
2001 Huntsville	AA Mil	24	23	0	0	131	571	143	67	65	18	3	2	8	35	0	115	3	0	10	5	.667	0	0	4.47
1998 Colorado	NL	2	2	1	0	13.1	57	16	7	7	2	0	1	2	2	0	8	0	0	1	0	1.000	1	0	4.73
1999 Colorado	NL	7	7	0	0	29.2	139	42	26	26	8	4	0	1	8	0	21	2	0	0	2	.000	0	0	7.89
2000 Philadelphia	NL	2	0	0	0	5	25	7	4	4	1	1	0	0	3	0	3	0	0	1	0	1.000	0	0	7.20
8 Min. YEARS		211	146	12	26	994.2	4254	1015	551	481	128	32	34	63	276	11	886	35	16	62	58	.517	0	8	4.35
3 Maj. YEARS		11	9	1	0	48	221	65	37	37	11	5	0	2	13	0	32	2	0	2	2	.500	1	0	6.94

Matt Bruback

Pitches: Right **Bats:** Right **Pos:** SP-23   **Ht:** 6'7" **Wt:** 215 **Born:** 1/12/79 **Age:** 23

Year Team	Lg Org	G	GS	CG	GF	IP	BFP	H	R	ER	HR	SH	SF	HB	TBB	IBB	SO	WP	Bk	W	L	Pct.	ShO	Sv	ERA
1998 Williamsprt	A- ChC	14	14	0	0	66.1	304	62	46	29	2	2	3	4	45	0	43	7	0	2	7	.222	0	0	3.93
1999 Lansing	A ChC	25	25	0	0	135	633	151	92	81	15	5	3	10	87	0	118	10	1	9	8	.529	0	0	5.40
2000 Lansing	A ChC	9	9	2	0	55.1	237	49	23	18	2	1	0	4	19	0	36	3	1	4	2	.667	0	0	2.93
Daytona	A+ ChC	18	18	0	0	89	409	101	57	48	6	5	4	6	50	1	69	12	0	5	5	.500	0	0	4.85
2001 West Tenn	AA ChC	9	9	0	0	38	197	58	44	38	3	1	2	6	20	0	43	2	2	2	5	.286	0	0	9.00
Daytona	A+ ChC	14	14	0	0	84	346	70	33	28	3	1	3	7	21	0	87	3	0	6	3	.667	0	0	3.00
4 Min. YEARS		89	89	2	0	467.2	2126	491	295	242	31	15	15	37	242	1	396	37	4	28	30	.483	0	0	4.66

Mo Bruce

Bats: Right **Throws:** Right **Pos:** 2B-38; 3B-22; PH-5; PR-2; SS-1; DH-1   **Ht:** 5'10" **Wt:** 190 **Born:** 5/1/75 **Age:** 27

						BATTING										BASERUNNING				PERCENTAGES		
Year Team	Lg Org	G	AB	H	2B	3B	HR	TB	R	RBI	TBB	IBB	SO	HBP	SH	SF	SB	CS	SB%	GDP	Avg	OBP	SLG
1996 Kingsport	R+ NYM	11	38	7	0	1	0	9	5	4	0	0	7	1	0	1	2	1	.67	1	.184	.200	.237
Mets	R NYM	30	120	33	5	3	0	44	16	7	3	0	15	0	3	1	6	1	.86	1	.275	.290	.367
1997 Kingsport	R+ NYM	34	128	47	8	3	3	70	35	21	16	0	20	2	0	0	14	4	.78	1	.367	.445	.547
Pittsfield	A- NYM	29	115	40	7	3	4	65	26	14	11	0	23	2	0	2	12	2	.86	4	.348	.408	.565
1998 Capital Cty	A NYM	126	516	176	24	4	15	253	81	74	41	4	107	1	1	1	45	15	.75	5	.341	.390	.490
1999 Binghamton	AA NYM	133	500	135	25	4	9	195	80	76	61	2	134	4	5	5	33	11	.75	9	.270	.351	.390
2000 Binghamton	AA NYM	81	314	86	16	3	2	114	50	23	27	0	55	1	2	1	21	10	.68	8	.274	.332	.363
Norfolk	AAA NYM	43	151	35	5	1	2	48	24	10	10	1	46	2	0	0	8	3	.73	5	.232	.288	.318
2001 Ottawa	AAA Mon	6	15	2	0	0	0	2	1	0	2	0	7	0	0	0	0	0	—	0	.133	.235	.133
Harrisburg	AA Mon	45	136	31	6	0	3	46	19	15	8	0	36	1	1	1	14	2	.88	2	.228	.274	.338
Altoona	AA Pit	10	34	4	1	0	0	5	4	2	4	0	11	0	1	0	0	2	.00	1	.118	.211	.147
6 Min. YEARS		548	2067	596	97	22	38	851	341	246	183	7	461	14	13	12	155	51	.75	37	.288	.348	.412

Sean Brummett

Pitches: Left **Bats:** Left **Pos:** RP-21; SP-11   **Ht:** 6'0" **Wt:** 200 **Born:** 1/10/78 **Age:** 24

Year Team	Lg Org	G	GS	CG	GF	IP	BFP	H	R	ER	HR	SH	SF	HB	TBB	IBB	SO	WP	Bk	W	L	Pct.	ShO	Sv	ERA
1999 Boise	A- Ana	17	3	0	2	32.1	148	41	25	24	3	1	0	1	12	1	26	1	0	1	2	.333	0	0	6.68
2000 Cedar Rapds	A Ana	32	5	1	17	72.1	290	58	16	8	0	5	0	3	23	3	53	4	1	7	4	.636	0	5	1.00
Erie	AA Ana	9	9	1	0	49	225	63	33	29	6	1	2	1	25	0	30	0	0	0	7	.000	0	0	5.33
2001 Arkansas	AA Ana	25	5	2	7	65.2	302	65	46	41	8	4	2	12	28	0	45	4	0	2	4	.333	0	0	5.62
Rancho Cuca	A+ Ana	7	6	1	0	38.1	169	46	24	21	4	1	1	3	10	0	28	4	0	2	4	.333	0	0	4.93
3 Min. YEARS		90	28	5	26	257.2	1134	273	144	123	21	12	5	20	98	4	182	13	1	12	21	.364	0	5	4.30

Justin Brunette

Pitches: Left **Bats:** Left **Pos:** RP-47   **Ht:** 6'1" **Wt:** 200 **Born:** 10/7/75 **Age:** 26

Year Team	Lg Org	G	GS	CG	GF	IP	BFP	H	R	ER	HR	SH	SF	HB	TBB	IBB	SO	WP	Bk	W	L	Pct.	ShO	Sv	ERA
1997 New Jersey	A- StL	6	0	0	2	5.2	29	13	6	5	0	0	0	0	0	0	6	1	1	1	0	1.000	0	0	7.94
1999 Peoria	A StL	38	0	0	12	44.2	181	34	9	9	2	2	1	1	16	1	44	2	1	3	1	.750	0	2	1.81
Arkansas	AA StL	18	0	0	3	18.1	82	21	12	4	3	0	0	0	7	0	23	1	0	1	2	.333	0	0	1.96
2000 Arkansas	AA StL	3	0	0	1	3	13	5	4	1	1	0	0	0	0	0	1	0	0	0	0	—	0	0	3.00
Memphis	AAA StL	30	0	0	7	33.2	159	42	27	23	4	3	2	1	14	2	27	1	0	1	2	.333	0	0	6.15
2001 Norfolk	AAA NYM	24	0	0	6	26	132	42	32	28	5	3	0	0	15	3	23	1	0	2	2	.500	0	0	9.69
Binghamton	AA NYM	23	0	0	12	29.2	132	43	20	18	4	1	0	0	7	0	33	0	1	3	1	.750	0	4	5.46
2000 St. Louis	NL	4	0	0	2	4.2	27	8	3	3	0	0	0	0	5	0	2	1	1	0	0	—	0	0	5.79
4 Min. YEARS		142	0	0	43	161	728	200	110	88	19	9	3	2	59	6	157	6	3	11	8	.579	0	6	4.92

Will Brunson

Pitches: Left **Bats:** Left **Pos:** RP-38; SP-1   **Ht:** 6'5" **Wt:** 185 **Born:** 3/20/70 **Age:** 32

Year Team	Lg Org	G	GS	CG	GF	IP	BFP	H	R	ER	HR	SH	SF	HB	TBB	IBB	SO	WP	Bk	W	L	Pct.	ShO	Sv	ERA
1992 Princeton	R+ Cin	13	13	0	0	72.2	313	68	34	29	6	4	2	3	28	0	48	2	0	5	5	.500	0	0	3.59
1993 Chston-WV	A Cin	37	15	0	4	123.2	545	119	68	54	10	4	4	11	50	1	103	7	2	5	6	.455	0	0	3.93
1994 Winston-Sal	A+ Cin	30	22	3	0	165	711	161	83	73	22	5	7	12	58	2	129	6	4	12	7	.632	0	0	3.98
1995 San Berndno	A+ LA	13	13	0	0	83.1	334	68	24	19	4	3	5	5	21	0	70	3	0	10	0	1.000	0	0	2.05
San Antonio	AA LA	14	14	0	0	80	356	105	46	44	4	3	1	4	22	0	44	5	1	4	5	.444	0	0	4.95
1996 San Antonio	AA LA	11	5	0	1	42	166	32	13	10	2	2	0	1	15	0	38	2	1	3	1	.750	0	0	2.14
Albuquerque	AAA LA	9	9	1	0	54.1	239	53	29	27	7	2	1	2	23	1	47	2	0	3	4	.429	0	0	4.47
1997 Albuquerque	AAA LA	27	0	0	9	26.1	125	39	19	19	3	1	1	1	10	1	25	0	0	1	1	.500	0	0	6.49
San Antonio	AA LA	17	11	2	4	72.2	299	68	30	28	8	3	1	6	13	0	71	2	0	5	5	.500	1	0	3.47
1998 Albuquerque	AAA LA	34	15	1	5	120	520	135	69	62	11	5	3	4	40	1	100	3	1	5	8	.385	0	2	4.65
1999 Toledo	AAA Det	38	1	0	15	47.2	201	45	28	24	5	3	0	2	17	1	41	2	1	3	1	.750	0	3	4.53
2000 Sacramento	AAA Oak	18	0	0	5	24.2	111	26	12	10	0	2	0	1	11	1	22	0	0	3	0	1.000	0	0	3.65
2001 Salt Lake	AAA Ana	39	1	0	12	69.2	294	73	37	34	9	3	1	1	20	2	52	0	1	2	2	.500	0	0	4.39
1998 Los Angeles	NL	2	0	0	1	2.1	12	3	3	3	0	0	0	0	2	0	1	0	0	0	1	.000	0	0	11.57
Detroit	AL	8	0	0	1	3	11	2	0	0	0	0	0	0	1	0	1	0	0	0	0	—	0	0	0.00
1999 Detroit	AL	17	0	0	1	12	58	18	9	8	3	1	2	0	6	1	9	0	0	1	0	1.000	0	0	6.00
10 Min. YEARS		300	119	7	58	982	4214	992	492	433	91	40	26	53	328	10	790	34	11	61	45	.575	1	5	3.97
2 Maj. YEARS		27	0	0	3	17.1	80	23	12	11	3	1	2	0	9	1	11	0	0	1	1	.500	0	0	5.71

40

Eric Bruntlett

Bats: Right **Throws:** Right **Pos:** SS-115; DH-10; PH-4 **Ht:** 6'0" **Wt:** 200 **Born:** 3/29/78 **Age:** 24

			BATTING														BASERUNNING				PERCENTAGES		
Year Team	Lg Org	G	AB	H	2B	3B	HR	TB	R	RBI	TBB	IBB	SO	HBP	SH	SF	SB	CS	SB%	GDP	Avg	OBP	SLG
2000 Martinsvlle	R+ Hou	50	172	47	11	4	1	69	40	21	30	0	22	11	1	0	14	1	.93	2	.273	.413	.401
2001 Round Rock	AA Hou	123	503	134	23	3	3	172	84	40	50	1	76	8	5	3	23	7	.77	7	.266	.340	.342
New Orleans	AAA Hou	5	16	2	0	0	0	2	3	1	2	0	1	0	1	0	0	0	—	1	.125	.222	.125
2 Min. YEARS		178	691	183	34	7	4	243	127	62	82	1	99	19	7	3	37	8	.82	10	.265	.357	.352

Jim Bruske

Pitches: Right **Bats:** Right **Pos:** RP-24; SP-13 **Ht:** 6'1" **Wt:** 200 **Born:** 10/7/64 **Age:** 37

		HOW MUCH HE PITCHED						WHAT HE GAVE UP										THE RESULTS					
Year Team	Lg Org	G	GS	CG	GF	IP	BFP	H	R	ER	HR	SH	SF	HB	TBB	IBB	SO	WP	Bk	W	L	Pct.	ShO	Sv	ERA
1986 Batavia	A- Cle	1	0	0	1	1	7	1	2	2	0	0	0	0	3	0	3	2	0	0	0	—	0	0	18.00
1989 Canton-Akrn	AA Cle	2	0	0	2	2	11	3	3	3	0	0	0	0	2	0	1	1	0	0	0	—	0	0	13.50
1990 Canton-Akrn	AA Cle	32	13	3	6	118	511	118	53	43	6	2	3	4	42	2	62	5	0	9	3	.750	2	0	3.28
1991 Canton-Akrn	AA Cle	17	11	0	3	80.1	337	73	36	31	3	0	1	2	27	3	35	2	0	5	2	.714	0	1	3.47
Colo Spngs	AAA Cle	7	1	0	3	25.2	100	19	9	7	3	0	1	0	8	0	13	1	1	4	0	1.000	0	2	2.45
1992 Colo Spngs	AAA Cle	7	0	0	1	17.2	83	24	11	9	2	0	0	2	6	1	8	2	0	2	0	1.000	0	0	4.58
Jackson	AA Hou	13	9	1	1	61.2	258	54	23	18	2	2	2	4	14	1	48	1	1	4	3	.571	0	0	2.63
1993 Jackson	AA Hou	15	15	1	0	97.1	391	86	34	25	6	1	1	2	22	1	83	2	0	9	5	.643	0	0	2.31
Tucson	AAA Hou	12	9	0	1	66.2	290	77	36	28	4	2	1	0	18	2	42	3	0	4	2	.667	0	1	3.78
1994 Tucson	AAA Hou	7	7	0	0	39	170	47	22	18	2	1	0	1	8	0	25	2	0	3	1	.750	0	0	4.15
1995 Albuquerque	AAA LA	43	6	0	13	114	492	128	54	52	6	4	4	3	41	2	99	3	0	7	5	.583	0	4	4.11
1996 Albuquerque	AAA LA	36	0	0	21	62	270	63	34	28	3	3	4	3	21	6	51	1	0	5	2	.714	0	4	4.06
1997 Las Vegas	AAA SD	16	9	0	0	68	294	73	41	37	8	2	1	3	22	1	67	2	0	5	4	.556	0	0	4.90
1998 Las Vegas	AAA SD	5	0	0	4	6	25	8	4	4	1	0	0	0	1	0	2	0	0	0	1	.000	0	1	6.00
Columbus	AAA NYY	4	0	0	3	7.2	31	7	1	1	0	0	0	0	2	0	9	0	0	0	0	—	0	1	1.17
2000 Indianaplis	AAA Mil	19	2	0	4	32	159	47	36	33	9	3	2	3	14	2	22	2	0	2	4	.333	0	1	9.28
2001 Salt Lake	AAA Ana	27	5	0	8	57	255	70	35	31	9	2	2	4	10	0	58	3	0	3	1	.750	0	1	4.89
Las Vegas	AAA LA	10	8	0	1	49.1	220	59	31	30	6	0	2	5	15	0	49	1	0	2	2	.500	0	0	5.47
1995 Los Angeles	NL	9	0	0	3	10	45	12	7	5	0	0	0	1	4	0	5	1	0	0	0	—	0	1	4.50
1996 Los Angeles	NL	11	0	0	5	12.2	58	17	8	8	2	0	0	1	3	1	12	1	0	0	0	—	0	0	5.68
1997 San Diego	NL	28	0	0	6	44.2	193	37	22	18	4	2	3	1	25	1	32	4	0	4	1	.800	0	0	3.63
1998 Los Angeles	NL	35	0	0	10	44	195	47	18	17	2	0	0	3	19	1	31	3	0	3	0	1.000	0	1	3.48
San Diego	NL	4	0	0	1	7	34	10	4	3	1	0	0	0	4	2	4	0	0	0	0	—	0	0	3.86
New York	AL	3	1	0	0	9	36	9	3	3	2	0	0	0	1	0	3	0	0	1	0	1.000	0	0	3.00
2000 Milwaukee	NL	15	0	0	1	16.2	85	22	15	12	5	0	1	2	12	1	8	0	0	1	0	1.000	0	0	6.48
13 Min. YEARS		273	95	5	72	905.1	3904	957	465	400	70	22	24	36	276	21	677	33	2	64	35	.646	2	16	3.98
5 Maj. YEARS		105	1	0	26	144	646	154	77	66	16	2	4	8	68	6	95	9	0	9	1	.900	0	2	4.13

Mark Budzinski

Bats: Left **Throws:** Left **Pos:** OF-121; DH-1; PR-1 **Ht:** 6'2" **Wt:** 175 **Born:** 8/26/73 **Age:** 28

			BATTING														BASERUNNING				PERCENTAGES		
Year Team	Lg Org	G	AB	H	2B	3B	HR	TB	R	RBI	TBB	IBB	SO	HBP	SH	SF	SB	CS	SB%	GDP	Avg	OBP	SLG
1995 Watertown	A- Cle	70	253	64	12	8	3	101	50	25	52	1	49	8	3	2	15	5	.75	3	.253	.394	.399
1996 Columbus	A Cle	74	260	68	12	4	3	97	42	38	59	4	68	4	2	1	12	3	.80	5	.262	.404	.373
1997 Kinston	A+ Cle	68	241	69	13	3	7	109	43	39	48	1	61	1	2	0	6	4	.60	3	.286	.407	.452
1998 Akron	AA Cle	127	478	125	21	5	10	186	68	62	50	2	125	1	4	2	12	8	.60	9	.262	.331	.389
1999 Akron	AA Cle	86	297	84	17	6	6	131	58	46	48	0	63	5	2	0	9	4	.69	3	.283	.391	.441
Buffalo	AAA Cle	47	133	38	7	3	2	57	24	17	22	2	36	0	2	0	4	2	.67	3	.286	.387	.429
2000 Akron	AA Cle	18	71	17	2	0	1	22	7	5	6	1	20	1	1	0	3	2	.60	0	.239	.308	.310
Buffalo	AAA Cle	118	427	124	21	7	6	177	68	37	49	3	81	1	5	0	12	4	.75	2	.290	.365	.415
2001 Buffalo	AAA Cle	122	438	112	26	4	2	152	69	39	28	2	125	7	9	4	13	4	.76	4	.256	.308	.347
7 Min. YEARS		730	2598	701	131	40	40	1032	429	308	362	16	628	28	30	9	86	36	.70	32	.270	.364	.397

Ryan Bukvich

Pitches: Right **Bats:** Right **Pos:** RP-44 **Ht:** 6'3" **Wt:** 237 **Born:** 5/13/78 **Age:** 24

		HOW MUCH HE PITCHED						WHAT HE GAVE UP										THE RESULTS					
Year Team	Lg Org	G	GS	CG	GF	IP	BFP	H	R	ER	HR	SH	SF	HB	TBB	IBB	SO	WP	Bk	W	L	Pct.	ShO	Sv	ERA
2000 Spokane	A- KC	10	0	0	8	14	56	5	1	1	0	1	0	1	9	0	15	1	0	2	0	1.000	0	2	0.64
Chston-WV	A KC	11	0	0	9	14.1	57	6	3	3	0	2	0	1	7	0	17	1	0	0	0	—	0	4	1.88
Wilmington	A+ KC	2	0	0	0	2	15	3	4	4	0	1	0	1	5	2	3	1	0	0	1	.000	0	0	18.00
2001 Wilmington	A+ KC	37	0	0	29	57.2	248	41	16	11	1	0	2	4	31	0	80	5	1	0	1	.000	0	13	1.72
Wichita	AA KC	7	0	0	3	12	47	9	6	5	2	0	0	0	2	0	14	2	0	0	0	—	0	0	3.75
2 Min. YEARS		67	0	0	49	100	423	64	30	24	3	4	2	7	54	2	129	10	1	2	2	.500	0	19	2.16

Sean Buller

Pitches: Left **Bats:** Left **Pos:** RP-21 **Ht:** 6'5" **Wt:** 235 **Born:** 11/28/75 **Age:** 26

		HOW MUCH HE PITCHED						WHAT HE GAVE UP										THE RESULTS					
Year Team	Lg Org	G	GS	CG	GF	IP	BFP	H	R	ER	HR	SH	SF	HB	TBB	IBB	SO	WP	Bk	W	L	Pct.	ShO	Sv	ERA
1998 Jamestown	A- Det	13	5	0	4	37.1	167	42	30	25	3	0	2	1	12	0	26	1	0	2	2	.500	0	0	6.03
1999 Lakeland	A+ Det	1	0	0	1	3	15	4	3	3	0	0	1	0	2	0	2	0	0	0	0	—	0	0	9.00
W Michigan	A Det	31	17	2	2	120.1	528	133	78	66	11	3	6	5	55	1	72	9	0	10	10	.500	0	0	4.94
2000 Lakeland	A+ Det	29	1	0	13	49.2	212	45	19	11	3	0	1	0	18	1	29	3	0	5	2	.714	0	1	1.99
2001 Toledo	AAA Det	5	0	0	1	10.2	44	8	2	2	0	0	0	0	5	0	9	0	0	1	0	1.000	0	0	1.69
Erie	AA Det	16	0	0	8	21.2	96	27	15	14	2	1	0	0	4	1	11	0	0	2	1	.667	0	2	5.82
4 Min. YEARS		95	23	2	29	242.2	1062	259	147	121	19	4	10	6	96	3	149	13	0	20	15	.571	0	3	4.49

Scott Bullett

Bats: Left **Throws:** Left **Pos:** OF-20; PH-2   **Ht:** 6'2" **Wt:** 225 **Born:** 12/25/68 **Age:** 33

		BATTING																BASERUNNING				PERCENTAGES		
Year Team	Lg Org	G	AB	H	2B	3B	HR	TB	R	RBI	TBB	IBB	SO	HBP	SH	SF	SB	CS	SB%	GDP	Avg	OBP	SLG
1988 Pirates	R Pit	21	61	11	1	0	0	12	6	8	7	1	9	0	1	1	2	5	.29	0	.180	.261	.197
1989 Pirates	R Pit	46	165	42	7	3	1	58	24	16	12	2	31	5	1	0	15	5	.75	2	.255	.324	.352
1990 Welland	A- Pit	74	256	77	11	4	3	105	46	33	13	2	50	2	1	0	30	6	.83	7	.301	.339	.410
1991 Augusta	A Pit	95	384	109	21	6	1	145	61	36	27	2	79	2	1	1	48	17	.74	1	.284	.333	.378
Salem	A+ Pit	39	156	52	7	5	2	75	22	15	8	1	29	0	1	0	15	7	.68	0	.333	.366	.481
1992 Carolina	AA Pit	132	518	140	20	5	8	194	59	45	28	5	98	10	2	7	29	21	.58	7	.270	.316	.375
Buffalo	AAA Pit	3	10	4	0	2	0	8	1	0	0	0	2	0	0	0	0	0	—	0	.400	.400	.800
1993 Buffalo	AAA Pit	110	408	117	13	6	1	145	62	30	39	0	67	1	8	0	28	17	.62	5	.287	.350	.355
1994 Iowa	AAA ChC	135	530	163	28	4	13	238	75	69	19	4	110	5	11	6	27	16	.63	5	.308	.334	.449
1996 Orlando	AA ChC	3	11	2	0	0	0	2	2	0	1	0	2	0	0	0	2	0	1.00	0	.182	.250	.182
1997 Rochester	AAA Bal	136	512	128	24	8	9	195	73	58	45	2	112	7	0	2	19	11	.63	17	.250	.318	.381
1999 Allentown	IND —	22	83	30	8	1	3	49	17	28	4	2	9	3	0	1	7	1	.88	1	.361	.407	.590
2000 Colo Sprngs	AAA Col	11	40	19	3	0	0	22	6	8	2	0	5	0	0	0	2	3	.40	1	.475	.500	.550
2001 Colo Sprngs	AAA Col	21	78	20	4	1	2	32	7	11	0	0	17	0	0	1	1	0	1.00	1	.256	.253	.410
1991 Pittsburgh	NL	11	4	0	0	0	0	0	2	0	0	0	3	1	0	0	1	1	.50	0	.000	.200	.000
1993 Pittsburgh	NL	23	55	11	0	2	0	15	2	4	3	0	15	0	0	1	3	2	.60	1	.200	.237	.273
1995 Chicago	NL	104	150	41	5	7	3	69	19	22	12	2	30	1	1	0	8	3	.73	4	.273	.331	.460
1996 Chicago	NL	109	165	35	5	0	3	49	26	16	10	0	54	0	1	1	7	3	.70	2	.212	.256	.297
12 Min. YEARS		848	3212	914	147	45	43	1280	461	357	205	21	620	35	25	19	225	109	.67	47	.285	.332	.399
4 Maj. YEARS		247	374	87	10	9	6	133	49	42	25	2	102	2	2	2	19	9	.68	7	.233	.283	.356

Jim Bullinger

Pitches: Right **Bats:** Right **Pos:** SP-19   **Ht:** 6'2" **Wt:** 180 **Born:** 8/21/65 **Age:** 36

		HOW MUCH HE PITCHED						WHAT HE GAVE UP											THE RESULTS					
Year Team	Lg Org	G	GS	CG	GF	IP	BFP	H	R	ER	HR	SH	SF	HB	TBB	IBB	SO	WP	Bk	W	L	Pct.	ShO	Sv	ERA
1989 Charlotte	AA ChC	2	0	0	2	3	14	2	0	0	0	0	0	0	3	0	5	1	0	0	0	—	0	0	0.00
1990 Winston-Sal	A+ ChC	14	13	3	0	90	392	81	43	37	5	3	2	7	46	0	85	6	1	7	6	.538	0	0	3.70
Charlotte	AA ChC	9	9	0	0	44	194	42	30	25	7	1	1	3	18	0	33	3	1	3	4	.429	0	0	5.11
1991 Charlotte	AA ChC	20	20	8	0	142.2	595	132	62	56	5	5	1	6	61	2	128	5	3	9	9	.500	0	0	3.53
Iowa	AAA ChC	8	8	0	0	46.2	203	47	32	28	6	1	1	0	23	0	30	7	0	3	4	.429	0	0	5.40
1992 Iowa	AAA ChC	20	0	0	20	22	91	17	6	6	0	1	1	0	12	3	15	2	1	1	2	.333	0	14	2.45
1993 Iowa	AAA ChC	49	3	0	37	73.2	326	64	29	28	3	2	3	4	43	5	74	13	0	4	6	.400	0	20	3.42
1995 Orlando	AA ChC	1	1	0	0	4	16	3	0	0	0	0	0	0	1	0	2	0	0	0	0	—	0	0	0.00
1998 Tacoma	AAA Sea	20	16	0	2	101.2	459	106	64	57	13	1	1	8	58	1	73	4	0	8	7	.533	0	0	5.05
1999 Vero Beach	A+ LA	6	6	0	0	19	90	23	17	16	5	1	1	0	10	0	18	1	0	0	2	.000	0	0	7.58
2000 Waterbury	IND —	5	5	0	0	25	118	29	19	11	3	1	0	1	13	0	20	1	0	1	3	.250	0	0	3.96
Adirondack	IND —	2	2	0	0	12	56	17	10	8	2	0	0	4	1	0	8	0	0	1	0	1.000	0	0	6.00
2001 Long Island	IND —	9	9	1	0	47.1	202	42	15	12	5	1	1	4	14	0	25	3	0	6	1	.857	1	0	2.28
Memphis	AAA StL	10	10	0	0	53	251	68	47	41	11	2	1	3	30	1	36	1	0	1	8	.111	0	0	6.96
1992 Chicago	NL	39	9	1	15	85	380	72	49	44	9	9	4	4	54	6	36	4	0	2	8	.200	0	7	4.66
1993 Chicago	NL	15	0	0	6	16.2	75	18	9	8	1	0	1	0	9	0	10	0	0	1	0	1.000	0	1	4.32
1994 Chicago	NL	33	10	1	10	100	412	87	43	40	6	3	3	1	34	2	72	4	1	6	2	.750	0	2	3.60
1995 Chicago	NL	24	24	1	0	150	665	152	80	69	14	12	5	9	65	7	93	5	1	12	8	.600	1	0	4.14
1996 Chicago	NL	37	20	1	6	129.1	598	144	101	94	15	8	5	8	68	5	90	7	0	6	10	.375	1	1	6.54
1997 Montreal	NL	36	25	2	4	155.1	697	165	106	96	17	8	6	12	74	5	87	7	0	7	12	.368	2	0	5.56
1998 Seattle	AL	2	1	0	0	5.2	33	13	10	10	3	0	1	0	2	0	4	0	0	0	1	.000	0	0	15.88
10 Min. YEARS		175	102	12	61	684	3007	673	374	325	65	19	13	40	333	12	552	47	6	43	53	.448	1	34	4.28
7 Maj. YEARS		186	89	6	41	642	2860	651	398	361	65	40	25	34	306	25	392	27	2	34	41	.453	4	11	5.06

Kirk Bullinger

Pitches: Right **Bats:** Right **Pos:** RP-40; SP-1   **Ht:** 6'2" **Wt:** 170 **Born:** 10/28/69 **Age:** 32

		HOW MUCH HE PITCHED						WHAT HE GAVE UP											THE RESULTS					
Year Team	Lg Org	G	GS	CG	GF	IP	BFP	H	R	ER	HR	SH	SF	HB	TBB	IBB	SO	WP	Bk	W	L	Pct.	ShO	Sv	ERA
1992 Hamilton	A- StL	35	0	0	7	48.2	191	24	7	6	0	1	1	2	15	4	61	3	1	2	2	.500	0	2	1.11
1993 Springfield	A StL	50	0	0	46	51.1	208	26	19	13	5	3	2	2	21	1	72	6	0	1	3	.250	0	33	2.28
1994 St. Pete	A+ StL	39	0	0	18	53.2	220	37	16	7	0	4	0	1	20	5	50	4	3	2	0	1.000	0	6	1.17
1995 Harrisburg	AA Mon	56	0	0	39	67	282	61	22	18	4	4	1	0	25	5	42	2	2	5	3	.625	0	7	2.42
1996 Ottawa	AAA Mon	10	0	0	4	15.1	62	10	6	6	3	0	0	0	9	1	9	1	0	2	1	.667	0	0	3.52
Harrisburg	AA Mon	47	0	0	40	45.2	193	46	16	10	5	3	1	1	18	3	29	3	0	3	4	.429	0	22	1.97
1997 Wst Plm Bch	A+ Mon	2	0	0	0	3.2	15	3	0	0	0	0	0	0	0	0	7	1	0	2	0	1.000	0	0	0.00
Harrisburg	AA Mon	21	0	0	12	27	106	22	9	8	4	1	0	1	6	0	21	0	0	3	0	1.000	0	6	2.67
Ottawa	AAA Mon	22	0	0	14	31.2	119	17	7	6	0	2	1	0	10	0	15	1	0	3	4	.429	0	5	1.71
1998 Expos	R Mon	2	2	0	0	4	14	2	0	0	0	0	0	0	0	0	7	0	0	0	0	—	0	0	0.00
Jupiter	A+ Mon	8	0	0	1	10	42	9	7	6	1	0	0	0	2	0	12	2	0	0	0	—	0	0	5.40
Ottawa	AAA Mon	13	0	0	4	17	72	16	2	2	0	1	0	0	6	1	7	0	0	0	0	—	0	3	1.06
1999 Trenton	AA Bos	17	0	0	17	17	66	6	2	1	1	1	0	0	5	1	16	1	0	1	1	.500	0	10	0.53
Pawtucket	AAA Bos	35	0	0	30	37.2	160	37	14	10	3	1	1	2	13	4	27	0	0	0	2	.000	0	15	2.39
2000 Reading	AA Phi	2	1	0	0	3	12	3	0	0	0	0	0	1	1	0	1	0	0	0	0	—	0	0	0.00
Phillies	R Phi	1	1	0	0	1	3	0	0	0	0	0	0	0	0	0	0	0	0	0	0	—	0	0	0.00
Scranton-WB	AAA Phi	26	0	0	21	25	99	19	4	2	0	3	0	1	10	2	16	0	0	0	1	.000	0	12	0.72
2001 Akron	AA Cle	3	0	0	3	3.2	16	5	2	2	0	1	1	0	1	1	4	0	0	0	1	.000	0	0	4.91
Somerset	IND —	2	0	0	0	4	12	0	0	0	0	0	0	0	0	0	0	0	0	0	0	—	0	0	0.00
Charlotte	AAA CWS	36	1	0	16	50.1	212	44	23	20	5	5	4	4	21	6	34	3	0	0	3	.000	0	5	3.58
1998 Montreal	NL	8	0	0	1	7	35	14	8	7	1	0	0	0	3	0	1	0	0	1	0	1.000	0	0	9.00
1999 Boston	AL	4	0	0	0	2	9	2	1	1	0	0	0	0	2	0	2	0	0	0	0	—	0	0	4.50
2000 Philadelphia	NL	3	0	0	1	3.1	14	4	2	2	0	0	0	0	0	0	3	0	0	0	0	—	0	0	5.40
10 Min. YEARS		427	5	0	272	516.2	2099	387	156	117	31	30	12	15	183	34	437	27	6	24	25	.490	0	127	2.04
3 Maj. YEARS		15	0	0	2	12.1	58	20	11	10	1	0	1	0	2	0	6	0	0	1	0	1.000	0	0	7.30

Nate Bump

Pitches: Right Bats: Right Pos: SP-8; RP-3   Ht: 6'2" Wt: 185 Born: 7/24/76 Age: 25

Year Team	Lg Org	G	GS	CG	GF	IP	BFP	H	R	ER	HR	SH	SF	HB	TBB	IBB	SO	WP	Bk	W	L	Pct.	ShO	Sv	ERA
1998 Salem-Keizr	A- SF	2	2	0	0	8	31	5	0	0	0	0	0	2	3	0	8	1	0	0	0	—	0	0	0.00
San Jose	A+ SF	11	11	0	0	61.2	240	37	13	12	2	1	1	2	24	0	61	2	0	6	1	.857	0	0	1.75
1999 Shreveport	AA SF	17	17	1	0	92.1	394	85	40	34	9	6	0	5	32	0	59	2	0	4	10	.286	1	0	3.31
Portland	AA Fla	8	8	0	0	43	203	57	38	29	3	1	2	5	12	0	33	1	0	2	6	.250	0	0	6.07
2000 Portland	AA Fla	26	26	3	0	149.2	663	169	85	76	16	5	4	15	49	1	98	5	0	8	9	.471	1	0	4.57
2001 Portland	AA Fla	11	8	0	2	54.2	228	55	41	32	10	2	1	3	10	0	41	0	0	4	5	.444	0	0	5.27
4 Min. YEARS		75	72	4	2	409.1	1759	408	217	183	40	15	8	32	130	1	300	11	0	24	31	.436	2	0	4.02

Kevin Burford

Bats: Left Throws: Left Pos: 1B-77; DH-20; PH-5   Ht: 6'0" Wt: 190 Born: 11/7/77 Age: 24

Year Team	Lg Org	G	AB	H	2B	3B	HR	TB	R	RBI	TBB	IBB	SO	HBP	SH	SF	SB	CS	SB%	GDP	Avg	OBP	SLG
1997 Padres	R SD	47	167	65	15	2	4	96	42	50	49	1	25	4	0	5	12	5	.71	3	.389	.524	.575
Idaho Falls	R+ SD	7	29	6	0	1	1	11	2	3	1	0	5	0	0	0	0	0	—	1	.207	.233	.379
1998 Clinton	A SD	123	446	115	26	4	6	167	68	55	62	2	125	10	1	4	15	4	.79	8	.258	.358	.374
1999 Portland	A- Col	64	216	66	22	2	7	113	55	33	52	3	45	5	0	2	9	6	.60	3	.306	.447	.523
2000 Salem	A+ Col	127	465	136	40	4	16	232	73	80	58	2	79	10	0	4	11	4	.73	6	.292	.380	.499
2001 Carolina	AA Col	101	363	105	21	4	6	152	51	35	45	2	79	8	0	3	4	1	.80	5	.289	.377	.419
5 Min. YEARS		469	1686	493	124	17	40	771	291	256	267	10	358	37	1	18	51	20	.72	26	.292	.397	.457

Lance Burkhart

Bats: Right Throws: Right Pos: C-79; 1B-13; DH-13; 3B-8; PH-6; PR-1   Ht: 5'9" Wt: 220 Born: 12/16/74 Age: 27

Year Team	Lg Org	G	AB	H	2B	3B	HR	TB	R	RBI	TBB	IBB	SO	HBP	SH	SF	SB	CS	SB%	GDP	Avg	OBP	SLG
1997 Vermont	A- Mon	38	143	24	6	1	0	32	15	12	17	0	40	1	0	0	3	3	.50	3	.168	.261	.224
1998 Vermont	A- Mon	16	44	13	4	1	0	19	13	5	13	0	13	1	1	1	0	0	—	0	.295	.458	.432
Cape Fear	A Mon	17	50	12	3	1	1	20	10	11	16	1	17	2	1	1	1	3	.25	0	.240	.435	.400
1999 Cape Fear	A Mon	2	6	1	1	0	0	2	2	0	2	0	4	0	0	0	0	0	—	0	.167	.375	.333
Ottawa	AAA Mon	2	8	1	0	0	0	1	1	0	0	0	5	0	0	0	0	0	—	0	.125	.125	.125
Jupiter	A+ Mon	45	131	28	8	0	5	51	19	21	13	1	35	2	0	2	1	1	.50	1	.214	.291	.389
2000 Beloit	A Mil	58	202	57	18	0	17	126	42	64	34	4	42	4	0	5	0	2	.00	1	.282	.388	.624
Huntsville	AA Mil	51	155	30	6	1	6	56	17	19	19	3	43	1	4	0	0	0	—	2	.194	.286	.361
2001 High Desert	A+ Mil	65	234	73	23	1	20	158	57	55	44	2	58	8	1	2	4	2	.67	0	.312	.434	.675
Huntsville	AA Mil	52	170	40	10	0	12	86	34	38	21	2	54	3	1	2	0	1	.00	5	.235	.327	.506
5 Min. YEARS		346	1143	279	79	5	61	551	210	225	179	13	311	22	8	13	9	12	.43	16	.244	.354	.482

Gary Burnham

Bats: Left Throws: Left Pos: 1B-79; DH-22; PH-11; P-2   Ht: 5'11" Wt: 200 Born: 10/13/74 Age: 27

Year Team	Lg Org	G	AB	H	2B	3B	HR	TB	R	RBI	TBB	IBB	SO	HBP	SH	SF	SB	CS	SB%	GDP	Avg	OBP	SLG
1997 Batavia	A- Phi	73	289	94	22	4	5	139	44	45	30	0	47	5	1	2	3	1	.75	8	.325	.396	.481
1998 Clearwater	A+ Phi	139	513	152	33	10	8	229	93	70	63	8	76	14	0	7	10	4	.71	9	.296	.384	.446
1999 Reading	AA Phi	116	354	88	20	0	12	144	47	49	41	3	49	15	6	1	11	3	.79	16	.249	.350	.407
2000 Reading	AA Phi	111	355	95	28	0	13	162	53	61	40	2	47	14	0	2	1	0	1.00	16	.268	.363	.456
2001 Reading	AA Phi	109	371	118	25	2	15	192	59	77	35	2	43	11	0	9	1	2	.33	14	.318	.385	.518
5 Min. YEARS		548	1882	547	128	16	53	866	296	302	209	15	262	59	7	21	25	11	.69	57	.291	.375	.460

Kevin Burns

Bats: Left Throws: Left Pos: 1B-70; DH-45; PH-10   Ht: 6'5" Wt: 220 Born: 9/9/75 Age: 26

Year Team	Lg Org	G	AB	H	2B	3B	HR	TB	R	RBI	TBB	IBB	SO	HBP	SH	SF	SB	CS	SB%	GDP	Avg	OBP	SLG
1995 Astros	R Hou	42	136	34	4	1	3	49	17	23	12	1	24	0	0	1	8	3	.73	5	.250	.309	.360
1996 Auburn	A- Hou	71	269	71	19	3	11	129	27	55	15	1	77	4	0	5	2	1	.67	1	.264	.307	.480
1997 Quad City	A Hou	131	477	129	28	1	20	219	72	86	53	8	114	6	0	4	1	2	.33	12	.270	.348	.459
1998 Kissimmee	A+ Hou	128	470	127	24	4	19	216	69	81	69	5	124	5	0	3	11	3	.79	8	.270	.367	.460
1999 Jackson	AA Hou	113	352	99	21	2	12	160	55	58	42	4	74	4	0	4	6	3	.67	2	.281	.361	.455
2000 New Orleans	AAA Hou	4	14	3	1	1	0	6	3	1	1	0	2	0	0	0	0	0	—	3	.214	.267	.429
Round Rock	AA Hou	87	255	81	17	2	8	126	48	46	28	5	58	3	0	3	1	2	.33	5	.318	.388	.494
2001 New Orleans	AAA Hou	34	99	26	5	3	1	40	19	11	15	0	18	3	0	1	0	1	.00	2	.263	.376	.404
Round Rock	AA Hou	89	305	83	20	2	20	167	57	56	45	6	79	7	0	4	2	0	1.00	6	.272	.374	.548
7 Min. YEARS		699	2377	653	139	19	94	1112	367	417	280	30	570	32	0	24	31	15	.67	41	.275	.356	.468

Adrian Burnside

Pitches: Left Bats: Right Pos: SP-18; RP-1   Ht: 6'3" Wt: 168 Born: 3/15/77 Age: 25

Year Team	Lg Org	G	GS	CG	GF	IP	BFP	H	R	ER	HR	SH	SF	HB	TBB	IBB	SO	WP	Bk	W	L	Pct.	ShO	Sv	ERA
1996 Great Falls	R+ LA	14	5	0	1	41	204	44	35	31	3	2	4	0	38	0	33	6	0	1	3	.250	0	0	6.80
1997 Yakima	A- LA	15	13	0	0	65.2	314	67	53	36	9	1	3	5	49	1	66	4	4	6	3	.667	0	0	4.93
1998 San Berndno	A+ LA	21	12	0	2	78.1	381	97	79	68	6	5	8	8	48	0	65	8	0	1	10	.091	0	0	7.81
Yakima	A- LA	8	6	0	1	33.1	156	27	21	15	0	1	2	2	30	0	34	8	1	1	4	.200	0	0	4.05
1999 San Berndno	A+ LA	26	22	0	0	131.2	571	124	69	61	7	3	4	11	55	1	129	10	2	10	9	.526	0	0	4.17
2000 San Antonio	AA LA	17	17	0	0	90	400	73	40	30	6	7	4	7	55	3	82	3	0	5	5	.545	0	0	2.90
2001 Jacksnville	AA LA	13	12	0	0	67.2	280	44	21	20	6	2	0	5	30	0	67	4	2	4	3	.571	0	0	2.66
Altoona	AA Pit	6	6	0	0	32.1	138	28	15	13	3	2	1	2	14	0	32	2	2	0	2	.000	0	0	3.62
6 Min. YEARS		120	93	0	4	543	2444	504	333	274	40	21	22	46	319	4	508	45	11	29	39	.426	0	0	4.54

Sean Burroughs

Bats: Left **Throws:** Right **Pos:** 3B-96; DH-4; PH-3; PR-1   **Ht:** 6'2" **Wt:** 200 **Born:** 9/12/80 **Age:** 21

Year Team	Lg Org	G	AB	H	2B	3B	HR	TB	R	RBI	TBB	IBB	SO	HBP	SH	SF	SB	CS	SB%	GDP	Avg	OBP	SLG
1999 Fort Wayne	A SD	122	426	153	30	3	5	204	65	80	74	7	59	14	2	5	17	15	.53	10	.359	.464	.479
Rancho Cuca	A+ SD	6	23	10	3	0	1	16	3	5	3	0	3	1	0	0	0	1	.00	1	.435	.519	.696
2000 Okla	AA SD	108	392	114	29	4	2	157	46	42	58	6	45	3	4	4	6	8	.43	10	.291	.383	.401
2001 Portland	AAA SD	104	394	127	28	1	9	184	60	55	37	2	54	4	4	0	9	2	.82	13	.322	.386	.467
3 Min. YEARS		340	1235	404	90	8	17	561	174	182	172	15	161	22	10	9	32	26	.55	34	.327	.416	.454

Terry Burrows

Pitches: Left **Bats:** Left **Pos:** RP-6   **Ht:** 6'1" **Wt:** 190 **Born:** 11/28/68 **Age:** 33

Year Team	Lg Org	G	GS	CG	GF	IP	BFP	H	R	ER	HR	SH	SF	HB	TBB	IBB	SO	WP	Bk	W	L	Pct.	ShO	Sv	ERA
1990 Butte	R+ Tex	14	11	1	1	62.2	275	56	35	28	1	3	1	0	35	0	64	6	2	3	6	.333	0	0	4.02
1991 Gastonia	A Tex	27	26	0	0	147.2	614	107	79	73	11	3	0	5	78	0	151	6	6	12	8	.600	0	0	4.45
1992 Charlotte	A+ Tex	14	14	0	0	80	327	71	22	18	2	2	1	4	25	1	66	5	4	4	2	.667	0	0	2.03
Tulsa	AA Tex	14	13	1	0	76	314	66	22	18	3	0	0	0	35	0	59	4	0	6	3	.667	0	0	2.13
Okla City	AAA Tex	1	1	0	0	8	30	3	1	1	1	0	0	0	5	0	5	0	0	1	0	1.000	0	0	1.13
1993 Okla City	AAA Tex	27	25	1	0	138	645	171	101	98	19	8	7	2	76	0	74	8	5	7	15	.318	0	0	6.39
1994 Okla City	AAA Tex	44	5	0	15	82.1	353	75	43	39	9	4	3	4	37	3	57	4	5	3	5	.375	0	1	4.26
1995 Okla City	AAA Tex	5	0	0	0	2.2	16	5	4	3	0	0	0	0	2	0	4	1	0	0	1	.000	0	0	10.13
1996 New Orleans	AAA Mil	18	0	0	9	28.2	108	19	9	8	1	0	1	0	8	0	17	1	1	3	0	1.000	0	6	2.51
Columbus	AAA NYY	23	0	0	5	22.2	102	24	16	15	1	1	1	2	11	0	20	1	0	1	0	1.000	0	0	5.96
1997 Las Vegas	AAA SD	31	1	0	10	33.2	160	44	24	24	3	1	0	1	19	3	26	1	1	1	5	.167	0	2	6.42
Edmonton	AAA Oak	13	0	0	3	27	127	35	18	17	2	1	2	0	15	2	24	2	0	2	2	.500	0	0	5.67
1998 Rochester	AAA Bal	29	15	1	3	132.1	531	104	49	43	8	1	7	2	42	0	112	2	1	9	6	.600	0	0	2.92
1999 Orioles	R Bal	2	2	0	0	5	17	0	1	0	0	0	0	0	1	0	4	0	0	0	0	—	0	0	0.00
Rochester	AAA Bal	17	17	0	0	93	382	74	49	41	9	2	6	7	39	0	75	1	2	1	6	.143	0	0	3.97
2000 Sacramento	AAA Oak	2	2	0	0	13	51	8	2	2	1	0	1	1	4	1	7	0	0	1	0	1.000	0	0	1.38
2001 Ottawa	AAA Mon	6	0	0	1	8.1	38	7	7	3	0	1	0	1	5	1	6	1	0	0	1	.000	0	0	3.24
1994 Texas	AL	1	0	0	0	1	5	1	1	1	1	0	0	0	1	0	0	0	0	0	0	—	0	0	9.00
1995 Texas	AL	28	3	0	6	44.2	207	60	37	32	11	0	0	2	19	0	22	4	0	2	2	.500	0	1	6.45
1996 Milwaukee	AL	8	0	0	4	12.2	58	12	4	4	2	1	0	1	10	0	5	0	0	2	0	1.000	0	0	2.84
1997 San Diego	NL	13	0	0	4	10.1	52	12	13	12	1	1	0	1	8	1	8	0	0	0	2	.000	0	0	10.45
12 Min. YEARS		287	132	5	47	961	4090	869	488	431	71	27	30	30	437	11	766	43	28	53	61	.465	0	9	4.04
4 Maj. YEARS		50	3	0	14	68.2	322	85	55	49	15	2	0	4	38	1	35	4	0	4	4	.500	0	1	6.42

Darren Burton

Bats: Both **Throws:** Right **Pos:** OF-74; DH-8; PH-4; P-1   **Ht:** 6'1" **Wt:** 185 **Born:** 9/16/72 **Age:** 29

Year Team	Lg Org	G	AB	H	2B	3B	HR	TB	R	RBI	TBB	IBB	SO	HBP	SH	SF	SB	CS	SB%	GDP	Avg	OBP	SLG
1990 Royals	R KC	15	58	12	0	1	0	14	10	2	4	0	17	0	1	2	6	0	1.00	0	.207	.250	.241
1991 Appleton	A KC	134	532	143	32	6	2	193	78	51	45	4	122	1	3	6	37	12	.76	18	.269	.324	.363
1992 Baseball Cy	A+ KC	123	431	106	15	6	4	145	54	36	49	7	93	6	4	3	16	14	.53	7	.246	.329	.336
1993 Wilmington	A+ KC	134	549	152	23	5	10	215	82	45	48	1	111	1	13	4	30	10	.75	7	.277	.334	.392
1994 Memphis	AA KC	97	373	95	12	3	3	122	55	37	35	4	53	1	4	5	10	6	.63	5	.255	.316	.327
1995 Omaha	AAA KC	2	5	0	0	0	0	0	0	0	0	0	1	0	0	0	0	0	—	0	.000	.000	.000
Wichita	AA KC	41	163	39	9	1	1	53	13	20	12	0	27	1	9	0	6	6	.50	2	.239	.295	.325
Orlando	AA ChC	62	222	68	16	2	4	100	40	21	27	2	42	0	0	7	4	4	.64	5	.306	.382	.450
1996 Omaha	AAA KC	129	463	125	28	5	15	208	75	67	59	6	82	6	9	4	7	7	.50	10	.270	.357	.449
1997 Scranton-WB	AAA Phi	70	253	63	16	3	8	109	34	39	19	1	40	3	1	4	3	0	1.00	6	.249	.305	.431
Reading	AA Phi	45	184	58	11	3	8	99	23	34	9	2	39	3	2	3	1	1	.50	1	.315	.352	.538
1998 Scranton-WB	AAA Phi	117	394	105	21	3	18	186	56	64	53	1	83	6	2	3	9	0	1.00	10	.266	.360	.472
1999 Scranton-WB	AAA Phi	118	409	107	30	3	13	182	61	63	44	2	96	5	3	4	7	2	.78	9	.262	.338	.445
2000 Scranton-WB	AAA Phi	14	29	7	4	0	0	11	0	1	7	2	8	0	1	0	2	0	1.00	2	.241	.389	.379
Altoona	AA Pit	63	229	75	8	2	5	102	44	33	23	0	42	5	3	3	8	0	1.00	3	.328	.396	.445
2001 Altoona	AA Pit	85	299	86	15	2	7	126	36	32	23	2	62	5	1	1	5	1	.83	3	.288	.348	.421
12 Min. YEARS		1249	4593	1241	240	45	98	1865	661	545	457	34	918	43	56	42	149	63	.70	88	.270	.339	.406

Mike Byas

Bats: Both **Throws:** Right **Pos:** OF-92; PH-9; DH-1; PR-1   **Ht:** 6'0" **Wt:** 170 **Born:** 4/21/76 **Age:** 26

Year Team	Lg Org	G	AB	H	2B	3B	HR	TB	R	RBI	TBB	IBB	SO	HBP	SH	SF	SB	CS	SB%	GDP	Avg	OBP	SLG
1997 Salem-Keizr	A- SF	71	290	80	9	1	0	91	68	16	48	0	44	2	1	0	51	9	.85	4	.276	.382	.314
1998 San Jose	A+ SF	135	521	131	10	2	1	148	87	36	81	1	98	0	2	3	30	22	.58	8	.251	.349	.284
1999 Shreveport	AA SF	129	487	132	9	1	0	143	76	41	68	0	79	1	3	3	31	15	.67	7	.271	.362	.294
Fresno	AAA SF	5	22	8	2	0	0	10	4	2	5	1	4	0	0	0	2	1	.67	0	.364	.481	.455
2000 Fresno	AAA SF	135	516	136	10	1	2	154	84	34	78	0	89	1	5	2	36	18	.67	5	.264	.360	.298
2001 Fresno	AAA SF	17	21	4	1	0	0	5	4	1	7	0	5	0	0	0	0	0	—	0	.190	.393	.238
Shreveport	AA SF	83	316	84	13	2	0	101	55	25	49	0	57	3	5	3	21	10	.68	4	.266	.367	.320
5 Min. YEARS		575	2173	575	54	7	3	652	378	155	336	2	376	7	19	10	171	75	.70	28	.265	.363	.300

Mike Bynum

Pitches: Left **Bats:** Left **Pos:** SP-15; RP-1   **Ht:** 6'4" **Wt:** 200 **Born:** 3/20/78 **Age:** 24

Year Team	Lg Org	G	GS	CG	GF	IP	BFP	H	R	ER	HR	SH	SF	HB	TBB	IBB	SO	WP	Bk	W	L	Pct.	ShO	Sv	ERA
1999 Idaho Falls	R+ SD	5	3	0	0	17	60	7	0	0	0	1	0	0	4	0	21	0	0	1	0	1.000	0	0	0.00
Rancho Cuca	A+ SD	7	7	0	0	38.1	159	35	17	14	1	1	1	2	8	0	44	2	2	3	1	.750	0	0	3.29
2000 Rancho Cuca	A+ SD	21	21	0	0	126	517	101	55	42	4	3	5	8	51	0	129	7	1	9	6	.600	0	0	3.00
Mobile	AA SD	6	6	0	0	34	144	31	12	11	2	1	2	2	16	0	27	1	1	3	1	.750	0	0	2.91
2001 Mobile	AA SD	16	15	0	0	84.1	368	90	53	47	14	4	3	3	35	0	69	0	0	2	7	.222	0	0	5.02
3 Min. YEARS		55	52	0	0	299.2	1248	264	137	114	21	10	11	15	114	0	290	10	4	18	15	.545	0	0	3.42

44

Marlon Byrd

Bats: Right **Throws:** Right **Pos:** OF-134; DH-2; PH-2   **Ht:** 6'0" **Wt:** 225 **Born:** 8/30/77 **Age:** 24

Year Team	Lg Org	G	AB	H	2B	3B	HR	TB	R	RBI	TBB	IBB	SO	HBP	SH	SF	SB	CS	SB%	GDP	Avg	OBP	SLG
1999 Batavia	A- Phi	65	243	72	7	6	13	130	40	50	28	1	70	5	0	3	8	2	.80	3	.296	.376	.535
2000 Piedmont	A Phi	133	515	159	29	13	17	265	104	93	51	0	110	10	1	5	41	5	.89	7	.309	.379	.515
2001 Reading	AA Phi	137	510	161	22	8	28	283	108	89	52	3	93	11	2	7	32	5	.86	7	.316	.386	.555
3 Min. YEARS		335	1268	392	58	27	58	678	252	232	131	4	273	26	3	15	81	12	.87	17	.309	.381	.535

Tim Byrdak

Pitches: Left **Bats:** Left **Pos:** SP-3; RP-1   **Ht:** 5'11" **Wt:** 190 **Born:** 10/31/73 **Age:** 28

Year Team	Lg Org	G	GS	CG	GF	IP	BFP	H	R	ER	HR	SH	SF	HB	TBB	IBB	SO	WP	Bk	W	L	Pct.	ShO	Sv	ERA
1994 Eugene	A- KC	15	15	0	0	73.1	302	60	33	25	6	2	2	4	20	0	77	1	1	4	5	.444	0	0	3.07
1995 Wilmington	A+ KC	27	26	0	0	166.1	657	118	46	40	7	3	3	10	45	2	127	1	0	11	5	.688	0	0	2.16
1996 Wichita	AA KC	15	15	0	0	84.2	388	112	73	65	15	5	1	0	44	0	47	8	0	5	7	.417	0	0	6.91
1997 Wilmington	A+ KC	22	2	0	15	41	169	34	17	16	3	5	1	2	12	4	47	4	0	4	3	.571	0	3	3.51
1998 Wichita	AA KC	34	0	0	10	52	242	58	29	24	3	4	4	2	28	1	37	2	3	3	5	.375	0	2	4.15
Omaha	AAA KC	26	0	0	8	36.2	161	31	13	10	3	4	0	2	20	0	32	2	0	2	1	.667	0	1	2.45
1999 Omaha	AAA KC	33	0	0	17	49.2	216	39	19	10	2	2	0	6	28	2	51	2	0	3	1	.750	0	4	1.81
2000 Omaha	AA KC	4	0	0	1	6.2	29	9	4	4	1	0	0	0	3	0	1	0	0	0	0	—	0	0	5.40
Omaha	AAA KC	34	1	0	17	52.2	244	59	27	26	5	4	1	4	29	3	47	3	2	6	2	.750	0	4	4.44
2001 Buffalo	AAA Cle	4	3	0	0	17.1	75	18	10	9	1	1	0	1	5	0	17	1	0	2	0	1.000	0	0	4.67
1998 Kansas City	AL	3	0	0	0	1.2	9	5	1	1	1	0	0	0	0	0	1	0	0	0	0	—	0	0	5.40
1999 Kansas City	AL	33	0	0	5	24.2	128	32	24	21	5	3	0	1	20	2	17	3	1	0	3	.000	0	1	7.66
2000 Kansas City	AL	12	0	0	1	6.1	34	11	8	8	3	0	0	0	4	0	8	1	0	0	1	.000	0	0	11.37
8 Min. YEARS		214	62	0	68	580.1	2483	538	271	229	44	30	14	31	234	12	483	24	6	40	29	.580	0	14	3.55
3 Maj. YEARS		48	0	0	6	32.2	171	48	33	30	9	3	0	1	24	2	26	4	1	0	4	.000	0	0	8.27

Wilmy Caceres

Bats: Both **Throws:** Right **Pos:** SS-70; 2B-17   **Ht:** 6'0" **Wt:** 165 **Born:** 10/2/78 **Age:** 23

Year Team	Lg Org	G	AB	H	2B	3B	HR	TB	R	RBI	TBB	IBB	SO	HBP	SH	SF	SB	CS	SB%	GDP	Avg	OBP	SLG
1997 Billings	R+ Cin		38	10	2	0	0	12	10	9	2	0	3	1	0	0	1	1	.50	0	.263	.317	.316
1998 Chston-WV	A Cin	103	394	102	12	7	0	128	48	27	18	0	62	9	7	0	24	14	.63	9	.259	.306	.325
Burlington	A Cin	35	150	44	8	0	1	55	23	14	4	0	24	3	1	0	7	5	.58	3	.293	.325	.367
1999 Reds	R Cin	2	9	3	0	0	0	3	2	0	0	0	1	0	0	0	0	0	—	0	.333	.333	.333
Clinton	A Cin	117	476	124	18	5	1	155	77	30	30	1	65	2	2	2	52	22	.70	6	.261	.306	.326
2000 Chattanooga	AA Cin	130	534	143	23	4	2	180	69	33	37	3	71	4	5	5	36	19	.65	10	.268	.317	.337
2001 Salt Lake	AAA Ana	87	325	81	5	4	0	94	38	21	12	1	45	3	4	2	12	6	.67	8	.249	.281	.289
5 Min. YEARS		489	1926	507	68	20	4	627	267	134	103	5	271	22	19	9	132	67	.66	36	.263	.307	.326

Brett Cadiente

Bats: Left **Throws:** Left **Pos:** OF-123; DH-11; PH-6   **Ht:** 5'11" **Wt:** 180 **Born:** 6/17/77 **Age:** 25

Year Team	Lg Org	G	AB	H	2B	3B	HR	TB	R	RBI	TBB	IBB	SO	HBP	SH	SF	SB	CS	SB%	GDP	Avg	OBP	SLG
1999 Pulaski	R+ Tex	68	274	97	16	7	7	148	69	49	38	1	51	3	1	3	18	2	.90	3	.354	.434	.540
2000 Savannah	A Tex	129	499	154	15	9	6	205	83	50	51	1	112	1	7	8	31	15	.67	6	.309	.369	.411
2001 Charlotte	A+ Tex	68	272	76	14	5	1	103	39	21	26	4	44	1	1	1	10	8	.56	2	.279	.343	.379
Oklahoma	AAA Tex	2	5	2	0	0	0	2	0	0	0	0	2	0	0	0	0	0	—	0	.400	.400	.400
Tulsa	AA Tex	67	262	73	16	5	3	108	32	24	15	1	66	1	3	2	8	5	.62	3	.279	.318	.412
3 Min. YEARS		334	1312	402	61	26	17	566	223	144	130	7	275	6	12	14	67	30	.69	14	.306	.368	.431

Henry Calderon

Bats: Right **Throws:** Right **Pos:** 3B-94; PH-3; OF-1; DH-1   **Ht:** 6'1" **Wt:** 170 **Born:** 8/3/77 **Age:** 24

Year Team	Lg Org	G	AB	H	2B	3B	HR	TB	R	RBI	TBB	IBB	SO	HBP	SH	SF	SB	CS	SB%	GDP	Avg	OBP	SLG
1997 Royals	R KC	43	139	34	5	3	1	48	17	15	10	0	31	2	2	2	3	1	.75	3	.245	.301	.345
1998 Spokane	A- KC	72	282	95	17	2	9	143	58	48	25	3	66	5	3	4	19	4	.83	4	.337	.396	.507
1999 Chston-WV	A KC	130	459	104	29	1	7	156	49	56	21	1	106	9	9	4	33	14	.70	9	.227	.272	.340
2000 Wilmington	A+ KC	122	419	110	11	4	4	141	52	45	19	0	76	8	10	4	14	6	.70	14	.263	.304	.337
2001 Wichita	AA KC	97	327	86	21	5	5	132	50	49	18	0	51	10	3	4	4	8	.33	10	.263	.318	.404
5 Min. YEARS		464	1626	429	83	15	26	620	226	213	93	4	330	34	27	18	73	33	.69	40	.264	.314	.381

Kiko Calero

Pitches: Right **Bats:** Right **Pos:** SP-19; RP-8   **Ht:** 6'1" **Wt:** 170 **Born:** 1/9/75 **Age:** 27

Year Team	Lg Org	G	GS	CG	GF	IP	BFP	H	R	ER	HR	SH	SF	HB	TBB	IBB	SO	WP	Bk	W	L	Pct.	ShO	Sv	ERA
1996 Spokane	A- KC	17	11	0	3	75	318	77	34	21	5	0	6	3	18	0	61	2	2	4	2	.667	0	1	2.52
1997 Wichita	AA KC	23	22	2	0	127.2	541	120	78	63	15	4	6	4	44	0	100	2	2	11	9	.550	0	0	4.44
1998 Lansing	A KC	4	4	0	0	16.2	76	19	7	7	1	0	0	2	7	0	10	1	1	1	0	1.000	0	0	3.78
Wichita	AA KC	3	3	0	0	14	72	23	16	15	2	1	0	1	6	0	5	0	0	1	0	1.000	0	0	9.64
Wilmington	A+ KC	17	17	0	0	97.2	409	74	33	31	7	1	3	7	51	1	90	6	0	7	3	.700	0	0	2.86
1999 Wichita	AA KC	26	23	1	1	129.1	579	143	67	59	14	2	2	6	57	3	92	7	2	9	3	.750	1	1	4.11
2000 Wichita	AA KC	28	25	0	0	153.2	648	141	74	62	16	7	3	10	66	2	130	7	1	10	7	.588	0	0	3.63
2001 Wichita	AA KC	27	19	0	1	124.1	531	110	57	46	10	3	6	7	51	1	94	7	1	14	5	.737	0	0	3.33
6 Min. YEARS		145	124	3	5	738.1	3174	707	366	304	70	18	26	40	300	7	582	32	9	57	29	.663	1	2	3.71

Jeremy Callier

Pitches: Right **Bats:** Right **Pos:** RP-17; SP-1 **Ht:** 6'0" **Wt:** 195 **Born:** 11/18/75 **Age:** 26

Year Team	Lg Org	HOW MUCH HE PITCHED						WHAT HE GAVE UP											THE RESULTS				
		G	GS	CG	GF	IP	BFP	H	R	ER	HR	SH	SF	HB	TBB	IBB	SO	WP	Bk	W	L	Pct.	ShO	Sv	ERA
1998 Butte	R+ Ana	19	11	2	1	101.2	433	102	51	40	7	1	2	8	26	0	78	3	2	3	9	.250	0	0	3.54
1999 Erie	AA Ana	1	0	0	1	1	7	2	2	2	0	0	0	0	2	0	2	0	0	0	0	—	0	0	18.00
Lk Elsinore	A+ Ana	34	7	0	9	95.2	418	107	48	41	5	5	0	3	33	2	69	6	1	5	3	.625	0	2	3.86
2000 Erie	AA Ana	41	0	0	28	58	238	52	30	26	5	0	2	2	24	1	44	2	0	2	3	.400	0	11	4.03
Edmonton	AAA Ana	9	2	0	3	22.1	104	29	14	14	0	2	1	1	7	1	16	0	0	2	2	.500	0	0	5.64
2001 Arkansas	AA Ana	16	0	0	7	24	114	31	19	19	3	1	4	1	10	0	6	2	1	2	0	1.000	0	1	7.13
Rancho Cuca	A+ Ana	2	1	0	0	4	13	1	0	0	0	0	0	0	0	0	3	0	0	0	0	—	0	0	0.00
4 Min. YEARS		122	21	2	49	306.2	1327	324	164	142	20	9	9	15	102	4	218	13	4	14	17	.452	0	14	4.17

Ron Calloway

Bats: Left **Throws:** Left **Pos:** OF-119; DH-13; PH-3 **Ht:** 6'0" **Wt:** 190 **Born:** 9/4/76 **Age:** 25

Year Team	Lg Org	BATTING														BASERUNNING				PERCENTAGES		
		G	AB	H	2B	3B	HR	TB	R	RBI	TBB	IBB	SO	HBP	SH	SF	SB	CS	SB%	GDP	Avg	OBP	SLG
1997 Lethbridge	R+ Ari	43	148	37	5	0	0	42	23	9	14	0	29	3	0	2	5	8	.38	4	.250	.323	.284
South Bend	A Ari	9	25	7	1	0	0	8	3	1	2	0	8	0	0	0	1	0	1.00	1	.280	.333	.320
1998 High Desert	A+ Ari	44	156	44	8	2	3	65	30	27	12	0	38	2	2	2	2	4	.33	3	.282	.337	.417
South Bend	A Ari	69	251	66	12	2	3	91	29	33	25	1	50	2	1	3	7	5	.58	3	.263	.331	.363
1999 High Desert	A+ Ari	60	196	62	14	1	3	87	41	23	30	0	34	2	2	0	22	7	.76	3	.316	.412	.444
El Paso	AA Ari	11	32	7	0	0	0	7	4	1	7	0	7	0	0	0	1	2	.33	0	.219	.359	.219
Jupiter	A+ Mon	54	211	57	8	4	3	82	30	25	15	0	45	2	4	0	5	6	.45	9	.270	.325	.389
2000 Jupiter	A+ Mon	135	530	147	24	6	6	201	78	65	55	3	89	4	1	6	34	14	.71	13	.277	.346	.379
2001 Harrisburg	AA Mon	74	279	92	22	4	9	149	48	47	24	2	46	3	5	3	25	7	.78	2	.330	.385	.534
Ottawa	AAA Mon	61	239	63	12	0	10	105	27	35	16	2	64	6	2	2	11	1	.92	6	.264	.323	.439
5 Min. YEARS		560	2067	582	106	19	37	837	313	266	200	8	410	24	17	18	113	54	.68	44	.282	.349	.405

Ryan Cameron

Pitches: Right **Bats:** Right **Pos:** SP-15; RP-5 **Ht:** 6'1" **Wt:** 180 **Born:** 9/13/77 **Age:** 24

Year Team	Lg Org	HOW MUCH HE PITCHED						WHAT HE GAVE UP											THE RESULTS				
		G	GS	CG	GF	IP	BFP	H	R	ER	HR	SH	SF	HB	TBB	IBB	SO	WP	Bk	W	L	Pct.	ShO	Sv	ERA
1998 Portland	A- Col	18	2	0	9	40.1	193	45	30	27	7	2	0	1	24	0	47	2	0	0	6	.000	0	1	6.02
1999 Portland	A- Col	4	0	0	3	5	18	1	0	0	0	1	0	0	1	1	4	0	0	1	0	1.000	0	1	0.00
Asheville	A Col	17	0	0	5	34.2	140	18	10	9	1	0	0	1	18	1	40	4	0	3	1	.750	0	2	2.34
2000 Salem	A+ Col	26	26	1	0	160.1	715	152	81	64	9	7	5	9	78	0	168	12	2	13	7	.650	0	0	3.59
2001 Salem	A+ Col	2	2	0	0	8	36	5	4	2	1	0	1	0	5	0	12	0	0	0	1	.000	0	0	2.25
Carolina	AA Col	18	13	0	1	89.2	427	112	64	52	10	3	3	4	45	0	74	4	0	7	6	.538	0	0	5.22
4 Min. YEARS		85	43	1	18	338	1529	333	189	154	28	13	9	15	171	2	345	22	2	24	21	.533	0	4	4.10

Jason Camilli

Bats: Right **Throws:** Right **Pos:** 2B-73; SS-11; PH-7; 3B-6; DH-6 **Ht:** 6'0" **Wt:** 190 **Born:** 10/18/75 **Age:** 26

Year Team	Lg Org	BATTING														BASERUNNING				PERCENTAGES		
		G	AB	H	2B	3B	HR	TB	R	RBI	TBB	IBB	SO	HBP	SH	SF	SB	CS	SB%	GDP	Avg	OBP	SLG
1994 Expos	R Mon	53	212	54	4	3	0	64	33	13	31	1	44	0	0	1	5	6	.45	4	.255	.348	.302
1995 Albany	A Mon	53	181	34	5	0	3	48	28	16	38	0	50	3	0	2	13	10	.57	0	.188	.335	.265
Vermont	A- Mon	63	243	59	10	2	1	76	37	21	30	1	52	2	3	2	17	10	.63	4	.243	.329	.313
1996 Delmarva	A Mon	119	426	95	13	2	3	121	53	36	63	1	89	5	9	2	26	17	.60	4	.223	.329	.284
1997 Cape Fear	A Mon	98	396	118	35	2	3	166	57	43	31	0	64	5	7	2	22	11	.67	7	.298	.355	.419
Wst Plm Bch	A+ Mon	15	47	6	3	0	0	9	1	1	2	0	12	0	1	0	0	1	.00	1	.128	.163	.191
1998 Jupiter	A+ Mon	89	314	81	15	1	2	104	45	33	35	2	55	2	1	1	9	10	.47	2	.258	.335	.331
Harrisburg	AA Mon	6	18	2	0	0	0	2	1	1	3	0	5	0	0	0	0	0	—	0	.111	.238	.111
1999 Ottawa	AAA Mon	35	102	27	6	0	0	33	12	8	11	0	19	0	0	0	4	1	.80	3	.265	.336	.324
Harrisburg	AA Mon	63	154	33	7	0	4	52	26	16	23	0	31	2	0	1	0	2	.00	3	.214	.322	.338
2000 Expos	R Mon	5	15	4	1	0	0	5	1	2	2	0	3	0	1	2	1	0	1.00	0	.267	.316	.333
Ottawa	AAA Mon	21	77	12	4	1	0	18	7	11	3	0	21	0	0	1	0	0	—	1	.156	.185	.234
Harrisburg	AA Mon	65	240	51	10	3	3	76	27	19	24	1	51	3	4	2	3	6	.33	5	.213	.290	.317
2001 El Paso	AA Ari	13	39	13	1	0	0	14	7	3	2	0	8	0	0	0	0	2	.00	0	.333	.357	.359
St. Paul	IND —	24	85	21	2	0	2	29	7	9	5	0	10	0	2	0	0	2	.00	0	.247	.289	.341
Tulsa	AA Tex	55	174	42	8	1	3	61	21	24	32	1	36	4	4	1	4	1	.80	5	.241	.370	.351
8 Min. YEARS		777	2723	652	124	15	24	878	363	256	335	7	550	26	32	18	104	79	.57	41	.239	.327	.322

Juan Camilo

Bats: Left **Throws:** Right **Pos:** OF-84; PH-4; PR-2; DH-1 **Ht:** 6'0" **Wt:** 205 **Born:** 6/24/78 **Age:** 24

Year Team	Lg Org	BATTING														BASERUNNING				PERCENTAGES		
		G	AB	H	2B	3B	HR	TB	R	RBI	TBB	IBB	SO	HBP	SH	SF	SB	CS	SB%	GDP	Avg	OBP	SLG
1997 Athletics	R Oak	50	191	66	11	5	8	111	48	47	41	0	41	2	0	0	12	2	.86	6	.346	.466	.581
Sou Oregon	A- Oak	4	13	3	0	0	0	3	0	2	1	0	4	0	0	0	0	1	.00	0	.231	.286	.231
1998 Visalia	A+ Oak	85	220	49	9	0	4	70	29	27	35	3	75	3	2	0	5	4	.56	1	.223	.337	.318
Sou Oregon	A- Oak	31	108	37	8	3	4	63	25	29	22	0	32	1	0	5	5	2	.71	0	.343	.441	.583
1999 Visalia	A+ Oak	82	285	81	17	2	17	153	58	52	34	0	89	4	0	1	7	6	.54	8	.284	.367	.537
2000 Lakeland	A+ Det	114	373	92	18	2	12	145	49	45	46	5	102	2	2	3	4	9	.31	4	.247	.330	.389
2001 Lakeland	A+ Det	55	193	58	10	5	8	102	34	37	26	3	52	4	0	1	7	2	.78	1	.301	.393	.528
Erie	AA Det	33	110	31	3	1	5	51	14	17	7	0	27	0	0	1	1	1	.50	1	.282	.322	.464
5 Min. YEARS		454	1493	417	71	18	58	698	257	256	212	11	462	16	4	11	41	27	.60	21	.279	.372	.468

Jared Camp

Pitches: Right **Bats:** Right **Pos:** RP-44　　　　　　　　　　　**Ht:** 6'2" **Wt:** 195 **Born:** 5/4/75 **Age:** 27

			HOW MUCH HE PITCHED						WHAT HE GAVE UP									THE RESULTS					
Year Team	Lg Org	G	GS	CG	GF	IP	BFP	H	R	ER	HR	SH	SF	HB	TBB	IBB	SO	WP	Bk	W	L	Pct.	ShO	Sv	ERA
1995 Helena	R+ Mil	8	8	0	0	34.1	166	44	39	33	1	1	3	3	20	0	26	6	2	1	4	.200	0	0	8.65
1996 Beloit	A Mil	11	11	0	0	53	251	56	42	32	4	3	9	2	39	0	47	10	1	3	5	.375	0	0	5.43
Watertown	A- Cle	15	15	1	0	95.2	380	68	29	18	2	1	1	7	30	0	99	6	0	10	2	.833	1	0	1.69
1997 Akron	AA Cle	12	12	1	0	64	293	79	49	44	13	4	1	1	26	1	39	4	0	2	8	.200	0	0	6.19
Kinston	A+ Cle	13	12	0	0	73.2	297	57	36	31	11	5	1	2	20	0	64	1	1	5	4	.556	0	0	3.79
1998 Akron	AA Cle	18	16	0	2	85.2	364	84	37	36	8	3	5	5	31	0	42	2	1	6	2	.750	0	0	3.78
1999 Kinston	A+ Cle	18	6	1	7	54.2	224	48	15	12	2	0	3	4	16	0	59	4	0	3	2	.600	0	4	1.98
Buffalo	AAA Cle	10	0	0	7	10.2	51	4	2	1	0	0	1	1	13	0	14	4	0	0	0	—	0	1	0.84
Akron	AA Cle	17	0	0	13	18	92	22	17	13	0	2	3	2	16	0	18	2	1	1	2	.333	0	7	6.50
2000 Akron	AA Cle	9	0	0	1	17.1	88	28	21	18	6	0	1	1	7	0	13	2	0	0	0	—	0	0	9.35
Buffalo	AAA Cle	3	0	0	2	4	20	5	2	1	0	1	0	1	2	0	1	1	0	0	0	—	0	1	2.25
Tulsa	AA Tex	7	0	0	3	10	48	10	6	0	1	1	0	1	7	0	4	2	0	0	0	—	0	1	0.00
Omaha	AAA KC	13	0	0	2	12.2	71	19	24	19	4	0	0	2	13	0	13	1	0	1	2	.333	0	0	13.50
2001 Wichita	AA KC	33	0	0	21	46.1	214	44	28	26	7	1	0	1	35	2	44	6	0	1	2	.333	0	4	5.05
Erie	AA Det	11	0	0	5	18.2	86	16	11	10	1	2	1	0	16	1	18	3	0	1	1	.500	0	1	4.82
7 Min. YEARS		198	80	3	63	598.2	2645	584	358	294	60	24	29	33	291	4	500	54	6	34	34	.500	1	19	4.42

Shawn Camp

Pitches: Right **Bats:** Right **Pos:** RP-53; SP-5　　　　　　　　　**Ht:** 6'1" **Wt:** 200 **Born:** 11/18/75 **Age:** 26

			HOW MUCH HE PITCHED						WHAT HE GAVE UP									THE RESULTS					
Year Team	Lg Org	G	GS	CG	GF	IP	BFP	H	R	ER	HR	SH	SF	HB	TBB	IBB	SO	WP	Bk	W	L	Pct.	ShO	Sv	ERA
1997 Idaho Falls	R+ SD	30	0	0	24	32.2	150	41	22	20	3	1	1	2	14	0	41	4	0	2	1	.667	0	12	5.51
1998 Clinton	A SD	47	0	0	39	55	240	48	19	16	0	3	3	7	20	4	62	6	1	3	5	.375	0	13	2.62
1999 Rancho Cuca	A+ SD	53	0	0	28	66	285	68	37	29	4	4	4	1	25	3	78	7	1	1	5	.167	0	6	3.95
2000 Rancho Cuca	A+ SD	14	0	0	13	18.2	72	10	3	3	0	0	0	2	5	0	18	2	0	1	0	1.000	0	6	1.45
Mobile	AA SD	45	0	0	11	59.1	252	47	23	16	4	2	2	1	30	2	53	4	0	3	3	.500	0	1	2.43
2001 Portland	AAA SD	4	1	0	1	7	22	2	0	0	0	0	0	0	1	0	6	0	0	1	0	1.000	0	0	0.00
Mobile	AA SD	35	1	0	0	48.2	204	46	24	24	2	5	2	6	15	1	55	2	0	6	2	.750	0	0	4.44
Altoona	AA Pit	8	3	0	1	23.1	103	25	14	11	3	0	2	3	8	1	19	1	1	4	0	1.000	0	0	4.24
Nashville	AAA Pit	11	0	0	1	17	67	11	4	4	1	0	1	0	8	1	15	0	0	0	0	—	0	0	2.12
5 Min. YEARS		247	5	0	118	327.2	1395	298	146	123	17	15	15	22	126	12	347	26	3	21	16	.568	0	38	3.38

Carlos Campusano

Bats: Right **Throws:** Right **Pos:** PH-16; SS-14; DH-11; 3B-5; 2B-3; PR-3　　**Ht:** 5'11" **Wt:** 160 **Born:** 9/2/75 **Age:** 26

			BATTING														BASERUNNING				PERCENTAGES		
Year Team	Lg Org	G	AB	H	2B	3B	HR	TB	R	RBI	TBB	IBB	SO	HBP	SH	SF	SB	CS	SB%	GDP	Avg	OBP	SLG
1995 Brewers	R Mil	54	173	43	4	1	1	52	25	15	14	1	27	5	1	1	7	3	.70	6	.249	.321	.301
1996 Beloit	A Mil	108	337	83	17	4	1	111	33	20	10	0	63	5	5	1	4	3	.57	7	.246	.278	.329
1997 Bakersfield	A+ SF	61	191	38	8	3	1	55	17	15	7	0	49	4	3	2	2	0	1.00	3	.199	.240	.288
1998 San Jose	A+ SF	34	98	18	1	2	0	23	11	7	5	0	29	3	1	1	0	0	—	3	.184	.243	.235
1999 San Jose	A+ SF	27	84	26	2	1	1	33	13	7	6	0	15	4	3	1	4	1	.80	1	.310	.379	.393
Shreveport	AA SF	15	39	6	0	2	1	13	5	6	3	0	10	0	0	0	1	0	1.00	1	.154	.214	.333
Bakersfield	A+ SF	14	51	18	2	0	1	23	7	4	1	0	13	2	0	0	2	2	.50	0	.353	.389	.451
Fresno	AAA SF	16	46	13	2	0	0	15	2	3	2	0	9	3	0	1	0	0	—	4	.283	.346	.326
2000 Shreveport	AA SF	11	25	5	1	0	0	6	5	1	0	0	9	0	0	0	0	0	—	0	.200	.200	.240
San Jose	A+ SF	1	3	1	0	0	0	1	0	0	0	0	1	0	0	0	0	0	—	0	.333	.333	.333
Fresno	AAA SF	2	3	0	0	0	0	0	0	0	0	0	1	0	0	0	0	0	—	0	.000	.000	.000
Bakersfield	A+ SF	68	246	62	10	4	1	83	33	26	11	0	47	7	7	1	13	3	.81	5	.252	.302	.337
2001 San Jose	A+ SF	11	40	8	3	0	1	14	2	7	0	0	9	0	0	0	0	1	.00	4	.200	.200	.350
Shreveport	AA SF	27	63	9	3	0	0	12	6	1	5	0	18	1	1	0	0	1	.00	1	.143	.217	.190
Fresno	AAA SF	13	22	3	1	0	0	4	1	3	0	0	5	0	0	0	0	0	—	1	.136	.136	.182
7 Min. YEARS		462	1421	333	54	17	8	445	160	115	64	1	304	34	22	8	33	14	.70	36	.234	.282	.313

Robinson Cancel

Bats: Right **Throws:** Right **Pos:** C-67; PH-11; DH-3; 3B-2　　　　**Ht:** 6'0" **Wt:** 195 **Born:** 5/4/76 **Age:** 26

			BATTING														BASERUNNING				PERCENTAGES		
Year Team	Lg Org	G	AB	H	2B	3B	HR	TB	R	RBI	TBB	IBB	SO	HBP	SH	SF	SB	CS	SB%	GDP	Avg	OBP	SLG
1994 Brewers	R Mil	29	70	12	0	0	0	12	6	8	9	1	19	2	0	2	0	2	.00	2	.171	.277	.171
1995 Helena	R+ Mil	46	154	37	9	0	0	46	18	24	9	0	20	2	1	2	8	3	.73	3	.240	.287	.299
1996 Beloit	A Mil	72	218	48	3	1	1	56	26	29	14	0	31	1	5	1	13	5	.72	7	.220	.269	.257
1997 Beloit	A Mil	17	50	15	3	0	0	18	9	4	7	0	9	3	0	0	0	2	.00	1	.300	.417	.360
Stockton	A+ Mil	64	211	59	11	0	1	73	25	16	13	0	40	2	7	1	9	3	.75	6	.280	.326	.346
1998 Stockton	A+ Mil	11	32	6	1	0	0	7	3	2	4	0	8	0	0	0	2	1	.67	0	.188	.278	.219
El Paso	AA Mil	58	158	51	10	0	1	64	17	30	22	1	32	0	4	1	2	2	.50	5	.323	.403	.405
1999 Huntsville	AA Mil	66	223	56	10	1	5	83	35	32	23	0	38	3	0	1	8	5	.62	10	.251	.328	.372
Louisville	AAA Mil	39	117	43	8	0	5	66	22	28	14	0	28	1	1	1	6	2	.75	6	.368	.436	.564
2000 Huntsville	AA Mil	22	71	19	3	0	1	25	11	12	11	0	16	0	0	1	5	1	.83	2	.268	.361	.352
2001 Huntsville	AA Mil	29	86	15	2	0	0	17	8	5	6	0	17	1	2	1	0	5	.00	5	.174	.234	.198
Indianapolis	AAA Mil	51	172	37	5	0	1	45	16	18	9	2	38	1	1	3	0	0	—	5	.215	.254	.262
1999 Milwaukee	NL	15	44	8	2	0	0	10	5	5	2	0	12	1	1	0	0	0	—	0	.182	.234	.227
8 Min. YEARS		504	1562	398	65	2	15	512	196	208	141	4	296	16	21	14	53	31	.63	55	.255	.320	.328

Ben Candelaria

Bats: Left   **Throws:** Right   **Pos:** OF-70; PH-16; DH-4; PR-4   **Ht:** 5'11"   **Wt:** 167   **Born:** 1/29/75   **Age:** 27

				BATTING													BASERUNNING				PERCENTAGES		
Year Team	Lg Org	G	AB	H	2B	3B	HR	TB	R	RBI	TBB	IBB	SO	HBP	SH	SF	SB	CS	SB%	GDP	Avg	OBP	SLG
1992 Blue Jays	R Tor	29	77	12	2	1	0	16	10	3	6	0	16	0	1	1	4	3	.57	0	.156	.214	.208
1993 Medcine Hat	R+ Tor	62	208	55	7	1	5	79	24	34	27	1	49	3	5	4	3	3	.50	3	.264	.351	.380
1994 Hagerstown	A Tor	3	13	3	0	0	1	6	2	3	0	0	4	0	0	0	0	0	—	0	.231	.231	.462
St.Cathrnes	A- Tor	71	250	66	15	1	2	89	36	37	35	1	55	1	3	1	8	4	.67	6	.264	.355	.356
1995 Dunedin	A+ Tor	125	471	122	21	5	5	168	66	49	53	1	98	0	3	5	11	4	.73	11	.259	.331	.357
1996 Knoxville	AA Tor	55	162	45	11	2	3	69	16	14	18	0	40	2	2	0	3	3	.50	7	.278	.357	.426
Dunedin	A+ Tor	39	125	25	5	0	1	33	13	6	12	0	25	0	1	0	1	4	.20	1	.200	.270	.264
1997 Knoxville	AA Tor	120	472	139	32	5	15	226	81	67	42	2	89	5	4	6	4	3	.57	9	.294	.354	.479
1998 Knoxville	AA Tor	36	156	52	8	3	10	96	33	31	9	0	31	1	1	1	0	3	.00	2	.333	.371	.615
Syracuse	AAA Tor	69	251	62	13	2	7	100	28	32	23	2	68	2	0	3	2	0	1.00	5	.247	.312	.398
1999 Jacksnville	AA Det	120	464	125	31	3	18	216	65	77	35	3	93	1	0	5	6	7	.46	13	.269	.319	.466
2000 St. Paul	IND —	60	223	66	12	0	6	96	31	35	27	3	24	4	1	0	8	2	.80	5	.296	.382	.430
Portland	AA Fla	20	66	17	3	0	2	26	8	15	7	1	16	1	1	2	0	0	—	0	.258	.329	.394
2001 Portland	AA Fla	29	95	29	6	1	2	43	15	16	11	1	13	1	1	1	0	1	.00	4	.305	.407	.453
Calgary	AAA Fla	61	163	52	17	1	5	86	23	29	7	3	19	0	0	2	0	0	—	3	.319	.343	.528
10 Min. YEARS		899	3196	870	183	25	82	1349	447	447	317	18	640	21	23	31	50	37	.57	69	.272	.339	.422

Jon Cannon

Pitches: Left   **Bats:** Right   **Pos:** RP-37; SP-2   **Ht:** 6'3"   **Wt:** 200   **Born:** 1/1/75   **Age:** 27

		HOW MUCH HE PITCHED						WHAT HE GAVE UP											THE RESULTS				
Year Team	Lg Org	G	GS	CG	GF	IP	BFP	H	R	ER	HR	SH	SF	HB	TBB	IBB	SO	WP	Bk	W	L	Pct.	ShO	Sv	ERA
1996 Williamsprt	A- ChC	14	13	0	1	83.1	329	61	31	28	6	0	0	3	26	0	66	2	5	6	4	.600	0	0	3.02
1997 Rockford	A ChC	24	20	1	3	129.1	548	110	53	45	13	2	3	7	50	1	130	16	3	9	6	.600	0	0	3.13
Daytona	A+ ChC	2	2	0	0	13.2	55	7	2	2	1	2	1	0	10	1	13	0	0	1	0	1.000	0	0	1.32
1998 Daytona	A+ ChC	7	7	1	0	31.1	142	37	22	13	1	2	2	0	12	0	28	1	0	0	3	.000	0	0	3.73
1999 Daytona	A+ ChC	33	11	1	12	95.2	424	83	55	47	8	7	5	10	66	3	77	6	2	3	5	.375	0	0	4.42
2000 Daytona	A+ ChC	7	1	0	3	16.1	62	7	0	0	0	0	0	0	7	0	11	1	0	0	1		0	1	0.00
West Tenn	AA ChC	32	1	0	9	53	225	35	19	18	4	4	2	2	31	1	44	1	0	1	2	.333	0	1	3.06
2001 Shreveport	AA SF	17	2	0	4	36.2	155	23	15	13	4	3	1	2	19	1	39	1	1	2	0	1.000	0	1	3.19
San Jose	A+ SF	22	0	0	6	41.2	174	36	17	15	2	1	1	3	18	0	48	4	0	3	1	.750	0	2	3.24
6 Min. YEARS		158	57	3	38	501	2114	399	214	181	39	21	15	27	239	7	456	32	11	25	21	.543	0	5	3.25

Jorge Cantu

Bats: Right   **Throws:** Right   **Pos:** SS-121; DH-9; PR-1   **Ht:** 6'1"   **Wt:** 178   **Born:** 1/30/82   **Age:** 20

				BATTING													BASERUNNING				PERCENTAGES		
Year Team	Lg Org	G	AB	H	2B	3B	HR	TB	R	RBI	TBB	IBB	SO	HBP	SH	SF	SB	CS	SB%	GDP	Avg	OBP	SLG
1999 Hudson Val	A- TB	72	281	73	17	2	1	97	33	33	20	0	59	2	4	1	3	4	.43	8	.260	.313	.345
2000 Chston-SC	A TB	46	186	55	13	2	2	78	25	24	11	1	39	3	1	1	3	2	.60	3	.296	.343	.419
St. Pete	A+ TB	36	130	38	5	2	1	50	18	14	3	0	13	1	3	0	4	2	.67	3	.292	.313	.385
2001 Orlando	AA TB	130	512	131	26	3	4	175	58	45	17	0	93	8	5	7	4	9	.31	13	.256	.287	.342
3 Min. YEARS		284	1109	297	61	9	8	400	134	116	51	1	204	14	13	9	14	17	.45	27	.268	.306	.361

Aaron Capista

Bats: Both   **Throws:** Right   **Pos:** SS-78; 3B-39; 2B-6; PR-1   **Ht:** 6'2"   **Wt:** 189   **Born:** 5/31/79   **Age:** 23

				BATTING													BASERUNNING				PERCENTAGES		
Year Team	Lg Org	G	AB	H	2B	3B	HR	TB	R	RBI	TBB	IBB	SO	HBP	SH	SF	SB	CS	SB%	GDP	Avg	OBP	SLG
1997 Red Sox	R Bos	38	134	32	6	1	0	40	16	14	16	1	17	0	0	2	6	2	.75	3	.239	.316	.299
1998 Michigan	A Bos	127	471	123	25	5	5	173	58	68	23	0	47	6	2	6	5	3	.63	16	.261	.300	.367
1999 Sarasota	A+ Bos	130	518	137	18	3	5	176	64	47	45	2	60	3	8	4	25	10	.71	9	.264	.325	.340
2000 Trenton	AA Bos	126	434	103	20	3	2	135	52	36	37	0	68	4	2	2	9	4	.69	6	.237	.302	.311
2001 Trenton	AA Bos	117	404	86	25	4	2	125	48	40	20	2	48	3	3	6	2	1	.67	8	.213	.252	.309
5 Min. YEARS		538	1961	481	94	16	14	649	238	205	141	5	240	16	15	20	47	20	.70	42	.245	.298	.331

Chris Capuano

Pitches: Left   **Bats:** Left   **Pos:** SP-28   **Ht:** 6'3"   **Wt:** 215   **Born:** 8/19/78   **Age:** 23

		HOW MUCH HE PITCHED						WHAT HE GAVE UP											THE RESULTS				
Year Team	Lg Org	G	GS	CG	GF	IP	BFP	H	R	ER	HR	SH	SF	HB	TBB	IBB	SO	WP	Bk	W	L	Pct.	ShO	Sv	ERA
2000 South Bend	A Ari	18	18	0	0	101.2	408	68	35	25	2	4	1	5	45	0	105	2	2	10	4	.714	0	0	2.21
2001 El Paso	AA Ari	28	28	2	0	159.1	733	184	109	94	13	4	8	11	75	0	167	9	2	10	11	.476	2	0	5.31
2 Min. YEARS		46	46	2	0	261	1141	252	144	119	15	8	9	16	120	0	272	11	4	20	15	.571	2	0	4.10

Angel Caraballo

Pitches: Right   **Bats:** Right   **Pos:** RP-31; SP-7   **Ht:** 6'0"   **Wt:** 180   **Born:** 1/20/80   **Age:** 22

		HOW MUCH HE PITCHED						WHAT HE GAVE UP											THE RESULTS				
Year Team	Lg Org	G	GS	CG	GF	IP	BFP	H	R	ER	HR	SH	SF	HB	TBB	IBB	SO	WP	Bk	W	L	Pct.	ShO	Sv	ERA
1998 White Sox	R CWS	14	13	0	0	63.2	328	90	71	53	5	1	7	8	36	0	57	11	8	3	5	.375	0	0	7.49
1999 Bristol	R+ CWS	13	13	1	0	81	352	88	40	36	11	2	0	4	27	0	88	10	5	8	2	.800	0	0	4.00
2000 Bristol	R+ CWS	13	13	0	0	77.1	319	67	39	27	8	3	2	2	27	0	61	6	0	7	4	.636	0	0	3.14
2001 Tennessee	AA Tor	26	5	1	4	52.2	227	51	36	32	7	0	2	2	21	1	36	1	0	3	3	.500	0	1	5.47
Dunedin	A+ Tor	12	2	0	2	30	135	30	19	16	3	1	1	2	18	2	21	2	1	3	1	.750	0	0	4.80
4 Min. YEARS		78	46	2	6	304.2	1361	326	205	164	34	7	12	18	129	3	263	30	14	24	15	.615	0	1	4.84

Lance Caraccioli

Pitches: Left **Bats:** Left **Pos:** SP-23; RP-10   **Ht:** 6'4" **Wt:** 190 **Born:** 12/14/77 **Age:** 24

Year Team	Lg Org	G	GS	CG	GF	IP	BFP	H	R	ER	HR	SH	SF	HB	TBB	IBB	SO	WP	Bk	W	L	Pct.	ShO	Sv	ERA
1998 Yakima	A- LA	11	7	0	3	41.2	193	43	26	24	7	0	0	1	28	0	44	5	1	0	5	.000	0	0	5.18
1999 San Berndno	A+ LA	28	26	0	0	140	645	124	90	78	9	7	10	10	126	0	98	8	1	6	7	.462	0	0	5.01
2000 San Berndno	A+ LA	34	9	0	12	105.2	476	105	56	46	8	3	3	6	68	1	95	4	2	10	3	.769	0	4	3.92
2001 Vero Beach	A+ LA	5	5	0	0	29.2	114	23	6	6	2	0	0	2	7	0	22	0	0	2	1	.667	0	0	1.82
Jacksnville	AA LA	28	18	0	4	130	561	139	76	67	7	8	5	8	45	0	87	7	0	8	4	.667	0	1	4.64
4 Min. YEARS		106	65	0	19	447	1989	434	254	221	33	18	18	27	274	1	346	24	4	26	20	.565	0	5	4.45

Brett Caradonna

Bats: Left **Throws:** Right **Pos:** OF-58; DH-41; PH-8   **Ht:** 6'1" **Wt:** 185 **Born:** 12/3/78 **Age:** 23

Year Team	Lg Org	G	AB	H	2B	3B	HR	TB	R	RBI	TBB	IBB	SO	HBP	SH	SF	SB	CS	SB%	GDP	Avg	OBP	SLG
1997 White Sox	R CWS	36	123	34	5	3	2	51	15	16	11	1	21	1	0	3	3	0	1.00	2	.276	.333	.415
Bristol	R+ CWS	22	80	25	3	0	1	31	16	12	13	1	16	1	0	0	3	2	.60	3	.313	.415	.388
1998 Hickory	A CWS	116	447	119	21	1	3	151	43	35	45	2	84	5	1	3	15	11	.58	11	.266	.338	.338
1999 Winston-Sal	A+ CWS	128	505	127	28	4	9	190	68	62	48	2	108	2	4	5	18	7	.72	5	.251	.316	.376
2000 Winston-Sal	A+ CWS	103	365	76	20	2	2	106	39	32	29	2	70	2	1	0	3	1	.75	11	.208	.270	.290
2001 Birmingham	AA CWS	1	1	0	0	0	0	0	0	0	0	0	0	0	0	0	0	0	—	1	.000	.000	.000
Winston-Sal	A+ CWS	104	345	81	14	1	2	103	34	25	29	2	66	5	3	4	7	7	.50	12	.235	.300	.299
5 Min. YEARS		510	1866	462	91	11	19	632	215	182	175	10	365	16	9	15	49	28	.64	45	.248	.315	.339

Dan Carlson

Pitches: Right **Bats:** Right **Pos:** RP-36; SP-3   **Ht:** 6'0" **Wt:** 185 **Born:** 1/26/70 **Age:** 32

Year Team	Lg Org	G	GS	CG	GF	IP	BFP	H	R	ER	HR	SH	SF	HB	TBB	IBB	SO	WP	Bk	W	L	Pct.	ShO	Sv	ERA
1990 Everett	A- SF	17	11	0	3	62.1	279	60	42	37	5	1	4	1	33	1	77	9	5	2	6	.250	0	0	5.34
1991 Clinton	A SF	27	27	5	0	181.1	740	149	69	62	11	3	3	2	76	0	164	18	5	16	7	.696	3	0	3.08
1992 Shreveport	AA SF	27	27	4	0	186	765	166	85	66	15	5	3	1	60	3	157	4	0	15	9	.625	1	0	3.19
1993 Phoenix	AAA SF	13	12	0	0	70	320	79	54	51	12	2	1	5	32	1	48	4	0	5	6	.455	0	0	6.56
Shreveport	AA SF	15	15	2	0	100.1	397	86	30	25	9	4	4	0	26	3	81	5	0	7	4	.636	1	0	2.24
1994 Phoenix	AAA SF	31	22	0	2	151.1	665	173	80	78	21	3	9	1	55	1	117	10	0	13	6	.684	0	1	4.64
1995 Phoenix	AAA SF	23	22	2	1	132.2	582	138	67	63	11	7	7	3	66	0	93	6	1	9	5	.643	0	0	4.27
1996 Phoenix	AAA SF	33	15	2	3	146.2	604	135	61	56	18	5	5	2	46	0	123	3	0	13	6	.684	0	1	3.44
1997 Bakersfield	A+ SF	2	2	0	0	6	22	3	0	0	0	0	0	0	1	0	7	0	0	0	0	—	0	0	0.00
Phoenix	AAA SF	29	14	0	7	109	451	102	53	47	12	3	3	2	36	1	108	6	1	13	3	.813	0	3	3.88
1998 Durham	AAA TB	19	11	0	3	68	316	87	52	48	8	1	1	3	28	0	59	4	1	3	5	.375	0	0	6.35
1999 Tucson	AAA Ari	32	18	0	5	117.2	527	130	82	71	19	3	1	6	52	6	118	4	2	4	9	.308	0	0	5.43
2000 Tucson	AAA Ari	4	3	0	1	22	96	25	9	4	1	1	2	0	7	0	12	1	0	0	1	.000	0	0	1.64
2001 Memphis	AAA StL	7	3	0	2	21	94	25	13	11	3	1	0	0	8	0	21	1	0	1	0	1.000	0	0	4.71
El Paso	AA Ari	32	0	0	12	51.1	214	53	22	21	4	0	3	1	12	3	55	3	1	4	2	.667	0	5	3.68
1996 San Francisco	NL	5	0	0	3	10	46	13	6	3	2	0	2	0	2	0	4	0	0	1	0	1.000	0	0	2.70
1997 San Francisco	NL	6	0	0	2	15.1	72	20	14	13	5	0	1	0	8	1	14	0	0	0	0	—	0	0	7.63
1998 Tampa Bay	AL	10	0	0	1	17.2	86	25	15	15	3	2	1	3	8	0	16	0	0	0	0	—	0	0	7.64
1999 Arizona	NL	2	0	0	1	4	18	5	4	4	0	0	0	0	0	0	3	0	0	0	0	—	0	0	9.00
12 Min. YEARS		311	202	15	39	1425.2	6072	1411	719	640	149	39	46	27	538	19	1240	78	16	105	69	.603	5	10	4.04
4 Maj. YEARS		23	0	0	7	47	222	63	39	35	10	2	4	3	18	1	37	0	0	1	0	1.000	0	0	6.70

Matt Carnes

Pitches: Right **Bats:** Right **Pos:** RP-21; SP-7   **Ht:** 6'3" **Wt:** 208 **Born:** 8/18/75 **Age:** 26

Year Team	Lg Org	G	GS	CG	GF	IP	BFP	H	R	ER	HR	SH	SF	HB	TBB	IBB	SO	WP	Bk	W	L	Pct.	ShO	Sv	ERA
1997 Elizabethtn	R+ Min	8	7	1	0	38	156	33	17	13	3	2	0	1	5	0	42	7	1	3	0	1.000	0	0	3.08
Fort Wayne	A Min	1	1	0	0	4	18	2	4	4	1	0	0	0	5	0	3	1	1	0	1	.000	0	0	9.00
1998 Fort Wayne	A Min	47	10	1	18	104	473	119	74	63	5	8	8	7	36	5	92	8	1	8	5	.615	0	5	5.45
1999 Fort Myers	A+ Min	52	1	0	20	81	343	74	48	33	4	8	7	2	26	0	67	6	1	4	4	.500	0	4	3.67
2000 Fort Myers	A+ Min	19	9	0	1	54.1	228	54	20	16	1	1	3	1	19	3	48	4	0	2	2	.000	0	0	2.65
New Britain	AA Min	14	14	0	0	88.2	392	99	59	51	7	1	6	4	37	1	63	4	0	1	8	.111	0	0	5.18
2001 New Britain	AA Min	28	7	0	10	64.2	276	64	31	27	4	3	1	1	20	4	63	1	0	4	5	.444	0	2	3.76
5 Min. YEARS		169	49	2	49	434.2	1886	445	253	207	25	23	25	16	148	13	378	31	4	20	25	.444	0	11	4.29

Bubba Carpenter

Bats: Left **Throws:** Left **Pos:** OF-85; PH-20; DH-9; PR-1   **Ht:** 6'1" **Wt:** 185 **Born:** 7/23/68 **Age:** 33

Year Team	Lg Org	G	AB	H	2B	3B	HR	TB	R	RBI	TBB	IBB	SO	HBP	SH	SF	SB	CS	SB%	GDP	Avg	OBP	SLG
1991 Pr William	A+ NYY	69	236	66	10	3	6	100	33	34	40	3	50	2	1	3	4	1	.80	7	.280	.384	.424
1992 Albany-Col	AA NYY	60	221	51	11	5	4	84	24	31	25	0	41	2	0	1	2	3	.40	8	.231	.313	.380
Pr William	A+ NYY	68	240	76	15	2	5	110	41	41	35	2	44	1	1	6	4	4	.50	4	.317	.397	.458
1993 Albany-Col	AA NYY	14	53	17	4	0	2	27	8	14	7	0	4	0	0	1	2	2	.50	2	.321	.393	.509
Columbus	AAA NYY	70	199	53	9	0	5	77	29	17	29	3	35	3	0	1	2	2	.50	4	.266	.360	.387
1994 Albany-Col	AA NYY	116	378	109	14	1	13	164	47	51	58	5	65	3	3	3	9	5	.64	3	.288	.385	.434
Columbus	AAA NYY	7	15	4	0	0	0	4	0	2	0	0	7	0	0	0	0	0	—	1	.267	.267	.267
1995 Columbus	AAA NYY	116	374	92	12	3	11	143	57	49	40	2	70	1	2	3	13	6	.68	2	.246	.318	.382
1996 Columbus	AAA NYY	132	466	114	23	3	7	164	55	48	48	1	80	0	2	1	10	7	.59	7	.245	.315	.352
1997 Columbus	AAA NYY	85	271	76	12	4	6	114	47	39	48	0	46	0	3	1	4	8	.33	3	.280	.388	.421
1998 Yankees	R NYY	5	17	4	0	2	1	11	3	7	2	0	2	0	0	0	0	0	—	0	.235	.316	.647
Columbus	AAA NYY	63	198	45	14	2	7	84	28	24	36	2	48	1	2	0	3	2	.60	9	.227	.349	.424
1999 Columbus	AAA NYY	101	325	92	20	2	22	182	78	81	75	7	68	4	1	4	7	3	.70	4	.283	.419	.560
2000 Colo Sprngs	AAA Col	53	157	35	7	2	4	58	23	19	33	3	37	0	1	1	3	2	.60	2	.223	.356	.369

49

Year Team	Lg Org	G	AB	H	2B	3B	HR	TB	R	RBI	TBB	IBB	SO	HBP	SH	SF	SB	CS	SB%	GDP	Avg	OBP	SLG
2001 Norfolk	AAA NYM	28	82	20	3	1	1	28	12	13	13	1	19	2	0	2	2	3	.40	3	.244	.354	.341
Colo Sprngs	AAA Col	49	125	33	14	0	2	53	22	10	18	2	23	3	0	0	3	2	.60	2	.264	.370	.424
Carolina	AA Col	32	100	23	7	0	1	33	12	12	16	0	17	1	0	0	3	1	.75	0	.230	.342	.330
2000 Colorado	NL	15	27	6	0	0	3	15	4	5	4	0	13	0	0	0	0	0	—	0	.222	.323	.556
11 Min. YEARS		1068	3457	910	175	30	97	1436	519	492	523	31	656	23	16	27	71	51	.58	61	.263	.361	.415

Dustin Carr

Bats: Right Throws: Right Pos: 3B-20; OF-20; DH-19; 1B-8; 2B-5; PH-3; PR-2   Ht: 5'11" Wt: 189 Born: 6/7/75 Age: 27

Year Team	Lg Org	G	AB	H	2B	3B	HR	TB	R	RBI	TBB	IBB	SO	HBP	SH	SF	SB	CS	SB%	GDP	Avg	OBP	SLG
1997 Hudson Val	A- TB	74	281	81	12	2	5	112	46	47	42	2	42	2	0	3	4	2	.67	10	.288	.381	.399
1998 St. Pete	A+ TB	138	516	132	23	5	6	183	85	52	70	4	86	11	8	3	11	4	.73	9	.256	.355	.355
1999 Orlando	AA TB	125	461	139	22	3	6	185	76	63	70	0	62	4	8	3	7	2	.78	12	.302	.396	.401
2000 Orlando	AA TB	2	11	3	0	0	0	3	1	1	0	0	2	0	0	0	0	0	—	0	.273	.273	.273
Durham	AAA TB	111	365	80	14	2	3	107	38	36	49	0	61	3	7	3	9	2	.82	9	.219	.314	.293
2001 Durham	AAA TB	73	227	55	6	1	4	75	25	26	25	0	47	5	6	1	5	2	.71	5	.242	.329	.330
5 Min. YEARS		523	1861	490	77	13	24	665	271	225	256	6	300	25	29	13	36	12	.75	45	.263	.358	.357

Danny Carrasco

Pitches: Right Bats: Right Pos: RP-48; SP-1   Ht: 6'2" Wt: 191 Born: 4/12/77 Age: 25

		HOW MUCH HE PITCHED						WHAT HE GAVE UP												THE RESULTS					
Year Team	Lg Org	G	GS	CG	GF	IP	BFP	H	R	ER	HR	SH	SF	HB	TBB	IBB	SO	WP	Bk	W	L	Pct.	ShO	Sv	ERA
1998 Watertown	A- Cle	13	1	0	6	31.2	145	36	23	19	3	1	0	2	14	0	38	1	0	1	1	.500	0	2	5.40
1999 Williamsprt	A- Pit	18	4	0	6	51.2	212	43	20	17	2	1	3	3	23	0	49	7	4	4	2	.667	0	0	2.96
Lynchburg	A+ Pit	2	0	0	0	5.2	29	9	8	4	0	1	0	0	3	0	4	0	0	1	0	1.000	0	0	6.35
2000 Hickory	A Pit	27	0	0	25	40.1	176	35	10	6	0	1	0	7	20	1	40	2	0	5	4	.556	0	6	1.34
Lynchburg	A+ Pit	8	0	0	6	10.1	45	8	5	4	1	1	0	0	8	0	10	1	0	1	0	1.000	0	2	3.48
Altoona	AA Pit	9	0	0	3	14	68	16	14	13	0	0	0	1	13	0	10	1	0	1	1	.500	0	0	8.36
2001 Lynchburg	A+ Pit	22	0	0	11	36	141	18	7	6	0	1	0	2	14	1	40	1	2	4	0	1.000	0	7	1.50
Altoona	AA Pit	27	1	0	11	37	169	34	22	17	2	2	0	0	25	2	35	2	0	2	2	.500	0	1	4.14
4 Min. YEARS		126	6	0	68	226.2	985	199	109	86	8	8	3	15	120	4	226	15	6	18	11	.621	0	18	3.41

Jose Carreno

Bats: Right Throws: Right Pos: C-37; PH-3   Ht: 5'11" Wt: 190 Born: 4/23/78 Age: 24

Year Team	Lg Org	G	AB	H	2B	3B	HR	TB	R	RBI	TBB	IBB	SO	HBP	SH	SF	SB	CS	SB%	GDP	Avg	OBP	SLG
1998 Expos	R Mon	40	134	38	4	0	1	45	14	16	5	0	21	2	1	2	5	5	.50	3	.284	.315	.336
Jupiter	A+ Pit	10	28	7	1	0	2	14	2	6	2	0	6	0	1	0	0	0	—	0	.250	.300	.500
1999 Cape Fear	A Mon	41	140	31	2	0	0	33	11	10	5	0	16	1	1	1	4	3	.57	3	.221	.252	.236
Jupiter	A+ Mon	2	6	0	0	0	0	0	0	0	0	0	2	0	0	0	0	0	—	0	.000	.000	.000
2000 Cape Fear	A Mon	18	58	19	2	0	0	21	3	8	10	0	4	1	0	3	0	0	—	1	.328	.417	.362
Jupiter	A+ Mon	38	125	32	3	0	0	35	6	3	10	0	18	2	3	0	0	1	.00	2	.256	.321	.280
2001 Harrisburg	AA Mon	40	120	19	1	0	0	20	3	8	12	2	24	1	0	2	0	2	.00	2	.158	.237	.167
4 Min. YEARS		189	611	146	13	0	3	168	39	51	44	2	91	7	6	8	9	11	.45	11	.239	.294	.275

Jamey Carroll

Bats: Right Throws: Right Pos: 2B-28; SS-23; 3B-22; PH-7; DH-4   Ht: 5'10" Wt: 175 Born: 2/18/74 Age: 28

Year Team	Lg Org	G	AB	H	2B	3B	HR	TB	R	RBI	TBB	IBB	SO	HBP	SH	SF	SB	CS	SB%	GDP	Avg	OBP	SLG
1996 Vermont	A- Mon	54	203	56	6	1	0	64	40	17	29	0	25	0	3	2	16	11	.59	1	.276	.363	.315
1997 Wst Plm Bch	A+ Mon	121	407	99	19	1	0	120	56	38	43	0	48	4	8	4	17	11	.61	4	.243	.319	.295
1998 Jupiter	A+ Mon	55	222	58	5	0	0	63	40	14	24	1	26	5	2	1	11	4	.73	2	.261	.345	.284
Harrisburg	AA Mon	75	261	66	11	3	0	83	43	20	41	0	29	5	5	0	11	5	.69	4	.253	.365	.318
1999 Harrisburg	AA Mon	141	561	164	34	5	5	223	78	63	48	2	58	5	5	4	21	10	.68	13	.292	.351	.398
2000 Harrisburg	AA Mon	45	169	49	5	3	0	60	23	18	12	0	13	0	1	1	8	2	.80	5	.290	.335	.355
Ottawa	AAA Mon	91	349	97	17	2	2	124	53	23	33	1	32	2	6	2	6	3	.67	9	.278	.342	.355
2001 Ottawa	AAA Mon	83	267	64	8	2	0	76	26	16	18	1	41	2	2	1	5	5	.50	8	.240	.292	.285
6 Min. YEARS		665	2439	653	105	17	7	813	359	209	248	5	272	23	32	15	95	51	.65	46	.268	.339	.333

Charley Carter

Bats: Right Throws: Right Pos: 1B-100; OF-20; DH-14; PH-1   Ht: 6'2" Wt: 205 Born: 12/11/75 Age: 26

Year Team	Lg Org	G	AB	H	2B	3B	HR	TB	R	RBI	TBB	IBB	SO	HBP	SH	SF	SB	CS	SB%	GDP	Avg	OBP	SLG
1998 Auburn	A- Hou	61	218	72	24	1	8	122	32	42	22	1	35	1	1	4	1	1	.50	5	.330	.388	.560
1999 Kissimmee	A+ Hou	115	416	114	19	2	12	173	62	56	28	2	77	3	0	4	0	3	.00	7	.274	.322	.416
2000 Kissimmee	A+ Hou	106	398	110	32	0	10	172	51	66	21	0	64	1	0	8	2	1	.67	16	.276	.308	.432
Round Rock	AA Hou	24	90	24	7	0	3	40	12	21	6	0	15	0	0	1	0	0	—	2	.267	.309	.444
2001 Round Rock	AA Hou	133	525	138	26	1	25	241	65	97	35	3	106	2	0	5	1	1	.50	11	.263	.309	.459
4 Min. YEARS		439	1647	458	108	4	58	748	222	282	112	6	297	7	1	22	4	6	.40	41	.278	.323	.454

Mike Carter

Bats: Right Throws: Right Pos: OF-96; PH-8; PR-2; P-1   Ht: 5'9" Wt: 170 Born: 5/5/69 Age: 33

Year Team	Lg Org	G	AB	H	2B	3B	HR	TB	R	RBI	TBB	IBB	SO	HBP	SH	SF	SB	CS	SB%	GDP	Avg	OBP	SLG
1990 Helena	R+ Mil	61	241	74	11	3	0	91	45	30	16	0	20	6	2	5	22	7	.76	0	.307	.358	.378
1991 Beloit	A Mil	123	452	126	24	4	2	164	62	40	26	5	42	4	2	3	46	13	.78	5	.279	.322	.363

Year Team	Lg Org	G	AB	H	2B	3B	HR	TB	R	RBI	TBB	IBB	SO	HBP	SH	SF	SB	CS	SB%	GDP	Avg	OBP	SLG
1992 Stockton	A+ Mil	67	252	66	9	1	3	86	38	26	17	1	26	2	3	5	31	8	.79	4	.262	.308	.341
El Paso	AA Mil	50	165	42	4	4	1	57	20	15	16	2	31	0	3	1	10	8	.56	3	.255	.319	.345
1993 El Paso	AA Mil	17	73	27	4	1	2	39	16	16	3	0	7	0	0	0	6	4	.60	1	.370	.395	.534
New Orleans	AAA Mil	104	369	102	18	5	3	139	49	31	17	0	52	4	11	4	20	11	.65	6	.276	.312	.377
1994 Iowa	AAA ChC	122	421	122	24	3	6	170	56	30	14	1	43	4	12	4	16	14	.53	7	.290	.316	.404
1995 Iowa	AAA ChC	107	421	137	16	3	8	183	57	40	14	3	46	6	3	3	12	12	.50	5	.325	.354	.435
1996 Iowa	AAA ChC	113	384	102	13	1	2	123	41	18	10	0	42	1	5	1	4	6	.40	5	.266	.285	.320
1997 Midland	AA Ana	15	65	18	3	1	0	23	9	2	2	0	8	0	1	0	5	2	.71	1	.277	.299	.354
1998 Sioux Falls	IND —	13	56	19	6	0	4	37	15	15	1	0	7	1	1	2	3	1	.75	2	.339	.350	.661
1999 Scranton-WB	AAA Phi	9	31	5	1	1	1	11	2	4	0	0	8	2	0	0	0	1	.00	0	.161	.212	.355
Sioux Falls	IND —	15	65	16	1	1	0	19	10	4	3	0	10	0	0	0	1	2	.33	1	.246	.279	.292
2000 Somerset	IND —	33	128	24	4	0	1	31	12	15	5	0	11	1	1	0	6	2	.75	1	.188	.224	.242
Bridgeport	IND —	83	335	109	14	3	10	159	66	64	19	2	26	5	3	6	18	5	.78	9	.325	.364	.475
2001 Richmond	AAA Atl	104	388	114	16	3	2	142	55	20	10	1	45	4	15	3	10	10	.50	5	.294	.316	.366
12 Min. YEARS		1036	3846	1103	168	34	45	1474	553	370	173	15	424	40	62	37	210	106	.66	55	.287	.321	.383

Shannon Carter

Bats: Left **Throws:** Left **Pos:** OF-50; DH-2; PH-2; PR-2   **Ht:** 6'0" **Wt:** 180 **Born:** 3/23/79 **Age:** 23

Year Team	Lg Org	G	AB	H	2B	3B	HR	TB	R	RBI	TBB	IBB	SO	HBP	SH	SF	SB	CS	SB%	GDP	Avg	OBP	SLG
1997 Orioles	R Bal	50	159	31	3	2	0	38	22	11	12	0	45	4	0	0	13	5	.72	1	.195	.269	.239
1998 Bluefield	R+ Bal	36	150	37	2	0	1	42	23	10	9	0	35	0	0	0	14	3	.82	1	.247	.289	.280
St.Cathrnes	A- Tor	24	61	16	3	0	1	22	8	7	4	0	14	1	1	0	2	0	1.00	1	.262	.318	.361
1999 St.Cathrnes	A- Tor	61	215	60	5	4	1	76	38	16	11	0	54	2	1	1	15	6	.71	1	.279	.319	.353
Syracuse	AAA Tor	2	9	1	0	0	0	1	0	0	0	0	2	0	0	0	0	0	—	2	.111	.111	.111
2000 Hagerstown	A Tor	123	443	121	15	7	0	150	74	39	45	0	129	11	1	0	33	6	.85	5	.273	.355	.339
2001 Syracuse	AAA Tor	4	9	1	1	0	0	2	1	1	1	0	2	1	0	0	0	0	—	0	.111	.273	.222
Dunedin	A+ Tor	48	161	44	7	1	0	53	25	17	5	0	44	3	0	1	6	6	.50	4	.273	.306	.329
5 Min. YEARS		348	1207	311	36	14	3	384	191	101	87	0	325	22	3	2	83	26	.76	15	.258	.319	.318

Joe Caruso

Bats: Right **Throws:** Right **Pos:** OF-68; 2B-21; SS-16; 3B-16; PH-7; DH-6; C-1; 1B-1; P-1   **Ht:** 5'9" **Wt:** 190 **Born:** 12/30/74 **Age:** 27

Year Team	Lg Org	G	AB	H	2B	3B	HR	TB	R	RBI	TBB	IBB	SO	HBP	SH	SF	SB	CS	SB%	GDP	Avg	OBP	SLG
1997 Spokane	A- KC	57	194	58	12	3	5	91	48	36	29	1	30	6	8	0	10	4	.71	1	.299	.406	.469
1998 Lansing	A KC	120	417	112	23	7	9	176	73	60	60	1	61	13	1	5	24	9	.73	8	.269	.374	.422
1999 Wilmington	A+ KC	102	361	85	13	6	5	125	60	37	34	0	68	8	6	3	6	4	.60	7	.235	.313	.346
2000 Wichita	AA KC	108	400	125	26	1	13	192	69	66	34	3	45	16	5	5	10	5	.67	4	.313	.385	.480
2001 Wichita	AA KC	120	424	112	26	1	8	164	75	59	50	4	65	23	5	5	12	6	.67	8	.264	.369	.387
5 Min. YEARS		507	1796	492	100	18	40	748	325	258	207	9	269	66	25	18	62	28	.69	28	.274	.367	.416

Mike Caruso

Bats: Left **Throws:** Right **Pos:** 2B-59; SS-52; PH-2   **Ht:** 6'1" **Wt:** 172 **Born:** 5/27/77 **Age:** 25

Year Team	Lg Org	G	AB	H	2B	3B	HR	TB	R	RBI	TBB	IBB	SO	HBP	SH	SF	SB	CS	SB%	GDP	Avg	OBP	SLG
1996 Bellingham	A- SF	73	312	91	13	1	2	112	48	24	16	2	23	2	3	6	24	10	.71	2	.292	.324	.359
1997 San Jose	A+ SF	108	441	147	24	11	2	199	76	50	38	3	19	6	4	3	11	16	.41	3	.333	.391	.451
Winston-Sal	A+ CWS	28	119	27	3	2	0	34	12	14	4	0	8	2	0	0	3	0	1.00	0	.227	.264	.286
2000 Charlotte	AAA CWS	88	309	76	11	5	0	97	38	26	22	0	23	3	8	2	5	7	.42	7	.246	.301	.314
2001 Durham	AAA TB	110	387	113	10	9	0	141	62	35	22	0	22	7	9	2	11	9	.55	4	.292	.340	.364
1998 Chicago	AL	133	523	160	17	6	5	204	81	55	14	0	38	7	8	3	22	6	.79	8	.306	.331	.390
1999 Chicago	AL	136	529	132	11	4	2	157	60	35	20	0	36	3	11	1	12	14	.46	6	.250	.280	.297
4 Min. YEARS		407	1568	454	61	28	4	583	236	149	102	5	95	20	24	13	54	42	.56	16	.290	.338	.372
2 Maj. YEARS		269	1052	292	28	10	7	361	141	90	34	0	74	10	19	4	34	20	.63	14	.278	.305	.343

Joe Casey

Pitches: Right **Bats:** Right **Pos:** RP-42   **Ht:** 6'0" **Wt:** 192 **Born:** 1/25/79 **Age:** 23

Year Team	Lg Org	G	GS	CG	GF	IP	BFP	H	R	ER	HR	SH	SF	HB	TBB	IBB	SO	WP	Bk	W	L	Pct.	ShO	Sv	ERA
1997 St.Cathrnes	A- Tor	14	11	0	1	64	279	59	42	31	6	0	1	3	23	0	43	11	0	7	4	.636	0	0	4.36
1998 Hagerstown	A Tor	22	16	0	1	77.1	346	84	53	40	6	6	3	6	41	2	62	4	1	2	7	.222	0	0	4.66
St.Cathrnes	A- Tor	4	3	0	0	11	65	18	19	15	1	0	1	2	11	0	9	2	0	1	2	.333	0	0	12.27
1999 Hagerstown	A Tor	28	28	0	0	142	637	150	99	74	10	4	3	10	64	0	79	25	3	7	14	.333	0	0	4.69
2000 Dunedin	A+ Tor	27	27	0	0	158.1	677	151	88	74	7	1	5	14	74	2	96	21	2	10	8	.556	0	0	4.21
2001 Tennessee	AA Tor	42	0	0	12	61	275	74	36	32	8	7	1	5	16	1	42	6	0	4	3	.571	0	1	4.72
5 Min. YEARS		137	85	0	14	513.2	2279	536	337	266	38	18	14	40	229	5	331	69	6	31	38	.449	0	2	4.66

Uriel Casillas

Bats: Right **Throws:** Right **Pos:** 3B-81; SS-18; 2B-9; PH-7; 1B-1; PR-1   **Ht:** 5'11" **Wt:** 185 **Born:** 8/22/75 **Age:** 26

Year Team	Lg Org	G	AB	H	2B	3B	HR	TB	R	RBI	TBB	IBB	SO	HBP	SH	SF	SB	CS	SB%	GDP	Avg	OBP	SLG
1997 Martinsvlle	R+ Phi	60	220	59	12	1	1	76	42	26	12	3	29	12	3	2	5	3	.63	6	.268	.346	.345
1998 Batavia	A- Phi	60	219	49	9	0	4	70	37	31	32	0	47	7	3	4	3	2	.60	4	.224	.336	.320
1999 Piedmont	A Phi	73	225	51	11	2	0	66	30	20	48	0	33	7	2	1	4	5	.44	7	.227	.377	.293
Clearwater	A+ Phi	32	113	32	5	0	0	37	23	24	17	0	10	9	4	1	4	2	.67	2	.283	.414	.327
2000 Clearwater	A+ Phi	48	140	43	7	1	0	55	17	14	32	0	17	3	2	1	0	3	.00	3	.307	.443	.393
2001 Reading	AA Phi	113	384	92	17	2	5	128	46	40	27	0	47	10	7	4	4	5	.44	9	.240	.304	.333
5 Min. YEARS		386	1301	326	61	6	11	432	195	155	179	0	183	48	21	13	20	20	.50	31	.251	.359	.332

Carlos Casimiro

Bats: Right **Throws:** Right **Pos:** 3B-65; OF-57; DH-7; SS-2; PR-2; 2B-1; PH-1   **Ht:** 5'11" **Wt:** 179 **Born:** 11/8/76 **Age:** 25

							BATTING												BASERUNNING				PERCENTAGES		
Year Team	Lg Org	G	AB	H	2B	3B	HR	TB	R	RBI	TBB	IBB	SO	HBP	SH	SF		SB	CS	SB%	GDP		Avg	OBP	SLG
1995 Orioles	R Bal	32	107	27	4	2	2	41	14	11	10	0	22	1	1	2		1	3	.25	3		.252	.317	.383
1996 Bluefield	R+ Bal	62	239	66	16	0	10	112	51	33	20	1	52	2	2	2		22	9	.71	3		.276	.335	.469
1997 Delmarva	A Bal	122	457	111	21	8	9	175	54	51	26	1	108	5	4	2		20	13	.61	11		.243	.290	.383
1998 Frederick	A+ Bal	131	478	113	23	9	15	199	44	61	25	2	98	1	4	6		10	7	.59	16		.236	.273	.416
1999 Bowie	AA Bal	139	526	116	23	1	18	195	73	64	39	0	101	3	5	5		7	12	.37	10		.221	.276	.371
2000 Bowie	AA Bal	87	290	76	12	2	6	110	44	32	23	0	66	1	3	1		2	4	.33	5		.262	.317	.379
Rochester	AAA Bal	24	81	18	4	0	4	34	9	10	4	0	16	0	0	0		0	0	—	1		.222	.259	.420
2001 Rochester	AAA Bal	48	166	39	9	1	4	62	21	14	7	0	41	2	1	0		5	1	.83	4		.235	.274	.373
Bowie	AA Bal	80	302	67	15	1	4	96	22	24	18	2	81	1	1	0		2	5	.29	6		.222	.268	.318
2000 Baltimore	AL	2	8	1	1	0	0	2	0	3	0	0	2	0	0	0		0	0	—	0		.125	.125	.250
7 Min. YEARS		725	2646	633	127	24	72	1024	332	300	172	6	585	16	21	18		69	54	.56	59		.239	.288	.387

Brett Casper

Bats: Right **Throws:** Right **Pos:** OF-8; DH-1; PH-1   **Ht:** 6'3" **Wt:** 215 **Born:** 11/24/75 **Age:** 26

							BATTING												BASERUNNING				PERCENTAGES		
Year Team	Lg Org	G	AB	H	2B	3B	HR	TB	R	RBI	TBB	IBB	SO	HBP	SH	SF		SB	CS	SB%	GDP		Avg	OBP	SLG
1997 Salem-Keizr	A- SF	61	229	51	14	1	7	88	31	34	31	0	86	3	0	1		17	3	.85	2		.223	.322	.384
1998 Salem-Keizr	A- SF	7	26	8	1	1	0	11	2	3	2	0	7	0	0	0		0	1	.00	0		.308	.357	.423
Bakersfield	A+ SF	74	237	46	10	3	2	68	27	18	23	0	75	7	0	0		5	4	.56	8		.194	.285	.287
1999 San Jose	A+ SF	121	436	116	22	2	16	190	71	77	56	2	135	6	4	3		20	10	.67	12		.266	.355	.436
2000 Bakersfield	A+ SF	128	436	106	27	3	15	184	85	70	97	1	146	13	2	3		22	4	.85	8		.243	.393	.422
2001 Shreveport	AA SF	10	26	2	0	0	0	2	1	1	5	0	15	1	1	1		0	0	—	0		.077	.242	.077
5 Min. YEARS		401	1390	329	74	10	40	543	217	203	214	3	464	30	7	8		64	22	.74	30		.237	.349	.391

Scott Cassidy

Pitches: Right **Bats:** Right **Pos:** SP-26; RP-1   **Ht:** 6'2" **Wt:** 175 **Born:** 10/3/75 **Age:** 26

		HOW MUCH HE PITCHED						WHAT HE GAVE UP												THE RESULTS					
Year Team	Lg Org	G	GS	CG	GF	IP	BFP	H	R	ER	HR	SH	SF	HB	TBB	IBB	SO	WP	Bk	W	L	Pct.	ShO	Sv	ERA
1998 Medcine Hat	R+ Tor	15	14	0	0	81.1	325	71	31	22	4	2	3	5	14	0	82	2	0	8	1	.889	0	0	2.43
1999 Hagerstown	A Tor	27	27	1	0	170.2	694	151	78	62	13	2	1	21	30	0	178	3	2	13	7	.650	0	0	3.27
2000 Dunedin	A+ Tor	14	13	1	1	88	342	53	15	13	4	3	2	3	34	2	89	4	0	9	3	.750	0	0	1.33
Tennessee	AA Tor	8	7	0	0	42.2	190	48	30	28	7	1	4	4	15	0	39	3	0	2	2	.500	0	0	5.91
2001 Tennessee	AA Tor	16	15	4	0	96.2	394	78	45	37	10	3	0	7	27	0	81	1	0	6	6	.500	3	0	3.44
Syracuse	AAA Tor	11	11	0	0	63	276	60	24	19	6	0	1	6	26	0	48	1	0	3	3	.500	0	0	2.71
4 Min. YEARS		91	87	6	1	542.1	2221	461	223	181	44	11	11	46	146	2	517	14	2	41	22	.651	3	0	3.00

Hugo Castellanos

Pitches: Right **Bats:** Right **Pos:** RP-43   **Ht:** 6'4" **Wt:** 204 **Born:** 6/30/80 **Age:** 22

		HOW MUCH HE PITCHED						WHAT HE GAVE UP												THE RESULTS					
Year Team	Lg Org	G	GS	CG	GF	IP	BFP	H	R	ER	HR	SH	SF	HB	TBB	IBB	SO	WP	Bk	W	L	Pct.	ShO	Sv	ERA
2000 Hagerstown	A Tor	29	0	0	19	38.1	155	16	11	7	1	2	0	5	18	1	30	5	0	0	3	.000	0	7	1.64
Dunedin	A+ Tor	4	0	0	4	8	37	5	4	4	1	1	1	0	10	1	5	0	0	0	0	—	0	1	4.50
2001 Tennessee	AA Tor	43	0	0	24	64.2	282	53	24	18	4	4	1	8	33	4	47	2	0	5	2	.714	0	2	2.51
2 Min. YEARS		76	0	0	47	111	474	74	39	29	6	7	2	13	61	6	82	7	0	5	5	.500	0	10	2.35

Carlos Castillo

Bats: Right **Throws:** Right **Pos:** C-5; 1B-3; 3B-2; DH-1; PR-1   **Ht:** 6'0" **Wt:** 175 **Born:** 5/6/81 **Age:** 21

							BATTING												BASERUNNING				PERCENTAGES		
Year Team	Lg Org	G	AB	H	2B	3B	HR	TB	R	RBI	TBB	IBB	SO	HBP	SH	SF		SB	CS	SB%	GDP		Avg	OBP	SLG
1999 Athletics	R Oak	31	88	18	4	1	1	27	9	13	3	0	23	2	0	1		0	0	—	2		.205	.245	.307
2001 Sacramento	AAA Oak	1	1	0	0	0	0	0	0	0	0	0	1	0	0	0		0	0	—	0		.000	.000	.000
Athletics	R Oak	7	21	4	0	0	0	4	4	3	3	0	4	1	1	0		0	0	—	1		.190	.320	.190
Modesto	A+ Oak	3	7	1	0	0	0	1	3	0	2	0	3	0	0	0		0	0	—	0		.143	.333	.143
2 Min. YEARS		42	117	23	4	1	1	32	16	16	8	0	31	3	1	1		0	0	—	3		.197	.264	.274

Ruben Castillo

Bats: Right **Throws:** Right **Pos:** SS-116; PR-1   **Ht:** 6'2" **Wt:** 155 **Born:** 8/16/80 **Age:** 21

							BATTING												BASERUNNING				PERCENTAGES		
Year Team	Lg Org	G	AB	H	2B	3B	HR	TB	R	RBI	TBB	IBB	SO	HBP	SH	SF		SB	CS	SB%	GDP		Avg	OBP	SLG
1998 Mariners	R Sea	26	75	16	0	0	0	16	8	6	10	0	23	0	2	0		2	1	.67	1		.213	.306	.213
1999 Wisconsin	A Sea	20	44	9	0	0	0	9	7	4	5	0	9	0	0	1		1	1	.50	3		.205	.286	.205
Everett	A- Sea	62	226	65	10	2	2	85	38	27	19	0	48	2	3	1		11	2	.85	3		.288	.347	.376
2000 Wisconsin	A Sea	123	416	89	14	4	2	117	57	46	29	0	101	2	8	4		21	6	.78	3		.214	.266	.281
2001 San Berndno	A+ Sea	76	270	60	7	2	1	74	31	26	5	0	53	3	7	2		10	2	.83	5		.222	.243	.274
San Antonio	AA Sea	40	126	25	4	0	0	29	12	7	7	0	27	1	2	1		1	0	1.00	1		.198	.244	.230
4 Min. YEARS		347	1157	264	35	8	5	330	153	116	75	0	261	8	22	8		46	12	.79	16		.228	.278	.285

Nelson Castro

Bats: Right **Throws:** Right **Pos:** SS-124; 2B-4   **Ht:** 5'10" **Wt:** 190 **Born:** 6/4/76 **Age:** 26

Year Team	Lg Org	G	AB	H	2B	3B	HR	TB	R	RBI	TBB	IBB	SO	HBP	SH	SF	SB	CS	SB%	GDP	Avg	OBP	SLG
1995 Angels	R Ana	55	190	37	1	2	0	42	34	22	27	0	50	4	4	1	15	7	.68	2	.195	.306	.221
1996 Boise	A- Ana	1	1	0	0	0	0	0	0	0	0	0	0	0	0	0	0	0	—	0	.000	.000	.000
Angels	R Ana	53	186	38	4	3	3	57	31	14	32	0	42	2	1	0	25	8	.76	3	.204	.327	.306
1997 Boise	A- Ana	69	293	86	16	1	7	125	74	37	38	1	53	4	1	1	26	6	.81	1	.294	.381	.427
1998 Lk Elsinore	A+ Ana	131	470	110	16	7	4	152	73	41	40	1	101	6	0	3	36	12	.75	5	.234	.301	.323
1999 Lk Elsinore	A+ Ana	125	444	111	16	12	1	154	68	50	36	1	75	3	5	4	53	19	.74	5	.250	.308	.347
2000 Bakersfield	A+ SF	53	218	62	14	3	5	97	38	41	20	0	40	0	4	6	27	8	.77	5	.284	.336	.445
Fresno	AAA SF	67	244	62	7	2	5	88	27	20	14	0	51	0	1	1	10	4	.71	7	.254	.291	.361
2001 Shreveport	AA SF	122	479	142	27	6	11	214	76	60	42	0	122	7	8	4	38	11	.78	7	.296	.359	.447
Fresno	AAA SF	6	23	3	1	0	0	4	3	1	1	0	5	0	0	0	0	0	—	1	.130	.167	.174
7 Min. YEARS		682	2548	651	102	36	36	933	424	286	250	3	539	26	24	20	230	75	.75	36	.255	.326	.366

Ramon Castro

Bats: Right **Throws:** Right **Pos:** SS-91; 2B-15; 3B-6; PH-2; PR-1   **Ht:** 6'0" **Wt:** 195 **Born:** 10/23/79 **Age:** 22

Year Team	Lg Org	G	AB	H	2B	3B	HR	TB	R	RBI	TBB	IBB	SO	HBP	SH	SF	SB	CS	SB%	GDP	Avg	OBP	SLG
1997 Eugene	A- Atl	71	226	45	8	3	1	62	20	23	24	0	56	6	4	3	7	1	.88	5	.199	.290	.274
1998 Eugene	A- Atl	74	296	77	10	1	3	98	33	33	22	0	49	5	5	2	8	1	.89	1	.260	.320	.331
1999 Macon	A Atl	105	350	91	12	4	3	120	32	33	24	0	55	2	7	2	13	5	.72	4	.260	.310	.343
2000 Myrtle Bch	A+ Atl	108	385	97	20	3	5	138	52	44	44	0	76	12	3	1	13	5	.72	4	.252	.346	.358
2001 Greenville	AA Atl	76	261	80	19	5	6	127	35	31	25	0	56	9	7	3	5	8	.38	5	.307	.383	.487
Richmond	AAA Atl	36	135	30	8	2	1	45	14	15	7	0	30	1	3	0	1	2	.33	5	.222	.266	.333
5 Min. YEARS		470	1653	420	77	18	19	590	186	179	146	0	322	35	29	11	47	22	.68	24	.254	.326	.357

Mike Cather

Pitches: Right **Bats:** Right **Pos:** RP-15   **Ht:** 6'2" **Wt:** 205 **Born:** 12/17/70 **Age:** 31

Year Team	Lg Org	G	GS	CG	GF	IP	BFP	H	R	ER	HR	SH	SF	HB	TBB	IBB	SO	WP	Bk	W	L	Pct.	ShO	Sv	ERA
1993 Rangers	R Tex	25	0	0	17	30.2	124	20	7	6	0	0	0	3	9	0	30	2	1	1	1	.500	0	4	1.76
1994 Charlotte	A+ Tex	44	0	0	37	60.1	270	56	33	26	2	3	2	3	40	3	53	1	0	8	6	.571	0	6	3.88
1995 Tulsa	AA Tex	18	0	0	12	21.2	90	20	11	8	0	4	1	1	7	5	15	0	0	0	2	.000	0	0	3.32
Winnipeg	IND —	27	0	0	24	31	123	18	6	5	1	2	0	0	12	3	35	2	0	4	2	.667	0	8	1.45
1996 Greenville	AA Atl	53	0	0	18	87.2	384	89	42	36	2	6	2	8	29	5	61	2	1	3	4	.429	0	5	3.70
1997 Greenville	AA Atl	22	0	0	2	37.1	153	37	18	18	2	1	2	6	7	1	29	0	0	5	2	.714	0	1	4.34
Richmond	AAA Atl	13	0	0	10	26	102	17	6	5	1	2	0	1	9	1	22	0	0	0	0	—	0	3	1.73
1998 Richmond	AAA Atl	11	0	0	2	15.1	72	22	12	10	1	2	1	0	6	0	10	2	0	0	1	.000	0	0	5.87
1999 Richmond	AAA Atl	45	0	0	20	67.2	308	71	57	51	4	8	5	1	34	2	60	5	3	2	7	.222	0	1	6.78
2000 Calgary	AAA Fla	43	0	0	28	63.1	280	66	34	28	6	4	3	3	27	2	62	0	0	4	5	.444	0	8	3.98
2001 Memphis	AAA StL	15	0	0	4	21.2	102	27	14	14	3	0	1	1	9	1	21	0	0	1	1	.500	0	0	5.82
1997 Atlanta	NL	35	0	0	10	37.2	155	23	12	10	1	2	0	2	19	4	29	0	0	2	4	.333	0	0	2.39
1998 Atlanta	NL	36	0	0	11	41.1	173	39	21	18	7	4	2	2	12	1	33	0	0	2	2	.500	0	0	3.92
1999 Atlanta	NL	4	0	0	0	2.2	13	5	3	3	2	0	0	0	1	0	1	0	0	0	0	1.000	0	0	10.13
9 Min. YEARS		316	0	0	174	462.2	2008	443	240	207	22	32	16	27	189	23	398	14	5	28	31	.475	0	36	4.03
3 Maj. YEARS		75	0	0	21	81.2	341	67	36	31	10	6	2	4	32	5	62	0	0	5	6	.455	0	0	3.42

Blas Cedeno

Pitches: Right **Bats:** Right **Pos:** RP-42   **Ht:** 6'0" **Wt:** 165 **Born:** 11/15/72 **Age:** 29

Year Team	Lg Org	G	GS	CG	GF	IP	BFP	H	R	ER	HR	SH	SF	HB	TBB	IBB	SO	WP	Bk	W	L	Pct.	ShO	Sv	ERA
1991 Bristol	R+ Det	14	2	0	6	45	202	47	36	19	7	0	3	2	18	1	37	3	4	1	4	.200	0	0	3.80
1992 Bristol	R+ Det	13	13	3	0	80.2	335	64	21	18	2	3	1	5	41	0	77	6	0	8	2	.800	2	0	2.01
Fayettevlle	A Det	2	1	1	1	9	32	3	3	3	0	0	0	0	4	0	12	0	0	1	0	1.000	0	1	3.00
1993 Fayettevlle	A Det	28	22	1	3	148.2	621	145	64	52	11	5	3	11	55	0	103	6	0	6	6	.500	1	0	3.15
1994 Lakeland	A+ Det	5	0	0	3	14	52	9	3	2	1	1	1	0	4	0	16	1	0	1	0	1.000	0	1	1.29
Trenton	AA Det	34	0	0	18	52.1	228	50	18	15	5	4	0	2	27	2	40	4	0	1	3	.250	0	3	2.58
1995 Jacksnville	AA Det	48	5	0	13	80.2	329	71	34	31	7	1	1	1	36	1	53	2	1	3	2	.600	0	4	3.46
1996 Lakeland	A+ Det	10	0	0	5	16.1	72	17	10	10	3	0	0	1	7	0	11	2	0	1	1	.500	0	0	5.51
Jacksnville	AA Det	26	2	0	8	46.2	219	63	34	28	7	2	3	3	26	0	30	3	0	0	0	—	0	0	5.40
1997 Rockford	A ChC	22	0	0	13	40.1	168	36	19	13	3	1	1	1	14	2	25	0	0	3	3	.500	0	0	2.90
1998 New Jersey	IND —	12	7	0	2	48.1	224	62	34	24	3	0	0	3	14	1	37	7	0	1	6	.143	0	0	4.47
1999 Clearwater	A+ Phi	34	0	0	8	57.2	243	63	33	27	5	2	4	1	17	1	42	4	0	4	4	.500	0	1	4.21
Reading	AA Phi	19	0	0	5	31.2	131	30	16	15	5	2	1	0	12	3	18	0	0	2	2	.500	0	0	4.26
2000 Reading	AA Phi	36	0	0	20	54.2	228	47	31	29	4	0	1	1	24	1	34	3	0	3	1	.750	0	7	4.77
2001 Reading	AA Phi	7	0	0	4	12	50	12	4	3	1	0	0	0	3	0	10	0	0	1	0	1.000	0	0	2.25
Scranton-WB	AAA Phi	35	0	0	17	58.2	254	56	29	29	9	2	3	4	23	3	52	2	1	3	4	.429	0	1	4.45
11 Min. YEARS		345	52	5	126	796.2	3388	775	389	318	73	23	22	35	325	15	597	43	6	38	39	.494	3	15	3.59

Tony Cento

Pitches: Left **Bats:** Left **Pos:** RP-47; SP-1   **Ht:** 5'11" **Wt:** 170 **Born:** 8/16/77 **Age:** 24

Year Team	Lg Org	G	GS	CG	GF	IP	BFP	H	R	ER	HR	SH	SF	HB	TBB	IBB	SO	WP	Bk	W	L	Pct.	ShO	Sv	ERA
1999 Elizabethtn	R+ Min	18	0	0	14	19.1	90	22	6	4	1	1	0	1	6	1	35	1	0	1	2	.333	0	5	1.86
Quad City	A Min	11	0	0	3	8.1	34	6	2	1	0	0	1	1	3	1	11	1	0	1	0	1.000	0	0	1.08
2000 Quad City	A Min	52	1	0	14	82.1	335	56	31	18	3	4	3	2	34	9	72	1	2	6	7	.462	0	5	1.97
2001 New Britain	AA Min	9	0	0	6	10	50	19	14	10	1	0	0	0	3	0	8	0	0	0	1	.000	0	0	9.00
Fort Myers	A+ Min	39	1	0	7	57.2	238	49	27	22	3	1	4	3	21	0	47	2	0	3	2	.600	0	0	3.43
3 Min. YEARS		129	2	0	44	177.2	747	152	76	55	8	6	8	7	67	11	173	5	2	11	12	.478	0	10	2.79

Matt Cepicky

Bats: Left   Throws: Right   Pos: OF-104; DH-18; PH-1   Ht: 6'2"   Wt: 215   Born: 11/10/77   Age: 24

Year Team	Lg Org	G	AB	H	2B	3B	HR	TB	R	RBI	TBB	IBB	SO	HBP	SH	SF	SB	CS	SB%	GDP	Avg	OBP	SLG
1999 Vermont	A- Mon	74	323	99	15	5	12	160	50	53	20	1	49	1	0	0	10	9	.53	6	.307	.349	.495
2000 Jupiter	A+ Mon	131	536	160	32	7	5	221	61	88	24	4	64	2	1	5	32	13	.71	9	.299	.328	.412
2001 Harrisburg	AA Mon	122	459	121	23	8	19	217	59	77	21	2	97	2	2	4	5	12	.29	6	.264	.296	.473
3 Min. YEARS		327	1318	380	70	20	36	598	170	218	65	7	210	5	3	9	47	34	.58	21	.288	.322	.454

Jaime Cerda

Pitches: Left   Bats: Left   Pos: RP-43   Ht: 6'0"   Wt: 175   Born: 10/26/78   Age: 23

Year Team	Lg Org	G	GS	CG	GF	IP	BFP	H	R	ER	HR	SH	SF	HB	TBB	IBB	SO	WP	Bk	W	L	Pct.	ShO	Sv	ERA
2000 Pittsfield	A- NYM	20	1	0	6	47	176	33	6	3	0	2	0	0	6	1	51	2	0	4	1	.800	0	5	0.57
2001 St. Lucie	A+ NYM	28	0	0	15	55.2	213	40	8	6	3	3	1	1	12	0	56	0	0	2	1	.667	0	6	0.97
Binghamton	AA NYM	12	0	0	9	20.1	82	17	7	7	1	1	1	1	6	0	22	2	0	1	0	1.000	0	3	3.10
Norfolk	AAA NYM	3	0	0	1	4.2	18	2	2	2	0	0	0	0	2	0	4	1	0	0	0	—	0	0	3.86
2 Min. YEARS		63	1	0	31	127.2	489	92	23	18	4	6	2	2	26	1	133	5	0	7	2	.778	0	14	1.27

Juan Cerros

Pitches: Right   Bats: Right   Pos: RP-50; SP-1   Ht: 6'1"   Wt: 203   Born: 9/25/76   Age: 25

Year Team	Lg Org	G	GS	CG	GF	IP	BFP	H	R	ER	HR	SH	SF	HB	TBB	IBB	SO	WP	Bk	W	L	Pct.	ShO	Sv	ERA
1999 St. Lucie	A+ NYM	5	0	0	2	7.2	32	5	1	0	0	0	0	1	4	0	6	0	1	2	0	1.000	0	0	0.00
2000 Binghamton	AA NYM	50	2	0	23	74.2	327	71	33	29	8	0	3	4	30	1	52	6	0	10	4	.714	0	3	3.50
2001 Binghamton	AA NYM	13	0	0	7	18.1	86	24	10	10	2	0	0	0	7	0	14	3	0	1	2	.333	0	0	4.91
Norfolk	AAA NYM	38	1	0	8	57	257	65	33	25	5	1	6	4	22	3	32	5	0	1	3	.250	0	1	3.95
3 Min. YEARS		106	3	0	40	157.2	702	165	77	64	15	1	9	9	63	4	104	14	1	14	9	.609	0	4	3.65

Chris Cervantes

Pitches: Left   Bats: Left   Pos: RP-38; SP-7   Ht: 6'1"   Wt: 165   Born: 2/4/79   Age: 23

Year Team	Lg Org	G	GS	CG	GF	IP	BFP	H	R	ER	HR	SH	SF	HB	TBB	IBB	SO	WP	Bk	W	L	Pct.	ShO	Sv	ERA
1998 South Bend	A Ari	21	0	0	10	33.2	137	29	8	5	0	3	2	1	6	1	37	4	0	2	2	.500	0	2	1.34
1999 South Bend	A Ari	38	10	0	14	115	490	109	49	40	9	5	1	4	34	0	89	10	1	8	5	.615	0	3	3.13
High Desert	A+ Ari	1	0	0	0	1	7	5	6	6	1	0	0	0	1	0	1	0	0	0	0	—	0	0	162.00
2000 South Bend	A Ari	11	11	0	0	59.1	247	62	29	20	3	0	3	2	11	0	54	2	0	5	4	.556	0	0	3.03
El Paso	AA Ari	16	15	0	0	95	411	108	50	46	13	5	1	7	21	0	72	3	2	7	5	.583	0	0	4.36
2001 El Paso	AA Ari	45	7	0	9	96	436	110	68	58	14	3	4	7	36	2	87	10	0	3	7	.300	0	1	5.44
4 Min. YEARS		132	43	0	33	399.1	1728	423	210	175	40	16	11	21	109	3	340	29	3	25	23	.521	0	6	3.94

Mike Cervenak

Bats: Right   Throws: Right   Pos: 3B-40; 1B-33; 2B-27; DH-20; SS-18; PH-10   Ht: 6'0"   Wt: 187   Born: 8/17/76   Age: 25

Year Team	Lg Org	G	AB	H	2B	3B	HR	TB	R	RBI	TBB	IBB	SO	HBP	SH	SF	SB	CS	SB%	GDP	Avg	OBP	SLG
1999 Chillicothe	IND —	68	301	92	17	4	3	126	59	46	13	0	21	3	2	2	6	2	.75	4	.306	.339	.419
2000 Chillicothe	IND —	40	171	61	9	0	12	106	33	43	14	2	13	3	1	0	2	1	.67	5	.357	.415	.620
Greensboro	A NYY	38	155	51	4	5	3	74	19	20	7	0	21	4	3	1	3	4	.43	1	.329	.371	.477
2001 Norwich	AA NYY	128	463	127	37	1	11	199	63	60	44	1	75	9	2	2	2	4	.33	8	.274	.347	.430
3 Min. YEARS		274	1090	331	67	10	29	505	174	169	78	3	130	19	8	5	13	11	.54	18	.304	.359	.463

Dionys Cesar

Bats: Both   Throws: Right   Pos: SS-80; 3B-10; 2B-6; PH-3; OF-1; PR-1   Ht: 5'10"   Wt: 155   Born: 9/27/76   Age: 25

Year Team	Lg Org	G	AB	H	2B	3B	HR	TB	R	RBI	TBB	IBB	SO	HBP	SH	SF	SB	CS	SB%	GDP	Avg	OBP	SLG
1995 Athletics	R Oak	48	171	55	11	4	2	80	41	21	23	0	29	2	3	2	17	10	.63	0	.322	.404	.468
1996 Modesto	A+ Oak	22	60	12	2	0	0	14	5	4	7	0	19	0	6	0	1	3	.25	0	.200	.284	.233
Sou Oregon	A- Oak	52	203	55	7	4	1	73	37	12	19	0	46	4	7	1	18	6	.75	3	.271	.344	.360
1997 Visalia	A+ Oak	97	285	68	16	2	1	91	60	11	43	1	79	1	6	0	10	12	.45	5	.239	.340	.319
1998 Visalia	A+ Oak	130	501	141	34	8	7	212	87	54	56	2	98	1	6	3	31	12	.72	6	.281	.353	.423
1999 Midland	AA Oak	35	105	20	4	3	3	39	15	15	18	0	28	1	1	1	1	4	.20	0	.190	.312	.371
Visalia	A+ Oak	77	320	103	21	5	7	155	59	62	41	3	51	3	2	5	21	11	.66	8	.322	.398	.484
2000 Visalia	A+ Oak	5	22	5	2	0	2	13	3	6	1	0	4	0	0	1	0	0	—	2	.227	.250	.591
Midland	AA Oak	111	433	120	21	2	4	157	62	37	38	0	65	0	4	3	13	10	.57	7	.277	.333	.363
2001 Huntsville	AA Mil	60	227	64	12	1	8	102	38	31	25	0	50	0	4	2	4	3	.57	6	.282	.350	.449
Indianapolis	AAA Mil	35	129	40	11	1	1	56	12	17	10	1	23	3	1	2	1	0	1.00	3	.310	.368	.434
7 Min. YEARS		672	2456	683	141	30	36	992	419	270	281	7	492	15	40	20	117	71	.62	40	.278	.353	.404

Gustavo Chacin

Pitches: Left   Bats: Left   Pos: SP-23; RP-2   Ht: 5'11"   Wt: 185   Born: 12/4/80   Age: 21

Year Team	Lg Org	G	GS	CG	GF	IP	BFP	H	R	ER	HR	SH	SF	HB	TBB	IBB	SO	WP	Bk	W	L	Pct.	ShO	Sv	ERA
1999 Medcine Hat	R+ Tor	15	9	0	2	64	280	68	33	22	6	4	4	7	23	0	50	4	3	4	3	.571	0	1	3.09
2000 Tennessee	AA Tor	2	2	0	0	5	31	10	7	7	1	0	0	0	6	0	5	0	1	0	2	.000	0	0	12.60
Dunedin	A+ Tor	25	21	0	1	127.2	584	138	69	57	14	1	2	3	64	0	77	9	0	9	5	.643	0	0	4.02
2001 Tennessee	AA Tor	25	23	1	0	140.1	588	138	66	62	17	2	3	7	39	0	86	5	0	11	8	.579	1	0	3.98
3 Min. YEARS		67	55	1	3	337	1483	354	175	148	38	7	9	18	132	0	218	18	4	24	18	.571	1	1	3.95

Jim Chamblee

Bats: Right **Throws:** Right **Pos:** 2B-91; OF-14; PH-4; 3B-3; 1B-3; DH-2; SS-1; PR-1   **Ht:** 6'4" **Wt:** 176 **Born:** 5/6/75 **Age:** 27

		BATTING															BASERUNNING				PERCENTAGES		
Year Team	Lg Org	G	AB	H	2B	3B	HR	TB	R	RBI	TBB	IBB	SO	HBP	SH	SF	SB	CS	SB%	GDP	Avg	OBP	SLG
1995 Utica	A- Bos	62	200	51	9	1	2	68	36	16	23	0	45	6	1	1	9	7	.56	5	.255	.348	.340
1996 Michigan	A Bos	100	303	66	15	2	1	88	31	39	16	0	75	7	4	4	2	2	.50	1	.218	.270	.290
1997 Michigan	A Bos	133	487	146	29	5	22	251	72	73	53	3	107	17	0	5	18	4	.82	8	.300	.384	.515
1998 Trenton	AA Bos	136	489	118	33	3	17	208	71	65	62	1	144	16	6	4	9	5	.64	2	.241	.343	.425
1999 Pawtucket	AAA Bos	127	464	127	21	3	24	226	84	88	43	2	126	13	4	3	5	3	.63	4	.274	.350	.487
2000 Pawtucket	AAA Bos	127	407	105	26	4	17	190	72	56	50	1	129	7	2	2	8	3	.73	4	.258	.348	.467
2001 Pawtucket	AAA Bos	103	378	91	22	0	10	143	40	32	31	4	104	6	5	1	8	5	.62	4	.241	.308	.378
New Orleans	AAA Hou	11	35	9	2	0	1	14	3	4	4	0	13	1	1	0	0	0	—	1	.257	.350	.400
7 Min. YEARS		799	2763	713	157	18	94	1188	449	373	282	11	743	73	23	20	59	29	.67	29	.258	.340	.430

Mike Chaney

Pitches: Left **Bats:** Both **Pos:** RP-29; SP-3   **Ht:** 6'3" **Wt:** 200 **Born:** 10/3/74 **Age:** 27

		HOW MUCH HE PITCHED						WHAT HE GAVE UP										THE RESULTS					
Year Team	Lg Org	G	GS	CG	GF	IP	BFP	H	R	ER	HR	SH	SF	HB	TBB	IBB	SO	WP	Bk	W	L	Pct.	ShO	Sv	ERA
1996 Erie	A- Pit	10	5	0	2	29	125	27	20	17	1	2	3	1	14	1	21	1	3	1	1	.500	0	0	5.28
1997 Augusta	A Pit	31	14	0	2	125.1	525	129	58	49	8	4	4	5	28	1	95	7	0	8	7	.533	0	0	3.52
2000 Evansville	IND —	4	4	1	0	27	103	17	5	3	0	3	0	1	5	0	24	3	0	2	0	1.000	0	0	1.00
2001 Lynchburg	A+ Pit	28	3	0	9	68	289	69	31	28	5	2	0	3	22	0	44	2	2	3	3	.500	0	2	3.71
Altoona	AA Pit	4	0	0	1	9.1	47	18	7	7	1	0	1	1	2	1	2	2	0	0	0	—	0	0	6.75
4 Min. YEARS		77	26	1	14	258.2	1089	260	121	104	15	11	8	11	71	3	186	15	5	14	11	.560	0	2	3.62

Carlos Chantres

Pitches: Right **Bats:** Right **Pos:** SP-28   **Ht:** 6'3" **Wt:** 175 **Born:** 4/1/76 **Age:** 26

		HOW MUCH HE PITCHED						WHAT HE GAVE UP										THE RESULTS					
Year Team	Lg Org	G	GS	CG	GF	IP	BFP	H	R	ER	HR	SH	SF	HB	TBB	IBB	SO	WP	Bk	W	L	Pct.	ShO	Sv	ERA
1994 White Sox	R CWS	16	2	0	3	35	150	28	21	14	2	1	0	3	13	0	29	6	1	0	1	.000	0	1	3.60
1995 White Sox	R CWS	11	11	2	0	61.2	257	65	32	22	2	1	1	1	14	0	47	1	2	2	3	.400	0	0	3.21
1996 Hickory	A CWS	18	18	0	0	119.2	497	108	63	50	10	6	3	1	38	0	93	8	5	6	7	.462	0	0	3.76
South Bend	A CWS	10	9	1	0	65	274	61	31	26	3	1	2	2	19	0	41	3	1	4	5	.444	0	0	3.60
1997 Winston-Sal	A+ CWS	26	26	2	0	164.2	712	152	94	86	21	6	5	4	71	1	158	10	2	9	11	.450	0	0	4.70
1998 Birmingham	AA CWS	20	5	0	7	52.2	251	58	35	34	5	6	6	0	42	1	49	3	0	2	4	.333	0	1	5.81
Winston-Sal	A+ CWS	13	13	1	0	88.1	370	71	43	37	10	3	6	8	41	0	86	5	0	5	5	.500	0	0	3.77
1999 Birmingham	AA CWS	28	21	1	5	141.1	596	122	64	55	13	1	7	7	61	0	105	9	1	6	8	.429	0	2	3.50
2000 Charlotte	AAA CWS	29	22	0	2	142.2	601	136	59	56	12	4	4	8	54	2	85	8	2	10	4	.714	0	0	3.53
2001 Indianapols	AAA Mil	28	28	0	0	167.1	760	176	93	82	15	8	8	8	93	1	87	6	1	7	11	.389	0	0	4.41
8 Min. YEARS		199	155	7	17	1038.1	4468	977	535	462	93	37	42	42	446	5	780	59	15	51	59	.464	0	4	4.00

Jake Chapman

Pitches: Left **Bats:** Right **Pos:** RP-53   **Ht:** 6'1" **Wt:** 190 **Born:** 1/11/74 **Age:** 28

		HOW MUCH HE PITCHED						WHAT HE GAVE UP										THE RESULTS					
Year Team	Lg Org	G	GS	CG	GF	IP	BFP	H	R	ER	HR	SH	SF	HB	TBB	IBB	SO	WP	Bk	W	L	Pct.	ShO	Sv	ERA
1996 Spokane	A- KC	19	7	0	3	68.1	274	44	19	18	2	2	2	6	20	1	71	3	1	7	1	.875	0	1	2.37
1997 Wilmington	A+ KC	27	26	0	0	154.1	673	163	83	66	7	3	5	5	59	5	122	4	0	8	9	.471	0	0	3.85
1998 Wilmington	A+ KC	27	26	1	0	162.1	665	158	72	59	4	6	3	6	37	1	113	5	2	13	9	.591	1	0	3.27
1999 Wichita	AA KC	52	0	0	13	69.2	316	87	38	34	5	0	3	3	29	6	53	4	0	3	0	1.000	0	3	4.39
2000 Ottawa	AAA Mon	7	1	0	0	8.2	40	9	2	2	0	0	0	0	5	0	8	0	0	1	0	1.000	0	0	2.08
Harrisburg	AA Mon	49	0	0	11	66.1	295	73	34	28	4	3	2	1	26	1	53	1	0	4	5	.444	0	1	3.80
2001 Harrisburg	AA Mon	53	0	0	10	67.2	286	55	26	18	5	3	1	3	27	4	69	1	0	7	3	.700	0	2	2.39
6 Min. YEARS		234	60	1	37	597.1	2549	589	274	225	25	22	13	24	203	18	489	18	3	43	27	.614	1	7	3.39

Scott Chapman

Bats: Right **Throws:** Right **Pos:** OF-23; DH-12; C-2; PH-2   **Ht:** 6'2" **Wt:** 200 **Born:** 1/30/78 **Age:** 24

		BATTING															BASERUNNING				PERCENTAGES		
Year Team	Lg Org	G	AB	H	2B	3B	HR	TB	R	RBI	TBB	IBB	SO	HBP	SH	SF	SB	CS	SB%	GDP	Avg	OBP	SLG
1995 Astros	R Hou	14	28	8	1	0	0	9	3	1	4	0	4	0	1	0	1	1	.50	2	.286	.375	.321
1996 Astros	R Hou	45	142	37	8	1	2	53	17	19	18	1	25	0	1	2	3	1	.75	3	.261	.340	.373
1997 Kissimmee	A+ Hou	2	7	2	0	0	0	2	1	0	0	0	3	0	0	0	0	0	—	0	.286	.286	.286
Auburn	A- Hou	53	205	67	11	0	6	96	32	39	6	0	23	0	0	1	1	2	.33	14	.327	.344	.468
1998 Quad City	A Hou	82	277	66	14	1	5	97	28	28	9	1	67	6	2	1	7	5	.58	11	.238	.276	.350
1999 Michigan	A Hou	64	226	61	17	1	11	113	37	36	14	0	32	7	0	1	1	2	.33	7	.270	.331	.500
2000 Kissimmee	A+ Hou	107	373	95	26	1	8	147	51	59	50	1	85	3	0	6	0	1	.00	9	.255	.343	.394
2001 Round Rock	AA Hou	3	10	3	1	0	0	4	2	1	0	0	3	0	0	0	0	0	—	1	.300	.300	.400
Daytona	A+ ChC	18	66	4	0	0	0	4	3	2	5	0	15	0	0	0	0	0	—	2	.061	.127	.061
Yuma	IND —	14	51	8	2	1	0	12	1	8	1	0	13	1	1	1	0	0	—	1	.157	.185	.235
7 Min. YEARS		402	1385	351	80	5	32	537	175	193	107	3	270	17	5	12	13	12	.52	50	.253	.312	.388

Travis Chapman

Bats: Right **Throws:** Right **Pos:** 3B-94; DH-9   **Ht:** 6'2" **Wt:** 185 **Born:** 6/5/78 **Age:** 24

		BATTING															BASERUNNING				PERCENTAGES		
Year Team	Lg Org	G	AB	H	2B	3B	HR	TB	R	RBI	TBB	IBB	SO	HBP	SH	SF	SB	CS	SB%	GDP	Avg	OBP	SLG
2000 Phillies	R Phi	9	32	6	3	1	0	11	3	5	4	0	4	2	0	1	0	1	.00	0	.188	.308	.344
Batavia	A- Phi	49	174	55	10	2	1	72	23	28	12	0	24	7	2	2	0	1	.00	1	.316	.379	.414
2001 Clearwater	A+ Phi	96	329	101	22	0	4	135	39	50	44	3	39	11	2	6	3	1	.75	12	.307	.400	.410
Reading	AA Phi	7	22	4	0	0	1	7	3	3	0	0	5	2	0	0	0	0	—	0	.182	.250	.318
2 Min. YEARS		161	557	166	35	3	6	225	68	86	60	3	72	22	4	9	3	3	.50	13	.298	.383	.404

Frank Charles

Bats: Right **Throws:** Right **Pos:** C-69; PH-2; 1B-1   **Ht:** 6'4" **Wt:** 210 **Born:** 2/23/69 **Age:** 33

Year Team	Lg Org	G	AB	H	2B	3B	HR	TB	R	RBI	TBB	IBB	SO	HBP	SH	SF	SB	CS	SB%	GDP	Avg	OBP	SLG
1991 Everett	A- SF	62	239	76	17	1	9	122	31	49	21	0	55	1	0	1	1	2	.33	5	.318	.374	.510
1992 Clinton	A SF	2	5	0	0	0	0	0	1	0	0	0	3	0	0	0	0	0	—	0	.000	.000	.000
San Jose	A+ SF	87	286	83	16	1	0	101	27	34	11	2	61	4	1	0	4	4	.50	12	.290	.326	.353
1993 St. Paul	IND —	58	216	59	13	0	2	78	27	37	11	0	33	3	5	1	5	3	.63	9	.273	.316	.361
1994 Charlotte	A+ Tex	79	254	67	17	1	2	92	23	33	16	1	52	3	5	2	2	3	.40	2	.264	.313	.362
1995 Tulsa	AA Tex	126	479	121	24	3	13	190	51	72	22	0	92	4	1	4	1	0	1.00	19	.253	.289	.397
1996 Okla City	AAA Tex	35	113	21	7	2	1	35	10	8	4	0	29	1	0	2	0	3	.00	3	.186	.217	.310
Tulsa	AA Tex	41	147	39	6	0	5	60	18	15	10	0	28	0	0	0	2	0	1.00	1	.265	.312	.408
1997 Tulsa	AA Tex	95	335	77	18	2	9	126	38	49	24	1	81	3	1	1	2	2	.50	9	.230	.287	.376
1998 Fresno	AAA SF	4	10	5	0	0	1	8	2	1	1	0	2	0	0	0	0	0	—	0	.500	.545	.800
Shreveport	AA SF	108	411	118	39	1	12	195	49	66	18	0	93	6	0	5	0	2	.00	10	.287	.323	.474
1999 Las Vegas	AAA SD	80	272	67	19	2	2	96	25	28	10	2	61	3	0	2	2	0	1.00	16	.246	.279	.353
2000 New Orleans	AAA Hou	84	284	74	10	3	5	105	29	37	21	1	62	3	2	3	1	3	.25	9	.261	.315	.370
2001 New Orleans	AAA Hou	3	3	1	0	0	0	1	0	0	0	0	0	1	0	0	0	0	—	0	.333	.500	.333
Rochester	AAA Bal	68	240	58	12	0	1	73	15	24	11	0	56	3	2	4	1	1	.50	6	.242	.279	.304
2000 Houston	NL	4	7	3	1	0	0	4	1	2	0	0	2	0	0	0	0	0	—	0	.429	.429	.571
11 Min. YEARS		932	3294	866	198	16	62	1282	346	453	180	7	708	35	17	25	21	23	.48	101	.263	.306	.389

Anthony Chavez

Pitches: Right **Bats:** Right **Pos:** RP-43; SP-8   **Ht:** 5'11" **Wt:** 190 **Born:** 10/22/70 **Age:** 31

Year Team	Lg Org	G	GS	CG	GF	IP	BFP	H	R	ER	HR	SH	SF	HB	TBB	IBB	SO	WP	Bk	W	L	Pct.	ShO	Sv	ERA
1992 Boise	A- Ana	14	0	0	2	16	75	22	13	7	0	0	0	0	4	2	21	3	0	1	1	.500	0	0	3.94
1993 Cedar Rapds	A Ana	41	0	0	35	59.1	252	44	17	10	1	6	2	2	24	2	87	3	1	4	5	.444	0	16	1.52
Midland	AA Ana	5	0	0	3	8.2	41	11	5	4	1	0	1	0	4	1	9	3	0	0	0	—	0	1	4.15
1994 Lk Elsinore	A+ Ana	12	0	0	7	13.1	75	21	19	15	0	2	1	2	11	2	12	2	0	0	5	.000	0	1	10.13
Cedar Rapds	A Ana	39	1	0	34	50	227	48	33	24	0	3	2	2	28	4	52	7	0	4	3	.571	0	16	4.32
1995 Vancouver	AAA Ana	8	0	0	5	12	46	7	4	2	0	1	0	0	4	0	8	0	0	2	0	1.000	0	1	1.50
Midland	AA Ana	7	0	0	6	9	42	13	9	8	1	0	0	1	1	0	4	1	0	0	1	.000	0	2	8.00
Lk Elsinore	A+ Ana	33	0	0	14	44.2	206	51	28	21	2	2	3	4	19	2	49	5	0	4	2	.667	0	2	4.23
1996 Lk Elsinore	A+ Ana	10	0	0	8	13.2	53	8	4	3	0	0	0	3	3	0	16	0	0	3	0	1.000	0	4	1.98
Midland	AA Ana	31	0	0	16	72.2	322	81	40	34	4	6	7	2	24	2	55	3	1	2	4	.333	0	1	4.21
1997 Midland	AA Ana	33	1	0	15	47	200	53	23	22	1	3	2	3	15	1	35	4	0	1	2	.333	0	6	4.21
Vancouver	AAA Ana	28	0	0	26	28.1	111	21	8	8	2	0	2	1	6	0	22	3	0	4	1	.800	0	15	2.54
1998 Vancouver	AAA Ana	53	0	0	51	51.1	218	44	20	15	5	4	2	6	17	0	42	0	0	1	4	.200	0	22	2.63
1999 Vancouver	AAA Oak	54	0	0	36	69	315	67	42	30	8	8	3	3	37	5	72	2	0	4	6	.400	0	14	3.91
2001 Tucson	AAA Ari	51	8	1	9	86.2	406	109	59	44	5	7	2	6	37	2	76	4	0	7	6	.538	0	1	4.57
1997 Anaheim	AL	7	0	0	2	9.2	41	7	1	1	1	1	1	0	5	1	10	0	0	0	0	—	0	0	0.93
9 Min. YEARS		419	10	1	267	581.2	2589	600	324	247	30	42	26	35	234	23	560	40	2	37	40	.481	0	100	3.82

Raul Chavez

Bats: Right **Throws:** Right **Pos:** C-82; PH-4; 3B-1; 1B-1   **Ht:** 5'11" **Wt:** 210 **Born:** 3/18/73 **Age:** 29

Year Team	Lg Org	G	AB	H	2B	3B	HR	TB	R	RBI	TBB	IBB	SO	HBP	SH	SF	SB	CS	SB%	GDP	Avg	OBP	SLG
1990 Astros	R Hou	48	155	50	8	1	0	60	23	23	7	0	12	2	2	1	5	3	.63	7	.323	.358	.387
1991 Burlington	A Hou	114	420	108	17	0	3	134	54	41	25	1	64	10	3	4	1	4	.20	13	.257	.312	.319
1992 Asheville	A Hou	95	348	99	22	1	2	129	37	40	16	1	39	4	1	4	1	0	1.00	16	.284	.320	.371
1993 Osceola	A+ Hou	58	197	45	5	1	0	52	13	16	8	0	19	1	1	1	1	1	.50	12	.228	.261	.264
1994 Jackson	AA Hou	89	251	55	7	0	1	65	17	22	17	3	41	2	2	1	1	0	1.00	5	.219	.273	.259
1995 Jackson	AA Hou	58	188	54	8	0	4	74	16	25	8	1	17	3	4	2	0	4	.00	7	.287	.323	.394
Tucson	AAA Hou	32	103	27	5	0	0	32	14	10	8	0	13	2	1	1	0	1	.00	7	.262	.325	.311
1996 Ottawa	AAA Mon	60	198	49	10	0	2	65	15	24	11	0	31	1	4	0	0	2	.00	7	.247	.290	.328
1997 Ottawa	AAA Mon	92	310	76	17	0	4	105	31	46	18	1	42	4	3	3	1	3	.25	9	.245	.293	.339
1998 Ottawa	AAA Mon	11	31	7	0	0	0	7	2	1	5	0	5	0	1	0	0	0	—	1	.226	.333	.226
Tacoma	AAA Sea	76	233	52	6	0	4	70	27	34	22	1	41	4	2	2	1	2	.33	7	.223	.294	.300
1999 Tacoma	AAA Sea	102	354	95	20	1	3	126	39	40	28	1	63	6	0	2	1	3	.25	11	.268	.331	.356
2000 New Orleans	AAA Hou	99	303	74	13	0	2	93	31	36	34	5	44	4	4	4	3	0	1.00	12	.244	.325	.307
2001 New Orleans	AAA Hou	85	278	84	17	0	8	125	38	40	19	2	34	7	4	1	1	1	.50	9	.302	.361	.450
1996 Montreal	NL	4	5	1	0	0	0	1	1	0	1	0	1	0	0	0	1	0	1.00	1	.200	.333	.200
1997 Montreal	NL	13	26	7	0	0	0	7	0	2	0	0	5	0	0	1	1	0	1.00	0	.269	.259	.269
1998 Seattle	AL	1	1	0	0	0	0	0	0	0	0	0	0	0	0	0	0	0	—	0	.000	.000	.000
2000 Houston	NL	14	43	11	2	0	1	16	3	5	3	2	6	0	0	0	0	0	—	0	.256	.298	.372
12 Min. YEARS		1019	3369	875	155	4	33	1137	357	398	226	16	465	50	32	30	16	24	.40	118	.260	.313	.337
4 Maj. YEARS		32	75	19	2	0	1	24	4	7	4	2	12	0	0	2	2	0	1.00	6	.253	.284	.320

Chin-Feng Chen

Bats: Right **Throws:** Right **Pos:** OF-61; DH-61; PH-6   **Ht:** 6'1" **Wt:** 189 **Born:** 10/28/77 **Age:** 24

Year Team	Lg Org	G	AB	H	2B	3B	HR	TB	R	RBI	TBB	IBB	SO	HBP	SH	SF	SB	CS	SB%	GDP	Avg	OBP	SLG
1999 San Berndno	A+ LA	131	510	161	22	10	31	296	98	123	75	6	129	5	0	7	31	7	.82	5	.316	.404	.580
2000 San Antonio	AA LA	133	516	143	27	4	6	194	66	67	61	3	131	3	1	3	23	15	.61	7	.277	.355	.376
2001 Vero Beach	A+ LA	62	235	63	15	3	5	99	38	41	28	2	56	6	0	1	2	0	1.00	3	.268	.359	.421
Jacksnville	AA LA	66	224	70	16	2	17	141	47	50	41	4	65	2	1	1	5	4	.56	7	.313	.422	.629
3 Min. YEARS		392	1485	437	80	18	59	730	249	281	205	15	381	16	2	12	61	26	.70	24	.294	.383	.492

Virgil Chevalier

Bats: Right **Throws:** Right **Pos:** 1B-81; OF-29; DH-16; PH-3; C-1   **Ht:** 6'2" **Wt:** 240 **Born:** 10/31/73 **Age:** 28

Year Team	Lg Org	G	AB	H	2B	3B	HR	TB	R	RBI	TBB	IBB	SO	HBP	SH	SF	SB	CS	SB%	GDP	Avg	OBP	SLG
1995 Utica	A- Bos	64	250	77	12	2	7	114	34	46	11	0	35	3	0	3	15	6	.71	6	.308	.341	.456
Michigan	A Bos	2	6	4	1	0	0	5	2	0	1	0	0	0	0	0	1	0	1.00	0	.667	.714	.833
1996 Michigan	A Bos	126	483	120	31	3	8	181	61	62	33	1	69	1	1	5	11	4	.73	11	.248	.295	.375
1997 Sarasota	A+ Bos	94	289	60	13	1	6	93	31	37	19	0	43	3	2	3	8	7	.53	6	.208	.261	.322
1998 Sarasota	A+ Bos	81	327	107	22	4	8	161	59	59	27	3	59	1	1	6	13	4	.76	5	.327	.374	.492
Trenton	AA Bos	30	117	32	7	2	2	49	19	16	4	0	17	0	3	1	2	2	.50	2	.274	.295	.419
1999 Trenton	AA Bos	131	509	149	29	4	13	225	81	76	50	0	73	2	8	8	9	9	.50	11	.293	.353	.442
2000 Pawtucket	AAA Bos	8	24	3	0	0	0	3	1	0	1	0	0	0	0	0	0	0	—	1	.125	.160	.125
Trenton	AA Bos	89	346	107	25	1	7	155	58	67	34	1	35	2	0	8	3	2	.60	11	.309	.367	.448
2001 Trenton	AA Bos	121	456	119	25	1	16	194	59	67	43	2	58	3	0	7	3	3	.50	12	.261	.324	.425
Pawtucket	AAA Bos	7	27	7	2	0	0	9	2	4	0	0	3	0	0	0	0	0	—	0	.259	.259	.333
7 Min. YEARS		753	2834	785	167	18	67	1189	407	434	223	7	392	15	15	41	65	37	.64	65	.277	.329	.420

Paul Chiaffredo

Bats: Right **Throws:** Right **Pos:** C-39; DH-28; 1B-3; PH-2   **Ht:** 6'2" **Wt:** 206 **Born:** 5/30/76 **Age:** 26

Year Team	Lg Org	G	AB	H	2B	3B	HR	TB	R	RBI	TBB	IBB	SO	HBP	SH	SF	SB	CS	SB%	GDP	Avg	OBP	SLG
1997 St.Cathrnes	A- Tor	48	163	39	8	1	2	55	20	15	9	0	42	9	1	1	5	2	.71	1	.239	.313	.337
1998 Dunedin	A+ Tor	89	290	68	19	0	4	99	34	41	16	0	68	6	6	3	1	3	.25	8	.234	.286	.341
1999 Knoxville	AA Tor	11	39	3	1	0	1	7	3	3	0	0	10	2	2	0	0	0	—	2	.077	.122	.179
Dunedin	A+ Tor	88	261	66	22	2	3	101	39	21	17	0	44	12	4	4	1	4	.20	12	.253	.323	.387
2000 Hagerstown	A Tor	13	45	16	6	0	1	25	9	5	9	0	6	3	0	0	0	0	—	0	.356	.491	.556
Tennessee	AA Tor	18	63	7	1	0	0	8	6	2	5	0	16	1	0	0	0	1	.00	0	.111	.188	.127
Dunedin	A+ Tor	11	38	11	1	0	2	18	7	6	5	0	9	1	0	0	0	0	—	0	.289	.386	.474
2001 Tennessee	AA Tor	42	132	33	7	1	1	45	11	16	22	2	33	2	1	1	2	2	.50	1	.250	.363	.341
Dunedin	A+ Tor	28	94	20	6	1	3	37	13	20	5	0	26	5	0	2	0	0	—	2	.213	.283	.394
5 Min. YEARS		348	1125	263	71	5	17	395	142	129	88	2	254	41	14	11	9	12	.43	26	.234	.310	.351

Giuseppe Chiaramonte

Bats: Right **Throws:** Right **Pos:** DH-22; C-15; PH-13   **Ht:** 6'0" **Wt:** 200 **Born:** 2/19/76 **Age:** 26

Year Team	Lg Org	G	AB	H	2B	3B	HR	TB	R	RBI	TBB	IBB	SO	HBP	SH	SF	SB	CS	SB%	GDP	Avg	OBP	SLG
1997 San Jose	A+ SF	64	223	51	11	1	12	100	29	44	25	1	58	4	0	3	0	0	—	7	.229	.314	.448
1998 San Jose	A+ SF	129	502	137	33	3	22	242	87	87	47	4	139	4	0	12	5	2	.71	7	.273	.333	.482
1999 Shreveport	AA SF	114	400	98	20	2	19	179	54	74	40	1	88	6	0	5	4	2	.67	5	.245	.319	.448
2000 Fresno	AAA SF	122	443	113	30	6	24	227	70	79	47	1	81	3	1	3	2	1	.67	7	.255	.329	.512
2001 Fresno	AAA SF	37	100	21	6	0	2	33	11	12	4	0	19	4	0	1	0	1	.00	2	.210	.266	.330
Shreveport	AA SF	13	44	9	2	0	0	11	3	3	4	0	6	0	0	1	0	1	.00	2	.205	.265	.250
5 Min. YEARS		479	1712	429	102	12	79	792	254	299	167	7	391	21	1	25	11	7	.61	30	.251	.321	.463

Ron Chiavacci

Pitches: Right **Bats:** Right **Pos:** SP-25   **Ht:** 6'2" **Wt:** 220 **Born:** 9/5/77 **Age:** 24

Year Team	Lg Org	G	GS	CG	GF	IP	BFP	H	R	ER	HR	SH	SF	HB	TBB	IBB	SO	WP	Bk	W	L	Pct.	ShO	Sv	ERA
1998 Expos	R Mon	13	6	0	0	55	218	43	17	13	1	3	0	2	13	0	42	3	2	6	3	.667	0	0	2.13
Jupiter	A+ Mon	4	0	0	1	7.2	29	5	2	2	0	2	0	2	2	0	5	0	0	0	1	.000	0	1	2.35
1999 Cape Fear	A Mon	20	8	0	6	62.2	295	60	39	25	5	3	3	6	34	0	67	1	0	5	3	.625	0	1	3.59
Jupiter	A+ Mon	8	8	0	0	48.1	198	36	15	12	5	0	0	5	17	0	32	3	0	4	4	.500	0	0	2.23
2000 Jupiter	A+ Mon	28	26	1	2	158	674	145	80	64	12	4	7	7	59	0	131	7	0	11	11	.500	0	0	3.65
2001 Harrisburg	AA Mon	25	25	2	0	147.1	648	137	77	65	12	7	5	7	76	2	161	9	1	3	11	.214	1	0	3.97
4 Min. YEARS		98	73	3	9	479	2062	426	230	181	35	19	15	29	201	2	438	23	3	29	33	.468	1	2	3.40

Jason Childers

Pitches: Right **Bats:** Right **Pos:** RP-38; SP-2   **Ht:** 6'0" **Wt:** 165 **Born:** 1/13/75 **Age:** 27

Year Team	Lg Org	G	GS	CG	GF	IP	BFP	H	R	ER	HR	SH	SF	HB	TBB	IBB	SO	WP	Bk	W	L	Pct.	ShO	Sv	ERA
1997 Helena	R+ Mil	10	0	0	6	16.1	69	14	9	6	2	2	0	0	7	0	25	0	0	1	1	.500	0	2	3.31
1998 Beloit	A Mil	34	14	1	4	117	477	104	48	25	8	6	2	1	22	2	110	7	2	8	6	.571	0	0	1.92
1999 Ogden	R+ Mil	3	3	0	0	13	50	10	4	2	1	0	0	0	3	0	14	1	0	0	0	—	0	0	1.38
Stockton	A+ Mil	12	12	1	0	73.1	314	78	39	29	12	2	2	3	11	0	73	3	1	2	8	.200	0	0	3.56
2000 Mudville	A Mil	28	28	0	0	157.1	646	140	71	61	12	3	3	0	54	0	177	6	0	12	10	.545	0	0	3.49
2001 Huntsville	AA Mil	40	2	0	10	87.2	364	76	32	28	7	2	2	2	30	3	85	2	0	7	6	.538	0	2	2.87
5 Min. YEARS		127	59	2	20	464.2	1920	422	203	151	42	15	9	7	127	5	484	19	3	30	31	.492	0	4	2.92

Matt Childers

Pitches: Right **Bats:** Right **Pos:** SP-27   **Ht:** 6'5" **Wt:** 195 **Born:** 12/3/78 **Age:** 23

Year Team	Lg Org	G	GS	CG	GF	IP	BFP	H	R	ER	HR	SH	SF	HB	TBB	IBB	SO	WP	Bk	W	L	Pct.	ShO	Sv	ERA
1997 Helena	R+ Mil	14	10	0	1	61	285	81	44	42	5	2	4	0	24	0	19	1	0	1	4	.200	0	1	6.20
1998 Helena	R+ Mil	2	2	1	0	14	53	9	1	1	0	0	0	0	4	1	4	0	0	1	0	1.000	1	0	0.64
Beloit	A Mil	14	12	3	0	67	303	89	55	38	5	3	2	4	20	0	49	2	0	3	7	.300	0	0	5.10
1999 Beloit	A Mil	20	19	0	0	100	448	129	72	66	9	1	5	5	30	1	52	0	0	3	10	.231	0	0	5.94
2000 Beloit	A Mil	12	12	1	0	73	300	64	33	22	4	0	0	4	17	0	47	2	1	8	2	.800	1	0	2.71
Mudville	A Mil	15	15	0	0	85.1	388	103	59	45	10	2	2	3	32	0	43	3	2	3	9	.250	0	0	4.75
2001 High Desert	A+ Mil	20	20	0	0	117.1	529	155	95	84	19	3	7	6	29	0	76	5	0	6	11	.353	0	0	6.44
Huntsville	AA Mil	7	7	0	0	39.1	172	41	19	15	3	1	1	5	12	0	21	3	0	2	2	.500	0	0	3.43
5 Min. YEARS		104	97	5	1	557	2478	671	383	313	55	12	21	24	168	2	311	16	5	27	45	.375	2	1	5.06

Jin Ho Cho

Pitches: Right **Bats:** Right **Pos:** RP-21; SP-16   **Ht:** 6'3" **Wt:** 220 **Born:** 8/16/75 **Age:** 26

		HOW MUCH HE PITCHED						WHAT HE GAVE UP										THE RESULTS					
Year Team	Lg Org	G	GS	CG	GF	IP	BFP	H	R	ER	HR	SH	SF	HB	TBB	IBB	SO	WP	Bk	W	L	Pct.	ShO	Sv	ERA
1998 Sarasota	A+ Bos	5	5	0	0	32	132	33	14	11	1	0	4	0	5	0	30	2	0	3	1	.750	0	0	3.09
Trenton	AA Bos	13	13	1	0	74	299	59	21	18	4	3	4	3	19	2	62	0	0	5	2	.714	1	0	2.19
1999 Pawtucket	AAA Bos	17	17	4	0	109.2	447	99	46	42	12	2	3	4	29	1	80	1	0	9	3	.750	0	0	3.45
2000 Sarasota	A+ Bos	3	3	0	0	15	60	13	5	4	1	0	0	0	0	0	15	0	0	1	1	.500	0	0	2.40
Trenton	AA Bos	10	10	0	0	58.2	260	76	45	38	8	2	3	3	8	0	32	0	0	3	5	.375	0	0	5.83
Pawtucket	AAA Bos	13	9	1	2	71.2	298	77	37	37	9	3	2	0	13	3	37	0	0	4	3	.571	0	0	4.65
2001 Pawtucket	AAA Bos	37	16	0	17	117.2	492	133	62	59	14	4	4	5	17	3	77	2	0	3	10	.231	0	10	4.51
1998 Boston	AL	4	4	0	0	18.2	87	28	17	17	4	0	1	1	3	0	15	1	0	0	3	.000	0	0	8.20
1999 Boston	AL	9	7	0	1	39.1	171	45	26	25	7	1	3	2	8	0	16	0	0	2	3	.400	0	0	5.72
4 Min. YEARS		98	73	6	19	478.2	1988	490	230	209	49	14	20	15	91	9	333	5	0	28	25	.528	1	10	3.93
2 Maj. YEARS		13	11	0	1	58	258	73	43	42	11	1	4	3	11	0	31	1	0	2	6	.250	0	0	6.52

Hee Seop Choi

Bats: Left **Throws:** Left **Pos:** 1B-72; DH-2; PH-2; PR-1   **Ht:** 6'5" **Wt:** 235 **Born:** 3/16/79 **Age:** 23

		BATTING														BASERUNNING				PERCENTAGES		
Year Team	Lg Org	G	AB	H	2B	3B	HR	TB	R	RBI	TBB	IBB	SO	HBP	SH	SF	SB	CS	SB%	GDP	Avg	OBP	SLG
1999 Lansing	A ChC	79	290	93	18	6	18	177	71	70	50	0	68	2	0	2	2	1	.67	8	.321	.422	.610
2000 Daytona	A+ ChC	96	345	102	25	6	15	184	60	70	37	5	78	6	0	5	4	1	.80	7	.296	.369	.533
West Tenn	AA ChC	36	122	37	9	0	10	76	25	25	25	0	38	0	0	1	3	1	.75	5	.303	.419	.623
2001 Iowa	AAA ChC	77	266	61	11	0	13	111	38	45	34	1	67	0	0	4	5	1	.83	5	.229	.313	.417
3 Min. YEARS		288	1023	293	63	12	56	548	194	210	146	6	251	8	0	12	14	4	.78	25	.286	.376	.536

Ben Christensen

Pitches: Right **Bats:** Right **Pos:** SP-3   **Ht:** 6'4" **Wt:** 205 **Born:** 2/7/78 **Age:** 24

		HOW MUCH HE PITCHED						WHAT HE GAVE UP										THE RESULTS					
Year Team	Lg Org	G	GS	CG	GF	IP	BFP	H	R	ER	HR	SH	SF	HB	TBB	IBB	SO	WP	Bk	W	L	Pct.	ShO	Sv	ERA
1999 Cubs	R ChC	3	3	0	0	9	39	8	3	3	0	0	0	1	5	0	10	1	1	0	1	.000	0	0	3.00
Eugene	A- ChC	5	5	0	0	21.1	100	21	14	14	2	0	1	0	14	0	21	2	0	0	2	.000	0	0	5.91
Daytona	A+ ChC	4	4	0	0	22.2	106	25	16	16	4	1	1	3	11	0	18	1	1	1	3	.250	0	0	6.35
2000 Daytona	A+ ChC	10	10	1	0	64.1	253	43	18	15	6	0	0	3	15	0	63	2	0	4	2	.667	0	0	2.10
West Tenn	AA ChC	7	7	0	0	42.1	177	36	18	13	2	2	3	1	15	0	42	1	0	3	1	.750	0	0	2.76
2001 West Tenn	AA ChC	3	3	0	0	16.2	74	20	12	12	2	1	0	0	9	0	9	1	0	2	1	.667	0	0	6.48
3 Min. YEARS		32	32	1	0	176.1	749	153	81	73	16	4	5	8	69	0	163	8	2	10	10	.500	0	0	3.73

Mike Christensen

Bats: Right **Throws:** Right **Pos:** 3B-81; DH-4; 1B-1   **Ht:** 6'2" **Wt:** 190 **Born:** 5/24/76 **Age:** 26

		BATTING														BASERUNNING				PERCENTAGES		
Year Team	Lg Org	G	AB	H	2B	3B	HR	TB	R	RBI	TBB	IBB	SO	HBP	SH	SF	SB	CS	SB%	GDP	Avg	OBP	SLG
1998 Boise	A- Ana	70	286	75	22	0	9	124	47	47	18	2	63	1	1	2	1	0	1.00	9	.262	.306	.434
1999 Cedar Rapds	A Ana	127	504	142	36	2	18	236	68	71	42	3	102	5	0	4	1	2	.33	12	.282	.341	.468
2000 Lk Elsinore	A+ Ana	129	523	141	30	2	14	217	66	95	26	1	101	3	2	5	3	3	.50	14	.270	.305	.415
2001 Arkansas	AA Ana	86	298	70	23	2	6	115	32	33	19	0	76	1	0	2	4	2	.67	2	.235	.281	.386
4 Min. YEARS		412	1611	428	111	6	47	692	213	246	105	6	342	10	3	13	9	7	.56	37	.266	.312	.430

Clint Chrysler

Pitches: Left **Bats:** Left **Pos:** RP-58   **Ht:** 6'0" **Wt:** 190 **Born:** 11/4/75 **Age:** 26

		HOW MUCH HE PITCHED						WHAT HE GAVE UP										THE RESULTS					
Year Team	Lg Org	G	GS	CG	GF	IP	BFP	H	R	ER	HR	SH	SF	HB	TBB	IBB	SO	WP	Bk	W	L	Pct.	ShO	Sv	ERA
1997 Everett	A- Sea	18	0	0	10	22.2	83	11	3	2	0	0	0	0	7	0	25	3	0	3	0	1.000	0	2	0.79
1998 Wisconsin	A Sea	17	0	0	4	27	123	33	19	16	1	2	1	2	9	1	30	2	0	0	2	.000	0	1	5.33
Everett	A- Sea	24	0	0	20	34	156	30	11	8	2	1	1	2	18	0	44	5	0	4	2	.667	0	9	2.12
Orlando	AA Sea	3	0	0	2	4.2	19	4	2	2	2	0	0	0	1	0	6	0	0	0	0	—	0	0	3.86
1999 Wisconsin	A Sea	51	0	0	28	56.2	243	47	22	13	4	4	4	3	22	3	59	5	1	5	7	.417	0	8	2.06
2000 Lynchburg	A+ Pit	51	0	0	32	63	260	48	20	18	1	0	1	0	22	2	63	4	0	5	1	.833	0	14	2.57
2001 Altoona	AA Pit	51	0	0	15	49.1	216	52	24	18	3	2	0	4	12	1	31	2	0	4	3	.571	0	3	3.28
Nashville	AAA Pit	7	0	0	2	10	48	14	4	3	2	0	0	1	4	0	6	0	0	0	0	—	0	0	2.70
5 Min. YEARS		222	0	0	113	267.1	1148	239	105	80	15	9	7	11	95	7	264	21	1	21	15	.583	0	37	2.69

Vinny Chulk

Pitches: Right **Bats:** Right **Pos:** RP-43; SP-2   **Ht:** 6'2" **Wt:** 185 **Born:** 12/19/78 **Age:** 23

		HOW MUCH HE PITCHED						WHAT HE GAVE UP										THE RESULTS					
Year Team	Lg Org	G	GS	CG	GF	IP	BFP	H	R	ER	HR	SH	SF	HB	TBB	IBB	SO	WP	Bk	W	L	Pct.	ShO	Sv	ERA
2000 Medcine Hat	R+ Tor	14	13	0	0	68.2	295	75	36	29	5	0	2	2	20	0	51	3	0	2	4	.333	0	0	3.80
2001 Syracuse	AAA Tor	5	0	0	2	6	25	5	1	1	0	0	0	0	4	0	3	3	0	1	0	1.000	0	0	1.50
Dunedin	A+ Tor	16	1	0	4	34.2	157	38	16	12	2	2	2	0	13	1	50	4	0	1	2	.333	0	1	3.12
Tennessee	AA Tor	24	1	0	7	43	169	34	15	15	5	5	4	2	8	1	43	1	0	2	5	.286	0	2	3.14
2 Min. YEARS		59	15	0	13	152.1	646	152	68	57	12	7	8	4	45	2	147	11	0	6	11	.353	0	3	3.37

Mark Cisar

Pitches: Right Bats: Right Pos: RP-48   Ht: 5'11" Wt: 176 Born: 5/22/75 Age: 27

Year Team	Lg Org	G	GS	CG	GF	IP	BFP	H	R	ER	HR	SH	SF	HB	TBB	IBB	SO	WP	Bk	W	L	Pct.	ShO	Sv	ERA
1998 Lowell	A- Bos	22	0	0	22	38	151	22	11	6	1	0	1	2	10	0	42	1	0	2	1	.667	0	9	1.42
Michigan	A Bos	6	0	0	2	7.1	37	8	4	4	0	0	1	0	8	0	4	2	0	1	1	.500	0	1	4.91
1999 Augusta	A Bos	52	0	0	49	68.1	288	57	22	17	0	3	2	4	22	3	64	4	0	3	6	.333	0	27	2.24
2000 Sarasota	A+ Bos	10	0	0	1	16.1	70	15	8	5	1	0	0	1	4	1	14	0	0	0	0	—	0	0	2.76
2001 Sarasota	A+ Bos	27	0	0	14	38	170	41	21	19	4	3	1	3	15	1	39	0	0	1	1	.500	0	6	4.50
Trenton	AA Bos	21	0	0	12	31.1	123	30	15	15	2	1	0	1	7	0	21	2	0	1	1	.500	0	3	4.31
4 Min. YEARS		138	0	0	98	199.1	839	173	81	66	8	7	5	11	66	5	184	9	0	8	10	.444	0	46	2.98

Chris Clapinski

Bats: Both Throws: Right Pos: 2B-20; 3B-17; OF-17; SS-11; PH-5; DH-4; PR-2   Ht: 6'0" Wt: 175 Born: 8/20/71 Age: 30

Year Team	Lg Org	G	AB	H	2B	3B	HR	TB	R	RBI	TBB	IBB	SO	HBP	SH	SF	SB	CS	SB%	GDP	Avg	OBP	SLG
1992 Marlins	R Fla	59	212	51	8	1	1	64	36	15	49	2	42	4	3	2	5	6	.45	4	.241	.390	.302
1993 Kane County	A Fla	82	214	45	12	1	0	59	22	27	31	0	55	1	8	4	3	8	.27	3	.210	.308	.276
1994 Brevard Cty	A+ Fla	65	157	45	12	3	1	66	33	13	23	2	28	3	7	1	3	2	.60	2	.287	.386	.420
1995 Portland	AA Fla	87	208	49	9	3	4	76	32	30	28	2	44	2	5	5	5	2	.71	4	.236	.325	.365
1996 Portland	AA Fla	23	73	19	7	0	3	35	15	11	13	1	13	2	1	1	3	1	.75	2	.260	.382	.479
Charlotte	AAA Fla	105	362	103	20	1	10	155	74	39	47	0	54	3	8	5	13	6	.68	7	.285	.367	.428
1997 Charlotte	AAA Fla	110	340	89	24	2	12	153	62	52	48	4	64	9	6	2	14	2	.88	9	.262	.366	.450
1998 Brevard Cty	A+ Fla	5	14	1	0	1	0	3	1	4	7	2	2	0	0	1	0	0	—	1	.071	.364	.214
Charlotte	AAA Fla	100	312	84	18	1	9	131	53	35	39	0	53	5	7	1	11	3	.79	7	.269	.359	.420
1999 Calgary	AAA Fla	81	267	86	21	6	8	143	51	35	30	0	53	2	3	1	5	1	.83	6	.322	.393	.536
2000 Calgary	AAA Fla	62	214	60	10	3	6	94	41	24	33	0	36	2	1	2	3	3	.50	4	.280	.378	.439
Brevard Cty	A+ Fla	4	17	6	0	0	1	9	4	1	0	0	2	0	0	0	0	0	—	0	.353	.353	.529
2001 Brevard Cty	A+ Fla	10	29	10	0	0	1	13	10	6	14	2	5	1	0	0	0	0	—	0	.345	.568	.448
Portland	AA Fla	5	18	4	0	0	1	7	6	2	4	0	2	0	2	0	1	0	1.00	1	.222	.364	.389
Calgary	AAA Fla	58	199	50	10	1	7	83	31	20	17	0	43	2	0	0	1	2	.33	2	.251	.317	.417
1999 Florida	NL	36	56	13	1	2	0	18	6	2	9	0	12	1	0	0	1	0	1.00	1	.232	.348	.321
2000 Florida	NL	34	49	15	4	1	1	24	12	7	5	0	7	0	1	0	0	0	—	1	.306	.370	.490
10 Min. YEARS		856	2636	702	151	23	64	1091	471	314	383	15	496	36	51	25	67	36	.65	52	.266	.364	.414
2 Maj. YEARS		70	105	28	5	3	1	42	18	9	14	0	19	1	1	0	1	0	1.00	2	.267	.358	.400

Chris Clark

Pitches: Right Bats: Right Pos: RP-30; SP-6   Ht: 6'1" Wt: 180 Born: 10/29/74 Age: 27

Year Team	Lg Org	G	GS	CG	GF	IP	BFP	H	R	ER	HR	SH	SF	HB	TBB	IBB	SO	WP	Bk	W	L	Pct.	ShO	Sv	ERA
1994 Padres	R SD	17	1	0	6	33.2	153	35	17	12	2	1	0	2	18	0	25	5	0	0	0	—	0	1	3.21
1995 Padres	R SD	13	12	1	0	73	313	52	30	17	1	1	1	7	38	0	82	5	0	5	5	.500	0	0	2.10
Idaho Falls	R+ SD	1	1	0	0	6	24	3	3	3	1	0	0	0	4	0	9	1	0	0	0	—	0	0	4.50
1996 Clinton	A SD	24	11	0	7	82	385	96	58	46	5	4	3	7	51	1	74	9	1	3	8	.273	0	1	5.05
1997 Clinton	A SD	32	11	0	5	89	395	89	50	41	5	0	3	3	46	0	91	15	0	5	5	.500	0	3	4.15
1998 Brevard Cty	A+ Fla	40	2	0	30	60.2	288	52	38	29	1	3	7	4	46	3	58	12	0	2	3	.400	0	9	4.30
1999 Portland	AA Fla	4	0	0	1	6	29	5	5	5	1	1	1	0	7	0	4	1	0	1	0	1.000	0	0	7.50
Brevard Cty	A+ Fla	28	12	0	10	86	395	93	60	53	5	3	5	6	48	1	48	12	0	3	8	.273	0	1	5.55
2000 Portland	AA Fla	32	8	0	2	86.2	381	83	42	37	5	3	3	2	48	0	54	6	0	7	3	.700	0	3	3.84
2001 Arkansas	AA Ana	28	6	0	9	66.1	303	74	53	50	2	1	9	9	35	1	34	12	0	3	3	.500	0	0	6.78
Brevard Cty	A+ Fla	4	0	0	3	6.1	34	6	5	4	0	1	0	0	9	0	7	1	0	0	1	.000	0	1	5.68
Portland	AA Fla	4	0	0	2	5.2	25	3	2	2	1	0	0	0	5	0	6	0	0	1	0	1.000	0	0	3.18
8 Min. YEARS		227	64	1	75	601.1	2725	591	363	299	35	19	21	40	355	6	492	79	1	30	36	.455	0	16	4.48

Doug Clark

Bats: Left Throws: Right Pos: OF-110; PH-8; DH-7; PR-1   Ht: 6'2" Wt: 205 Born: 3/5/76 Age: 26

Year Team	Lg Org	G	AB	H	2B	3B	HR	TB	R	RBI	TBB	IBB	SO	HBP	SH	SF	SB	CS	SB%	GDP	Avg	OBP	SLG
1998 Salem-Keizr	A- SF	59	227	76	8	6	3	105	49	41	32	0	31	3	1	1	12	8	.60	1	.335	.422	.463
1999 Bakersfield	A+ SF	118	420	137	17	2	11	191	67	58	59	4	89	5	0	0	17	11	.61	5	.326	.415	.455
Shreveport	AA SF	15	50	11	3	0	1	17	6	6	4	0	9	0	0	0	0	0	—	2	.220	.278	.340
2000 Shreveport	AA SF	131	492	134	20	7	10	198	68	75	43	5	102	5	1	7	12	4	.75	13	.272	.333	.402
2001 Shreveport	AA SF	123	414	114	16	4	6	156	53	51	45	4	83	3	6	4	20	5	.80	8	.275	.348	.377
4 Min. YEARS		446	1603	472	64	19	31	667	243	231	183	13	314	16	8	12	61	28	.69	29	.294	.370	.416

Brandon Claussen

Pitches: Left Bats: Left Pos: SP-29   Ht: 6'2" Wt: 175 Born: 5/1/79 Age: 23

Year Team	Lg Org	G	GS	CG	GF	IP	BFP	H	R	ER	HR	SH	SF	HB	TBB	IBB	SO	WP	Bk	W	L	Pct.	ShO	Sv	ERA
1999 Yankees	R NYY	2	2	0	0	11.1	42	7	4	4	2	0	0	0	2	0	16	0	0	0	0	.000	0	0	3.18
Staten Ilnd	A- NYY	12	12	1	0	72	295	70	30	27	4	3	0	3	12	2	89	4	4	6	4	.600	0	0	3.38
Greensboro	A NYY	1	1	0	0	6	29	8	7	7	1	0	0	0	2	0	5	1	1	0	1	.000	0	0	10.50
2000 Greensboro	A NYY	17	17	1	0	97.2	416	91	49	44	9	4	4	1	44	0	98	3	0	8	5	.615	0	0	4.05
Tampa	A+ NYY	9	9	1	0	52.1	220	49	24	18	1	1	0	2	17	0	44	2	1	2	5	.286	1	0	3.10
2001 Tampa	A+ NYY	8	8	0	0	56	227	47	21	17	2	2	2	0	13	0	69	1	2	5	2	.714	0	0	2.73
Norwich	AA NYY	21	21	1	0	131	554	101	42	31	6	7	6	5	55	0	151	5	3	9	2	.818	1	0	2.13
3 Min. YEARS		70	70	5	0	426.1	1783	373	177	148	25	17	12	11	145	2	472	16	11	30	20	.600	2	0	3.12

Edgard Clemente

Bats: Right **Throws:** Right **Pos:** OF-94; PH-2; DH-1   **Ht:** 5'11" **Wt:** 188 **Born:** 12/15/75 **Age:** 26

Year Team	Lg Org	G	AB	H	2B	3B	HR	TB	R	RBI	TBB	IBB	SO	HBP	SH	SF	SB	CS	SB%	GDP	Avg	OBP	SLG
1993 Rockies	R Col	39	147	36	4	2	2	50	20	20	16	0	35	0	2	2	7	5	.58	2	.245	.315	.340
1994 Asheville	A Col	119	447	106	22	3	11	167	50	39	23	0	120	3	3	2	9	9	.50	14	.237	.278	.374
1995 Salem	A+ Col	131	497	149	25	6	13	225	74	69	40	4	102	4	3	7	7	10	.41	17	.300	.352	.453
1996 New Haven	AA Col	132	486	141	29	4	19	235	72	62	53	5	114	4	0	0	6	2	.75	7	.290	.365	.484
1997 Colo Sprngs	AAA Col	120	438	123	24	10	17	218	70	73	34	2	119	6	1	2	6	3	.67	8	.281	.340	.498
1998 Colo Sprngs	AAA Col	135	493	124	21	7	22	225	79	82	40	0	117	4	1	5	5	5	.50	6	.252	.310	.456
1999 Colo Sprngs	AAA Col	75	276	84	24	1	17	161	46	60	20	1	55	2	0	1	5	5	.50	7	.304	.355	.583
2000 Edmonton	AAA Ana	22	87	21	4	1	2	33	14	10	9	0	23	2	0	0	0	2	.00	2	.241	.327	.379
2001 Trenton	AA Bos	11	45	16	3	1	3	30	7	7	2	0	6	0	0	0	0	1	.00	1	.356	.383	.667
Pawtucket	AAA Bos	86	300	74	14	0	12	124	32	35	25	0	84	5	2	3	2	0	1.00	8	.247	.312	.413
1998 Colorado	NL	11	17	6	0	1	0	8	2	2	2	0	8	0	0	0	0	0	—	0	.353	.421	.471
1999 Colorado	NL	57	162	41	10	2	8	79	24	25	7	0	46	0	1	1	0	0	—	4	.253	.282	.488
2000 Anaheim	AL	46	78	17	2	0	0	19	4	5	0	0	27	1	1	0	1	0	1.00	0	.218	.228	.244
9 Min. YEARS		870	3216	874	170	35	118	1468	464	457	262	12	775	30	12	22	47	42	.53	73	.272	.330	.456
3 Maj. YEARS		114	257	64	12	3	8	106	30	32	9	0	81	1	2	1	0	1	.00	4	.249	.276	.412

Brad Clontz

Pitches: Right **Bats:** Right **Pos:** RP-30   **Ht:** 6'1" **Wt:** 203 **Born:** 4/25/71 **Age:** 31

Year Team	Lg Org	G	GS	CG	GF	IP	BFP	H	R	ER	HR	SH	SF	HB	TBB	IBB	SO	WP	Bk	W	L	Pct.	ShO	Sv	ERA
1992 Pulaski	R+ Atl	4	0	0	3	5.2		3	1	1	0	0	0	2	2	0	7	1	0			—	0	1	1.59
Macon	A Atl	17	0	0	14	23	103	19	14	10	2	2	1	3	10	0	18	1	0	2	1	.667	0	2	3.91
1993 Durham	A+ Atl	51	0	0	38	75.1	325	69	32	23	5	8	0	4	26	1	79	6	0	1	7	.125	0	10	2.75
1994 Greenville	AA Atl	39	0	0	38	45	178	32	13	6	5	3	1	1	10	2	49	2	0	1	2	.333	0	27	1.20
Richmond	AAA Atl	24	0	0	22	25.2	101	19	6	6	1	0	1	0	9	2	21	0	0	0	0	—	0	11	2.10
1997 Richmond	AAA Atl	16	0	0	11	22	77	10	1	0	0	2	0	1	2	1	24	0	0	0	0	—	0	6	0.00
1998 Albuquerque	AAA LA	6	0	0	2	7	38	11	10	6	2	0	0	0	5	0	12	3	0	1	2	.333	0	0	7.71
Norfolk	AAA NYM	28	0	0	7	42	185	43	26	16	4	0	1	1	16	3	49	2	0	2	4	.333	0	0	3.43
1999 Nashville	AAA Pit	12	0	0	12	18	73	18	8	7	3	2	1	1	6	0	23	0	0	0	2	.000	0	7	3.50
2000 Nashville	AAA Pit	4	0	0	2	4.2	17	1	0	0	0	0	0	0	2	0	5	0	0	0	0	—	0	1	0.00
Altoona	AA Pit	4	0	0	0	4.2	19	4	2	1	1	1	1	1	1	0	4	0	0	0	0	—	0	1	1.93
2001 Colo Sprngs	AAA Col	21	0	0	10	23	120	37	26	23	7	3	1	4	10	0	23	1	0	2	1	.667	0	0	9.00
Myrtle Bch	A+ Atl	9	0	0	6	11.1	51	8	4	2	1	0	0	3	5	1	12	0	0	0	1	.000	0	0	1.59
1995 Atlanta	NL	59	0	0	14	69	295	71	29	28	5	3	2	4	22	4	55	0	0	8	1	.889	0	4	3.65
1996 Atlanta	NL	81	0	0	11	80.2	350	78	53	51	11	5	4	2	33	8	49	0	1	6	3	.667	0	1	5.69
1997 Atlanta	NL	51	0	0	16	48	203	52	24	20	3	0	2	1	18	3	42	1	0	5	1	.833	0	1	3.75
1998 Los Angeles	NL	18	0	0	6	20.2	87	15	13	13	3	0	0	2	10	4	14	0	0	2	0	1.000	0	0	5.66
New York	NL	2	0	0	0	3	14	4	3	3	1	0	0	0	2	0	2	0	0	0	0	—	0	0	9.00
1999 Pittsburgh	NL	56	0	0	16	49.1	223	49	21	15	6	2	1	3	24	5	40	2	0	1	3	.250	0	2	2.74
2000 Pittsburgh	NL	5	0	0	0	7	37	7	4	4	1	0	0	0	11	2	8	1	0	0	0	—	0	0	5.14
8 Min. YEARS		235	0	0	165	307.1	1310	268	143	101	30	21	7	21	104	10	326	16	0	9	20	.310	0	65	2.96
6 Maj. YEARS		272	0	0	63	277.2	1209	276	147	134	30	10	9	12	120	26	210	4	1	22	8	.733	0	8	4.34

Ivanon Coffie

Bats: Left **Throws:** Right **Pos:** DH-33; 3B-16; 1B-12; PH-1   **Ht:** 6'1" **Wt:** 192 **Born:** 5/16/77 **Age:** 25

Year Team	Lg Org	G	AB	H	2B	3B	HR	TB	R	RBI	TBB	IBB	SO	HBP	SH	SF	SB	CS	SB%	GDP	Avg	OBP	SLG
1996 Orioles	R Bal	56	193	42	8	4	0	58	29	20	23	1	26	2	0	0	6	2	.75	4	.218	.307	.301
1997 Delmarva	A Bal	90	305	84	14	5	3	117	41	48	23	1	45	4	1	6	19	10	.66	5	.275	.328	.384
1998 Frederick	A+ Bal	130	473	121	19	2	16	192	62	75	48	2	109	3	3	9	17	12	.59	11	.256	.323	.406
1999 Bowie	AA Bal	57	195	36	9	3	3	60	21	23	20	0	46	1	1	3	2	2	.50	3	.185	.260	.308
Frederick	A+ Bal	73	276	78	18	4	11	137	35	53	28	3	62	4	0	3	7	4	.64	5	.283	.354	.496
2000 Bowie	AA Bal	87	341	91	21	3	9	145	49	44	36	3	53	4	0	3	1	4	.20	6	.267	.341	.425
Rochester	AAA Bal	21	78	17	2	1	0	21	4	10	2	0	21	1	1	1	0	0	—	1	.218	.244	.269
2001 Orioles	R Bal	6	18	5	1	0	1	9	2	2	2	0	5	0	0	0	0	0	—	0	.278	.350	.500
Rochester	AAA Bal	56	206	55	10	1	8	91	33	35	15	1	47	1	0	2	3	0	1.00	4	.267	.317	.442
2000 Baltimore	AL	23	60	13	4	1	0	19	6	6	5	0	11	1	0	1	1	0	1.00	3	.217	.284	.317
6 Min. YEARS		576	2085	529	102	23	51	830	276	310	197	11	414	20	6	27	55	34	.62	39	.254	.320	.398

Eric Cole

Bats: Right **Throws:** Right **Pos:** OF-112; PH-8; DH-1; PR-1   **Ht:** 6'0" **Wt:** 185 **Born:** 11/15/75 **Age:** 26

Year Team	Lg Org	G	AB	H	2B	3B	HR	TB	R	RBI	TBB	IBB	SO	HBP	SH	SF	SB	CS	SB%	GDP	Avg	OBP	SLG
1995 Astros	R Hou	39	122	33	3	1	0	38	17	12	7	0	21	2	3	0	7	5	.58	0	.270	.321	.311
1996 Auburn	A- Hou	46	151	26	4	0	1	33	9	10	6	0	46	3	1	4	5	15	.75	7	.172	.213	.219
1997 Auburn	A- Hou	71	222	61	20	3	8	111	29	34	19	1	46	5	2	3	4	4	.50	3	.275	.341	.500
1998 Quad City	A Hou	132	500	140	30	6	11	215	73	83	24	0	104	5	0	1	32	15	.68	7	.280	.319	.430
1999 Kissimmee	A+ Hou	120	460	122	27	5	13	198	62	67	39	3	120	7	0	4	23	13	.64	12	.265	.329	.430
Jackson	AA Hou	15	54	9	1	0	2	16	4	8	1	0	11	0	1	0	0	0	—	3	.167	.182	.296
2000 Round Rock	AA Hou	132	543	158	46	0	22	270	90	94	43	3	98	9	0	6	21	10	.68	12	.291	.349	.497
2001 New Orleans	AAA Hou	121	397	105	25	2	3	143	47	41	38	1	94	7	5	0	1	4	.20	18	.264	.339	.360
7 Min. YEARS		676	2449	654	156	17	60	1024	331	349	177	8	540	38	12	18	91	52	.64	62	.267	.324	.418

Victor Cole

Pitches: Right **Bats:** Both **Pos:** RP-3   **Ht:** 5'10" **Wt:** 160 **Born:** 1/23/68 **Age:** 34

			HOW MUCH HE PITCHED					WHAT HE GAVE UP									THE RESULTS					
Year Team	Lg Org	G	GS	CG	GF	IP	BFP	H	R	ER	HR	SH	SF	HB	TBB	IBB	SO	WP	Bk	W	L	Pct.	ShO	Sv	ERA
1988 Eugene	A- KC	15	0	0	13	23.2	94	16	6	4	0	0	0	2	8	0	39	3	0	1	0	1.000	0	9	1.52
Baseball Cy	A+ KC	10	5	0	2	35	149	27	9	8	0	1	1	1	21	0	29	2	0	5	0	1.000	0	1	2.06
1989 Memphis	AA KC	13	13	0	0	63.2	303	67	53	45	4	4	1	5	51	1	52	4	1	1	9	.100	0	0	6.36
Baseball Cy	A+ KC	9	9	0	0	42	186	43	23	18	2	1	1	0	22	0	30	2	1	3	1	.750	0	0	3.86
1990 Memphis	AA KC	46	6	0	15	107.2	479	91	61	52	6	4	1	3	70	2	102	2	2	3	8	.273	0	4	4.35
1991 Omaha	AAA KC	6	0	0	1	13	54	9	6	6	1	0	0	0	9	1	12	0	0	1	1	.500	0	0	4.15
Carolina	AA Pit	20	0	0	17	28.1	116	13	8	6	1	0	1	2	19	1	32	3	2	0	2	.000	0	12	1.91
Buffalo	AAA Pit	19	1	0	9	24	115	23	11	10	2	0	1	1	20	0	23	3	0	1	2	.333	0	0	3.75
1992 Buffalo	AAA Pit	19	19	3	0	115.2	498	102	46	40	8	3	3	4	61	0	69	8	0	11	6	.647	1	0	3.11
1993 Buffalo	AAA Pit	6	6	0	0	26.1	134	35	25	25	5	2	1	0	24	0	14	1	0	1	3	.250	0	0	8.54
Carolina	AA Pit	27	0	0	13	41	189	39	30	27	5	1	0	2	31	2	35	6	0	0	4	.000	0	8	5.93
New Orleans	AAA Mil	6	1	0	0	6	34	9	7	7	0	0	1	1	7	0	5	0	0	0	2	.000	0	0	10.50
1994 El Paso	AA Mil	8	0	0	2	8	50	18	17	16	4	0	0	1	9	1	3	0	1	0	1	.000	0	0	18.00
Memphis	AA KC	6	6	0	0	35.2	162	32	22	19	3	0	4	0	23	0	22	2	0	2	1	.667	0	0	4.79
1995 Las Vegas	AAA SD	4	4	0	0	19.2	86	19	17	14	4	1	1	0	10	0	12	1	1	0	2	.000	0	0	6.41
Salinas	IND —	4	4	0	0	22.2	104	25	16	9	0	2	2	0	13	0	22	2	0	1	1	.500	0	0	3.57
Memphis	AA SD	8	2	0	3	20	81	15	5	3	0	0	0	0	8	1	17	0	0	1	0	1.000	0	0	1.35
1996 Pine Bluff	IND —	8	0	0	2	23.1	89	16	2	2	0	1	0	2	4	0	27	2	0	3	0	1.000	0	1	0.77
Memphis	AA SD	8	1	0	4	15	65	11	3	2	0	0	0	1	8	0	13	0	0	1	0	1.000	0	1	1.20
1998 West Tenn	AA ChC	19	0	0	2	30	127	26	12	8	1	1	1	1	11	1	31	2	0	2	2	.500	0	0	2.40
Iowa	AAA ChC	38	2	0	6	67.1	296	77	35	28	4	3	1	1	25	0	69	7	1	2	2	.500	0	0	3.74
1999 Iowa	AAA ChC	19	2	0	2	40.1	188	41	24	21	3	2	0	3	23	1	33	5	2	2	1	.667	0	0	4.69
West Tenn	AA ChC	17	0	0	8	23	103	21	11	10	2	0	1	0	18	0	17	2	0	3	1	.750	0	0	3.91
2000 Memphis	AAA StL	5	3	0	1	18.2	74	13	6	6	0	0	0	1	8	1	16	0	1	1	0	1.000	0	0	2.89
2001 Memphis	AAA StL	3	0	0	0	5.1	29	7	6	4	1	0	0	0	4	0	4	0	0	0	1	.000	0	0	6.75
1992 Pittsburgh	NL	8	4	0	2	23	104	23	14	14	1	1	1	0	14	0	12	1	0	0	2	.000	0	0	5.48
13 Min. YEARS		343	84	3	100	855.1	3805	795	461	390	56	26	21	32	507	12	728	57	12	45	50	.474	1	35	4.10

Javier Colina

Bats: Right **Throws:** Right **Pos:** 2B-114; 3B-7; PH-1   **Ht:** 6'1" **Wt:** 180 **Born:** 2/15/79 **Age:** 23

					BATTING												BASERUNNING				PERCENTAGES		
Year Team	Lg Org	G	AB	H	2B	3B	HR	TB	R	RBI	TBB	IBB	SO	HBP	SH	SF	SB	CS	SB%	GDP	Avg	OBP	SLG
1998 Rockies	R Col	44	169	54	6	2	6	82	28	39	18	0	30	3	1	4	9	4	.69	5	.320	.387	.485
1999 Asheville	A Col	124	516	156	37	3	6	217	70	81	26	0	101	6	2	6	12	11	.52	12	.302	.339	.421
2000 Carolina	AA Col	130	429	93	12	1	2	113	34	35	44	2	81	3	10	4	5	2	.71	8	.217	.292	.263
2001 Carolina	AA Col	7	24	1	0	0	0	1	0	2	0	0	10	0	1	0	0	1	.00	1	.042	.042	.042
Salem	A+ Col	113	439	125	33	7	9	199	67	58	22	1	61	9	5	12	9	4	.69	8	.285	.324	.453
4 Min. YEARS		418	1577	429	88	13	23	612	199	215	110	3	283	21	19	26	35	22	.61	34	.272	.323	.388

Mike Collins

Bats: Right **Throws:** Right **Pos:** SS-59; 2B-18; 3B-10; PH-4; DH-3   **Ht:** 5'10" **Wt:** 172 **Born:** 1/29/77 **Age:** 25

					BATTING												BASERUNNING				PERCENTAGES		
Year Team	Lg Org	G	AB	H	2B	3B	HR	TB	R	RBI	TBB	IBB	SO	HBP	SH	SF	SB	CS	SB%	GDP	Avg	OBP	SLG
1998 Yakima	A- LA	18	67	19	2	0	0	21	5	2	4	0	6	1	3	0	2	6	.25	0	.284	.333	.313
Great Falls	R+ LA	44	143	44	10	3	0	60	23	18	13	0	19	3	10	2	4	2	.67	2	.308	.373	.420
1999 San Antonio	AA LA	7	12	4	0	0	0	4	1	0	5	0	2	0	1	0	0	1	.00	0	.333	.529	.333
Vero Beach	A+ LA	101	356	95	10	2	3	118	37	31	34	0	68	1	9	3	8	12	.40	7	.267	.330	.331
2000 San Berndno	A+ LA	103	342	100	12	0	0	112	50	36	44	0	45	1	6	8	11	6	.65	6	.292	.367	.327
2001 Jacksnville	AA LA	17	39	5	0	0	0	5	1	3	5	0	9	0	0	2	2	1	.67	2	.128	.217	.128
Vero Beach	A+ LA	74	268	74	11	0	2	91	29	24	37	0	26	2	6	2	5	3	.63	6	.276	.366	.340
4 Min. YEARS		364	1227	341	45	5	5	411	146	114	142	0	175	8	35	17	32	31	.51	23	.278	.352	.335

Mark Comolli

Pitches: Right **Bats:** Right **Pos:** RP-13; SP-6   **Ht:** 6'0" **Wt:** 190 **Born:** 3/11/79 **Age:** 23

					HOW MUCH HE PITCHED					WHAT HE GAVE UP									THE RESULTS					
Year Team	Lg Org	G	GS	CG	GF	IP	BFP	H	R	ER	HR	SH	SF	HB	TBB	IBB	SO	WP	Bk	W	L	Pct.	ShO	Sv	ERA
2001 Syracuse	AAA Tor	1	1	0	0	4	15	4	1	0	0	0	0	0	1	0	1	0	0	0	0	—	0	0	0.00
Auburn	A- Tor	10	0	0	6	19	81	21	11	10	1	2	0	0	6	0	21	6	0	2	1	.667	0	1	4.74
Chston-WV	A Tor	8	5	0	0	32.1	132	28	16	14	2	0	1	5	6	0	27	2	0	1	2	.333	0	0	3.90
1 Min. YEAR		19	6	0	6	55.1	228	53	28	24	3	2	1	5	13	0	49	8	0	3	3	.500	0	1	3.90

Clay Condrey

Pitches: Right **Bats:** Right **Pos:** RP-66   **Ht:** 6'3" **Wt:** 195 **Born:** 11/19/75 **Age:** 26

					HOW MUCH HE PITCHED					WHAT HE GAVE UP									THE RESULTS					
Year Team	Lg Org	G	GS	CG	GF	IP	BFP	H	R	ER	HR	SH	SF	HB	TBB	IBB	SO	WP	Bk	W	L	Pct.	ShO	Sv	ERA
1998 Padres	R SD	5	0	0	4	5.1	26	6	4	2	0	0	0	0	5	1	1	1	1	0	1	.000	0	0	3.38
Idaho Falls	R+ SD	18	0	0	17	24.2	111	31	12	7	2	1	1	1	4	0	19	3	0	2	1	.667	0	5	2.55
1999 Fort Wayne	A SD	42	0	0	39	47.2	202	40	24	20	5	0	2	0	19	4	47	4	1	2	3	.400	0	20	3.78
Rancho Cuca	A+ SD	6	0	0	1	7.1	29	4	3	3	1	0	0	0	3	0	9	0	0	0	0	—	0	0	3.68
2000 Rancho Cuca	A+ SD	18	0	0	9	20.2	85	18	9	8	1	1	0	2	7	0	21	2	1	1	1	.500	0	4	3.48
Mobile	AA SD	35	0	0	19	43.2	195	41	27	26	4	3	2	5	20	0	25	1	0	2	2	.500	0	6	5.36
2001 Mobile	AA SD	27	0	0	23	33.2	144	33	23	17	1	4	2	0	15	4	21	0	0	2	2	.500	0	12	4.54
Portland	AAA SD	39	0	0	13	53	231	63	37	28	7	4	3	4	13	1	45	2	0	1	3	.250	0	2	4.75
4 Min. YEARS		190	0	0	125	236	1023	236	139	111	21	13	10	12	86	10	191	13	3	10	13	.435	0	49	4.23

61

Steve Connelly

Pitches: Right Bats: Right Pos: RP-33

Ht: 6'4" Wt: 210 Born: 4/27/74 Age: 28

Year Team	Lg Org	G	GS	CG	GF	IP	BFP	H	R	ER	HR	SH	SF	HB	TBB	IBB	SO	WP	Bk	W	L	Pct.	ShO	Sv	ERA
1995 Sou Oregon	A- Oak	17	0	0	10	28.1	133	29	17	12	1	3	2	4	14	4	19	6	0	2	4	.333	0	2	3.81
1996 Modesto	A+ Oak	52	0	0	42	64.2	283	58	33	27	5	1	1	5	32	1	65	5	2	4	7	.364	0	14	3.76
1997 Huntsville	AA Oak	43	0	0	22	69.2	297	74	33	29	3	2	1	4	20	2	49	5	0	3	3	.500	0	7	3.75
1998 Edmonton	AAA Oak	55	0	0	27	76	310	64	34	32	7	1	2	2	24	2	62	5	0	6	0	1.000	0	13	3.79
1999 Fresno	AAA SF	54	0	0	20	72	338	93	58	42	8	2	2	5	32	3	47	14	1	6	4	.600	0	2	5.25
2000 Fresno	AAA SF	43	0	0	36	59.2	264	63	33	29	9	3	1	2	20	0	44	1	0	4	3	.571	0	9	4.37
2001 Fresno	AAA SF	33	0	0	12	58.2	244	47	26	24	2	4	2	5	23	0	40	1	0	2	3	.400	0	4	3.68
1998 Oakland	AL	3	0	0	1	4.2	28	10	1	1	0	0	0	1	4	0	1	0	0	0	0	—	0	0	1.93
7 Min. YEARS		297	0	0	169	429	1859	428	234	195	35	16	11	27	165	12	326	37	3	31	27	.534	0	51	4.09

Greg Connors

Bats: Right Throws: Right Pos: 1B-85; DH-23; OF-9; C-5; 3B-2; PH-2; PR-2; 2B-1; P-1

Ht: 6'2" Wt: 185 Born: 8/22/74 Age: 27

Year Team	Lg Org	G	AB	H	2B	3B	HR	TB	R	RBI	TBB	IBB	SO	HBP	SH	SF	SB	CS	SB%	GDP	Avg	OBP	SLG
1997 Everett	A- Sea	54	230	67	18	1	6	105	41	43	16	0	44	3	0	4	6	2	.75	3	.291	.340	.457
Lancaster	A+ Sea	10	37	9	2	0	1	14	5	5	4	0	10	0	0	0	1		.00	0	.243	.317	.378
1998 Lancaster	A+ Sea	27	101	29	11	1	6	60	17	26	3	0	16	2	0	1	0	0	—	1	.287	.318	.594
Wisconsin	A Sea	94	364	103	31	3	12	176	45	57	22	0	95	1	0	5	8	8	.50	5	.283	.321	.484
1999 Lancaster	A+ Sea	117	448	120	20	7	16	202	72	84	40	2	91	6	1	5	10	7	.59	3	.268	.333	.451
2000 New Haven	AA Sea	123	452	126	29	3	9	188	64	58	47	0	83	7	2	5	0	1	.00	7	.279	.352	.416
2001 San Antonio	AA Sea	121	455	109	14	6	11	168	68	69	32	0	94	5	1	5	5	5	.50	19	.240	.294	.369
5 Min. YEARS		546	2087	563	125	21	61	913	312	342	164	2	433	24	4	25	29	24	.55	38	.270	.327	.437

Patrick Coogan

Pitches: Right Bats: Right Pos: SP-23; RP-10

Ht: 6'3" Wt: 195 Born: 9/12/75 Age: 26

Year Team	Lg Org	G	GS	CG	GF	IP	BFP	H	R	ER	HR	SH	SF	HB	TBB	IBB	SO	WP	Bk	W	L	Pct.	ShO	Sv	ERA
1997 New Jersey	A- StL	10	10	0	0	56	231	56	27	23	4	1	0	3	14	0	37	0	2	2	5	.286	0	0	3.70
1998 Pr William	A+ StL	14	14	0	0	74.1	340	94	55	46	7	3	4	4	25	0	57	5	2	4	5	.444	0	0	5.57
1999 Potomac	A+ StL	19	19	2	0	101	457	112	73	65	14	4	5	7	43	0	67	5	0	4	7	.364	0	0	5.79
2000 Arkansas	AA StL	27	26	1	1	150	661	164	96	85	21	6	6	9	62	0	79	7	1	9	13	.409	0	0	5.10
2001 New Haven	AA StL	33	23	1	6	148.2	648	168	91	84	19	3	6	8	43	0	115	15	1	8	8	.500	1	0	5.09
5 Min. YEARS		103	92	4	7	530	2337	594	342	303	65	17	21	31	187	0	355	32	6	27	38	.415	1	0	5.15

Andy Cook

Pitches: Right Bats: Right Pos: RP-30; SP-8

Ht: 6'5" Wt: 195 Born: 2/26/77 Age: 25

Year Team	Lg Org	G	GS	CG	GF	IP	BFP	H	R	ER	HR	SH	SF	HB	TBB	IBB	SO	WP	Bk	W	L	Pct.	ShO	Sv	ERA
1998 Pittsfield	A- NYM	15	11	0	1	70	304	78	36	29	6	2	4	3	20	1	54	5	2	5	3	.625	0	0	3.73
1999 Capital Cty	A NYM	27	26	0	1	149.2	628	150	66	47	16	4	4	3	42	0	124	10	1	12	7	.632	0	1	2.83
2000 St. Lucie	A+ NYM	28	16	1	7	126	537	123	51	47	7	3	4	11	37	1	94	2	1	10	4	.714	1	4	3.36
2001 St. Lucie	A+ NYM	16	6	0	4	51	218	39	16	13	2	3	1	4	22	2	50	1	0	5	2	.714	0	0	2.29
Binghamton	AA NYM	22	2	1	3	47.1	207	51	28	25	3	0	3	3	16	0	33	2	0	2	2	.500	0	1	4.75
4 Min. YEARS		108	61	2	16	444	1894	441	197	161	34	12	16	24	137	4	355	20	4	34	18	.654	1	6	3.26

B.R. Cook

Pitches: Right Bats: Right Pos: SP-28

Ht: 6'4" Wt: 200 Born: 3/2/78 Age: 24

Year Team	Lg Org	G	GS	CG	GF	IP	BFP	H	R	ER	HR	SH	SF	HB	TBB	IBB	SO	WP	Bk	W	L	Pct.	ShO	Sv	ERA
1999 New Jersey	A- StL	9	8	0	0	44.1	189	42	19	14	2	0	0	1	16	0	42	5	2	5	1	.833	0	0	2.84
2000 Peoria	A StL	18	18	0	0	97.2	438	90	66	40	7	3	1	3	52	2	83	7	1	5	7	.417	0	0	3.69
Potomac	A+ StL	8	8	0	0	42.1	193	48	31	26	3	3	3	2	27	0	23	3	0	0	4	.000	0	0	5.53
2001 Potomac	A+ StL	8	8	0	0	50.1	198	35	20	16	2	1	1	3	12	0	36	1	1	4	2	.667	0	0	2.86
New Haven	AA StL	20	20	0	0	121.2	515	115	68	54	11	5	4	3	37	0	84	7	2	5	8	.385	0	0	3.99
3 Min. YEARS		63	62	0	0	356.1	1533	330	204	150	25	12	9	12	144	2	268	23	6	19	22	.463	0	0	3.79

Derrick Cook

Pitches: Right Bats: Right Pos: RP-11; SP-2

Ht: 6'2" Wt: 195 Born: 8/6/75 Age: 26

Year Team	Lg Org	G	GS	CG	GF	IP	BFP	H	R	ER	HR	SH	SF	HB	TBB	IBB	SO	WP	Bk	W	L	Pct.	ShO	Sv	ERA
1996 Rangers	R Tex	6	5	1	0	23	100	25	14	12	1	0	1	2	11	0	13	1	0	2	1	.667	1	0	4.70
1997 Pulaski	R+ Tex	6	6	0	0	33.2	141	32	15	14	1	0	1	2	12	0	32	4	0	2	2	.500	0	0	3.74
Charlotte	A+ Tex	8	8	2	0	58.2	243	54	21	15	5	0	1	2	15	0	35	4	0	5	2	.714	0	0	2.30
1998 Charlotte	A+ Tex	26	26	1	0	167.1	710	170	81	68	13	8	2	5	64	1	111	13	1	13	7	.650	1	0	3.66
1999 Tulsa	AA Tex	21	21	0	0	114.1	524	137	81	72	12	3	6	4	45	3	71	17	0	7	6	.538	0	0	5.67
2000 Tulsa	AA Tex	21	20	0	0	113.2	498	111	91	58	12	0	3	8	54	1	72	8	0	5	8	.385	0	0	4.59
2001 Charlotte	A+ Tex	2	2	0	0	8	32	7	2	0	0	0	0	0	1	0	5	0	0	0	0	—	0	0	0.00
Tulsa	AA Tex	7	0	0	4	10	50	15	12	10	2	2	0	0	6	0	4	1	0	0	1	.000	0	1	9.00
West Tenn	AA ChC	4	0	0	2	6.2	33	9	6	6	2	2	0	0	5	1	3	0	0	0	2	.000	0	0	8.10
6 Min. YEARS		101	88	6	6	535.1	2331	560	303	255	48	15	14	23	213	6	346	48	1	34	29	.540	2	1	4.29

Brent Cookson

Bats: Right **Throws:** Right **Pos:** OF-44; DH-11; PH-4   **Ht:** 6'1" **Wt:** 200 **Born:** 9/7/69 **Age:** 32

					BATTING													BASERUNNING				PERCENTAGES		
Year Team	Lg Org	G	AB	H	2B	3B	HR	TB	R	RBI	TBB	IBB	SO	HBP	SH	SF	SB	CS	SB%	GDP	Avg	OBP	SLG
1991 Sou Oregon	A- Oak	6	9	0	0	0	0	0	0	0	0	0	7	0	0	0	0	0	—	1	.000	.000	.000
Athletics	R Oak	1	1	0	0	0	0	0	0	0	0	0	1	0	0	0	0	0	—	0	.000	.000	.000
1992 Clinton	A SF	46	145	31	5	1	8	62	30	20	22	0	48	3	1	1	9	3	.75	4	.214	.327	.428
San Jose	A+ SF	68	255	74	8	4	12	126	44	49	25	0	69	3	0	2	9	5	.64	8	.290	.358	.494
1993 San Jose	A+ SF	67	234	60	10	1	17	123	43	50	43	1	73	3	2	5	14	6	.70	5	.256	.372	.526
1994 Shreveport	AA SF	62	207	67	21	3	11	127	32	41	18	2	57	1	2	2	4	1	.80	4	.324	.377	.614
Phoenix	AAA SF	14	43	12	0	1	1	17	7	6	5	0	14	1	0	0	0	1	.00	1	.279	.367	.395
1995 Phoenix	AAA SF	68	210	63	9	3	15	123	38	46	25	2	36	1	1	2	3	3	.50	4	.300	.374	.586
Omaha	AAA KC	40	137	55	13	0	4	80	28	20	17	0	24	4	0	0	0	0	—	3	.401	.475	.584
1996 Pawtucket	AAA Bos	73	255	69	13	1	19	141	51	50	24	1	72	5	0	2	2	4	.33	9	.271	.328	.553
Rochester	AAA Bal	30	113	30	7	0	6	55	22	21	9	0	20	2	0	1	2	1	.67	5	.265	.328	.487
1998 Tucson	AAA Ari	36	100	36	12	0	6	66	24	19	18	0	26	2	0	0	0	0	—	1	.360	.463	.660
1999 Albuquerque	AAA LA	85	277	89	18	1	28	193	57	70	38	2	56	2	1	4	7	1	.88	5	.321	.402	.697
2000 Albuquerque	AAA LA	34	115	36	5	0	11	74	30	38	22	2	22	0	0	1	4	2	.67	4	.313	.420	.643
2001 Las Vegas	AAA LA	59	190	54	13	2	12	107	30	48	22	0	34	5	0	2	1	1	.50	7	.284	.370	.563
1995 Kansas City	AL	22	35	5	1	0	0	6	2	5	2	0	7	0	1	0	1	0	1.00	0	.143	.189	.171
1999 Los Angeles	NL	3	5	1	0	0	0	1	0	0	0	0	1	0	0	0	0	0	—	0	.200	.200	.200
10 Min. YEARS		689	2291	676	134	17	150	1294	436	478	288	10	559	32	7	25	55	28	.66	61	.295	.378	.565
2 Maj. YEARS		25	40	6	1	0	0	7	2	5	2	0	8	0	1	0	1	0	1.00	0	.150	.190	.175

Chris Cooper

Pitches: Left **Bats:** Left **Pos:** RP-27   **Ht:** 5'11" **Wt:** 190 **Born:** 10/31/78 **Age:** 23

		HOW MUCH HE PITCHED					WHAT HE GAVE UP											THE RESULTS					
Year Team	Lg Org	G	GS	CG	GF	IP	BFP	H	R	ER	HR	SH	SF	HB	TBB	IBB	SO	WP	Bk	W	L	Pct.	ShO	Sv	ERA
2001 Akron	AA Cle	2	0	0	0	2	8	2	1	1	0	0	0	0	0	0	3	0	0	0	0	—	0	0	4.50
Mahoning Vy	A- Cle	25	0	0	18	34	153	34	24	9	1	4	2	0	10	2	40	1	0	0	5	.000	0	11	2.38
1 Min. YEAR		27	0	0	18	36	161	36	25	10	1	4	2	0	10	2	43	1	0	0	5	.000	0	11	2.50

Trace Coquillette

Bats: Right **Throws:** Right **Pos:** OF-46; 2B-23; DH-11; 3B-4; PH-4   **Ht:** 5'11" **Wt:** 185 **Born:** 6/4/74 **Age:** 28

					BATTING													BASERUNNING				PERCENTAGES		
Year Team	Lg Org	G	AB	H	2B	3B	HR	TB	R	RBI	TBB	IBB	SO	HBP	SH	SF	SB	CS	SB%	GDP	Avg	OBP	SLG
1993 Wst Plm Bch	A+ Mon	6	18	5	3	0	0	8	2	3	2	0	5	0	1	0	0	0	—	0	.278	.350	.444
Expos	R Mon	44	159	40	4	3	2	56	27	11	37	0	28	7	1	3	16	3	.84	0	.252	.408	.352
1994 Burlington	A Mon	5	17	3	1	0	0	4	2	0	1	0	4	0	0	0	1	0	1.00	0	.176	.222	.235
Vermont	A- Mon	70	252	77	11	5	9	125	54	52	23	0	40	8	1	6	7	2	.78	5	.306	.374	.496
1995 Albany	A Mon	128	458	123	27	4	3	167	67	57	64	2	91	9	4	6	17	16	.52	8	.269	.365	.365
1996 Expos	R Mon	7	25	4	1	0	0	5	4	0	4	0	6	0	0	0	1	0	1.00	0	.160	.276	.200
Wst Plm Bch	A+ Mon	72	266	67	17	4	1	95	39	27	27	1	72	8	0	3	9	7	.56	5	.252	.336	.357
1997 Wst Plm Bch	A+ Mon	53	188	60	18	2	8	106	34	33	27	0	27	6	1	1	8	7	.53	1	.319	.419	.564
Harrisburg	AA Mon	81	293	76	17	3	10	129	46	51	25	0	40	14	1	1	9	4	.69	5	.259	.345	.440
1998 Harrisburg	AA Mon	49	187	62	10	0	9	99	40	23	15	0	41	6	0	1	10	3	.77	2	.332	.397	.529
Ottawa	AAA Mon	74	252	64	14	0	7	99	30	40	17	1	38	7	2	3	3	3	.50	9	.254	.315	.393
1999 Ottawa	AAA Mon	98	334	109	32	3	14	189	56	55	44	1	68	24	0	6	10	4	.71	6	.326	.434	.566
2000 Ottawa	AAA Mon	75	267	64	19	1	1	88	30	27	24	1	58	11	2	4	2	2	.00	6	.240	.324	.330
2001 Buffalo	AAA Cle	55	178	37	5	3	6	66	27	22	19	0	38	5	0	2	1	2	.33	3	.208	.299	.371
Toledo	AAA Det	28	85	17	6	1	3	34	13	10	13	1	29	1	2	1	0	0	—	0	.200	.310	.400
1999 Montreal	NL	17	49	13	3	0	0	16	2	4	4	0	7	1	1	0	1	0	1.00	3	.265	.333	.327
2000 Montreal	NL	34	59	12	4	0	1	19	6	8	7	0	19	0	0	1	0	0	—	2	.203	.284	.322
9 Min. YEARS		845	2979	808	185	29	73	1270	471	411	342	7	585	106	15	37	92	53	.63	50	.271	.363	.426
2 Maj. YEARS		51	108	25	7	0	1	35	8	12	11	0	26	1	1	1	1	0	1.00	5	.231	.306	.324

Archie Corbin

Pitches: Right **Bats:** Right **Pos:** RP-58   **Ht:** 6'4" **Wt:** 230 **Born:** 12/30/67 **Age:** 34

		HOW MUCH HE PITCHED					WHAT HE GAVE UP											THE RESULTS					
Year Team	Lg Org	G	GS	CG	GF	IP	BFP	H	R	ER	HR	SH	SF	HB	TBB	IBB	SO	WP	Bk	W	L	Pct.	ShO	Sv	ERA
1986 Kingsport	R+ NYM	18	1	0	9	30.1	149	31	23	16	3	0	1	0	28	0	30	8	1	1	1	.500	0	0	4.75
1987 Kingsport	R+ NYM	6	6	0	0	25.2	128	24	21	18	3	0	0	2	26	0	17	6	0	2	3	.400	0	0	6.31
1988 Kingsport	R+ NYM	11	10	4	0	69.1	277	47	23	12	5	2	0	3	17	0	47	1	1	7	2	.778	1	0	1.56
1989 Columbia	A NYM	27	23	4	3	153.2	664	149	86	77	16	4	4	5	72	0	130	2	0	9	9	.500	2	1	4.51
1990 St. Lucie	A+ NYM	20	18	3	2	118	494	97	47	39	2	4	3	7	59	0	105	10	0	7	8	.467	2	0	2.97
1991 Memphis	AA KC	28	25	1	0	156.1	692	139	90	81	7	4	6	8	90	1	166	13	0	8	8	.500	0	0	4.66
1992 Memphis	AA KC	27	20	2	1	112.1	503	115	64	59	7	3	1	1	73	0	100	11	0	7	8	.467	0	0	4.73
Harrisburg	AA Mon	1	1	0	0	3	11	2	0	0	0	0	0	0	1	0	3	0	0	0	0	—	0	0	0.00
1993 Harrisburg	AA Mon	42	2	0	21	73.1	314	43	31	30	0	1	5	2	59	1	91	5	1	5	3	.625	0	4	3.68
1994 Buffalo	AAA Pit	14	1	0	3	22.2	99	14	13	12	0	1	1	1	18	0	23	2	0	0	0	—	0	0	4.76
1995 Calgary	AAA Pit	47	1	0	13	61	309	76	63	58	6	0	5	3	55	0	54	7	0	1	5	.167	0	1	8.56
1996 Rochester	AAA Bal	20	5	0	10	43.2	197	44	25	23	5	1	1	1	25	0	47	4	0	0	2	.000	0	1	4.74
1997 Rochester	AAA Bal	43	1	0	22	69.2	314	47	32	31	5	2	3	1	62	0	66	10	0	4	3	.571	0	5	4.00
1998 Las Vegas	AAA SD	6	0	0	1	4	36	7	16	13	0	1	0	3	13	0	3	3	0	0	0	—	0	0	27.00
Charlotte	AAA Fla	34	0	0	12	48.2	212	25	15	14	2	1	2	0	46	1	55	0	0	2	2	.500	0	3	2.59
1999 Calgary	AAA Fla	12	0	0	7	13.1	61	13	11	10	3	0	1	0	10	0	16	3	0	1	0	1.000	0	0	6.75
2000 Omaha	AAA KC	32	0	0	15	43.1	221	56	44	39	5	3	2	0	40	1	29	9	0	1	5	.167	0	6	8.10
Charlotte	AAA CWS	8	0	0	2	10.2	50	13	8	5	1	0	1	0	6	0	11	1	0	2	0	1.000	0	0	4.22
2001 Charlotte	AAA CWS	58	0	0	20	77.1	336	58	29	27	3	4	1	0	54	6	64	13	0	6	7	.462	0	1	3.14
1991 Kansas City	AL	2	0	0	2	2.1	12	3	1	1	0	0	0	0	2	0	1	0	0	0	0	—	0	0	3.86
1996 Baltimore	AL	18	0	0	5	27.1	123	22	7	7	2	0	1	1	22	0	20	2	0	2	0	1.000	0	0	2.30
1999 Florida	NL	17	0	0	4	21	104	25	20	17	2	1	1	1	15	0	30	3	0	0	1	.000	0	0	7.29
16 Min. YEARS		454	114	14	141	1136.2	5067	1000	641	564	73	31	37	46	754	10	1057	115	3	62	67	.481	3	25	4.47
3 Maj. YEARS		37	0	0	11	50.2	239	50	28	25	4	1	2	2	39	0	51	5	1	2	1	.667	0	0	4.44

Tim Corcoran

Pitches: Right **Bats:** Right **Pos:** RP-40 **Ht:** 6'2" **Wt:** 195 **Born:** 4/15/78 **Age:** 24

Year Team	Lg Org	HOW MUCH HE PITCHED						WHAT HE GAVE UP										THE RESULTS				
		G	GS	CG	GF	IP	BFP	H	R	ER	HR	SH	SF	HB	TBB	IBB	SO	WP	Bk	W	L	Pct.	ShO	Sv	ERA
1997 Mets	R NYM	10	0	0	4	21	94	16	8	7	0	2	0	0	15	0	20	4	0	3	0	1.000	0	3	3.00
Kingsport	R+ NYM	7	0	0	3	17	75	12	10	8	2	0	2	3	8	2	14	2	1	2	0	1.000	0	0	4.24
1998 St. Lucie	A+ NYM	4	0	0	2	7.2	35	10	7	7	1	0	0	0	2	0	8	0	0	0	0	—	0	0	8.22
Capital Cty	A NYM	20	1	0	10	48.1	204	43	21	14	4	1	1	5	15	0	38	3	0	2	3	.400	0	4	2.61
1999 Capital Cty	A NYM	40	3	0	10	75	332	62	43	37	5	4	3	9	41	0	89	8	1	0	3	.000	0	3	4.44
2000 Capital Cty	A NYM	31	0	0	13	53.1	230	46	28	24	7	0	0	4	27	2	58	11	0	3	5	.375	0	1	4.05
2001 Frederick	A+ Bal	33	0	0	25	50.1	205	37	16	15	4	5	1	2	19	3	42	5	0	6	5	.545	0	6	2.68
Bowie	AA Bal	7	0	0	4	11.2	41	4	1	1	0	0	0	0	3	0	13	1	0	1	0	1.000	0	0	0.77
5 Min. YEARS		152	4	0	71	284.1	1216	230	134	113	23	12	7	23	130	7	282	34	2	17	16	.515	0	17	3.58

Julio Cordido

Bats: Right **Throws:** Right **Pos:** 3B-118; 2B-2; PH-1 **Ht:** 6'1" **Wt:** 192 **Born:** 7/30/80 **Age:** 21

Year Team	Lg Org	BATTING													BASERUNNING				PERCENTAGES		
		G	AB	H	2B	3B	HR	TB	R	RBI	TBB	IBB	SO	HBP	SH	SF	SB	CS	SB%	GDP	Avg	OBP	SLG
1999 Salem-Keizr	A- SF	70	242	64	10	2	1	81	36	28	29	0	44	4	2	1	8	4	.67	3	.264	.351	.335
2000 Bakersfield	A+ SF	130	460	116	17	3	10	169	70	64	46	0	99	7	5	6	13	12	.52	3	.252	.326	.367
2001 Shreveport	AA SF	121	433	94	14	2	1	115	45	47	31	1	68	3	1	4	11	3	.79	15	.217	.272	.266
3 Min. YEARS		321	1135	274	41	7	12	365	151	139	106	1	211	14	8	11	32	19	.63	21	.241	.311	.322

Francisco Cordova

Pitches: Right **Bats:** Right **Pos:** SP-2 **Ht:** 6'1" **Wt:** 197 **Born:** 4/26/72 **Age:** 30

Year Team	Lg Org	HOW MUCH HE PITCHED						WHAT HE GAVE UP										THE RESULTS				
		G	GS	CG	GF	IP	BFP	H	R	ER	HR	SH	SF	HB	TBB	IBB	SO	WP	Bk	W	L	Pct.	ShO	Sv	ERA
1999 Altoona	AA Pit	2	2	0	0	9.2	48	13	8	5	0	0	0	0	4	0	12	1	1	1	1	.500	0	0	4.66
Nashville	AAA Pit	2	2	0	0	12	47	10	2	1	1	0	1	0	1	0	7	0	0	2	0	1.000	0	0	0.75
2001 Altoona	AA Pit	1	1	0	0	4.1	19	6	2	2	0	0	0	0	1	0	4	0	0	0	0	—	0	0	4.15
Nashville	AAA Pit	1	1	0	0	1	5	2	2	2	1	0	0	0	0	0	1	0	0	0	0	—	0	0	18.00
1996 Pittsburgh	NL	59	6	0	41	99	414	103	49	45	11	1	0	2	20	6	95	2	1	4	7	.364	0	12	4.09
1997 Pittsburgh	NL	29	29	2	0	178.2	744	175	80	72	14	3	7	9	49	4	121	4	0	11	8	.579	2	0	3.63
1998 Pittsburgh	NL	33	33	3	0	220.1	921	204	91	81	22	9	6	3	69	5	157	1	1	13	14	.481	2	0	3.31
1999 Pittsburgh	NL	27	27	2	0	160.2	682	166	83	79	16	7	4	4	59	6	98	5	0	8	10	.444	0	0	4.43
2000 Pittsburgh	NL	18	17	0	0	95	421	107	63	55	12	3	3	2	38	4	66	3	1	6	8	.429	0	0	5.21
2 Min. YEARS		6	6	0	0	27	119	31	14	10	2	0	1	0	6	0	24	1	1	3	1	.750	0	0	3.33
5 Maj. YEARS		166	112	7	41	753.2	3182	755	366	332	75	23	20	20	235	25	537	15	3	42	47	.472	4	12	3.96

Bryan Corey

Pitches: Right **Bats:** Right **Pos:** RP-35; SP-12 **Ht:** 6'0" **Wt:** 170 **Born:** 10/21/73 **Age:** 28

Year Team	Lg Org	HOW MUCH HE PITCHED						WHAT HE GAVE UP										THE RESULTS				
		G	GS	CG	GF	IP	BFP	H	R	ER	HR	SH	SF	HB	TBB	IBB	SO	WP	Bk	W	L	Pct.	ShO	Sv	ERA
1995 Jamestown	A- Det	29	0	0	28	28	116	21	14	12	2	0	1	1	12	1	41	4	0	2	2	.500	0	10	3.86
1996 Fayettevlle	A Det	60	0	0	53	82	315	50	19	11	2	4	6	2	17	3	101	6	2	6	4	.600	0	34	1.21
1997 Jacksnville	AA Det	52	0	0	36	68	298	74	42	36	8	5	3	1	21	3	37	4	0	3	8	.273	0	9	4.76
1998 Tucson	AAA Ari	39	10	0	14	87.2	401	116	61	53	14	1	2	6	24	0	50	2	2	4	6	.400	0	2	5.44
1999 Toledo	AAA Det	48	0	0	17	69.1	303	63	27	22	6	4	1	2	34	4	36	2	1	5	2	.714	0	2	2.86
2000 Sacramento	AAA Oak	47	6	0	16	85	362	88	43	40	11	4	3	3	29	2	55	2	1	8	3	.727	0	4	4.24
2001 Portland	AAA SD	47	12	0	25	106	455	124	55	55	12	3	5	3	31	3	66	1	1	8	7	.533	0	6	4.67
1998 Arizona	NL	3	0	0	2	4	20	6	4	4	1	1	0	1	2	0	1	0	0	0	0	—	0	0	9.00
7 Min. YEARS		322	28	0	189	526	2250	536	261	229	55	21	21	18	168	16	386	21	7	36	32	.529	0	67	3.92

Brad Cornett

Pitches: Right **Bats:** Right **Pos:** RP-37; SP-4 **Ht:** 6'3" **Wt:** 188 **Born:** 2/4/69 **Age:** 33

Year Team	Lg Org	HOW MUCH HE PITCHED						WHAT HE GAVE UP										THE RESULTS				
		G	GS	CG	GF	IP	BFP	H	R	ER	HR	SH	SF	HB	TBB	IBB	SO	WP	Bk	W	L	Pct.	ShO	Sv	ERA
1992 St.Cathrnes	A- Tor	25	0	0	13	60	241	54	30	24	6	1	0	3	10	0	64	5	0	4	1	.800	0	1	3.60
1993 Hagerstown	A Tor	31	21	3	7	172.1	711	164	77	46	6	5	5	5	31	2	161	6	1	10	8	.556	1	3	2.40
1994 Knoxville	AA Tor	7	7	1	0	37.1	151	34	18	10	2	1	0	1	6	0	26	3	0	2	3	.400	0	0	2.41
Syracuse	AAA Tor	3	3	0	0	19	85	18	8	3	0	0	1	0	9	1	12	0	0	1	2	.333	0	0	1.42
1995 Syracuse	AAA Tor	3	3	0	0	11	49	13	6	6	1	0	1	0	4	0	3	0	0	1	0	1.000	0	0	4.91
1996 Dunedin	A+ Tor	4	0	0	2	7.1	41	15	7	7	1	0	0	1	3	0	5	1	1	0	1	.000	0	0	8.59
1998 Tucson	AAA Ari	6	6	0	0	26.1	127	44	25	23	6	1	2	0	6	0	12	1	0	1	2	.333	0	0	7.86
El Paso	AA Mil	3	3	0	0	15.2	75	22	16	9	4	1	0	0	5	0	10	3	1	0	2	.000	0	0	5.17
Louisville	AAA Mil	12	8	0	0	61.2	256	64	30	25	9	4	1	2	14	0	34	1	0	3	3	.500	0	0	3.65
1999 Lehigh Val	IND —	23	23	3	0	162.1	679	172	84	71	17	2	4	3	37	1	118	0	0	11	9	.550	0	0	3.94
2000 Lehigh Val	IND —	5	4	0	0	26.1	122	33	15	14	0	0	0	0	10	0	20	2	0	2	1	.667	0	0	4.78
Durham	AAA TB	19	12	0	3	88.2	383	100	46	42	7	1	2	2	24	1	72	1	1	4	5	.444	0	0	4.26
2001 Syracuse	AAA Tor	6	0	0	2	11.1	53	17	8	8	0	0	1	0	5	1	6	1	0	1	0	1.000	0	0	6.35
Bridgeport	IND —	2	2	0	0	12	46	10	4	3	0	0	1	0	1	0	9	0	0	0	1	.000	0	0	2.25
Durham	AAA TB	33	2	0	6	61.1	255	56	22	14	3	4	0	2	12	0	55	6	0	4	2	.667	0	2	2.05
1994 Toronto	AL	9	4	0	0	31	141	40	25	23	1	4	2	3	11	2	22	2	0	1	3	.250	0	0	6.68
1995 Toronto	AL	5	0	0	2	5	25	9	6	5	1	0	0	1	3	0	4	1	0	0	0	—	0	0	9.00
9 Min. YEARS		182	94	7	33	772.2	3274	816	396	305	62	20	17	19	177	6	607	30	4	43	41	.512	1	6	3.55
2 Maj. YEARS		14	4	0	2	36	166	49	31	28	2	4	2	4	14	2	26	3	0	1	3	.250	0	0	7.00

David Cortes

Pitches: Right **Bats:** Right **Pos:** RP-33

Ht: 5'11" **Wt:** 195 **Born:** 10/15/73 **Age:** 28

		HOW MUCH HE PITCHED						WHAT HE GAVE UP										THE RESULTS					
Year Team	Lg Org	G	GS	CG	GF	IP	BFP	H	R	ER	HR	SH	SF	HB	TBB	IBB	SO	WP	Bk	W	L	Pct.	ShO	Sv	ERA
1996 Eugene	A- Atl	15	0	0	11	24.2	95	13	2	2	0	1	0	0	6	0	33	0	0	2	1	.667	0	4	0.73
1997 Macon	A Atl	27	0	0	24	31.1	114	16	3	2	0	2	1	2	4	0	32	0	0	3	0	1.000	0	15	0.57
Durham	A+ Atl	19	0	0	16	19.1	76	15	5	5	1	0	1	0	5	0	16	1	0	2	0	1.000	0	8	2.33
Greenville	AA Atl	3	0	0	1	5	20	4	1	1	0	0	0	0	1	0	7	0	0	1	0	1.000	0	0	1.80
1998 Richmond	AAA Atl	29	0	0	17	44.2	181	37	15	14	2	3	1	0	14	3	46	1	0	3	3	.500	0	4	2.82
Colo Sprngs	AAA Col	6	0	0	0	7	37	14	6	6	0	0	0	0	2	0	5	0	0	1	0	1.000	0	0	7.71
1999 Richmond	AAA Atl	47	0	0	42	45.2	198	50	19	17	2	2	1	0	14	5	42	2	0	2	3	.400	0	22	3.35
2001 Myrtle Bch	A+ Atl	9	0	0	2	10.2	49	11	7	7	2	1	0	0	5	0	9	2	0	0	2	.000	0	2	5.91
Greenville	AA Atl	14	0	0	6	17.2	85	19	18	16	2	1	0	1	11	2	10	3	1	0	3	.000	0	0	8.15
Macon	A Atl	10	0	0	4	12.2	61	14	11	10	1	0	1	1	5	0	8	2	0	1	0	1.000	0	0	7.11
1999 Atlanta	NL	4	0	0	4	3.2	18	3	3	2	0	0	0	0	4	0	2	2	0	0	0	—	0	0	4.91
5 Min. YEARS		179	0	0	123	218.2	916	193	87	80	11	10	5	4	67	10	208	11	1	15	12	.556	0	55	3.29

Tony Cosentino

Bats: Right **Throws:** Right **Pos:** C-51; DH-6; PH-2

Ht: 6'0" **Wt:** 195 **Born:** 12/7/78 **Age:** 23

		BATTING													BASERUNNING				PERCENTAGES		
Year Team	Lg Org	G	AB	H	2B	3B	HR	TB	R	RBI	TBB	IBB	SO	HBP	SH	SF	SB	CS	SB%	GDP	Avg	OBP	SLG
1997 Padres	R SD	33	106	29	3	1	1	37	11	14	18	0	20	1	0	0	1	0	1.00	6	.274	.384	.349
1998 Padres	R SD	42	148	39	9	1	0	50	29	24	39	1	31	3	0	4	1	2	.33	5	.264	.418	.338
1999 Idaho Falls	R+ SD	20	88	33	5	2	2	48	14	30	6	1	11	0	0	2	0	0	—	5	.375	.406	.545
Fort Wayne	A SD	37	127	31	5	0	0	36	11	11	22	0	33	1	0	1	1	1	.50	3	.244	.358	.283
2000 Fort Wayne	A SD	80	276	72	19	1	3	102	25	38	32	0	50	5	0	2	1	0	1.00	13	.261	.346	.370
2001 Mobile	AA SD	5	10	0	0	0	0	0	0	0	2	0	2	0	0	0	0	0	—	1	.000	.167	.000
Lk Elsinore	A+ SD	53	174	37	9	1	4	60	21	21	20	0	32	1	1	3	1	1	.50	6	.213	.293	.345
5 Min. YEARS		270	929	241	50	6	10	333	111	138	139	2	179	11	1	12	5	4	.56	39	.259	.358	.358

Caonabo Cosme

Bats: Right **Throws:** Right **Pos:** SS-66; 3B-24; PR-3; DH-1; PH-1

Ht: 6'2" **Wt:** 160 **Born:** 3/18/79 **Age:** 23

		BATTING													BASERUNNING				PERCENTAGES		
Year Team	Lg Org	G	AB	H	2B	3B	HR	TB	R	RBI	TBB	IBB	SO	HBP	SH	SF	SB	CS	SB%	GDP	Avg	OBP	SLG
1997 Athletics	R Oak	37	130	28	6	1	1	39	28	17	19	0	28	2	1	1	7	1	.88	2	.215	.322	.300
1998 Modesto	A+ Oak	124	414	114	24	3	2	150	48	41	27	0	137	2	10	3	16	7	.70	6	.275	.321	.362
1999 Modesto	A+ Oak	122	444	95	21	2	2	126	55	47	45	1	148	4	3	3	14	7	.67	12	.214	.290	.284
2000 Modesto	A+ Oak	133	548	132	33	2	2	175	73	53	56	0	163	2	12	3	44	15	.75	9	.241	.312	.319
2001 Modesto	A+ Oak	58	236	69	16	1	1	90	43	21	20	1	54	2	6	2	22	6	.79	2	.292	.350	.381
Midland	AA Oak	34	99	19	2	2	0	25	9	4	4	0	32	0	5	0	1	2	.33	0	.192	.223	.253
5 Min. YEARS		508	1871	457	102	11	8	605	256	183	171	2	562	12	37	12	104	38	.73	31	.244	.310	.323

Chris Coste

Bats: Right **Throws:** Right **Pos:** C-37; 1B-19; OF-12; DH-12; 3B-1; PH-1

Ht: 6'1" **Wt:** 205 **Born:** 2/4/73 **Age:** 29

		BATTING													BASERUNNING				PERCENTAGES		
Year Team	Lg Org	G	AB	H	2B	3B	HR	TB	R	RBI	TBB	IBB	SO	HBP	SH	SF	SB	CS	SB%	GDP	Avg	OBP	SLG
1995 Brandon	IND —	24	94	24	7	0	0	31	12	13	3	—	10	—	—	—	2	1	.67		.255		.330
1996 Fargo-Mh	IND —	81	315	99	30	0	6	147	40	56	17	0	56	10	4	4	2	3	.40	6	.314	.364	.467
1997 Fargo-Mh	IND —	84	337	105	22	0	12	163	45	50	23	0	53	7	0	1	7	1	.88	10	.312	.367	.484
1998 Fargo-Mh	IND —	85	326	107	17	2	10	158	59	55	31	0	30	3	0	2	6	3	.67	14	.328	.390	.485
1999 Fargo-Mh	IND —	85	352	118	18	2	16	188	67	60	31	1	42	2	0	3	4	1	.80	17	.335	.389	.534
2000 Buffalo	AAA Cle	31	96	29	2	0	4	43	15	8	3	0	12	1	1	0	0	1	.00	4	.302	.330	.448
Akron	AA Cle	65	240	80	20	4	2	114	32	31	15	2	33	4	0	1	1	2	.33	7	.333	.381	.475
2001 Akron	AA Cle	6	24	3	0	0	0	3	1	0	1	0	3	0	0	0	0	1	.00	0	.125	.160	.125
Buffalo	AAA Cle	75	271	78	16	2	7	119	31	50	15	1	50	4	1	4	0	1	.00	11	.288	.330	.439
7 Min. YEARS		536	2055	643	132	10	57	966	302	323	139	—	289				22	14	.61		.313		.470

Joe Cotton

Pitches: Right **Bats:** Right **Pos:** RP-53

Ht: 6'2" **Wt:** 185 **Born:** 3/25/75 **Age:** 27

		HOW MUCH HE PITCHED						WHAT HE GAVE UP										THE RESULTS					
Year Team	Lg Org	G	GS	CG	GF	IP	BFP	H	R	ER	HR	SH	SF	HB	TBB	IBB	SO	WP	Bk	W	L	Pct.	ShO	Sv	ERA
1996 Batavia	A- Phi	9	9	0	0	46.1	196	43	23	22	2	3	1	1	19	0	37	4	0	2	4	.333	0	0	4.27
1997 Batavia	A- Phi	15	15	0	0	96.1	402	90	38	32	10	2	2	7	29	0	74	6	0	7	4	.636	0	0	2.99
1998 Piedmont	A Phi	44	0	0	20	77.1	322	73	48	38	14	4	6	6	16	1	79	3	0	6	8	.429	0	5	4.42
1999 Clearwater	A+ Phi	38	3	0	5	69.1	263	41	17	15	5	1	3	1	15	2	43	1	0	5	3	.625	0	1	1.95
2000 Clearwater	A+ Phi	9	0	0	4	16	65	16	7	7	1	1	0	0	2	0	14	0	0	0	1	.000	0	0	3.94
2001 Midland	AA Phi	33	2	0	18	72	273	48	17	16	5	0	2	1	19	1	51	0	0	4	1	.800	0	6	2.00
Reading	AA Phi	47	0	0	19	65	272	50	21	20	4	2	3	2	28	3	63	1	1	6	1	.857	0	7	2.77
Sacramento	AAA Oak	6	0	0	0	6.1	31	7	6	6	1	1	1	0	5	0	7	0	0	0	2	.000	0	0	8.53
6 Min. YEARS		201	29	0	66	448.2	1824	368	177	156	42	14	18	18	133	7	368	15	1	30	24	.556	0	19	3.13

John Cotton

Bats: Left **Throws:** Right **Pos:** 3B-31; 1B-28; PH-19; 2B-15; DH-14; OF-5

Ht: 6'0" **Wt:** 190 **Born:** 10/30/70 **Age:** 31

		BATTING													BASERUNNING				PERCENTAGES		
Year Team	Lg Org	G	AB	H	2B	3B	HR	TB	R	RBI	TBB	IBB	SO	HBP	SH	SF	SB	CS	SB%	GDP	Avg	OBP	SLG
1989 Burlington	R+ Cle	64	227	47	5	1	2	60	36	22	22	0	56	3	4	1	20	3	.87	5	.207	.285	.264
1990 Watertown	A- Cle	73	286	60	9	4	2	83	53	27	40	3	71	2	2	1	24	7	.77	4	.210	.310	.290
1991 Columbus	A Cle	122	405	92	11	9	13	160	88	42	93	1	135	3	3	3	56	15	.79	6	.227	.373	.395
1992 Kinston	A+ Cle	103	360	72	7	3	11	118	67	39	48	1	106	2	1	2	23	7	.77	3	.200	.296	.328

Year Team	Lg Org	G	AB	H	2B	3B	HR	TB	R	RBI	TBB	IBB	SO	HBP	SH	SF	SB	CS	SB%	GDP	Avg	OBP	SLG
1993 Kinston	A+ Cle	127	454	120	16	3	13	181	81	51	59	1	130	11	5	2	28	24	.54	3	.264	.361	.399
1994 Springfield	A SD	24	82	19	5	3	1	33	14	8	12	0	19	0	0	0	7	1	.88	0	.232	.330	.402
Wichita	AA SD	34	85	16	4	0	3	29	9	14	13	3	20	1	0	2	2	0	1.00	3	.188	.297	.341
Rancho Cuca	A+ SD	48	171	35	3	2	4	54	35	19	22	0	48	2	0	0	9	3	.75	3	.205	.303	.316
1995 Memphis	AA SD	121	407	103	19	8	12	174	60	47	38	0	101	4	6	4	15	6	.71	2	.253	.320	.428
1996 Toledo	AAA Det	50	171	32	7	1	4	53	14	19	7	0	64	2	2	0	4	4	.50	1	.187	.228	.310
Jacksnville	AA Det	63	217	52	7	4	13	106	34	39	19	2	66	2	0	1	15	3	.83	2	.240	.305	.488
1997 Birmingham	AA CWS	33	124	36	10	2	7	71	23	26	9	0	33	2	0	1	1	2	.33	3	.290	.346	.573
Nashville	AAA CWS	94	323	87	14	3	11	140	45	50	24	1	94	0	1	2	8	2	.80	7	.269	.318	.433
1998 Daytona	A+ ChC	12	48	14	4	0	3	27	8	11	3	0	8	1	0	0	0	0	—	3	.292	.346	.563
West Tenn	AA ChC	90	319	93	14	3	13	152	46	53	19	1	68	4	0	5	10	3	.77	3	.292	.334	.476
1999 Carolina	AA Col	42	163	46	9	0	10	85	27	21	10	1	48	1	0	0	0	1	.00	3	.282	.328	.521
Colo Sprngs	AAA Col	70	235	74	18	1	15	139	50	48	14	4	64	2	1	3	4	2	.67	6	.315	.354	.591
2000 Colo Sprngs	AAA Col	103	314	103	21	5	16	182	58	62	30	3	97	1	0	2	13	0	1.00	6	.328	.386	.580
2001 Nashville	AAA Pit	30	80	16	4	0	1	23	7	9	5	1	22	0	1	0	2	0	.00	3	.200	.247	.288
Las Vegas	AAA LA	42	127	26	2	0	8	52	15	17	11	3	44	2	0	1	1	1	.50	2	.205	.279	.409
Harrisburg	AA Mon	5	17	5	0	0	3	14	5	8	1	0	5	0	0	0	0	0	—	0	.294	.333	.824
Ottawa	AAA Mon	24	93	26	8	1	5	51	11	15	6	2	25	1	0	0	2	1	.67	1	.280	.330	.548
13 Min. YEARS		1374	4708	1174	197	53	170	1987	786	647	505	27	1324	46	26	29	242	87	.74	69	.249	.326	.422

Darron Cox

Bats: Right **Throws:** Right **Pos:** C-56; PH-16; DH-6; PR-2 **Ht:** 6'1" **Wt:** 205 **Born:** 11/21/67 **Age:** 34

Year Team	Lg Org	G	AB	H	2B	3B	HR	TB	R	RBI	TBB	IBB	SO	HBP	SH	SF	SB	CS	SB%	GDP	Avg	OBP	SLG
1989 Billings	R+ Cin	49	157	43	6	0	0	49	20	18	21	0	34	5	2	0	11	3	.79	1	.274	.377	.312
1990 Chston-WV	A Cin	103	367	93	11	3	1	113	53	44	40	2	75	7	4	3	14	3	.82	12	.253	.336	.308
1991 Cedar Rapds	A Cin	21	60	16	4	0	0	20	12	4	8	0	11	4	1	0	7	1	.88	2	.267	.389	.333
Chattanooga	AA Cin	13	38	7	1	0	0	8	2	3	2	0	9	0	1	1	0	0	—	1	.184	.220	.211
Chston-WV	A Cin	79	294	71	14	1	2	93	37	28	24	0	40	2	1	7	8	4	.67	7	.241	.297	.316
1992 Chattanooga	AA Cin	98	331	84	19	1	1	108	29	38	15	0	63	5	1	6	8	3	.73	7	.254	.291	.326
1993 Chattanooga	AA Cin	89	300	65	9	5	3	93	35	26	38	2	63	3	7	1	7	4	.64	7	.217	.310	.310
1994 Iowa	AAA ChC	99	301	80	15	1	3	106	26	26	28	4	47	4	3	0	5	2	.71	12	.266	.336	.352
1995 Orlando	AA ChC	33	102	29	5	0	4	46	8	15	8	0	16	1	2	2	3	3	.50	3	.284	.336	.451
Iowa	AAA ChC	33	94	22	6	0	1	31	7	14	8	0	21	2	2	4	0	0	—	0	.234	.296	.330
1996 Richmond	AAA Atl	55	168	40	9	0	3	58	19	20	5	0	22	3	2	2	1	0	1.00	5	.238	.270	.345
1997 Orlando	AA ChC	3	9	2	1	0	1	6	2	4	1	0	1	0	0	0	1	0	—	1	.222	.273	.667
1998 Durham	AAA TB	84	278	84	16	1	9	129	45	35	23	0	41	5	8	0	2	2	.50	6	.302	.366	.464
1999 Ottawa	AAA Mon	3	9	0	0	0	0	0	0	0	1	0	2	0	0	0	0	0	—	0	.000	.100	.000
2000 Colo Sprngs	AAA Col	78	244	78	14	0	3	101	37	46	27	2	34	4	2	7	3	3	.50	10	.320	.387	.414
2001 Colo Sprngs	AAA Col	76	209	58	10	1	3	79	33	25	24	1	42	6	1	2	3	1	.75	8	.278	.364	.378
1999 Montreal	NL	15	25	6	1	0	1	10	2	2	0	0	5	2	0	0	0	0	—	0	.240	.296	.400
13 Min. YEARS		916	2961	772	140	13	34	1040	374	346	273	11	521	50	38	35	72	29	.71	82	.261	.330	.351

Ryan Cox

Pitches: Right **Bats:** Right **Pos:** SP-24 **Ht:** 6'3" **Wt:** 210 **Born:** 12/25/76 **Age:** 25

Year Team	Lg Org	G	GS	CG	GF	IP	BFP	H	R	ER	HR	SH	SF	HB	TBB	IBB	SO	WP	Bk	W	L	Pct.	ShO	Sv	ERA
1999 Salem-Keizr	A- SF	8	8	0	0	34.1	139	39	15	12	1	2	1	1	10	0	20	0	2	2	1	.667	0	0	3.15
Bakersfield	A+ SF	7	7	0	0	33.1	151	46	22	18	6	1	0	1	3	0	30	2	0	1	4	.200	0	0	4.86
2000 San Jose	A+ SF	19	19	0	0	107.1	463	122	67	55	12	3	7	5	28	0	54	5	0	5	8	.385	0	0	4.61
Shreveport	AA SF	7	7	0	0	33.1	158	53	35	30	5	0	1	3	5	0	24	0	0	2	2	.500	0	0	8.10
Fresno	AAA SF	1	0	0	0	1	6	3	2	2	0	0	0	0	0	0	1	1	0	0	0	—	0	0	18.00
2001 Shreveport	AA SF	24	24	1	0	136.2	575	145	70	56	8	3	6	6	24	0	61	2	0	8	8	.500	0	0	3.69
3 Min. YEARS		66	65	1	0	346	1492	408	209	173	32	9	15	16	70	0	190	10	2	18	23	.439	0	0	4.50

Robbie Crabtree

Pitches: Right **Bats:** Right **Pos:** RP-63 **Ht:** 6'1" **Wt:** 175 **Born:** 11/25/72 **Age:** 29

Year Team	Lg Org	G	GS	CG	GF	IP	BFP	H	R	ER	HR	SH	SF	HB	TBB	IBB	SO	WP	Bk	W	L	Pct.	ShO	Sv	ERA
1996 Bellingham	A- SF	28	0	0	13	52	206	38	18	16	8	2	1	6	14	1	72	3	0	3	3	.500	0	4	2.77
1997 Bakersfield	A+ SF	45	9	1	9	112.1	506	124	77	64	10	1	0	5	59	1	116	12	1	7	7	.500	0	1	5.13
1998 San Jose	A+ SF	24	0	0	10	54.1	213	39	6	6	0	4	0	3	8	0	67	1	0	6	1	.857	0	2	0.99
Shreveport	AA SF	26	0	0	13	54	205	30	11	10	4	1	0	2	16	2	56	2	0	2	0	1.000	0	1	1.67
Fresno	AAA SF	3	1	0	2	4.2	26	8	7	6	1	0	0	1	2	0	10	0	0	0	0	—	0	0	11.57
1999 Fresno	AAA SF	22	1	0	11	34.1	150	37	23	20	2	0	0	0	10	1	40	0	0	1	4	.200	0	1	5.24
Shreveport	AA SF	36	0	0	14	63.1	251	50	21	18	2	0	1	0	18	2	65	3	0	4	2	.667	0	2	2.56
2000 Fresno	AAA SF	63	0	0	21	127.2	544	126	67	54	8	7	4	7	31	5	116	2	0	5	6	.455	0	8	3.81
2001 Fresno	AAA SF	63	0	0	31	114.2	474	115	56	47	11	7	3	1	34	5	99	3	0	8	10	.444	0	6	3.69
6 Min. YEARS		310	11	1	124	617.1	2575	567	286	241	46	22	9	19	192	17	641	29	1	36	33	.522	0	28	3.51

Kevin Crafton

Pitches: Right **Bats:** Right **Pos:** RP-13 **Ht:** 6'1" **Wt:** 185 **Born:** 5/10/74 **Age:** 28

Year Team	Lg Org	G	GS	CG	GF	IP	BFP	H	R	ER	HR	SH	SF	HB	TBB	IBB	SO	WP	Bk	W	L	Pct.	ShO	Sv	ERA
1996 New Jersey	A- StL	23	0	0	10	33	132	28	8	8	1	3	1		6	2	43	2	0	2	3	.400	0	2	2.18
1997 Peoria	A StL	50	0	0	35	55	219	40	16	12	1	2	5	2	18	7	59	2	1	7	2	.778	0	29	1.96
1998 Arkansas	AA StL	46	0	0	13	55.2	227	52	23	20	8	12	2	0	7	0	44	2	0	5	1	.833	0	1	3.23
1999 Memphis	AAA StL	4	0	0	0	4.1	26	12	12	11	2	0	1	1	0	0	2	0	0	0	1	.000	0	0	22.85
Arkansas	AA StL	42	0	0	14	46.1	209	57	41	39	9	2	1	1	16	1	41	2	0	7	2	.778	0	2	7.58

	HOW MUCH HE PITCHED						WHAT HE GAVE UP												THE RESULTS					
Year Team	Lg Org	G	GS	CG	GF	IP	BFP	H	R	ER	HR	SH	SF	HB	TBB	IBB	SO	WP	Bk	W	L	Pct.	ShO	Sv	ERA
2000 Memphis	AAA StL	2	0	0	1	2.2	12	4	2	2	0	0	0	0	1	0	0	0	0	0	0	—	0	0	6.75
Arkansas	AA StL	57	0	0	28	70.2	302	69	24	20	5	4	4	2	28	4	48	1	0	9	5	.643	0	4	2.55
2001 Memphis	AAA StL	13	0	0	2	19	100	34	20	17	2	1	1	1	6	0	13	1	0	1	1	.500	0	0	8.05
6 Min. YEARS		237	0	0	113	286.2	1227	296	146	129	29	18	12	8	82	14	250	10	1	31	15	.674	0	38	4.05

Carl Crawford

Bats: Left **Throws:** Left **Pos:** OF-130; DH-2   **Ht:** 6'2" **Wt:** 203 **Born:** 8/5/81 **Age:** 20

		BATTING													BASERUNNING				PERCENTAGES		
Year Team	Lg Org	G	AB	H	2B	3B	HR	TB	R	RBI	TBB	IBB	SO	HBP	SH	SF	SB	CS	SB%	GDP	Avg	OBP	SLG
1999 Princeton	R+ TB	84	260	83	14	4	0	105	62	25	13	0	47	1	1	3	17	3	.85	5	.319	.350	.404
2000 Chston-SC	A TB	135	564	170	21	11	6	231	99	57	32	1	102	3	9	1	55	9	.86	1	.301	.342	.410
2001 Orlando	AA TB	132	537	147	24	3	4	189	64	51	36	2	90	4	6	2	36	20	.64	3	.274	.323	.352
3 Min. YEARS		327	1361	400	59	18	10	525	225	133	81	3	239	8	16	6	108	32	.77	9	.294	.336	.386

Joe Crawford

Pitches: Left **Bats:** Left **Pos:** SP-22; RP-1   **Ht:** 6'3" **Wt:** 225 **Born:** 5/2/70 **Age:** 32

		HOW MUCH HE PITCHED						WHAT HE GAVE UP												THE RESULTS					
Year Team	Lg Org	G	GS	CG	GF	IP	BFP	H	R	ER	HR	SH	SF	HB	TBB	IBB	SO	WP	Bk	W	L	Pct.	ShO	Sv	ERA
1991 Kingsport	R+ NYM	19	0	0	16	32.1	118	16	5	4	0	0	0	1	8	0	43	3	1	0	0	—	0	11	1.11
Columbia	A NYM	3	0	0	2	3	9	0	0	0	0	0	0	0	0	0	6	0	0	0	0	—	0	0	0.00
1992 St. Lucie	A+ NYM	25	1	0	16	43.2	174	29	18	10	1	1	3	0	15	3	32	1	3	3	3	.500	0	3	2.06
1993 St. Lucie	A+ NYM	34	0	0	19	37	156	38	15	15	0	2	0	2	14	5	24	0	0	3	3	.500	0	5	3.65
1994 St. Lucie	A+ NYM	33	0	0	15	42.2	155	22	8	7	1	1	2	2	9	2	31	1	0	1	1	.500	0	5	1.48
Binghamton	AA NYM	13	0	0	6	14.2	70	20	10	9	2	0	2	0	8	0	9	0	0	1	0	1.000	0	0	5.52
1995 Binghamton	AA NYM	42	1	0	15	60.2	239	48	17	15	4	3	7	5	17	4	43	3	1	7	2	.778	0	0	2.23
Norfolk	AAA NYM	8	0	0	1	18.2	70	9	5	4	0	1	0	0	4	0	13	0	0	1	1	.500	0	0	1.93
1996 Binghamton	AA NYM	7	7	1	0	49.2	190	34	10	8	4	2	0	0	9	1	34	1	2	5	1	.833	1	0	1.45
Norfolk	AAA NYM	20	16	2	2	96.2	403	98	45	37	10	3	1	4	20	1	68	0	1	6	5	.545	1	0	3.44
1997 Norfolk	AAA NYM	16	16	0	0	99.2	431	109	45	39	6	5	5	1	31	0	72	4	2	8	2	.800	1	0	3.52
2000 Indianapolis	AAA Mil	3	0	0	0	0.2	6	3	2	2	1	0	0	1	0	0	1	1	0	0	0	—	0	0	27.00
Bridgeport	IND —	16	15	2	0	97	420	106	52	42	7	4	0	3	25	0	57	2	0	9	1	.900	1	0	3.90
2001 Bridgeport	IND —	8	8	1	0	41.2	200	52	32	27	4	0	3	3	15	1	28	3	0	2	2	.500	0	0	5.83
El Paso	AAA Ari	7	7	0	0	40.2	181	49	30	24	1	6	1	2	12	0	30	1	0	0	4	.000	0	0	5.31
Tucson	AAA Ari	8	7	1	0	41.1	193	58	30	24	7	1	2	2	12	1	32	0	0	2	4	.333	0	0	5.23
1997 New York	NL	19	2	0	9	46.1	182	36	18	17	7	2	0	0	13	1	25	0	1	4	3	.571	0	0	3.30
9 Min. YEARS		262	78	7	92	720	3015	691	324	267	48	29	26	26	199	18	523	20	10	48	29	.623	3	24	3.34

Brad Cresse

Bats: Right **Throws:** Right **Pos:** C-96; DH-22   **Ht:** 6'4" **Wt:** 215 **Born:** 7/31/78 **Age:** 23

		BATTING													BASERUNNING				PERCENTAGES		
Year Team	Lg Org	G	AB	H	2B	3B	HR	TB	R	RBI	TBB	IBB	SO	HBP	SH	SF	SB	CS	SB%	GDP	Avg	OBP	SLG
2000 High Desert	A+ Ari	48	173	56	7	0	17	114	35	56	17	1	50	7	0	2	0	0	—	3	.324	.402	.659
El Paso	AA Ari	15	42	11	1	0	1	15	9	10	6	0	12	3	0	1	0	0	—	1	.262	.385	.357
2001 El Paso	AA Ari	118	429	124	39	1	14	207	55	81	44	0	116	18	0	7	0	1	.00	11	.289	.373	.483
2 Min. YEARS		181	644	191	47	1	32	336	99	147	67	1	178	28	0	10	0	1	.00	15	.297	.382	.522

Mark Cridland

Bats: Left **Throws:** Right **Pos:** OF-73; PH-6; DH-4; PR-2   **Ht:** 6'3" **Wt:** 205 **Born:** 5/15/75 **Age:** 27

		BATTING													BASERUNNING				PERCENTAGES		
Year Team	Lg Org	G	AB	H	2B	3B	HR	TB	R	RBI	TBB	IBB	SO	HBP	SH	SF	SB	CS	SB%	GDP	Avg	OBP	SLG
1998 Beloit	A Mil	79	296	77	16	2	6	115	35	37	14	3	63	3	5	4	0	1	.00	4	.260	.297	.389
1999 Stockton	A+ Mil	124	437	114	26	5	13	189	51	87	33	3	64	6	5	16	14	7	.67	6	.261	.311	.432
2000 Mudville	A+ Mil	131	503	131	25	6	21	231	78	66	49	4	101	9	1	3	20	9	.69	11	.260	.335	.459
2001 Huntsville	AA Mil	70	234	54	8	1	7	85	25	31	12	1	56	1	1	0	3	4	.43	1	.231	.271	.363
High Desert	A+ Mil	12	46	15	5	1	3	31	13	8	6	0	15	0	0	0	4	1	.80	0	.326	.404	.674
4 Min. YEARS		416	1516	391	80	15	50	651	202	229	114	11	299	19	12	23	41	22	.65	22	.258	.313	.429

Bubba Crosby

Bats: Left **Throws:** Left **Pos:** OF-112; PH-8; DH-1   **Ht:** 5'11" **Wt:** 185 **Born:** 8/11/76 **Age:** 25

		BATTING													BASERUNNING				PERCENTAGES		
Year Team	Lg Org	G	AB	H	2B	3B	HR	TB	R	RBI	TBB	IBB	SO	HBP	SH	SF	SB	CS	SB%	GDP	Avg	OBP	SLG
1998 San Berndno	A+ LA	56	199	43	9	2	0	56	25	14	17	0	38	0	4	3	3	5	.38	3	.216	.274	.281
1999 San Berndno	A+ LA	96	371	110	21	3	1	140	53	37	42	3	71	6	4	1	19	8	.70	6	.296	.376	.377
2000 Vero Beach	A+ LA	73	274	73	13	8	8	126	50	51	31	3	41	7	3	1	27	10	.73	9	.266	.355	.460
San Berndno	A+ LA	3	12	3	0	0	0	3	2	2	0	0	4	0	0	0	1	0	1.00	0	.250	.250	.250
2001 Las Vegas	AAA LA	13	42	9	2	1	0	13	5	5	1	0	8	0	0	0	1	1	.50	0	.214	.233	.310
Jacksnville	AA LA	107	384	116	22	5	6	166	68	47	37	2	60	8	7	7	22	6	.79	7	.302	.369	.432
4 Min. YEARS		348	1282	354	67	19	15	504	203	156	128	8	222	21	18	12	73	30	.71	26	.276	.349	.393

Rick Croushore

Pitches: Right **Bats:** Right **Pos:** RP-9; SP-3   **Ht:** 6'4" **Wt:** 210 **Born:** 8/7/70 **Age:** 31

		HOW MUCH HE PITCHED						WHAT HE GAVE UP												THE RESULTS					
Year Team	Lg Org	G	GS	CG	GF	IP	BFP	H	R	ER	HR	SH	SF	HB	TBB	IBB	SO	WP	Bk	W	L	Pct.	ShO	Sv	ERA
1993 Glens Falls	A- StL	31	0	0	11	41.1	184	38	16	14	1	4	1	2	22	4	36	6	0	4	1	.800	0	1	3.05
1994 Madison	A StL	62	0	0	14	94.1	410	90	49	43	5	4	2	5	46	2	103	10	4	6	6	.500	0	0	4.10
1995 St. Pete	A+ StL	12	11	0	0	59	251	44	25	23	2	3	1	4	32	0	57	5	0	6	4	.600	0	0	3.51

Year Team	Lg Org	G	GS	CG	GF	IP	BFP	H	R	ER	HR	SH	SF	HB	TBB	IBB	SO	WP	Bk	W	L	Pct	ShO	Sv	ERA
1996 Arkansas	AA StL	34	17	2	11	108	486	113	75	59	18	4	1	2	51	1	85	7	0	5	10	.333	0	3	4.92
1997 Arkansas	AA StL	17	16	1	1	92.2	421	111	52	43	7	1	5	4	37	0	67	8	2	7	5	.583	0	0	4.18
Louisville	AAA StL	14	6	0	3	43.2	173	37	14	12	3	0	0	0	13	0	41	4	0	1	2	.333	0	1	2.47
1998 Memphis	AAA StL	23	0	0	9	28.2	115	21	16	15	3	1	0	1	9	0	40	2	0	0	3	.000	0	2	4.71
1999 Memphis	AAA StL	7	0	0	5	6.2	34	8	5	5	1	0	1	0	6	0	11	1	0	1	0	1.000	0	0	6.75
2000 Colo Sprngs	AAA Col	33	2	0	12	36.2	178	40	31	30	4	2	4	2	32	1	30	6	0	2	4	.333	0	0	7.36
Pawtucket	AAA Bos	11	0	0	5	21	87	16	8	8	1	0	1	0	10	0	23	2	0	0	1	.000	0	0	3.43
2001 St. Lucie	A+ NYM	2	2	0	0	3	10	1	0	0	0	0	0	0	0	0	5	0	0	0	0	—	0	0	0.00
Norfolk	AAA NYM	10	1	0	3	13.1	55	8	5	5	1	0	2	4	5	0	10	2	0	0	0	—	0	0	3.38
1998 St. Louis	NL	41	0	0	15	54.1	243	44	31	30	6	2	1	4	29	2	47	6	0	0	3	.000	0	8	4.97
1999 St. Louis	NL	59	0	0	12	71.2	329	68	42	33	9	7	1	3	43	4	88	9	0	3	7	.300	0	3	4.14
2000 Colorado	NL	6	0	0	1	11.1	56	15	11	11	1	0	1	1	6	1	11	1	0	0	0	—	0	0	8.74
Boston	AL	5	0	0	3	4.2	24	4	3	3	0	1	1	1	5	1	3	1	0	0	1	1.000	0	0	5.79
9 Min. YEARS		256	55	3	74	548.1	2404	527	296	257	46	19	18	24	263	8	508	53	6	32	36	.471	0	11	4.22
3 Maj. YEARS		111	0	0	31	142	652	131	87	77	16	10	4	9	83	8	149	17	0	5	11	.313	0	11	4.88

Chuck Crowder

Pitches: Left **Bats:** Left **Pos:** RP-18; SP-14 **Ht:** 6'2" **Wt:** 200 **Born:** 9/30/76 **Age:** 25

Year Team	Lg Org	G	GS	CG	GF	IP	BFP	H	R	ER	HR	SH	SF	HB	TBB	IBB	SO	WP	Bk	W	L	Pct	ShO	Sv	ERA
1999 Portland	A- Col	6	6	0	0	27	119	24	14	13	2	0	0	2	16	0	39	2	0	2	1	.667	0	0	4.33
2000 Salem	A+ Col	28	28	0	0	168.2	710	124	78	66	6	10	9	10	86	0	154	8	0	14	9	.609	0	0	3.52
2001 Carolina	AA Col	32	14	0	3	101	482	126	64	60	7	1	4	7	63	1	71	8	2	6	6	.500	0	0	5.35
3 Min. YEARS		66	48	0	3	296.2	1311	274	156	139	15	11	13	19	165	1	264	18	8	22	16	.579	0	0	4.22

Jim Crowell

Pitches: Left **Bats:** Right **Pos:** RP-14; SP-2 **Ht:** 6'4" **Wt:** 230 **Born:** 5/14/74 **Age:** 28

Year Team	Lg Org	G	GS	CG	GF	IP	BFP	H	R	ER	HR	SH	SF	HB	TBB	IBB	SO	WP	Bk	W	L	Pct	ShO	Sv	ERA
1995 Watertown	A- Cle	12	9	0	0	56.2	241	50	22	18	1	0	2	1	27	1	48	2	1	5	2	.714	0	0	2.86
1996 Columbus	A Cle	28	28	3	0	165.1	710	163	89	76	16	9	5	9	69	0	104	12	0	7	10	.412	0	0	4.14
1997 Kinston	A+ Cle	17	17	0	0	114	461	96	41	30	4	3	2	1	26	0	94	3	0	9	4	.692	0	0	2.37
Akron	AA Cle	3	3	0	0	18	80	13	12	9	2	1	1	1	11	0	7	1	0	1	0	1.000	0	0	4.50
Chattanooga	AA Cin	3	3	0	0	19	75	19	6	6	2	1	1	0	5	0	14	0	0	2	1	.667	0	0	2.84
Indianapols	AAA Cin	3	3	1	0	19.2	85	19	7	6	1	0	2	0	8	0	6	1	0	1	1	.500	1	0	2.75
1998 Chattanooga	AA Cin	5	5	0	0	24.1	129	38	27	23	2	0	3	0	17	0	10	2	2	0	4	.000	0	0	8.51
Chston-WV	A Cin	5	5	0	0	15	83	28	23	22	1	0	2	2	9	0	9	1	0	0	4	.000	0	0	13.20
Indianapols	AAA Cin	1	1	0	0	4	19	7	3	3	0	0	0	0	0	0	2	0	0	0	0	—	0	0	6.75
1999 Chattanooga	AA Cin	27	27	0	0	148.1	690	173	98	84	12	5	6	4	85	0	80	3	0	10	5	.667	0	0	5.10
2000 Chattanooga	AA StL	23	0	0	6	29	148	35	23	19	3	1	0	3	22	2	20	0	0	1	0	—	0	1	5.90
Arkansas	AA StL	12	0	0	6	15	68	16	10	9	1	1	0	1	8	1	10	0	0	1	0	.500	0	1	5.40
2001 Portland	AAA SD	11	2	0	2	19.2	93	22	15	12	3	1	1	1	15	0	7	1	0	1	0	—	0	0	5.49
Mobile	AA SD	5	0	0	1	4.1	18	2	1	1	0	1	0	0	4	0	0	0	0	1	0	1.000	0	0	2.08
1997 Cincinnati	NL	2	1	0	1	6.1	36	12	7	7	2	2	0	0	5	0	3	0	0	1	0	.000	0	0	9.95
7 Min. YEARS		155	103	4	14	652.1	2900	681	377	318	48	23	25	30	306	4	411	25	4	37	32	.536	1	1	4.39

Mike Crudale

Pitches: Right **Bats:** Right **Pos:** RP-62 **Ht:** 6'0" **Wt:** 205 **Born:** 1/3/77 **Age:** 25

Year Team	Lg Org	G	GS	CG	GF	IP	BFP	H	R	ER	HR	SH	SF	HB	TBB	IBB	SO	WP	Bk	W	L	Pct	ShO	Sv	ERA
1999 Johnson Cty	R+ StL	24	0	0	8	33	142	29	15	12	1	1	0	1	14	0	36	5	0	0	1	.000	0	1	3.27
2000 Peoria	A StL	38	0	0	14	50.2	209	40	17	13	2	5	0	3	16	3	45	4	0	6	1	.857	0	5	2.31
Potomac	A+ StL	21	0	0	9	25.2	120	31	17	13	3	2	2	1	11	1	28	0	0	2	4	.333	0	2	4.56
2001 New Haven	AA StL	62	0	0	30	80.1	338	76	42	29	7	2	2	0	22	4	85	7	0	4	9	.308	0	9	3.25
3 Min. YEARS		145	0	0	61	189.2	809	176	91	67	13	10	4	5	63	8	194	16	0	12	15	.444	0	17	3.18

Chuck Crumpton

Pitches: Right **Bats:** Right **Pos:** RP-55 **Ht:** 6'4" **Wt:** 210 **Born:** 12/30/76 **Age:** 25

Year Team	Lg Org	G	GS	CG	GF	IP	BFP	H	R	ER	HR	SH	SF	HB	TBB	IBB	SO	WP	Bk	W	L	Pct	ShO	Sv	ERA
1999 Vermont	A- Mon	19	0	0	13	23.1	102	24	11	5	0	1	1	3	6	0	24	2	1	1	2	.333	0	5	1.93
Cape Fear	A Mon	13	0	0	13	19	74	15	3	1	0	0	0	1	3	0	15	0	0	2	1	.667	0	7	0.47
2000 Jupiter	A+ Mon	16	0	0	13	18.1	82	20	13	12	1	0	2	0	6	1	12	0	0	0	0	—	0	7	5.89
Harrisburg	AA Mon	31	11	0	7	77.2	340	90	43	37	7	0	1	5	23	0	34	7	0	3	2	.600	0	1	4.29
2001 Jupiter	A+ Mon	3	0	0	2	6	24	4	2	1	0	1	0	0	3	1	3	0	0	1	0	1.000	0	0	1.50
Harrisburg	AA Mon	52	0	0	24	66.2	292	73	39	32	6	3	4	5	25	5	44	3	1	2	6	.250	0	4	4.32
3 Min. YEARS		134	11	0	72	211	914	226	111	88	14	5	8	14	66	7	132	12	2	8	12	.400	0	24	3.75

Jose Cueto

Pitches: Right **Bats:** Right **Pos:** SP-22; RP-8 **Ht:** 6'2" **Wt:** 175 **Born:** 9/13/78 **Age:** 23

Year Team	Lg Org	G	GS	CG	GF	IP	BFP	H	R	ER	HR	SH	SF	HB	TBB	IBB	SO	WP	Bk	W	L	Pct	ShO	Sv	ERA
1999 Cubs	R ChC	11	9	0	0	56.2	247	49	32	18	1	1	3	4	22	0	66	2	1	3	4	.429	0	0	2.86
Eugene	A- ChC	4	4	0	0	24	101	26	13	12	2	2	1	4	5	0	21	1	0	0	2	.000	0	0	4.50
2000 Lansing	A ChC	16	1	0	6	26.2	132	26	19	17	1	3	2	0	25	1	35	9	1	0	4	.000	0	0	5.74
Eugene	A- ChC	13	7	0	0	44.2	200	43	27	26	1	0	1	4	24	0	51	5	1	2	5	.286	0	0	5.24
2001 Lansing	A ChC	22	14	2	1	95	399	71	50	40	4	3	3	8	44	0	105	9	3	4	4	.500	2	0	3.79
Daytona	A+ ChC	6	6	0	0	38.2	165	31	19	13	6	1	2	2	13	0	41	3	1	1	2	.333	0	0	3.03
West Tenn	AA ChC	2	2	0	0	9.1	44	10	9	9	5	1	0	2	6	0	10	1	0	0	1	.000	0	0	8.68
3 Min. YEARS		74	43	2	9	295	1288	256	169	135	20	11	12	24	139	1	329	30	7	10	22	.313	2	1	4.12

Chris Cumberland

Pitches: Left **Bats:** Right **Pos:** SP-21; RP-12
Ht: 6'1" **Wt:** 189 **Born:** 1/15/73 **Age:** 29

Year Team	Lg Org	G	GS	CG	GF	IP	BFP	H	R	ER	HR	SH	SF	HB	TBB	IBB	SO	WP	Bk	W	L	Pct.	ShO	Sv	ERA
1993 Oneonta	A- NYY	15	15	0	0	89	393	109	43	33	2	1	5	0	28	0	62	6	2	4	4	.500	0	0	3.34
1994 Greensboro	A NYY	22	22	1	0	137.2	559	123	55	45	9	4	2	4	41	0	95	11	2	14	5	.737	1	0	2.94
1995 Yankees	R NYY	4	4	0	0	7	26	3	1	1	0	0	0	0	1	0	7	0	0	0	1	.000	0	0	1.29
Tampa	A+ NYY	5	5	0	0	24.2	104	28	10	5	1	1	0	1	5	0	10	1	0	1	2	.333	0	0	1.82
1996 Columbus	AAA NYY	12	12	1	0	58	272	86	45	42	9	4	1	4	23	0	35	3	0	2	7	.222	0	0	6.52
Norwich	AA NYY	16	16	2	0	95.2	427	112	73	56	13	2	5	4	37	2	44	4	0	5	7	.417	1	0	5.27
1997 Norwich	AA NYY	25	25	3	0	154.2	686	188	100	69	12	5	3	5	59	1	81	10	4	11	10	.524	1	0	4.02
New Britain	AA Min	1	1	0	0	5.2	22	5	2	2	0	0	0	0	2	0	2	2	0	1	0	1.000	0	0	3.18
1998 New Britain	AA Min	37	2	0	10	54.2	220	44	24	16	1	1	2	0	17	2	48	6	0	3	4	.429	0	1	2.63
Salt Lake	AAA Min	17	1	1	4	30.1	142	37	21	20	2	3	1	1	18	1	19	5	3	3	2	.600	1	0	5.93
1999 Trenton	AA Bos	14	0	0	6	21	84	12	1	1	0	1	1	0	13	1	18	1	0	2	0	1.000	0	1	0.43
Pawtucket	AAA Bos	36	1	0	16	62.2	266	56	33	31	4	2	3	2	30	0	35	4	0	4	3	.571	0	0	4.45
2000 Fresno	AAA SF	9	4	0	0	29	137	40	32	32	12	1	2	1	15	0	10	1	0	0	3	.000	0	0	9.93
Greenville	AA Atl	12	2	0	3	21.2	97	19	12	11	1	1	0	1	10	1	10	0	0	2	1	.667	0	0	4.57
2001 Richmond	AAA Atl	13	1	0	3	16.2	76	23	11	9	1	0	1	0	7	1	10	1	1	2	3	.400	0	1	4.86
Greenville	AA Atl	20	20	2	0	125	529	126	51	48	5	9	4	3	40	0	85	2	1	3	7	.300	1	0	3.46
9 Min. YEARS		258	131	10	42	933.1	4040	1011	514	421	72	35	30	26	346	9	571	57	13	57	59	.491	5	3	4.06

Ryan Cummings

Pitches: Right **Bats:** Right **Pos:** RP-42
Ht: 6'0" **Wt:** 210 **Born:** 6/3/76 **Age:** 26

Year Team	Lg Org	G	GS	CG	GF	IP	BFP	H	R	ER	HR	SH	SF	HB	TBB	IBB	SO	WP	Bk	W	L	Pct.	ShO	Sv	ERA
1997 Boise	A- Ana	14	13	0	0	70	297	73	38	24	3	2	1	7	10	0	79	4	2	6	2	.750	0	0	3.09
1998 Lk Elsinore	A+ Ana	1	1	0	0	5	23	5	3	3	0	0	0	2	3	0	4	1	0	0	1	.000	0	0	5.40
1999 Cedar Rapds	A Ana	19	19	3	0	121	511	104	69	59	14	4	10	6	35	0	97	18	2	5	8	.385	1	0	4.39
Lk Elsinore	A+ Ana	7	7	0	0	46.2	203	43	19	17	3	1	0	4	15	1	41	1	0	3	1	.750	0	0	3.28
Erie	AA Ana	3	3	0	0	17.2	81	18	12	10	3	0	1	3	10	0	7	0	0	1	1	.500	0	0	5.09
2000 Erie	AA Ana	26	16	0	5	99.2	465	122	80	69	14	0	2	10	45	1	53	6	2	4	9	.308	0	0	6.23
2001 Arkansas	AA Ana	42	0	0	18	65.2	286	61	34	26	3	2	2	6	21	0	42	4	0	6	3	.667	0	6	3.56
5 Min. YEARS		112	59	3	23	425.2	1866	426	255	208	40	9	16	38	139	2	323	34	6	25	25	.500	1	6	4.40

John Curl

Bats: Left **Throws:** Right **Pos:** 1B-40; DH-19; OF-13; PH-4; 3B-1; PR-1
Ht: 6'3" **Wt:** 205 **Born:** 11/10/72 **Age:** 29

Year Team	Lg Org	G	AB	H	2B	3B	HR	TB	R	RBI	TBB	IBB	SO	HBP	SH	SF	SB	CS	SB%	GDP	Avg	OBP	SLG
1995 Medcine Hat	R+ Tor	69	270	86	26	1	7	135	47	63	31	8	61	0	0	3	5	1	.83	11	.319	.385	.500
1996 Dunedin	A+ Tor	125	447	110	20	2	18	188	52	62	44	1	133	1	2	5	7	4	.64	6	.246	.312	.421
1997 Knoxville	AA Tor	10	29	6	1	0	0	7	0	1	3	0	6	0	0	0	0	0	—	0	.207	.281	.241
Dunedin	A+ Tor	74	231	59	14	0	15	118	36	48	24	4	53	0	0	1	3	2	.60	4	.255	.324	.511
1998 Mobile	AA SD	104	363	100	22	2	16	174	47	66	40	1	108	0	0	1	3	2	.60	4	.275	.347	.479
1999 Mobile	AA SD	133	474	135	30	3	22	237	79	76	77	3	137	1	0	8	9	5	.64	0	.285	.380	.500
2000 Las Vegas	AAA SD	111	292	85	25	4	5	133	43	53	35	1	80	0	0	4	4	2	.67	4	.291	.363	.455
2001 Somerset	IND —	22	78	20	4	0	1	27	7	13	14	0	21	0	0	2	4	2	.67	1	.256	.362	.346
San Antonio	AA Sea	52	174	45	7	0	6	70	23	20	23	2	47	2	0	1	3	1	.75	0	.259	.350	.402
7 Min. YEARS		700	2358	646	149	12	90	1089	334	402	291	20	646	4	2	25	39	17	.70	30	.274	.351	.462

Joe Curreri

Pitches: Right **Bats:** Right **Pos:** RP-34
Ht: 6'1" **Wt:** 190 **Born:** 6/29/77 **Age:** 25

Year Team	Lg Org	G	GS	CG	GF	IP	BFP	H	R	ER	HR	SH	SF	HB	TBB	IBB	SO	WP	Bk	W	L	Pct.	ShO	Sv	ERA
1999 Bristol	R+ CWS	16	0	0	12	24.2	103	17	10	8	2	0	1	3	9	0	24	0	0	1	0	1.000	0	5	2.92
2000 Burlington	A CWS	41	0	0	29	53.2	237	46	24	22	5	2	4	3	35	5	56	3	1	4	4	.500	0	12	3.69
2001 Charlotte	AAA CWS	1	0	0	0	3	12	4	0	0	0	0	0	0	0	0	3	0	0	1	0	1.000	0	0	0.00
Winston-Sal	A+ CWS	33	0	0	7	48.2	209	46	27	26	5	4	2	3	19	0	44	1	0	3	3	.500	0	1	4.81
3 Min. YEARS		91	0	0	48	130	561	113	61	56	12	6	7	9	63	5	127	4	1	9	7	.563	0	18	3.88

Chris Curry

Bats: Right **Throws:** Right **Pos:** C-61; DH-13; PH-8; OF-2; 1B-1
Ht: 6'1" **Wt:** 205 **Born:** 11/17/77 **Age:** 24

Year Team	Lg Org	G	AB	H	2B	3B	HR	TB	R	RBI	TBB	IBB	SO	HBP	SH	SF	SB	CS	SB%	GDP	Avg	OBP	SLG
1999 Eugene	A- ChC	41	132	30	6	0	2	42	18	9	5	0	35	3	0	0	0	2	.00	4	.227	.271	.318
2000 Daytona	A+ ChC	20	59	9	0	0	0	9	5	3	4	0	17	1	1	0	0	0	—	4	.153	.219	.153
Lansing	A ChC	48	131	27	3	1	6	50	17	23	12	0	41	1	0	1	0	0	—	3	.206	.276	.382
2001 West Tenn	AA ChC	42	108	23	3	0	1	29	9	11	12	0	34	0	4	1	0	0	—	5	.213	.289	.269
Lansing	A ChC	29	95	11	4	0	0	15	7	8	9	0	21	2	1	3	0	0	—	5	.116	.202	.158
Daytona	A+ ChC	12	38	10	4	0	0	14	2	5	4	0	12	0	0	0	0	0	—	0	.263	.333	.368
3 Min. YEARS		192	563	110	20	1	9	159	58	59	46	0	160	7	6	5	0	2	.00	15	.195	.262	.282

Mike Curry

Bats: Left **Throws:** Right **Pos:** OF-107; PH-7; DH-4; PR-2
Ht: 5'10" **Wt:** 190 **Born:** 2/15/77 **Age:** 25

Year Team	Lg Org	G	AB	H	2B	3B	HR	TB	R	RBI	TBB	IBB	SO	HBP	SH	SF	SB	CS	SB%	GDP	Avg	OBP	SLG
1998 Spokane	A- KC	67	227	57	8	2	1	72	53	25	46	2	41	3	2	6	30	7	.81	1	.251	.376	.317
1999 Chston-WV	A KC	85	318	99	13	3	0	118	70	25	48	0	58	9	6	3	61	13	.82	4	.311	.413	.371
Wilmington	A+ KC	54	200	46	4	2	1	57	31	16	34	1	39	1	3	2	24	9	.73	2	.230	.342	.285

Year Team	Lg Org	G	AB	H	2B	3B	HR	TB	R	RBI	TBB	IBB	SO	HBP	SH	SF	SB	CS	SB%	GDP	Avg	OBP	SLG
2000 Wichita	AA KC	123	461	133	18	6	4	175	104	52	94	2	99	5	4	2	52	16	.76	4	.289	.413	.380
2001 Norfolk	AAA NYM	12	33	4	0	0	1	7	3	1	10	0	17	0	1	0	2	1	.67	0	.121	.326	.212
Binghamton	AA NYM	107	400	116	16	4	5	155	65	28	40	1	100	5	1	2	24	16	.60	4	.290	.360	.388
4 Min. YEARS		448	1639	455	59	17	12	584	326	147	272	6	354	23	17	15	193	62	.76	15	.278	.385	.356

Derek Dace

Pitches: Left **Bats:** Left **Pos:** RP-50   **Ht:** 6'7" **Wt:** 200 **Born:** 4/11/75 **Age:** 27

Year Team	Lg Org	G	GS	CG	GF	IP	BFP	H	R	ER	HR	SH	SF	HB	TBB	IBB	SO	WP	Bk	W	L	Pct.	ShO	Sv	ERA
1994 Astros	R Hou	11	11	1	0	59	245	55	26	22	2	5	2	1	21	0	52	2	3	3	5	.400	0	0	3.36
1995 Astros	R Hou	11	10	2	1	69.1	274	60	20	15	2	3	1	1	6	0	77	5	2	3	4	.429	1	0	1.95
Kissimmee	A+ Hou	1	1	0	0	2.2	17	4	5	5	0	0	1	0	5	0	1	0	0	0	1	.000	0	0	16.88
1996 Kissimmee	A+ Hou	12	0	0	3	18.1	73	19	6	6	0	0	0	0	7	0	11	1	0	0	0	—	0	1	2.95
Jackson	AA Hou	1	1	0	0	4	21	5	1	1	1	0	0	0	5	0	0	0	0	0	0	—	0	0	2.25
Auburn	A- Hou	15	15	0	0	97	400	89	41	35	7	2	1	2	35	2	87	1	0	9	4	.692	0	0	3.25
1997 Lakeland	A+ Det	2	0	0	1	2.1	9	2	1	1	1	0	0	0	1	0	0	0	0	0	0	—	0	0	3.86
W Michigan	A Det	10	2	0	3	25	100	23	2	2	0	0	0	1	4	0	24	0	0	1	0	1.000	0	2	0.72
Toledo	AAA Det	5	0	0	3	10	48	13	8	4	0	1	0	1	6	0	6	1	0	0	0	—	0	0	3.60
1998 Jacksnville	AA Det	40	0	0	15	67	277	51	32	31	8	0	2	2	29	0	48	2	0	5	3	.625	0	3	4.16
1999 El Paso	AA Ari	40	0	0	14	52	232	58	33	30	4	2	2	3	23	2	34	0	0	2	2	.500	0	0	5.19
2000 El Paso	AA Ari	28	0	0	12	33.1	139	28	15	13	1	3	1	1	19	3	25	1	0	2	2	.500	0	0	3.51
Tucson	AAA Ari	31	1	0	11	35	155	37	17	16	2	2	0	0	15	1	21	1	0	2	0	1.000	0	1	4.11
2001 Tucson	AAA Ari	17	0	0	6	21.2	104	29	19	13	2	0	2	2	7	0	14	0	0	0	3	.000	0	0	5.40
Somerset	IND —	33	0	0	13	52.2	207	44	19	17	3	1	0	2	12	1	28	3	0	7	3	.700	0	4	2.91
8 Min. YEARS		257	41	3	82	549.1	2301	517	245	211	33	19	12	16	195	9	428	17	5	33	25	.569	1	11	3.46

Brian Dallimore

Bats: Right **Throws:** Right **Pos:** 3B-106; 2B-19; DH-2; PR-2   **Ht:** 6'1" **Wt:** 185 **Born:** 11/15/73 **Age:** 28

Year Team	Lg Org	G	AB	H	2B	3B	HR	TB	R	RBI	TBB	IBB	SO	HBP	SH	SF	SB	CS	SB%	GDP	Avg	OBP	SLG
1996 Auburn	A- Hou	74	290	77	17	3	5	115	50	30	18	0	38	10	0	4	7	5	.58	5	.266	.326	.397
1997 Quad City	A Hou	130	492	128	23	3	6	175	80	48	38	0	76	20	6	5	24	8	.75	19	.260	.335	.356
Kissimmee	A+ Hou	1	3	0	0	0	0	0	0	0	0	0	2	0	0	0	0	0	—	0	.000	.000	.000
1998 Kissimmee	A+ Hou	62	240	61	11	1	0	74	34	19	19	0	42	5	4	1	7	5	.58	6	.254	.321	.308
1999 Kissimmee	A+ Hou	19	74	20	2	0	0	22	12	3	4	0	10	3	1	1	2	1	.67	1	.270	.329	.297
Jackson	AA Hou	70	251	67	13	1	5	97	38	19	16	0	44	10	2	1	13	3	.81	12	.267	.335	.386
2000 Round Rock	AA Hou	5	11	2	1	0	0	6	1	3	1	0	3	0	0	0	0	0	—	0	.182	.250	.545
El Paso	AA Ari	107	356	99	16	1	4	129	50	53	25	3	55	6	3	5	17	3	.85	13	.278	.332	.362
2001 El Paso	AA Ari	127	517	169	38	6	8	243	74	67	30	1	56	13	12	1	11	13	.46	9	.327	.378	.470
6 Min. YEARS		595	2234	623	121	15	29	861	339	242	151	4	326	67	28	18	81	38	.68	65	.279	.340	.385

Jeff D'Amico

Pitches: Right **Bats:** Right **Pos:** SP-20; RP-12   **Ht:** 6'3" **Wt:** 200 **Born:** 11/9/74 **Age:** 27

Year Team	Lg Org	G	GS	CG	GF	IP	BFP	H	R	ER	HR	SH	SF	HB	TBB	IBB	SO	WP	Bk	W	L	Pct.	ShO	Sv	ERA
1996 Athletics	R Oak	8	0	0	2	19	72	14	3	3	0	0	0	3	2	0	15	0	1	3	0	1.000	0	0	1.42
Modesto	A+ Oak	1	0	0	0	1	7	3	3	2	0	0	0	1	0	0	0	0	0	0	0	—	0	0	18.00
1997 Modesto	A+ Oak	20	13	0	5	97	442	115	50	41	5	1	4	7	34	1	89	9	1	7	3	.700	0	1	3.80
Edmonton	AAA Oak	10	7	0	1	30.2	141	42	29	28	7	1	2	2	6	0	19	3	0	1	2	.333	0	1	8.22
1998 Athletics	R Oak	4	1	0	0	9.1	34	6	4	4	2	0	0	1	1	0	8	0	0	0	0	—	0	0	3.86
Huntsville	AA Oak	24	8	0	4	61	295	77	57	52	12	1	6	3	34	0	46	6	5	5	5	.500	0	0	7.67
1999 Midland	AA Oak	32	0	0	18	45.1	207	53	31	25	4	3	3	3	16	2	38	3	0	1	2	.333	0	3	4.96
Vancouver	AAA Oak	14	0	0	11	17	76	16	6	5	1	1	0	0	10	1	10	2	0	2	2	.500	0	3	2.65
Omaha	AAA KC	12	0	0	10	18.2	88	29	13	9	1	0	0	1	3	0	12	3	1	1	3	.250	0	2	4.34
2000 Omaha	AAA KC	16	16	1	0	91.2	386	87	39	39	16	1	0	7	26	1	66	6	2	3	3	.500	0	0	3.83
2001 Omaha	AAA KC	32	20	0	5	140	595	151	65	55	19	8	3	5	40	2	92	5	2	5	7	.417	0	0	3.54
2000 Kansas City	AL	7	1	0	1	13.2	71	19	14	14	2	1	0	0	15	1	9	1	2	0	1	.000	0	0	9.22
6 Min. YEARS		173	65	1	56	530.2	2342	593	307	263	67	16	18	33	172	7	395	37	12	28	27	.509	0	10	4.46

Pat Daneker

Pitches: Right **Bats:** Right **Pos:** RP-19; SP-10   **Ht:** 6'3" **Wt:** 195 **Born:** 1/14/76 **Age:** 26

Year Team	Lg Org	G	GS	CG	GF	IP	BFP	H	R	ER	HR	SH	SF	HB	TBB	IBB	SO	WP	Bk	W	L	Pct.	ShO	Sv	ERA
1997 Bristol	R+ CWS	12	12	0	0	63.2	294	83	55	46	5	2	3	5	20	1	53	4	5	3	6	.333	0	0	6.50
1998 Hickory	A CWS	17	17	2	0	117	474	115	50	41	14	2	0	1	16	0	95	2	6	6	6	.500	0	0	3.15
Winston-Sal	A+ CWS	7	7	2	0	53	210	51	13	12	3	2	0	2	5	1	43	1	4	5	0	1.000	0	0	2.04
1999 Birmingham	AA CWS	16	16	3	0	109	451	106	46	39	6	2	2	2	30	1	71	4	2	6	8	.429	0	0	3.22
Charlotte	AAA CWS	9	9	1	0	49.1	230	64	36	36	10	1	2	3	16	0	36	4	0	4	4	.500	0	0	6.57
2000 Charlotte	AAA CWS	27	25	0	0	144	633	168	102	92	26	2	3	4	49	1	69	4	4	8	12	.400	0	0	5.75
Syracuse	AAA Tor	2	2	0	0	13.2	58	18	6	5	2	0	1	1	2	0	4	1	0	1	1	.500	0	0	3.29
2001 Syracuse	AAA Tor	10	10	1	0	50.1	237	75	53	50	9	3	2	3	17	0	14	3	0	2	5	.286	0	0	8.94
West Tenn	AA ChC	2	0	0	0	1.1	9	2	2	2	0	0	0	0	2	0	1	0	0	0	0	—	0	0	13.50
Iowa	AAA ChC	16	0	0	10	21.2	115	41	26	22	2	2	3	2	9	2	9	3	1	3	1	.750	0	0	9.14
St. George	IND —	1	0	0	0	1	6	2	1	1	0	0	0	0	1	0	1	0	0	0	0	—	0	0	9.00
1999 Chicago	AL	3	2	0	1	15	64	14	8	7	1	2	1	0	6	0	5	0	0	0	0	—	0	0	4.20
5 Min. YEARS		119	98	9	10	624	2717	726	390	346	77	16	16	23	167	6	396	26	22	38	43	.469	0	0	4.99

Dave Daniels

Pitches: Right **Bats:** Right **Pos:** RP-13 | **Ht:** 6'2" **Wt:** 182 **Born:** 7/25/73 **Age:** 28

Year Team	Lg Org	G	GS	CG	GF	IP	BFP	H	R	ER	HR	SH	SF	HB	TBB	IBB	SO	WP	Bk	W	L	Pct.	ShO	Sv	ERA
1995 Johnstown	IND —	28	0	0	9	44	186	36	22	16	1	3	1	4	15	1	40	1	3	4	1	.800	0	3	3.27
1996 Augusta	A Pit	11	0	0	7	12.1	58	21	8	7	0	1	0	0	3	1	14	0	1	0	1	.000	0	3	5.11
Erie	A- Pit	31	0	0	19	36.1	150	33	12	11	3	3	1	4	5	3	45	0	0	1	3	.250	0	7	2.72
1997 Augusta	A Pit	44	0	0	39	55	231	51	22	16	0	1	0	1	13	3	51	0	1	6	3	.667	0	18	2.62
Lynchburg	A+ Pit	10	0	0	8	10	36	6	2	2	1	0	0	0	1	0	6	1	0	1	1	.500	0	4	1.80
1998 Lynchburg	A+ Pit	14	0	0	12	18.1	65	9	3	3	2	1	0	0	3	0	19	0	0	0	0	—	0	9	1.47
Carolina	AA Pit	35	0	0	32	39.1	163	34	15	13	0	1	3	2	16	1	37	2	2	4	3	.571	0	16	2.97
Nashville	AAA Pit	2	0	0	0	1	4	0	0	0	0	0	0	0	2	0	1	0	0	0	0	—	0	0	0.00
1999 Altoona	AA Pit	55	0	0	29	67.1	276	55	21	20	6	3	1	2	19	2	63	1	0	2	2	.500	0	8	2.67
2000 Mobile	AA SD	9	0	0	0	11.1	50	10	7	5	0	0	0	0	5	0	11	0	0	0	1	.000	0	0	3.97
Potomac	A+ StL	31	0	0	3	42.1	158	27	8	6	1	0	1	3	8	0	36	3	0	2	2	.500	0	1	1.28
2001 New Haven	AA StL	13	0	0	2	22	91	19	7	7	1	1	1	1	8	2	17	0	1	1	1	.500	0	0	2.86
7 Min. YEARS		283	0	0	160	359.1	1468	301	127	106	15	14	8	17	98	13	340	8	8	21	18	.538	0	68	2.65

Paul Darnell

Pitches: Left **Bats:** Right **Pos:** RP-38; SP-9 | **Ht:** 6'5" **Wt:** 190 **Born:** 6/4/76 **Age:** 26

Year Team	Lg Org	G	GS	CG	GF	IP	BFP	H	R	ER	HR	SH	SF	HB	TBB	IBB	SO	WP	Bk	W	L	Pct.	ShO	Sv	ERA
1999 Billings	R+ Cin	9	9	0	0	48.1	226	55	37	28	5	1	4	3	22	0	39	4	0	3	3	.500	0	0	5.21
Clinton	A Cin	6	6	0	0	35.1	152	35	19	12	4	0	0	3	13	0	23	1	0	3	2	.600	0	0	3.06
2000 Clinton	A Cin	26	25	3	0	161.2	679	131	81	63	11	10	4	7	67	1	164	12	1	9	10	.474	1	0	3.51
2001 Mudville	A+ Cin	5	5	0	0	32	131	27	13	12	4	0	0	2	8	0	33	0	0	2	1	.667	0	0	3.38
Chattanooga	AA Cin	21	4	0	1	38.1	169	39	13	11	1	4	1	2	13	0	43	0	1	3	1	.750	0	0	2.58
Louisville	AAA Cin	21	0	0	5	21	90	15	6	6	3	2	0	0	11	1	32	1	0	2	0	1.000	0	0	2.57
3 Min. YEARS		88	49	3	6	336.2	1447	302	169	132	28	17	9	17	134	2	334	18	2	22	17	.564	1	0	3.53

Tommy Darrell

Pitches: Right **Bats:** Right **Pos:** RP-34; SP-1 | **Ht:** 6'6" **Wt:** 220 **Born:** 7/21/76 **Age:** 25

Year Team	Lg Org	G	GS	CG	GF	IP	BFP	H	R	ER	HR	SH	SF	HB	TBB	IBB	SO	WP	Bk	W	L	Pct.	ShO	Sv	ERA
1995 Angels	R Ana	18	5	0	7	63	254	51	18	12	1	1	3	4	14	0	49	3	1	4	3	.571	0	2	1.71
1996 Boise	A- Ana	15	15	1	0	101	433	114	56	39	11	2	2	4	13	2	76	2	0	8	1	.889	1	0	3.48
1997 Cedar Rapids	A Ana	27	26	5	0	191.2	810	212	108	86	18	7	0	6	40	1	106	7	2	12	10	.545	0	0	4.04
1998 Lk Elsinore	A+ Ana	21	16	0	2	97.2	465	120	76	62	7	2	2	11	44	3	56	14	4	4	11	.267	0	0	5.71
Cedar Rapids	A Ana	9	5	0	0	66.2	281	68	35	30	7	0	3	2	17	0	44	7	0	3	4	.429	0	0	4.05
1999 Sarasota	A+ Bos	30	12	1	6	101	455	118	75	74	8	5	7	5	30	5	67	11	0	4	10	.286	0	3	4.99
2000 Sarasota	A+ Bos	44	3	0	21	96.2	422	98	53	44	8	3	4	9	34	6	71	2	0	4	4	.500	0	5	4.10
Trenton	AA Bos	2	0	0	1	2	8	2	0	0	0	0	0	0	1	0	1	1	0	0	0	—	0	1	0.00
2001 Jupiter	A+ Mon	11	0	0	4	21	91	14	6	6	0	1	0	0	16	0	16	2	0	1	1	.500	0	0	2.57
Harrisburg	AA Mon	24	1	0	9	34.2	173	45	37	30	4	1	1	3	19	0	15	5	0	0	2	.000	0	0	7.79
7 Min. YEARS		201	87	10	50	775.1	3392	842	464	365	64	22	22	44	228	17	501	54	7	40	46	.465	1	11	4.24

Bobby Darula

Bats: Left **Throws:** Right **Pos:** DH-52; OF-34; 1B-5; PH-5 | **Ht:** 5'10" **Wt:** 175 **Born:** 10/29/74 **Age:** 27

Year Team	Lg Org	G	AB	H	2B	3B	HR	TB	R	RBI	TBB	IBB	SO	HBP	SH	SF	SB	CS	SB%	GDP	Avg	OBP	SLG
1996 Ogden	R+ Mil	45	106	29	4	0	4	45	19	23	17	0	22	2	0	1	2	0	1.00	2	.274	.381	.425
1997 Ogden	R+ Mil	69	262	87	26	4	6	139	61	52	42	0	23	5	1	4	11	2	.85	5	.332	.428	.531
1998 Stockton	A+ Mil	18	45	13	4	1	1	22	10	8	8	1	6	1	1	0	2	0	1.00	1	.289	.407	.489
1999 Beloit	A Mil	120	438	133	24	8	4	185	63	75	62	4	57	7	1	4	19	5	.79	7	.304	.395	.422
2000 Huntsville	AA Mil	35	117	28	7	0	1	38	17	10	14	0	17	3	0	1	3	1	.75	1	.239	.333	.325
Beloit	A Mil	71	237	91	18	3	3	124	56	43	44	2	25	9	0	3	16	2	.89	2	.384	.491	.523
2001 Huntsville	AA Mil	22	65	18	2	1	2	28	6	7	4	0	7	1	1	0	1	1	.50	0	.277	.329	.431
High Desert	A+ Mil	74	254	77	10	6	2	105	42	39	42	2	26	9	3	2	15	4	.79	8	.303	.417	.413
6 Min. YEARS		454	1524	476	95	23	23	686	274	257	233	9	183	37	7	15	69	15	.82	26	.312	.412	.450

Dave Darwin

Pitches: Left **Bats:** Left **Pos:** RP-13; SP-10 | **Ht:** 6'0" **Wt:** 185 **Born:** 12/19/73 **Age:** 28

Year Team	Lg Org	G	GS	CG	GF	IP	BFP	H	R	ER	HR	SH	SF	HB	TBB	IBB	SO	WP	Bk	W	L	Pct.	ShO	Sv	ERA
1996 Fayetteville	A Det	17	9	0	0	59	234	54	22	21	2	0	1	2	12	1	49	5	3	5	2	.714	0	0	3.20
1997 W Michigan	A Det	21	4	0	10	40.1	164	23	7	4	2	0	2	2	20	2	31	0	1	1	0	1.000	0	3	0.89
Lakeland	A+ Det	12	12	1	0	82.2	326	70	23	23	2	3	2	0	18	0	41	1	1	10	1	.909	0	0	2.50
1998 Toledo	AAA Det	1	1	1	0	7	25	4	1	1	1	0	0	1	0	0	5	0	0	1	0	1.000	0	0	1.29
Jacksonville	AA Det	24	23	2	1	139.2	612	152	94	83	22	3	2	6	52	0	76	2	2	12	6	.667	1	0	5.35
1999 Jacksnville	AA Det	28	28	3	0	187.1	813	194	95	74	19	1	6	11	58	1	100	2	0	14	12	.538	1	0	3.56
2000 Toledo	AAA Det	24	5	0	8	64.2	292	70	44	42	11	1	3	2	41	0	47	3	0	1	6	.143	0	0	5.85
2001 Buffalo	AAA Cle	4	3	0	0	17.2	82	20	12	6	1	0	0	0	8	0	13	0	0	1	0	1.000	0	0	3.06
Akron	AA Cle	19	7	0	3	56.1	245	62	34	26	6	2	2	3	18	3	43	3	0	3	2	.600	0	0	4.15
6 Min. YEARS		150	92	7	22	654.2	2793	649	332	280	66	10	18	31	227	7	405	16	7	47	30	.610	2	3	3.85

Cleatus Davidson

Bats: Both **Throws:** Right **Pos:** SS-117; 2B-7; PR-2; DH-1 **Ht:** 5'10" **Wt:** 180 **Born:** 11/1/76 **Age:** 25

Year Team	Lg Org	G	AB	H	2B	3B	HR	TB	R	RBI	TBB	IBB	SO	HBP	SH	SF	SB	CS	SB%	GDP	Avg	OBP	SLG
1994 Twins	R Min	24	85	15	1	0	0	16	8	5	9	0	19	0	1	1	3	1	.75	0	.176	.253	.188
1995 Twins	R Min	21	75	15	2	1	0	19	11	5	10	0	17	0	0	0	8	3	.73	0	.200	.294	.253
Elizabethtn	R+ Min	39	152	45	6	2	3	64	27	27	11	0	31	3	0	0	10	4	.71	2	.296	.355	.421
1996 Fort Wayne	A Min	59	203	36	8	3	0	50	20	30	23	0	45	0	1	2	2	3	.40	4	.177	.259	.246
Elizabethtn	R+ Min	65	248	71	10	6	6	111	53	31	39	2	45	2	3	1	17	6	.74	5	.286	.386	.448
1997 Fort Wayne	A Min	124	478	122	16	8	6	172	80	52	52	1	100	1	5	4	39	9	.81	7	.255	.327	.360
1998 Fort Myers	A+ Min	130	527	127	12	7	2	159	97	45	45	0	99	3	13	3	44	16	.73	8	.241	.303	.302
1999 New Britain	AA Min	127	491	120	16	10	2	162	88	40	53	1	110	3	10	6	40	14	.74	8	.244	.318	.330
2000 New Britain	AA Min	119	445	102	13	7	0	129	42	31	28	0	93	3	10	1	15	7	.68	6	.229	.279	.290
2001 Mobile	AA SD	125	467	102	18	4	2	134	39	34	23	0	101	0	9	2	13	6	.62	4	.218	.254	.287
1999 Minnesota	AL	12	22	3	0	0	0	3	3	3	0	0	4	0	2	0	2	0	1.00	2	.136	.136	.136
8 Min. YEARS		833	3171	755	102	48	21	1016	465	300	293	4	660	15	52	20	191	71	.73	42	.238	.304	.320

Allen Davis

Pitches: Left **Bats:** Left **Pos:** SP-8 **Ht:** 6'4" **Wt:** 195 **Born:** 10/1/75 **Age:** 26

Year Team	Lg Org	G	GS	CG	GF	IP	BFP	H	R	ER	HR	SH	SF	HB	TBB	IBB	SO	WP	Bk	W	L	Pct.	ShO	Sv	ERA
1998 Yakima	A- LA	4	2	0	1	16	61	10	4	2	0	0	0	0	3	0	14	1	0	2	0	1.000	0	0	1.13
San Berndno	A+ LA	5	5	0	0	31	127	30	13	10	2	1	1	0	7	0	34	1	2	1	2	.333	0	0	2.90
San Antonio	AA LA	6	5	0	0	31.1	132	31	13	11	2	1	0	1	9	0	33	0	1	2	2	.500	0	0	3.16
1999 San Antonio	AA LA	29	20	1	3	130	574	140	81	61	13	5	4	4	46	1	87	4	0	7	10	.412	1	0	4.22
2000 San Antonio	AA LA	29	26	3	0	163	706	187	91	82	18	6	6	6	51	0	123	1	0	10	8	.556	1	0	4.53
2001 Harrisburg	AA Mon	8	8	1	0	53	216	48	20	17	4	2	1	4	9	0	36	1	0	2	2	.500	0	0	2.89
4 Min. YEARS		81	66	5	4	424.1	1816	446	224	183	39	15	12	15	125	1	327	8	3	24	24	.500	2	0	3.88

Glenn Davis

Bats: Both **Throws:** Left **Pos:** 1B-132; PH-2 **Ht:** 6'1" **Wt:** 200 **Born:** 11/25/75 **Age:** 26

Year Team	Lg Org	G	AB	H	2B	3B	HR	TB	R	RBI	TBB	IBB	SO	HBP	SH	SF	SB	CS	SB%	GDP	Avg	OBP	SLG
1997 San Berndno	A+ LA	64	228	56	16	0	9	99	44	36	46	0	77	2	0	0	7	3	.70	3	.246	.377	.434
1998 Vero Beach	A+ LA	102	376	89	14	2	20	167	63	63	70	1	106	2	0	5	13	4	.76	7	.237	.355	.444
San Antonio	AA LA	20	69	20	2	0	6	40	14	15	10	0	22	0	0	0	2	0	1.00	0	.290	.380	.580
1999 San Antonio	AA LA	134	492	128	33	4	10	199	72	63	69	4	130	0	1	2	6	7	.46	12	.260	.350	.404
2000 San Antonio	AA LA	113	377	78	17	6	9	134	54	40	58	2	113	3	2	1	2	0	1.00	11	.207	.317	.355
2001 Jacksnville	AA LA	134	478	116	29	4	20	221	62	89	67	2	142	3	0	8	14	5	.74	11	.243	.335	.462
5 Min. YEARS		567	2020	487	111	20	74	860	309	306	320	9	590	10	3	16	44	19	.70	46	.241	.345	.426

J.J. Davis

Bats: Right **Throws:** Right **Pos:** OF-63; DH-7; PH-1 **Ht:** 6'4" **Wt:** 250 **Born:** 10/25/78 **Age:** 23

Year Team	Lg Org	G	AB	H	2B	3B	HR	TB	R	RBI	TBB	IBB	SO	HBP	SH	SF	SB	CS	SB%	GDP	Avg	OBP	SLG
1997 Pirates	R Pit	45	166	42	10	2	1	59	19	18	14	2	44	2	0	3	0	0	—	4	.255	.315	.358
Erie	A- Pit	4	13	1	0	0	0	1	1	0	0	0	4	0	0	0	0	0	—	0	.077	.077	.077
1998 Erie	A- Pit	52	196	53	12	2	8	93	25	39	20	1	54	2	0	2	4	1	.80	3	.270	.341	.474
Augusta	A Pit	30	106	21	6	0	4	39	11	11	3	0	24	0	0	0	1	1	.50	4	.198	.220	.368
1999 Hickory	A Pit	86	317	84	26	1	19	169	58	65	44	3	99	4	0	2	2	5	.29	3	.265	.360	.533
2000 Lynchburg	A+ Pit	130	485	118	36	1	20	216	77	80	52	2	171	4	0	4	9	4	.69	11	.243	.319	.445
2001 Pirates	R Pit	4	17	8	1	0	2	15	3	6	1	0	2	0	0	0	0	0	—	1	.471	.500	.882
Altoona	AA Pit	67	228	57	13	3	4	88	21	26	21	0	79	2	0	1	2	5	.29	1	.250	.317	.386
5 Min. YEARS		418	1527	384	104	9	58	680	215	245	155	8	477	14	0	12	18	16	.53	27	.251	.324	.445

Tim Davis

Pitches: Left **Bats:** Left **Pos:** RP-28 **Ht:** 5'11" **Wt:** 165 **Born:** 7/14/70 **Age:** 31

Year Team	Lg Org	G	GS	CG	GF	IP	BFP	H	R	ER	HR	SH	SF	HB	TBB	IBB	SO	WP	Bk	W	L	Pct.	ShO	Sv	ERA
1993 Appleton	A Sea	16	16	3	4	77.2	313	54	20	16	5	1	2	2	33	0	89	4	2	10	2	.833	2	2	1.85
Riverside	A+ Sea	18	0	0	17	30.2	117	14	6	6	1	0	1	1	9	0	56	1	0	3	0	1.000	0	7	1.76
1994 Calgary	AAA Sea	6	6	1	0	39.2	161	35	13	8	1	1	1	0	8	0	43	0	0	3	1	.750	0	0	1.82
1995 Tacoma	AAA Sea	2	2	0	0	13.1	57	15	8	8	2	0	0	0	4	0	13	0	0	0	0	—	0	0	5.40
1996 Everett	A- Sea	1	1	0	0	2	7	0	0	0	0	0	0	0	0	0	5	0	0	0	0	—	0	0	0.00
Tacoma	AAA Sea	8	1	0	1	17	78	19	12	10	1	3	1	0	10	2	19	1	0	0	1	.000	0	0	5.29
1997 Tacoma	AAA Sea	1	1	0	0	5	22	4	2	2	0	1	0	0	3	0	5	0	0	1	0	1.000	0	0	3.60
1998 Orlando	AA Sea	14	5	0	2	22	86	18	9	6	2	0	2	1	4	0	19	3	0	1	1	.500	0	0	2.45
1999 Durham	AAA TB	3	0	0	1	2	11	2	2	2	0	0	0	2	1	0	1	0	0	0	0	—	0	0	9.00
St. Pete	A+ TB	1	0	0	0	0.2	6	3	2	2	0	0	0	0	1	0	1	1	0	0	0	—	0	0	27.00
2001 Huntsville	AA Mil	28	0	0	11	37.2	167	36	15	12	1	2	1	5	18	3	32	1	0	1	2	.333	0	2	2.87
1994 Seattle	AL	42	1	0	12	49.1	225	57	25	22	4	3	3	1	25	5	28	6	0	2	2	.500	0	2	4.01
1995 Seattle	AL	5	5	0	0	24	117	30	21	17	2	0	1	0	18	2	19	0	0	2	1	.667	0	0	6.38
1996 Seattle	AL	40	0	0	4	42.2	187	43	21	19	4	1	1	2	17	1	34	0	0	2	2	.500	0	0	4.01
1997 Seattle	AL	2	0	0	1	6.2	31	6	5	5	1	0	0	1	4	0	10	0	0	0	0	—	0	0	6.75
8 Min. YEARS		98	26	4	36	247.2	1025	200	89	72	13	8	8	11	92	5	283	11	2	19	8	.704	2	12	2.62
4 Maj. YEARS		89	6	0	17	122.2	560	136	72	63	11	4	5	4	64	8	91	6	0	6	5	.545	0	2	4.62

Tommy Davis

Bats: Right **Throws:** Right **Pos:** 1B-73; 3B-17; C-12; DH-8; OF-6; PH-4 **Ht:** 6'1" **Wt:** 210 **Born:** 5/21/73 **Age:** 29

		BATTING															BASERUNNING				PERCENTAGES		
Year Team	Lg Org	G	AB	H	2B	3B	HR	TB	R	RBI	TBB	IBB	SO	HBP	SH	SF	SB	CS	SB%	GDP	Avg	OBP	SLG
1994 Albany	A Bal	61	216	59	10	1	5	86	35	35	18	0	52	2	0	3	2	4	.33	6	.273	.331	.398
1995 Frederick	A+ Bal	130	496	133	26	3	15	210	62	57	41	7	105	4	1	3	7	1	.88	14	.268	.327	.423
Bowie	AA Bal	9	32	10	3	0	3	22	5	10	1	0	9	1	0	0	0	0	—	1	.313	.353	.688
1996 Bowie	AA Bal	137	524	137	32	2	14	215	75	54	41	4	113	10	3	3	5	8	.38	16	.261	.325	.410
1997 Rochester	AAA Bal	119	438	133	22	2	15	204	74	62	43	2	90	2	3	1	6	1	.86	16	.304	.368	.466
1998 Bowie	AA Bal	37	132	37	11	0	1	51	12	15	13	2	27	3	0	1	0	0	—	1	.280	.356	.386
1999 Rochester	AAA Bal	110	413	106	18	0	11	157	49	56	24	2	65	0	2	4	1	4	.20	11	.257	.295	.380
2000 Rochester	AAA Bal	122	456	131	27	0	15	203	65	64	45	2	93	7	0	6	2	1	.67	17	.287	.356	.445
2001 Louisville	AAA Cin	112	396	107	25	2	6	154	48	47	27	3	97	3	0	5	1	1	.50	14	.270	.318	.389
1999 Baltimore	AL	5	6	1	0	0	0	1	0	0	0	0	2	0	0	0	0	0	—	1	.167	.167	.167
8 Min. YEARS		837	3103	853	174	10	85	1302	425	400	253	22	651	32	9	26	24	20	.55	96	.275	.333	.420

Scott Davison

Pitches: Right **Bats:** Right **Pos:** RP-30 **Ht:** 6'0" **Wt:** 190 **Born:** 10/16/70 **Age:** 31

		HOW MUCH HE PITCHED						WHAT HE GAVE UP												THE RESULTS					
Year Team	Lg Org	G	GS	CG	GF	IP	BFP	H	R	ER	HR	SH	SF	HB	TBB	IBB	SO	WP	Bk	W	L	Pct.	ShO	Sv	ERA
1994 Bellingham	A- Sea	13	0	0	11	15	66	11	5	3	0	1	0	1	6	1	21	3	2	0	1	.000	0	7	1.80
Appleton	A Sea	4	0	0	2	7.1	30	7	4	3	0	2	0	0	2	0	7	0	2	0	1	.000	0	0	3.68
Calgary	AAA Sea	11	0	0	3	14.2	67	20	10	10	1	0	0	1	6	0	17	2	1	0	1	.000	0	0	6.14
1995 Tacoma	AAA Sea	8	3	0	2	22	91	21	14	13	1	1	1	0	4	0	12	1	1	1	1	.500	0	0	5.32
Port City	AA Sea	34	0	0	28	40.2	156	22	4	4	1	6	2	1	16	1	50	2	0	2	0	1.000	0	10	0.89
1996 Tacoma	AAA Sea	17	0	0	16	23	90	13	2	1	1	0	1	0	6	1	23	0	0	1	1	.500	0	9	0.39
2001 St. George	IND —	28	0	0	20	36	148	38	14	13	2	1	2	2	7	1	30	0	0	3	0	1.000	0	8	3.25
Durham	AAA TB	2	0	0	1	3.1	20	9	7	7	0	0	0	0	2	0	3	0	0	0	0	—	0	0	18.90
1995 Seattle	AL	3	0	0	3	4.1	21	7	3	3	1	0	0	0	1	0	3	0	0	0	0	—	0	0	6.23
1996 Seattle	AL	5	0	0	3	9	40	11	9	9	4	0	0	0	3	0	9	0	0	0	0	—	0	0	9.00
4 Min. YEARS		117	3	0	83	162	668	141	60	54	5	10	7	6	49	4	163	11	6	7	5	.583	0	34	3.00
2 Maj. YEARS		8	0	0	6	13.1	61	18	12	12	7	0	0	0	4	0	12	0	0	0	0	—	0	0	8.10

Gookie Dawkins

Bats: Right **Throws:** Right **Pos:** SS-98; PH-6; PR-1 **Ht:** 6'1" **Wt:** 180 **Born:** 5/12/79 **Age:** 23

		BATTING															BASERUNNING				PERCENTAGES		
Year Team	Lg Org	G	AB	H	2B	3B	HR	TB	R	RBI	TBB	IBB	SO	HBP	SH	SF	SB	CS	SB%	GDP	Avg	OBP	SLG
1997 Billings	R+ Cin	70	253	61	5	0	4	78	47	37	30	0	38	0	3	6	16	6	.73	6	.241	.315	.308
1998 Burlington	A Cin	102	367	97	7	6	1	119	52	30	37	0	60	1	2	2	37	10	.79	10	.264	.332	.324
1999 Rockford	A Cin	76	305	83	10	6	6	129	56	32	35	2	38	0	1	1	38	13	.75	5	.272	.346	.423
Chattanooga	AA Cin	32	129	47	7	0	2	60	24	13	14	0	17	0	2	0	15	5	.75	5	.364	.427	.465
2000 Chattanooga	AA Cin	95	368	85	20	6	6	135	54	31	40	0	71	3	2	2	22	10	.69	3	.231	.310	.367
2001 Chattanooga	AA Cin	104	394	89	16	3	8	135	59	40	32	1	88	2	4	3	14	4	.78	9	.226	.285	.343
1999 Cincinnati	NL	7	7	1	0	0	0	1	1	0	0	0	4	1	0	0	0	0	—	0	.143	.250	.143
2000 Cincinnati	NL	14	41	9	2	0	0	11	5	3	2	1	7	0	1	0	0	0	—	3	.220	.256	.268
5 Min. YEARS		479	1816	462	65	21	29	656	292	183	188	3	312	6	14	14	142	48	.75	38	.254	.324	.361
2 Maj. YEARS		21	48	10	2	0	0	12	6	3	2	1	11	1	1	0	0	0	—	3	.208	.255	.250

Joey Dawley

Pitches: Right **Bats:** Right **Pos:** SP-21; RP-9 **Ht:** 6'4" **Wt:** 205 **Born:** 9/19/71 **Age:** 30

		HOW MUCH HE PITCHED						WHAT HE GAVE UP												THE RESULTS					
Year Team	Lg Org	G	GS	CG	GF	IP	BFP	H	R	ER	HR	SH	SF	HB	TBB	IBB	SO	WP	Bk	W	L	Pct.	ShO	Sv	ERA
1993 Bluefield	R+ Bal	20	0	0	15	30.2	143	34	20	12	1	2	1	1	14	3	30	3	1	3	1	.750	0	3	3.52
1994 Bluefield	R+ Bal	11	2	0	5	23.2	110	20	18	15	2	0	1	1	18	0	18	4	0	1	2	.333	0	2	5.70
Albany	A Bal	5	0	0	4	7.1	37	7	6	5	0	0	1	1	7	1	4	1	0	0	0	—	0	0	6.14
1995 Frederick	A+ Bal	24	0	0	8	32.2	163	41	28	23	4	1	1	3	22	1	29	5	1	1	2	.333	0	1	6.34
Palm Spring	IND —	15	0	0	1	28	128	28	14	12	2	0	1	2	9	0	20	1	1	1	0	1.000	0	0	3.86
1996 Palm Spring	IND —	27	0	0	18	33.2	146	26	14	6	3	0	0	1	18	1	29	2	1	2	1	.667	0	4	1.60
1997 Chico	IND —	41	0	0	35	41.1	186	42	24	20	2	0	2	2	18	2	51	2	1	1	4	.200	0	14	4.35
1998 Chico	IND —	45	0	0	41	43	196	32	20	16	2	2	2	0	27	2	36	5	0	2	4	.333	0	26	3.35
1999 Greenville	AA Atl	26	11	0	2	91.2	387	76	54	41	5	3	4	3	37	3	89	3	2	5	3	.625	0	0	4.03
Richmond	AAA Atl	7	7	1	0	40	174	43	26	23	5	3	2	0	12	0	31	4	0	0	3	.000	0	0	5.18
2001 Myrtle Bch	A+ Atl	5	0	0	2	10	34	4	2	2	0	0	0	0	0	0	16	0	0	1	0	1.000	0	0	1.80
Richmond	AAA Atl	3	0	0	1	6.1	22	3	2	2	1	0	0	0	1	0	5	0	0	1	0	1.000	0	0	2.84
Greenville	AA Atl	22	21	1	0	127.1	518	95	50	43	15	6	4	4	46	0	130	3	1	7	5	.583	0	0	3.04
8 Min. YEARS		251	41	2	132	515.2	2244	462	280	220	42	17	19	18	229	13	488	34	8	25	25	.500	0	50	3.84

Zach Day

Pitches: Right **Bats:** Right **Pos:** SP-28; RP-1 **Ht:** 6'4" **Wt:** 185 **Born:** 6/15/78 **Age:** 24

		HOW MUCH HE PITCHED						WHAT HE GAVE UP												THE RESULTS					
Year Team	Lg Org	G	GS	CG	GF	IP	BFP	H	R	ER	HR	SH	SF	HB	TBB	IBB	SO	WP	Bk	W	L	Pct.	ShO	Sv	ERA
1996 Yankees	R NYY	7	5	0	1	33.2	139	41	26	21	3	0	0	4	3	0	23	0	0	5	2	.714	0	0	5.61
1997 Oneonta	A- NYY	14	14	0	0	92	372	82	26	22	2	2	4	1	23	0	92	3	0	7	2	.778	0	0	2.15
1998 Tampa	A+ NYY	18	17	0	0	100	479	142	89	61	5	3	2	6	32	4	69	5	0	5	8	.385	0	0	5.49
Greensboro	A NYY	7	6	1	0	36	155	35	22	11	1	2	1	3	6	0	37	4	0	1	2	.333	0	0	2.75
1999 Yankees	R NYY	5	4	0	0	16.2	74	20	10	7	1	0	0	1	4	0	17	0	0	1	1	.500	0	0	3.78
Greensboro	A NYY	2	2	0	0	8	42	14	11	2	0	0	0	1	1	0	4	0	0	0	1	.000	0	0	2.25
2000 Greensboro	A NYY	13	13	1	0	85.1	343	72	29	18	6	0	0	3	31	0	101	11	1	9	3	.750	1	0	1.90
Tampa	A+ NYY	7	7	0	0	34.1	150	33	22	16	2	0	0	1	15	1	36	1	0	2	4	.333	0	0	4.19
Akron	AA Cle	8	8	0	0	46	192	38	20	18	1	4	0	3	21	0	43	4	0	4	2	.667	0	0	3.52

Year Team	Lg Org	HOW MUCH HE PITCHED						WHAT HE GAVE UP												THE RESULTS					
		G	GS	CG	GF	IP	BFP	H	R	ER	HR	SH	SF	HB	TBB	IBB	SO	WP	Bk	W	L	Pct.	ShO	Sv	ERA
2001 Akron	AA Cle	22	22	2	0	136.2	572	123	57	47	8	3	1	4	45	1	94	7	0	9	10	.474	0	0	3.10
Buffalo	AAA Cle	1	1	0	0	6	22	3	1	1	0	0	0	0	1	0	4	0	0	1	0	1.000	0	0	1.50
Ottawa	AAA Mon	6	5	0	0	26.2	120	38	23	22	2	0	1	2	8	0	15	3	0	2	2	.500	0	0	7.43
6 Min. YEARS		110	104	4	1	621.1	2660	641	336	246	31	14	10	27	190	6	535	38	1	46	37	.554	1	0	3.56

Jeff Deardorff

Bats: Right **Throws:** Right **Pos:** OF-81; 1B-37; DH-5; PH-4; 3B-3; PR-1   **Ht:** 6'3" **Wt:** 220 **Born:** 8/14/78 **Age:** 23

Year Team	Lg Org	BATTING														BASERUNNING				PERCENTAGES		
		G	AB	H	2B	3B	HR	TB	R	RBI	TBB	IBB	SO	HBP	SH	SF	SB	CS	SB%	GDP	Avg	OBP	SLG
1997 Ogden	R+ Mil	63	222	61	17	3	2	90	33	27	24	0	74	5	1	0	2	2	.50	1	.275	.359	.405
1998 Beloit	A Mil	88	326	83	17	1	11	135	41	45	27	1	125	4	2	1	3	1	.75	5	.255	.318	.414
1999 Stockton	A+ Mil	126	436	116	22	2	10	172	59	47	40	1	150	6	1	2	7	7	.22	5	.266	.335	.394
2000 Mudville	A+ Mil	111	421	103	20	7	10	167	48	54	32	2	120	1	0	6	7	10	.41	9	.245	.296	.397
2001 High Desert	A+ Mil	69	260	79	18	1	15	144	40	57	22	1	70	3	0	4	5	4	.56	4	.304	.360	.554
Huntsville	AA Mil	58	201	56	11	1	14	111	30	43	13	0	66	2	2	1	1	1	.50	4	.279	.327	.552
5 Min. YEARS		515	1866	498	105	15	62	819	251	273	158	5	605	21	6	14	20	25	.44	28	.267	.329	.439

Tim DeCinces

Bats: Left **Throws:** Right **Pos:** C-55; PH-5; DH-3; 1B-1; P-1   **Ht:** 6'2" **Wt:** 195 **Born:** 4/26/74 **Age:** 28

Year Team	Lg Org	BATTING														BASERUNNING				PERCENTAGES		
		G	AB	H	2B	3B	HR	TB	R	RBI	TBB	IBB	SO	HBP	SH	SF	SB	CS	SB%	GDP	Avg	OBP	SLG
1996 Bluefield	R+ Bal	39	128	38	8	0	7	67	24	32	24	0	28	2	0	5	3	1	.75	5	.297	.403	.523
1997 Delmarva	A Bal	127	416	107	20	0	13	166	65	70	97	1	117	0	1	3	3	4	.43	10	.257	.395	.399
1998 Rochester	AAA Bal	7	21	2	1	0	0	3	1	0	2	0	6	0	0	0	0	0	—	0	.095	.174	.143
Frederick	A+ Bal	110	374	100	25	0	16	173	50	64	59	2	90	4	1	2	3	4	.43	8	.267	.371	.463
Bowie	AA Bal	5	18	6	1	0	1	10	5	4	1	0	5	0	0	0	0	0	—	0	.333	.368	.556
1999 Bowie	AA Bal	84	258	67	15	0	12	118	38	36	54	3	52	0	0	1	0	2	.00	7	.260	.387	.457
Rochester	AAA Bal	16	53	14	5	0	2	25	7	8	0	0	12	0	0	0	0	0	—	2	.264	.264	.472
2000 Mobile	AA SD	72	207	56	9	0	11	98	34	44	42	1	28	0	0	7	1	0	1.00	4	.271	.383	.473
2001 Portland	AAA SD	7	18	1	0	0	0	1	1	0	1	0	8	0	0	0	0	0	—	0	.056	.105	.056
Mobile	AA SD	56	180	37	4	1	4	55	11	25	19	0	29	0	0	3	0	0	—	8	.206	.277	.306
6 Min. YEARS		523	1673	428	88	1	66	716	236	283	299	7	375	6	2	21	10	11	.48	44	.256	.367	.428

Kory DeHaan

Bats: Left **Throws:** Right **Pos:** OF-122; PH-6; PR-1   **Ht:** 6'2" **Wt:** 187 **Born:** 7/16/76 **Age:** 25

Year Team	Lg Org	BATTING														BASERUNNING				PERCENTAGES		
		G	AB	H	2B	3B	HR	TB	R	RBI	TBB	IBB	SO	HBP	SH	SF	SB	CS	SB%	GDP	Avg	OBP	SLG
1997 Erie	A- Pit	58	205	49	7	6	1	72	43	18	38	2	43	2	6	4	14	9	.61	4	.239	.357	.351
1998 Augusta	A Pit	132	475	149	39	8	8	228	85	75	69	3	114	8	8	7	33	13	.72	4	.314	.404	.480
1999 Lynchburg	A+ Pit	78	295	96	19	5	7	146	55	42	36	3	63	4	4	1	32	10	.76	4	.325	.405	.495
Altoona	AA Pit	47	190	51	13	2	3	77	26	24	11	0	46	2	5	3	14	6	.70	3	.268	.311	.405
2000 Rancho Cuca	A+ SD	4	14	3	1	0	1	7	2	1	1	0	4	0	0	0	0	0	—	0	.214	.267	.500
Las Vegas	AAA SD	10	41	12	4	0	0	16	7	3	2	0	11	1	1	1	3	0	1.00	1	.293	.333	.390
2001 Portland	AAA SD	87	304	77	9	5	7	117	35	28	20	1	71	2	1	1	12	9	.57	4	.253	.303	.385
Mobile	AA SD	42	159	47	8	2	4	71	29	23	22	1	27	2	2	3	12	4	.75	2	.296	.382	.447
2000 San Diego	NL	90	103	21	7	0	2	34	19	13	5	0	39	0	1	1	4	2	.67	2	.204	.239	.330
5 Min. YEARS		458	1683	484	101	28	31	734	282	214	199	10	379	21	27	20	120	51	.70	22	.288	.366	.436

Rick DeHart

Pitches: Left **Bats:** Left **Pos:** RP-18   **Ht:** 6'1" **Wt:** 180 **Born:** 3/21/70 **Age:** 32

Year Team	Lg Org	HOW MUCH HE PITCHED						WHAT HE GAVE UP												THE RESULTS					
		G	GS	CG	GF	IP	BFP	H	R	ER	HR	SH	SF	HB	TBB	IBB	SO	WP	Bk	W	L	Pct.	ShO	Sv	ERA
1992 Albany	A Mon	38	10	1	15	117	476	91	42	32	11	5	5	4	40	1	133	5	6	9	6	.600	1	3	2.46
1993 San Berndno	A+ Mon	9	9	0	0	53.1	237	56	28	18	4	3	1	0	25	0	44	0	0	4	3	.571	0	0	3.04
Harrisburg	AA Mon	12	7	0	1	34	163	45	31	29	5	1	2	2	19	0	18	2	0	2	4	.333	0	0	7.68
Wst Plm Bch	A+ Mon	7	7	1	0	42	175	42	14	14	0	1	1	1	17	0	33	2	0	1	3	.250	1	0	3.00
1994 Wst Plm Bch	A+ Mon	30	20	3	5	136.1	566	132	61	51	12	7	2	3	34	0	88	7	1	9	7	.563	2	0	3.37
1995 Harrisburg	AA Mon	35	12	0	4	93	417	94	62	50	13	4	6	5	39	3	64	4	4	6	7	.462	0	0	4.84
1996 Harrisburg	AA Mon	30	2	0	14	43.2	190	46	19	13	4	1	2	3	19	0	30	1	0	1	2	.333	0	1	2.68
1997 Ottawa	AAA Mon	43	0	0	14	63	264	60	33	28	6	2	1	4	22	2	57	1	0	0	0	.000	0	4	4.00
1998 Ottawa	AAA Mon	38	0	0	18	53	220	46	19	19	5	1	0	2	17	2	48	1	0	7	1	.875	0	2	3.23
1999 Ottawa	AAA Mon	15	2	0	5	26.1	127	33	19	14	4	3	0	2	11	1	22	1	0	2	4	.333	0	0	4.78
2001 Wilmington	A+ KC	5	0	0	1	5.2	23	5	2	1	0	0	0	0	3	1	2	0	0	0	1	.000	0	0	1.59
Wichita	AA KC	13	0	0	3	23.1	107	30	20	17	3	0	0	1	7	0	16	0	0	2	2	.500	0	0	6.56
1997 Montreal	NL	23	0	0	7	29.1	130	33	21	21	7	1	2	0	14	4	29	2	0	2	1	.667	0	0	5.52
1998 Montreal	NL	26	0	0	6	28	134	34	22	15	3	3	1	0	13	1	14	1	1	0	0	—	0	1	4.82
1999 Montreal	NL	3	0	0	0	1.2	14	6	4	4	2	0	0	0	3	1	1	0	0	0	0	—	0	0	21.60
9 Min. YEARS		275	69	5	80	690.2	2971	680	350	286	67	28	20	27	253	10	555	24	11	43	44	.494	4	10	3.73
3 Maj. YEARS		52	0	0	13	59	278	73	47	37	12	4	3	0	30	6	44	3	1	2	1	.667	0	1	5.64

Jose de la Cruz

Bats: Right **Throws:** Right **Pos:** C-36; PH-6; 3B-3; 1B-2; DH-2; P-1   **Ht:** 6'0" **Wt:** 170 **Born:** 1/27/78 **Age:** 24

Year Team	Lg Org	BATTING														BASERUNNING				PERCENTAGES		
		G	AB	H	2B	3B	HR	TB	R	RBI	TBB	IBB	SO	HBP	SH	SF	SB	CS	SB%	GDP	Avg	OBP	SLG
1998 Athletics	R Oak	46	156	37	5	2	2	52	19	26	21	0	29	0	0	4	1	0	1.00	2	.237	.320	.333
1999 Visalia	A+ Oak	43	115	24	5	1	4	43	17	17	12	0	32	2	0	2	3	1	.75	4	.209	.290	.374
Sou Oregon	A- Oak	18	51	8	4	0	1	15	7	8	9	0	16	1	0	0	0	0	—	1	.157	.295	.294
2000 Modesto	A+ Oak	59	164	29	7	0	1	39	17	20	30	1	47	1	1	2	1	5	.17	5	.177	.305	.238

74

			BATTING															BASERUNNING				PERCENTAGES		
Year Team	Lg Org	G	AB	H	2B	3B	HR	TB	R	RBI	TBB	IBB	SO	HBP	SH	SF	SB	CS	SB%	GDP	Avg	OBP	SLG
2001 Sacramento	AAA Oak	2	1	0	0	0	0	0	0	0	0	0	1	0	0	0	0	0	—	0	.000	.000	.000
Visalia	A+ Oak	45	130	23	7	0	1	33	10	23	15	0	32	1	0	1	4	1	.80	0	.177	.265	.254
4 Min. YEARS		213	617	121	28	3	9	182	70	94	87	1	157	5	1	9	9	7	.56	12	.196	.297	.295

Jorge de la Rosa

Pitches: Left **Bats:** Left **Pos:** RP-41   **Ht:** 6'1" **Wt:** 192 **Born:** 4/5/81 **Age:** 21

		HOW MUCH HE PITCHED						WHAT HE GAVE UP										THE RESULTS					
Year Team	Lg Org	G	GS	CG	GF	IP	BFP	H	R	ER	HR	SH	SF	HB	TBB	IBB	SO	WP	Bk	W	L	Pct.	ShO	Sv	ERA
1999 High Desert	A+ Ari	2	0	0	2	3	12	1	0	0	0	0	0	0	2	0	3	0	0	0	0	—	0	0	0.00
Diamondbcks	R Ari	8	0	0	6	14	56	12	5	5	1	0	0	0	3	0	17	2	1	0	0	.000	0	2	3.21
Missoula	R+ Ari	13	0	0	6	14.2	75	22	17	13	2	0	0	0	9	0	14	4	0	0	1	.000	0	2	7.98
2001 Sarasota	A+ Bos	12	0	0	10	29.2	114	13	7	4	0	0	0	0	12	0	27	2	0	1	1	.000	0	2	1.21
Trenton	AA Bos	29	0	0	4	37	187	56	35	24	4	1	1	4	20	1	27	6	0	1	3	.250	0	0	5.84
2 Min. YEARS		64	0	0	28	98.1	444	104	64	46	7	1	1	4	46	1	88	14	1	1	5	.167	0	6	4.21

Maximo de la Rosa

Pitches: Right **Bats:** Right **Pos:** RP-38   **Ht:** 5'11" **Wt:** 170 **Born:** 7/12/71 **Age:** 30

		HOW MUCH HE PITCHED						WHAT HE GAVE UP										THE RESULTS					
Year Team	Lg Org	G	GS	CG	GF	IP	BFP	H	R	ER	HR	SH	SF	HB	TBB	IBB	SO	WP	Bk	W	L	Pct.	ShO	Sv	ERA
1993 Burlington	R+ Cle	14	14	2	0	76.1	319	53	38	32	3	3	2	5	37	2	69	3	2	7	2	.778	1	0	3.77
1994 Columbus	A Cle	14	14	0	0	75.1	310	49	33	28	2	1	1	10	38	0	71	5	2	4	2	.667	0	0	3.35
Kinston	A+ Cle	13	13	0	0	69.2	324	82	56	39	7	2	4	4	38	0	53	3	2	0	11	.000	0	0	5.04
1995 Canton-Akrn	AA Cle	1	0	0	0	0.1	3	1	2	2	1	0	0	0	1	0	0	0	0	0	0	—	0	0	54.00
Kinston	A+ Cle	43	0	0	21	61.2	266	46	23	15	0	5	2	4	37	3	61	7	1	5	2	.714	0	8	2.19
1996 Canton-Akrn	AA Cle	40	15	0	17	119.2	530	104	60	52	7	2	4	3	81	3	109	12	2	11	5	.688	0	3	3.91
1997 Buffalo	AAA Cle	15	4	0	3	43	208	43	34	31	10	2	3	9	33	0	31	1	0	2	2	.500	0	0	6.49
Akron	AA Cle	17	13	5	2	97.1	435	112	63	48	11	8	4	5	32	3	70	2	4	4	9	.308	0	0	4.44
1998 Orlando	AA Sea	42	0	0	29	62.1	260	47	23	21	2	4	4	5	24	1	51	5	0	6	4	.600	0	8	3.03
Tacoma	AAA Sea	9	0	0	8	10.2	45	6	4	4	0	0	3	1	8	0	4	0	0	2	1	.667	0	0	3.38
1999 New Haven	AA Sea	10	0	0	9	10.2	45	9	4	3	1	0	0	1	3	0	7	2	0	0	1	.000	0	4	2.53
Tacoma	AAA Sea	15	0	0	5	22	112	34	18	15	3	0	2	3	10	1	24	0	0	0	2	.000	0	1	6.14
Colo Sprngs	AAA Col	8	0	0	2	11	48	12	3	3	1	1	0	2	4	1	5	2	0	0	1	.000	0	1	2.45
2000 Nashua	IND —	6	0	0	1	14.1	55	8	4	3	1	1	1	1	3	0	14	0	0	1	0	1.000	0	1	1.88
2001 Chattanooga	AA Cin	38	0	0	17	46.2	213	57	31	27	4	1	4	2	13	1	52	1	0	2	6	.250	0	2	5.21
9 Min. YEARS		285	73	7	114	721	3173	663	396	323	53	30	34	53	362	15	621	45	13	44	48	.478	1	27	4.03

Jorge DeLeon

Bats: Right **Throws:** Right **Pos:** 3B-36; SS-11; 2B-3; P-1   **Ht:** 6'2" **Wt:** 164 **Born:** 9/26/74 **Age:** 27

			BATTING															BASERUNNING				PERCENTAGES		
Year Team	Lg Org	G	AB	H	2B	3B	HR	TB	R	RBI	TBB	IBB	SO	HBP	SH	SF	SB	CS	SB%	GDP	Avg	OBP	SLG
1997 Lowell	A- Bos	3	12	4	0	0	0	4	1	2	0	0	0	0	0	0	0	0	—	0	.333	.333	.333
Michigan	A Bos	20	59	16	3	0	0	19	10	4	0	0	19	0	0	1	2	0	1.00	3	.271	.258	.322
1998 Michigan	A Bos	50	185	49	8	1	2	65	23	19	15	0	19	0	3	2	4	0	1.00	4	.265	.317	.351
Trenton	AA Bos	29	86	25	7	0	0	32	11	10	5	0	3	0	5	0	2	1	.67	5	.291	.330	.372
1999 Sarasota	A+ Bos	66	219	60	11	2	1	78	33	18	24	0	33	0	5	0	3	2	.60	5	.274	.341	.425
2000 Sarasota	A+ Bos	10	40	11	4	1	0	17	5	3	4	0	7	0	0	0	1	0	1.00	1	.275	.341	.425
Trenton	AA Bos	88	339	104	16	1	2	128	47	38	24	1	51	5	2	0	1	8	.11	8	.307	.361	.378
Pawtucket	AAA Bos	5	16	2	1	0	0	3	0	0	0	0	4	0	0	0	0	0	—	0	.125	.125	.188
2001 Pawtucket	AAA Bos	9	30	5	2	0	0	7	3	3	3	0	8	0	0	0	0	0	—	0	.167	.235	.233
Trenton	AA Bos	29	111	28	6	2	1	41	14	10	12	0	12	0	1	0	2	1	.67	4	.252	.325	.369
Red Sox	R Bos	10	24	5	2	0	0	7	3	0	4	0	4	1	0	0	1	0	1.00	0	.208	.345	.292
5 Min. YEARS		319	1121	309	60	7	6	401	153	107	91	1	160	6	17	6	16	12	.57	31	.276	.332	.358

Ernie Delgado

Pitches: Right **Bats:** Right **Pos:** RP-6   **Ht:** 6'2" **Wt:** 190 **Born:** 7/21/75 **Age:** 26

		HOW MUCH HE PITCHED						WHAT HE GAVE UP										THE RESULTS					
Year Team	Lg Org	G	GS	CG	GF	IP	BFP	H	R	ER	HR	SH	SF	HB	TBB	IBB	SO	WP	Bk	W	L	Pct.	ShO	Sv	ERA
1993 Marlins	R Fla	11	11	0	0	61.1	261	61	27	21	0	0	2	4	19	0	46	5	2	4	3	.571	0	0	3.08
1994 Brevard Cty	A+ Fla	1	1	0	0	6	25	3	3	2	0	1	2	0	4	0	1	1	0	1	1	.000	0	0	3.00
Marlins	R Fla	4	2	0	2	16	71	15	10	6	0	0	0	0	5	0	18	1	0	1	1	.500	0	0	3.38
1995 Brevard Cty	A+ Fla	18	10	0	4	62.1	308	74	51	49	4	1	4	7	59	0	36	7	2	1	6	.143	0	0	7.07
1996 Hagerstown	A Tor	35	2	0	16	85.1	386	89	50	34	2	5	3	7	45	1	70	12	2	4	7	.364	0	2	3.59
1997 Hagerstown	A Tor	32	17	0	5	134.1	618	163	96	78	10	6	6	10	56	0	103	12	0	5	10	.333	0	0	5.23
1998 Dunedin	A+ Tor	44	9	2	13	118.2	532	119	57	48	5	6	1	6	59	4	97	6	2	7	10	.412	1	1	3.64
1999 Knoxville	AA Tor	31	0	0	12	51.1	219	49	27	20	1	1	3	1	23	0	33	5	0	4	1	.800	0	0	3.51
Syracuse	AAA Tor	14	4	0	2	27.2	139	38	29	29	3	1	1	0	19	0	15	2	0	0	4	.000	0	0	9.43
2000 Kinston	A+ Cle	9	0	0	2	17	71	11	3	3	0	0	0	1	10	0	22	1	0	1	0	1.000	0	0	1.59
Akron	AA Cle	34	0	0	22	44.1	210	43	26	23	5	0	1	0	40	1	31	6	0	3	4	.429	0	6	4.67
2001 Akron	AA Cle	6	0	0	3	8.1	31	5	3	3	1	1	1	0	1	0	5	1	0	1	0	.000	0	1	3.24
9 Min. YEARS		239	56	2	81	632.2	2871	670	382	316	31	22	24	36	340	6	481	60	8	30	48	.385	1	12	4.50

Jason Dellaero

Bats: Both **Throws:** Right **Pos:** SS-114; PR-1   **Ht:** 6'2" **Wt:** 195 **Born:** 12/17/76 **Age:** 25

			BATTING															BASERUNNING				PERCENTAGES		
Year Team	Lg Org	G	AB	H	2B	3B	HR	TB	R	RBI	TBB	IBB	SO	HBP	SH	SF	SB	CS	SB%	GDP	Avg	OBP	SLG
1997 White Sox	R CWS	5	15	3	2	0	0	5	1	1	1	0	2	0	0	1	0	0	—	1	.200	.235	.333
Hickory	A CWS	55	191	53	10	3	6	87	37	29	17	0	49	3	0	3	3	1	.75	6	.277	.341	.455
1998 Winston-Sal	A+ CWS	121	428	89	23	3	10	148	45	49	25	2	147	5	3	2	12	4	.75	5	.208	.259	.346

Year Team	Lg Org	G	AB	H	2B	3B	HR	TB	R	RBI	TBB	IBB	SO	HBP	SH	SF	SB	CS	SB%	GDP	Avg	OBP	SLG
1999 Winston-Sal	A+ CWS	54	184	41	13	0	2	60	22	19	18	1	59	3	4	0	9	4	.69	2	.223	.302	.326
Birmingham	AA CWS	81	272	73	13	3	10	122	40	44	14	0	76	3	8	3	6	8	.43	5	.268	.308	.449
2000 Birmingham	AA CWS	122	438	81	18	1	7	122	36	42	20	0	142	6	7	2	9	6	.60	7	.185	.230	.279
2001 Charlotte	AAA CWS	115	377	67	10	0	11	110	32	28	17	0	113	2	8	0	4	4	.50	4	.178	.217	.292
1999 Chicago	AL	11	33	3	0	0	0	3	1	2	1	0	13	0	0	1	0	0	—	0	.091	.114	.091
5 Min. YEARS		553	1905	407	89	10	46	654	213	212	112	3	588	22	30	11	43	27	.61	30	.214	.264	.343

Pete Della Ratta

Pitches: Right **Bats:** Right **Pos:** RP-52; SP-1 **Ht:** 6'4" **Wt:** 223 **Born:** 2/14/74 **Age:** 28

Year Team	Lg Org	G	GS	CG	GF	IP	BFP	H	R	ER	HR	SH	SF	HB	TBB	IBB	SO	WP	Bk	W	L	Pct.	ShO	Sv	ERA
1996 Sou Oregon	A- Oak	22	0	0	6	41.1	194	45	34	33	10	2	2	4	24	4	41	3	1	0	5	.000	0	2	7.19
1997 Modesto	A+ Oak	45	0	0	19	83.2	362	73	45	31	5	5	4	6	31	8	81	6	0	6	7	.462	0	3	3.33
1998 Huntsville	AA Oak	5	0	0	2	8	49	21	12	10	2	0	1	0	4	2	3	0	0	0	1	.000	0	0	11.25
Visalia	A+ Oak	36	0	0	28	59	249	43	24	16	5	3	1	1	25	6	73	4	0	5	1	.833	0	13	2.44
1999 Binghamton	AA NYM	41	3	0	9	82.2	329	75	22	20	4	2	3	3	13	1	68	2	0	1	4	.200	0	0	2.18
2000 Binghamton	AA NYM	13	0	0	5	17.1	79	18	16	13	3	1	0	0	8	0	8	1	0	1	2	.333	0	0	6.75
St. Lucie	A+ NYM	2	0	0	1	1.1	7	2	0	0	0	0	0	0	0	0	2	0	0	0	0	—	0	0	0.00
2001 Binghamton	AA NYM	22	0	0	9	30	139	36	25	21	3	1	2	3	8	0	30	1	0	4	2	.667	0	0	6.30
Bridgeport	IND —	31	1	0	13	47.2	200	42	18	16	0	0	2	4	12	0	43	4	0	1	1	.500	0	4	3.02
6 Min. YEARS		217	4	0	91	371	1608	355	196	160	32	14	15	21	125	21	349	21	1	18	23	.439	0	22	3.88

Eddy de los Santos

Bats: Right **Throws:** Right **Pos:** 2B-91; SS-19; DH-5; PR-3; PH-1 **Ht:** 6'2" **Wt:** 170 **Born:** 2/24/78 **Age:** 24

Year Team	Lg Org	G	AB	H	2B	3B	HR	TB	R	RBI	TBB	IBB	SO	HBP	SH	SF	SB	CS	SB%	GDP	Avg	OBP	SLG
1996 Devil Rays	R TB	50	184	48	6	1	0	56	18	20	13	0	58	3	2	0	11	3	.79	4	.245	.302	.286
Butte	R+ TB	16	59	16	0	0	0	16	15	12	6	0	17	0	2	2	1	1	.50	1	.271	.328	.271
1997 Chston-SC	A TB	127	432	101	11	2	2	122	46	40	20	0	101	2	5	4	8	9	.47	3	.234	.269	.282
1998 St. Pete	A TB	111	393	94	11	1	0	107	33	32	17	1	64	3	5	3	6	4	.60	7	.239	.274	.272
Durham	AAA TB	4	11	3	2	0	0	5	2	2	0	0	6	1	0	0	0	0	—	0	.273	.333	.455
1999 Orlando	AA TB	128	448	123	24	4	3	164	53	49	29	0	69	2	5	7	3	2	.60	9	.275	.317	.366
2000 Orlando	AA TB	48	171	40	6	1	0	48	11	8	5	0	26	2	1	1	2	3	.40	2	.234	.263	.281
Durham	AAA TB	78	271	68	4	1	3	83	27	32	21	0	50	2	5	1	3	2	.60	9	.251	.308	.306
2001 Orlando	AA TB	114	415	107	13	1	2	128	33	38	22	0	60	5	10	2	14	11	.56	10	.258	.302	.308
6 Min. YEARS		676	2396	600	77	11	10	729	238	233	133	1	451	20	35	20	48	35	.58	45	.250	.293	.304

Emmanuel del Rosario

Bats: Both **Throws:** Right **Pos:** 2B-76; 3B-31; SS-6; DH-5; PH-4; PR-4; OF-1 **Ht:** 5'11" **Wt:** 149 **Born:** 7/8/81 **Age:** 20

Year Team	Lg Org	G	AB	H	2B	3B	HR	TB	R	RBI	TBB	IBB	SO	HBP	SH	SF	SB	CS	SB%	GDP	Avg	OBP	SLG
1999 Orioles	R Bal	40	123	30	2	0	0	32	19	8	22	0	10	2	4	1	10	5	.67	2	.244	.365	.260
2000 Bluefield	R+ Bal	54	185	46	6	1	0	54	23	15	27	1	23	3	4	2	11	1	.92	8	.249	.350	.292
2001 Delmarva	A Bal	106	313	70	9	2	1	86	44	24	35	0	38	7	11	2	16	1	.94	5	.224	.314	.275
Bowie	AA Bal	7	14	5	0	0	0	5	0	1	0	0	2	0	0	0	0	0	—	0	.357	.357	.357
3 Min. YEARS		207	635	151	17	3	1	177	86	48	84	1	73	12	21	5	37	7	.84	15	.238	.336	.279

Rich DeLucia

Pitches: Right **Bats:** Right **Pos:** RP-28 **Ht:** 6'0" **Wt:** 190 **Born:** 10/7/64 **Age:** 37

Year Team	Lg Org	G	GS	CG	GF	IP	BFP	H	R	ER	HR	SH	SF	HB	TBB	IBB	SO	WP	Bk	W	L	Pct.	ShO	Sv	ERA
1986 Bellingham	A- Sea	13	11	1	1	74	0	44	20	14	4	0	0	4	24	0	69	3	0	8	1	.800	1	0	1.70
1988 San Berndno	A+ Sea	22	22	0	0	127.2	541	110	57	44	4	2	6	7	59	3	118	6	2	7	8	.467	0	0	3.10
1989 Williamsprt	AA Sea	10	10	0	0	54.2	234	59	28	23	5	3	2	1	13	0	41	5	0	3	4	.429	0	0	3.79
1990 San Berndno	A+ Sea	5	5	1	0	30.2	116	19	9	7	4	1	0	4	3	0	35	1	0	4	1	.800	0	0	2.05
Williamsprt	AA Sea	18	18	2	0	115	447	92	30	27	7	3	3	2	30	2	76	1	0	6	6	.500	1	0	2.11
Calgary	AAA Sea	5	5	1	0	32.1	139	30	17	13	2	0	3	2	12	0	23	3	0	2	2	.500	0	0	3.62
1992 Calgary	AAA Sea	8	5	2	3	40.1	162	32	11	11	2	0	1	0	14	0	38	2	0	4	2	.667	1	1	2.45
1993 Calgary	AAA Sea	8	7	0	1	44	192	45	30	28	6	0	3	0	20	1	38	4	0	1	5	.167	0	1	5.73
1994 Indianapols	AAA Cin	36	0	0	31	43	172	22	12	11	2	3	0	1	24	1	52	1	0	5	1	.833	0	19	2.30
1996 San Jose	A+ Sea	5	4	0	0	7.1	24	2	0	0	0	0	0	0	3	0	11	0	0	0	0	—	0	0	2.45
1999 Buffalo	AAA Cle	44	0	0	33	47.1	210	39	24	22	6	1	1	2	29	3	46	4	0	2	3	.400	0	19	4.18
2000 Sacramento	AAA Oak	10	10	0	0	50	212	50	27	22	4	0	1	0	18	0	34	3	0	3	1	.750	0	0	3.96
2001 Toledo	AAA Det	28	0	0	12	39	156	27	11	11	3	1	1	0	15	0	45	1	0	1	1	.500	0	5	2.54
1990 Seattle	AL	5	5	1	0	36	144	30	9	8	2	2	0	0	9	0	20	0	0	1	2	.333	0	0	2.00
1991 Seattle	AL	32	31	0	0	182	779	176	107	103	31	5	14	4	78	4	98	10	0	12	13	.480	1	0	5.09
1992 Seattle	AL	30	11	0	6	83.2	382	100	55	51	13	2	2	2	35	1	66	1	0	3	6	.333	0	1	5.49
1993 Seattle	AL	30	1	0	11	42.2	195	46	24	22	5	1	1	1	23	3	48	4	0	3	6	.333	0	0	4.64
1994 Cincinnati	NL	8	0	0	2	10.2	47	9	6	5	4	0	0	0	5	0	15	1	0	0	0	—	0	0	4.22
1995 St. Louis	NL	56	1	0	8	82.1	342	63	38	31	9	5	2	3	36	2	76	5	0	8	7	.533	0	0	3.39
1996 San Francisco	NL	56	0	0	20	61.2	279	62	44	40	8	4	2	3	31	6	55	7	0	3	6	.333	0	0	5.84
1997 San Francisco	NL	3	0	0	1	1.2	12	6	3	2	0	0	0	0	2	0	2	0	0	0	0	—	0	0	10.80
Anaheim	AL	33	0	0	13	42.1	174	29	18	17	5	2	2	1	27	2	42	1	0	6	4	.600	0	3	3.61
1998 Anaheim	AL	61	0	0	18	71.2	314	56	36	34	10	5	7	3	46	5	73	8	1	2	6	.250	0	3	4.27
1999 Cleveland	AL	6	0	0	2	9.1	50	13	7	7	4	0	0	0	9	2	7	1	0	0	1	.000	0	0	6.75
11 Min. YEARS		212	97	7	81	705.1	2609	574	278	235	52	14	20	20	264	10	626	34	2	46	36	.561	3	45	3.00
10 Maj. YEARS		320	49	1	80	624	2718	590	347	320	91	26	30	17	299	25	502	39	1	38	51	.427	0	7	4.62

Chris Demetral

Bats: Left **Throws:** Right **Pos:** 2B-50; DH-22; 3B-15; PH-5; OF-4; SS-1; 1B-1 **Ht:** 5'11" **Wt:** 175 **Born:** 12/8/69 **Age:** 32

Year Team	Lg Org	G	AB	H	2B	3B	HR	TB	R	RBI	TBB	IBB	SO	HBP	SH	SF	SB	CS	SB%	GDP	Avg	OBP	SLG
1991 Yakima	A- LA	65	226	64	11	0	2	81	43	41	34	2	32	1	6	0	4	3	.57	2	.283	.379	.358
1992 Bakersfield	A+ LA	90	306	84	14	1	4	112	38	36	33	7	45	1	4	3	7	8	.47	3	.275	.344	.366
1993 Vero Beach	A+ LA	122	437	142	22	3	5	185	63	48	69	2	47	2	6	3	6	6	.50	9	.325	.417	.423
1994 San Antonio	AA LA	108	368	96	26	3	6	146	44	39	34	5	44	1	11	2	5	2	.71	8	.261	.323	.397
1995 Albuquerque	AAA LA	87	187	52	7	1	3	70	34	19	24	2	28	0	3	0	1	6	.14	7	.278	.360	.374
1996 San Berndno	A+ LA	11	32	9	3	0	1	15	5	4	6	1	5	0	0	0	0	3	.00	0	.281	.395	.469
Albuquerque	AAA LA	99	209	55	8	0	4	75	30	26	40	5	35	0	5	5	4	3	.57	6	.263	.374	.359
1997 Albuquerque	AAA LA	12	24	6	2	0	1	11	1	1	6	0	3	0	0	0	0	1	.00	1	.250	.400	.458
Vero Beach	A+ LA	86	278	77	13	3	12	132	52	45	48	0	40	2	2	4	5	2	.71	6	.277	.383	.475
1998 Tulsa	AA Tex	45	147	40	9	3	4	67	22	18	33	0	24	1	2	0	2	3	.40	4	.272	.409	.456
Oklahoma	AAA Tex	57	157	47	6	0	4	65	26	16	20	0	31	0	4	2	3	2	.60	1	.299	.374	.414
1999 Oklahoma	AAA Tex	65	183	48	7	1	4	69	29	18	28	0	35	0	7	1	1	2	.33	3	.262	.358	.377
2000 Oklahoma	AAA Tex	106	355	85	9	5	8	128	55	47	55	2	53	1	9	3	2	3	.40	5	.239	.341	.361
2001 Oklahoma	AAA Tex	92	322	76	11	1	2	95	33	27	34	0	32	0	7	2	1	1	.50	8	.236	.307	.295
11 Min. YEARS		1045	3231	881	148	21	60	1251	475	385	464	26	454	9	66	25	41	45	.48	63	.273	.363	.387

Chris Demouy

Pitches: Left **Bats:** Right **Pos:** RP-31 **Ht:** 6'1" **Wt:** 205 **Born:** 11/3/75 **Age:** 26

Year Team	Lg Org	G	GS	CG	GF	IP	BFP	H	R	ER	HR	SH	SF	HB	TBB	IBB	SO	WP	Bk	W	L	Pct.	ShO	Sv	ERA
1998 Boise	A- Ana	20	0	0	17	23.1	96	11	5	4	0	3	1	1	11	0	29	2	2	5	1	.833	0	9	1.54
1999 Cedar Rapds	A Ana	46	0	0	28	48.2	212	39	18	13	3	7	3	0	28	2	51	8	0	2	1	.667	0	16	2.40
2000 Lk Elsinore	A+ Ana	40	1	0	17	59.1	264	62	21	15	0	1	2	3	26	0	44	3	0	7	2	.778	0	2	2.28
Edmonton	AAA Ana	1	0	0	0	3	11	1	1	1	0	0	0	0	1	0	0	0	0	0	0	—	0	0	3.00
Erie	AA Ana	9	0	0	8	17.2	83	22	12	10	2	1	2	0	7	1	11	0	0	0	1	.000	0	0	5.09
2001 Arkansas	AA Ana	24	0	0	10	35.1	167	42	25	24	4	1	3	2	22	0	16	2	0	2	0	1.000	0	0	6.11
Rancho Cuca	A+ Ana	7	0	0	2	10	39	7	3	3	1	0	0	0	3	0	6	1	0	0	1	.000	0	0	2.70
4 Min. YEARS		147	1	0	82	197.1	872	184	85	70	10	13	11	6	98	3	157	16	2	16	6	.727	0	27	3.19

Darrell Dent

Bats: Left **Throws:** Left **Pos:** OF-105; PH-8; DH-3; PR-2 **Ht:** 6'2" **Wt:** 175 **Born:** 5/26/77 **Age:** 25

Year Team	Lg Org	G	AB	H	2B	3B	HR	TB	R	RBI	TBB	IBB	SO	HBP	SH	SF	SB	CS	SB%	GDP	Avg	OBP	SLG
1995 Orioles	R Bal	36	125	35	7	3	0	48	24	6	21	0	22	2	0	1	6	2	.75	2	.280	.389	.384
1996 Bluefield	R+ Bal	59	193	43	6	2	0	53	40	14	28	1	49	0	1	4	30	9	.77	2	.223	.316	.275
1997 Delmarva	A Bal	128	441	103	17	4	1	131	69	37	63	2	110	4	7	6	60	15	.80	2	.234	.331	.297
1998 Frederick	A+ Bal	131	456	112	19	1	0	133	65	24	43	1	95	4	13	3	33	16	.67	4	.246	.314	.292
1999 Bowie	AA Bal	108	250	53	9	2	0	66	41	17	37	0	58	2	12	4	24	5	.83	4	.212	.314	.264
Rochester	AAA Bal	9	30	4	0	0	2	10	4	5	3	0	8	0	1	1	4	0	1.00	0	.133	.206	.333
2000 Bowie	AA Bal	115	362	94	11	1	0	107	52	25	56	0	63	2	7	2	20	11	.65	4	.260	.360	.296
2001 Jacksnville	AA LA	117	376	105	15	2	4	136	50	32	42	0	91	6	4	2	31	12	.72	5	.279	.359	.362
7 Min. YEARS		703	2233	549	84	15	7	684	345	160	293	4	496	20	45	23	208	70	.75	23	.246	.336	.306

Doug Dent

Pitches: Right **Bats:** Right **Pos:** RP-23; SP-4 **Ht:** 6'8" **Wt:** 210 **Born:** 3/23/77 **Age:** 25

Year Team	Lg Org	G	GS	CG	GF	IP	BFP	H	R	ER	HR	SH	SF	HB	TBB	IBB	SO	WP	Bk	W	L	Pct.	ShO	Sv	ERA
1998 Braves	R Atl	4	4	0	0	14.2	61	14	11	7	1	0	2	2	4	0	16	1	2	0	2	.000	0	0	4.30
Danville	R+ Atl	9	9	1	0	47.1	212	57	28	19	4	2	1	3	19	0	29	1	1	5	3	.625	0	0	3.61
1999 Macon	A Atl	17	17	0	0	89	375	78	42	34	8	1	3	2	30	0	64	5	1	4	5	.444	0	0	3.44
Fort Wayne	A SD	8	8	0	0	48.2	201	43	23	19	2	0	1	1	17	0	32	4	1	4	1	.800	0	0	3.51
2000 Rancho Cuca	A+ SD	10	7	0	1	40.2	176	34	17	11	2	1	1	3	19	0	31	4	0	2	1	.667	0	0	2.43
Mobile	AA SD	18	16	0	0	82.2	392	97	65	54	8	3	5	11	44	0	47	10	1	4	9	.308	0	0	5.88
2001 Mobile	AA SD	3	1	0	0	5.1	31	10	6	6	0	0	0	1	5	0	2	0	0	0	1	.000	0	0	10.13
Mudville	A+ Cin	24	3	0	6	64.1	286	69	34	28	4	2	3	7	24	0	63	5	1	6	3	.667	0	2	3.92
4 Min. YEARS		93	65	1	7	392.2	1734	402	226	178	31	9	16	30	162	0	284	30	7	25	25	.500	0	2	4.08

Sean DePaula

Pitches: Right **Bats:** Right **Pos:** RP-6 **Ht:** 6'4" **Wt:** 220 **Born:** 11/7/73 **Age:** 28

Year Team	Lg Org	G	GS	CG	GF	IP	BFP	H	R	ER	HR	SH	SF	HB	TBB	IBB	SO	WP	Bk	W	L	Pct.	ShO	Sv	ERA
1996 Burlington	R+ Cle	23	0	0	11	35.1	151	31	16	15	3	2	2	2	13	0	42	4	3	4	2	.667	0	1	3.82
Watertown	A- Cle	1	0	0	1	2	6	0	0	0	0	0	0	0	0	0	5	0	0	0	0	—	0	0	0.00
1997 Watertown	A- Cle	9	0	0	2	19	86	21	6	6	1	1	1	1	8	0	17	0	0	1	1	.500	0	0	2.84
Columbus	A Cle	29	1	0	7	71	336	71	56	41	4	3	7	4	43	3	75	9	0	4	5	.444	0	0	5.20
1998 Kinston	A+ Cle	28	1	0	14	49.2	226	50	20	13	0	2	1	3	18	3	59	6	0	3	2	.600	0	1	2.36
Akron	AA Cle	8	1	0	1	17	81	16	10	9	0	1	0	0	15	0	17	3	0	1	1	.500	0	0	4.76
1999 Kinston	A+ Cle	23	0	0	14	51.1	208	36	17	13	6	0	0	3	17	0	75	4	0	4	2	.667	0	7	2.28
Akron	AA Cle	14	0	0	6	28	122	20	11	11	2	2	0	2	17	0	31	2	0	1	0	1.000	0	3	3.54
Buffalo	AAA Cle	5	0	0	5	5	19	0	0	0	0	0	0	1	3	0	7	1	0	0	0	—	0	2	0.00
2000 Akron	AA Cle	4	0	0	1	5	18	1	1	1	0	0	1	0	2	0	4	0	0	0	0	—	0	0	1.80
Buffalo	AAA Cle	9	0	0	4	13	62	16	10	8	1	0	1	1	7	0	11	2	0	1	0	1.000	0	0	5.54
2001 Buffalo	AAA Cle	6	0	0	4	8.2	32	2	1	1	0	0	1	0	6	0	6	0	0	1	0	1.000	0	0	1.04
1999 Cleveland	AL	11	0	0	4	11.2	45	8	6	6	0	2	0	0	3	0	18	0	0	0	0	—	0	0	4.63
2000 Cleveland	AL	13	0	0	3	16.2	83	20	11	11	3	0	1	0	14	2	16	0	0	0	0	—	0	0	5.94
6 Min. YEARS		159	3	0	69	305	1347	264	148	118	17	11	15	17	147	6	349	31	3	20	13	.606	0	14	3.48
2 Maj. YEARS		24	0	0	7	28.1	128	28	17	17	3	2	1	0	17	2	34	0	0	0	0	—	0	0	5.40

Jeff DePippo

Bats: Right **Throws:** Right **Pos:** C-64; DH-9; PH-7; OF-6; PR-2   **Ht:** 5'7" **Wt:** 170 **Born:** 4/29/76 **Age:** 26

Year Team	Lg Org	G	AB	H	2B	3B	HR	TB	R	RBI	TBB	IBB	SO	HBP	SH	SF	SB	CS	SB%	GDP	Avg	OBP	SLG
1998 Burlington	R+ Cle	39	115	24	6	0	1	33	16	9	10	0	33	6	0	1	0	2	.00	2	.209	.303	.287
1999 Kinston	A+ Cle	68	174	37	8	1	2	53	33	19	29	0	51	17	8	3	3	1	.75	1	.213	.372	.305
2000 Akron	AA Cle	57	172	39	6	1	3	56	20	19	13	0	60	6	7	2	2	1	.67	2	.227	.301	.326
2001 Akron	AA Cle	82	240	63	10	2	6	95	32	28	14	0	51	14	3	4	5	8	.38	9	.263	.335	.396
4 Min. YEARS		246	701	163	30	4	12	237	101	75	66	0	195	43	18	10	10	12	.45	14	.233	.332	.338

Keoni DeRenne

Bats: Right **Throws:** Right **Pos:** 2B-94; SS-31; PH-5   **Ht:** 5'7" **Wt:** 162 **Born:** 4/30/79 **Age:** 23

Year Team	Lg Org	G	AB	H	2B	3B	HR	TB	R	RBI	TBB	IBB	SO	HBP	SH	SF	SB	CS	SB%	GDP	Avg	OBP	SLG
2000 Jamestown	A- Atl	20	66	20	6	0	1	29	9	9	11	0	5	2	0	1	6	1	.86	3	.303	.413	.439
Macon	A Atl	38	145	38	9	1	1	52	13	11	11	0	20	2	0	2	3	3	.50	1	.262	.319	.359
2001 Greenville	AA Atl	130	453	108	15	2	3	136	42	42	44	3	57	5	6	3	4	2	.67	8	.238	.311	.300
2 Min. YEARS		188	664	166	30	3	5	217	74	62	66	3	82	9	6	6	13	6	.68	12	.250	.323	.327

Tony DeRosso

Bats: Right **Throws:** Right **Pos:** 3B-78; PH-11; DH-6; 1B-3   **Ht:** 6'3" **Wt:** 226 **Born:** 11/7/75 **Age:** 26

Year Team	Lg Org	G	AB	H	2B	3B	HR	TB	R	RBI	TBB	IBB	SO	HBP	SH	SF	SB	CS	SB%	GDP	Avg	OBP	SLG
1994 Red Sox	R Bos	46	168	42	6	0	4	60	23	22	12	0	33	5	0	3	1	0	1.00	2	.250	.314	.357
1995 Michigan	A Bos	106	382	89	20	1	13	150	57	50	38	2	93	11	1	2	9	1	.90	5	.233	.319	.393
1996 Sarasota	A+ Bos	116	416	107	19	5	14	178	64	60	31	2	84	8	2	5	15	2	.88	10	.257	.317	.428
1997 Trenton	AA Bos	102	357	77	18	1	14	139	50	40	26	0	94	2	3	2	13	1	.93	5	.216	.271	.389
1998 Trenton	AA Bos	9	28	3	0	0	1	6	3	3	2	0	12	0	0	1	0	0	—	0	.107	.161	.214
Red Sox	R Bos	4	15	7	2	0	0	9	4	3	1	0	3	0	0	0	0	0	—	0	.467	.500	.600
Sarasota	A+ Bos	4	13	4	3	0	0	7	1	5	3	1	1	0	0	0	0	0	—	0	.308	.438	.538
1999 Red Sox	R Bos	5	18	5	3	0	1	11	3	7	2	0	2	0	0	1	0	1	.00	1	.278	.333	.611
Augusta	A Bos	36	128	38	7	1	6	65	19	27	16	0	21	1	0	2	0	0	—	3	.297	.374	.508
2000 Trenton	AA Bos	120	449	126	28	4	20	222	77	85	45	1	91	5	0	2	0	1	.00	14	.281	.351	.494
2001 Huntsville	AA Mil	65	218	51	17	0	6	86	21	25	19	1	36	2	2	4	0	1	.00	12	.234	.296	.394
Mobile	AA SD	28	94	22	5	0	3	36	8	18	9	0	20	3	0	1	0	0	—	2	.234	.318	.383
8 Min. YEARS		641	2286	571	128	12	82	969	330	345	204	7	490	37	8	23	38	7	.84	54	.250	.318	.424

Marc Deschenes

Pitches: Right **Bats:** Right **Pos:** RP-44   **Ht:** 6'0" **Wt:** 175 **Born:** 1/6/73 **Age:** 29

Year Team	Lg Org	G	GS	CG	GF	IP	BFP	H	R	ER	HR	SH	SF	HB	TBB	IBB	SO	WP	Bk	W	L	Pct.	ShO	Sv	ERA
1996 Columbus	A Cle	16	16	0	0	76.2	343	70	38	29	7	3	1	3	41	0	67	6	0	5	2	.714	0	0	3.40
1997 Columbus	A Cle	40	0	0	39	42.2	180	31	11	9	2	0	1	1	21	0	69	3	0	2	2	.500	0	19	1.90
Kinston	A+ Cle	20	0	0	19	22.1	79	9	2	2	2	0	0	0	4	0	39	1	0	2	0	1.000	0	10	0.81
1998 Kinston	A+ Cle	1	0	0	1	1	4	0	0	0	0	0	0	0	1	0	2	0	0	0	0	—	0	0	0.00
Akron	AA Cle	47	0	0	26	58.1	259	52	36	25	4	2	4	0	34	6	52	5	0	4	6	.400	0	5	3.86
1999 Akron	AA Cle	43	0	0	26	65.1	277	57	28	24	5	5	2	2	31	6	64	3	0	3	2	.600	0	3	3.31
2000 Akron	AA Cle	41	0	0	31	54.1	238	43	27	24	3	3	2	4	31	3	64	4	0	2	4	.333	0	2	3.98
2001 Buffalo	AAA Cle	22	0	0	6	29.2	149	38	23	21	4	2	0	2	23	1	29	2	1	2	2	.500	0	0	6.37
Akron	AA Cle	22	0	0	8	31.1	140	25	9	6	1	4	2	5	18	2	30	0	0	2	2	.500	0	0	1.72
6 Min. YEARS		252	16	0	156	381.2	1669	325	174	140	30	17	14	15	204	18	416	24	1	22	20	.524	0	39	3.30

John DeSilva

Pitches: Right **Bats:** Right **Pos:** RP-37; SP-3   **Ht:** 6'0" **Wt:** 195 **Born:** 9/30/67 **Age:** 34

Year Team	Lg Org	G	GS	CG	GF	IP	BFP	H	R	ER	HR	SH	SF	HB	TBB	IBB	SO	WP	Bk	W	L	Pct.	ShO	Sv	ERA
1989 Niagara Fal	A- Det	4	4	0	0	24	95	15	5	5	0	1	0	2	8	0	24	3	1	3	0	1.000	0	0	1.88
Fayetteville	A Det	9	9	1	0	52.2	215	40	23	16	4	1	2	0	21	0	54	2	3	2	2	.500	0	0	2.73
1990 Lakeland	A+ Det	14	14	0	0	91	349	54	18	15	4	1	2	4	25	0	113	3	1	8	1	.889	0	0	1.48
London	AA Det	14	14	1	0	89	372	87	47	37	4	1	4	2	27	0	76	3	0	5	6	.455	1	0	3.74
1991 London	AA Det	11	11	2	0	73.2	294	51	24	23	4	2	2	0	24	0	80	1	0	5	4	.556	1	0	2.81
Toledo	AAA Det	11	11	1	0	58.2	254	62	33	30	10	0	1	1	21	0	56	1	0	5	4	.556	0	0	4.60
1992 Toledo	AAA Det	7	2	0	3	19	89	26	18	18	5	1	0	0	8	0	21	0	0	0	3	.000	0	0	8.53
London	AA Det	9	9	1	0	52.1	216	51	24	24	4	1	2	1	13	0	53	2	1	2	4	.333	1	0	4.13
1993 Toledo	AAA Det	25	24	1	0	161	675	145	76	66	13	2	5	0	60	2	136	3	1	7	10	.412	0	0	3.69
1994 Albuquerque	AAA LA	25	6	0	4	66.2	317	90	62	58	7	1	3	4	27	0	39	3	0	3	5	.375	0	1	7.83
San Antonio	AA LA	25	2	0	7	46	202	46	29	26	3	2	1	1	18	2	46	2	1	1	3	.250	0	2	5.09
1995 Rochester	AAA Bal	26	25	2	1	150.2	644	156	78	70	19	3	3	6	51	0	82	2	1	11	9	.550	0	0	4.18
1996 Palm Spring	IND —	1	1	0	0	5	18	1	2	2	1	0	0	0	2	0	7	0	0	1	0	1.000	0	0	3.60
Pawtucket	AAA Bos	16	16	0	0	84.2	373	99	55	49	12	2	1	0	27	0	68	1	0	4	3	.571	0	0	5.21
1998 New Jersey	IND —	11	11	4	0	80.2	315	53	17	14	4	5	0	3	24	2	90	8	0	8	1	.889	0	0	1.56
Ottawa	AAA Mon	7	7	0	0	48.1	191	42	15	14	5	1	2	2	12	0	25	1	0	4	2	.667	0	0	2.61
1999 Ottawa	AAA Mon	22	15	0	0	90.1	377	73	35	29	4	6	5	1	41	1	75	5	0	4	1	.800	0	0	2.89
2000 Calgary	AAA Fla	29	19	3	5	140.1	613	150	78	73	21	6	8	5	43	2	94	3	2	10	9	.526	0	2	4.68
2001 Calgary	AAA Fla	26	3	0	7	38.2	189	59	33	29	5	1	0	4	9	1	29	1	0	1	2	.333	0	1	6.75
Las Vegas	AAA LA	14	0	0	7	25	98	23	7	6	2	0	1	0	6	2	27	1	0	1	0	.500	0	0	2.16
1993 Detroit	AL	1	0	0	1	1	4	2	1	1	0	0	1	0	0	0	0	0	0	0	0	—	0	0	9.00
Los Angeles	NL	3	0	0	2	5.1	23	6	4	4	0	0	0	0	1	0	6	0	0	0	0	—	0	0	6.75
1995 Baltimore	AL	2	2	0	0	8.2	41	8	7	7	3	1	1	1	7	0	1	0	0	1	0	1.000	0	0	7.27
12 Min. YEARS		306	203	16	37	1397.2	5896	1323	676	604	131	37	42	37	467	12	1195	45	12	85	70	.548	4	6	3.89
2 Maj. YEARS		6	2	0	3	15	68	16	12	12	3	1	2	1	8	0	7	0	0	1	0	1.000	0	0	7.20

Phil Devey

Pitches: Left **Bats:** Left **Pos:** SP-20; RP-10 **Ht:** 6'0" **Wt:** 170 **Born:** 5/31/77 **Age:** 25

Year Team	Lg Org	G	GS	CG	GF	IP	BFP	H	R	ER	HR	SH	SF	HB	TBB	IBB	SO	WP	Bk	W	L	Pct.	ShO	Sv	ERA
1999 Yakima	A- LA	13	13	1	0	78.1	330	70	43	34	6	2	0	9	27	0	56	6	1	5	4	.556	0	0	3.91
2000 San Berndno	A+ LA	29	24	1	1	172.1	737	179	86	72	13	5	7	13	54	1	112	3	1	6	11	.353	0	0	3.76
2001 Vero Beach	A+ LA	3	0	0	1	7	29	8	2	2	1	0	0	0	0	0	6	0	0	0	0	—	0	1	2.57
Las Vegas	AAA LA	3	3	0	0	14.2	74	25	18	18	1	1	0	1	9	0	7	1	1	0	2	.000	0	0	11.05
Jacksnville	AA LA	24	17	0	2	112.1	482	121	56	47	12	3	4	8	21	0	76	4	2	8	2	.800	0	0	3.77
3 Min. YEARS		72	57	2	4	384.2	1652	403	205	173	33	11	11	31	111	1	257	14	5	19	19	.500	0	2	4.05

Doug Devore

Bats: Left **Throws:** Left **Pos:** OF-120; DH-6; PH-3 **Ht:** 6'4" **Wt:** 200 **Born:** 12/14/77 **Age:** 24

Year Team	Lg Org	G	AB	H	2B	3B	HR	TB	R	RBI	TBB	IBB	SO	HBP	SH	SF	SB	CS	SB%	GDP	Avg	OBP	SLG
1999 Missoula	R+ Ari	32	115	27	4	4	3	48	22	22	14	0	36	4	0	2	2	0	1.00	5	.235	.333	.417
2000 South Bend	A Ari	127	452	132	27	4	15	212	64	60	47	5	101	2	2	4	9	6	.60	9	.292	.358	.469
2001 El Paso	AA Ari	128	476	140	32	11	15	239	67	74	46	7	118	4	1	4	11	3	.79	7	.294	.358	.502
3 Min. YEARS		287	1043	299	63	19	33	499	153	156	107	12	255	10	3	10	22	9	.71	18	.287	.356	.478

Jason Dewey

Bats: Right **Throws:** Right **Pos:** C-69; PH-2; PR-1 **Ht:** 6'1" **Wt:** 200 **Born:** 4/18/77 **Age:** 25

Year Team	Lg Org	G	AB	H	2B	3B	HR	TB	R	RBI	TBB	IBB	SO	HBP	SH	SF	SB	CS	SB%	GDP	Avg	OBP	SLG
1997 Boise	A- Ana	68	272	88	17	2	13	148	55	64	41	4	70	2	1	2	5	2	.71	2	.324	.413	.544
1998 Lk Elsinore	A+ Ana	111	391	115	30	3	15	196	64	66	66	0	118	0	0	2	8	8	.50	10	.294	.394	.501
1999 Erie	AA Ana	40	139	31	7	0	4	50	17	14	17	1	50	0	0	0	0	1	.00	2	.223	.308	.360
Lk Elsinore	A+ Ana	66	242	78	23	0	10	131	48	31	30	0	62	2	0	2	0	0	—	6	.322	.399	.541
2000 Carolina	AA Col	96	318	72	24	0	9	123	29	44	34	1	101	6	6	2	1	3	.25	9	.226	.311	.387
2001 Carolina	AA Col	71	243	58	21	0	5	94	24	27	23	1	78	2	1	2	1	0	1.00	4	.239	.307	.387
5 Min. YEARS		452	1605	442	122	5	56	742	237	246	211	7	479	12	8	10	15	14	.52	35	.275	.362	.462

Mark Dewey

Pitches: Right **Bats:** Right **Pos:** RP-11 **Ht:** 6'0" **Wt:** 216 **Born:** 1/3/65 **Age:** 37

Year Team	Lg Org	G	GS	CG	GF	IP	BFP	H	R	ER	HR	SH	SF	HB	TBB	IBB	SO	WP	Bk	W	L	Pct.	ShO	Sv	ERA
1987 Everett	A- SF	19	10	1	5	84.2	365	88	39	31	2	2	6	2	26	1	67	1	2	7	3	.700	0	1	3.30
1988 Clinton	A SF	37	7	1	11	119.1	474	95	36	19	5	2	1	8	14	0	76	1	5	10	4	.714	0	7	1.43
1989 San Jose	A+ SF	59	0	0	57	68.2	301	62	35	24	2	5	1	7	23	5	60	3	0	1	6	.143	0	30	3.15
1990 Shreveport	AA SF	33	0	0	32	38.1	157	37	11	8	1	3	0	1	10	2	23	1	0	1	5	.167	0	13	1.88
Phoenix	AAA SF	19	0	0	17	30.1	130	26	14	9	2	2	1	2	10	2	27	1	0	2	3	.400	0	8	2.67
1991 Phoenix	AAA SF	10	0	0	10	11.1	59	16	7	5	0	2	1	1	7	5	4	0	0	1	2	.333	0	4	3.97
Tidewater	AAA NYM	48	0	0	32	64.2	286	61	30	24	2	5	6	0	36	6	38	4	1	12	3	.800	0	9	3.34
1992 Tidewater	AAA NYM	43	0	0	32	54.1	238	61	29	26	5	6	0	0	18	6	55	5	0	5	7	.417	0	9	4.31
1993 Buffalo	AAA Pit	22	0	0	11	29.1	114	21	9	4	2	0	1	0	5	0	17	0	0	2	0	1.000	0	6	1.23
2001 Nashville	AAA Pit	11	0	0	2	10.1	43	9	3	2	0	1	1	0	2	0	3	1	0	1	1	.500	0	0	1.74
1990 San Francisco	NL	14	0	0	5	22.2	92	22	7	7	1	2	0	0	5	1	11	0	1	1	1	.500	0	0	2.78
1992 New York	NL	20	0	0	6	33.1	143	37	16	16	2	1	0	0	10	2	24	0	1	1	0	1.000	0	0	4.32
1993 Pittsburgh	NL	21	0	0	17	26.2	108	14	8	7	0	3	3	3	10	1	14	0	0	1	2	.333	0	7	2.36
1994 Pittsburgh	NL	45	0	0	18	51.1	226	61	22	21	4	2	1	3	17	6	32	1	0	2	1	.667	0	1	3.68
1995 San Francisco	NL	27	0	0	5	31.2	137	30	12	11	2	1	1	0	17	6	32	1	0	1	0	1.000	0	0	3.13
1996 San Francisco	NL	78	0	0	16	83.1	360	79	40	39	9	4	5	4	19	6	57	4	0	6	3	.667	0	0	4.21
8 Min. YEARS		301	17	2	209	511.1	2167	476	213	152	21	28	13	24	151	27	370	17	8	42	34	.553	0	87	2.68
6 Maj. YEARS		205	0	0	70	249	1066	243	105	101	18	12	9	11	102	22	168	5	2	12	7	.632	0	8	3.65

Scott DeWitt

Pitches: Left **Bats:** Right **Pos:** RP-42; SP-1 **Ht:** 6'4" **Wt:** 200 **Born:** 10/6/74 **Age:** 27

Year Team	Lg Org	G	GS	CG	GF	IP	BFP	H	R	ER	HR	SH	SF	HB	TBB	IBB	SO	WP	Bk	W	L	Pct.	ShO	Sv	ERA
1995 Marlins	R Fla	11	10	1	0	63.2	245	48	15	14	1	3	2	2	9	0	70	1	1	5	3	.625	0	0	1.98
Kane County	A Fla	1	1	0	0	3	10	0	0	0	0	0	0	1	0	0	2	0	0	0	0	—	0	0	0.00
1996 Kane County	A Fla	27	27	1	0	148.2	667	151	96	78	8	5	4	19	59	0	119	2	2	10	11	.476	1	0	4.72
1997 Brevard Cty	A+ Fla	25	24	0	1	132	585	145	80	61	13	6	3	8	51	0	121	3	1	4	10	.286	0	0	4.16
1998 Portland	AA Fla	50	3	0	13	59.2	278	61	35	30	7	2	3	4	36	0	64	4	1	4	4	.500	0	1	4.53
1999 Carolina	AA Col	45	0	0	15	66.2	309	84	34	29	2	3	2	4	21	1	65	6	1	1	2	.333	0	2	3.92
2000 Carolina	AA Col	34	0	0	12	51.1	224	44	22	18	5	2	2	7	19	1	36	4	0	5	2	.714	0	1	3.16
2001 Carolina	AA Col	43	1	0	17	63	286	66	36	25	5	5	3	7	28	0	52	1	0	2	6	.250	0	1	3.57
7 Min. YEARS		236	66	2	58	588	2604	599	318	255	41	26	19	52	224	2	529	21	6	31	38	.449	1	5	3.90

Alejandro Diaz

Bats: Right **Throws:** Right **Pos:** OF-23; PH-3 **Ht:** 5'9" **Wt:** 190 **Born:** 7/9/78 **Age:** 23

Year Team	Lg Org	G	AB	H	2B	3B	HR	TB	R	RBI	TBB	IBB	SO	HBP	SH	SF	SB	CS	SB%	GDP	Avg	OBP	SLG
1999 Clinton	A Cin	55	221	63	14	3	6	101	39	41	12	1	35	2	0	4	28	11	.72	6	.285	.322	.457
Chattanooga	AA Cin	55	220	58	9	8	7	104	27	35	8	0	31	3	2	2	6	2	.75	3	.264	.296	.473
2000 Chattanooga	AA Cin	122	491	131	19	8	13	205	69	66	14	1	77	4	0	5	18	20	.47	5	.267	.290	.418
2001 Chattanooga	AA Cin	25	87	26	2	0	3	37	13	10	2	0	12	1	0	1	0	1	.00	2	.299	.319	.425
3 Min. YEARS		257	1019	278	44	19	29	447	148	152	36	2	155	10	2	12	52	34	.60	16	.273	.301	.439

Angel Diaz

Bats: Right **Throws:** Right **Pos:** C-43; DH-22; PH-3; OF-1; 1B-1   **Ht:** 6'0" **Wt:** 198 **Born:** 7/27/76 **Age:** 25

						BATTING												BASERUNNING				PERCENTAGES		
Year Team	Lg Org	G	AB	H	2B	3B	HR	TB	R	RBI	TBB	IBB	SO	HBP	SH	SF	SB	CS	SB%	GDP	Avg	OBP	SLG
1998 Boise	A- Ana	3	10	2	0	0	1	5	3	1	3	0	4	0	0	0	0	1	.00	0	.200	.385	.500
Butte	R+ Ana	50	160	49	10	3	6	83	38	33	28	0	36	3	0	3	0	1	.00	6	.306	.412	.519
Cedar Rapds	A Ana	5	15	5	0	0	2	11	2	3	3	0	7	1	0	0	0	0	—	0	.333	.474	.733
1999 Cedar Rapds	A Ana	81	281	68	11	1	10	111	43	42	34	0	85	6	0	0	0	3	.00	4	.242	.336	.395
2000 Lk Elsinore	A+ Ana	45	133	47	11	1	3	69	24	18	19	0	29	4	1	2	7	3	.70	2	.353	.443	.519
2001 Rancho Cuca	A+ Ana	26	84	14	4	1	0	20	9	5	7	1	27	2	0	0	1	0	1.00	3	.167	.247	.238
Arkansas	AA Ana	35	117	31	9	0	4	52	17	15	8	0	23	3	1	0	0	1	.00	1	.265	.328	.444
Salt Lake	AAA Ana	7	26	6	2	0	0	8	5	4	0	0	7	1	0	0	0	0	—	0	.231	.259	.308
4 Min. YEARS		252	826	222	47	6	26	359	141	121	102	1	218	20	2	5	8	9	.47	18	.269	.361	.435

Edwin Diaz

Bats: Right **Throws:** Right **Pos:** 2B-75; 3B-33; SS-5; PR-3; PH-2   **Ht:** 5'11" **Wt:** 170 **Born:** 1/15/75 **Age:** 27

						BATTING												BASERUNNING				PERCENTAGES		
Year Team	Lg Org	G	AB	H	2B	3B	HR	TB	R	RBI	TBB	IBB	SO	HBP	SH	SF	SB	CS	SB%	GDP	Avg	OBP	SLG
1993 Rangers	R Tex	43	154	47	10	5	1	70	27	23	19	1	21	4	0	2	12	5	.71	4	.305	.391	.455
1994 Chston-SC	A Tex	122	413	109	22	7	11	178	52	60	22	0	107	8	8	9	11	14	.44	7	.264	.308	.431
1995 Charlotte	A+ Tex	115	450	128	26	5	8	188	46	56	33	0	94	7	3	2	8	13	.38	10	.284	.341	.418
1996 Tulsa	AA Tex	121	499	132	33	6	16	225	70	65	25	4	122	9	8	4	8	9	.47	9	.265	.309	.451
1997 Okla City	AAA Tex	20	73	8	3	1	1	16	6	4	2	0	27	2	1	0	1	1	.50	1	.110	.156	.219
Tulsa	AA Tex	105	440	121	31	1	15	199	65	46	33	0	102	8	2	5	6	9	.40	6	.275	.335	.452
1998 Tucson	AAA Ari	131	510	134	31	12	2	195	61	49	27	0	105	4	2	5	9	6	.60	9	.263	.302	.382
1999 Tucson	AAA Ari	107	415	129	24	1	11	188	72	50	17	3	77	7	3	4	6	7	.46	7	.311	.345	.453
2000 Oklahoma	AAA Tex	55	198	45	10	0	6	73	27	28	11	0	43	1	3	4	1	0	1.00	2	.227	.266	.369
2001 Edmonton	AAA Min	113	381	104	26	3	11	169	59	56	25	0	65	5	5	3	3	6	.33	5	.273	.324	.444
1998 Arizona	NL	3	7	0	0	0	0	0	0	0	0	0	2	0	0	0	0	0	—	0	.000	.000	.000
1999 Arizona	NL	4	5	2	2	0	0	4	2	1	3	1	1	0	0	0	0	0	—	0	.400	.625	.800
9 Min. YEARS		932	3533	957	216	41	82	1501	487	437	214	8	763	55	35	35	65	70	.48	60	.271	.320	.425
2 Maj. YEARS		7	12	2	2	0	0	4	2	1	3	1	3	0	0	0	0	0	—	0	.167	.333	.333

Juan Diaz

Bats: Right **Throws:** Right **Pos:** DH-37; 1B-36; PH-1   **Ht:** 6'2" **Wt:** 228 **Born:** 2/19/76 **Age:** 26

						BATTING												BASERUNNING				PERCENTAGES		
Year Team	Lg Org	G	AB	H	2B	3B	HR	TB	R	RBI	TBB	IBB	SO	HBP	SH	SF	SB	CS	SB%	GDP	Avg	OBP	SLG
1997 Savannah	A LA	127	460	106	24	2	25	209	63	83	48	2	155	4	1	4	2	2	.50	10	.230	.306	.454
Vero Beach	A+ LA	1	3	2	0	0	1	5	2	3	0	0	1	1	0	0	0	0	—	0	.667	.750	1.667
1998 Vero Beach	A+ LA	67	250	73	12	1	17	138	33	51	21	2	52	4	0	3	1	2	.33	4	.292	.353	.552
San Antonio	AA LA	56	188	50	13	0	13	102	26	30	15	1	45	2	0	0	0	0	—	4	.266	.327	.543
1999 San Antonio	AA LA	66	254	77	21	1	9	127	42	52	26	1	77	3	0	4	0	0	—	4	.303	.369	.500
2000 Sarasota	A+ Bos	14	51	14	2	1	4	30	7	12	4	0	15	1	0	1	0	0	—	1	.275	.333	.588
Trenton	AA Bos	50	198	62	14	1	17	129	36	53	10	0	56	0	0	2	0	0	—	6	.313	.343	.652
Pawtucket	AAA Bos	13	43	12	0	0	7	33	11	17	6	0	9	0	0	2	0	1	1.00	1	.279	.353	.767
2001 Pawtucket	AAA Bos	74	279	75	17	1	20	154	45	51	17	2	85	6	0	1	0	0	—	10	.269	.323	.552
5 Min. YEARS		468	1726	471	103	7	113	927	265	352	147	8	495	21	1	17	4	4	.50	41	.273	.334	.537

Miguel Diaz

Bats: Right **Throws:** Right **Pos:** OF-31; PH-21; DH-5; PR-4   **Ht:** 5'11" **Wt:** 160 **Born:** 9/29/77 **Age:** 24

						BATTING												BASERUNNING				PERCENTAGES		
Year Team	Lg Org	G	AB	H	2B	3B	HR	TB	R	RBI	TBB	IBB	SO	HBP	SH	SF	SB	CS	SB%	GDP	Avg	OBP	SLG
1997 Johnson Cty	R+ StL	59	223	63	17	1	4	94	33	28	7	0	32	2	0	4	1	3	.25	7	.283	.305	.422
1998 Peoria	A StL	53	139	29	7	0	1	39	21	16	0	0	19	1	2	0	4	6	.40	6	.209	.214	.281
1999 Peoria	A StL	105	343	87	18	6	3	126	44	34	8	0	59	7	6	1	10	6	.63	6	.254	.284	.367
2000 Potomac	A+ StL	105	312	78	23	2	0	105	35	32	14	0	47	5	4	3	5	3	.63	6	.250	.290	.337
2001 New Haven	AA StL	58	117	32	4	1	0	38	7	6	4	1	20	2	0	0	2	5	.29	1	.274	.309	.325
5 Min. YEARS		380	1134	289	69	10	8	402	140	116	33	1	177	17	12	8	22	23	.49	28	.255	.284	.354

Jason Dickson

Pitches: Right **Bats:** Left **Pos:** SP-20   **Ht:** 6'0" **Wt:** 195 **Born:** 3/30/73 **Age:** 29

		HOW MUCH HE PITCHED					WHAT HE GAVE UP										THE RESULTS					
Year Team	Lg Org	G	GS	CG	GF	IP	BFP	H	R	ER	HR	SH	SF	HB	TBB	IBB	SO	WP	Bk	W	L	Pct.	ShO	Sv	ERA
1994 Boise	A- Ana	9	7	0	1	44.1	190	40	22	19	3	1	0	2	18	1	37	3	2	3	1	.750	0	0	3.86
1995 Cedar Rapds	A Ana	25	25	9	0	173	708	151	71	55	12	4	3	8	45	0	134	7	2	14	6	.700	1	0	2.86
1996 Midland	AA Ana	8	8	3	0	55.1	228	55	27	22	3	2	0	0	10	0	40	3	0	5	2	.714	1	0	3.58
Vancouver	AAA Ana	18	18	7	0	130.1	553	134	73	55	9	2	4	5	40	1	70	4	4	7	11	.389	0	0	3.80
1998 Vancouver	AAA Ana	4	4	0	0	25.1	100	26	5	5	2	2	0	1	4	0	18	0	1	2	1	.667	0	0	1.78
2000 Edmonton	AAA Ana	2	2	0	0	8	38	13	9	9	1	0	0	0	4	0	4	1	0	0	2	.000	0	0	10.13
2001 Dunedin	A+ Tor	4	4	0	0	18	73	14	3	3	1	0	0	1	1	0	20	1	1	1	1	.500	0	0	1.50
Tennessee	AA Tor	5	5	0	0	32.2	138	30	12	12	1	1	0	2	11	0	21	0	0	2	1	.667	0	0	3.31
Syracuse	AAA Tor	11	11	0	0	57.2	267	75	52	46	11	5	3	6	19	0	40	0	0	4	7	.364	0	0	7.18
1996 California	AL	7	7	0	0	43.1	192	52	22	22	6	2	1	1	18	1	20	1	1	1	4	.200	0	0	4.57
1997 Anaheim	AL	33	32	2	1	203.2	888	236	111	97	32	4	5	7	56	3	115	4	1	13	9	.591	1	0	4.29
1998 Anaheim	AL	27	18	0	5	122	545	147	89	82	17	4	9	6	41	1	61	6	0	10	10	.500	0	0	6.05
2000 Anaheim	AL	6	6	0	0	28	125	39	20	19	5	1	0	1	7	0	18	0	0	2	2	.500	0	0	6.11
6 Min. YEARS		86	84	19	1	544.2	2295	538	274	226	43	17	10	25	152	2	384	19	9	38	32	.543	2	1	3.73
4 Maj. YEARS		73	63	2	6	397	1750	474	242	220	60	11	15	15	122	5	214	11	2	26	25	.510	1	0	4.99

80

Mark DiFelice

Pitches: Right **Bats:** Right **Pos:** SP-26; RP-1   **Ht:** 6'2" **Wt:** 190 **Born:** 8/23/76 **Age:** 25

Year Team	Lg Org	G	GS	CG	GF	IP	BFP	H	R	ER	HR	SH	SF	HB	TBB	IBB	SO	WP	Bk	W	L	Pct.	ShO	Sv	ERA
1998 Portland	A- Col	15	13	0	2	81.2	343	83	45	30	6	1	2	3	11	0	62	3	1	4	6	.400	0	0	3.31
1999 Salem	A+ Col	27	23	3	1	156.1	642	142	71	67	20	4	6	4	36	0	142	3	1	8	12	.400	0	0	3.86
2000 Carolina	AA Col	23	22	2	0	133	556	152	58	53	15	2	3	0	19	0	98	2	0	7	5	.583	0	0	3.59
2001 Carolina	AA Col	19	18	2	0	123	498	108	47	43	13	3	5	3	23	0	98	1	0	6	4	.600	1	0	3.15
Colo Sprngs	AAA Col	8	8	0	0	46	207	56	29	27	11	2	1	8	8	3	43	1	0	3	2	.600	0	0	5.28
4 Min. YEARS		92	84	7	3	540	2246	541	250	220	65	12	17	18	97	3	443	10	2	28	29	.491	1	0	3.67

John Dillinger

Pitches: Right **Bats:** Right **Pos:** SP-26   **Ht:** 6'5" **Wt:** 240 **Born:** 8/28/73 **Age:** 28

Year Team	Lg Org	G	GS	CG	GF	IP	BFP	H	R	ER	HR	SH	SF	HB	TBB	IBB	SO	WP	Bk	W	L	Pct.	ShO	Sv	ERA
1992 Pirates	R Pit	13	10	0	1	52.1	250	43	37	20	1	0	5	6	42	0	45	6	2	3	3	.500	0	0	3.44
1993 Lethbridge	R+ Pit	15	15	3	0	80.1	367	65	51	35	2	3	5	5	60	1	94	9	3	3	10	.231	0	0	3.92
1994 Augusta	A Pit	23	22	1	1	119.2	524	107	77	57	5	6	2	3	54	1	118	8	5	5	9	.357	0	0	4.29
1995 Lynchburg	A+ Pit	27	22	0	1	123	540	111	62	55	10	5	5	7	67	4	97	9	7	6	6	.500	0	0	4.02
1996 Lynchburg	A+ Pit	33	15	2	0	132.1	554	101	65	55	11	3	3	4	58	0	113	11	1	10	5	.667	0	0	3.74
1997 Carolina	AA Pit	23	11	0	3	81	382	88	66	54	8	3	4	5	52	0	64	7	1	6	4	.600	0	0	6.00
1998 Carolina	AA Pit	4	0	0	0	5.2	32	11	9	9	4	1	0	2	4	0	4	0	0	1	0	1.000	0	0	14.29
Allentown	IND —	14	14	0	0	88.1	397	96	46	35	7	7	5	3	47	0	66	5	0	7	3	.700	0	0	3.57
2000 Somerset	IND —	3	0	0	0	5.1	30	9	8	6	0	1	1	0	5	1	4	1	0	0	1	.000	0	0	10.13
2001 Syracuse	AAA Tor	26	26	1	0	155.2	669	150	79	69	10	4	5	15	58	1	108	15	0	11	7	.611	0	0	3.99
9 Min. YEARS		181	135	7	6	843.2	3745	781	500	395	58	33	35	50	447	8	713	71	19	51	49	.510	1	1	4.21

Joe Dillon

Bats: Right **Throws:** Right **Pos:** 1B-54; 3B-31; 2B-11; DH-7; PH-3; SS-1   **Ht:** 6'2" **Wt:** 205 **Born:** 8/2/75 **Age:** 26

Year Team	Lg Org	G	AB	H	2B	3B	HR	TB	R	RBI	TBB	IBB	SO	HBP	SH	SF	SB	CS	SB%	GDP	Avg	OBP	SLG
1997 Spokane	A- KC	19	70	15	3	0	2	24	6	6	5	0	13	1	0	0	1	0	1.00	2	.214	.276	.343
1998 Lansing	A KC	73	268	70	17	2	15	136	37	43	36	1	57	0	4	0	9	2	.82	5	.261	.349	.507
1999 Wilmington	A+ KC	134	503	133	31	2	16	216	73	90	59	4	124	7	2	5	9	6	.60	12	.264	.347	.429
2000 Wichita	AA KC	62	220	70	16	2	10	120	35	43	39	1	38	7	2	5	0	0	—	6	.318	.428	.545
Omaha	AAA KC	45	149	42	11	2	1	60	19	11	17	0	26	2	0	0	1	0	1.00	6	.282	.363	.403
2001 Wichita	AA KC	101	369	106	19	3	15	176	62	59	36	1	60	8	1	3	4	3	.57	10	.287	.361	.477
5 Min. YEARS		434	1579	436	97	11	59	732	232	252	192	7	318	25	9	13	24	11	.69	41	.276	.361	.464

Doug Dimma

Pitches: Left **Bats:** Right **Pos:** RP-41; SP-2   **Ht:** 5'11" **Wt:** 175 **Born:** 7/3/78 **Age:** 23

Year Team	Lg Org	G	GS	CG	GF	IP	BFP	H	R	ER	HR	SH	SF	HB	TBB	IBB	SO	WP	Bk	W	L	Pct.	ShO	Sv	ERA
1999 St.Cathrnes	A- Tor	17	2	0	5	47.2	214	48	29	20	1	1	0	3	28	1	42	4	2	3	1	.750	0	1	3.78
Syracuse	AAA Tor	1	0	0	0	1	4	2	1	1	0	0	0	0	0	1	0	0	0	0	0	—	0	0	9.00
2000 Dunedin	A+ Tor	43	0	0	17	79.2	361	74	46	34	6	1	3	9	48	4	42	7	0	6	3	.667	0	1	3.84
2001 Tennessee	AA Tor	19	0	0	4	13.1	61	16	8	8	2	1	1	2	9	1	5	0	0	0	2	.000	0	1	5.40
Dunedin	A+ Tor	24	2	0	12	48	231	58	31	26	4	1	1	3	30	2	27	6	0	1	2	.333	0	0	4.88
3 Min. YEARS		104	4	0	38	189.2	871	198	115	89	14	4	5	17	115	8	117	17	2	10	8	.556	0	3	4.22

Allen Dina

Bats: Right **Throws:** Right **Pos:** OF-86; PH-16; DH-7   **Ht:** 5'10" **Wt:** 190 **Born:** 9/28/73 **Age:** 28

Year Team	Lg Org	G	AB	H	2B	3B	HR	TB	R	RBI	TBB	IBB	SO	HBP	SH	SF	SB	CS	SB%	GDP	Avg	OBP	SLG
1998 Pittsfield	A- NYM	68	278	83	16	5	5	124	47	39	24	0	34	1	1	4	18	5	.78	1	.299	.352	.446
Capital Cty	A NYM	2	8	3	2	0	0	5	1	3	0	0	1	0	0	0	0	0	—	0	.375	.375	.625
1999 St. Lucie	A+ NYM	85	343	118	16	4	12	178	65	47	25	0	54	6	4	3	34	10	.77	2	.344	.395	.519
Binghamton	AA NYM	49	192	44	10	3	0	60	25	15	9	0	46	1	0	2	9	3	.75	6	.229	.265	.313
2000 Binghamton	AA NYM	121	419	108	22	4	7	159	58	46	22	0	78	11	9	3	21	10	.68	7	.258	.310	.379
2001 Norfolk	AAA NYM	7	12	0	0	0	0	0	0	2	0	0	2	0	0	2	0	0	—	0	.000	.000	.000
St. Lucie	A+ NYM	16	61	22	6	1	3	39	13	12	2	0	10	0	0	0	4	0	1.00	0	.361	.381	.639
Binghamton	AA NYM	85	269	74	17	1	3	102	33	35	17	1	53	2	6	3	9	6	.60	4	.275	.320	.379
4 Min. YEARS		433	1582	452	89	18	30	667	242	199	99	1	278	21	20	17	95	34	.74	20	.286	.333	.422

Mike Diorio

Pitches: Right **Bats:** Right **Pos:** RP-43   **Ht:** 6'2" **Wt:** 215 **Born:** 3/1/73 **Age:** 29

Year Team	Lg Org	G	GS	CG	GF	IP	BFP	H	R	ER	HR	SH	SF	HB	TBB	IBB	SO	WP	Bk	W	L	Pct.	ShO	Sv	ERA
1993 Auburn	A- Hou	15	15	0	0	79	356	98	57	45	6	2	2	3	27	0	57	6	0	3	7	.300	0	0	5.13
1994 Astros	R Hou	2	0	0	0	2.1	15	5	6	6	1	0	0	0	3	0	2	0	0	0	1	.000	0	0	23.14
Osceola	A+ Hou	13	7	0	0	44	191	48	24	14	4	1	2	0	11	0	27	2	0	3	2	.600	0	0	2.86
1995 Quad City	A Hou	33	11	0	4	91.2	391	82	39	33	6	4	0	4	36	1	81	13	2	6	4	.600	0	0	3.24
1997 Jackson	AA Hou	8	0	0	2	11.1	63	18	17	12	1	1	0	2	6	1	9	1	2	1	3	.250	0	1	9.53
Kissimmee	A+ Hou	36	0	0	30	39.1	161	33	15	13	1	1	0	1	10	1	30	1	1	3	2	.600	0	19	2.97
1998 Jackson	AA Hou	32	0	0	24	43	182	35	16	10	0	3	2	0	21	4	31	2	0	2	3	.400	0	11	2.09
New Orleans	AAA Hou	21	0	0	8	29.1	134	38	24	17	3	2	2	1	11	4	14	1	0	4	2	.667	0	2	5.22
1999 New Orleans	AAA Hou	50	0	0	14	70.1	333	85	59	50	10	2	2	1	31	6	32	6	0	2	3	.400	0	1	6.40
2000 Nashville	AAA Pit	6	3	0	1	16.1	76	11	7	7	2	0	1	1	17	1	12	1	0	0	0	—	0	0	3.86
2001 Newark	IND —	25	0	0	10	30	120	20	9	9	1	1	1	0	10	1	26	1	0	1	1	.500	0	1	2.70
Altoona	AA Pit	18	0	0	2	33	155	40	34	29	5	0	2	2	19	0	14	0	0	1	4	.200	0	0	7.91
8 Min. YEARS		259	36	0	95	489.2	2177	513	307	245	40	17	12	23	202	19	335	34	5	26	32	.448	0	36	4.50

Dan DiPace

Bats: Left **Throws:** Right **Pos:** OF-11; DH-9; PH-6; 1B-3   **Ht:** 6'2" **Wt:** 215 **Born:** 4/24/75 **Age:** 27

Year Team	Lg Org	G	AB	H	2B	3B	HR	TB	R	RBI	TBB	IBB	SO	HBP	SH	SF	SB	CS	SB%	GDP	Avg	OBP	SLG
1996 Lafayette	IND —	40	104	24	2	0	5	41	13	24	14	1	24	3	1	0	6	1	.86	1	.231	.339	.394
1997 Duluth-Sup	IND —	5	17	3	1	0	0	4	1	0	3	0	5	0	0	0	0	0	—	1	.176	.300	.235
Tyler	IND —	42	115	33	6	0	5	54	22	24	16	0	31	2	1	1	4	3	.57	0	.287	.381	.470
1998 Lansing	A KC	20	49	13	1	0	1	17	11	7	11	1	14	2	0	2	1	0	1.00	1	.265	.406	.347
Wilmington	A+ KC	16	41	5	0	0	0	5	5	2	7	0	20	1	0	0	0	0	—	2	.122	.265	.122
Spokane	A- KC	44	113	31	11	0	6	60	12	34	18	1	28	4	0	4	0	0	—	1	.274	.381	.531
1999 Chston-WV	A KC	65	192	43	11	0	2	60	23	19	34	1	67	6	1	0	8	3	.73	3	.224	.358	.313
Huntsville	AA Mil	11	26	3	1	0	0	4	2	2	3	0	9	0	0	0	0	0	—	0	.115	.207	.154
2000 Aberdeen	IND —	5	15	5	1	0	0	6	1	1	0	0	5	1	0	0	1	0	1.00	0	.333	.375	.400
2001 Trenton	AA Bos	12	31	4	1	0	0	5	1	1	1	0	14	1	0	0	0	0	—	0	.129	.182	.161
Nashua	IND —	15	39	9	0	0	0	9	3	4	8	0	14	2	0	0	0	0	—	0	.231	.388	.231
6 Min. YEARS		275	742	173	35	0	19	265	94	118	115	4	231	22	3	7	20	7	.74	10	.233	.350	.357

Nate Dishington

Bats: Left **Throws:** Right **Pos:** OF-28; DH-7; PH-6   **Ht:** 6'3" **Wt:** 290 **Born:** 1/8/75 **Age:** 27

Year Team	Lg Org	G	AB	H	2B	3B	HR	TB	R	RBI	TBB	IBB	SO	HBP	SH	SF	SB	CS	SB%	GDP	Avg	OBP	SLG
1993 Johnson Cty	R+ StL	36	121	19	5	1	1	29	13	7	16	0	52	2	0	2	4	2	.67	3	.157	.262	.240
1994 Cardinals	R StL	51	179	51	15	3	4	84	36	36	22	2	58	5	0	2	1	1	.50	2	.285	.375	.469
1995 Savannah	A StL	124	444	95	17	5	11	155	56	44	62	4	154	17	0	6	13	7	.65	14	.214	.329	.349
1996 Peoria	A StL	75	208	47	12	3	3	74	22	30	25	0	73	7	0	4	1	1	.50	6	.226	.324	.356
1997 Pr William	A+ StL	133	448	122	20	6	28	238	75	106	81	11	121	7	1	6	8	5	.62	3	.272	.387	.531
1998 Arkansas	AA StL	75	237	60	6	1	17	119	40	49	40	1	91	3	0	1	6	1	.86	3	.253	.367	.502
Memphis	AAA StL	60	200	53	15	1	10	100	30	34	24	1	88	8	0	0	1	1	.50	2	.265	.366	.500
1999 Memphis	AAA StL	72	196	41	11	1	8	78	34	32	25	1	96	0	0	2	1	4	.20	1	.209	.296	.398
Akron	AA Cle	17	59	14	2	0	5	31	12	14	6	0	30	3	0	0	0	0	—	1	.237	.338	.525
2001 New Haven	AA StL	39	129	25	5	0	7	51	12	22	7	1	61	4	0	3	1	0	1.00	2	.194	.252	.395
8 Min. YEARS		682	2221	527	108	21	94	959	330	374	308	21	824	56	1	26	36	22	.62	37	.237	.341	.432

Jeremy Dodson

Bats: Left **Throws:** Right **Pos:** OF-100; PH-8; DH-2   **Ht:** 6'2" **Wt:** 200 **Born:** 5/3/77 **Age:** 25

Year Team	Lg Org	G	AB	H	2B	3B	HR	TB	R	RBI	TBB	IBB	SO	HBP	SH	SF	SB	CS	SB%	GDP	Avg	OBP	SLG
1998 Spokane	A- KC	69	268	90	19	5	9	146	56	59	25	2	59	6	0	5	8	4	.67	5	.336	.398	.545
1999 Wichita	AA KC	133	452	116	20	1	21	201	63	58	51	2	95	2	1	0	9	5	.64	12	.257	.335	.445
2000 Wichita	AA KC	128	450	107	16	4	18	185	69	57	52	2	111	7	5	0	17	8	.68	7	.238	.326	.411
2001 Wichita	AA KC	35	113	23	1	1	1	29	13	7	11	1	31	2	1	0	3	0	1.00	4	.204	.286	.257
Wilmington	A+ KC	70	215	46	8	2	5	73	27	30	32	3	78	7	0	1	7	0	1.00	4	.214	.333	.340
4 Min. YEARS		435	1498	382	64	13	54	634	228	211	171	10	374	24	7	6	44	17	.72	32	.255	.340	.423

Andy Dominique

Bats: Right **Throws:** Right **Pos:** C-52; 1B-47; DH-9; 3B-5; PH-3   **Ht:** 6'0" **Wt:** 224 **Born:** 10/30/75 **Age:** 26

Year Team	Lg Org	G	AB	H	2B	3B	HR	TB	R	RBI	TBB	IBB	SO	HBP	SH	SF	SB	CS	SB%	GDP	Avg	OBP	SLG
1997 Batavia	A- Phi	72	277	77	17	0	14	136	52	48	26	0	60	10	0	5	4	1	.80	6	.278	.355	.491
1998 Piedmont	A Phi	133	514	145	38	4	24	255	82	102	61	4	97	12	0	4	0	2	.00	9	.282	.369	.496
1999 Clearwater	A+ Phi	130	487	124	29	5	14	205	77	92	69	4	84	10	3	8	3	3	.50	13	.255	.354	.421
2000 Reading	AA Phi	104	327	78	27	0	13	144	46	50	35	0	56	8	3	4	0	1	.00	9	.239	.324	.440
2001 Reading	AA Phi	76	261	73	16	0	12	125	43	49	37	2	45	1	0	2	3	1	.75	6	.280	.369	.479
Scranton-WB	AAA Phi	40	135	23	6	0	3	38	16	18	12	0	34	1	1	0	0	0	—	4	.170	.243	.281
5 Min. YEARS		555	2001	520	133	5	80	903	316	359	240	10	376	42	7	23	10	8	.56	47	.260	.348	.451

Bo Donaldson

Pitches: Right **Bats:** Right **Pos:** RP-34; SP-2   **Ht:** 6'0" **Wt:** 200 **Born:** 10/10/74 **Age:** 27

Year Team	Lg Org	G	GS	CG	GF	IP	BFP	H	R	ER	HR	SH	SF	HB	TBB	IBB	SO	WP	Bk	W	L	Pct.	ShO	Sv	ERA
1997 Boise	A- Ana	27	0	0	25	52	208	31	10	7	0	3	1	2	20	1	88	10	2	3	1	.750	0	15	1.21
1998 Lk Elsinore	A+ Ana	54	3	0	42	76.1	340	65	38	32	7	5	3	9	40	4	99	12	4	4	6	.400	0	20	3.77
1999 Rockford	A Cin	19	0	0	7	30	119	17	7	4	0	4	0	0	12	3	50	2	1	2	1	.667	0	1	1.20
Chattanooga	AA Cin	38	0	0	19	51.1	199	50	18	17	2	3	1	1	16	2	67	2	1	5	3	.625	0	6	2.98
2000 Chattanooga	AA Cin	57	0	0	46	61.2	284	50	31	25	7	4	1	4	48	6	78	6	2	1	4	.200	0	24	3.65
2001 Altoona	AA Pit	17	0	0	12	20.1	81	12	7	7	2	0	0	3	7	0	22	0	0	3	1	.750	0	5	3.10
Nashville	AAA Pit	11	0	0	3	14	60	9	4	1	0	1	0	2	9	0	17	2	0	1	1	.500	0	0	0.64
Portland	AAA SD	8	2	0	3	19.2	69	6	2	1	0	0	0	2	2	0	18	0	0	2	0	1.000	0	0	0.46
5 Min. YEARS		231	5	0	157	325.1	1360	220	117	94	19	19	7	23	154	16	439	34	10	21	17	.553	0	71	2.60

Brendan Donnelly

Pitches: Right **Bats:** Right **Pos:** RP-56   **Ht:** 6'3" **Wt:** 205 **Born:** 7/4/71 **Age:** 30

Year Team	Lg Org	G	GS	CG	GF	IP	BFP	H	R	ER	HR	SH	SF	HB	TBB	IBB	SO	WP	Bk	W	L	Pct.	ShO	Sv	ERA
1992 White Sox	R CWS	9	7	0	1	41.2	191	41	25	17	0	0	2	8	21	0	31	6	0	0	3	.000	0	1	3.67
1993 Geneva	A- ChC	21	3	0	7	43	198	39	34	30	4	1	1	6	29	0	29	7	3	4	0	1.000	0	1	6.28
1994 Ohio Valley	IND —	10	0	0	1	13.2	59	13	5	4	1	0	0	3	4	0	20	1	0	1	1	.500	0	0	2.63
1995 Chston-WV	A Cin	24	0	0	22	30.1	112	14	4	4	0	1	2	1	7	1	33	1	0	1	1	.500	0	12	1.19
Winston-Sal	A+ Cin	23	0	0	14	35.1	138	20	6	4	1	2	0	2	14	2	32	0	1	1	2	.333	0	2	1.02
Indianapols	AAA Cin	3	0	0	0	2.2	18	7	8	7	2	0	1	1	2	0	1	2	0	1	1	.500	0	0	23.63

		HOW	MUCH	HE	PITCHED			WHAT	HE	GAVE	UP									THE	RESULTS				
Year Team	Lg Org	G	GS	CG	GF	IP	BFP	H	R	ER	HR	SH	SF	HB	TBB	IBB	SO	WP	Bk	W	L	Pct.	ShO	Sv	ERA
1996 Chattanooga	AA Cin	22	0	0	10	29.1	133	27	21	18	4	0	1	1	17	2	22	1	0	1	2	.333	0	0	5.52
1997 Chattanooga	AA Cin	62	0	0	21	82.2	359	71	43	30	6	4	3	4	37	4	64	9	0	6	4	.600	0	6	3.27
1998 Chattanooga	AA Cin	38	0	0	35	45.1	203	43	16	15	4	1	1	3	24	5	47	8	0	2	5	.286	0	13	2.98
Indianapols	AAA Cin	19	1	0	6	37.1	157	29	16	11	3	1	0	3	16	3	39	2	0	4	1	.800	0	0	2.65
1999 Nashua	IND —	3	0	0	3	3	11	1	1	1	1	0	0	0	3	0	4	0	0	0	0	—	0	0	3.00
Durham	AAA TB	37	1	0	10	62	247	53	23	21	5	0	4	4	18	1	61	5	0	5	5	.500	0	2	3.05
Altoona	AA Pit	2	0	0	2	2.1	12	4	2	2	0	1	2	0	2	0	0	0	0	0	0	—	0	1	7.71
Syracuse	AAA Tor	5	0	0	2	9.1	39	8	4	3	1	2	0	0	4	1	9	1	0	0	1	.000	0	0	2.89
2000 Syracuse	AAA Tor	37	0	0	7	42.2	203	47	34	26	5	4	1	1	27	2	34	1	0	4	6	.400	0	0	5.48
Iowa	AAA ChC	9	0	0	3	16.2	83	25	19	14	3	0	1	2	6	1	14	2	0	0	3	.000	0	1	7.56
2001 Arkansas	AA Ana	27	0	0	24	29	120	21	8	8	2	0	1	1	13	1	37	1	0	4	1	.800	0	12	2.48
Salt Lake	AAA Ana	29	0	0	12	41.1	165	38	11	11	4	1	1	0	8	0	50	2	0	5	1	.833	0	1	2.40
10 Min. YEARS		380	12	0	180	567.2	2448	501	280	226	46	18	21	40	252	23	527	49	4	39	37	.513	0	52	3.58

Randey Dorame

Pitches: Left **Bats:** Left **Pos:** SP-19; RP-3   **Ht:** 6'2" **Wt:** 205 **Born:** 1/23/79 **Age:** 23

		HOW	MUCH	HE	PITCHED			WHAT	HE	GAVE	UP									THE	RESULTS				
Year Team	Lg Org	G	GS	CG	GF	IP	BFP	H	R	ER	HR	SH	SF	HB	TBB	IBB	SO	WP	Bk	W	L	Pct.	ShO	Sv	ERA
1999 Vero Beach	A+ LA	3	2	0	0	11	48	15	9	7	2	0	0	0	1	0	5	0	0	0	2	.000	0	0	5.73
San Berndno	A+ LA	24	24	1	0	154.1	613	130	52	43	9	3	6	3	37	0	159	7	1	14	3	.824	1	0	2.51
2000 Vero Beach	A+ LA	9	9	2	0	57	226	50	15	14	3	3	2	2	13	0	49	2	0	7	1	.875	0	0	2.21
San Antonio	AA LA	9	9	0	0	58.1	238	53	29	25	5	3	3	1	18	0	28	2	1	3	4	.429	0	0	3.86
Carolina	AA Col	2	2	0	0	10.2	46	7	6	6	3	0	0	2	4	0	9	0	0	0	2	.000	0	0	5.06
2001 Carolina	AA Col	5	5	0	0	28	120	33	17	15	3	0	3	0	6	0	17	1	0	0	4	.000	0	0	4.82
Salem	A+ Col	17	14	0	2	78.2	353	95	50	46	10	4	3	4	28	0	57	4	1	2	5	.286	0	0	5.26
3 Min. YEARS		69	65	3	2	398	1644	383	178	156	35	13	17	12	107	0	324	16	3	26	21	.553	1	0	3.53

Jim Dougherty

Pitches: Right **Bats:** Right **Pos:** RP-59   **Ht:** 6'1" **Wt:** 225 **Born:** 3/8/68 **Age:** 34

		HOW	MUCH	HE	PITCHED			WHAT	HE	GAVE	UP									THE	RESULTS				
Year Team	Lg Org	G	GS	CG	GF	IP	BFP	H	R	ER	HR	SH	SF	HB	TBB	IBB	SO	WP	Bk	W	L	Pct.	ShO	Sv	ERA
1991 Asheville	A Hou	61	0	0	48	82	324	63	17	14	0	7	0	3	24	6	76	0	2	3	1	.750	0	27	1.54
1992 Osceola	A+ Hou	57	0	0	52	81	325	66	21	14	1	4	2	2	22	4	77	0	1	5	2	.714	0	31	1.56
1993 Jackson	AA Hou	52	0	0	50	53	207	39	15	11	3	0	0	1	21	0	55	0	0	2	2	.500	0	36	1.87
1994 Tucson	AAA Hou	55	0	0	48	59	276	74	32	27	9	1	1	2	30	6	49	4	0	5	4	.556	0	21	4.12
1995 Tucson	AAA Hou	8	0	0	3	11	46	11	4	4	1	0	0	0	5	0	12	0	1	1	0	1.000	0	1	3.27
1996 Tucson	AAA Hou	46	0	0	23	61.2	269	65	35	24	0	1	1	2	27	3	53	2	1	4	3	.571	0	1	3.50
1997 Norfolk	AAA NYM	49	0	0	24	62	259	45	11	10	3	4	2	2	43	3	59	4	0	10	1	.909	0	4	1.45
1998 Edmonton	AAA Oak	45	0	0	26	57.2	254	57	24	24	7	2	1	2	33	4	45	1	0	2	1	.667	0	6	3.75
1999 Nashville	AAA Pit	53	0	0	20	59.2	274	69	38	36	9	3	4	0	27	5	55	0	0	3	3	.500	0	10	5.43
2000 Memphis	AAA StL	60	0	0	24	81.1	342	76	33	30	5	6	4	5	29	5	82	3	2	3	7	.300	0	6	3.32
2001 Las Vegas	AAA LA	59	0	0	45	81	344	82	39	38	8	2	2	0	34	7	85	2	0	4	5	.444	0	14	4.22
1995 Houston	NL	56	0	0	11	67.2	294	76	37	37	7	3	3	3	25	1	49	1	0	8	4	.667	0	0	4.92
1996 Houston	NL	12	0	0	2	13	64	14	14	13	2	1	1	1	11	1	6	0	0	0	2	.000	0	0	9.00
1998 Oakland	AL	9	0	0	4	12	59	17	11	11	2	1	0	1	7	0	3	0	0	0	2	.000	0	0	8.25
1999 Pittsburgh	NL	2	0	0	0	2	12	3	3	2	0	0	0	0	3	0	1	0	0	0	0	—	0	0	9.00
11 Min. YEARS		545	0	0	363	689.1	2920	643	269	232	46	30	17	19	295	43	648	16	7	42	29	.592	0	157	3.03
4 Maj. YEARS		79	0	0	17	94.2	429	110	65	63	11	5	4	5	46	2	59	1	0	8	8	.500	0	0	5.99

Ryan Doumit

Bats: Both **Throws:** Right **Pos:** C-28; DH-19; PH-2   **Ht:** 6'0" **Wt:** 180 **Born:** 4/3/81 **Age:** 21

		BATTING														BASERUNNING				PERCENTAGES		
Year Team	Lg Org	G	AB	H	2B	3B	HR	TB	R	RBI	TBB	IBB	SO	HBP	SH	SF	SB	CS	SB%	GDP	Avg	OBP	SLG
1999 Pirates	R Pit	29	85	24	5	0	1	32	17	7	15	0	14	4	0	1	4	2	.67	0	.282	.410	.376
2000 Williamsprt	A- Pit	66	246	77	15	5	2	108	25	40	23	1	33	4	0	7	2	2	.50	7	.313	.371	.439
2001 Pirates	R Pit	7	17	4	2	0	0	6	2	3	2	1	0	0	0	0	0	0	—	0	.235	.316	.353
Altoona	AA Pit	2	4	1	0	0	0	1	0	2	1	0	1	0	0	0	0	0	—	0	.250	.400	.250
Hickory	A Pit	39	148	40	6	0	2	52	14	14	10	0	32	4	0	0	2	1	.67	2	.270	.333	.351
3 Min. YEARS		143	500	146	28	5	5	199	58	66	51	2	80	12	0	8	8	5	.62	9	.292	.366	.398

Travis Driskill

Pitches: Right **Bats:** Right **Pos:** SP-28   **Ht:** 6'0" **Wt:** 185 **Born:** 8/1/71 **Age:** 30

		HOW	MUCH	HE	PITCHED			WHAT	HE	GAVE	UP									THE	RESULTS				
Year Team	Lg Org	G	GS	CG	GF	IP	BFP	H	R	ER	HR	SH	SF	HB	TBB	IBB	SO	WP	Bk	W	L	Pct.	ShO	Sv	ERA
1993 Watertown	A- Cle	21	8	0	7	63	276	62	38	29	4	3	6	5	21	0	53	6	0	5	4	.556	0	3	4.14
1994 Columbus	A Cle	62	0	0	59	64.1	267	51	25	18	2	5	2	1	30	4	88	6	0	5	5	.500	0	35	2.52
1995 Canton-Akrn	AA Cle	33	0	0	22	46.1	200	46	24	24	3	1	1	1	19	1	39	0	1	3	4	.429	0	4	4.66
Kinston	A+ Cle	15	0	0	9	23	90	17	7	7	2	0	3	1	5	1	24	1	0	0	2	.000	0	0	2.74
1996 Canton-Akrn	AA Cle	29	24	4	0	172	732	169	89	69	8	6	6	3	63	0	148	10	2	13	7	.650	2	0	3.61
1997 Buffalo	AAA Cle	29	24	1	1	147	645	159	86	76	22	2	6	3	60	0	102	15	1	8	7	.533	0	0	4.65
1998 Akron	AA Cle	5	4	0	1	26.1	109	27	12	10	4	0	1	1	7	0	16	0	0	3	0	1.000	0	0	3.42
Buffalo	AAA Cle	1	1	0	0	6	28	9	6	6	0	0	0	0	1	0	5	0	0	0	0	—	0	0	9.00
1999 Buffalo	AAA Cle	31	18	0	3	132.1	561	146	78	71	21	5	5	6	32	2	90	4	1	9	8	.529	0	0	4.83
2000 New Orleans	AAA Hou	28	28	0	0	179.1	774	201	101	80	15	5	3	7	45	0	113	6	0	12	11	.522	1	0	4.01
2001 New Orleans	AAA Hou	28	28	1	0	178.2	735	175	83	75	21	6	5	6	33	2	145	5	1	11	5	.688	0	0	3.78
9 Min. YEARS		282	135	8	102	1038.1	4417	1062	549	465	102	33	38	34	316	10	823	53	6	69	53	.566	3	42	4.03

Mike Drumright

Pitches: Right **Bats:** Left **Pos:** RP-21; SP-16   **Ht:** 6'4" **Wt:** 210 **Born:** 4/19/74 **Age:** 28

Year Team	Lg Org	G	GS	CG	GF	IP	BFP	H	R	ER	HR	SH	SF	HB	TBB	IBB	SO	WP	Bk	W	L	Pct.	ShO	Sv	ERA
1995 Lakeland	A+ Det	5	5	0	0	21	87	19	11	10	2	1	0	0	9	0	19	1	2	1	1	.500	0	0	4.29
Jacksnville	AA Det	5	5	0	0	31.2	137	30	13	13	4	0	0	2	15	1	34	1	5	0	1	.000	0	0	3.69
1996 Jacksnville	AA Det	18	18	1	0	99.2	418	80	51	44	11	1	3	3	48	0	109	10	6	6	4	.600	1	0	3.97
1997 Jacksnville	AA Det	5	5	0	0	28.2	112	16	7	5	0	1	1	3	13	0	24	2	0	1	1	.500	0	0	1.57
Toledo	AAA Det	23	23	0	0	133.1	612	134	78	75	22	8	8	4	91	1	115	5	4	5	10	.333	0	0	5.06
1998 Toledo	AAA Det	29	27	1	1	154	733	188	130	119	21	3	13	7	94	0	91	16	1	4	19	.174	0	0	6.95
1999 Toledo	AAA Det	21	21	1	0	120.2	535	116	88	80	17	2	7	7	59	2	76	8	0	6	10	.375	0	0	5.97
Calgary	AAA Fla	12	0	0	1	21	113	39	33	32	5	1	0	1	13	0	15	2	0	0	2	.000	0	0	13.71
2000 Calgary	AAA Fla	34	22	1	3	131.1	641	164	105	91	10	3	5	4	101	0	87	12	1	9	8	.529	0	0	6.24
2001 Portland	AA Fla	18	16	1	0	102	416	100	54	46	13	2	0	0	27	0	85	6	0	5	8	.385	0	0	4.06
Calgary	AAA Fla	19	0	0	10	31.1	143	30	15	13	1	4	3	0	24	2	39	4	0	0	5	.000	0	1	3.73
7 Min. YEARS		189	142	5	15	874.2	3947	916	585	528	106	26	40	31	494	6	694	67	19	37	69	.349	1	1	5.43

Scott Dunn

Pitches: Right **Bats:** Right **Pos:** SP-27   **Ht:** 6'3" **Wt:** 180 **Born:** 5/23/78 **Age:** 24

Year Team	Lg Org	G	GS	CG	GF	IP	BFP	H	R	ER	HR	SH	SF	HB	TBB	IBB	SO	WP	Bk	W	L	Pct.	ShO	Sv	ERA
1999 Billings	R+ Cin	9	8	0	0	39.2	178	36	24	19	3	0	1	3	24	0	36	3	2	1	3	.250	0	0	4.31
2000 Clinton	A Cin	26	26	2	0	147.2	638	123	78	65	9	2	3	4	89	1	159	20	0	11	3	.786	1	0	3.96
2001 Mudville	A+ Cin	10	10	1	0	59.2	248	45	17	14	2	0	0	1	31	0	73	4	0	5	3	.625	1	0	2.11
Chattanooga	AA Cin	17	17	0	0	98.1	450	96	51	45	10	8	2	2	71	0	87	8	0	7	2	.778	0	0	4.12
3 Min. YEARS		62	61	3	0	345.1	1514	300	170	143	24	10	6	10	215	1	355	35	2	24	11	.686	2	0	3.73

Bill Duplissea

Bats: Right **Throws:** Right **Pos:** C-50; PH-5; DH-1; PR-1; P-1   **Ht:** 6'0" **Wt:** 200 **Born:** 9/27/77 **Age:** 24

Year Team	Lg Org	G	AB	H	2B	3B	HR	TB	R	RBI	TBB	IBB	SO	HBP	SH	SF	SB	CS	SB%	GDP	Avg	OBP	SLG
1999 Yakima	A- LA	13	33	5	2	0	1	10	5	4	5	0	7	3	0	1	2	1	.67	1	.152	.310	.303
2000 San Berndno	A+ LA	7	9	2	0	0	0	2	1	1	2	0	4	0	0	0	1	0	1.00	0	.222	.364	.222
Great Falls	R+ LA	5	13	2	0	0	0	2	1	1	2	0	3	0	0	1	0	0	—	0	.154	.250	.154
Albuquerque	AAA LA	9	19	5	2	0	1	10	3	4	0	0	8	1	0	0	0	0	—	0	.263	.300	.526
Vero Beach	A+ LA	3	7	1	1	0	0	2	1	0	2	0	1	0	0	0	0	0	—	0	.143	.333	.286
2001 Jacksnville	AA LA	17	40	6	2	0	0	8	1	4	5	1	14	3	1	0	0	0	—	1	.150	.292	.200
Vero Beach	A+ LA	39	107	20	4	2	0	28	8	6	11	0	37	7	3	0	1	0	1.00	2	.187	.304	.262
3 Min. YEARS		93	228	41	11	2	2	62	20	20	27	1	74	14	4	2	4	1	.80	4	.180	.303	.272

Jayson Durocher

Pitches: Right **Bats:** Right **Pos:** RP-34   **Ht:** 6'3" **Wt:** 195 **Born:** 8/18/74 **Age:** 27

Year Team	Lg Org	G	GS	CG	GF	IP	BFP	H	R	ER	HR	SH	SF	HB	TBB	IBB	SO	WP	Bk	W	L	Pct.	ShO	Sv	ERA
1993 Expos	R Mon	7	7	3	0	39	150	32	23	15	0	2	0	3	13	0	21	3	1	2	3	.400	2	0	3.46
1994 Vermont	A- Mon	15	15	3	0	99	422	92	40	34	0	0	3	2	44	1	74	11	1	9	2	.818	1	0	3.09
1995 Albany	A Mon	24	22	1	1	122	526	105	67	53	5	4	11	5	56	1	88	11	1	3	7	.300	0	0	3.91
1996 Wst Plm Bch	A+ Mon	23	23	1	0	129.1	557	118	65	48	5	4	3	7	44	0	101	15	3	7	6	.538	1	0	3.34
1997 Wst Plm Bch	A+ Mon	25	17	0	2	87	385	84	58	37	6	3	3	4	39	0	71	10	2	6	4	.600	0	0	3.83
1998 Jupiter	A+ Mon	23	0	0	12	36.1	162	47	21	17	3	1	2	1	8	0	27	4	0	2	1	.667	0	5	4.21
Harrisburg	AA Mon	10	0	0	4	11.1	48	10	8	5	0	1	1	0	6	0	12	1	0	0	1	.000	0	1	3.97
1999 Harrisburg	AA Mon	29	1	0	11	51.2	224	44	29	20	5	2	2	6	25	1	36	3	1	1	3	.250	0	4	3.48
Ottawa	AAA Mon	17	0	0	6	35.2	146	17	12	6	2	3	1	1	20	2	22	3	0	1	3	.250	0	4	1.51
2000 Mobile	AA SD	27	0	0	23	30.1	132	26	7	7	4	2	1	3	12	1	43	3	0	1	1	.500	0	14	2.08
Las Vegas	AAA SD	31	0	0	18	40	187	44	25	22	2	2	2	3	25	3	38	6	0	3	5	.375	0	7	4.95
2001 Tulsa	AA Tex	3	0	0	2	3.2	15	0	0	0	0	0	0	1	3	0	4	2	0	0	0	—	0	0	0.00
Oklahoma	AAA Tex	31	0	0	20	39.2	176	34	25	22	5	3	0	3	23	1	52	1	0	4	1	.800	0	6	4.99
9 Min. YEARS		265	85	8	99	725	3130	653	380	286	37	27	29	39	318	10	589	73	9	39	37	.513	4	41	3.55

Trent Durrington

Bats: Right **Throws:** Right **Pos:** 2B-71; OF-12; PH-11; SS-9; 3B-9; DH-9; P-1   **Ht:** 5'10" **Wt:** 188 **Born:** 8/27/75 **Age:** 26

Year Team	Lg Org	G	AB	H	2B	3B	HR	TB	R	RBI	TBB	IBB	SO	HBP	SH	SF	SB	CS	SB%	GDP	Avg	OBP	SLG
1994 Angels	R Ana	16	52	14	3	0	1	20	13	2	11	0	16	1	0	0	5	1	.83	1	.269	.406	.385
1995 Boise	A- Ana	50	140	24	4	1	3	39	23	19	17	0	35	2	2	2	2	0	1.00	4	.171	.267	.279
1996 Boise	A- Ana	40	154	43	7	2	0	54	38	14	31	1	32	13	0	0	24	5	.83	4	.279	.439	.351
Cedar Rapds	A Ana	25	76	19	1	0	0	20	12	4	33	0	20	2	2	1	15	2	.88	2	.250	.482	.263
1997 Lk Elsinore	A+ Ana	123	409	101	21	3	3	137	60	36	51	1	90	11	17	3	52	18	.74	8	.247	.344	.335
1998 Midland	AA Ana	112	351	79	10	1	1	94	62	30	50	0	74	17	7	4	24	12	.67	5	.225	.346	.268
1999 Erie	AA Ana	107	396	114	26	1	3	151	84	34	52	1	66	9	12	5	59	16	.79	4	.288	.379	.381
2000 Edmonton	AAA Ana	28	105	23	4	1	3	38	19	14	16	0	25	1	3	1	8	6	.57	3	.219	.325	.362
2001 Las Vegas	AAA LA	22	55	12	4	1	1	21	10	2	8	0	19	1	0	0	3	1	.75	0	.218	.328	.382
Arkansas	AA Ana	51	182	53	12	0	10	95	37	35	26	0	47	7	1	1	22	2	.92	2	.291	.398	.522
Salt Lake	AAA Ana	39	122	40	11	4	3	68	20	21	11	0	24	2	2	2	7	4	.64	3	.328	.387	.557
1999 Anaheim	AL	43	122	22	2	0	0	24	14	2	9	0	28	0	5	0	4	3	.57	1	.180	.237	.197
2000 Anaheim	AL	4	3	0	0	0	0	0	0	0	0	0	0	0	0	0	0	0	—	1	.000	.000	.000
8 Min. YEARS		613	2042	522	103	14	28	737	378	211	306	3	448	66	46	19	221	67	.77	36	.256	.367	.361
2 Maj. YEARS		47	125	22	2	0	0	24	14	2	9	0	28	0	5	0	4	3	.57	2	.176	.231	.192

84

Radhames Dykhoff

Pitches: Left   Bats: Left   Pos: SP-14; RP-13   Ht: 6'1"   Wt: 210   Born: 9/27/74   Age: 27

Year Team	Lg Org	G	GS	CG	GF	IP	BFP	H	R	ER	HR	SH	SF	HB	TBB	IBB	SO	WP	Bk	W	L	Pct.	ShO	Sv	ERA
1993 Orioles	R Bal	14	3	0	1	45	184	37	22	17	2	3	3	2	11	0	29	3	0	1	2	.333	0	1	3.40
1994 Orioles	R Bal	12	12	1	0	73	307	69	34	27	2	0	5	0	17	0	67	4	1	3	6	.333	0	0	3.33
1995 High Desert	A+ Bal	34	2	0	10	80.2	389	95	68	45	8	7	7	0	44	2	88	0	2	1	5	.167	0	3	5.02
1996 Frederick	A+ Bal	33	0	0	15	62	290	77	45	39	7	4	4	1	22	2	75	0	0	2	6	.250	0	3	5.66
1997 Bowie	AA Bal	7	0	0	4	8.2	43	10	9	8	2	0	0	0	7	0	7	0	0	0	0	—	0	1	8.31
Delmarva	A Bal	1	0	0	1	3	12	3	0	0	0	0	0	0	0	0	3	0	0	0	0	—	0	0	0.00
Frederick	A+ Bal	31	0	0	18	67	282	48	19	18	4	6	1	0	38	3	98	0	1	3	3	.500	0	5	2.42
1998 Bowie	AA Bal	38	8	0	9	93.2	411	83	51	49	10	2	3	4	52	1	98	3	0	3	7	.300	0	1	4.71
1999 Rochester	AAA Bal	47	0	0	6	82.1	341	69	42	36	11	3	2	3	31	0	57	1	0	2	0	1.000	0	1	3.94
2000 Norfolk	AAA NYM	32	0	0	11	38.1	176	40	23	21	5	1	3	1	21	3	43	3	0	2	3	.400	0	0	4.93
Binghamton	AA NYM	17	1	0	2	25.2	104	16	7	6	2	0	0	1	8	0	30	0	0	3	0	1.000	0	0	2.10
2001 Arkansas	AA Ana	27	14	0	7	80.2	357	85	46	41	4	1	5	5	35	0	37	1	0	2	3	.400	0	0	4.57
1998 Baltimore	AL	1	0	0	1	1	6	2	2	2	0	0	0	0	1	0	1	0	0	0	0	—	0	0	18.00
9 Min. YEARS		293	40	1	84	660	2896	632	366	307	57	27	33	17	286	11	632	15	4	22	35	.386	0	16	4.19

Matt Easterday

Bats: Right   Throws: Right   Pos: 2B-41; OF-38; PR-8; DH-3; 3B-1   Ht: 6'1"   Wt: 188   Born: 5/3/79   Age: 23

Year Team	Lg Org	G	AB	H	2B	3B	HR	TB	R	RBI	TBB	IBB	SO	HBP	SH	SF	SB	CS	SB%	GDP	Avg	OBP	SLG
2000 Utica	A- Fla	60	220	56	14	1	3	81	36	26	22	0	45	6	1	6	8	4	.67	6	.255	.331	.368
2001 Calgary	AAA Fla	15	46	9	1	1	0	12	6	3	2	0	10	1	0	0	0	1	.00	1	.196	.245	.261
Kane County	A Fla	72	195	51	7	2	2	68	42	16	33	0	37	4	1	3	10	3	.77	6	.262	.374	.349
2 Min. YEARS		147	461	116	22	4	5	161	84	45	57	0	92	11	2	9	18	8	.69	13	.252	.342	.349

Derrin Ebert

Pitches: Left   Bats: Right   Pos: SP-27; RP-3   Ht: 6'3"   Wt: 200   Born: 8/21/76   Age: 25

Year Team	Lg Org	G	GS	CG	GF	IP	BFP	H	R	ER	HR	SH	SF	HB	TBB	IBB	SO	WP	Bk	W	L	Pct.	ShO	Sv	ERA
1994 Braves	R Atl	10	7	1	2	43	176	40	18	14	4	0	0	1	8	0	25	1	3	1	3	.250	1	0	2.93
1995 Macon	A Atl	28	28	0	0	182	766	184	87	67	12	5	4	7	46	0	124	3	2	14	5	.737	0	0	3.31
1996 Durham	A+ Atl	27	27	2	0	166.1	711	189	102	74	13	8	9	4	37	1	99	5	0	12	9	.571	0	0	4.00
1997 Greenville	AA Atl	27	25	0	1	175.2	743	191	95	80	24	9	6	4	48	1	101	10	0	11	8	.579	0	0	4.10
1998 Richmond	AAA Atl	29	29	0	0	163.2	710	195	94	82	14	5	3	3	49	1	88	4	0	9	9	.500	0	0	4.51
1999 Richmond	AAA Atl	25	24	2	0	150.2	646	173	79	72	13	5	6	2	44	0	82	7	0	8	7	.533	1	0	4.30
2000 Richmond	AAA Atl	32	23	0	2	150.2	670	192	94	80	21	4	7	4	44	0	91	4	0	5	9	.357	0	0	4.78
2001 Pawtucket	AAA Bos	10	7	1	0	43.2	192	50	29	22	4	1	1	1	10	0	34	2	0	2	3	.400	0	0	4.53
Trenton	AA Bos	20	20	0	0	116.1	496	134	67	60	12	3	2	7	23	0	89	6	1	7	9	.438	0	0	4.64
1999 Atlanta	NL	5	0	0	3	8	35	9	5	5	2	0	0	0	5	1	4	0	0	0	1	.000	0	1	5.63
8 Min. YEARS		208	190	6	4	1192	5110	1348	665	551	117	40	38	33	309	3	733	42	6	69	62	.527	2	0	4.16

Kevin Eberwein

Bats: Right   Throws: Right   Pos: 3B-19; 1B-14; DH-3   Ht: 6'4"   Wt: 200   Born: 3/30/77   Age: 25

Year Team	Lg Org	G	AB	H	2B	3B	HR	TB	R	RBI	TBB	IBB	SO	HBP	SH	SF	SB	CS	SB%	GDP	Avg	OBP	SLG
1998 Clinton	A SD	65	247	73	20	3	10	129	42	38	26	0	66	6	2	2	4	2	.67	6	.296	.374	.522
1999 Mobile	AA SD	10	35	6	1	0	1	10	5	2	3	0	16	0	0	1	0	0	—	0	.171	.231	.286
Rancho Cuca	A+ SD	110	417	108	30	4	18	200	69	69	42	0	139	12	2	2	7	5	.58	7	.259	.342	.480
2000 Mobile	AA SD	100	372	98	16	2	18	172	57	71	45	3	77	2	0	4	2	2	.50	8	.263	.343	.462
2001 Lk Elsinore	A+ SD	9	30	10	4	0	2	20	6	4	6	1	6	1	0	0	0	0	—	1	.333	.459	.667
Portland	AAA SD	27	94	25	8	1	3	44	16	11	10	2	22	2	0	0	0	2	.00	2	.266	.349	.468
4 Min. YEARS		321	1195	320	79	10	52	575	195	195	132	6	326	23	4	9	13	11	.54	24	.268	.350	.481

Alex Eckelman

Bats: Right   Throws: Right   Pos: 2B-58; 3B-34; OF-20; SS-13; PH-7; DH-4; P-2; PR-1   Ht: 5'11"   Wt: 190   Born: 7/16/74   Age: 27

Year Team	Lg Org	G	AB	H	2B	3B	HR	TB	R	RBI	TBB	IBB	SO	HBP	SH	SF	SB	CS	SB%	GDP	Avg	OBP	SLG
1997 Richmond	IND —	3	12	6	1	1	1	12	1	5	1	0	2	1	0	0	0	0	—	1	.500	.571	1.000
Johnson Cty	R+ StL	49	165	53	13	1	1	89	30	27	10	0	23	7	1	2	3	1	.75	3	.321	.380	.539
1998 Peoria	A StL	16	52	17	4	1	1	26	7	11	5	0	9	0	0	0	2	2	.50	2	.327	.386	.500
Pr William	A+ StL	38	89	26	1	1	2	35	15	9	9	0	14	0	1	1	2	2	.50	2	.292	.354	.393
1999 Potomac	A+ StL	52	161	31	5	2	4	52	20	14	13	0	39	5	1	0	3	3	.50	2	.193	.274	.323
Arkansas	AA StL	41	116	28	4	3	1	41	5	13	5	0	20	4	2	3	0	0	—	4	.241	.289	.353
2000 Memphis	AAA StL	6	16	6	0	0	0	6	2	1	0	0	1	0	0	0	0	0	—	0	.375	.375	.375
Arkansas	AA StL	85	280	87	16	3	4	121	42	33	24	1	27	8	7	3	4	1	.80	2	.311	.378	.432
2001 New Haven	AA StL	130	411	87	17	0	5	119	33	38	20	3	68	6	7	3	14	5	.74	8	.212	.257	.290
5 Min. YEARS		420	1302	341	61	12	25	501	155	151	87	4	203	31	19	12	26	14	.65	26	.262	.321	.385

Eric Eckenstahler

Pitches: Left   Bats: Left   Pos: RP-50   Ht: 6'7"   Wt: 210   Born: 12/17/76   Age: 25

Year Team	Lg Org	G	GS	CG	GF	IP	BFP	H	R	ER	HR	SH	SF	HB	TBB	IBB	SO	WP	Bk	W	L	Pct.	ShO	Sv	ERA
2000 Oneonta	A- Det	8	0	0	4	11	46	7	3	2	0	0	1	2	3	0	13	1	0	0	0	—	0	0	1.64
W Michigan	A Det	10	3	0	4	18.2	89	21	15	12	4	1	1	0	11	0	22	0	1	0	2	.000	0	1	5.79
2001 Lakeland	A+ Det	4	0	0	2	6	22	3	1	1	0	0	0	1	2	0	7	2	0	1	0	1.000	0	1	1.50
Erie	AA Det	46	0	0	18	64.2	289	65	32	28	7	1	1	3	31	4	73	3	1	4	2	.667	0	4	3.90
2 Min. YEARS		68	3	0	28	100.1	446	96	51	43	11	2	3	7	47	4	115	6	2	5	4	.556	0	6	3.86

Brian Edmondson

Pitches: Right **Bats:** Right **Pos:** RP-53 **Ht:** 6'2" **Wt:** 175 **Born:** 1/29/73 **Age:** 29

Year Team	Lg Org	G	GS	CG	GF	IP	BFP	H	R	ER	HR	SH	SF	HB	TBB	IBB	SO	WP	Bk	W	L	Pct.	ShO	Sv	ERA
1991 Bristol	R+ Det	12	12	1	0	69	289	72	38	35	7	1	2	3	23	1	42	5	2	4	4	.500	0	0	4.57
1992 Fayetteville	A Det	28	27	3	0	155.1	665	145	69	58	10	5	3	6	67	0	125	6	2	10	6	.625	1	0	3.36
1993 Lakeland	A+ Det	19	19	1	0	114.1	483	115	44	38	6	1	0	3	43	0	64	7	0	8	5	.615	0	0	2.99
London	AA Det	5	5	1	0	23	109	30	23	16	2	1	0	0	13	0	17	1	0	0	4	.000	0	0	6.26
1994 Trenton	AA Det	26	26	2	0	162	703	171	89	82	12	2	6	6	61	1	90	11	2	11	9	.550	0	0	4.56
1995 Binghamton	AA NYM	23	22	1	0	134.1	601	150	82	71	17	5	5	6	59	2	69	7	0	7	11	.389	1	0	4.76
1996 Binghamton	AA NYM	39	13	1	9	114.1	502	130	69	54	16	7	7	4	38	5	83	3	1	6	6	.500	0	0	4.25
1997 Binghamton	AA NYM	14	0	0	7	22	85	17	4	3	0	2	0	0	7	0	18	1	0	2	0	1.000	0	3	1.23
Norfolk	AAA NYM	31	4	0	8	68.1	296	62	27	22	5	3	3	4	37	2	65	4	1	4	3	.571	0	1	2.90
2001 Brevard Cty	A+ Fla	16	0	0	7	26	104	23	8	5	0	1	2	2	4	1	21	0	0	5	2	.714	0	0	1.73
Portland	AA Fla	14	0	0	6	26	97	16	7	5	3	3	1	1	5	1	16	1	0	3	3	.400	0	1	1.73
Calgary	AAA Fla	23	0	0	12	29.2	148	43	33	28	7	2	2	1	15	2	20	4	0	2	5	.286	0	0	8.49
1998 Atlanta	NL	10	0	0	3	16.2	73	14	10	8	2	0	0	0	8	1	8	4	0	0	1	.000	0	0	4.32
Florida	NL	43	0	0	10	59.1	261	62	28	25	8	5	3	3	29	4	32	1	0	4	3	.571	0	0	3.79
1999 Florida	NL	68	0	0	14	94	428	106	65	61	11	6	7	6	44	5	58	5	0	5	8	.385	0	1	5.84
8 Min. YEARS		250	128	11	49	944.1	4082	974	493	417	85	33	31	36	372	15	630	50	8	61	58	.513	2	8	3.97
2 Maj. YEARS		121	0	0	27	170	762	182	103	94	21	11	10	9	81	10	98	10	0	9	12	.429	0	1	4.98

Mike Edwards

Bats: Right **Throws:** Right **Pos:** 1B-22; 3B-20; DH-13 **Ht:** 6'1" **Wt:** 185 **Born:** 11/24/76 **Age:** 25

Year Team	Lg Org	G	AB	H	2B	3B	HR	TB	R	RBI	TBB	IBB	SO	HBP	SH	SF	SB	CS	SB%	GDP	Avg	OBP	SLG
1995 Burlington	R+ Cle	43	130	22	2	0	0	24	20	5	17	0	35	2	0	0	5	2	.71	2	.169	.275	.185
1996 Burlington	R+ Cle	58	206	58	13	1	1	76	31	17	37	0	26	3	3	3	5	4	.56	4	.282	.394	.369
1997 Burlington	R+ Cle	60	236	68	16	2	4	100	50	41	38	1	53	1	0	2	10	5	.67	2	.288	.386	.424
1998 Columbus	A Cle	124	497	146	34	4	8	212	82	81	66	2	95	3	3	2	16	6	.73	13	.294	.379	.427
1999 Kinston	A+ Cle	133	456	132	25	4	16	213	76	89	93	6	117	9	0	9	8	3	.73	12	.289	.413	.467
2000 Akron	AA Cle	136	481	142	25	2	11	204	72	63	68	2	86	5	3	3	7	3	.70	9	.295	.386	.424
2001 Mahoning Vy	A- Cle	20	71	26	5	0	6	49	19	24	12	0	7	1	0	0	0	1	.00	0	.366	.464	.690
Akron	AA Cle	29	111	37	7	3	6	68	21	24	13	1	26	0	0	0	0	0	—	3	.333	.403	.613
Buffalo	AAA Cle	3	9	2	0	0	0	2	1	1	1	0	3	0	0	0	0	0	—	1	.222	.300	.222
7 Min. YEARS		606	2197	633	127	16	52	948	372	345	345	12	448	24	9	19	51	24	.68	46	.288	.388	.431

Scott Eibey

Pitches: Left **Bats:** Left **Pos:** RP-38 **Ht:** 6'4" **Wt:** 208 **Born:** 1/19/74 **Age:** 28

Year Team	Lg Org	G	GS	CG	GF	IP	BFP	H	R	ER	HR	SH	SF	HB	TBB	IBB	SO	WP	Bk	W	L	Pct.	ShO	Sv	ERA
1995 Bluefield	R+ Bal	14	6	0	3	43.2	196	51	32	27	4	2	0	2	24	0	26	6	1	3	1	.750	0	2	5.56
1996 High Desert	A+ Bal	11	0	0	1	11.2	66	17	16	11	0	0	1	0	10	2	7	2	0	1	0	1.000	0	0	8.49
Bluefield	R+ Bal	24	0	0	10	45	187	30	19	14	3	0	3	3	17	0	59	4	1	5	1	.833	0	2	2.80
1997 Delmarva	A Bal	47	0	0	19	93.1	371	65	25	19	3	7	0	2	33	5	82	4	0	10	4	.714	0	7	1.83
1998 Bowie	AA Bal	24	0	0	8	36.1	159	40	20	17	5	0	1	0	14	0	29	1	1	1	1	.500	0	0	4.21
Frederick	A+ Bal	21	0	0	5	35	152	47	17	15	3	4	1	0	8	0	20	3	0	1	2	.333	0	1	3.86
1999 Frederick	A+ Bal	15	0	0	6	29	120	26	14	12	2	0	1	0	10	1	27	0	0	0	2	.000	0	0	3.72
Bowie	AA Bal	27	4	0	3	51.1	222	49	17	15	2	1	1	1	25	2	29	5	2	2	0	1.000	0	2	2.63
2000 Frederick	A+ Bal	4	0	0	3	6.2	30	9	4	3	1	0	0	0	0	0	5	1	0	1	1	.500	0	0	4.05
Bowie	AA Bal	37	0	0	15	57	256	59	34	32	8	4	4	2	25	4	32	0	0	4	4	.500	0	0	5.05
2001 Bowie	AA Bal	38	0	0	21	69	318	84	53	47	9	4	5	2	22	4	48	2	0	0	3	.000	0	0	6.13
7 Min. YEARS		262	10	0	94	478	2076	477	251	212	40	22	17	12	188	18	364	28	5	28	19	.596	0	12	3.99

Dave Elder

Pitches: Right **Bats:** Right **Pos:** SP-21; RP-7 **Ht:** 6'0" **Wt:** 180 **Born:** 9/23/75 **Age:** 26

Year Team	Lg Org	G	GS	CG	GF	IP	BFP	H	R	ER	HR	SH	SF	HB	TBB	IBB	SO	WP	Bk	W	L	Pct.	ShO	Sv	ERA
1997 Pulaski	R+ Tex	20	0	0	17	32.1	127	18	8	7	2	0	0	0	12	0	57	4	0	2	2	.500	0	6	1.95
1999 Charlotte	A+ Tex	24	1	0	16	44.1	186	33	15	14	2	4	0	2	25	0	42	4	0	4	2	.667	0	4	2.84
Tulsa	AA Tex	3	0	0	1	6.2	32	8	7	6	0	0	0	0	6	1	7	0	0	1	0	1.000	0	0	8.10
2000 Tulsa	AA Tex	33	21	0	8	116.2	554	121	80	64	9	4	4	4	88	0	104	11	0	7	6	.538	0	2	4.94
2001 Tulsa	AA Tex	13	13	0	0	72	308	64	28	24	1	0	3	2	43	0	78	3	0	4	6	.400	0	0	3.00
Oklahoma	AAA Tex	15	8	0	3	57.2	266	54	36	32	4	2	0	4	43	0	56	4	1	5	4	.556	0	0	4.99
4 Min. YEARS		108	43	0	45	329.2	1473	298	174	147	18	10	7	12	217	1	344	26	1	23	20	.535	0	13	4.01

Mark Ellis

Bats: Right **Throws:** Right **Pos:** SS-131; DH-1; PH-1 **Ht:** 5'11" **Wt:** 180 **Born:** 6/6/77 **Age:** 25

Year Team	Lg Org	G	AB	H	2B	3B	HR	TB	R	RBI	TBB	IBB	SO	HBP	SH	SF	SB	CS	SB%	GDP	Avg	OBP	SLG
1999 Spokane	A- KC	71	281	92	14	0	7	127	67	47	47	3	40	3	5	4	21	7	.75	1	.327	.424	.452
2000 Wilmington	A+ KC	132	484	146	27	4	6	199	83	62	78	0	72	7	4	3	25	7	.78	11	.302	.404	.411
Wichita	AA KC	7	22	7	1	0	0	8	4	4	5	0	5	0	0	0	1	0	1.00	0	.318	.444	.364
2001 Sacramento	AAA Oak	132	472	129	38	0	10	197	71	53	54	4	78	5	5	5	21	7	.75	13	.273	.351	.417
3 Min. YEARS		342	1259	374	80	4	23	531	225	166	184	7	195	15	14	12	68	21	.76	25	.297	.390	.422

Jason Ellison

Pitches: Right **Bats:** Right **Pos:** RP-45; SP-1   **Ht:** 6'4" **Wt:** 188 **Born:** 7/24/75 **Age:** 26

Year Team	Lg Org	G	GS	CG	GF	IP	BFP	H	R	ER	HR	SH	SF	HB	TBB	IBB	SO	WP	Bk	W	L	Pct.	ShO	Sv	ERA
1996 Yankees	R NYY	21	3	0	17	36	151	24	8	5	0	1	0	3	15	0	42	2	1	3	2	.600	0	7	1.25
Oneonta	A- NYY	1	0	0	1	1	5	2	1	1	0	0	0	0	0	0	2	0	0	0	0	—	0	0	9.00
1997 Oneonta	A- NYY	11	0	0	3	20.2	82	19	6	4	0	0	0	1	4	0	19	2	0	1	0	.000	0	0	1.74
Greensboro	A NYY	9	0	0	4	13	60	16	10	7	1	0	0	1	3	0	11	1	0	1	0	1.000	0	1	4.85
1998 Greensboro	A NYY	54	0	0	49	65.1	279	56	30	23	5	5	0	2	27	3	71	6	0	4	6	.400	0	28	3.17
1999 Tampa	A+ NYY	49	0	0	42	54.1	226	42	15	13	0	4	2	4	19	1	56	0	0	0	2	.000	0	35	2.15
2000 Norwich	AA NYY	10	0	0	8	9.1	48	18	11	9	1	2	0	0	2	1	5	0	1	1	1	.500	0	4	8.68
2001 San Antonio	AA Sea	46	1	0	26	65	296	76	30	27	3	6	2	4	28	7	57	5	0	2	8	.200	0	9	3.74
6 Min. YEARS		201	4	0	150	264.2	1147	253	111	89	10	18	5	14	98	12	263	16	2	11	20	.355	0	84	3.03

Chris Elmore

Pitches: Left **Bats:** Left **Pos:** SP-18; RP-13   **Ht:** 6'1" **Wt:** 195 **Born:** 4/28/77 **Age:** 25

Year Team	Lg Org	G	GS	CG	GF	IP	BFP	H	R	ER	HR	SH	SF	HB	TBB	IBB	SO	WP	Bk	W	L	Pct.	ShO	Sv	ERA
2000 Lowell	A- Bos	15	10	1	3	71.1	279	55	20	15	0	1	1	6	14	0	46	3	2	3	3	.500	1	2	1.89
2001 Sarasota	A+ Bos	17	5	0	5	59.2	247	58	25	16	1	3	1	3	12	1	40	0	0	6	2	.750	0	1	2.41
Trenton	AA Bos	14	13	0	0	78.2	328	76	34	20	4	2	1	8	19	0	56	9	0	5	3	.625	0	0	2.29
2 Min. YEARS		46	28	1	8	209.2	854	189	79	51	5	6	3	17	45	1	142	12	2	14	8	.636	1	3	2.19

Jamie Emiliano

Pitches: Right **Bats:** Right **Pos:** RP-50   **Ht:** 5'10" **Wt:** 210 **Born:** 8/2/74 **Age:** 27

Year Team	Lg Org	G	GS	CG	GF	IP	BFP	H	R	ER	HR	SH	SF	HB	TBB	IBB	SO	WP	Bk	W	L	Pct.	ShO	Sv	ERA
1995 Portland	A- Col	28	0	0	22	38.2	165	31	16	15	0	2	1	4	16	2	41	5	0	4	1	.800	0	11	3.49
1996 Asheville	A Col	6	0	0	4	5.2	25	7	6	6	1	0	0	0	2	0	7	1	1	1	1	.500	0	1	9.53
1997 Asheville	A Col	18	0	0	12	20	96	24	15	13	1	0	0	0	12	0	20	3	0	0	1	.000	0	0	5.85
1998 Salem	A+ Col	4	0	0	1	7.2	36	9	3	3	0	0	1	0	5	0	6	1	0	1	1	.500	0	0	3.52
Asheville	A Col	41	0	0	38	43.2	208	56	22	17	2	4	1	5	21	0	35	1	0	3	4	.429	0	18	3.50
1999 Salem	A+ Col	45	0	0	23	53.2	240	50	26	21	4	3	2	5	29	1	47	8	0	5	1	.833	0	7	3.52
2000 Carolina	AA Col	47	0	0	11	58	250	52	27	17	1	4	1	4	23	3	37	3	0	3	4	.429	0	2	2.64
2001 Carolina	AA Col	50	0	0	25	64.2	281	56	29	24	4	5	0	6	30	3	38	1	0	3	6	.333	0	2	3.34
7 Min. YEARS		239	0	0	136	292	1301	285	146	116	13	18	6	24	138	9	231	23	1	20	19	.513	0	41	3.58

Scott Emmons

Bats: Right **Throws:** Right **Pos:** C-7; 1B-3; PH-3   **Ht:** 6'4" **Wt:** 205 **Born:** 12/25/73 **Age:** 28

Year Team	Lg Org	G	AB	H	2B	3B	HR	TB	R	RBI	TBB	IBB	SO	HBP	SH	SF	SB	CS	SB%	GDP	Avg	OBP	SLG
1995 Oneonta	A- NYY	67	242	48	15	3	2	75	25	32	25	0	62	3	2	5	1	1	.50	5	.198	.276	.310
1996 Greensboro	A NYY	15	46	11	1	0	1	15	7	9	2	0	6	1	1	1	0	1	.00	0	.239	.280	.326
Tampa	A+ NYY	36	98	20	2	1	1	27	6	10	10	1	26	2	3	0	0	1	.00	1	.204	.291	.276
1997 Tampa	A+ NYY	51	118	21	5	0	2	32	19	14	9	0	28	6	2	1	0	0	—	2	.178	.269	.271
Greensboro	A NYY	3	7	2	1	0	0	3	1	0	1	0	1	0	0	0	0	0	—	0	.286	.375	.429
1998 Tampa	A+ NYY	13	24	6	2	0	0	8	3	4	4	0	6	1	0	0	1	0	1.00	0	.250	.379	.333
Norwich	AA NYY	48	145	25	6	0	1	34	12	5	14	0	43	4	0	2	2	1	.67	4	.172	.261	.234
1999 Norwich	AA NYY	37	102	24	1	0	3	34	13	16	6	0	25	4	1	0	0	0	—	4	.235	.304	.333
2001 Norwich	AA NYY	10	15	2	1	0	0	3	2	0	1	0	4	0	0	0	1	0	1.00	0	.133	.188	.200
6 Min. YEARS		280	797	159	34	4	10	231	88	90	72	1	201	21	9	9	5	4	.56	18	.199	.280	.290

Angelo Encarnacion

Bats: Right **Throws:** Right **Pos:** C-48; DH-2; PR-1   **Ht:** 5'9" **Wt:** 190 **Born:** 4/18/73 **Age:** 29

Year Team	Lg Org	G	AB	H	2B	3B	HR	TB	R	RBI	TBB	IBB	SO	HBP	SH	SF	SB	CS	SB%	GDP	Avg	OBP	SLG
1991 Welland	A- Pit	50	181	46	3	2	0	53	21	15	5	0	27	1	0	0	4	3	.57	5	.254	.278	.293
1992 Augusta	A Pit	94	314	80	14	3	1	103	39	29	25	1	37	1	4	2	2	4	.33	5	.255	.310	.328
1993 Salem	A+ Pit	70	238	61	12	1	3	84	20	24	13	1	27	0	0	1	1	4	.20	5	.256	.294	.353
Buffalo	AAA Pit	3	9	3	0	0	0	3	1	2	0	0	0	0	0	0	0	0	—	0	.333	.333	.333
1994 Carolina	AA Pit	67	227	66	17	0	3	92	26	32	11	1	28	2	0	4	2	2	.50	4	.291	.324	.405
1995 Calgary	AAA Pit	21	80	20	3	0	1	26	8	6	1	1	12	0	0	0	1	0	1.00	2	.250	.259	.325
1996 Calgary	AAA Pit	75	263	84	18	0	4	114	38	31	10	2	19	3	0	2	6	2	.75	10	.319	.349	.433
1997 Las Vegas	AAA SD	79	253	62	12	1	3	85	27	23	15	1	32	1	1	0	1	5	.17	9	.245	.290	.336
1998 Vancouver	AAA Ana	8	25	6	2	0	0	8	3	2	0	0	2	0	0	0	0	1	.00	1	.240	.240	.320
Midland	AA Ana	28	93	20	1	0	2	27	9	7	8	0	11	1	2	0	0	0	—	2	.215	.284	.290
1999 Akron	AA Cle	34	127	27	7	0	1	37	9	21	6	0	19	0	1	0	1	1	.50	5	.213	.248	.291
West Tenn	AA ChC	30	101	26	6	1	1	37	11	10	4	0	12	1	0	0	2	0	1.00	1	.257	.292	.366
2000 Iowa	AAA ChC	10	24	6	1	0	0	7	2	1	1	0	3	0	0	0	0	0	—	0	.250	.280	.292
Newark	IND —	30	107	29	6	0	1	38	15	7	6	0	13	0	1	0	2	2	.50	0	.271	.310	.355
Pawtucket	AAA Bos	19	59	18	4	0	0	22	7	3	4	0	4	0	2	0	0	0	—	3	.305	.349	.373
2001 Red Sox	R Bos	3	5	1	1	0	0	2	1	0	2	0	0	0	0	0	1	0	1.00	0	.200	.429	.400
Pawtucket	AAA Bos	47	155	41	5	1	1	51	16	11	8	0	17	1	2	0	1	0	1.00	6	.265	.305	.329
1995 Pittsburgh	NL	58	159	36	7	2	2	53	18	10	13	5	28	0	3	0	1	1	.50	3	.226	.285	.333
1996 Pittsburgh	NL	7	22	7	2	0	0	9	3	1	0	0	5	0	0	0	0	0	—	1	.318	.318	.409
1997 Anaheim	AL	11	17	7	1	0	1	11	2	4	0	0	1	0	0	0	2	0	1.00	0	.412	.412	.647
11 Min. YEARS		668	2261	596	112	9	21	789	253	224	119	7	263	11	13	9	24	24	.50	62	.264	.303	.349
3 Maj. YEARS		76	198	50	10	2	3	73	23	15	13	5	34	0	3	0	3	1	.75	4	.253	.299	.369

Bienvenido Encarnacion

Bats: Right **Throws:** Right **Pos:** 2B-19; SS-10; 3B-9; DH-2; PH-2; OF-1; PR-1 **Ht:** 5'11" **Wt:** 180 **Born:** 2/24/78 **Age:** 24

Year Team	Lg Org	G	AB	H	2B	3B	HR	TB	R	RBI	TBB	IBB	SO	HBP	SH	SF	SB	CS	SB%	GDP	Avg	OBP	SLG
1997 Butte	R+ Ana	26	81	21	5	0	0	26	11	9	2	0	14	1	2	0	2	2	.50	2	.259	.286	.321
1998 Butte	R+ Ana	69	291	91	10	2	5	120	46	44	27	0	40	3	2	2	13	6	.68	5	.313	.375	.412
1999 Cedar Rapds	A Ana	57	206	54	3	2	1	64	28	23	11	0	33	0	6	2	4	2	.67	8	.262	.297	.311
2000 Lk Elsinore	A+ Ana	76	266	60	9	0	0	69	24	33	11	0	40	3	7	0	5	4	.56	6	.226	.264	.259
2001 Salt Lake	AAA Ana	6	23	7	0	0	0	7	6	3	2	0	6	0	0	0	0	0	—	0	.304	.360	.304
Rancho Cuca	A+ Ana	35	104	21	4	1	0	27	13	4	8	1	31	2	2	0	0	1	.00	3	.202	.272	.260
5 Min. YEARS		269	971	254	31	5	6	313	128	116	61	1	164	9	19	4	24	15	.62	24	.262	.310	.322

Trevor Enders

Pitches: Left **Bats:** Right **Pos:** RP-36; SP-9 **Ht:** 6'0" **Wt:** 214 **Born:** 12/22/74 **Age:** 27

Year Team	Lg Org	G	GS	CG	GF	IP	BFP	H	R	ER	HR	SH	SF	HB	TBB	IBB	SO	WP	Bk	W	L	Pct.	ShO	Sv	ERA
1996 Butte	R+ TB	19	0	0	6	27.2	132	34	22	15	1	2	2	2	13	1	24	2	0	0	1	.000	0	1	4.88
1997 Chston-SC	A TB	44	0	0	24	67	271	55	18	14	2	2	1	2	17	3	73	2	1	4	3	.571	0	2	1.88
1998 St. Pete	A+ TB	51	0	0	16	68.2	267	48	20	17	4	2	3	3	15	3	61	5	0	10	1	.909	0	1	2.23
1999 Orlando	AA TB	60	0	0	11	95.1	394	86	37	35	4	3	5	2	33	1	63	5	0	8	2	.800	0	1	3.30
2000 Orlando	AA TB	29	5	0	8	67	264	63	26	24	7	0	1	1	11	0	41	3	3	6	3	.667	0	0	3.22
Durham	AAA TB	15	0	0	5	26.2	104	22	8	8	3	1	0	1	6	0	16	2	0	0	1	.000	0	0	2.70
2001 Durham	AAA TB	32	1	0	10	47	201	51	26	26	8	4	5	3	14	2	26	1	0	2	5	.286	0	0	4.98
Orlando	AA TB	13	8	0	0	47.1	196	51	26	26	9	1	0	3	5	0	38	2	0	3	3	.500	0	0	4.94
2000 Tampa Bay	AL	9	0	0	4	9.1	46	14	13	11	2	2	0	0	5	0	5	0	0	0	1	.000	0	0	10.61
6 Min. YEARS		263	14	0	80	446.2	1829	410	183	165	38	15	16	17	114	10	342	22	4	33	19	.635	0	5	3.32

Chris Enochs

Pitches: Right **Bats:** Right **Pos:** RP-29; SP-10 **Ht:** 6'3" **Wt:** 225 **Born:** 10/11/75 **Age:** 26

Year Team	Lg Org	G	GS	CG	GF	IP	BFP	H	R	ER	HR	SH	SF	HB	TBB	IBB	SO	WP	Bk	W	L	Pct.	ShO	Sv	ERA
1997 Sou Oregon	A- Oak	3	3	0	0	10.1	45	12	4	4	0	0	0	1	2	0	10	1	0	0	0	—	0	0	3.48
Modesto	A+ Oak	10	9	0	1	45.1	203	51	20	14	0	3	2	3	12	0	45	7	0	3	0	1.000	0	0	2.78
1998 Huntsville	AA Oak	26	26	0	0	148	660	159	101	78	12	2	6	9	64	2	100	5	0	9	10	.474	0	0	4.74
1999 Midland	AA Oak	13	11	0	0	45	238	69	57	50	9	0	5	2	34	1	33	11	0	3	5	.375	0	0	10.00
Visalia	A+ Oak	4	4	0	0	18.1	87	24	10	10	4	0	1	0	10	0	19	2	0	0	0	—	0	0	4.91
2000 Visalia	A+ Oak	18	18	0	0	97	429	116	61	50	6	5	5	0	38	0	75	6	1	2	5	.286	0	0	4.64
2001 Midland	AA Oak	39	10	0	9	99.2	440	102	57	48	9	3	2	4	39	3	67	6	0	5	4	.556	0	1	4.33
5 Min. YEARS		113	81	0	10	463.2	2102	533	310	254	40	13	20	20	199	6	349	38	1	22	24	.478	0	1	4.93

Morgan Ensberg

Bats: Right **Throws:** Right **Pos:** 3B-81; DH-6; SS-1 **Ht:** 6'2" **Wt:** 210 **Born:** 8/26/75 **Age:** 26

Year Team	Lg Org	G	AB	H	2B	3B	HR	TB	R	RBI	TBB	IBB	SO	HBP	SH	SF	SB	CS	SB%	GDP	Avg	OBP	SLG
1998 Auburn	A- Hou	59	196	45	10	1	5	72	39	31	46	1	51	6	0	2	15	3	.83	5	.230	.388	.367
1999 Kissimmee	A+ Hou	123	427	102	25	2	15	176	72	69	68	0	90	9	1	3	17	6	.74	9	.239	.353	.412
2000 Round Rock	AA Hou	137	483	145	34	0	28	263	95	90	92	3	107	8	3	6	9	12	.43	15	.300	.416	.545
2001 New Orleans	AAA Hou	87	316	98	20	0	23	187	65	61	45	0	60	3	0	4	6	3	.67	12	.310	.397	.592
2000 Houston	NL	4	7	2	0	0	0	2	0	0	0	0	1	0	0	0	0	0	—	0	.286	.286	.286
4 Min. YEARS		406	1422	390	89	3	71	698	271	251	251	4	308	26	4	15	47	24	.66	41	.274	.389	.491

Brian Epke

Bats: Right **Throws:** Right **Pos:** C-22; PH-4; DH-2 **Ht:** 6'0" **Wt:** 195 **Born:** 5/2/79 **Age:** 23

Year Team	Lg Org	G	AB	H	2B	3B	HR	TB	R	RBI	TBB	IBB	SO	HBP	SH	SF	SB	CS	SB%	GDP	Avg	OBP	SLG
2001 Tucson	AAA Ari	2	3	0	0	0	0	0	1	0	1	0	2	1	0	0	0	0	—	0	.000	.400	.000
Yakima	A- Ari	5	12	1	0	0	0	1	2	4	1	0	3	0	0	1	0	0	—	0	.083	.143	.083
South Bend	A Ari	18	56	14	1	0	0	15	5	5	3	0	11	2	0	0	1	0	1.00	0	.250	.311	.268
1 Min. YEAR		25	71	15	1	0	0	16	8	9	5	0	16	3	0	1	1	0	1.00	1	.211	.288	.225

Vince Eppolito

Pitches: Right **Bats:** Right **Pos:** RP-27 **Ht:** 6'5" **Wt:** 225 **Born:** 7/29/77 **Age:** 24

Year Team	Lg Org	G	GS	CG	GF	IP	BFP	H	R	ER	HR	SH	SF	HB	TBB	IBB	SO	WP	Bk	W	L	Pct.	ShO	Sv	ERA
2000 Missoula	R+ Ari	20	0	0	8	32.1	153	30	28	26	1	0	1	8	25	0	35	9	0	4	0	1.000	0	0	7.24
2001 Tucson	AAA Ari	2	0	0	2	2	10	1	1	1	0	0	0	0	3	0	3	0	0	0	0	—	0	0	4.50
South Bend	A Ari	25	0	0	11	36.2	173	34	24	22	2	3	1	2	28	0	31	8	0	2	1	.667	0	1	5.40
2 Min. YEARS		47	0	0	21	71	336	65	53	49	3	3	2	10	56	0	69	17	0	6	1	.857	0	1	6.21

Corey Erickson

Bats: Right **Throws:** Right **Pos:** 3B-118; 2B-13; 1B-10; DH-4; PH-3; PR-1 **Ht:** 5'11" **Wt:** 190 **Born:** 1/10/77 **Age:** 25

Year Team	Lg Org	G	AB	H	2B	3B	HR	TB	R	RBI	TBB	IBB	SO	HBP	SH	SF	SB	CS	SB%	GDP	Avg	OBP	SLG
1995 Mets	R NYM	53	178	50	6	1	7	79	38	35	37	3	40	4	0	5	10	3	.77	2	.281	.406	.444
Kingsport	R+ NYM	2	9	3	0	0	1	6	1	4	0	0	3	0	0	0	0	0	—	0	.333	.333	.667
1996 Capital Cty	A NYM	58	209	46	14	0	1	63	16	17	19	0	57	3	3	4	5	3	.63	2	.220	.289	.301
Pittsfield	A- NYM	73	258	68	19	1	11	122	49	49	43	2	71	4	0	4	6	3	.67	3	.264	.372	.473

Year Team	Lg Org	G	AB	H	2B	3B	HR	TB	R	RBI	TBB	IBB	SO	HBP	SH	SF	SB	CS	SB%	GDP	Avg	OBP	SLG
1997 St. Lucie	A+ NYM	46	134	27	3	0	3	39	10	11	22	0	43	3	1	2	0	2	.00	1	.201	.323	.291
Capital Cty	A NYM	49	173	37	11	2	2	58	18	16	11	0	49	1	1	3	3	1	.75	2	.214	.261	.335
1998 St. Lucie	A+ NYM	100	346	78	23	4	6	127	49	33	16	0	88	9	0	1	5	2	.71	6	.225	.277	.367
1999 Capital Cty	A NYM	129	424	100	21	1	23	192	64	57	46	0	120	14	0	6	9	3	.75	4	.236	.327	.453
2000 Kinston	A+ Cle	120	422	113	27	0	22	206	66	72	51	3	109	11	0	5	9	2	.82	3	.268	.358	.488
Akron	AA Cle	7	28	6	2	0	3	17	4	9	2	0	11	0	0	0	0	0	—	0	.214	.267	.607
2001 Akron	AA Cle	133	483	110	28	2	22	208	67	65	33	3	132	8	1	5	7	4	.64	8	.228	.285	.431
Buffalo	AAA Cle	3	6	0	0	0	0	0	1	0	0	0	3	0	0	0	0	0	—	0	.000	.000	.000
7 Min. YEARS		773	2670	638	154	11	101	1117	383	368	280	11	726	57	6	35	54	23	.70	31	.239	.321	.418

Matt Erickson

Bats: Left **Throws:** Right **Pos:** SS-56; 2B-56; PH-3; PR-2; 3B-1   **Ht:** 5'11" **Wt:** 190 **Born:** 7/30/75 **Age:** 26

Year Team	Lg Org	G	AB	H	2B	3B	HR	TB	R	RBI	TBB	IBB	SO	HBP	SH	SF	SB	CS	SB%	GDP	Avg	OBP	SLG
1997 Utica	A- Fla	69	238	78	10	0	5	103	44	44	48	3	36	11	2	4	9	3	.75	7	.328	.455	.433
1998 Kane County	A Fla	124	441	143	32	2	4	191	83	64	72	1	62	18	7	3	17	7	.71	8	.324	.436	.433
1999 Portland	AA Fla	107	361	97	20	2	0	121	38	35	51	0	65	3	5	5	2	3	.40	9	.269	.360	.335
2000 Portland	AA Fla	100	335	101	23	4	2	138	56	41	59	3	62	9	1	3	8	3	.73	9	.301	.416	.412
2001 Calgary	AAA Fla	115	413	128	21	1	2	157	66	29	39	0	69	12	8	0	11	4	.73	13	.310	.386	.380
5 Min. YEARS		515	1788	547	106	9	13	710	287	213	269	7	294	53	23	15	47	20	.70	46	.306	.409	.397

Mark Ernster

Bats: Right **Throws:** Right **Pos:** SS-26; PH-2   **Ht:** 6'0" **Wt:** 190 **Born:** 12/10/77 **Age:** 24

Year Team	Lg Org	G	AB	H	2B	3B	HR	TB	R	RBI	TBB	IBB	SO	HBP	SH	SF	SB	CS	SB%	GDP	Avg	OBP	SLG
1999 Ogden	R+ Mil	5	22	5	1	1	0	8	3	2	1	0	1	1	1	0	1	0	1.00	1	.227	.292	.364
2000 Mudville	A+ Mil	61	204	47	9	1	3	67	30	22	13	0	40	3	3	1	4	2	.67	8	.230	.285	.328
Huntsville	AA Mil	57	205	50	9	0	5	74	27	26	35	2	46	1	3	1	10	6	.63	6	.244	.355	.361
2001 Huntsville	AA Mil	28	81	12	4	0	1	19	6	4	4	1	23	3	1	0	0	1	.00	2	.148	.216	.235
3 Min. YEARS		151	512	114	23	2	9	168	66	54	53	3	110	8	8	2	15	9	.63	17	.223	.304	.328

Vaughn Eshelman

Pitches: Left **Bats:** Left **Pos:** RP-6; SP-1   **Ht:** 6'3" **Wt:** 205 **Born:** 5/22/69 **Age:** 33

Year Team	Lg Org	G	GS	CG	GF	IP	BFP	H	R	ER	HR	SH	SF	HB	TBB	IBB	SO	WP	Bk	W	L	Pct.	ShO	Sv	ERA
1991 Bluefield	R+ Bal	3	3	0	0	14	59	10	4	1	1	0	1	0	9	0	15	1	0	1	0	1.000	0	0	0.64
Kane County	A Bal	11	11	2	0	77.2	319	57	23	20	3	3	1	3	35	0	90	2	2	5	3	.625	1	0	2.32
1993 Frederick	A+ Bal	24	24	2	0	143.1	608	128	70	62	10	4	3	7	59	0	122	7	1	7	10	.412	1	0	3.89
1994 Bowie	AA Bal	27	25	2	0	166.1	713	175	81	74	13	7	3	3	60	1	133	8	0	11	9	.550	2	0	4.00
1995 Trenton	AA Bos	2	2	0	0	7	25	3	1	0	0	0	0	1	0	0	7	0	0	0	1	.000	0	0	0.00
1996 Pawtucket	AAA Bos	7	7	1	0	43.2	190	40	21	21	6	3	0	3	19	1	28	1	0	1	2	.333	0	0	4.33
1997 Pawtucket	AAA Bos	14	13	0	1	66.2	281	63	38	36	4	7	4	5	22	0	57	3	0	3	4	.429	0	1	4.86
2000 Reds	R Cin	2	2	0	0	9.2	35	1	2	2	0	1	0	0	4	0	6	0	0	0	1	.000	0	0	1.86
Louisville	AAA Cin	1	1	0	0	4	21	7	7	4	0	1	0	1	3	0	2	0	0	0	1	.000	0	0	9.00
Dayton	A Cin	2	2	0	0	7	32	8	5	5	0	0	0	1	4	0	4	1	0	0	1	.000	0	0	6.43
2001 Norfolk	AAA NYM	7	1	0	4	11.1	56	13	6	4	0	2	1	3	7	1	4	0	0	2	0	1.000	0	0	3.18
1995 Boston	AL	23	14	0	4	81.2	356	86	47	44	3	0	3	1	36	0	41	4	0	6	3	.667	0	0	4.85
1996 Boston	AL	39	10	0	1	87.2	428	112	79	69	13	3	5	2	58	4	59	4	0	6	3	.667	0	0	7.08
1997 Boston	AL	21	6	0	6	42.2	198	58	32	30	3	1	2	2	17	5	18	2	0	3	3	.500	0	0	6.33
8 Min. YEARS		100	91	7	5	550.2	2339	505	258	229	37	27	14	26	222	3	468	23	3	30	32	.484	4	1	3.74
3 Maj. YEARS		83	30	0	11	212	982	256	158	143	19	4	10	5	111	9	118	10	0	15	9	.625	0	0	6.07

Josue Espada

Bats: Right **Throws:** Right **Pos:** SS-75; 2B-5; 3B-3; PH-3; PR-1   **Ht:** 5'10" **Wt:** 175 **Born:** 8/30/75 **Age:** 26

Year Team	Lg Org	G	AB	H	2B	3B	HR	TB	R	RBI	TBB	IBB	SO	HBP	SH	SF	SB	CS	SB%	GDP	Avg	OBP	SLG
1996 Sou Oregon	A- Oak	15	54	12	1	0	1	16	7	5	5	0	10	1	1	0	0	0	—	1	.222	.300	.296
W Michigan	A Oak	23	74	20	2	0	0	22	9	4	13	0	11	2	0	0	3	1	.75	2	.270	.393	.297
1997 Visalia	A+ Oak	118	445	122	7	3	3	144	90	39	72	1	69	9	7	3	46	17	.73	6	.274	.384	.324
1998 Huntsville	AA Oak	51	161	41	7	1	1	53	29	22	27	0	15	4	5	1	7	4	.64	4	.255	.373	.329
1999 Midland	AA Oak	113	435	147	15	2	6	184	85	51	62	0	51	2	2	3	22	16	.58	5	.338	.420	.423
Vancouver	AAA Oak	6	26	8	1	0	0	9	2	0	3	0	4	0	0	0	1	2	.33	0	.308	.379	.346
2000 Sacramento	AAA Oak	40	145	34	7	0	0	41	21	10	27	0	23	1	3	0	7	2	.78	5	.234	.358	.283
Midland	AA Oak	23	98	26	7	0	0	33	17	7	12	0	12	2	0	0	2	2	.50	4	.265	.357	.337
2001 Calgary	AAA Fla	79	290	87	20	2	3	120	61	30	39	0	49	4	3	3	13	7	.65	4	.300	.387	.414
Colo Sprngs	AAA Col	7	27	7	2	0	1	12	8	2	5	0	0	0	0	0	3	2	.60	0	.259	.375	.444
6 Min. YEARS		475	1755	504	69	8	15	634	329	170	265	1	250	25	21	10	104	53	.66	31	.287	.386	.361

Rendy Espina

Pitches: Left **Bats:** Left **Pos:** RP-39; SP-1   **Ht:** 6'0" **Wt:** 180 **Born:** 5/11/78 **Age:** 24

Year Team	Lg Org	G	GS	CG	GF	IP	BFP	H	R	ER	HR	SH	SF	HB	TBB	IBB	SO	WP	Bk	W	L	Pct.	ShO	Sv	ERA
1995 Twins	R Min	4	2	0	1	10	50	7	10	1	0	1	0	0	6	0	3	3	2	0	1	.000	0	0	0.90
1996 Twins	R Min	7	1	0	2	11.2	54	18	12	12	0	1	0	1	8	0	10	1	1	0	0	.000	0	0	9.26
1997 Twins	R Min	8	7	0	0	34.2	132	24	11	5	0	1	0	2	6	0	34	4	0	2	2	.500	0	0	1.30
Elizabethtn	R+ Min	8	3	0	1	17	86	25	21	15	2	0	0	3	9	0	15	3	1	0	3	.000	0	0	7.94
1999 Batavia	A- Phi	1	0	0	0	1	9	5	4	4	1	0	0	0	1	0	1	0	0	0	1	.000	0	0	36.00
Phillies	R Phi	2	0	0	2	1	4	1	0	0	0	0	0	0	0	0	1	0	0	1	0	1.000	0	1	0.00
Piedmont	A Phi	15	0	0	7	35	143	35	20	18	1	2	2	1	10	1	31	3	1	0	2	.000	0	3	4.63

Year Team	Lg Org	G	GS	CG	GF	IP	BFP	H	R	ER	HR	SH	SF	HB	TBB	IBB	SO	WP	Bk	W	L	Pct.	ShO	Sv	ERA
2000 Tennessee	AA Tor	53	0	0	19	59.2	264	49	22	14	1	2	2	5	35	1	41	2	1	6	1	.857	0	3	2.11
2001 Rancho Cuca	A+ Ana	2	1	0	0	1.2	11	4	4	4	1	0	1	2	0	0	2	0	0	0	0	—	0	0	21.60
Salt Lake	AAA Ana	2	0	0	2	2.1	7	1	1	1	1	0	0	0	0	0	1	0	0	0	0	—	0	0	3.86
Syracuse	AAA Tor	36	0	0	11	47	199	41	26	19	4	1	1	5	17	1	33	1	1	6	1	.857	0	0	3.64
6 Min. YEARS		136	14	0	45	221	959	214	131	93	11	7	6	19	92	3	172	17	7	15	13	.536	0	7	3.79

Cam Esslinger

Pitches: Right **Bats:** Right **Pos:** RP-40 **Ht:** 6'0" **Wt:** 170 **Born:** 12/28/76 **Age:** 25

Year Team	Lg Org	G	GS	CG	GF	IP	BFP	H	R	ER	HR	SH	SF	HB	TBB	IBB	SO	WP	Bk	W	L	Pct.	ShO	Sv	ERA
1999 Portland	A- Col	14	14	0	0	80	351	76	37	34	1	4	2	10	35	1	68	3	2	6	3	.667	0	0	3.83
2000 Asheville	A Col	47	2	0	39	64.2	271	55	23	22	2	2	2	3	23	1	84	4	0	4	2	.667	0	24	3.06
2001 Carolina	AA Col	40	0	0	29	42	192	32	26	23	0	4	2	2	31	1	51	8	0	1	1	.500	0	16	4.93
3 Min. YEARS		101	16	0	68	186.2	814	163	86	79	3	10	6	15	89	3	203	15	2	11	6	.647	0	40	3.81

Leo Estrella

Pitches: Right **Bats:** Right **Pos:** RP-36; SP-9 **Ht:** 6'1" **Wt:** 185 **Born:** 2/20/75 **Age:** 27

Year Team	Lg Org	G	GS	CG	GF	IP	BFP	H	R	ER	HR	SH	SF	HB	TBB	IBB	SO	WP	Bk	W	L	Pct.	ShO	Sv	ERA
1996 Kingsport	R+ NYM	15	7	1	3	58	248	54	32	25	3	4	1	1	24	0	52	6	2	6	3	.667	0	0	3.88
1997 Pittsfield	A- NYM	15	15	0	0	92	395	91	48	31	0	2	1	3	27	0	55	3	2	7	6	.538	0	0	3.03
1998 Capital Cty	A NYM	20	20	3	0	119	502	120	66	52	10	7	3	8	23	0	97	1	1	10	8	.556	0	0	3.93
Hagerstown	A Tor	5	5	0	0	30	133	34	19	15	0	2	3	3	13	1	27	2	1	1	3	.250	0	0	4.50
1999 Dunedin	A+ Tor	27	24	2	0	168	666	166	74	60	11	6	5	17	47	0	116	6	1	14	7	.667	2	0	3.21
2000 Tennessee	AA Tor	13	13	3	0	76	324	68	36	31	6	4	3	10	30	1	63	2	0	5	5	.500	2	0	3.67
Syracuse	AAA Tor	15	15	3	0	89.2	364	68	42	40	8	1	4	2	40	0	48	2	1	5	4	.556	1	0	4.01
2001 Chattanooga	AA Cin	3	3	0	0	14.2	59	13	6	6	0	0	1	0	4	0	14	0	0	0	1	.000	0	0	3.68
Norfolk	AAA NYM	8	1	0	0	17.1	77	23	7	6	1	0	1	3	8	0	10	3	0	2	0	1.000	0	0	3.12
Louisville	AAA Cin	34	5	0	9	62.2	273	67	36	34	8	2	1	1	27	0	37	3	0	1	1	.500	0	1	4.88
2000 Toronto	AL	2	0	0	1	4.2	21	9	3	3	1	0	1	0	0	0	3	0	0	0	0	—	0	0	5.79
6 Min. YEARS		155	108	12	12	727.1	3071	704	366	300	47	28	22	49	243	2	519	28	8	51	38	.573	5	1	3.71

Luis Estrella

Pitches: Right **Bats:** Right **Pos:** RP-20; SP-17 **Ht:** 6'1" **Wt:** 220 **Born:** 10/7/74 **Age:** 27

Year Team	Lg Org	G	GS	CG	GF	IP	BFP	H	R	ER	HR	SH	SF	HB	TBB	IBB	SO	WP	Bk	W	L	Pct.	ShO	Sv	ERA
1996 Bellingham	A- SF	23	0	0	6	55.1	213	35	13	11	3	1	0	0	22	1	52	6	0	4	0	1.000	0	1	1.79
1997 San Jose	A+ SF	42	0	0	15	77	332	84	39	29	3	1	0	2	25	3	59	7	6	5	5	.500	0	2	3.39
1998 San Jose	A+ SF	36	2	0	12	72	315	79	41	38	5	3	1	2	27	0	57	9	1	5	6	.455	0	2	4.75
1999 Fresno	AAA SF	8	0	0	7	11.2	62	23	16	16	4	1	1	0	7	0	5	1	0	0	1	.000	0	0	12.34
Shreveport	AA SF	40	5	0	15	92.1	375	77	33	31	2	2	1	2	33	1	75	7	1	6	4	.600	0	4	3.02
2000 Fresno	AAA SF	16	7	0	0	57	267	75	52	47	9	1	1	2	31	0	32	4	0	1	5	.167	0	0	7.42
Shreveport	AA SF	21	6	0	7	59	237	51	24	18	2	6	1	1	22	3	31	5	0	1	4	.200	0	1	2.75
2001 Shreveport	AA SF	7	0	0	1	8.2	41	10	6	3	1	1	0	0	5	0	8	1	0	1	0	1.000	0	0	3.12
Fresno	AAA SF	30	17	0	2	115.2	501	123	60	58	19	3	1	2	52	2	73	3	1	8	3	.727	0	0	4.51
6 Min. YEARS		223	37	0	65	548.2	2344	557	284	251	48	19	6	11	224	10	392	43	9	31	28	.525	0	10	4.12

Dave Evans

Pitches: Right **Bats:** Right **Pos:** RP-18; SP-8 **Ht:** 6'3" **Wt:** 205 **Born:** 1/1/68 **Age:** 34

Year Team	Lg Org	G	GS	CG	GF	IP	BFP	H	R	ER	HR	SH	SF	HB	TBB	IBB	SO	WP	Bk	W	L	Pct.	ShO	Sv	ERA
1990 San Berndno	A+ Sea	26	26	4	0	155	673	135	83	72	9	4	7	7	74	0	143	10	0	14	9	.609	0	0	4.18
1991 Jacksnville	AA Sea	21	20	1	0	115.2	507	118	74	67	15	2	7	9	49	0	76	12	0	5	9	.357	0	0	5.21
1993 Appleton	A Sea	5	5	0	0	27.2	117	21	9	7	0	2	0	0	15	0	23	5	2	2	1	.667	0	0	2.28
Riverside	A+ Sea	8	8	1	0	41.2	187	41	22	21	5	1	1	5	23	0	42	2	0	3	2	.600	1	0	4.54
1994 Jacksnville	AA Sea	31	6	0	8	81.1	354	86	59	50	11	3	4	5	31	2	62	4	0	3	5	.375	0	0	5.53
1995 Jackson	AA Hou	49	0	0	37	67.2	278	50	29	25	2	5	3	4	28	6	54	0	1	2	9	.182	0	18	3.33
Tucson	AAA Hou	2	0	0	0	3	12	2	0	0	0	0	0	0	1	0	4	0	0	0	0	—	0	0	0.00
1996 Tucson	AAA Hou	43	15	0	12	111.2	511	120	77	65	8	8	3	12	47	3	80	11	0	6	12	.333	0	0	5.24
1998 Carolina	AA Pit	26	3	0	6	56.2	254	56	36	33	8	3	1	0	30	1	52	8	3	5	4	.556	0	0	5.24
Nashville	AAA Pit	7	1	0	4	11.2	67	19	12	11	2	2	0	3	8	1	8	4	0	0	2	.000	0	0	8.49
Bowie	AA Bal	14	0	0	6	18.1	84	17	9	4	1	1	1	5	6	0	26	2	0	1	1	.500	0	0	1.96
1999 Rochester	AAA Bal	60	0	0	32	70.2	309	70	48	42	11	5	2	5	27	2	65	9	1	2	11	.154	0	2	5.35
2000 Tucson	AAA Ari	41	3	0	15	74.2	343	82	47	41	11	4	2	0	41	2	60	8	0	4	6	.600	0	2	4.94
2001 Round Rock	AAA Hou	1	1	0	0	4.2	20	6	5	5	2	0	0	0	0	0	4	0	0	0	0	—	0	0	9.64
New Orleans	AAA Hou	25	7	1	7	42.1	201	50	37	30	11	1	1	2	27	1	40	4	0	2	1	.667	1	1	6.38
10 Min. YEARS		359	95	7	127	882.2	3917	873	547	473	96	39	32	59	407	18	739	79	7	51	70	.421	2	26	4.82

Keith Evans

Pitches: Right **Bats:** Right **Pos:** RP-43; SP-2 **Ht:** 6'5" **Wt:** 220 **Born:** 11/2/75 **Age:** 26

Year Team	Lg Org	G	GS	CG	GF	IP	BFP	H	R	ER	HR	SH	SF	HB	TBB	IBB	SO	WP	Bk	W	L	Pct.	ShO	Sv	ERA
1997 Cape Fear	A Mon	21	21	3	0	138	551	113	56	40	6	2	4	10	18	0	102	1	0	12	7	.632	1	0	2.61
Wst Plm Bch	A+ Mon	7	7	2	0	43.2	185	42	23	21	4	2	2	5	11	0	20	1	0	4	3	.333	2	0	4.33
1998 Jupiter	A+ Mon	8	8	1	0	50.1	194	45	18	16	1	0	1	3	5	0	25	1	0	5	2	.714	0	0	2.86
Harrisburg	AA Mon	20	20	1	0	124	520	133	59	49	13	6	2	8	30	2	76	2	0	8	9	.471	0	0	3.56
1999 Harrisburg	AA Mon	5	5	0	0	27	120	29	14	11	5	1	0	3	5	0	21	1	0	0	2	.000	0	0	3.67
Ottawa	AAA Mon	24	18	2	0	122	525	143	79	65	17	3	1	10	22	0	74	2	0	2	13	.133	0	0	4.80

Year Team	Lg Org	HOW MUCH HE PITCHED						WHAT HE GAVE UP											THE RESULTS					
		G	GS	CG	GF	IP	BFP	H	R	ER	HR	SH	SF	HB	TBB	IBB	SO	WP	Bk	W	L	Pct.	ShO	Sv	ERA
2000 Ottawa	AAA Mon	15	8	0	1	52	240	64	29	23	3	3	2	4	20	0	22	3	0	2	4	.333	0	0	3.98
2001 Ottawa	AAA Mon	45	2	0	10	83.2	357	94	40	37	7	2	2	4	13	0	72	1	1	7	3	.700	0	1	3.98
5 Min. YEARS		145	89	9	11	640.2	2692	663	318	262	56	19	14	47	124	2	412	12	1	38	44	.463	3	1	3.68

Lee Evans

Bats: Both **Throws:** Right **Pos:** C-49; 3B-30; OF-26; DH-9; 1B-7; PH-1   **Ht:** 6'1" **Wt:** 185 **Born:** 7/20/77 **Age:** 24

Year Team	Lg Org	BATTING														BASERUNNING				PERCENTAGES		
		G	AB	H	2B	3B	HR	TB	R	RBI	TBB	IBB	SO	HBP	SH	SF	SB	CS	SB%	GDP	Avg	OBP	SLG
1996 Pirates	R Pit	32	111	31	5	2	3	49	27	20	18	1	26	3	1	0	3	0	1.00	2	.279	.394	.441
1997 Augusta	A Pit	54	186	36	9	2	2	55	19	23	14	1	52	1	0	1	6	3	.67	1	.194	.252	.296
Erie	A- Pit	40	141	42	6	0	5	63	20	16	11	1	30	2	1	1	1	2	.33	3	.298	.355	.447
1998 Augusta	A Pit	98	337	75	19	1	5	111	43	43	28	0	90	3	0	4	6	3	.67	4	.223	.285	.329
1999 Lynchburg	A+ Pit	117	413	93	18	2	11	148	44	58	37	2	129	5	2	8	3	6	.33	4	.225	.292	.358
2000 Lynchburg	A+ Pit	90	305	79	15	3	9	127	45	37	43	0	88	2	2	2	16	1	.94	6	.259	.352	.416
Altoona	AA Pit	32	118	28	4	1	1	37	18	8	14	2	28	1	4	0	1	1	.50	3	.237	.323	.314
2001 Altoona	AA Pit	118	428	106	21	8	11	176	53	48	37	3	116	5	4	2	12	5	.71	4	.248	.314	.411
6 Min. YEARS		581	2039	490	97	19	47	766	269	253	202	10	559	22	14	18	48	21	.70	33	.240	.313	.376

Tom Evans

Bats: Right **Throws:** Right **Pos:** 3B-49; SS-1; PH-1   **Ht:** 6'1" **Wt:** 200 **Born:** 7/9/74 **Age:** 27

Year Team	Lg Org	BATTING														BASERUNNING				PERCENTAGES		
		G	AB	H	2B	3B	HR	TB	R	RBI	TBB	IBB	SO	HBP	SH	SF	SB	CS	SB%	GDP	Avg	OBP	SLG
1992 Medcine Hat	R+ Tor	52	166	36	3	0	1	42	17	21	33	0	29	1	1	1	4	3	.57	4	.217	.348	.253
1993 Hagerstown	A Tor	119	389	100	25	1	7	148	47	54	53	2	61	3	0	4	9	2	.82	7	.257	.347	.380
1994 Hagerstown	A Tor	95	322	88	16	2	13	147	52	48	51	1	80	1	1	1	2	1	.67	3	.273	.373	.457
1995 Dunedin	A+ Tor	130	444	124	29	3	9	186	63	66	51	0	80	8	3	7	7	2	.78	10	.279	.359	.419
1996 Knoxville	AA Tor	120	394	111	27	1	17	191	87	65	115	0	113	9	0	2	4	0	1.00	7	.282	.452	.485
1997 Dunedin	A+ Tor	15	42	11	2	0	2	19	8	4	11	0	10	4	0	1	0	0	—	0	.262	.448	.452
Syracuse	AAA Tor	107	396	99	17	1	15	163	60	65	53	1	104	9	1	3	1	2	.33	4	.263	.365	.434
1998 Syracuse	AAA Tor	109	400	120	32	1	15	199	57	55	50	1	74	8	0	1	11	7	.61	10	.300	.388	.498
1999 Oklahoma	AAA Tex	128	439	123	35	3	12	200	84	68	66	1	100	9	1	1	5	4	.56	10	.280	.384	.456
2001 Toledo	AAA Det	50	169	45	12	2	5	76	26	19	26	0	33	4	0	0	1	3	.25	4	.266	.377	.450
1997 Toronto	AL	12	38	11	2	0	1	16	7	2	2	0	10	1	0	0	0	1	.00	1	.289	.341	.421
1998 Toronto	AL	7	10	0	0	0	0	0	0	0	1	0	2	0	0	0	0	0	—	1	.000	.091	.000
2000 Texas	AL	23	54	15	4	0	0	19	10	5	10	0	13	1	1	1	0	3	.00	1	.278	.394	.352
9 Min. YEARS		925	3141	857	198	14	96	1371	501	465	509	6	684	56	7	21	44	24	.65	62	.273	.382	.436
3 Maj. YEARS		42	102	26	6	0	1	35	17	7	13	0	25	2	1	1	0	4	.00	2	.255	.347	.343

Alex Fajardo

Bats: Right **Throws:** Right **Pos:** OF-46; PH-23; DH-11; 2B-3; PR-2   **Ht:** 6'0" **Wt:** 180 **Born:** 2/6/76 **Age:** 26

Year Team	Lg Org	BATTING														BASERUNNING				PERCENTAGES		
		G	AB	H	2B	3B	HR	TB	R	RBI	TBB	IBB	SO	HBP	SH	SF	SB	CS	SB%	GDP	Avg	OBP	SLG
1997 Batavia	A- Phi	52	200	54	7	4	2	75	35	29	7	1	34	3	3	1	9	2	.82	5	.270	.303	.375
1998 Piedmont	A Phi	115	457	128	24	1	5	169	83	46	44	1	88	1	12	4	38	4	.90	6	.280	.342	.370
1999 Piedmont	A Phi	118	444	108	16	6	6	154	66	43	52	0	91	6	10	3	44	10	.81	7	.243	.329	.347
2000 San Jose	A+ SF	93	331	93	9	3	0	108	47	39	54	0	67	3	4	4	23	6	.79	8	.281	.383	.326
Fresno	AAA SF	4	12	3	0	1	0	5	1	1	0	0	3	0	1	0	0	0	—	0	.250	.250	.417
2001 Hagerstown	A SF	12	37	6	0	0	0	6	4	3	10	0	14	1	1	0	3	0	1.00	0	.162	.354	.162
San Jose	A+ SF	40	136	33	9	2	1	49	22	12	16	0	30	0	3	0	9	4	.69	1	.243	.322	.360
Fresno	AAA SF	27	32	9	1	0	0	10	5	3	4	0	14	0	1	0	0	0	—	0	.281	.361	.313
5 Min. YEARS		461	1649	434	66	17	14	576	243	176	187	2	341	14	35	12	126	26	.83	27	.263	.341	.349

Brian Falkenborg

Pitches: Right **Bats:** Right **Pos:** SP-20   **Ht:** 6'6" **Wt:** 195 **Born:** 1/18/78 **Age:** 24

Year Team	Lg Org	HOW MUCH HE PITCHED						WHAT HE GAVE UP												THE RESULTS					
		G	GS	CG	GF	IP	BFP	H	R	ER	HR	SH	SF	HB	TBB	IBB	SO	WP	Bk	W	L	Pct.	ShO	Sv	ERA
1996 Orioles	R Bal	8	6	0	1	28	116	21	13	8	1	0	0	1	8	0	36	2	1	0	3	.000	0	0	2.57
High Desert	A+ Bal	1	0	0	0	1	3	1	0	0	0	0	0	0	0	0	1	0	0	0	0	—	0	0	0.00
1997 Bowie	AA Bal	1	1	0	0	1.2	11	3	3	3	0	0	0	0	3	0	0	0	0	0	1	.000	0	0	16.20
Delmarva	A Bal	25	25	0	0	127	547	122	73	63	6	3	2	13	46	2	107	17	0	7	9	.438	0	0	4.46
1998 Frederick	A+ Bal	15	14	1	0	78	338	83	42	39	6	3	2	4	18	0	70	8	0	5	5	.500	1	0	4.50
1999 Orioles	R Bal	3	2	0	0	9	37	6	2	2	0	0	0	0	3	0	11	1	0	1	0	1.000	0	0	2.00
Bowie	AA Bal	16	16	0	0	83.1	361	77	40	35	11	2	0	5	36	0	77	1	0	3	6	.333	0	0	3.78
2001 San Antonio	AA Sea	12	12	2	0	66	296	80	47	40	9	2	3	5	24	0	56	5	0	5	6	.455	1	0	5.45
Tacoma	AAA Sea	8	8	0	0	48.1	206	50	25	24	6	1	2	2	18	0	27	1	0	2	4	.333	0	0	4.47
1999 Baltimore	AL	2	0	0	0	3	12	2	0	0	0	0	0	0	2	0	1	0	0	0	0	—	0	0	0.00
5 Min. YEARS		89	84	3	1	442.1	1915	443	245	214	39	11	9	30	156	2	385	35	1	23	34	.404	2	0	4.35

Steve Falteisek

Pitches: Right **Bats:** Right **Pos:** SP-16; RP-6   **Ht:** 6'2" **Wt:** 200 **Born:** 1/28/72 **Age:** 30

Year Team	Lg Org	HOW MUCH HE PITCHED						WHAT HE GAVE UP												THE RESULTS					
		G	GS	CG	GF	IP	BFP	H	R	ER	HR	SH	SF	HB	TBB	IBB	SO	WP	Bk	W	L	Pct.	ShO	Sv	ERA
1992 Jamestown	A- Mon	15	15	2	0	96	407	84	47	38	3	4	1	5	31	2	82	9	10	3	8	.273	0	0	3.56
1993 Burlington	A Mon	14	14	0	0	76.1	345	86	59	50	4	4	1	2	35	0	63	4	1	3	5	.375	0	0	5.90
1994 Wst Plm Bch	A+ Mon	27	24	1	0	159.2	658	144	72	45	3	0	6	3	49	0	91	11	4	9	4	.692	0	0	2.54
1995 Harrisburg	AA Mon	25	25	5	0	168	707	152	74	55	3	7	5	11	64	4	112	6	1	9	6	.600	0	0	2.95
Ottawa	AAA Mon	3	3	1	0	23	86	17	4	3	0	0	0	1	5	0	18	0	1	2	0	1.000	1	0	1.17

Year Team	Lg Org	G	GS	CG	GF	IP	BFP	H	R	ER	HR	SH	SF	HB	TBB	IBB	SO	WP	Bk	W	L	Pct.	ShO	Sv	ERA
1996 Ottawa	AAA Mon	12	12	0	0	58	272	75	45	41	10	1	0	5	25	0	26	3	0	2	5	.286	0	0	6.36
Harrisburg	AA Mon	17	17	1	0	115.2	492	111	60	49	9	7	0	5	48	1	62	5	3	6	5	.545	0	0	3.81
1997 Ottawa	AAA Mon	22	22	1	0	125	555	135	67	55	10	7	7	5	54	1	56	12	1	6	9	.400	0	0	3.96
1998 Ottawa	AAA Mon	34	22	1	1	161.2	719	186	110	98	17	4	4	11	59	1	83	10	0	10	11	.476	0	0	5.46
1999 Louisville	AAA Mil	42	4	0	8	76.1	359	98	65	58	13	2	2	4	41	4	34	7	1	5	11	.313	0	0	6.84
2000 Calgary	AAA Fla	5	1	0	0	7.2	53	23	18	17	2	0	0	1	5	0	5	1	0	0	1	.000	0	0	19.96
2001 Long Island	IND —	11	11	1	0	64.1	271	69	34	28	9	0	1	0	10	0	39	0	2	4	5	.444	0	0	3.92
Bowie	AA Bal	11	5	0	4	42.1	198	59	45	37	11	2	4	0	15	1	25	7	0	1	6	.143	0	0	7.87
1997 Montreal	NL	5	0	0	2	8	34	8	4	3	0	0	2	1	3	0	2	0	0	0	0	—	0	0	3.38
1999 Milwaukee	NL	10	0	0	3	12	52	18	10	10	3	0	1	0	3	0	5	0	0	0	0	—	0	0	7.50
10 Min. YEARS		238	175	13	13	1174	5122	1239	700	574	94	38	31	53	441	14	696	75	24	60	76	.441	1	0	4.40
2 Maj. YEARS		15	0	0	5	20	86	26	14	13	3	0	3	1	6	0	7	0	0	0	0	—	0	0	5.85

Tom Farmer

Pitches: Right **Bats:** Right **Pos:** SP-12   **Ht:** 6'3" **Wt:** 185 **Born:** 7/27/79 **Age:** 22

Year Team	Lg Org	G	GS	CG	GF	IP	BFP	H	R	ER	HR	SH	SF	HB	TBB	IBB	SO	WP	Bk	W	L	Pct.	ShO	Sv	ERA
2001 Oneonta	A- Det	4	4	0	0	22	95	24	13	7	1	0	1	0	4	0	11	0	2	1	1	.500	0	0	2.86
W Michigan	A Det	6	6	0	0	38	144	30	10	10	2	0	0	0	8	0	28	4	1	3	2	.600	0	0	2.37
Erie	AA Det	2	2	0	0	10.2	45	12	3	3	1	1	0	0	4	0	8	1	0	0	0	—	0	0	2.53
1 Min. YEAR		12	12	0	0	70.2	284	66	26	20	4	1	1	0	16	0	47	5	3	4	3	.571	0	0	2.55

Jeff Farnsworth

Pitches: Right **Bats:** Right **Pos:** SP-27   **Ht:** 6'2" **Wt:** 190 **Born:** 10/6/75 **Age:** 26

Year Team	Lg Org	G	GS	CG	GF	IP	BFP	H	R	ER	HR	SH	SF	HB	TBB	IBB	SO	WP	Bk	W	L	Pct.	ShO	Sv	ERA
1996 Everett	A- Sea	10	7	0	1	39.1	158	33	19	18	4	0	1	0	13	0	42	6	5	3	3	.500	0	0	4.12
1997 Lancaster	A+ Sea	5	5	0	0	20.2	93	24	20	16	2	1	1	3	8	0	18	2	0	1	1	.500	0	0	6.97
1999 Lancaster	A+ Sea	26	9	0	6	72	351	91	61	52	7	1	10	15	43	1	43	10	0	3	6	.333	0	3	6.50
2000 New Haven	AA Sea	39	8	0	6	101.1	414	91	40	39	6	2	2	9	25	1	70	3	1	9	3	.750	0	2	3.46
2001 San Antonio	AA Sea	27	27	0	0	155.1	688	182	92	75	10	4	3	8	47	0	113	3	3	11	10	.524	0	0	4.35
5 Min. YEARS		107	56	0	13	388.2	1704	421	232	200	29	8	17	35	136	2	286	24	9	27	23	.540	0	5	4.63

Troy Farnsworth

Bats: Right **Throws:** Right **Pos:** 3B-93; 1B-27; PH-2; DH-1   **Ht:** 6'2" **Wt:** 200 **Born:** 2/4/76 **Age:** 26

Year Team	Lg Org	G	AB	H	2B	3B	HR	TB	R	RBI	TBB	IBB	SO	HBP	SH	SF	SB	CS	SB%	GDP	Avg	OBP	SLG
1998 New Jersey	A- StL	65	218	56	14	1	6	90	33	37	25	0	64	6	2	3	2	4	.33	2	.257	.345	.413
1999 Peoria	A StL	134	500	125	33	3	19	221	76	78	54	4	124	12	0	4	3	2	.60	10	.250	.336	.442
2000 Potomac	A+ StL	137	512	123	24	3	23	222	67	113	44	1	133	11	0	11	7	2	.78	7	.240	.308	.434
2001 New Haven	AA StL	115	422	98	21	1	18	175	47	70	28	3	104	15	1	4	4	7	.36	8	.232	.301	.415
4 Min. YEARS		451	1652	402	92	8	66	708	223	298	152	8	425	44	3	22	16	15	.52	27	.243	.320	.429

Jim Farrell

Pitches: Right **Bats:** Right **Pos:** RP-2   **Ht:** 6'1" **Wt:** 174 **Born:** 11/1/73 **Age:** 28

Year Team	Lg Org	G	GS	CG	GF	IP	BFP	H	R	ER	HR	SH	SF	HB	TBB	IBB	SO	WP	Bk	W	L	Pct.	ShO	Sv	ERA
1995 Red Sox	R Bos	1	1	0	0	6	20	2	1	1	0	0	0	0	1	0	3	0	0	1	0	1.000	0	0	1.50
Michigan	A Bos	13	13	1	0	69	291	62	34	28	10	1	1	5	23	0	70	3	1	3	2	.600	0	0	3.65
1996 Michigan	A Bos	7	7	2	0	44	185	39	15	12	2	1	0	1	17	1	32	1	0	6	1	.857	0	0	2.45
Sarasota	A+ Bos	21	21	3	0	133.1	539	116	58	52	11	4	5	4	34	0	92	9	0	9	8	.529	1	0	3.51
1997 Trenton	AA Bos	26	26	0	0	162.2	706	173	93	79	24	1	5	7	57	0	110	11	0	12	7	.632	0	0	4.37
Pawtucket	AAA Bos	1	1	0	0	5	21	4	0	0	0	1	0	0	2	0	6	1	0	0	0	—	0	0	0.00
1998 Pawtucket	AAA Bos	28	25	2	0	163.1	709	176	106	100	31	2	5	5	52	0	142	8	1	14	8	.636	1	0	5.51
1999 Pawtucket	AAA Bos	14	5	0	2	43	190	45	25	20	7	2	3	1	16	0	35	2	0	2	3	.400	0	0	4.19
Trenton	AA Bos	7	5	0	0	27	116	26	13	10	1	0	1	1	9	1	26	1	0	2	2	.500	0	0	3.33
2001 Pawtucket	AAA Bos	1	0	0	0	1	4	1	0	0	0	0	0	0	0	0	0	0	0	0	0	—	0	0	0.00
Trenton	AA Bos	1	0	0	0	2	8	1	0	0	0	0	0	0	1	0	2	0	0	0	0	—	0	0	0.00
6 Min. YEARS		120	104	8	2	656.1	2790	645	345	302	87	12	20	24	212	2	518	36	2	49	31	.613	2	0	4.14

Danny Fatheree

Bats: Right **Throws:** Right **Pos:** C-22; DH-13; PH-7   **Ht:** 5'11" **Wt:** 232 **Born:** 8/25/78 **Age:** 23

Year Team	Lg Org	G	AB	H	2B	3B	HR	TB	R	RBI	TBB	IBB	SO	HBP	SH	SF	SB	CS	SB%	GDP	Avg	OBP	SLG
1997 Astros	R Hou	21	38	9	1	0	0	10	4	3	3	0	0	0	1	1	0	1	.00	0	.237	.286	.263
1998 Auburn	A- Hou	52	196	51	10	0	2	67	26	27	19	1	40	1	1	3	1	4	.20	4	.260	.324	.342
1999 Michigan	A Hou	38	118	24	5	2	1	36	13	18	11	0	19	1	0	1	2	1	.67	3	.203	.275	.305
2000 Michigan	A Hou	46	132	35	4	0	3	48	18	17	19	0	18	1	1	1	1	1	.50	5	.265	.359	.364
2001 Lexington	A Hou	21	61	14	3	0	1	20	8	9	7	0	13	1	1	0	0	0	—	1	.230	.319	.328
Round Rock	AA Hou	8	23	3	0	0	1	6	3	2	2	0	2	0	0	0	0	0	—	0	.130	.200	.261
Michigan	A Hou	9	27	8	4	1	0	14	5	3	3	0	6	0	1	1	0	0	—	1	.296	.355	.519
5 Min. YEARS		195	595	144	27	3	8	201	77	79	64	1	98	4	4	7	4	7	.36	14	.242	.316	.338

Pedro Feliciano

Pitches: Left **Bats:** Left **Pos:** RP-60   **Ht:** 5'11" **Wt:** 165 **Born:** 8/25/76 **Age:** 25

Year Team	Lg Org	G	GS	CG	GF	IP	BFP	H	R	ER	HR	SH	SF	HB	TBB	IBB	SO	WP	Bk	W	L	Pct.	ShO	Sv	ERA
		HOW MUCH HE PITCHED						**WHAT HE GAVE UP**												**THE RESULTS**					
1995 Great Falls	R+ LA	6	0	0	3	6.2	43	12	12	10	0	0	0	0	7	1	9	4	2	0	0	—	0	0	13.50
1996 Great Falls	R+ LA	22	1	0	10	41	206	50	36	26	1	0	5	3	26	2	39	4	3	2	3	.400	0	3	5.71
1997 Savannah	A LA	36	9	1	8	105.2	437	90	45	31	11	3	3	1	39	0	94	6	4	3	7	.300	0	4	2.64
Vero Beach	A+ LA	1	0	0	0	2	7	3	1	1	1	0	0	0	0	0	1	0	0	0	0	—	0	0	4.50
1998 Vero Beach	A+ LA	22	10	0	8	68.1	300	68	44	35	8	0	1	2	30	1	51	2	0	2	5	.286	0	2	4.61
2000 Vero Beach	A+ LA	25	2	0	7	61.1	289	76	31	26	4	4	4	5	24	1	48	3	0	4	5	.444	0	2	3.82
San Antonio	AA LA	9	0	0	3	9.1	37	7	2	2	0	1	0	1	4	1	11	0	2	0	0	—	0	2	1.93
Albuquerque	AAA LA	1	0	0	1	1	9	3	3	2	2	0	0	0	1	0	2	0	0	0	0	—	0	0	18.00
2001 Las Vegas	AAA LA	6	0	0	1	8.2	49	16	11	7	2	1	0	1	5	1	5	1	0	0	1	.000	0	0	7.27
Jacksnville	AA LA	54	0	0	38	60.1	229	41	14	13	3	4	0	3	11	1	55	2	0	5	4	.556	0	17	1.94
6 Min. YEARS		182	22	1	79	364.1	1606	366	199	153	32	13	13	16	147	8	315	22	11	16	25	.390	0	28	3.78

Hersy Felix

Bats: Right **Throws:** Right **Pos:** C-41; DH-2   **Ht:** 6'3" **Wt:** 180 **Born:** 4/11/78 **Age:** 24

Year Team	Lg Org	G	AB	R	2B	3B	HR	TB	R	RBI	TBB	IBB	SO	HBP	SH	SF	SB	CS	SB%	GDP	Avg	OBP	SLG
		BATTING															**BASERUNNING**				**PERCENTAGES**		
1998 Royals	R KC	48	173	45	5	0	5	65	23	25	21	0	34	2	0	3	0	1	.00	4	.260	.342	.376
Wilmington	A+ KC	3	3	1	0	0	0	1	0	0	0	0	2	0	0	0	0	0	—	0	.333	.333	.333
1999 Chston-WV	A KC	23	80	23	7	0	1	33	6	4	3	0	17	0	0	0	2	0	1.00	2	.288	.313	.413
2000 Spokane	A- KC	50	131	18	6	0	2	30	17	10	11	0	39	4	1	0	0	0	—	5	.137	.226	.229
2001 Wichita	AA KC	3	9	2	0	0	1	5	1	1	0	0	5	0	1	0	0	0	—	0	.222	.222	.556
Wilmington	A+ KC	4	14	1	0	0	0	1	1	1	1	0	1	0	0	0	0	0	—	0	.071	.125	.071
Omaha	AAA KC	1	4	1	1	0	0	2	1	1	0	0	0	0	0	0	0	0	—	0	.250	.250	.500
Burlington	A KC	35	114	24	4	0	1	31	9	8	12	0	23	0	1	0	0	0	—	3	.211	.286	.272
4 Min. YEARS		167	528	115	23	0	10	168	58	50	48	0	121	6	3	4	2	1	.67	14	.218	.288	.318

Miguel Felix

Pitches: Right **Bats:** Right **Pos:** SP-15; RP-1   **Ht:** 6'3" **Wt:** 180 **Born:** 12/30/76 **Age:** 25

Year Team	Lg Org	G	GS	CG	GF	IP	BFP	H	R	ER	HR	SH	SF	HB	TBB	IBB	SO	WP	Bk	W	L	Pct.	ShO	Sv	ERA
		HOW MUCH HE PITCHED						**WHAT HE GAVE UP**												**THE RESULTS**					
1994 White Sox	R CWS	5	0	0	2	5	30	9	8	5	1	0	1	1	5	0	3	0	2	0	1	.000	0	0	9.00
1996 White Sox	R CWS	12	12	1	0	73.1	317	73	39	27	2	0	3	5	19	0	64	2	3	3	6	.333	0	0	3.31
1997 White Sox	R CWS	3	2	0	1	12	45	10	3	2	0	0	0	0	2	0	10	1	0	0	0	—	0	0	1.50
Bristol	R+ CWS	11	10	0	0	50.1	256	78	52	42	7	0	4	7	22	0	38	5	2	2	5	.286	0	0	7.51
1998 Hickory	A CWS	21	19	1	0	97.1	468	111	90	70	13	1	1	6	64	0	86	13	1	3	11	.214	0	0	6.47
Bristol	R+ CWS	5	4	0	0	21.2	100	20	16	11	2	1	1	4	15	0	23	3	0	1	1	.500	0	0	4.57
1999 Burlington	A CWS	30	0	0	11	44.2	237	60	52	39	3	0	4	7	39	0	29	15	1	0	2	.000	0	0	7.86
Winston-Sal	A+ CWS	9	0	0	4	14	62	11	8	3	1	0	1	5	7	0	7	2	0	1	0	1.000	0	1	1.93
2000 Winston-Sal	A+ CWS	27	0	0	10	35.1	167	39	32	30	2	1	2	6	21	0	32	9	0	0	0	—	0	0	7.64
Frederick	A+ Bal	10	0	0	4	11.1	65	18	17	17	3	0	0	6	11	0	5	0	0	0	0	—	0	0	13.50
2001 Rochester	AAA Bal	1	1	0	0	4.2	24	5	6	6	1	0	0	0	5	0	3	1	0	0	1	.000	0	0	11.57
Bowie	AA Bal	15	14	1	0	80	337	73	44	39	7	1	1	7	32	1	58	6	2	5	5	.500	1	0	4.39
7 Min. YEARS		147	62	3	32	449.2	2108	507	367	291	42	4	18	54	242	1	358	57	11	15	32	.319	1	1	5.82

Sid Fernandez

Pitches: Left **Bats:** Left **Pos:** SP-1   **Ht:** 6'1" **Wt:** 230 **Born:** 10/12/62 **Age:** 39

Year Team	Lg Org	G	GS	CG	GF	IP	BFP	H	R	ER	HR	SH	SF	HB	TBB	IBB	SO	WP	Bk	W	L	Pct.	ShO	Sv	ERA
		HOW MUCH HE PITCHED						**WHAT HE GAVE UP**												**THE RESULTS**					
1981 Lethbridge	R+ LA	11	11	2	0	76	—	43	21	13	1	—	—	1	31	0	128	3	—	5	1	.833	1	0	1.54
1982 Vero Beach	A+ LA	12	12	5	0	84.2	—	38	19	18	3	—	—	5	38	0	137	1	—	8	1	.889	4	0	1.91
Albuquerque	AAA LA	13	13	5	0	88	—	76	54	53	13	—	—	5	52	2	86	4	—	6	5	.545	0	0	5.42
1983 San Antonio	AA LA	24	24	4	0	153	—	111	61	48	11	—	—	8	96	0	209	4	—	13	4	.765	1	0	2.82
1984 Tidewater	AAA NYM	17	17	3	0	105.2	451	69	39	30	2	5	3	3	63	1	123	8	0	6	5	.545	0	0	2.56
1985 Tidewater	AAA NYM	5	5	1	0	35.1	142	17	8	8	2	0	1	0	21	0	42	1	0	4	1	.800	1	0	2.04
1991 St. Lucie	A+ NYM	1	1	0	0	3	11	1	0	0	0	0	0	0	1	0	4	0	0	0	0	—	0	0	0.00
Williamsprt	A NYM	1	1	0	0	6	23	3	0	0	0	0	0	0	1	0	5	0	0	0	0	—	0	0	0.00
Tidewater	AAA NYM	3	3	0	0	15.2	58	9	2	2	0	0	1	0	6	0	22	0	0	1	0	1.000	0	0	1.15
1993 St. Lucie	A+ NYM	1	1	0	0	4	16	3	2	2	1	0	0	0	1	0	7	0	0	0	1	.000	0	0	4.50
Binghamton	AA NYM	2	2	0	0	10	36	6	2	2	0	0	0	0	3	0	11	0	0	1	0	1.000	0	0	1.80
1994 Albany	A Bal	1	1	0	0	3	11	0	0	0	0	0	0	0	2	0	4	0	0	0	0	—	0	0	0.00
Rochester	AAA Bal	1	1	0	0	4	16	3	2	2	0	0	0	0	1	0	4	0	0	0	0	—	0	0	4.50
1995 Bowie	AA Bal	2	2	1	0	12	41	4	2	1	0	0	0	0	3	0	10	1	0	1	0	1.000	1	0	0.75
1996 Clearwater	A+ Phi	1	1	0	0	3	9	0	0	0	0	0	0	0	0	0	4	0	0	0	0	—	0	0	0.00
1997 New Orleans	AAA Hou	2	2	0	0	8.1	34	7	4	4	0	0	0	0	3	0	7	2	0	0	1	.000	0	0	4.32
2001 Columbus	AAA NYY	1	1	0	0	2	10	3	3	3	1	0	0	0	2	0	1	0	0	0	0	—	0	0	13.50
1983 Los Angeles	NL	2	1	0	0	6	33	7	4	4	0	0	0	1	7	0	9	0	0	0	1	.000	0	0	6.00
1984 New York	NL	15	15	0	0	90	371	74	40	35	8	5	5	0	34	3	62	1	4	6	6	.500	0	0	3.50
1985 New York	NL	26	26	3	0	170.1	685	108	56	53	14	4	4	3	80	3	180	3	2	9	9	.500	0	0	2.80
1986 New York	NL	32	31	2	1	204.1	855	161	82	80	13	9	7	2	91	1	200	6	0	16	6	.727	1	1	3.52
1987 New York	NL	28	27	3	0	156	665	130	75	66	16	3	6	8	67	8	134	2	0	12	8	.600	1	0	3.81
1988 New York	NL	31	31	1	0	187	751	127	69	63	15	2	7	6	70	1	189	4	9	12	10	.545	1	0	3.03
1989 New York	NL	35	32	6	0	219.1	883	157	73	69	21	4	4	6	75	3	198	1	3	14	5	.737	2	0	2.83
1990 New York	NL	30	30	2	0	179.1	735	130	79	69	18	7	6	5	67	4	181	1	0	9	14	.391	1	0	3.46
1991 New York	NL	8	8	0	0	44	177	36	18	14	4	5	1	0	9	0	31	0	0	1	3	.250	0	0	2.86
1992 New York	NL	32	32	5	0	214.2	865	162	67	65	12	12	11	4	67	4	193	0	0	14	11	.560	2	0	2.73
1993 New York	NL	18	18	1	0	119.2	469	82	42	39	17	3	1	3	36	0	81	2	0	5	6	.455	1	0	2.93
1994 Baltimore	AL	19	19	2	0	115.1	494	109	66	66	27	4	3	2	46	2	95	1	0	6	6	.500	0	0	5.15
1995 Baltimore	AL	8	7	0	1	28	137	36	26	23	9	1	0	1	17	2	31	0	0	0	4	.000	0	0	7.39
Philadelphia	NL	11	11	0	0	64.2	263	48	25	24	11	1	0	1	21	0	79	0	1	6	1	.857	0	0	3.34

93

Year Team	Lg Org	G	GS	CG	GF	IP	BFP	H	R	ER	HR	SH	SF	HB	TBB	IBB	SO	WP	Bk	W	L	Pct.	ShO	Sv	ERA
		HOW MUCH HE PITCHED						**WHAT HE GAVE UP**												**THE RESULTS**					
1996 Philadelphia	NL	11	11	0	0	63	264	50	25	24	5	2	2	1	26	2	77	1	0	3	6	.333	0	0	3.43
1997 Houston	NL	1	1	0	0	5	21	4	2	2	1	0	0	0	2	0	3	0	0	1	0	1.000	0	0	3.60
12 Min. YEARS		98	98	21	0	613.2	—	393	219	186	34	—	—	22	324	3	807	24	—	44	19	.698	7	0	2.73
15 Maj. YEARS		307	300	25	2	1866.2	7668	1421	749	696	191	62	57	41	715	33	1743	22	19	114	96	.543	9	1	3.36

Luke Field

Pitches: Right **Bats:** Right **Pos:** SP-15   **Ht:** 5'11" **Wt:** 178 **Born:** 1/27/79 **Age:** 23

Year Team	Lg Org	G	GS	CG	GF	IP	BFP	H	R	ER	HR	SH	SF	HB	TBB	IBB	SO	WP	Bk	W	L	Pct.	ShO	Sv	ERA
		HOW MUCH HE PITCHED						**WHAT HE GAVE UP**												**THE RESULTS**					
2000 Mahoning Vy	A- Cle	22	1	0	6	49.2	221	56	36	27	3	0	3	3	21	0	31	4	2	2	3	.400	0	0	4.89
2001 Mahoning Vy	A- Cle	14	14	0	0	69.1	310	80	48	30	5	3	2	3	25	1	53	6	0	4	5	.444	0	0	3.89
Akron	AA Cle	1	1	0	0	5	25	8	6	6	1	0	1	0	2	0	1	1	0	0	1	.000	0	0	10.80
2 Min. YEARS		37	16	0	6	124	556	144	90	63	9	3	6	6	48	1	85	11	2	6	9	.400	0	0	4.57

Nathan Field

Pitches: Right **Bats:** Right **Pos:** RP-52   **Ht:** 6'2" **Wt:** 185 **Born:** 12/11/75 **Age:** 26

Year Team	Lg Org	G	GS	CG	GF	IP	BFP	H	R	ER	HR	SH	SF	HB	TBB	IBB	SO	WP	Bk	W	L	Pct.	ShO	Sv	ERA
		HOW MUCH HE PITCHED						**WHAT HE GAVE UP**												**THE RESULTS**					
1998 Vermont	A- Mon	25	0	0	16	35	150	32	16	12	1	1	0	3	11	0	39	5	1	3	1	.750	0	2	3.09
1999 Ottawa	AAA Mon	2	0	0	1	3	16	4	1	1	0	0	0	0	4	0	4	0	0	0	0	—	0	0	3.00
Cape Fear	A Mon	42	0	0	21	65	300	75	49	39	8	2	3	7	22	2	55	4	0	4	8	.333	0	2	5.40
2000 Sioux City	IND —	11	0	0	3	23.1	100	17	10	5	1	1	1	0	15	3	19	3	0	3	0	1.000	0	1	1.93
Chston-WV	A KC	17	0	0	4	36.1	152	28	10	9	2	4	1	2	15	0	31	3	1	1	2	.333	0	0	2.23
2001 Wichita	AA KC	52	0	0	44	73	300	61	16	12	3	3	2	2	18	3	67	5	0	4	2	.667	0	19	1.48
4 Min. YEARS		149	0	0	89	235.2	1018	217	102	78	15	11	7	14	85	8	215	20	2	15	13	.536	0	23	2.98

Mike Figga

Bats: Right **Throws:** Right **Pos:** C-63; PH-4; DH-3   **Ht:** 6'0" **Wt:** 200 **Born:** 7/31/70 **Age:** 31

Year Team	Lg Org	G	AB	H	2B	3B	HR	TB	R	RBI	TBB	IBB	SO	HBP	SH	SF	SB	CS	SB%	GDP	Avg	OBP	SLG
		BATTING															**BASERUNNING**				**PERCENTAGES**		
1990 Yankees	R NYY	40	123	35	1	1	2	44	19	18	17	2	33	1	0	1	4	2	.67	2	.285	.373	.358
1991 Pr William	A+ NYY	55	174	34	6	0	3	49	15	17	19	0	51	0	2	1	2	1	.67	9	.195	.273	.282
1992 Pr William	A+ NYY	3	10	2	1	0	0	3	0	0	2	0	3	0	0	0	1	0	1.00	0	.200	.333	.300
Ft. Laud	A+ NYY	80	249	44	13	0	1	60	12	15	13	1	78	2	3	0	3	1	.75	7	.177	.223	.241
1993 San Berndno	A+ NYY	83	308	82	17	1	25	176	48	71	17	0	84	2	2	3	2	3	.40	7	.266	.306	.571
Albany-Col	AA NYY	6	22	5	0	0	0	5	3	2	2	0	9	0	0	0	1	0	1.00	0	.227	.292	.227
1994 Albany-Col	AA NYY	1	2	1	1	0	0	2	1	0	0	0	1	0	0	0	0	0	—	0	.500	.500	1.000
Tampa	A+ NYY	111	420	116	17	5	15	188	48	75	22	1	94	2	1	5	3	0	1.00	12	.276	.312	.448
1995 Norwich	AA NYY	109	399	108	22	4	13	177	59	61	43	3	90	1	2	6	1	0	1.00	10	.271	.339	.444
Columbus	AAA NYY	8	25	7	1	0	1	11	2	3	3	0	5	0	1	0	0	0	—	0	.280	.357	.440
1996 Columbus	AAA NYY	4	11	3	1	0	0	4	3	0	1	0	3	0	0	0	0	0	—	0	.273	.333	.364
1997 Columbus	AAA NYY	110	390	95	14	4	12	153	48	54	18	0	104	2	1	3	3	3	.50	9	.244	.278	.392
1998 Columbus	AAA NYY	123	461	129	30	3	26	243	57	95	35	4	109	2	0	1	2	2	.50	15	.280	.333	.527
2000 Trenton	AA Bos	8	27	5	0	0	1	8	1	2	2	0	8	0	0	0	0	0	—	0	.185	.241	.296
Pawtucket	AAA Bos	2	8	0	0	0	0	0	0	0	1	0	2	0	0	0	0	0	—	0	.000	.111	.000
San Antonio	AA LA	43	148	35	5	0	8	64	16	21	12	0	37	1	0	0	0	0	—	5	.236	.298	.432
Albuquerque	AAA LA	15	35	13	4	0	0	17	10	8	2	0	12	0	0	1	0	0	—	2	.371	.395	.486
2001 Columbus	AAA NYY	1	5	0	0	0	0	0	0	0	0	0	2	0	0	0	0	0	—	0	.000	.000	.000
St. Lucie	A+ NYM	25	90	25	3	1	4	42	10	11	4	0	22	0	0	1	0	0	.00	2	.278	.305	.467
Binghamton	AA NYM	8	31	10	2	0	1	15	2	7	0	0	8	0	0	1	0	0	—	0	.323	.313	.484
Norfolk	AAA NYM	36	110	21	4	0	5	40	13	16	4	1	26	1	1	1	0	1	.00	2	.191	.224	.364
1997 New York	AL	2	4	0	0	0	0	0	0	0	0	0	3	0	0	0	0	0	—	0	.000	.000	.000
1998 New York	AL	1	4	1	0	0	0	1	1	0	0	0	1	0	0	0	0	0	—	0	.250	.250	.250
1999 New York	AL	2	0	0	0	0	0	0	0	0	0	0	0	0	0	0	0	0	—	0	—	—	—
Baltimore	AL	41	86	19	4	0	1	26	12	5	2	0	27	0	2	1	0	2	.00	1	.221	.236	.302
11 Min. YEARS		871	3048	770	142	19	117	1301	367	476	217	12	781	14	13	24	22	14	.61	82	.253	.303	.427
3 Maj. YEARS		46	94	20	4	0	1	27	13	5	2	0	31	0	2	1	0	2	.00	1	.213	.227	.287

Chone Figgins

Bats: Both **Throws:** Right **Pos:** 2B-111; SS-13; 3B-1; DH-1; PH-1   **Ht:** 5'8" **Wt:** 155 **Born:** 1/22/78 **Age:** 24

Year Team	Lg Org	G	AB	H	2B	3B	HR	TB	R	RBI	TBB	IBB	SO	HBP	SH	SF	SB	CS	SB%	GDP	Avg	OBP	SLG
		BATTING															**BASERUNNING**				**PERCENTAGES**		
1997 Rockies	R Col	53	210	59	5	6	1	79	41	23	34	0	50	3	0	2	30	12	.71	2	.281	.386	.376
1998 Portland	A- Col	69	269	76	9	3	1	94	41	26	24	0	56	2	6	1	25	4	.86	3	.283	.345	.349
1999 Salem	A+ Col	123	444	106	12	3	0	124	65	22	41	0	86	3	14	2	27	13	.68	5	.239	.306	.279
2000 Salem	A+ Col	134	522	145	26	4	3	208	92	48	67	0	107	1	6	5	37	19	.66	7	.278	.358	.398
2001 Carolina	AA Col	86	332	73	14	5	2	103	41	25	40	2	73	2	6	2	27	8	.77	0	.220	.306	.310
Arkansas	AA Ana	39	138	37	12	2	0	53	21	12	14	0	26	0	3	3	7	2	.78	0	.268	.329	.384
5 Min. YEARS		504	1915	496	78	33	7	661	301	156	220	2	398	11	35	15	153	58	.73	17	.259	.336	.345

Carlos Figueroa

Pitches: Left **Bats:** Left **Pos:** RP-47   **Ht:** 6'1" **Wt:** 190 **Born:** 10/5/79 **Age:** 22

Year Team	Lg Org	G	GS	CG	GF	IP	BFP	H	R	ER	HR	SH	SF	HB	TBB	IBB	SO	WP	Bk	W	L	Pct.	ShO	Sv	ERA
		HOW MUCH HE PITCHED						**WHAT HE GAVE UP**												**THE RESULTS**					
1997 Rangers	R Tex	5	1	0	0	5.2	27	7	2	2	1	0	0	0	2	0	9	0	1	0	0	—	0	0	3.18
1998 Rangers	R Tex	19	0	0	8	40.1	162	34	17	16	4	0	0	1	11	0	39	3	2	6	1	.857	0	1	3.57
1999 Rangers	R Tex	6	0	0	2	10.2	39	5	1	1	0	0	0	1	3	0	17	0	4	4	0	1.000	0	0	0.84
Savannah	A Tex	10	0	0	2	20	97	19	14	13	2	0	0	3	16	0	30	5	1	0	0	—	0	1	5.85

Year Team	Lg Org	G	GS	CG	GF	IP	BFP	H	R	ER	HR	SH	SF	HB	TBB	IBB	SO	WP	Bk	W	L	Pct.	ShO	Sv	ERA
						HOW MUCH HE PITCHED						**WHAT HE GAVE UP**									**THE RESULTS**				
2000 Charlotte	A+ Tex	33	1	0	7	58	270	53	41	37	0	2	1	5	44	1	51	6	1	6	3	.667	0	1	5.74
2001 Tulsa	AA Tex	3	0	0	2	4.1	19	3	1	1	0	0	0	1	3	0	2	2	0	0	1	.000	0	0	2.08
Charlotte	A+ Tex	44	0	0	17	69	296	50	27	19	1	11	7	3	39	6	51	7	2	2	4	.333	0	3	2.48
5 Min. YEARS		120	2	0	39	208	910	171	103	89	8	14	8	14	118	7	199	23	11	18	9	.667	0	7	3.85

Franky Figueroa

Bats: Right **Throws:** Right **Pos:** 1B-120; DH-13; 3B-5 **Ht:** 6'6" **Wt:** 239 **Born:** 2/9/77 **Age:** 25

Year Team	Lg Org	G	AB	H	2B	3B	HR	TB	R	RBI	TBB	IBB	SO	HBP	SH	SF	SB	CS	SB%	GDP	Avg	OBP	SLG
							BATTING											**BASERUNNING**			**PERCENTAGES**		
1996 Orioles	R Bal	43	150	51	8	1	0	61	22	23	8	0	25	3	0	2	3	0	1.00	7	.340	.380	.407
1997 Delmarva	A Bal	7	28	5	1	0	0	6	2	3	0	0	8	0	0	0	0	0	—	2	.179	.179	.214
Bluefield	R+ Bal	63	243	65	14	1	8	105	32	41	14	0	70	2	0	1	4	2	.67	3	.267	.312	.432
1998 Delmarva	A Bal	137	515	142	29	4	13	218	61	94	14	1	113	14	0	11	8	0	1.00	15	.276	.307	.423
Frederick	A+ Bal	4	19	3	1	0	1	7	2	3	0	0	4	1	0	0	0	0	—	0	.158	.200	.368
1999 Frederick	A+ Bal	132	527	132	20	3	17	209	59	78	32	0	138	7	0	5	2	3	.40	21	.250	.299	.397
2000 Frederick	A+ Bal	126	490	125	23	0	17	199	58	87	22	3	109	6	1	7	1	3	.25	15	.255	.291	.406
2001 Bowie	AA Bal	137	534	160	32	0	14	234	61	72	21	2	138	2	1	4	0	4	.00	23	.300	.326	.438
6 Min. YEARS		649	2506	683	128	9	70	1039	297	401	111	6	605	35	2	30	18	12	.60	86	.273	.309	.415

Juan Figueroa

Pitches: Right **Bats:** Right **Pos:** SP-24; RP-1 **Ht:** 6'3" **Wt:** 150 **Born:** 6/24/79 **Age:** 23

Year Team	Lg Org	G	GS	CG	GF	IP	BFP	H	R	ER	HR	SH	SF	HB	TBB	IBB	SO	WP	Bk	W	L	Pct.	ShO	Sv	ERA
						HOW MUCH HE PITCHED						**WHAT HE GAVE UP**									**THE RESULTS**				
1997 White Sox	R CWS	11	10	0	0	64.1	274	66	31	24	4	0	3	7	14	0	43	1	0	1	4	.200	0	0	3.36
1998 Bristol	R+ CWS	13	13	2	0	80	353	87	58	45	14	2	3	4	22	0	102	4	1	5	5	.500	1	0	5.06
1999 Burlington	A CWS	17	16	2	0	115.1	491	100	51	40	8	0	6	5	44	0	139	4	1	8	4	.667	0	0	3.12
Winston-Sal	A+ CWS	10	10	1	0	56.1	252	67	47	33	2	3	2	2	19	0	50	3	0	2	5	.286	0	0	5.27
2000 Winston-Sal	A+ CWS	9	7	1	2	52	224	58	30	27	3	3	1	0	8	0	65	3	0	4	4	.500	0	0	4.67
Birmingham	AA CWS	10	9	0	0	55.2	241	57	25	21	4	1	3	6	24	0	42	3	1	2	3	.400	0	0	3.40
Bowie	AA Bal	7	7	0	0	39	183	46	24	24	3	2	2	2	21	2	42	3	0	2	2	.500	0	0	5.54
2001 Bowie	AA Bal	18	17	1	1	99.1	443	126	63	54	14	6	8	1	26	4	52	2	0	3	10	.231	0	0	4.89
Frederick	A+ Bal	7	7	0	0	39.2	158	37	8	7	0	0	2	0	3	0	26	0	0	5	0	1.000	0	0	1.59
5 Min. YEARS		102	96	7	3	601.2	2619	644	337	275	52	17	30	30	181	6	561	23	3	32	37	.464	1	0	4.11

Luis Figueroa

Bats: Right **Throws:** Right **Pos:** 3B-39; 2B-19; DH-12; SS-5 **Ht:** 6'0" **Wt:** 175 **Born:** 3/2/77 **Age:** 25

Year Team	Lg Org	G	AB	H	2B	3B	HR	TB	R	RBI	TBB	IBB	SO	HBP	SH	SF	SB	CS	SB%	GDP	Avg	OBP	SLG
							BATTING											**BASERUNNING**			**PERCENTAGES**		
1995 Mariners	R Sea	32	120	35	2	0	0	37	14	11	12	0	9	2	0	1	1	2	.33	4	.292	.363	.308
1996 Lancaster	A+ Sea	9	31	12	4	1	0	18	5	6	2	0	6	0	0	0	0	1	.00	0	.387	.424	.581
Everett	A- Sea	4	13	6	1	1	0	9	4	3	2	0	1	0	0	0	0	0	—	1	.462	.533	.692
Wisconsin	A Sea	36	137	40	9	0	2	55	18	19	6	0	14	3	1	2	1	1	.50	6	.292	.331	.401
1997 Wisconsin	A Sea	125	482	138	27	2	3	178	56	60	33	1	21	6	2	1	3	3	.50	18	.286	.339	.369
1998 Wisconsin	A Sea	96	306	89	18	0	1	110	41	48	42	5	18	8	0	1	7	1	.88	13	.291	.389	.359
1999 Lancaster	A+ Sea	39	146	52	8	1	4	74	21	20	18	2	8	2	0	2	2	2	.50	10	.356	.429	.507
Mariners	R Sea	3	10	5	1	0	0	6	2	1	0	0	0	0	0	0	0	0	—	1	.500	.500	.600
2000 New Haven	AA Sea	117	427	116	24	1	1	145	49	37	34	1	39	2	2	2	0	1	.00	14	.272	.327	.340
2001 San Antonio	AA Sea	18	64	9	2	0	0	11	5	4	1	0	6	1	0	0	1	0	1.00	2	.141	.167	.172
San Berndno	A+ Sea	32	124	40	10	1	0	52	24	16	17	0	15	2	0	1	2	0	1.00	1	.323	.410	.419
Tacoma	AAA Sea	24	76	26	4	0	0	30	9	9	3	0	8	0	0	1	0	1	.00	4	.342	.363	.395
7 Min. YEARS		535	1936	568	110	7	11	725	248	234	170	9	145	26	5	11	17	12	.59	74	.293	.357	.374

Curt Fiore

Bats: Right **Throws:** Right **Pos:** 3B-69; OF-26; DH-9; 2B-7; PH-7; 1B-2; P-1 **Ht:** 6'2" **Wt:** 195 **Born:** 7/28/77 **Age:** 24

Year Team	Lg Org	G	AB	H	2B	3B	HR	TB	R	RBI	TBB	IBB	SO	HBP	SH	SF	SB	CS	SB%	GDP	Avg	OBP	SLG
							BATTING											**BASERUNNING**			**PERCENTAGES**		
1999 Danville	R+ Atl	53	198	66	13	0	3	88	35	24	22	1	39	7	0	1	0	5	.00	4	.333	.417	.444
2000 Macon	A Atl	108	360	102	17	1	8	145	64	47	42	0	56	14	2	2	8	1	.89	11	.283	.378	.403
2001 Greenville	AA Atl	13	39	6	2	0	0	8	2	0	0	0	13	2	1	0	0	0	—	1	.154	.199	.205
Myrtle Bch	A+ Atl	100	329	93	20	2	6	135	56	42	47	2	69	19	3	5	5	1	.83	13	.283	.398	.410
3 Min. YEARS		274	926	267	52	3	17	376	157	113	111	3	177	42	6	8	13	7	.65	29	.288	.386	.406

Mark Fischer

Bats: Right **Throws:** Right **Pos:** OF-120; DH-5; PR-2; PH-1 **Ht:** 6'1" **Wt:** 205 **Born:** 4/15/76 **Age:** 26

Year Team	Lg Org	G	AB	H	2B	3B	HR	TB	R	RBI	TBB	IBB	SO	HBP	SH	SF	SB	CS	SB%	GDP	Avg	OBP	SLG
							BATTING											**BASERUNNING**			**PERCENTAGES**		
1997 Lowell	A- Bos	48	179	59	15	1	5	91	25	25	15	0	38	3	0	1	13	2	.87	4	.330	.389	.508
1998 Red Sox	R Bos	7	26	5	0	0	2	11	5	5	4	1	8	0	0	0	2	0	1.00	0	.192	.300	.423
Michigan	A Bos	102	379	96	19	2	8	143	52	50	36	2	93	1	0	3	9	6	.60	5	.253	.317	.377
1999 Sarasota	A+ Bos	106	359	91	14	3	5	126	42	40	28	0	85	1	4	1	11	6	.65	11	.253	.308	.351
2000 Sarasota	A+ Bos	51	180	54	15	0	9	96	31	30	21	1	45	1	0	2	5	2	.71	1	.300	.373	.533
Trenton	AA Bos	34	108	22	6	1	1	33	15	15	12	0	39	1	0	4	1	1	.50	1	.204	.280	.306
2001 Trenton	AA Bos	127	463	103	22	2	11	162	48	55	25	1	148	0	1	4	3	1	.75	9	.222	.260	.350
5 Min. YEARS		475	1694	430	91	9	41	662	218	220	141	5	456	7	5	15	44	18	.71	31	.254	.311	.391

Mike Fischer

Pitches: Right Bats: Right Pos: RP-34; SP-4   Ht: 6'4" Wt: 200 Born: 12/10/76 Age: 25

Year Team	Lg Org	G	GS	CG	GF	IP	BFP	H	R	ER	HR	SH	SF	HB	TBB	IBB	SO	WP	Bk	W	L	Pct.	ShO	Sv	ERA
1998 San Berndno	A+ LA	12	12	0	0	51.1	229	57	35	26	6	0	2	1	15	0	38	2	3	1	3	.250	0	0	4.56
1999 San Berndno	A+ LA	3	3	0	0	11	47	13	6	6	1	0	0	0	4	0	7	1	0	1	0	1.000	0	0	4.91
2000 San Berndno	A+ LA	11	10	0	0	45.1	198	53	24	20	4	0	1	2	17	0	33	3	0	2	2	.500	0	0	3.97
2001 Vero Beach	A+ LA	26	0	0	10	45.1	183	31	8	8	2	0	0	2	18	0	44	10	0	1	0	1.000	0	2	1.59
Jacksnville	AA LA	12	4	0	1	28	124	30	18	16	7	2	0	4	8	1	28	1	0	1	0	1.000	0	0	5.14
4 Min. YEARS		64	29	0	11	181	781	184	91	76	20	2	3	9	62	1	150	17	3	6	5	.545	0	2	3.78

Pete Fisher

Pitches: Right Bats: Right Pos: RP-23; SP-17   Ht: 6'3" Wt: 215 Born: 7/7/77 Age: 24

Year Team	Lg Org	G	GS	CG	GF	IP	BFP	H	R	ER	HR	SH	SF	HB	TBB	IBB	SO	WP	Bk	W	L	Pct.	ShO	Sv	ERA
1998 Elizabethtn	R+ Min	12	12	0	0	66.1	290	82	43	38	9	5	1	3	9	0	57	2	2	5	3	.625	0	0	5.16
1999 Fort Myers	A+ Min	25	24	0	0	146.2	639	171	74	61	10	3	6	9	38	0	91	14	3	5	10	.333	0	0	3.74
2000 New Britain	AA Min	15	12	0	2	60.2	286	89	55	45	4	1	3	5	14	0	36	2	1	2	5	.286	0	0	6.68
Fort Myers	A+ Min	14	14	2	0	88.2	370	75	34	31	9	3	0	7	37	0	67	2	0	8	3	.727	0	0	3.15
2001 Fort Myers	A+ Min	31	9	0	8	91.2	402	91	48	34	5	4	2	5	32	5	77	7	0	4	5	.444	0	2	3.34
New Britain	AA Min	9	8	0	0	52.1	219	52	20	11	3	1	0	4	11	0	39	1	0	5	2	.714	0	0	1.89
4 Min. YEARS		106	79	2	10	506.1	2206	560	274	220	40	17	12	33	141	5	367	28	6	29	28	.509	0	2	3.91

Steve Fitch

Pitches: Right Bats: Right Pos: SP-16; RP-2   Ht: 6'1" Wt: 180 Born: 2/15/78 Age: 24

Year Team	Lg Org	G	GS	CG	GF	IP	BFP	H	R	ER	HR	SH	SF	HB	TBB	IBB	SO	WP	Bk	W	L	Pct.	ShO	Sv	ERA
2000 Mahoning Vy	A- Cle	12	10	0	0	61	255	68	30	29	3	4	1	0	12	0	38	1	0	5	1	.833	0	0	4.28
2001 Columbus	A Cle	4	4	0	0	27	106	23	7	3	1	0	0	0	3	0	16	2	0	2	0	1.000	0	0	1.00
Akron	AA Cle	1	1	0	0	2.1	14	4	4	2	1	0	0	0	1	0	2	0	0	0	0	—	0	0	7.71
Kinston	A+ Cle	13	11	0	1	65	290	77	36	30	3	2	2	2	22	0	45	2	1	4	4	.500	0	0	4.15
2 Min. YEARS		30	26	0	1	155.1	665	172	77	64	8	6	3	3	38	0	101	5	1	11	5	.688	0	0	3.71

Brian Fitzgerald

Pitches: Left Bats: Left Pos: RP-49; SP-1   Ht: 5'11" Wt: 175 Born: 12/26/74 Age: 27

Year Team	Lg Org	G	GS	CG	GF	IP	BFP	H	R	ER	HR	SH	SF	HB	TBB	IBB	SO	WP	Bk	W	L	Pct.	ShO	Sv	ERA
1996 Everett	A- Sea	21	1	0	8	39	181	56	36	28	2	1	1	0	8	0	31	1	2	1	2	.333	0	1	6.46
1997 Wisconsin	A Sea	41	0	0	28	69.2	263	63	16	15	4	1	0	0	19	2	68	2	1	3	1	.750	0	10	1.94
1998 Lancaster	A+ Sea	41	0	0	18	70.2	315	79	39	33	5	2	1	2	24	2	48	1	0	1	2	.333	0	1	4.20
Orlando	AA Sea	2	0	0	1	4.1	18	5	1	1	0	0	0	0	1	0	4	0	0	0	0	—	0	1	2.08
1999 Lancaster	A+ Sea	6	6	0	0	34	153	50	35	27	3	0	2	0	4	0	23	1	0	1	3	.250	0	0	7.15
New Haven	AA Sea	29	1	0	13	54	228	58	24	23	2	2	2	1	18	0	37	0	0	2	2	.500	0	3	3.83
2000 New Haven	AA Sea	44	2	0	18	79	331	84	33	31	7	1	1	3	19	0	62	1	1	6	4	.600	0	4	3.53
2001 San Antonio	AA Sea	30	0	0	10	41.1	174	33	10	9	0	3	0	3	16	4	26	1	0	4	1	.800	0	1	1.96
Tacoma	AAA Sea	20	1	0	9	34.2	153	40	19	15	5	0	0	0	11	0	26	2	0	2	1	.667	0	0	3.89
6 Min. YEARS		234	11	0	105	426.2	1834	468	213	182	28	10	7	9	120	8	325	9	4	20	16	.556	0	21	3.84

Jason Fitzgerald

Bats: Left Throws: Left Pos: OF-55; DH-5; PH-2   Ht: 6'1" Wt: 190 Born: 9/16/75 Age: 26

Year Team	Lg Org	G	AB	H	2B	3B	HR	TB	R	RBI	TBB	IBB	SO	HBP	SH	SF	SB	CS	SB%	GDP	Avg	OBP	SLG
1997 Watertown	A- Cle	34	112	22	8	0	1	33	11	13	17	0	31	0	1	2	2	0	1.00	4	.196	.298	.295
1998 Columbus	A Cle	132	490	134	28	3	16	216	60	80	38	1	117	4	1	9	21	6	.78	1	.273	.325	.441
1999 Kinston	A+ Cle	82	310	74	17	3	4	109	26	39	22	1	77	1	1	3	15	7	.68	5	.239	.289	.352
2000 Kinston	A+ Cle	82	318	80	16	3	4	114	42	44	29	2	55	2	1	4	21	4	.84	3	.252	.314	.358
Akron	AA Cle	56	208	58	8	4	4	86	27	30	23	1	38	1	1	2	7	6	.54	0	.279	.350	.413
2001 Akron	AA Cle	61	239	65	12	1	4	91	23	19	10	1	38	0	1	1	10	2	.83	4	.272	.300	.381
5 Min. YEARS		447	1677	433	89	14	33	649	189	225	139	6	356	8	6	21	76	25	.75	17	.258	.314	.387

Kevin Flanagan

Bats: Right Throws: Right Pos: PH-2; DH-1   Ht: 6'0" Wt: 195 Born: 12/23/76 Age: 25

Year Team	Lg Org	G	AB	H	2B	3B	HR	TB	R	RBI	TBB	IBB	SO	HBP	SH	SF	SB	CS	SB%	GDP	Avg	OBP	SLG
2000 Staten Ilnd	A- NYY	5	3	0	0	0	0	0	0	0	0	0	2	0	0	0	0	0	—	0	.000	.000	.000
2001 Columbus	AAA NYY	3	5	0	0	0	0	0	1	0	2	0	2	0	0	0	0	0	—	0	.000	.286	.000
2 Min. YEARS		8	8	0	0	0	0	0	1	0	2	0	4	0	0	0	0	0	—	0	.000	.200	.000

Ryan Fleming

Bats: Left Throws: Left Pos: OF-97; PH-8; PR-4; DH-3   Ht: 5'11" Wt: 180 Born: 2/11/76 Age: 26

Year Team	Lg Org	G	AB	H	2B	3B	HR	TB	R	RBI	TBB	IBB	SO	HBP	SH	SF	SB	CS	SB%	GDP	Avg	OBP	SLG
1998 Medcine Hat	R+ Tor	70	255	78	20	1	2	106	46	41	37	0	29	4	2	4	17	3	.85	0	.306	.397	.416
1999 Dunedin	A+ Tor	51	123	28	7	1	0	37	17	9	10	1	19	4	3	1	4	3	.57	3	.228	.304	.301
Hagerstown	A Tor	61	227	76	9	2	4	101	34	35	23	1	26	0	2	4	7	6	.54	4	.335	.390	.445
2000 Syracuse	AAA Tor	3	11	2	0	0	0	2	1	1	0	0	0	0	0	0	0	0	—	0	.182	.182	.182
Dunedin	A+ Tor	90	309	94	18	1	4	126	42	32	28	1	38	1	6	5	6	8	.43	1	.304	.359	.408

Year Team	Lg Org	G	AB	H	2B	3B	HR	TB	R	RBI	TBB	IBB	SO	HBP	SH	SF	SB	CS	SB%	GDP	Avg	OBP	SLG
Tennessee	AA Tor	37	105	18	4	0	2	28	16	9	20	0	17	1	3	0	2	1	.67	1	.171	.310	.267
2001 Tennessee	AA Tor	106	349	97	19	4	10	154	57	35	38	5	49	2	4	5	6	6	.50	6	.278	.348	.441
4 Min. YEARS		418	1379	393	77	9	22	554	231	162	156	8	178	12	20	19	42	27	.61	15	.285	.358	.402

Travis Fleming

Pitches: Right Bats: Right Pos: RP-47   Ht: 6'4" Wt: 190 Born: 9/26/76 Age: 25

		HOW MUCH HE PITCHED						WHAT HE GAVE UP												THE RESULTS					
Year Team	Lg Org	G	GS	CG	GF	IP	BFP	H	R	ER	HR	SH	SF	HB	TBB	IBB	SO	WP	Bk	W	L	Pct.	ShO	Sv	ERA
1999 Orioles	R Bal	4	3	0	0	16	62	12	2	2	0	0	0	0	2	0	21	1	1	1	1	.500	0	0	1.13
Delmarva	A Bal	14	1	0	4	38.1	159	36	24	20	4	1	1	1	14	0	33	3	0	2	1	.667	0	1	4.70
2000 Delmarva	A Bal	53	0	0	32	72	308	74	32	31	7	0	0	2	21	3	85	2	0	7	2	.778	0	11	3.88
2001 Bowie	AA Bal	3	0	0	2	4	30	15	11	4	2	0	0	2	0	0	2	0	0	0	0	—	0	0	9.00
Frederick	A+ Bal	44	0	0	40	57.1	249	53	18	16	2	1	2	6	20	1	59	2	0	1	3	.250	0	23	2.51
3 Min. YEARS		118	4	0	78	187.2	808	190	87	73	15	2	3	11	57	4	200	8	1	11	7	.611	0	35	3.50

Adam Flohr

Pitches: Left Bats: Left Pos: RP-25; SP-14   Ht: 6'2" Wt: 185 Born: 3/29/77 Age: 25

		HOW MUCH HE PITCHED						WHAT HE GAVE UP												THE RESULTS					
Year Team	Lg Org	G	GS	CG	GF	IP	BFP	H	R	ER	HR	SH	SF	HB	TBB	IBB	SO	WP	Bk	W	L	Pct.	ShO	Sv	ERA
1998 Hudson Val	A- TB	15	14	0	1	79.1	316	69	28	23	3	1	1	4	11	0	70	3	0	5	1	.833	0	0	2.61
1999 St. Pete	A+ TB	31	18	0	2	135	587	164	78	57	10	6	1	9	30	0	64	9	2	6	6	.500	1	0	3.80
2000 St. Pete	A+ TB	27	27	2	0	173.1	729	173	88	68	7	5	2	9	51	0	134	10	0	6	11	.353	1	0	3.53
2001 Fort Myers	A+ Min	21	2	0	5	40.2	177	47	31	23	5	1	4	2	9	1	40	0	2	1	2	.333	0	1	5.09
New Britain	AA Min	18	12	0	1	74	321	94	43	40	8	3	0	3	15	0	49	4	0	3	5	.375	0	0	4.86
4 Min. YEARS		112	73	2	9	502.1	2130	547	268	211	33	16	8	27	116	1	357	26	4	21	25	.457	1	1	3.78

Javier Flores

Bats: Right Throws: Right Pos: C-33; DH-13; 1B-5   Ht: 6'0" Wt: 185 Born: 12/20/75 Age: 26

		BATTING												BASERUNNING				PERCENTAGES		
Year Team	Lg Org	G	AB	H	2B	3B	HR	TB	R	RBI	TBB	IBB	SO	HBP	SH	SF	SB	CS	SB%	GDP	Avg	OBP	SLG
1997 Sou Oregon	A- Oak	45	160	53	11	3	1	73	25	25	17	0	22	9	1	3	2	1	.67	2	.331	.418	.456
1998 Visalia	A+ Oak	49	163	41	7	1	2	56	19	17	12	0	32	8	3	1	0	0	—	4	.252	.332	.344
1999 Visalia	A+ Oak	103	362	107	22	1	5	146	48	63	27	0	59	9	2	6	6	3	.67	8	.296	.354	.403
2000 Midland	AA Oak	12	33	8	4	0	0	12	3	4	5	0	5	0	1	0	0	0	—	0	.242	.342	.364
Visalia	A+ Oak	77	257	66	9	1	4	89	35	41	33	1	34	4	1	4	2	3	.40	5	.257	.346	.346
2001 Tulsa	AA Tex	32	116	28	4	1	0	34	8	11	9	0	10	2	0	1	2	2	.50	6	.241	.305	.293
Charlotte	A+ Tex	19	52	9	3	0	0	12	3	2	7	0	3	2	1	0	0	0	—	2	.173	.295	.231
5 Min. YEARS		337	1143	312	60	7	12	422	141	163	110	1	165	34	9	15	12	9	.57	27	.273	.350	.369

Jose Flores

Bats: Right Throws: Right Pos: SS-35; 3B-26; 2B-23; PH-11; OF-7; 1B-4   Ht: 5'11" Wt: 180 Born: 6/28/73 Age: 29

		BATTING												BASERUNNING				PERCENTAGES		
Year Team	Lg Org	G	AB	H	2B	3B	HR	TB	R	RBI	TBB	IBB	SO	HBP	SH	SF	SB	CS	SB%	GDP	Avg	OBP	SLG
1994 Batavia	A- Phi	68	229	58	7	3	0	71	41	16	41	0	31	6	2	2	23	8	.74	3	.253	.378	.310
1995 Clearwater	A+ Phi	49	185	41	4	3	1	54	25	19	15	0	27	4	7	1	12	5	.71	4	.222	.293	.292
Piedmont	A Phi	61	186	49	7	0	0	56	22	19	24	0	29	3	5	4	11	8	.58	6	.263	.350	.301
1996 Scranton-WB	AAA Phi	26	70	18	1	0	0	19	10	3	12	0	10	2	1	1	0	1	.00	2	.257	.376	.271
Clearwater	A+ Phi	84	281	64	6	5	1	83	39	39	34	0	42	3	5	1	15	2	.88	6	.228	.317	.295
1997 Scranton-WB	AAA Phi	71	204	51	14	1	1	70	32	18	28	1	51	2	5	2	3	1	.75	2	.250	.343	.343
1998 Scranton-WB	AAA Phi	98	345	104	18	2	6	144	53	34	49	1	45	2	7	2	12	6	.67	7	.301	.389	.417
1999 Scranton-WB	AAA Phi	64	228	56	6	2	0	66	35	18	37	1	43	7	4	0	13	3	.81	1	.246	.346	.289
Tacoma	AAA Sea	42	143	44	6	1	3	61	33	15	37	1	23	5	2	2	4	3	.57	2	.308	.460	.427
2000 New Haven	AA Sea	12	38	7	3	0	0	10	5	1	7	0	5	2	1	0	0	0	—	0	.184	.340	.263
Tacoma	AAA Sea	91	328	93	14	4	3	124	53	30	53	0	44	5	1	3	19	7	.73	6	.284	.388	.378
2001 Colo Spngs	AAA Col	100	316	93	21	5	2	130	61	36	48	1	57	3	4	1	8	2	.80	1	.294	.391	.411
8 Min. YEARS		766	2553	678	107	26	17	888	409	248	385	5	407	44	44	19	120	46	.72	40	.266	.369	.348

Neomar Flores

Pitches: Right Bats: Right Pos: RP-9; SP-5   Ht: 6'2" Wt: 180 Born: 3/12/82 Age: 20

		HOW MUCH HE PITCHED						WHAT HE GAVE UP												THE RESULTS					
Year Team	Lg Org	G	GS	CG	GF	IP	BFP	H	R	ER	HR	SH	SF	HB	TBB	IBB	SO	WP	Bk	W	L	Pct.	ShO	Sv	ERA
2000 Medcine Hat	R+ Tor	1	1	0	0	3	14	6	4	4	1	0	0	0	1	0	2	0	0	0	0	—	0	0	12.00
2001 Auburn	A- Tor	12	4	0	2	54.1	232	45	33	29	6	0	3	5	19	0	51	3	0	3	1	.750	0	0	4.80
Syracuse	AAA Tor	2	1	0	0	7	27	4	3	3	1	0	0	0	2	0	2	0	0	0	0	—	0	0	3.86
2 Min. YEARS		15	6	0	2	64.1	273	55	40	36	8	0	3	5	22	0	55	3	0	3	1	.750	0	0	5.04

Randy Flores

Pitches: Left Bats: Left Pos: SP-25; RP-3   Ht: 6'0" Wt: 180 Born: 7/31/75 Age: 26

		HOW MUCH HE PITCHED						WHAT HE GAVE UP												THE RESULTS					
Year Team	Lg Org	G	GS	CG	GF	IP	BFP	H	R	ER	HR	SH	SF	HB	TBB	IBB	SO	WP	Bk	W	L	Pct.	ShO	Sv	ERA
1997 Oneonta	A- NYY	13	13	2	0	74.2	308	64	32	27	3	0	1	4	23	1	70	5	1	4	4	.500	1	0	3.25
1998 Tampa	A+ NYY	5	5	0	0	23.2	115	28	23	17	2	2	2	1	16	2	15	0	4	1	2	.333	0	0	6.46
Greensboro	A NYY	21	20	2	0	130.2	535	119	48	38	6	2	3	7	33	0	139	2	4	12	7	.632	1	0	2.62
1999 Norwich	AA NYY	4	4	0	0	25	120	32	20	18	0	2	0	1	11	1	19	1	1	0	1	.000	0	0	6.48
Tampa	A+ NYY	21	20	1	1	135	555	118	56	43	4	4	7		38	0	99	5	0	11	4	.733	1	0	2.87

Year Team	Lg Org	G	GS	CG	GF	IP	BFP	H	R	ER	HR	SH	SF	HB	TBB	IBB	SO	WP	Bk	W	L	Pct.	ShO	Sv	ERA
2000 Norwich	AA NYY	31	20	3	3	141	601	138	64	46	8	4	2	5	58	1	97	8	1	10	9	.526	0	1	2.94
Columbus	AAA NYY	4	4	0	0	23.1	117	43	21	19	3	0	0	0	7	0	16	1	1	1	2	.333	0	0	7.33
2001 Columbus	AAA NYY	3	0	0	1	5.2	23	5	4	3	2	0	0	0	2	0	4	1	0	0	1	.000	0	0	4.76
Norwich	AA NYY	25	25	3	0	158.2	677	156	64	49	13	5	3	1	63	0	115	3	3	14	6	.700	2	0	2.78
5 Min. YEARS		127	111	11	5	717.2	3051	703	332	260	41	19	15	26	251	5	574	26	15	53	36	.596	5	1	3.26

Pat Flury

Pitches: Right **Bats:** Right **Pos:** RP-48 ···· **Ht:** 6'2" **Wt:** 215 **Born:** 3/14/73 **Age:** 29

Year Team	Lg Org	G	GS	CG	GF	IP	BFP	H	R	ER	HR	SH	SF	HB	TBB	IBB	SO	WP	Bk	W	L	Pct.	ShO	Sv	ERA
1993 Eugene	A- KC	27	0	0	19	33	144	25	15	12	0	2	2	1	22	1	34	4	0	2	2	.500	0	7	3.27
1994 Rockford	A KC	34	0	0	18	55	254	61	27	24	3	2	2	5	33	2	41	3	2	1	3	.250	0	2	3.93
1995 Wilmington	A+ KC	15	0	0	6	22	89	18	6	6	2	0	1	1	9	1	14	1	1	1	0	1.000	0	1	2.45
Springfield	A KC	34	0	0	19	54.1	246	65	32	26	5	4	1	1	24	0	35	2	0	2	6	.250	0	1	4.31
1996 Wilmington	A+ KC	45	0	0	19	84.1	339	66	22	18	2	2	1	0	29	4	67	9	0	7	2	.778	0	5	1.92
1997 Wichita	AA KC	42	0	0	19	48	215	47	26	19	4	2	3	4	18	3	47	1	0	8	3	.727	0	5	3.56
Omaha	AAA KC	18	0	0	7	26.2	124	29	18	18	5	2	0	2	16	2	24	1	0	1	0	1.000	0	0	6.08
1998 Wichita	AA KC	8	0	0	2	11.2	59	14	11	7	0	1	0	3	7	0	13	1	0	1	1	.500	0	1	5.40
Trenton	AA Bos	26	0	0	24	30.2	122	24	6	6	2	0	0	0	11	1	37	3	0	0	0	—	0	16	1.76
Pawtucket	AAA Bos	17	0	0	5	22.1	100	23	15	14	3	1	0	0	16	0	22	4	0	0	0	—	0	0	5.64
1999 Chattanooga	AA Cin	43	0	0	21	53.1	221	36	20	17	2	5	0	1	31	0	69	4	1	1	1	.500	0	15	2.87
Indianapolis	AAA Cin	23	0	0	14	23	115	27	18	18	4	0	1	1	20	0	20	6	0	1	1	.500	0	6	7.04
2000 Calgary	AAA Fla	12	0	0	4	19.1	100	28	18	17	5	2	0	1	14	0	15	6	0	1	0	1.000	0	1	7.91
Ottawa	AAA Mon	40	0	0	25	57	232	40	10	9	0	2	2	3	26	1	46	2	1	4	3	.571	0	5	1.42
2001 Ottawa	AAA Mon	10	0	0	5	11.2	49	8	6	6	3	0	1	1	8	0	9	1	0	1	0	.000	0	0	4.63
Norwich	AA NYY	4	0	0	1	5.2	21	2	1	1	1	0	0	0	2	0	9	0	0	1	0	1.000	0	1	1.59
Columbus	AAA NYY	34	0	0	19	47.1	193	31	13	13	2	3	2	1	19	1	66	1	0	3	2	.600	0	3	2.47
9 Min. YEARS		432	0	0	227	605.1	2623	544	264	231	43	28	14	25	305	16	568	49	5	34	25	.576	0	67	3.43

Steve Foley

Bats: Right **Throws:** Right **Pos:** OF-91; PR-6; DH-1 ···· **Ht:** 5'9" **Wt:** 200 **Born:** 4/6/75 **Age:** 27

Year Team	Lg Org	G	AB	H	2B	3B	HR	TB	R	RBI	TBB	IBB	SO	HBP	SH	SF	SB	CS	SB%	GDP	Avg	OBP	SLG
2000 Schaumburg	IND —	71	284	88	14	2	9	133	42	51	15	1	33	7	0	1	12	4	.75	4	.310	.358	.468
2001 Schaumburg	IND —	28	120	35	8	0	5	58	17	18	6	0	20	1	0	2	5	1	.83	3	.292	.326	.483
San Antonio	AA Sea	30	87	20	5	1	0	27	9	10	6	1	14	2	2	1	4	1	.80	1	.230	.292	.310
San Berndno	A+ Sea	34	127	32	4	1	1	41	20	9	10	0	25	7	3	3	2	0	1.00	0	.252	.333	.323
2 Min. YEARS		163	618	175	31	4	15	259	88	88	37	2	92	17	5	7	23	6	.79	8	.283	.337	.419

Chad Fonville

Bats: Both **Throws:** Right **Pos:** 2B-65; OF-3; SS-2; PH-2; PR-1 ···· **Ht:** 5'6" **Wt:** 155 **Born:** 3/5/71 **Age:** 31

Year Team	Lg Org	G	AB	H	2B	3B	HR	TB	R	RBI	TBB	IBB	SO	HBP	SH	SF	SB	CS	SB%	GDP	Avg	OBP	SLG
1992 Everett	A- SF	63	260	71	9	1	1	85	56	33	31	1	39	3	1	0	36	14	.72	2	.273	.357	.327
1993 Clinton	A SF	120	447	137	16	10	1	176	80	44	40	2	48	9	5	2	52	16	.76	0	.306	.373	.394
1994 San Jose	A+ SF	68	283	87	9	6	0	108	58	26	34	0	34	4	5	0	22	8	.73	5	.307	.389	.382
1996 Albuquerque	AAA LA	25	96	23	1	0	0	24	17	5	8	0	13	0	4	0	7	0	1.00	0	.240	.292	.250
1997 Albuquerque	AAA LA	102	371	81	5	2	0	90	49	22	30	0	39	3	3	2	23	10	.70	3	.218	.281	.243
1998 New Haven	AA Col	54	189	47	0	1	0	49	26	9	23	0	24	1	2	2	16	5	.76	7	.249	.330	.259
1999 Pawtucket	AAA Bos	74	257	65	3	2	1	75	31	14	20	0	31	2	4	0	6	4	.60	4	.253	.312	.292
2001 Nashua	IND —	55	200	68	6	0	0	74	36	16	35	2	23	5	6	1	13	3	.81	1	.340	.448	.370
Columbus	AAA NYY	16	58	13	3	1	0	18	9	7	4	1	13	1	0	0	1	1	.50	2	.224	.286	.310
1995 Montreal	NL	14	12	4	0	0	0	4	2	0	0	0	3	0	0	0	2	0	1.00	0	.333	.333	.333
Los Angeles	NL	88	308	85	6	1	0	93	41	16	23	1	39	1	6	0	20	5	.80	5	.276	.328	.302
1996 Los Angeles	NL	103	201	41	4	1	0	47	34	13	17	1	31	0	3	0	7	2	.78	1	.204	.266	.234
1997 Los Angeles	NL	9	14	2	0	0	0	2	1	1	2	0	3	0	0	0	1	0	1.00	0	.143	.250	.143
Chicago	AL	9	9	1	0	0	0	1	1	1	1	0	1	0	1	0	2	0	1.00	0	.111	.200	.111
1999 Boston	AL	3	2	0	0	0	0	0	1	0	2	0	0	0	0	0	0	1	.00	0	.000	.500	.000
8 Min. YEARS		577	2161	592	54	22	3	699	362	176	225	6	264	28	30	9	176	61	.74	24	.274	.349	.323
4 Maj. YEARS		226	546	133	10	2	0	147	80	31	45	2	77	1	10	0	30	10	.75	4	.244	.302	.269

Ben Ford

Pitches: Right **Bats:** Right **Pos:** SP-8 ···· **Ht:** 6'7" **Wt:** 225 **Born:** 8/15/75 **Age:** 26

Year Team	Lg Org	G	GS	CG	GF	IP	BFP	H	R	ER	HR	SH	SF	HB	TBB	IBB	SO	WP	Bk	W	L	Pct.	ShO	Sv	ERA
1994 Yankees	R NYY	18	0	0	11	34	143	27	13	9	0	0	0	6	8	0	31	3	0	2	2	.500	0	3	2.38
1995 Greensboro	A NYY	7	0	0	2	7	31	4	4	4	1	1	0	0	5	1	8	2	0	0	0	—	0	0	5.14
Oneonta	A- NYY	29	0	0	10	52	209	39	23	5	1	0	2	5	16	0	50	8	0	5	0	1.000	0	0	0.87
1996 Greensboro	A NYY	43	0	0	16	82.1	359	75	48	39	3	4	1	11	33	6	84	9	0	2	6	.250	0	2	4.26
1997 Tampa	A+ NYY	32	0	0	30	37.1	155	27	8	8	1	2	0	6	14	1	37	4	0	4	0	1.000	0	18	1.93
Norwich	AA NYY	28	0	0	14	42.2	183	35	28	20	1	1	2	3	19	1	38	4	0	4	3	.571	0	1	4.22
1998 Tucson	AAA Ari	48	0	0	36	68.1	313	68	41	33	6	3	3	2	33	5	63	7	1	2	5	.286	0	13	4.35
1999 Columbus	AAA NYY	53	0	0	23	70.1	318	69	42	37	4	2	1	9	39	1	40	11	0	6	3	.667	0	3	4.73
2000 Columbus	AAA NYY	20	2	0	5	44	194	37	15	15	3	0	1	4	24	0	41	8	0	3	0	1.000	0	0	3.07
Iowa	AAA ChC	8	8	0	0	36.2	178	36	30	27	4	2	4	3	31	0	30	2	0	1	3	.250	0	0	6.63
2001 Cubs	R ChC	3	3	0	0	9	41	10	4	2	0	0	1	1	2	0	9	0	0	1	0	1.000	0	0	2.00
Iowa	AAA ChC	5	5	0	0	23.1	108	31	15	15	3	1	0	3	9	1	16	0	0	2	3	.400	0	0	5.79
1998 Arizona	NL	8	0	0	2	10	49	13	12	11	2	0	0	2	3	0	5	1	0	0	0	—	0	0	9.90
2000 New York	AL	4	2	0	0	11	52	14	11	11	1	0	0	3	7	0	5	0	0	0	1	.000	0	0	9.00
8 Min. YEARS		294	18	0	147	507	2247	458	271	214	27	16	15	53	233	15	447	58	1	31	26	.544	0	40	3.80
2 Maj. YEARS		12	2	0	2	21	101	27	23	22	3	0	0	5	10	0	10	1	0	0	1	.000	0	0	9.43

Lew Ford

Bats: Right **Throws:** Right **Pos:** OF-126; DH-2; PH-2 **Ht:** 6'0" **Wt:** 190 **Born:** 8/12/76 **Age:** 25

Year Team	Lg Org	G	AB	H	2B	3B	HR	TB	R	RBI	TBB	IBB	SO	HBP	SH	SF	SB	CS	SB%	GDP	Avg	OBP	SLG
1999 Lowell	A- Bos	62	250	70	17	4	7	116	48	34	19	1	35	5	0	3	15	2	.88	6	.280	.339	.464
2000 Augusta	A Bos	126	514	162	35	11	9	246	122	74	52	3	83	12	3	2	52	4	.93	12	.315	.390	.479
2001 Fort Myers	A+ Min	67	265	79	15	2	2	104	42	24	21	3	30	12	1	2	19	9	.68	3	.298	.373	.392
New Britain	AA Min	62	252	55	9	3	7	91	30	25	20	0	35	6	1	2	5	5	.50	4	.218	.289	.361
3 Min. YEARS		317	1281	366	76	20	25	557	242	157	112	7	183	35	5	9	91	20	.82	25	.286	.357	.435

Tom Fordham

Pitches: Left **Bats:** Left **Pos:** RP-13; SP-5 **Ht:** 6'2" **Wt:** 205 **Born:** 2/20/74 **Age:** 28

Year Team	Lg Org	G	GS	CG	GF	IP	BFP	H	R	ER	HR	SH	SF	HB	TBB	IBB	SO	WP	Bk	W	L	Pct.	ShO	Sv	ERA
1993 White Sox	R CWS	3	0	0	1	10	41	9	2	2	0	0	0	0	3	0	12	1	0	1	1	.500	0	0	1.80
Sarasota	A+ CWS	2	0	0	1	5	21	3	1	0	0	0	0	0	3	2	5	1	1	0	0	—	0	0	0.00
Hickory	A CWS	8	8	1	0	48.2	194	36	21	21	3	1	6	0	21	0	27	3	2	4	3	.571	0	0	3.88
1994 Hickory	A CWS	17	17	1	0	109	452	101	47	38	10	1	1	3	30	1	121	5	4	10	5	.667	1	0	3.14
South Bend	A CWS	11	11	1	0	74.2	315	82	46	36	4	4	3	0	14	0	48	4	0	4	4	.500	1	0	4.34
1995 Pr William	A+ CWS	13	13	1	0	84	340	66	20	19	7	2	1	2	35	2	78	1	0	9	0	1.000	1	0	2.04
Birmingham	AA CWS	14	14	2	0	82.2	348	79	35	31	9	2	2	0	28	2	61	3	0	6	3	.667	1	0	3.38
1996 Birmingham	AA CWS	6	6	0	0	37.1	147	26	13	11	4	0	2	0	14	1	37	2	0	2	1	.667	0	0	2.65
Nashville	AAA CWS	22	22	3	0	140.2	589	117	60	54	15	4	2	4	69	1	118	7	1	10	8	.556	2	0	3.45
1997 Nashville	AAA CWS	21	20	2	0	114	493	113	64	60	14	1	5	1	53	1	90	6	1	6	7	.462	0	0	4.74
1998 Calgary	AAA CWS	9	9	0	0	56.2	225	38	21	19	6	1	3	0	26	0	39	3	0	4	2	.667	0	0	3.02
1999 Charlotte	AAA CWS	29	21	0	2	112	538	144	101	91	25	2	4	3	66	0	101	10	0	4	7	.364	0	0	7.31
2000 Indianapols	AAA Mil	48	3	0	11	66	295	48	29	26	2	2	2	0	49	0	64	6	0	3	6	.333	0	0	3.55
2001 Indianapols	AAA Mil	18	5	1	5	38.1	152	25	15	11	6	1	1	0	13	0	35	2	1	1	2	.333	0	0	2.58
1997 Chicago	AL	7	1	0	1	17.1	78	17	13	12	2	1	2	1	10	2	10	0	0	0	1	.000	0	0	6.23
1998 Chicago	AL	29	5	0	5	48	228	51	36	36	7	1	1	1	42	0	23	1	0	1	2	.333	0	0	6.75
9 Min. YEARS		221	149	12	20	979	4150	887	475	419	105	21	32	13	424	10	836	54	10	64	49	.566	6	0	3.85
2 Maj. YEARS		36	6	0	6	65.1	306	68	49	48	9	2	3	2	52	2	33	1	0	1	3	.250	0	0	6.61

Scott Forster

Pitches: Left **Bats:** Right **Pos:** RP-14; SP-1 **Ht:** 6'1" **Wt:** 194 **Born:** 10/27/71 **Age:** 30

Year Team	Lg Org	G	GS	CG	GF	IP	BFP	H	R	ER	HR	SH	SF	HB	TBB	IBB	SO	WP	Bk	W	L	Pct.	ShO	Sv	ERA
1994 Vermont	A- Mon	12	9	0	0	52.2	236	38	32	19	0	0	1	4	34	0	39	6	2	1	6	.143	0	0	3.25
1995 Wst Plm Bch	A+ Mon	26	26	1	0	146.2	643	129	78	66	6	5	4	7	80	1	92	16	0	6	11	.353	0	0	4.05
1996 Harrisburg	AA Mon	28	28	0	0	176.1	755	164	92	74	15	3	4	7	67	2	97	5	0	10	7	.588	0	0	3.78
1997 Harrisburg	AA Mon	17	15	0	2	79.1	365	77	45	20	7	7	6	6	48	0	71	4	0	3	6	.333	0	0	2.27
1998 Jupiter	A+ Mon	6	0	0	1	8	38	9	1	0	8	0	0	1	5	0	7	2	0	0	0	—	0	0	9.00
Harrisburg	AA Mon	25	11	0	5	77.2	360	90	50	42	8	2	1	6	47	1	54	5	0	7	3	.700	0	0	4.87
1999 Harrisburg	AA Mon	2	0	0	1	5	16	3	0	0	0	0	0	1	0	0	1	0	0	0	0	—	0	0	0.00
Ottawa	AAA Mon	53	0	0	27	52.1	249	49	32	30	3	2	1	2	47	2	32	8	0	0	4	.000	0	6	5.16
2000 Ottawa	AAA Mon	23	0	0	9	31	135	24	11	8	0	1	1	1	22	1	22	5	0	1	0	1.000	0	2	2.32
2001 Huntsville	AA Mil	6	1	0	1	8.2	43	10	8	6	1	1	2	0	7	0	6	1	0	1	1	.500	0	0	6.23
Louisville	AAA Cin	9	0	0	2	10.1	46	7	3	2	0	0	0	0	9	1	9	2	0	1	0	1.000	0	0	1.74
2000 Montreal	NL	42	0	0	10	32	154	28	31	28	5	2	3	2	25	1	23	2	0	0	1	.000	0	0	7.88
8 Min. YEARS		207	90	1	48	648	2886	600	361	275	40	22	21	35	366	8	430	54	2	30	38	.441	0	4	3.82

John Foster

Pitches: Left **Bats:** Left **Pos:** RP-50 **Ht:** 6'0" **Wt:** 200 **Born:** 5/17/78 **Age:** 24

Year Team	Lg Org	G	GS	CG	GF	IP	BFP	H	R	ER	HR	SH	SF	HB	TBB	IBB	SO	WP	Bk	W	L	Pct.	ShO	Sv	ERA
1999 Danville	R+ Atl	18	0	0	7	39	148	28	10	6	0	5	0	2	6	0	36	4	0	4	1	.800	0	1	1.38
2000 Myrtle Bch	A+ Atl	38	0	0	17	48.2	204	48	13	10	2	4	2	2	14	4	46	4	0	2	1	.667	0	3	1.85
2001 Greenville	AA Atl	50	0	0	21	68.2	303	71	30	23	6	11	3	2	33	7	63	5	0	8	7	.533	0	7	3.01
3 Min. YEARS		106	0	0	45	156.1	655	147	53	39	8	20	5	6	53	11	145	13	0	14	9	.609	0	11	2.25

Quincy Foster

Bats: Left **Throws:** Right **Pos:** OF-100; PR-7; PH-4 **Ht:** 6'2" **Wt:** 175 **Born:** 10/30/74 **Age:** 27

Year Team	Lg Org	G	AB	H	2B	3B	HR	TB	R	RBI	TBB	IBB	SO	HBP	SH	SF	SB	CS	SB%	GDP	Avg	OBP	SLG
1996 Utica	A- Fla	73	240	53	7	1	1	65	34	22	30	0	71	4	3	4	24	6	.80	3	.221	.313	.271
1997 Brevard Cty	A+ Fla	61	186	46	8	2	1	61	25	11	14	0	47	3	2	5	12	4	.75	0	.247	.310	.328
1998 Kane County	A Fla	134	545	138	14	10	0	172	90	37	51	4	114	8	8	4	73	19	.79	7	.253	.324	.316
1999 Brevard Cty	A+ Fla	134	568	167	13	6	3	201	78	54	36	1	96	8	1	9	56	23	.71	4	.294	.344	.354
2000 Marlins	R Fla	5	16	4	1	0	0	5	2	1	1	0	0	1	0	0	0	1	.00	0	.250	.333	.313
Portland	AA Fla	65	248	77	7	4	2	98	60	21	23	0	42	7	3	2	25	8	.76	2	.310	.382	.395
2001 Portland	AA Fla	68	200	43	2	3	2	57	34	14	25	0	31	2	4	0	23	9	.72	4	.215	.308	.285
Brevard Cty	A+ Fla	41	154	46	6	1	0	54	29	12	19	0	25	2	0	1	16	5	.76	2	.299	.381	.351
6 Min. YEARS		581	2157	574	58	27	9	713	352	172	199	5	426	35	22	13	229	75	.75	22	.266	.336	.331

Jason Fox

Bats: Both **Throws:** Right **Pos:** OF-86; PH-7; PR-1 **Ht:** 6'2" **Wt:** 185 **Born:** 3/30/77 **Age:** 25

Year Team	Lg Org	G	AB	H	2B	3B	HR	TB	R	RBI	TBB	IBB	SO	HBP	SH	SF	SB	CS	SB%	GDP	Avg	OBP	SLG
1998 Helena	R+ Mil	43	179	54	13	1	5	84	40	23	15	1	36	1	2	1	21	4	.84	1	.302	.357	.469

(Batting — continued)

Year Team	Lg Org	G	AB	H	2B	3B	HR	TB	R	RBI	TBB	IBB	SO	HBP	SH	SF	SB	CS	SB%	GDP	Avg	OBP	SLG
1999 Stockton	A+ Mil	70	248	58	8	3	1	75	34	18	14	0	63	2	10	2	15	4	.79	7	.234	.278	.302
Beloit	A Mil	41	163	36	3	1	1	44	18	6	11	0	34	1	1	0	8	3	.73	2	.221	.274	.270
2000 Mudville	A+ Mil	130	493	123	17	2	2	150	58	43	52	1	92	3	10	5	53	17	.76	4	.249	.322	.304
2001 Huntsville	AA Mil	90	289	71	10	2	3	94	32	28	18	0	74	1	8	2	19	7	.73	3	.246	.290	.325
4 Min. YEARS		374	1372	342	51	9	12	447	182	118	110	2	299	8	31	10	116	35	.77	17	.249	.307	.326

Aaron France

Pitches: Right **Bats:** Left **Pos:** SP-5; RP-2 **Ht:** 6'3" **Wt:** 188 **Born:** 4/17/74 **Age:** 28

	HOW MUCH HE PITCHED						WHAT HE GAVE UP												THE RESULTS					
Year Team	Lg Org	G	GS	CG	GF	IP	BFP	H	R	ER	HR	SH	SF	HB	TBB	IBB	SO	WP	Bk	W	L	Pct.	ShO	Sv	ERA
1994 Welland	A- Pit	7	5	0	1	24	98	22	12	6	1	0	1	3	6	0	16	1	1	0	2	.000	0	0	2.25
1995 Augusta	A Pit	18	15	0	0	94.2	388	80	29	26	4	3	3	5	26	0	77	6	2	6	6	.500	0	0	2.47
1996 Lynchburg	A+ Pit	13	13	0	0	60.1	286	79	53	43	6	1	0	3	32	1	40	8	3	0	8	.000	0	0	6.41
Augusta	A Pit	5	5	0	0	25	105	23	9	7	2	2	0	1	7	0	24	0	1	2	1	.667	0	0	2.52
1997 Augusta	A Pit	26	17	1	2	107.1	458	98	48	42	5	7	0	8	44	0	89	6	3	7	4	.636	0	0	3.52
1998 Lynchburg	A+ Pit	26	20	0	2	129	529	99	51	39	9	3	1	12	45	0	110	7	0	6	5	.545	0	0	2.72
1999 Altoona	AA Pit	33	11	0	7	95.2	414	79	50	39	8	5	3	5	48	1	70	7	3	4	5	.444	0	0	3.67
2000 Altoona	AA Pit	22	12	0	0	81	355	83	41	31	4	0	5	1	27	1	57	6	0	5	2	.714	0	0	3.44
2001 Altoona	AA Pit	7	5	0	0	25.1	120	36	19	16	4	3	2	3	10	0	17	1	0	1	2	.333	0	0	5.68
8 Min. YEARS		157	103	1	12	642.1	2753	599	312	249	43	17	17	41	245	3	500	42	13	31	35	.470	0	0	3.49

David Francia

Bats: Left **Throws:** Left **Pos:** OF-82; PH-20; DH-9 **Ht:** 6'0" **Wt:** 167 **Born:** 4/16/75 **Age:** 27

Year Team	Lg Org	G	AB	H	2B	3B	HR	TB	R	RBI	TBB	IBB	SO	HBP	SH	SF	SB	CS	SB%	GDP	Avg	OBP	SLG
1996 Batavia	A- Phi	69	280	81	14	5	4	117	45	29	8	0	25	6	2	2	16	6	.73	1	.289	.321	.418
1997 Piedmont	A Phi	112	424	127	24	7	9	192	72	65	25	2	61	19	4	8	39	12	.76	5	.300	.359	.453
Clearwater	A+ Phi	21	75	21	3	1	0	26	5	10	6	0	7	1	3	0	5	2	.71	1	.280	.341	.347
1998 Clearwater	A+ Phi	48	194	54	13	0	6	85	33	23	12	0	30	7	2	2	13	4	.76	4	.278	.340	.438
Reading	AA Phi	68	269	64	12	4	3	93	29	20	13	0	41	2	3	2	6	7	.46	3	.238	.276	.346
1999 Reading	AA Phi	107	339	92	22	5	4	136	41	43	21	3	57	13	6	1	13	4	.76	5	.271	.337	.401
2000 Reading	AA Phi	56	210	61	8	3	3	84	36	26	11	0	29	10	8	2	16	7	.70	2	.290	.352	.400
Scranton-WB	AAA Phi	48	117	34	9	0	2	49	16	15	18	1	17	2	2	0	7	4	.64	0	.291	.394	.419
2001 Scranton-WB	AAA Phi	110	347	79	13	2	3	105	34	37	25	3	58	7	2	4	19	7	.73	2	.228	.290	.303
6 Min. YEARS		639	2255	613	118	27	34	887	311	268	139	9	325	67	32	21	134	53	.72	23	.272	.330	.393

Matt Franco

Bats: Left **Throws:** Right **Pos:** 3B-85; 1B-40; DH-3; PH-3; OF-1; PR-1 **Ht:** 6'1" **Wt:** 210 **Born:** 8/19/69 **Age:** 32

Year Team	Lg Org	G	AB	H	2B	3B	HR	TB	R	RBI	TBB	IBB	SO	HBP	SH	SF	SB	CS	SB%	GDP	Avg	OBP	SLG
1987 Wytheville	R+ ChC	62	202	50	10	1	1	65	25	26	26	1	41	0	0	0	4	1	.80	3	.248	.333	.322
1988 Wytheville	R+ ChC	20	79	31	9	1	0	42	14	16	7	0	5	0	0	0	0	1	.00	1	.392	.442	.532
Geneva	A- ChC	44	164	42	2	0	3	53	19	21	19	3	13	0	0	1	2	0	1.00	7	.256	.332	.323
1989 Chston-WV	A ChC	109	377	102	16	1	5	135	42	48	57	0	40	0	5	4	2	2	.50	10	.271	.363	.358
Peoria	A ChC	16	58	13	4	0	0	17	4	9	5	0	5	1	0	1	0	1	.00	1	.224	.292	.293
1990 Peoria	A ChC	123	443	125	33	2	6	180	52	65	43	2	39	1	1	2	4	4	.50	19	.282	.346	.406
1991 Winston-Sal	A+ ChC	104	307	66	12	1	4	92	47	40	46	2	41	2	2	6	4	1	.80	6	.215	.316	.300
1992 Charlotte	AA ChC	108	343	97	18	3	2	127	35	31	26	1	46	1	0	3	3	3	.50	4	.283	.332	.370
1993 Orlando	AA ChC	68	237	75	20	1	7	118	31	37	29	2	30	2	1	2	3	6	.33	2	.316	.393	.498
Iowa	AAA ChC	62	199	58	17	4	5	98	24	29	16	3	30	1	0	3	4	1	.80	6	.291	.342	.492
1994 Iowa	AAA ChC	128	437	121	32	4	11	194	63	71	52	5	66	2	2	5	3	3	.50	7	.277	.353	.444
1995 Iowa	AAA ChC	121	455	128	28	5	6	184	51	58	37	5	44	0	1	6	1	1	.50	11	.281	.331	.404
1996 Norfolk	AAA NYM	133	508	164	40	2	7	229	74	81	36	3	55	3	1	9	5	2	.71	10	.323	.365	.451
1997 Norfolk	AAA NYM	7	26	7	2	0	0	9	5	0	2	1	2	1	0	0	0	0	—	0	.269	.345	.346
1998 Norfolk	AAA NYM	5	19	7	1	0	0	8	2	1	3	0	1	0	0	0	2	0	1.00	0	.368	.455	.421
2000 Norfolk	AAA NYM	14	51	7	1	0	0	8	3	1	3	0	10	0	0	0	0	0	—	0	.137	.185	.157
2001 Norfolk	AAA NYM	124	433	106	25	1	8	157	49	47	52	7	72	2	0	5	5	2	.71	16	.245	.325	.363
1995 Chicago	NL	16	17	5	1	0	0	6	3	1	0	0	4	0	0	0	0	0	—	0	.294	.294	.353
1996 New York	NL	14	31	6	1	0	1	10	3	2	1	0	5	1	0	1	0	0	—	1	.194	.235	.323
1997 New York	NL	112	163	45	5	0	5	65	21	21	13	4	23	1	0	0	1	0	1.00	4	.276	.330	.399
1998 New York	NL	103	161	44	7	2	1	58	20	13	23	6	26	1	1	1	0	1	.00	8	.273	.366	.360
1999 New York	NL	122	132	31	5	0	4	48	18	21	28	3	21	0	0	1	0	0	—	3	.235	.366	.364
2000 New York	NL	101	134	32	4	0	2	42	9	14	21	3	22	0	0	1	0	0	—	3	.239	.340	.313
14 Min. YEARS		1248	4338	1199	270	26	65	1716	540	576	459	35	540	16	13	47	42	28	.60	105	.276	.344	.396
6 Maj. YEARS		468	638	163	23	2	13	229	74	72	86	16	101	2	2	4	1	1	.50	25	.255	.344	.359

Mike Frank

Bats: Left **Throws:** Left **Pos:** OF-91; DH-11; PH-3; PR-2; P-1 **Ht:** 6'2" **Wt:** 195 **Born:** 1/14/75 **Age:** 27

Year Team	Lg Org	G	AB	H	2B	3B	HR	TB	R	RBI	TBB	IBB	SO	HBP	SH	SF	SB	CS	SB%	GDP	Avg	OBP	SLG
1997 Billings	R+ Cin	69	266	100	22	6	10	164	62	62	35	5	24	2	0	3	18	8	.69	7	.376	.448	.617
1998 Indianapols	AAA Cin	22	88	30	4	0	0	34	8	13	7	0	9	0	0	0	1	0	1.00	3	.341	.389	.386
Chattanooga	AA Cin	58	231	75	12	4	12	131	43	43	19	1	28	1	0	3	5	2	.71	3	.325	.374	.567
1999 Indianapols	AAA Cin	121	433	128	36	7	9	205	73	62	36	2	55	8	2	3	10	6	.63	10	.296	.358	.473
2000 Chattanooga	AA Cin	8	30	8	1	2	0	13	6	5	1	0	1	0	0	0	0	0	—	1	.267	.290	.433
Louisville	AAA Cin	62	197	54	16	2	6	92	30	28	20	2	26	4	1	1	8	1	.89	5	.274	.351	.467
Columbus	AAA NYY	45	138	33	5	3	2	50	19	12	16	1	13	3	1	1	5	3	.63	5	.239	.329	.362
2001 Columbus	AAA NYY	106	356	90	20	2	10	144	45	53	41	3	52	5	4	7	11	3	.79	10	.253	.333	.404
1998 Cincinnati	NL	28	89	20	6	0	0	26	14	7	7	0	12	0	1	0	0	0	—	3	.225	.278	.292
5 Min. YEARS		491	1739	518	116	26	49	833	286	278	175	14	208	23	8	18	58	23	.72	43	.298	.366	.479

Micah Franklin

Bats: Both **Throws:** Right **Pos:** OF-43; 3B-30; PH-21; DH-18; 1B-3; PR-2   **Ht:** 6'0" **Wt:** 195 **Born:** 4/25/72 **Age:** 30

					BATTING												BASERUNNING				PERCENTAGES		
Year Team	Lg Org	G	AB	H	2B	3B	HR	TB	R	RBI	TBB	IBB	SO	HBP	SH	SF	SB	CS	SB%	GDP	Avg	OBP	SLG
1990 Kingsport	R+ NYM	39	158	41	9	2	7	75	29	25	8	0	44	1	0	2	4	1	.80	2	.259	.296	.475
1991 Pittsfield	A- NYM	26	94	27	4	2	0	35	17	14	21	0	20	1	2	1	12	3	.80	3	.287	.419	.372
Erie	A- NYM	39	153	37	4	0	2	47	28	8	25	0	35	2	0	1	4	5	.44	3	.242	.354	.307
1992 Billings	R+ Cin	75	251	84	13	2	11	134	58	60	53	3	65	15	0	3	18	17	.51	3	.335	.472	.534
1993 Winston-Sal	A+ Cin	20	69	16	1	1	3	28	10	6	10	1	19	2	1	0	0	1	.00	0	.232	.346	.406
Chston-WV	A Cin	102	343	90	14	4	17	163	56	68	47	4	109	18	3	6	6	1	.86	4	.262	.374	.475
1994 Winston-Sal	A+ Cin	42	150	45	7	0	21	115	44	44	27	5	48	6	0	1	7	0	1.00	1	.300	.424	.767
Chattanooga	AA Cin	79	279	77	17	0	10	124	46	40	33	3	79	13	0	3	2	2	.50	3	.276	.375	.444
1995 Calgary	AAA Pit	110	358	105	28	0	21	196	64	71	47	8	95	1	0	5	3	3	.50	7	.293	.372	.547
1996 Toledo	AAA Det	53	179	44	10	1	7	77	32	21	27	0	60	3	0	0	3	2	.60	1	.246	.354	.430
Louisville	AAA StL	86	289	67	18	3	15	136	43	53	40	2	71	8	1	3	2	3	.40	4	.232	.338	.471
1997 Louisville	AAA StL	99	326	72	14	1	12	124	49	48	51	4	74	3	0	3	2	0	1.00	9	.221	.329	.380
1998 Iowa	AAA ChC	118	359	118	26	2	29	235	74	95	59	8	72	13	0	4	5	3	.63	10	.329	.437	.655
2001 Indianapolis	AAA Mil	110	331	76	12	4	23	165	54	63	47	3	73	12	0	2	1	3	.25	7	.230	.344	.498
1997 St. Louis	NL	17	34	11	0	0	2	17	6	2	3	0	10	0	0	0	0	0	—	0	.324	.378	.500
10 Min. YEARS		998	3339	899	177	22	178	1654	604	616	495	41	864	98	7	34	69	44	.61	57	.269	.376	.495

Lance Franks

Pitches: Right **Bats:** Right **Pos:** RP-17; SP-11   **Ht:** 5'11" **Wt:** 180 **Born:** 8/20/75 **Age:** 26

		HOW MUCH HE PITCHED					WHAT HE GAVE UP									THE RESULTS				
Year Team	Lg Org	G	GS	CG	GF	IP	BFP	H	R	ER	HR	SH	SF	HB	TBB	IBB	SO	WP	Bk	W	L	Pct.	ShO	Sv	ERA
1997 Johnson Cty	R+ StL	26	0	0	23	30.2	113	16	4	4	1	0	0	0	7	1	40	2	0	0	0	—	0	12	1.17
Pr William	A+ StL	2	0	0	0	4.1	16	3	1	1	1	0	0	0	1	0	4	0	0	1	0	1.000	0	0	2.08
1998 Peoria	A StL	58	0	0	23	75	295	57	23	19	4	4	3	3	20	4	68	5	0	4	6	.400	0	4	2.28
1999 Potomac	A+ StL	54	0	0	6	78.2	308	63	25	23	5	2	2	3	17	0	61	2	0	5	1	.833	0	0	2.63
2000 Arkansas	AA StL	43	7	0	5	89	396	90	59	51	16	5	3	3	44	4	56	3	1	6	4	.600	0	0	5.16
2001 New Haven	AA StL	28	11	0	4	90.1	409	86	60	41	11	3	3	9	48	0	72	5	0	2	8	.200	0	0	4.08
5 Min. YEARS		211	18	0	61	368	1537	315	172	139	38	14	11	18	137	9	301	17	1	18	19	.486	0	16	3.40

Kevin Frederick

Pitches: Right **Bats:** Left **Pos:** RP-53   **Ht:** 6'1" **Wt:** 208 **Born:** 11/4/76 **Age:** 25

		HOW MUCH HE PITCHED					WHAT HE GAVE UP									THE RESULTS				
Year Team	Lg Org	G	GS	CG	GF	IP	BFP	H	R	ER	HR	SH	SF	HB	TBB	IBB	SO	WP	Bk	W	L	Pct.	ShO	Sv	ERA
1998 Elizabethtn	R+ Min	17	0	0	10	29.2	130	28	21	14	4	1	0	0	10	1	46	4	0	1	4	.200	0	1	4.25
1999 Twins	R Min	2	0	0	0	2.1	14	6	5	4	0	0	1	0	1	0	3	0	0	0	0	—	0	0	15.43
2000 Quad City	A Min	27	0	0	11	46	193	34	17	12	1	3	1	4	23	4	51	4	0	5	0	1.000	0	4	2.35
Fort Myers	A+ Min	19	0	0	7	30	123	20	11	9	0	1	1	1	14	1	37	4	2	2	1	.667	0	3	2.70
2001 Fort Myers	A+ Min	9	0	0	4	18	65	9	2	2	1	0	0	0	3	1	19	0	0	2	0	1.000	0	1	1.00
New Britain	AA Min	44	0	0	18	82.2	331	56	17	15	5	6	2	8	28	7	109	4	0	6	2	.750	0	7	1.63
4 Min. YEARS		118	0	0	50	208.2	856	153	73	56	11	11	5	13	79	14	265	16	2	16	7	.696	0	16	2.42

Corey Freeman

Bats: Right **Throws:** Right **Pos:** SS-53; 2B-5; PH-5; 3B-4; OF-4; P-3; PR-2   **Ht:** 5'11" **Wt:** 165 **Born:** 10/13/79 **Age:** 22

					BATTING												BASERUNNING				PERCENTAGES		
Year Team	Lg Org	G	AB	H	2B	3B	HR	TB	R	RBI	TBB	IBB	SO	HBP	SH	SF	SB	CS	SB%	GDP	Avg	OBP	SLG
1998 Mariners	R Sea	37	122	35	2	0	0	37	21	15	9	1	20	2	1	2	9	1	.90	1	.287	.341	.303
1999 Mariners	R Sea	28	103	28	9	0	0	37	20	13	8	0	25	2	0	0	8	2	.80	1	.272	.336	.359
Wisconsin	A Sea	18	63	12	6	0	0	18	6	9	1	0	18	1	1	2	0	0	—	1	.190	.215	.286
2000 Lancaster	A+ Sea	27	112	24	6	1	0	32	19	7	8	0	23	2	0	1	5	6	.45	2	.214	.276	.286
Everett	A- Sea	65	216	47	12	2	0	63	32	11	24	0	64	0	6	3	12	6	.67	3	.218	.292	.292
2001 San Antonio	AA Sea	26	74	13	3	0	1	19	6	3	5	0	18	0	4	0	1	0	1.00	3	.176	.228	.257
Tacoma	AAA Sea	7	14	3	0	0	0	3	3	1	0	0	5	0	0	0	0	0	—	0	.214	.214	.214
Wisconsin	A Sea	37	106	16	4	0	1	23	14	10	8	0	24	5	4	2	3	6	.33	2	.151	.240	.217
4 Min. YEARS		245	810	178	42	3	2	232	121	69	63	1	197	12	17	8	38	21	.64	13	.220	.283	.286

Kai Freeman

Pitches: Right **Bats:** Right **Pos:** RP-18; SP-10   **Ht:** 6'2" **Wt:** 182 **Born:** 3/11/77 **Age:** 25

		HOW MUCH HE PITCHED					WHAT HE GAVE UP									THE RESULTS				
Year Team	Lg Org	G	GS	CG	GF	IP	BFP	H	R	ER	HR	SH	SF	HB	TBB	IBB	SO	WP	Bk	W	L	Pct.	ShO	Sv	ERA
1998 White Sox	R CWS	1	0	0	0	2	8	1	1	1	0	0	1	0	1	0	2	1	0	0	0	—	0	0	4.50
Bristol	R+ CWS	11	9	1	0	57.2	252	56	28	21	1	2	0	4	21	0	44	5	3	6	2	.750	0	0	3.28
1999 Winston-Sal	A+ CWS	32	8	0	5	95.1	417	100	58	52	13	6	4	5	32	1	64	1	1	2	6	.250	0	1	4.91
2000 Birmingham	AA CWS	30	2	0	8	52.2	238	57	32	23	5	3	4	1	22	1	31	4	0	3	2	.600	0	0	3.93
2001 Birmingham	AA CWS	28	10	0	6	83.1	375	100	53	47	4	2	3	9	33	2	38	4	0	5	3	.625	0	0	5.08
4 Min. YEARS		102	29	1	19	291	1290	314	172	144	23	13	12	19	109	4	179	15	4	16	13	.552	0	1	4.45

Alejandro Freire

Bats: Right **Throws:** Right **Pos:** DH-105; OF-18; 1B-10   **Ht:** 6'2" **Wt:** 185 **Born:** 8/23/74 **Age:** 27

					BATTING												BASERUNNING				PERCENTAGES		
Year Team	Lg Org	G	AB	H	2B	3B	HR	TB	R	RBI	TBB	IBB	SO	HBP	SH	SF	SB	CS	SB%	GDP	Avg	OBP	SLG
1994 Astros	R Hou	29	83	25	4	0	1	32	8	13	5	0	17	3	2	2	5	1	.83	0	.301	.345	.386
1995 Quad City	A Hou	125	417	127	23	1	15	197	71	65	50	1	83	6	2	7	9	5	.64	9	.305	.381	.472
1996 Kissimmee	A+ Hou	115	384	98	24	1	12	160	40	42	24	1	66	7	1	1	11	7	.61	11	.255	.309	.417
1997 Lakeland	A+ Det	130	477	154	30	2	24	260	85	92	50	1	84	12	0	7	13	4	.76	10	.323	.396	.545
1998 Jacksnville	AA Det	129	494	136	30	0	16	214	79	78	33	1	83	17	1	9	3	1	.75	16	.275	.336	.433

Year Team	Lg Org	G	AB	H	2B	3B	HR	TB	R	RBI	TBB	IBB	SO	HBP	SH	SF	SB	CS	SB%	GDP	Avg	OBP	SLG
1999 Lakeland	A+ Det	13	41	9	3	0	1	15	6	5	10	0	7	3	1	1	0	0	—	1	.220	.400	.366
Jacksnville	AA Det	66	243	72	20	0	10	122	45	43	23	0	44	6	0	4	2	0	1.00	8	.296	.366	.502
2000 Jacksnville	AA Det	135	471	129	16	0	25	220	73	77	69	1	111	16	0	6	2	4	.33	13	.274	.381	.467
2001 Erie	AA Det	133	501	148	33	0	17	232	73	82	46	1	113	11	0	3	2	3	.40	17	.295	.365	.463
8 Min. YEARS		875	3111	898	183	4	121	1452	480	497	310	6	608	81	7	41	47	25	.65	85	.289	.364	.467

Nate Frese

Bats: Right **Throws:** Right **Pos:** SS-70; PH-2 **Ht:** 6'3" **Wt:** 200 **Born:** 7/10/77 **Age:** 24

Year Team	Lg Org	G	AB	H	2B	3B	HR	TB	R	RBI	TBB	IBB	SO	HBP	SH	SF	SB	CS	SB%	GDP	Avg	OBP	SLG
1998 Williamsprt	A- ChC	54	174	38	8	0	2	52	28	18	16	0	38	2	3	7	5	2	.71	1	.218	.281	.299
1999 Lansing	A ChC	107	373	99	27	4	4	146	68	49	58	2	67	5	1	8	10	4	.71	13	.265	.365	.391
2000 Daytona	A+ ChC	117	425	126	24	5	7	181	70	52	64	0	84	6	8	4	10	6	.63	9	.296	.393	.426
2001 West Tenn	AA ChC	72	233	42	5	1	4	61	25	19	38	1	62	5	2	2	0	1	.00	7	.180	.306	.262
4 Min. YEARS		350	1205	305	64	10	17	440	191	138	176	3	251	18	14	21	25	13	.66	30	.253	.351	.365

Hanley Frias

Bats: Both **Throws:** Right **Pos:** SS-58; 2B-47; PH-3; PR-3; 3B-1 **Ht:** 6'0" **Wt:** 173 **Born:** 12/5/73 **Age:** 28

Year Team	Lg Org	G	AB	H	2B	3B	HR	TB	R	RBI	TBB	IBB	SO	HBP	SH	SF	SB	CS	SB%	GDP	Avg	OBP	SLG
1992 Rangers	R Tex	58	205	50	9	2	0	63	37	28	27	0	30	2	2	2	28	6	.82	1	.244	.335	.307
1993 Chston-SC	A Tex	132	473	109	20	4	4	149	61	37	40	0	108	3	4	4	27	14	.66	8	.230	.292	.315
1994 High Desert	A+ Mon	124	452	115	17	6	3	153	70	59	41	1	74	2	5	3	37	12	.76	9	.254	.317	.338
1995 Charlotte	A+ Tex	33	120	40	6	3	0	52	23	14	15	0	11	1	3	1	8	6	.57	0	.333	.409	.433
Tulsa	AA Tex	93	360	101	18	4	0	127	44	27	45	0	53	1	8	2	14	12	.54	6	.281	.360	.353
1996 Tulsa	AA Tex	134	505	145	24	12	3	199	73	41	30	2	73	0	5	3	9	9	.50	19	.287	.325	.394
1997 Okla City	AAA Tex	132	484	128	17	4	5	168	64	46	56	2	72	1	8	3	35	15	.70	8	.264	.340	.347
1998 Tucson	AAA Ari	63	253	73	10	4	1	94	32	21	24	0	41	0	2	3	16	7	.70	4	.289	.346	.372
1999 Tucson	AAA Ari	23	80	24	3	0	0	27	15	6	7	0	15	0	1	0	3	1	.75	2	.300	.356	.338
2001 Edmonton	AAA Min	49	142	26	6	0	0	32	15	7	10	0	28	0	1	0	2	3	.40	3	.183	.237	.225
Memphis	AAA StL	58	240	58	8	2	2	76	27	19	16	0	44	2	0	1	6	4	.60	3	.242	.293	.317
1997 Texas	AL	14	26	5	1	0	0	6	4	1	1	0	4	0	0	0	0	0	—	1	.192	.222	.231
1998 Arizona	NL	15	23	3	0	1	1	8	4	2	0	0	5	0	0	0	0	0	—	1	.130	.130	.348
1999 Arizona	NL	69	150	41	3	2	1	51	27	16	29	2	18	0	1	0	4	3	.57	2	.273	.391	.340
2000 Arizona	NL	75	112	23	5	0	2	34	18	6	17	0	18	0	0	0	2	2	.50	3	.205	.310	.304
9 Min. YEARS		899	3314	869	138	41	17	1140	461	305	311	5	549	12	39	22	185	89	.68	63	.262	.326	.344
4 Maj. YEARS		173	311	72	9	3	4	99	53	25	47	2	45	0	1	0	6	5	.55	7	.232	.332	.318

Javier Fuentes

Bats: Right **Throws:** Right **Pos:** 3B-11; DH-5; PH-4; 2B-1; 1B-1 **Ht:** 6'1" **Wt:** 182 **Born:** 9/27/74 **Age:** 27

Year Team	Lg Org	G	AB	H	2B	3B	HR	TB	R	RBI	TBB	IBB	SO	HBP	SH	SF	SB	CS	SB%	GDP	Avg	OBP	SLG
1996 Lowell	A- Bos	46	157	45	6	1	2	59	21	21	21	0	23	2	0	0	2	1	.67	4	.287	.378	.376
1997 Michigan	A Bos	30	77	13	1	1	0	16	10	8	7	0	18	4	2	0	1	1	.50	2	.169	.273	.208
Sarasota	A+ Bos	47	147	42	6	2	2	58	16	22	12	0	19	1	2	0	4	6	.40	2	.286	.344	.395
1998 Sarasota	A+ Bos	82	251	69	14	1	4	97	45	29	38	1	38	7	1	0	5	2	.71	5	.275	.385	.386
1999 Augusta	A Bos	39	130	33	4	1	1	42	16	13	22	0	13	4	1	1	6	1	.86	0	.254	.376	.323
Sarasota	A+ Bos	64	176	51	4	0	0	55	28	13	33	0	17	6	3	3	6	1	.86	2	.290	.413	.313
2000 Sarasota	A+ Bos	4	10	3	1	0	0	4	2	3	1	0	1	0	1	0	0	0	—	0	.300	.364	.400
Trenton	AA Bos	2	6	1	0	0	0	1	0	0	1	0	0	0	1	0	0	1	.00	0	.167	.286	.167
El Paso	AA Ari	5	7	2	0	0	0	2	1	0	2	0	0	0	0	0	0	0	—	0	.286	.444	.286
South Bend	A Ari	80	278	80	9	1	3	100	38	33	32	0	24	7	6	4	7	2	.78	3	.288	.371	.360
2001 Harrisburg	AA Mon	22	50	14	3	1	0	19	7	6	7	0	4	1	0	0	0	0	—	1	.280	.379	.380
6 Min. YEARS		421	1289	353	48	8	12	453	184	148	176	1	157	32	16	8	31	15	.67	22	.274	.373	.351

Jody Fuller

Pitches: Right **Bats:** Right **Pos:** RP-49; SP-1 **Ht:** 6'3" **Wt:** 225 **Born:** 9/12/76 **Age:** 25

		HOW MUCH HE PITCHED						WHAT HE GAVE UP												THE RESULTS				
Year Team	Lg Org	G	GS	CG	GF	IP	BFP	H	R	ER	HR	SH	SF	HB	TBB	IBB	SO	WP	Bk	W	L	Pct.	ShO	Sv	ERA
1998 Lethbridge	R+ Ari	18	7	0	5	54.2	225	45	26	24	5	2	0	2	24	0	41	3	0	5	1	.833	0	0	3.95
1999 South Bend	A Ari	36	11	0	10	116.1	524	133	68	58	6	1	7	4	43	0	83	7	0	7	4	.636	0	0	4.49
2000 Tucson	AAA Ari	1	0	0	0	5	18	3	2	2	1	0	0	0	0	0	4	0	0	1	0	1.000	0	0	3.60
South Bend	A Ari	20	20	1	0	123.2	516	116	58	43	8	4	6	6	37	3	76	9	0	9	6	.600	0	0	3.13
El Paso	AA Ari	8	1	0	3	22.1	89	24	12	12	1	0	3	1	5	0	10	1	0	0	0	—	0	0	4.84
2001 Lancaster	A+ Ari	23	1	0	8	36	168	43	23	18	4	3	0	1	19	0	27	3	0	2	3	.400	0	0	4.50
El Paso	AA Ari	12	0	0	3	19.1	90	23	13	12	1	0	0	1	12	1	12	1	0	0	2	.000	0	0	5.59
Wilmington	A+ KC	15	0	0	9	17.2	80	20	8	8	1	2	0	1	10	3	11	2	0	1	1	.500	0	0	4.08
4 Min. YEARS		133	40	1	38	395	1710	407	210	177	27	12	16	16	150	7	264	26	0	25	17	.595	0	1	4.03

Eddy Furniss

Bats: Left **Throws:** Left **Pos:** DH-110; 1B-7; PH-1 **Ht:** 6'2" **Wt:** 225 **Born:** 9/18/75 **Age:** 26

Year Team	Lg Org	G	AB	H	2B	3B	HR	TB	R	RBI	TBB	IBB	SO	HBP	SH	SF	SB	CS	SB%	GDP	Avg	OBP	SLG
1998 Augusta	A Pit	24	86	40	7	0	9	74	32	31	24	1	20	0	0	2	1	1	.50	2	.465	.571	.860
Carolina	AA Pit	16	44	6	1	0	0	7	1	3	4	0	13	0	0	2	0	0	—	1	.136	.200	.159
Lynchburg	A+ Pit	31	109	21	7	0	2	34	7	11	17	0	38	1	0	1	1	0	1.00	1	.193	.305	.312
1999 Lynchburg	A+ Pit	128	444	116	33	1	23	220	96	87	94	5	113	6	0	5	5	4	.56	13	.261	.393	.495
2000 Altoona	AA Pit	121	348	83	16	1	11	134	50	52	68	3	82	3	1	5	4	4	.50	4	.239	.363	.385

				BATTING														BASERUNNING				PERCENTAGES		
Year Team	Lg Org	G	AB	H	2B	3B	HR	TB	R	RBI	TBB	IBB	SO	HBP	SH	SF	SB	CS	SB%	GDP	Avg	OBP	SLG
2001 Visalia	A+ Oak	80	294	102	20	2	16	174	54	49	49	7	72	3	0	4	4	0	1.00	5	.347	.440	.592
Midland	AA Oak	38	132	33	10	2	1	50	11	13	19	0	43	1	0	0	0	0	—	2	.250	.349	.379
4 Min. YEARS		438	1457	401	94	6	62	693	251	246	275	16	381	14	1	19	15	9	.63	28	.275	.391	.476

Chris Fussell

Pitches: Right **Bats:** Right **Pos:** SP-9   **Ht:** 6'2" **Wt:** 200 **Born:** 5/19/76 **Age:** 26

		HOW MUCH HE PITCHED						WHAT HE GAVE UP										THE RESULTS					
Year Team	Lg Org	G	GS	CG	GF	IP	BFP	H	R	ER	HR	SH	SF	HB	TBB	IBB	SO	WP	Bk	W	L	Pct.	ShO	Sv	ERA
1994 Orioles	R Bal	14	8	0	2	56.1	245	53	30	26	2	1	4	4	24	0	65	6	1	2	3	.400	0	0	4.15
1995 Bluefield	R+ Bal	12	12	1	0	65.2	265	37	18	16	4	1	1	7	32	0	98	3	1	9	1	.900	1	0	2.19
1996 Frederick	A+ Bal	15	14	1	0	86.1	369	71	36	27	8	1	1	5	44	0	94	5	0	5	2	.714	1	0	2.81
1997 Bowie	AA Bal	19	18	0	0	82.1	398	102	71	65	12	1	5	10	58	3	71	7	0	1	8	.111	0	0	7.11
Frederick	A+ Bal	9	9	1	0	50	218	42	23	22	5	2	3	3	31	2	54	3	0	3	3	.500	1	0	3.96
1998 Bowie	AA Bal	18	18	0	0	93	413	87	54	44	13	1	6	4	52	1	84	4	0	3	7	.300	0	0	4.26
Rochester	AAA Bal	10	10	0	0	58.2	249	50	30	26	4	1	3	5	28	0	51	5	0	5	2	.714	0	0	3.99
1999 Omaha	AAA KC	14	13	1	1	81.1	332	66	35	32	11	2	0	2	27	0	80	4	0	10	3	.769	1	0	3.54
2000 Royals	R KC	2	2	0	0	3.2	23	6	5	1	0	0	0	2	2	0	6	0	0	0	1	.000	0	0	2.45
Omaha	AAA KC	6	6	0	0	21.2	99	22	13	12	5	1	0	3	12	0	12	0	0	1	1	.500	0	0	4.98
2001 Omaha	AAA KC	9	9	0	0	39.1	197	58	47	42	15	0	0	3	24	0	35	2	0	2	6	.250	0	0	9.61
1998 Baltimore	AL	3	2	0	0	9.2	47	11	9	9	1	1	1	0	9	1	8	0	0	0	1	.000	0	0	8.38
1999 Kansas City	AL	17	8	0	3	56	265	72	51	46	9	1	4	5	36	3	37	6	0	0	5	.000	0	2	7.39
2000 Kansas City	AL	20	9	0	2	70	320	76	52	49	18	3	5	2	44	2	46	3	0	5	3	.625	0	0	6.30
8 Min. YEARS		128	119	4	3	638.1	2808	594	362	313	79	11	23	48	334	6	650	39	2	41	37	.526	4	0	4.41
3 Maj. YEARS		40	19	0	5	135.2	632	159	112	104	28	5	10	7	89	6	91	9	0	5	9	.357	0	2	6.90

Steve Gagliano

Pitches: Right **Bats:** Right **Pos:** RP-51; SP-1   **Ht:** 6'4" **Wt:** 200 **Born:** 8/4/77 **Age:** 24

		HOW MUCH HE PITCHED						WHAT HE GAVE UP										THE RESULTS					
Year Team	Lg Org	G	GS	CG	GF	IP	BFP	H	R	ER	HR	SH	SF	HB	TBB	IBB	SO	WP	Bk	W	L	Pct.	ShO	Sv	ERA
1997 Marlins	R Fla	12	12	1	0	56	234	56	28	23	1	2	1	3	16	0	50	4	1	3	4	.429	0	0	3.70
Utica	A- Fla	1	1	0	0	3.2	20	6	4	4	0	0	1	0	3	0	6	0	1	0	1	.000	0	0	9.82
1998 Brevard Cty	A+ Fla	8	0	0	3	13	63	15	12	7	3	1	0	1	10	0	7	1	1	0	0	—	0	0	4.85
Utica	A- Fla	13	12	1	0	68	292	67	33	25	4	2	1	1	27	1	66	5	1	6	4	.600	0	0	3.31
Kane County	A Fla	8	3	0	3	22.1	109	33	21	19	2	1	3	1	10	0	17	2	0	1	1	.500	0	0	7.66
1999 Brevard Cty	A+ Fla	15	7	0	5	48.2	227	59	38	25	6	0	4	4	14	0	29	3	0	2	5	.286	0	0	4.62
Beloit	A Mil	15	9	1	2	74.2	314	71	40	34	8	4	1	6	23	0	45	9	0	5	3	.625	1	1	4.10
2000 Lansing	A ChC	12	2	0	3	32	145	34	18	15	0	0	1	1	13	0	13	1	0	2	0	1.000	0	0	4.22
Daytona	A+ ChC	16	3	0	3	39	161	29	14	12	4	1	0	4	10	0	40	7	1	1	1	.500	0	3	2.77
2001 Daytona	A+ ChC	17	0	0	11	21.1	98	23	11	10	0	1	0	0	14	2	16	2	0	1	2	.333	0	7	4.22
West Tenn	AA ChC	35	1	0	3	48.2	217	49	24	23	5	3	2	1	23	3	44	2	1	1	2	.333	0	0	4.25
5 Min. YEARS		152	50	3	33	427.1	1880	442	243	197	33	15	14	22	163	6	333	36	6	22	23	.489	1	11	4.15

Shawn Gallagher

Bats: Right **Throws:** Right **Pos:** DH-50; 1B-36; OF-9; PH-3; PR-1   **Ht:** 6'0" **Wt:** 205 **Born:** 11/8/76 **Age:** 25

				BATTING														BASERUNNING				PERCENTAGES		
Year Team	Lg Org	G	AB	H	2B	3B	HR	TB	R	RBI	TBB	IBB	SO	HBP	SH	SF	SB	CS	SB%	GDP	Avg	OBP	SLG
1995 Rangers	R Tex	58	210	71	13	3	7	111	34	40	19	0	44	1	0	3	17	4	.81	7	.338	.391	.529
Hudson Val	A- Tex	5	20	3	2	0	0	5	1	4	1	0	4	1	0	0	0	0	—	2	.150	.227	.250
1996 Chston-SC	A Tex	88	303	68	11	4	7	108	29	32	18	0	104	6	3	2	6	1	.86	6	.224	.280	.356
Hudson Val	A- Tex	44	176	48	10	2	4	74	15	29	7	0	48	2	0	1	8	5	.62	5	.273	.306	.420
1997 Charlotte	A+ Tex	27	99	14	4	0	0	18	7	8	5	0	35	1	0	1	0	0	—	0	.141	.189	.182
Pulaski	R+ Tex	50	199	64	13	3	15	128	41	52	10	0	49	4	0	4	2	0	1.00	5	.322	.359	.643
1998 Charlotte	A+ Tex	137	520	160	37	4	26	283	111	121	66	3	116	7	0	10	18	6	.75	4	.308	.386	.544
1999 Tulsa	AA Tex	112	452	128	30	3	18	218	61	78	26	2	84	4	0	2	1	0	1.00	9	.283	.326	.482
2000 Tulsa	AA Tex	29	113	32	8	0	5	55	22	24	12	0	30	1	0	2	0	0	—	3	.283	.352	.487
Oklahoma	AAA Tex	64	219	52	9	3	6	85	27	30	23	1	43	1	1	5	1	4	.20	6	.237	.306	.388
Harrisburg	AA Mon	21	68	13	3	0	0	16	7	5	7	0	14	4	0	1	3	1	.75	3	.191	.300	.235
2001 Wichita	AA KC	96	345	91	19	4	12	154	44	48	25	1	62	2	2	3	5	7	.42	7	.264	.315	.446
7 Min. YEARS		731	2724	744	159	26	100	1255	399	471	219	7	633	34	6	34	61	28	.69	53	.273	.331	.461

Claudio Galva

Pitches: Left **Bats:** Left **Pos:** RP-59   **Ht:** 6'2" **Wt:** 205 **Born:** 11/28/79 **Age:** 22

		HOW MUCH HE PITCHED						WHAT HE GAVE UP										THE RESULTS					
Year Team	Lg Org	G	GS	CG	GF	IP	BFP	H	R	ER	HR	SH	SF	HB	TBB	IBB	SO	WP	Bk	W	L	Pct.	ShO	Sv	ERA
1999 Athletics	R Oak	14	11	0	0	68	275	64	23	18	0	3	2	2	16	0	59	4	1	6	2	.750	0	0	2.38
2000 Visalia	A+ Oak	48	7	0	30	97.1	421	103	54	39	9	1	3	1	29	0	98	3	1	7	4	.636	0	15	3.61
2001 Midland	AA Oak	55	0	0	24	60.2	268	56	24	19	5	6	2	1	27	6	44	2	1	1	2	.333	0	11	2.82
Sacramento	AAA Oak	4	0	0	0	5	26	7	2	2	1	2	0	0	5	2	6	0	0	1	0	1.000	0	0	3.60
3 Min. YEARS		121	18	0	54	231	990	230	103	78	15	11	7	4	77	8	207	9	3	15	8	.652	0	26	3.04

Randy Galvez

Pitches: Right **Bats:** Right **Pos:** SP-15   **Ht:** 6'2" **Wt:** 167 **Born:** 7/26/78 **Age:** 23

		HOW MUCH HE PITCHED						WHAT HE GAVE UP										THE RESULTS					
Year Team	Lg Org	G	GS	CG	GF	IP	BFP	H	R	ER	HR	SH	SF	HB	TBB	IBB	SO	WP	Bk	W	L	Pct.	ShO	Sv	ERA
1997 Great Falls	R+ LA	16	1	0	5	29.2	128	29	14	9	0	1	1	3	10	0	29	1	0	3	1	.750	0	0	3.64
2000 San Antonio	AA LA	12	12	0	0	63.1	281	74	40	36	5	1	1	4	30	0	35	3	0	4	4	.500	0	0	5.12
2001 Altoona	AA Pit	15	15	0	0	86	359	93	40	33	3	4	1	1	22	1	45	5	0	5	6	.455	0	0	3.45
3 Min. YEARS		43	28	0	5	179	768	196	94	81	8	5	3	8	62	1	109	9	0	12	11	.522	0	0	4.07

Jamie Gann

Bats: Right **Throws:** Right **Pos:** OF-80; P-9; PH-3; DH-1; PR-1 **Ht:** 6'1" **Wt:** 197 **Born:** 5/1/75 **Age:** 27

Year Team	Lg Org	G	AB	H	2B	3B	HR	TB	R	RBI	TBB	IBB	SO	HBP	SH	SF	SB	CS	SB%	GDP	Avg	OBP	SLG
1996 Lethbridge	R+ Ari	49	129	37	10	1	2	55	19	22	10	0	42	2	0	1	3	3	.50	4	.287	.345	.426
1997 South Bend	A Ari	12	36	6	1	0	0	7	4	3	1	0	9	0	1	0	0	1	.00	0	.167	.189	.194
High Desert	A+ Ari	91	267	60	12	2	6	94	33	32	17	2	71	1	2	2	2	1	.67	6	.225	.272	.352
1998 Diamondbcks	R Ari	2	7	3	1	0	0	4	1	1	0	0	2	0	0	0	0	0	—	0	.429	.429	.571
High Desert	A+ Ari	59	217	48	8	3	6	80	25	25	8	0	59	5	0	1	9	4	.69	4	.221	.264	.369
1999 El Paso	AA Ari	109	443	116	24	6	9	179	69	56	32	0	141	8	3	2	7	11	.39	8	.262	.322	.404
2000 El Paso	AA Ari	42	153	31	5	0	4	48	19	10	6	0	35	2	0	0	4	2	.67	4	.203	.242	.314
Diamondbcks	R Ari	6	19	9	3	0	0	12	5	7	0	0	1	1	0	0	2	0	1.00	0	.474	.500	.632
Tucson	AAA Ari	65	208	52	12	2	5	83	35	33	3	0	44	4	1	3	3	1	.75	6	.250	.271	.399
2001 Tucson	AAA Ari	7	15	4	1	0	1	8	2	4	0	0	0	0	0	0	0	0	—	0	.267	.267	.533
El Paso	AA Ari	55	190	41	5	0	2	52	20	18	7	0	44	4	2	0	5	3	.63	9	.216	.259	.274
Lancaster	A+ Ari	31	90	18	2	0	1	23	14	10	5	0	21	2	0	0	1	2	.33	2	.200	.253	.256
6 Min. YEARS		528	1774	425	84	14	36	645	246	221	89	2	469	29	9	11	36	28	.56	43	.240	.285	.364

Eddy Garabito

Bats: Both **Throws:** Right **Pos:** 2B-106; SS-24; DH-3; PH-1; PR-1 **Ht:** 5'8" **Wt:** 172 **Born:** 12/2/78 **Age:** 23

Year Team	Lg Org	G	AB	H	2B	3B	HR	TB	R	RBI	TBB	IBB	SO	HBP	SH	SF	SB	CS	SB%	GDP	Avg	OBP	SLG
1997 Delmarva	A Bal	2	4	0	0	0	0	0	0	0	0	0	0	0	0	0	0	0	—	0	.000	.000	.000
Bluefield	R+ Bal	61	231	70	12	3	5	103	47	44	21	0	30	3	2	7	26	9	.74	5	.303	.359	.446
1998 Delmarva	A Bal	135	481	119	20	8	9	182	81	66	44	3	93	5	4	12	25	15	.63	9	.247	.310	.378
Frederick	A+ Bal	4	19	4	1	1	0	7	4	2	1	0	5	0	0	0	1	1	.00	0	.211	.250	.368
1999 Frederick	A+ Bal	132	539	138	24	4	6	188	76	77	52	1	68	4	8	10	38	18	.68	7	.256	.321	.349
2000 Rochester	AAA Bal	9	35	3	1	0	0	4	3	0	2	0	10	0	0	0	1	0	1.00	2	.086	.135	.114
Bowie	AA Bal	116	482	121	21	3	6	166	72	52	27	1	55	5	8	7	22	9	.71	7	.251	.294	.344
2001 Rochester	AAA Bal	127	517	138	29	6	3	188	65	34	31	2	76	3	17	2	24	11	.69	7	.267	.311	.364
5 Min. YEARS		586	2308	593	108	25	29	838	348	275	178	7	337	20	39	38	136	63	.68	37	.257	.311	.363

Amaury Garcia

Bats: Right **Throws:** Right **Pos:** 2B-27; DH-5; SS-1; PH-1 **Ht:** 5'10" **Wt:** 160 **Born:** 5/20/75 **Age:** 27

Year Team	Lg Org	G	AB	H	2B	3B	HR	TB	R	RBI	TBB	IBB	SO	HBP	SH	SF	SB	CS	SB%	GDP	Avg	OBP	SLG
1994 Marlins	R Fla	58	208	65	9	3	0	80	46	25	33	0	49	2	1	2	10	3	.77	4	.313	.408	.385
1995 Kane County	A Fla	26	58	14	4	1	1	23	19	5	18	0	12	1	0	0	5	2	.71	1	.241	.429	.397
Elmira	A- Fla	62	231	63	7	3	0	76	40	17	34	2	50	4	3	0	41	12	.77	1	.273	.375	.329
1996 Kane County	A Fla	105	391	103	19	7	6	154	65	36	62	2	83	5	7	2	37	19	.66	8	.263	.370	.394
1997 Brevard Cty	A+ Fla	124	479	138	30	2	7	193	77	44	49	2	97	5	14	3	45	11	.80	4	.288	.358	.403
1998 Portland	AA Fla	137	544	147	19	6	13	217	79	62	45	0	126	2	14	1	23	15	.61	7	.270	.328	.399
1999 Calgary	AAA Fla	119	479	152	37	9	17	258	94	53	44	0	79	6	7	1	17	11	.61	9	.317	.381	.539
2000 Calgary	AAA Fla	120	479	140	26	3	13	211	83	47	41	0	79	4	7	3	35	15	.70	15	.292	.351	.441
2001 Charlotte	AAA CWS	34	118	28	4	1	0	34	9	7	7	0	26	1	4	0	4	0	1.00	2	.237	.286	.288
1999 Florida	NL	10	24	6	0	1	2	14	6	2	3	0	11	0	0	0	0	0	—	0	.250	.333	.583
8 Min. YEARS		785	2987	850	155	35	57	1246	512	296	333	6	601	30	57	12	217	88	.71	51	.285	.361	.417

Carlos Garcia

Bats: Right **Throws:** Right **Pos:** 3B-18; SS-16; 2B-10; DH-9; 1B-8; PH-3; P-1 **Ht:** 6'1" **Wt:** 195 **Born:** 10/15/67 **Age:** 34

Year Team	Lg Org	G	AB	H	2B	3B	HR	TB	R	RBI	TBB	IBB	SO	HBP	SH	SF	SB	CS	SB%	GDP	Avg	OBP	SLG
1987 Macon	A Pit	110	373	95	14	3	3	124	44	38	23	2	80	6	2	2	20	10	.67	6	.255	.307	.332
1988 Augusta	A Pit	73	269	78	13	2	1	98	32	45	22	0	46	1	2	1	11	6	.65	5	.290	.345	.364
Salem	A+ Pit	62	236	65	9	3	1	83	21	28	10	0	32	1	0	3	8	2	.80	9	.275	.304	.352
1989 Salem	A+ Pit	81	304	86	12	4	7	127	45	49	18	0	51	4	1	5	19	6	.76	3	.283	.326	.418
Harrisburg	AA Pit	54	188	53	5	5	3	77	28	25	8	0	36	0	0	1	6	4	.60	4	.282	.310	.410
1990 Harrisburg	AA Pit	65	242	67	11	2	5	97	36	25	16	0	36	3	1	1	12	1	.92	6	.277	.328	.401
Buffalo	AAA Pit	63	197	52	10	0	5	77	23	18	16	2	40	2	1	2	7	4	.64	5	.264	.323	.391
1991 Buffalo	AAA Pit	127	463	123	21	6	7	177	62	60	33	5	78	7	6	3	30	7	.81	6	.266	.322	.382
1992 Buffalo	AAA Pit	113	426	129	28	9	13	214	73	70	24	2	64	4	4	5	21	7	.75	7	.303	.342	.502
1996 Calgary	AAA Pit	2	6	2	0	1	0	4	0	0	0	0	0	0	0	0	0	0	—	0	.333	.333	.667
1998 Vancouver	AAA Ana	44	161	41	6	0	3	56	18	15	8	1	22	2	0	1	2	5	.29	2	.255	.297	.348
1999 Las Vegas	AAA SD	78	274	77	19	0	3	105	36	28	17	1	61	3	0	0	5	0	1.00	10	.281	.330	.383
2000 Columbus	AAA NYY	93	280	76	17	1	2	101	35	39	27	0	53	0	4	2	7	6	.54	7	.271	.333	.361
2001 Columbus	AAA NYY	61	215	54	12	0	3	75	22	19	14	0	39	2	1	0	8	1	.89	4	.251	.303	.349
1990 Pittsburgh	NL	4	4	2	0	0	0	2	1	0	0	0	2	0	0	0	0	0	—	0	.500	.500	.500
1991 Pittsburgh	NL	12	24	6	1	0	0	10	2	1	1	0	8	0	0	0	1	0	1.00	0	.250	.280	.417
1992 Pittsburgh	NL	22	39	8	1	0	0	9	4	4	0	0	9	0	1	2	0	0	—	1	.205	.195	.231
1993 Pittsburgh	NL	141	546	147	25	5	12	218	77	47	31	2	67	9	6	5	18	11	.62	9	.269	.316	.399
1994 Pittsburgh	NL	98	412	114	15	2	6	151	49	28	16	2	67	4	1	1	18	9	.67	4	.277	.309	.367
1995 Pittsburgh	NL	104	367	108	24	2	6	154	41	50	25	5	55	2	5	3	8	4	.67	4	.294	.340	.420
1996 Pittsburgh	NL	101	390	111	18	4	6	155	66	44	23	3	58	4	3	2	16	6	.73	3	.285	.329	.397
1997 Toronto	AL	103	350	77	18	2	3	108	29	23	15	0	60	2	10	4	11	3	.79	7	.220	.253	.309
1998 Anaheim	AL	19	35	5	1	0	0	6	4	0	3	0	11	1	1	0	2	0	1.00	4	.143	.231	.171
1999 San Diego	NL	6	11	2	0	0	0	2	1	0	1	0	3	0	0	0	0	0	—	2	.182	.250	.182
11 Min. YEARS		1026	3634	998	177	36	56	1415	475	459	236	13	638	35	22	26	156	59	.73	74	.275	.323	.389
10 Maj. YEARS		610	2178	580	102	17	33	815	274	197	115	12	340	22	27	17	73	33	.69	33	.266	.307	.374

Guillermo Garcia

Bats: Right **Throws:** Right **Pos:** C-56; DH-18; 1B-9; PH-5; 3B-3
Ht: 6'3" **Wt:** 215 **Born:** 4/4/72 **Age:** 30

						BATTING											BASERUNNING				PERCENTAGES		
Year Team	Lg Org	G	AB	H	2B	3B	HR	TB	R	RBI	TBB	IBB	SO	HBP	SH	SF	SB	CS	SB%	GDP	Avg	OBP	SLG
1990 Mets	R NYM	42	136	25	1	2	0	30	9	6	7	1	34	1	2	1	1	1	.50	2	.184	.228	.221
1991 Kingsport	R+ NYM	15	33	8	1	1	0	11	9	2	4	0	4	0	0	0	0	0	—	1	.242	.324	.333
Pittsfield	A- NYM	45	157	43	13	2	0	60	22	24	15	0	38	1	3	3	4	1	.80	5	.274	.335	.382
1992 Pittsfield	A- NYM	73	272	54	11	1	2	73	36	26	20	0	52	2	0	3	3	4	.43	5	.199	.256	.268
1993 Capital Cty	A NYM	119	429	124	28	2	3	165	64	72	49	1	60	10	1	3	10	8	.56	11	.289	.373	.385
1994 St. Lucie	A+ NYM	55	203	48	9	1	1	62	22	23	13	1	24	3	2	0	0	2	.00	6	.236	.292	.305
1995 Winston-Sal	A+ Cin	78	245	58	10	2	3	81	26	29	28	0	32	1	1	2	2	2	.50	7	.237	.315	.331
1996 Indianapols	AAA Cin	16	47	12	2	0	0	14	4	0	2	2	6	0	0	0	0	0	—	5	.255	.286	.298
Chattanooga	AA Cin	60	203	64	12	0	6	94	25	36	12	2	32	1	2	1	3	3	.50	3	.315	.355	.463
1997 Chattanooga	AA Cin	20	74	21	1	1	4	36	11	19	8	0	13	0	0	1	0	0	—	1	.284	.349	.486
Indianapols	AAA Cin	55	151	36	2	0	10	68	16	20	9	0	46	1	0	2	0	2	.00	2	.238	.282	.450
1998 Indianapols	AAA Cin	93	334	85	20	0	19	162	48	60	22	1	81	0	1	0	0	2	.00	9	.254	.301	.485
1999 Chattanooga	AA Cin	10	42	13	3	3	1	25	11	7	2	0	6	1	0	0	0	0	—	3	.310	.356	.595
Indianapols	AAA Cin	65	233	67	9	0	10	106	30	28	22	2	44	5	0	5	1	1	.50	12	.288	.355	.455
2000 Louisville	AAA Cin	102	327	89	24	2	14	159	38	55	25	1	54	2	1	5	2	2	.50	9	.272	.323	.486
2001 New Haven	AA StL	7	18	3	0	0	1	6	2	1	0	0	5	0	1	0	0	0	—	0	.167	.167	.333
Rochester	AAA Bal	5	19	1	0	0	0	1	1	0	2	0	5	0	0	0	0	0	—	1	.053	.143	.053
Camden	IND —	76	273	86	16	0	17	153	47	68	36	3	48	6	1	9	0	0	—	11	.315	.395	.560
1998 Cincinnati	NL	12	36	7	2	0	2	15	3	4	2	0	13	0	0	0	0	0	—	2	.194	.237	.417
1999 Florida	NL	4	4	1	0	0	0	1	0	0	0	0	2	0	0	0	0	0	—	0	.250	.250	.250
12 Min. YEARS		936	3196	837	162	17	91	1306	421	476	276	14	584	34	16	35	26	28	.48	95	.262	.324	.409
2 Maj. YEARS		16	40	8	2	0	2	16	3	4	2	0	15	0	0	0	0	0	—	2	.200	.238	.400

Jose Garcia

Pitches: Right **Bats:** Right **Pos:** SP-21
Ht: 6'3" **Wt:** 195 **Born:** 4/29/78 **Age:** 24

		HOW MUCH HE PITCHED						WHAT HE GAVE UP										THE RESULTS					
Year Team	Lg Org	G	GS	CG	GF	IP	BFP	H	R	ER	HR	SH	SF	HB	TBB	IBB	SO	WP	Bk	W	L	Pct.	ShO	Sv	ERA
1996 Helena	R+ Mil	2	0	0	0	1.2	9	1	3	3	0	0	0	0	3	0	2	1	0	0	0	—	0	0	16.20
1997 Beloit	A Mil	27	26	2	0	155.1	682	145	89	69	9	7	3	5	70	1	126	12	4	6	11	.353	0	0	4.00
1998 Stockton	A+ Mil	28	28	1	0	169.1	749	147	89	69	12	3	9	10	91	1	167	16	0	11	12	.478	0	0	3.67
2000 Huntsville	AA Mil	19	18	0	0	103	463	107	52	43	8	3	4	5	54	0	78	6	0	4	8	.333	0	0	3.76
2001 Huntsville	AA Mil	21	21	1	0	111	481	99	52	46	6	4	7	8	49	1	84	6	0	6	5	.545	0	0	3.73
5 Min. YEARS		97	93	4	0	540.1	2384	499	285	230	35	17	23	28	267	3	457	41	4	27	36	.429	0	0	3.83

Luis Garcia

Bats: Right **Throws:** Right **Pos:** SS-87; 3B-15; PH-12; DH-3; 2B-1; OF-1
Ht: 6'0" **Wt:** 175 **Born:** 5/20/75 **Age:** 27

						BATTING											BASERUNNING				PERCENTAGES		
Year Team	Lg Org	G	AB	H	2B	3B	HR	TB	R	RBI	TBB	IBB	SO	HBP	SH	SF	SB	CS	SB%	GDP	Avg	OBP	SLG
1993 Bristol	R+ Det	24	57	12	1	0	1	16	7	7	3	0	11	0	1	0	3	1	.75	1	.211	.250	.281
1994 Jamestown	A- Det	67	239	47	8	2	1	62	21	19	8	0	48	1	6	3	6	9	.40	4	.197	.223	.259
1995 Lakeland	A+ Det	102	361	101	10	4	2	125	39	35	8	0	42	1	4	4	9	10	.47	6	.280	.294	.346
Jacksnville	AA Det	17	47	13	0	0	0	13	6	5	1	0	8	1	0	0	2	1	.67	0	.277	.306	.277
1996 Jacksnville	AA Det	131	522	128	22	4	9	185	68	46	12	1	90	2	7	2	15	12	.56	9	.245	.264	.354
1997 Jacksnville	AA Det	126	456	122	19	1	5	158	55	48	10	0	59	3	6	6	3	2	.60	15	.268	.284	.346
1998 Toledo	AAA Det	114	407	105	19	4	3	141	37	31	8	0	59	1	3	3	3	2	.60	11	.258	.272	.346
1999 Toledo	AAA Det	89	308	82	19	1	3	112	30	34	5	0	41	1	3	5	3	3	.50	12	.266	.276	.364
2000 Memphis	AAA StL	112	386	112	17	3	11	168	53	44	13	0	65	5	4	2	5	5	.50	11	.290	.320	.435
2001 Memphis	AAA StL	118	422	108	20	1	7	151	42	44	8	0	71	4	1	3	2	1	.67	20	.256	.275	.358
1999 Detroit	AL	8	9	1	1	0	0	2	0	0	0	0	2	0	0	0	0	0	—	0	.111	.111	.222
9 Min. YEARS		900	3205	830	135	20	42	1131	358	313	76	1	494	19	35	28	51	46	.53	89	.259	.278	.353

Luis Garcia

Bats: Right **Throws:** Right **Pos:** 1B-111; OF-10; DH-6; 3B-1; PH-1
Ht: 6'4" **Wt:** 184 **Born:** 11/5/78 **Age:** 23

						BATTING											BASERUNNING				PERCENTAGES		
Year Team	Lg Org	G	AB	H	2B	3B	HR	TB	R	RBI	TBB	IBB	SO	HBP	SH	SF	SB	CS	SB%	GDP	Avg	OBP	SLG
1997 Red Sox	R Bos	8	0	0	0	0	0	0	0	0	0	0	0	0	0	0	0	0	—	0	—	—	—
1999 Mexico	R —	50	188	62	9	6	13	122	35	40	22	1	31	0	0	1	1	2	.33	2	.330	.398	.649
2000 Augusta	A Bos	128	493	128	27	5	20	225	72	77	51	6	112	1	0	2	8	1	.89	8	.260	.329	.456
2001 Sarasota	A+ Bos	65	267	81	14	1	12	133	38	44	18	2	61	1	0	1	2	2	.50	8	.303	.348	.498
Trenton	AA Bos	63	229	71	20	1	14	135	35	45	28	1	68	0	0	1	0	1	.00	3	.310	.384	.590
4 Min. YEARS		314	1177	342	70	13	59	615	180	206	119	10	272	2	0	5	11	6	.65	21	.291	.355	.523

Mike Garcia

Pitches: Right **Bats:** Right **Pos:** RP-18
Ht: 6'2" **Wt:** 220 **Born:** 5/11/68 **Age:** 34

		HOW MUCH HE PITCHED						WHAT HE GAVE UP										THE RESULTS					
Year Team	Lg Org	G	GS	CG	GF	IP	BFP	H	R	ER	HR	SH	SF	HB	TBB	IBB	SO	WP	Bk	W	L	Pct.	ShO	Sv	ERA
1989 Bristol	R+ Det	8	0	0	0	15.2	68	17	9	8	0	1	0	0	4	1	13	1	1	0	3	.000	0	0	4.60
Niagara Fal	A- Det	7	6	1	0	40.1	151	27	12	7	3	1	0	3	7	0	39	0	0	5	1	.833	0	0	1.56
1990 Fayettevlle	A Det	28	28	6	0	180.1	726	152	69	51	7	6	2	6	41	0	113	3	0	12	8	.600	2	0	2.55
1991 Lakeland	A+ Det	25	24	0	0	144	596	130	63	50	5	4	2	6	41	2	109	3	2	6	8	.429	0	0	3.13
1992 London	AA Det	27	20	1	3	136.2	581	149	69	59	10	4	5	4	35	1	92	2	0	8	8	.500	1	0	3.89
1993 London	AA Det	6	6	0	0	11.1	55	12	8	7	0	1	0	0	6	0	12	1	0	1	0	1.000	0	0	5.56
Rochester	IND —	16	16	1	0	94.2	396	89	36	31	8	1	4	1	27	0	100	5	0	9	2	.818	0	0	2.95
1999 Nashville	AAA Pit	23	0	0	10	27.1	114	24	12	12	3	3	1	1	10	2	35	0	0	0	0	.000	0	2	3.95
2000 Nashville	AAA Pit	24	0	0	3	33	137	31	17	13	3	1	2	0	8	0	31	0	0	2	2	.500	0	0	3.55
2001 Altoona	AA Pit	18	0	0	14	20	76	15	1	1	0	0	0	1	4	0	15	0	0	2	0	1.000	0	4	0.45

Year Team	Lg Org	G	GS	CG	GF	IP	BFP	H	R	ER	HR	SH	SF	HB	TBB	IBB	SO	WP	Bk	W	L	Pct.	ShO	Sv	ERA
1999 Pittsburgh	NL	7	0	0	2	7	25	2	1	1	1	0	0	0	3	0	9	0	0	1	0	1.000	0	0	1.29
2000 Pittsburgh	NL	13	0	0	2	11.1	59	21	15	14	1	0	3	0	7	1	9	1	0	0	2	.000	0	0	11.12
8 Min. YEARS		182	94	9	32	703.1	2900	646	296	239	39	22	16	22	183	6	559	15	3	45	34	.570	3	6	3.06
2 Maj. YEARS		20	0	0	4	18.1	84	23	16	15	2	0	3	0	10	1	18	1	0	1	2	.333	0	0	7.36

Osmani Garcia

Bats: Right **Throws:** Right **Pos:** 3B-106; DH-6; 1B-4; PH-3; SS-1; 2B-1 **Ht:** 6'0" **Wt:** 210 **Born:** 9/6/74 **Age:** 27

Year Team	Lg Org	G	AB	H	2B	3B	HR	TB	R	RBI	TBB	IBB	SO	HBP	SH	SF	SB	CS	SB%	GDP	Avg	OBP	SLG
2000 Charlotte	A+ Tex	44	170	57	12	1	6	89	26	34	5	0	14	1	4	2	1	2	.33	3	.335	.354	.524
Oklahoma	AAA Tex	43	148	40	7	0	2	53	17	20	10	0	14	1	1	1	1	2	.33	2	.270	.319	.358
2001 Tulsa	AA Tex	71	260	67	14	4	6	107	29	35	10	1	27	1	2	4	0	2	.00	4	.258	.284	.412
Oklahoma	AAA Tex	47	173	41	11	0	1	55	15	21	3	0	19	1	4	3	1	2	.33	6	.237	.250	.318
2 Min. YEARS		205	751	205	44	5	15	304	87	110	28	1	74	4	11	10	3	8	.27	15	.273	.299	.405

Rosman Garcia

Pitches: Right **Bats:** Right **Pos:** RP-19; SP-8 **Ht:** 6'2" **Wt:** 165 **Born:** 1/3/79 **Age:** 23

Year Team	Lg Org	G	GS	CG	GF	IP	BFP	H	R	ER	HR	SH	SF	HB	TBB	IBB	SO	WP	Bk	W	L	Pct.	ShO	Sv	ERA
1998 Yankees	R NYY	12	12	0	0	67	284	70	38	19	1	3	0	3	9	0	47	1	2	4	3	.571	0	0	2.55
1999 Greensboro	A NYY	9	9	0	0	42.1	204	60	33	30	4	0	1	2	20	0	31	12	3	2	3	.400	0	0	6.38
Staten IInd	A- NYY	18	10	0	1	69.2	310	86	40	33	3	3	3	4	14	2	40	4	1	2	6	.250	0	1	4.26
2000 Greensboro	A NYY	23	15	1	1	104.1	454	115	67	53	12	3	1	4	35	0	73	5	1	6	6	.500	0	0	4.57
Tampa	A+ NYY	4	3	0	1	18	77	18	13	11	1	0	3	2	4	0	6	0	1	0	2	.000	0	1	5.50
2001 Norwich	AA NYY	1	1	0	0	6	28	5	4	0	0	0	0	1	2	0	6	2	0	1	0	1.000	0	0	0.00
Tampa	A+ NYY	26	7	0	4	59.2	263	56	30	23	2	4	2	5	22	6	42	4	2	2	6	.250	0	1	3.47
4 Min. YEARS		93	57	1	7	367	1620	410	225	169	23	13	10	21	106	8	245	28	8	17	26	.395	0	3	4.14

Sonny Garcia

Pitches: Right **Bats:** Right **Pos:** SP-25; RP-5 **Ht:** 6'3" **Wt:** 215 **Born:** 9/10/76 **Age:** 25

Year Team	Lg Org	G	GS	CG	GF	IP	BFP	H	R	ER	HR	SH	SF	HB	TBB	IBB	SO	WP	Bk	W	L	Pct.	ShO	Sv	ERA
1998 Bluefield	R+ Bal	12	8	0	2	57.1	226	39	15	13	2	0	2	1	19	0	77	3	4	4	2	.667	0	0	2.04
Delmarva	A Bal	4	4	1	0	25	100	17	9	7	2	2	0	1	9	0	21	5	1	2	0	1.000	0	0	2.52
1999 Delmarva	A Bal	13	12	0	0	62	271	68	46	40	6	1	2	8	19	0	44	5	0	3	5	.375	0	0	5.81
2000 Delmarva	A Bal	26	21	1	0	110.2	478	106	55	46	12	2	2	5	38	1	123	2	1	6	7	.462	0	0	3.74
2001 Frederick	A+ Bal	25	20	2	3	143	593	132	67	52	9	8	2	10	33	3	139	4	1	8	9	.471	0	1	3.27
Bowie	AA Bal	5	5	1	0	28.1	130	33	22	18	4	0	0	0	9	2	21	3	0	1	3	.250	0	0	5.72
4 Min. YEARS		85	70	5	5	426.1	1798	395	214	176	35	13	8	25	127	6	425	22	7	24	26	.480	0	1	3.72

Tony Garcia

Bats: Right **Throws:** Right **Pos:** C-54; DH-5; PH-4; 1B-3 **Ht:** 6'1" **Wt:** 213 **Born:** 3/12/78 **Age:** 24

Year Team	Lg Org	G	AB	H	2B	3B	HR	TB	R	RBI	TBB	IBB	SO	HBP	SH	SF	SB	CS	SB%	GDP	Avg	OBP	SLG
1998 White Sox	R CWS	36	120	30	5	2	3	48	21	21	15	1	31	5	0	1	5	4	.56	3	.250	.355	.400
1999 Burlington	A CWS	73	230	54	10	0	2	70	35	20	22	0	76	13	5	1	3	4	.43	4	.235	.335	.304
2000 Winston-Sal	A+ CWS	77	238	66	14	1	3	91	33	32	20	0	55	14	4	1	5	1	.83	7	.277	.366	.382
2001 Birmingham	AA CWS	2	7	1	0	0	1	4	1	1	0	0	3	0	0	0	0	0	—	0	.143	.143	.571
Winston-Sal	A+ CWS	63	206	46	6	3	1	61	12	18	7	0	45	7	1	2	4	4	.50	4	.223	.270	.296
4 Min. YEARS		251	801	197	35	6	10	274	102	92	64	1	210	39	10	5	17	13	.57	18	.246	.330	.342

Lee Gardner

Pitches: Right **Bats:** Right **Pos:** RP-57 **Ht:** 6'0" **Wt:** 219 **Born:** 1/16/75 **Age:** 27

Year Team	Lg Org	G	GS	CG	GF	IP	BFP	H	R	ER	HR	SH	SF	HB	TBB	IBB	SO	WP	Bk	W	L	Pct.	ShO	Sv	ERA
1998 St. Pete	A+ TB	3	0	0	1	4	15	3	0	0	0	0	0	0	1	0	2	0	0	0	0	—	0	0	0.00
Chston-SC	A TB	28	0	0	13	35.2	154	38	18	16	3	2	0	1	4	0	55	1	0	0	3	.000	0	3	4.04
1999 Orlando	AA TB	1	0	0	0	2	9	3	2	2	0	0	0	0	1	0	1	0	0	0	0	—	0	0	9.00
St. Pete	A+ TB	20	0	0	13	23	96	20	7	5	1	1	1	2	5	0	22	0	0	2	0	1.000	0	7	1.96
2000 Orlando	AA TB	36	0	0	24	45	186	34	19	17	0	4	3	2	14	1	48	6	0	3	2	.600	0	12	3.40
Durham	AAA TB	21	0	0	9	18.2	75	12	7	7	1	1	0	0	9	1	8	1	0	1	0	1.000	0	5	3.38
2001 Orlando	AA TB	1	0	0	0	1.2	4	0	0	0	0	0	0	0	0	0	0	0	0	0	0	—	0	0	0.00
Durham	AAA TB	56	0	0	18	76	324	76	27	23	10	3	2	2	23	2	55	4	0	5	2	.714	0	2	2.72
4 Min. YEARS		166	0	0	78	206	863	186	80	70	15	11	6	7	57	4	191	12	0	11	7	.611	0	29	3.06

Cecilio Garibaldi

Pitches: Right **Bats:** Right **Pos:** RP-23; SP-12 **Ht:** 6'2" **Wt:** 214 **Born:** 1/5/78 **Age:** 24

Year Team	Lg Org	G	GS	CG	GF	IP	BFP	H	R	ER	HR	SH	SF	HB	TBB	IBB	SO	WP	Bk	W	L	Pct.	ShO	Sv	ERA
1998 Devil Rays	R TB	22	0	0	16	26.2	116	30	16	15	2	1	3	1	9	1	20	2	0	1	3	.250	0	5	5.06
1999 St. Pete	A+ TB	21	15	0	1	99	429	109	56	48	7	3	4	12	28	2	52	6	1	6	6	.500	0	0	4.36
2000 St. Pete	A+ TB	25	17	2	2	110	465	101	59	45	9	1	7	10	36	2	73	6	0	5	7	.417	0	0	3.68
2001 Orlando	AA TB	35	12	0	5	104.1	448	111	57	52	16	2	2	6	37	0	66	6	0	5	6	.455	0	1	4.49
4 Min. YEARS		103	44	2	24	340	1458	351	188	160	34	7	16	29	110	5	211	20	1	17	22	.436	0	6	4.24

Hal Garrett

Pitches: Right **Bats:** Right **Pos:** RP-9; SP-2   **Ht:** 6'2" **Wt:** 175 **Born:** 4/27/75 **Age:** 27

Year Team	Lg Org	G	GS	CG	GF	IP	BFP	H	R	ER	HR	SH	SF	HB	TBB	IBB	SO	WP	Bk	W	L	Pct.	ShO	Sv	ERA
1993 Padres	R SD	14	14	0	0	72.1	317	64	40	26	3	0	1	5	31	2	83	6	0	6	5	.545	0	0	3.24
1994 Springfield	A SD	21	20	0	0	102.1	454	93	67	54	8	2	5	6	54	2	79	9	2	7	4	.636	0	0	4.75
1995 Clinton	A SD	11	11	1	0	58	268	58	43	36	4	5	2	4	34	3	41	5	0	3	8	.273	0	0	5.59
Rancho Cuca	A+ SD	23	1	0	5	42	196	40	21	13	2	2	5	2	25	0	43	7	1	0	4	.000	0	0	2.79
1996 Clinton	A SD	25	3	0	11	49.2	229	45	28	25	4	2	2	5	31	2	60	3	0	2	3	.400	0	1	4.53
Rancho Cuca	A+ SD	24	1	0	3	51	214	41	12	11	3	1	2	3	20	0	56	6	0	4	1	.800	0	0	1.94
1997 Carolina	AA Pit	6	0	0	2	13.1	64	19	14	13	6	1	0	0	6	1	7	2	0	1	2	.333	0	0	8.78
Lynchburg	A+ Pit	29	5	0	11	56	250	56	36	30	5	4	3	4	22	3	45	5	0	2	5	.286	0	5	4.82
Savannah	A LA	8	1	0	4	16	78	21	15	15	0	1	0	2	7	0	13	4	0	0	3	.000	0	0	8.44
1998 Vero Beach	A+ LA	20	20	1	0	112.1	506	111	75	62	11	1	3	7	57	0	86	10	0	6	6	.500	0	0	4.97
San Antonio	AA LA	11	2	0	6	22.1	95	21	9	9	1	0	0	0	13	0	13	2	0	2	1	.667	0	2	3.63
1999 San Antonio	AA LA	42	4	0	13	94.2	404	70	47	38	8	7	2	1	55	4	76	9	0	5	9	.357	0	2	3.61
Albuquerque	AAA LA	1	0	0	0	2.1	11	3	4	4	1	0	0	0	2	0	1	0	0	0	1	.000	0	0	15.43
2000 Albuquerque	AAA LA	27	2	0	8	40	182	42	27	24	4	1	0	2	23	0	29	5	0	3	4	.429	0	1	5.40
San Antonio	AA LA	21	5	0	0	47.1	236	57	39	33	3	2	1	5	40	1	32	5	1	1	6	.143	0	0	6.27
2001 Akron	AA Cle	11	2	0	7	25.2	113	21	17	16	5	2	0	2	14	0	19	2	0	1	4	.200	0	0	5.61
9 Min. YEARS		294	91	2	76	805.1	3617	762	494	409	68	31	26	48	434	18	683	80	4	43	66	.394	0	11	4.57

Josh Garrett

Pitches: Right **Bats:** Right **Pos:** RP-42; SP-4   **Ht:** 6'4" **Wt:** 205 **Born:** 1/12/78 **Age:** 24

Year Team	Lg Org	G	GS	CG	GF	IP	BFP	H	R	ER	HR	SH	SF	HB	TBB	IBB	SO	WP	Bk	W	L	Pct.	ShO	Sv	ERA
1996 Red Sox	R Bos	7	5	0	0	27	108	22	8	5	0	2	0	5	5	0	17	0	0	1	1	.500	0	0	1.67
1997 Michigan	A Bos	22	22	2	0	138.2	619	142	94	74	13	7	4	13	35	0	64	23	3	8	10	.444	0	0	4.80
1998 Sarasota	A+ Bos	26	25	5	0	155.1	692	182	108	90	17	3	5	14	40	1	68	4	1	8	12	.400	2	0	5.21
1999 Sarasota	A+ Bos	26	26	0	0	149	683	189	87	76	9	1	6	17	50	2	95	7	0	8	10	.444	0	0	4.59
2000 Trenton	AA Bos	13	5	0	0	37.1	198	69	48	37	3	2	4	2	16	1	22	2	1	1	3	.250	0	0	8.92
Sarasota	A+ Bos	16	8	0	1	54	248	68	46	41	9	4	1	8	9	2	36	1	1	2	6	.250	0	0	6.83
2001 Trenton	AA Bos	46	4	0	13	81.1	379	84	61	51	10	2	3	14	44	2	68	11	0	3	6	.333	0	0	5.64
6 Min. YEARS		156	95	7	14	642.2	2927	778	452	374	61	21	23	73	199	8	370	48	6	31	48	.392	2	0	5.24

Matt Garrick

Bats: Right **Throws:** Right **Pos:** C-34; PH-4; DH-2   **Ht:** 6'0" **Wt:** 185 **Born:** 8/19/75 **Age:** 26

Year Team	Lg Org	G	AB	H	2B	3B	HR	TB	R	RBI	TBB	IBB	SO	HBP	SH	SF	SB	CS	SB%	GDP	Avg	OBP	SLG
1997 Boise	A- Ana	5	20	6	0	0	0	6	1	4	3	0	2	0	0	0	0	0	—	1	.300	.391	.300
Cedar Rapds	A Ana	28	95	21	6	1	0	29	11	14	12	0	23	2	1	0	1	0	1.00	7	.221	.321	.305
1998 Cedar Rapds	A Ana	61	212	52	13	0	4	77	27	25	29	0	55	1	2	0	5	1	.83	2	.245	.339	.363
1999 Potomac	A+ StL	70	216	36	10	1	3	57	17	17	32	0	57	0	3	1	1	5	.17	4	.167	.273	.264
2000 Arkansas	AA StL	101	325	76	17	0	4	105	33	35	36	3	71	2	1	1	1	2	.33	12	.234	.313	.323
2001 New Haven	AA StL	40	127	28	6	0	2	40	10	10	9	0	25	0	0	1	1	0	1.00	3	.220	.270	.315
5 Min. YEARS		305	995	219	52	2	13	314	99	105	121	3	233	5	7	3	9	8	.53	29	.220	.307	.316

Chris Garza

Pitches: Left **Bats:** Left **Pos:** RP-16   **Ht:** 5'11" **Wt:** 180 **Born:** 7/23/75 **Age:** 26

Year Team	Lg Org	G	GS	CG	GF	IP	BFP	H	R	ER	HR	SH	SF	HB	TBB	IBB	SO	WP	Bk	W	L	Pct.	ShO	Sv	ERA
1996 Elizabethtn	R+ Min	22	0	0	12	36.1	145	26	8	8	3	1	1	2	12	0	44	3	3	4	0	1.000	0	5	1.98
1997 Fort Wayne	A Min	60	0	0	32	95	385	67	28	21	2	3	2	3	38	1	90	11	0	5	2	.714	0	15	1.99
1998 Fort Myers	A+ Min	58	0	0	43	82	358	73	33	25	3	9	4	4	46	3	63	9	0	5	5	.500	0	14	2.74
1999 Fort Myers	A+ Min	21	1	0	10	40.1	169	36	16	14	1	1	1	3	18	0	30	3	1	1	2	.333	0	4	3.12
New Britain	AA Min	31	0	0	8	30.1	129	14	10	7	0	2	1	4	19	0	40	4	0	1	0	1.000	0	0	2.08
2000 New Britain	AA Min	39	0	0	10	43.2	195	34	21	17	1	2	2	2	26	2	52	1	0	2	4	.333	0	0	3.50
Salt Lake	AAA Min	19	0	0	11	20.2	101	28	19	14	1	2	1	0	13	1	19	2	0	1	1	.500	0	0	6.10
2001 Tulsa	AA Tex	16	0	0	4	23.1	100	15	11	8	1	0	1	1	16	0	23	1	0	0	1	.000	0	0	3.09
6 Min. YEARS		266	1	0	130	371.2	1582	293	146	114	12	20	13	19	188	7	361	34	4	19	15	.559	0	36	2.76

Jake Gautreau

Bats: Left **Throws:** Right **Pos:** 3B-46; DH-4   **Ht:** 6'0" **Wt:** 185 **Born:** 11/14/79 **Age:** 22

Year Team	Lg Org	G	AB	H	2B	3B	HR	TB	R	RBI	TBB	IBB	SO	HBP	SH	SF	SB	CS	SB%	GDP	Avg	OBP	SLG
2001 Portland	AAA SD	2	7	2	0	0	1	5	2	2	2	1	2	0	0	0	0	0	—	0	.286	.444	.714
Eugene	A- SD	48	178	55	19	0	6	92	28	36	22	0	47	4	0	4	1	1	.50	2	.309	.389	.517
1 Min. YEAR		50	185	57	19	0	7	97	30	38	24	1	49	4	0	4	1	1	.50	2	.308	.392	.524

Marty Gazarek

Bats: Right **Throws:** Right **Pos:** OF-44; PR-5; DH-2   **Ht:** 6'2" **Wt:** 205 **Born:** 6/1/73 **Age:** 29

Year Team	Lg Org	G	AB	H	2B	3B	HR	TB	R	RBI	TBB	IBB	SO	HBP	SH	SF	SB	CS	SB%	GDP	Avg	OBP	SLG
1994 Williamsprt	A- ChC	45	181	68	13	0	2	87	22	18	6	0	17	2	3	0	14	7	.67	2	.376	.402	.481
Peoria	A ChC	23	89	29	6	0	1	38	18	12	2	0	14	3	0	2	2	3	.40	4	.326	.354	.427
1995 Rockford	A ChC	107	399	104	24	1	3	139	57	53	27	1	58	8	2	3	7	5	.58	8	.261	.318	.348
1996 Daytona	A+ ChC	129	472	131	31	4	11	203	68	77	28	0	52	12	0	5	15	13	.54	10	.278	.331	.430
1997 Orlando	AA ChC	76	290	96	23	0	10	149	55	52	20	2	31	5	0	2	10	3	.77	3	.331	.382	.514
1998 West Tenn	AA ChC	21	64	21	4	2	1	32	14	11	13	1	10	2	0	1	6	2	.75	3	.328	.450	.500
Iowa	AAA ChC	88	238	61	16	0	4	89	33	16	16	0	38	5	2	0	4	3	.57	5	.256	.317	.374

Year Team	Lg Org	G	AB	H	2B	3B	HR	TB	R	RBI	TBB	IBB	SO	HBP	SH	SF	SB	CS	SB%	GDP	Avg	OBP	SLG
1999 Iowa	AAA ChC	40	128	41	12	0	5	68	13	16	5	1	13	1	0	1	0	1	.00	2	.320	.348	.531
West Tenn	AA ChC	35	128	38	9	1	6	67	16	27	4	1	7	3	0	1	2	5	.29	3	.297	.331	.523
2000 Greenville	AA Atl	61	202	58	10	0	7	89	27	28	18	0	32	8	0	2	5	3	.63	4	.287	.365	.441
2001 Toledo	AAA Det	17	56	12	4	0	1	19	10	3	5	0	5	0	0	0	2	0	1.00	1	.214	.279	.339
Erie	AA Det	31	101	27	4	0	0	31	13	6	8	0	16	4	1	1	1	1	.50	1	.267	.342	.307
8 Min. YEARS		673	2348	686	156	8	51	1011	346	319	152	6	293	53	8	18	68	46	.60	46	.292	.347	.431

Geoff Geary

Pitches: Right **Bats:** Right **Pos:** RP-20; SP-16   **Ht:** 6'0" **Wt:** 175 **Born:** 8/26/76 **Age:** 25

Year Team	Lg Org	G	GS	CG	GF	IP	BFP	H	R	ER	HR	SH	SF	HB	TBB	IBB	SO	WP	Bk	W	L	Pct.	ShO	Sv	ERA
1998 Batavia	A- Phi	16	15	1	1	95.1	368	78	20	17	6	3	0	6	14	0	101	3	0	9	1	.900	1	0	1.60
1999 Clearwater	A+ Phi	24	19	2	0	139	611	175	77	61	11	6	4	5	31	1	77	6	3	10	5	.667	0	0	3.95
2000 Reading	AA Phi	22	22	1	0	129.1	553	141	66	59	15	4	2	7	22	0	112	1	2	7	6	.538	0	0	4.11
2001 Reading	AA Phi	29	13	0	10	112.1	449	101	48	45	14	7	5	3	21	3	88	4	3	9	7	.563	0	2	3.61
Scranton-WB	AAA Phi	7	3	0	0	22	101	35	17	17	2	1	0	1	6	1	21	0	1	0	3	.000	0	0	6.95
4 Min. YEARS		98	72	4	11	498	2082	530	228	199	48	19	13	16	94	5	399	14	9	35	22	.614	1	2	3.60

Esteban German

Bats: Right **Throws:** Right **Pos:** 2B-113; DH-18; PR-1   **Ht:** 5'10" **Wt:** 180 **Born:** 12/26/78 **Age:** 23

Year Team	Lg Org	G	AB	H	2B	3B	HR	TB	R	RBI	TBB	IBB	SO	HBP	SH	SF	SB	CS	SB%	GDP	Avg	OBP	SLG
1998 Athletics	R Oak	55	202	62	3	10	2	91	52	28	33	0	43	4	2	1	40	8	.83	1	.307	.413	.450
1999 Modesto	A+ Oak	128	501	156	16	12	4	208	107	52	102	0	128	5	5	7	40	16	.71	3	.311	.428	.415
2000 Midland	AA Oak	24	75	16	1	0	1	20	13	6	18	0	21	2	2	0	5	3	.63	1	.213	.379	.267
Visalia	A+ Oak	109	428	113	14	10	2	153	82	35	61	0	86	5	4	2	78	8	.91	4	.264	.361	.357
2001 Midland	AA Oak	92	335	95	20	3	6	139	79	30	63	0	66	12	4	0	31	11	.74	6	.284	.415	.415
Sacramento	AAA Oak	38	150	56	8	0	4	76	40	14	18	0	20	6	2	1	17	2	.89	4	.373	.457	.507
4 Min. YEARS		446	1691	498	62	35	19	687	373	165	295	0	364	34	19	11	211	48	.81	19	.295	.407	.406

Mark Gibbs

Bats: Right **Throws:** Right **Pos:** 2B-51; SS-11; 3B-8; PR-6; PH-5; 1B-1; P-1   **Ht:** 6'0" **Wt:** 185 **Born:** 8/16/77 **Age:** 24

Year Team	Lg Org	G	AB	H	2B	3B	HR	TB	R	RBI	TBB	IBB	SO	HBP	SH	SF	SB	CS	SB%	GDP	Avg	OBP	SLG
2000 Orioles	R Bal	44	143	37	8	0	1	48	23	12	23	1	33	7	1	2	13	2	.87	1	.259	.383	.336
2001 Frederick	A+ Bal	42	121	25	4	0	3	38	12	12	8	0	42	3	3	0	1	1	.67	1	.207	.273	.314
Bowie	AA Bal	32	79	18	2	0	0	20	7	6	4	0	23	0	0	1	1	1	.00	1	.228	.262	.253
2 Min. YEARS		118	343	80	14	0	4	106	42	30	35	1	98	10	4	3	15	4	.79	3	.233	.320	.309

David Gibralter

Bats: Right **Throws:** Right **Pos:** OF-64; 1B-52; DH-8; PH-3   **Ht:** 6'3" **Wt:** 224 **Born:** 6/19/75 **Age:** 27

Year Team	Lg Org	G	AB	H	2B	3B	HR	TB	R	RBI	TBB	IBB	SO	HBP	SH	SF	SB	CS	SB%	GDP	Avg	OBP	SLG
1993 Red Sox	R Bos	48	177	48	14	0	3	71	23	27	11	1	34	6	1	2	1	1	.50	0	.271	.332	.401
1994 Sarasota	A+ Bos	51	184	35	5	1	4	54	20	18	6	1	41	1	0	0	1	2	.33	2	.190	.220	.293
Utica	A- Bos	62	222	57	11	0	5	83	31	32	14	2	40	5	1	2	3	1	.75	5	.257	.313	.374
1995 Michigan	A Bos	121	456	115	34	1	16	199	48	82	20	2	79	8	3	4	3	4	.43	7	.252	.293	.436
1996 Sarasota	A+ Bos	120	452	129	34	3	12	205	47	70	30	3	101	9	0	4	8	7	.53	9	.285	.339	.454
1997 Trenton	AA Bos	123	478	131	25	1	14	200	70	86	44	3	103	9	1	4	3	5	.38	10	.274	.344	.418
1998 Trenton	AA Bos	100	385	100	16	0	15	161	48	61	25	2	91	7	1	6	2	3	.40	5	.260	.312	.418
1999 Trenton	AA Bos	124	448	134	22	1	24	230	76	97	32	3	68	13	2	5	5	5	.50	13	.299	.359	.513
2000 Bowie	AA Bal	134	497	141	20	1	19	220	70	87	39	0	81	12	2	9	3	1	.75	18	.284	.345	.443
2001 Huntsville	AA Mil	95	354	96	19	0	13	154	48	36	44	4	48	10	0	3	1	2	.33	5	.271	.352	.435
Indianapolis	AAA Mil	27	98	32	9	0	3	50	10	17	6	0	10	1	1	3	0	1	.00	2	.327	.361	.510
9 Min. YEARS		1005	3751	1018	209	8	128	1627	497	625	263	21	696	81	12	42	30	32	.48	79	.271	.329	.434

Steve Gibralter

Bats: Right **Throws:** Right **Pos:** OF-87; 3B-2; DH-1   **Ht:** 6'0" **Wt:** 195 **Born:** 10/9/72 **Age:** 29

Year Team	Lg Org	G	AB	H	2B	3B	HR	TB	R	RBI	TBB	IBB	SO	HBP	SH	SF	SB	CS	SB%	GDP	Avg	OBP	SLG
1990 Reds	R Cin	52	174	45	11	3	4	74	26	27	23	1	30	3	3	1	8	2	.80	5	.259	.353	.425
1991 Chston-WV	A Cin	140	544	145	36	7	6	213	72	71	31	2	117	5	2	6	11	13	.46	14	.267	.309	.392
1992 Cedar Rapds	A Cin	137	529	162	32	3	19	257	92	99	51	4	99	12	1	3	12	9	.57	8	.306	.378	.486
1993 Chattanooga	AA Cin	132	477	113	25	3	11	177	65	47	20	2	108	7	3	4	7	12	.37	6	.237	.276	.371
1994 Chattanooga	AA Cin	133	460	124	28	3	14	200	71	63	47	0	114	9	4	5	10	8	.56	5	.270	.345	.435
1995 Indianapolis	AAA Cin	79	263	83	19	3	18	162	49	63	25	3	70	4	1	2	0	0	.00	6	.316	.381	.616
1996 Indianapolis	AAA Cin	126	447	114	29	2	11	180	58	54	26	6	114	2	1	3	2	3	.40	10	.255	.297	.403
1997 Chattanooga	AA Cin	30	97	25	9	0	2	40	20	12	13	1	22	2	1	3	0	0	—	0	.258	.348	.412
1998 Huntsville	AA Cin	17	67	18	4	0	1	25	8	4	6	0	13	1	1	0	1	0	1.00	3	.269	.338	.373
Indianapolis	AAA Cin	68	226	58	12	4	11	111	34	31	10	0	66	2	0	1	2	3	.33	3	.257	.293	.491
1999 Omaha	AAA KC	110	417	111	21	1	28	218	77	78	27	1	97	13	2	2	6	3	.67	9	.266	.329	.523
2000 Charlotte	AAA CWS	65	237	60	9	2	11	106	33	37	17	3	54	1	1	0	2	0	1.00	8	.253	.304	.447
2001 Long Island	IND —	8	30	11	1	1	1	17	6	6	2	0	2	2	0	0	5	1	.83	1	.367	.441	.567
Chattanooga	AA Cin	82	306	84	21	1	16	155	51	53	25	1	66	6	2	4	10	2	.83	7	.275	.337	.507
1995 Cincinnati	NL	4	3	1	0	0	0	1	0	0	0	0	0	0	0	0	0	0	—	0	.333	.333	.333
1996 Cincinnati	NL	2	2	0	0	0	0	0	0	0	0	0	2	0	0	0	0	0	—	0	.000	.000	.000
12 Min. YEARS		1179	4274	1153	257	33	153	1935	662	645	323	24	972	69	22	36	80	57	.58	85	.270	.329	.453
2 Maj. YEARS		6	5	1	0	0	0	1	0	0	0	0	2	0	0	0	0	0	—	0	.200	.200	.200

Derrick Gibson

Bats: Right Throws: Right Pos: OF-46; PH-5   Ht: 6'2" Wt: 244 Born: 2/5/75 Age: 27

				BATTING														BASERUNNING				PERCENTAGES		
Year Team	Lg Org	G	AB	H	2B	3B	HR	TB	R	RBI	TBB	IBB	SO	HBP	SH	SF	SB	CS	SB%	GDP	Avg	OBP	SLG
1993 Rockies	R Col	34	119	18	2	2	0	24	13	10	5	0	55	3	0	1	3	0	1.00	1	.151	.203	.202
1994 Bend	A- Col	73	284	75	19	5	12	140	47	57	29	5	102	9	0	1	14	4	.78	4	.264	.350	.493
1995 Asheville	A Col	135	506	148	16	10	32	280	91	115	29	5	136	19	1	6	31	13	.70	10	.292	.350	.553
1996 New Haven	AA Col	122	449	115	21	4	15	189	58	62	31	1	125	8	1	4	3	12	.20	15	.256	.313	.421
1997 New Haven	AA Col	119	461	146	24	2	23	243	91	75	36	7	100	10	0	2	20	13	.61	8	.317	.377	.527
Colo Sprngs	AAA Col	21	78	33	7	0	3	49	14	12	5	1	9	0	0	0	0	2	.00	1	.423	.458	.628
1998 Colo Sprngs	AAA Col	126	497	145	20	3	14	213	84	81	35	2	110	3	0	2	14	6	.70	17	.292	.341	.429
1999 Colo Sprngs	AAA Col	110	385	106	19	6	17	188	68	67	30	0	82	6	0	2	12	6	.67	5	.275	.336	.488
2000 Calgary	AAA Fla	100	340	95	12	2	10	141	43	43	18	2	84	9	1	2	13	7	.65	5	.279	.331	.415
2001 El Paso	AA Ari	18	72	25	4	0	2	35	13	16	6	1	18	2	0	1	3	1	.75	2	.347	.407	.486
Tucson	AAA Ari	32	97	24	8	1	2	40	8	15	5	0	19	4	0	0	5	0	1.00	0	.247	.311	.412
1998 Colorado	NL	7	21	9	1	0	0	10	4	2	1	0	4	1	0	0	0	0	—	0	.429	.478	.476
1999 Colorado	NL	10	28	5	1	0	2	12	2	6	0	0	7	1	0	0	0	0	—	2	.179	.207	.429
9 Min. YEARS		890	3288	930	152	35	130	1542	530	553	229	24	840	73	3	21	118	64	.65	70	.283	.341	.469
2 Maj. YEARS		17	49	14	2	0	2	22	6	8	1	0	11	2	0	0	0	0	—	2	.286	.327	.449

David Gil

Pitches: Right Bats: Right Pos: SP-16; RP-1   Ht: 6'4" Wt: 215 Born: 10/1/78 Age: 23

		HOW MUCH HE PITCHED						WHAT HE GAVE UP									THE RESULTS					
Year Team	Lg Org	G	GS	CG	GF	IP	BFP	H	R	ER	HR	SH	SF	HB	TBB	IBB	SO	WP	Bk	W	L	Pct.	ShO	Sv	ERA
2000 Dayton	A Cin	4	4	0	0	26.2	109	20	13	8	1	2	0	1	11	0	15	1	0	1	1	.500	0	0	2.70
Chattanooga	AA Cin	6	3	0	1	25	105	15	7	6	1	0	0	8	13	0	25	3	0	2	0	1.000	0	1	2.16
2001 Reds	R Cin	4	4	0	0	11	61	19	15	9	1	1	1	2	6	0	14	0	0	0	2	.000	0	0	7.36
Dayton	A Cin	2	2	0	0	11.2	47	11	1	1	0	1	0	0	3	0	15	0	0	1	0	1.000	0	0	0.77
Chattanooga	AA Cin	11	10	0	1	61	269	65	23	21	4	1	2	2	30	0	55	4	1	6	1	.857	0	1	3.10
2 Min. YEARS		27	23	0	2	135.1	591	130	59	45	7	5	3	13	63	0	124	8	1	10	4	.714	0	2	2.99

Shawn Gilbert

Bats: Right Throws: Right Pos: 2B-25; SS-23; OF-13; 3B-2; 1B-1   Ht: 5'9" Wt: 185 Born: 3/12/68 Age: 34

				BATTING														BASERUNNING				PERCENTAGES		
Year Team	Lg Org	G	AB	H	2B	3B	HR	TB	R	RBI	TBB	IBB	SO	HBP	SH	SF	SB	CS	SB%	GDP	Avg	OBP	SLG
1987 Visalia	A+ Min	82	272	61	5	0	5	81	39	27	34	0	59	7	4	4	6	4	.60	8	.224	.322	.298
1988 Visalia	A+ Min	14	43	16	3	2	0	23	10	8	10	0	7	1	0	0	1	1	.50	0	.372	.500	.535
Kenosha	A Min	108	402	112	21	2	3	146	80	44	63	2	61	2	0	5	49	10	.83	6	.279	.375	.363
1989 Visalia	A+ Min	125	453	113	17	1	2	138	52	43	54	1	70	3	6	3	42	16	.72	11	.249	.331	.305
1990 Orlando	AA Min	123	433	110	18	2	4	144	68	44	61	0	69	5	4	3	31	9	.78	10	.254	.351	.333
1991 Orlando	AA Min	138	529	135	12	5	3	166	69	38	53	1	70	11	6	6	43	19	.69	18	.255	.332	.314
1992 Portland	AAA Min	138	444	109	17	2	3	139	60	52	36	2	55	4	5	2	31	8	.79	10	.245	.307	.313
1993 Nashville	AAA CWS	104	278	63	17	2	0	84	28	17	12	0	41	2	2	1	6	2	.75	4	.227	.263	.302
1994 Scranton-WB	AAA Phi	141	547	139	33	4	7	201	81	52	66	3	86	7	3	3	20	15	.57	9	.254	.340	.367
1995 Scranton-WB	AAA Phi	136	536	141	26	2	3	177	84	42	64	0	102	6	4	4	17	9	.65	8	.263	.346	.330
1996 Norfolk	AAA NYM	131	493	126	28	1	9	183	76	50	46	0	97	5	14	4	16	4	.80	2	.256	.323	.371
1997 Norfolk	AAA NYM	78	288	76	13	1	8	115	53	33	43	1	64	2	3	1	7	2	.78	2	.264	.362	.399
1998 Norfolk	AAA NYM	39	133	36	8	0	2	50	21	12	16	1	28	2	0	2	3	1	.75	2	.271	.350	.376
Memphis	AAA StL	62	216	58	15	2	7	98	37	32	29	1	53	6	0	3	7	4	.64	3	.269	.366	.454
1999 Albuquerque	AAA LA	114	421	128	35	3	10	199	88	52	62	0	84	4	8	4	25	8	.76	3	.304	.395	.473
2000 Albuquerque	AAA LA	86	297	99	19	4	14	168	67	49	60	1	69	5	0	1	11	10	.52	3	.333	.452	.566
2001 Las Vegas	AAA LA	59	224	74	14	2	8	116	25	36	20	0	43	1	4	3	11	4	.73	2	.330	.383	.518
1997 New York	NL	29	22	3	0	0	1	6	3	1	1	0	8	0	0	0	1	0	1.00	0	.136	.174	.273
1998 New York	NL	3	3	0	0	0	0	0	1	0	0	0	1	0	0	0	0	0	—	0	.000	.000	.000
St. Louis	NL	4	2	1	0	0	0	1	0	0	0	0	1	0	0	0	1	0	1.00	0	.500	.500	.500
2000 Los Angeles	NL	15	20	3	1	0	1	7	5	3	2	0	7	0	1	0	0	0	—	0	.150	.227	.350
15 Min. YEARS		1678	6009	1596	301	35	87	2228	938	631	729	13	1058	73	63	49	339	136	.71	104	.266	.350	.371
3 Maj. YEARS		51	47	7	1	0	2	14	9	4	3	0	17	0	1	0	2	0	1.00	0	.149	.200	.298

Jason Gilfillan

Pitches: Right Bats: Right Pos: RP-44   Ht: 6'6" Wt: 215 Born: 8/31/76 Age: 25

		HOW MUCH HE PITCHED						WHAT HE GAVE UP									THE RESULTS					
Year Team	Lg Org	G	GS	CG	GF	IP	BFP	H	R	ER	HR	SH	SF	HB	TBB	IBB	SO	WP	Bk	W	L	Pct.	ShO	Sv	ERA
1997 Spokane	A- KC	16	0	0	5	16	82	16	13	9	0	1	0	1	16	1	22	3	0	2	1	.667	0	0	5.06
1998 Royals	R KC	7	6	0	0	9	42	10	8	8	1	0	0	1	4	0	6	1	0	1	1	.500	0	0	8.00
Spokane	A- KC	6	0	0	0	7.1	36	7	5	4	0	0	1	1	6	0	8	0	0	0	0	—	0	0	4.91
1999 Chston-WV	A KC	8	0	0	1	11.2	66	22	19	19	2	0	0	1	6	0	9	1	0	0	1	.000	0	0	14.66
Spokane	A- KC	25	0	0	7	34.2	161	31	23	22	6	3	4	6	22	0	37	3	1	4	1	.800	0	1	5.71
2000 Chston-WV	A KC	30	0	0	19	45	202	45	24	21	3	0	3	4	21	0	44	4	0	1	2	.333	0	7	4.20
Wilmington	A+ KC	12	0	0	3	15.1	74	13	6	3	0	0	0	1	13	0	20	2	0	3	1	.750	0	1	1.76
Omaha	AAA KC	1	0	0	1	1	4	0	0	0	0	0	0	0	1	0	2	0	0	0	0	—	0	0	0.00
2001 Wilmington	A+ KC	33	0	0	23	55	219	35	8	6	0	3	0	4	17	1	68	3	0	4	1	.800	0	9	0.98
Wichita	AA KC	11	0	0	3	17.1	89	23	13	12	0	0	1	1	13	2	13	4	0	0	0	—	0	0	6.23
5 Min. YEARS		149	6	0	62	212.1	975	202	121	104	12	7	9	20	119	5	229	21	1	15	8	.652	0	18	4.41

Eric Gillespie

Bats: Left Throws: Right Pos: OF-25; 1B-21; 3B-18; DH-16; PH-11 Ht: 5'10" Wt: 200 Born: 6/6/75 Age: 27

Year Team	Lg Org	G	AB	H	2B	3B	HR	TB	R	RBI	TBB	IBB	SO	HBP	SH	SF	SB	CS	SB%	GDP	Avg	OBP	SLG
1996 Boise	A- Ana	61	192	53	11	5	3	83	28	38	25	1	50	1	1	3	0	1	.00	4	.276	.357	.432
1997 Cedar Rapids	A Ana	122	421	107	26	7	18	201	78	72	55	0	80	4	0	4	8	0	1.00	1	.254	.343	.477
1998 Lk Elsinore	A+ Ana	30	98	31	12	0	3	52	13	11	14	1	21	1	0	0	2	1	.67	1	.316	.407	.531
1999 Jacksnville	AA Det	118	474	145	28	6	19	242	80	88	53	2	89	2	0	5	12	2	.86	12	.306	.375	.511
2000 Toledo	AAA Det	69	239	62	17	0	8	103	25	39	19	0	49	0	0	2	0	2	.00	3	.259	.312	.431
2001 Portland	AA Fla	82	240	54	16	2	4	86	28	35	29	3	45	1	1	2	3	1	.75	6	.225	.309	.358
6 Min. YEARS		482	1664	452	110	20	55	767	252	283	195	7	334	9	2	16	25	7	.78	33	.272	.348	.461

Troy Gingrich

Bats: Left Throws: Left Pos: OF-69; DH-10; PR-6; PH-4 Ht: 5'10" Wt: 175 Born: 1/17/77 Age: 25

Year Team	Lg Org	G	AB	H	2B	3B	HR	TB	R	RBI	TBB	IBB	SO	HBP	SH	SF	SB	CS	SB%	GDP	Avg	OBP	SLG
2000 Vermont	A- Mon	16	65	19	3	1	1	27	12	5	9	0	16	1	0	1	5	2	.71	4	.292	.382	.415
Cape Fear	A Mon	44	144	36	8	1	0	46	21	12	31	1	32	4	1	0	13	3	.81	1	.250	.397	.319
2001 Harrisburg	AA Mon	13	34	0	0	0	0	0	0	0	3	0	10	0	0	0	0	0	—	0	.000	.081	.000
Jupiter	A+ Mon	70	199	48	9	3	0	63	30	15	37	1	37	8	2	1	6	7	.46	7	.241	.380	.317
2 Min. YEARS		143	442	103	20	5	1	136	63	32	80	2	95	13	3	2	24	12	.67	12	.233	.365	.308

Isabel Giron

Pitches: Right Bats: Right Pos: RP-58 Ht: 6'2" Wt: 170 Born: 11/17/77 Age: 24

Year Team	Lg Org	G	GS	CG	GF	IP	BFP	H	R	ER	HR	SH	SF	HB	TBB	IBB	SO	WP	Bk	W	L	Pct.	ShO	Sv	ERA
1998 Hagerstown	A Tor	21	21	4	0	126.1	517	110	57	35	11	6	3	7	27	1	129	7	2	10	9	.526	3	0	2.49
Knoxville	AA Tor	6	5	0	0	35.1	145	29	15	15	5	0	1	0	13	1	35	3	0	1	1	.500	0	0	3.82
1999 Knoxville	AA Tor	17	16	0	0	95.2	423	97	59	52	12	3	6	7	39	0	81	1	1	7	5	.583	0	0	4.89
Mobile	AA SD	11	11	0	0	62.2	273	71	49	44	17	1	3	1	15	1	45	2	0	4	7	.364	0	0	6.32
2000 Mobile	AA SD	69	0	0	21	79	339	71	52	49	9	5	1	7	32	2	77	4	1	5	5	.500	0	5	5.58
2001 Mobile	AA SD	14	0	0	2	18.1	74	15	5	4	2	1	0	1	4	0	20	0	0	0	0	—	0	0	1.96
Portland	AAA SD	44	0	0	14	64.2	293	74	36	35	14	0	2	4	27	0	69	1	0	4	1	.800	0	0	4.87
4 Min. YEARS		182	53	4	37	482	2064	467	273	234	70	16	16	27	157	5	456	18	4	31	28	.525	3	5	4.37

Chris Gissell

Pitches: Right Bats: Right Pos: SP-27; RP-1 Ht: 6'5" Wt: 210 Born: 1/4/78 Age: 24

Year Team	Lg Org	G	GS	CG	GF	IP	BFP	H	R	ER	HR	SH	SF	HB	TBB	IBB	SO	WP	Bk	W	L	Pct.	ShO	Sv	ERA
1996 Cubs	R ChC	11	10	0	0	61.1	246	54	23	16	1	0	1	4	8	0	64	1	3	4	2	.667	0	0	2.35
1997 Rockford	A ChC	26	24	3	1	143.2	646	155	89	71	7	5	4	11	62	1	105	11	3	6	11	.353	1	0	4.45
1998 Rockford	A ChC	5	5	0	0	33.2	138	27	8	3	0	1	1	1	15	0	23	1	0	3	0	1.000	0	0	0.80
Daytona	A+ ChC	22	21	1	0	136	597	149	80	63	12	3	5	11	38	1	123	7	0	7	6	.538	0	0	4.17
West Tenn	AA ChC	1	1	0	0	4	21	5	7	6	2	0	0	0	4	2	4	0	0	0	1	.000	0	0	13.50
1999 West Tenn	AA ChC	20	18	0	0	97.2	470	121	76	65	10	4	6	10	62	3	57	9	2	3	8	.273	0	0	5.99
2000 West Tenn	AA ChC	16	16	0	0	93	395	80	39	32	6	3	2	6	41	1	65	2	0	7	5	.583	0	0	3.10
2001 West Tenn	AA ChC	28	27	0	0	159.2	695	159	91	80	13	5	8	9	63	0	136	7	0	5	11	.313	0	0	4.51
6 Min. YEARS		129	122	4	1	729	3208	750	413	336	51	21	27	52	293	8	577	38	8	35	44	.443	1	0	4.15

Josh Glassey

Bats: Left Throws: Right Pos: C-12; DH-3; PH-2 Ht: 6'1" Wt: 190 Born: 5/6/77 Age: 25

Year Team	Lg Org	G	AB	H	2B	3B	HR	TB	R	RBI	TBB	IBB	SO	HBP	SH	SF	SB	CS	SB%	GDP	Avg	OBP	SLG
1996 Yakima	A- LA	50	137	30	5	0	0	35	11	20	26	1	44	0	0	0	0	0	—	3	.219	.344	.255
1997 Savannah	A LA	73	207	38	5	0	0	43	17	20	35	0	72	0	3	1	3	1	.75	3	.184	.300	.208
1998 Albuquerque	AAA LA	6	8	1	1	0	0	2	1	1	1	0	3	0	0	0	1	0	1.00	0	.125	.222	.250
Vero Beach	A+ LA	58	159	36	7	0	2	49	19	16	35	1	27	1	3	1	1	2	.33	4	.226	.367	.308
1999 Yakima	A- LA	28	92	21	4	0	2	31	13	14	19	0	24	0	4	1	0	1	.00	5	.228	.357	.337
2000 San Berndno	A+ LA	20	60	11	7	0	0	18	10	4	18	1	20	1	0	0	0	0	—	2	.183	.380	.300
High Desert	A+ Ari	23	69	18	7	0	0	25	8	6	11	0	16	0	0	0	1	0	.00	0	.261	.363	.362
2001 Lancaster	A+ Ari	8	20	3	0	0	0	3	6	1	8	0	2	1	0	0	1	1	.50	0	.150	.414	.150
El Paso	AA Ari	8	18	3	0	0	0	3	1	0	3	0	5	0	0	0	0	0	—	1	.167	.286	.167
6 Min. YEARS		274	770	161	36	0	4	209	86	82	156	3	213	3	10	3	6	6	.50	18	.209	.343	.271

Keith Glauber

Pitches: Right Bats: Right Pos: RP-41; SP-4 Ht: 6'2" Wt: 190 Born: 1/18/72 Age: 30

Year Team	Lg Org	G	GS	CG	GF	IP	BFP	H	R	ER	HR	SH	SF	HB	TBB	IBB	SO	WP	Bk	W	L	Pct.	ShO	Sv	ERA
1994 New Jersey	A- StL	17	10	0	3	68.2	289	67	36	32	3	4	2	2	26	1	51	8	0	4	6	.400	0	0	4.19
1995 Savannah	A StL	40	0	0	3	62.2	277	50	29	26	2	2	3	5	36	3	62	9	1	2	1	.667	0	0	3.73
1996 Peoria	A StL	54	0	0	36	64	276	54	31	22	2	2	5	1	26	2	80	2	1	3	3	.500	0	14	3.09
1997 Arkansas	AA StL	50	0	0	22	59	245	48	22	18	3	2	4	2	25	2	53	5	0	5	7	.417	0	3	2.75
Louisville	AAA StL	15	0	0	12	15.2	71	18	14	9	2	1	0	1	4	0	14	0	0	1	3	.250	0	5	5.17
1998 Burlington	A Cin	7	1	0	1	14	73	13	9	6	1	0	0	2	6	0	13	2	0	0	1	.000	0	0	3.86
Chattanooga	AA Cin	2	2	0	0	9	35	3	4	4	1	0	0	0	6	0	5	0	0	1	1	.500	0	0	4.00
Indianapols	AAA Cin	4	4	0	0	16	78	20	17	16	1	3	2	1	14	0	15	3	0	1	3	.250	0	0	9.00
1999 Chattanooga	AA Cin	7	7	0	0	50	193	42	12	11	0	1	1	2	6	0	26	3	1	5	0	1.000	1	0	1.98
Indianapols	AAA Cin	12	12	1	0	68	305	84	49	44	8	1	6	6	20	0	51	1	0	3	3	.500	0	0	5.82

Year Team	Lg Org	G	GS	CG	GF	IP	BFP	H	R	ER	HR	SH	SF	HB	TBB	IBB	SO	WP	Bk	W	L	Pct.	ShO	Sv	ERA
2000 Chattanooga	AA Cin	32	0	0	9	41	176	42	19	16	2	5	2	4	12	3	27	2	1	0	4	.000	0	2	3.51
Louisville	AAA Cin	18	0	0	10	29.2	116	26	5	5	1	1	1	0	6	1	15	1	0	1	2	.333	0	4	1.52
2001 Louisville	AAA Cin	23	0	0	6	36.2	167	45	30	23	8	2	1	5	10	1	24	4	0	3	3	.500	0	0	5.65
Chattanooga	AA Cin	22	4	0	5	44.1	188	53	21	21	9	3	2	1	8	0	30	0	0	2	1	.667	0	0	4.26
1998 Cincinnati	NL	3	0	0	2	7.2	31	6	2	2	0	0	0	1	1	0	4	2	0	0	0	.000	0	0	2.35
2000 Cincinnati	NL	4	0	0	0	7.1	30	5	3	3	0	0	0	1	2	0	4	0	0	0	0	.000	0	0	3.68
8 Min. YEARS		303	40	1	107	578.2	2489	565	298	253	43	28	29	32	207	13	466	40	4	31	38	.449	1	28	3.93
2 Maj. YEARS		7	0	0	2	15	61	11	5	5	0	0	0	2	3	0	8	2	0	0	0	.000	0	0	3.00

Mike Glavine

Bats: Left **Throws:** Left **Pos:** 1B-71; PH-11; DH-9 **Ht:** 6'3" **Wt:** 210 **Born:** 1/24/73 **Age:** 29

Year Team	Lg Org	G	AB	H	2B	3B	HR	TB	R	RBI	TBB	IBB	SO	HBP	SH	SF	SB	CS	SB%	GDP	Avg	OBP	SLG
1995 Burlington	R+ Cle	46	155	38	10	0	11	81	28	28	22	0	37	1	0	2	1	0	1.00	0	.245	.339	.523
1996 Columbus	A Cle	38	119	33	5	0	6	56	17	16	28	2	33	1	0	1	0	0	.00	2	.277	.416	.471
1997 Columbus	A Cle	114	397	95	16	0	28	195	62	75	80	1	127	3	0	1	0	1	.00	9	.239	.370	.491
1998 Kinston	A+ Cle	125	398	87	23	1	22	178	61	76	73	4	117	5	2	6	1	4	.20	4	.219	.342	.447
1999 Greenville	AA Atl	107	305	82	24	0	17	157	47	52	49	0	65	1	0	2	1	0	.00	3	.269	.370	.515
2000 Greenville	AA Atl	128	423	99	26	0	11	158	37	81	36	3	83	5	0	7	1	1	.50	8	.234	.297	.374
2001 Richmond	AAA Atl	23	44	6	2	0	0	8	1	4	6	2	11	0	0	1	0	0	—	1	.136	.235	.182
Somerset	IND —	68	254	62	14	0	11	109	24	41	27	0	55	1	1	4	2	3	.40	6	.244	.315	.429
7 Min. YEARS		649	2095	502	120	1	106	942	277	373	321	12	528	17	3	24	5	12	.29	33	.240	.342	.450

Mike Glendenning

Bats: Right **Throws:** Right **Pos:** DH-53; OF-47; PH-9; 1B-1 **Ht:** 6'0" **Wt:** 225 **Born:** 8/26/76 **Age:** 25

Year Team	Lg Org	G	AB	H	2B	3B	HR	TB	R	RBI	TBB	IBB	SO	HBP	SH	SF	SB	CS	SB%	GDP	Avg	OBP	SLG
1996 Bellingham	A- SF	73	265	69	19	4	12	132	54	48	39	0	80	1	1	2	4	6	.40	6	.260	.355	.498
1997 Bakersfield	A+ SF	134	503	130	27	0	33	256	95	100	63	1	150	4	0	7	1	4	.20	15	.258	.341	.509
1998 Shreveport	AA SF	78	254	62	12	2	7	99	27	33	35	1	57	4	0	1	0	0	—	2	.244	.344	.390
San Jose	A+ SF	48	176	44	9	0	10	83	26	33	24	0	66	0	0	0	1	1	.50	5	.250	.340	.472
1999 San Jose	A+ SF	104	368	90	26	1	23	187	71	80	71	2	112	11	0	3	7	4	.64	10	.245	.380	.508
Shreveport	AA SF	32	106	28	6	0	5	49	14	19	12	0	30	1	0	1	1	1	.50	2	.264	.342	.462
2000 Fresno	AAA SF	40	139	27	7	0	6	52	17	18	13	0	41	1	0	2	0	1	.00	5	.194	.265	.374
Shreveport	AA SF	85	291	76	14	0	16	138	50	54	36	4	87	5	0	2	1	1	.50	5	.261	.350	.474
2001 Shreveport	AA SF	60	207	38	3	0	7	62	20	18	21	0	71	2	0	1	0	0	—	7	.184	.264	.300
Lancaster	A+ Ari	9	33	8	4	0	2	18	2	6	4	0	13	0	0	0	1	0	1.00	1	.242	.324	.545
El Paso	AA Ari	40	140	33	9	0	3	51	17	18	18	1	46	2	1	1	1	0	1.00	3	.236	.329	.364
6 Min. YEARS		703	2482	605	136	7	124	1127	393	427	336	9	753	31	2	20	16	18	.47	58	.244	.339	.454

Ross Gload

Bats: Left **Throws:** Left **Pos:** OF-72; 1B-50; DH-11; PH-9 **Ht:** 6'0" **Wt:** 185 **Born:** 4/5/76 **Age:** 26

Year Team	Lg Org	G	AB	H	2B	3B	HR	TB	R	RBI	TBB	IBB	SO	HBP	SH	SF	SB	CS	SB%	GDP	Avg	OBP	SLG
1997 Utica	A- Fla	68	245	64	15	2	3	92	28	43	28	0	57	2	0	5	1	1	.50	5	.261	.336	.376
1998 Kane County	A Fla	132	501	157	41	3	12	240	77	92	58	7	84	3	2	3	7	6	.54	13	.313	.386	.479
1999 Brevard Cty	A+ Fla	133	490	146	26	3	10	208	80	74	53	3	76	5	2	5	3	1	.75	8	.298	.369	.424
2000 Portland	AA Fla	100	401	114	28	4	16	198	60	65	29	3	53	2	3	4	4	1	.80	4	.284	.333	.494
Iowa	AAA ChC	28	104	42	10	2	14	98	24	39	9	1	13	1	0	1	1	1	.50	2	.404	.452	.942
2001 Iowa	AAA ChC	133	475	141	32	10	15	238	70	93	35	3	88	3	4	7	9	7	.56	8	.297	.344	.501
2000 Chicago	NL	18	31	6	0	1	1	11	4	3	3	0	10	0	0	1	0	0	—	1	.194	.257	.355
5 Min. YEARS		594	2216	664	152	24	70	1074	339	406	212	17	371	16	11	25	25	17	.60	40	.300	.361	.485

Jim Goelz

Bats: Right **Throws:** Right **Pos:** SS-59; 2B-19; OF-13; PR-11; 3B-7; PH-2; 1B-1; DH-1 **Ht:** 5'10" **Wt:** 170 **Born:** 2/13/76 **Age:** 26

Year Team	Lg Org	G	AB	H	2B	3B	HR	TB	R	RBI	TBB	IBB	SO	HBP	SH	SF	SB	CS	SB%	GDP	Avg	OBP	SLG
1998 Yakima	A- LA	69	213	39	6	0	0	45	20	15	28	0	36	3	6	4	9	0	1.00	6	.183	.282	.211
1999 Yakima	A- LA	42	142	40	3	1	1	48	19	17	12	0	22	2	3	2	2	5	.29	4	.282	.342	.338
2000 Vero Beach	A+ LA	75	241	59	7	2	0	70	36	19	25	1	45	2	4	4	2	4	.33	2	.245	.316	.290
Yakima	A- LA	1	2	1	0	0	0	1	1	0	0	0	0	1	0	0	0	0	—	0	.500	.667	.500
2001 Buffalo	AAA Cle	4	4	1	0	0	0	1	0	0	0	0	2	0	0	0	0	0	—	0	.250	.250	.250
Akron	AA Cle	101	283	74	20	2	1	101	30	28	13	0	43	0	4	2	6	3	.67	8	.261	.292	.357
4 Min. YEARS		292	885	214	36	5	2	266	106	79	78	1	148	8	17	12	19	12	.61	24	.242	.305	.301

Geoff Goetz

Pitches: Left **Bats:** Left **Pos:** RP-25 **Ht:** 5'11" **Wt:** 163 **Born:** 4/3/79 **Age:** 23

Year Team	Lg Org	G	GS	CG	GF	IP	BFP	H	R	ER	HR	SH	SF	HB	TBB	IBB	SO	WP	Bk	W	L	Pct.	ShO	Sv	ERA
1997 Mets	R NYM	8	6	0	1	26.1	112	23	11	8	0	2	0	6	18	0	28	1	2	0	2	.000	0	1	2.73
1998 Capital Cty	A NYM	15	15	0	0	77.1	336	68	45	34	3	0	1	6	37	0	68	12	1	5	4	.556	0	0	3.96
Kane County	A Fla	9	9	0	0	42.2	189	44	22	22	4	1	2	2	24	1	36	5	0	1	4	.200	0	0	4.64
1999 Kane County	A Fla	16	12	0	0	50.2	223	52	28	24	9	4	0	4	24	0	43	7	0	5	3	.625	0	0	4.26
2000 Brevard Cty	A+ Fla	27	0	0	15	67	270	43	19	13	1	3	1	0	36	1	61	6	0	6	2	.750	0	5	1.75
Portland	AA Fla	17	0	0	7	22.2	105	27	15	15	3	4	0	1	11	0	21	1	0	1	2	.333	0	1	5.96
2001 Portland	AA Fla	25	0	0	0	29.1	120	22	10	5	2	0	1	0	12	0	24	3	0	2	2	.500	0	0	1.53
5 Min. YEARS		117	42	0	29	316	1355	279	150	121	17	9	10	15	162	2	281	35	3	20	19	.513	0	7	3.45

Jeff Goldbach

Bats: Right **Throws:** Right **Pos:** C-60; DH-14; PH-5

Ht: 6'0" **Wt:** 190 **Born:** 12/20/79 **Age:** 22

Year Team	Lg Org	G	AB	H	2B	3B	HR	TB	R	RBI	TBB	IBB	SO	HBP	SH	SF	SB	CS	SB%	GDP	Avg	OBP	SLG
1998 Cubs	R ChC	38	136	36	11	2	4	63	22	25	11	0	41	2	0	0	5	2	.71	1	.265	.329	.463
1999 Lansing	A ChC	112	399	108	27	3	18	195	82	72	64	2	66	7	0	5	1	4	.20	5	.271	.377	.489
2000 Daytona	A+ ChC	119	420	84	15	1	10	131	49	60	31	1	76	8	0	7	6	5	.55	1	.200	.264	.312
2001 West Tenn	AA ChC	32	98	20	4	1	3	35	11	6	9	1	17	1	1	0	1	0	1.00	1	.204	.278	.357
Daytona	A+ ChC	46	145	28	5	1	4	47	14	17	15	0	28	2	1	1	0	0	—	1	.193	.276	.324
4 Min. YEARS		347	1198	276	62	8	39	471	178	180	130	4	228	20	2	13	13	11	.54	9	.230	.313	.393

Tony Gomes

Pitches: Right **Bats:** Right **Pos:** RP-28

Ht: 6'0" **Wt:** 190 **Born:** 9/10/77 **Age:** 24

Year Team	Lg Org	G	GS	CG	GF	IP	BFP	H	R	ER	HR	SH	SF	HB	TBB	IBB	SO	WP	Bk	W	L	Pct.	ShO	Sv	ERA
1998 Yakima	A- LA	16	11	0	2	72.2		76	53	33	6	0	4	4	34	0	52	11	2	2	8	.200	0	1	4.09
1999 Vero Beach	A+ LA	37	0	0	17	61.2	285	67	45	43	7	7	2	2	32	3	70	5	1	4	5	.444	0	2	6.28
2001 Vero Beach	A+ LA	11	0	0	7	23.1	94	13	6	6	0	3	0	2	11	1	26	2	0	1	1	.500	0	4	2.31
Jacksnville	AA LA	17	0	0	5	28.1	129	30	13	9	1	1	1	0	15	2	31	1	1	1	1	.500	0	2	2.86
3 Min. YEARS		81	11	0	31	186	829	186	117	91	14	11	7	8	92	6	179	19	4	8	15	.348	0	9	4.40

Alexis Gomez

Bats: Left **Throws:** Left **Pos:** OF-131; PH-1; PR-1

Ht: 6'2" **Wt:** 160 **Born:** 8/6/80 **Age:** 21

Year Team	Lg Org	G	AB	H	2B	3B	HR	TB	R	RBI	TBB	IBB	SO	HBP	SH	SF	SB	CS	SB%	GDP	Avg	OBP	SLG
1999 Royals	R KC	56	214	59	12	1	5	88	44	31	32	0	48	1	1	1	13	5	.72	1	.276	.371	.411
2000 Wilmington	A+ KC	121	461	117	13	4	1	141	63	33	45	1	121	2	7	1	21	10	.68	8	.254	.322	.306
2001 Wilmington	A+ KC	48	169	51	8	2	1	66	29	9	11	2	43	1	2	0	7	3	.70	4	.302	.348	.391
Wichita	AA KC	83	342	96	15	6	4	135	55	34	27	1	70	4	1	4	16	10	.62	4	.281	.337	.395
3 Min. YEARS		308	1186	323	48	13	11	430	191	107	115	4	282	8	11	6	57	28	.67	17	.272	.339	.363

Heber Gomez

Bats: Right **Throws:** Right **Pos:** 3B-5; SS-2; 2B-2; PH-1

Ht: 5'10" **Wt:** 190 **Born:** 11/3/77 **Age:** 24

Year Team	Lg Org	G	AB	H	2B	3B	HR	TB	R	RBI	TBB	IBB	SO	HBP	SH	SF	SB	CS	SB%	GDP	Avg	OBP	SLG
2001 Chattanooga	AA Cin	10	37	7	2	0	0	9	2	1	1	1	7	2	0	0	1	0	1.00	1	.189	.250	.243

Ramon Gomez

Bats: Right **Throws:** Right **Pos:** OF-46; PH-8; DH-6; PR-2

Ht: 6'2" **Wt:** 175 **Born:** 10/6/75 **Age:** 26

Year Team	Lg Org	G	AB	H	2B	3B	HR	TB	R	RBI	TBB	IBB	SO	HBP	SH	SF	SB	CS	SB%	GDP	Avg	OBP	SLG
1995 Hickory	A CWS	76	231	53	6	0	0	59	26	9	18	0	64	2	3	0	17	9	.65	5	.229	.291	.255
White Sox	R CWS	30	103	27	3	0	1	33	16	6	12	0	22	3	0	0	12	4	.75	2	.262	.356	.320
1996 Hickory	A CWS	116	418	104	8	3	1	121	73	30	44	0	99	2	11	2	57	19	.75	5	.249	.322	.289
1997 Winston-Sal	A+ CWS	118	477	132	23	12	2	185	78	42	42	0	132	3	8	2	53	21	.72	9	.277	.338	.388
1998 Winston-Sal	A+ CWS	43	124	27	5	2	0	36	21	10	12	1	36	2	1	0	13	3	.81	1	.218	.297	.290
1999 Birmingham	AA CWS	99	274	78	10	5	0	98	47	26	31	1	81	2	6	1	26	10	.72	1	.285	.360	.358
2000 High Desert	A+ Ari	41	130	40	3	4	2	57	21	9	11	0	30	1	1	0	10	4	.71	1	.308	.366	.438
El Paso	AA Ari	74	264	75	8	8	2	105	42	37	26	0	50	2	1	2	18	2	.90	2	.284	.350	.398
2001 Clearwater	A+ Phi	21	77	26	3	2	1	36	16	8	13	0	21	0	1	0	13	3	.81	1	.338	.433	.468
Reading	AA Phi	38	105	20	7	3	0	33	7	10	5	0	42	3	0	1	2	2	.50	1	.190	.246	.314
7 Min. YEARS		656	2203	582	76	39	9	763	347	187	214	2	577	20	34	8	221	77	.74	28	.264	.334	.346

Rich Gomez

Bats: Right **Throws:** Right **Pos:** OF-92; DH-1; PR-1

Ht: 5'11" **Wt:** 190 **Born:** 8/19/77 **Age:** 24

Year Team	Lg Org	G	AB	H	2B	3B	HR	TB	R	RBI	TBB	IBB	SO	HBP	SH	SF	SB	CS	SB%	GDP	Avg	OBP	SLG
1998 Tigers	R Det	47	162	54	11	4	6	91	42	40	21	3	37	5	0	0	20	2	.91	3	.333	.426	.562
1999 W Michigan	A Det	130	479	145	26	12	8	219	89	81	54	1	122	10	0	1	66	10	.87	1	.303	.384	.457
2000 Lakeland	A+ Det	128	455	126	20	10	8	190	78	57	50	1	102	8	6	3	48	8	.86	4	.277	.357	.418
2001 Erie	AA Det	93	346	93	21	2	14	160	60	44	25	0	75	16	1	2	26	7	.79	4	.269	.344	.462
4 Min. YEARS		398	1442	418	78	28	36	660	269	222	150	5	336	39	7	6	160	27	.86	12	.290	.371	.458

Gabe Gonzalez

Pitches: Left **Bats:** Left **Pos:** RP-40

Ht: 6'1" **Wt:** 150 **Born:** 5/24/72 **Age:** 30

Year Team	Lg Org	G	GS	CG	GF	IP	BFP	H	R	ER	HR	SH	SF	HB	TBB	IBB	SO	WP	Bk	W	L	Pct.	ShO	Sv	ERA
1995 Kane County	A Fla	32	0	0	10	43.1	181	32	18	11	0	2	1	2	14	2	41	1	0	4	4	.500	0	1	2.28
1996 Charlotte	AAA Fla	2	0	0	1	3	15	4	1	1	0	0	0	0	2	0	3	0	0	0	0	—	0	0	3.00
Brevard Cty	A+ Fla	47	0	0	32	76.1	308	56	20	15	2	9	1	3	23	7	62	2	0	2	7	.222	0	9	1.77
1997 Portland	AA Fla	29	0	0	10	42.2	171	43	12	10	1	3	3	0	5	1	28	1	0	3	2	.600	0	3	2.11
Charlotte	AAA Fla	37	1	0	11	42.2	176	38	15	13	3	1	2	2	14	1	24	0	0	2	2	.500	0	3	2.74
1998 Charlotte	AAA Fla	57	4	0	13	87	412	101	67	53	3	8	7	1	53	5	41	2	1	3	9	.250	0	2	5.48
1999 Portland	AA Fla	26	0	0	11	38	161	38	19	15	2	4	1	3	8	1	34	2	0	2	4	.333	0	0	3.55
Calgary	AAA Fla	24	0	0	10	28	123	27	15	13	2	0	2	2	9	1	23	0	0	1	1	.500	0	0	4.18
2000 Ottawa	AAA Mon	14	0	0	5	25	130	34	21	19	3	0	2	1	20	0	11	2	0	1	2	.333	0	1	6.84
Harrisburg	AA Mon	44	0	0	8	44.2	188	46	24	19	4	2	3	0	12	1	25	0	1	2	0	1.000	0	0	3.83

			HOW MUCH HE PITCHED						WHAT HE GAVE UP								THE RESULTS					
Year Team	Lg Org	G	GS	CG	GF	IP	BFP	H	R	ER	HR	SH	SF	HB	TBB	IBB	SO	WP	Bk	W	L	Pct.	ShO	Sv	ERA
2001 Long Beach	IND —	29	0	0	19	43	178	38	15	7	1	6	2	0	9	2	30	0	0	1	4	.200	0	5	1.47
Portland	AAA SD	3	0	0	2	4.1	25	9	6	6	1	0	2	0	3	0	1	0	0	0	1	.000	0	0	12.46
Mobile	AA SD	8	0	0	1	13.2	57	18	6	2	0	2	0	0	1	0	8	0	0	1	0	1.000	0	0	1.32
1998 Florida	NL	3	0	0	1	1	5	1	1	1	0	0	0	1	1	0	0	0	0	0	0	—	0	0	9.00
7 Min. YEARS		352	5	0	131	491.2	2125	484	239	184	22	37	26	14	173	21	331	10	2	22	36	.379	0	24	3.37

Jimmy Gonzalez

Bats: Right Throws: Right Pos: C-57; PH-1   Ht: 6'3" Wt: 235 Born: 3/8/73 Age: 29

							BATTING										BASERUNNING				PERCENTAGES		
Year Team	Lg Org	G	AB	H	2B	3B	HR	TB	R	RBI	TBB	IBB	SO	HBP	SH	SF	SB	CS	SB%	GDP	Avg	OBP	SLG
1991 Astros	R Hou	34	103	21	3	0	0	24	7	3	7	0	33	0	1	0	3	5	.38	1	.204	.255	.233
1992 Burlington	A Hou	91	301	53	13	0	4	78	32	21	34	0	119	1	0	0	0	3	.00	6	.176	.262	.259
1993 Quad City	A Hou	47	154	35	9	1	0	46	20	15	14	1	36	4	1	1	2	2	.50	4	.227	.306	.299
Asheville	A Hou	43	149	33	5	0	4	50	16	15	7	0	37	0	2	1	3	1	.75	3	.221	.255	.336
1994 Jackson	AA Hou	4	6	0	0	0	0	0	0	0	0	0	0	0	0	0	0	0	—	0	.000	.000	.000
Osceola	A+ Hou	99	321	74	18	0	5	107	33	38	20	0	80	4	2	2	2	0	1.00	10	.231	.282	.333
1995 Quad City	A Hou	35	78	19	3	1	1	27	4	14	8	0	13	1	0	1	1	2	.33	2	.244	.318	.346
1996 Jackson	AA Hou	2	5	1	0	0	0	1	1	0	1	0	1	0	0	0	0	0	—	0	.200	.333	.200
Kissimmee	A+ Hou	73	208	35	4	1	6	59	19	17	25	0	59	3	2	3	1	0	1.00	8	.168	.264	.284
1997 Kissimmee	A+ Hou	12	44	15	6	2	2	31	7	6	1	0	9	3	0	1	0	0	—	1	.341	.388	.705
Jackson	AA Hou	97	342	87	18	0	14	147	49	58	37	1	91	8	0	3	2	1	.67	7	.254	.338	.430
1998 Mobile	AA SD	26	85	25	8	0	6	51	14	17	13	0	22	0	0	0	0	0	—	2	.294	.388	.600
Las Vegas	AAA SD	51	160	38	9	0	5	62	22	21	15	1	44	1	1	2	1	0	1.00	1	.238	.303	.388
1999 Mobile	AA SD	21	68	18	3	0	2	27	15	8	7	1	16	3	0	1	0	0	—	2	.265	.354	.397
Las Vegas	AAA SD	40	112	33	9	1	3	53	10	19	14	1	29	0	0	3	0	0	—	1	.295	.364	.473
2000 Binghamton	AA NYM	73	234	65	13	1	8	104	32	30	21	0	52	5	0	1	1	2	.33	3	.278	.349	.444
2001 Ottawa	AAA Mon	58	215	38	8	1	6	66	18	19	8	0	49	2	0	1	0	0	—	4	.177	.212	.307
11 Min. YEARS		806	2585	590	129	8	66	933	299	301	232	5	690	35	9	20	16	16	.50	54	.228	.298	.361

Lariel Gonzalez

Pitches: Right Bats: Right Pos: RP-12   Ht: 6'4" Wt: 228 Born: 5/25/76 Age: 26

			HOW MUCH HE PITCHED						WHAT HE GAVE UP								THE RESULTS					
Year Team	Lg Org	G	GS	CG	GF	IP	BFP	H	R	ER	HR	SH	SF	HB	TBB	IBB	SO	WP	Bk	W	L	Pct.	ShO	Sv	ERA
1994 Rockies	R Col	16	1	0	7	28.2	135	28	24	15	1	1	2	2	21	2	23	9	0	3	2	.600	0	0	4.71
1995 Portland	A- Col	15	11	0	2	57.2	258	44	31	26	4	1	1	7	43	0	48	9	5	3	4	.429	0	2	4.06
1996 Asheville	A Col	35	0	0	24	45	208	37	21	18	2	0	0	1	37	0	53	4	2	1	1	.500	0	4	3.60
1997 Salem	A+ Col	44	0	0	25	57	237	42	19	16	3	2	2	3	23	1	79	4	0	5	0	1.000	0	8	2.53
1998 New Haven	AA Col	58	0	0	45	58	255	46	30	27	5	3	3	3	40	2	63	11	0	0	4	.000	0	22	4.19
1999 Colo Sprngs	AAA Col	11	0	0	4	13.1	66	18	16	15	2	1	1	0	12	2	9	1	0	0	1	.000	0	0	10.13
Carolina	AA Col	30	0	0	24	34	167	39	27	20	4	4	1	1	22	0	41	8	0	2	1	.667	0	14	5.29
2000 Norfolk	AAA NYM	52	0	0	19	66.2	304	68	33	31	4	3	6	4	38	3	61	8	0	5	5	.500	0	5	4.19
2001 West Tenn	AA ChC	11	0	0	3	11.2	59	15	11	6	1	2	0	0	7	0	8	0	0	1	0	1.000	0	0	4.63
Camden	IND —	1	0	0	0	0.2	6	3	2	2	0	0	0	0	1	0	1	0	1	0	0	—	0	0	27.00
1998 Colorado	NL	1	0	0	1	1	3	3	2	2	0	0	0	0	0	0	0	0	0	0	0	—	0	0	0.00
8 Min. YEARS		273	12	0	153	372.2	1695	340	214	176	26	17	16	21	244	10	385	55	7	20	18	.526	0	55	4.25

Luis Gonzalez

Bats: Right Throws: Right Pos: 2B-61; 3B-23; SS-10; DH-9; PH-2; PR-1   Ht: 5'11" Wt: 170 Born: 6/26/79 Age: 23

							BATTING										BASERUNNING				PERCENTAGES		
Year Team	Lg Org	G	AB	H	2B	3B	HR	TB	R	RBI	TBB	IBB	SO	HBP	SH	SF	SB	CS	SB%	GDP	Avg	OBP	SLG
1998 Columbus	A Cle	101	320	87	14	1	3	112	48	32	28	0	63	8	10	1	10	3	.77	0	.272	.345	.350
1999 Kinston	A+ Cle	1	1	0	0	0	0	0	0	0	0	0	0	0	0	0	0	0	—	0	.000	.000	.000
Columbus	A Cle	83	299	88	18	2	7	131	41	50	26	0	40	5	4	5	6	5	.55	5	.294	.355	.438
2000 Kinston	A+ Cle	79	284	70	11	0	2	87	32	33	21	0	54	6	12	2	6	6	.50	6	.246	.310	.306
2001 Kinston	A+ Cle	52	183	59	14	0	5	88	31	19	14	0	36	8	1	2	3	5	.38	1	.322	.391	.481
Akron	AA Cle	52	199	60	12	2	5	91	41	17	7	0	26	2	0	2	2	3	.40	3	.302	.329	.457
4 Min. YEARS		368	1286	364	69	5	22	509	193	151	96	0	219	29	27	12	27	22	.55	20	.283	.344	.396

Manny Gonzalez

Bats: Both Throws: Right Pos: OF-64; DH-4; PH-4; PR-1   Ht: 6'2" Wt: 195 Born: 5/5/76 Age: 26

							BATTING										BASERUNNING				PERCENTAGES		
Year Team	Lg Org	G	AB	H	2B	3B	HR	TB	R	RBI	TBB	IBB	SO	HBP	SH	SF	SB	CS	SB%	GDP	Avg	OBP	SLG
1995 Great Falls	R+ LA	59	197	71	9	3	4	98	35	30	9	1	27	0	1	3	16	7	.70	2	.360	.383	.497
1996 San Berndno	A+ LA	43	168	51	7	3	0	64	29	21	12	0	32	0	2	0	10	8	.56	2	.304	.350	.381
Savannah	A LA	65	231	53	10	2	1	70	30	19	20	0	52	1	1	2	15	8	.65	3	.229	.291	.303
1997 Hickory	A CWS	116	469	129	21	2	11	187	70	54	28	1	78	1	7	5	31	12	.72	11	.275	.314	.399
1998 Birmingham	AA CWS	102	371	112	24	2	2	146	51	35	23	0	52	4	8	1	9	7	.56	11	.302	.348	.394
1999 Charlotte	AAA CWS	48	129	40	6	1	1	51	14	25	5	1	20	0	8	0	1	4	.20	1	.310	.336	.395
St. Paul	IND —	18	83	24	4	1	2	36	13	12	5	0	9	1	0	0	5	4	.56	1	.289	.337	.434
2000 Charlotte	AAA CWS	2	4	1	0	0	0	1	0	0	0	0	0	0	0	0	0	1	.00	0	.250	.250	.250
Solano	IND —	83	347	109	26	1	13	176	58	78	17	0	55	3	2	6	13	10	.57	8	.314	.346	.507
2001 El Paso	AA Ari	9	26	5	1	0	0	6	3	1	1	0	4	0	0	0	0	1	.00	0	.192	.222	.231
Reading	AA Phi	64	238	70	19	0	3	98	32	24	13	0	37	3	5	2	2	3	.40	4	.294	.336	.412
7 Min. YEARS		609	2263	665	127	15	37	933	335	299	133	3	366	13	34	19	102	65	.61	43	.294	.334	.412

Mike Gonzalez

Pitches: Left **Bats:** Right **Pos:** SP-16; RP-12   **Ht:** 6'2" **Wt:** 217 **Born:** 5/23/78 **Age:** 24

Year Team	Lg Org	G	GS	CG	GF	IP	BFP	H	R	ER	HR	SH	SF	HB	TBB	IBB	SO	WP	Bk	W	L	Pct.	ShO	Sv	ERA
1997 Pirates	R Pit	7	3	0	0	29	115	21	9	8	0	1	0	1	8	0	33	3	3	2	0	1.000	0	0	2.48
Augusta	A Pit	4	3	0	1	19.1	76	11	5	4	1	1	0	0	8	0	22	3	0	1	1	.500	0	0	1.86
1998 Lynchburg	A+ Pit	7	7	0	0	28.1	131	40	21	21	5	0	1	3	13	0	22	1	0	0	3	.000	0	0	6.67
Augusta	A Pit	11	9	0	0	50.2	221	43	24	16	2	1	1	7	26	0	72	3	4	4	2	.667	0	0	2.84
1999 Lynchburg	A+ Pit	20	20	0	0	112	478	98	55	50	10	2	1	4	63	0	119	10	0	10	4	.714	0	0	4.02
Altoona	AA Pit	7	5	0	0	26.2	133	34	25	24	4	2	1	2	19	0	31	3	3	2	3	.400	0	0	8.10
2000 Pirates	R Pit	2	1	0	1	6	35	8	6	3	1	0	0	1	4	0	7	3	0	1	0	1.000	0	0	4.50
Lynchburg	A+ Pit	12	10	0	1	56	256	57	34	29	6	5	2	3	34	0	53	1	0	4	3	.571	0	0	4.66
2001 Lynchburg	A+ Pit	14	2	0	7	30.2	127	28	14	10	3	3	1	0	7	1	32	5	1	2	2	.500	0	0	2.93
Altoona	AA Pit	14	14	1	0	87.1	367	81	38	36	5	6	2	0	36	0	66	2	1	5	4	.556	1	0	3.71
5 Min. YEARS		98	74	1	10	446	1939	421	231	201	37	21	9	21	218	1	457	34	12	31	22	.585	1	0	4.06

Arnie Gooch

Pitches: Right **Bats:** Right **Pos:** SP-26; RP-2   **Ht:** 6'2" **Wt:** 195 **Born:** 11/12/76 **Age:** 25

Year Team	Lg Org	G	GS	CG	GF	IP	BFP	H	R	ER	HR	SH	SF	HB	TBB	IBB	SO	WP	Bk	W	L	Pct.	ShO	Sv	ERA
1994 Rockies	R Col	15	9	0	1	58	238	45	28	17	2	0	2	2	16	0	66	12	1	2	4	.333	0	0	2.64
1995 Asheville	A Col	21	21	1	0	128.2	541	111	51	42	8	3	3	4	57	0	117	13	0	5	8	.385	1	0	2.94
Capital Cty	A NYM	6	6	0	0	38.1	169	39	25	19	3	0	1	2	15	0	34	5	0	2	3	.400	0	0	4.46
1996 St. Lucie	A+ NYM	26	26	2	0	167.2	680	131	74	48	7	6	4	4	51	3	141	11	0	12	12	.500	0	0	2.58
1997 Binghamton	AA NYM	27	27	4	0	161	727	179	106	91	12	4	7	5	76	3	98	12	0	10	12	.455	1	0	5.09
1998 Binghamton	AA NYM	27	27	2	0	163.2	705	164	92	71	15	5	5	1	60	4	116	14	0	11	14	.440	1	0	3.90
1999 Reds	R Cin	2	2	0	0	8	32	5	2	1	0	0	0	1	1	0	6	0	0	1	1	.500	0	0	1.13
Clinton	A Cin	2	2	0	0	8	36	8	5	4	1	0	0	0	3	0	5	0	0	1	1	.500	0	0	4.50
2000 Chattanooga	AA Cin	21	21	1	0	135.2	583	133	78	62	13	4	1	8	55	4	80	16	0	9	7	.563	0	0	4.11
2001 Louisville	AAA Cin	28	26	1	1	148.2	657	175	101	93	16	6	6	6	43	1	95	8	0	7	10	.412	0	1	5.63
8 Min. YEARS		175	167	11	2	1017.2	4368	990	562	448	77	28	29	33	377	15	758	91	1	60	72	.455	3	1	3.96

Andrew Good

Pitches: Right **Bats:** Right **Pos:** SP-27; RP-2   **Ht:** 6'2" **Wt:** 166 **Born:** 9/19/79 **Age:** 22

Year Team	Lg Org	G	GS	CG	GF	IP	BFP	H	R	ER	HR	SH	SF	HB	TBB	IBB	SO	WP	Bk	W	L	Pct.	ShO	Sv	ERA
1998 Diamondbcks	R Ari	9	8	0	0	33.2	152	46	25	16	1	0	1	2	7	0	25	3	0	1	3	.250	0	0	4.28
South Bend	A Ari	2	0	0	1	6	28	7	4	2	0	0	0	2	1	0	6	0	1	0	1	.000	0	0	3.00
1999 South Bend	A Ari	27	27	0	0	153.2	662	160	80	70	9	3	9	9	42	0	146	7	0	11	10	.524	0	0	4.10
2001 Lancaster	A+ Ari	19	18	0	0	101.1	454	108	63	54	12	6	4	13	27	0	104	5	0	8	6	.571	0	0	4.80
El Paso	AA Ari	10	9	0	0	56.2	270	79	44	37	2	1	2	3	20	0	46	3	0	2	3	.400	0	0	5.88
3 Min. YEARS		67	62	0	1	351.1	1566	400	216	179	24	10	16	29	97	0	327	18	1	22	23	.489	0	0	4.59

Steve Goodell

Bats: Right **Throws:** Right **Pos:** DH-30; 1B-20; OF-4; 2B-2; 3B-2   **Ht:** 6'3" **Wt:** 196 **Born:** 4/23/75 **Age:** 27

Year Team	Lg Org	G	AB	H	2B	3B	HR	TB	R	RBI	TBB	IBB	SO	HBP	SH	SF	SB	CS	SB%	GDP	Avg	OBP	SLG
1995 Elmira	A- Fla	69	253	64	14	4	7	107	42	30	36	0	50	14	1	2	4	5	.44	8	.253	.374	.423
Kane County	A Fla	2	7	2	0	0	0	2	0	1	2	0	2	0	0	0	0	0	—	0	.286	.444	.286
1996 Brevard Cty	A+ Fla	1	4	1	0	0	0	1	0	0	0	0	0	0	0	0	0	0	—	0	.250	.250	.250
Kane County	A Fla	86	282	79	17	2	9	127	34	39	30	2	68	13	2	5	1	1	.50	8	.280	.370	.450
1997 Brevard Cty	A+ Fla	117	381	103	18	2	11	158	48	61	60	0	67	14	6	7	1	1	.50	7	.270	.383	.415
1998 Portland	AA Fla	48	118	22	6	0	1	31	13	11	26	1	35	4	2	0	0	1	.00	3	.186	.351	.263
Danville	A+ Atl	54	198	59	14	2	5	92	21	20	17	1	42	6	4	3	3	4	.43	5	.298	.366	.465
Greenville	AA Atl	5	18	5	1	0	3	15	7	6	3	0	3	1	0	0	0	0	—	1	.278	.409	.833
1999 Greenville	AA Atl	102	338	101	25	2	15	175	69	58	55	2	61	12	0	3	8	6	.57	5	.299	.412	.518
2000 Atlantic Ct	IND —	4	10	2	0	0	1	5	2	1	0	0	2	0	0	0	0	0	—	0	.200	.200	.500
Carolina	AA Col	76	229	59	13	1	11	107	39	42	48	2	48	10	0	1	2	1	.67	7	.258	.406	.467
2001 Winnipeg	IND —	15	57	13	4	1	0	19	7	1	9	0	11	0	0	1	1	0	1.00	3	.228	.328	.333
St. George	IND —	2	6	1	0	0	1	4	2	2	1	0	1	0	0	0	0	0	—	0	.167	.250	.667
Bowie	AA Bal	41	135	33	6	1	6	59	27	26	24	0	36	5	0	2	1	3	.25	5	.244	.373	.437
7 Min. YEARS		622	2036	544	118	15	70	902	311	298	311	8	426	79	15	25	21	22	.49	52	.267	.381	.443

Randy Goodrich

Pitches: Right **Bats:** Right **Pos:** RP-21; SP-13   **Ht:** 6'4" **Wt:** 210 **Born:** 11/8/76 **Age:** 25

Year Team	Lg Org	G	GS	CG	GF	IP	BFP	H	R	ER	HR	SH	SF	HB	TBB	IBB	SO	WP	Bk	W	L	Pct.	ShO	Sv	ERA
1998 Salem-Keizr	A- SF	17	10	0	1	62.1	274	74	43	36	5	0	3	4	17	1	38	2	3	4	5	.444	0	0	5.20
1999 San Jose	A+ SF	38	18	0	4	136.2	623	174	95	73	6	5	6	11	34	0	82	6	3	8	8	.500	0	1	4.81
2000 Shreveport	AA SF	51	1	0	25	75	331	90	36	31	10	7	1	0	17	4	48	2	1	4	5	.444	0	12	3.72
2001 Shreveport	AA SF	19	0	0	7	33.1	155	46	28	28	7	1	0	1	12	0	19	1	0	1	1	.500	0	0	7.56
San Jose	A+ SF	15	13	0	1	56.1	282	89	58	54	7	1	3	6	23	0	34	1	0	0	9	.000	0	0	8.63
4 Min. YEARS		140	42	0	38	363.2	1665	473	260	222	35	14	13	22	103	5	221	12	7	17	28	.378	0	13	5.49

Curtis Goodwin

Bats: Left **Throws:** Left **Pos:** OF-93; PR-4; DH-1   **Ht:** 5'11" **Wt:** 180 **Born:** 9/30/72 **Age:** 29

								BATTING									BASERUNNING				PERCENTAGES		
Year Team	Lg Org	G	AB	H	2B	3B	HR	TB	R	RBI	TBB	IBB	SO	HBP	SH	SF	SB	CS	SB%	GDP	Avg	OBP	SLG
1991 Orioles	R Bal	48	151	39	5	0	0	44	32	9	38	0	25	1	5	0	26	5	.84	3	.258	.411	.291
1992 Kane County	A Bal	134	542	153	7	5	1	173	85	42	38	0	106	2	14	0	52	18	.74	1	.282	.332	.319
1993 Frederick	A+ Bal	138	555	156	15	10	2	197	98	42	52	0	90	1	7	1	61	15	.80	8	.281	.343	.355
1994 Bowie	AA Bal	142	597	171	18	8	2	211	105	37	40	0	78	3	13	2	59	10	.86	7	.286	.333	.353
1995 Rochester	AAA Bal	36	140	37	3	3	0	46	24	7	12	0	15	1	3	0	17	3	.85	4	.264	.327	.329
1996 Indianapols	AAA Cin	91	337	88	19	4	2	121	57	30	54	2	67	1	5	1	40	12	.77	2	.261	.364	.359
1997 Indianapols	AAA Cin	30	116	32	4	1	1	41	14	7	15	0	20	0	1	0	11	8	.58	0	.276	.359	.353
2000 Atlantic Ct	IND —	12	41	7	0	0	0	7	5	3	5	0	9	1	1	0	5	0	1.00	1	.171	.277	.171
Sonoma Cty	IND —	10	39	14	2	0	0	16	5	4	9	0	3	0	1	0	0	1	.00	0	.359	.479	.410
Solano	IND —	27	111	33	7	4	0	48	28	9	13	0	21	2	4	0	7	0	1.00	0	.297	.381	.432
Wichita	AA KC	10	38	10	1	0	0	11	8	2	6	0	5	0	0	0	2	1	.67	1	.263	.364	.289
2001 Oklahoma	AAA Tex	73	236	54	3	1	2	65	24	19	10	0	45	0	9	2	3	3	.50	1	.229	.258	.275
Solano	IND —	22	93	31	6	1	0	39	19	5	6	0	16	0	3	1	9	3	.75	2	.333	.370	.419
1995 Baltimore	AL	87	289	76	11	3	1	96	40	24	15	0	53	2	7	3	22	4	.85	5	.263	.301	.332
1996 Cincinnati	NL	49	136	31	3	0	0	34	20	5	19	0	34	0	1	0	15	6	.71	1	.228	.323	.250
1997 Cincinnati	NL	85	265	67	11	0	1	81	27	12	24	0	53	1	6	1	22	13	.63	6	.253	.316	.306
1998 Colorado	NL	119	159	39	7	0	1	49	27	6	16	0	40	0	10	1	5	1	.83	3	.245	.313	.308
1999 Chicago	NL	89	157	38	6	1	0	46	15	9	13	1	38	0	4	1	2	4	.33	7	.242	.298	.293
Toronto	AL	2	8	0	0	0	0	0	0	0	0	0	3	0	0	0	0	0	—	0	.000	.000	.000
9 Min. YEARS		774	2996	825	90	37	10	1019	504	216	298	2	500	12	66	7	292	79	.79	30	.275	.343	.340
5 Maj. YEARS		431	1014	251	38	4	3	306	129	56	87	1	221	3	28	6	66	28	.70	22	.248	.307	.302

Jaime Goudie

Bats: Right **Throws:** Right **Pos:** 2B-88; DH-4; PH-4; PR-1   **Ht:** 5'10" **Wt:** 180 **Born:** 3/8/79 **Age:** 23

								BATTING									BASERUNNING				PERCENTAGES		
Year Team	Lg Org	G	AB	H	2B	3B	HR	TB	R	RBI	TBB	IBB	SO	HBP	SH	SF	SB	CS	SB%	GDP	Avg	OBP	SLG
1997 Yakima	A- LA	56	230	55	10	6	0	77	33	16	16	0	38	2	1	0	21	5	.81	2	.239	.294	.335
1998 San Berndno	A+ LA	49	175	32	5	3	0	43	16	4	11	1	36	5	2	1	4	2	.67	6	.183	.250	.246
Yakima	A- LA	35	138	38	8	2	0	50	15	16	6	0	16	0	2	2	6	1	.86	5	.275	.301	.362
Vero Beach	A+ LA	35	115	37	7	1	1	49	15	8	12	1	24	3	2	1	7	4	.64	3	.322	.397	.426
1999 Reds	R Cin	1	2	1	0	0	0	1	0	1	0	0	0	0	0	0	0	0	—	0	.500	.500	.500
Clinton	A Cin	84	340	109	20	4	3	146	56	50	21	2	46	2	0	2	16	6	.73	8	.321	.362	.429
2000 Hagerstown	A Tor	116	412	100	19	3	6	143	53	51	36	0	68	9	8	3	26	10	.72	6	.243	.315	.347
2001 Dunedin	A+ Tor	47	174	47	9	1	2	64	23	23	7	0	30	2	1	1	3	2	.60	3	.270	.304	.368
Tennessee	AA Tor	45	154	39	7	2	1	53	19	15	7	0	22	0	5	2	3	1	.75	3	.253	.282	.344
5 Min. YEARS		468	1740	458	85	22	13	626	230	184	116	4	280	23	21	12	86	31	.74	36	.263	.316	.360

John Grabow

Pitches: Left **Bats:** Left **Pos:** SP-23   **Ht:** 6'2" **Wt:** 189 **Born:** 11/4/78 **Age:** 23

		HOW MUCH HE PITCHED					WHAT HE GAVE UP									THE RESULTS					
Year Team	Lg Org	G	GS	CG	GF	IP	BFP	H	R	ER	HR	SH	SF	HB	TBB	IBB	SO	WP	Bk	W	L	Pct.	ShO	Sv	ERA
1997 Pirates	R Pit	11	8	0	0	45.1	204	57	32	23	0	1	2	0	14	0	28	3	0	2	7	.222	0	0	4.57
1998 Augusta	A Pit	17	16	0	0	71.2	329	84	59	46	7	1	5	3	34	0	67	9	0	6	3	.667	0	0	5.78
1999 Hickory	A Pit	26	26	0	0	156.1	654	152	82	66	16	3	3	5	32	0	164	3	0	9	10	.474	0	0	3.80
2000 Altoona	AA Pit	24	24	1	0	145.1	637	145	81	70	10	1	6	5	65	0	109	8	1	8	7	.533	0	0	4.33
2001 Pirates	R Pit	6	6	0	0	12	50	11	6	5	1	0	0	1	4	0	9	2	0	0	1	.000	0	0	3.75
Lynchburg	A+ Pit	7	7	0	0	36.2	174	42	30	26	3	3	0	2	26	0	35	2	0	1	3	.250	0	0	6.38
Altoona	AA Pit	10	10	0	0	50.2	214	30	23	19	1	2	0	2	39	0	42	5	3	2	5	.286	0	0	3.38
5 Min. YEARS		101	97	1	0	518	2262	521	313	255	38	11	16	18	214	0	454	32	4	28	36	.438	0	0	4.43

Jason Grabowski

Bats: Left **Throws:** Right **Pos:** 3B-58; OF-23; 1B-20; DH-14; SS-1; PH-1; PR-1   **Ht:** 6'3" **Wt:** 200 **Born:** 5/24/76 **Age:** 26

								BATTING									BASERUNNING				PERCENTAGES		
Year Team	Lg Org	G	AB	H	2B	3B	HR	TB	R	RBI	TBB	IBB	SO	HBP	SH	SF	SB	CS	SB%	GDP	Avg	OBP	SLG
1997 Pulaski	R+ Tex	50	174	51	14	0	4	77	36	24	40	2	32	0	1	1	6	1	.86	2	.293	.423	.443
1998 Savannah	A Tex	104	352	95	13	6	14	162	63	52	57	0	93	1	0	1	16	9	.64	7	.270	.372	.460
1999 Charlotte	A+ Tex	123	434	136	31	6	12	215	68	87	65	3	66	5	1	2	13	10	.57	8	.313	.407	.495
Tulsa	AA Tex	2	6	1	0	0	0	1	1	0	2	1	2	0	0	0	0	0	—	0	.167	.375	.167
2000 Tulsa	AA Tex	135	493	135	33	5	19	235	93	90	88	1	106	4	0	7	8	7	.53	12	.274	.383	.477
2001 Tacoma	AAA Sea	114	394	117	32	3	9	182	60	58	61	5	94	2	0	5	7	4	.64	8	.297	.390	.462
5 Min. YEARS		528	1853	535	123	20	58	872	321	311	313	12	393	12	2	16	50	31	.62	37	.289	.392	.471

Mike Grace

Pitches: Right **Bats:** Right **Pos:** RP-20; SP-1   **Ht:** 6'4" **Wt:** 210 **Born:** 6/20/70 **Age:** 32

		HOW MUCH HE PITCHED					WHAT HE GAVE UP									THE RESULTS					
Year Team	Lg Org	G	GS	CG	GF	IP	BFP	H	R	ER	HR	SH	SF	HB	TBB	IBB	SO	WP	Bk	W	L	Pct.	ShO	Sv	ERA
1991 Batavia	A- Phi	6	6	0	0	32.1	123	20	9	5	3	2	0	1	14	1	36	1	2	1	2	.333	0	0	1.39
Spartanburg	A Phi	6	6	0	0	33.1	127	24	7	7	1	2	1	0	9	0	23	1	0	3	1	.750	0	0	1.89
1992 Spartanburg	A Phi	6	6	0	0	27.1	114	25	16	15	3	0	0	1	8	0	21	2	0	0	1	.000	0	0	4.94
1994 Spartanburg	A Phi	15	15	0	0	80.1	345	84	50	43	6	4	1	8	20	1	45	0	0	5	5	.500	0	0	4.82
1995 Reading	AA Phi	24	24	2	0	147.1	606	137	65	58	13	5	0	6	35	0	118	3	2	13	6	.684	0	0	3.54
Scranton-WB	AAA Phi	2	2	1	0	17	68	17	3	3	0	0	0	0	2	0	13	2	0	2	0	1.000	0	0	1.59
1997 Reading	AA Phi	4	4	0	0	20.1	93	28	17	13	1	0	0	0	6	0	10	1	0	1	3	.250	0	0	5.75
Scranton-WB	AAA Phi	12	12	4	0	75	331	84	43	38	0	3	5	3	17	1	55	1	0	5	6	.455	0	0	4.56
1998 Scranton-WB	AAA Phi	11	10	2	0	75	327	92	44	42	8	9	3	5	18	1	39	2	0	3	6	.333	0	0	5.04
1999 Scranton-WB	AAA Phi	10	9	0	0	46.2	202	52	25	23	6	2	1	2	17	0	27	1	0	2	2	.500	0	0	4.44
2000 Rochester	AAA Bal	34	3	0	5	76.1	317	66	36	34	5	3	0	6	16	1	43	1	0	4	3	.571	0	0	4.01

115

Year Team	Lg Org	G	GS	CG	GF	IP	BFP	H	R	ER	HR	SH	SF	HB	TBB	IBB	SO	WP	Bk	W	L	Pct.	ShO	Sv	ERA
2001 Chattanooga	AA Cin	21	1	0	7	33.1	161	44	26	21	1	1	4		15	3	27	3	0	3	2	.600	0	4	5.67
1995 Philadelphia	NL	2	2	0	0	11.1	47	10	4	4	0	1	0	0	4	0	7	0	0	1	1	.500	0	0	3.18
1996 Philadelphia	NL	12	12	1	0	80	323	72	33	31	9	4	0	1	16	1	49	0	1	7	2	.778	1	0	3.49
1997 Philadelphia	NL	6	6	1	0	39	151	32	16	15	3	0	1	1	10	1	26	2	0	3	2	.600	1	0	3.46
1998 Philadelphia	NL	21	15	0	1	90.1	418	116	61	55	10	7	1	8	30	1	46	1	1	4	7	.364	0	0	5.48
1999 Philadelphia	NL	27	5	0	1	55	273	80	48	47	5	3	3	6	30	0	28	4	0	1	4	.200	0	0	7.69
9 Min. YEARS		151	98	9	12	664.1	2814	673	341	302	51	32	12	38	187	8	457	20	4	42	37	.532	0	1	4.09
5 Maj. YEARS		68	40	2	2	275.2	1212	310	162	152	27	15	5	16	90	3	156	7	2	16	16	.500	2	0	4.96

Jess Graham

Bats: Left **Throws:** Left **Pos:** OF-57; PH-8; DH-1; PR-1   **Ht:** 6'0" **Wt:** 180 **Born:** 10/12/75 **Age:** 26

Year Team	Lg Org	G	AB	H	2B	3B	HR	TB	R	RBI	TBB	IBB	SO	HBP	SH	SF	SB	CS	SB%	GDP	Avg	OBP	SLG
1997 Chillicothe	IND —	48	146	51	7	2	3	71	41	17	23	0	16	4	2	1	12	5	.71	4	.349	.448	.486
1998 Michigan	A Bos	113	414	108	22	5	8	164	73	61	50	1	96	12	2	2	10	4	.71	12	.261	.356	.396
1999 Sarasota	A+ Bos	129	462	124	33	5	7	188	66	65	49	3	77	19	6	2	5	4	.56	8	.268	.361	.407
2000 Sarasota	A+ Bos	13	42	7	1	0	1	11	4	2	6	0	7	1	0	1	2	1	.67	2	.167	.280	.262
Trenton	AA Bos	75	256	61	11	3	5	93	28	33	20	2	61	5	2	2	0	3	.00	4	.238	.304	.363
2001 Sarasota	A+ Bos	17	47	12	2	0	1	17	6	2	6	0	11	0	0	0	0	1	.00	0	.255	.340	.362
Trenton	AA Bos	49	124	34	7	0	4	53	9	18	15	2	36	0	1	0	0	1	.00	2	.274	.350	.427
5 Min. YEARS		444	1491	397	83	15	29	597	227	198	169	8	304	41	13	9	29	19	.60	36	.266	.355	.400

Alex Graman

Pitches: Left **Bats:** Left **Pos:** SP-28   **Ht:** 6'4" **Wt:** 200 **Born:** 11/17/77 **Age:** 24

Year Team	Lg Org	G	GS	CG	GF	IP	BFP	H	R	ER	HR	SH	SF	HB	TBB	IBB	SO	WP	Bk	W	L	Pct.	ShO	Sv	ERA
1999 Staten Ilnd	A- NYY	14	14	0	0	81.1	324	74	30	27	7	3	1	1	16	0	85	1	1	6	3	.667	0	0	2.99
2000 Tampa	A+ NYY	28	28	3	0	143	598	120	64	58	6	5	2	3	58	1	111	9	1	8	9	.471	1	0	3.65
Norwich	AA NYY	1	1	0	0	5.1	25	6	7	7	3	0	1	0	4	0	3	0	0	0	1	.000	0	0	11.81
2001 Norwich	AA NYY	28	28	1	0	166.1	723	174	83	65	10	3	6	2	60	0	138	6	0	12	9	.571	0	0	3.52
3 Min. YEARS		71	71	4	0	396	1670	374	184	157	26	11	9	7	138	1	337	16	2	26	22	.542	1	0	3.57

Mike Gray

Pitches: Left **Bats:** Left **Pos:** RP-54   **Ht:** 6'1" **Wt:** 170 **Born:** 12/6/76 **Age:** 25

Year Team	Lg Org	G	GS	CG	GF	IP	BFP	H	R	ER	HR	SH	SF	HB	TBB	IBB	SO	WP	Bk	W	L	Pct.	ShO	Sv	ERA
1999 Macon	A Atl	46	1	0	22	81.1	349	88	45	33	6	3	2	7	12	1	57	2	1	5	4	.556	0	8	3.65
2000 Myrtle Bch	A+ Atl	30	0	0	17	52.2	212	50	24	22	7	2	2	0	10	1	53	0	0	2	3	.400	0	1	3.76
2001 Greenville	AA Atl	25	0	0	10	40.1	177	41	23	17	4	2	2	2	13	2	22	0	0	3	1	.750	0	0	3.79
El Paso	AA Ari	29	0	0	18	31.1	132	32	11	6	1	1	1	1	8	0	13	0	0	3	1	.750	0	4	1.72
3 Min. YEARS		130	1	0	67	205.2	870	211	103	78	18	8	7	10	43	4	145	2	1	13	9	.591	0	13	3.41

Chad Green

Bats: Both **Throws:** Right **Pos:** OF-92; PH-8; PR-3; DH-2   **Ht:** 5'10" **Wt:** 180 **Born:** 6/28/75 **Age:** 27

Year Team	Lg Org	G	AB	H	2B	3B	HR	TB	R	RBI	TBB	IBB	SO	HBP	SH	SF	SB	CS	SB%	GDP	Avg	OBP	SLG
1996 Ogden	R+ Mil	21	81	29	4	1	3	44	22	8	15	0	23	1	1	2	12	3	.80	0	.358	.455	.543
1997 Stockton	A+ Mil	127	513	128	26	14	2	188	78	43	37	2	138	2	11	4	37	16	.70	3	.250	.300	.366
1998 Stockton	A+ Mil	40	151	52	13	2	0	69	30	17	12	3	22	1	1	1	22	5	.81	2	.344	.394	.457
El Paso	AA Mil	7	6	0	0	0	0	0	0	0	1	0	3	0	0	0	0	0	—	0	.000	.143	.000
1999 Huntsville	AA Mil	116	422	104	22	3	10	162	56	46	2	109		2	2	3	28	13	.68	6	.246	.321	.384
2000 Indianapols	AAA Mil	43	123	25	8	2	3	46	18	10	10	0	36	1	2	1	6	2	.75	2	.203	.267	.374
Huntsville	AA Mil	85	317	74	22	2	3	109	44	27	29	1	85	1	1	3	19	6	.76	2	.233	.297	.344
2001 Portland	AAA SD	21	67	15	4	1	2	27	12	2	9	0	28	0	0	0	4	1	.80	0	.224	.316	.403
Mobile	AA SD	42	137	31	8	3	1	48	14	15	11	1	42	0	1	1	3	2	.60	0	.226	.282	.350
Akron	AA Cle	37	127	33	8	2	3	54	23	16	11	0	28	0	2	1	8	2	.80	0	.260	.317	.425
6 Min. YEARS		539	1944	491	115	30	27	747	297	184	181	9	514	8	21	16	139	50	.74	15	.253	.316	.384

Nick Green

Bats: Right **Throws:** Right **Pos:** 2B-75; SS-3; DH-3; PH-3; PR-1   **Ht:** 6'0" **Wt:** 178 **Born:** 9/10/78 **Age:** 23

Year Team	Lg Org	G	AB	H	2B	3B	HR	TB	R	RBI	TBB	IBB	SO	HBP	SH	SF	SB	CS	SB%	GDP	Avg	OBP	SLG
1999 Jamestown	A- Atl	73	273	81	15	0	11	129	52	41	26	0	66	4	0	3	14	4	.78	4	.297	.363	.473
Macon	A Atl	3	10	2	0	0	1	5	1	3	0	0	4	0	0	0	1	0	1.00	0	.200	.200	.500
2000 Macon	A Atl	91	339	83	19	4	11	143	47	43	22	0	75	5	1	6	10	4	.71	4	.245	.296	.422
Myrtle Bch	A+ Atl	27	91	22	6	0	1	31	13	6	10	0	23	3	1	0	3	2	.60	0	.242	.337	.341
2001 Richmond	AAA Atl	2	5	1	0	0	0	1	0	0	0	0	3	0	0	0	0	0	—	0	.200	.200	.200
Myrtle Bch	A+ Atl	80	297	79	18	1	10	129	49	42	32	0	70	7	1	3	9	2	.82	2	.266	.348	.432
3 Min. YEARS		276	1015	268	58	5	34	438	162	136	90	0	241	19	3	12	37	12	.76	10	.264	.332	.432

Scarborough Green

Bats: Both **Throws:** Right **Pos:** OF-91; PH-18; PR-5   **Ht:** 5'10" **Wt:** 180 **Born:** 6/9/74 **Age:** 28

Year Team	Lg Org	G	AB	H	2B	3B	HR	TB	R	RBI	TBB	IBB	SO	HBP	SH	SF	SB	CS	SB%	GDP	Avg	OBP	SLG
1993 Cardinals	R StL	33	95	21	3	1	0	26	16	11	7	0	17	3	1	0	3	2	.60	1	.221	.295	.274
1994 Johnson Cty	R+ StL	54	199	48	5	0	0	53	32	11	25	1	61	0	4	2	22	7	.76	0	.241	.323	.266

116

Year Team	Lg Org	G	AB	H	2B	3B	HR	TB	R	RBI	TBB	IBB	SO	HBP	SH	SF	SB	CS	SB%	GDP	Avg	OBP	SLG
1995 Savannah	A StL	132	429	98	7	6	1	120	48	25	55	0	101	3	9	1	26	9	.74	6	.228	.320	.280
1996 St. Pete	A+ StL	36	140	41	4	1	1	50	26	11	21	1	22	2	2	0	13	9	.59	1	.293	.393	.357
Arkansas	AA StL	92	300	60	6	3	3	81	45	24	38	1	58	3	3	1	21	8	.72	3	.200	.295	.270
1997 Arkansas	AA StL	76	251	77	14	4	2	105	45	29	36	4	48	2	3	1	11	5	.69	2	.307	.397	.418
Louisville	AAA StL	52	209	53	11	2	3	77	26	13	22	0	55	0	1	0	10	7	.59	3	.254	.325	.368
1998 Memphis	AAA StL	26	81	16	5	0	0	21	11	2	8	1	22	0	1	0	1	4	.20	2	.198	.270	.259
Arkansas	AA StL	18	75	27	2	1	2	37	16	9	6	0	12	0	0	0	9	2	.82	0	.360	.407	.493
1999 Oklahoma	AAA Tex	104	359	89	16	6	3	126	68	29	34	1	86	3	4	3	26	11	.70	3	.248	.316	.351
2000 Oklahoma	AAA Tex	27	99	31	6	0	1	40	20	10	22	0	24	1	3	0	14	2	.88	0	.313	.443	.404
2001 Altoona	AA Pit	27	91	23	1	0	0	24	10	6	6	1	19	1	0	1	10	0	1.00	1	.253	.303	.264
Nashville	AAA Pit	33	58	9	2	1	0	13	8	4	8	2	16	0	2	1	2	1	.67	1	.155	.254	.224
New Haven	AA StL	47	160	40	7	1	0	49	14	10	21	0	38	1	3	2	12	4	.75	2	.250	.337	.306
1997 St. Louis	NL	20	31	3	0	0	0	3	5	1	2	0	5	0	0	0	0	0	—	0	.097	.152	.097
1999 Texas	AL	18	13	4	0	0	0	4	4	0	1	0	2	0	0	0	0	1	.00	0	.308	.357	.308
2000 Texas	AL	79	124	29	1	1	0	32	21	9	10	0	26	0	5	0	10	6	.63	3	.234	.291	.258
9 Min. YEARS		757	2546	633	89	26	16	822	385	194	309	12	579	19	36	12	180	71	.72	25	.249	.333	.323
3 Maj. YEARS		117	168	36	1	1	0	39	30	10	13	0	33	0	5	0	10	7	.59	3	.214	.271	.232

Charlie Greene

Bats: Right **Throws:** Right **Pos:** C-86; PH-4; OF-1; DH-1   **Ht:** 6'2" **Wt:** 190 **Born:** 1/23/71 **Age:** 31

Year Team	Lg Org	G	AB	H	2B	3B	HR	TB	R	RBI	TBB	IBB	SO	HBP	SH	SF	SB	CS	SB%	GDP	Avg	OBP	SLG
1991 Padres	R SD	49	183	52	15	1	5	84	27	39	16	0	23	3	2	6	6	1	.86	7	.284	.341	.459
1992 Chston-SC	A SD	98	298	55	9	1	1	69	22	24	11	0	60	5	3	2	1	2	.33	7	.185	.225	.232
1993 Waterloo	A SD	84	213	38	8	0	2	52	19	20	13	0	33	3	6	3	0	0	—	5	.178	.233	.244
1994 Binghamton	AA NYM	30	106	18	4	0	0	22	13	2	6	1	18	1	0	1	0	0	—	3	.170	.219	.208
St. Lucie	A+ NYM	69	224	57	4	0	0	61	23	21	9	0	31	4	4	1	0	1	.00	3	.254	.294	.272
1995 Binghamton	AA NYM	100	346	82	13	0	2	101	26	34	15	4	47	5	3	4	2	1	.67	10	.237	.276	.292
Norfolk	AAA NYM	27	88	17	3	0	0	20	6	4	3	0	28	0	1	0	0	1	.00	1	.193	.220	.227
1996 Binghamton	AA NYM	100	336	82	17	0	2	105	35	27	17	0	52	0	2	4	2	0	1.00	8	.244	.277	.313
1997 Norfolk	AAA NYM	76	238	49	7	0	8	80	27	28	9	0	54	2	0	2	1	0	1.00	4	.206	.239	.336
1998 Rochester	AAA Bal	77	250	53	10	0	4	75	23	28	9	0	54	3	5	0	1	1	.50	4	.212	.248	.300
1999 Louisville	AAA Mil	56	161	34	8	0	4	54	16	15	7	1	26	0	0	0	0	0	—	2	.211	.244	.335
2000 Syracuse	AAA Tor	77	267	60	12	0	5	87	23	26	17	0	46	3	3	0	1	3	.25	5	.225	.279	.326
2001 Portland	AAA SD	67	211	29	2	0	1	34	11	10	9	0	47	1	4	4	0	0	—	4	.137	.173	.161
Richmond	AAA Atl	23	66	11	1	0	0	12	4	3	1	1	17	0	1	0	0	0	—	4	.167	.203	.182
1996 New York	NL	2	1	0	0	0	0	0	0	0	0	0	0	0	0	0	0	0	—	0	.000	.000	.000
1997 Baltimore	AL	5	2	0	0	0	0	0	0	1	0	0	1	0	0	0	0	0	—	0	.000	.000	.000
1998 Baltimore	AL	13	21	4	1	0	0	5	1	0	0	0	8	0	1	0	0	0	—	1	.190	.190	.238
1999 Milwaukee	NL	32	42	8	1	0	0	9	4	1	5	0	11	0	1	1	0	0	—	0	.190	.271	.214
2000 Toronto	AL	3	9	1	0	0	0	1	0	0	0	0	5	0	0	0	0	0	—	0	.111	.111	.111
11 Min. YEARS		933	2987	637	113	2	34	856	275	282	144	7	536	30	34	27	14	10	.58	68	.213	.254	.287
5 Maj. YEARS		55	75	13	2	0	0	15	5	2	5	0	25	0	2	1	0	0	—	1	.173	.222	.200

Kevin Gregg

Pitches: Right **Bats:** Right **Pos:** RP-43; SP-1   **Ht:** 6'6" **Wt:** 200 **Born:** 6/20/78 **Age:** 24

		HOW MUCH HE PITCHED						WHAT HE GAVE UP												THE RESULTS					
Year Team	Lg Org	G	GS	CG	GF	IP	BFP	H	R	ER	HR	SH	SF	HB	TBB	IBB	SO	WP	Bk	W	L	Pct.	ShO	Sv	ERA
1996 Athletics	R Oak	11	9	0	0	40.2	169	30	14	14	1	1	1	2	21	0	48	11	0	3	3	.500	0	0	3.10
1997 Visalia	A+ Oak	25	24	0	0	115.1	534	116	81	73	8	2	3	5	74	0	136	6	0	8	7	.533	0	1	5.70
1998 Modesto	A+ Oak	30	24	0	3	144	640	139	72	61	7	9	2	6	76	2	141	7	0	8	7	.533	0	1	3.81
1999 Visalia	A+ Oak	13	11	1	2	64	271	60	34	27	3	1	2	4	23	0	48	7	1	4	4	.500	1	1	3.80
Midland	AA Oak	16	16	2	0	91.1	380	75	45	38	7	0	3	6	31	1	66	6	0	4	7	.364	0	0	3.74
Vancouver	AAA Oak	1	1	0	0	5	21	6	2	2	0	0	0	0	2	0	4	2	0	1	0	1.000	0	0	3.60
2000 Midland	AA Oak	28	27	0	0	140.2	655	171	120	100	18	5	6	8	73	0	97	6	0	5	14	.263	0	0	6.40
2001 Midland	AA Oak	44	1	0	10	81.1	366	88	48	41	5	1	5	4	40	4	72	8	1	5	5	.500	0	1	4.54
6 Min. YEARS		168	113	3	15	682.1	3036	685	416	356	49	19	17	35	340	7	612	75	2	36	48	.429	1	3	4.70

Tom Gregorio

Bats: Right **Throws:** Right **Pos:** C-46; DH-3   **Ht:** 6'2" **Wt:** 200 **Born:** 5/5/77 **Age:** 25

Year Team	Lg Org	G	AB	H	2B	3B	HR	TB	R	RBI	TBB	IBB	SO	HBP	SH	SF	SB	CS	SB%	GDP	Avg	OBP	SLG
1999 Boise	A- Ana	52	186	55	10	1	5	82	29	36	11	0	33	2	0	2	0	1	.00	3	.296	.338	.441
2000 Cedar Rapds	A Ana	106	379	93	17	0	6	128	46	41	35	4	79	7	3	2	2	1	.67	13	.245	.319	.338
2001 Angels	R Ana	4	11	3	0	0	0	3	1	1	3	0	2	0	0	0	0	0	—	0	.273	.429	.273
Arkansas	AA Ana	45	157	30	10	0	1	43	15	23	7	0	37	4	2	1	0	0	—	3	.191	.243	.274
3 Min. YEARS		207	733	181	37	1	12	256	91	101	56	4	151	13	5	5	2	2	.50	19	.247	.310	.349

Dan Grice

Bats: Right **Throws:** Right **Pos:** SS-54; 3B-9; 2B-1; PH-1; PR-1   **Ht:** 5'11" **Wt:** 180 **Born:** 10/5/75 **Age:** 26

Year Team	Lg Org	G	AB	H	2B	3B	HR	TB	R	RBI	TBB	IBB	SO	HBP	SH	SF	SB	CS	SB%	GDP	Avg	OBP	SLG
1997 Bend	IND —	50	139	37	1	1	0	40	26	14	18	0	29	3	5	2	5	0	1.00	7	.266	.358	.288
1998 Madison	IND —	74	243	52	10	1	1	67	36	26	34	0	49	1	0	1	10	2	.83	8	.214	.312	.276
1999 Madison	IND —	84	290	72	8	0	2	86	46	33	31	0	61	2	4	1	2	6	.25	14	.248	.324	.297
2000 Madison	IND —	74	241	59	7	2	3	79	33	33	28	0	42	6	6	2	9	7	.56	5	.245	.336	.328
2001 Albany-Col	IND —	30	111	27	8	0	1	38	16	13	9	0	20	0	6	2	3	3	.50	1	.243	.295	.342
Daytona	A+ ChC	28	94	12	2	0	0	14	7	7	6	0	16	0	2	1	2	0	1.00	2	.128	.178	.149
West Tenn	AA ChC	7	14	2	1	0	0	3	1	1	1	0	3	1	1	0	0	0	—	0	.143	.235	.214
5 Min. YEARS		347	1132	261	37	4	7	327	165	127	127	0	220	13	24	10	31	18	.63	37	.231	.313	.289

Jeremy Griffiths

Pitches: Right **Bats:** Right **Pos:** SP-22; RP-3 **Ht:** 6'6" **Wt:** 230 **Born:** 3/22/78 **Age:** 24

		HOW MUCH HE PITCHED						WHAT HE GAVE UP												THE RESULTS					
Year Team	Lg Org	G	GS	CG	GF	IP	BFP	H	R	ER	HR	SH	SF	HB	TBB	IBB	SO	WP	Bk	W	L	Pct.	ShO	Sv	ERA
1999 Kingsport	R+ NYM	14	14	1	0	76.1	321	68	40	28	6	1	3	1	36	1	74	5	1	3	5	.375	0	0	3.30
2000 Capital Cty	A NYM	26	26	0	0	128.2	548	120	78	62	12	1	4	8	39	0	138	8	0	7	12	.368	0	0	4.34
2001 St. Lucie	A+ NYM	23	20	2	0	132	551	126	63	55	9	9	3	5	35	1	95	11	3	7	8	.467	0	0	3.75
Binghamton	AA NYM	2	2	1	0	13	51	8	3	1	0	1	0	0	4	0	12	1	0	2	0	1.000	0	0	0.69
3 Min. YEARS		65	62	4	0	350	1471	322	184	146	27	12	10	14	114	2	319	25	4	19	25	.432	0	0	3.75

Kevin Grijak

Bats: Left **Throws:** Right **Pos:** 1B-23; OF-18; DH-4; PH-4 **Ht:** 6'2" **Wt:** 215 **Born:** 8/6/70 **Age:** 31

		BATTING															BASERUNNING				PERCENTAGES		
Year Team	Lg Org	G	AB	H	2B	3B	HR	TB	R	RBI	TBB	IBB	SO	HBP	SH	SF	SB	CS	SB%	GDP	Avg	OBP	SLG
1991 Idaho Falls	R+ Atl	52	202	68	9	1	10	109	33	58	16	1	15	1	2	4	4	1	.80	5	.337	.381	.540
1992 Pulaski	R+ Atl	10	31	11	3	0	0	14	1	6	6	0	0	0	0	0	2	2	.50	1	.355	.459	.452
Macon	A Atl	47	157	41	13	0	5	69	20	21	15	2	16	3	0	2	3	0	1.00	3	.261	.333	.439
1993 Macon	A Atl	120	389	115	26	5	7	172	50	59	37	4	37	6	2	12	9	5	.64	9	.296	.356	.442
1994 Durham	A+ Atl	22	68	25	3	0	11	61	18	22	12	4	6	3	0	1	1	1	.50	1	.368	.476	.897
Greenville	AA Atl	100	348	94	19	1	11	148	40	58	20	1	40	6	0	7	2	3	.40	11	.270	.315	.425
1995 Greenville	AA Atl	21	74	32	5	0	2	43	14	11	7	0	9	2	0	2	0	1	.00	1	.432	.482	.581
Richmond	AAA Atl	106	309	92	16	5	12	154	35	56	25	4	47	4	0	4	1	3	.25	10	.298	.354	.498
1996 Richmond	AAA Atl	13	30	11	3	0	1	17	3	8	5	0	7	1	0	0	0	1	.00	1	.367	.472	.567
1997 Greenville	AA Atl	72	240	60	12	1	13	113	35	48	18	2	35	5	1	3	0	1	.00	8	.250	.312	.471
1998 Carolina	AA Pit	46	146	51	8	0	9	86	29	33	18	2	15	4	0	3	1	0	1.00	4	.349	.427	.589
Nashville	AAA Pit	67	227	65	17	0	15	127	32	40	23	0	34	3	1	1	4	2	.20	8	.286	.358	.559
1999 Albuquerque	AAA LA	119	401	127	28	1	18	211	58	80	19	2	50	3	2	3	2	6	.25	4	.317	.350	.526
2000 Albuquerque	AAA LA	112	337	96	20	3	17	173	61	79	31	5	55	3	0	5	10	9	.53	8	.285	.346	.513
2001 Calgary	AAA Fla	45	142	35	7	0	5	57	17	27	12	0	13	4	0	3	1	0	1.00	6	.246	.317	.401
11 Min. YEARS		952	3101	923	189	17	136	1554	446	605	264	27	379	48	8	50	37	37	.50	79	.298	.357	.501

Nate Grindell

Bats: Right **Throws:** Right **Pos:** 3B-51; OF-40; 1B-32; DH-12; PH-1 **Ht:** 6'1" **Wt:** 180 **Born:** 4/9/77 **Age:** 25

		BATTING															BASERUNNING				PERCENTAGES		
Year Team	Lg Org	G	AB	H	2B	3B	HR	TB	R	RBI	TBB	IBB	SO	HBP	SH	SF	SB	CS	SB%	GDP	Avg	OBP	SLG
1998 Burlington	R+ Cle	14	41	10	2	0	1	15	6	7	2	0	6	0	0	0	0	0	—	0	.244	.279	.366
Watertown	A- Cle	27	81	21	7	0	1	31	13	13	15	0	9	0	0	2	1	2	.33	1	.259	.367	.383
1999 Mahoning Vy	A Cle	71	267	84	20	2	5	123	42	47	24	1	39	4	0	4	6	5	.55	3	.315	.375	.461
2000 Columbus	A Cle	132	500	143	36	3	18	239	80	98	55	3	74	9	0	7	17	2	.89	8	.286	.363	.478
2001 Kinston	A+ Cle	69	272	75	17	1	6	112	41	41	16	3	42	3	0	5	1	3	.25	6	.276	.318	.412
Akron	AA Cle	63	229	65	17	1	10	114	34	45	10	0	45	4	0	6	6	4	.60	3	.284	.317	.498
4 Min. YEARS		376	1390	398	99	7	41	634	216	251	122	7	215	20	0	24	31	16	.66	21	.286	.347	.456

Ryan Gripp

Bats: Right **Throws:** Right **Pos:** 3B-123; DH-12; 1B-1 **Ht:** 6'1" **Wt:** 210 **Born:** 4/20/78 **Age:** 24

		BATTING															BASERUNNING				PERCENTAGES		
Year Team	Lg Org	G	AB	H	2B	3B	HR	TB	R	RBI	TBB	IBB	SO	HBP	SH	SF	SB	CS	SB%	GDP	Avg	OBP	SLG
1999 Eugene	A- ChC	73	266	82	18	1	12	138	40	48	27	0	65	10	0	3	2	1	.67	7	.308	.389	.519
2000 Lansing	A ChC	135	498	166	36	0	20	262	87	92	68	2	86	5	0	3	4	0	1.00	13	.333	.416	.526
2001 Daytona	A+ ChC	67	241	71	19	0	5	105	35	49	27	1	57	7	0	5	6	5	.55	5	.295	.375	.436
West Tenn	AA ChC	68	255	58	19	0	8	101	31	45	25	0	60	7	0	1	2	0	1.00	2	.227	.313	.396
3 Min. YEARS		343	1260	377	92	1	45	606	193	234	147	3	268	29	0	12	14	6	.70	27	.299	.382	.481

Lee Gronkiewicz

Pitches: Right **Bats:** Right **Pos:** RP-27 **Ht:** 5'11" **Wt:** 183 **Born:** 8/21/78 **Age:** 23

		HOW MUCH HE PITCHED						WHAT HE GAVE UP												THE RESULTS					
Year Team	Lg Org	G	GS	CG	GF	IP	BFP	H	R	ER	HR	SH	SF	HB	TBB	IBB	SO	WP	Bk	W	L	Pct.	ShO	Sv	ERA
2001 Burlington	R+ Cle	25	0	0	23	31.2	124	18	11	9	1	1	1	2	8	0	47	2	0	3	3	.500	0	10	2.56
Akron	AA Cle	2	0	0	2	2	10	4	0	0	0	0	0	0	0	0	1	0	0	0	0	—	0	0	0.00
1 Min. YEAR		27	0	0	25	33.2	134	22	11	9	1	1	1	2	8	0	48	2	0	3	3	.500	0	10	2.41

Gabe Gross

Bats: Left **Throws:** Right **Pos:** OF-44; DH-2 **Ht:** 6'3" **Wt:** 205 **Born:** 10/21/79 **Age:** 22

		BATTING															BASERUNNING				PERCENTAGES		
Year Team	Lg Org	G	AB	H	2B	3B	HR	TB	R	RBI	TBB	IBB	SO	HBP	SH	SF	SB	CS	SB%	GDP	Avg	OBP	SLG
2001 Dunedin	A+ Tor	35	126	38	9	2	4	63	23	15	26	1	29	2	0	1	4	2	.67	2	.302	.426	.500
Tennessee	AA Tor	11	41	10	1	0	3	20	8	11	6	1	12	3	0	1	0	1	.00	1	.244	.373	.488
1 Min. YEAR		46	167	48	10	2	7	83	31	26	32	2	41	5	0	2	4	3	.57	3	.287	.413	.497

Kip Gross

Pitches: Right **Bats:** Right **Pos:** RP-16; SP-12 **Ht:** 6'2" **Wt:** 195 **Born:** 8/24/64 **Age:** 37

		HOW MUCH HE PITCHED						WHAT HE GAVE UP												THE RESULTS					
Year Team	Lg Org	G	GS	CG	GF	IP	BFP	H	R	ER	HR	SH	SF	HB	TBB	IBB	SO	WP	Bk	W	L	Pct.	ShO	Sv	ERA
1987 Lynchburg	A+ NYM	16	15	2	0	89.1	379	92	37	27	1	2	3	6	22	1	39	1	1	7	4	.636	0	0	2.72
1988 St. Lucie	A+ NYM	28	27	7	1	178.1	736	153	72	52	1	3	7	7	53	6	124	10	11	13	9	.591	3	0	2.62
1989 Jackson	AA NYM	16	16	4	0	112	444	96	47	31	9	4	2	2	13	0	60	4	1	5	5	.545	0	0	2.49
Tidewater	AAA NYM	12	12	0	0	70.1	289	72	33	31	3	5	2	1	17	0	39	1	1	4	4	.500	0	0	3.97

Year Team	Lg Org	G	GS	CG	GF	IP	BFP	H	R	ER	HR	SH	SF	HB	TBB	IBB	SO	WP	Bk	W	L	Pct.	ShO	Sv	ERA
1990 Nashville	AAA Cin	40	11	2	11	127	521	113	54	47	6	6	2	7	47	3	62	6	3	12	7	.632	1	3	3.33
1991 Nashville	AAA Cin	14	6	1	3	47.2	195	39	13	11	3	2	1	4	16	0	28	3	1	5	3	.625	1	0	2.08
1992 Albuquerque	AAA LA	31	14	2	16	107.2	437	96	48	42	1	4	4	2	36	5	58	3	1	6	5	.545	0	8	3.51
1993 Albuquerque	AAA LA	59	7	0	25	124.1	521	115	58	56	7	7	1	2	41	6	96	9	3	13	7	.650	0	13	4.05
1994 Albuquerque	AAA LA	10	0	0	3	16	65	14	9	9	0	0	1	1	6	1	11	1	0	1	1	.500	0	1	5.06
1999 Pawtucket	AAA Bos	10	2	0	2	21.2	98	24	14	13	3	0	1	2	12	0	16	2	0	1	0	1.000	0	0	5.40
2000 New Orleans	AAA Hou	25	25	2	0	157.2	664	156	80	69	20	10	6	4	44	1	94	3	0	8	7	.533	0	0	3.94
2001 Las Vegas	AAA LA	10	0	0	7	17.2	81	26	11	10	5	0	2	0	4	0	8	1	0	3	1	.750	0	0	5.09
Colo Sprngs	AAA Col	18	12	1	1	82	360	112	65	55	10	0	2	4	12	1	48	2	0	1	7	.125	1	0	6.04
1990 Cincinnati	NL	5	0	0	2	6.1	25	6	3	3	0	0	1	0	2	0	3	0	0	0	0	—	0	0	4.26
1991 Cincinnati	NL	29	9	1	6	85.2	381	93	43	33	8	6	2	0	40	2	40	5	1	6	4	.600	0	0	3.47
1992 Los Angeles	NL	16	1	0	7	23.2	109	32	14	11	1	0	0	0	10	1	14	1	1	1	1	.500	0	0	4.18
1993 Los Angeles	NL	10	0	0	0	15	59	13	1	1	0	0	0	0	4	0	12	0	0	0	0	—	0	0	0.60
1999 Boston	AL	11	1	0	7	12.2	64	15	11	11	3	1	1	3	8	2	9	1	0	0	2	.000	0	0	7.82
2000 Houston	NL	2	1	0	0	4.1	23	9	8	5	2	0	0	2	2	0	3	0	0	1	0	1.000	0	0	10.38
11 Min. YEARS		289	147	21	69	1151.2	4790	1108	541	453	69	41	30	42	323	24	683	46	25	80	60	.571	6	25	3.54
6 Maj. YEARS		73	12	1	22	147.2	661	168	80	64	14	7	4	3	66	5	81	7	2	7	8	.467	0	0	3.90

Dan Grummitt

Bats: Right **Throws:** Right **Pos:** 1B-90; DH-27 **Ht:** 6'5" **Wt:** 233 **Born:** 6/16/76 **Age:** 26

Year Team	Lg Org	G	AB	H	2B	3B	HR	TB	R	RBI	TBB	IBB	SO	HBP	SH	SF	SB	CS	SB%	GDP	Avg	OBP	SLG
1998 Princeton	R+ TB	44	106	28	3	2	4	47	25	19	15	0	39	8	1	1	2	1	.67	2	.264	.392	.443
1999 Chston-SC	A TB	8	30	4	1	0	1	8	6	4	1	0	12	2	0	0	0	0	—	0	.133	.212	.267
Hudson Val	A- TB	73	287	73	13	1	22	154	44	58	30	1	78	5	0	2	3	1	.75	4	.254	.333	.537
2000 Chston-SC	A TB	111	410	107	22	2	19	190	70	74	37	1	116	22	0	5	6	3	.67	7	.261	.350	.463
2001 Bakersfield	A+ TB	46	165	53	22	0	9	102	31	28	18	0	50	9	0	0	3	2	.60	1	.321	.417	.618
Orlando	AA TB	71	244	58	11	1	11	104	37	41	23	1	74	11	0	0	2	2	.50	7	.238	.331	.426
4 Min. YEARS		353	1242	323	72	6	66	605	213	224	124	3	369	57	1	8	16	9	.64	21	.260	.352	.487

Kevin Gryboski

Pitches: Right **Bats:** Right **Pos:** RP-58 **Ht:** 6'5" **Wt:** 220 **Born:** 11/15/73 **Age:** 28

Year Team	Lg Org	G	GS	CG	GF	IP	BFP	H	R	ER	HR	SH	SF	HB	TBB	IBB	SO	WP	Bk	W	L	Pct.	ShO	Sv	ERA
1995 Everett	A- Sea	25	0	0	14	36	156	27	18	14	2	3	1	3	18	2	25	3	0	1	5	.167	0	2	3.50
1996 Wisconsin	A Sea	32	21	3	5	138.2	630	146	90	73	7	9	6	12	62	2	100	12	0	10	5	.667	0	1	4.74
1997 Lancaster	A+ Sea	21	15	0	4	67.1	332	113	82	74	13	2	8	1	26	0	41	7	0	0	7	.000	0	0	9.89
1998 Orlando	AA Sea	2	0	0	0	5	23	8	5	5	1	0	0	0	1	0	4	2	0	0	0	—	0	0	9.00
Lancaster	A+ Sea	37	3	0	17	85	351	75	35	25	4	1	2	4	31	1	73	3	0	5	5	.500	0	8	2.65
1999 New Haven	AA Sea	47	0	0	32	62.1	267	67	27	20	5	5	2	3	20	4	41	3	0	2	5	.286	0	10	2.89
2000 New Haven	AA Sea	16	0	0	14	18	78	15	5	5	0	1	0	1	8	1	20	4	0	1	1	.500	0	2	2.50
Tacoma	AAA Sea	31	0	0	18	41	181	45	23	22	3	2	0	0	23	4	35	7	0	2	2	.500	0	2	4.83
2001 Tacoma	AAA Sea	58	0	0	50	60	256	64	29	26	8	5	1	0	19	2	50	2	0	2	5	.286	0	22	3.90
7 Min. YEARS		269	39	3	154	513.1	2274	560	314	264	43	28	20	24	208	16	389	43	0	23	35	.397	0	54	4.63

Creighton Gubanich

Bats: Right **Throws:** Right **Pos:** C-35; DH-19; PH-7; 1B-2 **Ht:** 6'3" **Wt:** 200 **Born:** 3/27/72 **Age:** 30

Year Team	Lg Org	G	AB	H	2B	3B	HR	TB	R	RBI	TBB	IBB	SO	HBP	SH	SF	SB	CS	SB%	GDP	Avg	OBP	SLG
1991 Sou Oregon	A- Oak	43	132	30	7	2	4	53	23	18	19	0	35	6	0	0	0	4	.00	2	.227	.350	.402
1992 Madison	A Oak	121	404	100	19	3	9	152	46	55	41	1	102	16	8	1	0	7	.00	8	.248	.340	.376
1993 Madison	A Oak	119	373	100	19	2	19	180	65	78	63	2	105	11	2	12	3	3	.50	7	.268	.379	.483
1994 Modesto	A+ Oak	108	375	88	20	3	15	159	53	55	54	0	102	7	5	2	5	4	.56	9	.235	.340	.424
1995 Huntsville	AA Oak	94	274	60	7	1	13	108	37	43	48	0	82	7	2	5	1	0	1.00	2	.219	.344	.394
1996 Huntsville	AA Oak	62	217	60	19	0	6	106	40	43	31	1	71	4	3	2	1	0	1.00	5	.276	.374	.488
1997 Edmonton	AAA Oak	43	145	48	13	0	7	82	23	34	14	0	42	2	1	1	0	2	.00	4	.331	.395	.566
Tucson	AAA Mil	24	85	29	5	0	5	49	13	17	1	0	19	1	0	0	1	0	1.00	1	.341	.356	.576
Colo Sprngs	AAA Col	14	47	9	1	0	3	19	4	6	4	0	18	0	0	0	0	0	—	4	.191	.255	.404
1998 Las Vegas	AAA SD	86	292	85	22	0	19	164	48	70	30	3	85	3	0	6	1	1	.50	4	.291	.356	.562
1999 Pawtucket	AAA Bos	27	92	26	3	0	5	44	12	10	6	0	23	0	0	1	0	0	—	4	.283	.323	.478
2000 Indianapols	AAA Mil	109	380	108	34	0	16	190	48	71	35	6	95	2	2	3	0	0	.00	11	.284	.345	.500
2001 Indianapols	AAA Mil	30	83	15	5	0	2	26	6	4	4	1	19	1	0	0	0	0	—	3	.181	.227	.313
Charlotte	AAA CWS	32	114	28	3	0	7	52	19	19	13	1	32	0	0	0	0	0	—	1	.246	.318	.456
1999 Boston	AL	18	47	13	2	1	1	20	4	7	1	0	13	0	0	0	0	0	—	3	.277	.346	.426
11 Min. YEARS		946	3130	815	184	12	137	1434	451	542	369	15	863	61	23	36	15	22	.41	71	.260	.346	.458

Mark Guerra

Pitches: Right **Bats:** Right **Pos:** SP-19; RP-18 **Ht:** 6'2" **Wt:** 200 **Born:** 11/4/71 **Age:** 30

Year Team	Lg Org	G	GS	CG	GF	IP	BFP	H	R	ER	HR	SH	SF	HB	TBB	IBB	SO	WP	Bk	W	L	Pct.	ShO	Sv	ERA
1994 Pittsfield	A- NYM	14	14	2	0	94	392	105	47	36	4	4	5	4	21	1	62	2	2	7	6	.538	0	0	3.45
1995 St. Lucie	A+ NYM	23	23	4	0	160	644	148	55	47	5	4	4	4	33	1	110	2	3	9	9	.500	3	0	2.64
Binghamton	AA NYM	6	5	1	0	32.2	139	35	24	21	6	1	0	0	9	1	24	0	0	2	1	.667	0	0	5.79
1996 Binghamton	AA NYM	27	20	1	3	140.1	577	143	60	55	23	5	2	2	34	3	84	1	1	7	6	.538	0	0	3.53
1997 Binghamton	AA NYM	48	7	1	17	94.2	403	96	46	34	10	3	2	1	30	1	74	2	0	4	8	.333	0	7	3.23
1998 Norfolk	AAA NYM	18	0	0	8	30.2	142	40	24	22	6	2	3	1	14	1	19	0	0	2	1	.667	0	0	6.46
Binghamton	AA NYM	30	2	0	21	41.1	171	38	17	13	5	1	3	0	11	1	30	0	0	3	3	.500	0	12	2.83
1999 Norfolk	AAA NYM	63	2	0	11	89	391	90	45	29	5	3	2	0	39	8	70	2	0	8	3	.727	0	0	2.93
2000 Norfolk	AAA NYM	36	0	0	16	48.2	219	55	29	26	5	3	0	2	23	7	29	3	0	1	4	.200	0	1	4.81
New Orleans	AAA Hou	9	8	0	1	45	199	58	32	30	2	4	1	4	5	1	25	0	0	1	4	.200	0	0	6.00

119

Year Team	Lg Org	G	GS	CG	GF	IP	BFP	H	R	ER	HR	SH	SF	HB	TBB	IBB	SO	WP	Bk	W	L	Pct.	ShO	Sv	ERA
2001 Round Rock	AA Hou	9	4	1	0	36	133	21	8	7	3	1	2	1	5	0	27	0	0	2	0	1.000	0	0	1.75
New Orleans	AAA Hou	28	15	1	4	108.1	466	129	56	47	9	1	3	2	21	1	56	4	0	7	8	.467	1	0	3.90
8 Min. YEARS		311	100	11	81	920.2	3876	958	443	367	84	30	27	21	245	26	610	16	6	53	53	.500	4	20	3.59

Junior Guerrero

Pitches: Right **Bats:** Right **Pos:** RP-15; SP-14   **Ht:** 6'2" **Wt:** 175 **Born:** 8/21/79 **Age:** 22

Year Team	Lg Org	G	GS	CG	GF	IP	BFP	H	R	ER	HR	SH	SF	HB	TBB	IBB	SO	WP	Bk	W	L	Pct.	ShO	Sv	ERA
1998 Royals	R KC	13	6	0	3	61.1	257	57	24	22	2	4	2	2	19	0	58	5	1	4	4	.500	0	0	3.23
1999 Chston-WV	A KC	19	19	0	0	104.1	441	90	39	32	6	4	5	3	45	0	113	10	2	7	3	.700	0	0	2.76
Wilmington	A+ KC	9	9	0	0	51.1	206	30	10	8	2	1	1	0	26	0	68	4	0	4	2	.667	0	0	1.40
2000 Wichita	AA KC	28	24	0	2	131	603	153	93	83	25	1	6	3	69	2	79	8	3	4	10	.286	0	0	5.70
2001 Wichita	AA KC	15	0	0	7	15.2	92	30	18	15	1	0	2	0	14	1	11	1	0	1	2	.333	0	1	8.62
Wilmington	A+ KC	14	14	0	0	83.2	345	78	35	34	7	3	2	12	24	0	59	4	1	5	4	.556	0	0	3.66
4 Min. YEARS		98	72	0	12	447.1	1944	438	219	194	43	13	18	20	197	3	388	32	7	25	25	.500	0	1	3.90

Matt Guerrier

Pitches: Right **Bats:** Right **Pos:** SP-27   **Ht:** 6'3" **Wt:** 190 **Born:** 8/2/78 **Age:** 23

Year Team	Lg Org	G	GS	CG	GF	IP	BFP	H	R	ER	HR	SH	SF	HB	TBB	IBB	SO	WP	Bk	W	L	Pct.	ShO	Sv	ERA
1999 Bristol	R+ CWS	21	0	0	19	25.2	109	18	9	3	1	0	2	1	14	2	37	1	1	5	0	1.000	0	10	1.05
Winston-Sal	A+ CWS	4	0	0	4	3.1	15	3	2	2	0	0	0	1	0	0	5	2	0	0	0	—	0	2	5.40
2000 Winston-Sal	A+ CWS	30	0	0	28	34.2	147	25	13	5	0	2	1	3	12	0	35	2	0	0	3	.000	0	19	1.30
Birmingham	AA CWS	23	0	0	19	23.1	95	17	9	7	1	0	0	1	12	1	19	3	0	3	1	.750	0	7	2.70
2001 Birmingham	AA CWS	15	15	1	0	98.2	402	85	42	34	8	5	0	5	32	1	75	5	0	11	3	.786	1	0	3.10
Charlotte	AAA CWS	12	12	3	0	81.1	328	75	33	32	7	4	2	4	18	0	43	2	0	7	1	.875	0	0	3.54
3 Min. YEARS		105	27	4	70	267	1096	223	108	83	17	11	5	15	88	4	214	15	1	26	8	.765	1	38	2.80

Giomar Guevara

Bats: Both **Throws:** Right **Pos:** SS-108; PR-1; P-1   **Ht:** 5'8" **Wt:** 150 **Born:** 10/23/72 **Age:** 29

Year Team	Lg Org	G	AB	H	2B	3B	HR	TB	R	RBI	TBB	IBB	SO	HBP	SH	SF	SB	CS	SB%	GDP	Avg	OBP	SLG
1993 Bellingham	A- Sea	62	211	48	8	3	1	65	31	23	34	2	46	2	4	0	4	7	.36	3	.227	.340	.308
1994 Appleton	A Sea	110	385	116	23	3	8	169	57	46	42	1	77	2	5	1	9	16	.36	6	.301	.372	.439
Jacksnville	AA Sea	7	20	4	2	0	1	9	2	3	2	0	9	0	1	0	0	0	—	0	.200	.273	.450
1995 Riverside	A+ Sea	83	292	71	12	3	2	95	53	34	30	1	71	1	6	6	7	4	.64	4	.243	.310	.325
1996 Port City	AA Sea	119	414	110	18	2	2	138	60	41	54	1	102	4	9	4	21	7	.75	12	.266	.353	.333
1997 Tacoma	AAA Sea	54	176	43	5	1	2	56	29	13	5	0	39	1	5	0	3	7	.30	2	.244	.269	.318
Memphis	AA Sea	65	228	60	10	4	4	90	30	28	20	0	42	0	0	1	5	5	.50	3	.263	.321	.395
1998 Lancaster	A+ Sea	19	61	15	4	0	0	19	15	3	14	0	20	1	0	0	1	1	.50	1	.246	.395	.311
Orlando	AA Sea	14	45	15	5	1	0	22	13	6	8	0	11	0	1	0	0	0	—	3	.333	.434	.489
1999 Tacoma	AAA Sea	32	116	34	13	0	3	56	15	15	12	0	22	2	1	0	0	1	.00	3	.293	.369	.483
2000 Toledo	AAA Det	109	383	108	23	2	7	156	61	33	44	0	65	4	5	3	4	5	.44	10	.282	.359	.407
2001 Toledo	AAA Det	109	400	94	15	3	6	133	50	36	33	1	97	2	13	4	8	2	.80	7	.235	.294	.333
1997 Seattle	AL	5	4	0	0	0	0	0	0	0	0	0	2	0	0	0	1	0	1.00	0	.000	.000	.000
1998 Seattle	AL	11	13	3	2	0	0	5	4	0	4	0	4	1	0	0	0	0	—	1	.231	.444	.385
1999 Seattle	AL	10	12	3	2	0	0	5	2	2	0	0	2	0	0	0	0	0	—	0	.250	.250	.417
9 Min. YEARS		783	2731	718	138	22	36	1008	416	281	298	6	601	19	50	19	62	55	.53	54	.263	.337	.369
3 Maj. YEARS		26	29	6	4	0	0	10	6	2	4	0	8	1	0	0	1	0	1.00	1	.207	.324	.345

Aaron Guiel

Bats: Left **Throws:** Right **Pos:** OF-113; DH-8; PH-1   **Ht:** 5'10" **Wt:** 190 **Born:** 10/5/72 **Age:** 29

Year Team	Lg Org	G	AB	H	2B	3B	HR	TB	R	RBI	TBB	IBB	SO	HBP	SH	SF	SB	CS	SB%	GDP	Avg	OBP	SLG
1993 Boise	A- Ana	35	104	31	6	4	2	51	24	12	26	1	21	4	2	0	3	0	1.00	1	.298	.455	.490
1994 Cedar Rapds	A Ana	127	454	122	30	1	18	208	84	82	64	2	93	6	5	3	21	7	.75	7	.269	.364	.458
1995 Lk Elsinore	A+ Ana	113	409	110	25	7	7	170	73	58	69	0	96	7	4	4	7	6	.54	7	.269	.380	.416
1996 Midland	AA Ana	129	439	118	29	7	10	191	72	48	56	0	71	10	2	1	11	7	.61	6	.269	.364	.435
1997 Midland	AA Ana	116	419	138	37	7	22	255	91	85	59	3	94	18	2	3	14	10	.58	9	.329	.431	.609
Mobile	AA SD	8	26	10	2	0	1	15	9	9	5	0	4	1	0	0	1	0	1.00	0	.385	.500	.577
1998 Padres	R SD	8	16	8	3	1	1	16	8	6	5	1	5	3	0	0	1	1	.50	0	.500	.667	1.000
Las Vegas	AAA SD	60	183	57	15	4	5	95	33	31	28	2	51	4	1	2	5	1	.83	4	.311	.410	.519
1999 Las Vegas	AAA SD	84	257	63	25	2	12	128	46	39	44	3	86	5	0	3	5	4	.56	6	.245	.362	.498
2000 Omaha	AAA KC	73	258	74	15	2	13	132	47	40	35	0	54	8	0	0	6	0	1.00	3	.287	.389	.512
2001 Omaha	AAA KC	121	442	118	27	3	21	214	78	73	51	3	92	13	1	6	6	4	.60	12	.267	.355	.484
9 Min. YEARS		874	3007	849	214	38	112	1475	565	483	442	15	667	79	17	22	80	40	.67	55	.282	.386	.491

Jeff Guiel

Bats: Left **Throws:** Right **Pos:** OF-60; DH-32; 3B-12; 1B-7; PH-6   **Ht:** 5'11" **Wt:** 195 **Born:** 1/12/74 **Age:** 28

Year Team	Lg Org	G	AB	H	2B	3B	HR	TB	R	RBI	TBB	IBB	SO	HBP	SH	SF	SB	CS	SB%	GDP	Avg	OBP	SLG
1997 Cedar Rapds	A Ana	41	132	42	7	0	10	79	32	26	35	5	28	3	0	2	13	2	.87	0	.318	.465	.598
1998 Lk Elsinore	A+ Ana	101	315	85	24	7	16	171	64	60	83	5	87	8	0	3	19	9	.68	3	.270	.430	.543
1999 Lk Elsinore	A+ Ana	15	58	19	4	2	3	36	12	12	11	0	18	0	0	0	2	1	.67	0	.328	.435	.621
Erie	AA Ana	57	175	46	10	3	6	80	34	24	33	0	33	2	1	3	3	3	.50	3	.263	.380	.457
2000 Erie	AA Ana	118	410	104	25	3	16	183	55	59	49	3	97	10	1	9	2	4	.33	8	.254	.341	.446
2001 Arkansas	AA Ana	55	176	55	12	4	13	110	33	36	21	2	52	4	0	4	3	2	.60	2	.313	.390	.625
Salt Lake	AAA Ana	61	224	72	14	1	10	118	37	35	17	1	39	1	1	1	2	0	1.00	2	.321	.370	.527
5 Min. YEARS		448	1490	423	96	18	74	777	267	252	249	16	354	28	3	22	44	21	.68	18	.284	.391	.521

120

Lindsay Gulin

Pitches: Left **Bats:** Left **Pos:** SP-21; RP-5   **Ht:** 6'3" **Wt:** 175 **Born:** 11/22/76 **Age:** 25

Year Team	Lg Org	G	GS	CG	GF	IP	BFP	H	R	ER	HR	SH	SF	HB	TBB	IBB	SO	WP	Bk	W	L	Pct.	ShO	Sv	ERA
1995 Mets	R NYM	10	4	0	3	47.1	182	36	11	9	4	0	1	1	13	0	48	2	2	6	0	1.000	0	0	1.71
Pittsfield	A- NYM	1	1	0	0	7	29	4	4	3	1	1	0	0	3	0	3	1	1	1	0	1.000	0	0	3.86
1996 Capital Cty	A NYM	19	19	1	0	112.1	470	88	40	33	6	0	2	6	57	0	134	5	6	7	7	.500	0	0	2.64
1997 St. Lucie	A+ NYM	9	6	0	0	26.1	136	36	31	27	2	0	2	1	21	1	11	6	1	0	3	.000	0	0	9.23
Capital Cty	A NYM	17	15	1	2	99	421	77	37	32	2	2	2	5	60	0	118	9	1	8	1	.889	1	0	2.91
1998 St. Lucie	A+ NYM	6	4	0	0	27	106	16	9	7	2	2	0	1	11	1	19	1	0	1	1	.500	0	0	2.33
Lancaster	A+ Sea	9	3	0	3	24.2	118	32	17	16	3	0	0	1	15	0	18	1	2	2	2	.500	0	0	5.84
Wisconsin	A Sea	13	8	0	2	48.1	207	47	24	20	5	3	1	3	20	0	51	6	0	1	3	.250	0	1	3.72
1999 St. Paul	IND —	16	16	0	0	102	419	83	41	36	8	1	3	5	46	0	83	6	6	8	2	.800	0	0	3.18
Daytona	A+ ChC	3	1	0	0	13.2	53	7	0	0	0	1	0	0	7	0	19	0	0	2	0	1.000	0	0	0.00
2000 Daytona	A+ ChC	19	17	0	1	109.2	447	93	34	30	8	5	1	3	43	0	97	5	3	11	2	.846	0	0	2.46
West Tenn	AA ChC	9	9	1	0	52.1	237	49	33	29	4	1	3	4	30	0	54	4	2	5	2	.714	1	0	4.99
2001 Jacksonville	AA LA	26	21	1	0	126.1	541	128	46	37	10	5	3	6	46	0	111	0	2	7	5	.583	1	0	2.64
7 Min. YEARS		157	124	4	11	796	3366	696	327	279	55	21	18	36	372	2	766	46	26	59	28	.678	3	1	3.15

Eric Gunderson

Pitches: Left **Bats:** Right **Pos:** RP-58   **Ht:** 6'0" **Wt:** 190 **Born:** 3/29/66 **Age:** 36

Year Team	Lg Org	G	GS	CG	GF	IP	BFP	H	R	ER	HR	SH	SF	HB	TBB	IBB	SO	WP	Bk	W	L	Pct.	ShO	Sv	ERA
1987 Everett	A- SF	15	15	5	0	98.2	406	80	34	27	4	2	2	3	34	1	99	4	3	8	4	.667	3	0	2.46
1988 San Jose	A+ SF	20	20	5	0	149.1	640	131	56	44	2	7	3	17	52	0	151	14	6	12	5	.706	4	0	2.65
Shreveport	AA SF	7	6	0	1	36.2	166	45	25	21	1	1	1	1	13	0	28	0	1	1	2	.333	0	0	5.15
1989 Shreveport	AA SF	11	11	2	0	72.2	298	68	24	22	1	1	3	1	23	0	61	1	1	8	2	.800	1	0	2.72
Phoenix	AAA SF	14	14	2	0	85.2	375	93	51	48	7	5	6	2	36	2	56	7	1	2	4	.333	1	0	5.04
1990 Phoenix	AAA SF	16	16	0	0	82	418	137	87	75	11	5	3	3	46	1	41	4	2	5	7	.417	0	0	8.23
Shreveport	AA SF	8	8	1	0	52.2	225	51	24	19	7	1	3	2	17	1	44	1	0	2	2	.500	1	0	3.25
1991 Phoenix	AAA SF	40	14	0	8	107	511	153	85	73	10	3	4	3	44	4	53	3	0	7	6	.538	0	3	6.14
1992 Jacksonville	AA Sea	15	0	0	8	23.1	93	18	10	6	2	1	0	0	7	0	23	0	0	2	0	1.000	0	2	2.31
Calgary	AAA Sea	27	1	0	12	52.1	244	57	37	35	6	4	3	5	31	3	50	5	0	0	2	.000	0	5	6.02
1993 Calgary	AAA Sea	5	0	0	1	6.2	40	14	15	14	1	0	2	2	8	0	3	1	0	0	1	.000	0	0	18.90
Binghamton	AA NYM	20	1	0	7	22.1	104	20	14	13	1	3	1	2	14	0	26	1	0	2	1	.667	0	1	5.24
Norfolk	AAA NYM	6	5	1	0	34	149	41	16	14	5	0	0	2	9	1	26	1	0	3	2	.600	0	0	3.71
1994 St. Lucie	A+ NYM	3	0	0	1	4.2	17	4	0	0	0	0	0	0	0	0	6	0	0	1	0	1.000	0	1	0.00
Norfolk	AAA NYM	19	2	1	2	36.2	151	25	16	15	0	1	0	1	17	2	31	2	0	3	1	.750	1	1	3.68
1996 Pawtucket	AAA Bos	26	1	0	3	33.2	144	38	15	13	2	0	1	0	9	1	34	3	0	2	1	.667	0	2	3.48
1999 Oklahoma	AAA Tex	5	0	0	2	6.2	32	11	6	6	2	0	0	0	1	0	3	1	0	0	1	.000	0	0	8.10
2000 Syracuse	AAA Tor	33	0	0	10	27	117	26	12	8	2	2	1	1	11	0	17	4	1	0	3	.000	0	2	2.67
Fresno	AAA SF	13	0	0	7	23.1	109	34	18	13	2	1	0	1	7	1	14	0	0	2	1	.667	0	2	5.01
2001 Buffalo	AAA Cle	2	0	0	1	2	9	2	1	0	0	0	0	0	0	0	3	0	0	0	0	—	0	1	0.00
Columbus	AAA NYY	56	0	0	17	73.2	307	70	32	25	6	4	2	3	24	1	60	3	0	2	4	.333	0	6	3.05
1990 San Francisco	NL	7	4	0	1	19.2	94	24	14	12	2	1	0	0	11	1	14	0	0	1	2	.333	0	0	5.49
1991 San Francisco	NL	2	0	0	1	3.1	18	6	4	2	0	0	0	0	1	0	2	0	0	0	0	—	0	1	5.40
1992 Seattle	AL	9	0	0	4	9.1	45	12	12	9	1	0	2	1	5	3	2	0	2	2	1	.667	0	0	8.68
1994 New York	NL	14	0	0	3	9	31	5	0	0	0	0	0	0	4	0	4	0	0	0	0	—	0	0	0.00
1995 New York	NL	30	0	0	7	24.1	103	25	10	10	2	0	1	1	8	3	19	1	0	1	1	.500	0	0	3.70
Boston	AL	19	0	0	1	12.1	58	13	7	7	0	2	1	2	9	1	9	0	0	2	1	.667	0	0	5.11
1996 Boston	AL	28	0	0	2	17.1	82	21	17	16	5	0	2	2	8	2	7	3	0	0	0	.000	0	0	8.31
1997 Texas	AL	60	0	0	11	49.2	209	45	19	18	5	2	3	2	15	3	31	2	1	2	1	.667	0	1	3.26
1998 Texas	AL	68	1	0	13	67.2	303	88	43	39	13	1	3	1	19	4	41	4	0	0	3	.000	0	0	5.19
1999 Texas	AL	11	0	0	3	10	51	20	8	8	1	0	1	0	2	0	6	3	0	0	0	—	0	0	7.20
2000 Toronto	AL	6	0	0	1	6.1	37	15	6	5	0	0	1	0	2	1	2	0	0	1	0	1.000	0	0	7.11
12 Min. YEARS		361	114	17	80	1031	4555	1118	578	491	72	41	35	49	403	18	829	55	15	62	49	.559	11	27	4.29
10 Maj. YEARS		254	5	0	47	229	1031	274	140	126	29	6	14	10	84	18	137	13	3	8	11	.421	0	2	4.95

Rick Guttormson

Pitches: Right **Bats:** Right **Pos:** SP-24; RP-4   **Ht:** 6'2" **Wt:** 185 **Born:** 1/11/77 **Age:** 25

Year Team	Lg Org	G	GS	CG	GF	IP	BFP	H	R	ER	HR	SH	SF	HB	TBB	IBB	SO	WP	Bk	W	L	Pct.	ShO	Sv	ERA
1997 Padres	R SD	5	0	0	4	11	55	17	11	6	3	0	1	0	4	0	19	0	0	1	1	.500	0	1	4.91
Idaho Falls	R+ SD	18	2	0	8	28	129	34	25	20	2	5	2	2	11	2	19	5	0	3	2	.600	0	3	6.43
1998 Clinton	A SD	30	25	0	0	159	673	155	66	46	9	1	4	12	41	1	141	7	1	10	7	.588	0	2	2.60
1999 Rancho Cuca	A+ SD	28	28	1	0	174.1	714	165	83	72	15	4	1	9	36	0	125	6	2	14	8	.636	0	0	3.72
2000 Mobile	AA SD	17	15	0	0	81.1	361	88	44	36	9	4	2	5	35	0	36	1	2	4	4	.500	0	0	3.98
2001 Portland	AAA SD	1	0	0	0	5	26	9	6	6	0	0	2	1	1	0	1	0	0	0	1	.000	0	0	10.80
Mobile	AA SD	27	24	0	2	143.1	624	146	84	75	18	4	4	13	51	0	78	5	0	5	16	.238	0	0	4.71
5 Min. YEARS		126	94	1	18	602	2582	614	319	261	56	18	16	42	179	3	419	24	5	37	39	.487	0	6	3.90

Brad Guy

Pitches: Right **Bats:** Right **Pos:** RP-44; SP-6   **Ht:** 6'2" **Wt:** 192 **Born:** 10/25/75 **Age:** 26

Year Team	Lg Org	G	GS	CG	GF	IP	BFP	H	R	ER	HR	SH	SF	HB	TBB	IBB	SO	WP	Bk	W	L	Pct.	ShO	Sv	ERA
1997 Erie	A- Pit	25	0	0	6	52.2	201	37	12	11	3	3	0	2	7	0	53	9	1	5	1	.833	0	1	1.88
1998 Augusta	A Pit	56	0	0	24	86.1	363	75	39	29	7	6	0	4	26	4	94	10	3	6	4	.600	0	4	3.02
1999 Lynchburg	A+ Pit	49	0	0	27	72.1	308	77	35	33	2	5	2	1	17	2	60	7	1	6	6	.500	0	10	4.11
2000 Altoona	AA Pit	54	1	0	27	81.2	354	82	35	32	3	2	1	1	25	1	37	6	0	4	6	.400	0	7	3.53
2001 Altoona	AA Pit	28	4	0	16	51.1	226	59	32	23	3	1	2	3	17	2	30	4	1	3	4	.429	0	4	4.03
Nashville	AAA Pit	22	2	0	3	46.2	196	47	26	22	3	1	2	1	16	3	35	1	0	2	2	.500	0	0	4.24
5 Min. YEARS		234	7	0	103	391	1648	377	179	150	21	19	7	12	108	12	309	37	6	26	23	.531	0	26	3.45

121

Domingo Guzman

Pitches: Right **Bats:** Right **Pos:** RP-11 **Ht:** 6'0" **Wt:** 210 **Born:** 4/5/75 **Age:** 27

Year Team	Lg Org	G	GS	CG	GF	IP	BFP	H	R	ER	HR	SH	SF	HB	TBB	IBB	SO	WP	Bk	W	L	Pct.	ShO	Sv	ERA
1994 Padres	R SD	13	13	0	0	70	309	65	39	32	1	1	2	11	25	0	55	5	2	8	4	.667	0	0	4.11
1995 Idaho Falls	R+ SD	27	0	0	23	25.2	127	25	22	19	2	3	1	1	25	1	33	6	3	2	1	.667	0	11	6.66
1996 Clinton	A SD	6	5	0	1	20.2	112	32	33	29	2	0	1	2	19	0	18	5	0	0	5	.000	0	0	12.63
Idaho Falls	R+ SD	15	10	1	1	65.1	278	52	41	30	7	2	1	7	29	0	75	13	0	4	2	.667	1	0	4.13
1997 Clinton	A SD	12	12	5	0	79	320	66	36	28	7	2	2	3	25	0	91	5	2	4	5	.444	0	0	3.19
Rancho Cuca	A+ SD	6	6	0	0	38	168	42	23	23	6	2	1	2	16	0	39	2	0	3	2	.600	0	0	5.45
1998 Rancho Cuca	A+ SD	4	4	0	0	21.2	91	22	11	9	1	0	1	1	6	0	16	3	0	1	1	.500	0	0	3.74
Mobile	AA SD	12	8	0	2	48	217	51	34	24	7	3	0	3	26	0	39	8	0	5	2	.714	0	1	4.50
1999 Mobile	AA SD	41	0	0	21	51	240	60	33	31	2	3	3	5	25	1	38	3	0	1	2	.333	0	0	5.47
2000 Mobile	AA SD	14	1	0	4	17.1	76	13	8	4	2	1	1	2	11	0	14	4	0	0	0	—	0	0	2.08
Las Vegas	AAA SD	43	3	0	10	63.1	282	56	47	42	10	3	6	8	35	3	54	6	2	3	5	.375	0	1	5.97
2001 Portland	AAA SD	11	0	0	4	17.1	78	20	13	13	0	2	1	2	5	1	16	1	0	1	2	.333	0	1	6.75
1999 San Diego	NL	7	0	0	2	5	33	13	12	12	1	2	0	0	3	2	4	0	0	0	1	.000	0	0	21.60
2000 San Diego	NL	1	0	0	0	1	6	1	1	1	0	0	0	2	1	0	0	0	0	0	0	—	0	0	9.00
8 Min. YEARS		204	62	6	66	517.1	2298	504	340	284	47	22	20	47	247	6	488	61	9	32	31	.508	1	20	4.94
2 Maj. YEARS		8	0	0	2	6	39	14	13	13	1	2	0	2	4	2	4	0	0	0	1	.000	0	0	19.50

Elpidio Guzman

Bats: Left **Throws:** Left **Pos:** OF-110; DH-7 **Ht:** 6'2" **Wt:** 165 **Born:** 2/24/79 **Age:** 23

		BATTING															BASERUNNING				PERCENTAGES		
Year Team	Lg Org	G	AB	H	2B	3B	HR	TB	R	RBI	TBB	IBB	SO	HBP	SH	SF	SB	CS	SB%	GDP	Avg	OBP	SLG
1997 Butte	R+ Ana	17	43	13	2	1	3	26	12	13	5	0	5	0	0	0	3	0	1.00	5	.302	.375	.605
1998 Butte	R+ Ana	69	299	99	16	5	9	152	70	61	24	2	44	2	1	1	40	9	.82	8	.331	.383	.508
1999 Cedar Rapds	A Ana	130	526	144	26	13	4	208	74	48	41	4	84	2	5	3	52	17	.75	11	.274	.327	.395
2000 Lk Elsinore	A+ Ana	135	532	150	20	16	9	229	96	72	61	2	116	3	5	11	53	14	.79	6	.282	.353	.430
2001 Arkansas	AA Ana	117	459	112	21	8	7	170	58	46	17	1	89	2	2	3	18	14	.56	6	.244	.272	.370
5 Min. YEARS		468	1859	518	85	43	32	785	310	240	148	9	338	9	13	18	166	54	.75	31	.279	.332	.422

Juan Guzman

Pitches: Right **Bats:** Right **Pos:** SP-12 **Ht:** 5'11" **Wt:** 195 **Born:** 10/28/66 **Age:** 35

Year Team	Lg Org	G	GS	CG	GF	IP	BFP	H	R	ER	HR	SH	SF	HB	TBB	IBB	SO	WP	Bk	W	L	Pct.	ShO	Sv	ERA
1985 Dodgers	R LA	21	3	0	12	42	189	39	26	18	2	3	2	1	25	3	43	15	3	5	1	.833	0	4	3.86
1986 Vero Beach	A+ LA	26	24	3	0	131.1	594	114	69	51	3	4	3	4	90	4	96	16	2	10	9	.526	0	0	3.49
1987 Bakersfield	A+ LA	22	21	0	0	110	508	106	71	58	4	0	1	1	84	0	113	19	1	5	6	.455	0	0	4.75
1988 Knoxville	AA Tor	46	2	0	23	84	363	52	29	22	1	4	4	1	61	5	90	6	6	4	5	.444	0	6	2.36
1989 Syracuse	AAA Tor	14	0	0	4	20.1	99	13	9	9	0	0	1	4	30	0	28	5	0	1	1	.500	0	0	3.98
Knoxville	AA Tor	22	8	0	7	47.2	232	34	36	33	2	2	1	2	60	0	50	8	5	1	4	.200	0	0	6.23
1990 Knoxville	AA Tor	37	21	2	7	157	685	145	84	74	10	6	11	3	80	6	138	21	8	11	9	.550	0	1	4.24
1991 Syracuse	AAA Tor	12	11	0	0	67	287	46	39	30	4	1	3	2	42	0	67	7	2	4	5	.444	0	0	4.03
1992 Syracuse	AAA Tor	1	1	0	0	3	16	6	2	2	0	0	0	0	1	0	3	0	0	0	0	—	0	0	6.00
1995 Syracuse	AAA Tor	1	1	0	0	5	18	1	0	0	0	0	0	0	3	0	5	1	0	0	0	—	0	0	0.00
1997 Dunedin	A+ Tor	2	2	0	0	4	15	3	0	0	0	0	0	0	1	0	3	0	0	0	0	—	0	0	0.00
2000 St. Pete	A+ TB	1	1	0	0	5	21	4	0	0	0	0	0	0	2	0	6	0	0	1	0	1.000	0	0	0.00
Orlando	AA TB	1	1	0	0	5.1	26	6	6	5	1	1	0	1	3	0	5	0	0	0	1	.000	0	0	8.44
Durham	AAA TB	2	2	0	0	9.2	42	13	6	6	3	0	0	0	1	0	7	0	0	0	2	.000	0	0	5.59
2001 Orlando	AA TB	2	2	0	0	12	45	8	1	1	0	0	0	0	4	0	9	0	0	2	0	1.000	0	0	0.75
Durham	AAA TB	10	10	0	0	60.1	259	50	35	32	7	5	4	5	30	0	42	4	0	4	2	.667	0	0	4.77
1991 Toronto	AL	23	23	1	0	138.2	574	98	53	46	6	2	5	4	66	0	123	10	0	10	3	.769	0	0	2.99
1992 Toronto	AL	28	28	1	0	180.2	733	135	56	53	6	5	3	1	72	2	165	14	2	16	5	.762	0	0	2.64
1993 Toronto	AL	33	33	2	0	221	963	211	107	98	17	5	9	3	110	2	194	26	1	14	3	.824	1	0	3.99
1994 Toronto	AL	25	25	2	0	147.1	671	165	102	93	20	1	6	3	76	1	124	13	1	12	11	.522	0	0	5.68
1995 Toronto	AL	24	24	3	0	135.1	619	151	101	95	15	3	2	3	73	6	94	8	0	4	14	.222	0	0	6.32
1996 Toronto	AL	27	27	4	0	187.2	756	158	68	61	20	2	2	7	53	3	165	7	0	11	8	.579	1	0	2.93
1997 Toronto	AL	13	13	0	0	60	261	48	42	33	14	1	2	2	31	0	52	4	0	3	6	.333	0	0	4.95
1998 Toronto	AL	22	22	2	0	145	632	133	83	71	19	2	3	6	65	1	113	6	0	6	12	.333	0	0	4.41
Baltimore	AL	11	11	0	0	66	286	60	34	31	4	0	2	2	33	1	55	5	0	4	4	.500	0	0	4.23
1999 Baltimore	AL	21	21	1	0	122.2	544	124	63	57	18	4	3	3	65	3	95	7	2	5	9	.357	1	0	4.18
Cincinnati	NL	12	12	1	0	77.1	320	70	33	26	10	3	1	1	21	3	60	5	0	6	3	.667	0	0	3.03
2000 Tampa Bay	AL	1	1	0	0	1.2	14	7	8	8	2	1	0	0	2	0	3	0	0	0	1	.000	0	0	43.20
12 Min. YEARS		220	110	5	53	763.2	3399	640	413	341	37	26	30	20	517	18	705	102	27	48	45	.516	0	11	4.02
10 Maj. YEARS		240	240	17	0	1483.1	6373	1360	750	672	149	29	38	35	667	22	1243	105	6	91	79	.535	3	0	4.08

Leiby Guzman

Pitches: Right **Bats:** Right **Pos:** RP-36 **Ht:** 6'5" **Wt:** 160 **Born:** 9/27/76 **Age:** 25

Year Team	Lg Org	G	GS	CG	GF	IP	BFP	H	R	ER	HR	SH	SF	HB	TBB	IBB	SO	WP	Bk	W	L	Pct.	ShO	Sv	ERA
1999 Rangers	R Tex	1	1	0	0	2	11	2	0	0	0	0	0	0	0	0	1	0	0	0	0	—	0	0	0.00
Charlotte	A+ Tex	19	18	0	1	93.1	420	114	67	61	16	0	5	9	40	0	45	5	0	5	6	.455	0	0	5.88
2000 Tulsa	AA Tex	24	20	0	2	115.1	544	143	86	73	15	1	4	8	58	1	84	4	0	7	9	.438	0	0	5.70
2001 Tulsa	AA Tex	25	0	0	13	48.1	209	48	30	29	7	2	3	1	15	0	31	1	0	2	0	1.000	0	1	5.40
Shreveport	AA SF	11	0	0	5	14.1	67	17	9	5	0	1	1	0	2	0	14	2	0	2	1	.667	0	0	3.14
3 Min. YEARS		80	39	0	21	274.1	1251	324	192	168	38	4	13	18	115	1	175	12	0	16	16	.500	0	1	5.51

Yamid Haad

Bats: Right **Throws:** Right **Pos:** C-41; PH-9; DH-3; 1B-2; P-1   **Ht:** 6'2" **Wt:** 204 **Born:** 9/2/77 **Age:** 24

Year Team	Lg Org	G	AB	H	2B	3B	HR	TB	R	RBI	TBB	IBB	SO	HBP	SH	SF	SB	CS	SB%	GDP	Avg	OBP	SLG
1997 Erie	A- Pit	43	155	45	7	3	1	61	27	19	7	0	27	0	1	6	3	3	.50	5	.290	.310	.394
1998 Lynchburg	A+ Pit	88	299	76	8	2	5	103	32	34	13	0	54	3	4	4	1	7	.13	11	.254	.288	.344
1999 Lynchburg	A+ Pit	59	209	53	11	1	5	81	31	33	33	1	42	1	2	3	5	2	.71	8	.254	.354	.388
Altoona	AA Pit	43	137	25	3	0	6	46	20	10	19	0	32	0	1	1	7	2	.78	4	.182	.280	.336
2000 Altoona	AA Pit	59	183	36	7	0	4	55	24	13	18	0	44	0	1	1	1	1	.50	4	.197	.267	.301
Lynchburg	A+ Pit	25	91	23	8	0	3	40	14	9	11	0	16	0	0	1	2	0	1.00	4	.253	.330	.440
2001 Lynchburg	A+ Pit	3	11	2	1	0	0	3	0	1	0	0	3	0	0	0	1	0	1.00	0	.182	.182	.273
Altoona	AA Pit	1	3	0	0	0	0	0	0	0	0	0	0	0	0	0	0	0	—	0	.000	.000	.000
Nashville	AAA Pit	51	144	37	5	0	2	48	14	10	7	0	27	0	2	0	0	3	.00	2	.257	.291	.333
1999 Pittsburgh	NL	1	1	0	0	0	0	0	0	0	0	0	0	0	0	0	0	0	—	0	.000	.000	.000
5 Min. YEARS		372	1232	297	50	6	26	437	162	129	108	1	245	4	11	16	20	18	.53	38	.241	.301	.355

Chris Haas

Bats: Left **Throws:** Right **Pos:** 1B-100; 3B-13; PH-8; DH-5; OF-2; 2B-1   **Ht:** 6'2" **Wt:** 210 **Born:** 10/15/76 **Age:** 25

Year Team	Lg Org	G	AB	H	2B	3B	HR	TB	R	RBI	TBB	IBB	SO	HBP	SH	SF	SB	CS	SB%	GDP	Avg	OBP	SLG
1995 Johnson Cty	R+ StL	67	242	65	15	3	7	107	43	50	52	0	93	1	0	0	1	3	.25	8	.269	.400	.442
1996 Peoria	A StL	124	421	101	19	1	11	155	56	65	64	3	169	7	1	3	3	2	.60	4	.240	.347	.368
1997 Peoria	A StL	36	115	36	11	0	5	62	23	22	22	1	38	3	0	2	3	0	1.00	4	.313	.430	.539
Pr William	A+ StL	100	361	86	10	2	14	142	58	54	42	2	144	4	1	2	1	1	.50	7	.238	.323	.393
1998 Arkansas	AA StL	132	445	122	27	4	20	217	75	83	73	5	129	8	0	5	1	2	.33	5	.274	.382	.488
1999 Memphis	AAA StL	114	397	91	19	2	18	168	63	73	66	3	155	2	3	5	4	4	.50	4	.229	.338	.423
2000 Memphis	AAA StL	23	56	12	1	0	1	16	7	9	9	0	11	0	0	0	0	0	—	2	.214	.323	.286
Arkansas	AA StL	82	291	79	14	2	17	148	52	59	40	2	84	4	1	3	0	1	.00	11	.271	.364	.509
2001 West Tenn	AA ChC	126	417	102	16	4	25	201	64	72	65	5	151	3	1	4	2	2	.50	6	.245	.348	.482
7 Min. YEARS		804	2745	694	132	18	118	1216	441	487	433	21	974	32	7	24	15	15	.50	51	.253	.358	.443

Danny Haas

Bats: Left **Throws:** Right **Pos:** OF-22; DH-15; PH-4   **Ht:** 5'11" **Wt:** 180 **Born:** 1/4/76 **Age:** 26

Year Team	Lg Org	G	AB	H	2B	3B	HR	TB	R	RBI	TBB	IBB	SO	HBP	SH	SF	SB	CS	SB%	GDP	Avg	OBP	SLG
1997 Lowell	A- Bos	9	28	5	3	0	0	8	6	0	2	0	8	1	2	0	3	0	1.00	0	.179	.258	.286
1998 Michigan	A Bos	96	299	70	14	1	3	95	39	29	22	1	55	5	2	2	1	2	.33	7	.234	.296	.318
1999 Sarasota	A+ Bos	87	241	58	8	5	0	76	18	24	22	1	54	6	2	2	4	3	.57	5	.241	.317	.315
2000 Sarasota	A+ Bos	118	398	101	12	1	4	127	44	39	30	2	63	7	1	2	5	8	.38	5	.254	.316	.319
2001 Red Sox	R Bos	11	28	3	1	0	0	4	6	1	9	1	1	0	0	1	0	0	—	1	.107	.316	.143
Trenton	AA Bos	29	80	14	3	0	0	17	10	5	8	0	20	1	0	0	1	0	1.00	4	.175	.258	.213
5 Min. YEARS		350	1074	251	41	7	7	327	123	98	93	5	201	20	7	7	14	13	.52	22	.234	.305	.304

Richard Hackett

Bats: Right **Throws:** Right **Pos:** OF-43; PH-11; DH-1   **Ht:** 6'1" **Wt:** 200 **Born:** 4/30/79 **Age:** 23

Year Team	Lg Org	G	AB	H	2B	3B	HR	TB	R	RBI	TBB	IBB	SO	HBP	SH	SF	SB	CS	SB%	GDP	Avg	OBP	SLG
2001 Orioles	R Bal	7	21	5	1	0	0	6	2	1	2	0	4	0	0	0	0	1	.00	1	.238	.304	.286
Bluefield	R+ Bal	39	97	24	4	0	5	43	19	20	18	0	32	4	0	2	1	4	.20	0	.247	.380	.443
Bowie	AA Bal	3	8	1	0	0	0	1	0	0	1	0	5	0	0	0	0	1	.00	0	.125	.222	.125
1 Min. YEAR		49	126	30	5	0	5	50	21	21	21	0	41	4	0	2	1	6	.14	1	.238	.359	.397

Travis Hafner

Bats: Left **Throws:** Right **Pos:** 1B-78; DH-10   **Ht:** 6'3" **Wt:** 240 **Born:** 6/3/77 **Age:** 25

Year Team	Lg Org	G	AB	H	2B	3B	HR	TB	R	RBI	TBB	IBB	SO	HBP	SH	SF	SB	CS	SB%	GDP	Avg	OBP	SLG
1997 Rangers	R Tex	55	189	54	14	0	5	83	38	24	24	1	45	3	0	0	7	2	.78	3	.286	.375	.439
1998 Savannah	A Tex	123	405	96	15	4	16	167	62	84	68	2	139	6	0	5	7	3	.70	8	.237	.351	.412
1999 Savannah	A Tex	134	480	140	30	4	28	262	94	111	67	6	151	11	0	5	5	4	.56	11	.292	.387	.546
2000 Charlotte	A+ Tex	122	436	151	34	1	22	253	90	109	67	2	86	18	0	7	0	4	.00	9	.346	.447	.580
2001 Tulsa	AA Tex	88	323	91	25	0	20	176	59	74	59	5	82	4	0	3	3	1	.75	10	.282	.396	.545
5 Min. YEARS		522	1833	532	118	9	91	941	343	402	285	16	503	42	0	20	22	14	.61	41	.290	.394	.513

Talley Haines

Pitches: Right **Bats:** Right **Pos:** RP-59   **Ht:** 6'5" **Wt:** 203 **Born:** 11/16/76 **Age:** 25

Year Team	Lg Org	G	GS	CG	GF	IP	BFP	H	R	ER	HR	SH	SF	HB	TBB	IBB	SO	WP	Bk	W	L	Pct.	ShO	Sv	ERA
1998 Princeton	R+ TB	27	1	0	9	43.1	197	54	32	25	4	0	1	2	17	0	37	5	1	2	3	.400	0	2	5.19
1999 St. Pete	A+ TB	2	0	0	1	4.1	13	1	0	0	0	0	0	2	0	0	4	0	0	0	0	—	0	0	0.00
Chston-SC	A TB	47	0	0	34	61	248	51	33	22	2	2	0	3	12	4	68	5	1	3	2	.600	0	18	3.25
2000 St. Pete	A+ TB	16	0	0	10	22.2	94	22	10	7	1	0	0	0	2	1	22	0	0	2	1	.667	0	3	2.78
Durham	AAA TB	1	0	0	0	1.1	10	6	4	4	1	0	0	0	1	0	2	1	0	0	1	.000	0	0	27.00
Orlando	AA TB	33	0	0	21	54.1	222	36	18	9	2	6	2	1	21	5	47	3	0	3	3	.500	0	1	1.49
2001 Orlando	AA TB	58	0	0	38	71.2	316	73	32	29	7	8	1	2	29	3	73	6	0	6	6	.500	0	8	3.64
Durham	AAA TB	1	0	0	1	2	6	0	0	0	0	0	0	0	1	0	1	0	0	0	0	—	0	1	0.00
4 Min. YEARS		185	1	0	114	260.2	1106	243	129	96	17	16	4	10	82	13	254	20	2	16	16	.500	0	35	3.31

Beau Hale

Pitches: Right **Bats:** Right **Pos:** SP-17 **Ht:** 6'2" **Wt:** 220 **Born:** 12/1/78 **Age:** 23

		HOW MUCH HE PITCHED						WHAT HE GAVE UP										THE RESULTS				
Year Team	Lg Org	G	GS	CG	GF	IP	BFP	H	R	ER	HR	SH	SF	HB	TBB	IBB	SO	WP	Bk	W	L	Pct.	ShO	Sv	ERA
2001 Frederick	A+ Bal	5	5	1	0	34	133	30	8	5	1	1	0	1	4	0	30	0	1	1	2	.333	0	0	1.32
Bowie	AA Bal	12	12	0	0	61.2	268	74	39	35	8	3	5	3	15	1	40	4	2	1	5	.167	0	0	5.11
1 Min. YEAR		17	17	1	0	95.2	401	104	47	40	9	4	5	4	19	1	70	4	3	2	7	.222	0	0	3.76

Bill Hall

Bats: Right **Throws:** Right **Pos:** SS-130; DH-1; PH-1 **Ht:** 6'0" **Wt:** 175 **Born:** 12/28/79 **Age:** 22

		BATTING														BASERUNNING				PERCENTAGES		
Year Team	Lg Org	G	AB	H	2B	3B	HR	TB	R	RBI	TBB	IBB	SO	HBP	SH	SF	SB	CS	SB%	GDP	Avg	OBP	SLG
1998 Helena	R+ Mil	29	85	15	3	0	0	18	11	5	9	0	27	1	1	0	5	5	.50	2	.176	.263	.212
1999 Ogden	R+ Mil	69	280	81	15	2	6	118	41	31	15	1	61	2	2	1	19	8	.70	6	.289	.329	.421
2000 Beloit	A Mil	130	470	123	30	6	3	174	57	41	18	0	127	1	12	5	10	11	.48	12	.262	.287	.370
2001 High Desert	A+ Mil	89	346	105	21	6	15	183	61	51	22	0	78	3	4	3	18	9	.67	3	.303	.348	.529
Huntsville	AA Mil	41	160	41	8	1	3	60	14	14	5	0	46	0	3	0	5	3	.63	5	.256	.279	.375
4 Min. YEARS		358	1341	365	77	15	27	553	184	142	69	1	339	7	22	9	57	36	.61	28	.272	.309	.412

Justin Hall

Bats: Right **Throws:** Right **Pos:** 2B-51; DH-16; PH-8; 3B-5; SS-1 **Ht:** 5'10" **Wt:** 175 **Born:** 9/23/76 **Age:** 25

		BATTING														BASERUNNING				PERCENTAGES		
Year Team	Lg Org	G	AB	H	2B	3B	HR	TB	R	RBI	TBB	IBB	SO	HBP	SH	SF	SB	CS	SB%	GDP	Avg	OBP	SLG
1998 Sou Oregon	A- Oak	69	265	76	12	8	3	113	56	33	35	0	39	6	2	2	5	3	.63	9	.287	.380	.426
1999 Athletics	R Oak	7	20	7	1	0	0	8	5	4	5	0	5	2	0	1	0	1	.00	0	.350	.500	.400
Sou Oregon	A- Oak	5	20	6	3	0	0	9	2	2	1	0	4	1	1	1	1	0	1.00	0	.300	.348	.450
2000 Modesto	A+ Oak	90	341	87	17	3	3	119	59	38	56	0	65	6	2	4	12	3	.80	7	.255	.366	.349
2001 Modesto	A+ Oak	33	87	22	3	0	1	28	10	9	9	0	20	3	1	0	2	2	.50	1	.253	.343	.322
San Jose	A+ SF	42	151	40	11	1	2	59	22	13	24	0	39	1	1	0	1	0	1.00	3	.265	.369	.391
Fresno	AAA SF	1	4	2	0	0	0	2	1	1	0	0	0	0	0	0	0	0	—	0	.500	.500	.500
4 Min. YEARS		247	888	240	47	12	9	338	155	100	130	0	172	19	7	8	21	9	.70	20	.270	.372	.381

Noah Hall

Bats: Right **Throws:** Right **Pos:** OF-84; 2B-17 **Ht:** 5'11" **Wt:** 200 **Born:** 6/9/77 **Age:** 25

		BATTING														BASERUNNING				PERCENTAGES		
Year Team	Lg Org	G	AB	H	2B	3B	HR	TB	R	RBI	TBB	IBB	SO	HBP	SH	SF	SB	CS	SB%	GDP	Avg	OBP	SLG
1996 Expos	R Mon	41	134	32	5	3	1	46	24	18	19	2	22	5	1	2	6	2	.75	2	.239	.350	.343
1997 Wst Plm Bch	A+ Mon	1	1	0	0	0	0	0	0	0	0	0	1	0	0	0	0	0	—	0	.000	.000	.000
Vermont	A- Mon	73	266	73	12	8	2	107	43	45	45	2	48	3	0	2	22	5	.81	1	.274	.383	.402
1998 Cape Fear	A Mon	127	447	142	21	7	11	210	84	90	52	2	69	14	3	3	33	9	.79	16	.318	.403	.470
Jupiter	A+ Mon	4	8	2	0	0	0	2	2	0	3	0	1	1	0	0	1	1	.50	0	.250	.500	.250
1999 Jupiter	A+ Mon	119	398	94	10	3	8	134	57	49	49	1	60	8	6	7	32	11	.74	12	.236	.327	.337
2000 Jupiter	A+ Mon	90	310	89	8	2	3	110	64	40	57	1	36	8	1	2	26	11	.70	3	.287	.408	.355
Harrisburg	AA Mon	45	147	38	8	2	3	59	25	24	35	2	19	3	2	2	8	5	.62	3	.259	.406	.401
2001 St. Paul	IND —	88	352	110	19	4	8	161	61	47	45	0	45	5	0	4	37	6	.86	9	.313	.394	.457
Louisville	AAA Cin	1	2	0	0	0	0	0	0	0	0	0	0	0	0	1	0	0	—	1	.000	.000	.000
6 Min. YEARS		589	2065	580	83	29	36	829	360	313	305	10	301	47	13	22	165	50	.77	47	.281	.382	.401

Pat Hallmark

Bats: Right **Throws:** Right **Pos:** OF-24; DH-6; PH-2; PR-1 **Ht:** 6'0" **Wt:** 170 **Born:** 12/31/73 **Age:** 28

		BATTING														BASERUNNING				PERCENTAGES		
Year Team	Lg Org	G	AB	H	2B	3B	HR	TB	R	RBI	TBB	IBB	SO	HBP	SH	SF	SB	CS	SB%	GDP	Avg	OBP	SLG
1995 Spokane	A- KC	56	227	69	11	0	4	92	36	25	13	0	37	2	2	2	5	3	.63	5	.304	.344	.405
1996 Lansing	A KC	118	453	127	23	5	1	163	68	53	34	2	80	3	6	1	33	9	.79	3	.280	.334	.360
1997 Lansing	A KC	88	306	87	13	6	0	112	49	39	28	0	43	7	1	5	22	5	.81	8	.284	.353	.366
Wilmington	A+ KC	27	100	30	5	0	2	41	22	11	12	0	16	3	1	2	8	3	.73	0	.300	.385	.410
1998 Wilmington	A+ KC	103	364	99	19	1	5	135	59	35	46	0	71	5	6	5	33	19	.63	6	.272	.357	.371
1999 Wichita	AA KC	75	242	69	7	2	5	95	35	24	21	0	62	5	3	2	14	7	.67	3	.285	.352	.393
2000 Wichita	AA KC	132	479	156	26	3	10	218	80	79	52	6	74	20	5	6	41	14	.75	10	.326	.409	.455
2001 Omaha	AAA KC	32	93	23	5	0	0	28	10	10	7	0	17	5	2	1	3	0	1.00	2	.247	.330	.301
7 Min. YEARS		631	2264	660	109	17	27	884	359	276	213	8	400	50	26	24	159	60	.73	37	.292	.362	.390

Matt Halloran

Bats: Right **Throws:** Right **Pos:** 2B-37; PH-7; 3B-5; DH-5; 1B-3 **Ht:** 6'2" **Wt:** 185 **Born:** 3/3/78 **Age:** 24

		BATTING														BASERUNNING				PERCENTAGES		
Year Team	Lg Org	G	AB	H	2B	3B	HR	TB	R	RBI	TBB	IBB	SO	HBP	SH	SF	SB	CS	SB%	GDP	Avg	OBP	SLG
1996 Padres	R SD	39	134	35	7	4	0	50	22	15	10	0	22	2	0	0	2	1	.67	3	.261	.322	.373
1997 Clinton	A SD	46	154	31	7	0	1	41	19	22	8	0	37	4	1	2	9	3	.75	5	.201	.256	.266
1998 Clinton	A SD	123	459	103	21	3	1	133	48	42	33	0	92	10	5	3	19	12	.61	15	.224	.289	.290
1999 Rancho Cuca	A+ SD	95	309	67	11	2	0	82	39	22	17	0	75	7	4	1	15	9	.63	17	.217	.272	.265
2000 Charlotte	A+ Tex	5	14	2	2	0	0	4	1	5	1	0	4	1	0	1	0	0	—	2	.143	.235	.286
Savannah	A Tex	35	82	14	3	0	0	17	5	5	8	0	15	1	0	2	2	1	.67	1	.171	.247	.207
2001 Charlotte	A+ Tex	26	88	20	9	0	1	32	12	8	3	0	20	2	2	0	1	1	.50	0	.227	.269	.364
Tulsa	AA Tex	27	70	15	5	0	1	23	7	4	4	0	15	2	3	0	1	0	1.00	3	.214	.276	.329
6 Min. YEARS		396	1310	287	65	9	4	382	153	123	84	0	280	29	15	9	49	27	.64	46	.219	.279	.292

124

Garrick Haltiwanger

Bats: Right **Throws:** Left **Pos:** OF-52; PH-12; DH-11; PR-1 **Ht:** 6'0" **Wt:** 195 **Born:** 3/3/75 **Age:** 27

Year Team	Lg Org	G	AB	H	2B	3B	HR	TB	R	RBI	TBB	IBB	SO	HBP	SH	SF	SB	CS	SB%	GDP	Avg	OBP	SLG
1996 Pittsfield	A- NYM	60	203	52	9	2	9	92	36	37	24	3	55	4	1	2	9	4	.69	3	.256	.343	.453
1997 Capital Cty	A NYM	125	441	115	19	2	14	180	59	73	45	0	107	10	1	2	20	7	.74	4	.261	.341	.408
1998 St. Lucie	A+ NYM	108	344	64	11	1	11	110	35	42	34	0	69	7	5	3	7	6	.54	5	.186	.271	.320
1999 Binghamton	AA NYM	4	11	3	0	0	1	6	1	2	1	0	1	0	0	0	0	0	—	0	.273	.333	.545
Norfolk	AAA NYM	6	13	0	0	0	0	0	2	0	0	0	8	0	0	0	0	0	—	1	.000	.000	.000
St. Lucie	A+ NYM	111	423	112	18	6	10	172	67	71	31	3	77	13	0	5	20	12	.63	6	.265	.331	.407
2000 Dunedin	A+ Tor	100	354	103	27	3	10	166	57	56	37	1	67	3	0	1	18	4	.82	10	.291	.362	.469
2001 Syracuse	AAA Tor	23	73	17	1	1	2	26	8	12	11	0	21	2	0	1	2	2	.50	0	.233	.345	.356
Tennessee	AA Tor	46	133	35	9	1	3	55	23	15	18	0	33	1	3	1	8	4	.67	5	.263	.353	.414
6 Min. YEARS		583	1995	501	94	16	60	807	288	308	201	7	438	40	10	15	84	39	.68	34	.251	.330	.405

Jimmy Hamilton

Pitches: Left **Bats:** Left **Pos:** RP-48; SP-1 **Ht:** 6'3" **Wt:** 205 **Born:** 8/1/75 **Age:** 26

Year Team	Lg Org	G	GS	CG	GF	IP	BFP	H	R	ER	HR	SH	SF	HB	TBB	IBB	SO	WP	Bk	W	L	Pct.	ShO	Sv	ERA
1996 Burlington	R+ Cle	10	10	0	0	45	193	45	22	20	7	1	2	3	16	0	50	8	0	1	3	.250	0	0	4.00
1997 Columbus	A Cle	22	22	0	0	123	547	123	68	61	10	3	2	0	66	0	137	11	0	5	7	.417	0	0	4.46
1998 Kinston	A+ Cle	44	0	0	15	75.1	305	61	25	23	5	8	3	4	21	5	83	4	0	4	6	.400	0	4	2.75
1999 Akron	AA Cle	25	0	0	10	31.1	134	19	14	13	1	1	1	1	24	2	27	4	0	0	2	.000	0	2	3.73
Buffalo	AAA Cle	26	0	0	4	24.1	122	24	22	14	3	1	3	1	27	0	25	1	0	1	2	.333	0	0	5.18
Rochester	AAA Bal	3	0	0	0	2	11	1	3	3	0	0	1	0	4	0	2	0	0	0	0	—	0	0	13.50
2000 Rochester	AAA Bal	2	0	0	2	1	4	0	0	0	0	0	0	0	1	0	1	0	0	0	0	—	0	0	0.00
Bowie	AA Bal	51	0	0	14	57.2	252	53	26	24	6	1	4	1	29	1	49	3	0	5	4	.556	0	4	3.75
2001 Rochester	AAA Bal	36	1	0	9	55.2	248	58	29	28	4	5	3	2	27	1	49	5	0	3	3	.000	0	1	4.53
Bowie	AA Bal	13	0	0	0	29.2	120	30	11	11	1	2	1	0	8	0	22	1	0	3	1	.750	0	1	3.34
6 Min. YEARS		232	33	0	60	445	1936	414	220	197	37	22	20	12	223	9	445	37	0	19	28	.404	0	12	3.98

Jon Hamilton

Bats: Left **Throws:** Left **Pos:** OF-134; PH-3; DH-1; PR-1 **Ht:** 6'1" **Wt:** 195 **Born:** 10/23/77 **Age:** 24

Year Team	Lg Org	G	AB	H	2B	3B	HR	TB	R	RBI	TBB	IBB	SO	HBP	SH	SF	SB	CS	SB%	GDP	Avg	OBP	SLG
1997 Burlington	R+ Cle	64	247	60	11	3	4	89	50	20	51	3	69	5	1	2	25	5	.83	0	.243	.380	.360
1998 Columbus	A Cle	133	487	127	22	10	15	214	88	71	79	1	130	7	3	4	22	9	.71	4	.261	.369	.439
1999 Kinston	A+ Cle	131	473	132	29	5	13	210	74	65	61	1	114	1	5	4	9	4	.69	3	.279	.360	.444
2000 Akron	AA Cle	137	493	123	28	3	7	178	57	56	62	2	117	3	0	4	12	6	.67	8	.249	.335	.361
2001 Akron	AA Cle	134	471	132	24	4	17	215	60	65	42	4	118	3	4	3	9	12	.43	3	.280	.341	.456
Buffalo	AAA Cle	2	4	0	0	0	0	0	0	0	1	0	1	0	0	0	0	0	—	0	.000	.200	.000
5 Min. YEARS		601	2175	574	114	25	56	906	329	277	296	11	549	19	13	17	77	36	.68	18	.264	.355	.417

Josh Hamilton

Bats: Left **Throws:** Left **Pos:** OF-24; DH-3 **Ht:** 6'4" **Wt:** 209 **Born:** 5/21/81 **Age:** 21

Year Team	Lg Org	G	AB	H	2B	3B	HR	TB	R	RBI	TBB	IBB	SO	HBP	SH	SF	SB	CS	SB%	GDP	Avg	OBP	SLG
1999 Princeton	R+ TB	56	236	82	20	4	10	140	49	48	13	0	43	0	1	2	18	3	.86	0	.347	.378	.593
Hudson Val	A- TB	16	72	14	3	0	0	17	7	7	1	0	14	1	0	1	1	1	.50	2	.194	.213	.236
2000 Chston-SC	A TB	96	392	118	23	3	13	186	62	61	26	3	72	2	0	3	14	6	.70	5	.301	.345	.474
2001 Orlando	AA TB	23	89	16	5	0	1	24	5	4	5	2	22	0	0	1	2	0	1.00	0	.180	.221	.236
Chston-SC	A TB	4	11	4	1	0	1	8	3	2	2	0	3	0	0	0	0	0	—	1	.364	.462	.727
3 Min. YEARS		195	800	234	52	7	24	372	126	122	47	5	154	3	1	7	35	10	.78	8	.293	.331	.465

Rob Hammock

Bats: Right **Throws:** Right **Pos:** OF-53; C-35; 3B-11; 1B-10; DH-3; PH-3; PR-2; 2B-1 **Ht:** 5'11" **Wt:** 190 **Born:** 5/13/77 **Age:** 25

Year Team	Lg Org	G	AB	H	2B	3B	HR	TB	R	RBI	TBB	IBB	SO	HBP	SH	SF	SB	CS	SB%	GDP	Avg	OBP	SLG
1998 Lethbridge	R+ Ari	62	227	65	14	2	10	113	46	56	28	1	34	2	0	2	5	4	.56	3	.286	.367	.498
1999 High Desert	A+ Ari	114	379	126	20	7	9	187	80	72	47	2	63	2	0	6	3	6	.33	8	.332	.403	.493
2000 High Desert	A+ Ari	40	136	48	15	1	3	74	25	23	27	1	24	1	0	3	3	3	.50	5	.353	.455	.544
El Paso	AA Ari	45	140	35	5	1	1	45	22	15	11	1	25	1	0	2	1	2	.33	1	.250	.305	.321
2001 South Bend	A Ari	34	125	31	3	2	2	44	16	14	14	0	21	0	1	0	5	6	.45	2	.248	.324	.352
El Paso	AA Ari	26	74	12	5	0	0	17	6	4	7	0	18	0	1	0	2	2	.50	1	.162	.235	.230
Lancaster	A+ Ari	45	190	59	11	3	4	88	33	36	16	1	42	7	0	4	3	2	.60	6	.311	.378	.463
4 Min. YEARS		366	1271	376	73	16	29	568	228	220	150	6	227	13	2	17	22	25	.47	26	.296	.371	.447

Chris Hammond

Pitches: Left **Bats:** Left **Pos:** RP-45; SP-4 **Ht:** 6'1" **Wt:** 195 **Born:** 1/21/66 **Age:** 36

Year Team	Lg Org	G	GS	CG	GF	IP	BFP	H	R	ER	HR	SH	SF	HB	TBB	IBB	SO	WP	Bk	W	L	Pct.	ShO	Sv	ERA
1986 Reds	R Cin	7	7	1	0	41.2	176	27	21	13	0	1	0	0	17	1	53	5	0	3	2	.600	0	0	2.81
Tampa	A+ Cin	5	5	0	0	21.2	100	25	8	8	0	0	0	1	13	1	5	1	0	0	2	.000	0	0	3.32
1987 Tampa	A+ Cin	25	24	6	1	170	745	174	81	67	10	4	4	3	60	1	126	6	3	11	11	.500	0	0	3.55
1988 Chattanooga	AA Cin	26	26	4	0	182.2	743	127	48	35	2	1	3	3	77	3	127	5	4	16	5	.762	2	0	1.72
1989 Nashville	AAA Cin	24	24	3	0	157.1	697	144	69	59	7	6	4	9	96	1	142	9	2	11	7	.611	1	0	3.38
1990 Nashville	AAA Cin	24	24	5	0	149	611	118	43	36	7	1	3	5	63	1	149	8	7	15	1	.938	3	0	2.17
1994 Portland	AA Fla	1	1	0	0	2	7	0	0	0	0	0	0	0	0	0	2	0	0	0	0	—	0	0	0.00
Brevard Cty	A+ Fla	2	2	0	0	7.1	30	4	3	1	0	0	2	0	3	0	5	0	0	0	0	—	0	0	1.23

125

Year Team	Lg Org	G	GS	CG	GF	IP	BFP	H	R	ER	HR	SH	SF	HB	TBB	IBB	SO	WP	Bk	W	L	Pct.	ShO	Sv	ERA
		HOW MUCH HE PITCHED						WHAT HE GAVE UP												THE RESULTS					
1995 Brevard Cty	A+ Fla	1	1	0	0	4	16	3	1	0	0	1	0	0	0	0	4	0	0	0	0	—	0	0	0.00
Charlotte	AAA Fla	1	1	0	0	4	19	3	1	0	0	0	0	0	2	0	3	1	0	0	0	—	0	0	0.00
1996 Brevard Cty	A+ Fla	1	1	0	0	4	14	3	0	0	0	0	0	0	0	0	8	1	0	0	0	—	0	0	0.00
Charlotte	AAA Fla	1	1	0	0	5	20	5	4	4	0	0	0	0	0	0	3	0	0	1	0	1.000	0	0	7.20
1998 Charlotte	AAA Fla	5	5	0	0	28	129	35	17	15	2	3	1	0	14	2	22	0	0	1	3	.250	0	0	4.82
2001 Buffalo	AAA Cle	28	4	0	3	51.2	225	53	22	19	5	0	0	2	20	1	54	1	0	7	3	.700	0	0	3.31
Richmond	AAA Atl	21	0	0	4	30.2	120	32	9	8	0	2	0	0	4	0	29	0	0	3	1	.750	0	0	2.35
1990 Cincinnati	NL	3	3	0	0	11.1	50	13	9	8	2	1	0	0	12	1	4	1	3	0	2	.000	0	0	6.35
1991 Cincinnati	NL	20	18	0	0	99.2	425	92	51	45	4	6	1	2	48	3	50	3	0	7	7	.500	0	0	4.06
1992 Cincinnati	NL	28	26	0	1	147.1	627	149	75	69	13	5	3	3	55	6	79	6	0	7	10	.412	0	0	4.21
1993 Florida	NL	32	32	1	0	191	826	207	106	99	18	10	2	1	66	2	108	10	5	11	12	.478	0	0	4.66
1994 Florida	NL	13	13	1	0	73.1	312	79	30	25	5	5	2	1	23	1	40	3	0	4	4	.500	1	0	3.07
1995 Florida	NL	25	24	3	0	161	683	157	73	68	17	7	7	9	47	2	126	3	1	9	6	.600	2	0	3.80
1996 Florida	NL	38	9	0	5	81	368	104	65	59	14	3	4	4	27	3	50	1	0	5	8	.385	0	0	6.56
1997 Boston	AL	29	8	0	6	65.1	293	81	45	43	5	0	3	2	27	4	48	2	0	3	4	.429	0	0	5.92
1998 Florida	NL	3	3	0	0	13.2	67	20	11	10	3	2	0	1	8	0	8	0	0	0	2	.000	0	0	6.59
10 Min. YEARS		172	126	19	8	859	3652	753	327	265	33	19	17	17	369	11	732	37	16	68	35	.660	6	1	2.78
9 Maj. YEARS		191	136	5	12	843.2	3657	902	465	426	81	39	22	23	313	22	513	29	9	46	55	.455	3	1	4.54

Joey Hammond

Bats: Right **Throws:** Right **Pos:** SS-78; 3B-29; 2B-17; PR-4; DH-2; P-2; OF-1; 1B-1; PH-1 **Ht:** 6'1" **Wt:** 184 **Born:** 10/27/77 **Age:** 24

Year Team	Lg Org	G	AB	H	2B	3B	HR	TB	R	RBI	TBB	IBB	SO	HBP	SH	SF	SB	CS	SB%	GDP	Avg	OBP	SLG
		BATTING															BASERUNNING				PERCENTAGES		
1998 Bluefield	R+ Bal	31	129	50	5	0	1	58	23	16	12	0	15	1	0	1	4	2	.67	4	.388	.441	.450
Delmarva	A Bal	38	135	32	6	1	1	43	19	15	16	0	21	1	0	0	1	2	.33	5	.237	.322	.319
Frederick	A+ Bal	3	10	3	1	0	0	4	3	2	3	0	2	0	0	0	1	0	1.00	0	.300	.462	.400
1999 Delmarva	A Bal	21	81	21	1	2	1	29	10	7	13	0	22	0	0	0	0	0	—	4	.259	.362	.358
Frederick	A+ Bal	79	245	71	14	1	3	96	41	37	57	0	66	0	5	2	3	3	.50	8	.290	.421	.392
2000 Frederick	A+ Bal	126	432	111	22	2	0	137	47	39	65	3	88	5	4	5	5	8	.38	7	.257	.357	.317
2001 Frederick	A+ Bal	25	94	30	5	1	0	37	12	8	16	0	18	0	1	1	1	3	.25	1	.319	.414	.394
Bowie	AA Bal	102	342	95	13	2	1	115	49	26	42	1	59	6	2	2	2	3	.40	8	.278	.365	.336
4 Min. YEARS		425	1468	413	67	9	7	519	204	150	224	4	291	13	12	11	17	21	.45	37	.281	.379	.354

Josh Hancock

Pitches: Right **Bats:** Right **Pos:** SP-24 **Ht:** 6'3" **Wt:** 217 **Born:** 4/11/78 **Age:** 24

Year Team	Lg Org	G	GS	CG	GF	IP	BFP	H	R	ER	HR	SH	SF	HB	TBB	IBB	SO	WP	Bk	W	L	Pct.	ShO	Sv	ERA
		HOW MUCH HE PITCHED						WHAT HE GAVE UP												THE RESULTS					
1998 Red Sox	R Bos	5	1	0	1	13.1	51	9	5	5	1	2	0	0	3	0	21	0	0	0	1	.500	0	0	3.38
Lowell	A- Bos	1	1	0	0	4	20	5	2	1	0	0	1	0	4	0	4	1	0	0	1	.000	0	0	2.25
1999 Augusta	A Bos	25	25	0	0	139.2	607	154	79	59	12	4	2	4	46	0	106	10	1	9	8	.429	0	0	3.80
2000 Sarasota	A+ Bos	26	24	1	0	143.2	628	164	89	71	9	5	6	6	37	0	95	8	2	5	10	.333	0	0	4.45
2001 Trenton	AA Bos	24	24	0	0	130.2	553	138	60	53	8	3	2	4	37	0	119	11	0	8	6	.571	0	0	3.65
4 Min. YEARS		81	75	1	1	431.1	1859	470	235	189	30	14	11	14	127	0	345	30	3	20	26	.435	0	0	3.94

Shawn Hannah

Pitches: Right **Bats:** Right **Pos:** SP-18; RP-17 **Ht:** 6'3" **Wt:** 205 **Born:** 3/22/77 **Age:** 25

Year Team	Lg Org	G	GS	CG	GF	IP	BFP	H	R	ER	HR	SH	SF	HB	TBB	IBB	SO	WP	Bk	W	L	Pct.	ShO	Sv	ERA
		HOW MUCH HE PITCHED						WHAT HE GAVE UP												THE RESULTS					
2000 Oneonta	A- Det	16	1	1	5	41.1	157	31	8	6	0	1	1	0	7	1	25	3	0	6	1	.857	0	0	1.31
W Michigan	A Det	2	0	0	1	8	27	3	0	0	0	0	0	0	1	0	5	0	0	1	0	1.000	0	1	0.00
2001 Toledo	AAA Det	1	1	0	0	6	24	6	5	5	1	0	0	0	1	0	1	0	0	0	0	—	0	0	7.50
Lakeland	A+ Det	34	17	0	7	129	558	128	63	48	9	5	5	10	54	1	55	4	1	7	5	.583	0	0	3.35
2 Min. YEARS		53	19	1	13	184.1	766	168	76	59	10	6	6	10	63	2	86	7	1	14	6	.700	0	1	2.88

Jed Hansen

Bats: Right **Throws:** Right **Pos:** OF-77; 3B-21; DH-13; 2B-5; SS-3; C-1 **Ht:** 6'1" **Wt:** 195 **Born:** 8/19/72 **Age:** 29

Year Team	Lg Org	G	AB	H	2B	3B	HR	TB	R	RBI	TBB	IBB	SO	HBP	SH	SF	SB	CS	SB%	GDP	Avg	OBP	SLG
		BATTING															BASERUNNING				PERCENTAGES		
1994 Eugene	A- KC	66	235	57	8	2	3	78	26	17	24	2	56	8	2	1	6	4	.60	1	.243	.332	.332
1995 Springfield	A KC	122	414	107	27	7	9	175	86	50	78	0	73	7	6	1	44	10	.81	8	.258	.384	.423
1996 Wichita	AA KC	99	405	116	27	4	12	187	60	50	29	0	72	4	4	2	14	8	.64	6	.286	.339	.462
Omaha	AAA KC	29	99	23	4	0	3	36	14	9	12	0	22	3	1	1	2	0	1.00	1	.232	.330	.364
1997 Omaha	AAA KC	114	380	102	20	2	11	159	43	44	32	0	78	2	5	2	8	1	.89	9	.268	.327	.418
1998 Omaha	AAA KC	127	417	116	19	7	16	197	63	56	44	0	125	4	4	7	17	9	.65	7	.278	.347	.472
1999 Omaha	AAA KC	54	175	48	8	5	7	87	35	22	32	2	72	3	3	0	8	3	.73	2	.274	.395	.497
2000 Las Vegas	AAA SD	14	24	5	1	0	2	12	3	5	5	0	11	0	1	0	1	0	1.00	2	.208	.345	.500
Norfolk	AAA NYM	39	96	14	2	0	4	28	13	9	18	1	31	1	3	1	2	4	.33	2	.146	.284	.292
Louisville	AAA Cin	16	51	9	1	0	1	13	7	2	4	0	15	0	1	1	1	1	.50	2	.176	.236	.255
2001 Wilmington	A+ KC	17	64	21	3	1	5	41	8	20	10	1	18	0	1	2	2	2	.50	1	.328	.413	.641
Wichita	AA KC	17	57	21	8	0	3	38	17	6	9	0	10	1	1	2	5	2	.71	0	.368	.463	.667
Omaha	AAA KC	80	288	73	14	1	10	119	37	22	34	0	86	3	5	3	10	6	.63	3	.253	.335	.413
1997 Kansas City	AL	34	94	29	6	1	1	40	11	14	13	0	29	1	2	1	3	2	.60	2	.309	.394	.426
1998 Kansas City	AL	4	3	0	0	0	0	0	0	0	0	0	3	0	0	0	0	0	—	0	.000	.000	.000
1999 Kansas City	AL	49	79	16	1	0	3	26	16	5	10	0	32	0	4	1	0	1	.00	0	.203	.289	.329
8 Min. YEARS		794	2705	712	142	29	86	1170	412	312	331	6	669	36	37	19	120	50	.71	44	.263	.349	.433
3 Maj. YEARS		87	176	45	7	1	4	66	27	19	23	0	64	1	6	2	3	3	.50	2	.256	.342	.375

Aaron Harang

Pitches: Right **Bats:** Right **Pos:** SP-27   **Ht:** 6'7" **Wt:** 240 **Born:** 5/9/78 **Age:** 24

Year Team	Lg Org	G	GS	CG	GF	IP	BFP	H	R	ER	HR	SH	SF	HB	TBB	IBB	SO	WP	Bk	W	L	Pct.	ShO	Sv	ERA
1999 Pulaski	R+ Tex	16	10	1	6	78.1	309	64	22	20	5	2	3	4	17	1	87	2	1	9	2	.818	1	1	2.30
2000 Charlotte	A+ Tex	28	27	3	0	157	642	128	68	58	10	1	3	7	50	0	136	5	1	13	5	.722	2	0	3.32
2001 Midland	AA Oak	27	27	0	0	150	654	173	81	69	9	0	3	6	37	1	112	3	0	10	8	.556	0	0	4.14
3 Min. YEARS		71	64	4	6	385.1	1605	365	171	147	24	3	9	17	104	2	335	10	2	32	15	.681	3	1	3.43

Jason Hardtke

Bats: Both **Throws:** Right **Pos:** 2B-41; OF-24; DH-16; 3B-15; PH-4; PR-3; 1B-1   **Ht:** 5'10" **Wt:** 175 **Born:** 9/15/71 **Age:** 30

Year Team	Lg Org	G	AB	H	2B	3B	HR	TB	R	RBI	TBB	IBB	SO	HBP	SH	SF	SB	CS	SB%	GDP	Avg	OBP	SLG
1990 Burlington	R+ Cle	39	142	38	7	0	4	57	18	16	23	0	19	2	0	0	11	1	.92	3	.268	.377	.401
1991 Columbus	A Cle	139	534	155	26	8	12	233	104	81	75	5	48	7	6	6	22	4	.85	6	.290	.381	.436
1992 Kinston	A+ Cle	6	19	4	0	0	0	4	3	1	4	0	4	0	0	0	0	0	—	0	.211	.348	.211
Waterloo	A SD	110	411	125	27	4	8	184	75	47	38	3	33	5	1	5	9	7	.56	9	.304	.366	.448
High Desert	A+ SD	10	41	11	1	0	2	18	9	8	4	0	4	1	0	1	1	1	.50	1	.268	.340	.439
1993 Rancho Cuca	A+ SD	130	523	167	38	7	11	252	98	85	61	2	54	2	2	6	7	8	.47	12	.319	.389	.482
1994 Wichita	AA SD	75	255	60	15	1	5	92	26	29	21	1	44	0	2	4	1	2	.33	4	.235	.289	.361
Rancho Cuca	A+ SD	4	13	4	0	0	0	4	2	0	3	0	2	0	0	0	1	0	1.00	0	.308	.438	.308
1995 Norfolk	AAA NYM	4	7	2	1	0	0	3	1	0	2	0	0	0	0	0	1	1	.50	0	.286	.444	.429
Binghamton	AA NYM	121	455	130	42	4	4	192	65	52	66	1	58	4	2	9	6	8	.43	7	.286	.375	.422
1996 Binghamton	AA NYM	35	137	36	11	0	3	56	23	16	16	1	16	0	1	0	1	0	1.00	3	.263	.340	.409
Norfolk	AAA NYM	71	257	77	17	2	9	125	49	35	29	1	29	0	4	2	4	6	.40	4	.300	.368	.486
1997 Binghamton	AA NYM	97	388	107	23	3	11	169	46	45	40	1	54	0	0	4	3	6	.33	9	.276	.343	.436
Binghamton	AA NYM	6	26	10	2	0	1	15	3	4	2	0	2	0	0	0	0	0	—	0	.385	.429	.577
1998 Iowa	AAA ChC	91	333	96	20	1	11	151	67	53	35	1	46	4	1	2	7	7	.50	7	.288	.361	.453
1999 Indianapols	AAA Cin	101	416	137	37	2	12	214	74	61	35	1	43	2	1	4	7	4	.64	7	.329	.381	.514
2000 Colo Sprngs	AAA Col	5	20	4	0	0	0	4	3	1	2	1	3	0	0	0	0	0	—	1	.200	.273	.200
2001 Buffalo	AAA Cle	39	128	33	7	3	0	46	19	14	16	1	16	1	2	0	0	1	.00	3	.258	.345	.359
Charlotte	AAA CWS	57	208	54	14	0	10	98	33	25	18	0	27	4	2	0	2	1	.67	0	.260	.330	.471
1996 New York	NL	19	57	11	5	0	0	16	3	6	2	0	12	1	0	0	0	0	—	1	.193	.233	.281
1997 New York	NL	30	56	15	2	0	2	23	9	8	4	1	6	1	0	1	1	1	.50	3	.268	.323	.411
1998 Chicago	NL	18	21	5	0	0	0	5	2	2	2	0	6	0	0	0	0	0	—	0	.238	.304	.238
12 Min. YEARS		1140	4313	1250	288	35	103	1917	718	573	490	19	502	32	28	40	81	59	.58	75	.290	.363	.444
3 Maj. YEARS		67	134	31	7	0	2	44	14	16	8	1	24	2	0	1	1	1	.50	4	.231	.283	.328

Tim Harikkala

Pitches: Right **Bats:** Right **Pos:** SP-27; RP-4   **Ht:** 6'2" **Wt:** 185 **Born:** 7/15/71 **Age:** 30

Year Team	Lg Org	G	GS	CG	GF	IP	BFP	H	R	ER	HR	SH	SF	HB	TBB	IBB	SO	WP	Bk	W	L	Pct.	ShO	Sv	ERA
1992 Bellingham	A- Sea	15	2	0	2	33.1	145	37	15	10	2	3	2	0	16	0	18	1	2	2	0	1.000	0	1	2.70
1993 Bellingham	A- Sea	4	0	0	0	8	30	3	1	1	0	0	0	1	2	0	12	0	0	1	0	1.000	0	1	1.13
Appleton	A Sea	15	4	0	5	38.2	175	50	30	28	3	2	1	2	12	2	33	4	3	3	3	.500	0	0	6.52
1994 Appleton	A Sea	13	13	3	0	93.2	373	69	31	20	6	2	3	5	24	0	63	5	0	8	3	.727	0	0	1.92
Riverside	A+ Sea	4	4	0	0	29	108	16	6	2	1	0	1	0	10	0	30	1	0	4	0	1.000	0	0	0.62
Jacksnville	AA Sea	9	9	0	0	54.1	245	70	30	24	4	1	3	1	19	0	22	4	0	4	1	.800	0	0	3.98
1995 Tacoma	AAA Sea	25	24	4	0	146.1	638	151	78	69	13	3	4	2	55	3	73	7	0	5	12	.294	1	0	4.24
1996 Tacoma	AAA Sea	27	27	1	0	158.1	715	204	98	85	12	3	6	5	48	2	115	5	1	8	12	.400	1	0	4.83
1997 Tacoma	AAA Sea	21	21	0	0	113.1	538	160	93	81	11	3	5	4	50	2	86	7	0	6	8	.429	0	0	6.43
Memphis	AA Sea	5	5	1	0	33.2	146	39	18	14	3	0	1	3	4	0	26	1	0	3	1	.750	0	0	3.74
1998 Orlando	AA Sea	15	15	3	0	103.1	429	112	56	52	9	5	2	7	14	0	55	0	0	5	7	.417	2	0	4.53
Tacoma	AAA Sea	18	4	1	9	57	257	74	32	31	6	1	1	1	13	0	44	0	0	2	3	.400	1	1	4.89
1999 Pawtucket	AAA Bos	14	1	0	4	30	141	44	19	18	2	0	1	2	7	1	19	0	0	1	2	.333	0	0	5.40
2000 Huntsville	AA Mil	22	4	0	5	48.1	205	54	20	16	1	3	1	1	8	0	34	0	0	5	3	.625	0	0	2.98
Indianapols	AAA Mil	14	10	0	3	63.2	271	73	36	32	5	0	0	3	15	0	22	3	0	4	2	.667	0	1	4.52
2001 Indianapols	AAA Mil	31	27	1	3	172	757	210	104	91	15	8	10	7	42	1	96	2	1	11	10	.524	0	0	4.76
1995 Seattle	AL	1	0	0	1	3.1	18	7	6	6	1	0	0	0	1	0	1	0	0	0	0	—	0	0	16.20
1996 Seattle	AL	1	1	0	0	4.1	20	4	6	6	1	1	0	1	2	0	1	0	0	0	1	.000	0	0	12.46
1999 Boston	AL	7	0	0	2	13	58	15	9	9	2	0	2	1	6	1	7	1	0	1	1	.500	0	0	6.23
10 Min. YEARS		252	170	14	31	1183	5173	1366	667	574	93	34	41	41	339	11	748	40	7	72	67	.518	5	3	4.37
3 Maj. YEARS		9	1	0	3	20.2	96	26	21	21	2	3	0	2	9	1	9	1	0	1	2	.333	0	0	9.15

Brandon Harper

Bats: Right **Throws:** Right **Pos:** C-98; DH-7   **Ht:** 6'4" **Wt:** 200 **Born:** 4/29/76 **Age:** 26

Year Team	Lg Org	G	AB	H	2B	3B	HR	TB	R	RBI	TBB	IBB	SO	HBP	SH	SF	SB	CS	SB%	GDP	Avg	OBP	SLG
1997 Marlins	R Fla	2	6	0	0	0	0	0	1	0	1	0	1	0	0	0	0	0	—	1	.000	.000	.000
Utica	A- Fla	47	152	39	7	2	2	56	27	22	19	2	32	1	0	2	1	1	.50	9	.257	.339	.368
1998 Kane County	A Fla	113	412	95	22	2	4	133	34	50	42	3	64	4	1	5	1	3	.25	16	.231	.305	.323
1999 Brevard Cty	A+ Fla	81	280	75	9	0	4	96	35	40	30	2	31	3	4	3	1	1	.50	4	.268	.342	.343
2000 Marlins	R Fla	8	27	8	1	0	0	9	8	2	7	0	4	0	0	0	0	0	—	0	.296	.441	.333
Portland	AA Fla	37	125	26	3	0	5	44	15	17	12	0	23	1	0	0	0	0	—	4	.208	.283	.352
2001 Brevard Cty	A+ Fla	29	101	24	6	0	2	36	14	16	12	0	14	2	1	0	0	1	.00	0	.238	.330	.356
Portland	AA Fla	76	247	59	13	0	3	81	21	24	27	3	52	5	1	3	0	0	—	7	.239	.323	.328
5 Min. YEARS		393	1350	326	61	4	20	455	154	172	149	10	221	16	7	13	3	6	.33	45	.241	.321	.337

Tim Harrell

Pitches: Right **Bats:** Right **Pos:** RP-48; SP-1 **Ht:** 6'4" **Wt:** 215 **Born:** 10/31/75 **Age:** 26

Year Team	Lg Org	G	GS	CG	GF	IP	BFP	H	R	ER	HR	SH	SF	HB	TBB	IBB	SO	WP	Bk	W	L	Pct.	ShO	Sv	ERA
1998 Yakima	A- LA	13	6	0	3	53.1	237	53	30	23	4	2	1	4	24	0	50	4	1	5	3	.625	0	0	3.88
1999 San Berndno	A+ LA	44	0	0	14	74.2	324	78	40	40	10	4	4	0	36	2	78	13	0	5	2	.714	0	2	4.82
2000 Vero Beach	A+ LA	30	18	1	5	117	508	121	77	65	9	1	7	3	44	1	89	8	1	7	7	.500	1	2	5.00
2001 Vero Beach	A+ LA	2	0	0	0	4	14	1	0	0	0	0	0	0	1	0	3	0	0	0	0	—	0	0	0.00
Jacksonville	AA LA	47	1	0	23	81	338	70	32	27	11	3	1	3	29	2	71	4	0	5	4	.556	0	5	3.00
4 Min. YEARS		136	25	1	45	330	1421	323	179	155	34	10	13	10	134	5	291	29	2	22	16	.579	1	9	4.23

Mark Harriger

Pitches: Right **Bats:** Right **Pos:** SP-9; RP-1 **Ht:** 6'2" **Wt:** 196 **Born:** 4/29/75 **Age:** 27

Year Team	Lg Org	G	GS	CG	GF	IP	BFP	H	R	ER	HR	SH	SF	HB	TBB	IBB	SO	WP	Bk	W	L	Pct.	ShO	Sv	ERA
1996 Boise	A- Ana	7	0	0	0	4.1	26	9	5	4	1	1	0	0	3	0	3	1	1	0	0	—	0	0	8.31
1997 Cedar Rapids	A Ana	12	11	1	1	50.2	251	70	50	44	4	3	3	1	33	1	50	10	4	1	6	.143	1	0	7.82
Boise	A- Ana	13	12	0	0	51	243	51	52	45	2	1	5	1	36	1	42	15	0	3	4	.429	0	0	7.94
1998 Cedar Rapids	A Ana	16	16	3	0	117	472	86	37	29	3	3	2	4	38	0	105	14	1	8	4	.667	0	0	2.23
Lk Elsinore	A+ Ana	13	12	3	0	81.1	350	86	43	37	5	3	2	2	23	0	68	6	0	5	5	.500	1	0	4.09
1999 Erie	AA Ana	6	6	0	0	30.2	135	31	16	16	4	0	0	0	15	0	13	4	0	2	1	.667	0	0	4.70
2001 Arkansas	AA Ana	10	9	0	0	50.1	223	52	33	26	7	0	2	3	23	0	31	3	1	2	3	.400	0	0	4.65
5 Min. YEARS		77	66	7	2	385.1	1700	385	236	201	26	11	14	11	171	2	312	53	7	21	23	.477	3	0	4.69

Brian Harris

Bats: Both **Throws:** Right **Pos:** 2B-75; SS-55; 3B-5; PH-1 **Ht:** 5'10" **Wt:** 171 **Born:** 4/28/75 **Age:** 27

Year Team	Lg Org	G	AB	H	2B	3B	HR	TB	R	RBI	TBB	IBB	SO	HBP	SH	SF	SB	CS	SB%	GDP	Avg	OBP	SLG
1997 Batavia	A- Phi	51	148	46	7	1	0	55	31	19	31	0	27	4	3	1	11	6	.65	1	.311	.440	.372
1998 Clearwater	A+ Phi	118	437	121	17	6	5	165	55	65	47	2	56	9	6	9	20	13	.61	13	.277	.353	.378
Reading	AA Phi	11	40	10	0	1	0	12	5	4	5	0	7	0	0	1	0	1	.00	0	.250	.326	.300
1999 Reading	AA Phi	119	380	84	13	3	5	118	42	41	46	1	58	1	7	6	9	5	.64	10	.221	.303	.311
2000 Reading	AA Phi	110	351	94	22	3	10	152	46	41	38	0	48	4	10	4	12	5	.71	7	.268	.343	.433
2001 Reading	AA Phi	135	511	125	27	5	13	201	71	58	45	2	62	7	7	3	20	9	.69	7	.245	.313	.393
5 Min. YEARS		544	1867	480	86	19	33	703	250	228	212	5	258	25	33	24	72	39	.65	38	.257	.337	.377

Cedrick Harris

Bats: Right **Throws:** Right **Pos:** OF-95; PR-6; PH-5; DH-1 **Ht:** 6'2" **Wt:** 190 **Born:** 11/14/77 **Age:** 24

Year Team	Lg Org	G	AB	H	2B	3B	HR	TB	R	RBI	TBB	IBB	SO	HBP	SH	SF	SB	CS	SB%	GDP	Avg	OBP	SLG
2000 High Desert	A+ Ari	34	129	34	6	4	0	48	27	14	12	0	29	1	1	1	10	4	.71	1	.264	.329	.372
2001 El Paso	AA Ari	16	49	10	1	0	1	14	4	4	2	0	15	0	0	1	1	0	1.00	0	.204	.231	.286
Lancaster	A+ Ari	84	319	88	13	1	6	121	63	34	26	0	77	3	4	3	21	8	.72	2	.276	.333	.379
2 Min. YEARS		134	497	132	20	5	7	183	94	52	40	0	121	4	5	5	32	12	.73	3	.266	.322	.368

Corey Hart

Bats: Both **Throws:** Right **Pos:** SS-63; 3B-21; DH-7; P-3; PH-2 **Ht:** 6'0" **Wt:** 180 **Born:** 9/5/75 **Age:** 26

Year Team	Lg Org	G	AB	H	2B	3B	HR	TB	R	RBI	TBB	IBB	SO	HBP	SH	SF	SB	CS	SB%	GDP	Avg	OBP	SLG
1998 Spokane	A- KC	58	157	38	6	0	3	53	25	21	50	0	38	2	2	0	8	4	.67	1	.242	.431	.338
1999 Chston-WV	A KC	92	295	56	16	3	0	78	43	39	58	1	62	3	4	5	13	7	.65	3	.190	.324	.264
2000 Wilmington	A+ KC	88	243	53	6	2	1	66	45	22	64	0	62	2	6	1	6	6	.50	7	.218	.384	.272
2001 Wichita	AA KC	17	41	9	2	0	0	11	8	1	10	0	5	0	1	0	0	1	.00	0	.220	.373	.268
Wilmington	A+ KC	75	282	81	14	0	4	107	53	26	55	4	62	3	4	1	1	6	.14	9	.287	.408	.379
4 Min. YEARS		330	1018	237	44	5	8	315	174	109	237	5	229	10	17	7	28	24	.54	20	.233	.381	.309

Jason Hart

Bats: Right **Throws:** Right **Pos:** 1B-132; DH-1; PH-1 **Ht:** 6'4" **Wt:** 240 **Born:** 9/5/77 **Age:** 24

Year Team	Lg Org	G	AB	H	2B	3B	HR	TB	R	RBI	TBB	IBB	SO	HBP	SH	SF	SB	CS	SB%	GDP	Avg	OBP	SLG
1998 Sou Oregon	A- Oak	75	295	76	19	1	20	157	58	69	36	2	67	3	0	8	0	1	.00	4	.258	.336	.532
1999 Modesto	A+ Oak	135	550	168	48	2	19	277	96	123	56	1	105	4	0	7	2	5	.29	18	.305	.370	.504
2000 Midland	AA Oak	135	546	178	44	3	30	318	98	121	67	5	112	6	0	7	4	0	1.00	18	.326	.401	.582
Sacramento	AAA Oak	5	18	5	1	0	1	9	4	4	3	0	7	0	0	0	0	0	—	0	.278	.381	.500
2001 Sacramento	AAA Oak	134	494	122	26	1	19	207	71	75	57	0	102	4	0	8	3	3	.50	11	.247	.325	.419
4 Min. YEARS		484	1903	549	138	7	89	968	327	392	219	8	393	17	0	30	9	9	.50	56	.288	.362	.509

Pete Hartmann

Pitches: Left **Bats:** Left **Pos:** RP-16; SP-3 **Ht:** 6'2" **Wt:** 200 **Born:** 5/13/71 **Age:** 31

Year Team	Lg Org	G	GS	CG	GF	IP	BFP	H	R	ER	HR	SH	SF	HB	TBB	IBB	SO	WP	Bk	W	L	Pct.	ShO	Sv	ERA
1993 Erie	A- Tex	15	15	1	0	88.1	380	74	51	41	5	1	0	3	43	0	98	6	1	6	7	.462	0	0	4.18
1994 Charlotte	A+ Tex	26	24	0	1	128.1	575	132	70	65	8	4	5	4	77	0	107	15	6	5	11	.313	0	0	4.56
1995 Charlotte	A+ Tex	15	2	0	9	35.2	180	46	34	29	7	4	2	0	26	0	30	3	4	2	4	.333	0	2	7.32
Stockton	A+ Mil	12	0	0	5	14	61	9	7	7	1	1	2	0	11	0	9	1	1	2	0	1.000	0	1	4.50
1996 Grays Harbr	IND —	5	5	0	0	25.1	125	33	23	22	0	1	1	0	22	1	10	0	0	3	0	.000	0	0	7.82
Bangor	IND —	9	8	1	0	59.1	256	48	28	17	6	1	0	1	30	0	57	4	0	5	1	.833	0	0	2.58

	HOW MUCH HE PITCHED						WHAT HE GAVE UP								THE RESULTS						
Year Team	Lg Org	G	GS	CG	GF	IP	BFP	H	R	ER	HR	SH	SF	HB	TBB	IBB	SO	WP	Bk	W	L	Pct.	ShO	Sv	ERA
1997 Bangor	IND —	17	17	5	0	119.2	519	120	60	46	8	6	2	1	55	2	118	7	4	8	6	.571	1	0	3.46
1998 New Jersey	IND —	7	7	2	0	47.2	185	34	11	9	2	1	1	1	15	2	41	2	0	4	0	1.000	0	0	1.70
1999 Bowie	AA Bal	11	0	0	1	15.2	66	11	4	3	1	2	0	0	8	0	12	2	1	1	1	.500	0	0	1.72
Rochester	AAA Bal	34	3	0	8	44.1	215	56	45	44	14	0	1	3	27	1	43	7	0	1	5	.167	0	0	8.93
2000 Allentown	IND —	7	7	1	0	46.1	202	46	27	21	1	3	1	1	22	0	49	6	0	2	3	.400	1	0	4.08
2001 El Paso	AA Ari	19	3	0	6	31.1	174	46	32	27	3	1	1	1	31	3	27	2	0	0	4	.000	0	0	7.76
9 Min. YEARS		177	91	10	30	656	2938	655	392	331	56	25	14	15	367	9	601	55	17	36	45	.444	2	3	4.54

Derek Hasselhoff

Pitches: Right **Bats:** Right **Pos:** RP-59 **Ht:** 6'2" **Wt:** 185 **Born:** 10/10/73 **Age:** 28

	HOW MUCH HE PITCHED						WHAT HE GAVE UP								THE RESULTS						
Year Team	Lg Org	G	GS	CG	GF	IP	BFP	H	R	ER	HR	SH	SF	HB	TBB	IBB	SO	WP	Bk	W	L	Pct.	ShO	Sv	ERA
1995 Bristol	R+ CWS	12	11	0	1	66.1	281	66	32	27	4	1	1	2	14	0	46	2	2	7	3	.700	0	0	3.66
1996 South Bend	A CWS	35	0	0	29	47.2	205	46	19	17	4	4	1	2	17	0	39	5	0	6	3	.667	0	10	3.21
Pr William	A+ CWS	5	0	0	4	10.1	49	14	7	6	1	0	0	0	6	2	9	0	0	0	1	.000	0	1	5.23
1997 Winston-Sal	A+ CWS	20	0	0	11	34.2	138	22	10	6	1	2	1	0	15	3	41	4	0	3	2	.600	0	3	1.56
Birmingham	AA CWS	18	0	0	10	33.2	141	35	10	9	3	0	1	1	11	0	22	1	0	5	2	.714	0	3	2.41
Nashville	AAA CWS	6	0	0	1	7.1	37	9	8	8	2	0	0	0	7	0	2	0	0	1	1	.500	0	0	9.82
1998 Calgary	AAA CWS	13	0	0	5	19	89	23	15	14	3	1	1	1	8	0	24	0	1	2	0	1.000	0	0	6.63
White Sox	R CWS	6	1	0	1	10	36	6	1	0	0	0	0	0	0	0	16	0	0	0	0	—	0	0	0.00
Winston-Sal	A+ CWS	1	0	0	0	2	9	3	0	0	0	0	0	0	0	0	3	0	0	0	0	—	0	0	0.00
1999 Charlotte	AAA CWS	49	0	0	18	71	311	83	46	38	7	1	0	0	25	1	65	3	0	6	0	1.000	0	4	4.82
2000 Charlotte	AAA CWS	46	1	0	23	65.2	281	62	32	27	6	2	2	2	23	2	51	1	0	7	4	.636	0	6	3.70
2001 Charlotte	AAA CWS	34	0	0	17	44.1	173	29	14	10	4	2	1	0	12	2	41	0	1	6	1	.857	0	6	2.03
Fresno	AAA SF	25	0	0	17	28	122	24	19	12	6	2	1	1	14	1	24	0	0	2	0	1.000	0	8	3.86
7 Min. YEARS		270	13	0	137	440	1872	422	213	174	41	15	9	9	152	11	383	16	4	45	17	.726	0	41	3.56

Chris Hatcher

Bats: Right **Throws:** Right **Pos:** DH-41; OF-27; PH-1 **Ht:** 6'3" **Wt:** 235 **Born:** 1/7/69 **Age:** 33

	BATTING															BASERUNNING				PERCENTAGES		
Year Team	Lg Org	G	AB	H	2B	3B	HR	TB	R	RBI	TBB	IBB	SO	HBP	SH	SF	SB	CS	SB%	GDP	Avg	OBP	SLG
1990 Auburn	A- Hou	72	259	64	10	0	9	101	37	45	27	3	86	5	0	5	8	2	.80	4	.247	.324	.390
1991 Burlington	A Hou	129	497	117	23	6	13	191	69	65	46	4	180	9	0	4	10	5	.67	6	.235	.309	.384
1992 Osceola	A+ Hou	97	367	103	19	6	17	185	49	68	20	1	97	5	0	5	11	0	1.00	5	.281	.322	.504
1993 Jackson	AA Hou	101	367	95	15	3	15	161	45	64	11	0	104	11	0	3	5	8	.38	8	.259	.298	.439
1994 Tucson	AAA Hou	108	349	104	28	4	12	176	55	73	19	0	90	4	0	6	5	1	.83	6	.298	.336	.504
1995 Jackson	AA Hou	11	39	12	1	0	1	16	5	3	4	0	6	1	0	1	0	2	.00	1	.308	.378	.410
Tucson	AAA Hou	94	290	83	19	2	14	148	59	50	42	2	107	4	1	2	7	3	.70	9	.286	.382	.510
1996 Jackson	AA Hou	41	156	48	9	1	13	98	29	36	9	2	39	4	0	1	2	1	.67	5	.308	.359	.628
Tucson	AAA Hou	95	348	105	21	4	18	188	53	61	14	1	87	5	0	5	10	8	.56	9	.302	.333	.540
1997 Wichita	AA KC	11	42	11	0	0	5	26	7	7	4	0	16	1	0	0	1	0	1.00	0	.262	.340	.619
Omaha	AAA KC	68	222	51	9	0	11	93	34	24	17	2	68	6	0	3	0	1	.00	4	.230	.298	.419
1998 Omaha	AAA KC	126	485	150	21	2	46	313	84	106	25	3	125	3	0	3	8	6	.57	9	.309	.345	.645
1999 Colo Sprngs	AAA Col	98	334	115	24	2	21	206	63	69	23	1	89	10	0	5	12	4	.75	12	.344	.398	.617
2000 Iowa	AAA ChC	86	288	80	15	1	24	169	46	71	26	1	64	10	0	2	4	4	.50	4	.278	.356	.587
Edmonton	AAA Ana	30	115	39	8	4	7	76	19	24	8	1	24	3	0	1	1	0	1.00	3	.339	.394	.661
2001 Durham	AAA TB	69	251	67	12	0	11	112	31	38	19	0	63	3	0	4	4	2	.67	3	.267	.321	.446
1998 Kansas City	AL	8	15	1	0	0	0	1	0	1	1	0	7	0	0	0	0	0	—	0	.067	.125	.067
12 Min. YEARS		1236	4409	1244	234	35	237	2259	685	804	314	21	1245	84	1	50	88	47	.65	88	.282	.338	.512

Kevin Haverbusch

Bats: Right **Throws:** Right **Pos:** 2B-32; OF-28; PH-17; DH-14; 1B-6 **Ht:** 6'3" **Wt:** 199 **Born:** 6/16/76 **Age:** 26

	BATTING															BASERUNNING				PERCENTAGES		
Year Team	Lg Org	G	AB	H	2B	3B	HR	TB	R	RBI	TBB	IBB	SO	HBP	SH	SF	SB	CS	SB%	GDP	Avg	OBP	SLG
1997 Erie	A- Pit	67	241	75	15	2	10	124	37	55	13	1	37	4	2	4	4	4	.50	6	.311	.351	.515
1998 Lynchburg	A+ Pit	49	181	60	12	1	8	98	25	39	9	0	33	6	0	2	4	2	.67	5	.331	.379	.541
Carolina	AA Pit	46	168	63	10	0	3	82	28	29	13	1	20	3	0	0	1	3	.25	3	.375	.429	.488
1999 Altoona	AA Pit	93	332	95	22	2	14	163	57	61	12	0	60	19	1	9	6	3	.67	9	.286	.339	.491
2000 Altoona	AA Pit	43	140	39	3	1	5	59	23	21	11	0	15	2	0	0	2	2	.50	5	.279	.340	.421
2001 Altoona	AA Pit	43	153	40	10	2	2	60	17	19	5	1	23	2	1	4	1	2	.33	6	.261	.287	.392
Nashville	AAA Pit	50	147	49	7	2	7	81	24	30	4	0	34	6	0	1	3	1	.75	0	.333	.373	.551
5 Min. YEARS		391	1362	421	79	10	49	667	211	254	67	3	222	42	4	20	21	17	.55	34	.309	.355	.490

Nathan Haynes

Bats: Left **Throws:** Left **Pos:** OF-71; DH-7; PH-1 **Ht:** 5'9" **Wt:** 170 **Born:** 9/7/79 **Age:** 22

	BATTING															BASERUNNING				PERCENTAGES		
Year Team	Lg Org	G	AB	H	2B	3B	HR	TB	R	RBI	TBB	IBB	SO	HBP	SH	SF	SB	CS	SB%	GDP	Avg	OBP	SLG
1997 Athletics	R Oak	17	54	15	1	0	0	16	8	6	7	0	9	2	1	0	5	1	.83	3	.278	.381	.296
Sou Oregon	A- Oak	24	82	23	1	1	0	26	18	9	26	0	21	2	0	1	19	3	.86	1	.280	.459	.317
1998 Modesto	A+ Oak	125	507	128	18	7	1	158	89	41	54	2	139	4	6	2	42	18	.70	10	.252	.328	.312
1999 Visalia	A+ Oak	35	145	45	7	1	1	57	28	14	17	0	27	3	2	1	12	10	.55	1	.310	.392	.393
Lk Elsinore	A+ Ana	26	110	36	5	5	1	54	19	15	12	0	19	1	0	1	10	5	.67	2	.327	.395	.491
Erie	AA Ana	5	19	3	1	0	0	4	3	0	5	0	5	1	0	0	0	0	—	2	.158	.360	.211
2000 Erie	AA Ana	118	457	116	16	4	6	158	56	43	33	0	107	9	8	2	37	20	.65	3	.254	.315	.346
2001 Arkansas	AA Ana	79	316	98	11	5	5	134	49	23	32	2	65	3	2	0	33	15	.69	4	.310	.379	.424
5 Min. YEARS		429	1690	464	55	23	14	607	270	151	186	4	392	25	19	7	158	72	.69	26	.275	.354	.359

Andy Hazlett

Pitches: Left   Bats: Left   Pos: RP-15; SP-8   Ht: 6'3"   Wt: 187   Born: 8/27/75   Age: 26

Year Team	Lg Org	G	GS	CG	GF	IP	BFP	H	R	ER	HR	SH	SF	HB	TBB	IBB	SO	WP	Bk	W	L	Pct.	ShO	Sv	ERA
1997 Lowell	A- Bos	19	3	0	12	50.1	206	44	16	9	1	0	1	0	7	0	66	0	0	5	0	1.000	0	4	1.61
Michigan	A Bos	2	2	0	0	12	50	15	7	7	2	0	0	0	1	0	12	0	0	1	0	1.000	0	0	5.25
1998 Sarasota	A+ Bos	30	22	4	1	160.2	662	154	76	57	4	2	7	3	25	2	135	3	1	11	7	.611	2	1	3.19
1999 Trenton	AA Bos	27	26	2	1	164.1	674	155	84	76	15	5	2	8	41	0	123	7	3	9	9	.500	1	1	4.16
2000 Pawtucket	AAA Bos	3	0	0	0	3	20	11	8	8	1	0	1	0	0	0	4	0	0	0	0	—	0	0	24.00
Trenton	AA Bos	42	4	0	18	92.1	389	85	43	34	9	5	1	5	23	4	84	1	0	6	6	.500	0	6	3.31
2001 Trenton	AA Bos	14	7	0	4	52	213	51	24	22	4	0	1	4	13	0	39	1	0	6	1	.857	0	1	3.81
Pawtucket	AAA Bos	9	1	0	3	22.2	83	14	4	4	3	0	0	0	3	0	18	0	0	2	0	1.000	0	1	1.59
5 Min. YEARS		146	65	6	39	557.1	2297	529	262	217	39	12	13	20	113	6	481	12	4	40	23	.635	3	14	3.50

Daniel Head

Pitches: Right   Bats: Right   Pos: RP-36; SP-3   Ht: 6'2"   Wt: 215   Born: 10/7/78   Age: 23

Year Team	Lg Org	G	GS	CG	GF	IP	BFP	H	R	ER	HR	SH	SF	HB	TBB	IBB	SO	WP	Bk	W	L	Pct.	ShO	Sv	ERA
2000 Everett	A- Sea	10	0	0	3	16	78	21	10	8	1	1	1	2	7	0	17	0	0	0	0	—	0	0	4.50
2001 Wisconsin	A Sea	16	1	0	6	32.2	139	24	15	11	2	0	1	5	11	1	27	1	1	3	1	.750	0	1	3.03
Tacoma	AAA Sea	2	0	0	2	2	7	1	0	0	0	0	0	0	1	0	1	0	0	1	0	1.000	0	0	0.00
Everett	A- Sea	21	2	0	7	50.2	212	40	14	11	5	1	2	4	14	4	44	2	0	4	4	.500	0	2	1.95
2 Min. YEARS		49	3	0	18	101.1	436	86	39	30	8	2	4	11	33	5	89	3	1	8	5	.615	0	3	2.66

Shane Heams

Pitches: Right   Bats: Right   Pos: RP-50   Ht: 6'1"   Wt: 175   Born: 9/29/75   Age: 26

Year Team	Lg Org	G	GS	CG	GF	IP	BFP	H	R	ER	HR	SH	SF	HB	TBB	IBB	SO	WP	Bk	W	L	Pct.	ShO	Sv	ERA
1996 Mariners	R Sea	9	0	0	5	15.1	64	10	7	5	0	0	0	1	6	0	12	3	1	1	1	.500	0	2	2.93
1997 Mariners	R Sea	21	0	0	14	37	168	30	20	7	2	3	0	5	22	0	42	7	0	6	2	.750	0	4	1.70
1998 Jamestown	A- Det	24	0	0	14	47.1	202	43	27	21	1	0	1	2	16	0	73	5	0	2	2	.500	0	6	3.99
1999 W Michigan	A Det	51	0	0	30	69	294	41	26	18	1	3	4	1	39	2	101	15	1	5	4	.556	0	10	2.35
2000 Jacksnville	AA Det	39	0	0	19	55.2	238	35	17	16	4	3	1	2	34	2	67	2	0	6	2	.750	0	5	2.59
Toledo	AAA Det	6	0	0	2	9.2	52	13	12	12	3	0	2	1	12	0	7	3	0	0	0	—	0	0	11.17
2001 Erie	AA Det	36	0	0	20	54.1	226	22	15	13	1	3	1	5	37	2	57	6	0	5	3	.625	0	6	2.15
Toledo	AAA Det	14	0	0	5	18	100	20	19	18	4	1	0	1	27	0	21	9	0	1	2	.333	0	0	9.00
6 Min. YEARS		200	0	0	109	306.1	1344	214	143	110	16	13	9	18	193	6	380	50	2	26	16	.619	0	31	3.23

Jeff Heaverlo

Pitches: Right   Bats: Right   Pos: SP-27   Ht: 6'1"   Wt: 185   Born: 1/13/78   Age: 24

Year Team	Lg Org	G	GS	CG	GF	IP	BFP	H	R	ER	HR	SH	SF	HB	TBB	IBB	SO	WP	Bk	W	L	Pct.	ShO	Sv	ERA
1999 Everett	A- Sea	3	0	0	1	8.2	35	5	5	2	1	1	0	1	2	0	9	1	0	1	0	1.000	0	0	2.08
Wisconsin	A Sea	3	3	1	0	17.2	75	15	6	5	1	1	0	1	7	0	24	0	1	1	0	1.000	1	0	2.55
2000 Tacoma	AAA Sea	2	2	0	0	13	54	14	7	7	2	0	1	0	6	0	4	1	0	1	0	1.000	0	0	4.85
Lancaster	A+ Sea	27	27	0	0	155.2	685	170	84	73	18	4	5	6	52	0	159	9	2	14	6	.700	0	0	4.22
2001 San Antonio	AA Sea	27	27	4	0	178.2	744	164	75	62	12	8	2	9	40	0	173	8	0	11	6	.647	4	0	3.12
3 Min. YEARS		62	59	5	1	373.2	1593	368	177	149	34	14	8	17	107	0	369	19	3	27	13	.675	5	0	3.59

Bryan Hebson

Pitches: Right   Bats: Right   Pos: RP-18; SP-8   Ht: 6'5"   Wt: 210   Born: 3/12/76   Age: 26

Year Team	Lg Org	G	GS	CG	GF	IP	BFP	H	R	ER	HR	SH	SF	HB	TBB	IBB	SO	WP	Bk	W	L	Pct.	ShO	Sv	ERA
1998 Expos	R Mon	4	4	0	0	17	64	10	1	1	0	0	0	0	7	0	16	2	0	2	0	1.000	0	0	0.53
Cape Fear	A Mon	16	16	0	0	72.2	323	71	42	38	8	1	4	0	29	0	57	1	0	4	5	.444	0	0	4.71
1999 Cape Fear	A Mon	6	6	0	0	33.2	142	22	13	10	2	1	1	3	17	0	34	2	0	0	1	.000	0	0	2.67
Jupiter	A+ Mon	17	16	0	1	103.1	414	85	33	23	5	2	3	5	26	0	79	3	0	7	6	.538	0	0	2.00
2000 Harrisburg	AA Mon	29	29	3	0	171.1	753	175	102	87	23	7	2	14	66	2	90	3	0	7	15	.318	1	0	4.57
2001 Harrisburg	AA Mon	26	8	2	6	75	320	78	40	37	12	3	4	7	19	0	54	2	0	2	8	.200	0	0	4.44
4 Min. YEARS		98	79	5	7	473	2016	441	231	196	50	14	14	40	164	2	330	13	0	22	35	.386	1	0	3.73

Chris Heintz

Bats: Right   Throws: Right   Pos: C-41; 3B-1; PH-1   Ht: 6'1"   Wt: 200   Born: 8/6/74   Age: 27

Year Team	Lg Org	G	AB	H	2B	3B	HR	TB	R	RBI	TBB	IBB	SO	HBP	SH	SF	SB	CS	SB%	GDP	Avg	OBP	SLG
1996 Bristol	R+ CWS	8	29	10	7	0	2	23	7	8	4	0	2	0	0	0	1	1	.50	0	.345	.424	.793
South Bend	A CWS	64	230	61	12	1	1	78	25	22	23	1	46	3	1	1	1	1	.50	3	.265	.339	.339
1997 Hickory	A CWS	107	388	110	28	1	2	146	57	54	28	0	57	9	2	5	1	3	.25	6	.284	.342	.376
1998 Winston-Sal	A+ CWS	130	508	147	21	4	8	200	66	79	31	0	87	5	3	9	10	8	.56	17	.289	.331	.394
1999 Winston-Sal	A+ CWS	118	417	122	33	2	7	180	55	60	40	1	72	4	3	2	6	3	.67	7	.293	.359	.432
2000 Harrisburg	AA CWS	73	239	64	15	1	2	87	27	34	21	0	33	0	1	6	4	1	.80	2	.268	.320	.364
2001 Charlotte	AAA CWS	5	10	1	1	0	0	2	1	1	0	0	3	0	0	0	0	0	—	0	.100	.091	.200
Birmingham	AA CWS	37	119	28	8	0	2	42	14	8	10	0	23	2	2	1	0	2	.00	2	.235	.303	.353
6 Min. YEARS		542	1940	543	125	9	24	758	252	266	157	2	323	23	12	25	23	19	.55	37	.280	.337	.391

Rick Heiserman

Pitches: Right **Bats:** Right **Pos:** RP-28; SP-4   **Ht:** 6'7" **Wt:** 225 **Born:** 2/22/73 **Age:** 29

		HOW MUCH HE PITCHED						WHAT HE GAVE UP										THE RESULTS				
Year Team	Lg Org	G	GS	CG	GF	IP	BFP	H	R	ER	HR	SH	SF	HB	TBB	IBB	SO	WP	Bk	W	L	Pct.	ShO	Sv	ERA
1994 Watertown	A- Cle	7	0	0	2	11.2	48	6	3	3	0	0	1	1	5	0	6	2	2	1	0	1.000	0	0	2.31
1995 Kinston	A+ Cle	19	19	1	0	113	470	97	55	47	13	3	4	9	42	1	86	6	1	9	3	.750	0	0	3.74
St. Pete	A+ StL	6	5	0	1	28	118	28	18	17	2	0	2	1	11	0	18	4	0	2	3	.400	0	0	5.46
1996 St. Pete	A+ StL	26	26	1	0	155.1	663	168	68	56	8	6	3	9	41	0	104	4	0	10	8	.556	1	0	3.24
1997 Arkansas	AA StL	34	20	1	9	131.2	569	151	73	61	19	6	2	8	36	2	90	8	0	5	8	.385	1	4	4.17
Louisville	AAA StL	1	0	0	1	2	10	2	1	1	1	0	0	0	1	0	0	0	0	0	0	—	0	0	4.50
1998 Arkansas	AA StL	18	0	0	18	16.1	76	20	11	9	1	1	0	1	5	0	9	2	0	0	3	.000	0	9	4.96
Memphis	AAA StL	40	0	0	16	40.1	185	54	21	18	2	2	1	2	14	1	28	1	0	2	3	.400	0	6	4.02
1999 Memphis	AAA StL	52	0	0	38	61.2	266	67	37	35	7	1	1	4	21	1	57	6	0	2	3	.400	0	20	5.11
2000 Memphis	AAA StL	55	1	0	22	77	340	85	36	35	10	6	3	2	29	3	55	6	0	6	3	.667	0	6	4.09
2001 Pawtucket	AAA Bos	3	0	0	0	4.1	20	4	3	3	1	0	0	0	4	0	2	0	0	0	0	—	0	0	6.23
New Haven	AA StL	5	0	0	2	7.2	33	7	4	3	1	1	0	0	3	0	5	1	0	0	0	—	0	0	3.52
Memphis	AAA StL	24	4	0	1	49	213	61	26	25	9	0	0	5	11	0	33	1	0	1	1	.500	0	0	4.59
1999 St. Louis	NL	3	0	0	0	4.1	24	8	4	4	2	0	0	0	4	0	4	2	0	0	0	—	0	0	8.31
8 Min. YEARS		290	75	3	110	698	3011	750	356	313	74	26	17	42	223	8	493	41	3	38	35	.521	2	45	4.04

Matthew Hellman

Bats: Right **Throws:** Right **Pos:** OF-58; PH-1   **Ht:** 5'11" **Wt:** 185 **Born:** 11/18/78 **Age:** 23

		BATTING														BASERUNNING				PERCENTAGES		
Year Team	Lg Org	G	AB	H	2B	3B	HR	TB	R	RBI	TBB	IBB	SO	HBP	SH	SF	SB	CS	SB%	GDP	Avg	OBP	SLG
2001 Portland	AAA SD	1	3	0	0	0	0	0	0	0	0	0	1	0	0	0	0	0	—	0	.000	.000	.000
* Eugene	A- SD	57	200	44	6	1	3	61	28	15	24	0	41	1	0	3	2	2	.50	5	.220	.303	.305
1 Min. YEAR		58	203	44	6	1	3	61	28	15	24	0	42	1	0	3	2	2	.50	5	.217	.299	.300

Rod Henderson

Pitches: Right **Bats:** Right **Pos:** SP-23   **Ht:** 6'4" **Wt:** 195 **Born:** 3/11/71 **Age:** 31

		HOW MUCH HE PITCHED						WHAT HE GAVE UP										THE RESULTS				
Year Team	Lg Org	G	GS	CG	GF	IP	BFP	H	R	ER	HR	SH	SF	HB	TBB	IBB	SO	WP	Bk	W	L	Pct.	ShO	Sv	ERA
1992 Jamestown	A- Mon	1	1	0	0	3	13	2	3	2	0	0	0	0	5	0	2	0	0	0	0	—	0	0	6.00
1993 Wst Plm Bch	A+ Mon	22	22	1	0	143	580	110	50	46	3	4	5	6	44	0	127	8	6	12	7	.632	1	0	2.90
Harrisburg	AA Mon	5	5	0	0	29.2	125	20	10	6	0	1	0	0	15	0	25	2	1	5	0	1.000	0	0	1.82
1994 Harrisburg	AA Mon	2	2	0	0	12	44	5	2	2	1	0	0	0	4	0	16	0	0	2	0	1.000	0	0	1.50
Ottawa	AAA Mon	23	21	0	1	122.2	545	123	67	63	16	2	5	2	67	3	100	1	0	6	9	.400	0	1	4.62
1995 Harrisburg	AA Mon	12	12	0	0	56.1	240	51	28	27	4	0	1	5	18	0	53	1	0	3	6	.333	0	0	4.31
1996 Ottawa	AAA Mon	25	23	3	0	121.1	528	117	75	70	12	1	4	4	52	1	83	2	0	4	11	.267	1	0	5.19
1997 Ottawa	AAA Mon	26	20	2	3	123.2	542	136	72	68	18	4	2	6	49	3	103	6	0	5	9	.357	1	1	4.95
1998 Ottawa	AAA Mon	6	0	0	1	11	66	23	17	11	3	1	0	0	12	0	12	0	0	0	1	.000	0	0	9.00
Louisville	AAA Mil	22	19	1	1	121.1	493	100	45	40	4	2	1	4	39	0	68	1	0	11	5	.688	0	0	2.97
1999 Louisville	AAA Mil	28	22	0	1	120.2	550	119	109	85	20	5	5	7	64	0	76	6	0	7	11	.389	0	0	6.34
2000 Binghamton	AA NYM	5	0	0	7	12.1	50	7	6	6	0	0	1	0	5	0	10	1	0	1	0	1.000	0	0	4.38
Long Island	IND —	14	12	1	1	78	303	48	20	19	3	0	4	3	28	0	66	4	0	9	1	.900	1	0	2.19
Tacoma	AAA Sea	4	4	0	0	16.1	77	19	11	11	1	0	0	1	14	0	12	0	0	2	1	.667	0	0	6.06
2001 Long Island	IND —	15	15	2	0	103	411	88	36	29	7	2	4	0	24	2	96	2	0	8	4	.667	1	0	2.53
Sacramento	AAA Oak	8	8	0	0	36.2	175	50	33	32	9	1	2	1	18	0	30	2	0	4	1	.800	0	0	7.85
1994 Montreal	NL	3	2	0	0	6.2	37	9	9	7	1	3	0	0	7	0	3	0	0	0	1	.000	0	0	9.45
1998 Milwaukee	NL	2	0	0	0	3.2	17	5	4	4	2	0	0	1	0	0	1	0	0	0	0	—	0	0	9.82
10 Min. YEARS		222	186	10	15	1111	4742	1018	584	517	101	23	34	39	458	9	879	36	7	79	66	.545	5	2	4.19
2 Maj. YEARS		5	2	0	0	10.1	54	14	13	11	3	3	0	1	7	0	4	0	0	0	1	.000	0	0	9.58

Scott Henderson

Pitches: Right **Bats:** Right **Pos:** RP-39   **Ht:** 6'3" **Wt:** 195 **Born:** 2/27/75 **Age:** 27

		HOW MUCH HE PITCHED						WHAT HE GAVE UP										THE RESULTS				
Year Team	Lg Org	G	GS	CG	GF	IP	BFP	H	R	ER	HR	SH	SF	HB	TBB	IBB	SO	WP	Bk	W	L	Pct.	ShO	Sv	ERA
1997 Utica	A- Fla	15	1	0	6	39.2	151	28	11	10	1	2	1	1	7	0	51	3	0	5	1	.833	0	4	2.27
1998 Kane County	A Fla	40	1	0	19	81.1	337	64	29	27	2	4	2	4	27	7	96	2	0	10	7	.588	0	4	2.99
1999 Portland	AA Fla	46	1	0	21	85	343	67	32	28	4	4	2	8	26	4	83	7	0	6	3	.667	0	7	2.96
2000 Calgary	AAA Fla	8	0	0	2	10.2	51	10	10	6	1	0	1	1	6	0	12	4	0	0	1	.000	0	0	5.06
Portland	AA Fla	39	0	0	20	63.1	266	47	23	22	5	1	1	1	25	0	73	6	1	7	2	.778	0	4	3.13
2001 Portland	AA Fla	39	0	0	15	56.2	238	52	31	30	9	6	1	0	23	2	55	5	0	5	7	.417	0	4	4.76
5 Min. YEARS		187	3	0	83	336.2	1386	268	136	123	22	17	8	15	114	13	370	27	1	33	21	.611	0	23	3.29

Mark Hendrickson

Pitches: Left **Bats:** Left **Pos:** RP-32; SP-6   **Ht:** 6'9" **Wt:** 230 **Born:** 6/23/74 **Age:** 28

		HOW MUCH HE PITCHED						WHAT HE GAVE UP										THE RESULTS				
Year Team	Lg Org	G	GS	CG	GF	IP	BFP	H	R	ER	HR	SH	SF	HB	TBB	IBB	SO	WP	Bk	W	L	Pct.	ShO	Sv	ERA
1998 Dunedin	A+ Tor	16	5	0	1	49.1	207	44	16	13	2	2	2	0	26	1	38	2	0	4	3	.571	0	1	2.37
1999 Knoxville	AA Tor	12	11	0	0	55.2	254	73	46	41	4	2	0	2	21	0	39	2	1	2	7	.222	0	0	6.63
2000 Dunedin	A+ Tor	12	12	1	0	51.1	235	63	34	32	7	1	5	0	29	0	38	1	0	2	2	.500	0	0	5.61
Tennessee	AA Tor	6	6	0	0	39.2	161	32	17	16	5	1	0	0	12	0	29	4	0	3	1	.750	0	0	3.63
2001 Syracuse	AAA Tor	38	6	0	7	73.1	315	80	43	38	13	2	0	3	18	1	33	2	0	2	9	.182	0	0	4.66
4 Min. YEARS		84	40	1	8	269.1	1172	292	156	140	31	8	7	5	106	2	177	11	1	13	22	.371	0	1	4.68

131

Oscar Henriquez

Pitches: Right **Bats:** Right **Pos:** RP-39   **Ht:** 6'6" **Wt:** 220 **Born:** 1/28/74 **Age:** 28

			HOW MUCH HE PITCHED					WHAT HE GAVE UP									THE RESULTS				
Year Team	Lg Org	G	GS	CG	GF	IP	BFP	H	R	ER	HR	SH	SF	HB	TBB	IBB	SO	WP	Bk	W	L	Pct.	ShO	Sv	ERA
1993 Asheville	A Hou	27	26	2	0	150	679	154	95	74	12	6	5	10	70	2	117	7	3	9	10	.474	1	0	4.44
1995 Kissimmee	A+ Hou	20	0	0	7	44.2	207	40	29	25	2	2	2	6	30	0	36	3	0	3	4	.429	0	1	5.04
1996 Kissimmee	A+ Hou	37	0	0	33	34	162	28	18	15	0	1	1	3	29	2	40	4	0	0	4	.000	0	15	3.97
1997 New Orleans	AAA Hou	60	0	0	37	74	313	65	28	23	4	6	3	5	27	3	80	7	1	4	5	.444	0	12	2.80
1998 Charlotte	AAA Fla	26	0	0	19	31.2	134	29	12	9	3	0	1	2	12	0	37	4	0	1	0	1.000	0	11	2.56
1999 Norfolk	AAA NYM	53	0	0	41	54	254	54	31	24	8	4	3	3	38	4	65	8	1	3	4	.429	0	23	4.00
2000 Norfolk	AAA NYM	16	0	0	11	14	65	12	10	10	2	2	1	1	11	1	14	2	0	0	1	.000	0	4	6.43
2001 Norfolk	AAA NYM	39	0	0	32	38.1	162	30	13	12	1	5	1	2	19	0	44	0	0	2	4	.333	0	19	2.82
1997 Houston	NL	4	0	0	1	4	17	2	2	2	0	1	0	1	3	0	3	0	0	0	1	.000	0	0	4.50
1998 Florida	NL	15	0	0	4	20	100	26	22	19	4	0	2	1	12	0	19	1	0	0	0	—	0	0	8.55
8 Min. YEARS		278	26	2	180	440.2	1976	412	236	192	32	26	17	32	236	12	433	35	5	22	32	.407	1	85	3.92
2 Maj. YEARS		19	0	0	5	24	117	28	24	21	4	1	2	2	15	0	22	1	0	0	1	.000	0	0	7.88

Butch Henry

Pitches: Left **Bats:** Left **Pos:** SP-18   **Ht:** 6'1" **Wt:** 205 **Born:** 10/7/68 **Age:** 33

			HOW MUCH HE PITCHED					WHAT HE GAVE UP									THE RESULTS				
Year Team	Lg Org	G	GS	CG	GF	IP	BFP	H	R	ER	HR	SH	SF	HB	TBB	IBB	SO	WP	Bk	W	L	Pct.	ShO	Sv	ERA
1987 Billings	R+ Cin	9	5	0	2	35	151	37	21	18	3	0	1	1	12	1	38	4	1	4	0	1.000	0	1	4.63
1988 Cedar Rapds	A Cin	27	27	1	0	187	745	144	59	47	14	7	4	6	56	2	163	6	8	16	2	.889	1	0	2.26
1989 Chattanooga	AA Cin	7	7	0	0	26.1	110	22	12	10	2	1	1	0	12	1	19	2	0	1	3	.250	0	0	3.42
1990 Chattanooga	AA Cin	24	22	2	0	143	622	151	74	67	15	9	5	3	58	0	95	12	2	8	8	.500	0	0	4.22
1991 Tucson	AAA Hou	27	27	2	0	153.2	671	192	92	82	10	8	5	1	42	2	97	5	4	10	11	.476	0	0	4.80
1993 Ottawa	AAA Mon	5	5	1	0	31.1	125	34	15	13	2	0	1	0	1	0	25	0	0	3	1	.750	0	0	3.73
1994 Ottawa	AAA Mon	2	2	1	0	14	54	11	0	0	0	0	0	0	2	1	11	2	0	2	0	1.000	1	0	0.00
1997 Sarasota	A+ Bos	2	2	0	0	8.1	33	8	5	5	1	0	0	0	0	0	7	0	0	0	1	.000	0	0	5.40
1998 Sarasota	A+ Bos	1	1	0	0	6.2	23	4	2	1	0	0	0	0	0	0	5	0	0	0	1	.000	0	0	1.35
1999 Tacoma	AAA Sea	4	0	0	1	5	18	4	0	0	0	0	0	0	1	0	3	0	0	2	0	1.000	0	0	0.00
2001 Syracuse	AAA Tor	12	12	1	0	78.1	323	91	38	35	5	2	3	2	9	1	49	0	0	6	4	.600	0	0	4.02
Indianapols	AAA Mil	5	5	1	0	36	152	39	25	24	8	0	1	1	9	0	27	0	1	2	3	.400	0	0	6.00
Columbus	AAA NYY	1	1	0	0	2	16	10	7	6	1	0	0	0	0	0	1	0	0	0	1	.000	0	0	27.00
1992 Houston	NL	28	28	2	0	165.2	710	185	81	74	16	12	7	1	41	7	96	2	2	6	9	.400	1	0	4.02
1993 Colorado	NL	20	15	1	1	84.2	390	117	66	62	14	6	5	1	24	2	39	1	0	2	8	.200	0	0	6.59
Montreal	NL	10	1	0	3	18.1	77	18	10	8	1	0	1	0	4	0	8	0	0	1	1	.500	0	0	3.93
1994 Montreal	NL	24	15	0	1	107.1	433	97	30	29	10	5	3	2	20	1	70	1	0	8	3	.727	0	1	2.43
1995 Montreal	NL	21	21	1	0	126.2	524	133	47	40	11	7	3	2	28	3	60	0	1	7	9	.438	1	0	2.84
1997 Boston	AL	36	5	0	13	84.1	345	89	36	33	6	2	3	0	19	2	51	0	0	7	3	.700	0	6	3.52
1998 Boston	AL	2	2	0	0	9	38	8	4	4	2	0	0	1	3	0	6	0	0	0	0	—	0	0	4.00
1999 Seattle	AL	7	4	0	0	25	112	30	15	14	1	0	1	2	10	0	15	0	0	2	0	1.000	0	0	5.04
11 Min. YEARS		126	116	9	3	726.2	3043	747	350	308	61	27	21	14	202	8	540	31	16	54	35	.607	2	1	3.81
7 Maj. YEARS		148	91	4	18	621	2629	677	289	264	61	32	23	9	149	15	345	4	3	33	33	.500	2	7	3.83

Drew Henson

Bats: Right **Throws:** Right **Pos:** 3B-78; DH-3   **Ht:** 6'5" **Wt:** 222 **Born:** 2/13/80 **Age:** 22

					BATTING											BASERUNNING				PERCENTAGES		
Year Team	Lg Org	G	AB	H	2B	3B	HR	TB	R	RBI	TBB	IBB	SO	HBP	SH	SF	SB	CS	SB%	GDP	Avg	OBP	SLG
1998 Yankees	R NYY	10	38	12	3	0	1	18	5	2	3	1	9	0	0	0	0	0	—	1	.316	.366	.474
1999 Tampa	A+ NYY	69	254	71	12	0	13	122	37	37	26	0	71	1	0	3	3	1	.75	6	.280	.345	.480
2000 Tampa	A+ NYY	5	21	7	2	0	1	12	4	1	1	0	7	0	0	0	1	0	1.00	0	.333	.364	.571
Norwich	AA NYY	59	223	64	9	2	7	98	39	39	20	1	75	1	0	1	0	5	.00	6	.287	.347	.439
Chattanooga	AA Cin	16	64	11	8	0	1	22	7	9	4	0	25	0	0	0	2	0	1.00	2	.172	.221	.344
2001 Tampa	A+ NYY	5	14	2	0	0	1	5	2	3	2	0	7	2	0	1	1	0	1.00	1	.143	.316	.357
Norwich	AA NYY	5	19	7	1	0	0	8	2	2	1	1	4	1	0	0	1	0	1.00	1	.368	.429	.421
Columbus	AAA NYY	71	270	60	6	0	11	99	29	38	10	1	85	0	0	1	2	1	.67	5	.222	.249	.367
4 Min. YEARS		240	903	234	41	2	35	384	125	131	67	4	283	5	0	6	8	9	.47	24	.259	.312	.425

John Herbert

Pitches: Right **Bats:** Right **Pos:** RP-31   **Ht:** 6'8" **Wt:** 230 **Born:** 10/23/77 **Age:** 24

			HOW MUCH HE PITCHED					WHAT HE GAVE UP									THE RESULTS				
Year Team	Lg Org	G	GS	CG	GF	IP	BFP	H	R	ER	HR	SH	SF	HB	TBB	IBB	SO	WP	Bk	W	L	Pct.	ShO	Sv	ERA
2000 Idaho Falls	R+ SD	17	0	0	7	21.2	114	17	14	11	2	2	0	0	6	0	24	5	0	2	2	.500	0	0	4.57
2001 Fort Wayne	A SD	2	0	0	0	5	28	6	5	4	0	0	0	0	4	0	2	1	0	1	0	1.000	0	0	7.20
Portland	AAA SD	1	0	0	0	1	3	0	0	0	0	0	0	0	0	0	1	0	0	0	0	—	0	0	0.00
Eugene	A- SD	28	0	0	15	36	146	25	13	11	2	2	1	3	11	0	39	3	3	3	1	.750	0	4	2.75
2 Min. YEARS		48	0	0	22	63.2	268	48	32	26	4	4	1	3	21	0	66	9	3	6	3	.667	0	4	3.68

Carlos Hernandez

Bats: Right **Throws:** Right **Pos:** 2B-109; SS-9; 3B-6; DH-4; PH-2; OF-1; PR-1   **Ht:** 5'9" **Wt:** 175 **Born:** 12/12/75 **Age:** 26

					BATTING											BASERUNNING				PERCENTAGES		
Year Team	Lg Org	G	AB	H	2B	3B	HR	TB	R	RBI	TBB	IBB	SO	HBP	SH	SF	SB	CS	SB%	GDP	Avg	OBP	SLG
1994 Astros	R Hou	51	192	62	10	1	0	74	45	23	19	0	22	4	2	1	25	7	.78	1	.323	.394	.385
1995 Quad City	A Hou	126	470	122	19	6	4	165	74	40	39	1	68	11	9	1	58	21	.73	4	.260	.330	.351
1996 Quad City	A Hou	112	456	123	15	7	5	167	67	49	27	0	71	4	9	5	41	14	.75	6	.270	.313	.366
1997 Jackson	AA Hou	92	363	106	12	1	4	132	62	33	33	2	59	4	6	3	17	8	.68	7	.292	.355	.364
1998 New Orleans	AAA Hou	134	494	147	23	2	1	177	64	54	21	3	81	12	7	1	29	11	.73	10	.298	.341	.358
1999 New Orleans	AAA Hou	94	355	104	14	0	0	118	56	43	27	1	65	10	3	3	22	13	.63	5	.293	.357	.332
2000 Tacoma	AAA Sea	62	210	50	10	1	0	62	21	15	15	0	38	3	4	0	9	0	1.00	5	.238	.298	.295
2001 Binghamton	AA NYM	70	266	84	18	1	5	119	49	32	22	2	42	6	2	1	20	9	.69	5	.316	.380	.447
Norfolk	AAA NYM	56	194	44	5	0	0	49	22	10	15	0	31	7	5	2	4	1	.80	6	.227	.303	.253

Year Team	Lg Org	G	AB	H	2B	3B	HR	TB	R	RBI	TBB	IBB	SO	HBP	SH	SF	SB	CS	SB%	GDP	Avg	OBP	SLG
						BATTING												**BASERUNNING**				**PERCENTAGES**		
1999 Houston	NL	16	14	2	0	0	0	2	4	1	0	0	0	0	0	1	0	3	1	.75	0	.143	.143	.143
2000 Seattle	AL	2	1	0	0	0	0	0	0	0	0	0	1	0	0	0	0	1	.00	0	.000	.000	.000
8 Min. YEARS		797	3000	842	126	19	19	1063	460	299	218	9	477	61	47	17	225	84	.73	52	.281	.340	.354
2 Maj. YEARS		18	15	2	0	0	0	2	4	1	0	0	1	0	1	0	3	2	.60	0	.133	.133	.133

Carlos Hernandez

Bats: Right **Throws:** Right **Pos:** C-2   **Ht:** 5'10" **Wt:** 215 **Born:** 5/24/67 **Age:** 35

Year Team	Lg Org	G	AB	H	2B	3B	HR	TB	R	RBI	TBB	IBB	SO	HBP	SH	SF	SB	CS	SB%	GDP	Avg	OBP	SLG
1985 Dodgers	R LA	22	49	12	1	0	0	13	3	6	3	0	8	0	0	0	0	0	—	4	.245	.288	.265
1986 Dodgers	R LA	57	205	64	7	0	1	74	19	31	5	2	18	2	1	1	1	2	.33	7	.312	.333	.361
1987 Bakersfield	A+ LA	48	162	37	6	1	3	54	22	22	14	0	23	3	1	2	8	4	.67	6	.228	.298	.333
1988 Bakersfield	A+ LA	92	333	103	15	2	5	137	37	52	16	2	39	1	3	4	3	2	.60	18	.309	.339	.411
Albuquerque	AAA LA	3	8	1	0	0	0	1	0	1	0	0	0	0	0	0	0	0	—	1	.125	.125	.125
1989 San Antonio	AA LA	99	370	111	16	3	8	157	37	41	12	0	46	7	1	3	2	3	.40	12	.300	.332	.424
Albuquerque	AAA LA	4	14	3	0	0	0	3	1	1	2	1	1	0	0	0	0	0	—	1	.214	.313	.214
1990 Albuquerque	AAA LA	52	143	45	8	1	0	55	11	16	8	1	25	1	0	3	2	2	.50	5	.315	.348	.385
1991 Albuquerque	AAA LA	95	345	119	24	2	8	171	60	44	24	5	36	1	0	4	5	5	.50	10	.345	.387	.496
1996 Albuquerque	AAA LA	66	233	56	11	0	5	82	19	30	11	0	49	2	1	3	5	4	.56	1	.240	.277	.352
1997 Rancho Cuca	A+ SD	1	4	1	0	0	0	1	0	0	0	0	0	1	0	0	0	0	—	1	.250	.250	.250
Las Vegas	AAA SD	3	10	4	0	0	1	7	1	5	1	0	3	0	0	1	0	0	—	0	.400	.417	.700
2001 Memphis	AAA StL	2	4	2	0	0	1	5	1	1	0	0	0	0	0	0	0	0	—	0	.500	.500	1.250
1990 Los Angeles	NL	10	20	4	1	0	0	5	2	1	0	0	2	0	0	0	0	0	—	0	.200	.200	.250
1991 Los Angeles	NL	15	14	3	1	0	0	4	1	1	0	0	5	1	0	1	1	0	1.00	1	.214	.250	.286
1992 Los Angeles	NL	69	173	45	4	0	3	58	11	17	11	1	21	4	0	0	0	1	.00	8	.260	.316	.335
1993 Los Angeles	NL	50	99	25	5	0	2	36	6	7	2	0	11	0	1	0	0	0	—	0	.253	.267	.364
1994 Los Angeles	NL	32	64	14	2	0	2	22	6	6	1	0	14	0	0	0	0	0	—	5	.219	.231	.344
1995 Los Angeles	NL	45	94	14	1	0	2	21	3	8	7	0	25	1	1	0	0	0	—	5	.149	.216	.223
1996 Los Angeles	NL	13	14	4	0	0	0	4	1	0	2	0	2	0	0	0	0	0	—	0	.286	.375	.286
1997 San Diego	NL	50	134	42	7	1	3	60	15	14	3	0	27	0	1	0	0	2	.00	5	.313	.328	.448
1998 San Diego	NL	129	390	102	15	0	9	144	34	52	16	2	54	9	0	2	2	2	.50	19	.262	.305	.369
2000 San Diego	NL	58	191	48	11	0	2	65	16	25	16	1	26	3	0	2	1	3	.25	4	.251	.316	.340
St. Louis	NL	17	51	14	4	0	1	21	7	10	5	0	9	1	0	1	1	0	1.00	0	.275	.345	.412
10 Min. YEARS		544	1880	558	88	9	32	760	211	250	96	11	249	17	7	19	26	22	.54	69	.297	.333	.404
10 Maj. YEARS		488	1244	315	51	1	24	440	102	141	63	4	196	19	3	8	5	8	.38	43	.253	.298	.354

Jesus Hernandez

Bats: Left **Throws:** Left **Pos:** OF-21; DH-4; PH-2   **Ht:** 6'2" **Wt:** 170 **Born:** 6/6/77 **Age:** 25

Year Team	Lg Org	G	AB	H	2B	3B	HR	TB	R	RBI	TBB	IBB	SO	HBP	SH	SF	SB	CS	SB%	GDP	Avg	OBP	SLG
1996 Burlington	R+ Cle	19	66	15	2	0	2	23	15	6	13	0	8	0	1	0	5	0	1.00	1	.227	.354	.348
1997 Watertown	A- Cle	16	45	10	4	0	0	14	4	3	6	0	10	0	0	2	1	0	1.00	1	.222	.302	.311
Burlington	R+ Cle	50	192	58	12	0	7	91	37	40	25	1	36	4	0	4	7	2	.78	1	.302	.387	.474
1998 Watertown	A- Cle	70	257	62	13	5	5	100	42	43	39	2	49	0	2	2	15	0	1.00	5	.241	.339	.389
1999 Columbus	A Cle	70	255	78	22	3	12	142	43	56	30	3	53	4	0	2	8	2	.80	6	.306	.385	.557
2000 Kinston	A+ Cle	62	222	62	12	5	4	96	30	30	33	0	57	1	1	2	11	7	.61	1	.279	.372	.432
2001 Akron	AA Cle	4	14	5	1	0	0	6	1	0	3	0	5	0	0	0	1	1	.50	0	.357	.471	.429
Kinston	A+ Cle	23	82	13	3	2	3	29	15	7	10	0	20	2	1	1	1	1	.50	0	.159	.263	.354
6 Min. YEARS		314	1133	303	69	15	33	501	187	185	159	6	238	11	5	13	49	13	.79	15	.267	.359	.442

John Hernandez

Bats: Right **Throws:** Right **Pos:** C-48; PH-3; 1B-1; P-1   **Ht:** 6'2" **Wt:** 205 **Born:** 9/1/79 **Age:** 22

Year Team	Lg Org	G	AB	H	2B	3B	HR	TB	R	RBI	TBB	IBB	SO	HBP	SH	SF	SB	CS	SB%	GDP	Avg	OBP	SLG
1997 Yakima	A- LA	29	77	14	3	0	1	20	7	8	9	0	22	1	1	0	1	1	.50	3	.182	.276	.260
1998 Great Falls	R+ LA	40	133	38	7	0	3	54	21	15	6	0	23	5	1	1	3	0	1.00	1	.286	.338	.406
1999 San Berndno	A+ LA	61	199	52	17	0	7	90	31	25	21	1	44	3	4	0	0	1	.00	8	.261	.341	.452
2000 San Berndno	A+ LA	80	273	68	14	0	2	91	30	20	14	1	53	12	7	1	6	2	.75	5	.249	.313	.333
2001 Las Vegas	AAA LA	5	15	1	1	0	0	2	1	1	0	0	3	0	0	0	1	0	1.00	0	.067	.067	.133
Vero Beach	A+ LA	38	114	23	9	0	0	32	8	22	5	0	19	3	0	3	1	1	.50	2	.202	.248	.281
El Paso	AA Ari	8	21	3	1	0	0	4	1	0	0	0	6	0	0	0	0	0	—	1	.143	.143	.190
5 Min. YEARS		261	832	199	55	0	13	293	99	91	55	2	170	24	13	5	12	5	.71	20	.239	.303	.352

Michel Hernandez

Bats: Right **Throws:** Right **Pos:** C-49; DH-2; PH-2   **Ht:** 6'0" **Wt:** 211 **Born:** 8/12/78 **Age:** 23

Year Team	Lg Org	G	AB	H	2B	3B	HR	TB	R	RBI	TBB	IBB	SO	HBP	SH	SF	SB	CS	SB%	GDP	Avg	OBP	SLG
1998 Oneonta	A- NYY	61	205	52	8	2	0	64	29	24	20	0	19	0	1	1	4	4	.50	10	.254	.319	.312
1999 Tampa	A+ NYY	82	281	69	10	1	2	87	26	23	18	0	49	3	3	2	2	2	.50	8	.246	.296	.310
2000 Norwich	AA NYY	21	66	14	2	0	0	16	7	4	4	0	13	0	2	1	1	0	1.00	1	.212	.254	.242
Tampa	A+ NYY	75	231	51	12	0	1	66	17	28	29	0	23	3	4	3	0	4	.43	4	.221	.312	.286
2001 Yankees	R NYY	2	5	0	0	0	0	0	0	0	0	0	1	1	0	0	0	0	—	1	.000	.167	.000
Norwich	AA NYY	51	128	29	6	0	2	41	10	10	10	0	20	2	2	1	1	0	1.00	5	.227	.291	.320
4 Min. YEARS		292	916	215	38	3	5	274	89	89	81	0	125	9	12	8	11	10	.52	29	.235	.301	.299

Alex Herrera

Pitches: Left **Bats:** Left **Pos:** RP-43   **Ht:** 5'11" **Wt:** 175 **Born:** 11/5/79 **Age:** 22

		HOW MUCH HE PITCHED						WHAT HE GAVE UP											THE RESULTS					
Year Team	Lg Org	G	GS	CG	GF	IP	BFP	H	R	ER	HR	SH	SF	HB	TBB	IBB	SO	WP	Bk	W	L	Pct.	ShO	Sv	ERA
2000 Columbus	A Cle	20	0	0	2	42	186	41	25	16	1	3	3	3	21	1	41	2	1	4	3	.571	0	0	3.43
Kinston	A+ Cle	17	0	0	6	31	138	28	11	8	1	0	1	1	19	0	40	3	1	0	1	.000	0	1	2.32
Akron	AA Cle	2	0	0	1	1.1	6	2	1	0	0	0	0	0	1	0	1	0	0	0	0	—	0	0	0.00
2001 Kinston	A+ Cle	28	0	0	8	59.2	231	36	6	4	1	0	0	2	18	0	83	2	0	4	0	1.000	0	3	0.60
Akron	AA Cle	15	0	0	9	28.2	114	24	9	9	1	0	0	0	9	0	22	2	0	3	0	1.000	0	2	2.83
2 Min. YEARS		82	0	0	26	162.2	675	131	52	37	4	3	4	6	68	1	187	9	2	11	4	.733	0	6	2.05

Mike Hessman

Bats: Right **Throws:** Right **Pos:** 3B-113; OF-18; 1B-5; DH-2; P-1   **Ht:** 6'5" **Wt:** 215 **Born:** 3/5/78 **Age:** 24

		BATTING														BASERUNNING				PERCENTAGES		
Year Team	Lg Org	G	AB	H	2B	3B	HR	TB	R	RBI	TBB	IBB	SO	HBP	SH	SF	SB	CS	SB%	GDP	Avg	OBP	SLG
1996 Braves	R Atl	53	190	41	10	1	1	56	13	15	12	1	41	4	4	0	1	1	.50	0	.216	.277	.295
1997 Macon	A Atl	122	459	108	25	0	21	196	69	74	41	0	167	6	0	2	0	2	.00	6	.235	.305	.427
1998 Danville	A+ Atl	118	445	89	21	0	20	170	47	63	30	0	172	6	0	2	3	3	.50	6	.200	.259	.382
1999 Myrtle Bch	A+ Atl	103	365	90	25	0	23	184	62	54	47	3	135	11	0	3	0	3	.00	3	.247	.347	.504
2000 Greenville	AA Atl	127	437	80	23	1	19	162	52	50	37	0	178	8	0	2	3	1	.75	9	.183	.258	.371
2001 Greenville	AA Atl	129	478	110	23	2	26	215	66	80	39	2	124	7	0	0	2	4	.33	5	.230	.298	.450
6 Min. YEARS		652	2374	518	127	4	110	983	309	336	206	6	817	42	4	9	9	14	.39	29	.218	.291	.414

Joe Hietpas

Bats: Right **Throws:** Right **Pos:** C-11; DH-1; PH-1   **Ht:** 6'3" **Wt:** 220 **Born:** 5/1/79 **Age:** 23

		BATTING														BASERUNNING				PERCENTAGES		
Year Team	Lg Org	G	AB	H	2B	3B	HR	TB	R	RBI	TBB	IBB	SO	HBP	SH	SF	SB	CS	SB%	GDP	Avg	OBP	SLG
2001 Kingsport	R+ NYM	11	27	5	1	0	0	6	3	1	6	0	11	1	0	0	0	0	—	0	.185	.353	.222
Binghamton	AA NYM	2	3	0	0	0	0	0	0	0	0	0	1	0	0	0	0	0	—	0	.000	.000	.000
1 Min. YEAR		13	30	5	1	0	0	6	3	1	6	0	12	1	0	0	0	0	—	0	.167	.324	.200

Andy High

Pitches: Left **Bats:** Left **Pos:** SP-19; RP-1   **Ht:** 6'4" **Wt:** 220 **Born:** 5/22/74 **Age:** 28

		HOW MUCH HE PITCHED						WHAT HE GAVE UP											THE RESULTS					
Year Team	Lg Org	G	GS	CG	GF	IP	BFP	H	R	ER	HR	SH	SF	HB	TBB	IBB	SO	WP	Bk	W	L	Pct.	ShO	Sv	ERA
1996 Bangor	IND —	14	14	4	0	92.2	403	94	55	40	6	11	3	1	22	1	53	6	1	7	3	.700	2	0	3.88
1997 Bangor	IND —	15	8	0	3	54.2	258	73	38	28	2	1	2	1	23	2	42	3	0	3	4	.429	0	0	4.61
1998 New Jersey	IND —	23	0	0	4	39	153	29	13	12	4	2	1	3	7	0	47	0	0	4	2	.667	0	1	2.77
1999 New Jersey	IND —	36	3	0	8	48.2	217	54	30	23	5	3	0	3	19	1	51	3	1	4	3	.571	0	0	4.25
2000 New Jersey	IND —	31	0	0	13	39	171	38	18	14	0	2	0	1	20	7	50	1	1	1	6	.143	0	4	3.23
Atlantic Ct	IND —	7	0	0	3	10	40	6	1	1	0	0	0	1	4	0	13	0	1	1	1	.500	0	0	0.90
2001 Atlantic Ct	IND —	14	14	2	0	90	373	89	34	32	8	1	2	1	20	0	75	2	1	9	2	.818	0	0	3.20
Huntsville	AA Mil	6	5	0	0	29.2	117	22	9	7	4	3	2	0	6	0	28	1	0	2	1	.667	0	0	2.12
6 Min. YEARS		146	44	6	31	403.2	1732	405	198	157	29	23	10	11	121	11	359	16	5	31	22	.585	2	5	3.50

Cary Hiles

Pitches: Right **Bats:** Right **Pos:** RP-51   **Ht:** 5'10" **Wt:** 173 **Born:** 11/29/75 **Age:** 26

		HOW MUCH HE PITCHED						WHAT HE GAVE UP											THE RESULTS					
Year Team	Lg Org	G	GS	CG	GF	IP	BFP	H	R	ER	HR	SH	SF	HB	TBB	IBB	SO	WP	Bk	W	L	Pct.	ShO	Sv	ERA
1998 Batavia	A- Phi	25	0	0	23	30.1	134	27	11	10	0	0	0	1	13	0	45	4	1	2	2	.500	0	10	2.97
1999 Piedmont	A Phi	44	0	0	40	61	255	52	20	15	3	6	0	3	12	0	84	9	0	3	2	.600	0	26	2.21
2000 Clearwater	A+ Phi	46	0	0	41	62.2	280	76	27	22	0	5	1	3	22	2	41	3	1	8	3	.727	0	20	3.16
2001 Reading	AA Phi	51	0	0	30	81.2	325	60	24	22	6	2	2	7	21	3	62	5	2	2	3	.400	0	11	2.42
4 Min. YEARS		166	0	0	134	235.2	994	215	82	69	9	13	3	14	68	5	232	21	4	15	10	.600	0	67	2.64

Bobby Hill

Bats: Both **Throws:** Right **Pos:** 2B-56; PH-3; SS-1; DH-1   **Ht:** 5'10" **Wt:** 180 **Born:** 4/3/78 **Age:** 24

		BATTING														BASERUNNING				PERCENTAGES		
Year Team	Lg Org	G	AB	H	2B	3B	HR	TB	R	RBI	TBB	IBB	SO	HBP	SH	SF	SB	CS	SB%	GDP	Avg	OBP	SLG
2000 Newark	IND —	132	481	157	22	9	13	236	109	82	101	2	57	4	1	7	81	15	.84	8	.326	.442	.491
2001 Cubs	R ChC	3	9	2	0	0	0	2	1	2	1	0	3	0	0	0	1	0	1.00	0	.222	.364	.222
West Tenn	AA ChC	57	209	63	8	1	3	82	30	21	32	1	39	2	1	2	20	8	.71	7	.301	.396	.392
2 Min. YEARS		192	699	222	30	10	16	320	140	104	135	3	99	6	2	9	102	23	.82	15	.318	.428	.458

Jason Hill

Bats: Right **Throws:** Right **Pos:** C-84; DH-6; OF-3; 1B-2; 3B-1; PH-1; PR-1   **Ht:** 6'3" **Wt:** 210 **Born:** 3/17/77 **Age:** 25

		BATTING														BASERUNNING				PERCENTAGES		
Year Team	Lg Org	G	AB	H	2B	3B	HR	TB	R	RBI	TBB	IBB	SO	HBP	SH	SF	SB	CS	SB%	GDP	Avg	OBP	SLG
1998 Boise	A- Ana	57	203	53	17	0	7	91	30	39	22	0	45	3	0	1	1	0	1.00	5	.261	.341	.448
1999 Cedar Rapds	A Ana	111	390	112	22	0	9	161	59	52	36	4	59	12	4	5	3	2	.60	5	.287	.361	.413
2000 Lk Elsinore	A+ Ana	70	233	58	12	0	4	82	23	33	23	1	44	4	4	2	0	1	.00	5	.249	.324	.352
2001 Salt Lake	AAA Ana	8	27	10	1	1	0	13	3	3	2	0	4	0	0	0	0	0	—	1	.370	.414	.481
Arkansas	AA Ana	85	298	77	18	0	11	128	42	45	18	1	58	4	1	4	1	1	.50	9	.258	.306	.430
4 Min. YEARS		331	1151	310	70	1	31	475	157	172	101	6	210	23	9	12	5	4	.56	27	.269	.337	.413

Terry Hill

Pitches: Left **Bats:** Left **Pos:** RP-25   **Ht:** 5'10" **Wt:** 179 **Born:** 10/17/75 **Age:** 26

Year Team	Lg Org	G	GS	CG	GF	IP	BFP	H	R	ER	HR	SH	SF	HB	TBB	IBB	SO	WP	Bk	W	L	Pct.	ShO	Sv	ERA
1998 Lowell	A- Bos	19	7	0	6	63	282	60	28	14	2	0	2	2	33	3	61	6	0	0	4	.000	0	0	2.00
1999 Augusta	A Bos	53	0	0	15	92.1	383	77	30	28	6	5	3	3	25	2	95	11	0	3	6	.333	0	1	2.73
2000 Sarasota	A+ Bos	34	0	0	13	60.1	246	50	20	20	3	2	2	5	18	3	54	1	0	4	0	1.000	0	2	2.98
Trenton	AA Bos	18	0	0	9	24.2	112	25	15	12	1	1	0	3	13	3	28	2	0	2	3	.400	0	1	4.38
2001 Red Sox	R Bos	3	0	0	0	7.1	25	2	1	1	0	0	0	1	0	0	11	0	0	2	0	1.000	0	0	1.23
Trenton	AA Bos	22	0	0	7	38	167	38	25	16	3	0	0	5	10	2	42	3	0	3	1	.750	0	0	3.79
4 Min. YEARS		149	7	0	50	285.2	1215	252	119	91	15	8	7	19	99	13	291	23	0	14	14	.500	0	4	2.87

Eric Hinske

Bats: Left **Throws:** Right **Pos:** 3B-120; 2B-1; DH-1   **Ht:** 6'2" **Wt:** 225 **Born:** 8/5/77 **Age:** 24

Year Team	Lg Org	G	AB	H	2B	3B	HR	TB	R	RBI	TBB	IBB	SO	HBP	SH	SF	SB	CS	SB%	GDP	Avg	OBP	SLG
1998 Williamsprt	A- ChC	68	248	74	20	0	9	121	46	57	35	3	61	2	0	4	19	3	.86	2	.298	.384	.488
Rockford	A ChC	6	20	9	4	0	1	16	8	4	5	0	6	0	0	1	1	0	1.00	0	.450	.538	.800
1999 Daytona	A+ ChC	130	445	132	28	6	19	229	76	79	62	7	90	5	1	5	16	10	.62	5	.297	.385	.515
Iowa	AAA ChC	4	15	4	0	1	1	9	3	2	1	0	4	0	0	0	0	0	—	0	.267	.313	.600
2000 West Tenn	AA ChC	131	436	113	21	9	20	212	76	73	78	3	133	3	0	3	14	5	.74	7	.259	.373	.486
2001 Sacramento	AAA Oak	121	436	123	27	1	25	227	71	79	54	3	113	10	2	2	20	7	.74	6	.282	.373	.521
4 Min. YEARS		460	1600	455	100	17	75	814	280	294	235	16	407	20	3	15	70	25	.74	20	.284	.380	.509

Brian Hitchcox

Bats: Left **Throws:** Right **Pos:** DH-12; 3B-9; SS-8; 2B-8; PR-4; OF-1; PH-1   **Ht:** 5'11" **Wt:** 175 **Born:** 7/21/78 **Age:** 23

Year Team	Lg Org	G	AB	H	2B	3B	HR	TB	R	RBI	TBB	IBB	SO	HBP	SH	SF	SB	CS	SB%	GDP	Avg	OBP	SLG
1999 Batavia	A- Phi	54	166	37	5	1	2	50	22	18	19	0	14	8	1	3	7	1	.88	2	.223	.327	.301
2000 Piedmont	A Phi	112	407	109	19	2	3	141	48	42	25	1	35	16	2	3	10	8	.56	5	.268	.333	.346
2001 Reading	AA Phi	9	25	3	0	0	0	3	1	1	0	0	5	0	0	0	1	0	1.00	1	.120	.120	.120
Clearwater	A+ Phi	32	87	17	2	1	1	24	9	6	8	0	6	1	3	1	2	3	.40	3	.195	.268	.276
3 Min. YEARS		207	685	166	26	4	6	218	80	67	52	1	60	25	6	7	20	12	.63	11	.242	.316	.318

Brent Hoard

Pitches: Left **Bats:** Right **Pos:** SP-16; RP-2   **Ht:** 6'4" **Wt:** 210 **Born:** 11/3/76 **Age:** 25

Year Team	Lg Org	G	GS	CG	GF	IP	BFP	H	R	ER	HR	SH	SF	HB	TBB	IBB	SO	WP	Bk	W	L	Pct.	ShO	Sv	ERA
1998 Fort Wayne	A Min	15	2	0	2	31	141	32	19	18	0	0	0	0	20	2	37	9	0	2	1	.667	0	0	5.23
1999 Quad City	A Min	28	28	1	0	149.2	643	143	68	57	9	4	3	2	64	1	139	7	1	12	7	.632	0	0	3.43
2000 Quad City	A Min	6	6	1	0	28.1	130	34	22	17	5	0	0	0	11	0	14	2	0	0	3	.000	0	0	5.40
Fort Myers	A+ Min	19	18	0	1	92	412	98	57	44	6	3	2	3	44	2	55	8	0	5	9	.357	0	0	4.30
2001 Fort Myers	A+ Min	17	15	0	1	80.1	336	78	31	30	5	4	4	3	28	0	70	7	0	7	4	.636	0	0	3.36
New Britain	AA Min	1	1	0	0	6	21	2	1	0	0	0	1	0	1	0	2	1	0	1	0	1.000	0	0	0.00
4 Min. YEARS		86	70	2	4	387.1	1683	387	198	166	25	11	10	8	168	5	317	34	1	27	24	.529	0	0	3.86

Josh Hochgesang

Bats: Right **Throws:** Right **Pos:** 3B-74; DH-8; PH-1   **Ht:** 6'3" **Wt:** 210 **Born:** 4/16/77 **Age:** 25

Year Team	Lg Org	G	AB	H	2B	3B	HR	TB	R	RBI	TBB	IBB	SO	HBP	SH	SF	SB	CS	SB%	GDP	Avg	OBP	SLG
1999 Sou Oregon	A- Oak	21	71	11	2	0	1	16	10	8	14	0	23	4	1	0	0	1	.00	1	.155	.326	.225
2000 Visalia	A+ Oak	126	443	109	23	3	20	198	78	80	90	4	135	7	2	9	20	9	.69	11	.246	.375	.447
2001 Midland	AA Oak	83	303	70	18	3	6	112	48	33	30	1	84	10	1	1	8	3	.73	2	.231	.320	.370
3 Min. YEARS		230	817	190	43	6	27	326	136	121	134	5	242	21	4	10	28	13	.68	14	.233	.351	.399

Kevin Hodge

Bats: Right **Throws:** Right **Pos:** 2B-52; 3B-45; SS-18; OF-5; P-2; PH-1; PR-1   **Ht:** 5'11" **Wt:** 182 **Born:** 10/28/76 **Age:** 25

Year Team	Lg Org	G	AB	H	2B	3B	HR	TB	R	RBI	TBB	IBB	SO	HBP	SH	SF	SB	CS	SB%	GDP	Avg	OBP	SLG
1998 Elizabethtn	R+ Min	55	194	56	16	1	12	110	37	54	29	1	55	2	0	3	4	4	.50	2	.289	.382	.567
1999 Quad City	A Min	125	425	102	30	3	13	177	65	73	78	1	85	7	1	8	6	6	.50	12	.240	.361	.416
2000 Fort Myers	A+ Min	130	450	125	29	3	10	190	60	56	54	2	91	5	5	4	6	3	.67	12	.278	.359	.422
2001 New Britain	AA Min	44	139	24	4	1	1	33	16	6	14	0	39	2	0	0	1	2	.33	2	.173	.258	.237
Fort Myers	A+ Min	61	221	52	13	0	7	86	35	27	36	1	51	4	0	1	3	1	.75	3	.235	.351	.389
4 Min. YEARS		415	1429	359	92	8	43	596	213	216	211	5	321	20	6	16	20	16	.56	31	.251	.352	.417

Kerry Hodges

Bats: Right **Throws:** Right **Pos:** OF-45; DH-5; 2B-2   **Ht:** 6'4" **Wt:** 220 **Born:** 11/7/79 **Age:** 22

Year Team	Lg Org	G	AB	H	2B	3B	HR	TB	R	RBI	TBB	IBB	SO	HBP	SH	SF	SB	CS	SB%	GDP	Avg	OBP	SLG
2001 Martinsvlle	R+ Hou	49	179	44	15	0	1	62	19	16	8	0	43	8	3	2	5	5	.50	2	.246	.305	.346
Round Rock	AA Hou	1	3	0	0	0	0	0	0	0	0	0	2	0	0	0	0	0	—	0	.000	.000	.000
1 Min. YEAR		50	182	44	15	0	1	62	19	16	8	0	45	8	3	2	5	5	.50	2	.242	.300	.341

Kevin Hodges

Pitches: Right **Bats:** Right **Pos:** SP-14   **Ht:** 6'4" **Wt:** 200 **Born:** 6/24/73 **Age:** 29

Year Team	Lg Org	G	GS	CG	GF	IP	BFP	H	R	ER	HR	SH	SF	HB	TBB	IBB	SO	WP	Bk	W	L	Pct.	ShO	Sv	ERA
1991 Royals	R KC	9	3	0	0	23	104	22	14	11	0	1	1	4	11	0	13	2	0	1	2	.333	0	0	4.30
1992 Royals	R KC	11	9	0	0	49.2	232	60	30	26	1	2	2	4	25	0	24	1	1	5	3	.625	0	0	4.71
1993 Royals	R KC	12	10	0	2	71	299	52	25	16	0	5	0	7	25	0	40	3	0	7	2	.778	0	0	2.03
Wilmington	A+ KC	3	0	0	1	4.2	18	2	0	0	0	1	0	1	3	0	1	0	0	1	0	1.000	0	0	0.00
1994 Rockford	A KC	24	17	2	6	114.1	466	96	53	43	5	3	0	9	35	1	83	7	3	9	6	.600	1	3	3.38
1995 Wilmington	A+ KC	12	10	0	1	53.2	232	53	31	27	1	1	1	3	25	1	27	4	0	2	3	.400	0	0	4.53
1996 Lansing	A KC	9	9	0	0	48.1	208	47	32	25	3	2	1	6	19	0	23	3	1	1	2	.333	0	0	4.66
Wilmington	A+ KC	8	8	0	0	38.2	172	45	30	23	2	0	3	1	18	0	15	5	1	2	4	.333	0	0	5.35
1997 Wilmington	A+ KC	28	20	0	4	124.2	563	150	78	62	11	3	6	5	44	7	63	5	2	8	11	.421	0	1	4.48
1998 Jackson	AA Hou	29	15	0	4	107.1	462	108	55	43	8	5	2	7	38	3	70	6	2	4	5	.444	0	0	3.61
1999 Jackson	AA Hou	8	8	0	0	49	211	48	22	16	0	2	2	3	16	0	21	0	0	1	4	.200	0	0	2.94
New Orleans	AAA Hou	5	5	0	0	27.1	126	34	23	22	6	0	2	1	11	1	16	0	0	1	3	.250	0	0	7.24
Tacoma	AAA Sea	18	1	0	1	83	358	88	31	30	3	3	1	9	27	1	42	3	0	3	3	.500	0	1	3.25
2000 Tacoma	AAA Sea	30	11	2	6	98	393	87	32	30	3	3	3	8	21	1	73	1	0	4	3	.571	1	3	2.76
2001 Tacoma	AAA Sea	14	14	2	0	86.2	374	97	50	40	8	0	2	6	25	0	55	1	1	5	5	.500	1	0	4.15
2000 Seattle	AL	13	0	0	7	17.1	73	18	10	10	4	0	1	2	12	0	7	1	0	0	0	—	0	0	5.19
11 Min. YEARS		216	151	6	25	979.1	4218	989	506	410	51	31	26	74	343	15	566	41	11	54	56	.491	3	8	3.80

Scott Hodges

Bats: Left **Throws:** Right **Pos:** 3B-76; DH-6; PH-4   **Ht:** 6'0" **Wt:** 190 **Born:** 12/26/78 **Age:** 23

						BATTING											BASERUNNING				PERCENTAGES		
Year Team	Lg Org	G	AB	H	2B	3B	HR	TB	R	RBI	TBB	IBB	SO	HBP	SH	SF	SB	CS	SB%	GDP	Avg	OBP	SLG
1997 Expos	R Mon	57	198	47	13	2	2	70	27	23	24	1	48	2	1	3	2	2	.50	2	.237	.322	.354
1998 Vermont	A- Mon	67	266	74	13	3	3	102	35	35	11	1	59	1	2	4	8	1	.89	3	.278	.305	.383
1999 Cape Fear	A Mon	127	449	116	31	2	8	175	62	59	45	2	105	3	1	9	8	15	.35	11	.258	.324	.390
2000 Jupiter	A+ Mon	111	422	129	32	1	14	205	75	83	49	6	66	3	2	11	8	2	.80	8	.306	.373	.486
Harrisburg	AA Mon	6	17	3	0	0	1	6	2	5	2	2	4	0	0	2	1	0	1.00	1	.176	.238	.353
2001 Harrisburg	AA Mon	85	305	84	11	2	5	114	30	32	25	5	56	0	0	2	3	2	.60	4	.275	.328	.374
5 Min. YEARS		453	1657	453	100	10	33	672	231	237	156	17	338	9	6	31	30	22	.58	28	.273	.334	.406

Aaron Holbert

Bats: Right **Throws:** Right **Pos:** 2B-29; 3B-13; DH-12; SS-2; OF-1   **Ht:** 6'0" **Wt:** 160 **Born:** 1/9/73 **Age:** 29

						BATTING											BASERUNNING				PERCENTAGES		
Year Team	Lg Org	G	AB	H	2B	3B	HR	TB	R	RBI	TBB	IBB	SO	HBP	SH	SF	SB	CS	SB%	GDP	Avg	OBP	SLG
1990 Johnson Cty	R+ StL	54	176	30	4	1	1	39	27	18	24	1	33	3	1	1	3	5	.38	2	.170	.279	.222
1991 Springfield	A StL	59	215	48	5	1	1	58	22	24	15	0	26	6	1	2	5	8	.38	3	.223	.290	.270
1992 Savannah	A StL	119	438	117	17	4	1	145	53	34	40	0	57	8	6	3	62	25	.71	4	.267	.337	.331
1993 St. Pete	A+ StL	121	457	121	18	3	2	151	60	31	28	2	61	4	15	1	45	22	.67	6	.265	.312	.330
1994 Cardinals	R StL	5	12	2	0	0	0	2	3	0	2	0	2	0	0	0	2	0	1.00	0	.167	.286	.167
Arkansas	AA StL	59	233	69	10	6	2	97	41	19	14	0	25	2	4	1	9	7	.56	5	.296	.340	.416
1995 Louisville	AAA StL	112	401	103	16	4	9	154	57	40	20	1	60	5	3	5	14	6	.70	10	.257	.297	.384
1996 Louisville	AAA StL	112	436	115	16	6	4	155	54	32	21	0	61	2	5	4	20	14	.59	8	.264	.298	.356
1997 Louisville	AAA StL	93	314	80	14	3	4	112	32	32	15	1	56	2	3	4	9	5	.64	9	.255	.290	.357
1998 Orlando	AA Sea	68	251	72	13	5	3	104	46	34	22	0	41	5	4	1	10	14	.42	3	.287	.355	.414
Tacoma	AAA Sea	56	229	72	12	0	9	111	38	31	12	0	40	3	2	1	6	6	.50	3	.314	.355	.485
1999 Durham	AAA TB	100	347	108	18	4	12	170	77	56	25	0	56	5	5	8	14	5	.74	4	.311	.361	.490
2000 Pawtucket	AAA Bos	80	294	74	13	2	3	100	38	23	15	0	54	4	1	0	8	6	.57	4	.252	.297	.340
Calgary	AAA Fla	29	104	29	5	1	4	48	18	18	10	0	12	1	0	0	3	4	.43	2	.279	.348	.462
2001 Syracuse	AAA Tor	55	212	52	10	2	2	72	25	19	8	1	33	2	5	3	9	0	1.00	4	.245	.276	.340
1996 St. Louis	NL	1	3	0	0	0	0	0	0	0	0	0	0	0	0	0	0	0	—	0	.000	.000	.000
12 Min. YEARS		1122	4119	1092	171	42	57	1518	591	411	271	6	617	52	40	31	219	127	.63	67	.265	.316	.369

Damon Hollins

Bats: Right **Throws:** Left **Pos:** OF-90; DH-19; PH-4   **Ht:** 5'11" **Wt:** 180 **Born:** 6/12/74 **Age:** 28

						BATTING											BASERUNNING				PERCENTAGES		
Year Team	Lg Org	G	AB	H	2B	3B	HR	TB	R	RBI	TBB	IBB	SO	HBP	SH	SF	SB	CS	SB%	GDP	Avg	OBP	SLG
1992 Braves	R Atl	49	179	41	12	1	1	58	35	15	30	0	22	2	2	0	15	2	.88	3	.229	.346	.324
1993 Danville	R+ Atl	62	240	77	15	2	7	117	37	51	19	0	30	1	0	3	10	2	.83	5	.321	.369	.488
1994 Durham	A+ Atl	131	485	131	28	6	23	228	76	88	45	0	115	4	2	3	12	7	.63	9	.270	.335	.470
1995 Greenville	AA Atl	129	466	115	26	2	18	199	64	77	44	6	120	4	0	6	6	6	.50	7	.247	.313	.427
1996 Richmond	AAA Atl	42	146	29	9	0	0	38	16	8	16	1	37	0	1	0	2	3	.40	2	.199	.278	.260
1997 Richmond	AAA Atl	134	498	132	31	3	20	229	73	63	45	4	84	3	6	1	7	2	.78	18	.265	.329	.460
1998 Richmond	AAA Atl	119	436	115	26	3	13	186	61	48	45	2	85	0	1	4	10	2	.83	16	.264	.330	.427
1999 Indianapolis	AAA Cin	106	328	86	19	0	9	132	58	43	31	1	44	1	1	0	11	2	.85	13	.262	.328	.402
2000 Indianapolis	AAA Mil	87	287	82	16	3	2	110	33	32	21	0	35	1	0	2	5	3	.63	5	.286	.334	.383
2001 Edmonton	AAA Min	69	232	64	8	2	6	94	29	30	22	0	44	2	2	1	3	3	.50	8	.276	.342	.405
Richmond	AAA Atl	43	160	42	10	2	5	71	27	24	14	2	34	0	0	0	2	2	.50	7	.263	.318	.444
1998 Atlanta	NL	3	6	1	0	0	0	1	0	0	0	0	1	0	0	0	0	0	—	0	.167	.167	.167
Los Angeles	NL	5	9	2	0	0	0	2	1	2	0	0	2	0	0	0	0	1	.00	0	.222	.222	.222
10 Min. YEARS		971	3457	914	200	18	104	1462	509	479	332	16	650	18	15	22	83	34	.71	93	.264	.330	.423

Heath Honeycutt

Bats: Right **Throws:** Right **Pos:** 3B-125; DH-4; PH-3   **Ht:** 6'4" **Wt:** 210 **Born:** 7/30/76 **Age:** 25

						BATTING											BASERUNNING				PERCENTAGES		
Year Team	Lg Org	G	AB	H	2B	3B	HR	TB	R	RBI	TBB	IBB	SO	HBP	SH	SF	SB	CS	SB%	GDP	Avg	OBP	SLG
1998 Utica	A- Fla	68	245	59	8	2	7	92	40	33	25	2	67	6	0	0	11	2	.85	4	.241	.326	.376
1999 Brevard Cty	A+ Fla	103	376	107	18	8	5	156	58	50	25	1	78	9	0	3	6	1	.86	10	.285	.341	.415

Year Team	Lg Org	G	AB	H	2B	3B	HR	TB	R	RBI	TBB	IBB	SO	HBP	SH	SF	SB	CS	SB%	GDP	Avg	OBP	SLG
2000 Portland	AA Fla	50	170	31	4	1	2	43	19	15	12	0	58	4	0	3	3	0	1.00	3	.182	.249	.253
Brevard Cty	A+ Fla	16	54	14	2	0	1	19	8	3	6	1	13	1	0	0	1	0	1.00	3	.259	.344	.352
2001 Portland	AA Fla	132	475	115	24	2	9	170	56	59	41	1	129	12	0	3	10	8	.56	16	.242	.316	.358
4 Min. YEARS		369	1320	326	56	13	24	480	181	160	109	5	345	32	0	9	31	11	.74	36	.247	.318	.364

Jay Hood

Bats: Right **Throws:** Right **Pos:** 3B-12; SS-3; 2B-1; PH-1   **Ht:** 6'0" **Wt:** 185 **Born:** 3/8/77 **Age:** 25

Year Team	Lg Org	G	AB	H	2B	3B	HR	TB	R	RBI	TBB	IBB	SO	HBP	SH	SF	SB	CS	SB%	GDP	Avg	OBP	SLG
1998 Boise	A- Ana	41	132	26	6	0	3	41	20	19	23	0	22	5	0	2	1	1	.50	2	.197	.333	.311
1999 Lk Elsinore	A+ Ana	102	374	88	14	5	3	121	48	43	24	0	81	2	5	6	8	9	.47	7	.235	.281	.324
2000 Lk Elsinore	A+ Ana	26	103	19	3	0	0	22	9	9	4	0	25	2	1	1	1	2	.33	0	.184	.227	.214
Erie	AA Ana	71	240	51	16	0	4	79	25	29	16	0	50	2	1	0	3	0	1.00	6	.213	.267	.329
2001 Arkansas	AA Ana	17	55	16	2	0	1	21	8	9	3	1	15	0	0	0	0	1	.00	2	.291	.328	.382
4 Min. YEARS		257	904	200	41	5	11	284	110	109	70	1	193	11	7	9	13	13	.50	17	.221	.283	.314

Kevin Hooper

Bats: Right **Throws:** Right **Pos:** 2B-134   **Ht:** 5'10" **Wt:** 160 **Born:** 12/7/76 **Age:** 25

Year Team	Lg Org	G	AB	H	2B	3B	HR	TB	R	RBI	TBB	IBB	SO	HBP	SH	SF	SB	CS	SB%	GDP	Avg	OBP	SLG
1999 Utica	A- Fla	73	289	81	18	6	0	111	52	22	39	0	35	4	2	3	14	8	.64	2	.280	.370	.384
2000 Kane County	A Fla	123	457	114	25	6	3	160	73	38	73	2	83	6	9	1	17	2	.89	6	.249	.359	.350
2001 Kane County	A Fla	17	65	19	2	0	0	21	11	4	11	0	13	0	1	0	3	1	.75	0	.292	.390	.323
Portland	AA Fla	117	468	144	19	6	2	181	70	39	59	4	78	7	7	2	24	12	.67	8	.308	.392	.387
3 Min. YEARS		330	1279	358	64	18	5	473	206	103	182	6	209	17	18	7	58	23	.72	16	.280	.375	.370

Dave Hooten

Pitches: Right **Bats:** Right **Pos:** RP-20; SP-9   **Ht:** 6'0" **Wt:** 176 **Born:** 5/8/75 **Age:** 27

Year Team	Lg Org	G	GS	CG	GF	IP	BFP	H	R	ER	HR	SH	SF	HB	TBB	IBB	SO	WP	Bk	W	L	Pct.	ShO	Sv	ERA
1996 Elizabethtn	R+ Min	6	0	0	5	8.1	37	6	4	4	0	0	2	1	5	0	15	0	2	1	0	1.000	0	1	4.32
Fort Wayne	A Min	21	0	0	14	37.1	155	30	11	10	0	2	4	2	13	1	39	3	1	4	1	.800	0	2	2.41
1997 Fort Wayne	A Min	28	27	2	0	165.2	675	134	57	48	5	4	2	9	54	0	138	4	6	11	8	.579	2	0	2.61
1998 Fort Myers	A+ Min	28	28	0	0	158.1	714	185	94	79	7	0	10	11	57	0	136	4	0	9	11	.450	0	0	4.49
1999 New Britain	AA Min	52	5	0	17	103.2	450	94	55	41	10	3	6	1	49	2	89	3	0	6	6	.500	0	1	3.56
2000 New Britain	AA Min	37	2	0	8	61.1	264	59	38	36	6	1	4	4	26	1	64	1	0	4	3	.571	0	1	5.28
Salt Lake	AAA Min	13	0	0	4	27.2	112	26	14	12	7	0	0	0	10	0	15	0	0	1	2	.333	0	1	3.90
2001 Edmonton	AAA Min	7	0	0	1	10	49	17	10	10	1	0	0	1	4	0	4	0	0	1	0	1.000	0	0	9.00
Sonoma Cty	IND —	4	2	0	0	12.2	55	12	6	2	0	0	0	1	3	0	9	0	0	1	0	1.000	0	0	1.42
Akron	AA Cle	17	6	0	8	46	181	43	7	7	3	2	0	1	12	0	31	3	0	4	0	1.000	0	4	1.37
Buffalo	AAA Cle	1	1	0	0	5	20	5	1	1	0	0	0	0	1	0	2	0	0	1	0	1.000	0	0	1.80
6 Min. YEARS		214	71	2	57	636	2712	611	297	250	40	12	28	31	234	4	542	21	9	43	32	.573	2	10	3.54

Shane Hopper

Bats: Right **Throws:** Right **Pos:** OF-68; PH-16; DH-15; 3B-7; 1B-1; PR-1   **Ht:** 6'1" **Wt:** 205 **Born:** 9/22/75 **Age:** 26

Year Team	Lg Org	G	AB	H	2B	3B	HR	TB	R	RBI	TBB	IBB	SO	HBP	SH	SF	SB	CS	SB%	GDP	Avg	OBP	SLG
1999 Johnstown	IND —	83	328	122	27	3	8	179	65	83	34	1	66	4	0	7	12	1	.92	14	.372	.429	.546
2000 Las Vegas	AAA SD	5	21	8	3	0	0	11	3	5	0	0	5	0	0	0	0	0	—	0	.381	.381	.524
Rancho Cuca	A+ SD	108	447	135	28	7	11	210	77	58	28	1	110	5	1	3	15	11	.58	15	.302	.348	.470
2001 Lk Elsinore	A+ SD	31	126	34	7	1	4	55	24	21	11	2	33	0	0	1	5	3	.63	5	.270	.326	.437
Mobile	AA SD	69	191	49	10	0	2	65	27	23	16	2	52	4	2	1	5	4	.56	4	.257	.325	.340
3 Min. YEARS		296	1113	348	75	11	25	520	196	190	89	6	266	13	3	12	37	19	.66	38	.313	.367	.467

Joe Horgan

Pitches: Left **Bats:** Left **Pos:** RP-19; SP-15   **Ht:** 6'1" **Wt:** 200 **Born:** 6/7/77 **Age:** 25

Year Team	Lg Org	G	GS	CG	GF	IP	BFP	H	R	ER	HR	SH	SF	HB	TBB	IBB	SO	WP	Bk	W	L	Pct.	ShO	Sv	ERA
1996 Burlington	R+ Cle	23	0	0	18	34.1	157	37	25	16	1	0	0	4	9	0	48	4	0	1	2	.333	0	7	4.19
1997 Watertown	A- Cle	15	4	0	2	38.1	179	48	31	26	4	2	2	1	18	1	31	4	1	0	1	.000	0	0	6.10
Kinston	A+ Cle	4	2	0	0	17.1	83	23	15	14	1	1	0	1	9	0	9	0	0	1	2	.333	0	0	7.27
1998 Columbus	A Cle	22	1	0	9	34	134	19	9	9	3	0	0	0	21	0	27	7	0	2	1	.667	0	0	2.38
1999 Bakersfield	A+ SF	25	19	1	1	117.1	520	129	76	68	18	2	2	10	43	0	101	5	2	6	10	.375	0	0	5.22
2000 San Jose	A+ SF	27	27	1	0	166.1	739	190	104	85	15	5	6	14	66	0	92	14	0	14	10	.583	0	0	4.60
Shreveport	AA SF	1	0	0	1	5.1	20	2	2	2	0	0	0	0	1	0	3	0	0	0	0	—	0	0	3.38
2001 Shreveport	AA SF	31	14	0	3	103.2	438	97	51	42	10	6	7	4	27	1	61	2	0	3	5	.375	0	1	3.65
Fresno	AAA SF	3	1	0	0	7.2	36	11	5	5	1	0	0	0	3	0	5	0	0	0	0	—	0	0	5.87
6 Min. YEARS		151	68	2	34	524.1	2306	556	318	267	53	16	17	34	198	3	377	36	3	27	31	.466	0	8	4.58

Jeff Horn

Bats: Right **Throws:** Right **Pos:** C-48; PH-17; 1B-7; 3B-2; DH-1   **Ht:** 6'1" **Wt:** 213 **Born:** 8/23/70 **Age:** 31

Year Team	Lg Org	G	AB	H	2B	3B	HR	TB	R	RBI	TBB	IBB	SO	HBP	SH	SF	SB	CS	SB%	GDP	Avg	OBP	SLG
1992 Elizabethtn	R+ Min	41	144	35	6	0	1	44	20	26	25	1	25	4	0	2	2	0	1.00	2	.243	.366	.306
1993 Fort Wayne	A Min	66	200	39	7	0	5	61	19	23	18	0	51	4	1	4	1	2	.33	3	.195	.270	.305
1994 Fort Myers	A+ Min	34	100	28	3	0	0	31	10	9	8	1	11	3	0	1	0	2	.00	6	.280	.348	.310

Year Team	Lg Org	G	AB	H	2B	3B	HR	TB	R	RBI	TBB	IBB	SO	HBP	SH	SF	SB	CS	SB%	GDP	Avg	OBP	SLG
								BATTING									BASERUNNING				PERCENTAGES		
1995 Salt Lake	AAA Min	3	10	5	1	0	0	6	0	2	0	0	1	0	0	0	0	0	—	0	.500	.500	.600
Fort Myers	A+ Min	66	199	53	5	1	0	60	25	20	38	1	30	4	1	3	2	3	.40	4	.266	.389	.302
1996 Salt Lake	AAA Min	25	83	28	5	0	3	42	14	13	12	1	5	2	2	2	0	1	.00	4	.337	.424	.506
Hardware Cy	AA Min	12	45	12	2	0	0	14	4	3	6	1	7	0	0	0	0	1	.00	0	.267	.353	.311
1997 New Britain	AA Min	56	184	47	10	0	4	69	17	26	19	0	24	7	2	2	2	4	.33	7	.255	.344	.375
Salt Lake	AAA Min	23	78	26	6	0	1	35	16	13	11	0	22	1	0	0	0	0	—	0	.333	.422	.449
1998 Salt Lake	AAA Min	24	72	22	5	0	1	30	14	6	12	0	18	1	2	0	1	2	.33	0	.306	.412	.417
1999 Greenville	AA Atl	66	166	38	6	0	2	50	19	27	16	0	28	4	0	3	1	2	.33	0	.229	.307	.301
2000 Richmond	AAA Atl	13	32	6	3	0	1	12	2	5	3	0	11	1	1	0	0	0	—	0	.188	.278	.375
2001 Greenville	AA Atl	72	187	48	10	0	2	64	18	16	26	0	42	1	1	0	1	0	1.00	8	.257	.347	.342
10 Min. YEARS		501	1500	387	69	1	20	518	178	189	194	5	275	32	9	19	9	16	.36	41	.258	.351	.345

Jim Horner

Bats: Right Throws: Right Pos: C-65
Ht: 6'0" Wt: 210 Born: 11/11/73 Age: 28

Year Team	Lg Org	G	AB	H	2B	3B	HR	TB	R	RBI	TBB	IBB	SO	HBP	SH	SF	SB	CS	SB%	GDP	Avg	OBP	SLG
								BATTING									BASERUNNING				PERCENTAGES		
1996 Everett	A- Sea	18	60	9	2	0	2	17	6	5	10	1	16	1	0	0	0	0	—	0	.150	.282	.283
1997 Wisconsin	A Sea	47	161	40	10	1	5	67	19	24	17	0	53	5	1	1	0	1	.00	4	.248	.337	.416
Lancaster	A+ Sea	45	163	42	6	0	9	75	26	27	16	0	48	2	0	1	2	0	1.00	4	.258	.330	.460
1998 Orlando	AA Sea	73	247	54	9	1	9	92	29	36	33	0	59	3	1	5	2	1	.67	5	.219	.313	.372
1999 New Haven	AA Sea	76	278	75	17	0	6	110	29	50	17	0	51	4	1	2	1	1	.50	10	.270	.319	.396
2000 New Haven	AA Sea	65	245	59	11	2	6	101	36	33	20	1	42	5	0	2	4	1	.80	7	.241	.309	.412
2001 Tacoma	AAA Sea	65	236	67	16	0	6	101	45	29	10	1	41	12	2	2	1	0	1.00	7	.284	.342	.428
6 Min. YEARS		389	1390	346	71	4	46	563	190	204	123	3	310	32	5	13	10	4	.71	38	.249	.322	.405

Craig House

Pitches: Right Bats: Right Pos: RP-54
Ht: 6'2" Wt: 221 Born: 7/8/77 Age: 24

Year Team	Lg Org	G	GS	CG	GF	IP	BFP	H	R	ER	HR	SH	SF	HB	TBB	IBB	SO	WP	Bk	W	L	Pct.	ShO	Sv	ERA
		HOW MUCH HE PITCHED						WHAT HE GAVE UP												THE RESULTS					
1999 Portland	A- Col	26	0	0	19	34.2	154	28	14	8	0	1	0	5	14	0	58	4	2	2	1	.667	0	11	2.08
2000 Salem	A+ Col	13	0	0	12	16	69	7	4	4	0	1	0	2	10	0	24	7	0	2	0	1.000	0	8	2.25
Carolina	AA Col	18	0	0	14	21.1	96	14	11	9	0	1	1	0	15	0	28	6	0	0	2	.000	0	9	3.80
Colo Sprngs	AAA Col	8	0	0	8	8.1	32	6	4	3	0	0	1	1	2	0	8	1	0	0	0	—	0	4	3.24
2001 Colo Sprngs	AAA Col	54	0	0	21	58.2	260	50	32	29	4	4	3	6	31	1	62	9	0	2	2	.500	0	6	4.45
2000 Colorado	NL	16	0	0	3	13.2	69	13	11	11	3	0	1	2	17	0	8	0	0	1	1	.500	0	0	7.24
3 Min. YEARS		119	0	0	74	139	611	105	65	53	4	6	6	14	72	1	180	27	2	6	5	.545	0	38	3.43

J.R. House

Bats: Right Throws: Right Pos: C-88; 1B-12; DH-10; PH-2
Ht: 6'1" Wt: 202 Born: 11/11/79 Age: 22

Year Team	Lg Org	G	AB	H	2B	3B	HR	TB	R	RBI	TBB	IBB	SO	HBP	SH	SF	SB	CS	SB%	GDP	Avg	OBP	SLG
								BATTING									BASERUNNING				PERCENTAGES		
1999 Pirates	R Pit	33	113	37	9	3	5	67	13	23	11	0	23	2	0	1	1	0	1.00	1	.327	.394	.593
Williamsprt	A- Pit	26	100	36	6	0	1	39	11	13	9	0	21	0	0	0	0	1	.00	2	.360	.358	.390
Hickory	A Pit	4	11	3	0	0	0	3	1	0	0	0	3	0	0	0	0	0	—	0	.273	.273	.273
2000 Hickory	A Pit	110	420	146	29	1	23	246	78	90	46	2	91	6	0	6	1	2	.33	7	.348	.414	.586
2001 Altoona	AA Pit	112	426	110	25	1	11	170	51	56	37	2	103	5	0	2	1	1	.50	12	.258	.323	.399
3 Min. YEARS		285	1070	326	69	5	40	525	154	182	103	4	241	13	0	9	3	4	.43	22	.305	.370	.491

Ben Howard

Pitches: Right Bats: Right Pos: SP-23; RP-2
Ht: 6'2" Wt: 190 Born: 1/15/79 Age: 23

Year Team	Lg Org	G	GS	CG	GF	IP	BFP	H	R	ER	HR	SH	SF	HB	TBB	IBB	SO	WP	Bk	W	L	Pct.	ShO	Sv	ERA
		HOW MUCH HE PITCHED						WHAT HE GAVE UP												THE RESULTS					
1997 Padres	R SD	13	12	0	1	54.1	281	54	53	45	3	1	0	2	63	0	59	19	7	1	4	.200	0	0	7.45
1998 Idaho Falls	R+ SD	15	15	0	0	68.2	354	67	61	46	2	4	1	4	87	0	79	17	6	4	5	.444	0	0	6.03
1999 Fort Wayne	A SD	28	28	0	0	144.2	666	123	100	76	17	4	3	5	110	0	131	19	1	6	10	.375	0	0	4.73
2000 Rancho Cuca	A+ SD	32	19	0	4	107.1	506	88	87	76	8	2	2	2	111	1	150	14	1	5	11	.313	0	0	6.37
2001 Lk Elsinore	A+ SD	18	18	0	0	101.2	414	86	37	32	4	3	2	1	32	0	107	3	0	8	2	.800	0	0	2.83
Mobile	AA SD	7	5	0	1	30	117	17	9	8	3	0	0	0	15	0	29	3	0	2	0	1.000	0	0	2.40
5 Min. YEARS		113	97	0	6	506.2	2338	435	347	283	37	14	8	14	418	1	555	75	15	26	32	.448	0	0	5.03

David Howard

Bats: Both Throws: Right Pos: 2B-2; PH-2
Ht: 6'0" Wt: 175 Born: 2/26/67 Age: 35

Year Team	Lg Org	G	AB	H	2B	3B	HR	TB	R	RBI	TBB	IBB	SO	HBP	SH	SF	SB	CS	SB%	GDP	Avg	OBP	SLG
								BATTING									BASERUNNING				PERCENTAGES		
1987 Fort Myers	A+ KC	89	289	56	9	4	1	76	26	19	30	0	68	0	7	0	11	10	.52	3	.194	.270	.263
1988 Appleton	A KC	110	368	82	9	4	1	102	48	22	25	0	80	2	4	3	7	5	.58	3	.223	.274	.277
1989 Baseball Cy	A+ KC	83	267	63	7	3	3	85	36	30	23	1	44	1	3	2	12	2	.86	1	.236	.297	.318
1990 Memphis	AA KC	116	384	96	10	4	5	129	41	44	39	0	73	1	10	6	15	4	.79	2	.250	.316	.336
1991 Omaha	AAA KC	14	41	5	0	0	0	5	2	2	7	0	11	1	2	0	1	1	.50	0	.122	.265	.122
1992 Baseball Cy	A+ KC	3	9	4	1	0	0	5	3	0	2	0	0	0	0	0	0	0	—	0	.444	.545	.556
Omaha	AAA KC	19	68	8	1	0	0	9	5	5	3	0	8	0	2	2	1	0	1.00	0	.118	.151	.132
1993 Omaha	AAA KC	47	157	40	8	2	0	52	15	18	7	0	20	1	4	3	3	1	.75	3	.255	.286	.331
1999 Memphis	AAA StL	8	19	5	0	0	0	5	3	2	1	0	6	1	0	1	2	1	1.00	0	.263	.318	.263
2001 Norfolk	AAA NYM	8	16	2	1	0	0	2	0	0	0	0	4	0	0	0	0	0	—	0	.125	.125	.250
1991 Kansas City	AL	94	236	51	7	0	1	61	20	17	16	0	45	1	9	2	5	3	.60	1	.216	.267	.258
1992 Kansas City	AL	74	219	49	6	2	1	62	19	18	15	0	43	0	8	2	3	4	.43	0	.224	.271	.283
1993 Kansas City	AL	15	24	8	0	1	0	10	5	2	2	0	5	0	2	1	1	0	1.00	0	.333	.370	.417
1994 Kansas City	AL	46	83	19	4	0	1	26	9	13	11	0	23	0	3	1	3	2	.60	1	.229	.309	.313

Year Team	Lg Org	G	AB	H	2B	3B	HR	TB	R	RBI	TBB	IBB	SO	HBP	SH	SF	SB	CS	SB%	GDP	Avg	OBP	SLG
																	BASERUNNING				PERCENTAGES		
1995 Kansas City	AL	95	255	62	13	4	0	83	23	19	24	1	41	1	6	1	6	1	.86	7	.243	.310	.325
1996 Kansas City	AL	143	420	92	14	5	4	128	51	48	40	1	74	4	17	4	5	6	.45	6	.219	.291	.305
1997 Kansas City	AL	80	162	39	8	1	1	52	24	13	10	1	31	1	3	1	2	2	.50	1	.241	.287	.321
1998 St. Louis	NL	46	102	25	1	1	2	34	15	12	12	2	22	0	2	1	0	0	—	0	.245	.322	.333
1999 St. Louis	NL	52	82	17	4	0	1	24	3	6	7	3	27	2	1	0	0	2	.00	0	.207	.286	.293
9 Min. YEARS		493	1610	360	46	17	10	470	179	142	137	1	314	7	32	17	52	23	.69	23	.224	.285	.292
9 Maj. YEARS		645	1583	362	57	14	11	480	169	148	137	7	311	9	51	15	23	19	.55	21	.229	.291	.303

Thomas Howard

Bats: Both   Throws: Right   Pos: OF-26; DH-23; PH-8

Ht: 6'2"   Wt: 205   Born: 12/11/64   Age: 37

Year Team	Lg Org	G	AB	H	2B	3B	HR	TB	R	RBI	TBB	IBB	SO	HBP	SH	SF	SB	CS	SB%	GDP	Avg	OBP	SLG
																	BASERUNNING				PERCENTAGES		
1986 Spokane	A- SD	13	55	23	3	3	2	38	16	17	3	0	9	1	0	0	2	1	.67	0	.418	.458	.691
Reno	A+ SD	61	223	57	7	3	10	100	35	39	34	1	49	0	1	3	10	2	.83	3	.256	.350	.448
1987 Wichita	AA SD	113	401	133	27	4	14	210	72	60	36	9	72	1	8	1	26	8	.76	8	.332	.387	.524
1988 Las Vegas	AAA SD	44	167	42	9	1	0	53	29	15	12	2	31	1	1	0	3	4	.43	5	.251	.306	.317
Wichita	AA SD	29	103	31	9	2	0	44	15	16	13	0	14	0	0	0	6	3	.67	3	.301	.379	.427
1989 Las Vegas	AAA SD	80	303	91	18	3	3	124	45	31	30	1	56	0	3	1	22	11	.67	6	.300	.362	.409
1990 Las Vegas	AAA SD	89	341	112	26	8	5	169	58	51	44	5	63	0	4	4	27	5	.84	5	.328	.401	.496
1991 Las Vegas	AAA SD	25	94	29	3	1	2	40	22	16	10	3	16	0	1	0	11	5	.69	1	.309	.368	.426
1996 Chattanooga	AA Cin	8	30	10	1	0	1	14	4	2	2	0	7	0	0	0	1	1	.50	0	.333	.375	.467
Indianapols	AAA Cin	1	5	2	0	0	1	5	2	2	0	0	0	0	0	0	0	0	—	0	.400	.400	1.000
1999 Memphis	AAA StL	35	119	43	10	2	2	63	24	21	13	0	21	1	1	1	1	2	.33	2	.361	.425	.529
2000 Memphis	AAA StL	17	34	9	2	0	0	11	7	5	7	1	6	2	0	0	0	1	.00	0	.265	.419	.324
2001 Nashville	AAA Pit	13	30	6	2	0	0	8	2	1	2	0	7	1	0	0	0	0	—	0	.200	.273	.267
Camden	IND —	43	150	46	12	0	4	70	20	23	22	0	18	0	0	1	1	0	1.00	5	.307	.393	.467
1990 San Diego	NL	20	44	12	2	0	0	14	4	0	0	0	11	0	1	0	0	1	.00	1	.273	.273	.318
1991 San Diego	NL	106	281	70	12	3	4	100	30	22	24	4	57	1	2	1	10	7	.59	4	.249	.309	.356
1992 San Diego	NL	5	3	1	0	0	0	1	1	0	0	0	0	0	1	0	0	0	—	0	.333	.333	.333
Cleveland	AL	117	358	99	15	2	2	124	36	32	17	1	60	0	10	2	15	8	.65	4	.277	.308	.346
1993 Cleveland	AL	74	178	42	7	0	3	58	26	23	12	0	42	0	0	4	5	1	.83	5	.236	.278	.326
Cincinnati	NL	38	141	39	8	3	4	65	22	13	12	0	21	0	0	1	5	6	.45	4	.277	.331	.461
1994 Cincinnati	NL	83	178	47	11	0	5	73	24	24	10	1	30	0	3	1	4	2	.67	2	.264	.302	.410
1995 Cincinnati	NL	113	281	85	15	2	3	113	42	26	20	0	37	1	1	1	17	8	.68	3	.302	.350	.402
1996 Cincinnati	NL	121	360	98	19	10	6	155	50	42	17	3	51	3	2	0	6	5	.55	5	.272	.307	.431
1997 Houston	NL	107	255	63	16	1	3	90	24	22	26	1	48	3	1	1	2	4	.33	3	.247	.323	.353
1998 Los Angeles	NL	47	76	14	4	0	2	24	9	4	3	0	15	0	0	0	1	0	1.00	3	.184	.215	.316
1999 St. Louis	NL	98	195	57	10	0	6	85	16	28	17	0	26	2	0	1	1	1	.50	3	.292	.353	.436
2000 St. Louis	NL	86	133	28	4	1	6	52	13	28	7	0	34	1	0	0	1	0	1.00	3	.211	.255	.391
10 Min. YEARS		571	2055	634	129	27	44	949	351	299	228	22	369	7	19	13	110	43	.72	40	.309	.377	.462
11 Maj. YEARS		1015	2483	655	123	22	44	954	297	264	165	10	432	11	21	16	66	41	.62	39	.264	.311	.384

Tom Howard

Pitches: Left   Bats: Right   Pos: RP-36; SP-1

Ht: 6'5"   Wt: 211   Born: 7/29/75   Age: 26

Year Team	Lg Org	G	GS	CG	GF	IP	BFP	H	R	ER	HR	SH	SF	HB	TBB	IBB	SO	WP	Bk	W	L	Pct.	ShO	Sv	ERA
1993 Marlins	R Fla	8	6	1	0	34	151	35	16	12	0	0	2	0	20	0	31	5	0	2	4	.333	0	0	3.18
1994 Marlins	R Fla	11	4	0	2	32	157	28	22	21	0	1	0	2	34	0	37	8	0	1	2	.333	0	1	5.91
1995 Elmira	A- Fla	10	0	0	0	13.1	69	9	13	11	0	0	1	0	21	0	7	0	0	0	0	—	0	0	7.43
1998 Chston-SC	A TB	33	0	0	8	51.1	234	55	25	18	2	3	0	2	25	1	39	8	0	3	3	.500	0	0	3.16
1999 Quad City	A Min	15	1	0	4	29.1	118	26	6	5	1	0	0	0	4	0	22	2	0	2	1	.667	0	0	1.53
Fort Myers	A+ Min	22	0	0	14	42.2	194	43	28	24	3	1	3	2	25	0	22	4	0	1	2	.333	0	0	5.06
2000 Fort Myers	A+ Min	27	2	0	3	59	268	65	32	27	2	1	3	2	21	0	52	3	0	2	2	.500	0	2	4.12
New Britain	AA Min	13	2	0	5	24.2	114	32	12	10	1	0	0	1	13	0	8	1	0	0	1	.000	0	0	3.65
2001 New Britain	AA Min	4	0	0	2	4	21	6	4	4	0	0	0	1	4	0	2	0	0	0	0	—	0	0	9.00
Fort Myers	A+ Min	33	1	0	12	58.1	286	58	45	39	6	3	4	1	64	1	57	14	1	6	3	.667	0	0	6.02
7 Min. YEARS		176	16	1	54	348.2	1612	357	203	171	15	9	13	11	231	2	277	51	1	17	18	.486	0	3	4.41

Ty Howington

Pitches: Left   Bats: Both   Pos: SP-20

Ht: 6'4"   Wt: 225   Born: 11/4/80   Age: 21

Year Team	Lg Org	G	GS	CG	GF	IP	BFP	H	R	ER	HR	SH	SF	HB	TBB	IBB	SO	WP	Bk	W	L	Pct.	ShO	Sv	ERA
2000 Dayton	A Cin	27	26	0	0	141.2	656	150	91	83	7	3	8	13	86	1	119	19	1	5	15	.250	0	0	5.27
2001 Dayton	A Cin	6	6	1	0	39	141	15	7	5	0	0	2	1	9	0	47	0	0	4	0	1.000	0	0	1.15
Mudville	A+ Cin	7	7	0	0	37	168	33	18	10	2	2	1	4	20	0	44	2	0	3	2	.600	0	0	2.43
Chattanooga	AA Cin	7	7	0	0	41.1	181	36	18	15	3	3	2	2	24	1	38	4	1	1	3	.250	0	0	3.27
2 Min. YEARS		47	46	1	0	259	1146	234	134	113	12	8	13	20	139	2	248	25	2	13	20	.394	0	0	3.93

Travis Hubbel

Pitches: Right   Bats: Right   Pos: SP-9; RP-9

Ht: 6'0"   Wt: 190   Born: 6/27/79   Age: 23

Year Team	Lg Org	G	GS	CG	GF	IP	BFP	H	R	ER	HR	SH	SF	HB	TBB	IBB	SO	WP	Bk	W	L	Pct.	ShO	Sv	ERA
1999 St.Cathrnes	A- Tor	5	3	0	2	20	83	16	5	4	1	0	0	1	7	0	19	0	0	0	0	—	0	1	1.80
2000 Hagerstown	A Tor	19	19	0	0	113.1	478	103	62	50	7	3	3	10	55	0	75	13	0	8	6	.571	0	0	3.97
Dunedin	A+ Tor	3	0	0	0	5.1	20	4	2	2	2	1	0	0	2	0	3	1	0	0	0	—	0	0	3.38
2001 Tennessee	AA Tor	6	5	0	0	26.2	114	20	11	10	3	1	1	3	18	0	12	2	0	1	0	1.000	0	0	3.38
Dunedin	A+ Tor	12	4	0	2	29.1	146	26	31	20	3	0	2	6	25	0	20	11	0	1	3	.250	0	0	6.14
3 Min. YEARS		45	31	0	5	194.2	841	169	111	86	16	5	6	20	107	0	129	27	0	10	9	.526	0	1	3.98

Luke Hudson

Pitches: Right Bats: Right Pos: SP-28; RP-1   Ht: 6'3" Wt: 195 Born: 5/2/77 Age: 25

Year Team	Lg Org	G	GS	CG	GF	IP	BFP	H	R	ER	HR	SH	SF	HB	TBB	IBB	SO	WP	Bk	W	L	Pct.	ShO	Sv	ERA
1998 Portland	A- Col	15	15	0	0	79.2	361	68	46	42	8	1	4	4	51	0	82	8	3	3	6	.333	0	0	4.74
1999 Asheville	A Col	21	20	1	1	88	372	89	47	42	10	2	2	8	24	0	96	3	3	6	5	.545	0	0	4.30
2000 Salem	A+ Col	19	19	2	0	110	462	101	47	40	9	3	4	10	34	0	80	5	1	5	8	.385	2	0	3.27
2001 Carolina	AA Col	29	28	1	0	165	729	159	90	77	19	5	4	15	68	0	145	18	1	7	12	.368	0	0	4.20
4 Min. YEARS		84	82	4	1	442.2	1924	417	230	201	46	11	14	37	177	0	403	34	8	21	31	.404	2	0	4.09

Orlando Hudson

Bats: Both Throws: Right Pos: 2B-125; 3B-18; PR-2; PH-1   Ht: 6'0" Wt: 175 Born: 12/12/77 Age: 24

Year Team	Lg Org	G	AB	H	2B	3B	HR	TB	R	RBI	TBB	IBB	SO	HBP	SH	SF	SB	CS	SB%	GDP	Avg	OBP	SLG
1998 Medcine Hat	R+ Tor	65	242	71	18	1	8	115	50	42	22	0	36	7	0	2	6	5	.55	3	.293	.366	.475
1999 Hagerstown	A Tor	132	513	137	36	6	7	206	66	74	42	3	85	2	1	5	8	6	.57	10	.267	.322	.402
2000 Dunedin	A+ Tor	96	358	102	16	2	7	143	54	48	37	1	42	2	4	1	9	5	.64	15	.285	.354	.399
Tennessee	AA Tor	39	134	32	4	3	2	48	17	15	15	1	18	2	1	2	3	2	.60	3	.239	.320	.358
2001 Tennessee	AA Tor	84	306	94	22	8	4	144	51	52	37	3	42	3	1	2	8	3	.73	12	.307	.385	.471
Syracuse	AAA Tor	55	194	59	14	3	4	91	31	27	23	1	34	2	2	3	11	3	.79	1	.304	.378	.469
4 Min. YEARS		471	1747	495	110	23	32	747	269	258	176	9	257	18	9	15	45	24	.65	44	.283	.352	.428

B.J. Huff

Bats: Right Throws: Right Pos: OF-22; DH-8; 1B-6; PH-3; PR-1   Ht: 6'1" Wt: 189 Born: 8/1/75 Age: 26

Year Team	Lg Org	G	AB	H	2B	3B	HR	TB	R	RBI	TBB	IBB	SO	HBP	SH	SF	SB	CS	SB%	GDP	Avg	OBP	SLG
1996 Pittsfield	A- NYM	42	138	27	4	2	2	41	19	14	7	0	36	1	1	1	3	1	.75	2	.196	.238	.297
1997 Capital Cty	A NYM	99	363	92	20	5	7	143	44	41	19	1	78	4	1	2	11	3	.79	8	.253	.296	.394
1998 St. Lucie	A+ NYM	118	451	117	23	3	11	179	60	60	25	0	108	7	1	6	8	10	.44	14	.259	.305	.397
1999 Binghamton	AA NYM	57	205	51	9	1	7	83	26	32	19	1	46	1	0	2	9	2	.82	4	.249	.313	.405
2000 Binghamton	AA NYM	73	208	44	8	1	4	66	18	24	22	0	79	1	1	1	2	1	.33	3	.212	.289	.317
2001 Binghamton	AA NYM	7	20	1	0	0	0	1	0	0	0	0	13	0	0	0	0	1	.00	0	.050	.050	.050
St. Lucie	A+ NYM	31	106	24	7	0	1	34	12	13	7	0	35	1	0	1	5	4	.56	3	.226	.278	.321
6 Min. YEARS		427	1491	356	71	12	32	547	184	184	99	2	395	15	4	13	37	23	.62	34	.239	.290	.367

Larry Huff

Bats: Right Throws: Right Pos: 2B-12; OF-11; 3B-5; PR-4; PH-3   Ht: 6'0" Wt: 175 Born: 1/24/72 Age: 30

Year Team	Lg Org	G	AB	H	2B	3B	HR	TB	R	RBI	TBB	IBB	SO	HBP	SH	SF	SB	CS	SB%	GDP	Avg	OBP	SLG
1994 Martinsvlle	R+ Phi	39	143	36	2	1	1	43	24	7	29	0	20	6	1	0	17	4	.81	3	.252	.399	.301
Batavia	A- Phi	20	67	15	1	0	0	16	13	2	12	1	10	0	2	0	5	0	1.00	1	.224	.342	.239
1995 Piedmont	A Phi	130	481	131	26	4	1	168	86	51	74	5	64	10	7	4	26	8	.76	9	.272	.378	.349
1996 Clearwater	A+ Phi	128	483	132	17	5	0	159	73	37	60	1	65	6	10	4	37	11	.77	4	.273	.358	.329
1997 Reading	AA Phi	124	425	112	21	3	5	154	58	41	36	3	57	6	6	0	24	7	.77	10	.264	.330	.362
1998 Reading	AA Phi	40	136	46	7	2	7	78	26	25	19	0	15	5	1	1	10	2	.83	4	.338	.435	.574
1999 Reading	AA Phi	121	427	111	28	3	3	154	72	54	60	1	69	10	6	8	28	6	.82	11	.260	.358	.361
Scranton-WB	AAA Phi	9	17	4	2	0	0	6	4	1	5	0	2	1	0	0	0	0	—	0	.235	.435	.353
2000 Wichita	AA KC	83	290	87	14	1	3	112	48	43	51	0	48	3	7	3	13	8	.62	9	.300	.406	.386
2001 Edmonton	AAA Min	27	67	21	2	2	1	30	10	11	7	0	13	0	2	2	2	1	.67	3	.313	.368	.448
8 Min. YEARS		721	2536	695	120	21	21	920	414	272	353	11	363	47	42	22	162	47	.78	54	.274	.370	.363

Royce Huffman

Bats: Right Throws: Right Pos: 3B-134; DH-2; 1B-1; PH-1; PR-1   Ht: 6'0" Wt: 195 Born: 1/11/77 Age: 25

Year Team	Lg Org	G	AB	H	2B	3B	HR	TB	R	RBI	TBB	IBB	SO	HBP	SH	SF	SB	CS	SB%	GDP	Avg	OBP	SLG
1999 Martinsvlle	R+ Hou	53	196	58	16	7	2	94	39	36	31	0	29	4	0	4	18	2	.90	2	.296	.396	.480
2000 Kissimmee	A+ Hou	129	450	134	32	4	5	189	82	55	84	2	49	6	1	6	31	4	.89	12	.298	.410	.420
Round Rock	AA Hou	4	17	6	1	0	0	7	2	2	0	0	2	1	0	0	1	1	.50	1	.353	.389	.412
2001 Round Rock	AA Hou	137	511	158	35	1	4	207	75	49	51	0	90	12	3	4	13	8	.62	6	.309	.382	.405
3 Min. YEARS		323	1174	356	84	12	11	497	198	142	166	2	170	23	4	14	63	15	.81	21	.303	.396	.423

Bobby Hughes

Bats: Right Throws: Right Pos: C-1   Ht: 6'4" Wt: 229 Born: 3/10/71 Age: 31

Year Team	Lg Org	G	AB	H	2B	3B	HR	TB	R	RBI	TBB	IBB	SO	HBP	SH	SF	SB	CS	SB%	GDP	Avg	OBP	SLG
1992 Helena	R+ Mil	11	40	7	1	1	0	10	5	6	4	0	14	2	0	0	0	0	—	0	.175	.283	.250
1993 Beloit	A Mil	98	321	89	11	3	17	157	42	56	23	0	77	6	5	0	1	3	.25	0	.277	.337	.489
1994 El Paso	AA Mil	12	36	10	4	1	0	16	3	12	5	0	7	1	0	2	0	1	.00	1	.278	.364	.444
Stockton	A+ Mil	95	322	81	24	3	11	144	54	53	33	0	83	9	1	2	2	1	.67	8	.252	.336	.447
1995 Stockton	A+ Mil	52	179	42	9	2	8	79	22	31	17	1	41	1	0	3	2	2	.50	10	.235	.300	.441
El Paso	AA Mil	51	173	46	12	0	7	79	11	27	12	1	30	2	0	2	0	2	.00	4	.266	.317	.457
1996 New Orleans	AAA Mil	37	125	25	5	0	4	42	11	15	4	0	31	3	0	0	1	1	.50	2	.200	.242	.336
El Paso	AA Mil	67	237	72	18	1	15	137	43	39	30	1	40	2	0	3	3	3	.50	5	.304	.382	.578
1997 Tucson	AAA Mil	89	290	90	29	2	7	144	43	51	24	1	46	9	0	4	0	0	—	9	.310	.376	.497
1999 Louisville	AAA Mil	10	32	6	2	0	1	11	5	2	2	0	7	1	0	0	0	0	—	0	.188	.257	.344
2000 Buffalo	AAA Cle	69	224	57	13	0	7	91	30	32	15	0	44	6	1	2	2	2	.50	3	.254	.316	.406
2001 Rochester	AAA Bal	1	3	0	0	0	0	0	0	0	0	0	0	0	0	0	0	0	—	0	.000	.000	.000
1998 Milwaukee	NL	85	218	50	7	2	9	88	28	29	16	1	54	1	1	1	1	2	.33	3	.229	.284	.404
1999 Milwaukee	NL	48	101	26	2	0	3	37	10	8	5	0	28	0	0	0	0	0	—	3	.257	.292	.366
9 Min. YEARS		592	1982	525	128	13	77	910	269	324	169	4	420	42	7	18	11	15	.42	44	.265	.333	.459
2 Maj. YEARS		133	319	76	9	2	12	125	38	37	21	1	82	1	1	1	1	2	.33	6	.238	.287	.392

140

Travis Hughes

Pitches: Right **Bats:** Right **Pos:** RP-42; SP-5

Ht: 6'5" Wt: 215 Born: 5/25/78 Age: 24

		HOW MUCH HE PITCHED						WHAT HE GAVE UP										THE RESULTS					
Year Team	Lg Org	G	GS	CG	GF	IP	BFP	H	R	ER	HR	SH	SF	HB	TBB	IBB	SO	WP	Bk	W	L	Pct.	ShO	Sv	ERA
1998 Pulaski	R+ Tex	22	3	0	17	41.2	188	30	25	18	2	0	0	4	25	1	48	8	3	2	6	.250	0	2	3.89
1999 Savannah	A Tex	30	23	1	5	157	646	127	60	49	9	3	3	11	54	0	150	9	2	11	7	.611	0	2	2.81
2000 Charlotte	A+ Tex	39	14	1	19	126.1	553	122	76	62	9	6	1	12	54	3	96	11	0	9	9	.500	0	9	4.42
2001 Tulsa	AA Tex	47	5	0	29	87.1	393	91	52	45	8	3	4	4	45	2	86	2	1	5	7	.417	0	8	4.64
4 Min. YEARS		138	45	2	70	412.1	1780	370	213	174	28	12	8	31	178	6	380	30	6	27	29	.482	0	21	3.80

Jason Huisman

Bats: Right **Throws:** Right **Pos:** 2B-57; OF-26; DH-14; 3B-9; 1B-5; SS-2; PH-2; PR-1

Ht: 6'3" Wt: 195 Born: 4/16/76 Age: 26

		BATTING													BASERUNNING				PERCENTAGES		
Year Team	Lg Org	G	AB	H	2B	3B	HR	TB	R	RBI	TBB	IBB	SO	HBP	SH	SF	SB	CS	SB%	GDP	Avg	OBP	SLG
1998 Boise	A- Ana	73	292	95	20	2	5	134	47	59	27	2	52	9	0	1	5	0	1.00	7	.325	.398	.459
1999 Lk Elsinore	A+ Ana	91	346	95	17	3	3	127	50	43	24	0	64	8	0	4	10	5	.67	8	.275	.332	.367
2000 Erie	AA Ana	120	441	121	23	4	3	161	52	42	40	1	75	9	3	1	14	4	.78	9	.274	.346	.365
2001 Arkansas	AA Ana	109	371	103	22	0	10	155	55	51	39	0	63	4	1	4	4	9	.31	5	.278	.349	.418
4 Min. YEARS		393	1450	414	82	9	21	577	204	195	130	3	254	30	4	10	33	18	.65	29	.286	.354	.398

Rick Huisman

Pitches: Right **Bats:** Right **Pos:** RP-23

Ht: 6'3" Wt: 210 Born: 5/17/69 Age: 33

		HOW MUCH HE PITCHED						WHAT HE GAVE UP										THE RESULTS					
Year Team	Lg Org	G	GS	CG	GF	IP	BFP	H	R	ER	HR	SH	SF	HB	TBB	IBB	SO	WP	Bk	W	L	Pct.	ShO	Sv	ERA
1990 Everett	A- SF	1	0	0	0	2	10	3	1	1	0	0	0	0	2	0	2	1	0	0	0	—	0	0	4.50
Clinton	A SF	14	13	0	0	79	315	57	19	18	2	1	2	0	33	0	103	5	4	6	5	.545	0	0	2.05
1991 San Jose	A+ SF	26	26	7	0	182.1	720	126	45	37	5	11	3	3	73	1	216	13	3	16	4	.800	4	0	1.83
1992 Shreveport	AA SF	17	16	1	0	103.1	403	79	33	27	3	2	0	5	31	1	100	3	1	7	4	.636	1	0	2.35
Phoenix	AAA SF	9	8	0	0	56	230	45	16	15	3	1	1	1	24	0	44	1	0	3	2	.600	0	0	2.41
1993 San Jose	A+ SF	4	4	1	0	23.1	97	19	6	6	0	2	1	2	12	0	15	1	0	2	1	.667	0	0	2.31
Phoenix	AAA SF	14	14	0	0	72.1	333	78	54	48	5	1	1	1	45	0	59	8	4	3	4	.429	0	0	5.97
Tucson	AAA Hou	2	0	0	0	3.2	18	6	5	3	0	0	0	0	1	0	4	5	0	1	0	1.000	0	0	7.36
1994 Jackson	AA Hou	49	0	0	46	50.1	204	32	10	9	1	1	1	2	24	2	63	1	0	3	0	1.000	0	31	1.61
1995 Tucson	AAA Hou	42	0	0	28	54.2	246	58	33	27	1	0	3	1	28	3	47	3	1	6	1	.857	0	6	4.45
Omaha	AAA KC	5	0	0	3	5	19	3	1	1	1	0	0	0	1	0	13	0	0	0	0	—	0	1	1.80
1996 Omaha	AAA KC	27	4	0	6	57.1	243	52	31	31	9	0	1	2	24	0	50	0	1	2	4	.333	0	0	4.87
1997 Omaha	AAA KC	37	1	0	8	59.2	268	59	29	24	7	1	3	3	35	1	57	7	0	1	5	.167	0	2	3.62
1998 Fresno	AAA SF	44	0	0	17	72	309	65	46	43	18	0	2	1	34	2	80	4	0	2	6	.250	0	0	5.38
1999 New Orleans	AAA Hou	35	0	0	15	52.1	217	42	23	21	6	0	1	1	16	2	67	0	0	3	1	.750	0	3	3.61
2000 New Orleans	AAA Hou	48	0	0	27	54.1	217	36	26	21	5	1	2	0	20	1	64	5	0	3	5	.375	0	10	3.48
2001 Rochester	AAA Bal	15	0	0	8	17	84	24	13	12	4	1	1	0	9	1	13	2	0	0	1	.000	0	1	6.35
Memphis	AAA StL	3	0	0	2	15	71	18	17	12	4	1	0	0	9	0	16	1	0	0	0	—	0	0	7.20
1995 Kansas City	AL	7	0	0	2	9.2	44	14	8	8	2	1	0	0	1	0	12	0	0	0	0	—	0	0	7.45
1996 Kansas City	AL	22	0	0	5	29.1	130	25	15	15	4	2	2	0	18	2	23	0	0	2	1	.667	0	1	4.60
12 Min. YEARS		397	86	9	161	959.2	4004	804	406	356	74	23	22	22	421	14	1013	60	14	58	44	.569	5	54	3.34
2 Maj. YEARS		29	0	0	7	39	174	39	23	23	6	3	2	0	19	2	35	0	0	2	1	.667	0	1	5.31

Tim Hummel

Bats: Right **Throws:** Right **Pos:** 2B-93; SS-36; 3B-5

Ht: 6'2" Wt: 195 Born: 11/18/78 Age: 23

		BATTING													BASERUNNING				PERCENTAGES		
Year Team	Lg Org	G	AB	H	2B	3B	HR	TB	R	RBI	TBB	IBB	SO	HBP	SH	SF	SB	CS	SB%	GDP	Avg	OBP	SLG
2000 Burlington	A CWS	39	144	47	9	1	1	61	22	21	21	0	20	1	0	2	8	3	.73	2	.326	.411	.424
Winston-Sal	A+ CWS	27	98	32	7	0	1	42	15	9	13	1	12	2	0	1	1	1	.50	4	.327	.416	.429
2001 Birmingham	AA CWS	134	524	152	33	6	7	218	83	63	62	2	69	5	8	10	14	3	.82	12	.290	.364	.416
2 Min. YEARS		200	766	231	49	7	9	321	120	93	96	3	101	8	8	12	23	7	.77	18	.302	.380	.419

Jeff Hundley

Pitches: Left **Bats:** Left **Pos:** SP-16; RP-7

Ht: 6'2" Wt: 205 Born: 2/19/77 Age: 25

		HOW MUCH HE PITCHED						WHAT HE GAVE UP										THE RESULTS					
Year Team	Lg Org	G	GS	CG	GF	IP	BFP	H	R	ER	HR	SH	SF	HB	TBB	IBB	SO	WP	Bk	W	L	Pct.	ShO	Sv	ERA
1998 Boise	A- Ana	16	16	0	0	92.2	376	77	42	35	7	1	4	2	27	1	89	7	2	8	3	.727	0	0	3.40
1999 Cedar Rapds	A Ana	25	25	6	0	158	698	163	99	71	17	5	8	8	62	0	140	10	2	9	9	.500	1	0	4.04
2000 Edmonton	AAA Ana	2	1	0	0	9.1	47	14	12	12	0	0	3	2	4	0	2	2	0	0	0	.000	0	0	11.57
Erie	AA Ana	10	9	0	0	45	230	74	51	46	10	1	2	2	27	0	21	2	0	0	8	.000	0	0	9.20
Lk Elsinore	A+ Ana	18	15	0	1	97	403	85	48	30	3	5	2	2	36	1	69	6	0	5	5	.500	0	0	2.78
2001 Rancho Cuca	A+ Ana	13	7	0	0	53.2	222	48	25	25	10	3	2	3	17	1	38	1	0	2	1	.667	0	0	4.19
Arkansas	AA Ana	10	9	0	1	54	254	63	48	37	7	4	2	6	25	0	31	2	0	2	6	.250	0	0	6.17
4 Min. YEARS		94	82	6	2	509.2	2230	524	325	256	54	19	23	25	198	3	390	30	4	26	34	.433	1	0	4.52

Brian Hunter

Bats: Right **Throws:** Left **Pos:** 1B-55; DH-13; OF-6; PH-1

Ht: 6'0" Wt: 195 Born: 3/4/68 Age: 34

		BATTING													BASERUNNING				PERCENTAGES		
Year Team	Lg Org	G	AB	H	2B	3B	HR	TB	R	RBI	TBB	IBB	SO	HBP	SH	SF	SB	CS	SB%	GDP	Avg	OBP	SLG
1987 Pulaski	R+ Atl	65	251	58	10	2	8	96	38	30	18	0	47	5	0	1	3	2	.60	7	.231	.295	.382
1988 Burlington	A Atl	117	417	108	17	0	22	191	58	71	45	2	90	8	1	7	7	2	.78	7	.259	.338	.458
Durham	A+ Atl	13	49	17	3	0	3	29	13	9	7	0	9	2	0	0	2	0	1.00	0	.347	.429	.592
1989 Greenville	AA Atl	124	451	114	19	2	19	194	57	82	33	2	61	7	1	9	5	4	.56	4	.253	.308	.430
1990 Richmond	AAA Atl	43	137	27	4	0	5	46	13	16	18	0	37	0	1	2	1	1	.67	0	.197	.288	.336
Greenville	AA Atl	88	320	77	13	1	14	134	45	55	43	1	62	3	0	4	3	4	.43	6	.241	.332	.419

BATTING / BASERUNNING / PERCENTAGES

Year Team	Lg Org	G	AB	H	2B	3B	HR	TB	R	RBI	TBB	IBB	SO	HBP	SH	SF	SB	CS	SB%	GDP	Avg	OBP	SLG
1991 Richmond	AAA Atl	48	181	47	7	0	10	84	28	30	11	1	24	1	2	3	3	2	.60	6	.260	.301	.464
1993 Richmond	AAA Atl	30	99	24	7	0	6	49	16	26	10	0	21	3	0	0	0	1	.00	1	.242	.330	.495
1995 Indianapols	AAA Cin	9	36	13	5	0	4	30	7	11	6	1	11	0	0	0	0	1	.00	0	.361	.452	.833
1996 Tacoma	AAA Sea	25	92	32	6	1	7	61	19	24	9	0	11	0	0	3	1	0	1.00	3	.348	.394	.663
1997 Indianapols	AAA Cin	139	506	142	36	4	21	249	74	85	42	2	76	4	2	8	9	6	.60	3	.281	.336	.492
1998 Calgary	AAA CWS	11	31	3	1	0	0	4	1	6	2	1	9	2	0	2	0	0	—	1	.097	.189	.129
2000 Richmond	AAA Atl	2	8	1	0	0	1	4	2	1	1	0	1	0	0	0	0	1	1.00	1	.125	.222	.500
2001 Atlantic Ct	IND —	42	153	50	14	0	12	100	38	38	19	0	28	3	0	0	0	0	—	1	.327	.411	.654
Syracuse	AAA Tor	30	105	25	5	0	3	39	21	16	15	0	21	3	1	0	1	0	1.00	2	.238	.350	.371
1991 Atlanta	NL	97	271	68	16	1	12	122	32	50	17	0	48	1	0	2		2	.00	6	.251	.296	.450
1992 Atlanta	NL	102	238	57	13	2	14	116	34	41	21	3	50	0	1	8	1	2	.33	2	.239	.292	.487
1993 Atlanta	NL	37	80	11	3	1	0	16	4	8	2	1	15	0	0	3	0	0	—	1	.138	.153	.200
1994 Pittsburgh	NL	76	233	53	15	1	11	103	28	47	15	2	55	0	0	4	0	0	—	3	.227	.270	.442
Cincinnati	NL	9	23	7	1	0	4	20	6	10	2	0	1	0	0	0	0	0	—	0	.304	.346	.870
1995 Cincinnati	NL	40	79	17	6	0	1	26	9	9	11	1	21	1	0	2	2	1	.67	2	.215	.312	.329
1996 Seattle	AL	75	198	53	10	0	7	84	21	28	15	2	43	4	1	3	0	1	.00	6	.268	.327	.424
1998 St. Louis	NL	62	112	23	9	1	4	46	11	13	7	0	23	1	3	0	1	1	.50	4	.205	.258	.411
1999 Atlanta	NL	114	181	45	12	1	6	77	28	30	31	1	40	4	5	2	1	1	.00	6	.249	.367	.425
2000 Atlanta	NL	2	2	1	0	0	1	4	1	1	0	0	0	0	0	0	0	0	—	0	.500	.500	2.000
Philadelphia	NL	85	138	29	5	0	7	55	13	22	20	1	39	0	0	0	0	1	.00	2	.210	.310	.399
12 Min. YEARS		786	2836	738	147	10	135	1310	430	500	279	10	507	39	8	38	41	24	.63	49	.260	.331	.462
9 Maj. YEARS		699	1555	364	90	7	67	669	187	259	141	11	335	11	10	25	4	9	.31	32	.234	.298	.430

Johnny Hunter

Pitches: Right **Bats:** Right **Pos:** SP-21; RP-5   **Ht:** 6'1" **Wt:** 190 **Born:** 6/14/75 **Age:** 27

Year Team	Lg Org	G	GS	CG	GF	IP	BFP	H	R	ER	HR	SH	SF	HB	TBB	IBB	SO	WP	Bk	W	L	Pct.	ShO	Sv	ERA
1997 Idaho Falls	R+ SD	4	0	0	3	5.1	25	4	1	1	0	0	0	0	2	0	0	0	0	0	0	—	0	1	1.69
1998 Clinton	A SD	1	0	0	1	0.1	2	0	0	0	0	0	0	0	0	0	0	0	0	0	0	—	0	0	0.00
1999 Idaho Falls	R+ SD	29	0	0	14	49	240	55	41	30	5	1	0	4	34	0	54	10	0	3	4	.429	0	3	5.51
2000 Fort Wayne	A SD	4	0	0	2	7	32	7	5	4	1	1	0	0	4	0	10	1	0	1	1	.500	0	0	5.14
Rancho Cuca	A+ SD	47	8	0	7	106	469	92	68	55	7	3	6	2	65	0	87	14	4	5	5	.500	0	0	4.67
2001 Lk Elsinore	A+ SD	7	5	0	0	33	134	27	19	14	1	0	0	0	11	0	29	1	0	3		1.000	0	0	3.82
Mobile	AA SD	19	16	1	1	98.1	428	105	57	53	7	5	2	6	37	1	61	1	0	3	6	.333	0	0	4.85
5 Min. YEARS		111	29	1	28	299	1330	290	191	157	21	11	8	12	154	1	241	27	4	15	16	.484	0	4	4.73

Scott Hunter

Bats: Right **Throws:** Right **Pos:** OF-103; DH-19; PH-9   **Ht:** 6'1" **Wt:** 210 **Born:** 12/17/75 **Age:** 26

Year Team	Lg Org	G	AB	H	2B	3B	HR	TB	R	RBI	TBB	IBB	SO	HBP	SH	SF	SB	CS	SB%	GDP	Avg	OBP	SLG
1994 Great Falls	R+ LA	64	237	75	12	4	2	101	45	28	25	1	40	5	4	3	17	5	.77	1	.316	.389	.426
1995 San Berndo	A+ LA	113	379	108	19	3	11	166	68	59	36	1	83	6	4	1	27	8	.77	0	.285	.355	.438
Capital Cty	A NYM	12	40	10	0	0	0	10	2	1	2	0	13	1	1	1	2	1	.67	2	.250	.295	.250
1996 St. Lucie	A+ NYM	127	475	122	19	1	2	149	71	38	38	4	68	8	3	3	49	12	.80	6	.257	.321	.314
1997 Binghamton	AA NYM	80	289	74	12	2	10	120	45	31	25	1	52	4	1	4	24	9	.73	6	.256	.320	.415
1998 Norfolk	AAA NYM	7	21	3	0	0	0	3	2	3	3	0	5	2	1	0	1	2	.33	1	.143	.308	.143
Binghamton	AA NYM	130	487	153	25	3	14	226	80	65	47	2	75	7	1	8	39	15	.72	6	.314	.377	.464
1999 Norfolk	AAA NYM	50	180	41	4	0	8	69	20	23	8	0	42	3	1	2	6	6	.50	2	.228	.269	.383
Ottawa	AAA Mon	78	280	63	13	0	8	100	22	41	21	0	64	3	2	5	2	5	.29	1	.225	.282	.357
2000 Ottawa	AAA Mon	7	20	4	2	0	0	6	2	3	1	0	5	1	1	1	1	0	1.00	0	.200	.261	.300
Akron	AA Cle	94	347	79	16	3	5	116	35	33	14	0	61	8	3	5	11	6	.65	5	.228	.270	.334
Buffalo	AAA Cle	1	1	0	0	0	0	0	0	0	1	0	1	0	0	0	0	0	—	0	.000	.500	.000
2001 Binghamton	AA NYM	65	253	68	9	0	15	122	44	41	7	0	47	3	3	2	13	6	.68	5	.269	.294	.482
Norfolk	AAA NYM	65	239	67	12	4	2	93	23	31	8	1	40	2	10	3	6	3	.67	6	.280	.306	.389
8 Min. YEARS		893	3248	867	143	20	77	1281	459	397	236	10	596	53	35	38	198	78	.72	41	.267	.323	.394

Butch Huskey

Bats: Right **Throws:** Right **Pos:** 1B-107; DH-7; OF-5; PH-4   **Ht:** 6'3" **Wt:** 244 **Born:** 11/10/71 **Age:** 30

Year Team	Lg Org	G	AB	H	2B	3B	HR	TB	R	RBI	TBB	IBB	SO	HBP	SH	SF	SB	CS	SB%	GDP	Avg	OBP	SLG
1989 Mets	R NYM	54	190	50	14	2	6	86	27	34	14	0	36	1	0	0	4	1	.80	2	.263	.317	.453
1990 Kingsport	R+ NYM	72	279	75	12	0	14	129	39	53	24	1	74	2	0	5	4	3	.57	2	.269	.326	.462
1991 Columbia	A NYM	134	492	141	27	5	26	256	88	99	54	6	90	4	1	7	22	10	.69	11	.287	.357	.520
1992 St. Lucie	A+ NYM	134	493	125	17	1	18	198	65	75	33	6	74	1	0	5	7	3	.70	5	.254	.299	.402
1993 Binghamton	AA NYM	139	526	132	23	1	25	232	72	98	48	3	102	2	0	8	11	2	.85	14	.251	.312	.441
1994 Norfolk	AAA NYM	127	474	108	23	3	10	167	59	57	37	2	88	3	4	5	16	7	.70	9	.228	.285	.352
1995 Norfolk	AAA NYM	109	394	112	18	1	28	216	66	87	39	4	88	6	0	3	8	6	.57	9	.284	.355	.548
1998 Norfolk	AAA NYM	2	8	2	0	0	0	2	0	3	0	0	1	0	0	0	0	0	—	0	.250	.222	.250
2000 Salt Lake	AAA Min	2	9	3	0	0	0	3	2	5	1	0	2	0	0	0	0	0	—	0	.333	.400	1.000
2001 Colo Sprngs	AAA Col	122	458	148	29	1	19	236	76	87	42	2	95	1	0	12	2	2	.50	18	.323	.372	.515
1993 New York	NL	13	41	6	1	0	0	7	2	3	1	1	13	0	0	0	0	0	—	0	.146	.159	.171
1995 New York	NL	28	90	17	1	0	3	27	8	11	10	0	16	0	1	1	1	0	1.00	0	.189	.267	.300
1996 New York	NL	118	414	115	16	2	15	180	43	60	27	3	77	0	0	4	1	2	.33	10	.278	.319	.435
1997 New York	NL	142	471	135	26	2	24	237	61	81	25	5	84	1	0	8	8	5	.62	21	.287	.319	.503
1998 New York	NL	113	369	93	18	0	13	150	43	59	26	3	66	1	2	4	7	6	.54	13	.252	.300	.407
1999 Seattle	AL	74	262	76	9	0	15	130	44	49	27	0	45	0	0	3	3	1	.75	3	.290	.353	.496
Boston	AL	45	124	33	6	0	7	60	18	28	7	1	20	0	0	0	0	0	—	0	.266	.305	.484
2000 Minnesota	AL	64	215	48	13	0	5	76	22	27	25	1	49	2	0	3	0	2	.00	5	.223	.306	.353
Colorado	NL	45	92	32	8	0	4	52	18	14	11	0	14	0	0	1	1	1	.50	5	.348	.432	.565
10 Min. YEARS		895	3323	896	163	14	148	1531	494	598	292	24	650	20	5	46	74	34	.69	70	.270	.328	.461
7 Maj. YEARS		642	2078	555	98	4	86	919	259	336	164	15	384	4	3	28	21	17	.55	66	.267	.318	.442

Brent Husted

Pitches: Right **Bats:** Right **Pos:** RP-37   **Ht:** 6'3" **Wt:** 198 **Born:** 3/30/76 **Age:** 26

			HOW MUCH HE PITCHED						WHAT HE GAVE UP									THE RESULTS					
Year Team	Lg Org	G	GS	CG	GF	IP	BFP	H	R	ER	HR	SH	SF	HB	TBB	IBB	SO	WP	Bk	W	L	Pct.	ShO	Sv	ERA
1997 Yakima	A- LA	10	6	0	1	29.2	145	45	32	23	0	0	0	1	11	3	22	2	0	1	5	.167	0	0	6.98
1998 San Berndno	A+ LA	49	0	0	20	85	360	77	41	34	6	4	2	2	24	4	68	6	0	3	6	.333	0	1	3.60
1999 Vero Beach	A+ LA	47	0	0	44	54	222	42	30	25	9	2	3	1	17	0	41	2	0	4	4	.333	0	27	4.17
2000 San Antonio	AA LA	52	0	0	26	70.1	300	64	37	32	7	5	3	4	22	2	48	0	0	4	9	.308	0	3	4.09
2001 Jacksnville	AA LA	23	0	0	6	37.2	171	52	25	23	6	1	1	3	13	0	21	1	0	3	3	.500	0	1	5.50
Las Vegas	AAA LA	14	0	0	8	19.2	89	25	9	8	1	0	0	2	7	0	11	2	0	0	0	—	0	0	3.66
5 Min. YEARS		195	6	0	105	296.1	1287	305	174	145	29	12	9	13	94	9	211	13	0	13	27	.325	0	32	4.40

Norm Hutchins

Bats: Both **Throws:** Left **Pos:** OF-105; DH-2; PR-1   **Ht:** 5'11" **Wt:** 198 **Born:** 11/20/75 **Age:** 26

			BATTING												BASERUNNING				PERCENTAGES		
Year Team	Lg Org	G	AB	H	2B	3B	HR	TB	R	RBI	TBB	IBB	SO	HBP	SH	SF	SB	CS	SB%	GDP	Avg	OBP	SLG
1994 Angels	R Ana	43	136	26	4	1	0	32	8	7	3	0	44	1	1	1	5	2	.71	0	.191	.213	.235
1995 Angels	R Ana	14	59	16	1	1	0	19	9	7	4	0	10	1	2	1	8	4	.67	1	.271	.323	.322
Boise	A- Ana	45	176	44	6	2	2	60	34	11	15	0	44	2	4	1	10	6	.63	2	.250	.314	.341
1996 Cedar Rapds	A Ana	126	466	105	13	16	2	156	59	52	28	0	110	6	8	2	22	8	.73	5	.225	.277	.335
1997 Lk Elsinore	A+ Ana	132	564	163	31	12	15	263	82	69	23	4	147	6	5	6	39	17	.70	2	.289	.321	.466
1998 Midland	AA Ana	89	394	123	20	10	10	193	74	50	14	0	84	4	0	1	32	10	.76	8	.312	.341	.490
Vancouver	AAA Ana	7	29	6	0	0	1	9	4	3	2	0	9	1	0	1	1	2	.33	0	.207	.273	.310
1999 Edmonton	AAA Ana	126	521	130	27	6	7	190	80	51	40	1	127	8	4	4	25	17	.60	8	.250	.311	.365
2000 Colo Sprngs	AAA Col	15	44	10	1	2	1	18	8	4	2	0	15	1	1	1	2	1	.67	1	.227	.271	.409
Carolina	AA Col	77	281	68	13	4	4	101	31	29	21	0	69	6	3	2	19	6	.76	2	.242	.306	.359
2001 Durham	AAA TB	78	261	60	10	1	7	93	32	28	9	0	64	5	2	2	15	2	.88	4	.230	.267	.356
Orlando	AA TB	30	105	23	1	1	2	32	14	9	6	0	30	3	1	0	4	2	.67	0	.219	.281	.305
8 Min. YEARS		782	3036	774	127	56	51	1166	435	320	167	5	753	44	31	22	182	77	.70	35	.255	.301	.384

Omar Infante

Bats: Right **Throws:** Right **Pos:** SS-132   **Ht:** 6'0" **Wt:** 150 **Born:** 12/26/81 **Age:** 20

			BATTING												BASERUNNING				PERCENTAGES		
Year Team	Lg Org	G	AB	H	2B	3B	HR	TB	R	RBI	TBB	IBB	SO	HBP	SH	SF	SB	CS	SB%	GDP	Avg	OBP	SLG
1999 Tigers	R Det	21	75	20	0	0	0	20	9	4	3	0	9	0	0	1	4	0	1.00	1	.267	.291	.267
2000 Lakeland	A+ Det	79	259	71	11	0	2	88	35	24	20	0	29	1	5	4	11	5	.69	4	.274	.324	.340
W Michigan	A Det	12	48	11	0	0	0	11	7	5	5	0	7	2	4	0	1	0	1.00	2	.229	.327	.229
2001 Erie	AA Det	132	540	163	21	4	2	198	86	62	46	1	87	2	4	7	27	12	.69	9	.302	.355	.367
3 Min. YEARS		244	922	265	32	4	4	317	137	95	74	1	132	5	9	12	43	17	.72	16	.287	.340	.344

Jeff Inglin

Bats: Right **Throws:** Right **Pos:** DH-65; OF-63   **Ht:** 5'11" **Wt:** 185 **Born:** 10/8/75 **Age:** 26

			BATTING												BASERUNNING				PERCENTAGES		
Year Team	Lg Org	G	AB	H	2B	3B	HR	TB	R	RBI	TBB	IBB	SO	HBP	SH	SF	SB	CS	SB%	GDP	Avg	OBP	SLG
1996 Bristol	R+ CWS	50	193	56	10	0	8	90	27	24	11	0	25	9	0	0	9	6	.60	8	.290	.357	.466
Hickory	A CWS	22	83	30	6	2	2	46	12	15	4	0	11	1	0	1	2	1	.67	3	.361	.393	.554
1997 Hickory	A CWS	135	536	179	34	6	16	273	100	102	49	4	87	4	0	9	31	8	.79	12	.334	.388	.509
1998 Birmingham	AA CWS	139	494	121	22	6	24	227	75	100	78	3	101	4	0	9	3	2	.60	12	.245	.347	.460
1999 Charlotte	AAA CWS	14	39	8	0	0	3	17	8	8	4	0	9	1	0	0	0	1	.00	0	.205	.295	.436
Birmingham	AA CWS	117	432	126	26	4	15	205	63	63	58	3	62	6	2	2	20	2	.91	13	.292	.382	.475
2000 Birmingham	AA CWS	65	244	71	12	3	5	104	43	40	34	0	43	4	2	4	5	2	.71	7	.291	.381	.426
Charlotte	AAA CWS	45	146	44	8	1	5	69	19	31	12	0	17	2	1	1	3	0	1.00	3	.301	.360	.473
2001 Charlotte	AAA CWS	128	481	131	25	6	24	240	66	75	43	0	103	6	0	3	3	4	.43	13	.272	.338	.499
6 Min. YEARS		715	2648	766	143	28	102	1271	413	458	293	10	458	37	5	29	76	26	.75	75	.289	.364	.480

Darron Ingram

Bats: Right **Throws:** Right **Pos:** OF-77; DH-58; PH-1   **Ht:** 6'3" **Wt:** 226 **Born:** 6/7/76 **Age:** 26

			BATTING												BASERUNNING				PERCENTAGES		
Year Team	Lg Org	G	AB	H	2B	3B	HR	TB	R	RBI	TBB	IBB	SO	HBP	SH	SF	SB	CS	SB%	GDP	Avg	OBP	SLG
1994 Princeton	R+ Cin	46	131	26	5	1	2	39	13	11	19	0	50	1	3	1	1	4	.20	2	.198	.303	.298
1995 Princeton	R+ Cin	60	233	64	6	3	14	118	37	53	11	0	78	1	0	2	3	1	.75	5	.275	.308	.506
1996 Chston-WV	A Cin	15	48	9	3	0	1	15	5	6	8	1	19	0	0	1	0	0	—	0	.188	.298	.313
Billings	R+ Cin	65	251	74	13	6	17	138	49	56	34	2	88	2	0	1	7	3	.70	1	.295	.382	.550
1997 Burlington	A Cin	134	510	135	25	4	29	255	74	97	46	1	195	0	0	3	8	5	.62	9	.265	.324	.500
1998 Chattanooga	AA Cin	125	466	108	21	9	17	198	62	65	43	1	169	0	0	7	4	3	.57	8	.232	.293	.425
1999 Chattanooga	AA Cin	85	267	59	11	3	11	109	42	40	28	0	95	0	0	1	5	7	.42	5	.221	.294	.408
Clinton	A Cin	22	76	27	5	0	5	47	15	18	14	0	20	0	0	0	1	1	.50	0	.355	.456	.618
2000 San Berndno	A+ LA	100	396	105	16	6	15	178	58	71	37	1	136	0	0	2	5	5	.50	10	.265	.326	.449
2001 Birmingham	AA CWS	136	514	135	34	4	22	243	77	91	52	3	188	4	0	8	6	6	.50	7	.263	.330	.473
8 Min. YEARS		788	2892	742	139	30	133	1340	432	508	292	10	1038	8	3	26	40	35	.53	47	.257	.324	.463

Eric Ireland

Pitches: Right **Bats:** Right **Pos:** SP-28; RP-1   **Ht:** 6'1" **Wt:** 170 **Born:** 3/11/77 **Age:** 25

			HOW MUCH HE PITCHED						WHAT HE GAVE UP									THE RESULTS					
Year Team	Lg Org	G	GS	CG	GF	IP	BFP	H	R	ER	HR	SH	SF	HB	TBB	IBB	SO	WP	Bk	W	L	Pct.	ShO	Sv	ERA
1996 Astros	R Hou	12	11	0	1	53.2	235	54	33	28	1	3	1	3	23	1	43	13	1	3	4	.429	0	0	4.70
1997 Auburn	A- Hou	16	16	2	0	107	458	111	55	44	4	2	0	12	21	1	78	3	0	5	7	.417	0	0	3.70
1998 Quad City	A Hou	29	28	6	1	206	860	172	80	66	15	5	4	15	71	2	191	7	3	14	9	.609	2	0	2.88
1999 Jackson	AA Hou	3	3	0	0	14.2	64	19	9	7	1	1	0	2	1	0	15	2	0	0	1	.000	0	0	4.30
Kissimmee	A+ Hou	24	24	5	0	170.1	684	145	59	39	12	7	1	8	30	1	133	13	2	10	7	.588	2	0	2.06

Year Team	Lg Org	G	GS	CG	GF	IP	BFP	H	R	ER	HR	SH	SF	HB	TBB	IBB	SO	WP	Bk	W	L	Pct.	ShO	Sv	ERA
		HOW MUCH HE PITCHED						WHAT HE GAVE UP												THE RESULTS					
2000 Round Rock	AA Hou	29	29	2	0	179.2	754	171	84	68	14	7	4	5	64	0	123	12	0	11	9	.550	2	0	3.41
2001 Sacramento	AAA Oak	29	28	0	0	168.1	771	215	120	98	24	5	4	10	56	3	102	6	0	8	11	.421	0	0	5.24
6 Min. YEARS		142	139	15	2	899.2	3826	887	440	350	71	30	14	53	267	9	685	56	6	51	48	.515	6	0	3.50

Chairon Isenia

Bats: Right **Throws:** Right **Pos:** C-54; DH-32; 1B-3; PH-3   **Ht:** 5'11" **Wt:** 216 **Born:** 1/23/79 **Age:** 23

Year Team	Lg Org	G	AB	H	2B	3B	HR	TB	R	RBI	TBB	IBB	SO	HBP	SH	SF	SB	CS	SB%	GDP	Avg	OBP	SLG
		BATTING															BASERUNNING				PERCENTAGES		
1998 St. Pete	A+ TB	1	0	0	0	0	0	0	0	0	0	0	0	0	0	0	0	0	—	0	.000	.000	.000
Devil Rays	R TB	42	132	39	10	2	0	53	25	14	8	0	20	0	0	2	7	6	.54	1	.295	.331	.402
1999 Princeton	R+ TB	30	101	28	7	2	2	45	19	12	8	0	15	2	0	1	5	2	.71	2	.277	.339	.446
Hudson Val	A- TB	33	118	31	9	0	3	49	17	16	4	0	22	1	0	2	0	1	.00	4	.263	.288	.415
2000 Chston-SC	A TB	102	384	104	21	0	6	143	37	59	16	1	53	6	2	5	5	3	.63	9	.271	.307	.372
2001 Orlando	AA TB	15	43	7	1	0	0	8	2	4	3	0	7	0	1	0	0	0	—	0	.163	.217	.186
Bakersfield	A+ TB	76	290	84	16	0	8	124	42	50	16	1	41	4	1	1	2	3	.40	4	.290	.334	.428
4 Min. YEARS		299	1068	293	64	4	19	422	142	155	55	2	158	13	4	11	19	15	.56	20	.274	.315	.395

Hansel Izquierdo

Pitches: Right **Bats:** Right **Pos:** RP-23; SP-15   **Ht:** 6'2" **Wt:** 205 **Born:** 1/2/77 **Age:** 25

Year Team	Lg Org	G	GS	CG	GF	IP	BFP	H	R	ER	HR	SH	SF	HB	TBB	IBB	SO	WP	Bk	W	L	Pct.	ShO	Sv	ERA
		HOW MUCH HE PITCHED						WHAT HE GAVE UP												THE RESULTS					
1995 Marlins	R Fla	1	0	0	0	2	10	3	3	0	0	1	0	0	2	0	0	1	0	0	0	—	0	0	0.00
1996 Marlins	R Fla	12	0	0	10	13.1	52	7	4	4	0	0	0	3	5	0	17	3	1	0	1	.000	0	3	2.70
1997 White Sox	R CWS	5	0	0	2	10.1	45	9	4	4	0	1	0	0	8	0	15	1	0	0	0	—	0	0	3.48
Bristol	R+ CWS	9	2	0	2	23	104	25	14	11	5	0	0	4	8	0	24	0	1	2	2	.500	0	0	4.30
1998 Hickory	A CWS	28	27	2	1	175	771	159	104	85	14	6	2	22	76	0	186	15	1	9	11	.450	1	0	4.37
Winston-Sal	A+ CWS	1	0	0	1	2	7	1	0	0	0	0	0	0	1	0	2	0	0	0	0	—	0	0	0.00
1999 Winston-Sal	A+ CWS	18	13	0	4	82.2	371	76	46	38	5	5	2	8	46	1	72	13	1	3	5	.375	0	0	4.14
2000 Birmingham	AA CWS	8	0	0	5	12	53	12	11	10	2	1	1	0	5	1	5	1	0	2	1	.333	0	1	7.50
Kinston	A+ Cle	10	5	0	2	41.1	178	39	29	22	4	2	2	5	13	0	34	1	0	1	3	.250	0	1	4.79
Sonoma Cty	IND —	4	3	0	0	13	72	16	14	14	0	1	1	3	17	1	10	2	0	0	1	.000	0	0	9.69
2001 Kane County	A Fla	24	2	0	5	47.2	181	27	8	7	1	1	0	3	13	0	42	1	2	7	1	.875	0	2	1.32
Brevard Cty	A+ Fla	4	4	0	0	26.2	105	15	8	8	3	1	0	4	6	0	22	0	0	2	0	1.000	0	0	2.70
Portland	AA Fla	10	9	1	0	56.2	224	47	24	24	10	0	1	4	10	0	45	4	0	7	2	.778	1	0	3.81
7 Min. YEARS		134	65	3	32	505.2	2173	436	269	227	44	19	9	56	210	3	474	42	6	32	28	.533	2	7	4.04

Brandon Jackson

Bats: Right **Throws:** Right **Pos:** SS-58; 2B-15; 3B-10; PR-3; PH-1   **Ht:** 6'1" **Wt:** 180 **Born:** 10/28/75 **Age:** 26

Year Team	Lg Org	G	AB	H	2B	3B	HR	TB	R	RBI	TBB	IBB	SO	HBP	SH	SF	SB	CS	SB%	GDP	Avg	OBP	SLG
		BATTING															BASERUNNING				PERCENTAGES		
1998 St.Cathrnes	A- Tor	57	171	45	5	0	1	53	30	11	18	0	26	2	4	0	6	0	1.00	5	.263	.340	.310
1999 St.Cathrnes	A- Tor	62	214	71	13	1	2	92	37	25	28	0	45	8	0	5	3	8	.27	4	.332	.420	.430
2000 Hagerstown	A Tor	110	391	122	17	8	5	170	71	52	43	0	83	13	1	8	5	6	.45	6	.312	.391	.435
Dunedin	A+ Tor	6	16	5	2	0	0	7	6	2	3	0	0	1	0	1	2	0	1.00	0	.313	.429	.438
2001 Greensboro	A NYY	5	20	5	0	0	0	5	3	2	2	1	5	0	0	1	2	0	1.00	0	.250	.304	.250
Tampa	A+ NYY	69	225	52	8	0	3	69	23	26	25	0	45	3	0	4	3	7	.30	7	.231	.311	.307
Norwich	AA NYY	11	38	12	1	0	1	16	5	5	2	0	7	0	1	0	0	2	.00	0	.316	.350	.421
4 Min. YEARS		320	1075	312	46	9	12	412	175	123	121	1	211	27	6	19	21	23	.48	22	.290	.370	.383

Ryan Jacobs

Pitches: Left **Bats:** Right **Pos:** RP-10   **Ht:** 6'2" **Wt:** 215 **Born:** 2/3/74 **Age:** 28

Year Team	Lg Org	G	GS	CG	GF	IP	BFP	H	R	ER	HR	SH	SF	HB	TBB	IBB	SO	WP	Bk	W	L	Pct.	ShO	Sv	ERA
		HOW MUCH HE PITCHED						WHAT HE GAVE UP												THE RESULTS					
1992 Braves	R Atl	12	2	0	6	35	148	30	18	10	1	3	2	1	8	2	40	2	0	1	3	.250	0	1	2.57
1993 Danville	R+ Atl	10	10	0	0	42.2	188	35	24	19	5	1	2	1	25	0	32	6	0	4	3	.571	0	0	4.01
1994 Macon	A Atl	27	18	1	2	121.2	532	105	54	39	9	4	2	3	62	2	81	6	1	8	7	.533	1	1	2.88
1995 Durham	A+ Atl	29	25	1	0	148.2	640	145	72	58	12	6	5	3	57	3	99	10	0	11	6	.647	0	0	3.51
1996 Greenville	AA Atl	21	21	0	0	99.2	468	127	83	74	19	3	4	4	57	1	64	8	0	3	9	.250	0	0	6.68
1997 Greenville	AA Atl	28	6	0	3	68.2	328	84	61	55	8	1	5	2	43	1	52	6	0	1	8	.111	0	1	7.21
1998 Richmond	AAA Atl	2	0	0	0	4.1	28	9	9	9	1	0	0	0	6	0	1	1	0	0	0	—	0	0	18.69
Greenville	AA Atl	35	15	0	7	101	478	104	73	60	14	3	8	2	72	3	74	12	1	6	9	.400	0	0	5.35
1999 Carolina	AA Col	28	21	1	2	114	535	120	76	67	10	6	8	2	68	1	89	5	0	6	12	.333	0	0	5.29
2000 Mudville	A+ Mil	26	1	0	4	36	175	41	35	30	4	2	1	1	29	0	31	6	0	2	3	.400	0	0	7.50
Huntsville	AA Mil	18	0	0	8	29	134	32	18	14	1	0	1	1	16	0	23	2	0	0	1	.000	0	1	4.34
2001 Huntsville	AA Mil	10	0	0	2	13	58	10	6	4	0	1	0	1	5	1	15	0	0	0	1	.000	0	0	2.77
10 Min. YEARS		246	119	3	37	813.2	3712	842	529	439	88	31	34	26	448	14	601	64	2	42	62	.404	1	4	4.86

Bucky Jacobsen

Bats: Right **Throws:** Right **Pos:** 1B-104; DH-5; PH-4   **Ht:** 6'4" **Wt:** 220 **Born:** 8/30/75 **Age:** 26

Year Team	Lg Org	G	AB	H	2B	3B	HR	TB	R	RBI	TBB	IBB	SO	HBP	SH	SF	SB	CS	SB%	GDP	Avg	OBP	SLG
		BATTING															BASERUNNING				PERCENTAGES		
1997 Ogden	R+ Mil	67	238	78	17	2	8	123	57	52	41	0	44	3	0	4	6	6	.50	4	.328	.427	.517
1998 Beloit	A Mil	135	499	146	31	1	27	260	96	100	83	3	133	8	0	4	5	2	.71	10	.293	.399	.521
1999 Huntsville	AA Mil	47	150	29	6	1	3	46	20	19	20	0	32	3	0	5	4	1	.80	4	.193	.292	.307
Stockton	A+ Mil	46	156	39	8	0	5	62	22	22	21	1	40	4	0	1	3	3	.50	4	.250	.352	.397
2000 Huntsville	AA Mil	81	268	74	14	0	18	142	44	50	51	2	69	4	0	4	4	2	.67	8	.276	.394	.530
2001 Huntsville	AA Mil	27	93	41	9	0	10	80	21	28	15	2	14	1	0	1	1	2	.33	3	.441	.518	.860
Indianapolis	AAA Mil	86	300	74	18	1	12	130	42	53	26	1	78	4	1	3	0	0	—	13	.247	.312	.433
5 Min. YEARS		489	1704	481	103	5	83	843	302	324	257	9	410	27	1	22	23	16	.59	46	.282	.381	.495

Jason Jacome

Pitches: Left **Bats:** Left **Pos:** RP-19; SP-16   **Ht:** 6'1" **Wt:** 185 **Born:** 11/24/70 **Age:** 31

		HOW MUCH HE PITCHED						WHAT HE GAVE UP											THE RESULTS				
Year Team	Lg Org	G	GS	CG	GF	IP	BFP	H	R	ER	HR	SH	SF	HB	TBB	IBB	SO	WP	Bk	W	L	Pct.	ShO	Sv	ERA
1991 Kingsport	R+ NYM	12	7	3	5	55.1	210	35	18	10	1	3	2	0	13	2	48	6	1	5	4	.556	1	2	1.63
1992 Columbia	A NYM	8	8	1	0	52.2	209	40	7	6	2	0	0	0	15	0	49	4	1	4	1	.800	0	0	1.03
St. Lucie	A+ NYM	17	17	5	0	114.1	454	98	45	36	7	4	3	3	30	0	66	6	0	6	7	.462	1	0	2.83
1993 St. Lucie	A+ NYM	14	14	2	0	99.1	409	106	37	34	2	1	1	0	23	1	66	2	4	8	4	.667	2	0	3.08
Binghamton	AA NYM	14	14	0	0	87	374	85	36	31	6	5	2	4	38	1	56	3	0	8	4	.667	0	0	3.21
1994 Norfolk	AAA NYM	19	19	4	0	126.2	540	138	57	40	8	3	5	3	42	1	80	3	0	8	6	.571	1	0	2.84
1995 Norfolk	AAA NYM	8	8	0	0	43.2	181	40	21	19	5	4	1	1	13	0	31	1	0	2	4	.333	0	0	3.92
1997 Buffalo	AAA Cle	7	7	1	0	37	151	41	14	13	7	1	3	1	10	0	23	0	1	3	1	.750	0	0	3.16
1998 Buffalo	AAA Cle	24	24	2	0	154.2	642	161	62	56	13	2	2	3	38	0	109	5	1	14	2	.875	0	0	3.26
2001 Tucson	AAA Ari	35	16	0	7	120	532	149	78	71	11	1	9	2	37	3	72	5	2	1	8	.111	0	0	5.33
1994 New York	NL	8	8	1	0	54	222	54	17	16	3	3	1	0	17	2	30	2	0	4	3	.571	1	0	2.67
1995 New York	NL	5	5	0	0	21	110	33	24	24	3	1	1	1	15	0	11	1	0	0	4	.000	0	0	10.29
Kansas City	AL	15	14	1	0	84	364	101	52	50	15	2	3	1	21	2	39	0	1	4	6	.400	0	0	5.36
1996 Kansas City	AL	49	2	0	21	47.2	220	67	27	25	5	3	0	2	22	5	32	1	0	0	4	.000	0	0	4.72
1997 Kansas City	AL	7	0	0	0	6.2	35	13	7	7	2	0	0	1	5	1	3	0	0	0	0	—	0	0	9.45
Cleveland	AL	21	4	0	2	42.2	183	45	26	25	8	0	1	0	15	4	24	2	0	2	0	1.000	0	0	5.27
1998 Cleveland	AL	1	1	0	0	5	26	10	8	8	2	0	0	0	3	0	2	0	0	0	1	.000	0	0	14.40
8 Min. YEARS		158	134	18	12	890.2	3702	893	375	316	62	24	28	17	259	8	600	35	10	57	40	.588	5	2	3.19
5 Maj. YEARS		106	34	2	23	261	1166	323	161	155	38	9	6	5	98	14	141	6	1	10	18	.357	1	1	5.34

Tom Jacquez

Pitches: Left **Bats:** Left **Pos:** RP-24; SP-9   **Ht:** 6'2" **Wt:** 195 **Born:** 12/29/75 **Age:** 26

		HOW MUCH HE PITCHED						WHAT HE GAVE UP											THE RESULTS				
Year Team	Lg Org	G	GS	CG	GF	IP	BFP	H	R	ER	HR	SH	SF	HB	TBB	IBB	SO	WP	Bk	W	L	Pct.	ShO	Sv	ERA
1997 Batavia	A- Phi	4	4	0	0	22.1	93	20	6	6	0	2	2	3	2	0	20	0	0	2	1	.667	0	0	2.42
Piedmont	A Phi	8	8	0	0	41.2	183	45	29	23	2	2	3	3	13	0	26	1	0	2	4	.333	0	0	4.97
1998 Clearwater	A+ Phi	29	28	2	0	169.2	740	215	102	81	12	6	9	3	31	3	108	5	4	9	11	.450	1	0	4.30
1999 Reading	AA Phi	38	14	0	8	122.2	555	149	84	72	20	3	2	11	32	1	68	1	0	6	5	.545	0	1	5.28
Scranton-WB	AAA Phi	3	0	0	1	3.2	15	4	1	1	0	0	0	0	0	0	4	0	0	1	0	1.000	0	0	2.45
2000 Reading	AA Phi	13	0	0	8	27.1	115	26	11	9	2	2	0	0	9	0	21	1	0	0	3	.000	0	3	2.96
Scranton-WB	AAA Phi	35	1	0	8	54.2	229	53	15	12	3	2	4	3	20	1	34	1	0	5	1	.833	0	1	1.98
2001 Scranton-WB	AAA Phi	33	9	1	6	109.1	443	100	43	38	8	3	2	3	29	0	86	0	0	10	6	.625	0	0	3.13
2000 Philadelphia	NL	9	0	0	2	7.1	34	10	9	9	2	0	1	0	3	1	6	0	0	0	0	—	0	1	11.05
5 Min. YEARS		163	64	3	31	551.1	2373	612	291	242	47	18	22	26	136	5	367	9	4	34	32	.515	1	5	3.95

Delvin James

Pitches: Right **Bats:** Right **Pos:** RP-22; SP-16   **Ht:** 6'4" **Wt:** 222 **Born:** 1/3/78 **Age:** 24

		HOW MUCH HE PITCHED						WHAT HE GAVE UP											THE RESULTS				
Year Team	Lg Org	G	GS	CG	GF	IP	BFP	H	R	ER	HR	SH	SF	HB	TBB	IBB	SO	WP	Bk	W	L	Pct.	ShO	Sv	ERA
1996 Devil Rays	R TB	11	11	1	0	47.2	236	64	52	47	0	1	3	11	21	0	40	11	2	2	8	.200	0	0	8.87
1997 Princeton	R+ TB	20	5	0	2	58.1	276	71	57	32	11	1	2	4	24	1	46	4	2	4	4	.500	0	0	4.94
1998 St. Pete	A TB	1	0	0	0	1.2	7	2	2	2	0	0	0	1	0	0	0	0	0	0	0	—	0	0	10.80
Chston-SC	A TB	7	0	0	2	8.1	40	12	5	5	0	0	2	1	2	0	8	0	0	2	0	1.000	0	0	5.40
Hudson Val	A- TB	15	15	0	0	81.2	345	71	39	27	2	1	1	5	32	0	64	6	0	7	4	.636	0	0	2.98
1999 Chston-SC	A TB	25	25	1	0	158.1	654	142	76	64	13	9	4	8	33	1	106	8	1	8	8	.500	0	0	3.64
St. Pete	A+ TB	3	2	0	1	17	71	18	6	6	0	0	0	3	4	0	6	1	0	3	0	1.000	0	0	3.18
2000 St. Pete	A+ TB	22	22	3	0	137.1	576	142	74	65	10	2	2	7	27	2	74	5	0	7	9	.438	1	0	4.26
Orlando	AA TB	6	6	1	0	37	153	31	15	12	3	0	3	3	7	0	26	1	0	1	3	.250	0	0	2.92
2001 Orlando	AA TB	7	7	0	0	43.2	163	25	8	8	1	2	1	2	9	0	31	2	1	2	0	1.000	0	0	1.65
Durham	AAA TB	31	9	1	8	84.1	373	99	51	45	8	4	2	5	27	1	51	6	0	3	7	.300	0	0	4.80
6 Min. YEARS		148	102	7	13	675.1	2894	677	385	313	48	20	20	50	186	5	452	44	6	39	43	.476	1	0	4.17

Kenny James

Bats: Both **Throws:** Right **Pos:** OF-94; PH-13; DH-6; PR-5   **Ht:** 6'0" **Wt:** 198 **Born:** 10/9/76 **Age:** 25

		BATTING														BASERUNNING				PERCENTAGES		
Year Team	Lg Org	G	AB	H	2B	3B	HR	TB	R	RBI	TBB	IBB	SO	HBP	SH	SF	SB	CS	SB%	GDP	Avg	OBP	SLG
1995 Expos	R Mon	43	156	33	1	0	0	34	20	3	20	0	43	3	0	0	11	8	.58	1	.212	.313	.218
1996 Expos	R Mon	44	165	35	5	2	0	44	24	12	15	1	33	3	2	0	4	3	.57	0	.212	.290	.267
1997 Vermont	A- Mon	71	301	70	4	5	2	90	61	23	13	1	52	11	2	1	37	4	.90	0	.233	.288	.299
1998 Cape Fear	A Mon	114	451	114	10	3	2	136	73	32	21	0	68	11	12	1	41	6	.87	6	.253	.302	.302
1999 Harrisburg	AA Mon	29	102	26	4	2	0	34	8	6	1	0	19	1	5	0	7	3	.70	1	.255	.269	.333
Jupiter	A+ Mon	99	372	88	9	1	2	105	68	32	31	2	57	6	8	1	37	7	.84	8	.237	.305	.282
2000 Harrisburg	AA Mon	91	321	77	12	4	2	103	47	32	42	0	54	4	4	2	31	5	.86	7	.240	.333	.321
Ottawa	AAA Mon	48	180	44	7	3	1	60	26	11	9	0	28	3	5	0	9	0	1.00	3	.244	.292	.333
2001 Harrisburg	AA Mon	41	95	18	3	1	0	23	17	3	6	0	13	2	2	1	9	3	.75	0	.189	.250	.242
Jupiter	A+ Mon	74	282	77	8	5	2	101	49	19	17	2	40	5	9	0	22	8	.73	1	.273	.326	.358
7 Min. YEARS		654	2425	582	63	26	11	730	393	173	175	6	407	49	49	6	208	47	.82	27	.240	.304	.301

Ryan Jamison

Pitches: Right **Bats:** Right **Pos:** SP-17; RP-2   **Ht:** 6'3" **Wt:** 185 **Born:** 1/5/78 **Age:** 24

		HOW MUCH HE PITCHED						WHAT HE GAVE UP											THE RESULTS				
Year Team	Lg Org	G	GS	CG	GF	IP	BFP	H	R	ER	HR	SH	SF	HB	TBB	IBB	SO	WP	Bk	W	L	Pct.	ShO	Sv	ERA
1999 Auburn	A- Hou	15	15	0	0	87.2	374	83	45	40	7	1	3	6	36	0	83	6	4	5	3	.625	0	0	4.11
2000 Michigan	A Hou	41	7	0	15	98.2	402	66	32	23	3	4	3	10	38	3	95	8	1	8	3	.727	0	7	2.10
2001 Lexington	A Hou	9	8	0	1	55.1	215	40	17	14	3	1	2	6	9	0	63	6	0	4	2	.667	0	0	2.28
Round Rock	AA Hou	10	9	0	0	46.1	211	49	25	18	5	0	3	2	23	0	32	5	0	5	2	.714	0	0	3.50
3 Min. YEARS		75	39	0	16	288	1202	238	119	95	18	6	11	24	106	3	273	24	5	22	10	.688	0	7	2.97

145

Cheyenne Janke

Pitches: Right **Bats:** Right **Pos:** RP-22; SP-10   **Ht:** 6'5" **Wt:** 235 **Born:** 2/16/77 **Age:** 25

Year Team	Lg Org	G	GS	CG	GF	IP	BFP	H	R	ER	HR	SH	SF	HB	TBB	IBB	SO	WP	Bk	W	L	Pct.	ShO	Sv	ERA
						HOW MUCH HE PITCHED					**WHAT HE GAVE UP**											**THE RESULTS**			
1999 New Jersey	A- StL	15	14	0	0	83.1	356	85	40	34	8	2	1	1	20	0	63	8	2	2	5	.286	0	0	3.67
2000 Peoria	A StL	28	27	0	0	167	734	169	97	75	8	7	4	10	53	3	90	11	0	10	10	.500	0	0	4.04
2001 Potomac	A+ StL	15	5	0	1	36.1	159	44	16	10	2	1	0	2	9	0	17	2	0	0	0	—	0	0	2.48
New Haven	AA StL	17	5	0	5	44	201	65	31	27	5	1	1	0	14	0	20	2	0	1	4	.200	0	0	5.52
3 Min. YEARS		75	51	0	6	330.2	1450	363	184	146	23	11	6	13	96	3	190	23	2	13	19	.406	0	0	3.97

Marty Janzen

Pitches: Right **Bats:** Right **Pos:** SP-13; RP-4   **Ht:** 6'3" **Wt:** 197 **Born:** 5/31/73 **Age:** 29

Year Team	Lg Org	G	GS	CG	GF	IP	BFP	H	R	ER	HR	SH	SF	HB	TBB	IBB	SO	WP	Bk	W	L	Pct.	ShO	Sv	ERA
						HOW MUCH HE PITCHED					**WHAT HE GAVE UP**											**THE RESULTS**			
1992 Yankees	R NYY	12	11	0	0	68.2	277	55	21	18	0	3	2	5	15	0	73	3	3	7	2	.778	0	0	2.36
Greensboro	A NYY	2	0	0	2	5	20	5	2	2	0	0	0	0	1	0	5	2	0	0	0	—	0	1	3.60
1993 Yankees	R NYY	5	5	0	0	22.1	93	20	5	3	0	0	0	1	3	0	19	0	0	0	1	.000	0	0	1.21
1994 Greensboro	A NYY	17	17	0	0	104	431	98	57	45	8	0	0	2	25	1	92	2	2	3	7	.300	0	0	3.89
1995 Tampa	A+ NYY	18	18	1	0	113.2	461	102	38	33	4	1	2	4	30	0	104	3	4	10	3	.769	0	0	2.61
Norwich	AA NYY	3	3	0	0	20	85	17	11	11	2	0	0	2	7	0	16	2	0	1	2	.333	0	0	4.95
Knoxville	AA Tor	7	7	2	0	48	188	35	14	14	2	0	2	1	14	0	44	1	1	5	1	.833	1	0	2.63
1996 Syracuse	AAA Tor	10	10	0	0	55.2	257	74	54	48	12	1	4	2	24	2	34	2	0	3	4	.429	0	0	7.76
1997 Syracuse	AAA Tor	22	9	0	6	65	304	76	58	52	12	3	3	3	36	0	56	8	0	0	5	.000	0	1	7.20
1998 Columbus	AAA NYY	16	12	1	0	68.2	318	78	48	44	8	0	3	1	38	0	54	6	0	5	6	.455	0	0	5.77
Yankees	R NYY	1	1	0	0	3	10	1	0	0	0	0	0	0	0	0	5	0	0	0	0	—	0	0	0.00
Norwich	AA NYY	11	7	1	2	34.2	168	42	28	15	3	2	3	2	19	1	38	2	0	1	7	.125	0	0	3.89
1999 Indianapols	AAA Cin	9	1	0	3	16.2	73	16	9	9	0	1	1	2	8	2	8	1	0	1	1	.500	0	0	4.86
Chattanooga	AA Cin	30	4	0	7	54.2	246	54	32	30	6	4	1	7	29	4	41	5	0	1	3	.250	0	0	4.94
2000 Tucson	AAA Ari	10	3	0	2	25.2	123	30	16	16	9	1	0	3	14	1	15	0	0	1	0	1.000	0	1	5.61
Nashua	IND —	4	4	0	0	25	96	16	3	3	0	0	0	2	6	0	30	1	1	3	0	1.000	0	0	1.08
2001 Salt Lake	AAA Ana	2	0	0	0	3.2	20	5	5	5	0	0	1	1	3	0	3	1	0	0	0	—	0	0	12.27
Nashua	IND —	15	13	0	0	75.1	318	69	32	24	3	0	4	6	27	1	59	4	0	5	5	.500	0	0	2.87
10 Min. YEARS		194	125	5	22	809.2	3488	793	433	372	69	16	26	44	299	12	696	43	11	46	47	.495	1	3	4.14
1996 Toronto	AL	15	11	0	3	73.2	344	95	65	60	16	1	3	2	38	3	47	7	0	4	6	.400	0	0	7.33
1997 Toronto	AL	12	0	0	6	25	105	23	11	10	4	0	0	0	13	0	17	0	0	2	1	.667	0	0	3.60
2 Maj. YEARS		27	11	0	9	98.2	449	118	76	70	20	1	3	2	51	3	64	7	0	6	7	.462	0	0	6.39

Matt Jarvis

Pitches: Left **Bats:** Right **Pos:** RP-35   **Ht:** 6'4" **Wt:** 185 **Born:** 2/22/72 **Age:** 30

Year Team	Lg Org	G	GS	CG	GF	IP	BFP	H	R	ER	HR	SH	SF	HB	TBB	IBB	SO	WP	Bk	W	L	Pct.	ShO	Sv	ERA
						HOW MUCH HE PITCHED					**WHAT HE GAVE UP**											**THE RESULTS**			
1991 Orioles	R Bal	11	5	0	0	37.1	163	44	22	18	2	1	2	0	17	0	30	2	1	3	1	.750	0	0	4.34
1992 Kane County	A Bal	34	7	0	8	71.1	327	84	53	36	3	2	1	1	35	2	43	7	3	4	4	.500	0	0	4.54
1993 Albany	A Bal	29	29	8	0	185.1	797	173	82	63	7	5	2	5	82	4	118	10	1	11	13	.458	1	0	3.06
1994 Frederick	A+ Bal	31	14	0	3	103.2	459	92	58	48	7	5	2	9	48	0	67	3	0	10	4	.714	0	1	4.17
1995 Bowie	AA Bal	26	21	0	1	118	531	154	71	67	11	4	4	4	42	1	60	5	3	9	8	.529	0	0	5.11
1996 Bowie	AA Bal	6	4	0	0	19.1	91	31	17	16	2	0	2	1	7	0	13	4	1	1	3	.250	0	0	7.45
Winnipeg	IND —	17	15	2	1	103	454	99	46	41	11	3	2	6	55	1	63	3	3	11	3	.786	0	0	3.58
1997 Arkansas	AA StL	50	4	0	16	80	344	70	24	17	0	9	1	3	45	4	52	4	0	8	5	.615	0	2	1.91
1998 Arkansas	AA StL	56	0	0	32	59.1	258	55	30	27	2	2	0	3	30	2	46	3	0	6	1	.857	0	15	4.10
1999 San Antonio	AA LA	3	0	0	0	3	20	10	10	9	0	0	0	0	3	1	1	0	0	0	1	.000	0	0	27.00
2001 San Antonio	AA Sea	23	0	0	15	23	103	23	14	13	1	0	1	3	11	1	18	0	0	1	1	.500	0	8	5.09
Tacoma	AAA Sea	12	0	0	5	17.1	73	12	3	3	0	2	1	2	7	0	9	0	0	2	0	1.000	0	0	1.56
10 Min. YEARS		298	99	10	83	820.2	3620	847	430	358	46	33	18	37	382	16	520	44	12	66	44	.600	1	27	3.93

Domingo Jean

Pitches: Right **Bats:** Right **Pos:** RP-56   **Ht:** 6'2" **Wt:** 175 **Born:** 1/9/69 **Age:** 33

Year Team	Lg Org	G	GS	CG	GF	IP	BFP	H	R	ER	HR	SH	SF	HB	TBB	IBB	SO	WP	Bk	W	L	Pct.	ShO	Sv	ERA
						HOW MUCH HE PITCHED					**WHAT HE GAVE UP**											**THE RESULTS**			
1990 White Sox	R CWS	13	13	1	0	78.2	312	55	32	20	1	0	1	6	16	0	65	10	2	2	5	.286	0	0	2.29
1991 South Bend	A CWS	25	25	2	0	158	680	121	75	58	7	3	7	10	65	0	141	17	5	12	8	.600	0	0	3.30
1992 Ft. Laud	A+ NYY	23	23	5	0	158.2	637	118	57	46	3	7	6	6	49	1	172	4	1	6	11	.353	1	0	2.61
Albany-Col	AA NYY	1	1	0	0	4	17	3	2	1	0	0	0	0	3	0	6	1	0	0	0	—	0	0	2.25
1993 Albany-Col	AA NYY	11	11	1	0	61	257	42	24	17	1	1	1	5	33	0	41	4	0	5	3	.625	0	0	2.51
Columbus	AAA NYY	7	7	1	0	44.2	180	40	15	14	2	0	2	0	13	1	39	3	0	2	2	.500	0	0	2.82
Pr William	A+ NYY	1	0	0	0	1.2	6	1	0	0	0	0	0	0	0	0	1	0	0	0	0	—	0	0	0.00
1994 Tucson	AAA Hou	6	3	0	1	19	88	20	13	12	3	0	1	2	11	1	16	0	0	0	0	—	0	0	5.68
1995 Tucson	AAA Hou	3	3	0	0	13.2	62	15	10	10	1	0	0	0	7	0	14	3	0	2	1	.667	0	0	6.59
Okla City	AAA Tex	24	13	1	9	88	418	102	70	60	12	4	2	1	61	0	72	14	3	3	8	.273	0	1	6.14
Indianapols	AAA Cin	2	0	0	0	2	7	1	0	0	1	0	0	0	0	1	1	0	0	1	0	1.000	0	0	0.00
1996 Indianapols	AAA Cin	7	0	0	2	9.1	49	13	11	9	2	0	0	0	8	1	5	0	0	1	1	.500	0	0	8.68
Chattanooga	AA Cin	39	0	0	37	39.2	169	34	19	18	1	3	0	0	17	2	33	5	0	2	3	.400	0	31	4.08
1997 Chattanooga	AA Cin	10	0	0	4	12	69	17	20	13	2	0	2	1	15	1	9	1	0	1	1	.500	0	1	9.75
1998 New Haven	AA Col	12	5	0	4	27	131	30	21	21	1	2	0	1	19	0	17	3	1	2	2	.500	0	1	7.00
Colo Sprngs	AAA Col	36	0	0	12	47.2	226	64	33	29	5	1	7	3	25	1	38	4	0	3	2	.600	0	0	5.48
1999 Bridgeport	IND —	42	0	0	19	48	227	55	43	36	8	0	3	6	25	0	38	7	0	2	1	.667	0	4	6.75
2000 Norwich	AA NYY	62	0	0	46	86.1	357	63	30	30	8	4	1	5	39	5	73	12	3	9	4	.692	0	28	3.13
2001 Columbus	AAA NYY	35	0	0	15	41.1	201	51	23	18	1	0	2	2	22	2	45	7	0	2	4	.333	0	3	3.92
Norwich	AA NYY	21	0	0	14	29.2	112	20	5	4	2	2	0	0	4	2	43	1	0	3	2	.600	0	6	1.21
1993 New York	AL	10	6	0	1	40.1	176	37	20	20	7	0	1	0	19	1	20	1	0	1	1	.500	0	0	4.46
12 Min. YEARS		380	104	11	163	970.1	4205	865	503	416	62	28	37	50	432	18	869	96	15	58	58	.500	1	75	3.86

Brian Jenkins

Bats: Right **Throws:** Right **Pos:** OF-50; DH-11; PR-2; PH-1 **Ht:** 5'11" **Wt:** 215 **Born:** 10/11/78 **Age:** 23

								BATTING								BASERUNNING				PERCENTAGES		
Year Team	Lg Org	G	AB	H	2B	3B	HR	TB	R	RBI	TBB	IBB	SO	HBP	SH	SF	SB	CS	SB%	GDP	Avg	OBP	SLG
1997 Mets	R NYM	36	109	38	6	1	1	49	17	15	4	0	16	0	0	1	1	1	.50	3	.349	.368	.450
1998 Kingsport	R+ NYM	55	201	52	10	2	5	81	31	25	18	0	17	5	1	1	8	5	.62	5	.259	.333	.403
1999 Capital Cty	A NYM	107	400	116	15	7	20	205	69	79	30	2	69	4	4	6	19	7	.73	7	.290	.341	.513
2000 Capital Cty	A NYM	60	217	58	12	2	3	83	25	23	14	2	41	3	0	2	5	2	.71	1	.267	.318	.382
2001 St. Lucie	A+ NYM	35	126	34	5	1	4	53	15	15	5	0	26	4	0	2	4	3	.57	2	.270	.314	.421
Kinston	A+ Cle	23	83	29	5	2	1	41	10	14	7	0	13	1	0	1	2	3	.40	1	.349	.402	.494
Akron	AA Cle	6	23	5	4	0	0	9	4	3	0	0	5	1	0	1	0	0	—	0	.217	.240	.391
5 Min. YEARS		322	1159	332	57	15	34	521	171	174	78	4	187	18	5	14	39	21	.65	19	.286	.337	.450

Bobby Jenks

Pitches: Right **Bats:** Right **Pos:** SP-23 **Ht:** 6'3" **Wt:** 225 **Born:** 3/14/81 **Age:** 21

			HOW	MUCH	HE	PITCHED					WHAT	HE	GAVE	UP						THE	RESULTS		
Year Team	Lg Org	G	GS	CG	GF	IP	BFP	H	R	ER	HR	SH	SF	HB	TBB	IBB	SO	WP	Bk	W	L	Pct.	ShO	Sv	ERA
2000 Butte	R+ Ana	14	12	0	0	52.2	265	61	57	46	2	2	4	5	44	0	42	19	1	1	7	.125	0	0	7.86
2001 Cedar Rapds	A Ana	21	21	0	0	99	450	90	74	58	10	2	4	12	64	0	98	13	1	3	7	.300	0	0	5.27
Arkansas	AA Ana	2	2	0	0	10	47	8	5	4	0	0	0	2	5	0	10	3	0	1	0	1.000	0	0	3.60
2 Min. YEARS		37	35	0	0	161.2	762	159	136	108	12	4	8	19	113	0	150	35	3	5	14	.263	0	0	6.01

Justin Jensen

Pitches: Left **Bats:** Left **Pos:** RP-39; SP-2 **Ht:** 6'3" **Wt:** 210 **Born:** 12/19/73 **Age:** 28

			HOW	MUCH	HE	PITCHED					WHAT	HE	GAVE	UP						THE	RESULTS		
Year Team	Lg Org	G	GS	CG	GF	IP	BFP	H	R	ER	HR	SH	SF	HB	TBB	IBB	SO	WP	Bk	W	L	Pct.	ShO	Sv	ERA
1994 Bristol	R+ Det	11	9	0	0	44	190	39	28	20	3	3	1	1	25	0	39	5	1	2	4	.333	0	0	4.09
1995 Jamestown	A- Det	14	14	0	0	74.1	332	73	53	40	7	0	5	4	41	0	63	9	3	2	8	.200	0	0	4.84
1996 Fayettevlle	A Det	26	26	2	0	153	646	127	78	55	8	4	4	13	58	0	148	11	1	7	11	.389	0	0	3.24
1997 Lakeland	A+ Det	25	25	1	0	143.1	624	143	78	66	10	1	8	4	68	0	112	9	0	7	10	.412	0	0	4.14
1998 Lakeland	A+ Det	30	13	0	7	104.2	477	106	57	47	6	6	7	4	62	0	86	12	0	5	7	.417	0	1	4.04
1999 Somerset	IND —	24	23	2	0	156.1	644	120	55	48	13	3	2	7	77	1	111	8	2	12	5	.706	0	0	2.76
2000 Trenton	AA Bos	10	0	0	7	14.1	64	13	12	12	3	1	1	1	8	0	6	2	0	1	1	.500	0	0	7.53
Sarasota	A+ Bos	12	1	0	5	16	79	24	12	12	2	1	1	0	5	0	15	0	0	1	1	.500	0	1	6.75
Somerset	IND —	9	9	0	0	47.1	210	47	25	23	7	3	0	1	22	1	44	3	0	3	1	.750	0	0	4.37
2001 Norwich	AA NYY	4	0	0	1	7.1	32	7	3	3	1	0	0	0	4	0	6	0	0	0	0	—	0	0	3.68
Tampa	A+ NYY	37	2	0	13	62	275	52	22	16	1	4	1	3	36	0	67	7	0	3	3	.500	0	0	2.32
8 Min. YEARS		202	122	5	33	822.2	3573	751	423	342	61	26	30	38	406	2	697	66	7	43	51	.457	0	2	3.74

Mike Jerzembeck

Pitches: Right **Bats:** Right **Pos:** RP-6; SP-4 **Ht:** 6'1" **Wt:** 185 **Born:** 5/18/72 **Age:** 30

			HOW	MUCH	HE	PITCHED					WHAT	HE	GAVE	UP						THE	RESULTS		
Year Team	Lg Org	G	GS	CG	GF	IP	BFP	H	R	ER	HR	SH	SF	HB	TBB	IBB	SO	WP	Bk	W	L	Pct.	ShO	Sv	ERA
1993 Oneonta	A- NYY	14	14	0	0	77.1	327	70	25	23	1	3	1	3	26	0	76	2	2	8	4	.667	0	0	2.68
1994 Tampa	A+ NYY	16	16	0	0	68.2	274	59	27	24	6	1	2	2	22	0	45	2	1	4	3	.571	0	0	3.15
1995 Tampa	A+ NYY	2	0	0	0	3	17	5	4	3	1	0	0	0	2	0	1	1	0	0	1	.000	0	0	9.00
1996 Columbus	AAA NYY	1	0	0	0	1.2	7	1	1	1	0	0	0	0	1	0	0	0	0	0	0	—	0	0	5.40
Norwich	AA NYY	14	13	1	0	69.2	303	74	38	35	9	4	2	3	26	0	65	2	4	3	6	.333	1	0	4.52
Tampa	A+ NYY	12	12	0	0	73.1	297	67	26	24	4	1	1	0	13	0	60	3	0	4	2	.667	0	0	2.95
1997 Norwich	AA NYY	8	8	0	0	42	164	21	10	8	1	2	0	0	16	0	42	2	1	2	1	.667	0	0	1.71
Columbus	AAA NYY	20	20	2	0	130.1	540	125	55	52	14	4	5	2	37	0	118	4	0	7	5	.583	0	0	3.59
1998 Columbus	AAA NYY	24	24	0	0	140.1	624	158	82	76	20	1	1	3	55	1	107	4	1	4	9	.308	0	0	4.87
2001 Norwich	AA NYY	10	4	0	1	28	119	30	20	16	5	0	3	0	8	0	31	2	0	1	2	.333	0	0	5.14
1998 New York	AL	3	2	0	0	6.1	31	9	9	9	2	0	1	0	4	0	1	1	1	0	1	.000	0	0	12.79
7 Min. YEARS		121	111	3	1	634.1	2672	610	288	262	61	16	15	13	206	1	545	22	9	33	33	.500	1	0	3.72

Joe Jester

Bats: Right **Throws:** Right **Pos:** 2B-114; 3B-3; DH-3; SS-1; PR-1 **Ht:** 5'10" **Wt:** 180 **Born:** 7/17/78 **Age:** 23

								BATTING								BASERUNNING				PERCENTAGES		
Year Team	Lg Org	G	AB	H	2B	3B	HR	TB	R	RBI	TBB	IBB	SO	HBP	SH	SF	SB	CS	SB%	GDP	Avg	OBP	SLG
1999 Salem-Keizr	A- SF	72	263	79	19	1	8	124	67	40	50	3	57	7	7	2	13	6	.68	2	.300	.422	.471
2000 San Jose	A+ SF	114	429	113	13	4	8	158	94	46	69	0	75	17	3	6	24	8	.75	7	.263	.382	.368
Fresno	AAA SF	4	15	3	1	0	0	4	1	0	2	0	4	0	0	0	0	0	—	1	.200	.294	.267
2001 San Jose	A+ SF	81	295	75	17	2	7	117	51	41	35	1	77	12	3	1	20	5	.80	4	.254	.356	.397
Shreveport	AA SF	40	150	48	14	2	6	84	26	27	12	0	33	3	1	1	4	1	.80	2	.320	.380	.560
3 Min. YEARS		311	1152	318	64	9	29	487	239	154	168	4	246	39	14	10	61	20	.75	16	.276	.383	.423

Jason Jimenez

Pitches: Left **Bats:** Right **Pos:** RP-46; SP-4 **Ht:** 6'2" **Wt:** 205 **Born:** 1/10/76 **Age:** 26

			HOW	MUCH	HE	PITCHED					WHAT	HE	GAVE	UP						THE	RESULTS		
Year Team	Lg Org	G	GS	CG	GF	IP	BFP	H	R	ER	HR	SH	SF	HB	TBB	IBB	SO	WP	Bk	W	L	Pct.	ShO	Sv	ERA
1997 Hudson Val	A- TB	19	0	0	5	31.2	121	16	5	1	1	0	0	2	10	0	31	0	1	3	0	1.000	0	0	0.28
1998 St. Pete	A+ TB	13	0	0	8	19	97	24	20	18	3	0	2	3	10	2	15	3	1	0	2	.000	0	0	8.53
Hudson Val	A- TB	29	0	0	6	39.1	154	20	13	7	1	3	0	5	13	1	55	2	1	5	2	.714	0	4	1.60
1999 St. Pete	A+ TB	41	1	0	19	56.2	229	46	23	15	2	2	0	3	21	2	47	2	0	4	4	.500	0	5	2.38
2000 Durham	AAA TB	19	1	0	7	31.2	147	33	17	17	4	0	0	1	25	0	28	1	0	1	1	.500	0	0	4.83
Orlando	AA TB	30	1	0	8	46.1	185	29	13	10	4	0	1	2	12	0	53	3	0	5	1	.833	0	0	1.94
2001 Durham	AAA TB	15	0	0	8	23	102	23	12	12	4	0	0	0	14	0	25	0	0	1	0	1.000	0	1	4.70
Orlando	AA TB	35	4	0	22	51	218	46	20	18	2	2	1	3	24	1	46	2	0	3	3	.500	0	10	3.18
5 Min. YEARS		201	7	0	83	298.2	1253	237	123	98	21	7	4	19	129	6	300	13	3	21	14	.600	0	20	2.95

147

Todd Johannes

Bats: Right **Throws:** Right **Pos:** C-19; DH-3; PH-3; PR-1   **Ht:** 6'3" **Wt:** 185 **Born:** 10/25/76 **Age:** 25

						BATTING										BASERUNNING				PERCENTAGES		
Year Team	Lg Org	G	AB	H	2B	3B	HR	TB	R	RBI	TBB	IBB	SO	HBP	SH	SF	SB	CS	SB%	GDP	Avg	OBP	SLG
1999 Harrisburg	AA Mon	1	4	1	0	0	0	1	0	0	0	0	2	0	0	0	0	0	—	0	.250	.250	.250
Vermont	A- Mon	24	84	25	2	0	0	27	5	11	10	0	15	0	0	2	1	0	1.00	2	.298	.365	.321
2000 Cape Fear	A Mon	38	102	20	2	0	0	22	8	10	9	0	20	5	2	1	0	1	.00	1	.196	.291	.216
2001 Ottawa	AAA Mon	4	10	0	0	0	0	0	0	0	0	0	5	0	0	0	0	0	—	0	.000	.000	.000
Jupiter	A+ Mon	22	58	5	0	0	1	8	5	2	7	0	23	1	0	0	0	0	—	1	.086	.197	.138
3 Min. YEARS		89	258	51	4	0	1	58	18	23	26	0	65	6	2	3	1	1	.50	4	.198	.283	.225

Adam Johnson

Bats: Left **Throws:** Left **Pos:** OF-24; DH-14; 1B-7; PH-3; PR-1; P-1   **Ht:** 6'0" **Wt:** 185 **Born:** 7/18/75 **Age:** 26

						BATTING										BASERUNNING				PERCENTAGES		
Year Team	Lg Org	G	AB	H	2B	3B	HR	TB	R	RBI	TBB	IBB	SO	HBP	SH	SF	SB	CS	SB%	GDP	Avg	OBP	SLG
1996 Eugene	A- Atl	76	318	100	22	9	7	161	58	56	19	3	32	4	1	2	4	1	.80	4	.314	.359	.506
1997 Durham	A+ Atl	133	502	141	39	3	26	264	80	92	50	9	94	4	0	16	18	8	.69	10	.281	.341	.526
1998 Greenville	AA Atl	121	411	104	21	3	19	188	67	77	42	6	71	4	0	7	7	7	.50	10	.253	.323	.457
1999 Richmond	AAA Atl	14	42	14	2	0	1	19	7	6	2	0	5	1	1	0	1	1	.50	0	.333	.378	.452
Greenville	AA Atl	104	394	114	27	2	14	187	50	72	31	1	74	4	0	5	1	6	.14	11	.289	.343	.475
2000 Birmingham	AA CWS	105	379	88	21	2	11	146	42	60	42	2	74	2	0	3	3	5	.38	10	.232	.310	.385
2001 Charlotte	AAA CWS	7	18	8	2	0	0	10	1	4	0	0	0	1	1	0	0	1	.00	0	.444	.474	.556
Birmingham	AA CWS	43	148	38	9	0	2	53	13	11	9	1	28	1	0	0	0	0	—	7	.257	.304	.358
6 Min. YEARS		603	2212	607	143	19	80	1028	318	378	195	22	378	21	3	33	34	29	.54	52	.274	.334	.465

Barry Johnson

Pitches: Right **Bats:** Right **Pos:** RP-45; SP-1   **Ht:** 6'4" **Wt:** 200 **Born:** 8/21/69 **Age:** 32

		HOW MUCH HE PITCHED						WHAT HE GAVE UP											THE RESULTS					
Year Team	Lg Org	G	GS	CG	GF	IP	BFP	H	R	ER	HR	SH	SF	HB	TBB	IBB	SO	WP	Bk	W	L	Pct.	ShO	Sv	ERA
1991 Expos	R Mon	7	1	0	3	12.2	55	10	9	5	0	0	0	4	6	0	10	2	0	0	2	.000	0	0	3.55
1992 South Bend	A CWS	16	16	5	0	109.1	463	111	56	46	5	1	5	6	23	0	74	8	1	7	5	.583	1	0	3.79
1993 Sarasota	A+ CWS	18	1	0	7	54.1	205	33	5	4	1	5	2	2	8	0	40	1	1	5	0	1.000	0	1	0.66
Birmingham	AA CWS	13	1	0	8	21.2	97	27	11	8	2	1	1	0	6	0	16	2	1	2	0	1.000	0	1	3.32
1994 Birmingham	AA CWS	51	0	0	12	97.2	427	100	51	35	7	8	3	2	30	3	67	2	0	6	2	.750	0	1	3.23
1995 Birmingham	AA CWS	47	0	0	10	78	308	64	21	16	1	2	1	2	15	1	53	2	1	7	4	.636	0	0	1.85
1996 Birmingham	AA CWS	9	0	0	7	10.2	35	2	0	0	0	1	0	0	1	0	15	0	0	0	0	—	0	4	0.00
Nashville	AAA CWS	38	8	0	8	103	430	93	38	32	11	2	3	1	39	3	68	4	0	7	2	.778	0	0	2.80
1997 Nashville	AAA CWS	14	0	0	5	25.1	108	24	10	10	1	1	1	0	11	1	10	3	0	4	1	.800	0	2	3.55
Calgary	AAA Pit	34	1	0	12	56.2	247	55	30	26	7	1	3	1	23	2	51	3	0	5	2	.714	0	1	4.13
1998 Oklahoma	AAA Tex	31	7	1	10	77.1	343	96	66	57	13	2	1	3	21	0	54	3	0	2	8	.200	0	1	6.63
Tucson	AAA Ari	5	1	0	0	11.2	56	16	12	9	2	0	0	1	5	1	10	1	0	0	1	.000	0	0	6.94
Norwich	AA NYY	7	0	0	3	12	53	13	6	5	1	1	1	0	5	0	12	1	0	1	0	1.000	0	0	3.75
1999 Scranton-WB	AAA Phi	31	18	1	5	136.1	602	157	83	76	12	1	5	1	49	2	88	7	0	6	10	.375	1	0	5.02
2000 Scranton-WB	AAA Phi	56	1	0	22	81	339	66	25	24	6	3	2	4	30	4	57	1	0	7	4	.636	0	3	2.67
2001 Columbus	AAA NYY	38	1	0	16	63.1	268	64	32	29	7	2	4	2	19	2	37	0	0	4	2	.667	0	1	4.12
Norwich	AA NYY	8	0	0	4	11.2	54	12	7	6	0	0	0	3	5	0	16	0	0	1	1	.500	0	0	4.63
11 Min. YEARS		423	60	7	132	962.2	4090	943	462	388	76	31	32	32	296	19	678	40	4	64	44	.593	2	15	3.63

Gary Johnson

Bats: Right **Throws:** Right **Pos:** OF-127; PH-7; DH-1   **Ht:** 6'4" **Wt:** 210 **Born:** 9/6/76 **Age:** 25

						BATTING										BASERUNNING				PERCENTAGES		
Year Team	Lg Org	G	AB	H	2B	3B	HR	TB	R	RBI	TBB	IBB	SO	HBP	SH	SF	SB	CS	SB%	GDP	Avg	OBP	SLG
1997 Cubs	R ChC	52	198	57	14	5	1	84	40	31	23	0	26	14	0	1	9	3	.75	4	.288	.398	.424
Rockford	A ChC	1	3	0	0	0	0	0	0	0	1	0	1	0	0	0	1	0	1.00	1	.000	.250	.000
1998 Daytona	A+ ChC	116	413	96	12	0	12	144	61	55	53	3	101	10	1	4	10	2	.83	7	.232	.331	.349
1999 Daytona	A+ ChC	108	323	74	16	1	7	113	46	38	39	1	53	10	3	5	4	6	.40	10	.229	.326	.350
2000 Daytona	A+ ChC	124	436	126	21	5	15	202	75	65	56	2	74	15	1	7	25	7	.78	11	.289	.382	.463
2001 West Tenn	AA ChC	135	463	121	28	5	8	183	87	64	58	1	105	15	0	8	15	5	.75	6	.261	.357	.395
5 Min. YEARS		536	1836	474	91	16	43	726	309	253	229	7	360	64	5	25	64	23	.74	39	.258	.356	.395

Gary Johnson

Bats: Left **Throws:** Left **Pos:** OF-105; DH-21; PH-3   **Ht:** 6'3" **Wt:** 210 **Born:** 10/29/75 **Age:** 26

						BATTING										BASERUNNING				PERCENTAGES		
Year Team	Lg Org	G	AB	H	2B	3B	HR	TB	R	RBI	TBB	IBB	SO	HBP	SH	SF	SB	CS	SB%	GDP	Avg	OBP	SLG
1999 Boise	A- Ana	71	264	83	17	1	2	108	56	48	34	3	44	2	0	3	6	2	.75	6	.314	.393	.409
2000 Lk Elsinore	A+ Ana	70	266	90	20	2	13	153	56	62	41	1	59	4	0	5	13	6	.68	6	.338	.427	.575
Erie	AA Ana	71	258	74	10	4	10	122	44	56	35	0	63	3	0	1	4	4	.50	4	.287	.377	.473
2001 Arkansas	AA Ana	128	466	114	24	2	11	175	63	72	60	4	93	7	0	5	8	7	.53	8	.245	.336	.376
3 Min. YEARS		340	1254	361	71	9	36	558	219	238	170	8	259	16	0	14	31	19	.62	24	.288	.376	.445

James Johnson

Pitches: Left **Bats:** Both **Pos:** RP-34; SP-1   **Ht:** 6'1" **Wt:** 175 **Born:** 8/7/76 **Age:** 25

		HOW MUCH HE PITCHED						WHAT HE GAVE UP											THE RESULTS					
Year Team	Lg Org	G	GS	CG	GF	IP	BFP	H	R	ER	HR	SH	SF	HB	TBB	IBB	SO	WP	Bk	W	L	Pct.	ShO	Sv	ERA
1998 Ogden	R+ Mil	13	13	0	0	68.1	305	75	51	37	10	0	2	0	27	0	77	11	1	5	6	.455	0	0	4.87
1999 Stockton	A+ Mil	29	23	1	1	129.1	568	146	83	68	13	6	5	2	47	1	135	22	1	5	6	.455	1	0	4.73
2000 Mudville	A+ Mil	11	11	0	0	58.2	241	45	25	20	1	1	2	0	20	0	66	4	0	3	5	.375	0	0	3.07
Huntsville	AA Mil	16	10	0	1	68	299	74	42	35	9	2	1	0	22	0	74	11	0	4	3	.571	0	0	4.63

148

Year Team	Lg Org	G	GS	CG	GF	IP	BFP	H	R	ER	HR	SH	SF	HB	TBB	IBB	SO	WP	Bk	W	L	Pct.	ShO	Sv	ERA
2001 Kinston	A+ Cle	4	1	0	0	12.1	45	8	2	1	1	0	1	0	2	0	13	1	0	0	0	—	0	0	0.73
Akron	AA Cle	31	0	0	6	46.1	193	35	15	15	2	1	1	2	19	0	55	9	0	4	0	1.000	0	0	2.91
4 Min. YEARS		104	58	1	8	383	1651	383	218	176	36	10	12	4	137	1	420	59	2	21	20	.512	1	0	4.14

Jason Johnson

Bats: Right **Throws:** Right **Pos:** OF-108; PH-2; PR-2; DH-1   **Ht:** 6'1" **Wt:** 170 **Born:** 8/21/77 **Age:** 24

Year Team	Lg Org	G	AB	H	2B	3B	HR	TB	R	RBI	TBB	IBB	SO	HBP	SH	SF	SB	CS	SB%	GDP	Avg	OBP	SLG
1996 Martinsville	R+ Phi	55	213	58	5	2	0	67	29	13	14	0	27	2	0	1	20	7	.74	2	.272	.322	.315
1997 Batavia	A- Phi	60	238	70	11	5	0	91	40	28	17	0	26	3	3	5	20	7	.74	3	.294	.342	.382
1998 Piedmont	A Phi	106	446	119	14	3	1	142	63	45	36	0	58	5	6	1	32	12	.73	9	.267	.328	.318
1999 Piedmont	A Phi	111	447	118	21	5	1	152	51	31	22	0	61	8	5	2	27	11	.71	7	.264	.309	.340
2000 Clearwater	A+ Phi	95	335	92	18	3	3	125	56	34	32	1	60	10	4	6	22	7	.76	6	.275	.350	.373
2001 Clearwater	A+ Phi	46	187	54	12	0	2	72	26	32	12	0	32	1	2	4	22	3	.88	0	.289	.328	.385
Reading	AA Phi	65	197	52	10	0	0	62	26	10	9	2	41	5	4	2	9	4	.69	4	.264	.310	.315
6 Min. YEARS		538	2063	563	91	18	7	711	291	193	142	3	305	34	24	21	152	51	.75	31	.273	.327	.345

Keith Johnson

Bats: Right **Throws:** Right **Pos:** SS-89; 3B-32; 1B-8; 2B-4; PH-2; PR-1   **Ht:** 5'11" **Wt:** 200 **Born:** 4/17/71 **Age:** 31

Year Team	Lg Org	G	AB	H	2B	3B	HR	TB	R	RBI	TBB	IBB	SO	HBP	SH	SF	SB	CS	SB%	GDP	Avg	OBP	SLG
1992 Yakima	A- LA	57	197	40	6	0	1	49	27	17	16	0	37	10	1	1	5	1	.83	4	.203	.295	.249
1993 Vero Beach	A+ LA	111	404	96	22	0	4	130	37	48	18	0	71	4	6	5	13	13	.50	8	.238	.274	.322
1994 Bakersfield	A+ LA	64	210	42	12	1	2	62	19	19	16	0	49	5	3	2	13	7	.65	3	.200	.270	.295
1995 San Berndno	A+ LA	111	417	101	26	1	17	180	64	68	17	0	83	4	11	2	20	12	.63	4	.242	.277	.432
1996 San Antonio	AA LA	127	521	143	28	6	10	213	74	57	17	1	82	4	9	3	15	8	.65	15	.274	.301	.409
Albuquerque	AAA LA	4	16	4	1	0	0	5	2	2	1	0	1	0	0	0	0	0	—	0	.250	.294	.313
1997 San Antonio	AA LA	96	298	80	9	3	9	122	43	52	17	0	48	4	8	3	7	6	.54	4	.268	.314	.409
1998 Albuquerque	AAA LA	82	254	59	5	1	6	84	32	26	10	0	51	4	6	1	6	3	.67	4	.232	.271	.331
San Antonio	AA LA	40	154	46	10	1	3	67	20	16	10	2	26	3	6	1	10	5	.67	3	.299	.351	.435
1999 El Paso	AA Ari	17	70	21	10	1	3	42	17	15	4	0	17	0	1	1	0	1	.00	4	.300	.333	.600
Tucson	AAA Ari	107	356	102	19	0	12	157	61	46	30	2	71	8	4	4	2	4	.33	11	.287	.352	.441
2000 Edmonton	AAA Ana	109	423	130	31	2	13	204	63	64	19	0	71	7	6	5	7	8	.47	11	.307	.344	.482
2001 Las Vegas	AAA LA	125	435	109	32	4	12	185	55	50	17	0	87	7	14	2	4	5	.44	11	.251	.289	.425
2000 Anaheim	AL	6	4	2	0	0	0	2	2	0	2	0	0	0	1	0	0	0	—	0	.500	.667	.500
10 Min. YEARS		1050	3755	973	211	20	92	1500	514	480	192	5	694	60	75	30	102	73	.58	85	.259	.303	.399

Lance Johnson

Bats: Left **Throws:** Left **Pos:** OF-51; PH-8; PR-2   **Ht:** 5'11" **Wt:** 165 **Born:** 7/6/63 **Age:** 38

Year Team	Lg Org	G	AB	H	2B	3B	HR	TB	R	RBI	TBB	IBB	SO	HBP	SH	SF	SB	CS	SB%	GDP	Avg	OBP	SLG
1984 Erie	A- StL	71	283	96	7	5	1	116	63	28	45	1	20	0	1	3	29	10	.74	6	.339	.426	.410
1985 St. Pete	A+ StL	129	497	134	17	10	2	177	68	55	58	5	39	0	2	9	33	19	.63	7	.270	.340	.356
1986 Arkansas	AA StL	127	445	128	24	6	2	170	82	33	59	2	57	1	3	2	49	15	.77	6	.288	.371	.382
1987 Louisville	AAA StL	116	477	159	21	11	5	217	89	50	49	7	45	0	3	2	42	16	.72	9	.333	.394	.455
1988 Vancouver	AAA CWS	100	411	126	12	6	2	156	71	36	42	4	52	0	2	5	49	16	.75	7	.307	.367	.380
1989 Vancouver	AAA CWS	106	408	124	11	7	0	149	69	28	46	0	36	0	0	4	33	18	.65	2	.304	.371	.365
2001 Newark	IND —	23	85	26	5	4	0	39	17	12	9	0	6	0	0	0	8	3	.73	2	.306	.372	.459
Colo Sprngs	AAA Col	35	135	46	8	2	2	64	26	16	4	0	14	0	1	2	9	4	.69	2	.341	.355	.474
1987 St. Louis	NL	33	59	13	2	1	0	17	4	7	4	1	6	0	0	0	6	1	.86	2	.220	.270	.288
1988 Chicago	AL	33	124	23	4	1	0	29	11	6	6	0	11	0	2	0	6	2	.75	1	.185	.223	.234
1989 Chicago	AL	50	180	54	8	2	0	66	28	16	17	0	24	0	2	0	16	3	.84	1	.300	.360	.367
1990 Chicago	AL	151	541	154	18	9	1	193	76	51	33	2	45	1	8	4	36	22	.62	12	.285	.325	.357
1991 Chicago	AL	160	588	161	14	13	0	201	72	49	26	2	58	1	6	3	26	11	.70	14	.274	.304	.342
1992 Chicago	AL	157	567	158	15	12	3	206	67	47	34	4	33	1	4	5	41	14	.75	20	.279	.318	.363
1993 Chicago	AL	147	540	168	18	14	0	214	75	47	36	1	33	0	3	0	35	7	.83	10	.311	.354	.396
1994 Chicago	AL	106	412	114	11	14	3	162	56	54	26	5	23	2	0	3	26	6	.81	8	.277	.321	.393
1995 Chicago	AL	142	607	186	18	12	10	258	98	57	32	2	31	1	2	3	40	6	.87	7	.306	.341	.425
1996 New York	NL	160	682	227	31	21	9	327	117	69	33	8	40	1	3	5	50	12	.81	6	.333	.362	.479
1997 New York	NL	72	265	82	10	6	1	107	43	24	33	2	21	0	1	0	15	10	.60	6	.309	.385	.404
Chicago	NL	39	204	44	6	2	4	66	17	15	9	1	10	0	0	1	5	2	.71	2	.303	.342	.455
1998 Chicago	NL	85	304	85	8	4	2	107	51	21	26	1	22	0	1	1	10	6	.63	5	.280	.335	.352
1999 Chicago	NL	95	335	87	11	6	1	113	46	21	37	0	20	0	4	1	13	3	.81	6	.260	.332	.337
2000 New York	AL	18	30	9	1	0	0	10	6	2	0	0	7	0	0	0	2	0	1.00	1	.300	.300	.333
7 Min. YEARS		707	2741	839	105	51	14	1088	485	258	312	18	269	1	12	27	252	101	.71	41	.306	.374	.397
14 Maj. YEARS		1448	5379	1565	175	117	34	2076	767	486	352	29	384	7	35	27	327	105	.76	103	.291	.334	.386

Mark Johnson

Pitches: Right **Bats:** Right **Pos:** SP-24   **Ht:** 6'3" **Wt:** 226 **Born:** 5/2/75 **Age:** 27

Year Team	Lg Org	G	GS	CG	GF	IP	BFP	H	R	ER	HR	SH	SF	HB	TBB	IBB	SO	WP	Bk	W	L	Pct.	ShO	Sv	ERA
1997 Kissimmee	A+ Hou	26	26	3	0	155.1	652	150	67	53	8	7	5	6	39	1	127	4	6	8	9	.471	1	0	3.07
1998 Portland	AA Fla	26	26	2	0	142.1	615	147	89	73	12	8	2	4	60	4	120	7	0	5	14	.263	0	0	4.62
1999 Yankees	R NYY	3	2	0	0	11	50	15	11	10	1	1	1	0	5	1	10	0	0	0	3	.000	0	0	8.18
Tampa	A+ NYY	1	1	0	0	6	22	4	1	1	0	0	0	1	0	0	6	0	0	1	0	1.000	0	0	1.50
Norwich	AA NYY	16	15	0	0	88	393	88	51	36	7	1	5	4	39	0	52	6	0	9	3	.750	0	0	3.68
2000 Toledo	AAA Det	17	17	1	0	100	454	142	81	73	15	3	8	6	26	2	48	1	0	2	11	.154	0	0	6.57
2001 Toledo	AAA Det	24	24	2	0	141	609	170	83	75	21	2	3	8	24	1	79	6	1	7	11	.389	1	0	4.79
2000 Detroit	AL	9	3	0	3	24	116	25	23	20	3	1	4	1	16	1	11	2	0	0	1	.000	0	0	7.50
5 Min. YEARS		113	111	8	0	643.2	2798	716	383	321	65	22	19	28	194	9	442	24	7	32	51	.386	2	0	4.49

149

Reed Johnson

Bats: Right **Throws:** Right **Pos:** OF-133; DH-2; PH-1; PR-1   **Ht:** 5'10" **Wt:** 180 **Born:** 12/8/76 **Age:** 25

Year Team	Lg Org	G	AB	H	2B	3B	HR	TB	R	RBI	TBB	IBB	SO	HBP	SH	SF	SB	CS	SB%	GDP	Avg	OBP	SLG
1999 St.Cathrnes	A- Tor	60	191	46	8	2	2	64	24	23	24	1	31	2	4	4	5	5	.50	1	.241	.326	.335
2000 Hagerstown	A Tor	95	324	94	24	5	8	152	66	70	62	1	49	14	2	3	14	2	.88	9	.290	.422	.469
Dunedin	A+ Tor	36	133	42	9	2	4	67	26	28	14	0	27	11	1	3	3	2	.60	1	.316	.416	.504
2001 Tennessee	AA Tor	136	554	174	29	4	13	250	104	74	45	2	79	18	5	2	42	12	.78	11	.314	.383	.451
3 Min. YEARS		327	1202	356	70	13	27	533	220	195	145	4	186	45	12	12	64	21	.75	25	.296	.389	.443

Rontrez Johnson

Bats: Right **Throws:** Right **Pos:** OF-115; PH-1; PR-1   **Ht:** 5'10" **Wt:** 165 **Born:** 12/8/76 **Age:** 25

Year Team	Lg Org	G	AB	H	2B	3B	HR	TB	R	RBI	TBB	IBB	SO	HBP	SH	SF	SB	CS	SB%	GDP	Avg	OBP	SLG
1995 Red Sox	R Bos	52	193	49	4	2	0	57	37	11	30	0	30	1	3	1	25	5	.83	1	.254	.356	.295
1996 Red Sox	R Bos	28	85	25	6	0	0	31	20	9	17	0	11	0	1	0	6	2	.75	2	.294	.412	.365
Lowell	A- Bos	35	135	30	4	0	4	46	27	12	21	1	30	0	0	2	7	3	.70	2	.222	.323	.341
1997 Michigan	A Bos	118	411	99	10	6	5	136	87	40	65	0	96	9	6	3	29	12	.71	2	.241	.355	.331
1998 Michigan	A Bos	85	306	83	15	5	5	123	65	32	66	0	46	4	1	5	24	8	.75	4	.271	.402	.402
1999 Sarasota	A+ Bos	132	494	148	30	4	8	210	97	59	74	0	63	8	8	7	18	15	.55	7	.300	.395	.425
2000 Trenton	AA Bos	134	524	141	21	2	6	184	83	53	55	1	73	6	3	4	30	19	.61	12	.269	.343	.351
2001 Trenton	AA Bos	73	255	72	15	1	10	119	48	31	22	0	40	9	2	3	17	7	.71	4	.282	.356	.467
Pawtucket	AAA Bos	44	187	56	16	3	4	90	32	22	10	0	35	7	1	0	8	4	.67	7	.299	.358	.481
7 Min. YEARS		701	2590	703	121	23	42	996	496	269	360	2	424	44	25	25	164	75	.69	41	.271	.367	.385

Bobby Jones

Pitches: Left **Bats:** Right **Pos:** SP-6; RP-1   **Ht:** 6'0" **Wt:** 178 **Born:** 4/11/72 **Age:** 30

Year Team	Lg Org	G	GS	CG	GF	IP	BFP	H	R	ER	HR	SH	SF	HB	TBB	IBB	SO	WP	Bk	W	L	Pct.	ShO	Sv	ERA
1992 Helena	R+ Mil	14	13	1	0	76.1	341	93	51	37	7	4	2	1	23	0	53	6	5	5	4	.556	0	0	4.36
1993 Beloit	A Mil	25	25	4	0	144.2	661	159	82	66	9	1	6	9	65	1	115	4	4	10	10	.500	0	0	4.11
1994 Stockton	A+ Mil	26	26	2	0	147.2	638	131	90	69	12	4	4	4	64	0	147	5	2	6	12	.333	0	0	4.21
1995 Colo Sprngs	AAA Col	11	8	0	0	40.2	204	50	38	33	5	4	1	2	33	1	48	4	1	1	2	.333	0	0	7.30
New Haven	AA Col	27	8	0	9	73.1	315	61	27	21	4	3	3	8	36	2	70	7	0	5	2	.714	0	3	2.58
1996 Colo Sprngs	AAA Col	57	0	0	17	88.2	410	88	54	49	8	5	2	4	63	4	78	7	2	2	8	.200	0	3	4.97
1997 Colo Sprngs	AAA Col	25	21	0	2	133	593	135	89	76	16	1	5	12	71	2	104	2	0	7	11	.389	0	0	5.14
1999 Colo Sprngs	AAA Col	3	3	0	0	16.2	82	17	13	10	1	0	0	3	15	0	14	1	0	2	1	.667	0	0	5.40
2000 Norfolk	AAA NYM	22	21	4	0	133.1	572	122	66	64	13	0	3	5	58	4	100	6	1	10	8	.556	1	0	4.32
2001 St. Lucie	A+ NYM	4	4	0	0	9.2	40	6	2	1	0	1	0	0	4	0	9	0	0	0	1	.000	0	0	0.93
Binghamton	AA NYM	2	1	0	0	5	15	0	0	0	0	0	0	0	0	0	6	0	0	0	0	—	0	0	0.00
Norfolk	AAA NYM	1	1	0	0	2	6	0	0	0	0	0	0	0	0	0	0	0	0	0	0	—	0	0	0.00
1997 Colorado	NL	4	4	0	0	19.1	96	30	18	18	2	2	3	0	12	0	5	0	0	1	1	.500	0	0	8.38
1998 Colorado	NL	35	20	1	1	141.1	630	153	87	82	12	9	6	6	66	0	109	4	1	7	8	.467	0	0	5.22
1999 Colorado	NL	30	20	0	1	112.1	546	132	91	79	24	7	4	6	77	0	74	4	0	6	10	.375	0	0	6.33
2000 New York	NL	11	1	0	4	21.2	99	18	11	10	2	0	1	3	14	1	20	0	0	0	1	.000	0	0	4.15
9 Min. YEARS		217	131	11	28	871	3877	862	512	426	75	23	26	48	432	14	744	42	15	48	59	.449	1	6	4.40
4 Maj. YEARS		80	45	1	6	294.2	1371	333	207	189	40	18	14	15	169	1	208	8	1	14	20	.412	0	0	5.77

Chris Jones

Bats: Right **Throws:** Right **Pos:** OF-79; DH-8; PR-8; 1B-5; PH-5   **Ht:** 6'1" **Wt:** 219 **Born:** 12/16/65 **Age:** 36

Year Team	Lg Org	G	AB	H	2B	3B	HR	TB	R	RBI	TBB	IBB	SO	HBP	SH	SF	SB	CS	SB%	GDP	Avg	OBP	SLG
1984 Billings	R+ Cin	21	73	11	2	0	2	19	8	13	2	0	24	0	0	1	4	0	1.00	0	.151	.171	.260
1985 Billings	R+ Cin	63	240	62	12	5	4	96	43	33	19	0	72	1	1	1	13	0	1.00	3	.258	.314	.400
1986 Cedar Rapds	A Cin	128	473	117	13	9	20	208	65	78	20	1	126	3	0	4	23	17	.58	7	.247	.280	.440
1987 Vermont	AA Cin	113	383	88	11	4	10	137	50	39	23	4	99	4	2	3	13	10	.57	12	.230	.278	.358
1988 Chattanooga	AA Cin	116	410	111	20	7	4	157	50	61	29	1	102	2	0	7	11	9	.55	4	.271	.317	.383
1989 Nashville	AAA Cin	21	49	8	1	0	2	15	8	5	0	0	16	0	1	0	2	0	1.00	0	.163	.163	.306
Chattanooga	AA Cin	103	378	95	18	2	10	147	47	54	23	1	68	3	0	1	10	2	.83	13	.251	.299	.389
1990 Nashville	AAA Cin	134	436	114	23	3	10	173	53	52	23	3	86	2	5	1	12	8	.60	18	.261	.301	.397
1991 Nashville	AAA Cin	73	267	65	5	4	9	105	29	33	19	1	65	2	0	1	10	5	.67	6	.243	.298	.393
1992 Tucson	AAA Hou	45	170	55	9	8	3	89	25	28	18	1	34	0	1	2	7	1	.88	7	.324	.384	.524
1993 Colo Sprngs	AAA Col	46	168	47	5	5	12	98	41	40	19	2	47	2	0	4	8	2	.80	2	.280	.352	.583
1994 Colo Sprngs	AAA Col	98	386	124	22	4	20	214	77	75	35	3	72	2	0	4	6	1	.86	3	.321	.380	.554
1995 Norfolk	AAA NYM	33	114	38	12	1	3	61	20	19	11	1	20	1	0	3	5	2	.71	2	.333	.388	.535
1998 Fresno	AAA SF	25	60	16	1	3	3	32	11	8	6	0	12	0	1	1	2	1	.67	0	.267	.333	.533
1999 Syracuse	AAA Tor	81	279	66	12	3	8	108	45	40	19	0	74	0	1	0	11	3	.79	12	.237	.285	.387
2000 Las Vegas	AAA SD	13	26	7	2	0	1	12	6	6	2	0	9	0	0	2	1	0	1.00	0	.269	.300	.462
Indianapols	AAA Mil	64	233	71	17	6	3	109	32	25	12	1	58	1	0	2	5	4	.56	3	.305	.339	.468
2001 Syracuse	AAA Tor	37	137	30	2	2	3	45	17	15	13	2	35	1	0	3	7	2	.78	2	.219	.286	.328
Richmond	AAA Atl	32	65	16	4	0	0	20	7	4	10	1	26	1	2	1	0	3	.00	0	.246	.351	.308
Indianapols	AAA Mil	31	113	32	2	1	7	57	20	21	9	0	25	1	1	1	0	0	—	2	.283	.339	.504
1991 Cincinnati	NL	52	89	26	1	2	2	37	14	6	2	0	31	0	0	1	2	1	.67	2	.292	.304	.416
1992 Houston	NL	54	63	12	2	1	1	19	7	4	7	0	21	0	0	3	3	0	1.00	1	.190	.271	.302
1993 Colorado	NL	86	209	57	11	4	6	94	29	31	10	1	48	0	0	5	9	4	.69	6	.273	.305	.450
1994 Colorado	NL	21	40	12	2	1	0	16	6	2	2	1	14	0	0	0	0	1	.00	1	.300	.333	.400
1995 New York	NL	79	182	51	6	2	8	85	33	31	13	1	45	1	2	3	2	1	.67	4	.280	.327	.467
1996 New York	NL	89	149	36	7	0	4	55	22	18	12	1	42	2	0	0	1	0	1.00	3	.242	.307	.369
1997 San Diego	NL	92	152	37	9	0	7	67	24	25	16	0	45	2	1	1	7	2	.78	4	.243	.322	.441
1998 Arizona	NL	20	31	6	1	0	0	7	3	3	3	0	9	0	0	0	0	0	—	2	.194	.265	.226
San Francisco	NL	43	90	17	2	2	2	27	14	10	8	0	28	0	0	2	1	1	.67	0	.189	.250	.300
2000 Milwaukee	NL	12	16	3	2	0	0	5	3	1	1	0	4	0	0	0	0	0	—	0	.188	.235	.313
16 Min. YEARS		1277	4460	1173	193	67	134	1902	654	649	312	23	1070	26	15	38	156	71	.69	102	.263	.312	.426
9 Maj. YEARS		548	1021	257	43	11	30	412	155	131	74	4	287	5	1	8	26	10	.72	21	.252	.303	.404

Jaime Jones

Bats: Left **Throws:** Left **Pos:** OF-23; DH-5; PH-3; PR-1 **Ht:** 6'3" **Wt:** 190 **Born:** 8/2/76 **Age:** 25

Year Team	Lg Org	G	AB	H	2B	3B	HR	TB	R	RBI	TBB	IBB	SO	HBP	SH	SF	SB	CS	SB%	GDP	Avg	OBP	SLG
1995 Marlins	R Fla	5	18	4	0	0	0	4	2	3	5	1	4	0	0	0	0	0	—	0	.222	.391	.222
Elmira	A- Fla	31	116	33	6	2	4	55	21	11	9	0	30	0	0	0	5	4	.56	2	.284	.336	.474
1996 Kane County	A Fla	62	237	59	17	1	8	102	29	45	19	0	74	0	0	5	7	2	.78	6	.249	.299	.430
1997 Brevard Cty	A+ Fla	95	373	101	27	4	10	166	63	60	44	2	86	1	0	4	6	1	.86	7	.271	.346	.445
1998 Portland	AA Fla	123	438	123	27	0	10	180	58	63	55	3	118	3	0	3	4	1	.80	11	.281	.363	.411
1999 Calgary	AAA Fla	41	138	34	6	0	0	40	12	7	10	1	30	0	0	0	1	3	.25	5	.246	.297	.290
Portland	AA Fla	73	244	62	16	0	7	99	39	31	47	1	81	2	0	2	2	0	1.00	3	.254	.376	.406
2000 Portland	AA Fla	50	185	42	6	2	6	70	25	30	13	0	47	3	0	2	0	4	.00	2	.227	.286	.378
2001 Portland	AA Fla	31	94	19	4	0	1	26	9	10	12	0	29	1	0	0	2	1	.67	2	.202	.299	.277
7 Min. YEARS		511	1843	477	109	9	46	742	258	260	214	8	499	10	0	16	27	16	.63	38	.259	.337	.403

Jason Jones

Bats: Both **Throws:** Right **Pos:** 1B-127; DH-3; PH-2; OF-1 **Ht:** 6'3" **Wt:** 210 **Born:** 10/17/76 **Age:** 25

Year Team	Lg Org	G	AB	H	2B	3B	HR	TB	R	RBI	TBB	IBB	SO	HBP	SH	SF	SB	CS	SB%	GDP	Avg	OBP	SLG
1999 Pulaski	R+ Tex	69	262	93	18	1	11	152	65	58	33	1	55	7	0	5	1	2	.33	5	.355	.433	.580
2000 Savannah	A Tex	132	466	125	34	6	9	198	59	61	65	1	97	4	1	5	9	5	.64	15	.268	.359	.425
2001 Tulsa	AA Tex	30	107	23	6	0	2	35	8	8	3	1	17	1	0	0	0	0	—	4	.215	.243	.327
Charlotte	A+ Tex	102	375	106	26	2	15	181	50	81	56	5	48	1	0	4	1	3	.25	12	.283	.374	.483
3 Min. YEARS		333	1210	347	90	9	37	566	182	208	157	8	217	13	1	14	11	10	.52	36	.287	.371	.468

Jeremy Jones

Bats: Right **Throws:** Right **Pos:** C-77; 1B-9; DH-6; PH-3 **Ht:** 6'3" **Wt:** 195 **Born:** 8/12/77 **Age:** 24

Year Team	Lg Org	G	AB	H	2B	3B	HR	TB	R	RBI	TBB	IBB	SO	HBP	SH	SF	SB	CS	SB%	GDP	Avg	OBP	SLG
1998 Pulaski	R+ Tex	26	101	28	3	1	3	42	11	14	10	0	18	0	0	1	0	0	—	5	.277	.339	.416
1999 Charlotte	A+ Tex	11	31	6	1	0	1	10	4	4	4	0	10	0	0	0	1	0	1.00	1	.194	.286	.323
Savannah	A Tex	43	133	32	6	2	0	42	18	16	15	0	27	1	2	3	0	1	.00	2	.241	.316	.316
2000 Charlotte	A+ Tex	50	155	45	11	2	2	66	17	24	17	1	24	4	0	1	1	1	.50	4	.290	.373	.426
Tulsa	AA Tex	30	97	28	6	1	2	42	18	13	13	0	19	0	3	2	0	2	.00	2	.289	.366	.433
2001 Tulsa	AA Tex	93	311	72	13	0	4	97	34	29	30	1	61	4	8	2	1	3	.25	9	.232	.305	.312
4 Min. YEARS		253	828	211	40	6	12	299	102	100	89	2	159	9	13	9	3	7	.30	23	.255	.330	.361

Marcus Jones

Pitches: Right **Bats:** Right **Pos:** RP-18; SP-9 **Ht:** 6'5" **Wt:** 235 **Born:** 3/29/75 **Age:** 27

Year Team	Lg Org	G	GS	CG	GF	IP	BFP	H	R	ER	HR	SH	SF	HB	TBB	IBB	SO	WP	Bk	W	L	Pct.	ShO	Sv	ERA
1997 Sou Oregon	A- Oak	14	10	0	0	56	246	58	37	28	4	0	3	2	22	0	49	4	0	3	3	.500	0	0	4.50
1998 Visalia	A+ Oak	29	20	0	8	131	587	155	79	68	8	2	4	7	45	3	112	2	3	7	9	.438	0	4	4.67
Edmonton	AAA Oak	2	2	0	0	10.2	50	14	7	3	1	0	0	0	5	0	4	1	0	1	0	1.000	0	0	2.53
1999 Visalia	A+ Oak	18	15	0	0	91	401	103	56	45	7	3	3	4	32	1	82	3	1	6	4	.600	0	0	4.45
Vancouver	AAA Oak	3	3	0	0	15	73	23	11	4	1	0	0	0	5	0	5	1	0	2	1	.667	0	0	2.40
Modesto	A+ Oak	7	5	0	0	32	137	29	18	10	5	2	0	3	14	0	36	1	0	2	1	.667	0	0	2.81
2000 Visalia	A+ Oak	3	2	0	1	11	49	15	8	8	1	1	0	1	3	0	11	0	0	1	0	1.000	0	0	6.55
Sacramento	AAA Oak	17	17	0	0	101.1	434	108	57	49	7	3	5	2	36	0	51	3	1	6	4	.600	0	0	4.35
Midland	AA Oak	5	5	0	0	23	92	24	8	7	0	2	1	0	1	0	12	0	1	2	0	1.000	0	0	2.74
2001 Sacramento	AAA Oak	27	9	1	6	73.1	316	81	39	37	4	3	1	4	20	1	51	1	0	2	3	.400	0	1	4.54
2000 Oakland	AL	1	1	0	0	2.1	15	5	4	4	1	0	0	0	3	0	1	0	0	0	0	—	0	0	15.43
5 Min. YEARS		125	88	1	15	544.1	2385	610	320	259	38	16	18	22	183	5	413	16	6	32	26	.552	0	5	4.28

Ryan Jorgensen

Bats: Right **Throws:** Right **Pos:** C-72; DH-13; PH-1 **Ht:** 6'2" **Wt:** 195 **Born:** 5/4/79 **Age:** 23

Year Team	Lg Org	G	AB	H	2B	3B	HR	TB	R	RBI	TBB	IBB	SO	HBP	SH	SF	SB	CS	SB%	GDP	Avg	OBP	SLG
2000 Eugene	A- ChC	41	130	39	10	2	1	56	17	23	17	0	27	1	2	2		4	.33	1	.300	.380	.431
2001 Daytona	A+ ChC	54	188	53	12	1	8	91	24	29	23	0	39	2	0	1		3	.25	6	.282	.366	.484
West Tenn	AA ChC	32	109	13	4	0	2	23	8	7	11	0	38	0	0	3	0	0	—	5	.119	.195	.211
2 Min. YEARS		127	427	105	26	3	11	170	49	59	51	0	104	3	2	5	3	7	.30	12	.246	.327	.398

Kevin Joseph

Pitches: Right **Bats:** Right **Pos:** RP-50 **Ht:** 6'4" **Wt:** 200 **Born:** 8/1/76 **Age:** 25

Year Team	Lg Org	G	GS	CG	GF	IP	BFP	H	R	ER	HR	SH	SF	HB	TBB	IBB	SO	WP	Bk	W	L	Pct.	ShO	Sv	ERA
1997 Salem-Keizr	A- SF	17	6	0	5	45	208	44	35	27	4	1	2	2	26	0	45	10	3	3	5	.375	0	0	5.40
1998 Bakersfield	A+ SF	6	6	0	0	21	120	35	26	19	3	1	1	2	20	0	17	7	0	0	4	.000	0	0	8.14
Salem-Keizr	A- SF	23	0	0	0	43.1	194	36	25	21	3	1	3	5	27	0	37	8	1	1	0	.500	0	0	4.36
1999 San Jose	A+ SF	20	0	0	9	30.2	122	17	9	8	1	3	0	0	13	0	30	2	1	1	2	.333	0	2	2.35
Shreveport	AA SF	7	0	0	3	12.2	52	8	4	2	0	1	0	1	5	0	16	0	0	2	0	.000	0	1	1.42
2000 Shreveport	AA SF	27	16	0	8	102.2	454	116	60	59	8	5	7	5	48	1	71	4	0	3	11	.214	0	1	5.17
2001 San Jose	A+ SF	9	0	0	4	13.1	53	12	6	5	0	0	3	2	1	0	15	2	0	0	0	—	0	3	3.38
Shreveport	AA SF	24	0	0	11	33.1	145	31	9	9	1	0	2	2	13	3	27	4	0	2	1	.667	0	1	2.43
Fresno	AAA SF	5	0	0	2	8.1	36	9	7	7	0	1	1	0	4	1	2	2	0	0	1	.000	0	0	7.56
Memphis	AAA StL	12	0	0	6	12	56	8	9	9	2	1	1	1	11	1	6	0	0	0	2	.000	0	0	6.75
5 Min. YEARS		150	28	0	48	322.1	1440	316	190	166	22	14	20	20	168	6	266	39	5	10	29	.256	0	8	4.63

Jimmy Journell

Pitches: Right **Bats:** Right **Pos:** SP-27 **Ht:** 6'4" **Wt:** 205 **Born:** 12/29/77 **Age:** 24

Year Team	Lg Org	G	GS	CG	GF	IP	BFP	H	R	ER	HR	SH	SF	HB	TBB	IBB	SO	WP	Bk	W	L	Pct.	ShO	Sv	ERA
2000 New Jersey	A- StL	13	1	0	3	32	136	12	12	7	0	0	2	2	24	0	39	8	0	1	0	1.000	0	0	1.97
2001 Potomac	A+ StL	26	26	0	0	151	620	121	54	42	8	6	5	18	42	0	156	7	0	14	6	.700	0	0	2.50
New Haven	AA StL	1	1	1	0	7	21	0	0	0	0	0	0	0	3	0	6	0	0	1	0	1.000	1	0	0.00
2 Min. YEARS		40	28	1	3	190	777	133	66	49	8	6	7	20	69	0	201	15	0	16	6	.727	1	0	2.32

Jeff Juden

Pitches: Right **Bats:** Both **Pos:** SP-12; RP-4 **Ht:** 6'8" **Wt:** 271 **Born:** 1/19/71 **Age:** 31

Year Team	Lg Org	G	GS	CG	GF	IP	BFP	H	R	ER	HR	SH	SF	HB	TBB	IBB	SO	WP	Bk	W	L	Pct.	ShO	Sv	ERA
1989 Astros	R Hou	9	8	0	0	39.2	177	33	21	15	0	1	3	3	17	0	49	7	2	1	4	.200	0	0	3.40
1990 Osceola	A+ Hou	15	15	2	0	91	390	72	37	23	2	3	1	5	42	0	85	7	4	10	1	.909	0	0	2.27
Columbus	AA Hou	11	11	0	0	52	250	55	36	31	2	2	1	4	42	2	40	9	2	1	3	.250	0	0	5.37
1991 Jackson	AA Hou	16	16	0	0	95.2	408	84	43	33	4	8	4	3	44	0	75	5	2	6	3	.667	0	0	3.10
Tucson	AAA Hou	10	10	0	0	56.2	245	56	28	20	2	4	3	0	25	0	51	7	0	3	2	.600	0	0	3.18
1992 Tucson	AAA Hou	26	26	0	0	147	655	149	84	66	11	12	7	7	71	1	120	12	7	9	10	.474	0	0	4.04
1993 Tucson	AAA Hou	27	27	0	0	169	755	174	102	87	8	5	5	9	76	0	156	15	0	11	6	.647	0	0	4.63
1994 Scranton-WB	AAA Phi	6	6	0	0	25.1	126	30	28	24	5	0	4	4	19	0	28	3	2	2	2	.500	0	0	8.53
1995 Scranton-WB	AAA Phi	14	13	0	0	83.1	354	73	43	38	4	4	3	9	33	1	65	4	1	6	4	.600	0	0	4.10
1999 Columbus	AAA NYY	27	26	4	0	176.1	768	164	124	109	24	6	7	17	76	2	151	14	4	11	12	.478	1	0	5.56
2001 Charlotte	AAA CWS	12	11	1	0	65	281	44	34	24	5	0	0	2	46	0	63	2	1	5	5	.500	0	0	3.32
Sioux City	IND —	4	1	0	1	10	60	13	13	13	1	1	2	0	6	0	10	2	0	0	2	.000	0	0	11.70
1991 Houston	NL	4	3	0	0	18	81	19	14	12	3	2	3	0	7	1	11	0	1	0	2	.000	0	0	6.00
1993 Houston	NL	2	0	0	1	5	23	4	3	3	1	0	1	0	4	1	7	0	0	0	1	.000	0	0	5.40
1994 Philadelphia	NL	6	5	0	0	27.2	121	29	25	19	4	1	2	1	12	0	22	0	2	1	4	.200	0	0	6.18
1995 Philadelphia	NL	13	10	1	0	62.2	271	53	31	28	6	5	4	5	31	0	47	4	1	2	4	.333	0	0	4.02
1996 San Francisco	NL	36	0	0	9	41.2	180	39	23	19	7	1	2	1	20	2	35	3	0	4	0	1.000	0	0	4.10
Montreal	NL	22	0	0	7	32.2	138	22	12	8	1	2	1	4	14	0	26	2	0	1	0	1.000	0	0	2.20
1997 Montreal	NL	22	22	3	0	130	565	125	64	61	17	5	4	9	57	2	107	7	1	11	5	.688	0	0	4.22
Cleveland	AL	8	5	0	0	31.1	141	32	21	19	6	2	2	1	15	0	29	1	0	0	1	.000	0	0	5.46
1998 Milwaukee	NL	24	24	2	0	138.1	629	149	91	85	20	9	7	10	66	0	109	6	0	7	11	.389	0	0	5.53
Anaheim	AL	8	6	0	1	40	172	33	32	30	7	0	0	2	18	0	39	4	0	1	3	.250	0	0	6.75
1999 New York	AL	2	1	0	0	5.2	29	5	9	1	1	0	0	1	3	0	9	0	0	0	1	.000	0	0	1.59
9 Min. YEARS		177	170	7	1	1011	4469	947	593	483	68	47	38	69	501	6	893	87	25	65	54	.546	1	0	4.30
8 Maj. YEARS		147	76	6	18	533	2350	510	325	285	73	27	26	34	247	6	441	27	5	27	32	.458	0	0	4.81

Eric Junge

Pitches: Right **Bats:** Right **Pos:** SP-27 **Ht:** 6'5" **Wt:** 215 **Born:** 1/5/77 **Age:** 25

Year Team	Lg Org	G	GS	CG	GF	IP	BFP	H	R	ER	HR	SH	SF	HB	TBB	IBB	SO	WP	Bk	W	L	Pct.	ShO	Sv	ERA
1999 Yakima	A- LA	15	15	0	0	82	363	98	60	53	10	3	6	0	31	0	55	3	0	5	7	.417	0	0	5.82
2000 San Berndno	A+ LA	29	24	0	2	158	666	159	69	59	8	3	5	9	53	0	116	8	2	8	1	.889	0	1	3.36
2001 Jacksnville	AA LA	27	27	1	0	164	686	143	72	63	19	11	3	13	56	2	116	6	0	10	11	.476	1	0	3.46
3 Min. YEARS		71	66	1	2	404	1715	400	201	175	37	17	14	22	140	2	287	17	2	23	19	.548	1	1	3.90

Josh Kalinowski

Pitches: Left **Bats:** Left **Pos:** SP-25 **Ht:** 6'2" **Wt:** 190 **Born:** 12/12/76 **Age:** 25

Year Team	Lg Org	G	GS	CG	GF	IP	BFP	H	R	ER	HR	SH	SF	HB	TBB	IBB	SO	WP	Bk	W	L	Pct.	ShO	Sv	ERA
1997 Portland	A- Col	6	6	0	0	18.2	78	15	6	5	0	0	0	0	10	0	27	3	0	0	1	.000	0	0	2.41
1998 Asheville	A Col	28	28	3	0	172.1	743	159	93	75	15	7	4	8	65	0	215	17	3	12	10	.545	1	0	3.92
1999 Salem	A+ Col	27	27	1	0	162.1	659	119	47	38	3	4	2	6	71	0	176	11	1	11	6	.647	0	0	2.11
2000 Carolina	AA Col	6	6	0	0	26	119	30	22	18	0	1	1	1	12	0	27	2	1	1	3	.250	0	0	6.23
2001 Carolina	AA Col	25	25	0	0	137.1	616	151	76	62	15	8	5	5	65	0	116	5	1	7	8	.467	0	0	4.06
5 Min. YEARS		92	92	4	0	516.2	2215	474	244	198	33	20	12	20	223	0	561	38	6	31	28	.525	1	0	3.45

Tim Kalita

Pitches: Left **Bats:** Right **Pos:** SP-29; RP-1 **Ht:** 6'2" **Wt:** 220 **Born:** 11/21/78 **Age:** 23

Year Team	Lg Org	G	GS	CG	GF	IP	BFP	H	R	ER	HR	SH	SF	HB	TBB	IBB	SO	WP	Bk	W	L	Pct.	ShO	Sv	ERA
1999 Oneonta	A- Det	3	3	0	0	12.1	44	3	1	0	0	0	0	0	5	0	15	1	0	0	0	—	0	0	0.00
W Michigan	A Det	9	9	0	0	47.1	213	46	26	22	2	1	1	5	27	0	35	4	1	4	1	.800	0	0	4.18
2000 Lakeland	A+ Det	27	25	1	0	149.2	672	146	93	76	7	3	4	16	73	0	107	11	0	7	12	.368	0	0	4.57
2001 Erie	AA Det	30	29	5	0	200	826	190	98	85	25	3	7	11	49	0	147	5	0	15	9	.625	0	0	3.83
3 Min. YEARS		69	66	6	0	409.1	1755	385	218	183	34	7	12	32	154	0	304	21	1	26	22	.542	0	0	4.02

Scott Kamieniecki

Pitches: Right **Bats:** Right **Pos:** SP-4; RP-4 **Ht:** 6'0" **Wt:** 200 **Born:** 4/19/64 **Age:** 38

Year Team	Lg Org	G	GS	CG	GF	IP	BFP	H	R	ER	HR	SH	SF	HB	TBB	IBB	SO	WP	Bk	W	L	Pct.	ShO	Sv	ERA
1987 Pr William	A+ NYY	19	19	1	0	112.1	499	91	61	52	7	1	2	5	78	3	84	9	2	9	5	.643	0	0	4.17
Albany-Col	AA NYY	10	7	0	1	37	176	41	25	22	0	5	0	1	33	3	19	3	1	1	3	.250	0	0	5.35
1988 Pr William	A+ NYY	15	15	7	0	100.1	451	115	62	49	3	2	0	2	50	1	72	10	1	6	7	.462	2	0	4.40
Ft. Laud	A+ NYY	12	11	0	0	77	329	71	36	31	0	1	2	1	40	1	51	7	0	3	6	.333	1	0	3.62
1989 Albany-Col	AA NYY	24	23	6	1	151	636	142	67	62	13	1	3	2	57	1	140	5	0	10	9	.526	3	1	3.70
1990 Albany-Col	AA NYY	22	21	3	1	132	562	113	55	47	5	6	6	0	61	2	99	4	1	10	9	.526	1	0	3.20

Year Team	Lg Org	G	GS	CG	GF	IP	BFP	H	R	ER	HR	SH	SF	HB	TBB	IBB	SO	WP	Bk	W	L	Pct.	ShO	Sv	ERA
1991 Columbus	AAA NYY	11	11	3	0	76.1	308	61	25	20	2	3	2	3	20	0	58	2	3	6	3	.667	1	0	2.36
1992 Ft. Laud	A+ NYY	1	1	1	0	7	28	8	1	1	0	0	0	0	0	0	3	0	0	1	0	1.000	0	0	1.29
Columbus	AAA NYY	2	2	0	0	13	50	6	1	1	1	0	0	0	4	0	12	0	0	1	0	1.000	0	0	0.69
1993 Columbus	AAA NYY	1	1	0	0	6	22	5	1	1	0	0	0	0	0	0	4	0	0	1	0	1.000	0	0	1.50
1995 Tampa	A+ NYY	1	1	0	0	5	22	6	2	1	0	0	0	0	1	0	2	1	0	1	0	1.000	0	0	1.80
Columbus	AAA NYY	1	1	0	0	6.2	23	2	0	0	0	0	0	0	1	0	10	0	0	1	0	1.000	0	0	0.00
1996 Tampa	A+ NYY	3	3	1	0	23	92	20	6	3	1	0	0	0	4	0	17	1	0	2	1	.667	0	0	1.17
Columbus	AAA NYY	5	5	2	0	30.1	131	33	21	19	4	0	0	1	8	0	27	2	0	2	1	.667	0	0	5.64
1998 Bowie	AA Bal	3	3	0	0	11.1	49	13	6	6	1	0	0	0	2	0	5	1	0	1	0	1.000	0	0	4.76
1999 Bowie	AA Bal	1	1	0	0	5	18	6	2	2	0	0	0	0	0	0	1	0	0	0	1	.000	0	0	3.60
Frederick	A+ Bal	1	1	0	0	4	14	0	0	0	0	0	0	0	1	0	3	0	0	0	0	—	0	0	0.00
Rochester	AAA Bal	4	4	0	0	23	95	23	13	13	5	0	1	1	6	0	14	0	0	1	2	.333	0	0	5.09
2001 Iowa	AAA ChC	8	4	0	1	37	150	34	16	15	3	4	1	2	10	0	38	6	0	1	4	.200	0	0	3.65
1991 New York	AL	9	9	0	0	55.1	239	54	24	24	8	2	1	3	22	1	34	1	0	4	4	.500	0	0	3.90
1992 New York	AL	28	28	4	0	188	804	193	100	91	13	3	5	5	74	9	88	9	1	6	14	.300	0	0	4.36
1993 New York	AL	30	20	2	4	154.1	659	163	73	70	17	3	5	3	59	7	72	2	0	10	7	.588	0	1	4.08
1994 New York	AL	22	16	1	2	117.1	509	115	53	49	13	4	3	3	59	5	71	4	0	8	6	.571	0	0	3.76
1995 New York	AL	17	16	1	1	89.2	391	83	43	40	8	1	0	3	49	1	43	4	0	7	6	.538	0	0	4.01
1996 New York	AL	7	5	0	0	22.2	120	36	30	28	6	0	0	2	19	1	15	1	0	1	2	.333	0	0	11.12
1997 Baltimore	AL	30	30	0	0	179.1	764	179	83	80	20	1	6	4	67	2	109	5	0	10	6	.625	0	0	4.01
1998 Baltimore	AL	12	11	0	1	54.2	249	67	41	41	7	3	2	4	26	0	25	2	0	2	6	.250	0	0	6.75
1999 Baltimore	AL	43	3	0	18	56.1	248	52	32	31	4	4	3	4	29	2	39	4	0	2	4	.333	0	2	4.95
2000 Cleveland	AL	26	0	0	7	33.1	157	42	22	21	6	1	0	1	20	5	29	3	0	1	3	.250	0	0	5.67
Atlanta	NL	26	0	0	4	24.2	117	22	18	15	3	0	0	0	22	1	17	0	0	1	0	.667	0	2	5.47
12 Min. YEARS		144	134	25	4	857.1	3655	790	400	345	45	23	17	18	376	11	659	51	8	57	51	.528	8	1	3.62
10 Maj. YEARS		250	138	8	37	975.2	4254	1006	519	490	105	22	25	32	446	34	542	35	1	53	59	.473	0	5	4.52

Kyle Kane

Pitches: Right **Bats:** Left **Pos:** RP-40; SP-1   **Ht:** 6'3" **Wt:** 215 **Born:** 2/4/76 **Age:** 26

Year Team	Lg Org	G	GS	CG	GF	IP	BFP	H	R	ER	HR	SH	SF	HB	TBB	IBB	SO	WP	Bk	W	L	Pct.	ShO	Sv	ERA
1998 Bristol	R+ CWS	13	0	0	3	23.2	115	34	21	14	3	1	2	3	8	0	17	6	0	1	0	1.000	0	0	5.32
1999 Bristol	R+ CWS	5	5	0	0	28	112	19	8	8	2	2	0	2	11	0	23	3	0	2	0	1.000	0	0	2.57
Burlington	A CWS	12	0	0	5	18	100	28	29	27	3	0	2	3	12	0	17	5	1	1	0	1.000	0	1	13.50
2000 Winston-Sal	A+ CWS	32	0	0	7	50.2	243	57	39	33	3	2	1	6	31	3	47	1	0	1	2	.333	0	0	5.86
2001 Winston-Sal	A+ CWS	14	0	0	5	21.2	81	10	5	5	1	0	0	3	8	0	32	0	0	1	0	1.000	0	0	2.08
Charlotte	AAA CWS	1	1	0	0	3	13	4	2	2	0	0	0	0	1	0	0	0	0	0	0	—	0	0	6.00
Birmingham	AA CWS	26	0	0	12	34	127	20	9	7	1	2	0	3	6	1	43	6	0	2	1	.667	0	3	1.85
4 Min. YEARS		103	6	0	32	179	791	172	113	96	13	7	5	20	77	4	179	21	1	8	3	.727	0	5	4.83

Scott Karl

Pitches: Left **Bats:** Left **Pos:** SP-14   **Ht:** 6'2" **Wt:** 209 **Born:** 8/9/71 **Age:** 30

Year Team	Lg Org	G	GS	CG	GF	IP	BFP	H	R	ER	HR	SH	SF	HB	TBB	IBB	SO	WP	Bk	W	L	Pct.	ShO	Sv	ERA
1992 Helena	R+ Mil	9	9	1	0	61.2	245	54	13	10	2	1	1	2	16	0	57	5	1	7	0	1.000	1	0	1.46
1993 El Paso	AA Mil	27	27	4	0	180	732	172	67	49	9	6	3	6	35	0	95	6	7	13	8	.619	2	0	2.45
1994 El Paso	AA Mil	8	8	3	0	54.2	219	44	21	18	2	2	1	1	15	1	51	3	0	5	1	.833	0	0	2.96
New Orleans	AAA Mil	15	13	2	0	89	375	92	38	38	10	3	2	4	33	1	54	2	0	5	5	.500	0	0	3.84
1995 New Orleans	AAA Mil	8	6	1	1	46.1	191	47	18	17	3	0	1	2	12	2	29	1	0	3	4	.429	1	0	3.30
2000 Colo Sprngs	AAA Col	3	2	0	1	20.2	88	21	17	13	2	1	0	0	4	1	16	0	0	0	3	.000	0	0	5.66
Lk Elsinore	A+ Ana	1	0	0	0	7	27	5	0	0	0	0	0	0	1	0	5	0	0	1	0	1.000	0	0	0.00
2001 Nashville	AAA Pit	14	14	0	0	84.2	356	79	40	36	9	3	2	1	29	0	54	1	0	4	3	.571	0	0	3.83
1995 Milwaukee	AL	25	18	1	3	124	548	141	65	57	10	3	3	3	50	6	59	0	0	6	7	.462	0	0	4.14
1996 Milwaukee	AL	32	32	3	0	207.1	905	220	124	112	29	2	7	11	72	0	121	5	1	13	9	.591	1	0	4.86
1997 Milwaukee	AL	32	32	1	0	193.1	839	212	103	96	23	5	2	4	67	1	119	6	0	10	13	.435	0	0	4.47
1998 Milwaukee	NL	33	33	0	0	192.1	843	219	104	94	21	14	3	4	66	4	102	6	0	10	11	.476	0	0	4.40
1999 Milwaukee	NL	33	33	0	0	197.2	885	246	121	105	21	12	7	8	69	4	74	4	2	11	11	.500	0	0	4.78
2000 Colorado	NL	17	9	0	1	65.2	319	95	56	56	14	3	3	3	33	3	29	3	0	2	3	.400	0	0	7.68
Anaheim	AL	6	4	0	0	21.2	105	31	21	16	2	1	0	0	12	0	9	2	0	2	2	.500	0	0	6.65
6 Min. YEARS		85	79	11	2	544	2233	514	214	181	37	16	10	16	145	5	361	18	8	38	24	.613	4	0	2.99
6 Maj. YEARS		178	161	5	4	1002	4444	1164	594	536	120	40	25	33	369	18	513	26	3	54	56	.491	1	0	4.81

Matt Kata

Bats: Both **Throws:** Right **Pos:** 2B-117; SS-6; PH-2   **Ht:** 6'1" **Wt:** 185 **Born:** 3/14/78 **Age:** 24

Year Team	Lg Org	G	AB	H	2B	3B	HR	TB	R	RBI	TBB	IBB	SO	HBP	SH	SF	SB	CS	SB%	GDP	Avg	OBP	SLG
1999 South Bend	A Ari	78	318	83	14	5	3	116	40	33	28	0	46	4	1	1	5	6	.45	5	.261	.328	.365
2000 South Bend	A Ari	133	521	133	22	9	6	191	82	59	52	2	58	6	3	5	38	12	.76	10	.255	.327	.367
2001 Lancaster	A+ Ari	119	494	146	19	6	10	207	80	54	41	3	79	5	4	1	30	8	.79	4	.296	.355	.419
El Paso	AA Ari	4	16	7	2	0	0	9	4	4	2	0	2	0	0	0	0	1	.00	0	.438	.500	.563
3 Min. YEARS		334	1349	369	57	20	19	523	206	150	123	5	185	15	8	7	73	27	.73	19	.274	.339	.388

Justin Kaye

Pitches: Right **Bats:** Right **Pos:** RP-56   **Ht:** 6'4" **Wt:** 185 **Born:** 6/9/76 **Age:** 26

Year Team	Lg Org	G	GS	CG	GF	IP	BFP	H	R	ER	HR	SH	SF	HB	TBB	IBB	SO	WP	Bk	W	L	Pct.	ShO	Sv	ERA
1995 Mariners	R Sea	12	0	0	4	19.1	116	33	28	23	1	0	2	1	19	0	13	4	0	0	1	.000	0	0	10.71
1996 Mariners	R Sea	20	0	0	12	32.1	156	34	23	13	4	0	1	5	19	1	36	7	2	1	0	1.000	0	3	3.62
1997 Wisconsin	A Sea	28	26	0	2	127	618	129	113	103	13	6	5	16	104	0	115	21	6	8	12	.400	0	0	7.30

Year Team	Lg Org	G	GS	CG	GF	IP	BFP	H	R	ER	HR	SH	SF	HB	TBB	IBB	SO	WP	Bk	W	L	Pct.	ShO	Sv	ERA
		HOW MUCH HE PITCHED						WHAT HE GAVE UP												THE RESULTS				
1998 Wisconsin	A Sea	28	0	0	23	47.1	196	25	11	9	2	6	0	2	30	4	79	6	0	6	2	.750	0	9	1.71
Lancaster	A+ Sea	16	0	0	7	30.1	139	37	24	23	4	2	1	0	13	2	34	9	0	1	2	.333	0	0	6.82
1999 Lancaster	A+ Sea	53	0	0	46	61	289	68	42	39	4	2	3	5	40	1	66	6	0	3	5	.375	0	14	5.75
2000 New Haven	AA Sea	50	0	0	23	84.1	368	80	32	25	3	3	3	5	36	4	109	4	3	2	5	.286	0	8	2.67
2001 Tacoma	AAA Sea	56	0	0	15	77	332	51	27	25	5	6	1	6	46	2	107	3	1	3	2	.600	0	4	2.92
7 Min. YEARS		263	26	0	132	478.2	2209	457	300	260	36	25	16	40	307	14	559	60	12	24	29	.453	0	38	4.89

Austin Kearns

Bats: Right **Throws:** Right **Pos:** OF-59; PH-4; DH-2   **Ht:** 6'3" **Wt:** 220 **Born:** 5/20/80 **Age:** 22

Year Team	Lg Org	G	AB	H	2B	3B	HR	TB	R	RBI	TBB	IBB	SO	HBP	SH	SF	SB	CS	SB%	GDP	Avg	OBP	SLG
		BATTING															BASERUNNING				PERCENTAGES		
1998 Billings	R+ Cin	30	108	34	9	0	1	46	17	14	23	0	22	1	0	2	1	1	.50	4	.315	.433	.426
1999 Rockford	A Cin	124	426	110	36	5	13	195	72	48	50	3	120	9	0	3	21	8	.72	9	.258	.346	.458
2000 Dayton	A Cin	136	484	148	37	2	27	270	110	104	90	5	93	7	0	9	18	5	.78	14	.306	.415	.558
2001 Reds	R Cin	6	17	3	2	0	0	5	2	4	2	0	7	0	0	3	0	0	—	0	.176	.227	.294
Chattanooga	AA Cin	59	205	55	11	2	6	88	30	36	26	0	43	6	2	2	7	5	.58	4	.268	.364	.429
4 Min. YEARS		355	1240	350	95	9	47	604	231	206	191	8	285	23	2	19	47	19	.71	31	.282	.383	.487

Brian Keck

Bats: Right **Throws:** Right **Pos:** SS-54; 3B-25; 1B-16; PH-11; 2B-2   **Ht:** 6'3" **Wt:** 185 **Born:** 1/15/74 **Age:** 28

Year Team	Lg Org	G	AB	H	2B	3B	HR	TB	R	RBI	TBB	IBB	SO	HBP	SH	SF	SB	CS	SB%	GDP	Avg	OBP	SLG
		BATTING															BASERUNNING				PERCENTAGES		
1996 Portland	A- Col	43	156	41	1	2	0	46	29	20	22	0	23	1	3	1	7	2	.78	1	.263	.356	.295
1997 Asheville	A Col	37	124	29	3	0	0	32	8	8	9	0	22	0	7	0	5	2	.71	5	.234	.286	.258
Salem	A+ Col	48	121	34	4	0	0	38	22	11	11	1	21	3	5	2	17	3	.85	3	.281	.350	.314
1998 Salem	A+ Col	85	263	72	8	3	1	89	30	24	24	0	39	1	11	2	10	11	.48	8	.274	.334	.338
1999 Salem	A+ Col	103	347	84	10	3	3	109	54	30	37	1	53	1	14	5	14	2	.88	9	.242	.313	.314
Carolina	AA Col	5	15	3	0	1	0	5	0	2	4	0	3	0	0	0	2	1	.67	1	.200	.368	.333
2000 Carolina	AA Col	63	203	53	10	1	3	74	22	28	18	1	44	3	6	3	9	5	.64	6	.261	.326	.365
2001 Carolina	AA Col	100	327	86	15	1	4	115	35	41	22	1	46	1	7	5	12	5	.71	6	.263	.307	.352
6 Min. YEARS		484	1556	402	51	11	11	508	200	164	147	4	251	10	53	18	76	31	.71	39	.258	.323	.326

Rusty Keith

Bats: Right **Throws:** Right **Pos:** OF-61; DH-22; PH-4; PR-4; P-1   **Ht:** 6'0" **Wt:** 209 **Born:** 9/18/77 **Age:** 24

Year Team	Lg Org	G	AB	H	2B	3B	HR	TB	R	RBI	TBB	IBB	SO	HBP	SH	SF	SB	CS	SB%	GDP	Avg	OBP	SLG
		BATTING															BASERUNNING				PERCENTAGES		
1998 Athletics	R Oak	48	179	57	18	4	3	92	37	39	20	0	21	2	1	6	6	3	.67	4	.318	.382	.514
1999 Visalia	A+ Oak	124	448	140	28	3	10	204	87	62	82	1	59	7	3	4	10	8	.56	13	.313	.423	.455
2000 Sacramento	AAA Oak	4	16	8	4	0	2	18	5	6	2	0	2	0	0	0	0	0	.500	0	.500	.556	1.125
Modesto	A+ Oak	104	389	123	22	1	8	171	84	61	82	1	72	3	4	3	10	3	.77	11	.316	.436	.440
Midland	AA Oak	18	61	12	2	0	1	17	8	6	9	0	11	1	0	0	0	0	—	2	.197	.310	.279
2001 Midland	AA Oak	89	291	76	20	1	3	107	39	31	46	0	43	0	4	2	1	4	.20	9	.261	.360	.368
4 Min. YEARS		387	1384	416	94	9	27	609	260	205	241	2	208	13	12	15	27	18	.60	39	.301	.405	.440

Kris Keller

Pitches: Right **Bats:** Right **Pos:** RP-52   **Ht:** 6'2" **Wt:** 225 **Born:** 3/1/78 **Age:** 24

Year Team	Lg Org	G	GS	CG	GF	IP	BFP	H	R	ER	HR	SH	SF	HB	TBB	IBB	SO	WP	Bk	W	L	Pct.	ShO	Sv	ERA
		HOW MUCH HE PITCHED						WHAT HE GAVE UP												THE RESULTS				
1996 Tigers	R Det	8	6	0	0	34	143	23	12	9	0	1	2	0	21	0	23	7	1	1	1	.500	0	0	2.38
1997 Jamestown	A- Det	16	0	0	10	27	143	37	33	26	3	1	3	3	20	0	18	5	2	0	2	.000	0	0	8.67
1998 Jamestown	A- Det	27	0	0	24	33	141	29	12	12	3	1	2	1	16	0	41	3	0	1	3	.250	0	8	3.27
1999 W Michigan	A Det	49	0	0	28	77	324	63	28	25	6	4	3	3	36	1	87	11	2	5	3	.625	0	8	2.92
2000 Jacksnville	AA Det	62	0	0	58	68	299	58	24	22	0	1	5	0	44	3	60	9	0	2	3	.400	0	26	2.91
2001 Toledo	AAA Det	52	0	0	23	68.1	302	64	42	34	10	0	4	3	38	3	60	10	0	5	2	.714	0	4	4.48
6 Min. YEARS		214	6	0	143	307.1	1352	274	151	128	22	8	19	10	175	7	289	45	5	14	14	.500	0	46	3.75

Rich Kelley

Pitches: Left **Bats:** Left **Pos:** SP-3; RP-2   **Ht:** 6'3" **Wt:** 210 **Born:** 5/27/70 **Age:** 32

Year Team	Lg Org	G	GS	CG	GF	IP	BFP	H	R	ER	HR	SH	SF	HB	TBB	IBB	SO	WP	Bk	W	L	Pct.	ShO	Sv	ERA
		HOW MUCH HE PITCHED						WHAT HE GAVE UP												THE RESULTS				
1991 Niagara Fal	A- Det	15	13	0	1	81.1	341	76	38	30	7	0	2	1	33	1	78	4	0	4	8	.333	0	0	3.32
1992 Fayettevlle	A Det	28	26	2	0	162.2	664	140	62	51	15	2	4	6	63	0	117	12	9	13	5	.722	0	0	2.82
1993 Lakeland	A+ Det	26	9	0	10	85.2	350	78	31	29	2	2	2	4	31	1	45	5	4	4	5	.444	0	2	3.05
London	AA Det	7	0	0		5	25	7	5	5	1	0	0	0	5	0	3	3	1	0	0	—	0	0	9.00
1994 Lakeland	A+ Det	13	0	0	10	38	156	32	15	10	2	2	5	0	15	1	23	0	0	4	2	.667	0	1	2.37
Trenton	AA Det	16	4	0	2	42.1	178	46	28	27	8	1	1	0	20	0	29	3	1	1	2	.333	0	0	5.74
1995 Jacksonville	AA Det	7	0	0	1	6	24	9	3	3	1	1	1	0	0	0	2	0	1	1	0	1.000	0	0	4.50
1998 Rochester	AAA Bal	15	3	0	4	38	156	34	28	23	6	0	1	1	17	0	24	2	1	1	3	.250	0	1	5.45
Bowie	AA Bal	18	13	0	1	85	355	80	38	35	12	1	3	2	34	2	56	2	2	8	2	.800	0	0	3.71
1999 Huntsville	AA Mil	25	0	0	12	28.1	123	30	19	18	3	2	0	3	8	0	26	1	1	1	3	.250	0	5	5.72
2000 Erie	AA Ana	44	4	1	18	97.1	428	120	58	48	12	3	8	3	32	1	72	3	3	5	6	.455	0	2	4.44
Edmonton	AAA Ana	7	2	0	3	20.1	100	29	17	15	4	0	1	1	10	0	12	0	1	0	1	.000	0	0	6.64
2001 Arkansas	AA Ana	5	3	0	0	19.1	85	19	13	8	0	1	0	0	8	0	14	2	0	1	1	.500	0	0	3.72
9 Min. YEARS		226	77	3	62	709.1	2985	700	355	302	73	15	28	21	276	6	501	37	24	43	38	.531	0	9	3.83

Ryan Kellner

Bats: Right **Throws:** Right **Pos:** C-91; PH-1   **Ht:** 6'2" **Wt:** 205 **Born:** 12/9/77 **Age:** 24

Year Team	Lg Org	G	AB	H	2B	3B	HR	TB	R	RBI	TBB	IBB	SO	HBP	SH	SF	SB	CS	SB%	GDP	Avg	OBP	SLG
1998 Yakima	A- LA	19	55	15	1	1	1	21	6	5	1	0	22	2	0	0	0	0	—	1	.273	.310	.382
1999 Vero Beach	A+ LA	54	179	37	1	1	2	46	21	14	10	0	51	2	3	0	1	1	.50	5	.207	.257	.257
2000 Vero Beach	A+ LA	62	221	58	13	0	3	80	23	24	18	1	44	3	1	4	0	4	.00	7	.262	.321	.362
San Antonio	AA LA	15	44	4	0	0	0	4	4	1	4	0	14	0	0	0	0	0	—	1	.091	.167	.091
2001 Jacksnville	AA LA	25	91	27	4	0	1	34	5	9	3	0	20	0	1	0	0	0	—	1	.297	.319	.374
Vero Beach	A+ LA	66	236	49	8	1	4	71	15	21	17	0	52	6	2	1	0	2	.00	6	.208	.277	.301
4 Min. YEARS		241	826	190	27	3	11	256	74	74	53	1	203	13	7	5	1	7	.13	21	.230	.285	.310

Heath Kelly

Bats: Right **Throws:** Right **Pos:** 2B-21; 3B-8; PH-3; SS-2; DH-2; OF-1; 1B-1   **Ht:** 6'1" **Wt:** 185 **Born:** 2/16/76 **Age:** 26

Year Team	Lg Org	G	AB	H	2B	3B	HR	TB	R	RBI	TBB	IBB	SO	HBP	SH	SF	SB	CS	SB%	GDP	Avg	OBP	SLG
1998 Utica	A- Fla	34	95	22	3	1	0	27	14	10	9	0	29	3	1	1	1	1	.50	3	.232	.315	.284
1999 Kane County	A Fla	69	189	47	8	2	1	62	34	31	36	1	69	4	1	3	7	3	.70	6	.249	.375	.328
2000 Brevard Cty	A+ Fla	50	152	35	8	0	5	58	17	25	9	1	54	2	2	0	2	1	.67	3	.230	.282	.382
2001 Utica	A- Fla	7	18	4	1	0	1	8	5	3	0	0	2	0	0	0	0	0	—	1	.222	.222	.444
Kane County	A Fla	11	34	6	0	0	0	6	1	3	1	0	10	0	0	0	1	0	.00	0	.176	.200	.176
Portland	AA Fla	17	37	6	2	1	1	13	3	1	1	0	13	0	0	0	0	1	.00	1	.162	.184	.351
4 Min. YEARS		188	525	120	22	4	8	174	74	73	56	2	177	9	4	4	10	7	.59	14	.229	.311	.331

Kenny Kelly

Bats: Right **Throws:** Right **Pos:** OF-121; PR-1   **Ht:** 6'3" **Wt:** 180 **Born:** 1/26/79 **Age:** 23

Year Team	Lg Org	G	AB	H	2B	3B	HR	TB	R	RBI	TBB	IBB	SO	HBP	SH	SF	SB	CS	SB%	GDP	Avg	OBP	SLG
1997 Devil Rays	R TB	27	99	21	2	1	2	31	21	7	11	0	24	2	0	0	6	3	.67	1	.212	.304	.313
1998 Chston-SC	A TB	54	218	61	7	5	3	87	46	17	19	0	52	4	0	1	19	4	.83	1	.280	.347	.399
1999 St. Pete	A+ TB	51	206	57	10	4	3	84	39	21	18	0	46	4	0	0	14	5	.74	1	.277	.346	.408
2000 Orlando	AA TB	124	489	123	17	8	3	165	73	29	59	1	119	6	4	2	31	21	.60	9	.252	.338	.337
2001 San Antonio	AA Sea	121	478	125	20	5	11	188	72	46	45	0	111	3	5	5	18	12	.60	9	.262	.326	.393
2000 Tampa Bay	AL	2	1	0	0	0	0	0	0	0	0	0	0	0	0	0	0	0	—	0	.000	.000	.000
5 Min. YEARS		377	1490	387	56	23	22	555	251	120	152	1	352	19	9	8	88	45	.66	21	.260	.334	.372

Roberto Kelly

Bats: Right **Throws:** Right **Pos:** OF-39; DH-16; PH-9   **Ht:** 6'2" **Wt:** 198 **Born:** 10/1/64 **Age:** 37

Year Team	Lg Org	G	AB	H	2B	3B	HR	TB	R	RBI	TBB	IBB	SO	HBP	SH	SF	SB	CS	SB%	GDP	Avg	OBP	SLG
1982 Yankees	R NYY	31	86	17	1	1	1	23	13	18	10	0	18	0	0	3	3	3	.50	—	.198	.273	.267
1983 Oneonta	A- NYY	20	49	13	0	0	0	13	6	3	3	0	5	2	0	0	3	4	.43	—	.265	.333	.265
Greensboro	A NYY	48	167	36	1	2	2	47	17	17	12	0	20	0	1	0	12	2	.86	—	.216	.268	.281
1984 Greensboro	A NYY	111	361	86	13	2	1	106	68	26	57	0	49	1	1	3	42	10	.81	1	.238	.341	.294
1985 Ft. Laud	A+ NYY	114	417	103	4	13	3	142	86	38	58	1	70	3	3	6	49	14	.78	6	.247	.339	.341
1986 Albany-Col	AA NYY	86	299	87	11	4	2	112	42	43	29	0	63	0	1	5	10	5	.67	5	.291	.348	.375
1987 Columbus	AAA NYY	118	471	131	19	8	13	205	77	62	33	0	116	3	1	8	51	10	.84	5	.278	.324	.435
1988 Columbus	AAA NYY	30	120	40	8	1	3	59	25	16	6	1	29	1	1	0	11	3	.79	3	.333	.370	.492
1997 Fort Myers	A+ Min	4	11	4	0	0	1	7	2	3	4	0	1	0	0	0	0	0	—	0	.364	.533	.636
2001 Colo Sprngs	AAA Col	63	212	61	10	0	12	107	32	48	18	2	48	4	0	5	1	2	.33	6	.288	.347	.505
1987 New York	AL	23	52	14	3	0	1	20	12	7	5	0	15	0	1	0	9	3	.75	0	.269	.328	.385
1988 New York	AL	38	77	19	4	1	1	28	9	7	3	0	15	0	3	1	5	2	.71	0	.247	.272	.364
1989 New York	AL	137	441	133	18	3	9	184	65	48	41	3	89	6	8	0	35	12	.74	9	.302	.369	.417
1990 New York	AL	162	641	183	32	4	15	268	85	61	33	0	148	4	4	4	42	17	.71	7	.285	.323	.418
1991 New York	AL	126	486	130	22	2	20	216	68	69	45	2	77	5	2	5	32	9	.78	14	.267	.333	.444
1992 New York	AL	152	580	158	31	2	10	223	81	66	41	4	96	4	1	6	28	5	.85	19	.272	.322	.384
1993 Cincinnati	NL	78	320	102	17	3	9	152	44	35	17	0	43	2	0	3	21	5	.81	10	.319	.354	.475
1994 Cincinnati	NL	47	179	54	8	0	3	71	29	21	11	1	35	3	0	1	9	8	.53	3	.302	.351	.397
Atlanta	NL	63	255	73	15	3	6	112	44	24	24	0	36	0	0	2	10	3	.77	5	.286	.345	.439
1995 Montreal	NL	24	95	26	4	0	1	33	11	9	7	1	14	2	0	0	4	3	.57	4	.274	.337	.347
Los Angeles	NL	112	409	114	19	2	6	155	47	48	15	5	65	4	0	7	15	7	.68	10	.279	.306	.379
1996 Minnesota	AL	98	322	104	17	4	6	147	41	47	23	0	53	7	0	5	10	2	.83	17	.323	.375	.457
1997 Minnesota	AL	75	247	71	19	2	5	109	39	37	17	0	50	2	1	2	7	4	.64	4	.287	.336	.441
Seattle	AL	30	121	36	7	0	7	64	19	22	5	0	17	1	1	1	2	1	.67	2	.298	.328	.529
1998 Texas	AL	75	257	83	7	3	16	144	48	46	8	0	46	3	1	1	0	2	.00	4	.323	.349	.560
1999 Texas	AL	87	290	87	17	1	8	130	41	37	21	0	57	5	0	2	6	1	.86	5	.300	.355	.448
2000 New York	AL	10	25	3	1	0	1	7	4	1	0	0	6	1	0	0	0	0	—	0	.120	.185	.280
9 Min. YEARS		625	2193	578	67	31	38	821	368	274	230	4	419	14	8	30	182	53	.77	—	.264	.333	.374
14 Maj. YEARS		1337	4797	1390	241	30	124	2063	687	585	317	16	862	49	22	41	235	84	.74	113	.290	.337	.430

Dave Kelton

Bats: Right **Throws:** Right **Pos:** 3B-54; DH-4   **Ht:** 6'3" **Wt:** 205 **Born:** 12/17/79 **Age:** 22

Year Team	Lg Org	G	AB	H	2B	3B	HR	TB	R	RBI	TBB	IBB	SO	HBP	SH	SF	SB	CS	SB%	GDP	Avg	OBP	SLG
1998 Cubs	R ChC	50	181	48	7	5	6	83	39	29	23	0	58	2	0	1	16	3	.84	2	.265	.353	.459
1999 Lansing	A ChC	124	509	137	17	4	13	201	75	68	39	1	121	2	0	3	22	9	.71	11	.269	.322	.395
2000 Daytona	A+ ChC	132	523	140	30	7	18	238	75	84	38	4	120	2	1	5	7	8	.47	9	.268	.317	.455
2001 West Tenn	AA ChC	58	224	70	9	4	12	123	33	45	24	0	55	1	0	2	1	3	.25	1	.313	.378	.549
4 Min. YEARS		364	1437	395	63	20	49	645	222	226	124	5	354	7	1	11	46	23	.67	23	.275	.333	.449

Nathan Kent

Pitches: Right **Bats:** Right **Pos:** SP-26 **Ht:** 6'6" **Wt:** 210 **Born:** 8/16/78 **Age:** 23

Year Team	Lg Org	G	GS	CG	GF	IP	BFP	H	R	ER	HR	SH	SF	HB	TBB	IBB	SO	WP	Bk	W	L	Pct.	ShO	Sv	ERA
1999 Jamestown	A- Atl	14	11	0	1	52.1	225	57	31	24	2	0	0	0	11	0	49	1	0	3	3	.500	0	1	4.13
Greenville	AA Atl	1	0	0	0	1	6	1	2	2	1	0	0	0	2	0	2	0	0	0	0	—	0	0	18.00
2000 Macon	A Atl	5	1	0	4	9.2	42	9	5	5	0	0	1	1	3	0	5	1	0	1	1	.500	0	0	4.66
Myrtle Bch	A+ Atl	24	20	1	0	137.2	537	97	50	39	3	4	3	4	30	0	89	3	1	10	6	.625	0	0	2.55
2001 Greenville	AA Atl	26	26	0	0	154.2	679	186	89	70	12	4	5	3	38	2	111	2	1	8	10	.444	0	0	4.07
3 Min. YEARS		70	58	1	5	355.1	1489	350	177	140	18	8	9	8	84	2	256	7	2	22	20	.524	0	1	3.55

Jason Kershner

Pitches: Left **Bats:** Left **Pos:** SP-20; RP-12 **Ht:** 6'2" **Wt:** 165 **Born:** 12/19/76 **Age:** 25

Year Team	Lg Org	G	GS	CG	GF	IP	BFP	H	R	ER	HR	SH	SF	HB	TBB	IBB	SO	WP	Bk	W	L	Pct.	ShO	Sv	ERA
1995 Martinsvlle	R+ Phi	13	13	0	0	63	278	67	42	36	10	0	2	5	29	0	64	6	0	4	2	.667	0	0	5.14
1996 Piedmont	A Phi	28	28	2	0	168	703	154	81	70	12	5	4	3	59	0	156	12	1	11	9	.550	1	0	3.75
1997 Clearwater	A+ Phi	22	16	0	3	99.1	417	113	49	43	9	2	4	4	21	0	51	2	0	5	10	.333	0	1	3.90
1998 Clearwater	A+ Phi	41	8	0	11	94.1	405	108	57	42	8	1	3	6	25	0	65	8	0	3	3	.500	0	3	4.01
1999 Reading	AA Phi	57	2	0	30	92.2	412	99	67	59	14	3	6	5	40	3	86	5	0	4	4	.500	0	8	5.73
2000 Clearwater	A+ Phi	2	2	0	0	14	52	7	1	1	1	0	0	0	5	0	15	0	0	1	0	1.000	0	0	0.64
Reading	AA Phi	27	19	0	3	119	501	125	49	48	15	6	1	5	25	0	80	3	0	9	2	.818	0	1	3.63
2001 Reading	AA Phi	26	19	0	2	123.2	525	147	75	66	18	5	5	3	26	1	70	4	0	5	9	.357	0	0	4.80
Scranton-WB	AAA Phi	6	1	0	1	15	63	12	8	6	3	0	2	0	3	0	7	0	0	1	0	1.000	0	0	3.60
7 Min. YEARS		222	108	2	50	789	3356	832	429	371	90	22	27	31	233	4	594	40	1	43	40	.518	1	13	4.23

Kyle Kessel

Pitches: Left **Bats:** Right **Pos:** SP-18; RP-13 **Ht:** 6'0" **Wt:** 160 **Born:** 6/2/76 **Age:** 26

Year Team	Lg Org	G	GS	CG	GF	IP	BFP	H	R	ER	HR	SH	SF	HB	TBB	IBB	SO	WP	Bk	W	L	Pct.	ShO	Sv	ERA
1995 Mets	R NYM	7	7	0	0	40	160	29	12	8	1	1	1	2	11	0	47	3	0	3	0	1.000	0	0	1.80
Kingsport	R+ NYM	5	5	0	0	30	134	33	11	6	1	0	0	4	10	1	23	0	0	4	0	1.000	0	0	1.80
1996 Pittsfield	A- NYM	13	13	0	0	79.2	332	80	44	42	6	0	1	4	19	0	67	4	2	2	6	.250	0	0	4.74
1997 Capital Cty	A NYM	27	27	5	0	168.2	685	131	63	51	8	9	5	9	53	3	151	8	0	11	11	.500	1	0	2.72
1998 Mets	R NYM	4	4	0	0	14	53	5	4	1	1	1	0	1	5	0	19	0	0	1	1	.500	0	0	0.64
St. Lucie	A+ NYM	16	16	0	0	89.1	394	101	58	51	11	2	1	7	27	0	61	3	1	2	7	.222	0	0	5.14
1999 Mets	R NYM	3	3	0	0	8	29	5	4	3	0	0	0	1	2	0	11	1	0	0	1	.000	0	0	3.38
St. Lucie	A+ Hou	8	8	0	0	35	157	35	22	18	4	2	1	1	16	0	24	0	0	1	2	.333	0	0	4.63
2000 Kissimmee	A+ Hou	12	12	0	0	75	315	74	37	28	3	3	0	2	24	1	56	1	0	4	5	.444	0	0	3.36
Round Rock	AA Hou	14	13	0	0	72	320	68	45	39	12	4	1	4	48	1	43	0	0	6	5	.545	0	0	4.88
2001 Round Rock	AA Hou	13	10	0	1	57.1	271	75	43	38	7	2	3	4	26	0	39	5	0	3	6	.333	0	0	5.97
New Orleans	AAA Hou	15	6	0	2	41	205	64	40	36	5	2	1	3	24	0	24	3	0	1	3	.250	0	0	7.90
Binghamton	AA NYM	3	2	0	1	9	41	12	10	8	2	0	0	0	2	0	7	0	0	0	1	.000	0	0	8.00
7 Min. YEARS		140	126	5	4	719	3096	712	393	329	61	26	14	42	267	6	572	28	3	38	48	.442	1	0	4.12

Cory Keylor

Bats: Left **Throws:** Right **Pos:** OF-60; DH-2; PH-2 **Ht:** 6'3" **Wt:** 200 **Born:** 8/25/79 **Age:** 22

Year Team	Lg Org	G	AB	H	2B	3B	HR	TB	R	RBI	TBB	IBB	SO	HBP	SH	SF	SB	CS	SB%	GDP	Avg	OBP	SLG
2001 Bluefield	R+ Bal	3	13	7	1	1	1	13	5	4	2	0	4	0	0	0	0	0	—	0	.538	.600	1.000
Bowie	AA Bal	3	7	1	1	0	0	2	0	1	0	0	2	0	0	1	0	0	—	0	.143	.125	.286
Delmarva	A Bal	56	191	44	13	0	5	72	28	19	19	1	64	5	0	0	4	2	.67	1	.230	.316	.377
1 Min. YEAR		62	211	52	15	1	6	87	33	24	21	1	70	5	0	1	4	2	.67	1	.246	.328	.412

Ryan Kibler

Pitches: Right **Bats:** Right **Pos:** SP-29 **Ht:** 6'2" **Wt:** 185 **Born:** 9/17/80 **Age:** 21

Year Team	Lg Org	G	GS	CG	GF	IP	BFP	H	R	ER	HR	SH	SF	HB	TBB	IBB	SO	WP	Bk	W	L	Pct.	ShO	Sv	ERA
1999 Rockies	R Col	14	14	2	0	81.1	337	77	35	23	3	2	0	10	14	1	55	2	0	6	2	.750	0	0	2.55
Portland	A- Col	1	1	0	0	3.1	21	8	8	8	1	0	0	0	4	0	4	0	0	0	0	—	0	0	21.60
2000 Asheville	A Col	26	26	0	0	155	711	173	107	76	9	3	1	14	67	0	110	7	0	10	14	.417	0	0	4.41
2001 Asheville	A Col	10	10	1	0	61.1	260	50	26	20	3	2	3	7	27	0	59	5	0	3	5	.375	0	0	2.93
Salem	A+ Col	11	11	0	0	75.2	300	53	19	13	0	1	0	9	16	0	61	2	0	7	0	1.000	0	0	1.55
Carolina	AA Col	8	8	1	0	47	198	38	17	11	0	1	1	1	19	0	41	6	0	4	1	.800	1	0	2.11
3 Min. YEARS		70	70	4	0	423.2	1827	399	212	151	16	9	5	41	147	1	330	22	0	30	22	.577	1	0	3.21

Mark Kiefer

Pitches: Right **Bats:** Right **Pos:** SP-17; RP-15 **Ht:** 6'4" **Wt:** 194 **Born:** 11/13/68 **Age:** 33

Year Team	Lg Org	G	GS	CG	GF	IP	BFP	H	R	ER	HR	SH	SF	HB	TBB	IBB	SO	WP	Bk	W	L	Pct.	ShO	Sv	ERA
1988 Helena	R+ Mil	15	9	4	2	68	296	76	30	20	3	0	6	6	17	0	51	4	3	4	4	.500	1	0	2.65
1989 Beloit	A Mil	30	15	7	5	131.2	533	106	44	34	4	1	4	8	32	2	100	6	0	9	6	.600	2	1	2.32
1990 Brewers	R Mil	1	1	0	0	2.1	10	3	1	1	0	0	0	0	1	0	2	0	0	0	0	—	0	0	3.86
Stockton	A+ Mil	11	10	0	1	60	261	65	23	22	5	0	0	8	17	0	37	3	1	5	2	.714	0	0	3.30
1991 El Paso	AA Mil	12	12	0	0	75.2	325	62	33	28	4	2	2	1	43	2	72	6	0	7	1	.875	0	0	3.33
Denver	AAA Mil	17	17	3	0	101.1	449	104	55	52	7	4	1	9	41	0	68	6	0	5	6	.455	0	0	4.62
1992 Denver	AAA Mil	27	26	1	0	162.2	706	168	95	83	25	3	4	9	65	1	145	8	3	7	13	.350	0	0	4.59
1993 El Paso	AA Mil	11	11	0	0	51.2	221	48	29	23	5	1	0	2	19	0	44	6	3	3	4	.429	0	0	4.01
New Orleans	AAA Mil	5	5	0	0	28.1	126	28	20	16	4	1	1	0	17	0	23	4	0	3	2	.600	0	0	5.08

156

Year Team	Lg Org	G	GS	CG	GF	IP	BFP	H	R	ER	HR	SH	SF	HB	TBB	IBB	SO	WP	Bk	W	L	Pct.	ShO	Sv	ERA
1994 New Orleans	AAA Mil	21	21	0	0	124.2	531	111	61	54	17	2	3	15	48	0	116	13	0	9	7	.563	0	0	3.90
1995 New Orleans	AAA Mil	12	12	1	0	70.1	290	60	22	22	5	1	0	5	19	0	52	6	0	8	2	.800	0	0	2.82
1996 New Orleans	AAA Mil	22	10	1	3	72.2	310	60	40	35	15	3	3	3	33	1	66	4	0	3	6	.333	0	0	4.33
Omaha	AAA KC	8	7	0	0	45.2	196	49	31	25	7	2	1	2	9	0	33	0	0	3	2	.600	0	0	4.93
2001 Las Vegas	AAA LA	32	17	2	5	145.2	623	126	75	68	21	3	4	12	46	5	174	4	0	11	7	.611	2	1	4.20
1993 Milwaukee	AL	6	0	0	4	9.1	37	3	0	0	0	0	0	1	5	0	7	0	0	0	0	—	0	1	0.00
1994 Milwaukee	AL	7	0	0	1	10.2	52	15	12	10	4	0	2	0	8	0	8	0	0	1	0	1.000	0	0	8.44
1995 Milwaukee	AL	24	0	0	7	49.2	209	37	20	19	6	0	0	0	27	2	41	4	0	4	1	.800	0	0	3.44
1996 Milwaukee	AL	7	0	0	2	10	48	15	9	9	1	1	1	0	5	1	5	1	1	0	0	—	0	0	8.10
10 Min. YEARS		224	173	17	18	1140.2	4877	1066	559	483	122	26	24	80	407	11	983	70	10	81	61	.570	6	2	3.81
4 Maj. YEARS		44	0	0	14	79.2	346	70	41	38	11	1	3	1	45	3	61	5	1	5	1	.833	0	1	4.29

Skip Kiil

Bats: Right **Throws:** Right **Pos:** OF-11; PH-2; PR-2   **Ht:** 6'0" **Wt:** 172 **Born:** 4/10/74 **Age:** 28

Year Team	Lg Org	G	AB	H	2B	3B	HR	TB	R	RBI	TBB	IBB	SO	HBP	SH	SF	SB	CS	SB%	GDP	Avg	OBP	SLG
1997 Piedmont	A Phi	82	261	59	15	3	7	101	48	34	35	0	74	13	3	3	13	2	.87	0	.226	.343	.387
1998 Clearwater	A+ Phi	116	397	109	31	3	14	188	90	70	70	3	109	5	6	4	23	6	.79	4	.275	.387	.474
1999 Clearwater	A+ Phi	86	305	91	15	8	14	164	74	55	70	0	101	7	5	3	24	5	.83	2	.298	.436	.538
2000 Reading	AA Phi	58	182	37	10	0	6	65	24	19	40	0	60	3	4	2	5	3	.63	2	.203	.352	.357
Clearwater	A+ Phi	40	148	40	13	0	4	65	25	25	23	0	46	4	1	1	7	2	.78	1	.270	.381	.439
2001 Norwich	AA NYY	10	16	3	2	0	1	8	5	5	5	0	8	1	0	1	1	0	1.00	0	.188	.391	.500
Mudville	A+ Cin	5	20	6	0	0	1	9	1	3	0	0	4	2	0	0	1	1	.50	0	.300	.364	.450
5 Min. YEARS		397	1329	345	86	14	47	600	267	211	243	3	402	35	19	14	74	19	.80	9	.260	.384	.451

Andy Kimball

Pitches: Right **Bats:** Right **Pos:** RP-48   **Ht:** 6'0" **Wt:** 190 **Born:** 8/23/75 **Age:** 26

Year Team	Lg Org	G	GS	CG	GF	IP	BFP	H	R	ER	HR	SH	SF	HB	TBB	IBB	SO	WP	Bk	W	L	Pct.	ShO	Sv	ERA
1997 Sou Oregon	A- Oak	13	7	0	0	54.2	230	37	29	22	4	1	1	3	17	0	75	8	2	3	2	.600	0	0	3.62
1998 Modesto	A+ Oak	42	8	0	24	97.1	440	113	62	48	7	3	8	6	29	5	96	6	2	5	6	.455	0	12	4.44
1999 Midland	AA Oak	47	0	0	15	89.1	412	112	64	54	14	2	4	2	40	4	87	13	4	9	5	.643	0	2	5.44
2000 Midland	AA Oak	29	0	0	11	47.1	223	60	42	39	9	1	1	6	20	0	38	2	0	3	4	.429	0	2	7.42
Modesto	A+ Oak	16	0	0	9	32.2	140	31	22	10	1	0	2	1	13	3	29	5	0	1	6	.143	0	0	2.76
2001 Huntsville	AA Mil	48	0	0	16	71.1	314	73	32	24	7	7	2	3	28	7	39	5	0	8	6	.571	0	2	3.03
5 Min. YEARS		195	15	0	75	392.2	1759	426	251	197	42	14	18	21	147	19	364	39	8	29	29	.500	0	18	4.52

Brad King

Bats: Right **Throws:** Right **Pos:** C-72; DH-7; PH-4; 1B-1   **Ht:** 6'2" **Wt:** 205 **Born:** 12/3/74 **Age:** 27

Year Team	Lg Org	G	AB	H	2B	3B	HR	TB	R	RBI	TBB	IBB	SO	HBP	SH	SF	SB	CS	SB%	GDP	Avg	OBP	SLG
1996 Williamsprt	A- ChC	23	70	12	2	1	0	16	7	8	4	0	20	4	0	1	0	1	.00	0	.171	.253	.229
1997 Rockford	A ChC	68	204	51	14	1	7	88	31	29	19	2	35	8	2	4	4	4	.50	5	.250	.332	.431
1998 Daytona	A+ ChC	84	276	81	17	0	1	101	49	37	30	0	37	7	2	2	5	6	.45	11	.293	.375	.366
1999 West Tenn	AA ChC	92	232	53	10	0	0	63	29	25	38	5	34	9	2	6	2	1	.67	7	.228	.351	.272
2000 Chattanooga	AA Cin	41	108	27	5	0	2	38	18	11	18	1	26	3	0	3	3	3	.50	2	.250	.364	.352
2001 San Antonio	AA Sea	80	262	82	16	0	10	128	34	56	33	1	33	5	1	2	4	4	.50	13	.313	.397	.489
6 Min. YEARS		388	1152	306	64	2	20	434	168	166	142	9	185	36	7	18	18	19	.49	38	.266	.359	.377

Cesar King

Bats: Right **Throws:** Right **Pos:** C-19   **Ht:** 6'0" **Wt:** 175 **Born:** 2/28/78 **Age:** 24

Year Team	Lg Org	G	AB	H	2B	3B	HR	TB	R	RBI	TBB	IBB	SO	HBP	SH	SF	SB	CS	SB%	GDP	Avg	OBP	SLG
1996 Chston-SC	A Tex	84	276	69	10	1	7	102	35	28	21	0	58	1	0	2	8	5	.62	5	.250	.303	.370
1997 Charlotte	A+ Tex	91	307	91	14	4	6	131	51	37	35	0	58	1	3	4	8	6	.57	5	.296	.366	.427
Tulsa	AA Tex	14	45	16	1	0	1	20	6	8	5	0	3	0	0	0	0	1	.00	2	.356	.420	.444
1998 Tulsa	AA Tex	90	316	70	16	2	3	99	40	39	30	2	68	2	3	6	1	1	.50	10	.222	.288	.313
1999 Tulsa	AA Tex	95	321	73	19	2	11	129	41	45	32	1	70	2	3	1	2	1	.67	7	.227	.301	.402
2000 Oklahoma	AAA Tex	13	42	6	2	1	0	10	3	7	4	0	10	1	0	0	0	1	.00	1	.143	.234	.238
Scranton-WB	AAA Phi	43	129	30	7	0	2	43	13	19	8	0	25	2	1	2	0	0	—	4	.233	.284	.333
2001 Omaha	AAA KC	19	56	16	6	0	2	28	5	12	1	0	5	0	0	2	1	0	1.00	2	.286	.288	.500
6 Min. YEARS		449	1492	371	75	10	32	562	194	195	136	3	297	9	10	17	20	15	.57	36	.249	.312	.377

Jarrod Kingrey

Pitches: Right **Bats:** Right **Pos:** RP-51   **Ht:** 6'1" **Wt:** 200 **Born:** 8/23/76 **Age:** 25

Year Team	Lg Org	G	GS	CG	GF	IP	BFP	H	R	ER	HR	SH	SF	HB	TBB	IBB	SO	WP	Bk	W	L	Pct.	ShO	Sv	ERA
1998 St.Cathrnes	A- Tor	25	0	0	24	37.2	148	21	7	2	1	1	0	0	17	0	58	5	1	0	0	—	0	16	0.48
Hagerstown	A Tor	1	0	0	0	2.1	10	3	2	1	0	1	0	0	0	0	3	0	0	0	1	.000	0	0	3.86
1999 Hagerstown	A Tor	56	0	0	48	61	259	49	24	21	5	1	0	6	26	0	69	0	4	3	2	.600	0	27	3.10
2000 Dunedin	A+ Tor	37	0	0	34	39.1	177	33	20	13	2	2	3	2	23	1	35	5	1	4	2	.667	0	23	2.97
Tennessee	AA Tor	16	0	0	15	17	76	11	6	4	0	2	1	1	15	2	16	1	0	2	0	1.000	0	7	2.12
2001 Tennessee	AA Tor	51	0	0	45	54.2	236	41	17	15	6	2	1	7	32	2	52	1	0	5	3	.625	0	27	2.47
4 Min. YEARS		186	0	0	166	212	906	158	76	56	14	9	4	17	113	5	233	12	6	14	8	.636	0	100	2.38

Matt Kinney

Pitches: Right **Bats:** Right **Pos:** SP-29   **Ht:** 6'5" **Wt:** 220 **Born:** 12/16/76 **Age:** 25

		HOW MUCH HE PITCHED						WHAT HE GAVE UP										THE RESULTS					
Year Team	Lg Org	G	GS	CG	GF	IP	BFP	H	R	ER	HR	SH	SF	HB	TBB	IBB	SO	WP	Bk	W	L	Pct.	ShO	Sv	ERA
1995 Red Sox	R Bos	8	2	0	4	27.2	119	29	13	9	0	1	2	2	10	0	11	5	0	1	3	.250	0	2	2.93
1996 Lowell	A- Bos	15	15	0	0	87.1	387	68	51	26	0	3	3	9	44	2	72	13	1	3	9	.250	0	0	2.68
1997 Michigan	A Bos	22	22	2	0	117.1	514	93	59	46	4	5	2	0	78	2	123	6	0	8	5	.615	1	0	3.53
1998 Sarasota	A+ Bos	22	20	2	1	121.1	536	109	70	54	5	5	2	2	75	3	96	19	2	9	6	.600	1	1	4.01
Fort Myers	A+ Min	7	7	0	0	37.1	162	31	18	13	0	2	1	0	18	0	39	6	0	3	2	.600	0	0	3.13
1999 Twins	R Min	3	3	0	0	5.2	24	6	4	3	0	0	0	0	3	0	8	0	0	0	1	.000	0	0	4.76
New Britain	AA Min	14	13	0	0	60.2	284	69	54	48	8	2	3	4	36	0	50	6	1	4	7	.364	0	0	7.12
2000 New Britain	AA Min	15	15	0	0	86.1	358	74	31	26	7	2	0	1	35	0	93	4	0	6	1	.857	0	0	2.71
Salt Lake	AAA Min	9	9	0	0	55	228	42	26	26	5	1	1	1	26	0	59	2	1	5	2	.714	0	0	4.25
2001 Edmonton	AAA Min	29	29	2	0	161.2	727	178	101	91	25	2	8	7	74	0	146	11	0	6	11	.353	0	0	5.07
2000 Minnesota	AL	8	8	0	0	42.1	186	41	26	24	7	0	4	0	25	1	24	4	0	2	2	.500	0	0	5.10
7 Min. YEARS		144	135	6	5	760.1	3339	699	427	342	54	23	22	26	399	7	697	72	5	45	47	.489	2	3	4.05

Scott Kirby

Bats: Right **Throws:** Right **Pos:** OF-62; PH-9   **Ht:** 6'2" **Wt:** 190 **Born:** 7/18/77 **Age:** 24

		BATTING														BASERUNNING				PERCENTAGES		
Year Team	Lg Org	G	AB	H	2B	3B	HR	TB	R	RBI	TBB	IBB	SO	HBP	SH	SF	SB	CS	SB%	GDP	Avg	OBP	SLG
1996 Helena	R+ Mil	47	145	29	4	0	4	45	26	21	19	0	42	4	1	2	0	3	.00	4	.200	.306	.310
1997 Helena	R+ Mil	68	248	65	10	1	11	110	65	47	53	0	65	7	0	4	8	6	.57	5	.262	.401	.444
1998 Beloit	A Mil	107	359	73	19	2	8	120	51	40	47	0	109	6	5	1	5	4	.56	7	.203	.305	.334
1999 Beloit	A Mil	68	247	75	14	1	17	142	54	47	47	0	59	3	0	3	3	1	.75	5	.304	.417	.575
Stockton	A+ Mil	60	202	58	15	3	10	109	35	36	25	2	59	7	0	4	3	3	.50	7	.287	.378	.540
2000 Huntsville	AA Mil	118	344	75	11	1	12	124	54	45	66	2	112	12	2	1	7	5	.58	4	.218	.362	.360
2001 Huntsville	AA Mil	68	184	42	13	0	6	73	27	23	22	1	63	4	1	1	3	0	1.00	0	.228	.322	.397
6 Min. YEARS		536	1729	417	86	8	68	723	312	259	279	5	509	43	9	16	29	22	.57	32	.241	.358	.418

Daron Kirkreit

Pitches: Right **Bats:** Right **Pos:** RP-20   **Ht:** 6'6" **Wt:** 225 **Born:** 8/7/72 **Age:** 29

		HOW MUCH HE PITCHED						WHAT HE GAVE UP										THE RESULTS					
Year Team	Lg Org	G	GS	CG	GF	IP	BFP	H	R	ER	HR	SH	SF	HB	TBB	IBB	SO	WP	Bk	W	L	Pct.	ShO	Sv	ERA
1993 Watertown	A- Cle	7	7	1	0	36.1	156	33	14	9	1	1	0	0	11	0	44	1	1	4	1	.800	0	0	2.23
1994 Kinston	A+ Cle	20	19	4	1	127.2	510	92	48	38	9	3	1	7	40	0	116	6	0	8	7	.533	0	0	2.68
Canton-Akrn	AA Cle	9	9	0	0	46.1	217	53	35	32	5	2	1	0	25	2	54	4	0	3	5	.375	0	0	6.22
1995 Canton-Akrn	AA Cle	14	14	1	0	80.2	360	74	54	51	13	5	5	6	46	1	67	2	0	2	9	.182	0	0	5.69
Kinston	A+ Cle	3	3	0	0	13.2	63	14	9	9	1	1	1	2	6	0	14	1	0	0	1	.000	0	0	5.93
1996 Kinston	A+ Cle	6	6	0	0	32.2	125	23	7	7	3	0	1	2	10	0	19	3	0	2	0	1.000	0	0	1.93
1997 Buffalo	AAA Cle	1	1	1	0	7	23	3	0	0	0	0	0	0	1	0	2	0	0	1	0	1.000	1	0	0.00
Akron	AA Cle	26	20	1	3	117.2	562	131	96	68	15	9	4	13	69	3	83	10	1	8	9	.471	0	0	5.20
1998 Wichita	AA KC	10	7	0	0	38	184	52	34	28	4	3	2	3	16	1	23	5	0	1	3	.250	0	0	6.63
El Paso	AA Mil	18	13	0	2	73.2	348	103	57	51	6	4	3	2	39	1	31	6	1	1	6	.143	0	0	6.23
1999 Nashua	IND —	7	7	0	0	39.2	194	53	36	26	5	0	1	1	18	0	24	3	0	1	2	.333	0	0	5.90
New Haven	AA Sea	5	4	0	1	24	107	33	8	7	0	1	1	0	7	0	15	3	0	2	2	.500	0	0	2.63
Lancaster	A+ Sea	9	9	0	0	47	212	65	34	28	5	0	1	1	17	0	35	4	1	4	4	.500	0	0	5.36
2000 Nashua	IND —	29	26	0	0	151.2	673	162	79	66	9	6	4	8	63	0	91	1	0	10	6	.625	0	0	3.92
2001 Arkansas	AA Ana	17	0	0	9	26	124	38	23	20	4	1	1	1	9	0	9	3	0	2	1	.667	0	0	6.92
Long Beach	IND —	3	0	0	3	4	13	2	0	0	0	0	1	0	0	0	3	0	0	0	0	—	0	0	0.00
9 Min. YEARS		184	145	8	19	866	3871	931	534	440	80	36	26	47	377	7	630	52	4	49	56	.467	1	0	4.57

Rick Kirsten

Pitches: Right **Bats:** Right **Pos:** SP-27; RP-1   **Ht:** 6'0" **Wt:** 165 **Born:** 7/23/78 **Age:** 23

		HOW MUCH HE PITCHED						WHAT HE GAVE UP										THE RESULTS					
Year Team	Lg Org	G	GS	CG	GF	IP	BFP	H	R	ER	HR	SH	SF	HB	TBB	IBB	SO	WP	Bk	W	L	Pct.	ShO	Sv	ERA
1999 Tigers	R Det	11	4	0	4	25.2	112	18	15	15	2	3	2	2	17	0	27	1	0	1	1	.500	0	0	5.26
Lakeland	A+ Det	2	1	0	0	16.2	60	7	1	1	0	0	0	0	6	0	8	1	0	2	0	1.000	1	0	0.54
2000 W Michigan	A Det	6	6	0	0	39.1	163	36	10	8	1	1	0	3	8	0	25	2	0	4	1	.800	0	0	1.83
Lakeland	A+ Det	14	13	2	0	87.1	364	80	42	32	8	4	4	11	23	0	45	3	1	5	4	.556	0	0	3.30
Jacksnville	AA Det	4	1	0	2	9.1	37	9	6	6	4	0	1	1	3	0	5	0	0	1	1	.500	0	0	5.79
2001 Erie	AA Det	28	27	1	0	161.2	709	161	93	83	22	3	4	22	53	0	143	6	0	14	8	.636	0	0	4.62
3 Min. YEARS		65	53	4	6	340	1445	311	167	145	37	11	11	39	110	0	253	13	1	27	15	.643	1	0	3.84

Danny Klassen

Bats: Right **Throws:** Right **Pos:** 3B-5; SS-1; 2B-1   **Ht:** 6'0" **Wt:** 190 **Born:** 9/22/75 **Age:** 26

		BATTING														BASERUNNING				PERCENTAGES		
Year Team	Lg Org	G	AB	H	2B	3B	HR	TB	R	RBI	TBB	IBB	SO	HBP	SH	SF	SB	CS	SB%	GDP	Avg	OBP	SLG
1993 Brewers	R Mil	38	117	26	5	0	2	37	26	20	24	3	28	8	1	4	14	3	.82	2	.222	.379	.316
Helena	R+ Mil	18	45	9	1	0	0	10	8	3	7	0	11	2	1	0	2	1	.67	2	.200	.333	.222
1994 Beloit	A Mil	133	458	119	20	3	6	163	61	54	58	0	123	12	17	3	28	14	.67	3	.260	.356	.356
1995 Beloit	A Mil	59	218	60	15	2	2	85	27	25	16	0	43	4	0	3	12	4	.75	4	.275	.332	.390
1996 Stockton	A+ Mil	118	432	116	22	4	2	152	58	46	34	0	77	10	5	2	14	8	.64	12	.269	.335	.352
1997 El Paso	AA Mil	135	519	172	30	6	14	256	112	81	48	1	104	10	4	4	16	9	.64	13	.331	.396	.493
1998 Tucson	AAA Ari	73	281	82	25	2	10	141	47	47	19	1	54	6	0	5	6	2	.75	11	.292	.344	.502
1999 Diamondbcks	R Ari	6	17	4	1	0	0	5	2	1	1	0	4	0	0	0	0	0	—	1	.235	.278	.294
Tucson	AAA Ari	64	245	66	16	3	6	106	38	33	20	1	51	1	0	2	5	3	.63	5	.269	.325	.433
2000 Tucson	AAA Ari	28	97	31	7	2	2	48	25	14	19	1	23	1	2	0	1	2	.33	2	.320	.436	.495
2001 Tucson	AAA Ari	7	18	4	0	0	1	7	5	3	2	0	3	1	0	0	0	0	—	0	.222	.333	.389

Year Team	Lg Org	G	AB	H	2B	3B	HR	TB	R	RBI	TBB	IBB	SO	HBP	SH	SF	SB	CS	SB%	GDP	Avg	OBP	SLG
1998 Arizona	NL	29	108	21	2	1	3	34	12	8	9	0	33	1	0	0	1	1	.50	5	.194	.263	.315
1999 Arizona	NL	1	1	1	0	0	0	1	0	0	0	0	0	0	0	0	0	0	—	0	1.000	1.000	1.000
2000 Arizona	NL	29	76	18	3	0	2	27	13	8	8	0	24	1	2	0	1	1	.50	0	.237	.318	.355
9 Min. YEARS		679	2447	689	142	22	45	1010	409	327	248	7	521	55	30	23	98	46	.68	55	.282	.358	.413
3 Maj. YEARS		59	185	40	5	1	5	62	25	16	17	0	57	2	2	0	2	2	.50	5	.216	.289	.335

Josh Klimek

Bats: Left **Throws:** Right **Pos:** 3B-69; OF-40; PH-11; DH-8; 1B-4; PR-1 **Ht:** 6'1" **Wt:** 175 **Born:** 2/2/74 **Age:** 28

Year Team	Lg Org	G	AB	H	2B	3B	HR	TB	R	RBI	TBB	IBB	SO	HBP	SH	SF	SB	CS	SB%	GDP	Avg	OBP	SLG
1996 Helena	R+ Mil	67	253	75	17	0	6	110	56	51	42	5	39	0	0	3	5	1	.83	4	.296	.393	.435
1997 Beloit	A Mil	121	443	118	31	3	12	191	62	66	39	1	56	5	2	6	4	8	.33	8	.266	.329	.431
1998 Stockton	A+ Mil	124	440	125	27	6	9	191	61	56	36	7	60	4	1	6	4	2	.67	6	.284	.340	.434
1999 Huntsville	AA Mil	123	431	103	28	0	14	173	46	71	33	6	78	4	2	8	3	2	.60	5	.239	.294	.401
2000 Huntsville	AA Mil	108	378	106	22	0	14	170	53	62	29	0	71	5	0	6	3	4	.43	4	.280	.335	.450
2001 Huntsville	AA Mil	96	310	88	12	2	18	158	48	51	45	8	65	1	3	4	2	1	.67	4	.284	.372	.510
Indianapolis	AAA Mil	30	104	27	6	0	1	36	13	4	10	0	26	1	2	0	0	0	—	0	.260	.330	.346
6 Min. YEARS		669	2359	642	143	11	74	1029	339	361	234	27	395	20	10	33	21	18	.54	31	.272	.339	.436

Brian Knoll

Pitches: Right **Bats:** Right **Pos:** RP-14; SP-10 **Ht:** 6'3" **Wt:** 200 **Born:** 8/4/73 **Age:** 28

Year Team	Lg Org	G	GS	CG	GF	IP	BFP	H	R	ER	HR	SH	SF	HB	TBB	IBB	SO	WP	Bk	W	L	Pct.	ShO	Sv	ERA
1995 Bellingham	A- SF	22	2	0	5	57	232	44	22	13	1	4	1	3	17	0	35	2	1	5	2	.714	0	0	2.05
1996 Burlington	A SF	52	0	0	16	79	342	76	43	32	5	6	2	4	34	2	56	4	0	3	8	.273	0	1	3.65
1997 Bakersfield	A+ SF	49	0	0	23	68	323	88	50	43	6	3	1	2	35	3	56	10	0	3	6	.333	0	2	5.69
1998 San Jose	A+ SF	42	6	1	15	114.2	490	135	47	44	4	3	3	5	21	0	109	5	0	7	7	.500	1	3	3.45
1999 Shreveport	AA SF	33	17	1	6	128.1	530	117	54	50	15	5	4	11	34	0	91	6	0	9	7	.563	1	1	3.51
2000 Shreveport	AA SF	21	10	1	5	79.2	346	80	34	30	8	4	7	4	26	2	62	0	0	7	5	.583	0	3	3.39
Fresno	AAA SF	10	10	0	0	62	277	76	46	43	13	5	4	5	19	0	36	1	0	3	4	.429	0	0	6.24
2001 Fresno	AAA SF	22	9	0	5	62.2	302	88	52	50	12	4	4	3	29	0	47	3	0	0	3	.000	0	0	7.18
Shreveport	AA SF	2	1	0	1	4	20	5	1	1	0	0	0	0	3	0	2	1	0	0	0	—	0	0	2.25
7 Min. YEARS		253	55	3	76	655.1	2862	709	349	306	64	34	26	37	218	7	494	32	1	37	42	.468	2	10	4.20

Ryan Knox

Bats: Right **Throws:** Right **Pos:** OF-103; PH-1 **Ht:** 6'0" **Wt:** 185 **Born:** 6/28/77 **Age:** 25

Year Team	Lg Org	G	AB	H	2B	3B	HR	TB	R	RBI	TBB	IBB	SO	HBP	SH	SF	SB	CS	SB%	GDP	Avg	OBP	SLG
1999 Helena	R+ Mil	72	275	96	17	1	2	121	58	25	25	1	27	4	3	4	44	11	.80	1	.349	.406	.440
2000 Beloit	A Mil	125	460	125	19	6	2	162	72	41	34	3	61	17	16	7	42	10	.81	5	.272	.340	.352
2001 High Desert	A+ Mil	75	304	97	17	5	4	136	65	29	45	0	57	7	0	1	37	13	.74	3	.319	.417	.447
Huntsville	AA Mil	28	96	18	2	0	0	20	11	4	5	0	15	1	1	0	8	2	.80	1	.188	.235	.208
3 Min. YEARS		300	1135	336	55	12	8	439	206	99	109	4	160	29	20	12	131	36	.78	10	.296	.369	.387

Jason Knupfer

Bats: Right **Throws:** Right **Pos:** 2B-51; 1B-18; 3B-14; PH-9; SS-3; PR-3 **Ht:** 6'0" **Wt:** 185 **Born:** 9/21/74 **Age:** 27

Year Team	Lg Org	G	AB	H	2B	3B	HR	TB	R	RBI	TBB	IBB	SO	HBP	SH	SF	SB	CS	SB%	GDP	Avg	OBP	SLG
1996 Batavia	A- Phi	66	218	61	5	1	1	71	32	24	25	0	43	4	3	2	5	5	.50	4	.280	.361	.326
1997 Clearwater	A+ Phi	108	365	94	15	0	1	112	56	40	49	1	70	4	7	5	5	6	.45	7	.258	.348	.307
1998 Reading	AA Phi	63	193	42	7	2	0	53	27	15	27	1	46	3	4	4	2	1	.67	7	.218	.317	.275
1999 Clearwater	A+ Phi	15	45	13	2	0	0	15	13	3	12	0	5	0	3	0	1	0	1.00	0	.289	.439	.333
2000 Reading	AA Phi	84	279	75	14	1	4	103	53	24	39	1	46	0	11	3	6	6	.50	4	.269	.355	.369
2001 Scranton-WB	AAA Phi	90	276	66	12	2	1	85	41	25	30	1	59	6	3	1	10	5	.67	6	.239	.326	.308
6 Min. YEARS		426	1376	351	55	6	7	439	222	131	182	4	269	17	31	15	29	23	.56	28	.255	.346	.319

Ed Kofler

Pitches: Right **Bats:** Right **Pos:** SP-27; RP-1 **Ht:** 6'2" **Wt:** 175 **Born:** 12/23/77 **Age:** 24

Year Team	Lg Org	G	GS	CG	GF	IP	BFP	H	R	ER	HR	SH	SF	HB	TBB	IBB	SO	WP	Bk	W	L	Pct.	ShO	Sv	ERA
1996 Devil Rays	R TB	10	10	0	0	41	189	49	30	24	2	0	4	4	11	0	36	2	2	1	4	.200	0	0	5.27
1997 Princeton	R+ TB	13	13	0	0	63	280	63	46	39	9	1	1	7	28	0	66	5	2	5	6	.455	0	0	5.57
1998 Hudson Val	A- TB	16	12	0	0	77.1	317	65	34	26	4	2	2	4	24	0	64	6	3	6	3	.667	0	1	3.03
1999 Chston-SC	A TB	27	27	2	0	157.1	661	153	85	70	10	4	7	11	37	0	136	10	4	9	11	.450	0	0	4.00
2000 St. Pete	A+ TB	28	26	1	1	148.1	658	180	98	87	11	3	9	8	46	0	98	11	2	9	10	.474	0	0	5.28
2001 Orlando	AA TB	13	13	0	0	59.2	290	81	57	52	7	0	4	5	26	0	39	3	0	2	7	.222	0	0	7.84
Bakersfield	A+ TB	15	14	0	0	78.2	344	88	43	37	11	1	1	1	25	0	74	0	1	5	6	.455	0	0	4.23
6 Min. YEARS		122	115	3	2	625.1	2739	679	393	335	54	11	28	40	197	0	513	37	14	37	47	.440	0	1	4.82

Graham Koonce

Bats: Left **Throws:** Left **Pos:** 1B-61; OF-27; DH-19; PH-11 **Ht:** 6'4" **Wt:** 225 **Born:** 5/15/75 **Age:** 27

Year Team	Lg Org	G	AB	H	2B	3B	HR	TB	R	RBI	TBB	IBB	SO	HBP	SH	SF	SB	CS	SB%	GDP	Avg	OBP	SLG
1994 Bristol	R+ Det	44	120	25	4	0	0	29	15	15	28	1	25	3	0	3	4	0	1.00	6	.208	.364	.242
1995 Jamestown	A- Det	73	289	81	16	1	3	108	37	34	35	0	63	2	0	1	8	3	.73	1	.280	.361	.374
1996 Fayetteville	A Det	133	487	116	22	3	8	168	61	59	58	2	97	5	2	4	7	7	.50	9	.238	.323	.345

Year Team	Lg Org	G	AB	H	2B	3B	HR	TB	R	RBI	TBB	IBB	SO	HBP	SH	SF	SB	CS	SB%	GDP	Avg	OBP	SLG
1997 Tri-City	IND —	89	286	82	15	3	3	112	46	34	67	4	55	3	2	4	13	6	.68	5	.287	.422	.392
1998 Chico	IND —	69	242	80	15	0	10	125	50	41	38	4	41	3	0	1	0	0	—	6	.331	.426	.517
1999 Rancho Cuca	A+ SD	132	474	135	16	1	19	210	76	79	76	5	110	11	0	6	4	1	.80	12	.285	.392	.443
2000 Rancho Cuca	A+ SD	137	475	140	40	3	18	240	92	93	107	7	105	4	0	4	0	0	—	4	.295	.425	.505
2001 Mobile	AA SD	109	320	85	18	0	13	142	52	48	89	1	83	4	1	2	0	0	—	3	.266	.429	.444
Portland	AAA SD	6	14	3	1	0	1	7	5	2	5	0	6	0	0	0	0	0	—	1	.214	.421	.500
8 Min. YEARS		792	2707	747	147	11	75	1141	434	405	503	24	585	35	5	25	36	17	.68	47	.276	.393	.421

Casey Kopitzke

Bats: Right **Throws:** Right **Pos:** C-37; PH-5; OF-1; DH-1 **Ht:** 6'2" **Wt:** 210 **Born:** 5/31/78 **Age:** 24

Year Team	Lg Org	G	AB	H	2B	3B	HR	TB	R	RBI	TBB	IBB	SO	HBP	SH	SF	SB	CS	SB%	GDP	Avg	OBP	SLG
1999 Eugene	A- ChC	37	110	23	3	0	0	26	19	12	15	0	25	4	0	2	3	3	.50	6	.209	.321	.236
2000 Lansing	A ChC	68	201	45	10	0	1	58	19	22	18	0	28	3	3	3	1	1	.50	8	.224	.293	.289
2001 Iowa	AAA ChC	4	5	1	0	0	0	1	1	2	0	0	1	0	0	0	0	0	—	0	.200	.200	.200
Daytona	A+ ChC	38	96	23	1	0	0	24	15	8	11	0	17	6	3	1	0	2	.00	2	.240	.351	.250
3 Min. YEARS		147	412	92	14	0	1	109	54	44	44	0	71	13	6	6	4	6	.40	16	.223	.314	.265

John Koronka

Pitches: Left **Bats:** Left **Pos:** SP-26 **Ht:** 6'1" **Wt:** 180 **Born:** 6/3/80 **Age:** 22

	HOW MUCH HE PITCHED						WHAT HE GAVE UP									THE RESULTS					
Year Team	Lg Org	G	GS	CG	GF	IP	BFP	H	R	ER	HR	SH	SF	HB	TBB	IBB	SO	WP	Bk	W	L	Pct.	ShO	Sv	ERA
1998 Billings	R+ Cin	12	3	0	3	31.1	177	47	43	28	2	1	3	3	26	0	36	4	1	0	3	.000	0	0	8.04
1999 Reds	R Cin	7	7	0	0	37.1	148	25	11	7	1	1	1	3	14	0	27	1	1	3	3	.500	0	0	1.69
Billings	R+ Cin	7	7	0	0	40.1	173	41	26	25	1	2	2	2	17	0	34	1	0	2	3	.400	0	0	5.58
2000 Clinton	A Cin	20	18	4	0	104	452	123	65	50	7	2	3	0	38	2	74	4	0	4	13	.235	0	0	4.33
2001 Dayton	A Cin	5	5	0	0	24	100	23	12	2	0	0	0	2	8	0	25	0	0	3	1	.750	0	0	0.75
Chattanooga	AA Cin	9	9	0	0	55	251	62	37	35	7	4	1	1	28	0	44	1	1	5	.167	0	0	5.73
Mudville	A+ Cin	12	12	0	0	71	321	78	44	39	10	1	1	2	39	0	66	3	3	5	2	.714	0	0	4.94
4 Min. YEARS		72	61	4	3	363	1622	399	238	186	28	11	11	13	170	2	306	14	6	18	30	.375	0	0	4.61

Aaron Kramer

Pitches: Right **Bats:** Both **Pos:** RP-21; SP-4 **Ht:** 6'1" **Wt:** 210 **Born:** 6/25/75 **Age:** 27

	HOW MUCH HE PITCHED						WHAT HE GAVE UP									THE RESULTS					
Year Team	Lg Org	G	GS	CG	GF	IP	BFP	H	R	ER	HR	SH	SF	HB	TBB	IBB	SO	WP	Bk	W	L	Pct.	ShO	Sv	ERA
1998 Idaho Falls	R+ SD	6	6	0	0	36.1	152	30	14	9	0	2	1	1	10	0	22	1	0	4	0	1.000	0	0	2.23
Clinton	A SD	3	2	0	0	9	40	13	4	2	0	1	0	0	2	0	7	0	0	1	0	1.000	0	0	2.00
1999 Rancho Cuca	A+ SD	23	23	0	0	139	592	154	73	56	14	1	5	3	31	0	98	6	4	9	9	.500	0	0	3.63
2001 Mobile	AA SD	23	4	0	5	49.2	218	53	32	29	11	4	2	3	12	1	41	3	0	2	7	.222	0	0	5.26
West Tenn	AA ChC	2	0	0	0	1.1	7	3	3	3	1	0	0	0	0	0	2	0	0	0	0	—	0	0	20.25
3 Min. YEARS		57	35	0	5	235.1	1009	253	126	99	26	7	9	7	55	1	170	10	4	16	16	.500	0	0	3.79

Scott Krause

Bats: Right **Throws:** Right **Pos:** DH-44; OF-42; PH-2; P-1 **Ht:** 6'1" **Wt:** 187 **Born:** 8/16/73 **Age:** 28

Year Team	Lg Org	G	AB	H	2B	3B	HR	TB	R	RBI	TBB	IBB	SO	HBP	SH	SF	SB	CS	SB%	GDP	Avg	OBP	SLG
1994 Helena	R+ Mil	63	252	90	18	3	4	126	51	52	18	2	49	9	1	2	13	6	.68	2	.357	.416	.500
1995 Beloit	A Mil	134	481	119	30	4	13	196	83	76	50	5	126	12	3	7	24	10	.71	7	.247	.329	.407
1996 El Paso	AA Mil	24	85	27	5	2	3	45	16	11	2	0	19	1	1	0	2	0	1.00	1	.318	.341	.529
Stockton	A+ Mil	108	427	128	22	4	19	215	82	83	32	0	101	16	1	3	25	6	.81	9	.300	.368	.504
1997 El Paso	AA Mil	125	474	171	33	11	16	274	97	88	20	3	108	7	4	7	13	4	.76	7	.361	.390	.578
1998 Louisville	AAA Mil	117	390	114	25	2	26	221	71	82	46	3	104	15	3	1	11	4	.73	16	.292	.387	.567
1999 Louisville	AAA Mil	133	499	138	26	7	15	223	57	89	33	2	104	13	7	8	10	6	.63	13	.277	.333	.447
2000 Indianapolis	AAA Mil	67	208	56	15	0	7	92	29	33	15	1	57	5	1	1	1	0	1.00	2	.269	.332	.442
Huntsville	AA Mil	11	28	9	3	0	0	12	2	5	0	0	8	0	0	0	0	1	—	1	.321	.321	.429
2001 Akron	AA Cle	87	303	77	16	1	15	140	47	52	26	1	84	4	1	5	0	3	.00	4	.254	.317	.462
8 Min. YEARS		869	3147	929	193	34	118	1544	535	571	242	17	760	82	22	34	99	39	.72	62	.295	.357	.491

Jack Krawczyk

Pitches: Right **Bats:** Right **Pos:** RP-47 **Ht:** 6'4" **Wt:** 210 **Born:** 8/12/75 **Age:** 26

	HOW MUCH HE PITCHED						WHAT HE GAVE UP									THE RESULTS					
Year Team	Lg Org	G	GS	CG	GF	IP	BFP	H	R	ER	HR	SH	SF	HB	TBB	IBB	SO	WP	Bk	W	L	Pct.	ShO	Sv	ERA
1998 Helena	R+ Mil	7	0	0	7	8.1	41	10	7	4	1	0	1	0	3	1	11	0	0	0	1	.000	0	0	4.32
Beloit	A Mil	19	3	0	5	40.1	165	37	23	21	3	2	0	1	11	1	42	0	0	3	1	.750	0	4	4.69
1999 Beloit	A Mil	6	0	0	6	6.1	24	5	0	0	0	0	0	0	1	0	11	0	0	0	0	—	0	3	0.00
Stockton	A+ Mil	41	1	0	13	77	331	87	48	40	8	5	3	1	19	2	74	3	0	5	4	.556	0	2	4.68
2000 Huntsville	AA Mil	1	0	0	0	4	16	4	2	2	1	0	0	1	0	0	4	0	0	0	0	—	0	0	4.50
Mudville	A+ Mil	49	0	0	42	86	321	62	14	14	2	5	1	1	9	1	80	1	0	7	1	.875	0	15	1.47
2001 Huntsville	AA Mil	47	0	0	19	81.1	321	67	33	31	9	3	0	4	16	3	66	6	1	6	2	.750	0	1	3.43
4 Min. YEARS		170	4	0	92	303.1	1219	272	127	112	24	15	5	7	60	8	286	10	1	21	9	.700	0	21	3.32

Mike Kremblas

Bats: Right **Throws:** Right **Pos:** C-27; OF-17; PH-8; DH-7; 1B-2; PR-1   **Ht:** 6'0" **Wt:** 180 **Born:** 10/1/75 **Age:** 26

						BATTING										BASERUNNING				PERCENTAGES		
Year Team	Lg Org	G	AB	H	2B	3B	HR	TB	R	RBI	TBB	IBB	SO	HBP	SH	SF	SB	CS	SB%	GDP	Avg	OBP	SLG
1998 Medcine Hat	R+ Tor	59	184	54	15	0	4	81	40	36	40	1	30	9	1	2	5	4	.56	4	.293	.438	.440
1999 Hagerstown	A Tor	58	165	34	7	0	0	41	22	7	15	0	28	14	1	1	2	0	1.00	5	.206	.323	.248
2000 Dunedin	A+ Tor	25	64	18	2	1	0	22	15	10	16	0	7	6	0	1	1	0	1.00	1	.281	.460	.344
Tennessee	AA Tor	30	69	19	4	0	1	26	16	6	9	0	14	10	5	2	1	1	.50	2	.275	.422	.377
2001 Syracuse	AAA Tor	4	9	2	0	0	0	2	3	0	1	0	4	1	0	0	0	0	—	0	.222	.364	.222
Dunedin	A+ Tor	49	141	27	6	1	0	35	17	15	18	0	34	6	1	2	0	3	.00	5	.191	.305	.248
4 Min. YEARS		225	632	154	34	2	5	207	113	74	99	1	117	46	8	8	9	8	.53	17	.244	.381	.328

Rick Krivda

Pitches: Left **Bats:** Right **Pos:** SP-13; RP-1   **Ht:** 6'1" **Wt:** 185 **Born:** 1/19/70 **Age:** 32

		HOW MUCH HE PITCHED						WHAT HE GAVE UP									THE RESULTS					
Year Team	Lg Org	G	GS	CG	GF	IP	BFP	H	R	ER	HR	SH	SF	HB	TBB	IBB	SO	WP	Bk	W	L	Pct.	ShO	Sv	ERA
1991 Bluefield	R+ Bal	15	8	0	2	67	265	48	20	14	0	2	1	0	24	0	79	1	4	7	1	.875	0	1	1.88
1992 Kane County	A Bal	18	18	2	0	121.2	502	108	53	41	6	0	3	1	41	0	124	5	1	12	5	.706	0	0	3.03
Frederick	A+ Bal	9	9	1	0	57.1	236	51	23	19	7	0	0	1	15	0	64	1	1	5	1	.833	1	0	2.98
1993 Bowie	AA Bal	22	22	0	0	125.2	522	114	46	43	10	2	1	2	50	0	108	1	2	7	5	.583	0	0	3.08
Rochester	AAA Bal	5	5	0	0	33.1	133	20	7	7	2	1	0	1	16	0	23	1	0	3	0	1.000	0	0	1.89
1994 Rochester	AAA Bal	28	26	3	2	163	688	149	75	64	12	1	6	4	73	4	122	9	1	9	10	.474	2	0	3.53
1995 Rochester	AAA Bal	16	16	1	0	101.2	429	96	44	36	11	6	4	2	32	0	74	3	3	6	5	.545	0	0	3.19
1996 Rochester	AAA Bal	8	8	0	0	44	191	51	24	21	6	0	1	1	15	0	34	2	2	3	1	.750	0	0	4.30
1997 Rochester	AAA Bal	22	21	6	0	146	589	122	61	55	13	0	2	5	34	0	128	2	2	14	2	.875	3	0	3.39
1999 Omaha	AAA KC	21	18	0	0	115.1	541	154	94	73	17	2	3	5	41	0	70	3	3	6	8	.429	0	0	5.70
2000 Rochester	AAA Bal	26	26	0	0	152.2	645	142	75	53	15	3	8	3	61	0	99	5	0	11	9	.550	0	0	3.12
2001 Memphis	AAA StL	14	13	0	0	80.2	345	87	50	39	9	3	7	3	20	0	46	1	0	4	6	.400	0	0	4.35
1995 Baltimore	AL	13	13	1	0	75.1	319	76	40	38	9	0	4	4	25	1	53	2	2	2	7	.222	0	0	4.54
1996 Baltimore	AL	22	11	0	4	81.2	359	89	48	45	14	2	2	1	39	2	54	3	1	3	5	.375	0	0	4.96
1997 Baltimore	AL	10	10	0	0	50	225	67	36	35	7	1	2	0	18	1	29	0	2	4	2	.667	0	0	6.30
1998 Cleveland	AL	11	1	0	5	25	112	24	10	9	2	0	0	0	16	1	10	1	1	2	0	1.000	0	0	3.24
Cincinnati	NL	16	1	0	1	26.1	138	41	34	33	7	3	1	3	19	1	19	1	1	0	2	.000	0	0	11.28
10 Min. YEARS		204	190	13	4	1208.1	5086	1142	572	465	108	20	36	28	422	4	971	34	19	87	53	.621	6	1	3.46
4 Maj. YEARS		72	36	1	10	258.1	1153	297	168	160	39	6	9	8	117	6	165	7	7	11	16	.407	0	0	5.57

Andy Kropf

Bats: Both **Throws:** Right **Pos:** C-28; 3B-25; P-1   **Ht:** 6'1" **Wt:** 195 **Born:** 7/19/78 **Age:** 23

						BATTING										BASERUNNING				PERCENTAGES		
Year Team	Lg Org	G	AB	H	2B	3B	HR	TB	R	RBI	TBB	IBB	SO	HBP	SH	SF	SB	CS	SB%	GDP	Avg	OBP	SLG
2000 Tigers	R Det	12	34	6	2	0	1	11	3	3	3	0	3	0	0	1	1	1	.50	0	.176	.237	.324
Lakeland	A+ Det	29	87	22	3	0	2	31	7	8	6	0	29	0	0	1	0	0	—	2	.253	.298	.356
2001 Erie	AA Det	5	15	5	2	0	0	7	1	1	1	0	4	0	0	0	0	0	—	0	.333	.375	.467
Lakeland	A+ Det	48	169	39	8	0	3	56	16	15	16	0	27	0	0	1	1	0	1.00	5	.231	.296	.331
2 Min. YEARS		94	305	72	15	0	6	105	27	27	26	0	63	0	0	3	2	1	.67	7	.236	.293	.344

Dustin Krug

Pitches: Right **Bats:** Right **Pos:** RP-27   **Ht:** 6'5" **Wt:** 225 **Born:** 3/6/77 **Age:** 25

		HOW MUCH HE PITCHED						WHAT HE GAVE UP									THE RESULTS					
Year Team	Lg Org	G	GS	CG	GF	IP	BFP	H	R	ER	HR	SH	SF	HB	TBB	IBB	SO	WP	Bk	W	L	Pct.	ShO	Sv	ERA
1998 Williamsprt	A- ChC	27	0	0	27	30.1	123	26	6	5	0	1	0	1	8	2	26	1	0	1	1	.500	0	4	1.48
1999 Lansing	A ChC	46	0	0	23	59	278	75	34	22	1	4	5	4	25	0	32	9	0	3	7	.300	0	5	3.36
2000 Daytona	A+ ChC	52	1	0	16	79.1	353	82	39	31	6	1	3	4	37	9	64	7	1	5	7	.417	0	0	3.52
2001 West Tenn	AA ChC	7	0	0	3	10	53	16	12	11	1	0	1	3	5	0	9	0	0	0	0	—	0	0	9.90
Daytona	A+ ChC	20	0	0	6	31	149	46	21	18	1	1	1	0	12	2	22	2	0	3	2	.600	0	1	5.23
4 Min. YEARS		152	1	0	75	209.2	956	245	112	87	9	7	10	12	87	13	153	19	1	12	17	.414	0	10	3.73

Greg Kubes

Pitches: Left **Bats:** Right **Pos:** SP-24; RP-2   **Ht:** 6'6" **Wt:** 205 **Born:** 11/10/76 **Age:** 25

		HOW MUCH HE PITCHED						WHAT HE GAVE UP									THE RESULTS					
Year Team	Lg Org	G	GS	CG	GF	IP	BFP	H	R	ER	HR	SH	SF	HB	TBB	IBB	SO	WP	Bk	W	L	Pct.	ShO	Sv	ERA
1998 Batavia	A- Phi	15	12	0	0	75.1	312	72	33	27	1	3	2	0	23	0	79	4	3	7	3	.700	0	0	3.23
1999 Piedmont	A Phi	27	27	4	0	164.2	705	162	65	48	4	8	3	3	47	0	147	4	0	11	12	.478	0	0	2.62
2000 Clearwater	A+ Phi	24	24	0	0	136.1	612	158	81	69	6	5	5	5	64	1	70	4	0	5	9	.357	0	0	4.56
2001 Reading	AA Phi	6	5	0	1	27	110	32	12	11	1	0	2	0	7	0	12	0	0	0	1	.000	0	0	3.67
Clearwater	A+ Phi	20	19	0	0	111.2	495	124	59	47	7	3	2	3	50	1	89	0	0	10	6	.625	0	0	3.79
4 Min. YEARS		92	87	4	1	515	2234	548	250	202	19	19	14	11	191	2	397	12	3	33	31	.516	0	0	3.53

Hector Kuilan

Bats: Right **Throws:** Right **Pos:** C-76; OF-4; PH-1   **Ht:** 5'11" **Wt:** 190 **Born:** 4/3/76 **Age:** 26

						BATTING										BASERUNNING				PERCENTAGES		
Year Team	Lg Org	G	AB	H	2B	3B	HR	TB	R	RBI	TBB	IBB	SO	HBP	SH	SF	SB	CS	SB%	GDP	Avg	OBP	SLG
1994 Marlins	R Fla	40	141	22	7	0	0	29	11	17	6	0	15	0	2	2	0	1	.00	4	.156	.188	.206
1995 Marlins	R Fla	48	153	38	8	0	0	46	14	27	17	1	20	1	2	2	4	1	.80	4	.248	.324	.301
Kane County	A Fla	2	7	0	0	0	0	0	0	0	0	0	1	0	0	0	0	0	—	0	.000	.000	.000
1996 Kane County	A Fla	94	308	62	12	1	6	94	28	30	22	0	52	3	3	2	1	3	.25	7	.201	.260	.305
1997 Brevard Cty	A+ Fla	77	265	60	16	0	0	76	18	25	7	0	41	4	3	3	0	1	.00	12	.226	.254	.287
Charlotte	AAA Fla	14	39	4	0	0	0	4	3	3	2	0	8	0	0	0	0	0	—	2	.103	.146	.103

161

(Batting — continued)

Year Team	Lg Org	G	AB	H	2B	3B	HR	TB	R	RBI	TBB	IBB	SO	HBP	SH	SF	SB	CS	SB%	GDP	Avg	OBP	SLG
1998 Portland	AA Fla	31	107	27	4	0	2	37	8	14	2	0	9	0	3	2	0	0	—	2	.252	.261	.346
Brevard Cty	A+ Fla	61	208	47	11	0	6	76	13	28	12	0	29	2	2	1	2	1	.67	3	.226	.274	.365
1999 Portland	AA Fla	76	245	64	11	0	2	81	22	32	11	0	42	2	3	4	0	0	—	9	.261	.294	.331
2001 Lehigh Val	IND —	68	265	75	11	0	8	110	32	37	8	0	30	1	0	4	0	1	.00	5	.283	.302	.415
Carolina	AA Col	12	43	8	2	0	1	13	3	3	3	0	6	0	0	0	0	0	—	1	.186	.239	.302
7 Min. YEARS		523	1781	407	82	1	25	566	152	216	90	1	253	13	18	20	7	8	.47	49	.229	.268	.318

Mike Kusiewicz

Pitches: Left Bats: Right Pos: SP-24; RP-2   Ht: 6'2" Wt: 190 Born: 11/1/76 Age: 25

Year Team	Lg Org	G	GS	CG	GF	IP	BFP	H	R	ER	HR	SH	SF	HB	TBB	IBB	SO	WP	Bk	W	L	Pct.	ShO	Sv	ERA
1995 Salem	A+ Col	1	1	0	0	6	26	7	1	1	0	0	0	2	0	0	7	0	1	0	0	—	0	0	1.50
Asheville	A Col	21	21	0	0	122.1	484	92	40	28	6	2	0	6	34	0	103	9	1	8	4	.667	0	0	2.06
1996 Salem	A+ Col	5	3	0	2	23	100	19	15	13	2	1	1	1	12	0	18	2	0	1	0	.000	0	1	5.09
New Haven	AA Col	14	14	0	0	76.1	326	83	38	28	4	2	3	2	27	2	64	0	1	2	4	.333	0	0	3.30
1997 New Haven	AA Col	10	4	0	0	28.1	138	41	28	20	2	2	2	6	10	1	11	1	0	2	4	.333	0	0	6.35
Salem	A+ Col	19	18	1	0	117.2	480	99	44	33	5	4	5	9	32	0	107	7	1	8	6	.571	1	0	2.52
1998 New Haven	AA Col	27	26	2	0	178.2	740	161	59	46	4	12	6	16	35	0	151	9	1	14	7	.667	0	0	2.32
1999 Rockies	R Col	6	6	0	0	24.2	112	26	16	15	0	1	1	2	9	0	27	1	1	1	3	.250	0	0	5.47
2000 Tennessee	AA Tor	27	26	1	1	156	684	149	83	63	14	8	4	9	59	1	115	10	0	7	9	.438	0	0	3.63
2001 Trenton	AA Bos	18	17	0	0	89	365	83	39	34	6	3	3	9	19	2	92	2	0	4	5	.444	0	0	3.44
Pawtucket	AAA Bos	8	7	0	0	36.2	162	42	23	19	3	1	0	2	12	0	31	1	0	2	2	.500	0	0	4.66
7 Min. YEARS		156	143	4	3	858.2	3617	802	386	300	46	36	25	64	249	6	726	42	6	48	45	.516	1	1	3.14

Craig Kuzmic

Bats: Both Throws: Right Pos: 2B-89; 3B-46; OF-9; DH-3; SS-1; PH-1   Ht: 6'0" Wt: 185 Born: 5/2/77 Age: 25

Year Team	Lg Org	G	AB	H	2B	3B	HR	TB	R	RBI	TBB	IBB	SO	HBP	SH	SF	SB	CS	SB%	GDP	Avg	OBP	SLG
1998 Everett	A- Sea	54	186	52	14	2	9	97	36	47	33	3	55	5	0	3	3	1	.75	3	.280	.396	.522
1999 Lancaster	A+ Sea	32	108	22	4	0	5	41	19	15	20	1	43	1	0	1	3	1	.75	1	.204	.331	.380
Wisconsin	A Sea	91	323	77	18	1	10	127	48	55	61	0	84	2	2	2	7	4	.64	10	.238	.361	.393
2000 Lancaster	A+ Sea	136	522	155	27	10	19	259	106	104	71	3	124	10	0	6	5	8	.38	10	.297	.388	.496
2001 San Antonio	AA Sea	131	479	135	31	5	15	221	79	91	67	2	133	6	1	5	7	4	.64	11	.282	.373	.461
4 Min. YEARS		444	1618	441	94	18	58	745	288	312	252	9	439	24	3	17	25	18	.58	35	.273	.375	.460

John Lackey

Pitches: Right Bats: Right Pos: SP-28   Ht: 6'6" Wt: 200 Born: 10/23/78 Age: 23

Year Team	Lg Org	G	GS	CG	GF	IP	BFP	H	R	ER	HR	SH	SF	HB	TBB	IBB	SO	WP	Bk	W	L	Pct.	ShO	Sv	ERA
1999 Boise	A- Ana	15	15	1	0	81.1	372	81	59	45	7	5	2	8	50	1	77	14	1	6	2	.750	0	0	4.98
2000 Cedar Rapds	A Ana	5	5	0	0	30.1	115	20	7	7	1	0	0	2	5	0	21	4	0	3	2	.600	0	0	2.08
Lk Elsinore	A+ Ana	15	15	2	0	100.2	433	94	56	38	9	0	5	9	42	0	74	12	3	6	6	.500	1	0	3.40
Erie	AA Ana	8	8	2	0	57.1	234	58	23	21	6	1	0	1	9	0	43	0	0	6	1	.857	0	0	3.30
2001 Arkansas	AA Ana	18	18	3	0	127.1	509	106	55	49	11	6	5	3	29	0	94	8	0	9	7	.563	2	0	3.46
Salt Lake	AAA Ana	10	10	1	0	57.2	253	75	44	43	5	2	1	1	16	0	42	3	1	3	4	.429	0	0	6.71
3 Min. YEARS		71	71	9	0	454.2	1916	434	244	203	39	14	13	24	151	1	351	41	5	33	22	.600	3	0	4.02

Steve Lackey

Bats: Right Throws: Right Pos: SS-10; PR-3   Ht: 5'11" Wt: 159 Born: 9/25/74 Age: 27

Year Team	Lg Org	G	AB	H	2B	3B	HR	TB	R	RBI	TBB	IBB	SO	HBP	SH	SF	SB	CS	SB%	GDP	Avg	OBP	SLG
1992 Mets	R NYM	12	47	9	1	0	0	10	6	3	3	0	7	1	1	0	0	1	.00	0	.191	.255	.213
Kingsport	R+ NYM	38	148	26	2	0	0	28	16	10	17	0	22	3	0	0	3	4	.43	5	.176	.274	.189
1993 Kingsport	R+ NYM	53	172	25	4	0	0	29	14	9	14	0	30	0	1	1	3	4	.43	4	.145	.209	.169
1994 Pittsfield	A- NYM	3	4	1	0	0	0	1	1	0	2	0	0	0	0	0	0	0	—	0	.250	.500	.250
Kingsport	R+ NYM	56	187	37	6	1	0	45	22	7	24	1	31	3	3	0	2	2	.50	2	.198	.299	.241
1995 Pittsfield	A- NYM	21	75	18	5	0	0	23	7	6	2	0	16	1	1	1	1	0	1.00	1	.240	.266	.307
Capital Cty	A NYM	67	178	34	8	0	1	45	21	21	11	1	42	2	5	3	9	2	.82	2	.191	.242	.253
1996 Fayettevlle	A Det	82	310	67	13	0	4	92	38	43	28	0	58	3	5	5	24	6	.80	4	.216	.283	.297
Visalia	A+ Det	46	184	49	11	1	4	74	27	29	16	0	44	1	2	2	7	1	.88	7	.266	.325	.402
1997 Jacksnville	AA Det	5	13	1	0	0	0	1	1	0	0	0	1	0	0	0	1	0	1.00	2	.077	.077	.077
Lakeland	A+ Det	71	247	55	14	0	0	69	24	22	10	0	58	1	6	2	5	4	.56	3	.223	.254	.279
1998 Jacksnville	AA Det	12	34	11	1	0	0	12	6	3	5	0	5	0	0	1	0	0	—	0	.324	.410	.353
Lakeland	A+ Det	102	415	118	14	3	3	147	68	39	31	0	73	4	9	5	19	7	.73	7	.284	.336	.354
1999 Myrtle Bch	A+ Atl	53	216	59	10	2	0	73	24	16	15	0	33	4	1	2	13	4	.76	1	.273	.329	.338
Greenville	AA Atl	80	315	92	18	3	4	128	50	38	21	0	55	0	6	3	9	8	.53	7	.292	.333	.406
2000 Greenville	AA Atl	129	489	114	9	0	3	132	61	33	39	0	95	3	10	2	24	8	.75	15	.233	.293	.270
2001 Akron	AA Cle	13	27	6	1	0	0	7	4	0	4	0	7	0	0	0	2	0	1.00	0	.222	.323	.259
10 Min. YEARS		843	3061	722	117	10	19	916	390	279	242	2	577	26	55	26	122	51	.71	60	.236	.295	.299

Pete LaForest

Bats: Left Throws: Right Pos: C-7   Ht: 6'2" Wt: 208 Born: 1/27/78 Age: 24

Year Team	Lg Org	G	AB	H	2B	3B	HR	TB	R	RBI	TBB	IBB	SO	HBP	SH	SF	SB	CS	SB%	GDP	Avg	OBP	SLG
1995 Expos	R Mon	2	6	0	0	0	0	0	1	0	2	0	4	0	0	0	0	0	—	0	.000	.250	.000
1997 Devil Rays	R TB	34	107	28	7	2	3	48	21	21	10	0	18	1	0	1	4	3	.57	1	.262	.328	.449
1998 Princeton	R+ TB	25	91	25	7	1	2	40	18	14	12	1	18	1	1	0	4	1	.80	0	.275	.365	.440
1999 Chston-SC	A TB	125	445	114	21	3	13	180	64	53	55	6	97	5	6	3	9	3	.75	11	.256	.343	.404

Year Team	Lg Org	G	AB	H	2B	3B	HR	TB	R	RBI	TBB	IBB	SO	HBP	SH	SF	SB	CS	SB%	GDP	Avg	OBP	SLG
2000 St. Pete	A+ TB	129	474	128	28	7	14	212	85	70	56	4	108	6	1	5	2	4	.33	4	.270	.351	.447
2001 Orlando	AA TB	7	21	2	0	0	1	5	3	1	5	0	9	0	0	0	0	0	—	0	.095	.269	.238
6 Min. YEARS		322	1144	297	63	13	33	485	192	159	140	11	254	13	8	9	19	11	.63	16	.260	.345	.424

Denny Lail

Pitches: Right **Bats:** Right **Pos:** SP-20; RP-13   **Ht:** 6'1" **Wt:** 172 **Born:** 9/10/74 **Age:** 27

Year Team	Lg Org	G	GS	CG	GF	IP	BFP	H	R	ER	HR	SH	SF	HB	TBB	IBB	SO	WP	Bk	W	L	Pct.	ShO	Sv	ERA
1995 Oneonta	A- NYY	13	13	0	0	68	309	66	38	30	3	1	4	5	31	0	59	1	0	5	6	.455	0	0	3.97
1996 Greensboro	A NYY	11	0	0	1	23	100	19	16	12	2	0	0	2	11	1	24	4	0	1	0	1.000	0	0	4.70
Tampa	A+ NYY	31	0	0	8	35.1	152	37	11	10	0	1	0	1	14	2	21	2	0	4	0	1.000	0	1	2.55
1997 Tampa	A+ NYY	44	1	0	13	62.1	267	67	38	27	2	1	5	0	23	7	40	4	0	3	5	.375	0	0	3.90
1998 Tampa	AA NYY	8	0	0	0	10	49	15	6	6	1	0	0	0	7	2	9	0	0	0	0	—	0	0	5.40
Tampa	A+ NYY	31	0	0	13	48.2	211	44	24	22	3	1	2	1	25	0	46	4	1	4	0	1.000	0	1	4.07
1999 Tampa	A+ NYY	22	4	0	6	60.2	237	45	17	14	2	0	1	1	16	0	53	1	0	1	3	.250	0	2	2.08
Norwich	AA NYY	6	6	0	0	41.1	156	24	12	8	1	1	0	0	11	0	29	1	1	5	0	1.000	0	0	1.74
2000 Columbus	AAA NYY	27	22	0	3	147.1	625	149	83	76	23	2	4	1	52	1	114	4	4	7	7	.500	0	0	4.64
2001 Columbus	AAA NYY	33	20	0	2	136.2	591	144	84	70	11	4	8	6	46	1	105	3	2	6	6	.500	0	1	4.61
7 Min. YEARS		226	66	0	46	633.1	2697	610	329	275	48	11	24	17	236	14	500	24	8	36	27	.571	0	5	3.91

Jason Lakman

Pitches: Right **Bats:** Right **Pos:** RP-39; SP-1   **Ht:** 6'4" **Wt:** 220 **Born:** 10/17/76 **Age:** 25

Year Team	Lg Org	G	GS	CG	GF	IP	BFP	H	R	ER	HR	SH	SF	HB	TBB	IBB	SO	WP	Bk	W	L	Pct.	ShO	Sv	ERA
1995 White Sox	R CWS	9	5	0	1	41.1	181	44	17	15	2	0	2	5	12	0	23	2	2	3	0	1.000	0	0	3.27
1996 Hickory	A CWS	13	13	0	0	63.2	302	66	55	48	7	0	1	4	43	0	43	7	3	0	6	.000	0	0	6.79
Bristol	R+ CWS	13	13	1	0	66.2	312	70	48	42	5	0	3	6	38	0	64	13	1	4	4	.500	0	0	5.67
1997 Hickory	A CWS	27	27	3	0	154.2	667	139	82	67	11	5	1	4	70	0	168	24	1	10	9	.526	0	0	3.90
1998 Winston-Sal	A+ CWS	13	13	1	0	86	363	62	37	36	0	2	2	17	30	0	98	3	0	3	2	.600	0	0	3.77
Birmingham	AA CWS	15	15	0	0	72.1	352	89	70	64	15	1	3	8	40	0	79	6	2	0	10	.000	0	0	7.96
1999 Birmingham	AA CWS	3	0	0	2	3	22	3	5	5	0	0	0	2	9	0	3	5	0	0	0	—	0	0	15.00
Winston-Sal	A+ CWS	20	20	2	0	119.2	531	108	69	58	4	3	4	8	55	1	110	14	0	9	8	.529	0	0	4.36
2000 Birmingham	AA CWS	27	2	0	12	45.2	210	49	25	21	2	0	2	3	30	0	44	7	0	2	2	.500	0	1	4.14
Bowie	AA Bal	17	0	0	5	22.1	102	18	17	14	5	5	0	0	15	2	24	3	0	1	3	.250	0	0	5.64
2001 Frederick	A+ Bal	3	0	0	1	5.1	22	4	1	1	0	0	0	1	0	0	8	0	0	1	0	1.000	0	0	1.69
Bowie	AA Bal	18	1	0	7	34.1	161	48	34	31	6	0	4	2	12	0	26	2	0	0	2	.000	0	0	8.13
Rochester	AAA Bal	19	0	0	9	26.1	119	32	13	10	1	1	2	2	9	1	12	3	1	1	0	1.000	0	0	3.42
7 Min. YEARS		197	109	7	37	741.1	3344	732	473	412	58	17	24	62	363	4	702	89	10	34	46	.425	0	2	5.00

David Lamb

Bats: Both **Throws:** Right **Pos:** SS-79; 2B-23; 3B-7; PH-5   **Ht:** 6'2" **Wt:** 165 **Born:** 6/6/75 **Age:** 27

Year Team	Lg Org	G	AB	H	2B	3B	HR	TB	R	RBI	TBB	IBB	SO	HBP	SH	SF	SB	CS	SB%	GDP	Avg	OBP	SLG
1993 Orioles	R Bal	16	56	10	1	0	0	11	4	6	10	0	8	0	0	0	2	0	1.00	1	.179	.303	.196
1994 Albany	A Bal	92	308	74	9	2	0	87	37	29	32	0	40	2	6	0	4	1	.80	4	.240	.316	.282
1995 Bowie	AA Bal	1	4	1	0	0	0	1	0	1	0	0	1	0	0	0	0	0	—	0	.250	.250	.250
Frederick	A+ Bal	124	436	97	14	2	2	121	39	34	38	5	81	10	8	5	6	7	.46	10	.222	.297	.278
1996 High Desert	A+ Bal	116	460	118	24	3	3	157	63	55	50	1	68	10	5	2	5	6	.45	19	.257	.341	.341
1997 Frederick	A+ Bal	70	249	65	21	1	2	94	30	39	25	2	32	6	3	3	3	1	.75	10	.261	.339	.378
Bowie	AA Bal	73	269	89	20	2	4	125	46	38	34	0	35	4	4	4	0	0	—	3	.331	.408	.465
1998 Bowie	AA Bal	66	241	73	10	1	2	91	29	25	27	1	33	1	4	1	1	3	.25	6	.303	.374	.378
Rochester	AAA Bal	48	178	53	7	1	1	65	24	16	17	1	25	3	1	2	1	5	.17	4	.298	.365	.365
1999 Durham	AAA TB	7	30	7	3	0	0	10	7	7	2	0	4	0	2	1	0	1	.00	0	.233	.273	.333
2000 Norfolk	AAA NYM	109	356	80	23	1	2	111	45	35	40	3	49	8	9	6	8	3	.73	9	.225	.312	.312
2001 Carolina	AA Col	82	287	78	16	0	5	109	32	32	37	4	39	4	11	2	2	3	.40	7	.272	.361	.380
Colo Sprngs	AAA Col	5	9	2	0	0	0	2	1	0	0	0	4	0	0	0	0	0	—	0	.222	.222	.222
Calgary	AAA Fla	23	67	20	6	0	1	29	15	6	11	0	11	2	4	0	0	0	—	3	.299	.413	.433
1999 Tampa Bay	AL	55	124	28	5	1	1	38	18	13	10	0	18	0	0	0	0	1	.00	4	.226	.284	.306
2000 New York	NL	7	5	1	0	0	0	1	1	0	1	0	1	0	0	0	0	0	—	0	.200	.333	.200
9 Min. YEARS		832	2950	767	154	13	22	1013	372	323	323	17	430	50	57	26	32	30	.52	76	.260	.340	.343
2 Maj. YEARS		62	129	29	5	1	1	39	19	13	11	0	19	0	0	0	0	1	.00	4	.225	.286	.302

Justin Lamber

Pitches: Left **Bats:** Right **Pos:** RP-38; SP-1   **Ht:** 6'0" **Wt:** 210 **Born:** 5/22/76 **Age:** 26

Year Team	Lg Org	G	GS	CG	GF	IP	BFP	H	R	ER	HR	SH	SF	HB	TBB	IBB	SO	WP	Bk	W	L	Pct.	ShO	Sv	ERA
1997 Spokane	A- KC	25	0	0	12	27.1	126	24	14	13	1	0	1	1	20	0	40	10	0	1	1	.500	0	4	4.28
1998 Wilmington	A+ KC	32	0	0	16	53.1	228	43	21	20	3	1	2	1	29	3	68	6	0	2	2	.500	0	2	3.38
1999 Wilmington	A+ KC	39	2	0	18	68.2	304	68	29	28	2	1	0	2	33	2	67	8	0	5	3	.625	0	6	3.67
2000 Wichita	AA KC	43	0	0	19	68.2	327	85	54	50	8	5	2	2	58	10	43	6	1	5	3	.625	0	2	6.55
2001 Wichita	AA KC	19	0	0	5	36	169	42	22	22	6	2	1	1	24	1	21	1	0	0	3	.000	0	1	5.50
Wilmington	A+ KC	20	1	0	9	47.1	189	32	11	9	2	0	0	3	13	0	39	1	1	4	4	.500	0	2	1.71
5 Min. YEARS		178	3	0	79	301.1	1343	294	151	142	22	9	6	10	177	16	278	32	2	17	15	.531	0	17	4.24

163

Jeremy Lambert

Pitches: Right **Bats:** Right **Pos:** RP-59 **Ht:** 6'1" **Wt:** 195 **Born:** 1/10/79 **Age:** 23

Year Team	Lg Org	G	GS	CG	GF	IP	BFP	H	R	ER	HR	SH	SF	HB	TBB	IBB	SO	WP	Bk	W	L	Pct.	ShO	Sv	ERA
1997 Johnson Cty	R+ StL	27	0	0	4	32.1	181	46	42	33	3	1	1	5	37	1	29	6	0	1	1	.500	0	1	9.19
1998 Johnson Cty	R+ StL	13	11	0	0	64	294	73	44	35	7	1	2	6	37	0	30	4	1	4	4	.500	0	0	4.92
1999 Peoria	A StL	21	0	0	1	34.1	175	48	36	34	5	0	2	2	27	0	27	3	0	2	1	.667	0	0	8.91
2000 Potomac	A+ StL	16	3	0	2	28.2	121	30	17	14	1	1	1	1	7	0	28	1	0	0	0	—	0	0	4.40
Arkansas	AA StL	39	0	0	5	47	207	41	27	20	1	2	1	1	28	7	63	0	0	0	2	.000	0	3	3.83
2001 New Haven	AA StL	31	0	0	27	33.1	150	32	17	11	4	2	2	4	17	2	48	1	0	2	2	.500	0	14	2.97
Memphis	AAA StL	28	0	0	16	30.2	123	23	14	11	7	3	1	2	8	0	39	0	0	5	1	.833	0	3	3.23
5 Min. YEARS		175	14	0	55	270.1	1251	293	197	158	28	10	10	21	161	10	264	15	1	14	11	.560	0	21	5.26

Luis Landaeta

Bats: Left **Throws:** Left **Pos:** OF-54; PH-9; DH-3 **Ht:** 6'0" **Wt:** 180 **Born:** 3/4/77 **Age:** 25

Year Team	Lg Org	G	AB	H	2B	3B	HR	TB	R	RBI	TBB	IBB	SO	HBP	SH	SF	SB	CS	SB%	GDP	Avg	OBP	SLG
1996 Rockies	R Col	44	176	49	9	1	0	60	27	20	5	0	22	4	1	4	7	2	.78	5	.278	.307	.341
1997 Rockies	R Col	37	144	42	6	3	0	54	24	13	7	0	9	1	1	0	4	3	.57	5	.292	.329	.375
1998 Portland	A- Col	29	111	33	3	2	0	40	19	12	8	1	16	2	0	0	4	4	.50	2	.297	.355	.360
Asheville	A Col	28	91	20	1	0	1	24	12	9	2	0	14	0	4	4	5	3	.63	0	.220	.227	.264
1999 Asheville	A Col	117	453	127	22	1	4	163	61	51	20	1	80	2	5	1	9	7	.56	9	.280	.313	.360
2000 Salem	A+ Col	89	288	73	11	0	9	111	34	33	9	0	51	2	3	3	10	5	.67	8	.253	.278	.385
2001 Carolina	AA Col	66	241	68	11	4	1	90	27	23	16	1	27	1	2	2	8	6	.57	2	.282	.327	.373
6 Min. YEARS		410	1504	412	63	11	15	542	204	161	67	3	219	12	16	14	47	30	.61	31	.274	.307	.360

Jacques Landry

Bats: Right **Throws:** Right **Pos:** OF-107; DH-16; 3B-10; 1B-3; SS-1; PR-1 **Ht:** 6'3" **Wt:** 205 **Born:** 8/15/73 **Age:** 28

Year Team	Lg Org	G	AB	H	2B	3B	HR	TB	R	RBI	TBB	IBB	SO	HBP	SH	SF	SB	CS	SB%	GDP	Avg	OBP	SLG
1996 Lakeland	A+ Det	11	35	3	1	0	0	4	2	2	3	0	15	0	0	1	0	0	—	0	.086	.154	.114
Fayetteville	A Det	31	101	19	4	0	1	26	10	3	5	0	36	1	0	0	1	0	1.00	1	.188	.234	.257
1997 W Michigan	A Det	103	369	101	18	5	16	177	51	52	21	1	99	8	0	5	15	3	.83	6	.274	.323	.480
1998 Lakeland	A+ Det	105	397	100	17	2	11	154	51	51	26	1	105	4	4	2	8	6	.57	4	.252	.303	.388
1999 Modesto	A+ Oak	133	508	158	46	6	27	297	92	111	47	2	128	10	3	12	18	4	.82	6	.311	.373	.585
2000 Midland	AA Oak	127	470	120	32	3	18	212	83	80	47	2	143	10	0	5	9	5	.64	5	.255	.333	.451
2001 Midland	AA Oak	134	506	122	14	4	36	252	102	95	64	2	184	15	0	4	37	7	.84	4	.241	.341	.498
6 Min. YEARS		644	2386	623	132	20	109	1122	391	394	213	8	710	48	7	29	88	25	.78	27	.261	.330	.470

Jason Lane

Bats: Right **Throws:** Left **Pos:** OF-134; DH-2; PH-2 **Ht:** 6'2" **Wt:** 220 **Born:** 12/22/76 **Age:** 25

Year Team	Lg Org	G	AB	H	2B	3B	HR	TB	R	RBI	TBB	IBB	SO	HBP	SH	SF	SB	CS	SB%	GDP	Avg	OBP	SLG
1999 Auburn	A- Hou	74	283	79	18	5	13	146	46	59	38	2	46	3	0	4	6	4	.60	2	.279	.366	.516
2000 Michigan	A Hou	133	511	153	38	0	23	260	98	104	62	7	91	8	0	13	20	7	.74	9	.299	.375	.509
2001 Round Rock	AA Hou	137	526	166	36	2	38	320	103	124	61	11	98	21	1	1	14	2	.88	6	.316	.407	.608
3 Min. YEARS		344	1320	398	92	7	74	726	247	287	161	20	235	32	1	18	40	13	.75	17	.302	.386	.550

Ryan Lane

Bats: Right **Throws:** Right **Pos:** OF-21; 2B-16; 3B-13; SS-10; PH-3; DH-2 **Ht:** 6'1" **Wt:** 185 **Born:** 7/6/74 **Age:** 27

Year Team	Lg Org	G	AB	H	2B	3B	HR	TB	R	RBI	TBB	IBB	SO	HBP	SH	SF	SB	CS	SB%	GDP	Avg	OBP	SLG
1993 Twins	R Min	43	138	20	3	2	0	27	15	5	15	0	38	2	3	1	3	1	.75	2	.145	.237	.196
1994 Elizabethtn	R+ Min	59	202	48	13	0	3	70	32	18	26	0	47	2	3	2	4	3	.57	4	.238	.328	.347
1995 Fort Wayne	A Min	115	432	115	37	1	6	172	69	56	65	0	92	7	6	4	17	9	.65	9	.266	.368	.398
1996 Fort Myers	A+ Min	106	404	110	20	7	9	171	74	62	60	0	96	6	6	9	21	9	.70	2	.272	.367	.423
Hardware Cy	A Min	33	117	26	5	1	2	39	13	12	8	0	29	0	2	1	3	4	.43	1	.222	.270	.333
1997 New Britain	AA Min	128	444	115	26	2	5	160	63	56	43	0	79	1	8	7	18	7	.72	5	.259	.321	.360
1998 Twins	R Min	18	65	19	5	1	2	32	9	10	4	0	13	0	1	0	2	1	.67	1	.292	.333	.492
1999 New Britain	AA Min	17	49	14	0	1	3	25	6	6	7	1	10	2	0	0	2	2	.50	1	.286	.397	.510
Tulsa	AA Tex	77	264	72	23	5	9	132	38	48	26	0	47	1	0	4	5	2	.71	9	.273	.336	.500
2000 Tulsa	AA Tex	117	425	137	29	2	16	218	75	79	69	4	94	3	0	5	15	7	.68	5	.322	.416	.513
2001 Sacramento	AAA Oak	56	186	39	8	0	4	59	17	14	21	0	39	1	1	1	6	1	.86	3	.210	.292	.317
9 Min. YEARS		769	2726	715	169	22	59	1105	411	366	344	5	584	25	30	34	96	46	.68	42	.262	.346	.405

Selwyn Langaigne

Bats: Left **Throws:** Left **Pos:** OF-50; 1B-31; PR-4; DH-2; PH-1 **Ht:** 6'0" **Wt:** 190 **Born:** 3/22/76 **Age:** 26

Year Team	Lg Org	G	AB	H	2B	3B	HR	TB	R	RBI	TBB	IBB	SO	HBP	SH	SF	SB	CS	SB%	GDP	Avg	OBP	SLG
1996 Medcine Hat	R+ Tor	32	100	26	4	1	2	38	19	11	17	0	20	1	2	0	8	2	.80	4	.260	.373	.380
Hagerstown	A Tor	4	14	2	0	0	0	2	1	1	1	0	5	0	0	0	2	0	1.00	0	.143	.200	.143
Dunedin	A+ Tor	31	117	26	2	3	0	34	16	4	9	0	30	2	4	0	1	3	.25	5	.222	.289	.291
1997 Dunedin	A+ Tor	42	90	17	3	0	1	23	9	7	10	0	26	0	4	0	4	1	.80	4	.189	.270	.256
St.Cathrnes	A- Tor	74	266	85	15	4	1	111	50	39	48	1	46	2	0	3	19	9	.68	5	.320	.423	.417
1998 Dunedin	A+ Tor	128	475	124	7	0	0	131	52	38	37	0	73	2	7	2	21	17	.55	12	.261	.316	.276
1999 Knoxville	AA Tor	40	123	30	4	1	0	36	18	10	10	0	25	0	2	0	3	4	.43	10	.244	.301	.293
Dunedin	A+ Tor	62	201	59	9	1	2	76	35	25	16	0	29	0	3	3	5	5	.50	2	.294	.341	.378
2000 Dunedin	A+ Tor	5	10	6	1	0	0	7	2	1	1	1	2	0	0	0	0	0	—	0	.600	.636	.700
Tennessee	AA Tor	76	213	52	4	1	0	58	26	22	21	1	43	1	2	1	1	5	.17	7	.244	.314	.272
Syracuse	AAA Tor	16	46	11	5	0	0	16	3	0	1	0	8	0	1	0	0	1	.00	1	.239	.255	.348

	BATTING																BASERUNNING				PERCENTAGES		
Year Team	Lg Org	G	AB	H	2B	3B	HR	TB	R	RBI	TBB	IBB	SO	HBP	SH	SF	SB	CS	SB%	GDP	Avg	OBP	SLG
2001 Tennessee	AA Tor	19	62	17	4	0	0	21	6	7	3	0	11	1	0	0	1	2	.33	2	.274	.318	.339
Syracuse	AAA Tor	62	201	48	7	1	3	66	31	23	17	0	53	1	2	2	4	2	.67	8	.239	.299	.328
6 Min. YEARS		591	1918	503	65	12	9	619	268	188	191	3	371	10	27	11	69	51	.58	60	.262	.331	.323

Steve Langone

Pitches: Right **Bats:** Right **Pos:** SP-14; RP-10   **Ht:** 6'2" **Wt:** 195 **Born:** 1/12/78 **Age:** 24

	HOW MUCH HE PITCHED						WHAT HE GAVE UP										THE RESULTS					
Year Team	Lg Org	G	GS	CG	GF	IP	BFP	H	R	ER	HR	SH	SF	HB	TBB	IBB	SO	WP	Bk	W	L	Pct.	ShO	Sv	ERA
2000 Yakima	A- LA	15	12	0	1	84.2	335	76	30	29	6	4	2	3	5	0	79	1	0	4	4	.500	1	0	3.08
2001 Jacksnville	AA LA	1	1	0	0	6	20	2	1	1	0	0	1	0	0	0	8	0	0	0	0	—	0	0	1.50
Vero Beach	A+ LA	23	13	1	5	98.2	400	94	32	27	8	1	2	3	18	0	89	3	2	9	3	.750	1	0	2.46
2 Min. YEARS		39	26	1	6	189.1	755	172	63	57	14	5	5	6	23	0	176	4	2	13	7	.650	1	1	2.71

James Langston

Bats: Both **Throws:** Right **Pos:** 3B-115; 1B-11; DH-3; PH-3; OF-1   **Ht:** 6'3" **Wt:** 198 **Born:** 3/23/78 **Age:** 24

	BATTING																BASERUNNING				PERCENTAGES		
Year Team	Lg Org	G	AB	H	2B	3B	HR	TB	R	RBI	TBB	IBB	SO	HBP	SH	SF	SB	CS	SB%	GDP	Avg	OBP	SLG
1999 Williamsprt	A- Pit	54	200	55	8	1	1	68	15	20	6	1	40	1	0	0	2	1	.67	6	.275	.300	.340
2000 Hickory	A Pit	113	435	127	23	3	8	180	62	77	27	2	99	2	3	4	3	1	.75	8	.292	.333	.414
2001 Lynchburg	A+ Pit	101	381	101	30	0	2	137	29	45	15	2	83	2	0	0	0	4	.00	7	.265	.294	.360
Altoona	AA Pit	28	103	29	3	1	0	34	9	7	2	0	22	0	0	0	0	1	.00	1	.282	.295	.330
3 Min. YEARS		296	1119	312	64	5	11	419	115	149	50	5	244	5	3	7	5	7	.42	22	.279	.311	.374

Derrick Lankford

Bats: Left **Throws:** Right **Pos:** 1B-24; OF-20; DH-11; PH-3   **Ht:** 6'2" **Wt:** 228 **Born:** 9/21/74 **Age:** 27

	BATTING																BASERUNNING				PERCENTAGES		
Year Team	Lg Org	G	AB	H	2B	3B	HR	TB	R	RBI	TBB	IBB	SO	HBP	SH	SF	SB	CS	SB%	GDP	Avg	OBP	SLG
1997 Erie	A- Pit	58	195	60	11	3	10	107	36	55	33	4	57	1	0	2	2	0	1.00	1	.308	.407	.549
1998 Augusta	A Pit	127	457	127	25	4	22	226	72	89	59	5	119	5	0	7	8	5	.62	11	.278	.362	.495
1999 Lynchburg	A+ Pit	123	456	133	28	8	20	237	80	88	52	1	124	7	0	6	4	0	1.00	7	.292	.369	.520
2000 Altoona	AA Pit	96	314	92	16	2	10	142	41	40	47	3	60	0	0	3	4	1	.80	7	.293	.382	.452
2001 Altoona	AA Pit	6	19	3	1	1	0	6	2	2	1	0	6	0	0	0	0	0	—	0	.158	.200	.316
Lakewood	A Phi	49	171	44	14	0	4	70	17	21	34	1	49	4	0	2	2	1	.67	1	.257	.389	.409
5 Min. YEARS		459	1612	459	95	18	66	788	248	295	226	14	415	17	0	20	20	7	.74	27	.285	.374	.489

Frank Lankford

Pitches: Right **Bats:** Right **Pos:** RP-40   **Ht:** 6'2" **Wt:** 190 **Born:** 3/26/71 **Age:** 31

	HOW MUCH HE PITCHED						WHAT HE GAVE UP										THE RESULTS					
Year Team	Lg Org	G	GS	CG	GF	IP	BFP	H	R	ER	HR	SH	SF	HB	TBB	IBB	SO	WP	Bk	W	L	Pct.	ShO	Sv	ERA
1993 Oneonta	A- NYY	16	7	0	1	64.2	276	60	41	24	3	3	2	1	22	0	61	5	0	4	5	.444	0	0	3.34
1994 Greensboro	A NYY	54	0	0	27	82.1	352	79	37	27	3	6	1	1	18	3	74	7	1	7	6	.538	0	7	2.95
1995 Tampa	A+ NYY	55	0	0	36	73	305	64	29	21	0	7	0	2	22	6	58	1	0	4	6	.400	0	15	2.59
1996 Norwich	AA NYY	61	0	0	25	88	392	82	42	26	4	9	1	2	40	6	61	3	0	7	8	.467	0	4	2.66
1997 Norwich	AA NYY	11	11	2	0	68.1	277	58	28	22	3	1	1	2	15	1	39	1	1	4	2	.667	0	0	2.90
Columbus	AAA NYY	15	13	1	2	93.2	374	84	33	28	2	3	1	2	22	1	40	1	0	7	4	.636	1	0	2.69
1998 Columbus	AAA NYY	15	15	3	0	94	413	110	60	53	12	3	0	1	32	0	58	3	0	5	9	.357	0	0	5.07
1999 Yankees	R NYY	1	1	0	0	2	8	2	1	1	0	0	0	0	1	0	2	1	0	0	0	—	0	0	4.50
2000 Modesto	A+ Oak	1	1	0	0	2	6	0	0	0	0	0	0	0	0	0	2	0	0	0	0	—	0	0	0.00
Sacramento	AAA Oak	29	7	0	4	67	284	68	32	28	4	1	2	3	25	1	33	3	1	1	5	.167	0	0	3.76
2001 Sacramento	AAA Oak	40	0	0	16	69.1	308	87	44	37	8	3	2	1	23	3	37	5	0	5	5	.500	0	2	4.80
1998 Los Angeles	NL	12	0	0	9	19.2	89	23	13	13	2	0	0	2	7	0	7	1	0	0	2	.000	0	1	5.95
9 Min. YEARS		298	55	6	111	704.1	2995	694	347	267	39	36	10	15	220	21	465	30	3	44	50	.468	1	28	3.41

Eduardo Lantigua

Pitches: Right **Bats:** Right **Pos:** SP-26; RP-3   **Ht:** 6'0" **Wt:** 176 **Born:** 1/5/80 **Age:** 22

	HOW MUCH HE PITCHED						WHAT HE GAVE UP										THE RESULTS					
Year Team	Lg Org	G	GS	CG	GF	IP	BFP	H	R	ER	HR	SH	SF	HB	TBB	IBB	SO	WP	Bk	W	L	Pct.	ShO	Sv	ERA
2000 Bristol	R+ CWS	12	12	1	0	59.1	273	63	42	35	4	3	5	10	30	2	59	6	0	2	7	.222	0	0	5.31
2001 Winston-Sal	A+ CWS	22	19	1	1	120.2	499	92	46	41	7	5	2	7	58	1	113	8	0	8	6	.571	1	0	3.06
Birmingham	AA CWS	7	7	2	0	43.2	183	40	19	18	2	0	4	0	18	0	34	2	0	4	0	1.000	1	0	3.71
2 Min. YEARS		41	38	4	1	223.2	955	195	107	94	13	8	11	17	106	3	206	16	0	14	13	.519	2	0	3.78

Doug Lantz

Pitches: Right **Bats:** Right **Pos:** SP-12   **Ht:** 6'1" **Wt:** 185 **Born:** 8/26/79 **Age:** 22

	HOW MUCH HE PITCHED						WHAT HE GAVE UP										THE RESULTS					
Year Team	Lg Org	G	GS	CG	GF	IP	BFP	H	R	ER	HR	SH	SF	HB	TBB	IBB	SO	WP	Bk	W	L	Pct.	ShO	Sv	ERA
2001 Mahoning Vy	A- Cle	11	11	0	0	55	235	65	28	21	2	2	1	6	11	1	33	2	0	4	6	.400	0	0	3.44
Akron	AA Cle	1	1	0	0	6	18	1	0	0	0	0	0	0	0	0	3	0	0	0	0	—	0	0	0.00
1 Min. YEAR		12	12	0	0	61	253	66	28	21	2	2	1	6	11	1	36	2	0	4	6	.400	0	0	3.10

Andy Larkin

Pitches: Right **Bats:** Right **Pos:** SP-18; RP-8   **Ht:** 6'4" **Wt:** 210 **Born:** 6/27/74 **Age:** 28

	HOW MUCH HE PITCHED						WHAT HE GAVE UP										THE RESULTS					
Year Team	Lg Org	G	GS	CG	GF	IP	BFP	H	R	ER	HR	SH	SF	HB	TBB	IBB	SO	WP	Bk	W	L	Pct.	ShO	Sv	ERA
1992 Marlins	R Fla	14	4	0	2	41.1	187	41	26	24	0	1	1	7	19	0	20	4	0	1	2	.333	0	2	5.23

165

Year Team	Lg Org	G	GS	CG	GF	IP	BFP	H	R	ER	HR	SH	SF	HB	TBB	IBB	SO	WP	Bk	W	L	Pct.	ShO	Sv	ERA
		HOW MUCH HE PITCHED						WHAT HE GAVE UP												THE RESULTS					
1993 Elmira	A- Fla	14	14	4	0	88	368	74	43	29	1	1	3	12	23	0	89	9	1	5	7	.417	1	0	2.97
1994 Kane County	A Fla	21	21	3	0	140	577	125	53	44	6	3	3	19	27	0	125	4	0	9	7	.563	1	0	2.83
1995 Portland	AA Fla	9	9	0	0	40	160	29	16	15	5	4	0	6	11	2	23	1	0	1	2	.333	0	0	3.38
1996 Brevard Cty	A+ Fla	6	6	0	0	27.2	126	34	20	13	0	0	1	7	7	0	18	3	0	4	0	.000	0	0	4.23
Portland	AA Fla	8	8	0	0	49.1	195	45	18	17	6	2	0	2	10	0	40	3	0	4	1	.800	0	0	3.10
1997 Charlotte	AAA Fla	28	27	3	0	144.1	669	166	109	97	23	3	3	15	76	2	103	4	1	6	11	.353	0	0	6.05
1998 Charlotte	AAA Fla	11	10	0	0	53.2	246	55	39	38	8	2	0	4	32	2	41	2	0	4	1	.800	0	0	6.37
1999 Brevard Cty	A+ Fla	4	4	0	0	15	66	16	5	4	0	0	2	3	3	0	7	0	0	0	1	.000	0	0	2.40
Portland	AA Fla	7	1	0	3	12.2	57	16	10	10	2	0	0	0	4	0	7	1	0	1	1	.500	0	0	7.11
2000 Louisville	AAA Cin	27	0	0	10	41.2	173	30	13	12	4	0	2	2	17	1	40	5	0	1	0	1.000	0	4	2.59
2001 Colo Sprngs	AAA Col	26	18	0	2	120	537	134	78	72	17	5	4	11	41	1	99	4	1	4	8	.333	0	0	5.40
1996 Florida	NL	1	1	0	0	5	22	3	1	1	0	0	0	1	4	0	2	0	0	0	0	—	0	0	1.80
1998 Florida	NL	17	14	0	0	74.2	373	101	87	80	12	5	2	4	55	3	43	3	0	3	8	.273	0	0	9.64
2000 Cincinnati	NL	3	0	0	2	6.2	30	6	4	4	1	0	0	0	5	0	7	0	0	0	0	—	0	0	5.40
Kansas City	AL	18	0	0	9	19.1	97	29	20	19	5	2	1	0	11	2	17	2	0	0	3	.000	0	0	8.84
10 Min. YEARS		175	122	10	17	773.2	3361	765	430	375	72	21	19	88	270	8	612	40	3	36	45	.444	2	6	4.36
3 Maj. YEARS		39	15	0	11	105.2	522	139	112	104	18	7	3	5	75	5	69	5	0	3	11	.214	0	1	8.86

Greg LaRocca

Bats: Right **Throws:** Right **Pos:** 3B-55; SS-33; DH-5; 2B-3; PH-1 **Ht:** 5'11" **Wt:** 185 **Born:** 11/10/72 **Age:** 29

Year Team	Lg Org	G	AB	H	2B	3B	HR	TB	R	RBI	TBB	IBB	SO	HBP	SH	SF	SB	CS	SB%	GDP	Avg	OBP	SLG
		BATTING															BASERUNNING				PERCENTAGES		
1994 Spokane	A- SD	42	158	46	9	2	0	59	20	14	14	0	18	2	2	0	7	2	.78	4	.291	.356	.373
Rancho Cuca	A+ SD	28	85	14	5	1	1	24	7	8	7	0	11	2	1	1	3	1	.75	2	.165	.242	.282
1995 Rancho Cuca	A+ SD	125	466	150	36	5	8	220	77	74	44	0	77	12	0	2	15	4	.79	13	.322	.393	.472
Memphis	AA SD	2	7	1	0	0	0	1	0	0	0	0	1	0	0	0	0	1	.00	1	.143	.143	.143
1996 Memphis	AA SD	128	445	122	22	5	6	172	66	42	51	4	58	10	5	5	5	9	.36	9	.274	.358	.387
1997 Mobile	AA SD	76	300	80	16	2	3	109	44	31	26	0	46	8	0	5	8	3	.73	4	.267	.336	.363
1998 Las Vegas	AAA SD	95	304	94	22	5	8	150	55	39	19	0	48	12	2	2	7	4	.64	3	.309	.371	.493
1999 Las Vegas	AAA SD	14	51	14	2	0	0	16	3	2	2	0	10	4	0	1	2	2	.50	3	.275	.345	.314
2000 Las Vegas	AAA SD	137	482	142	42	7	9	225	90	80	54	1	62	12	1	2	13	4	.76	9	.295	.378	.467
2001 Akron	AA Cle	31	104	33	9	0	3	51	16	19	18	1	11	2	0	2	2	0	1.00	1	.317	.421	.490
Buffalo	AAA Cle	61	216	67	12	1	12	117	39	37	12	0	35	6	2	1	2	1	.67	4	.310	.362	.542
2000 San Diego	NL	13	27	6	2	0	0	8	1	2	1	0	4	0	2	0	0	0	—	1	.222	.250	.296
8 Min. YEARS		739	2618	763	175	28	50	1144	417	346	247	6	377	70	13	21	62	33	.65	53	.291	.365	.437

Joe Lawrence

Bats: Right **Throws:** Right **Pos:** C-75; 3B-12; DH-8; SS-1; 1B-1; PH-1 **Ht:** 6'2" **Wt:** 200 **Born:** 2/13/77 **Age:** 25

Year Team	Lg Org	G	AB	H	2B	3B	HR	TB	R	RBI	TBB	IBB	SO	HBP	SH	SF	SB	CS	SB%	GDP	Avg	OBP	SLG
		BATTING															BASERUNNING				PERCENTAGES		
1996 St.Cathrnes	A- Tor	29	98	22	7	2	0	33	23	11	14	1	17	2	1	3	1	1	.50	1	.224	.325	.337
1997 Hagerstown	A Tor	116	446	102	24	1	8	152	63	38	49	0	107	5	3	2	10	12	.45	3	.229	.311	.341
1998 Dunedin	A+ Tor	125	454	140	31	6	11	216	102	44	105	2	88	4	5	1	15	12	.56	11	.308	.441	.476
1999 Knoxville	AA Tor	70	250	66	16	2	7	107	52	24	56	0	48	3	0	2	7	6	.54	10	.264	.402	.428
2000 Dunedin	A+ Tor	101	375	113	32	1	13	186	69	67	69	6	74	5	0	3	21	7	.75	9	.301	.414	.496
Tennessee	AA Tor	39	133	35	9	0	0	44	22	9	30	0	27	3	1	1	7	1	.88	2	.263	.407	.331
2001 Syracuse	AAA Tor	93	318	70	11	4	1	92	27	26	36	0	62	6	1	1	6	9	.40	6	.220	.310	.289
6 Min. YEARS		573	2074	548	130	16	40	830	358	219	359	9	423	28	11	13	67	48	.58	42	.264	.378	.400

Sean Lawrence

Pitches: Left **Bats:** Left **Pos:** RP-43 **Ht:** 6'4" **Wt:** 215 **Born:** 9/2/70 **Age:** 31

Year Team	Lg Org	G	GS	CG	GF	IP	BFP	H	R	ER	HR	SH	SF	HB	TBB	IBB	SO	WP	Bk	W	L	Pct.	ShO	Sv	ERA
		HOW MUCH HE PITCHED						WHAT HE GAVE UP												THE RESULTS					
1992 Welland	A- Pit	15	15	0	0	74	330	75	55	43	10	2	2	2	34	1	71	6	3	3	6	.333	0	0	5.23
1993 Augusta	A Pit	22	22	0	0	121	516	108	59	42	9	7	4	4	50	1	96	6	0	6	8	.429	0	0	3.12
Salem	A+ Pit	4	4	0	0	15	77	25	19	17	1	2	1	0	9	0	14	2	0	1	3	.250	0	0	10.20
1994 Salem	A+ Pit	12	12	0	0	72	312	76	38	21	8	1	2	3	18	0	66	2	0	4	2	.667	0	0	2.63
1995 Carolina	AA Pit	12	3	0	3	21.1	96	27	13	13	2	0	0	1	8	1	19	0	0	2	0	.000	0	0	5.48
Lynchburg	A+ Pit	20	19	0	0	111	465	115	56	52	16	3	3	1	25	0	82	3	0	5	8	.385	0	0	4.22
1996 Carolina	AA Pit	37	9	0	13	82	362	80	40	36	11	2	1	3	36	1	81	0	1	3	5	.375	0	2	3.95
1997 Calgary	AAA Pit	26	26	2	0	143.1	641	154	83	67	17	9	6	3	57	3	116	6	0	8	9	.471	0	0	4.21
1998 Nashville	AAA Pit	26	26	0	0	147	634	153	86	82	20	7	2	6	57	1	126	4	1	12	9	.571	0	0	5.02
1999 Vancouver	AAA Oak	25	2	0	7	39.1	188	51	25	21	4	2	1	1	21	1	37	1	0	2	2	.500	0	0	4.81
2000 Schaumburg	IND —	10	8	0	1	44.2	206	56	34	32	9	2	2	3	15	0	30	6	0	3	3	.500	0	0	6.45
2001 Portland	AAA SD	25	0	0	7	35.2	162	32	16	14	1	3	0	1	13	0	44	2	0	0	3	.000	0	0	3.53
Tucson	AAA Ari	18	0	0	8	22.2	101	20	15	9	2	0	1	2	9	3	32	1	0	1	3	.250	0	0	3.57
1998 Pittsburgh	NL	7	3	0	0	19.2	92	25	16	16	4	0	2	0	10	0	12	1	0	2	1	.667	0	0	7.32
10 Min. YEARS		252	146	2	39	929	4082	972	539	449	110	40	25	30	352	12	814	39	5	48	63	.432	0	2	4.35

Brett Laxton

Pitches: Right **Bats:** Left **Pos:** RP-40; SP-5 **Ht:** 6'1" **Wt:** 210 **Born:** 10/5/73 **Age:** 28

Year Team	Lg Org	G	GS	CG	GF	IP	BFP	H	R	ER	HR	SH	SF	HB	TBB	IBB	SO	WP	Bk	W	L	Pct.	ShO	Sv	ERA
		HOW MUCH HE PITCHED						WHAT HE GAVE UP												THE RESULTS					
1996 Sou Oregon	A- Oak	13	8	0	1	32.2	162	39	34	28	4	1	1	3	26	1	38	5	3	0	5	.000	0	0	7.71
1997 Visalia	A+ Oak	29	22	0	2	138.2	606	141	62	46	7	4	0	11	50	0	121	14	0	11	5	.688	0	0	2.99
1998 Huntsville	AA Oak	21	21	0	0	129.2	570	109	64	49	4	3	6	10	79	0	82	8	0	11	4	.733	0	0	3.40
Edmonton	AAA Oak	8	8	0	0	46.1	204	45	35	34	6	1	3	5	24	2	21	7	0	2	4	.333	0	0	6.60
1999 Vancouver	AAA Oak	25	25	3	0	161.1	662	158	68	62	8	5	4	6	49	0	112	10	0	13	8	.619	1	0	3.46
2000 Omaha	AAA KC	21	21	0	0	108.1	492	118	69	64	4	3	5	7	61	0	88	7	0	5	9	.357	0	0	5.32
2001 Omaha	AAA KC	45	5	0	16	96.1	414	92	49	43	7	2	5	7	35	1	75	5	0	3	7	.300	0	2	4.02
1999 Oakland	AL	3	2	0	0	9.2	50	12	12	8	1	0	3	2	7	1	9	3	0	0	1	.000	0	0	7.45

		HOW	MUCH	HE	PITCHED			WHAT	HE	GAVE	UP					THE	RESULTS			
Year Team	Lg Org	G	GS	CG	GF	IP	BFP	H	R	ER	HR	SH	SF	HB	TBB	IBB	SO	WP	Bk	W	L	Pct.	ShO	Sv	ERA
2000 Kansas City	AL	6	1	0	1	16.2	79	23	15	15	0	1	0	2	10	1	14	1	0	0	1	.000	—	0	8.10
6 Min. YEARS		162	110	3	19	713.1	3110	702	381	326	40	19	24	49	324	4	537	56	3	45	42	.517	1	2	4.11
2 Maj. YEARS		9	3	0	1	26.1	129	35	27	23	1	1	3	4	17	2	23	4	0	0	2	.000	0	0	7.86

B.J. Leach

Pitches: Right **Bats:** Right **Pos:** RP-28   **Ht:** 5'11" **Wt:** 175 **Born:** 8/3/77 **Age:** 24

		HOW	MUCH	HE	PITCHED			WHAT	HE	GAVE	UP					THE	RESULTS			
Year Team	Lg Org	G	GS	CG	GF	IP	BFP	H	R	ER	HR	SH	SF	HB	TBB	IBB	SO	WP	Bk	W	L	Pct.	ShO	Sv	ERA
1999 Red Sox	R Bos	1	0	0	1	2	9	2	1	0	0	0	0	0	1	0	1	1	0	0	0	—	0	0	0.00
Lowell	A- Bos	13	4	0	1	45.1	194	41	23	18	4	0	1	0	18	0	52	2	0	5	2	.714	0	0	3.57
2000 Augusta	A Bos	60	0	0	58	72.1	289	45	23	13	4	6	1	2	20	1	87	5	0	3	3	.500	0	40	1.62
2001 Red Sox	R Bos	5	0	0	4	8.1	31	6	2	2	0	0	0	0	1	0	10	1	0	2	0	1.000	0	2	2.16
Trenton	AA Bos	23	0	0	19	40	174	42	21	20	7	1	1	3	11	3	40	2	0	2	2	.500	0	1	4.50
3 Min. YEARS		102	4	0	83	168	697	136	70	53	15	7	3	5	51	4	190	11	0	12	7	.632	0	43	2.84

Nick Leach

Bats: Left **Throws:** Right **Pos:** 1B-110; PH-3; DH-2; P-1   **Ht:** 6'1" **Wt:** 190 **Born:** 12/7/77 **Age:** 24

		BATTING														BASERUNNING				PERCENTAGES		
Year Team	Lg Org	G	AB	H	2B	3B	HR	TB	R	RBI	TBB	IBB	SO	HBP	SH	SF	SB	CS	SB%	GDP	Avg	OBP	SLG
1996 Great Falls	R+ LA	58	199	50	8	1	9	87	42	25	36	2	33	3	0	0	2	4	.33	3	.251	.374	.437
1997 Savannah	A LA	37	131	35	6	0	0	41	14	13	14	0	23	4	0	0	1	2	.33	2	.267	.356	.313
Yakima	A- LA	54	192	60	18	1	7	101	33	47	32	4	37	6	0	1	5	0	1.00	4	.313	.424	.526
San Berndno	A+ LA	16	60	22	6	1	4	42	11	12	5	0	11	2	0	0	0	1	.00	1	.367	.433	.700
1998 San Berndno	A+ LA	131	469	110	30	2	6	162	49	48	44	4	96	5	2	1	6	11	.35	6	.235	.306	.345
1999 Vero Beach	A+ LA	128	449	127	21	0	20	208	58	74	62	3	73	6	0	3	10	5	.67	6	.283	.375	.463
2000 Norwich	AA NYY	113	354	98	23	1	7	144	44	49	56	3	79	3	2	1	5	3	.63	6	.277	.379	.407
2001 Norwich	AA NYY	55	167	35	13	0	3	57	17	22	28	1	39	0	0	0	2	2	.50	4	.210	.320	.341
Tampa	A+ NYY	59	201	54	6	2	8	88	24	33	19	2	42	5	1	6	0	6	.00	5	.269	.338	.438
6 Min. YEARS		651	2222	591	131	8	64	930	292	323	296	19	433	34	5	14	31	34	.48	37	.266	.359	.419

Juan LeBron

Bats: Right **Throws:** Right **Pos:** OF-95; DH-11; PH-8; PR-1   **Ht:** 6'4" **Wt:** 195 **Born:** 6/7/77 **Age:** 25

		BATTING														BASERUNNING				PERCENTAGES		
Year Team	Lg Org	G	AB	H	2B	3B	HR	TB	R	RBI	TBB	IBB	SO	HBP	SH	SF	SB	CS	SB%	GDP	Avg	OBP	SLG
1995 Royals	R KC	47	147	26	5	2	2	41	17	13	10	0	38	2	0	4	0	3	.00	6	.177	.233	.279
1996 Royals	R KC	58	215	62	9	2	3	84	19	30	6	0	34	2	0	0	1	2	.33	9	.288	.314	.391
1997 Lansing	A KC	35	113	24	7	0	3	40	12	20	0	0	32	1	0	2	0	0	—	4	.212	.216	.354
Spokane	A- KC	69	288	88	27	1	7	138	49	45	17	2	74	2	0	1	8	4	.67	5	.306	.347	.479
1998 Lansing	A KC	121	442	111	26	9	17	206	70	84	57	5	129	8	1	5	18	11	.62	11	.251	.344	.466
2000 Binghamton	AA NYM	72	238	54	17	0	6	89	26	25	16	0	82	3	0	2	2	4	.33	3	.227	.282	.374
St. Lucie	A+ NYM	24	90	18	2	0	2	26	6	8	6	0	25	1	0	1	0	0	—	3	.200	.255	.289
2001 Binghamton	AA NYM	113	363	89	16	4	18	167	43	52	39	3	121	9	0	2	2	4	.33	6	.245	.332	.460
6 Min. YEARS		539	1896	472	109	18	58	791	242	277	151	10	535	28	1	17	31	28	.53	47	.249	.311	.417

A.J. Leday

Bats: Right **Throws:** Right **Pos:** OF-22; DH-16; 1B-12   **Ht:** 6'3" **Wt:** 225 **Born:** 2/17/73 **Age:** 29

		BATTING														BASERUNNING				PERCENTAGES		
Year Team	Lg Org	G	AB	H	2B	3B	HR	TB	R	RBI	TBB	IBB	SO	HBP	SH	SF	SB	CS	SB%	GDP	Avg	OBP	SLG
1995 Lethbridge	R+ —	61	229	68	10	3	2	90	30	41	18	2	33	6	1	2	6	8	.43	9	.297	.361	.393
1996 Chston-WV	A Cin	9	26	6	1	0	1	10	3	5	6	0	9	1	0	0	1	2	.33	0	.231	.394	.385
Duluth-Sup	IND —	80	315	103	29	2	20	196	59	65	28	0	60	3	0	5	6	1	.86	4	.327	.382	.622
1997 Duluth-Sup	IND —	83	333	100	19	5	7	150	63	57	44	1	54	14	1	3	12	5	.71	8	.300	.369	.450
1998 Rancho Cuca	A+ SD	134	539	166	33	5	24	281	94	94	28	2	98	6	2	5	15	10	.60	15	.308	.346	.521
1999 Jackson	AA Hou	63	187	45	7	0	4	64	21	16	9	0	38	8	1	0	4	2	.67	3	.241	.301	.342
2000 Mobile	AA SD	44	136	33	7	0	4	52	12	18	6	0	35	2	0	0	1	3	.25	4	.243	.285	.382
2001 Arkansas	AA Ana	117	407	115	20	2	12	175	45	70	26	1	84	14	0	4	4	2	.67	9	.283	.344	.430
Winnipeg	IND —	4	16	2	0	0	0	2	1	2	2	0	8	0	0	1	0	0	—	0	.125	.211	.125
		45	185	79	12	3	9	124	36	46	8	0	17	7	0	1	3	2	.60	5	.427	.468	.670
7 Min. YEARS		640	2373	717	138	20	83	1144	364	414	155	6	436	61	5	23	52	35	.60	57	.302	.357	.482

Corey Lee

Pitches: Left **Bats:** Left **Pos:** SP-17; RP-10   **Ht:** 6'2" **Wt:** 185 **Born:** 12/26/74 **Age:** 27

		HOW	MUCH	HE	PITCHED			WHAT	HE	GAVE	UP					THE	RESULTS			
Year Team	Lg Org	G	GS	CG	GF	IP	BFP	H	R	ER	HR	SH	SF	HB	TBB	IBB	SO	WP	Bk	W	L	Pct.	ShO	Sv	ERA
1996 Hudson Val	A- TB	9	9	0	0	54.2	226	42	24	20	1	2	3	1	21	1	59	1	2	1	4	.200	0	0	3.29
1997 Charlotte	A+ Tex	23	23	6	0	160.2	654	132	66	62	9	5	3	7	60	0	147	7	0	15	5	.750	2	0	3.47
1998 Tulsa	AA Tex	26	25	1	0	143.2	625	105	81	72	16	3	5	5	102	1	132	12	1	10	9	.526	0	0	4.51
1999 Tulsa	AA Tex	22	22	0	0	127.2	549	132	76	63	11	1	1	4	44	0	121	3	1	8	5	.615	0	0	4.44
Oklahoma	AAA Tex	4	4	0	0	26.2	105	21	6	6	2	0	0	0	8	0	25	2	0	3	0	1.000	0	0	2.03
2000 Oklahoma	AAA Tex	26	21	0	0	112	569	163	128	109	15	3	3	2	87	1	84	3	2	2	12	.143	0	0	8.76
2001 Oklahoma	AAA Tex	2	0	0	1	3	19	5	7	6	1	0	0	0	4	0	1	0	0	0	0	—	0	0	18.00
Tulsa	AA Tex	25	17	1	4	125.1	532	117	78	74	14	2	5	7	51	2	103	2	2	5	12	.294	0	0	5.31
1999 Texas	AL	1	0	0	1	1	6	2	3	3	1	0	0	0	1	0	0	0	0	0	1	.000	0	0	27.00
6 Min. YEARS		137	121	8	5	753.2	3279	717	466	412	69	16	20	26	377	5	672	30	8	44	47	.484	2	0	4.92

Derek Lee

Pitches: Left **Bats:** Left **Pos:** SP-28   **Ht:** 6'4" **Wt:** 185 **Born:** 8/20/74 **Age:** 27

Year Team	Lg Org	G	GS	CG	GF	IP	BFP	H	R	ER	HR	SH	SF	HB	TBB	IBB	SO	WP	Bk	W	L	Pct.	ShO	Sv	ERA
1997 Ogden	R+ Mil	14	13	0	0	74.1	325	89	49	32	3	2	6	3	20	0	71	8	1	4	4	.500	0	0	3.87
1998 Stockton	A+ Mil	30	18	1	2	136	583	134	70	63	9	4	5	5	48	1	141	8	0	5	9	.357	1	1	4.17
1999 Huntsville	AA Mil	26	21	4	0	140	604	143	70	60	16	6	2	8	51	4	77	5	1	8	8	.500	2	0	3.86
2000 Indianapols	AAA Mil	3	2	0	0	13.1	62	16	7	7	2	0	1	0	6	0	9	0	0	2	0	1.000	0	0	4.73
Huntsville	AA Mil	28	20	1	2	131.1	544	121	48	37	6	2	5	6	41	0	87	6	2	11	3	.786	1	0	2.54
2001 Huntsville	AA Mil	28	28	0	0	162.1	695	173	76	61	10	5	8	2	39	2	109	4	0	7	11	.389	0	0	3.38
5 Min. YEARS		129	102	6	4	657.1	2813	676	320	260	46	19	27	24	205	7	494	31	4	37	35	.514	4	1	3.56

Garrett Lee

Pitches: Right **Bats:** Right **Pos:** RP-23; SP-9   **Ht:** 6'5" **Wt:** 210 **Born:** 8/17/76 **Age:** 25

Year Team	Lg Org	G	GS	CG	GF	IP	BFP	H	R	ER	HR	SH	SF	HB	TBB	IBB	SO	WP	Bk	W	L	Pct.	ShO	Sv	ERA
1996 Braves	R Atl	13	3	0	2	39	152	32	12	12	2	2	0	4	3	0	36	4	2	1	2	.333	0	1	2.77
1997 Danville	R+ Atl	14	14	1	0	84	360	87	57	46	8	3	2	7	17	1	72	3	1	5	5	.500	1	0	4.93
1998 Eugene	A- Atl	9	9	0	0	47	216	56	41	33	7	1	2	7	11	1	47	1	2	2	3	.400	0	0	6.32
1999 Jamestown	A- Atl	13	13	1	0	77.1	323	79	39	35	8	1	5	6	16	0	47	0	2	4	3	.571	0	0	4.07
Myrtle Bch	A+ Atl	3	3	0	0	17.2	77	21	12	10	1	1	0	0	3	0	12	0	0	1	1	.500	0	0	5.09
2000 Myrtle Bch	A+ Atl	29	6	0	5	79.2	322	61	19	18	2	3	1	7	21	0	60	2	1	7	3	.700	0	1	2.03
Richmond	AAA Atl	2	1	0	0	7	30	6	2	2	0	0	0	3	3	0	3	0	0	0	0	—	0	0	2.57
2001 Greenville	AA Atl	32	9	1	11	92	393	103	55	47	12	5	4	4	17	2	63	2	1	4	9	.308	1	0	4.60
6 Min. YEARS		115	58	3	18	443.2	1873	445	237	203	40	16	14	38	91	4	340	12	9	24	26	.480	2	2	4.12

Jon Lee

Pitches: Right **Bats:** Right **Pos:** RP-28   **Ht:** 6'5" **Wt:** 215 **Born:** 7/24/78 **Age:** 23

Year Team	Lg Org	G	GS	CG	GF	IP	BFP	H	R	ER	HR	SH	SF	HB	TBB	IBB	SO	WP	Bk	W	L	Pct.	ShO	Sv	ERA
2000 Diamondbcks	R Ari	9	0	0	2	24.1	106	30	15	9	0	1	1	0	8	1	19	4	1	0	1	.000	0	1	3.33
Tucson	AAA Ari	1	0	0	0	2.2	11	1	0	0	0	0	0	0	0	0	1	0	0	1	0	1.000	0	0	0.00
South Bend	A Ari	7	0	0	4	7	35	9	5	5	1	2	0	1	4	0	4	2	0	0	0	—	0	2	6.43
2001 El Paso	AA Ari	3	0	0	1	2.2	15	3	3	2	1	0	0	0	6	0	1	3	0	0	0	—	0	0	6.75
Tucson	AAA Ari	2	0	0	0	2.2	12	3	1	1	0	0	1	0	1	0	1	0	0	0	0	—	0	0	3.38
Lancaster	A+ Ari	5	0	0	1	6.1	35	14	12	8	0	1	1	1	1	1	4	1	1	0	1	.000	0	1	11.37
Yakima	A- Ari	18	0	0	9	30.2	132	32	17	15	4	1	0	1	10	1	23	8	0	2	3	.400	0	0	4.40
2 Min. YEARS		45	0	0	17	76.1	346	92	53	40	5	6	3	5	30	3	53	18	2	3	5	.375	0	4	4.72

Sang-Hoon Lee

Pitches: Left **Bats:** Left **Pos:** RP-43   **Ht:** 6'1" **Wt:** 190 **Born:** 3/11/71 **Age:** 31

Year Team	Lg Org	G	GS	CG	GF	IP	BFP	H	R	ER	HR	SH	SF	HB	TBB	IBB	SO	WP	Bk	W	L	Pct.	ShO	Sv	ERA
2000 Pawtucket	AAA Bos	45	1	0	18	71	287	51	23	16	5	3	0	1	24	2	73	1	4	5	2	.714	0	2	2.03
2001 Pawtucket	AAA Bos	43	0	0	21	53	227	52	33	32	11	2	2	1	16	3	44	3	2	3	5	.375	0	4	5.43
2000 Boston	AL	9	0	0	1	11.2	49	11	4	4	2	0	1	1	5	0	6	0	0	0	0	—	0	0	3.09
2 Min. YEARS		88	1	0	39	124	514	103	56	48	16	5	2	2	40	5	117	4	6	8	7	.533	0	6	3.48

Randy Leek

Pitches: Left **Bats:** Left **Pos:** SP-28; RP-2   **Ht:** 6'0" **Wt:** 175 **Born:** 4/18/77 **Age:** 25

Year Team	Lg Org	G	GS	CG	GF	IP	BFP	H	R	ER	HR	SH	SF	HB	TBB	IBB	SO	WP	Bk	W	L	Pct.	ShO	Sv	ERA
1999 Oneonta	A- Det	21	3	1	4	63.1	249	58	16	11	0	1	1	2	9	1	66	2	0	6	3	.667	0	1	1.56
2000 Lakeland	A+ Det	20	20	2	0	126.2	520	122	60	48	9	1	6	5	25	1	97	3	0	3	6	.333	0	0	3.41
Toledo	AAA Det	1	1	0	0	4.2	22	6	5	5	1	0	0	0	3	0	1	0	0	0	0	—	0	0	9.64
Jacksnville	AA Det	7	6	0	0	31	146	43	29	27	6	1	1	2	8	0	21	0	0	2	2	.500	0	0	7.84
2001 Toledo	AAA Det	1	1	0	0	7	27	7	3	3	0	0	0	0	0	0	3	0	0	0	0	—	0	0	3.86
Erie	AA Det	29	27	4	1	179.1	740	190	87	77	24	3	4	9	27	1	123	2	0	11	7	.611	1	1	3.86
3 Min. YEARS		79	58	7	5	412	1704	426	200	171	43	6	12	18	72	3	311	7	0	22	18	.550	1	2	3.74

Brandon Leese

Pitches: Right **Bats:** Right **Pos:** SP-9   **Ht:** 6'4" **Wt:** 205 **Born:** 10/8/75 **Age:** 26

Year Team	Lg Org	G	GS	CG	GF	IP	BFP	H	R	ER	HR	SH	SF	HB	TBB	IBB	SO	WP	Bk	W	L	Pct.	ShO	Sv	ERA
1996 Bellingham	A- SF	16	15	0	0	80.1	341	59	39	29	6	6	2	5	37	0	90	8	0	5	6	.455	0	0	3.25
1997 San Jose	A+ SF	19	19	0	0	112	475	99	44	38	11	1	0	4	46	2	99	15	0	7	5	.583	0	0	3.05
Kane County	A Fla	7	6	0	0	42.1	171	27	18	18	0	1	2	3	18	0	32	3	1	3	1	.750	0	0	3.83
1998 Brevard Cty	A+ Fla	8	8	0	0	47.1	209	63	36	30	3	1	1	2	7	0	30	2	0	1	5	.167	0	0	5.70
Portland	AA Fla	20	20	0	0	126.1	544	137	70	58	16	11	1	5	37	1	94	2	0	4	7	.364	0	0	4.13
1999 Portland	AA Fla	20	11	0	2	81.2	370	110	66	52	8	2	0	7	20	0	52	2	4	4	4	.500	0	0	5.73
2000 Portland	AA Fla	27	25	6	1	173.2	728	179	82	67	18	8	5	7	47	1	96	6	1	12	9	.571	1	1	3.47
2001 Calgary	AAA Fla	9	9	0	0	44	203	68	36	34	8	1	3	1	7	1	30	2	0	3	3	.500	0	0	6.95
6 Min. YEARS		126	113	6	3	707.2	3041	742	391	326	70	25	14	34	219	5	523	40	4	39	40	.494	1	1	4.15

Chuck Lehr

Pitches: Right **Bats:** Right **Pos:** SP-27; RP-2 **Ht:** 6'1" **Wt:** 200 **Born:** 8/3/77 **Age:** 24

Year Team	Lg Org	G	GS	CG	GF	IP	BFP	H	R	ER	HR	SH	SF	HB	TBB	IBB	SO	WP	Bk	W	L	Pct.	ShO	Sv	ERA
1999 Sou Oregon	A- Oak	14	4	0	7	42.1	207	62	36	28	3	5	1	2	17	3	40	9	0	2	6	.250	0	0	5.95
2000 Sacramento	AAA Oak	1	1	0	0	4	21	7	5	5	1	0	0	0	3	0	3	0	0	0	0	—	0	0	11.25
Modesto	A+ Oak	29	25	0	1	175	709	161	71	62	10	8	4	5	46	1	138	15	5	13	6	.684	0	0	3.19
2001 Midland	AA Oak	29	27	0	2	155.1	709	206	107	94	20	6	2	11	43	1	103	4	2	11	12	.478	0	0	5.45
3 Min. YEARS		73	57	0	10	376.2	1646	436	219	189	34	19	7	18	109	5	284	28	7	26	24	.520	0	0	4.52

Chris Lemonis

Bats: Left **Throws:** Right **Pos:** 2B-92; PH-10; DH-2; 1B-1; PR-1 **Ht:** 5'11" **Wt:** 185 **Born:** 8/21/73 **Age:** 28

Year Team	Lg Org	G	AB	H	2B	3B	HR	TB	R	RBI	TBB	IBB	SO	HBP	SH	SF	SB	CS	SB%	GDP	Avg	OBP	SLG
1995 Jamestown	A- Det	57	191	45	7	2	0	56	19	21	18	0	32	2	3	1	5	1	.83	4	.236	.307	.293
1996 Visalia	A+ Det	126	482	134	27	3	14	209	69	82	35	1	99	6	2	4	12	5	.71	12	.278	.332	.434
1997 W Michigan	A Det	48	158	48	10	1	3	69	27	30	9	1	31	1	0	0	2	5	.29	3	.304	.345	.437
1998 Lakeland	A+ Det	93	327	92	17	1	3	120	45	48	27	3	46	2	0	3	1	1	.50	10	.281	.337	.367
1999 Jacksnville	AA Det	75	265	75	16	1	5	108	35	38	19	0	45	6	0	0	1	2	.33	6	.283	.345	.408
2000 Toledo	AAA Det	84	288	62	21	3	3	98	30	23	17	2	53	1	1	0	1	1	.50	10	.215	.261	.340
2001 Calgary	AAA Fla	9	25	4	0	0	0	4	3	1	2	0	7	1	0	0	0	0	—	1	.160	.250	.160
Tucson	AAA Ari	9	23	5	2	0	0	7	3	0	1	0	3	0	0	0	0	0	—	1	.217	.250	.304
El Paso	AA Ari	87	333	103	19	2	2	132	45	52	23	1	51	4	2	4	8	3	.73	13	.309	.357	.396
7 Min. YEARS		588	2092	568	119	13	30	803	276	295	151	8	367	23	8	12	30	18	.63	60	.272	.326	.384

Patrick Lennon

Bats: Right **Throws:** Right **Pos:** DH-12; OF-2 **Ht:** 6'2" **Wt:** 200 **Born:** 4/27/68 **Age:** 34

Year Team	Lg Org	G	AB	H	2B	3B	HR	TB	R	RBI	TBB	IBB	SO	HBP	SH	SF	SB	CS	SB%	GDP	Avg	OBP	SLG
1986 Bellingham	A- Sea	51	169	41	5	2	3	59	35	27	36	0	50	0	1	1	8	6	.57	3	.243	.374	.349
1987 Wausau	A Sea	98	319	80	21	3	7	128	54	34	46	1	82	1	1	2	25	8	.76	10	.251	.345	.401
1988 Vermont	AA Sea	95	321	83	9	3	9	125	44	40	21	1	87	3	3	4	15	6	.71	9	.259	.307	.389
1989 Williamsprt	AA Sea	66	248	65	14	2	3	92	32	31	23	2	53	0	0	5	7	4	.64	9	.262	.319	.371
1990 San Berndno	A+ Sea	44	163	47	6	2	8	81	29	30	15	1	51	0	0	0	6	0	1.00	4	.288	.346	.497
Williamsprt	AA Sea	49	167	49	6	4	5	78	24	22	10	0	37	2	0	3	10	4	.71	2	.293	.335	.467
1991 Calgary	AAA Sea	112	416	137	29	5	15	221	75	74	46	4	68	4	1	1	12	5	.71	9	.329	.400	.531
1992 Calgary	AAA Sea	13	48	17	3	0	1	23	8	9	6	0	10	0	0	0	4	1	.80	1	.354	.426	.479
1993 Canton-Akrn	AA Cle	45	152	39	7	1	4	60	24	22	30	1	45	1	0	2	4	2	.67	4	.257	.378	.395
1994 New Britain	AA Bos	114	429	140	30	5	17	231	80	67	48	1	96	5	0	1	13	9	.59	10	.326	.400	.538
1995 Pawtucket	AAA Bos	40	128	35	6	2	3	54	20	20	16	0	42	1	0	0	6	4	.60	6	.273	.356	.422
Trenton	AA Bos	27	98	39	7	0	1	49	19	8	14	0	22	1	0	0	7	2	.78	3	.398	.478	.500
Salt Lake	AAA Min	34	115	46	15	0	6	79	26	29	12	2	29	1	0	1	2	1	.67	1	.400	.457	.687
1996 Edmonton	AAA Oak	68	251	82	16	2	12	138	37	42	28	2	82	2	0	0	3	3	.50	9	.327	.399	.550
1997 Edmonton	AAA Oak	39	134	46	7	0	9	80	28	35	22	4	34	2	0	2	0	0	—	5	.343	.438	.597
Modesto	A+ Oak	5	16	3	1	0	1	7	3	4	3	1	5	0	0	0	0	0	—	0	.188	.316	.438
1998 Syracuse	AAA Tor	126	438	127	22	4	27	238	87	95	87	3	121	2	0	2	12	4	.75	21	.290	.408	.543
1999 Syracuse	AAA Tor	37	134	45	5	0	9	77	26	33	22	0	40	1	0	1	3	3	.50	2	.336	.430	.575
Toledo	AAA Det	74	280	74	16	1	21	155	49	50	33	0	66	2	0	1	1	2	.33	10	.264	.345	.554
2000 Ottawa	AAA Mon	118	418	122	21	2	14	189	69	63	52	1	110	5	0	3	0	6	.00	12	.292	.374	.452
2001 Columbus	AAA NYY	14	44	6	1	1	1	12	6	2	9	0	14	1	0	0	0	0	—	0	.136	.296	.273
1991 Seattle	AL	9	8	1	1	0	0	2	2	1	3	0	1	0	0	0	0	0	—	0	.125	.364	.250
1992 Seattle	AL	1	2	0	0	0	0	0	0	0	0	0	0	0	0	0	0	0	—	0	.000	.000	.000
1996 Kansas City	AL	14	30	7	3	0	0	10	5	1	7	0	10	0	0	0	0	0	—	0	.233	.378	.333
1997 Oakland	AL	56	116	34	6	1	1	45	14	14	15	0	35	0	0	1	0	1	.00	3	.293	.374	.388
1998 Toronto	AL	2	4	2	2	0	0	4	1	0	0	0	1	0	0	0	0	0	—	0	.500	.500	1.000
1999 Toronto	AL	9	29	6	2	0	1	11	3	6	2	0	12	1	0	0	0	0	—	0	.207	.281	.379
16 Min. YEARS		1269	4488	1323	247	39	176	2176	775	737	579	24	1144	34	6	31	138	70	.66	130	.295	.377	.485
6 Maj. YEARS		91	189	50	14	1	2	72	25	22	27	0	59	1	0	1	0	1	.00	3	.265	.359	.381

Carlos Leon

Bats: Both **Throws:** Right **Pos:** SS-11; PR-2; 2B-1 **Ht:** 5'10" **Wt:** 169 **Born:** 8/31/79 **Age:** 22

Year Team	Lg Org	G	AB	H	2B	3B	HR	TB	R	RBI	TBB	IBB	SO	HBP	SH	SF	SB	CS	SB%	GDP	Avg	OBP	SLG
1997 Red Sox	R Bos	44	126	31	5	3	0	42	18	15	14	0	25	1	3	0	10	3	.77	4	.246	.324	.333
1998 Michigan	A Bos	107	372	93	7	3	3	115	59	37	50	0	81	11	10	3	10	10	.50	4	.250	.353	.309
1999 Sarasota	A+ Bos	47	154	24	1	1	0	27	16	14	12	0	16	3	5	0	9	1	.90	3	.156	.231	.175
Augusta	A Bos	60	210	49	7	0	1	59	34	19	23	0	42	10	0	1	13	4	.76	2	.233	.336	.281
2000 Sarasota	A+ Bos	88	302	93	14	4	1	118	61	31	37	2	24	6	4	3	12	10	.55	14	.308	.391	.391
2001 Trenton	AA Bos	15	49	10	4	0	0	14	4	5	4	0	13	1	2	0	1	2	.33	1	.204	.291	.286
Trenton	AA Bos	11	27	6	0	2	0	10	4	2	1	0	4	1	2	0	2	2	.50	1	.222	.276	.370
5 Min. YEARS		372	1240	306	38	13	5	385	196	122	142	2	205	33	26	7	57	32	.64	29	.247	.338	.310

Donny Leon

Bats: Both **Throws:** Right **Pos:** 3B-74; DH-47; 1B-12; PH-3; OF-1 **Ht:** 6'2" **Wt:** 185 **Born:** 5/7/76 **Age:** 26

Year Team	Lg Org	G	AB	H	2B	3B	HR	TB	R	RBI	TBB	IBB	SO	HBP	SH	SF	SB	CS	SB%	GDP	Avg	OBP	SLG
1995 Yankees	R NYY	16	41	7	1	0	0	8	3	5	3	0	14	0	0	0	0	1	.00	0	.171	.227	.195
1996 Yankees	R NYY	53	191	69	14	4	6	109	30	46	9	2	30	4	1	4	1	2	.33	2	.361	.394	.571
1997 Greensboro	A NYY	137	516	131	32	1	12	201	45	74	15	2	106	5	2	7	6	4	.60	13	.254	.278	.390
1998 Tampa	A+ NYY	100	385	112	24	1	10	168	54	59	23	1	64	7	1	2	0	0	—	9	.291	.341	.436
1999 Norwich	AA NYY	118	457	138	34	2	21	239	69	100	34	2	102	3	1	7	0	0	—	10	.302	.349	.523

Year Team	Lg Org	G	AB	H	2B	3B	HR	TB	R	RBI	TBB	IBB	SO	HBP	SH	SF	SB	CS	SB%	GDP	Avg	OBP	SLG
2000 Columbus	AAA NYY	59	204	51	10	1	9	90	30	26	20	0	49	2	2	2	3	3	.50	6	.250	.320	.441
Yankees	R NYY	5	18	3	0	0	2	9	3	4	0	0	6	1	0	0	0	0	—	0	.167	.190	.500
Tampa	A+ NYY	23	79	17	6	0	1	26	5	14	6	2	23	1	0	1	0	0	—	1	.215	.276	.329
2001 Columbus	AAA NYY	12	43	7	1	0	0	8	4	3	3	1	14	0	0	1	1	0	1.00	1	.163	.213	.186
Norwich	AA NYY	116	436	111	26	2	15	186	45	74	19	2	115	5	0	6	0	2	.00	10	.255	.290	.427
7 Min. YEARS		639	2370	646	148	11	76	1044	288	405	132	12	523	28	7	32	11	12	.48	52	.273	.315	.441

Jose Leon

Bats: Right **Throws:** Right **Pos:** 3B-132; DH-3; PR-1 **Ht:** 6'0" **Wt:** 175 **Born:** 12/8/76 **Age:** 25

Year Team	Lg Org	G	AB	H	2B	3B	HR	TB	R	RBI	TBB	IBB	SO	HBP	SH	SF	SB	CS	SB%	GDP	Avg	OBP	SLG
1994 Cardinals	R StL	46	161	37	3	2	0	44	16	17	11	0	51	3	1	4	1	4	.20	4	.230	.285	.273
1995 Savannah	A StL	41	133	22	4	1	0	28	15	11	10	1	46	1	1	0	0	1	.00	6	.165	.229	.211
1996 Johnson Cty	R+ StL	59	222	55	9	3	10	100	29	36	17	0	92	2	2	1	5	3	.63	1	.248	.306	.450
New Jersey	A- StL	7	28	8	3	1	1	16	4	3	0	0	7	2	0	0	0	0	—	0	.286	.333	.571
1997 Peoria	A StL	118	399	92	21	2	20	177	50	54	32	1	122	9	2	2	6	5	.55	10	.231	.301	.444
1998 Pr William	A+ StL	124	436	127	31	3	21	227	77	74	53	4	137	9	2	4	5	3	.63	6	.291	.376	.521
1999 Arkansas	AA StL	112	335	78	17	0	18	149	37	54	25	0	114	6	1	1	3	3	.50	5	.233	.297	.445
2000 Arkansas	AA StL	90	297	80	16	3	14	144	41	41	16	0	66	5	2	0	2	1	.67	7	.269	.318	.485
Bowie	AA Bal	18	68	17	1	0	1	21	7	6	4	0	13	2	0	0	5	2	.71	2	.250	.311	.309
2001 Bowie	AA Bal	26	95	34	9	1	4	57	18	20	8	0	21	1	0	0	1	1	.50	2	.358	.413	.600
Rochester	AAA Bal	109	416	116	20	4	12	180	54	53	25	0	96	4	2	1	7	3	.70	14	.279	.325	.433
8 Min. YEARS		750	2590	666	134	20	101	1143	348	369	201	6	765	44	13	13	35	26	.57	57	.257	.320	.441

Brian Lesher

Bats: Right **Throws:** Left **Pos:** OF-78; DH-9; 1B-6; PH-1 **Ht:** 6'5" **Wt:** 222 **Born:** 3/5/71 **Age:** 31

Year Team	Lg Org	G	AB	H	2B	3B	HR	TB	R	RBI	TBB	IBB	SO	HBP	SH	SF	SB	CS	SB%	GDP	Avg	OBP	SLG
1992 Sou Oregon	A- Oak	46	136	26	7	1	3	44	21	18	12	0	35	2	0	1	3	7	.30	3	.191	.265	.324
1993 Madison	A Oak	119	394	108	13	5	5	146	63	47	46	0	102	9	6	6	20	9	.69	13	.274	.358	.371
1994 Modesto	A+ Oak	117	393	114	21	0	14	177	76	68	81	5	84	8	0	8	11	11	.50	8	.290	.414	.450
1995 Huntsville	AA Oak	127	471	123	23	2	19	207	78	71	64	2	110	2	0	1	7	8	.47	7	.261	.351	.439
1996 Edmonton	AAA Oak	109	414	119	29	2	18	206	57	75	36	0	108	7	2	3	6	5	.55	9	.287	.352	.498
1997 Edmonton	AAA Oak	110	415	134	27	5	21	234	85	78	64	3	86	3	0	2	14	3	.82	14	.323	.415	.564
1998 Edmonton	AAA Oak	99	360	108	31	1	11	174	62	60	46	1	96	2	0	2	3	4	.43	11	.300	.380	.483
1999 Vancouver	AAA Oak	103	387	113	29	2	14	188	66	64	41	0	71	6	2	5	8	2	.80	6	.292	.364	.486
2000 Tacoma	AAA Sea	132	489	141	33	3	25	255	77	92	70	5	104	2	2	4	4	4	.50	10	.288	.377	.521
2001 Indianapols	AAA Mil	93	346	98	17	4	7	144	51	63	40	0	78	2	0	5	1	1	.50	5	.283	.356	.416
1996 Oakland	AL	26	82	19	3	0	5	37	11	16	5	0	17	1	1	1	0	0	—	2	.232	.281	.451
1997 Oakland	AL	46	131	30	4	1	4	48	17	16	9	0	30	0	0	2	4	1	.80	4	.229	.275	.366
1998 Oakland	AL	7	7	1	1	0	0	2	0	1	0	0	3	0	0	0	0	0	—	0	.143	.143	.286
2000 Seattle	AL	5	5	4	1	1	0	7	1	3	1	0	0	0	0	0	1	0	1.00	0	.800	.833	1.400
10 Min. YEARS		1055	3805	1084	230	25	137	1775	636	636	500	16	874	43	12	37	77	54	.59	96	.285	.371	.466
4 Maj. YEARS		84	225	54	9	2	9	94	29	36	15	0	50	1	1	3	5	1	.83	6	.240	.287	.418

Matt Levan

Pitches: Left **Bats:** Left **Pos:** RP-19 **Ht:** 6'3" **Wt:** 200 **Born:** 6/24/75 **Age:** 27

Year Team	Lg Org	G	GS	CG	GF	IP	BFP	H	R	ER	HR	SH	SF	HB	TBB	IBB	SO	WP	Bk	W	L	Pct.	ShO	Sv	ERA
1996 Marlins	R Fla	9	6	0	2	26.1	108	24	14	10	1	0	0	0	11	0	26	0	3	1	3	.250	0	0	3.42
1997 Utica	A- Fla	1	1	0	0	4	20	5	3	3	1	0	0	1	1	0	6	1	0	0	0	—	0	0	6.75
Kane County	A Fla	11	9	0	0	43.2	183	44	16	15	5	1	0	3	16	0	45	5	2	2	3	.400	0	0	3.09
1998 Kane County	A Fla	30	9	0	7	91.2	410	111	72	65	10	4	1	3	36	2	87	2	0	1	7	.125	0	0	6.38
1999 Brevard Cty	A+ Fla	35	2	0	14	66.1	291	52	39	30	6	4	2	1	39	3	84	9	0	2	3	.400	0	2	4.07
2000 Brevard Cty	A+ Fla	4	0	0	3	8.2	40	10	8	8	1	0	0	0	5	0	12	0	0	0	1	.000	0	2	8.31
2001 Portland	AA Fla	4	0	0	0	8.2	42	8	5	4	1	0	0	1	7	1	8	0	0	0	0	—	0	0	4.15
Brevard Cty	A+ Fla	15	0	0	6	20.2	94	21	10	8	2	0	1	0	10	0	18	2	0	1	0	1.000	0	1	3.48
6 Min. YEARS		109	27	0	32	270	1188	275	167	143	27	9	4	9	125	6	286	19	5	7	17	.292	0	5	4.77

Colby Lewis

Pitches: Right **Bats:** Right **Pos:** SP-25; RP-1 **Ht:** 6'4" **Wt:** 215 **Born:** 8/2/79 **Age:** 22

Year Team	Lg Org	G	GS	CG	GF	IP	BFP	H	R	ER	HR	SH	SF	HB	TBB	IBB	SO	WP	Bk	W	L	Pct.	ShO	Sv	ERA
1999 Pulaski	R+ Tex	14	11	1	0	64.2	280	46	24	14	3	0	3	7	27	0	84	3	4	7	3	.700	1	0	1.95
2000 Charlotte	A+ Tex	28	27	3	0	163.2	692	169	83	74	11	4	7	10	45	0	153	11	2	11	10	.524	1	0	4.07
2001 Charlotte	A+ Tex	1	0	0	0	4.1	13	0	0	0	0	0	0	0	0	0	8	0	0	1	0	1.000	0	0	0.00
Tulsa	AA Tex	25	25	1	0	156	686	150	85	78	15	8	6	16	62	2	162	16	0	10	10	.500	0	0	4.50
3 Min. YEARS		68	63	5	0	388.2	1671	365	192	166	29	12	16	33	134	2	407	30	6	29	23	.558	2	0	3.84

Derrick Lewis

Pitches: Right **Bats:** Right **Pos:** SP-12 **Ht:** 6'5" **Wt:** 215 **Born:** 5/7/76 **Age:** 26

Year Team	Lg Org	G	GS	CG	GF	IP	BFP	H	R	ER	HR	SH	SF	HB	TBB	IBB	SO	WP	Bk	W	L	Pct.	ShO	Sv	ERA
1997 Danville	R+ Atl	16	9	0	2	49.2	241	59	48	35	5	1	1	2	31	0	46	8	0	2	4	.333	0	0	6.34
1998 Macon	A Atl	23	23	0	0	113.1	502	108	64	48	7	1	4	8	55	0	100	15	2	5	6	.455	0	0	3.81
1999 Myrtle Bch	A+ Atl	24	23	0	0	131	551	100	44	35	9	1	3	3	81	0	102	6	1	8	4	.667	0	0	2.40
2000 Greenville	AA Atl	27	27	1	0	163.2	706	146	70	60	5	4	4	6	83	2	143	10	0	7	9	.438	1	0	3.30
2001 Richmond	AAA Atl	12	12	0	0	60.2	256	50	34	30	2	1	1	1	37	2	50	5	0	4	4	.500	0	0	4.45
5 Min. YEARS		102	94	1	2	518.1	2256	463	260	208	28	8	13	20	287	4	441	44	3	26	27	.491	1	0	3.61

Richie Lewis

Pitches: Right **Bats:** Right **Pos:** SP-21; RP-3   **Ht:** 5'10" **Wt:** 175 **Born:** 1/25/66 **Age:** 36

Year	Team	Lg Org	G	GS	CG	GF	IP	BFP	H	R	ER	HR	SH	SF	HB	TBB	IBB	SO	WP	Bk	W	L	Pct.	ShO	Sv	ERA
1987	Indianapolis	AAA Mon	2	0	0	2	3.2	19	6	4	4	2	0	0	0	2	0	3	0	0	0	0	—	0	0	9.82
1988	Jacksonville	AA Mon	12	12	1	0	61.1	275	37	32	23	2	0	3	3	56	0	60	7	4	5	3	.625	0	0	3.38
1989	Jacksonville	AA Mon	17	17	0	0	94.1	414	80	37	27	2	7	1	2	55	0	105	8	2	5	4	.556	0	0	2.58
1990	Wst Plm Bch	A+ Mon	10	0	0	6	15	68	12	8	5	0	1	0	0	11	0	14	1	0	0	1	.000	0	2	3.00
	Jacksonville	AA Mon	11	0	0	8	14.1	54	7	2	2	0	0	1	0	5	0	14	3	0	0	0	—	0	5	1.26
1991	Harrisburg	AA Mon	34	6	0	16	74.2	318	67	33	31	2	3	2	2	40	1	82	5	2	6	5	.545	0	5	3.74
	Indianapols	AAA Mon	5	4	0	0	27.2	131	35	12	11	1	0	1	0	20	1	22	2	0	1	0	1.000	0	0	3.58
	Rochester	AAA Bal	2	2	0	0	16	62	13	5	5	1	0	0	0	7	0	18	1	0	1	0	1.000	0	0	2.81
1992	Rochester	AAA Bal	24	23	6	1	159.1	668	136	63	58	15	1	4	3	61	2	154	13	2	10	9	.526	1	0	3.28
1995	Charlotte	AAA Fla	17	8	1	4	59	243	50	22	21	5	2	4	0	20	0	45	4	2	5	2	.714	0	0	3.20
1996	Toledo	AAA Det	2	0	0	0	4	13	1	1	1	1	0	0	0	1	0	4	0	0	0	0	—	0	0	2.25
1997	Edmonton	AAA Oak	11	1	0	4	20	96	24	13	13	2	1	1	1	14	1	25	3	0	1	1	.500	0	1	5.85
	Indianapols	AAA Cin	27	0	0	17	29.2	120	22	7	5	0	1	2	2	7	2	33	3	0	0	1	.000	0	9	1.52
1998	Rochester	AAA Bal	21	21	2	0	124	526	107	77	69	17	1	3	7	42	0	131	10	0	5	7	.417	0	0	5.01
1999	Norfolk	AAA NYM	20	20	3	0	122.2	542	128	82	69	19	6	2	5	49	7	101	4	2	7	8	.467	1	0	5.06
2000	Norfolk	AAA NYM	9	9	0	0	53.1	221	49	20	19	0	3	0	2	17	1	40	2	0	3	4	.429	0	0	3.21
	Buffalo	AAA Cle	2	2	0	0	8	32	8	4	4	2	0	0	0	3	0	5	0	0	1	0	1.000	0	0	4.50
2001	Buffalo	AAA Cle	7	5	0	1	30	119	19	8	7	3	0	0	2	13	1	11	3	0	2	0	1.000	0	0	2.10
	Norfolk	AAA NYM	17	16	0	0	91.2	397	83	46	41	8	2	0	1	47	1	66	4	0	7	4	.636	0	0	4.03
1992	Baltimore	AL	2	2	0	0	6.2	40	13	8	8	1	0	1	0	7	0	4	0	0	1	1	.500	0	0	10.80
1993	Florida	NL	57	0	0	14	77.1	341	68	37	28	7	8	4	1	43	6	65	9	1	6	3	.667	0	0	3.26
1994	Florida	NL	45	0	0	9	54	261	62	44	34	7	3	1	1	38	9	45	10	1	1	4	.200	0	0	5.67
1995	Florida	NL	21	1	0	6	36	152	30	15	15	9	2	0	1	15	5	32	1	2	0	1	.000	0	0	3.75
1996	Detroit	AL	72	0	0	19	90.1	412	78	45	42	9	5	10	4	65	9	78	14	2	4	6	.400	0	2	4.18
1997	Oakland	AL	14	0	0	5	18.2	94	24	21	20	7	1	1	1	15	0	12	2	0	2	0	1.000	0	0	9.64
	Cincinnati	NL	4	0	0	0	5.2	25	4	5	4	3	2	0	0	3	0	4	0	0	0	0	—	0	0	6.35
1998	Baltimore	AL	2	1	0	0	4.2	25	8	8	8	2	0	1	0	5	0	4	1	0	0	0	—	0	0	15.43
13 Min. YEARS			250	146	13	59	1008.2	4318	884	476	415	82	28	24	33	470	17	933	73	14	59	49	.546	2	23	3.70
7 Maj. YEARS			217	4	0	53	293.1	1350	287	183	159	45	21	18	8	191	29	244	37	6	14	15	.483	0	2	4.88

Jim Leyritz

Bats: Right **Throws:** Right **Pos:** 1B-17; 3B-8; C-3; OF-3; DH-3; PH-3   **Ht:** 5'11" **Wt:** 220 **Born:** 12/27/63 **Age:** 38

Year	Team	Lg Org	G	AB	H	2B	3B	HR	TB	R	RBI	TBB	IBB	SO	HBP	SH	SF	SB	CS	SB%	GDP	Avg	OBP	SLG
1986	Ft. Laud	A+ NYY	12	34	10	1	1	0	13	3	1	4	1	5	1	0	0	0	0	—	1	.294	.385	.382
	Oneonta	A- NYY	23	91	33	3	1	4	50	12	15	5	1	10	0	2	3	1	0	1.00	0	.363	.384	.549
1987	Ft. Laud	A+ NYY	102	374	115	22	0	6	155	48	51	38	1	54	6	7	4	2	1	.67	8	.307	.377	.414
1988	Albany-Col	AA NYY	112	382	92	18	3	5	131	40	50	43	5	60	6	3	2	3	3	.50	6	.241	.326	.343
1989	Albany-Col	AA NYY	114	375	118	18	2	10	170	53	66	65	5	51	9	2	5	2	1	.67	8	.315	.423	.453
1990	Columbus	AAA NYY	59	204	59	11	1	8	96	36	32	37	1	33	3	2	1	4	2	.67	6	.289	.404	.471
1991	Columbus	AAA NYY	79	270	72	24	1	11	131	50	48	38	1	49	8	1	3	1	2	.33	5	.267	.370	.485
1999	Rancho Cuca	A+ SD	1	4	0	0	0	0	0	0	0	0	0	1	0	0	0	0	0	—	0	.000	.000	.000
	Las Vegas	AAA SD	2	8	0	0	0	0	0	0	0	0	0	5	0	0	0	0	0	—	0	.000	.000	.000
2001	Newark	IND —	19	71	21	3	0	4	36	15	15	9	1	14	1	0	0	1	1	.50	2	.296	.383	.507
	Portland	AAA SD	16	46	12	1	0	0	28	8	10	5	0	13	1	0	1	1	0	1.00	1	.261	.340	.609
1990	New York	AL	92	303	78	13	1	5	108	28	25	27	1	51	7	1	1	2	3	.40	11	.257	.331	.356
1991	New York	AL	32	77	14	3	0	0	17	8	4	13	0	15	0	1	0	0	1	.00	0	.182	.300	.221
1992	New York	AL	63	144	37	6	0	7	64	17	26	14	1	22	6	0	3	0	1	.00	2	.257	.341	.444
1993	New York	AL	95	259	80	14	0	14	136	43	53	37	3	59	8	0	1	0	0	—	12	.309	.410	.525
1994	New York	AL	75	249	66	12	0	17	129	47	58	35	1	61	6	0	3	0	0	—	9	.265	.365	.518
1995	New York	AL	77	264	71	12	0	7	104	37	37	37	2	73	6	0	1	1	1	.50	4	.269	.374	.394
1996	New York	AL	88	265	70	10	0	7	101	23	40	30	3	68	9	2	3	2	0	1.00	11	.264	.355	.381
1997	Anaheim	AL	84	294	81	7	0	11	121	47	50	37	2	56	3	3	5	1	1	.50	11	.276	.357	.412
	Texas	AL	37	85	24	4	0	0	28	11	14	23	0	22	3	1	1	1	0	1.00	2	.282	.446	.329
1998	Boston	AL	52	129	37	6	0	8	67	17	24	21	1	34	2	0	4	0	0	—	4	.287	.385	.519
	San Diego	NL	62	143	38	10	0	4	60	17	18	21	0	40	7	0	1	0	0	—	2	.266	.384	.420
1999	San Diego	NL	50	134	32	5	0	8	61	17	21	15	1	37	4	0	1	0	0	—	3	.239	.331	.455
	New York	NL	31	66	15	4	1	0	21	8	5	13	1	17	0	0	0	0	0	—	3	.227	.354	.318
2000	New York	AL	24	55	12	0	0	1	15	2	4	7	0	14	1	0	0	0	0	—	2	.218	.317	.273
	Los Angeles	NL	41	60	12	0	0	1	16	3	8	7	0	12	1	0	1	0	0	—	2	.200	.294	.267
8 Min. YEARS			539	1859	532	101	9	53	810	265	288	244	16	295	35	17	19	15	10	.60	38	.286	.376	.436
11 Maj. YEARS			903	2527	667	107	2	90	1048	325	387	337	16	581	65	8	24	7	7	.50	79	.264	.362	.415

Brad Lidge

Pitches: Right **Bats:** Right **Pos:** SP-5   **Ht:** 6'5" **Wt:** 200 **Born:** 12/23/76 **Age:** 25

Year	Team	Lg Org	G	GS	CG	GF	IP	BFP	H	R	ER	HR	SH	SF	HB	TBB	IBB	SO	WP	Bk	W	L	Pct.	ShO	Sv	ERA
1998	Quad City	A Hou	4	4	0	0	11	50	10	5	4	0	0	0	1	5	0	6	1	0	0	1	.000	0	0	3.27
1999	Kissimmee	A+ Hou	6	6	0	0	21.1	82	13	8	8	0	0	0	0	11	0	19	2	0	0	2	.000	0	0	3.38
2000	Kissimmee	A+ Hou	8	8	0	0	41.2	164	28	14	13	3	1	0	1	15	0	46	1	2	2	1	.667	0	0	2.81
2001	Round Rock	AA Hou	5	5	0	0	26	107	21	5	5	1	1	1	2	7	0	42	1	0	2	0	1.000	0	0	1.73
4 Min. YEARS			23	23	0	0	100	403	72	32	30	4	2	1	4	38	0	113	5	2	4	4	.500	0	0	2.70

Kevin Lidle

Bats: Both **Throws:** Right **Pos:** C-40; PH-2; P-2   **Ht:** 5'11" **Wt:** 170 **Born:** 3/22/72 **Age:** 30

Year Team	Lg Org	G	AB	H	2B	3B	HR	TB	R	RBI	TBB	IBB	SO	HBP	SH	SF	SB	CS	SB%	GDP	Avg	OBP	SLG
1992 Niagara Fal	A- Det	58	140	34	6	2	1	47	21	18	8	0	42	1	6	3	3	2	.60	1	.243	.283	.336
1993 Fayettevlle	A Det	58	197	42	14	1	5	73	29	25	34	0	42	1	0	1	2	0	1.00	0	.213	.330	.371
1994 Lakeland	A+ Det	56	187	49	13	2	6	84	26	30	19	0	46	4	1	1	1	1	.50	2	.262	.341	.449
1995 Jacksnville	AA Det	36	80	13	7	0	1	23	12	5	1	0	31	0	1	0	1	0	1.00	1	.163	.173	.288
Fayettevlle	A Det	36	113	16	4	1	4	34	15	13	16	0	44	1	3	2	0	1	.00	1	.142	.250	.301
1996 Lakeland	A+ Det	97	320	69	18	1	8	113	37	41	30	0	90	3	0	1	1	1	.50	4	.216	.288	.353
Jacksnville	AA Det	4	8	2	0	0	1	5	2	2	1	0	2	0	0	0	1	0	1.00	0	.250	.333	.625
1997 Jacksnville	AA Det	59	186	28	7	0	1	38	18	16	17	0	77	2	3	2	0	0	—	4	.151	.227	.204
1998 Salem	A+ Col	31	59	7	4	0	2	17	6	7	3	0	14	0	0	0	0	0	—	0	.119	.161	.288
New Haven	AA Col	11	35	5	2	0	2	13	5	5	3	0	13	0	1	0	0	0	—	0	.143	.211	.371
Colo Sprngs	AAA Col	5	15	4	1	1	0	7	2	1	1	0	8	1	0	0	0	0	—	0	.267	.353	.467
1999 Mobile	AA SD	63	180	40	8	0	6	66	23	26	30	2	40	5	2	2	1	3	.25	4	.222	.346	.367
Las Vegas	AAA SD	10	29	8	3	0	2	17	5	5	3	0	8	0	0	1	0	0	—	2	.276	.333	.586
2000 Somerset	IND —	20	60	10	2	1	0	14	3	8	5	0	20	2	1	1	2	1	.67	1	.167	.250	.233
Erie	AA Ana	29	82	18	2	0	0	20	11	3	10	2	14	2	0	0	1	2	.33	0	.220	.319	.244
2001 Salt Lake	AAA Ana	30	88	26	7	0	1	36	10	10	9	0	27	3	2	1	2	1	.67	0	.295	.376	.409
Memphis	AAA StL	13	35	2	1	0	0	3	1	2	2	0	14	0	0	0	0	0	—	0	.057	.108	.086
10 Min. YEARS		616	1814	373	99	9	40	610	226	217	192	4	532	25	20	15	15	12	.56	22	.206	.288	.336

Rod Lindsey

Bats: Right **Throws:** Right **Pos:** OF-111; PH-1   **Ht:** 5'8" **Wt:** 175 **Born:** 1/28/76 **Age:** 26

Year Team	Lg Org	G	AB	H	2B	3B	HR	TB	R	RBI	TBB	IBB	SO	HBP	SH	SF	SB	CS	SB%	GDP	Avg	OBP	SLG
1994 Padres	R SD	48	172	46	3	0	0	49	29	19	11	0	59	9	0	0	15	8	.65	2	.267	.344	.285
1995 Idaho Falls	R+ SD	35	155	41	4	4	0	53	30	14	13	0	37	4	0	1	21	7	.75	1	.265	.335	.342
1996 Clinton	A SD	23	87	14	2	0	0	16	11	4	11	0	30	3	0	1	12	8	.60	2	.161	.275	.184
Idaho Falls	R+ SD	48	185	56	4	6	5	87	45	17	23	0	53	2	0	0	16	3	.84	1	.303	.386	.470
1997 Clinton	A SD	130	502	107	15	8	6	156	80	49	62	0	161	7	3	2	70	23	.75	8	.213	.307	.311
1998 Clinton	A SD	40	155	42	4	4	4	66	32	17	17	1	54	3	1	1	36	4	.90	2	.271	.352	.426
W Michigan	A Det	45	158	43	7	4	3	67	37	17	22	1	42	10	0	1	24	8	.75	1	.272	.393	.424
1999 Jacksnville	AA Det	7	27	5	1	0	0	6	3	2	1	0	6	0	1	0	0	0	—	0	.185	.214	.222
Lakeland	A+ Det	120	485	129	20	8	7	186	81	51	25	0	129	18	4	5	61	20	.75	6	.266	.323	.384
2000 Jacksnville	AA Det	114	393	88	11	4	0	107	57	20	38	0	100	10	10	1	46	14	.77	4	.224	.308	.272
2001 Erie	AA Det	111	385	97	14	1	2	119	51	34	23	0	77	12	3	5	29	12	.71	6	.252	.311	.309
2000 Detroit	AL	11	3	1	1	0	0	2	6	0	0	0	1	1	1	0	2	1	.67	0	.333	.500	.667
8 Min. YEARS		721	2704	668	85	39	27	912	456	244	246	2	748	78	22	17	330	107	.76	33	.247	.326	.337

Dave Lindstrom

Bats: Right **Throws:** Right **Pos:** C-54; 2B-6; OF-3   **Ht:** 5'10" **Wt:** 185 **Born:** 8/6/74 **Age:** 27

Year Team	Lg Org	G	AB	H	2B	3B	HR	TB	R	RBI	TBB	IBB	SO	HBP	SH	SF	SB	CS	SB%	GDP	Avg	OBP	SLG
1996 Jamestown	A- Det	52	165	41	10	0	5	66	19	13	10	0	29	2	5	0	1	0	1.00	3	.248	.299	.400
1997 Lakeland	A+ Det	76	213	44	8	0	3	61	25	14	24	0	25	3	5	2	1	0	1.00	9	.207	.293	.286
1998 Toledo	AAA Det	1	3	0	0	0	0	0	0	0	0	0	1	0	0	0	0	0	—	0	.000	.000	.000
Lakeland	A+ Det	103	337	83	20	2	5	122	52	42	50	1	46	11	3	7	0	3	.00	8	.246	.356	.362
1999 Jacksnville	AA Det	66	214	58	17	1	7	98	30	35	24	0	35	6	1	5	1	3	.25	9	.271	.353	.458
2000 Toledo	AAA Det	12	36	10	0	0	2	16	6	6	2	0	3	1	1	0	0	0	—	3	.278	.333	.444
Jacksnville	AA Det	68	222	52	11	0	7	84	26	36	19	0	17	4	0	3	1	0	1.00	8	.234	.302	.378
2001 Toledo	AAA Det	61	203	52	16	1	1	73	21	22	10	0	24	3	9	1	1	1	.50	8	.256	.300	.360
6 Min. YEARS		439	1393	340	82	4	30	520	179	168	139	1	180	30	24	18	5	7	.42	46	.244	.322	.373

Cole Liniak

Bats: Right **Throws:** Right **Pos:** 3B-82; DH-18; 2B-5; PH-1; PR-1   **Ht:** 6'1" **Wt:** 190 **Born:** 8/23/76 **Age:** 25

Year Team	Lg Org	G	AB	H	2B	3B	HR	TB	R	RBI	TBB	IBB	SO	HBP	SH	SF	SB	CS	SB%	GDP	Avg	OBP	SLG
1995 Red Sox	R Bos	23	79	21	7	0	1	31	9	8	4	0	8	1	2	0	2	0	1.00	2	.266	.310	.392
1996 Michigan	A Bos	121	437	115	26	2	3	154	65	46	59	1	59	10	3	8	7	6	.54	12	.263	.358	.352
1997 Sarasota	A+ Bos	64	217	73	16	0	6	107	32	42	22	1	31	3	3	2	1	2	.33	2	.336	.402	.493
Trenton	AA Bos	53	200	56	11	0	2	73	20	18	17	0	29	1	1	.00	6	.280	.338	.365
1998 Red Sox	R Bos	2	8	0	0	0	0	0	1	0	0	0	1	0	0	0	0	0	—	0	.000	.111	.000
Pawtucket	AAA Bos	112	429	112	31	1	17	196	65	59	39	1	71	5	4	3	4	4	.50	11	.261	.328	.457
1999 Pawtucket	AAA Bos	95	348	92	25	0	12	153	55	42	40	1	57	1	3	1	0	5	.00	7	.264	.341	.440
2000 Iowa	AAA ChC	123	411	97	24	1	19	180	63	58	39	0	77	3	4	4	5	3	.63	16	.236	.304	.438
2001 Syracuse	AAA Tor	103	344	83	21	1	10	136	40	49	32	3	55	3	5	5	1	2	.33	8	.241	.307	.395
1999 Chicago	NL	12	29	7	2	0	0	9	3	2	1	0	4	0	0	0	0	1	.00	2	.241	.267	.310
2000 Chicago	NL	3	3	0	0	0	0	0	0	0	0	0	2	0	0	0	0	0	—	0	.000	.000	.000
7 Min. YEARS		696	2473	649	161	5	70	1030	350	322	252	7	388	28	27	24	20	23	.47	64	.262	.335	.416
2 Maj. YEARS		15	32	7	2	0	0	9	3	2	1	0	6	0	0	0	0	1	.00	2	.219	.242	.281

Doug Linton

Pitches: Right **Bats:** Right **Pos:** SP-12   **Ht:** 6'1" **Wt:** 190 **Born:** 2/9/65 **Age:** 37

Year Team	Lg Org	G	GS	CG	GF	IP	BFP	H	R	ER	HR	SH	SF	HB	TBB	IBB	SO	WP	Bk	W	L	Pct.	ShO	Sv	ERA
1987 Myrtle Bch	A Tor	20	19	2	1	122	480	94	36	21	9	0	2	2	25	0	155	8	1	14	2	.875	0	1	1.55
Knoxville	AA Tor	1	1	0	0	3	15	5	3	3	0	0	0	1	1	0	1	0	0	0	0	—	0	0	9.00
1988 Dunedin	A+ Tor	12	0	0	6	27.2	111	19	5	5	0	1	1	0	9	1	28	2	2	2	1	.667	0	2	1.63

172

Year Team	Lg Org	G	GS	CG	GF	IP	BFP	H	R	ER	HR	SH	SF	HB	TBB	IBB	SO	WP	Bk	W	L	Pct.	ShO	Sv	ERA
1989 Dunedin	A+ Tor	9	1	0	5	27.1	117	27	12	9	1	0	1	0	9	0	35	1	0	1	2	.333	0	2	2.96
Knoxville	AA Tor	14	13	3	0	90	355	68	28	26	2	3	1	2	23	2	93	6	1	5	4	.556	2	0	2.60
1990 Syracuse	AAA Tor	26	26	8	0	177.1	753	174	77	67	14	2	10	8	67	3	113	4	1	10	10	.500	3	0	3.40
1991 Syracuse	AAA Tor	30	26	3	1	161.2	710	181	108	90	21	6	10	10	56	2	93	5	0	10	12	.455	1	0	5.01
1992 Syracuse	AAA Tor	25	25	7	0	170.2	741	176	83	71	17	5	4	7	70	3	126	12	1	12	10	.545	1	0	3.74
1993 Syracuse	AAA Tor	13	7	0	4	47.1	206	48	29	28	11	2	1	3	14	3	42	2	0	2	6	.250	0	2	5.32
1994 Norfolk	AAA NYM	3	3	0	0	18	66	11	6	4	1	0	0	1	1	0	15	0	0	2	1	.667	0	0	2.00
1995 Omaha	AAA KC	18	18	2	0	108.1	472	129	60	53	9	5	3	7	24	2	85	3	1	7	7	.500	1	0	4.40
1996 Omaha	AAA KC	4	4	0	0	22.2	99	26	13	12	1	0	1	2	7	0	14	2	0	1	1	.500	0	0	4.76
1998 Salt Lake	AAA Min	18	14	0	2	79.2	348	106	57	53	19	1	3	1	14	1	60	5	2	4	4	.500	0	0	5.99
1999 Rochester	AAA Bal	18	18	1	0	118.1	510	120	58	48	13	3	4	10	27	1	97	3	0	7	5	.583	0	0	3.65
2000 Colo Sprngs	AAA Col	28	28	6	0	174	753	189	109	104	15	11	10	12	42	2	136	7	1	10	13	.435	3	0	5.38
2001 Norfolk	AAA NYM	12	12	0	0	75.2	302	74	28	27	8	4	3	2	10	0	67	2	1	7	3	.700	0	0	3.21
1992 Toronto	AL	8	3	0	2	24	116	31	23	23	5	1	2	0	17	0	16	2	0	1	3	.250	0	0	8.63
1993 Toronto	AL	4	1	0	0	11	55	11	8	8	0	0	2	1	9	0	4	0	0	0	1	.000	0	0	6.55
California	AL	19	0	0	6	25.2	123	35	22	22	8	0	1	0	14	1	19	2	0	2	0	1.000	0	0	7.71
1994 New York	NL	32	3	0	8	50.1	241	74	27	25	4	3	1	0	20	3	29	2	0	6	2	.750	0	0	4.47
1995 Kansas City	AL	7	2	0	0	22.1	98	22	21	18	4	0	0	2	10	1	13	0	0	0	1	.000	0	0	7.25
1996 Kansas City	AL	21	18	0	0	104	452	111	65	58	13	6	2	8	26	1	87	3	1	7	9	.438	0	0	5.02
1999 Baltimore	AL	14	8	0	0	59	264	69	41	39	14	4	0	2	25	1	31	4	0	1	4	.200	0	0	5.95
14 Min. YEARS		251	215	32	19	1423.2	6038	1447	710	621	141	43	54	68	399	20	1160	62	13	94	81	.537	11	7	3.93
6 Maj. YEARS		105	35	0	16	296.1	1349	353	207	193	48	14	8	13	121	7	199	13	1	17	20	.459	0	0	5.86

Nathan Lipowicz

Bats: Right **Throws:** Right **Pos:** OF-32; DH-2; PH-1 **Ht:** 5'10" **Wt:** 175 **Born:** 2/9/78 **Age:** 24

Year Team	Lg Org	G	AB	H	2B	3B	HR	TB	R	RBI	TBB	IBB	SO	HBP	SH	SF	SB	CS	SB%	GDP	Avg	OBP	SLG
2000 Great Falls	R+ LA	43	145	35	5	3	3	55	22	12	7	0	36	1	0	2	2	2	.50	2	.241	.277	.379
2001 Vero Beach	A+ LA	33	101	24	4	0	0	28	8	9	7	0	22	2	1	1	0	0	—	0	.238	.297	.277
Las Vegas	AAA LA	2	8	1	1	0	0	2	0	0	0	0	3	0	0	0	0	0	—	0	.125	.125	.250
2 Min. YEARS		78	254	60	10	3	3	85	30	21	14	0	61	3	1	3	2	2	.50	4	.236	.281	.335

James Lira

Pitches: Right **Bats:** Right **Pos:** RP-52 **Ht:** 6'1" **Wt:** 160 **Born:** 5/19/78 **Age:** 24

Year Team	Lg Org	G	GS	CG	GF	IP	BFP	H	R	ER	HR	SH	SF	HB	TBB	IBB	SO	WP	Bk	W	L	Pct.	ShO	Sv	ERA
1998 Princeton	R+ TB	29	0	0	22	36	161	36	18	15	3	2	1	1	19	2	51	3	0	4	1	.800	0	14	3.75
1999 St. Pete	A+ TB	36	0	0	13	44.1	191	45	18	15	1	2	2	2	17	1	25	4	0	4	1	.800	0	0	3.05
2000 St. Pete	A+ TB	42	0	0	22	52.1	214	47	15	13	2	1	2	1	15	0	39	2	0	2	4	.333	0	2	2.24
Orlando	AA TB	2	0	0	0	3	17	4	4	4	1	0	0	0	3	0	4	0	0	0	0	—	0	0	12.00
2001 Michigan	A Hou	25	0	0	23	31.1	123	17	7	6	2	4	1	1	12	2	33	2	0	2	2	.500	0	12	1.72
Round Rock	AA Hou	27	0	0	13	39	158	32	16	13	2	1	3	2	10	0	27	2	1	1	0	.000	0	2	3.00
4 Min. YEARS		161	0	0	93	206	864	181	78	66	11	10	9	7	76	5	179	13	1	12	9	.571	0	30	2.88

Mike Lockwood

Bats: Left **Throws:** Left **Pos:** OF-127; PH-4; DH-2 **Ht:** 6'0" **Wt:** 190 **Born:** 12/27/76 **Age:** 25

Year Team	Lg Org	G	AB	H	2B	3B	HR	TB	R	RBI	TBB	IBB	SO	HBP	SH	SF	SB	CS	SB%	GDP	Avg	OBP	SLG
1999 Sou Oregon	A- Oak	69	255	92	18	5	7	141	48	51	39	1	49	8	0	6	6	5	.55	5	.361	.451	.553
2000 Modesto	A+ Oak	47	159	50	12	0	6	80	42	35	46	6	25	4	3	7	9	1	.90	3	.314	.463	.503
Sacramento	AAA Oak	36	126	32	3	0	1	38	14	13	17	1	14	1	2	3	0	2	.00	1	.254	.340	.302
Midland	AA Oak	56	236	73	16	1	4	103	45	31	21	0	33	6	2	1	1	1	.50	4	.309	.377	.436
2001 Midland	AA Oak	131	493	128	36	3	6	188	71	69	49	1	80	8	4	5	9	4	.69	8	.260	.333	.381
3 Min. YEARS		339	1269	375	85	9	24	550	220	199	172	9	201	27	11	23	25	13	.66	21	.296	.385	.433

Kyle Logan

Bats: Left **Throws:** Right **Pos:** OF-68; PH-4; DH-2 **Ht:** 6'0" **Wt:** 196 **Born:** 7/11/75 **Age:** 26

Year Team	Lg Org	G	AB	H	2B	3B	HR	TB	R	RBI	TBB	IBB	SO	HBP	SH	SF	SB	CS	SB%	GDP	Avg	OBP	SLG
1997 Auburn	A- Hou	71	260	76	16	4	0	100	27	29	20	3	60	1	0	0	5	10	.33	3	.292	.345	.385
1998 Quad City	A Hou	110	352	93	22	2	4	131	50	49	36	3	50	2	2	5	22	13	.63	4	.264	.332	.372
1999 Kissimmee	A+ Hou	113	399	116	33	7	7	184	57	62	33	4	62	3	1	3	16	5	.76	5	.291	.347	.461
2000 Round Rock	AA Hou	109	343	75	17	0	6	110	44	31	35	2	63	4	1	5	13	5	.72	4	.219	.295	.321
Kissimmee	A+ Hou	17	51	14	1	2	0	19	8	4	13	2	6	2	0	2	7	0	1.00	0	.275	.426	.373
2001 Round Rock	AA Hou	73	258	81	22	3	6	127	36	32	19	3	44	4	1	1	12	3	.80	4	.314	.369	.492
5 Min. YEARS		493	1663	455	111	18	23	671	222	207	156	17	285	16	5	16	75	36	.68	20	.274	.339	.403

Matt Logan

Bats: Left **Throws:** Right **Pos:** 1B-93; DH-2; PH-2 **Ht:** 6'3" **Wt:** 210 **Born:** 7/22/79 **Age:** 22

Year Team	Lg Org	G	AB	H	2B	3B	HR	TB	R	RBI	TBB	IBB	SO	HBP	SH	SF	SB	CS	SB%	GDP	Avg	OBP	SLG
1998 Medcine Hat	R+ Tor	47	173	46	12	1	3	69	29	30	23	0	41	4	0	1	1	1	.50	5	.266	.363	.399
1999 Hagerstown	A Tor	119	453	110	21	1	9	160	55	57	32	1	130	2	2	4	3	2	.60	6	.243	.293	.353
2000 Dunedin	A+ Tor	124	373	104	26	1	9	159	58	55	36	0	93	7	2	6	4	1	.80	13	.279	.348	.426
2001 Tennessee	AA Tor	96	277	57	12	1	9	98	32	34	28	1	82	5	1	2	3	1	.75	10	.206	.288	.354
4 Min. YEARS		386	1276	317	71	4	30	486	174	176	119	2	346	18	5	13	11	5	.69	34	.248	.318	.381

Josh Loggins

Bats: Right **Throws:** Right **Pos:** OF-67; DH-10; PR-7; PH-6; C-2   **Ht:** 6'1" **Wt:** 190 **Born:** 11/29/76 **Age:** 25

							BATTING										BASERUNNING				PERCENTAGES		
Year Team	Lg Org	G	AB	H	2B	3B	HR	TB	R	RBI	TBB	IBB	SO	HBP	SH	SF	SB	CS	SB%	GDP	Avg	OBP	SLG
1998 Idaho Falls	R+ SD	71	299	102	20	5	8	156	66	64	35	0	60	2	1	2	8	8	.50	7	.341	.411	.522
1999 Fort Wayne	A SD	136	522	155	29	7	14	240	75	85	60	4	119	12	2	5	24	12	.67	13	.297	.379	.460
2000 Rancho Cuca	A+ SD	78	293	88	13	4	6	127	52	43	30	2	84	6	0	4	9	4	.69	5	.300	.372	.433
2001 Mobile	AA SD	34	89	17	3	0	2	26	10	6	6	1	27	1	0	1	0	0	—	4	.191	.247	.292
Norwich	AA NYY	52	176	47	12	0	2	65	24	27	16	0	52	2	1	2	2	2	.50	3	.267	.332	.369
4 Min. YEARS		371	1379	409	77	16	32	614	227	225	147	7	342	23	4	14	43	26	.62	32	.297	.370	.445

Dave Lohrman

Pitches: Right **Bats:** Right **Pos:** RP-35   **Ht:** 6'6" **Wt:** 200 **Born:** 9/16/75 **Age:** 26

		HOW MUCH HE PITCHED						WHAT HE GAVE UP											THE RESULTS				
Year Team	Lg Org	G	GS	CG	GF	IP	BFP	H	R	ER	HR	SH	SF	HB	TBB	IBB	SO	WP	Bk	W	L	Pct.	ShO	Sv	ERA
1997 Pittsfield	A- NYM	22	0	0	13	34	146	25	18	11	2	0	0	5	12	0	42	3	1	1	2	.333	0	4	2.91
1998 St. Lucie	A+ NYM	19	1	0	6	30.2	145	39	27	23	6	0	1	2	14	1	27	5	0	2	3	.400	0	0	6.75
Capital City	A NYM	21	0	0	12	42.1	180	27	14	5	2	2	1	0	20	1	53	3	0	3	1	.750	0	4	1.06
1999 St. Lucie	A+ NYM	43	1	0	16	76	325	64	33	26	3	4	1	4	46	4	75	5	0	4	0	1.000	0	0	3.08
2000 St. Lucie	A+ NYM	43	0	0	19	63	310	75	40	34	1	2	3	5	42	2	70	12	0	1	6	.143	0	3	4.86
2001 St. Lucie	A+ NYM	20	0	0	6	37.2	151	18	8	7	0	1	2	4	20	0	53	5	0	3	1	.750	0	2	1.67
Binghamton	AA NYM	13	0	0	8	25.2	109	20	9	6	2	1	1	1	12	1	26	1	0	2	1	.667	0	6	2.10
Norfolk	AAA NYM	2	0	0	1	3	12	4	2	2	1	0	0	0	0	0	3	0	0	0	0	—	0	0	6.00
5 Min. YEARS		183	2	0	81	312.1	1378	272	151	114	17	10	9	21	166	9	349	34	1	16	14	.533	0	19	3.28

Steve Lomasney

Bats: Right **Throws:** Right **Pos:** C-70; DH-5; PR-1   **Ht:** 6'0" **Wt:** 195 **Born:** 8/29/77 **Age:** 24

							BATTING										BASERUNNING				PERCENTAGES		
Year Team	Lg Org	G	AB	H	2B	3B	HR	TB	R	RBI	TBB	IBB	SO	HBP	SH	SF	SB	CS	SB%	GDP	Avg	OBP	SLG
1995 Red Sox	R Bos	29	92	15	6	0	0	21	10	7	8	1	16	5	1	0	2	1	.67	0	.163	.267	.228
1996 Lowell	A- Bos	59	173	24	10	0	4	46	26	21	42	0	63	2	0	0	2	0	1.00	2	.139	.313	.266
1997 Michigan	A Bos	102	324	89	27	3	12	158	50	51	32	0	98	9	3	3	3	4	.43	8	.275	.353	.488
1998 Sarasota	A+ Bos	122	443	106	22	1	22	196	74	63	59	3	145	16	1	2	13	4	.76	7	.239	.348	.442
1999 Sarasota	A+ Bos	55	189	51	10	0	8	85	35	28	26	0	57	8	0	0	5	2	.71	2	.270	.381	.450
Trenton	AA Bos	47	151	37	6	0	12	79	24	31	31	2	44	9	1	1	7	5	.58	5	.245	.401	.523
2000 Trenton	AA Bos	66	233	57	16	1	8	99	30	27	24	0	81	12	1	1	4	6	.40	8	.245	.343	.425
Red Sox	R Bos	6	15	4	2	0	0	6	2	1	4	0	6	0	0	0	1	0	1.00	1	.267	.421	.400
2001 Trenton	AA Bos	58	209	52	14	2	10	100	24	29	23	1	76	3	0	0	0	1	.00	8	.249	.332	.478
Pawtucket	AAA Bos	17	63	18	4	0	2	28	10	9	4	0	21	1	1	0	2	0	1.00	2	.286	.338	.444
1999 Boston	AL	1	2	0	0	0	0	0	0	0	0	0	2	0	0	0	0	0	—	0	.000	.000	.000
7 Min. YEARS		561	1892	453	117	7	78	818	285	267	253	7	607	65	8	8	38	24	.61	42	.239	.348	.432

George Lombard

Bats: Left **Throws:** Right **Pos:** OF-12; PH-1   **Ht:** 6'0" **Wt:** 212 **Born:** 9/14/75 **Age:** 26

							BATTING										BASERUNNING				PERCENTAGES		
Year Team	Lg Org	G	AB	H	2B	3B	HR	TB	R	RBI	TBB	IBB	SO	HBP	SH	SF	SB	CS	SB%	GDP	Avg	OBP	SLG
1994 Braves	R Atl	40	129	18	2	0	0	20	10	5	18	0	47	3	0	0	10	4	.71	1	.140	.260	.155
1995 Macon	A Atl	49	180	37	6	1	3	54	32	16	27	3	44	5	1	0	16	4	.80	4	.206	.325	.300
Eugene	A- Atl	68	262	66	5	3	5	92	38	19	23	0	91	5	2	1	35	13	.73	0	.252	.323	.351
1996 Macon	A Atl	116	444	109	16	8	15	186	76	51	36	0	122	7	8	2	24	17	.59	4	.245	.311	.419
1997 Durham	A+ Atl	131	462	122	25	7	14	203	65	72	66	9	145	9	2	2	35	7	.83	6	.264	.365	.439
1998 Greenville	AA Atl	122	422	130	25	4	22	229	84	65	71	10	140	5	5	4	35	5	.88	2	.308	.410	.543
1999 Richmond	AAA Atl	74	233	48	11	3	7	86	25	29	35	2	98	3	0	0	21	6	.78	2	.206	.317	.369
2000 Richmond	AAA Atl	112	424	117	25	7	10	186	72	48	55	3	130	6	5	3	32	9	.78	3	.276	.365	.439
2001 Richmond	AAA Atl	13	44	14	2	1	4	30	7	8	6	0	14	2	1	0	3	2	.60	1	.318	.423	.682
1998 Atlanta	NL	6	6	2	0	0	1	5	2	1	0	0	1	0	0	0	1	0	1.00	0	.333	.333	.833
1999 Atlanta	NL	6	6	2	0	0	0	2	1	0	1	0	2	0	0	0	2	0	1.00	0	.333	.429	.333
2000 Atlanta	NL	27	39	4	0	0	0	4	8	2	1	0	14	1	0	0	4	0	1.00	2	.103	.146	.103
8 Min. YEARS		725	2600	661	117	34	80	1086	409	313	337	27	831	45	24	12	211	67	.76	21	.254	.348	.418
3 Maj. YEARS		39	51	8	0	0	1	11	11	3	2	0	17	1	0	0	7	0	1.00	2	.157	.204	.216

Alex Lontayo

Pitches: Left **Bats:** Left **Pos:** RP-16; SP-13   **Ht:** 6'1" **Wt:** 195 **Born:** 12/12/75 **Age:** 26

		HOW MUCH HE PITCHED						WHAT HE GAVE UP											THE RESULTS				
Year Team	Lg Org	G	GS	CG	GF	IP	BFP	H	R	ER	HR	SH	SF	HB	TBB	IBB	SO	WP	Bk	W	L	Pct.	ShO	Sv	ERA
1999 Augusta	A Bos	40	0	0	14	58.2	255	55	31	28	7	1	2	4	26	0	80	3	1	2	0	1.000	0	0	4.30
2000 Lk Elsinore	A+ Ana	6	3	0	1	21.2	95	21	14	8	0	1	1	0	12	0	19	0	0	2	0	1.000	0	1	3.32
Erie	AA Ana	34	2	0	11	57	249	55	39	33	7	3	6	3	27	1	37	2	1	1	4	.200	0	2	5.21
2001 Greenville	AA Atl	9	9	0	0	50.1	232	59	34	29	3	3	1	0	26	2	43	1	2	3	5	.375	0	0	5.19
Myrtle Bch	A+ Atl	20	4	0	3	50.1	232	56	26	24	3	3	1	3	27	1	42	4	0	5	2	.714	0	0	4.29
3 Min. YEARS		109	18	0	29	238	1063	246	144	122	20	11	11	10	118	4	221	10	4	13	11	.542	0	3	4.61

Brian Looney

Pitches: Left **Bats:** Left **Pos:** RP-11   **Ht:** 5'10" **Wt:** 180 **Born:** 9/26/69 **Age:** 32

		HOW MUCH HE PITCHED						WHAT HE GAVE UP											THE RESULTS				
Year Team	Lg Org	G	GS	CG	GF	IP	BFP	H	R	ER	HR	SH	SF	HB	TBB	IBB	SO	WP	Bk	W	L	Pct.	ShO	Sv	ERA
1991 Jamestown	A- Mon	11	11	2	0	62.1	246	42	12	8	0	2	2	0	28	0	64	6	0	7	1	.875	1	0	1.16
1992 Rockford	A Mon	17	0	0	5	31.1	141	28	13	11	0	2	0	1	23	0	34	1	0	3	1	.750	0	0	3.16
Albany	A Mon	11	11	1	0	67.1	265	51	34	16	1	1	3	0	30	0	56	4	0	3	2	.600	1	0	2.14

174

Year Team	Lg Org	G	GS	CG	GF	IP	BFP	H	R	ER	HR	SH	SF	HB	TBB	IBB	SO	WP	Bk	W	L	Pct.	ShO	Sv	ERA
		HOW MUCH HE PITCHED						WHAT HE GAVE UP												THE RESULTS					
1993 Wst Plm Bch	A+ Mon	18	16	0	1	106	451	108	48	37	2	7	3	5	29	0	109	2	1	4	6	.400	0	0	3.14
Harrisburg	AA Mon	8	8	1	0	56.2	221	36	15	15	2	1	1	1	17	1	76	0	0	2	2	.600	1	0	2.38
1994 Ottawa	AAA Mon	27	16	0	2	124.2	565	134	71	60	10	3	6	3	67	4	90	2	0	7	7	.500	0	0	4.33
1995 Pawtucket	AAA Bos	18	18	1	0	100.2	438	106	44	39	9	2	0	3	33	0	78	7	2	4	7	.364	0	0	3.49
1996 Pawtucket	AAA Bos	27	9	1	7	82.1	357	78	55	44	14	0	2	4	27	2	78	3	0	5	6	.455	1	1	4.81
1997 Salt Lake	AAA Min	17	0	0	6	24.2	103	20	7	6	4	1	0	0	10	2	21	2	0	0	2	.000	0	1	2.19
1998 Columbus	AAA NYY	41	10	0	7	92.2	424	97	52	46	13	3	5	1	52	2	63	3	0	4	4	.500	0	0	4.47
1999 Toledo	AAA Det	47	1	0	11	55	255	51	38	38	7	5	4	2	44	0	52	7	0	3	0	1.000	0	2	6.22
Scranton-WB	AAA Phi	3	3	0	0	16	74	19	9	7	3	0	0	1	6	0	12	1	1	1	0	1.000	0	0	3.94
2000 Buffalo	AAA Cle	8	0	0	3	12.2	63	15	13	12	1	1	2	2	8	1	8	0	0	1	0	1.000	0	0	8.53
Calgary	AAA Fla	3	2	0	1	9	39	11	7	7	1	1	1	0	2	0	6	0	0	0	2	.000	0	0	7.00
2001 Norwich	AA NYY	11	0	0	5	16	84	23	18	15	2	0	3	1	10	0	16	0	0	0	0	—	0	0	8.44
1993 Montreal	NL	3	1	0	1	6	28	8	2	2	0	0	0	0	2	0	7	0	1	0	0	—	0	0	3.00
1994 Montreal	NL	1	0	0	0	2	11	4	5	5	1	0	0	1	0	0	2	0	0	0	0	—	0	0	22.50
1995 Boston	AL	3	1	0	0	4.2	29	12	9	9	1	1	2	0	4	1	2	0	0	0	1	.000	0	0	17.36
11 Min. YEARS		267	105	6	48	857.1	3726	819	424	361	69	29	32	24	386	12	763	38	4	45	40	.529	4	4	3.79
3 Maj. YEARS		7	2	0	1	12.2	68	24	16	16	2	1	2	1	6	1	11	0	1	0	1	.000	0	0	11.37

Aquilino Lopez

Pitches: Right Bats: Right Pos: RP-42 Ht: 6'3" Wt: 165 Born: 7/30/80 Age: 21

Year Team	Lg Org	G	GS	CG	GF	IP	BFP	H	R	ER	HR	SH	SF	HB	TBB	IBB	SO	WP	Bk	W	L	Pct.	ShO	Sv	ERA
		HOW MUCH HE PITCHED						WHAT HE GAVE UP												THE RESULTS					
1999 Everett	A- Sea	15	15	1	0	87.2	365	76	44	37	8	1	2	2	30	2	93	2	0	7	6	.538	0	0	3.80
2000 Wisconsin	A Sea	39	5	1	29	68	268	47	16	14	1	0	1	4	20	4	67	3	0	6	1	.857	1	17	1.85
2001 San Antonio	AA Sea	42	0	0	13	62.2	265	48	24	21	4	2	2	6	25	2	79	5	0	4	3	.571	0	2	3.02
3 Min. YEARS		96	20	2	42	218.1	898	171	84	72	13	3	5	12	75	8	239	10	0	17	10	.630	1	19	2.97

Javier Lopez

Pitches: Left Bats: Left Pos: RP-38; SP-1 Ht: 6'4" Wt: 220 Born: 7/11/77 Age: 24

Year Team	Lg Org	G	GS	CG	GF	IP	BFP	H	R	ER	HR	SH	SF	HB	TBB	IBB	SO	WP	Bk	W	L	Pct.	ShO	Sv	ERA
		HOW MUCH HE PITCHED						WHAT HE GAVE UP												THE RESULTS					
1998 South Bend	A Ari	16	9	0	1	44	218	60	36	32	2	2	3	0	30	0	31	7	0	2	4	.333	0	0	6.55
1999 South Bend	A Ari	20	20	0	0	99	458	122	74	66	9	1	4	3	43	0	70	9	0	4	6	.400	0	0	6.00
2000 High Desert	A+ Ari	30	21	0	4	136.1	602	152	87	79	14	4	7	6	57	0	98	8	2	4	8	.333	0	2	5.22
2001 Lancaster	A+ Ari	17	0	0	10	24	103	30	9	7	2	2	0	0	5	0	18	1	1	1	3	.250	0	1	2.63
El Paso	AA Ari	22	1	0	4	40	191	64	39	33	6	2	1	0	14	2	21	1	0	1	0	1.000	0	0	7.43
4 Min. YEARS		105	51	0	19	343.1	1572	428	245	217	33	11	15	9	149	2	238	26	3	12	21	.364	0	3	5.69

Johan Lopez

Pitches: Right Bats: Right Pos: RP-3 Ht: 6'2" Wt: 210 Born: 4/4/75 Age: 27

Year Team	Lg Org	G	GS	CG	GF	IP	BFP	H	R	ER	HR	SH	SF	HB	TBB	IBB	SO	WP	Bk	W	L	Pct.	ShO	Sv	ERA
		HOW MUCH HE PITCHED						WHAT HE GAVE UP												THE RESULTS					
1992 Astros	R Hou	17	0	0	4	34	160	42	28	17	1	0	3	3	13	0	19	7	4	1	1	.500	0	0	4.50
1994 Auburn	A- Hou	14	14	2	0	76.2	339	86	49	41	4	2	4	4	24	0	74	7	3	7	5	.583	1	0	4.81
1995 Kissimmee	A+ Hou	18	12	0	3	69	283	55	30	20	3	1	2	3	25	0	67	5	3	5	5	.500	0	1	2.61
1996 Kissimmee	A+ Hou	19	19	2	0	98.1	434	114	50	41	5	0	5	1	35	1	70	9	3	3	10	.231	1	0	3.75
1997 Jackson	AA Hou	35	19	0	5	133.2	586	131	79	65	18	7	2	6	57	3	109	11	4	6	8	.429	0	1	4.38
1998 New Orleans	AAA Hou	45	6	0	7	80.1	357	84	52	50	11	6	1	2	28	1	77	3	0	7	2	.778	0	5	5.60
1999 Binghamton	AA NYM	2	0	0	1	2	11	3	3	3	0	1	0	0	3	0	1	0	0	0	0	—	0	0	13.50
Norfolk	AAA NYM	33	8	0	6	102	438	98	49	47	13	6	0	2	44	6	84	10	1	3	5	.375	0	1	4.15
2000 Oklahoma	AAA Tex	29	0	0	16	56.1	230	44	28	26	6	0	3	2	20	2	42	3	0	6	2	.750	0	5	4.15
2001 Oklahoma	AAA Tex	3	0	0	0	7.2	32	8	4	3	1	0	0	0	2	0	4	0	0	0	0	—	0	0	3.52
9 Min. YEARS		215	78	4	42	660	2870	665	372	313	62	24	17	23	251	13	547	55	18	38	38	.500	2	8	4.27

Jose Lopez

Pitches: Right Bats: Right Pos: SP-18; RP-1 Ht: 5'11" Wt: 195 Born: 1/28/76 Age: 26

Year Team	Lg Org	G	GS	CG	GF	IP	BFP	H	R	ER	HR	SH	SF	HB	TBB	IBB	SO	WP	Bk	W	L	Pct.	ShO	Sv	ERA
		HOW MUCH HE PITCHED						WHAT HE GAVE UP												THE RESULTS					
2000 Hickory	A Pit	29	7	2	10	76.2	315	54	27	20	3	2	3	1	35	3	73	6	1	3	4	.429	1	1	2.35
Lynchburg	A+ Pit	6	6	1	0	37.2	161	29	14	13	2	0	0	1	19	2	38	0	0	4	1	.800	1	0	3.11
2001 Lynchburg	A+ Pit	13	13	0	0	76	316	63	28	20	5	3	4	4	23	0	70	2	0	5	4	.556	0	0	2.37
Altoona	AA Pit	6	5	0	0	31.2	145	38	20	17	3	1	2	2	11	1	23	1	0	1	2	.333	0	0	4.83
2 Min. YEARS		54	31	3	10	222	937	184	89	70	13	6	9	8	88	6	204	9	1	13	11	.542	2	1	2.84

Mickey Lopez

Bats: Both Throws: Right Pos: 2B-48; SS-36; OF-20; PH-3; PR-3 Ht: 5'10" Wt: 165 Born: 11/17/73 Age: 28

Year Team	Lg Org	G	AB	H	2B	3B	HR	TB	R	RBI	TBB	IBB	SO	HBP	SH	SF	SB	CS	SB%	GDP	Avg	OBP	SLG
		BATTING															BASERUNNING				PERCENTAGES		
1995 Helena	R+ Mil	57	225	73	19	2	1	99	66	41	38	3	20	5	2	4	12	8	.60	1	.324	.426	.440
1996 Beloit	A Mil	61	236	64	10	2	0	78	35	14	28	0	36	1	10	0	12	8	.60	8	.271	.351	.331
Stockton	A+ Mil	64	217	61	10	1	0	73	30	25	23	0	36	4	9	1	6	4	.60	0	.281	.359	.336
1997 El Paso	AA Mil	134	483	145	21	10	3	195	79	58	48	2	60	5	9	5	20	10	.67	10	.300	.366	.404
1998 El Paso	AA Mil	120	459	127	24	9	2	175	81	64	46	1	61	2	4	5	12	10	.55	11	.277	.342	.381
Louisville	AAA Mil	3	4	1	0	0	0	1	1	0	2	1	0	0	0	0	0	0	.00	0	.250	.500	.250
1999 Huntsville	AA Mil	83	315	94	16	5	5	135	58	40	46	2	46	5	3	4	31	4	.89	9	.298	.392	.429
Louisville	AAA Mil	49	181	58	17	2	5	94	43	31	37	0	25	2	2	1	11	7	.61	1	.320	.439	.519
2000 Indianapols	AAA Mil	67	208	54	14	1	2	76	38	22	37	0	26	4	1	4	14	7	.67	5	.260	.375	.365
Huntsville	AAA Mil	53	212	71	22	4	4	113	42	26	30	0	32	0	6	1	7	1	.70	5	.335	.416	.533
2001 Reading	AA Phi	107	382	104	18	6	11	167	71	47	63	2	58	7	6	2	21	6	.78	6	.272	.383	.437
7 Min. YEARS		798	2922	852	171	42	33	1206	544	368	398	11	400	35	52	27	155	71	.69	56	.292	.380	.413

Norberto Lopez

Bats: Right **Throws:** Right **Pos:** C-13; PH-1   **Ht:** 5'8" **Wt:** 190 **Born:** 12/9/76 **Age:** 25

Year Team	Lg Org	G	AB	H	2B	3B	HR	TB	R	RBI	TBB	IBB	SO	HBP	SH	SF	SB	CS	SB%	GDP	Avg	OBP	SLG
1999 Butte	R+ Ana	8	17	2	0	0	0	2	1	0	0	0	8	1	0	0	0	0	—	0	.118	.167	.118
Boise	A- Ana	5	13	3	1	0	0	4	1	0	2	0	5	0	0	0	0	0	—	0	.231	.333	.308
Lk Elsinore	A+ Ana	2	4	0	0	0	0	0	0	0	0	0	2	0	0	0	0	0	—	0	.000	.000	.000
Cedar Rapds	A Ana	2	6	1	0	0	0	1	0	1	1	0	2	0	0	0	0	0	—	0	.167	.286	.167
2000 Lk Elsinore	A+ Ana	30	79	3	1	0	0	4	2	2	9	0	29	0	2	0	0	0	—	3	.038	.136	.051
2001 Arkansas	AA Ana	2	6	1	1	0	0	2	0	0	1	0	3	0	0	0	0	0	—	0	.167	.286	.333
Salt Lake	AAA Ana	2	5	0	0	0	0	0	0	0	0	0	1	0	0	0	0	0	—	0	.000	.000	.000
Rancho Cuca	A+ Ana	9	20	3	0	0	0	3	0	0	0	0	8	0	0	0	0	0	—	0	.150	.150	.150
3 Min. YEARS		60	150	13	3	0	0	16	4	3	13	0	58	1	2	0	0	0	—	3	.087	.165	.107

Pee Wee Lopez

Bats: Right **Throws:** Right **Pos:** C-35; PH-7; DH-4; OF-1   **Ht:** 6'0" **Wt:** 200 **Born:** 10/22/76 **Age:** 25

Year Team	Lg Org	G	AB	H	2B	3B	HR	TB	R	RBI	TBB	IBB	SO	HBP	SH	SF	SB	CS	SB%	GDP	Avg	OBP	SLG
1996 Kingsport	R+ NYM	65	250	79	22	4	7	130	53	58	31	1	25	4	0	2	0	1	.00	4	.316	.397	.520
Pittsfield	A- NYM	5	14	6	0	1	0	8	2	3	1	0	1	0	0	0	0	0	—	1	.429	.467	.571
1997 St. Lucie	A+ NYM	113	375	93	19	0	3	121	40	30	39	3	56	0	1	1	3	2	.60	10	.248	.318	.323
1998 Mariners	R Sea	5	15	5	2	0	0	7	1	2	1	0	2	0	0	0	0	0	—	1	.333	.375	.467
Wisconsin	A Sea	35	121	27	5	1	1	37	11	12	9	0	18	1	0	0	0	0	—	1	.223	.282	.306
1999 New Haven	AA ChC	8	32	6	1	0	0	7	1	1	0	0	5	0	0	0	0	0	—	0	.188	.188	.219
Lancaster	A+ Sea	72	247	71	10	3	5	102	37	28	15	0	36	5	2	1	5	4	.56	11	.287	.340	.413
2000 West Tenn	AA ChC	69	227	59	12	1	1	76	19	26	14	1	33	1	2	1	0	1	.00	13	.260	.305	.335
2001 West Tenn	AA ChC	22	69	23	4	1	1	32	8	12	5	0	9	0	1	0	0	0	—	2	.333	.378	.464
Iowa	AAA ChC	24	54	9	3	0	0	12	6	2	3	0	12	0	0	0	0	0	—	2	.167	.211	.222
6 Min. YEARS		418	1404	378	78	11	18	532	178	174	118	5	197	11	6	5	8	8	.50	50	.269	.330	.379

Rodrigo Lopez

Pitches: Right **Bats:** Right **Pos:** RP-12; SP-8   **Ht:** 6'1" **Wt:** 180 **Born:** 12/14/75 **Age:** 26

Year Team	Lg Org	G	GS	CG	GF	IP	BFP	H	R	ER	HR	SH	SF	HB	TBB	IBB	SO	WP	Bk	W	L	Pct.	ShO	Sv	ERA
1995 Padres	R SD	11	7	0	3	34.2	162	41	29	21	0	1	2	2	14	0	33	3	1	1	1	.500	0	1	5.45
1996 Idaho Falls	R+ SD	15	14	0	1	71	314	76	52	45	3	4	3	4	34	0	72	8	4	4	4	.500	0	1	5.70
1997 Clinton	A SD	37	14	2	19	121.2	508	103	49	43	6	7	4	3	42	1	123	3	4	6	8	.429	0	9	3.18
1998 Mobile	AA SD	4	4	2	0	25.2	101	21	11	4	1	0	1	0	4	0	20	0	0	3	0	1.000	1	0	1.40
1999 Mobile	AA SD	28	28	2	0	169.1	728	187	91	83	14	4	6	7	58	3	138	5	1	10	8	.556	1	0	4.41
2000 Las Vegas	AAA SD	20	20	1	0	109.1	483	123	66	57	9	3	7	2	45	1	100	0	0	8	7	.533	0	0	4.69
Portland	AAA SD	11	8	0	1	52.1	214	45	22	20	7	1	1	1	15	0	37	1	0	2	2	.500	0	0	3.44
2000 San Diego	NL	6	6	0	0	24.2	120	40	24	24	5	0	1	0	13	0	17	0	0	0	3	.000	0	0	8.76
7 Min. YEARS		135	95	7	26	597	2570	611	327	274	41	21	25	19	216	5	532	20	10	34	31	.523	2	11	4.13

Mike Lopez-Cao

Bats: Left **Throws:** Right **Pos:** C-51; DH-14; PH-11; 3B-3; 2B-1   **Ht:** 5'9" **Wt:** 187 **Born:** 8/14/75 **Age:** 26

Year Team	Lg Org	G	AB	H	2B	3B	HR	TB	R	RBI	TBB	IBB	SO	HBP	SH	SF	SB	CS	SB%	GDP	Avg	OBP	SLG
1997 Hudson Val	A- TB	14	44	13	3	0	1	19	6	7	3	0	10	0	0	1	2	0	1.00	2	.295	.333	.432
Princeton	R+ TB	17	53	12	0	1	1	17	7	7	5	0	8	0	0	1	0	0	—	0	.226	.288	.321
1998 Chston-SC	A TB	14	24	6	0	0	0	6	2	4	4	0	4	1	0	1	2	0	1.00	0	.250	.367	.250
1999 Delmarva	A Bal	2	6	1	0	0	1	4	2	3	1	0	0	0	0	1	0	0	—	0	.167	.250	.667
Frederick	A+ Bal	29	88	21	4	0	2	31	12	11	9	0	16	0	1	1	1	0	1.00	1	.239	.306	.352
Bowie	AA Bal	16	47	12	1	0	2	19	5	7	2	0	8	0	0	0	0	0	—	1	.255	.286	.404
2000 Frederick	A+ Bal	49	117	23	8	0	7	52	15	24	14	0	23	5	1	2	0	1	.00	5	.197	.304	.444
Bowie	AA Bal	17	49	11	3	0	0	14	7	4	4	0	7	1	0	0	0	0	—	1	.224	.296	.286
2001 Rochester	AAA Bal	2	1	0	0	0	0	0	0	0	0	0	0	1	0	0	0	0	—	0	.000	.500	.000
Frederick	A+ Bal	15	43	16	1	0	3	26	4	8	4	1	10	1	0	0	0	1	.00	0	.372	.438	.605
Bowie	AA Bal	61	174	35	11	0	4	58	18	20	17	1	34	5	1	1	0	2	.00	4	.201	.289	.333
5 Min. YEARS		236	646	150	31	1	21	246	78	95	63	2	120	14	3	8	5	4	.56	14	.232	.311	.381

Luis Lorenzana

Bats: Right **Throws:** Right **Pos:** SS-67; 2B-8; PR-3; PH-2   **Ht:** 6'2" **Wt:** 193 **Born:** 11/9/78 **Age:** 23

Year Team	Lg Org	G	AB	H	2B	3B	HR	TB	R	RBI	TBB	IBB	SO	HBP	SH	SF	SB	CS	SB%	GDP	Avg	OBP	SLG
1996 Pirates	R Pit	18	53	8	1	0	0	9	4	5	12	0	8	1	1	1	0	1	.00	1	.151	.313	.170
Erie	A- Pit	44	128	25	8	1	0	35	19	12	16	0	26	3	4	3	1	4	.20	4	.195	.293	.273
1997 Augusta	A Pit	92	288	68	11	1	0	81	36	20	31	0	66	2	4	1	4	5	.44	5	.236	.314	.281
1998 Lynchburg	A+ Pit	95	283	67	7	2	2	84	27	24	35	1	62	5	9	2	2	2	.50	8	.237	.329	.297
1999 Lynchburg	A+ Pit	49	156	40	7	0	2	53	15	14	11	0	37	4	0	1	2	3	.40	5	.256	.320	.340
Altoona	AA Pit	34	74	16	2	1	2	26	9	8	14	0	17	4	1	3	0	0	—	2	.216	.358	.351
2000 Altoona	AA Pit	24	51	8	2	0	0	10	7	2	4	0	15	0	2	0	0	0	—	0	.157	.218	.196
Lynchburg	A+ Pit	58	170	39	3	4	1	53	22	9	20	0	35	2	9	1	3	3	.50	0	.229	.316	.312
2001 Portland	AAA SD	2	4	0	0	0	0	0	0	0	0	0	1	0	0	0	0	0	—	0	.000	.000	.000
Mobile	AA SD	5	11	2	0	0	0	2	1	0	1	0	5	0	1	0	0	0	—	0	.182	.250	.182
Lk Elsinore	A+ SD	70	234	63	7	1	0	72	32	17	24	0	48	8	4	0	5	1	.83	6	.269	.357	.308
6 Min. YEARS		491	1452	336	48	10	7	425	172	111	168	1	320	29	35	12	17	19	.47	33	.231	.321	.293

Juan Lorenzo

Bats: Both **Throws:** Right **Pos:** SS-53; 3B-46; 2B-6; PR-3   **Ht:** 5'11" **Wt:** 172 **Born:** 6/10/78 **Age:** 24

Year Team	Lg Org	G	AB	H	2B	3B	HR	TB	R	RBI	TBB	IBB	SO	HBP	SH	SF	SB	CS	SB%	GDP	Avg	OBP	SLG
1995 Twins	R Min	14	46	10	0	0	0	10	3	2	4	0	6	0	0	1	0	0	—	0	.217	.275	.217
1996 Twins	R Min	37	134	34	5	0	3	48	23	15	2	0	20	2	2	0	4	1	.80	1	.254	.275	.358
1997 Fort Wayne	A Min	4	7	1	0	0	0	1	0	0	0	0	1	1	1	0	0	0	—	0	.143	.250	.143
Elizabethtn	R+ Min	52	210	63	10	2	7	98	41	34	12	1	38	6	3	0	4	2	.67	6	.300	.355	.467
1998 Elizabethtn	R+ Min	44	176	46	8	1	6	74	33	23	7	0	17	3	1	2	4	1	.80	3	.261	.298	.420
1999 Fort Myers	A+ Min	119	421	108	11	1	3	130	51	48	9	0	68	6	4	4	8	3	.73	8	.257	.280	.309
2000 Fort Myers	A+ Min	119	431	122	25	1	3	158	57	44	20	0	33	6	7	4	8	3	.73	10	.283	.321	.367
2001 New Britain	AA Min	101	319	75	9	3	3	99	32	24	5	0	32	6	7	7	2	2	.50	8	.235	.255	.310
7 Min. YEARS		490	1744	459	68	8	25	618	240	190	59	1	215	30	25	18	30	12	.71	36	.263	.296	.354

Andrew Lorraine

Pitches: Left **Bats:** Left **Pos:** SP-25; RP-5   **Ht:** 6'3" **Wt:** 200 **Born:** 8/11/72 **Age:** 29

Year Team	Lg Org	G	GS	CG	GF	IP	BFP	H	R	ER	HR	SH	SF	HB	TBB	IBB	SO	WP	Bk	W	L	Pct.	ShO	Sv	ERA
1993 Boise	A- Ana	6	6	3	0	42	159	33	6	6	3	0	0	2	6	0	39	0	0	4	1	.800	1	0	1.29
1994 Vancouver	AAA Ana	22	22	4	0	142	599	156	63	54	13	2	4	11	34	1	90	1	1	12	4	.750	2	0	3.42
1995 Vancouver	AAA Ana	18	18	4	0	97.2	420	105	49	43	7	4	3	3	30	0	51	4	0	6	6	.500	1	0	3.96
Nashville	AAA CWS	7	7	0	0	39	184	51	29	26	4	1	3	1	12	0	26	2	0	4	1	.800	0	0	6.00
1996 Edmonton	AAA Oak	30	25	0	0	141	640	181	95	89	19	4	5	4	46	2	73	5	1	8	10	.444	0	0	5.68
1997 Edmonton	AAA Oak	23	20	2	2	117.2	520	143	72	62	12	3	7	2	34	1	75	3	0	8	6	.571	2	0	4.74
1998 Tacoma	AAA Sea	52	4	0	10	80.1	359	93	44	43	10	3	3	2	36	2	70	2	0	7	4	.636	0	2	4.82
1999 Iowa	AAA ChC	22	21	1	0	143	603	149	67	59	16	4	2	6	34	0	96	5	0	9	8	.529	0	0	3.71
2000 Buffalo	AAA Cle	14	13	0	0	90.2	378	97	37	35	8	0	2	2	24	0	51	1	1	8	3	.727	0	0	3.47
2001 Calgary	AAA Fla	30	25	1	0	150	685	209	100	90	19	5	5	7	36	4	101	4	0	9	5	.643	1	0	5.40
1994 California	AL	4	3	0	0	18.2	96	30	23	22	7	2	1	0	11	0	10	0	0	0	2	.000	0	0	10.61
1995 Chicago	AL	5	0	0	2	8	30	3	3	3	0	0	0	1	2	0	5	0	0	0	0	—	0	0	3.38
1997 Oakland	AL	12	6	0	1	29.2	146	45	22	21	2	0	3	1	15	0	18	0	0	3	1	.750	0	0	6.37
1998 Seattle	AL	4	0	0	1	3.2	16	3	1	1	0	0	0	0	4	0	1	1	0	0	0	—	0	0	2.45
1999 Chicago	NL	11	11	2	0	61.2	272	71	42	38	9	6	2	0	22	3	40	3	0	2	5	.286	1	0	5.55
2000 Chicago	NL	8	5	0	0	32	148	36	25	23	5	2	2	0	18	1	25	0	1	1	2	.333	0	0	6.47
Cleveland	AL	10	0	0	3	9.1	41	8	4	4	1	0	0	0	5	0	5	0	0	0	0	—	0	0	3.86
9 Min. YEARS		224	161	15	12	1043.1	4547	1217	562	507	111	26	34	40	292	10	672	27	3	75	48	.610	7	2	4.37
6 Maj. YEARS		54	25	2	7	163	749	196	120	112	24	10	8	2	77	4	103	4	1	6	10	.375	1	0	6.18

Shane Loux

Pitches: Right **Bats:** Right **Pos:** SP-27; RP-1   **Ht:** 6'2" **Wt:** 205 **Born:** 8/13/79 **Age:** 22

Year Team	Lg Org	G	GS	CG	GF	IP	BFP	H	R	ER	HR	SH	SF	HB	TBB	IBB	SO	WP	Bk	W	L	Pct.	ShO	Sv	ERA
1997 Tigers	R Det	10	9	1	0	43	158	19	7	4	0	0	0	1	10	0	33	2	1	4	1	.800	1	0	0.84
1998 W Michigan	A Det	28	28	2	0	157	698	184	96	81	13	2	4	8	52	0	88	12	2	7	13	.350	1	0	4.64
1999 W Michigan	A Det	8	8	0	0	47.1	215	55	39	33	5	1	2	8	16	1	43	4	0	1	3	.250	0	0	6.27
Lakeland	A+ Det	17	17	0	0	91	412	92	48	41	8	2	5	10	47	0	52	7	1	6	5	.545	0	0	4.05
2000 Lakeland	A+ Det	1	1	0	0	5	19	2	1	1	0	1	0	0	3	0	6	0	0	0	1	.000	0	0	1.80
Jacksnville	AA Det	26	26	2	0	157.2	670	150	78	67	12	3	7	14	55	0	130	7	0	12	9	.571	0	0	3.82
2001 Toledo	AAA Det	28	27	2	1	151	727	203	111	97	22	4	10	15	73	0	72	14	1	10	11	.476	0	0	5.78
5 Min. YEARS		118	116	7	1	652	2899	705	380	324	60	13	28	56	256	1	424	46	5	40	43	.482	2	0	4.47

Kevin Lovingier

Pitches: Left **Bats:** Left **Pos:** RP-60   **Ht:** 6'1" **Wt:** 190 **Born:** 8/29/71 **Age:** 30

Year Team	Lg Org	G	GS	CG	GF	IP	BFP	H	R	ER	HR	SH	SF	HB	TBB	IBB	SO	WP	Bk	W	L	Pct.	ShO	Sv	ERA
1994 New Jersey	A- StL	35	0	0	5	52.1	211	36	13	9	3	3	0	2	19	1	71	3	0	1	0	1.000	0	1	1.55
1995 Savannah	A StL	38	0	0	18	47	195	35	14	7	1	3	1	1	21	5	54	3	0	6	3	.667	0	1	1.34
St. Pete	A+ StL	22	0	0	6	21.2	82	9	4	4	0	1	1	2	10	1	14	1	0	1	0	1.000	0	0	1.66
1996 Arkansas	AA StL	60	0	0	19	63.2	295	60	30	29	4	6	2	1	48	6	73	3	0	2	3	.400	0	1	4.10
1997 Arkansas	AA StL	59	0	0	22	74.1	314	68	27	21	4	3	0	0	26	2	82	5	1	4	3	.571	0	0	2.54
1998 Arkansas	AA StL	19	0	0	6	24	104	20	9	7	2	0	0	0	13	1	26	3	0	1	0	1.000	0	0	2.63
Memphis	AAA StL	39	0	0	8	59	245	38	22	20	7	3	0	2	33	0	63	2	1	5	1	.833	0	0	3.05
1999 Memphis	AAA StL	51	0	0	11	78	338	66	44	42	8	1	1	0	40	0	66	4	0	3	4	.429	0	0	4.85
2000 Nashua	IND	60	0	0	37	77.2	315	46	23	22	7	2	2	2	37	2	110	5	0	8	2	.800	0	12	2.55
2001 Columbus	AAA NYY	7	0	0	2	10	51	13	9	5	1	1	0	0	7	0	9	1	0	0	2	.000	0	0	4.50
Norwich	AA NYY	53	0	0	14	89.2	348	56	22	19	0	2	2	0	31	2	94	6	0	3	5	.375	0	0	1.91
8 Min. YEARS		443	0	0	148	597.1	2498	447	217	185	37	25	9	13	285	20	662	36	2	34	23	.596	0	18	2.79

Benny Lowe

Pitches: Left **Bats:** Left **Pos:** RP-43; SP-1   **Ht:** 5'10" **Wt:** 185 **Born:** 6/13/74 **Age:** 28

Year Team	Lg Org	G	GS	CG	GF	IP	BFP	H	R	ER	HR	SH	SF	HB	TBB	IBB	SO	WP	Bk	W	L	Pct.	ShO	Sv	ERA
1994 Blue Jays	R Tor	22	1	0	5	22.1	104	20	16	11	0	4	0	2	14	1	27	1	1	2	1	.667	0	1	4.43
1995 St.Cathrnes	A- Tor	15	15	0	1	78.2	358	89	43	38	3	3	3	9	40	1	61	10	1	4	5	.444	0	1	4.35
1996 Hagerstown	A Tor	46	1	0	34	65.2	289	60	24	17	2	2	1	7	52	0	89	2	0	2	3	.400	0	9	2.33
1997 Knoxville	AA Tor	18	0	0	8	26	124	33	21	16	6	1	1	2	14	1	29	2	2	3	1	.750	0	0	5.54
Dunedin	A+ Tor	13	0	0	13	14.2	57	7	3	3	0	0	1	1	3	0	19	1	0	2	1	.667	0	5	1.84
Hagerstown	A Tor	2	0	0	2	2	10	3	3	0	0	0	0	0	0	0	4	0	0	0	0	—	0	0	0.00
1998 Dunedin	A+ Tor	9	0	0	3	9.1	46	8	5	2	0	1	1	2	6	0	13	1	0	0	0	—	0	0	1.93
1999 Knoxville	AA Tor	58	0	0	19	68.1	309	68	44	39	8	6	4	3	40	0	70	7	0	4	6	.400	0	3	5.14

	HOW MUCH HE PITCHED						WHAT HE GAVE UP												THE RESULTS					
Year Team	Lg Org	G	GS	CG	GF	IP	BFP	H	R	ER	HR	SH	SF	HB	TBB	IBB	SO	WP	Bk	W	L	Pct.	ShO	Sv	ERA
2000 Lakeland	A+ Det	20	0	0	19	19	78	11	6	5	1	1	0	0	10	0	17	0	0	0	2	.000	0	11	2.37
Jacksnville	AA Det	17	0	0	17	23.1	117	28	21	21	3	2	0	1	17	1	25	5	0	0	0	—	0	0	8.10
2001 Camden	IND —	14	0	0	3	21.1	79	7	0	0	0	2	0	1	11	0	19	2	0	1	0	1.000	0	0	0.00
Mudville	A+ Cin	4	0	0	3	6.2	27	4	3	3	0	0	1	1	3	0	7	1	0	1	1	.500	0	0	4.05
Chattanooga	AA Cin	26	1	0	8	38.2	168	29	21	18	1	3	2	1	24	0	35	1	0	3	2	.600	0	0	4.19
8 Min. YEARS		264	18	0	120	396	1766	347	210	173	24	25	14	30	234	3	415	33	4	22	22	.500	0	29	3.93

Terrell Lowery

Bats: Right **Throws:** Right **Pos:** OF-69; DH-1; PH-1 **Ht:** 6'3" **Wt:** 195 **Born:** 10/25/70 **Age:** 31

	BATTING															BASERUNNING				PERCENTAGES		
Year Team	Lg Org	G	AB	H	2B	3B	HR	TB	R	RBI	TBB	IBB	SO	HBP	SH	SF	SB	CS	SB%	GDP	Avg	OBP	SLG
1991 Butte	R+ Tex	54	214	64	10	7	3	97	38	33	29	0	44	1	0	2	23	12	.66	2	.299	.382	.453
1993 Charlotte	A+ Tex	65	257	77	7	9	3	111	46	36	46	2	47	2	1	1	14	15	.48	2	.300	.408	.432
Tulsa	AA Tex	66	258	62	5	1	3	78	29	14	28	1	50	1	1	1	10	12	.45	5	.240	.316	.302
1994 Tulsa	AA Tex	129	496	142	34	8	8	216	89	54	59	0	113	5	5	5	33	15	.69	7	.286	.365	.435
1995 Rangers	R Tex	10	34	9	3	1	3	23	10	7	6	0	7	0	0	0	1	0	1.00	1	.265	.375	.676
Charlotte	A+ Tex	11	35	9	2	2	0	15	4	4	6	0	6	1	0	0	1	0	1.00	2	.257	.381	.429
1996 Binghamton	AA NYM	62	211	58	13	4	7	100	34	32	44	2	44	2	2	3	5	6	.45	4	.275	.400	.474
Norfolk	AAA NYM	62	193	45	7	2	4	68	25	21	22	0	44	1	3	2	6	3	.67	1	.233	.312	.352
1997 Iowa	AAA ChC	110	386	116	28	3	17	201	69	71	65	2	97	1	1	2	9	8	.53	8	.301	.401	.521
1998 Iowa	AAA ChC	65	246	73	14	1	12	125	41	49	27	0	63	2	1	2	5	2	.71	10	.297	.368	.508
1999 Durham	AAA TB	71	275	92	20	5	15	167	69	57	43	1	62	1	8	2	10	5	.67	3	.335	.424	.607
2000 Fresno	AAA SF	84	301	60	9	1	16	119	48	44	36	0	88	3	1	2	6	1	.86	12	.199	.289	.395
2001 Durham	AAA TB	71	253	66	14	3	1	89	28	18	28	0	69	1	3	2	6	3	.67	6	.261	.335	.352
1997 Chicago	NL	9	14	4	0	0	0	4	2	0	3	0	3	0	0	0	1	0	1.00	1	.286	.412	.286
1998 Chicago	NL	24	15	3	1	0	0	4	2	1	3	0	7	0	0	0	0	0	—	0	.200	.333	.267
1999 Tampa Bay	AL	66	185	48	15	1	2	71	25	17	19	0	53	1	0	1	0	2	.00	1	.259	.330	.384
2000 San Francisco	NL	24	34	15	4	0	1	22	13	5	7	0	8	1	0	0	1	0	1.00	1	.441	.548	.647
10 Min. YEARS		860	3159	873	166	47	92	1409	530	440	439	8	734	21	26	24	129	82	.61	63	.276	.366	.446
4 Maj. YEARS		123	248	70	20	1	3	101	42	23	32	0	71	2	0	1	2	2	.50	2	.282	.367	.407

Brian Loyd

Bats: Right **Throws:** Right **Pos:** C-46; DH-7; PH-3 **Ht:** 6'2" **Wt:** 205 **Born:** 12/3/73 **Age:** 28

	BATTING															BASERUNNING				PERCENTAGES		
Year Team	Lg Org	G	AB	H	2B	3B	HR	TB	R	RBI	TBB	IBB	SO	HBP	SH	SF	SB	CS	SB%	GDP	Avg	OBP	SLG
1996 Clinton	A SD	10	37	11	2	0	0	13	3	2	0	0	6	2	0	0	0	0	—	0	.297	.333	.351
1997 Clinton	A SD	73	259	71	10	0	2	87	35	33	25	2	41	8	4	5	6	4	.60	12	.274	.350	.336
1998 Rancho Cuca	A+ SD	87	318	97	19	1	4	130	55	35	42	1	45	10	2	2	1	4	.20	8	.305	.401	.409
Dunedin	A+ Tor	16	49	10	0	0	1	13	8	5	5	0	10	1	1	2	1	0	1.00	3	.204	.281	.265
1999 Knoxville	AA Tor	104	364	102	18	1	11	155	53	65	46	3	57	4	4	6	9	2	.82	11	.280	.362	.426
2000 Tennessee	AA Tor	58	194	58	10	1	1	73	21	23	29	1	22	2	0	2	7	3	.70	6	.299	.392	.376
Syracuse	AAA Tor	22	52	7	0	0	1	10	2	4	3	0	9	1	0	1	0	2	.00	2	.135	.193	.192
2001 Tennessee	AA Tor	15	50	11	3	0	0	14	4	2	2	0	11	2	0	0	2	0	1.00	2	.220	.278	.280
Lk Elsinore	A+ SD	14	46	14	3	0	0	17	8	10	3	0	6	1	1	1	0	0	—	4	.304	.353	.370
Portland	AAA SD	25	88	21	3	0	3	33	7	10	4	0	11	1	0	0	0	0	—	1	.239	.280	.375
6 Min. YEARS		424	1457	402	68	3	23	545	196	189	159	7	218	32	12	19	26	15	.63	49	.276	.356	.374

Lou Lucca

Bats: Right **Throws:** Right **Pos:** 3B-108; 2B-18; PH-7; SS-5; DH-4 **Ht:** 5'11" **Wt:** 210 **Born:** 10/13/70 **Age:** 31

	BATTING															BASERUNNING				PERCENTAGES		
Year Team	Lg Org	G	AB	H	2B	3B	HR	TB	R	RBI	TBB	IBB	SO	HBP	SH	SF	SB	CS	SB%	GDP	Avg	OBP	SLG
1992 Erie	A- Fla	76	263	74	16	1	13	131	51	44	33	0	40	5	0	2	6	3	.67	8	.281	.370	.498
1993 Kane County	A Fla	127	419	116	25	2	6	163	52	53	60	0	58	9	2	7	4	10	.29	9	.277	.374	.389
1994 Brevard Cty	A+ Fla	130	441	125	29	1	8	180	62	76	72	2	73	4	0	6	3	7	.30	18	.283	.384	.408
1995 Portland	AA Fla	112	388	107	28	1	9	164	57	64	59	5	77	5	0	2	4	4	.50	18	.276	.377	.423
1996 Charlotte	AAA Fla	87	273	71	14	1	7	108	26	35	11	0	62	4	0	3	0	3	.00	11	.260	.296	.396
1997 Charlotte	AAA Fla	96	292	83	22	1	18	161	40	51	22	4	56	2	0	3	5	4	.56	7	.284	.335	.551
1998 Charlotte	AAA Fla	112	397	115	32	0	11	180	47	51	13	2	75	5	0	2	2	6	.25	10	.290	.319	.453
1999 Scranton-WB	AAA Phi	136	533	143	33	2	12	216	61	70	22	0	94	9	0	5	4	6	.40	15	.268	.306	.405
2000 Memphis	AAA StL	122	462	131	31	2	14	208	70	70	32	3	61	9	2	3	7	4	.64	10	.284	.340	.450
2001 Memphis	AAA StL	135	479	127	32	1	9	188	58	64	27	4	67	10	2	2	2	3	.40	12	.265	.317	.392
10 Min. YEARS		1133	3947	1092	262	12	107	1699	524	578	351	20	663	62	6	35	37	50	.43	118	.277	.342	.430

Brian Luderer

Bats: Right **Throws:** Right **Pos:** C-73; DH-13; PH-1 **Ht:** 5'11" **Wt:** 160 **Born:** 8/19/78 **Age:** 23

	BATTING															BASERUNNING				PERCENTAGES		
Year Team	Lg Org	G	AB	H	2B	3B	HR	TB	R	RBI	TBB	IBB	SO	HBP	SH	SF	SB	CS	SB%	GDP	Avg	OBP	SLG
1996 Athletics	R Oak	6	13	4	0	0	0	4	1	2	0	0	1	0	1	0	0	0	—	0	.308	.308	.308
1997 Athletics	R Oak	39	123	33	4	0	3	46	21	26	17	0	12	6	1	1	3	4	.43	6	.268	.381	.374
1998 Modesto	A+ Oak	19	45	6	2	2	0	12	3	3	4	0	6	0	2	0	0	0	—	0	.133	.204	.267
Sou Oregon	A- Oak	10	37	11	2	1	2	21	9	7	2	0	7	0	0	0	0	0	—	0	.297	.333	.568
Huntsville	AA Oak	17	38	11	1	1	0	14	4	5	3	0	7	1	1	0	0	0	—	1	.289	.357	.368
1999 Vancouver	AAA Oak	10	28	9	1	0	0	10	6	4	4	0	2	1	0	0	0	0	—	0	.321	.424	.357
Modesto	A+ Oak	55	182	52	13	2	1	72	22	22	16	1	25	2	2	2	3	3	.50	5	.286	.347	.396
2000 Modesto	A+ Oak	40	136	41	2	0	4	55	22	23	22	0	22	3	2	1	1	1	.50	4	.301	.407	.404
Midland	AA Oak	33	108	34	6	0	4	52	18	16	15	0	11	0	0	3	0	1	.00	4	.315	.389	.481
2001 Midland	AA Oak	86	307	79	20	1	5	116	30	34	23	1	49	4	6	4	1	1	.50	10	.257	.314	.378
6 Min. YEARS		315	1017	280	51	7	19	402	136	142	106	2	142	17	15	11	8	10	.44	30	.275	.350	.395

Ryan Ludwick

Bats: Right **Throws:** Left **Pos:** OF-133; DH-3; PR-1   **Ht:** 6'3" **Wt:** 203 **Born:** 7/13/78 **Age:** 23

Year Team	Lg Org	G	AB	H	2B	3B	HR	TB	R	RBI	TBB	IBB	SO	HBP	SH	SF	SB	CS	SB%	GDP	Avg	OBP	SLG
1999 Modesto	A+ Oak	43	171	47	11	3	4	76	28	34	19	0	45	3	0	5	2	1	.67	0	.275	.348	.444
2000 Modesto	A+ Oak	129	493	130	26	3	29	249	86	102	68	0	128	9	1	7	10	6	.63	6	.264	.359	.505
2001 Midland	AA Oak	119	443	119	23	3	25	223	82	96	56	1	113	7	1	5	9	10	.47	6	.269	.356	.503
Sacramento	AAA Oak	17	57	13	3	0	1	19	10	7	2	0	16	0	1	2	2	0	1.00	0	.228	.246	.333
3 Min. YEARS		308	1164	309	63	9	59	567	206	239	145	1	302	19	3	19	23	17	.58	12	.265	.351	.487

Larry Luebbers

Pitches: Right **Bats:** Right **Pos:** SP-26; RP-3   **Ht:** 6'6" **Wt:** 210 **Born:** 10/11/69 **Age:** 32

Year Team	Lg Org	G	GS	CG	GF	IP	BFP	H	R	ER	HR	SH	SF	HB	TBB	IBB	SO	WP	Bk	W	L	Pct.	ShO	Sv	ERA
1990 Billings	R+ Cin	13	13	1	0	72.1	319	74	46	36	3	2	3	6	31	0	48	7	1	5	4	.556	1	0	4.48
1991 Cedar Rapids	A Cin	28	28	3	0	184.2	781	177	85	64	8	12	6	10	64	5	98	11	4	8	10	.444	0	0	3.12
1992 Cedar Rapids	A Cin	14	14	1	0	82.1	355	71	33	24	2	4	3	8	33	0	56	1	1	7	0	1.000	0	0	2.62
Chattanooga	AA Cin	14	14	1	0	87.1	368	86	34	22	5	2	1	4	34	1	56	5	2	6	5	.545	0	0	2.27
1993 Indianapolis	AAA Cin	15	15	0	0	84.1	380	81	45	39	7	6	2	6	47	5	51	1	0	4	7	.364	0	0	4.16
1994 Iowa	AAA ChC	27	26	0	0	138.2	630	149	100	93	22	4	7	5	87	3	90	7	4	10	12	.455	0	0	6.04
1995 Chattanooga	AA Cin	28	21	0	4	118	514	112	71	61	7	6	6	7	59	1	87	1	0	10	6	.625	0	0	4.65
1996 Chattanooga	AA Cin	11	11	0	0	69.1	292	64	32	28	6	3	1	3	26	0	38	5	0	3	5	.375	0	0	3.63
Indianapolis	AAA Cin	14	11	0	0	71.1	301	76	44	31	8	1	2	1	23	2	35	1	0	5	4	.556	0	0	3.91
1997 Richmond	AAA Atl	27	26	2	1	144	634	180	101	86	20	2	6	3	44	2	91	6	0	3	14	.176	0	0	5.38
1998 Memphis	AAA StL	29	29	2	0	173.1	732	183	90	79	23	5	2	7	47	1	110	2	0	11	11	.500	2	0	4.10
1999 Memphis	AAA StL	21	19	1	0	129.2	547	134	61	58	15	7	3	5	33	1	84	3	0	13	4	.765	1	0	4.03
2000 Louisville	AAA Cin	18	17	2	1	114.2	472	97	50	45	9	4	0	6	40	1	69	2	0	7	6	.538	1	0	3.53
2001 Chattanooga	AA Cin	8	8	1	0	54.1	222	48	23	18	2	1	2	2	12	0	48	1	0	2	3	.400	1	0	2.98
Louisville	AAA Cin	21	18	2	1	121	494	129	54	48	8	5	2	6	24	1	60	3	0	7	6	.538	1	0	3.57
1993 Cincinnati	NL	14	14	0	0	77.1	332	74	49	39	7	4	5	1	38	3	38	4	0	2	5	.286	0	0	4.54
1999 St. Louis	NL	8	8	1	0	45.2	199	46	27	26	8	4	0	3	16	0	16	1	1	3	3	.500	0	0	5.12
2000 Cincinnati	NL	14	1	0	4	20.1	94	27	15	14	1	1	0	0	12	2	9	1	0	0	2	.000	0	1	6.20
12 Min. YEARS		288	270	16	7	1645.1	7041	1661	869	732	145	64	46	79	604	23	1021	56	12	101	97	.510	7	0	4.00
3 Maj. YEARS		36	23	1	4	143.1	625	147	91	79	16	9	5	4	66	5	63	6	1	5	10	.333	0	1	4.96

Spike Lundberg

Pitches: Right **Bats:** Both **Pos:** SP-16; RP-15   **Ht:** 6'1" **Wt:** 185 **Born:** 5/4/77 **Age:** 25

Year Team	Lg Org	G	GS	CG	GF	IP	BFP	H	R	ER	HR	SH	SF	HB	TBB	IBB	SO	WP	Bk	W	L	Pct.	ShO	Sv	ERA
1997 Rangers	R Tex	14	1	0	11	32.1	115	13	4	3	1	0	1	0	11	0	32	0	1	1	1	.500	0	5	0.84
1998 Savannah	A Tex	50	0	0	43	87.2	396	105	69	54	9	7	2	7	27	1	70	5	1	6	9	.400	0	14	5.54
1999 Charlotte	A+ Tex	30	21	4	1	156	656	162	63	49	4	2	6	9	44	1	81	4	4	14	7	.667	1	0	2.83
2000 Tulsa	AA Tex	40	13	0	16	150.2	637	148	61	51	9	5	5	8	54	4	102	5	1	14	7	.667	0	4	3.05
2001 Oklahoma	AAA Tex	13	8	0	2	55	257	72	51	41	8	2	3	3	15	1	31	1	0	3	5	.375	0	0	6.71
Tulsa	AA Tex	18	8	1	8	67.1	282	75	27	26	4	2	2	6	9	0	41	2	0	5	3	.625	1	6	3.48
5 Min. YEARS		165	51	5	81	549	2343	575	275	224	35	18	19	33	160	7	357	17	7	43	32	.573	2	29	3.67

Jeremy Luster

Bats: Both **Throws:** Right **Pos:** 1B-119; DH-8; PH-3; OF-2; P-1   **Ht:** 6'4" **Wt:** 210 **Born:** 6/10/77 **Age:** 25

Year Team	Lg Org	G	AB	H	2B	3B	HR	TB	R	RBI	TBB	IBB	SO	HBP	SH	SF	SB	CS	SB%	GDP	Avg	OBP	SLG
1998 Salem-Keizr	A- SF	51	181	55	13	3	6	92	32	48	23	1	30	2	0	3	6	4	.60	3	.304	.383	.508
1999 Bakersfield	A+ SF	52	184	37	4	3	0	47	26	19	22	1	54	0	0	1	9	4	.69	6	.201	.285	.255
Salem-Keizr	A- SF	39	146	32	7	1	1	44	22	14	16	0	48	3	1	0	7	1	.88	0	.219	.309	.301
2000 Bakersfield	A+ SF	137	517	146	35	5	14	233	86	99	77	6	104	10	0	8	17	2	.89	11	.282	.381	.451
2001 Shreveport	AA SF	130	506	138	33	2	4	187	54	76	33	3	94	7	0	5	6	3	.67	11	.273	.323	.370
4 Min. YEARS		409	1534	408	92	14	25	603	220	256	171	11	330	22	1	17	45	14	.76	31	.266	.345	.393

Ryan Luther

Bats: Right **Throws:** Right **Pos:** 2B-93; C-31; PH-9; OF-1; PR-1   **Ht:** 6'0" **Wt:** 185 **Born:** 1/21/77 **Age:** 25

Year Team	Lg Org	G	AB	H	2B	3B	HR	TB	R	RBI	TBB	IBB	SO	HBP	SH	SF	SB	CS	SB%	GDP	Avg	OBP	SLG
1999 Salem-Keizr	A- SF	61	220	66	12	1	4	92	34	38	18	1	35	9	0	2	12	4	.75	5	.300	.373	.418
2000 Bakersfield	A+ SF	110	414	124	25	2	7	174	78	48	48	1	94	10	5	6	14	8	.64	6	.300	.381	.420
2001 Shreveport	AA SF	127	453	127	26	2	4	169	54	42	32	0	78	15	8	2	6	8	.43	9	.280	.347	.373
3 Min. YEARS		298	1087	317	63	5	15	435	166	128	98	2	207	34	13	10	32	20	.62	20	.292	.365	.400

Keith Luuloa

Bats: Right **Throws:** Right **Pos:** 2B-28; 1B-26; SS-21; 3B-12; PH-10; OF-4; DH-4   **Ht:** 6'1" **Wt:** 175 **Born:** 12/24/74 **Age:** 27

Year Team	Lg Org	G	AB	H	2B	3B	HR	TB	R	RBI	TBB	IBB	SO	HBP	SH	SF	SB	CS	SB%	GDP	Avg	OBP	SLG
1994 Angels	R Ana	28	97	29	4	1	1	38	14	10	8	0	14	4	1	3	3	4	.43	0	.299	.366	.392
1995 Lk Elsinore	A+ Ana	102	380	100	22	7	5	151	50	53	24	0	47	6	7	1	1	5	.17	9	.263	.316	.397
1996 Midland	AA Ana	134	531	138	24	2	7	187	80	44	47	0	54	6	8	3	4	6	.40	14	.260	.325	.352
1997 Midland	AA Ana	120	421	115	29	5	9	181	67	59	36	0	59	5	10	6	7	4	.64	18	.273	.333	.430
1998 Midland	AA Ana	130	479	160	43	2	17	274	85	102	75	5	54	7	2	16	6	5	.55	15	.334	.419	.572
Vancouver	AAA Ana	8	30	10	1	0	0	11	4	3	4	0	3	0	0	1	1	1	.50	1	.333	.400	.367
1999 Edmonton	AAA Ana	115	396	113	23	1	4	150	54	46	44	0	53	5	4	2	7	7	.50	14	.285	.362	.379

Year Team	Lg Org	G	AB	H	2B	3B	HR	TB	R	RBI	TBB	IBB	SO	HBP	SH	SF	SB	CS	SB%	GDP	Avg	OBP	SLG
2000 Edmonton	AAA Ana	76	270	66	17	2	8	111	39	44	30	1	30	2	1	4	2	4	.33	11	.244	.320	.411
Iowa	AAA ChC	4	16	6	1	0	1	10	4	4	2	0	1	0	0	0	1	0	1.00	1	.375	.444	.625
2001 Portland	AAA SD	64	217	59	13	2	4	88	31	16	13	0	24	5	2	2	1	1	.50	9	.272	.325	.406
New Orleans	AAA Hou	36	93	19	7	0	2	32	14	11	13	1	17	2	1	1	0	0	—	3	.204	.312	.344
2000 Anaheim	AL	6	18	6	0	0	0	6	3	0	1	0	1	0	0	0	0	0	—	0	.333	.368	.333
8 Min. YEARS		817	2930	815	184	30	58	1233	442	392	296	7	356	42	36	39	33	37	.47	95	.278	.349	.421

Scott Lydy

Bats: Right **Throws:** Right **Pos:** OF-49; 1B-25; DH-15; PH-13; 3B-2   **Ht:** 6'5" **Wt:** 195 **Born:** 10/26/68 **Age:** 33

Year Team	Lg Org	G	AB	H	2B	3B	HR	TB	R	RBI	TBB	IBB	SO	HBP	SH	SF	SB	CS	SB%	GDP	Avg	OBP	SLG
1989 Sou Oregon	A- Oak	67	230	48	11	2	3	72	37	28	31	0	72	3	3	4	8	5	.62	—	.209	.306	.313
1990 Madison	A Oak	54	174	33	6	2	4	55	33	19	25	1	62	1	0	2	7	5	.58	1	.190	.292	.316
Athletics	R Oak	18	50	17	6	0	2	29	8	11	10	0	14	0	0	0	0	0	—	1	.340	.450	.580
1991 Madison	A Oak	127	464	120	26	2	12	186	64	69	66	5	109	5	0	4	24	9	.73	10	.259	.354	.401
1992 Reno	A+ Oak	33	124	49	13	2	2	72	29	27	26	2	30	0	1	0	9	4	.69	1	.395	.500	.581
Huntsville	AA Oak	109	387	118	20	3	9	171	64	65	67	5	95	4	0	4	16	5	.76	4	.305	.409	.442
1993 Tacoma	AAA Oak	95	341	100	22	6	9	161	70	41	50	3	87	1	2	3	12	4	.75	8	.293	.382	.472
1994 Tacoma	AAA Oak	135	508	160	37	3	17	254	98	73	58	1	108	6	1	6	22	6	.79	14	.315	.388	.500
1995 Edmonton	AAA Oak	104	400	116	29	7	16	207	78	65	33	3	66	6	3	5	15	4	.79	11	.290	.349	.518
1998 Rochester	AAA Bal	20	66	9	5	0	1	17	3	8	4	0	15	1	0	1	1	0	1.00	2	.136	.194	.258
Winnipeg	IND —	3	10	1	1	0	0	2	1	2	1	0	7	1	0	0	0	0	—	0	.100	.250	.200
1999 Charlotte	AAA CWS	19	66	14	2	0	2	22	11	13	8	0	15	0	0	2	1	0	1.00	1	.212	.289	.333
Birmingham	AA CWS	111	400	106	25	1	20	193	74	65	67	3	61	3	1	1	18	3	.86	5	.265	.374	.483
2000 Charlotte	AAA CWS	116	368	100	15	4	14	165	66	45	69	3	70	8	0	3	15	2	.88	9	.272	.395	.448
2001 New Orleans	AAA Hou	95	283	75	20	1	7	118	37	43	47	1	62	2	2	2	8	5	.62	3	.265	.371	.417
1993 Oakland	AL	41	102	23	5	0	2	34	11	7	8	0	39	1	0	0	2	0	1.00	1	.225	.288	.333
11 Min. YEARS		1106	3871	1066	238	33	118	1724	673	574	562	27	873	41	12	37	156	52	.75	—	.275	.370	.445

Albenis Machado

Bats: Both **Throws:** Right **Pos:** 2B-81; SS-16; 3B-4; DH-4; PH-3; PR-1   **Ht:** 6'0" **Wt:** 175 **Born:** 3/20/79 **Age:** 23

Year Team	Lg Org	G	AB	H	2B	3B	HR	TB	R	RBI	TBB	IBB	SO	HBP	SH	SF	SB	CS	SB%	GDP	Avg	OBP	SLG
1998 Jupiter	A+ Mon	3	8	1	0	1	0	3	1	0	0	0	1	0	0	0	0	0	—	0	.125	.125	.375
Vermont	A- Mon	58	197	55	5	2	1	67	31	23	32	0	33	3	3	4	11	13	.46	4	.279	.381	.340
1999 Cape Fear	A Mon	124	434	107	16	5	2	139	84	34	102	2	77	6	7	1	19	28	.40	1	.247	.396	.320
2000 Jupiter	A+ Mon	128	428	105	10	4	1	126	79	39	79	2	67	5	1	8	16	11	.59	6	.245	.363	.294
2001 Harrisburg	AA Mon	99	341	89	13	3	3	117	57	33	44	2	56	4	1	5	10	7	.59	5	.261	.352	.343
4 Min. YEARS		412	1408	357	44	15	7	452	252	129	257	6	234	18	43	14	56	59	.49	16	.254	.372	.321

Andy Machado

Bats: Both **Throws:** Right **Pos:** SS-112; PR-2   **Ht:** 5'11" **Wt:** 165 **Born:** 1/25/81 **Age:** 21

Year Team	Lg Org	G	AB	H	2B	3B	HR	TB	R	RBI	TBB	IBB	SO	HBP	SH	SF	SB	CS	SB%	GDP	Avg	OBP	SLG
1999 Clearwater	A+ Phi	1	2	0	0	0	0	0	0	0	0	0	1	0	0	0	0	0	—	0	.000	.000	.000
Phillies	R Phi	43	143	37	6	3	2	55	26	12	15	1	38	2	7	1	6	3	.67	5	.259	.335	.385
Piedmont	A Phi	20	60	14	4	2	0	22	7	7	7	0	20	1	1	0	2	1	.67	0	.233	.324	.367
2000 Clearwater	A+ Phi	117	417	102	19	7	1	138	55	35	54	0	103	0	5	2	32	18	.64	7	.245	.330	.331
Reading	AA Phi	3	11	4	1	0	1	8	2	2	0	0	4	0	0	0	0	0	—	0	.364	.364	.727
2001 Clearwater	A+ Phi	82	272	71	5	8	5	107	49	36	31	2	66	4	10	3	23	9	.72	3	.261	.342	.393
Reading	AA Phi	31	101	15	2	0	1	20	13	8	12	0	25	0	3	1	5	2	.71	1	.149	.237	.198
3 Min. YEARS		297	1006	243	37	20	10	350	152	100	119	3	257	7	26	7	68	33	.67	16	.242	.324	.348

Garry Maddox Jr.

Bats: Left **Throws:** Right **Pos:** OF-51; DH-37; PH-5   **Ht:** 6'3" **Wt:** 180 **Born:** 10/24/74 **Age:** 27

Year Team	Lg Org	G	AB	H	2B	3B	HR	TB	R	RBI	TBB	IBB	SO	HBP	SH	SF	SB	CS	SB%	GDP	Avg	OBP	SLG
1997 High Desert	A+ Ari	101	409	125	22	12	7	192	89	44	52	2	94	0	3	0	25	8	.76	8	.306	.384	.469
1998 High Desert	A+ Ari	2	8	5	2	0	1	10	3	4	1	0	1	0	0	1	1	0	1.00	0	.625	.600	1.250
Jackson	AA Hou	25	94	33	3	2	3	49	20	14	5	0	20	0	0	1	3	2	.60	0	.351	.384	.521
Tucson	AAA Ari	81	269	71	13	4	4	104	36	18	15	0	57	3	0	1	4	3	.57	6	.264	.309	.387
1999 El Paso	AA Ari	127	492	145	35	9	15	243	80	75	31	2	106	8	1	4	22	5	.81	5	.295	.344	.494
2000 Trenton	AA Bos	100	363	100	13	3	4	131	58	40	36	0	87	2	2	2	7	5	.58	2	.275	.342	.361
2001 Pawtucket	AAA Bos	8	27	3	0	0	0	3	1	1	0	0	8	0	0	0	0	0	—	1	.111	.111	.111
Trenton	AA Bos	84	287	86	25	5	11	154	47	48	40	1	76	3	0	4	4	5	.44	2	.300	.386	.537
5 Min. YEARS		528	1949	568	113	35	45	886	334	244	180	5	449	16	6	12	66	28	.70	24	.291	.354	.455

Chris Madonna

Bats: Left **Throws:** Right **Pos:** C-36; 1B-9; 3B-7; PH-5; DH-4; PR-2   **Ht:** 5'11" **Wt:** 190 **Born:** 3/13/73 **Age:** 29

Year Team	Lg Org	G	AB	H	2B	3B	HR	TB	R	RBI	TBB	IBB	SO	HBP	SH	SF	SB	CS	SB%	GDP	Avg	OBP	SLG
1994 Zanesville	IND —	49	139	29	5	0	1	37	20	22	33	1	26	1	0	1	12	5	.71	3	.209	.362	.266
1995 St. Lucie	A+ NYM	3	5	0	0	0	0	0	0	0	0	0	1	0	0	0	0	0	—	0	.000	.000	.000
1996 Tri-City	IND —	63	150	41	11	3	4	70	21	22	17	1	36	0	2	2	1	1	.50	2	.273	.343	.467
1997 Trenton	AA Bos	14	41	14	3	0	0	17	7	6	6	0	11	0	0	0	2	2	.50	1	.341	.426	.415
Michigan	A Bos	16	34	5	2	0	0	7	4	1	6	0	9	1	0	1	1	0	1.00	0	.147	.286	.206
1998 Tri-City	IND —	83	262	81	18	5	6	127	47	43	55	4	47	2	1	1	9	3	.75	10	.309	.431	.485
1999 Tri-City	IND —	79	263	80	13	3	12	135	53	49	58	2	54	1	2	1	12	2	.86	4	.304	.430	.513

Year Team	Lg Org	BATTING															BASERUNNING				PERCENTAGES		
		G	AB	H	2B	3B	HR	TB	R	RBI	TBB	IBB	SO	HBP	SH	SF	SB	CS	SB%	GDP	Avg	OBP	SLG
2000 Aberdeen	IND —	5	19	8	2	0	1	13	4	4	0	0	4	1	0	0	1	0	1.00	0	.421	.450	.684
2001 Bridgeport	IND —	21	61	21	5	1	1	31	9	15	15	0	11	0	1	0	0	1	1.00	2	.344	.474	.508
Midland	AA Oak	40	106	25	2	1	4	41	21	16	17	1	31	2	2	3	0	1	.00	3	.236	.344	.387
8 Min. YEARS		373	1080	304	61	13	29	478	186	178	207	9	230	8	8	9	39	14	.74	25	.281	.398	.443

Jim Magrane

Pitches: Right **Bats:** Right **Pos:** SP-28; RP-1   **Ht:** 6'2" **Wt:** 208 **Born:** 7/23/78 **Age:** 23

Year Team	Lg Org	HOW MUCH HE PITCHED						WHAT HE GAVE UP											THE RESULTS					
		G	GS	CG	GF	IP	BFP	H	R	ER	HR	SH	SF	HB	TBB	IBB	SO	WP	Bk	W	L	Pct.	ShO	Sv	ERA
2000 Chston-SC	A TB	27	27	1	0	173	710	158	64	53	9	3	0	4	43	0	162	14	1	12	5	.706	1	0	2.76
2001 Orlando	AA TB	29	28	1	0	182	755	166	87	60	15	6	7	4	56	1	126	13	1	8	12	.400	0	0	2.97
2 Min. YEARS		56	55	2	0	355	1465	324	151	113	24	9	7	8	99	1	288	27	2	20	17	.541	1	0	2.86

Mike Mahoney

Bats: Right **Throws:** Right **Pos:** C-85; DH-6; PH-3; 3B-1; 1B-1; PR-1   **Ht:** 6'1" **Wt:** 200 **Born:** 12/5/72 **Age:** 29

Year Team	Lg Org	BATTING															BASERUNNING				PERCENTAGES		
		G	AB	H	2B	3B	HR	TB	R	RBI	TBB	IBB	SO	HBP	SH	SF	SB	CS	SB%	GDP	Avg	OBP	SLG
1995 Eugene	A- Atl	43	112	27	6	0	1	36	14	15	15	1	17	3	1	1	6	2	.75	5	.241	.344	.321
1996 Durham	A+ Atl	101	363	94	24	2	9	149	52	46	23	0	64	7	4	4	4	3	.57	8	.259	.312	.410
1997 Greenville	AA Atl	87	298	68	17	0	8	109	46	46	28	1	75	3	5	2	1	0	1.00	10	.228	.299	.366
1998 Greenville	AA Atl	20	74	16	5	0	1	24	3	6	1	0	20	2	0	2	1	1	.50	1	.216	.241	.324
Richmond	AAA Atl	71	208	44	10	0	5	69	26	28	24	3	49	5	6	5	1	1	.50	10	.212	.302	.332
1999 Richmond	AAA Atl	55	145	33	7	0	2	46	10	20	6	1	25	1	2	3	0	1	.00	2	.228	.258	.317
2000 West Tenn	AA ChC	24	76	23	7	0	0	30	12	7	7	0	16	2	0	1	0	0	—	0	.303	.372	.395
Iowa	AAA ChC	63	181	55	14	0	6	87	29	28	16	0	28	6	1	3	2	1	.67	2	.304	.374	.481
2001 Iowa	AAA ChC	95	289	65	14	1	3	90	22	27	22	0	63	4	6	2	1	3	.25	8	.225	.287	.311
2000 Chicago	NL	4	7	2	1	0	0	3	1	1	1	0	1	0	0	0	0	0	—	0	.286	.444	.429
7 Min. YEARS		559	1746	425	104	3	35	640	214	223	142	6	357	33	25	23	16	12	.57	46	.243	.309	.367

T.J. Maier

Bats: Right **Throws:** Right **Pos:** 2B-78; PH-2; PR-1   **Ht:** 6'0" **Wt:** 180 **Born:** 2/24/75 **Age:** 27

Year Team	Lg Org	BATTING															BASERUNNING				PERCENTAGES		
		G	AB	H	2B	3B	HR	TB	R	RBI	TBB	IBB	SO	HBP	SH	SF	SB	CS	SB%	GDP	Avg	OBP	SLG
1997 New Jersey	A- StL	50	155	33	9	1	2	50	19	22	20	0	30	2	1	1	6	2	.75	2	.213	.309	.323
1998 Peoria	A StL	84	271	73	14	1	2	95	47	28	45	0	52	6	4	1	6	5	.55	5	.269	.384	.351
1999 Potomac	A+ StL	102	353	93	15	0	2	114	53	38	55	0	61	3	0	4	12	7	.63	6	.263	.364	.323
2000 Arkansas	AA StL	110	364	107	16	3	6	147	59	42	49	1	42	6	1	2	13	7	.65	7	.294	.385	.404
2001 Memphis	AAA StL	6	17	4	0	0	0	4	4	1	2	0	3	0	0	1	0	0	—	0	.235	.300	.235
New Haven	AA StL	74	255	72	20	2	4	108	46	35	38	2	58	6	1	2	9	4	.69	2	.282	.385	.424
5 Min. YEARS		426	1415	382	74	7	16	518	228	166	209	3	246	23	7	11	46	25	.65	22	.270	.370	.366

Oswaldo Mairena

Pitches: Left **Bats:** Left **Pos:** RP-53   **Ht:** 5'11" **Wt:** 165 **Born:** 7/30/75 **Age:** 26

Year Team	Lg Org	HOW MUCH HE PITCHED						WHAT HE GAVE UP											THE RESULTS					
		G	GS	CG	GF	IP	BFP	H	R	ER	HR	SH	SF	HB	TBB	IBB	SO	WP	Bk	W	L	Pct.	ShO	Sv	ERA
1997 Tampa	A+ NYY	3	0	0	0	4.1	19	6	2	2	1	0	0	0	6	0	0	0	0	0	0	—	0	0	4.15
Greensboro	A NYY	49	0	0	20	60.1	241	43	24	17	2	3	1	1	16	3	75	0	3	6	1	.857	0	8	2.54
1998 Tampa	A+ NYY	52	0	0	11	54	238	53	24	19	5	2	2	3	23	3	50	0	2	1	5	.167	0	0	3.17
1999 Norwich	AA NYY	49	0	0	16	57.1	252	48	24	17	3	4	4	1	27	4	47	4	0	4	3	.571	0	2	2.67
2000 Columbus	AAA NYY	5	1	0	2	9	43	12	3	3	2	1	0	0	5	1	4	0	0	1	1	.500	0	0	3.00
Norwich	AA NYY	35	0	0	5	32.1	137	29	16	10	0	1	2	1	11	3	30	0	0	0	4	.000	0	0	2.78
West Tenn	AA ChC	2	0	0	1	2	10	3	1	0	0	1	0	1	1	1	0	0	0	0	1	.000	0	0	0.00
Iowa	AAA ChC	11	0	0	3	14.2	62	13	9	8	1	1	0	0	2	0	4	3	0	1	0	1.000	0	0	4.91
2001 Portland	AAA Fla	22	0	0	7	34.1	134	27	12	6	3	5	0	0	8	0	27	2	0	4	2	.667	0	3	1.57
Calgary	AAA Fla	31	0	0	8	39.1	179	52	33	33	4	2	2	0	13	5	44	2	0	3	2	.600	0	0	7.55
2000 Chicago	NL	2	0	0	1	2	14	7	4	4	1	0	0	0	2	0	0	0	0	0	0	—	0	0	18.00
5 Min. YEARS		259	1	0	73	307.2	1315	286	148	115	21	20	12	7	106	20	287	11	5	20	19	.513	0	13	3.36

Dennis Malave

Bats: Left **Throws:** Left **Pos:** OF-44; PH-1   **Ht:** 5'9" **Wt:** 165 **Born:** 1/6/80 **Age:** 22

Year Team	Lg Org	BATTING															BASERUNNING				PERCENTAGES		
		G	AB	H	2B	3B	HR	TB	R	RBI	TBB	IBB	SO	HBP	SH	SF	SB	CS	SB%	GDP	Avg	OBP	SLG
1998 Burlington	R+ Cle	60	208	58	3	5	4	83	40	19	34	0	59	1	2	0	27	13	.68	6	.279	.383	.399
Watertown	A- Cle	6	20	5	0	0	1	8	1	6	0	0	4	0	0	0	2	1	.67	0	.250	.250	.400
1999 Mahoning Vy	A- Cle	12	41	10	0	0	1	13	11	9	7	0	9	1	0	1	1	1	.50	0	.244	.360	.317
Columbus	A Cle	44	150	40	6	1	3	57	16	15	14	0	44	1	2	0	8	8	.50	5	.267	.333	.380
2000 Kinston	A+ Cle	19	46	16	4	2	1	27	8	11	6	0	10	0	1	0	4	0	1.00	0	.348	.423	.587
Mahoning Vy	A- Cle	42	178	53	4	8	2	79	39	26	23	1	30	2	4	1	15	5	.75	3	.298	.382	.444
2001 Mahoning Vy	A- Cle	40	128	25	3	1	0	30	19	8	21	0	23	3	1	3	4	8	.33	2	.195	.316	.234
Akron	AA Cle	4	7	0	0	0	0	0	0	0	0	0	2	0	0	0	0	0	—	0	.000	.000	.000
4 Min. YEARS		227	778	207	20	17	12	297	134	93	105	1	179	8	10	5	61	36	.63	16	.266	.357	.382

Jaime Malave

Bats: Right **Throws:** Right **Pos:** C-9   **Ht:** 6'0" **Wt:** 215 **Born:** 3/22/75 **Age:** 27

		BATTING															BASERUNNING				PERCENTAGES		
Year Team	Lg Org	G	AB	H	2B	3B	HR	TB	R	RBI	TBB	IBB	SO	HBP	SH	SF	SB	CS	SB%	GDP	Avg	OBP	SLG
1995 Yakima	A- LA	44	137	37	13	2	1	57	12	15	6	0	41	1	1	2	1	1	.50	1	.270	.301	.416
1996 Savannah	A LA	6	16	4	0	0	0	4	2	5	0	0	3	1	0	1	0	0	—	0	.250	.278	.250
Yakima	A- LA	40	108	22	6	0	5	43	14	16	6	0	33	0	1	0	0	0	—	2	.204	.246	.398
1997 Savannah	A LA	58	206	52	11	1	9	92	23	32	4	0	54	1	1	1	2	1	.67	2	.252	.269	.447
San Berndno	A+ LA	1	4	1	0	0	0	1	0	0	0	0	0	0	0	0	0	0	—	0	.250	.250	.250
1998 Vero Beach	A+ LA	28	89	24	6	1	4	44	12	9	10	0	16	0	0	0	1	0	1.00	1	.270	.343	.494
San Antonio	AA LA	28	55	14	5	0	1	22	3	4	6	1	10	0	2	0	0	0	—	2	.255	.328	.400
1999 Waterbury	IND —	19	72	19	2	0	3	30	12	9	10	0	17	1	0	0	0	0	—	1	.264	.361	.417
Jupiter	A+ Mon	3	10	4	2	0	0	6	2	2	2	0	1	0	0	0	0	0	—	0	.400	.462	.600
Ottawa	AAA Mon	3	8	2	0	0	0	2	2	0	1	0	4	0	0	0	0	0	—	0	.250	.333	.250
Harrisburg	AA Mon	12	18	4	0	0	3	13	4	4	2	0	4	0	1	0	0	0	—	0	.222	.300	.722
2000 Ottawa	AAA Mon	1	3	2	0	0	0	2	0	0	0	0	0	0	0	0	0	0	—	0	.667	.667	.667
Harrisburg	AA Mon	77	192	49	13	0	13	101	26	36	17	1	63	3	0	3	0	0	—	4	.255	.321	.526
2001 Binghamton	AA NYM	7	19	2	1	0	0	3	2	1	1	0	4	1	0	0	0	0	—	0	.105	.190	.158
St. Lucie	A+ NYM	2	9	4	0	0	0	4	2	0	0	0	5	0	1	0	0	1	.00	0	.444	.444	.444
7 Min. YEARS		329	946	240	59	4	39	424	116	133	65	2	255	8	7	8	4	3	.57	13	.254	.305	.448

Carlos Maldonado

Bats: Right **Throws:** Right **Pos:** C-74; DH-1; PH-1   **Ht:** 6'2" **Wt:** 185 **Born:** 1/3/79 **Age:** 23

		BATTING															BASERUNNING				PERCENTAGES		
Year Team	Lg Org	G	AB	H	2B	3B	HR	TB	R	RBI	TBB	IBB	SO	HBP	SH	SF	SB	CS	SB%	GDP	Avg	OBP	SLG
1996 Mariners	R Sea	29	100	22	0	0	2	28	10	18	6	0	10	1	1	4	0	1	.00	7	.220	.261	.280
1997 Wisconsin	A Sea	97	316	60	8	2	0	72	15	25	17	1	33	3	8	3	2	3	.40	8	.190	.236	.228
1998 Wisconsin	A Sea	7	23	4	0	0	0	4	4	1	2	0	1	0	0	0	0	0	—	1	.174	.240	.174
Tacoma	AAA Sea	3	9	0	0	0	0	0	0	0	0	0	1	0	0	0	0	0	—	0	.000	.000	.000
Everett	A- Sea	42	150	43	10	0	5	68	19	24	10	0	17	2	0	2	1	0	1.00	5	.287	.335	.453
1999 Wisconsin	A Sea	92	302	93	13	0	0	106	35	33	43	1	32	0	2	2	4	6	.40	10	.308	.392	.351
2000 Round Rock	AA Hou	116	423	114	24	2	5	157	46	52	35	3	71	5	5	6	5	4	.56	15	.270	.328	.371
2001 Round Rock	AA Hou	76	262	75	14	0	4	101	29	33	27	0	55	3	0	3	1	2	.33	11	.286	.356	.385
6 Min. YEARS		462	1585	411	69	4	16	536	158	186	140	5	220	14	16	20	13	16	.45	57	.259	.321	.338

Randi Mallard

Pitches: Right **Bats:** Right **Pos:** RP-51   **Ht:** 6'1" **Wt:** 180 **Born:** 8/11/75 **Age:** 26

		HOW MUCH HE PITCHED						WHAT HE GAVE UP												THE RESULTS					
Year Team	Lg Org	G	GS	CG	GF	IP	BFP	H	R	ER	HR	SH	SF	HB	TBB	IBB	SO	WP	Bk	W	L	Pct.	ShO	Sv	ERA
1996 Princeton	R+ Cin	13	11	1	1	66	302	66	42	27	2	0	3	4	38	0	72	16	1	2	7	.222	0	0	3.68
1997 Chston-WV	A Cin	13	12	0	0	56.1	238	51	25	24	0	2	3	5	23	0	61	8	0	3	3	.500	0	0	3.83
1998 Burlington	A Cin	14	13	2	0	82.2	356	79	41	31	3	2	1	1	32	0	71	6	1	9	3	.750	0	0	3.38
Chattanooga	AA Cin	13	12	0	0	60.1	294	65	37	29	3	1	1	3	58	1	34	7	1	1	4	.200	0	0	4.33
1999 Chattanooga	AA Cin	14	14	0	0	71.2	342	92	61	54	7	2	2	2	45	0	45	15	2	4	5	.444	0	0	6.78
Clinton	A Cin	6	1	0	1	15.2	70	18	12	12	0	0	0	3	3	0	21	4	0	0	1	.000	0	0	6.89
2000 St. Paul	IND —	30	0	0	17	43.2	209	55	39	30	3	3	1	2	19	0	35	8	0	2	4	.333	0	1	6.18
2001 Atlantic Ct	IND —	43	0	0	29	52	237	52	30	20	3	2	2	5	24	4	47	9	0	6	5	.545	0	11	3.46
West Tenn	AA ChC	8	0	0	1	10	54	13	12	11	1	2	0	3	9	2	7	0	0	0	1	.000	0	0	9.90
6 Min. YEARS		154	63	3	49	458.1	2102	491	299	238	22	14	13	28	251	7	393	73	5	27	33	.450	0	12	4.67

Brian Mallette

Pitches: Right **Bats:** Right **Pos:** RP-56   **Ht:** 6'0" **Wt:** 185 **Born:** 1/19/75 **Age:** 27

		HOW MUCH HE PITCHED						WHAT HE GAVE UP												THE RESULTS					
Year Team	Lg Org	G	GS	CG	GF	IP	BFP	H	R	ER	HR	SH	SF	HB	TBB	IBB	SO	WP	Bk	W	L	Pct.	ShO	Sv	ERA
1997 Helena	R+ Mil	23	0	0	13	35.1	156	33	19	17	1	3	2	1	20	2	58	7	0	6	2	.750	0	5	4.33
1998 Beloit	A Mil	50	0	0	44	55.1	234	40	23	19	2	1	0	3	29	2	76	2	0	2	1	.667	0	23	3.09
1999 Stockton	A+ Mil	28	0	0	14	36	162	38	16	6	1	0	1	3	16	1	34	0	0	2	0	1.000	0	4	1.50
2000 Mudville	A+ Mil	50	0	0	15	71	316	52	35	26	6	1	3	5	52	1	94	11	0	4	4	.500	0	2	3.30
2001 Huntsville	AA Mil	44	0	0	39	55	232	43	13	12	4	4	1	3	23	4	71	4	0	7	2	.778	0	17	1.96
Indianapols	AAA Mil	12	0	0	6	17	96	10	4	2	2	0	1	1	8	0	23	1	0	0	1	.000	0	2	1.06
5 Min. YEARS		207	0	0	131	269.2	1169	216	110	82	16	9	8	16	148	10	356	25	0	21	10	.677	0	53	2.74

Marty Malloy

Bats: Left **Throws:** Right **Pos:** 2B-69; SS-38; PH-14; DH-12; 3B-2; PR-2   **Ht:** 5'10" **Wt:** 165 **Born:** 7/6/72 **Age:** 29

		BATTING															BASERUNNING				PERCENTAGES		
Year Team	Lg Org	G	AB	H	2B	3B	HR	TB	R	RBI	TBB	IBB	SO	HBP	SH	SF	SB	CS	SB%	GDP	Avg	OBP	SLG
1992 Idaho Falls	R+ Atl	62	251	79	18	1	2	105	45	28	11	0	43	2	0	1	8	4	.67	3	.315	.347	.418
1993 Macon	A Atl	109	376	110	19	3	2	141	55	36	39	3	70	2	3	3	24	8	.75	4	.293	.360	.375
1994 Durham	A+ Atl	118	428	113	22	1	6	155	53	35	52	2	69	2	2	3	18	12	.60	9	.264	.344	.362
1995 Greenville	AA Atl	124	461	128	20	3	10	184	73	59	39	1	58	0	7	8	11	12	.48	6	.278	.329	.399
1996 Richmond	AAA Atl	18	64	13	2	1	0	17	7	8	5	1	7	0	2	1	3	0	1.00	1	.203	.257	.266
Greenville	AA Atl	111	429	134	27	2	4	177	82	36	54	6	50	4	6	2	11	10	.52	11	.312	.393	.413
1997 Richmond	AAA Atl	108	414	118	19	5	2	153	66	25	41	1	61	1	5	1	17	7	.71	6	.285	.351	.370
1998 Richmond	AAA Atl	124	483	140	25	3	7	192	75	54	51	2	65	5	5	4	20	7	.74	12	.290	.361	.398
1999 Richmond	AAA Atl	114	407	119	23	1	7	165	58	36	53	2	52	2	4	3	19	15	.56	2	.292	.374	.405
2000 Tigers	R Det	2	1	1	0	0	0	1	0	1	2	0	0	0	0	0	0	0	—	0	1.000	1.000	1.000
Lakeland	A+ Det	7	26	6	1	0	1	10	4	4	1	0	1	0	0	0	1	0	1.00	0	.231	.286	.385
Toledo	AAA Det	30	115	27	8	0	4	47	16	16	7	0	18	0	1	1	0	0	—	0	.235	.276	.409
2001 Louisville	AAA Cin	126	468	142	36	4	6	204	69	49	27	0	51	2	7	6	8	7	.53	8	.303	.340	.436
1998 Atlanta	NL	11	28	5	1	0	1	9	3	1	2	0	2	0	0	0	0	0	—	0	.179	.233	.321
10 Min. YEARS		1053	3923	1130	220	24	51	1551	603	387	382	18	545	21	42	32	140	82	.63	61	.288	.352	.395

Corwin Malone

Pitches: Left **Bats:** Right **Pos:** SP-27 **Ht:** 6'3" **Wt:** 200 **Born:** 7/3/80 **Age:** 21

Year Team	Lg Org	G	GS	CG	GF	IP	BFP	H	R	ER	HR	SH	SF	HB	TBB	IBB	SO	WP	Bk	W	L	Pct.	ShO	Sv	ERA
1999 White Sox	R CWS	10	0	0	3	18	90	16	19	16	1	0	0	1	16	0	24	5	4	0	2	.000	0	0	8.00
2000 Burlington	A CWS	38	1	0	16	71.2	345	67	52	39	4	4	4	2	60	4	82	17	2	2	3	.400	0	0	4.90
2001 Kannapolis	A CWS	18	18	2	0	112.1	450	83	30	25	2	2	3	0	44	3	119	4	1	11	4	.733	0	0	2.00
Winston-Sal	A+ CWS	5	5	0	0	36.2	143	25	10	7	1	3	0	0	10	1	38	0	0	0	1	.000	0	0	1.72
Birmingham	AA CWS	4	4	0	0	19.1	76	8	5	5	2	0	0	1	12	0	20	1	0	2	0	1.000	0	0	2.33
3 Min. YEARS		75	28	2	19	258	1104	199	116	92	10	9	7	4	142	8	283	27	7	15	10	.600	0	0	3.21

Nick Maness

Pitches: Right **Bats:** Right **Pos:** SP-26; RP-2 **Ht:** 6'4" **Wt:** 210 **Born:** 10/17/78 **Age:** 23

Year Team	Lg Org	G	GS	CG	GF	IP	BFP	H	R	ER	HR	SH	SF	HB	TBB	IBB	SO	WP	Bk	W	L	Pct.	ShO	Sv	ERA
1997 Mets	R NYM	11	6	0	2	44.2	205	52	25	15	3	1	1	1	20	0	54	2	2	3	2	.600	0	0	3.02
1998 Kingsport	R+ NYM	13	13	0	0	64.1	289	68	41	32	7	2	5	1	30	0	76	7	1	5	3	.625	0	0	4.48
1999 Capital Cty	A NYM	23	22	0	0	107.1	469	92	74	59	8	3	5	6	57	0	99	20	2	5	6	.455	0	0	4.95
2000 Binghamton	AA NYM	2	1	0	0	9.1	38	8	2	2	1	0	0	0	4	0	3	0	1	1	0	1.000	0	0	1.93
St. Lucie	A+ NYM	26	25	0	1	145.1	602	116	58	52	14	5	4	5	68	1	124	3	5	11	7	.611	0	0	3.22
2001 Binghamton	AA NYM	28	26	1	1	143	654	168	94	79	13	5	7	6	65	4	107	5	0	6	12	.333	0	0	4.97
5 Min. YEARS		103	93	1	4	514	2257	504	294	239	46	16	22	19	244	5	463	37	11	31	30	.508	0	0	4.18

Mark Mangum

Pitches: Right **Bats:** Right **Pos:** SP-26 **Ht:** 6'2" **Wt:** 180 **Born:** 8/24/78 **Age:** 23

Year Team	Lg Org	G	GS	CG	GF	IP	BFP	H	R	ER	HR	SH	SF	HB	TBB	IBB	SO	WP	Bk	W	L	Pct.	ShO	Sv	ERA
1997 Rockies	R Col	13	13	0	0	60.2	286	66	45	35	1	0	3	7	35	0	72	9	1	3	6	.333	0	0	5.19
1998 Vermont	A- Mon	14	12	0	1	70.2	303	78	39	35	3	2	2	6	15	0	59	4	0	3	9	.250	0	1	4.46
1999 Cape Fear	A Mon	26	26	1	0	159.1	677	156	85	62	14	1	7	16	54	0	107	15	0	10	11	.476	0	0	3.50
2000 Jupiter	A+ Mon	20	19	1	1	114	487	109	62	52	11	4	3	5	30	0	55	4	0	6	8	.429	0	0	4.11
2001 Harrisburg	AA Mon	26	26	2	0	140.1	613	161	88	72	14	6	5	14	36	1	59	3	0	7	8	.467	1	0	4.62
5 Min. YEARS		99	96	4	2	545	2366	570	319	256	43	13	22	55	170	1	352	35	1	29	42	.408	1	1	4.23

Jim Manias

Pitches: Left **Bats:** Left **Pos:** RP-48 **Ht:** 6'4" **Wt:** 190 **Born:** 10/21/74 **Age:** 27

Year Team	Lg Org	G	GS	CG	GF	IP	BFP	H	R	ER	HR	SH	SF	HB	TBB	IBB	SO	WP	Bk	W	L	Pct.	ShO	Sv	ERA
1996 Butte	R+ TB	16	13	0	1	72	336	98	64	42	8	2	5	3	22	0	55	5	1	5	4	.556	0	0	5.25
1997 St. Pete	A+ TB	28	28	2	0	171.1	710	163	84	72	16	3	4	11	40	0	119	6	0	13	5	.722	0	0	3.78
1998 St. Pete	A+ TB	30	21	0	3	137	618	167	99	85	27	3	11	9	37	0	79	7	0	6	13	.316	0	0	5.58
1999 Chattanooga	AA Cin	1	0	0	0	0.2	0	0	0	0	0	0	0	0	0	0	0	0	0	0	0	—	0	0	0.00
Rockford	A Cin	30	10	4	1	90.2	391	84	46	37	5	1	1	2	36	2	103	5	0	9	7	.563	1	0	3.67
2000 Dayton	A Cin	17	16	6	0	120.1	496	112	53	43	11	0	4	2	25	0	109	5	0	6	6	.500	1	0	3.22
Chattanooga	AA Cin	15	5	1	3	45.2	200	41	23	21	6	2	1	0	23	6	45	3	0	1	4	.200	0	0	4.14
2001 Mudville	A+ Cin	24	0	0	7	45.1	187	38	16	14	5	2	0	2	12	0	45	2	0	3	2	.600	0	2	2.78
Chattanooga	AA Cin	24	0	0	5	26	101	13	9	9	2	3	2	4	6	0	23	1	0	1	1	.500	0	0	3.12
6 Min. YEARS		185	93	13	20	709	3041	716	394	323	80	16	28	33	201	8	578	34	1	44	42	.512	4	2	4.10

Derek Mann

Bats: Left **Throws:** Right **Pos:** 2B-16; DH-12; SS-7; PR-4; PH-1 **Ht:** 6'0" **Wt:** 166 **Born:** 3/8/78 **Age:** 24

Year Team	Lg Org	G	AB	H	2B	3B	HR	TB	R	RBI	TBB	IBB	SO	HBP	SH	SF	SB	CS	SB%	GDP	Avg	OBP	SLG
1997 Devil Rays	R TB	50	168	48	2	1	1	55	34	17	29	0	24	5	2	0	8	11	.42	3	.286	.406	.327
1998 Princeton	R+ TB	68	280	91	10	6	1	116	63	32	32	1	46	1	2	0	16	7	.70	4	.325	.396	.414
1999 Chston-SC	A TB	124	449	127	20	1	5	164	86	45	71	0	88	9	12	4	22	10	.69	6	.283	.388	.365
2000 St. Pete	A+ TB	65	195	48	7	3	2	67	25	14	21	0	28	2	8	2	5	3	.63	3	.246	.323	.344
2001 Altoona	AA Pit	1	3	0	0	0	0	0	0	0	0	0	1	0	0	0	0	0	—	0	.000	.000	.000
Lynchburg	A+ Pit	38	102	28	3	2	0	35	14	11	9	0	25	0	2	0	4	2	.67	3	.275	.333	.343
5 Min. YEARS		346	1197	342	42	13	9	437	222	119	162	1	212	17	26	6	55	33	.63	19	.286	.377	.365

Julio Manon

Pitches: Right **Bats:** Left **Pos:** SP-21; RP-4 **Ht:** 6'0" **Wt:** 200 **Born:** 6/10/73 **Age:** 29

Year Team	Lg Org	G	GS	CG	GF	IP	BFP	H	R	ER	HR	SH	SF	HB	TBB	IBB	SO	WP	Bk	W	L	Pct.	ShO	Sv	ERA
1993 Cardinals	R StL	15	4	0	1	33.1	151	44	21	19	2	0	3	0	12	0	22	5	4	2	3	.400	0	0	5.13
1994 Johnson Cty	R+ StL	5	0	0	2	8.2	43	11	8	8	2	0	0	0	5	0	7	0	0	1	2	.333	0	0	8.31
Cardinals	R StL	14	0	0	4	16	69	20	9	9	0	0	0	0	1	0	18	1	2	0	1	.000	0	1	5.06
1995 River City	R+ StL	16	8	2	3	74	319	75	34	30	4	0	3	2	30	2	77	10	0	3	4	.429	0	1	3.65
1997 Chston-SC	A TB	27	9	0	4	88.2	392	95	53	44	8	5	3	3	22	1	98	7	0	3	5	.375	0	0	4.47
1998 Orlando	AA TB	13	0	0	5	20.2	96	22	19	14	3	0	1	0	9	0	22	3	0	0	2	.000	0	0	6.10
St. Pete	A+ TB	38	0	0	14	55.2	219	41	25	23	7	0	0	2	19	1	73	4	1	5	5	.500	0	1	3.72
1999 Orlando	AA TB	30	5	0	8	67	303	80	43	38	9	0	1	0	23	0	53	3	0	3	3	.500	0	0	5.10
St. Paul	IND —	4	3	0	0	20.1	85	18	9	5	0	0	1	0	7	0	21	1	0	1	1	.500	0	0	2.21
2000 R Mon	R Mon	4	0	0	1	10.1	36	4	1	1	0	2	0	1	2	0	10	0	0	2	0	1.000	0	0	0.87
Harrisburg	AA Mon	14	4	0	4	31.1	136	32	19	18	7	1	2	2	8	0	25	1	0	2	1	.667	0	1	5.17
2001 Harrisburg	AA Mon	10	7	0	3	52	207	50	20	18	6	1	1	0	16	0	44	1	0	4	3	.571	0	0	3.12
Ottawa	AAA Mon	15	14	0	1	84	339	71	31	29	11	2	0	0	34	0	67	2	0	1	4	.200	0	0	3.11
8 Min. YEARS		205	54	2	50	562	2395	563	292	256	59	11	15	12	188	4	537	38	7	27	34	.443	0	5	4.10

183

Roberto Manzueta

Pitches: Right **Bats:** Left **Pos:** RP-27 **Ht:** 6'1" **Wt:** 197 **Born:** 12/28/78 **Age:** 23

		HOW MUCH HE PITCHED						WHAT HE GAVE UP											THE RESULTS				
Year Team	Lg Org	G	GS	CG	GF	IP	BFP	H	R	ER	HR	SH	SF	HB	TBB	IBB	SO	WP	Bk	W	L	Pct.	ShO	Sv	ERA
1999 High Desert	A+ Ari	40	0	0	19	66.2	294	63	29	26	4	1	2	8	31	2	59	8	0	2	2	.500	0	2	3.51
2000 Altoona	AA Pit	8	2	0	0	21.1	104	26	16	12	0	0	1	0	13	0	14	2	0	0	1	.000	0	0	5.06
Lynchburg	A+ Pit	23	2	0	9	42.2	194	49	28	23	3	2	1	1	13	0	38	6	0	0	4	.000	0	0	4.85
2001 Lynchburg	A+ Pit	15	0	0	11	23.2	103	18	11	7	2	1	1	1	12	0	30	0	0	3	0	.000	0	1	2.66
Altoona	AA Pit	12	0	0	4	20	88	19	13	12	0	0	1	2	11	2	14	0	0	1	1	.500	0	0	5.40
3 Min. YEARS		98	4	0	43	174.1	783	175	97	80	9	4	6	12	80	4	155	16	0	3	11	.214	0	3	4.13

T.R. Marcinczyk

Bats: Right **Throws:** Right **Pos:** 1B-70; 3B-28; DH-3; PH-2; C-1; OF-1 **Ht:** 6'2" **Wt:** 210 **Born:** 10/11/73 **Age:** 28

		BATTING															BASERUNNING				PERCENTAGES		
Year Team	Lg Org	G	AB	H	2B	3B	HR	TB	R	RBI	TBB	IBB	SO	HBP	SH	SF	SB	CS	SB%	GDP	Avg	OBP	SLG
1996 Sou Oregon	A- Oak	63	216	48	13	2	7	86	29	38	22	0	57	5	5	4	3	3	.50	3	.222	.304	.398
1997 Modesto	A+ Oak	133	463	128	41	2	23	242	89	91	71	5	107	11	1	6	4	4	.50	7	.276	.381	.523
1998 Huntsville	AA Oak	131	501	135	25	2	26	242	90	88	51	3	127	9	0	7	2	6	.25	15	.269	.343	.483
1999 Midland	AA Oak	127	477	133	39	1	23	243	87	111	62	2	109	12	0	7	2	0	1.00	12	.279	.371	.509
2000 Sacramento	AAA Oak	11	39	9	1	0	1	13	4	3	4	0	7	1	0	0	0	0	—	0	.231	.318	.333
Modesto	A+ Oak	10	40	13	5	0	1	21	9	11	3	0	6	1	0	0	1	0	1.00	1	.325	.386	.525
Fort Myers	A+ Min	4	16	3	0	0	0	3	1	1	0	0	3	1	0	1	0	0	—	2	.188	.222	.188
New Britain	AA Min	60	191	48	9	0	7	73	21	23	27	1	53	2	0	0	1	2	.33	6	.225	.327	.382
2001 New Britain	AA Min	7	16	2	0	0	0	2	0	1	3	0	5	0	0	0	0	0	—	0	.125	.263	.125
Fargo-Mh	IND —	89	361	93	17	1	20	172	64	71	20	0	65	6	0	2	13	4	.76	4	.258	.306	.476
6 Min. YEARS		635	2320	607	150	8	108	1097	394	438	263	11	539	48	6	27	26	19	.58	50	.262	.345	.473

Alex Marconi

Bats: Right **Throws:** Right **Pos:** C-19; 1B-7; DH-7; PH-6; 3B-2 **Ht:** 6'0" **Wt:** 187 **Born:** 3/25/78 **Age:** 24

		BATTING															BASERUNNING				PERCENTAGES		
Year Team	Lg Org	G	AB	H	2B	3B	HR	TB	R	RBI	TBB	IBB	SO	HBP	SH	SF	SB	CS	SB%	GDP	Avg	OBP	SLG
2000 Princeton	R+ TB	19	65	22	10	0	0	32	8	9	4	0	10	0	1	0	0	0	—	5	.338	.377	.492
Hudson Val	A- TB	24	86	25	1	2	1	33	11	10	7	1	15	0	0	1	2	2	.50	3	.291	.340	.384
2001 Bakersfield	A+ TB	34	109	26	3	0	1	32	11	11	6	0	27	0	0	0	0	0	—	5	.239	.278	.294
Durham	AAA TB	1	4	0	0	0	0	0	0	0	0	0	1	0	0	0	0	0	—	0	.000	.000	.000
2 Min. YEARS		78	264	73	14	2	2	97	30	30	17	1	53	0	1	1	2	2	.50	13	.277	.319	.367

Mike Maroth

Pitches: Left **Bats:** Left **Pos:** SP-23; RP-1 **Ht:** 6'0" **Wt:** 180 **Born:** 8/17/77 **Age:** 24

		HOW MUCH HE PITCHED						WHAT HE GAVE UP											THE RESULTS				
Year Team	Lg Org	G	GS	CG	GF	IP	BFP	H	R	ER	HR	SH	SF	HB	TBB	IBB	SO	WP	Bk	W	L	Pct.	ShO	Sv	ERA
1998 Red Sox	R Bos	4	2	0	1	12.2	49	9	3	0	0	0	0	0	2	0	14	0	0	1	1	.500	0	0	0.00
Lowell	A- Bos	6	6	0	0	31	127	22	13	10	1	0	1	3	13	0	34	3	0	2	3	.400	0	0	2.90
1999 Sarasota	A+ Bos	20	19	0	0	111.1	497	124	65	50	3	6	4	10	35	1	64	11	2	11	6	.647	0	0	4.04
Lakeland	A+ Det	3	3	0	0	16.2	71	18	7	6	1	1	0	0	7	0	11	2	0	2	1	.667	0	0	3.24
Jacksnville	AA Det	4	4	0	0	20.2	96	27	15	11	2	1	1	0	7	0	10	1	0	1	2	.333	0	0	4.79
2000 Jacksnville	AA Det	27	26	2	0	164.1	689	176	79	72	14	9	9	3	58	0	85	6	1	9	14	.391	1	0	3.94
2001 Toledo	AAA Det	24	23	0	0	131.2	587	158	80	68	11	5	5	4	50	1	63	4	0	7	10	.412	0	0	4.65
4 Min. YEARS		88	83	2	1	488.1	2116	534	262	217	32	22	20	20	172	2	281	27	3	33	37	.471	1	0	4.00

Rob Marquez

Pitches: Right **Bats:** Right **Pos:** RP-34 **Ht:** 6'0" **Wt:** 200 **Born:** 4/21/73 **Age:** 29

		HOW MUCH HE PITCHED						WHAT HE GAVE UP											THE RESULTS				
Year Team	Lg Org	G	GS	CG	GF	IP	BFP	H	R	ER	HR	SH	SF	HB	TBB	IBB	SO	WP	Bk	W	L	Pct.	ShO	Sv	ERA
1995 Vermont	A- Mon	29	0	0	29	32	122	15	5	3	0	1	0	1	11	0	32	1	0	1	1	.500	0	21	0.84
1996 Wst Plm Bch	A+ Mon	11	0	0	7	11	54	14	10	9	0	0	1	0	5	0	8	0	0	1	1	.500	0	6	7.36
Delmarva	A Mon	29	0	0	14	46.2	210	44	23	19	4	2	5	3	22	0	49	5	0	1	2	.333	0	1	3.66
1997 Cape Fear	A Mon	12	0	0	5	18.1	81	15	6	6	0	0	1	0	12	0	18	0	2	0	0	—	0	2	2.95
Wst Plm Bch	A+ Mon	21	0	0	13	28	117	28	12	8	3	1	0	0	3	0	22	0	0	1	1	.500	0	6	2.57
1998 Jupiter	A+ Mon	39	0	0	14	51.1	234	60	28	22	4	4	0	7	16	0	46	0	0	5	4	.556	0	3	3.86
Harrisburg	AA Mon	4	0	0	3	6	22	4	2	2	2	0	0	0	2	0	5	0	0	0	0	—	0	1	3.00
1999 Jupiter	A+ Mon	13	0	0	9	15.2	62	5	2	0	0	2	0	1	6	0	15	0	1	3	0	1.000	0	3	0.00
Harrisburg	AA Mon	18	0	0	11	25.2	116	31	15	13	3	1	1	2	8	1	22	0	0	2	2	.500	0	1	4.56
Ottawa	AAA Mon	18	0	0	7	27.2	131	33	19	15	3	1	1	1	14	2	16	1	1	1	1	.500	0	1	4.88
2000 Ottawa	AAA Mon	53	0	0	15	96	435	116	61	54	7	5	5	11	34	1	63	6	0	4	4	.500	0	3	5.06
2001 Ottawa	AAA Mon	34	0	0	7	60.2	245	57	23	20	5	0	3	4	12	2	27	3	0	6	0	1.000	0	0	2.97
7 Min. YEARS		281	0	0	134	419	1827	422	206	171	31	17	15	35	145	6	323	16	4	25	16	.610	0	48	3.67

Jason Marr

Pitches: Right **Bats:** Right **Pos:** RP-51 **Ht:** 6'1" **Wt:** 195 **Born:** 9/9/75 **Age:** 26

		HOW MUCH HE PITCHED						WHAT HE GAVE UP											THE RESULTS				
Year Team	Lg Org	G	GS	CG	GF	IP	BFP	H	R	ER	HR	SH	SF	HB	TBB	IBB	SO	WP	Bk	W	L	Pct.	ShO	Sv	ERA
1998 Johnson Cty	R+ StL	25	0	0	20	34	142	23	11	8	3	1	0	2	10	1	36	5	0	2	2	.500	0	10	2.12
1999 Potomac	A+ StL	50	0	0	45	53	237	57	36	31	5	2	3	1	21	3	40	6	0	1	6	.143	0	21	5.26
2000 Potomac	A+ StL	48	0	0	46	55.2	235	52	24	22	5	2	2	3	17	0	45	0	1	2	4	.333	0	30	3.56
2001 New Haven	AA StL	51	0	0	23	61.2	275	68	36	34	5	3	3	1	25	3	27	1	0	3	4	.429	0	0	4.96
4 Min. YEARS		174	0	0	134	204.1	889	200	107	95	18	8	8	7	73	7	148	12	1	8	16	.333	0	61	4.18

Lee Marshall

Pitches: Right **Bats:** Right **Pos:** RP-50   **Ht:** 6'5" **Wt:** 217 **Born:** 9/25/76 **Age:** 25

Year Team	Lg Org	G	GS	CG	GF	IP	BFP	H	R	ER	HR	SH	SF	HB	TBB	IBB	SO	WP	Bk	W	L	Pct.	ShO	Sv	ERA
1995 Twins	R Min	6	1	0	0	11	57	16	10	6	1	1	1	2	8	0	7	2	0	0	1	.000	0	0	4.91
1996 Twins	R Min	12	12	3	0	70	283	59	31	18	0	1	1	2	18	2	39	2	1	4	4	.500	1	0	2.31
1997 Elizabethtn	R+ Min	14	14	1	0	84	369	93	56	36	6	4	1	5	16	0	41	2	0	5	3	.625	0	0	3.86
1998 Fort Wayne	A Min	46	12	0	9	104	481	133	74	60	5	1	2	5	33	1	71	9	2	8	5	.615	0	1	5.19
1999 Fort Myers	A+ Min	28	0	0	18	36.2	144	32	10	6	1	4	3	0	5	0	25	1	0	2	2	.500	0	5	1.47
2000 New Britain	AA Min	59	0	0	43	69.1	308	82	35	31	4	8	2	2	27	2	52	5	0	5	4	.556	0	8	4.02
2001 New Britain	AA Min	11	0	0	5	18.2	85	20	6	4	1	1	1	0	4	0	15	0	0	1	3	.250	0	2	1.93
Edmonton	AAA Min	39	0	0	30	53.2	229	50	18	14	2	2	0	2	20	1	37	1	0	4	2	.667	0	11	2.35
7 Min. YEARS		215	39	4	105	447.1	1956	485	240	175	20	22	11	18	131	6	287	22	3	29	24	.547	1	27	3.52

Brandon Marsters

Bats: Right **Throws:** Right **Pos:** C-75; DH-22; PH-3   **Ht:** 5'11" **Wt:** 190 **Born:** 3/14/75 **Age:** 27

Year Team	Lg Org	G	AB	H	2B	3B	HR	TB	R	RBI	TBB	IBB	SO	HBP	SH	SF	SB	CS	SB%	GDP	Avg	OBP	SLG
1996 Batavia	A- Phi	42	151	35	8	2	1	50	15	13	8	0	46	1	0	0	1	0	1.00	1	.232	.275	.331
1997 Piedmont	A Phi	61	212	43	8	0	2	57	25	20	22	2	51	0	2	0	0	0	—	4	.203	.278	.269
Clearwater	A+ Phi	44	141	26	3	0	0	29	10	18	15	0	26	4	1	2	1	0	1.00	3	.184	.278	.206
1998 Clearwater	A+ Phi	76	265	75	12	1	6	107	33	39	16	0	41	2	4	2	2	1	.67	4	.283	.326	.404
Reading	AA Phi	38	143	33	4	2	1	44	9	7	11	0	34	1	0	1	0	1	.00	5	.231	.288	.308
1999 Salt Lake	AAA Min	11	25	5	1	0	1	9	4	8	2	0	6	0	0	0	0	0	—	0	.200	.259	.360
Fort Myers	A+ Min	54	173	41	11	0	2	58	18	28	19	0	33	1	0	5	1	0	1.00	7	.237	.308	.335
2000 Fort Myers	A+ Min	118	407	126	25	4	7	180	46	77	31	6	61	4	2	3	2	1	.67	9	.310	.362	.442
2001 New Britain	AA Min	100	349	77	16	1	9	122	35	36	29	2	75	3	3	1	2	1	.67	8	.221	.285	.350
6 Min. YEARS		544	1866	461	88	10	29	656	195	246	153	10	373	16	12	14	9	4	.69	42	.247	.307	.352

Billy Martin

Bats: Right **Throws:** Right **Pos:** 1B-60; 3B-47; DH-29   **Ht:** 6'2" **Wt:** 200 **Born:** 6/10/76 **Age:** 26

Year Team	Lg Org	G	AB	H	2B	3B	HR	TB	R	RBI	TBB	IBB	SO	HBP	SH	SF	SB	CS	SB%	GDP	Avg	OBP	SLG
1998 Kingsport	R+ NYM	61	214	66	19	0	7	106	43	42	22	0	58	6	0	2	1	1	.50	5	.308	.385	.495
1999 Capital Cty	A NYM	64	220	52	19	1	8	97	38	30	24	0	82	6	0	3	1	1	.50	3	.236	.324	.441
2000 South Bend	A Ari	123	415	116	26	4	25	225	78	90	83	6	130	11	0	3	7	1	.88	6	.280	.410	.542
2001 Lancaster	A+ Ari	130	472	141	33	4	26	260	98	106	95	2	130	7	0	4	0	4	.00	1	.299	.420	.551
El Paso	AA Ari	4	17	3	0	1	0	5	3	1	1	0	4	0	0	0	0	0	—	0	.176	.222	.294
4 Min. YEARS		382	1338	378	97	10	66	693	260	269	225	8	404	30	0	12	9	7	.56	15	.283	.394	.518

Justin Martin

Bats: Both **Throws:** Right **Pos:** OF-62; 2B-44; PR-6; PH-5; DH-3; 3B-1   **Ht:** 5'8" **Wt:** 160 **Born:** 2/19/76 **Age:** 26

Year Team	Lg Org	G	AB	H	2B	3B	HR	TB	R	RBI	TBB	IBB	SO	HBP	SH	SF	SB	CS	SB%	GDP	Avg	OBP	SLG
1999 Williamsprt	A- Pit	31	109	27	2	0	0	29	26	8	21	0	26	0	2	1	16	1	.94	1	.248	.366	.266
Hickory	A Pit	23	85	25	1	0	0	26	14	5	17	0	19	1	1	0	12	2	.86	0	.294	.417	.306
2000 Lynchburg	A+ Pit	98	355	93	9	1	0	104	52	26	58	0	70	8	4	1	37	10	.79	6	.262	.377	.293
2001 Lynchburg	A+ Pit	50	181	52	8	1	0	62	25	7	17	1	34	2	2	1	4	9	.31	1	.287	.353	.343
Altoona	AA Pit	63	161	53	7	0	0	60	20	13	14	1	21	2	1	1	16	6	.73	2	.329	.388	.373
3 Min. YEARS		265	891	250	27	2	0	281	137	59	127	2	170	13	10	4	85	28	.75	10	.281	.377	.315

Paco Martin

Bats: Right **Throws:** Right **Pos:** 2B-39; OF-25; SS-10; 3B-10; DH-7; PH-7   **Ht:** 5'10" **Wt:** 164 **Born:** 12/10/66 **Age:** 35

Year Team	Lg Org	G	AB	H	2B	3B	HR	TB	R	RBI	TBB	IBB	SO	HBP	SH	SF	SB	CS	SB%	GDP	Avg	OBP	SLG
1984 White Sox	R CWS	56	205	56	8	2	1	71	36	30	21	0	31	4	1	4	18	5	.78	3	.273	.346	.346
1985 Appleton	A CWS	30	96	19	2	0	0	21	15	5	9	0	23	0	3	0	2	2	.50	1	.198	.267	.219
Niagara Fal	A- CWS	60	217	55	9	0	1	67	22	13	7	0	41	1	5	0	6	4	.60	2	.253	.280	.309
1986 Appleton	A CWS	9	33	10	2	0	0	12	4	2	2	0	5	0	0	0	1	0	1.00	1	.303	.343	.364
1987 Chston-WV	A CWS	68	250	78	14	1	5	109	44	35	17	1	40	4	4	3	14	4	.78	1	.312	.361	.436
Peninsula	A+ CWS	41	162	42	6	1	1	53	21	18	18	0	19	1	0	4	11	6	.65	3	.259	.330	.327
1988 Tampa	A+ CWS	101	360	93	10	4	2	117	44	33	17	0	49	3	7	3	24	5	.83	13	.258	.295	.325
1990 Vancouver	AAA CWS	130	508	135	20	4	3	172	77	45	27	0	63	5	8	6	10	7	.59	14	.266	.306	.339
1991 Vancouver	AAA CWS	93	338	94	9	0	0	103	39	20	21	0	38	3	10	2	11	7	.61	14	.278	.324	.305
1992 Vancouver	AAA CWS	135	497	143	12	7	0	169	72	29	29	1	44	2	14	2	29	12	.71	11	.288	.328	.340
1993 Nashville	AAA CWS	137	580	179	21	6	9	239	87	74	26	0	59	2	12	6	31	5	.86	15	.309	.337	.412
1994 Nashville	AAA CWS	43	172	44	8	0	2	58	26	12	10	2	14	1	3	2	4	6	.40	6	.256	.297	.337
1996 Nashville	AAA CWS	17	68	14	3	0	2	23	9	8	4	0	10	1	1	1	0	1	.00	1	.206	.257	.338
1999 Syracuse	AAA Tor	81	319	94	11	2	5	124	45	34	12	0	33	2	3	2	14	1	.93	9	.295	.322	.389
2000 Indianapols	AAA Mil	117	406	114	26	3	1	149	51	41	22	0	38	3	11	3	10	3	.77	13	.281	.320	.367
2001 Calgary	AAA Fla	93	333	102	20	4	5	145	45	38	14	3	41	1	1	2	8	3	.73	13	.306	.334	.435
1993 Chicago	AL	8	14	5	0	0	0	5	3	2	1	0	1	0	0	0	0	0	—	0	.357	.400	.357
1994 Chicago	AL	45	131	36	7	1	1	48	19	16	9	0	16	0	3	2	4	2	.67	2	.275	.317	.366
1995 Chicago	AL	72	160	43	7	4	2	64	17	17	3	0	25	1	2	3	5	0	1.00	5	.269	.281	.400
1996 Chicago	AL	70	140	49	7	0	1	59	30	14	6	0	17	0	4	1	10	2	.83	4	.350	.374	.421
1997 Chicago	AL	71	213	64	7	1	2	79	24	27	6	0	31	0	0	0	1	4	.20	2	.300	.320	.371
1998 Anaheim	AL	79	195	42	2	0	1	47	20	13	6	0	29	0	3	2	3	1	.75	9	.215	.236	.241
1999 Toronto	AL	9	27	6	0	0	0	8	3	0	4	0	4	2	0	0	0	0	—	0	.222	.364	.296
14 Min. YEARS		1211	4544	1272	181	34	37	1632	637	437	256	7	548	33	83	40	194	70	.73	122	.280	.320	.359
7 Maj. YEARS		354	880	245	32	6	7	310	116	89	35	0	123	3	12	8	23	9	.72	24	.278	.306	.352

Chris Martine

Bats: Right Throws: Right Pos: C-54; DH-6; PH-3; PR-2; P-1 Ht: 6'2" Wt: 190 Born: 7/10/75 Age: 26

Year Team	Lg Org	G	AB	H	2B	3B	HR	TB	R	RBI	TBB	IBB	SO	HBP	SH	SF	SB	CS	SB%	GDP	Avg	OBP	SLG
1997 New Jersey	A- StL	47	142	30	5	0	0	35	22	12	22	0	37	2	0	3	0	0	—	3	.211	.320	.246
1998 Pr William	A+ StL	96	279	52	13	0	2	71	29	25	38	0	77	4	5	3	2	6	.25	4	.186	.290	.254
1999 Potomac	A+ StL	42	136	28	7	2	1	42	11	14	16	0	42	2	3	2	1	2	.33	3	.206	.295	.309
Arkansas	AA StL	18	40	6	1	0	0	7	3	1	2	0	12	4	2	0	0	0	—	1	.150	.261	.175
2000 Arkansas	AA StL	5	16	1	0	0	0	1	1	0	0	0	6	0	0	0	0	0	—	0	.063	.063	.063
2001 New Haven	AA StL	62	180	38	6	0	0	44	21	5	12	0	46	2	2	1	2	2	.50	3	.211	.267	.244
5 Min. YEARS		270	793	155	32	2	3	200	87	57	90	0	220	14	12	9	5	10	.33	14	.195	.286	.252

Jason Martines

Pitches: Right Bats: Left Pos: RP-63 Ht: 6'2" Wt: 190 Born: 1/21/76 Age: 26

Year Team	Lg Org	G	GS	CG	GF	IP	BFP	H	R	ER	HR	SH	SF	HB	TBB	IBB	SO	WP	Bk	W	L	Pct.	ShO	Sv	ERA
1997 Lethbridge	R+ Ari	22	0	0	6	43	180	45	15	15	4	1	1	2	11	0	34	1	0	3	3	.500	0	0	3.14
1998 Tucson	AAA Ari	1	0	0	0	1.1	6	0	0	0	0	0	0	0	2	0	2	0	0	0	0	—	0	0	0.00
High Desert	A+ Ari	5	0	0	1	10.2	50	16	10	9	3	1	2	0	3	0	7	1	0	0	1	.000	0	0	7.59
South Bend	A Ari	21	0	0	16	33.1	148	33	16	13	1	0	1	1	15	0	31	4	1	0	2	.000	0	0	3.51
1999 High Desert	A+ Ari	43	0	0	37	71.2	306	68	33	18	5	2	1	2	28	4	73	1	1	9	7	.563	0	9	2.26
2000 El Paso	AA Ari	55	0	0	20	86.1	356	72	32	27	3	2	6	4	27	3	77	0	0	9	1	.900	0	2	2.81
2001 Tucson	AAA Ari	12	0	0	5	18	94	31	19	18	4	2	1	2	7	1	15	1	1	0	3	.000	0	1	9.00
El Paso	AA Ari	51	0	0	15	69	290	62	32	23	3	4	5	8	20	3	49	0	0	4	3	.571	0	1	3.00
5 Min. YEARS		210	0	0	100	333.1	1430	327	157	123	23	12	17	19	113	11	288	8	3	25	20	.556	0	13	3.32

Belvani Martinez

Bats: Right Throws: Right Pos: OF-76; 2B-35; PH-7 Ht: 5'11" Wt: 172 Born: 12/14/78 Age: 23

Year Team	Lg Org	G	AB	H	2B	3B	HR	TB	R	RBI	TBB	IBB	SO	HBP	SH	SF	SB	CS	SB%	GDP	Avg	OBP	SLG
1997 Diamondbcks	R Ari	30	134	43	11	2	0	58	25	11	3	0	18	3	2	2	7	2	.78	3	.321	.345	.433
Lethbridge	R+ Ari	25	90	31	4	1	6	55	21	13	5	0	13	4	1	1	4	1	.80	2	.344	.400	.611
1998 South Bend	A Ari	18	80	20	2	0	0	22	11	6	3	0	22	2	0	0	5	1	.83	3	.250	.294	.275
Lethbridge	R+ Ari	63	256	78	11	3	5	110	56	25	12	0	30	4	2	3	30	10	.75	7	.305	.342	.430
1999 High Desert	A+ Ari	109	477	159	23	9	8	224	84	55	18	1	69	9	3	4	35	30	.54	7	.333	.366	.470
2000 Carolina	AA Col	115	406	101	18	4	3	136	50	36	11	2	63	5	6	0	25	10	.71	11	.249	.277	.335
2001 Carolina	AA Col	115	430	112	21	7	5	162	46	37	7	1	59	10	11	3	29	13	.69	9	.260	.287	.377
5 Min. YEARS		475	1873	544	90	26	27	767	293	183	59	4	274	37	25	13	135	67	.67	42	.290	.323	.410

Casey Martinez

Bats: Right Throws: Right Pos: C-26; DH-8; PH-6; 1B-2; P-1 Ht: 5'11" Wt: 200 Born: 8/31/77 Age: 24

Year Team	Lg Org	G	AB	H	2B	3B	HR	TB	R	RBI	TBB	IBB	SO	HBP	SH	SF	SB	CS	SB%	GDP	Avg	OBP	SLG
2000 Medcine Hat	R Tor	9	25	7	3	0	1	13	5	3	6	0	7	1	0	0	0	0	—	1	.280	.438	.520
Queens	A- Tor	7	22	3	0	0	0	3	2	0	1	0	7	1	1	0	0	0	—	0	.136	.208	.136
2001 Dunedin	A+ Tor	7	17	3	1	0	0	4	1	3	0	0	2	0	1	0	0	0	—	0	.176	.176	.235
Syracuse	AAA Tor	5	5	3	0	0	0	3	1	1	0	0	1	0	0	0	0	0	—	0	.600	.600	.600
Chston-WV	A Tor	27	83	12	2	0	1	17	7	4	2	0	23	1	0	0	1	0	1.00	1	.145	.174	.205
2 Min. YEARS		55	152	28	6	0	2	40	16	11	9	0	40	3	2	0	1	0	1.00	2	.184	.244	.263

Eddy Martinez

Bats: Right Throws: Right Pos: SS-92; 3B-16; 2B-13; PR-2; DH-1; PH-1 Ht: 6'2" Wt: 173 Born: 10/23/77 Age: 24

Year Team	Lg Org	G	AB	H	2B	3B	HR	TB	R	RBI	TBB	IBB	SO	HBP	SH	SF	SB	CS	SB%	GDP	Avg	OBP	SLG
1995 Bluefield	R+ Bal	57	185	57	11	3	1	77	42	35	23	0	42	5	1	1	5	5	.50	1	.308	.397	.416
1996 Frederick	A+ Bal	74	244	54	4	0	2	64	21	25	21	0	48	2	1	1	13	8	.62	5	.221	.287	.262
Bluefield	R+ Bal	37	122	27	3	0	1	33	18	15	13	0	29	2	3	0	15	5	.75	1	.221	.307	.270
1997 Bowie	AA Bal	16	45	7	3	0	0	10	3	1	6	0	12	0	3	0	2	0	1.00	0	.156	.255	.222
Frederick	A+ Bal	54	174	42	6	0	1	51	14	14	19	0	43	2	3	2	6	7	.46	9	.241	.320	.293
Rochester	AAA Bal	12	27	2	1	0	0	3	0	3	1	0	8	0	1	0	0	0	—	0	.074	.107	.111
1998 Delmarva	A Bal	113	361	95	16	1	2	119	46	39	33	0	66	2	13	3	21	7	.75	9	.263	.326	.330
Bowie	AA Bal	5	14	4	0	0	0	4	1	1	1	0	3	0	1	0	0	0	—	0	.286	.333	.286
1999 Frederick	A+ Bal	127	416	121	21	1	2	150	68	55	52	1	99	13	5	5	8	4	.67	6	.291	.383	.361
2000 Rochester	AAA Bal	13	36	8	2	0	0	10	7	1	5	0	7	0	0	0	1	0	1.00	1	.222	.317	.278
Frederick	A+ Bal	40	152	46	10	1	0	58	23	15	24	0	34	2	5	0	7	6	.54	2	.303	.404	.382
Bowie	AA Bal	41	127	32	2	2	1	41	17	20	17	1	21	5	3	1	0	2	—	2	.252	.360	.323
2001 Bowie	AA Bal	32	122	35	1	0	1	39	21	10	14	0	31	1	1	2	5	3	.63	2	.287	.360	.320
Rochester	AAA Bal	90	314	85	14	1	7	122	42	33	21	0	66	4	10	1	7	0	1.00	6	.271	.324	.389
7 Min. YEARS		711	2339	615	94	9	18	781	323	267	250	2	509	38	50	16	90	45	.67	48	.263	.342	.334

Gabby Martinez

Bats: Right Throws: Right Pos: 2B-39; OF-14; SS-11; PH-11; 3B-3; DH-3; PR-2; 1B-1 Ht: 6'2" Wt: 170 Born: 1/7/74 Age: 28

Year Team	Lg Org	G	AB	H	2B	3B	HR	TB	R	RBI	TBB	IBB	SO	HBP	SH	SF	SB	CS	SB%	GDP	Avg	OBP	SLG
1992 Brewers	R Mil	48	165	43	7	2	0	54	29	24	12	0	19	3	2	2	7	5	.58	3	.261	.319	.327
1993 Beloit	A Mil	94	285	69	14	5	0	93	40	24	14	0	52	1	15	4	22	10	.69	2	.242	.276	.326
1994 Stockton	A+ Mil	112	364	90	18	3	0	114	37	32	17	1	66	4	4	4	19	11	.63	8	.247	.285	.313
1995 Stockton	A+ Mil	64	213	55	13	3	1	77	25	20	10	0	25	2	9	3	13	6	.68	6	.258	.294	.362
El Paso	AA Mil	44	133	37	3	2	0	44	13	11	2	0	22	2	3	1	5	1	.83	2	.278	.297	.331

186

Year Team	Lg Org	G	AB	H	2B	3B	HR	TB	R	RBI	TBB	IBB	SO	HBP	SH	SF	SB	CS	SB%	GDP	Avg	OBP	SLG
								BATTING									BASERUNNING				PERCENTAGES		
1996 El Paso	AA Mil	91	338	85	11	8	0	112	44	37	18	1	57	2	13	4	8	9	.47	8	.251	.290	.331
1997 Yankees	R NYY	2	5	2	0	0	1	5	3	2	1	0	0	0	0	0	2	0	1.00	0	.400	.500	1.000
Norwich	AA NYY	77	312	100	12	5	6	140	49	54	11	0	44	5	10	3	21	6	.78	5	.321	.350	.449
1998 Columbus	AAA NYY	36	131	31	3	1	0	36	17	8	4	0	22	1	2	1	5	3	.63	6	.237	.263	.275
Tampa	A+ NYY	44	166	53	8	1	5	78	26	24	5	2	20	3	1	0	21	6	.78	5	.319	.351	.470
1999 Charlotte	AAA CWS	16	49	14	1	0	4	27	8	5	5	0	6	0	3	0	3	3	.50	2	.286	.352	.551
2000 Long Island	IND —	10	42	11	3	0	1	17	7	6	2	0	6	1	1	0	9	0	1.00	0	.262	.311	.405
West Tenn	AA ChC	13	42	9	1	0	2	16	5	5	3	1	6	0	2	0	5	2	.71	1	.214	.267	.381
Iowa	AAA ChC	25	65	11	1	0	1	15	6	5	1	0	9	1	1	0	2	1	.67	1	.169	.194	.231
Binghamton	AA NYM	48	165	41	4	3	2	57	22	12	11	0	22	0	6	0	8	8	.50	8	.248	.295	.345
2001 Binghamton	AA NYM	25	87	23	6	2	1	36	6	10	3	0	14	2	1	0	8	2	.80	0	.264	.304	.414
Norfolk	AAA NYM	48	149	39	6	1	0	47	23	6	12	0	19	1	4	0	9	5	.64	1	.262	.321	.315
10 Min. YEARS		797	2711	713	111	36	24	968	360	285	131	5	409	28	77	22	167	78	.68	56	.263	.302	.357

Greg Martinez

Bats: Both **Throws:** Right **Pos:** OF-81; DH-5   **Ht:** 5'10" **Wt:** 168 **Born:** 1/27/72 **Age:** 30

Year Team	Lg Org	G	AB	H	2B	3B	HR	TB	R	RBI	TBB	IBB	SO	HBP	SH	SF	SB	CS	SB%	GDP	Avg	OBP	SLG
								BATTING									BASERUNNING				PERCENTAGES		
1993 Brewers	R Mil	5	19	12	0	0	0	12	6	3	4	0	0	1	0	0	7	1	.88	0	.632	.708	.632
Helena	R+ Mil	52	183	53	4	2	0	61	45	19	30	0	26	6	3	5	30	6	.83	0	.290	.397	.333
1994 Beloit	A Mil	81	224	62	8	1	0	72	39	20	25	1	32	3	6	1	27	11	.71	4	.277	.356	.321
1995 Stockton	A+ Mil	114	410	113	8	2	0	125	80	43	69	1	64	2	10	1	55	9	.86	7	.276	.382	.305
1996 Stockton	A+ Mil	73	286	82	5	1	0	89	51	26	29	0	34	0	8	2	30	9	.77	3	.287	.350	.311
El Paso	AA Mil	41	166	52	2	2	1	61	27	21	13	0	19	3	6	1	14	4	.78	1	.313	.372	.367
1997 El Paso	AA Mil	95	381	111	10	10	1	144	75	29	32	0	55	3	9	2	39	7	.85	5	.291	.349	.378
Tucson	AAA Mil	3	12	5	2	0	0	7	2	3	0	0	1	0	0	0	1	0			.417	.417	.583
1998 Louisville	AAA Mil	115	376	98	4	11	4	136	65	25	51	0	80	0	10	0	43	7	.86	3	.261	.349	.362
1999 Huntsville	AA Mil	25	98	27	3	2	0	34	18	6	12	1	13	0	1	0	8	2	.80	2	.276	.355	.347
Louisville	AAA Mil	107	419	111	13	4	4	144	79	29	53	0	50	4	5	1	48	7	.87	10	.265	.352	.344
2000 Athletics	R Oak	6	22	5	0	0	0	5	4	2	4	0	5	1	0	0	2	0	1.00	1	.227	.370	.227
Modesto	A+ Oak	3	11	4	0	0	0	4	1	0	2	0	1	0	0	0	1	1	.50	0	.364	.500	.364
Midland	AA Oak	28	81	22	1	1	0	25	13	7	12	0	14	0	2	0	10	1	.91	2	.272	.366	.309
2001 St. George	IND —	24	101	46	11	4	0	65	27	22	13	0	9	0	2	1	15	2	.88	3	.455	.513	.644
Durham	AAA TB	62	242	71	6	2	1	84	36	21	29	0	46	4	5	1	14	7	.67	3	.293	.377	.347
1998 Milwaukee	NL	13	3	0	0	0	0	0	0	0	2	0	1	0	2	0	2	0	1.00	0	.000	.250	.000
9 Min. YEARS		834	3031	874	77	42	11	1068	568	276	378	3	448	28	67	15	343	74	.82	47	.288	.371	.352

Gustavo Martinez

Pitches: Right **Bats:** Right **Pos:** SP-16; RP-3   **Ht:** 6'0" **Wt:** 175 **Born:** 11/9/80 **Age:** 21

Year Team	Lg Org	G	GS	CG	GF	IP	BFP	H	R	ER	HR	SH	SF	HB	TBB	IBB	SO	WP	Bk	W	L	Pct.	ShO	Sv	ERA
		HOW MUCH HE PITCHED						WHAT HE GAVE UP												THE RESULTS					
2000 Mariners	R Sea	17	1	0	4	42.2	197	42	27	17	0	0	0	3	25	0	53	3	0	6	3	.667	0	1	3.59
2001 San Antonio	AA Sea	3	0	0	2	9.1	34	5	2	2	2	0	1	2	6	0	6	0	0	0	0	—	0	0	1.93
Tacoma	AAA Sea	1	1	0	0	6	24	2	1	1	0	0	1	0	4	0	7	0	0	1	0	1.000	0	0	1.50
Everett	A- Sea	15	15	0	0	84.1	356	62	30	25	4	3	2	18	34	0	100	8	0	5	3	.625	0	0	2.67
2 Min. YEARS		36	17	0	6	142.1	611	111	60	45	6	3	2	23	65	0	166	11	0	12	6	.667	0	1	2.85

Javier Martinez

Pitches: Right **Bats:** Right **Pos:** RP-17   **Ht:** 6'2" **Wt:** 235 **Born:** 2/5/77 **Age:** 25

Year Team	Lg Org	G	GS	CG	GF	IP	BFP	H	R	ER	HR	SH	SF	HB	TBB	IBB	SO	WP	Bk	W	L	Pct.	ShO	Sv	ERA
		HOW MUCH HE PITCHED						WHAT HE GAVE UP												THE RESULTS					
1994 Huntington	R+ ChC	9	8	0	1	35	147	24	20	15	1	1	2	3	21	0	31	9	2	2	1	.667	0	0	3.86
1995 Rockford	A ChC	18	18	1	0	104.2	455	100	56	46	6	5	4	12	39	0	53	15	2	6	6	.500	0	0	3.96
1996 Cubs	R ChC	3	3	0	0	15	62	11	4	1	0	0	0	1	6	0	15	1	0	2	1	.667	0	0	0.60
Rockford	A ChC	10	10	3	0	59	250	49	26	22	5	2	2	1	30	0	53	9	0	4	3	.571	0	0	3.36
1997 Daytona	A+ ChC	9	9	2	0	51.1	238	65	40	33	8	1	3	3	26	0	34	3	2	2	6	.250	0	0	5.79
Rockford	A ChC	17	17	1	0	79	369	85	61	50	7	3	2	3	50	1	70	10	0	1	7	.125	0	0	5.70
1999 Hickory	A Pit	6	0	0	0	7.2	36	6	6	3	0	1	0	0	6	0	13	1	0	0	0	—	0	0	3.52
Altoona	AA Pit	10	0	0	3	10.1	55	11	8	7	1	0	1	0	14	0	16	0	0	0	0	—	0	0	6.10
2000 Dayton	A Cin	16	1	0	7	19	82	20	13	12	3	0	1	1	10	1	24	1	0	4	1	.800	0	0	6.35
2001 Mudville	A+ Cin	16	0	0	8	16.2	68	14	4	4	2	0	0	1	6	0	21	1	0	3	0	1.000	0	0	2.16
Chattanooga	AA Cin	1	0	0	0	0.1	7	2	6	5	1	1	0	0	3	0	0	0	0	0	0	—	0	0	135.00
1998 Pittsburgh	NL	37	0	0	13	41	199	39	32	22	5	1	3	4	34	1	42	5	0	0	1	.000	0	0	4.83
7 Min. YEARS		115	66	7	19	396	1769	387	244	198	34	14	14	25	211	2	330	50	6	24	25	.490	0	1	4.50

Jesus Martinez

Pitches: Left **Bats:** Left **Pos:** RP-17   **Ht:** 6'2" **Wt:** 145 **Born:** 3/13/74 **Age:** 28

Year Team	Lg Org	G	GS	CG	GF	IP	BFP	H	R	ER	HR	SH	SF	HB	TBB	IBB	SO	WP	Bk	W	L	Pct.	ShO	Sv	ERA
		HOW MUCH HE PITCHED						WHAT HE GAVE UP												THE RESULTS					
1992 Great Falls	R+ LA	6	6	0	0	18.1	112	36	30	27	4	0	0	2	21	0	23	9	0	0	3	.000	0	0	13.25
Dodgers	R LA	7	7	1	0	41	174	38	19	15	1	2	0	1	11	0	39	5	0	1	4	.200	0	0	3.29
1993 Bakersfield	A+ LA	30	21	0	2	145.2	653	144	95	67	12	5	11	5	75	0	108	6	5	4	13	.235	0	0	4.14
1994 San Antonio	AA LA	1	1	0	0	4	14	3	2	2	0	0	0	0	2	0	3	0	0	1	0	1.000	0	0	4.50
Vero Beach	A+ LA	18	18	1	0	87.2	386	91	65	61	7	2	3	6	43	0	69	3	0	7	9	.438	1	0	6.26
1995 San Antonio	AA LA	24	24	1	0	139.2	603	129	64	55	6	7	4	7	71	0	83	16	4	6	9	.400	0	0	3.54
Albuquerque	AAA LA	2	0	0	0	4	20	4	2	2	0	1	1	1	4	2	5	0	0	1	1	.500	0	0	4.50
1996 San Antonio	AA LA	27	27	0	0	161.2	706	157	90	79	7	5	1	5	92	0	124	20	0	10	13	.435	0	0	4.40
1997 Albuquerque	AAA LA	26	12	0	6	84	404	112	64	58	8	3	1	1	52	0	80	15	1	7	1	.875	0	0	6.21
1998 Indianapols	AAA Cin	22	18	0	0	93.1	425	119	78	71	10	4	4	5	42	0	39	7	3	7	6	.538	0	0	6.85
1999 Sarasota	A+ Bos	16	2	0	8	32.2	151	36	20	19	2	2	6	3	17	1	20	5	0	1	2	.333	0	0	5.23

187

Year Team	Lg Org	G	GS	CG	GF	IP	BFP	H	R	ER	HR	SH	SF	HB	TBB	IBB	SO	WP	Bk	W	L	Pct.	ShO	Sv	ERA
2000 Akron	AA Cle	7	0	0	1	14.2	68	17	8	6	2	0	0	1	10	0	5	1	0	0	1	.000	0	0	3.68
Kinston	A+ Cle	2	0	0	2	4	17	3	0	0	0	0	0	0	3	0	3	0	0	0	0	—	0	0	0.00
Binghamton	AA NYM	6	4	0	0	20	90	20	11	10	1	0	2	2	12	0	16	2	1	1	1	.500	0	0	4.50
2001 Binghamton	AA NYM	17	0	0	7	30	136	33	17	17	2	2	0	0	16	3	24	5	0	2	0	1.000	0	0	5.10
10 Min. YEARS		211	140	3	27	880.2	3959	942	565	489	62	33	39	39	471	6	641	94	14	47	64	.423	1	0	5.00

Jose Martinez

Pitches: Right **Bats:** Right **Pos:** SP-14; RP-11   **Ht:** 6'0" **Wt:** 165 **Born:** 2/4/75 **Age:** 27

Year Team	Lg Org	G	GS	CG	GF	IP	BFP	H	R	ER	HR	SH	SF	HB	TBB	IBB	SO	WP	Bk	W	L	Pct.	ShO	Sv	ERA
1996 Chston-SC	A Tex	11	1	0	3	21	105	34	24	23	7	0	1	2	7	1	17	6	2	1	2	.333	0	0	9.86
Hudson Val	A- Tex	16	5	0	4	54.2	233	56	35	23	3	3	2	0	11	0	38	6	3	2	3	.400	0	0	3.79
1997 Charlotte	A+ Tex	26	0	0	13	57.2	229	52	25	24	6	3	0	0	13	0	48	4	1	3	1	.750	0	2	3.75
1998 Tulsa	AA Tex	7	7	0	0	34.1	160	46	34	29	6	1	2	2	14	0	21	3	2	2	2	.500	0	0	7.60
Charlotte	A+ Tex	19	19	2	0	123.2	521	120	55	38	12	3	3	5	28	3	86	5	3	7	5	.583	0	0	2.77
1999 Tulsa	AA Tex	33	9	0	10	98	441	112	69	59	16	2	6	2	36	0	70	2	1	4	4	.500	0	3	5.42
2000 Tulsa	AA Tex	18	13	1	1	103.1	431	97	44	36	7	6	2	0	21	0	79	10	0	5	6	.455	1	0	3.14
Oklahoma	AAA Tex	11	10	0	0	53	248	77	49	43	10	2	2	4	14	0	23	6	0	2	5	.286	0	0	7.30
2001 Oklahoma	AAA Tex	1	1	0	0	6.2	22	1	0	0	0	0	0	0	1	0	3	0	0	0	0	—	0	0	0.00
Tulsa	AA Tex	24	13	0	3	93.1	419	98	61	49	12	2	4	5	39	0	58	11	1	6	6	.500	0	0	4.73
6 Min. YEARS		166	78	3	34	645.2	2809	693	396	324	79	22	22	20	184	4	443	53	13	32	34	.485	1	5	4.52

Louis Martinez

Bats: Right **Throws:** Right **Pos:** 2B-32; PH-13; 3B-9; SS-6; PR-2   **Ht:** 6'0" **Wt:** 175 **Born:** 11/1/76 **Age:** 25

Year Team	Lg Org	G	AB	H	2B	3B	HR	TB	R	RBI	TBB	IBB	SO	HBP	SH	SF	SB	CS	SB%	GDP	Avg	OBP	SLG
1999 Braves	R Atl	23	87	28	4	1	0	34	8	14	8	0	13	1	2	0	0	2	.00	1	.322	.385	.391
Myrtle Bch	A+ Atl	5	15	2	1	0	0	3	1	0	1	0	2	0	0	0	0	0	—	0	.133	.188	.200
2000 Macon	A Atl	33	114	25	3	0	0	28	16	4	11	0	10	2	2	0	4	1	.80	2	.219	.299	.246
Richmond	AAA Atl	28	71	12	3	1	0	17	3	2	2	1	12	0	3	1	2	0	1.00	0	.169	.189	.239
2001 Myrtle Bch	A+ Atl	2	7	1	0	0	0	1	0	0	0	0	0	1	0	0	0	0	—	0	.143	.143	.143
Richmond	AAA Atl	9	24	1	0	0	0	1	2	0	3	0	1	1	0	0	0	1	.00	1	.042	.040	.042
Greenville	AA Atl	46	99	18	3	0	0	21	11	2	4	0	14	2	2	0	1	0	1.00	4	.182	.229	.212
3 Min. YEARS		146	417	87	14	2	0	105	40	24	26	1	54	5	11	2	7	4	.64	8	.209	.262	.252

Luis Martinez

Pitches: Left **Bats:** Left **Pos:** SP-22; RP-7   **Ht:** 6'1" **Wt:** 183 **Born:** 1/20/80 **Age:** 22

Year Team	Lg Org	G	GS	CG	GF	IP	BFP	H	R	ER	HR	SH	SF	HB	TBB	IBB	SO	WP	Bk	W	L	Pct.	ShO	Sv	ERA
1998 Helena	R+ Mil	17	10	0	2	48	275	64	73	54	5	1	2	5	66	0	47	14	4	0	9	.000	0	0	10.13
1999 Ogden	R+ Mil	15	7	0	4	50.1	259	66	65	39	3	1	3	3	34	0	43	13	0	0	7	.000	0	1	6.97
2000 Beloit	A Mil	28	13	0	7	92.2	412	71	49	39	8	0	6	5	61	1	77	7	1	5	7	.417	0	0	3.79
2001 Huntsville	AA Mil	7	0	0	0	9.1	48	13	7	7	0	0	0	0	9	0	13	0	0	0	0	—	0	0	6.75
High Desert	A+ Mil	22	22	0	0	112.2	498	112	67	65	9	2	2	4	64	0	121	9	1	8	9	.471	0	0	5.19
4 Min. YEARS		89	52	0	13	313	1492	326	261	204	25	4	13	17	234	1	301	43	6	13	32	.289	0	1	5.87

Willie Martinez

Pitches: Right **Bats:** Right **Pos:** SP-20; RP-1   **Ht:** 6'2" **Wt:** 180 **Born:** 1/4/78 **Age:** 24

Year Team	Lg Org	G	GS	CG	GF	IP	BFP	H	R	ER	HR	SH	SF	HB	TBB	IBB	SO	WP	Bk	W	L	Pct.	ShO	Sv	ERA
1995 Burlington	R+ Cle	11	11	0	0	40	209	64	50	42	1	2	2	4	25	0	36	6	3	0	7	.000	0	0	9.45
1996 Watertown	A- Cle	14	14	1	0	90	358	79	25	24	5	2	0	0	21	2	92	6	0	6	5	.545	1	0	2.40
1997 Kinston	A+ Cle	23	23	1	0	137	568	125	61	47	13	4	3	4	42	2	120	4	0	8	2	.800	0	0	3.09
1998 Akron	AA Cle	26	26	2	0	154	661	169	92	75	15	6	2	6	44	0	117	10	1	9	7	.563	1	0	4.38
1999 Akron	AA Cle	24	24	0	0	147.1	639	163	83	67	20	5	2	3	45	0	91	8	0	9	8	.529	0	0	4.09
Buffalo	AAA Cle	4	4	0	0	22.1	101	28	17	17	3	1	0	2	7	1	12	0	0	2	2	.500	0	0	6.85
2000 Buffalo	AAA Cle	28	22	0	3	135.1	598	132	72	67	16	6	3	5	67	1	95	11	1	8	5	.615	0	1	4.46
2001 Edmonton	AAA Min	21	20	0	0	112.1	512	147	80	70	18	1	5	4	39	1	86	8	0	7	8	.467	0	0	5.61
2000 Cleveland	AL	1	0	0	0	3	11	1	1	1	1	0	0	0	1	0	1	0	0	0	0	—	0	0	3.00
7 Min. YEARS		151	144	4	3	838.1	3645	907	480	409	91	27	17	28	290	7	649	53	5	49	44	.527	2	1	4.39

Onan Masaoka

Pitches: Left **Bats:** Right **Pos:** RP-40; SP-5   **Ht:** 6'0" **Wt:** 188 **Born:** 10/27/77 **Age:** 24

Year Team	Lg Org	G	GS	CG	GF	IP	BFP	H	R	ER	HR	SH	SF	HB	TBB	IBB	SO	WP	Bk	W	L	Pct.	ShO	Sv	ERA
1995 Yakima	A- LA	15	7	0	5	49.1	225	28	25	20	2	1	0	4	47	0	75	12	4	2	4	.333	0	3	3.65
1996 Savannah	A LA	13	13	0	0	65	283	55	35	31	7	1	0	6	35	0	80	3	2	2	5	.286	0	0	4.29
1997 Vero Beach	A+ LA	28	24	2	3	148.2	612	113	72	64	16	6	4	10	55	1	132	10	1	6	8	.429	1	0	3.87
1998 San Antonio	AA LA	27	20	1	2	110	500	114	79	65	11	2	5	6	63	0	94	3	1	6	6	.500	1	1	5.32
2000 Albuquerque	AAA LA	18	5	0	4	37.1	172	31	17	16	1	1	1	0	36	1	22	2	0	3	1	.750	0	0	3.86
2001 Las Vegas	AAA LA	31	5	0	4	73	331	87	49	45	9	3	6	3	28	4	61	5	0	8	4	.667	0	1	5.55
Charlotte	AAA CWS	14	0	0	4	14.2	59	11	8	7	2	1	0	1	23	1	22	0	0	0	1	.000	0	5	4.30
1999 Los Angeles	NL	54	0	0	12	66.2	300	55	33	32	8	1	2	2	47	3	61	3	0	2	4	.333	0	2	4.32
2000 Los Angeles	NL	29	0	0	3	27	116	23	12	12	2	0	0	1	15	1	27	2	0	1	1	.500	0	0	4.00
6 Min. YEARS		146	74	3	26	498	2182	439	285	248	48	15	16	30	269	6	486	35	8	27	29	.482	2	11	4.48
2 Maj. YEARS		83	0	0	15	93.2	416	78	45	44	10	1	2	3	62	4	88	5	0	3	5	.375	0	1	4.23

Damon Mashore

Bats: Right **Throws:** Right **Pos:** OF-72; PH-8; PR-1 **Ht:** 5'11" **Wt:** 209 **Born:** 10/31/69 **Age:** 32

Year Team	Lg Org	G	AB	H	2B	3B	HR	TB	R	RBI	TBB	IBB	SO	HBP	SH	SF	SB	CS	SB%	GDP	Avg	OBP	SLG
1991 Sou Oregon	A- Oak	73	264	72	17	6	6	119	48	31	34	1	94	2	2	3	15	5	.75	6	.273	.356	.451
1992 Modesto	A+ Oak	124	471	133	22	3	18	215	91	64	73	3	136	6	5	1	29	17	.63	6	.282	.385	.456
1993 Huntsville	AA Oak	70	253	59	7	2	3	79	35	20	25	0	64	4	1	2	18	4	.82	5	.233	.310	.312
1994 Athletics	R Oak	11	34	14	2	0	0	16	6	6	4	0	3	1	0	1	1	1	.50	3	.412	.475	.471
Huntsville	AA Oak	59	210	47	11	2	3	71	24	21	13	1	53	0	1	3	6	1	.86	3	.224	.265	.338
1995 Edmonton	AAA Oak	117	337	101	19	5	1	133	50	37	42	0	77	5	3	3	17	5	.77	9	.300	.382	.395
1996 Edmonton	AAA Oak	50	183	49	9	1	8	84	32	29	19	0	48	5	2	2	6	2	.75	3	.268	.349	.459
1998 Vancouver	AAA Ana	42	143	39	7	0	2	52	19	15	18	0	28	1	2	0	1	1	.50	2	.273	.358	.364
1999 Fresno	AAA SF	110	347	91	20	1	20	173	62	69	38	0	98	4	4	2	7	3	.70	15	.262	.340	.499
2000 Tucson	AAA Ari	23	66	12	2	1	0	16	10	3	14	0	11	1	0	0	2	1	.67	3	.182	.333	.242
Yuma	IND —	16	63	27	10	0	1	40	17	15	8	1	13	1	0	0	6	1	.86	1	.429	.500	.635
2001 Memphis	AAA StL	79	289	86	17	1	7	126	35	37	18	0	62	5	0	2	3	4	.43	5	.298	.347	.436
1996 Oakland	AL	50	105	28	7	1	3	46	20	12	16	0	31	1	1	1	4	0	1.00	2	.267	.366	.438
1997 Oakland	AL	92	279	69	10	2	3	92	55	18	50	1	82	5	7	1	5	4	.56	5	.247	.370	.330
1998 Anaheim	AL	43	98	23	6	0	2	35	13	11	9	0	22	3	1	0	1	0	1.00	3	.235	.318	.357
10 Min. YEARS		774	2660	730	143	22	69	1124	429	347	306	6	687	35	20	19	111	45	.71	61	.274	.355	.423
3 Maj. YEARS		185	482	120	23	3	8	173	88	41	75	1	135	9	9	2	10	4	.71	10	.249	.359	.359

Justin Mashore

Bats: Right **Throws:** Right **Pos:** OF-43; PH-11; DH-4 **Ht:** 5'9" **Wt:** 190 **Born:** 2/14/72 **Age:** 30

Year Team	Lg Org	G	AB	H	2B	3B	HR	TB	R	RBI	TBB	IBB	SO	HBP	SH	SF	SB	CS	SB%	GDP	Avg	OBP	SLG
1991 Bristol	R+ Det	58	177	36	3	0	3	48	29	11	28	1	65	0	2	0	17	6	.74	1	.203	.312	.271
1992 Fayettevlle	A Det	120	401	96	18	3	4	132	54	43	36	2	117	3	9	1	31	8	.79	3	.239	.306	.329
1993 Lakeland	A+ Det	118	442	113	11	4	3	141	64	30	37	4	92	6	16	5	26	13	.67	9	.256	.318	.319
1994 Trenton	AA Det	131	450	100	13	5	7	144	63	45	36	0	120	3	8	3	31	7	.82	9	.222	.283	.320
1995 Toledo	AAA Det	72	223	49	4	3	4	71	32	21	14	1	62	3	9	2	12	9	.57	1	.220	.273	.318
Jacksnville	AA Det	40	148	36	8	2	4	60	26	15	6	0	41	3	3	0	5	1	.83	2	.243	.287	.405
1996 Jacksnville	AA Det	120	453	129	27	8	7	193	67	50	33	1	97	4	7	2	17	13	.57	10	.285	.337	.426
1997 Padres	R SD	7	26	7	3	0	0	10	4	3	5	1	13	0	1	0	1	1	.50	1	.269	.387	.385
Mobile	AA SD	90	281	67	10	5	11	120	53	41	32	2	70	5	3	3	11	8	.58	8	.238	.324	.427
1998 Chico	IND —	87	369	107	18	5	14	177	88	69	31	3	91	5	4	2	45	15	.75	6	.290	.351	.480
1999 Trenton	AA Bos	5	16	6	2	2	0	12	3	5	1	1	4	0	0	0	1	0	1.00	0	.375	.412	.750
Sarasota	A+ Bos	17	49	8	3	0	2	17	6	4	5	0	13	0	1	0	1	0	1.00	1	.163	.241	.347
St. Lucie	A+ NYM	28	104	22	4	2	1	33	13	10	7	1	25	2	0	1	1	4	.20	3	.212	.272	.317
Binghamton	AA NYM	13	42	9	2	0	1	14	4	3	0	0	13	1	1	0	1	0	1.00	2	.214	.233	.333
2000 Yuma	IND —	66	269	91	19	6	8	146	61	47	30	2	55	4	3	3	13	4	.76	5	.338	.408	.543
Carolina	AA Col	17	43	10	1	1	1	16	4	4	4	1	8	2	0	0	2	1	.67	2	.233	.327	.372
2001 Carolina	AA Col	57	172	43	12	0	4	67	21	23	11	1	42	1	1	2	4	3	.57	3	.250	.296	.390
11 Min. YEARS		1046	3665	929	158	46	74	1401	592	424	316	21	928	42	68	24	219	93	.70	66	.253	.318	.382

Jared Mathis

Bats: Right **Throws:** Right **Pos:** OF-37; PH-23; 3B-15; C-8; 2B-8; SS-3; PR-1; P-1 **Ht:** 5'10" **Wt:** 180 **Born:** 8/8/75 **Age:** 26

Year Team	Lg Org	G	AB	H	2B	3B	HR	TB	R	RBI	TBB	IBB	SO	HBP	SH	SF	SB	CS	SB%	GDP	Avg	OBP	SLG
1997 Lafayette	IND —	10	41	12	0	0	1	15	4	1	2	0	3	0	1	0	1	2	.33	1	.293	.326	.366
Ogden	R+ Mil	54	197	55	14	0	0	69	30	29	6	0	20	4	4	1	7	3	.70	3	.279	.313	.350
1998 Beloit	A Mil	24	90	24	5	0	0	29	12	3	1	0	8	1	4	0	1	0	1.00	4	.267	.283	.322
Stockton	A+ Mil	69	204	59	6	0	0	65	24	17	3	0	17	4	8	3	8	0	1.00	3	.289	.308	.319
1999 Stockton	A+ Mil	23	61	14	1	0	0	15	7	10	2	0	3	2	0	1	1	3	.25	1	.230	.273	.246
Huntsville	AA Mil	74	218	49	5	1	2	62	23	24	8	0	32	1	9	1	2	3	.40	2	.225	.254	.284
2000 Huntsville	AA Mil	101	351	91	23	1	2	122	49	21	12	1	49	13	9	1	5	9	.36	6	.259	.308	.348
2001 Huntsville	AA Mil	87	204	50	11	1	2	69	15	17	6	1	25	5	8	0	1	1	.50	4	.245	.284	.338
5 Min. YEARS		442	1366	354	65	3	7	446	164	122	40	2	157	30	43	7	25	22	.53	24	.259	.294	.327

Julius Matos

Bats: Right **Throws:** Right **Pos:** SS-109; 2B-17; PH-3; PR-2 **Ht:** 5'11" **Wt:** 175 **Born:** 12/12/74 **Age:** 27

Year Team	Lg Org	G	AB	H	2B	3B	HR	TB	R	RBI	TBB	IBB	SO	HBP	SH	SF	SB	CS	SB%	GDP	Avg	OBP	SLG
1994 Watertown	A- Cle	43	138	34	2	2	0	40	13	18	13	0	33	0	0	2	3	2	.60	6	.246	.307	.290
1995 Columbus	A Cle	52	155	38	7	3	0	51	16	13	11	1	21	3	1	0	2	2	.50	8	.245	.308	.329
1996 Thunder Bay	IND —	82	295	81	13	0	3	103	33	32	14	0	48	2	5	1	8	7	.53	9	.275	.311	.349
1997 Sioux City	IND —	83	353	94	12	3	6	130	64	44	20	0	38	4	1	2	8	7	.53	4	.266	.311	.368
1998 High Desert	A+ Ari	111	439	132	27	4	4	179	70	60	23	0	40	2	7	8	19	13	.59	9	.301	.333	.408
1999 El Paso	AA Ari	120	425	119	17	5	5	161	54	41	13	0	37	1	4	3	5	2	.71	10	.280	.301	.379
2000 Mobile	AA SD	135	546	144	30	4	5	189	61	35	31	0	57	2	7	0	11	9	.55	13	.264	.306	.346
2001 Mobile	AA SD	19	67	22	6	0	0	28	13	2	1	0	5	1	2	1	1	2	.33	2	.328	.343	.418
Portland	AAA SD	106	383	107	12	2	7	144	40	34	15	2	48	6	3	3	6	8	.43	6	.279	.314	.376
8 Min. YEARS		751	2801	771	126	19	30	1025	364	279	141	3	327	21	30	20	63	52	.55	67	.275	.313	.366

Pascual Matos

Bats: Right **Throws:** Right **Pos:** C-74; 1B-5; PH-2 **Ht:** 6'2" **Wt:** 160 **Born:** 12/23/74 **Age:** 27

Year Team	Lg Org	G	AB	H	2B	3B	HR	TB	R	RBI	TBB	IBB	SO	HBP	SH	SF	SB	CS	SB%	GDP	Avg	OBP	SLG
1992 Braves	R Atl	13	33	5	1	0	0	6	3	0	10	0	12	0	0	0	0	1	.00	1	.152	.349	.182
1993 Braves	R Atl	36	119	27	5	1	0	34	12	15	3	0	32	2	1	1	3	1	.75	1	.227	.256	.286

BATTING																	BASERUNNING				PERCENTAGES		
Year Team	Lg Org	G	AB	H	2B	3B	HR	TB	R	RBI	TBB	IBB	SO	HBP	SH	SF	SB	CS	SB%	GDP	Avg	OBP	SLG
1994 Macon	A Atl	11	29	5	2	0	0	7	1	2	0	0	10	1	0	0	1	0	1.00	0	.172	.200	.241
Idaho Falls	R+ Atl	43	157	40	7	1	7	70	22	29	2	0	39	0	1	2	7	2	.78	7	.255	.261	.446
1995 Macon	A Atl	72	238	44	11	1	5	72	23	26	11	0	86	1	0	0	2	2	.50	4	.185	.224	.303
1996 Durham	A+ Atl	67	219	49	9	3	6	82	24	28	7	0	70	3	0	1	6	0	1.00	2	.224	.257	.374
1997 Durham	A+ Atl	117	430	104	18	3	18	182	51	50	14	3	122	2	0	1	5	4	.44	12	.242	.268	.423
1998 Greenville	AA Atl	98	338	84	16	1	12	138	40	58	14	2	102	4	3	2	4	1	.80	6	.249	.285	.408
1999 Richmond	AAA Atl	66	224	47	7	0	3	63	17	21	6	0	47	1	3	2	3	1	.75	6	.210	.232	.281
2000 Richmond	AAA Atl	70	230	55	9	2	4	80	21	21	8	0	65	3	3	0	1	1	.50	5	.239	.274	.348
Greenville	AA Atl	24	84	14	7	0	0	21	7	5	5	0	26	1	0	1	1	0	1.00	5	.167	.220	.250
2001 Columbus	AAA NYY	77	256	56	12	1	4	82	23	26	12	0	60	2	3	1	1	3	.25	6	.219	.258	.320
1999 Atlanta	NL	6	8	1	0	0	0	1	0	2	0	0	1	0	0	0	0	0	—	1	.125	.125	.125
10 Min. YEARS		694	2357	530	104	13	59	837	244	281	92	5	671	20	14	11	33	17	.66	55	.225	.259	.355

Dave Matranga

Bats: Right **Throws:** Right **Pos:** 2B-102; PH-4; SS-2; DH-1 **Ht:** 6'0" **Wt:** 196 **Born:** 1/8/77 **Age:** 25

BATTING																	BASERUNNING				PERCENTAGES		
Year Team	Lg Org	G	AB	H	2B	3B	HR	TB	R	RBI	TBB	IBB	SO	HBP	SH	SF	SB	CS	SB%	GDP	Avg	OBP	SLG
1998 Auburn	A- Hou	40	144	44	13	1	4	71	34	24	25	1	38	5	1	1	16	3	.84	0	.306	.423	.493
1999 Kissimmee	A+ Hou	124	472	109	20	4	6	155	70	48	68	0	118	12	9	2	17	10	.63	3	.231	.341	.328
2000 Round Rock	AA Hou	120	373	87	14	3	6	125	50	44	48	0	99	17	2	1	5	5	.50	1	.233	.346	.335
2001 New Orleans	AAA Hou	4	16	5	1	0	1	9	3	3	0	0	5	1	0	1	1	0	1.00	0	.313	.333	.563
Round Rock	AA Hou	103	387	117	34	2	10	185	78	60	45	1	91	14	7	4	17	7	.71	2	.302	.391	.478
4 Min. YEARS		391	1392	362	82	10	27	545	235	179	186	2	351	49	19	9	56	25	.69	6	.260	.365	.392

Lamont Matthews

Bats: Left **Throws:** Left **Pos:** OF-122; PH-2; DH-1; P-1 **Ht:** 6'2" **Wt:** 210 **Born:** 6/15/78 **Age:** 24

BATTING																	BASERUNNING				PERCENTAGES		
Year Team	Lg Org	G	AB	H	2B	3B	HR	TB	R	RBI	TBB	IBB	SO	HBP	SH	SF	SB	CS	SB%	GDP	Avg	OBP	SLG
1999 Yakima	A- LA	66	249	56	11	2	17	122	46	52	34	1	87	2	2	2	4	4	.50	1	.225	.321	.490
San Berndno	A+ LA	4	15	4	1	0	1	8	2	3	2	0	7	0	0	0	0	1	.00	0	.267	.353	.533
2000 San Berndno	A+ LA	131	473	116	28	9	24	234	79	90	88	2	170	6	1	6	12	13	.48	5	.245	.366	.495
2001 Jacksnville	AA LA	18	55	8	4	0	0	12	4	7	12	0	25	0	0	1	0	1	.00	2	.145	.294	.218
Vero Beach	A+ LA	107	349	107	26	3	10	169	61	57	95	4	106	4	0	2	1	3	.25	5	.307	.458	.484
3 Min. YEARS		326	1141	291	70	14	52	545	192	209	231	7	395	12	3	11	17	22	.44	13	.255	.383	.478

Brian Matz

Pitches: Left **Bats:** Left **Pos:** RP-24; SP-13 **Ht:** 6'1" **Wt:** 205 **Born:** 9/23/74 **Age:** 27

HOW MUCH HE PITCHED								WHAT HE GAVE UP												THE RESULTS					
Year Team	Lg Org	G	GS	CG	GF	IP	BFP	H	R	ER	HR	SH	SF	HB	TBB	IBB	SO	WP	Bk	W	L	Pct.	ShO	Sv	ERA
1996 Vermont	A- Mon	14	9	0	3	55.1	224	41	20	16	3	1	0	2	18	0	53	2	0	5	3	.625	0	0	2.60
1997 Cape Fear	A Mon	44	5	1	12	96.1	424	102	54	47	9	5	6	8	41	0	64	13	1	4	6	.400	1	0	4.39
1998 Cape Fear	A Mon	17	16	0	0	98.2	391	75	35	31	5	4	1	3	28	0	63	11	0	3	5	.375	0	0	2.83
Jupiter	A+ Mon	15	6	0	4	41.2	196	54	31	28	3	1	0	2	19	0	29	2	0	1	2	.333	0	2	6.05
1999 Jupiter	A+ Mon	41	1	0	17	91.1	375	77	30	24	3	7	0	6	31	1	46	4	1	5	2	.714	0	7	2.36
2000 Harrisburg	AA Mon	41	13	0	15	94	409	95	62	48	10	3	4	4	34	0	57	2	1	7	6	.538	0	2	4.60
2001 Harrisburg	AA Mon	37	13	0	9	96.2	431	116	68	59	22	3	3	3	28	1	62	7	1	1	8	.111	0	0	5.49
6 Min. YEARS		209	63	1	60	574	2450	560	300	253	55	24	14	28	199	2	374	41	4	26	32	.448	1	11	3.97

Brian Matzenbacher

Pitches: Right **Bats:** Right **Pos:** RP-49 **Ht:** 6'3" **Wt:** 190 **Born:** 3/23/77 **Age:** 25

HOW MUCH HE PITCHED								WHAT HE GAVE UP												THE RESULTS					
Year Team	Lg Org	G	GS	CG	GF	IP	BFP	H	R	ER	HR	SH	SF	HB	TBB	IBB	SO	WP	Bk	W	L	Pct.	ShO	Sv	ERA
1999 Missoula	R+ Ari	24	0	0	22	26	113	22	13	9	0	1	0	1	13	2	28	1	1	3	3	.500	0	11	3.12
2000 South Bend	A Ari	51	0	0	22	65.2	282	56	25	22	3	2	1	3	31	2	61	4	0	5	6	.455	0	5	3.02
2001 Lancaster	A+ Ari	48	0	0	16	78.2	340	85	39	30	4	6	2	5	23	1	85	7	0	5	4	.556	0	3	3.43
El Paso	AA Ari	1	0	0	1	5	22	5	1	1	0	1	0	0	2	0	4	0	0	1	0	1.000	0	0	1.80
3 Min. YEARS		124	0	0	61	175.1	757	168	78	62	7	10	3	9	69	5	178	12	1	14	13	.519	0	19	3.18

Scott Maynard

Bats: Right **Throws:** Right **Pos:** C-70 **Ht:** 6'2" **Wt:** 215 **Born:** 8/28/77 **Age:** 24

BATTING																	BASERUNNING				PERCENTAGES		
Year Team	Lg Org	G	AB	H	2B	3B	HR	TB	R	RBI	TBB	IBB	SO	HBP	SH	SF	SB	CS	SB%	GDP	Avg	OBP	SLG
1995 Tacoma	AAA Sea	1	1	0	0	0	0	0	0	0	0	0	0	0	0	0	0	0	—	1	.000	.000	.000
Mariners	R Sea	21	72	17	2	0	1	22	6	12	9	0	21	0	1	2	0	0	—	3	.236	.313	.306
1996 Mariners	R Sea	47	164	46	7	1	1	58	20	17	15	0	53	1	1	0	1	3	.25	3	.280	.344	.354
1997 Everett	A- Sea	24	86	19	3	0	2	28	11	13	5	0	30	0	2	0	0	1	1.00	0	.221	.264	.326
Memphis	AA Sea	14	38	6	0	0	0	6	3	3	1	0	12	1	0	0	0	0	—	0	.158	.200	.158
1998 Wisconsin	A Sea	81	236	41	8	1	2	57	29	17	30	0	70	0	3	2	4	4	.50	6	.174	.265	.242
1999 Lancaster	A+ Sea	8	27	7	4	0	1	14	6	3	4	0	8	0	0	0	0	0	—	0	.259	.355	.519
Wisconsin	A Sea	50	135	27	4	0	2	37	16	15	10	0	29	0	1	1	1	3	.25	9	.200	.253	.274
2000 Lancaster	A+ Sea	94	342	89	15	0	7	125	43	59	39	0	96	2	1	3	2	1	.67	7	.260	.337	.365
2001 San Antonio	AA Sea	70	229	42	11	0	0	53	17	19	21	0	59	1	6	0	3	0	1.00	3	.183	.255	.231
7 Min. YEARS		410	1330	294	54	2	16	400	151	158	134	0	378	5	15	8	16	12	.57	23	.221	.293	.301

Bryan Mazur

Pitches: Left **Bats:** Left **Pos:** RP-54 **Ht:** 6'0" **Wt:** 175 **Born:** 7/26/77 **Age:** 24

Year Team	Lg Org	G	GS	CG	GF	IP	BFP	H	R	ER	HR	SH	SF	HB	TBB	IBB	SO	WP	Bk	W	L	Pct.	ShO	Sv	ERA
1999 Sou Oregon	A- Oak	23	0	0	20	40.1	172	36	20	15	5	2	1	1	17	2	29	3	0	5	2	.714	0	8	3.35
2000 Modesto	A+ Oak	36	2	0	19	76.2	333	81	34	31	3	3	2	3	23	3	68	9	0	5	3	.625	0	7	3.64
2001 Midland	AA Oak	6	0	0	3	4.2	23	10	1	1	1	0	0	0	1	0	2	0	0	0	0	—	0	0	1.93
Visalia	A+ Oak	48	0	0	19	62	292	81	48	41	4	8	2	5	27	2	45	3	0	3	7	.300	0	5	5.95
3 Min. YEARS		113	2	0	61	183.2	820	208	103	88	13	13	7	9	68	7	144	15	0	13	12	.520	0	20	4.31

Chris McBride

Pitches: Right **Bats:** Left **Pos:** SP-4 **Ht:** 6'5" **Wt:** 210 **Born:** 10/13/73 **Age:** 28

Year Team	Lg Org	G	GS	CG	GF	IP	BFP	H	R	ER	HR	SH	SF	HB	TBB	IBB	SO	WP	Bk	W	L	Pct.	ShO	Sv	ERA
1994 St.Cathrnes	A- Tor	13	13	1	0	69.2	302	81	39	33	4	1	1	4	12	0	30	5	0	4	4	.500	0	0	4.26
1995 Hagerstown	A Tor	19	19	2	0	107	461	121	61	51	4	5	3	5	27	1	52	3	1	5	10	.333	0	0	4.29
1996 St.Cathrnes	A- Tor	6	6	1	0	43	169	37	14	12	2	0	0	4	7	0	28	2	0	3	1	.750	0	0	2.51
Hagerstown	A Tor	8	8	3	0	58.2	222	42	13	11	4	0	2	4	9	0	34	0	0	5	2	.714	2	0	1.69
1997 Dunedin	A+ Tor	10	4	0	1	31	153	44	25	21	4	0	0	3	17	0	25	5	0	3	0	1.000	0	0	6.10
Knoxville	AA Tor	10	10	0	0	60.2	256	61	30	25	5	2	1	3	14	0	33	3	1	4	4	.500	0	0	3.71
1998 Knoxville	AA Tor	35	21	1	5	155.1	681	185	102	76	18	4	11	6	37	1	90	1	0	10	5	.667	0	2	4.40
2000 Tennessee	AA Tor	22	4	0	9	60.1	240	51	18	16	5	2	2	4	9	0	37	5	0	2	2	.500	0	1	2.39
2001 Jacksnville	AA LA	4	4	0	0	19	81	24	12	10	2	0	0	0	3	0	19	1	0	2	1	.667	0	0	4.74
7 Min. YEARS		127	89	8	15	604.2	2565	646	314	255	48	14	20	33	135	2	348	25	2	38	29	.567	2	3	3.80

Tim McClaskey

Pitches: Right **Bats:** Right **Pos:** RP-63 **Ht:** 5'10" **Wt:** 170 **Born:** 1/11/76 **Age:** 26

Year Team	Lg Org	G	GS	CG	GF	IP	BFP	H	R	ER	HR	SH	SF	HB	TBB	IBB	SO	WP	Bk	W	L	Pct.	ShO	Sv	ERA
1996 Marlins	R Fla	12	12	2	0	73	288	58	28	21	3	5	3	2	13	0	63	2	0	4	3	.571	2	0	2.59
1997 Utica	A- Fla	1	0	0	1	5	16	1	0	0	0	0	0	0	0	0	8	0	0	1	0	1.000	0	0	0.00
Kane County	A Fla	18	2	0	7	37	151	29	18	13	3	1	2	3	8	2	38	3	1	2	1	.667	0	1	3.16
1998 Kane County	A Fla	34	2	0	18	74	326	87	45	35	5	3	4	5	16	3	70	4	0	5	2	.714	0	2	4.26
1999 New Haven	AA Sea	4	0	0	2	8	27	4	2	2	1	0	0	0	1	0	7	0	0	0	0	—	0	0	2.25
Lancaster	A+ Sea	30	0	0	9	58	260	83	51	41	9	1	1	6	11	0	54	3	0	3	3	.500	0	0	6.36
2000 Brevard Cty	A+ Fla	46	0	0	38	84	333	72	26	21	6	2	2	5	18	4	97	2	1	7	4	.636	0	13	2.25
2001 Brevard Cty	A+ Fla	26	0	0	24	30.2	124	21	3	3	0	1	0	3	8	3	41	0	0	3	1	.750	0	14	0.88
Portland	AA Fla	37	0	0	13	50.1	201	38	17	16	5	4	1	3	10	2	52	1	0	2	2	.500	0	2	2.86
6 Min. YEARS		208	16	2	112	420	1726	393	190	152	32	17	13	27	85	14	430	15	2	27	16	.628	2	32	3.26

Matt McClellan

Pitches: Right **Bats:** Right **Pos:** RP-47; SP-1 **Ht:** 6'7" **Wt:** 220 **Born:** 8/13/76 **Age:** 25

Year Team	Lg Org	G	GS	CG	GF	IP	BFP	H	R	ER	HR	SH	SF	HB	TBB	IBB	SO	WP	Bk	W	L	Pct.	ShO	Sv	ERA
1997 Medcine Hat	R+ Tor	14	6	0	1	39	192	50	36	30	7	0	3	3	24	0	43	2	0	2	5	.286	0	0	6.92
1998 Hagerstown	A Tor	25	25	1	0	139.2	589	109	65	48	8	5	4	14	58	3	126	6	5	8	7	.533	0	0	3.09
1999 Dunedin	A+ Tor	26	25	1	0	147.1	612	114	69	62	15	1	5	10	61	0	146	6	3	13	5	.722	0	0	3.79
2000 Tennessee	AA Tor	28	27	0	0	168.2	743	174	100	90	16	2	4	11	69	1	140	11	3	6	12	.333	0	0	4.80
2001 Tennessee	AA Tor	19	0	0	9	18.2	83	17	10	5	3	0	2	0	8	0	20	1	0	2	2	.500	0	1	2.41
Syracuse	AAA Tor	29	1	0	12	52.1	228	49	21	19	4	1	3	2	20	1	44	6	0	1	2	.333	0	2	3.27
5 Min. YEARS		141	84	2	22	565.2	2447	513	301	254	53	9	21	40	240	5	519	32	11	32	33	.492	0	3	4.04

Matt McClendon

Pitches: Right **Bats:** Right **Pos:** SP-15; RP-8 **Ht:** 6'6" **Wt:** 220 **Born:** 10/13/77 **Age:** 24

Year Team	Lg Org	G	GS	CG	GF	IP	BFP	H	R	ER	HR	SH	SF	HB	TBB	IBB	SO	WP	Bk	W	L	Pct.	ShO	Sv	ERA
1999 Jamestown	A- Atl	7	7	0	0	23	94	18	11	10	2	0	0	1	11	0	24	2	0	1	1	.500	0	0	3.91
2000 Myrtle Bch	A+ Atl	6	6	0	0	39.2	147	24	7	7	1	1	0	0	8	0	43	1	0	3	1	.750	0	0	1.59
Greenville	AA Atl	22	21	1	1	131	561	124	59	55	6	4	8	5	54	0	90	12	0	7	6	.538	1	0	3.78
2001 Richmond	AAA Atl	10	10	0	0	46.1	219	50	45	42	5	3	3	2	31	4	31	0	2	0	6	.000	0	0	8.16
Greenville	AA Atl	2	2	0	0	10.2	48	10	7	7	1	1	1	0	7	0	9	2	0	0	1	.000	0	0	5.91
Braves	R Atl	3	3	0	0	6.2	33	3	2	1	0	0	0	0	10	0	15	3	0	0	0	—	0	0	1.35
Myrtle Bch	A+ Atl	8	0	0	1	9.1	48	7	10	9	0	1	1	4	9	0	10	8	0	1	2	.333	0	0	8.68
3 Min. YEARS		58	49	1	2	266.2	1150	236	141	131	15	10	13	12	130	4	222	28	2	12	17	.414	1	0	4.42

Brian McClure

Bats: Left **Throws:** Right **Pos:** 3B-35; 2B-29; SS-6; OF-2; DH-2; P-2; PH-1 **Ht:** 6'0" **Wt:** 170 **Born:** 1/15/74 **Age:** 28

Year Team	Lg Org	G	AB	H	2B	3B	HR	TB	R	RBI	TBB	IBB	SO	HBP	SH	SF	SB	CS	SB%	GDP	Avg	OBP	SLG
1996 Idaho Falls	R+ SD	72	308	99	18	6	6	147	62	45	38	0	63	3	0	4	10	2	.83	6	.321	.397	.477
1997 Clinton	A SD	118	416	115	18	11	4	167	75	55	90	4	64	1	3	6	12	11	.52	7	.276	.402	.401
1998 Rancho Cuca	A+ SD	129	492	130	25	11	9	204	89	57	66	2	98	1	7	5	4	3	.57	8	.264	.357	.415
1999 Rancho Cuca	A+ SD	36	116	26	5	1	2	39	26	15	26	0	22	1	3	2	4	1	.80	1	.224	.366	.336
Mobile	AA SD	51	169	35	10	3	1	54	17	27	17	1	34	2	1	2	0	0	—	4	.207	.284	.320
2000 Toledo	AAA Det	16	48	15	2	1	0	19	7	3	9	0	8	0	0	0	1	0	1.00	0	.313	.421	.396
Jacksonville	AA Det	81	246	70	17	0	1	90	33	18	40	0	46	0	1	1	2	1	.67	4	.285	.383	.366
2001 Erie	AA Det	75	255	64	14	2	1	85	29	22	23	0	45	2	1	1	0	0	—	13	.251	.317	.333
6 Min. YEARS		578	2050	554	109	35	24	805	338	242	309	7	380	16	14	20	33	18	.65	43	.270	.367	.393

191

Sam McConnell

Pitches: Left **Bats:** Left **Pos:** SP-23; RP-3   **Ht:** 6'1" **Wt:** 213 **Born:** 12/31/75 **Age:** 26

Year Team	Lg Org	G	GS	CG	GF	IP	BFP	H	R	ER	HR	SH	SF	HB	TBB	IBB	SO	WP	Bk	W	L	Pct.	ShO	Sv	ERA
1997 Erie	A- Pit	17	10	0	0	58.2	261	56	38	33	7	1	3	3	24	0	45	6	0	2	2	.500	0	0	5.06
1998 Augusta	A Pit	8	8	1	0	45	183	36	22	16	2	1	0	1	13	1	35	1	1	4	3	.571	0	0	3.20
Lynchburg	A+ Pit	19	19	3	0	121	483	118	48	39	4	2	1	1	20	0	80	2	0	8	5	.615	1	0	2.90
Carolina	AA Pit	2	1	0	0	12	53	15	7	6	2	1	1	0	3	0	5	0	0	0	1	.000	0	0	4.50
1999 Lynchburg	A+ Pit	15	15	4	0	101.2	402	84	41	36	8	3	5	5	27	1	70	6	0	7	3	.700	2	0	3.19
Altoona	AA Pit	13	12	1	0	62.1	299	82	52	46	7	6	3	4	33	1	40	5	1	1	7	.125	0	0	6.64
2000 Altoona	AA Pit	20	13	3	0	106	422	83	24	19	3	2	2	2	26	0	61	1	1	9	2	.818	1	0	1.61
Nashville	AAA Pit	8	8	0	0	49	216	58	36	35	8	1	2	4	16	0	22	1	0	1	4	.200	0	0	6.43
2001 Nashville	AAA Pit	26	23	1	1	134.1	600	159	103	90	20	3	7	3	41	2	98	7	1	7	10	.412	0	0	6.03
5 Min. YEARS		128	109	13	1	690	2919	691	371	320	61	20	24	23	203	5	456	29	4	39	37	.513	4	0	4.17

Paul McCurtain

Pitches: Right **Bats:** Right **Pos:** RP-17   **Ht:** 6'1" **Wt:** 190 **Born:** 2/5/76 **Age:** 26

Year Team	Lg Org	G	GS	CG	GF	IP	BFP	H	R	ER	HR	SH	SF	HB	TBB	IBB	SO	WP	Bk	W	L	Pct.	ShO	Sv	ERA
1998 Portland	AA Fla	1	0	0	0	1.2	8	0	1	1	0	1	0	0	2	0	2	1	0	0	0	—	0	0	5.40
Utica	A- Fla	17	2	0	5	39	173	35	25	19	1	5	0	3	19	2	33	7	0	0	1	.000	0	1	4.38
1999 Brevard Cty	A+ Fla	40	0	0	32	57.2	261	59	32	22	1	0	1	2	25	0	49	2	1	3	2	.600	0	12	3.43
2000 Brevard Cty	A+ Fla	3	0	0	0	6	24	6	2	2	0	0	0	0	2	1	8	1	0	0	0	—	0	0	3.00
Portland	AA Fla	41	2	0	16	85.1	382	98	46	39	9	4	3	5	34	2	56	1	0	6	1	.857	0	2	4.11
2001 Brevard Cty	A+ Fla	7	0	0	2	10.1	47	11	10	8	0	0	0	0	6	0	10	0	0	0	1	.000	0	1	6.97
Portland	AA Fla	10	0	0	2	14.1	71	17	9	8	2	0	0	0	13	0	14	1	1	0	0	—	0	0	5.02
4 Min. YEARS		119	4	0	57	214.1	966	226	125	99	13	10	4	10	101	5	172	13	2	9	5	.643	0	16	4.16

Neal McDade

Pitches: Right **Bats:** Right **Pos:** RP-18; SP-9   **Ht:** 6'3" **Wt:** 170 **Born:** 6/16/76 **Age:** 26

Year Team	Lg Org	G	GS	CG	GF	IP	BFP	H	R	ER	HR	SH	SF	HB	TBB	IBB	SO	WP	Bk	W	L	Pct.	ShO	Sv	ERA
1996 Erie	A- Pit	13	13	3	0	76.2	319	76	33	29	3	4	3	4	21	0	67	5	2	7	3	.700	0	0	3.40
Lynchburg	A+ Pit	1	1	0	0	5	23	6	6	5	1	1	0	1	1	0	2	0	0	1	0	1.000	0	0	9.00
1997 Augusta	A Pit	36	12	0	8	112.1	466	105	42	35	4	3	3	5	24	3	104	5	2	10	4	.714	0	3	2.80
Lynchburg	A+ Pit	3	3	0	0	18.2	77	16	8	6	3	1	0	1	6	0	15	2	0	2	0	1.000	0	0	2.89
1998 Lynchburg	A+ Pit	25	11	0	6	90	369	87	35	33	7	3	3	5	20	0	74	5	1	5	3	.625	0	3	3.30
2000 Lynchburg	A+ Pit	7	7	0	0	29	131	35	18	15	2	1	3	1	11	1	24	0	0	1	2	.333	0	0	4.66
2001 Altoona	AA Pit	19	9	0	3	73.1	323	85	38	33	3	2	0	3	24	0	55	3	1	2	5	.286	0	0	4.05
Nashville	AAA Pit	8	0	0	2	15	64	14	5	5	1	0	1	1	7	1	8	2	0	1	1	.500	0	0	3.00
5 Min. YEARS		112	56	3	19	420	1772	424	185	161	24	14	14	23	114	5	349	22	6	28	19	.596	0	6	3.45

Denny McDaniel

Pitches: Left **Bats:** Left **Pos:** RP-50   **Ht:** 6'3" **Wt:** 215 **Born:** 8/12/76 **Age:** 25

Year Team	Lg Org	G	GS	CG	GF	IP	BFP	H	R	ER	HR	SH	SF	HB	TBB	IBB	SO	WP	Bk	W	L	Pct.	ShO	Sv	ERA
1996 Royals	R KC	7	5	0	1	19.1	84	15	11	8	0	2	0	3	10	0	25	2	1	1	1	.500	0	0	3.72
1998 Spokane	A- KC	29	0	0	7	36	173	42	25	17	2	0	1	2	19	4	43	4	1	1	5	.167	0	1	4.25
1999 Abilene	IND —	36	0	0	33	41.2	192	47	24	19	4	3	2	4	21	1	39	5	0	0	2	.000	0	9	4.10
2000 Lancaster	A+ Sea	43	0	0	14	44.1	208	42	29	20	2	0	6	5	25	2	37	5	0	5	0	1.000	0	1	4.06
2001 Birmingham	AA CWS	18	0	0	7	21	100	30	18	18	2	1	1	2	9	0	13	1	0	1	2	.333	0	0	7.71
Winston-Sal	A+ CWS	32	0	0	5	46	198	43	18	15	1	2	1	1	21	3	25	6	0	1	3	.250	0	0	2.93
5 Min. YEARS		165	5	0	67	208.1	956	219	125	97	11	8	11	17	105	10	182	23	2	9	13	.409	0	11	4.19

Darnell McDonald

Bats: Right **Throws:** Right **Pos:** OF-131; DH-2; PR-1   **Ht:** 5'11" **Wt:** 201 **Born:** 11/17/78 **Age:** 23

Year Team	Lg Org	G	AB	H	2B	3B	HR	TB	R	RBI	TBB	IBB	SO	HBP	SH	SF	SB	CS	SB%	GDP	Avg	OBP	SLG
1998 Delmarva	A Bal	134	528	138	24	5	6	190	87	44	33	0	117	5	4	5	35	11	.76	5	.261	.308	.360
Frederick	A+ Bal	4	18	4	2	0	1	9	3	2	3	0	6	0	0	0	2	0	1.00	1	.222	.333	.500
1999 Frederick	A+ Bal	130	507	135	23	5	6	186	81	73	61	0	92	5	7	7	26	9	.74	13	.266	.347	.367
2000 Bowie	AA Bal	116	459	111	13	5	6	152	59	43	29	0	87	4	6	4	11	4	.73	7	.242	.290	.331
2001 Bowie	AA Bal	30	117	33	7	1	3	51	16	21	9	0	28	1	0	1	3	3	.50	1	.282	.336	.436
Rochester	AAA Bal	104	391	93	19	2	2	122	37	35	29	0	75	1	2	2	13	9	.59	8	.238	.291	.312
4 Min. YEARS		518	2020	514	88	18	24	710	283	218	164	0	405	16	19	19	90	36	.71	35	.254	.313	.351

Jon McDonald

Pitches: Right **Bats:** Right **Pos:** SP-26   **Ht:** 6'3" **Wt:** 195 **Born:** 10/16/77 **Age:** 24

Year Team	Lg Org	G	GS	CG	GF	IP	BFP	H	R	ER	HR	SH	SF	HB	TBB	IBB	SO	WP	Bk	W	L	Pct.	ShO	Sv	ERA
2000 Fort Myers	A+ Min	10	10	0	0	49.2	207	42	24	22	1	1	1	6	16	0	33	3	1	3	3	.500	0	0	3.99
2001 Fort Myers	A+ Min	9	9	0	0	50	206	44	15	11	0	0	0	1	15	1	44	8	1	4	2	.667	0	0	1.98
New Britain	AA Min	17	17	0	0	96.2	407	88	47	37	7	1	0	8	34	0	68	5	2	8	3	.727	0	0	3.44
2 Min. YEARS		36	36	0	0	196.1	820	174	86	70	8	2	1	15	65	1	145	16	4	15	8	.652	0	0	3.21

Tom McGee

Bats: Right Throws: Right Pos: C-46; 3B-2; DH-1   Ht: 5'11" Wt: 193 Born: 1/29/75 Age: 27

					BATTING												BASERUNNING				PERCENTAGES		
Year Team	Lg Org	G	AB	H	2B	3B	HR	TB	R	RBI	TBB	IBB	SO	HBP	SH	SF	SB	CS	SB%	GDP	Avg	OBP	SLG
1997 Bluefield	R+ Bal	27	86	21	5	0	1	29	14	8	11	0	22	5	0	0	2	1	.67	3	.244	.363	.337
1998 Delmarva	A Bal	50	123	33	5	0	2	44	16	14	9	0	23	3	2	2	4	2	.67	2	.268	.328	.358
1999 Frederick	A+ Bal	7	30	6	1	0	0	7	2	3	1	0	6	0	0	1	0	0	—	2	.200	.219	.233
Delmarva	A Bal	71	218	59	16	2	4	91	37	27	34	2	52	4	2	5	0	4	.00	5	.271	.372	.417
2000 Frederick	A+ Bal	85	252	56	12	1	2	76	29	27	25	0	74	4	6	2	5	1	.83	9	.222	.300	.302
2001 Bowie	AA Bal	48	156	25	6	0	2	37	15	14	12	0	32	3	2	0	0	1	.00	5	.160	.234	.237
5 Min. YEARS		288	865	200	45	3	11	284	113	93	92	2	209	19	12	10	11	9	.55	26	.231	.315	.328

Sean McGowan

Bats: Right Throws: Right Pos: OF-55; 1B-47; DH-33; PH-4   Ht: 6'6" Wt: 240 Born: 5/15/77 Age: 25

					BATTING												BASERUNNING				PERCENTAGES		
Year Team	Lg Org	G	AB	H	2B	3B	HR	TB	R	RBI	TBB	IBB	SO	HBP	SH	SF	SB	CS	SB%	GDP	Avg	OBP	SLG
1999 Salem-Keizr	A- SF	63	257	86	12	1	15	145	40	62	20	4	56	1	0	0	3	1	.75	6	.335	.385	.564
San Jose	A+ SF	2	8	3	1	0	0	4	1	1	0	0	3	0	0	0	0	1	.00	0	.375	.375	.500
2000 San Jose	A+ SF	114	456	149	32	2	12	221	58	106	43	1	71	6	0	3	4	3	.57	12	.327	.390	.485
Shreveport	AA SF	18	69	24	4	0	0	28	5	12	1	0	8	0	0	0	0	0	—	2	.348	.357	.406
2001 Shreveport	AA SF	31	125	38	6	0	3	53	11	17	5	0	19	0	0	2	1	1	.00	3	.304	.326	.424
Fresno	AAA SF	104	391	112	30	2	14	188	59	65	23	0	95	2	0	2	1	0	1.00	10	.286	.328	.481
3 Min. YEARS		332	1306	412	85	5	44	639	174	263	92	5	252	9	0	7	8	6	.57	33	.315	.363	.489

Cody McKay

Bats: Left Throws: Right Pos: C-78; DH-12; 3B-8; PH-2; OF-1   Ht: 6'0" Wt: 212 Born: 1/11/74 Age: 28

					BATTING												BASERUNNING				PERCENTAGES		
Year Team	Lg Org	G	AB	H	2B	3B	HR	TB	R	RBI	TBB	IBB	SO	HBP	SH	SF	SB	CS	SB%	GDP	Avg	OBP	SLG
1996 Sou Oregon	A- Oak	69	254	68	13	0	3	90	33	30	25	0	42	6	1	3	0	5	.00	7	.268	.344	.354
1997 Modesto	A+ Oak	125	390	97	20	1	7	140	47	50	46	2	69	16	3	4	4	2	.67	9	.249	.349	.359
1998 Huntsville	AA Oak	9	21	6	0	0	1	9	5	1	6	0	5	2	0	0	0	0	—	0	.286	.483	.429
Edmonton	AAA Oak	19	57	13	3	0	0	16	6	5	7	0	5	3	2	0	1	0	1.00	2	.228	.343	.281
Modesto	A+ Oak	107	402	114	25	1	6	159	59	58	40	1	62	17	3	3	2	4	.33	12	.284	.370	.396
1999 Midland	AA Oak	94	333	98	21	1	6	139	59	43	38	5	40	8	1	5	1	2	.33	11	.294	.375	.417
2000 Midland	AA Oak	115	427	136	35	2	5	190	70	89	67	6	54	10	0	10	1	5	.17	15	.319	.414	.445
Sacramento	AAA Oak	16	58	13	4	0	1	20	8	7	5	1	14	1	0	0	0	0	—	0	.224	.297	.345
2001 Sacramento	AAA Oak	99	350	92	19	0	6	129	36	41	27	1	64	5	2	1	1	0	1.00	12	.263	.324	.369
6 Min. YEARS		653	2292	637	140	5	35	892	323	324	261	16	355	68	12	26	10	18	.36	68	.278	.365	.389

Walt McKeel

Bats: Right Throws: Right Pos: C-36; 1B-7; PH-7; DH-5   Ht: 6'0" Wt: 200 Born: 1/17/72 Age: 30

					BATTING												BASERUNNING				PERCENTAGES		
Year Team	Lg Org	G	AB	H	2B	3B	HR	TB	R	RBI	TBB	IBB	SO	HBP	SH	SF	SB	CS	SB%	GDP	Avg	OBP	SLG
1990 Red Sox	R Bos	13	44	11	3	0	0	14	2	6	3	0	8	0	0	1	0	2	.00	2	.250	.292	.318
1991 Red Sox	R Bos	35	113	15	0	1	2	23	10	12	17	0	20	1	0	4	0	0	—	5	.133	.244	.204
1992 Lynchburg	A+ Bos	96	288	64	11	0	12	111	33	33	22	0	77	3	5	1	2	1	.67	3	.222	.283	.385
1993 Lynchburg	A+ Bos	80	247	59	17	2	5	95	28	32	26	0	40	3	6	3	0	1	.00	6	.239	.315	.385
1994 Sarasota	A+ Bos	37	137	38	8	1	2	54	15	15	8	1	19	1	0	0	1	0	1.00	1	.277	.322	.394
New Britain	AA Bos	50	164	30	6	1	1	41	10	17	7	1	35	3	1	2	0	0	—	5	.183	.227	.250
1995 Trenton	AA Bos	29	84	20	3	1	2	31	11	11	8	0	15	0	0	2	2	1	.67	1	.238	.298	.369
Sarasota	A+ Bos	62	198	66	14	0	8	104	26	35	25	0	28	3	0	5	6	3	.67	4	.333	.407	.525
1996 Trenton	AA Bos	128	464	140	19	1	16	209	86	78	60	3	52	7	5	7	2	4	.33	13	.302	.385	.450
1997 Pawtucket	AAA Bos	66	237	60	15	0	6	93	34	30	34	3	39	1	1	2	0	1	.00	8	.253	.347	.392
Trenton	AA Bos	7	25	4	2	0	0	6	0	4	1	0	2	0	1	0	0	0	—	0	.160	.192	.240
1998 Red Sox	R Bos	13	36	9	2	0	1	14	1	4	4	0	8	0	0	0	0	0	—	1	.250	.317	.389
Pawtucket	AAA Bos	48	170	49	10	1	4	73	26	26	21	0	27	1	0	0	1	2	.33	8	.288	.370	.429
1999 Toledo	AAA Det	67	215	52	9	1	7	84	21	37	26	0	32	4	1	2	2	2	.50	6	.242	.332	.391
Sonoma Cty	IND —	2	9	4	0	0	1	7	1	1	0	0	3	0	0	0	0	0	—	0	.444	.444	.778
2000 Carolina	AA Col	72	227	51	15	0	8	90	29	26	31	0	45	8	2	2	3	3	.50	7	.225	.336	.396
2001 Colo Sprngs	AAA Col	28	79	19	4	1	1	28	13	4	6	1	22	0	0	0	0	0	—	2	.241	.294	.354
Carolina	AA Col	24	68	15	2	0	3	26	11	9	14	1	14	4	3	0	0	0	—	2	.221	.384	.382
1996 Boston	AL	1	0	0	0	0	0	0	0	0	0	0	0	0	0	0	0	0	—	0	.000	—	.000
1997 Boston	AL	5	3	0	0	0	0	0	0	0	0	0	1	0	0	0	0	0	—	0	.000	.000	.000
12 Min. YEARS		857	2805	706	140	10	79	1103	357	380	313	10	486	39	25	32	19	20	.49	72	.252	.332	.393
2 Maj. YEARS		6	3	0	0	0	0	0	0	0	0	0	1	0	0	0	0	0	—	0	.000	.000	.000

Dan McKinley

Bats: Left Throws: Right Pos: OF-91; PH-10; DH-4; PR-1   Ht: 6'0" Wt: 185 Born: 5/15/76 Age: 26

					BATTING												BASERUNNING				PERCENTAGES		
Year Team	Lg Org	G	AB	H	2B	3B	HR	TB	R	RBI	TBB	IBB	SO	HBP	SH	SF	SB	CS	SB%	GDP	Avg	OBP	SLG
1998 Shreveport	AA SF	33	112	20	3	3	0	29	16	11	11	1	30	3	0	1	2	3	.40	3	.179	.268	.259
Bakersfield	A+ SF	94	379	114	16	4	6	156	58	44	30	2	84	10	4	2	19	6	.76	8	.301	.366	.412
1999 San Jose	A+ SF	15	53	12	2	1	1	19	7	3	7	1	13	1	1	0	2	0	1.00	1	.226	.328	.358
Akron	AA Cle	111	463	119	20	6	3	160	70	37	24	0	87	4	8	3	3	5	.38	8	.257	.298	.346
2000 Kinston	A+ Cle	13	62	20	5	0	0	25	8	7	2	0	11	1	0	0	4	1	.80	1	.323	.354	.403
Harrisburg	AA Mon	131	517	145	20	14	4	205	66	57	25	1	75	9	8	3	23	7	.77	3	.280	.323	.397
2001 Ottawa	AAA Mon	105	360	101	18	6	5	146	31	39	20	0	85	4	4	1	12	6	.67	7	.281	.325	.406
4 Min. YEARS		502	1946	531	84	34	19	740	256	198	119	5	385	32	26	10	65	28	.70	31	.273	.324	.380

Marty McLeary

Pitches: Right Bats: Right Pos: RP-53 Ht: 6'5" Wt: 220 Born: 10/26/74 Age: 27

Year Team	Lg Org	G	GS	CG	GF	IP	BFP	H	R	ER	HR	SH	SF	HB	TBB	IBB	SO	WP	Bk	W	L	Pct.	ShO	Sv	ERA
1997 Lowell	A- Bos	13	13	0	0	62.1	275	53	38	26	2	3	3	5	36	1	43	6	2	3	6	.333	0	0	3.75
1998 Michigan	A Bos	37	7	0	11	88.2	396	99	58	41	4	1	3	5	35	2	54	5	1	5	7	.417	0	0	4.16
1999 Sarasota	A+ Bos	8	0	0	0	12.2	73	29	20	17	1	2	1	1	7	0	11	2	0	1	0	1.000	0	0	12.08
Augusta	A Bos	35	9	0	16	80.2	338	73	34	28	8	3	2	4	25	1	90	5	2	5	6	.455	0	3	3.12
2000 Trenton	AA Bos	43	8	0	22	96.2	449	114	66	49	5	2	6	2	53	3	53	8	1	2	9	.182	0	5	4.56
2001 Trenton	AA Bos	35	0	0	14	54.2	252	58	30	21	2	4	1	5	30	5	42	2	0	9	6	.600	0	2	3.46
Pawtucket	AAA Bos	18	0	0	7	30	127	28	13	10	4	2	1	1	15	1	20	1	0	1	2	.333	0	0	3.00
5 Min. YEARS		189	37	0	70	425.2	1910	454	259	192	26	17	17	23	201	13	313	29	6	26	36	.419	0	10	4.06

Mike McMullen

Pitches: Right Bats: Right Pos: RP-27; SP-1 Ht: 6'6" Wt: 230 Born: 10/13/73 Age: 28

Year Team	Lg Org	G	GS	CG	GF	IP	BFP	H	R	ER	HR	SH	SF	HB	TBB	IBB	SO	WP	Bk	W	L	Pct.	ShO	Sv	ERA
1993 Giants	R SF	14	14	0	0	64	306	70	60	45	1	3	2	5	53	0	44	12	0	1	6	.143	0	0	6.33
1994 Clinton	A SF	14	1	0	5	24.1	122	34	25	17	5	1	1	1	14	0	22	4	2	1	3	.250	0	0	6.29
Giants	R SF	10	9	0	0	49	205	47	21	18	2	2	3	3	15	1	40	3	0	3	3	.500	0	0	3.31
1995 Burlington	A SF	29	11	2	6	83.2	410	98	76	51	5	2	4	9	54	3	53	9	2	4	10	.286	0	0	5.49
1996 Burlington	A SF	38	0	0	7	56.1	241	47	22	18	3	4	2	5	28	0	33	5	0	2	0	.000	0	0	2.88
1997 San Jose	A+ SF	56	0	0	23	91	377	85	37	27	1	9	4	5	33	3	71	6	0	6	4	.600	0	7	2.67
1998 Shreveport	AA SF	52	0	0	37	67.2	296	47	23	16	1	5	1	6	41	9	76	5	0	6	4	.600	0	9	2.13
Fresno	AAA SF	2	0	0	0	3.1	14	2	2	2	0	0	0	0	2	0	2	0	0	1	0	1.000	0	0	5.40
1999 Fresno	AAA SF	41	0	0	13	66	290	52	36	32	5	1	1	10	41	2	56	4	2	2	2	.500	0	1	4.36
2000 Fresno	AAA SF	36	0	0	12	50.1	246	37	35	27	2	3	5	12	52	1	41	12	1	4	2	.667	0	1	4.83
2001 Edmonton	AAA Min	14	0	0	5	16	72	12	10	6	1	0	2	1	15	0	11	3	0	0	0	—	0	0	3.38
Solano	IND —	8	0	0	2	9.2	52	14	6	6	0	1	1	1	9	0	6	1	0	1	1	.500	0	1	5.59
Wichita	AA KC	6	1	0	2	8.2	53	13	11	11	3	1	0	2	12	1	5	1	1	0	0	—	0	0	11.42
9 Min. YEARS		320	36	2	112	590	2684	558	364	276	29	32	26	60	369	20	460	65	8	29	37	.439	0	18	4.21

Sean McNally

Bats: Right Throws: Right Pos: 3B-101; 1B-17; DH-7; SS-6; PH-2 Ht: 6'4" Wt: 210 Born: 12/14/72 Age: 29

Year Team	Lg Org	G	AB	H	2B	3B	HR	TB	R	RBI	TBB	IBB	SO	HBP	SH	SF	SB	CS	SB%	GDP	Avg	OBP	SLG
1994 Eugene	A- KC	74	278	69	16	2	3	98	44	30	24	1	66	4	2	2	4	7	.36	5	.248	.315	.353
1995 Springfield	A KC	132	479	130	28	8	12	210	60	79	35	6	119	8	0	6	6	3	.67	10	.271	.328	.438
1996 Wilmington	A+ KC	126	428	118	27	1	8	171	49	63	57	2	83	5	1	8	3	3	.50	8	.276	.361	.400
1997 Wichita	AA KC	18	53	13	4	0	0	17	9	2	11	0	12	0	0	0	1	2	.33	2	.245	.375	.321
Wilmington	A+ KC	95	323	86	22	2	17	163	51	68	40	4	98	2	3	1	2	1	.67	6	.266	.350	.505
1998 Wichita	AA KC	98	319	84	21	3	6	129	43	44	39	0	86	1	2	5	2	4	.33	9	.263	.341	.404
1999 Wichita	AA KC	129	440	124	24	2	36	260	97	109	93	2	132	6	1	3	7	3	.70	12	.282	.411	.591
2000 Calgary	AAA Fla	112	374	98	22	4	12	164	58	41	42	0	104	5	3	3	2	4	.33	12	.262	.342	.439
2001 Buffalo	AAA Cle	51	178	40	10	1	8	76	24	29	24	1	71	2	0	2	0	1	.00	3	.225	.320	.427
Tucson	AAA Ari	74	249	60	5	2	6	87	24	28	24	2	77	3	0	1	4	1	.80	1	.241	.314	.349
8 Min. YEARS		909	3121	822	179	25	108	1375	459	493	389	18	848	36	12	31	31	29	.52	68	.263	.349	.441

Rusty McNamara

Bats: Right Throws: Right Pos: DH-46; PH-7; 1B-1 Ht: 5'9" Wt: 190 Born: 1/23/75 Age: 27

Year Team	Lg Org	G	AB	H	2B	3B	HR	TB	R	RBI	TBB	IBB	SO	HBP	SH	SF	SB	CS	SB%	GDP	Avg	OBP	SLG
1997 Batavia	A- Phi	72	295	92	17	0	6	127	55	54	15	0	33	10	0	6	3	3	.50	4	.312	.359	.431
1998 Clearwater	A+ Phi	134	529	154	36	1	9	219	78	94	23	1	44	14	3	9	14	7	.67	20	.291	.332	.414
1999 Clearwater	A+ Phi	69	274	88	12	2	3	113	40	43	29	1	22	9	2	2	5	3	.63	8	.321	.401	.412
Reading	AA Phi	50	177	44	9	1	5	70	26	20	17	0	22	4	4	0	0	2	.00	6	.249	.328	.395
2000 Reading	AA Phi	125	466	137	24	6	14	215	79	76	43	1	41	18	1	6	3	3	.50	10	.294	.371	.461
2001 Phillies	R Phi	1	4	0	0	0	0	0	0	0	0	0	3	0	0	0	0	0	—	0	.000	.000	.000
Clearwater	A+ Phi	9	28	12	6	0	0	18	5	11	6	0	2	2	0	0	2	0	1.00	1	.429	.556	.643
Lakewood	A Phi	5	17	3	1	0	0	4	4	1	4	0	3	0	0	0	1	0	1.00	1	.176	.333	.235
Reading	AA Phi	33	118	33	10	0	1	46	18	16	6	1	10	0	0	1	1	0	.00	4	.280	.312	.390
Scranton-WB	AAA Phi	5	14	2	0	0	1	5	2	2	1	0	1	2	0	1	0	0	—	0	.143	.278	.357
5 Min. YEARS		503	1922	565	115	10	39	817	307	317	144	4	181	59	10	25	28	19	.60	55	.294	.357	.425

Troy McNaughton

Bats: Left Throws: Left Pos: OF-104; PH-12; DH-6; 2B-1 Ht: 6'0" Wt: 195 Born: 1/27/75 Age: 27

Year Team	Lg Org	G	AB	H	2B	3B	HR	TB	R	RBI	TBB	IBB	SO	HBP	SH	SF	SB	CS	SB%	GDP	Avg	OBP	SLG
1998 New Jersey	A- StL	53	157	40	7	4	1	58	27	14	20	0	45	2	3	1	6	5	.55	4	.255	.344	.369
1999 Peoria	A StL	125	484	132	25	6	14	211	57	84	37	1	123	4	0	4	5	4	.56	11	.273	.327	.436
2000 Potomac	A+ StL	125	458	126	26	2	13	195	63	70	41	2	124	2	2	3	16	9	.64	8	.275	.335	.426
2001 Memphis	AAA StL	6	23	3	2	0	1	8	5	1	2	0	5	0	0	0	0	0	—	0	.130	.200	.348
New Haven	AA StL	115	387	91	29	3	8	150	57	39	37	3	108	3	2	0	6	10	.38	8	.235	.307	.388
4 Min. YEARS		424	1509	392	89	15	37	622	209	208	137	6	405	11	7	8	33	28	.54	33	.260	.324	.412

Aaron McNeal

Bats: Right **Throws:** Right **Pos:** 1B-108; DH-16; PH-5   **Ht:** 6'3" **Wt:** 230 **Born:** 4/28/78 **Age:** 24

Year Team	Lg Org	G	AB	H	2B	3B	HR	TB	R	RBI	TBB	IBB	SO	HBP	SH	SF	SB	CS	SB%	GDP	Avg	OBP	SLG
1996 Astros	R Hou	55	200	50	10	2	2	70	22	31	13	1	52	4	0	2	0	2	.00	5	.250	.306	.350
1997 Auburn	A- Hou	12	40	10	3	0	0	13	5	3	4	0	10	0	0	0	1	0	1.00	1	.250	.318	.325
Astros	R Hou	46	164	48	12	0	3	69	22	26	11	0	28	0	0	2	0	5	.00	4	.293	.333	.421
1998 Quad City	A Hou	112	370	105	15	1	14	164	54	61	31	2	112	5	1	0	3	3	.50	12	.284	.347	.443
1999 Michigan	A Hou	133	536	166	29	3	38	315	95	131	40	4	121	2	0	3	7	1	.88	13	.310	.358	.588
2000 Round Rock	AA Hou	97	361	112	20	2	11	169	40	69	24	3	91	1	1	3	0	4	.00	11	.310	.352	.468
2001 Mobile	AA SD	59	220	64	13	1	6	97	27	29	16	1	53	2	0	1	0	1	.00	14	.291	.343	.441
Binghamton	AA NYM	70	264	53	7	0	11	93	26	25	12	0	77	0	0	0	1	3	.25	13	.201	.236	.352
6 Min. YEARS		584	2155	608	109	9	85	990	291	375	151	11	544	14	2	11	12	19	.39	73	.282	.332	.459

Brian McNichol

Pitches: Left **Bats:** Left **Pos:** RP-46; SP-1   **Ht:** 6'5" **Wt:** 225 **Born:** 5/20/74 **Age:** 28

		HOW MUCH HE PITCHED						WHAT HE GAVE UP									THE RESULTS					
Year Team	Lg Org	G	GS	CG	GF	IP	BFP	H	R	ER	HR	SH	SF	HB	TBB	IBB	SO	WP	Bk	W	L	Pct.	ShO	Sv	ERA
1995 Williamsprt	A- ChC	9	9	0	0	49.2	215	57	28	17	1	1	1	2	8	0	35	1	1	3	1	.750	0	0	3.08
1996 Daytona	A+ ChC	8	7	0	0	34.2	162	39	24	18	4	0	1	0	14	0	22	1	0	1	2	.333	0	0	4.67
Cubs	R ChC	1	1	0	0	3.1	16	4	2	0	0	0	0	0	0	0	2	0	0	0	0	—	0	0	0.00
1997 Daytona	A+ ChC	6	6	0	0	39	161	32	14	10	1	1	2	3	10	1	40	1	0	2	2	.500	0	0	2.31
Orlando	AA ChC	22	22	0	0	119.1	544	153	89	77	18	3	7	2	42	6	97	9	0	7	10	.412	0	0	5.81
1998 West Tenn	AA ChC	28	26	4	0	179	753	170	88	74	14	5	6	7	62	5	168	9	1	12	9	.571	1	0	3.72
Iowa	AAA ChC	1	1	0	0	7	31	12	6	6	2	0	0	0	1	0	5	0	0	0	0	—	0	0	7.71
1999 Iowa	AAA ChC	28	28	2	0	161.1	720	194	108	100	21	7	2	7	55	0	120	6	0	10	11	.476	1	0	5.58
2000 Iowa	AAA ChC	43	13	0	14	115	519	131	81	75	20	2	6	4	52	1	105	2	1	3	8	.273	0	1	5.87
2001 Chattanooga	AA Cin	21	1	0	5	26	106	19	4	3	0	4	0	1	9	1	32	1	0	4	0	1.000	0	0	1.04
Louisville	AAA Cin	26	0	0	6	28.1	112	23	8	5	1	1	2	1	5	0	22	0	0	4	1	.800	0	1	1.59
1999 Chicago	NL	4	2	0	1	10.2	54	15	8	8	4	0	1	1	7	0	12	0	0	0	2	.000	0	0	6.75
7 Min. YEARS		193	114	6	25	762.2	3339	834	452	385	82	24	27	27	258	14	648	30	3	46	44	.511	2	1	4.54

Randy Meadows

Bats: Right **Throws:** Right **Pos:** 2B-36; PH-18; 3B-13; SS-6; PR-4; OF-3; DH-3; P-2   **Ht:** 6'0" **Wt:** 185 **Born:** 8/15/76 **Age:** 25

Year Team	Lg Org	G	AB	H	2B	3B	HR	TB	R	RBI	TBB	IBB	SO	HBP	SH	SF	SB	CS	SB%	GDP	Avg	OBP	SLG
1998 Dubois Cty	IND —	39	96	14	2	0	0	16	10	6	3	0	16	3	0	1	1	2	.33	4	.146	.194	.167
1999 Vermont	A- Mon	9	30	6	0	0	0	6	4	2	3	0	7	0	1	0	1	2	.33	0	.200	.273	.200
Cape Fear	A Mon	50	141	32	5	1	0	39	18	9	7	0	35	5	4	0	2	5	.29	2	.227	.288	.277
2000 Jupiter	A+ Mon	47	142	33	5	1	0	40	16	9	4	0	27	1	3	0	2	1	.67	3	.232	.259	.282
2001 Jupiter	A+ Mon	5	14	1	0	0	0	1	1	0	0	0	5	0	1	0	0	0	—	0	.071	.071	.071
Camden	IND —	2	5	0	0	0	0	0	0	0	0	0	3	0	0	0	0	0	—	0	.000	.000	.000
Daytona	A+ ChC	5	20	2	0	0	0	2	0	0	1	0	6	0	0	0	1	0	1.00	0	.100	.143	.100
West Tenn	AA ChC	64	140	36	7	1	0	45	16	15	6	0	35	3	6	1	1	3	.25	0	.257	.300	.321
4 Min. YEARS		221	588	124	19	3	0	149	65	41	24	0	134	12	15	2	8	13	.38	9	.211	.256	.253

Tydus Meadows

Bats: Right **Throws:** Right **Pos:** OF-59; PH-8; DH-7; PR-1   **Ht:** 6'2" **Wt:** 215 **Born:** 9/5/77 **Age:** 24

Year Team	Lg Org	G	AB	H	2B	3B	HR	TB	R	RBI	TBB	IBB	SO	HBP	SH	SF	SB	CS	SB%	GDP	Avg	OBP	SLG
1998 Cubs	R ChC	27	98	36	8	4	3	61	25	26	17	1	17	2	0	0	6	5	.55	1	.367	.470	.622
Rockford	A ChC	35	134	39	5	0	7	65	35	24	15	1	32	4	0	1	6	1	.86	1	.291	.377	.485
1999 Lansing	A ChC	126	449	135	32	6	17	230	80	74	66	2	85	11	0	4	18	10	.64	13	.301	.400	.512
2000 Daytona	A+ ChC	46	167	52	11	2	6	85	30	24	17	0	36	4	1	2	11	4	.73	1	.311	.384	.509
West Tenn	AA ChC	80	249	65	14	4	5	102	33	32	20	0	72	4	2	5	4	2	.67	2	.261	.320	.410
2001 Daytona	A+ ChC	5	20	7	1	0	1	11	5	4	3	0	4	2	0	0	0	0	—	1	.350	.480	.550
Cubs	R ChC	1	2	0	0	0	0	0	0	0	0	0	1	0	0	0	0	0	—	0	.000	.000	.000
West Tenn	AA ChC	67	197	53	10	3	10	99	42	29	40	2	57	8	0	0	2	2	.00	5	.269	.412	.503
4 Min. YEARS		387	1316	387	81	19	49	653	250	213	178	6	304	35	3	12	45	24	.65	24	.294	.389	.496

Carlos Medina

Pitches: Left **Bats:** Left **Pos:** RP-24   **Ht:** 6'2" **Wt:** 160 **Born:** 5/16/77 **Age:** 25

		HOW MUCH HE PITCHED						WHAT HE GAVE UP									THE RESULTS					
Year Team	Lg Org	G	GS	CG	GF	IP	BFP	H	R	ER	HR	SH	SF	HB	TBB	IBB	SO	WP	Bk	W	L	Pct.	ShO	Sv	ERA
1996 Marlins	R Fla	4	1	0	1	9.2	48	16	7	4	0	1	0	2	1	0	9	3	0	0	1	.000	0	0	3.72
1998 Delmarva	A Bal	22	11	0	5	80.2	343	70	41	34	7	10	3	6	39	1	85	5	3	4	6	.400	0	0	3.79
Bowie	AA Bal	1	1	0	0	5	16	1	0	0	0	0	0	0	0	0	6	1	0	1	0	1.000	0	0	0.00
1999 Frederick	A+ Bal	5	5	0	0	31.1	127	22	6	6	1	2	0	3	13	0	30	1	1	4	0	1.000	0	0	1.72
Bowie	AA Bal	15	15	0	0	78	350	86	52	48	6	2	2	7	37	0	70	6	4	3	6	.333	0	0	5.54
2000 St. Lucie	A+ NYM	11	1	0	2	21.1	87	22	10	8	0	1	0	1	9	0	16	0	2	1	2	.333	0	0	3.38
2001 Binghamton	AA NYM	24	0	0	5	33	151	36	15	13	2	3	2	1	13	2	17	4	0	0	1	.000	0	1	3.55
5 Min. YEARS		82	34	0	13	259	1122	253	131	113	16	19	7	20	112	3	233	20	10	13	16	.448	0	1	3.93

195

Rafael Medina

Pitches: Right **Bats:** Right **Pos:** RP-27   **Ht:** 6'3" **Wt:** 240 **Born:** 2/15/75 **Age:** 27

Year Team	Lg Org	G	GS	CG	GF	IP	BFP	H	R	ER	HR	SH	SF	HB	TBB	IBB	SO	WP	Bk	W	L	Pct.	ShO	Sv	ERA
1993 Yankees	R NYY	5	5	0	0	27.1	107	16	6	2	0	1	1	1	12	0	21	1	1	2	0	1.000	0	0	0.66
1994 Oneonta	A- NYY	14	14	1	0	73.1	319	67	54	38	7	2	1	1	35	0	59	7	3	3	7	.300	0	0	4.66
1995 Greensboro	A NYY	19	19	1	0	98.2	418	86	48	44	8	0	5	6	38	0	108	6	3	4	4	.500	0	0	4.01
Tampa	A+ NYY	6	6	0	0	30.1	131	29	12	8	0	0	0	1	12	0	25	0	2	2	2	.500	0	0	2.37
1996 Norwich	AA NYY	19	19	1	0	103	446	78	48	35	7	5	1	6	55	2	112	11	4	5	8	.385	0	0	3.06
1997 Rancho Cuca	A+ SD	3	3	0	0	18	68	13	4	4	1	1	0	0	5	0	14	1	0	2	0	1.000	0	0	2.00
Las Vegas	AAA SD	13	13	0	0	66.2	321	90	60	56	12	1	1	2	39	1	50	8	2	4	5	.444	0	0	7.56
1998 Charlotte	AAA Fla	11	9	3	1	57.2	245	53	27	25	8	0	2	2	26	1	41	4	1	4	2	.667	1	0	3.90
1999 Calgary	AAA Fla	25	0	0	9	35	153	29	15	13	1	1	0	2	21	0	34	3	0	1	2	.333	0	1	3.34
2000 Syracuse	AAA Tor	33	2	0	16	54.2	235	37	18	17	2	0	2	3	35	1	33	4	0	3	1	.750	0	1	2.80
2001 Memphis	AAA StL	27	0	0	9	38.2	165	30	17	16	6	1	1	3	16	0	36	2	0	3	1	.750	0	0	3.72
1998 Florida	NL	12	12	0	0	67.1		76	50	45	8	5	4	3	52	3	49	5	0	2	6	.250	0	0	6.01
1999 Florida	NL	20	0	0	4	23.1	110	20	15	15	3	1	0	1	20	2	16	2	1	1	1	.500	0	0	5.79
9 Min. YEARS		175	90	6	35	603.1	2608	528	309	258	52	12	18	27	294	5	533	47	16	33	32	.508	1	2	3.85
2 Maj. YEARS		32	12	0	4	90.2	437	96	65	60	11	6	4	4	72	5	65	7	1	3	7	.300	0	0	5.96

Anthony Medrano

Bats: Right **Throws:** Right **Pos:** 2B-48; OF-37; SS-26; 3B-17; DH-2   **Ht:** 5'10" **Wt:** 175 **Born:** 12/8/74 **Age:** 27

Year Team	Lg Org	G	AB	H	2B	3B	HR	TB	R	RBI	TBB	IBB	SO	HBP	SH	SF	SB	CS	SB%	GDP	Avg	OBP	SLG
1993 Blue Jays	R Tor	39	158	42	9	0	0	51	20	9	10	0	9	3	0	0	6	2	.75	1	.266	.322	.323
1994 Blue Jays	R Tor	6	22	8	4	0	1	15	2	5	1	0	0	0	0	0	0	0	—	2	.364	.391	.682
Dunedin	A+ Tor	60	199	47	6	4	4	73	20	21	12	0	26	3	3	1	3	3	.50	4	.236	.288	.367
1995 Wichita	AA KC	1	5	0	0	0	0	0	0	0	0	0	3	0	0	0	0	0	—	0	.000	.000	.000
Wilmington	A+ KC	123	460	131	20	6	3	172	69	43	34	2	42	5	15	4	11	6	.65	10	.285	.338	.374
1996 Wichita	AA KC	125	474	130	26	1	8	182	59	55	18	0	36	2	7	2	10	8	.56	8	.274	.302	.384
1997 Wichita	AA KC	108	349	86	9	1	4	109	45	42	26	1	32	1	9	4	8	2	.80	10	.246	.297	.312
Omaha	AAA KC	17	59	12	0	0	4	24	10	9	4	1	5	0	0	2	0	1	.00	1	.203	.242	.407
1998 Wichita	AA KC	95	301	92	14	2	10	140	48	46	28	0	36	9	8	3	3	3	.50	7	.306	.378	.465
1999 Wichita	AA KC	73	257	87	15	1	5	119	45	32	21	0	23	4	5	6	4	2	.67	3	.339	.389	.463
Omaha	AAA KC	33	112	35	6	1	2	49	14	23	10	0	15	1	3	2	0	1	.00	3	.313	.368	.438
2000 Omaha	AAA KC	128	485	129	23	1	8	178	65	55	33	0	45	3	7	4	18	8	.69	14	.266	.314	.367
2001 Buffalo	AAA Cle	121	466	135	28	1	7	186	68	52	54	1	40	6	9	6	21	7	.75	12	.290	.367	.399
9 Min. YEARS		929	3347	934	160	18	56	1298	465	392	251	5	312	37	66	35	84	43	.66	75	.279	.333	.388

Steve Medrano

Bats: Both **Throws:** Right **Pos:** SS-73; 2B-14; PR-2   **Ht:** 6'0" **Wt:** 150 **Born:** 10/8/77 **Age:** 24

Year Team	Lg Org	G	AB	H	2B	3B	HR	TB	R	RBI	TBB	IBB	SO	HBP	SH	SF	SB	CS	SB%	GDP	Avg	OBP	SLG
1996 Royals	R KC	46	154	42	10	0	1	55	24	11	19	2	21	2	3	0	3	1	.75	4	.273	.360	.357
1997 Lansing	A KC	97	321	71	7	5	0	88	35	29	34	0	39	3	3	3	10	5	.67	8	.221	.299	.274
1998 Lansing	A KC	106	340	88	14	5	0	112	45	29	34	2	39	4	13	3	15	3	.83	4	.259	.332	.329
1999 Wilmington	A+ KC	98	362	91	4	3	0	101	41	24	30	1	66	1	8	1	12	10	.55	5	.251	.310	.279
2000 Chston-WV	A KC	44	163	35	3	0	0	38	30	9	24	0	28	1	4	1	5	1	.83	6	.215	.317	.233
Wilmington	A+ KC	3	13	2	0	0	0	2	1	0	0	0	0	0	1	0	0	0	—	0	.154	.154	.154
Wichita	AA KC	16	49	11	0	0	0	11	5	4	2	0	9	0	1	1	0	2	.00	1	.224	.250	.224
2001 Wichita	AA KC	46	140	34	5	0	0	39	16	15	14	0	22	0	3	0	3	2	.60	5	.243	.312	.279
Wilmington	A+ KC	42	146	30	3	0	0	33	22	7	14	0	37	4	4	0	2	2	.50	1	.205	.293	.226
6 Min. YEARS		498	1688	404	46	13	1	479	219	128	171	5	261	15	40	8	50	26	.66	34	.239	.313	.284

Dan Meier

Bats: Left **Throws:** Left **Pos:** OF-59; 1B-40; DH-18; PH-7   **Ht:** 6'0" **Wt:** 202 **Born:** 8/13/77 **Age:** 24

Year Team	Lg Org	G	AB	H	2B	3B	HR	TB	R	RBI	TBB	IBB	SO	HBP	SH	SF	SB	CS	SB%	GDP	Avg	OBP	SLG
1998 South Bend	A Ari	22	56	10	3	0	0	13	7	5	11	0	20	0	0	0	0	0	—	1	.179	.313	.232
Tucson	AAA Ari	10	29	6	3	0	0	9	5	2	1	0	9	0	0	1	0	0	—	1	.207	.226	.310
Diamondbcks	R Ari	12	35	12	3	0	1	18	10	5	11	0	8	0	0	1	1	0	1.00	0	.343	.489	.514
1999 High Desert	A+ Ari	129	418	112	25	4	24	217	85	89	70	3	138	9	1	1	0	0	—	6	.268	.384	.519
2000 El Paso	AA Ari	25	62	12	1	1	2	21	8	7	3	0	25	0	0	1	0	1	.00	3	.194	.227	.339
High Desert	A+ Ari	11	30	8	1	0	2	15	6	4	7	0	8	0	0	1	0	0	—	1	.267	.395	.500
Lynchburg	A+ Pit	57	202	62	12	2	14	120	45	43	29	1	46	7	0	1	2	2	.50	5	.307	.410	.594
2001 Lynchburg	A+ Pit	20	73	21	7	0	3	37	11	12	10	0	21	0	0	1	1	1	.50	2	.288	.369	.507
Altoona	AA Pit	97	312	80	14	4	13	141	43	38	45	0	80	3	3	1	1	1	.50	7	.256	.355	.452
4 Min. YEARS		383	1217	323	69	11	59	591	220	205	187	4	355	19	4	8	5	5	.50	26	.265	.370	.486

Dave Meliah

Bats: Left **Throws:** Right **Pos:** 2B-30; DH-28; 3B-21; 1B-13; OF-11; PH-8; SS-5; PR-1   **Ht:** 6'3" **Wt:** 185 **Born:** 3/11/77 **Age:** 25

Year Team	Lg Org	G	AB	H	2B	3B	HR	TB	R	RBI	TBB	IBB	SO	HBP	SH	SF	SB	CS	SB%	GDP	Avg	OBP	SLG
1998 Pulaski	R+ Tex	48	183	48	8	0	5	71	21	28	13	1	26	2	1	3	5	3	.63	0	.262	.313	.388
1999 Savannah	A Tex	93	358	106	21	3	8	157	53	49	16	0	80	3	0	2	3	6	.33	8	.296	.330	.439
2000 Tulsa	AA Tex	10	36	9	1	2	0	14	2	5	1	1	7	0	0	1	0	0	—	0	.250	.263	.389
Charlotte	A+ Tex	104	407	118	24	7	6	174	65	50	16	2	53	3	3	5	2	2	.50	7	.290	.318	.428
2001 Oklahoma	AAA Tex	20	63	16	5	0	1	24	9	7	9	0	13	0	0	0	2	2	.50	0	.254	.347	.381
Tulsa	AA Tex	90	307	89	17	4	12	150	40	47	24	2	47	1	1	1	4	4	.50	4	.290	.342	.489
4 Min. YEARS		365	1354	386	76	16	32	590	190	186	79	6	226	9	5	12	16	17	.48	19	.285	.326	.436

Jackson Melian

Bats: Right **Throws:** Right **Pos:** OF-114; PH-4; DH-2   **Ht:** 6'2" **Wt:** 190 **Born:** 1/20/80 **Age:** 22

Year Team	Lg Org	G	AB	H	2B	3B	HR	TB	R	RBI	TBB	IBB	SO	HBP	SH	SF	SB	CS	SB%	GDP	Avg	OBP	SLG
1997 Yankees	R NYY	57	213	56	11	2	3	80	32	36	20	0	52	0	0	2	9	1	.90	8	.263	.323	.376
1998 Greensboro	A NYY	135	467	119	18	2	8	165	66	45	41	0	120	7	1	4	15	12	.56	12	.255	.322	.353
1999 Tampa	A+ NYY	128	467	132	17	13	6	193	65	61	49	1	98	10	1	8	11	8	.58	8	.283	.358	.413
2000 Norwich	AA NYY	81	290	73	8	4	9	116	34	38	18	1	69	3	2	3	17	1	.94	6	.252	.299	.400
Chattanooga	AA Cin	2	6	1	0	0	0	1	0	0	0	0	0	0	0	0	0	0	—	0	.167	.167	.167
2001 Chattanooga	AA Cin	120	426	101	22	0	16	171	64	52	36	1	95	10	0	1	10	7	.59	11	.237	.311	.401
5 Min. YEARS		523	1869	482	76	21	42	726	261	232	164	3	434	30	4	18	62	29	.68	45	.258	.325	.388

Juan Melo

Bats: Both **Throws:** Right **Pos:** 2B-94; 3B-4; SS-2; PH-2   **Ht:** 6'1" **Wt:** 180 **Born:** 5/11/76 **Age:** 26

Year Team	Lg Org	G	AB	H	2B	3B	HR	TB	R	RBI	TBB	IBB	SO	HBP	SH	SF	SB	CS	SB%	GDP	Avg	OBP	SLG
1994 Spokane	A- SD	3	11	4	1	0	1	8	4	2	1	0	3	0	0	0	0	0	—	1	.364	.417	.727
Padres	R SD	37	145	41	3	3	0	50	20	15	10	0	36	6	0	1	3	2	.60	5	.283	.352	.345
1995 Clinton	A SD	134	479	135	32	1	5	184	65	46	33	0	88	5	5	2	12	10	.55	11	.282	.333	.384
1996 Rancho Cuca	A+ SD	128	503	153	27	6	8	216	75	75	22	0	102	10	0	1	6	8	.43	10	.304	.345	.429
1997 Las Vegas	AAA SD	12	48	13	4	0	1	20	6	6	1	0	10	1	0	1	0	0	—	0	.271	.294	.417
Mobile	AA SD	113	456	131	22	2	7	178	52	67	29	4	90	0	0	2	7	9	.44	16	.287	.329	.390
1998 Las Vegas	AAA SD	130	467	127	26	1	6	173	61	47	24	2	91	4	2	3	9	8	.53	15	.272	.311	.370
1999 Las Vegas	AAA SD	45	169	34	3	2	2	47	17	13	7	0	34	2	0	0	1	1	.50	5	.201	.242	.278
Syracuse	AAA Tor	41	141	33	9	1	3	53	21	13	10	0	31	1	0	1	8	4	.67	2	.234	.288	.376
Indianapols	AAA Cin	3	9	3	0	0	1	6	2	3	0	0	2	0	0	0	1	0	1.00	0	.333	.333	.667
2000 Fresno	AAA SF	123	417	123	26	6	12	197	58	50	35	3	89	3	4	1	13	13	.50	8	.295	.353	.472
2001 Fresno	AAA SF	100	375	117	22	4	9	174	46	55	19	1	64	5	1	5	9	9	.50	8	.312	.349	.464
2000 San Francisco	NL	11	13	1	0	0	0	1	0	1	0	0	5	0	0	0	0	0	—	0	.077	.077	.077
8 Min. YEARS		869	3220	914	175	26	55	1306	427	392	191	10	640	37	12	17	69	64	.52	81	.284	.330	.406

John Melton

Bats: Right **Throws:** Right **Pos:** DH-21; C-20; PH-5   **Ht:** 6'2" **Wt:** 200 **Born:** 9/17/78 **Age:** 23

Year Team	Lg Org	G	AB	H	2B	3B	HR	TB	R	RBI	TBB	IBB	SO	HBP	SH	SF	SB	CS	SB%	GDP	Avg	OBP	SLG
2000 Diamondbcks	R Ari	22	59	20	7	1	0	29	12	9	5	0	24	3	0	1	0	1	.00	1	.339	.412	.492
Missoula	R+ Ari	2	5	1	0	0	0	1	2	0	3	0	3	0	0	0	0	0	—	0	.200	.500	.200
2001 Lancaster	A+ Ari	31	85	17	3	1	1	25	10	8	13	0	36	2	2	0	0	1	.00	1	.200	.320	.294
El Paso	AA Ari	2	4	2	1	0	0	3	0	2	1	0	2	0	0	0	0	0	—	0	.500	.600	.750
Missoula	R+ Ari	13	32	9	1	0	2	16	5	6	7	0	11	0	0	0	1	0	1.00	1	.281	.410	.500
2 Min. YEARS		70	185	49	12	2	3	74	29	25	29	0	76	5	2	1	1	2	.33	3	.265	.377	.400

Lou Melucci

Bats: Right **Throws:** Right **Pos:** 3B-32; 2B-16; SS-13; DH-8; PR-4; PH-3; OF-2   **Ht:** 5'9" **Wt:** 175 **Born:** 9/20/77 **Age:** 24

Year Team	Lg Org	G	AB	H	2B	3B	HR	TB	R	RBI	TBB	IBB	SO	HBP	SH	SF	SB	CS	SB%	GDP	Avg	OBP	SLG
1999 Vermont	A- Mon	33	123	24	3	1	0	29	13	7	10	0	34	1	1	0	6	1	.86	2	.195	.261	.236
2000 Cape Fear	A Mon	68	198	46	9	2	2	65	27	18	20	0	58	4	0	1	8	0	1.00	1	.232	.314	.328
2001 Jupiter	A+ Mon	65	201	44	6	1	1	55	20	16	25	0	61	1	6	0	3	4	.43	4	.219	.308	.274
Harrisburg	AA Mon	6	15	3	0	0	0	3	1	2	0	0	7	0	0	1	1	0	1.00	0	.200	.188	.200
3 Min. YEARS		172	537	117	18	4	3	152	61	43	55	0	160	6	7	2	18	5	.78	7	.218	.297	.283

Kevin Mench

Bats: Right **Throws:** Right **Pos:** OF-117; DH-2; PH-1   **Ht:** 6'0" **Wt:** 215 **Born:** 1/7/78 **Age:** 24

Year Team	Lg Org	G	AB	H	2B	3B	HR	TB	R	RBI	TBB	IBB	SO	HBP	SH	SF	SB	CS	SB%	GDP	Avg	OBP	SLG
1999 Pulaski	R+ Tex	65	260	94	22	1	16	166	63	60	28	0	48	2	0	5	12	2	.86	2	.362	.420	.638
Savannah	A Tex	6	23	7	1	1	2	16	4	8	2	0	4	0	0	0	0	0	—	0	.304	.360	.696
2000 Charlotte	A+ Tex	132	491	164	39	9	27	302	118	121	78	3	72	7	0	7	19	7	.73	9	.334	.427	.615
2001 Tulsa	AA Tex	120	475	126	34	2	26	242	78	83	34	0	76	6	0	6	4	6	.40	7	.265	.319	.509
3 Min. YEARS		323	1249	391	96	13	71	726	263	272	142	3	200	15	0	18	35	15	.70	19	.313	.385	.581

Carlos Mendez

Bats: Right **Throws:** Right **Pos:** 1B-55; C-41; DH-8; PH-3   **Ht:** 6'0" **Wt:** 210 **Born:** 6/18/74 **Age:** 28

Year Team	Lg Org	G	AB	H	2B	3B	HR	TB	R	RBI	TBB	IBB	SO	HBP	SH	SF	SB	CS	SB%	GDP	Avg	OBP	SLG
1992 Royals	R KC	49	200	61	16	1	3	88	34	33	8	2	13	2	0	3	2	1	.67	2	.305	.333	.440
1993 Royals	R KC	50	163	51	10	0	4	73	18	27	4	1	15	2	0	4	6	1	.86	2	.313	.329	.448
1994 Rockford	A KC	104	363	129	26	2	5	174	45	51	13	2	50	5	4	4	0	2	.00	11	.355	.382	.479
1995 Wilmington	A+ KC	107	396	108	19	2	7	152	46	61	18	1	36	0	1	5	0	4	.00	17	.273	.301	.384
1996 Wilmington	A+ KC	109	406	119	25	3	4	162	40	59	22	4	39	3	3	7	3	1	.75	6	.293	.329	.399
1997 Wichita	AA KC	129	507	165	32	1	12	235	72	90	19	2	43	1	0	8	4	7	.36	19	.325	.346	.464
1998 Omaha	AAA KC	50	173	47	13	0	2	66	23	18	10	0	24	1	0	2	3	0	1.00	4	.272	.312	.382
Wichita	AA KC	52	207	66	14	0	9	107	37	39	7	1	20	0	1	5	4	1	.80	10	.319	.333	.517
1999 Omaha	AAA KC	84	293	82	25	0	10	137	38	37	6	0	32	0	3	3	4	3	.57	8	.280	.291	.468
2000 Toledo	AAA Det	100	374	108	21	0	19	186	49	72	12	0	37	3	0	7	0	0	—	11	.289	.311	.497
2001 Toledo	AAA Det	102	398	98	27	1	18	181	45	76	9	0	53	5	3	6	0	0	—	13	.246	.268	.455
10 Min. YEARS		936	3480	1034	228	10	93	1561	447	563	128	13	362	22	15	54	26	20	.57	103	.297	.321	.449

Geronimo Mendoza

Pitches: Right **Bats:** Left **Pos:** SP-27; RP-2   **Ht:** 6'4" **Wt:** 180 **Born:** 1/23/78 **Age:** 24

		HOW MUCH HE PITCHED					WHAT HE GAVE UP										THE RESULTS					
Year Team	Lg Org	G	GS	CG	GF	IP	BFP	H	R	ER	HR	SH	SF	HB	TBB	IBB	SO	WP	Bk	W	L	Pct.	ShO	Sv	ERA
1995 White Sox	R CWS	10	0	0	8	14.2	59	8	9	7	3	0	2	1	7	0	11	1	0	0	1	.000	0	0	4.30
1996 White Sox	R CWS	12	7	0	0	38.2	202	55	49	42	2	3	3	3	26	0	29	6	1	1	8	.111	0	0	9.78
1997 White Sox	R CWS	12	8	0	1	54	241	51	32	22	3	5	2	3	28	0	41	4	0	2	7	.222	0	0	3.67
1998 Bristol	R+ CWS	13	13	0	0	80	350	78	40	34	5	2	1	4	30	0	70	6	0	5	2	.714	0	0	3.83
1999 Burlington	A CWS	28	28	0	0	157.1	713	186	96	81	10	3	3	8	60	5	119	7	0	9	8	.529	0	0	4.63
2000 Winston-Sal	A+ CWS	31	19	4	4	145	635	146	65	55	7	5	3	4	65	0	117	13	0	11	6	.647	3	0	3.41
2001 Birmingham	AA CWS	12	12	0	0	69.1	312	84	51	39	7	2	3	2	28	0	38	3	0	5	4	.556	0	0	5.06
Charlotte	AAA CWS	17	15	0	1	96.1	407	103	57	53	16	2	5	1	31	2	68	6	0	5	8	.385	0	0	4.95
7 Min. YEARS		135	102	4	14	655.1	2919	711	399	333	53	22	22	26	275	7	493	46	1	38	44	.463	3	0	4.57

Hatuey Mendoza

Pitches: Right **Bats:** Right **Pos:** SP-21; RP-11   **Ht:** 6'1" **Wt:** 175 **Born:** 3/16/80 **Age:** 22

		HOW MUCH HE PITCHED					WHAT HE GAVE UP										THE RESULTS					
Year Team	Lg Org	G	GS	CG	GF	IP	BFP	H	R	ER	HR	SH	SF	HB	TBB	IBB	SO	WP	Bk	W	L	Pct.	ShO	Sv	ERA
1997 Diamondbcks	R Ari	17	0	0	5	29.2	151	29	27	25	0	2	0	8	25	1	24	3	0	1	5	.167	0	0	7.58
1998 Lethbridge	R+ Ari	1	1	0	0	0.2	8	2	4	2	0	0	0	0	3	0	1	1	0	0	1	.000	0	0	27.00
Diamondbcks	R Ari	11	10	0	0	44.1	209	43	30	18	1	0	1	5	23	0	54	13	0	2	3	.400	0	0	3.65
South Bend	A Ari	4	4	0	0	24	116	29	21	14	1	0	1	1	15	0	20	3	1	0	4	.000	0	0	5.25
1999 South Bend	A Ari	13	11	0	2	57.2	283	64	57	53	5	0	1	8	45	0	36	20	2	3	9	.250	0	0	8.27
Diamondbcks	R Ari	13	13	0	0	71.2	338	83	64	45	3	1	6	5	31	0	69	14	3	2	7	.222	0	0	5.65
Missoula	R+ Ari	1	0	0	1	3	15	3	5	0	0	0	0	0	2	0	3	3	0	0	0	—	0	0	0.00
2000 High Desert	A+ Ari	29	27	0	0	150.2	710	170	140	110	17	1	4	12	98	0	107	19	0	8	12	.400	0	0	6.57
2001 El Paso	AA Ari	8	5	0	0	28.2	135	29	25	20	3	1	1	3	17	0	20	1	1	1	5	.167	0	0	6.28
Lancaster	A+ Ari	24	16	1	1	105.1	455	114	69	55	17	2	5	4	43	0	72	7	3	8	5	.615	1	0	4.70
5 Min. YEARS		121	87	1	9	515.2	2420	566	442	342	47	7	19	46	302	1	406	84	10	25	51	.329	1	0	5.97

Todd Mensik

Bats: Left **Throws:** Left **Pos:** 1B-130; OF-3; DH-1; PH-1   **Ht:** 6'2" **Wt:** 195 **Born:** 2/27/75 **Age:** 27

		BATTING															BASERUNNING				PERCENTAGES		
Year Team	Lg Org	G	AB	H	2B	3B	HR	TB	R	RBI	TBB	IBB	SO	HBP	SH	SF	SB	CS	SB%	GDP	Avg	OBP	SLG
1996 Sou Oregon	A- Oak	59	192	46	8	0	0	54	21	14	19	2	39	2	0	4	2	0	1.00	6	.240	.309	.281
1997 Visalia	A+ Oak	15	45	9	1	0	1	13	3	6	6	0	11	1	0	1	0	0	—	2	.200	.302	.289
1998 Modesto	A+ Oak	111	379	104	26	2	14	176	56	59	63	2	103	2	2	1	1	4	.20	2	.274	.380	.464
1999 Visalia	A+ Oak	134	505	147	29	4	29	271	93	123	79	11	114	9	0	3	5	1	.83	8	.291	.394	.537
2000 Midland	AA Oak	124	414	109	24	2	23	206	56	84	72	6	114	5	2	5	0	0	—	11	.263	.375	.498
2001 Midland	AA Oak	132	502	142	35	1	21	242	69	79	60	2	104	4	0	5	0	1	.00	16	.283	.361	.482
6 Min. YEARS		575	2037	557	123	9	88	962	298	365	299	23	485	23	4	19	8	6	.57	45	.273	.370	.472

Jorge Meran

Bats: Right **Throws:** Right **Pos:** C-40; DH-2   **Ht:** 6'1" **Wt:** 168 **Born:** 6/18/77 **Age:** 25

		BATTING															BASERUNNING				PERCENTAGES		
Year Team	Lg Org	G	AB	H	2B	3B	HR	TB	R	RBI	TBB	IBB	SO	HBP	SH	SF	SB	CS	SB%	GDP	Avg	OBP	SLG
1996 Tigers	R Det	51	168	53	13	3	2	78	25	32	13	0	42	5	1	2	7	2	.78	3	.315	.378	.464
1997 Jamestown	A- Det	51	183	32	11	0	4	55	21	15	11	1	50	0	0	1	2	1	.67	3	.175	.221	.301
1998 Lakeland	A+ Det	7	20	4	3	0	0	7	0	1	0	0	7	0	0	0	0	0	—	0	.200	.200	.350
Jamestown	A- Det	30	110	30	7	1	4	51	13	20	15	2	24	2	0	0	3	1	.75	3	.273	.370	.464
1999 W Michigan	A Det	44	152	30	9	4	2	53	18	23	7	0	38	1	1	2	1	3	.25	1	.197	.235	.349
2000 Jacksnville	AA Det	4	13	2	0	0	0	2	2	0	0	0	1	1	0	0	0	0	—	2	.154	.214	.154
Lakeland	A+ Det	63	224	60	10	3	7	97	22	19	10	0	45	0	0	0	2	3	.40	2	.268	.299	.433
2001 Toledo	AAA Det	7	21	4	0	0	0	4	0	2	2	0	7	0	1	1	1	0	1.00	1	.190	.250	.190
Erie	AA Det	35	117	31	4	0	3	44	11	17	4	0	39	4	1	1	0	0	—	2	.265	.310	.376
6 Min. YEARS		292	1008	246	57	11	22	391	112	129	62	3	253	13	4	7	16	10	.62	15	.244	.294	.388

Ronnie Merrill

Bats: Both **Throws:** Right **Pos:** SS-88; 2B-32; DH-1; PH-1   **Ht:** 6'1" **Wt:** 185 **Born:** 11/13/78 **Age:** 23

		BATTING															BASERUNNING				PERCENTAGES		
Year Team	Lg Org	G	AB	H	2B	3B	HR	TB	R	RBI	TBB	IBB	SO	HBP	SH	SF	SB	CS	SB%	GDP	Avg	OBP	SLG
2000 Oneonta	A- Det	33	135	42	5	2	1	54	21	21	12	1	23	2	0	0	6	3	.67	1	.311	.376	.400
2001 W Michigan	A Det	83	309	98	11	3	8	139	53	53	36	2	47	7	2	6	15	7	.68	5	.317	.394	.450
Erie	AA Det	37	147	43	14	0	4	69	22	18	12	1	27	0	2	2	0	1	.00	3	.293	.342	.469
2 Min. YEARS		153	591	183	30	5	13	262	96	92	60	4	97	9	4	8	21	11	.66	9	.310	.377	.443

Joey Messman

Pitches: Right **Bats:** Right **Pos:** RP-34; SP-1   **Ht:** 6'2" **Wt:** 175 **Born:** 7/29/75 **Age:** 26

		HOW MUCH HE PITCHED					WHAT HE GAVE UP										THE RESULTS					
Year Team	Lg Org	G	GS	CG	GF	IP	BFP	H	R	ER	HR	SH	SF	HB	TBB	IBB	SO	WP	Bk	W	L	Pct.	ShO	Sv	ERA
1997 Auburn	A- Hou	25	0	0	10	28	132	26	13	10	1	3	0	6	21	3	31	8	0	1	2	.333	0	1	3.21
1998 Quad City	A Hou	63	0	0	16	87.2	359	70	36	30	2	2	3	4	33	4	74	9	0	6	3	.667	0	5	3.08
1999 Kissimmee	A+ Hou	45	0	0	40	59.1	251	38	20	16	6	4	0	4	35	2	47	6	2	3	4	.429	0	15	2.43
San Jose	A+ SF	2	0	0	2	1.2	13	6	5	5	0	0	0	0	3	0	3	3	0	0	0	—	0	0	27.00
2000 Shreveport	AA SF	38	0	0	11	60.2	248	51	27	23	7	2	4	0	23	2	46	8	1	5	2	.714	0	1	3.41
2001 Shreveport	AA SF	12	1	0	3	26.1	119	24	15	12	3	4	3	2	14	0	13	1	1	1	1	.500	0	2	4.10
San Jose	A+ SF	23	0	0	8	42	186	47	28	18	3	2	2	2	15	0	24	7	2	3	1	.750	0	2	3.86
5 Min. YEARS		208	1	0	90	305.2	1308	262	144	114	22	17	12	18	144	11	235	42	6	19	13	.594	0	24	3.36

198

Mike Metcalfe

Bats: Both **Throws:** Right **Pos:** 2B-90; OF-32; PH-7; DH-2   **Ht:** 5'10" **Wt:** 175 **Born:** 1/2/73 **Age:** 29

					BATTING												BASERUNNING				PERCENTAGES		
Year Team	Lg Org	G	AB	H	2B	3B	HR	TB	R	RBI	TBB	IBB	SO	HBP	SH	SF	SB	CS	SB%	GDP	Avg	OBP	SLG
1994 Bakersfield	A+ LA	69	275	78	10	0	0	88	44	18	28	0	34	1	4	2	41	13	.76	6	.284	.350	.320
1995 San Antonio	AA LA	10	41	10	1	0	0	11	10	2	7	0	2	0	1	1	1	2	.33	0	.244	.347	.268
Vero Beach	A+ LA	120	435	131	13	3	3	159	86	35	60	2	37	3	6	5	60	27	.69	8	.301	.386	.366
1996 Vero Beach	A+ LA	2	5	0	0	0	0	0	0	0	0	0	0	0	0	0	0	0	—	0	.000	.000	.000
1997 San Berndno	A+ LA	132	519	147	28	7	3	198	83	47	55	0	79	4	6	1	67	32	.68	5	.283	.356	.382
1998 San Antonio	AA LA	57	213	60	5	5	3	84	35	19	30	1	24	1	3	2	19	15	.56	3	.282	.370	.394
1999 San Antonio	AA LA	123	461	135	25	3	3	175	78	57	65	1	47	3	9	4	57	21	.73	3	.293	.381	.380
2000 San Antonio	AA LA	52	196	48	5	3	2	65	42	25	30	1	18	1	4	1	34	9	.79	0	.245	.346	.332
Albuquerque	AAA LA	35	149	45	6	3	0	57	22	21	10	0	16	2	2	2	9	11	.45	2	.302	.350	.383
2001 Louisville	AAA Cin	6	20	3	0	0	0	3	1	0	4	0	5	0	0	0	2	1	.67	0	.150	.292	.150
Chattanooga	AA Cin	123	474	137	25	4	3	179	68	47	38	2	59	2	6	1	32	10	.76	9	.289	.344	.378
1998 Los Angeles	NL	4	1	0	0	0	0	0	0	0	0	0	1	0	0	0	2	0	1.00	0	.000	.000	.000
2000 Los Angeles	NL	4	12	1	0	0	0	1	0	0	1	0	2	0	0	0	0	0	—	0	.083	.154	.083
8 Min. YEARS		729	2788	794	118	28	17	1019	469	271	327	7	321	17	41	19	322	141	.70	36	.285	.361	.365
2 Maj. YEARS		8	13	1	0	0	0	1	0	0	1	0	3	0	0	0	2	0	1.00	0	.077	.143	.077

Rod Metzler

Bats: Both **Throws:** Right **Pos:** 2B-102; OF-10; PR-4; PH-2   **Ht:** 5'11" **Wt:** 185 **Born:** 11/19/74 **Age:** 27

					BATTING												BASERUNNING				PERCENTAGES		
Year Team	Lg Org	G	AB	H	2B	3B	HR	TB	R	RBI	TBB	IBB	SO	HBP	SH	SF	SB	CS	SB%	GDP	Avg	OBP	SLG
1997 Spokane	A- KC	62	224	55	5	5	3	75	37	31	18	0	48	1	5	2	9	2	.82	1	.228	.286	.335
1998 Lansing	A KC	88	323	81	17	4	2	112	45	34	36	0	77	3	4	0	17	6	.74	2	.251	.331	.347
1999 Chston-WV	A KC	130	462	122	23	7	7	180	64	60	48	0	98	9	5	1	29	14	.67	7	.264	.344	.390
Wichita	AA KC	3	10	5	2	0	2	13	5	4	0	0	3	1	1	0	0	0	—	0	.500	.545	1.300
2000 Wichita	AA KC	111	361	96	15	3	5	132	50	44	28	4	74	5	5	1	7	8	.47	4	.266	.327	.366
2001 Wichita	AA KC	110	381	108	20	3	4	146	62	62	46	3	81	5	4	3	13	11	.54	10	.283	.366	.383
5 Min. YEARS		504	1761	463	82	22	23	658	263	235	176	7	381	24	24	7	75	41	.65	24	.263	.337	.374

Jake Meyer

Pitches: Right **Bats:** Right **Pos:** RP-32; SP-2   **Ht:** 6'1" **Wt:** 195 **Born:** 1/7/75 **Age:** 27

		HOW MUCH HE PITCHED					WHAT HE GAVE UP										THE RESULTS					
Year Team	Lg Org	G	GS	CG	GF	IP	BFP	H	R	ER	HR	SH	SF	HB	TBB	IBB	SO	WP	Bk	W	L	Pct.	ShO	Sv	ERA
1997 Bristol	R+ CWS	17	0	0	15	20	84	15	7	5	3	1	0	0	7	0	25	4	0	1	1	.500	0	5	2.25
1998 Hickory	A CWS	35	0	0	24	56	244	58	30	20	5	2	1	0	22	1	47	7	1	0	6	.000	0	11	3.21
Winston-Sal	A+ CWS	11	0	0	10	12.1	51	12	6	4	1	0	0	0	3	2	13	2	0	0	1	.000	0	2	2.92
1999 Rockford	A Cin	33	0	0	31	46	197	40	16	13	1	4	0	3	18	4	51	2	0	3	2	.600	0	16	2.54
Chattanooga	AA Cin	20	0	0	10	22.2	102	24	17	15	1	0	1	0	14	0	16	4	0	2	2	.500	0	0	5.96
2000 New Haven	AA Sea	15	0	0	10	19.2	81	17	5	5	0	0	0	1	8	0	20	4	0	1	0	1.000	0	4	2.29
Mariners	R Sea	3	3	0	0	4	19	4	2	2	0	0	0	0	3	0	6	0	0	0	0	—	0	0	4.50
Tacoma	AAA Sea	8	0	0	4	12.2	52	9	5	5	2	1	0	0	5	1	14	3	0	0	1	.000	0	0	3.55
2001 Tacoma	AAA Sea	9	1	0	2	15.2	69	15	11	11	0	0	1	0	7	0	18	1	0	0	0	—	0	0	6.32
San Antonio	AA Sea	25	1	0	9	36.1	167	43	26	24	7	2	1	0	17	1	35	3	1	1	4	.200	0	1	5.94
5 Min. YEARS		176	5	0	115	245.1	1066	237	125	104	20	10	4	4	104	9	245	30	2	8	17	.320	0	37	3.82

Mike Meyers

Pitches: Right **Bats:** Right **Pos:** SP-25   **Ht:** 6'2" **Wt:** 210 **Born:** 10/18/77 **Age:** 24

		HOW MUCH HE PITCHED					WHAT HE GAVE UP										THE RESULTS					
Year Team	Lg Org	G	GS	CG	GF	IP	BFP	H	R	ER	HR	SH	SF	HB	TBB	IBB	SO	WP	Bk	W	L	Pct.	ShO	Sv	ERA
1997 Cubs	R ChC	12	2	0	4	38.1	166	34	15	6	2	1	1	2	13	0	45	0	0	3	1	.750	0	3	1.41
Williamsprt	A- ChC	1	1	0	0	4	15	3	0	0	1	0	0	0	1	0	2	0	0	0	0	—	0	0	0.00
1998 Rockford	A ChC	17	16	0	0	85.2	363	75	37	32	3	2	0	3	32	2	86	5	1	7	5	.583	0	0	3.36
1999 Daytona	A+ ChC	19	17	2	2	107.1	436	68	30	23	9	2	3	9	40	0	122	4	0	10	3	.769	0	0	1.93
West Tenn	AA ChC	5	5	0	0	33	128	21	5	4	1	1	1	0	10	1	51	1	0	4	0	1.000	0	0	1.09
2000 West Tenn	AA ChC	9	9	3	0	59	242	41	18	16	4	5	2	4	26	0	51	2	0	5	2	.714	1	0	2.44
Iowa	AAA ChC	13	12	0	0	59.1	278	74	51	48	9	2	5	6	30	2	44	2	0	2	6	.250	0	0	7.28
2001 Iowa	AAA ChC	25	25	0	0	147.2	631	129	58	53	9	3	6	2	64	3	124	8	0	7	4	.636	0	0	3.23
5 Min. YEARS		101	87	5	6	534.1	2259	445	214	182	37	17	18	26	216	8	525	22	2	38	21	.644	1	3	3.07

Jose Mieses

Pitches: Right **Bats:** Right **Pos:** SP-10; RP-1   **Ht:** 6'1" **Wt:** 165 **Born:** 10/14/79 **Age:** 22

		HOW MUCH HE PITCHED					WHAT HE GAVE UP										THE RESULTS					
Year Team	Lg Org	G	GS	CG	GF	IP	BFP	H	R	ER	HR	SH	SF	HB	TBB	IBB	SO	WP	Bk	W	L	Pct.	ShO	Sv	ERA
1999 Helena	R+ Mil	15	15	3	0	108	425	79	36	32	5	1	0	1	28	0	87	6	3	10	2	.833	1	0	2.67
2000 Beloit	A Mil	21	21	2	0	135	530	107	43	38	8	5	1	3	37	1	132	6	1	13	6	.684	2	0	2.53
Mudville	A+ Mil	6	6	0	0	34	144	25	11	10	1	1	1	2	18	0	40	3	1	4	1	.800	0	0	2.65
2001 Huntsville	AA Mil	5	4	0	1	24.1	97	21	7	6	2	0	1	2	3	0	35	2	0	0	0	—	0	0	2.22
Indianapols	AAA Mil	3	3	0	0	13.1	72	23	12	9	4	1	0	0	7	0	13	2	0	0	3	.000	0	0	6.08
Brewers	R Mil	2	2	0	0	4.1	19	3	1	0	0	0	0	0	1	0	5	1	0	0	1	.000	0	0	0.00
Ogden	R+ Mil	1	1	0	0	1	7	3	3	3	0	0	0	0	1	0	2	0	0	0	1	.000	0	0	27.00
3 Min. YEARS		53	52	5	1	320	1294	261	113	98	20	8	3	8	95	1	314	20	5	27	14	.659	3	0	2.76

199

Aaron Miles

Bats: Both   **Throws:** Right   **Pos:** DH-43; 3B-23; 2B-16; PH-2   **Ht:** 5'8"   **Wt:** 170   **Born:** 12/15/76   **Age:** 25

Year Team	Lg Org	G	AB	H	2B	3B	HR	TB	R	RBI	TBB	IBB	SO	HBP	SH	SF	SB	CS	SB%	GDP	Avg	OBP	SLG
1995 Astros	R Hou	47	171	44	9	3	0	59	32	18	14	0	14	0	4	1	9	6	.60	3	.257	.312	.345
1996 Astros	R Hou	55	214	63	3	2	0	70	48	15	20	0	18	1	5	0	14	7	.67	3	.294	.357	.327
1997 Quad City	A Hou	97	370	97	13	2	1	117	55	35	30	0	45	2	7	4	18	11	.62	8	.262	.318	.316
1998 Quad City	A Hou	108	369	90	22	6	2	130	42	37	25	3	52	1	7	1	28	13	.68	6	.244	.293	.352
1999 Michigan	A Hou	112	470	149	28	8	10	223	72	71	28	3	33	2	6	7	17	12	.59	8	.317	.353	.474
2000 Kissimmee	A+ Hou	75	295	86	20	1	2	114	40	36	28	0	29	0	2	1	11	6	.65	7	.292	.352	.386
2001 Birmingham	AA CWS	84	343	89	16	3	8	135	53	42	26	0	35	2	3	3	3	5	.38	10	.259	.313	.394
7 Min. YEARS		578	2232	618	111	25	23	848	342	254	171	6	226	8	34	17	100	60	.63	45	.277	.328	.380

Benji Miller

Pitches: Right   **Bats:** Right   **Pos:** RP-38   **Ht:** 6'2"   **Wt:** 180   **Born:** 5/2/76   **Age:** 26

	HOW MUCH HE PITCHED						WHAT HE GAVE UP										THE RESULTS					
Year Team	Lg Org	G	GS	CG	GF	IP	BFP	H	R	ER	HR	SH	SF	HB	TBB	IBB	SO	WP	Bk	W	L	Pct.	ShO	Sv	ERA
1998 Salem-Keizr	A- SF	30	0	0	27	44	180	33	13	11	1	0	0	0	20	0	51	4	0	4	3	.571	0	17	2.25
1999 San Jose	A+ SF	47	0	0	38	59.2	248	53	26	20	3	2	4	1	17	0	61	6	2	3	2	.600	0	20	3.02
2000 Shreveport	AA SF	58	0	0	29	86	372	81	44	32	10	6	2	2	37	7	71	3	4	3	9	.308	0	4	3.35
2001 Shreveport	AA SF	37	0	0	20	66	296	63	33	31	7	2	3	3	35	2	39	5	1	1	6	.143	0	2	4.23
San Jose	A+ SF	1	0	0	0	1	3	0	0	0	0	0	0	0	0	0	2	0	0	0	0	—	0	0	0.00
4 Min. YEARS		173	0	0	114	256.2	1099	230	116	94	21	10	9	6	109	9	224	18	6	12	20	.375	0	43	3.30

Greg Miller

Pitches: Left   **Bats:** Left   **Pos:** SP-14   **Ht:** 6'5"   **Wt:** 215   **Born:** 9/30/79   **Age:** 22

	HOW MUCH HE PITCHED						WHAT HE GAVE UP										THE RESULTS					
Year Team	Lg Org	G	GS	CG	GF	IP	BFP	H	R	ER	HR	SH	SF	HB	TBB	IBB	SO	WP	Bk	W	L	Pct.	ShO	Sv	ERA
1997 Red Sox	R Bos	4	4	0	0	9.2	40	8	6	4	0	0	0	0	6	0	6	0	2	0	2	.000	0	0	3.72
1998 Red Sox	R Bos	11	7	0	0	43.1	187	33	18	12	2	2	2	4	18	0	47	3	2	6	0	1.000	0	0	2.49
1999 Augusta	A Bos	25	25	1	0	136.2	558	109	54	47	8	1	0	5	56	0	146	4	3	10	6	.625	0	0	3.10
2000 Kissimmee	A+ Hou	24	24	1	0	146	604	131	63	60	13	4	5	2	46	1	109	5	2	10	8	.556	0	0	3.70
Round Rock	AA Hou	2	0	0	0	2.1	8	0	0	0	0	0	0	0	1	0	2	0	0	0	0	—	0	0	0.00
2001 Round Rock	AA Hou	14	14	0	0	55.1	236	38	22	20	3	1	4	3	35	0	37	1	0	5	3	.625	0	0	3.25
5 Min. YEARS		80	74	2	0	393.1	1633	319	163	143	26	8	11	14	162	1	347	13	9	31	19	.620	0	0	3.27

Justin Miller

Pitches: Right   **Bats:** Right   **Pos:** SP-28; RP-1   **Ht:** 6'2"   **Wt:** 195   **Born:** 8/27/77   **Age:** 24

	HOW MUCH HE PITCHED						WHAT HE GAVE UP										THE RESULTS					
Year Team	Lg Org	G	GS	CG	GF	IP	BFP	H	R	ER	HR	SH	SF	HB	TBB	IBB	SO	WP	Bk	W	L	Pct.	ShO	Sv	ERA
1997 Portland	A- Col	14	11	0	1	67.1	288	68	26	16	3	2	2	4	20	0	54	6	0	4	2	.667	0	0	2.14
1998 Asheville	A Col	27	27	3	0	163.1	705	177	89	67	14	4	3	15	40	0	142	5	0	13	8	.619	1	0	3.69
1999 Salem	A+ Col	8	8	0	0	37	159	35	18	17	3	0	0	5	11	0	35	5	0	1	2	.333	0	0	4.14
2000 Midland	AA Oak	18	18	0	0	87	371	74	49	44	8	2	0	6	41	1	82	9	1	5	4	.556	0	0	4.55
Sacramento	AAA Oak	9	9	0	0	54.2	217	42	18	15	3	0	1	3	13	0	34	2	0	4	1	.800	0	0	2.47
2001 Sacramento	AAA Oak	29	28	1	0	165	718	174	94	87	26	4	4	16	64	1	134	11	0	7	10	.412	0	0	4.75
5 Min. YEARS		105	101	4	1	574.1	2458	570	294	246	57	12	10	49	189	2	481	38	1	34	27	.557	1	0	3.85

Matt Miller

Pitches: Right   **Bats:** Right   **Pos:** RP-44   **Ht:** 6'3"   **Wt:** 215   **Born:** 11/23/71   **Age:** 30

	HOW MUCH HE PITCHED						WHAT HE GAVE UP										THE RESULTS					
Year Team	Lg Org	G	GS	CG	GF	IP	BFP	H	R	ER	HR	SH	SF	HB	TBB	IBB	SO	WP	Bk	W	L	Pct.	ShO	Sv	ERA
1996 Greenville	IND —	19	6	0	5	69.2	331	77	51	47	2	1	3	8	50	0	54	3	2	5	2	.714	0	1	6.07
1997 Greenville	IND —	15	15	5	0	107.1	433	76	34	27	0	3	2	4	49	0	129	10	1	12	3	.800	3	0	2.26
1998 Greenville	IND —	8	8	4	0	53.2	228	46	26	17	1	6	2	1	19	1	49	2	0	1	7	.125	0	0	2.85
Savannah	A Tex	17	0	0	10	35.1	137	25	9	9	0	2	0	2	10	0	46	2	0	3	1	.750	0	3	2.29
1999 Charlotte	A+ Tex	22	0	0	20	29.2	132	27	12	10	0	0	1	1	13	1	39	2	0	1	2	.333	0	8	3.03
Tulsa	AA Tex	34	0	0	25	56	235	42	24	21	2	4	5	1	28	2	83	5	0	6	4	.600	0	7	3.38
2000 Rangers	R Tex	1	0	0	0	2	9	2	1	1	0	0	0	1	0	0	4	0	0	0	0	—	0	0	4.50
Tulsa	AA Tex	3	0	0	0	3.2	22	7	7	6	0	0	1	0	4	0	4	1	0	0	0	—	0	0	14.73
Oklahoma	AAA Tex	39	0	0	25	60.1	276	61	29	24	6	4	4	3	34	4	69	4	0	3	3	.500	0	4	3.58
2001 Portland	AAA SD	44	0	0	31	44.2	192	44	22	18	1	3	0	2	14	2	43	5	0	1	7	.125	0	17	3.63
6 Min. YEARS		202	29	9	116	462.1	1995	407	215	180	12	23	18	23	221	10	520	34	3	32	29	.525	3	40	3.50

Ryan Miller

Bats: Right   **Throws:** Right   **Pos:** SS-19; 2B-13; 3B-7; PH-7; DH-1; PR-1; P-1   **Ht:** 6'0"   **Wt:** 175   **Born:** 10/22/72   **Age:** 29

Year Team	Lg Org	G	AB	H	2B	3B	HR	TB	R	RBI	TBB	IBB	SO	HBP	SH	SF	SB	CS	SB%	GDP	Avg	OBP	SLG
1994 Pittsfield	A- NYM	68	277	71	11	1	1	87	37	23	16	1	37	4	3	2	3	3	.50	0	.256	.304	.314
1995 St. Lucie	A+ NYM	89	279	68	10	3	2	90	32	23	13	0	42	7	8	2	5	3	.63	7	.244	.292	.323
Binghamton	AA NYM	9	19	1	0	0	0	1	3	0	2	0	4	0	1	0	1	0	1.00	0	.053	.143	.053
1996 St. Lucie	A+ NYM	86	310	79	8	3	2	99	32	23	22	1	51	3	13	1	8	5	.62	5	.255	.310	.319
1997 St. Lucie	A+ NYM	61	193	49	12	1	2	69	27	28	11	0	38	1	2	2	5	5	.50	3	.254	.295	.358
Kissimmee	A+ Hou	13	34	9	0	0	0	9	5	1	5	0	3	0	2	0	1	0	1.00	1	.265	.359	.265
Jackson	AA Hou	20	55	11	0	2	1	18	6	8	5	0	10	0	1	1	1	0	1.00	1	.200	.262	.327
1998 New Orleans	AAA Hou	8	17	5	1	0	0	6	4	3	1	0	3	1	0	0	1	0	1.00	0	.294	.368	.353
Jackson	AA Hou	102	293	90	20	0	3	119	36	26	9	0	43	9	3	4	6	4	.60	10	.307	.343	.406
1999 Jackson	AA Hou	27	75	11	0	1	0	13	5	4	2	0	11	2	0	0	5	0	1.00	4	.147	.190	.173
New Orleans	AAA Hou	64	174	48	8	0	1	59	19	25	5	0	29	1	0	1	0	2	.00	3	.276	.298	.339

Year Team	Lg Org	G	AB	H	2B	3B	HR	TB	R	RBI	TBB	IBB	SO	HBP	SH	SF	SB	CS	SB%	GDP	Avg	OBP	SLG
								BATTING									**BASERUNNING**				**PERCENTAGES**		
2000 New Orleans	AAA Hou	111	299	75	18	1	3	104	31	35	18	1	58	10	3	5	1	5	.17	7	.251	.310	.348
2001 Norfolk	AAA NYM	22	56	10	3	0	0	13	5	3	3	0	14	2	1	0				1	.179	.246	.232
Binghamton	AA NYM	22	60	10	2	0	2	18	5	3	0	0	17	1	0	0	1	0	1.00	0	.167	.180	.300
8 Min. YEARS		702	2141	537	93	12	17	705	247	205	112	3	360	41	37	18	38	27	.58	41	.251	.298	.329

Trever Miller

Pitches: Left **Bats:** Right **Pos:** RP-19; SP-17 **Ht:** 6'4" **Wt:** 195 **Born:** 5/29/73 **Age:** 29

Year Team	Lg Org	G	GS	CG	GF	IP	BFP	H	R	ER	HR	SH	SF	HB	TBB	IBB	SO	WP	Bk	W	L	Pct.	ShO	Sv	ERA
			HOW	**MUCH**	**HE**	**PITCHED**					**WHAT**	**HE**	**GAVE**	**UP**								**THE**	**RESULTS**		
1991 Bristol	R+ Det	13	13	0	0	54	253	60	44	34	7	3	3	2	29	0	46	9	1	2	7	.222	0	0	5.67
1992 Bristol	R+ Det	12	12	1	0	69.1	311	75	45	38	4	3	3	1	27	0	64	4	1	3	8	.273	0	0	4.93
1993 Fayettevlle	A Det	28	28	2	0	161	699	151	99	75	7	2	8	5	67	0	116	10	0	8	13	.381	0	0	4.19
1994 Trenton	AA Det	26	26	6	0	174.1	754	198	95	85	9	10	8	3	51	0	73	3	1	7	16	.304	0	0	4.39
1995 Jacksnville	AA Det	31	16	3	4	122.1	512	122	46	37	5	4	2	5	34	0	77	1	0	8	2	.800	2	0	2.72
1996 Toledo	AAA Det	27	27	0	0	165.1	722	167	98	90	19	4	1	9	65	1	115	3	2	13	6	.684	0	0	4.90
1997 New Orleans	AAA Hou	29	27	2	0	163.2	694	177	71	60	15	8	4	3	54	1	99	6	0	6	7	.462	0	0	3.30
2000 Albuquerque	AAA LA	12	9	1	0	58	248	60	29	22	5	2	1	1	20	0	39	2	0	4	2	.667	1	0	3.41
2001 Sarasota	A+ Bos	3	2	0	0	8	29	3	2	2	0	1	0	1	1	0	6	0	0	0	0	—	0	0	2.25
Pawtucket	AAA Bos	33	15	0	8	116	514	142	79	67	16	4	6	7	34	2	93	2	1	3	11	.214	0	0	5.20
1996 Detroit	AL	5	4	0	0	16.2	88	28	17	17	3	2	2	2	9	0	8	0	0	0	4	.000	0	0	9.18
1998 Houston	NL	37	1	0	15	53.1	235	57	21	18	4	0	0	1	20	1	30	1	0	2	0	1.000	0	1	3.04
1999 Houston	NL	47	0	0	11	49.2	232	58	29	28	6	2	2	5	29	1	37	4	0	3	2	.600	0	1	5.07
2000 Philadelphia	NL	14	0	0	2	14	72	19	16	13	3	1	1	1	9	1	10	1	0	0	0	—	0	0	8.36
Los Angeles	NL	2	0	0	0	2.1	18	8	6	6	0	0	0	1	3	0	1	0	0	0	0	—	0	0	23.14
9 Min. YEARS		214	175	15	12	1092	4736	1155	608	510	87	41	36	37	382	4	728	40	6	54	72	.429	3	0	4.20
4 Maj. YEARS		105	5	0	28	136	645	170	89	82	16	5	5	10	70	3	86	6	0	5	6	.455	0	2	5.43

Ralph Milliard

Bats: Right **Throws:** Right **Pos:** 2B-5 **Ht:** 5'11" **Wt:** 175 **Born:** 12/30/73 **Age:** 28

Year Team	Lg Org	G	AB	H	2B	3B	HR	TB	R	RBI	TBB	IBB	SO	HBP	SH	SF	SB	CS	SB%	GDP	Avg	OBP	SLG
							BATTING										**BASERUNNING**				**PERCENTAGES**		
1993 Marlins	R Fla	53	192	45	15	0	0	60	35	25	30	0	17	6	0	1	11	5	.69	8	.234	.354	.313
1994 Kane County	A Fla	133	515	153	34	2	8	215	97	67	68	2	63	9	4	7	10	10	.50	6	.297	.384	.417
1995 Portland	AA Fla	128	464	124	22	3	11	185	104	40	85	3	83	14	13	4	22	10	.69	5	.267	.393	.399
1996 Charlotte	AAA Fla	69	250	69	15	2	6	106	47	26	38	0	43	5	1	1	8	4	.67	5	.276	.381	.424
Portland	AA Fla	6	20	4	0	1	0	6	2	2	1	0	5	0	0	0	1	0	1.00	0	.200	.238	.300
1997 Charlotte	AAA Fla	33	132	35	5	1	4	54	19	18	9	0	21	3	4	0	5	3	.63	1	.265	.326	.409
Portland	AA Fla	19	69	19	1	2	0	24	13	5	7	0	8	1	3	0	3	2	.60	2	.275	.351	.348
1998 Norfolk	AAA NYM	127	417	108	24	4	15	185	73	52	79	0	59	8	5	2	17	6	.74	4	.259	.385	.444
1999 Chattanooga	AA Cin	32	102	30	3	1	4	47	19	23	20	1	13	3	1	2	2	3	.40	1	.294	.417	.461
2000 Las Vegas	AAA SD	108	371	104	26	3	5	151	61	40	63	2	63	5	7	2	18	9	.67	7	.280	.390	.407
2001 Buffalo	AAA Cle	5	15	4	1	0	0	5	2	1	2	0	2	0	0	0	0	0	—	0	.267	.353	.333
1996 Florida	NL	24	62	10	2	0	0	12	7	1	14	1	16	0	0	1	2	0	1.00	1	.161	.312	.194
1997 Florida	NL	8	30	6	0	0	0	6	2	2	3	0	3	2	1	0	1	1	.50	2	.200	.314	.200
1998 New York	NL	10	1	0	0	0	0	0	3	0	0	0	1	0	0	0	0	0	—	0	.000	.000	.000
9 Min. YEARS		713	2547	695	146	19	53	1038	472	299	402	8	377	54	38	19	97	52	.65	39	.273	.381	.408
3 Maj. YEARS		42	93	16	2	0	0	18	12	3	17	1	20	2	1	1	3	1	.75	3	.172	.310	.194

Ryan Mills

Pitches: Left **Bats:** Right **Pos:** SP-8 **Ht:** 6'5" **Wt:** 205 **Born:** 7/21/77 **Age:** 24

Year Team	Lg Org	G	GS	CG	GF	IP	BFP	H	R	ER	HR	SH	SF	HB	TBB	IBB	SO	WP	Bk	W	L	Pct.	ShO	Sv	ERA
			HOW	**MUCH**	**HE**	**PITCHED**					**WHAT**	**HE**	**GAVE**	**UP**								**THE**	**RESULTS**		
1998 Fort Myers	A+ Min	2	2	0	0	5	20	2	3	1	0	0	0	0	1	0	3	3	0	0	0	—	0	0	1.80
1999 Fort Myers	A+ Min	27	21	0	3	95.1	499	121	107	94	6	0	6	16	87	1	70	20	0	3	10	.231	0	0	8.87
2000 Quad City	A Min	20	20	0	0	119.2	518	101	54	47	5	7	3	15	64	0	110	9	0	3	6	.333	0	0	3.53
New Britain	AA Min	8	8	0	0	32	185	47	49	33	6	1	2	6	34	0	21	3	0	0	7	.000	0	0	9.28
2001 New Britain	AA Min	8	8	0	0	40.2	182	45	31	29	3	1	1	5	14	0	29	2	0	2	5	.286	0	0	6.42
4 Min. YEARS		65	59	0	3	292.2	1404	316	244	204	20	9	12	42	200	1	233	37	0	8	28	.222	0	0	6.27

Tony Milo

Pitches: Left **Bats:** Left **Pos:** RP-41; SP-2 **Ht:** 6'5" **Wt:** 225 **Born:** 5/5/78 **Age:** 24

Year Team	Lg Org	G	GS	CG	GF	IP	BFP	H	R	ER	HR	SH	SF	HB	TBB	IBB	SO	WP	Bk	W	L	Pct.	ShO	Sv	ERA
			HOW	**MUCH**	**HE**	**PITCHED**					**WHAT**	**HE**	**GAVE**	**UP**								**THE**	**RESULTS**		
2000 Butte	R+ Ana	12	2	0	3	35.2	166	44	25	18	2	1	2	2	10	0	44	2	0	1	3	.250	0	2	4.54
Boise	A- Ana	9	4	0	0	32	130	26	9	9	2	0	1	0	11	0	51	0	0	4	0	1.000	0	0	2.53
2001 Rancho Cuca	A+ Ana	24	0	0	8	37	150	24	5	4	0	4	1	0	17	4	45	3	0	3	1	.750	0	2	0.97
Arkansas	AA Ana	19	2	0	6	30.1	136	29	18	18	5	1	0	2	17	0	35	1	0	1	2	.333	0	1	5.34
2 Min. YEARS		64	8	0	17	135	582	123	57	49	9	6	3	6	55	4	175	6	0	9	6	.600	0	5	3.27

Steve Mintz

Pitches: Right **Bats:** Left **Pos:** RP-10; SP-3 **Ht:** 5'11" **Wt:** 195 **Born:** 11/24/68 **Age:** 33

Year Team	Lg Org	G	GS	CG	GF	IP	BFP	H	R	ER	HR	SH	SF	HB	TBB	IBB	SO	WP	Bk	W	L	Pct.	ShO	Sv	ERA
			HOW	**MUCH**	**HE**	**PITCHED**					**WHAT**	**HE**	**GAVE**	**UP**								**THE**	**RESULTS**		
1990 Yakima	A- LA	20	0	0	12	26	113	21	9	7	1	3	1	1	16	1	38	2	1	2	3	.400	0	3	2.42
1991 Bakersfield	A+ LA	28	11	0	6	92	419	85	56	44	2	5	4	4	58	1	101	9	1	6	6	.500	0	3	4.30
1992 Vero Beach	A+ LA	43	2	0	21	77.2	323	66	29	27	7	5	3	3	30	2	66	7	3	3	6	.333	0	8	3.13
1993 New Britain	AA Bos	43	1	0	20	69.1	287	52	22	16	3	5	1	2	30	5	51	7	0	2	4	.333	0	7	2.08

Year Team	Lg Org	G	GS	CG	GF	IP	BFP	H	R	ER	HR	SH	SF	HB	TBB	IBB	SO	WP	Bk	W	L	Pct.	ShO	Sv	ERA
		HOW MUCH HE PITCHED						WHAT HE GAVE UP												THE RESULTS					
1994 Phoenix	AAA SF	24	0	0	13	36	161	40	24	22	8	1	3	1	13	3	27	3	0	0	1	.000	0	3	5.50
Shreveport	AA SF	30	0	0	12	65.1	261	45	29	16	5	2	1	2	22	1	42	8	0	10	2	.833	0	0	2.20
1995 Phoenix	AAA SF	31	0	0	19	49	205	42	16	13	4	3	0	2	21	4	36	4	0	5	2	.714	0	7	2.39
1996 Phoenix	AAA SF	59	0	0	45	57	256	63	39	34	6	1	3	2	25	3	35	5	2	5	2	.375	0	27	5.37
1997 Las Vegas	AAA SD	27	0	0	16	34.2	171	50	31	31	7	1	2	2	17	3	28	2	0	5	2	.714	0	5	8.05
1998 Nashville	AAA Pit	56	0	0	18	72.2	334	85	48	44	7	4	4	3	32	2	45	3	0	4	4	.500	0	1	5.45
1999 Erie	AA Ana	26	0	0	14	32.1	135	26	12	8	3	1	1	2	12	0	33	0	0	1	1	.500	0	9	2.23
Edmonton	AAA Ana	31	0	0	27	30.2	127	31	11	8	2	0	1	2	6	0	17	2	0	4	3	.571	0	9	2.35
2000 Edmonton	AAA Ana	32	2	0	19	41.2	210	60	42	35	4	4	3	0	28	1	24	3	0	4	4	.500	0	2	7.56
2001 Salt Lake	AAA Ana	13	3	0	6	37.1	175	50	28	24	5	2	2	3	11	0	21	0	1	1	2	.333	0	0	5.79
1995 San Francisco	NL	14	0	0	3	19.1	96	26	16	16	4	2	1	2	12	3	7	0	0	1	2	.333	0	0	7.45
1999 Anaheim	AL	3	0	0	2	5	23	8	2	2	1	0	0	0	2	0	2	0	0	0	0	—	0	0	3.60
12 Min. YEARS		463	19	0	248	721.2	3177	716	396	329	64	37	29	29	321	26	564	55	8	50	45	.526	0	82	4.10
2 Maj. YEARS		17	0	0	5	24.1	119	34	18	18	5	2	1	2	14	3	9	0	0	1	2	.333	0	0	6.66

Dean Mitchell

Pitches: Right **Bats:** Right **Pos:** RP-5; SP-2 **Ht:** 5'11" **Wt:** 175 **Born:** 3/19/74 **Age:** 28

Year Team	Lg Org	G	GS	CG	GF	IP	BFP	H	R	ER	HR	SH	SF	HB	TBB	IBB	SO	WP	Bk	W	L	Pct.	ShO	Sv	ERA
		HOW MUCH HE PITCHED						WHAT HE GAVE UP												THE RESULTS					
1996 Yakima	A- LA	15	5	0	3	52.1	233	53	25	20	4	1	5	0	25	1	61	3	1	2	2	.500	0	2	3.44
1997 Savannah	A LA	52	7	1	38	122	499	110	50	39	6	5	3	1	25	1	118	2	1	11	5	.688	0	16	2.88
San Berndno	A+ LA	1	0	0	1	1	4	0	0	0	0	0	0	0	1	0	1	0	0	0	0	—	0	0	0.00
1998 San Antonio	AA LA	46	3	0	29	79	331	74	31	29	8	5	1	3	22	2	76	4	0	2	5	.286	0	14	3.30
1999 Albuquerque	AAA LA	31	0	0	15	47.2	232	61	41	39	9	1	3	1	28	2	42	6	0	2	1	.667	0	0	7.36
San Antonio	AA LA	10	7	0	2	31.2	144	36	20	11	2	0	2	0	14	0	28	3	0	1	2	.333	0	0	3.13
2000 Oklahoma	AAA Tex	45	0	0	18	59	272	69	43	39	5	2	4	2	32	3	39	6	0	3	4	.429	0	3	5.95
2001 Oklahoma	AAA Tex	4	0	0	4	6.1	27	9	6	5	1	0	0	1	1	0	2	1	0	0	0	—	0	0	7.11
Somerset	IND —	3	2	0	0	8	33	4	2	2	0	0	0	0	5	0	2	0	0	1	0	1.000	0	0	2.25
6 Min. YEARS		207	24	1	110	407	1775	416	218	184	35	14	18	8	153	9	369	25	2	22	19	.537	0	35	4.07

Derek Mitchell

Bats: Right **Throws:** Right **Pos:** SS-72; 2B-6; 3B-4; PR-1 **Ht:** 6'2" **Wt:** 170 **Born:** 3/9/75 **Age:** 27

Year Team	Lg Org	G	AB	H	2B	3B	HR	TB	R	RBI	TBB	IBB	SO	HBP	SH	SF	SB	CS	SB%	GDP	Avg	OBP	SLG
		BATTING															BASERUNNING				PERCENTAGES		
1996 Jamestown	A- Det	56	184	45	10	2	2	65	25	18	0	38	2	7	2	7	4	.64	1	.245	.316	.353
1997 W Michigan	A Det	110	353	70	14	2	1	91	47	31	50	1	91	5	8	3	11	8	.58	5	.198	.304	.258
1998 Jacksnville	AA Det	128	421	93	21	2	2	124	58	54	68	1	94	6	4	8	6	3	.67	9	.221	.332	.295
1999 Jacksnville	AA Det	124	422	102	17	1	7	142	56	49	53	0	117	2	4	5	4	2	.67	3	.242	.326	.336
2000 Jacksnville	AA Det	116	330	65	14	0	1	82	38	27	54	0	76	0	7	1	3	3	.50	4	.197	.309	.248
2001 Birmingham	AA CWS	82	237	50	8	1	2	66	37	21	34	1	68	3	8	4	5	4	.56	5	.211	.313	.278
6 Min. YEARS		616	1947	425	84	8	15	570	261	207	277	3	484	18	38	23	36	24	.60	27	.218	.318	.293

Scott Mitchell

Pitches: Right **Bats:** Right **Pos:** RP-9; SP-6 **Ht:** 6'0" **Wt:** 185 **Born:** 3/19/73 **Age:** 29

Year Team	Lg Org	G	GS	CG	GF	IP	BFP	H	R	ER	HR	SH	SF	HB	TBB	IBB	SO	WP	Bk	W	L	Pct.	ShO	Sv	ERA
		HOW MUCH HE PITCHED						WHAT HE GAVE UP												THE RESULTS					
1995 Vermont	A- Mon	18	1	0	5	40.1	171	35	18	10	1	2	2	4	15	0	30	2	4	3	1	.750	0	1	2.23
1996 Delmarva	A Mon	33	5	1	10	76.2	320	69	29	20	7	3	1	5	24	1	76	3	3	5	6	.455	0	1	2.35
1997 Wst Plm Bch	A+ Mon	39	3	0	15	73.2	291	61	21	21	4	3	1	3	18	0	56	4	0	5	3	.625	0	3	2.57
Harrisburg	AA Mon	4	3	0	0	17.1	67	11	7	7	3	1	0	1	3	0	13	1	0	1	0	1.000	0	0	3.63
1998 Harrisburg	AA Mon	32	17	2	5	135	558	136	58	57	13	3	6	6	37	1	81	0	0	9	3	.750	1	2	3.80
Ottawa	AAA Mon	18	9	0	1	62.1	282	78	43	39	11	1	3	3	25	0	28	0	1	4	4	.500	0	0	5.63
1999 Harrisburg	AA Mon	3	3	0	0	19	74	16	9	9	5	0	1	0	3	0	10	1	1	2	0	1.000	0	0	4.26
2000 Ottawa	AAA Mon	28	13	0	0	89.1	397	109	63	60	13	5	4	5	28	2	52	5	1	6	5	.545	0	0	6.04
2001 Ottawa	AAA Mon	6	2	0	2	19.2	81	17	10	9	1	0	0	0	10	0	10	3	0	0	1	.000	0	0	4.12
Harrisburg	AA Mon	9	4	0	2	21.2	95	24	11	10	4	1	2	1	6	0	14	1	0	1	2	.333	0	0	4.15
7 Min. YEARS		190	60	4	40	555	2336	556	269	242	62	19	20	28	169	4	370	20	10	36	25	.590	1	7	3.92

Greg Mix

Pitches: Right **Bats:** Right **Pos:** RP-41; SP-1 **Ht:** 6'4" **Wt:** 225 **Born:** 8/21/71 **Age:** 30

Year Team	Lg Org	G	GS	CG	GF	IP	BFP	H	R	ER	HR	SH	SF	HB	TBB	IBB	SO	WP	Bk	W	L	Pct.	ShO	Sv	ERA
		HOW MUCH HE PITCHED						WHAT HE GAVE UP												THE RESULTS					
1993 Elmira	A- Fla	17	1	0	8	45.1	205	51	26	21	4	0	1	4	17	0	38	4	0	3	3	.500	0	2	4.17
1994 Brevard Cty	A+ Fla	44	0	0	22	78	314	65	29	27	2	4	4	2	20	2	51	1	0	6	2	.750	0	4	3.12
1995 Brevard Cty	A+ Fla	5	4	1	0	29.2	119	27	13	13	1	0	0	3	10	0	17	1	1	3	1	.750	0	0	3.94
Portland	AA Fla	24	13	0	1	92.1	401	98	51	48	9	2	4	4	25	5	56	3	0	6	4	.600	0	0	4.68
1996 Charlotte	AAA Fla	4	4	0	0	18.1	87	27	15	14	4	2	0	2	7	1	9	1	0	1	3	.250	0	0	6.87
Portland	AA Fla	25	5	0	8	65.2	296	80	40	33	8	4	5	5	19	5	57	6	2	3	0	1.000	0	1	4.52
1997 Portland	AA Fla	30	13	0	4	102.2	461	121	70	54	16	7	5	8	32	0	74	5	0	7	7	.500	0	0	4.73
1998 Greenville	AA Atl	22	0	0	9	25	119	32	19	14	2	0	3	0	11	0	18	3	0	1	1	.500	0	2	5.04
Richmond	AAA Atl	28	2	0	13	64.2	268	52	24	21	8	1	2	4	19	0	59	1	0	2	4	.333	0	2	2.92
1999 Pawtucket	AAA Bos	46	4	0	13	85.1	388	89	45	35	9	3	5	4	40	0	79	9	1	4	4	.500	0	1	3.69
2000 Indianapols	AAA Mil	38	0	0	10	54.1	240	57	33	28	8	4	6	2	18	2	42	7	0	3	2	.600	0	2	4.64
2001 Long Island	IND —	27	0	0	22	29.2	112	17	9	8	1	1	1	1	11	1	31	2	0	0	2	.000	0	10	2.43
Pawtucket	AAA Bos	8	1	0	1	12.2	59	15	12	12	3	0	1	0	7	0	15	0	0	0	0	—	0	0	8.53
Edmonton	AAA Min	7	0	0	1	11	44	12	6	3	2	1	1	0	5	0	5	1	0	1	0	.500	0	1	2.45
9 Min. YEARS		325	47	1	112	714.2	3115	743	392	331	77	29	38	39	236	16	551	44	4	40	34	.541	0	25	4.17

Kevin Mobley

Pitches: Right Bats: Right Pos: RP-35; SP-1   Ht: 6'7" Wt: 245 Born: 1/26/75 Age: 27

Year Team	Lg Org	G	GS	CG	GF	IP	BFP	H	R	ER	HR	SH	SF	HB	TBB	IBB	SO	WP	Bk	W	L	Pct.	ShO	Sv	ERA
1997 Jamestown	A- Det	18	0	0	9	25.2	115	27	10	9	1	4	2	1	11	1	24	0	0	2	1	.667	0	0	3.16
1998 Lakeland	A+ Det	34	8	1	10	79.1	345	80	44	42	9	0	3	5	36	2	58	4	0	4	3	.571	1	2	4.76
1999 Lakeland	A+ Det	46	5	0	12	96.2	414	107	48	41	11	5	8	3	26	1	73	5	0	7	4	.636	0	2	3.82
2000 Jacksnville	AA Det	43	5	1	8	90	368	62	31	27	5	0	4	3	42	2	72	7	0	6	0	1.000	1	0	2.70
2001 Tulsa	AA Tex	36	1	0	10	75	325	71	40	33	6	4	3	9	32	2	58	6	0	3	0	1.000	0	0	3.96
5 Min. YEARS		177	19	2	49	366.2	1567	347	173	152	32	13	20	21	147	8	285	22	0	22	8	.733	2	4	3.73

Gabe Molina

Pitches: Right Bats: Right Pos: RP-24; SP-16   Ht: 6'1" Wt: 220 Born: 5/3/75 Age: 27

Year Team	Lg Org	G	GS	CG	GF	IP	BFP	H	R	ER	HR	SH	SF	HB	TBB	IBB	SO	WP	Bk	W	L	Pct.	ShO	Sv	ERA
1996 Bluefield	R+ Bal	23	0	0	19	30	131	29	12	12	1	1	0	2	13	1	33	5	3	4	0	1.000	0	7	3.60
1997 Delmarva	A Bal	46	0	0	31	91	364	59	24	22	3	6	1	3	32	5	119	7	2	8	6	.571	0	7	2.18
1998 Bowie	AA Bal	47	0	0	38	61.2	256	48	24	23	5	3	1	1	27	0	75	5	1	3	2	.600	0	24	3.36
1999 Rochester	AAA Bal	45	0	0	36	57.1	241	45	22	20	3	2	1	2	23	1	58	6	1	2	2	.500	0	18	3.14
2000 Rochester	AAA Bal	18	4	0	9	27.1	120	30	16	15	3	2	0	0	10	0	26	2	1	1	2	.333	0	5	4.94
Richmond	AAA Atl	9	0	0	8	10	41	7	5	4	2	0	2	0	3	0	9	0	1	1	0	1.000	0	3	3.60
2001 Calgary	AAA Fla	40	16	0	4	107	483	126	75	70	14	2	1	5	39	1	105	13	4	5	9	.357	0	0	5.89
1999 Baltimore	AL	20	0	0	7	23	102	22	19	17	4	0	0	0	16	1	14	4	0	1	2	.333	0	0	6.65
2000 Baltimore	AL	9	0	0	3	13	74	25	14	13	2	0	2	0	9	0	8	0	0	0	0	—	0	0	9.00
Atlanta	NL	2	0	0	1	2	11	3	4	2	1	0	1	1	1	0	1	0	0	0	0	—	0	0	9.00
6 Min. YEARS		228	20	0	145	384.1	1636	344	178	166	31	16	6	13	147	8	425	38	13	24	21	.533	0	64	3.89
2 Maj. YEARS		31	0	0	11	38	187	50	37	32	7	0	3	1	26	1	23	4	0	1	2	.333	0	0	7.58

Izzy Molina

Bats: Right Throws: Right Pos: C-70; DH-3   Ht: 6'1" Wt: 224 Born: 6/3/71 Age: 31

Year Team	Lg Org	G	AB	H	2B	3B	HR	TB	R	RBI	TBB	IBB	SO	HBP	SH	SF	SB	CS	SB%	GDP	Avg	OBP	SLG
1990 Athletics	R Oak	38	122	43	12	2	0	59	19	18	9	1	21	2	1	3	5	0	1.00	6	.352	.397	.484
1991 Madison	A Oak	95	316	89	16	1	3	116	35	45	15	1	40	6	1	4	6	4	.60	9	.282	.323	.367
1992 Reno	A+ Oak	116	436	113	17	2	10	164	71	75	39	0	57	7	7	6	8	7	.53	20	.259	.326	.376
Tacoma	AAA Oak	10	36	7	0	1	0	9	3	5	2	0	6	0	0	0	1	0	1.00	1	.194	.237	.250
1993 Modesto	A+ Oak	125	444	116	26	5	6	170	61	69	44	0	85	3	4	11	2	8	.20	11	.261	.325	.383
1994 Huntsville	AA Oak	116	388	84	17	2	8	129	31	50	16	0	47	5	7	7	5	1	.83	10	.216	.252	.332
1995 Edmonton	AAA Oak	2	6	1	0	0	0	1	0	0	0	0	2	0	0	0	0	0	—	0	.167	.167	.167
Huntsville	AA Oak	83	301	78	16	1	8	120	38	26	26	0	62	8	0	2	3	4	.43	6	.259	.332	.399
1996 Edmonton	AAA Oak	98	342	90	12	3	12	144	45	56	25	4	55	3	5	2	2	5	.29	9	.263	.317	.421
1997 Edmonton	AAA Oak	61	218	57	11	3	6	92	33	34	12	0	27	0	1	0	2	0	1.00	4	.261	.300	.422
1998 Edmonton	AAA Oak	86	303	73	15	2	8	116	29	38	17	0	60	4	1	3	3	0	1.00	16	.241	.287	.383
1999 Columbus	AAA NYY	97	338	83	16	1	4	113	44	51	18	0	47	1	2	6	4	2	.67	9	.246	.281	.334
2000 Omaha	AAA KC	90	311	73	9	1	10	114	39	36	14	0	55	2	0	5	5	4	.56	6	.235	.268	.367
2001 Syracuse	AAA Tor	73	256	78	20	1	16	148	34	38	18	0	52	1	1	0	1	0	1.00	7	.305	.353	.578
1996 Oakland	AL	14	25	5	2	0	0	7	0	1	1	0	3	0	0	0	0	0	—	0	.200	.231	.280
1997 Oakland	AL	48	111	22	3	1	3	36	6	7	3	0	17	0	1	0	0	0	—	1	.198	.219	.324
1998 Oakland	AL	6	2	1	0	0	0	1	1	0	0	0	0	0	0	0	0	0	—	0	.500	.500	.500
12 Min. YEARS		1090	3817	985	187	25	91	1495	482	541	255	6	616	42	30	49	47	35	.57	108	.258	.308	.392
3 Maj. YEARS		68	138	28	5	1	3	44	7	8	4	0	20	0	1	0	0	0	—	1	.203	.225	.319

Shane Monahan

Bats: Left Throws: Right Pos: OF-68; 1B-8; PH-7; DH-4; PR-1; P-1   Ht: 6'0" Wt: 195 Born: 8/12/74 Age: 27

Year Team	Lg Org	G	AB	H	2B	3B	HR	TB	R	RBI	TBB	IBB	SO	HBP	SH	SF	SB	CS	SB%	GDP	Avg	OBP	SLG
1995 Wisconsin	A Sea	59	233	66	9	6	1	90	34	32	11	0	40	2	7	3	9	2	.82	4	.283	.317	.386
1996 Lancaster	A+ Sea	132	585	164	31	12	14	261	107	97	30	2	124	4	3	8	19	5	.79	8	.280	.316	.446
1997 Memphis	AA Sea	107	401	121	24	6	12	193	52	76	30	2	100	2	1	2	14	7	.67	4	.302	.352	.481
Tacoma	AAA Sea	21	85	25	4	0	2	35	15	12	5	0	21	1	2	0	5	1	.83	1	.294	.341	.412
1998 Tacoma	AAA Sea	69	277	69	8	5	4	99	32	33	19	3	47	0	4	2	6	4	.60	3	.249	.295	.357
1999 Tacoma	AAA Sea	108	399	102	21	2	7	148	51	32	19	2	81	3	1	2	9	3	.75	4	.256	.293	.371
2000 Tacoma	AAA Sea	8	27	8	1	1	1	14	3	8	1	0	4	1	0	1	1	1	.50	0	.296	.333	.519
Las Vegas	AAA SD	13	39	7	2	0	0	9	5	5	5	0	6	0	1	0	0	2	.00	0	.179	.273	.231
Chattanooga	AA Cin	25	80	20	8	0	4	40	10	16	7	0	18	1	1	0	3	0	1.00	1	.250	.315	.500
Louisville	AAA Cin	18	62	20	3	2	3	36	12	11	3	0	12	1	1	0	1	0	1.00	0	.323	.364	.581
Colo Spmgs	AAA Col	21	66	15	3	1	1	23	8	13	6	0	10	1	1	1	1	3	.25	0	.227	.297	.348
2001 Solano	IND —	47	180	61	16	0	10	107	45	43	18	3	27	1	2	3	8	0	1.00	3	.339	.396	.594
Altoona	AA Pit	21	71	21	6	1	2	35	9	10	4	1	12	0	1	0	1	2	.33	1	.296	.333	.493
Nashville	AAA Pit	16	41	9	0	0	1	12	3	3	2	0	9	0	0	1	0	0	—	0	.220	.250	.293
1998 Seattle	AL	62	211	51	8	1	4	73	17	28	8	0	53	0	4	0	1	2	.33	0	.242	.269	.346
1999 Seattle	AL	16	15	2	0	0	0	2	3	0	0	0	6	0	0	0	0	0	—	0	.133	.133	.133
7 Min. YEARS		665	2546	708	136	36	62	1102	386	391	160	13	511	17	24	24	78	30	.72	29	.278	.322	.433
2 Maj. YEARS		78	226	53	8	1	4	75	20	28	8	0	59	0	4	0	1	2	.33	0	.235	.261	.332

Greg Montalbano

Pitches: Left **Bats:** Left **Pos:** SP-25; RP-2 **Ht:** 6'2" **Wt:** 185 **Born:** 8/24/77 **Age:** 24

Year Team	Lg Org	G	GS	CG	GF	IP	BFP	H	R	ER	HR	SH	SF	HB	TBB	IBB	SO	WP	Bk	W	L	Pct.	ShO	Sv	ERA
2000 Red Sox	R Bos	4	4	0	0	12	51	13	6	5	1	0	0	0	3	0	14	1	0	0	2	.000	0	0	3.75
Lowell	A- Bos	2	2	0	0	10.1	39	4	3	2	0	1	1	0	4	0	15	0	0	0	1	.000	0	0	1.74
2001 Sarasota	A+ Bos	17	15	0	0	91.1	367	66	36	30	11	4	5	4	25	1	77	3	3	9	3	.750	0	0	2.96
Trenton	AA Bos	10	10	0	0	48	199	50	25	24	8	1	0	1	14	0	45	0	3	3	3	.500	0	0	4.50
2 Min. YEARS		33	31	0	0	161.2	656	133	70	61	20	6	6	5	46	1	151	4	6	12	9	.571	0	0	3.40

Ivan Montane

Pitches: Right **Bats:** Right **Pos:** RP-34; SP-2 **Ht:** 6'2" **Wt:** 195 **Born:** 6/3/73 **Age:** 29

Year Team	Lg Org	G	GS	CG	GF	IP	BFP	H	R	ER	HR	SH	SF	HB	TBB	IBB	SO	WP	Bk	W	L	Pct.	ShO	Sv	ERA
1992 Mariners	R Sea	13	11	0	1	46	224	44	39	29	0	0	0	3	41	0	48	18	4	1	3	.250	0	0	5.67
1993 Bellingham	A- Sea	15	15	1	0	73.1	305	55	36	32	7	2	1	3	37	0	53	9	3	5	4	.556	0	0	3.93
1994 Appleton	A Sea	29	26	1	0	159	680	132	79	68	13	4	6	12	82	0	155	19	2	8	9	.471	1	0	3.85
1995 Riverside	A+ Sea	24	16	0	6	92.2	442	101	67	58	3	3	6	10	71	0	79	19	0	5	5	.500	0	0	5.63
1996 Lancaster	A+ Sea	11	11	0	0	59.1	273	57	37	24	2	5	3	2	43	0	54	9	0	2	2	.500	0	0	3.64
Port City	AA Sea	18	18	0	0	100.1	461	96	67	57	6	1	2	9	75	0	81	16	2	3	8	.273	0	0	5.11
1997 Memphis	AA Sea	22	12	0	6	71.2	347	83	70	60	16	1	5	6	51	0	63	11	0	0	8	.000	0	0	7.53
Lancaster	A+ Sea	6	6	0	0	32.1	150	40	25	19	2	1	2	2	13	1	34	8	1	1	2	.333	0	0	5.29
1998 Orlando	AA Sea	2	0	0	0	2.1	12	3	3	3	0	0	0	0	2	0	0	0	0	0	0	—	0	0	11.57
1999 Wisconsin	A Sea	10	0	0	9	12.2	49	5	1	1	0	0	0	0	5	0	18	2	0	0	0	—	0	3	0.71
New Haven	AA Sea	41	0	0	25	54.2	219	38	16	15	2	3	2	2	22	2	70	5	0	4	2	.667	0	10	2.47
2000 New Haven	AA Sea	26	0	0	15	38.2	189	50	36	32	3	1	0	4	22	1	39	6	1	2	5	.286	0	2	7.45
Tacoma	AAA Sea	16	0	0	5	24.1	124	29	18	16	2	0	2	3	23	0	24	1	0	0	2	.000	0	0	5.92
2001 Norfolk	AAA NYM	15	2	0	1	37	174	40	23	17	4	2	1	4	23	1	26	2	0	1	4	.200	0	0	4.14
Binghamton	AA NYM	21	0	0	14	33.1	140	31	13	11	1	1	1	0	11	0	32	4	0	2	2	.500	0	2	2.97
10 Min. YEARS		269	117	2	82	837.2	3789	804	530	442	61	24	29	60	521	6	776	129	13	34	56	.378	1	15	4.75

Ricardo Montas

Bats: Right **Throws:** Right **Pos:** SS-36; 3B-34; 2B-31; 1B-4; PR-4; PH-3; DH-2 **Ht:** 6'1" **Wt:** 170 **Born:** 3/9/77 **Age:** 25

Year Team	Lg Org	G	AB	H	2B	3B	HR	TB	R	RBI	TBB	IBB	SO	HBP	SH	SF	SB	CS	SB%	GDP	Avg	OBP	SLG
1995 Royals	R KC	22	28	2	0	0	1	5	2	3	3	0	6	1	0	0	0	0	—	1	.071	.188	.179
1996 Lansing	A KC	8	24	7	0	0	0	7	1	0	2	0	4	0	0	0	0	0	—	0	.292	.346	.292
Royals	R KC	50	182	48	6	1	2	62	25	22	20	2	31	3	2	1	5	1	.83	7	.264	.345	.341
1997 Lansing	A KC	4	10	3	0	0	0	3	0	1	0	0	2	0	0	1	0	0	—	0	.300	.273	.300
Spokane	A- KC	66	217	65	5	3	2	82	42	20	35	1	39	2	2	2	5	3	.63	5	.300	.398	.378
1998 Lansing	A KC	51	140	32	4	1	1	41	21	14	22	2	28	1	1	0	4	2	.67	4	.229	.337	.293
Spokane	A- KC	63	211	64	10	0	1	77	45	27	30	1	28	1	4	4	10	1	.91	10	.303	.386	.365
1999 Wilmington	A+ KC	98	349	86	15	0	2	107	46	31	47	0	60	3	5	2	4	2	.67	7	.246	.339	.307
2000 Wichita	AA KC	11	37	8	2	0	0	10	5	3	0	0	5	0	0	0	0	0	—	1	.216	.216	.270
Wilmington	A+ KC	93	314	87	17	0	0	104	43	36	42	0	49	5	2	4	6	1	.86	9	.277	.367	.331
2001 El Paso	AA Ari	28	96	24	5	0	1	32	5	9	10	0	17	0	1	0	0	1	.00	3	.250	.321	.333
Lancaster	A+ Ari	70	205	60	8	0	1	71	28	16	24	1	46	2	2	1	3	4	.43	2	.293	.371	.346
7 Min. YEARS		564	1813	486	72	5	11	601	263	182	235	7	315	18	19	15	37	15	.71	49	.268	.355	.331

Matt Montgomery

Pitches: Right **Bats:** Right **Pos:** RP-29 **Ht:** 6'4" **Wt:** 210 **Born:** 5/13/76 **Age:** 26

Year Team	Lg Org	G	GS	CG	GF	IP	BFP	H	R	ER	HR	SH	SF	HB	TBB	IBB	SO	WP	Bk	W	L	Pct.	ShO	Sv	ERA
1997 Yakima	A- LA	11	9	0	0	55.1	229	48	23	15	3	2	0	1	17	0	38	2	2	2	2	.500	0	0	2.44
Great Falls	R+ LA	4	4	0	0	23	92	24	11	10	1	0	0	0	3	0	6	1	0	1	1	.500	0	0	3.91
1998 San Berndno	A+ LA	63	0	0	58	79	331	69	31	28	6	4	3	1	27	4	81	5	1	4	6	.400	0	26	3.19
Albuquerque	AAA LA	3	0	0	3	3	11	0	0	0	0	1	0	1	2	0	3	0	0	0	0	—	0	2	0.00
1999 San Antonio	AA LA	58	0	0	56	55.1	254	65	35	16	1	3	2	3	17	2	39	5	1	5	6	.455	0	26	2.60
2000 Albuquerque	AAA LA	7	0	0	1	10	51	15	8	8	3	0	0	0	7	0	6	2	0	1	0	1.000	0	0	7.20
San Antonio	AA LA	41	4	0	19	89	402	98	55	39	5	8	5	5	37	0	82	5	0	5	5	.500	0	5	3.94
2001 Las Vegas	AAA LA	1	0	0	0	2.1	10	1	0	0	0	0	0	0	2	0	3	0	0	0	0	—	0	0	0.00
Jacksnville	AA LA	14	0	0	3	25.1	103	20	9	9	1	2	1	1	8	0	17	4	1	1	0	1.000	0	1	3.20
Bakersfield	A+ TB	14	0	0	3	22.2	94	20	13	12	3	1	2	0	7	1	29	3	0	2	3	.400	0	1	4.76
5 Min. YEARS		216	17	0	143	365	1577	360	185	137	23	21	13	12	127	7	304	27	5	20	24	.455	0	60	3.38

Ray Montgomery

Bats: Right **Throws:** Right **Pos:** OF-35; DH-16; 1B-4; PH-4 **Ht:** 6'3" **Wt:** 225 **Born:** 8/8/70 **Age:** 31

Year Team	Lg Org	G	AB	H	2B	3B	HR	TB	R	RBI	TBB	IBB	SO	HBP	SH	SF	SB	CS	SB%	GDP	Avg	OBP	SLG
1990 Auburn	A- Hou	61	193	45	8	1	0	55	19	13	23	1	32	1	4	1	11	5	.69	5	.233	.317	.285
1991 Burlington	A Hou	120	433	109	24	3	3	148	60	57	37	1	66	8	11	2	17	14	.55	10	.252	.321	.342
1992 Jackson	AA Hou	51	148	31	4	1	1	40	13	10	7	2	27	0	1	1	4	1	.80	5	.209	.244	.270
1993 Tucson	AAA Hou	15	50	17	3	1	2	28	9	6	5	0	7	1	1	0	1	2	.33	1	.340	.411	.560
Jackson	AA Hou	100	338	95	16	3	10	147	50	59	36	1	54	6	1	6	12	6	.67	7	.281	.355	.435
1994 Tucson	AAA Hou	103	332	85	19	6	7	137	51	51	35	6	54	2	2	3	5	3	.63	9	.256	.328	.413
1995 Jackson	AA Hou	35	127	38	8	1	10	78	24	24	13	2	13	5	0	1	6	3	.67	3	.299	.384	.614
Tucson	AAA Hou	88	291	88	19	0	11	140	48	68	24	1	58	2	1	8	5	3	.63	3	.302	.351	.481
1996 Tucson	AAA Hou	100	360	110	20	0	22	196	70	75	59	7	54	3	0	1	7	1	.88	12	.306	.407	.544
1997 New Orleans	AAA Hou	20	73	21	5	0	6	44	17	13	11	0	15	0	0	0	1	1	.50	2	.288	.381	.603
1998 New Orleans	AAA Hou	75	272	79	18	1	9	126	42	45	26	0	48	0	0	4	4	2	.67	8	.290	.354	.463
1999 Nashville	AAA Pit	90	272	90	23	2	16	165	57	52	24	0	49	5	1	5	5	3	.63	9	.331	.389	.607

Year Team	Lg Org	BATTING															BASERUNNING				PERCENTAGES		
		G	AB	H	2B	3B	HR	TB	R	RBI	TBB	IBB	SO	HBP	SH	SF	SB	CS	SB%	GDP	Avg	OBP	SLG
2000 Nashville	AAA Pit	71	228	59	10	1	7	92	36	29	19	1	38	7	0	0	3	5	.38	8	.259	.335	.404
2001 Norfolk	AAA NYM	57	194	62	7	1	7	92	37	33	27	2	36	1	0	3	4	2	.67	2	.320	.400	.474
1996 Houston	NL	12	14	3	1	0	1	7	4	4	1	0	5	0	0	0	0	0	—	0	.214	.267	.500
1997 Houston	NL	29	68	16	4	1	0	22	8	4	5	0	18	0	0	3	0	0	—	2	.235	.276	.324
1998 Houston	NL	6	5	2	0	0	0	2	2	0	0	0	0	0	0	0	0	0	—	0	.400	.400	.400
12 Min. YEARS		986	3311	929	184	21	111	1488	533	535	346	24	551	44	22	35	85	51	.63	80	.281	.353	.449
3 Maj. YEARS		47	87	21	5	1	1	31	14	8	6	0	23	0	0	3	0	0	—	2	.241	.281	.356

Eric Moody

Pitches: Right **Bats:** Right **Pos:** RP-34; SP-8   **Ht:** 6'6" **Wt:** 185 **Born:** 1/6/71 **Age:** 31

Year Team	Lg Org	HOW MUCH HE PITCHED						WHAT HE GAVE UP												THE RESULTS					
		G	GS	CG	GF	IP	BFP	H	R	ER	HR	SH	SF	HB	TBB	IBB	SO	WP	Bk	W	L	Pct.	ShO	Sv	ERA
1993 Erie	A- Tex	17	7	0	4	54	229	54	30	23	3	0	1	2	13	1	33	3	1	3	3	.500	0	0	3.83
1994 Hudson Val	A- Tex	15	12	1	1	89	355	82	32	28	2	2	3	2	18	1	68	3	4	7	3	.700	0	0	2.83
1995 Charlotte	A+ Tex	13	13	2	0	88.1	353	84	30	27	2	3	1	5	13	0	57	0	0	5	5	.500	2	0	2.75
1996 Tulsa	AA Tex	44	5	0	29	95.2	395	92	40	38	4	1	3	1	23	2	80	4	0	8	4	.667	0	16	3.57
1997 Okla City	AAA Tex	35	10	1	10	112	469	114	49	43	13	5	1	4	21	1	72	1	0	5	6	.455	1	1	3.46
1998 Oklahoma	AAA Tex	45	6	0	29	101.1	436	112	51	38	9	2	4	6	23	4	73	4	1	6	6	.500	0	12	3.38
1999 Charlotte	A+ Tex	1	1	0	0	2	9	2	2	2	0	0	1	0	0	1	0	1	0	0	0	—	0	0	9.00
Oklahoma	AAA Tex	39	1	0	20	73.2	309	78	33	28	5	3	3	4	13	3	31	3	0	7	4	.636	0	4	3.42
2000 Las Vegas	AAA SD	4	1	0	0	7.1	34	12	4	4	1	0	0	0	0	0	4	0	0	0	1	.000	0	0	4.91
Calgary	AAA Fla	35	1	0	12	50.1	226	75	37	35	12	1	0	1	8	1	26	0	0	1	3	.250	0	2	6.26
2001 Nashville	AAA Pit	42	8	1	9	112.1	456	112	47	43	15	5	2	3	14	1	50	2	0	5	6	.455	1	0	3.45
1997 Texas	AL	10	1	0	3	19	82	26	10	9	4	0	1	0	2	0	12	0	0	0	1	.000	0	0	4.26
9 Min. YEARS		290	65	5	114	786	3271	817	355	309	66	22	19	28	146	14	495	20	6	47	41	.534	4	35	3.54

Brian Moon

Bats: Both **Throws:** Right **Pos:** C-94; PH-2; DH-1; PR-1   **Ht:** 6'0" **Wt:** 190 **Born:** 7/15/77 **Age:** 24

Year Team	Lg Org	BATTING															BASERUNNING				PERCENTAGES		
		G	AB	H	2B	3B	HR	TB	R	RBI	TBB	IBB	SO	HBP	SH	SF	SB	CS	SB%	GDP	Avg	OBP	SLG
1997 Helena	R+ Mil	49	170	48	5	0	0	53	15	22	8	0	23	5	4	2	2	1	.67	4	.282	.330	.312
1998 Beloit	A Mil	118	438	112	20	1	1	137	62	54	46	4	62	23	9	7	0	1	.00	9	.256	.352	.313
1999 Stockton	A+ Mil	116	385	102	14	2	2	126	52	30	37	4	40	7	2	4	6	6	.50	9	.265	.337	.327
2000 Huntsville	AA Mil	106	312	57	13	1	1	75	34	33	45	5	49	10	3	4	2	4	.33	9	.183	.302	.240
2001 Huntsville	AA Mil	97	287	45	11	2	0	60	17	16	20	0	50	2	10	1	0	2	.00	7	.157	.216	.209
5 Min. YEARS		486	1592	364	63	6	4	451	180	155	156	13	224	47	28	18	10	14	.42	38	.229	.313	.283

Mike Moore

Bats: Right **Throws:** Right **Pos:** OF-57; PH-12; DH-7; PR-1   **Ht:** 6'4" **Wt:** 225 **Born:** 3/7/71 **Age:** 31

Year Team	Lg Org	BATTING															BASERUNNING				PERCENTAGES		
		G	AB	H	2B	3B	HR	TB	R	RBI	TBB	IBB	SO	HBP	SH	SF	SB	CS	SB%	GDP	Avg	OBP	SLG
1992 Yakima	A- LA	18	58	12	1	0	2	19	12	6	9	1	25	0	0	0	3	2	.60	1	.207	.313	.328
1993 Bakersfield	A LA	100	403	116	25	1	13	182	61	58	29	0	103	3	0	4	23	10	.70	6	.288	.337	.452
1994 San Antonio	AA LA	72	254	57	12	1	5	86	32	32	22	0	75	6	0	1	11	7	.61	2	.224	.300	.339
Bakersfield	A+ LA	21	81	24	5	0	2	35	17	8	13	1	21	0	0	0	2	0	1.00	3	.296	.394	.432
1995 Vero Beach	A+ LA	7	22	6	1	0	0	7	3	1	6	0	8	0	0	0	0	1	.00	1	.273	.429	.318
1996 San Antonio	AA LA	64	200	48	10	4	2	72	21	21	17	0	64	2	0	1	8	4	.67	4	.240	.305	.360
1997 Binghamton	AA NYM	50	130	39	11	1	2	58	19	13	18	1	47	1	0	1	7	3	.70	2	.300	.387	.446
Norfolk	AAA NYM	34	83	20	4	0	2	30	10	6	9	0	33	0	0	0	1	0	1.00	3	.241	.315	.361
1998 Lancaster	A+ Sea	19	63	13	3	1	3	27	12	11	5	0	27	1	0	2	0	1	.00	0	.206	.268	.429
Missn Viejo	IND —	35	133	30	7	1	6	57	26	16	15	0	41	3	0	2	8	0	1.00	1	.226	.314	.429
Nashua	IND —	35	132	33	10	0	8	67	25	19	17	0	48	1	0	0	4	0	1.00	2	.250	.340	.508
1999 Nashua	IND —	105	390	110	22	1	26	212	65	82	44	2	110	3	1	1	6	2	.75	3	.282	.358	.544
2000 Huntsville	AA Mil	26	76	14	2	1	2	24	5	8	5	0	37	1	0	0	1	0	.00	1	.184	.244	.316
Greenville	AA Atl	29	104	23	3	1	7	49	12	14	6	0	50	2	0	0	1	0	1.00	2	.221	.277	.471
Richmond	AAA Atl	24	63	11	5	0	2	22	10	5	6	0	28	1	0	0	0	0	.00	2	.175	.257	.349
2001 Greenville	AA Atl	27	63	10	2	0	2	18	8	6	4	0	33	2	0	0	0	0	—	0	.159	.232	.286
Long Island	IND —	44	141	30	9	1	4	53	18	14	21	1	59	5	0	0	2	0	1.00	4	.213	.335	.376
10 Min. YEARS		710	2396	596	132	13	88	1018	356	320	246	6	809	31	1	12	76	31	.71	37	.249	.325	.425

David Moraga

Pitches: Left **Bats:** Left **Pos:** SP-15; RP-11   **Ht:** 6'0" **Wt:** 185 **Born:** 7/8/75 **Age:** 26

Year Team	Lg Org	HOW MUCH HE PITCHED						WHAT HE GAVE UP												THE RESULTS					
		G	GS	CG	GF	IP	BFP	H	R	ER	HR	SH	SF	HB	TBB	IBB	SO	WP	Bk	W	L	Pct.	ShO	Sv	ERA
1994 Expos	R Mon	14	0	0	7	23.2	100	23	11	4	0	3	1	0	8	1	13	4	2	3	5	.375	0	2	1.52
1995 Wst Plm Bch	A+ Mon	3	3	0	0	16	75	20	7	7	0	0	0	0	10	0	10	0	0	1	1	.500	0	0	3.94
Albany	A Mon	25	24	1	0	147.2	620	136	63	44	6	6	4	1	46	0	109	10	0	8	8	.500	0	0	2.68
1996 Wst Plm Bch	A+ Mon	29	20	1	1	125.2	560	138	74	64	6	4	7	4	50	0	96	12	0	7	10	.412	0	0	4.58
1997 Wst Plm Bch	A+ Mon	13	7	0	3	47.2	207	50	27	26	3	1	2	1	18	0	37	6	0	1	4	.200	0	0	4.91
1998 Jupiter	A+ Mon	25	0	0	11	45	180	37	16	14	2	5	2	1	9	0	38	3	0	5	2	.714	0	0	2.80
Harrisburg	AA Mon	19	4	0	5	40	182	42	27	22	3	2	1	3	22	2	23	5	0	1	4	.200	0	1	4.95
1999 Ottawa	AAA Mon	4	3	0	0	16	76	24	14	11	4	1	2	0	5	0	10	1	0	1	2	.333	0	0	6.19
Jupiter	A+ Mon	23	23	2	0	137.2	575	124	63	56	8	4	0	4	44	0	91	6	0	8	6	.571	2	0	3.66
Harrisburg	AA Mon	1	0	0	0	3	11	1	0	0	0	0	0	0	0	0	0	0	0	0	1	.000	0	0	0.00
2000 Harrisburg	AA Mon	22	12	1	0	71.1	299	67	28	27	2	2	1	1	24	1	39	0	2	7	3	.700	0	0	3.41
Carolina	AA Col	8	8	3	0	59.1	243	52	18	7	3	3	1	3	11	0	53	2	0	3	3	.500	0	0	1.06
Colo Spngs	AAA Col	6	6	2	0	31.1	147	50	27	27	6	1	0	1	7	0	6	0	0	4	1	.800	0	0	7.76
2001 Colo Spngs	AAA Col	3	3	0	0	12.1	65	21	16	15	4	0	0	0	8	0	9	0	0	0	1	.000	0	0	10.95
West Tenn	AA ChC	23	12	1	2	83.1	349	82	44	38	11	2	5	0	21	2	58	8	0	4	5	.444	0	0	4.10
2000 Montreal	NL	3	0	0	1	1.2	14	6	7	7	0	1	0	0	2	0	2	1	0	0	0	—	0	0	37.80
Colorado	NL	1	0	0	1	1	8	4	5	5	1	0	1	1	0	0	0	0	0	0	0	—	0	0	45.00
8 Min. YEARS		208	125	11	29	860	3689	867	435	362	58	34	26	20	283	6	592	57	6	54	55	.495	2	3	3.79

Andy Morales

Bats: Right **Throws:** Right **Pos:** 3B-25; DH-23; PH-3   **Ht:** 6'2" **Wt:** 208 **Born:** 12/3/74 **Age:** 27

Year Team	Lg Org	G	AB	H	2B	3B	HR	TB	R	RBI	TBB	IBB	SO	HBP	SH	SF	SB	CS	SB%	GDP	Avg	OBP	SLG
2001 Norwich	AA NYY	48	160	37	3	1	1	45	15	14	10	1	25	3	0	1	1	1	.50	2	.231	.287	.281

Steve Morales

Bats: Both **Throws:** Right **Pos:** C-45; PH-5; DH-1   **Ht:** 5'10" **Wt:** 195 **Born:** 5/4/78 **Age:** 24

Year Team	Lg Org	G	AB	H	2B	3B	HR	TB	R	RBI	TBB	IBB	SO	HBP	SH	SF	SB	CS	SB%	GDP	Avg	OBP	SLG
1997 Marlins	R Fla	20	62	13	1	0	2	20	7	13	6	0	10	1	0	2	1	1	.50	3	.210	.282	.323
1998 Portland	AA Fla	3	10	3	0	0	0	3	0	3	0	0	2	0	0	0	0	0	—	1	.300	.300	.300
Utica	A- Fla	26	85	21	2	0	3	32	14	14	5	0	18	0	0	2	2	1	.67	2	.247	.283	.376
1999 Kane County	A Fla	28	96	26	5	0	2	37	12	11	4	0	16	1	2	0	0	0	—	2	.271	.307	.385
2000 Kane County	A Fla	42	114	25	3	0	4	40	9	19	11	0	24	3	2	1	0	0	—	2	.219	.302	.351
Calgary	AAA Fla	3	3	0	0	0	0	0	0	0	0	0	0	0	0	0	0	0	—	1	.000	.000	.000
2001 Calgary	AAA Fla	2	2	1	0	0	0	1	0	0	0	0	1	0	0	0	0	0	—	0	.500	.500	.500
Brevard Cty	A+ Fla	48	157	39	7	0	4	58	19	15	10	0	15	5	3	1	0	0	—	4	.248	.312	.369
5 Min. YEARS		172	529	128	18	0	15	191	61	75	36	0	86	10	7	6	3	2	.60	15	.242	.299	.361

Willie Morales

Bats: Right **Throws:** Right **Pos:** C-67; 3B-1; PH-1; PR-1   **Ht:** 5'11" **Wt:** 185 **Born:** 9/7/72 **Age:** 29

Year Team	Lg Org	G	AB	H	2B	3B	HR	TB	R	RBI	TBB	IBB	SO	HBP	SH	SF	SB	CS	SB%	GDP	Avg	OBP	SLG
1993 Sou Oregon	A- Oak	60	208	56	16	0	1	75	34	27	19	2	36	4	1	4	0	3	.00	2	.269	.336	.361
Tacoma	AAA Oak	2	3	0	0	0	0	0	0	0	1	0	1	0	0	0	0	0	—	0	.000	.250	.000
1994 W Michigan	A Oak	111	380	101	26	0	13	166	47	51	36	4	64	3	3	2	3	5	.38	12	.266	.333	.437
1995 Modesto	A+ Oak	109	419	116	32	0	4	160	49	60	28	1	75	7	2	4	1	4	.20	13	.277	.330	.382
1996 Huntsville	AA Oak	108	377	110	24	0	18	188	54	73	38	2	67	7	4	6	0	2	.00	11	.292	.362	.499
1997 Huntsville	AA Oak	36	136	37	11	0	3	57	19	24	17	0	24	0	0	3	1	0	1.00	2	.272	.346	.419
Edmonton	AAA Oak	56	179	52	12	0	5	79	23	35	11	0	27	0	3	3	0	2	.00	4	.291	.326	.441
1998 Edmonton	AAA Oak	73	242	47	13	0	5	75	25	30	17	0	47	1	1	1	0	1	.00	8	.194	.249	.310
1999 Vancouver	AAA Oak	5	14	2	1	0	0	3	2	2	1	0	4	0	1	1	0	0	—	2	.143	.188	.214
Midland	AA Oak	102	343	96	27	0	16	171	43	71	24	0	54	6	2	4	2	0	1.00	8	.280	.334	.499
2000 Rochester	AAA Bal	73	249	62	12	1	6	94	21	23	12	0	58	0	2	1	0	3	.00	3	.249	.282	.378
2001 Rochester	AAA Bal	52	164	38	7	0	1	48	18	11	5	0	32	1	3	2	2	1	.67	2	.232	.256	.293
Colo Sprngs	AAA Col	17	51	8	1	0	1	12	4	2	1	0	8	0	1	1	2	0	1.00	1	.157	.170	.235
2000 Baltimore	AL	3	11	3	1	0	0	4	1	0	0	0	3	0	0	0	0	0	—	0	.273	.273	.364
9 Min. YEARS		804	2765	725	182	1	73	1128	339	409	210	9	497	29	23	32	11	21	.34	68	.262	.318	.408

Julio Moreno

Pitches: Right **Bats:** Right **Pos:** RP-27; SP-5   **Ht:** 6'1" **Wt:** 180 **Born:** 10/23/75 **Age:** 26

Year Team	Lg Org	G	GS	CG	GF	IP	BFP	H	R	ER	HR	SH	SF	HB	TBB	IBB	SO	WP	Bk	W	L	Pct.	ShO	Sv	ERA
1994 Orioles	R Bal	4	2	0	0	8.1	41	14	14	11	2	0	2	0	1	0	6	0	0	0	2	.000	0	0	11.88
1995 Orioles	R Bal	5	5	1	0	34	131	17	9	6	0	1	2	1	7	0	29	1	1	3	2	.600	1	0	1.59
Bluefield	R+ Bal	9	8	0	1	49.1	214	61	31	23	3	1	3	0	12	0	36	3	1	4	3	.571	0	0	4.20
1996 Frederick	A+ Bal	28	26	0	1	162	682	167	80	63	14	8	0	9	38	0	147	9	3	9	10	.474	0	0	3.50
1997 Bowie	AA Bal	27	25	1	0	138.2	596	141	76	59	20	2	3	6	64	4	106	6	3	9	6	.600	0	0	3.83
1999 Orioles	R Bal	4	2	0	0	10	39	8	4	2	1	0	1	0	1	0	5	0	0	1	0	1.000	0	0	1.80
Bowie	AA Bal	10	10	0	0	44.1	202	46	29	26	9	1	2	1	27	0	25	4	0	2	2	.500	0	0	5.28
2000 Orioles	R Bal	3	0	0	0	6	27	6	3	0	0	0	0	0	3	0	6	0	0	0	0	—	0	0	0.00
Frederick	A+ Bal	2	0	0	0	4	15	2	2	2	0	0	0	0	1	0	1	0	0	0	0	—	0	0	4.50
Bowie	AA Bal	13	0	0	4	31	144	43	21	19	6	0	2	1	10	1	14	3	0	1	1	.500	0	0	5.52
2001 Binghamton	AA NYM	12	0	0	3	20.1	91	21	13	11	3	0	3	0	9	0	17	1	0	3	2	.600	0	0	4.87
St. Lucie	A+ NYM	20	5	1	7	55.1	230	52	22	19	3	1	1	3	9	0	43	0	0	5	4	.556	0	2	3.09
7 Min. YEARS		137	83	3	16	563.1	2412	578	304	241	63	14	19	21	182	5	435	27	8	37	32	.536	1	2	3.85

Orber Moreno

Pitches: Right **Bats:** Right **Pos:** RP-29; SP-1   **Ht:** 6'3" **Wt:** 200 **Born:** 4/27/77 **Age:** 25

Year Team	Lg Org	G	GS	CG	GF	IP	BFP	H	R	ER	HR	SH	SF	HB	TBB	IBB	SO	WP	Bk	W	L	Pct.	ShO	Sv	ERA
1995 Royals	R KC	8	3	0	1	22	89	15	9	6	0	0	0	2	7	0	21	2	0	1	1	.500	0	0	2.45
1996 Royals	R KC	12	7	0	5	46.1	187	37	15	7	2	2	0	1	10	0	50	1	2	5	1	.833	0	1	1.36
1997 Lansing	A KC	27	25	0	0	138.1	603	150	83	74	15	6	4	8	45	0	128	9	0	4	8	.333	0	0	4.81
1998 Wilmington	A+ KC	23	0	0	17	33	115	8	3	3	1	1	0	0	10	1	50	1	0	3	2	.600	0	7	0.82
Wichita	AA KC	24	0	0	19	34.1	144	28	13	11	1	2	0	0	12	3	40	3	0	0	1	.000	0	2	2.88
1999 Omaha	AAA KC	16	0	0	15	25.2	97	17	6	6	2	0	0	0	4	0	30	0	0	3	1	.750	0	4	2.10
Royals	R KC	1	1	0	0	1	3	0	0	0	0	0	0	0	0	0	1	0	0	0	0	—	0	0	0.00
2001 Wilmington	A+ KC	8	1	0	2	10.2	48	12	5	3	1	0	0	1	1	0	16	1	0	1	1	.500	0	0	2.53
Wichita	AA KC	5	0	0	2	8.2	31	3	0	0	0	0	0	1	2	0	10	0	1	0	0	—	0	1	0.00
Omaha	AAA KC	17	0	0	11	21	90	19	11	11	4	0	0	0	8	0	25	1	0	1	1	.500	0	4	4.71
1999 Kansas City	AL	7	0	0	3	8	34	4	5	5	1	0	0	0	6	0	7	0	0	0	0	—	0	0	5.63
6 Min. YEARS		141	37	0	72	341	1407	289	145	121	26	11	4	13	99	4	371	18	3	18	16	.529	0	23	3.19

206

Ramon Moreta

Bats: Right **Throws:** Right **Pos:** OF-99; PH-2   **Ht:** 5'11" **Wt:** 185 **Born:** 9/5/75 **Age:** 26

Year Team	Lg Org	G	AB	H	2B	3B	HR	TB	R	RBI	TBB	IBB	SO	HBP	SH	SF	SB	CS	SB%	GDP	Avg	OBP	SLG
1997 Great Falls	R+ LA	68	265	89	6	2	1	102	45	20	18	0	38	1	6	0	29	17	.63	5	.336	.380	.385
1998 San Berndno	A+ LA	134	536	138	19	7	1	174	67	24	44	1	109	2	11	0	46	23	.67	8	.257	.316	.325
Albuquerque	AAA LA	8	27	10	1	2	0	15	5	3	1	0	9	0	0	1	2	2	.50	0	.370	.379	.556
1999 San Antonio	AA LA	117	397	121	13	3	2	146	56	42	18	0	66	0	11	2	26	16	.62	12	.305	.333	.368
2000 San Antonio	AA LA	126	468	112	16	2	11	165	61	31	37	1	86	5	7	2	26	20	.57	8	.239	.301	.353
2001 Tacoma	AAA Sea	23	69	15	3	1	1	23	8	13	6	0	31	2	0	3	3	3	.50	3	.217	.288	.333
Salt Lake	AAA Ana	2	7	2	0	0	0	2	0	1	0	0	0	0	0	0	0	1	.00	0	.286	.286	.286
Rancho Cuca	A+ Ana	34	137	44	13	1	1	62	23	13	9	0	32	1	1	0	19	7	.73	5	.321	.367	.453
San Jose	A+ SF	11	40	8	0	0	0	8	5	2	3	0	9	0	2	0	3	3	.50	0	.200	.256	.200
Shreveport	AA SF	30	109	31	4	0	2	41	14	14	6	1	15	2	0	1	9	6	.60	3	.284	.331	.376
5 Min. YEARS		553	2055	570	75	18	19	738	284	163	142	3	395	13	38	9	163	98	.62	44	.277	.327	.359

Scott Morgan

Bats: Right **Throws:** Right **Pos:** OF-118; DH-10; PH-2; 1B-1   **Ht:** 6'7" **Wt:** 230 **Born:** 7/19/73 **Age:** 28

Year Team	Lg Org	G	AB	H	2B	3B	HR	TB	R	RBI	TBB	IBB	SO	HBP	SH	SF	SB	CS	SB%	GDP	Avg	OBP	SLG
1995 Watertown	A- Cle	66	244	64	18	0	2	88	42	33	26	0	63	8	0	4	6	5	.55	11	.262	.348	.361
1996 Columbus	A Cle	87	305	95	25	1	22	188	62	80	46	0	70	11	0	4	9	5	.64	5	.311	.415	.616
1997 Kinston	A+ Cle	95	368	116	32	3	23	223	86	67	47	3	87	5	0	4	4	2	.67	8	.315	.396	.606
Akron	AA Cle	21	69	12	3	0	2	21	11	6	8	0	20	1	0	1	1	0	1.00	0	.174	.266	.304
1998 Akron	AA Cle	119	456	134	31	4	25	248	95	89	56	1	124	8	0	4	4	5	.44	9	.294	.378	.544
1999 Akron	AA Cle	88	344	97	26	2	26	205	72	70	38	5	96	2	0	1	6	1	.86	4	.282	.356	.596
Buffalo	AAA Cle	48	171	44	9	0	8	77	32	31	18	0	38	3	0	3	2	3	.40	2	.257	.333	.450
2000 Buffalo	AAA Cle	11	33	12	3	0	0	15	5	4	7	0	7	1	0	0	1	0	1.00	1	.364	.476	.455
Edmonton	AAA Ana	90	320	79	25	2	9	135	53	54	32	1	74	3	0	2	8	3	.73	5	.247	.319	.422
2001 Salt Lake	AAA Ana	128	501	133	39	3	28	262	93	83	41	4	117	5	0	2	2	0	1.00	10	.265	.326	.523
7 Min. YEARS		753	2811	786	211	15	145	1462	551	517	319	14	696	47	0	26	43	24	.64	55	.280	.360	.520

Mike Moriarty

Bats: Right **Throws:** Right **Pos:** SS-125; 3B-3; PH-2; PR-2; 2B-1; P-1   **Ht:** 6'0" **Wt:** 195 **Born:** 3/8/74 **Age:** 28

Year Team	Lg Org	G	AB	H	2B	3B	HR	TB	R	RBI	TBB	IBB	SO	HBP	SH	SF	SB	CS	SB%	GDP	Avg	OBP	SLG
1995 Fort Wayne	A Min	62	203	46	6	3	4	70	26	26	27	1	44	2	2	3	8	0	1.00	1	.227	.319	.345
1996 Fort Myers	A+ Min	133	428	107	18	2	3	138	76	39	59	0	67	8	5	4	14	15	.48	2	.250	.349	.322
1997 New Britain	AA Min	135	421	93	22	5	6	143	60	48	53	1	68	3	10	5	12	5	.71	10	.221	.309	.340
1998 New Britain	AA Min	38	112	32	8	0	4	52	22	15	17	0	16	3	3	1	0	4	.00	1	.286	.391	.464
Salt Lake	AAA Min	64	161	36	8	2	3	57	21	19	22	0	39	1	2	1	2	1	.67	1	.224	.319	.354
1999 Salt Lake	AAA Min	128	380	98	21	7	4	145	63	51	56	1	62	6	11	5	6	4	.60	9	.258	.358	.382
2000 Salt Lake	AAA Min	127	390	97	23	4	13	167	73	55	63	0	58	5	9	4	1	2	.33	9	.249	.357	.428
2001 Edmonton	AAA Min	131	404	98	17	2	13	158	66	50	58	0	94	13	5	2	5	4	.56	12	.243	.354	.391
7 Min. YEARS		818	2499	607	123	25	50	930	407	303	355	3	448	41	47	25	48	35	.58	45	.243	.343	.372

Cesar Morillo

Bats: Both **Throws:** Right **Pos:** DH-18; PH-10; 2B-3; 3B-2   **Ht:** 5'11" **Wt:** 180 **Born:** 7/21/73 **Age:** 28

Year Team	Lg Org	G	AB	H	2B	3B	HR	TB	R	RBI	TBB	IBB	SO	HBP	SH	SF	SB	CS	SB%	GDP	Avg	OBP	SLG
1990 Royals	R KC	55	185	50	6	2	1	63	21	17	22	0	45	2	3	0	7	4	.64	4	.270	.354	.341
1991 Baseball Cy	A+ KC	62	226	39	8	0	0	47	11	13	13	0	68	2	7	2	6	5	.55	4	.173	.222	.208
Appleton	A KC	63	236	59	9	3	1	77	35	17	38	0	54	1	1	0	9	8	.53	2	.250	.355	.326
1992 Baseball Cy	A+ KC	35	102	17	5	1	0	24	8	7	10	0	23	1	3	1	1	0	1.00	1	.167	.246	.235
Eugene	A- KC	51	180	44	9	1	1	58	28	17	21	0	40	1	3	0	6	4	.60	1	.244	.327	.322
1993 Rockford	A KC	101	327	85	13	3	3	113	47	36	30	3	65	3	5	2	4	1	.80	4	.260	.326	.346
1994 Wilmington	A+ KC	16	55	9	1	0	0	10	3	4	5	1	17	1	0	1	1	0	1.00	1	.164	.242	.182
Rockford	A KC	70	242	68	11	2	2	89	23	25	15	2	35	2	1	2	4	3	.57	6	.281	.326	.368
1995 Bakersfield	A+ KC	108	371	113	25	1	1	143	41	37	31	2	71	4	5	1	4	12	.25	6	.305	.364	.385
1996 Wichita	AA KC	45	119	28	3	1	2	39	8	7	7	0	18	0	5	0	3	0	1.00	3	.235	.278	.328
1997 Tulsa	AA Tex	84	288	76	18	1	1	99	38	23	28	2	53	0	4	1	0	4	.00	3	.264	.328	.344
1998 Bakersfield	A+ SF	14	38	7	0	0	0	7	3	6	3	0	10	0	1	1	0	0	—	1	.184	.238	.184
Shreveport	AA SF	10	18	2	0	0	0	2	1	2	1	0	3	0	0	1	0	0	—	0	.111	.158	.111
Newark	IND —	11	36	10	1	0	0	11	5	4	1	0	3	1	1	1	1	2	.33	1	.278	.308	.306
Nashua	IND —	28	98	28	3	2	1	38	16	18	9	0	15	1	1	0	9	3	.75	3	.286	.352	.388
Atlantic Ct	IND —	31	123	43	10	0	1	56	16	13	8	0	20	0	3	0	7	2	.78	2	.350	.389	.455
1999 Newark	IND —	91	338	99	21	2	6	142	60	42	24	0	55	1	8	1	19	6	.76	9	.293	.341	.420
2000 El Paso	AA Ari	10	21	4	1	0	0	5	0	1	0	0	6	0	0	0	0	0	—	0	.190	.190	.238
Round Rock	AA Hou	88	281	83	15	0	3	107	43	37	25	4	56	5	0	2	9	7	.56	9	.295	.361	.381
2001 Round Rock	AA Hou	33	93	17	1	2	1	25	11	8	6	1	12	0	3	0	2	0	1.00	3	.183	.232	.269
12 Min. YEARS		1006	3377	881	160	21	24	1155	418	334	297	15	669	25	54	16	92	61	.60	65	.261	.324	.342

Justin Morneau

Bats: Left **Throws:** Right **Pos:** 1B-116; DH-11   **Ht:** 6'4" **Wt:** 205 **Born:** 5/15/81 **Age:** 21

Year Team	Lg Org	G	AB	H	2B	3B	HR	TB	R	RBI	TBB	IBB	SO	HBP	SH	SF	SB	CS	SB%	GDP	Avg	OBP	SLG
1999 Twins	R Min	17	53	16	5	0	0	21	3	9	2	0	6	1	1	1	0	1	.00	2	.302	.333	.396
2000 Twins	R Min	52	194	78	21	0	10	129	47	58	30	7	18	0	0	2	3	1	.75	5	.402	.478	.665
Elizabethtn	R+ Min	6	23	5	0	0	1	8	4	3	1	0	6	0	0	0	0	0	—	0	.217	.250	.348

Year Team	Lg Org	G	AB	H	2B	3B	HR	TB	R	RBI	TBB	IBB	SO	HBP	SH	SF	SB	CS	SB%	GDP	Avg	OBP	SLG
								BATTING										BASERUNNING			PERCENTAGES		
2001 Quad City	A Min	64	236	84	17	2	12	141	50	53	26	1	38	3	0	4	0	0	—	4	.356	.420	.597
Fort Myers	A+ Min	53	197	58	10	3	4	86	25	40	24	1	41	8	0	5	0	0	—	4	.294	.385	.437
New Britain	AA Min	10	38	6	1	0	0	7	3	4	3	0	8	0	0	1	0	0	—	0	.158	.214	.184
3 Min. YEARS		202	741	247	54	5	27	392	132	167	86	9	117	12	1	13	3	2	.60	16	.333	.405	.529

Bobby Morris

Bats: Left **Throws:** Right **Pos:** PH-26; 2B-21; OF-20; 1B-9; DH-9; PR-1   **Ht:** 6'0" **Wt:** 175 **Born:** 11/22/72 **Age:** 29

Year Team	Lg Org	G	AB	H	2B	3B	HR	TB	R	RBI	TBB	IBB	SO	HBP	SH	SF	SB	CS	SB%	GDP	Avg	OBP	SLG
								BATTING										BASERUNNING			PERCENTAGES		
1993 Huntington	R+ ChC	50	170	49	8	3	1	66	29	24	24	0	29	1	2	3	6	7	.46	2	.288	.374	.388
1994 Peoria	A ChC	101	362	128	33	1	7	184	61	64	53	4	63	7	10	2	7	7	.50	10	.354	.443	.508
1995 Daytona	A+ ChC	95	344	106	18	2	2	134	44	55	38	6	46	8	2	5	22	8	.73	5	.308	.385	.390
1996 Orlando	AA ChC	131	465	122	29	3	8	181	72	62	65	4	73	6	0	8	12	14	.46	12	.262	.355	.389
1997 Orlando	AA ChC	4	16	5	1	0	0	6	3	1	2	0	3	0	0	0	0	0	—	0	.313	.389	.375
Kinston	A+ Cle	10	32	5	1	0	2	12	6	10	4	0	6	2	0	1	0	0	—	0	.156	.282	.375
Akron	AA Cle	42	119	30	9	1	1	44	17	15	22	0	21	2	2	1	1	2	.33	3	.252	.375	.370
1998 Kinston	A+ Cle	25	65	17	2	1	2	27	11	14	6	0	12	3	3	1	2	1	.67	1	.262	.347	.415
1999 Tulsa	AA Tex	6	21	7	2	0	0	9	0	2	4	0	1	1	0	0	0	0	—	1	.333	.462	.429
2000 Chattanooga	AA Cin	87	245	67	14	1	5	98	34	35	32	0	42	2	1	3	6	2	.75	9	.273	.358	.400
2001 Chattanooga	AA Cin	85	224	63	18	1	9	110	35	44	41	2	41	3	0	4	4	4	.50	2	.281	.393	.491
9 Min. YEARS		636	2063	599	135	13	37	871	312	326	291	16	337	35	20	28	60	45	.57	47	.290	.383	.422

Cody Morrison

Pitches: Right **Bats:** Right **Pos:** RP-8   **Ht:** 6'2" **Wt:** 200 **Born:** 9/26/74 **Age:** 27

Year Team	Lg Org	G	GS	CG	GF	IP	BFP	H	R	ER	HR	SH	SF	HB	TBB	IBB	SO	WP	Bk	W	L	Pct.	ShO	Sv	ERA
				HOW MUCH HE PITCHED							WHAT HE GAVE UP											THE RESULTS			
1998 Boise	A- Ana	30	0	0	20	35.1	154	25	10	7	0	1	0	3	16	0	40	9	1	5	1	.833	0	6	1.78
1999 Lk Elsinore	A+ Ana	45	0	0	27	67.2	332	65	57	40	2	3	1	11	50	7	64	7	1	4	8	.333	0	3	5.32
2000 Lancaster	A+ Sea	52	0	0	21	82	342	78	42	39	5	2	1	6	29	3	60	5	2	8	7	.533	0	3	4.28
2001 San Antonio	AA Sea	8	0	0	4	9.2	48	15	14	14	2	1	0	1	4	0	8	0	0	0	0	—	0	1	13.03
4 Min. YEARS		135	0	0	72	194.2	876	183	123	100	9	7	2	21	99	10	172	21	4	17	16	.515	0	13	4.62

Mark Mortimer

Bats: Right **Throws:** Right **Pos:** C-33; DH-28; PH-13; 1B-7; OF-4; 3B-1; P-1   **Ht:** 6'1" **Wt:** 215 **Born:** 9/15/75 **Age:** 26

Year Team	Lg Org	G	AB	H	2B	3B	HR	TB	R	RBI	TBB	IBB	SO	HBP	SH	SF	SB	CS	SB%	GDP	Avg	OBP	SLG
								BATTING										BASERUNNING			PERCENTAGES		
1997 Danville	R+ Atl	5	13	1	0	0	0	1	3	3	4	0	1	0	1	1	0	0	—	1	.077	.278	.077
Eugene	A- Atl	53	174	53	7	2	2	70	25	21	16	0	24	2	0	2	1	1	.50	3	.305	.366	.402
1998 Macon	A Atl	28	94	28	7	0	5	50	21	26	18	0	11	2	0	0	1	0	1.00	2	.298	.421	.532
Danville	A+ Atl	98	338	80	11	2	6	113	32	33	41	4	53	5	0	2	4	4	.00	12	.237	.326	.334
1999 Greenville	AA Atl	11	30	7	1	0	0	8	4	5	3	0	7	0	0	1	0	0	—	0	.233	.294	.267
Myrtle Bch	A+ Atl	73	250	69	13	0	3	91	29	31	28	0	48	5	3	4	1	0	1.00	6	.276	.355	.364
2000 Greenville	AA Atl	41	118	21	3	0	4	36	14	12	12	0	15	1	1	0	0	1	.00	5	.178	.260	.305
Myrtle Bch	A+ Atl	41	135	36	4	1	1	45	17	14	22	0	26	2	1	0	0	1	.00	5	.267	.377	.333
Richmond	AAA Atl	4	10	2	0	0	0	2	1	1	1	0	1	0	0	0	0	0	—	0	.200	.333	.200
2001 Greenville	AA Atl	33	87	22	2	1	3	35	9	8	6	0	13	2	0	0	0	0	—	0	.253	.316	.402
Myrtle Bch	A+ Atl	50	181	35	4	0	2	45	18	17	17	0	31	5	0	3	0	0	—	7	.193	.277	.249
5 Min. YEARS		437	1430	354	52	6	26	496	171	171	168	4	230	25	6	13	3	6	.33	39	.248	.334	.347

Ryan Moskau

Pitches: Left **Bats:** Right **Pos:** RP-29; SP-10   **Ht:** 6'3" **Wt:** 210 **Born:** 8/22/77 **Age:** 24

Year Team	Lg Org	G	GS	CG	GF	IP	BFP	H	R	ER	HR	SH	SF	HB	TBB	IBB	SO	WP	Bk	W	L	Pct.	ShO	Sv	ERA
				HOW MUCH HE PITCHED							WHAT HE GAVE UP											THE RESULTS			
1998 Yakima	A- LA	9	6	0	3	36.2	156	22	11	5	3	2	0	3	13	0	42	0	1	3	0	1.000	0	2	1.23
San Berndno	A+ LA	6	6	1	0	39	163	37	18	15	2	1	4	4	16	1	31	1	1	3	3	.500	1	0	3.46
1999 Vero Beach	A+ LA	17	17	0	0	104	443	99	54	48	8	3	4	7	40	0	68	6	4	5	5	.500	0	0	4.15
Brevard Cty	A+ Fla	9	9	2	0	63.2	261	50	22	19	4	4	0	1	21	0	40	0	0	4	3	.571	0	0	2.69
2000 Portland	AA Fla	16	16	2	0	84.2	377	96	58	52	9	8	2	3	38	0	53	3	0	3	8	.273	0	0	5.53
Brevard Cty	A+ Fla	10	9	1	0	52.2	245	74	40	38	6	0	2	2	15	0	43	1	0	2	5	.286	0	0	6.49
2001 Portland	AA Fla	39	10	0	9	103.1	430	103	45	40	12	8	4	5	29	3	78	2	0	3	2	.600	0	2	3.48
4 Min. YEARS		106	73	6	12	484	2075	481	248	217	44	26	12	25	172	4	355	13	6	23	26	.469	1	4	4.04

Julio Mosquera

Bats: Right **Throws:** Right **Pos:** C-98; PH-5; DH-4; 1B-1; PR-1   **Ht:** 6'0" **Wt:** 190 **Born:** 1/29/72 **Age:** 30

Year Team	Lg Org	G	AB	H	2B	3B	HR	TB	R	RBI	TBB	IBB	SO	HBP	SH	SF	SB	CS	SB%	GDP	Avg	OBP	SLG
								BATTING										BASERUNNING			PERCENTAGES		
1993 Blue Jays	R Tor	35	108	28	3	2	0	35	9	15	8	0	16	1	2	1	3	2	.60	3	.259	.314	.324
1994 Medcine Hat	R+ Tor	59	229	78	17	1	2	103	33	44	18	3	35	3	0	2	3	3	.50	4	.341	.393	.450
1995 Hagerstown	A Tor	108	406	118	22	5	3	159	64	46	29	2	53	13	3	5	5	5	.50	13	.291	.353	.392
1996 Knoxville	AA Tor	92	318	73	17	0	2	96	36	31	29	1	55	4	3	1	6	5	.55	16	.230	.301	.302
Syracuse	AAA Tor	23	72	18	1	0	0	19	6	5	6	0	14	1	0	0	0	0	—	1	.250	.316	.264
1997 Syracuse	AAA Tor	10	35	8	1	0	0	9	5	1	2	0	5	1	0	0	0	0	—	2	.229	.289	.257
Knoxville	AA Tor	87	309	90	23	1	5	130	47	50	22	0	56	5	2	3	3	4	.43	10	.291	.345	.421
1998 Syracuse	AAA Tor	28	94	20	6	0	2	32	10	4	5	0	12	4	1	1	1	0	1.00	3	.213	.279	.340
Knoxville	AA Tor	12	43	12	1	0	0	13	4	8	4	0	7	0	0	1	0	0	—	0	.279	.333	.302
1999 Orlando	AA TB	80	259	79	13	1	4	106	36	37	15	2	40	3	1	4	1	0	1.00	14	.305	.345	.409
2000 Columbus	AAA NYY	35	101	24	6	2	1	37	17	14	8	0	20	6	1	1	6	0	1.00	5	.238	.328	.366
Norwich	AA NYY	29	74	17	3	2	0	24	9	3	8	0	12	1	2	1	2	2	.50	2	.230	.310	.324

208

Year Team	Lg Org	G	AB	H	2B	3B	HR	TB	R	RBI	TBB	IBB	SO	HBP	SH	SF	SB	CS	SB%	GDP	Avg	OBP	SLG
2001 Columbus	AAA NYY	16	41	10	2	0	0	12	6	2	1	0	10	3	1	0	0	0	—	2	.244	.311	.293
Norwich	AA NYY	88	268	72	18	0	9	117	31	33	14	2	64	7	1	4	2	1	.67	3	.269	.317	.437
1996 Toronto	AL	8	22	5	2	0	0	7	2	2	0	0	3	1	0	0	0	1	.00	0	.227	.261	.318
1997 Toronto	AL	3	8	2	1	0	0	3	0	0	0	0	2	0	0	0	0	0	—	0	.250	.250	.375
9 Min. YEARS		702	2357	647	133	14	28	892	313	293	169	10	399	52	17	24	32	22	.59	75	.275	.334	.378
2 Maj. YEARS		11	30	7	3	0	0	10	2	2	0	0	5	1	0	0	0	1	.00	0	.233	.258	.333

Danny Mota

Pitches: Right **Bats:** Right **Pos:** RP-46 **Ht:** 6'0" **Wt:** 180 **Born:** 10/9/75 **Age:** 26

Year Team	Lg Org	G	GS	CG	GF	IP	BFP	H	R	ER	HR	SH	SF	HB	TBB	IBB	SO	WP	Bk	W	L	Pct.	ShO	Sv	ERA
1995 Yankees	R NYY	14	0	0	9	32.2	133	27	9	8	2	4	0	2	4	0	35	6	3	2	3	.400	0	0	2.20
1996 Oneonta	A- NYY	10	0	0	8	10	42	10	5	5	0	0	0	0	2	0	11	0	1	0	1	.000	0	7	4.50
1997 Greensboro	A NYY	20	0	0	9	29.2	111	17	6	6	1	0	0	0	11	1	30	0	0	2	0	1.000	0	1	1.82
Oneonta	A- NYY	27	0	0	25	28.1	119	21	8	7	0	1	0	0	16	0	40	0	0	1	0	1.000	0	17	2.22
1998 Fort Wayne	A Min	25	0	0	20	32	153	24	14	8	2	3	0	2	8	1	39	0	1	4	3	.571	0	7	2.25
Fort Myers	A+ Min	19	4	0	9	47.1	206	45	21	15	3	1	3	0	22	0	49	6	1	3	5	.375	0	0	2.85
1999 Fort Myers	A+ Min	11	0	0	3	18.2	79	19	5	5	0	1	1	0	5	0	22	0	0	1	1	.500	0	0	2.41
New Britain	AA Min	6	0	0	5	12.2	52	11	5	5	2	1	0	0	5	1	12	0	0	1	0	1.000	0	0	3.55
2000 Fort Myers	A+ Min	29	1	0	13	48.1	209	38	20	11	0	1	3	1	23	5	52	5	0	2	2	.500	0	4	2.05
New Britain	AA Min	24	0	0	16	28.1	110	19	13	9	1	0	1	0	8	1	40	0	0	3	1	.750	0	4	2.86
Salt Lake	AAA Min	4	0	0	1	5.2	23	5	1	1	0	1	0	0	1	0	5	0	0	0	0	—	0	0	1.59
2001 Edmonton	AAA Min	34	0	0	15	47.1	210	52	31	31	7	3	2	1	23	1	43	4	0	3	3	.500	0	2	5.89
Las Vegas	AAA LA	12	0	0	5	11.2	55	16	10	10	1	1	1	0	8	1	7	0	0	1	2	.333	0	1	7.71
2000 Minnesota	AL	4	0	0	3	5.1	28	10	5	5	1	0	0	0	1	0	3	1	0	0	0	—	0	0	8.44
7 Min. YEARS		235	5	0	138	352.2	1484	304	148	121	19	17	11	6	136	11	385	21	6	22	22	.500	0	43	3.09

Tony Mota

Bats: Both **Throws:** Right **Pos:** OF-111; DH-5; PH-5; PR-1 **Ht:** 6'1" **Wt:** 170 **Born:** 10/31/77 **Age:** 24

Year Team	Lg Org	G	AB	H	2B	3B	HR	TB	R	RBI	TBB	IBB	SO	HBP	SH	SF	SB	CS	SB%	GDP	Avg	OBP	SLG
1996 Yakima	A- LA	60	225	62	11	3	3	88	29	29	13	0	37	1	3	1	13	7	.65	0	.276	.317	.391
1997 San Berndno	A+ LA	111	420	101	14	13	4	153	53	49	30	2	97	4	6	2	11	8	.58	9	.240	.296	.364
1998 Vero Beach	A+ LA	61	254	81	18	5	7	130	45	35	18	3	27	2	0	0	13	8	.62	6	.319	.369	.512
San Antonio	AA LA	59	222	54	10	6	2	82	20	22	12	1	36	0	2	3	16	8	.67	6	.243	.278	.369
1999 San Antonio	AA LA	98	345	112	31	2	15	192	65	75	41	6	56	0	4	2	13	5	.72	14	.325	.394	.557
2000 Albuquerque	AAA LA	102	372	100	11	4	6	137	57	47	28	2	61	0	0	2	8	6	.57	9	.269	.318	.368
2001 Las Vegas	AAA LA	120	442	131	29	8	8	200	62	57	40	1	79	1	3	2	16	7	.70	12	.296	.355	.452
6 Min. YEARS		611	2280	641	124	41	45	982	331	314	182	15	393	8	18	12	90	49	.65	56	.281	.335	.431

Bill Mott

Bats: Left **Throws:** Right **Pos:** OF-35; DH-11; PH-1 **Ht:** 6'2" **Wt:** 180 **Born:** 1/2/76 **Age:** 26

Year Team	Lg Org	G	AB	H	2B	3B	HR	TB	R	RBI	TBB	IBB	SO	HBP	SH	SF	SB	CS	SB%	GDP	Avg	OBP	SLG
1998 Boise	A- Ana	63	207	63	11	0	7	95	54	37	48	1	41	5	1	3	21	1	.95	1	.304	.441	.459
1999 Lk Elsinore	A+ Ana	25	88	28	5	1	1	38	16	12	10	0	18	1	2	2	6	3	.67	1	.318	.386	.432
2000 Lk Elsinore	A+ Ana	115	396	119	20	9	11	190	83	82	76	5	78	10	1	5	29	8	.78	5	.301	.421	.480
2001 Arkansas	AA Ana	25	94	30	5	4	0	43	9	9	9	1	21	0	0	0	10	4	.71	0	.319	.379	.457
Angels	R Ana	5	12	1	0	1	0	3	2	2	4	0	4	1	0	1	0	0	—	0	.083	.333	.250
Rancho Cuca	A+ Ana	17	69	21	5	1	3	37	14	16	8	0	11	0	1	2	5	1	.83	0	.304	.367	.536
4 Min. YEARS		250	866	262	46	16	22	406	178	158	155	7	169	17	5	13	71	17	.81	7	.303	.413	.469

Sean Mulligan

Bats: Right **Throws:** Right **Pos:** C-33; DH-2 **Ht:** 6'2" **Wt:** 210 **Born:** 4/25/70 **Age:** 32

Year Team	Lg Org	G	AB	H	2B	3B	HR	TB	R	RBI	TBB	IBB	SO	HBP	SH	SF	SB	CS	SB%	GDP	Avg	OBP	SLG
1991 Chston-SC	A SD	60	215	56	9	3	4	83	24	30	17	0	56	6	1	1	4	1	.80	5	.260	.331	.386
1992 High Desert	A+ SD	35	118	19	4	0	4	35	14	14	11	1	38	3	0	1	0	0	—	3	.161	.248	.297
Waterloo	A SD	79	278	70	13	1	5	100	24	43	20	0	62	5	2	4	0	1	1.00	10	.252	.309	.360
1993 Rancho Cuca	A+ SD	79	268	75	10	3	6	109	29	36	34	0	33	3	0	4	1	3	.25	16	.280	.362	.407
1994 Rancho Cuca	A+ SD	66	243	74	18	1	9	121	45	49	24	1	39	5	1	8	1	0	1.00	4	.305	.368	.498
Wichita	AA SD	56	208	73	14	0	1	90	29	30	11	2	25	5	0	3	2	3	.40	9	.351	.392	.433
1995 Las Vegas	AAA SD	101	339	93	20	1	7	136	34	43	27	2	61	8	1	3	0	0	—	7	.274	.340	.401
1996 Las Vegas	AAA SD	102	358	103	24	3	19	190	55	75	30	4	68	7	0	2	1	2	.33	8	.288	.353	.531
1997 Akron	AA Cle	2	7	3	1	0	0	4	1	1	1	0	0	0	0	0	0	0	—	0	.429	.500	.571
1998 St. Paul	IND —	3	12	2	0	0	0	2	1	2	0	0	5	1	0	0	0	0	—	1	.167	.231	.167
1999 Duluth-Sup	IND —	52	200	50	10	0	5	75	23	25	14	2	21	4	0	0	1	0	1.00	1	.250	.312	.375
Bridgeport	IND —	18	62	11	3	0	1	17	7	6	5	0	20	2	0	0	0	0	—	1	.177	.257	.274
2000 Ottawa	AAA Mon	15	50	11	4	0	0	15	3	3	0	0	7	1	0	1	0	0	—	0	.220	.231	.300
Bridgeport	IND —	90	305	101	26	0	13	166	46	75	28	1	36	9	5	4	0	1	.00	8	.331	.399	.544
2001 Camden	IND —	22	73	13	2	0	2	21	7	6	5	0	13	4	1	1	0	0	—	5	.178	.265	.288
Rochester	AAA Bal	7	27	9	2	0	1	14	5	4	1	0	5	0	0	0	0	0	1.00	0	.333	.357	.519
Bowie	AA Bal	6	23	5	0	0	2	11	2	7	0	0	6	0	0	0	0	0	—	1	.217	.217	.478
1996 San Diego	NL	2	1	0	0	0	0	0	0	0	0	0	0	0	0	0	0	0	—	0	.000	.000	.000
11 Min. YEARS		793	2786	768	160	12	79	1189	349	449	228	13	495	63	11	33	11	11	.50	85	.276	.341	.427

Billy Munoz

Bats: Left **Throws:** Left **Pos:** 1B-39; DH-5; PH-3 　　　　**Ht:** 6'2" **Wt:** 220 **Born:** 6/30/75 **Age:** 27

				BATTING													BASERUNNING				PERCENTAGES		
Year Team	Lg Org	G	AB	H	2B	3B	HR	TB	R	RBI	TBB	IBB	SO	HBP	SH	SF	SB	CS	SB%	GDP	Avg	OBP	SLG
1998 Columbus	A Cle	120	417	111	24	1	12	173	61	60	68	2	104	1	0	1	3	2	.60	6	.266	.370	.415
1999 Kinston	A+ Cle	106	378	96	25	1	9	150	46	55	48	2	108	1	1	1	3	2	.60	9	.254	.339	.397
2000 Kinston	A+ Cle	63	213	67	13	1	11	115	28	39	21	0	46	3	0	3	0	1	.00	5	.315	.379	.540
Akron	AA Cle	74	281	77	15	4	14	142	41	48	29	2	66	4	1	1	1	0	1.00	3	.274	.349	.505
2001 Mahoning Vy	A- Cle	12	43	13	3	1	0	18	3	8	3	0	6	0	0	0	0	0	—	3	.302	.348	.419
Akron	AA Cle	34	114	21	4	0	4	37	5	12	12	0	21	0	0	0	0	0	—	0	.184	.260	.325
4 Min. YEARS		409	1446	385	84	8	50	635	184	222	181	6	351	9	2	7	7	5	.58	26	.266	.350	.439

Juan Munoz

Bats: Left **Throws:** Left **Pos:** 1B-123; DH-2; PH-2; OF-1; P-1 　　　　**Ht:** 5'9" **Wt:** 170 **Born:** 3/27/74 **Age:** 28

				BATTING													BASERUNNING				PERCENTAGES		
Year Team	Lg Org	G	AB	H	2B	3B	HR	TB	R	RBI	TBB	IBB	SO	HBP	SH	SF	SB	CS	SB%	GDP	Avg	OBP	SLG
1995 Johnson Cty	R+ StL	57	190	66	12	1	7	101	43	31	27	0	17	0	0	2	13	2	.87	1	.347	.425	.532
1996 Peoria	A StL	31	111	38	9	0	0	47	19	19	14	0	14	1	0	0	4	1	.80	2	.342	.411	.423
St. Pete	A+ StL	90	330	80	12	3	1	101	41	46	38	0	35	1	3	3	6	5	.55	8	.242	.320	.306
1997 Pr William	A+ StL	66	256	80	16	7	4	122	41	48	19	3	25	0	0	4	3	1	.75	5	.313	.355	.477
Arkansas	AA StL	58	215	60	9	2	6	91	28	31	16	0	26	1	2	1	6	10	.38	2	.279	.330	.423
1998 Arkansas	AA StL	28	119	32	9	0	0	41	16	18	3	0	15	0	0	3	0	0	—	4	.269	.280	.345
Memphis	AAA StL	117	399	107	17	5	4	146	54	44	29	5	58	0	5	2	9	4	.69	9	.268	.316	.366
1999 Arkansas	AA StL	2	3	2	0	0	0	2	1	0	0	0	0	0	0	0	0	0	—	0	.667	.667	.667
2000 Arkansas	AA StL	68	247	85	14	1	5	116	41	31	16	0	16	1	1	1	5	2	.71	7	.344	.385	.470
Memphis	AAA StL	32	79	17	7	0	0	24	6	7	2	0	10	0	0	1	2	1	.67	2	.215	.232	.304
2001 New Haven	AA StL	126	456	126	19	2	9	176	39	56	24	4	48	0	1	3	9	7	.56	15	.276	.311	.386
7 Min. YEARS		675	2405	693	124	21	36	967	329	331	188	12	264	4	12	23	57	33	.63	55	.288	.338	.402

Peter Munro

Pitches: Right **Bats:** Right **Pos:** RP-25; SP-8 　　　　**Ht:** 6'3" **Wt:** 210 **Born:** 6/14/75 **Age:** 27

		HOW MUCH HE PITCHED						WHAT HE GAVE UP										THE RESULTS					
Year Team	Lg Org	G	GS	CG	GF	IP	BFP	H	R	ER	HR	SH	SF	HB	TBB	IBB	SO	WP	Bk	W	L	Pct.	ShO	Sv	ERA
1995 Utica	A- Bos	14	14	0	0	90	389	79	38	26	3	3	3	7	33	1	74	4	0	5	4	.556	0	0	2.60
1996 Sarasota	A+ Bos	27	25	2	1	155	667	153	76	62	4	3	2	7	62	1	115	7	1	11	6	.647	2	1	3.60
1997 Trenton	AA Bos	22	22	1	0	116.1	506	113	76	64	12	10	6	8	47	0	109	6	3	7	10	.412	0	0	4.95
1998 Pawtucket	AAA Bos	18	17	0	0	106.2	450	111	49	48	10	2	5	4	35	2	75	8	0	5	4	.556	0	0	4.05
Syracuse	AAA Tor	8	8	0	0	44.2	213	58	42	37	7	2	0	2	23	2	42	4	0	2	5	.286	0	0	7.46
1999 Syracuse	AAA Tor	18	11	0	3	69.2	312	70	29	24	6	0	3	4	33	1	68	3	0	6	1	.857	0	0	3.10
2000 Dunedin	A+ Tor	3	3	0	0	11.1	47	11	7	7	0	0	0	0	4	0	12	1	0	0	1	.000	0	0	5.56
Syracuse	AAA Tor	10	10	0	0	61.2	251	52	20	17	1	2	1	2	25	0	45	2	0	4	3	.571	0	0	2.48
Oklahoma	AAA Tex	5	5	1	0	31	136	27	17	16	3	0	1	3	14	0	15	1	0	1	2	.333	1	0	4.65
2001 Oklahoma	AAA Tex	33	8	0	9	88.2	390	89	50	46	12	2	4	4	43	1	73	3	0	8	6	.571	0	0	4.67
1999 Toronto	AL	31	2	0	9	55.1	250	70	38	37	6	1	4	2	23	0	38	3	0	0	2	.000	0	0	6.02
2000 Toronto	AL	9	3	0	2	25.2	127	38	22	17	1	1	0	3	16	0	16	1	0	1	1	.500	0	0	5.96
7 Min. YEARS		158	123	6	13	775	3361	763	404	347	58	24	25	41	319	8	628	39	4	49	42	.538	3	1	4.03
2 Maj. YEARS		40	5	0	11	81	377	108	60	54	7	2	4	5	39	0	54	4	0	1	3	.250	0	0	6.00

Mike Murphy

Bats: Right **Throws:** Right **Pos:** OF-102; DH-7; 1B-4; PH-2 　　　　**Ht:** 6'2" **Wt:** 185 **Born:** 1/23/72 **Age:** 30

				BATTING													BASERUNNING				PERCENTAGES		
Year Team	Lg Org	G	AB	H	2B	3B	HR	TB	R	RBI	TBB	IBB	SO	HBP	SH	SF	SB	CS	SB%	GDP	Avg	OBP	SLG
1990 Martinsvlle	R+ Phi	9	31	3	0	0	0	3	4	1	7	0	17	0	0	0	1	2	.33	1	.097	.263	.097
1991 Martinsvlle	R+ Phi	44	156	34	3	0	0	37	15	7	11	1	40	1	2	0	9	2	.82	5	.218	.274	.237
1992 Batavia	A- Phi	63	228	58	6	2	2	74	32	27	21	0	48	4	3	0	15	8	.65	6	.254	.328	.325
1993 Spartanburg	A Phi	133	509	147	29	6	3	197	70	60	35	1	91	9	9	2	33	14	.70	15	.289	.344	.387
1994 Dunedin	A+ Tor	125	469	129	11	4	1	151	57	34	55	3	106	9	4	3	31	10	.76	9	.275	.360	.322
1995 Canton-Akrn	AA Cle	10	23	1	0	0	0	1	3	0	4	0	3	0	0	0	0	1	.00	0	.043	.185	.043
Kinston	A+ Cle	67	177	41	6	0	1	50	26	15	15	1	30	3	1	1	13	4	.76	2	.232	.301	.282
1996 Charlotte	A+ Tex	87	358	119	20	7	7	174	73	52	32	1	94	3	3	0	22	9	.71	5	.332	.392	.486
Tulsa	AA Tex	34	121	28	7	2	4	51	22	16	21	0	29	3	1	1	1	0	1.00	2	.231	.356	.421
1997 Tulsa	AA Tex	46	156	40	10	1	4	64	30	19	35	0	45	4	0	0	6	3	.67	3	.256	.405	.410
Okla City	AAA Tex	73	243	80	13	5	5	118	37	25	38	1	66	4	4	2	14	5	.74	1	.329	.425	.486
1998 Charlotte	A+ Tex	3	7	2	1	0	0	3	4	1	3	0	1	0	0	0	1	0	1.00	0	.286	.500	.429
Tulsa	AA Tex	58	196	49	8	2	4	73	26	22	27	1	56	2	0	2	6	2	.75	8	.250	.344	.372
Oklahoma	AAA Tex	24	74	16	1	0	0	17	10	5	6	0	23	0	1	0	3	1	.75	1	.216	.275	.230
Rochester	AAA Bal	8	29	11	0	0	1	14	3	2	3	0	7	0	0	0	1	1	.50	0	.379	.438	.483
1999 Rochester	AAA Bal	70	217	49	6	3	1	64	35	21	34	0	63	1	3	3	7	3	.70	6	.226	.329	.295
Tacoma	AAA Sea	38	129	38	7	3	2	57	22	22	13	0	36	2	1	3	10	4	.71	2	.295	.361	.442
2000 Tacoma	AAA Sea	97	360	102	18	4	6	146	54	38	32	0	86	3	1	1	10	3	.77	4	.283	.346	.406
2001 Carolina	AA Col	114	410	108	19	1	7	150	57	43	62	3	114	8	1	4	21	5	.81	13	.263	.368	.366
12 Min. YEARS		1103	3893	1055	165	40	48	1444	580	410	454	12	955	56	34	22	204	77	.73	83	.271	.354	.371

Nate Murphy

Bats: Left **Throws:** Left **Pos:** OF-72; DH-15; PH-6 　　　　**Ht:** 6'0" **Wt:** 195 **Born:** 4/15/75 **Age:** 27

				BATTING													BASERUNNING				PERCENTAGES		
Year Team	Lg Org	G	AB	H	2B	3B	HR	TB	R	RBI	TBB	IBB	SO	HBP	SH	SF	SB	CS	SB%	GDP	Avg	OBP	SLG
1996 Boise	A- Ana	67	266	76	18	1	7	117	58	41	41	1	63	1	0	1	12	4	.75	4	.286	.382	.440
1997 Cedar Rapds	A Ana	51	149	33	4	2	0	41	21	13	19	1	43	1	0	1	4	2	.67	2	.221	.312	.275
1998 Lk Elsinore	A+ Ana	40	120	20	2	0	5	37	15	10	9	1	46	0	1	0	5	2	.71	2	.167	.225	.308

	BATTING																BASERUNNING				PERCENTAGES		
Year Team	Lg Org	G	AB	H	2B	3B	HR	TB	R	RBI	TBB	IBB	SO	HBP	SH	SF	SB	CS	SB%	GDP	Avg	OBP	SLG
1999 Lk Elsinore	A+ Ana	28	107	38	8	1	5	63	21	20	11	1	27	2	0	1	9	4	.69	0	.355	.421	.589
Erie	AA Ana	104	359	96	17	8	14	171	48	56	54	3	85	3	4	2	6	5	.55	7	.267	.366	.476
2000 Edmonton	AAA Ana	119	393	101	17	6	8	154	60	38	52	3	91	2	3	2	6	4	.60	11	.257	.345	.392
2001 Salt Lake	AAA Ana	53	177	44	8	1	5	69	28	21	16	1	53	2	2	0	1	3	.25	2	.249	.318	.390
El Paso	AA Ari	38	122	32	8	3	4	58	22	18	19	0	29	0	0	1	6	1	.86	1	.262	.359	.475
6 Min. YEARS		500	1693	440	82	22	48	710	273	217	221	11	437	11	10	8	49	25	.66	29	.260	.348	.419

Dan Murray

Pitches: Right **Bats:** Right **Pos:** RP-47; SP-1 **Ht:** 6'1" **Wt:** 195 **Born:** 11/21/73 **Age:** 28

	HOW MUCH HE PITCHED						WHAT HE GAVE UP												THE RESULTS					
Year Team	Lg Org	G	GS	CG	GF	IP	BFP	H	R	ER	HR	SH	SF	HB	TBB	IBB	SO	WP	Bk	W	L	Pct.	ShO	Sv	ERA
1995 Pittsfield	A- NYM	22	0	0	19	32	145	24	7	7	1	2	0	1	16	3	34	3	0	0	6	.000	0	6	1.97
1996 St. Lucie	A+ NYM	33	13	0	5	101.2	465	114	60	48	2	3	3	8	53	3	56	11	0	7	5	.583	0	4	4.25
1997 St. Lucie	A+ NYM	30	24	4	3	156.1	682	150	75	60	4	5	3	10	55	3	91	13	0	12	10	.545	2	0	3.45
1998 Binghamton	AA NYM	27	27	1	0	164.1	681	153	64	58	13	3	2	8	54	2	159	5	0	11	6	.647	1	0	3.18
1999 Norfolk	AAA NYM	29	27	3	1	145	650	149	91	80	22	7	5	7	70	5	96	11	3	12	10	.545	1	0	4.97
2000 Omaha	AAA KC	27	22	1	3	140.2	618	148	99	87	22	2	9	7	60	3	102	9	1	10	9	.526	1	1	5.57
2001 Omaha	AAA KC	48	1	0	25	98	418	105	49	43	10	2	2	4	30	3	70	4	0	3	3	.500	0	3	3.95
1999 New York	NL	1	0	0	1	2	12	4	3	3	0	0	1	0	2	0	1	1	0	0	0	—	0	0	13.50
Kansas City	AL	4	0	0	0	8.1	39	14	9	6	4	0	0	1	4	0	8	0	0	0	0	—	0	0	6.48
2000 Kansas City	AL	10	0	0	3	19.1	86	20	10	10	7	2	1	1	10	0	16	2	0	0	0	—	0	0	4.66
7 Min. YEARS		216	114	9	56	838	3659	843	455	383	74	24	24	45	338	22	608	56	4	55	49	.529	5	15	4.11
2 Maj. YEARS		15	0	0	4	29.2	137	33	21	19	11	2	2	2	16	0	25	3	0	0	0	—	0	0	5.76

Aaron Myers

Pitches: Right **Bats:** Right **Pos:** RP-27; SP-7 **Ht:** 6'2" **Wt:** 205 **Born:** 5/14/76 **Age:** 26

	HOW MUCH HE PITCHED						WHAT HE GAVE UP												THE RESULTS					
Year Team	Lg Org	G	GS	CG	GF	IP	BFP	H	R	ER	HR	SH	SF	HB	TBB	IBB	SO	WP	Bk	W	L	Pct.	ShO	Sv	ERA
1998 Ogden	R+ Mil	4	4	0	0	26	114	32	16	10	2	1	1	1	8	0	8	0	1	2	0	1.000	0	0	3.46
Beloit	A Mil	11	10	0	0	57.2	258	65	36	30	3	3	1	5	19	0	41	5	1	4	5	.444	0	0	4.68
1999 Stockton	A+ Mil	22	10	0	2	83	360	88	52	42	7	3	6	8	25	2	81	3	4	3	4	.429	0	1	4.55
2000 Mudville	A+ Mil	50	0	0	19	88.1	374	64	36	35	9	2	3	6	44	0	104	3	0	2	3	.400	0	2	3.57
2001 Huntsville	AA Mil	34	7	0	9	70	304	53	31	28	4	2	1	3	40	0	68	3	1	3	4	.429	0	2	3.60
4 Min. YEARS		121	31	0	30	325	1410	302	171	145	25	11	12	23	136	2	302	14	7	14	16	.467	0	5	4.02

Adrian Myers

Bats: Right **Throws:** Right **Pos:** OF-98; DH-5; PH-1; PR-1 **Ht:** 5'10" **Wt:** 175 **Born:** 5/10/75 **Age:** 27

	BATTING																BASERUNNING				PERCENTAGES		
Year Team	Lg Org	G	AB	H	2B	3B	HR	TB	R	RBI	TBB	IBB	SO	HBP	SH	SF	SB	CS	SB%	GDP	Avg	OBP	SLG
1996 Hudson Val	A- Tex	54	142	24	5	4	1	40	22	15	17	0	44	8	0	2	19	2	.90	2	.169	.290	.282
1997 Charlotte	A+ Tex	90	287	71	7	4	0	86	40	21	36	0	73	3	1	1	18	15	.55	5	.247	.336	.300
1998 Charlotte	A+ Tex	122	454	122	20	7	6	174	84	64	55	1	98	3	7	9	51	23	.69	11	.269	.345	.383
1999 Tulsa	AA Tex	99	357	84	12	4	1	107	60	28	44	0	63	3	1	1	33	7	.83	14	.235	.323	.300
2000 New Haven	AA Sea	92	334	95	19	3	2	126	60	34	59	1	69	2	0	1	8	10	.44	5	.284	.394	.377
2001 Tacoma	AAA Sea	71	260	66	10	8	0	92	30	33	18	0	59	1	1	1	4	4	.50	5	.254	.304	.354
San Antonio	AA Sea	33	129	30	4	2	0	38	14	15	17	0	30	1	2	3	6	4	.60	4	.233	.320	.295
6 Min. YEARS		561	1963	492	77	32	10	663	310	210	246	2	436	21	12	18	139	65	.68	46	.251	.338	.338

Brett Myers

Pitches: Right **Bats:** Right **Pos:** SP-23; RP-3 **Ht:** 6'4" **Wt:** 215 **Born:** 8/17/80 **Age:** 21

	HOW MUCH HE PITCHED						WHAT HE GAVE UP												THE RESULTS					
Year Team	Lg Org	G	GS	CG	GF	IP	BFP	H	R	ER	HR	SH	SF	HB	TBB	IBB	SO	WP	Bk	W	L	Pct.	ShO	Sv	ERA
1999 Phillies	R Phi	7	5	0	0	27	105	17	8	7	0	0	0	2	7	0	30	2	0	2	1	.667	0	0	2.33
2000 Piedmont	A Phi	27	27	2	0	175.1	738	165	78	62	7	1	4	9	69	0	140	8	0	13	7	.650	1	0	3.18
2001 Reading	AA Phi	26	23	1	0	156	661	156	71	67	21	3	1	10	43	1	130	5	0	13	4	.765	1	0	3.87
3 Min. YEARS		60	55	3	0	358.1	1504	338	157	136	28	4	5	21	119	1	300	15	0	28	12	.700	2	0	3.42

Randy Myers

Pitches: Left **Bats:** Left **Pos:** RP-1 **Ht:** 6'1" **Wt:** 210 **Born:** 9/19/62 **Age:** 39

	HOW MUCH HE PITCHED						WHAT HE GAVE UP												THE RESULTS					
Year Team	Lg Org	G	GS	CG	GF	IP	BFP	H	R	ER	HR	SH	SF	HB	TBB	IBB	SO	WP	Bk	W	L	Pct.	ShO	Sv	ERA
1982 Kingsport	A+ NYM	13	13	1	0	74.1	—	68	49	34	1	—	—	4	69	0	86	12	—	6	3	.667	0	0	4.12
1983 Columbia	A NYM	28	28	3	0	173.1	—	146	94	70	15	—	—	4	108	0	164	19	—	14	10	.583	0	0	3.63
1984 Lynchburg	A+ NYM	23	22	7	1	157	641	123	46	36	7	5	1	3	61	0	171	11	0	13	5	.722	1	0	2.06
Jackson	AA NYM	5	5	1	0	35	148	29	14	8	2	2	2	0	16	1	35	2	1	2	1	.667	0	0	2.06
1985 Jackson	AA NYM	19	19	2	0	120.1	517	99	61	53	4	5	5	1	69	1	116	8	1	4	8	.333	1	0	3.96
Tidewater	AAA NYM	8	7	0	0	44	184	40	13	9	1	1	1	1	20	1	25	4	0	1	1	.500	0	0	1.84
1986 Tidewater	AAA NYM	45	0	0	35	65	278	44	19	17	2	3	0	2	44	3	79	2	0	6	7	.462	0	12	2.35
1987 Tidewater	AAA NYM	5	0	0	4	7.1	33	6	4	4	0	1	0	1	4	0	13	3	0	0	0	—	0	3	4.91
2001 Tacoma	AAA Sea	1	0	0	0	0	4	3	4	4	1	0	0	0	1	0	0	0	0	0	0	—	0	0	
1985 New York	NL	1	0	0	1	2	7	0	0	0	0	0	0	0	1	0	2	0	0	0	0	—	0	0	0.00
1986 New York	NL	10	0	0	5	10.2	53	11	5	5	1	0	0	0	9	1	13	0	0	0	0	—	0	0	4.22
1987 New York	NL	54	0	0	18	75	314	61	36	33	6	7	6	0	30	5	92	3	0	3	6	.333	0	6	3.96
1988 New York	NL	55	0	0	44	68	261	45	15	13	5	3	2	2	17	2	69	2	0	7	3	.700	0	26	1.72
1989 New York	NL	65	0	0	47	84.1	349	62	23	22	4	6	2	2	40	4	88	3	0	7	4	.636	0	24	2.35
1990 Cincinnati	NL	66	0	0	59	86.2	353	59	24	20	6	4	2	3	38	0	98	2	1	4	6	.400	0	31	2.08
1991 Cincinnati	NL	58	12	1	18	132	575	116	61	52	8	8	6	1	80	5	108	2	1	6	13	.316	0	6	3.55

Year Team	Lg Org	G	GS	CG	GF	IP	BFP	H	R	ER	HR	SH	SF	HB	TBB	IBB	SO	WP	Bk	W	L	Pct.	ShO	Sv	ERA
1992 San Diego	NL	66	0	0	57	79.2	348	84	38	38	7	7	5	1	34	3	66	5	0	3	6	.333	0	38	4.29
1993 Chicago	NL	73	0	0	69	75.1	313	65	26	26	7	1	2	1	26	2	86	3	0	2	4	.333	0	53	3.11
1994 Chicago	NL	38	0	0	34	40.1	174	40	18	17	3	3	1	0	16	1	32	2	0	1	5	.167	0	21	3.79
1995 Chicago	NL	57	0	0	47	55.2	240	49	25	24	7	2	3	0	28	1	59	0	0	1	2	.333	0	38	3.88
1996 Baltimore	AL	62	0	0	50	58.2	262	60	24	23	7	3	3	1	29	4	74	3	0	4	4	.500	0	31	3.53
1997 Baltimore	AL	61	0	0	57	59.2	241	47	12	10	2	2	0		22	2	56	3	0	2	3	.400	0	45	1.51
1998 Toronto	AL	41	0	0	37	42.1	190	44	21	21	4	2	1	2	19	4	32	2	0	3	4	.429	0	28	4.46
San Diego	NL	21	0	0	5	14.1	64	15	10	10	2	2	0	0	7	1	9	2	0	1	3	.250	0	0	6.28
7 Min. YEARS		147	94	14	40	676.1	—	558	304	235	33	—	—	16	392	6	689	61	—	46	35	.568	2	15	3.13
14 Maj. YEARS		728	12	1	548	884.2	3744	758	338	314	69	50	33	12	396	43	884	32	2	44	63	.411	0	347	3.19

Tootie Myers

Bats: Right **Throws:** Left **Pos:** OF-77; 2B-32; DH-13; PH-10; PR-1 **Ht:** 5'11" **Wt:** 178 **Born:** 9/8/78 **Age:** 23

Year Team	Lg Org	G	AB	H	2B	3B	HR	TB	R	RBI	TBB	IBB	SO	HBP	SH	SF	SB	CS	SB%	GDP	Avg	OBP	SLG
1997 Expos	R Mon	54	217	50	9	2	0	63	26	13	11	0	58	4	1	0	24	8	.75	3	.230	.280	.290
1998 Vermont	A- Mon	73	271	65	15	3	0	86	33	24	29	0	86	6	3	3	14	7	.67	5	.240	.324	.317
1999 Cape Fear	A Mon	137	515	115	19	8	11	183	61	52	35	1	147	10	6	1	30	16	.65	9	.223	.285	.355
2000 Jupiter	A+ Mon	110	449	109	16	9	7	164	70	43	41	1	111	3	9	2	26	16	.62	3	.243	.309	.365
2001 Harrisburg	AA Mon	123	396	104	15	8	10	165	49	49	34	1	118	6	4	2	17	7	.71	7	.263	.329	.417
5 Min. YEARS		497	1848	443	74	30	28	661	239	181	150	3	520	29	23	8	111	54	.67	27	.240	.306	.358

Rick Nadeau

Bats: Right **Throws:** Right **Pos:** OF-84; DH-13; PH-6 **Ht:** 6'0" **Wt:** 195 **Born:** 11/20/75 **Age:** 26

Year Team	Lg Org	G	AB	H	2B	3B	HR	TB	R	RBI	TBB	IBB	SO	HBP	SH	SF	SB	CS	SB%	GDP	Avg	OBP	SLG
1999 London	IND —	80	349	118	32	6	8	186	69	82	34	1	57	5	0	8	17	9	.65	7	.338	.407	.549
2000 London	IND —	80	312	103	21	1	19	183	78	71	42	2	64	5	0	6	11	6	.65	5	.330	.411	.587
2001 Trenton	AA Bos	6	18	3	1	0	0	4	1	1	0	0	5	0	0	0	0	0	—	1	.167	.167	.222
Sarasota	A+ Bos	96	348	91	17	2	5	127	32	45	33	0	55	3	1	3	6	5	.55	13	.261	.328	.365
3 Min. YEARS		262	1017	315	71	9	32	500	180	199	109	3	181	13	1	17	34	20	.63	26	.310	.378	.492

Mike Nakamura

Pitches: Right **Bats:** Right **Pos:** RP-47; SP-1 **Ht:** 5'10" **Wt:** 171 **Born:** 9/6/76 **Age:** 25

Year Team	Lg Org	G	GS	CG	GF	IP	BFP	H	R	ER	HR	SH	SF	HB	TBB	IBB	SO	WP	Bk	W	L	Pct.	ShO	Sv	ERA
1998 Fort Wayne	A Min	29	0	0	6	80	347	82	41	29	8	4	3	3	29	0	70	3	2	2	5	.286	0	1	3.26
Fort Myers	A+ Min	8	6	1	1	28.2	123	28	15	11	3	2	0	2	10	0	21	1	0	1	3	.250	0	0	3.45
1999 Fort Myers	A+ Min	14	0	0	6	19.2	74	9	5	4	1	2	2	0	5	0	18	1	0	2	0	1.000	0	2	1.83
2000 Fort Myers	A+ Min	32	0	0	19	41.1	162	33	9	7	0	2	1	0	11	1	46	2	0	1	0	1.000	0	12	1.52
2001 New Britain	AA Min	48	1	0	19	86.1	357	75	20	17	3	3	1	2	24	5	109	3	0	5	1	.833	0	5	1.77
4 Min. YEARS		131	16	1	51	256	1063	227	90	68	15	13	7	9	79	6	264	10	2	11	9	.550	0	20	2.39

Shane Nance

Pitches: Left **Bats:** Left **Pos:** RP-49 **Ht:** 5'8" **Wt:** 180 **Born:** 9/7/77 **Age:** 24

Year Team	Lg Org	G	GS	CG	GF	IP	BFP	H	R	ER	HR	SH	SF	HB	TBB	IBB	SO	WP	Bk	W	L	Pct.	ShO	Sv	ERA
2000 Yakima	A- LA	12	9	0	0	58	228	41	19	16	1	2	0	2	22	0	66	2	0	2	4	.333	0	0	2.48
2001 Vero Beach	A+ LA	21	0	0	13	48	196	28	15	14	3	1	0	3	21	1	63	2	0	6	3	.667	0	4	2.63
Jacksnville	AA LA	28	0	0	11	45.1	179	31	11	8	4	2	1	0	17	1	44	1	0	7	0	1.000	0	1	1.59
2 Min. YEARS		61	9	0	24	151.1	603	100	45	38	8	5	1	5	60	2	173	5	0	15	7	.682	0	5	2.26

Joe Nathan

Pitches: Right **Bats:** Right **Pos:** SP-17; RP-14 **Ht:** 6'4" **Wt:** 195 **Born:** 11/22/74 **Age:** 27

Year Team	Lg Org	G	GS	CG	GF	IP	BFP	H	R	ER	HR	SH	SF	HB	TBB	IBB	SO	WP	Bk	W	L	Pct.	ShO	Sv	ERA
1997 Salem-Keizr	A- SF	18	5	0	4	62	254	53	22	17	7	4	2	4	26	0	44	2	0	2	1	.667	0	2	2.47
1998 Shreveport	AA SF	4	4	0	0	15.1	74	20	15	15	4	0	0	2	9	0	10	0	0	1	3	.250	0	0	8.80
San Jose	A+ SF	22	22	0	0	122	506	100	51	45	13	1	1	10	48	0	118	1	0	8	6	.571	0	0	3.32
1999 Shreveport	AA SF	2	2	0	0	8.2	38	5	4	3	0	1	1	1	7	0	7	2	1	0	1	.000	0	0	3.12
Fresno	AAA SF	13	13	1	0	74.2	324	68	44	37	11	3	1	5	36	0	82	6	1	6	4	.600	0	0	4.46
2000 San Jose	A+ SF	1	1	0	0	5	19	4	2	2	1	0	1	0	1	0	2	1	0	0	1	.000	0	0	3.60
Bakersfield	A+ SF	1	1	0	0	5.1	25	2	3	3	0	0	0	1	7	0	6	1	0	1	0	1.000	0	0	5.06
Fresno	AAA SF	3	3	0	0	14.1	64	15	8	7	4	1	0	0	7	0	9	1	0	2	0	1.000	0	0	4.40
2001 Fresno	AAA SF	10	10	0	0	46.1	236	63	47	40	13	4	5	5	33	0	21	6	0	0	5	.000	0	0	7.77
Shreveport	AA SF	21	7	0	6	62.1	294	73	49	48	11	7	2	0	37	5	33	7	1	3	6	.333	0	0	6.28
1999 San Francisco	NL	19	14	0	2	90.1	395	84	45	42	17	2	0	1	46	0	54	2	0	7	4	.636	0	1	4.18
2000 San Francisco	NL	20	15	0	0	93.1	426	89	63	54	12	5	5	4	63	4	61	5	0	5	2	.714	0	0	5.21
5 Min. YEARS		95	68	1	10	416	1834	403	245	217	64	21	13	32	211	5	332	27	3	21	29	.420	0	2	4.69
2 Maj. YEARS		39	29	0	2	183.2	821	173	108	96	29	7	5	5	109	4	115	7	0	12	6	.667	0	1	4.70

212

Joey Nation

Pitches: Left **Bats:** Left **Pos:** SP-9; RP-5   **Ht:** 6'2" **Wt:** 205 **Born:** 9/28/78 **Age:** 23

		HOW MUCH HE PITCHED						WHAT HE GAVE UP										THE RESULTS					
Year Team	Lg Org	G	GS	CG	GF	IP	BFP	H	R	ER	HR	SH	SF	HB	TBB	IBB	SO	WP	Bk	W	L	Pct.	ShO	Sv	ERA
1997 Danville	R+ Atl	8	8	0	0	26.1	107	24	11	8	1	0	0	1	5	0	41	1	0	1	2	.333	0	0	2.73
1998 Macon	A Atl	29	28	1	0	143	640	179	102	80	15	6	6	1	39	0	141	10	2	6	12	.333	0	0	5.03
1999 Macon	A Atl	6	6	0	0	27.1	118	27	10	9	1	0	1	1	9	0	31	2	1	1	1	.500	0	0	2.96
Myrtle Bch	A+ Atl	19	17	0	0	96.1	401	88	51	47	7	2	4	2	37	0	87	4	0	5	4	.556	0	0	4.39
Daytona	A+ ChC	2	2	0	0	13	47	8	2	2	0	0	0	0	2	0	11	0	0	2	0	1.000	0	0	1.38
2000 West Tenn	AA ChC	27	27	1	0	166	695	137	72	61	17	6	6	6	65	2	165	9	0	11	10	.524	1	0	3.31
2001 Iowa	AAA ChC	14	9	0	0	44.2	181	39	16	15	5	0	0	1	13	0	48	0	0	3	2	.600	0	0	3.02
2000 Chicago	NL	2	2	0	0	11.2	55	12	9	9	2	1	1	2	8	0	8	0	0	0	2	.000	0	0	6.94
5 Min. YEARS		105	97	2	0	516.2	2189	502	264	222	46	14	17	12	170	2	524	26	3	29	31	.483	1	0	3.87

Jason Navarro

Pitches: Left **Bats:** Left **Pos:** RP-52   **Ht:** 6'4" **Wt:** 225 **Born:** 7/5/75 **Age:** 26

		HOW MUCH HE PITCHED						WHAT HE GAVE UP										THE RESULTS					
Year Team	Lg Org	G	GS	CG	GF	IP	BFP	H	R	ER	HR	SH	SF	HB	TBB	IBB	SO	WP	Bk	W	L	Pct.	ShO	Sv	ERA
1997 New Jersey	A- StL	10	10	1	0	44.2	211	60	40	34	4	0	1	1	22	0	41	7	3	1	6	.143	0	0	6.85
1998 Pr William	A+ StL	30	24	0	3	136.1	600	143	79	66	12	1	8	5	66	1	105	9	1	6	7	.462	0	0	4.36
1999 Potomac	A+ StL	39	14	0	3	111.1	508	134	82	75	12	3	6	5	49	0	66	7	1	5	13	.278	0	0	6.06
2000 Potomac	A+ StL	23	0	0	8	27.2	114	22	11	10	3	1	2	4	10	2	24	0	0	1	2	.333	0	0	3.25
Arkansas	AA StL	33	0	0	8	34.2	154	36	25	22	1	3	5	3	18	2	35	2	0	2	2	.500	0	2	5.71
2001 New Haven	AA StL	52	0	0	17	61.2	291	64	47	36	11	2	1	11	37	2	48	3	0	1	2	.333	0	0	5.25
5 Min. YEARS		187	48	1	39	416.1	1878	459	284	243	44	8	21	31	202	7	319	28	5	16	32	.333	0	2	5.25

Papy Ndungidi

Bats: Left **Throws:** Right **Pos:** OF-64; DH-37; PR-3; PH-2   **Ht:** 6'2" **Wt:** 199 **Born:** 3/15/79 **Age:** 23

		BATTING															BASERUNNING				PERCENTAGES		
Year Team	Lg Org	G	AB	H	2B	3B	HR	TB	R	RBI	TBB	IBB	SO	HBP	SH	SF	SB	CS	SB%	GDP	Avg	OBP	SLG
1997 Orioles	R Bal	18	54	10	2	1	2	20	10	7	12	0	15	1	0	0	4	0	1.00	1	.185	.343	.370
1998 Bluefield	R+ Bal	59	210	62	10	5	7	103	26	35	35	2	52	1	0	0	6	5	.55	3	.295	.398	.490
Frederick	A+ Bal	1	2	0	0	0	0	0	0	0	0	0	1	0	0	0	0	0	—	0	.000	.000	.000
1999 Delmarva	A Bal	64	217	42	8	2	0	54	33	24	49	2	54	3	1	1	18	2	.90	7	.194	.348	.249
Frederick	A+ Bal	60	192	51	10	3	0	67	40	18	39	0	43	3	1	1	4	2	.67	6	.266	.396	.349
2000 Frederick	A+ Bal	90	313	89	16	4	10	143	53	59	60	2	83	3	3	5	16	5	.76	4	.284	.399	.457
Bowie	AA Bal	41	136	32	6	0	3	47	17	14	25	0	33	3	0	0	2	2	.50	5	.235	.366	.346
2001 Bowie	AA Bal	104	339	72	17	1	3	100	34	35	37	0	90	4	1	2	3	5	.38	8	.212	.296	.295
5 Min. YEARS		437	1463	358	69	16	25	534	213	192	257	6	371	18	6	9	53	21	.72	34	.245	.362	.365

Steve Neal

Bats: Left **Throws:** Left **Pos:** 1B-126; PH-2; DH-1   **Ht:** 6'0" **Wt:** 260 **Born:** 2/14/77 **Age:** 25

		BATTING															BASERUNNING				PERCENTAGES		
Year Team	Lg Org	G	AB	H	2B	3B	HR	TB	R	RBI	TBB	IBB	SO	HBP	SH	SF	SB	CS	SB%	GDP	Avg	OBP	SLG
1998 Diamondbcks	R Ari	12	47	15	4	0	0	19	8	8	6	1	13	3	0	0	4	0	1.00	4	.319	.429	.404
Lethbridge	R+ Ari	43	148	37	8	0	3	54	16	20	28	0	50	2	0	0	5	4	.56	4	.250	.376	.365
1999 High Desert	A+ Ari	6	20	5	0	0	2	11	3	2	1	0	7	0	0	0	0	0	—	0	.250	.286	.550
South Bend	A Ari	69	249	70	14	2	7	109	41	53	40	2	72	1	0	3	6	2	.75	3	.281	.379	.438
2000 High Desert	A+ Ari	111	395	117	27	3	15	195	59	70	56	1	92	3	0	1	11	4	.73	8	.296	.387	.494
2001 El Paso	AA Ari	7	29	5	3	0	0	8	0	1	1	0	10	0	0	0	0	0	—	0	.172	.200	.276
South Bend	A Ari	121	453	116	23	3	20	205	71	92	39	6	137	8	0	3	7	1	.88	10	.256	.324	.453
4 Min. YEARS		369	1341	365	79	8	47	601	198	246	171	10	381	17	0	7	33	11	.75	27	.272	.360	.448

Mike Neill

Bats: Left **Throws:** Left **Pos:** OF-54; PH-6; DH-5; C-2; PR-2; 2B-1   **Ht:** 6'2" **Wt:** 200 **Born:** 4/27/70 **Age:** 32

		BATTING															BASERUNNING				PERCENTAGES		
Year Team	Lg Org	G	AB	H	2B	3B	HR	TB	R	RBI	TBB	IBB	SO	HBP	SH	SF	SB	CS	SB%	GDP	Avg	OBP	SLG
1991 Sou Oregon	A- Oak	63	240	84	14	0	5	113	42	42	35	3	54	0	4	1	9	3	.75	1	.350	.431	.471
1992 Reno	A+ Oak	130	473	159	26	7	5	214	101	76	81	2	96	5	6	2	23	11	.68	15	.336	.437	.452
Huntsville	AA Oak	5	16	5	0	0	0	5	4	2	2	0	7	0	1	1	1	0	1.00	0	.313	.368	.313
1993 Huntsville	AA Oak	54	179	44	8	0	1	55	30	15	34	0	45	1	0	1	3	4	.43	4	.246	.367	.307
Modesto	A+ Oak	17	62	12	3	0	0	15	4	4	12	0	12	0	1	0	0	1	.00	0	.194	.324	.242
1994 Tacoma	AAA Oak	7	22	5	1	0	0	6	1	2	3	0	7	0	0	0	0	0	—	2	.227	.320	.273
Modesto	A+ Oak	47	165	48	4	1	2	60	22	18	26	1	50	1	2	1	1	1	.50	4	.291	.389	.364
1995 Modesto	A+ Oak	71	257	71	17	1	6	108	39	36	34	2	65	2	5	1	4	4	.50	6	.276	.364	.420
Huntsville	AA Oak	33	107	32	6	1	2	46	11	16	12	1	29	0	1	1	1	0	1.00	1	.299	.367	.430
1996 Edmonton	AAA Oak	6	20	3	1	0	1	7	4	4	2	0	3	0	1	0	0	0	—	0	.150	.227	.350
Modesto	A+ Oak	114	442	150	20	6	19	239	101	78	68	4	123	4	2	2	28	7	.80	3	.339	.430	.541
1997 Edmonton	AAA Oak	7	21	4	0	0	0	4	3	3	7	0	7	0	2	0	1	1	.50	1	.190	.393	.190
Huntsville	AA Oak	122	486	165	30	2	14	241	129	80	72	0	113	4	3	3	16	7	.70	8	.340	.427	.496
1998 Edmonton	AAA Oak	99	371	112	18	4	10	168	72	48	65	0	91	2	6	1	6	5	.55	12	.302	.408	.453
Huntsville	AA Oak	12	35	9	5	0	0	14	1	2	4	1	13	0	1	0	0	0	—	0	.257	.333	.400
1999 Vancouver	AAA Oak	96	365	108	23	2	10	165	61	61	57	3	97	2	2	4	10	5	.67	11	.296	.390	.452
2000 Tacoma	AAA Sea	112	397	123	38	1	11	196	69	63	75	6	105	6	6	4	9	4	.69	10	.310	.423	.494
2001 Pawtucket	AAA Bos	67	208	51	10	2	5	80	27	22	31	0	70	0	6	1	2	1	.67	4	.245	.342	.385
1998 Oakland	AL	6	15	4	1	0	0	5	2	0	2	0	4	0	0	0	0	0	—	0	.267	.353	.333
11 Min. YEARS		1062	3866	1185	224	27	91	1736	721	572	620	23	987	27	48	23	114	54	.68	82	.307	.404	.449

213

Bry Nelson

Bats: Both **Throws:** Right **Pos:** 3B-64; 2B-57; PH-7; OF-5; DH-3; 1B-1   **Ht:** 5'10" **Wt:** 205 **Born:** 1/27/74 **Age:** 28

						BATTING										BASERUNNING				PERCENTAGES		
Year Team	Lg Org	G	AB	H	2B	3B	HR	TB	R	RBI	TBB	IBB	SO	HBP	SH	SF	SB	CS	SB%	GDP	Avg	OBP	SLG
1994 Quad City	A Hou	45	156	38	6	0	1	47	20	6	11	0	15	0	0	0	3	5	.38	3	.244	.293	.301
Auburn	A- Hou	65	261	84	16	7	6	132	53	35	11	0	13	1	3	1	2	1	.67	9	.322	.350	.506
1995 Kissimmee	A+ Hou	105	395	129	34	5	3	182	47	52	20	0	37	1	1	6	14	10	.58	8	.327	.355	.461
Quad City	A Hou	6	26	1	1	0	0	2	1	2	0	0	3	0	0	0	0	0	—	2	.038	.038	.077
1996 Kissimmee	A+ Hou	89	345	87	21	6	3	129	38	52	19	3	27	1	1	4	8	2	.80	13	.252	.290	.374
1997 Orlando	AA ChC	110	382	110	33	2	8	171	54	58	45	4	43	1	1	6	5	7	.42	15	.288	.359	.448
1998 West Tenn	AA ChC	32	102	29	6	2	2	45	10	18	12	2	12	0	0	1	4	2	.67	5	.284	.357	.441
1999 West Tenn	AA ChC	129	471	126	24	5	16	208	66	78	42	4	52	2	1	4	10	7	.59	13	.268	.328	.442
2000 Tucson	AAA Ari	69	261	81	21	0	5	117	34	31	16	0	20	0	0	2	4	2	.67	8	.310	.348	.448
2001 Tucson	AAA Ari	85	326	98	15	0	6	131	37	41	16	2	20	1	1	3	9	5	.64	12	.301	.332	.402
Nashville	AAA Pit	49	185	58	7	0	5	80	23	15	10	0	16	1	4	2	3	3	.50	7	.314	.348	.432
8 Min. YEARS		784	2910	841	184	27	55	1244	380	388	202	15	258	8	12	29	62	44	.58	95	.289	.334	.427

Jeff Nettles

Bats: Right **Throws:** Right **Pos:** 3B-75; SS-8; OF-7; 1B-3; DH-3; PH-3; 2B-1   **Ht:** 6'2" **Wt:** 200 **Born:** 8/20/78 **Age:** 23

						BATTING										BASERUNNING				PERCENTAGES		
Year Team	Lg Org	G	AB	H	2B	3B	HR	TB	R	RBI	TBB	IBB	SO	HBP	SH	SF	SB	CS	SB%	GDP	Avg	OBP	SLG
1998 Yankees	R NYY	12	24	3	1	0	0	4	1	1	5	0	4	0	0	0	0	1	.00	1	.125	.276	.167
1999 Yankees	R NYY	44	142	39	8	1	6	67	24	31	15	0	27	3	1	5	1	2	.33	4	.275	.345	.472
2000 Greensboro	A NYY	84	283	73	14	0	8	111	34	45	22	0	43	6	2	3	2	3	.40	8	.258	.322	.392
2001 Tampa	A+ NYY	77	253	51	14	0	4	77	28	31	24	1	53	1	1	3	0	2	.00	6	.202	.270	.304
Columbus	AAA NYY	12	27	5	0	0	0	5	1	1	5	0	9	0	0	0	2	1	.67	1	.185	.313	.185
Norwich	AA NYY	6	17	2	0	0	0	2	1	0	1	0	8	0	0	0	0	1	.00	0	.118	.167	.118
4 Min. YEARS		235	746	173	37	1	18	266	89	109	72	1	144	10	4	11	5	10	.33	20	.232	.304	.357

Scott Neuberger

Bats: Right **Throws:** Right **Pos:** OF-120   **Ht:** 6'3" **Wt:** 213 **Born:** 8/14/77 **Age:** 24

						BATTING										BASERUNNING				PERCENTAGES		
Year Team	Lg Org	G	AB	H	2B	3B	HR	TB	R	RBI	TBB	IBB	SO	HBP	SH	SF	SB	CS	SB%	GDP	Avg	OBP	SLG
1997 P+ TB	R+ TB	67	254	70	11	2	9	112	46	53	30	0	59	2	0	3	7	1	.88	5	.276	.353	.441
1998 Chston-SC	A TB	132	475	115	18	1	4	147	53	58	41	2	134	3	3	4	5	7	.42	16	.242	.304	.309
1999 St. Pete	A+ TB	127	442	115	14	3	10	165	55	63	24	0	104	8	1	6	1	2	.33	12	.260	.306	.373
2000 Orlando	AA TB	118	418	91	15	1	8	132	36	40	31	0	75	10	8	2	4	5	.44	8	.218	.286	.316
2001 Orlando	AA TB	120	419	111	25	1	4	150	49	43	36	1	83	4	3	1	5	3	.63	9	.265	.328	.358
5 Min. YEARS		564	2008	502	83	8	35	706	239	257	162	3	455	27	15	16	22	18	.55	50	.250	.312	.352

Tom Nevers

Bats: Right **Throws:** Right **Pos:** 3B-62; SS-41; PH-14; 2B-7; DH-3; 1B-2; P-1   **Ht:** 6'1" **Wt:** 190 **Born:** 9/13/71 **Age:** 30

						BATTING										BASERUNNING				PERCENTAGES		
Year Team	Lg Org	G	AB	H	2B	3B	HR	TB	R	RBI	TBB	IBB	SO	HBP	SH	SF	SB	CS	SB%	GDP	Avg	OBP	SLG
1990 Astros	R Hou	50	185	44	10	5	2	70	23	32	27	0	38	3	0	3	13	3	.81	3	.238	.339	.378
1991 Asheville	A Hou	129	441	111	26	2	16	189	59	71	53	0	124	3	2	5	10	12	.45	11	.252	.333	.429
1992 Osceola	A+ Hou	125	455	114	24	6	8	174	49	55	22	1	124	3	2	1	6	2	.75	10	.251	.289	.382
1993 Jackson	AA Hou	55	184	50	8	2	1	65	21	10	16	2	36	2	1	1	5	2	.78	5	.272	.335	.353
1994 Jackson	AA Hou	125	449	120	25	2	8	173	54	62	31	2	101	4	1	7	10	5	.67	8	.267	.316	.385
1995 Jackson	AA Hou	83	298	72	7	3	8	109	36	35	24	2	58	2	0	2	5	2	.71	10	.242	.301	.366
Stockton	A+ Mil	4	14	4	0	0	0	4	2	3	0	0	6	2	0	0	1	0	1.00	0	.286	.375	.286
El Paso	AA Mil	35	118	30	5	1	1	40	19	12	11	0	21	3	0	0	2	1	.67	6	.254	.333	.339
1996 Hardware Cy	AA Min	127	459	121	27	7	7	183	65	44	46	1	87	3	2	3	3	10	.23	18	.264	.333	.399
1997 Louisville	AAA StL	71	227	53	9	0	8	86	22	27	12	0	48	2	2	2	1	3	.25	12	.233	.276	.379
1998 Vancouver	AAA Ana	30	89	18	0	0	1	21	7	4	5	0	18	0	0	1	1	0	1.00	3	.202	.242	.236
Chattanooga	AA Cin	58	221	48	9	4	7	86	30	31	17	3	53	2	4	1	1	0	1.00	6	.217	.278	.389
1999 Chattanooga	AA Cin	111	380	112	23	2	17	190	61	65	15	0	74	2	2	2	3	5	.38	14	.295	.323	.500
2000 Louisville	AAA Cin	76	221	52	9	0	5	76	28	22	20	1	59	3	0	2	2	2	.50	7	.235	.305	.344
2001 Louisville	AAA Cin	5	19	2	1	0	0	3	0	3	1	0	5	0	0	1	0	0	—	1	.105	.143	.158
Chattanooga	AA Cin	120	402	101	33	1	17	187	63	67	43	2	101	4	0	4	4	5	.44	17	.251	.327	.465
12 Min. YEARS		1204	4162	1052	216	35	106	1656	539	543	343	14	953	38	16	35	69	52	.57	131	.253	.313	.398

Eric Newman

Pitches: Right **Bats:** Right **Pos:** RP-13; SP-1   **Ht:** 6'4" **Wt:** 205 **Born:** 8/27/72 **Age:** 29

		HOW MUCH HE PITCHED					WHAT HE GAVE UP											THE RESULTS				
Year Team	Lg Org	G	GS	CG	GF	IP	BFP	H	R	ER	HR	SH	SF	HB	TBB	IBB	SO	WP	Bk	W	L	Pct.	ShO	Sv	ERA
1995 Clinton	A SD	11	10	1	0	42.1	212	52	41	36	5	1	2	2	38	2	31	3	3	1	7	.125	0	0	7.65
Idaho Falls	R+ SD	15	14	0	0	81.2	365	91	49	40	3	5	4	7	35	0	65	3	1	8	4	.667	0	0	4.41
1996 Clinton	A SD	34	14	0	6	113.1	501	101	71	54	9	3	7	7	67	0	108	13	1	5	7	.417	0	1	4.29
1997 Rancho Cuca	A+ SD	35	15	0	3	123.2	542	104	64	57	12	1	3	7	73	1	141	12	0	13	6	.684	0	0	4.15
1998 Mobile	AA SD	27	25	1	0	140	632	152	100	87	14	5	9	6	71	1	120	17	0	9	12	.429	1	0	5.59
1999 West Tenn	AA ChC	58	0	0	15	84.1	359	61	37	30	5	5	2	5	49	6	90	8	0	5	3	.625	0	8	3.20
2000 Iowa	AAA ChC	30	8	0	10	79	350	74	54	48	12	6	3	1	52	4	68	5	0	3	5	.375	0	0	5.47
2001 El Paso	AA Ari	13	0	0	7	18.1	93	26	19	18	5	0	4	1	13	0	20	5	0	1	0	.000	0	0	8.84
Sonoma Cty	IND —	1	1	0	0	4	21	5	5	5	0	0	0	1	3	0	3	0	0	0	1	.000	0	0	11.25
7 Min. YEARS		224	87	2	39	686.2	3075	666	440	375	65	26	34	37	401	14	646	66	5	44	46	.489	1	10	4.92

Derek Nicholson

Bats: Left **Throws:** Right **Pos:** OF-37; 1B-13; 3B-9; DH-7; PH-5; PR-2 **Ht:** 6'0" **Wt:** 205 **Born:** 6/17/76 **Age:** 26

Year Team	Lg Org	G	AB	H	2B	3B	HR	TB	R	RBI	TBB	IBB	SO	HBP	SH	SF	SB	CS	SB%	GDP	Avg	OBP	SLG
1998 Auburn	A- Hou	50	168	52	9	1	4	75	28	34	23	1	34	2	0	3	3	2	.60	1	.310	.393	.446
1999 Michigan	A Hou	66	216	69	8	5	3	96	40	39	30	0	25	1	1	2	3	4	.43	6	.319	.402	.444
2000 Michigan	A Hou	116	408	127	25	4	7	181	62	69	65	2	54	5	0	8	9	7	.56	6	.311	.405	.444
2001 Lakeland	A+ Det	39	116	31	4	1	0	37	12	18	16	2	16	2	0	3	2	0	1.00	5	.267	.358	.319
Erie	AA Det	30	94	31	8	3	2	51	19	13	13	1	13	2	0	0	0	0	—	4	.330	.422	.543
4 Min. YEARS		301	1002	310	54	14	16	440	161	173	147	6	142	12	1	16	17	13	.57	22	.309	.398	.439

Kevin Nicholson

Bats: Both **Throws:** Right **Pos:** SS-13; 3B-12; 2B-6; PH-3 **Ht:** 5'10" **Wt:** 190 **Born:** 3/29/76 **Age:** 26

Year Team	Lg Org	G	AB	H	2B	3B	HR	TB	R	RBI	TBB	IBB	SO	HBP	SH	SF	SB	CS	SB%	GDP	Avg	OBP	SLG
1997 Padres	R SD	7	34	9	1	0	2	16	7	8	2	0	5	0	0	0	0	2	.00	2	.265	.306	.471
Rancho Cuca	A+ SD	17	65	21	5	0	1	29	7	9	4	0	15	2	2	0	2	1	.67	1	.323	.380	.446
1998 Mobile	AA SD	132	488	105	27	3	5	153	64	52	47	7	114	3	5	6	9	5	.64	10	.215	.285	.314
1999 Mobile	AA SD	127	489	141	38	3	13	224	84	81	46	1	92	5	1	6	16	5	.76	15	.288	.352	.458
2000 Las Vegas	AAA SD	91	326	91	26	3	6	141	48	44	35	0	62	3	1	5	4	4	.50	5	.279	.350	.433
2001 Portland	AAA SD	11	31	6	1	0	0	7	1	1	4	0	3	0	0	0	1	0	1.00	0	.194	.286	.226
Colo Sprngs	AAA Col	23	78	30	5	0	1	38	14	11	5	1	7	0	1	0	1	1	.50	2	.385	.422	.487
2000 San Diego	NL	37	97	21	6	1	1	32	7	8	4	0	31	1	3	0	1	0	1.00	2	.216	.255	.330
5 Min. YEARS		408	1511	403	103	9	28	608	225	206	143	9	298	13	10	17	32	19	.63	35	.267	.332	.402

Aaron Nieckula

Bats: Right **Throws:** Right **Pos:** C-66; 1B-7; DH-6; PH-4; OF-2; PR-2; 3B-1 **Ht:** 5'11" **Wt:** 200 **Born:** 9/7/76 **Age:** 25

Year Team	Lg Org	G	AB	H	2B	3B	HR	TB	R	RBI	TBB	IBB	SO	HBP	SH	SF	SB	CS	SB%	GDP	Avg	OBP	SLG
1998 Sou Oregon	A- Oak	41	126	26	6	0	0	32	17	21	18	0	31	2	2	2	2	0	1.00	1	.206	.311	.254
1999 Sou Oregon	A- Oak	15	50	13	4	0	1	20	11	9	9	0	12	2	0	1	2	1	.67	2	.260	.387	.400
Visalia	A+ Oak	25	65	18	4	0	0	22	13	10	8	0	17	4	2	2	2	0	1.00	0	.277	.380	.338
2000 Visalia	A+ Oak	72	212	55	8	0	2	69	45	29	39	1	54	13	0	2	14	6	.70	3	.259	.402	.325
Modesto	A+ Oak	15	48	13	2	0	0	15	6	5	12	0	12	1	0	0	3	1	.75	1	.271	.426	.313
2001 Modesto	A+ Oak	26	83	24	1	1	3	36	12	11	8	0	19	5	2	0	1	0	1.00	2	.289	.385	.434
Visalia	A+ Oak	43	129	38	6	0	4	56	26	15	11	0	34	10	0	3	2	1	.67	1	.295	.386	.434
Midland	AA Oak	12	39	15	5	0	1	23	8	10	2	0	7	2	1	1	0	0	—	0	.385	.432	.590
4 Min. YEARS		249	752	202	36	1	11	273	138	110	107	1	186	39	7	11	25	10	.71	10	.269	.383	.363

Melvin Nieves

Bats: Both **Throws:** Right **Pos:** OF-13 **Ht:** 6'2" **Wt:** 220 **Born:** 12/28/71 **Age:** 30

Year Team	Lg Org	G	AB	H	2B	3B	HR	TB	R	RBI	TBB	IBB	SO	HBP	SH	SF	SB	CS	SB%	GDP	Avg	OBP	SLG
1988 Braves	R Atl	56	176	30	6	0	1	39	16	12	20	0	53	2	1	1	5	4	.56	2	.170	.261	.222
1989 Pulaski	R+ Atl	64	231	64	16	3	9	113	43	46	30	4	59	1	3	4	6	4	.60	2	.277	.357	.489
1990 Sumter	A Atl	126	459	130	24	7	9	195	60	59	53	4	125	9	1	9	10	6	.63	7	.283	.362	.425
1991 Durham	A+ Atl	64	201	53	11	0	9	91	31	25	40	2	53	5	0	1	3	8	.27	1	.264	.397	.453
1992 Durham	A+ Atl	31	106	32	9	1	8	67	18	32	17	3	33	2	0	4	2	2	.67	1	.302	.395	.632
Greenville	AA Atl	100	350	99	23	5	18	186	61	76	52	2	98	6	2	4	6	4	.60	4	.283	.381	.531
1993 Richmond	AAA Atl	78	273	76	10	3	10	122	38	36	25	4	84	2	1	1	4	3	.57	4	.278	.342	.447
Las Vegas	AAA SD	43	159	49	10	1	7	82	31	24	18	0	42	2	0	0	2	2	.50	1	.308	.385	.516
1994 Las Vegas	AAA SD	111	406	125	17	6	25	229	81	92	58	3	138	8	0	2	1	2	.33	10	.308	.403	.564
1998 Indianapols	AAA Cin	15	53	15	4	0	2	25	10	13	9	0	11	0	0	0	0	0	—	0	.283	.387	.472
2001 Colo Sprngs	AAA Col	13	43	10	5	1	1	20	7	4	8	0	20	1	0	0	1	0	1.00	0	.233	.365	.465
1992 Atlanta	NL	12	19	4	1	0	0	5	0	1	2	0	7	0	0	0	0	0	—	0	.211	.286	.263
1993 San Diego	NL	19	47	9	0	0	2	15	4	3	3	0	21	1	0	0	0	0	—	0	.191	.255	.319
1994 San Diego	NL	10	19	5	1	0	1	9	2	4	3	0	10	0	0	0	0	0	—	0	.263	.364	.474
1995 San Diego	NL	98	234	48	6	1	14	98	32	38	19	0	88	5	1	3	2	3	.40	9	.205	.276	.419
1996 Detroit	AL	120	431	106	23	4	24	209	71	60	44	2	158	6	0	3	1	2	.33	10	.246	.322	.485
1997 Detroit	AL	116	359	82	18	1	20	162	46	64	39	6	157	5	0	2	1	7	.13	3	.228	.311	.451
1998 Cincinnati	NL	83	119	30	4	0	2	40	8	17	26	1	42	0	0	2	0	0	—	3	.252	.381	.336
9 Min. YEARS		701	2457	683	135	27	99	1169	396	419	330	22	716	38	8	26	42	35	.55	32	.278	.369	.476
7 Maj. YEARS		458	1228	284	53	6	63	538	163	187	136	9	483	17	1	10	4	12	.25	25	.231	.314	.438

Wil Nieves

Bats: Right **Throws:** Right **Pos:** C-91; PH-4; PR-2 **Ht:** 5'11" **Wt:** 190 **Born:** 9/25/77 **Age:** 24

Year Team	Lg Org	G	AB	H	2B	3B	HR	TB	R	RBI	TBB	IBB	SO	HBP	SH	SF	SB	CS	SB%	GDP	Avg	OBP	SLG
1996 Padres	R SD	43	113	39	5	0	2	50	23	22	13	0	19	0	2	0	3	4	.43	1	.345	.413	.442
1997 Clinton	A SD	18	55	12	1	1	1	18	6	7	6	0	10	0	1	1	2	1	.67	0	.218	.290	.327
Padres	R SD	8	27	8	2	0	0	10	2	2	5	0	5	0	1	0	1	0	1.00	0	.296	.406	.370
1998 Clinton	A SD	115	380	97	22	0	3	128	47	55	47	4	69	7	4	6	7	9	.44	16	.255	.343	.337
1999 Rancho Cuca	A+ SD	120	427	140	26	2	7	191	58	61	40	1	54	5	1	4	2	7	.22	12	.328	.389	.447
2000 Rancho Cuca	A+ SD	31	101	26	5	0	0	31	16	9	15	0	17	0	2	1	2	0	1.00	3	.257	.350	.307
Las Vegas	AAA SD	1	1	0	0	0	0	0	0	0	0	0	0	0	0	0	0	0	—	0	.000	.000	.000
Mobile	AA SD	68	214	57	4	0	4	73	18	30	16	4	22	1	2	1	1	1	.50	9	.266	.319	.341
2001 Mobile	AA SD	95	330	99	24	0	3	132	28	41	18	2	40	2	2	1	1	0	1.00	8	.300	.336	.400
6 Min. YEARS		499	1648	478	89	3	20	633	198	227	160	11	236	15	15	17	19	22	.46	49	.290	.355	.384

Drew Niles

Bats: Both **Throws:** Right **Pos:** SS-26; 2B-21; PH-15; 3B-7; DH-6; PR-4; OF-1 **Ht:** 6'1" **Wt:** 175 **Born:** 3/17/77 **Age:** 25

Year Team	Lg Org	G	AB	H	2B	3B	HR	TB	R	RBI	TBB	IBB	SO	HBP	SH	SF	SB	CS	SB%	GDP	Avg	OBP	SLG
1998 Kane County	A Fla	26	87	24	4	0	0	28	12	9	12	1	20	0	0	4	2	1	.67	1	.276	.350	.322
Charlotte	AAA Fla	16	49	13	1	0	1	17	5	5	6	0	12	1	0	1	0	1	.00	1	.265	.351	.347
1999 Brevard Cty	A+ Fla	40	117	20	1	1	1	26	12	12	15	0	30	1	0	2	0	0	—	2	.171	.267	.222
Utica	A- Fla	18	66	15	3	0	0	18	4	7	9	0	15	0	2	0	3	.00	1	.227	.320	.273
Portland	AA Fla	46	135	31	3	0	0	34	12	9	21	0	34	0	3	2	0	2	.00	7	.230	.329	.252
2000 Kane County	A Fla	14	40	7	0	2	0	11	4	5	4	0	9	0	1	2	1	1	.50	1	.175	.239	.275
Portland	AA Fla	39	124	30	3	1	0	35	14	10	9	0	21	1	1	0	2	0	1.00	3	.242	.299	.282
Brevard Cty	A+ Fla	32	94	22	2	1	0	26	9	5	13	0	22	0	3	1	2	1	.67	3	.234	.324	.277
2001 Portland	AA Fla	71	194	46	7	2	4	69	22	18	17	0	55	3	2	2	2	7	.22	7	.237	.306	.356
4 Min. YEARS		302	906	208	24	7	6	264	94	80	106	1	218	6	12	14	9	16	.36	26	.230	.310	.291

Elvin Nina

Pitches: Right **Bats:** Right **Pos:** SP-28; RP-1 **Ht:** 6'0" **Wt:** 185 **Born:** 11/25/75 **Age:** 26

Year Team	Lg Org	G	GS	CG	GF	IP	BFP	H	R	ER	HR	SH	SF	HB	TBB	IBB	SO	WP	Bk	W	L	Pct.	ShO	Sv	ERA
1997 Sou Oregon	A- Oak	18	2	0	8	31	150	36	24	18	4	0	0	2	18	1	26	2	2	1	3	.250	0	1	5.23
1998 Visalia	A+ Oak	30	21	1	5	130.1	583	135	77	65	9	2	6	5	62	1	131	13	2	8	8	.500	1	0	4.49
Edmonton	AAA Oak	1	0	0	0	0.1	4	1	0	0	0	1	0	0	2	1	0	1	0	0	0	—	0	0	0.00
1999 Modesto	A+ Oak	17	12	0	0	73.1	319	59	31	17	2	3	0	6	41	1	74	5	0	5	2	.714	0	0	2.09
Midland	AA Oak	7	4	0	2	30	140	36	21	16	0	0	1	2	18	0	18	2	0	3	2	.600	0	0	4.80
Erie	AA Ana	4	4	0	0	24.1	103	20	12	11	2	1	1	0	15	0	19	1	0	3	0	1.000	0	0	4.07
2000 Erie	AA Ana	12	10	0	0	57.1	243	51	31	27	3	4	1	3	24	0	30	2	0	2	4	.333	0	0	4.24
Edmonton	AAA Ana	3	2	0	0	9.1	44	11	6	3	0	0	1	0	6	0	3	0	1	0	0	—	0	0	2.89
2001 Salt Lake	AAA Ana	29	28	1	0	158	730	195	112	96	19	3	5	7	79	1	101	10	0	10	11	.476	0	0	5.47
5 Min. YEARS		121	83	4	15	514	2316	544	314	253	39	14	15	25	265	5	402	36	5	32	30	.516	1	1	4.43

Wayne Nix

Pitches: Right **Bats:** Right **Pos:** SP-28; RP-1 **Ht:** 6'5" **Wt:** 210 **Born:** 9/16/76 **Age:** 25

Year Team	Lg Org	G	GS	CG	GF	IP	BFP	H	R	ER	HR	SH	SF	HB	TBB	IBB	SO	WP	Bk	W	L	Pct.	ShO	Sv	ERA
1995 Athletics	R Oak	6	3	0	0	14	57	15	10	9	3	1	0	1	4	0	14	1	0	0	2	.000	0	0	5.79
1997 Athletics	R Oak	15	4	0	1	32.1	162	32	28	21	2	0	1	2	29	1	32	8	4	1	3	.250	0	0	5.85
1998 Sou Oregon	A- Oak	16	15	0	1	71	320	76	56	42	7	0	2	1	37	0	56	10	2	6	6	.500	0	0	5.32
1999 Modesto	A+ Oak	34	18	0	4	119.1	532	109	76	56	10	3	5	9	69	2	105	8	3	9	6	.600	0	2	4.22
2000 Visalia	A+ Oak	30	24	1	2	139.1	615	125	99	82	7	3	4	7	76	2	146	19	1	9	5	.643	1	1	5.30
2001 Visalia	A+ Oak	27	26	1	1	148	628	149	81	66	18	3	2	6	36	0	167	12	1	9	7	.563	0	0	4.01
Midland	AA Oak	2	2	0	0	10.1	54	24	15	10	1	0	1	0	1	0	12	0	0	0	2	.000	0	0	8.71
6 Min. YEARS		130	92	2	9	534.1	2368	530	365	286	48	10	15	26	252	5	532	58	11	34	31	.523	1	3	4.82

Ray Noriega

Pitches: Left **Bats:** Right **Pos:** RP-30 **Ht:** 5'10" **Wt:** 170 **Born:** 3/28/74 **Age:** 28

Year Team	Lg Org	G	GS	CG	GF	IP	BFP	H	R	ER	HR	SH	SF	HB	TBB	IBB	SO	WP	Bk	W	L	Pct.	ShO	Sv	ERA
1996 Sou Oregon	A- Oak	17	14	0	0	61	263	61	28	24	3	2	0	2	22	0	50	4	0	4	4	.500	0	0	3.54
1997 Modesto	A+ Oak	28	28	0	0	156	698	161	101	70	17	8	2	4	69	1	119	10	3	5	8	.385	0	0	4.04
1998 Visalia	A+ Oak	36	6	0	10	71.1	328	91	55	49	8	2	4	2	24	1	77	6	0	3	5	.375	0	2	6.18
1999 Visalia	A+ Oak	60	0	0	34	69.1	308	67	36	31	6	4	4	2	32	2	62	6	0	5	3	.625	0	11	4.02
2000 Modesto	A+ Oak	24	0	0	18	26.1	114	22	8	3	0	2	1	0	15	2	20	5	0	0	3	.000	0	12	1.03
Midland	AA Oak	21	0	0	7	26.2	113	21	13	11	1	1	2	2	11	0	17	0	1	3	0	1.000	0	1	3.71
2001 Modesto	A+ Oak	13	0	0	8	21.1	83	13	4	4	1	1	0	3	7	2	19	1	0	3	1	.750	0	2	1.69
Midland	AA Oak	17	0	0	3	22	119	34	24	23	5	1	0	4	16	3	20	0	0	0	1	.000	0	0	9.41
6 Min. YEARS		216	48	0	80	454	2026	470	269	215	41	21	13	19	196	11	384	32	4	23	25	.479	0	28	4.26

Ben Norris

Pitches: Left **Bats:** Left **Pos:** SP-12; RP-6 **Ht:** 6'3" **Wt:** 185 **Born:** 12/6/77 **Age:** 24

Year Team	Lg Org	G	GS	CG	GF	IP	BFP	H	R	ER	HR	SH	SF	HB	TBB	IBB	SO	WP	Bk	W	L	Pct.	ShO	Sv	ERA
1996 Diamondbcks	R Ari	8	7	0	0	31.1	133	33	21	16	3	3	0	4	4	0	37	2	0	2	2	.500	0	0	4.60
Lethbridge	R+ Ari	3	3	0	0	11.1	54	14	9	8	0	0	2	0	5	0	12	2	1	0	0	—	0	0	6.35
1997 South Bend	A Ari	14	13	0	0	60.1	291	69	44	27	7	2	2	6	31	0	40	2	1	1	8	.111	0	0	4.03
Lethbridge	R+ Ari	14	14	0	0	83.1	373	93	61	45	6	1	3	8	23	0	54	4	0	7	3	.700	0	0	4.86
1998 South Bend	A Ari	15	15	0	0	89.1	389	98	44	33	6	1	5	10	27	0	53	7	0	1	5	.167	0	0	3.32
High Desert	A+ Ari	9	6	0	2	40.2	180	48	27	25	7	2	0	0	18	0	17	1	0	2	2	.500	0	1	5.53
1999 High Desert	A+ Ari	8	8	0	0	40.2	181	39	27	20	4	0	3	4	24	0	45	0	0	2	2	.500	0	0	4.43
El Paso	AA Ari	20	20	0	0	119	535	132	61	55	13	3	2	8	53	0	87	6	2	10	6	.625	0	0	4.16
2000 Tucson	AAA Ari	12	10	0	0	55.1	275	88	56	49	7	5	2	2	29	1	28	2	1	2	6	.250	0	0	7.97
El Paso	AA Ari	7	7	1	0	45	192	41	14	11	1	2	0	3	18	1	24	1	0	4	1	.800	0	0	2.20
2001 El Paso	AA Ari	16	10	0	1	58.1	299	104	61	47	1	1	5	5	30	0	25	2	0	1	6	.143	0	0	7.25
Lancaster	A+ Ari	2	2	0	0	12.2	55	16	9	8	2	0	0	1	2	1	18	0	0	1	0	1.000	0	0	5.68
6 Min. YEARS		128	115	1	3	647.1	2957	775	434	344	57	20	24	51	264	3	440	29	5	33	41	.446	0	1	4.78

Dax Norris

Bats: Right Throws: Right Pos: C-74; DH-12; PH-6; 1B-4; PR-1   Ht: 5'10" Wt: 190 Born: 1/14/73 Age: 29

Year Team	Lg Org	G	AB	H	2B	3B	HR	TB	R	RBI	TBB	IBB	SO	HBP	SH	SF	SB	CS	SB%	GDP	Avg	OBP	SLG
1996 Eugene	A- Atl	60	232	67	17	0	7	105	31	37	18	0	32	3	3	1	2	0	1.00	4	.289	.346	.453
1997 Greenville	AA Atl	2	9	3	0	0	1	6	3	3	0	0	1	0	0	0	0	0	—	0	.333	.333	.667
Durham	A+ Atl	95	338	80	19	0	7	120	29	45	32	1	49	4	0	3	2	5	.29	10	.237	.308	.355
1998 Danville	A+ Atl	28	92	30	12	1	3	53	9	21	7	1	15	2	0	3	1	2	.33	1	.326	.375	.576
Greenville	AA Atl	64	199	46	15	0	6	79	30	26	15	0	43	4	1	1	1	2	.33	7	.231	.297	.397
1999 Greenville	AA Atl	120	403	112	27	0	15	184	59	66	41	2	59	7	0	4	2	1	.67	10	.278	.352	.457
2000 Greenville	AA Atl	132	484	122	27	0	13	188	56	72	50	5	74	8	0	5	1	1	.50	12	.252	.329	.388
2001 Richmond	AAA Atl	95	317	89	25	0	3	123	26	38	16	0	44	5	1	2	2	2	.50	5	.281	.324	.388
6 Min. YEARS		596	2074	549	142	1	55	858	243	308	179	9	317	33	5	19	11	13	.46	49	.265	.330	.414

Jason Norton

Pitches: Right Bats: Right Pos: SP-4; RP-2   Ht: 6'3" Wt: 205 Born: 4/9/76 Age: 26

		HOW MUCH HE PITCHED						WHAT HE GAVE UP												THE RESULTS					
Year Team	Lg Org	G	GS	CG	GF	IP	BFP	H	R	ER	HR	SH	SF	HB	TBB	IBB	SO	WP	Bk	W	L	Pct.	ShO	Sv	ERA
1998 Red Sox	R Bos	3	0	0	3	6	20	2	1	1	1	0	0	0	1	0	9	1	0	1	1	.500	0	0	1.50
Lowell	A- Bos	6	4	0	0	25.1	105	22	17	13	1	0	0	1	7	0	33	1	3	1	1	.500	0	0	4.62
Michigan	A Bos	7	7	0	0	42	173	34	14	9	1	1	1	1	12	2	36	3	0	3	1	.750	0	0	1.93
1999 Augusta	A Bos	30	17	2	5	136	544	106	50	35	11	1	2	4	28	1	150	7	0	9	6	.600	1	0	2.32
2000 Sarasota	A+ Bos	40	5	0	12	91	405	102	53	39	6	4	2	3	29	3	89	4	2	7	7	.500	0	1	3.86
Trenton	AA Bos	1	1	0	0	7	26	3	0	0	0	0	0	0	3	0	10	1	0	1	0	1.000	0	0	0.00
2001 Trenton	AA Bos	6	4	0	0	16.1	81	24	25	22	5	2	1	1	8	0	17	1	0	0	2	.000	0	0	12.12
4 Min. YEARS		93	38	2	20	323.2	1354	293	160	119	25	8	6	10	88	6	344	18	5	22	18	.550	1	1	3.31

Phil Norton

Pitches: Left Bats: Right Pos: RP-43; SP-3   Ht: 6'1" Wt: 190 Born: 2/1/76 Age: 26

		HOW MUCH HE PITCHED						WHAT HE GAVE UP												THE RESULTS					
Year Team	Lg Org	G	GS	CG	GF	IP	BFP	H	R	ER	HR	SH	SF	HB	TBB	IBB	SO	WP	Bk	W	L	Pct.	ShO	Sv	ERA
1996 Cubs	R ChC	1	0	0	1	3	10	1	0	0	0	0	0	0	0	0	6	0	1	0	0	—	0	0	0.00
Williamsprt	A- ChC	15	13	2	1	85	364	68	33	24	1	3	2	3	33	2	77	7	3	7	4	.636	1	0	2.54
1997 Rockford	A ChC	18	18	3	0	109	460	92	51	39	4	3	3	1	44	1	114	12	1	9	3	.750	0	0	3.22
Daytona	A+ ChC	7	6	3	0	42.1	171	40	11	11	5	1	0	0	12	0	44	0	0	3	2	.600	0	0	2.34
Orlando	AA ChC	2	1	0	1	7	28	8	2	2	0	0	0	0	2	1	7	0	0	1	0	1.000	0	0	2.57
1998 Daytona	A+ ChC	10	10	0	0	66	275	57	30	24	4	1	1	2	26	1	54	4	1	4	3	.571	0	0	3.27
West Tenn	AA ChC	19	19	1	0	120.1	515	118	60	47	11	4	3	5	50	1	119	6	1	6	6	.500	1	0	3.52
1999 West Tenn	AA ChC	14	13	0	0	86.2	365	72	32	23	5	3	4	3	42	4	81	9	0	7	4	.636	0	0	2.39
Iowa	AAA ChC	14	14	0	0	79.2	361	98	63	59	20	0	2	5	33	0	61	3	1	5	6	.455	0	0	6.67
2000 Iowa	AAA ChC	28	26	2	0	159.2	733	166	100	88	16	9	6	2	104	4	126	8	2	8	13	.381	1	0	4.96
2001 Iowa	AAA ChC	46	3	0	14	73.2	318	65	27	22	3	9	3	6	41	7	75	8	1	6	3	.667	0	2	2.69
2000 Chicago	NL	2	2	0	0	8.2	47	14	10	9	5	0	0	0	7	0	6	0	0	0	1	.000	0	0	9.35
6 Min. YEARS		174	123	11	17	832.1	3600	785	409	339	69	33	24	27	387	21	764	57	11	56	44	.560	3	2	3.67

Dave Noyce

Pitches: Left Bats: Left Pos: RP-42; SP-8   Ht: 6'5" Wt: 195 Born: 3/2/77 Age: 25

		HOW MUCH HE PITCHED						WHAT HE GAVE UP												THE RESULTS					
Year Team	Lg Org	G	GS	CG	GF	IP	BFP	H	R	ER	HR	SH	SF	HB	TBB	IBB	SO	WP	Bk	W	L	Pct.	ShO	Sv	ERA
1998 Utica	A- Fla	17	0	0	5	30.2	128	23	15	12	1	4	1	4	11	1	28	1	1	4	2	.667	0	2	3.52
1999 Kane County	A Fla	16	16	2	0	101	419	82	43	37	5	3	5	3	29	0	86	6	1	7	3	.700	2	0	3.30
2000 Brevard Cty	A+ Fla	18	17	1	0	93	413	91	53	40	12	3	4	12	35	0	63	4	1	6	5	.545	1	0	3.87
Daytona	A+ ChC	3	3	0	0	12.1	56	9	6	3	0	0	0	0	9	0	6	0	0	1	0	1.000	0	0	2.19
2001 West Tenn	AA ChC	50	8	0	12	96	437	98	53	43	9	4	6	7	48	3	87	5	1	3	8	.273	0	1	4.03
4 Min. YEARS		104	44	3	17	333	1453	303	170	135	27	14	16	26	132	4	270	16	4	21	18	.538	3	3	3.65

Abraham Nunez

Bats: Both Throws: Right Pos: OF-134; PH-2   Ht: 6'2" Wt: 186 Born: 2/5/80 Age: 22

Year Team	Lg Org	G	AB	H	2B	3B	HR	TB	R	RBI	TBB	IBB	SO	HBP	SH	SF	SB	CS	SB%	GDP	Avg	OBP	SLG
1997 Diamondbcks	R Ari	54	213	65	17	4	0	90	52	21	26	0	40	2	2	1	3	3	.50	4	.305	.384	.423
Lethbridge	R+ Ari	2	6	1	0	0	0	1	2	1	1	0	0	0	0	0	0	0	—	0	.167	.286	.167
1998 South Bend	A Ari	110	364	93	14	2	9	138	44	47	67	4	81	3	3	5	12	14	.46	4	.255	.371	.379
1999 High Desert	A+ Ari	130	488	133	29	6	22	240	106	93	86	2	122	2	1	8	40	13	.75	10	.273	.378	.492
2000 Brevard Cty	A+ Fla	31	103	20	4	0	1	27	17	9	28	1	34	2	0	0	11	3	.79	3	.194	.376	.262
Portland	AA Fla	74	221	61	17	3	6	102	39	42	44	1	64	0	0	3	8	6	.57	3	.276	.392	.462
2001 Portland	AA Fla	136	467	112	14	9	17	195	75	53	83	3	155	3	5	2	26	19	.58	4	.240	.357	.418
5 Min. YEARS		537	1862	485	95	24	55	793	335	266	335	11	496	12	11	19	100	58	.63	28	.260	.373	.426

Franklin Nunez

Pitches: Right Bats: Right Pos: RP-25; SP-14   Ht: 6'0" Wt: 175 Born: 1/18/77 Age: 25

		HOW MUCH HE PITCHED						WHAT HE GAVE UP												THE RESULTS					
Year Team	Lg Org	G	GS	CG	GF	IP	BFP	H	R	ER	HR	SH	SF	HB	TBB	IBB	SO	WP	Bk	W	L	Pct.	ShO	Sv	ERA
1998 Martinsvlle	R+ Phi	6	4	0	0	25.1	109	23	10	7	0	0	0	2	8	0	19	2	3	2	2	.500	0	0	2.49
1999 Piedmont	A Phi	13	13	1	0	77	326	69	39	29	4	4	1	6	25	0	88	2	1	4	8	.333	0	0	3.39
2000 Clearwater	A+ Phi	23	14	1	6	112	492	112	54	45	4	1	3	7	57	0	81	9	1	10	4	.714	0	2	3.62
2001 Reading	AA Phi	39	14	0	10	110	486	107	68	54	9	3	2	6	51	3	112	9	0	8	7	.533	0	3	4.42
4 Min. YEARS		81	45	2	16	324.1	1413	311	171	135	17	8	6	21	141	3	300	22	5	24	21	.533	0	5	3.75

Jorge Nunez

Bats: Right **Throws:** Right **Pos:** SS-111; 2B-9; PH-2; PR-1   **Ht:** 5'10" **Wt:** 158 **Born:** 3/3/78 **Age:** 24

Year Team	Lg Org	G	AB	H	2B	3B	HR	TB	R	RBI	TBB	IBB	SO	HBP	SH	SF	SB	CS	SB%	GDP	Avg	OBP	SLG
1998 Hagerstown	A Tor	4	16	4	0	0	0	4	0	1	0	0	1	0	0	0	1	0	1.00	0	.250	.250	.250
Medcine Hat	R+ Tor	74	317	101	9	11	6	150	74	52	28	0	45	1	1	0	31	2	.94	3	.319	.376	.473
1999 Hagerstown	A Tor	133	564	151	28	11	14	243	116	61	40	1	103	2	1	2	51	8	.86	8	.268	.317	.431
2000 Vero Beach	A+ LA	128	534	154	17	8	4	199	86	39	38	0	104	2	5	2	54	22	.71	5	.288	.337	.373
Albuquerque	AAA LA	1	3	0	0	0	0	0	0	0	0	0	0	0	0	0	0	0	—	0	.000	.000	.000
2001 Jacksnville	AA LA	123	473	123	15	2	4	154	63	28	33	3	88	2	10	1	44	11	.80	6	.260	.310	.326
4 Min. YEARS		463	1907	533	69	32	28	750	339	181	139	4	341	7	17	5	181	43	.81	22	.279	.330	.393

Jose Nunez

Bats: Right **Throws:** Right **Pos:** PH-11; 3B-10; DH-10; SS-7; 2B-2; PR-1   **Ht:** 5'10" **Wt:** 175 **Born:** 12/8/78 **Age:** 23

Year Team	Lg Org	G	AB	H	2B	3B	HR	TB	R	RBI	TBB	IBB	SO	HBP	SH	SF	SB	CS	SB%	GDP	Avg	OBP	SLG
1998 New Jersey	A- StL	55	162	35	6	2	1	48	17	14	9	0	22	3	1	0	5	4	.56	4	.216	.270	.296
1999 New Jersey	A- StL	45	157	48	11	1	1	64	29	13	20	1	18	2	3	0	6	3	.67	4	.306	.391	.408
2000 Potomac	A+ StL	87	242	61	18	0	2	85	25	24	11	0	36	4	2	0	4	2	.67	5	.252	.296	.351
2001 New Haven	AA StL	39	82	13	2	0	0	15	7	1	5	0	20	1	0	0	5	1	.83	1	.159	.216	.183
4 Min. YEARS		226	643	157	37	3	4	212	78	52	45	1	96	10	6	0	20	10	.67	14	.244	.304	.330

Jon Nunnally

Bats: Left **Throws:** Right **Pos:** OF-84; DH-10; PH-4   **Ht:** 5'10" **Wt:** 190 **Born:** 11/9/71 **Age:** 30

Year Team	Lg Org	G	AB	H	2B	3B	HR	TB	R	RBI	TBB	IBB	SO	HBP	SH	SF	SB	CS	SB%	GDP	Avg	OBP	SLG
1992 Watertown	A- Cle	69	246	59	10	4	5	92	39	43	32	2	55	1	0	4	12	3	.80	3	.240	.325	.374
1993 Columbus	A Cle	125	438	110	15	2	15	174	81	56	63	0	108	3	4	6	17	11	.61	5	.251	.345	.397
1994 Kinston	A+ Cle	132	483	129	29	4	22	228	70	74	64	3	125	3	1	3	23	11	.68	5	.267	.354	.472
1996 Omaha	AAA KC	103	345	97	21	4	25	201	76	77	47	8	100	8	0	6	10	9	.53	2	.281	.374	.583
1997 Omaha	AAA KC	68	230	64	11	1	15	122	35	33	39	2	67	3	0	2	8	3	.73	3	.278	.387	.530
1998 Indianapols	AAA Cin	79	290	73	18	2	11	128	53	53	47	0	71	2	1	6	7	4	.64	3	.252	.354	.441
1999 Pawtucket	AAA Bos	133	494	132	24	3	23	231	90	76	85	5	103	3	1	7	26	4	.87	7	.267	.374	.468
2001 Omaha	AAA KC	97	316	66	9	0	18	129	50	53	54	2	109	3	0	1	11	3	.79	3	.209	.329	.408
1995 Kansas City	AL	119	303	74	15	6	14	143	51	42	51	5	86	2	4	0	6	4	.60	4	.244	.357	.472
1996 Kansas City	AL	35	90	19	5	1	5	41	16	17	13	2	25	0	0	1	0	0	—	0	.211	.308	.456
1997 Kansas City	AL	13	29	7	0	1	1	12	8	4	5	0	7	0	0	0	0	0	—	0	.241	.353	.414
Cincinnati	NL	65	201	64	12	3	13	121	38	35	26	0	51	2	1	1	7	3	.70	2	.318	.400	.602
1998 Cincinnati	NL	74	174	36	9	0	7	66	29	20	34	3	38	1	1	3	3	4	.43	4	.207	.335	.379
1999 Boston	AL	10	14	4	1	0	0	5	4	1	0	0	6	0	0	0	0	0	—	0	.286	.286	.357
2000 New York	NL	48	74	14	5	1	2	27	16	6	17	0	26	0	0	1	3	1	.75	1	.189	.337	.365
8 Min. YEARS		806	2842	730	137	18	134	1305	494	465	431	22	738	26	7	35	114	48	.70	31	.257	.356	.459
6 Maj. YEARS		364	885	218	47	12	42	415	162	125	146	10	239	5	6	6	19	12	.61	11	.246	.354	.469

Talmadge Nunnari

Bats: Left **Throws:** Left **Pos:** 1B-65; DH-20; PH-20; OF-17   **Ht:** 6'1" **Wt:** 200 **Born:** 4/9/75 **Age:** 27

Year Team	Lg Org	G	AB	H	2B	3B	HR	TB	R	RBI	TBB	IBB	SO	HBP	SH	SF	SB	CS	SB%	GDP	Avg	OBP	SLG
1997 Vermont	A- Mon	62	236	75	11	3	4	104	30	42	31	4	37	3	0	4	6	3	.67	4	.318	.398	.441
Cape Fear	A Mon	9	35	13	1	1	1	19	8	6	1	0	5	0	0	0	2	0	1.00	5	.371	.389	.543
1998 Cape Fear	A Mon	79	289	88	18	0	2	112	51	51	42	2	44	1	0	0	4	4	.50	5	.304	.395	.388
Jupiter	A+ Mon	56	201	59	14	0	2	79	18	34	30	1	39	0	0	6	1	2	.33	2	.294	.376	.393
1999 Jupiter	A+ Mon	71	261	93	17	1	5	127	41	44	27	1	36	3	1	0	10	0	1.00	5	.356	.423	.487
Harrisburg	AA Mon	63	239	79	17	1	6	116	45	29	39	3	46	1	2	2	7	2	.78	3	.331	.423	.485
2000 Harrisburg	AA Mon	92	317	85	16	2	5	120	46	54	48	1	66	2	0	5	10	6	.63	6	.268	.363	.379
Ottawa	AAA Mon	44	135	38	12	1	0	52	17	12	23	1	31	2	0	1	0	1	.00	1	.281	.391	.385
2001 Ottawa	AAA Mon	110	343	75	15	1	4	104	35	35	38	3	81	4	4	4	13	2	.87	3	.219	.301	.303
Harrisburg	AA Mon	9	32	5	2	0	1	10	4	4	1	0	6	1	0	1	0	0	—	1	.156	.200	.313
2000 Montreal	NL	18	5	1	0	0	0	2	2	1	6	1	2	0	0	1	0	0	—	0	.200	.583	.200
5 Min. YEARS		595	2088	610	123	10	30	843	295	311	280	16	391	17	7	23	53	20	.73	30	.292	.377	.404

Rodney Nye

Bats: Right **Throws:** Right **Pos:** 3B-107; 1B-5; PH-1   **Ht:** 6'4" **Wt:** 215 **Born:** 12/2/76 **Age:** 25

Year Team	Lg Org	G	AB	H	2B	3B	HR	TB	R	RBI	TBB	IBB	SO	HBP	SH	SF	SB	CS	SB%	GDP	Avg	OBP	SLG
1999 Pittsfield	A- NYM	70	255	78	30	2	7	133	45	48	32	1	36	5	0	4	10	4	.71	5	.306	.389	.522
2000 St. Lucie	A+ NYM	132	464	126	28	1	6	174	70	62	58	4	74	10	0	4	8	8	.50	15	.272	.362	.375
2001 Binghamton	AA NYM	109	366	99	23	0	7	143	45	45	49	1	82	2	1	2	5	5	.50	6	.270	.358	.391
3 Min. YEARS		311	1085	303	81	3	20	450	160	155	139	6	192	17	1	10	23	17	.58	26	.279	.367	.415

Pablo Ochoa

Pitches: Right **Bats:** Right **Pos:** SP-13; RP-6   **Ht:** 6'1" **Wt:** 185 **Born:** 10/21/75 **Age:** 26

		HOW MUCH HE PITCHED						WHAT HE GAVE UP										THE RESULTS				
Year Team	Lg Org	G	GS	CG	GF	IP	BFP	H	R	ER	HR	SH	SF	HB	TBB	IBB	SO	WP	Bk	W	L	Pct.	ShO	Sv	ERA
1999 Capital Cty	A NYM	3	0	0	2	5.2	19	2	0	0	0	0	0	0	1	0	4	0	0	0	0	—	0	1	0.00
2000 Binghamton	AA NYM	26	26	1	0	146.2	659	171	94	85	10	6	9	4	75	0	106	8	1	9	12	.429	1	0	5.22
2001 Norfolk	AAA NYM	19	13	0	0	73.2	315	71	38	30	7	1	1	4	27	0	49	1	2	3	4	.429	0	0	3.67
3 Min. YEARS		48	39	1	2	226	993	244	132	115	17	7	10	8	103	0	159	9	3	12	16	.429	1	1	4.58

Brian O'Connor

Pitches: Left **Bats:** Left **Pos:** RP-21; SP-16   **Ht:** 6'2" **Wt:** 170 **Born:** 1/4/77 **Age:** 25

Year Team	Lg Org	G	GS	CG	GF	IP	BFP	H	R	ER	HR	SH	SF	HB	TBB	IBB	SO	WP	Bk	W	L	Pct.	ShO	Sv	ERA
1995 Pirates	R Pit	14	5	0	5	43	183	33	22	9	1	0	1	0	13	0	43	4	2	2	2	.500	0	1	1.88
1996 Augusta	A Pit	19	0	0	5	35.1	147	33	13	12	2	3	1	1	8	0	37	6	0	0	1	.000	0	1	3.06
Erie	A- Pit	15	15	0	0	67.2	329	75	60	44	4	3	2	3	47	0	60	10	1	4	10	.286	0	0	5.85
1997 Augusta	A Pit	25	14	0	3	85.2	385	90	54	42	6	4	1	2	39	1	91	11	0	2	7	.222	0	0	4.41
Lynchburg	A+ Pit	11	0	0	6	13	55	11	5	5	0	0	0	1	6	1	14	3	0	2	1	.667	0	2	3.46
1998 Lynchburg	A+ Pit	14	14	1	0	86.2	371	86	34	25	3	3	1	1	22	1	84	7	0	6	2	.750	0	0	2.60
Carolina	AA Pit	14	13	0	0	64.1	318	86	65	59	11	3	2	3	53	1	41	12	0	2	4	.333	0	0	8.25
1999 Altoona	AA Pit	28	27	1	0	153.1	698	152	98	77	10	11	3	6	92	2	106	21	0	7	11	.389	0	0	4.52
2000 Altoona	AA Pit	22	22	4	0	129.1	562	120	69	54	4	4	2	7	61	0	76	12	0	12	4	.750	0	0	3.76
Nashville	AAA Pit	5	5	0	0	26.1	121	30	23	20	2	1	2	1	14	0	19	5	0	2	2	.500	0	0	6.84
2001 Nashville	AAA Pit	37	16	0	7	111.2	512	124	87	77	15	5	2	3	58	3	74	12	1	6	9	.400	0	1	6.21
2000 Pittsburgh	NL	6	1	0	2	12.1	62	12	11	7	2	1	1	1	11	0	7	4	0	0	0	—	0	0	5.11
7 Min. YEARS		204	131	6	26	816.1	3681	840	530	424	58	37	17	28	413	9	645	103	4	45	53	.459	0	5	4.67

Chad Ogea

Pitches: Right **Bats:** Right **Pos:** SP-8   **Ht:** 6'2" **Wt:** 220 **Born:** 11/9/70 **Age:** 31

Year Team	Lg Org	G	GS	CG	GF	IP	BFP	H	R	ER	HR	SH	SF	HB	TBB	IBB	SO	WP	Bk	W	L	Pct.	ShO	Sv	ERA
1992 Kinston	A+ Cle	21	21	5	0	139.1	573	135	61	54	6	6	4	5	29	0	123	7	4	13	3	.813	2	0	3.49
Canton-Akrn	AA Cle	7	7	1	0	49	195	38	12	12	2	1	0	4	12	0	40	3	0	6	1	.857	1	0	2.20
1993 Charlotte	AAA Cle	29	29	2	0	181.2	751	169	91	77	26	4	3	2	54	0	135	6	4	13	8	.619	0	0	3.81
1994 Charlotte	AAA Cle	24	23	6	1	163.2	658	146	80	70	21	4	8	4	34	0	113	3	1	9	10	.474	0	1	3.85
1995 Buffalo	AAA Cle	4	4	0	0	17.2	79	16	12	9	1	0	0	2	8	0	11	0	0	0	1	.000	0	0	4.58
1996 Buffalo	AAA Cle	5	5	0	0	25.2	108	27	15	15	4	0	0	1	6	0	20	0	0	1	1	.000	0	0	5.26
1997 Buffalo	AAA Cle	4	4	0	0	21	88	24	10	10	2	0	0	0	6	0	11	0	0	1	1	.500	0	0	4.29
1998 Buffalo	AAA Cle	9	9	1	0	42.1	178	42	19	17	2	1	1	4	5	0	34	1	0	2	1	.667	0	0	3.61
2000 Akron	AA Cle	4	4	0	0	25.1	111	26	17	13	4	1	2	3	5	0	16	0	0	2	1	.667	0	0	4.62
Buffalo	AAA Cle	1	1	0	0	1.1	13	8	6	6	2	0	0	0	1	0	0	0	0	0	0	—	0	0	40.50
2001 Tampa	A+ NYY	2	2	0	0	9	42	10	3	3	0	2	1	1	3	0	6	1	0	0	0	—	0	0	3.00
Columbus	AAA NYY	6	6	0	0	27.2	127	34	24	24	6	1	0	0	15	1	21	0	0	0	4	.000	0	0	7.81
1994 Cleveland	AL	4	1	0	0	16.1	80	21	11	11	2	0	0	1	10	2	11	0	0	0	1	.000	0	0	6.06
1995 Cleveland	AL	20	14	1	3	106.1	442	95	38	36	11	0	5	1	29	0	57	3	1	8	3	.727	0	0	3.05
1996 Cleveland	AL	29	21	1	2	146.2	620	151	82	78	22	3	3	5	42	3	101	2	0	10	6	.625	1	0	4.79
1997 Cleveland	AL	21	21	1	0	126.1	532	139	79	70	13	3	5	5	47	4	80	4	2	8	9	.471	0	0	4.99
1998 Cleveland	AL	19	9	0	1	69	307	74	44	43	9	1	3	7	25	1	43	0	0	5	4	.556	0	0	5.61
1999 Philadelphia	NL	36	28	0	3	168	746	192	110	105	36	10	4	4	61	1	77	5	2	6	12	.333	0	0	5.63
9 Min. YEARS		116	115	15	1	703.2	2923	675	350	310	76	20	19	26	178	1	530	21	9	46	31	.597	3	1	3.96
6 Maj. YEARS		129	94	3	9	632.2	2747	672	364	343	93	17	20	23	214	11	369	14	5	37	35	.514	1	0	4.88

Teuris Olivares

Bats: Right **Throws:** Right **Pos:** SS-132; PR-1   **Ht:** 6'0" **Wt:** 164 **Born:** 12/15/78 **Age:** 23

Year Team	Lg Org	G	AB	H	2B	3B	HR	TB	R	RBI	TBB	IBB	SO	HBP	SH	SF	SB	CS	SB%	GDP	Avg	OBP	SLG
1996 Yankees	R NYY	9	20	6	1	0	0	7	3	4	1	0	2	0	1	0	0	0	—	0	.300	.333	.350
1997 Yankees	R NYY	38	153	40	4	7	0	58	33	17	14	0	40	1	0	0	7	2	.78	1	.261	.327	.379
1998 Oneonta	A- NYY	73	271	75	15	6	4	114	44	43	26	0	60	2	0	5	14	7	.67	5	.277	.339	.421
1999 Greensboro	A NYY	110	451	126	18	6	11	189	78	52	26	0	78	6	3	4	14	7	.67	10	.279	.324	.419
2000 Tampa	A+ NYY	121	468	118	22	3	7	167	56	47	39	0	70	0	3	5	20	11	.65	10	.252	.307	.357
2001 Tampa	A+ NYY	4	15	4	2	0	0	6	2	0	2	0	3	0	0	0	1	0	1.00	1	.267	.353	.400
Norwich	AA NYY	128	439	93	15	3	4	126	55	30	22	0	93	3	4	3	5	4	.56	8	.212	.253	.287
6 Min. YEARS		483	1817	462	77	25	26	667	271	193	130	0	346	12	11	17	61	31	.66	35	.254	.306	.367

Brian Oliver

Bats: Right **Throws:** Right **Pos:** 2B-9; DH-8; PR-2; PH-1   **Ht:** 5'10" **Wt:** 170 **Born:** 11/7/76 **Age:** 25

Year Team	Lg Org	G	AB	H	2B	3B	HR	TB	R	RBI	TBB	IBB	SO	HBP	SH	SF	SB	CS	SB%	GDP	Avg	OBP	SLG
1998 Boise	A- Ana	17	54	14	3	1	0	19	6	5	8	0	6	1	3	0	0	1	.00	3	.259	.365	.352
1999 Cedar Rapds	A Ana	66	252	69	16	1	6	105	43	29	26	0	30	6	4	4	12	1	.92	3	.274	.351	.417
2000 Erie	AA Ana	17	59	12	0	0	0	12	3	3	4	0	9	4	2	0	2	1	.67	0	.203	.299	.203
2001 Tulsa	AA Tex	12	40	9	1	1	0	12	5	5	6	0	8	1	1	2	0	0	—	0	.225	.327	.300
Charlotte	A+ Tex	8	21	5	0	0	0	5	2	1	0	0	0	0	0	0	0	0	—	0	.238	.238	.238
4 Min. YEARS		120	426	109	20	3	6	153	59	43	44	0	53	12	10	6	14	3	.82	6	.256	.338	.359

Miguel Olivo

Bats: Right **Throws:** Right **Pos:** C-90; DH-2; PH-1; PR-1   **Ht:** 6'1" **Wt:** 215 **Born:** 7/15/78 **Age:** 23

Year Team	Lg Org	G	AB	H	2B	3B	HR	TB	R	RBI	TBB	IBB	SO	HBP	SH	SF	SB	CS	SB%	GDP	Avg	OBP	SLG
1998 Athletics	R Oak	46	164	51	11	3	2	74	30	23	8	0	43	4	0	1	2	2	.50	5	.311	.356	.451
1999 Modesto	A+ Oak	73	243	74	13	6	9	126	46	42	21	1	60	2	1	1	4	5	.44	6	.305	.363	.519
2000 Midland	AA Oak	19	59	14	2	0	1	19	8	9	5	0	15	0	1	0	0	0	—	3	.237	.297	.322
Modesto	A+ Oak	58	227	64	11	5	5	100	40	35	16	0	53	2	0	2	5	2	.71	8	.282	.332	.441
2001 Birmingham	AA CWS	93	316	82	23	1	14	149	45	55	37	4	62	7	5	3	6	3	.67	4	.259	.347	.472
4 Min. YEARS		289	1009	285	60	15	31	468	169	164	87	5	233	15	7	7	17	12	.59	26	.282	.346	.464

Tim Olson

Bats: Right **Throws:** Right **Pos:** SS-79; 3B-28; OF-1; PH-1   **Ht:** 6'2" **Wt:** 200 **Born:** 8/1/78 **Age:** 23

Year Team	Lg Org	G	AB	H	2B	3B	HR	TB	R	RBI	TBB	IBB	SO	HBP	SH	SF	SB	CS	SB%	GDP	Avg	OBP	SLG
2000 South Bend	A Ari	68	261	57	14	2	2	81	37	26	15	0	49	8	0	1	15	3	.83	5	.218	.281	.310
2001 Lancaster	A+ Ari	61	239	69	12	4	6	107	36	32	14	0	49	3	2	0	13	9	.59	4	.289	.336	.448
El Paso	AA Ari	46	167	53	13	0	2	72	29	24	11	0	36	6	0	1	4	4	.50	4	.317	.378	.431
2 Min. YEARS		175	667	179	39	6	10	260	102	82	40	0	134	17	2	2	32	16	.67	13	.268	.325	.390

Steve Ontiveros

Pitches: Right **Bats:** Right **Pos:** SP-22; RP-1   **Ht:** 6'0" **Wt:** 190 **Born:** 3/5/61 **Age:** 41

Year Team	Lg Org	G	GS	CG	GF	IP	BFP	H	R	ER	HR	SH	SF	HB	TBB	IBB	SO	WP	Bk	W	L	Pct.	ShO	Sv	ERA
1982 Medford	A- Oak	4	0	0	3	8	—	3	0	0	0	—	—	0	4	0	9	0	0	1	0	1.000	0	0	0.00
West Haven	AA Oak	16	2	0	5	27	—	34	26	19	4	—	—	3	12	0	28	1	0	2	2	.500	0	0	6.33
1983 Albany	AA Oak	32	13	5	12	129.2	—	131	62	54	11	—	—	0	36	2	91	3	0	8	4	.667	0	5	3.75
1984 Tacoma	AAA Oak	2	2	0	0	11.1	0	18	11	10	3	0	0	1	5	0	6	0	0	1	1	.500	0	0	7.94
Madison	A Oak	5	5	2	0	30.2	122	23	10	7	0	1	1	1	6	0	26	1	0	3	1	.750	0	0	2.05
1985 Tacoma	AAA Oak	15	0	0	7	33.2	0	26	13	11	1	0	0	2	21	2	30	1	0	3	0	1.000	0	2	2.94
1987 Tacoma	AAA Oak	1	1	0	0	3	12	1	1	1	0	0	1	0	2	0	1	1	0	0	0	—	0	0	3.00
1989 Scranton-WB	AAA Phi	1	1	0	0	3.1	15	3	0	0	0	0	0	0	3	0	0	0	0	0	0	—	0	0	0.00
1990 Clearwater	A+ Phi	3	3	0	0	7.2	29	4	2	2	0	0	0	0	3	0	2	0	1	0	0	—	0	0	2.35
Reading	AA Phi	2	2	0	0	6	29	7	6	6	0	0	0	2	2	0	8	0	0	0	2	.000	0	0	9.00
1991 Scranton-WB	AAA Phi	7	7	0	0	31	127	29	11	10	2	0	1	0	10	0	21	2	0	1	2	.667	0	0	2.90
1993 Portland	AAA Min	20	16	2	2	103.1	418	90	40	33	5	2	6	4	20	0	73	5	2	7	6	.538	1	0	2.87
1996 Lk Elsinore	A+ Ana	2	2	0	0	8	35	12	3	2	0	0	0	0	0	0	8	1	0	1	1	.500	0	0	2.25
1997 Lk Elsinore	A+ Ana	1	1	0	0	0.1	2	0	1	1	0	0	0	0	1	0	0	0	0	0	1	.000	0	0	27.00
1998 Memphis	AAA StL	3	3	0	0	9.2	45	14	11	9	1	0	0	0	2	0	10	0	1	0	1	.000	0	0	8.38
Rochester	AAA Bal	16	14	0	0	80.2	333	77	35	33	10	2	2	2	25	0	64	1	0	5	1	.833	0	1	3.68
1999 Louisville	AAA Mil	8	8	0	0	48.2	203	47	26	24	5	3	1	0	12	1	33	1	0	5	1	.833	0	0	4.44
2000 Valley	IND —	9	9	2	0	62.2	262	56	31	25	5	1	0	4	16	0	55	0	0	4	4	.500	1	0	3.59
Colo Sprngs	AAA Col	8	8	0	0	43.1	177	36	15	14	6	1	0	3	10	1	33	2	0	4	1	.800	0	0	2.91
2001 Norfolk	AAA NYM	7	7	1	0	41.1	166	32	13	13	2	0	0	5	9	0	28	3	1	2	2	.500	1	0	2.83
Sacramento	AAA Oak	16	15	0	0	85	375	94	50	43	11	2	6	4	28	1	64	3	1	7	6	.538	0	0	4.55
1985 Oakland	AL	39	0	0	18	74.2	284	45	17	16	4	2	2	2	19	2	36	1	0	1	3	.250	0	8	1.93
1986 Oakland	AL	46	0	0	27	72.2	305	72	40	38	10	1	6	1	25	3	54	4	0	2	2	.500	0	10	4.71
1987 Oakland	AL	35	22	2	6	150.2	645	141	78	67	19	6	2	4	50	3	97	4	1	10	8	.556	1	1	4.00
1988 Oakland	AL	10	10	0	0	54.2	241	57	32	28	4	5	0	0	21	1	30	5	5	3	4	.429	0	0	4.61
1989 Philadelphia	NL	6	5	0	0	30.2	134	34	15	13	2	1	0	0	15	1	12	2	0	2	1	.667	0	0	3.82
1990 Philadelphia	NL	5	0	0	1	10	43	9	3	3	1	0	0	0	3	0	6	0	0	0	0	—	0	0	2.70
1993 Seattle	AL	14	0	0	8	18	72	18	3	2	0	1	0	0	6	2	13	1	0	0	2	.000	0	0	1.00
1994 Oakland	AL	27	13	2	5	115.1	463	93	39	34	7	2	1	6	26	1	56	5	0	6	4	.600	0	0	2.65
1995 Oakland	AL	22	22	2	0	129.2	558	144	75	63	12	2	6	4	38	0	77	5	0	9	6	.600	1	0	4.37
2000 Boston	AL	3	1	0	0	5.1	29	9	6	6	1	0	0	0	4	0	1	2	0	1	1	.500	0	0	10.13
15 Min. YEARS		178	119	12	31	774.1	—	737	367	317	66	—	—	31	227	7	590	25	6	55	35	.611	2	8	3.68
10 Maj. YEARS		207	73	6	65	661.2	2773	622	308	270	60	20	17	17	207	13	382	29	6	34	31	.523	2	19	3.67

Mike Oquist

Pitches: Right **Bats:** Right **Pos:** SP-20; RP-1   **Ht:** 6'2" **Wt:** 190 **Born:** 5/30/68 **Age:** 34

Year Team	Lg Org	G	GS	CG	GF	IP	BFP	H	R	ER	HR	SH	SF	HB	TBB	IBB	SO	WP	Bk	W	L	Pct.	ShO	Sv	ERA
1989 Erie	A- Bal	15	15	1	0	97.2	402	86	43	39	7	2	1	3	25	0	109	1	1	7	4	.636	1	0	3.59
1990 Frederick	A+ Bal	25	25	3	0	166.1	678	134	64	52	11	6	6	4	48	3	170	9	1	9	8	.529	1	0	2.81
1991 Hagerstown	AA Bal	27	26	1	1	166.1	717	168	82	75	15	4	7	0	62	4	136	7	1	10	9	.526	0	0	4.06
1992 Rochester	AAA Bal	26	24	5	0	153.1	665	164	80	70	17	5	4	5	45	1	111	6	1	10	12	.455	0	0	4.11
1993 Rochester	AAA Bal	28	21	2	1	149.1	617	144	62	58	20	5	1	2	41	1	128	5	1	9	8	.529	1	0	3.50
1994 Rochester	AAA Bal	13	8	0	4	50.2	213	54	23	21	5	0	1	1	15	0	36	3	1	3	2	.600	0	3	3.73
1995 Rochester	AAA Bal	7	0	0	3	12	56	17	8	7	0	0	0	0	5	1	11	0	0	0	0	—	0	2	5.25
1996 Las Vegas	AAA SD	27	20	2	4	140.1	586	136	55	45	12	6	6	3	44	2	110	4	0	9	4	.692	0	1	2.89
1997 Edmonton	AAA Oak	9	9	1	0	52.2	225	57	23	19	3	2	1	0	16	0	37	0	0	6	1	.857	0	0	3.25
Modesto	A+ Oak	2	2	0	0	3.2	17	5	2	2	1	0	0	0	1	0	5	0	0	0	0	—	0	0	4.91
1999 Vancouver	AAA Oak	1	1	0	0	6	22	2	0	0	0	0	0	0	1	0	2	1	0	1	0	1.000	0	0	0.00
2000 Toledo	AAA Det	29	28	3	0	161	723	214	106	93	18	4	7	8	43	1	97	8	0	7	15	.318	1	0	5.20
2001 Edmonton	AAA Min	21	20	2	1	110.2	482	132	62	51	12	1	1	3	29	0	76	1	0	5	8	.385	0	0	4.15
1993 Baltimore	AL	5	0	0	2	11.2	50	12	5	5	0	0	0	0	4	1	8	0	0	0	0	—	0	0	3.86
1994 Baltimore	AL	15	9	0	3	58.1	278	75	41	40	7	3	4	6	30	4	39	3	0	3	3	.500	0	0	6.17
1995 Baltimore	AL	27	0	0	2	54	255	51	27	25	6	1	4	2	41	3	27	2	0	2	1	.667	0	0	4.17
1996 San Diego	NL	8	0	0	3	7.2	30	6	2	2	0	0	0	0	4	2	4	1	0	0	0	—	0	0	2.35
1997 Oakland	AL	19	17	1	0	107.2	473	111	62	60	15	3	3	6	43	3	72	2	0	4	6	.400	0	0	5.02
1998 Oakland	AL	31	29	0	2	175	777	210	125	121	27	5	6	5	57	1	112	4	0	7	11	.389	0	0	6.22
1999 Oakland	AL	28	24	0	1	140.2	629	158	86	84	18	3	1	2	64	5	89	2	0	9	10	.474	0	0	5.37
12 Min. YEARS		230	199	20	14	1270	5403	1313	610	532	121	35	35	29	375	13	1028	45	6	76	71	.517	4	6	3.77
7 Maj. YEARS		133	79	1	13	555	2492	623	348	337	73	15	18	21	243	19	351	14	0	25	31	.446	0	0	5.46

Kevin Orie

Bats: Right **Throws:** Right **Pos:** 3B-133; DH-1   **Ht:** 6'4" **Wt:** 215 **Born:** 9/1/72 **Age:** 29

Year Team	Lg Org	G	AB	H	2B	3B	HR	TB	R	RBI	TBB	IBB	SO	HBP	SH	SF	SB	CS	SB%	GDP	Avg	OBP	SLG
1993 Peoria	A ChC	65	238	64	17	1	7	104	28	45	21	1	51	10	2	2	3	5	.38	7	.269	.351	.437
1994 Daytona	A+ ChC	6	17	7	3	1	1	15	4	5	8	1	4	1	0	0	0	1	.00	0	.412	.615	.882
1995 Daytona	A+ ChC	119	409	100	17	4	9	152	54	51	42	2	71	15	0	6	5	4	.56	11	.244	.333	.372
1996 Orlando	AA ChC	82	296	93	25	0	8	142	42	58	48	3	52	0	0	6	2	0	1.00	7	.314	.403	.480
Iowa	AAA ChC	14	48	10	1	0	2	17	5	6	6	1	10	0	0	0	0	0	—	1	.208	.296	.354

Year Team	Lg Org	G	AB	H	2B	3B	HR	TB	R	RBI	TBB	IBB	SO	HBP	SH	SF	SB	CS	SB%	GDP	Avg	OBP	SLG
1997 Orlando	AA ChC	3	13	5	2	0	2	13	3	6	2	1	1	0	0	0	0	0	—	1	.385	.467	1.000
Iowa	AAA ChC	9	32	12	4	0	1	19	7	8	5	0	5	0	0	0	0	0	—	0	.375	.459	.594
1998 Iowa	AAA ChC	24	92	34	8	0	9	69	27	24	12	1	15	2	0	0	1	0	1.00	3	.370	.453	.750
1999 Calgary	AAA Fla	23	72	23	9	0	3	41	10	8	13	0	7	1	0	0	0	0	—	0	.319	.430	.569
2000 Omaha	AAA KC	54	175	49	11	2	5	79	30	23	28	0	24	5	0	2	3	3	.50	8	.280	.390	.451
Columbus	AAA NYY	41	149	43	13	0	4	68	19	19	12	0	28	3	0	0	1	0	1.00	4	.289	.354	.456
2001 Scranton-WB	AAA Phi	134	509	149	34	2	13	226	77	45	77	5	63	9	0	2	11	6	.65	8	.293	.394	.444
1997 Chicago	NL	114	364	100	23	5	8	157	40	44	39	3	57	5	3	4	2	2	.50	13	.275	.350	.431
1998 Chicago	NL	64	204	37	14	0	2	57	24	21	18	0	35	3	1	4	1	1	.50	4	.181	.253	.279
Florida	NL	48	175	46	8	1	6	74	23	17	14	2	24	5	1	0	1	0	1.00	4	.263	.335	.423
1999 Florida	NL	77	240	61	16	0	6	95	26	29	22	1	43	3	0	2	1	0	1.00	8	.254	.322	.396
9 Min. YEARS		574	2050	589	144	10	64	945	306	298	274	15	331	46	2	18	26	19	.58	50	.287	.381	.461
3 Maj. YEARS		303	983	244	61	6	22	383	113	111	93	6	159	16	5	10	5	3	.63	29	.248	.320	.390

Rod Ormond

Pitches: Right **Bats:** Right **Pos:** RP-17; SP-8   **Ht:** 6'4" **Wt:** 210 **Born:** 6/17/77 **Age:** 25

		HOW MUCH HE PITCHED						WHAT HE GAVE UP												THE RESULTS					
Year Team	Lg Org	G	GS	CG	GF	IP	BFP	H	R	ER	HR	SH	SF	HB	TBB	IBB	SO	WP	Bk	W	L	Pct.	ShO	Sv	ERA
1999 Bluefield	R+ Bal	4	0	0	4	9.1	36	2	4	0	0	0	1	0	3	0	11	1	0	1	0	1.000	0	0	0.00
Delmarva	A Bal	17	1	0	7	37.1	156	29	16	12	1	0	0	4	19	0	38	5	2	1	2	.333	0	3	2.89
2000 Frederick	A+ Bal	39	0	0	12	67	294	66	38	27	3	5	2	3	25	0	59	4	0	2	5	.286	0	2	3.63
2001 Bowie	AA Bal	1	0	0	0	1.2	10	4	4	4	0	0	1	0	1	0	0	0	0	0	0	—	0	0	21.60
Delmarva	A Bal	24	8	0	3	56	250	59	37	26	6	2	1	4	14	1	59	3	0	4	4	.500	0	0	4.18
3 Min. YEARS		85	9	0	26	171.1	746	160	99	69	10	7	5	11	62	1	167	13	2	8	11	.421	0	5	3.62

Luis Ortiz

Bats: Right **Throws:** Right **Pos:** 1B-53; DH-5; 3B-2; PH-2   **Ht:** 6'0" **Wt:** 195 **Born:** 5/25/70 **Age:** 32

Year Team	Lg Org	G	AB	H	2B	3B	HR	TB	R	RBI	TBB	IBB	SO	HBP	SH	SF	SB	CS	SB%	GDP	Avg	OBP	SLG
1991 Red Sox	R Bos	42	153	51	11	2	4	78	21	29	7	0	9	2	1	1	2	1	.67	1	.333	.368	.510
1992 Lynchburg	A+ Bos	94	355	103	27	1	10	162	43	61	22	3	55	2	0	5	4	2	.67	8	.290	.331	.456
1993 Pawtucket	AAA Bos	102	402	118	28	1	18	202	45	81	13	3	74	2	0	4	1	1	.50	10	.294	.316	.502
1994 Pawtucket	AAA Bos	81	317	99	15	3	6	138	47	36	29	5	29	0	0	0	1	4	.20	9	.312	.370	.435
1995 Okla City	AAA Tex	47	170	52	10	5	2	78	19	20	8	2	20	0	1	3	1	1	.50	7	.306	.331	.459
1996 Okla City	AAA Tex	124	501	159	25	0	14	226	70	73	22	2	36	4	0	6	0	5	.00	17	.317	.347	.451
1997 Okla City	AAA Tex	22	82	25	5	0	1	33	9	11	5	0	7	0	0	3	1	1	.50	2	.305	.333	.402
1998 Omaha	AAA KC	44	138	42	13	0	5	70	27	22	10	1	11	0	0	2	0	2	.00	6	.304	.351	.507
1999 Louisville	AAA Mil	96	304	80	11	0	11	124	36	33	23	0	41	0	0	4	0	2	.00	8	.263	.311	.408
2000 Diamondbcks	R Ari	1	3	3	1	0	0	4	3	2	1	0	0	0	0	0	0	0	—	0	1.000	1.000	1.333
Tucson	AAA Ari	92	308	93	26	3	10	155	50	65	16	0	17	4	3	6	0	0	—	17	.302	.338	.503
2001 Winnipeg	IND —	45	189	66	10	2	9	107	38	42	18	3	12	0	0	3	0	0	—	7	.349	.400	.566
Ottawa	AAA Mon	16	57	16	5	1	0	23	4	8	3	0	6	0	0	1	0	0	—	2	.281	.311	.404
1993 Boston	AL	9	12	3	0	0	0	3	0	1	0	0	2	0	0	0	0	0	—	0	.250	.250	.250
1994 Boston	AL	7	18	3	2	0	0	5	3	6	1	0	5	0	1	3	0	0	—	0	.167	.182	.278
1995 Texas	AL	41	108	25	5	2	1	37	10	18	6	0	18	0	0	1	0	1	.00	7	.231	.270	.343
1996 Texas	AL	3	7	2	0	1	1	7	1	1	0	0	1	0	0	0	0	0	—	0	.286	.286	1.000
11 Min. YEARS		806	2979	907	187	18	90	1400	412	483	177	19	317	14	5	36	10	19	.34	94	.304	.342	.470
4 Maj. YEARS		60	145	33	7	3	2	52	14	26	7	0	26	0	1	4	0	1	.00	7	.228	.256	.359

Matt Ortiz

Bats: Right **Throws:** Right **Pos:** DH-44; C-16; OF-8; SS-1; PH-1   **Ht:** 5'11" **Wt:** 195 **Born:** 4/18/78 **Age:** 24

Year Team	Lg Org	G	AB	H	2B	3B	HR	TB	R	RBI	TBB	IBB	SO	HBP	SH	SF	SB	CS	SB%	GDP	Avg	OBP	SLG
2000 New Jersey	A- StL	28	87	16	3	1	2	27	6	8	5	0	16	0	0	0	0	0	—	2	.184	.228	.310
Peoria	A StL	9	23	4	0	0	1	7	2	3	2	0	6	0	0	0	0	0	—	1	.174	.240	.304
2001 New Haven	AA StL	4	12	2	2	0	0	4	0	2	2	1	2	0	0	0	0	0	—	0	.167	.286	.333
Peoria	A StL	65	216	53	13	1	0	68	23	23	19	0	31	2	1	3	4	3	.57	5	.245	.308	.315
2 Min. YEARS		106	338	75	18	2	3	106	31	36	28	1	55	2	1	3	4	3	.57	8	.222	.283	.314

Nicky Ortiz

Bats: Right **Throws:** Right **Pos:** SS-98; PH-2; DH-1   **Ht:** 6'0" **Wt:** 160 **Born:** 7/9/73 **Age:** 28

Year Team	Lg Org	G	AB	H	2B	3B	HR	TB	R	RBI	TBB	IBB	SO	HBP	SH	SF	SB	CS	SB%	GDP	Avg	OBP	SLG
1991 Red Sox	R Bos	35	100	26	3	1	0	31	16	13	22	0	24	4	1	0	1	2	.33	1	.260	.413	.310
1992 Red Sox	R Bos	50	163	43	9	3	0	58	25	15	28	0	36	0	2	1	3	2	.60	4	.264	.370	.356
Elmira	A- Bos	9	28	5	0	0	0	8	2	1	5	0	13	0	0	0	0	0	—	0	.179	.303	.286
1993 Ft. Laud	A+ Bos	36	112	23	9	1	1	37	9	14	9	0	39	0	4	0	2	1	.67	1	.205	.264	.330
Utica	A- Bos	63	197	53	14	1	2	75	31	26	19	0	56	6	1	2	4	1	.80	3	.269	.348	.381
1994 Sarasota	A+ Bos	81	283	76	18	3	2	106	34	40	21	1	57	3	6	3	7	2	.78	11	.269	.323	.375
1995 Sarasota	A+ Bos	91	304	75	20	1	5	112	38	38	27	0	68	4	1	1	6	4	.60	3	.247	.315	.368
1996 Michigan	A Bos	73	242	73	14	4	2	101	37	25	20	1	44	5	1	1	1	1	.50	4	.302	.366	.417
Trenton	AA Bos	38	130	29	4	0	3	42	20	13	13	2	28	0	1	0	2	2	.50	3	.223	.294	.323
1997 Trenton	AA Bos	87	288	81	17	2	8	126	47	53	27	1	55	5	6	5	3	2	.60	8	.281	.348	.438
1998 Ottawa	AAA Mon	12	32	3	1	0	0	4	1	0	6	0	10	0	1	0	0	0	—	0	.094	.237	.125
Harrisburg	AA Mon	56	163	44	11	2	6	77	18	24	18	0	37	2	7	2	2	3	.40	7	.270	.346	.472
Trenton	AA Bos	39	131	30	6	0	1	39	17	9	14	0	27	1	3	0	0	0	—	2	.229	.308	.298
1999 Buffalo	AAA Cle	22	51	13	4	0	0	17	7	1	3	0	10	0	0	0	0	0	—	2	.255	.296	.333
Akron	AA Cle	55	195	52	15	2	2	77	24	13	17	0	40	4	0	3	1	2	.33	5	.267	.333	.395
San Antonio	AA LA	14	40	7	1	0	0	8	4	2	3	0	7	0	0	0	0	0	—	2	.175	.233	.200

			BATTING															BASERUNNING				PERCENTAGES		
Year Team	Lg Org	G	AB	H	2B	3B	HR	TB	R	RBI	TBB	IBB	SO	HBP	SH	SF	SB	CS	SB%	GDP	Avg	OBP	SLG
2000 Wichita	AA KC	111	381	112	19	2	10	165	59	62	52	1	66	1	9	2	14	6	.70	13	.294	.378	.433
Norwich	AA NYY	11	37	6	0	0	0	6	4	1	7	0	8	1	0	0	0	0	—	2	.162	.311	.162
2001 Omaha	AAA KC	99	316	79	20	1	6	119	39	40	33	0	65	3	5	4	2	6	.25	11	.250	.323	.377
11 Min. YEARS		982	3193	830	188	23	48	1208	432	390	344	6	690	39	48	24	48	34	.59	86	.260	.337	.378

Willis Otanez

Bats: Right **Throws:** Right **Pos:** 1B-53; 3B-19; PH-10; OF-8; DH-6   **Ht:** 6'1" **Wt:** 215 **Born:** 4/19/73 **Age:** 29

			BATTING															BASERUNNING				PERCENTAGES		
Year Team	Lg Org	G	AB	H	2B	3B	HR	TB	R	RBI	TBB	IBB	SO	HBP	SH	SF	SB	CS	SB%	GDP	Avg	OBP	SLG
1991 Great Falls	R+ LA	58	222	64	9	2	6	95	38	39	19	0	34	2	1	4	3	3	.50	7	.288	.344	.428
1992 Vero Beach	A+ LA	117	390	86	18	0	3	113	27	27	24	0	60	4	5	3	2	4	.33	10	.221	.271	.290
1993 Bakersfield	A+ LA	95	325	85	11	2	10	130	34	39	29	1	63	2	4	2	1	4	.20	9	.262	.324	.400
1994 Vero Beach	A+ LA	131	476	132	27	1	19	218	77	72	53	2	98	4	0	7	4	2	.67	10	.277	.350	.458
1995 Vero Beach	A+ LA	92	354	92	24	0	10	146	39	53	28	3	59	2	0	5	1	1	.50	15	.260	.314	.412
San Antonio	AA LA	27	100	24	4	1	1	33	8	7	6	0	25	0	0	2	0	1	.00	3	.240	.278	.330
1996 Bowie	AA Bal	138	506	134	27	2	24	237	60	75	45	2	97	1	2	5	3	7	.30	17	.265	.323	.468
1997 Orioles	R Bal	8	25	8	2	0	2	16	5	3	2	0	4	1	0	0	0	0	—	1	.320	.393	.640
Bowie	AA Bal	19	78	26	9	0	3	44	13	13	9	0	19	0	0	1	0	1	.00	3	.333	.398	.564
Rochester	AAA Bal	49	168	35	9	0	5	59	20	25	15	0	35	0	0	3	0	0	—	8	.208	.269	.351
1998 Rochester	AAA Bal	124	481	137	24	2	27	246	87	100	41	6	104	6	1	8	1	0	1.00	8	.285	.343	.511
2000 Tennessee	AA Tor	27	103	33	5	0	5	53	13	19	10	1	16	1	0	1	0	0	—	6	.320	.383	.515
Syracuse	AAA Tor	22	76	13	3	0	2	22	6	14	6	0	15	0	0	1	0	0	—	4	.171	.229	.289
2001 Greenville	AA Atl	93	308	82	14	2	12	136	39	43	42	3	60	4	0	5	2	2	.50	14	.266	.357	.442
1998 Baltimore	AL	3	5	1	0	0	0	1	0	0	0	0	2	0	0	0	0	0	—	0	.200	.200	.200
1999 Baltimore	AL	29	80	17	3	0	2	26	7	11	6	0	16	1	1	1	0	0	—	3	.213	.273	.325
Toronto	AL	42	127	32	8	0	5	55	21	13	9	0	30	1	0	0	0	0	—	3	.252	.307	.433
10 Min. YEARS		1000	3612	951	186	12	129	1548	466	529	329	18	689	27	13	47	17	25	.40	111	.263	.326	.429
2 Maj. YEARS		74	212	50	11	0	7	82	28	24	15	0	48	2	1	1	0	0	—	6	.236	.291	.387

Paul Ottavinia

Bats: Left **Throws:** Left **Pos:** 1B-59; OF-58; DH-3; PH-1; PR-1   **Ht:** 6'1" **Wt:** 190 **Born:** 4/22/73 **Age:** 29

			BATTING															BASERUNNING				PERCENTAGES		
Year Team	Lg Org	G	AB	H	2B	3B	HR	TB	R	RBI	TBB	IBB	SO	HBP	SH	SF	SB	CS	SB%	GDP	Avg	OBP	SLG
1994 Burlington	A Mon	49	187	38	8	0	2	52	17	21	7	0	28	0	0	2	5	1	.83	2	.203	.230	.278
1995 Wst Plm Bch	A+ Mon	112	395	93	20	2	1	120	35	37	34	2	44	2	5	2	13	6	.68	10	.235	.298	.304
1996 Expos	R Mon	3	10	4	0	0	0	4	1	1	2	0	1	0	0	0	0	0	—	0	.400	.500	.400
Wst Plm Bch	A+ Mon	45	141	30	2	1	1	37	15	10	12	0	20	0	3	1	2	1	.67	2	.213	.273	.262
1997 Fargo-Mh	IND —	42	168	56	16	3	0	78	45	22	16	0	16	2	0	0	12	4	.75	2	.333	.398	.464
1998 Fargo-Mh	IND —	10	44	18	4	3	1	31	11	19	1	0	6	0	0	0	1	1	.50	0	.409	.422	.705
Tampa	A+ NYY	57	174	44	13	3	5	78	25	28	14	2	20	0	0	5	2	0	1.00	3	.253	.301	.448
1999 Norwich	AA NYY	59	191	55	11	3	7	93	26	31	14	1	40	1	0	1	5	3	.63	5	.288	.338	.487
2000 Norwich	AA NYY	127	477	144	27	8	8	211	80	58	56	7	50	10	0	5	15	5	.75	10	.302	.383	.442
2001 Columbus	AAA NYY	42	147	40	11	4	2	65	20	14	14	0	16	3	0	1	3	4	.43	6	.272	.345	.442
Norwich	AA NYY	76	302	78	19	2	6	119	52	34	30	2	45	6	0	2	11	1	.92	7	.258	.335	.394
8 Min. YEARS		622	2236	600	131	29	33	888	327	275	200	14	286	24	8	19	69	26	.73	47	.268	.332	.397

Mark Outlaw

Pitches: Left **Bats:** Left **Pos:** RP-46; SP-3   **Ht:** 5'11" **Wt:** 180 **Born:** 1/2/77 **Age:** 25

		HOW MUCH HE PITCHED					WHAT HE GAVE UP										THE RESULTS					
Year Team	Lg Org	G	GS	CG	GF	IP	BFP	H	R	ER	HR	SH	SF	HB	TBB	IBB	SO	WP	Bk	W	L	Pct.	ShO	Sv	ERA
1999 Batavia	A- Phi	23	0	0	10	33.1	134	26	10	6	1	2	3	0	9	2	45	5	0	1	1	.500	0	4	1.62
2000 Piedmont	A Phi	48	0	0	25	48	197	28	15	5	1	1	3	2	18	2	61	2	0	5	2	.714	0	11	0.94
2001 Reading	AA Phi	49	3	0	24	64.2	292	74	38	36	5	4	2	2	28	5	59	2	0	4	6	.400	0	7	5.01
3 Min. YEARS		120	3	0	59	146	623	128	63	47	7	7	8	4	55	9	165	9	0	10	9	.526	0	22	2.90

Jeremy Owens

Bats: Right **Throws:** Right **Pos:** OF-119; DH-11; PR-1   **Ht:** 6'1" **Wt:** 200 **Born:** 12/9/76 **Age:** 25

			BATTING															BASERUNNING				PERCENTAGES		
Year Team	Lg Org	G	AB	H	2B	3B	HR	TB	R	RBI	TBB	IBB	SO	HBP	SH	SF	SB	CS	SB%	GDP	Avg	OBP	SLG
1998 Idaho Falls	R+ SD	69	284	79	16	4	8	127	61	52	36	0	81	8	0	3	30	7	.81	2	.278	.372	.447
1999 Fort Wayne	A SD	129	513	144	26	12	9	221	111	66	63	2	153	9	4	6	65	14	.82	5	.281	.365	.431
Rancho Cuca	A+ SD	9	38	6	1	0	0	7	2	1	1	0	13	1	0	1	2	1	.67	1	.158	.195	.184
2000 Rancho Cuca	A+ SD	138	570	146	29	10	16	243	99	63	63	1	183	5	8	4	54	12	.82	5	.256	.333	.426
2001 Mobile	AA SD	107	395	85	20	6	7	138	46	26	55	1	149	2	5	5	33	12	.73	2	.215	.311	.349
Lk Elsinore	A+ SD	24	91	18	1	1	3	30	8	9	7	0	39	1	0	1	4	2	.67	0	.198	.260	.330
4 Min. YEARS		476	1891	478	93	33	43	766	327	217	225	4	618	26	17	20	188	48	.80	15	.253	.337	.405

Ryan Owens

Bats: Right **Throws:** Right **Pos:** 3B-119; SS-7; PH-3   **Ht:** 6'2" **Wt:** 200 **Born:** 3/18/78 **Age:** 24

			BATTING															BASERUNNING				PERCENTAGES		
Year Team	Lg Org	G	AB	H	2B	3B	HR	TB	R	RBI	TBB	IBB	SO	HBP	SH	SF	SB	CS	SB%	GDP	Avg	OBP	SLG
1999 El Paso	AA Ari	31	113	36	5	1	1	46	11	18	8	0	36	2	0	1	1	2	.33	1	.319	.371	.407
High Desert	A+ Ari	26	103	41	7	3	4	66	19	28	9	0	30	1	1	1	2	3	.33	0	.398	.447	.641
2000 El Paso	AA Ari	60	208	45	7	4	5	75	30	24	21	1	60	2	1	0	5	4	.56	3	.216	.294	.361
South Bend	A Ari	71	270	67	20	0	9	114	52	43	47	1	76	4	1	7	15	4	.79	6	.248	.368	.422
2001 El Paso	AA Ari	16	56	13	2	0	0	15	4	1	5	0	18	0	0	0	1	0	1.00	2	.232	.295	.268
Carolina	AA Col	111	392	105	20	2	8	153	66	47	63	1	107	8	1	2	12	4	.75	7	.268	.378	.390
3 Min. YEARS		315	1142	307	61	10	27	469	182	161	153	3	327	17	4	11	34	17	.67	19	.269	.362	.411

Todd Ozias

Pitches: Right **Bats:** Right **Pos:** RP-39   **Ht:** 6'1" **Wt:** 185 **Born:** 8/19/76 **Age:** 25

Year Team	Lg Org	G	GS	CG	GF	IP	BFP	H	R	ER	HR	SH	SF	HB	TBB	IBB	SO	WP	Bk	W	L	Pct.	ShO	Sv	ERA
1998 Salem-Keizr	A- SF	27	0	0	15	45.2	184	38	23	20	6	5	1	2	12	1	51	6	0	3	4	.429	0	2	3.94
1999 Bakersfield	A+ SF	52	0	0	49	56.1	235	47	21	16	6	0	2	1	25	1	67	6	0	5	5	.500	0	26	2.56
2000 San Jose	A+ SF	47	0	0	44	52	227	49	28	20	4	2	3	1	17	0	61	7	0	2	1	.667	0	21	3.46
Shreveport	AA SF	1	0	0	0	2	12	5	2	2	1	0	0	0	1	0	1	0	0	0	0	—	0	0	9.00
2001 Shreveport	AA SF	30	0	0	11	56	240	47	21	17	6	2	1	6	22	4	32	2	0	3	3	.500	0	0	2.73
Tulsa	AA Tex	9	0	0	3	12.1	57	15	10	10	2	0	0	1	8	1	10	3	0	0	0	—	0	0	7.30
4 Min. YEARS		166	0	0	122	224.1	955	201	105	85	25	9	7	11	85	7	222	24	0	13	13	.500	0	49	3.41

Francisco Ozuna

Pitches: Left **Bats:** Left **Pos:** RP-30   **Ht:** 6'2" **Wt:** 180 **Born:** 5/17/81 **Age:** 21

Year Team	Lg Org	G	GS	CG	GF	IP	BFP	H	R	ER	HR	SH	SF	HB	TBB	IBB	SO	WP	Bk	W	L	Pct.	ShO	Sv	ERA
2001 Chston-WV	A Tor	18	0	0	6	35	134	25	13	10	2	1	1	3	4	0	16	3	1	2	1	.667	0	2	2.57
Tennessee	AA Tor	12	0	0	5	12	51	11	3	2	0	0	1	2	4	0	7	0	0	1	0	1.000	0	0	1.50
1 Min. YEAR		30	0	0	11	47	185	36	16	12	2	1	2	5	8	0	23	3	1	3	1	.750	0	2	2.30

Alex Pacheco

Pitches: Right **Bats:** Right **Pos:** RP-43   **Ht:** 6'3" **Wt:** 200 **Born:** 7/19/73 **Age:** 28

Year Team	Lg Org	G	GS	CG	GF	IP	BFP	H	R	ER	HR	SH	SF	HB	TBB	IBB	SO	WP	Bk	W	L	Pct.	ShO	Sv	ERA
1990 Expos	R Mon	6	0	0	0	8.2	41	11	7	5	0	0	0	0	4	0	5	2	1	1	0	1.000	0	0	5.19
1991 Expos	R Mon	15	4	0	3	44.1	209	56	32	25	0	1	2	1	26	0	19	6	0	3	0	1.000	0	1	5.08
1992 Jamestown	A- Mon	16	5	0	4	50.1	229	53	36	31	5	2	2	3	29	1	32	2	1	3	3	.500	0	1	5.54
1993 Jamestown	A- Mon	6	1	0	1	14	60	11	7	5	0	0	1	0	4	0	15	4	0	0	1	.000	0	0	3.21
Burlington	A Mon	13	7	0	2	43	194	47	31	20	3	2	2	3	12	0	24	3	0	3	5	.375	0	1	4.19
1994 Burlington	A Mon	37	4	0	19	68.1	302	79	51	39	6	7	2	6	22	1	69	5	0	3	8	.273	0	5	5.14
Wst Plm Bch	A+ Mon	9	0	0	0	12	47	9	3	3	1	0	1	0	4	0	12	2	0	1	0	1.000	0	0	2.25
1995 Harrisburg	AA Mon	45	0	0	29	86.1	371	76	45	41	8	1	1	8	31	4	88	4	0	9	7	.563	0	4	4.27
Ottawa	AAA Mon	4	0	0	0	8.2	35	8	6	6	2	0	0	0	5	0	4	0	0	1	0	1.000	0	0	6.23
1996 Harrisburg	AA Mon	18	0	0	4	26.1	113	26	10	8	2	1	1	1	12	1	27	0	0	5	2	.714	0	0	2.73
Ottawa	AAA Mon	33	0	0	12	41.2	191	47	32	30	6	5	1	6	18	0	34	2	0	2	2	.500	0	6	6.48
1997 Tacoma	AAA Sea	15	2	0	4	27.2	143	45	27	27	4	0	0	3	15	1	21	1	0	0	2	.000	0	0	8.78
Memphis	AAA Sea	9	0	0	6	12	50	7	5	5	0	0	0	0	9	0	13	2	0	1	1	.500	0	1	3.75
1998 Durham	AAA TB	1	0	0	1	2	7	1	1	1	1	0	0	0	0	0	2	0	0	0	0	—	0	0	4.50
2001 Norwich	AA NYY	43	0	0	41	50	192	25	9	7	2	0	1	0	16	2	65	5	0	5	4	.556	0	26	1.26
1996 Montreal	NL	5	0	0	0	5.2	26	8	7	7	2	0	0	0	1	0	7	0	0	0	0	—	0	0	11.12
10 Min. YEARS		270	23	0	126	495.1	2184	501	302	253	40	19	14	31	207	10	430	38	2	37	35	.514	0	43	4.60

Delvis Pacheco

Pitches: Right **Bats:** Right **Pos:** RP-13; SP-11   **Ht:** 6'2" **Wt:** 180 **Born:** 6/25/78 **Age:** 24

Year Team	Lg Org	G	GS	CG	GF	IP	BFP	H	R	ER	HR	SH	SF	HB	TBB	IBB	SO	WP	Bk	W	L	Pct.	ShO	Sv	ERA
1995 Braves	R Atl	13	13	0	0	60	260	47	26	17	1	0	3	38	0	52	5	2	1	8	.111	0	0	2.55
1996 Danville	R+ Atl	13	12	0	0	64.2	271	56	28	19	1	1	1	2	21	0	60	5	0	8	1	.889	0	0	2.64
1997 Macon	A Atl	35	4	0	7	80	335	77	39	36	8	1	2	3	23	0	74	1	0	1	3	.250	0	2	4.05
1998 Macon	A Atl	18	10	0	3	63.1	272	67	39	35	12	1	2	6	14	0	42	5	1	7	4	.636	0	0	4.97
1999 Myrtle Bch	A+ Atl	40	3	0	16	99.1	429	87	47	38	9	5	2	6	42	3	87	7	0	6	5	.545	0	2	3.44
2000 Richmond	AAA Atl	25	0	0	6	58.2	238	61	32	31	6	3	4	2	18	2	44	2	0	1	2	.333	0	0	4.76
Greenville	AA Atl	11	10	0	0	58.2	245	55	22	20	9	0	0	1	23	0	51	2	0	6	2	.750	0	0	3.07
2001 Myrtle Bch	A+ Atl	2	2	0	0	10	36	4	0	0	0	0	0	0	2	0	7	0	0	1	0	1.000	0	0	0.00
Richmond	AAA Atl	22	9	1	5	58	269	78	36	34	4	2	2	1	24	2	51	2	1	1	4	.200	0	4	5.28
7 Min. YEARS		179	63	1	37	552.2	2355	532	269	230	50	13	14	24	205	7	468	29	4	32	29	.525	0	4	3.75

John Pachot

Bats: Right **Throws:** Right **Pos:** C-46; PH-7; DH-2   **Ht:** 6'2" **Wt:** 168 **Born:** 11/11/74 **Age:** 27

Year Team	Lg Org	G	AB	H	2B	3B	HR	TB	R	RBI	TBB	IBB	SO	HBP	SH	SF	SB	CS	SB%	GDP	Avg	OBP	SLG
1993 Expos	R Mon	35	121	37	4	1	0	43	13	16	2	0	7	0	4	2	0	1	.00	5	.306	.312	.355
1994 Burlington	A Mon	100	351	89	17	0	1	109	37	26	13	1	46	3	5	4	1	2	.33	12	.254	.283	.311
1995 Wst Plm Bch	A+ Mon	67	227	57	10	0	0	67	17	23	12	0	38	2	3	1	1	2	.33	4	.251	.293	.295
1996 Expos	R Mon	8	30	9	1	1	0	12	3	3	1	0	0	1	1	0	0	0	—	0	.300	.344	.400
Wst Plm Bch	A+ Mon	44	163	31	9	0	0	40	8	19	2	0	19	0	1	0	0	1	.00	1	.190	.200	.245
1997 Harrisburg	AA Mon	94	323	90	23	3	7	140	40	50	22	0	42	3	2	5	6	6	.50	10	.279	.326	.433
1998 Ottawa	AAA Mon	100	344	78	18	1	2	104	33	39	15	1	45	3	3	3	2	2	.50	13	.227	.263	.302
1999 Ottawa	AAA Mon	17	56	12	4	0	0	16	7	6	6	1	9	0	1	1	0	0	—	2	.214	.286	.286
Tucson	AAA Ari	35	102	27	4	0	1	34	10	11	3	0	10	0	0	0	1	0	1.00	5	.265	.286	.333
2000 El Paso	AA Ari	5	14	2	1	0	0	3	1	1	0	0	1	0	0	0	0	0	—	1	.143	.143	.214
Portland	AA Fla	97	323	94	19	0	3	122	35	57	22	0	41	2	5	4	0	4	.00	6	.291	.336	.378
2001 Las Vegas	AAA LA	6	22	7	1	0	1	11	3	1	0	0	3	0	0	0	1	0	1.00	2	.318	.318	.500
Dodgers	R LA	1	5	1	0	0	1	4	1	1	0	0	0	0	0	0	0	0	—	0	.200	.200	.800
Jacksnville	AA LA	46	152	37	15	1	4	66	12	22	4	0	20	0	0	2	0	2	.00	4	.243	.259	.434
9 Min. YEARS		655	2233	571	126	7	20	771	220	275	102	3	282	14	25	22	12	20	.38	60	.256	.290	.345

Pete Paciorek

Bats: Left **Throws:** Left **Pos:** 1B-38; PH-33; DH-28; OF-13   **Ht:** 6'3" **Wt:** 205 **Born:** 5/19/76 **Age:** 26

Year Team	Lg Org	G	AB	H	2B	3B	HR	TB	R	RBI	TBB	IBB	SO	HBP	SH	SF	SB	CS	SB%	GDP	Avg	OBP	SLG
1995 Padres	R SD	54	183	47	11	3	5	79	32	24	33	1	58	1	1	0	6	4	.60	1	.257	.373	.432
1996 Idaho Falls	R+ SD	72	283	84	15	2	15	148	56	69	36	1	64	4	0	6	6	1	.86	6	.297	.377	.523
1997 Clinton	A SD	126	435	102	19	11	7	164	70	52	70	5	113	4	1	5	10	4	.71	6	.234	.342	.377
1998 Rancho Cuca	A+ SD	137	481	133	28	6	17	224	82	86	63	3	135	4	6	6	8	7	.53	4	.277	.361	.466
1999 Mobile	AA SD	83	226	50	9	2	4	75	38	17	38	1	60	4	0	4	2	3	.40	6	.221	.343	.332
2000 San Berndno	A+ LA	134	499	139	29	9	12	222	80	83	76	6	106	7	1	5	10	10	.50	6	.279	.378	.445
2001 Jacksnville	AA LA	65	150	32	8	1	4	54	17	20	15	0	42	1	2	0	3	1	.75	6	.213	.289	.360
Vero Beach	A+ LA	46	143	28	5	1	4	47	13	17	13	1	33	0	2	1	0	0	—	5	.196	.261	.329
7 Min. YEARS		717	2400	615	124	35	68	1013	388	368	344	18	611	25	13	23	45	30	.60	40	.256	.352	.422

Geraldo Padua

Pitches: Right **Bats:** Right **Pos:** RP-16; SP-3   **Ht:** 6'2" **Wt:** 165 **Born:** 2/9/77 **Age:** 25

Year Team	Lg Org	G	GS	CG	GF	IP	BFP	H	R	ER	HR	SH	SF	HB	TBB	IBB	SO	WP	Bk	W	L	Pct.	ShO	Sv	ERA
1997 Yankees	R NYY	11	8	1	1	61.2	237	46	24	20	5	2	0	1	8	0	36	5	1	8	0	1.000	1	0	2.92
1998 Oneonta	A- NYY	15	14	0	0	86	362	79	40	30	3	1	2	3	29	0	75	2	1	8	0	1.000	0	0	3.14
1999 Greensboro	A NYY	21	21	1	0	139.2	569	120	53	44	12	0	1	2	35	0	155	13	1	9	4	.692	1	0	2.84
Rancho Cuca	A+ SD	7	7	0	0	40.2	174	43	21	21	4	0	0	0	18	0	41	6	0	3	3	.500	0	0	4.65
2000 Altoona	AA Pit	9	9	0	0	41.1	202	59	42	32	3	3	1	2	20	0	31	3	0	1	6	.143	0	0	6.97
Lynchburg	A+ Pit	17	14	0	2	92	396	102	57	43	11	5	2	1	22	0	57	7	0	4	9	.308	0	0	4.21
2001 Altoona	AA Pit	10	0	0	5	13	61	17	14	14	5	2	1	1	6	0	10	1	0	0	1	.000	0	0	9.69
Tampa	A+ NYY	1	0	0	1	1	3	0	0	0	0	0	0	0	1	0	1	0	0	0	0	—	0	0	0.00
Greensboro	A NYY	3	3	0	0	18.2	73	20	8	8	0	0	0	0	3	0	14	0	0	1	1	.500	0	0	3.86
Norwich	AA NYY	5	0	0	1	9.1	36	5	3	3	0	0	0	1	3	0	11	0	0	1	0	1.000	0	0	2.89
5 Min. YEARS		99	76	2	10	503.1	2113	491	262	215	43	13	7	11	145	0	431	37	3	35	24	.593	2	0	3.84

Jeromy Palki

Pitches: Right **Bats:** Right **Pos:** RP-41; SP-2   **Ht:** 6'0" **Wt:** 215 **Born:** 4/14/76 **Age:** 26

Year Team	Lg Org	G	GS	CG	GF	IP	BFP	H	R	ER	HR	SH	SF	HB	TBB	IBB	SO	WP	Bk	W	L	Pct.	ShO	Sv	ERA
1995 Mariners	R Sea	4	0	0	1	5.2	29	7	7	5	0	1	1	0	5	0	2	1	0	0	0	—	0	0	7.94
1996 Mariners	R Sea	18	0	0	12	47.1	194	31	14	13	3	1	1	2	17	0	56	2	0	1	1	.500	0	6	2.47
1997 Wisconsin	A Sea	44	0	0	35	64.2	255	50	22	20	2	5	2	2	18	2	75	2	0	9	3	.750	0	8	2.78
1998 Fort Myers	A+ Min	40	0	0	17	58.2	263	51	39	31	3	4	3	2	29	1	48	7	0	0	4	.000	0	4	4.76
1999 Twins	R Min	3	1	0	0	5	16	0	0	0	0	0	0	0	1	0	3	0	0	0	0	—	0	0	0.00
2000 Fort Myers	A+ Min	42	0	0	16	73	314	72	32	26	6	0	2	3	30	1	75	4	0	6	3	.667	0	3	3.21
2001 Fort Myers	A+ Min	12	0	0	6	20	82	15	5	4	1	0	1	0	10	0	24	2	0	1	1	.500	0	1	1.80
New Britain	AA Min	31	2	0	17	60.1	247	50	19	19	1	2	0	0	22	4	59	2	0	3	1	.750	0	1	2.83
7 Min. YEARS		194	3	0	104	334.2	1400	274	138	118	16	13	10	9	132	8	342	20	0	20	13	.606	0	23	3.17

Rick Palma

Pitches: Left **Bats:** Left **Pos:** RP-57   **Ht:** 6'1" **Wt:** 160 **Born:** 9/26/79 **Age:** 22

Year Team	Lg Org	G	GS	CG	GF	IP	BFP	H	R	ER	HR	SH	SF	HB	TBB	IBB	SO	WP	Bk	W	L	Pct.	ShO	Sv	ERA
1997 Williamsprt	A- ChC	14	14	1	0	77.2	336	77	36	30	6	1	3	2	36	1	47	2	5	4	7	.364	0	0	3.48
1998 Rockford	A ChC	21	19	0	0	103	451	114	59	51	6	3	4	3	36	0	65	9	1	7	6	.538	0	0	4.46
1999 Lansing	A ChC	22	22	2	0	134.2	571	134	61	44	6	1	4	3	44	0	79	8	4	7	7	.500	0	0	2.94
2000 Daytona	A+ ChC	20	19	0	1	99.2	446	109	61	52	9	5	5	0	44	0	72	9	5	4	8	.333	0	1	4.70
2001 West Tenn	AA ChC	57	0	0	21	70.2	292	61	29	24	6	4	4	0	25	1	70	2	0	4	9	.308	0	0	3.06
5 Min. YEARS		134	74	3	22	485.2	2096	495	246	201	33	17	19	9	185	2	333	30	15	26	37	.413	0	1	3.72

Mike Paradis

Pitches: Right **Bats:** Right **Pos:** SP-26; RP-1   **Ht:** 6'3" **Wt:** 190 **Born:** 5/3/78 **Age:** 24

Year Team	Lg Org	G	GS	CG	GF	IP	BFP	H	R	ER	HR	SH	SF	HB	TBB	IBB	SO	WP	Bk	W	L	Pct.	ShO	Sv	ERA
1999 Delmarva	A Bal	2	2	0	0	3	18	3	5	5	0	1	2	0	4	0	6	0	1	0	1	.000	0	0	15.00
2000 Delmarva	A Bal	18	18	0	0	97	438	95	53	43	5	1	2	7	49	0	81	10	2	6	5	.545	0	0	3.99
Frederick	A+ Bal	8	8	1	0	45.1	212	55	24	21	1	0	2	4	24	0	32	2	0	2	5	.286	0	0	4.17
2001 Bowie	AA Bal	27	26	1	0	137.2	634	157	98	72	13	4	2	4	62	1	108	14	1	8	13	.381	0	0	4.71
3 Min. YEARS		55	54	2	0	283	1300	310	180	141	19	6	6	15	139	1	227	26	4	16	24	.400	0	0	4.48

Christian Parra

Pitches: Right **Bats:** Right **Pos:** SP-18   **Ht:** 6'1" **Wt:** 255 **Born:** 2/28/78 **Age:** 24

Year Team	Lg Org	G	GS	CG	GF	IP	BFP	H	R	ER	HR	SH	SF	HB	TBB	IBB	SO	WP	Bk	W	L	Pct.	ShO	Sv	ERA
1999 Jamestown	A- Atl	9	9	0	0	49.1	207	46	21	17	2	0	0	1	19	0	62	1	1	1	2	.333	0	0	3.10
Macon	A Atl	6	6	0	0	32.1	139	33	15	12	3	0	1	1	12	0	37	1	1	1	1	.500	0	0	3.31
2000 Myrtle Bch	A+ Atl	26	25	2	1	157.2	608	98	46	40	6	2	5	3	56	0	163	8	2	17	4	.810	2	0	2.28
2001 Greenville	AA Atl	18	18	0	0	89.1	404	87	58	54	9	3	4	3	56	2	82	8	1	3	8	.273	0	0	5.44
3 Min. YEARS		59	58	2	1	329	1358	264	140	123	20	5	10	10	143	2	344	18	5	22	15	.595	2	0	3.36

Wade Parrish

Pitches: Left **Bats:** Left **Pos:** RP-42; SP-1   **Ht:** 6'1" **Wt:** 205 **Born:** 11/13/77 **Age:** 24

Year Team	Lg Org	G	GS	CG	GF	IP	BFP	H	R	ER	HR	SH	SF	HB	TBB	IBB	SO	WP	Bk	W	L	Pct.	ShO	Sv	ERA
1999 Yakima	A- LA	17	8	0	5	60	261	57	30	27	4	0	2	1	24	0	48	2	0	4	3	.571	0	2	4.05
2000 San Berndno	A+ LA	29	0	0	12	51	221	39	22	18	3	1	0	0	32	3	56	3	0	2	3	.400	0	2	3.18
2001 Vero Beach	A+ LA	23	0	0	15	39	153	34	9	8	3	0	0	1	7	0	42	4	0	4	1	.800	0	6	1.85
Jacksnville	AA LA	4	0	0	3	7	34	7	4	4	0	1	0	1	5	1	5	0	0	1	1	.500	0	0	5.14
Birmingham	AA CWS	16	1	0	4	26	98	19	4	4	1	1	1	2	5	0	15	3	0	4	0	1.000	0	0	1.38
3 Min. YEARS		89	9	0	39	183	767	156	69	61	11	3	3	5	73	4	166	12	0	15	8	.652	0	10	3.00

Val Pascucci

Bats: Right **Throws:** Right **Pos:** OF-119; 1B-19; DH-5; PH-2   **Ht:** 6'6" **Wt:** 235 **Born:** 11/17/78 **Age:** 23

Year Team	Lg Org	G	AB	H	2B	3B	HR	TB	R	RBI	TBB	IBB	SO	HBP	SH	SF	SB	CS	SB%	GDP	Avg	OBP	SLG
1999 Vermont	A- Mon	72	259	91	26	1	7	140	62	48	53	3	46	14	0	2	17	2	.89	5	.351	.482	.541
2000 Cape Fear	A Mon	20	69	22	4	0	3	35	17	10	16	0	15	0	0	1	5	0	1.00	2	.319	.442	.507
Jupiter	A+ Mon	113	405	115	30	2	14	191	70	66	66	0	98	11	0	5	14	6	.70	9	.284	.394	.472
2001 Harrisburg	AA Mon	138	476	116	17	1	21	198	79	67	65	1	114	11	1	6	8	8	.50	8	.244	.344	.416
3 Min. YEARS		343	1209	344	77	4	45	564	228	191	200	4	273	36	1	14	44	16	.73	24	.285	.398	.467

John Patterson

Pitches: Right **Bats:** Right **Pos:** SP-19; RP-1   **Ht:** 6'5" **Wt:** 183 **Born:** 1/30/78 **Age:** 24

Year Team	Lg Org	G	GS	CG	GF	IP	BFP	H	R	ER	HR	SH	SF	HB	TBB	IBB	SO	WP	Bk	W	L	Pct.	ShO	Sv	ERA
1997 South Bend	A Ari	18	18	0	0	78	327	63	32	28	3	1	2	5	34	0	95	8	0	1	9	.100	0	0	3.23
1998 High Desert	A+ Ari	25	25	0	0	127	519	102	54	40	12	0	3	4	42	0	148	5	0	8	7	.533	0	0	2.83
1999 El Paso	AA Ari	18	18	2	0	100	429	98	61	53	16	3	1	0	42	0	117	3	0	8	6	.571	0	0	4.77
Tucson	AAA Ari	7	6	0	0	30.2	148	43	26	24	3	0	0	0	18	0	29	0	0	1	5	.167	0	0	7.04
2000 Tucson	AAA Ari	3	2	0	0	15	76	21	14	13	1	1	1	0	9	0	10	2	0	0	2	.000	0	0	7.80
2001 Lancaster	A+ Ari	2	2	0	0	9.1	40	9	6	6	3	0	0	0	3	0	9	0	0	0	0	—	0	0	5.79
El Paso	AA Ari	5	5	0	0	25.1	112	30	15	12	2	0	0	2	9	0	19	1	0	1	2	.333	0	0	4.26
Tucson	AAA Ari	13	12	0	0	67.2	313	82	50	44	9	2	5	3	31	3	40	2	1	2	7	.222	0	0	5.85
5 Min. YEARS		91	88	2	0	453	1964	448	258	220	49	7	12	14	188	3	467	21	1	21	38	.356	0	0	4.37

Brad Pautz

Pitches: Right **Bats:** Right **Pos:** RP-49   **Ht:** 6'3" **Wt:** 190 **Born:** 1/3/77 **Age:** 25

Year Team	Lg Org	G	GS	CG	GF	IP	BFP	H	R	ER	HR	SH	SF	HB	TBB	IBB	SO	WP	Bk	W	L	Pct.	ShO	Sv	ERA
1999 Batavia	A- Phi	13	13	2	0	77.2	326	77	37	35	4	2	1	1	30	1	58	4	1	8	4	.667	2	0	4.06
2000 Piedmont	A Phi	13	11	1	0	65.2	272	53	20	17	2	0	5	4	24	0	33	3	0	3	2	.600	0	0	2.33
2001 Clearwater	A+ Phi	44	0	0	37	64	273	62	29	24	1	4	4	1	24	3	51	6	0	3	2	.600	0	16	3.38
Reading	AA Phi	5	0	0	3	4.2	20	3	2	1	0	0	0	0	4	1	4	1	0	0	0	—	0	0	1.93
3 Min. YEARS		75	24	3	40	212	891	195	88	77	7	6	10	6	82	5	146	14	1	14	8	.636	2	16	3.27

Dave Pavlas

Pitches: Right **Bats:** Right **Pos:** RP-40; SP-1   **Ht:** 6'7" **Wt:** 205 **Born:** 8/12/62 **Age:** 39

Year Team	Lg Org	G	GS	CG	GF	IP	BFP	H	R	ER	HR	SH	SF	HB	TBB	IBB	SO	WP	Bk	W	L	Pct.	ShO	Sv	ERA
1985 Peoria	A ChC	17	15	3	2	110	452	90	40	32	7	3	1	3	32	0	86	6	1	8	3	.727	1	1	2.62
1986 Winston-Sal	A+ ChC	28	26	5	0	173.1	739	172	91	74	8	6	4	6	57	2	143	11	1	14	6	.700	2	0	3.84
1987 Pittsfield	AA ChC	7	7	0	0	45	199	49	25	19	6	0	3	3	17	0	27	1	1	6	1	.857	0	0	3.80
Tulsa	AA Tex	13	12	0	1	59.2	280	79	51	51	9	1	0	3	27	0	46	7	0	1	6	.143	0	0	7.69
1988 Tulsa	AA Tex	26	5	1	9	77.1	299	52	26	17	3	6	2	5	18	1	69	4	6	5	2	.714	0	2	1.98
Okla City	AAA Tex	13	8	0	2	52.1	237	59	29	26	1	1	2	3	28	0	40	2	1	3	1	.750	0	0	4.47
1989 Okla City	AAA Tex	29	21	4	4	143.2	652	175	89	75	7	6	7	7	67	4	94	8	1	2	14	.125	0	0	4.70
1990 Iowa	AAA ChC	53	3	0	22	99.1	421	84	38	36	4	4	3	10	48	6	96	8	1	8	3	.727	0	8	3.26
1991 Iowa	AAA ChC	61	0	0	29	97.1	418	92	49	43	5	10	5	5	43	9	54	13	0	5	6	.455	0	7	3.98
1992 Iowa	AAA ChC	12	4	0	6	37.1	166	43	20	14	5	2	0	0	8	0	34	0	0	3	3	.500	0	0	3.38
1995 Columbus	AAA NYY	48	0	0	32	58.2	233	43	19	17	2	4	1	1	20	2	51	4	0	3	3	.500	0	18	2.61
1996 Columbus	AAA NYY	57	0	0	46	77	306	64	20	17	5	1	0	0	13	1	65	3	0	8	2	.800	0	26	1.99
1997 Columbus	AAA NYY	26	0	0	25	25.1	116	33	14	13	3	2	1	0	4	2	34	0	0	1	3	.250	0	12	4.62
1998 Tucson	AAA Ari	9	0	0	8	8.1	46	15	11	8	3	0	1	1	5	1	8	0	0	0	2	.000	0	1	8.64
Edmonton	AAA Oak	26	3	0	10	58	239	51	23	20	4	0	3	1	12	1	41	2	0	2	2	.500	0	1	3.10
1999 Columbus	AAA NYY	38	2	0	13	62.1	256	69	32	28	5	0	3	2	9	1	49	1	0	4	2	.667	0	1	4.04
2000 Nashville	AAA Pit	45	0	0	17	71.2	311	71	36	27	8	7	3	4	23	3	61	2	0	4	2	.667	0	0	3.39
2001 Nashville	AAA Pit	41	1	0	18	41.1	167	34	12	12	4	1	1	1	8	2	40	3	0	1	4	.200	0	6	2.61
1990 Chicago	NL	13	0	0	3	21.1	93	23	7	5	2	0	2	0	6	2	12	3	0	2	0	1.000	0	0	2.11
1991 Chicago	NL	1	0	0	1	1	5	3	2	2	1	1	0	0	0	0	0	0	0	0	0	—	0	0	18.00
1995 New York	AL	4	0	0	1	5.2	24	8	2	2	0	0	0	0	0	0	3	0	0	0	0	—	0	0	3.18
1996 New York	AL	16	0	0	8	23	97	23	7	6	0	2	0	1	7	2	18	3	0	0	0	—	0	1	2.35
15 Min. YEARS		549	107	13	244	1298	5537	1275	630	529	89	54	40	56	439	35	1038	75	12	78	65	.545	3	88	3.67
4 Maj. YEARS		34	0	0	13	51	219	57	18	15	3	3	2	1	13	4	33	6	0	2	0	1.000	0	1	2.65

Tony Pavlovich

Pitches: Right **Bats:** Right **Pos:** RP-51   **Ht:** 5'10" **Wt:** 191 **Born:** 8/23/74 **Age:** 27

		HOW MUCH HE PITCHED						WHAT HE GAVE UP										THE RESULTS				
Year Team	Lg Org	G	GS	CG	GF	IP	BFP	H	R	ER	HR	SH	SF	HB	TBB	IBB	SO	WP	Bk	W	L	Pct.	ShO	Sv	ERA
1994 Brewers	R Mil	19	0	0	15	27.1	109	24	7	5	1	1	2	1	8	0	29	3	0	2	1	.667	0	8	1.65
1995 Brewers	R Mil	19	0	0	18	18	78	20	10	8	0	2	1	0	3	0	20	1	0	0	2	.000	0	10	4.00
Helena	R+ Mil	9	0	0	9	9.2	37	4	1	1	1	0	0	1	3	0	14	1	0	0	0	—	0	4	0.93
1996 Beloit	A Mil	28	0	0	15	33.2	141	26	12	12	1	4	0	0	15	1	31	2	0	2	3	.400	0	4	3.21
1997 Springfield	IND —	30	0	0	20	43.1	197	52	23	20	2	6	1	1	19	4	44	1	0	3	5	.375	0	4	4.15
1998 Springfield	IND —	20	0	0	9	28.2	108	14	5	4	2	1	0	1	7	1	40	2	1	1	2	.333	0	4	1.26
Erie	A- Pit	8	0	0	3	11	42	6	3	2	1	0	0	0	2	0	17	0	0	0	2	.000	0	1	1.64
1999 Hickory	A Pit	56	0	0	39	73.1	287	55	29	19	8	1	3	1	16	4	78	1	0	5	1	.833	0	20	2.33
2000 Lynchburg	A+ Pit	36	0	0	27	40	171	38	18	16	0	1	0	3	13	1	33	1	0	2	1	.667	0	14	3.60
2001 Lynchburg	A+ Pit	20	0	0	20	23	86	13	1	1	0	1	1	0	5	0	27	0	0	1	0	1.000	0	13	0.39
Altoona	AA Pit	31	0	0	26	42.1	174	38	15	14	0	2	1	3	13	5	26	1	0	3	.000	0	12	2.98
8 Min. YEARS		276	0	0	201	350.1	1430	290	124	102	16	19	9	11	104	16	359	13	1	16	20	.444	0	94	2.62

Jerrod Payne

Pitches: Right **Bats:** Right **Pos:** RP-43   **Ht:** 5'10" **Wt:** 198 **Born:** 8/27/77 **Age:** 24

		HOW MUCH HE PITCHED						WHAT HE GAVE UP										THE RESULTS				
Year Team	Lg Org	G	GS	CG	GF	IP	BFP	H	R	ER	HR	SH	SF	HB	TBB	IBB	SO	WP	Bk	W	L	Pct.	ShO	Sv	ERA
2000 Queens	A- Tor	2	0	0	1	2	8	3	2	2	1	0	0	0	0	0	1	1	0	0	0	—	0	0	9.00
Hagerstown	A Tor	19	0	0	17	17	70	15	9	7	0	0	2	0	6	0	6	2	0	0	2	.000	0	8	3.71
2001 Dunedin	A+ Tor	21	0	0	16	27.1	118	25	13	7	2	0	1	0	8	1	22	0	0	2	2	.500	0	8	2.30
Tennessee	AA Tor	22	0	0	6	29.1	135	37	22	20	4	2	2	0	9	1	18	1	0	2	3	.400	0	1	6.14
2 Min. YEARS		64	0	0	40	75.2	331	80	46	36	7	2	5	0	23	2	47	4	0	4	7	.364	0	17	4.28

Rich Paz

Bats: Right **Throws:** Right **Pos:** 2B-48; 3B-30; SS-6; PH-6; DH-1; P-1   **Ht:** 5'8" **Wt:** 172 **Born:** 7/30/77 **Age:** 24

		BATTING															BASERUNNING				PERCENTAGES		
Year Team	Lg Org	G	AB	H	2B	3B	HR	TB	R	RBI	TBB	IBB	SO	HBP	SH	SF	SB	CS	SB%	GDP	Avg	OBP	SLG
1996 High Desert	A+ Bal	7	17	3	1	0	0	4	2	0	1	0	4	0	2	0	0	0	—	1	.176	.222	.235
Bluefield	R+ Bal	50	170	50	7	0	1	60	42	21	42	0	24	3	1	4	9	4	.69	1	.294	.434	.353
1997 Delmarva	A Bal	111	389	94	14	4	2	122	60	48	38	1	60	5	15	4	15	5	.75	8	.242	.314	.314
1998 Delmarva	A Bal	98	325	104	10	4	5	137	55	56	75	2	42	8	2	5	22	7	.76	6	.320	.453	.422
Frederick	A+ Bal	40	143	35	10	0	3	54	31	8	21	0	22	4	3	0	6	3	.67	3	.245	.357	.378
1999 Frederick	A+ Bal	54	163	41	9	0	0	50	27	18	47	0	27	2	3	5	15	6	.71	2	.252	.415	.307
Bowie	AA Bal	79	273	78	12	2	2	100	39	20	51	0	35	6	8	2	11	3	.79	4	.286	.407	.366
2000 Frederick	A+ Bal	79	268	82	13	0	4	107	53	45	71	0	47	3	6	6	15	8	.65	5	.306	.448	.399
Bowie	AA Bal	40	137	39	9	3	1	57	18	17	27	0	28	2	4	1	3	2	.60	0	.285	.407	.416
2001 Altoona	AA Pit	85	248	59	15	1	4	88	30	30	52	2	55	3	1	2	7	6	.54	7	.238	.374	.355
6 Min. YEARS		643	2133	585	100	14	22	779	357	263	425	5	344	36	45	29	103	44	.70	37	.274	.399	.365

Josh Pearce

Pitches: Right **Bats:** Right **Pos:** SP-28   **Ht:** 6'3" **Wt:** 215 **Born:** 8/20/77 **Age:** 24

		HOW MUCH HE PITCHED						WHAT HE GAVE UP										THE RESULTS				
Year Team	Lg Org	G	GS	CG	GF	IP	BFP	H	R	ER	HR	SH	SF	HB	TBB	IBB	SO	WP	Bk	W	L	Pct.	ShO	Sv	ERA
1999 New Jersey	A- StL	14	14	1	0	77.2	336	78	45	43	8	2	6	5	20	0	78	14	1	3	7	.300	1	0	4.98
2000 Potomac	A+ StL	10	10	1	0	62.2	259	70	25	24	5	0	1	1	10	0	42	0	0	5	3	.625	0	0	3.45
Arkansas	AA StL	17	17	0	0	97.1	441	117	68	59	13	6	2	6	35	2	63	5	1	5	6	.455	0	0	5.46
2001 New Haven	AA StL	18	18	0	0	115.1	484	111	55	48	11	4	2	6	34	1	96	5	0	6	8	.429	0	0	3.75
Memphis	AAA StL	10	10	0	0	69.2	291	72	43	33	11	2	5	1	12	1	36	3	0	4	4	.500	0	0	4.26
3 Min. YEARS		69	69	2	0	422.2	1811	448	236	207	48	14	16	19	111	4	315	27	2	23	28	.451	1	0	4.41

J.J. Pearsall

Pitches: Left **Bats:** Left **Pos:** RP-43   **Ht:** 6'2" **Wt:** 202 **Born:** 9/9/73 **Age:** 28

		HOW MUCH HE PITCHED						WHAT HE GAVE UP										THE RESULTS				
Year Team	Lg Org	G	GS	CG	GF	IP	BFP	H	R	ER	HR	SH	SF	HB	TBB	IBB	SO	WP	Bk	W	L	Pct.	ShO	Sv	ERA
1995 San Berndno	A+ LA	6	0	0	2	10.2	54	15	10	10	3	3	0	0	7	0	5	1	0	0	1	.000	0	0	8.44
Yakima	A- LA	20	1	0	8	38.2	167	39	18	14	1	1	2	2	14	0	26	5	0	2	3	.400	0	1	3.26
1996 Savannah	A LA	45	2	0	13	87.2	398	76	48	32	6	3	2	7	46	3	88	8	3	6	5	.545	0	3	3.29
1997 San Berndno	A+ LA	31	28	0	1	160.2	696	145	91	81	12	4	4	8	93	0	112	9	2	14	11	.560	0	0	4.54
1998 San Antonio	AA LA	46	4	0	11	72	320	71	38	35	8	0	2	2	37	2	63	5	0	6	5	.545	0	0	4.38
Albuquerque	AAA LA	8	0	0	4	13	62	16	10	9	1	1	1	1	8	0	7	1	0	1	1	.500	0	1	6.23
1999 San Antonio	AA LA	10	0	0	3	16	75	14	11	8	1	0	1	1	8	0	13	0	0	0	0	—	0	0	4.50
Chattanooga	AA Cin	32	0	0	7	39.2	184	40	31	26	5	0	1	0	28	3	36	2	0	3	1	.750	0	0	5.90
2000 Chattanooga	AA Cin	22	0	0	10	18.1	88	18	16	14	5	1	1	0	15	2	23	1	1	4	1	.800	0	1	6.87
Tulsa	AA Tex	28	0	0	10	43.1	197	42	22	16	3	4	0	6	20	1	37	1	0	4	0	1.000	0	3	3.32
2001 Tulsa	AA Tex	43	0	0	27	58	245	54	27	21	7	3	1	4	18	3	58	2	0	6	4	.600	0	9	3.26
7 Min. YEARS		291	35	0	96	558	2485	528	322	266	52	20	15	32	294	14	469	35	6	46	32	.590	0	19	4.29

Jason Pearson

Pitches: Left **Bats:** Left **Pos:** RP-49; SP-5   **Ht:** 6'0" **Wt:** 195 **Born:** 12/29/75 **Age:** 26

		HOW MUCH HE PITCHED						WHAT HE GAVE UP										THE RESULTS				
Year Team	Lg Org	G	GS	CG	GF	IP	BFP	H	R	ER	HR	SH	SF	HB	TBB	IBB	SO	WP	Bk	W	L	Pct.	ShO	Sv	ERA
1998 Marlins	R Fla	11	3	0	5	34.1	144	28	8	6	0	0	1	1	5	0	36	2	0	4	0	1.000	0	2	1.57
Kane County	A Fla	2	0	0	2	2.2	14	3	3	1	0	0	1	1	1	0	1	0	0	0	0	—	0	0	3.38
1999 Sioux Falls	IND —	27	2	0	11	63.1	271	57	29	21	6	3	5	3	28	2	48	2	0	2	3	.400	0	0	2.98
2000 Fargo-Mh	IND —	18	16	1	0	107.2	455	90	45	36	6	3	2	3	49	1	82	4	1	10	2	.833	0	0	3.01
2001 Mobile	AA SD	54	5	0	16	86.1	371	88	40	40	5	4	6	3	30	3	67	3	0	5	5	.500	0	1	4.17
4 Min. YEARS		112	26	1	34	294.1	1245	266	125	104	17	10	14	11	113	6	234	11	1	21	10	.677	0	3	3.18

Terry Pearson

Pitches: Right **Bats:** Right **Pos:** RP-59 **Ht:** 6'0" **Wt:** 200 **Born:** 11/10/71 **Age:** 30

		HOW MUCH HE PITCHED					WHAT HE GAVE UP													THE RESULTS					
Year Team	Lg Org	G	GS	CG	GF	IP	BFP	H	R	ER	HR	SH	SF	HB	TBB	IBB	SO	WP	Bk	W	L	Pct.	ShO	Sv	ERA
1995 Zanesville	IND —	14	14	0	0	83.2	367	80	45	30	5	5	4	5	37	0	55	2	0	6	2	.750	0	0	3.23
1996 Zanesville	IND —	31	0	0	30	35.2	152	30	12	2	0	2	0	3	8	0	43	2	0	4	1	.800	0	20	0.50
1997 Sioux Falls	IND —	41	0	0	15	62.2	298	85	54	29	5	4	4	3	30	3	46	6	0	2	3	.400	0	1	4.16
2000 Sioux Falls	IND —	19	0	0	13	22.1	103	27	17	11	1	2	0	2	7	2	14	4	0	2	2	.500	0	6	4.43
Duluth-Sup	IND —	18	0	0	8	20.1	94	28	18	15	0	4	0	0	4	0	18	6	0	2	2	.500	0	3	6.64
2001 Erie	AA Det	59	0	0	47	61.1	273	65	26	20	1	4	1	3	16	2	62	5	1	4	4	.500	0	23	2.93
5 Min. YEARS		182	14	0	113	286	1287	315	172	107	12	21	9	16	102	7	238	25	1	20	14	.588	0	53	3.37

Jake Peavy

Pitches: Right **Bats:** Right **Pos:** SP-24 **Ht:** 6'1" **Wt:** 180 **Born:** 5/31/81 **Age:** 21

		HOW MUCH HE PITCHED					WHAT HE GAVE UP													THE RESULTS					
Year Team	Lg Org	G	GS	CG	GF	IP	BFP	H	R	ER	HR	SH	SF	HB	TBB	IBB	SO	WP	Bk	W	L	Pct.	ShO	Sv	ERA
1999 Padres	R SD	13	11	1	0	73.2	286	52	16	11	4	2	0	3	23	0	90	5	3	7	1	.875	0	0	1.34
Idaho Falls	R+ SD	2	2	0	0	11	40	5	0	0	0	0	0	0	1	0	13	0	0	2	0	1.000	0	0	0.00
2000 Fort Wayne	A SD	26	25	0	0	133.2	565	107	61	43	6	4	3	9	53	0	164	8	2	13	8	.619	0	0	2.90
2001 Lk Elsinore	A+ SD	19	19	0	0	105.1	422	76	41	36	6	2	1	6	33	1	144	5	0	7	5	.583	0	0	3.08
Mobile	AA SD	5	5	0	0	28	114	19	8	8	3	0	0	3	12	1	44	1	0	2	1	.667	0	0	2.57
3 Min. YEARS		65	62	1	0	351.2	1427	259	126	98	19	8	4	21	122	2	455	19	5	31	15	.674	0	0	2.51

Jay Pecci

Bats: Both **Throws:** Right **Pos:** 2B-52; SS-47; DH-14; 3B-12; PH-3; PR-1 **Ht:** 5'11" **Wt:** 185 **Born:** 9/26/76 **Age:** 25

		BATTING																BASERUNNING				PERCENTAGES		
Year Team	Lg Org	G	AB	H	2B	3B	HR	TB	R	RBI	TBB	IBB	SO	HBP	SH	SF	SB	CS	SB%	GDP	Avg	OBP	SLG
1998 Sou Oregon	A- Oak	39	130	38	2	0	0	40	21	14	22	0	22	4	1	1	3	4	.43	0	.292	.408	.308
Modesto	A+ Oak	21	73	23	2	1	1	30	9	6	4	0	11	1	2	0	2	1	.67	1	.315	.359	.411
1999 Visalia	A+ Oak	119	377	95	14	2	1	116	60	43	42	0	56	10	7	1	12	7	.63	9	.252	.342	.308
2000 Visalia	A+ Oak	26	102	38	9	0	3	56	21	23	15	2	12	2	0	1	6	4	.60	3	.373	.458	.549
Midland	AA Oak	102	353	87	15	3	2	114	52	36	44	1	50	15	4	5	5	7	.42	13	.246	.350	.323
2001 Midland	AA Oak	125	469	122	31	7	3	176	72	49	42	1	56	26	8	2	16	7	.70	11	.260	.353	.375
4 Min. YEARS		432	1504	403	73	13	10	532	235	171	169	4	207	58	22	10	44	30	.59	37	.268	.362	.354

Mike Peeples

Bats: Right **Throws:** Right **Pos:** OF-84; DH-13; PH-11; 3B-10 **Ht:** 6'0" **Wt:** 175 **Born:** 9/3/76 **Age:** 25

		BATTING																BASERUNNING				PERCENTAGES		
Year Team	Lg Org	G	AB	H	2B	3B	HR	TB	R	RBI	TBB	IBB	SO	HBP	SH	SF	SB	CS	SB%	GDP	Avg	OBP	SLG
1994 Blue Jays	R Tor	47	172	40	5	3	0	51	22	11	13	1	25	4	3	2	17	5	.77	0	.233	.298	.297
1995 Medcine Hat	R+ Tor	72	285	89	14	4	3	120	55	50	35	1	46	5	2	3	27	5	.84	14	.312	.393	.421
1996 Hagerstown	A Tor	74	268	63	15	1	3	89	30	31	37	0	55	3	4	3	15	5	.75	5	.235	.331	.332
1997 Dunedin	A+ Tor	129	477	122	29	2	2	161	73	42	54	1	83	3	9	7	26	16	.62	8	.256	.331	.338
1998 Knoxville	AA Tor	113	395	99	16	3	7	142	58	42	36	0	62	2	17	3	20	10	.67	5	.251	.314	.359
1999 Dunedin	A+ Tor	132	541	156	34	6	20	262	100	68	49	1	80	7	5	5	20	11	.65	7	.288	.352	.484
2000 Tennessee	AA Tor	123	475	133	26	4	18	221	70	73	46	1	71	7	9	4	11	8	.58	14	.280	.350	.465
2001 Colo Sprngs	AAA Col	115	424	127	23	4	19	215	71	69	27	0	63	6	0	5	9	9	.50	11	.300	.346	.507
8 Min. YEARS		805	3037	829	162	27	72	1261	479	386	297	5	485	37	49	32	145	69	.68	64	.273	.342	.415

Alex Pelaez

Bats: Right **Throws:** Right **Pos:** 3B-89; 1B-17; PH-10; P-8; 2B-4; DH-2 **Ht:** 5'9" **Wt:** 190 **Born:** 4/6/76 **Age:** 26

		BATTING																BASERUNNING				PERCENTAGES		
Year Team	Lg Org	G	AB	H	2B	3B	HR	TB	R	RBI	TBB	IBB	SO	HBP	SH	SF	SB	CS	SB%	GDP	Avg	OBP	SLG
1998 Idaho Falls	R+ SD	63	262	89	17	1	8	132	52	51	29	0	32	1	0	2	3	1	.75	10	.340	.405	.504
1999 Las Vegas	AAA SD	5	13	4	0	0	0	4	1	0	0	0	0	0	0	0	0	0	—	1	.308	.308	.308
Rancho Cuca	A+ SD	117	443	132	21	4	4	173	62	54	35	3	53	1	1	2	7	3	.70	24	.298	.349	.391
2000 Rancho Cuca	A+ SD	62	235	66	20	0	2	92	29	28	23	0	27	0	0	4	2	2	.50	11	.281	.340	.391
Las Vegas	AAA SD	34	108	27	3	0	1	33	13	15	4	1	20	1	5	0	0	0	—	2	.250	.281	.306
Mobile	AA SD	28	90	24	3	0	2	33	8	11	10	0	15	0	0	1	0	0	—	5	.267	.337	.367
2001 Mobile	AA SD	114	416	117	22	1	10	171	44	53	32	3	52	2	2	5	2	0	1.00	5	.281	.332	.411
4 Min. YEARS		423	1567	459	86	6	27	638	209	212	133	7	201	5	8	15	14	6	.70	67	.293	.347	.407

Kit Pellow

Bats: Right **Throws:** Right **Pos:** 1B-121; DH-6; PH-2 **Ht:** 6'1" **Wt:** 205 **Born:** 8/28/73 **Age:** 28

		BATTING																BASERUNNING				PERCENTAGES		
Year Team	Lg Org	G	AB	H	2B	3B	HR	TB	R	RBI	TBB	IBB	SO	HBP	SH	SF	SB	CS	SB%	GDP	Avg	OBP	SLG
1996 Spokane	A- KC	71	279	80	18	2	18	156	48	66	20	0	52	8	1	7	8	3	.73	5	.287	.344	.559
1997 Lansing	A KC	65	256	76	17	2	11	130	39	52	24	1	74	6	0	4	2	0	1.00	5	.297	.366	.508
Wichita	AA KC	68	241	60	12	1	10	104	40	41	21	1	72	2	2	3	5	2	.71	5	.249	.311	.432
1998 Wichita	AA KC	103	374	100	24	3	29	217	70	73	27	3	107	6	1	3	4	3	.57	5	.267	.324	.580
Omaha	AAA KC	14	54	10	3	0	2	19	8	6	2	0	19	0	0	1	2	0	1.00	1	.185	.207	.352
1999 Omaha	AAA KC	131	475	136	28	4	35	277	88	99	20	3	117	18	1	7	6	5	.55	11	.286	.335	.583
2000 Omaha	AAA KC	117	421	105	17	3	22	194	61	75	38	1	89	16	1	5	6	4	.60	5	.249	.331	.461
2001 Omaha	AAA KC	129	484	141	15	0	20	216	81	81	37	1	101	13	2	7	4	3	.57	3	.291	.353	.446
6 Min. YEARS		698	2584	708	134	15	147	1313	435	493	189	9	631	69	8	38	37	20	.65	37	.274	.335	.508

Jesus Pena

Pitches: Left **Bats:** Left **Pos:** RP-30; SP-10   **Ht:** 6'0" **Wt:** 170 **Born:** 3/8/75 **Age:** 27

Year Team	Lg Org	G	GS	CG	GF	IP	BFP	H	R	ER	HR	SH	SF	HB	TBB	IBB	SO	WP	Bk	W	L	Pct.	ShO	Sv	ERA
1995 Erie	A- Pit	3	3	0	0	10.2	56	18	16	15	1	1	0	2	7	0	5	0	1	0	3	.000	0	0	12.66
Pirates	R Pit	7	6	0	0	35	138	20	11	10	0	0	0	0	19	0	36	4	0	0	0	—	0	0	2.57
1996 Erie	A- Pit	21	3	0	5	35.2	164	32	24	19	3	2	0	2	24	1	34	2	0	2	5	.286	0	0	4.79
1997 Hickory	A CWS	43	0	0	32	65	263	55	24	16	3	4	3	0	19	1	57	3	0	5	3	.625	0	8	2.22
1998 Winston-Sal	A+ CWS	23	0	0	13	31.2	125	20	11	11	2	2	2	1	12	1	37	0	1	3	4	.429	0	7	3.13
Birmingham	AA CWS	22	0	0	12	23.1	100	20	12	10	3	2	1	0	10	0	28	2	2	0	2	.000	0	2	3.86
1999 Birmingham	AA CWS	40	0	0	18	45.2	183	31	12	12	2	1	1	0	18	1	49	2	1	3	2	.600	0	5	2.36
2000 Charlotte	AAA CWS	21	0	0	9	17.1	69	10	6	6	1	0	0	0	10	0	19	1	1	0	0	—	0	4	3.12
Birmingham	AA CWS	23	0	0	20	21.1	89	19	9	8	2	1	0	2	6	2	25	0	1	1	2	.333	0	10	3.38
2001 Pawtucket	AAA Bos	26	8	0	4	72.1	341	92	59	53	10	2	5	4	38	3	42	3	3	3	5	.375	0	0	6.59
Trenton	AA Bos	14	2	0	7	32	147	46	20	18	6	1	0	0	7	0	35	2	1	2	4	.333	0	1	5.06
1999 Chicago	AL	26	0	0	1	20.1	106	21	15	12	3	1	1	0	23	5	20	3	0	0	0	—	0	0	5.31
2000 Chicago	AL	20	0	0	7	23.1	109	25	18	14	6	0	2	1	16	0	19	1	0	2	1	.667	0	0	5.40
Boston	AL	2	0	0	0	3	14	3	1	1	1	0	0	1	3	0	1	0	0	0	0	—	0	0	3.00
7 Min. YEARS		243	22	0	120	390	1675	363	204	178	33	16	12	11	170	9	367	19	11	19	30	.388	0	37	4.11
2 Maj. YEARS		48	0	0	8	46.2	229	49	34	27	10	1	2	2	42	5	40	4	0	2	1	.667	0	1	5.21

Juan Pena

Pitches: Left **Bats:** Left **Pos:** SP-27   **Ht:** 6'3" **Wt:** 189 **Born:** 6/4/79 **Age:** 23

Year Team	Lg Org	G	GS	CG	GF	IP	BFP	H	R	ER	HR	SH	SF	HB	TBB	IBB	SO	WP	Bk	W	L	Pct.	ShO	Sv	ERA
1997 Athletics	R Oak	14	13	0	0	65	290	54	38	21	0	5	0	2	33	0	67	5	5	6	2	.750	0	0	2.91
1998 Sou Oregon	A- Oak	8	8	0	0	46	194	46	21	11	2	1	1	2	10	1	38	0	3	1	2	.333	0	0	2.15
Modesto	A+ Oak	6	6	0	0	33	154	50	25	19	2	2	1	1	7	0	32	3	0	3	2	.600	0	0	5.18
1999 Visalia	A+ Oak	33	18	0	4	131.1	609	168	106	84	10	3	3	0	61	2	107	9	3	9	5	.643	0	1	5.76
2000 Modesto	A+ Oak	29	27	0	0	154	659	132	85	66	7	5	4	1	75	2	177	16	3	6	9	.400	0	0	3.86
2001 Midland	AA Oak	27	27	0	0	148.1	645	164	88	67	13	4	2	5	46	0	106	4	1	11	9	.550	0	0	4.07
5 Min. YEARS		117	99	0	4	577.2	2551	614	363	268	34	20	11	11	232	5	527	37	15	36	29	.554	0	1	4.18

Mike Penney

Pitches: Right **Bats:** Right **Pos:** RP-33; SP-10   **Ht:** 6'1" **Wt:** 190 **Born:** 3/29/77 **Age:** 25

Year Team	Lg Org	G	GS	CG	GF	IP	BFP	H	R	ER	HR	SH	SF	HB	TBB	IBB	SO	WP	Bk	W	L	Pct.	ShO	Sv	ERA
1998 Helena	R+ Mil	10	10	0	0	46.1	217	63	47	38	8	1	4	2	20	0	36	4	1	1	5	.167	0	0	7.38
1999 Beloit	A Mil	27	27	4	0	170	740	171	94	80	16	2	3	7	70	2	109	11	2	9	12	.429	2	0	4.24
2000 Mudville	A+ Mil	13	13	0	0	66.2	287	63	31	24	3	2	4	6	28	0	45	6	0	2	4	.333	0	0	3.24
Huntsville	AA Mil	20	0	0	11	20.1	83	19	7	6	0	0	0	1	6	0	22	4	0	0	1	.000	0	7	2.66
Indianapolis	AAA Mil	17	0	0	10	18.1	80	16	9	7	2	2	0	0	10	1	13	1	0	1	1	.500	0	1	3.44
2001 Indianapolis	AAA Mil	22	5	0	5	57	254	70	38	34	8	2	2	1	23	0	35	0	0	4	3	.571	0	1	5.37
Huntsville	AA Mil	21	5	0	13	49	222	50	24	18	4	4	2	1	22	0	30	1	0	4	3	.571	0	7	3.31
4 Min. YEARS		130	60	4	39	427.2	1883	452	250	207	41	13	15	18	179	3	290	27	3	21	29	.420	2	16	4.36

Danny Peoples

Bats: Right **Throws:** Right **Pos:** 1B-87; OF-10; DH-8; PH-1   **Ht:** 6'1" **Wt:** 225 **Born:** 1/20/75 **Age:** 27

Year Team	Lg Org	G	AB	H	2B	3B	HR	TB	R	RBI	TBB	IBB	SO	HBP	SH	SF	SB	CS	SB%	GDP	Avg	OBP	SLG
1996 Watertown	A- Cle	35	117	28	7	0	3	44	20	26	28	2	36	2	0	1	3	1	.75	2	.239	.392	.376
1997 Kinston	A+ Cle	121	409	102	21	1	34	227	82	84	84	4	145	6	0	6	8	1	.89	6	.249	.380	.555
1998 Akron	AA Cle	60	222	62	19	0	8	105	30	32	29	1	61	1	0	2	1	1	.50	7	.279	.362	.473
1999 Akron	AA Cle	127	494	124	23	3	21	216	75	78	55	1	142	4	0	2	2	1	.67	9	.251	.330	.437
2000 Buffalo	AAA Cle	124	420	109	19	2	21	195	68	74	63	1	122	4	0	4	2	4	.33	8	.260	.358	.464
2001 Buffalo	AAA Cle	106	370	82	20	1	17	155	62	48	56	1	133	3	0	6	0	3	.00	4	.222	.324	.419
6 Min. YEARS		573	2032	507	109	7	104	942	337	342	315	10	639	20	0	21	16	11	.59	36	.250	.353	.464

Joel Peralta

Pitches: Right **Bats:** Right **Pos:** RP-50   **Ht:** 5'11" **Wt:** 155 **Born:** 3/23/80 **Age:** 22

Year Team	Lg Org	G	GS	CG	GF	IP	BFP	H	R	ER	HR	SH	SF	HB	TBB	IBB	SO	WP	Bk	W	L	Pct.	ShO	Sv	ERA
2000 Butte	R+ Ana	10	1	0	8	19	87	24	15	14	2	1	2	2	10	1	17	2	1	2	1	.667	0	1	6.63
Boise	A- Ana	4	0	0	1	8.1	41	12	6	6	0	0	1	1	5	0	9	0	0	0	0	—	0	0	6.48
2001 Cedar Rapds	A Ana	41	0	0	39	42.1	166	27	13	10	3	2	1	4	5	0	53	0	0	0	0	—	0	23	2.13
Arkansas	AA Ana	9	0	0	9	10	53	15	10	7	2	0	1	2	5	0	14	0	1	0	1	.000	0	2	6.30
2 Min. YEARS		64	1	0	57	79.2	347	78	44	37	7	3	5	9	25	1	93	2	2	2	2	.500	0	26	4.18

Juan Peralta

Bats: Both **Throws:** Right **Pos:** SS-66; DH-5; 2B-2; PR-2; PH-1   **Ht:** 5'11" **Wt:** 155 **Born:** 6/24/83 **Age:** 19

Year Team	Lg Org	G	AB	H	2B	3B	HR	TB	R	RBI	TBB	IBB	SO	HBP	SH	SF	SB	CS	SB%	GDP	Avg	OBP	SLG
2001 Tennessee	AA Tor	3	2	1	0	0	0	1	1	2	0	0	0	0	0	0	0	0	—	0	.500	.500	.500
Medcine Hat	R+ Tor	71	299	69	8	3	0	83	45	13	26	1	47	0	2	2	18	8	.69	3	.231	.291	.278
1 Min. YEAR		74	301	70	8	3	0	84	46	15	26	1	47	0	2	2	18	8	.69	3	.233	.292	.279

Antonio Perez

Bats: Right **Throws:** Right **Pos:** SS-5   **Ht:** 5'11" **Wt:** 175 **Born:** 7/26/81 **Age:** 20

		BATTING															BASERUNNING				PERCENTAGES		
Year Team	Lg Org	G	AB	H	2B	3B	HR	TB	R	RBI	TBB	IBB	SO	HBP	SH	SF	SB	CS	SB%	GDP	Avg	OBP	SLG
1999 Rockford	A Cin	119	385	111	20	3	7	158	69	41	43	0	80	13	8	3	35	24	.59	3	.288	.376	.410
2000 Lancaster	A+ Sea	98	395	109	36	6	17	208	90	63	58	1	99	8	9	4	28	16	.64	3	.276	.376	.527
2001 San Antonio	AA Sea	5	21	3	0	0	0	3	3	0	0	0	7	0	0	0	0	0	—	0	.143	.143	.143
3 Min. YEARS		222	801	223	56	9	24	369	162	104	101	1	186	21	17	7	63	40	.61	6	.278	.371	.461

Carlos Perez

Pitches: Left **Bats:** Left **Pos:** SP-6   **Ht:** 6'3" **Wt:** 210 **Born:** 1/14/71 **Age:** 31

		HOW MUCH HE PITCHED					WHAT HE GAVE UP										THE RESULTS					
Year Team	Lg Org	G	GS	CG	GF	IP	BFP	H	R	ER	HR	SH	SF	HB	TBB	IBB	SO	WP	Bk	W	L	Pct.	ShO	Sv	ERA
1990 Expos	R Mon	13	2	0	6	35.2	145	24	14	10	0	1	1	1	15	0	38	1	0	3	1	.750	0	2	2.52
1991 Sumter	A Mon	16	12	0	2	73.2	306	57	29	20	3	0	7	0	32	0	69	3	1	2	2	.500	0	0	2.44
1992 Rockford	A Mon	7	1	0	2	9.1	43	12	7	6	3	1	0	1	5	0	8	1	0	0	1	.000	0	0	5.79
1993 Burlington	A Mon	12	1	0	5	16.2	69	13	6	6	0	3	0	0	9	0	21	0	1	1	0	1.000	0	0	3.24
San Berndno	A+ Mon	20	18	3	0	131	550	120	57	50	12	3	2	0	44	0	98	9	6	8	7	.533	0	0	3.44
1994 Harrisburg	AA Mon	12	11	2	1	79	307	55	27	17	5	3	0	2	18	0	69	5	0	7	2	.778	2	1	1.94
Ottawa	AAA Mon	17	17	3	0	119	511	130	50	44	8	5	3	3	41	2	82	4	1	7	5	.583	0	0	3.33
1998 Expos	R Mon	1	0	0	0	5	20	5	2	0	1	0	0	1	1	0	2	0	0	1	0	1.000	0	0	0.00
1999 Albuquerque	AAA LA	6	6	2	0	38	168	46	28	25	6	2	1	3	10	0	14	0	1	3	3	.500	0	0	5.92
2001 Las Vegas	AAA LA	6	6	0	0	30.1	142	44	22	22	3	0	0	1	11	0	20	1	0	2	1	.667	0	0	6.53
1995 Montreal	NL	28	23	2	2	141.1	592	142	61	58	18	6	1	5	28	2	106	8	4	10	8	.556	1	0	3.69
1997 Montreal	NL	33	32	8	0	206.2	857	206	109	89	21	5	7	4	48	1	110	2	1	12	13	.480	5	0	3.88
1998 Montreal	NL	23	23	3	0	163.1	690	177	79	68	12	11	3	3	33	3	82	5	1	7	10	.412	0	0	3.75
Los Angeles	NL	11	11	4	0	77.2	319	67	30	28	9	3	0	0	30	1	46	2	0	4	4	.500	2	0	3.24
1999 Los Angeles	NL	17	16	0	0	89.2	420	116	77	74	23	6	3	6	39	1	40	2	3	2	10	.167	0	0	7.43
2000 Los Angeles	NL	30	22	0	1	144	641	192	95	89	25	6	2	8	33	1	64	3	1	5	8	.385	0	0	5.56
8 Min. YEARS		110	74	10	16	537.2	2261	504	244	200	41	18	14	11	186	2	421	24	10	34	22	.607	2	4	3.35
5 Maj. YEARS		142	127	17	3	822.2	3519	900	451	406	108	37	16	26	211	9	448	22	10	40	53	.430	8	0	4.44

Jerson Perez

Bats: Right **Throws:** Right **Pos:** SS-113; 2B-7; PH-2; PR-1   **Ht:** 5'10" **Wt:** 185 **Born:** 1/20/76 **Age:** 26

		BATTING															BASERUNNING				PERCENTAGES		
Year Team	Lg Org	G	AB	H	2B	3B	HR	TB	R	RBI	TBB	IBB	SO	HBP	SH	SF	SB	CS	SB%	GDP	Avg	OBP	SLG
1996 Mets	R NYM	40	151	42	5	3	0	53	24	12	17	1	18	1	0	0	7	2	.78	2	.278	.355	.351
Kingsport	R+ NYM	6	17	3	0	0	0	3	4	3	5	0	6	0	0	2	0	0	—	2	.176	.333	.176
Pittsfield	A- NYM	1	3	1	0	0	0	1	1	0	1	0	1	0	0	0	0	0	—	0	.333	.500	.333
1997 Kingsport	R+ NYM	65	258	69	10	2	3	92	45	29	7	0	41	3	0	2	12	7	.63	4	.267	.293	.357
Capital Cty	A NYM	2	6	4	3	0	0	7	3	2	0	0	0	1	0	0	1	0	1.00	0	.667	.714	1.167
1998 Capital Cty	A NYM	120	488	136	18	10	7	195	72	64	18	0	128	3	5	11	14	4	.78	6	.279	.302	.400
1999 St. Lucie	A+ NYM	128	468	120	15	7	7	170	60	45	27	0	117	8	9	3	7	5	.58	10	.256	.306	.363
2000 Dunedin	A+ Tor	126	509	138	35	7	8	211	69	64	20	0	106	4	8	5	8	4	.67	11	.271	.301	.415
2001 Syracuse	AAA Tor	5	16	2	1	0	0	3	1	0	1	0	7	0	1	0	0	0	—	0	.125	.176	.188
Tennessee	AA Tor	116	422	119	23	4	4	162	60	49	30	0	96	5	5	4	14	3	.82	7	.282	.334	.384
6 Min. YEARS		609	2338	634	110	33	29	897	339	268	126	1	520	25	28	27	63	25	.72	42	.271	.312	.384

Jhonny Perez

Bats: Right **Throws:** Right **Pos:** 2B-89; SS-27; PH-1   **Ht:** 5'10" **Wt:** 180 **Born:** 10/23/76 **Age:** 25

		BATTING															BASERUNNING				PERCENTAGES		
Year Team	Lg Org	G	AB	H	2B	3B	HR	TB	R	RBI	TBB	IBB	SO	HBP	SH	SF	SB	CS	SB%	GDP	Avg	OBP	SLG
1994 Astros	R Hou	36	144	46	12	2	1	65	37	27	15	1	16	1	1	1	18	3	.86	4	.319	.385	.451
1995 Kissimmee	A+ Hou	65	214	58	12	0	4	82	24	31	22	1	37	7	0	0	23	7	.77	5	.271	.358	.383
1996 Kissimmee	A+ Hou	90	322	87	20	2	12	147	54	49	26	1	70	2	3	0	16	16	.50	3	.270	.329	.457
1997 Kissimmee	A+ Hou	69	273	72	16	5	3	107	40	22	12	0	38	1	2	3	8	6	.57	5	.264	.294	.392
Jackson	AA Hou	48	154	39	7	0	3	55	16	17	12	0	26	1	1	0	4	3	.57	2	.253	.311	.357
1998 Jackson	AA Hou	130	439	125	20	0	10	175	65	39	45	4	72	1	6	0	22	11	.67	9	.285	.353	.399
1999 Jackson	AA Hou	76	276	69	16	4	4	105	37	25	19	0	44	1	6	2	7	8	.47	8	.250	.299	.380
2000 Kissimmee	A+ Hou	13	51	18	1	0	0	19	6	4	5	0	8	0	1	0	5	2	.71	1	.353	.411	.373
Round Rock	AA Hou	79	273	81	9	1	7	113	44	31	17	0	40	1	5	0	14	4	.78	6	.297	.340	.414
2001 Erie	AA Det	83	293	78	13	3	5	112	42	30	20	0	46	2	4	3	10	4	.71	9	.266	.314	.382
Toledo	AAA Det	32	120	30	7	2	1	44	19	14	9	0	24	1	3	1	7	2	.78	2	.250	.305	.367
8 Min. YEARS		721	2559	703	133	19	50	1024	384	289	202	7	421	18	32	10	134	66	.67	54	.275	.331	.400

Josue Perez

Bats: Both **Throws:** Right **Pos:** OF-58; PH-3   **Ht:** 6'0" **Wt:** 180 **Born:** 8/12/77 **Age:** 24

		BATTING															BASERUNNING				PERCENTAGES		
Year Team	Lg Org	G	AB	H	2B	3B	HR	TB	R	RBI	TBB	IBB	SO	HBP	SH	SF	SB	CS	SB%	GDP	Avg	OBP	SLG
1999 Vero Beach	A+ LA	62	201	56	14	1	2	78	24	22	21	0	29	2	1	2	14	11	.56	5	.279	.350	.388
Clearwater	A+ Phi	23	93	23	2	0	0	25	15	6	7	0	17	1	0	2	6	1	.86	3	.247	.301	.269
2000 Clearwater	A+ Phi	70	279	83	9	8	3	117	41	32	28	2	48	6	3	3	18	14	.56	2	.297	.370	.419
Reading	AA Phi	32	96	23	5	1	1	33	10	8	9	0	19	0	1	1	2	5	.29	1	.240	.302	.344
2001 Reading	AA Phi	50	167	28	4	0	1	35	12	6	14	1	38	1	1	0	3	3	.50	2	.168	.236	.210
Phillies	R Phi	10	39	12	3	1	0	17	9	3	5	0	4	0	0	0	3	1	.75	2	.308	.386	.436
3 Min. YEARS		247	875	225	37	11	7	305	111	77	84	3	155	10	6	8	46	35	.57	15	.257	.327	.349

229

Dan Perkins

Pitches: Right **Bats:** Right **Pos:** SP-1　　　　　　　　　**Ht:** 6'2" **Wt:** 193 **Born:** 3/15/75 **Age:** 27

Year Team	Lg Org	G	GS	CG	GF	IP	BFP	H	R	ER	HR	SH	SF	HB	TBB	IBB	SO	WP	Bk	W	L	Pct.	ShO	Sv	ERA
1993 Elizabethtn	R+ Min	10	10	0	0	45	210	46	33	25	3	1	1	5	25	0	30	5	1	3	3	.500	0	0	5.00
1994 Fort Wayne	A Min	12	12	0	0	50.2	229	61	38	35	3	3	1	4	22	1	34	4	1	1	8	.111	0	0	6.22
Elizabethtn	R+ Min	10	9	1	0	54	223	51	31	22	2	2	1	7	14	0	34	9	1	0	2	.000	0	0	3.67
1995 Fort Wayne	A Min	29	22	0	2	121.1	562	133	86	74	3	3	4	13	69	1	89	22	2	7	12	.368	0	0	5.49
1996 Fort Myers	A+ Min	39	13	3	10	136.2	557	125	52	45	5	4	6	11	37	1	111	9	1	13	7	.650	1	2	2.96
1997 New Britain	AA Min	24	24	2	0	144.2	644	158	94	79	17	8	2	11	53	1	114	10	0	7	10	.412	0	0	4.91
1998 New Britain	AA Min	20	19	1	0	117.2	508	140	64	52	8	3	3	3	31	1	79	6	0	13	5	.722	1	0	3.98
Salt Lake	AAA Min	7	7	1	0	46.2	205	48	30	25	8	0	2	2	20	1	33	2	0	5	0	1.000	0	0	4.82
1999 Salt Lake	AAA Min	3	2	0	0	12.2	57	11	6	6	3	0	0	2	4	0	7	3	0	0	0	—	0	0	4.26
2000 Salt Lake	AAA Min	33	22	0	3	141	667	207	131	115	26	1	7	5	51	0	97	6	3	9	10	.474	0	1	7.34
2001 Akron	AA Cle	1	1	0	0	3	16	7	5	5	1	0	0	0	0	0	4	0	0	0	0	—	0	0	15.00
1999 Minnesota	AL	29	12	0	7	86.2	413	117	69	63	14	2	4	5	43	0	44	6	2	1	7	.125	0	0	6.54
9 Min. YEARS		188	141	8	15	873.1	3878	987	570	483	79	25	27	63	326	6	632	76	9	58	57	.504	2	3	4.98

Mike Perkins

Pitches: Right **Bats:** Right **Pos:** RP-13; SP-6　　　　　　　**Ht:** 6'1" **Wt:** 195 **Born:** 5/29/79 **Age:** 23

Year Team	Lg Org	G	GS	CG	GF	IP	BFP	H	R	ER	HR	SH	SF	HB	TBB	IBB	SO	WP	Bk	W	L	Pct.	ShO	Sv	ERA
1999 Johnson Cty	R+ StL	15	11	0	1	61.2	270	71	34	28	2	0	2	2	19	0	50	1	2	6	1	.857	0	0	4.09
2000 Peoria	A StL	8	6	0	0	23.2	116	31	23	12	1	0	2	0	14	0	28	4	0	2	3	.400	0	0	4.56
New Jersey	A- StL	15	15	0	0	84.1	376	85	47	40	4	1	4	7	41	0	77	3	0	5	6	.455	0	0	4.27
2001 New Haven	AA StL	1	1	0	0	3	17	6	4	4	1	0	0	2	2	0	2	0	0	0	1	.000	0	0	12.00
Peoria	A StL	7	0	0	0	11.1	43	3	2	1	0	0	1	0	2	0	8	1	0	0	0	—	0	0	0.79
Potomac	A+ StL	11	5	0	1	29.2	130	32	15	13	2	1	0	1	13	0	25	3	0	1	3	.250	0	0	3.94
3 Min. YEARS		57	38	0	2	213.2	952	228	125	98	10	2	9	12	91	0	190	12	2	14	14	.500	0	0	4.13

Marco Pernalete

Bats: Both **Throws:** Right **Pos:** 2B-32; 3B-31; SS-16; DH-13; 1B-11; PH-9; PR-1　　**Ht:** 6'0" **Wt:** 155 **Born:** 10/12/78 **Age:** 23

Year Team	Lg Org	G	AB	H	2B	3B	HR	TB	R	RBI	TBB	IBB	SO	HBP	SH	SF	SB	CS	SB%	GDP	Avg	OBP	SLG
1997 Bakersfield	A+ SF	17	37	10	0	0	0	10	6	2	2	0	7	1	1	0	0	1	.00	0	.270	.325	.270
1998 Bakersfield	A+ SF	73	190	44	6	0	0	50	19	12	11	0	52	2	4	0	5	1	.83	1	.232	.281	.263
1999 San Jose	A+ SF	99	370	88	19	0	3	116	50	32	30	1	105	5	5	2	10	3	.77	2	.238	.302	.314
2000 Bakersfield	A+ SF	91	301	77	16	1	5	110	53	27	57	2	88	3	6	1	15	3	.83	5	.256	.378	.365
2001 Fresno	AAA SF	32	101	31	7	2	2	48	9	11	10	1	22	0	0	1	1	0	1.00	1	.307	.366	.475
Shreveport	AA SF	29	93	26	5	1	2	39	9	12	9	0	17	2	1	5	1	0	1.00	1	.280	.339	.419
San Jose	A+ SF	48	171	60	11	1	2	79	25	22	17	1	45	2	0	2	3	1	.75	0	.351	.411	.462
5 Min. YEARS		389	1263	336	64	5	14	452	171	118	136	5	336	15	17	11	34	10	.77	10	.266	.342	.358

Chan Perry

Bats: Right **Throws:** Right **Pos:** 1B-68; OF-14; DH-11; PH-6; 3B-5　　**Ht:** 6'2" **Wt:** 200 **Born:** 9/13/72 **Age:** 29

Year Team	Lg Org	G	AB	H	2B	3B	HR	TB	R	RBI	TBB	IBB	SO	HBP	SH	SF	SB	CS	SB%	GDP	Avg	OBP	SLG
1994 Burlington	R+ Cle	52	185	58	16	1	5	91	28	32	18	0	28	1	0	4	6	0	1.00	9	.314	.370	.492
1995 Columbus	A Cle	113	411	117	30	4	9	182	64	50	53	1	49	2	2	4	7	2	.78	6	.285	.366	.443
1996 Kinston	A+ Cle	96	358	104	27	1	10	163	44	62	36	3	33	2	3	3	2	3	.40	9	.291	.356	.455
1997 Akron	AA Cle	119	476	150	34	2	20	248	74	96	28	0	61	5	1	6	3	3	.50	14	.315	.355	.521
1998 Buffalo	AAA Cle	13	49	11	4	0	0	15	8	3	6	0	10	2	0	0	1	0	1.00	0	.224	.333	.306
Akron	AA Cle	54	203	57	17	2	5	93	36	27	23	1	43	0	0	1	3	2	.60	2	.281	.352	.458
1999 Akron	AA Cle	37	154	43	14	0	7	78	24	30	11	0	27	1	0	1	1	0	1.00	3	.279	.329	.506
Buffalo	AAA Cle	79	273	77	17	0	10	124	44	59	19	0	34	3	3	7	5	1	.83	9	.282	.328	.454
2000 Buffalo	AAA Cle	92	362	107	18	1	10	157	48	65	21	0	55	3	0	4	1	2	.33	9	.296	.336	.434
2001 Richmond	AAA Atl	98	350	96	15	3	8	141	38	39	19	2	60	3	1	1	6	14	.13	14	.274	.316	.403
2000 Cleveland	AL	13	14	1	0	0	0	1	1	0	0	0	5	0	0	0	0	0	—	1	.071	.071	.071
8 Min. YEARS		753	2821	820	192	14	84	1292	408	463	234	7	400	22	10	31	30	19	.61	74	.291	.346	.458

Mark Persails

Pitches: Right **Bats:** Right **Pos:** RP-13; SP-12　　　　　　**Ht:** 6'3" **Wt:** 190 **Born:** 10/25/75 **Age:** 26

Year Team	Lg Org	G	GS	CG	GF	IP	BFP	H	R	ER	HR	SH	SF	HB	TBB	IBB	SO	WP	Bk	W	L	Pct.	ShO	Sv	ERA
1995 Tigers	R Det	11	10	0	0	51	237	50	37	25	4	3	5	4	25	0	30	8	1	1	4	.200	0	0	4.41
1996 Jamestown	A- Det	13	13	0	0	63.2	275	53	35	30	6	1	0	6	29	0	37	6	0	1	4	.200	0	0	4.24
1997 Jamestown	A- Det	15	14	2	1	84.2	384	103	64	54	5	1	3	3	33	1	56	13	0	3	7	.300	0	0	5.74
1998 W Michigan	A Det	39	3	0	15	92.1	372	75	33	29	7	7	1	3	29	0	64	4	0	11	5	.688	0	2	2.83
1999 Kissimmee	A+ Hou	10	0	0	2	20.1	92	26	9	5	1	0	0	1	4	0	15	3	0	1	1	.500	0	0	2.21
Jackson	AA Hou	12	0	0	2	19.2	82	15	5	3	1	1	0	1	10	0	20	2	0	1	0	1.000	0	0	1.37
2000 Round Rock	AA Hou	50	2	0	16	78.1	375	101	64	55	10	7	3	4	41	4	63	8	0	3	2	.600	0	3	6.32
2001 Round Rock	AA Hou	1	0	0	0	1.1	6	2	2	2	0	0	0	0	0	0	1	2	0	0	0	—	0	0	13.50
Lakeland	A+ Det	3	0	0	2	6.2	26	6	2	2	1	0	0	1	0	0	6	0	0	0	1	.000	0	1	2.84
Erie	AA Det	9	7	0	1	38.1	188	62	37	31	5	1	5	1	18	0	15	3	0	1	4	.200	0	0	7.28
Toledo	AAA Det	12	5	0	4	48.1	218	53	37	31	5	2	3	2	21	0	24	1	0	2	3	.400	0	0	5.77
7 Min. YEARS		175	54	2	43	504.1	2255	546	325	267	45	25	18	25	211	5	331	50	1	24	30	.444	0	6	4.76

Tommy Peterman

Bats: Left **Throws:** Left **Pos:** 1B-76; DH-9; PH-5   **Ht:** 6'0" **Wt:** 228 **Born:** 5/21/75 **Age:** 27

Year Team	Lg Org	BATTING																BASERUNNING				PERCENTAGES		
		G	AB	H	2B	3B	HR	TB	R	RBI	TBB	IBB	SO	HBP	SH	SF	SB	CS	SB%	GDP	Avg	OBP	SLG
1996 Elizabethtn	R+ Min	3	10	3	0	0	1	6	5	4	5	0	1	0	0	0	0	0	—	0	.300	.533	.600
Fort Wayne	A Min	58	176	45	11	0	3	65	17	28	10	3	30	2	0	3	0	1	.00	1	.256	.298	.369
1997 Fort Wayne	A Min	113	417	122	22	0	7	165	46	57	28	4	69	1	1	5	0	4	.00	9	.293	.335	.396
1998 Fort Myers	A+ Min	135	519	162	36	2	20	262	71	110	63	13	86	4	1	6	2	0	1.00	11	.312	.387	.505
1999 New Britain	AA Min	140	538	141	28	0	20	229	68	84	61	5	84	3	0	4	1	2	.33	10	.262	.338	.426
2000 New Britain	AA Min	118	394	107	18	1	9	154	54	43	34	2	54	3	1	2	2	1	.67	13	.272	.333	.391
2001 New Britain	AA Min	88	302	72	16	1	3	99	35	34	21	1	40	2	2	1	1	1	.50	11	.238	.291	.328
6 Min. YEARS		655	2356	652	131	4	63	980	296	360	222	28	364	15	5	21	6	9	.40	55	.277	.340	.416

Tony Peters

Bats: Right **Throws:** Right **Pos:** OF-66; 1B-19; PH-14; 3B-7; PR-7; C-3   **Ht:** 6'2" **Wt:** 210 **Born:** 10/28/74 **Age:** 27

Year Team	Lg Org	BATTING																BASERUNNING				PERCENTAGES		
		G	AB	H	2B	3B	HR	TB	R	RBI	TBB	IBB	SO	HBP	SH	SF	SB	CS	SB%	GDP	Avg	OBP	SLG
1995 Brewers	R Mil	51	172	42	8	2	2	60	25	24	29	0	55	2	1	0	9	3	.75	2	.244	.360	.349
1996 Beloit	A Mil	71	179	46	13	3	2	71	20	23	18	0	47	0	1	1	5	1	.83	3	.257	.323	.397
1997 Beloit	A Mil	113	375	88	16	6	9	143	50	43	31	0	110	1	5	1	21	7	.75	8	.235	.294	.381
1998 Hagerstown	A Tor	104	327	99	12	1	10	143	58	35	25	0	72	3	3	0	15	7	.68	8	.303	.358	.437
1999 Dunedin	A+ Tor	116	316	77	12	2	14	135	58	50	44	1	97	6	4	3	15	4	.79	3	.244	.344	.427
2000 Dunedin	A+ Tor	127	455	122	30	2	15	201	97	61	71	1	164	7	4	3	23	8	.74	9	.268	.373	.442
2001 Tennessee	AA Tor	91	256	63	9	1	11	107	46	33	25	0	83	4	4	1	8	1	.89	5	.246	.322	.418
7 Min. YEARS		673	2080	537	100	17	63	860	354	269	243	2	628	23	22	9	96	31	.76	38	.258	.341	.413

Chris Petersen

Bats: Right **Throws:** Right **Pos:** 2B-50; SS-43; PH-9; 3B-8   **Ht:** 5'11" **Wt:** 175 **Born:** 11/6/70 **Age:** 31

Year Team	Lg Org	BATTING																BASERUNNING				PERCENTAGES		
		G	AB	H	2B	3B	HR	TB	R	RBI	TBB	IBB	SO	HBP	SH	SF	SB	CS	SB%	GDP	Avg	OBP	SLG
1992 Geneva	A- ChC	71	244	55	8	0	1	66	36	23	32	0	69	4	9	2	11	7	.61	4	.225	.323	.270
1993 Daytona	A+ ChC	130	473	101	10	0	0	111	66	28	58	0	105	9	17	1	19	11	.63	10	.214	.311	.235
1994 Orlando	AA ChC	117	376	85	12	3	1	106	34	26	37	0	89	2	16	1	8	11	.42	7	.226	.298	.282
1995 Orlando	AA ChC	125	382	81	10	3	4	109	48	36	45	3	97	4	5	3	7	3	.70	14	.212	.300	.285
1996 Orlando	AA ChC	47	152	45	3	4	2	62	21	12	18	0	31	5	0	1	3	5	.38	5	.296	.386	.408
Iowa	AAA ChC	63	194	48	6	3	2	66	12	23	12	1	46	1	2	1	1	2	.33	4	.247	.293	.340
1997 Iowa	AAA ChC	119	391	94	16	2	3	123	49	33	32	4	89	6	4	3	1	6	.14	15	.240	.306	.315
1998 Iowa	AAA ChC	118	389	91	16	2	8	135	54	41	21	3	100	7	5	2	2	4	.33	12	.234	.284	.347
1999 Colo Sprngs	AAA Col	107	370	96	21	1	6	137	56	34	29	1	85	7	3	2	4	0	1.00	12	.259	.324	.370
2000 Iowa	AAA ChC	9	18	1	1	0	0	2	1	0	2	0	5	0	0	0	0	0	—	1	.056	.150	.111
Richmond	AAA Atl	79	252	57	10	0	0	67	12	21	14	0	42	2	6	1	2	4	.33	4	.226	.271	.266
2001 Altoona	AA Pit	38	100	21	6	0	0	27	7	11	17	0	20	2	1	1	1	2	.33	4	.210	.333	.270
Nashville	AAA Pit	21	55	21	5	0	2	32	9	18	3	0	15	3	1	1	0	2	.00	0	.382	.435	.582
Tucson	AAA Ari	43	123	26	2	0	2	34	16	8	8	1	18	3	5	1	2	0	1.00	6	.211	.274	.276
1999 Colorado	NL	7	13	2	0	0	0	2	1	2	2	0	3	0	0	0	0	0	—	0	.154	.267	.154
10 Min. YEARS		1087	3519	822	126	18	31	1077	421	314	328	13	811	55	74	20	61	57	.52	98	.234	.307	.306

Tommy Phelps

Pitches: Left **Bats:** Left **Pos:** RP-42; SP-2   **Ht:** 6'3" **Wt:** 192 **Born:** 3/4/74 **Age:** 28

Year Team	Lg Org	HOW MUCH HE PITCHED						WHAT HE GAVE UP											THE RESULTS					
		G	GS	CG	GF	IP	BFP	H	R	ER	HR	SH	SF	HB	TBB	IBB	SO	WP	Bk	W	L	Pct.	ShO	Sv	ERA
1993 Burlington	A Mon	8	8	0	0	41	173	36	18	17	4	1	1	1	13	0	33	2	0	2	4	.333	0	0	3.73
Jamestown	A- Mon	16	15	1	0	92.1	416	102	62	47	4	4	3	5	37	1	74	7	1	3	8	.273	0	0	4.58
1994 Burlington	A Mon	23	23	1	0	118.1	534	143	91	73	9	7	7	5	48	1	82	7	0	8	8	.500	1	0	5.55
1995 Wst Plm Bch	A+ Mon	2	2	0	0	5	33	10	10	9	0	0	0	0	11	0	5	2	0	0	2	.000	0	0	16.20
Albany	A Mon	24	24	1	0	135.1	597	142	76	50	6	0	4	5	45	0	119	5	1	10	9	.526	0	0	3.33
1996 Wst Plm Bch	A+ Mon	18	18	1	0	112	468	105	42	36	5	4	1	2	35	0	71	8	0	10	2	.833	1	0	2.89
Harrisburg	AA Mon	8	8	2	0	47.1	195	43	16	13	3	2	0	1	19	2	23	0	0	2	2	.500	2	0	2.47
1997 Harrisburg	AA Mon	18	18	0	0	101.1	462	115	68	53	14	8	5	5	39	1	86	3	1	10	6	.625	0	0	4.71
1998 Jupiter	A+ Mon	7	7	0	0	41	181	42	21	20	3	0	2	2	15	0	21	1	0	2	2	.500	0	0	4.39
Harrisburg	AA Mon	12	10	0	0	59.2	247	57	29	24	5	4	3	0	26	0	26	2	0	5	4	.556	0	0	3.62
1999 Harrisburg	AA Mon	13	13	1	0	64.2	306	73	53	41	13	3	6	7	26	0	36	2	0	3	6	.333	0	0	5.71
2000 Jacksnville	AA Det	38	11	0	0	102	435	111	59	56	17	1	0	7	26	2	62	1	0	6	6	.500	0	0	4.94
2001 Toledo	AAA Det	29	0	0	8	59.2	271	74	30	24	4	0	1	3	19	3	53	1	0	3	2	.600	0	1	3.62
Erie	AA Det	15	2	0	5	32.2	139	33	14	13	1	3	2	3	8	2	31	2	0	1	1	.500	0	2	3.58
9 Min. YEARS		231	159	7	20	1012.1	4457	1089	589	476	88	37	35	46	367	12	722	43	3	65	62	.512	4	3	4.23

Andy Phillips

Bats: Right **Throws:** Right **Pos:** 2B-120; DH-6   **Ht:** 6'0" **Wt:** 205 **Born:** 4/6/77 **Age:** 25

Year Team	Lg Org	BATTING																BASERUNNING				PERCENTAGES		
		G	AB	H	2B	3B	HR	TB	R	RBI	TBB	IBB	SO	HBP	SH	SF	SB	CS	SB%	GDP	Avg	OBP	SLG
1999 Staten Ilnd	A- NYY	64	233	75	11	7	7	121	35	48	37	1	40	3	0	3	3	3	.50	4	.322	.417	.519
2000 Tampa	A+ NYY	127	478	137	33	2	13	213	66	58	46	0	98	2	0	8	2	0	1.00	9	.287	.346	.446
Norwich	AA NYY	7	28	7	2	1	0	11	5	3	3	0	11	0	1	0	1	0	1.00	1	.250	.323	.393
2001 Norwich	AA NYY	51	183	49	9	2	6	80	23	25	21	2	54	0	0	2	1	0	1.00	6	.268	.340	.437
Tampa	A+ NYY	75	288	82	17	4	11	145	43	50	25	1	55	3	1	10	3	3	.50	6	.302	.353	.503
3 Min. YEARS		324	1210	355	72	16	37	570	172	184	132	4	258	8	2	23	10	6	.63	26	.293	.361	.471

Brandon Phillips

Bats: Right **Throws:** Right **Pos:** SS-121; 2B-1; 3B-1; DH-1   **Ht:** 5'11" **Wt:** 185 **Born:** 6/28/81 **Age:** 21

		BATTING														BASERUNNING				PERCENTAGES		
Year Team	Lg Org	G	AB	H	2B	3B	HR	TB	R	RBI	TBB	IBB	SO	HBP	SH	SF	SB	CS	SB%	GDP	Avg	OBP	SLG
1999 Expos	R Mon	47	169	49	11	3	1	69	23	21	15	0	35	3	0	0	12	3	.80	6	.290	.358	.408
2000 Cape Fear	A Mon	126	484	117	17	8	11	183	74	72	38	3	97	9	0	5	23	8	.74	11	.242	.306	.378
2001 Jupiter	A+ Mon	55	194	55	12	2	4	83	36	23	38	0	45	6	0	1	17	3	.85	3	.284	.414	.428
Harrisburg	AA Mon	67	265	79	19	0	7	119	35	36	12	0	42	4	1	1	13	6	.68	9	.298	.337	.449
3 Min. YEARS		295	1112	300	59	13	23	454	168	152	103	3	219	22	1	7	65	20	.76	29	.270	.342	.408

J.R. Phillips

Bats: Left **Throws:** Left **Pos:** 1B-29; OF-1; PH-1   **Ht:** 6'1" **Wt:** 205 **Born:** 4/29/70 **Age:** 32

		BATTING														BASERUNNING				PERCENTAGES		
Year Team	Lg Org	G	AB	H	2B	3B	HR	TB	R	RBI	TBB	IBB	SO	HBP	SH	SF	SB	CS	SB%	GDP	Avg	OBP	SLG
1988 Bend	A- Ana	56	210	40	8	0	4	60	24	23	21	1	70	1	1	3	3	1	.75	5	.190	.264	.286
1989 Quad City	A Ana	125	442	85	29	1	8	140	41	50	49	2	146	4	4	4	3	3	.50	5	.192	.277	.317
1990 Palm Spring	A+ Ana	46	162	32	4	1	1	41	14	15	10	1	58	1	1	1	3	1	.75	7	.198	.247	.253
Boise	A- Ana	68	238	46	6	0	10	82	30	34	19	0	78	0	1	2	1	1	.50	4	.193	.251	.345
1991 Palm Spring	A+ Ana	130	471	117	22	2	20	203	64	70	57	4	144	3	1	2	15	13	.54	8	.248	.332	.431
1992 Midland	AA Ana	127	449	118	32	4	14	200	58	77	32	4	165	2	1	4	5	3	.63	9	.237	.284	.402
1993 Phoenix	AAA SF	134	506	133	35	2	27	253	80	94	53	9	127	6	0	6	7	5	.58	2	.263	.336	.500
1994 Phoenix	AAA SF	95	360	108	28	5	27	227	69	79	45	4	96	4	0	2	4	5	.44	4	.300	.382	.631
1996 Scranton-WB	AAA Phi	53	200	57	14	2	13	114	33	42	19	0	53	1	0	2	2	2	.50	9	.285	.347	.570
1997 New Orleans	AAA Hou	104	411	119	28	0	21	210	59	71	39	3	112	0	0	4	0	1	.00	11	.290	.348	.511
1998 New Orleans	AAA Hou	56	225	68	18	0	21	149	51	60	21	2	65	1	0	2	1	1	.50	4	.302	.361	.662
1999 Colo Sprngs	AAA Col	124	479	149	22	0	41	294	87	100	54	6	143	1	0	4	4	3	.57	13	.311	.380	.614
2000 Charlotte	AAA CWS	59	210	46	9	0	10	85	22	35	18	1	65	1	0	2	3	0	1.00	6	.219	.281	.405
New Orleans	AAA Hou	73	269	72	8	0	14	122	35	52	28	4	77	4	0	3	1	0	1.00	4	.268	.342	.454
2001 Carolina	AA Col	31	119	35	8	0	8	67	18	23	12	3	33	1	0	0	1	0	.00	1	.294	.364	.563
1993 San Francisco	NL	11	16	5	1	1	1	11	1	4	0	0	5	0	0	0	0	0	—	0	.313	.313	.688
1994 San Francisco	NL	15	38	5	0	0	1	8	1	3	1	0	13	0	0	1	0	1	1.00	1	.132	.150	.211
1995 San Francisco	NL	92	231	45	9	0	9	81	27	28	19	2	69	0	2	0	1	1	.50	3	.195	.256	.351
1996 San Francisco	NL	15	25	5	0	0	2	11	3	5	1	0	13	0	0	0	0	0	—	0	.200	.231	.440
Philadelphia	NL	35	79	12	5	0	5	32	9	10	10	1	38	1	0	0	0	0	—	0	.152	.256	.405
1997 Houston	NL	13	15	2	0	0	1	5	2	4	0	0	7	0	0	1	0	0	—	0	.133	.125	.333
1998 Houston	NL	36	58	11	0	0	2	17	4	9	7	1	22	0	0	0	0	0	—	1	.190	.277	.293
1999 Colorado	NL	25	39	9	4	0	2	19	5	4	0	0	13	1	0	0	0	0	—	1	.231	.250	.487
13 Min. YEARS		1281	4799	1225	271	17	239	2247	685	825	477	44	1432	30	9	40	52	40	.57	92	.255	.324	.468
7 Maj. YEARS		242	501	94	19	1	23	184	52	67	38	4	180	2	2	2	2	1	.67	6	.188	.247	.367

Jason Phillips

Pitches: Right **Bats:** Right **Pos:** RP-14; SP-10   **Ht:** 6'6" **Wt:** 225 **Born:** 3/22/74 **Age:** 28

		HOW MUCH HE PITCHED						WHAT HE GAVE UP											THE RESULTS					
Year Team	Lg Org	G	GS	CG	GF	IP	BFP	H	R	ER	HR	SH	SF	HB	TBB	IBB	SO	WP	Bk	W	L	Pct.	ShO	Sv	ERA
1992 Pirates	R Pit	4	4	0	0	17	88	21	21	16	0	1	1	0	13	0	10	4	4	1	2	.333	0	0	8.47
1993 Welland	A- Pit	14	14	0	0	71.1	323	60	44	28	2	1	2	9	36	0	66	15	4	4	6	.400	0	0	3.53
1994 Augusta	A Pit	23	23	1	0	108.1	531	118	97	81	4	3	4	12	88	1	108	21	3	6	12	.333	0	0	6.73
1995 Augusta	A Pit	30	6	0	3	80	354	76	46	32	2	2	2	0	53	1	65	10	0	4	3	.571	0	0	3.60
1996 Augusta	A Pit	14	14	1	0	89.2	366	79	35	24	3	2	3	6	29	1	75	9	1	5	4	.556	1	0	2.41
Lynchburg	A+ Pit	13	13	1	0	73.2	343	82	47	37	3	2	2	5	35	0	63	6	1	5	6	.455	1	0	4.52
1997 Lynchburg	A+ Pit	23	23	2	0	138.2	577	129	66	58	10	4	2	6	35	0	140	9	1	11	6	.647	1	0	3.76
Carolina	AA Pit	4	4	2	0	31	127	21	8	8	1	1	2	4	9	0	22	2	0	1	2	.333	1	0	2.32
1998 Carolina	AA Pit	25	25	1	0	151	663	161	89	79	14	8	1	9	52	3	114	10	3	7	13	.350	1	0	4.71
Nashville	AAA Pit	5	5	0	0	31.1	136	38	10	9	3	3	0	1	12	0	21	3	0	2	0	1.000	0	0	2.59
1999 Nashville	AAA Pit	1	1	0	0	3	19	6	6	5	0	0	0	0	5	1	5	1	0	0	0	—	0	0	15.00
2000 Nashville	AAA Pit	6	6	0	0	30.2	138	30	20	16	4	2	0	3	18	0	18	0	0	2	4	.333	0	0	4.70
2001 Altoona	AA Pit	6	1	0	2	9	48	18	11	10	0	0	0	1	4	0	4	2	0	0	1	.000	0	0	10.00
Akron	AA Cle	10	3	0	1	24	102	18	11	11	2	0	2	1	15	0	20	2	0	2	1	.667	0	0	4.13
Buffalo	AAA Cle	8	6	1	1	35	138	27	15	13	3	0	1	2	8	0	25	0	0	2	2	.500	0	0	3.34
1999 Pittsburgh	NL	6	0	0	0	7	37	11	9	9	2	2	1	0	6	1	7	2	0	0	0	—	0	0	11.57
10 Min. YEARS		186	148	9	7	893.2	3953	884	526	427	51	29	22	59	412	7	756	94	17	52	62	.456	5	0	4.30

Paul Phillips

Bats: Right **Throws:** Right **Pos:** C   **Ht:** 5'11" **Wt:** 180 **Born:** 4/15/77 **Age:** 25

		BATTING														BASERUNNING				PERCENTAGES		
Year Team	Lg Org	G	AB	H	2B	3B	HR	TB	R	RBI	TBB	IBB	SO	HBP	SH	SF	SB	CS	SB%	GDP	Avg	OBP	SLG
1998 Spokane	A- KC	59	234	72	12	2	4	100	55	25	18	0	19	4	0	1	12	1	.92	2	.308	.366	.427
Wilmington	A+ KC	2	5	2	0	0	0	2	0	2	0	0	1	0	0	1	0	0	—	0	.400	.333	.400
1999 Wichita	AA KC	108	393	105	20	2	3	138	58	56	26	0	38	2	3	3	8	9	.47	8	.267	.314	.351
2000 Wichita	AA KC	82	291	85	11	5	4	118	49	30	21	1	22	1	1	4	4	5	.44	11	.292	.338	.405
2001	KC							DNP—Elbow Injury															
3 Min. YEARS		251	923	264	43	9	11	358	162	113	65	1	80	7	4	9	24	15	.62	21	.286	.335	.388

Wynter Phoenix

Bats: Left **Throws:** Left **Pos:** OF-90; PH-9; PR-4; DH-3   **Ht:** 6'2" **Wt:** 208 **Born:** 12/7/74 **Age:** 27

		BATTING														BASERUNNING				PERCENTAGES		
Year Team	Lg Org	G	AB	H	2B	3B	HR	TB	R	RBI	TBB	IBB	SO	HBP	SH	SF	SB	CS	SB%	GDP	Avg	OBP	SLG
1997 Yakima	A- LA	56	186	47	14	2	3	74	29	17	23	2	36	3	5	1	11	4	.73	1	.253	.343	.398
1998 San Berndno	A+ LA	110	318	79	16	3	7	122	38	47	35	2	67	3	3	2	20	11	.65	2	.248	.327	.384
1999 Vero Beach	A+ LA	62	202	70	10	2	5	99	43	31	42	4	30	8	1	1	5	5	.55	1	.347	.474	.490
San Antonio	AA LA	60	169	42	6	1	5	65	22	22	21	1	41	2	4	2	1	2	.33	3	.249	.335	.385
2000 Portland	AA Fla	121	385	99	23	6	10	164	69	62	61	3	95	7	2	2	10	7	.59	6	.257	.367	.426

Year Team	Lg Org	BATTING															BASERUNNING				PERCENTAGES		
		G	AB	H	2B	3B	HR	TB	R	RBI	TBB	IBB	SO	HBP	SH	SF	SB	CS	SB%	GDP	Avg	OBP	SLG
2001 Portland	AA Fla	24	60	15	2	0	2	23	9	6	3	0	15	0	0	0	0	1	.00	2	.250	.286	.383
Bowie	AA Bal	81	267	60	17	4	4	97	32	20	26	2	62	3	0	4	11	5	.69	5	.225	.297	.363
5 Min. YEARS		514	1587	412	88	18	36	644	242	205	211	14	346	26	15	12	59	35	.63	20	.260	.353	.406

Jeff Pickler

Bats: Left   **Throws:** Right   **Pos:** 2B-132; DH-1; PH-1   **Ht:** 5'10"   **Wt:** 180   **Born:** 1/6/76   **Age:** 26

Year Team	Lg Org	BATTING															BASERUNNING				PERCENTAGES		
		G	AB	H	2B	3B	HR	TB	R	RBI	TBB	IBB	SO	HBP	SH	SF	SB	CS	SB%	GDP	Avg	OBP	SLG
1998 Ogden	R+ Mil	71	280	102	22	0	4	136	55	49	39	0	25	2	4	2	20	8	.71	4	.364	.443	.486
1999 Stockton	A+ Mil	80	311	105	14	3	1	128	40	42	23	2	29	0	1	1	7	6	.54	6	.338	.382	.412
Huntsville	AA Mil	51	183	51	8	1	1	64	20	23	15	0	25	0	2	2	9	4	.69	11	.279	.330	.350
2000 Huntsville	AA Mil	71	254	77	11	0	0	88	34	26	30	0	28	1	4	2	15	12	.56	7	.303	.374	.346
Indianapolis	AAA Mil	56	189	58	6	1	1	69	34	20	24	0	27	1	1	0	14	3	.82	6	.307	.388	.365
2001 Huntsville	AA Mil	134	523	150	17	2	0	171	74	32	60	3	51	1	6	2	34	14	.71	2	.287	.360	.327
4 Min. YEARS		463	1740	543	78	7	7	656	257	192	191	5	185	5	18	9	99	47	.68	36	.312	.380	.377

Jorge Piedra

Bats: Left   **Throws:** Left   **Pos:** OF-118; PH-7   **Ht:** 6'0"   **Wt:** 195   **Born:** 4/17/79   **Age:** 23

Year Team	Lg Org	BATTING															BASERUNNING				PERCENTAGES		
		G	AB	H	2B	3B	HR	TB	R	RBI	TBB	IBB	SO	HBP	SH	SF	SB	CS	SB%	GDP	Avg	OBP	SLG
1998 Great Falls	R+ LA	72	282	108	22	7	2	150	72	33	39	3	29	1	3	0	16	7	.70	4	.383	.460	.532
1999 San Berndno	A+ LA	8	30	9	2	0	0	11	6	3	3	0	3	0	1	2	1	0	1.00	0	.300	.343	.367
Vero Beach	A+ LA	15	59	17	3	1	1	25	13	6	7	1	9	0	0	1	2	2	.50	0	.288	.358	.424
2000 Vero Beach	A+ LA	92	360	102	11	6	6	143	59	52	29	1	57	5	3	7	21	5	.81	6	.283	.339	.397
Daytona	A+ ChC	34	139	48	11	1	1	64	24	17	6	0	15	0	2	2	8	4	.67	0	.345	.367	.460
2001 West Tenn	AA ChC	124	441	108	26	6	8	170	55	54	37	2	80	8	2	7	12	5	.71	8	.245	.310	.385
4 Min. YEARS		345	1311	392	75	21	18	563	229	165	121	7	193	14	11	19	60	23	.72	18	.299	.360	.429

Kirk Pierce

Bats: Right   **Throws:** Right   **Pos:** C-66; DH-2; PH-1   **Ht:** 6'3"   **Wt:** 200   **Born:** 5/26/73   **Age:** 29

Year Team	Lg Org	BATTING															BASERUNNING				PERCENTAGES		
		G	AB	H	2B	3B	HR	TB	R	RBI	TBB	IBB	SO	HBP	SH	SF	SB	CS	SB%	GDP	Avg	OBP	SLG
1995 Batavia	A- Phi	30	101	22	5	1	0	29	18	7	10	0	23	6	1	0	0	0	—	4	.218	.325	.287
1996 Piedmont	A Phi	67	198	50	12	0	2	68	22	28	22	0	43	12	1	2	0	1	.00	6	.253	.359	.343
1997 Clearwater	A+ Phi	24	68	18	1	1	1	24	9	5	3	0	13	3	1	0	0	0	—	3	.265	.324	.353
1998 Reading	AA Phi	80	265	67	12	0	6	97	31	29	41	2	63	4	2	1	0	0	—	3	.253	.360	.366
Scranton-WB	AAA Phi	4	13	1	0	0	0	1	2	0	3	0	2	1	2	0	0	0	—	0	.077	.294	.077
1999 Reading	AA Phi	83	255	66	10	0	9	103	37	40	42	1	56	10	0	5	4	3	.57	9	.259	.378	.404
2000 Fargo-Mh	IND —	81	269	73	18	1	13	132	59	48	45	1	48	13	1	1	0	0	—	6	.271	.399	.491
2001 Norwich	AA NYY	12	28	8	2	0	1	13	5	4	0	0	8	5	0	0	0	0	—	5	.286	.459	.464
Fargo-Mh	IND —	57	216	60	10	0	8	94	28	33	18	0	62	9	0	0	0	0	—	5	.278	.358	.435
7 Min. YEARS		438	1413	365	70	3	40	561	211	194	188	4	318	63	8	9	4	4	.50	39	.258	.368	.397

Anthony Pigott

Bats: Right   **Throws:** Right   **Pos:** OF-74; PR-6; DH-3   **Ht:** 6'1"   **Wt:** 194   **Born:** 6/13/76   **Age:** 26

Year Team	Lg Org	BATTING															BASERUNNING				PERCENTAGES		
		G	AB	H	2B	3B	HR	TB	R	RBI	TBB	IBB	SO	HBP	SH	SF	SB	CS	SB%	GDP	Avg	OBP	SLG
1997 Hudson Val	A- TB	1	4	0	0	0	0	0	0	1	0	0	1	0	0	0	0	0	—	0	.000	.000	.000
Princeton	R+ TB	46	151	35	4	1	0	41	20	14	8	0	34	1	1	1	2	1	.67	3	.232	.273	.272
1998 Hudson Val	A- TB	9	16	4	1	0	0	5	3	3	1	0	2	0	0	0	1	0	1.00	1	.250	.294	.313
Chston-SC	A TB	29	100	17	3	1	2	29	9	11	2	0	26	0	0	1	1	0	1.00	4	.170	.184	.280
1999 St. Pete	A+ TB	105	339	91	9	4	2	114	41	33	11	0	84	4	3	1	16	8	.67	5	.268	.299	.336
Orlando	AA TB	4	8	2	1	0	0	3	0	0	0	0	2	0	0	0	0	0	—	0	.250	.250	.375
2000 Orlando	AA TB	43	125	30	5	0	0	35	13	9	6	0	29	0	3	0	2	3	.40	4	.240	.275	.280
St. Pete	A+ TB	62	243	65	12	1	2	85	36	17	6	0	50	1	1	0	11	5	.69	2	.267	.288	.350
2001 Orlando	AA TB	82	250	60	10	1	2	78	29	28	7	1	39	2	11	2	8	3	.73	8	.240	.264	.312
5 Min. YEARS		381	1236	304	45	8	8	389	151	116	41	1	267	8	19	5	40	21	.66	27	.246	.274	.315

Rafael Pina

Pitches: Right   **Bats:** Right   **Pos:** RP-12; SP-10   **Ht:** 6'1"   **Wt:** 170   **Born:** 8/16/71   **Age:** 30

Year Team	Lg Org	HOW MUCH HE PITCHED						WHAT HE GAVE UP												THE RESULTS					
		G	GS	CG	GF	IP	BFP	H	R	ER	HR	SH	SF	HB	TBB	IBB	SO	WP	Bk	W	L	Pct.	ShO	Sv	ERA
1991 Elizabethtn	R+ Min	16	13	3	1	89.1	394	79	42	25	1	3	2	5	44	0	64	8	10	4	5	.444	1	0	2.52
1992 Elizabethtn	R+ Min	11	10	1	0	66	292	68	39	27	2	3	0	2	22	0	43	7	1	6	2	.750	0	0	3.68
1999 Rochester	AAA Bal	48	10	0	18	111.1	488	113	60	54	15	1	3	2	48	2	88	7	1	8	10	.444	0	5	4.37
2000 Rochester	AAA Bal	14	9	0	1	56.2	247	64	44	37	9	3	1	4	19	1	34	3	0	0	6	.000	0	0	5.88
El Paso	AA Ari	12	11	0	0	71	318	82	40	31	6	3	1	4	21	0	65	3	1	3	3	.500	0	0	3.93
2001 Sonoma Cty	IND —	5	4	0	0	25.1	117	31	20	12	2	0	3	2	4	0	12	1	0	2	2	.500	0	0	4.26
Bowie	AA Bal	4	0	0	2	8.2	36	6	3	2	0	0	0	0	1	0	5	1	0	1	0	1.000	0	0	2.08
Rochester	AAA Bal	13	6	1	2	40	173	45	17	11	2	1	1	1	12	0	30	2	0	1	3	.250	0	0	2.48
5 Min. YEARS		123	63	5	24	468.1	2065	488	265	199	37	14	11	20	171	3	341	32	13	24	32	.429	1	5	3.82

Aquiles Pinales

Pitches: Right **Bats:** Right **Pos:** RP-41
Ht: 5'11" **Wt:** 165 **Born:** 9/5/74 **Age:** 27

Year Team	Lg Org	G	GS	CG	GF	IP	BFP	H	R	ER	HR	SH	SF	HB	TBB	IBB	SO	WP	Bk	W	L	Pct.	ShO	Sv	ERA
1996 Macon	A Atl	18	0	0	6	28.1	135	26	23	18	3	0	1	1	21	0	22	4	2	3	1	.750	0	0	5.72
Eugene	A- Atl	3	0	0	3	5.1	20	4	3	2	1	1	0	0	2	0	4	0	0	0	0	—	0	1	3.38
2001 Akron	AA Cle	5	0	0	2	8	40	13	9	8	1	0	0	0	4	0	6	1	1	0	0	—	0	0	9.00
Kinston	A+ Cle	36	0	0	15	58.1	268	65	34	29	2	3	1	5	25	3	55	4	1	4	5	.444	0	3	4.47
2 Min. YEARS		62	0	0	26	100	463	108	69	57	7	4	2	6	52	3	87	9	4	7	6	.538	0	4	5.13

Chris Pine

Pitches: Right **Bats:** Right **Pos:** RP-19
Ht: 6'2" **Wt:** 205 **Born:** 9/25/76 **Age:** 25

Year Team	Lg Org	G	GS	CG	GF	IP	BFP	H	R	ER	HR	SH	SF	HB	TBB	IBB	SO	WP	Bk	W	L	Pct.	ShO	Sv	ERA
1998 Ogden	R+ Mil	3	1	0	1	8	37	9	10	10	1	1	0	0	4	0	11	1	1	0	1	.000	0	0	11.25
1999 Beloit	A Mil	7	0	0	4	14.1	65	.13	7	5	1	0	2	1	10	0	17	2	0	0	1	.000	0	0	3.14
2001 Angels	R Ana	3	0	0	0	4	18	5	3	2	0	0	0	0	0	0	2	0	0	0	1	.000	0	0	4.50
Cedar Rapids	A Ana	12	0	0	7	15.1	59	6	3	3	1	1	0	0	7	0	24	2	0	1	1	.500	0	2	1.76
Arkansas	AA Ana	4	0	0	1	4.1	25	6	3	2	0	0	0	2	6	0	4	0	0	1	0	1.000	0	1	4.15
3 Min. YEARS		29	1	0	13	46	204	39	26	22	3	2	2	3	27	0	58	5	1	2	4	.333	0	3	4.30

Juan Piniella

Bats: Right **Throws:** Right **Pos:** OF-98; DH-11; PH-6; PR-1
Ht: 5'10" **Wt:** 160 **Born:** 3/13/78 **Age:** 24

Year Team	Lg Org	G	AB	H	2B	3B	HR	TB	R	RBI	TBB	IBB	SO	HBP	SH	SF	SB	CS	SB%	GDP	Avg	OBP	SLG
1996 Rangers	R Tex	55	223	53	6	2	0	63	38	18	15	0	54	5	4	2	19	5	.79	1	.238	.298	.283
1997 Pulaski	R+ Tex	33	126	34	4	3	1	47	20	17	8	0	22	0	3	2	9	4	.69	1	.270	.309	.373
1998 Savannah	A Tex	72	255	87	13	6	3	121	51	39	30	0	48	4	7	2	28	11	.72	0	.341	.416	.475
Charlotte	A+ Tex	61	222	68	8	3	2	88	37	23	25	0	38	1	1	0	23	6	.79	0	.306	.379	.396
1999 Tulsa	AA Tex	124	458	121	23	2	9	175	69	46	61	0	120	7	1	8	15	6	.71	6	.264	.354	.382
2000 Tulsa	AA Tex	126	447	110	17	1	5	144	68	40	67	0	105	4	12	1	24	8	.75	5	.246	.349	.322
2001 Tulsa	AA Tex	110	373	97	24	2	3	134	51	34	38	1	98	5	10	4	13	3	.81	0	.260	.333	.359
6 Min. YEARS		581	2104	570	95	19	23	772	334	217	244	1	485	26	38	19	131	43	.75	13	.271	.351	.367

Ryan Poe

Pitches: Right **Bats:** Right **Pos:** SP-7
Ht: 6'2" **Wt:** 220 **Born:** 9/3/77 **Age:** 24

Year Team	Lg Org	G	GS	CG	GF	IP	BFP	H	R	ER	HR	SH	SF	HB	TBB	IBB	SO	WP	Bk	W	L	Pct.	ShO	Sv	ERA
1998 Helena	R+ Mil	14	5	0	2	46.1	202	52	30	24	3	1	1	3	15	0	43	1	1	3	3	.500	0	1	4.66
1999 Beloit	A Mil	49	5	0	28	96	398	94	46	38	9	1	2	3	16	3	108	5	1	6	10	.375	0	9	3.56
2000 Mudville	A+ Mil	33	7	0	21	82.2	323	56	19	18	5	1	3	3	21	1	98	2	1	7	5	.583	0	9	1.96
Huntsville	AA Mil	9	0	0	8	21.1	94	18	8	8	1	2	1	2	9	2	20	1	0	1	3	.250	0	3	3.38
2001 Huntsville	AA Mil	7	7	0	0	35	137	30	15	15	5	0	0	1	7	0	40	0	0	1	2	.333	0	0	3.86
4 Min. YEARS		112	24	0	59	281.1	1154	250	118	103	23	5	7	12	68	6	309	9	3	18	23	.439	0	22	3.30

Jamie Pogue

Bats: Right **Throws:** Right **Pos:** C-91; DH-21; PR-2; PH-1
Ht: 6'4" **Wt:** 235 **Born:** 8/17/77 **Age:** 24

Year Team	Lg Org	G	AB	H	2B	3B	HR	TB	R	RBI	TBB	IBB	SO	HBP	SH	SF	SB	CS	SB%	GDP	Avg	OBP	SLG
1999 London	IND —	68	237	64	14	1	5	95	42	30	33	0	61	9	0	0	3	2	.60	5	.270	.380	.401
2000 New Jersey	A- StL	28	90	21	6	0	0	27	12	9	24	1	18	1	0	1	1	0	1.00	4	.233	.397	.300
Peoria	A StL	22	66	11	1	1	1	17	8	6	12	0	20	3	2	0	0	1	.00	2	.167	.321	.258
2001 New Haven	AA StL	5	15	3	0	1	0	5	3	0	2	0	1	0	0	0	0	0	—	0	.200	.294	.333
Potomac	A+ StL	108	354	85	15	0	8	124	48	42	55	1	61	7	1	1	11	7	.61	6	.240	.353	.350
3 Min. YEARS		231	762	184	36	3	14	268	113	87	126	2	161	20	4	2	15	10	.60	17	.241	.363	.352

Kevin Polcovich

Bats: Right **Throws:** Right **Pos:** 2B-26; PH-24; SS-21; 3B-7; DH-1
Ht: 5'9" **Wt:** 182 **Born:** 6/28/70 **Age:** 32

Year Team	Lg Org	G	AB	H	2B	3B	HR	TB	R	RBI	TBB	IBB	SO	HBP	SH	SF	SB	CS	SB%	GDP	Avg	OBP	SLG
1992 Carolina	AA Pit	13	35	6	0	0	0	6	1	1	4	0	4	2	0	0	0	2	.00	1	.171	.293	.171
Augusta	A Pit	46	153	40	6	2	0	50	24	10	18	0	30	8	3	0	7	7	.50	1	.261	.369	.327
1993 Augusta	A Pit	14	48	13	2	0	0	15	9	4	7	0	8	0	2	1	2	1	.67	1	.271	.357	.313
Carolina	AA Pit	4	11	3	0	0	0	3	1	1	1	0	1	0	2	0	0	0	—	1	.273	.333	.273
Salem	A+ Pit	94	282	72	10	3	1	91	44	25	49	0	42	12	6	3	13	6	.68	7	.255	.384	.323
1994 Carolina	AA Pit	125	406	95	14	2	2	119	46	33	38	4	70	11	10	8	9	4	.69	6	.234	.311	.293
1995 Carolina	AA Pit	64	221	70	8	0	3	87	27	18	14	1	29	5	3	1	10	5	.67	3	.317	.369	.394
Calgary	AAA Pit	62	213	60	8	1	3	79	31	27	11	0	32	8	2	3	5	6	.45	7	.282	.336	.371
1996 Calgary	AAA Pit	104	336	92	21	3	1	122	53	46	18	3	49	14	5	2	7	6	.54	9	.274	.335	.363
1997 Carolina	AA Pit	17	50	16	5	0	3	30	13	7	10	0	4	2	2	0	4	2	.67	1	.320	.452	.600
Calgary	AAA Pit	17	62	19	4	0	1	26	7	9	1	0	7	1	0	1	0	0	—	1	.306	.323	.419
1999 Nashville	AAA Pit	80	233	56	10	1	.3	77	37	25	20	1	52	4	7	4	6	4	.60	4	.240	.307	.330
2001 Memphis	AAA StL	72	183	54	10	2	3	77	35	20	12	2	39	8	1	1	4	0	1.00	1	.295	.363	.421
1997 Pittsburgh	NL	84	245	67	16	1	4	97	37	21	21	4	45	9	2	2	2	2	.50	11	.273	.350	.396
1998 Pittsburgh	NL	81	212	40	12	0	0	52	18	14	15	2	33	5	3	3	4	3	.57	7	.189	.255	.245
8 Min. YEARS		712	2233	596	98	14	20	782	328	226	203	11	367	75	43	24	67	43	.61	43	.267	.345	.350
2 Maj. YEARS		165	457	107	28	1	4	149	55	35	36	6	78	14	5	5	6	5	.55	18	.234	.307	.326

Simon Pond

Bats: Left **Throws:** Right **Pos:** 1B-97; DH-26; PH-12; OF-8; 3B-3   **Ht:** 6'1" **Wt:** 190 **Born:** 10/27/76 **Age:** 25

						BATTING											BASERUNNING				PERCENTAGES		
Year Team	Lg Org	G	AB	H	2B	3B	HR	TB	R	RBI	TBB	IBB	SO	HBP	SH	SF	SB	CS	SB%	GDP	Avg	OBP	SLG
1994 Expos	R Mon	40	147	38	7	0	0	45	18	15	16	1	25	1	0	3	1	1	.50	4	.259	.329	.306
1995 Albany	A Mon	23	80	17	5	0	0	22	4	7	4	0	25	2	0	0	1	0	1.00	3	.213	.267	.275
Expos	R Mon	45	133	20	6	1	0	28	13	12	22	0	34	1	0	0	2	3	.40	3	.150	.276	.211
1996 Vermont	A- Mon	69	253	76	16	1	3	103	37	40	26	2	26	3	1	3	9	3	.75	7	.300	.368	.407
1997 Cape Fear	A Mon	118	444	120	11	0	3	140	48	47	37	1	46	2	1	4	12	8	.60	22	.270	.326	.315
1998 Jupiter	A+ Mon	105	344	82	15	1	1	102	40	32	24	2	58	6	2	4	1	4	.20	7	.238	.296	.297
Harrisburg	AA Mon	2	3	0	0	0	0	0	0	0	1	0	1	0	0	0	0	0	—	0	.000	.250	.000
1999 Jupiter	A+ Mon	127	434	111	25	1	10	168	47	77	48	3	83	14	1	11	4	8	.33	10	.256	.341	.387
2000 Jupiter	A+ Mon	19	63	13	1	0	3	23	7	8	9	0	13	1	0	0	1	0	1.00	0	.206	.315	.365
Kinston	A+ Cle	64	237	76	18	0	6	112	40	37	22	1	49	3	0	2	14	3	.82	9	.321	.383	.473
2001 Kinston	A+ Cle	25	97	33	8	1	4	55	13	24	10	0	12	1	0	2	1	1	.50	0	.340	.400	.567
Akron	AA Cle	114	388	104	29	3	11	172	46	46	30	2	70	2	2	5	2	3	.40	9	.268	.320	.443
8 Min. YEARS		751	2623	690	141	8	41	970	313	345	249	12	442	36	7	34	48	34	.59	74	.263	.331	.370

Colin Porter

Bats: Left **Throws:** Left **Pos:** OF-114; PH-12; DH-1; PR-1   **Ht:** 6'2" **Wt:** 200 **Born:** 11/23/75 **Age:** 26

						BATTING											BASERUNNING				PERCENTAGES		
Year Team	Lg Org	G	AB	H	2B	3B	HR	TB	R	RBI	TBB	IBB	SO	HBP	SH	SF	SB	CS	SB%	GDP	Avg	OBP	SLG
1998 Auburn	A- Hou	67	240	68	18	4	4	106	40	30	19	0	61	5	2	1	14	11	.56	3	.283	.447	.442
1999 Michigan	A Hou	127	453	132	28	9	18	232	91	68	53	2	123	7	3	8	23	13	.64	4	.291	.369	.512
2000 Round Rock	AA Hou	124	435	119	25	5	14	196	76	57	56	4	130	6	0	1	17	9	.65	6	.274	.363	.451
2001 Round Rock	AA Hou	25	100	32	5	5	2	53	14	12	5	2	25	1	0	0	1	3	.25	0	.320	.358	.530
New Orleans	AAA Hou	101	312	74	14	1	7	111	48	33	34	2	105	3	0	4	11	6	.65	2	.237	.314	.356
4 Min. YEARS		444	1540	425	90	24	45	698	269	200	167	10	444	22	5	14	66	42	.61	15	.276	.352	.453

Mike Porzio

Pitches: Left **Bats:** Left **Pos:** SP-25; RP-8   **Ht:** 6'3" **Wt:** 190 **Born:** 8/20/72 **Age:** 29

		HOW MUCH HE PITCHED						WHAT HE GAVE UP									THE RESULTS					
Year Team	Lg Org	G	GS	CG	GF	IP	BFP	H	R	ER	HR	SH	SF	HB	TBB	IBB	SO	WP	Bk	W	L	Pct.	ShO	Sv	ERA
1993 Cubs	R ChC	10	8	0	2	42.1	200	42	26	18	1	3	2	3	30	0	30	1	2	1	3	.250	0	0	3.83
1994 Cubs	R ChC	7	0	0	6	13.2	64	19	10	9	0	0	0	1	6	0	5	0	0	0	3	.000	0	1	5.93
1995 Mobile	IND —	16	2	0	4	28.1	131	32	19	17	2	4	1	3	13	2	15	2	0	0	3	.000	0	0	5.40
Ogden	R+ —	8	8	2	0	48	220	66	39	34	4	0	3	2	15	0	26	6	0	4	3	.571	0	0	6.38
1996 Tennessee	IND —	15	15	3	0	98.2	428	94	55	40	9	2	4	9	30	1	54	4	0	7	4	.636	0	0	3.65
1997 Sioux City	IND —	27	5	1	6	61.1	284	75	32	29	6	0	3	5	27	1	63	2	0	2	2	.500	1	0	4.26
1998 Danville	A+ Atl	26	11	1	8	97	384	74	34	27	7	5	3	1	30	5	95	1	0	3	2	.600	0	2	2.51
Salem	A+ Col	7	7	0	0	42.1	173	40	20	13	6	1	0	2	12	0	46	1	0	2	3	.400	0	0	2.76
1999 Colo Sprngs	AAA Col	35	0	0	6	42.2	198	44	16	16	5	3	0	3	30	4	33	4	1	5	1	.833	0	0	3.38
2000 Colo Sprngs	AAA Col	6	6	0	0	26	133	39	30	29	7	3	2	0	20	0	26	0	1	0	3	.000	0	0	10.04
Carolina	AA Col	20	18	1	2	121.1	502	111	53	46	11	5	4	5	31	0	90	5	0	7	4	.636	1	0	3.41
2001 Birmingham	AA CWS	2	2	0	0	13	49	3	2	2	1	0	0	1	5	0	10	2	0	1	0	1.000	0	0	1.38
Charlotte	AAA CWS	31	23	0	2	134.1	592	138	76	65	14	6	6	8	55	2	107	9	1	6	6	.500	0	0	4.35
1999 Colorado	NL	16	0	0	3	14.2	75	21	14	14	5	1	0	0	10	0	10	0	0	0	0	—	0	0	8.59
9 Min. YEARS		210	105	8	36	769	3358	777	412	345	73	32	28	43	304	15	600	37	5	38	37	.507	2	3	4.04

Scott Pose

Bats: Left **Throws:** Right **Pos:** OF-16; PH-3   **Ht:** 5'11" **Wt:** 190 **Born:** 2/11/67 **Age:** 35

						BATTING											BASERUNNING				PERCENTAGES		
Year Team	Lg Org	G	AB	H	2B	3B	HR	TB	R	RBI	TBB	IBB	SO	HBP	SH	SF	SB	CS	SB%	GDP	Avg	OBP	SLG
1989 Billings	R+ Cin	60	210	74	7	2	0	85	52	25	54	3	31	1	1	1	26	3	.90	2	.352	.485	.405
1990 Chston-WV	A Cin	135	486	143	13	5	0	166	106	46	114	8	56	7	5	6	49	21	.70	5	.298	.435	.346
1991 Nashville	AAA Cin	15	52	10	0	0	0	10	7	3	2	0	9	2	2	0	3	1	.75	0	.192	.250	.192
Chattanooga	AA Cin	117	402	110	8	5	1	131	61	31	69	3	50	2	7	3	17	13	.57	7	.274	.380	.326
1992 Chattanooga	AA Cin	136	526	180	22	8	2	224	87	45	63	5	66	4	4	3	21	27	.44	8	.342	.414	.426
1993 Edmonton	AAA Fla	109	398	113	8	6	0	133	61	27	42	3	36	1	5	1	19	9	.68	8	.284	.353	.334
1994 New Orleans	AAA Mil	124	429	121	13	7	0	148	60	52	47	2	52	2	9	4	20	8	.71	7	.282	.353	.345
1995 Albuquerque	AAA LA	7	16	3	1	0	0	4	5	1	2	0	0	0	0	0	2	0	1.00	0	.188	.278	.250
Salt Lake	AAA Min	70	203	63	9	1	0	74	41	19	29	2	28	1	3	3	13	4	.76	2	.310	.394	.365
1996 Syracuse	AAA Tor	113	419	114	11	6	0	137	71	39	58	0	71	3	9	4	30	16	.65	3	.272	.362	.327
1997 Columbus	AAA NYY	57	227	70	10	7	2	100	50	32	32	0	29	5	2	0	13	5	.72	2	.308	.405	.441
1998 Columbus	AAA NYY	133	489	145	23	10	3	197	78	46	53	0	72	6	7	4	47	14	.77	8	.297	.370	.403
2001 New Orleans	AAA Hou	17	59	16	2	0	0	18	5	3	4	0	6	0	0	1	6	2	.75	2	.271	.317	.305
1993 Florida	NL	15	41	8	2	0	0	10	0	3	2	0	4	0	0	0	2	0	.00	1	.195	.233	.244
1997 New York	AL	54	87	19	2	1	0	23	19	5	9	0	11	0	0	0	3	1	.75	1	.218	.292	.264
1999 Kansas City	AL	86	137	39	3	0	0	42	27	12	21	1	22	0	0	1	6	2	.75	3	.285	.377	.307
2000 Kansas City	AL	47	48	9	0	0	0	9	6	1	6	0	13	0	0	0	1	0	.00	0	.188	.278	.188
11 Min. YEARS		1093	3910	1162	127	57	8	1427	684	369	569	26	506	34	54	29	266	123	.68	54	.297	.389	.365
4 Maj. YEARS		202	313	75	7	1	0	84	52	21	38	1	50	0	1	1	9	6	.60	5	.240	.321	.268

Dave Post

Bats: Right **Throws:** Right **Pos:** 1B-24; OF-16; 3B-15; PH-13; 2B-8; DH-2; P-1   **Ht:** 5'11" **Wt:** 170 **Born:** 9/3/73 **Age:** 28

						BATTING											BASERUNNING				PERCENTAGES		
Year Team	Lg Org	G	AB	H	2B	3B	HR	TB	R	RBI	TBB	IBB	SO	HBP	SH	SF	SB	CS	SB%	GDP	Avg	OBP	SLG
1992 Great Falls	R+ LA	41	138	40	8	0	1	51	23	25	23	0	16	4	3	2	10	5	.67	4	.290	.401	.370
1993 Yakima	A- LA	60	210	53	8	1	1	66	34	22	35	1	27	4	3	3	7	4	.64	3	.252	.365	.314
1994 Bakersfield	A+ LA	31	106	25	5	1	0	32	16	9	13	0	9	3	0	0	6	4	.60	2	.236	.336	.302
Yakima	A- LA	70	263	77	14	1	1	96	46	27	56	3	42	5	1	5	18	5	.78	3	.293	.419	.365

					BATTING												BASERUNNING			PERCENTAGES		
Year Team	Lg Org	G	AB	H	2B	3B	HR	TB	R	RBI	TBB	IBB	SO	HBP	SH	SF	SB	CS	SB%	GDP	Avg	OBP	SLG
1995 Vero Beach	A+ LA	52	114	27	2	1	0	31	16	11	23	0	11	2	3	1	3	0	1.00	5	.237	.371	.272
1996 Expos	R Mon	8	25	2	0	0	1	5	3	1	4	1	6	0	1	0	1	0	1.00	1	.080	.207	.200
Wst Plm Bch	A+ Mon	79	258	72	15	6	5	114	42	35	37	1	32	5	5	4	8	4	.67	6	.279	.375	.442
1997 Harrisburg	AA Mon	48	156	41	10	0	3	60	26	18	24	0	24	5	3	1	5	1	.83	1	.263	.376	.385
1998 Harrisburg	AA Mon	19	58	20	3	1	1	28	9	9	7	0	3	1	0	0	1	1	.50	0	.345	.424	.483
Ottawa	AAA Mon	93	330	99	23	2	6	144	59	35	28	1	50	6	1	0	7	7	.50	5	.300	.365	.436
1999 Harrisburg	AA Mon	5	21	8	1	0	1	12	5	3	1	0	2	0	1	0	0	0	—	0	.381	.409	.571
Ottawa	AAA Mon	108	375	97	17	2	10	148	49	36	34	3	56	8	2	3	12	8	.60	9	.259	.331	.395
2000 Ottawa	AAA Mon	115	362	92	22	5	4	136	45	43	56	2	44	7	4	1	8	3	.73	10	.254	.364	.376
Buffalo	AAA Cle	5	16	5	0	0	0	5	1	0	5	0	2	0	0	0	0	0	—	0	.313	.476	.313
2001 Jacksnville	AA LA	5	14	4	1	1	0	7	3	3	1	0	3	0	0	0	0	0	—	0	.286	.333	.500
Dodgers	R LA	1	2	0	0	0	0	0	0	0	0	0	1	0	0	0	0	0	—	0	.000	.000	.000
Las Vegas	AAA LA	67	180	53	14	1	2	75	24	31	26	2	21	1	3	1	2	3	.40	7	.294	.385	.417
10 Min. YEARS		807	2628	715	143	22	36	1010	401	308	373	14	349	51	30	21	88	45	.66	55	.272	.371	.384

Rick Powalski

Pitches: Left **Bats:** Left **Pos:** RP-31; SP-6 **Ht:** 6'11" **Wt:** 190 **Born:** 5/9/78 **Age:** 24

		HOW MUCH HE PITCHED						WHAT HE GAVE UP											THE RESULTS					
Year Team	Lg Org	G	GS	CG	GF	IP	BFP	H	R	ER	HR	SH	SF	HB	TBB	IBB	SO	WP	Bk	W	L	Pct.	ShO	Sv	ERA
1997 Cubs	R ChC	6	0	0	0	11.1	51	11	4	2	0	0	0	0	7	0	13	0	0	0	0	—	0	0	1.59
1998 Williamsprt	A- ChC	18	0	0	3	34.1	150	36	24	20	1	1	3	2	19	1	20	5	0	1	2	.333	0	0	5.24
1999 Reno	IND —	45	2	1	8	69	335	76	50	47	6	2	1	6	52	1	71	6	0	4	6	.400	0	0	6.13
2000 Macon	A Atl	43	0	0	26	58.2	258	57	31	23	3	2	1	6	23	3	58	3	1	2	5	.286	0	8	3.53
2001 Albany	IND —	34	6	3	27	89.1	360	59	31	18	4	6	4	4	16	0	132	3	0	8	4	.667	0	10	1.81
Orlando	AA TB	3	0	0	0	3.1	20	6	2	2	0	0	0	2	3	0	5	0	0	0	0	—	0	0	5.40
5 Min. YEARS		149	8	4	64	266	1174	245	142	112	14	11	9	20	120	5	299	17	1	15	17	.469	0	18	3.79

Jeremy Powell

Pitches: Right **Bats:** Right **Pos:** SP-11 **Ht:** 6'5" **Wt:** 230 **Born:** 6/18/76 **Age:** 26

		HOW MUCH HE PITCHED						WHAT HE GAVE UP											THE RESULTS					
Year Team	Lg Org	G	GS	CG	GF	IP	BFP	H	R	ER	HR	SH	SF	HB	TBB	IBB	SO	WP	Bk	W	L	Pct.	ShO	Sv	ERA
1994 Expos	R Mon	9	9	1	0	43	171	37	16	14	1	0	1	2	14	0	36	2	2	2	2	.500	0	0	2.93
1995 Albany	A Mon	1	1	0	0	5.2	20	4	1	1	0	0	0	0	1	0	6	1	0	1	0	1.000	0	0	1.59
Vermont	A- Mon	15	15	0	0	87	373	88	48	42	5	2	2	6	34	1	47	6	2	5	5	.500	0	0	4.34
1996 Delmarva	A Mon	27	27	1	0	157.2	665	127	68	53	9	1	6	15	66	0	109	11	4	12	9	.571	0	0	3.03
1997 Wst Plm Bch	A+ Mon	26	26	1	0	155	675	162	75	52	3	9	5	12	62	0	121	12	2	9	10	.474	0	0	3.02
1998 Oklahoma	AAA Tex	1	0	0	0	2	13	3	5	3	1	0	0	1	2	0	4	0	0	0	0	—	0	0	13.50
Harrisburg	AA Mon	22	22	1	0	131.2	546	115	54	44	13	7	2	9	37	0	77	6	1	9	7	.563	0	0	3.01
1999 Ottawa	AAA Mon	16	16	0	0	91	382	85	37	30	5	3	3	4	37	0	72	6	0	3	5	.375	0	0	2.97
2000 Ottawa	AAA Mon	25	24	0	1	126.1	592	160	101	97	17	3	2	9	55	1	99	8	3	5	13	.278	0	0	6.91
2001 Portland	AAA SD	11	11	0	0	73.2	273	43	14	13	2	2	1	2	14	0	63	2	0	4	2	.667	0	1	1.59
1998 Montreal	NL	7	6	0	1	25	112	27	25	22	5	2	2	4	11	0	14	0	0	1	5	.167	0	0	7.92
1999 Montreal	NL	17	17	0	0	97	438	113	60	51	14	9	3	8	44	2	44	4	1	4	8	.333	0	0	4.73
2000 Montreal	NL	11	4	0	6	26	121	35	27	23	6	2	1	0	9	0	19	1	0	0	3	.000	0	0	7.96
8 Min. YEARS		153	151	4	1	873	3710	824	419	349	56	27	22	60	322	2	634	54	14	50	53	.485	0	0	3.60
3 Maj. YEARS		35	27	0	7	148	671	175	112	96	25	13	6	12	64	2	77	5	1	5	16	.238	0	0	5.84

Jeff Powers

Bats: Left **Throws:** Right **Pos:** SS-42; 2B-32; 3B-16; PH-14; PR-3; 1B-1 **Ht:** 6'0" **Wt:** 175 **Born:** 3/20/76 **Age:** 26

					BATTING												BASERUNNING			PERCENTAGES		
Year Team	Lg Org	G	AB	H	2B	3B	HR	TB	R	RBI	TBB	IBB	SO	HBP	SH	SF	SB	CS	SB%	GDP	Avg	OBP	SLG
1998 Watertown	A- Cle	18	67	20	5	0	1	28	10	11	5	0	10	1	1	1	1	0	1.00	3	.299	.351	.418
1999 Columbus	A Cle	76	233	62	10	0	2	78	34	30	24	2	24	4	3	4	2	3	.40	0	.266	.340	.335
2000 High Desert	A+ Ari	112	408	126	20	3	2	158	55	52	34	0	29	4	5	4	3	6	.33	2	.309	.364	.387
2001 Asheville	A Col	19	72	17	3	0	2	26	11	6	2	0	11	0	0	4	0	0	—	2	.236	.257	.361
Colo Sprngs	AAA Col	7	16	2	0	0	1	5	1	3	1	0	3	0	1	0	0	0	—	2	.125	.176	.313
Salem	A+ Col	44	118	22	4	1	0	28	9	6	7	0	15	1	6	0	0	2	.00	3	.186	.238	.237
Carolina	AA Col	30	84	16	2	1	0	20	5	5	6	0	12	1	3	0	0	1	.00	2	.190	.253	.238
4 Min. YEARS		306	998	265	44	5	8	343	125	113	79	2	104	11	19	9	6	12	.33	14	.266	.324	.344

John Powers

Bats: Left **Throws:** Right **Pos:** 2B-43; 3B-37; PH-14; DH-7 **Ht:** 5'9" **Wt:** 165 **Born:** 6/2/74 **Age:** 28

					BATTING												BASERUNNING			PERCENTAGES		
Year Team	Lg Org	G	AB	H	2B	3B	HR	TB	R	RBI	TBB	IBB	SO	HBP	SH	SF	SB	CS	SB%	GDP	Avg	OBP	SLG
1996 Clinton	A SD	64	237	61	8	4	1	80	29	21	34	0	38	4	3	3	1	4	.20	5	.257	.356	.338
1997 Mobile	AA SD	14	48	12	0	0	1	15	8	8	8	0	9	2	0	2	2	0	1.00	1	.250	.367	.313
Rancho Cuca	A+ SD	107	402	102	28	5	10	170	77	44	63	0	90	11	5	3	7	8	.47	9	.254	.367	.423
1998 Mobile	AA SD	127	476	144	27	4	12	215	92	52	76	1	76	8	4	2	9	6	.60	8	.303	.406	.452
2000 Mobile	AA SD	93	305	80	23	1	3	114	61	22	50	0	56	6	1	2	3	3	.67	2	.262	.375	.374
2001 Mobile	AA SD	96	315	87	15	6	4	126	41	35	37	1	58	3	4	6	7	5	.58	4	.276	.352	.400
5 Min. YEARS		501	1783	486	101	20	31	720	308	182	268	2	327	34	17	18	32	26	.55	29	.273	.375	.404

Scott Prather

Pitches: Left **Bats:** Left **Pos:** RP-39; SP-4 **Ht:** 6'2" **Wt:** 185 **Born:** 10/8/76 **Age:** 25

		HOW MUCH HE PITCHED						WHAT HE GAVE UP											THE RESULTS					
Year Team	Lg Org	G	GS	CG	GF	IP	BFP	H	R	ER	HR	SH	SF	HB	TBB	IBB	SO	WP	Bk	W	L	Pct.	ShO	Sv	ERA
1998 New Jersey	A- StL	15	14	0	0	71.1	295	55	30	25	2	2	0	1	30	0	73	6	0	4	6	.400	0	0	3.15
1999 Peoria	A StL	27	27	0	0	147.1	642	134	81	63	10	4	4	11	77	0	132	5	0	9	10	.474	0	0	3.85

Year Team	Lg Org	G	GS	CG	GF	IP	BFP	H	R	ER	HR	SH	SF	HB	TBB	IBB	SO	WP	Bk	W	L	Pct.	ShO	Sv	ERA
		HOW MUCH HE PITCHED						**WHAT HE GAVE UP**												**THE RESULTS**					
2000 Potomac	A+ StL	42	7	0	7	75.2	339	61	50	42	6	3	6	1	56	0	70	5	0	5	3	.625	0	2	5.00
2001 Potomac	A+ StL	20	0	0	7	25	112	24	15	10	1	1	1	1	7	0	27	1	0	2	1	.667	0	0	3.60
New Haven	AA StL	23	4	0	5	48.2	215	52	20	20	5	2	2	2	17	2	38	2	0	1	3	.250	0	0	3.70
4 Min. YEARS		127	52	0	19	368	1603	326	196	160	24	12	13	16	187	2	340	19	0	21	23	.477	0	2	3.91

Andy Pratt

Pitches: Left   **Bats:** Left   **Pos:** SP-26; RP-1   **Ht:** 5'11"   **Wt:** 160   **Born:** 8/27/79   **Age:** 22

Year Team	Lg Org	G	GS	CG	GF	IP	BFP	H	R	ER	HR	SH	SF	HB	TBB	IBB	SO	WP	Bk	W	L	Pct.	ShO	Sv	ERA
		HOW MUCH HE PITCHED						**WHAT HE GAVE UP**												**THE RESULTS**					
1998 Rangers	R Tex	12	8	0	1	56	225	49	25	24	4	1	3	1	14	0	49	0	1	4	3	.571	0	0	3.86
1999 Savannah	A Tex	13	13	1	0	71.2	299	66	30	23	4	4	2	4	16	0	100	4	0	4	4	.500	1	0	2.89
2000 Charlotte	A+ Tex	16	16	2	0	92.2	365	68	37	28	8	1	2	1	26	0	95	1	2	7	4	.636	1	0	2.72
Tulsa	AA Tex	11	11	0	0	52.1	255	66	48	42	7	0	2	2	33	0	42	5	1	1	6	.143	0	0	7.22
2001 Tulsa	AA Tex	27	26	3	0	168	730	175	99	86	18	8	5	6	57	0	132	9	1	8	10	.444	1	0	4.61
4 Min. YEARS		79	74	6	1	440.2	1874	424	239	203	41	14	14	14	146	0	418	19	5	24	27	.471	3	0	4.15

Scott Pratt

Bats: Left   **Throws:** Right   **Pos:** 2B-55; OF-8; DH-6; SS-3; PH-1   **Ht:** 5'10"   **Wt:** 185   **Born:** 2/4/77   **Age:** 25

Year Team	Lg Org	G	AB	H	2B	3B	HR	TB	R	RBI	TBB	IBB	SO	HBP	SH	SF	SB	CS	SB%	GDP	Avg	OBP	SLG
		BATTING															**BASERUNNING**				**PERCENTAGES**		
1998 Watertown	A- Cle	47	174	61	12	3	2	85	37	14	34	1	26	5	1	1	15	10	.60	4	.351	.467	.489
1999 Kinston	A+ Cle	133	486	120	27	6	9	186	86	54	77	3	95	6	1	3	47	11	.81	6	.247	.355	.383
2000 Akron	AA Cle	129	500	118	18	6	7	169	67	51	39	1	98	1	7	3	22	12	.65	7	.236	.291	.338
Buffalo	AAA Cle	4	12	1	0	0	0	1	0	1	0	0	4	0	0	1	0	0	—	1	.083	.077	.083
2001 Akron	AA Cle	68	264	74	13	4	4	107	33	24	26	0	48	2	2	0	16	11	.59	0	.280	.349	.405
4 Min. YEARS		381	1436	374	70	19	22	548	223	144	176	5	271	14	11	8	100	44	.69	18	.260	.345	.382

Josh Pressley

Bats: Left   **Throws:** Right   **Pos:** 1B-18; DH-12   **Ht:** 6'6"   **Wt:** 223   **Born:** 4/2/80   **Age:** 22

Year Team	Lg Org	G	AB	H	2B	3B	HR	TB	R	RBI	TBB	IBB	SO	HBP	SH	SF	SB	CS	SB%	GDP	Avg	OBP	SLG
		BATTING															**BASERUNNING**				**PERCENTAGES**		
1998 Devil Rays	R TB	36	125	38	6	0	1	47	22	16	20	1	29	4	0	0	2	1	.67	0	.304	.416	.376
1999 Chston-SC	A TB	118	437	106	22	0	9	155	50	64	49	5	80	5	0	4	1	4	.20	11	.243	.323	.355
2000 Chston-SC	A TB	130	488	148	44	0	6	210	61	60	49	3	62	4	0	3	2	1	.67	17	.303	.369	.430
2001 Orlando	AA TB	30	111	31	2	1	1	38	10	12	6	0	22	0	0	0	0	0	—	4	.279	.316	.342
4 Min. YEARS		314	1161	323	74	1	17	450	143	152	124	9	193	13	0	7	5	6	.45	32	.278	.352	.388

Eddie Priest

Pitches: Left   **Bats:** Right   **Pos:** SP-15; RP-8   **Ht:** 6'1"   **Wt:** 200   **Born:** 4/8/74   **Age:** 28

Year Team	Lg Org	G	GS	CG	GF	IP	BFP	H	R	ER	HR	SH	SF	HB	TBB	IBB	SO	WP	Bk	W	L	Pct.	ShO	Sv	ERA
		HOW MUCH HE PITCHED						**WHAT HE GAVE UP**												**THE RESULTS**					
1994 Billings	R+ Cin	13	13	2	0	85	333	74	31	24	3	1	0	1	14	0	82	2	1	7	4	.636	0	0	2.54
1995 Winston-Sal	A+ Cin	12	12	1	0	67	275	60	32	27	7	2	2	0	22	0	60	2	0	5	5	.500	1	0	3.63
1996 Winston-Sal	A+ Cin	4	4	0	0	12.1	48	5	2	1	1	0	0	0	6	0	9	1	0	1	0	1.000	0	0	0.73
1997 Chston-WV	A Cin	14	14	0	0	77	321	79	38	31	6	2	3	2	10	0	70	5	0	5	3	.625	0	0	3.62
Chattanooga	AA Cin	14	14	1	0	91.2	379	101	39	35	7	2	2	0	17	1	63	3	1	4	6	.400	0	0	3.44
1998 Chattanooga	AA Cin	4	4	0	0	26	105	15	6	5	1	1	0	0	10	1	29	1	0	1	2	.333	0	0	1.73
Indianapols	AAA Cin	6	6	0	0	34	147	36	19	18	6	2	0	1	7	0	21	2	0	4	1	.800	0	0	4.76
Buffalo	AAA Cle	16	16	0	0	88	390	103	56	48	10	2	1	2	28	1	44	2	0	3	5	.375	0	2	4.91
1999 Indianapols	AAA Cin	18	12	0	2	69	303	86	41	41	10	3	3	2	20	1	35	3	1	6	5	.545	0	0	5.35
Chattanooga	AA Cin	12	12	0	0	77	337	99	42	34	6	3	1	3	14	0	60	1	2	4	3	.571	0	0	3.97
2000 Chattanooga	AA Cin	27	27	3	0	180	770	182	78	56	5	10	5	8	59	1	149	11	0	11	7	.611	1	0	2.80
2001 Las Vegas	AAA LA	23	15	0	1	93.1	431	132	75	64	14	5	2	6	31	1	67	7	0	4	8	.333	0	0	6.17
1998 Cincinnati	NL	2	2	0	0	6	29	12	8	7	2	0	1	0	1	0	0	1	0	0	1	.000	0	0	10.50
8 Min. YEARS		163	149	7	3	900.1	3839	972	459	384	76	33	19	25	238	6	689	40	5	55	49	.529	2	2	3.84

Alejandro Prieto

Bats: Right   **Throws:** Right   **Pos:** 3B-44; 2B-39; SS-21; OF-3; DH-2   **Ht:** 5'11"   **Wt:** 175   **Born:** 6/19/76   **Age:** 26

Year Team	Lg Org	G	AB	H	2B	3B	HR	TB	R	RBI	TBB	IBB	SO	HBP	SH	SF	SB	CS	SB%	GDP	Avg	OBP	SLG
		BATTING															**BASERUNNING**				**PERCENTAGES**		
1993 Royals	R KC	45	114	28	3	0	0	31	14	6	9	1	13	0	4	0	4	2	.67	1	.246	.301	.272
1994 Royals	R KC	18	60	18	5	0	2	29	15	17	2	1	5	4	0	1	1	0	1.00	0	.300	.358	.483
1995 Springfield	A KC	124	431	108	9	3	2	129	61	44	40	1	69	6	12	2	11	7	.61	10	.251	.322	.299
1996 Wilmington	A+ KC	119	447	127	19	6	1	160	65	40	31	0	66	3	8	5	26	15	.63	7	.284	.331	.360
1997 Wilmington	A+ KC	129	437	94	13	3	3	122	52	38	41	1	59	2	11	6	20	8	.71	6	.215	.282	.279
1998 Wichita	AA KC	113	384	101	18	7	2	139	61	35	31	0	54	2	8	0	4	8	.33	13	.263	.321	.362
1999 Wichita	AA KC	114	360	106	23	4	6	155	56	41	35	1	47	1	13	3	12	6	.67	10	.294	.356	.431
2000 Omaha	AAA KC	118	384	101	19	0	7	141	54	37	26	0	40	6	8	2	14	6	.70	12	.263	.318	.367
2001 Omaha	AAA KC	105	376	106	21	3	8	157	45	44	36	0	59	1	4	3	9	2	.82	12	.282	.344	.418
9 Min. YEARS		885	2993	789	130	26	31	1064	423	302	251	5	412	25	68	22	101	54	.65	71	.264	.324	.355

Chris Prieto

Bats: Left   **Throws:** Left   **Pos:** OF-115; PH-3   **Ht:** 5'11"   **Wt:** 180   **Born:** 8/24/72   **Age:** 29

Year Team	Lg Org	G	AB	H	2B	3B	HR	TB	R	RBI	TBB	IBB	SO	HBP	SH	SF	SB	CS	SB%	GDP	Avg	OBP	SLG
1993 Spokane	A- SD	73	280	81	17	5	1	111	64	28	47	0	30	5	0	3	36	3	.92	4	.289	.397	.396
1994 Rancho Cuca	A+ SD	102	353	87	10	3	1	106	64	29	52	1	49	5	6	4	29	11	.73	3	.246	.348	.300
1995 Rancho Cuca	A+ SD	114	366	100	12	6	2	130	80	35	64	2	55	5	8	5	39	14	.74	10	.273	.384	.355
1996 Rancho Cuca	A+ SD	55	217	52	11	2	2	73	36	23	39	1	36	0	1	0	23	8	.74	2	.240	.355	.336
Las Vegas	AAA SD	5	7	0	0	0	0	0	1	0	0	0	0	0	0	0	0	0	—	0	.000	.000	.000
Memphis	AA SD	7	12	4	0	1	0	6	1	0	1	0	2	0	0	0	2	0	1.00	0	.333*	.385	.500
1997 Rancho Cuca	A+ SD	22	82	23	4	0	4	39	21	12	19	1	16	0	3	0	4	3	.57	0	.280	.416	.476
Mobile	AA SD	109	388	124	22	9	2	170	80	58	59	0	55	10	1	5	26	6	.81	2	.320	.418	.438
1998 Las Vegas	AAA SD	92	352	107	18	6	2	143	65	35	40	1	48	1	1	0	20	11	.65	4	.304	.377	.406
1999 Las Vegas	AAA SD	108	348	84	14	6	6	128	66	29	46	0	51	6	2	2	21	6	.78	2	.241	.338	.368
2000 Albuquerque	AAA LA	85	248	69	13	3	8	112	53	31	50	1	42	4	3	1	25	5	.83	3	.278	.406	.452
2001 Las Vegas	AAA LA	118	446	130	27	6	19	226	98	58	67	3	79	13	2	1	25	7	.78	6	.291	.398	.507
9 Min. YEARS		890	3099	861	148	47	47	1244	629	338	484	10	463	49	27	21	250	74	.77	36	.278	.382	.401

Rick Prieto

Bats: Both   **Throws:** Right   **Pos:** OF-86; 2B-13; PH-7; 3B-2; PR-2   **Ht:** 5'10"   **Wt:** 175   **Born:** 8/24/72   **Age:** 29

Year Team	Lg Org	G	AB	H	2B	3B	HR	TB	R	RBI	TBB	IBB	SO	HBP	SH	SF	SB	CS	SB%	GDP	Avg	OBP	SLG
1993 Watertown	A- Cle	68	219	64	15	4	4	99	53	40	39	2	61	8	1	1	11	1	.92	3	.292	.416	.452
1994 Columbus	A Cle	124	378	81	14	8	8	135	67	39	65	3	87	15	4	0	21	10	.68	6	.214	.352	.357
1995 Kinston	A+ Cle	26	88	17	2	1	1	24	12	10	13	0	20	0	1	0	3	1	.75	2	.193	.297	.273
Bakersfield	A+ Cle	74	248	55	12	2	2	77	34	22	29	0	46	3	6	0	15	2	.88	1	.222	.311	.310
Columbus	A Cle	4	18	4	0	0	1	7	1	2	0	0	4	0	0	0	0	0	—	0	.222	.222	.389
1996 Salinas	IND —	88	364	123	27	10	5	185	83	49	38	1	42	7	0	1	30	1	.97	6	.338	.410	.508
1997 Salinas	IND —	22	98	35	6	2	1	48	14	10	5	0	12	2	0	1	15	0	1.00	1	.357	.396	.490
Rancho Cuca	A+ SD	68	281	82	12	3	5	115	47	31	44	0	45	6	2	0	11	6	.65	0	.292	.399	.409
1998 Las Vegas	AAA SD	32	79	21	6	1	0	29	15	8	12	0	22	2	0	1	4	2	.67	0	.266	.372	.367
Mobile	AA SD	72	218	52	9	2	4	77	30	25	21	1	49	3	0	0	9	2	.82	0	.239	.314	.353
1999 Mobile	AA SD	118	359	103	14	4	6	143	61	43	57	0	55	5	5	1	28	5	.85	6	.287	.391	.398
2000 Birmingham	AA CWS	118	432	110	15	3	1	134	65	40	86	1	59	2	14	3	30	5	.86	7	.255	.379	.310
2001 Birmingham	AA CWS	92	313	75	12	4	4	107	51	34	52	0	47	3	4	1	9	6	.60	8	.240	.352	.342
Charlotte	AAA CWS	11	26	6	0	0	0	6	4	1	6	0	6	0	1	0	0	0	—	2	.231	.375	.231
9 Min. YEARS		917	3121	828	144	44	42	1186	537	354	467	8	555	56	38	9	186	41	.82	42	.265	.370	.380

Chris Pritchett

Bats: Left   **Throws:** Right   **Pos:** DH-67; 1B-55; PH-2; 3B-1   **Ht:** 6'4"   **Wt:** 212   **Born:** 1/31/70   **Age:** 32

Year Team	Lg Org	G	AB	H	2B	3B	HR	TB	R	RBI	TBB	IBB	SO	HBP	SH	SF	SB	CS	SB%	GDP	Avg	OBP	SLG
1991 Boise	A- Ana	70	255	68	10	3	9	111	41	50	47	3	41	2	0	3	1	0	1.00	7	.267	.381	.435
1992 Quad City	A Ana	128	448	130	19	1	13	190	79	72	71	6	88	5	2	5	9	4	.69	7	.290	.389	.424
1993 Midland	AA Ana	127	464	143	30	6	2	191	61	66	61	2	72	2	6	7	3	7	.30	17	.308	.386	.412
1994 Midland	AA Ana	127	460	142	25	4	6	193	86	91	92	8	87	2	3	7	5	3	.63	8	.309	.421	.420
1995 Vancouver	AAA Ana	123	434	120	27	4	8	179	66	53	56	6	79	5	2	1	2	3	.40	7	.276	.365	.412
1996 Vancouver	AAA Ana	130	485	143	39	1	16	232	78	73	71	11	96	6	0	6	5	4	.56	7	.295	.387	.478
1997 Vancouver	AAA Ana	109	383	107	30	3	7	164	60	47	42	6	72	5	5	2	5	3	.63	9	.279	.356	.428
1998 Vancouver	AAA Ana	104	374	97	21	1	7	141	42	41	37	3	72	0	3	5	2	2	.50	14	.259	.322	.377
1999 Edmonton	AAA Ana	34	118	33	15	1	12	150	60	45	47	3	70	3	1	2	1	1	.50	7	.279	.368	.431
2000 Scranton-WB	AAA Phi	117	391	93	18	2	6	133	55	60	56	3	65	5	1	6	5	2	.71	6	.238	.336	.340
2001 Salt Lake	AAA Ana	125	476	144	36	3	17	237	66	75	45	5	102	1	2	3	3	2	.60	7	.303	.362	.498
1996 California	AL	5	13	2	0	0	0	2	1	1	0	0	3	0	0	0	0	0	—	0	.154	.154	.154
1998 Anaheim	AL	31	80	23	2	1	2	33	12	8	4	0	16	0	0	0	2	0	1.00	0	.288	.321	.413
1999 Anaheim	AL	20	45	7	1	0	1	11	3	2	2	0	9	0	1	1	1	1	.50	0	.156	.188	.244
2000 Philadelphia	NL	5	11	1	0	0	0	1	0	0	1	0	3	0	0	0	0	0	—	0	.091	.167	.091
11 Min. YEARS		1256	4518	1284	270	29	103	1921	694	673	625	57	844	36	25	47	41	31	.57	96	.284	.372	.425
4 Maj. YEARS		61	149	33	3	1	3	47	16	11	7	0	31	0	1	1	3	1	.75	4	.221	.255	.315

Alan Probst

Bats: Right   **Throws:** Right   **Pos:** C-55; PH-5   **Ht:** 6'4"   **Wt:** 215   **Born:** 10/24/70   **Age:** 31

Year Team	Lg Org	G	AB	H	2B	3B	HR	TB	R	RBI	TBB	IBB	SO	HBP	SH	SF	SB	CS	SB%	GDP	Avg	OBP	SLG
1992 Auburn	A- Hou	66	224	53	14	1	5	84	24	34	23	1	48	3	1	2	1	0	1.00	5	.237	.313	.375
1993 Asheville	A Hou	40	124	32	4	0	5	51	14	21	12	0	34	0	0	1	0	2	.00	5	.258	.321	.411
Quad City	A Hou	49	176	48	9	2	3	70	18	28	16	1	48	3	0	3	2	0	1.00	1	.273	.338	.398
1994 Quad City	A Hou	113	375	87	14	4	9	130	50	41	37	3	98	2	3	3	2	5	.29	2	.232	.302	.347
1995 Quad City	A Hou	52	151	39	12	1	7	74	23	27	13	0	28	1	1	1	2	0	1.00	3	.258	.319	.490
Jackson	AA Hou	28	89	21	5	0	1	29	11	8	7	0	25	1	0	2	0	0	—	3	.236	.293	.326
1996 Tucson	AAA Hou	2	7	2	1	0	0	3	0	1	1	0	3	0	0	0	0	0	—	0	.286	.375	.429
Jackson	AA Hou	63	180	44	9	1	7	76	20	33	16	1	43	2	2	2	1	0	1.00	0	.244	.310	.422
1997 Jackson	AA Hou	8	24	8	2	0	1	13	2	7	3	0	7	0	0	0	0	0	—	0	.333	.407	.542
New Orleans	AAA Hou	46	112	25	6	0	2	37	8	10	9	0	27	0	1	2	0	0	—	4	.223	.276	.330
1998 Knoxville	AA Tor	79	261	68	22	0	10	120	53	44	35	0	81	2	1	3	2	1	.67	5	.261	.349	.460
Syracuse	AAA Tor	12	33	11	1	0	1	15	2	4	2	0	6	0	0	0	0	0	—	2	.333	.371	.455
1999 Syracuse	AAA Tor	23	59	13	2	0	1	18	6	5	4	0	18	0	0	1	0	0	—	1	.220	.266	.305
Knoxville	AA Tor	21	66	14	3	0	1	20	5	7	5	0	23	0	1	0	0	0	—	3	.212	.260	.303
2000 Norfolk	AAA NYM	36	104	28	5	0	2	39	11	13	10	0	38	0	1	0	0	0	—	1	.269	.333	.375
2001 Norfolk	AAA NYM	23	60	9	2	0	1	14	4	5	4	0	19	0	0	2	0	0	—	3	.150	.197	.233
St. Lucie	A+ NYM	37	112	17	6	0	1	26	6	9	12	0	38	3	2	0	0	1	.00	6	.152	.252	.232
10 Min. YEARS		698	2157	519	117	6	57	819	257	297	209	6	584	17	13	24	10	9	.53	53	.241	.310	.380

Scott Proctor

Pitches: Right Bats: Right Pos: SP-24; RP-1 Ht: 6'1" Wt: 198 Born: 1/2/77 Age: 25

Year Team	Lg Org	G	GS	CG	GF	IP	BFP	H	R	ER	HR	SH	SF	HB	TBB	IBB	SO	WP	Bk	W	L	Pct.	ShO	Sv	ERA
1998 Yakima	A- LA	3	1	0	2	5	26	9	8	6	1	1	1	0	1	0	4	1	2	0	1	.000	0	2	10.80
1999 Yakima	A- LA	16	6	0	5	50	235	57	45	40	4	1	4	5	26	0	41	7	1	4	2	.667	0	0	7.20
2000 Vero Beach	A+ LA	35	5	0	15	89	413	93	65	51	13	2	4	6	54	1	70	6	1	3	7	.300	0	1	5.16
2001 Vero Beach	A+ LA	15	15	0	0	90.2	366	73	30	25	8	2	2	9	30	1	79	3	0	6	4	.600	0	0	2.48
Jacksnville	AA LA	10	9	0	0	49.2	215	39	26	23	6	3	2	2	31	1	48	2	0	4	3	.571	0	0	4.17
4 Min. YEARS		79	36	0	22	284.1	1255	271	174	145	32	9	13	22	142	3	242	19	4	17	17	.500	0	3	4.59

Jason Pruett

Pitches: Left Bats: Left Pos: RP-39 Ht: 6'3" Wt: 186 Born: 1/21/79 Age: 23

Year Team	Lg Org	G	GS	CG	GF	IP	BFP	H	R	ER	HR	SH	SF	HB	TBB	IBB	SO	WP	Bk	W	L	Pct.	ShO	Sv	ERA
1999 Hudson Val	A- TB	25	0	0	5	40.2	166	32	13	9	1	6	1	1	8	0	29	1	1	4	2	.667	0	1	1.99
2000 Chston-SC	A TB	49	0	0	25	68.2	290	55	30	19	4	6	4	1	20	0	73	2	0	6	4	.600	0	13	2.49
2001 St. Pete	A+ TB	8	0	0	8	10.2	45	11	2	1	0	3	0	0	3	0	7	1	0	2	1	.667	0	2	0.84
Bluefield	R+ Bal	1	0	0	0	1.2	10	2	1	1	0	0	0	2	1	0	2	1	0	0	0	—	0	0	5.40
Orlando	AA TB	38	0	0	13	51	236	59	38	29	5	3	5	2	19	0	29	3	0	2	5	.286	0	1	5.12
3 Min. YEARS		121	0	0	51	172.2	747	159	84	59	10	18	10	6	51	0	140	8	1	14	12	.538	0	17	3.08

Brandon Puffer

Pitches: Right Bats: Right Pos: RP-56 Ht: 6'3" Wt: 190 Born: 10/5/75 Age: 26

Year Team	Lg Org	G	GS	CG	GF	IP	BFP	H	R	ER	HR	SH	SF	HB	TBB	IBB	SO	WP	Bk	W	L	Pct.	ShO	Sv	ERA
1994 Twins	R Min	18	0	0	16	35.1	157	33	18	12	1	0	1	4	19	0	40	6	1	2	2	.500	0	2	3.06
1995 Twins	R Min	14	5	0	6	40.2	175	29	21	13	0	0	0	2	21	0	35	5	0	0	3	.000	0	1	2.88
1996 Angels	R Ana	1	1	0	0	5	23	7	2	2	0	0	0	0	1	0	3	1	0	0	1	.000	0	0	3.60
Boise	A- Ana	16	0	0	8	30.1	129	27	19	15	3	1	3	1	11	0	22	3	0	2	0	1.000	0	1	4.45
1997 Boise	A- Ana	6	0	0	2	15.1	63	10	5	4	0	0	1	1	2	0	15	1	0	0	0	—	0	1	2.35
Cedar Rapds	A Ana	10	0	0	2	17.1	66	8	6	5	0	0	0	0	10	0	11	3	1	0	0	—	0	0	2.60
1998 Chattanooga	AA Cin	7	0	0	4	8.2	32	2	3	3	2	0	0	1	3	0	6	0	0	0	0	—	0	0	3.12
Chston-WV	A Cin	29	0	0	12	50.2	242	68	45	39	4	2	1	7	23	4	36	5	0	2	7	.222	0	1	6.93
1999 Clinton	A Cin	59	0	0	55	63.1	277	53	20	14	2	2	2	11	24	3	60	4	1	1	2	.333	0	34	1.99
2000 Asheville	A Col	14	0	0	9	14.1	75	19	16	13	3	2	0	3	11	3	15	3	0	0	0	—	0	5	8.16
Somerset	IND —	15	0	0	7	23	104	25	12	9	1	0	1	1	9	2	21	2	1	2	2	.500	0	1	3.52
Kissimmee	A+ Hou	18	0	0	18	21.1	95	18	6	3	0	3	0	1	11	4	26	3	0	2	3	.400	0	9	1.27
2001 Round Rock	AA Hou	56	0	0	33	82.2	331	52	19	19	4	1	1	7	35	2	91	3	0	6	1	.857	0	8	2.07
8 Min. YEARS		263	6	0	172	408	1769	351	192	151	20	11	10	39	180	18	381	39	4	17	21	.447	0	63	3.33

Denis Pujals

Pitches: Right Bats: Right Pos: RP-9 Ht: 6'3" Wt: 228 Born: 2/5/73 Age: 29

Year Team	Lg Org	G	GS	CG	GF	IP	BFP	H	R	ER	HR	SH	SF	HB	TBB	IBB	SO	WP	Bk	W	L	Pct.	ShO	Sv	ERA
1996 Butte	R+ TB	15	15	0	0	87.1	392	110	65	49	9	1	0	5	19	0	82	6	3	2	7	.222	0	0	5.05
1997 St. Pete	A+ TB	24	24	2	0	140.1	588	156	74	69	14	6	8	8	27	1	69	1	0	9	4	.692	1	0	4.43
1998 St. Pete	A+ TB	42	0	0	9	72.2	308	73	30	23	1	2	1	2	22	2	46	2	0	5	2	.714	0	1	2.85
1999 Orlando	AA TB	42	0	0	9	72.1	316	82	35	31	6	2	6	6	19	3	39	6	0	5	3	.625	0	0	3.86
2000 Durham	AAA TB	20	3	0	6	48	215	59	32	28	4	1	1	1	19	1	18	0	1	4	2	.667	0	0	5.25
Orlando	AA TB	6	2	0	0	19	75	14	6	5	1	0	1	2	4	0	7	1	0	1	2	.333	0	0	2.37
2001 Durham	AAA TB	2	0	0	0	5	23	5	5	3	2	0	2	1	2	0	2	0	0	0	0	—	0	0	5.40
Orlando	AA TB	7	0	0	2	11	56	19	9	9	3	0	1	1	4	0	3	0	0	0	0	—	0	0	7.36
6 Min. YEARS		158	44	2	26	455.2	1973	518	256	217	40	12	20	26	116	7	266	16	4	26	20	.565	1	1	4.29

Rafael Pujols

Bats: Right Throws: Right Pos: C-53; 1B-30; DH-12; PH-4; OF-1 Ht: 6'0" Wt: 165 Born: 1/20/78 Age: 24

Year Team	Lg Org	G	AB	H	2B	3B	HR	TB	R	RBI	TBB	IBB	SO	HBP	SH	SF	SB	CS	SB%	GDP	Avg	OBP	SLG
1998 Sou Oregon	A- Oak	54	183	41	6	1	3	58	24	24	21	0	34	0	0	1	3	0	1.00	4	.224	.302	.317
1999 Modesto	A+ Oak	71	233	55	16	0	3	80	28	32	24	0	34	1	0	2	5	6	.45	4	.236	.308	.343
2000 Visalia	A+ Oak	117	422	136	16	2	9	183	61	74	50	5	57	1	0	8	11	6	.65	8	.322	.389	.434
2001 Midland	AA Oak	19	59	13	3	1	0	18	5	6	4	0	13	1	0	1	0	0	—	1	.220	.277	.305
Sacramento	AAA Oak	9	30	7	1	0	1	11	4	3	3	0	5	0	0	0	0	0	—	0	.233	.303	.367
Modesto	A+ Oak	64	223	60	13	1	1	78	33	23	45	3	34	1	3	1	4	1	.80	6	.269	.393	.350
4 Min. YEARS		334	1150	312	55	5	17	428	155	162	147	8	177	4	3	13	23	13	.64	25	.271	.352	.372

Kenny Pumphrey

Pitches: Right Bats: Right Pos: SP-21; RP-8 Ht: 6'6" Wt: 208 Born: 9/10/76 Age: 25

Year Team	Lg Org	G	GS	CG	GF	IP	BFP	H	R	ER	HR	SH	SF	HB	TBB	IBB	SO	WP	Bk	W	L	Pct.	ShO	Sv	ERA
1994 Mets	R NYM	10	8	0	0	57.1	244	51	27	23	6	1	4	3	16	0	42	6	3	1	3	.250	0	0	3.61
1995 Kingsport	R+ NYM	12	12	0	0	65.1	283	50	32	28	3	3	0	6	42	0	76	7	0	7	3	.700	0	0	3.86
1996 Pittsfield	A- NYM	14	14	1	0	87	373	68	41	31	1	1	2	4	41	0	61	10	2	7	2	.778	1	0	3.21
1997 Capital Cty	A NYM	27	27	3	0	165.2	708	137	66	57	11	7	3	20	72	0	133	11	1	12	6	.667	2	0	3.10
1998 St. Lucie	A+ NYM	25	25	1	0	142.1	606	126	66	50	7	2	6	7	57	0	99	9	1	10	6	.625	0	0	3.16
Binghamton	AA NYM	3	2	0	0	8	36	10	4	4	0	0	0	0	3	0	6	0	0	1	0	1.000	0	0	4.50
1999 Binghamton	AA NYM	25	23	0	1	131.1	617	146	95	70	10	4	4	15	71	0	84	5	0	6	9	.400	0	0	4.80
2000 New Britain	AA Min	12	12	0	0	63.1	289	68	54	50	7	1	1	8	31	0	39	3	0	0	5	.000	0	0	7.11
Fort Myers	A+ Min	14	13	1	0	83.1	343	68	32	28	1	1	3	6	35	0	58	3	0	4	6	.400	0	0	3.02

Year Team	Lg Org	G	GS	CG	GF	IP	BFP	H	R	ER	HR	SH	SF	HB	TBB	IBB	SO	WP	Bk	W	L	Pct.	ShO	Sv	ERA
2001 Edmonton	AAA Min	7	7	0	0	38.2	186	55	39	31	3	1	0	4	18	1	17	1	0	1	6	.143	0	0	7.22
New Britain	AA Min	22	14	2	3	103	415	89	38	33	5	1	2	7	26	0	52	4	0	8	2	.800	1	1	2.88
8 Min. YEARS		171	157	9	4	945.1	4100	868	498	405	54	22	25	80	412	1	667	59	7	57	52	.523	4	1	3.86

Rob Purvis

Pitches: Right **Bats:** Right **Pos:** SP-23; RP-1   **Ht:** 6'2" **Wt:** 200 **Born:** 8/11/77 **Age:** 24

Year Team	Lg Org	G	GS	CG	GF	IP	BFP	H	R	ER	HR	SH	SF	HB	TBB	IBB	SO	WP	Bk	W	L	Pct.	ShO	Sv	ERA
1999 White Sox	R CWS	4	0	0	3	9	48	12	10	4	0	0	0	0	6	0	7	1	0	0	1	.000	0	2	4.00
Burlington	A CWS	6	0	0	3	11.1	50	10	5	3	1	0	0	1	4	0	8	0	1	0	0	—	0	1	2.38
2000 Winston-Sal	A+ CWS	27	27	2	0	167.2	727	139	81	63	6	2	2	11	87	0	114	22	0	11	10	.524	0	0	3.38
Birmingham	AA CWS	1	1	0	0	4	24	6	8	2	1	0	1	0	3	0	3	0	0	1	0	1.000	0	0	4.50
2001 Birmingham	AA CWS	24	23	0	1	140	629	165	96	82	9	2	6	4	70	0	53	14	2	5	9	.357	0	0	5.27
3 Min. YEARS		62	51	2	7	332	1478	332	200	154	17	4	9	16	170	0	185	37	7	16	21	.432	0	3	4.17

J.J. Putz

Pitches: Right **Bats:** Right **Pos:** SP-26; RP-1   **Ht:** 6'5" **Wt:** 220 **Born:** 2/22/77 **Age:** 25

Year Team	Lg Org	G	GS	CG	GF	IP	BFP	H	R	ER	HR	SH	SF	HB	TBB	IBB	SO	WP	Bk	W	L	Pct.	ShO	Sv	ERA
1999 Everett	A- Sea	10	0	0	3	22.1	99	23	13	12	2	1	4	2	11	1	17	0	1	0	0	—	0	2	4.84
2000 Wisconsin	A Sea	26	25	3	0	142.2	611	130	71	50	4	6	7	9	63	2	105	8	0	12	6	.667	2	0	3.15
2001 San Antonio	AA Sea	27	26	0	0	148	642	145	80	63	11	10	5	9	59	2	135	12	0	7	9	.438	0	0	3.83
3 Min. YEARS		63	51	3	3	313	1352	298	164	125	17	17	16	20	133	5	257	20	1	19	15	.559	2	2	3.59

Matt Quatraro

Bats: Right **Throws:** Right **Pos:** C-48; 1B-22; OF-11; DH-3; PH-2; PR-1   **Ht:** 6'2" **Wt:** 208 **Born:** 11/14/73 **Age:** 28

Year Team	Lg Org	G	AB	H	2B	3B	HR	TB	R	RBI	TBB	IBB	SO	HBP	SH	SF	SB	CS	SB%	GDP	Avg	OBP	SLG
1996 Butte	R+ TB	59	244	84	16	4	1	111	53	59	25	0	29	8	0	3	3	1	.75	4	.344	.418	.455
1997 Chston-SC	A TB	78	294	88	18	2	7	131	45	42	18	0	55	2	1	5	15	5	.75	7	.299	.339	.446
1998 St. Pete	A+ TB	73	270	67	14	2	4	97	36	31	31	1	67	2	1	3	4	0	1.00	6	.248	.327	.359
1999 Orlando	AA TB	1	4	1	0	0	1	4	1	2	0	0	2	0	1	0	0	0	—	0	.250	.250	1.000
St. Pete	A+ TB	73	218	57	14	2	3	84	20	23	14	1	47	1	2	0	3	1	.75	6	.261	.309	.385
2000 St. Pete	A+ TB	15	49	10	1	1	1	16	6	3	2	0	14	0	0	0	0	0	—	2	.204	.235	.327
2001 Orlando	AA TB	81	271	88	24	2	6	134	38	35	17	0	60	7	1	4	4	1	.80	2	.325	.375	.494
6 Min. YEARS		380	1350	395	87	13	23	577	189	195	107	2	274	20	6	15	29	8	.78	35	.293	.350	.427

Robb Quinlan

Bats: Right **Throws:** Right **Pos:** 1B-113; OF-8; DH-7; PH-2   **Ht:** 6'1" **Wt:** 195 **Born:** 3/17/77 **Age:** 25

Year Team	Lg Org	G	AB	H	2B	3B	HR	TB	R	RBI	TBB	IBB	SO	HBP	SH	SF	SB	CS	SB%	GDP	Avg	OBP	SLG
1999 Boise	A- Ana	73	295	95	20	1	9	144	51	77	35	2	52	4	0	1	5	3	.63	5	.322	.400	.488
2000 Lk Elsinore	A+ Ana	127	482	153	35	5	5	213	79	85	67	1	82	2	2	9	6	4	.60	7	.317	.396	.442
2001 Arkansas	AA Ana	129	492	145	33	7	14	234	82	79	53	9	84	6	0	7	4	4	.00	12	.295	.366	.476
3 Min. YEARS		329	1269	393	88	13	28	591	212	241	155	12	218	12	2	17	11	11	.50	24	.310	.385	.466

Humberto Quintero

Bats: Right **Throws:** Right **Pos:** C-105; PH-2; DH-1   **Ht:** 5'10" **Wt:** 190 **Born:** 8/2/79 **Age:** 22

Year Team	Lg Org	G	AB	H	2B	3B	HR	TB	R	RBI	TBB	IBB	SO	HBP	SH	SF	SB	CS	SB%	GDP	Avg	OBP	SLG
1999 Bristol	R+ CWS	48	155	43	5	2	0	52	30	15	9	0	19	6	3	0	11	1	.92	8	.277	.341	.335
2000 Burlington	A CWS	75	248	59	12	2	0	75	23	24	15	1	31	3	4	2	10	6	.63	8	.238	.287	.302
White Sox	R CWS	15	56	22	2	2	0	28	13	8	0	0	3	2	0	0	1	0	1.00	2	.393	.414	.500
2001 Kannapolis	A CWS	60	197	53	7	1	1	65	32	20	8	1	20	7	8	0	7	3	.70	5	.269	.321	.330
Winston-Sal	A+ CWS	43	154	37	6	0	0	43	15	12	5	0	19	2	2	3	9	3	.75	3	.240	.268	.279
Birmingham	AA CWS	5	19	4	0	0	0	4	0	2	0	0	2	1	0	0	0	0	—	0	.211	.250	.211
3 Min. YEARS		246	829	218	32	7	1	267	113	81	37	2	94	21	17	5	38	13	.75	26	.263	.309	.322

Ryan Radmanovich

Bats: Left **Throws:** Right **Pos:** OF-111; PH-8; DH-6; PR-1   **Ht:** 6'2" **Wt:** 200 **Born:** 8/9/71 **Age:** 30

Year Team	Lg Org	G	AB	H	2B	3B	HR	TB	R	RBI	TBB	IBB	SO	HBP	SH	SF	SB	CS	SB%	GDP	Avg	OBP	SLG
1993 Fort Wayne	A Min	62	204	59	7	5	8	100	36	38	30	2	60	7	2	2	8	2	.80	4	.289	.395	.490
1994 Fort Myers	A+ Min	26	85	16	4	0	2	26	11	9	7	0	19	2	0	0	3	1	.75	0	.188	.266	.306
Fort Wayne	A Min	101	383	105	20	6	19	194	64	69	45	3	98	3	1	1	19	14	.58	7	.274	.354	.507
1995 Fort Myers	A+ Min	12	41	13	2	0	0	15	3	5	2	0	8	1	0	0	0	0	—	0	.317	.364	.366
1996 Hardware Cy	AA Min	125	453	127	31	2	25	237	77	86	49	6	122	3	3	2	4	11	.27	12	.280	.353	.523
1997 Salt Lake	AAA Min	133	485	128	25	4	28	245	92	78	67	7	138	4	1	5	11	4	.73	4	.264	.355	.505
1998 Tacoma	AAA Sea	110	397	119	33	2	15	201	73	65	46	3	83	1	5	7	2	4	.33	6	.300	.368	.506
1999 Tacoma	AAA Sea	109	420	120	24	3	17	201	69	80	53	5	83	4	3	6	10	4	.71	8	.286	.366	.479
2000 Las Vegas	AAA SD	120	399	109	31	3	11	179	74	59	60	3	84	0	0	5	4	3	.57	9	.273	.364	.449
2001 Portland	AAA SD	92	296	78	17	1	14	139	44	52	59	3	82	0	2	4	2	4	.33	6	.264	.382	.470
Nashville	AAA Pit	31	94	27	8	0	5	50	17	14	11	0	26	0	0	1	1	0	1.00	6	.287	.358	.532
1998 Seattle	AL	25	69	15	4	0	2	25	5	10	4	1	25	0	2	0	1	1	.50	0	.217	.260	.362
9 Min. YEARS		921	3257	901	202	26	144	1587	560	555	429	32	803	25	17	33	64	47	.58	56	.277	.362	.487

Steve Rain

Pitches: Right **Bats:** Right **Pos:** RP-34   **Ht:** 6'6" **Wt:** 260 **Born:** 6/2/75 **Age:** 27

Year Team	Lg Org	G	GS	CG	GF	IP	BFP	H	R	ER	HR	SH	SF	HB	TBB	IBB	SO	WP	Bk	W	L	Pct.	ShO	Sv	ERA
1993 Cubs	R ChC	10	6	0	3	37	162	37	20	16	0	1	1	2	17	0	29	5	1	1	3	.250	0	0	3.89
1994 Huntington	R+ ChC	14	10	1	1	68	272	55	26	20	2	2	2	2	19	0	55	4	4	3	3	.500	1	0	2.65
1995 Rockford	A ChC	53	0	0	51	59.1	234	38	12	8	0	3	2	2	23	3	66	8	0	5	2	.714	0	23	1.21
1996 Orlando	AA ChC	35	0	0	29	38.2	163	32	15	11	4	0	0	3	12	1	48	2	1	1	0	1.000	0	10	2.56
Iowa	AAA ChC	26	0	0	26	26	103	17	9	9	3	3	3	0	8	3	23	1	0	2	1	.667	0	10	3.12
1997 Iowa	AAA ChC	40	0	0	17	44.1	217	51	30	29	8	2	1	0	34	4	50	4	1	7	1	.875	0	1	5.89
Orlando	AA ChC	14	0	0	12	14.2	69	16	7	5	2	0	0	1	8	0	11	0	0	1	2	.333	0	4	3.07
1998 Iowa	AAA ChC	29	14	1	4	103.2	487	118	82	77	14	6	2	7	64	0	83	16	0	4	6	.400	0	0	6.68
1999 West Tenn	AA ChC	40	0	0	39	45.1	188	32	9	8	3	0	2	1	16	3	55	5	1	3	1	.750	0	24	1.59
Iowa	AAA ChC	8	0	0	7	9	38	7	2	2	1	0	0	0	4	0	9	0	0	0	1	.000	0	2	2.00
2000 Iowa	AAA ChC	28	0	0	21	31.1	132	31	14	12	4	2	1	0	6	1	34	2	0	0	2	.000	0	0	3.45
2001 Iowa	AAA ChC	9	0	0	6	7.2	40	10	12	10	3	1	0	2	6	0	9	2	0	0	1	—	0	1	11.74
Indianapols	AAA Mil	25	0	0	11	35.1	180	35	34	29	4	2	0	5	34	2	34	5	0	2	2	.500	0	1	7.39
1999 Chicago	NL	16	0	0	5	14.2	79	28	17	15	1	3	1	1	7	0	12	1	0	0	1	.000	0	0	9.20
2000 Chicago	NL	37	0	0	6	49.2	214	46	25	24	10	1	1	1	27	0	54	4	0	3	4	.429	0	0	4.35
9 Min. YEARS		331	30	2	227	520.1	2285	479	272	236	48	22	14	25	251	17	506	54	8	29	24	.547	1	82	4.08
2 Maj. YEARS		53	0	0	11	64.1	293	74	42	39	11	4	2	2	34	0	66	5	0	3	5	.375	0	0	5.46

Aaron Rakers

Pitches: Right **Bats:** Right **Pos:** RP-51   **Ht:** 6'3" **Wt:** 205 **Born:** 1/22/77 **Age:** 25

Year Team	Lg Org	G	GS	CG	GF	IP	BFP	H	R	ER	HR	SH	SF	HB	TBB	IBB	SO	WP	Bk	W	L	Pct.	ShO	Sv	ERA
1999 Bluefield	R+ Bal	3	0	0	1	7	28	5	2	2	1	0	0	0	3	0	12	0	0	0	0	—	0	0	2.57
Delmarva	A Bal	18	0	0	16	25.1	97	9	6	4	0	0	1	0	13	0	38	1	1	4	1	.800	0	8	1.42
2000 Frederick	A+ Bal	26	0	0	19	40.2	157	23	8	7	2	0	2	2	12	1	57	1	0	1	1	.500	0	8	1.55
Bowie	AA Bal	24	0	0	18	29	118	20	11	9	5	1	3	1	10	0	21	0	0	3	2	.600	0	8	2.79
2001 Bowie	AA Bal	51	0	0	39	60.1	257	53	21	16	8	1	1	2	20	1	74	4	0	4	4	.500	0	14	2.39
3 Min. YEARS		122	0	0	93	162.1	657	110	48	38	16	2	7	5	58	2	202	6	1	12	8	.600	0	38	2.11

Jason Rakers

Pitches: Right **Bats:** Right **Pos:** RP-39; SP-5   **Ht:** 6'2" **Wt:** 200 **Born:** 6/29/73 **Age:** 29

Year Team	Lg Org	G	GS	CG	GF	IP	BFP	H	R	ER	HR	SH	SF	HB	TBB	IBB	SO	WP	Bk	W	L	Pct.	ShO	Sv	ERA
1995 Watertown	A- Cle	14	14	1	0	75	315	72	27	25	3	0	2	0	24	1	73	6	2	4	3	.571	1	0	3.00
1996 Columbus	A Cle	14	14	1	0	77.1	319	84	37	31	5	1	1	3	17	0	64	8	1	5	4	.556	1	0	3.61
1997 Kinston	A+ Cle	17	17	2	0	102.2	405	93	41	35	10	1	0	1	18	0	105	2	1	8	5	.615	2	0	3.07
Buffalo	AAA Cle	1	1	0	0	7	26	5	0	0	0	0	0	0	1	0	3	0	0	1	0	1.000	0	0	0.00
Akron	AA Cle	7	7	1	0	41	168	36	21	20	3	1	2	4	11	0	31	1	0	1	4	.200	1	0	4.39
1998 Akron	AA Cle	5	5	0	0	31.1	130	35	10	9	2	2	1	0	7	0	27	2	0	3	1	.750	0	0	2.59
Buffalo	AAA Cle	21	21	1	0	126	542	134	70	64	13	2	6	8	38	0	89	7	1	8	6	.571	1	0	4.57
1999 Buffalo	AAA Cle	23	20	1	1	131.2	577	151	83	72	17	4	2	6	31	2	85	4	3	7	8	.467	0	0	4.92
2000 Omaha	AAA KC	32	6	0	9	75	319	83	49	46	14	0	2	1	17	2	68	2	1	3	2	.600	0	2	5.52
2001 Omaha	AAA KC	44	5	0	24	97	401	100	50	48	16	1	3	3	16	0	99	2	0	6	4	.600	0	5	4.45
1998 Cleveland	AL	1	0	0	0	1	6	0	1	1	0	1	0	0	3	0	0	0	0	0	0	—	0	0	9.00
1999 Cleveland	AL	1	0	0	0	2	9	2	1	1	0	0	0	0	1	0	0	0	0	0	0	—	0	0	4.50
2000 Kansas City	AL	11	0	0	3	21.2	102	33	22	22	5	0	1	0	7	0	16	3	0	2	0	1.000	0	0	9.14
7 Min. YEARS		178	110	7	34	764	3202	793	388	350	83	12	19	26	180	5	644	34	9	46	37	.554	5	7	4.12
3 Maj. YEARS		13	0	0	4	24.2	117	35	24	24	6	0	2	0	11	0	16	3	0	2	0	1.000	0	0	8.76

Erasmo Ramirez

Pitches: Left **Bats:** Left **Pos:** RP-50; SP-1   **Ht:** 6'0" **Wt:** 180 **Born:** 4/29/76 **Age:** 26

Year Team	Lg Org	G	GS	CG	GF	IP	BFP	H	R	ER	HR	SH	SF	HB	TBB	IBB	SO	WP	Bk	W	L	Pct.	ShO	Sv	ERA
1998 Bakersfield	A+ SF	14	0	0	9	21.1	80	10	8	8	0	2	0	2	6	0	17	1	3	1	1	.500	0	3	3.38
Salem-Keizr	A- SF	9	2	0	0	19.1	81	19	11	8	3	1	0	1	2	0	23	0	0	0	1	.000	0	0	3.72
1999 San Jose	A+ SF	31	0	0	12	57.1	219	42	18	17	2	2	4	1	8	0	52	2	0	2	0	1.000	0	5	2.67
2000 Shreveport	AA SF	39	2	0	13	58.2	269	80	45	42	7	6	4	3	21	5	46	0	0	0	5	.000	0	1	6.44
2001 San Jose	A+ SF	17	0	0	6	31.2	126	23	14	12	2	2	0	0	5	0	33	2	0	3	2	.600	0	1	3.41
Shreveport	AA SF	22	1	0	6	33.1	130	25	10	8	1	0	0	3	5	0	39	2	0	2	1	1.000	0	0	2.16
Tulsa	AA Tex	12	0	0	6	16.1	68	17	8	8	3	0	0	0	5	0	18	0	0	2	1	.667	0	0	4.41
4 Min. YEARS		144	5	0	52	238	973	216	114	103	18	13	8	10	52	5	228	7	3	10	10	.500	0	11	3.89

Horacio Ramirez

Pitches: Left **Bats:** Left **Pos:** SP-3   **Ht:** 6'1" **Wt:** 170 **Born:** 11/24/79 **Age:** 22

Year Team	Lg Org	G	GS	CG	GF	IP	BFP	H	R	ER	HR	SH	SF	HB	TBB	IBB	SO	WP	Bk	W	L	Pct.	ShO	Sv	ERA
1997 Braves	R Atl	11	8	0	2	44	175	30	13	11	1	0	1	0	18	0	61	4	0	3	3	.500	0	0	2.25
1998 Macon	A Atl	12	12	0	0	55.1	249	70	50	36	8	2	3	2	16	0	38	2	0	1	7	.125	0	0	5.86
Eugene	A- Atl	16	8	0	3	55.2	273	84	51	39	4	3	6	4	17	0	39	4	2	2	7	.222	0	0	6.31
1999 Macon	A Atl	17	14	1	0	77.2	316	70	30	23	6	2	5	2	25	0	43	1	1	6	3	.667	1	0	2.67
2000 Myrtle Bch	A+ Atl	27	26	3	0	148.1	609	136	57	53	14	1	1	2	42	0	125	6	4	15	8	.652	2	0	3.22
2001 Greenville	AA Atl	3	3	0	0	14.2	66	17	8	8	2	2	0	1	8	0	17	0	0	1	1	.500	0	0	4.91
5 Min. YEARS		86	71	4	5	395.2	1688	407	209	170	35	10	16	11	126	0	323	17	7	28	29	.491	3	0	3.87

241

Joslin Ramirez

Pitches: Right **Bats:** Right **Pos:** SP-18; RP-4   **Ht:** 5'11" **Wt:** 182 **Born:** 11/19/80 **Age:** 21

Year Team	Lg Org	G	GS	CG	GF	IP	BFP	H	R	ER	HR	SH	SF	HB	TBB	IBB	SO	WP	Bk	W	L	Pct.	ShO	Sv	ERA
2000 Diamondbcks	R Ari	15	4	0	2	50.1	245	70	50	36	2	0	1	1	28	0	47	3	1	4	5	.444	0	0	6.44
2001 El Paso	AA Ari	4	0	0	2	6.1	27	5	2	1	0	0	1	0	2	0	9	0	1	1	0	1.000	0	0	1.42
South Bend	A Ari	18	18	0	0	104.1	444	109	48	38	10	4	6	4	28	0	73	5	2	6	5	.545	0	0	3.28
2 Min. YEARS		37	22	0	4	161	716	184	100	75	12	4	8	5	58	0	129	8	4	11	10	.524	0	0	4.19

Omar Ramirez

Bats: Right **Throws:** Right **Pos:** OF-104; PH-19   **Ht:** 5'9" **Wt:** 170 **Born:** 11/2/70 **Age:** 31

Year Team	Lg Org	G	AB	H	2B	3B	HR	TB	R	RBI	TBB	IBB	SO	HBP	SH	SF	SB	CS	SB%	GDP	Avg	OBP	SLG
1990 Indians	R Cle	18	58	10	0	0	0	10	6	2	11	0	11	0	0	0	2	4	.33	2	.172	.304	.172
1991 Watertown	A- Cle	56	210	56	17	0	2	79	30	17	30	0	30	1	3	1	12	2	.86	2	.267	.360	.376
1992 Kinston	A+ Cle	110	411	123	20	5	13	192	73	49	38	1	53	3	8	2	19	12	.61	5	.299	.361	.467
1993 Canton-Akrn	AA Cle	125	516	162	24	6	7	219	116	53	53	2	49	5	4	1	24	6	.80	9	.314	.383	.424
1994 Charlotte	AAA Cle	134	419	97	20	2	8	145	66	45	54	0	43	1	2	3	15	7	.68	11	.232	.319	.346
1995 Canton-Akrn	AA Cle	10	34	11	0	0	0	11	6	3	3	0	3	0	1	0	0	0	—	0	.324	.378	.324
1996 Kinston	A+ Cle	2	5	2	0	0	1	5	1	3	1	0	0	0	0	0	0	0	—	1	.400	.500	1.000
1998 Rio Grande	IND —	71	284	96	18	4	12	158	66	58	37	1	24	3	1	2	26	3	.90	10	.338	.417	.556
1999 New Orleans	AAA Hou	110	379	96	15	2	6	133	56	51	30	2	49	2	2	2	8	3	.73	13	.253	.310	.351
2000 New Orleans	AAA Hou	133	469	150	24	2	2	184	73	53	69	1	36	6	5	4	19	13	.59	23	.320	.411	.392
2001 New Orleans	AAA Hou	118	363	91	20	0	2	117	40	39	29	1	42	3	2	6	9	4	.69	4	.251	.307	.322
11 Min. YEARS		887	3148	894	158	21	53	1253	533	373	355	8	340	24	28	21	134	54	.71	80	.284	.359	.398

Kelly Ramos

Bats: Both **Throws:** Right **Pos:** C-77; PH-1   **Ht:** 6'0" **Wt:** 168 **Born:** 10/15/76 **Age:** 25

Year Team	Lg Org	G	AB	H	2B	3B	HR	TB	R	RBI	TBB	IBB	SO	HBP	SH	SF	SB	CS	SB%	GDP	Avg	OBP	SLG
1996 Mets	R NYM	20	59	11	0	1	0	13	3	7	3	0	10	0	1	0	0	2	.00	2	.186	.226	.220
1997 Kingsport	R+ NYM	50	170	38	3	1	7	64	25	32	17	3	33	1	4	0	2	3	.40	5	.224	.298	.376
1998 Pittsfield	A- NYM	63	215	64	10	6	3	95	31	34	13	1	36	1	0	4	0	1	.00	6	.298	.335	.442
1999 St. Lucie	A+ NYM	24	80	15	3	1	2	26	6	11	8	1	16	0	4	3	0	0	—	4	.188	.253	.325
Capital Cty	A NYM	82	262	67	14	0	10	111	31	34	9	0	52	10	2	1	4	2	.67	5	.256	.305	.424
2000 Trenton	AA Bos	8	25	5	1	0	0	6	2	0	2	0	8	0	1	0	0	0	—	0	.200	.259	.240
Augusta	A Bos	73	260	65	17	1	7	105	27	37	24	1	54	6	1	0	0	1	.33	9	.250	.328	.404
2001 Sarasota	A+ Bos	17	66	11	2	0	0	13	4	3	1	0	15	1	0	0	0	0	—	1	.167	.191	.197
Pawtucket	AAA Bos	5	13	3	0	0	0	3	0	0	0	0	3	0	0	0	0	0	—	0	.231	.231	.231
Trenton	AA Bos	56	182	38	6	1	7	67	14	27	6	0	49	1	1	2	0	0	—	4	.209	.236	.368
6 Min. YEARS		398	1332	317	56	11	36	503	143	185	83	6	276	20	14	10	7	10	.41	36	.238	.291	.378

Mario Ramos

Pitches: Left **Bats:** Left **Pos:** SP-28   **Ht:** 5'11" **Wt:** 165 **Born:** 10/19/77 **Age:** 24

Year Team	Lg Org	G	GS	CG	GF	IP	BFP	H	R	ER	HR	SH	SF	HB	TBB	IBB	SO	WP	Bk	W	L	Pct.	ShO	Sv	ERA
2000 Modesto	A+ Oak	26	24	1	1	152	624	131	63	49	6	9	3	3	50	4	134	3	1	12	5	.706	1	0	2.90
Midland	AA Oak	4	4	0	0	27.1	107	24	6	4	0	1	1	0	6	0	19	0	0	2	0	1.000	0	0	1.32
2001 Midland	AA Oak	15	15	0	0	93.2	384	71	37	32	7	3	1	4	28	0	68	1	2	8	1	.889	0	0	3.07
Sacramento	AAA Oak	13	13	1	0	80.1	340	74	32	28	5	2	2	2	27	0	82	4	0	8	3	.727	1	0	3.14
2 Min. YEARS		58	56	2	1	353.1	1455	300	138	113	18	15	7	9	111	4	303	8	3	30	9	.769	2	0	2.88

Rob Ramsay

Pitches: Left **Bats:** Left **Pos:** SP-26   **Ht:** 6'5" **Wt:** 215 **Born:** 12/3/73 **Age:** 28

Year Team	Lg Org	G	GS	CG	GF	IP	BFP	H	R	ER	HR	SH	SF	HB	TBB	IBB	SO	WP	Bk	W	L	Pct.	ShO	Sv	ERA
1996 Red Sox	R Bos	2	0	0	1	3.2	19	5	2	2	0	0	0	1	3	0	5	0	0	0	1	.000	0	0	4.91
Sarasota	A+ Bos	12	7	0	0	34	165	42	23	23	1	1	1	1	27	0	32	2	2	2	2	.500	0	0	6.09
1997 Sarasota	A+ Bos	23	22	1	0	135.2	603	134	90	72	16	1	3	5	63	0	115	7	0	9	9	.500	0	0	4.78
1998 Trenton	AA Bos	27	27	1	0	162.2	659	137	67	63	10	5	5	3	50	1	166	8	3	12	6	.667	1	0	3.49
1999 Pawtucket	AAA Bos	20	20	0	0	114.1	498	114	81	68	21	9	4	4	36	1	79	5	3	6	6	.500	0	0	5.35
Tacoma	AAA Sea	5	5	0	0	33.1	130	20	6	4	2	0	1	0	14	1	37	1	0	4	1	.800	0	0	1.08
2000 Tacoma	AAA Sea	3	3	0	0	16	68	16	8	8	1	0	0	0	6	0	6	0	0	0	1	.000	0	0	4.50
Everett	A- Sea	1	1	0	0	2	8	2	0	0	0	0	0	0	0	0	4	0	0	0	0	—	0	0	0.00
2001 Tacoma	AAA Sea	26	26	0	0	149.1	667	160	98	80	26	4	10	2	60	0	113	2	0	10	11	.476	0	0	4.82
1999 Seattle	AL	6	3	0	1	18.1	81	23	13	13	3	0	1	0	9	1	11	1	0	0	2	.000	0	0	6.38
2000 Seattle	AL	37	1	0	6	50.1	230	43	22	19	3	2	3	1	40	3	32	4	0	1	1	.500	0	0	3.40
6 Min. YEARS		119	111	2	1	651	2817	630	375	320	77	20	24	16	259	3	557	25	8	43	37	.538	1	0	4.42
2 Maj. YEARS		43	4	0	7	68.2	311	66	35	32	6	2	4	1	49	4	43	5	0	1	3	.250	0	0	4.19

Brad Ramsey

Bats: Right **Throws:** Right **Pos:** DH-39; C-33; 1B-27; PH-7   **Ht:** 6'4" **Wt:** 225 **Born:** 11/7/76 **Age:** 25

Year Team	Lg Org	G	AB	H	2B	3B	HR	TB	R	RBI	TBB	IBB	SO	HBP	SH	SF	SB	CS	SB%	GDP	Avg	OBP	SLG
1997 Cubs	R ChC	51	200	63	10	3	8	103	50	34	22	0	33	13	0	2	8	0	1.00	3	.315	.414	.515
1998 Daytona	A+ ChC	89	312	90	25	1	6	135	49	37	32	0	64	13	0	2	4	1	.80	6	.288	.376	.433
1999 Daytona	A+ ChC	105	330	70	15	0	9	112	47	44	40	1	67	16	2	6	1	3	.25	17	.212	.321	.339
2000 Cubs	R ChC	5	15	5	2	1	1	12	5	3	5	0	2	0	0	0	0	0	—	0	.333	.500	.800
Lansing	A ChC	4	12	1	0	0	0	1	0	0	3	0	5	0	1	0	0	0	—	0	.083	.267	.083

			BATTING															BASERUNNING				PERCENTAGES		
Year Team	Lg Org	G	AB	H	2B	3B	HR	TB	R	RBI	TBB	IBB	SO	HBP	SH	SF	SB	CS	SB%	GDP	Avg	OBP	SLG
2001 Daytona	A+ ChC	96	332	75	16	0	7	112	28	41	23	3	75	7	1	2	2	3	.40	9	.226	.288	.337
West Tenn	AA ChC	9	20	5	1	0	2	12	5	4	3	0	6	1	0	0	0	0	—	1	.250	.375	.600
5 Min. YEARS		359	1221	309	69	5	33	487	184	163	128	4	252	50	4	12	15	7	.68	36	.253	.345	.399

Scott Randall

Pitches: Right **Bats:** Right **Pos:** SP-13; RP-9 **Ht:** 6'3" **Wt:** 190 **Born:** 10/29/75 **Age:** 26

		HOW MUCH HE PITCHED						WHAT HE GAVE UP										THE RESULTS					
Year Team	Lg Org	G	GS	CG	GF	IP	BFP	H	R	ER	HR	SH	SF	HB	TBB	IBB	SO	WP	Bk	W	L	Pct.	ShO	Sv	ERA
1995 Portland	A- Col	15	15	1	0	95	391	76	35	21	2	2	2	8	28	1	78	7	2	7	3	.700	0	0	1.99
1996 Asheville	A Col	24	24	1	0	154.1	615	121	53	47	11	5	1	7	50	3	136	4	0	14	4	.778	1	0	2.74
1997 Salem	A+ Col	27	26	2	1	176	763	167	93	75	8	8	6	11	66	3	128	14	0	9	10	.474	1	0	3.84
1998 New Haven	AA Col	29	29	7	0	202	863	210	102	86	14	9	10	9	62	1	135	10	1	10	14	.417	2	0	3.83
1999 Colo Sprngs	AAA Col	9	9	0	0	42	205	62	41	37	5	3	1	1	22	1	25	5	1	1	4	.200	0	0	7.93
Carolina	AA Col	16	16	3	0	99.2	432	101	52	38	6	3	5	8	34	2	102	3	0	5	8	.385	1	0	3.43
2000 Salt Lake	AAA Min	14	14	0	0	75.2	344	105	52	46	9	1	1	1	22	0	54	5	0	5	3	.625	0	0	5.47
Oklahoma	AAA Tex	16	10	0	2	74.2	339	96	49	45	8	3	6	4	33	1	35	2	0	2	3	.400	0	0	5.42
2001 Salem	A+ Col	2	0	0	0	6	27	9	3	3	0	0	0	0	1	0	7	0	0	0	0	—	0	0	4.50
Carolina	AA Col	1	1	0	0	6	21	5	0	0	0	0	0	0	0	0	3	0	0	0	0	—	0	0	0.00
Colo Sprngs	AAA Col	19	12	0	2	70.2	319	74	48	43	11	0	1	3	34	3	47	3	1	6	5	.545	0	0	5.48
7 Min. YEARS		172	156	14	5	1002	4319	1026	528	441	74	34	33	52	352	15	750	53	5	59	54	.522	5	0	3.96

Jaisen Randolph

Bats: Both **Throws:** Right **Pos:** OF-104; PH-5; DH-4 **Ht:** 6'0" **Wt:** 180 **Born:** 1/19/79 **Age:** 23

			BATTING															BASERUNNING				PERCENTAGES		
Year Team	Lg Org	G	AB	H	2B	3B	HR	TB	R	RBI	TBB	IBB	SO	HBP	SH	SF	SB	CS	SB%	GDP	Avg	OBP	SLG
1997 Cubs	R ChC	53	218	58	1	4	0	67	42	26	26	0	45	5	0	2	24	5	.83	3	.266	.355	.307
1998 Rockford	A ChC	128	491	142	18	9	1	181	78	33	40	2	113	5	9	2	32	21	.60	4	.289	.348	.369
1999 Daytona	A+ ChC	130	511	139	16	5	2	171	70	37	43	1	86	8	4	0	25	26	.49	4	.272	.338	.335
2000 West Tenn	AA ChC	126	490	119	15	5	1	147	76	31	56	2	96	2	3	3	46	20	.70	3	.243	.321	.300
2001 West Tenn	AA ChC	102	365	84	11	1	0	97	43	17	50	1	61	3	6	1	23	15	.61	4	.230	.327	.266
Binghamton	AA NYM	11	39	7	1	0	0	8	7	0	6	0	5	0	0	0	0	4	.00	0	.179	.289	.205
5 Min. YEARS		550	2114	549	62	24	4	671	316	144	221	6	406	23	22	8	150	91	.62	18	.260	.335	.317

Steve Randolph

Pitches: Left **Bats:** Left **Pos:** RP-22; SP-14 **Ht:** 6'3" **Wt:** 185 **Born:** 5/1/74 **Age:** 28

		HOW MUCH HE PITCHED						WHAT HE GAVE UP										THE RESULTS					
Year Team	Lg Org	G	GS	CG	GF	IP	BFP	H	R	ER	HR	SH	SF	HB	TBB	IBB	SO	WP	Bk	W	L	Pct.	ShO	Sv	ERA
1995 Yankees	R NYY	8	3	0	1	24.1	94	11	7	6	1	0	0	1	16	0	34	3	1	4	0	1.000	0	0	2.22
Oneonta	A- NYY	6	6	0	0	21.2	109	19	22	18	0	0	2	1	23	0	31	5	0	0	3	.000	0	0	7.48
1996 Greensboro	A NYY	32	17	0	7	100.1	451	64	46	42	8	4	5	5	96	1	111	13	3	4	7	.364	0	0	3.77
1997 Tampa	A+ NYY	34	13	1	6	95.1	417	74	55	41	8	7	3	3	63	5	108	4	1	4	7	.364	0	1	3.87
Tucson	AAA Ari	17	17	0	0	85.1	357	71	44	34	6	3	2	3	42	0	104	0	0	4	4	.500	0	0	3.59
1998 High Desert	A+ Ari	17	1	0	3	22.2	99	16	11	8	1	0	2	0	19	2	23	3	0	1	3	.250	0	0	3.18
1999 El Paso	AA Ari	8	8	0	0	44.1	186	39	14	13	1	2	0	1	23	0	38	1	1	2	2	.500	0	0	2.64
Diamondbcks	R Ari	2	2	0	0	6	25	5	3	3	0	0	0	0	2	0	7	0	0	0	0	—	0	0	4.50
Tucson	AAA Ari	11	10	1	0	41.2	204	47	37	32	7	1	2	2	32	1	26	1	0	0	7	.000	0	0	6.91
2000 Tucson	AAA Ari	5	3	0	1	13.1	69	11	13	13	3	1	1	0	19	0	6	0	0	0	0	—	0	0	8.78
2001 Tucson	AAA Ari	18	0	0	7	21.1	109	24	15	15	2	1	2	2	19	1	16	2	0	2	0	1.000	0	0	6.33
El Paso	AA Ari	18	14	1	0	75	342	69	50	43	11	1	2	3	53	1	66	7	1	5	6	.455	1	0	5.16
7 Min. YEARS		176	94	3	25	551.1	2462	450	317	268	48	20	21	21	407	11	570	39	7	26	39	.400	1	1	4.37

Fred Rath

Pitches: Right **Bats:** Right **Pos:** RP-18; SP-10 **Ht:** 6'3" **Wt:** 220 **Born:** 1/5/73 **Age:** 29

		HOW MUCH HE PITCHED						WHAT HE GAVE UP										THE RESULTS					
Year Team	Lg Org	G	GS	CG	GF	IP	BFP	H	R	ER	HR	SH	SF	HB	TBB	IBB	SO	WP	Bk	W	L	Pct.	ShO	Sv	ERA
1995 Elizabethtn	R+ Min	27	0	0	25	33.1	134	20	8	5	2	2	0	1	11	1	50	3	0	1	1	.500	0	12	1.35
1996 Fort Wayne	A Min	32	0	0	29	41.2	163	26	12	7	1	0	2	0	10	0	63	3	0	1	2	.333	0	14	1.51
Fort Myers	A+ Min	22	0	0	16	29	123	25	10	9	1	1	0	2	10	0	29	3	0	2	5	.286	0	4	2.79
1997 Fort Myers	A+ Min	17	0	0	11	22	87	18	4	4	2	1	1	0	3	1	22	1	0	4	0	1.000	0	2	1.64
New Britain	AA Min	33	0	0	23	50.1	200	43	17	15	1	1	3	1	13	0	33	3	0	3	3	.500	0	12	2.68
1998 Salt Lake	AAA Min	10	0	0	9	11	46	11	2	2	1	0	0	0	2	0	11	0	0	0	1	.000	0	3	1.64
Salt Lake	AAA Min	27	0	0	22	31.2	133	35	16	16	4	1	0	2	8	0	15	3	0	1	2	.333	0	8	4.55
Colo Sprngs	AAA Col	23	0	0	14	28.1	132	37	17	16	2	1	2	2	15	1	20	4	0	5	1	.833	0	4	5.08
1999 Salt Lake	AAA Min	56	0	0	18	82.2	350	88	41	36	9	3	5	6	24	0	36	6	0	7	5	.583	0	3	3.92
2000 Salt Lake	AAA Min	12	0	0	1	18	80	21	12	6	1	0	0	0	5	0	14	1	0	2	1	.667	0	0	3.00
Memphis	AAA StL	18	9	0	2	63	274	72	40	36	9	4	1	2	24	0	33	2	0	2	3	.400	0	0	5.14
Nashville	AAA Pit	7	7	0	0	43.1	193	42	31	24	8	2	1	2	23	1	15	2	0	3	4	.429	0	0	4.98
2001 New Haven	AA StL	1	0	0	0	1.2	11	3	3	3	1	0	0	0	3	0	0	0	0	0	0	—	0	0	16.20
Memphis	AAA StL	27	10	0	4	78	369	103	60	58	12	4	1	4	33	0	57	2	0	4	5	.444	0	0	6.69
1998 Colorado	NL	2	0	0	1	5.1	23	6	1	1	0	0	1	0	2	0	2	0	0	0	0	—	0	0	1.69
7 Min. YEARS		312	26	0	174	534	2295	544	273	237	54	20	16	23	184	4	398	33	0	35	33	.515	0	62	3.99

Jon Ratliff

Pitches: Right **Bats:** Right **Pos:** SP-14; RP-8 **Ht:** 6'4" **Wt:** 195 **Born:** 12/22/71 **Age:** 30

		HOW MUCH HE PITCHED						WHAT HE GAVE UP										THE RESULTS					
Year Team	Lg Org	G	GS	CG	GF	IP	BFP	H	R	ER	HR	SH	SF	HB	TBB	IBB	SO	WP	Bk	W	L	Pct.	ShO	Sv	ERA
1993 Geneva	A- ChC	3	3	0	0	14	65	12	8	5	0	0	0	2	8	0	7	0	0	1	1	.500	0	0	3.21
Daytona	A+ ChC	8	8	0	0	41	194	50	29	18	2	4	3	5	23	0	15	3	1	2	4	.333	0	0	3.95

243

Year Team	Lg Org	HOW MUCH HE PITCHED						WHAT HE GAVE UP												THE RESULTS					
		G	GS	CG	GF	IP	BFP	H	R	ER	HR	SH	SF	HB	TBB	IBB	SO	WP	Bk	W	L	Pct.	ShO	Sv	ERA
1994 Daytona	A+ ChC	8	8	1	0	54	227	64	23	21	5	2	1	4	5	0	17	4	0	3	2	.600	0	0	3.50
Iowa	AAA ChC	5	4	0	0	28.1	131	39	19	17	7	1	1	2	7	0	10	3	0	1	3	.250	0	0	5.40
Orlando	AA ChC	12	12	1	0	62.1	292	78	44	39	4	4	5	8	26	1	19	5	0	1	9	.100	0	0	5.63
1995 Orlando	AA ChC	26	25	1	1	140	599	143	67	54	9	2	8	10	42	1	94	13	0	10	5	.667	1	0	3.47
1996 Iowa	AAA ChC	32	13	0	5	93.2	419	107	63	55	10	3	6	6	31	2	59	3	0	4	8	.333	0	0	5.28
1997 Iowa	AAA ChC	9	4	0	1	32.1	134	30	20	20	6	1	0	2	7	0	25	2	0	1	3	.250	0	0	5.57
Orlando	AA ChC	18	15	0	1	101.1	443	112	59	49	10	5	2	1	32	3	68	12	1	6	4	.600	0	0	4.35
1998 Richmond	AAA Atl	29	29	2	0	151.1	671	167	90	83	18	4	9	4	65	0	143	9	0	12	13	.480	0	0	4.94
1999 Richmond	AAA Atl	27	27	0	0	157.2	660	154	88	78	24	3	6	3	44	2	129	5	0	5	12	.294	0	0	4.45
2000 Sacramento	AAA Oak	20	18	0	1	107.1	442	102	48	41	12	2	3	4	31	2	72	7	1	8	4	.667	0	0	3.44
2001 Modesto	A+ Oak	4	0	0	2	7	28	4	1	1	0	0	0	0	3	0	6	1	0	0	0	—	0	0	1.29
Sacramento	AAA Oak	18	14	0	1	63	306	84	58	55	9	1	3	1	38	1	41	5	0	1	7	.125	0	0	7.86
2000 Oakland	AL	1	0	0	1	1	3	0	0	0	0	0	0	0	0	0	0	0	0	0	0	—	0	0	0.00
9 Min. YEARS		219	180	5	12	1053.1	4611	1146	617	536	114	30	47	52	362	12	705	72	3	55	75	.423	1	3	4.58

Jon Rauch

Pitches: Right   **Bats:** Right   **Pos:** SP-6   **Ht:** 6'10"   **Wt:** 230   **Born:** 9/27/78   **Age:** 23

Year Team	Lg Org	HOW MUCH HE PITCHED						WHAT HE GAVE UP												THE RESULTS					
		G	GS	CG	GF	IP	BFP	H	R	ER	HR	SH	SF	HB	TBB	IBB	SO	WP	Bk	W	L	Pct.	ShO	Sv	ERA
1999 Bristol	R+ CWS	14	9	0	3	56.2	264	65	44	28	4	1	2	3	16	1	66	6	2	4	4	.500	0	2	4.45
Winston-Sal	A+ CWS	1	1	0	0	6	26	4	3	2	1	0	0	0	3	0	7	1	0	0	0	—	0	0	3.00
2000 Winston-Sal	A+ CWS	18	18	1	0	110	456	102	49	35	10	4	3	5	33	0	124	4	1	11	3	.786	0	0	2.86
Birmingham	AA CWS	8	8	2	0	56	220	36	18	14	4	1	0	2	16	0	63	2	0	5	1	.833	2	0	2.25
2001 Charlotte	AAA CWS	6	6	0	0	28	121	28	20	18	8	0	0	1	7	0	27	1	0	1	3	.250	0	0	5.79
3 Min. YEARS		47	42	3	3	256.2	1087	235	134	97	27	6	5	11	75	1	287	14	3	21	11	.656	2	2	3.40

Kenny Rayborn

Pitches: Right   **Bats:** Right   **Pos:** RP-14   **Ht:** 6'4"   **Wt:** 210   **Born:** 11/22/74   **Age:** 27

Year Team	Lg Org	HOW MUCH HE PITCHED						WHAT HE GAVE UP												THE RESULTS					
		G	GS	CG	GF	IP	BFP	H	R	ER	HR	SH	SF	HB	TBB	IBB	SO	WP	Bk	W	L	Pct.	ShO	Sv	ERA
1997 Lowell	A- Bos	11	7	0	1	46	197	39	18	14	0	1	2	6	15	0	35	8	0	2	2	.500	0	1	2.74
1998 Michigan	A Bos	17	8	0	5	49.1	217	62	27	25	5	1	3	1	13	0	34	8	0	4	2	.667	0	0	4.56
1999 Greenville	IND —	18	18	2	0	115	532	140	86	62	5	7	4	10	43	0	80	9	0	6	9	.400	0	0	4.85
2000 Lancaster	A+ Sea	21	1	0	3	55.2	228	47	24	18	2	0	4	1	19	3	43	4	0	5	1	.833	0	0	2.91
New Haven	AA Sea	13	7	0	3	46.1	207	54	25	25	1	2	1	5	19	0	26	1	0	4	3	.571	0	0	4.86
2001 San Antonio	AA Sea	14	0	0	8	19.2	93	26	15	15	1	0	1	5	8	1	11	1	0	1	1	1.000	0	0	6.86
5 Min. YEARS		94	41	2	20	332	1474	368	195	159	14	11	15	28	117	4	229	31	0	22	17	.564	0	1	4.31

Josh Reding

Bats: Right   **Throws:** Right   **Pos:** SS-71; 3B-41; 2B-10; PH-6; OF-5; DH-1; PR-1   **Ht:** 6'3"   **Wt:** 175   **Born:** 3/7/77   **Age:** 25

Year Team	Lg Org	BATTING														BASERUNNING				PERCENTAGES		
		G	AB	H	2B	3B	HR	TB	R	RBI	TBB	IBB	SO	HBP	SH	SF	SB	CS	SB%	GDP	Avg	OBP	SLG
1997 Expos	R Mon	56	196	50	11	1	2	69	34	19	22	0	31	4	2	2	14	3	.82	3	.255	.339	.352
Vermont	A- Mon	8	24	4	2	1	0	8	2	0	3	0	11	0	0	0	0	0	—	0	.167	.259	.333
1998 Expos	R Mon	2	8	3	1	0	0	4	2	0	0	0	3	0	0	0	1	1	.50	1	.375	.375	.500
Cape Fear	A Mon	73	253	59	6	0	1	68	32	21	22	1	71	4	9	0	13	4	.76	8	.233	.305	.269
Jupiter	A+ Mon	4	12	3	1	0	0	4	2	2	0	0	3	0	0	0	1	0	.00	0	.250	.250	.333
1999 Jupiter	A+ Mon	121	415	109	10	2	2	129	54	31	22	0	73	1	12	6	30	9	.77	6	.263	.297	.311
2000 Harrisburg	AA Mon	137	457	100	11	5	2	127	58	48	58	0	110	10	9	4	25	6	.81	10	.219	.318	.278
2001 Ottawa	AAA Mon	6	18	2	1	0	0	3	0	2	1	0	6	2	0	1	0	0	—	1	.111	.227	.167
Harrisburg	AA Mon	117	372	75	9	4	3	101	25	34	18	2	94	1	7	2	10	5	.67	17	.202	.239	.272
5 Min. YEARS		524	1755	405	52	13	10	513	209	157	146	3	402	22	39	15	93	29	.76	46	.231	.296	.292

Brandon Reed

Pitches: Right   **Bats:** Right   **Pos:** RP-24   **Ht:** 6'4"   **Wt:** 195   **Born:** 12/18/74   **Age:** 27

Year Team	Lg Org	HOW MUCH HE PITCHED						WHAT HE GAVE UP												THE RESULTS					
		G	GS	CG	GF	IP	BFP	H	R	ER	HR	SH	SF	HB	TBB	IBB	SO	WP	Bk	W	L	Pct.	ShO	Sv	ERA
1994 Bristol	R+ Det	13	13	0	0	78	337	82	41	31	3	1	3	9	10	0	68	4	0	3	5	.375	0	0	3.58
1995 Fayettevlle	A Det	55	0	0	53	64.2	252	40	11	7	1	1	0	3	18	1	78	8	0	3	0	1.000	0	41	0.97
1996 Tigers	R Det	1	1	0	0	2	6	0	0	0	0	0	0	0	0	0	2	0	0	0	0	—	0	0	0.00
Jacksnville	AA Det	7	3	0	1	26	94	18	6	6	1	0	1	1	3	0	18	0	0	1	0	1.000	0	1	2.08
1997 Jacksnville	AA Det	27	27	2	0	176	754	190	100	89	25	6	10	8	54	0	90	9	0	11	9	.550	0	0	4.55
1998 Toledo	AAA Det	39	17	0	6	117.1	540	159	84	78	17	4	4	5	46	1	70	2	0	5	7	.417	0	0	5.98
1999 Toledo	AAA Det	44	6	1	21	91.1	401	101	53	42	6	1	7	5	26	3	59	1	0	8	5	.615	0	3	4.14
2000 Toledo	AAA Det	45	4	0	26	73.1	330	80	52	49	13	2	3	2	36	4	56	3	2	7	6	.538	0	6	6.01
2001 Columbus	AAA NYY	24	0	0	8	33.2	140	27	18	13	2	2	1	2	8	1	30	1	0	1	2	.333	0	1	3.48
8 Min. YEARS		255	71	3	115	662.1	2854	697	365	315	68	17	29	36	201	10	471	28	2	39	34	.534	0	52	4.28

Jeff Reed

Bats: Left   **Throws:** Right   **Pos:** C-29; PH-5   **Ht:** 6'2"   **Wt:** 200   **Born:** 11/12/62   **Age:** 39

Year Team	Lg Org	BATTING														BASERUNNING				PERCENTAGES		
		G	AB	H	2B	3B	HR	TB	R	RBI	TBB	IBB	SO	HBP	SH	SF	SB	CS	SB%	GDP	Avg	OBP	SLG
1980 Elizabethtn	A+ Min	65	225	64	15	1	1	84	39	20	51	—	23	4	2	2	2	2	.50	—	.284	.422	.373
1981 Wisc Rapids	A Min	106	312	73	12	1	4	99	63	34	86	1	36	4	7	0	4	4	.50	—	.234	.405	.317
Orlando	AA Min	3	4	1	0	0	0	1	0	0	1	0	0	0	0	0	0	0	—	—	.250	.400	.250
1982 Visalia	A+ Min	125	395	130	19	2	5	168	69	54	78	3	32	7	4	4	1	2	.33	—	.329	.444	.425
1983 Orlando	AA Min	118	379	100	16	5	6	144	52	45	76	6	40	8	5	5	2	3	.40	—	.264	.393	.380
Toledo	AAA Min	14	41	7	1	1	0	10	5	3	5	0	9	2	0	0	0	0	—	—	.171	.292	.244

Year Team	Lg Org	G	AB	H	2B	3B	HR	TB	R	RBI	TBB	IBB	SO	HBP	SH	SF	SB	CS	SB%	GDP	Avg	OBP	SLG
1984 Toledo	AAA Min	94	301	80	16	3	3	111	30	35	37	3	35	2	4	1	1	3	.25	7	.266	.349	.369
1985 Toledo	AAA Min	122	404	100	15	3	5	136	53	36	59	3	49	5	9	6	1	1	.50	13	.248	.346	.337
1986 Toledo	AAA Min	25	71	22	5	3	1	36	10	14	17	0	9	0	3	1	0	0	—	3	.310	.438	.507
1987 Indianapols	AAA Mon	5	17	3	0	0	0	3	0	0	1	0	2	0	1	0	0	0	—	0	.176	.222	.176
1988 Indianapols	AAA Mon	8	22	7	3	0	0	10	1	1	2	0	2	0	0	0	0	0	—	0	.318	.375	.455
1992 Nashville	AAA Cin	14	25	6	1	0	1	10	1	2	2	1	7	0	1	1	0	0	—	2	.240	.286	.400
1993 San Jose	A+ SF	4	10	5	1	0	0	6	2	2	1	0	0	0	0	0	0	0	—	0	.500	.545	.600
2001 Scranton-WB	AAA Phi	31	98	23	1	0	4	36	12	8	14	0	24	0	1	1	0	0	—	0	.235	.327	.367
1984 Minnesota	AL	18	21	3	3	0	0	6	3	1	2	0	6	0	1	0	0	0	—	0	.143	.217	.286
1985 Minnesota	AL	7	10	2	0	0	0	2	2	0	0	0	3	0	0	0	0	0	—	0	.200	.200	.200
1986 Minnesota	AL	68	165	39	6	1	2	53	13	9	16	0	19	1	3	0	1	0	1.00	2	.236	.308	.321
1987 Montreal	NL	75	207	44	11	0	1	58	15	21	12	1	20	1	4	4	1		.00	1	.213	.254	.280
1988 Montreal	NL	43	123	27	3	2	0	34	10	9	13	1	22	0	1	1	1	1	1.00	3	.220	.292	.276
Cincinnati	NL	49	142	33	6	0	1	42	10	7	15	0	19	0	0	0	0	0	—	2	.232	.306	.296
1989 Cincinnati	NL	102	287	64	11	0	3	84	16	23	34	5	46	2	3	4	0	0	—	6	.223	.306	.293
1990 Cincinnati	NL	72	175	44	8	1	3	63	12	16	24	5	26	0	5	1	0	0	—	6	.251	.340	.360
1991 Cincinnati	NL	91	270	72	15	2	3	100	20	31	23	3	38	1	1	5	0	1	.00	6	.267	.321	.370
1992 Cincinnati	NL	15	25	4	0	0	0	4	2	2	1	1	4	0	0	0	0	0	—	1	.160	.192	.160
1993 San Francisco	NL	66	119	31	3	0	6	52	10	12	16	4	22	0	0	1	0	1	.00	2	.261	.346	.437
1994 San Francisco	NL	50	103	18	3	0	1	24	11	7	11	4	21	0	0	0	0	0	—	3	.175	.254	.233
1995 San Francisco	NL	66	113	30	2	0	0	32	12	9	20	3	17	0	1	0	0	0	—	3	.265	.376	.283
1996 Colorado	NL	116	341	97	20	1	8	143	34	37	43	8	65	2	6	3	2	2	.50	8	.284	.365	.419
1997 Colorado	NL	90	256	76	10	0	17	137	43	47	35	1	55	2	5	0	2	1	.67	8	.297	.386	.535
1998 Colorado	NL	113	259	75	17	1	9	121	43	39	37	4	57	1	3	3	0	0	—	6	.290	.377	.467
1999 Colorado	NL	46	106	27	5	0	2	38	11	11	17	1	24	1	0	1	0	1	.00	3	.255	.360	.358
Chicago	NL	57	150	39	11	2	1	57	18	17	28	0	34	2	0	1	1	1	.50	4	.260	.381	.380
2000 Chicago	NL	90	229	49	10	0	4	71	26	25	44	2	68	1	2	1	0	1	.00	5	.214	.342	.310
12 Min. YEARS		734	2304	621	105	19	30	854	337	254	430	—	268	32	37	21	11	15	.42	—	.270	.389	.371
17 Maj. YEARS		1234	3101	774	144	10	61	1121	311	323	391	43	566	14	35	25	7	9	.44	74	.250	.334	.361

Keith Reed

Bats: Right Throws: Right Pos: OF-104; DH-5; PR-1   Ht: 6'4" Wt: 215 Born: 10/8/78 Age: 23

Year Team	Lg Org	G	AB	H	2B	3B	HR	TB	R	RBI	TBB	IBB	SO	HBP	SH	SF	SB	CS	SB%	GDP	Avg	OBP	SLG
1999 Bluefield	R+ Bal	4	16	3	0	0	0	3	2	0	1	0	3	0	0	0	0	1	.00	0	.188	.235	.188
Delmarva	A Bal	61	240	62	14	3	4	94	36	25	22	0	53	3	2	2	3	2	.60	4	.258	.326	.392
2000 Delmarva	A Bal	70	269	78	16	1	11	129	43	59	25	5	56	5	1	3	20	4	.83	3	.290	.358	.480
Frederick	A+ Bal	65	243	57	10	1	8	93	33	31	21	2	58	4	0	3	9	1	.90	4	.235	.303	.383
2001 Frederick	A+ Bal	72	267	72	14	0	7	107	28	29	13	1	57	1	1	1	8	6	.57	7	.270	.305	.401
Bowie	AA Bal	18	67	17	3	0	1	23	7	8	6	0	10	0	0	0	2	2	.50	0	.254	.315	.343
Rochester	AAA Bal	20	74	23	7	1	2	38	11	11	5	0	14	0	0	0	1	1	.50	1	.311	.354	.514
3 Min. YEARS		310	1176	312	64	6	33	487	160	163	93	8	251	13	4	9	43	17	.72	22	.265	.324	.414

Maximo Regalado

Pitches: Right Bats: Right Pos: RP-18   Ht: 6'1" Wt: 198 Born: 11/18/76 Age: 25

Year Team	Lg Org	G	GS	CG	GF	IP	BFP	H	R	ER	HR	SH	SF	HB	TBB	IBB	SO	WP	Bk	W	L	Pct.	ShO	Sv	ERA
1997 Great Falls	R+ LA	9	6	0	0	36.2	158	27	12	8	0	1	1	2	21	0	24	1	0	2	1	.667	0	0	1.96
1998 Vero Beach	A+ LA	4	4	0	0	16	78	17	15	12	3	0	1	0	13	0	14	1	0	0	2	.000	0	0	6.75
Great Falls	R+ LA	3	0	0	2	5.2	21	2	0	0	0	0	0	1	3	0	7	1	0	0	0	—	0	0	0.00
San Berndno	A+ LA	14	3	0	1	47.1	212	45	30	22	4	0	1	3	24	0	42	4	0	3	3	.500	0	0	4.18
1999 Vero Beach	A+ LA	20	19	1	0	90	429	110	65	58	16	5	3	12	49	0	58	7	0	2	12	.143	0	0	5.80
2000 Vero Beach	A+ LA	30	0	0	29	30.2	114	15	4	3	0	0	0	1	8	1	45	2	0	0	0	—	0	21	0.88
San Antonio	AA LA	26	0	0	22	23.1	103	22	8	8	1	0	0	1	15	0	27	2	0	1	2	.333	0	9	3.09
2001 Jacksnville	AA LA	18	0	0	5	22.2	110	20	18	16	3	0	0	2	22	0	33	1	0	2	3	.400	0	1	6.35
5 Min. YEARS		124	32	1	59	272.1	1225	258	152	127	27	6	5	22	155	1	250	19	0	10	23	.303	0	31	4.20

Nick Regilio

Pitches: Right Bats: Right Pos: SP-21   Ht: 6'2" Wt: 185 Born: 9/4/78 Age: 23

Year Team	Lg Org	G	GS	CG	GF	IP	BFP	H	R	ER	HR	SH	SF	HB	TBB	IBB	SO	WP	Bk	W	L	Pct.	ShO	Sv	ERA
1999 Pulaski	R+ Tex	11	8	1	0	49.2	194	30	12	9	2	0	1	3	16	0	58	4	1	4	2	.667	1	0	1.63
2000 Charlotte	A+ Tex	20	20	0	0	85.2	369	94	54	43	8	3	1	7	29	0	63	10	2	4	3	.571	0	0	4.52
2001 Charlotte	A+ Tex	11	11	1	0	64	254	47	16	11	5	1	1	6	16	0	60	0	1	6	2	.750	1	0	1.55
Tulsa	AA Tex	10	10	0	0	52	236	62	34	32	2	2	1	4	20	0	40	2	0	1	3	.250	0	0	5.54
3 Min. YEARS		52	49	2	0	251.1	1053	233	116	95	17	6	4	15	81	0	221	16	4	15	10	.600	2	0	3.40

Justin Reid

Pitches: Right Bats: Right Pos: SP-24; RP-1   Ht: 6'6" Wt: 200 Born: 6/30/77 Age: 25

Year Team	Lg Org	G	GS	CG	GF	IP	BFP	H	R	ER	HR	SH	SF	HB	TBB	IBB	SO	WP	Bk	W	L	Pct.	ShO	Sv	ERA
1999 Williamsprt	A- Pit	16	11	0	4	62.1	277	71	41	32	4	0	3	3	23	0	68	0	4	2	6	.250	0	0	4.62
2000 Hickory	A Pit	27	22	5	4	170	694	146	82	57	12	3	4	3	30	0	176	5	0	9	8	.529	0	3	3.02
2001 Lynchburg	A+ Pit	8	8	1	0	56	221	50	15	14	4	0	1	2	6	0	48	2	0	2	4	.333	0	0	2.25
Altoona	AA Pit	17	16	1	0	110	452	104	38	31	5	7	1	5	14	0	70	2	0	5	5	.500	1	0	2.54
3 Min. YEARS		68	57	7	8	398.1	1644	371	176	134	25	10	9	13	73	0	362	9	4	18	23	.439	1	4	3.03

Cameron Reimers

Pitches: Right Bats: Right Pos: SP-26; RP-1   Ht: 6'5" Wt: 205 Born: 9/15/78 Age: 23

Year Team	Lg Org	G	GS	CG	GF	IP	BFP	H	R	ER	HR	SH	SF	HB	TBB	IBB	SO	WP	Bk	W	L	Pct.	ShO	Sv	ERA
1999 Medcine Hat	R+ Tor	13	5	0	3	44.1	184	39	21	16	2	1	3	2	12	0	29	7	3	1	5	.167	0	2	3.25
2000 Hagerstown	A Tor	26	26	2	0	154.1	671	158	79	64	10	5	4	21	45	0	112	14	2	7	11	.389	0	0	3.73
2001 Dunedin	A+ Tor	22	22	3	0	141	604	150	81	69	13	4	5	20	24	1	88	2	2	10	6	.625	0	0	4.40
Tennessee	AA Tor	5	4	0	0	30	126	32	22	22	8	0	1	3	5	0	19	1	0	1	2	.333	0	0	6.60
3 Min. YEARS		66	57	5	3	369.2	1585	379	203	171	33	10	13	46	86	1	248	24	7	19	24	.442	0	2	4.16

Chris Reinike

Pitches: Right Bats: Right Pos: RP-28   Ht: 6'0" Wt: 195 Born: 11/16/76 Age: 25

Year Team	Lg Org	G	GS	CG	GF	IP	BFP	H	R	ER	HR	SH	SF	HB	TBB	IBB	SO	WP	Bk	W	L	Pct.	ShO	Sv	ERA
1998 Watertown	A- Cle	15	15	0	0	89.2	367	64	21	19	1	0	2	8	33	1	92	2	0	7	3	.833	0	0	1.91
1999 Columbus	A Cle	11	11	0	0	48	222	55	28	23	3	0	1	4	21	0	41	1	1	3	4	.429	0	0	4.31
2000 Columbus	A Cle	7	0	0	1	12	49	6	2	2	0	0	0	2	4	0	19	2	0	0	0	—	0	0	1.50
Kinston	A+ Cle	11	0	0	3	20.2	83	13	7	5	0	1	1	2	8	0	25	2	0	0	1	.000	0	0	2.18
Akron	AA Cle	1	0	0	0	2	8	1	1	1	0	0	0	0	2	0	3	0	0	0	0	—	0	0	4.50
2001 Buffalo	AAA Cle	1	0	0	0	1	6	1	1	1	0	0	0	0	3	0	1	2	0	0	0	—	0	0	9.00
Akron	AA Cle	27	0	0	13	52.1	226	55	34	31	5	0	0	2	18	0	40	6	1	1	3	.250	0	5	5.33
4 Min. YEARS		73	26	0	17	225.2	961	194	94	82	9	1	4	18	89	1	221	15	2	14	10	.583	0	5	3.27

Tyler Renwick

Pitches: Right Bats: Right Pos: RP-22   Ht: 6'4" Wt: 206 Born: 8/12/78 Age: 23

Year Team	Lg Org	G	GS	CG	GF	IP	BFP	H	R	ER	HR	SH	SF	HB	TBB	IBB	SO	WP	Bk	W	L	Pct.	ShO	Sv	ERA
1998 Medcine Hat	R+ Tor	9	0	0	3	8	57	10	20	19	2	0	0	2	20	0	7	2	1	1	1	.500	0	0	21.38
1999 St.Cathrnes	A- Tor	16	5	0	6	39	182	35	28	23	2	1	2	1	33	0	32	10	0	2	4	.333	0	0	5.31
2000 Queens	A- Tor	7	7	0	0	35.1	156	26	19	10	1	0	0	1	23	0	31	5	0	2	2	.500	0	0	2.55
Hagerstown	A Tor	7	7	0	0	35	170	44	28	21	2	2	1	5	21	0	17	11	0	3	2	.600	0	0	5.40
2001 Chston-WV	A Tor	7	0	0	2	11.2	63	17	16	15	1	2	2	0	13	1	8	5	0	1	2	.333	0	0	11.57
Syracuse	AAA Tor	2	0	0	0	5.2	26	7	2	2	1	0	1	0	4	0	2	0	0	0	0	—	0	0	3.18
Auburn	A- Tor	13	0	0	7	31	139	35	18	17	4	0	2	1	10	0	24	5	0	1	0	1.000	0	0	4.94
4 Min. YEARS		61	19	0	18	165.2	793	174	131	107	13	5	8	10	124	1	121	38	1	10	11	.476	0	0	5.81

Michael Restovich

Bats: Right Throws: Right Pos: OF-140; 1B-2; PH-1   Ht: 6'4" Wt: 233 Born: 1/3/79 Age: 23

Year Team	Lg Org	G	AB	H	2B	3B	HR	TB	R	RBI	TBB	IBB	SO	HBP	SH	SF	SB	CS	SB%	GDP	Avg	OBP	SLG
1998 Elizabethtn	R+ Min	65	242	86	20	1	13	147	68	64	54	0	58	9	0	0	5	2	.71	10	.355	.489	.607
Fort Wayne	A Min	11	45	20	5	2	0	29	9	6	4	0	12	0	0	0	0	0	—	1	.444	.490	.644
1999 Quad City	A Min	131	493	154	30	6	19	253	91	107	74	4	100	13	0	5	7	9	.44	9	.312	.412	.513
2000 Fort Myers	A+ Min	135	475	125	27	9	8	194	73	64	61	1	100	4	0	3	19	7	.73	11	.263	.350	.408
2001 New Britain	AA Min	140	501	135	33	4	23	245	69	84	54	8	125	6	0	4	15	7	.68	8	.269	.345	.489
4 Min. YEARS		482	1756	520	115	22	63	868	310	325	247	13	395	32	0	12	46	25	.65	39	.296	.390	.494

Todd Revenig

Pitches: Right Bats: Right Pos: RP-46   Ht: 6'1" Wt: 185 Born: 6/28/69 Age: 33

Year Team	Lg Org	G	GS	CG	GF	IP	BFP	H	R	ER	HR	SH	SF	HB	TBB	IBB	SO	WP	Bk	W	L	Pct.	ShO	Sv	ERA
1990 Sou Oregon	A- Oak	24	0	0	14	44.2	176	33	13	4	2	4	1	0	9	2	46	1	2	3	2	.600	0	6	0.81
1991 Madison	A Oak	26	0	0	22	28.2	109	13	6	3	1	3	0	0	10	2	27	1	1	1	0	1.000	0	13	0.94
Huntsville	AA Oak	12	0	0	6	18.1	68	11	3	2	1	0	1	2	4	0	10	0	0	1	2	.333	0	0	0.98
1992 Huntsville	AA Oak	53	0	0	48	63.2	233	33	14	12	8	2	2	0	11	0	49	1	0	1	1	.500	0	33	1.70
1994 Athletics	R Oak	4	4	0	0	7.2	33	7	4	3	1	1	0	0	2	0	6	0	0	0	0	—	0	0	3.52
1995 Edmonton	AAA Oak	45	0	0	30	54.1	230	53	32	26	5	3	3	2	15	1	28	2	0	4	5	.444	0	10	4.31
1996 Rochester	AAA Bal	3	0	0	0	6	25	8	5	5	2	0	0	0	0	0	4	0	0	2	0	1.000	0	0	7.50
Bowie	AA Bal	38	0	0	29	61.2	238	42	18	18	6	0	2	2	18	0	39	2	0	3	4	.429	0	7	2.63
2000 El Paso	AA Ari	12	11	0	0	60.1	276	90	50	42	7	3	3	6	14	0	50	0	0	0	0	.333	0	0	6.27
Diamondbcks	R Ari	2	2	0	0	2	9	2	0	0	0	0	0	0	0	0	1	1	0	0	0	—	0	0	0.00
Tucson	AAA Ari	17	0	0	9	26.1	110	29	8	8	1	1	0	0	4	0	28	1	0	2	1	.667	0	2	2.73
2001 Tucson	AAA Ari	46	0	0	16	65.2	287	82	39	37	9	1	1	1	12	7	42	1	0	4	5	.444	0	0	5.07
1992 Oakland	AL	2	0	0	2	2	7	2	0	0	0	0	0	0	0	0	1	0	0	0	0	—	0	0	0.00
8 Min. YEARS		282	17	0	174	439.1	1794	403	192	160	43	18	13	13	99	12	330	10	3	23	24	.489	0	71	3.28

Carlos Reyes

Pitches: Right Bats: Both Pos: RP-25   Ht: 6'0" Wt: 190 Born: 4/4/69 Age: 33

Year Team	Lg Org	G	GS	CG	GF	IP	BFP	H	R	ER	HR	SH	SF	HB	TBB	IBB	SO	WP	Bk	W	L	Pct.	ShO	Sv	ERA
1991 Braves	R Atl	20	0	0	13	45.2	195	44	15	9	0	1	1	0	9	1	37	1	3	3	2	.600	0	5	1.77
1992 Macon	A Atl	23	0	0	7	60	241	57	16	14	2	1	1	5	11	1	57	2	0	2	3	.400	0	2	2.10
Durham	A+ Atl	21	0	0	12	40.2	158	31	11	11	1	2	0	1	10	0	33	2	0	1	2	.667	0	5	2.43
1993 Greenville	AA Atl	33	2	0	10	70	290	64	22	16	5	2	2	3	24	1	57	2	0	8	1	.889	0	2	2.06
Richmond	AAA Atl	18	1	0	11	28.2	130	30	12	12	2	2	0	3	11	3	30	2	1	1	0	1.000	0	1	3.77
1994 Modesto	A+ Oak	3	3	0	0	5	17	2	0	0	0	0	0	0	0	0	3	1	0	0	0	—	0	0	0.00
1997 Columbus	AAA NYY	1	1	0	0	2	12	5	4	4	0	0	0	0	2	0	0	0	0	0	0	—	0	0	18.00
Edmonton	AAA Oak	5	4	1	0	31	123	30	14	12	2	0	2	0	3	1	23	0	0	2	0	1.000	0	0	3.48
1998 Las Vegas	AAA SD	1	0	0	0	1.2	6	1	0	0	0	0	0	0	0	0	2	0	0	0	0	—	0	0	0.00

		HOW MUCH HE PITCHED						WHAT HE GAVE UP												THE RESULTS					
Year Team	Lg Org	G	GS	CG	GF	IP	BFP	H	R	ER	HR	SH	SF	HB	TBB	IBB	SO	WP	Bk	W	L	Pct.	ShO	Sv	ERA
2000 Reading	AA Phi	2	0	0	0	3	9	1	0	0	0	0	0	0	0	0	3	0	0	0	0	—	0	0	0.00
Las Vegas	AAA SD	16	0	0	5	28.1	125	28	13	9	5	2	1	0	9	1	24	1	0	0	2	.000	0	1	2.86
2001 Sacramento	AAA Oak	17	0	0	9	30.1	135	31	21	21	5	1	2	1	14	1	26	1	0	2	0	1.000	0	0	6.23
Tucson	AAA Ari	8	0	0	4	9.1	45	13	10	9	1	0	1	0	5	1	7	3	0	0	1	.000	0	0	8.68
1994 Oakland	AL	27	9	0	8	78	344	71	38	36	10	2	3	2	44	1	57	3	0	0	3	.000	0	1	4.15
1995 Oakland	AL	40	1	0	19	69	306	71	43	39	10	4	0	5	28	4	48	5	0	4	6	.400	0	4	5.09
1996 Oakland	AL	46	10	0	14	122.1	550	134	71	65	19	2	8	2	61	8	78	2	1	7	10	.412	0	0	4.78
1997 Oakland	AL	37	6	0	9	77.1	352	101	52	50	13	3	2	2	25	2	43	2	1	3	4	.429	0	0	5.82
1998 San Diego	NL	22	0	0	8	27.2	109	23	11	11	4	2	1	2	6	0	24	0	1	2	2	.500	0	1	3.58
Boston	AL	24	0	0	10	38.1	158	35	15	15	2	0	1	1	14	2	23	3	0	1	1	.500	0	0	3.52
1999 San Diego	NL	65	0	0	23	77.1	331	76	38	32	11	5	3	0	24	4	57	7	1	2	4	.333	0	1	3.72
2000 Philadelphia	NL	10	0	0	5	10.1	44	10	6	6	2	2	0	0	5	0	4	1	0	0	2	.000	0	0	5.23
San Diego	NL	12	0	0	4	18	77	15	12	12	5	0	0	1	8	0	13	0	1	1	1	.500	0	0	6.00
8 Min. YEARS		168	11	1	71	355.2	1486	337	138	117	23	11	11	13	96	10	304	15	4	20	10	.667	0	16	2.96
7 Maj. YEARS		283	26	0	100	518.1	2271	536	286	266	76	20	18	15	215	21	347	23	5	20	33	.377	0	4	4.62

Eddy Reyes

Pitches: Right Bats: Right Pos: RP-44   Ht: 6'4" Wt: 204 Born: 4/24/76 Age: 26

		HOW MUCH HE PITCHED						WHAT HE GAVE UP												THE RESULTS					
Year Team	Lg Org	G	GS	CG	GF	IP	BFP	H	R	ER	HR	SH	SF	HB	TBB	IBB	SO	WP	Bk	W	L	Pct.	ShO	Sv	ERA
1997 Hudson Val	A- TB	31	0	0	29	32.2	144	24	12	10	1	2	0	4	18	0	29	0	5	0	2	.000	0	14	2.76
1998 Chston-SC	A TB	56	0	0	52	61.2	255	60	23	15	2	2	1	3	12	1	49	6	0	4	6	.400	0	24	2.19
1999 St. Pete	A+ TB	37	0	0	33	38.1	172	31	13	8	0	4	1	6	23	1	30	0	0	2	0	.000	0	25	1.88
Orlando	AA TB	18	0	0	11	28.2	133	31	16	13	3	1	1	6	11	2	25	2	3	1	3	.250	0	2	4.08
2000 Orlando	AA TB	50	0	0	35	59.1	280	52	32	26	5	1	1	11	48	0	44	3	0	2	5	.286	0	14	3.94
2001 Orlando	AA TB	31	0	0	7	43	202	45	30	26	2	3	1	4	27	1	28	0	0	2	3	.400	0	1	5.44
Brevard Cty	A+ Fla	13	0	0	9	15	71	13	13	6	1	0	1	3	10	1	9	1	0	2	0	1.000	0	2	3.60
5 Min. YEARS		236	0	0	176	278.2	1257	256	139	104	14	13	6	37	149	6	214	12	8	11	21	.344	0	82	3.36

Edison Reynoso

Pitches: Right Bats: Right Pos: SP-5; RP-2   Ht: 6'1" Wt: 170 Born: 11/10/75 Age: 26

		HOW MUCH HE PITCHED						WHAT HE GAVE UP												THE RESULTS					
Year Team	Lg Org	G	GS	CG	GF	IP	BFP	H	R	ER	HR	SH	SF	HB	TBB	IBB	SO	WP	Bk	W	L	Pct.	ShO	Sv	ERA
2001 Tampa	A+ NYY	1	1	0	0	3.2	12	1	0	0	0	0	0	0	0	0	5	0	0	0	0	—	0	0	0.00
Norwich	AA NYY	5	3	0	0	18.1	80	19	12	8	2	0	0	1	5	0	17	0	0	1	0	1.000	0	0	3.93
Staten IInd	A- NYY	1	1	0	0	5	21	3	1	0	0	0	0	0	2	0	9	1	0	1	0	1.000	0	0	0.00
1 Min. YEAR		7	5	0	0	27	113	23	13	8	2	0	0	1	7	0	31	1	0	2	0	1.000	0	0	2.67

Chad Ricketts

Pitches: Right Bats: Right Pos: RP-48   Ht: 6'5" Wt: 225 Born: 2/12/75 Age: 27

		HOW MUCH HE PITCHED						WHAT HE GAVE UP												THE RESULTS					
Year Team	Lg Org	G	GS	CG	GF	IP	BFP	H	R	ER	HR	SH	SF	HB	TBB	IBB	SO	WP	Bk	W	L	Pct.	ShO	Sv	ERA
1995 Cubs	R ChC	2	2	0	0	9	32	1	0	0	0	0	0	1	1	0	5	0	0	1	0	1.000	0	0	0.00
Williamsprt	A- ChC	12	12	0	0	68.2	312	89	46	32	4	0	3	8	16	0	37	1	3	4	5	.444	0	0	4.19
1996 Rockford	A ChC	37	9	0	17	87.2	389	89	60	49	8	5	2	7	29	2	70	5	1	3	8	.273	0	4	5.03
1997 Rockford	A ChC	16	0	0	10	29	116	19	9	8	1	1	1	1	11	2	32	1.	0	4	0	1.000	0	3	2.48
Daytona	A+ ChC	20	0	0	17	20.1	82	13	4	1	0	0	1	0	6	0	18	1	0	3	1	.750	0	4	0.44
Orlando	AA ChC	2	0	0	0	2	15	7	4	4	0	0	0	0	2	0	3	0	0	0	0	—	0	0	18.00
1998 Daytona	A+ ChC	47	0	0	41	49	204	41	15	10	0	3	0	3	11	1	59	2	0	2	1	.667	0	19	1.84
West Tenn	AA ChC	13	0	0	11	15.1	65	19	7	6	0	0	1	1	4	2	13	1	0	0	2	.000	0	6	3.52
1999 West Tenn	AA ChC	57	0	0	26	67	275	55	25	23	8	3	1	2	21	4	80	1	0	6	4	.600	0	8	3.09
2000 Albuquerque	AAA LA	54	0	0	27	67.2	294	59	35	26	7	5	2	5	36	2	75	3	0	6	2	.750	0	7	3.46
2001 Las Vegas	AAA LA	48	0	0	17	58.2	253	49	24	19	5	4	5	2	25	4	70	3	0	1	3	.250	0	3	2.91
7 Min. YEARS		308	23	0	166	474.1	2037	441	230	178	33	21	15	31	162	17	462	18	4	30	26	.536	0	58	3.38

Jim Rickon

Bats: Right Throws: Right Pos: C-26; 1B-8; PH-6; DH-4   Ht: 6'4" Wt: 225 Born: 6/1/76 Age: 26

		BATTING															BASERUNNING				PERCENTAGES		
Year Team	Lg Org	G	AB	H	2B	3B	HR	TB	R	RBI	TBB	IBB	SO	HBP	SH	SF	SB	CS	SB%	GDP	Avg	OBP	SLG
1999 Burlington	R+ Cle	31	96	29	5	0	4	46	16	17	19	0	25	1	0	0	2	1	.67	2	.302	.422	.479
Mahoning Vy	A- Cle	8	25	5	0	0	1	8	3	4	2	0	7	0	1	0	0	0	—	2	.200	.259	.320
2000 Columbus	A Cle	17	40	8	2	1	0	12	3	1	5	0	17	0	0	0	0	0	—	1	.200	.289	.300
Mahoning Vy	A- Cle	3	10	3	0	0	0	3	0	3	2	0	2	0	0	0	0	0	—	0	.300	.417	.300
Akron	AA Cle	3	4	2	1	0	0	3	1	0	0	0	0	0	0	0	0	0	—	0	.500	.500	.750
Kinston	A+ Cle	8	26	10	3	0	1	16	6	2	1	0	6	2	0	0	0	0	—	1	.385	.448	.615
2001 Kinston	A+ Cle	29	80	18	3	0	4	33	13	13	6	0	23	2	0	0	0	1	.00	3	.225	.295	.413
Akron	AA Cle	12	26	4	1	0	0	5	0	0	1	0	9	0	0	0	1	0	1.00	0	.154	.185	.192
3 Min. YEARS		111	307	79	15	1	10	126	42	40	36	0	89	5	1	0	3	2	.60	2	.257	.345	.410

Auntwan Riggins

Bats: Both Throws: Right Pos: OF-42; SS-17; PH-3; DH-2; PR-2   Ht: 6'1" Wt: 170 Born: 6/17/76 Age: 26

		BATTING															BASERUNNING				PERCENTAGES		
Year Team	Lg Org	G	AB	H	2B	3B	HR	TB	R	RBI	TBB	IBB	SO	HBP	SH	SF	SB	CS	SB%	GDP	Avg	OBP	SLG
1998 St.Cathrnes	A- Tor	5	12	2	0	0	0	2	1	0	1	0	3	0	0	0	0	0	—	0	.167	.231	.167
Medcine Hat	R+ Tor	41	153	38	6	1	0	46	30	18	10	0	34	3	3	1	16	1	.94	0	.248	.305	.301
1999 St.Cathrnes	A- Tor	44	105	25	3	1	0	30	16	11	12	0	34	5	0	0	12	2	.86	0	.238	.344	.286
2000 Hagerstown	A Tor	67	195	43	5	0	0	48	25	9	12	0	56	2	4	0	16	4	.80	4	.221	.273	.246

Year Team	Lg Org	BATTING															BASERUNNING				PERCENTAGES		
		G	AB	H	2B	3B	HR	TB	R	RBI	TBB	IBB	SO	HBP	SH	SF	SB	CS	SB%	GDP	Avg	OBP	SLG
2001 Lk Elsinore	A+ SD	17	66	15	0	0	0	15	7	5	4	0	22	1	1	0	2	2	.50	1	.227	.282	.227
Mobile	AA SD	14	34	5	0	0	0	5	0	1	2	0	8	1	0	0	1	1	.50	1	.147	.216	.147
Portland	AAA SD	1	1	0	0	0	0	0	0	0	0	0	1	0	0	0	0	0	—	0	.000	.000	.000
Fort Wayne	A SD	32	117	28	4	0	0	32	15	5	16	0	29	1	2	0	12	3	.80	5	.239	.336	.274
4 Min. YEARS		221	683	156	18	2	0	178	94	49	57	0	187	13	10	1	59	13	.82	8	.228	.300	.261

Eric Riggs

Bats: Both **Throws:** Right **Pos:** 3B-85; SS-19; PH-12; 2B-5; OF-1; DH-1   **Ht:** 6'2" **Wt:** 190 **Born:** 8/19/76 **Age:** 25

Year Team	Lg Org	BATTING															BASERUNNING				PERCENTAGES		
		G	AB	H	2B	3B	HR	TB	R	RBI	TBB	IBB	SO	HBP	SH	SF	SB	CS	SB%	GDP	Avg	OBP	SLG
1998 Vero Beach	A+ LA	61	230	57	12	3	3	84	30	17	23	0	46	0	3	1	3	4	.43	1	.248	.315	.365
1999 San Berndno	A+ LA	130	523	144	18	10	16	230	105	69	70	2	92	6	7	5	27	11	.71	6	.275	.364	.440
2000 San Antonio	AA LA	117	421	94	19	4	7	142	56	39	54	2	85	2	15	2	18	6	.75	8	.223	.313	.337
2001 Jacksonville	AA LA	118	394	101	28	1	6	149	52	36	42	3	49	5	11	3	7	4	.64	2	.256	.333	.378
4 Min. YEARS		426	1568	396	77	18	32	605	243	161	189	7	272	13	36	11	55	25	.69	17	.253	.336	.386

Mike Riley

Pitches: Left **Bats:** Left **Pos:** RP-23; SP-12   **Ht:** 6'1" **Wt:** 162 **Born:** 1/2/75 **Age:** 27

Year Team	Lg Org	HOW MUCH HE PITCHED						WHAT HE GAVE UP											THE RESULTS					
		G	GS	CG	GF	IP	BFP	H	R	ER	HR	SH	SF	HB	TBB	IBB	SO	WP	Bk	W	L	Pct.	ShO	Sv	ERA
1996 Bellingham	A- SF	17	3	0	2	36.2	181	38	26	17	3	1	1	2	29	0	38	5	2	1	3	.250	0	0	4.17
1997 Bakersfield	A+ SF	6	4	0	0	20.1	94	25	20	19	4	0	1	0	8	0	17	0	0	1	2	.333	0	0	8.41
Salem-Keizr	A- SF	15	15	1	0	88.1	375	76	39	34	9	2	2	4	28	0	96	6	1	9	2	.818	0	0	3.46
1998 Bakersfield	A+ SF	40	15	2	7	128	555	130	73	64	8	3	3	3	58	1	110	9	1	6	12	.333	0	2	4.50
1999 Shreveport	AA SF	30	13	1	4	111	456	80	35	26	6	2	2	1	53	0	107	2	1	8	3	.727	1	1	2.11
2000 Fresno	AAA SF	24	24	0	0	128	578	141	92	84	21	5	3	4	54	0	114	6	0	6	8	.429	0	0	5.91
2001 Fresno	AAA SF	28	5	0	7	53.1	255	59	41	36	9	1	0	4	33	0	52	3	1	2	4	.333	0	0	6.08
Shreveport	AA SF	7	7	2	0	43	189	55	26	23	6	3	2	4	12	0	34	1	0	3	2	.600	0	0	4.81
6 Min. YEARS		167	86	6	20	608.2	2683	604	352	303	66	17	14	22	275	1	568	32	6	36	36	.500	1	3	4.48

Brian Rios

Bats: Right **Throws:** Right **Pos:** 3B-59; DH-19; SS-15; 2B-9; PH-4; PR-1; P-1   **Ht:** 6'3" **Wt:** 190 **Born:** 7/25/74 **Age:** 27

Year Team	Lg Org	BATTING															BASERUNNING				PERCENTAGES		
		G	AB	H	2B	3B	HR	TB	R	RBI	TBB	IBB	SO	HBP	SH	SF	SB	CS	SB%	GDP	Avg	OBP	SLG
1996 Jamestown	A- Det	36	102	31	6	2	1	44	19	17	19	0	15	0	0	1	4	1	.80	3	.304	.410	.431
1997 Jamestown	A- Det	45	167	44	6	1	4	64	23	23	14	0	22	4	0	2	3	0	1.00	6	.263	.332	.383
1998 W Michigan	A Det	100	343	91	18	1	3	120	44	46	23	2	60	3	3	3	5	4	.56	6	.265	.315	.350
1999 Lakeland	A+ Det	119	430	121	27	7	6	180	60	44	24	1	47	5	0	6	7	3	.70	13	.281	.323	.419
2000 Jacksonville	AA Det	95	315	82	23	3	5	126	42	36	29	0	59	8	3	4	1	1	.50	3	.260	.334	.400
2001 Toledo	AAA Det	104	372	121	29	5	14	202	47	62	22	2	66	4	2	2	2	4	.33	17	.325	.368	.543
6 Min. YEARS		499	1729	490	109	19	33	736	235	228	131	5	269	24	8	18	22	13	.63	48	.283	.339	.426

Carlos Rivera

Bats: Left **Throws:** Left **Pos:** 1B-100; PH-8; DH-3; OF-1   **Ht:** 5'11" **Wt:** 230 **Born:** 6/10/78 **Age:** 24

Year Team	Lg Org	BATTING															BASERUNNING				PERCENTAGES		
		G	AB	H	2B	3B	HR	TB	R	RBI	TBB	IBB	SO	HBP	SH	SF	SB	CS	SB%	GDP	Avg	OBP	SLG
1996 Pirates	R Pit	48	183	52	8	3	3	75	24	26	15	1	22	1	0	2	1	1	.50	8	.284	.338	.410
1997 Augusta	A Pit	120	415	113	16	5	9	166	52	65	19	2	82	10	0	6	4	1	.80	9	.272	.316	.400
1998 Lynchburg	A+ Pit	29	113	26	4	0	4	42	11	16	0	0	19	1	0	1	0	1	.00	3	.230	.235	.372
Augusta	A Pit	87	316	90	17	1	5	124	38	53	11	2	46	6	0	3	3	5	.38	9	.285	.318	.392
1999 Hickory	A Pit	119	457	147	30	1	13	218	63	86	15	2	45	11	0	4	2	1	.67	13	.322	.355	.477
2000 Pirates	R Pit	6	24	7	0	0	0	7	2	0	1	0	2	0	0	0	0	0	—	1	.292	.320	.292
Lynchburg	A+ Pit	64	233	63	17	0	5	95	20	47	6	1	34	2	0	9	0	1	.00	7	.270	.284	.408
2001 Altoona	AA Pit	111	389	91	30	0	10	151	44	50	13	2	71	1	1	4	0	2	.00	11	.234	.258	.388
6 Min. YEARS		584	2130	589	122	10	49	878	254	343	80	10	321	32	1	29	10	12	.45	61	.277	.309	.412

Homero Rivera

Pitches: Left **Bats:** Right **Pos:** RP-49; SP-2   **Ht:** 5'10" **Wt:** 165 **Born:** 8/13/78 **Age:** 23

Year Team	Lg Org	HOW MUCH HE PITCHED						WHAT HE GAVE UP											THE RESULTS					
		G	GS	CG	GF	IP	BFP	H	R	ER	HR	SH	SF	HB	TBB	IBB	SO	WP	Bk	W	L	Pct.	ShO	Sv	ERA
1997 Tigers	R Det	15	9	0	1	51	231	67	36	28	3	1	0	3	10	0	47	6	1	4	4	.500	0	0	4.94
1998 Tigers	R Det	16	7	1	4	57.1	250	64	40	34	6	0	1	3	17	1	53	5	3	3	6	.333	0	2	5.34
1999 Oneonta	A- Det	23	0	0	8	49.2	218	44	19	15	3	6	4	4	22	3	47	5	1	5	2	.714	0	0	2.72
2000 W Michigan	A Det	36	0	0	10	47.1	202	45	23	18	4	2	2	3	15	1	40	1	0	3	4	.429	0	2	3.42
2001 Lakeland	A+ Det	35	0	0	13	49.1	193	30	13	12	1	4	0	2	18	2	31	3	0	3	4	.429	0	3	2.19
Erie	AA Det	16	2	0	8	30.1	132	35	16	16	4	0	2	2	11	1	19	3	0	1	2	.333	0	2	4.75
5 Min. YEARS		141	18	1	44	285	1226	285	147	123	21	13	9	17	93	8	237	23	5	19	22	.463	0	9	3.88

Roberto Rivera

Bats: Both **Throws:** Right **Pos:** OF-99; PH-18; DH-7; PR-3   **Ht:** 6'2" **Wt:** 180 **Born:** 11/25/76 **Age:** 25

Year Team	Lg Org	BATTING															BASERUNNING				PERCENTAGES		
		G	AB	H	2B	3B	HR	TB	R	RBI	TBB	IBB	SO	HBP	SH	SF	SB	CS	SB%	GDP	Avg	OBP	SLG
1995 Orioles	R Bal	42	150	44	7	3	3	66	21	26	10	0	38	2	0	2	6	3	.67	5	.293	.341	.440
1996 Orioles	R Bal	4	8	5	1	1	0	8	7	2	3	0	1	0	0	1	3	0	1.00	0	.625	.667	1.000
Bluefield	R+ Bal	46	158	34	8	0	5	57	20	26	10	0	54	0	0	0	14	4	.78	3	.215	.262	.361

Saul Rivera (partial top table - unnamed batting player)

	BATTING															BASERUNNING				PERCENTAGES		
Year Team	Lg Org	G	AB	H	2B	3B	HR	TB	R	RBI	TBB	IBB	SO	HBP	SH	SF	SB	CS	SB%	GDP	Avg	OBP	SLG
1997 Delmarva	A Bal	17	59	9	0	1	2	17	6	5	1	0	20	0	0	0	1	2	.33	0	.153	.167	.288
Frederick	A+ Bal	16	53	12	1	0	1	16	8	8	3	0	16	1	0	0	1	1	.50	0	.226	.281	.302
Bluefield	R+ Bal	50	192	61	20	2	3	94	28	27	13	1	43	1	2	1	6	6	.50	3	.318	.362	.490
1998 Frederick	A+ Bal	3	6	2	0	0	1	5	1	1	1	1	1	0	0	0	0	0	—	0	.333	.429	.833
Delmarva	A Bal	110	390	93	21	5	7	145	55	50	25	1	99	4	3	5	17	4	.81	5	.238	.288	.372
1999 Frederick	A+ Bal	118	460	126	21	4	12	191	70	53	39	0	89	3	0	3	18	9	.67	4	.274	.333	.415
Bowie	AA Bal	9	36	8	0	0	0	8	0	1	1	0	9	0	0	0	2	0	1.00	1	.222	.243	.222
2000 Bowie	AA Bal	80	272	61	13	3	4	92	31	34	31	1	62	1	1	4	10	2	.83	10	.224	.302	.338
Frederick	A+ Bal	36	116	29	5	3	1	43	14	18	12	3	30	2	1	2	4	0	1.00	0	.250	.326	.371
2001 Greenville	AA Atl	121	392	93	19	1	6	132	49	27	30	0	78	6	3	2	9	4	.69	11	.237	.300	.337
7 Min. YEARS		652	2292	577	116	23	45	874	310	278	179	7	540	20	10	20	91	35	.72	42	.252	.309	.381

Saul Rivera

Pitches: Right **Bats:** Right **Pos:** RP-36 **Ht:** 5'11" **Wt:** 155 **Born:** 12/7/77 **Age:** 24

	HOW MUCH HE PITCHED						WHAT HE GAVE UP											THE RESULTS				
Year Team	Lg Org	G	GS	CG	GF	IP	BFP	H	R	ER	HR	SH	SF	HB	TBB	IBB	SO	WP	Bk	W	L	Pct.	ShO	Sv	ERA
1998 Elizabethtn	R+ Min	23	0	0	21	36	147	19	10	9	4	2	0	0	19	2	65	1	0	3	3	.500	0	7	2.25
1999 Quad City	A Min	60	0	0	54	69.2	283	42	12	11	0	2	0	0	36	5	102	2	0	4	1	.800	0	23	1.42
2000 New Britain	AA Min	22	0	0	7	37	163	28	16	16	0	2	1	2	22	0	47	8	0	1	0	1.000	0	0	3.89
Fort Myers	A+ Min	29	0	0	22	37.2	166	34	15	15	0	2	0	0	19	3	45	6	1	8	1	.889	0	5	3.58
2001 Twins	R Min	3	0	0	0	3	13	2	0	0	0	0	0	0	1	0	4	0	0	0	0	—	0	0	0.00
New Britain	AA Min	33	0	0	27	42.2	181	35	16	15	3	2	1	1	18	1	55	1	0	5	2	.714	0	13	3.16
4 Min. YEARS		170	0	0	131	226	953	160	69	66	7	10	2	3	115	11	318	18	1	21	7	.750	0	48	2.63

Todd Rizzo

Pitches: Left **Bats:** Right **Pos:** RP-49 **Ht:** 6'2" **Wt:** 220 **Born:** 5/24/71 **Age:** 31

	HOW MUCH HE PITCHED						WHAT HE GAVE UP											THE RESULTS				
Year Team	Lg Org	G	GS	CG	GF	IP	BFP	H	R	ER	HR	SH	SF	HB	TBB	IBB	SO	WP	Bk	W	L	Pct.	ShO	Sv	ERA
1992 Yakima	A- LA	15	0	0	8	26	121	21	13	13	3	0	1	2	24	0	26	6	0	2	0	1.000	0	0	4.50
Dodgers	R LA	3	1	0	1	7	31	4	4	3	0	0	0	1	8	0	7	0	0	0	1	.000	0	0	3.86
1994 San Antonio	IND —	17	0	0	—	28.2	—	30	32	24	—	—	—	—	41	—	20	—	—	0	2	.000	0	1	7.53
Tyler	IND —	14	1	0	—	18.1	—	24	23	17	—	—	—	—	21	—	13	—	—	0	0	—	0	0	8.35
1995 Pr William	A+ CWS	36	0	0	10	68	307	68	30	21	2	2	1	3	39	8	59	13	0	3	5	.375	0	1	2.78
1996 Birmingham	AA CWS	46	0	0	19	68.2	300	61	28	21	0	3	2	1	40	7	48	7	0	4	4	.500	0	10	2.75
1997 Nashville	AAA CWS	54	0	0	23	70.2	318	63	39	28	6	3	1	3	33	3	60	9	0	4	5	.444	0	6	3.57
1998 Calgary	AAA CWS	50	0	0	19	72	358	102	62	54	6	3	3	3	39	3	58	10	1	7	3	.700	0	4	6.75
1999 Charlotte	AAA CWS	53	0	0	16	71	308	68	37	32	5	6	5	2	31	2	46	6	0	4	5	.444	0	8	4.06
2000 Salt Lake	AAA Min	61	0	0	14	71.2	315	76	31	27	1	3	1	0	27	1	43	4	0	6	4	.600	0	1	3.39
2001 Las Vegas	AAA LA	13	0	0	3	17.1	83	17	9	7	1	0	1	2	14	1	19	1	0	1	0	1.000	0	0	3.63
Fresno	AAA SF	36	0	0	14	46	207	49	26	23	5	1	4	3	22	0	39	5	1	3	4	.429	0	6	4.50
1998 Chicago	AL	9	0	0	1	6.2	38	12	12	10	0	1	0	1	6	0	3	2	0	0	0	—	0	0	13.50
1999 Chicago	AL	3	0	0	2	1.1	12	4	2	1	0	1	0	0	3	1	2	0	0	0	2	.000	0	0	6.75
9 Min. YEARS		398	2	0	127	565.1	—	583	334	270	—	—	—	—	339	—	438	—	—	34	33	.507	0	37	4.30
2 Maj. YEARS		12	0	0	3	8	50	16	14	11	0	1	0	1	9	1	5	2	0	0	2	.000	0	0	12.38

Joe Roa

Pitches: Right **Bats:** Right **Pos:** SP-26 **Ht:** 6'1" **Wt:** 194 **Born:** 10/11/71 **Age:** 30

	HOW MUCH HE PITCHED						WHAT HE GAVE UP											THE RESULTS				
Year Team	Lg Org	G	GS	CG	GF	IP	BFP	H	R	ER	HR	SH	SF	HB	TBB	IBB	SO	WP	Bk	W	L	Pct.	ShO	Sv	ERA
1989 Braves	R Atl	13	4	0	4	37.1	156	40	18	12	2	0	1	0	10	1	21	3	0	2	2	.500	0	0	2.89
1990 Pulaski	R+ Atl	14	11	3	1	75.2	313	55	29	25	3	2	1	2	26	0	49	2	2	4	2	.667	1	0	2.97
1991 Macon	A Atl	30	18	4	2	141	556	106	46	33	6	0	3	5	33	4	96	3	0	13	3	.813	2	1	2.11
1992 St. Lucie	A+ NYM	26	24	2	0	156.1	647	176	80	63	9	6	6	6	15	1	61	0	1	9	7	.563	1	0	3.63
1993 Binghamton	AA NYM	32	23	2	0	167.1	693	190	80	72	9	2	4	10	24	0	73	3	2	12	7	.632	1	0	3.87
1994 Binghamton	AA NYM	3	3	0	0	20	82	18	6	4	0	2	2	1	1	0	11	1	2	2	1	.667	0	0	1.80
Norfolk	AAA NYM	25	25	5	0	167.2	703	184	82	65	16	3	12	4	34	1	74	4	0	8	8	.500	0	0	3.49
1995 Buffalo	AAA Cle	25	24	3	1	164.2	678	168	71	64	9	2	5	7	28	1	93	1	2	17	3	.850	0	0	3.50
1996 Buffalo	AAA Cle	26	24	5	0	165.1	676	161	66	60	19	5	3	6	36	0	82	6	1	11	8	.579	0	0	3.27
1997 Phoenix	AAA SF	6	5	0	0	36	158	43	21	19	4	1	0	1	11	0	16	0	0	3	1	.750	0	0	4.75
1998 Fresno	AAA SF	27	27	2	0	162	702	192	102	93	26	9	2	4	32	0	97	3	2	12	9	.571	1	0	5.17
2000 Akron	AA Cle	19	14	1	2	103	439	91	48	39	7	5	2	7	38	0	59	3	0	6	5	.545	0	0	3.41
2001 Portland	AA Fla	7	7	0	0	36	143	36	15	12	2	2	1	2	3	1	26	0	0	2	2	.500	0	0	3.00
Calgary	AAA Fla	19	19	1	0	124	508	134	58	54	16	5	1	4	12	2	81	1	1	6	6	.500	0	0	3.92
1995 Cleveland	AL	1	1	0	0	6	28	9	4	4	1	1	0	0	2	0	5	0	0	0	1	.000	0	0	6.00
1996 Cleveland	AL	1	0	0	0	1.2	11	4	2	2	0	0	0	0	3	0	0	0	0	0	0	—	0	0	10.80
1997 San Francisco	NL	28	3	0	4	65.2	289	86	40	38	8	5	4	2	20	5	34	0	1	5	5	.286	0	0	5.21
12 Min. YEARS		272	228	28	10	1556.1	6454	1594	722	615	128	44	43	59	303	11	839	30	13	105	64	.621	6	1	3.56
3 Maj. YEARS		30	4	0	4	73.1	328	99	46	44	9	6	4	2	25	5	34	0	1	2	6	.250	0	0	5.40

Jason Roach

Pitches: Right **Bats:** Right **Pos:** SP-25; RP-1 **Ht:** 6'4" **Wt:** 199 **Born:** 4/20/76 **Age:** 26

	HOW MUCH HE PITCHED						WHAT HE GAVE UP											THE RESULTS				
Year Team	Lg Org	G	GS	CG	GF	IP	BFP	H	R	ER	HR	SH	SF	HB	TBB	IBB	SO	WP	Bk	W	L	Pct.	ShO	Sv	ERA
1998 Capital Cty	A NYM	1	0	0	1	1	5	1	0	0	0	0	0	0	1	0	1	0	0	0	0	—	0	0	0.00
1999 St. Lucie	A+ NYM	2	0	0	1	2	7	1	0	0	0	0	0	0	1	0	3	0	0	0	0	—	0	0	0.00
2000 Pittsfield	A- NYM	5	5	0	0	26.2	108	18	11	7	0	0	0	2	7	0	26	0	1	1	1	.500	0	0	2.36
Binghamton	AA NYM	1	1	0	0	5	24	7	3	2	0	1	0	0	3	0	3	0	0	0	0	—	0	0	3.60
St. Lucie	A+ NYM	9	9	0	0	48.2	191	42	15	14	2	1	2	0	12	0	22	1	0	5	3	.625	0	0	2.59
2001 Binghamton	AA NYM	22	21	0	0	116	500	129	54	42	7	6	4	4	28	1	70	1	2	8	7	.533	0	0	3.26
Norfolk	AAA NYM	4	4	0	0	16.1	77	21	13	13	1	2	1	1	7	1	7	0	0	1	2	.333	0	0	7.16
4 Min. YEARS		44	40	0	2	215.2	912	219	96	78	10	10	7	7	58	2	132	2	3	15	13	.536	0	0	3.26

Jake Robbins

Pitches: Right **Bats:** Right **Pos:** RP-57   **Ht:** 6'5" **Wt:** 190 **Born:** 5/23/76 **Age:** 26

		HOW MUCH HE PITCHED					WHAT HE GAVE UP													THE RESULTS					
Year Team	Lg Org	G	GS	CG	GF	IP	BFP	H	R	ER	HR	SH	SF	HB	TBB	IBB	SO	WP	Bk	W	L	Pct.	ShO	Sv	ERA
1994 Yankees	R NYY	8	3	0	0	23	102	21	16	13	2	1	3	1	15	0	14	2	1	0	2	.000	0	0	5.09
1995 Yankees	R NYY	14	3	0	3	37.1	159	32	26	23	2	2	1	1	18	1	17	4	0	2	3	.400	0	0	5.54
Oneonta	A- NYY	1	0	0	1	1	3	0	0	0	0	0	0	0	0	0	1	0	0	0	0	—	0	0	0.00
1996 Greensboro	A NYY	18	12	0	2	74	349	80	59	53	5	4	5	7	49	0	50	10	4	1	8	.111	0	0	6.45
Oneonta	A- NYY	11	11	0	0	66	298	64	42	33	3	5	1	2	35	1	47	6	1	3	4	.429	0	0	4.50
1997 Greensboro	A NYY	20	19	0	0	101.1	462	114	81	65	6	2	3	2	55	1	72	7	0	6	4	.600	0	0	5.77
Tampa	A+ NYY	3	3	0	0	16	73	18	14	9	2	0	2	0	10	1	5	2	0	1	1	.500	0	0	5.06
1998 Tampa	A+ NYY	26	25	2	0	152.1	674	167	83	65	5	5	6	1	72	2	87	4	1	11	6	.647	2	0	3.84
1999 Norwich	AA NYY	20	19	2	0	111	508	118	80	67	7	4	8	3	60	3	63	2	2	3	12	.200	1	0	5.43
Tampa	A+ NYY	7	7	0	0	41.2	187	44	30	22	3	1	2	2	19	2	31	5	0	3	3	.500	0	0	4.75
2000 Columbus	AAA NYY	1	0	0	1	1	7	3	1	1	0	0	0	0	1	0	0	0	0	0	0	—	0	0	9.00
Norwich	AA NYY	48	4	0	13	71.1	326	68	45	22	4	2	3	6	40	1	53	5	0	3	5	.375	0	0	2.78
2001 Richmond	AAA Atl	57	0	0	17	78.1	352	73	51	48	1	4	1	6	51	3	53	9	0	5	3	.625	0	1	5.51
8 Min. YEARS		234	106	4	37	774.1	3500	802	528	421	40	30	35	31	425	15	493	56	9	38	51	.427	3	1	4.89

J.P. Roberge

Bats: Right **Throws:** Right **Pos:** 3B-40; 1B-37; OF-23; 2B-18; DH-4; PH-1   **Ht:** 6'0" **Wt:** 177 **Born:** 9/12/72 **Age:** 29

		BATTING															BASERUNNING				PERCENTAGES		
Year Team	Lg Org	G	AB	H	2B	3B	HR	TB	R	RBI	TBB	IBB	SO	HBP	SH	SF	SB	CS	SB%	GDP	Avg	OBP	SLG
1994 Great Falls	R+ LA	63	256	82	17	1	1	104	55	42	20	0	22	5	2	5	24	4	.86	7	.320	.374	.406
Yakima	A- LA	4	8	3	1	0	0	4	1	0	0	0	3	1	0	0	0	1	.00	0	.375	.444	.500
1995 Vero Beach	A+ LA	3	9	0	0	0	0	0	1	0	0	0	2	0	0	0	0	0	—	0	.000	.000	.000
San Berndno	A+ LA	116	450	129	22	1	17	204	92	59	34	0	62	8	2	3	31	8	.79	9	.287	.345	.453
1996 San Berndno	A+ LA	12	44	16	3	1	1	24	8	6	3	0	9	2	0	1	1	2	.33	0	.364	.420	.545
San Antonio	AA LA	62	232	68	14	2	6	104	28	27	14	1	39	2	2	2	9	3	.75	5	.293	.336	.448
Albuquerque	AAA LA	53	156	50	6	1	4	70	17	17	14	1	28	1	3	0	3	0	1.00	1	.321	.380	.449
1997 San Antonio	AA LA	134	516	166	26	4	17	251	94	105	39	3	70	7	2	5	18	9	.67	13	.322	.374	.486
1998 Albuquerque	AAA LA	136	475	144	30	1	10	206	83	67	31	1	64	5	2	5	22	6	.79	17	.303	.349	.434
1999 Omaha	AAA KC	116	437	137	31	3	13	213	77	66	26	0	59	5	5	0	16	5	.76	15	.314	.359	.487
2000 Columbus	AAA NYY	29	77	9	3	0	1	15	7	6	5	0	10	1	1	0	0	0	—	1	.117	.181	.195
Omaha	AAA KC	6	23	9	4	0	1	16	5	1	1	0	3	0	0	0	0	0	—	0	.391	.417	.696
Wichita	AA KC	36	124	30	6	0	1	39	20	13	10	1	17	1	0	0	1	1	.50	3	.242	.304	.315
2001 Reading	AA Phi	87	343	110	13	1	19	182	61	71	25	6	40	4	1	3	12	4	.75	14	.321	.371	.531
Scranton-WB	AAA Phi	26	96	26	8	0	0	34	10	10	9	1	18	1	1	1	0	1	.00	5	.271	.336	.354
8 Min. YEARS		883	3246	979	184	15	91	1466	559	490	231	14	446	43	21	25	137	44	.76	90	.302	.353	.452

Chris Roberts

Pitches: Left **Bats:** Right **Pos:** SP-7; RP-5   **Ht:** 6'0" **Wt:** 190 **Born:** 6/25/71 **Age:** 31

		HOW MUCH HE PITCHED						WHAT HE GAVE UP												THE RESULTS					
Year Team	Lg Org	G	GS	CG	GF	IP	BFP	H	R	ER	HR	SH	SF	HB	TBB	IBB	SO	WP	Bk	W	L	Pct.	ShO	Sv	ERA
1993 St. Lucie	A+ NYM	25	25	3	0	173.1	703	162	64	53	3	2	4	7	36	0	111	2	1	13	5	.722	2	0	2.75
1994 Binghamton	AA NYM	27	27	2	0	175.1	751	164	77	64	11	8	5	6	77	1	128	12	1	13	8	.619	2	0	3.29
1995 Norfolk	AAA NYM	25	25	2	0	150	676	197	99	92	24	6	4	8	58	0	88	5	0	7	13	.350	0	0	5.52
1996 Mets	R NYM	3	3	0	0	13	48	11	2	2	0	0	0	1	0	0	12	1	0	0	0	—	0	0	1.38
St. Lucie	A+ NYM	1	1	0	0	6	21	1	0	0	0	0	0	0	3	0	2	0	0	1	0	1.000	0	0	0.00
Binghamton	AA NYM	9	9	1	0	46	225	55	40	37	6	6	2	1	37	0	30	1	0	2	7	.222	0	0	7.24
1997 Binghamton	AA NYM	19	19	1	0	105.1	448	103	69	58	18	6	2	8	33	0	66	1	1	5	8	.385	0	0	4.96
Norfolk	AAA NYM	7	6	0	1	37.1	164	38	17	12	2	2	1	2	17	0	21	0	1	0	4	.000	0	0	2.89
1998 Edmonton	AAA Oak	18	8	0	2	50.2	234	55	39	33	5	3	3	5	28	0	44	5	1	0	4	.000	0	0	5.86
Newburgh	IND —	9	9	2	0	53.1	230	58	28	27	4	0	1	3	19	1	37	1	0	5	2	.714	1	0	4.56
1999 Carolina	AA Col	43	1	0	17	81	360	76	46	34	10	5	2	6	36	0	52	3	0	5	4	.556	0	1	3.78
2001 Indianapols	AAA Mil	5	0	0	1	8.1	43	12	6	6	0	2	0	3	5	1	5	1	0	0	0	—	0	0	6.48
Camden	IND —	7	7	1	0	43.1	200	58	29	27	1	3	1	3	14	0	21	0	0	1	3	.250	0	0	5.61
8 Min. YEARS		198	140	12	21	943	4103	990	516	445	84	43	25	53	363	3	617	32	5	52	58	.473	5	1	4.25

Mark Roberts

Pitches: Right **Bats:** Right **Pos:** RP-33   **Ht:** 6'2" **Wt:** 205 **Born:** 9/29/75 **Age:** 26

		HOW MUCH HE PITCHED						WHAT HE GAVE UP												THE RESULTS					
Year Team	Lg Org	G	GS	CG	GF	IP	BFP	H	R	ER	HR	SH	SF	HB	TBB	IBB	SO	WP	Bk	W	L	Pct.	ShO	Sv	ERA
1996 Hickory	A CWS	13	13	0	0	72	298	70	42	39	12	3	2	3	19	0	62	4	3	4	6	.400	0	0	4.88
1997 Hickory	A CWS	4	4	0	0	22	96	23	12	9	3	1	1	0	9	0	14	1	0	2	0	.000	0	0	3.68
Winston-Sal	A+ CWS	14	14	3	0	91.1	379	78	48	41	10	1	3	3	45	0	64	4	0	5	9	.357	0	0	4.04
1998 Winston-Sal	A+ CWS	27	25	2	0	165.1	706	165	88	72	15	6	8	10	50	1	142	6	0	9	9	.500	1	0	3.92
1999 Birmingham	AA CWS	33	17	0	7	124.1	525	108	64	47	11	3	7	3	41	0	84	3	0	5	8	.385	0	2	3.40
2000 Birmingham	AA CWS	17	8	0	7	60	256	65	27	25	4	1	1	1	17	1	46	1	0	6	3	.667	0	3	3.75
Charlotte	AAA CWS	14	10	1	1	64.1	262	58	16	15	7	1	3	3	20	1	38	2	1	7	2	.778	0	0	2.10
2001 Calgary	AAA Fla	33	0	0	21	36	167	47	21	18	5	2	0	0	15	3	35	3	0	6	3	.667	0	8	4.50
6 Min. YEARS		155	91	6	36	635.1	2689	614	318	266	67	18	25	23	216	6	485	24	4	42	42	.500	1	13	3.77

Nick Roberts

Pitches: Right **Bats:** Right **Pos:** SP-27; RP-1   **Ht:** 6'2" **Wt:** 185 **Born:** 11/6/76 **Age:** 25

		HOW MUCH HE PITCHED						WHAT HE GAVE UP												THE RESULTS					
Year Team	Lg Org	G	GS	CG	GF	IP	BFP	H	R	ER	HR	SH	SF	HB	TBB	IBB	SO	WP	Bk	W	L	Pct.	ShO	Sv	ERA
1999 Martinsvlle	R+ Hou	10	7	1	1	47.1	188	43	11	10	0	1	0	1	6	0	56	2	3	4	2	.667	0	1	1.90
2000 Michigan	A Hou	22	20	2	0	139.1	587	121	53	48	10	1	5	5	61	1	107	5	1	13	6	.684	1	0	3.10
2001 Lexington	A Hou	20	20	3	0	137.1	540	118	49	45	10	3	4	4	21	0	128	3	0	10	1	.909	1	0	2.95
Round Rock	AA Hou	8	7	0	0	45.1	198	52	27	26	6	3	5	3	10	0	26	0	0	2	4	.333	0	0	5.16
3 Min. YEARS		60	54	6	2	369.1	1513	334	140	129	26	8	14	13	98	1	317	10	4	29	13	.690	2	1	3.14

Jeriome Robertson

Pitches: Left **Bats:** Left **Pos:** RP-57   **Ht:** 6'1" **Wt:** 190 **Born:** 3/30/77 **Age:** 25

Year Team	Lg Org	HOW MUCH HE PITCHED						WHAT HE GAVE UP												THE RESULTS					
		G	GS	CG	GF	IP	BFP	H	R	ER	HR	SH	SF	HB	TBB	IBB	SO	WP	Bk	W	L	Pct.	ShO	Sv	ERA
1996 Astros	R Hou	13	13	1	0	78.1	304	51	20	15	2	3	0	4	15	0	98	6	2	5	3	.625	1	0	1.72
Kissimmee	A+ Hou	1	1	0	0	7	27	4	4	2	0	0	0	0	1	0	2	0	0	0	0	—	0	0	2.57
1997 Quad City	A Hou	26	25	2	1	146	647	151	86	66	12	1	4	8	56	1	135	5	3	11	8	.579	1	1	4.07
1998 Kissimmee	A+ Hou	28	28	2	0	175	740	185	83	72	13	3	5	7	53	3	131	5	6	10	10	.500	0	0	3.70
1999 Jackson	AA Hou	28	28	1	0	191	791	184	81	65	22	6	4	8	45	2	133	5	7	15	7	.682	0	0	3.06
2000 Kissimmee	A+ Hou	5	5	1	0	29	121	28	19	15	1	1	0	2	5	0	13	0	0	2	1	.667	1	0	4.66
Round Rock	AA Hou	11	10	0	1	61	265	62	36	28	8	3	1	2	18	1	30	4	1	2	2	.500	0	0	4.13
New Orleans	AAA Hou	9	9	0	0	49.2	228	64	42	39	10	2	2	3	23	1	27	1	0	1	7	.125	0	0	7.07
2001 Round Rock	AA Hou	57	0	0	11	73.2	326	89	33	32	10	2	1	1	21	0	72	6	0	5	1	.833	0	3	3.91
6 Min. YEARS		178	119	7	13	810.2	3449	818	404	334	78	21	17	35	237	8	641	32	19	51	39	.567	3	4	3.71

Mike Robertson

Bats: Left **Throws:** Left **Pos:** 1B-71; DH-25; OF-21; PH-11   **Ht:** 6'0" **Wt:** 189 **Born:** 10/9/70 **Age:** 31

Year Team	Lg Org	BATTING															BASERUNNING				PERCENTAGES		
		G	AB	H	2B	3B	HR	TB	R	RBI	TBB	IBB	SO	HBP	SH	SF	SB	CS	SB%	GDP	Avg	OBP	SLG
1991 Utica	A- CWS	13	54	9	2	1	0	13	6	8	5	0	10	0	0	0	2	1	.67	0	.167	.237	.241
South Bend	A CWS	54	210	69	16	2	1	92	30	26	18	3	24	3	3	3	7	6	.54	5	.329	.385	.438
1992 Sarasota	A+ CWS	106	395	99	21	3	10	156	50	59	50	3	55	7	1	3	5	7	.42	8	.251	.343	.395
Birmingham	AA CWS	27	90	17	8	1	1	30	6	9	10	1	19	0	1	1	0	1	.00	2	.189	.267	.333
1993 Birmingham	AA CWS	138	511	138	31	3	11	208	73	73	59	4	97	3	0	8	10	5	.67	10	.270	.344	.407
1994 Birmingham	AA CWS	53	196	62	20	2	3	95	32	30	31	4	34	2	0	2	6	3	.67	5	.316	.411	.485
Nashville	AAA CWS	67	213	48	8	1	8	82	21	21	15	4	27	3	0	0	0	3	.00	4	.225	.286	.385
1995 Nashville	AAA CWS	139	499	124	17	4	19	206	55	52	50	7	72	11	3	2	2	4	.33	8	.248	.329	.413
1996 Nashville	AAA CWS	138	450	116	16	4	21	203	64	74	38	4	83	5	9	2	1	2	.33	10	.258	.321	.451
1997 Scranton-WB	AAA Phi	121	416	124	17	3	12	183	61	72	58	4	67	4	1	6	0	2	.00	9	.298	.384	.440
1998 Tucson	AAA Ari	111	411	112	14	3	13	171	49	70	33	1	56	7	0	3	1	0	1.00	15	.273	.335	.416
1999 Altoona	AA Pit	46	175	49	12	0	9	88	31	28	24	2	26	1	3	0	0	3	.00	1	.280	.370	.503
Nashville	AAA Pit	74	220	68	16	1	9	113	34	31	10	1	32	3	1	3	2	1	.67	5	.309	.343	.514
2000 New Orleans	AAA Hou	121	401	97	23	5	9	157	57	49	45	8	56	6	1	2	1	3	.25	13	.242	.326	.392
2001 Richmond	AAA Atl	127	434	118	19	5	6	165	42	40	30	3	56	2	1	2	4	12	.25	11	.272	.321	.380
1996 Chicago	AL	6	7	1	1	0	0	2	0	0	0	0	1	0	0	0	0	0	—	0	.143	.143	.286
1997 Philadelphia	NL	22	38	8	2	1	0	12	3	4	0	0	6	3	0	0	1	0	1.00	0	.211	.268	.316
1998 Arizona	NL	11	13	2	0	0	0	2	0	0	0	0	2	0	0	0	0	0	—	0	.154	.154	.154
11 Min. YEARS		1335	4675	1250	240	38	132	1962	611	642	476	49	714	57	24	37	41	53	.44	106	.267	.340	.420
3 Maj. YEARS		39	58	11	3	1	0	16	3	4	0	0	9	3	0	0	1	0	1.00	0	.190	.230	.276

Bo Robinson

Bats: Right **Throws:** Right **Pos:** 3B-99; 1B-20; DH-17; PH-3   **Ht:** 6'2" **Wt:** 195 **Born:** 8/21/75 **Age:** 26

Year Team	Lg Org	BATTING															BASERUNNING				PERCENTAGES		
		G	AB	H	2B	3B	HR	TB	R	RBI	TBB	IBB	SO	HBP	SH	SF	SB	CS	SB%	GDP	Avg	OBP	SLG
1998 Everett	A- Sea	60	204	55	14	1	4	83	33	27	24	0	34	2	0	2	1	0	1.00	4	.270	.349	.407
1999 Wisconsin	A Sea	138	499	164	50	3	13	259	101	102	108	4	75	4	0	8	4	1	.80	18	.329	.446	.519
2000 Lancaster	A+ Sea	136	515	161	33	0	10	224	93	97	65	2	69	5	1	9	2	5	.29	23	.313	.389	.435
2001 San Antonio	AA Sea	133	474	139	23	1	13	203	75	74	81	4	56	3	1	7	3	0	1.00	7	.293	.395	.428
4 Min. YEARS		467	1692	519	120	5	40	769	302	300	278	10	234	14	2	26	10	6	.63	52	.307	.403	.454

Dustin Robinson

Pitches: Right **Bats:** Right **Pos:** RP-49   **Ht:** 6'6" **Wt:** 225 **Born:** 9/13/75 **Age:** 26

Year Team	Lg Org	HOW MUCH HE PITCHED						WHAT HE GAVE UP												THE RESULTS					
		G	GS	CG	GF	IP	BFP	H	R	ER	HR	SH	SF	HB	TBB	IBB	SO	WP	Bk	W	L	Pct.	ShO	Sv	ERA
1997 Billings	R+ Cin	16	9	2	5	73.1	311	91	38	30	5	3	1	1	6	0	48	6	0	6	2	.750	0	4	3.68
1998 Chston-WV	A Cin	25	24	2	0	141	616	153	85	70	13	6	8	9	44	1	92	7	1	5	10	.333	0	0	4.47
1999 Clinton	A Cin	44	1	0	11	70	312	67	51	37	8	7	6	4	29	3	53	4	0	3	6	.333	0	0	4.76
2000 Clinton	A Cin	40	4	0	12	89	374	81	49	39	9	3	4	2	30	4	61	5	0	7	4	.636	0	1	3.94
2001 Mudville	A+ Cin	30	0	0	8	54.1	234	53	28	24	3	4	1	2	19	0	43	2	0	2	4	.333	0	3	3.98
Daytona	A+ ChC	2	0	0	1	4.1	16	2	1	1	1	0	0	0	1	0	7	0	0	0	0	—	0	0	2.08
West Tenn	AA ChC	17	0	0	10	20.2	94	24	10	10	3	1	1	2	9	3	18	3	0	1	1	.500	0	1	4.35
5 Min. YEARS		174	38	4	47	452.2	1957	471	262	211	42	24	21	20	138	11	322	27	1	24	27	.471	0	9	4.20

Bobby Rodgers

Pitches: Right **Bats:** Right **Pos:** RP-42; SP-2   **Ht:** 6'3" **Wt:** 225 **Born:** 7/22/74 **Age:** 27

Year Team	Lg Org	HOW MUCH HE PITCHED						WHAT HE GAVE UP												THE RESULTS					
		G	GS	CG	GF	IP	BFP	H	R	ER	HR	SH	SF	HB	TBB	IBB	SO	WP	Bk	W	L	Pct.	ShO	Sv	ERA
1996 Lowell	A- Bos	14	14	2	0	90	363	60	33	19	2	2	3		31	0	108	9	2	7	4	.636	1	0	1.90
1997 Kane County	A Fla	27	27	2	0	165.2	699	154	81	71	9	6	4	14	61	0	138	7	1	8	10	.444	0	0	3.86
1998 Brevard Cty	A+ Fla	7	7	0	0	35.1	143	24	17	16	2	2	1	1	7	0	35	1	0	1	1	.500	0	0	4.08
Portland	AA Fla	14	14	2	0	82	339	68	37	34	8	5	3	3	28	0	72	2	1	6	5	.545	1	0	3.73
1999 Portland	AA Fla	26	22	0	1	122.2	576	147	85	74	13	4	3	6	70	0	109	8	0	5	10	.333	0	0	5.43
2000 Portland	AA Fla	48	0	0	46	55.1	234	38	23	20	3	4	1	2	31	2	58	3	0	3	5	.375	0	22	3.25
2001 Portland	AA Fla	26	0	0	15	40	159	30	9	9	4	0	0	0	11	0	39	2	0	3	2	.600	0	4	2.03
Calgary	AAA Fla	18	2	0	3	37.1	166	35	25	25	7	3	3	2	20	0	28	4	0	1	3	.250	0	0	6.03
6 Min. YEARS		180	86	6	65	628.1	2679	566	310	268	49	26	17	31	259	2	587	36	4	34	40	.459	2	26	3.84

Fernando Rodney

Pitches: Right **Bats:** Right **Pos:** RP-11; SP-10   **Ht:** 5'11" **Wt:** 170 **Born:** 3/17/81 **Age:** 21

Year Team	Lg Org	G	GS	CG	GF	IP	BFP	H	R	ER	HR	SH	SF	HB	TBB	IBB	SO	WP	Bk	W	L	Pct.	ShO	Sv	ERA
1999 Tigers	R Det	22	0	0	20	30	129	20	8	8	1	3	2	3	21	0	39	1	1	3	3	.500	0	9	2.40
Lakeland	A+ Det	4	0	0	4	6.1	25	7	1	1	0	0	0	1	1	0	5	0	0	1	0	1.000	0	2	1.42
2000 W Michigan	A Det	22	10	0	1	82.2	353	74	34	27	2	5	0	2	35	0	56	3	0	6	4	.600	0	0	2.94
2001 Tigers	R Det	1	1	0	0	1	3	0	0	0	0	0	0	0	1	0	1	0	0	0	0	—	0	0	0.00
Lakeland	A+ Det	16	9	0	4	55.1	235	53	26	21	2	2	0	1	19	1	44	1	1	4	2	.667	0	0	3.42
Erie	AA Det	4	0	0	2	6.1	30	7	3	3	1	0	1	2	3	0	8	0	0	0	0	—	0	1	4.26
3 Min. YEARS		69	20	0	31	181.2	775	161	72	60	6	10	3	9	80	1	153	5	2	14	9	.609	0	12	2.97

Eddy Rodriguez

Pitches: Right **Bats:** Right **Pos:** RP-46   **Ht:** 6'1" **Wt:** 170 **Born:** 8/8/81 **Age:** 20

Year Team	Lg Org	G	GS	CG	GF	IP	BFP	H	R	ER	HR	SH	SF	HB	TBB	IBB	SO	WP	Bk	W	L	Pct.	ShO	Sv	ERA
2000 Orioles	R Bal	18	0	0	14	27	116	17	8	6	0	3	0	2	19	1	31	0	0	2	1	.667	0	6	2.00
Delmarva	A Bal	4	0	0	1	5	21	5	1	1	0	0	0	0	2	0	3	0	0	0	0	—	0	0	1.80
2001 Delmarva	A Bal	41	0	0	6	61	261	58	27	23	4	0	1	2	23	0	64	4	0	5	3	.625	0	1	3.39
Bowie	AA Bal	5	0	0	3	8.2	37	7	2	2	0	1	1	0	6	1	10	0	0	1	1	.500	0	2	2.08
2 Min. YEARS		68	0	0	24	101.2	435	87	38	32	5	4	2	4	50	2	108	4	0	8	5	.615	0	9	2.83

Frank Rodriguez

Pitches: Right **Bats:** Right **Pos:** RP-13   **Ht:** 5'9" **Wt:** 160 **Born:** 1/6/73 **Age:** 29

Year Team	Lg Org	G	GS	CG	GF	IP	BFP	H	R	ER	HR	SH	SF	HB	TBB	IBB	SO	WP	Bk	W	L	Pct.	ShO	Sv	ERA
1992 Brewers	R Mil	9	7	0	0	49	193	35	9	6	1	0	1	1	14	0	37	1	0	3	1	.750	0	0	1.10
Helena	R+ Mil	6	1	0	2	10.2	46	14	6	3	1	0	0	1	3	0	3	3	0	1	1	.500	0	0	2.53
1993 Helena	R+ Mil	18	1	0	9	41	176	31	19	11	0	2	0	1	17	3	63	8	1	2	1	.667	0	5	2.41
1994 Stockton	A+ Mil	26	24	3	0	151	627	139	67	57	6	6	9	13	52	1	124	6	0	10	9	.526	1	0	3.40
1995 El Paso	AA Mil	28	27	1	1	142.2	650	157	90	79	9	9	9	5	80	2	129	16	1	9	8	.529	0	0	4.98
1996 New Orleans	AAA Mil	13	1	0	7	18.2	87	24	15	14	1	1	1	0	11	3	16	0	0	0	2	.000	0	0	6.75
El Paso	AA Mil	16	7	0	3	34.1	169	45	32	26	1	0	2	2	24	0	39	1	0	3	4	.429	0	0	6.82
1997 El Paso	AA Mil	31	0	0	16	50.1	210	46	23	19	2	2	7	3	13	0	40	4	0	2	2	.500	0	4	3.40
Tucson	AAA Mil	12	6	1	1	47	204	53	25	23	1	2	1	2	19	1	41	1	0	3	1	.750	1	0	4.40
1998 El Paso	AA Mil	4	0	0	2	6	26	7	2	1	0	0	0	0	2	1	5	0	0	0	0	—	0	0	1.50
Louisville	AAA Mil	47	3	0	10	90.2	385	88	39	38	11	2	1	4	38	3	88	6	1	4	3	.571	0	2	3.77
2001 Altoona	AA Pit	7	0	0	3	9.1	47	9	6	5	0	0	1	1	8	1	5	1	0	0	0	—	0	0	4.82
Solano	IND —	6	0	0	2	7.2	47	15	8	7	0	0	0	1	8	0	10	2	0	2	0	1.000	0	1	8.22
8 Min. YEARS		223	77	5	56	658.1	2867	663	341	289	33	25	32	34	289	15	600	49	3	39	32	.549	2	12	3.95

Guillermo Rodriguez

Bats: Right **Throws:** Right **Pos:** C-93; 1B-7; DH-2; P-1   **Ht:** 5'11" **Wt:** 195 **Born:** 5/15/78 **Age:** 24

Year Team	Lg Org	G	AB	H	2B	3B	HR	TB	R	RBI	TBB	IBB	SO	HBP	SH	SF	SB	CS	SB%	GDP	Avg	OBP	SLG
1996 Bellingham	A- SF	3	4	0	0	0	0	0	1	0	0	0	1	0	0	0	0	0	—	0	.000	.000	.000
1997 Salem-Keizr	A- SF	11	39	9	3	0	0	12	3	3	5	0	12	0	0	0	0	1	.00	1	.231	.318	.308
San Jose	A+ SF	13	27	4	3	1	0	9	2	2	0	0	9	0	2	0	0	0	—	1	.148	.148	.333
1998 Salem-Keizr	A- SF	1	4	1	0	0	0	1	0	0	0	0	1	0	0	0	0	1	.00	0	.250	.250	.250
San Jose	A+ SF	1	1	0	0	0	0	0	0	0	0	0	0	0	0	0	0	0	—	0	.000	.000	.000
1999 Bakersfield	A+ SF	41	93	27	5	0	1	35	10	11	3	0	18	4	3	2	4	0	1.00	2	.290	.333	.376
Salem-Keizr	A- SF	33	114	29	5	0	6	52	16	34	9	1	28	3	0	0	1	3	.25	2	.254	.325	.456
2000 Bakersfield	A+ SF	118	437	105	27	1	10	164	63	58	30	0	101	13	4	3	20	8	.71	11	.240	.306	.375
2001 Shreveport	AA SF	65	216	44	7	0	5	66	21	25	8	0	40	6	5	3	3	0	1.00	5	.204	.249	.306
San Jose	A+ SF	35	126	34	10	0	2	50	18	21	9	0	26	8	4	1	2	2	.50	4	.270	.354	.397
6 Min. YEARS		321	1061	253	60	2	24	389	134	154	64	1	236	34	18	9	30	15	.67	26	.238	.301	.367

John Rodriguez

Bats: Left **Throws:** Left **Pos:** OF-103; DH-2   **Ht:** 6'0" **Wt:** 185 **Born:** 1/20/78 **Age:** 24

Year Team	Lg Org	G	AB	H	2B	3B	HR	TB	R	RBI	TBB	IBB	SO	HBP	SH	SF	SB	CS	SB%	GDP	Avg	OBP	SLG
1997 Yankees	R NYY	45	153	47	10	2	3	70	31	23	30	1	31	0	0	3	7	0	1.00	3	.307	.414	.458
1998 Greensboro	A NYY	119	408	103	18	4	10	159	64	49	64	1	93	4	0	3	14	3	.82	7	.252	.357	.390
1999 Yankees	R NYY	3	7	2	0	1	0	4	1	1	3	0	0	0	0	0	0	0	—	0	.286	.500	.571
Tampa	A+ NYY	71	269	82	14	3	8	126	37	43	41	7	52	3	1	3	2	5	.29	5	.305	.399	.468
2000 Norwich	AA NYY	17	56	11	4	0	1	18	4	10	8	0	22	1	0	0	1	0	—	0	.196	.308	.321
Tampa	A+ NYY	105	362	97	14	2	16	163	59	44	40	5	81	8	1	0	3	2	.60	6	.268	.354	.450
2001 Yankees	R NYY	2	6	5	0	0	0	5	2	2	0	0	0	0	0	0	0	0	—	0	.833	.833	.833
Norwich	AA NYY	103	393	112	31	1	22	211	64	66	26	2	117	11	3	2	2	3	.40	1	.285	.345	.537
5 Min. YEARS		465	1654	459	91	13	60	756	262	238	212	16	396	27	5	11	28	13	.68	29	.278	.367	.457

Jose Rodriguez

Pitches: Left **Bats:** Left **Pos:** RP-54   **Ht:** 6'1" **Wt:** 215 **Born:** 12/18/74 **Age:** 27

Year Team	Lg Org	G	GS	CG	GF	IP	BFP	H	R	ER	HR	SH	SF	HB	TBB	IBB	SO	WP	Bk	W	L	Pct.	ShO	Sv	ERA
1997 Johnson Cty	R+ StL	4	0	1	0	6.2	27	4	3	3	1	0	0	0	3	1	8	1	0	0	0	—	0	0	4.05
1998 Peoria	A StL	40	0	0	12	39.1	191	47	32	20	0	6	1	2	19	1	30	3	0	2	4	.333	0	0	4.58
1999 Arkansas	AA StL	30	0	0	9	36	173	38	16	13	6	2	0	0	25	0	30	4	0	1	2	.333	0	0	3.25
Peoria	A StL	15	0	0	2	16.1	74	14	7	6	1	3	0	0	8	0	15	0	0	2	3	.400	0	0	3.31

Year Team	Lg Org	G	GS	CG	GF	IP	BFP	H	R	ER	HR	SH	SF	HB	TBB	IBB	SO	WP	Bk	W	L	Pct.	ShO	Sv	ERA
						HOW MUCH HE PITCHED				WHAT HE GAVE UP											THE RESULTS				
2000 Arkansas	AA StL	10	0	0	2	11	47	7	3	3	0	2	0	0	4	2	8	0	0	1	0	1.000	0	1	2.45
Memphis	AAA StL	40	0	0	17	47.1	200	48	21	20	4	5	1	0	19	1	37	0	1	4	2	.667	0	3	3.80
2001 Memphis	AAA StL	54	0	0	17	60.2	262	52	25	24	7	2	2	2	31	0	54	0	0	2	1	.667	0	1	3.56
2000 St. Louis	NL	6	0	0	1	4	19	2	2	0	0	0	1	1	3	0	2	0	0	0	0	—	0	0	0.00
5 Min. YEARS		193	0	0	60	217.1	974	210	107	89	19	21	4	5	109	5	182	8	1	12	12	.500	0	5	3.69

Liu Rodriguez

Bats: Both **Throws:** Right **Pos:** 2B-94; SS-19; DH-4; PH-4; PR-2 **Ht:** 5'9" **Wt:** 170 **Born:** 11/5/76 **Age:** 25

Year Team	Lg Org	G	AB	H	2B	3B	HR	TB	R	RBI	TBB	IBB	SO	HBP	SH	SF	SB	CS	SB%	GDP	Avg	OBP	SLG
				BATTING													BASERUNNING				PERCENTAGES		
1995 White Sox	R CWS	36	119	27	6	1	1	38	18	11	23	0	19	0	2	0	4	2	.67	2	.227	.352	.319
1996 Hickory	A CWS	122	430	107	18	0	0	125	57	30	60	2	77	9	8	2	15	14	.52	3	.249	.351	.291
1997 Hickory	A CWS	129	450	130	21	6	1	166	72	62	65	0	56	5	10	7	12	13	.48	13	.289	.380	.369
1998 Winston-Sal	A+ CWS	112	420	117	27	3	2	156	62	43	45	0	40	9	10	7	15	10	.60	13	.279	.356	.371
1999 Birmingham	AA CWS	64	244	71	11	1	3	93	42	37	22	0	35	3	8	3	5	3	.63	2	.291	.353	.381
2000 Charlotte	AAA CWS	126	396	108	20	3	4	146	44	46	54	1	39	7	16	5	3	7	.30	10	.273	.366	.369
2001 Charlotte	AAA CWS	118	444	129	25	0	0	154	53	37	41	0	60	3	11	3	7	4	.64	8	.291	.352	.347
1999 Chicago	AL	39	93	22	2	2	1	31	8	12	12	0	11	3	3	0	0	0	—	5	.237	.343	.333
7 Min. YEARS		707	2503	689	128	14	11	878	348	266	310	3	326	36	65	27	61	53	.54	51	.275	.360	.351

Luis Rodriguez

Bats: Right **Throws:** Right **Pos:** C-66; PH-8; 3B-7; OF-6; 1B-3; DH-2; 2B-1 **Ht:** 5'11" **Wt:** 185 **Born:** 1/3/74 **Age:** 28

Year Team	Lg Org	G	AB	H	2B	3B	HR	TB	R	RBI	TBB	IBB	SO	HBP	SH	SF	SB	CS	SB%	GDP	Avg	OBP	SLG
				BATTING													BASERUNNING				PERCENTAGES		
1994 Blue Jays	R Tor	28	83	22	2	2	2	34	16	15	13	0	21	0	1	2	6	1	.86	1	.265	.357	.410
1995 St.Cathrnes	A- Tor	66	257	71	16	2	1	94	22	20	10	1	49	1	2	1	2	4	.33	7	.276	.305	.366
1996 Hagerstown	A Tor	79	256	53	8	1	1	66	19	25	24	0	58	1	5	1	6	4	.60	3	.207	.277	.258
1997 Syracuse	AAA Tor	3	2	0	0	0	0	0	0	0	0	0	2	0	0	0	0	0	—	0	.000	.000	.000
Hagerstown	A Tor	27	94	25	6	0	2	37	13	14	2	0	20	1	3	2	3	0	1.00	1	.266	.283	.394
Knoxville	AA Tor	24	78	21	3	1	0	26	6	6	3	0	20	1	0	0	0	1	.00	1	.269	.305	.333
1998 Syracuse	AAA Tor	5	15	2	0	0	0	2	1	2	0	0	6	0	1	1	0	0	—	0	.133	.125	.133
Dunedin	A+ Tor	67	196	57	15	0	4	84	34	41	10	0	39	2	5	4	11	2	.85	3	.291	.325	.429
Knoxville	AA Tor	8	17	7	0	1	0	9	6	1	7	0	5	0	0	0	1	0	1.00	1	.412	.583	.529
1999 Pawtucket	AAA Bos	2	3	0	0	0	0	0	0	0	0	0	1	0	0	0	0	0	—	0	.000	.000	.000
Sarasota	A+ Bos	31	114	33	8	0	3	50	19	14	8	0	17	1	1	2	5	1	.83	2	.289	.336	.439
Trenton	AA Bos	32	114	31	7	4	0	50	10	14	3	0	25	1	0	0	2	1	.67	4	.272	.297	.439
2000 Sarasota	A+ Bos	53	190	45	10	4	3	72	26	34	17	2	36	3	0	2	10	4	.71	6	.237	.307	.379
Pawtucket	AAA Bos	28	83	16	4	0	1	23	7	3	3	0	30	0	1	0	1	1	.50	1	.193	.221	.277
Trenton	AA Bos	27	93	26	1	0	6	45	14	14	7	0	23	1	0	1	2	0	1.00	6	.280	.333	.484
2001 Trenton	AA Bos	51	163	34	7	2	6	63	21	22	6	0	36	0	2	0	2	1	.67	2	.209	.237	.387
Pawtucket	AAA Bos	33	99	26	4	0	3	39	17	5	6	0	27	0	0	0	1	0	1.00	3	.263	.305	.394
8 Min. YEARS		564	1857	469	91	13	36	694	231	230	119	3	415	12	23	16	52	20	.72	42	.253	.299	.374

Mike Rodriguez

Bats: Right **Throws:** Right **Pos:** 1B-8; PH-5; 3B-4; OF-4; C-3; DH-3 **Ht:** 5'11" **Wt:** 185 **Born:** 4/1/75 **Age:** 27

Year Team	Lg Org	G	AB	H	2B	3B	HR	TB	R	RBI	TBB	IBB	SO	HBP	SH	SF	SB	CS	SB%	GDP	Avg	OBP	SLG
				BATTING													BASERUNNING				PERCENTAGES		
1996 St.Cathrnes	A- Tor	46	145	39	2	1	0	43	14	12	7	3	14	1	0	1	4	4	.50	4	.269	.303	.297
1997 Hagerstown	A Tor	43	123	28	3	0	0	31	17	12	18	0	25	1	3	3	0	2	.00	1	.228	.324	.252
St.Cathrnes	A- Tor	2	7	2	1	0	0	3	0	1	0	0	1	0	0	0	0	0	—	0	.286	.286	.429
1998 Hagerstown	A Tor	50	132	40	10	0	1	53	20	17	8	0	20	4	6	1	1	1	.50	3	.303	.359	.402
Dunedin	A+ Tor	15	37	8	2	0	0	10	4	2	3	0	4	2	2	0	0	0	—	2	.216	.310	.270
1999 Dunedin	A+ Tor	80	260	73	17	1	4	104	36	30	17	0	40	2	3	0	3	2	.60	9	.281	.330	.400
2000 Dunedin	A+ Tor	73	223	61	11	1	1	77	34	23	28	2	44	4	2	4	1	3	.25	6	.274	.359	.345
2001 Tennessee	AA Tor	12	40	12	6	0	2	24	5	13	3	0	3	0	0	1	1	0	1.00	0	.300	.341	.600
Dunedin	A+ Tor	13	38	7	0	0	0	7	4	6	0	0	5	0	0	1	0	0	—	0	.184	.179	.184
6 Min. YEARS		334	1005	270	52	3	8	352	134	116	84	5	156	14	16	12	10	12	.45	25	.269	.330	.350

Nerio Rodriguez

Pitches: Right **Bats:** Right **Pos:** SP-16; RP-7 **Ht:** 6'1" **Wt:** 205 **Born:** 3/22/73 **Age:** 29

Year Team	Lg Org	G	GS	CG	GF	IP	BFP	H	R	ER	HR	SH	SF	HB	TBB	IBB	SO	WP	Bk	W	L	Pct.	ShO	Sv	ERA
						HOW MUCH HE PITCHED				WHAT HE GAVE UP											THE RESULTS				
1995 High Desert	A+ Bal	7	0	0	3	10	44	8	2	2	0	0	0	0	7	0	10	0	0	0	0	—	0	0	1.80
1996 Frederick	A+ Bal	24	17	1	7	111.1	462	83	42	28	10	5	0	4	40	0	114	6	1	8	7	.533	0	2	2.26
Rochester	AAA Bal	2	2	0	0	15	58	10	3	3	0	0	0	0	2	0	6	2	0	1	0	1.000	0	0	1.80
1997 Rochester	AAA Bal	27	27	1	0	168.1	688	124	82	73	23	6	0	8	62	0	160	4	3	11	10	.524	1	0	3.90
1998 Rochester	AAA Bal	5	5	0	0	24.2	108	24	16	15	6	1	1	1	10	0	19	0	1	1	4	.200	0	0	5.47
Bowie	AA Bal	2	2	0	0	4	18	6	2	2	0	0	0	0	0	0	7	0	0	1	0	1.000	0	0	4.50
1999 Syracuse	AAA Tor	27	27	1	0	162.2	688	161	84	82	17	3	5	7	53	0	137	5	2	10	8	.556	1	0	4.54
2000 Pawtucket	AAA Bos	5	1	0	2	24.2	118	38	28	26	9	0	1	0	9	0	23	3	0	0	1	.000	0	0	9.49
Trenton	AA Bos	19	19	1	0	109.1	466	115	64	58	9	4	5	3	34	0	93	0	0	7	7	.500	0	0	4.77
2001 Norfolk	AAA NYM	1	0	0	0	0	2	2	2	2	0	0	0	0	0	0	0	0	0	0	0	—	0	0	
Akron	AA Cle	11	11	2	0	71.1	286	64	34	31	10	1	1	4	17	0	49	4	1	6	2	.750	1	0	3.91
Buffalo	AAA Cle	11	5	0	0	38.2	169	41	24	23	5	0	3	3	15	1	21	1	0	2	3	.400	0	1	5.35
1996 Baltimore	AL	8	1	0	2	16.2	77	18	11	8	2	0	1	1	7	0	12	0	0	1	0	1.000	0	0	4.32
1997 Baltimore	AL	6	2	0	1	22	98	21	15	12	2	1	4	1	8	0	11	1	0	2	1	.667	0	0	4.91
1998 Baltimore	AL	6	4	0	0	19	89	25	17	17	0	0	1	0	9	0	8	1	0	1	3	.250	0	0	8.05
Toronto	AL	7	0	0	3	8.44	44	10	9	9	1	0	0	1	8	0	3	0	0	1	0	1.000	0	0	9.72
1999 Toronto	AL	2	0	0	1	2	10	2	3	3	2	0	0	0	2	0	2	0	0	0	1	.000	0	0	13.50
7 Min. YEARS		148	116	6	14	740	3107	676	383	345	89	20	16	30	249	1	639	28	8	46	43	.517	3	3	4.20
4 Maj. YEARS		29	7	0	7	68	318	76	55	49	7	1	7	3	34	0	36	2	0	4	6	.400	0	0	6.49

Sammy Rodriguez

Bats: Right **Throws:** Right **Pos:** C-70; PH-6   **Ht:** 5'9" **Wt:** 196 **Born:** 8/20/75 **Age:** 26

		BATTING															BASERUNNING				PERCENTAGES		
Year Team	Lg Org	G	AB	H	2B	3B	HR	TB	R	RBI	TBB	IBB	SO	HBP	SH	SF	SB	CS	SB%	GDP	Avg	OBP	SLG
1995 Mets	R NYM	6	18	5	0	0	0	5	1	1	2	0	4	0	0	0	0	1	.00	1	.278	.350	.278
Butte	R+ NYM	17	57	14	1	0	1	18	7	6	4	0	13	0	0	0	2	1	.67	0	.246	.295	.316
1996 Pittsfield	A- NYM	32	93	18	3	0	1	24	8	10	11	0	25	1	0	1	1	0	1.00	3	.194	.283	.258
1997 Pittsfield	A- NYM	36	110	27	6	2	5	52	15	20	21	1	33	2	1	2	2	1	.67	1	.245	.370	.473
1998 Binghamton	AA NYM	3	8	1	0	0	0	1	2	1	1	0	0	0	0	0	0	0	—	0	.125	.222	.125
St. Lucie	A+ NYM	53	152	39	9	1	2	56	20	24	20	0	36	2	4	2	3	1	.75	1	.257	.347	.368
1999 Norfolk	AAA NYM	5	9	2	0	0	2	8	2	4	3	0	2	0	0	0	0	0	—	0	.222	.417	.889
Binghamton	AA NYM	69	203	46	10	0	3	65	15	24	21	0	49	3	2	0	2	2	.50	2	.227	.308	.320
2000 Norfolk	AAA NYM	26	64	12	1	0	0	13	4	3	5	0	11	1	0	0	0	4	.00	3	.188	.257	.203
Binghamton	AA NYM	2	8	2	2	0	0	4	1	3	0	0	1	0	0	0	0	0	—	0	.250	.250	.500
St. Lucie	A+ NYM	17	53	14	2	0	1	19	11	5	8	1	9	4	0	1	0	0	—	2	.264	.394	.358
2001 St. Lucie	A+ NYM	21	63	10	4	0	1	17	2	6	5	0	14	0	0	1	0	0	—	2	.159	.217	.270
Binghamton	AA NYM	53	159	39	12	0	5	66	20	13	18	0	39	1	1	0	1	0	1.00	9	.245	.326	.415
7 Min. YEARS		340	997	229	50	3	21	348	108	120	119	2	236	14	8	7	11	10	.52	23	.230	.318	.349

Tony Rodriguez

Bats: Right **Throws:** Right **Pos:** SS-108; 2B-4; OF-1   **Ht:** 5'11" **Wt:** 178 **Born:** 8/15/70 **Age:** 31

		BATTING															BASERUNNING				PERCENTAGES		
Year Team	Lg Org	G	AB	H	2B	3B	HR	TB	R	RBI	TBB	IBB	SO	HBP	SH	SF	SB	CS	SB%	GDP	Avg	OBP	SLG
1991 Elmira	A- Bos	77	272	70	10	2	1	87	48	23	32	0	45	3	2	4	29	4	.88	6	.257	.338	.320
1992 Lynchburg	A+ Bos	128	516	115	14	4	1	140	59	27	25	0	84	3	7	3	11	6	.65	11	.223	.261	.271
1993 New Britain	AA Bos	99	355	81	16	4	0	105	37	31	16	0	52	4	4	5	7	7	.50	8	.228	.266	.296
1994 Sarasota	A+ Bos	15	49	11	0	0	0	11	4	5	4	0	9	0	2	0	1	0	1.00	3	.224	.283	.224
New Britain	AA Bos	6	20	3	0	1	0	5	1	0	0	0	7	0	0	0	0	0	—	1	.150	.150	.250
Pawtucket	AAA Bos	64	169	43	4	1	4	61	16	18	5	0	22	0	7	2	3	3	.50	9	.254	.273	.361
1995 Pawtucket	AAA Bos	96	317	85	15	2	0	104	37	21	15	0	39	6	11	4	11	5	.69	8	.268	.310	.328
1996 Sarasota	A+ Bos	8	21	6	0	0	0	6	0	1	0	1	2	0	0	0	0	0	—	2	.286	.318	.286
Pawtucket	AAA Bos	72	265	65	14	1	3	90	37	28	15	1	32	3	10	0	3	1	.75	10	.245	.293	.340
1997 Pawtucket	AAA Bos	82	285	71	12	0	2	89	27	19	9	0	47	2	2	0	5	2	.71	12	.249	.277	.312
1998 Orlando	AA Sea	13	41	9	0	0	0	9	5	3	3	0	6	0	0	0	0	0	—	1	.220	.273	.220
Nashua	IND —	99	352	100	18	1	6	138	60	47	36	1	35	7	10	8	36	7	.84	5	.284	.355	.392
1999 Nashua	IND —	36	153	49	9	3	6	82	30	25	10	0	21	7	1	3	11	5	.69	3	.320	.382	.536
2000 Nashua	IND —	85	318	79	16	1	5	112	33	34	13	0	44	3	5	3	6	1	.86	9	.248	.282	.352
2001 West Tenn	AA ChC	33	131	37	5	0	1	45	13	15	4	0	23	5	3	2	3	3	.50	2	.282	.324	.344
Nashua	IND —	80	307	87	12	2	7	124	46	29	11	0	40	3	7	2	7	1	.88	8	.283	.313	.404
1996 Boston	AL	27	67	16	1	0	1	20	7	9	4	0	8	1	5	0	0	0	—	3	.239	.292	.299
11 Min. YEARS		993	3571	911	145	22	36	1208	453	325	199	2	508	46	71	36	133	45	.75	96	.255	.300	.338

Victor Rodriguez

Bats: Right **Throws:** Right **Pos:** 2B-97; PH-2   **Ht:** 6'0" **Wt:** 205 **Born:** 10/25/76 **Age:** 25

		BATTING															BASERUNNING				PERCENTAGES		
Year Team	Lg Org	G	AB	H	2B	3B	HR	TB	R	RBI	TBB	IBB	SO	HBP	SH	SF	SB	CS	SB%	GDP	Avg	OBP	SLG
1994 Marlins	R Fla	24	96	31	2	0	0	33	13	17	7	0	7	0	0	3	2	0	1.00	3	.323	.358	.344
1995 Kane County	A Fla	127	472	111	9	1	0	122	65	43	40	0	47	2	16	4	18	6	.75	17	.235	.295	.258
1996 Brevard Cty	A+ Fla	114	438	120	14	4	0	142	54	26	32	0	42	2	8	3	20	7	.74	13	.274	.324	.324
1997 Portland	AA Fla	113	401	111	18	4	3	146	63	38	30	0	43	0	10	3	13	7	.65	15	.277	.325	.364
1998 Portland	AA Fla	66	222	63	9	1	4	86	28	19	18	0	26	5	4	0	5	4	.56	7	.284	.351	.387
1999 Portland	AA Fla	38	97	20	3	1	1	28	13	12	10	0	9	2	3	1	0	1	.00	3	.206	.291	.289
2000 Kinston	A+ Cle	96	382	125	31	2	4	172	59	42	37	1	48	5	7	1	24	9	.73	7	.327	.393	.450
Akron	AA Cle	35	132	32	7	0	2	45	20	14	9	0	14	2	1	1	1	2	.33	2	.242	.299	.341
2001 Tampa	A+ NYY	41	151	41	10	2	1	58	22	15	21	0	15	5	1	2	5	3	.63	3	.272	.374	.384
Norwich	AA NYY	57	218	64	9	1	3	84	33	17	15	0	18	1	7	0	2	3	.40	7	.294	.342	.385
8 Min. YEARS		711	2609	718	112	16	18	916	370	243	219	1	269	24	57	18	90	42	.68	77	.275	.335	.351

Brian Rogers

Pitches: Right **Bats:** Right **Pos:** SP-29   **Ht:** 6'6" **Wt:** 200 **Born:** 2/13/77 **Age:** 25

		HOW MUCH HE PITCHED						WHAT HE GAVE UP										THE RESULTS					
Year Team	Lg Org	G	GS	CG	GF	IP	BFP	H	R	ER	HR	SH	SF	HB	TBB	IBB	SO	WP	Bk	W	L	Pct.	ShO	Sv	ERA
1998 Oneonta	A- NYY	6	6	0	0	35	135	23	9	9	3	1	1	1	10	0	34	2	1	2	2	.500	0	0	2.31
Tampa	A+ NYY	3	3	0	0	15	70	12	7	7	1	0	0	0	14	0	13	0	1	0	0	—	0	0	4.20
Greensboro	A NYY	3	3	0	0	16	71	18	15	14	6	0	1	1	6	0	19	3	0	1	1	.667	0	0	7.88
1999 Tampa	A+ NYY	25	23	1	0	134	577	141	62	57	13	2	1	2	43	1	129	7	0	8	10	.444	1	0	3.83
2000 Norwich	AA NYY	27	27	1	0	164.1	717	155	90	72	10	5	7	10	70	0	132	14	2	11	6	.647	0	0	3.94
2001 Norwich	AA NYY	29	29	1	0	177.1	775	187	97	78	21	7	4	8	63	1	150	10	0	10	9	.526	0	0	3.96
4 Min. YEARS		93	91	3	0	541.2	2345	536	280	237	54	15	14	22	206	2	477	36	4	33	28	.541	1	0	3.94

Ed Rogers

Bats: Right **Throws:** Right **Pos:** SS-126   **Ht:** 6'1" **Wt:** 150 **Born:** 8/10/81 **Age:** 20

		BATTING															BASERUNNING				PERCENTAGES		
Year Team	Lg Org	G	AB	H	2B	3B	HR	TB	R	RBI	TBB	IBB	SO	HBP	SH	SF	SB	CS	SB%	GDP	Avg	OBP	SLG
1999 Orioles	R Bal	53	177	51	5	1	1	61	34	19	23	0	22	4	4	2	20	3	.87	2	.288	.379	.345
2000 Delmarva	A Bal	80	332	91	14	5	5	130	46	42	22	0	63	0	10	3	27	6	.82	3	.274	.317	.392
Bowie	AA Bal	13	49	14	3	0	1	20	4	8	3	0	15	0	0	1	1	1	.50	0	.286	.321	.408
2001 Bowie	AA Bal	53	191	38	10	1	0	50	11	13	6	0	40	2	4	0	10	2	.83	4	.199	.231	.262
Frederick	A+ Bal	73	292	76	20	3	8	126	39	41	14	0	47	8	2	2	18	6	.75	8	.260	.310	.432
3 Min. YEARS		272	1041	270	52	10	15	387	134	123	68	0	187	14	20	8	76	18	.81	17	.259	.311	.372

Nate Rolison

Bats: Left **Throws:** Right **Pos:** 1B-21; DH-2; PH-1   **Ht:** 6'6" **Wt:** 240 **Born:** 3/27/77 **Age:** 25

Year Team	Lg	Org	G	AB	H	2B	3B	HR	TB	R	RBI	TBB	IBB	SO	HBP	SH	SF	SB	CS	SB%	GDP	Avg	OBP	SLG
1995 Marlins	R	Fla	37	134	37	10	2	1	54	22	19	15	1	34	8	0	1	0	0	—	1	.276	.380	.403
1996 Kane County	A	Fla	131	474	115	28	1	14	187	63	75	66	9	170	8	1	0	3	3	.50	9	.243	.345	.395
1997 Brevard Cty	A+	Fla	122	473	121	22	0	16	191	59	65	38	1	143	2	0	1	3	1	.75	16	.256	.313	.404
1998 Portland	AA	Fla	131	484	134	35	2	16	221	80	83	64	6	150	7	0	6	5	0	1.00	9	.277	.365	.457
1999 Portland	AA	Fla	124	438	131	20	1	17	204	71	69	68	3	112	6	0	2	0	1	.00	16	.299	.399	.466
2000 Calgary	AAA	Fla	123	443	146	37	3	23	258	88	88	70	5	117	3	0	2	3	1	.75	7	.330	.423	.582
2001 Marlins	R	Fla	2	4	2	0	0	0	2	1	1	3	0	1	0	0	0	0	0	—	0	.500	.714	.500
Portland	AA	Fla	5	19	4	1	0	0	5	1	2	1	0	7	0	0	0	0	0	—	2	.211	.250	.263
Calgary	AAA	Fla	3	12	2	0	0	0	2	1	1	1	0	3	0	0	0	0	0	—	1	.167	.231	.167
Brevard Cty	A+	Fla	14	45	17	3	0	1	23	7	6	10	1	7	1	0	1	0	0	—	4	.378	.491	.511
2000 Florida	NL		8	13	1	0	0	0	1	0	2	1	0	4	0	0	2	0	0	—	0	.077	.125	.077
7 Min. YEARS			692	2526	709	156	9	88	1147	393	409	336	26	744	35	1	13	14	6	.70	65	.281	.371	.454

Adam Roller

Pitches: Right **Bats:** Right **Pos:** RP-53   **Ht:** 6'3" **Wt:** 208 **Born:** 6/27/78 **Age:** 24

Year Team	Lg	Org	G	GS	CG	GF	IP	BFP	H	R	ER	HR	SH	SF	HB	TBB	IBB	SO	WP	Bk	W	L	Pct.	ShO	Sv	ERA
1997 Red Sox	R	Bos	10	0	0	2	17	78	7	9	6	0	1	1	6	14	0	21	5	0	1	1	.500	0	0	3.18
1998 Red Sox	R	Bos	15	2	0	3	39	194	51	31	21	3	1	1	2	22	1	27	10	0	0	2	.000	0	1	4.85
1999 Sarasota	A+	Bos	1	0	0	0	2.2	14	5	5	5	1	0	0	0	2	0	2	0	0	0	0	—	0	0	16.88
Lowell	A-	Bos	23	0	0	23	39	186	30	16	11	1	3	2	9	29	2	41	7	1	4	5	.444	0	2	2.54
2000 Greensboro	A	NYY	13	0	0	5	20.2	87	16	3	3	1	1	1	1	5	1	22	6	0	0	1	.000	0	1	1.31
Tampa	A+	NYY	19	0	0	14	25.2	118	29	17	12	1	1	3	3	9	0	26	5	0	1	4	.200	0	1	4.21
2001 Norwich	AA	NYY	2	0	0	1	3	11	3	0	0	0	1	0	0	0	0	2	0	0	0	0	—	0	0	0.00
Tampa	A+	NYY	51	0	0	36	67.2	264	42	14	9	0	2	2	3	15	3	76	3	2	2	3	.400	0	23	1.20
5 Min. YEARS			134	2	0	84	214.2	952	182	98	67	7	10	10	24	96	7	217	36	3	8	16	.333	0	28	2.81

Jason Romano

Bats: Right **Throws:** Right **Pos:** 2B-66; OF-18; DH-11   **Ht:** 6'0" **Wt:** 185 **Born:** 6/24/79 **Age:** 23

Year Team	Lg	Org	G	AB	H	2B	3B	HR	TB	R	RBI	TBB	IBB	SO	HBP	SH	SF	SB	CS	SB%	GDP	Avg	OBP	SLG
1997 Rangers	R	Tex	34	109	28	5	3	2	45	27	11	13	0	19	3	1	1	13	4	.76	1	.257	.349	.413
1998 Savannah	A	Tex	134	524	142	19	4	7	190	72	52	46	1	94	8	5	5	40	17	.70	6	.271	.336	.363
Charlotte	A+	Tex	7	24	5	1	0	0	6	3	1	2	0	2	0	1	1	1	2	.33	0	.208	.259	.250
1999 Charlotte	A+	Tex	120	459	143	27	14	13	237	84	71	39	2	72	13	4	7	34	16	.68	4	.312	.376	.516
2000 Tulsa	AA	Tex	131	535	145	35	2	8	208	87	70	56	0	84	6	16	7	25	10	.71	13	.271	.343	.389
2001 Tulsa	AA	Tex	46	186	45	9	1	1	59	19	19	16	0	31	1	3	1	8	3	.73	8	.242	.304	.317
Rangers	R	Tex	5	21	3	0	0	0	3	2	0	1	0	8	0	0	0	1	0	1.00	0	.143	.182	.143
Charlotte	A+	Tex	3	10	4	2	0	0	6	3	1	4	0	1	0	0	0	1	0	1.00	0	.400	.571	.600
Oklahoma	AAA	Tex	41	149	47	6	1	4	67	32	13	20	1	28	0	6	1	3	4	.43	4	.315	.394	.450
5 Min. YEARS			521	2017	562	104	25	35	821	329	238	197	4	339	31	36	23	126	56	.69	36	.279	.348	.407

Mandy Romero

Bats: Both **Throws:** Right **Pos:** C-48; DH-2; PH-2   **Ht:** 5'11" **Wt:** 196 **Born:** 10/29/67 **Age:** 34

Year Team	Lg	Org	G	AB	H	2B	3B	HR	TB	R	RBI	TBB	IBB	SO	HBP	SH	SF	SB	CS	SB%	GDP	Avg	OBP	SLG
1988 Princeton	R+	Pit	30	71	22	6	0	2	34	7	11	13	0	15	1	0	0	1	0	1.00	0	.310	.424	.479
1989 Augusta	A	Pit	121	388	87	26	3	4	131	58	55	67	4	74	6	3	6	8	5	.62	10	.224	.343	.338
1990 Salem	A+	Pit	124	460	134	31	3	17	222	62	90	55	3	68	5	2	4	2	0	.00	10	.291	.370	.483
1991 Carolina	AA	Pit	98	323	70	12	0	3	91	28	31	45	4	53	1	2	2	1	2	.33	4	.217	.313	.282
1992 Carolina	AA	Pit	80	269	58	16	0	3	83	28	27	29	0	39	1	1	2	0	3	.00	10	.216	.292	.309
1993 Buffalo	AAA	Pit	42	136	31	6	1	2	45	11	14	6	1	12	0	1	1	1	0	1.00	5	.228	.259	.331
1994 Buffalo	AAA	Pit	7	23	3	0	0	0	3	3	1	2	0	1	0	1	0	0	0	—	0	.130	.200	.130
1995 Wichita	AA	KC	121	440	133	32	1	21	230	73	82	69	10	60	5	0	1	1	3	.25	15	.302	.402	.523
1996 Memphis	AA	SD	88	297	80	15	0	10	125	40	46	41	2	52	1	1	2	3	1	.75	15	.269	.358	.421
1997 Mobile	AA	SD	61	222	71	22	0	13	132	50	52	38	3	31	2	0	1	0	1	.00	4	.320	.422	.595
Las Vegas	AAA	SD	33	91	28	4	1	3	43	19	13	11	1	19	1	0	1	0	0	—	4	.308	.385	.473
1998 Las Vegas	AAA	SD	40	131	38	8	0	8	70	25	22	20	1	25	1	1	0	0	1	.00	9	.290	.388	.534
Pawtucket	AAA	Bos	45	139	46	5	0	8	75	20	27	24	6	15	0	2	4	0	0	—	1	.331	.419	.540
1999 Pawtucket	AAA	Bos	46	143	31	7	0	3	47	8	22	13	0	26	0	2	1	0	0	—	6	.217	.280	.329
Norfolk	AAA	NYM	28	97	25	6	0	1	34	7	9	9	0	18	1	1	1	0	0	—	5	.258	.324	.351
2000 Buffalo	AAA	Cle	4	17	7	2	0	0	9	1	4	0	0	2	0	0	0	0	0	—	1	.412	.412	.529
Akron	AA	Cle	79	280	87	19	2	12	146	55	46	43	3	34	2	1	4	1	1	.50	6	.311	.401	.521
2001 Calgary	AAA	Fla	3	6	0	0	0	0	0	0	0	3	0	3	0	0	0	0	0	—	0	.000	.333	.000
Midland	AA	Oak	29	103	32	8	0	1	43	12	12	11	0	10	1	1	1	0	0	—	1	.311	.379	.417
Sacramento	AAA	Oak	19	60	11	4	0	1	18	4	5	5	0	13	0	0	0	0	0	—	2	.183	.246	.300
1997 San Diego	NL		21	48	10	0	0	2	16	7	4	2	0	18	0	0	0	1	0	1.00	1	.208	.240	.333
1998 San Diego	NL		6	9	0	0	0	0	0	1	0	1	0	3	0	0	0	0	0	—	0	.000	.100	.000
Boston	AL		12	13	3	1	0	0	4	2	1	3	0	3	0	0	0	0	0	—	1	.231	.375	.308
14 Min. YEARS			1098	3696	994	229	11	112	1581	511	569	504	38	570	28	19	31	16	19	.46	114	.269	.358	.428
2 Maj. YEARS			39	70	13	1	0	2	20	10	5	6	0	24	0	0	0	1	0	1.00	2	.186	.250	.286

Willie Romero

Bats: Right **Throws:** Right **Pos:** OF-6; PH-2; DH-1   **Ht:** 5'9" **Wt:** 192 **Born:** 8/5/74 **Age:** 27

						BATTING									BASERUNNING				PERCENTAGES		
Year Team	Lg Org	G	AB	H	2B	3B	HR	TB	R	RBI	TBB	IBB	SO	HBP	SH	SF	SB	CS	SB%	GDP	Avg	OBP	SLG
1993 Great Falls	R+ LA	15	58	16	5	0	0	21	12	9	2	0	9	0	0	0	2	1	.67	2	.276	.300	.362
Yakima	A- LA	13	51	13	0	0	0	13	8	1	1	0	12	2	0	1	3	0	1.00	1	.255	.291	.255
Bakersfield	A+ LA	20	77	27	5	0	1	35	8	12	5	0	16	0	0	0	4	2	.67	2	.351	.390	.455
1994 Vero Beach	A+ LA	38	126	29	6	0	2	41	15	13	9	0	19	1	2	0	0	2	.00	2	.230	.287	.325
Bakersfield	A+ LA	70	260	71	19	1	7	113	36	36	19	0	53	3	1	0	15	5	.75	3	.273	.330	.435
1995 San Antonio	AA LA	105	376	100	20	1	7	143	46	44	40	1	69	5	0	6	10	12	.45	7	.266	.340	.380
1996 San Antonio	AA LA	122	444	131	36	6	6	197	66	48	34	2	52	3	2	8	21	15	.58	11	.295	.344	.444
Albuquerque	AAA LA	4	13	5	0	0	1	8	1	3	1	0	1	0	0	0	1	0	1.00	0	.385	.429	.615
1997 San Antonio	AA LA	30	108	35	8	1	1	48	22	16	15	0	11	2	2	5	7	4	.64	1	.324	.400	.444
1998 Albuquerque	AAA LA	114	403	115	21	3	10	172	50	61	25	2	68	5	4	5	23	15	.61	14	.285	.331	.427
2001 Tucson	AAA Ari	9	26	6	1	0	0	7	2	1	2	0	7	0	0	0	0	1	.00	0	.231	.286	.269
7 Min. YEARS		540	1942	548	121	12	35	798	266	244	153	5	317	21	11	25	86	57	.60	43	.282	.337	.411

Brett Roneberg

Bats: Left **Throws:** Left **Pos:** OF-112; 1B-13; DH-11; PH-2   **Ht:** 6'2" **Wt:** 205 **Born:** 2/5/79 **Age:** 23

						BATTING									BASERUNNING				PERCENTAGES		
Year Team	Lg Org	G	AB	H	2B	3B	HR	TB	R	RBI	TBB	IBB	SO	HBP	SH	SF	SB	CS	SB%	GDP	Avg	OBP	SLG
1996 Marlins	R Fla	49	172	36	8	0	1	47	23	15	10	0	39	4	2	1	0	0	—	3	.209	.267	.273
1997 Marlins	R Fla	53	185	49	11	2	0	64	25	13	28	1	35	0	1	1	6	5	.55	7	.265	.360	.346
1998 Kane County	A Fla	68	240	65	7	0	3	81	35	35	25	0	50	1	3	1	2	5	.29	11	.271	.341	.338
1999 Kane County	A Fla	132	511	147	32	4	8	211	88	68	79	4	82	4	0	5	3	2	.60	11	.288	.384	.413
2000 Brevard Cty	A+ Fla	125	446	116	18	2	2	144	51	45	77	5	60	1	4	4	4	2	.67	13	.261	.368	.324
2001 Brevard Cty	A+ Fla	88	331	99	20	4	11	160	49	63	50	2	54	4	1	9	5	3	.63	6	.299	.388	.483
Portland	AA Fla	49	164	43	11	0	5	69	17	19	17	0	25	1	0	0	1	0	1.00	6	.262	.335	.421
6 Min. YEARS		564	2048	555	107	12	30	776	288	258	286	12	345	15	11	21	21	17	.55	57	.271	.361	.379

Rafael Roque

Pitches: Left **Bats:** Left **Pos:** SP-19; RP-1   **Ht:** 6'4" **Wt:** 189 **Born:** 10/27/73 **Age:** 28

		HOW MUCH HE PITCHED					WHAT HE GAVE UP											THE RESULTS					
Year Team	Lg Org	G	GS	CG	GF	IP	BFP	H	R	ER	HR	SH	SF	HB	TBB	IBB	SO	WP	Bk	W	L	Pct.	ShO	Sv	ERA
1992 Mets	R NYM	20	0	0	18	33.2	149	28	13	8	0	4	0	1	16	2	33	3	1	3	1	.750	0	8	2.14
1993 Kingsport	R+ NYM	14	7	0	4	45.1	222	58	44	31	9	3	2	7	26	0	36	8	1	1	3	.250	0	0	6.15
1994 St. Lucie	A+ NYM	2	0	0	2	3	15	2	1	0	0	1	1	1	3	1	2	0	0	0	0	—	0	0	0.00
Capital Cty	A NYM	15	15	1	0	86.1	353	73	26	23	6	1	3	4	30	1	74	7	1	6	3	.667	0	0	2.40
1995 St. Lucie	A+ NYM	24	24	2	0	136.2	582	114	65	54	7	2	4	4	72	1	81	11	4	6	9	.400	1	0	3.56
1996 Binghamton	AA NYM	13	13	0	0	60.2	291	71	57	49	8	2	1	2	39	0	46	4	0	0	4	.000	0	0	7.27
St. Lucie	A+ NYM	14	12	1	1	76.1	311	57	22	18	2	5	0	3	39	0	59	8	0	6	4	.600	0	0	2.12
1997 Binghamton	AA NYM	16	0	0	5	26.1	126	35	26	20	7	2	0	1	17	1	23	1	0	1	1	.500	0	1	6.84
St. Lucie	A+ NYM	17	13	1	1	77.2	325	81	42	37	8	3	4	1	25	0	54	2	1	2	10	.167	0	0	4.29
1998 El Paso	AA Mil	16	16	1	0	94	432	113	56	46	8	2	0	4	35	2	70	4	0	5	6	.455	0	0	4.40
Louisville	AAA Mil	9	8	0	0	49.2	207	42	21	20	2	2	2	4	19	1	43	1	0	5	2	.714	0	0	3.62
1999 Louisville	AAA Mil	2	2	0	0	10	35	4	0	0	0	1	0	0	3	0	3	0	0	1	0	1.000	0	0	0.00
2000 Indianapols	AAA Mil	25	20	1	0	132.1	576	127	66	61	18	7	2	6	63	1	111	2	0	9	4	.692	1	0	4.15
2001 Pawtucket	AAA Bos	20	19	0	0	98.2	427	101	52	46	15	1	2	3	35	1	68	1	2	8	5	.615	0	0	4.20
1998 Milwaukee	NL	9	9	0	0	48	206	42	28	26	9	4	0	1	24	0	34	3	1	4	2	.667	0	0	4.88
1999 Milwaukee	NL	43	9	0	7	84.1	386	96	52	50	16	1	3	4	42	1	66	4	1	1	6	.143	0	1	5.34
2000 Milwaukee	NL	4	0	0	1	5.1	29	7	6	6	1	0	1	0	7	1	4	0	0	0	0	—	0	0	10.13
10 Min. YEARS		207	149	7	31	930.2	4051	906	491	413	90	36	21	42	422	11	703	52	10	53	52	.505	2	8	3.99
3 Maj. YEARS		56	18	0	8	137.2	621	145	86	82	26	5	4	5	73	2	104	7	2	5	8	.385	0	1	5.36

Mike Rosamond

Bats: Right **Throws:** Right **Pos:** OF-132   **Ht:** 6'5" **Wt:** 220 **Born:** 4/18/78 **Age:** 24

						BATTING									BASERUNNING				PERCENTAGES		
Year Team	Lg Org	G	AB	H	2B	3B	HR	TB	R	RBI	TBB	IBB	SO	HBP	SH	SF	SB	CS	SB%	GDP	Avg	OBP	SLG
1999 Auburn	A- Hou	61	230	61	9	4	6	96	34	24	23	0	63	3	0	1	22	6	.79	5	.265	.339	.417
Michigan	A Hou	4	10	1	0	0	0	1	0	2	2	0	3	0	0	1	0	1	.00	0	.100	.231	.100
2000 Kissimmee	A+ Hou	129	446	92	14	7	16	168	60	60	60	3	151	2	2	6	17	13	.57	4	.206	.300	.377
2001 Lexington	A Hou	101	394	105	19	3	16	178	62	55	37	3	112	4	0	0	32	13	.71	7	.266	.336	.452
Round Rock	AA Hou	31	107	31	5	2	1	43	14	12	12	0	27	0	4	1	3	5	.38	2	.290	.358	.402
3 Min. YEARS		326	1187	290	47	16	39	486	170	153	134	6	356	9	6	9	74	38	.66	20	.244	.323	.409

Juan Rosario

Pitches: Right **Bats:** Right **Pos:** RP-44   **Ht:** 6'4" **Wt:** 219 **Born:** 11/17/75 **Age:** 26

		HOW MUCH HE PITCHED					WHAT HE GAVE UP											THE RESULTS					
Year Team	Lg Org	G	GS	CG	GF	IP	BFP	H	R	ER	HR	SH	SF	HB	TBB	IBB	SO	WP	Bk	W	L	Pct.	ShO	Sv	ERA
1993 Great Falls	R+ LA	2	2	0	0	5.1	37	11	13	13	3	0	0	5	6	0	4	0	0	0	1	.000	0	0	21.94
1995 Marlins	R Fla	1	0	0	0	1.1	10	4	2	2	0	0	0	0	1	0	3	1	0	0	0	—	0	0	13.50
1996 Devil Rays	R TB	3	0	0	1	3	10	0	3	0	0	0	0	0	3	0	3	2	1	0	0	—	0	0	0.00
1998 Hudson Val	A- TB	22	2	0	4	34.2	161	39	33	29	2	1	2	6	20	0	27	7	1	1	4	.200	0	1	7.53
1999 St. Pete	A+ TB	15	15	0	0	94.1	391	80	34	28	2	5	3	11	25	0	37	2	1	5	3	.625	0	0	2.67
2000 Orlando	AA TB	28	0	0	12	44.2	202	43	26	19	4	3	1	10	18	0	21	4	1	1	3	.250	0	6	3.83
2001 Orlando	AA TB	44	0	0	16	68.1	310	69	36	27	3	6	4	14	27	1	55	5	2	1	3	.250	0	3	3.56
7 Min. YEARS		115	19	0	33	251.2	1127	246	147	118	14	15	11	47	100	1	150	21	6	8	14	.364	0	10	4.22

Mel Rosario

Bats: Both **Throws:** Right **Pos:** C-61; PH-15; DH-6; OF-2; 1B-1   **Ht:** 6'0" **Wt:** 200 **Born:** 5/25/73 **Age:** 29

Year Team	Lg Org	G	AB	H	2B	3B	HR	TB	R	RBI	TBB	IBB	SO	HBP	SH	SF	SB	CS	SB%	GDP	Avg	OBP	SLG
1992 Spokane	A- SD	66	237	54	13	1	10	99	38	40	20	2	62	4	0	4	5	3	.63	6	.228	.294	.418
1993 Waterloo	A SD	32	105	22	6	2	5	47	15	15	7	1	37	2	0	0	5	2	.71	0	.210	.272	.448
Spokane	A- SD	41	140	32	5	0	4	49	17	19	8	2	36	0	0	0	2	1	.67	1	.229	.270	.350
1995 South Bend	A CWS	118	450	123	30	6	15	210	58	57	30	7	109	4	1	3	1	8	.11	0	.273	.322	.467
1996 Rancho Cuca	A+ SD	10	33	9	3	0	3	21	7	10	3	0	8	0	0	0	1	0	1.00	0	.273	.333	.636
High Desert	A+ Bal	42	163	52	9	1	10	93	35	34	21	0	45	9	0	0	4	0	1.00	3	.319	.425	.571
Bowie	AA Bal	47	162	34	10	0	2	50	14	17	6	1	43	5	1	2	3	2	.60	4	.210	.257	.309
Rochester	AAA Bal	3	2	0	0	0	0	0	0	0	0	0	1	0	0	0	0	0	—	0	.000	.000	.000
1997 Bowie	AA Bal	123	430	113	26	1	12	177	68	60	27	2	106	9	1	4	4	7	.36	5	.263	.317	.412
1998 Rochester	AAA Bal	34	113	28	4	0	3	41	10	10	6	0	24	1	0	1	5	2	.71	1	.248	.289	.363
Bowie	AA Bal	39	130	35	5	4	3	63	22	25	9	0	31	3	1	2	2	1	.67	3	.269	.326	.485
1999 Altoona	AA Pit	26	87	21	9	0	1	33	11	11	6	0	15	0	0	1	0	0	—	6	.241	.287	.379
Oklahoma	AAA Tex	7	26	5	1	0	0	6	2	3	0	0	8	0	0	0	1	0	1.00	0	.192	.192	.231
Tulsa	AA Tex	28	96	20	3	0	8	47	12	19	3	0	28	1	1	1	1	0	1.00	0	.208	.238	.490
2000 Birmingham	AA CWS	83	289	75	23	3	6	122	34	42	21	1	63	5	2	2	2	2	.50	3	.260	.319	.422
2001 Omaha	AAA KC	41	151	38	10	2	6	70	18	25	7	1	42	1	1	1	1	1	.50	1	.252	.288	.464
Tucson	AAA Ari	19	37	9	3	0	0	12	1	3	1	0	8	0	1	0	0	0	—	2	.243	.263	.324
Las Vegas	AAA LA	24	77	20	2	1	4	36	11	15	2	0	19	3	0	2	1	5	.17	1	.260	.298	.468
1997 Baltimore	AL	4	3	0	0	0	0	0	0	0	0	0	1	0	0	0	0	0	—	0	.000	.000	.000
9 Min. YEARS		783	2728	690	162	21	94	1176	373	405	177	17	685	47	9	23	38	34	.53	37	.253	.307	.431

Omar Rosario

Bats: Left **Throws:** Left **Pos:** OF-105; PH-5; DH-4; 1B-3; PR-3   **Ht:** 6'1" **Wt:** 170 **Born:** 1/14/78 **Age:** 24

Year Team	Lg Org	G	AB	H	2B	3B	HR	TB	R	RBI	TBB	IBB	SO	HBP	SH	SF	SB	CS	SB%	GDP	Avg	OBP	SLG
1997 Athletics	R Oak	56	216	52	9	3	0	67	48	28	38	0	51	7	1	3	40	3	.93	1	.241	.367	.310
1998 Visalia	A+ Oak	82	212	47	8	1	1	60	33	24	33	0	68	4	5	2	18	4	.82	2	.222	.335	.283
Sou Oregon	A- Oak	29	101	26	4	0	3	39	18	13	15	0	26	2	1	0	5	2	.71	0	.257	.364	.386
1999 Modesto	A+ Oak	116	419	125	23	6	5	175	82	57	70	1	94	6	4	4	19	12	.61	4	.298	.403	.418
2000 Sacramento	AAA Oak	8	27	8	1	0	0	9	4	1	2	0	5	1	0	0	0	0	—	0	.296	.367	.333
Visalia	A+ Oak	102	333	84	16	2	4	116	56	39	73	2	76	4	2	2	24	14	.63	5	.252	.391	.348
2001 Visalia	A+ Oak	30	113	31	4	0	2	41	17	12	26	0	27	3	0	0	10	3	.77	4	.274	.423	.363
Sacramento	AAA Oak	21	59	14	3	0	1	20	6	8	7	0	18	1	1	0	1	2	.33	2	.237	.328	.339
Modesto	A+ Oak	60	188	35	9	1	1	49	24	17	40	3	61	6	1	0	9	1	.90	4	.186	.346	.261
5 Min. YEARS		504	1668	422	77	13	17	576	288	199	304	6	426	34	15	11	126	41	.75	22	.253	.377	.345

Mike Rose

Bats: Both **Throws:** Right **Pos:** C-51; DH-20; OF-11; PH-11; 3B-1; PR-1; P-1   **Ht:** 6'1" **Wt:** 185 **Born:** 8/25/76 **Age:** 25

Year Team	Lg Org	G	AB	H	2B	3B	HR	TB	R	RBI	TBB	IBB	SO	HBP	SH	SF	SB	CS	SB%	GDP	Avg	OBP	SLG
1995 Astros	R Hou	35	89	23	2	1	1	30	13	9	11	0	18	3	0	0	2	1	.67	1	.258	.359	.337
1996 Kissimmee	A+ Hou	2	1	0	0	0	0	0	0	0	0	0	1	0	0	0	0	0	—	0	.000	.000	.000
Auburn	A- Hou	61	180	45	5	1	2	58	20	11	30	0	41	1	4	0	9	3	.75	5	.250	.360	.322
1997 Quad City	A Hou	79	234	60	6	1	3	77	22	27	28	0	62	4	8	3	3	1	.75	1	.256	.342	.329
1998 Kissimmee	A+ Hou	18	62	14	4	0	3	27	9	9	8	0	14	0	1	0	1	0	1.00	2	.226	.314	.435
Quad City	A Hou	88	267	81	13	2	7	119	48	40	52	3	56	1	3	1	10	8	.56	5	.303	.417	.446
1999 Jackson	AA Hou	15	45	11	0	0	3	20	8	8	13	1	10	0	1	0	0	2	.00	1	.244	.414	.444
Kissimmee	A+ Hou	95	303	84	16	2	11	137	61	32	59	0	64	3	0	2	12	6	.67	7	.277	.398	.452
2000 El Paso	AA Ari	117	352	100	22	1	10	154	58	62	68	2	70	1	1	4	8	11	.42	16	.284	.398	.438
2001 Tucson	AAA Ari	20	55	10	1	2	0	15	9	8	12	1	16	0	1	1	0	0	—	3	.182	.324	.273
El Paso	AA Ari	62	205	53	13	1	3	77	28	23	37	1	40	0	0	0	4	4	.50	8	.259	.370	.376
Trenton	AA Bos	9	24	4	0	0	1	7	3	2	6	1	10	0	0	0	0	1	.00	0	.167	.333	.292
7 Min. YEARS		601	1817	485	82	11	44	721	279	231	324	9	402	13	19	12	49	37	.57	49	.267	.380	.397

Teddy Rose

Pitches: Right **Bats:** Left **Pos:** RP-22; SP-15   **Ht:** 6'1" **Wt:** 185 **Born:** 8/23/73 **Age:** 28

Year Team	Lg Org	G	GS	CG	GF	IP	BFP	H	R	ER	HR	SH	SF	HB	TBB	IBB	SO	WP	Bk	W	L	Pct.	ShO	Sv	ERA
1996 Princeton	R+ Cin	11	11	1	0	59.1	262	70	44	41	9	2	3	3	21	0	53	9	2	3	5	.375	1	0	6.22
1997 Chston-WV	A Cin	38	13	2	0	129.1	525	108	44	36	7	9	3	6	27	0	132	3	2	11	6	.647	2	4	2.51
1998 Chattanooga	AA Cin	29	29	1	0	168.1	745	191	97	86	12	1	6	6	66	3	108	6	4	11	10	.524	0	0	4.60
1999 Reds	R Cin	1	0	0	1	2	11	4	2	2	0	0	0	0	1	0	3	0	0	0	0	—	0	0	9.00
Chattanooga	AA Cin	13	0	0	4	17	75	17	8	8	2	0	1	2	9	1	23	0	0	2	0	1.000	0	2	4.24
2000 Chattanooga	AA Cin	31	0	0	17	44	154	24	8	5	1	1	3	0	9	2	51	1	2	4	2	.667	0	8	1.10
Louisville	AAA Cin	23	0	0	6	38	158	36	23	21	5	1	2	1	13	0	33	1	0	2	2	.500	0	2	4.97
2001 Ottawa	AAA Mon	37	15	1	8	120.2	514	125	59	54	9	10	3	4	35	0	98	6	2	7	9	.438	0	0	4.03
6 Min. YEARS		183	68	5	45	575.2	2444	575	285	253	45	24	21	22	181	6	501	26	12	40	34	.541	3	16	3.96

Pete Rose Jr.

Bats: Left **Throws:** Right **Pos:** DH-16; PH-15; 3B-11; 1B-3   **Ht:** 6'1" **Wt:** 180 **Born:** 11/16/69 **Age:** 32

Year Team	Lg Org	G	AB	H	2B	3B	HR	TB	R	RBI	TBB	IBB	SO	HBP	SH	SF	SB	CS	SB%	GDP	Avg	OBP	SLG
1989 Frederick	A+ Bal	24	67	12	3	0	0	15	3	7	0	0	15	1	0	0	1	1	.50	1	.179	.191	.224
Erie	A- Bal	58	228	63	13	5	2	92	30	26	12	1	34	1	2	0	1	2	.33	3	.276	.315	.404
1990 Frederick	A+ Bal	97	323	75	14	2	1	96	32	41	26	0	33	1	7	5	0	3	.00	6	.232	.287	.297
1991 Sarasota	A+ CWS	99	323	70	12	2	0	86	31	35	36	3	35	2	8	3	5	6	.45	3	.217	.297	.266
1992 Columbus	A Cle	131	510	129	24	6	9	192	67	54	48	2	53	6	8	3	4	3	.57	9	.253	.323	.376

Year Team	Lg Org	G	AB	H	2B	3B	HR	TB	R	RBI	TBB	IBB	SO	HBP	SH	SF	SB	CS	SB%	GDP	Avg	OBP	SLG
1993 Kinston	A+ Cle	74	284	62	10	1	7	95	33	30	25	0	34	2	6	1	1	3	.25	5	.218	.285	.335
1994 Hickory	A CWS	32	114	25	4	1	0	31	14	12	13	2	18	2	3	2	0	0	—	3	.219	.305	.272
White Sox	R CWS	2	4	2	0	0	0	2	1	1	0	0	0	0	0	0	0	0	—	0	.500	.500	.500
Pr William	A+ CWS	45	146	41	3	1	4	58	18	22	18	0	15	0	2	3	0	1	.00	2	.281	.353	.397
1995 Birmingham	AA CWS	5	13	5	1	0	0	6	1	2	3	0	3	0	0	0	0	0	—	0	.385	.500	.462
South Bend	A CWS	116	423	117	24	6	4	165	56	65	54	0	45	5	2	7	2	0	1.00	6	.277	.360	.390
1996 Birmingham	AA CWS	108	399	97	13	1	3	121	40	44	32	1	54	2	5	3	1	3	.25	9	.243	.300	.303
1997 Indianapols	AAA Cin	12	40	9	2	0	0	11	2	1	2	0	11	0	0	0	0	0	—	1	.225	.262	.275
Chattanooga	AA Cin	112	445	137	31	0	25	243	75	98	34	1	63	3	1	3	0	1	.00	5	.308	.359	.546
1998 Indianapols	AAA Cin	43	133	37	7	1	3	55	19	13	8	0	10	2	0	1	1	0	1.00	3	.278	.326	.414
Nashville	AAA Pit	28	72	15	1	0	1	19	8	12	3	0	13	0	1	1	0	0	—	3	.208	.237	.264
New Jersey	IND —	12	33	14	4	1	1	23	2	8	3	0	4	0	0	0	0	0	—	2	.424	.472	.697
1999 New Jersey	IND —	81	303	91	27	1	15	165	70	53	42	7	29	5	0	7	7	0	1.00	6	.300	.387	.545
2000 Reading	AA Phi	109	356	88	22	1	8	136	56	56	56	4	47	2	1	3	8	2	.80	6	.247	.350	.382
2001 Reading	AA Phi	9	30	15	3	0	0	18	4	0	1	1	3	0	0	0	0	0	—	0	.500	.516	.600
Chattanooga	AA Cin	35	91	24	6	0	1	33	8	14	7	0	16	0	0	0	0	0	—	5	.264	.313	.363
1997 Cincinnati	NL	11	14	2	0	0	0	2	2	0	2	0	9	0	0	0	0	0	—	0	.143	.250	.143
13 Min. YEARS		1232	4337	1128	224	29	84	1662	570	594	423	22	535	34	46	43	31	25	.55	78	.260	.328	.383

John Roskos

Bats: Right **Throws:** Right **Pos:** 1B-35; PH-19; DH-17; OF-14; C-1; PR-1 **Ht:** 5'11" **Wt:** 195 **Born:** 11/19/74 **Age:** 27

Year Team	Lg Org	G	AB	H	2B	3B	HR	TB	R	RBI	TBB	IBB	SO	HBP	SH	SF	SB	CS	SB%	GDP	Avg	OBP	SLG
1993 Marlins	R Fla	11	40	7	1	0	1	11	6	3	5	0	11	1	0	0	1	1	.50	0	.175	.283	.275
1994 Elmira	A- Fla	39	136	38	7	0	4	57	11	23	27	0	37	0	0	2	0	1	.00	0	.279	.394	.419
1995 Kane County	A Fla	114	418	124	36	3	12	202	74	88	42	1	86	6	0	6	2	0	1.00	6	.297	.364	.483
1996 Portland	AA Fla	121	396	109	26	3	9	168	53	58	67	4	102	5	0	2	3	4	.43	5	.275	.385	.424
1997 Portland	AA Fla	123	451	139	31	1	24	244	66	84	50	2	81	0	2	6	4	6	.40	17	.308	.373	.541
1998 Charlotte	AAA Fla	115	416	118	23	1	10	173	54	62	43	0	84	3	0	3	0	4	.00	15	.284	.353	.416
1999 Calgary	AAA Fla	134	506	162	44	0	24	278	85	90	52	2	112	3	0	9	2	1	.67	18	.320	.381	.549
2000 Las Vegas	AAA SD	99	377	120	29	0	18	203	75	74	53	1	67	2	0	4	2	5	.29	14	.318	.401	.538
2001 Portland	AAA SD	46	134	32	9	1	3	52	15	20	11	1	31	0	0	3	0	0	—	6	.239	.291	.388
Iowa	AAA ChC	34	90	23	5	0	2	34	10	14	12	1	20	1	0	1	0	0	—	0	.256	.346	.378
1998 Florida	NL	10	10	1	0	0	0	1	1	0	0	0	5	0	0	0	0	0	—	0	.100	.100	.100
1999 Florida	NL	13	12	2	2	0	0	4	0	1	1	0	7	0	0	0	0	0	—	0	.167	.231	.333
2000 San Diego	NL	14	27	1	1	0	0	2	0	1	3	0	7	0	0	0	0	0	—	1	.037	.133	.074
9 Min. YEARS		836	2964	872	211	9	107	1422	449	516	362	12	631	21	2	36	14	22	.39	81	.294	.371	.480
3 Maj. YEARS		37	49	4	3	0	0	7	1	2	4	0	19	0	0	0	0	0	—	1	.082	.151	.143

Dave Ross

Bats: Right **Throws:** Right **Pos:** C-70; PH-5 **Ht:** 6'2" **Wt:** 205 **Born:** 3/19/77 **Age:** 25

Year Team	Lg Org	G	AB	H	2B	3B	HR	TB	R	RBI	TBB	IBB	SO	HBP	SH	SF	SB	CS	SB%	GDP	Avg	OBP	SLG
1998 Yakima	A- LA	59	191	59	14	1	6	93	31	25	34	0	49	1	2	2	2	2	.50	5	.309	.412	.487
1999 Vero Beach	A+ LA	114	375	85	19	1	7	127	47	39	46	1	111	7	1	6	5	10	.33	10	.227	.318	.339
2000 San Antonio	AA LA	24	67	14	2	1	3	27	11	12	9	1	17	1	1	1	1	0	1.00	0	.209	.308	.403
San Berndno	A+ LA	51	191	49	11	1	7	83	27	21	17	1	43	1	3	1	3	2	.60	3	.257	.319	.435
2001 Jacksnville	AA LA	74	246	65	13	1	11	113	35	45	34	0	72	10	0	3	1	1	.50	5	.264	.372	.459
4 Min. YEARS		322	1070	272	59	5	34	443	151	142	140	3	292	20	7	13	12	15	.44	23	.254	.348	.414

Jason Ross

Bats: Right **Throws:** Right **Pos:** OF-105; PH-10; PR-4 **Ht:** 6'4" **Wt:** 215 **Born:** 6/10/74 **Age:** 28

Year Team	Lg Org	G	AB	H	2B	3B	HR	TB	R	RBI	TBB	IBB	SO	HBP	SH	SF	SB	CS	SB%	GDP	Avg	OBP	SLG
1996 Danville	R+ Atl	43	149	40	8	1	3	59	26	20	11	0	42	4	0	0	6	3	.67	2	.268	.335	.396
Macon	A Atl	5	19	3	0	0	1	6	2	3	2	0	7	0	0	0	1	0	1.00	0	.158	.238	.316
1997 Macon	A Atl	112	430	111	20	5	9	168	70	59	37	0	121	9	0	3	16	7	.70	7	.258	.328	.391
1998 Danville	A+ Atl	115	378	80	14	3	6	118	36	34	15	0	107	3	2	2	11	5	.69	5	.212	.246	.312
1999 Myrtle Bch	A+ Atl	133	482	129	23	13	12	214	80	64	43	2	136	8	1	2	31	5	.86	11	.268	.336	.444
2000 Richmond	AAA Atl	73	251	63	16	0	12	115	32	26	22	3	91	3	0	0	13	5	.72	7	.251	.319	.458
2001 Richmond	AAA Atl	49	125	26	5	1	5	48	15	7	7	0	45	3	0	1	3	2	.60	3	.208	.265	.384
Greenville	AA Atl	63	187	48	7	1	11	90	27	30	33	0	55	8	2	2	15	6	.71	5	.257	.387	.481
6 Min. YEARS		593	2021	500	93	24	59	818	288	243	170	5	604	38	5	10	96	33	.74	40	.247	.316	.405

Aaron Royster

Bats: Right **Throws:** Right **Pos:** OF-38; DH-8; PH-6 **Ht:** 6'1" **Wt:** 215 **Born:** 11/30/72 **Age:** 29

Year Team	Lg Org	G	AB	H	2B	3B	HR	TB	R	RBI	TBB	IBB	SO	HBP	SH	SF	SB	CS	SB%	GDP	Avg	OBP	SLG
1994 Martinsvlle	R+ Phi	54	168	46	11	2	7	82	31	39	28	1	47	2	0	1	7	4	.64	2	.274	.382	.488
1995 Piedmont	A Phi	126	489	129	23	3	8	182	73	58	39	1	106	7	0	4	22	9	.71	16	.264	.325	.372
1996 Clearwater	A+ Phi	72	289	81	10	2	11	127	35	60	23	1	56	3	3	2	4	3	.57	7	.280	.338	.443
Reading	AA Phi	65	230	59	11	0	4	82	42	20	30	2	56	5	3	1	4	5	.44	3	.257	.353	.357
1997 Reading	AA Phi	112	412	106	18	5	15	179	59	62	53	0	104	1	0	2	2	3	.40	12	.257	.342	.434
1998 Reading	AA Phi	112	430	110	27	4	7	166	67	55	57	1	117	0	0	2	3	1	.75	13	.256	.342	.386
1999 Clearwater	A+ Phi	11	41	13	2	0	1	19	6	5	3	0	10	0	0	0	1	0	1.00	3	.317	.364	.463
Reading	AA Phi	91	310	90	17	2	8	135	53	48	48	2	90	3	2	3	11	5	.69	3	.290	.387	.435
2000 Scranton-WB	AAA Phi	14	29	4	1	0	0	5	3	2	1	0	14	0	0	0	1	0	1.00	1	.138	.156	.172
Reading	AA Phi	27	102	36	8	0	5	59	19	15	14	0	27	1	0	1	3	0	1.00	2	.353	.432	.578
2001 Scranton-WB	AAA Phi	8	19	6	1	0	0	7	3	1	0	0	9	0	0	0	0	0	—	0	.316	.316	.368
Reading	AA Phi	42	146	38	3	3	7	68	19	19	11	1	37	2	0	0	6	0	1.00	0	.260	.321	.466
8 Min. YEARS		734	2665	718	132	23	72	1112	410	384	307	9	669	26	8	16	64	30	.68	63	.269	.349	.417

Wilkin Ruan

Bats: Right **Throws:** Right **Pos:** OF-100; DH-1; PH-1 **Ht:** 6'0" **Wt:** 170 **Born:** 11/18/79 **Age:** 22

										BATTING									BASERUNNING				PERCENTAGES		
Year Team	Lg Org	G	AB	H	2B	3B	HR	TB	R	RBI	TBB	IBB	SO	HBP	SH	SF	SB	CS	SB%	GDP	Avg	OBP	SLG
1998 Jupiter	A+ Mon	5	18	3	0	0	0	3	2	0	1	0	3	0	0	0	2	0	1.00	0	.167	.211	.167
Expos	R Mon	54	201	48	9	3	1	66	22	19	5	0	43	2	3	2	13	13	.50	1	.239	.262	.328
1999 Cape Fear	A Mon	112	397	89	16	4	1	116	43	47	18	0	79	6	7	0	29	17	.63	5	.224	.268	.292
2000 Cape Fear	A Mon	134	574	165	29	10	0	214	95	51	24	1	75	8	2	5	64	10	.86	6	.287	.323	.373
2001 Jupiter	A+ Mon	72	293	83	8	2	2	101	41	26	10	2	35	3	7	1	25	14	.64	3	.283	.313	.345
Harrisburg	AA Mon	30	117	29	7	0	0	36	14	6	3	0	18	2	1	0	6	0	1.00	1	.248	.279	.308
4 Min. YEARS		407	1600	417	69	19	4	536	217	149	61	3	253	21	20	6	139	54	.72	14	.261	.296	.335

Nathan Ruhl

Pitches: Right **Bats:** Right **Pos:** RP-37; SP-6 **Ht:** 6'4" **Wt:** 236 **Born:** 7/16/76 **Age:** 25

		HOW MUCH HE PITCHED						WHAT HE GAVE UP										THE RESULTS						
Year Team	Lg Org	G	GS	CG	GF	IP	BFP	H	R	ER	HR	SH	SF	HB	TBB	IBB	SO	WP	Bk	W	L	Pct.	ShO	Sv	ERA
1996 Devil Rays	R TB	16	0	0	7	27	109	18	9	7	0	3	1	1	11	1	25	4	0	2	2	.500	0	0	2.33
1998 Princeton	R+ TB	14	0	0	6	17	76	12	10	9	2	1	0	1	11	0	25	6	0	1	1	.500	0	3	4.76
1999 Chston-SC	A TB	36	0	0	13	55.1	234	31	20	18	3	2	3	1	34	1	82	9	1	4	4	.500	0	2	2.93
St. Pete	A+ TB	4	0	0	4	7	32	9	2	2	0	0	0	1	3	0	5	0	0	2	0	1.000	0	0	2.57
2000 St. Pete	A+ TB	40	5	1	22	72.2	346	82	58	47	5	1	5	3	41	1	53	9	1	4	6	.400	0	7	5.82
2001 Bakersfield	A+ TB	12	4	0	2	31	149	37	17	17	3	3	0	2	21	1	31	2	1	1	2	.333	0	1	4.94
Orlando	AA TB	31	2	0	20	51	227	54	25	22	7	3	1	2	23	2	54	4	0	3	3	.500	0	6	3.88
5 Min. YEARS		153	11	1	74	261	1173	243	141	122	20	13	10	11	144	6	275	34	3	17	18	.486	0	19	4.21

Toby Rumfield

Bats: Right **Throws:** Right **Pos:** 1B-108; DH-13 **Ht:** 6'3" **Wt:** 190 **Born:** 9/4/72 **Age:** 29

										BATTING									BASERUNNING				PERCENTAGES		
Year Team	Lg Org	G	AB	H	2B	3B	HR	TB	R	RBI	TBB	IBB	SO	HBP	SH	SF	SB	CS	SB%	GDP	Avg	OBP	SLG
1991 Princeton	R+ Cin	59	226	62	13	3	3	90	22	30	9	0	43	5	2	3	1	7	.13	6	.274	.313	.398
1992 Billings	R+ Cin	66	253	68	15	3	4	101	34	50	7	0	34	4	0	4	5	2	.71	4	.269	.295	.399
1993 Chston-WV	A Cin	97	333	75	20	1	5	112	36	50	26	1	74	3	0	4	6	4	.60	7	.225	.284	.336
1994 Winston-Sal	A+ Cin	123	462	115	11	4	29	221	79	88	48	1	107	2	0	7	2	3	.40	9	.249	.318	.478
1995 Chattanooga	AA Cin	92	273	72	12	1	8	110	32	53	26	2	47	3	3	5	0	3	.00	14	.264	.329	.403
1996 Chattanooga	AA Cin	113	364	102	25	1	9	156	49	53	37	1	51	6	3	6	2	1	.67	12	.280	.351	.429
1997 Chattanooga	AA Cin	101	331	95	22	1	5	134	35	38	18	3	32	2	4	2	0	1	.00	12	.287	.326	.405
1998 Greenville	AA Atl	125	462	134	32	0	10	196	61	66	43	1	67	3	1	8	9	4	.69	17	.290	.349	.424
1999 Richmond	AAA Atl	111	383	105	23	1	15	175	57	62	31	1	57	6	2	2	1	2	.33	13	.274	.336	.457
2000 Richmond	AAA Atl	127	430	116	18	0	19	191	61	70	32	1	59	4	3	7	4	7	.36	9	.270	.324	.444
2001 Charlotte	AAA CWS	121	463	126	28	0	20	214	49	69	28	2	64	5	1	3	0	0	—	16	.272	.319	.462
11 Min. YEARS		1135	3980	1070	219	15	127	1700	515	629	305	13	635	43	19	47	30	34	.47	119	.269	.324	.427

Sean Runyan

Pitches: Left **Bats:** Left **Pos:** RP-11 **Ht:** 6'3" **Wt:** 210 **Born:** 6/21/74 **Age:** 28

		HOW MUCH HE PITCHED						WHAT HE GAVE UP										THE RESULTS						
Year Team	Lg Org	G	GS	CG	GF	IP	BFP	H	R	ER	HR	SH	SF	HB	TBB	IBB	SO	WP	Bk	W	L	Pct.	ShO	Sv	ERA
1992 Astros	R Hou	10	10	0	0	45	203	54	19	16	0	1	0	5	16	0	30	8	1	3	3	.500	0	0	3.20
1993 Astros	R Hou	12	12	0	0	66.1	302	66	35	22	2	1	3	2	24	0	52	4	0	4	3	.571	0	0	2.98
1994 Auburn	A- Hou	14	14	2	0	95.1	396	90	49	37	5	1	1	2	19	0	66	12	1	7	5	.583	1	0	3.49
1995 Quad City	A Hou	22	11	0	2	76.1	327	67	37	31	10	1	2	3	29	0	65	4	0	4	6	.400	0	0	3.66
1996 Quad City	A Hou	29	17	0	3	132.1	551	128	61	57	10	1	5	14	30	0	104	4	1	9	4	.692	0	0	3.88
1997 Mobile	AA SD	40	1	0	15	61.2	261	54	25	16	4	2	1	3	28	3	52	1	1	5	2	.714	0	1	2.34
1999 Toledo	AAA Det	10	0	0	2	10.1	45	7	4	4	1	0	0	2	6	0	7	0	0	0	0	—	0	0	3.48
2000 Jacksnville	AA Det	3	0	0	1	1.2	11	4	4	4	0	0	0	0	2	0	1	0	0	0	0	—	0	0	21.60
Toledo	AAA Det	44	0	0	11	49.1	238	58	36	32	8	1	4	4	35	1	32	6	0	1	2	.333	0	1	5.84
2001 Toledo	AAA Det	11	0	0	0	10.2	61	15	17	10	3	2	2	0	11	0	6	1	0	0	1	.000	0	0	8.44
1998 Detroit	AL	88	0	0	11	50.1	223	47	23	20	7	2	7	2	28	3	39	5	0	1	4	.200	0	1	3.58
1999 Detroit	AL	12	0	0	2	10.2	45	9	4	4	2	1	2	1	3	1	6	2	0	0	1	.000	0	0	3.38
2000 Detroit	AL	3	0	0	0	3	12	2	2	2	0	0	0	0	2	0	1	0	0	0	0	—	0	0	6.00
9 Min. YEARS		195	65	2	34	549	2395	543	287	229	43	10	18	35	200	4	415	40	4	33	26	.559	1	2	3.75
3 Maj. YEARS		103	0	0	13	64	280	58	29	26	9	3	10	3	33	4	46	7	0	1	5	.167	0	1	3.66

Jim Rushford

Bats: Left **Throws:** Left **Pos:** OF-84; 1B-26; DH-7; PH-7 **Ht:** 6'1" **Wt:** 190 **Born:** 3/24/74 **Age:** 28

										BATTING									BASERUNNING				PERCENTAGES		
Year Team	Lg Org	G	AB	H	2B	3B	HR	TB	R	RBI	TBB	IBB	SO	HBP	SH	SF	SB	CS	SB%	GDP	Avg	OBP	SLG
1996 Dubois Cty	IND —	40	44	15	2	0	2	23	9	6	6	0	10	3	1	1	6	0	1.00	1	.341	.444	.523
1997 Missn Viejo	IND —	8	0	0	0	0	0	0	0	0	0	0	0	0	0	0	0	0	—	0	—	—	—
1999 Schaumburg	IND —	47	166	48	12	2	2	70	26	28	23	3	27	3	2	3	7	2	.78	3	.289	.379	.422
2000 Duluth-Sup	IND —	75	289	95	16	3	12	153	53	53	25	2	32	4	0	0	13	5	.72	6	.329	.390	.529
2001 High Desert	A+ Mil	65	259	94	22	2	14	162	68	61	38	4	35	5	0	3	3	3	.50	5	.363	.449	.625
Huntsville	AA Mil	57	187	64	16	1	7	103	35	30	23	0	22	5	0	3	3	2	.60	3	.342	.422	.551
5 Min. YEARS		292	945	316	68	8	37	511	191	178	115	9	126	20	3	10	32	12	.73	18	.334	.414	.541

Brian Rust

Bats: Right **Throws:** Right **Pos:** 1B-31; OF-30; 3B-14; DH-14; PR-5; PH-4; 2B-2   **Ht:** 6'2" **Wt:** 205 **Born:** 8/1/74 **Age:** 27

Year Team	Lg Org	G	AB	H	2B	3B	HR	TB	R	RBI	TBB	IBB	SO	HBP	SH	SF	SB	CS	SB%	GDP	Avg	OBP	SLG
1995 Eugene	A- Atl	53	157	32	7	1	4	53	18	19	7	0	43	2	2	2	2	1	.67	2	.204	.244	.338
1996 Macon	A Atl	7	9	1	0	0	0	1	2	2	2	0	2	0	0	0	0	0	—	0	.111	.273	.111
Eugene	A- Atl	71	275	79	24	3	10	139	52	43	20	2	74	3	0	0	4	2	.67	4	.287	.342	.505
1997 Durham	A+ Atl	122	430	111	29	2	12	180	67	71	43	0	104	3	1	5	10	4	.71	8	.258	.326	.419
1998 Greenville	AA Atl	95	265	68	19	1	9	116	43	39	35	2	93	4	1	2	10	1	.91	5	.257	.350	.438
1999 Delmarva	A Bal	21	77	20	9	1	1	34	11	16	6	1	27	0	1	3	0	0	—	5	.260	.302	.442
Frederick	A+ Bal	9	27	4	1	0	0	5	7	1	5	0	7	2	0	0	0	0	—	0	.148	.324	.185
Bowie	AA Bal	52	149	46	11	0	4	69	24	21	17	0	29	3	2	3	2	0	1.00	3	.309	.384	.463
Rochester	AAA Bal	1	3	0	0	0	0	0	0	1	0	0	0	0	0	1	0	0	—	0	.000	.000	.000
2000 Frederick	A+ Bal	70	252	73	22	1	12	133	53	46	45	1	50	7	0	1	15	4	.79	5	.290	.410	.528
Rochester	AAA Bal	14	43	6	3	0	0	9	2	5	3	0	17	1	0	1	0	0	—	2	.140	.208	.209
Bowie	AA Bal	30	103	34	14	0	5	63	16	24	13	1	21	1	0	2	5	2	.71	2	.330	.403	.612
2001 Bowie	AA Bal	38	129	39	6	0	5	60	16	19	6	0	33	2	0	2	1	1	.17	4	.302	.338	.465
Rochester	AAA Bal	55	186	38	12	0	9	77	24	29	22	0	50	4	1	0	4	0	1.00	1	.204	.302	.414
7 Min. YEARS		638	2105	551	157	9	71	939	335	336	224	7	550	32	8	22	53	19	.74	41	.262	.339	.446

Jason Ryan

Pitches: Right **Bats:** Both **Pos:** SP-14   **Ht:** 6'3" **Wt:** 195 **Born:** 1/23/76 **Age:** 26

Year Team	Lg Org	G	GS	CG	GF	IP	BFP	H	R	ER	HR	SH	SF	HB	TBB	IBB	SO	WP	Bk	W	L	Pct.	ShO	Sv	ERA
1994 Cubs	R ChC	7	7	0	0	33	143	32	19	15	2	1	1	2	4	0	30	5	0	1	2	.333	0	0	4.09
Huntington	R+ ChC	4	4	1	0	26	93	7	1	1	0	1	0	1	8	0	32	0	0	2	0	1.000	1	0	0.35
Orlando	AA ChC	2	2	0	0	11	45	6	3	3	1	0	0	1	6	0	12	0	0	2	0	1.000	0	0	2.45
1995 Daytona	A+ ChC	26	26	0	0	134.2	579	128	61	52	10	3	2	9	54	0	98	13	1	11	5	.688	0	0	3.48
1996 Orlando	AA ChC	7	7	0	0	34.2	169	39	30	22	6	1	0	4	24	0	25	2	0	2	5	.286	0	0	5.71
Daytona	A+ ChC	17	10	0	3	67	298	72	42	39	8	5	2	4	33	0	49	1	0	1	8	.111	0	1	5.24
1997 Daytona	A+ ChC	27	27	5	0	170.1	740	168	105	84	22	3	10	6	55	2	140	12	0	9	8	.529	0	0	4.44
1998 West Tenn	AA ChC	30	25	2	3	147.2	661	172	97	80	20	7	4	10	57	3	121	10	1	3	13	.188	0	0	4.88
1999 West Tenn	AA ChC	8	7	0	0	44.2	185	29	12	7	1	1	1	4	15	1	53	1	0	5	0	1.000	0	0	1.41
New Britain	AA Min	8	8	0	0	50.2	217	48	29	27	6	1	0	1	24	0	42	3	0	2	4	.333	0	0	4.80
Salt Lake	AAA Min	9	9	0	0	54.1	240	57	36	31	8	1	3	1	24	1	34	0	0	4	4	.500	0	0	5.13
2000 Salt Lake	AAA Min	17	17	2	0	96.2	419	94	52	47	16	1	2	6	31	0	66	6	0	9	2	.818	1	0	4.38
2001 Nashville	AAA Pit	9	9	1	0	53.2	235	52	34	27	7	6	2	3	19	0	25	1	0	3	5	.375	0	0	4.53
Las Vegas	AAA LA	5	5	0	0	13.2	78	28	25	21	2	1	2	2	7	0	6	2	0	0	3	.000	0	0	13.83
1999 Minnesota	AL	8	8	1	0	40.2	182	46	23	22	9	0	1	3	17	0	15	0	0	1	4	.200	0	0	4.87
2000 Minnesota	AL	16	1	0	6	26	125	37	24	22	8	0	2	1	10	0	19	2	0	0	1	.000	0	0	7.62
8 Min. YEARS		176	163	11	6	938	4102	932	546	456	110	32	29	54	361	7	733	56	2	54	59	.478	2	1	4.38
2 Maj. YEARS		24	9	1	6	66.2	307	83	47	44	17	0	3	4	27	0	34	2	0	1	5	.167	0	0	5.94

Mike Ryan

Bats: Left **Throws:** Right **Pos:** OF-94; 2B-39; DH-4; PH-4   **Ht:** 5'10" **Wt:** 182 **Born:** 7/6/77 **Age:** 24

Year Team	Lg Org	G	AB	H	2B	3B	HR	TB	R	RBI	TBB	IBB	SO	HBP	SH	SF	SB	CS	SB%	GDP	Avg	OBP	SLG
1996 Twins	R Min	43	157	31	8	2	0	43	12	13	13	1	20	1	1	2	3	0	1.00	3	.197	.260	.274
1997 Elizabethtn	R+ Min	62	220	66	10	0	3	85	44	29	38	3	39	3	1	4	2	2	.50	8	.300	.404	.386
1998 Fort Wayne	A Min	113	412	131	24	6	9	194	69	71	44	2	92	2	3	5	7	3	.70	8	.318	.382	.471
1999 Fort Myers	A+ Min	131	507	139	26	5	8	199	85	71	63	2	60	5	4	6	3	4	.43	11	.274	.356	.393
2000 New Britain	AA Min	122	481	133	23	8	11	205	64	69	34	1	79	2	3	6	4	3	.57	13	.277	.323	.426
Salt Lake	AAA Min	3	9	2	0	0	0	2	1	2	3	0	2	0	0	0	0	0	—	1	.222	.417	.222
2001 Edmonton	AAA Min	135	527	152	36	7	18	256	89	73	52	1	121	2	1	3	1	6	.14	17	.288	.353	.486
6 Min. YEARS		609	2313	654	127	28	49	984	364	328	247	10	413	15	13	26	20	18	.53	61	.283	.352	.425

Carl Sadler

Pitches: Left **Bats:** Left **Pos:** RP-36; SP-2   **Ht:** 6'2" **Wt:** 180 **Born:** 10/11/76 **Age:** 25

Year Team	Lg Org	G	GS	CG	GF	IP	BFP	H	R	ER	HR	SH	SF	HB	TBB	IBB	SO	WP	Bk	W	L	Pct.	ShO	Sv	ERA
1996 Expos	R Mon	17	3	0	6	37	170	41	24	16	2	2	0	2	12	0	24	3	3	2	2	.500	0	1	3.89
1997 Expos	R Mon	9	3	0	0	20.2	91	26	11	10	0	0	1	2	5	0	14	2	0	0	2	.000	0	0	4.35
Vermont	A- Mon	7	6	0	0	36.1	167	33	20	17	2	1	2	2	23	0	27	4	1	2	2	.500	0	0	4.21
1999 Burlington	R+ Cle	5	5	0	0	23	93	18	10	8	0	1	0	0	10	0	22	5	0	1	0	1.000	0	0	3.13
Mahoning Vy	A- Cle	1	1	0	0	2	17	8	7	7	0	0	0	0	3	0	3	1	0	0	1	.000	0	0	31.50
2000 Mahoning Vy	A- Cle	5	0	0	1	6	25	5	2	2	0	1	0	0	3	0	3	0	0	0	0	—	0	0	3.00
Columbus	A Cle	10	0	0	3	16.1	73	20	13	12	0	0	0	0	7	0	21	5	0	1	3	.250	0	0	6.61
2001 Kinston	A+ Cle	27	2	0	10	62.1	258	51	19	13	2	0	0	3	18	1	78	1	0	6	0	1.000	0	2	1.88
Akron	AA Cle	11	0	0	6	18	85	23	16	13	1	0	0	0	9	0	14	0	1	2	3	.400	0	0	6.50
5 Min. YEARS		92	20	0	26	221.2	979	225	122	98	7	5	3	9	90	1	206	21	5	14	13	.519	0	3	3.98

Jason Saenz

Pitches: Left **Bats:** Left **Pos:** SP-23; RP-5   **Ht:** 6'2" **Wt:** 190 **Born:** 2/13/77 **Age:** 25

Year Team	Lg Org	G	GS	CG	GF	IP	BFP	H	R	ER	HR	SH	SF	HB	TBB	IBB	SO	WP	Bk	W	L	Pct.	ShO	Sv	ERA
1998 Pittsfield	A- NYM	12	7	0	1	44	199	56	37	33	6	1	2	2	23	1	34	4	2	2	3	.400	0	0	6.75
1999 Capital Cty	A NYM	27	27	0	0	134	617	147	89	81	16	0	5	18	68	0	125	16	2	10	8	.556	0	0	5.44
2000 St. Lucie	A+ NYM	28	28	0	0	153.1	684	155	98	75	7	4	10	8	83	0	107	14	4	6	9	.400	0	0	4.40
2001 Binghamton	AA NYM	28	23	0	1	143	662	167	97	90	16	3	6	8	80	8	95	16	2	8	15	.348	0	0	5.66
4 Min. YEARS		95	85	0	2	474.1	2162	535	321	279	45	8	23	36	254	9	361	50	10	26	35	.426	0	0	5.29

Marc Sagmoen

Bats: Left **Throws:** Left **Pos:** OF-64; 1B-11; DH-6   **Ht:** 5'11" **Wt:** 185 **Born:** 4/16/71 **Age:** 31

Year Team	Lg Org	G	AB	H	2B	3B	HR	TB	R	RBI	TBB	IBB	SO	HBP	SH	SF	SB	CS	SB%	GDP	Avg	OBP	SLG
1993 Erie	A- Tex	6	23	7	1	1	0	10	6	2	3	0	7	1	0	1	0	0	—	0	.304	.393	.435
Chston-SC	A Tex	63	234	69	13	4	6	108	44	34	23	0	39	3	3	3	16	4	.80	2	.295	.361	.462
1994 Charlotte	A+ Tex	122	475	139	25	10	3	193	74	47	37	2	56	3	1	3	15	10	.60	15	.293	.346	.406
1995 Okla City	AAA Tex	56	188	42	11	3	3	68	20	25	16	0	31	2	1	4	5	2	.71	2	.223	.286	.362
Tulsa	AA Tex	63	242	56	8	5	6	92	36	22	23	0	23	4	1	2	5	4	.56	2	.231	.306	.380
1996 Tulsa	AA Tex	96	387	109	21	6	10	172	58	62	33	4	58	2	0	7	5	8	.38	7	.282	.336	.444
Okla City	AAA Tex	32	116	34	6	0	5	55	16	16	4	0	20	1	0	1	1	0	1.00	0	.293	.320	.474
1997 Okla City	AAA Tex	111	418	110	32	6	5	169	47	44	26	4	95	1	1	2	4	3	.57	10	.263	.306	.404
1998 Oklahoma	AAA Tex	113	403	108	26	6	14	188	61	65	35	0	86	4	3	3	6	2	.75	7	.268	.330	.467
1999 Oklahoma	AAA Tex	83	268	73	11	3	13	129	42	43	24	3	58	0	1	1	3	2	.60	7	.272	.331	.481
2000 New Orleans	AAA Hou	122	414	111	15	7	12	176	65	43	40	1	82	1	4	4	20	5	.80	3	.268	.331	.425
2001 Edmonton	AAA Min	9	37	3	1	0	0	4	2	1	2	0	8	0	0	0	0	0	—	1	.081	.128	.108
Memphis	AAA StL	12	52	13	4	0	0	17	7	9	4	0	15	0	0	0	1	0	1.00	2	.250	.304	.327
Oklahoma	AAA Tex	59	235	56	10	1	4	80	22	16	8	0	53	0	2	2	3	2	.60	1	.238	.261	.340
1997 Texas	AL	21	43	6	2	0	1	11	2	4	2	0	13	0	0	1	0	0	—	1	.140	.174	.256
9 Min. YEARS		947	3492	930	184	52	81	1461	500	429	278	14	631	22	17	33	84	42	.67	59	.266	.322	.418

Mike Saipe

Pitches: Right **Bats:** Right **Pos:** SP-20; RP-1   **Ht:** 6'1" **Wt:** 188 **Born:** 9/10/73 **Age:** 28

Year Team	Lg Org	G	GS	CG	GF	IP	BFP	H	R	ER	HR	SH	SF	HB	TBB	IBB	SO	WP	Bk	W	L	Pct.	ShO	Sv	ERA
1994 Bend	A- Col	16	16	0	0	84.1	363	73	52	39	7	3	4	7	34	0	74	6	2	3	7	.300	0	0	4.16
1995 Salem	A+ Col	21	9	0	7	85.1	347	68	35	33	7	1	1	2	32	4	90	9	1	4	5	.444	0	3	3.48
1996 New Haven	AA Col	32	19	1	5	138	562	114	53	47	12	4	3	4	42	6	126	4	4	10	7	.588	1	3	3.07
1997 New Haven	AA Col	19	19	4	0	136.2	550	127	57	47	18	3	1	5	29	2	123	4	1	8	5	.615	2	0	3.10
Colo Sprngs	AAA Col	10	10	1	0	60.1	278	74	42	37	10	1	0	4	24	3	40	2	3	4	3	.571	0	0	5.52
1998 Colo Sprngs	AAA Col	24	24	2	0	139.2	632	167	96	80	19	3	5	8	51	1	124	4	2	5	11	.313	0	0	5.16
1999 Colo Sprngs	AAA Col	11	11	0	0	54	232	62	36	29	11	0	4	1	20	0	39	3	0	1	5	.167	0	0	4.83
2000 Carolina	AA Col	4	4	1	0	26.1	118	29	17	16	2	3	0	1	12	1	13	1	0	1	3	.250	0	0	5.47
Colo Sprngs	AAA Col	15	8	0	1	54.1	270	94	67	58	18	3	5	4	16	0	37	1	0	4	5	.444	0	0	9.61
Las Vegas	AAA SD	2	2	0	0	7.1	39	13	11	11	4	0	0	0	6	0	4	0	0	0	0	—	0	0	13.50
Edmonton	AAA Ana	3	3	0	1	18.2	90	26	15	15	2	0	1	0	10	0	14	0	0	0	1	.000	0	0	7.23
2001 Long Beach	IND —	14	13	4	0	92	383	87	39	32	2	3	2	6	23	1	69	1	0	8	4	.667	2	0	3.13
Greenville	AA Atl	7	7	0	0	49	193	43	13	13	2	2	0	0	13	1	36	2	0	4	2	.667	0	0	2.39
1998 Colorado	NL	2	2	0	0	10	54	22	12	12	5	1	0	2	0	0	2	0	0	0	1	.000	0	0	10.80
8 Min. YEARS		179	145	13	14	946	4057	977	533	457	114	26	26	42	312	19	789	37	13	52	58	.473	5	7	4.35

Jeremy Salazar

Bats: Right **Throws:** Right **Pos:** C-47   **Ht:** 6'0" **Wt:** 190 **Born:** 3/18/76 **Age:** 26

Year Team	Lg Org	G	AB	H	2B	3B	HR	TB	R	RBI	TBB	IBB	SO	HBP	SH	SF	SB	CS	SB%	GDP	Avg	OBP	SLG
1998 Batavia	A- Phi	20	68	19	5	0	2	30	6	18	4	0	21	1	0	0	0	0	—	1	.279	.329	.441
Piedmont	A Phi	41	158	45	10	0	2	61	20	19	23	0	39	4	0	1	1	0	1.00	3	.285	.387	.386
1999 Piedmont	A Phi	98	345	87	17	0	10	134	37	36	27	0	90	7	1	4	1	0	1.00	9	.252	.316	.388
Clearwater	A+ Phi	2	10	3	1	0	0	4	1	1	0	0	2	0	0	0	0	0	—	0	.300	.300	.400
2000 Clearwater	A+ Phi	45	164	41	11	1	1	57	18	25	13	0	37	1	1	1	0	0	—	6	.250	.307	.348
2001 Scranton-WB	AAA Phi	47	160	37	13	0	1	53	16	16	10	0	35	0	2	1	0	0	—	6	.231	.275	.331
4 Min. YEARS		253	905	232	57	1	16	339	98	115	77	0	224	13	4	7	2	0	1.00	25	.256	.321	.375

Oscar Salazar

Bats: Right **Throws:** Right **Pos:** SS-77; 3B-35; 2B-17; DH-5; PH-2; OF-1   **Ht:** 5'11" **Wt:** 178 **Born:** 6/27/78 **Age:** 24

Year Team	Lg Org	G	AB	H	2B	3B	HR	TB	R	RBI	TBB	IBB	SO	HBP	SH	SF	SB	CS	SB%	GDP	Avg	OBP	SLG
1998 Athletics	R Oak	26	102	33	7	5	2	56	29	18	12	0	15	1	0	0	4	1	.80	1	.324	.400	.549
Sou Oregon	A- Oak	28	101	32	4	1	5	53	19	28	16	0	22	0	1	3	5	2	.71	0	.317	.400	.525
1999 Modesto	A+ Oak	130	525	155	26	18	18	271	100	105	39	1	106	1	0	9	14	6	.70	10	.295	.340	.516
2000 Midland	AA Oak	111	427	128	27	1	13	196	70	57	39	0	71	2	2	3	4	4	.50	9	.300	.359	.459
2001 Sacramento	AAA Oak	4	13	2	1	0	0	3	0	1	1	0	1	0	0	0	1	0	1.00	2	.154	.214	.231
Sacramento	AAA Oak	5	16	1	0	0	0	1	0	1	1	0	5	0	0	0	0	0	—	0	.063	.118	.063
Midland	AA Oak	130	521	139	31	4	18	232	75	95	49	2	100	2	1	6	10	3	.77	11	.267	.329	.445
4 Min. YEARS		434	1705	490	96	29	56	812	293	305	157	3	320	6	4	21	38	16	.70	34	.287	.346	.476

Ruben Salazar

Bats: Right **Throws:** Right **Pos:** 2B-115; DH-15; 3B-6; PH-3   **Ht:** 5'10" **Wt:** 186 **Born:** 1/16/78 **Age:** 24

Year Team	Lg Org	G	AB	H	2B	3B	HR	TB	R	RBI	TBB	IBB	SO	HBP	SH	SF	SB	CS	SB%	GDP	Avg	OBP	SLG
1998 Twins	R Min	50	161	40	5	1	3	56	16	25	9	0	29	1	2	3	10	3	.77	4	.248	.287	.348
1999 Elizabethtn	R+ Min	64	262	105	24	2	14	175	66	65	48	3	43	5	1	2	11	4	.73	8	.401	.498	.668
2000 Fort Myers	A+ Min	124	499	155	25	0	11	213	80	64	37	1	81	2	0	3	3	5	.38	18	.311	.359	.427
2001 New Britain	AA Min	137	530	158	29	2	10	221	70	66	37	4	77	7	2	6	6	1	.86	17	.298	.348	.417
4 Min. YEARS		375	1452	458	83	5	38	665	232	220	131	8	230	15	5	14	30	13	.70	47	.315	.375	.458

Jeremy Salyers

Pitches: Right **Bats:** Right **Pos:** RP-25; SP-3   **Ht:** 6'3" **Wt:** 200 **Born:** 1/31/76 **Age:** 26

		HOW MUCH HE PITCHED						WHAT HE GAVE UP										THE RESULTS				
Year Team	Lg Org	G	GS	CG	GF	IP	BFP	H	R	ER	HR	SH	SF	HB	TBB	IBB	SO	WP	Bk	W	L	Pct.	ShO	Sv	ERA
1996 Expos	R Mon	11	9	2	1	57	246	47	36	27	4	3	1	8	26	0	30	1	0	1	4	.200	0	1	4.26
1997 Vermont	A- Mon	16	14	0	0	77.1	346	87	53	43	4	3	6	5	31	0	32	6	2	3	4	.429	0	0	5.00
1998 Cape Fear	A Mon	42	2	0	18	71.2	310	70	41	30	8	5	1	8	23	0	32	8	2	4	4	.500	0	3	3.77
1999 Cape Fear	A Mon	22	7	0	6	63	257	62	22	16	3	3	2	3	18	0	37	2	0	2	3	.400	0	1	2.29
Ottawa	AAA Mon	1	1	0	0	6	24	6	2	1	0	1	0	0	2	0	2	1	0	0	0	—	0	0	1.50
Harrisburg	AA Mon	12	1	0	8	25.2	105	20	9	8	1	1	0	2	11	0	9	1	0	1	0	1.000	0	0	2.81
2000 Ottawa	AAA Mon	1	1	0	0	5	24	5	5	5	0	0	1	0	5	0	1	1	0	0	1	.000	0	0	9.00
Jupiter	A+ Mon	14	6	0	3	41	201	55	35	25	0	2	3	1	23	0	22	1	0	3	4	.429	0	0	5.49
Harrisburg	AA Mon	20	4	0	3	33.1	166	44	27	22	3	2	1	4	19	0	20	3	0	1	3	.250	0	0	5.94
2001 Jupiter	A+ Mon	9	1	0	2	22.2	98	22	10	9	0	3	1	2	6	1	10	0	0	3	1	.750	0	0	3.57
Harrisburg	AA Mon	16	1	0	7	22.2	99	24	15	14	4	2	1	2	6	2	13	1	0	4	2	.667	0	0	5.56
St. Paul	IND —	3	1	0	1	4.2	26	9	9	9	3	0	1	1	2	0	1	0	0	0	1	.000	0	0	17.36
6 Min. YEARS		167	48	2	49	430	1902	451	264	209	30	25	18	36	172	3	209	25	4	22	27	.449	0	5	4.37

Jerry Salzano

Bats: Right **Throws:** Right **Pos:** 3B-68; DH-52; PH-4; 1B-3   **Ht:** 6'0" **Wt:** 175 **Born:** 10/27/74 **Age:** 27

		BATTING														BASERUNNING				PERCENTAGES		
Year Team	Lg Org	G	AB	H	2B	3B	HR	TB	R	RBI	TBB	IBB	SO	HBP	SH	SF	SB	CS	SB%	GDP	Avg	OBP	SLG
1992 Brewers	R Mil	51	177	43	5	0	0	48	18	20	23	0	31	4	2	3	1	3	.25	4	.243	.338	.271
1993 Helena	R+ Mil	66	227	59	12	2	1	78	30	18	25	0	39	3	4	2	6	3	.67	2	.260	.339	.344
1994 Beloit	A Mil	19	57	10	2	0	0	12	10	1	7	0	12	4	0	0	1	3	.25	2	.175	.309	.211
Williamsprt	A- ChC	75	283	80	15	3	2	107	33	37	15	0	44	8	1	2	5	5	.50	4	.283	.334	.378
1995 Williamsprt	A- ChC	62	218	65	13	2	0	82	28	23	22	0	28	4	0	1	4	3	.57	6	.298	.371	.376
Rockford	A ChC	6	21	6	1	1	0	9	0	2	1	0	1	0	0	0	0	1	.00	1	.286	.318	.429
1996 Lakeland	A+ Det	123	426	113	28	4	6	167	52	60	38	0	66	9	2	4	6	7	.46	10	.265	.335	.392
1997 Lakeland	A+ Det	40	135	30	4	1	2	42	20	8	22	2	27	2	1	0	1	1	.50	1	.222	.340	.311
Durham	A+ Atl	68	226	63	20	0	1	86	29	24	26	2	42	12	2	1	6	4	.60	10	.279	.381	.381
1998 Greenville	AA Atl	101	324	98	19	3	7	144	48	49	46	1	67	8	2	2	14	8	.64	8	.302	.400	.444
1999 Indianapols	AAA Cin	7	11	1	0	0	0	1	0	2	0	0	6	0	0	1	0	0	—	0	.091	.083	.091
Chattanooga	AA Cin	72	263	86	19	1	4	119	44	38	39	1	38	5	2	4	14	10	.58	5	.327	.418	.452
2000 Greenville	AA Atl	24	83	13	4	0	2	23	7	11	8	0	17	3	0	1	5	0	1.00	0	.157	.253	.277
2001 Trenton	AA Bos	125	453	128	31	1	7	182	65	54	50	1	90	12	1	2	15	6	.71	6	.283	.368	.402
10 Min. YEARS		839	2904	795	173	18	32	1100	384	347	322	7	508	74	17	23	78	54	.59	59	.274	.358	.379

Scott Samuels

Bats: Left **Throws:** Right **Pos:** OF-66; PH-3; DH-2; 1B-1   **Ht:** 5'11" **Wt:** 190 **Born:** 5/19/71 **Age:** 31

		BATTING														BASERUNNING				PERCENTAGES		
Year Team	Lg Org	G	AB	H	2B	3B	HR	TB	R	RBI	TBB	IBB	SO	HBP	SH	SF	SB	CS	SB%	GDP	Avg	OBP	SLG
1992 Erie	A- Fla	43	128	26	7	1	0	35	17	14	19	0	39	2	0	0	7	3	.70	2	.203	.315	.273
1993 High Desert	A+ Fla	76	219	65	10	4	6	101	43	40	45	0	55	1	0	1	12	4	.75	7	.297	.417	.461
1994 Brevard Cty	A+ Fla	89	281	65	11	0	3	85	35	25	46	1	70	4	1	1	11	5	.69	7	.231	.346	.302
1995 Beloit	AA ChC	5	21	6	1	0	1	10	3	4	3	0	4	0	0	0	2	0	1.00	0	.286	.375	.476
Daytona	A+ ChC	112	388	127	29	12	2	186	92	42	69	7	63	8	3	4	38	14	.73	8	.327	.435	.479
1996 Orlando	AA ChC	106	342	89	19	5	2	124	62	33	62	2	81	0	3	5	21	10	.68	3	.260	.373	.363
1997 Orlando	AA ChC	34	127	36	7	3	3	58	30	17	18	0	34	1	1	0	5	4	.56	4	.283	.377	.457
Ottawa	AAA Mon	20	55	19	3	0	1	25	6	7	7	3	12	0	1	0	2	0	1.00	1	.345	.419	.455
Harrisburg	AA Mon	64	223	66	19	1	5	102	32	32	34	3	43	1	1	0	13	4	.76	0	.296	.391	.457
1998 Harrisburg	AA Mon	20	58	16	3	0	4	31	9	11	7	0	13	1	0	0	4	1	.80	1	.276	.364	.534
Ottawa	AAA Mon	43	94	22	4	2	2	36	15	15	19	1	24	0	1	1	4	3	.57	2	.234	.360	.383
Winnipeg	IND —	8	30	9	1	1	2	18	7	4	6	0	5	3	0	0	3	0	1.00	0	.300	.462	.600
1999 Rio Grande	IND —	39	140	55	8	0	19	120	51	53	44	6	27	4	0	0	21	5	.81	1	.393	.548	.857
2000 Allentown	IND —	84	293	103	29	2	16	184	67	74	61	6	55	6	0	6	24	5	.83	1	.352	.464	.628
2001 Pawtucket	AAA Bos	38	125	32	9	1	4	55	14	14	14	0	21	0	1	0	5	2	.71	2	.256	.331	.440
Allentown	IND —	32	116	31	11	1	4	56	23	25	24	0	25	5	0	1	10	2	.83	2	.267	.411	.483
10 Min. YEARS		813	2640	767	171	33	74	1226	506	410	478	29	571	36	12	15	182	62	.75	42	.291	.404	.464

Brian Sanches

Pitches: Right **Bats:** Right **Pos:** SP-21; RP-8   **Ht:** 6'1" **Wt:** 195 **Born:** 8/8/78 **Age:** 23

		HOW MUCH HE PITCHED						WHAT HE GAVE UP										THE RESULTS				
Year Team	Lg Org	G	GS	CG	GF	IP	BFP	H	R	ER	HR	SH	SF	HB	TBB	IBB	SO	WP	Bk	W	L	Pct.	ShO	Sv	ERA
1999 Spokane	A- KC	9	9	0	0	34	146	32	19	18	2	0	0	1	12	0	51	0	0	1	1	.500	0	0	4.76
2000 Wilmington	A+ KC	28	27	2	0	158	665	132	77	62	9	5	7	15	69	0	122	11	3	6	12	.333	1	0	3.53
2001 Wichita	AA KC	29	21	0	3	134	610	152	96	89	12	7	3	13	61	4	95	12	1	7	9	.438	0	0	5.98
3 Min. YEARS		66	57	2	3	326	1421	316	192	169	23	12	10	29	142	4	268	23	4	14	22	.389	1	0	4.67

Duaner Sanchez

Pitches: Right **Bats:** Right **Pos:** SP-23   **Ht:** 6'0" **Wt:** 160 **Born:** 10/14/79 **Age:** 22

		HOW MUCH HE PITCHED						WHAT HE GAVE UP										THE RESULTS				
Year Team	Lg Org	G	GS	CG	GF	IP	BFP	H	R	ER	HR	SH	SF	HB	TBB	IBB	SO	WP	Bk	W	L	Pct.	ShO	Sv	ERA
1999 High Desert	A+ Ari	3	3	0	0	14.1	63	15	13	12	2	0	1	1	9	0	9	0	0	0	0	—	0	0	7.53
Missoula	R+ Ari	13	11	0	0	63.1	269	54	34	22	3	1	1	3	23	0	51	8	0	5	3	.625	0	0	3.13
2000 South Bend	A Ari	28	28	4	0	165.1	700	152	80	67	6	5	5	11	54	1	121	6	2	8	9	.471	0	0	3.65
2001 El Paso	AA Ari	13	13	0	0	70.1	323	92	56	53	5	1	7	6	25	1	41	5	0	3	7	.300	0	0	6.78
Lancaster	A+ Ari	10	10	1	0	59	270	65	44	30	7	4	4	7	18	0	49	3	4	2	4	.333	0	0	4.58
3 Min. YEARS		67	65	5	0	372.1	1625	378	227	184	23	11	18	28	129	2	271	22	6	18	23	.439	0	0	4.45

Freddy Sanchez

Bats: Right Throws: Right Pos: SS-113   Ht: 5'11" Wt: 185 Born: 12/21/77 Age: 24

Year Team	Lg Org	G	AB	H	2B	3B	HR	TB	R	RBI	TBB	IBB	SO	HBP	SH	SF	SB	CS	SB%	GDP	Avg	OBP	SLG
2000 Lowell	A- Bos	34	132	38	13	2	1	58	24	14	9	0	16	3	2	0	2	4	.33	1	.288	.347	.439
Augusta	A Bos	30	109	33	7	0	0	40	17	15	11	0	19	1	4	0	4	0	1.00	1	.303	.372	.367
2001 Sarasota	A+ Bos	69	280	95	19	4	1	125	40	24	22	1	30	2	3	3	5	3	.63	3	.339	.388	.446
Trenton	AA Bos	44	178	58	20	0	2	84	25	19	9	0	21	2	2	1	3	1	.75	6	.326	.363	.472
2 Min. YEARS		177	699	224	59	6	4	307	106	72	51	1	86	8	11	4	14	8	.64	11	.320	.371	.439

Wellington Sanchez

Bats: Right Throws: Right Pos: SS-27; PH-22; OF-21; 3B-16; PR-5; DH-2; 2B-1   Ht: 6'0" Wt: 162 Born: 5/27/77 Age: 25

Year Team	Lg Org	G	AB	H	2B	3B	HR	TB	R	RBI	TBB	IBB	SO	HBP	SH	SF	SB	CS	SB%	GDP	Avg	OBP	SLG
1997 Helena	R+ Mil	61	236	64	13	0	2	83	46	20	14	0	47	1	3	0	10	7	.59	3	.271	.315	.352
1998 Beloit	A Mil	39	137	34	5	2	0	43	23	15	19	2	24	1	5	0	3	2	.60	4	.248	.344	.314
1999 Beloit	A Mil	71	261	68	14	3	0	88	35	23	25	0	58	4	4	0	9	3	.75	5	.261	.334	.337
2000 Huntsville	AA Mil	85	244	63	9	2	1	79	26	28	34	0	47	2	5	0	1	6	.14	5	.258	.354	.324
2001 Huntsville	AA Mil	89	212	48	10	0	1	61	28	14	22	0	56	0	3	0	4	3	.57	3	.226	.299	.288
5 Min. YEARS		345	1090	277	51	7	4	354	158	100	114	2	232	8	20	0	27	21	.56	20	.254	.329	.325

Dave Sanders

Pitches: Left Bats: Left Pos: RP-36   Ht: 6'0" Wt: 200 Born: 8/29/79 Age: 22

Year Team	Lg Org	G	GS	CG	GF	IP	BFP	H	R	ER	HR	SH	SF	HB	TBB	IBB	SO	WP	Bk	W	L	Pct.	ShO	Sv	ERA
1999 White Sox	R CWS	7	1	0	2	16.1	66	12	3	2	0	1	0	1	6	3	26	1	0	1	0	1.000	0	1	1.10
2000 Winston-Sal	A+ CWS	51	0	0	20	48.1	228	39	35	28	4	2	2	4	39	1	50	12	1	3	2	.600	0	6	5.21
2001 Birmingham	AA CWS	36	0	0	12	34	150	27	12	10	1	1	2	3	25	1	25	2	0	3	0	1.000	0	0	2.65
3 Min. YEARS		94	1	0	34	98.2	444	78	50	40	5	4	4	8	70	5	101	15	1	7	2	.778	0	7	3.65

Frankie Sanders

Pitches: Right Bats: Right Pos: RP-10; SP-4   Ht: 5'11" Wt: 165 Born: 8/27/75 Age: 26

Year Team	Lg Org	G	GS	CG	GF	IP	BFP	H	R	ER	HR	SH	SF	HB	TBB	IBB	SO	WP	Bk	W	L	Pct.	ShO	Sv	ERA
1995 Burlington	R+ Cle	12	12	3	0	70	292	48	31	23	2	1	0	3	32	0	80	2	1	3	5	.375	0	0	2.96
Columbus	A Cle	2	0	0	1	9	39	9	3	3	0	1	0	1	4	0	9	1	0	1	1	.500	0	0	3.00
1996 Columbus	A Cle	22	22	0	0	121.1	508	103	52	34	8	3	2	6	37	1	109	13	4	9	3	.750	0	0	2.52
1997 Kinston	A+ Cle	25	25	2	0	146.1	611	130	72	66	10	6	2	2	66	1	127	8	0	11	5	.688	0	0	4.06
1998 Akron	AA Cle	29	29	2	0	186.1	781	175	82	72	15	8	6	11	71	0	108	6	0	11	8	.579	1	0	3.48
1999 Buffalo	AAA Cle	1	1	0	0	5	25	6	5	5	2	0	0	0	4	0	3	0	0	0	1	.000	0	0	9.00
Akron	AA Cle	33	13	0	6	120.2	546	139	72	65	12	6	7	6	51	2	72	9	0	6	6	.500	0	2	4.85
2000 Buffalo	AAA Cle	5	3	0	0	17.1	86	26	16	16	3	0	0	2	8	0	7	0	0	0	3	.000	0	0	8.31
Akron	AA Cle	19	9	0	3	69.1	312	77	47	40	9	5	3	6	29	2	50	2	0	5	5	.500	0	1	5.19
2001 Akron	AA Cle	1	1	0	0	0.1	8	3	7	7	1	0	0	1	3	0	0	0	0	0	0	—	0	0	189.00
Camden	IND —	8	4	0	1	26.2	119	24	20	20	6	1	0	0	16	0	14	1	0	0	1	.000	0	0	6.75
Chico	IND —	5	0	0	2	5.2	23	3	3	2	0	0	0	1	5	0	4	0	0	1	0	1.000	0	0	3.18
7 Min. YEARS		162	118	7	13	778	3350	743	410	353	68	31	20	39	326	6	583	42	5	46	39	.541	1	3	4.08

Danny Sandoval

Bats: Right Throws: Right Pos: SS-69; OF-21; 3B-16; PH-3   Ht: 5'11" Wt: 180 Born: 4/7/79 Age: 23

Year Team	Lg Org	G	AB	H	2B	3B	HR	TB	R	RBI	TBB	IBB	SO	HBP	SH	SF	SB	CS	SB%	GDP	Avg	OBP	SLG
1998 Hickory	A CWS	126	430	99	12	2	0	115	43	30	29	0	88	5	14	2	13	15	.46	10	.230	.285	.267
1999 Burlington	A CWS	76	255	58	5	1	3	74	34	37	17	0	39	0	6	2	8	5	.62	7	.227	.274	.290
2000 Burlington	A CWS	75	269	87	9	3	0	102	34	34	18	1	22	2	8	1	37	18	.67	6	.323	.369	.379
Winston-Sal	A+ CWS	52	199	53	11	2	2	74	29	17	18	1	21	1	7	0	11	7	.61	7	.266	.330	.372
Charlotte	AAA CWS	2	8	1	0	0	0	1	0	1	1	0	1	0	0	0	0	0	—	0	.125	.222	.125
2001 Winston-Sal	A+ CWS	48	176	48	11	0	3	68	25	14	11	1	31	3	6	2	11	2	.85	3	.273	.323	.386
Birmingham	AA CWS	58	203	57	7	1	0	66	24	29	17	1	26	1	6	3	17	4	.81	5	.281	.335	.325
4 Min. YEARS		437	1540	403	55	9	8	500	189	162	111	4	228	12	47	10	97	51	.66	38	.262	.314	.325

Scott Sandusky

Bats: Right Throws: Right Pos: C-108; 1B-7; PH-1   Ht: 6'0" Wt: 200 Born: 3/6/76 Age: 26

Year Team	Lg Org	G	AB	H	2B	3B	HR	TB	R	RBI	TBB	IBB	SO	HBP	SH	SF	SB	CS	SB%	GDP	Avg	OBP	SLG
1998 Cape Fear	A Mon	53	189	54	5	0	1	62	16	19	11	0	54	0	5	0	3	1	.75	3	.286	.325	.328
1999 Jupiter	A+ Mon	108	354	90	9	1	1	104	31	22	20	0	72	8	7	0	4	5	.44	6	.254	.309	.294
2000 Jupiter	A+ Mon	43	140	36	4	1	2	48	18	25	8	0	29	1	4	2	1	0	1.00	0	.257	.298	.343
Harrisburg	AA Mon	47	127	16	3	0	0	19	11	11	7	0	33	1	1	1	3	1	.75	2	.126	.176	.150
2001 Harrisburg	AA Mon	114	387	96	20	1	2	124	36	23	35	5	76	7	3	1	7	2	.78	9	.248	.321	.320
4 Min. YEARS		365	1197	292	41	3	6	357	112	100	81	5	264	17	20	4	17	10	.63	20	.244	.300	.298

Trevor Sansom

Pitches: Right **Bats:** Right **Pos:** RP-51 **Ht:** 6'4" **Wt:** 190 **Born:** 5/6/76 **Age:** 26

Year Team	Lg Org	G	GS	CG	GF	IP	BFP	H	R	ER	HR	SH	SF	HB	TBB	IBB	SO	WP	Bk	W	L	Pct.	ShO	Sv	ERA
1999 New Jersey	A- StL	20	0	0	7	23.1	121	34	28	20	3	1	1	1	16	2	18	4	0	1	3	.250	0	0	7.71
2000 Peoria	A StL	44	5	0	13	87.1	378	81	42	28	2	4	2	6	33	4	45	4	0	2	8	.200	0	3	2.89
2001 Potomac	A+ StL	50	0	0	12	69.2	307	72	33	21	2	5	3	4	22	3	45	0	0	6	4	.600	0	0	2.71
New Haven	AA StL	1	0	0	0	2	8	1	1	1	0	0	0	0	1	0	1	0	0	0	0	—	0	0	4.50
3 Min. YEARS		115	5	0	32	182.1	814	188	104	70	7	10	6	11	72	9	109	8	0	9	15	.375	0	3	3.46

Julio Santana

Pitches: Right **Bats:** Right **Pos:** SP-25 **Ht:** 6'0" **Wt:** 225 **Born:** 1/20/74 **Age:** 28

Year Team	Lg Org	G	GS	CG	GF	IP	BFP	H	R	ER	HR	SH	SF	HB	TBB	IBB	SO	WP	Bk	W	L	Pct.	ShO	Sv	ERA
1993 Rangers	R Tex	26	0	0	12	39	153	31	9	6	0	0	0	1	7	0	50	1	0	4	1	.800	0	7	1.38
1994 Chston-SC	A Tex	16	16	0	0	91.1	383	65	38	25	3	0	4	7	44	0	103	7	1	6	7	.462	0	0	2.46
Tulsa	AA Tex	11	11	2	0	71.1	290	50	26	23	1	1	2	2	41	0	45	2	0	7	2	.778	0	0	2.90
1995 Okla City	AAA Tex	2	2	0	0	3	25	9	14	13	3	0	0	0	7	0	6	1	1	0	2	.000	0	0	39.00
Charlotte	A+ Tex	5	5	1	0	31.1	136	32	16	13	1	1	1	0	16	0	27	7	2	0	3	.000	0	0	3.73
Tulsa	AA Tex	15	15	3	0	103	438	91	40	36	8	2	4	0	52	2	71	8	1	6	4	.600	0	0	3.15
1996 Okla City	AAA Tex	29	29	4	0	185.2	787	171	102	83	12	5	9	5	66	1	113	12	1	11	12	.478	1	0	4.02
1997 Okla City	AAA Tex	1	1	0	0	3	20	9	6	5	0	0	0	0	2	0	1	0	0	0	0	—	0	0	15.00
2000 Pawtucket	AAA Bos	12	12	0	0	65	271	61	34	34	7	1	0	2	23	0	55	0	2	5	3	.625	0	0	4.71
2001 Fresno	AAA SF	25	25	0	0	132.2	601	160	94	86	28	4	2	9	50	0	125	9	1	8	8	.500	0	0	5.83
1997 Texas	AL	30	14	0	3	104	496	141	86	78	16	1	5	4	49	2	64	8	1	4	6	.400	0	0	6.75
1998 Texas	AL	3	0	0	0	5.1	27	7	5	5	0	0	0	0	4	1	1	0	0	0	0	—	0	0	8.44
Tampa Bay	AL	32	19	1	5	140.1	603	144	72	66	18	2	5	5	58	2	60	3	0	5	6	.455	0	0	4.23
1999 Tampa Bay	AL	22	5	0	7	55.1	261	66	49	45	10	1	1	7	32	0	34	0	0	1	4	.200	0	0	7.32
2000 Montreal	NL	36	4	0	9	66.2	293	69	45	42	11	1	2	2	33	2	58	2	0	1	5	.167	0	0	5.67
7 Min. YEARS		142	116	10	12	725.1	3104	679	379	324	63	14	22	26	308	3	596	47	9	47	42	.528	1	7	4.02
4 Maj. YEARS		123	42	1	24	371.2	1680	427	257	236	55	5	13	18	176	7	217	13	1	11	21	.344	0	0	5.71

Osmany Santana

Bats: Left **Throws:** Left **Pos:** OF-11 **Ht:** 5'11" **Wt:** 185 **Born:** 8/9/76 **Age:** 25

Year Team	Lg Org	G	AB	H	2B	3B	HR	TB	R	RBI	TBB	IBB	SO	HBP	SH	SF	SB	CS	SB%	GDP	Avg	OBP	SLG
1998 Watertown	A- Cle	19	78	22	4	3	2	38	17	13	11	0	8	0	0	0	3	2	.60	2	.282	.371	.487
1999 Columbus	A Cle	38	133	43	6	0	0	49	23	17	10	1	21	1	1	1	15	6	.71	0	.323	.372	.368
Kinston	A+ Cle	43	145	35	8	0	3	52	16	20	8	0	26	1	1	0	7	0	1.00	1	.241	.286	.359
2000 Kinston	A+ Cle	44	190	62	12	2	0	78	27	14	15	0	27	0	2	1	13	4	.76	2	.326	.374	.411
Akron	AA Cle	51	191	54	6	0	1	63	16	23	11	0	23	1	5	0	14	1	.93	3	.283	.325	.330
2001 Akron	AA Cle	11	40	5	0	0	0	5	1	1	2	0	10	0	0	0	1	0	1.00	1	.125	.167	.125
4 Min. YEARS		206	777	221	36	5	6	285	100	88	57	1	115	3	13	2	53	13	.80	9	.284	.335	.367

Jack Santora

Bats: Both **Throws:** Right **Pos:** SS-52; 2B-24; PH-7; 3B-5; PR-1 **Ht:** 5'7" **Wt:** 145 **Born:** 10/6/76 **Age:** 25

Year Team	Lg Org	G	AB	H	2B	3B	HR	TB	R	RBI	TBB	IBB	SO	HBP	SH	SF	SB	CS	SB%	GDP	Avg	OBP	SLG
1999 Missoula	R+ Ari	51	195	51	9	1	1	65	46	31	34	0	33	2	6	2	36	7	.84	3	.262	.373	.333
2000 South Bend	A Ari	102	316	78	16	3	1	103	38	28	59	1	61	4	18	2	20	13	.61	6	.247	.370	.326
2001 El Paso	AA Ari	86	265	62	14	0	0	76	35	13	35	1	48	2	7	1	4	5	.44	2	.234	.327	.287
3 Min. YEARS		239	776	191	39	4	2	244	119	72	128	2	142	8	31	5	60	25	.71	11	.246	.357	.314

Rob Sasser

Bats: Right **Throws:** Right **Pos:** 3B-41; DH-9; PH-3 **Ht:** 6'3" **Wt:** 205 **Born:** 3/9/75 **Age:** 27

Year Team	Lg Org	G	AB	H	2B	3B	HR	TB	R	RBI	TBB	IBB	SO	HBP	SH	SF	SB	CS	SB%	GDP	Avg	OBP	SLG
1993 Braves	R Atl	33	113	27	4	0	0	31	19	7	6	0	25	4	0	2	2	1	.67	1	.239	.296	.274
1994 Idaho Falls	R+ Atl	58	219	50	9	6	2	77	32	26	19	3	58	1	0	1	13	1	.93	3	.228	.292	.352
1995 Danville	R+ Atl	12	47	15	2	1	0	19	8	7	4	1	7	0	0	0	5	1	.83	1	.319	.365	.404
Eugene	A- Atl	57	216	58	9	1	9	96	40	32	23	1	51	3	0	2	14	4	.78	2	.269	.344	.444
1996 Macon	A Atl	135	465	122	35	3	8	187	64	64	65	4	108	5	3	6	38	8	.83	4	.262	.355	.402
1997 Cedar Rapds	A Ana	134	497	135	26	5	17	222	103	77	69	6	92	8	0	3	37	13	.74	11	.272	.367	.447
1998 Charlotte	A+ Tex	4	13	4	2	0	0	6	1	3	3	0	5	0	0	0	1	0	1.00	1	.308	.438	.462
Tulsa	AA Tex	111	417	117	25	2	8	170	57	62	60	0	98	3	1	4	18	12	.60	11	.281	.372	.408
1999 Tulsa	AA Tex	5	19	5	2	0	0	7	3	0	1	0	2	0	0	0	0	0	—	0	.263	.300	.368
Jacksnville	AA Det	117	424	120	38	1	7	181	60	61	57	1	101	0	0	3	9	5	.64	5	.283	.370	.427
2000 Toledo	AAA Det	137	487	131	29	1	25	237	77	63	52	1	106	2	0	3	7	5	.58	9	.269	.340	.487
2001 Ottawa	AAA Mon	52	181	42	9	3	3	66	20	25	22	3	41	1	0	1	7	1	.88	2	.232	.317	.365
1998 Texas	AL	1	1	0	0	0	0	0	0	0	0	0	0	0	0	0	0	0	—	0	.000	.000	.000
9 Min. YEARS		855	3098	826	190	23	79	1299	484	427	381	20	694	30	4	26	151	51	.75	50	.267	.350	.419

Chris Saunders

Bats: Right **Throws:** Right **Pos:** 3B-97; DH-23; 1B-8; OF-2 **Ht:** 6'1" **Wt:** 203 **Born:** 7/19/70 **Age:** 31

Year Team	Lg Org	G	AB	H	2B	3B	HR	TB	R	RBI	TBB	IBB	SO	HBP	SH	SF	SB	CS	SB%	GDP	Avg	OBP	SLG
1992 Pittsfield	A- NYM	72	254	64	11	2	2	85	34	32	34	0	50	1	1	5	5	2	.71	5	.252	.337	.335
1993 St. Lucie	A+ NYM	123	456	115	14	4	4	149	45	64	40	4	89	1	1	4	6	7	.46	10	.252	.311	.327
1994 Binghamton	AA NYM	132	499	134	29	0	10	193	68	70	43	0	96	4	2	7	6	6	.50	12	.269	.327	.387

(Batting — continued)

Year Team	Lg Org	G	AB	H	2B	3B	HR	TB	R	RBI	TBB	IBB	SO	HBP	SH	SF	SB	CS	SB%	GDP	Avg	OBP	SLG
1995 Norfolk	AAA NYM	16	56	13	3	1	3	27	9	7	9	0	15	0	0	0	1	1	.50	1	.232	.338	.482
Binghamton	AA NYM	122	441	114	22	5	8	170	58	66	45	1	98	5	5	7	3	6	.33	7	.259	.329	.385
1996 Binghamton	AA NYM	141	510	152	27	3	17	236	82	105	73	3	88	8	2	11	5	4	.56	11	.298	.387	.463
1997 Binghamton	AA NYM	30	111	36	13	0	3	58	16	22	12	1	20	2	0	4	3	1	.75	2	.324	.388	.523
Norfolk	AAA NYM	68	173	43	9	0	0	52	24	24	37	2	37	2	2	1	2	2	.50	6	.249	.385	.301
1998 Ottawa	AAA Mon	131	478	131	26	2	9	188	58	58	46	1	98	7	0	5	1	1	.50	10	.274	.343	.393
1999 Chattanooga	AA Cin	58	216	68	13	1	7	104	31	35	34	1	42	0	0	5	0	1	.00	6	.315	.400	.481
2000 Chattanooga	AA Cin	61	200	70	15	1	9	114	30	37	28	1	53	3	0	2	1	6	.14	2	.350	.433	.570
Louisville	AAA Cin	26	69	12	1	1	0	15	6	2	3	0	12	2	1	1	0	0	—	2	.174	.227	.217
2001 Charlotte	AAA CWS	12	39	8	1	0	2	15	3	3	5	0	7	1	0	0	0	0	—	0	.205	.311	.385
Birmingham	AA CWS	118	442	130	33	0	10	193	74	68	60	1	85	8	0	7	4	1	.80	15	.294	.383	.437
10 Min. YEARS		1110	3944	1090	217	20	84	1599	538	593	469	15	790	44	14	59	37	38	.49	89	.276	.355	.405

Jamie Saylor

Bats: Left **Throws:** Right **Pos:** 2B-26; PH-19; SS-11; 3B-11; OF-5; DH-3; PR-2; C-1   **Ht:** 5'11" **Wt:** 185 **Born:** 9/11/74 **Age:** 27

Year Team	Lg Org	G	AB	H	2B	3B	HR	TB	R	RBI	TBB	IBB	SO	HBP	SH	SF	SB	CS	SB%	GDP	Avg	OBP	SLG
1993 Astros	R Hou	51	162	38	5	2	0	47	29	14	23	0	28	0	1	0	5	3	.63	1	.235	.330	.290
1994 Quad City	A Hou	92	321	84	16	2	2	110	57	22	28	2	65	7	7	1	14	5	.74	0	.262	.333	.343
1995 Kissimmee	A+ Hou	89	289	66	4	1	2	78	38	19	22	1	58	6	0	2	13	6	.68	5	.228	.295	.270
1996 Kissimmee	A+ Hou	59	181	37	3	3	1	49	17	6	10	0	43	0	3	2	8	6	.57	3	.204	.244	.271
Quad City	A Hou	23	58	7	1	0	0	8	8	5	3	0	13	2	2	2	4	2	.67	0	.121	.185	.138
1997 Quad City	A Hou	20	61	15	5	0	0	20	10	2	11	1	16	0	2	0	3	2	.60	3	.246	.361	.328
New Orleans	AAA Hou	2	0	0	0	0	0	0	0	0	0	0	0	0	0	0	0	0	—	0	—	—	—
Jackson	AA Hou	63	205	52	12	3	5	85	23	21	18	1	43	3	3	0	3	2	.60	1	.254	.323	.415
1998 New Orleans	AAA Hou	4	11	4	0	1	1	9	3	3	0	0	0	0	0	0	0	0	—	0	.364	.364	.818
Jackson	AA Hou	122	462	135	21	6	17	219	80	66	39	1	91	5	7	3	15	10	.60	4	.292	.352	.474
1999 New Orleans	AAA Hou	113	330	74	14	5	4	110	38	36	34	1	83	3	2	4	8	10	.44	6	.224	.299	.333
2000 New Orleans	AAA Hou	25	60	14	5	0	0	19	3	7	8	0	17	1	1	1	1	2	.33	2	.233	.329	.317
El Paso	AA Ari	90	286	61	12	10	1	96	50	28	44	2	71	6	2	2	14	2	.88	3	.213	.328	.336
2001 Calgary	AAA Fla	15	27	3	0	0	1	6	5	3	3	0	11	0	0	0	0	0	—	1	.111	.200	.222
Binghamton	AA NYM	56	156	35	6	1	4	55	18	21	16	0	42	2	2	2	2	4	.33	3	.224	.301	.353
9 Min. YEARS		824	2609	625	104	34	38	911	379	253	259	9	581	35	32	19	90	54	.63	32	.240	.315	.349

Gene Schall

Bats: Right **Throws:** Right **Pos:** 1B-54; DH-16; PH-3   **Ht:** 6'3" **Wt:** 201 **Born:** 6/5/70 **Age:** 32

Year Team	Lg Org	G	AB	H	2B	3B	HR	TB	R	RBI	TBB	IBB	SO	HBP	SH	SF	SB	CS	SB%	GDP	Avg	OBP	SLG
1991 Batavia	A- Phi	13	44	15	1	0	2	22	5	8	3	2	16	0	0	0	0	1	.00	1	.341	.383	.500
1992 Spartanburg	A Phi	77	276	74	13	1	8	113	44	41	29	0	52	3	2	2	2	2	.60	8	.268	.342	.409
Clearwater	A+ Phi	40	133	33	4	2	4	53	16	19	14	0	29	4	1	3	1	2	.33	2	.248	.331	.398
1993 Reading	AA Phi	82	285	93	12	4	15	158	51	60	24	0	56	10	0	3	2	1	.67	15	.326	.394	.554
Scranton-WB	AAA Phi	40	139	33	6	1	4	53	16	16	19	1	38	7	1	1	4	2	.67	2	.237	.355	.381
1994 Scranton-WB	AAA Phi	127	463	132	35	4	16	223	54	89	50	5	86	6	0	6	9	1	.90	11	.285	.358	.482
1995 Scranton-WB	AAA Phi	92	320	100	25	4	12	169	52	63	49	2	54	10	0	4	3	3	.50	14	.313	.415	.528
1996 Scranton-WB	AAA Phi	104	371	107	16	5	17	184	66	67	48	2	92	9	0	5	1	0	1.00	9	.288	.379	.496
1997 Nashville	AAA CWS	33	112	22	0	1	5	39	11	17	11	0	32	1	1	0	1	1	.50	1	.196	.274	.348
1998 Richmond	AAA Atl	100	340	102	22	0	22	190	60	73	37	3	80	9	0	6	1	3	.25	5	.300	.378	.559
1999 Richmond	AAA Atl	100	355	104	25	1	12	167	49	53	35	1	84	8	1	3	0	1	.00	7	.293	.367	.470
2000 Richmond	AAA Atl	124	430	123	25	1	21	213	72	80	49	1	94	18	0	3	0	5	.00	21	.286	.380	.495
2001 Scranton-WB	AAA Phi	73	263	74	20	1	14	138	40	54	31	2	57	7	0	2	0	0	—	11	.281	.370	.525
1995 Philadelphia	NL	24	65	15	2	0	0	17	2	5	6	1	16	1	0	0	0	0	—	1	.231	.306	.262
1996 Philadelphia	NL	28	66	18	5	1	2	31	7	10	12	0	15	1	0	0	0	0	—	2	.273	.392	.470
11 Min. YEARS		1005	3531	1012	204	25	152	1722	536	640	399	19	770	92	6	38	25	22	.53	107	.287	.370	.488
2 Maj. YEARS		52	131	33	7	1	2	48	9	15	18	1	31	2	0	0	0	0	—	3	.252	.351	.366

Aaron Scheffer

Pitches: Right **Bats:** Left **Pos:** RP-27   **Ht:** 6'2" **Wt:** 165 **Born:** 10/15/75 **Age:** 26

Year Team	Lg Org	G	GS	CG	GF	IP	BFP	H	R	ER	HR	SH	SF	HB	TBB	IBB	SO	WP	Bk	W	L	Pct.	ShO	Sv	ERA
1994 Bellingham	A- Sea	2	0	0	0	3	16	4	4	2	0	0	1	0	3	0	5	0	0	0	0	—	0	0	6.00
Mariners	R Sea	24	0	0	20	32.1	127	18	11	7	1	1	1	2	10	0	26	4	1	2	2	.500	0	6	1.95
1995 Wisconsin	A Sea	9	0	0	6	13.2	65	17	14	10	2	1	0	0	5	1	8	2	0	0	1	.000	0	0	6.59
Everett	A- Sea	24	0	0	9	43.1	185	44	23	18	4	1	0	2	16	1	38	2	1	2	5	.286	0	1	3.74
1996 Wisconsin	A Sea	45	1	0	28	67.2	292	55	35	28	5	2	2	3	34	4	89	16	5	8	1	.889	0	14	3.72
1997 Lancaster	A+ Sea	37	3	0	9	92.2	410	93	58	56	17	4	3	7	42	1	103	10	0	11	3	.786	0	4	5.44
1998 Lancaster	A+ Sea	25	0	0	19	43	189	46	19	15	0	2	1	1	12	3	65	5	0	2	2	.500	0	10	3.14
Orlando	AA Sea	19	0	0	11	32.2	132	23	8	8	3	2	0	0	13	0	33	1	1	1	0	1.000	0	5	2.20
1999 New Haven	AA Sea	10	0	0	4	17	79	19	9	7	3	1	0	1	8	0	24	1	0	2	0	1.000	0	3	3.71
Tacoma	AAA Sea	35	1	0	16	59.2	248	47	25	19	6	3	0	4	23	2	62	3	0	2	3	.400	0	9	2.87
2000 New Haven	AA Sea	29	0	0	22	38.2	173	33	15	15	4	5	3	4	19	5	53	5	0	2	2	.500	0	14	3.49
Tacoma	AAA Sea	21	0	0	6	32	141	26	22	18	5	6	5	1	15	1	21	2	0	1	6	.143	0	0	5.06
2001 Brevard Cty	A+ Fla	3	0	0	1	1	0	0	0	0	0	0	0	0	1	0	4	0	0	0	0	—	0	0	0.00
Portland	AA Fla	24	0	0	14	35.1	125	16	4	4	2	2	0	1	9	0	39	0	0	2	1	.667	0	1	1.02
1999 Seattle	AL	4	0	0	3	4.2	24	6	5	1	0	3	1	1	3	0	4	0	0	0	0	—	0	0	1.93
8 Min. YEARS		307	5	0	165	516	2199	442	247	207	52	30	16	26	210	18	570	51	8	35	26	.574	0	64	3.61

John Scheschuk

Bats: Left **Throws:** Left **Pos:** DH-66; 1B-49; PH-3   **Ht:** 6'2" **Wt:** 208 **Born:** 2/2/77 **Age:** 25

Year Team	Lg Org	G	AB	H	2B	3B	HR	TB	R	RBI	TBB	IBB	SO	HBP	SH	SF	SB	CS	SB%	GDP	Avg	OBP	SLG
1999 Fort Wayne	A SD	66	242	61	14	0	3	84	35	36	43	4	34	2	1	6	3	1	.75	4	.252	.362	.347
2000 Las Vegas	AAA SD	2	7	3	1	0	0	4	2	1	1	0	0	0	0	0	0	0	—	0	.429	.500	.571
Fort Wayne	A SD	131	461	129	25	0	8	178	72	85	80	5	51	6	0	5	6	1	.86	13	.280	.389	.386
2001 Lk Elsinore	A+ SD	96	346	98	28	2	7	151	48	46	55	1	60	1	1	2	3	3	.50	10	.283	.381	.436
Mobile	AA SD	21	83	15	4	0	1	22	8	9	5	0	14	2	0	0	1	0	1.00	1	.181	.244	.265
3 Min. YEARS		316	1139	306	72	2	19	439	165	177	184	10	159	11	2	13	13	5	.72	28	.269	.372	.385

Tony Schifano

Bats: Right **Throws:** Right **Pos:** 3B-36; DH-14; PH-12; 2B-10; SS-2; OF-2; PR-2; 1B-1   **Ht:** 6'1" **Wt:** 195 **Born:** 11/11/74 **Age:** 27

Year Team	Lg Org	G	AB	H	2B	3B	HR	TB	R	RBI	TBB	IBB	SO	HBP	SH	SF	SB	CS	SB%	GDP	Avg	OBP	SLG
1997 Brevard Cty	A+ Fla	1	1	0	0	0	0	0	0	0	0	0	1	0	0	0	0	0	—	0	.000	.000	.000
Utica	A- Fla	48	153	40	7	0	1	50	26	14	11	0	28	2	8	1	5	5	.50	3	.261	.317	.327
1998 Brevard Cty	A+ Fla	91	304	71	3	4	1	85	28	14	14	0	46	6	4	0	8	1	.89	9	.234	.281	.280
1999 Brevard Cty	A+ Fla	45	141	35	3	1	2	46	21	15	12	0	36	2	3	2	2	2	.50	1	.248	.312	.326
Portland	AA Fla	29	67	16	1	1	0	19	9	6	5	0	9	1	1	0	0	0	—	3	.239	.301	.284
Knoxville	AA Tor	27	92	25	4	1	0	31	12	15	3	0	15	1	1	1	5	3	.63	3	.272	.299	.337
2000 Tennessee	AA Tor	87	275	64	11	0	1	78	24	24	19	2	53	7	8	2	6	4	.60	4	.233	.297	.284
2001 New Orleans	AAA Hou	11	9	2	0	0	0	2	2	1	1	0	3	0	0	0	0	0	—	0	.222	.300	.222
Vero Beach	A+ LA	62	199	56	12	0	4	80	23	23	15	1	39	4	2	2	6	1	.86	5	.281	.341	.402
5 Min. YEARS		401	1241	309	41	7	9	391	145	112	80	3	230	23	27	8	32	16	.67	31	.249	.305	.315

Brian Schmack

Pitches: Right **Bats:** Right **Pos:** RP-40   **Ht:** 6'2" **Wt:** 195 **Born:** 12/7/73 **Age:** 28

Year Team	Lg Org	G	GS	CG	GF	IP	BFP	H	R	ER	HR	SH	SF	HB	TBB	IBB	SO	WP	Bk	W	L	Pct.	ShO	Sv	ERA
1995 Newark	IND —	7	4	0	2	30.1	135	40	21	18	3	5	0	2	10	0	16	1	0	2	1	.667	0	0	5.34
1996 Hickory	A CWS	43	0	0	25	62.1	264	61	24	16	4	9	0	4	16	5	56	3	1	6	4	.600	0	5	2.31
1997 Winston-Sal	A+ CWS	42	0	0	18	75.1	325	65	32	23	0	5	3	2	36	4	71	6	1	2	5	.286	0	6	2.75
1998 Winston-Sal	A+ CWS	42	0	0	34	61.1	256	48	23	15	3	5	0	9	17	0	52	2	1	5	5	.500	0	10	2.20
1999 Birmingham	AA CWS	43	0	0	26	63	270	60	31	24	3	2	1	8	18	0	56	6	0	4	4	.500	0	6	3.43
2000 Charlotte	AAA CWS	51	0	0	13	90.2	379	82	32	28	10	4	1	1	29	5	84	4	0	11	7	.611	0	1	2.78
2001 Oklahoma	AAA Tex	40	0	0	15	53	231	56	31	24	5	1	1	1	14	1	34	0	0	2	2	.500	0	1	4.08
7 Min. YEARS		268	4	0	133	436	1860	412	194	148	28	31	6	27	140	15	369	22	3	32	28	.533	0	29	3.06

Brent Schoening

Pitches: Right **Bats:** Right **Pos:** SP-22; RP-7   **Ht:** 6'1" **Wt:** 195 **Born:** 4/7/78 **Age:** 24

Year Team	Lg Org	G	GS	CG	GF	IP	BFP	H	R	ER	HR	SH	SF	HB	TBB	IBB	SO	WP	Bk	W	L	Pct.	ShO	Sv	ERA
1999 Quad City	A Min	6	1	0	1	11	45	7	3	3	1	0	0	0	5	0	11	1	1	0	1	.000	0	1	2.45
2000 Twins	R Min	2	2	0	0	7	25	2	1	1	1	0	0	0	3	0	8	0	0	0	0	—	0	0	1.29
Fort Myers	A+ Min	12	12	0	0	70	295	61	27	25	3	2	4	4	27	2	57	4	0	6	4	.600	0	0	3.21
2001 New Britain	AA Min	12	6	0	3	45.2	195	48	25	24	6	1	1	1	16	1	37	2	0	2	6	.250	0	0	4.73
Fort Myers	A+ Min	17	16	0	0	86.2	373	97	54	47	5	0	3	5	32	0	69	3	1	5	9	.357	0	0	4.88
3 Min. YEARS		49	37	0	4	220.1	933	215	110	100	16	3	8	10	83	3	182	10	2	13	20	.394	0	1	4.08

Tony Schrager

Bats: Right **Throws:** Right **Pos:** 2B-92; SS-12; 3B-5; PH-3; DH-2; PR-2; 1B-1   **Ht:** 6'1" **Wt:** 185 **Born:** 6/14/77 **Age:** 25

Year Team	Lg Org	G	AB	H	2B	3B	HR	TB	R	RBI	TBB	IBB	SO	HBP	SH	SF	SB	CS	SB%	GDP	Avg	OBP	SLG
1998 Williamsprt	A- ChC	8	26	5	0	0	0	5	4	3	5	0	9	0	0	0	3	1	.75	0	.192	.323	.192
Rockford	A ChC	50	167	42	12	1	6	74	38	19	43	1	32	3	3	2	3	2	.60	4	.251	.409	.443
1999 Lansing	A ChC	122	392	106	31	4	16	193	83	73	103	2	101	5	1	8	8	3	.73	8	.270	.421	.492
2000 Daytona	A+ ChC	116	378	87	19	3	9	139	48	49	56	0	83	4	3	3	7	3	.70	2	.230	.333	.368
2001 West Tenn	AA ChC	26	78	19	4	0	1	26	9	10	7	0	16	1	0	0	0	0	—	1	.244	.314	.333
Daytona	A+ ChC	89	299	94	22	2	14	162	55	56	54	1	49	5	0	4	10	6	.63	5	.314	.423	.542
4 Min. YEARS		411	1340	353	88	10	46	599	237	210	268	4	290	18	7	17	31	15	.67	20	.263	.389	.447

Steve Schrenk

Pitches: Right **Bats:** Right **Pos:** RP-46   **Ht:** 6'3" **Wt:** 215 **Born:** 11/20/68 **Age:** 33

Year Team	Lg Org	G	GS	CG	GF	IP	BFP	H	R	ER	HR	SH	SF	HB	TBB	IBB	SO	WP	Bk	W	L	Pct.	ShO	Sv	ERA
1987 White Sox	R CWS	8	6	1	0	28.1	115	23	10	3	0	3	0	2	12	0	19	2	1	1	2	.333	1	0	0.95
1988 South Bend	A CWS	21	18	1	1	90	417	95	63	50	4	0	3	13	37	0	58	7	2	3	7	.300	0	0	5.00
1989 South Bend	A CWS	16	16	1	0	79	353	71	44	38	6	2	0	8	44	1	49	9	0	5	2	.714	1	0	4.33
1990 South Bend	A CWS	20	14	2	2	103.2	419	79	44	34	7	3	3	11	25	0	92	7	1	7	6	.538	1	0	2.95
1991 White Sox	R CWS	11	7	0	2	37	144	30	20	12	0	1	0	5	6	0	39	1	0	1	3	.250	0	0	2.92
1992 Sarasota	A+ CWS	25	22	4	2	154	621	130	48	35	1	4	6	7	40	2	113	7	6	15	2	.882	2	1	2.05
Birmingham	AA CWS	2	2	0	0	12.1	59	13	5	5	0	0	1	1	11	0	9	1	0	1	1	.500	0	0	3.65
1993 Birmingham	AA CWS	8	8	2	0	61.2	224	31	11	8	2	1	1	1	7	0	51	3	0	5	1	.833	1	0	1.17
Nashville	AAA CWS	21	20	0	0	122.1	526	117	61	53	11	5	2	3	47	3	78	6	3	6	8	.429	0	0	3.90
1994 Nashville	AAA CWS	29	28	2	0	178.2	769	175	82	69	15	10	4	6	69	3	134	14	1	14	6	.700	1	0	3.48
1995 White Sox	R CWS	2	2	0	0	7	27	5	2	0	0	0	0	0	0	0	6	0	0	0	1	.000	0	0	0.00
1996 Nashville	AAA CWS	16	15	1	1	95.2	395	93	54	47	12	3	1	3	29	2	58	3	0	4	10	.286	0	0	4.42
1997 Rochester	AAA Bal	25	24	1	0	125.2	539	127	73	65	21	2	1	6	36	0	99	3	2	4	7	.364	0	0	4.66

Year Team	Lg Org	G	GS	CG	GF	IP	BFP	H	R	ER	HR	SH	SF	HB	TBB	IBB	SO	WP	Bk	W	L	Pct.	ShO	Sv	ERA
1998 Pawtucket	AAA Bos	34	0	0	6	60.2	265	60	27	19	8	4	2	2	23	1	45	6	0	8	3	.727	0	1	2.82
1999 Scranton-WB	AAA Phi	32	0	0	13	43	185	38	17	14	2	3	2	0	21	6	34	2	0	3	1	.750	0	2	2.93
2000 Scranton-WB	AAA Phi	26	0	0	15	34.1	126	18	5	5	2	2	1	2	5	2	27	0	0	2	1	.667	0	3	1.31
2001 Sacramento	AAA Oak	16	0	0	10	21.2	91	21	9	6	1	0	1	1	6	1	22	0	0	2	1	.667	0	3	2.49
Charlotte	AAA CWS	30	0	0	14	39	166	38	13	13	4	1	2	1	13	2	43	1	0	5	3	.625	0	2	3.00
1999 Philadelphia	NL	32	2	0	8	50.1	209	41	24	24	6	3	1	7	14	4	36	2	0	1	3	.250	0	1	4.29
2000 Philadelphia	NL	20	0	0	6	23.1	109	25	20	19	3	1	1	1	13	0	19	0	0	2	3	.400	0	0	7.33
15 Min. YEARS		342	182	15	66	1294	5441	1164	588	476	96	44	30	72	431	23	976	72	16	86	65	.570	7	12	3.31
2 Maj. YEARS		52	2	0	14	73.2	318	66	44	43	9	4	2	8	27	4	55	2	0	3	6	.333	0	1	5.25

Shawn Schumacher

Bats: Left **Throws:** Right **Pos:** C-72; DH-29; PH-10　　　　**Ht:** 6'1" **Wt:** 200 **Born:** 8/18/76 **Age:** 25

		BATTING														BASERUNNING				PERCENTAGES		
Year Team	Lg Org	G	AB	H	2B	3B	HR	TB	R	RBI	TBB	IBB	SO	HBP	SH	SF	SB	CS	SB%	GDP	Avg	OBP	SLG
1999 New Jersey	A- StL	47	154	35	6	0	3	50	14	23	11	0	8	4	0	3	2	3	.40	9	.227	.291	.325
2000 Peoria	A StL	13	46	13	5	0	0	18	5	5	2	0	6	0	0	0	0	0	—	0	.283	.313	.391
2001 Potomac	A+ StL	68	249	71	8	1	2	87	15	38	13	1	20	6	2	4	2	1	.67	8	.285	.331	.349
New Haven	AA StL	41	122	26	5	0	1	34	7	10	3	1	10	1	3	0	3	1	.75	6	.213	.238	.279
3 Min. YEARS		169	571	145	24	1	6	189	41	76	29	2	44	11	5	7	7	5	.58	23	.254	.299	.331

Tim Scott

Pitches: Right **Bats:** Right **Pos:** RP-41　　　　**Ht:** 6'2" **Wt:** 205 **Born:** 11/16/66 **Age:** 35

		HOW MUCH HE PITCHED						WHAT HE GAVE UP												THE RESULTS				
Year Team	Lg Org	G	GS	CG	GF	IP	BFP	H	R	ER	HR	SH	SF	HB	TBB	IBB	SO	WP	Bk	W	L	Pct.	ShO	Sv	ERA
1984 Great Falls	R+ LA	13	13	3	0	78	0	90	58	38	4	0	0	2	38	1	44	5	2	5	4	.556	2	0	4.38
1985 Bakersfield	A+ LA	12	10	2	1	63.2	0	84	46	41	4	0	0	1	34	0	31	2	4	3	4	.429	0	0	5.80
1986 Vero Beach	A+ LA	20	13	3	2	95.1	418	113	44	36	2	4	9	2	34	2	37	5	5	5	4	.556	1	0	3.40
1987 San Antonio	AA LA	2	2	0	0	5.1	33	14	10	10	2	0	0	1	2	0	6	1	0	0	1	.000	0	0	16.88
Bakersfield	A+ LA	7	5	1	1	32.1	137	33	19	16	2	0	1	1	10	1	29	2	0	2	3	.400	0	0	4.45
1988 Bakersfield	A+ LA	36	2	0	25	64.1	272	52	34	26	3	4	4	2	26	5	59	2	0	4	7	.364	0	7	3.64
1989 San Antonio	AA LA	48	0	0	28	68	308	71	30	28	3	5	3	0	36	5	64	1	4	4	2	.667	0	4	3.71
1990 Albuquerque	AAA LA	17	0	0	8	15	73	14	9	7	1	0	0	0	14	2	15	0	0	2	1	.667	0	3	4.20
San Antonio	AA LA	30	0	0	20	47.1	186	35	17	15	5	0	1	1	14	0	52	0	0	3	3	.500	0	7	2.85
1991 Las Vegas	AAA SD	41	11	0	9	111	497	133	78	64	8	5	2	1	39	8	74	1	0	8	8	.500	0	1	5.19
1992 Las Vegas	AAA SD	24	0	0	23	28	106	20	8	7	1	1	1	3	3	0	28	2	0	1	2	.333	0	15	2.25
1997 Colo Sprngs	AAA Col	12	0	0	9	14.2	52	7	2	2	1	1	1	0	3	0	18	1	1	0	0	—	0	3	1.23
1998 San Berndno	A+ LA	2	2	0	0	4	15	4	2	2	1	0	0	0	1	0	2	0	0	1	0	1.000	0	0	4.50
1999 San Antonio	IND —	17	0	0	17	19	65	11	3	3	1	2	0	0	3	0	23	0	0	1	3	.250	0	9	1.59
Nashville	AAA Pit	19	0	0	7	23	105	29	14	13	3	0	0	2	7	1	21	0	0	1	3	.250	0	5	5.09
2000 Solano	IND —	23	0	0	21	27	104	19	6	5	2	1	2	0	5	0	35	1	0	0	0	—	0	8	1.67
Louisville	AAA Cin	16	0	0	2	26	113	26	13	8	1	2	0	1	9	0	25	0	0	0	1	.000	0	0	2.77
2001 Sonoma Cty	IND —	27	0	0	25	29.2	116	20	4	3	1	1	1	2	3	0	44	0	0	3	0	1.000	0	15	0.91
Columbus	AAA NYY	14	0	0	5	23.1	102	24	14	13	3	0	1	0	6	1	28	0	0	2	3	.400	0	0	5.01
1991 San Diego	NL	2	0	0	0	1	5	2	2	1	0	0	0	0	0	0	1	0	0	0	0	—	0	0	9.00
1992 San Diego	NL	34	0	0	16	37.2	173	39	24	22	4	4	1	1	21	6	30	0	1	4	1	.800	0	0	5.26
1993 San Diego	NL	24	0	0	2	37.2	169	38	13	10	1	2	2	4	15	0	30	1	1	2	0	1.000	0	0	2.39
Montreal	NL	32	0	0	16	34	148	31	15	14	3	1	0	0	19	2	35	1	0	5	2	.714	0	1	3.71
1994 Montreal	NL	40	0	0	8	53.1	223	51	17	16	0	0	0	2	18	3	37	1	1	5	2	.714	0	1	2.70
1995 Montreal	NL	62	0	0	15	63.1	268	52	30	28	6	4	1	6	23	2	57	4	0	2	0	1.000	0	2	3.98
1996 Montreal	NL	45	0	0	14	46.1	198	41	18	16	3	1	2	2	21	2	37	1	0	3	5	.375	0	1	3.11
San Francisco	NL	20	0	0	2	19.2	90	24	18	18	5	3	1	1	9	0	10	2	0	2	2	.500	0	0	8.24
1997 San Diego	NL	14	0	0	2	18.1	87	25	17	16	2	0	1	3	5	0	14	0	0	1	1	.500	0	0	7.85
Colorado	NL	3	0	0	0	2	14	5	3	3	0	1	0	0	2	0	2	0	0	0	0	—	0	0	10.13
14 Min. YEARS		380	58	9	203	773	2702	799	411	337	48	26	26	19	281	26	635	23	16	44	48	.478	3	68	3.92
7 Maj. YEARS		276	0	0	75	314	1375	308	157	144	24	16	8	19	133	15	253	10	3	24	13	.649	0	5	4.13

Marcos Scutaro

Bats: Right **Throws:** Right **Pos:** 2B-122; 3B-5; SS-4; PH-3; PR-1　　　　**Ht:** 5'10" **Wt:** 170 **Born:** 10/30/75 **Age:** 26

		BATTING														BASERUNNING				PERCENTAGES		
Year Team	Lg Org	G	AB	H	2B	3B	HR	TB	R	RBI	TBB	IBB	SO	HBP	SH	SF	SB	CS	SB%	GDP	Avg	OBP	SLG
1996 Columbus	A Cle	85	315	79	12	3	10	127	66	45	38	0	86	4	4	5	6	3	.67	6	.251	.334	.403
1997 Buffalo	AAA Cle	21	57	15	3	0	1	21	8	6	6	0	8	0	1	1	0	1	.00	4	.263	.328	.368
Kinston	A+ Cle	97	378	103	17	6	10	162	58	59	35	0	72	9	2	3	23	7	.77	3	.272	.346	.429
1998 Buffalo	AAA Cle	8	26	6	3	0	0	9	3	4	0	0	2	1	0	0	0	0	—	0	.231	.231	.346
Akron	AA Cle	124	462	146	27	6	11	218	68	62	47	0	71	10	4	6	33	16	.67	8	.316	.387	.472
1999 Buffalo	AAA Cle	129	462	126	24	2	8	178	76	51	61	2	69	6	6	4	21	6	.78	5	.273	.362	.385
2000 Buffalo	AAA Cle	124	425	117	20	5	5	162	67	54	61	0	53	9	7	7	9	6	.60	8	.275	.373	.381
Indianapols	AAA Mil	4	13	7	1	1	1	13	5	3	1	0	2	0	0	0	1	0	1.00	1	.538	.571	1.000
2001 Indianapols	AAA Mil	132	495	146	29	3	11	214	87	50	62	2	83	10	5	3	11	11	.50	9	.295	.382	.432
6 Min. YEARS		724	2633	745	136	26	57	1104	438	334	311	4	446	48	30	29	104	50	.68	44	.283	.365	.419

Scott Seal

Bats: Left **Throws:** Left **Pos:** OF-78; PH-23; 1B-5; DH-3; PR-2　　　　**Ht:** 6'1" **Wt:** 205 **Born:** 8/16/75 **Age:** 26

		BATTING														BASERUNNING				PERCENTAGES		
Year Team	Lg Org	G	AB	H	2B	3B	HR	TB	R	RBI	TBB	IBB	SO	HBP	SH	SF	SB	CS	SB%	GDP	Avg	OBP	SLG
1997 Idaho Falls	R+ SD	30	120	43	8	3	3	66	18	30	22	1	24	1	0	1	0	3	.00	4	.358	.458	.550
Clinton	A SD	29	114	29	6	0	5	50	20	23	10	0	37	2	0	1	0	1	.67	3	.254	.323	.439
1998 Rancho Cuca	A+ SD	121	427	105	23	4	4	150	52	62	48	1	113	11	0	2	8	5	.62	9	.246	.336	.351
1999 Rancho Cuca	A+ SD	123	439	109	23	2	13	175	67	70	45	5	96	10	3	2	7	3	.70	13	.248	.331	.399
2000 Salem	A+ Col	103	344	92	31	3	6	147	55	35	23	0	75	9	0	1	10	5	.67	6	.267	.329	.427

Year Team	Lg Org	BATTING																BASERUNNING				PERCENTAGES		
		G	AB	H	2B	3B	HR	TB	R	RBI	TBB	IBB	SO	HBP	SH	SF	SB	CS	SB%	GDP	Avg	OBP	SLG
2001 Carolina	AA Col	70	186	38	7	1	4	59	24	26	33	2	34	4	4	3	2	2	.50	8	.204	.332	.317
Salem	A+ Col	34	94	17	4	0	2	27	9	9	8	2	20	2	2	0	1	1	.50	1	.181	.260	.287
5 Min. YEARS		510	1724	433	102	14	37	674	245	255	189	11	399	39	9	10	30	20	.60	44	.251	.337	.391

Todd Sears

Bats: Right **Throws:** Right **Pos:** 1B-107; PH-6; DH-4; 3B-1   **Ht:** 6'5" **Wt:** 215 **Born:** 10/23/75 **Age:** 26

Year Team	Lg Org	BATTING																BASERUNNING				PERCENTAGES		
		G	AB	H	2B	3B	HR	TB	R	RBI	TBB	IBB	SO	HBP	SH	SF	SB	CS	SB%	GDP	Avg	OBP	SLG
1997 Portland	A- Col	55	200	54	13	1	2	75	37	29	41	7	49	0	1	1	2	0	1.00	4	.270	.393	.375
1998 Asheville	A Col	130	459	133	26	2	11	196	71	82	72	1	89	5	1	6	10	4	.71	9	.290	.387	.427
1999 Salem	A+ Col	109	385	108	21	0	14	171	58	59	58	1	99	4	0	1	11	2	.85	9	.281	.379	.444
2000 Carolina	AA Col	86	299	90	21	0	12	147	54	72	72	1	76	2	0	5	12	3	.80	7	.301	.434	.492
New Britain	AA Min	40	140	44	8	1	3	63	15	15	18	1	40	1	0	0	1	0	1.00	1	.314	.396	.450
Salt Lake	AAA Min	3	11	4	1	0	1	8	2	4	1	0	2	0	0	0	0	0	—	1	.364	.417	.727
2001 Edmonton	AAA Min	118	408	127	25	2	13	195	61	50	41	2	71	3	1	3	2	1	.67	16	.311	.376	.478
5 Min. YEARS		541	1902	560	115	6	56	855	298	311	303	23	426	15	3	16	38	10	.79	51	.294	.393	.450

Jason Secoda

Pitches: Right **Bats:** Right **Pos:** SP-20; RP-14   **Ht:** 6'1" **Wt:** 195 **Born:** 9/2/74 **Age:** 27

Year Team	Lg Org	HOW MUCH HE PITCHED						WHAT HE GAVE UP												THE RESULTS					
		G	GS	CG	GF	IP	BFP	H	R	ER	HR	SH	SF	HB	TBB	IBB	SO	WP	Bk	W	L	Pct.	ShO	Sv	ERA
1995 Bristol	R+ CWS	13	12	0	0	65.2	307	78	57	39	3	1	3	1	33	0	63	8	1	2	8	.200	0	0	5.35
1996 South Bend	A CWS	32	22	0	6	133.2	605	132	84	59	9	2	3	3	75	0	94	18	1	6	12	.333	0	1	3.97
1997 Winston-Sal	A+ CWS	29	15	1	5	119.2	525	118	67	55	11	3	5	4	57	1	85	16	1	7	4	.636	0	2	4.14
1998 Winston-Sal	A+ CWS	6	0	0	4	11.1	43	8	2	2	0	1	0	0	2	1	8	1	0	2	0	1.000	0	0	1.59
Birmingham	AA CWS	39	0	0	20	65.1	307	78	50	46	6	2	4	2	39	2	45	7	1	2	3	.400	1	6	6.34
1999 Birmingham	AA CWS	22	17	1	0	115	477	100	49	44	7	2	4	8	39	0	94	8	1	8	7	.533	1	0	3.44
Charlotte	AAA CWS	7	7	3	0	44.1	201	54	35	26	10	0	1	3	10	0	33	4	0	2	5	.286	0	0	5.28
2000 Charlotte	AAA CWS	32	11	0	4	100.1	461	122	76	67	20	4	1	3	49	3	75	8	1	2	7	.222	0	0	6.01
2001 Charlotte	AAA CWS	34	20	1	4	139	628	168	90	80	17	7	8	2	56	1	105	11	1	3	9	.250	0	1	5.18
7 Min. YEARS		214	104	6	43	794.1	3554	858	510	418	83	22	29	26	360	8	602	81	7	34	55	.382	1	5	4.74

Reed Secrist

Bats: Left **Throws:** Right **Pos:** 3B-45; OF-24; C-23; 1B-19; PH-7; DH-2   **Ht:** 6'1" **Wt:** 205 **Born:** 5/7/70 **Age:** 32

Year Team	Lg Org	BATTING																BASERUNNING				PERCENTAGES		
		G	AB	H	2B	3B	HR	TB	R	RBI	TBB	IBB	SO	HBP	SH	SF	SB	CS	SB%	GDP	Avg	OBP	SLG
1992 Welland	A- Pit	42	117	25	6	0	1	34	16	13	19	0	36	2	2	1	4	3	.57	2	.214	.331	.291
1993 Augusta	A Pit	90	266	71	16	3	6	111	38	47	27	1	43	1	2	4	4	1	.80	10	.267	.332	.417
1994 Salem	A+ Pit	80	221	54	12	0	10	96	29	35	22	0	58	1	2	1	2	2	.50	4	.244	.314	.434
1995 Lynchburg	A+ Pit	112	380	107	18	3	19	188	60	75	54	7	88	3	1	4	3	4	.43	6	.282	.372	.495
1996 Calgary	AAA Pit	128	420	129	30	0	17	210	68	66	52	11	105	4	3	5	2	4	.33	8	.307	.385	.500
1997 Calgary	AAA Pit	40	121	32	7	3	5	60	19	18	14	0	32	0	1	0	1	0	1.00	3	.264	.341	.496
1998 Memphis	AAA StL	75	214	46	10	0	6	74	34	29	31	1	57	1	0	3	1	2	.33	3	.215	.313	.346
Knoxville	AA Tor	15	50	12	4	1	2	24	9	8	4	1	14	0	0	0	0	0	—	6	.240	.296	.480
1999 Altoona	AA Pit	36	95	16	5	0	0	21	9	10	13	1	23	1	1	1	0	0	—	6	.168	.273	.221
Nashville	AAA Pit	46	102	27	8	1	2	43	12	15	8	1	22	2	1	1	1	1	.50	1	.265	.327	.422
2000 Tulsa	AA Tex	42	133	43	10	1	3	64	19	20	13	2	28	4	0	1	3	0	1.00	3	.323	.397	.481
Oklahoma	AAA Tex	31	104	25	2	1	4	41	13	14	13	0	24	1	1	0	0	0	—	1	.240	.331	.394
2001 Altoona	AA Pit	4	14	1	0	0	0	1	0	1	1	0	6	0	0	0	0	0	—	1	.071	.133	.071
Nashville	AAA Pit	104	338	103	20	1	22	191	61	61	48	3	81	5	1	1	4	0	1.00	3	.305	.398	.565
10 Min. YEARS		845	2575	691	148	14	97	1158	387	412	319	28	617	25	15	22	24	18	.57	52	.268	.352	.450

Shawn Sedlacek

Pitches: Right **Bats:** Right **Pos:** SP-27; RP-1   **Ht:** 6'4" **Wt:** 200 **Born:** 6/29/77 **Age:** 25

Year Team	Lg Org	HOW MUCH HE PITCHED						WHAT HE GAVE UP												THE RESULTS					
		G	GS	CG	GF	IP	BFP	H	R	ER	HR	SH	SF	HB	TBB	IBB	SO	WP	Bk	W	L	Pct.	ShO	Sv	ERA
1998 Spokane	A- KC	16	13	0	0	86	371	89	43	33	2	1	4	6	18	0	62	4	5	9	2	.818	0	0	3.45
1999 Wilmington	A+ KC	17	17	1	0	92	411	111	61	54	7	6	3	6	26	0	69	4	0	4	6	.400	0	0	5.28
2000 Wichita	AA KC	35	16	1	11	140.1	612	153	69	57	10	5	2	12	43	4	81	8	2	15	6	.714	0	3	3.66
2001 Omaha	AAA KC	14	13	0	0	81	348	98	49	45	13	4	2	3	22	2	44	3	1	5	4	.556	0	0	5.00
Wichita	AA KC	14	14	1	0	86.2	360	85	37	35	7	1	2	8	14	1	66	3	0	6	7	.462	1	0	3.63
4 Min. YEARS		96	73	3	12	486	2102	536	259	224	39	17	13	35	123	7	322	22	8	39	25	.609	1	3	4.15

Ryan Seifert

Pitches: Right **Bats:** Right **Pos:** RP-21; SP-12   **Ht:** 6'5" **Wt:** 215 **Born:** 8/14/75 **Age:** 26

Year Team	Lg Org	HOW MUCH HE PITCHED						WHAT HE GAVE UP												THE RESULTS					
		G	GS	CG	GF	IP	BFP	H	R	ER	HR	SH	SF	HB	TBB	IBB	SO	WP	Bk	W	L	Pct.	ShO	Sv	ERA
1997 Portland	A- Col	16	15	0	0	74.1	337	89	49	40	8	0	4	4	31	0	52	3	0	1	7	.125	0	0	4.84
1998 Asheville	A Col	36	0	0	19	87.1	363	66	44	40	8	12	4	6	37	0	90	1	0	7	6	.538	0	5	4.12
1999 Colo Sprngs	AAA Col	1	1	0	0	4	18	4	2	2	1	0	0	0	2	0	2	0	0			—	0	0	4.50
Salem	A+ Col	24	0	0	5	46.1	196	40	24	18	0	2	3	3	21	0	51	0	0	3	5	.375	0	0	3.50
2000 Carolina	AA Col	32	9	0	0	97.2	422	97	49	44	6	1	6	4	37	1	95	3	0	3	6	.333	0	0	4.05
2001 Carolina	AA Col	33	12	1	9	103.1	433	103	42	36	10	4	4	3	28	0	88	2	0	4	6	.400	1	1	3.14
5 Min. YEARS		142	37	1	41	413	1769	399	210	180	33	19	20	20	156	1	378	9	0	18	30	.375	1	6	3.92

Jason Sekany

Pitches: Right **Bats:** Right **Pos:** RP-13; SP-9   **Ht:** 6'4" **Wt:** 214 **Born:** 7/20/75 **Age:** 26

Year Team	Lg Org	G	GS	CG	GF	IP	BFP	H	R	ER	HR	SH	SF	HB	TBB	IBB	SO	WP	Bk	W	L	Pct.	ShO	Sv	ERA
1996 Red Sox	R Bos	5	2	0	2	11.2	50	14	3	3	1	0	0	1	3	0	16	2	0	0	1	—	0	1	2.31
1997 Michigan	A Bos	16	16	3	0	106	448	92	55	48	5	2	4	4	41	1	103	14	0	5	6	.455	0	0	4.08
Sarasota	A+ Bos	10	9	0	1	64.2	290	56	43	40	8	2	2	2	41	0	32	3	2	4	4	.500	0	0	5.57
1998 Trenton	AA Bos	28	28	1	0	148.2	643	151	101	86	21	4	5	5	57	0	113	14	0	10	10	.500	0	0	5.21
1999 Pawtucket	AAA Bos	1	1	0	0	5.2	27	7	4	3	2	0	0	0	4	0	1	0	0	0	1	.000	0	0	4.76
Trenton	AA Bos	27	22	3	1	161.1	674	143	65	60	8	3	4	6	64	0	116	10	1	14	4	.778	2	0	3.35
2000 Pawtucket	AAA Bos	17	7	1	2	52.2	229	59	34	32	8	0	5	2	16	2	29	4	0	3	3	.500	0	0	5.47
Chattanooga	AA Cin	10	9	0	1	43.1	200	49	36	34	8	3	1	1	28	1	28	5	0	1	6	.143	0	0	7.06
2001 Pawtucket	AAA Bos	7	2	0	2	15.2	76	22	16	15	4	1	0	1	7	0	8	0	2	0	3	.000	0	0	8.62
Trenton	AA Bos	15	7	0	3	56.1	247	71	40	38	10	2	4	0	19	1	41	0	1	1	5	.167	0	0	6.07
6 Min. YEARS		136	103	8	12	666	2884	664	397	359	75	17	25	22	280	5	487	52	6	38	42	.475	2	1	4.85

Chip Sell

Bats: Left **Throws:** Right **Pos:** OF-78; 1B-35; PH-22; DH-2; 3B-1; PR-1   **Ht:** 6'2" **Wt:** 205 **Born:** 6/19/71 **Age:** 31

Year Team	Lg Org	G	AB	H	2B	3B	HR	TB	R	RBI	TBB	IBB	SO	HBP	SH	SF	SB	CS	SB%	GDP	Avg	OBP	SLG
1994 Yakima	A- LA	54	172	52	12	3	3	79	29	21	16	1	37	0	1	0	12	3	.80	6	.302	.362	.459
1995 Vero Beach	A+ LA	80	222	60	6	1	1	71	21	23	18	0	33	4	2	2	1	3	.25	5	.270	.333	.320
1996 San Berndno	A+ LA	95	321	90	12	0	1	105	47	23	27	2	68	5	3	1	13	5	.72	6	.280	.345	.327
1997 Vero Beach	A+ LA	111	342	97	21	7	7	153	50	46	29	2	67	4	2	3	25	8	.76	4	.284	.344	.447
1998 Albuquerque	AAA LA	37	136	43	2	2	0	49	22	10	11	0	23	0	1	1	9	6	.60	1	.316	.365	.360
San Antonio	AA LA	64	218	55	12	6	3	88	36	37	22	1	40	3	3	4	6	0	1.00	6	.252	.324	.404
1999 El Paso	AA Ari	92	329	101	16	1	8	143	50	35	20	0	66	3	0	1	19	6	.76	5	.307	.348	.435
Tucson	AAA Ari	30	84	30	5	2	1	42	12	18	3	0	14	3	2	0	4	3	.57	2	.357	.400	.500
2000 Tucson	AAA Ari	112	405	132	23	7	4	181	65	54	28	2	71	8	5	2	8	6	.57	1	.326	.379	.447
2001 El Paso	AA Ari	17	62	12	5	0	0	17	8	11	2	0	15	0	0	1	0	0	—	2	.194	.215	.274
Tucson	AAA Ari	94	248	65	10	2	6	97	34	28	12	3	49	2	3	2	3	2	.60	6	.262	.299	.391
Indianapols	AAA Mil	17	56	18	4	1	0	24	4	5	4	1	14	1	0	2	3	0	1.00	1	.321	.365	.429
8 Min. YEARS		803	2595	755	128	32	34	1049	378	311	192	12	497	33	22	22	103	42	.71	43	.291	.345	.404

Jae Weong Seo

Pitches: Right **Bats:** Right **Pos:** SP-24; RP-3   **Ht:** 6'1" **Wt:** 215 **Born:** 5/24/77 **Age:** 25

Year Team	Lg Org	G	GS	CG	GF	IP	BFP	H	R	ER	HR	SH	SF	HB	TBB	IBB	SO	WP	Bk	W	L	Pct.	ShO	Sv	ERA
1998 Mets	R NYM	2	0	0	0	5	17	4	0	0	0	0	0	0	0	0	5	0	0	0	0	—	0	0	0.00
St. Lucie	A+ NYM	8	7	0	0	35	141	26	13	9	2	2	0	3	10	0	37	1	6	3	1	.750	0	0	2.31
1999 St. Lucie	A+ NYM	3	3	0	0	14.2	55	8	3	3	0	0	1	0	2	0	14	0	0	2	0	1.000	0	0	1.84
2001 St. Lucie	A+ NYM	6	5	0	0	25.1	104	21	11	10	2	0	1	1	6	0	19	0	0	2	3	.400	0	0	3.55
Binghamton	AA NYM	12	10	0	1	60.1	235	44	14	13	3	3	1	6	11	1	47	0	0	5	1	.833	0	0	1.94
Norfolk	AAA NYM	9	9	0	0	47.1	191	53	18	18	4	4	0	2	6	1	25	0	1	2	2	.500	0	0	3.42
3 Min. YEARS		40	34	0	1	187.2	743	156	59	53	11	9	3	12	35	2	147	1	7	14	7	.667	0	0	2.54

Dan Serafini

Pitches: Left **Bats:** Both **Pos:** RP-41; SP-6   **Ht:** 6'1" **Wt:** 195 **Born:** 1/25/74 **Age:** 28

Year Team	Lg Org	G	GS	CG	GF	IP	BFP	H	R	ER	HR	SH	SF	HB	TBB	IBB	SO	WP	Bk	W	L	Pct.	ShO	Sv	ERA
1992 Twins	R Min	8	6	0	0	29.2	130	27	16	12	0	1	1	1	15	0	33	3	1	1	0	1.000	0	0	3.64
1993 Fort Wayne	A Min	27	27	1	0	140.2	606	117	72	57	5	2	2	6	83	0	147	12	2	10	8	.556	1	0	3.65
1994 Fort Myers	A+ Min	23	23	2	0	136.2	600	149	84	70	11	7	5	6	57	1	130	7	1	9	9	.500	1	0	4.61
1995 Hardware Cy	AA Min	27	27	1	0	162.2	692	155	74	61	7	3	4	12	72	0	123	3	4	12	9	.571	1	0	3.38
Salt Lake	AAA Min	1	0	0	1	4	17	4	3	3	2	0	0	0	1	0	4	0	0	0	0	—	0	1	6.75
1996 Salt Lake	AAA Min	25	23	1	1	130.2	588	164	84	81	20	5	6	2	58	1	109	9	2	7	7	.500	0	0	5.58
1997 Salt Lake	AAA Min	28	24	2	1	152	660	166	87	84	18	4	3	8	55	0	118	3	0	9	7	.563	0	0	4.97
1998 Salt Lake	AAA Min	9	8	0	1	53.1	233	56	29	22	4	0	0	3	21	0	39	4	0	2	4	.333	0	0	3.71
1999 Iowa	AAA ChC	2	2	0	0	13	56	12	6	4	1	1	0	0	5	0	11	0	0	0	0	—	0	0	2.77
2000 Las Vegas	AAA SD	26	4	0	1	51	255	74	44	39	6	3	4	6	23	1	45	4	0	2	4	.333	0	0	6.88
Nashville	AAA Pit	7	7	0	0	47	193	39	17	14	4	2	1	1	18	1	22	0	0	4	3	.571	0	0	2.68
2001 Fresno	AAA SF	7	0	0	2	11.1	59	17	14	13	2	1	2	1	9	1	9	0	0	1	1	.500	0	0	10.32
Norfolk	AAA NYM	31	2	0	0	49	210	48	18	18	3	1	2	4	16	3	38	1	0	5	2	.714	0	1	3.31
Indianapols	AAA Mil	9	4	0	0	22.2	102	30	17	15	2	1	0	2	9	0	18	2	0	2	2	.500	0	0	5.96
1996 Minnesota	AL	1	1	0	0	4.1	23	7	5	5	1	0	1	1	2	0	1	0	0	0	1	.000	0	0	10.38
1997 Minnesota	AL	6	4	1	1	26.1	111	27	11	10	1	1	0	1	11	0	15	1	0	2	1	.667	0	0	3.42
1998 Minnesota	AL	28	9	0	3	75	345	95	58	54	10	3	6	1	29	1	46	2	0	7	4	.636	0	0	6.48
1999 Chicago	NL	42	4	0	8	62.1	302	86	51	48	8	3	1	4	32	3	17	3	0	3	2	.600	0	0	6.93
2000 San Diego	NL	3	0	0	0	3	20	9	6	6	2	0	0	0	2	0	3	1	0	0	0	—	0	0	18.00
Pittsburgh	NL	11	11	0	0	62.1	280	70	35	34	9	8	2	1	26	1	32	2	0	2	5	.286	0	0	4.91
10 Min. YEARS		230	157	7	11	1003.2	4401	1058	565	493	85	31	30	52	435	8	846	48	10	64	56	.533	3	2	4.42
5 Maj. YEARS		91	29	1	13	233.1	1081	294	166	157	32	20	12	7	102	5	114	9	0	14	13	.519	0	0	6.06

Elio Serrano

Pitches: Right **Bats:** Right **Pos:** RP-46; SP-1   **Ht:** 6'3" **Wt:** 215 **Born:** 12/4/78 **Age:** 23

Year Team	Lg Org	G	GS	CG	GF	IP	BFP	H	R	ER	HR	SH	SF	HB	TBB	IBB	SO	WP	Bk	W	L	Pct.	ShO	Sv	ERA
1997 Martinsvlle	R+ Phi	21	0	0	8	41	187	46	34	27	10	2	1	2	16	0	40	3	1	1	5	.167	0	1	5.93
1998 Batavia	A- Phi	13	3	0	2	35.1	144	28	13	10	1	1	2	2	10	0	26	2	1	3	2	.600	0	1	2.55
1999 Batavia	A- Phi	19	3	0	2	39.1	176	38	22	18	3	0	2	3	20	1	29	2	0	0	4	.000	0	1	4.12
2000 Piedmont	A Phi	38	0	0	13	67.1	287	67	26	17	5	4	1	10	15	0	56	3	0	4	2	.667	0	5	2.27

269

Year Team	Lg Org	G	GS	CG	GF	IP	BFP	H	R	ER	HR	SH	SF	HB	TBB	IBB	SO	WP	Bk	W	L	Pct.	ShO	Sv	ERA
2001 Clearwater	A+ Phi	17	1	0	5	35.1	140	34	14	13	0	3	0	2	7	0	22	0	1	2	2	.500	0	1	3.31
Reading	AA Phi	30	0	0	14	37.1	146	22	12	12	3	3	1	1	9	2	30	2	0	1	1	.500	0	2	2.89
5 Min. YEARS		138	7	0	45	255.2	1080	235	121	97	22	13	7	20	77	3	203	12	3	11	16	.407	0	11	3.41

Jim Serrano

Pitches: Right **Bats:** Right **Pos:** RP-56   **Ht:** 5'10" **Wt:** 170 **Born:** 5/9/76 **Age:** 26

Year Team	Lg Org	G	GS	CG	GF	IP	BFP	H	R	ER	HR	SH	SF	HB	TBB	IBB	SO	WP	Bk	W	L	Pct.	ShO	Sv	ERA
1998 Vermont	A- Mon	7	0	0	7	7.2	28	3	1	1	0	0	0	0	1	0	12	1	0	0	0		0	5	1.17
Cape Fear	A Mon	15	0	0	8	24.2	116	22	11	10	2	1	2	1	15	0	29	5	0	2	0	1.000	0	3	3.65
1999 Jupiter	A+ Mon	44	1	0	24	93	365	59	25	22	4	2	5	7	27	4	118	8	0	8	5	.615	0	8	2.13
2000 Harrisburg	AA Mon	55	0	0	34	75	335	64	39	35	6	6	5	7	43	2	80	6	0	4	5	.444	0	16	4.20
2001 Harrisburg	AA Mon	47	0	0	42	53.2	216	30	20	13	4	2	3	0	24	4	73	0	0	6	3	.667	0	20	2.18
Ottawa	AAA Mon	9	0	0	5	8	42	11	5	4	0	0	0	1	6	0	11	1	0	0	1	.000	0	0	4.50
4 Min. YEARS		177	1	0	120	262	1102	189	101	85	16	11	15	16	116	10	323	21	0	20	14	.588	0	52	2.92

Scott Service

Pitches: Right **Bats:** Right **Pos:** RP-24   **Ht:** 6'6" **Wt:** 240 **Born:** 2/26/67 **Age:** 35

Year Team	Lg Org	G	GS	CG	GF	IP	BFP	H	R	ER	HR	SH	SF	HB	TBB	IBB	SO	WP	Bk	W	L	Pct.	ShO	Sv	ERA
1986 Spartanburg	A Phi	14	9	1	1	58.2	281	68	44	38	3	2	1	7	34	0	49	6	1	1	6	.143	0	0	5.83
Utica	A- Phi	10	10	2	0	70.2	299	65	30	21	1	3	2	5	18	0	43	5	1	5	4	.556	0	0	2.67
Clearwater	A+ Phi	4	4	1	0	25.1	105	20	10	9	2	1	0	0	15	0	19	1	1	1	2	.333	1	0	3.20
1987 Reading	AA Phi	5	4	0	0	19.2	95	22	19	17	5	0	0	0	16	1	12	1	0	0	3	.000	0	0	7.78
Clearwater	A+ Phi	21	21	5	0	137.2	557	127	46	38	8	2	3	4	32	0	73	1	1	13	4	.765	2	0	2.48
1988 Reading	AA Phi	10	9	1	1	56.2	240	52	25	18	4	1	1	0	22	2	39	1	6	3	4	.429	1	0	2.86
Maine	AAA Phi	19	18	1	0	110.1	470	109	51	45	10	6	6	2	31	3	87	0	2	8	8	.500	0	0	3.67
1989 Reading	AA Phi	23	10	1	9	85.2	349	71	36	31	8	1	3	8	23	0	82	3	0	6	6	.500	1	1	3.26
Scranton-WB	AAA Phi	23	0	0	15	33.1	148	27	8	8	2	4	0	2	23	6	23	0	0	3	1	.750	0	6	2.16
1990 Scranton-WB	AAA Phi	45	9	0	11	96.1	427	95	56	51	10	4	2	5	44	1	94	4	0	5	4	.556	0	2	4.76
1991 Indianapls	AAA Mon	18	17	3	1	121.1	477	83	42	40	7	2	3	6	39	0	91	5	1	6	7	.462	1	0	2.97
1992 Indianapls	AAA Cin	13	0	0	7	24.1	95	12	3	2	0	2	0	3	9	0	25	0	0	2	0	1.000	0	2	0.74
Nashville	AAA Cin	39	2	0	15	70.2	299	54	22	18	2	4	0	2	35	3	87	2	0	6	2	.750	0	4	2.29
1993 Indianapls	AAA Cin	21	1	0	13	30.1	133	25	16	15	5	3	1	0	17	3	28	1	0	4	2	.667	0	2	4.45
1994 Indianapls	AAA Cin	40	0	0	31	58.1	239	35	16	15	1	4	2	3	27	9	67	3	0	5	5	.500	0	13	2.31
1995 Indianapls	AAA Cin	36	0	0	32	41.1	175	33	13	10	4	2	1	3	15	2	48	1	0	4	1	.800	0	18	2.18
1996 Indianapls	AAA Cin	35	1	0	26	48	193	34	18	16	5	2	1	1	10	2	58	2	0	1	4	.200	0	15	3.00
1997 Indianapls	AAA Cin	33	0	0	28	34	148	30	15	14	5	4	0	2	12	1	53	2	0	3	2	.600	0	15	3.71
Omaha	AAA KC	16	0	0	14	14.2	57	9	0	0	0	0	0	0	4	0	16	0	0	0	0		0	9	0.00
2000 Sacramento	AAA Oak	33	0	0	31	41.2	166	27	8	6	1	1	0	0	11	4	50	5	1	6	2	.750	0	13	1.30
2001 Dayton	A Cin	4	0	0	3	5.2	21	2	0	0	0	0	0	0	0	0	6	0	0	0	0		0	2	0.00
Louisville	AAA Cin	20	0	0	11	24.2	106	22	13	13	6	1	1	3	10	1	27	1	0	2	0	1.000	0	5	4.74
1988 Philadelphia	NL	5	0	0	1	5.1	23	7	1	1	0	0	0	1	1	0	6	0	0	0	0		0	0	1.69
1992 Montreal	NL	5	0	0	0	7	41	15	11	11	1	0	0	0	5	0	11	0	0	0	0		0	0	14.14
1993 Colorado	NL	3	0	0	0	4.2	24	8	5	5	1	0	2	1	1	0	3	0	0	0	0		0	0	9.64
Cincinnati	NL	26	0	0	7	41.1	173	36	19	17	5	2	2	1	15	4	40	0	0	2	2	.500	0	2	3.70
1994 Cincinnati	NL	6	0	0	2	7.1	35	8	9	6	2	2	0	0	3	0	5	0	0	1	2	.333	0	0	7.36
1995 San Francisco	NL	28	0	0	6	31	129	18	11	11	4	3	2	2	20	4	30	3	0	3	1	.750	0	0	3.19
1996 Cincinnati	NL	34	1	0	5	48	213	51	21	21	7	4	1	6	18	4	46	5	0	1	0	1.000	0	0	3.94
1997 Cincinnati	NL	4	0	0	2	5.1	26	11	7	7	1	1	0	0	1	0	3	2	0	0	0		0	0	11.81
Kansas City	AL	12	0	0	1	17	69	17	9	9	1	1	1	0	5	0	19	0	0	0	3	.000	0	0	4.76
1998 Kansas City	AL	73	0	0	26	82.2	353	70	35	32	7	2	5	9	34	4	95	10	1	6	4	.600	0	4	3.48
1999 Kansas City	AL	68	0	0	29	75.1	352	87	51	51	13	4	7	3	42	8	68	3	0	5	5	.500	0	8	6.09
2000 Kansas City	AL	20	0	0	6	36.2	172	51	31	26	5	1	2	1	19	1	35	0	0	1	2	.333	0	1	6.38
14 Min. YEARS		482	115	15	249	1209.1	5080	1022	491	425	89	49	27	56	447	38	1077	44	14	84	67	.556	6	107	3.16
10 Maj. YEARS		284	1	0	85	361.2	1610	373	210	197	47	20	22	24	164	25	361	23	1	19	19	.500	0	15	4.90

Doug Sessions

Pitches: Right **Bats:** Right **Pos:** RP-32; SP-9   **Ht:** 6'1" **Wt:** 192 **Born:** 9/28/76 **Age:** 25

Year Team	Lg Org	G	GS	CG	GF	IP	BFP	H	R	ER	HR	SH	SF	HB	TBB	IBB	SO	WP	Bk	W	L	Pct.	ShO	Sv	ERA
1998 Auburn	A- Hou	26	0	0	24	31.1	125	22	10	8	2	2	1	0	10	0	41	0	1	1	0	1.000	0	14	2.30
1999 Michigan	A Hou	12	0	0	12	13	44	6	1	1	1	1	0	1	1	0	18	0	0	0	0		0	5	0.69
Kissimmee	A+ Hou	35	0	0	27	45.2	183	35	11	10	1	1	0	1	14	1	55	2	0	3	0	1.000	0	13	1.97
2000 Round Rock	AA Hou	56	0	0	34	82.1	351	78	35	31	7	5	2	1	37	4	80	1	0	6	4	.600	0	10	3.39
2001 Round Rock	AA Hou	41	9	0	4	103	433	98	53	50	13	3	6	3	33	0	78	0	0	6	4	.600	0	1	4.37
4 Min. YEARS		170	9	0	101	275.1	1136	239	110	100	24	12	9	6	95	5	272	3	1	16	8	.667	0	43	3.27

Ronni Severino

Pitches: Left **Bats:** Left **Pos:** RP-27; SP-11   **Ht:** 6'1" **Wt:** 199 **Born:** 8/6/75 **Age:** 26

Year Team	Lg Org	G	GS	CG	GF	IP	BFP	H	R	ER	HR	SH	SF	HB	TBB	IBB	SO	WP	Bk	W	L	Pct.	ShO	Sv	ERA
1996 Devil Rays	R TB	18	6	0	8	52	215	50	24	20	2	2	2	2	15	0	49	10	1	4	2	.667	0	1	3.46
1997 Princeton	R+ TB	14	14	0	0	65.1	292	71	39	23	3	0	1	1	28	0	57	6	2	4	4	.500	0	0	3.17
1998 Hudson Val	A- TB	22	5	0	1	52	223	47	29	24	2	1	5	2	24	0	61	12	2	3	2	.600	0	4	4.15
1999 Chston-SC	A TB	50	0	0	11	74.2	315	57	29	22	5	0	4	0	38	3	73	10	1	6	2	.750	0	4	2.65
2000 St. Pete	A+ TB	33	1	0	13	39.1	166	30	17	12	0	0	4	0	20	1	33	2	0	6	0	1.000	0	4	2.75
Orlando	AA TB	4	0	0	1	8.2	36	6	2	2	0	2	0	0	6	0	6	3	0	0	0		0	0	2.08
Durham	AAA TB	12	0	0	4	17	74	6	9	4	3	1	0	1	14	0	14	4	0	1	0	1.000	0	1	2.12
2001 Orlando	AA TB	38	11	0	9	90	419	116	58	50	12	1	5	2	47	0	63	12	1	3	8	.273	0	0	5.00
6 Min. YEARS		191	37	0	47	399	1740	383	205	157	27	7	23	9	192	4	356	59	7	27	18	.600	0	6	3.54

Chris Sexton

Bats: Right **Throws:** Right **Pos:** SS-93; 3B-7; 2B-4; DH-1; PH-1; PR-1   **Ht:** 5'11" **Wt:** 185 **Born:** 8/3/71 **Age:** 30

Year Team	Lg Org	G	AB	H	2B	3B	HR	TB	R	RBI	TBB	IBB	SO	HBP	SH	SF	SB	CS	SB%	GDP	Avg	OBP	SLG
1993 Billings	R+ Cin	72	273	91	14	4	4	125	63	46	35	1	27	1	0	8	13	4	.76	6	.333	.401	.458
1994 Chston-WV	A Cin	133	467	140	21	4	5	184	82	59	91	3	67	2	6	6	18	11	.62	9	.300	.412	.394
1995 Winston-Sal	A+ Cin	4	15	6	0	0	1	9	3	5	4	0	0	0	0	0	0	0	—	0	.400	.526	.600
Salem	A+ Cin	123	461	123	16	6	4	163	81	32	93	2	55	1	12	1	14	11	.56	11	.267	.390	.354
New Haven	AA Col	1	3	0	0	0	0	0	0	0	0	0	0	0	0	0	0	0	—	0	.000	.000	.000
1996 New Haven	AA Col	127	444	96	12	2	0	112	50	28	71	2	68	1	7	3	8	5	.62	10	.216	.324	.252
1997 New Haven	AA Col	98	360	107	22	4	1	140	65	38	62	0	37	2	11	4	8	16	.33	8	.297	.400	.389
Colo Sprngs	AAA Col	33	112	30	3	1	1	38	18	8	16	0	21	0	1	0	1	1	.50	4	.268	.359	.339
1998 Colo Sprngs	AAA Col	132	462	131	22	6	2	171	88	43	72	2	67	1	6	4	7	3	.70	17	.284	.378	.370
1999 Colo Sprngs	AAA Col	60	171	58	9	0	0	67	23	17	28	0	22	0	5	1	5	1	.83	7	.339	.430	.392
2000 Louisville	AAA Cin	99	389	126	19	1	7	168	79	50	63	0	45	0	1	2	8	4	.67	14	.324	.416	.432
2001 Louisville	AAA Cin	105	409	114	25	3	2	151	59	47	40	2	57	1	4	8	5	5	.50	13	.279	.338	.369
1999 Colorado	NL	35	59	14	0	1	1	19	9	7	11	1	10	0	0	0	4	2	.67	2	.237	.357	.322
2000 Cincinnati	NL	35	100	21	4	0	0	25	9	10	13	1	12	2	2	1	4	2	.67	5	.210	.310	.250
9 Min. YEARS		987	3566	1022	163	31	27	1328	611	373	575	12	466	9	53	37	87	61	.59	99	.287	.384	.372
2 Maj. YEARS		70	159	35	4	1	1	44	18	17	24	2	22	2	2	1	8	4	.67	7	.220	.328	.277

Jeff Sexton

Pitches: Right **Bats:** Right **Pos:** RP-31; SP-3   **Ht:** 6'2" **Wt:** 190 **Born:** 10/4/71 **Age:** 30

Year Team	Lg Org	G	GS	CG	GF	IP	BFP	H	R	ER	HR	SH	SF	HB	TBB	IBB	SO	WP	Bk	W	L	Pct.	ShO	Sv	ERA
1993 Watertown	A- Cle	17	1	1	9	33.2	145	35	15	10	1	1	0	1	10	3	30	3	0	1	1	.500	1	2	2.67
1994 Watertown	A- Cle	10	0	0	5	23	95	19	3	1	0	1	0	0	7	2	16	3	1	1	0	1.000	0	3	0.39
Columbus	A Cle	14	2	0	6	30	121	17	13	12	2	1	0	3	9	2	35	1	0	1	0	1.000	0	1	3.60
1995 Columbus	A Cle	14	13	2	0	82.1	318	66	27	20	2	1	1	3	16	0	71	0	1	6	2	.750	2	0	2.19
Kinston	A+ Cle	8	8	2	0	57	226	52	17	16	3	0	0	2	7	0	41	6	1	5	1	.833	1	0	2.53
1996 Canton-Akrn	AA Cle	9	9	0	0	49.1	210	45	29	28	6	2	0	2	23	1	34	1	0	2	4	.333	0	0	5.11
1997 Akron	AA Cle	16	3	0	5	47.1	215	55	27	25	4	4	4	5	15	1	38	1	2	2	0	1.000	0	1	4.75
Buffalo	AAA Cle	15	0	0	11	23.2	100	17	14	14	3	1	0	0	12	0	15	2	0	2	1	.667	0	0	5.32
1998 Akron	AA Cle	27	0	0	19	57.1	232	41	12	10	2	2	0	3	19	3	49	2	0	4	2	.667	0	11	1.57
Buffalo	AAA Cle	21	0	0	5	24.1	111	25	16	11	1	2	3	1	15	1	15	3	2	0	0	—	0	1	4.07
1999 Akron	AA Cle	15	0	0	11	20	89	24	10	8	1	2	5	1	9	0	16	1	0	1	0	1.000	0	2	3.60
Buffalo	AAA Cle	23	1	0	11	29	149	47	24	21	3	1	2	1	14	3	22	3	0	0	1	.000	0	1	6.52
2000 Carolina	AA Col	17	9	0	5	67.1	306	78	41	38	3	4	1	2	31	0	58	4	0	5	4	.556	0	1	5.08
Newark	IND —	19	0	0	11	20.2	95	23	16	15	4	0	0	0	11	0	20	3	0	1	1	.500	0	0	6.53
2001 Greenville	IND —	23	3	0	20	43.2	173	32	16	13	3	2	3	0	10	0	54	0	0	2	3	.400	0	6	2.68
Akron	AA Cle	11	0	0	4	17.2	78	22	7	4	1	0	0	0	5	0	14	1	0	0	1	.000	0	1	2.04
9 Min. YEARS		259	49	5	122	626.1	2663	598	287	246	39	24	19	24	213	16	528	35	6	33	21	.611	4	29	3.53

Adam Shabala

Bats: Left **Throws:** Right **Pos:** OF-84; DH-1; PR-1   **Ht:** 6'1" **Wt:** 190 **Born:** 2/6/78 **Age:** 24

Year Team	Lg Org	G	AB	H	2B	3B	HR	TB	R	RBI	TBB	IBB	SO	HBP	SH	SF	SB	CS	SB%	GDP	Avg	OBP	SLG
2000 Salem-Keizr	A- SF	59	176	38	6	3	4	62	27	19	30	0	60	2	0	1	2	1	.67	4	.216	.335	.352
2001 San Jose	A+ SF	3	7	1	0	0	0	1	1	0	2	0	4	0	0	0	0	0	—	0	.143	.333	.143
Shreveport	AA SF	12	35	12	0	0	1	15	9	4	7	0	10	0	1	0	2	0	1.00	0	.343	.452	.429
Hagerstown	A SF	70	256	80	16	2	1	103	37	29	37	0	37	6	5	0	11	4	.73	9	.313	.411	.402
2 Min. YEARS		144	474	131	22	5	6	181	74	52	76	0	111	8	6	1	15	5	.75	13	.276	.385	.382

Brian Shackelford

Bats: Left **Throws:** Left **Pos:** OF-96; PH-14; DH-6; 1B-1; P-1   **Ht:** 6'1" **Wt:** 190 **Born:** 8/30/76 **Age:** 25

Year Team	Lg Org	G	AB	H	2B	3B	HR	TB	R	RBI	TBB	IBB	SO	HBP	SH	SF	SB	CS	SB%	GDP	Avg	OBP	SLG
1998 Spokane	A- KC	70	266	78	21	1	10	131	35	55	35	1	52	3	4	3	3	1	.75	6	.293	.378	.492
1999 Chston-WV	A KC	73	260	52	14	2	10	100	25	30	26	0	80	1	1	1	1	1	.50	3	.200	.274	.385
2000 Wilmington	A+ KC	113	423	99	23	1	11	157	44	63	30	4	83	5	2	4	4	1	.80	10	.234	.290	.371
2001 Wichita	AA KC	110	366	95	18	3	20	179	62	72	33	3	79	6	4	6	4	4	.50	4	.260	.326	.489
4 Min. YEARS		366	1315	324	76	7	51	567	166	220	124	8	294	15	11	14	12	7	.63	23	.246	.315	.431

Jon Shave

Bats: Right **Throws:** Right **Pos:** SS-49; 2B-30; PH-5; 1B-3; DH-1   **Ht:** 6'0" **Wt:** 185 **Born:** 11/4/67 **Age:** 34

Year Team	Lg Org	G	AB	H	2B	3B	HR	TB	R	RBI	TBB	IBB	SO	HBP	SH	SF	SB	CS	SB%	GDP	Avg	OBP	SLG
1990 Butte	R+ Tex	64	250	88	9	3	2	109	41	42	25	0	27	3	2	4	21	7	.75	8	.352	.411	.436
1991 Gastonia	A Tex	55	213	62	11	0	2	79	29	24	20	0	26	1	3	0	11	9	.55	3	.291	.355	.371
Charlotte	A+ Tex	56	189	43	4	1	1	52	17	20	18	1	30	5	2	4	7	7	.50	3	.228	.306	.275
1992 Tulsa	AA Tex	118	453	130	23	5	2	169	57	36	37	1	59	4	7	5	6	7	.46	10	.287	.343	.373
1993 Okla City	AAA Tex	100	399	105	17	3	4	140	58	41	20	0	60	2	9	1	4	3	.57	12	.263	.301	.351
1994 Okla City	AAA Tex	95	332	73	15	2	1	95	29	31	14	1	61	5	12	5	6	2	.75	6	.220	.258	.286
1995 Okla City	AAA Tex	32	83	17	1	0	0	18	10	5	7	0	28	1	1	0	1	0	1.00	1	.205	.275	.217
1996 Okla City	AAA Tex	116	414	110	20	2	7	155	54	41	41	0	97	10	4	4	8	6	.57	7	.266	.343	.374
1997 Salt Lake	AAA Min	103	395	130	27	3	7	184	75	60	39	0	62	6	1	8	6	6	.50	9	.329	.391	.466
1998 Salt Lake	AAA Min	90	317	107	20	1	4	141	63	41	34	1	46	13	5	1	8	9	.47	7	.338	.422	.445
2000 Oklahoma	AAA Tex	131	510	148	21	5	10	209	85	54	40	3	65	17	3	3	12	5	.71	16	.290	.360	.410
2001 Pawtucket	AAA Bos	84	308	79	10	0	6	107	35	27	22	0	49	8	5	1	3	3	.50	6	.256	.322	.347
1993 Texas	AL	17	47	15	2	0	0	17	3	7	0	0	8	0	3	2	1	3	.25	0	.319	.306	.362
1998 Minnesota	AL	19	40	10	3	0	1	16	7	5	2	0	10	0	0	0	1	2	.33	0	.250	.302	.400

271

Year Team	Lg Org	G	AB	H	2B	3B	HR	TB	R	RBI	TBB	IBB	SO	HBP	SH	SF	SB	CS	SB%	GDP	Avg	OBP	SLG
1999 Texas	AL	43	73	21	4	0	0	25	10	9	5	0	17	2	3	0	1	0	1.00	0	.288	.350	.342
11 Min. YEARS		1044	3863	1092	178	25	46	1458	553	422	317	7	610	75	54	36	93	64	.59	88	.283	.346	.377
3 Maj. YEARS		79	160	46	9	0	1	58	20	21	8	0	35	2	6	2	3	5	.38	0	.288	.326	.363

Tom Shearn

Pitches: Right **Bats:** Right **Pos:** RP-35; SP-8 **Ht:** 6'4" **Wt:** 200 **Born:** 8/28/77 **Age:** 24

Year Team	Lg Org	G	GS	CG	GF	IP	BFP	H	R	ER	HR	SH	SF	HB	TBB	IBB	SO	WP	Bk	W	L	Pct.	ShO	Sv	ERA
1996 Astros	R Hou	17	3	0	3	41.2	162	34	13	8	2	1	2	2	10	0	43	3	1	5	2	.714	0	0	1.73
1997 Auburn	A- Hou	14	14	2	0	82.1	349	79	42	32	4	1	4	9	26	3	59	7	1	4	6	.400	2	0	3.50
1998 Quad City	A Hou	21	21	2	0	120	487	88	38	30	8	4	0	6	52	1	93	3	0	7	7	.500	1	0	2.25
1999 Kissimmee	A+ Hou	24	24	0	0	145.1	624	144	75	63	11	5	5	4	53	2	107	15	1	10	6	.625	0	0	3.90
2000 Round Rock	AA Hou	25	23	0	0	136.1	602	134	79	71	14	4	5	8	67	1	102	7	0	9	6	.600	0	0	4.69
2001 Round Rock	AA Hou	43	8	0	7	110	470	94	54	47	7	5	5	7	51	0	136	10	0	5	6	.455	0	1	3.85
6 Min. YEARS		144	93	4	10	635.2	2694	573	301	251	46	20	21	36	259	7	540	45	3	40	33	.548	3	1	3.55

Chris Sheff

Bats: Right **Throws:** Right **Pos:** OF-63; DH-25; PH-6; 1B-2; PR-1 **Ht:** 6'3" **Wt:** 215 **Born:** 2/4/71 **Age:** 31

Year Team	Lg Org	G	AB	H	2B	3B	HR	TB	R	RBI	TBB	IBB	SO	HBP	SH	SF	SB	CS	SB%	GDP	Avg	OBP	SLG
1992 Erie	A- Fla	57	193	46	8	2	3	67	29	16	32	1	47	1	1	1	15	2	.88	8	.238	.348	.347
1993 Kane County	A Fla	129	456	124	22	5	5	171	79	50	58	2	100	2	3	5	33	10	.77	11	.272	.353	.375
1994 Brevard Cty	A+ Fla	32	118	44	8	3	1	61	21	19	17	0	23	0	0	1	7	2	.78	2	.373	.449	.517
Portland	AA Fla	106	395	101	19	1	5	137	50	30	31	0	76	0	3	2	18	4	.82	13	.256	.308	.347
1995 Portland	AA Fla	131	471	130	25	7	12	205	85	91	72	6	84	5	1	8	23	6	.79	10	.276	.372	.435
1996 Portland	AA Fla	27	105	31	12	2	2	53	16	17	13	3	23	0	0	0	3	2	.60	3	.295	.373	.505
Charlotte	AAA Fla	92	284	75	15	1	12	128	41	49	21	1	55	0	0	1	7	1	.88	10	.264	.314	.451
1997 Charlotte	AAA Fla	120	322	82	23	1	11	140	54	43	43	1	76	1	2	3	16	4	.80	5	.255	.341	.435
1998 Edmonton	AAA Oak	120	402	120	24	4	10	182	74	55	67	0	82	5	0	1	17	5	.77	13	.299	.404	.453
1999 Vancouver	AAA Oak	118	421	121	24	1	15	192	62	70	45	1	87	1	3	3	9	6	.60	15	.287	.355	.456
2000 Norfolk	AAA NYM	114	340	88	18	1	7	129	46	43	45	1	73	6	0	0	9	4	.69	10	.259	.355	.379
2001 Louisville	AAA Cin	94	312	86	19	1	9	134	54	51	40	0	73	7	1	1	4	3	.57	7	.276	.369	.429
10 Min. YEARS		1140	3819	1048	217	29	92	1599	611	534	484	16	799	28	14	26	161	49	.77	107	.274	.358	.419

Anthony Shelby

Pitches: Left **Bats:** Left **Pos:** RP-19 **Ht:** 6'3" **Wt:** 230 **Born:** 12/11/73 **Age:** 28

Year Team	Lg Org	G	GS	CG	GF	IP	BFP	H	R	ER	HR	SH	SF	HB	TBB	IBB	SO	WP	Bk	W	L	Pct.	ShO	Sv	ERA
1993 Yankees	R NYY	10	10	1	0	54	223	46	25	16	0	1	0	3	22	0	48	2	3	4	1	.800	0	0	2.67
Oneonta	A- NYY	3	0	0	0	5.2	37	14	12	11	0	0	0	0	6	0	0	0	1	0	0	—	0	0	17.47
1994 Yankees	R NYY	8	8	0	0	42.1	177	33	19	5	1	2	0	0	16	0	51	1	1	3	1	.750	0	0	1.06
Oneonta	A- NYY	5	5	1	0	25.1	115	33	16	13	0	0	2	1	7	0	13	2	0	1	3	.250	0	0	4.62
1995 Greensboro	A NYY	27	13	0	3	89.2	381	87	54	40	5	2	4	6	28	0	81	6	0	3	8	.273	0	0	4.01
1996 Greensboro	A NYY	16	0	0	6	26	105	16	5	4	0	1	1	2	10	2	25	1	0	2	1	.667	0	1	1.38
Tampa	A+ NYY	24	0	0	8	30	124	26	12	6	1	1	1	1	7	1	18	1	0	2	2	.500	0	1	1.80
1997 Tampa	A+ NYY	48	0	0	11	69.1	285	68	23	20	4	4	4	0	16	5	57	3	1	4	3	.571	0	2	2.60
1998 Norwich	AA NYY	1	0	0	0	2	7	1	0	0	0	0	0	0	1	0	1	1	0	0	0	—	0	0	0.00
Columbus	AAA NYY	23	5	0	3	48	205	47	19	17	1	1	2	4	13	0	39	2	0	2	2	.500	0	0	3.19
2001 Orlando	AA TB	4	0	0	0	4.1	20	6	2	2	1	0	0	0	2	0	2	1	0	0	0	—	0	0	4.15
Nashua	IND —	4	0	0	1	4	25	10	5	5	1	0	0	0	4	0	4	0	0	0	0	—	0	0	11.25
Long Island	IND —	6	0	0	0	10.2	40	7	2	2	0	0	0	0	3	0	6	0	0	1	0	1.000	0	0	1.69
Atlantic Ct	IND —	5	0	0	1	7.1	25	3	1	1	1	0	0	0	2	0	8	0	0	0	0	—	0	0	1.23
7 Min. YEARS		184	41	2	33	418.2	1769	397	195	142	15	12	14	17	137	8	353	20	6	22	21	.512	0	4	3.05

Kevin Sheredy

Pitches: Right **Bats:** Right **Pos:** RP-48 **Ht:** 6'4" **Wt:** 210 **Born:** 1/3/75 **Age:** 27

Year Team	Lg Org	G	GS	CG	GF	IP	BFP	H	R	ER	HR	SH	SF	HB	TBB	IBB	SO	WP	Bk	W	L	Pct.	ShO	Sv	ERA
1996 New Jersey	A- StL	8	5	0	0	23	100	21	15	11	2	2	1	1	13	0	13	1	0	0	1	.000	0	0	4.30
1998 Peoria	A StL	13	13	0	0	68	304	75	38	30	6	6	4	4	24	0	39	13	0	4	4	.500	0	0	3.97
1999 Potomac	A+ StL	41	12	0	12	104	462	100	58	46	6	3	6	6	53	1	69	13	0	5	5	.500	0	0	3.98
2000 Arkansas	AA StL	21	0	0	4	26.2	154	42	45	42	7	1	1	6	29	0	12	5	2	0	2	.000	0	0	14.18
Potomac	A+ StL	30	1	0	15	40.1	193	46	25	23	2	1	2	5	26	1	24	2	0	2	5	.286	0	4	5.13
2001 New Haven	AA StL	48	0	0	12	64	267	46	29	21	6	5	2	2	34	3	58	6	0	0	7	.000	0	1	2.95
5 Min. YEARS		161	31	0	43	326	1480	330	210	173	29	18	16	24	179	5	215	40	2	11	24	.314	0	5	4.78

Jason Shiell

Pitches: Right **Bats:** Right **Pos:** RP-43; SP-2 **Ht:** 6'0" **Wt:** 180 **Born:** 10/19/76 **Age:** 25

Year Team	Lg Org	G	GS	CG	GF	IP	BFP	H	R	ER	HR	SH	SF	HB	TBB	IBB	SO	WP	Bk	W	L	Pct.	ShO	Sv	ERA
1995 Braves	R Atl	12	0	0	9	22.1	101	23	16	11	0	0	0	2	10	1	13	3	0	1	3	.250	0	2	4.43
1996 Danville	R+ Atl	12	12	0	0	59.1	231	44	14	13	1	0	1	1	19	0	57	3	0	3	1	.750	0	0	1.97
1997 Macon	A Atl	27	24	0	0	129	523	113	53	41	12	3	5	8	32	0	101	6	0	10	5	.667	0	0	2.86
1998 Macon	A Atl	4	3	0	0	8	32	7	4	4	2	0	0	0	1	0	4	1	0	0	1	.000	0	0	4.50
1999 Myrtle Bch	A+ Atl	26	17	0	1	114.2	485	118	51	48	5	4	2	3	36	0	90	9	0	6	7	.462	0	0	3.77
2000 Rancho Cuca	A+ SD	16	14	0	0	81	356	73	54	48	9	0	3	6	41	0	80	10	2	7	5	.583	0	0	5.33
2001 Mobile	AA SD	45	2	0	8	81	353	91	46	40	5	4	8	1	32	2	60	4	0	2	3	.400	0	0	4.44
7 Min. YEARS		142	72	0	18	495.1	2081	469	238	205	34	11	19	21	171	3	409	36	2	29	25	.537	0	2	3.72

Rick Short

Bats: Right **Throws:** Right **Pos:** 3B-92; PH-14; 2B-7; 1B-6; OF-3; PR-2   **Ht:** 6'0" **Wt:** 200 **Born:** 12/6/72 **Age:** 29

Year Team	Lg Org	G	AB	H	2B	3B	HR	TB	R	RBI	TBB	IBB	SO	HBP	SH	SF	SB	CS	SB%	GDP	Avg	OBP	SLG
1994 Bluefield	R+ Bal	64	229	69	8	0	4	89	39	35	22	1	23	2	0	2	4	6	.40	3	.301	.365	.389
1995 Frederick	A+ Bal	5	13	1	0	0	0	1	1	2	1	0	2	0	0	0	1	0	1.00	0	.077	.143	.077
Bluefield	R+ Bal	11	39	11	2	0	2	19	9	12	2	0	1	1	0	1	2	1	.67	2	.282	.326	.487
High Desert	A+ Bal	29	98	41	3	0	4	56	14	12	10	0	5	2	0	0	1	2	.33	2	.418	.482	.571
1996 Frederick	A+ Bal	126	474	148	33	0	3	190	68	54	29	2	44	5	5	4	12	7	.63	14	.312	.355	.401
1997 Frederick	A+ Bal	126	480	153	29	1	10	214	73	72	38	2	44	12	7	1	10	7	.59	20	.319	.382	.446
1998 Frederick	A+ Bal	59	221	68	14	0	6	100	36	28	18	1	29	8	1	3	3	2	.60	12	.308	.376	.452
Bowie	AA Bal	34	87	20	4	0	2	30	12	18	13	0	18	0	1	4	0	0	—	2	.230	.317	.345
Rochester	AAA Bal	13	34	6	1	0	1	10	3	4	4	0	4	1	0	1	0	0	—	0	.176	.275	.294
1999 Bowie	AA Bal	112	392	123	19	0	16	190	60	62	43	2	48	9	0	5	6	0	1.00	9	.314	.390	.485
2000 Rochester	AAA Bal	13	37	9	1	0	1	13	3	3	4	0	4	2	0	0	0	0	—	0	.243	.349	.351
Bowie	AA Bal	116	447	148	39	1	9	216	63	82	44	2	54	8	0	8	3	3	.50	14	.331	.394	.483
2001 West Tenn	AA ChC	8	19	5	0	0	0	5	5	0	5	0	1	1	0	0	0	1	.00	0	.263	.440	.263
Iowa	AAA ChC	105	313	86	19	1	5	122	38	34	22	0	42	3	5	1	2	1	.67	13	.275	.327	.390
8 Min. YEARS		821	2883	888	172	3	63	1255	424	418	255	10	319	54	19	30	44	30	.59	91	.308	.372	.435

Brian Shouse

Pitches: Left **Bats:** Left **Pos:** RP-55; SP-1   **Ht:** 5'11" **Wt:** 180 **Born:** 9/26/68 **Age:** 33

Year Team	Lg Org	G	GS	CG	GF	IP	BFP	H	R	ER	HR	SH	SF	HB	TBB	IBB	SO	WP	Bk	W	L	Pct.	ShO	Sv	ERA
1990 Welland	A- Pit	17	1	0	7	39.2	177	50	27	23	2	3	2	3	7	0	39	1	2	4	3	.571	0	2	5.22
1991 Augusta	A Pit	26	0	0	25	31	124	22	13	11	1	1	1	3	9	1	32	5	0	2	3	.400	0	8	3.19
Salem	A+ Pit	17	0	0	9	33.2	147	35	12	11	2	2	0	0	15	2	25	1	0	2	1	.667	0	3	2.94
1992 Carolina	AA Pit	59	0	0	33	77.1	323	71	31	21	3	8	2	2	28	4	79	4	1	5	6	.455	0	4	2.44
1993 Buffalo	AAA Pit	48	0	0	14	51.2	218	54	24	22	7	0	3	2	17	2	25	1	0	1	0	1.000	0	3	3.83
1994 Buffalo	AAA Pit	43	0	0	20	52	212	44	22	21	6	4	2	1	15	4	31	0	0	3	4	.429	0	0	3.63
1995 Calgary	AAA Pit	8	8	1	0	39.1	185	62	35	27	2	1	1	1	7	0	17	3	0	4	4	.500	0	0	6.18
Carolina	AA Pit	21	20	0	0	114.2	480	126	64	57	14	5	3	4	19	2	76	1	1	7	6	.538	0	0	4.47
1996 Calgary	AAA Pit	12	1	0	2	12.2	65	22	15	15	4	0	1	0	4	1	12	1	0	1	0	1.000	0	0	10.66
Rochester	AAA Bal	32	0	0	10	50	217	53	27	25	6	2	2	1	16	1	45	5	0	1	2	.333	0	2	4.50
1997 Rochester	AAA Bal	54	0	0	29	71.1	282	48	21	18	6	5	1	3	21	4	81	2	0	6	2	.750	0	9	2.27
1998 Pawtucket	AAA Bos	22	1	0	15	31	121	21	11	10	7	1	1	0	7	0	25	0	0	2	0	1.000	0	0	2.90
1999 Tucson	AAA Ari	30	0	0	8	44.2	213	63	35	31	4	6	2	1	18	3	32	2	0	3	4	.429	0	0	6.25
2000 Norfolk	AAA NYM	4	0	0	0	3.1	16	6	5	5	2	0	0	0	2	0	1	0	0	0	1	.000	0	0	13.50
Rochester	AAA Bal	43	0	0	14	57.2	244	63	20	18	4	0	2	2	14	1	52	2	0	4	4	.500	0	2	2.81
2001 New Orleans	AAA Hou	56	1	0	17	53	225	51	21	17	4	0	2	3	15	0	56	2	0	2	2	.500	0	1	2.89
1993 Pittsburgh	NL	6	0	0	1	4	22	7	4	4	1	0	1	0	2	0	3	1	0	0	0	—	0	0	9.00
1998 Boston	AL	7	0	0	4	8	36	9	5	5	2	0	0	0	4	0	5	0	0	0	1	.000	0	0	5.63
12 Min. YEARS		492	32	1	203	763	3249	791	383	332	74	38	25	26	214	25	628	30	4	47	42	.528	0	39	3.92
2 Maj. YEARS		13	0	0	5	12	58	16	9	9	3	0	1	0	6	0	8	1	0	0	1	.000	0	0	6.75

Allen Shrum

Bats: Right **Throws:** Right **Pos:** C-23; DH-9; PH-5   **Ht:** 6'3" **Wt:** 215 **Born:** 5/13/76 **Age:** 26

Year Team	Lg Org	G	AB	H	2B	3B	HR	TB	R	RBI	TBB	IBB	SO	HBP	SH	SF	SB	CS	SB%	GDP	Avg	OBP	SLG
1998 Twins	R Min	42	127	42	10	0	10	82	17	25	13	1	27	3	0	0	3	2	.60	2	.331	.406	.646
Fort Wayne	A Min	5	16	1	0	0	0	1	0	0	0	0	7	0	0	0	0	0	—	0	.063	.063	.063
1999 Quad City	A Min	68	191	45	12	0	1	60	14	22	16	0	52	3	1	2	0	0	—	8	.236	.302	.314
2000 Fort Myers	A+ Min	25	73	20	4	0	0	24	12	10	8	0	17	1	0	0	0	0	—	2	.274	.354	.329
New Britain	AA Min	41	127	28	5	0	2	39	13	20	9	0	32	0	0	1	0	0	—	8	.220	.270	.307
2001 New Britain	AA Min	7	12	0	0	0	0	0	0	0	0	0	4	0	0	0	0	0	—	1	.000	.000	.000
Hagerstown	A SF	29	106	23	7	0	2	36	12	12	6	0	30	1	1	0	0	1	.00	3	.217	.265	.340
4 Min. YEARS		217	652	159	38	0	15	242	68	89	52	1	169	8	2	3	3	3	.50	24	.244	.306	.371

Anthony Shumaker

Pitches: Left **Bats:** Left **Pos:** RP-53   **Ht:** 6'5" **Wt:** 219 **Born:** 5/14/73 **Age:** 29

Year Team	Lg Org	G	GS	CG	GF	IP	BFP	H	R	ER	HR	SH	SF	HB	TBB	IBB	SO	WP	Bk	W	L	Pct.	ShO	Sv	ERA
1995 Martinsville	R+ Phi	6	4	0	0	28	120	31	16	14	0	2	0	1	8	0	26	3	0	1	3	.250	0	0	4.50
Batavia	A- Phi	9	4	1	0	39	157	38	10	7	0	0	0	0	4	0	31	2	0	2	2	.500	1	0	1.62
1996 Piedmont	A Phi	20	0	0	13	32.2	120	16	7	5	2	0	0	0	10	1	51	3	0	3	0	1.000	0	4	1.38
Clearwater	A+ Phi	31	0	0	13	29.1	137	42	18	18	1	3	0	0	12	5	25	1	0	5	3	.625	0	3	5.52
1997 Clearwater	A+ Phi	61	0	0	28	72	295	64	22	17	1	2	0	2	17	1	77	5	0	5	4	.556	0	9	2.13
1998 Reading	AA Phi	38	21	1	9	166.2	689	152	75	62	20	9	7	4	44	2	129	3	0	7	10	.412	1	2	3.35
1999 Reading	AA Phi	10	10	1	0	60.2	249	48	17	12	3	3	2	2	17	1	60	1	1	4	3	.571	0	0	1.78
Scranton-WB	AAA Phi	14	14	1	0	89.2	403	119	60	57	15	3	6	2	32	2	49	2	0	3	5	.375	0	0	5.72
2000 Scranton-WB	AAA Phi	1	1	0	0	4	20	6	4	4	0	0	2	0	3	0	1	0	0	1	0	1.000	0	0	9.00
Norfolk	AAA NYM	21	17	1	1	101	451	121	58	56	12	6	5	6	35	2	55	5	1	4	5	.444	0	0	4.99
Rochester	AAA Bal	10	5	0	1	33	151	41	27	25	5	1	1	1	13	0	26	0	0	3	2	.600	0	0	6.82
2001 Rochester	AAA Bal	53	0	0	20	72.2	311	70	35	32	7	4	1	3	31	2	53	3	0	8	7	.533	0	4	3.96
1999 Philadelphia	NL	8	4	0	2	22.2	105	23	17	15	3	2	0	1	14	0	17	1	1	0	3	.000	0	0	5.96
7 Min. YEARS		274	76	5	85	728.2	3103	748	349	309	67	33	24	19	226	16	583	28	2	45	45	.500	2	22	3.82

Jacob Shumate

Pitches: Right **Bats:** Right **Pos:** RP-8   **Ht:** 6'2" **Wt:** 190 **Born:** 1/22/76 **Age:** 26

Year Team	Lg Org	G	GS	CG	GF	IP	BFP	H	R	ER	HR	SH	SF	HB	TBB	IBB	SO	WP	Bk	W	L	Pct.	ShO	Sv	ERA
1994 Danville	R+ Atl	12	7	0	1	31.2	175	30	34	29	0	1	5	8	52	0	29	15	0	0	4	.000	0	0	8.24
1995 Macon	A Atl	17	14	0	0	56	296	38	56	45	7	1	3	9	87	0	57	19	2	0	8	.000	0	0	7.23
Danville	R+ Atl	7	2	0	2	13.1	80	6	21	16	1	0	2	2	32	0	16	14	0	1	2	.333	0	0	10.80
1996 Macon	A Atl	1	1	0	0	3	16	5	5	4	0	0	1	0	2	0	2	1	0	0	0	—	0	0	12.00
1997 Eugene	A- Atl	19	0	0	7	20.2	126	19	32	25	1	0	0	2	43	0	23	7	0	0	2	.000	0	0	10.89
1998 Macon	A Atl	44	0	0	10	50.2	280	44	54	38	5	2	3	13	75	0	65	39	1	5	4	.556	0	0	6.75
Greenville	AA Atl	2	0	0	0	2.1	13	3	4	4	0	0	0	0	4	0	1	1	0	0	1	.000	0	0	15.43
1999 Myrtle Bch	A+ Atl	20	0	0	6	22.2	116	15	19	18	0	3	1	1	33	0	31	8	0	3	3	.500	0	0	7.15
Greenville	AA Atl	14	12	0	1	57	270	43	30	30	6	1	3	5	61	1	48	9	1	3	4	.429	0	0	4.74
2000 Greenville	AA Atl	47	0	0	39	45.2	208	32	23	21	3	1	0	2	41	0	41	10	0	2	1	.667	0	18	4.14
2001 Huntsville	AA Mil	8	0	0	3	9.1	52	18	17	16	3	1	2	1	6	0	10	2	0	0	1	.000	0	0	15.43
8 Min. YEARS		191	36	0	69	312.1	1632	253	295	246	26	10	20	43	436	1	323	125	4	14	30	.318	0	18	7.09

Wilson Sido

Pitches: Right **Bats:** Right **Pos:** SP-19; RP-1   **Ht:** 6'2" **Wt:** 178 **Born:** 6/18/76 **Age:** 26

Year Team	Lg Org	G	GS	CG	GF	IP	BFP	H	R	ER	HR	SH	SF	HB	TBB	IBB	SO	WP	Bk	W	L	Pct.	ShO	Sv	ERA
1998 Columbus	A Cle	4	4	0	0	24.2	101	17	7	7	1	0	0	3	8	1	27	0	1	2	0	1.000	0	0	2.55
1999 Kinston	A+ Cle	9	7	0	0	36.1	163	33	26	24	4	1	1	5	22	1	22	6	0	1	2	.333	0	0	5.94
Columbus	A Cle	13	12	0	0	49	232	63	43	40	5	2	2	3	23	0	51	4	3	3	7	.300	0	0	7.35
2000 Akron	AA Cle	1	1	1	0	7	25	4	2	1	0	0	0	2	0	0	6	0	0	1	0	1.000	0	0	1.29
Buffalo	AAA Cle	1	0	0	1	2	9	2	1	1	0	0	0	0	2	0	0	0	0	0	0	—	0	0	4.50
Kinston	A+ Cle	29	19	1	3	126.1	550	131	58	52	9	8	1	7	51	2	105	4	0	11	6	.647	1	0	3.70
2001 Akron	AA Cle	3	2	0	0	15.2	67	15	4	4	0	0	1	0	9	0	13	2	0	1	0	1.000	0	0	2.30
Kinston	A+ Cle	17	17	1	0	92.1	367	69	29	24	7	1	3	5	20	0	96	3	3	9	2	.818	0	0	2.33
4 Min. YEARS		77	62	3	4	353.2	1514	334	170	153	27	12	8	25	135	4	320	19	7	28	17	.622	2	0	3.89

Pete Sikaras

Pitches: Right **Bats:** Right **Pos:** RP-38   **Ht:** 6'2" **Wt:** 204 **Born:** 5/5/79 **Age:** 23

Year Team	Lg Org	G	GS	CG	GF	IP	BFP	H	R	ER	HR	SH	SF	HB	TBB	IBB	SO	WP	Bk	W	L	Pct.	ShO	Sv	ERA
2000 South Bend	A Ari	20	0	0	2	29.1	146	33	25	20	1	1	2	2	22	0	17	0	0	0	3	.000	0	1	6.14
2001 Tucson	AAA Ari	4	0	0	1	6	34	11	10	8	2	0	1	1	4	0	4	4	0	1	0	1.000	0	0	12.00
Lancaster	A+ Ari	18	0	0	7	24.2	112	25	22	17	2	0	1	1	18	1	20	4	0	1	1	.500	0	1	6.20
Yakima	A- Ari	16	0	0	13	30.1	137	31	16	12	2	2	0	0	15	2	24	4	1	2	5	.286	0	3	3.56
2 Min. YEARS		58	0	0	23	90.1	429	100	73	57	7	1	4	4	59	3	65	12	1	3	10	.231	0	5	5.68

Brian Sikorski

Pitches: Right **Bats:** Right **Pos:** SP-14   **Ht:** 6'1" **Wt:** 200 **Born:** 7/27/74 **Age:** 27

Year Team	Lg Org	G	GS	CG	GF	IP	BFP	H	R	ER	HR	SH	SF	HB	TBB	IBB	SO	WP	Bk	W	L	Pct.	ShO	Sv	ERA
1995 Auburn	A- Hou	23	0	0	19	34.1	137	22	8	8	1	0	1	0	14	2	35	1	0	1	2	.333	0	12	2.10
Quad City	A Hou	2	0	0	1	3	11	1	0	0	0	0	0	0	0	0	4	0	0	1	0	1.000	0	0	0.00
1996 Quad City	A Hou	26	25	1	0	166.2	704	140	79	58	12	4	7	10	70	2	150	7	9	11	8	.579	0	0	3.13
1997 Kissimmee	A+ Hou	11	11	0	0	67.2	279	64	29	23	2	0	1	6	16	0	46	0	3	8	2	.800	0	0	3.06
Jackson	AA Hou	17	17	0	0	93.1	402	91	55	48	8	5	2	4	31	2	74	0	2	5	5	.500	0	0	4.63
1998 Jackson	AA Hou	15	15	0	0	97.1	419	83	50	44	13	3	2	6	44	1	80	3	1	6	4	.600	0	0	4.07
New Orleans	AAA Hou	15	14	1	0	84	371	86	57	54	9	2	4	6	32	1	64	2	1	5	8	.385	0	0	5.79
1999 New Orleans	AAA Hou	28	27	2	0	158.1	690	169	92	87	25	8	1	9	58	1	122	6	2	7	10	.412	1	0	4.95
2000 Oklahoma	AAA Tex	24	23	5	1	140.1	591	131	73	63	9	2	8	3	60	1	99	3	5	10	9	.526	2	1	4.04
2001 Oklahoma	AAA Tex	14	14	1	0	87.1	360	79	37	35	8	2	4	2	23	0	73	0	1	6	4	.600	0	0	3.61
2000 Texas	AL	10	5	0	2	37.2	187	46	31	24	9	0	1	1	25	1	32	1	0	1	3	.250	0	0	5.73
7 Min. YEARS		175	146	10	21	932.1	3967	876	481	420	87	26	30	46	348	10	747	22	24	60	52	.536	3	13	4.05

Carlos Silva

Pitches: Right **Bats:** Right **Pos:** SP-28   **Ht:** 6'4" **Wt:** 225 **Born:** 4/23/79 **Age:** 23

Year Team	Lg Org	G	GS	CG	GF	IP	BFP	H	R	ER	HR	SH	SF	HB	TBB	IBB	SO	WP	Bk	W	L	Pct.	ShO	Sv	ERA
1996 Martinsvlle	R+ Phi	7	1	0	1	18	78	20	11	8	1	4	1	1	5	0	16	0	0	0	0	—	0	0	4.00
1997 Martinsvlle	R+ Phi	11	11	0	0	57.2	252	66	46	33	9	3	2	1	14	0	31	6	3	2	2	.500	0	0	5.15
1998 Martinsvlle	R+ Phi	7	7	1	0	41	180	48	24	23	2	2	3	2	4	0	21	3	2	1	4	.200	0	0	5.05
Batavia	A- Phi	9	7	0	0	45.1	206	61	37	32	4	0	1	2	9	0	27	2	0	2	3	.400	0	0	6.35
1999 Piedmont	A Phi	26	26	3	0	164.1	708	176	79	57	6	8	6	9	41	2	99	8	2	11	8	.579	1	0	3.12
2000 Clearwater	A+ Phi	26	24	4	0	176.1	778	229	99	70	7	6	5	11	26	1	82	4	2	8	13	.381	1	0	3.57
2001 Reading	AA Phi	28	28	4	0	180	740	197	85	78	20	6	2	11	27	0	100	3	0	15	8	.652	1	0	3.90
6 Min. YEARS		114	104	12	1	682.2	2942	797	381	301	49	29	20	37	126	3	376	26	9	39	38	.506	2	0	3.97

Doug Silva

Pitches: Right **Bats:** Right **Pos:** RP-36; SP-1   **Ht:** 6'3" **Wt:** 190 **Born:** 7/8/79 **Age:** 22

Year Team	Lg Org	G	GS	CG	GF	IP	BFP	H	R	ER	HR	SH	SF	HB	TBB	IBB	SO	WP	Bk	W	L	Pct.	ShO	Sv	ERA
1997 Rangers	R Tex	11	9	1	0	62	271	69	34	26	4	1	2	0	18	1	46	4	3	5	4	.556	0	0	3.77
1998 Savannah	A Tex	38	0	0	22	65	280	72	34	33	6	0	4	2	13	0	60	7	0	3	4	.429	0	7	4.57
1999 Savannah	A Tex	7	0	0	4	17.2	72	15	5	4	2	0	0	0	3	0	18	1	0	0	1	.000	0	1	2.04
Charlotte	A+ Tex	24	12	0	6	94.2	404	103	58	41	8	2	2	1	25	1	55	5	1	4	4	.500	0	0	3.90

Year Team	Lg Org	G	GS	CG	GF	IP	BFP	H	R	ER	HR	SH	SF	HB	TBB	IBB	SO	WP	Bk	W	L	Pct.	ShO	Sv	ERA
		HOW MUCH HE PITCHED						WHAT HE GAVE UP												THE RESULTS					
2000 Charlotte	A+ Tex	45	0	0	28	67.1	299	74	37	34	7	4	3	1	24	1	55	5	0	5	5	.500	0	10	4.54
2001 Charlotte	A+ Tex	23	1	0	6	55	211	45	16	14	3	3	1	0	10	0	50	2	0	3	1	.750	0	1	2.29
Tulsa	AA Tex	14	0	0	8	19	82	19	10	7	1	0	2	0	5	0	15	1	0	0	1	.000	0	1	3.32
5 Min. YEARS		162	22	1	75	380.2	1619	397	194	159	31	10	14	4	98	3	299	25	4	20	20	.500	0	20	3.76

Juan Silvestre

Bats: Right **Throws:** Right **Pos:** OF-65; DH-33; PH-5   **Ht:** 5'11" **Wt:** 180 **Born:** 1/10/78 **Age:** 24

Year Team	Lg Org	G	AB	H	2B	3B	HR	TB	R	RBI	TBB	IBB	SO	HBP	SH	SF	SB	CS	SB%	GDP	Avg	OBP	SLG
		BATTING															BASERUNNING				PERCENTAGES		
1997 Mariners	R Sea	34	135	46	11	3	7	84	32	36	15	1	31	2	0	3	4	2	.67	1	.341	.406	.622
Tacoma	AAA Sea	8	28	7	3	0	0	10	5	0	2	0	9	0	0	0	0	0	—	0	.250	.300	.357
Everett	A- Sea	14	54	17	3	1	3	31	9	9	4	0	19	2	0	1	1	0	1.00	0	.315	.377	.574
1998 Wisconsin	A Sea	106	401	101	20	5	15	176	44	56	22	1	98	7	2	2	7	2	.78	9	.252	.301	.439
1999 Wisconsin	A Sea	137	534	154	34	4	21	259	89	107	47	1	124	6	0	8	5	4	.56	17	.288	.348	.485
2000 Lancaster	A+ Sea	127	506	154	15	3	30	265	104	137	60	1	126	7	0	7	9	6	.60	5	.304	.381	.524
2001 San Antonio	AA Sea	101	372	85	13	0	8	122	29	39	21	0	113	1	0	3	0	2	.00	4	.228	.270	.328
5 Min. YEARS		527	2030	564	99	16	84	947	312	384	171	4	520	25	2	24	26	16	.62	36	.278	.338	.467

Ben Simon

Pitches: Right **Bats:** Right **Pos:** SP-24; RP-3   **Ht:** 6'1" **Wt:** 185 **Born:** 11/12/74 **Age:** 27

Year Team	Lg Org	G	GS	CG	GF	IP	BFP	H	R	ER	HR	SH	SF	HB	TBB	IBB	SO	WP	Bk	W	L	Pct.	ShO	Sv	ERA
		HOW MUCH HE PITCHED						WHAT HE GAVE UP												THE RESULTS					
1996	A- LA	15	10	0	1	66.1	275	59	34	27	5	3	5	3	21	2	62	0	1	2	6	.250	0	1	3.66
1997 Savannah	A LA	18	17	2	1	93.1	398	84	35	32	2	6	4	7	27	0	93	3	0	7	5	.583	1	0	3.09
1998 Vero Beach	A+ LA	7	5	0	1	18.2	81	22	14	14	1	0	0	0	7	0	16	2	0	1	2	.333	0	0	6.75
1999 Vero Beach	A+ LA	38	5	0	12	88.2	382	79	44	34	5	4	2	10	29	2	89	7	1	7	4	.636	0	2	3.45
2000 Vero Beach	A+ LA	4	4	0	0	23.2	97	23	12	10	4	1	1	3	5	0	16	0	1	1	0	1.000	0	0	3.80
San Antonio	AA LA	29	16	0	5	108.1	460	102	58	54	15	5	2	8	44	2	91	4	1	8	8	.500	0	2	4.49
2001 Jacksnville	AA LA	15	15	0	0	81.1	328	64	34	30	12	5	2	7	21	0	76	1	0	7	6	.538	0	0	3.32
Las Vegas	AAA LA	12	9	0	2	52.2	243	61	48	43	8	8	2	7	23	1	43	1	0	2	6	.250	0	0	7.35
6 Min. YEARS		138	81	2	22	533	2264	494	279	244	52	32	18	45	177	7	486	18	4	35	37	.486	1	5	4.12

Mitch Simons

Bats: Right **Throws:** Right **Pos:** 2B-33; PR-1   **Ht:** 5'9" **Wt:** 172 **Born:** 12/13/68 **Age:** 33

Year Team	Lg Org	G	AB	H	2B	3B	HR	TB	R	RBI	TBB	IBB	SO	HBP	SH	SF	SB	CS	SB%	GDP	Avg	OBP	SLG
		BATTING															BASERUNNING				PERCENTAGES		
1991 Jamestown	A- Mon	41	153	47	12	0	1	62	38	16	39	1	20	0	2	2	23	5	.82	1	.307	.443	.405
Wst Plm Bch	A+ Mon	15	50	9	2	1	0	13	3	4	5	0	8	0	0	0	1	0	1.00	0	.180	.255	.260
1992 Albany	A Mon	130	481	136	26	5	1	175	57	61	60	0	47	7	2	10	34	12	.74	6	.283	.364	.364
1993 Wst Plm Bch	A+ Mon	45	156	40	4	1	1	49	24	13	19	0	9	3	1	2	14	8	.64	3	.256	.344	.314
Harrisburg	AA Mon	29	77	18	1	1	0	21	5	5	7	0	14	0	2	1	2	0	1.00	1	.234	.294	.273
1994 Nashville	AA Min	102	391	124	26	0	3	159	46	48	39	0	38	6	3	5	30	9	.77	6	.317	.383	.407
1995 Salt Lake	AAA Min	130	480	156	34	4	3	207	87	46	47	2	45	10	4	2	32	16	.67	9	.325	.395	.431
1996 Salt Lake	AAA Min	129	512	135	27	8	5	193	76	59	43	3	59	8	3	4	35	11	.76	7	.264	.328	.377
1997 Salt Lake	AAA Min	115	462	138	34	10	5	207	87	59	47	4	48	5	9	5	26	5	.84	7	.299	.366	.448
1998 Rochester	AAA Bal	59	190	41	8	2	1	56	21	16	20	0	16	1	1	1	7	2	.78	4	.216	.292	.295
Tacoma	AAA Sea	47	180	42	6	2	2	58	27	21	15	0	23	4	2	1	10	1	.91	5	.233	.305	.322
1999 Charlotte	AAA CWS	119	474	137	32	1	7	192	85	52	45	0	67	11	6	2	22	6	.79	10	.289	.363	.405
2000 Norfolk	AAA NYM	113	409	109	22	4	0	139	52	48	37	1	55	4	7	2	16	13	.55	11	.267	.332	.340
2001 Oklahoma	AAA Tex	34	121	29	7	0	0	36	14	7	11	0	23	1	1	0	0	2	.00	1	.240	.308	.298
11 Min. YEARS		1108	4136	1161	241	39	29	1567	622	455	434	11	472	60	43	37	252	90	.74	71	.281	.355	.379

Jason Simontacchi

Pitches: Right **Bats:** Right **Pos:** SP-18; RP-14   **Ht:** 6'2" **Wt:** 185 **Born:** 11/13/73 **Age:** 28

Year Team	Lg Org	G	GS	CG	GF	IP	BFP	H	R	ER	HR	SH	SF	HB	TBB	IBB	SO	WP	Bk	W	L	Pct.	ShO	Sv	ERA
		HOW MUCH HE PITCHED						WHAT HE GAVE UP												THE RESULTS					
1996 Spokane	A- KC	14	6	0	3	47	214	59	37	27	8	3	3	3	21	0	43	1	0	2	5	.286	0	2	5.17
1997 Lansing	A KC	29	1	0	11	60.2	295	93	56	47	7	3	4	4	15	1	38	1	2	3	7	.300	0	2	6.97
1998 Springfield	IND —	16	16	3	0	110	451	103	43	36	14	7	0	6	21	3	92	4	1	10	2	.833	1	0	2.95
1999 Hickory	A Pit	23	7	0	8	69.1	297	71	34	31	8	2	1	6	19	1	66	5	3	4	6	.400	0	1	4.02
2001 Edmonton	AAA Min	32	18	2	3	143.1	627	192	97	85	21	3	7	6	23	1	83	4	0	7	13	.350	0	0	5.34
5 Min. YEARS		114	48	5	25	430.1	1884	518	267	226	58	18	15	25	93	6	322	15	6	26	33	.441	1	5	4.73

Allan Simpson

Pitches: Right **Bats:** Right **Pos:** RP-38   **Ht:** 6'4" **Wt:** 185 **Born:** 8/26/77 **Age:** 24

Year Team	Lg Org	G	GS	CG	GF	IP	BFP	H	R	ER	HR	SH	SF	HB	TBB	IBB	SO	WP	Bk	W	L	Pct.	ShO	Sv	ERA
		HOW MUCH HE PITCHED						WHAT HE GAVE UP												THE RESULTS					
1997 Everett	A- Sea	16	0	0	6	26.1	127	26	23	20	1	1	1	2	24	1	26	3	0	0	3	.000	0	0	6.84
1998 Wisconsin	A Sea	19	19	0	0	93.1	420	89	52	46	5	4	2	7	61	0	86	5	2	3	5	.375	0	0	4.44
Mariners	R Sea	3	0	0	1	9.1	37	8	2	1	1	0	0	0	3	0	12	0	0	1	0	1.000	0	1	0.96
1999 Wisconsin	A Sea	24	13	1	3	90.1	402	83	56	44	4	4	8	3	48	0	88	4	1	2	9	.182	0	4	4.38
Lancaster	A+ Sea	9	0	0	0	21.1	96	17	16	15	4	0	2	2	14	0	25	2	1	0	0	—	0	0	6.33
2000 Lancaster	A+ Sea	46	0	0	20	52	217	34	17	12	1	0	2	2	27	1	67	2	0	3	2	.600	0	6	2.08
2001 San Berndno	A+ Sea	16	0	0	5	30	121	19	7	6	1	1	1	1	12	1	40	2	0	1	0	1.000	0	1	1.80
San Antonio	AA Sea	22	0	0	16	38.2	157	25	8	8	1	1	3	2	15	1	37	2	0	2	1	.667	0	9	1.86
5 Min. YEARS		155	32	1	51	361.1	1577	301	181	152	18	11	19	18	204	4	381	20	4	12	20	.375	0	17	3.79

Ken Sims

Pitches: Right **Bats:** Right **Pos:** SP-14; RP-10   **Ht:** 6'4" **Wt:** 215 **Born:** 7/24/75 **Age:** 26

Year Team	Lg Org	G	GS	CG	GF	IP	BFP	H	R	ER	HR	SH	SF	HB	TBB	IBB	SO	WP	Bk	W	L	Pct.	ShO	Sv	ERA
1996 Orioles	R Bal	11	2	0	6	16.1	79	22	12	9	2	0	0	0	8	0	20	4	0	0	2	.000	0	2	4.96
1997 Bluefield	R+ Bal	18	2	0	10	35.1	158	30	18	12	2	0	1	3	22	0	33	1	1	1	2	.333	0	1	3.06
1998 Bluefield	R+ Bal	19	1	0	6	49.1	204	49	20	17	2	1	0	1	14	2	32	3	0	5	3	.625	0	0	3.10
Frederick	A+ Bal	3	0	0	2	6.2	26	6	2	1	1	0	0	0	0	0	8	0	0	0	0	—	0	1	1.35
1999 Frederick	A+ Bal	35	1	0	11	69	312	83	38	32	7	3	1	4	19	3	41	1	0	4	4	.500	0	2	4.17
2000 Frederick	A+ Bal	29	9	0	5	81	361	98	44	35	10	3	3	9	27	1	44	6	1	5	3	.625	0	0	3.89
2001 Bowie	AA Bal	24	14	1	3	112	479	123	54	51	9	5	4	10	26	0	51	4	0	8	4	.667	1	1	4.10
6 Min. YEARS		139	29	1	43	369.2	1619	411	188	157	33	12	9	27	116	6	229	19	2	23	18	.561	1	7	3.82

Steve Sinclair

Pitches: Left **Bats:** Left **Pos:** RP-53   **Ht:** 6'2" **Wt:** 190 **Born:** 8/2/71 **Age:** 30

Year Team	Lg Org	G	GS	CG	GF	IP	BFP	H	R	ER	HR	SH	SF	HB	TBB	IBB	SO	WP	Bk	W	L	Pct.	ShO	Sv	ERA
1991 Medcine Hat	R+ Tor	12	0	0	8	14.2	76	17	15	11	1	1	0	3	11	0	14	0	0	0	1	.000	0	0	6.75
1992 Blue Jays	R Tor	5	4	0	0	23	92	23	10	7	2	0	0	0	5	0	18	1	0	1	2	.333	0	0	2.74
Medcine Hat	R+ Tor	9	7	0	1	43	189	54	25	22	2	2	3	1	12	0	28	3	0	2	3	.400	0	0	4.60
1993 Dunedin	A+ Tor	15	12	0	0	78.1	335	87	41	29	5	2	2	1	16	0	45	5	1	5	2	.714	0	0	3.33
1994 Hagerstown	A Tor	38	1	0	16	105	458	127	53	44	9	4	5	2	25	0	75	3	0	9	2	.818	0	3	3.77
1995 Dunedin	A+ Tor	46	0	0	18	73	297	69	26	21	4	1	1	3	17	1	52	2	3	5	3	.625	0	2	2.59
1996 Dunedin	A+ Tor	3	0	0	1	2.2	12	4	2	1	1	0	0	0	0	0	1	0	0	0	1	.000	0	0	3.38
1997 Dunedin	A+ Tor	43	0	0	20	68.1	296	63	36	22	4	4	1	2	26	3	66	4	1	2	5	.286	0	3	2.90
Syracuse	AAA Tor	6	0	0	1	9	40	11	6	6	0	0	0	0	3	0	9	0	0	0	0	—	0	0	6.00
1998 Syracuse	AAA Tor	43	1	0	16	49.2	204	37	15	12	2	1	2	1	23	2	45	0	0	3	1	.750	0	3	2.18
1999 Syracuse	AAA Tor	34	0	0	30	39.1	156	24	11	9	3	0	0	4	12	1	31	1	0	2	2	.500	0	18	2.06
Tacoma	AAA Sea	2	0	0	0	2	9	2	1	1	0	0	0	0	1	0	1	1	0	1	0	1.000	0	0	4.50
2000 Tacoma	AAA Sea	45	0	0	8	58	265	68	36	29	6	3	2	1	27	5	45	3	1	4	3	.571	0	3	4.50
2001 Charlotte	AAA CWS	53	0	0	19	63.1	274	66	35	33	5	1	2	4	23	5	57	3	0	4	6	.400	0	1	4.69
1998 Toronto	AL	24	0	0	3	15	61	13	7	6	0	0	0	0	5	0	8	0	0	0	2	.000	0	0	3.60
1999 Toronto	AL	3	0	0	1	5.2	28	7	8	8	4	0	0	1	4	0	3	0	0	0	0	—	0	0	12.71
Seattle	AL	18	0	0	5	13.2	67	15	8	6	1	0	0	1	10	2	15	0	0	0	1	.000	0	0	3.95
11 Min. YEARS		354	25	0	138	629.1	2703	652	312	247	44	19	18	22	201	17	487	26	6	38	31	.551	0	33	3.53
2 Maj. YEARS		45	0	0	9	34.1	156	35	23	20	5	0	0	2	19	2	26	0	0	0	3	.000	0	0	5.24

Justin Singleton

Bats: Left **Throws:** Right **Pos:** OF-109; PR-5; PH-4; DH-1   **Ht:** 6'1" **Wt:** 190 **Born:** 4/10/79 **Age:** 23

Year Team	Lg Org	G	AB	H	2B	3B	HR	TB	R	RBI	TBB	IBB	SO	HBP	SH	SF	SB	CS	SB%	GDP	Avg	OBP	SLG
2001 Tennessee	AA Tor	15	36	10	0	0	0	10	5	3	4	0	13	0	1	1	1	1	.50	1	.278	.341	.278
Chston-WV	A Tor	100	345	80	15	5	2	111	51	25	33	0	138	0	6	0	24	7	.77	1	.232	.299	.322
1 Min. YEAR		115	381	90	15	5	2	121	56	28	37	0	151	0	7	1	25	8	.76	2	.236	.303	.318

Steve Sisco

Bats: Right **Throws:** Right **Pos:** 2B-42; 1B-27; 3B-17; OF-12; DH-3; PH-1   **Ht:** 5'10" **Wt:** 190 **Born:** 12/2/69 **Age:** 32

Year Team	Lg Org	G	AB	H	2B	3B	HR	TB	R	RBI	TBB	IBB	SO	HBP	SH	SF	SB	CS	SB%	GDP	Avg	OBP	SLG
1992 Eugene	A- KC	67	261	86	7	1	0	95	41	30	26	0	32	4	2	2	22	12	.65	7	.330	.396	.364
Appleton	A KC	1	4	1	0	0	0	1	1	0	0	0	1	0	0	0	0	0	—	0	.250	.250	.250
1993 Rockford	A KC	124	460	132	22	4	2	168	62	57	42	2	65	2	4	5	25	10	.71	14	.287	.346	.365
1994 Wilmington	A+ KC	76	270	74	11	4	3	102	41	32	37	0	39	2	6	4	5	6	.45	2	.274	.361	.378
1995 Omaha	AAA KC	7	24	5	1	0	0	6	4	0	2	0	8	0	1	0	0	0	—	0	.208	.269	.250
Wichita	AA KC	54	209	63	12	1	3	86	29	23	15	0	31	1	1	1	3	1	.75	5	.301	.350	.411
1996 Wichita	AA KC	122	462	137	24	1	13	202	80	74	40	0	69	3	5	5	4	2	.67	14	.297	.353	.437
1997 Wichita	AA KC	55	182	52	8	2	3	73	34	24	24	0	29	0	1	2	3	1	.75	5	.286	.365	.401
Omaha	AAA KC	54	188	49	8	0	3	66	23	12	8	0	34	0	3	1	2	1	.67	4	.261	.289	.351
1998 Omaha	AAA KC	109	371	104	20	0	20	184	58	58	26	1	58	0	5	3	4	6	.40	11	.280	.325	.496
1999 Richmond	AAA Atl	128	495	154	36	2	18	248	80	76	38	0	74	1	3	8	13	7	.65	7	.311	.356	.501
2000 Richmond	AAA Atl	75	275	81	16	0	12	133	46	35	21	2	46	2	3	2	3	2	.60	4	.295	.347	.484
2001 Rochester	AAA Bal	92	338	80	17	0	6	115	38	29	28	2	66	6	2	5	6	5	.55	10	.237	.302	.340
Scranton-WB	AAA Phi	3	13	3	0	0	0	3	0	0	0	0	4	0	0	0	1	0	1.00	0	.231	.231	.231
2000 Atlanta	NL	25	27	5	0	0	1	8	4	2	3	0	4	0	0	0	0	0	—	1	.185	.267	.296
10 Min. YEARS		967	3552	1021	182	15	83	1482	537	450	307	7	556	21	36	38	91	53	.63	83	.287	.344	.417

Bobby Sismondo

Pitches: Left **Bats:** Left **Pos:** RP-34; SP-6   **Ht:** 6'1" **Wt:** 180 **Born:** 11/14/76 **Age:** 25

Year Team	Lg Org	G	GS	CG	GF	IP	BFP	H	R	ER	HR	SH	SF	HB	TBB	IBB	SO	WP	Bk	W	L	Pct.	ShO	Sv	ERA
1998 Jamestown	A- Det	2	2	0	0	12.2	49	7	1	1	0	0	0	1	3	0	19	0	1	2	0	1.000	0	0	0.71
W Michigan	A Det	5	5	0	0	21.1	92	21	9	5	0	1	1	0	9	0	24	0	2	0	3	.000	0	0	2.11
1999 W Michigan	A Det	27	27	1	0	169.1	708	153	86	69	12	4	5	7	62	2	135	8	1	9	12	.429	1	0	3.67
2000 Clearwater	A+ Phi	32	6	0	11	87.2	375	85	49	39	7	2	2	3	35	0	62	5	1	5	7	.417	0	1	4.00
2001 Reading	AA Phi	26	0	0	9	34	152	32	20	16	5	2	1	1	19	0	27	2	0	0	1	.000	0	2	4.24
Clearwater	A+ Phi	6	4	1	0	30	123	26	13	10	2	0	0	1	10	0	15	1	1	2	2	.500	0	0	3.00
Huntsville	AA Mil	8	2	0	3	20.2	88	24	9	5	3	0	0	2	4	1	16	1	1	1	2	.333	0	1	2.18
4 Min. YEARS		106	46	2	23	375.2	1587	348	187	145	30	9	9	15	142	3	298	17	7	19	27	.413	1	4	3.47

Shaun Skrehot

Bats: Right **Throws:** Right **Pos:** SS-131; OF-6; DH-1   **Ht:** 5'9" **Wt:** 172 **Born:** 12/5/75 **Age:** 26

Year Team	Lg Org	G	AB	H	2B	3B	HR	TB	R	RBI	TBB	IBB	SO	HBP	SH	SF	SB	CS	SB%	GDP	Avg	OBP	SLG
1998 Erie	A- Pit	63	269	67	10	0	2	83	33	18	7	0	43	4	1	3	10	1	.91	3	.249	.276	.309
1999 Hickory	A Pit	115	461	108	17	5	1	138	53	37	16	0	72	5	7	4	12	8	.60	8	.234	.265	.299
2000 Lynchburg	A+ Pit	42	129	30	3	2	0	37	9	7	9	0	22	1	4	2	5	3	.63	2	.233	.284	.287
Altoona	AA Pit	57	158	36	4	1	0	42	14	9	16	0	32	3	1	0	7	2	.78	4	.228	.311	.266
2001 Altoona	AA Pit	117	468	125	30	6	6	185	61	45	30	2	63	5	6	5	24	15	.62	10	.267	.315	.395
Nashville	AAA Pit	18	58	13	3	0	1	19	8	7	8	0	12	1	1	0	1	2	.33	1	.224	.328	.328
4 Min. YEARS		412	1543	379	67	14	10	504	178	123	86	2	244	19	20	14	59	31	.66	28	.246	.291	.327

Matt Skrmetta

Pitches: Right **Bats:** Both **Pos:** RP-46   **Ht:** 6'3" **Wt:** 220 **Born:** 11/6/72 **Age:** 29

Year Team	Lg Org	G	GS	CG	GF	IP	BFP	H	R	ER	HR	SH	SF	HB	TBB	IBB	SO	WP	Bk	W	L	Pct.	ShO	Sv	ERA
1993 Bristol	R+ Det	8	5	0	1	35	158	30	23	19	1	0	3	3	22	1	29	6	3	2	3	.400	0	0	4.89
1994 Jamestown	A- Det	17	15	1	1	93.2	389	74	42	33	4	2	3	7	37	0	56	2	3	5	3	.625	0	0	3.17
1995 Fayettevlle	A Det	44	2	0	15	89.2	371	66	36	27	9	6	1	3	35	2	105	2	0	9	4	.692	0	2	2.71
1996 Jacksnville	AA Det	4	0	0	1	6	27	4	3	3	0	0	1	0	5	1	7	1	0	0	0	—	0	0	4.50
Lakeland	A+ Det	40	0	0	20	52.2	223	44	23	21	5	2	0	2	19	1	52	2	1	5	5	.500	0	5	3.59
1997 Mobile	AA SD	21	0	0	7	32.2	154	32	21	19	4	0	1	2	21	3	30	3	0	2	3	.400	0	1	5.23
Rancho Cuca	A+ SD	17	0	0	8	28.1	122	27	7	5	2	1	0	1	10	0	36	4	0	0	1	.000	0	1	1.59
1998 Mobile	AA SD	51	0	0	16	78	323	66	32	29	9	5	2	2	31	1	77	1	3	9	2	.818	0	0	3.35
1999 Mobile	AA SD	25	1	0	9	37.1	181	42	28	26	3	1	2	3	24	1	45	5	0	1	3	.250	0	1	6.27
Las Vegas	AAA SD	20	0	0	11	28.2	117	20	13	11	4	0	1	1	11	0	25	2	0	2	1	.667	0	1	3.45
2000 Ottawa	AAA Mon	32	0	0	27	34.2	154	32	23	21	4	1	1	2	19	0	38	2	0	0	3	.000	0	10	5.45
Nashville	AAA Pit	7	0	0	6	8.1	34	6	6	3	2	0	0	0	2	0	13	1	0	1	0	1.000	0	2	3.24
2001 Louisville	AAA Cin	46	0	0	23	54.1	220	41	17	15	5	1	1	3	20	3	58	5	0	2	4	.333	0	6	2.48
2000 Montreal	NL	6	0	0	3	5.1	29	6	10	9	1	0	1	0	6	0	4	2	0	0	0	—	0	0	15.19
Pittsburgh	NL	8	0	0	0	9.1	44	13	12	10	2	1	0	1	3	0	7	1	0	2	2	.500	0	0	9.64
9 Min. YEARS		332	23	1	145	579.1	2473	484	274	232	52	19	16	29	256	13	571	36	10	38	32	.543	0	28	3.60

Terrmel Sledge

Bats: Left **Throws:** Left **Pos:** 1B-120; PH-5; OF-3; DH-3   **Ht:** 6'0" **Wt:** 185 **Born:** 3/18/77 **Age:** 25

Year Team	Lg Org	G	AB	H	2B	3B	HR	TB	R	RBI	TBB	IBB	SO	HBP	SH	SF	SB	CS	SB%	GDP	Avg	OBP	SLG
1999 Everett	A- Sea	62	233	74	8	3	5	103	43	32	27	0	35	9	2	2	9	8	.53	2	.318	.406	.442
2000 Wisconsin	A Sea	7	23	5	2	0	0	11	5	3	3	0	3	1	0	0	1	0	1.00	1	.217	.333	.478
Lancaster	A+ Sea	103	384	130	22	7	11	199	90	75	72	3	49	17	1	5	35	11	.76	4	.339	.458	.518
2001 Harrisburg	AA Mon	129	448	124	22	6	9	185	66	48	51	0	72	9	3	5	30	8	.79	5	.277	.359	.413
3 Min. YEARS		301	1088	333	54	18	25	498	204	158	153	3	159	36	6	12	75	27	.74	12	.306	.405	.458

Aaron Small

Pitches: Right **Bats:** Right **Pos:** RP-33; SP-11   **Ht:** 6'5" **Wt:** 237 **Born:** 11/23/71 **Age:** 30

Year Team	Lg Org	G	GS	CG	GF	IP	BFP	H	R	ER	HR	SH	SF	HB	TBB	IBB	SO	WP	Bk	W	L	Pct.	ShO	Sv	ERA
1989 Medcine Hat	R+ Tor	15	14	0	0	70.2	326	80	55	46	2	3	2	3	31	1	40	9	5	1	7	.125	0	0	5.86
1990 Myrtle Bch	A Tor	27	27	1	0	147.2	643	150	72	46	6	2	7	4	56	2	96	16	5	9	9	.500	0	0	2.80
1991 Dunedin	A+ Tor	24	23	1	0	148.1	595	129	51	45	5	5	5	5	42	1	92	7	0	8	7	.533	0	0	2.73
1992 Knoxville	AA Tor	27	24	2	0	135	610	152	94	79	13	2	4	6	61	0	79	14	0	5	12	.294	1	0	5.27
1993 Knoxville	AA Tor	48	9	0	32	93	408	99	44	35	5	3	0	2	40	4	44	8	0	4	4	.500	0	16	3.39
1994 Syracuse	AAA Tor	13	0	0	6	24.1	99	19	8	6	2	2	0	1	9	2	15	2	0	3	2	.600	0	0	2.22
Knoxville	AA Tor	29	11	1	13	96.1	405	92	37	32	4	3	5	3	38	0	75	5	1	5	5	.500	1	5	2.99
1995 Syracuse	AAA Tor	1	0	0	0	1.2	9	3	1	1	1	0	0	0	1	0	2	0	0	0	0	—	0	0	5.40
Charlotte	AAA Fla	33	0	0	17	40.2	170	36	15	13	2	0	1	2	10	1	31	3	0	2	1	.667	0	10	2.88
1996 Edmonton	AAA Oak	25	19	1	4	119.2	492	111	65	57	9	2	2	5	28	0	83	9	0	8	6	.571	1	1	4.29
1997 Edmonton	AAA Oak	1	1	0	0	5	16	1	0	0	0	0	0	0	0	0	4	0	0	1	0	1.000	0	0	0.00
1999 Louisville	AAA Mil	11	0	0	3	21	111	38	23	22	3	1	0	0	15	1	11	4	0	1	1	.500	0	0	9.43
Durham	AAA TB	21	18	0	0	99.1	444	118	81	70	16	1	8	3	32	2	52	4	0	4	6	.400	0	0	6.34
2000 Colo Sprngs	AAA Col	36	18	0	2	131.2	596	152	87	82	14	1	6	13	43	0	85	3	0	11	6	.647	0	0	5.61
2001 Salt Lake	AAA Ana	3	0	0	0	5.1	23	8	1	1	1	0	0	0	0	1	5	0	0	1	0	1.000	0	0	1.69
Richmond	AAA Atl	41	11	0	10	96.1	412	97	50	41	14	1	1	1	31	5	61	2	0	10	7	.588	0	0	3.83
1994 Toronto	AL	1	0	0	1	2	13	5	2	2	1	0	1	0	2	0	0	0	0	0	0	—	0	0	9.00
1995 Florida	NL	7	0	0	1	6.1	32	7	2	1	1	0	0	0	6	0	5	1	0	1	0	1.000	0	0	1.42
1996 Oakland	AL	12	3	0	4	28.2	144	37	28	26	3	0	1	1	22	1	17	2	0	1	3	.250	0	0	8.16
1997 Oakland	AL	71	0	0	22	96.2	425	109	50	46	6	5	6	3	40	6	57	4	0	9	5	.643	0	4	4.28
1998 Oakland	AL	24	0	0	4	36	174	51	34	29	3	3	1	3	14	3	19	4	0	1	1	.500	0	0	7.25
Arizona	NL	23	0	0	9	31.2	130	32	14	13	5	2	0	1	8	1	14	0	0	3	1	.750	0	0	3.69
12 Min. YEARS		355	175	6	87	1236	5359	1285	684	576	97	26	41	48	438	19	775	86	11	72	74	.493	3	32	4.19
5 Maj. YEARS		138	3	0	41	201.1	918	241	130	117	19	10	9	8	92	11	112	10	0	15	10	.600	0	4	5.23

Brian Smith

Pitches: Right **Bats:** Right **Pos:** RP-38   **Ht:** 6'0" **Wt:** 190 **Born:** 9/17/72 **Age:** 29

Year Team	Lg Org	G	GS	CG	GF	IP	BFP	H	R	ER	HR	SH	SF	HB	TBB	IBB	SO	WP	Bk	W	L	Pct.	ShO	Sv	ERA
1994 Medcine Hat	R+ Tor	20	5	0	11	64	268	58	36	24	3	2	4	5	20	0	53	6	3	5	4	.556	0	4	3.38
1995 Hagerstown	A Tor	47	0	0	36	104	402	77	18	10	1	5	0	5	16	1	101	2	2	9	1	.900	0	21	0.87
1996 Knoxville	AA Tor	54	0	0	43	75.2	333	76	42	32	7	6	3	4	31	6	58	4	0	3	5	.375	0	16	3.81
1997 Knoxville	AA Tor	1	0	0	0	1	4	0	0	0	0	0	0	0	1	0	1	0	0	0	0	—	0	0	0.00
Syracuse	AAA Tor	31	21	0	2	137.1	619	169	89	82	12	2	6	8	51	1	73	4	3	7	11	.389	0	0	5.37

Year Team	Lg Org	HOW MUCH HE PITCHED						WHAT HE GAVE UP											THE RESULTS					
		G	GS	CG	GF	IP	BFP	H	R	ER	HR	SH	SF	HB	TBB	IBB	SO	WP	Bk	W	L	Pct.	ShO	Sv	ERA
1998 Dunedin	A+ Tor	4	0	0	2	10.2	42	8	4	4	0	0	0	1	3	1	9	0	0	1	0	1.000	0	2	3.38
Knoxville	AA Tor	42	0	0	15	71	307	72	39	32	7	2	4	3	25	3	50	2	0	4	2	.667	0	7	4.06
1999 Knoxville	AA Tor	29	0	0	21	35	154	42	25	20	4	0	1	3	6	0	27	2	1	1	2	.333	0	13	5.14
Syracuse	AAA Tor	29	0	0	23	46.1	210	45	22	18	7	5	1	2	24	4	46	2	0	7	4	.636	0	7	3.50
2000 Pirates	R Pit	5	2	0	1	6	19	0	0	0	0	0	0	0	1	0	5	0	0	0	0	—	0	0	0.00
Altoona	AA Pit	22	0	0	19	27.1	106	14	6	3	0	2	1	1	8	2	23	0	0	3	4	.429	0	12	0.99
2001 Altoona	AA Pit	2	0	0	1	4.1	16	3	0	0	0	0	0	0	0	0	3	0	0	1	0	1.000	0	0	0.00
Nashville	AAA Pit	36	0	0	34	39	164	37	22	16	5	0	1	1	7	0	34	2	0	1	2	.333	0	11	3.69
2000 Pittsburgh	NL	3	0	0	1	4.1	20	6	5	5	1	1	1	0	2	0	3	0	0	0	0	—	0	0	10.38
8 Min. YEARS		322	28	0	208	621.2	2644	601	303	241	46	24	21	33	193	18	483	24	9	42	35	.545	0	93	3.49

Bubba Smith

Bats: Right   Throws: Right   Pos: 1B-27; DH-4; 3B-1   Ht: 6'2"   Wt: 225   Born: 12/18/69   Age: 32

Year Team	Lg Org	BATTING															BASERUNNING				PERCENTAGES		
		G	AB	H	2B	3B	HR	TB	R	RBI	TBB	IBB	SO	HBP	SH	SF	SB	CS	SB%	GDP	Avg	OBP	SLG
1991 Bellingham	A- Sea	66	253	66	14	2	10	114	28	43	13	1	47	2	0	5	0	2	.00	9	.261	.300	.451
1992 Peninsula	A+ Sea	137	482	126	22	1	32	246	70	93	65	7	138	5	0	5	4	10	.29	13	.261	.352	.510
1993 Jacksonville	AA Sea	37	137	30	8	0	6	56	12	21	7	0	52	2	0	1	0	3	.00	1	.219	.265	.409
Riverside	A+ Sea	5	19	8	3	0	0	11	5	3	7	0	3	0	0	0	0	0	—	1	.421	.577	.579
Winston-Sal	A+ Cin	92	342	103	16	0	27	200	55	81	35	1	109	7	0	4	2	0	1.00	6	.301	.374	.585
1994 Chattanooga	AA Cin	4	9	0	0	0	0	0	0	0	0	0	7	0	0	0	0	0	—	0	.000	.000	.000
Chston-WV	A Cin	100	354	83	26	1	15	156	38	59	20	1	113	5	1	2	1	2	.33	8	.234	.283	.441
1995 Fort Myers	A+ Min	60	176	58	15	0	13	112	27	51	16	4	38	0	0	3	1	2	.33	8	.330	.379	.636
Hardware Cy	AA Min	42	148	36	11	0	6	65	20	21	6	1	41	0	0	1	0	0	—	5	.243	.271	.439
1996 Tulsa	AA Tex	134	513	150	28	0	32	274	82	94	48	5	121	5	0	3	0	1	.00	10	.292	.357	.534
1997 Okla City	AAA Tex	140	514	131	30	1	27	244	60	94	53	2	139	4	0	4	2	2	.50	16	.255	.327	.475
1998 Tucson	AAA Ari	9	27	4	0	0	1	7	3	6	6	2	7	0	0	1	0	0	—	1	.148	.294	.259
2001 Portland	AA Fla	31	122	22	4	0	6	44	11	22	6	0	29	1	0	1	0	2	—	2	.180	.223	.361
9 Min. YEARS		857	3096	817	177	5	175	1529	411	588	282	24	844	31	1	27	10	22	.31	83	.264	.329	.494

Cam Smith

Pitches: Right   Bats: Right   Pos: RP-36; SP-1   Ht: 6'3"   Wt: 190   Born: 9/20/73   Age: 28

Year Team	Lg Org	HOW MUCH HE PITCHED						WHAT HE GAVE UP											THE RESULTS					
		G	GS	CG	GF	IP	BFP	H	R	ER	HR	SH	SF	HB	TBB	IBB	SO	WP	Bk	W	L	Pct.	ShO	Sv	ERA
1993 Bristol	R+ Det	9	7	1	0	37.2	162	25	22	15	5	0	0	6	22	0	33	2	3	3	1	.750	0	0	3.58
Niagara Fal	A- Det	2	2	0	0	5	31	12	11	10	0	0	2	0	6	0	0	2	0	0	0	—	0	0	18.00
1994 Fayetteville	A Det	26	26	1	0	133.2	619	133	100	90	10	6	5	18	86	0	128	17	1	5	13	.278	0	0	6.06
1995 Fayetteville	A Det	29	29	2	0	149	652	110	75	63	6	3	3	18	87	0	166	21	1	13	8	.619	2	0	3.81
1996 Lakeland	A+ Det	22	21	0	1	113.2	500	93	64	58	10	1	5	7	71	0	114	8	0	5	8	.385	0	1	4.59
1997 Mobile	AA SD	26	15	0	4	79.1	390	85	70	62	5	1	1	3	73	0	88	14	0	3	5	.375	0	1	7.03
1998 Lancaster	A+ Sea	8	0	0	3	18	81	11	7	5	1	0	0	3	13	0	32	4	0	1	1	.500	0	2	2.50
Orlando	AA Sea	23	1	0	8	39	186	32	27	20	6	3	3	6	32	0	49	9	0	1	3	.250	0	0	4.62
1999 New Haven	AA Sea	41	0	0	10	55	267	42	39	31	3	1	5	9	61	0	59	20	0	1	4	.200	0	0	5.07
2000 San Antonio	AA LA	7	1	0	3	15.1	74	13	13	13	0	0	2	2	15	0	16	3	0	0	0	—	0	1	7.63
Albuquerque	AAA LA	39	0	0	12	61	297	61	43	29	3	5	6	12	48	0	56	5	0	7	3	.700	0	3	4.28
2001 Las Vegas	AAA LA	8	0	0	1	11.1	68	12	14	11	2	0	2	1	19	0	9	3	0	0	1	.000	0	0	8.74
Chattanooga	AA Cin	29	1	0	11	53.2	250	49	32	30	5	3	1	5	36	2	49	7	0	1	5	.167	0	1	5.03
9 Min. YEARS		269	103	4	53	771.2	3577	678	517	437	56	23	35	90	569	2	799	115	5	40	52	.435	2	7	5.10

Casey Smith

Bats: Right   Throws: Right   Pos: C-28; 1B-1; PH-1   Ht: 6'3"   Wt: 200   Born: 5/7/77   Age: 25

Year Team	Lg Org	BATTING															BASERUNNING				PERCENTAGES		
		G	AB	H	2B	3B	HR	TB	R	RBI	TBB	IBB	SO	HBP	SH	SF	SB	CS	SB%	GDP	Avg	OBP	SLG
1997 Burlington	R+ Cle	19	77	27	2	0	2	35	8	9	3	0	22	2	0	1	1	0	1.00	0	.351	.386	.455
Columbus	A Cle	13	36	12	0	0	1	15	6	3	8	0	15	1	0	0	0	0	—	0	.333	.467	.417
1998 Watertown	A- Cle	67	226	42	6	1	3	59	22	23	15	0	65	4	0	3	4	0	1.00	5	.186	.246	.261
1999 Columbus	A Cle	47	153	36	6	0	1	45	21	13	28	0	48	7	1	1	0	2	.00	1	.235	.376	.294
Kinston	A+ Cle	39	129	21	6	0	2	33	15	15	14	0	48	3	0	0	1	.00	0	.163	.260	.256
2000 Kinston	A+ Cle	69	230	52	14	0	3	75	27	21	28	0	60	5	2	1	3	0	1.00	10	.226	.322	.326
Akron	AA Cle	6	23	4	2	1	0	8	3	4	1	0	3	0	1	0	0	0	—	0	.174	.208	.348
2001 Akron	AA Cle	30	91	16	1	0	3	26	8	5	6	1	27	1	2	0	3	0	1.00	2	.176	.235	.286
5 Min. YEARS		290	965	210	37	2	15	296	110	93	103	1	288	23	6	6	11	.79	20	.218	.306	.307

Dan Smith

Pitches: Right   Bats: Right   Pos: SP-16; RP-5   Ht: 6'3"   Wt: 210   Born: 9/15/75   Age: 26

Year Team	Lg Org	HOW MUCH HE PITCHED						WHAT HE GAVE UP											THE RESULTS					
		G	GS	CG	GF	IP	BFP	H	R	ER	HR	SH	SF	HB	TBB	IBB	SO	WP	Bk	W	L	Pct.	ShO	Sv	ERA
1993 Rangers	R Tex	12	10	1	0	53.1	212	50	19	17	1	1	2	3	8	0	27	3	1	3	2	.600	0	0	2.87
1994 Chston-SC	A Tex	27	27	4	0	157.1	715	171	111	86	12	5	2	19	55	0	86	5	2	7	10	.412	0	0	4.92
1995 Rangers	R Tex	4	3	0	0	19	81	19	9	9	0	0	4	2	5	0	12	0	0	3	0	.000	0	0	4.26
Charlotte	A+ Tex	9	9	1	0	58	242	53	23	19	4	1	2	3	16	0	34	1	0	5	1	.833	1	0	2.95
1996 Charlotte	A+ Tex	18	18	1	0	87	403	100	61	49	6	5	4	5	38	0	55	3	0	3	7	.300	0	0	5.07
1997 Charlotte	A+ Tex	26	25	2	0	160.2	705	169	93	79	17	6	4	11	66	1	113	9	0	8	10	.444	0	0	4.43
1998 Tulsa	AA Tex	26	25	1	0	153.1	675	162	101	99	27	1	7	11	58	1	105	9	1	13	9	.591	0	0	5.81
Oklahoma	AAA Tex	1	1	0	0	6	25	6	4	4	2	1	0	1	1	0	3	0	0	0	0	—	0	0	6.00
1999 Ottawa	AAA Mon	11	11	0	0	71	298	61	31	29	7	3	0	7	27	0	59	3	0	5	4	.556	0	0	3.68
2000 Pawtucket	AAA Bos	24	21	2	1	124.2	546	134	72	67	15	2	3	9	41	1	70	7	0	7	10	.412	1	0	4.84
2001 Buffalo	AAA Cle	21	16	1	3	106	458	110	58	53	17	0	3	9	44	0	68	2	0	6	4	.600	0	0	4.50
1999 Montreal	NL	20	17	0	0	89.2	407	104	64	60	12	7	2	4	39	0	72	3	0	4	9	.308	0	0	6.02
2000 Boston	AL	2	0	0	0	3.1	15	2	3	3	0	1	0	0	3	0	1	0	0	0	0	—	0	0	8.10
9 Min. YEARS		179	166	13	4	996.1	4360	1035	582	511	108	25	29	79	359	3	632	42	4	57	60	.487	2	0	4.62
2 Maj. YEARS		22	17	0	0	93	422	106	67	63	12	8	5	4	42	0	73	3	0	4	9	.308	0	0	6.10

Jeff Smith

Bats: Left   **Throws:** Right   **Pos:** C-60; DH-33; PH-8; OF-2 | **Ht:** 6'3"   **Wt:** 216   **Born:** 6/17/74   **Age:** 28

Year Team	Lg Org	G	AB	H	2B	3B	HR	TB	R	RBI	TBB	IBB	SO	HBP	SH	SF	SB	CS	SB%	GDP	Avg	OBP	SLG
1996 Fort Wayne	A Min	63	208	49	6	0	2	61	20	26	22	0	32	0	1	2	2	1	.67	4	.236	.306	.293
1997 Fort Myers	A+ Min	49	121	34	5	0	4	51	17	26	12	0	18	0	0	6	0	2	.00	4	.281	.331	.421
New Britain	AA Min	5	18	4	1	0	0	5	1	3	2	0	4	0	0	0	0	0	—	0	.222	.300	.278
Salt Lake	AAA Min	7	12	3	2	0	0	5	2	2	1	0	3	0	0	0	0	0	—	0	.250	.308	.417
1998 Fort Myers	A+ Min	6	23	8	2	0	0	10	4	1	1	0	2	1	0	0	1	0	1.00	1	.348	.400	.435
Salt Lake	AAA Min	23	67	17	3	0	0	20	9	2	4	0	13	0	2	0	0	0	—	2	.254	.296	.299
New Britain	AA Min	27	84	23	11	0	1	37	11	12	5	2	21	1	1	2	0	0	—	3	.274	.315	.440
1999 New Britain	AA Min	79	265	67	13	0	6	98	25	31	23	0	40	3	3	4	1	0	1.00	4	.253	.315	.370
Salt Lake	AAA Min	5	18	7	3	0	1	13	5	3	0	0	1	0	0	0	0	0	—	0	.389	.389	.722
2000 New Britain	AA Min	37	140	54	13	1	5	84	23	30	7	0	17	0	0	0	1	1	.50	2	.386	.415	.600
Salt Lake	AAA Min	25	84	24	4	0	2	34	10	9	2	1	20	1	0	0	1	0	1.00	1	.286	.310	.405
2001 New Britain	AA Min	102	351	100	15	1	7	138	38	42	15	0	57	4	2	2	0	0	—	8	.285	.320	.393
6 Min. YEARS		428	1391	390	78	2	28	556	165	187	94	3	228	10	9	16	6	4	.60	30	.280	.327	.400

Mike Smith

Pitches: Right   **Bats:** Right   **Pos:** SP-28 | **Ht:** 5'11"   **Wt:** 195   **Born:** 9/19/77   **Age:** 24

Year Team	Lg Org	G	GS	CG	GF	IP	BFP	H	R	ER	HR	SH	SF	HB	TBB	IBB	SO	WP	Bk	W	L	Pct.	ShO	Sv	ERA
2000 Queens	A- Tor	14	12	0	0	51	205	41	18	13	1	4	2	0	17	0	55	9	1	2	2	.500	0	0	2.29
2001 Chston-WV	A Tor	14	14	2	0	94.1	378	78	32	22	2	1	2	6	21	0	85	6	0	5	5	.500	0	0	2.10
Tennessee	AA Tor	14	14	1	0	93	393	80	32	25	7	4	1	8	26	2	77	6	0	6	2	.750	0	0	2.42
2 Min. YEARS		42	40	3	0	238.1	976	199	82	60	10	6	5	16	64	2	217	21	1	13	9	.591	1	0	2.27

Nestor Smith

Bats: Both   **Throws:** Right   **Pos:** OF-72; PH-12; DH-8; PR-8 | **Ht:** 5'11"   **Wt:** 188   **Born:** 1/21/78   **Age:** 24

Year Team	Lg Org	G	AB	H	2B	3B	HR	TB	R	RBI	TBB	IBB	SO	HBP	SH	SF	SB	CS	SB%	GDP	Avg	OBP	SLG
1996 Yankees	R NYY	14	25	6	0	0	0	6	5	0	4	0	9	1	0	0	1	1	.50	0	.240	.367	.240
1998 Fort Myers	A Min	114	414	107	17	7	8	162	59	53	38	2	103	3	3	3	7	8	.47	10	.258	.338	.391
1999 Fort Myers	A+ Min	96	329	93	14	6	4	131	39	34	16	1	67	8	2	5	8	7	.53	3	.283	.327	.398
2000 Fort Myers	A+ Min	106	359	107	21	4	1	139	53	41	34	0	72	5	2	5	6	3	.67	6	.298	.362	.387
2001 New Britain	AA Min	95	294	73	5	8	3	103	29	17	8	0	74	2	6	2	5	6	.45	4	.248	.271	.350
5 Min. YEARS		425	1421	386	57	25	16	541	185	145	100	3	325	29	13	15	27	25	.52	23	.272	.329	.381

Travis Smith

Pitches: Right   **Bats:** Right   **Pos:** SP-22; RP-8 | **Ht:** 5'10"   **Wt:** 165   **Born:** 11/7/72   **Age:** 29

Year Team	Lg Org	G	GS	CG	GF	IP	BFP	H	R	ER	HR	SH	SF	HB	TBB	IBB	SO	WP	Bk	W	L	Pct.	ShO	Sv	ERA
1995 Helena	R+ Mil	20	7	0	11	56	224	41	16	15	4	0	0	7	19	0	63	4	2	4	2	.667	0	5	2.41
1996 Stockton	A+ Mil	14	6	0	3	58.2	241	56	17	12	4	1	0	4	21	0	48	2	4	6	1	.857	0	1	1.84
El Paso	AA Mil	17	17	3	0	107.2	478	119	56	50	6	4	5	6	39	0	68	2	0	7	4	.636	1	0	4.18
1997 El Paso	AA Mil	28	28	5	0	184.1	805	210	106	85	12	7	5	7	58	2	107	7	3	16	3	.842	1	0	4.15
1998 Louisville	AAA Mil	12	11	0	0	67.2	296	77	44	40	9	3	4	2	25	1	36	3	0	4	6	.400	0	0	5.32
1999 Ogden	R+ Mil	1	1	0	0	1	5	0	1	0	0	0	0	1	0	0	3	0	0	0	0	—	0	0	0.00
Stockton	A+ Mil	3	3	0	0	7.1	35	9	6	5	1	1	0	1	3	0	8	0	0	0	2	.000	0	0	6.14
Huntsville	AA Mil	7	7	0	0	38.1	171	40	27	25	3	2	2	0	18	0	23	6	1	3	2	.600	0	0	5.87
2000 Indianapolis	AAA Mil	3	3	0	0	10.2	58	19	18	15	6	1	1	1	9	1	5	0	0	1	1	.500	0	0	12.66
Huntsville	AA Mil	27	24	1	1	154.1	631	141	77	64	13	4	2	5	37	0	113	3	1	12	7	.632	1	0	3.73
2001 New Orleans	AAA Hou	1	0	0	0	2	10	3	0	0	0	0	0	0	1	0	0	0	0	0	0	—	0	0	0.00
Round Rock	AA Hou	29	22	1	1	160.1	653	154	66	55	7	5	4	5	26	0	85	2	0	15	8	.652	0	1	3.09
1998 Milwaukee	NL	1	0	0	0	2	7	1	0	0	0	0	0	0	0	0	1	0	0	0	0	—	0	0	0.00
7 Min. YEARS		162	129	10	16	848.1	3607	869	434	366	65	28	23	39	256	4	559	29	11	68	36	.654	3	7	3.88

Stewart Smothers

Bats: Right   **Throws:** Right   **Pos:** OF-38; PR-1 | **Ht:** 5'10"   **Wt:** 180   **Born:** 4/29/76   **Age:** 26

Year Team	Lg Org	G	AB	H	2B	3B	HR	TB	R	RBI	TBB	IBB	SO	HBP	SH	SF	SB	CS	SB%	GDP	Avg	OBP	SLG
1997 Eugene	A- Atl	59	233	64	11	6	2	93	31	27	21	0	57	1	3	0	12	4	.75	5	.275	.337	.399
1998 Macon	A Atl	139	506	103	17	3	9	153	61	60	46	1	145	5	7	8	17	12	.59	9	.204	.273	.302
1999 Myrtle Bch	A+ Atl	56	185	28	8	3	1	45	19	14	15	1	71	0	0	5	2	2	.50	3	.151	.210	.243
Macon	A Atl	63	219	62	12	0	7	95	32	39	16	0	61	0	2	5	2	3	.40	2	.283	.325	.434
2000 Myrtle Bch	A+ Atl	11	24	7	1	0	1	11	3	3	0	0	9	1	0	0	0	0	—	0	.292	.320	.458
Richmond	AAA Atl	5	18	1	0	0	0	1	3	0	1	0	9	0	0	0	0	0	—	0	.056	.105	.056
Greenville	AA Atl	57	158	35	6	2	4	57	28	11	31	1	51	0	2	1	7	0	1.00	7	.222	.347	.361
2001 Greenville	AA Atl	39	120	28	7	0	0	35	10	5	14	1	34	0	0	0	1	2	.33	0	.233	.313	.292
5 Min. YEARS		429	1463	328	62	14	24	490	187	159	144	4	437	7	14	19	41	23	.64	26	.224	.293	.335

Steve Smyth

Pitches: Left   **Bats:** Left   **Pos:** SP-18 | **Ht:** 6'1"   **Wt:** 220   **Born:** 6/3/78   **Age:** 24

Year Team	Lg Org	G	GS	CG	GF	IP	BFP	H	R	ER	HR	SH	SF	HB	TBB	IBB	SO	WP	Bk	W	L	Pct.	ShO	Sv	ERA
1999 Eugene	A- ChC	5	5	0	0	24.2	110	29	17	12	2	1	3	0	7	0	14	2	1	1	1	.500	0	0	4.38
Lansing	A ChC	10	10	0	0	50.2	238	68	40	39	5	0	2	2	30	0	46	6	0	5	3	.625	0	0	6.93
2000 Daytona	A+ ChC	24	23	1	0	138.1	589	134	62	50	9	0	2	5	57	0	100	9	1	8	8	.500	0	0	3.25
2001 West Tenn	AA ChC	18	18	3	0	120.1	497	110	38	34	9	4	1	5	40	1	93	6	0	9	3	.750	1	0	2.54
3 Min. YEARS		57	56	4	0	334	1434	341	157	135	25	5	8	12	134	1	253	23	2	23	15	.605	1	0	3.64

Esix Snead

Bats: Both **Throws:** Right **Pos:** OF-132; DH-1; PR-1   **Ht:** 5'10" **Wt:** 175 **Born:** 6/7/76 **Age:** 26

					BATTING											BASERUNNING				PERCENTAGES		
Year Team	Lg Org	G	AB	H	2B	3B	HR	TB	R	RBI	TBB	IBB	SO	HBP	SH	SF	SB	CS	SB%	GDP	Avg	OBP	SLG
1998 New Jersey	A- StL	58	193	45	4	4	1	60	38	16	33	0	54	7	1	0	42	11	.79	3	.233	.365	.311
1999 Potomac	A+ StL	67	249	45	8	5	0	63	37	14	32	0	57	4	3	3	35	12	.74	2	.181	.281	.253
Peoria	A StL	59	181	35	7	1	2	50	35	18	35	0	42	2	7	1	29	9	.76	3	.193	.329	.276
2000 Potomac	A+ StL	132	493	116	14	3	1	139	82	34	72	1	98	7	9	1	109	35	.76	7	.235	.340	.282
2001 New Haven	AA StL	133	520	121	21	6	1	157	71	33	44	0	115	12	5	1	64	23	.74	4	.233	.307	.302
4 Min. YEARS		449	1636	362	54	19	5	469	263	115	216	1	366	32	25	6	279	90	.76	19	.221	.323	.287

Chris Snopek

Bats: Right **Throws:** Right **Pos:** SS-71; 3B-45; 2B-14; PH-2; PR-1   **Ht:** 6'1" **Wt:** 190 **Born:** 9/20/70 **Age:** 31

					BATTING											BASERUNNING				PERCENTAGES		
Year Team	Lg Org	G	AB	H	2B	3B	HR	TB	R	RBI	TBB	IBB	SO	HBP	SH	SF	SB	CS	SB%	GDP	Avg	OBP	SLG
1992 Utica	A- CWS	73	245	69	15	1	2	92	49	29	52	4	44	2	1	4	14	4	.78	4	.282	.406	.376
1993 South Bend	A CWS	22	72	28	8	1	5	53	20	18	15	0	13	3	0	2	1	1	.50	1	.389	.500	.736
Sarasota	A+ CWS	107	371	91	21	4	10	150	61	50	65	2	67	1	3	6	3	2	.60	2	.245	.354	.404
1994 Birmingham	AA CWS	106	365	96	25	3	6	145	58	54	58	3	49	5	3	5	9	4	.69	7	.263	.367	.397
1995 Nashville	AAA CWS	113	393	127	23	4	12	194	56	55	50	1	72	4	6	3	2	5	.29	5	.323	.402	.494
1996 Nashville	AAA CWS	40	153	38	8	0	2	52	18	12	21	1	24	1	1	0	2	2	.50	0	.248	.343	.340
1997 Nashville	AAA CWS	20	73	17	4	0	3	30	8	8	7	0	13	0	0	0	0	0	—	4	.233	.300	.411
1999 Pawtucket	AAA Bos	24	81	20	7	0	3	36	10	10	5	0	15	0	1	0	2	0	1.00	2	.247	.291	.444
Indianapolis	AAA Cin	103	381	107	24	3	9	164	66	64	42	0	51	4	2	5	17	6	.74	10	.281	.354	.430
2000 Tacoma	AAA Sea	104	393	118	24	2	13	185	76	48	44	2	40	4	2	5	12	6	.67	5	.300	.372	.471
2001 Iowa	AAA ChC	130	470	130	33	0	14	205	65	57	32	0	67	2	4	5	6	5	.55	10	.277	.322	.436
1995 Chicago	AL	22	68	22	4	0	1	29	12	7	9	0	12	0	0	0	1	0	1.00	1	.324	.403	.426
1996 Chicago	AL	46	104	27	6	1	6	53	18	18	6	0	16	1	1	1	0	1	.00	5	.260	.304	.510
1997 Chicago	AL	86	298	65	15	0	5	95	27	35	18	0	51	1	4	2	3	2	.60	4	.218	.263	.319
1998 Chicago	AL	53	125	26	2	0	1	31	17	4	14	0	24	1	0	1	3	0	1.00	4	.208	.291	.248
Boston	AL	8	12	2	0	0	0	2	2	2	2	0	5	0	0	0	0	0	—	0	.167	.286	.167
9 Min. YEARS		842	2997	841	192	18	79	1306	487	405	391	13	455	26	23	35	68	35	.66	50	.281	.365	.436
4 Maj. YEARS		215	607	142	27	1	13	210	76	66	49	0	108	3	5	4	7	3	.70	15	.234	.293	.346

Chris Snusz

Bats: Right **Throws:** Right **Pos:** C-27; DH-11; 1B-5; PH-5; PR-1   **Ht:** 6'0" **Wt:** 190 **Born:** 11/8/72 **Age:** 29

					BATTING											BASERUNNING				PERCENTAGES		
Year Team	Lg Org	G	AB	H	2B	3B	HR	TB	R	RBI	TBB	IBB	SO	HBP	SH	SF	SB	CS	SB%	GDP	Avg	OBP	SLG
1995 Batavia	A- Phi	21	66	15	1	0	1	19	9	5	6	0	6	0	0	0	1	1	.50	4	.227	.292	.288
1996 Batavia	A- Phi	13	31	5	0	0	0	5	6	0	6	0	4	0	1	0	0	0	—	0	.161	.297	.161
Piedmont	A Phi	4	11	1	0	0	0	1	2	0	2	0	1	0	0	0	0	1	.00	0	.091	.231	.091
1997 Clearwater	A+ Phi	36	105	21	7	0	0	28	12	3	2	0	22	0	3	0	0	0	—	3	.200	.215	.267
1998 Scranton-WB	AAA Phi	3	9	1	1	0	0	2	0	0	0	0	2	0	0	0	0	0	—	1	.111	.111	.222
Clearwater	A+ Phi	19	56	11	1	0	0	12	6	6	1	0	9	1	1	1	0	0	—	0	.196	.220	.214
Reading	AA Phi	12	28	9	2	0	0	11	6	1	3	0	6	0	0	0	0	0	—	0	.321	.387	.393
1999 Chattanooga	AA Cin	2	6	3	1	0	0	4	0	2	1	0	0	0	0	0	0	0	—	0	.500	.571	.667
Clinton	A Cin	4	21	4	1	1	0	7	2	3	1	0	8	0	0	0	0	0	—	0	.190	.227	.333
Rockford	A Cin	19	53	9	1	0	1	13	6	2	3	0	13	1	1	0	1	0	1.00	4	.170	.228	.245
Harrisburg	AA Mon	5	13	4	1	0	0	5	2	3	1	0	3	0	0	0	0	0	—	1	.308	.357	.385
Ottawa	AAA Mon	21	63	18	3	0	3	30	6	9	1	0	18	0	1	0	0	0	—	2	.286	.297	.476
2000 Ottawa	AAA Mon	63	195	41	8	2	5	68	24	25	7	1	58	1	1	0	0	0	—	7	.210	.241	.349
2001 Buffalo	AAA Cle	1	1	0	0	0	0	0	0	0	0	0	0	0	0	0	0	0	—	0	.000	.000	.000
Akron	AA Cle	2	7	1	0	0	0	1	0	1	0	0	1	0	1	0	0	0	—	0	.143	.143	.143
Norwich	AA NYY	42	125	42	4	2	2	56	17	21	9	0	23	2	2	2	1	0	1.00	3	.336	.384	.448
7 Min. YEARS		267	790	185	31	5	12	262	98	81	43	1	174	5	11	3	3	2	.60	22	.234	.277	.332

Bill Snyder

Pitches: Right **Bats:** Right **Pos:** RP-31   **Ht:** 6'0" **Wt:** 190 **Born:** 1/29/75 **Age:** 27

		HOW MUCH HE PITCHED					WHAT HE GAVE UP											THE RESULTS					
Year Team	Lg Org	G	GS	CG	GF	IP	BFP	H	R	ER	HR	SH	SF	HB	TBB	IBB	SO	WP	Bk	W	L	Pct.	ShO	Sv	ERA
1997 Jamestown	A- Det	25	0	0	25	29	126	19	8	7	1	2	0	2	20	2	42	1	1	1	3	.250	0	9	2.17
1998 W Michigan	A Det	42	0	0	20	59.1	236	40	17	12	2	1	1	3	18	2	84	1	0	3	1	.750	0	2	1.82
1999 Lakeland	A+ Det	47	0	0	42	51.2	197	34	13	11	0	4	2	1	18	0	39	0	0	4	1	.800	0	16	1.92
Jacksnville	AA Det	14	0	0	8	18	80	16	6	5	0	1	0	3	5	1	17	0	0	1	0	1.000	0	2	2.50
2000 Toledo	AAA Det	18	0	0	5	22.2	119	28	26	26	5	1	4	2	24	0	10	1	0	0	0	—	0	0	10.32
Jacksnville	AA Det	29	0	0	13	40	177	33	16	16	4	2	2	2	23	2	38	1	1	1	2	.333	0	3	3.60
2001 Midland	AA Oak	31	0	0	14	42.1	203	59	32	26	9	0	1	2	21	2	24	2	0	1	3	.250	0	0	5.53
5 Min. YEARS		206	0	0	127	263	1138	229	118	103	21	11	10	15	129	9	254	6	2	11	10	.524	0	31	3.52

Earl Snyder

Bats: Right **Throws:** Right **Pos:** 1B-88; 3B-18; OF-8; DH-8; PH-1   **Ht:** 6'0" **Wt:** 207 **Born:** 5/6/76 **Age:** 26

					BATTING											BASERUNNING				PERCENTAGES		
Year Team	Lg Org	G	AB	H	2B	3B	HR	TB	R	RBI	TBB	IBB	SO	HBP	SH	SF	SB	CS	SB%	GDP	Avg	OBP	SLG
1998 Pittsfield	A- NYM	71	262	66	8	1	11	109	39	40	23	0	60	2	0	1	0	1	.00	6	.252	.316	.416
1999 Capital City	A NYM	136	486	130	25	4	28	247	73	97	55	0	117	2	0	9	2	2	.50	5	.267	.339	.508
2000 St. Lucie	A+ NYM	134	514	145	36	0	25	256	84	93	57	6	127	8	0	8	4	4	.50	8	.282	.358	.498
2001 Binghamton	AA NYM	114	405	114	35	2	20	213	69	75	58	5	111	4	0	3	4	2	.67	5	.281	.374	.526
Norfolk	AAA NYM	6	19	9	3	0	0	12	5	3	3	0	1	0	0	0	0	1	.00	0	.474	.565	.632
4 Min. YEARS		461	1686	464	107	7	84	837	270	308	196	11	416	17	0	21	10	10	.50	24	.275	.353	.496

280

John Snyder

Pitches: Right **Bats:** Right **Pos:** SP-23; RP-9   **Ht:** 6'3" **Wt:** 200 **Born:** 8/16/74 **Age:** 27

Year Team	Lg Org	G	GS	CG	GF	IP	BFP	H	R	ER	HR	SH	SF	HB	TBB	IBB	SO	WP	Bk	W	L	Pct.	ShO	Sv	ERA
1992 Angels	R Ana	15	0	0	7	44	195	40	27	16	0	2	5	3	16	1	38	1	4	2	4	.333	0	3	3.27
1993 Cedar Rapds	A Ana	21	16	1	0	99	467	126	88	65	13	7	5	8	39	1	79	6	4	5	6	.455	1	0	5.91
1994 Lk Elsinore	A+ Ana	26	26	2	0	159	698	181	101	79	16	5	5	6	56	0	108	11	2	10	11	.476	0	0	4.47
1995 Midland	AA Ana	21	21	4	0	133.1	591	158	93	85	12	3	6	10	48	1	81	7	3	8	9	.471	0	0	5.74
Birmingham	AA CWS	5	4	0	0	20.1	87	24	16	15	6	0	1	2	6	0	13	1	0	1	0	1.000	0	0	6.64
1996 White Sox	R CWS	4	4	0	0	16.1	58	5	3	3	1	1	0	0	4	0	23	0	0	1	0	1.000	0	0	1.65
Birmingham	AA CWS	9	9	0	0	54	236	59	35	29	10	2	2	1	16	1	58	4	3	3	5	.375	0	0	4.83
1997 Birmingham	AA CWS	20	20	2	0	114.1	510	130	76	59	9	1	3	6	43	0	90	6	2	7	8	.467	1	0	4.64
1998 Calgary	AAA CWS	15	15	1	0	97	429	112	49	47	11	5	2	5	34	1	63	2	2	7	3	.700	0	0	4.36
1999 Calgary	AAA CWS	3	3	0	0	17	75	17	9	8	2	0	0	2	5	0	9	0	0	3	0	1.000	0	0	4.24
2000 Huntsville	AA Mil	2	2	0	0	12.1	46	6	3	3	1	1	0	1	5	0	6	0	0	1	1	.500	0	0	2.19
Indianapols	AAA Mil	1	1	0	0	7	26	6	2	2	1	1	0	0	0	0	5	0	0	0	1	.000	0	0	2.57
2001 Indianapols	AAA Mil	32	23	0	4	147.1	683	202	115	91	15	4	4	12	37	0	84	8	1	3	11	.214	0	0	5.56
1998 Chicago	AL	15	14	1	0	86.1	367	96	49	46	14	2	4	2	23	1	52	2	0	7	2	.778	0	0	4.80
1999 Chicago	AL	25	25	1	0	129.1	602	167	103	96	27	3	7	6	49	0	67	11	0	9	12	.429	0	0	6.68
2000 Milwaukee	NL	23	23	0	0	127	556	147	95	87	8	6	7	9	77	10	69	6	0	3	10	.231	0	0	6.17
10 Min. YEARS		174	144	10	11	921	4101	1066	617	502	97	32	33	56	309	5	657	46	21	51	59	.464	2	3	4.91
3 Maj. YEARS		63	62	2	0	342.2	1565	410	247	229	49	11	18	17	149	11	188	19	0	19	24	.442	0	0	6.01

Matt Snyder

Pitches: Right **Bats:** Right **Pos:** RP-39; SP-1   **Ht:** 5'11" **Wt:** 201 **Born:** 7/7/74 **Age:** 27

Year Team	Lg Org	G	GS	CG	GF	IP	BFP	H	R	ER	HR	SH	SF	HB	TBB	IBB	SO	WP	Bk	W	L	Pct.	ShO	Sv	ERA
1995 Bluefield	R+ Bal	17	0	0	15	34.2	150	35	9	4	1	0	0	3	13	0	46	1	0	0	0	—	0	8	1.04
1996 High Desert	A+ Bal	58	0	0	49	72	317	60	34	30	6	5	2	1	38	2	93	9	1	6	2	.750	0	20	3.75
1997 Bowie	AA Bal	67	0	0	45	80	366	89	48	37	11	8	4	4	42	5	68	10	0	7	5	.583	0	19	4.16
1998 Rochester	AAA Bal	12	0	0	5	19.2	77	17	9	8	3	0	0	1	6	0	13	0	0	2	1	.667	0	0	3.66
Bowie	AA Bal	22	20	4	0	120	510	127	66	58	14	1	3	4	30	0	116	6	3	9	6	.600	1	0	4.35
1999 Rochester	AAA Bal	48	3	0	15	84.2	380	95	60	49	14	3	4	4	30	4	59	6	0	6	6	.500	0	1	5.21
2000 Bowie	AA Bal	23	12	0	3	90	385	84	50	39	9	4	6	5	38	1	77	1	0	2	7	.222	0	1	3.90
Rochester	AAA Bal	10	1	0	2	23	97	23	13	13	7	0	1	0	8	0	18	0	0	1	0	1.000	0	1	5.09
2001 Rochester	AAA Bal	9	0	0	4	11	56	13	8	6	1	1	1	1	10	0	9	4	1	0	0	—	0	1	4.91
Charlotte	A+ Tex	1	1	0	0	1.2	13	7	6	6	1	0	1	0	1	0	2	0	0	0	1	.000	0	0	32.40
Tulsa	AA Tex	4	0	0	2	10	47	14	9	9	1	0	0	0	3	0	6	2	0	1	0	1.000	0	0	8.10
Iowa	AAA ChC	1	0	0	1	1	5	1	1	1	0	0	0	0	1	0	3	0	0	0	0	—	0	0	9.00
West Tenn	AA ChC	25	0	0	9	31.1	147	36	33	31	6	0	2	3	17	1	31	3	0	2	1	.667	0	1	8.90
7 Min. YEARS		297	37	4	150	579	2550	601	346	291	73	23	24	26	237	13	541	42	5	36	29	.554	1	51	4.52

Tony Socarras

Bats: Left **Throws:** Right **Pos:** C-68; DH-6; PH-1; PR-1   **Ht:** 6'0" **Wt:** 200 **Born:** 11/8/78 **Age:** 23

Year Team	Lg Org	G	AB	H	2B	3B	HR	TB	R	RBI	TBB	IBB	SO	HBP	SH	SF	SB	CS	SB%	GDP	Avg	OBP	SLG
2000 Boise	A- Ana	55	161	41	9	0	5	65	26	28	24	1	47	4	0	3	0	4	.00	3	.255	.359	.404
2001 Arkansas	AA Ana	3	6	1	0	0	0	1	0	0	0	0	1	0	0	0	0	0	—	0	.167	.167	.167
Rancho Cuca	A+ Ana	56	176	23	4	0	5	42	10	9	14	1	68	0	3	0	1	1	.50	2	.131	.195	.239
Cedar Rapds	A Ana	16	51	11	1	0	2	18	10	11	7	0	20	3	0	1	0	0	—	1	.216	.339	.353
2 Min. YEARS		130	394	76	14	0	12	126	46	48	45	2	136	7	3	4	1	5	.17	6	.193	.284	.320

Clint Sodowsky

Pitches: Right **Bats:** Left **Pos:** RP-7   **Ht:** 6'4" **Wt:** 195 **Born:** 7/13/72 **Age:** 29

Year Team	Lg Org	G	GS	CG	GF	IP	BFP	H	R	ER	HR	SH	SF	HB	TBB	IBB	SO	WP	Bk	W	L	Pct.	ShO	Sv	ERA
1991 Bristol	R+ Det	14	8	0	3	55	253	49	34	23	3	2	1	2	34	0	44	8	4	0	5	.000	0	0	3.76
1992 Bristol	R+ Det	15	6	0	2	56	243	46	35	22	3	1	2	4	29	0	48	6	1	2	2	.500	0	0	3.54
1993 Fayettevlle	A Det	27	27	1	0	155.2	676	177	101	88	11	2	6	6	51	0	80	4	5	14	10	.583	0	0	5.09
1994 Lakeland	A+ Det	19	18	1	1	110.1	466	111	58	47	5	2	2	6	34	0	73	12	0	6	3	.667	1	0	3.83
1995 Jacksnville	AA Det	19	19	5	0	123.2	497	102	46	35	4	2	2	5	50	1	77	3	0	5	5	.500	3	0	2.55
Toledo	AAA Det	9	9	1	0	60	242	47	21	19	5	2	0	3	30	1	32	1	0	5	1	.833	0	0	2.85
1996 Toledo	AAA Det	19	19	1	0	118.2	525	128	67	52	8	8	3	6	51	0	59	3	2	6	8	.429	0	0	3.94
1997 Calgary	AAA Pit	8	0	0	1	13.2	64	19	10	10	1	0	0	0	6	0	9	1	0	0	1	.000	0	1	6.59
1998 Tucson	AAA Ari	2	2	0	0	9.1	42	11	4	4	0	0	0	0	3	0	7	0	1	0	1	.000	0	0	3.86
1999 Memphis	AAA StL	19	13	2	3	80.1	350	85	55	43	14	4	1	4	32	0	52	6	2	4	5	.444	1	3	4.82
2000 Akron	AA Cle	23	0	0	9	45.1	211	59	35	27	3	4	4	2	12	2	39	2	0	2	1	.667	0	3	5.36
Tulsa	AA Tex	6	0	0	3	9.1	41	6	6	5	0	1	0	0	6	0	8	0	1	0	0	—	0	0	4.82
Oklahoma	AA Tex	13	0	0	7	21.2	88	23	7	7	2	0	0	2	4	0	13	3	0	2	1	.667	0	2	2.91
2001 Scranton-WB	AAA Phi	7	0	0	4	7	33	8	4	3	0	0	0	0	3	1	8	0	0	0	0	—	0	3	3.86
1995 Detroit	AL	6	6	0	0	23.1	112	24	15	13	4	1	0	0	18	0	14	1	1	2	2	.500	0	0	5.01
1996 Detroit	AL	7	7	0	0	24.1	132	44	34	32	5	1	0	3	20	0	9	3	0	1	3	.250	0	0	11.84
1997 Pittsburgh	NL	45	0	0	8	52	236	49	22	21	6	1	2	2	34	7	51	6	0	2	2	.500	0	0	3.63
1998 Arizona	NL	45	6	0	10	77.2	357	86	56	49	5	5	2	7	39	5	42	4	2	3	6	.333	0	0	5.68
1999 St. Louis	NL	3	1	0	0	6.1	39	15	11	11	1	0	0	0	6	0	2	0	0	0	1	.000	0	0	15.63
11 Min. YEARS		200	121	11	33	866	3736	871	483	385	59	28	21	42	345	5	549	49	16	46	43	.517	5	12	4.00
5 Maj. YEARS		106	20	0	18	183.2	876	214	138	126	21	8	4	12	117	12	118	14	3	8	14	.364	0	0	6.17

Danny Solano

Bats: Right **Throws:** Right **Pos:** SS-113; 3B-7; PH-1 **Ht:** 5'9" **Wt:** 155 **Born:** 12/3/78 **Age:** 23

Year Team	Lg Org	G	AB	H	2B	3B	HR	TB	R	RBI	TBB	IBB	SO	HBP	SH	SF	SB	CS	SB%	GDP	Avg	OBP	SLG
1998 Charlotte	A+ Tex	84	262	68	15	0	1	86	46	30	42	0	54	2	9	4	9	6	.60	2	.260	.361	.328
1999 Oklahoma	AAA Tex	3	6	0	0	0	0	0	0	1	0	0	4	0	0	1	0	0	—	0	.000	.000	.000
Charlotte	A+ Tex	116	421	114	18	4	7	161	64	44	74	0	74	6	12	0	21	13	.62	3	.271	.387	.382
2000 Tulsa	AA Tex	109	359	90	13	3	7	130	36	33	40	0	66	6	10	2	10	6	.63	11	.251	.334	.362
2001 Tulsa	AA Tex	120	423	104	16	5	6	148	58	45	46	0	77	6	18	4	3	4	.43	6	.246	.326	.350
4 Min. YEARS		432	1471	376	62	12	21	525	204	153	202	0	275	20	49	11	43	29	.60	22	.256	.351	.357

Gabe Sollecito

Pitches: Right **Bats:** Both **Pos:** RP-42 **Ht:** 6'1" **Wt:** 190 **Born:** 3/3/72 **Age:** 30

Year Team	Lg Org	G	GS	CG	GF	IP	BFP	H	R	ER	HR	SH	SF	HB	TBB	IBB	SO	WP	Bk	W	L	Pct.	ShO	Sv	ERA
1993 Niagara Fal	A- Det	23	0	0	21	26.2	111	18	4	1	0	2	0	3	10	1	23	3	1	2	1	.667	0	14	0.34
1994 Fayetteville	A Det	46	0	0	45	57	238	47	21	18	1	2	2	10	15	2	52	1	0	4	3	.571	0	18	2.84
1996 Salinas	IND —	1	0	0	0	0.2	1	0	0	0	0	0	0	0	0	0	0	0	0	0	0	—	0	0	0.00
1997 Sioux Falls	IND —	13	0	0	8	13	65	19	12	11	0	0	0	1	8	2	9	1	0	0	4	.000	0	1	7.62
Salinas	IND —	24	0	0	19	32.1	132	23	6	5	1	0	2	2	9	2	37	2	0	4	1	.800	0	5	1.39
1998 Charlotte	A+ Tex	37	0	0	18	60	251	54	13	6	1	1	3	6	14	2	50	0	0	5	2	.714	0	2	0.90
Tulsa	AA Tex	5	0	0	3	9.1	39	5	3	2	0	0	0	1	4	0	10	2	0	1	0	1.000	0	0	1.93
1999 Tulsa	AA Tex	53	0	0	23	96.1	400	85	28	26	6	3	3	8	29	1	80	3	1	5	4	.556	0	11	2.43
2000 Oklahoma	AAA Tex	7	0	0	1	9.1	46	12	8	8	2	0	1	0	6	0	10	0	0	0	0	—	0	0	7.71
2001 Chico	IND —	35	0	0	17	51	199	36	14	6	0	1	0	2	8	1	55	2	0	3	2	.600	0	5	1.06
Iowa	AAA ChC	7	0	0	5	9.1	36	9	5	5	2	0	0	0	1	0	9	0	0	0	0	—	0	0	4.82
8 Min. YEARS		251	0	0	160	365	1518	308	114	88	13	9	11	33	104	11	335	14	2	24	17	.585	0	56	2.17

Scott Sollmann

Bats: Left **Throws:** Left **Pos:** OF-36; PH-12; PR-5; DH-2 **Ht:** 5'10" **Wt:** 167 **Born:** 5/2/75 **Age:** 27

Year Team	Lg Org	G	AB	H	2B	3B	HR	TB	R	RBI	TBB	IBB	SO	HBP	SH	SF	SB	CS	SB%	GDP	Avg	OBP	SLG
1996 Jamestown	A- Det	67	253	71	5	5	0	86	49	19	34	1	47	7	6	2	35	14	.71	2	.281	.378	.340
1997 W Michigan	A Det	121	460	144	13	4	0	165	89	33	79	5	81	11	8	3	40	14	.74	1	.313	.423	.359
1998 Jacksnville	AA Det	10	26	2	0	0	0	2	4	1	7	0	4	1	2	0	1	1	.50	0	.077	.294	.077
Lakeland	A+ Det	104	401	101	11	4	2	126	81	35	62	0	52	3	7	3	59	17	.78	1	.252	.354	.314
1999 Stockton	A+ Mil	67	249	87	10	5	0	107	61	33	52	3	38	1	1	1	32	14	.70	1	.349	.462	.430
Huntsville	AA Mil	55	191	60	4	5	1	77	34	9	34	0	31	3	0	0	17	8	.68	3	.314	.425	.403
2000 Tennessee	AA Tor	114	385	91	16	5	0	117	66	27	53	1	58	8	6	3	19	10	.66	6	.236	.339	.304
2001 Chattanooga	AA Cin	47	121	38	3	1	0	43	22	8	19	2	17	0	3	0	12	6	.67	1	.314	.407	.355
Mudville	A+ Cin	4	18	6	2	1	0	10	2	1	0	0	5	0	0	0	1	0	1.00	0	.333	.333	.556
6 Min. YEARS		589	2104	600	64	30	3	733	408	166	340	12	333	34	33	12	216	84	.72	15	.285	.391	.348

Shawn Sonnier

Pitches: Right **Bats:** Right **Pos:** RP-45; SP-2 **Ht:** 6'5" **Wt:** 210 **Born:** 7/5/76 **Age:** 25

Year Team	Lg Org	G	GS	CG	GF	IP	BFP	H	R	ER	HR	SH	SF	HB	TBB	IBB	SO	WP	Bk	W	L	Pct.	ShO	Sv	ERA
1998 Spokane	A- KC	7	0	0	3	6.2	27	7	1	1	0	0	0	0	1	0	10	1	0	0	0	—	0	1	1.35
1999 Wilmington	A+ KC	44	0	0	38	59	237	46	20	19	1	2	0	1	19	2	73	2	0	1	2	.333	0	13	2.88
2000 Wichita	AA KC	48	0	0	42	64	260	41	22	16	6	0	0	3	26	3	90	4	0	0	3	.000	0	21	2.25
2001 Omaha	AAA KC	47	2	0	28	71	313	69	41	38	15	0	3	0	33	0	63	2	0	5	5	.500	0	6	4.82
4 Min. YEARS		146	2	0	111	201	837	163	84	74	22	2	3	4	79	5	236	9	0	6	10	.375	0	41	3.31

Zach Sorensen

Bats: Both **Throws:** Right **Pos:** SS-53; DH-7; 2B-2 **Ht:** 6'0" **Wt:** 190 **Born:** 1/3/77 **Age:** 25

Year Team	Lg Org	G	AB	H	2B	3B	HR	TB	R	RBI	TBB	IBB	SO	HBP	SH	SF	SB	CS	SB%	GDP	Avg	OBP	SLG
1998 Watertown	A- Cle	53	200	60	7	8	4	95	38	26	35	0	35	0	2	0	14	4	.78	2	.300	.404	.475
1999 Kinston	A+ Cle	130	508	121	16	7	7	172	79	59	62	1	126	2	8	2	24	12	.67	6	.238	.322	.339
2000 Akron	AA Cle	96	382	99	17	4	6	142	62	38	42	0	62	2	4	3	16	6	.73	8	.259	.333	.372
Buffalo	AAA Cle	12	38	10	1	1	0	13	5	2	3	0	9	0	0	1	1	0	1.00	2	.263	.310	.342
2001 Mahoning Vy	A- Cle	14	53	13	0	1	1	18	10	11	2	0	8	0	1	2	2	0	1.00	3	.245	.263	.340
Akron	AA Cle	46	194	45	6	1	5	68	24	16	11	1	30	0	3	0	10	8	.56	3	.232	.273	.351
Buffalo	AAA Cle	2	7	2	0	0	0	2	2	1	0	0	0	0	0	0	0	0	—	0	.286	.286	.286
4 Min. YEARS		353	1382	350	47	22	23	510	220	153	155	2	270	4	18	8	67	30	.69	23	.253	.329	.369

Rafael Soriano

Pitches: Right **Bats:** Right **Pos:** SP-23 **Ht:** 6'1" **Wt:** 175 **Born:** 12/19/79 **Age:** 22

Year Team	Lg Org	G	GS	CG	GF	IP	BFP	H	R	ER	HR	SH	SF	HB	TBB	IBB	SO	WP	Bk	W	L	Pct.	ShO	Sv	ERA
1999 Everett	A- Sea	14	14	0	0	75.1	323	56	34	26	8	1	0	4	49	0	83	2	0	5	4	.556	0	0	3.11
2000 Wisconsin	A Sea	21	21	1	0	122.1	509	97	41	39	3	2	5	12	50	0	90	5	2	4	4	.667	0	2	2.87
2001 San Berndno	A+ Sea	15	15	2	0	89	346	49	28	25	4	2	2	4	39	0	98	2	0	6	3	.667	1	0	2.53
San Antonio	AA Sea	8	8	0	0	48.1	193	34	18	18	5	0	0	2	14	0	53	2	1	2	2	.500	0	0	3.35
3 Min. YEARS		58	58	3	0	335	1362	236	121	108	20	5	7	22	152	0	324	11	3	21	13	.618	1	0	2.90

Saul Soto

Bats: Right **Throws:** Right **Pos:** 1B-50; C-26; PH-4   **Ht:** 6'3" **Wt:** 225 **Born:** 8/11/78 **Age:** 23

					BATTING													BASERUNNING				PERCENTAGES		
Year Team	Lg Org	G	AB	H	2B	3B	HR	TB	R	RBI	TBB	IBB	SO	HBP	SH	SF	SB	CS	SB%	GDP	Avg	OBP	SLG
2000 Yakima	A- LA	55	192	49	12	0	6	79	26	26	19	1	46	9	2	0	1	3	.25	5	.255	.350	.411
2001 Jacksnville	AA LA	3	3	1	0	0	0	1	1	0	0	0	0	0	0	0	0	0	—	1	.333	.333	.333
Vero Beach	A+ LA	1	2	0	0	0	0	0	0	0	2	0	0	0	0	0	0	0	—	0	.000	.500	.000
Wilmington	A LA	75	252	66	17	0	6	101	32	34	33	0	34	9	1	1	4	4	.50	7	.262	.366	.401
2 Min. YEARS		134	449	116	29	0	12	181	59	60	54	1	80	18	3	1	5	7	.42	13	.258	.360	.403

Steve Sparks

Pitches: Right **Bats:** Right **Pos:** RP-22; SP-16   **Ht:** 6'4" **Wt:** 210 **Born:** 3/28/75 **Age:** 27

				HOW MUCH HE PITCHED						WHAT HE GAVE UP									THE RESULTS					
Year Team	Lg Org	G	GS	CG	GF	IP	BFP	H	R	ER	HR	SH	SF	HB	TBB	IBB	SO	WP	Bk	W	L	Pct.	ShO	Sv	ERA
1998 Erie	A- Pit	14	10	0	0	63	282	55	38	31	9	3	0	2	30	1	61	5	3	2	7	.222	0	0	4.43
Augusta	A Pit	2	2	0	0	8.2	43	11	9	6	1	0	1	0	4	0	12	1	0	0	1	.000	0	0	6.23
1999 Hickory	A Pit	25	12	1	2	88.2	407	97	60	44	3	3	3	5	51	0	72	7	0	4	6	.400	1	0	4.47
Lynchburg	A+ Pit	5	5	1	0	26	124	36	20	18	3	0	2	1	15	0	20	2	0	2	3	.400	0	0	6.23
2000 Altoona	AA Pit	23	17	3	3	109.1	484	103	66	58	6	3	4	11	54	0	66	8	0	6	7	.462	2	0	4.77
2001 Nashville	AAA Pit	31	10	1	9	74.2	358	77	50	42	10	5	0	3	64	2	63	6	0	3	5	.375	0	3	5.06
Altoona	AA Pit	7	6	1	0	38.1	166	31	19	16	2	0	2	1	25	0	32	5	0	1	4	.200	0	0	3.76
2000 Pittsburgh	NL	3	0	0	2	4	20	4	3	3	0	0	0	0	5	0	2	2	0	0	0	—	0	0	6.75
4 Min. YEARS		107	62	7	14	408.2	1864	410	262	215	28	11	14	30	243	3	326	34	3	18	33	.353	3	3	4.73

Brian Specht

Bats: Both **Throws:** Right **Pos:** SS-107; DH-2; PR-1   **Ht:** 5'11" **Wt:** 175 **Born:** 10/19/80 **Age:** 21

					BATTING													BASERUNNING				PERCENTAGES		
Year Team	Lg Org	G	AB	H	2B	3B	HR	TB	R	RBI	TBB	IBB	SO	HBP	SH	SF	SB	CS	SB%	GDP	Avg	OBP	SLG
2000 Lk Elsinore	A+ Ana	89	334	90	22	5	2	128	70	35	52	2	80	3	3	3	25	12	.68	6	.269	.370	.383
2001 Rancho Cuca	A+ Ana	65	264	64	13	6	7	110	45	31	24	1	78	3	3	1	17	3	.85	1	.242	.312	.417
Arkansas	AA Ana	45	155	41	9	2	2	60	14	15	13	0	32	1	1	0	2	2	.50	2	.265	.325	.387
2 Min. YEARS		199	753	195	44	13	11	298	129	81	89	3	190	7	7	4	44	17	.72	9	.259	.341	.396

Tim Spehr

Bats: Right **Throws:** Right **Pos:** C-48; PH-14; 1B-6; DH-2   **Ht:** 6'2" **Wt:** 200 **Born:** 7/2/66 **Age:** 35

					BATTING													BASERUNNING				PERCENTAGES		
Year Team	Lg Org	G	AB	H	2B	3B	HR	TB	R	RBI	TBB	IBB	SO	HBP	SH	SF	SB	CS	SB%	GDP	Avg	OBP	SLG
1988 Appleton	A KC	31	110	29	3	0	5	47	15	22	10	0	28	4	0	2	3	0	1.00	1	.264	.341	.427
1989 Baseball Cy	A+ KC	18	64	16	5	0	1	24	8	7	5	0	17	0	2	0	1	0	1.00	1	.250	.304	.375
Memphis	AA KC	61	216	42	9	0	8	75	22	23	16	0	59	2	1	1	1	3	.25	2	.194	.255	.347
1990 Omaha	AAA KC	102	307	69	10	2	6	101	42	34	41	0	88	10	6	2	5	5	.50	4	.225	.333	.329
1991 Omaha	AAA KC	72	215	59	14	2	6	95	27	26	25	1	48	4	3	3	3	2	.60	0	.274	.356	.442
1992 Omaha	AAA KC	109	336	85	22	0	15	152	48	42	61	0	89	11	4	1	4	2	.67	5	.253	.384	.452
1993 Ottawa	AAA Mon	46	141	28	6	1	4	48	15	13	14	1	35	6	0	1	2	1	.67	4	.199	.296	.340
1997 Richmond	AAA Atl	36	120	23	5	0	3	37	13	14	12	0	37	1	0	2	0	0	—	1	.192	.267	.308
1998 St. Lucie	A+ NYM	14	38	7	2	0	1	12	7	6	9	0	16	3	0	1	0	0	—	0	.184	.373	.316
Norfolk	AAA NYM	1	1	1	0	0	0	1	0	0	0	0	0	0	0	0	0	0	—	0	1.000	1.000	1.000
2000 Pawtucket	AAA Bos	77	227	34	7	1	5	58	25	25	36	0	85	4	3	3	0	1	.00	3	.150	.274	.256
2001 Louisville	AAA Cin	68	184	30	7	0	5	52	22	25	18	0	73	7	0	2	2	1	.67	3	.163	.261	.283
1991 Kansas City	AL	37	74	14	5	0	3	28	7	14	9	0	18	1	3	1	1	0	1.00	1	.189	.282	.378
1993 Montreal	NL	53	87	20	6	0	2	32	14	10	6	1	20	1	3	2	2	0	1.00	0	.230	.281	.368
1994 Montreal	NL	52	36	9	3	1	0	14	8	5	4	0	11	0	1	0	2	0	1.00	0	.250	.325	.389
1995 Montreal	NL	41	35	9	5	0	1	17	4	3	6	0	7	0	3	0	0	0	—	0	.257	.366	.486
1996 Montreal	NL	63	44	4	1	0	1	8	4	3	3	0	15	1	1	0	1	0	1.00	1	.091	.167	.182
1997 Kansas City	AL	17	35	6	0	0	1	9	3	2	2	0	12	1	0	0	1	0	1.00	0	.171	.237	.257
Atlanta	NL	8	14	3	1	0	1	7	2	4	0	0	4	0	0	0	1	0	1.00	0	.214	.214	.500
1998 New York	NL	21	51	7	1	0	0	8	3	3	7	1	16	2	0	0	1	0	1.00	0	.137	.267	.157
Kansas City	AL	11	25	6	2	0	1	11	5	2	8	0	3	2	1	0	0	0	—	1	.240	.457	.440
1999 Kansas City	AL	60	155	32	7	0	9	66	26	26	22	0	47	6	2	2	1	0	1.00	2	.206	.324	.426
10 Min. YEARS		635	1959	423	90	6	59	702	244	237	247	2	575	52	19	18	21	15	.58	24	.216	.317	.358
8 Maj. YEARS		363	556	110	31	1	19	200	76	72	67	2	153	14	14	5	9	0	1.00	6	.198	.298	.360

Corey Spencer

Pitches: Left **Bats:** Left **Pos:** RP-55   **Ht:** 6'1" **Wt:** 220 **Born:** 9/4/76 **Age:** 25

				HOW MUCH HE PITCHED						WHAT HE GAVE UP									THE RESULTS					
Year Team	Lg Org	G	GS	CG	GF	IP	BFP	H	R	ER	HR	SH	SF	HB	TBB	IBB	SO	WP	Bk	W	L	Pct.	ShO	Sv	ERA
1999 Lowell	A- Bos	19	0	0	3	29	127	33	12	8	0	0	0	0	7	0	38	1	0	1	0	1.000	0	1	2.48
Augusta	A Bos	7	1	0	2	11.2	49	13	6	6	1	0	0	0	5	0	13	0	0	1	0	1.000	0	1	4.63
2000 Augusta	A Bos	53	0	0	11	96.2	423	90	46	28	4	3	4	5	34	0	119	4	0	8	2	.800	0	2	2.61
2001 Trenton	AA Bos	55	0	0	43	77.2	349	85	41	39	9	5	4	1	31	5	82	5	0	3	5	.375	0	20	4.52
3 Min. YEARS		134	1	0	59	215	948	221	105	81	14	8	8	6	77	5	252	10	0	13	7	.650	0	24	3.39

Sean Spencer

Pitches: Left **Bats:** Left **Pos:** RP-52   **Ht:** 5'11" **Wt:** 185 **Born:** 5/29/75 **Age:** 27

				HOW MUCH HE PITCHED						WHAT HE GAVE UP									THE RESULTS					
Year Team	Lg Org	G	GS	CG	GF	IP	BFP	H	R	ER	HR	SH	SF	HB	TBB	IBB	SO	WP	Bk	W	L	Pct.	ShO	Sv	ERA
1997 Lancaster	A+ Sea	39	0	0	32	60.1	227	41	12	11	4	4	1	2	15	0	72	2	0	2	3	.400	0	18	1.64
1998 Orlando	AA Sea	37	0	0	32	42.2	178	33	18	14	3	3	1	1	18	1	43	5	1	2	1	.667	0	18	2.95
Tacoma	AAA Sea	9	0	0	3	13	56	10	7	7	0	0	0	1	7	0	16	1	0	2	0	1.000	0	1	4.85

Year Team	Lg Org	G	GS	CG	GF	IP	BFP	H	R	ER	HR	SH	SF	HB	TBB	IBB	SO	WP	Bk	W	L	Pct.	ShO	Sv	ERA
1999 Tacoma	AAA Sea	44	0	0	28	49.1	205	41	21	19	6	1	0	1	23	2	53	4	0	2	1	.667	0	7	3.47
2000 Tacoma	AAA Sea	42	0	0	20	45.1	208	35	21	17	3	5	2	1	37	3	46	3	2	3	2	.600	0	0	3.38
Ottawa	AAA Mon	10	0	0	5	10	52	15	12	11	2	0	1	1	6	0	8	0	0	1	1	.500	0	1	9.90
2001 Ottawa	AAA Mon	52	0	0	12	64.1	271	53	23	21	4	3	3	2	27	0	59	5	0	2	1	.667	0	0	2.94
1999 Seattle	AL	2	0	0	0	1.2	12	5	4	4	0	0	0	0	3	0	2	0	0	0	0	—	0	0	21.60
2000 Montreal	NL	8	0	0	1	6.2	28	7	4	4	2	0	1	0	3	0	6	4	0	0	0	—	0	0	5.40
5 Min. YEARS		233	0	0	132	285	1197	228	114	100	22	16	8	9	133	6	297	20	3	14	9	.609	0	45	3.16
2 Maj. YEARS		10	0	0	1	8.1	40	12	8	8	2	0	1	0	6	0	8	4	0	0	0	—	0	0	8.64

Stan Spencer

Pitches: Right **Bats:** Right **Pos:** SP-18; RP-2 **Ht:** 6'4" **Wt:** 223 **Born:** 8/7/69 **Age:** 32

Year Team	Lg Org	G	GS	CG	GF	IP	BFP	H	R	ER	HR	SH	SF	HB	TBB	IBB	SO	WP	Bk	W	L	Pct.	ShO	Sv	ERA
1991 Harrisburg	AA Mon	17	17	1	0	92	389	90	52	45	6	4	2	4	30	0	66	2	3	6	1	.857	0	0	4.40
1993 High Desert	A+ Fla	13	13	0	0	61.2	265	67	33	28	4	0	2	3	18	0	38	1	0	4	4	.500	0	0	4.09
1994 Brevard Cty	A+ Fla	6	5	0	1	20	84	20	9	7	0	0	1	1	6	0	22	1	0	1	0	1.000	0	0	3.15
Portland	AA Fla	20	20	1	0	124	505	113	52	48	12	4	6	2	30	2	96	3	1	9	4	.692	0	0	3.48
1995 Charlotte	AAA Fla	9	9	0	0	41.1	198	61	37	36	9	0	0	3	24	1	19	0	0	1	4	.200	0	0	7.84
Portland	AA Fla	8	8	0	0	39	193	57	39	32	9	0	4	2	19	0	32	0	0	1	4	.200	0	0	7.38
1997 Rancho Cuca	A+ SD	7	7	0	0	40.1	164	37	18	15	6	0	1	2	5	0	46	1	0	3	1	.750	0	0	3.35
Las Vegas	AAA SD	8	8	0	0	48	208	48	23	20	5	1	0	1	18	2	47	1	0	3	2	.600	0	0	3.75
1998 Las Vegas	AAA SD	22	22	0	0	137.1	570	120	67	60	17	3	3	5	42	2	136	6	1	12	6	.667	0	0	3.93
1999 Las Vegas	AAA SD	12	10	0	2	54.1	247	69	35	33	6	4	2	2	15	0	50	4	0	5	4	.556	0	0	5.47
2000 Las Vegas	AAA SD	6	6	0	0	36.2	146	29	9	7	2	1	3	1	7	0	40	3	1	4	0	1.000	0	0	1.72
2001 Portland	AAA SD	20	18	0	1	99	432	110	62	56	11	4	3	5	30	0	81	3	1	5	6	.455	0	0	5.09
1998 San Diego	NL	6	5	0	0	30.2	124	29	16	16	5	0	0	1	4	0	31	0	0	1	0	1.000	0	0	4.70
1999 San Diego	NL	9	8	0	1	38.1	172	56	44	39	11	4	0	1	11	1	36	1	1	0	7	.000	0	0	9.16
2000 San Diego	NL	8	8	0	0	49.2	208	44	22	18	7	2	1	2	19	1	40	0	1	2	2	.500	0	0	3.26
9 Min. YEARS		148	143	2	4	793.2	3401	821	436	387	87	21	27	31	244	7	673	25	7	54	36	.600	0	0	4.39
3 Maj. YEARS		23	21	0	1	118.2	515	129	82	73	23	6	1	4	34	2	107	1	2	3	9	.250	0	0	5.54

Mike Spiegel

Pitches: Left **Bats:** Left **Pos:** SP-18; RP-4 **Ht:** 6'5" **Wt:** 200 **Born:** 11/24/75 **Age:** 26

Year Team	Lg Org	G	GS	CG	GF	IP	BFP	H	R	ER	HR	SH	SF	HB	TBB	IBB	SO	WP	Bk	W	L	Pct.	ShO	Sv	ERA
1996 Burlington	R+ Cle	14	0	0	6	21.2	97	19	12	9	0	1	0	2	12	0	14	1	0	1	0	1.000	0	0	3.74
1997 Columbus	A Cle	2	2	0	0	10	39	6	4	4	1	0	0	1	5	0	6	0	0	0	0	—	0	0	3.60
1998 Watertown	A- Cle	1	1	0	0	6	25	2	1	0	0	0	0	2	5	0	7	0	1	1	0	1.000	0	0	0.00
Columbus	A Cle	13	13	0	0	65.1	297	75	53	45	7	2	1	6	34	0	61	6	2	5	6	.455	0	0	6.20
1999 Columbus	A Cle	7	7	0	0	35	145	27	13	11	4	1	0	1	14	0	38	2	2	1	0	1.000	0	0	2.83
Kinston	A+ Cle	18	18	0	0	96	405	69	46	33	8	6	4	7	51	0	103	11	0	5	3	.625	0	0	3.09
2000 Akron	AA Cle	9	7	0	1	36.2	182	48	32	29	6	0	3	2	24	1	18	2	0	1	3	.250	0	0	7.12
Kinston	A+ Cle	5	5	0	0	27	117	23	12	11	4	1	1	3	11	0	23	3	1	3	2	.600	0	0	3.67
2001 Akron	AA Cle	1	1	0	0	5.2	30	10	6	6	0	2	1	1	3	0	0	0	0	0	0	—	0	0	9.53
Kinston	A+ Cle	21	17	0	1	108.2	448	83	37	34	9	5	3	11	38	2	90	1	0	7	7	.500	0	0	2.82
6 Min. YEARS		91	71	0	8	412	1785	362	216	182	39	18	13	36	197	3	360	26	6	25	21	.543	0	0	3.98

Paul Spoljaric

Pitches: Left **Bats:** Right **Pos:** RP-7 **Ht:** 6'3" **Wt:** 210 **Born:** 9/24/70 **Age:** 31

Year Team	Lg Org	G	GS	CG	GF	IP	BFP	H	R	ER	HR	SH	SF	HB	TBB	IBB	SO	WP	Bk	W	L	Pct.	ShO	Sv	ERA
1990 Medcine Hat	R+ Tor	15	13	0	2	66.1	291	57	43	32	6	0	3	0	35	0	62	3	3	3	7	.300	0	1	4.34
1991 St.Cathrnes	A- Tor	4	4	0	0	18.2	77	21	14	10	1	0	0	1	9	0	21	0	0	0	2	.000	0	0	4.82
1992 Myrtle Bch	A Tor	26	26	1	0	162.2	647	111	68	51	7	4	4	5	58	0	161	7	1	10	8	.556	0	0	2.82
1993 Dunedin	A+ Tor	4	4	0	0	26	99	16	5	4	1	0	0	2	12	0	29	2	0	3	0	1.000	0	0	1.38
Knoxville	AA Tor	7	7	0	0	43.1	175	30	12	11	3	1	0	1	22	0	51	2	1	4	1	.800	0	0	2.28
Syracuse	AAA Tor	18	18	1	0	95.1	424	97	63	56	14	1	6	2	52	0	88	8	1	8	7	.533	1	0	5.29
1994 Syracuse	AAA Tor	8	8	0	0	47.1	226	47	37	30	7	1	3	2	28	1	38	4	0	1	5	.167	0	0	5.70
Knoxville	AA Tor	17	16	0	0	102	446	88	50	41	12	2	5	7	48	0	79	4	1	6	5	.545	0	0	3.62
1995 Syracuse	AAA Tor	43	9	0	27	87.2	382	69	51	48	13	3	1	2	54	3	108	8	0	2	10	.167	0	10	4.93
1996 Syracuse	AAA Tor	17	0	0	9	22	91	20	9	8	2	2	1	1	6	1	24	1	0	3	0	1.000	0	4	3.27
St.Cathrnes	A- Tor	2	2	0	0	5	18	3	0	0	0	0	0	0	0	0	7	1	0	0	0	—	0	0	0.00
1997 Dunedin	A+ Tor	4	3	0	1	10.2	43	10	3	2	1	0	0	2	2	0	10	1	0	0	0	—	0	0	1.69
2000 Omaha	AAA KC	43	0	0	25	51	210	44	17	16	5	1	4	0	19	0	56	4	0	1	2	.333	0	7	2.82
2001 Akron	AA Cle	3	0	0	0	3.1	12	4	0	0	0	0	0	0	0	0	3	0	0	0	0	—	0	0	0.00
Buffalo	AAA Cle	4	0	0	2	4.2	31	11	11	9	1	2	0	1	4	0	3	1	0	1	0	1.000	0	0	17.36
1994 Toronto	AL	2	1	0	0	2.1	21	5	10	10	3	0	0	0	9	1	2	0	0	0	1	.000	0	0	38.57
1996 Toronto	AL	28	0	0	12	38	163	30	17	13	6	1	1	2	19	1	38	0	0	2	2	.500	0	1	3.08
1997 Toronto	AL	37	0	0	10	48	198	37	17	17	3	1	2	2	21	4	43	5	1	0	3	.000	0	3	3.19
Seattle	AL	20	0	0	0	22.2	104	24	13	12	1	1	0	1	15	2	27	1	2	0	0	—	0	0	4.76
1998 Seattle	AL	53	6	0	10	83.1	387	85	67	60	14	5	3	5	55	3	89	10	0	4	6	.400	0	0	6.48
1999 Philadelphia	NL	5	3	0	1	11.1	64	23	24	19	1	1	1	1	7	0	10	0	0	0	3	.000	0	0	15.09
Toronto	AL	37	2	0	7	62	282	62	41	32	9	5	3	2	32	2	63	1	0	2	2	.500	0	0	4.65
2000 Kansas City	AL	13	0	0	4	9.2	40	9	7	7	4	1	0	0	5	0	6	0	0	0	0	—	0	0	6.52
10 Min. YEARS		215	110	2	66	746	3178	628	383	318	73	17	27	22	349	5	740	46	7	41	48	.461	1	22	3.84
6 Maj. YEARS		195	12	0	44	277.1	1259	275	196	170	41	15	10	9	163	13	278	17	3	8	17	.320	0	4	5.52

Jerry Spradlin

Pitches: Right **Bats:** Both **Pos:** RP-29 **Ht:** 6'7" **Wt:** 246 **Born:** 6/14/67 **Age:** 35

Year Team	Lg Org	G	GS	CG	GF	IP	BFP	H	R	ER	HR	SH	SF	HB	TBB	IBB	SO	WP	Bk	W	L	Pct.	ShO	Sv	ERA
1988 Billings	R+ Cin	17	5	0	2	47.2	201	45	25	17	2	1	2	2	14	1	23	3	0	4	1	.800	0	0	3.21
1989 Greensboro	A Cin	42	1	0	22	94.2	389	88	35	29	5	3	7	3	23	0	56	4	0	7	2	.778	0	2	2.76
1990 Cedar Rapids	A Cin	5	0	0	0	12	57	13	8	4	1	1	0	0	5	1	6	0	0	0	1	.000	0	0	3.00
Chston-WV	A Cin	43	1	1	34	74.1	308	74	23	21	1	4	1	2	17	5	39	3	1	3	4	.429	0	17	2.54
1991 Chattanooga	AA Cin	48	1	0	22	96	406	95	38	33	2	1	5	4	32	7	73	9	0	7	3	.700	0	4	3.09
1992 Cedar Rapids	A Cin	1	0	0	0	2.1	11	5	2	2	0	0	0	0	0	0	4	0	0	1	0	1.000	0	0	7.71
Chattanooga	AA Cin	59	0	0	53	65.1	248	52	11	10	1	6	1	0	13	3	35	3	0	3	3	.500	0	34	1.38
1993 Indianapolis	AAA Cin	34	0	0	8	56.2	239	58	24	22	4	2	0	0	12	2	46	2	0	3	2	.600	0	1	3.49
1994 Indianapolis	AAA Cin	28	5	0	7	73.1	319	87	36	30	5	3	2	5	16	1	49	3	1	3	3	.500	0	3	3.68
Edmonton	AAA Fla	6	0	0	1	10.2	45	12	3	3	0	2	1	0	4	0	3	0	0	1	0	1.000	0	0	2.53
1995 Charlotte	AAA Fla	41	0	0	14	59.1	244	59	26	20	6	2	3	3	15	1	38	5	0	3	3	.500	0	1	3.03
1996 Indianapolis	AAA Cin	49	8	0	28	100	415	94	49	37	14	3	1	4	23	3	79	3	0	6	8	.429	0	15	3.33
2001 Memphis	AAA StL	29	0	0	26	32.2	118	17	8	8	2	1	1	1	7	1	28	1	0	4	1	.800	0	14	2.20
1993 Cincinnati	NL	37	0	0	16	49	193	44	20	19	4	3	4	0	9	0	24	3	1	2	1	.667	0	2	3.49
1994 Cincinnati	NL	6	0	0	2	8	38	12	11	9	2	0	2	0	2	0	4	0	0	0	0	—	0	0	10.13
1996 Cincinnati	NL	1	0	0	1	0.1	1	0	0	0	0	0	0	0	0	0	0	1	0	0	0	—	0	0	0.00
1997 Philadelphia	NL	76	0	0	23	81.2	345	86	45	43	9	1	2	1	27	3	67	5	2	4	8	.333	0	1	4.74
1998 Philadelphia	NL	69	0	0	20	81.2	319	63	34	32	9	4	2	2	20	1	76	6	1	4	4	.500	0	1	3.53
1999 Cleveland	AL	4	0	0	1	3	18	6	6	6	1	0	0	0	3	0	2	0	0	0	0	—	0	0	18.00
San Francisco	NL	59	0	0	14	58	268	59	31	27	4	1	0	10	29	6	52	2	0	3	1	.750	0	0	4.19
2000 Kansas City	AL	50	0	0	30	75	320	81	49	46	9	3	1	3	27	2	54	1	0	4	4	.500	0	7	5.52
Chicago	NL	8	1	0	2	15	70	20	15	14	2	1	2	1	5	1	13	1	0	0	1	.000	0	0	8.40
10 Min. YEARS		402	21	1	217	725	3000	699	288	236	43	29	24	24	181	25	479	36	2	45	31	.592	0	92	2.93
7 Maj. YEARS		310	1	0	109	371.2	1572	371	211	196	40	13	13	17	122	13	292	19	4	17	19	.472	0	11	4.75

Kevin Sprague

Pitches: Left **Bats:** Left **Pos:** SP-27 **Ht:** 6'4" **Wt:** 215 **Born:** 3/10/77 **Age:** 25

Year Team	Lg Org	G	GS	CG	GF	IP	BFP	H	R	ER	HR	SH	SF	HB	TBB	IBB	SO	WP	Bk	W	L	Pct.	ShO	Sv	ERA
1999 Johnson Cty	R+ StL	11	11	0	0	64	264	47	27	23	4	3	2	2	27	0	73	3	4	5	3	.625	0	0	3.23
2000 Peoria	A StL	24	24	0	0	120.2	520	117	60	54	5	3	4	6	53	1	117	15	1	8	9	.471	0	0	4.03
2001 New Haven	AA StL	1	1	0	0	6	25	4	3	2	0	0	0	0	2	0	4	0	0	1	0	1.000	0	0	3.00
Potomac	A+ StL	26	26	2	0	164.1	674	155	64	62	9	3	4	11	43	3	113	9	1	9	8	.529	0	0	3.40
3 Min. YEARS		62	62	2	0	355	1483	323	154	141	18	9	10	19	125	4	307	27	6	23	20	.535	0	0	3.57

Jay Spurgeon

Pitches: Right **Bats:** Right **Pos:** SP-15 **Ht:** 6'6" **Wt:** 211 **Born:** 7/5/76 **Age:** 25

Year Team	Lg Org	G	GS	CG	GF	IP	BFP	H	R	ER	HR	SH	SF	HB	TBB	IBB	SO	WP	Bk	W	L	Pct.	ShO	Sv	ERA
1997 Bluefield	R+ Bal	9	7	0	1	35	146	35	13	13	4	0	1	1	14	1	32	1	1	1	1	.500	0	0	3.34
1998 Delmarva	A Bal	27	20	0	0	136.1	547	112	49	40	8	5	5	6	48	0	103	3	0	11	3	.786	0	0	2.64
1999 Frederick	A+ Bal	26	26	1	0	146	659	176	99	77	14	4	4	4	53	2	87	12	2	6	9	.400	0	0	4.75
2000 Frederick	A+ Bal	16	15	1	0	91.2	379	75	47	42	8	3	7	3	31	0	92	8	0	8	2	.800	0	0	4.12
Bowie	AA Bal	6	6	2	0	39	152	32	10	7	3	0	1	2	7	0	27	0	0	3	1	.750	1	0	1.62
Rochester	AAA Bal	2	2	0	0	13.2	54	5	1	1	1	0	0	1	9	0	10	0	0	2	0	1.000	0	0	0.66
2001 Rochester	AAA Bal	15	15	1	0	87	373	85	48	44	12	3	3	5	27	0	61	1	1	3	5	.375	0	0	4.55
2000 Baltimore	AL	7	4	0	1	24	110	26	16	16	5	1	0	2	15	0	11	3	0	1	1	.500	0	0	6.00
5 Min. YEARS		101	91	5	1	548.2	2310	520	267	224	50	15	21	22	189	3	412	25	4	34	21	.618	1	0	3.67

Chris Spurling

Pitches: Right **Bats:** Right **Pos:** RP-19; SP-15 **Ht:** 6'6" **Wt:** 240 **Born:** 6/28/77 **Age:** 25

Year Team	Lg Org	G	GS	CG	GF	IP	BFP	H	R	ER	HR	SH	SF	HB	TBB	IBB	SO	WP	Bk	W	L	Pct.	ShO	Sv	ERA
1998 Yankees	R NYY	13	6	0	2	51.1	219	57	21	13	3	0	2	2	11	0	44	2	0	2	1	.667	0	1	2.28
Greensboro	A NYY	1	1	0	0	6	25	7	2	2	1	0	0	0	1	0	5	0	0	1	0	1.000	0	0	3.00
1999 Greensboro	A NYY	49	0	0	26	76.1	332	78	34	31	8	4	9	2	23	3	68	7	0	4	6	.400	0	4	3.66
2000 Tampa	A+ NYY	34	0	0	15	57	239	50	27	24	1	2	3	1	22	5	55	3	0	4	6	.400	0	1	3.79
Lynchburg	A+ Pit	9	0	0	6	18.1	66	8	2	2	1	0	1	0	3	0	17	0	0	1	0	1.000	0	5	0.98
2001 Altoona	AA Pit	34	15	0	11	121.2	512	133	48	42	9	1	3	4	28	1	63	2	0	5	7	.417	0	1	3.11
4 Min. YEARS		140	22	0	60	330.2	1393	333	134	114	23	7	18	9	88	9	252	14	0	17	20	.459	0	12	3.10

Jason Stanford

Pitches: Left **Bats:** Left **Pos:** SP-25 **Ht:** 6'2" **Wt:** 200 **Born:** 1/23/77 **Age:** 25

Year Team	Lg Org	G	GS	CG	GF	IP	BFP	H	R	ER	HR	SH	SF	HB	TBB	IBB	SO	WP	Bk	W	L	Pct.	ShO	Sv	ERA
2000 Columbus	A Cle	14	14	0	0	79	335	82	32	24	3	1	3	2	20	0	72	3	0	7	4	.636	0	0	2.73
Kinston	A+ Cle	11	11	1	0	70	294	68	22	20	2	1	2	2	17	0	58	0	0	4	3	.571	0	0	2.57
Akron	AA Cle	1	1	0	0	5.2	23	5	1	1	0	0	0	1	1	0	5	0	0	1	0	1.000	0	0	1.59
2001 Akron	AA Cle	24	24	1	0	141.2	602	152	71	64	11	3	7	10	32	4	108	2	1	6	11	.353	0	0	4.07
Buffalo	AAA Cle	1	1	0	0	9	29	3	0	0	0	0	0	0	0	0	10	0	0	1	0	1.000	1	0	0.00
2 Min. YEARS		51	51	3	0	305.1	1283	310	126	109	16	5	12	15	70	4	253	5	1	19	18	.514	1	0	3.21

Rob Stanifer

Pitches: Right **Bats:** Right **Pos:** RP-54   **Ht:** 6'2" **Wt:** 220 **Born:** 3/10/72 **Age:** 30

		HOW MUCH HE PITCHED						WHAT HE GAVE UP												THE RESULTS					
Year Team	Lg Org	G	GS	CG	GF	IP	BFP	H	R	ER	HR	SH	SF	HB	TBB	IBB	SO	WP	Bk	W	L	Pct.	ShO	Sv	ERA
1994 Elmira	A- Fla	9	8	1	0	49	211	54	17	14	2	0	1	2	12	1	38	2	3	2	1	.667	0	0	2.57
Brevard Cty	A+ Fla	5	5	0	0	24.1	115	32	20	17	2	1	1	3	10	0	12	2	1	1	2	.333	0	0	6.29
1995 Brevard Cty	A+ Fla	18	13	0	0	82.2	360	97	47	38	4	4	5	7	15	0	45	2	0	3	6	.333	0	0	4.14
1996 Brevard Cty	A+ Fla	22	0	0	4	49	206	54	17	13	3	0	1	1	9	0	32	1	0	4	2	.667	0	0	2.39
Portland	AA Fla	18	0	0	10	34.1	137	27	15	6	3	1	2	1	9	0	33	2	0	3	1	.750	0	2	1.57
1997 Charlotte	AAA Fla	22	0	0	16	27.2	123	34	16	15	3	1	1	1	7	0	25	2	0	4	0	1.000	0	5	4.88
1998 Charlotte	AAA Fla	21	1	0	10	39.2	166	39	20	19	1	1	5	1	13	2	29	1	0	4	2	.667	0	4	4.31
1999 Calgary	AAA Fla	16	0	0	8	16	87	32	23	22	7	1	1	4	6	0	15	0	0	1	2	.333	0	0	12.38
Trenton	AA Bos	5	0	0	3	9	36	6	0	0	0	1	0	0	4	2	11	0	0	0	0	—	0	1	0.00
Pawtucket	AAA Bos	31	0	0	20	39.2	168	34	21	9	5	0	0	0	15	1	29	4	0	3	1	.750	0	3	2.04
2000 Pawtucket	AAA Bos	41	0	0	35	52.1	204	40	13	11	6	4	1	1	20	1	42	4	0	3	4	.429	0	16	1.89
2001 Iowa	AAA ChC	54	0	0	19	74.1	330	85	38	35	9	7	5	2	28	6	79	4	0	7	8	.467	0	6	4.24
1997 Florida	NL	36	0	0	10	45	188	43	23	23	9	4	0	3	16	0	28	1	0	1	2	.333	0	1	4.60
1998 Florida	NL	38	0	0	11	48	222	54	33	30	5	2	3	0	22	2	30	1	0	2	4	.333	0	1	5.63
2000 Boston	AL	8	0	0	3	13	66	22	19	11	3	0	0	0	4	1	3	0	0	0	0	—	0	0	7.62
8 Min. YEARS		262	27	1	125	498	2143	534	247	199	45	21	23	23	148	13	390	24	4	35	29	.547	0	37	3.60
3 Maj. YEARS		82	0	0	24	106	476	119	75	64	17	6	3	3	42	3	61	2	0	3	6	.333	0	2	5.43

Andy Stankiewicz

Bats: Right **Throws:** Right **Pos:** 2B-61; PH-10   **Ht:** 5'9" **Wt:** 165 **Born:** 8/10/64 **Age:** 37

		BATTING														BASERUNNING				PERCENTAGES		
Year Team	Lg Org	G	AB	H	2B	3B	HR	TB	R	RBI	TBB	IBB	SO	HBP	SH	SF	SB	CS	SB%	GDP	Avg	OBP	SLG
1986 Oneonta	A- NYY	59	216	64	8	3	0	78	51	17	38	0	41	5	4	4	14	3	.82	2	.296	.407	.361
1987 Ft. Laud	A+ NYY	119	456	140	18	7	2	178	80	47	62	1	84	4	7	1	26	13	.67	9	.307	.394	.390
1988 Albany-Col	AA NYY	109	414	111	20	2	1	138	63	33	39	0	53	9	9	2	15	10	.60	6	.268	.343	.333
Columbus	AAA NYY	29	114	25	0	0	0	25	4	4	6	0	25	0	1	0	2	0	1.00	4	.219	.258	.219
1989 Albany-Col	AA NYY	133	498	133	26	2	4	175	74	49	57	2	59	8	3	11	41	9	.82	8	.267	.345	.351
1990 Columbus	AAA NYY	135	446	102	14	4	1	127	68	48	71	1	63	10	7	4	25	8	.76	11	.229	.345	.285
1991 Columbus	AAA NYY	125	372	101	12	4	1	124	47	41	29	0	45	8	8	5	29	16	.64	9	.272	.333	.333
1993 Columbus	AAA NYY	90	331	80	12	5	0	102	45	32	29	0	46	3	4	3	12	8	.60	5	.242	.306	.308
1994 Jackson	AA Hou	5	12	5	0	0	0	5	1	3	0	0	0	0	0	1	0	0	—	1	.417	.385	.417
1995 Tucson	AAA Hou	25	87	24	4	0	1	31	16	15	14	0	8	0	2	1	3	1	.75	3	.276	.373	.356
1998 Diamondbcks	R Ari	3	10	3	0	0	0	3	2	3	0	0	0	0	0	0	0	0	—	0	.300	.300	.300
Tucson	AAA Ari	5	20	6	0	0	0	6	1	2	0	0	0	1	0	0	0	0	—	1	.300	.333	.300
1999 Columbus	AAA NYY	50	163	45	8	3	1	62	34	20	23	0	27	3	4	1	6	1	.86	3	.276	.374	.380
2000 Yankees	R NYY	1	3	0	0	0	0	0	0	0	2	0	1	0	0	0	0	0	—	0	.000	.400	.000
Columbus	AAA NYY	23	64	15	2	1	0	19	13	5	6	0	21	2	0	0	0	1	.00	1	.234	.319	.297
2001 Las Vegas	AAA LA	66	202	53	7	0	0	60	18	13	25	3	29	3	9	1	5	2	.71	3	.262	.351	.297
1992 New York	AL	116	400	107	22	2	2	139	52	25	38	0	42	5	7	1	9	5	.64	13	.268	.338	.348
1993 New York	AL	16	9	0	0	0	0	0	5	0	1	0	1	0	0	0	0	0	—	0	.000	.100	.000
1994 Houston	NL	37	54	14	3	0	1	20	10	5	12	0	12	1	2	0	1	1	.50	2	.259	.403	.370
1995 Houston	NL	43	52	6	1	0	0	7	6	7	12	2	19	0	1	0	4	2	.67	1	.115	.281	.135
1996 Montreal	NL	64	77	22	5	1	0	29	12	9	6	1	12	3	1	1	1	0	1.00	1	.286	.356	.377
1997 Montreal	NL	76	107	24	9	0	1	36	11	5	4	0	22	0	7	1	1	1	.50	1	.224	.250	.336
1998 Arizona	NL	77	145	30	5	0	0	35	9	8	7	0	33	2	0	1	1	0	1.00		.207	.252	.241
13 Min. YEARS		977	3408	907	131	31	11	1133	517	332	401	7	502	56	58	34	178	72	.71	66	.266	.350	.332
7 Maj. YEARS		429	844	203	45	3	4	266	105	59	80	3	141	11	18	4	17	9	.65	21	.241	.313	.315

Dave Steed

Bats: Right **Throws:** Right **Pos:** C-52; 1B-13; PH-2; 3B-1; DH-1   **Ht:** 6'1" **Wt:** 205 **Born:** 2/25/73 **Age:** 29

		BATTING														BASERUNNING				PERCENTAGES		
Year Team	Lg Org	G	AB	H	2B	3B	HR	TB	R	RBI	TBB	IBB	SO	HBP	SH	SF	SB	CS	SB%	GDP	Avg	OBP	SLG
1993 Great Falls	R+ LA	42	120	24	4	2	0	32	13	16	27	0	28	3	4	3	1	0	1.00	3	.200	.353	.267
1994 Yakima	A- LA	48	147	37	5	2	5	61	21	24	28	0	43	5	1	0	1	2	.33	4	.252	.389	.415
1995 Vero Beach	A+ LA	59	195	49	16	0	0	65	11	24	18	0	53	3	1	1	0	0	—	5	.251	.323	.333
San Antonio	AA LA	40	123	31	10	1	3	52	13	16	11	0	32	1	0	2	0	1	.00	2	.252	.314	.423
1996 San Berndno	A+ LA	28	87	26	6	0	1	35	11	13	14	0	19	1	1	0	2	3	.40	2	.299	.398	.402
Vero Beach	A+ LA	23	73	21	3	0	1	27	6	10	6	0	15	0	1	0	1	0	1.00	1	.288	.342	.370
San Antonio	AA LA	7	17	2	1	0	0	3	0	2	1	0	6	0	0	0	0	0	—	1	.118	.167	.176
1997 Albuquerque	AAA LA	25	47	10	4	0	1	17	8	4	4	1	19	0	0	0	0	0	—	0	.213	.275	.362
1998 Albuquerque	AAA LA	57	151	42	7	1	4	63	18	21	10	0	39	2	0	2	0	1	.00	5	.278	.331	.417
1999 Albuquerque	AAA LA	30	62	13	4	0	0	17	8	5	7	1	17	0	4	1	0	1	.00	3	.210	.286	.274
2000 Aberdeen	IND —	130	452	145	38	1	22	251	98	87	80	4	90	6	0	6	6	4	.60	12	.321	.425	.555
2001 Oklahoma	AAA Tex	67	227	53	10	0	7	84	28	29	25	1	61	3	1	2	1	0	.00	6	.233	.315	.370
9 Min. YEARS		556	1701	453	108	7	44	707	235	251	232	7	422	24	12	18	11	13	.46	43	.266	.359	.416

Kennie Steenstra

Pitches: Right **Bats:** Right **Pos:** SP-28   **Ht:** 6'5" **Wt:** 215 **Born:** 10/13/70 **Age:** 31

		HOW MUCH HE PITCHED						WHAT HE GAVE UP												THE RESULTS					
Year Team	Lg Org	G	GS	CG	GF	IP	BFP	H	R	ER	HR	SH	SF	HB	TBB	IBB	SO	WP	Bk	W	L	Pct.	ShO	Sv	ERA
1992 Geneva	A- ChC	3	3	1	0	20	76	11	4	2	0	0	0	0	3	0	12	0	1	3	0	1.000	0	0	0.90
Peoria	A ChC	12	12	4	0	89.2	364	79	29	21	5	2	1	3	21	1	68	4	3	6	3	.667	2	0	2.11
1993 Daytona	A+ ChC	13	13	1	0	81.1	317	64	26	23	2	3	2	8	12	1	57	2	1	5	3	.625	1	0	2.55
Iowa	AAA ChC	1	1	0	0	6.2	32	9	5	5	2	0	0	0	4	0	6	0	0	1	0	1.000	0	0	6.75
Orlando	AA ChC	14	14	2	0	100.1	427	103	47	40	4	4	2	9	25	0	60	5	2	8	3	.727	2	0	3.59
1994 Iowa	AAA ChC	3	3	0	0	13	68	24	21	19	2	0	2	2	4	0	10	0	0	1	2	.333	0	0	13.15
Orlando	AA ChC	23	23	2	0	158.1	654	146	55	46	12	9	3	9	39	4	83	4	1	9	7	.563	1	0	2.62
1995 Iowa	AAA ChC	29	26	6	1	171.1	722	174	85	74	15	6	6	8	48	3	96	6	0	9	12	.429	0	0	3.89
1996 Iowa	AAA ChC	26	26	1	0	158	686	170	96	88	24	5	9	9	47	4	101	2	0	8	12	.400	0	0	5.01

Year Team	Lg Org	G	GS	CG	GF	IP	BFP	H	R	ER	HR	SH	SF	HB	TBB	IBB	SO	WP	Bk	W	L	Pct.	ShO	Sv	ERA
				HOW	MUCH	HE	PITCHED		WHAT	HE	GAVE	UP								THE	RESULTS				
1997 Iowa	AAA ChC	25	25	4	0	160.2	663	161	85	70	15	4	9	0	41	4	111	7	0	5	10	.333	0	0	3.92
1998 Iowa	AAA ChC	25	24	1	0	148	639	171	84	72	16	6	3	1	36	1	104	0	0	11	5	.688	1	0	4.38
1999 Tacoma	AAA Sea	13	10	0	1	51.2	231	60	40	32	5	1	7	3	15	0	24	1	0	1	4	.200	0	0	5.57
Greenville	AA Atl	8	0	0	1	19	80	25	8	8	1	0	1	0	1	0	12	2	0	2	1	.667	0	0	3.79
2000 Memphis	AAA StL	10	1	0	3	25.2	115	28	11	11	1	0	0	2	12	0	13	0	0	1	0	1.000	0	2	3.86
Tucson	AAA Ari	24	19	1	2	130.1	574	159	68	58	15	10	4	4	41	0	62	0	0	8	5	.615	0	0	4.01
2001 Tucson	AAA Ari	28	28	1	0	170	737	187	101	79	14	7	4	7	42	1	114	1	0	9	6	.600	0	0	4.18
1998 Chicago	NL	4	0	0	1	3.1	18	7	4	4	2	0	0	0	1	0	4	0	0	0	0	—	0	0	10.80
10 Min. YEARS		257	228	24	8	1504	6385	1571	765	648	133	57	53	65	391	19	933	34	8	87	73	.544	9	2	3.88

Mike Stefanski

Bats: Right **Throws:** Right **Pos:** C-52; PH-7; PR-3; 1B-2   **Ht:** 6'2" **Wt:** 202 **Born:** 9/12/69 **Age:** 32

Year Team	Lg Org	G	AB	H	2B	3B	HR	TB	R	RBI	TBB	IBB	SO	HBP	SH	SF	SB	CS	SB%	GDP	Avg	OBP	SLG
				BATTING													BASERUNNING				PERCENTAGES		
1991 Brewers	R Mil	56	206	76	5	5	0	91	43	43	22	0	22	5	0	6	3	2	.60	4	.369	.431	.442
1992 Beloit	A Mil	116	385	105	12	0	4	129	66	45	55	1	81	4	3	3	9	4	.69	11	.273	.367	.335
1993 Stockton	A+ Mil	97	345	111	22	2	10	167	58	57	49	2	45	5	1	2	6	1	.86	15	.322	.411	.484
1994 El Paso	AA Mil	95	312	82	7	6	8	125	59	56	32	0	80	0	2	5	4	3	.57	5	.263	.327	.401
1995 El Paso	AA Mil	6	27	11	3	0	1	17	5	6	0	0	3	0	0	0	1	0	1.00	0	.407	.407	.630
New Orleans	AAA Mil	78	228	56	10	2	2	76	30	24	14	0	28	1	5	5	2	0	1.00	8	.246	.286	.333
1996 Louisville	AAA StL	53	126	26	7	1	2	41	11	9	11	1	11	1	1	2	1	2	.33	4	.206	.271	.325
1997 Arkansas	AA StL	1	4	1	0	1	0	3	1	0	0	0	0	0	0	0	0	0	—	1	.250	.250	.750
Louisville	AAA StL	57	197	60	10	0	6	88	26	22	12	0	20	1	2	1	0	1	.00	6	.305	.346	.447
1998 Memphis	AAA StL	95	298	79	19	1	6	118	34	44	23	4	42	4	5	2	1	2	.33	11	.265	.324	.396
1999 Memphis	AAA StL	64	201	60	12	0	4	84	27	22	17	0	28	4	1	2	3	0	1.00	8	.299	.362	.418
2000 Louisville	AAA Cin	32	96	22	7	0	2	35	12	10	4	1	17	3	0	0	0	0	—	3	.229	.282	.365
2001 Memphis	AAA StL	61	164	43	8	1	6	71	25	26	13	0	31	2	4	1	1	2	.33	4	.262	.322	.433
11 Min. YEARS		811	2589	732	122	19	51	1045	397	364	252	9	408	30	24	29	31	17	.65	80	.283	.350	.404

Steve Stemle

Pitches: Right **Bats:** Right **Pos:** SP-25; RP-1   **Ht:** 6'4" **Wt:** 200 **Born:** 5/20/77 **Age:** 25

Year Team	Lg Org	G	GS	CG	GF	IP	BFP	H	R	ER	HR	SH	SF	HB	TBB	IBB	SO	WP	Bk	W	L	Pct.	ShO	Sv	ERA
				HOW	MUCH	HE	PITCHED		WHAT	HE	GAVE	UP								THE	RESULTS				
1998 New Jersey	A- StL	9	9	0	0	44.1	184	37	17	9	1	0	0	1	14	0	47	4	1	3	3	.500	0	0	1.83
1999 Peoria	A StL	28	28	0	0	148	688	177	104	90	11	3	5	6	67	0	113	12	0	7	10	.412	0	0	5.47
2000 Potomac	A+ StL	26	26	1	0	150	668	169	89	80	15	2	4	12	59	1	84	16	0	9	10	.474	0	0	4.80
2001 New Haven	AA StL	26	25	0	0	134	603	159	76	71	12	4	3	10	43	2	75	4	0	7	10	.412	0	0	4.77
4 Min. YEARS		89	88	1	0	476.1	2143	542	286	250	39	9	12	29	183	3	319	36	1	26	33	.441	0	0	4.72

Dernell Stenson

Bats: Left **Throws:** Left **Pos:** OF-120; DH-1; PH-1   **Ht:** 6'1" **Wt:** 230 **Born:** 6/17/78 **Age:** 24

Year Team	Lg Org	G	AB	H	2B	3B	HR	TB	R	RBI	TBB	IBB	SO	HBP	SH	SF	SB	CS	SB%	GDP	Avg	OBP	SLG
				BATTING													BASERUNNING				PERCENTAGES		
1996 Red Sox	R Bos	32	97	21	3	1	2	32	16	15	16	0	26	7	0	3	4	3	.57	0	.216	.358	.330
1997 Michigan	A Bos	131	471	137	35	2	15	221	79	80	72	6	105	19	0	8	6	4	.60	10	.291	.400	.469
1998 Trenton	AA Bos	138	505	130	21	1	24	225	90	71	84	3	135	14	1	4	5	3	.63	6	.257	.376	.446
1999 Red Sox	R Bos	6	23	5	0	0	2	11	2	7	3	0	5	0	0	0	0	0	—	0	.217	.308	.478
Pawtucket	AAA Bos	121	440	119	28	2	18	205	64	82	55	5	119	6	2	5	2	1	.67	7	.270	.356	.466
2000 Pawtucket	AAA Bos	98	380	102	14	0	23	185	59	71	45	6	99	4	0	4	0	0	—	8	.268	.349	.487
2001 Pawtucket	AAA Bos	122	464	110	18	1	16	178	53	69	43	3	116	2	0	5	0	0	—	6	.237	.302	.384
6 Min. YEARS		648	2380	624	119	7	100	1057	363	395	318	23	605	52	3	29	17	11	.61	37	.262	.358	.444

Brent Stentz

Pitches: Right **Bats:** Right **Pos:** RP-25   **Ht:** 6'5" **Wt:** 225 **Born:** 7/24/75 **Age:** 26

Year Team	Lg Org	G	GS	CG	GF	IP	BFP	H	R	ER	HR	SH	SF	HB	TBB	IBB	SO	WP	Bk	W	L	Pct.	ShO	Sv	ERA
				HOW	MUCH	HE	PITCHED		WHAT	HE	GAVE	UP								THE	RESULTS				
1995 Tigers	R Det	24	0	0	24	26.2	107	21	7	7	1	1	1	1	12	2	28	4	1	2	1	.667	0	16	2.36
Lakeland	A+ Det	2	0	0	1	2	6	0	0	0	0	0	0	0	0	0	4	0	0	0	0	—	0	0	0.00
1996 Fayetteville	A Det	45	8	0	7	98	413	91	51	38	4	4	1	6	27	1	92	5	2	7	8	.467	0	2	3.49
1997 Fort Myers	A+ Min	49	1	0	30	69.1	285	53	20	19	4	2	3	2	24	3	70	5	2	7	2	.778	0	17	2.47
1998 New Britain	AA Min	57	0	0	53	59	244	44	13	13	3	2	1	1	28	2	65	1	0	1	2	.333	0	43	1.98
1999 Salt Lake	AAA Min	23	0	0	15	25.2	139	43	34	32	6	2	2	0	21	1	23	3	1	0	3	.000	0	3	11.22
New Britain	AA Min	32	0	0	28	31.1	125	23	13	13	3	0	0	0	12	2	44	0	0	1	0	1.000	0	3	3.73
2000 New Britain	AA Min	24	0	0	18	25	110	32	14	12	2	0	1	0	5	0	27	2	0	1	2	.333	0	7	4.32
Salt Lake	AAA Min	42	0	0	35	46.2	183	31	14	10	6	1	1	0	13	1	47	1	1	4	2	.667	0	13	1.93
2001 Twins	R Min	8	0	0	2	9.1	41	7	3	2	0	0	0	0	7	0	6	1	0	2	1	.667	0	1	1.93
Edmonton	AAA Min	17	0	0	14	14.1	66	19	9	9	2	0	0	0	5	0	12	0	0	0	0	—	0	7	5.65
7 Min. YEARS		323	9	0	227	407.1	1719	364	178	155	31	12	10	10	154	12	418	22	7	24	22	.522	0	117	3.42

Jason Stephens

Pitches: Right **Bats:** Right **Pos:** SP-24; RP-3   **Ht:** 6'0" **Wt:** 180 **Born:** 9/10/75 **Age:** 26

Year Team	Lg Org	G	GS	CG	GF	IP	BFP	H	R	ER	HR	SH	SF	HB	TBB	IBB	SO	WP	Bk	W	L	Pct.	ShO	Sv	ERA
				HOW	MUCH	HE	PITCHED		WHAT	HE	GAVE	UP								THE	RESULTS				
1996 Boise	A- Ana	3	0	0	2	3.1	16	4	3	3	1	0	0	0	1	0	5	0	0	2	0	1.000	0	1	8.10
Cedar Rapds	A Ana	21	0	0	20	26	118	27	12	10	1	1	2	3	14	2	19	2	0	2	3	.400	0	6	3.46
1997 Lk Elsinore	A+ Ana	24	22	1	1	126.2	569	149	86	76	14	1	2	16	42	2	101	4	1	7	11	.389	0	0	5.40
1998 Lk Elsinore	A+ Ana	35	13	1	6	123	534	128	72	56	7	6	2	6	47	3	89	11	1	7	6	.538	1	0	4.10
1999 Lk Elsinore	A+ Ana	15	11	1	0	68.2	310	84	39	32	6	3	1	2	24	2	66	2	0	3	3	.500	0	0	4.19

Year Team	Lg Org	G	GS	CG	GF	IP	BFP	H	R	ER	HR	SH	SF	HB	TBB	IBB	SO	WP	Bk	W	L	Pct.	ShO	Sv	ERA
2001 Rancho Cuca	A+ Ana	8	5	0	0	32.2	135	35	11	8	1	1	1	2	4	0	19	0	0	3	2	.600	0	0	2.20
Arkansas	AA Ana	19	19	2	0	119.1	502	117	64	52	12	2	5	8	26	2	75	7	0	6	7	.462	0	0	3.92
5 Min. YEARS		125	70	5	29	499.2	2184	544	287	237	42	14	13	37	158	11	374	26	2	30	32	.484	1	7	4.27

John Stephens

Pitches: Right **Bats:** Right **Pos:** SP-26; RP-1   **Ht:** 6'1" **Wt:** 200 **Born:** 11/15/79 **Age:** 22

Year Team	Lg Org	G	GS	CG	GF	IP	BFP	H	R	ER	HR	SH	SF	HB	TBB	IBB	SO	WP	Bk	W	L	Pct.	ShO	Sv	ERA
1997 Orioles	R Bal	9	3	0	3	33	121	15	3	3	1	3	2	0	9	0	43	0	0	3	0	1.000	0	1	0.82
Bluefield	R+ Bal	4	4	0	0	24	93	17	6	6	4	0	0	1	5	0	34	1	1	2	0	1.000	0	0	2.25
1998 Delmarva	A Bal	6	6	1	0	34.2	141	25	11	10	3	1	0	1	13	0	40	3	0	1	2	.333	1	0	2.60
1999 Delmarva	A Bal	28	27	4	0	170.1	702	148	75	61	10	5	4	10	36	0	217	4	0	10	8	.556	2	0	3.22
2000 Frederick	A+ Bal	20	20	0	0	118	497	119	45	40	5	3	4	8	22	1	121	6	0	7	6	.538	0	0	3.05
2001 Bowie	AA Bal	18	17	3	0	132	502	95	32	27	10	2	1	6	21	1	130	2	0	11	4	.733	3	0	1.84
Rochester	AAA Bal	9	9	0	0	58	247	52	31	26	5	2	3	3	19	1	61	4	0	2	5	.286	0	0	4.03
5 Min. YEARS		94	86	8	3	570	2303	471	203	173	38	16	14	29	125	3	646	20	1	36	25	.590	6	1	2.73

Brian Stephenson

Pitches: Right **Bats:** Right **Pos:** RP-6; SP-1   **Ht:** 6'3" **Wt:** 210 **Born:** 7/17/73 **Age:** 28

Year Team	Lg Org	G	GS	CG	GF	IP	BFP	H	R	ER	HR	SH	SF	HB	TBB	IBB	SO	WP	Bk	W	L	Pct.	ShO	Sv	ERA
1994 Williamsprt	A- ChC	5	5	0	0	19	80	17	9	9	2	0	2	4	4	0	13	1	1	0	2	.000	0	0	4.26
Peoria	A ChC	6	6	2	0	42.1	180	41	18	15	3	3	0	6	6	1	29	1	0	3	1	.750	0	0	3.19
1995 Daytona	A+ ChC	26	26	0	0	150	640	145	79	66	7	6	3	7	58	2	109	14	2	10	9	.526	0	0	3.96
1996 Orlando	AA ChC	32	20	0	3	128.2	574	130	82	67	13	4	9	5	61	3	106	10	1	5	13	.278	0	1	4.69
1997 Orlando	AA ChC	6	0	0	2	9.1	42	10	10	10	4	0	1	0	5	0	9	4	0	0	2	.000	0	0	9.64
1999 Cubs	R ChC	1	0	0	0	2	6	1	0	0	0	0	0	0	0	0	2	0	0	0	0	—	0	0	0.00
Eugene	A- ChC	2	2	0	0	4	22	4	5	2	0	0	0	1	4	0	4	0	0	0	1	.000	0	0	4.50
2000 San Antonio	AA LA	4	3	0	0	16.1	73	19	11	9	1	0	4	0	8	0	14	1	0	1	0	1.000	0	0	4.96
2001 Jacksnville	AA LA	7	1	0	1	8	33	6	4	1	0	0	1	0	2	0	3	0	0	1	0	1.000	0	0	1.13
7 Min. YEARS		89	63	2	6	379.2	1650	373	218	179	30	13	20	23	148	6	289	31	4	20	28	.417	0	1	4.24

Garrett Stephenson

Pitches: Right **Bats:** Right **Pos:** SP-1   **Ht:** 6'5" **Wt:** 208 **Born:** 1/2/72 **Age:** 30

Year Team	Lg Org	G	GS	CG	GF	IP	BFP	H	R	ER	HR	SH	SF	HB	TBB	IBB	SO	WP	Bk	W	L	Pct.	ShO	Sv	ERA
1992 Bluefield	R+ Bal	12	3	0	0	32.1	141	35	22	17	4	0	1	1	7	0	30	4	1	3	1	.750	0	0	4.73
1993 Albany	A Bal	30	24	3	3	171.1	697	142	65	54	6	1	4	5	44	0	147	3	5	16	7	.696	2	1	2.84
1994 Frederick	A+ Bal	18	17	1	0	107.1	450	91	62	48	13	2	5	5	36	2	133	2	4	7	5	.583	0	0	4.02
Bowie	AA Bal	7	7	1	0	36.2	161	47	22	21	2	0	1	0	11	1	32	3	2	3	2	.600	1	0	5.15
1995 Bowie	AA Bal	29	29	1	0	175.1	743	154	87	71	23	5	7	18	47	0	139	4	2	7	10	.412	0	0	3.64
1996 Rochester	AAA Bal	23	21	3	1	121.2	515	123	66	65	13	2	5	10	44	0	86	3	2	7	6	.538	1	0	4.81
1997 Scranton-WB	AAA Phi	7	3	0	1	29	125	27	19	19	6	0	1	0	12	0	27	2	0	3	1	.750	0	0	5.90
1998 Scranton-WB	AAA Phi	13	11	2	1	73.2	314	81	49	43	15	0	5	2	16	0	48	1	0	1	8	.111	0	0	5.25
1999 Arkansas	AA StL	1	1	0	0	5.1	23	8	3	2	1	1	0	0	1	0	2	0	0	0	0	—	0	0	3.38
Memphis	AAA StL	4	4	0	0	25.2	102	22	9	9	2	0	0	1	7	0	19	0	0	1	1	.500	0	0	3.16
2001 Memphis	AAA StL	1	1	0	0	2	8	2	0	0	0	0	0	0	0	0	2	0	0	0	0	—	0	0	0.00
1996 Baltimore	AL	3	0	0	2	6.1	35	13	9	9	1	1	0	1	3	1	3	0	0	0	1	.000	0	0	12.79
1997 Philadelphia	NL	20	18	2	0	117	474	104	45	41	11	2	5	3	38	0	81	1	0	8	6	.571	0	0	3.15
1998 Philadelphia	NL	6	6	0	0	23	118	31	24	23	3	1	0	0	19	0	17	0	1	0	2	.000	0	0	9.00
1999 St. Louis	NL	18	12	0	1	85.1	371	90	43	40	11	5	5	5	29	1	59	0	0	6	3	.667	0	0	4.22
2000 St. Louis	NL	32	31	3	0	200.1	802	209	105	100	31	6	7	7	63	0	123	2	2	16	9	.640	2	0	4.49
9 Min. YEARS		145	121	11	6	780.1	3279	732	404	349	85	11	29	42	225	3	665	22	16	48	41	.539	4	1	4.03
5 Maj. YEARS		79	67	5	3	432	1856	447	226	213	57	15	17	16	152	2	283	3	3	30	21	.588	2	0	4.44

Dave Stevens

Pitches: Right **Bats:** Right **Pos:** RP-48   **Ht:** 6'3" **Wt:** 215 **Born:** 3/4/70 **Age:** 32

Year Team	Lg Org	G	GS	CG	GF	IP	BFP	H	R	ER	HR	SH	SF	HB	TBB	IBB	SO	WP	Bk	W	L	Pct.	ShO	Sv	ERA
1990 Huntington	R+ ChC	13	11	0	1	56.2	274	47	44	29	3	2	3	7	47	0	55	6	8	2	4	.333	0	0	4.61
1991 Geneva	A- ChC	9	9	1	0	47.1	197	49	20	15	3	4	3	2	14	0	44	2	0	2	3	.400	0	0	2.85
1992 Charlotte	AA ChC	26	26	2	0	149.2	642	147	79	65	16	5	6	5	53	1	89	8	1	9	13	.409	0	0	3.91
1993 Orlando	AA ChC	11	11	1	0	70.1	304	69	36	33	7	1	0	2	35	0	49	1	0	6	1	.857	1	0	4.22
Iowa	AAA ChC	24	0	0	15	34.1	137	24	16	16	3	2	1	1	14	2	29	1	0	4	0	1.000	0	4	4.19
1994 Salt Lake	AAA Min	23	0	0	20	43	183	41	13	8	2	2	2	1	16	1	30	1	0	6	2	.750	0	3	1.67
1997 Salt Lake	AAA Min	16	14	1	0	90	395	93	52	43	10	1	2	4	31	0	71	4	1	9	3	.750	0	0	4.30
Iowa	AAA ChC	6	0	0	5	7.2	34	8	4	4	0	1	0	0	5	1	8	0	0	1	1	.500	0	1	4.70
1998 Iowa	AAA ChC	26	0	0	10	49.2	198	41	19	17	2	0	0	0	16	1	39	1	0	4	1	.800	0	2	3.08
1999 Buffalo	AAA Cle	20	0	0	18	23.2	97	12	4	4	1	1	1	2	14	1	28	0	0	1	0	1.000	0	12	1.52
Tacoma	AAA Sea	7	0	0	1	10	54	14	14	14	2	0	0	2	6	1	8	1	0	1	1	.500	0	0	12.60
2000 Richmond	AAA Atl	51	0	0	32	72	318	73	44	40	10	1	6	2	31	3	50	7	1	1	9	.100	0	0	5.00
2001 Richmond	AAA Atl	39	0	0	10	58.2	270	67	49	45	14	4	4	4	31	6	47	3	0	2	1	.667	0	1	6.90
Greenville	AA Atl	9	0	0	6	11.2	46	4	5	4	1	1	2	0	6	1	8	2	0	0	1	.000	0	2	3.09
1994 Minnesota	AL	24	0	0	6	45	208	55	35	34	6	2	0	1	23	2	24	3	0	5	2	.714	0	0	6.80
1995 Minnesota	AL	56	0	0	34	65.2	302	74	40	37	14	4	5	1	32	1	47	2	0	5	4	.556	0	10	5.07
1996 Minnesota	AL	49	0	0	38	58	251	58	31	30	12	3	3	0	25	2	29	1	0	3	3	.500	0	11	4.66
1997 Minnesota	AL	6	6	0	0	23	124	41	23	23	8	0	0	0	17	0	16	1	2	1	3	.250	0	0	9.00
Chicago	NL	10	0	0	0	9.1	50	13	11	10	0	0	1	1	9	0	13	0	1	0	2	.000	0	0	9.64
1998 Chicago	NL	31	0	0	13	38	169	42	20	20	6	4	1	1	17	5	31	1	1	1	2	.333	0	0	4.74

Year Team	Lg Org	G	GS	CG	GF	IP	BFP	H	R	ER	HR	SH	SF	HB	TBB	IBB	SO	WP	Bk	W	L	Pct.	ShO	Sv	ERA
										WHAT HE GAVE UP										THE RESULTS					
1999 Cleveland	AL	5	0	0	0	9	44	10	10	10	1	0	1	0	8	1	6	1	0	0	0	—	0	0	10.00
2000 Atlanta	NL	2	0	0	2	3	15	5	4	4	2	0	0	0	1	0	4	0	0	0	0	—	0	0	12.00
10 Min. YEARS		280	71	5	118	724.2	3148	689	399	337	74	25	30	32	319	18	555	37	11	48	40	.545	1	32	4.19
7 Maj. YEARS		183	6	0	93	251	1163	298	174	168	49	13	11	4	132	11	170	9	4	15	16	.484	0	21	6.02

Tony Stevens

Bats: Both **Throws:** Right **Pos:** SS-137; PR-2; PH-1 **Ht:** 5'10" **Wt:** 160 **Born:** 9/18/78 **Age:** 23

Year Team	Lg Org	G	AB	H	2B	3B	HR	TB	R	RBI	TBB	IBB	SO	HBP	SH	SF	SB	CS	SB%	GDP	Avg	OBP	SLG
				BATTING													BASERUNNING				PERCENTAGES		
1997 Twins	R Min	47	170	41	3	0	1	47	23	17	9	0	21	2	1	2	9	2	.82	8	.241	.284	.276
1998 Twins	R Min	52	187	48	7	1	3	66	30	12	11	0	19	2	1	1	3	7	.30	1	.257	.303	.353
Fort Myers	A+ Min	3	7	2	0	0	0	2	0	1	0	0	0	0	0	0	0	0	—	0	.286	.286	.286
2000 Quad City	A Min	116	443	103	15	2	0	122	53	30	34	0	61	9	13	4	14	11	.56	4	.233	.298	.275
New Britain	AA Min	11	46	12	2	0	0	14	1	4	1	0	9	1	1	1	0	1	.00	2	.261	.286	.304
2001 Fort Myers	A+ Min	65	197	35	5	1	0	42	23	12	17	0	35	4	8	3	7	5	.58	4	.178	.253	.213
New Britain	AA Min	72	245	42	7	1	1	54	19	21	10	0	29	2	18	0	3	3	.50	1	.171	.210	.220
4 Min. YEARS		366	1295	283	39	5	5	347	149	97	82	0	174	20	42	11	36	29	.55	20	.219	.273	.268

Jason Stevenson

Pitches: Right **Bats:** Right **Pos:** RP-20; SP-1 **Ht:** 6'3" **Wt:** 180 **Born:** 8/11/74 **Age:** 27

Year Team	Lg Org	G	GS	CG	GF	IP	BFP	H	R	ER	HR	SH	SF	HB	TBB	IBB	SO	WP	Bk	W	L	Pct.	ShO	Sv	ERA
				HOW MUCH HE PITCHED							WHAT HE GAVE UP										THE RESULTS				
1994 Huntington	R+ ChC	5	1	0	1	10.2	47	12	5	5	2	3	1	0	6	0	5	1	0	1	1	.500	0	1	4.22
Cubs	R ChC	5	5	0	0	25	112	31	12	7	1	3	1	0	4	0	19	3	0	1	1	.500	0	0	2.52
1995 Rockford	A ChC	33	5	0	9	77.1	333	85	50	48	9	1	4	1	31	0	54	5	5	4	3	.571	0	2	5.59
Daytona	A+ ChC	8	0	0	3	18.1	71	11	6	6	0	1	0	1	6	0	15	1	0	2	0	1.000	0	1	2.95
1996 Daytona	A+ ChC	27	17	2	5	122	519	136	56	48	7	6	5	5	22	2	86	8	1	8	5	.615	1	0	3.54
1997 Knoxville	AA Tor	26	26	2	0	149.2	640	166	88	71	18	5	5	7	43	1	101	7	1	12	9	.571	2	0	4.27
1998 Knoxville	AA Tor	33	22	1	6	134.1	600	159	88	81	16	7	2	6	51	4	98	9	3	6	10	.375	0	1	5.43
1999 Knoxville	AA Tor	21	19	1	1	92.1	429	99	69	64	8	2	5	2	57	0	73	4	4	4	7	.364	0	0	6.24
Syracuse	AAA Tor	7	7	0	0	38.2	180	52	30	26	7	0	2	1	21	0	15	2	1	1	2	.333	0	0	6.05
2001 Lk Elsinore	A+ SD	11	0	0	3	14.1	71	25	12	9	2	1	1	0	4	0	14	0	1	1	1	.500	0	0	5.65
Mobile	AA SD	10	1	0	2	17.2	82	20	8	7	0	3	0	0	10	0	9	0	0	1	2	.333	0	0	3.57
7 Min. YEARS		186	103	6	30	700.1	3084	796	424	372	70	32	26	23	255	7	489	40	16	41	41	.500	3	4	4.78

Josh Stewart

Pitches: Left **Bats:** Left **Pos:** SP-28 **Ht:** 6'3" **Wt:** 205 **Born:** 12/5/78 **Age:** 23

Year Team	Lg Org	G	GS	CG	GF	IP	BFP	H	R	ER	HR	SH	SF	HB	TBB	IBB	SO	WP	Bk	W	L	Pct.	ShO	Sv	ERA
				HOW MUCH HE PITCHED							WHAT HE GAVE UP										THE RESULTS				
1999 Bristol	R+ CWS	5	0	0	2	18	71	13	5	3	0	1	0	2	5	0	25	0	0	1	0	1.000	0	1	1.50
Burlington	A CWS	16	0	0	3	29.2	138	32	25	24	6	0	2	2	21	0	35	1	0	2	0	1.000	0	1	7.28
2000 Burlington	A CWS	25	25	1	0	138	617	157	84	70	14	5	3	10	58	2	82	9	0	9	9	.500	1	0	4.57
2001 Winston-Sal	A+ CWS	12	12	1	0	63.2	287	64	41	27	6	3	4	4	28	1	38	3	0	4	6	.400	0	0	3.82
Birmingham	AA CWS	16	16	0	0	82.1	388	110	68	61	7	2	3	8	42	0	47	2	2	3	4	.429	0	0	6.67
3 Min. YEARS		74	53	2	5	331.2	1501	376	223	185	33	11	12	26	154	3	227	15	2	19	19	.500	1	2	5.02

Kevin Stocker

Bats: Both **Throws:** Right **Pos:** PR-1 **Ht:** 6'1" **Wt:** 180 **Born:** 2/13/70 **Age:** 32

Year Team	Lg Org	G	AB	H	2B	3B	HR	TB	R	RBI	TBB	IBB	SO	HBP	SH	SF	SB	CS	SB%	GDP	Avg	OBP	SLG
				BATTING													BASERUNNING				PERCENTAGES		
1991 Spartanburg	A Phi	70	250	55	11	1	0	68	26	20	31	1	37	2	6	1	15	3	.83		.220	.310	.272
1992 Clearwater	A+ Phi	63	244	69	13	4	1	93	43	33	27	2	31	4	5	3	15	9	.63	4	.283	.360	.381
Reading	AA Phi	62	240	60	9	2	1	76	31	13	22	1	30	2	3	0	17	4	.81	2	.250	.318	.317
1993 Scranton-WB	AAA Phi	83	313	73	14	1	3	98	54	17	29	2	56	7	8	0	17	6	.74	2	.233	.312	.313
1994 Scranton-WB	AAA Phi	4	13	4	1	0	0	5	1	2	1	0	4	1	1	0	0	0	—	0	.308	.357	.385
1996 Scranton-WB	AAA Phi	12	44	10	3	0	2	19	5	6	0	0	6	1	1	0	1	0	1.00	0	.227	.244	.432
1999 St. Pete	A+ TB	3	11	1	0	0	0	1	2	0	1	0	0	0	0	0	0	0	—	0	.091	.167	.091
2001 Las Vegas	AAA LA	1	0	0	0	0	0	0	1	0	0	0	0	0	0	0	0	0	—	0			
1993 Philadelphia	NL	70	259	84	12	3	2	108	46	31	30	11	43	8	4	1	5	0	1.00	3	.324	.409	.417
1994 Philadelphia	NL	82	271	74	11	2	2	95	38	28	44	8	41	7	4	4	2	2	.50	3	.273	.383	.351
1995 Philadelphia	NL	125	412	90	14	3	1	113	42	32	43	9	75	9	10	3	6	1	.86	7	.218	.304	.274
1996 Philadelphia	NL	119	394	100	22	6	5	149	46	41	43	9	89	8	3	4	6	4	.60	6	.254	.336	.378
1997 Philadelphia	NL	149	504	134	23	5	4	179	51	40	51	7	91	2	2	1	11	6	.65	14	.266	.335	.355
1998 Tampa Bay	AL	112	336	70	11	3	6	105	37	25	27	1	80	8	8	2	5	3	.63	7	.208	.282	.313
1999 Tampa Bay	AL	79	254	76	11	2	1	94	39	27	24	0	41	4	4	0	9	7	.56	4	.299	.369	.370
2000 Tampa Bay	AL	40	114	30	7	1	2	45	20	8	19	0	27	2	2	0	1	2	.33	3	.263	.372	.395
Anaheim	AL	70	229	45	13	3	0	64	21	19	32	0	54	2	8	1	0	3	.00	8	.197	.299	.279
7 Min. YEARS		298	1115	272	51	8	7	360	163	91	111	6	160	16	23	4	65	22	.75	—	.244	.320	.323
8 Maj. YEARS		846	2773	703	124	28	23	952	340	248	313	45	541	50	45	16	45	28	.62	60	.254	.338	.343

Nick Stocks

Pitches: Right **Bats:** Right **Pos:** SP-15; RP-1 **Ht:** 6'2" **Wt:** 185 **Born:** 8/27/78 **Age:** 23

Year Team	Lg Org	G	GS	CG	GF	IP	BFP	H	R	ER	HR	SH	SF	HB	TBB	IBB	SO	WP	Bk	W	L	Pct.	ShO	Sv	ERA
				HOW MUCH HE PITCHED							WHAT HE GAVE UP										THE RESULTS				
2000 Peoria	A StL	25	24	1	0	150	643	133	88	63	4	4	4	15	52	5	118	8	2	10	10	.500	0	0	3.78
2001 New Haven	AA StL	16	15	1	0	82	371	89	52	47	10	3	2	11	33	1	63	3	0	2	12	.143	0	0	5.16
2 Min. YEARS		41	39	2	0	232	1014	222	140	110	14	7	6	26	85	6	181	11	2	12	22	.353	0	0	4.27

Mike Stoner

Bats: Right **Throws:** Right **Pos:** OF-42; DH-20; 1B-18; PH-9   **Ht:** 6'0" **Wt:** 210 **Born:** 5/23/73 **Age:** 29

			BATTING													BASERUNNING				PERCENTAGES		
Year Team	Lg Org	G	AB	H	2B	3B	HR	TB	R	RBI	TBB	IBB	SO	HBP	SH	SF	SB	CS	SB%	GDP	Avg	OBP	SLG
1996 Lethbridge	R+ Ari	24	78	25	1	2	1	33	13	13	12	0	13	2	1	2	1	0	1.00	1	.321	.415	.423
Bakersfield	A+ Ari	36	147	43	6	1	6	69	25	22	8	0	18	0	0	1	1	1	.50	4	.293	.327	.469
1997 High Desert	A+ Ari	136	567	203	44	5	33	356	115	142	36	4	91	3	1	11	6	4	.60	17	.358	.392	.628
1998 Tucson	AAA Ari	106	394	123	22	3	5	166	46	49	27	4	52	4	0	3	3	0	1.00	10	.312	.360	.421
1999 Tucson	AAA Ari	14	21	9	1	0	0	10	2	6	2	0	3	0	0	1	0	0	—	0	.429	.458	.476
El Paso	AA Ari	1	0	0	0	0	0	0	1	0	1	0	0	0	0	0	0	0	—	0	—	1.000	—
Erie	AA Ana	14	62	21	4	0	3	34	10	15	2	1	8	0	0	0	0	1	.00	0	.339	.359	.548
Edmonton	AAA Ana	22	81	28	5	1	3	44	12	12	4	0	11	0	0	0	1	0	.00	2	.346	.376	.543
2000 Edmonton	AAA Ana	85	329	90	11	2	13	144	48	44	16	0	42	4	0	2	1	2	.33	9	.274	.313	.438
Iowa	AAA ChC	26	85	29	6	0	2	41	16	17	6	1	6	6	0	1	0	0	—	2	.341	.418	.482
2001 Carolina	AA Col	45	155	41	7	3	2	60	25	27	14	1	19	5	2	1	0	0	—	6	.265	.343	.387
Altoona	AA Pit	42	135	34	7	1	3	52	15	21	2	0	21	4	0	1	0	3	.00	6	.252	.282	.385
6 Min. YEARS		551	2054	646	114	18	71	1009	328	368	130	11	284	28	4	23	12	12	.50	57	.315	.360	.491

Jim Stoops

Pitches: Right **Bats:** Right **Pos:** RP-11   **Ht:** 6'2" **Wt:** 180 **Born:** 6/30/72 **Age:** 30

			HOW MUCH HE PITCHED					WHAT HE GAVE UP										THE RESULTS					
Year Team	Lg Org	G	GS	CG	GF	IP	BFP	H	R	ER	HR	SH	SF	HB	TBB	IBB	SO	WP	Bk	W	L	Pct.	ShO	Sv	ERA
1995 Bellingham	A- SF	24	0	0	14	42	178	32	23	16	1	2	1	5	17	0	58	2	0	6	5	.545	0	4	3.43
1996 Burlington	A SF	46	0	0	18	60.2	262	43	24	17	2	4	1	6	40	4	69	6	1	3	3	.500	0	2	2.52
1997 San Jose	A+ SF	50	0	0	16	91.2	401	92	56	53	3	2	3	7	45	2	114	7	1	2	5	.286	0	4	5.20
1998 San Jose	A+ SF	45	0	0	43	55.1	222	28	7	6	0	0	0	3	25	0	96	1	0	2	1	.667	0	31	0.98
Salem	A+ Col	3	0	0	1	4.1	16	2	0	0	0	1	0	0	1	0	8	0	0	0	0	—	0	0	0.00
Colo Sprngs	AAA Col	11	0	0	6	14.2	58	6	6	2	0	0	2	1	8	0	17	0	0	1	0	1.000	0	1	1.23
1999 Colo Sprngs	AAA Col	55	5	0	22	88.2	400	93	54	51	11	6	6	4	56	2	57	7	0	3	7	.300	0	5	5.18
2000 Colo Sprngs	AAA Col	3	0	0	0	3.2	20	6	2	1	0	0	0	0	6	0	4	2	0	0	0	—	0	0	2.45
Carolina	AA Col	33	0	0	15	52.1	222	37	20	16	3	4	4	5	33	2	47	4	0	5	3	.625	0	2	2.75
2001 Columbus	AAA NYY	5	0	0	2	12	50	8	4	3	2	0	0	0	5	0	10	3	0	0	0	—	0	0	2.25
Norwich	AA NYY	6	0	0	1	9	48	14	10	6	3	0	0	0	6	0	9	0	0	0	0	—	0	0	6.00
1998 Colorado	NL	3	0	0	0	4	17	5	1	1	0	0	0	1	3	0	1	0	0	1	0	1.000	0	0	2.25
7 Min. YEARS		281	5	0	138	434.1	1880	361	206	171	25	19	17	31	242	10	489	32	2	22	24	.478	0	50	3.54

Pat Strange

Pitches: Right **Bats:** Right **Pos:** SP-25; RP-2   **Ht:** 6'5" **Wt:** 243 **Born:** 8/23/80 **Age:** 21

			HOW MUCH HE PITCHED					WHAT HE GAVE UP										THE RESULTS					
Year Team	Lg Org	G	GS	CG	GF	IP	BFP	H	R	ER	HR	SH	SF	HB	TBB	IBB	SO	WP	Bk	W	L	Pct.	ShO	Sv	ERA
1998 Mets	R NYM	4	4	0	0	19	79	18	3	3	0	0	0	1	7	0	19	0	0	1	1	.500	0	0	1.42
1999 Capital Cty	A NYM	28	21	2	1	154	627	138	57	45	4	4	3	10	29	1	113	7	0	12	5	.706	0	1	2.63
2000 St. Lucie	A+ NYM	19	13	2	1	88	374	78	48	35	4	2	5	9	32	0	77	9	1	10	1	.909	0	0	3.58
Binghamton	AA NYM	10	10	0	0	55.1	252	62	30	28	2	3	2	1	30	0	36	3	0	4	3	.571	0	0	4.55
2001 Binghamton	AA NYM	26	24	1	1	153.1	669	171	94	83	18	5	6	12	52	1	106	7	0	11	6	.647	0	0	4.87
Norfolk	AAA NYM	1	1	0	0	6	23	4	0	0	0	0	0	0	1	0	6	0	0	1	0	1.000	0	0	0.00
4 Min. YEARS		88	73	5	3	475.2	2024	471	232	194	28	14	16	33	151	2	357	26	1	39	16	.709	0	1	3.67

Elliott Strankman

Bats: Right **Throws:** Right **Pos:** SS-32; 3B-9; 2B-5; PH-3; PR-1   **Ht:** 6'1" **Wt:** 185 **Born:** 1/13/77 **Age:** 25

			BATTING													BASERUNNING				PERCENTAGES		
Year Team	Lg Org	G	AB	H	2B	3B	HR	TB	R	RBI	TBB	IBB	SO	HBP	SH	SF	SB	CS	SB%	GDP	Avg	OBP	SLG
2000 Salem-Keizr	A- SF	3	6	1	0	1	0	3	2	0	0	0	2	0	0	0	0	0	—	0	.167	.167	.500
2001 Hagerstown	A SF	39	116	30	12	0	0	42	16	10	5	0	29	4	1	0	3	4	.43	3	.259	.312	.362
Shreveport	AA SF	9	13	1	0	0	0	1	1	0	1	0	9	1	0	0	0	0	—	0	.077	.200	.077
2 Min. YEARS		51	135	32	12	1	0	46	19	10	6	0	40	5	1	0	3	4	.43	3	.237	.295	.341

Robert Stratton

Bats: Right **Throws:** Right **Pos:** OF-112; DH-21; PH-2   **Ht:** 6'2" **Wt:** 251 **Born:** 10/7/77 **Age:** 24

			BATTING													BASERUNNING				PERCENTAGES		
Year Team	Lg Org	G	AB	H	2B	3B	HR	TB	R	RBI	TBB	IBB	SO	HBP	SH	SF	SB	CS	SB%	GDP	Avg	OBP	SLG
1996 Mets	R NYM	17	59	15	2	0	2	23	5	9	2	0	22	0	1	0	3	2	.60	0	.254	.279	.390
1997 Kingsport	R+ NYM	63	245	61	11	5	15	127	51	50	19	1	94	6	0	0	11	6	.65	2	.249	.319	.518
1998 Mets	R NYM	12	46	12	1	0	3	22	4	13	2	1	15	0	0	1	1	0	1.00	0	.261	.286	.478
Pittsfield	A- NYM	34	124	28	5	4	6	59	18	18	11	0	55	0	0	0	3	2	.60	2	.226	.289	.476
1999 Capital Cty	A NYM	95	318	87	17	3	21	173	58	60	48	4	112	5	0	3	7	1	.88	1	.274	.374	.544
2000 St. Lucie	A+ NYM	108	381	87	18	4	29	200	61	87	60	3	180	8	1	2	3	5	.38	3	.228	.344	.525
2001 Binghamton	AA NYM	133	483	120	30	1	29	239	70	83	53	6	201	8	0	2	9	5	.64	5	.248	.332	.495
Norfolk	AAA NYM	2	7	1	0	0	1	4	1	3	0	0	2	0	0	1	0	0	—	0	.143	.125	.571
6 Min. YEARS		464	1663	411	84	17	106	847	268	323	195	15	681	27	2	9	37	21	.64	13	.247	.334	.509

Everett Stull

Pitches: Right **Bats:** Right **Pos:** SP-6; RP-3   **Ht:** 6'3" **Wt:** 200 **Born:** 8/24/71 **Age:** 30

			HOW MUCH HE PITCHED					WHAT HE GAVE UP										THE RESULTS					
Year Team	Lg Org	G	GS	CG	GF	IP	BFP	H	R	ER	HR	SH	SF	HB	TBB	IBB	SO	WP	Bk	W	L	Pct.	ShO	Sv	ERA
1992 Jamestown	A- Mon	14	14	0	0	63.1	303	52	49	38	2	2	3	3	61	0	64	18	4	3	5	.375	0	0	5.40
1993 Burlington	A Mon	15	15	1	0	82.1	366	68	44	35	8	2	1	3	59	0	85	11	4	4	9	.308	0	0	3.83
1994 Wst Plm Bch	A+ Mon	27	26	3	0	147	627	116	60	54	3	7	3	12	78	0	165	15	6	10	10	.500	1	0	3.31
1995 Harrisburg	AA Mon	24	24	0	0	126.2	569	114	88	78	12	5	5	9	79	2	132	7	1	3	12	.200	0	0	5.54

Year Team	Lg Org	G	GS	CG	GF	IP	BFP	H	R	ER	HR	SH	SF	HB	TBB	IBB	SO	WP	Bk	W	L	Pct.	ShO	Sv	ERA
1996 Harrisburg	AA Mon	14	14	0	0	80	345	64	31	28	8	3	2	2	52	1	81	6	0	6	3	.667	0	0	3.15
Ottawa	AAA Mon	13	13	1	0	69.2	331	87	57	49	7	3	3	3	39	1	69	5	0	2	6	.250	0	0	6.33
1997 Ottawa	AAA Mon	27	27	1	0	159.1	710	166	110	103	25	4	4	13	86	0	130	9	0	8	10	.444	0	0	5.82
1998 Rochester	AAA Bal	21	7	0	6	42.2	222	49	44	42	9	0	3	5	45	0	39	6	0	1	4	.200	0	0	8.86
1999 Richmond	AAA Atl	30	22	0	5	139	603	124	75	69	17	4	7	8	73	0	126	12	2	8	8	.500	0	0	4.47
2000 Indianaplos	AAA Mil	16	16	1	0	103.2	439	95	41	34	3	3	5	4	43	0	74	5	2	7	5	.583	1	0	2.95
2001 Brewers	R Mil	2	1	0	0	4.1	16	2	0	0	0	0	0	0	0	0	4	0	0	0	0	—	0	0	0.00
High Desert	A+ Mil	1	1	0	0	2.2	15	6	5	5	1	0	0	0	1	0	1	0	0	0	1	.000	0	0	16.88
Huntsville	AA Mil	6	4	0	1	25.2	102	21	11	11	3	0	0	2	5	0	23	4	0	1	1	.500	0	0	3.86
1997 Montreal	NL	3	0	0	1	3.1	21	7	7	6	1	1	0	0	4	0	2	0	0	0	1	.000	0	0	16.20
1999 Atlanta	NL	1	0	0	0	0.2	7	2	3	1	0	0	1	0	2	0	0	0	0	0	0	—	0	0	13.50
2000 Milwaukee	NL	20	4	0	3	43.1	199	41	30	28	7	2	3	4	30	0	33	5	0	2	3	.400	0	0	5.82
10 Min. YEARS		210	184	7	12	1046.1	4648	964	615	546	98	33	36	64	621	4	993	98	19	53	74	.417	2	0	4.70
3 Maj. YEARS		24	4	0	4	47.1	227	50	40	35	8	3	4	4	36	3	35	5	0	2	4	.333	0	0	6.65

Tim Sturdy

Pitches: Right **Bats:** Right **Pos:** SP-21; RP-9 **Ht:** 6'2" **Wt:** 179 **Born:** 10/8/78 **Age:** 23

Year Team	Lg Org	G	GS	CG	GF	IP	BFP	H	R	ER	HR	SH	SF	HB	TBB	IBB	SO	WP	Bk	W	L	Pct.	ShO	Sv	ERA
1997 Twins	R Min	9	2	1	3	24	88	12	4	2	0	0	0	0	6	0	14	0	2	1	1	.500	1	0	0.75
1998 Elizabethtn	R+ Min	12	12	0	0	69.2	302	65	38	31	4	1	2	6	27	0	46	8	1	5	1	.833	0	0	4.00
1999 Quad City	A Min	13	13	0	0	60.1	282	85	48	42	4	3	0	5	16	0	39	2	1	2	7	.222	0	0	6.27
Elizabethtn	R+ Min	12	12	0	0	73.1	311	71	33	27	2	3	1	4	17	0	64	9	1	6	1	.857	0	0	3.31
2000 Quad City	A Min	23	21	2	0	133.2	552	121	61	44	6	1	1	8	39	3	73	11	2	9	7	.563	1	0	2.96
New Britain	AA Min	1	1	0	0	7	31	7	5	4	0	1	0	1	1	0	5	0	0	0	1	.000	0	0	5.14
2001 Edmonton	AAA Min	2	2	0	0	7	40	15	14	13	2	0	0	1	6	0	3	2	0	0	1	.000	0	0	16.71
Fort Myers	A+ Min	28	19	1	2	129.2	552	122	74	55	2	8	4	10	53	2	54	9	2	8	10	.444	0	0	3.82
5 Min. YEARS		100	82	4	5	504.2	2158	498	277	218	20	17	8	35	165	5	298	41	9	31	29	.517	2	0	3.89

Felipe Suarez

Pitches: Right **Bats:** Right **Pos:** RP-33; SP-1 **Ht:** 6'2" **Wt:** 185 **Born:** 3/12/76 **Age:** 26

Year Team	Lg Org	G	GS	CG	GF	IP	BFP	H	R	ER	HR	SH	SF	HB	TBB	IBB	SO	WP	Bk	W	L	Pct.	ShO	Sv	ERA
1998 Huntington	IND —	7	7	0	0	42.2	185	39	25	21	3	1	2	4	15	0	40	2	0	2	2	.500	0	0	4.43
Boise	A- Ana	11	0	0	3	16.1	69	15	7	7	2	0	0	1	3	1	18	0	0	0	0	—	0	1	3.86
1999 Boise	A- Ana	5	5	0	0	29.2	135	32	26	20	2	1	1	4	11	0	33	2	0	1	2	.333	0	0	6.07
Cedar Rapds	A Ana	4	4	0	0	18	91	25	19	14	3	0	4	1	9	0	15	2	0	1	1	.500	0	0	7.00
2000 Lk Elsinore	A+ Ana	31	0	0	17	57.1	248	51	24	14	3	2	5	1	18	3	40	1	1	5	5	.500	0	5	2.20
Edmonton	AAA Ana	1	0	0	0	1	5	2	2	2	0	0	1	0	0	0	0	1	0	0	0	—	0	0	18.00
Erie	AA Ana	20	0	0	10	37	161	46	22	20	5	1	5	1	7	0	23	2	1	2	0	1.000	0	1	4.86
2001 Arkansas	AA Ana	34	1	0	15	66.2	294	77	37	33	12	3	3	4	18	0	46	3	0	2	5	.286	0	3	4.46
4 Min. YEARS		113	17	0	45	268.2	1188	287	162	131	30	8	21	16	81	4	215	13	2	13	15	.464	0	10	4.39

Luis Suarez

Bats: Right **Throws:** Right **Pos:** 2B-6; PH-4; 3B-3 **Ht:** 6'1" **Wt:** 175 **Born:** 9/5/78 **Age:** 23

Year Team	Lg Org	G	AB	H	2B	3B	HR	TB	R	RBI	TBB	IBB	SO	HBP	SH	SF	SB	CS	SB%	GDP	Avg	OBP	SLG
1998 Bristol	R+ CWS	60	198	50	5	1	1	60	35	25	22	0	40	0	2	5	7	1	.88	3	.253	.320	.303
1999 Burlington	A CWS	51	173	42	10	0	4	64	24	25	19	0	32	3	3	2	5	4	.56	1	.243	.325	.370
Winston-Sal	A+ CWS	74	241	49	7	2	2	66	20	26	22	0	66	2	5	3	3	2	.60	4	.203	.272	.274
2000 Winston-Sal	A+ CWS	102	346	85	17	3	5	123	39	38	15	0	81	2	8	3	4	4	.50	7	.246	.279	.355
2001 Birmingham	AA CWS	6	17	2	2	0	0	4	4	2	1	0	6	1	0	0	0	0	—	1	.118	.211	.235
Winston-Sal	A+ CWS	6	15	2	1	0	0	3	0	1	0	0	7	0	0	1	0	0	—	1	.133	.133	.200
4 Min. YEARS		298	990	230	42	6	12	320	122	117	79	0	232	8	18	13	19	11	.63	17	.232	.291	.323

Pedro Swann

Bats: Left **Throws:** Right **Pos:** OF-124; DH-13; PH-3; PR-1 **Ht:** 6'0" **Wt:** 200 **Born:** 10/27/70 **Age:** 31

Year Team	Lg Org	G	AB	H	2B	3B	HR	TB	R	RBI	TBB	IBB	SO	HBP	SH	SF	SB	CS	SB%	GDP	Avg	OBP	SLG
1991 Idaho Falls	R+ Atl	55	174	48	6	1	3	65	35	28	33	0	45	2	1	2	8	5	.62	4	.276	.393	.374
1992 Pulaski	R+ Atl	59	203	61	18	1	5	96	36	34	32	3	33	7	0	1	13	6	.68	6	.300	.412	.473
1993 Durham	A+ Atl	61	182	63	8	2	6	93	27	27	19	0	38	1	0	0	6	12	.33	2	.346	.411	.511
Greenville	AA Atl	44	157	48	9	2	3	70	19	21	9	0	23	1	1	0	2	2	.50	5	.306	.347	.446
1994 Greenville	AA Atl	126	428	121	25	2	10	180	55	49	46	2	85	4	0	2	16	9	.64	14	.283	.356	.421
1995 Richmond	AAA Atl	15	38	8	1	0	0	9	2	3	1	0	2	1	0	0	0	2	.00	0	.211	.250	.237
Greenville	AA Atl	102	339	110	24	2	11	171	57	64	45	2	63	3	0	3	14	11	.56	8	.324	.405	.504
1996 Greenville	AA Atl	35	129	40	5	0	3	54	15	20	18	2	23	3	1	1	4	4	.50	3	.310	.404	.419
Richmond	AAA Atl	93	296	74	11	4	4	105	42	35	22	2	56	4	2	3	7	7	.50	14	.250	.308	.355
1997 Greenville	AA Atl	124	465	133	29	2	24	238	78	83	49	5	75	4	0	1	5	5	.50	11	.286	.358	.512
1998 Toledo	AAA Det	120	419	122	28	2	15	199	56	66	41	4	74	3	1	4	6	3	.67	11	.291	.355	.475
1999 Toledo	AAA Det	103	332	86	14	2	10	134	51	37	36	0	67	6	0	5	3	1	.75	7	.259	.338	.404
2000 Richmond	AAA Atl	125	442	135	22	2	9	188	70	57	54	6	68	5	2	1	6	5	.55	10	.305	.386	.425
2001 Richmond	AAA Atl	139	488	142	33	5	8	209	68	72	52	3	95	8	1	10	12	6	.67	14	.291	.362	.428
2000 Atlanta	NL	4	2	0	0	0	0	0	0	0	0	0	0	0	0	0	0	0	—	0	.000	.000	.000
11 Min. YEARS		1201	4092	1191	233	27	111	1811	611	596	457	29	747	52	9	33	102	78	.57	103	.291	.367	.443

Brian Sweeney

Pitches: Right **Bats:** Right **Pos:** RP-28; SP-9   **Ht:** 6'2" **Wt:** 185 **Born:** 6/13/74 **Age:** 28

Year Team	Lg Org	G	GS	CG	GF	IP	BFP	H	R	ER	HR	SH	SF	HB	TBB	IBB	SO	WP	Bk	W	L	Pct.	ShO	Sv	ERA
1997 Lancaster	A+ Sea	40	0	0	13	85.1	358	83	39	36	11	2	4	2	21	1	73	8	0	6	3	.667	0	1	3.80
1998 Lancaster	A+ Sea	17	4	0	3	52	211	41	26	21	6	0	1	1	21	1	48	2	1	6	0	1.000	0	0	3.63
1999 Lancaster	A+ Sea	5	0	0	1	9.1	44	14	7	7	4	0	0	0	3	0	14	1	0	0	0	—	0	0	6.75
Tacoma	AAA Sea	5	1	0	2	16	75	26	17	12	5	2	0	0	2	0	10	1	0	0	2	.000	0	0	6.75
New Haven	AA Sea	23	18	0	3	111.1	478	125	65	58	18	1	3	4	31	1	83	4	0	4	6	.400	0	1	4.69
2000 Tacoma	AAA Sea	2	1	0	0	6	26	9	4	4	2	0	0	0	1	0	1	1	0	0	1	.000	0	0	6.00
New Haven	AA Sea	19	7	0	5	47.2	207	49	20	18	3	1	2	2	19	0	27	5	0	4	3	.571	0	1	3.40
2001 San Antonio	AA Sea	37	9	0	8	104.1	448	117	47	44	8	3	3	5	23	1	96	7	0	7	4	.636	0	1	3.80
5 Min. YEARS		148	40	0	35	432	1847	464	225	200	57	9	13	14	121	4	352	29	1	27	19	.587	0	4	4.17

Jamie Sykes

Bats: Right **Throws:** Right **Pos:** OF-93; DH-9; PH-8; PR-3; C-1   **Ht:** 5'11" **Wt:** 198 **Born:** 1/14/75 **Age:** 27

Year Team	Lg Org	G	AB	H	2B	3B	HR	TB	R	RBI	TBB	IBB	SO	HBP	SH	SF	SB	CS	SB%	GDP	Avg	OBP	SLG
1997 Lethbridge	R+ Ari	58	223	68	8	6	4	100	45	37	25	0	40	3	1	0	9	2	.82	6	.305	.382	.448
1998 High Desert	A+ Ari	36	125	21	5	2	3	39	13	16	19	0	33	0	0	1	5	2	.71	1	.168	.276	.312
South Bend	A Ari	26	93	19	2	3	2	33	12	10	16	0	20	2	0	0	5	0	1.00	0	.204	.333	.355
1999 South Bend	A Ari	127	479	137	34	10	15	236	75	83	53	1	111	4	1	4	17	8	.68	9	.286	.359	.493
2000 El Paso	AA Ari	48	154	31	5	2	3	49	16	21	19	1	45	0	0	3	6	3	.67	1	.201	.284	.318
High Desert	A+ Ari	83	303	87	15	6	16	162	64	57	45	0	80	1	0	2	11	6	.65	3	.287	.379	.535
2001 El Paso	AA Ari	64	216	54	7	0	3	70	22	16	13	0	75	3	0	1	9	2	.82	3	.250	.300	.324
Lancaster	A+ Ari	43	155	38	11	0	4	61	21	19	10	0	42	1	2	0	4	5	.44	3	.245	.295	.394
5 Min. YEARS		485	1748	455	87	29	50	750	268	259	200	2	446	14	4	11	66	28	.70	26	.260	.339	.429

Billy Sylvester

Pitches: Right **Bats:** Right **Pos:** RP-62   **Ht:** 6'5" **Wt:** 218 **Born:** 10/1/76 **Age:** 25

Year Team	Lg Org	G	GS	CG	GF	IP	BFP	H	R	ER	HR	SH	SF	HB	TBB	IBB	SO	WP	Bk	W	L	Pct.	ShO	Sv	ERA
1997 Braves	R Atl	12	9	0	1	53	225	45	25	23	2	0	0	3	28	0	58	6	0	3	4	.429	0	0	3.91
1998 Eugene	A- Atl	16	16	0	0	55.1	273	73	61	40	7	0	4	7	24	0	42	5	1	0	11	.000	0	0	6.51
1999 Macon	A Atl	44	1	0	21	83.2	373	78	37	29	3	5	5	6	37	2	75	5	1	5	4	.556	0	2	3.12
2000 Myrtle Bch	A+ Atl	32	0	0	27	45.2	172	16	8	4	2	1	1	3	15	1	48	2	0	3	0	1.000	0	16	0.79
2001 Greenville	AA Atl	26	0	0	24	30.1	129	18	8	8	3	1	0	2	24	0	41	4	0	1	0	1.000	0	12	2.37
Richmond	AAA Atl	36	0	0	21	37	169	28	21	21	2	1	4	2	27	2	41	4	0	0	4	.000	0	11	5.11
5 Min. YEARS		166	26	0	94	305	1341	258	160	125	19	8	14	23	155	5	305	26	2	12	23	.343	0	41	3.69

Jeff Taglienti

Pitches: Right **Bats:** Right **Pos:** RP-51   **Ht:** 6'0" **Wt:** 210 **Born:** 11/13/75 **Age:** 26

Year Team	Lg Org	G	GS	CG	GF	IP	BFP	H	R	ER	HR	SH	SF	HB	TBB	IBB	SO	WP	Bk	W	L	Pct.	ShO	Sv	ERA
1997 Lowell	A- Bos	17	4	0	11	36.2	150	30	22	20	2	0	0	0	13	0	34	3	2	3	4	.429	0	6	4.91
1998 Michigan	A Bos	57	0	0	49	76.1	303	54	19	16	0	3	2	3	17	2	111	3	0	4	2	.667	0	30	1.89
1999 Sarasota	A+ Bos	14	0	0	5	30	128	26	12	10	1	2	2	2	12	1	27	4	0	1	1	.500	0	3	3.00
Trenton	AA Bos	10	0	0	4	19.1	72	9	6	6	2	1	1	0	5	0	17	0	0	0	0	—	0	2	2.79
2000 Trenton	AA Bos	38	0	0	31	51	216	59	26	21	3	3	0	0	7	0	33	2	0	3	1	.750	0	10	3.71
Carolina	AA Col	10	0	0	9	12.1	51	9	4	2	1	1	0	0	3	0	7	0	0	1	1	.500	0	1	1.46
2001 Chattanooga	AA Cin	51	0	0	22	55.1	235	64	30	29	3	3	1	1	14	1	45	1	0	5	5	.500	0	7	4.72
5 Min. YEARS		197	4	0	131	281	1155	251	119	104	12	13	6	6	71	4	274	13	2	17	14	.548	0	58	3.33

Kazuhiro Takeoka

Pitches: Right **Bats:** Right **Pos:** RP-45   **Ht:** 6'4" **Wt:** 190 **Born:** 1/25/75 **Age:** 27

Year Team	Lg Org	G	GS	CG	GF	IP	BFP	H	R	ER	HR	SH	SF	HB	TBB	IBB	SO	WP	Bk	W	L	Pct.	ShO	Sv	ERA
2001 Greenville	AA Atl	45	0	0	21	74	326	76	31	22	2	10	1	10	21	6	46	9	1	5	3	.625	0	3	2.68

John Tamargo Jr.

Bats: Both **Throws:** Right **Pos:** 2B-58; 3B-17; SS-10; PH-9; DH-2   **Ht:** 5'9" **Wt:** 165 **Born:** 5/3/75 **Age:** 27

Year Team	Lg Org	G	AB	H	2B	3B	HR	TB	R	RBI	TBB	IBB	SO	HBP	SH	SF	SB	CS	SB%	GDP	Avg	OBP	SLG
1996 Pittsfield	A- NYM	55	184	41	5	3	0	52	26	19	35	0	34	2	1	3	5	3	.63	5	.223	.348	.283
1997 Capital Cty	A NYM	113	393	98	17	2	1	122	44	47	45	2	72	2	5	1	13	7	.65	9	.249	.329	.310
1998 St. Lucie	A+ NYM	105	347	84	24	1	0	110	40	33	41	2	60	3	9	2	14	7	.67	3	.242	.326	.317
Norfolk	AAA NYM	3	8	0	0	0	0	0	0	0	1	0	3	0	0	0	0	0	—	0	.000	.111	.000
1999 Binghamton	AA NYM	112	363	78	13	3	4	109	27	37	40	1	55	4	5	3	7	5	.58	8	.215	.298	.300
2000 Norfolk	AAA NYM	4	11	2	1	0	0	3	2	0	2	0	1	0	0	1	0	1	.00	1	.182	.357	.273
Binghamton	AA NYM	96	291	75	18	1	1	98	47	29	43	0	47	2	8	0	5	6	.45	10	.258	.357	.337
2001 Binghamton	AA NYM	49	151	38	8	1	1	51	13	10	13	0	19	0	7	0	3	3	.50	7	.252	.311	.338
Norfolk	AAA NYM	40	111	32	3	0	1	38	11	11	12	0	16	1	3	2	0	0	—	2	.288	.357	.342
6 Min. YEARS		577	1859	448	89	11	8	583	210	186	232	5	307	15	38	11	47	32	.59	45	.241	.328	.314

Dennis Tankersley

Pitches: Right **Bats:** Right **Pos:** SP-24; RP-1   **Ht:** 6'2" **Wt:** 185 **Born:** 2/24/79 **Age:** 23

		HOW MUCH HE PITCHED						WHAT HE GAVE UP										THE RESULTS					
Year Team	Lg Org	G	GS	CG	GF	IP	BFP	H	R	ER	HR	SH	SF	HB	TBB	IBB	SO	WP	Bk	W	L	Pct.	ShO	Sv	ERA
1999 Red Sox	R Bos	11	6	0	2	35.2	133	14	7	3	2	0	0	3	9	1	57	0	0	1	0	1.000	0	1	0.76
2000 Augusta	A Bos	15	15	1	0	75.1	326	73	41	34	4	0	0	4	32	0	74	1	1	5	3	.625	1	0	4.06
Fort Wayne	A SD	12	12	0	0	66.1	265	48	25	21	5	2	2	2	25	0	87	2	0	5	2	.714	0	0	2.85
2001 Lk Elsinore	A+ SD	9	8	0	0	52.1	196	29	5	3	1	1	0	0	12	0	68	0	0	5	1	.833	0	0	0.52
Mobile	AA SD	13	13	0	0	69.2	282	44	23	16	6	1	0	4	24	1	89	2	1	4	1	.800	0	0	2.07
Portland	AAA SD	3	3	0	0	14.1	68	16	13	11	2	2	2	0	8	0	16	0	0	1	2	.333	0	0	6.91
3 Min. YEARS		63	57	1	2	313.2	1270	224	114	88	20	6	4	13	110	2	391	5	2	21	9	.700	1	1	2.52

Tony Tarasco

Bats: Left **Throws:** Right **Pos:** OF-100; DH-6; PH-4; PR-1   **Ht:** 6'0" **Wt:** 205 **Born:** 12/9/70 **Age:** 31

		BATTING														BASERUNNING				PERCENTAGES		
Year Team	Lg Org	G	AB	H	2B	3B	HR	TB	R	RBI	TBB	IBB	SO	HBP	SH	SF	SB	CS	SB%	GDP	Avg	OBP	SLG
1988 Idaho Falls	R+ Atl	7	10	0	0	0	0	0	1	1	5	0	2	0	0	0	1	0	1.00	1	.000	.333	.000
Braves	R Atl	21	64	15	6	1	0	23	10	4	7	0	7	1	1	0	3	2	.60	4	.234	.311	.359
1989 Pulaski	R+ Atl	49	156	53	8	2	2	71	22	22	21	2	20	0	2	2	7	2	.78	2	.340	.413	.455
1990 Sumter	A Atl	107	355	94	13	3	3	122	42	37	37	1	57	1	5	3	9	5	.64	6	.265	.333	.344
1991 Durham	A+ Atl	78	248	62	8	2	12	110	31	38	21	2	64	1	4	3	11	9	.55	3	.250	.308	.444
1992 Greenville	AA Atl	133	489	140	22	2	15	211	73	54	27	2	84	1	3	7	33	19	.63	9	.286	.321	.431
1993 Richmond	AAA Atl	93	370	122	15	7	15	196	73	53	36	3	54	1	4	3	19	11	.63	1	.330	.388	.530
1996 Rochester	AAA Bal	29	103	27	6	0	2	39	18	9	17	2	20	0	1	1	4	4	.50	2	.262	.364	.379
Orioles	R Bal	3	8	3	1	0	0	4	2	3	2	1	1	0	0	0	0	0	—	0	.375	.455	.500
Frederick	A+ Bal	9	35	8	3	0	1	14	6	5	4	1	4	1	0	0	0	1	.00	2	.229	.325	.400
1997 Rochester	AAA Bal	10	35	7	0	0	2	13	4	6	7	0	7	0	0	1	0	0	—	1	.200	.326	.371
1998 Indianapolis	AAA Cin	90	319	100	19	1	16	169	53	45	43	1	46	1	2	2	3	2	.60	4	.313	.395	.530
1999 Columbus	AAA NYY	95	346	102	23	0	19	182	72	61	49	6	39	2	0	3	9	5	.64	10	.295	.383	.526
2001 St. Lucie	A+ NYM	3	13	3	2	0	0	5	1	2	0	0	4	0	0	0	0	0	—	1	.231	.231	.385
Norfolk	AAA NYM	105	366	107	31	4	7	167	53	57	48	8	43	0	0	4	14	8	.64	5	.292	.371	.456
1993 Atlanta	NL	24	35	8	2	0	0	10	6	2	0	0	5	1	0	1	0	1	.00	1	.229	.243	.286
1994 Atlanta	NL	87	132	36	6	0	5	57	16	19	9	1	17	0	0	3	5	0	1.00	5	.273	.313	.432
1995 Montreal	NL	126	438	109	18	4	14	177	64	40	51	12	78	2	3	1	24	3	.89	2	.249	.329	.404
1996 Baltimore	AL	31	84	20	3	0	1	26	14	9	7	0	15	0	1	0	5	3	.63	1	.238	.297	.310
1997 Baltimore	AL	100	166	34	8	1	7	65	26	26	25	1	33	1	1	0	2	2	.50	3	.205	.313	.392
1998 Cincinnati	NL	15	24	5	2	0	1	10	5	4	3	0	5	0	1	0	0	0	—	0	.208	.296	.417
1999 New York	AL	14	31	5	2	0	0	7	5	3	3	0	5	0	0	1	1	0	1.00	1	.161	.229	.226
11 Min. YEARS		832	2917	843	157	22	94	1326	461	397	324	29	452	9	22	30	113	68	.62	51	.289	.359	.455
7 Maj. YEARS		397	910	217	41	5	28	352	136	103	98	14	158	4	6	6	37	9	.80	13	.238	.313	.387

Luis Taveras

Bats: Right **Throws:** Right **Pos:** C-67; PH-1   **Ht:** 5'10" **Wt:** 185 **Born:** 8/1/77 **Age:** 24

		BATTING														BASERUNNING				PERCENTAGES		
Year Team	Lg Org	G	AB	H	2B	3B	HR	TB	R	RBI	TBB	IBB	SO	HBP	SH	SF	SB	CS	SB%	GDP	Avg	OBP	SLG
1997 Rangers	R Tex	37	83	20	3	0	1	26	10	10	9	1	21	0	0	1	1	0	1.00	2	.241	.312	.313
1998 Charlotte	A+ Tex	76	246	40	4	2	3	57	21	24	14	0	70	0	2	4	4	6	.40	1	.163	.205	.232
1999 Charlotte	A+ Tex	95	308	81	18	4	6	125	36	46	30	0	69	3	3	4	10	4	.71	6	.263	.330	.406
2000 Tulsa	AA Tex	82	285	66	14	3	5	101	44	37	34	0	73	2	2	6	3	2	.60	8	.232	.312	.354
2001 Oklahoma	AAA Tex	12	33	6	0	0	0	6	3	3	3	0	12	0	2	0	0	1	.00	1	.182	.250	.182
Tulsa	AA Tex	55	180	37	4	2	5	60	31	22	18	0	35	1	4	2	5	0	1.00	5	.206	.279	.333
5 Min. YEARS		357	1135	250	43	11	20	375	145	142	108	1	280	6	13	17	23	13	.64	27	.220	.288	.330

Nate Tebbs

Bats: Both **Throws:** Right **Pos:** SS-27; 2B-21; OF-20; PH-6; PR-5; 3B-1; DH-1   **Ht:** 5'10" **Wt:** 170 **Born:** 12/14/72 **Age:** 29

		BATTING														BASERUNNING				PERCENTAGES		
Year Team	Lg Org	G	AB	H	2B	3B	HR	TB	R	RBI	TBB	IBB	SO	HBP	SH	SF	SB	CS	SB%	GDP	Avg	OBP	SLG
1993 Red Sox	R Bos	43	146	38	4	1	0	44	21	4	15	1	16	0	7	0	7	1	.88	1	.260	.329	.301
1994 Utica	A- Bos	70	219	44	5	0	0	49	18	23	11	0	34	1	4	1	9	4	.69	1	.201	.241	.224
1995 Sarasota	A+ Bos	118	440	128	15	4	2	157	58	52	39	0	80	3	4	1	25	15	.63	7	.291	.352	.357
1996 Sarasota	A+ Bos	116	420	105	11	2	1	123	44	34	24	1	68	3	10	1	17	4	.81	7	.250	.295	.293
1997 Sarasota	A+ Bos	111	375	98	14	3	5	133	52	39	27	3	65	0	2	3	15	9	.63	9	.261	.309	.355
Trenton	AA Bos	5	16	5	0	0	0	5	2	0	2	0	1	0	0	0	0	1	.00	0	.313	.389	.313
1998 Trenton	AA Bos	104	394	101	21	2	2	132	44	31	36	0	63	3	3	1	14	13	.52	10	.256	.323	.335
Pawtucket	AAA Bos	17	57	16	2	0	0	18	7	4	3	0	13	0	2	0	5	2	.71	0	.281	.317	.316
1999 Pawtucket	AAA Bos	4	5	3	1	0	0	4	1	1	2	0	1	0	0	0	1	0	1.00	0	.600	.750	.800
Trenton	AA Bos	107	365	99	14	1	4	127	49	35	29	1	67	5	11	7	21	10	.68	7	.271	.328	.348
2000 Rochester	AAA Bal	4	9	3	0	0	0	3	1	1	2	0	1	0	0	0	0	0	—	2	.333	.455	.333
Mobile	AA SD	37	136	39	6	2	3	58	16	10	7	1	29	1	2	1	3	3	.50	1	.287	.324	.426
Las Vegas	AAA SD	38	133	34	4	0	2	44	18	21	7	0	24	0	1	4	4	0	1.00	4	.256	.285	.331
Arkansas	AA StL	29	116	29	7	0	0	36	13	14	8	0	20	0	1	0	2	4	.33	2	.250	.298	.310
2001 Pawtucket	AAA Bos	46	136	32	7	0	0	39	15	6	9	0	35	0	3	0	5	2	.71	1	.235	.283	.287
Richmond	AAA Atl	28	83	8	0	0	0	8	2	2	5	0	24	0	1	0	1	0	1.00	1	.096	.148	.096
9 Min. YEARS		877	3050	782	111	15	19	980	361	277	226	7	541	17	51	19	128	69	.65	53	.256	.309	.321

Michael Tejera

Pitches: Left **Bats:** Left **Pos:** SP-25   **Ht:** 5'9" **Wt:** 175 **Born:** 10/18/76 **Age:** 25

		HOW MUCH HE PITCHED						WHAT HE GAVE UP										THE RESULTS					
Year Team	Lg Org	G	GS	CG	GF	IP	BFP	H	R	ER	HR	SH	SF	HB	TBB	IBB	SO	WP	Bk	W	L	Pct.	ShO	Sv	ERA
1995 Marlins	R Fla	11	3	0	4	34	142	28	13	10	2	4	1	2	16	1	28	3	0	3	1	.750	0	2	2.65
1996 Marlins	R Fla	2	0	0	0	5	21	6	2	2	0	0	0	0	0	0	2	0	0	1	0	1.000	0	0	3.60

		HOW MUCH HE PITCHED					WHAT HE GAVE UP									THE RESULTS					
Year Team	Lg Org	G	GS	CG	GF	IP	BFP	H	R	ER	HR	SH	SF	HB	TBB	IBB	SO	WP	Bk	W	L	Pct.	ShO	Sv	ERA
1997 Utica	A- Fla	12	12	0	0	69.1	279	65	36	29	8	3	1	2	11	0	67	6	0	3	3	.500	0	0	3.76
1998 Kane County	A Fla	10	10	0	0	55.1	218	44	20	17	3	3	1	2	13	0	47	2	0	6	1	.857	0	0	2.77
Portland	AA Fla	18	18	2	0	107.1	466	113	55	49	15	3	1	4	36	2	97	4	0	9	5	.643	2	0	4.11
1999 Calgary	AAA Fla	2	2	0	0	9	49	19	14	12	2	1	1	1	4	0	5	1	0	0	2	.000	0	0	12.00
Portland	AA Fla	25	25	0	0	154.2	640	137	55	45	13	9	3	7	45	1	152	6	1	13	4	.765	0	0	2.62
2001 Portland	AA Fla	25	25	0	0	141	595	143	61	56	17	7	1	8	41	0	131	6	0	9	8	.529	0	0	3.57
1999 Florida	NL	3	1	0	1	6.1	31	10	8	8	1	0	0	0	5	0	7	0	0	0	0	—	0	0	11.37
6 Min. YEARS		105	95	2	4	575.2	2410	555	256	220	60	30	9	26	166	4	529	28	1	44	24	.647	2	2	3.44

Nate Tekavec

Pitches: Right **Bats:** Right **Pos:** SP-12; RP-7   **Ht:** 6'5" **Wt:** 200 **Born:** 5/2/79 **Age:** 23

		HOW MUCH HE PITCHED					WHAT HE GAVE UP									THE RESULTS					
Year Team	Lg Org	G	GS	CG	GF	IP	BFP	H	R	ER	HR	SH	SF	HB	TBB	IBB	SO	WP	Bk	W	L	Pct.	ShO	Sv	ERA
2000 Oneonta	A- Det	11	11	0	0	60.2	270	75	38	31	6	1	4	1	9	1	44	4	1	4	4	.500	0	0	4.60
2001 Lakeland	A+ Det	18	11	0	3	79.1	325	77	27	25	5	3	4	3	17	1	56	4	0	8	1	.889	0	0	2.84
Erie	AA Det	1	1	0	0	1.1	7	3	1	1	1	0	0	0	0	0	2	0	0	0	1	.000	0	0	6.75
2 Min. YEARS		30	23	0	3	141.1	602	155	66	57	12	4	8	4	26	2	102	8	1	12	6	.667	0	0	3.63

Mike Terhune

Bats: Both **Throws:** Right **Pos:** 3B-62; 2B-19; DH-3; SS-2; PR-2; 1B-1   **Ht:** 6'1" **Wt:** 185 **Born:** 10/14/75 **Age:** 26

		BATTING														BASERUNNING				PERCENTAGES		
Year Team	Lg Org	G	AB	H	2B	3B	HR	TB	R	RBI	TBB	IBB	SO	HBP	SH	SF	SB	CS	SB%	GDP	Avg	OBP	SLG
1996 Danville	R+ Atl	56	214	60	9	5	2	85	32	27	23	0	26	2	2	7	6	3	.67	6	.280	.346	.397
1997 Eugene	A- Atl	14	61	13	1	0	0	14	4	3	4	1	6	0	2	0	—	—	—	2	.213	.262	.230
Macon	A Atl	92	328	74	11	4	1	96	33	28	25	0	45	5	6	2	8	3	.73	4	.226	.289	.293
1998 Danville	A+ Atl	107	368	81	9	0	3	99	44	26	17	0	67	4	6	2	8	5	.62	13	.220	.261	.269
1999 Myrtle Bch	A+ Atl	92	312	70	10	3	1	89	24	26	27	0	51	0	6	1	3	2	.60	11	.224	.285	.285
2000 Greenville	AA Atl	82	186	42	10	1	1	57	31	15	17	0	32	1	8	5	1	4	.20	5	.226	.287	.306
2001 Binghamton	AA NYM	5	15	2	1	0	0	3	3	3	2	0	4	0	0	0	0	0	—	1	.133	.235	.200
St. Lucie	A+ NYM	80	262	68	15	2	3	96	26	31	28	1	30	2	5	5	6	5	.55	7	.260	.330	.366
6 Min. YEARS		528	1746	410	66	15	11	539	197	159	143	2	261	14	35	22	32	22	.59	49	.235	.295	.309

Luis Terrero

Bats: Right **Throws:** Right **Pos:** OF-87; PH-1   **Ht:** 6'2" **Wt:** 193 **Born:** 5/18/80 **Age:** 22

		BATTING														BASERUNNING				PERCENTAGES		
Year Team	Lg Org	G	AB	H	2B	3B	HR	TB	R	RBI	TBB	IBB	SO	HBP	SH	SF	SB	CS	SB%	GDP	Avg	OBP	SLG
1999 Missoula	R+ Ari	71	272	78	13	7	8	129	74	40	32	1	91	5	3	6	27	10	.73	2	.287	.365	.474
2000 High Desert	A+ Ari	19	79	15	3	1	0	20	10	1	3	0	16	1	0	0	5	5	.50	2	.190	.229	.253
Missoula	R+ Ari	68	276	72	10	4	8	106	48	44	10	0	75	8	1	1	23	11	.68	5	.261	.305	.384
2001 South Bend	A Ari	24	89	14	2	0	1	19	4	8	0	0	29	2	0	0	3	0	1.00	2	.157	.176	.213
Yakima	A- Ari	11	41	13	2	1	0	17	7	0	2	0	8	0	0	0	3	0	.00	0	.317	.349	.415
Lancaster	A+ Ari	19	71	32	9	1	4	55	16	11	1	1	14	1	0	0	5	0	1.00	5	.451	.466	.775
El Paso	AA Ari	34	147	44	13	3	3	72	29	8	4	0	45	3	2	0	9	2	.82	2	.299	.331	.490
3 Min. YEARS		246	975	268	52	13	24	418	188	112	52	2	278	20	6	7	72	31	.70	16	.275	.323	.429

Jay Tessmer

Pitches: Right **Bats:** Right **Pos:** RP-45   **Ht:** 6'3" **Wt:** 188 **Born:** 12/26/71 **Age:** 30

		HOW MUCH HE PITCHED					WHAT HE GAVE UP									THE RESULTS					
Year Team	Lg Org	G	GS	CG	GF	IP	BFP	H	R	ER	HR	SH	SF	HB	TBB	IBB	SO	WP	Bk	W	L	Pct.	ShO	Sv	ERA
1995 Oneonta	A- NYY	34	0	0	33	38	156	27	8	4	0	0	0	3	12	2	52	3	2	2	0	1.000	0	20	0.95
1996 Tampa	A+ NYY	68	0	0	63	68	18	68	18	16	2	6	0	6	19	3	104	1	0	12	4	.750	0	35	1.48
1997 Norwich	AA NYY	55	0	0	49	62.2	289	78	41	37	7	3	2	2	24	2	51	4	0	3	6	.333	0	17	5.31
1998 Norwich	AA NYY	45	0	0	44	49.2	208	50	8	6	0	3	0	0	13	5	57	0	1	3	4	.429	0	29	1.09
Columbus	AAA NYY	12	0	0	11	18.1	74	8	2	1	1	0	1	1	1	0	14	0	0	1	1	.500	0	5	0.49
1999 Columbus	AAA NYY	51	0	0	48	56.2	232	52	22	21	4	5	0	1	12	1	42	3	0	3	3	.500	0	28	3.34
2000 Columbus	AAA NYY	60	0	0	53	66.1	293	73	36	28	5	8	2	1	19	7	40	1	1	4	8	.333	0	34	3.80
2001 Colo Sprngs	AAA Col	10	0	0	8	13.2	71	23	14	10	4	2	1	1	6	2	10	1	0	1	0	1.000	0	0	6.59
Indianapols	AAA Mil	35	0	0	23	58	240	56	23	18	3	4	1	2	9	2	39	1	1	7	5	.583	0	4	2.79
1998 New York	AL	7	0	0	3	8.2	33	4	3	3	1	0	1	0	4	0	6	1	0	1	0	1.000	0	0	3.12
1999 New York	AL	6	0	0	4	6.2	41	16	11	11	1	0	0	1	4	2	3	0	0	0	0	—	0	0	14.85
2000 New York	AL	7	0	0	5	6.2	31	9	6	5	3	0	0	0	1	1	5	0	0	0	0	—	0	0	6.75
7 Min. YEARS		370	0	0	332	460.2	1934	435	172	141	26	31	7	17	115	24	409	14	5	36	31	.537	0	172	2.75
3 Maj. YEARS		20	0	0	12	22	105	29	20	19	5	0	1	1	9	3	14	1	0	1	0	1.000	0	0	7.77

Nate Teut

Pitches: Left **Bats:** Right **Pos:** SP-29   **Ht:** 6'7" **Wt:** 220 **Born:** 3/11/76 **Age:** 26

		HOW MUCH HE PITCHED					WHAT HE GAVE UP									THE RESULTS					
Year Team	Lg Org	G	GS	CG	GF	IP	BFP	H	R	ER	HR	SH	SF	HB	TBB	IBB	SO	WP	Bk	W	L	Pct.	ShO	Sv	ERA
1997 Williamsprt	A- ChC	9	9	0	0	49	203	55	23	14	0	1	2	0	6	1	37	2	1	3	4	.429	0	0	2.57
Rockford	A ChC	2	2	0	0	10.2	52	18	12	12	1	0	0	1	2	0	6	0	0	1	0	1.000	0	0	10.13
1998 Rockford	A ChC	16	16	1	0	103.1	434	99	49	38	9	1	3	6	23	0	67	3	1	8	5	.615	0	0	3.31
Daytona	A+ ChC	11	11	1	0	65.2	302	88	48	40	7	0	0	3	19	0	54	5	1	5	3	.625	0	0	5.48
1999 Daytona	A+ ChC	26	26	1	0	132.2	613	180	113	94	16	3	9	9	41	0	91	13	1	5	12	.294	0	0	6.38
2000 West Tenn	AA ChC	27	21	1	2	138.1	583	133	53	47	13	4	2	10	44	0	106	4	0	11	6	.647	1	0	3.06
2001 Iowa	AAA ChC	29	29	0	0	167	753	184	109	95	28	4	6	5	69	3	125	3	1	13	8	.619	0	0	5.12
5 Min. YEARS		120	114	4	2	666.2	2940	757	407	340	74	13	22	34	204	4	486	30	5	45	39	.536	1	0	4.59

Damon Thames

Bats: Right   Throws: Right   Pos: 2B-41; SS-22; PR-11; PH-7; 3B-3; DH-3   Ht: 6'1"   Wt: 170   Born: 11/15/76   Age: 25

Year Team	Lg Org	G	AB	H	2B	3B	HR	TB	R	RBI	TBB	IBB	SO	HBP	SH	SF	SB	CS	SB%	GDP	Avg	OBP	SLG
1999 New Jersey	A- StL	47	180	41	5	1	0	48	22	16	7	0	42	4	4	1	10	5	.67	1	.228	.271	.267
2000 Peoria	A StL	82	280	65	11	2	3	89	23	29	17	1	59	2	3	4	9	3	.75	4	.232	.277	.318
Potomac	A+ StL	30	104	27	5	0	6	50	12	16	1	0	18	1	2	0	1	0	1.00	3	.260	.274	.481
2001 Potomac	A+ StL	44	116	22	4	0	1	29	16	6	3	0	28	3	2	1	6	1	.86	3	.190	.248	.250
New Haven	AA StL	34	65	13	0	1	2	21	9	6	4	0	21	1	2	0	0	1	.00	2	.200	.257	.323
3 Min. YEARS		237	745	168	25	4	12	237	82	73	32	1	168	11	13	6	26	10	.72	13	.226	.266	.318

Marcus Thames

Bats: Right   Throws: Right   Pos: OF-137; DH-2   Ht: 6'2"   Wt: 205   Born: 3/6/77   Age: 25

Year Team	Lg Org	G	AB	H	2B	3B	HR	TB	R	RBI	TBB	IBB	SO	HBP	SH	SF	SB	CS	SB%	GDP	Avg	OBP	SLG
1997 Yankees	R NYY	57	195	67	17	4	7	113	51	36	16	0	26	3	1	4	6	4	.60	3	.344	.394	.579
Greensboro	A NYY	4	16	5	1	0	0	6	2	2	0	0	3	0	0	0	1	0	1.00	0	.313	.313	.375
1998 Tampa	A+ NYY	122	457	130	18	3	11	187	62	59	24	1	78	8	1	5	13	6	.68	5	.284	.328	.409
1999 Norwich	AA NYY	51	182	41	6	2	4	63	25	26	22	0	40	3	1	2	0	1	.00	2	.225	.316	.346
Tampa	A+ NYY	69	266	65	12	4	11	118	47	38	33	1	58	3	1	2	3	0	1.00	1	.244	.332	.444
2000 Norwich	AA NYY	131	474	114	30	2	15	193	72	79	50	1	89	4	0	8	1	5	.17	13	.241	.313	.407
2001 Norwich	AA NYY	139	520	167	43	4	31	311	114	97	73	8	101	7	0	3	10	4	.71	6	.321	.410	.598
5 Min. YEARS		573	2110	589	127	19	79	991	373	337	218	11	395	28	4	24	34	20	.63	30	.279	.351	.470

Nick Theodorou

Bats: Both   Throws: Right   Pos: OF-28; PH-21; 3B-8; 2B-3; C-2; PR-2; 1B-1; DH-1   Ht: 5'11"   Wt: 182   Born: 6/7/75   Age: 27

Year Team	Lg Org	G	AB	H	2B	3B	HR	TB	R	RBI	TBB	IBB	SO	HBP	SH	SF	SB	CS	SB%	GDP	Avg	OBP	SLG
1998 Yakima	A- LA	46	133	37	12	0	0	49	24	11	26	0	26	0	1	0	7	5	.58	1	.278	.394	.368
1999 San Berndno	A+ LA	104	355	110	11	4	0	129	57	44	72	3	62	7	5	1	14	14	.50	7	.310	.434	.363
2000 San Antonio	AA LA	113	266	64	14	3	1	87	29	25	49	3	39	1	2	3	3	3	.50	9	.241	.357	.327
2001 Vero Beach	A+ LA	8	17	0	0	0	0	0	3	1	8	0	4	0	0	1	0	0	—	0	.000	.308	.000
Las Vegas	AAA LA	1	1	0	0	0	0	0	0	0	0	0	1	0	0	0	0	0	—	0	.000	.000	.000
Jacksnville	AA LA	55	102	30	5	0	0	35	15	11	25	2	15	2	6	1	2	1	.67	2	.294	.438	.343
4 Min. YEARS		327	874	241	42	7	1	300	128	92	180	8	147	10	14	6	26	23	.53	20	.276	.403	.343

E.J. t'Hoen

Bats: Right   Throws: Right   Pos: 2B-18; SS-17; 3B-11; DH-4; PH-1; PR-1   Ht: 6'2"   Wt: 185   Born: 11/8/75   Age: 26

Year Team	Lg Org	G	AB	H	2B	3B	HR	TB	R	RBI	TBB	IBB	SO	HBP	SH	SF	SB	CS	SB%	GDP	Avg	OBP	SLG
1996 Boise	A- Ana	18	60	12	1	0	2	19	6	4	4	0	17	1	1	0	0	0	—	2	.200	.262	.317
1997 Cedar Rapds	A Ana	123	384	78	19	3	3	112	41	46	31	0	114	7	7	3	2	3	.40	7	.203	.273	.292
1998 Cedar Rapds	A Ana	130	441	96	22	1	18	174	57	55	50	2	129	7	3	2	10	5	.67	5	.218	.306	.395
1999 Edmonton	AAA Ana	9	29	4	0	0	0	4	2	0	2	0	7	0	1	0	0	0	—	0	.138	.194	.138
Erie	AA Ana	56	187	38	12	1	2	58	18	21	13	0	52	3	5	1	6	2	.75	4	.203	.265	.310
2000 Erie	AA Ana	62	198	43	13	0	6	74	24	26	24	0	54	3	2	3	6	1	.86	4	.217	.307	.374
Edmonton	AAA Ana	39	120	25	6	0	3	40	13	10	8	0	36	1	1	1	1	1	.50	1	.208	.264	.333
2001 Arkansas	AA Ana	30	93	16	5	1	2	29	11	7	12	1	31	2	1	1	5	3	.63	1	.172	.278	.312
Salt Lake	AAA Ana	18	64	14	5	0	2	25	8	7	1	0	18	2	0	0	0	1	.00	3	.219	.254	.391
6 Min. YEARS		485	1576	326	83	6	38	535	180	176	145	3	458	26	21	10	30	16	.65	27	.207	.283	.339

Evan Thomas

Pitches: Right   Bats: Right   Pos: SP-18; RP-1   Ht: 5'10"   Wt: 171   Born: 6/14/74   Age: 28

Year Team	Lg Org	G	GS	CG	GF	IP	BFP	H	R	ER	HR	SH	SF	HB	TBB	IBB	SO	WP	Bk	W	L	Pct.	ShO	Sv	ERA
1996 Batavia	A- Phi	13	13	0	0	81	321	60	29	25	3	1	3	5	23	0	75	6	0	10	2	.833	0	0	2.78
1997 Clearwater	A+ Phi	13	12	2	0	84.2	340	68	30	23	7	1	1	3	23	0	89	3	2	5	5	.500	0	0	2.44
Reading	AA Phi	15	15	0	0	83	377	98	51	38	10	5	2	7	32	1	83	3	2	5	6	.333	0	0	4.12
1998 Scranton-WB	AAA Phi	2	2	0	0	9	42	9	8	8	1	0	1	0	6	0	5	0	0	0	1	.000	0	0	8.00
Reading	AA Phi	24	24	3	0	158.1	676	180	66	59	12	3	5	4	44	2	134	3	1	8	5	.615	3	0	3.35
1999 Reading	AA Phi	36	15	1	8	127.1	545	123	53	46	7	3	7	5	50	2	127	2	0	9	5	.643	0	3	3.25
2000 Scranton-WB	AAA Phi	29	27	3	1	171	720	163	70	67	17	4	0	6	50	1	127	7	0	13	10	.565	2	0	3.53
2001 Scranton-WB	AAA Phi	19	18	0	0	104	464	123	68	61	14	5	0	2	36	1	74	3	0	3	13	.188	0	0	5.28
6 Min. YEARS		151	126	9	9	818.1	3485	824	375	327	71	22	19	32	264	7	714	27	5	51	47	.520	5	3	3.60

Juan Thomas

Bats: Right   Throws: Right   Pos: DH-101; 1B-27; PH-2; P-2   Ht: 6'4"   Wt: 265   Born: 4/17/72   Age: 30

Year Team	Lg Org	G	AB	H	2B	3B	HR	TB	R	RBI	TBB	IBB	SO	HBP	SH	SF	SB	CS	SB%	GDP	Avg	OBP	SLG
1992 White Sox	R CWS	55	189	42	6	1	6	68	30	29	18	0	76	3	0	2	8	1	.89	4	.222	.297	.360
1993 White Sox	R CWS	20	59	18	3	2	1	28	12	9	12	0	12	1	0	0	5	4	.56	1	.305	.431	.475
Hickory	A CWS	90	328	75	14	6	12	137	51	46	35	1	124	7	1	3	2	4	.33	7	.229	.314	.418
1994 South Bend	A CWS	119	446	112	20	6	18	198	57	79	27	2	143	9	0	5	3	4	.43	13	.251	.304	.444
1995 Pr William	A+ CWS	132	464	109	20	4	26	215	64	69	40	4	156	8	1	2	4	5	.44	16	.235	.305	.463
1996 Pr William	A+ CWS	134	495	148	28	6	20	248	88	71	54	3	129	5	0	3	9	3	.75	15	.299	.372	.501
1997 Winston-Sal	A+ CWS	45	164	43	7	0	13	89	28	28	17	0	61	0	1	0	1	1	.50	5	.262	.335	.543
Birmingham	AA CWS	80	311	94	16	2	10	144	50	55	23	1	92	4	0	4	1	2	.33	4	.302	.354	.463
1998 Atlantic Ct	IND —	99	395	100	18	0	33	217	64	103	35	2	119	1	0	5	6	3	.67	6	.253	.312	.549

BATTING / BASERUNNING / PERCENTAGES

Year Team	Lg Org	G	AB	H	2B	3B	HR	TB	R	RBI	TBB	IBB	SO	HBP	SH	SF	SB	CS	SB%	GDP	Avg	OBP	SLG
1999 Atlantic Ct	IND —	41	154	48	12	0	10	90	30	35	14	1	50	1	0	5	2	1	.67	3	.312	.362	.584
New Haven	AA Sea	71	267	65	13	0	16	126	47	51	14	1	92	6	0	1	0	0	—	6	.243	.295	.472
2000 New Haven	AA Sea	127	495	136	28	3	27	251	66	100	44	2	128	9	0	3	5	0	1.00	16	.275	.343	.507
2001 Tacoma	AAA Sea	129	503	151	39	2	23	263	75	95	40	2	141	2	0	5	2	2	.50	9	.300	.351	.523
10 Min. YEARS		1142	4270	1141	224	32	215	2074	662	770	373	19	1323	57	2	37	48	30	.62	105	.267	.332	.486

Andy Thompson

Bats: Right **Throws:** Right **Pos:** OF-31; DH-26   **Ht:** 6'3" **Wt:** 215 **Born:** 10/8/75 **Age:** 26

BATTING / BASERUNNING / PERCENTAGES

Year Team	Lg Org	G	AB	H	2B	3B	HR	TB	R	RBI	TBB	IBB	SO	HBP	SH	SF	SB	CS	SB%	GDP	Avg	OBP	SLG
1995 Hagerstown	A Tor	124	461	110	19	2	6	151	48	57	29	2	108	8	1	3	2	3	.40	15	.239	.293	.328
1996 Dunedin	A+ Tor	129	425	120	26	5	11	189	64	50	60	1	108	1	1	3	16	4	.80	5	.282	.370	.445
1997 Knoxville	AA Tor	124	448	128	25	3	15	204	75	71	63	3	76	6	1	4	0	5	.00	18	.286	.378	.455
1998 Knoxville	AA Tor	125	481	137	33	2	14	216	74	88	54	2	69	3	0	5	8	3	.73	10	.285	.357	.449
1999 Knoxville	AA Tor	67	254	62	16	3	15	129	56	53	34	2	55	8	0	5	7	3	.70	2	.244	.346	.508
Syracuse	AAA Tor	62	229	67	17	2	16	136	42	42	21	0	45	2	0	0	5	0	1.00	4	.293	.357	.594
2000 Syracuse	AAA Tor	121	426	105	27	2	22	202	59	65	50	1	95	9	0	6	9	2	.82	4	.246	.334	.474
2001 Dunedin	A+ Tor	9	34	18	6	0	1	27	5	6	5	3	7	2	0	0	0	0	—	0	.529	.610	.794
Syracuse	AAA Tor	48	178	41	5	1	7	69	15	28	14	1	42	4	0	5	2	4	.33	3	.230	.294	.388
2000 Toronto	AL	2	6	1	0	0	0	1	2	1	3	0	2	0	0	0	0	0	—	0	.167	.444	.167
7 Min. YEARS		809	2936	788	174	20	107	1323	438	460	330	15	605	43	3	31	49	24	.67	61	.268	.348	.451

Doug Thompson

Pitches: Right **Bats:** Right **Pos:** RP-43   **Ht:** 6'1" **Wt:** 195 **Born:** 7/22/76 **Age:** 25

HOW MUCH HE PITCHED / WHAT HE GAVE UP / THE RESULTS

Year Team	Lg Org	G	GS	CG	GF	IP	BFP	H	R	ER	HR	SH	SF	HB	TBB	IBB	SO	WP	Bk	W	L	Pct.	ShO	Sv	ERA
1998 Asheville	A Col	9	1	0	0	15.1	74	17	9	8	4	1	0	1	7	0	17	0	2	0	0	—	0	0	4.70
1999 Asheville	A Col	25	0	0	12	56	250	56	29	27	9	1	2	6	18	0	72	5	3	0	0	—	0	3	4.34
2000 Salem	A+ Col	46	0	0	13	62	267	43	29	21	2	3	1	5	35	1	80	3	2	5	3	.625	0	1	3.05
2001 Salem	A+ Col	17	0	0	5	31.1	135	30	15	14	1	2	0	0	16	1	35	4	0	2	2	.500	0	1	4.02
Carolina	AA Col	26	0	0	8	38.1	167	33	16	16	2	4	3	5	19	1	33	2	1	2	5	.286	0	1	3.76
4 Min. YEARS		123	1	0	38	203	893	179	98	86	18	11	6	17	95	3	237	14	8	12	13	.480	0	6	3.81

Eric Thompson

Pitches: Right **Bats:** Right **Pos:** RP-30; SP-5   **Ht:** 6'2" **Wt:** 195 **Born:** 9/7/77 **Age:** 24

HOW MUCH HE PITCHED / WHAT HE GAVE UP / THE RESULTS

Year Team	Lg Org	G	GS	CG	GF	IP	BFP	H	R	ER	HR	SH	SF	HB	TBB	IBB	SO	WP	Bk	W	L	Pct.	ShO	Sv	ERA
1998 Sou Oregon	A- Oak	13	6	0	0	56.2	252	60	34	28	7	2	1	2	25	0	51	2	5	5	2	.714	0	0	4.45
1999 Visalia	A+ Oak	31	20	0	5	126.2	595	150	91	79	9	2	6	11	56	2	110	10	1	9	6	.600	0	1	5.61
2000 Visalia	A+ Oak	13	7	0	4	56	228	49	31	31	5	0	0	2	18	0	61	0	0	4	3	.571	0	1	4.98
Midland	AA Oak	18	15	0	1	101.1	425	107	52	44	5	2	1	0	23	0	79	0	1	6	6	.500	0	1	3.91
2001 Midland	AA Oak	35	5	0	8	64.2	292	74	32	31	9	3	4	5	21	3	69	3	0	1	4	.200	0	2	4.31
4 Min. YEARS		110	59	0	18	405.1	1792	440	240	213	35	9	11	21	143	5	370	15	7	25	21	.543	0	5	4.73

Mark Thompson

Pitches: Right **Bats:** Right **Pos:** SP-10; RP-2   **Ht:** 6'2" **Wt:** 212 **Born:** 4/7/71 **Age:** 31

HOW MUCH HE PITCHED / WHAT HE GAVE UP / THE RESULTS

Year Team	Lg Org	G	GS	CG	GF	IP	BFP	H	R	ER	HR	SH	SF	HB	TBB	IBB	SO	WP	Bk	W	L	Pct.	ShO	Sv	ERA
1992 Bend	A- Col	16	16	4	0	106.1	421	81	32	23	2	1	2	4	31	1	102	8	4	6	4	.667	0	0	1.95
1993 Central Val	A+ Col	11	11	0	0	69.2	279	46	19	17	3	1	4	5	18	0	72	3	2	3	2	.600	0	0	2.20
Colo Sprngs	AAA Col	4	4	2	0	33.1	137	31	13	10	1	1	0	1	11	0	22	3	0	3	0	1.000	0	0	2.70
1994 Colo Sprngs	AAA Col	23	23	4	0	140.1	629	169	83	70	11	2	5	8	57	2	82	6	2	8	9	.471	1	0	4.49
1995 Colo Sprngs	AAA Col	11	10	0	0	62	276	73	43	42	2	2	2	6	25	0	38	0	0	5	3	.625	0	0	6.10
1997 Asheville	A Col	4	4	0	0	13.1	58	11	5	4	0	0	0	2	5	0	9	0	0	0	2	.000	0	0	2.70
1998 Rockies	R Col	1	1	0	0	3	9	1	0	0	0	0	0	0	0	0	2	0	0	0	0	—	0	0	0.00
Salem	A+ Col	3	3	0	0	13.2	61	17	7	6	2	0	0	1	3	0	10	0	0	0	0	—	0	0	3.95
Colo Sprngs	AAA Col	1	1	0	0	3.1	19	10	7	7	3	0	0	0	1	0	1	0	0	0	1	.000	0	0	18.90
1999 Indianapols	AAA Col	11	10	0	0	54.1	237	50	31	31	5	1	4	6	29	1	28	0	0	2	6	.250	0	0	5.13
Memphis	AAA StL	9	8	0	0	52	225	50	22	17	3	4	3	0	20	0	27	1	0	4	2	.667	0	0	2.94
2000 Arkansas	AA StL	1	1	0	0	3.2	16	6	2	2	0	0	0	0	0	0	3	0	0	0	0	—	0	0	4.91
Memphis	AAA StL	6	5	0	0	31	126	31	9	7	1	2	0	2	5	0	15	0	0	2	0	1.000	0	0	2.03
2001 Tri-City	A- Col	4	2	0	2	14	55	9	3	2	0	0	0	0	5	0	7	0	0	1	1	.500	0	0	1.29
Carolina	AA Col	8	8	1	0	48	206	43	29	27	4	0	1	8	15	1	38	0	0	3	2	.600	1	0	5.06
1994 Colorado	NL	2	2	0	0	9	49	16	9	9	2	0	0	1	8	0	5	0	0	1	1	.500	0	0	9.00
1995 Colorado	NL	21	5	0	3	51	240	73	42	37	7	4	4	1	22	2	30	2	0	2	3	.400	0	0	6.53
1996 Colorado	NL	34	28	3	2	169.2	763	189	109	100	25	10	3	13	74	1	99	1	1	9	11	.450	1	0	5.30
1997 Colorado	NL	6	6	0	0	29.2	146	40	27	26	8	3	2	4	13	0	9	0	1	3	3	.500	0	0	7.89
1998 Colorado	NL	6	6	0	0	23.1	116	36	22	20	8	2	2	5	12	0	14	1	0	1	2	.333	0	0	7.71
1999 St. Louis	NL	5	5	0	0	29.1	130	26	12	9	1	3	0	2	17	1	22	1	0	1	3	.250	0	0	2.76
2000 St. Louis	NL	20	0	0	9	25	116	24	21	14	4	1	1	3	15	0	19	3	0	1	1	.500	0	0	5.04
9 Min. YEARS		114	108	11	2	651	2768	634	309	269	38	14	21	43	226	5	457	21	8	39	32	.549	2	0	3.72
7 Maj. YEARS		94	52	3	9	337	1560	404	242	215	55	23	12	29	161	4	198	8	2	18	24	.429	1	0	5.74

Rich Thompson

Bats: Left **Throws:** Right **Pos:** OF-125; DH-2; PH-2; PR-1 **Ht:** 6'3" **Wt:** 180 **Born:** 4/23/79 **Age:** 23

Year Team	Lg Org	G	AB	H	2B	3B	HR	TB	R	RBI	TBB	IBB	SO	HBP	SH	SF	SB	CS	SB%	GDP	Avg	OBP	SLG
2000 Queens	A- Tor	68	252	66	9	5	1	88	42	27	45	1	57	6	5	0	28	8	.78	6	.262	.386	.349
2001 Dunedin	A+ Tor	112	454	141	14	6	1	170	90	60	44	1	72	9	3	4	39	11	.78	3	.311	.380	.374
Syracuse	AAA Tor	17	53	13	0	1	0	15	5	3	4	0	12	0	3	1	5	1	.83	1	.245	.293	.283
2 Min. YEARS		197	759	220	23	12	2	273	137	90	93	2	141	15	11	5	72	20	.78	4	.290	.376	.360

Travis Thompson

Pitches: Right **Bats:** Right **Pos:** RP-37 **Ht:** 6'3" **Wt:** 189 **Born:** 1/10/75 **Age:** 27

Year Team	Lg Org	G	GS	CG	GF	IP	BFP	H	R	ER	HR	SH	SF	HB	TBB	IBB	SO	WP	Bk	W	L	Pct.	ShO	Sv	ERA
1996 Portland	A- Col	9	0	0	2	16.2	73	21	11	11	0	2	0	0	6	0	8	1	1	0	2	.000	0	0	5.94
Rockies	R Col	9	3	0	3	30	128	34	12	11	1	1	0	0	5	0	25	0	1	4	1	.800	0	0	3.30
1997 Portland	A- Col	18	11	0	2	74	328	88	51	37	6	2	2	6	16	0	51	2	0	5	5	.500	0	0	4.50
1998 Asheville	A Col	26	24	0	0	147.1	619	155	71	53	11	1	4	6	36	0	113	6	1	6	7	.462	0	0	3.24
1999 Salem	A+ Col	56	0	0	52	62	267	54	19	12	1	7	1	2	24	4	53	5	0	3	3	.500	0	27	1.74
2000 Carolina	AA Col	50	0	0	41	58.1	278	70	44	41	8	3	2	7	30	0	43	4	0	3	7	.300	0	17	6.33
2001 Colo Spmgs	AAA Col	9	0	0	3	8.2	53	20	19	17	2	2	1	2	6	0	9	0	0	0	2	.000	0	0	17.65
Carolina	AA Col	28	0	0	13	37.1	165	39	20	19	6	3	1	4	13	1	28	5	1	1	1	.500	0	5	4.58
6 Min. YEARS		205	38	0	116	434.1	1911	481	247	201	35	21	11	27	136	5	330	23	4	22	28	.440	0	49	4.17

Travis Thompson

Pitches: Right **Bats:** Right **Pos:** SP-28 **Ht:** 6'5" **Wt:** 215 **Born:** 7/3/77 **Age:** 24

Year Team	Lg Org	G	GS	CG	GF	IP	BFP	H	R	ER	HR	SH	SF	HB	TBB	IBB	SO	WP	Bk	W	L	Pct.	ShO	Sv	ERA
1999 Billings	R+ Cin	8	0	0	3	20.2	72	14	1	0	0	1	0	0	3	0	27	4	0	1	0	1.000	0	0	0.00
2000 Clinton	A Cin	6	6	1	0	40.2	153	21	8	8	3	1	0	0	13	0	42	2	0	5	1	.833	1	0	1.77
Chattanooga	AA Cin	2	2	0	0	11.2	51	12	6	6	0	0	0	1	8	0	6	0	0	1	1	.500	0	0	4.63
Dayton	A Cin	19	17	4	0	136.1	574	133	52	42	6	4	1	5	39	0	115	4	1	11	4	.733	1	0	2.77
2001 Chattanooga	AA Cin	28	28	3	0	167	708	170	82	72	10	10	2	6	46	3	118	3	0	12	10	.545	1	0	3.88
3 Min. YEARS		63	53	8	3	376.1	1558	350	149	128	19	16	3	12	109	3	308	13	1	30	16	.652	3	0	3.06

Jake Thrower

Bats: Both **Throws:** Right **Pos:** 2B-91; SS-18; 3B-10; PH-4; PR-1 **Ht:** 5'11" **Wt:** 180 **Born:** 11/19/75 **Age:** 26

Year Team	Lg Org	G	AB	H	2B	3B	HR	TB	R	RBI	TBB	IBB	SO	HBP	SH	SF	SB	CS	SB%	GDP	Avg	OBP	SLG
1997 Idaho Falls	R+ SD	35	141	48	10	4	3	75	37	28	31	2	16	4	0	1	10	1	.91	2	.340	.469	.532
Clinton	A SD	19	63	16	3	0	0	19	8	12	13	0	15	2	1	0	1	3	.25	0	.254	.397	.302
1998 Clinton	A SD	43	145	42	11	1	5	70	25	27	22	0	22	4	0	0	11	3	.79	5	.290	.398	.483
Rancho Cuca	A+ SD	37	127	34	7	0	1	44	24	10	19	0	19	1	0	2	4	1	.80	2	.268	.362	.346
1999 Mobile	AA SD	40	149	36	9	2	3	58	15	26	21	1	26	1	0	1	3	3	.50	2	.242	.337	.389
Las Vegas	AAA SD	72	267	77	17	4	4	114	40	30	27	2	56	2	3	2	4	4	.50	6	.288	.356	.427
2000 Las Vegas	AAA SD	4	16	5	0	0	0	5	4	2	2	0	2	0	0	0	0	0	—	0	.313	.389	.313
Mobile	AA SD	31	115	32	6	0	1	41	16	11	14	1	22	1	2	2	3	0	1.00	1	.278	.356	.357
2001 Portland	AAA SD	15	54	11	1	0	0	12	3	1	2	1	8	0	1	0	1	0	1.00	0	.204	.232	.222
Mobile	AA SD	103	386	105	25	1	4	144	46	31	45	1	66	5	4	1	3	3	.50	8	.272	.355	.373
5 Min. YEARS		399	1463	406	89	12	21	582	218	178	196	8	252	20	11	9	40	18	.69	26	.278	.368	.398

Corey Thurman

Pitches: Right **Bats:** Right **Pos:** SP-26 **Ht:** 6'1" **Wt:** 215 **Born:** 11/5/78 **Age:** 23

Year Team	Lg Org	G	GS	CG	GF	IP	BFP	H	R	ER	HR	SH	SF	HB	TBB	IBB	SO	WP	Bk	W	L	Pct.	ShO	Sv	ERA
1996 Royals	R KC	11	11	0	0	47.1	221	53	32	32	2	0	2	3	28	0	52	8	1	1	6	.143	0	0	6.08
1997 Royals	R KC	8	8	1	0	34	149	28	12	9	1	1	0	2	22	0	42	1	0	2	1	.667	0	0	2.38
Spokane	A- KC	5	5	0	0	22.2	106	23	19	13	2	0	2	2	13	0	24	2	1	1	2	.333	0	0	5.16
1998 Spokane	A- KC	12	11	0	0	60	278	72	35	27	3	1	3	5	31	0	49	6	0	3	3	.500	0	0	4.05
Lansing	A KC	14	11	0	2	62.1	261	47	31	25	6	0	1	4	30	0	61	10	0	5	6	.455	0	0	3.61
1999 Wilmington	A+ KC	27	27	0	0	149.1	667	160	89	81	11	4	5	9	64	0	131	11	1	8	11	.421	0	0	4.88
2000 Wilmington	A+ KC	19	19	1	0	115.2	468	97	33	29	6	1	5	4	46	0	96	7	0	10	5	.667	0	0	2.26
Wichita	AA KC	9	9	0	0	50.1	222	46	34	27	10	2	1	3	24	0	47	4	1	4	5	.444	0	0	4.83
2001 Omaha	AAA KC	1	1	0	0	5	24	6	4	3	0	0	0	0	2	0	4	1	0	0	0	—	0	0	5.40
Wichita	AA KC	25	25	0	0	155	636	117	66	58	16	2	2	1	65	1	148	8	0	13	5	.722	0	0	3.37
6 Min. YEARS		131	127	2	2	701.2	3032	649	355	304	57	11	21	33	325	1	654	58	4	47	44	.516	0	0	3.90

Jerrey Thurston

Bats: Right **Throws:** Right **Pos:** C-42; PH-6; 1B-1 **Ht:** 6'4" **Wt:** 200 **Born:** 4/17/72 **Age:** 30

Year Team	Lg Org	G	AB	H	2B	3B	HR	TB	R	RBI	TBB	IBB	SO	HBP	SH	SF	SB	CS	SB%	GDP	Avg	OBP	SLG
1990 Padres	R SD	42	144	33	6	1	0	41	22	16	14	0	37	0	2	0	4	1	.80	1	.229	.297	.285
1991 Chston-SC	A SD	42	137	14	2	0	0	16	5	4	9	0	50	0	1	1	1	1	.50	3	.102	.156	.117
Spokane	A- SD	60	201	43	9	0	1	55	26	20	20	1	61	2	2	2	2	2	.50	2	.214	.289	.274
1992 Waterloo	A SD	96	263	37	7	0	0	44	20	14	12	0	73	2	.6	2	1	0	1.00	4	.141	.183	.167
1993 Wichita	AA SD	78	197	48	10	0	2	64	22	22	14	0	62	6	3	0	2	0	1.00	3	.244	.313	.325
1994 Wichita	AA SD	77	238	51	10	4	2	77	30	28	19	1	73	8	2	1	1	4	.20	8	.214	.293	.324
1995 Las Vegas	AAA SD	5	20	4	1	0	0	5	2	0	0	0	5	1	0	0	0	0	—	0	.200	.238	.250
Rancho Cuca	A+ SD	76	200	44	9	0	1	56	24	13	21	0	64	7	4	3	1	0	1.00	5	.220	.312	.280
1996 Orlando	AA ChC	67	177	37	6	1	3	54	16	23	14	0	57	0	3	0	0	0	—	5	.209	.267	.305

Year Team	Lg Org	G	AB	H	2B	3B	HR	TB	R	RBI	TBB	IBB	SO	HBP	SH	SF	SB	CS	SB%	GDP	Avg	OBP	SLG
						BATTING												BASERUNNING				PERCENTAGES	
1997 Lk Elsinore	A+ Ana	2	6	3	1	0	0	4	1	1	0	0	2	0	0	0	0	0	—	0	.500	.500	.667
Vancouver	AAA Ana	65	195	46	3	1	4	63	17	19	8	0	59	4	8	2	3	2	.60	2	.236	.278	.323
1998 Midland	AA Ana	29	95	30	4	0	2	40	20	22	8	0	24	2	0	1	0	0	—	2	.316	.377	.421
Vancouver	AAA Ana	9	25	4	1	0	0	5	0	1	3	0	8	0	0	0	0	0	—	0	.160	.250	.200
Ottawa	AAA Mon	13	30	1	0	0	0	1	2	0	4	0	15	0	0	0	0	0	—	0	.033	.147	.033
1999 New Orleans	AAA Hou	21	59	13	0	0	0	13	7	4	4	0	15	2	1	0	0	1	.00	3	.220	.292	.220
2000 Round Rock	AA Hou	24	77	19	2	1	1	26	4	7	1	0	19	1	1	0	0	1	.00	2	.247	.266	.338
New Orleans	AAA Hou	13	30	5	2	0	0	7	3	0	0	0	10	0	0	0	0	0	—	1	.167	.167	.233
2001 Lk Elsinore	A+ SD	14	45	7	0	0	0	7	3	2	2	0	20	1	0	0	0	0	—	1	.156	.208	.156
Mudville	A+ Cin	7	21	4	0	0	0	4	2	0	3	0	7	0	0	0	0	0	—	1	.190	.292	.190
Chattanooga	AA Cin	28	81	13	2	0	2	21	11	3	4	0	29	1	2	0	0	0	—	1	.160	.209	.259
12 Min. YEARS		768	2241	456	75	6	20	603	237	199	160	2	690	37	35	12	15	12	.56	42	.203	.267	.269

Joe Thurston

Bats: Left **Throws:** Right **Pos:** 2B-121; SS-12; PR-2 | **Ht:** 5'11" **Wt:** 175 **Born:** 9/29/79 **Age:** 22

Year Team	Lg Org	G	AB	H	2B	3B	HR	TB	R	RBI	TBB	IBB	SO	HBP	SH	SF	SB	CS	SB%	GDP	Avg	OBP	SLG
						BATTING												BASERUNNING				PERCENTAGES	
1999 Yakima	A- LA	71	277	79	10	3	0	95	48	32	27	1	34	21	6	3	27	17	.61	3	.285	.387	.343
San Berndno	A+ LA	2	3	0	0	0	0	0	0	0	0	0	1	1	0	0	0	0	—	0	.000	.250	.000
2000 San Berndno	A+ LA	138	551	167	31	8	4	226	97	70	56	1	61	17	9	8	43	25	.63	8	.303	.380	.410
2001 Jacksnville	AA LA	134	544	145	25	7	7	205	80	46	48	0	65	12	9	3	20	18	.53	5	.267	.338	.377
3 Min. YEARS		345	1375	391	66	18	11	526	225	148	131	2	161	51	24	14	90	60	.60	16	.284	.365	.383

Kevin Tillman

Bats: Left **Throws:** Right **Pos:** 2B-32; DH-9; PH-2; P-1 | **Ht:** 5'10" **Wt:** 190 **Born:** 1/24/78 **Age:** 24

Year Team	Lg Org	G	AB	H	2B	3B	HR	TB	R	RBI	TBB	IBB	SO	HBP	SH	SF	SB	CS	SB%	GDP	Avg	OBP	SLG
						BATTING												BASERUNNING				PERCENTAGES	
2001 Burlington	R+ Cle	40	126	30	6	0	6	54	22	23	17	0	39	2	0	2	3	0	1.00	5	.238	.333	.429
Akron	AA Cle	2	7	2	0	0	0	2	1	1	0	0	2	0	0	0	1	0	1.00	0	.286	.286	.286
1 Min. YEAR		42	133	32	6	0	6	56	23	24	17	0	41	2	0	2	4	0	1.00	5	.241	.331	.421

Brian Tokarse

Pitches: Right **Bats:** Right **Pos:** RP-39 | **Ht:** 6'3" **Wt:** 200 **Born:** 2/28/75 **Age:** 27

Year Team	Lg Org	G	GS	CG	GF	IP	BFP	H	R	ER	HR	SH	SF	HB	TBB	IBB	SO	WP	Bk	W	L	Pct.	ShO	Sv	ERA
				HOW MUCH HE PITCHED							WHAT HE GAVE UP											THE RESULTS			
1997 Butte	R+ Ana	8	7	0	0	36.2	162	44	33	28	3	1	4	2	8	0	34	2	0	2	4	.333	0	0	6.87
1998 Lk Elsinore	A+ Ana	22	22	2	0	125.1	553	150	93	80	7	1	2	9	42	0	97	6	4	9	9	.500	0	0	5.74
Hickory	A CWS	2	2	0	0	3.2	17	3	3	3	1	0	0	2	3	0	3	1	0	1	0	1.000	0	0	7.36
1999 Winston-Sal	A+ CWS	40	0	0	37	46.2	201	37	15	12	2	4	1	3	22	3	55	2	0	5	4	.556	0	14	2.31
Birmingham	AA CWS	6	0	0	0	10.2	46	12	7	6	1	1	0	0	3	0	11	1	0	1	0	1.000	0	0	5.06
2000 Birmingham	AA CWS	34	0	0	15	41.2	188	40	26	26	5	5	1	3	28	3	52	7	1	6	3	.667	0	1	5.62
2001 Birmingham	AA CWS	39	0	0	14	65.2	293	56	33	29	4	4	2	4	39	1	81	7	0	2	6	.250	0	0	3.97
5 Min. YEARS		151	31	2	66	330.1	1460	342	210	184	23	16	10	23	145	7	333	26	5	24	28	.462	0	15	5.01

Juan Tolentino

Bats: Right **Throws:** Right **Pos:** OF-109; DH-4; PH-3; PR-1 | **Ht:** 6'0" **Wt:** 165 **Born:** 3/12/76 **Age:** 26

Year Team	Lg Org	G	AB	H	2B	3B	HR	TB	R	RBI	TBB	IBB	SO	HBP	SH	SF	SB	CS	SB%	GDP	Avg	OBP	SLG
						BATTING												BASERUNNING				PERCENTAGES	
1996 Angels	R Ana	49	170	48	9	6	2	75	30	14	11	0	33	1	0	0	21	2	.91	4	.282	.330	.441
1997 Butte	R+ Ana	61	213	64	16	4	10	118	44	53	24	0	53	2	0	4	21	2	.91	2	.300	.370	.554
1998 Cedar Rapds	A Ana	133	495	129	27	6	11	201	82	57	51	1	135	6	3	2	49	25	.66	6	.261	.336	.406
1999 Erie	AA Ana	136	489	123	19	5	9	179	61	61	47	0	116	2	8	2	47	14	.77	7	.252	.319	.366
2000 Edmonton	AAA Ana	122	432	106	30	3	11	175	58	58	37	0	106	3	3	4	16	14	.53	6	.245	.307	.405
2001 Salt Lake	AAA Ana	114	452	125	35	3	11	199	70	66	25	0	87	5	4	3	17	4	.81	7	.277	.320	.440
6 Min. YEARS		615	2251	595	136	27	54	947	345	309	195	1	530	19	18	15	171	61	.74	32	.264	.326	.421

Mike Tonis

Bats: Right **Throws:** Right **Pos:** C-92; DH-3; PH-1 | **Ht:** 6'3" **Wt:** 215 **Born:** 2/9/79 **Age:** 23

Year Team	Lg Org	G	AB	H	2B	3B	HR	TB	R	RBI	TBB	IBB	SO	HBP	SH	SF	SB	CS	SB%	GDP	Avg	OBP	SLG
						BATTING												BASERUNNING				PERCENTAGES	
2000 Chston-WV	A KC	28	100	20	8	0	0	28	10	17	9	1	22	1	1	2	1	0	1.00	1	.200	.268	.280
Omaha	AAA KC	2	8	4	0	0	0	4	1	3	0	0	3	0	0	0	0	0	—	0	.500	.500	.500
2001 Wilmington	A+ KC	33	123	31	8	0	3	48	15	18	15	0	34	2	2	0	0	0	—	6	.252	.343	.390
Wichita	AA KC	63	226	61	11	1	9	101	36	43	22	2	41	4	0	1	1	1	.50	7	.270	.344	.447
2 Min. YEARS		126	457	116	27	1	12	181	62	81	46	3	100	7	3	3	2	1	.67	14	.254	.329	.396

Tony Torcato

Bats: Left **Throws:** Right **Pos:** OF-85; DH-52; PH-1 | **Ht:** 6'1" **Wt:** 195 **Born:** 10/25/79 **Age:** 22

Year Team	Lg Org	G	AB	H	2B	3B	HR	TB	R	RBI	TBB	IBB	SO	HBP	SH	SF	SB	CS	SB%	GDP	Avg	OBP	SLG
						BATTING												BASERUNNING				PERCENTAGES	
1998 Salem-Keizr	A- SF	59	220	64	15	2	3	92	31	43	14	0	38	3	0	6	4	2	.67	0	.291	.333	.418
1999 Bakersfield	A+ SF	110	422	123	25	0	4	160	50	58	30	3	67	3	1	7	2	1	.67	6	.291	.338	.379
2000 San Jose	A+ SF	119	490	159	37	2	7	221	77	88	41	8	62	6	0	7	19	4	.83	2	.324	.379	.451
Shreveport	AA SF	2	8	4	0	0	0	4	1	2	0	0	1	0	0	0	0	0	—	0	.500	.500	.500
2001 San Jose	A+ SF	67	258	88	21	2	2	119	38	47	17	3	40	4	0	7	9	3	.75	5	.341	.381	.461
Shreveport	AA SF	36	147	43	9	1	1	57	13	23	9	3	15	4	0	3	0	1	.00	6	.293	.344	.388
Fresno	AAA SF	35	150	48	8	1	2	64	20	8	2	0	20	0	0	0	0	0	—	1	.320	.329	.427
4 Min. YEARS		428	1695	529	115	8	19	717	230	269	113	17	243	20	1	30	34	12	.74	24	.312	.356	.423

Andres Torres

Bats: Both **Throws:** Right **Pos:** OF-55; DH-8; PR-1   **Ht:** 5'10" **Wt:** 175 **Born:** 1/26/78 **Age:** 24

					BATTING												BASERUNNING				PERCENTAGES		
Year Team	Lg Org	G	AB	H	2B	3B	HR	TB	R	RBI	TBB	IBB	SO	HBP	SH	SF	SB	CS	SB%	GDP	Avg	OBP	SLG
1998 Jamestown	A- Det	48	192	45	2	6	1	62	28	21	25	0	50	1	1	2	13	2	.87	1	.234	.323	.323
1999 W Michigan	A Det	117	407	96	20	5	2	132	72	34	92	1	116	10	9	5	39	18	.68	2	.236	.385	.324
2000 Lakeland	A+ Det	108	398	118	11	11	3	160	82	33	63	2	82	5	10	0	65	16	.80	10	.296	.399	.402
Jacksnville	AA Det	14	54	8	0	0	0	8	3	0	5	0	14	0	0	0	2	0	1.00	1	.148	.220	.148
2001 Erie	AA Det	64	252	74	16	3	1	99	54	23	36	1	50	5	0	1	19	11	.63	1	.294	.391	.393
4 Min. YEARS		351	1303	341	49	25	7	461	239	111	221	4	312	21	20	8	138	47	.75	15	.262	.375	.354

Gabby Torres

Bats: Right **Throws:** Right **Pos:** DH-49; C-35; PH-8   **Ht:** 5'10" **Wt:** 200 **Born:** 3/22/78 **Age:** 24

					BATTING												BASERUNNING				PERCENTAGES		
Year Team	Lg Org	G	AB	H	2B	3B	HR	TB	R	RBI	TBB	IBB	SO	HBP	SH	SF	SB	CS	SB%	GDP	Avg	OBP	SLG
1996 Twins	R Min	22	66	23	4	1	1	32	9	5	7	0	10	1	0	0	1	3	.25	3	.348	.419	.485
1997 Twins	R Min	45	152	39	5	1	0	46	17	16	19	0	21	6	3	2	18	3	.86	7	.257	.358	.303
1998 Elizabethtn	R+ Min	46	161	40	7	0	4	59	19	25	19	0	23	4	1	1	1	2	.33	10	.248	.341	.366
1999 Elizabethtn	R+ Min	7	24	6	1	0	1	10	5	3	4	0	1	1	1	0	1	1	.50	3	.250	.379	.417
Fort Myers	A+ Min	22	68	15	3	0	1	21	7	6	3	0	8	2	1	1	0	0	—	5	.221	.270	.309
2000 Salt Lake	AAA Min	1	1	0	0	0	0	0	0	0	0	0	0	0	0	0	0	0	—	0	.000	.000	.000
Quad City	A Min	71	268	73	14	0	6	105	36	33	19	0	39	7	3	1	1	1	.50	8	.272	.336	.392
Fort Myers	A+ Min	20	46	9	3	0	0	12	5	3	6	0	5	1	0	1	0	0	—	3	.196	.296	.261
2001 Fort Myers	A+ Min	49	157	41	8	0	1	52	17	18	7	0	28	5	1	3	2	0	1.00	3	.261	.308	.331
New Britain	AA Min	41	133	41	12	1	2	61	24	13	10	0	11	5	0	0	0	2	.00	7	.308	.378	.459
6 Min. YEARS		324	1076	287	57	3	16	398	139	122	94	0	146	32	10	9	24	12	.67	49	.267	.341	.370

Billy Traber

Pitches: Left **Bats:** Left **Pos:** SP-27   **Ht:** 6'5" **Wt:** 205 **Born:** 9/18/79 **Age:** 22

		HOW MUCH HE PITCHED						WHAT HE GAVE UP									THE RESULTS					
Year Team	Lg Org	G	GS	CG	GF	IP	BFP	H	R	ER	HR	SH	SF	HB	TBB	IBB	SO	WP	Bk	W	L	Pct.	ShO	Sv	ERA
2001 St. Lucie	A+ NYM	18	18	0	0	101.2	415	85	36	30	2	3	2	5	23	0	79	4	1	6	5	.545	0	0	2.66
Binghamton	AA NYM	8	8	0	0	42.2	188	50	25	21	4	1	3	2	13	1	45	4	1	4	3	.571	0	0	4.43
Norfolk	AAA NYM	1	1	0	0	7	26	5	3	1	0	0	0	0	0	0	0	1	1	0	1	.000	0	0	1.29
1 Min. YEAR		27	27	0	0	151.1	629	140	64	52	6	4	5	7	36	1	124	9	3	10	9	.526	0	0	3.09

Matt Treanor

Bats: Right **Throws:** Right **Pos:** C-39; DH-6; 1B-1; PH-1   **Ht:** 6'2" **Wt:** 225 **Born:** 3/3/76 **Age:** 26

					BATTING												BASERUNNING				PERCENTAGES		
Year Team	Lg Org	G	AB	H	2B	3B	HR	TB	R	RBI	TBB	IBB	SO	HBP	SH	SF	SB	CS	SB%	GDP	Avg	OBP	SLG
1994 Royals	R KC	46	99	18	5	0	1	26	17	12	14	1	23	3	1	1	1	1	.50	2	.182	.299	.263
1995 Springfield	A KC	75	211	39	6	2	3	58	17	19	21	0	59	4	2	2	1	1	.50	1	.185	.269	.275
1996 Lansing	A KC	119	384	100	18	2	6	140	56	33	35	1	63	13	6	1	5	3	.63	9	.260	.342	.365
1997 Wilmington	A+ KC	80	257	51	6	1	5	74	22	25	25	0	59	2	6	0	1	6	.14	4	.198	.275	.288
Brevard Cty	A+ Fla	23	70	15	4	1	0	21	11	3	12	0	14	2	1	0	0	0	—	1	.214	.345	.300
1998 Brevard Cty	A+ Fla	80	243	57	8	0	3	74	24	28	38	0	45	5	1	3	3	2	.60	4	.235	.346	.305
1999 Kane County	A Fla	86	308	88	21	1	10	141	56	53	36	0	65	15	2	2	4	1	.80	9	.286	.385	.458
2000 Brevard Cty	A+ Fla	109	350	86	17	0	3	112	51	37	48	0	65	14	4	3	3	3	.50	6	.246	.357	.320
2001 Marlins	R Fla	11	34	14	4	0	1	21	10	4	7	0	7	0	0	0	3	0	1.00	1	.412	.512	.618
Kane County	A Fla	1	1	1	0	0	0	1	2	0	3	0	0	0	0	0	0	0	—	0	1.000	1.000	1.000
Portland	AA Fla	35	89	14	2	0	2	22	7	8	13	0	18	9	2	0	1	1	.50	2	.157	.324	.247
8 Min. YEARS		665	2046	483	91	7	34	690	273	222	252	2	418	67	25	12	22	18	.55	39	.236	.337	.337

Chris Tremie

Bats: Right **Throws:** Right **Pos:** C-68; 1B-4; PH-3; PR-1   **Ht:** 6'0" **Wt:** 215 **Born:** 10/17/69 **Age:** 32

					BATTING												BASERUNNING				PERCENTAGES		
Year Team	Lg Org	G	AB	H	2B	3B	HR	TB	R	RBI	TBB	IBB	SO	HBP	SH	SF	SB	CS	SB%	GDP	Avg	OBP	SLG
1992 Utica	A- CWS	6	16	1	0	0	0	1	1	0	0	0	5	0	0	0	0	0	—	0	.063	.063	.063
1993 White Sox	R CWS	2	4	0	0	0	0	0	0	0	0	0	0	0	0	0	0	0	—	0	.000	.000	.000
Sarasota	A+ CWS	14	37	6	1	0	0	7	2	5	2	0	4	3	0	0	0	0	—	1	.162	.262	.189
Hickory	A CWS	49	155	29	6	1	1	40	7	17	9	0	26	4	1	0	0	0	—	5	.187	.250	.258
1994 Birmingham	AA CWS	92	302	68	13	0	2	87	32	29	17	0	44	6	3	2	4	1	.80	3	.225	.278	.288
1995 Nashville	AAA CWS	67	190	38	4	0	2	48	13	16	13	0	37	2	4	0	0	0	—	6	.200	.259	.253
1996 Nashville	AAA CWS	70	215	47	10	1	0	59	17	26	18	0	48	2	6	3	2	0	1.00	4	.219	.282	.274
1997 Reading	AA Phi	97	295	60	11	1	2	79	20	31	36	0	61	5	5	5	0	5	.00	7	.203	.296	.268
1998 Oklahoma	AAA Tex	78	247	55	10	0	0	65	35	12	24	0	47	5	4	1	1	1	.50	12	.223	.303	.263
1999 Nashville	AAA Pit	47	121	30	7	0	3	46	20	16	14	0	29	2	3	2	4	0	1.00	4	.248	.331	.380
2000 Newark	IND —	11	33	6	0	0	0	6	4	6	8	0	8	1	0	1	0	0	—	2	.182	.349	.182
Atlantic Ct	IND —	2	7	2	0	0	1	5	1	1	0	0	1	0	0	0	0	0	—	0	.286	.286	.714
Calgary	AAA Fla	46	120	32	7	1	2	47	16	17	15	1	24	0	1	0	1	1	.00	4	.267	.348	.392
2001 New Orleans	AAA Hou	8	17	2	1	0	0	3	0	2	4	0	2	0	1	1	0	0	—	0	.118	.273	.176
Round Rock	AA Hou	66	220	50	7	0	5	72	28	28	22	0	33	2	3	1	0	4	.00	8	.227	.302	.327
1995 Chicago	AL	10	24	4	0	0	0	4	0	0	1	0	2	0	1	0	0	0	—	0	.167	.200	.167
1998 Texas	AL	2	3	1	1	0	0	2	2	0	1	0	1	0	0	0	0	0	—	0	.333	.500	.667
1999 Pittsburgh	NL	9	14	1	0	0	0	1	1	1	2	0	4	0	0	0	0	0	—	0	.071	.188	.071
10 Min. YEARS		655	1979	426	77	4	18	565	196	206	182	1	369	32	31	16	11	12	.48	56	.215	.290	.285
3 Maj. YEARS		21	41	6	1	0	0	7	3	1	4	0	7	0	1	0	0	0	—	0	.146	.222	.171

J.J. Trujillo

Pitches: Right **Bats:** Right **Pos:** RP-66   **Ht:** 6'0" **Wt:** 180 **Born:** 10/9/75 **Age:** 26

Year Team	Lg Org	G	GS	CG	GF	IP	BFP	H	R	ER	HR	SH	SF	HB	TBB	IBB	SO	WP	Bk	W	L	Pct.	ShO	Sv	ERA
1999 Johnstown	IND —	39	0	0	29	45.2	192	33	11	8	0	2	2	3	21	1	60	4	0	1	3	.250	0	14	1.58
2000 Fort Wayne	A SD	63	0	0	59	74.2	286	39	16	11	3	3	0	5	25	1	85	4	2	3	4	.429	0	42	1.33
2001 Lk Elsinore	A+ SD	23	0	0	21	29	119	20	7	6	1	0	0	2	13	2	31	1	0	4	1	.800	0	13	1.86
Mobile	AA SD	43	0	0	21	51	217	44	20	15	1	3	4	4	20	2	44	4	1	3	3	.500	0	6	2.65
3 Min. YEARS		168	0	0	130	200.1	814	136	54	40	5	8	6	14	79	6	220	13	3	11	11	.500	0	75	1.80

Pete Tucci

Bats: Right **Throws:** Right **Pos:** OF-74; DH-20; PH-1; PR-1   **Ht:** 6'2" **Wt:** 210 **Born:** 10/8/75 **Age:** 26

Year Team	Lg Org	G	AB	H	2B	3B	HR	TB	R	RBI	TBB	IBB	SO	HBP	SH	SF	SB	CS	SB%	GDP	Avg	OBP	SLG
1996 St.Cathrnes	A- Tor	54	205	52	8	7	7	95	28	33	23	1	58	1	2	3	5	3	.63	1	.254	.328	.463
1997 Hagerstown	A Tor	127	466	123	28	5	10	191	60	75	35	1	95	5	1	6	9	5	.64	9	.264	.318	.410
1998 Dunedin	A+ Tor	92	356	117	30	3	23	222	72	76	29	0	97	5	2	2	8	5	.62	6	.329	.385	.624
Knoxville	AA Tor	38	141	41	7	4	7	77	25	36	13	0	29	2	0	2	3	2	.60	2	.291	.354	.546
1999 Mobile	AA SD	83	312	78	15	0	11	126	45	35	26	3	83	4	0	1	11	6	.65	7	.250	.315	.404
2000 Mobile	AA SD	133	476	103	35	3	17	195	63	73	39	0	147	5	0	8	18	4	.82	4	.216	.278	.410
2001 Mobile	AA SD	18	65	12	0	0	0	12	3	7	3	0	22	0	0	1	1	1	.50	0	.185	.217	.185
St. Lucie	A+ NYM	77	264	68	17	2	9	116	43	49	42	0	56	2	0	5	15	9	.63	5	.258	.358	.439
6 Min. YEARS		622	2285	594	140	24	84	1034	339	384	210	5	587	24	5	28	70	35	.67	34	.260	.325	.453

Julien Tucker

Pitches: Right **Bats:** Left **Pos:** RP-27; SP-1   **Ht:** 6'7" **Wt:** 200 **Born:** 4/19/73 **Age:** 29

Year Team	Lg Org	G	GS	CG	GF	IP	BFP	H	R	ER	HR	SH	SF	HB	TBB	IBB	SO	WP	Bk	W	L	Pct.	ShO	Sv	ERA
1993 Astros	R Hou	11	10	1	1	54.2	251	55	36	24	2	0	1	8	22	0	33	5	3	2	3	.400	0	0	3.95
1994 Auburn	A- Hou	14	14	3	0	84.1	355	72	30	21	4	1	3	5	30	0	63	13	0	8	3	.727	1	0	2.24
1995 Kissimmee	A+ Hou	19	15	0	0	68.1	327	86	61	38	3	1	6	5	27	0	28	5	3	2	11	.154	0	0	5.00
1996 Kissimmee	A+ Hou	32	16	0	6	116	525	131	79	55	8	4	6	12	41	1	55	9	1	4	8	.333	1	1	4.27
1997 Kissimmee	A+ Hou	33	8	0	7	69	324	79	48	40	1	0	3	5	42	3	49	2	1	8	7	.533	0	2	5.22
Hickory	A CWS	4	0	0	1	7.1	35	11	7	3	1	0	1	1	2	0	7	0	0	0	0	—	0	0	3.68
1998 Birmingham	AA CWS	34	5	0	7	66	318	77	66	50	2	1	3	5	45	0	47	10	1	4	6	.400	0	0	6.82
1999 Birmingham	AA CWS	37	0	0	22	49	222	52	30	29	6	1	0	5	22	0	32	6	0	2	1	.667	0	5	5.33
2000 Aberdeen	IND —	49	0	0	15	74.1	338	71	38	29	2	2	3	5	43	5	64	7	0	6	3	.667	0	1	3.51
2001 Erie	AA Det	23	0	0	5	45.2	217	52	30	25	2	3	4	2	30	2	21	5	0	1	5	.167	0	3	4.93
Akron	AA Cle	5	1	0	3	8.1	39	10	9	9	0	0	0	1	5	0	6	2	0	0	1	.000	0	0	9.72
9 Min. YEARS		261	69	4	67	643	2951	696	434	323	31	13	30	54	309	11	405	64	9	37	48	.435	1	12	4.52

T.J. Tucker

Pitches: Right **Bats:** Right **Pos:** SP-27   **Ht:** 6'3" **Wt:** 245 **Born:** 8/20/78 **Age:** 23

Year Team	Lg Org	G	GS	CG	GF	IP	BFP	H	R	ER	HR	SH	SF	HB	TBB	IBB	SO	WP	Bk	W	L	Pct.	ShO	Sv	ERA
1997 Expos	R Mon	3	2	0	0	4.2	19	5	1	1	0	0	0	0	1	0	11	0	0	1	0	1.000	0	0	1.93
1998 Expos	R Mon	7	7	0	0	36	134	23	5	3	1	0	0	0	5	0	40	0	0	1	0	1.000	0	0	0.75
Vermont	A- Mon	6	6	0	0	33	135	24	9	8	0	1	0	2	15	0	34	3	0	3	1	.750	0	0	2.18
Jupiter	A+ Mon	2	1	0	1	9	32	5	1	1	0	1	1	0	0	0	10	1	0	1	1	.500	0	0	1.00
1999 Jupiter	A+ Mon	7	7	0	0	44	171	24	7	6	2	0	1	0	16	0	35	1	0	5	1	.833	0	0	1.23
Harrisburg	AA Mon	19	19	1	0	116.1	489	110	55	53	12	4	1	4	38	0	85	5	1	8	5	.615	1	0	4.10
2000 Harrisburg	AA Mon	8	8	0	0	45	182	33	19	18	7	2	1	3	17	0	24	1	0	2	1	.667	0	0	3.60
2001 Harrisburg	AA Mon	13	13	0	0	82	348	77	38	34	10	4	2	3	37	0	57	4	2	5	5	.500	0	0	3.73
Ottawa	AAA Mon	14	14	1	0	84	354	68	42	29	11	6	2	4	33	0	63	3	2	3	5	.375	0	0	3.11
2000 Montreal	NL	2	2	0	0	7	35	11	9	9	5	0	0	0	3	0	2	1	0	0	1	.000	0	0	11.57
5 Min. YEARS		79	77	2	1	454	1864	369	177	153	43	18	8	16	162	0	359	18	5	29	19	.604	1	0	3.03

Jason Turman

Pitches: Right **Bats:** Right **Pos:** RP-24; SP-5   **Ht:** 6'10" **Wt:** 210 **Born:** 11/10/75 **Age:** 26

Year Team	Lg Org	G	GS	CG	GF	IP	BFP	H	R	ER	HR	SH	SF	HB	TBB	IBB	SO	WP	Bk	W	L	Pct.	ShO	Sv	ERA
1997 Cape Fear	A Mon	19	15	1	1	88.1	374	84	45	41	4	1	1	6	35	0	72	8	0	5	7	.417	0	0	4.18
1998 Cape Fear	A Mon	21	20	1	0	111	490	126	69	57	11	1	4	9	30	0	76	8	0	8	5	.615	0	1	4.62
Jupiter	A+ Mon	8	6	1	0	35.1	149	37	20	13	1	2	3	1	12	0	15	3	0	3	2	.600	0	0	3.31
1999 Lancaster	A+ Sea	31	12	1	9	97	436	116	66	56	12	1	2	6	35	1	78	14	0	4	10	.286	0	1	5.20
2000 New Haven	AA Sea	39	7	0	11	100.2	429	102	53	49	7	3	2	4	34	1	94	8	0	3	4	.429	0	3	4.38
2001 Tacoma	AAA Sea	29	5	0	4	75.2	311	54	26	19	6	2	4	8	26	1	85	3	1	7	5	.583	0	1	2.26
5 Min. YEARS		147	65	3	26	508	2189	519	279	235	41	10	16	34	172	3	420	44	1	30	33	.476	0	6	4.16

Derrick Turnbow

Pitches: Right **Bats:** Right **Pos:** SP-3   **Ht:** 6'3" **Wt:** 200 **Born:** 1/25/78 **Age:** 24

Year Team	Lg Org	G	GS	CG	GF	IP	BFP	H	R	ER	HR	SH	SF	HB	TBB	IBB	SO	WP	Bk	W	L	Pct.	ShO	Sv	ERA
1997 Martinsvlle	R+ Phi	7	7	0	0	24.1	121	34	29	20	5	0	6	3	16	1	7	5	0	1	3	.250	0	0	7.40
1998 Martinsvlle	R+ Phi	13	13	1	0	70	300	66	44	39	7	3	5	1	26	1	45	5	0	2	6	.250	0	0	5.01
1999 Piedmont	A Phi	26	26	4	0	161	651	130	67	60	10	1	2	7	53	0	149	8	0	12	8	.600	1	0	3.35
2001 Arkansas	AA Ana	3	3	0	0	14	56	12	4	4	0	1	0	0	5	0	11	0	0	0	0	—	0	0	2.57
2000 Anaheim	AL	24	1	0	16	38	181	36	21	20	7	0	1	2	36	0	25	3	1	0	0	—	0	0	4.74
4 Min. YEARS		49	49	5	0	269.1	1128	242	144	123	22	5	13	11	100	2	212	18	0	15	17	.469	1	0	4.11

Mark Turnbow

Pitches: Right **Bats:** Right **Pos:** RP-22   **Ht:** 6'3" **Wt:** 205 **Born:** 11/26/78 **Age:** 23

Year Team	Lg Org	G	GS	CG	GF	IP	BFP	H	R	ER	HR	SH	SF	HB	TBB	IBB	SO	WP	Bk	W	L	Pct.	ShO	Sv	ERA
1997 Burlington	R+ Cle	13	13	0	0	74.1	297	49	25	23	1	4	2	4	18	0	53	2	0	8	2	.800	0	0	2.78
1998 Columbus	A Cle	16	16	1	0	90.2	386	94	47	41	9	4	1	3	26	1	73	6	1	6	5	.545	0	0	4.07
1999 Kinston	A+ Cle	12	12	0	0	60.1	279	76	48	43	5	2	4	4	25	0	42	1	0	5	4	.556	0	0	6.41
Columbus	A Cle	13	13	1	0	72.2	304	78	38	30	7	0	3	3	13	0	75	4	2	3	4	.429	0	0	3.72
Akron	AA Cle	1	1	0	0	6	25	4	3	2	0	0	0	0	3	0	4	0	0	1	0	1.000	0	0	3.00
2001 Mahoning Vy	A- Cle	21	0	0	5	31	134	30	15	13	1	2	0	2	8	1	34	4	1	1	3	.250	0	0	3.77
Akron	AA Cle	1	0	0	0	3	11	1	1	1	0	0	1	0	2	0	1	0	0	0	0	—	0	0	3.00
4 Min. YEARS		77	55	2	5	338	1436	332	177	153	23	12	11	16	95	2	282	17	4	24	18	.571	0	0	4.07

Brad Tyler

Bats: Left **Throws:** Right **Pos:** OF-18; 1B-4; PH-4; 3B-1; DH-1; PR-1   **Ht:** 6'2" **Wt:** 180 **Born:** 3/3/69 **Age:** 33

Year Team	Lg Org	G	AB	H	2B	3B	HR	TB	R	RBI	TBB	IBB	SO	HBP	SH	SF	SB	CS	SB%	GDP	Avg	OBP	SLG
1990 Wausau	A Bal	56	187	44	4	3	2	60	31	24	44	2	45	2	1	2	11	4	.73	2	.235	.383	.321
1991 Kane County	A Bal	60	199	54	10	3	3	79	35	29	44	1	25	1	1	2	5	3	.63	0	.271	.402	.397
Frederick	A+ Bal	56	187	48	6	0	4	66	26	26	33	3	33	2	1	1	3	2	.60	0	.257	.372	.353
1992 Frederick	A+ Bal	54	185	47	11	2	3	71	34	22	43	2	34	2	1	4	9	3	.75	2	.254	.393	.384
Hagerstown	AA Bal	83	256	57	9	1	2	74	41	21	34	2	45	1	1	0	23	5	.82	5	.223	.318	.289
1993 Bowie	AA Bal	129	437	103	23	17	10	190	85	44	84	2	89	1	1	3	24	11	.69	2	.236	.358	.435
1994 Rochester	AAA Bal	101	314	82	15	8	7	134	38	43	38	2	69	2	1	0	7	4	.64	4	.261	.345	.427
1995 Rochester	AAA Bal	114	361	93	17	3	17	167	60	52	71	4	63	4	0	5	10	5	.67	3	.258	.381	.463
1996 Rochester	AAA Bal	118	382	103	18	10	13	180	68	52	67	2	95	5	1	3	19	7	.73	2	.270	.383	.471
1997 Richmond	AAA Atl	129	383	101	15	10	18	190	69	77	55	2	110	3	3	7	13	6	.68	4	.264	.355	.496
1998 Edmonton	AAA Oak	131	430	115	24	4	18	201	68	75	62	1	107	0	0	6	10	1	.91	1	.267	.355	.467
1999 Richmond	AAA Atl	122	413	118	20	2	21	205	73	79	69	1	99	4	2	2	18	3	.86	6	.286	.391	.496
2000 Indianapols	AAA Mil	113	371	92	16	3	8	138	59	49	67	9	63	1	1	5	13	3	.81	4	.248	.360	.372
2001 Louisville	AAA Cin	13	36	10	5	0	1	18	7	2	2	0	16	0	0	0	0	1	.00	0	.278	.316	.500
Chattanooga	AA Cin	14	47	12	4	1	1	21	7	11	5	0	13	0	0	0	1	1	.50	0	.255	.327	.447
12 Min. YEARS		1293	4188	1079	197	67	128	1794	701	606	718	33	906	29	14	40	166	59	.74	33	.258	.367	.428

Josh Tyler

Bats: Right **Throws:** Right **Pos:** OF-31; 3B-18; 2B-17; PH-11; C-10; SS-10; 1B-1; PR-1; P-1   **Ht:** 6'1" **Wt:** 185 **Born:** 9/6/73 **Age:** 28

Year Team	Lg Org	G	AB	H	2B	3B	HR	TB	R	RBI	TBB	IBB	SO	HBP	SH	SF	SB	CS	SB%	GDP	Avg	OBP	SLG
1994 Wausau	R Mil	54	193	52	4	3	0	62	35	24	30	0	34	6	0	4	8	4	.67	6	.269	.378	.321
1995 Beloit	A Mil	77	186	44	5	0	2	55	24	27	36	0	40	2	7	3	3	6	.33	4	.237	.361	.296
1996 Stockton	A+ Mil	75	273	88	14	2	2	112	42	33	25	0	35	11	7	2	4	8	.33	6	.322	.399	.410
1997 Stockton	A+ Mil	114	416	129	28	4	4	177	63	46	20	0	54	10	5	3	21	7	.75	7	.310	.354	.425
1998 San Jose	A+ SF	50	194	48	10	2	1	65	24	21	10	0	29	0	3	2	7	8	.47	8	.247	.282	.335
Shreveport	AA SF	14	39	8	0	0	0	8	5	3	1	1	4	1	0	1	0	0	—	1	.205	.238	.205
Fresno	AAA SF	3	3	0	0	0	0	0	0	0	1	0	1	0	0	0	0	0	—	0	.000	.250	.000
Bakersfield	A+ SF	53	220	59	14	1	6	93	27	43	11	0	32	3	3	2	12	2	.86	2	.268	.309	.423
1999 Shreveport	AA SF	105	331	87	17	0	3	113	41	39	30	1	53	4	3	2	14	5	.74	10	.263	.330	.341
2000 Fresno	AAA SF	78	212	58	10	1	0	70	24	11	24	0	29	5	1	1	12	4	.75	11	.274	.360	.330
2001 Shreveport	AA SF	17	44	12	3	0	0	15	3	3	4	0	8	0	1	0	3	2	.60	1	.273	.333	.341
Fresno	AAA SF	77	230	66	15	1	3	92	21	26	16	4	40	5	3	2	5	3	.63	4	.287	.344	.400
8 Min. YEARS		717	2341	651	120	14	21	862	309	276	208	6	359	47	33	22	89	49	.64	60	.278	.346	.368

Torre Tyson

Bats: Both **Throws:** Right **Pos:** OF-73; 2B-14; PR-8; SS-7; DH-6; PH-6   **Ht:** 5'10" **Wt:** 185 **Born:** 12/31/75 **Age:** 26

Year Team	Lg Org	G	AB	H	2B	3B	HR	TB	R	RBI	TBB	IBB	SO	HBP	SH	SF	SB	CS	SB%	GDP	Avg	OBP	SLG
1998 Red Sox	R Bos	36	118	38	9	0	2	53	29	18	30	0	8	3	0	0	8	4	.67	3	.322	.470	.449
1999 Red Sox	R Bos	10	19	2	0	0	0	2	4	3	4	0	2	0	0	1	1	1	.50	1	.105	.250	.105
River City	IND —	35	143	42	6	1	1	53	30	17	20	0	22	1	0	1	26	5	.84	1	.294	.382	.371
2000 Greensboro	A NYY	124	475	138	15	3	3	168	87	41	76	2	70	5	7	1	33	14	.70	3	.291	.393	.354
2001 Norwich	AA NYY	71	224	55	8	0	0	63	43	14	34	2	49	4	2	1	9	3	.75	3	.246	.354	.281
Tampa	A+ NYY	31	114	29	6	2	0	39	28	10	24	1	19	2	1	1	6	4	.60	3	.254	.390	.342
4 Min. YEARS		307	1093	304	44	6	6	378	221	103	188	5	170	15	10	5	83	31	.73	14	.278	.390	.346

Dennis Ulacia

Pitches: Left **Bats:** Left **Pos:** SP-29   **Ht:** 6'1" **Wt:** 185 **Born:** 4/2/81 **Age:** 21

Year Team	Lg Org	G	GS	CG	GF	IP	BFP	H	R	ER	HR	SH	SF	HB	TBB	IBB	SO	WP	Bk	W	L	Pct.	ShO	Sv	ERA
1999 White Sox	R CWS	8	8	0	0	38	157	36	19	16	2	0	1	1	11	1	52	0	2	3	2	.600	0	0	3.79
2000 Burlington	A CWS	28	28	1	0	148.1	671	157	109	78	8	8	6	11	67	0	111	7	0	4	14	.222	0	0	4.73
2001 Kannapolis	A CWS	15	15	0	0	89	357	68	25	24	6	1	0	5	36	1	93	1	0	8	1	.889	0	0	2.43
Charlotte	AAA CWS	1	1	1	0	7	27	6	2	2	1	0	0	0	1	0	3	0	0	1	0	1.000	0	0	2.57
Winston-Sal	A+ CWS	10	10	4	0	64.1	265	57	27	26	2	2	2	5	26	1	47	1	0	5	3	.625	0	0	3.64
Birmingham	AA CWS	3	3	0	0	20	78	11	7	5	1	0	0	2	5	0	18	2	0	1	1	.500	0	0	2.25
3 Min. YEARS		65	65	6	0	366.2	1555	335	189	151	20	11	9	24	146	3	324	11	2	22	21	.512	0	0	3.71

Dave Ullery

Bats: Left   **Throws:** Right   **Pos:** C-35; 1B-5; 3B-4   **Ht:** 6'3"   **Wt:** 225   **Born:** 12/16/74   **Age:** 27

Year Team	Lg Org	G	AB	H	2B	3B	HR	TB	R	RBI	TBB	IBB	SO	HBP	SH	SF	SB	CS	SB%	GDP	Avg	OBP	SLG
1997 Anderson	IND —	6	16	5	2	0	0	7	5	2	4	0	4	0	0	0	0	0	—	1	.313	.450	.438
Spokane	A- KC	12	23	5	0	0	1	8	1	4	5	1	5	1	0	0	0	0	—	1	.217	.379	.348
Lansing	A KC	18	44	7	1	2	1	15	5	10	13	0	16	1	0	1	0	0	—	2	.159	.356	.341
1998 Wilmington	A+ KC	74	202	39	5	0	3	53	16	22	21	2	66	2	10	5	1	1	.50	5	.193	.270	.262
1999 Wilmington	A+ KC	60	199	46	18	0	2	70	20	27	18	1	70	2	0	4	0	0	—	3	.231	.296	.352
2000 Wichita	AA KC	62	202	58	9	0	5	82	22	42	15	1	47	1	2	7	1	2	.33	6	.287	.329	.406
2001 Wichita	AA KC	12	42	12	3	0	0	15	8	9	6	1	6	0	0	0	0	0	—	1	.286	.375	.357
Omaha	AAA KC	17	51	8	1	1	0	11	4	1	5	0	20	1	1	0	1	0	1.00	0	.157	.246	.216
Bowie	AA Bal	14	53	15	3	0	2	24	3	12	1	0	15	1	0	0	0	0	—	1	.283	.304	.453
5 Min. YEARS		275	832	195	42	3	14	285	84	129	88	6	249	9	13	18	3	3	.50	20	.234	.308	.343

Enmanuel Ulloa

Pitches: Right   **Bats:** Right   **Pos:** RP-44; SP-1   **Ht:** 6'2"   **Wt:** 170   **Born:** 11/26/78   **Age:** 23

Year Team	Lg Org	G	GS	CG	GF	IP	BFP	H	R	ER	HR	SH	SF	HB	TBB	IBB	SO	WP	Bk	W	L	Pct.	ShO	Sv	ERA
1998 Mariners	R Sea	19	0	0	14	41	144	21	6	4	1	1	0	0	1	0	61	0	2	4	0	1.000	0	7	0.88
Wisconsin	A Sea	3	0	0		5	20	4	1	1	0	1	0	0	1	0	5	0	0	0	0	—	0	0	1.80
1999 Wisconsin	A Sea	35	10	0	17	88	384	90	50	45	9	1	0	1	36	2	98	8	6	7	3	.700	0	5	4.60
2000 Lancaster	A+ Sea	27	27	0	0	155.2	642	134	90	75	20	1	4	4	55	1	145	4	2	9	5	.643	0	4	4.34
Tacoma	AAA Sea	1	1	0	0	5	21	2	3	3	0	0	0	0	4	0	4	0	0	0	1	.000	0	0	5.40
2001 San Antonio	AA Sea	45	1	0	15	80	345	81	32	27	3	4	4	2	21	5	64	3	1	2	2	.500	0	4	3.04
4 Min. YEARS		130	39	0	46	374.2	1556	332	182	155	33	8	9	7	118	8	377	15	11	22	11	.667	0	16	3.72

Jeff Urban

Pitches: Left   **Bats:** Right   **Pos:** SP-27   **Ht:** 6'8"   **Wt:** 215   **Born:** 1/25/77   **Age:** 25

Year Team	Lg Org	G	GS	CG	GF	IP	BFP	H	R	ER	HR	SH	SF	HB	TBB	IBB	SO	WP	Bk	W	L	Pct.	ShO	Sv	ERA
1998 Salem-Keizr	A- SF	5	3	0	0	21.2	95	21	14	12	1	2	0	0	8	0	22	2	0	1	2	.333	0	0	4.98
San Jose	A+ SF	4	4	0	0	23	103	27	13	9	2	2	1	3	5	0	23	2	0	4	0	1.000	0	0	3.52
1999 Shreveport	A+ SF	14	14	0	0	69.2	319	100	54	45	8	5	0	1	19	0	54	3	0	2	7	.222	0	0	5.81
San Jose	A+ SF	15	13	0	2	81.1	336	78	41	34	7	0	2	4	18	0	89	0	0	8	5	.615	0	0	3.76
2001 Shreveport	AA SF	27	27	0	0	156.2	675	178	85	68	16	9	6	9	32	0	117	7	0	7	11	.389	0	0	3.91
3 Min. YEARS		65	61	0	2	352.1	1528	404	207	168	34	18	9	17	82	0	305	14	0	22	25	.468	0	0	4.29

Derick Urquhart

Bats: Left   **Throws:** Left   **Pos:** OF-84; DH-13; PH-9; PR-2; P-1   **Ht:** 5'8"   **Wt:** 175   **Born:** 12/20/75   **Age:** 26

Year Team	Lg Org	G	AB	H	2B	3B	HR	TB	R	RBI	TBB	IBB	SO	HBP	SH	SF	SB	CS	SB%	GDP	Avg	OBP	SLG
1998 Vermont	A- Mon	76	243	60	15	2	0	79	32	26	31	0	43	1	4	1	13	7	.65	2	.247	.333	.325
1999 Jupiter	A+ Mon	23	44	8	1	0	0	9	5	5	7	0	7	0	0	0	2	0	1.00	0	.182	.294	.205
Cape Fear	A Mon	54	169	52	4	4	3	73	31	18	26	1	19	1	2	0	6	8	.43	1	.308	.403	.432
2000 Erie	AA Ana	57	189	45	8	2	4	69	30	21	34	0	23	0	2	2	4	4	.50	2	.238	.351	.365
2001 Rancho Cuca	A+ Ana	25	41	10	3	0	1	16	8	2	6	0	6	1	1	0	4	0	1.00	0	.244	.354	.390
Arkansas	AA Ana	81	250	66	11	2	5	96	42	45	33	0	37	0	1	5	4	1	.80	4	.264	.344	.384
4 Min. YEARS		316	936	241	42	10	13	342	148	117	137	1	135	3	10	8	33	20	.62	9	.257	.351	.365

Carlos Urquiola

Bats: Left   **Throws:** Right   **Pos:** OF-66; DH-17; PH-11; PR-3   **Ht:** 5'8"   **Wt:** 150   **Born:** 4/22/80   **Age:** 22

Year Team	Lg Org	G	AB	H	2B	3B	HR	TB	R	RBI	TBB	IBB	SO	HBP	SH	SF	SB	CS	SB%	GDP	Avg	OBP	SLG
1997 Diamondbcks	R Ari	2	2	0	0	0	0	0	1	0	0	0	0	1	0	1	0	1	0	1.00	0	.000	.000	.000
1998 Diamondbcks	R Ari	9	34	21	3	4	0	32	14	10	5	0	5	3	0	0	13	1	.93	0	.618	.690	.941
South Bend	A Ari	39	166	53	8	4	0	69	28	16	10	0	15	1	0	2	10	8	.56	1	.319	.358	.416
1999 South Bend	A Ari	93	384	139	13	3	0	158	66	35	22	0	32	5	1	3	20	14	.59	2	.362	.401	.411
2000 High Desert	A+ Ari	40	165	60	6	2	0	70	34	12	15	0	16	3	1	1	24	5	.83	1	.364	.424	.424
El Paso	AA Ari	68	225	68	8	1	0	78	33	18	20	1	17	3	5	1	13	8	.62	2	.302	.365	.347
2001 Lancaster	A+ Ari	14	61	20	5	0	0	25	9	12	6	0	3	1	0	0	5	2	.71	2	.328	.397	.410
El Paso	AA Ari	41	153	43	7	1	0	52	26	9	10	0	16	0	2	0	7	3	.70	2	.281	.325	.340
Greenville	AA Atl	40	132	40	5	0	0	45	18	10	15	0	15	1	0	2	6	4	.60	1	.303	.373	.341
5 Min. YEARS		346	1322	444	55	15	0	529	229	122	103	1	120	17	10	9	99	45	.69	11	.336	.389	.400

Brant Ust

Bats: Right   **Throws:** Right   **Pos:** 3B-90; DH-4   **Ht:** 6'2"   **Wt:** 200   **Born:** 7/17/78   **Age:** 23

Year Team	Lg Org	G	AB	H	2B	3B	HR	TB	R	RBI	TBB	IBB	SO	HBP	SH	SF	SB	CS	SB%	GDP	Avg	OBP	SLG
1999 Oneonta	A- Det	58	226	59	12	3	5	92	23	34	16	2	54	4	1	3	3	4	.43	3	.261	.317	.407
2000 Jacksnville	AA Det	111	383	83	15	4	4	118	37	28	33	2	95	9	7	1	2	4	.33	12	.217	.293	.308
2001 Tigers	R Det	7	26	8	1	0	0	9	4	5	2	0	4	0	0	0	1	0	1.00	0	.308	.357	.346
Erie	AA Det	87	323	77	16	1	6	113	36	31	15	0	81	6	3	3	1	1	.50	8	.238	.282	.350
3 Min. YEARS		263	958	227	44	8	15	332	100	98	66	4	234	19	11	7	7	9	.44	23	.237	.297	.347

Carlos Valderrama

Bats: Right **Throws:** Right **Pos:** OF-41 **Ht:** 5'11" **Wt:** 175 **Born:** 11/30/77 **Age:** 24

					BATTING												BASERUNNING				PERCENTAGES		
Year Team	Lg Org	G	AB	H	2B	3B	HR	TB	R	RBI	TBB	IBB	SO	HBP	SH	SF	SB	CS	SB%	GDP	Avg	OBP	SLG
1997 Salem-Keizr	A- SF	41	138	44	7	3	3	66	21	28	12	0	29	0	0	2	22	0	1.00	2	.319	.368	.478
1998 Salem-Keizr	A- SF	7	29	10	1	0	0	11	5	4	1	0	7	0	0	0	4	0	1.00	2	.345	.367	.379
1999 San Jose	A+ SF	26	90	23	2	0	0	25	12	12	4	0	19	0	2	0	8	4	.67	1	.256	.287	.278
Salem-Keizr	A- SF	40	134	39	3	1	2	50	27	18	12	0	34	0	3	0	17	2	.89	0	.291	.349	.373
2000 Bakersfield	A+ SF	121	435	137	21	5	13	207	78	81	39	1	96	4	5	8	54	11	.83	4	.315	.370	.476
2001 Shreveport	AA SF	41	159	49	12	2	1	68	29	8	18	0	29	0	2	0	11	5	.69	1	.308	.379	.428
5 Min. YEARS		276	985	302	46	11	19	427	172	151	86	1	214	4	12	10	116	22	.84	10	.307	.361	.434

Jerry Valdez

Bats: Right **Throws:** Right **Pos:** C-63; PH-11; DH-7 **Ht:** 5'11" **Wt:** 185 **Born:** 6/6/74 **Age:** 28

					BATTING												BASERUNNING				PERCENTAGES		
Year Team	Lg Org	G	AB	H	2B	3B	HR	TB	R	RBI	TBB	IBB	SO	HBP	SH	SF	SB	CS	SB%	GDP	Avg	OBP	SLG
1997 Martinsvlle	R+ Phi	34	125	34	7	0	1	44	21	11	7	0	27	4	0	0	0	2	.00	2	.272	.331	.352
1998 Batavia	A- Phi	60	214	58	13	1	8	97	29	40	24	0	41	6	0	2	0	1	.00	4	.271	.358	.453
1999 Piedmont	A Phi	39	126	28	5	0	2	39	11	13	11	1	26	1	1	2	0	0	—	2	.222	.286	.310
2000 Clearwater	A+ Phi	59	218	49	14	1	3	74	24	21	19	1	41	4	0	0	1	1	.50	4	.225	.299	.339
2001 Scranton-WB	AAA Phi	5	13	4	0	0	1	7	1	2	0	0	3	1	0	0	0	0	—	0	.308	.357	.538
Reading	AA Phi	74	242	60	14	2	9	105	32	39	11	1	47	5	2	3	1	2	.33	10	.248	.291	.434
5 Min. YEARS		271	938	233	53	4	24	366	118	126	72	3	185	21	3	7	2	6	.25	22	.248	.314	.390

Santo Valdez

Pitches: Right **Bats:** Right **Pos:** RP-14; SP-1 **Ht:** 6'1" **Wt:** 170 **Born:** 3/30/82 **Age:** 20

		HOW MUCH HE PITCHED						WHAT HE GAVE UP												THE RESULTS					
Year Team	Lg Org	G	GS	CG	GF	IP	BFP	H	R	ER	HR	SH	SF	HB	TBB	IBB	SO	WP	Bk	W	L	Pct.	ShO	Sv	ERA
2001 Syracuse	AAA Tor	1	1	0	0	5	18	5	1	1	0	1	0	0	1	0	2	0	0	0	0	—	0	0	1.80
Auburn	A- Tor	14	0	0	8	41.1	175	38	19	18	2	4	2	0	13	1	47	2	0	3	3	.500	0	1	3.92
1 Min. YEAR		15	1	0	8	46.1	193	43	20	19	2	5	2	0	14	1	49	2	0	3	3	.500	0	1	3.69

Vic Valencia

Bats: Right **Throws:** Right **Pos:** C-66; PH-9; 1B-3; 3B-1 **Ht:** 6'2" **Wt:** 185 **Born:** 5/13/77 **Age:** 25

					BATTING												BASERUNNING				PERCENTAGES		
Year Team	Lg Org	G	AB	H	2B	3B	HR	TB	R	RBI	TBB	IBB	SO	HBP	SH	SF	SB	CS	SB%	GDP	Avg	OBP	SLG
1995 Yankees	R NYY	25	58	14	1	0	1	18	5	8	6	0	22	0	0	0	0	0	—	1	.241	.313	.310
1996 Oneonta	A- NYY	72	261	51	8	0	3	68	30	25	21	0	86	0	3	3	3	0	1.00	4	.195	.253	.261
1997 Greensboro	A NYY	107	353	78	12	1	13	131	42	43	43	0	116	7	2	1	2	1	.67	6	.221	.317	.371
1998 Tampa	A+ NYY	122	411	92	18	1	16	160	53	43	26	2	139	3	5	4	0	1	.00	4	.224	.273	.389
1999 Norwich	AA NYY	119	396	88	18	0	22	172	57	72	45	0	142	5	4	3	0	0	—	4	.222	.307	.434
2000 Columbus	AAA NYY	15	48	12	1	0	4	25	6	9	2	0	19	0	0	0	0	0	—	4	.250	.280	.521
Norwich	AA NYY	84	256	51	12	0	8	87	23	36	40	2	74	2	6	1	1	1	.50	5	.199	.311	.340
2001 Chattanooga	AA Cin	76	230	53	8	2	6	83	24	33	27	2	59	3	3	3	2	0	1.00	8	.230	.316	.361
7 Min. YEARS		620	2013	439	78	4	73	744	240	269	210	6	657	20	23	15	8	3	.73	33	.218	.296	.370

Javier Valentin

Bats: Both **Throws:** Right **Pos:** C-49; DH-27; 3B-25; 1B-20; PH-8 **Ht:** 5'10" **Wt:** 192 **Born:** 9/19/75 **Age:** 26

					BATTING												BASERUNNING				PERCENTAGES		
Year Team	Lg Org	G	AB	H	2B	3B	HR	TB	R	RBI	TBB	IBB	SO	HBP	SH	SF	SB	CS	SB%	GDP	Avg	OBP	SLG
1993 Twins	R Min	32	103	27	6	1	1	38	18	19	14	0	19	1	0	4	0	2	.00	1	.262	.344	.369
Elizabethtn	R+ Min	9	24	5	1	0	0	6	3	3	4	0	2	1	0	0	0	0	—	0	.208	.345	.250
1994 Elizabethtn	R+ Min	54	210	44	5	0	9	76	23	27	15	0	44	2	0	5	0	1	.00	5	.210	.263	.362
1995 Fort Wayne	A Min	112	383	123	26	5	19	216	59	65	47	7	75	2	1	0	0	5	.00	7	.321	.398	.564
1996 Fort Myers	A+ Min	87	338	89	26	1	7	138	34	54	32	4	65	4	0	5	1	0	1.00	6	.263	.330	.408
Hardware Cy	AA Min	48	165	39	8	0	3	56	22	14	16	1	35	1	3	0	0	3	.00	2	.236	.308	.339
1997 New Britain	AA Min	102	370	90	17	0	8	131	41	50	30	1	61	1	2	6	2	3	.40	1	.243	.297	.354
2000 Salt Lake	AAA Min	39	140	50	16	2	7	91	25	35	9	0	27	1	0	1	1	0	1.00	1	.357	.397	.650
2001 Edmonton	AAA Min	121	431	121	29	2	17	205	53	71	47	5	108	4	0	7	0	1	.00	14	.281	.352	.476
1997 Minnesota	AL	4	7	2	0	0	0	2	1	0	0	0	3	0	0	0	0	0	—	0	.286	.286	.286
1998 Minnesota	AL	55	162	32	7	1	3	50	11	18	11	1	30	1	0	3	1	0	—	7	.198	.247	.309
1999 Minnesota	AL	78	218	54	12	1	5	83	22	28	22	0	39	1	1	1	0	0	—	2	.248	.313	.381
7 Min. YEARS		604	2164	588	134	11	71	957	278	338	214	18	436	17	6	28	4	15	.21	44	.272	.338	.442
3 Maj. YEARS		137	387	88	19	2	8	135	34	46	33	1	72	1	4	6	0	0	—	9	.227	.286	.349

Mario Valenzuela

Bats: Right **Throws:** Right **Pos:** OF-136; DH-1 **Ht:** 6'2" **Wt:** 190 **Born:** 3/10/77 **Age:** 25

					BATTING												BASERUNNING				PERCENTAGES		
Year Team	Lg Org	G	AB	H	2B	3B	HR	TB	R	RBI	TBB	IBB	SO	HBP	SH	SF	SB	CS	SB%	GDP	Avg	OBP	SLG
1996 White Sox	R CWS	21	73	19	3	2	1	29	6	8	4	0	20	1	0	1	0	0	—	2	.260	.304	.397
1998 Bristol	R+ CWS	61	233	77	13	1	10	122	44	46	24	1	49	3	0	2	6	4	.60	3	.330	.397	.524
1999 Burlington	A CWS	122	477	154	31	6	10	227	89	70	44	0	77	6	3	3	13	6	.68	16	.323	.385	.476
2000 Winston-Sal	A+ CWS	138	524	137	31	2	21	235	87	85	59	0	110	2	1	6	11	3	.79	8	.261	.335	.448
2001 Birmingham	AA CWS	88	341	99	17	3	12	158	50	53	21	2	61	2	3	6	4	5	.44	8	.290	.330	.463
Charlotte	AAA CWS	49	176	46	7	1	10	85	19	26	8	1	34	1	1	4	2	0	1.00	7	.261	.291	.483
5 Min. YEARS		479	1824	532	102	15	64	856	295	288	160	4	351	15	8	22	36	18	.67	44	.292	.350	.469

Yohanny Valera

Bats: Right **Throws:** Right **Pos:** C-75   **Ht:** 6'1" **Wt:** 196 **Born:** 8/17/76 **Age:** 25

		BATTING															BASERUNNING				PERCENTAGES		
Year Team	Lg Org	G	AB	H	2B	3B	HR	TB	R	RBI	TBB	IBB	SO	HBP	SH	SF	SB	CS	SB%	GDP	Avg	OBP	SLG
1995 Kingsport	R+ NYM	56	204	60	13	0	3	82	30	36	11	0	33	5	2	1	2	1	.67	6	.294	.344	.402
1996 Capital Cty	A NYM	108	372	79	18	0	6	115	38	38	17	3	78	13	1	7	2	4	.33	9	.212	.267	.309
1997 Capital Cty	A+ NYM	94	293	56	14	0	8	94	32	33	21	0	101	5	2	1	2	0	1.00	4	.191	.256	.321
1998 St. Lucie	A+ NYM	91	298	61	21	1	14	126	37	42	21	0	92	7	1	1	1	1	.50	7	.205	.272	.423
1999 Norfolk	AAA NYM	23	65	10	2	0	1	15	3	6	4	0	16	1	1	0	0	0	—	0	.154	.214	.231
Binghamton	AA NYM	57	204	59	14	3	9	106	33	39	17	1	57	2	0	2	2	1	.67	9	.289	.347	.520
2000 Ottawa	AAA Mon	21	68	10	1	0	2	17	6	10	4	0	19	2	0	0	0	0	—	0	.147	.216	.250
Harrisburg	AA Mon	92	281	66	8	3	3	89	28	34	24	1	56	9	5	2	1	3	.25	4	.235	.313	.317
2001 Orlando	AA TB	75	250	64	20	3	6	108	26	32	13	0	67	13	3	3	0	2	.00	6	.256	.323	.432
2000 Montreal	NL	7	10	0	0	0	0	0	1	1	1	0	5	1	1	0	0	0	—	0	.000	.167	.000
7 Min. YEARS		617	2035	465	111	10	52	752	233	270	132	5	519	57	15	17	10	12	.45	46	.229	.292	.370

Jose Valverde

Pitches: Right **Bats:** Right **Pos:** RP-39   **Ht:** 6'4" **Wt:** 220 **Born:** 7/24/79 **Age:** 22

		HOW MUCH HE PITCHED					WHAT HE GAVE UP											THE RESULTS					
Year Team	Lg Org	G	GS	CG	GF	IP	BFP	H	R	ER	HR	SH	SF	HB	TBB	IBB	SO	WP	Bk	W	L	Pct.	ShO	Sv	ERA
1999 Diamondbcks	R Ari	20	0	0	17	28.2	138	34	21	13	1	0	0	4	10	0	47	1	1	1	2	.333	0	8	4.08
South Bend	A Ari	2	0	0	2	2.2	11	2	0	0	0	0	0	1	2	0	3	1	1	0	0	—	0	0	0.00
2000 South Bend	A Ari	31	0	0	21	31.2	138	31	20	19	1	2	0	3	25	0	39	8	0	0	5	.000	0	14	5.40
Missoula	R+ Ari	12	0	0	11	11.2	44	3	0	0	0	0	0	0	4	0	24	2	0	1	0	1.000	0	4	0.00
2001 El Paso	AA Ari	39	0	0	28	41.1	193	36	19	18	1	1	1	4	27	0	72	6	1	2	2	.500	0	13	3.92
3 Min. YEARS		104	0	0	77	116	538	106	60	50	3	3	1	12	68	0	185	18	3	4	9	.308	0	39	3.88

Andy VanHekken

Pitches: Left **Bats:** Right **Pos:** SP-27   **Ht:** 6'3" **Wt:** 175 **Born:** 7/31/79 **Age:** 22

		HOW MUCH HE PITCHED					WHAT HE GAVE UP											THE RESULTS					
Year Team	Lg Org	G	GS	CG	GF	IP	BFP	H	R	ER	HR	SH	SF	HB	TBB	IBB	SO	WP	Bk	W	L	Pct.	ShO	Sv	ERA
1998 Mariners	R Sea	11	8	0	0	40.2	179	34	23	20	1	0	0	2	18	0	55	7	1	6	3	.667	0	0	4.43
1999 Oneonta	A- Det	11	10	0	0	50.1	210	44	17	12	3	0	0	3	16	0	50	1	0	4	2	.667	0	0	2.15
2000 W Michigan	A Det	26	25	3	1	158	648	139	46	43	3	3	2	7	37	0	126	3	0	16	6	.727	1	1	2.45
2001 Lakeland	A+ Det	19	19	2	0	110.2	460	105	43	39	8	3	2	5	33	0	82	1	0	10	4	.714	0	0	3.17
Erie	AA Det	8	8	0	0	48	210	63	29	25	5	1	3	1	8	0	29	1	0	5	0	1.000	0	0	4.69
4 Min. YEARS		75	70	5	1	407.2	1707	385	160	139	20	7	7	18	112	0	342	13	1	41	15	.732	1	1	3.07

Bobby Van Iten

Bats: Left **Throws:** Right **Pos:** C-41; 1B-40; OF-32; 3B-4; PH-3; DH-1   **Ht:** 6'1" **Wt:** 186 **Born:** 7/1/77 **Age:** 24

		BATTING															BASERUNNING				PERCENTAGES		
Year Team	Lg Org	G	AB	H	2B	3B	HR	TB	R	RBI	TBB	IBB	SO	HBP	SH	SF	SB	CS	SB%	GDP	Avg	OBP	SLG
1996 Martinsvlle	R+ Phi	33	113	27	4	0	1	34	9	9	4	0	21	2	0	2	0	1	.00	3	.239	.273	.301
1997 Martinsvlle	R+ Phi	55	204	63	9	0	5	87	29	35	5	0	27	3	0	3	3	2	.60	1	.309	.330	.426
1998 Piedmont	A Phi	121	461	120	18	2	4	154	60	58	53	2	69	8	1	2	0	1	.00	14	.260	.345	.334
1999 Clearwater	A+ Phi	98	345	91	16	1	5	124	48	51	31	1	63	4	4	7	3	4	.43	7	.264	.326	.359
2000 Clearwater	A+ Phi	108	390	92	22	0	5	129	52	33	36	4	80	4	4	3	0	0	—	7	.236	.305	.331
2001 Reading	AA Phi	113	404	92	23	1	7	138	46	52	36	2	120	8	1	2	1	1	.50	5	.228	.302	.342
6 Min. YEARS		528	1917	485	92	4	27	666	244	238	165	9	380	29	10	19	7	9	.44	37	.253	.319	.347

Chris Van Rossum

Bats: Left **Throws:** Left **Pos:** OF-70; DH-13; PH-12; PR-3   **Ht:** 6'1" **Wt:** 175 **Born:** 2/15/74 **Age:** 28

		BATTING															BASERUNNING				PERCENTAGES		
Year Team	Lg Org	G	AB	H	2B	3B	HR	TB	R	RBI	TBB	IBB	SO	HBP	SH	SF	SB	CS	SB%	GDP	Avg	OBP	SLG
1996 Bellingham	A- SF	23	42	6	0	0	0	6	3	4	3	0	12	2	0	2	5	1	.83	0	.143	.224	.143
San Jose	A+ SF	11	31	8	2	0	0	10	7	4	6	0	10	1	0	0	1	2	.33	0	.258	.395	.323
1997 Bakersfield	A+ SF	125	441	115	17	5	2	148	72	40	57	1	98	15	5	5	9	12	.43	6	.261	.362	.336
1998 San Jose	A+ SF	65	214	53	9	3	2	74	33	15	17	0	55	4	1	1	10	2	.83	6	.248	.314	.346
Shreveport	AA SF	23	62	10	2	1	0	14	5	3	9	0	15	0	1	0	2	2	.50	1	.161	.268	.226
1999 High Desert	A+ Ari	28	90	28	5	1	4	47	13	16	9	0	27	2	0	2	2	1	.67	1	.311	.379	.522
Diamondbcks	R Ari	6	16	4	0	0	0	4	1	0	1	0	3	0	0	0	1	0	1.00	0	.250	.294	.250
South Bend	A Ari	2	6	1	0	0	0	1	2	1	3	0	1	0	0	0	0	0	—	0	.167	.444	.167
El Paso	AA Ari	26	75	21	0	0	3	35	11	9	8	0	21	0	0	0	1	0	1.00	1	.280	.360	.467
2000 Duluth-Sup	IND —	9	26	2	0	0	0	2	2	1	4	0	5	0	0	0	2	1	.67	2	.077	.200	.077
Clinton	A Cin	59	216	55	6	2	5	80	28	34	15	0	52	6	0	1	11	3	.79	3	.255	.319	.370
2001 Chattanooga	AA Cin	18	27	6	2	0	0	8	5	3	1	0	12	0	0	0	0	0	—	0	.222	.250	.296
Mudville	A+ Cin	47	156	26	2	0	0	28	14	5	5	1	37	1	2	0	5	3	.63	0	.167	.198	.179
Lehigh Val	IND —	31	92	24	3	0	2	33	11	11	8	0	21	0	1	1	2	1	.67	5	.261	.317	.359
6 Min. YEARS		473	1494	359	53	12	18	490	209	146	146	2	369	33	10	11	51	28	.65	25	.240	.319	.328

Claudio Vargas

Pitches: Right **Bats:** Right **Pos:** SP-27   **Ht:** 6'3" **Wt:** 210 **Born:** 5/19/79 **Age:** 23

		HOW MUCH HE PITCHED					WHAT HE GAVE UP											THE RESULTS					
Year Team	Lg Org	G	GS	CG	GF	IP	BFP	H	R	ER	HR	SH	SF	HB	TBB	IBB	SO	WP	Bk	W	L	Pct.	ShO	Sv	ERA
1998 Brevard Cty	A+ Fla	2	2	0	0	9.2	46	15	5	5	1	1	0	0	4	0	9	0	0	0	1	.000	0	0	4.66
Marlins	R Fla	5	4	0	0	28.2	117	24	15	13	1	0	1	3	7	0	27	2	0	0	4	.000	0	0	4.08
1999 Kane County	A Fla	19	19	1	0	99.2	426	97	47	43	8	2	3	0	41	0	88	2	2	5	5	.500	0	0	3.88
2000 Brevard Cty	A+ Fla	24	23	0	0	145.1	596	126	64	53	10	4	2	7	44	3	143	3	0	10	5	.667	0	0	3.28
Portland	AA Fla	3	2	0	0	15	68	16	9	6	1	1	2	1	6	0	13	0	0	1	1	.500	0	0	3.60

Year Team	Lg Org	G	GS	CG	GF	IP	BFP	H	R	ER	HR	SH	SF	HB	TBB	IBB	SO	WP	Bk	W	L	Pct.	ShO	Sv	ERA
		HOW MUCH HE PITCHED						WHAT HE GAVE UP												THE RESULTS					
2001 Portland	AA Fla	27	27	0	0	159	666	122	77	74	25	8	2	11	67	1	151	2	1	8	9	.471	0	0	4.19
4 Min. YEARS		80	77	1	0	457.1	1919	400	217	194	46	16	10	22	169	4	431	9	3	24	25	.490	0	0	3.82

Martin Vargas

Pitches: Right **Bats:** Right **Pos:** RP-54   **Ht:** 6'0" **Wt:** 155 **Born:** 2/22/78 **Age:** 24

Year Team	Lg Org	G	GS	CG	GF	IP	BFP	H	R	ER	HR	SH	SF	HB	TBB	IBB	SO	WP	Bk	W	L	Pct.	ShO	Sv	ERA
		HOW MUCH HE PITCHED						WHAT HE GAVE UP												THE RESULTS					
1998 Columbus	A Cle	7	7	0	0	29.2	153	42	36	33	7	0	2	3	24	0	25	7	0	1	4	.200	0	0	10.01
Burlington	R+ Cle	13	13	1	0	73.2	324	78	49	39	5	1	0	4	35	0	64	7	3	3	7	.300	0	0	4.76
1999 Columbus	A Cle	15	12	0	0	67.1	311	80	46	37	5	1	2	6	20	0	51	5	0	6	3	.667	0	0	4.95
Kinston	A+ Cle	20	0	0	6	42.1	179	31	16	13	3	5	3	3	20	1	44	2	0	6	1	.857	0	2	2.76
2000 Akron	AA Cle	53	0	0	26	81.1	374	96	52	49	4	6	3	6	30	3	58	10	0	10	8	.556	0	7	5.42
2001 Akron	AA Cle	32	0	0	24	40	189	52	29	25	1	3	2	1	23	0	35	8	0	1	5	.167	0	9	5.63
Buffalo	AAA Cle	22	0	0	12	27.2	120	20	11	9	1	1	1	2	17	1	22	8	0	0	3	.000	0	4	2.93
4 Min. YEARS		162	32	1	68	362	1650	399	239	205	26	17	13	25	169	5	299	47	3	27	31	.466	0	22	5.10

Leo Vasquez

Pitches: Left **Bats:** Left **Pos:** RP-36   **Ht:** 6'4" **Wt:** 193 **Born:** 7/1/73 **Age:** 28

Year Team	Lg Org	G	GS	CG	GF	IP	BFP	H	R	ER	HR	SH	SF	HB	TBB	IBB	SO	WP	Bk	W	L	Pct.	ShO	Sv	ERA
		HOW MUCH HE PITCHED						WHAT HE GAVE UP												THE RESULTS					
1996 Aberdeen	IND —	19	16	2	1	105.1	429	79	39	26	7	2	0	1	39	0	106	4	0	11	2	.846	2	0	2.22
1997 Binghamton	AA NYM	1	1	0	0	5.1	26	7	6	6	3	1	2	0	2	0	2	0	0	0	1	.000	0	0	10.13
Capital Cty	A NYM	22	8	0	8	56	250	63	37	32	4	1	2	3	22	1	49	7	1	4	5	.444	0	1	5.14
1998 Binghamton	AA NYM	14	2	0	2	29.1	140	28	16	15	1	2	1	2	25	0	28	3	0	1	1	.500	0	1	4.60
St. Lucie	A+ NYM	24	6	0	10	69	264	44	20	17	3	3	4	3	24	0	46	5	0	3	2	.600	0	2	2.22
1999 Binghamton	AA NYM	27	0	0	7	42.1	190	39	18	18	4	0	1	2	28	0	43	2	1	1	2	.333	0	1	3.83
Midland	AA Oak	13	0	0	5	23.1	103	18	11	8	2	1	1	2	13	1	24	1	1	3	1	.750	0	1	3.09
Vancouver	AAA Oak	1	0	0	0	1.2	8	2	1	1	0	0	0	0	2	0	0	0	0	0	0	—	0	0	5.40
2000 Midland	AA Oak	36	1	0	13	53	239	48	21	16	3	1	0	5	33	4	59	7	0	6	5	.545	0	4	2.72
2001 Sacramento	AAA Oak	36	0	0	22	44.1	213	52	28	26	4	1	0	3	31	0	36	2	0	0	1	.000	0	2	5.28
6 Min. YEARS		193	34	2	68	429.2	1862	380	197	165	31	12	11	21	219	6	393	31	3	29	20	.592	2	12	3.46

Rene Vega

Pitches: Left **Bats:** Left **Pos:** RP-31; SP-10   **Ht:** 5'10" **Wt:** 175 **Born:** 8/4/76 **Age:** 25

Year Team	Lg Org	G	GS	CG	GF	IP	BFP	H	R	ER	HR	SH	SF	HB	TBB	IBB	SO	WP	Bk	W	L	Pct.	ShO	Sv	ERA
		HOW MUCH HE PITCHED						WHAT HE GAVE UP												THE RESULTS					
1998 Kingsport	R+ NYM	22	0	0	11	40	186	46	32	25	2	3	3	2	17	0	42	4	1	3	2	.600	0	5	5.63
Pittsfield	A- NYM	2	0	0	1	5.1	19	2	1	1	0	0	0	0	1	0	6	0	0	1	0	1.000	0	0	1.69
1999 Capital Cty	A NYM	29	22	1	2	146	593	101	57	51	8	3	2	12	50	1	148	6	4	11	7	.611	0	1	3.14
2000 St. Lucie	A+ NYM	27	26	1	0	147.1	648	150	88	72	12	3	4	14	62	1	97	8	2	11	6	.647	0	0	4.40
2001 Binghamton	AA NYM	41	10	0	8	106.1	456	117	48	43	12	3	5	9	32	1	69	5	2	3	6	.333	0	2	3.64
4 Min. YEARS		121	60	2	22	445	1902	416	226	192	34	12	14	37	162	3	362	23	9	29	21	.580	0	8	3.88

Gil Velazquez

Bats: Right **Throws:** Right **Pos:** SS-94; 2B-11; PH-1; PR-1   **Ht:** 6'2" **Wt:** 170 **Born:** 10/17/79 **Age:** 22

Year Team	Lg Org	G	AB	H	2B	3B	HR	TB	R	RBI	TBB	IBB	SO	HBP	SH	SF	SB	CS	SB%	GDP	Avg	OBP	SLG
		BATTING															BASERUNNING				PERCENTAGES		
1998 Kingsport	R+ NYM	12	29	3	1	0	0	4	2	4	2	0	7	0	3	1	2	0	1.00	0	.103	.156	.138
Mets	R NYM	33	97	18	3	0	0	21	7	7	8	0	10	2	3	1	2	1	.67	1	.186	.259	.216
1999 Kingsport	R+ NYM	62	225	59	8	0	1	70	24	19	19	0	43	3	2	4	4	0	1.00	5	.262	.323	.311
Capital Cty	A NYM	21	75	17	4	1	0	23	9	6	3	0	14	1	2	3	0	1	.00	2	.227	.256	.307
2000 St. Lucie	A+ NYM	125	440	101	16	1	1	122	37	43	25	0	69	9	4	3	3	9	.25	15	.230	.283	.277
2001 Binghamton	AA NYM	106	358	74	11	2	3	98	33	19	26	1	84	3	4	0	1	1	.50	12	.207	.266	.274
4 Min. YEARS		359	1224	272	43	4	5	338	112	98	83	1	227	18	18	12	12	12	.50	35	.222	.279	.276

Juan Ventura

Bats: Right **Throws:** Right **Pos:** OF-39; DH-5; PR-3; 2B-1; 1B-1   **Ht:** 6'1" **Wt:** 170 **Born:** 12/10/80 **Age:** 21

Year Team	Lg Org	G	AB	H	2B	3B	HR	TB	R	RBI	TBB	IBB	SO	HBP	SH	SF	SB	CS	SB%	GDP	Avg	OBP	SLG
		BATTING															BASERUNNING				PERCENTAGES		
1999 Rockies	R Col	46	193	77	9	4	0	94	35	23	12	0	24	2	0	5	25	9	.74	2	.399	.429	.487
2000 Portland	A- Col	56	195	43	9	1	1	57	24	15	14	0	36	2	6	2	14	6	.70	6	.221	.277	.292
2001 Colo Sprngs	AAA Col	2	6	1	0	0	0	1	1	1	0	0	2	1	0	0	0	1	.00	1	.167	.286	.167
Tri-City	A- Col	47	162	33	5	3	0	44	26	8	15	0	38	5	2	0	7	4	.64	2	.204	.291	.272
3 Min. YEARS		151	556	154	23	8	1	196	86	47	41	0	100	10	8	7	46	20	.70	11	.277	.334	.353

Dario Veras

Pitches: Right **Bats:** Right **Pos:** RP-48   **Ht:** 6'1" **Wt:** 155 **Born:** 3/13/73 **Age:** 29

Year Team	Lg Org	G	GS	CG	GF	IP	BFP	H	R	ER	HR	SH	SF	HB	TBB	IBB	SO	WP	Bk	W	L	Pct.	ShO	Sv	ERA
		HOW MUCH HE PITCHED						WHAT HE GAVE UP												THE RESULTS					
1993 Bakersfield	A+ LA	7	0	0	1	13.1	61	13	11	11	1	0	1	0	8	2	11	0	0	1	0	1.000	0	0	7.43
Vero Beach	A+ LA	24	0	0	8	54.2	229	59	23	17	2	3	1	1	14	5	31	3	0	2	2	.500	0	2	2.80
1994 Rancho Cuca	A+ SD	59	0	0	13	79	332	66	28	18	7	7	0	6	25	9	56	2	0	9	2	.818	0	3	2.05
1995 Memphis	AA SD	58	0	0	22	82.2	360	81	38	35	8	3	1	7	27	11	70	5	1	7	3	.700	0	1	3.81
1996 Memphis	AA SD	29	0	0	8	42.2	172	38	14	11	4	1	2	1	9	2	47	2	1	3	1	.750	0	1	2.32
Las Vegas	AAA SD	19	1	0	9	40.1	165	41	17	13	1	3	1	0	6	2	30	2	0	6	2	.750	0	1	2.90

Year Team	Lg Org	G	GS	CG	GF	IP	BFP	H	R	ER	HR	SH	SF	HB	TBB	IBB	SO	WP	Bk	W	L	Pct.	ShO	Sv	ERA
1997 Mobile	AA SD	5	2	0	2	5	25	8	5	5	1	0	0	0	3	0	5	0	0	0	0	—	0	0	9.00
Rancho Cuca	A+ SD	2	0	0	1	3	13	3	3	2	1	1	0	0	1	0	3	1	0	0	0	—	0	1	6.00
Las Vegas	AAA SD	12	0	0	5	14.1	59	14	8	8	1	0	0	0	6	0	13	3	0	0	2	.000	0	2	5.02
1998 Las Vegas	AAA SD	31	0	0	27	35.2	153	36	15	15	5	0	0	2	11	0	29	4	0	2	1	.667	0	9	3.79
Pawtucket	AAA Bos	23	0	0	21	29	138	30	12	12	4	1	1	0	11	3	27	0	0	2	0	1.000	0	7	3.72
1999 Royals	R KC	3	2	0	0	4	15	3	0	0	0	0	0	0	0	0	3	0	0	0	0	—	0	0	0.00
Omaha	AAA KC	12	0	0	3	20.2		19	10	10	5	1	0	1	3	0	17	0	0	1	2	.333	0	0	4.35
2000 Kinston	A+ Cle	17	0	0	10	34.1	134	27	13	13	5	2	0	5	4	0	29	0	0	3	0	1.000	0	3	3.41
Akron	AA Cle	4	0	0	1	4.2	23	7	8	8	1	0	0	1	1	0	6	0	0	0	0	—	0	1	15.43
2001 Buffalo	AAA Cle	48	0	0	23	67	289	69	35	34	10	1	2	5	21	1	69	0	1	5	1	.833	0	6	4.57
1996 San Diego	NL	23	0	0	6	29	117	24	10	9	3	1	1	1	10	4	23	1	0	3	1	.750	0	2	2.79
1997 San Diego	NL	23	0	0	7	24.2	114	28	18	14	5	0	0	2	12	3	21	0	0	2	1	.667	0	5	5.11
1998 Boston	AL	7	0	0	4	8	43	12	9	9	0	0	0	1	7	0	2	2	0	0	1	.000	0	0	10.13
9 Min. YEARS		353	5	0	154	530.1	2235	514	240	212	56	23	9	29	150	35	446	22	3	41	16	.719	0	37	3.60
3 Maj. YEARS		53	0	0	17	61.2	274	64	37	32	8	1	1	4	29	7	46	3	0	5	3	.625	0	0	4.67

Wilton Veras

Bats: Right **Throws:** Right **Pos:** 3B-131; DH-5 **Ht:** 6'2" **Wt:** 198 **Born:** 1/19/78 **Age:** 24

Year Team	Lg Org	G	AB	H	2B	3B	HR	TB	R	RBI	TBB	IBB	SO	HBP	SH	SF	SB	CS	SB%	GDP	Avg	OBP	SLG
1995 Red Sox	R Bos	31	91	24	1	0	0	25	7	5	7	0	9	3	0	0	1	2	.33	2	.264	.337	.275
1996 Lowell	A- Bos	67	250	60	15	0	0	75	22	19	13	0	29	0	1	2	2	1	.67	9	.240	.275	.300
1997 Michigan	A Bos	131	489	141	21	3	8	192	51	68	31	0	51	6	1	3	3	2	.60	19	.288	.336	.393
1998 Trenton	AA Bos	126	470	137	27	4	16	220	70	67	15	1	66	6	6	5	5	4	.56	14	.291	.319	.468
1999 Trenton	AA Bos	116	474	133	23	2	11	193	65	75	23	1	55	5	1	5	7	6	.54	23	.281	.318	.407
2000 Pawtucket	AAA Bos	60	218	46	9	0	3	64	18	25	12	1	18	2	1	1	0	1	.00	6	.211	.258	.294
2001 Pawtucket	AAA Bos	136	521	120	16	2	8	164	44	52	14	0	63	7	1	3	5	6	.45	24	.230	.259	.315
1999 Boston	AL	36	118	34	5	1	2	47	14	13	5	0	14	2	0	2	0	2	.00	5	.288	.323	.398
2000 Boston	AL	49	164	40	7	1	0	49	21	14	7	0	20	2	3	3	0	0	—	2	.244	.278	.299
7 Min. YEARS		667	2513	661	112	11	46	933	277	311	115	3	291	29	11	19	23	22	.51	97	.263	.301	.371
2 Maj. YEARS		85	282	74	12	2	2	96	35	27	12	0	34	4	3	5	0	2	.00	7	.262	.297	.340

Shanin Veronie

Pitches: Right **Bats:** Right **Pos:** RP-37 **Ht:** 6'1" **Wt:** 190 **Born:** 8/18/76 **Age:** 25

Year Team	Lg Org	G	GS	CG	GF	IP	BFP	H	R	ER	HR	SH	SF	HB	TBB	IBB	SO	WP	Bk	W	L	Pct.	ShO	Sv	ERA
1999 Danville	R+ Atl	18	0	0	15	25.1	91	12	4	2	2	0	0	1	4	0	41	0	0	2	2	.500	0	3	0.71
2000 Macon	A Atl	43	0	0	34	66.1	269	48	22	20	4	3	1	4	26	2	69	2	0	4	4	.500	0	13	2.71
2001 Greenville	AA Atl	2	0	0	1	3	13	4	0	0	0	0	0	0	0	0	4	0	0	0	0	—	0	0	0.00
Myrtle Bch	A+ Atl	35	0	0	21	54.1	224	47	17	15	2	1	2	2	10	3	57	2	0	1	2	.333	0	9	2.48
3 Min. YEARS		98	0	0	71	149	597	111	43	37	8	4	3	7	40	5	171	4	0	7	8	.467	0	25	2.23

Jeff Verplancke

Pitches: Right **Bats:** Right **Pos:** RP-51 **Ht:** 6'3" **Wt:** 200 **Born:** 11/18/77 **Age:** 24

Year Team	Lg Org	G	GS	CG	GF	IP	BFP	H	R	ER	HR	SH	SF	HB	TBB	IBB	SO	WP	Bk	W	L	Pct.	ShO	Sv	ERA
2000 San Jose	A+ SF	26	25	1	0	139.2	642	159	111	91	12	5	6	11	67	1	129	7	4	6	14	.300	0	0	5.86
Fresno	AAA SF	1	0	0	0	5	20	3	1	1	0	0	0	0	2	0	6	0	0	0	0	—	0	0	1.80
2001 Shreveport	AA SF	43	0	0	40	48.2	217	50	27	24	3	4	3	5	20	3	46	3	0	1	8	.111	0	22	4.44
Fresno	AAA SF	8	0	0	4	12.1	50	9	4	4	1	0	0	2	6	0	13	0	0	1	0	.667	0	1	2.92
2 Min. YEARS		78	25	1	44	205.2	929	221	143	120	16	9	9	18	95	4	194	10	4	9	23	.281	0	23	5.25

Mike Villano

Pitches: Right **Bats:** Right **Pos:** RP-42; SP-2 **Ht:** 6'0" **Wt:** 200 **Born:** 8/10/71 **Age:** 30

Year Team	Lg Org	G	GS	CG	GF	IP	BFP	H	R	ER	HR	SH	SF	HB	TBB	IBB	SO	WP	Bk	W	L	Pct.	ShO	Sv	ERA
1995 Burlington	A SF	16	0	0	7	25.1	120	20	12	8	1	2	1	4	21	0	29	5	0	3	1	.750	0	1	2.84
San Jose	A+ SF	21	0	0	16	32.2	137	27	7	6	2	0	1	3	11	0	42	3	0	1	0	1.000	0	1	1.65
1996 San Jose	A+ SF	39	2	0	21	88	341	48	12	7	2	1	1	0	33	4	133	7	1	7	1	.875	0	8	0.72
Shreveport	AA SF	2	2	0	0	12	47	6	4	4	0	0	0	0	8	0	7	0	0	2	0	1.000	0	0	3.00
1997 Shreveport	AA SF	30	0	0	15	34.1	158	41	25	24	5	2	0	0	20	2	26	4	1	3	1	.750	0	2	6.29
Phoenix	AAA SF	13	11	0	1	71.1	309	75	36	33	7	3	2	2	27	1	41	2	0	5	3	.625	0	0	4.16
1998 Charlotte	AAA Fla	13	10	0	1	59.2	277	82	55	51	14	1	4	3	18	0	47	3	2	3	5	.375	0	0	7.69
1999 Calgary	AAA Fla	36	1	0	11	58	273	87	43	40	18	1	0	5	17	0	48	7	1	1	5	.167	0	2	6.21
Norfolk	AAA NYM	2	0	0	2	2	10	3	1	1	0	0	0	0	2	0	1	0	0	0	0	—	0	0	4.50
2000 Nashville	AAA Pit	45	1	0	11	75.2	338	77	64	54	13	3	2	3	43	3	56	6	2	5	3	.625	0	6	6.42
2001 Wichita	AA KC	37	2	0	20	68	312	79	43	34	8	2	1	10	29	3	40	7	1	6	7	.462	0	4	4.50
Shreveport	AA SF	7	0	0	7	8.2	30	6	1	1	1	0	0	0	1	1	7	0	0	0	0	—	0	5	1.04
7 Min. YEARS		261	29	0	112	535.2	2352	551	303	263	71	15	12	30	230	14	477	44	8	35	27	.565	0	25	4.42

Oscar Villarreal

Pitches: Right **Bats:** Left **Pos:** SP-27 **Ht:** 6'1" **Wt:** 190 **Born:** 11/22/81 **Age:** 20

Year Team	Lg Org	G	GS	CG	GF	IP	BFP	H	R	ER	HR	SH	SF	HB	TBB	IBB	SO	WP	Bk	W	L	Pct.	ShO	Sv	ERA
1999 Diamondbcks	R Ari	14	11	0	1	64.1	286	64	39	27	1	2	3	10	25	0	51	6	4	1	5	.167	0	0	3.78
2000 Tucson	AAA Ari	2	0	0	0	4.1	19	6	1	1	0	0	0	0	2	0	4	0	0	1	0	1.000	0	0	2.08
South Bend	A Ari	13	5	0	5	32.2	155	37	19	16	0	0	0	3	17	3	30	2	1	1	3	.250	0	0	4.41
Diamondbcks	R Ari	1	0	0	0	1	5	2	1	1	0	0	0	0	0	0	1	0	0	0	0	—	0	0	9.00
High Desert	A+ Ari	9	4	0	0	24.2	117	24	20	10	4	4	1	3	14	0	18	2	0	0	2	.000	0	0	3.65

Year Team	Lg Org	G	GS	CG	GF	IP	BFP	H	R	ER	HR	SH	SF	HB	TBB	IBB	SO	WP	Bk	W	L	Pct.	ShO	Sv	ERA
2001 El Paso	AA Ari	27	27	0	0	140.2	644	154	96	69	10	4	7	8	63	1	108	14	11	6	9	.400	0	0	4.41
3 Min. YEARS		66	47	0	6	267.2	1226	287	176	124	15	10	11	24	121	4	212	24	16	9	19	.321	0	0	4.17

Ismael Villegas

Pitches: Right **Bats:** Right **Pos:** SP-20; RP-14 **Ht:** 6'0" **Wt:** 188 **Born:** 8/12/76 **Age:** 25

Year Team	Lg Org	G	GS	CG	GF	IP	BFP	H	R	ER	HR	SH	SF	HB	TBB	IBB	SO	WP	Bk	W	L	Pct.	ShO	Sv	ERA
1995 Cubs	R ChC	11	10	0	0	41.1	168	33	17	11	1	2	6	2	11	0	26	3	2	3	2	.600	0	0	2.40
1996 Rockford	A ChC	10	10	1	0	47.1	223	63	40	27	5	1	2	3	25	0	30	3	1	2	5	.286	0	0	5.13
Williamsprt	A- ChC	2	2	0	0	7	31	7	3	2	0	0	0	0	4	0	5	1	0	0	0	—	0	0	2.57
Danville	R+ Atl	1	0	0	0	3	11	2	1	1	0	0	0	0	1	0	4	1	0	0	0	—	0	0	3.00
Macon	A Atl	12	12	2	0	72	313	80	46	40	8	2	4	1	19	1	60	6	0	3	7	.300	1	0	5.00
1997 Durham	A+ Atl	30	1	0	5	55	255	60	33	31	5	2	2	4	32	0	44	5	0	2	5	.286	0	1	5.07
1998 Greenville	AA Atl	40	17	1	11	124.1	567	134	78	73	11	3	3	3	71	1	120	11	2	7	6	.538	0	3	5.28
1999 Richmond	AAA Atl	44	2	0	8	92	400	93	51	45	7	6	3	2	39	3	61	8	0	6	7	.462	0	1	4.40
2000 Richmond	AAA Atl	41	0	0	13	63.2	286	66	38	34	7	5	6	2	31	1	51	1	0	0	5	.000	0	3	4.81
Greenville	AA Atl	8	0	0	3	16	75	20	12	8	2	2	1	0	7	1	16	1	0	2	1	.667	0	1	4.50
2001 Richmond	AAA Atl	34	20	0	2	134.1	552	128	65	62	21	4	3	0	39	5	100	1	0	4	7	.364	0	1	4.15
2000 Atlanta	NL	1	0	0	0	2.2	15	4	4	4	2	0	0	1	2	0	2	0	0	0	0	—	0	0	13.50
7 Min. YEARS		233	74	4	45	656	2881	686	384	334	67	27	30	17	279	12	517	41	5	29	45	.392	1	10	4.58

Julio Vinas

Bats: Right **Throws:** Right **Pos:** 1B-23; DH-15; P-1 **Ht:** 6'1" **Wt:** 205 **Born:** 2/14/73 **Age:** 29

Year Team	Lg Org	G	AB	H	2B	3B	HR	TB	R	RBI	TBB	IBB	SO	HBP	SH	SF	SB	CS	SB%	GDP	Avg	OBP	SLG
1991 White Sox	R CWS	50	187	42	9	0	3	60	21	29	19	0	40	2	0	2	2	3	.40	5	.225	.300	.321
1992 South Bend	A CWS	33	94	16	3	0	0	19	7	10	9	0	17	1	0	2	1	3	.25	1	.170	.245	.202
Utica	A- CWS	47	151	37	6	4	0	51	22	24	11	0	29	2	1	5	1	2	.33	2	.245	.296	.338
1993 South Bend	A CWS	55	188	60	15	1	9	104	24	37	12	1	29	1	2	2	1	1	.50	2	.319	.360	.553
Sarasota	A+ CWS	18	65	16	2	1	1	23	5	7	5	0	13	0	0	0	0	0	—	2	.246	.300	.354
1994 South Bend	A CWS	121	466	118	31	1	9	178	68	75	43	4	75	4	6	6	0	2	.00	9	.253	.318	.382
1995 Birmingham	AA CWS	102	372	100	16	2	6	138	47	61	37	1	80	5	0	7	3	3	.50	6	.269	.337	.371
1996 Nashville	AAA CWS	104	338	80	18	2	11	135	48	52	36	2	63	2	0	4	1	4	.20	8	.237	.311	.399
1997 Nashville	AAA CWS	91	314	73	12	2	11	122	39	41	25	2	72	2	3	5	4	4	.50	6	.232	.289	.389
1998 Rochester	AAA Bal	62	199	70	15	4	6	111	26	40	12	0	30	1	1	2	2	1	.67	3	.352	.388	.558
1999 Rochester	AAA Bal	126	484	151	32	2	20	247	67	83	25	1	73	1	0	7	4	3	.57	13	.312	.342	.510
2000 Akron	AA Cle	20	63	16	3	1	1	24	12	8	11	0	10	3	0	1	0	0	—	2	.254	.385	.381
Pawtucket	AAA Bos	29	107	27	5	0	4	44	14	16	9	1	20	1	0	0	1	0	1.00	1	.252	.316	.411
2001 Rochester	AAA Bal	38	142	31	5	1	3	47	17	21	13	1	23	1	0	3	0	0	—	0	.218	.283	.331
11 Min. YEARS		896	3170	837	172	21	84	1303	417	504	267	13	574	26	13	46	20	26	.43	61	.264	.322	.411

Travis Wade

Pitches: Right **Bats:** Right **Pos:** RP-60 **Ht:** 6'3" **Wt:** 220 **Born:** 7/8/75 **Age:** 26

Year Team	Lg Org	G	GS	CG	GF	IP	BFP	H	R	ER	HR	SH	SF	HB	TBB	IBB	SO	WP	Bk	W	L	Pct.	ShO	Sv	ERA
1997 Kalamazoo	IND —	2	1	0	0	2.1	20	7	10	8	2	0	0	2	4	0	0	0	0	0	2	.000	0	0	30.86
1998 Rio Grande	IND —	20	0	0	10	21.2	116	33	27	27	3	0	2	4	18	1	16	4	1	1	3	.250	0	4	11.22
Lubbock	IND —	11	0	0	11	15	69	18	11	11	1	0	2	1	7	0	10	3	1	0	0	—	0	3	6.60
1999 Kissimmee	A+ Hou	1	0	0	1	1	4	1	0	0	0	0	0	0	0	0	2	0	0	0	0	—	0	0	0.00
Auburn	A- Hou	26	0	0	23	37.2	150	25	10	10	0	3	0	2	13	0	53	0	0	1	1	.500	0	11	2.39
Michigan	A Hou	10	0	0	5	14	78	22	18	15	2	0	0	2	11	1	9	1	0	0	0	—	0	2	9.64
2000 Kissimmee	A+ Hou	38	0	0	33	48.2	187	36	9	4	2	1	0	1	10	2	51	1	1	4	1	.800	0	18	0.74
Round Rock	AA Hou	23	0	0	17	31.2	135	33	18	15	2	0	3	5	7	0	26	1	0	2	1	.667	0	6	4.26
2001 Round Rock	AA Hou	60	0	0	54	65.2	286	67	33	23	7	4	0	5	22	3	56	2	2	2	3	.400	0	23	3.15
5 Min. YEARS		191	1	0	154	237.2	1045	242	136	113	19	8	7	22	92	7	223	12	5	10	11	.476	0	67	4.28

Paul Wagner

Pitches: Right **Bats:** Right **Pos:** SP-1; RP-1 **Ht:** 6'1" **Wt:** 210 **Born:** 11/14/67 **Age:** 34

Year Team	Lg Org	G	GS	CG	GF	IP	BFP	H	R	ER	HR	SH	SF	HB	TBB	IBB	SO	WP	Bk	W	L	Pct.	ShO	Sv	ERA
1989 Welland	A- Pit	13	10	0	1	50.1	220	54	34	25	4	1	1	1	15	0	34	4	0	4	5	.444	0	0	4.47
1990 Augusta	A Pit	35	4	0	20	72	313	71	30	22	3	3	3	2	30	3	71	7	0	7	7	.500	0	4	2.75
Salem	A+ Pit	11	4	0	3	36	159	39	22	20	7	0	0	0	17	1	28	3	0	0	1	.000	0	2	5.00
1991 Salem	A+ Pit	25	25	5	0	158.2	660	124	70	55	14	4	2	8	60	0	113	11	1	11	6	.647	2	0	3.12
1992 Carolina	AA Pit	19	19	2	0	121.2	513	104	52	41	3	6	5	3	47	1	101	6	0	6	6	.500	1	0	3.03
Buffalo	AAA Pit	8	8	0	0	39.1	181	51	27	24	1	2	1	1	14	0	19	2	0	3	3	.500	0	0	5.49
1996 Pirates	R Pit	1	1	0	0	3	11	2	0	0	0	0	0	1	0	0	4	0	0	0	0	—	0	0	0.00
1997 Carolina	AA Pit	12	3	0	1	16	90	25	20	18	3	1	1	1	16	0	20	3	1	0	1	.000	0	0	10.13
1998 Beloit	A Mil	1	1	0	0	5	21	7	4	4	0	0	1	1	0	0	3	1	0	0	1	.000	0	0	7.20
Louisville	AAA Mil	3	3	0	0	12.1	58	17	12	12	3	0	0	0	5	0	6	1	0	1	0	1.000	0	0	8.76
Richmond	AAA Atl	8	0	0	1	13.2	54	11	4	3	0	1	0	0	3	0	9	0	0	1	0	1.000	0	0	1.98
1999 Buffalo	AAA Cle	23	23	0	0	129.2	559	123	67	55	11	1	4	4	55	2	95	11	0	8	4	.667	0	0	3.82
2001 Norfolk	AAA NYM	2	1	0	0	6.2	33	12	6	6	2	0	0	0	2	0	2	1	0	1	1	.500	0	0	8.10
1992 Pittsburgh	NL	6	1	0	1	13	52	9	1	1	0	0	0	0	5	0	5	1	0	2	0	1.000	0	0	0.69
1993 Pittsburgh	NL	44	17	1	9	141.1	599	143	72	67	15	6	7	1	42	2	114	12	0	8	8	.500	1	2	4.27
1994 Pittsburgh	NL	29	17	1	4	119.2	534	136	69	61	7	8	4	8	50	4	86	4	0	7	8	.467	0	0	4.59
1995 Pittsburgh	NL	33	25	3	1	165	725	174	96	88	18	7	2	7	72	7	120	8	0	5	16	.238	1	1	4.80
1996 Pittsburgh	NL	16	15	1	0	81.2	361	86	49	49	10	5	1	3	39	2	81	7	0	4	8	.333	0	0	5.40
1997 Pittsburgh	NL	14	0	0	2	16	79	17	7	7	3	1	0	1	13	3	9	3	2	0	0	—	0	0	3.94
Milwaukee	AL	2	0	0	1	2	8	3	2	2	1	0	0	0	0	0	0	0	0	1	0	1.000	0	0	9.00

Year Team	Lg Org	G	GS	CG	GF	IP	BFP	H	R	ER	HR	SH	SF	HB	TBB	IBB	SO	WP	Bk	W	L	Pct.	ShO	Sv	ERA
1998 Milwaukee	NL	13	9	0	1	55.2	261	67	49	44	10	5	2	1	31	1	37	3	0	1	5	.167	0	0	7.11
1999 Cleveland	AL	3	0	0	1	4.1	24	5	4	2	0	0	0	2	3	0	0	0	0	1	0	1.000	0	0	4.15
9 Min. YEARS		161	99	7	26	664.1	2872	640	348	285	51	19	18	22	264	7	505	50	2	42	35	.545	3	6	3.86
8 Maj. YEARS		160	84	6	20	598.2	2643	640	349	321	64	34	17	22	255	19	452	38	2	29	45	.392	2	3	4.83

Dave Wainhouse

Pitches: Right **Bats:** Left **Pos:** RP-48; SP-1 **Ht:** 6'2" **Wt:** 200 **Born:** 11/7/67 **Age:** 34

Year Team	Lg Org	G	GS	CG	GF	IP	BFP	H	R	ER	HR	SH	SF	HB	TBB	IBB	SO	WP	Bk	W	L	Pct.	ShO	Sv	ERA
1989 Wst Plm Bch	A+ Mon	13	13	0	0	66.1	286	75	35	30	4	3	2	8	19	0	26	6	3	1	5	.167	0	0	4.07
1990 Wst Plm Bch	A+ Mon	12	12	2	0	76.2	327	68	28	18	1	0	3	5	34	0	58	2	3	6	3	.667	1	0	2.11
Jacksnville	AA Mon	17	16	2	0	95.2	428	97	59	46	8	2	3	7	47	2	59	2	0	7	7	.500	0	0	4.33
1991 Harrisburg	AA Mon	33	0	0	27	52	224	49	17	15	1	2	0	4	17	2	46	3	0	2	2	.500	0	11	2.60
Indianaplis	AAA Mon	14	0	0	8	28.2	127	28	14	13	1	2	1	3	15	1	13	3	0	2	0	1.000	0	1	4.08
1992 Indianaplis	AAA Mon	44	0	0	41	46	208	48	22	21	4	2	2	2	24	6	37	4	0	5	4	.556	0	21	4.11
1993 Calgary	AAA Sea	13	0	0	10	15.2	62	10	7	7	2	2	2	1	7	1	7	2	0	0	1	.000	0	5	4.02
1995 Syracuse	AAA Tor	26	0	0	21	24.1	110	29	13	10	1	1	1	2	11	3	18	4	0	3	2	.600	0	5	3.70
Portland	AA Fla	17	0	0	5	25	122	39	22	20	3	0	1	1	8	1	16	1	0	2	1	.667	0	0	7.20
Charlotte	AAA Fla	4	0	0	1	3.2	21	6	6	4	1	0	1	0	4	0	2	2	0	0	0	—	0	0	9.82
1996 Carolina	AA Pit	45	0	0	40	51.1	226	43	22	18	3	4	1	4	31	3	34	2	0	5	3	.625	0	25	3.16
1997 Calgary	AAA Pit	25	0	0	9	38	174	46	25	25	5	1	1	3	13	2	24	3	0	1	0	1.000	0	1	5.92
1998 Colo Sprngs	AAA Col	38	0	0	30	50	214	47	25	20	4	3	2	3	23	0	44	1	1	2	3	.400	0	4	3.60
1999 Colo Sprngs	AAA Col	38	0	0	35	42.1	175	42	19	15	6	1	0	2	7	1	42	0	0	1	3	.250	0	22	3.19
2000 Memphis	AAA StL	20	6	0	2	43	199	55	32	30	8	1	2	3	20	0	20	1	0	4	4	.500	0	0	6.28
2001 Iowa	AAA ChC	49	1	0	19	75.2	330	86	38	35	9	5	3	4	24	2	61	1	0	3	5	.375	0	6	4.16
1991 Montreal	NL	2	0	0	1	2.2	14	2	2	2	0	0	1	0	4	0	1	2	0	0	1	.000	0	0	6.75
1993 Seattle	AL	3	0	0	0	2.1	20	7	7	7	1	0	0	1	5	0	2	0	0	0	0	—	0	0	27.00
1996 Pittsburgh	NL	17	0	0	6	23.2	101	22	16	15	3	1	2	0	10	1	16	2	0	1	0	1.000	0	0	5.70
1997 Pittsburgh	NL	25	0	0	6	28	137	34	28	25	2	3	1	3	17	0	21	1	1	0	1	.000	0	0	8.04
1998 Colorado	NL	10	0	0	3	11	51	15	6	6	1	0	0	2	5	0	3	0	0	1	0	1.000	0	0	4.91
1999 Colorado	NL	19	0	0	11	28.2	131	37	22	22	6	0	3	0	16	0	18	1	0	0	0	—	0	0	6.91
2000 St. Louis	NL	9	0	0	4	8.2	44	13	10	9	2	1	0	2	4	1	5	1	0	0	1	.000	0	0	9.35
12 Min. YEARS		408	48	4	248	734.1	3234	768	384	327	61	29	26	51	304	24	507	37	7	45	43	.511	1	101	4.01
7 Maj. YEARS		85	0	0	31	105	498	130	91	86	15	5	7	8	61	2	66	7	1	2	3	.400	0	0	7.37

Tom Waligora

Pitches: Right **Bats:** Right **Pos:** RP-22 **Ht:** 6'8" **Wt:** 240 **Born:** 8/7/76 **Age:** 25

Year Team	Lg Org	G	GS	CG	GF	IP	BFP	H	R	ER	HR	SH	SF	HB	TBB	IBB	SO	WP	Bk	W	L	Pct.	ShO	Sv	ERA
1997 Cubs	R ChC	16	0	0	11	22.2	110	25	16	13	0	1	0	2	15	0	29	1	0	3	0	1.000	0	2	5.16
1998 Rockford	A ChC	35	0	0	28	33.2	150	36	22	18	3	1	3	1	14	2	32	6	0	0	4	.000	0	18	4.81
1999 Lansing	A ChC	50	1	0	20	82	365	78	44	39	8	5	5	4	38	1	56	8	0	2	6	.250	0	5	4.28
2000 Daytona	A+ ChC	55	0	0	18	78.2	345	78	51	46	8	5	3	6	29	1	61	7	0	10	4	.714	0	5	5.26
2001 West Tenn	AA ChC	22	0	0	8	31	129	22	13	12	3	0	0	2	13	0	36	3	0	4	1	.800	0	0	3.48
5 Min. YEARS		178	1	0	85	248	1099	239	146	128	22	12	11	15	109	4	214	25	0	19	15	.559	0	30	4.65

Adam Walker

Pitches: Left **Bats:** Left **Pos:** SP-17 **Ht:** 6'7" **Wt:** 205 **Born:** 5/28/76 **Age:** 26

Year Team	Lg Org	G	GS	CG	GF	IP	BFP	H	R	ER	HR	SH	SF	HB	TBB	IBB	SO	WP	Bk	W	L	Pct.	ShO	Sv	ERA
1997 Martinsvlle	R+ Phi	21	2	0	8	28.2	131	32	28	20	1	1	3	4	11	0	30	5	0	0	5	.000	0	2	6.28
1998 Piedmont	A Phi	15	15	0	0	84	337	60	21	19	2	2	1	3	21	0	114	7	1	9	1	1.000	0	0	2.04
1999 Clearwater	A+ Phi	26	25	3	1	149	646	156	80	65	7	6	3	3	52	0	100	9	2	9	7	.563	2	0	3.93
2000 Piedmont	A Phi	8	8	0	0	48.1	196	37	11	11	1	1	0	2	14	0	50	3	0	6	1	.857	0	0	2.05
Clearwater	A+ Phi	18	17	1	0	114	486	116	50	39	6	3	6	4	39	1	87	7	1	9	8	.529	0	0	3.08
2001 Reading	AA Phi	15	15	3	0	91	351	50	22	19	2	1	0	6	28	0	81	6	0	7	4	.636	3	0	1.88
Binghamton	AA NYM	2	2	0	0	4	17	3	0	0	0	0	0	0	2	0	7	0	0	0	0	—	0	0	0.00
5 Min. YEARS		105	84	7	9	519	2164	454	212	173	19	14	13	22	167	1	469	37	4	40	25	.615	5	2	3.00

Jamie Walker

Pitches: Left **Bats:** Left **Pos:** RP-30; SP-8 **Ht:** 6'2" **Wt:** 190 **Born:** 7/1/71 **Age:** 30

Year Team	Lg Org	G	GS	CG	GF	IP	BFP	H	R	ER	HR	SH	SF	HB	TBB	IBB	SO	WP	Bk	W	L	Pct.	ShO	Sv	ERA
1992 Auburn	A- Hou	15	14	0	0	83.1	341	75	35	29	4	4	1	6	21	0	67	4	1	4	6	.400	0	0	3.13
1993 Quad City	A Hou	25	24	1	1	131.2	585	140	92	75	12	10	5	6	48	1	121	12	0	3	11	.214	1	0	5.13
1994 Quad City	A Hou	32	18	0	4	125	569	133	80	58	10	14	3	16	42	2	104	5	1	8	10	.444	0	1	4.18
1995 Jackson	AA Hou	50	0	0	19	58	250	59	29	29	6	3	2	2	24	5	38	4	1	4	2	.667	0	2	4.50
1996 Jackson	AA Hou	45	7	0	13	101	424	94	34	28	7	3	1	8	35	2	79	2	0	5	1	.833	0	2	2.50
1997 Wichita	AA KC	5	0	0	0	6.2	32	6	8	7	1	1	1	2	5	0	6	0	0	0	1	.000	0	0	9.45
1998 Omaha	AAA KC	7	7	0	0	46.2	198	57	15	14	3	2	1	2	11	1	21	1	0	5	1	.833	0	0	2.70
1999 Royals	R KC	2	2	0	0	8	35	10	3	3	1	0	0	0	0	0	9	1	0	1	0	1.000	0	0	3.38
Omaha	AAA KC	4	4	0	0	17.1	79	22	12	9	1	1	2	2	4	0	11	0	0	0	1	.000	0	0	4.67
2000 Omaha	AAA KC	24	15	0	3	101.2	446	138	65	59	25	2	1	7	25	1	52	0	0	3	10	.231	0	0	5.22
2001 Buffalo	AAA Cle	38	8	0	5	93	406	104	44	40	12	1	2	7	27	1	51	4	2	7	2	.778	0	2	3.87
1997 Kansas City	AL	50	0	0	15	43	197	46	28	26	6	2	2	3	20	3	24	2	0	3	3	.500	0	0	5.44
1998 Kansas City	AL	6	2	0	2	17.1	86	30	20	19	5	1	1	2	3	0	15	0	0	0	1	.000	0	0	9.87
10 Min. YEARS		247	99	1	45	772.1	3365	838	417	351	82	41	19	58	242	13	559	33	5	40	45	.471	1	7	4.09
2 Maj. YEARS		56	2	0	17	60.1	283	76	48	45	11	3	3	5	23	3	39	2	0	3	4	.429	0	0	6.71

Mark Walker

Bats: Right **Throws:** Right **Pos:** OF-89; PH-8; DH-4 **Ht:** 6'1" **Wt:** 195 **Born:** 8/17/78 **Age:** 23

Year Team	Lg Org	G	AB	H	2B	3B	HR	TB	R	RBI	TBB	IBB	SO	HBP	SH	SF	SB	CS	SB%	GDP	Avg	OBP	SLG
2000 Salem-Keizr	A- SF	35	95	18	3	1	1	26	12	7	13	0	52	0	0	0	3	1	.75	0	.189	.287	.274
2001 Hagerstown	A SF	58	169	27	4	2	4	47	19	12	32	0	74	0	2	2	8	2	.80	5	.160	.291	.278
Shreveport	AA SF	43	90	21	6	1	3	38	14	9	8	0	36	0	0	1	2	1	.67	0	.233	.293	.422
2 Min. YEARS		136	354	66	13	4	8	111	45	28	53	0	162	0	2	3	13	4	.76	5	.186	.290	.314

Tyler Walker

Pitches: Right **Bats:** Right **Pos:** SP-15; RP-1 **Ht:** 6'3" **Wt:** 255 **Born:** 5/15/76 **Age:** 26

Year Team	Lg Org	G	GS	CG	GF	IP	BFP	H	R	ER	HR	SH	SF	HB	TBB	IBB	SO	WP	Bk	W	L	Pct.	ShO	Sv	ERA
1997 Mets	R NYM	5	0	0	5	9	37	8	1	1	0	1	0	0	2	1	9	0	0	0	0	—	0	3	1.00
Pittsfield	A- NYM	1	0	0	0	0.2	6	2	2	1	1	0	0	0	1	0	1	0	0	0	0	—	0	0	13.50
1998 Capital Cty	A NYM	34	13	0	3	115.2	503	122	63	53	9	3	4	3	38	0	110	8	1	5	5	.500	0	1	4.12
1999 St. Lucie	A+ NYM	13	13	2	0	79.2	329	64	31	26	6	3	2	3	29	2	64	4	1	6	5	.545	0	0	2.94
Binghamton	AA NYM	13	13	0	0	68	306	78	49	47	11	3	2	2	32	0	59	4	3	6	4	.600	0	0	6.22
2000 Binghamton	AA NYM	22	22	0	0	121	495	82	43	37	3	2	4	2	55	1	111	9	1	7	6	.538	0	0	2.75
Norfolk	AAA NYM	5	5	0	0	26.1	111	29	7	7	0	2	0	0	9	0	17	1	0	1	3	.250	0	0	2.39
2001 St. Lucie	A+ NYM	4	4	0	0	15.2	69	19	14	14	0	0	0	0	3	0	11	3	0	0	2	.000	0	0	8.04
Binghamton	AA NYM	4	3	0	0	22.1	88	9	2	1	1	3	1	0	13	1	13	1	0	1	0	1.000	0	0	0.40
Norfolk	AAA NYM	8	8	0	0	40.1	160	34	19	18	7	2	1	1	8	0	35	1	0	3	2	.600	0	0	4.02
5 Min. YEARS		109	81	2	8	498.2	2104	447	231	205	38	19	14	11	190	5	430	32	6	29	27	.518	0	4	3.70

Dave Walling

Pitches: Right **Bats:** Right **Pos:** SP-10 **Ht:** 6'6" **Wt:** 200 **Born:** 11/12/78 **Age:** 23

Year Team	Lg Org	G	GS	CG	GF	IP	BFP	H	R	ER	HR	SH	SF	HB	TBB	IBB	SO	WP	Bk	W	L	Pct.	ShO	Sv	ERA
1999 Staten Ilnd	A- NYY	14	14	0	0	80.1	331	76	31	28	3	1	2	2	18	1	82	1	3	8	2	.800	0	0	3.14
2000 Tampa	A+ NYY	9	9	2	0	58.2	237	48	17	13	1	1	2	4	12	0	45	2	0	7	2	.778	0	0	1.99
Norwich	AA NYY	14	14	2	0	85.1	378	101	54	50	10	3	3	6	26	0	70	2	5	3	9	.250	0	0	5.27
2001 Columbus	AAA NYY	1	1	0	0	6	25	5	5	4	1	0	2	1	0	0	7	0	0	0	1	.000	0	0	6.00
Norwich	AA NYY	5	5	1	0	31.2	140	44	23	19	1	0	1	1	4	0	24	2	0	3	2	.600	0	0	5.40
Tampa	A+ NYY	4	4	0	0	17.1	79	23	12	10	2	1	0	2	2	0	9	0	0	1	1	.500	0	0	5.19
3 Min. YEARS		47	47	5	0	279.1	1190	297	142	124	18	6	10	14	62	1	237	7	8	22	17	.564	0	0	4.00

Les Walrond

Pitches: Left **Bats:** Left **Pos:** SP-16 **Ht:** 6'0" **Wt:** 195 **Born:** 11/7/76 **Age:** 25

Year Team	Lg Org	G	GS	CG	GF	IP	BFP	H	R	ER	HR	SH	SF	HB	TBB	IBB	SO	WP	Bk	W	L	Pct.	ShO	Sv	ERA
1998 New Jersey	A- StL	13	10	0	0	51.2	228	52	31	23	1	1	2	0	24	0	52	3	0	2	4	.333	0	0	4.01
1999 Peoria	A StL	21	20	0	0	109	489	115	77	69	12	2	5	3	59	0	78	6	0	7	10	.412	0	0	5.70
2000 Potomac	A+ StL	27	27	0	0	151	632	134	66	56	9	1	3	7	54	0	153	12	1	10	5	.667	0	0	3.34
2001 New Haven	AA StL	16	16	1	0	81.1	354	68	41	35	5	3	3	2	46	0	67	6	0	2	8	.200	0	0	3.87
4 Min. YEARS		77	73	1	0	393	1703	369	215	183	27	7	13	12	183	0	350	27	1	21	27	.438	0	0	4.19

Trevor Wamback

Pitches: Right **Bats:** Right **Pos:** SP-10; RP-4 **Ht:** 6'3" **Wt:** 205 **Born:** 12/22/76 **Age:** 25

Year Team	Lg Org	G	GS	CG	GF	IP	BFP	H	R	ER	HR	SH	SF	HB	TBB	IBB	SO	WP	Bk	W	L	Pct.	ShO	Sv	ERA
1998 Expos	R Mon	12	7	1	3	43.2	176	39	16	12	2	1	0	1	2	0	33	1	0	5	1	.833	0	1	2.47
Vermont	A- Mon	3	2	0	1	10.1	46	8	8	7	2	0	0	1	4	0	7	1	0	0	1	.000	0	0	6.10
1999 Expos	R Mon	2	2	0	0	12.1	48	12	5	4	1	0	0	0	1	0	12	0	0	1	0	1.000	0	0	2.92
Cape Fear	A Mon	24	14	1	2	104.2	414	98	39	33	10	2	2	3	14	0	77	3	1	6	3	.667	0	1	2.84
2000 Jupiter	A+ Mon	19	18	2	1	112.1	471	113	54	48	10	4	0	6	21	0	62	3	0	7	7	.500	0	0	3.85
2001 Harrisburg	AA Mon	3	0	0	1	7.2	34	12	9	9	1	0	1	1	0	0	3	0	0	0	0	—	0	0	10.57
Quebec	IND —	9	8	1	0	46.2	201	52	28	20	5	4	4	5	13	1	19	3	1	5	1	.833	1	0	3.86
New Jersey	IND —	1	1	0	0	6	27	6	4	3	1	0	1	2	1	0	3	0	0	0	1	.000	0	0	4.50
Winnipeg	IND —	1	1	0	0	4	24	9	9	8	1	0	0	1	3	0	2	1	0	0	1	.000	0	0	18.00
4 Min. YEARS		74	53	5	8	347.2	1441	349	172	144	33	11	8	19	59	1	218	12	2	24	15	.615	1	2	3.73

Bryan Ward

Pitches: Left **Bats:** Left **Pos:** RP-20; SP-1 **Ht:** 6'2" **Wt:** 205 **Born:** 1/25/72 **Age:** 30

Year Team	Lg Org	G	GS	CG	GF	IP	BFP	H	R	ER	HR	SH	SF	HB	TBB	IBB	SO	WP	Bk	W	L	Pct.	ShO	Sv	ERA
1993 Elmira	A- Fla	14	11	0	2	61.1	291	82	41	34	6	2	4	4	26	2	63	5	5	2	5	.286	0	0	4.99
1994 Kane County	A Fla	47	0	0	40	55.2	235	46	27	21	4	3	4	2	21	2	62	2	0	3	4	.429	0	11	3.40
1995 Portland	AA Fla	12	11	1	5	72	321	70	42	36	9	1	1	2	31	3	71	7	3	7	3	.700	1	2	4.50
Brevard Cty	A+ Fla	11	11	0	0	72	296	68	27	23	5	4	0	2	17	0	65	1	1	5	1	.833	0	0	2.88
1996 Portland	AA Fla	28	25	2	0	146.2	633	170	97	80	23	9	6	7	32	3	124	0	2	9	9	.500	0	0	4.91
1997 Portland	AA Fla	12	12	0	0	76	316	77	42	33	17	2	2	2	19	1	69	6	0	6	3	.667	0	0	3.91
Charlotte	AAA Fla	15	14	2	0	75.1	349	102	62	58	17	5	4	4	30	4	48	5	1	2	9	.182	0	0	6.93
1998 Birmingham	AA CWS	29	0	0	24	68.2	187	33	19	11	0	2	3	1	25	3	40	5	0	2	3	.400	0	12	2.36
1999 Charlotte	AAA CWS	14	0	0	6	15.1	64	15	7	6	2	1	1	3	3	1	15	1	0	2	0	1.000	0	0	3.52
2000 Scranton-WB	AAA Phi	22	0	0	14	27.1	113	23	11	7	1	4	0	1	8	0	17	3	0	3	2	.600	0	6	2.30
Edmonton	AAA Ana	6	0	0	2	6.1	30	12	4	3	0	0	0	0	1	1	3	0	0	0	0	—	0	1	4.26
2001 Red Sox	R Bos	1	0	0	1	2	10	4	4	4	1	0	0	0	0	0	2	1	0	0	0	—	0	0	18.00
Sarasota	A+ Bos	1	0	0	0	1.1	13	7	7	5	2	0	0	0	1	0	1	0	0	0	1	.000	0	0	33.75
Pawtucket	AAA Bos	19	1	0	7	33.2	155	47	23	16	2	2	0	2	6	2	18	1	0	0	3	.000	0	0	4.28

Year Team	Lg Org	G	GS	CG	GF	IP	BFP	H	R	ER	HR	SH	SF	HB	TBB	IBB	SO	WP	Bk	W	L	Pct.	ShO	Sv	ERA
1998 Chicago	AL	28	0	0	9	27	116	30	13	10	4	0	1	0	7	0	17	0	0	1	2	.333	0	1	3.33
1999 Chicago	AL	40	0	0	8	39.1	183	63	36	33	10	0	1	0	11	1	35	2	0	0	1	.000	0	0	7.55
2000 Philadelphia	NL	20	0	0	8	19.1	79	14	5	5	2	1	2	0	8	0	11	1	0	0	0	—	0	0	2.33
Anaheim	AL	7	0	0	2	8	36	8	6	5	1	0	0	0	2	0	3	2	0	0	0	—	0	0	5.63
9 Min. YEARS		239	85	5	101	687	3013	750	410	337	89	35	25	28	220	22	598	37	12	41	43	.488	1	33	4.41
3 Maj. YEARS		95	0	0	27	93.2	414	115	60	53	17	1	4	0	28	1	66	5	0	1	3	.250	0	1	5.09

Jeremy Ward

Pitches: Right **Bats:** Right **Pos:** RP-46   **Ht:** 6'3" **Wt:** 220 **Born:** 2/24/78 **Age:** 24

		HOW MUCH HE PITCHED						WHAT HE GAVE UP												THE RESULTS					
Year Team	Lg Org	G	GS	CG	GF	IP	BFP	H	R	ER	HR	SH	SF	HB	TBB	IBB	SO	WP	Bk	W	L	Pct.	ShO	Sv	ERA
1999 High Desert	A+ Ari	4	4	0	0	8.2	35	5	2	2	0	0	0	1	3	0	12	0	0	0	0	—	0	0	2.08
El Paso	AA Ari	19	0	0	17	25.2	101	18	7	7	1	0	1	0	9	1	26	1	0	1	1	.500	0	7	2.45
Tucson	AAA Ari	1	0	0	0	1.2	8	2	0	0	0	0	0	0	2	0	1	1	0	0	0	—	0	0	0.00
2000 Diamondbcks	R Ari	2	2	0	0	2	6	0	0	0	0	0	0	0	0	0	2	0	0	0	0	—	0	0	0.00
Tucson	AAA Ari	5	0	0	2	3.1	17	3	2	2	0	0	0	1	5	0	1	0	0	0	1	.000	0	0	5.40
2001 El Paso	AA Ari	6	0	0	6	8	26	2	2	1	1	0	0	0	1	0	6	0	0	0	0	—	0	0	1.13
Tucson	AAA Ari	40	0	0	23	46	208	53	23	18	2	3	1	2	17	2	35	5	0	3	4	.429	0	13	3.52
3 Min. YEARS		77	6	0	48	95.1	401	83	36	30	4	3	2	4	37	3	83	7	4	4	6	.400	0	20	2.83

Jeremy Ware

Bats: Right **Throws:** Right **Pos:** OF-55; PH-20; DH-5; PR-1   **Ht:** 6'0" **Wt:** 205 **Born:** 10/23/75 **Age:** 26

		BATTING														BASERUNNING				PERCENTAGES		
Year Team	Lg Org	G	AB	H	2B	3B	HR	TB	R	RBI	TBB	IBB	SO	HBP	SH	SF	SB	CS	SB%	GDP	Avg	OBP	SLG
1995 Expos	R Mon	38	116	28	4	2	2	42	18	15	18	0	28	3	0	1	5	4	.56	2	.241	.355	.362
1996 Expos	R Mon	15	44	16	3	3	0	25	10	17	9	0	4	0	2	0	6	1	.86	0	.364	.472	.568
Vermont	A- Mon	32	94	18	2	0	0	20	12	6	15	0	25	0	1	0	5	3	.63	1	.191	.303	.213
1997 Cape Fear	A Mon	138	529	139	32	5	16	229	84	77	43	2	114	6	0	6	32	7	.82	6	.263	.322	.433
1998 Jupiter	A+ Mon	127	492	121	35	3	10	192	51	64	23	1	102	7	4	7	21	5	.81	16	.246	.285	.390
1999 Jupiter	A+ Mon	7	25	8	2	0	2	16	5	11	2	0	5	0	0	0	3	0	1.00	0	.320	.370	.640
Harrisburg	AA Mon	111	381	100	23	2	9	154	57	56	41	2	79	2	2	5	12	5	.71	19	.262	.333	.404
2000 Harrisburg	AA Mon	123	442	123	23	2	10	180	62	63	39	2	87	2	0	5	12	11	.52	10	.278	.336	.407
2001 Ottawa	AAA Mon	53	147	39	13	0	2	58	13	13	6	0	24	0	3	0	2	0	1.00	4	.265	.294	.395
Harrisburg	AA Mon	27	87	25	6	0	3	40	12	16	7	1	14	0	0	0	1	1	.50	0	.287	.340	.460
7 Min. YEARS		671	2357	617	143	17	54	956	324	338	203	8	482	20	12	24	99	37	.73	60	.262	.323	.406

Brandon Warriax

Bats: Right **Throws:** Right **Pos:** SS-120   **Ht:** 6'0" **Wt:** 165 **Born:** 6/23/79 **Age:** 23

		BATTING														BASERUNNING				PERCENTAGES		
Year Team	Lg Org	G	AB	H	2B	3B	HR	TB	R	RBI	TBB	IBB	SO	HBP	SH	SF	SB	CS	SB%	GDP	Avg	OBP	SLG
1997 Charlotte	A+ Tex	1	4	0	0	0	0	0	0	0	0	0	1	0	0	0	0	0	—	1	.000	.000	.000
Rangers	R Tex	47	166	36	5	2	0	45	21	14	13	0	47	1	4	2	6	3	.67	6	.217	.275	.271
1998 Savannah	A Tex	51	187	39	8	0	3	56	24	14	16	0	41	0	3	0	9	2	.82	2	.209	.271	.299
Pulaski	R+ Tex	61	209	53	11	0	1	67	33	20	20	0	42	3	0	1	2	4	.33	4	.254	.326	.321
Charlotte	A+ Tex	5	16	2	0	0	0	2	2	1	1	0	5	0	0	0	0	0	—	1	.125	.176	.125
1999 Savannah	A Tex	43	144	22	3	1	1	30	10	13	15	0	43	0	2	2	7	1	.88	1	.153	.230	.208
Pulaski	R+ Tex	65	232	59	9	2	9	99	44	35	18	0	68	3	6	2	11	1	.92	3	.254	.314	.427
2000 Rangers	R Tex	7	32	4	2	0	0	6	1	6	3	0	6	0	0	0	1	0	1.00	0	.125	.200	.188
Charlotte	A+ Tex	84	304	63	13	1	4	90	33	39	20	0	74	0	1	1	8	7	.53	7	.207	.255	.296
2001 Tulsa	AA Tex	23	74	10	5	0	0	15	4	3	3	0	31	0	5	0	0	0	—	0	.135	.169	.203
Charlotte	A+ Tex	97	320	61	13	4	6	100	34	28	22	0	84	3	7	1	4	6	.40	4	.191	.249	.313
5 Min. YEARS		484	1688	349	69	10	24	510	206	173	131	0	442	10	28	9	48	24	.67	29	.207	.267	.302

Rico Washington

Bats: Left **Throws:** Right **Pos:** 3B-49; 2B-23; C-2; SS-1; PH-1   **Ht:** 5'10" **Wt:** 182 **Born:** 5/30/78 **Age:** 24

		BATTING														BASERUNNING				PERCENTAGES		
Year Team	Lg Org	G	AB	H	2B	3B	HR	TB	R	RBI	TBB	IBB	SO	HBP	SH	SF	SB	CS	SB%	GDP	Avg	OBP	SLG
1997 Pirates	R Pit	28	98	24	6	0	1	33	12	11	4	1	13	4	0	1	1	0	1.00	2	.245	.299	.337
1998 Erie	A- Pit	51	197	65	14	2	6	101	31	31	17	2	33	7	0	0	1	2	.33	4	.330	.403	.513
Augusta	A Pit	12	50	15	2	1	2	25	12	12	7	0	9	2	0	1	2	0	1.00	0	.300	.400	.500
1999 Hickory	A Pit	76	287	102	15	1	13	158	70	50	48	7	45	8	0	6	5	1	.83	4	.355	.453	.551
Lynchburg	A+ Pit	57	205	58	7	0	7	86	31	32	30	0	45	4	1	2	4	1	.80	8	.283	.382	.420
2000 Altoona	AA Pit	135	503	130	22	7	8	190	74	59	55	1	74	5	9	4	4	9	.31	11	.258	.335	.378
2001 Altoona	AA Pit	75	291	88	17	0	4	117	31	29	21	3	49	5	1	0	5	5	.50	5	.302	.360	.402
5 Min. YEARS		434	1631	482	83	11	41	710	261	224	182	14	268	35	11	14	22	18	.55	34	.296	.375	.435

B.J. Waszgis

Bats: Right **Throws:** Right **Pos:** C-47; 1B-22; DH-21; PH-7   **Ht:** 6'2" **Wt:** 215 **Born:** 8/24/70 **Age:** 31

		BATTING														BASERUNNING				PERCENTAGES		
Year Team	Lg Org	G	AB	H	2B	3B	HR	TB	R	RBI	TBB	IBB	SO	HBP	SH	SF	SB	CS	SB%	GDP	Avg	OBP	SLG
1991 Bluefield	R+ Bal	12	35	8	1	0	3	18	8	8	5	0	11	1	0	0	3	0	1.00	1	.229	.341	.514
1992 Kane County	A Bal	111	340	73	18	1	11	126	39	47	54	2	94	4	3	2	3	2	.60	8	.215	.328	.371
1993 Frederick	A+ Bal	31	109	27	4	0	3	40	12	9	9	0	30	2	0	1	1	1	.50	2	.248	.314	.367
Albany	A Bal	86	300	92	25	3	8	147	45	52	27	0	55	6	0	5	4	0	1.00	8	.307	.370	.490
1994 Frederick	A+ Bal	122	426	120	16	3	21	205	76	100	65	2	94	5	3	4	6	1	.86	3	.282	.380	.481
1995 Bowie	AA Bal	130	438	111	22	0	10	163	53	50	70	1	91	9	1	3	2	4	.33	5	.253	.365	.372
1996 Rochester	AAA Bal	96	304	81	16	0	11	130	37	48	41	0	87	4	1	1	2	3	.40	7	.266	.360	.428
1997 Rochester	AAA Bal	100	315	82	15	1	13	138	61	48	56	1	78	9	4	4	1	1	.50	5	.260	.383	.438

Year Team	Lg Org	G	AB	H	2B	3B	HR	TB	R	RBI	TBB	IBB	SO	HBP	SH	SF	SB	CS	SB%	GDP	Avg	OBP	SLG
1998 Pawtucket	AAA Bos	66	208	42	9	0	9	78	31	41	26	0	52	0	4	3	2	4	.33	7	.202	.287	.375
1999 Columbus	AAA NYY	63	191	53	12	0	6	83	36	31	27	2	55	6	2	1	4	2	.67	4	.277	.382	.435
2000 Oklahoma	AAA Tex	77	259	68	11	3	13	124	45	62	55	0	68	4	0	1	2	2	.50	8	.263	.398	.479
2001 Calgary	AAA Fla	96	311	78	18	0	23	165	50	65	31	2	90	8	0	2	0	1	.00	10	.251	.332	.531
2000 Texas	AL	24	45	10	1	0	0	11	6	4	4	0	10	1	0	1	0	0	—	1	.222	.294	.244
11 Min. YEARS		990	3236	835	167	11	131	1417	493	561	466	10	805	58	18	27	30	21	.59	68	.258	.359	.438

Derek Wathan

Bats: Both   Throws: Right   Pos: SS-125; PH-2   Ht: 6'3"   Wt: 190   Born: 12/13/76   Age: 25

Year Team	Lg Org	G	AB	H	2B	3B	HR	TB	R	RBI	TBB	IBB	SO	HBP	SH	SF	SB	CS	SB%	GDP	Avg	OBP	SLG
1998 Utica	A- Fla	60	224	60	8	2	0	72	32	23	21	0	35	3	5	0	10	9	.53	6	.268	.339	.321
1999 Kane County	A Fla	125	469	119	18	4	1	148	71	49	53	2	54	5	10	3	33	12	.73	13	.254	.334	.316
2000 Brevard Cty	A+ Fla	91	364	94	18	6	6	142	53	49	45	4	54	2	5	2	19	11	.63	6	.258	.341	.390
Portland	AA Fla	41	141	31	3	2	0	38	13	17	13	0	20	1	0	2	3	1	.75	1	.220	.287	.270
2001 Portland	AA Fla	127	469	118	12	8	4	158	65	35	45	0	83	2	5	5	25	16	.61	12	.252	.317	.337
4 Min. YEARS		444	1667	422	59	22	11	558	234	173	177	6	246	13	25	12	90	49	.65	38	.253	.327	.335

Dusty Wathan

Bats: Right   Throws: Right   Pos: C-45; 1B-6; PH-4; DH-2; 3B-1   Ht: 6'4"   Wt: 215   Born: 8/22/73   Age: 28

Year Team	Lg Org	G	AB	H	2B	3B	HR	TB	R	RBI	TBB	IBB	SO	HBP	SH	SF	SB	CS	SB%	GDP	Avg	OBP	SLG
1994 Mariners	R Sea	35	86	18	2	0	1	23	14	7	11	0	13	3	0	0	0	0	—	0	.209	.320	.267
1995 Wisconsin	A Sea	5	11	1	0	0	1	4	1	3	0	0	3	1	0	0	0	0	—	0	.091	.167	.364
Everett	A- Sea	53	181	49	9	1	6	78	32	25	17	0	26	7	1	0	2	1	.67	4	.271	.356	.431
1996 Lancaster	A+ Sea	74	246	64	10	1	8	100	41	40	26	0	65	6	3	1	1	1	.50	5	.260	.344	.407
1997 Lancaster	A+ Sea	56	202	60	17	0	4	89	27	35	21	0	51	7	1	1	0	1	.00	7	.297	.381	.441
Memphis	AA Sea	49	149	40	4	1	4	58	20	19	19	0	28	5	0	1	1	1	.50	4	.268	.368	.389
1998 Tacoma	AAA Sea	19	51	15	1	1	0	18	6	8	6	0	10	2	2	0	0	0	—	4	.294	.390	.353
Orlando	AA Sea	69	234	60	10	0	2	76	32	21	28	2	39	15	2	2	3	1	.75	8	.256	.369	.325
1999 New Haven	AA Sea	96	333	93	16	2	4	125	37	37	24	1	60	12	4	1	4	1	.80	11	.279	.349	.375
2000 Tacoma	AAA Sea	64	203	66	12	0	3	87	25	29	15	1	28	12	4	1	0	2	.00	4	.325	.403	.429
2001 Portland	AA Fla	55	134	36	10	0	2	52	24	21	13	1	28	17	1	0	1	0	.00	3	.269	.402	.388
8 Min. YEARS		575	1830	502	91	6	35	710	259	245	180	5	351	87	18	7	11	9	.55	50	.274	.365	.388

Pat Watkins

Bats: Right   Throws: Right   Pos: OF-56; DH-10; PH-1; PR-1   Ht: 6'2"   Wt: 195   Born: 9/2/72   Age: 29

Year Team	Lg Org	G	AB	H	2B	3B	HR	TB	R	RBI	TBB	IBB	SO	HBP	SH	SF	SB	CS	SB%	GDP	Avg	OBP	SLG
1993 Billings	R+ Cin	66	235	63	10	3	6	97	46	30	22	0	44	2	1	1	15	4	.79	4	.268	.335	.413
1994 Winston-Sal	A+ Cin	132	524	152	24	5	27	267	107	83	62	3	84	7	1	6	31	13	.70	8	.290	.369	.510
1995 Winston-Sal	A+ Cin	27	107	22	3	1	4	39	14	13	10	0	24	0	1	2	1	0	1.00	5	.206	.269	.364
Chattanooga	AA Cin	105	358	104	26	2	12	170	57	57	33	4	53	3	0	4	5	5	.50	7	.291	.352	.475
1996 Chattanooga	AA Cin	127	492	136	31	2	8	195	63	59	30	0	64	7	2	4	15	11	.58	17	.276	.325	.396
1997 Chattanooga	AA Cin	46	177	62	15	1	7	100	35	30	15	1	16	2	0	1	9	3	.75	3	.350	.405	.565
Indianapols	AAA Cin	84	325	91	14	7	9	146	46	35	24	2	55	1	3	1	13	9	.59	10	.280	.330	.449
1998 Indianapols	AAA Cin	44	188	71	12	1	3	94	37	24	15	0	26	1	1	1	8	3	.73	5	.378	.424	.500
1999 Colo Sprngs	AAA Col	12	30	10	1	0	0	11	4	2	2	0	6	0	0	1	0	0	—	0	.333	.364	.367
Carolina	AA Col	88	312	93	27	1	3	131	38	40	24	0	49	6	1	3	6	5	.55	3	.298	.357	.420
2000 Chattanooga	AA Col	33	120	35	4	0	1	42	16	16	9	0	21	0	1	2	4	2	.67	3	.292	.336	.350
Toledo	AAA Det	77	304	76	12	0	8	112	50	36	19	0	28	2	3	2	2	4	.33	13	.250	.297	.368
2001 Omaha	AAA KC	67	245	62	12	1	7	97	29	29	13	0	41	4	4	3	2	7	.22	10	.253	.298	.396
1997 Cincinnati	NL	17	29	6	2	0	0	8	2	0	0	0	5	0	1	0	1	0	1.00	1	.207	.207	.276
1998 Cincinnati	NL	83	147	39	8	1	2	55	11	15	8	0	26	1	2	4	1	3	.25	1	.265	.300	.374
1999 Colorado	NL	16	19	1	0	0	0	1	2	0	2	0	5	0	1	0	0	0	—	1	.053	.143	.053
9 Min. YEARS		908	3417	977	191	24	95	1501	542	454	278	10	511	35	18	31	111	66	.63	88	.286	.343	.439
3 Maj. YEARS		116	195	46	10	1	2	64	15	15	10	0	36	1	4	4	2	3	.40	5	.236	.271	.328

Scott Watkins

Pitches: Left   Bats: Left   Pos: RP-10   Ht: 6'3"   Wt: 180   Born: 5/15/70   Age: 32

Year Team	Lg Org	G	GS	CG	GF	IP	BFP	H	R	ER	HR	SH	SF	HB	TBB	IBB	SO	WP	Bk	W	L	Pct.	ShO	Sv	ERA
1992 Kenosha	A Min	27	0	0	11	46.1	196	43	21	19	4	2	1	3	14	0	58	1	0	2	5	.286	0	1	3.69
1993 Fort Wayne	A Min	15	0	0	8	30.1	124	26	13	11	0	1	2	1	9	0	31	0	1	2	0	1.000	0	1	3.26
Fort Myers	A+ Min	20	0	0	10	27.2	125	27	14	9	0	2	0	1	12	0	41	0	1	2	2	.500	0	3	2.93
Nashville	AA Min	13	0	0	3	16.2	75	19	15	11	2	0	1	1	7	0	17	2	1	0	1	.000	0	0	5.94
1994 Nashville	AA Min	11	0	0	8	13.2	60	13	9	7	1	1	2	0	4	0	11	1	0	1	0	1.000	0	3	4.61
Salt Lake	AAA Min	46	0	0	26	57.1	269	73	46	43	10	4	5	1	28	5	47	1	1	2	6	.250	0	3	6.75
1995 Salt Lake	AAA Min	45	0	0	33	54.2	217	45	18	17	4	1	3	1	13	1	57	1	0	4	2	.667	0	20	2.80
1996 Salt Lake	AAA Min	47	0	0	29	50.1	244	60	46	43	6	5	3	2	34	5	43	3	1	4	6	.400	0	1	7.69
1997 Omaha	AAA KC	9	0	0	4	15.1	72	19	13	11	4	0	1	0	6	0	15	2	1	0	0	.---	0	0	6.46
New Haven	AA Col	13	0	0	8	15.1	58	9	6	6	1	1	1	1	3	0	8	3	0	2	0	1.000	0	0	3.52
1998 Tulsa	AA Tex	10	1	0	4	21	80	14	5	5	1	0	0	0	2	0	25	1	0	1	0	1.000	0	1	2.14
Oklahoma	AAA Tex	38	0	0	22	49.2	214	44	19	18	6	2	1	3	22	1	50	5	0	6	1	.857	0	2	3.26
1999 Iowa	AAA ChC	47	3	0	10	63	287	71	47	43	11	3	3	0	33	1	54	7	0	1	2	.333	0	0	6.14
2000 Colo Sprngs	AAA Col	43	7	0	7	81	364	93	51	39	6	3	4	3	43	1	42	6	2	3	1	.750	0	1	4.33
2001 Colo Sprngs	AAA Col	10	0	0	2	7.2	48	13	10	9	1	0	1	0	10	0	4	1	0	0	0	.000	0	0	10.57
1995 Minnesota	AL	27	0	0	7	21.2	94	22	14	13	2	1	3	0	11	1	11	0	0	0	0	.---	0	0	5.40
10 Min. YEARS		394	11	0	185	550	2433	569	333	291	57	25	27	19	240	14	503	36	8	30	27	.526	0	36	4.76

Steve Watkins

Pitches: Right **Bats:** Right **Pos:** SP-24; RP-4   **Ht:** 6'4" **Wt:** 190 **Born:** 7/19/78 **Age:** 23

		HOW MUCH HE PITCHED						WHAT HE GAVE UP												THE RESULTS					
Year Team	Lg Org	G	GS	CG	GF	IP	BFP	H	R	ER	HR	SH	SF	HB	TBB	IBB	SO	WP	Bk	W	L	Pct.	ShO	Sv	ERA
1998 Idaho Falls	R+ SD	2	1	0	0	2	21	10	12	9	3	1	0	0	4	0	0	0	0	0	1	.000	0	0	40.50
Padres	R SD	9	3	0	1	20.2	88	15	4	3	0	2	1	1	10	0	20	3	0	1	0	1.000	0	0	1.31
1999 Fort Wayne	A SD	4	4	0	0	17	83	24	17	16	3	1	0	2	9	0	21	1	0	0	3	.000	0	0	8.47
Idaho Falls	R+ SD	12	11	0	0	61.1	272	60	39	30	5	4	3	4	25	0	75	9	0	5	2	.714	0	0	4.40
2000 Rancho Cuca	A+ SD	27	27	0	0	151	652	118	75	62	10	8	6	1	90	0	163	10	2	7	6	.538	0	0	3.70
2001 Lk Elsinore	A+ SD	5	5	0	0	29.1	120	23	6	6	0	1	1	0	7	0	23	2	0	2	0	1.000	1	0	1.84
Mobile	AA SD	23	19	0	2	97.1	447	108	74	62	14	2	6	5	53	2	55	3	0	4	8	.333	0	0	5.73
4 Min. YEARS		82	70	1	3	378.2	1683	358	227	188	35	19	17	13	198	2	357	28	2	19	20	.487	1	0	4.47

Mark Watson

Pitches: Left **Bats:** Right **Pos:** RP-36   **Ht:** 6'4" **Wt:** 215 **Born:** 1/23/74 **Age:** 28

		HOW MUCH HE PITCHED						WHAT HE GAVE UP												THE RESULTS					
Year Team	Lg Org	G	GS	CG	GF	IP	BFP	H	R	ER	HR	SH	SF	HB	TBB	IBB	SO	WP	Bk	W	L	Pct.	ShO	Sv	ERA
1996 Helena	R+ Mil	13	13	0	0	60.1	262	59	43	32	2	1	2	1	28	0	68	7	0	5	2	.714	0	0	4.77
1997 Beloit	A Mil	8	7	0	0	32.1	153	40	33	24	3	0	3	1	20	0	33	3	0	0	3	.000	0	0	6.68
Ogden	R+ Mil	10	10	1	0	47.2	202	44	26	22	4	1	2	0	19	0	49	2	0	4	3	.571	0	0	4.15
1998 Columbus	A Cle	31	12	1	8	97.2	408	95	53	44	10	3	3	3	32	0	77	6	2	3	4	.429	0	0	4.05
Kinston	A+ Cle	1	1	0	0	6.1	26	3	4	0	0	0	1	0	2	0	8	0	0	0	1	.000	0	0	0.00
1999 Kinston	A+ Cle	11	4	0	1	43.1	163	28	7	5	1	0	0	0	10	0	40	1	1	6	0	1.000	0	0	1.04
Akron	AA Cle	19	17	0	1	110	500	143	64	53	9	6	7	6	38	0	57	6	2	9	8	.529	0	0	4.34
2000 Buffalo	AAA Cle	16	0	0	3	20.1	91	18	11	10	1	1	2	0	12	6	16	1	0	1	2	.333	0	1	4.43
Tacoma	AAA Sea	16	0	0	4	25	111	30	16	11	3	0	3	0	6	0	17	0	1	2	1	.667	0	0	3.96
2001 Tacoma	AAA Sea	3	0	0	2	4	20	4	2	1	1	0	0	0	2	0	1	0	0	0	1	.000	0	1	2.25
Akron	AA Cle	30	0	0	21	39.1	166	34	19	18	2	1	1	1	13	0	34	2	0	3	1	.750	0	4	4.12
Buffalo	AAA Cle	3	0	0	0	4	25	9	7	6	1	0	0	0	3	1	3	0	0	0	1	.000	0	0	13.50
2000 Cleveland	AL	6	0	0	1	6.1	33	12	7	6	0	0	0	1	2	0	4	0	0	0	1	.000	0	0	8.53
6 Min. YEARS		161	64	2	40	490.1	2127	507	285	226	37	13	24	12	185	7	403	28	6	33	27	.550	0	6	4.15

Justin Wayne

Pitches: Right **Bats:** Right **Pos:** SP-21; RP-1   **Ht:** 6'3" **Wt:** 200 **Born:** 4/16/79 **Age:** 23

		HOW MUCH HE PITCHED						WHAT HE GAVE UP												THE RESULTS					
Year Team	Lg Org	G	GS	CG	GF	IP	BFP	H	R	ER	HR	SH	SF	HB	TBB	IBB	SO	WP	Bk	W	L	Pct.	ShO	Sv	ERA
2000 Jupiter	A+ Mon	5	5	0	0	26.1	112	26	22	17	2	1	1	0	11	0	24	1	0	0	3	.000	0	0	5.81
2001 Jupiter	A+ Mon	8	7	0	0	41.2	166	31	16	14	0	0	2	3	9	0	35	2	0	2	3	.400	0	0	3.02
Harrisburg	AA Mon	14	14	2	0	92.2	398	87	28	27	4	3	1	9	34	0	70	5	0	9	2	.818	0	0	2.62
2 Min. YEARS		27	26	2	0	160.2	676	144	66	58	6	4	4	12	54	0	129	8	0	11	8	.579	0	0	3.25

Eric Weaver

Pitches: Right **Bats:** Right **Pos:** RP-24   **Ht:** 6'5" **Wt:** 230 **Born:** 8/4/73 **Age:** 28

		HOW MUCH HE PITCHED						WHAT HE GAVE UP												THE RESULTS					
Year Team	Lg Org	G	GS	CG	GF	IP	BFP	H	R	ER	HR	SH	SF	HB	TBB	IBB	SO	WP	Bk	W	L	Pct.	ShO	Sv	ERA
1992 Vero Beach	A+ LA	19	18	1	0	89.2	394	73	52	41	7	5	6	1	57	0	73	17	2	4	11	.267	0	0	4.12
1993 Bakersfield	A+ LA	28	27	0	0	157.2	703	135	89	75	10	2	9	2	118	2	110	16	0	6	11	.353	0	0	4.28
1994 Vero Beach	A+ LA	7	7	0	0	24	109	28	20	18	3	0	0	1	9	1	22	1	0	1	3	.250	0	0	6.75
1995 San Antonio	AA LA	27	26	1	1	141.2	635	147	83	64	10	9	7	7	72	1	105	8	2	8	11	.421	0	0	4.07
1996 San Antonio	AA LA	18	18	1	0	122.2	509	106	51	45	6	7	2	3	44	0	69	2	1	10	5	.667	1	0	3.30
Albuquerque	AAA LA	13	8	0	0	46.2	225	63	39	28	5	2	1	3	22	0	38	3	0	1	4	.200	0	0	5.40
1997 San Antonio	AA LA	13	13	2	0	84.2	363	80	43	34	4	1	4	5	38	0	60	2	0	7	2	.778	1	0	3.61
Albuquerque	AAA LA	21	8	0	5	68.2	335	101	53	49	6	3	4	2	38	1	54	4	0	0	3	.000	0	0	6.42
1998 Albuquerque	AAA LA	46	0	0	26	61.2	277	65	41	38	7	2	2	3	32	2	63	2	0	2	5	.286	0	3	5.55
1999 Tacoma	AAA Sea	16	3	0	5	25.2	105	22	11	11	4	0	1	1	7	0	22	1	0	1	2	.333	0	1	3.86
2000 Edmonton	AAA Ana	34	0	0	28	37	164	37	20	17	5	1	1	2	13	0	36	3	0	1	2	.333	0	13	4.14
2001 Birmingham	AA CWS	24	0	0	10	31.1	133	25	14	12	3	2	0	0	16	2	31	2	0	3	3	.500	0	2	3.45
1998 Los Angeles	NL	7	0	0	4	9.2	35	5	1	1	1	1	0	0	6	0	5	0	0	2	0	1.000	0	0	0.93
1999 Seattle	AL	8	0	0	2	9.1	52	14	12	11	2	0	0	0	8	1	14	5	0	0	1	.000	0	0	10.61
2000 Anaheim	AL	17	0	0	4	18.1	92	20	16	14	5	0	1	0	16	1	8	1	0	0	2	.000	0	0	6.87
10 Min. YEARS		266	128	5	75	891.1	3952	882	516	432	70	34	37	30	466	9	683	61	5	44	62	.415	2	19	4.36
3 Maj. YEARS		32	0	0	10	37.1	179	39	29	26	8	1	1	0	30	2	27	6	0	2	3	.400	0	0	6.27

Jake Weber

Bats: Left **Throws:** Right **Pos:** OF-122; DH-4; PH-4; PR-4; 2B-1   **Ht:** 5'11" **Wt:** 188 **Born:** 4/22/76 **Age:** 26

		BATTING															BASERUNNING				PERCENTAGES		
Year Team	Lg Org	G	AB	H	2B	3B	HR	TB	R	RBI	TBB	IBB	SO	HBP	SH	SF	SB	CS	SB%	GDP	Avg	OBP	SLG
1998 Everett	A- Sea	75	275	93	20	2	11	150	75	52	67	3	42	5	2	3	14	7	.67	3	.338	.471	.545
1999 New Haven	AA Sea	136	489	125	22	2	11	184	64	59	66	2	73	3	1	2	5	7	.42	7	.256	.346	.376
2000 New Haven	AA Sea	129	473	121	21	7	5	171	71	56	60	2	56	2	2	4	11	4	.73	9	.256	.340	.362
2001 San Antonio	AA Sea	126	451	132	28	4	4	180	66	58	40	1	53	8	3	4	11	6	.65	4	.293	.358	.399
4 Min. YEARS		466	1688	471	91	15	31	685	276	225	233	8	224	18	8	13	41	24	.63	23	.279	.370	.406

Jeremy Wedel

Pitches: Right **Bats:** Right **Pos:** RP-45　　　　**Ht:** 6'0" **Wt:** 195 **Born:** 11/27/76 **Age:** 25

		HOW MUCH HE PITCHED						WHAT HE GAVE UP												THE RESULTS				
Year Team	Lg Org	G	GS	CG	GF	IP	BFP	H	R	ER	HR	SH	SF	HB	TBB	IBB	SO	WP	Bk	W	L	Pct.	ShO	Sv	ERA
1998 Batavia	A- Phi	16	15	1	0	88.1	376	102	48	43	3	1	2	3	15	0	65	11	0	7	6	.538	0	0	4.38
1999 Piedmont	A Phi	23	0	0	17	50	202	46	19	12	2	1	1	3	8	0	40	2	0	5	3	.625	0	3	2.16
Clearwater	A+ Phi	4	0	0	1	5.1	21	4	1	1	0	0	0	0	1	0	3	1	0	—			0	0	1.69
2000 Clearwater	A+ Phi	39	0	0	23	71.2	283	43	19	17	1	7	2	3	30	1	45	4	0	5	4	.556	0	9	2.13
2001 Reading	AA Phi	45	0	0	18	63	278	67	33	26	4	3	0	6	16	2	43	1	1	5	3	.625	0	5	3.71
4 Min. YEARS		127	15	1	59	278.1	1160	262	120	99	10	12	5	15	70	3	196	19	1	22	16	.579	0	17	3.20

Chris Weekly

Bats: Left **Throws:** Right **Pos:** 1B-65; 3B-34; PH-10; DH-7; OF-3　　　　**Ht:** 6'2" **Wt:** 195 **Born:** 12/4/76 **Age:** 25

		BATTING															BASERUNNING				PERCENTAGES		
Year Team	Lg Org	G	AB	H	2B	3B	HR	TB	R	RBI	TBB	IBB	SO	HBP	SH	SF	SB	CS	SB%	GDP	Avg	OBP	SLG
1999 Medcine Hat	R+ Tor	71	257	77	18	2	6	117	43	42	29	0	43	1	1	2	12	2	.86	6	.300	.370	.455
2000 Hagerstown	A Tor	66	234	68	15	1	7	106	21	49	22	0	53	1	0	3	2	5	.29	8	.291	.350	.453
Dunedin	A+ Tor	34	120	30	7	0	5	52	23	22	14	0	30	3	1	1	0	2	.00	0	.250	.341	.433
2001 Dunedin	A+ Tor	67	240	61	12	1	4	87	33	47	26	1	68	4	2	3	2	2	.50	5	.254	.333	.363
Tennessee	AA Tor	45	131	34	4	1	4	52	16	23	14	1	35	4	2	0	0	2	.00	3	.260	.349	.397
3 Min. YEARS		283	982	270	56	5	26	414	136	183	105	2	229	13	6	9	16	13	.55	22	.275	.350	.422

Clint Weibl

Pitches: Right **Bats:** Right **Pos:** SP-2　　　　**Ht:** 6'3" **Wt:** 180 **Born:** 3/17/75 **Age:** 27

		HOW MUCH HE PITCHED						WHAT HE GAVE UP												THE RESULTS				
Year Team	Lg Org	G	GS	CG	GF	IP	BFP	H	R	ER	HR	SH	SF	HB	TBB	IBB	SO	WP	Bk	W	L	Pct.	ShO	Sv	ERA
1996 Johnson Cty	R+ StL	7	7	0	0	44	172	27	12	10	1	0	0	1	12	0	51	0	0	4	1	.800	0	0	2.05
Peoria	A StL	5	5	0	0	29.2	122	27	16	16	2	0	1	2	7	0	21	0	0	1	2	.333	0	0	4.85
1997 Pr William	A+ StL	29	29	0	0	163	718	185	90	84	18	5	2	9	62	2	135	3	1	12	11	.522	0	0	4.64
1998 Memphis	AAA StL	1	1	0	0	5.2	24	6	5	4	0	0	0	0	2	0	2	2	0	1	0	1.000	0	0	6.35
Arkansas	AA StL	25	23	0	0	139	616	161	86	83	22	4	9	5	53	2	85	3	0	12	10	.545	0	0	5.37
1999 Arkansas	AA StL	28	17	1	2	110	483	121	59	57	11	3	0	3	49	1	75	4	1	4	9	.308	0	0	4.66
Memphis	AAA StL	5	0	0	1	8.1	36	10	9	5	2	1	1	0	2	0	8	0	0	1	0	1.000	0	0	5.40
2000 Arkansas	AA StL	10	9	0	0	57	243	57	35	30	10	0	2	1	19	0	51	1	0	3	3	.500	0	0	4.74
Memphis	AAA StL	19	18	2	0	120.2	481	98	45	38	11	1	2	6	37	0	92	1	1	9	4	.692	2	0	2.83
2001 Memphis	AAA StL	2	2	0	0	12	48	10	3	3	0	0	1	2	2	0	9	0	0	1	0	1.000	0	0	2.25
6 Min. YEARS		131	111	3	3	689.1	2943	702	360	330	77	14	18	29	245	5	529	14	3	47	41	.534	2	0	4.31

Brad Weis

Pitches: Left **Bats:** Left **Pos:** RP-43　　　　**Ht:** 5'11" **Wt:** 185 **Born:** 11/29/77 **Age:** 24

		HOW MUCH HE PITCHED						WHAT HE GAVE UP												THE RESULTS				
Year Team	Lg Org	G	GS	CG	GF	IP	BFP	H	R	ER	HR	SH	SF	HB	TBB	IBB	SO	WP	Bk	W	L	Pct.	ShO	Sv	ERA
1999 Elizabethtn	R+ Min	26	0	0	12	33.1	147	24	15	8	2	0	1	1	17	0	39	3	0	0	1	.000	0	3	2.16
2000 Quad City	A Min	40	0	0	22	60	255	55	20	17	9	0	3	6	22	5	56	4	1	1	2	.333	0	0	2.55
2001 Quad City	A Min	22	0	0	7	39.1	181	38	15	3	0	1	1	2	19	2	43	5	0	4	0	1.000	0	2	0.69
Fort Myers	A+ Min	17	0	0	8	20.2	94	20	9	6	1	2	3	2	10	2	26	1	0	1	1	.500	0	0	2.61
New Britain	AA Min	4	0	0	2	7	32	9	5	4	0	0	1	2	1	0	8	4	0	0	0	—	0	0	5.14
3 Min. YEARS		109	0	0	51	160.1	709	146	64	38	12	3	9	13	69	9	172	17	1	6	4	.600	0	5	2.13

Eric Welsh

Bats: Left **Throws:** Left **Pos:** 1B-120; PH-5; DH-4; OF-2　　　　**Ht:** 6'3" **Wt:** 200 **Born:** 9/17/76 **Age:** 25

		BATTING															BASERUNNING				PERCENTAGES		
Year Team	Lg Org	G	AB	H	2B	3B	HR	TB	R	RBI	TBB	IBB	SO	HBP	SH	SF	SB	CS	SB%	GDP	Avg	OBP	SLG
1997 Billings	R+ Cin	67	260	82	13	2	11	132	41	54	18	1	38	2	0	3	2	4	.33	3	.315	.360	.508
1998 Burlington	A Cin	135	525	136	33	3	7	196	49	68	27	1	112	9	1	3	7	6	.54	5	.259	.305	.373
1999 Rockford	A Cin	101	368	103	23	0	16	174	52	64	23	3	57	1	0	2	3	2	.60	9	.280	.322	.473
2000 Dayton	A Cin	41	142	40	11	0	13	90	29	35	17	1	35	3	0	1	0	0	.00	2	.282	.368	.634
Chattanooga	AA Cin	53	171	48	12	0	5	75	23	29	15	0	44	2	1	2	5	5	.50	2	.281	.342	.439
2001 Chattanooga	AA Cin	25	69	14	2	0	3	25	5	11	3	0	24	0	0	2	0	2	.00	2	.203	.230	.362
Mudville	A+ Cin	105	399	103	24	0	20	187	65	64	38	8	107	10	1	6	0	0	—	11	.258	.333	.469
5 Min. YEARS		527	1934	526	118	5	75	879	264	325	141	14	417	27	3	19	17	19	.47	34	.272	.327	.454

Jayson Werth

Bats: Right **Throws:** Right **Pos:** C-55; DH-43; 1B-28; PR-1　　　　**Ht:** 6'5" **Wt:** 190 **Born:** 5/20/79 **Age:** 23

		BATTING															BASERUNNING				PERCENTAGES		
Year Team	Lg Org	G	AB	H	2B	3B	HR	TB	R	RBI	TBB	IBB	SO	HBP	SH	SF	SB	CS	SB%	GDP	Avg	OBP	SLG
1997 Orioles	R Bal	32	88	26	6	0	1	35	16	8	22	0	22	0	0	1	7	1	.88	0	.295	.432	.398
1998 Delmarva	A Bal	120	408	108	20	3	8	158	71	53	50	0	92	15	1	2	21	6	.78	14	.265	.364	.387
Bowie	AA Bal	5	19	3	2	0	0	5	2	1	2	0	6	0	0	0	1	0	1.00	0	.158	.238	.263
1999 Frederick	A+ Bal	66	236	72	10	1	3	93	41	30	37	2	37	3	1	2	16	3	.84	4	.305	.403	.394
Bowie	AA Bal	35	121	33	5	1	1	43	18	11	17	0	26	2	1	3	7	1	.88	5	.273	.364	.355
2000 Frederick	A+ Bal	24	83	23	3	0	2	32	16	18	10	1	15	0	1	2	5	1	.83	3	.277	.347	.386
Bowie	AA Bal	85	276	63	16	2	5	98	47	26	54	1	50	4	4	1	9	3	.75	10	.228	.361	.355
2001 Dunedin	A+ Tor	21	70	14	3	0	2	23	9	14	17	0	19	0	0	0	1	1	.50	2	.200	.356	.329
Tennessee	AA Tor	104	369	105	23	1	18	184	51	69	63	0	93	3	1	7	12	3	.80	5	.285	.387	.499
5 Min. YEARS		492	1670	447	88	8	40	671	271	230	272	4	360	27	9	18	79	19	.81	39	.268	.375	.402

313

Barry Wesson

Bats: Right **Throws:** Right **Pos:** OF-133; PH-2; PR-1 **Ht:** 6'2" **Wt:** 195 **Born:** 4/6/77 **Age:** 25

Year Team	Lg Org	G	AB	H	2B	3B	HR	TB	R	RBI	TBB	IBB	SO	HBP	SH	SF	SB	CS	SB%	GDP	Avg	OBP	SLG
1995 Astros	R Hou	45	138	26	2	2	2	38	14	18	19	0	40	1	1	1	4	0	1.00	2	.188	.289	.275
Jackson	AA Hou	4	3	2	0	1	0	4	2	1	0	0	0	0	0	0	0	0	—	0	.667	.667	1.333
1996 Auburn	A- Hou	55	176	28	7	0	0	35	11	12	12	1	46	1	1	3	5	3	.63	5	.159	.214	.199
1997 Auburn	A- Hou	58	208	54	7	3	3	76	24	26	10	0	45	1	1	1	8	4	.67	1	.260	.295	.365
1998 Quad City	A Hou	138	493	124	21	2	7	170	71	43	32	1	90	5	2	0	22	12	.65	10	.252	.304	.345
1999 Kissimmee	A+ Hou	115	352	76	15	1	4	105	32	34	26	0	84	4	2	2	8	7	.53	3	.216	.276	.298
2000 Kissimmee	A+ Hou	81	308	84	21	3	5	126	50	35	33	0	66	2	4	1	24	5	.83	2	.273	.346	.409
Round Rock	AA Hou	39	110	26	1	2	2	37	12	15	10	0	32	0	0	2	6	2	.75	2	.236	.295	.336
2001 Round Rock	AA Hou	133	472	119	23	7	16	204	67	54	41	0	135	6	7	4	20	10	.67	4	.252	.317	.432
7 Min. YEARS		668	2260	539	97	21	39	795	283	238	183	2	538	20	18	14	97	43	.69	29	.238	.300	.352

Marty Weymouth

Pitches: Right **Bats:** Right **Pos:** RP-10 **Ht:** 6'2" **Wt:** 180 **Born:** 8/6/77 **Age:** 24

Year Team	Lg Org	G	GS	CG	GF	IP	BFP	H	R	ER	HR	SH	SF	HB	TBB	IBB	SO	WP	Bk	W	L	Pct.	ShO	Sv	ERA
1995 Mariners	R Sea	9	4	0	1	31.2	144	37	23	14	2	1	1	2	10	0	26	3	1	2	3	.400	0	0	3.98
1996 Everett	A- Sea	10	10	0	0	41	185	46	28	22	3	0	2	0	16	0	35	9	0	2	3	.400	0	0	4.83
1997 Wisconsin	A Sea	23	19	0	0	110.1	484	116	75	62	14	2	3	3	33	1	83	5	2	5	7	.417	0	0	5.06
1998 Hickory	A CWS	31	14	0	10	112	499	125	74	54	7	3	5	7	32	0	99	9	0	5	4	.444	0	3	4.34
1999 Winston-Sal	A+ CWS	41	0	0	16	57.1	257	62	35	30	1	3	1	1	21	3	42	3	1	5	6	.455	0	2	4.71
2000 Valley	IND —	1	1	0	0	3.2	18	1	3	3	0	0	1	1	5	0	2	2	0	0	1	.000	0	0	7.36
Birmingham	AA CWS	37	0	0	23	44.1	194	47	26	18	3	6	3	3	15	3	33	2	0	0	5	.000	0	13	3.65
2001 Birmingham	AA CWS	10	0	0	4	9.2	47	13	9	8	0	1	0	0	5	1	5	2	0	0	0	—	0	0	7.45
7 Min. YEARS		162	48	0	54	410	1828	447	273	211	30	16	16	17	137	8	325	35	4	18	30	.375	0	18	4.63

Matt Whisenant

Pitches: Left **Bats:** Right **Pos:** RP-14; SP-10 **Ht:** 6'3" **Wt:** 215 **Born:** 6/8/71 **Age:** 31

Year Team	Lg Org	G	GS	CG	GF	IP	BFP	H	R	ER	HR	SH	SF	HB	TBB	IBB	SO	WP	Bk	W	L	Pct.	ShO	Sv	ERA
1990 Princeton	R+ Phi	9	2	0	2	15	85	16	27	19	3	0	1	3	20	0	25	7	0	0	0	—	0	0	11.40
1991 Batavia	A- Phi	11	10	0	1	47.2	208	31	19	13	2	1	1	2	42	0	55	4	2	2	1	.667	0	0	2.45
1992 Spartanburg	A Phi	27	27	2	0	150.2	652	117	69	54	9	5	6	10	85	0	151	10	6	11	7	.611	0	0	3.23
1993 Kane County	A Fla	15	15	0	0	71	331	68	45	37	3	8	2	3	56	0	74	8	3	2	6	.250	0	0	4.69
1994 Brevard Cty	A+ Fla	28	26	5	0	160	679	125	71	60	7	6	7	9	82	2	103	18	1	6	9	.400	1	0	3.38
1995 Portland	AA Fla	23	22	2	0	128.2	544	106	57	50	8	7	4	9	65	3	107	8	0	10	6	.625	0	0	3.50
1996 Charlotte	AAA Fla	28	22	1	1	121	590	149	107	93	15	8	2	3	101	3	97	30	0	8	10	.444	0	0	6.92
1997 Brevard Cty	A+ Fla	2	1	0	0	3.1	15	3	3	3	0	0	0	0	3	0	4	1	0	0	0	—	0	0	8.10
Charlotte	AAA Fla	16	0	0	4	15	73	16	12	12	0	0	0	0	12	0	19	4	0	2	1	.667	0	0	7.20
2000 Las Vegas	AAA SD	33	0	0	8	39	190	49	26	23	3	0	0	3	26	2	24	4	0	0	3	.000	0	0	5.31
2001 Las Vegas	AAA LA	24	10	0	4	60.1	287	83	49	49	5	2	4	3	36	2	42	3	0	1	7	.125	0	0	7.31
1997 Florida	NL	4	0	0	2	2.2	19	4	6	5	0	1	0	0	6	0	4	0	0	0	0	—	0	0	16.88
Kansas City	AL	24	0	0	3	19	86	15	7	6	0	0	0	3	12	0	16	3	0	1	0	1.000	0	0	2.84
1998 Kansas City	AL	70	0	0	23	60.2	267	61	37	33	3	1	5	3	33	2	45	9	0	2	1	.667	0	2	4.90
1999 Kansas City	AL	48	0	0	21	39.2	184	40	28	28	4	1	0	7	26	1	27	1	0	4	4	.500	0	1	6.35
San Diego	NL	19	0	0	4	14.2	60	10	6	6	0	0	0	0	10	1	10	0	0	0	1	.000	0	0	3.68
2000 San Diego	NL	24	0	0	12	21.1	95	16	12	9	1	1	2	0	17	1	12	5	0	2	2	.500	0	0	3.80
10 Min. YEARS		216	135	10	20	811.2	3654	763	485	413	55	37	27	43	528	12	701	97	12	42	50	.457	1	1	4.58
4 Maj. YEARS		189	0	0	65	158	711	146	96	87	8	4	7	13	104	5	114	18	0	9	8	.529	0	3	4.96

Chad Whitaker

Bats: Left **Throws:** Right **Pos:** OF-35; DH-13; PH-5; PR-1 **Ht:** 6'2" **Wt:** 190 **Born:** 9/16/76 **Age:** 25

Year Team	Lg Org	G	AB	H	2B	3B	HR	TB	R	RBI	TBB	IBB	SO	HBP	SH	SF	SB	CS	SB%	GDP	Avg	OBP	SLG
1995 Burlington	R+ Cle	47	181	43	13	1	5	73	20	27	14	1	59	1	0	1	2	3	.40	1	.238	.294	.403
1996 Columbus	A Cle	66	234	55	10	1	12	103	32	29	25	1	80	1	0	1	2	2	.50	4	.235	.310	.440
1997 Columbus	A Cle	109	432	118	25	2	12	183	48	72	23	3	144	5	0	2	3	0	1.00	6	.273	.316	.424
1998 Kinston	A+ Cle	127	455	98	25	0	10	153	46	48	34	1	148	1	0	0	16	10	.62	6	.215	.271	.336
1999 Kinston	A+ Cle	76	280	67	14	0	9	108	34	36	21	1	62	1	0	2	2	3	.40	14	.239	.293	.386
Akron	AA Cle	41	149	48	12	2	5	79	18	38	15	0	40	0	0	2	0	1	.00	3	.322	.380	.530
2000 Akron	AA Cle	104	367	86	11	3	7	124	44	50	40	0	96	1	1	4	3	4	.43	5	.234	.308	.338
2001 Akron	AA Cle	51	155	37	9	1	6	66	16	18	13	0	34	1	0	4	2	1	.67	0	.239	.295	.426
7 Min. YEARS		621	2253	552	119	10	66	889	258	318	185	7	663	11	1	16	30	24	.56	39	.245	.303	.395

Bill White

Pitches: Left **Bats:** Left **Pos:** SP-26 **Ht:** 6'3" **Wt:** 210 **Born:** 11/20/78 **Age:** 23

Year Team	Lg Org	G	GS	CG	GF	IP	BFP	H	R	ER	HR	SH	SF	HB	TBB	IBB	SO	WP	Bk	W	L	Pct.	ShO	Sv	ERA
2000 Diamondbcks	R Ari	4	1	0	0	6	25	3	4	4	0	0	1	0	5	0	9	3	0	0	1	.000	0	0	6.00
South Bend	A Ari	1	1	0	0	2.2	14	3	1	1	0	0	0	0	3	0	5	1	0	0	0	—	0	0	3.38
2001 South Bend	A Ari	19	19	0	0	111.1	465	90	53	47	9	4	2	4	53	0	103	5	1	9	3	.750	0	0	3.80
El Paso	AA Ari	7	7	0	0	37.2	165	38	23	19	2	2	2	3	20	0	26	6	1	0	4	.000	0	0	4.54
2 Min. YEARS		31	28	0	0	157.2	669	134	81	71	11	6	5	7	81	0	143	15	2	9	8	.529	0	0	4.05

Matt White

Pitches: Right **Bats:** Right **Pos:** SP-7   **Ht:** 6'5" **Wt:** 230 **Born:** 8/13/78 **Age:** 23

Year Team	Lg Org	G	GS	CG	GF	IP	BFP	H	R	ER	HR	SH	SF	HB	TBB	IBB	SO	WP	Bk	W	L	Pct.	ShO	Sv	ERA
1997 Hudson Val	A- TB	15	15	0	0	84	369	78	44	38	3	3	2	11	29	0	82	11	1	4	6	.400	0	0	4.07
1998 Chston-SC	A TB	12	12	0	0	75.1	316	72	41	32	1	3	2	5	21	0	59	10	1	4	3	.571	0	0	3.82
St. Pete	A+ TB	17	17	1	0	95.2	414	107	70	59	10	2	5	6	41	0	64	12	0	4	8	.333	0	0	5.55
1999 St. Pete	A+ TB	21	20	2	0	113	498	125	75	65	6	2	6	8	33	0	92	10	1	9	7	.563	0	0	5.18
2000 Orlando	AA TB	20	20	2	0	120	505	94	56	50	10	2	5	15	58	0	98	7	1	7	6	.538	0	0	3.75
Durham	AAA TB	6	6	0	0	35	153	36	14	11	1	0	0	3	16	1	28	3	0	3	2	.600	0	0	2.83
2001 Durham	AAA TB	7	7	0	0	30	144	33	28	26	4	1	4	4	25	0	16	9	0	0	5	.000	0	0	7.80
5 Min. YEARS		98	97	5	0	553	2418	545	328	281	35	13	24	52	223	1	439	62	4	31	37	.456	0	0	4.57

Matt White

Pitches: Left **Bats:** Right **Pos:** SP-25   **Ht:** 6'1" **Wt:** 180 **Born:** 8/19/77 **Age:** 24

Year Team	Lg Org	G	GS	CG	GF	IP	BFP	H	R	ER	HR	SH	SF	HB	TBB	IBB	SO	WP	Bk	W	L	Pct.	ShO	Sv	ERA
1998 Burlington	R+ Cle	8	8	0	0	46.1	190	34	14	10	2	0	2	0	24	0	47	4	4	4	1	.800	0	0	1.94
Watertown	A- Cle	6	6	0	0	27.1	120	31	19	13	4	0	2	2	11	1	24	1	2	3	2	.600	0	0	4.28
1999 Columbus	A Cle	19	18	1	0	95.1	414	99	67	56	12	3	3	5	31	0	75	7	1	3	10	.231	0	0	5.29
2000 Kinston	A+ Cle	28	26	2	1	143.2	616	136	76	65	14	7	7	10	63	0	115	7	1	11	9	.550	0	0	4.07
2001 Akron	AA Cle	25	25	0	0	144	618	151	84	77	18	6	3	3	60	1	72	7	2	8	10	.444	0	0	4.81
4 Min. YEARS		86	83	3	1	456.2	1958	451	260	221	48	18	17	20	189	2	333	26	10	29	32	.475	0	0	4.36

Walt White

Bats: Right **Throws:** Right **Pos:** 2B-35; SS-22; 3B-3; PH-3; PR-2   **Ht:** 6'0" **Wt:** 195 **Born:** 12/12/71 **Age:** 30

Year Team	Lg Org	G	AB	H	2B	3B	HR	TB	R	RBI	TBB	IBB	SO	HBP	SH	SF	SB	CS	SB%	GDP	Avg	OBP	SLG
1994 Elmira	A- Fla	70	215	57	7	0	0	64	41	19	27	0	45	4	2	1	0	2	.00	4	.265	.356	.298
1995 Kane County	A Fla	63	207	59	18	2	1	84	30	23	32	0	52	3	5	3	3	2	.60	3	.285	.384	.406
1996 Kane County	A Fla	95	308	54	15	3	1	78	26	24	35	0	90	4	5	1	1	4	.20	3	.175	.267	.253
1997 Brevard Cty	A+ Fla	54	163	33	8	0	1	44	18	15	14	1	41	1	0	1	0	0	—	4	.202	.268	.270
1998 Brevard Cty	A+ Fla	13	39	6	0	0	0	6	6	4	7	0	9	0	0	0	0	2	.00	2	.154	.283	.154
Portland	AA Fla	70	203	55	9	2	6	86	23	25	16	0	53	4	2	2	1	1	.50	5	.271	.333	.424
1999 El Paso	AA Ari	13	50	6	3	0	0	9	4	1	2	0	13	0	0	0	0	0	—	1	.120	.154	.180
Tucson	AAA Ari	54	153	31	8	1	3	50	18	13	14	1	39	0	1	1	0	0	—	1	.203	.268	.327
2000 Tucson	AAA Ari	23	55	15	4	0	1	22	4	10	5	1	10	0	2	0	1	0	1.00	1	.273	.333	.400
El Paso	AA Ari	53	158	45	9	1	1	59	20	19	15	1	37	3	4	1	3	2	.60	3	.285	.356	.373
2001 Tucson	AAA Ari	35	79	17	4	1	0	23	11	8	8	0	23	0	2	0	1	0	1.00	1	.215	.287	.291
El Paso	AA Ari	27	86	13	2	0	0	15	7	3	7	1	25	0	1	0		1	.00	1	.151	.215	.174
8 Min. YEARS		570	1716	391	87	10	14	540	208	164	182	5	437	19	24	10	10	14	.42	34	.228	.307	.315

Shad Whiteley

Pitches: Right **Bats:** Right **Pos:** RP-10   **Ht:** 6'6" **Wt:** 220 **Born:** 3/19/75 **Age:** 27

Year Team	Lg Org	G	GS	CG	GF	IP	BFP	H	R	ER	HR	SH	SF	HB	TBB	IBB	SO	WP	Bk	W	L	Pct.	ShO	Sv	ERA
1998 Oneonta	A- NYY	14	14	1	0	81	335	53	30	22	0	3	1	5	39	0	85	6	5	8	2	.800	0	0	2.44
1999 Greensboro	A NYY	15	8	0	1	55.1	276	67	52	47	7	1	0	6	42	0	62	5	4	1	9	.100	0	0	7.64
Staten Ilnd	A- NYY	12	12	0	0	61.2	279	69	39	34	1	1	3	2	26	0	71	9	0	3	4	.429	0	0	4.96
2000 Norwich	AA NYY	8	0	0	6	14	71	14	11	11	2	0	2	1	15	1	6	0	0	0	0	—	0	0	7.07
Tampa	A+ NYY	33	1	0	11	57	245	42	21	13	1	4	1	3	30	2	62	3	0	2	0	1.000	0	1	2.05
2001 Norwich	AA NYY	1	0	0	0	2	8	2	1	1	1	0	0	0	0	0	2	0	0	0	0	—	0	0	4.50
Tampa	A+ NYY	9	0	0	2	9.2	43	9	4	3	0	0	0	0	6	0	9	0	0	1	0	1.000	0	0	2.79
4 Min. YEARS		92	35	1	21	280.2	1257	256	158	131	12	9	5	18	158	3	297	23	9	15	15	.500	0	1	4.20

Tommy Whiteman

Bats: Right **Throws:** Right **Pos:** SS-114; DH-4   **Ht:** 6'3" **Wt:** 175 **Born:** 7/14/79 **Age:** 22

Year Team	Lg Org	G	AB	H	2B	3B	HR	TB	R	RBI	TBB	IBB	SO	HBP	SH	SF	SB	CS	SB%	GDP	Avg	OBP	SLG
2000 Auburn	A- Hou	70	232	58	10	3	1	77	33	22	22	1	52	1	1	0	7	5	.58	7	.250	.318	.332
2001 Lexington	A Hou	114	389	124	26	8	18	220	58	57	34	1	106	7	4	4	17	13	.57	4	.319	.380	.566
Round Rock	AA Hou	4	16	4	0	0	1	7	1	1	0	0	5	1	0	0	0	0	—	0	.250	.294	.438
2 Min. YEARS		188	637	186	36	11	20	304	92	80	56	2	163	9	5	4	24	18	.57	11	.292	.356	.477

Darrell Whitmore

Bats: Left **Throws:** Right **Pos:** OF-45; DH-34; PH-34   **Ht:** 6'1" **Wt:** 210 **Born:** 11/18/68 **Age:** 33

Year Team	Lg Org	G	AB	H	2B	3B	HR	TB	R	RBI	TBB	IBB	SO	HBP	SH	SF	SB	CS	SB%	GDP	Avg	OBP	SLG
1990 Burlington	R+ Cle	30	112	27	3	2	0	34	18	13	9	0	30	2	0	1	9	5	.64	9	.241	.306	.304
1991 Watertown	A- Cle	6	19	7	2	1	0	11	2	3	3	0	2	0	0	0	0	0	—	0	.368	.455	.579
1992 Kinston	A+ Cle	121	443	124	22	2	10	180	71	52	56	5	92	5	0	5	17	9	.65	8	.280	.363	.406
1993 Edmonton	AAA Fla	73	273	97	24	2	9	152	52	62	22	0	53	0	0	3	11	8	.58	12	.355	.399	.557
1994 Edmonton	AAA Fla	115	421	119	24	5	20	213	72	61	41	3	76	2	0	3	14	3	.82	12	.283	.347	.506
1996 Charlotte	AAA Fla	55	204	62	13	0	11	108	27	36	7	2	43	1	0	2	2	5	.29	2	.304	.327	.529
1997 Syracuse	AAA Tor	58	195	50	15	0	4	77	23	21	24	3	54	1	0	2	7	4	.64	4	.256	.338	.395
Carolina	AA Pit	2	9	3	2	0	0	5	1	2	0	0	2	0	0	0	0	0	—	0	.333	.333	.556
1998 Nashville	AAA Pit	105	311	96	19	1	21	180	58	50	36	1	87	6	0	2	3	4	.43	5	.309	.389	.579
1999 Indianapols	AAA Cin	83	238	67	17	1	10	116	39	42	24	2	64	3	0	3	2	1	.67	8	.282	.351	.487
2000 Memphis	AAA StL	89	256	72	14	2	10	120	36	34	13	0	64	1	0	2	4	2	.67	3	.281	.316	.469

Year Team	Lg Org	G	AB	H	2B	3B	HR	TB	R	RBI	TBB	IBB	SO	HBP	SH	SF	SB	CS	SB%	GDP	Avg	OBP	SLG
							BATTING										BASERUNNING				PERCENTAGES		
2001 Memphis	AAA StL	112	328	91	22	0	11	146	47	52	22	3	61	3	0	3	2	3	.40	6	.277	.326	.445
1993 Florida	NL	76	250	51	8	2	4	75	24	19	10	0	72	5	2	0	4	2	.67	8	.204	.249	.300
1994 Florida	NL	9	22	5	1	0	0	6	1	0	3	0	5	0	0	0	0	1	.00	0	.227	.320	.273
1995 Florida	NL	27	58	11	2	0	1	16	6	2	5	0	15	0	1	1	0	0		1	.190	.250	.276
11 Min. YEARS		849	2809	815	177	16	106	1342	446	428	257	19	628	24	0	26	71	44	.62	60	.290	.352	.478
3 Maj. YEARS		112	330	67	11	2	5	97	31	21	18	0	92	5	3	1	4	3	.57	9	.203	.254	.294

Scott Wiggins

Pitches: Left **Bats:** Left **Pos:** RP-35; SP-5   **Ht:** 6'3" **Wt:** 205 **Born:** 3/24/76 **Age:** 26

Year Team	Lg Org	G	GS	CG	GF	IP	BFP	H	R	ER	HR	SH	SF	HB	TBB	IBB	SO	WP	Bk	W	L	Pct.	ShO	Sv	ERA
			HOW MUCH HE PITCHED						WHAT HE GAVE UP											THE RESULTS					
1997 Oneonta	A- NYY	13	13	1	0	63.1	261	58	25	18	1	0	0	2	22	0	44	0	0	6	2	.750	1	0	2.56
1998 Greensboro	A NYY	14	4	0	6	42.1	171	37	17	14	4	0	0	2	11	0	56	0	0	2	2	.500	0	1	2.98
Yankees	R NYY	1	1	0	0	1.2	7	2	1	0	0	0	0	0	0	0	2	0	0	0	0	—	0	0	0.00
Tampa	A+ NYY	11	5	0	1	33.2	136	19	12	7	1	2	0	0	17	1	36	2	0	1	1	.500	0	0	1.87
1999 Greensboro	A NYY	17	17	0	0	93.1	395	84	45	41	15	1	0	6	32	0	110	7	0	7	1	.875	0	0	3.95
2000 Tampa	A+ NYY	28	15	1	1	100.2	444	106	61	46	4	2	3	5	46	0	68	4	1	2	8	.200	1	0	4.11
2001 Norwich	AA NYY	4	0	0	3	4	12	0	0	0	0	0	0	0	1	0	5	0	0	0	0	—	0	0	0.00
Tampa	A+ NYY	36	5	0	9	68.1	302	72	29	23	5	1	2	10	23	1	77	8	0	4	3	.571	0	1	3.03
5 Min. YEARS		124	60	2	20	407.1	1728	378	190	149	30	6	5	25	152	2	398	21	1	22	17	.564	2	2	3.29

Ty Wigginton

Bats: Right **Throws:** Right **Pos:** 3B-47; 2B-32; DH-8; PH-6; 1B-5; C-1; OF-1   **Ht:** 6'0" **Wt:** 200 **Born:** 10/11/77 **Age:** 24

Year Team	Lg Org	G	AB	H	2B	3B	HR	TB	R	RBI	TBB	IBB	SO	HBP	SH	SF	SB	CS	SB%	GDP	Avg	OBP	SLG
							BATTING										BASERUNNING				PERCENTAGES		
1998 Pittsfield	A- NYM	70	272	65	14	4	8	111	39	29	16	0	72	1	1	0	11	2	.85	4	.239	.284	.408
1999 St. Lucie	A+ NYM	123	456	133	23	5	21	229	69	73	56	4	82	4	4	2	9	12	.43	5	.292	.373	.502
2000 Binghamton	AA NYM	122	453	129	27	3	20	222	64	77	24	0	107	2	1	7	5	5	.50	4	.285	.319	.490
2001 St. Lucie	A+ NYM	3	9	3	1	0	0	4	1	1	4	0	2	1	0	0	0	0		0	.333	.571	.444
Binghamton	AA NYM	8	28	8	3	0	0	11	5	0	5	0	5	0	1	0	1	0	1.00	0	.286	.394	.393
Norfolk	AAA NYM	78	260	65	12	0	7	98	29	24	27	0	66	2	1	2	3	3	.50	4	.250	.323	.377
4 Min. YEARS		404	1478	403	80	12	56	675	207	204	132	4	334	10	8	11	29	22	.57	17	.273	.334	.457

Luke Wilcox

Bats: Left **Throws:** Right **Pos:** OF-52; DH-16; PH-12   **Ht:** 6'4" **Wt:** 225 **Born:** 11/15/73 **Age:** 28

Year Team	Lg Org	G	AB	H	2B	3B	HR	TB	R	RBI	TBB	IBB	SO	HBP	SH	SF	SB	CS	SB%	GDP	Avg	OBP	SLG
							BATTING										BASERUNNING				PERCENTAGES		
1995 Oneonta	A- NYY	59	223	73	16	7	1	106	25	28	20	3	28	1	0	2	9	3	.75	4	.327	.382	.475
1996 Tampa	A+ NYY	119	470	133	32	5	11	208	72	76	40	1	71	3	4	6	14	10	.58	14	.283	.339	.443
1997 Tampa	A+ NYY	12	40	12	4	0	0	16	7	4	7	2	6	1	0	1	1	1	.50	0	.300	.408	.400
Norwich	AA NYY	74	300	83	13	1	6	116	45	34	18	1	36	3	1	1	13	3	.81	6	.277	.323	.387
1998 Orlando	AA TB	88	331	95	23	3	17	175	57	69	39	5	54	5	0	6	2	3	.40	6	.287	.365	.529
Durham	AAA TB	43	151	34	11	0	2	51	17	17	16	0	27	1	0	1	0	0	—	6	.225	.302	.338
1999 Orlando	AA TB	90	333	90	24	1	20	176	60	64	35	0	54	3	0	4	3	2	.60	9	.270	.341	.529
Durham	AAA TB	39	134	44	12	5	9	93	32	34	22	4	18	1	1	0	1	3	.25	2	.328	.427	.694
2000 Columbus	AAA NYY	106	343	75	13	2	13	131	48	49	38	1	58	2	0	7	6	2	.75	7	.219	.295	.382
Norwich	AA NYY	18	70	19	7	0	2	32	10	18	10	1	10	0	0	2	2	2	.50	1	.271	.354	.457
2001 Columbus	AAA NYY	11	40	6	1	0	2	13	3	6	3	0	6	0	0	1	0	1	.00	1	.150	.205	.325
Portland	AA Fla	69	220	53	14	0	9	94	25	41	21	1	43	1	0	0	1	1	.50	6	.241	.310	.427
7 Min. YEARS		728	2655	717	170	24	92	1211	401	440	269	19	411	21	6	31	52	31	.63	62	.270	.338	.456

Brian Williams

Pitches: Right **Bats:** Right **Pos:** RP-10; SP-9   **Ht:** 6'3" **Wt:** 230 **Born:** 2/15/69 **Age:** 33

Year Team	Lg Org	G	GS	CG	GF	IP	BFP	H	R	ER	HR	SH	SF	HB	TBB	IBB	SO	WP	Bk	W	L	Pct.	ShO	Sv	ERA
			HOW MUCH HE PITCHED						WHAT HE GAVE UP											THE RESULTS					
1990 Auburn	A- Hou	3	3	0	0	6.2	34	6	5	3	0	1	0	1	6	0	7	1	1	0	0	—	0	0	4.05
1991 Osceola	A+ Hou	15	15	0	0	89.2	378	72	41	29	0	3	6	2	40	1	67	3	5	6	4	.600	0	0	2.91
Jackson	AA Hou	3	3	0	0	15	66	17	8	7	1	0	0	0	7	0	15	3	0	2	1	.667	0	0	4.20
Tucson	AAA Hou	7	7	0	0	38.1	177	39	25	21	3	4	0	2	22	0	29	3	4	0	1	.000	0	0	4.93
1992 Tucson	AAA Hou	12	12	0	0	70	315	78	37	35	3	3	4	6	26	0	58	5	4	6	1	.857	0	0	4.50
1993 Tucson	AAA Hou	2	0	0	0	3	11	1	0	0	0	0	0	0	0	0	3	0	0	1	0	1.000	0	0	0.00
1994 Tucson	AAA Hou	3	3	0	0	20.1	86	22	6	5	0	0	0	0	9	0	17	1	0	2	0	1.000	0	0	2.21
1996 Toledo	AAA Det	3	3	1	0	19.2	87	22	13	12	1	0	0	0	9	1	21	3	1	1	2	.333	0	0	5.49
1997 Rochester	AAA Bal	22	9	0	13	69.1	299	68	33	30	8	3	2	4	23	0	78	1	2	4	3	.571	0	8	3.89
2000 Buffalo	AAA Cle	18	0	0	8	21	95	23	7	6	1	4	1	0	11	2	21	2	0	4	3	.571	0	3	2.57
2001 Pawtucket	AAA Bos	3	0	0	2	4	14	2	0	0	0	0	0	0	1	0	3	0	0	0	0	—	0	0	0.00
Columbus	AAA NYY	16	9	0	3	58	267	72	43	35	5	3	0	4	26	1	33	3	0	5	6	.455	0	0	5.43
1991 Houston	NL	2	2	0	0	12	49	11	5	5	2	0	0	1	4	0	4	0	0	0	1	.000	0	0	3.75
1992 Houston	NL	16	16	0	0	96.1	413	92	44	42	10	7	3	0	42	1	54	2	1	7	6	.538	0	0	3.92
1993 Houston	NL	42	5	0	12	82	357	76	48	44	7	5	3	4	38	4	56	9	2	4	4	.500	0	3	4.83
1994 Houston	NL	20	13	0	2	78.1	344	112	64	50	9	7	5	4	41	4	49	3	1	6	5	.545	0	0	5.74
1995 San Diego	NL	44	6	0	7	72	337	79	54	48	3	7	1	8	38	4	75	7	1	3	10	.231	0	0	6.00
1996 Detroit	AL	40	17	2	17	121	579	145	107	91	21	5	6	6	85	2	72	8	0	3	10	.231	1	2	6.77
1997 Baltimore	AL	13	0	0	6	24	110	20	8	8	0	0	0	1	18	0	14	1	0	0	0	—	0	0	3.00
1999 Houston	NL	50	0	0	15	67.1	303	69	35	33	4	5	4	5	35	2	53	7	0	2	1	.667	0	0	4.41
2000 Chicago	NL	22	0	0	5	24.1	122	28	27	26	4	3	1	3	22	2	14	3	0	1	1	.500	0	1	9.62
Cleveland	AL	7	0	0	1	18	81	23	9	8	2	0	1	1	8	1	6	1	0	0	0	—	0	0	4.00
9 Min. YEARS		107	64	1	26	415	1829	422	218	183	22	21	13	19	180	5	352	25	17	31	21	.596	0	11	3.97
9 Maj. YEARS		256	59	2	67	595.1	2735	655	401	355	62	39	25	32	332	20	397	41	5	26	38	.406	1	6	5.37

George Williams

Bats: Both **Throws:** Right **Pos:** C-16; PH-2 — **Ht:** 5'10" **Wt:** 215 **Born:** 4/22/69 **Age:** 33

Year Team	Lg Org	G	AB	H	2B	3B	HR	TB	R	RBI	TBB	IBB	SO	HBP	SH	SF	SB	CS	SB%	GDP	Avg	OBP	SLG
1991 Sou Oregon	A- Oak	55	174	41	10	0	2	57	24	24	38	0	36	5	3	1	9	4	.69	1	.236	.385	.328
1992 Madison	A Oak	115	349	106	18	2	5	143	56	42	76	6	53	8	5	1	9	5	.64	10	.304	.438	.410
1993 Huntsville	AA Oak	124	434	128	26	2	14	200	80	77	67	0	66	14	1	6	6	3	.67	10	.295	.401	.461
1994 W Michigan	A Oak	63	221	67	20	1	8	113	40	48	44	3	47	8	1	0	6	3	.67	3	.303	.436	.511
1995 Edmonton	AAA Oak	81	290	90	20	0	13	149	53	55	50	6	52	2	3	2	0	4	.00	9	.310	.413	.514
1996 Edmonton	AAA Oak	14	57	23	5	0	5	43	10	18	6	0	11	2	0	1	0	1	.00	2	.404	.470	.754
1997 Edmonton	AAA Oak	3	7	0	0	0	0	0	0	0	1	0	1	0	0	0	0	0	—	0	.000	.125	.000
Modesto	A+ Oak	13	44	14	4	0	1	21	8	6	7	2	14	0	0	1	0	1	.00	0	.318	.404	.477
1998 Athletics	R Oak	1	2	1	0	0	0	1	0	0	1	0	0	0	0	0	0	0	—	0	.500	.667	.500
1999 Salt Lake	AAA Min	74	228	69	16	1	6	105	38	31	42	2	51	6	0	0	0	3	.00	9	.303	.424	.461
New Orleans	AAA Hou	29	100	24	5	0	3	38	18	14	13	2	19	2	0	1	1	1	.50	6	.240	.336	.380
2000 Las Vegas	AAA SD	63	176	42	8	2	8	78	27	35	36	1	44	3	0	3	0	1	.00	3	.239	.372	.443
2001 Pawtucket	AAA Bos	17	46	6	2	0	0	8	6	1	8	0	10	1	0	0	0	0	—	0	.130	.259	.174
1995 Oakland	AL	29	79	23	5	1	3	39	13	14	11	2	21	2	0	2	0	0	—	1	.291	.383	.494
1996 Oakland	AL	56	132	20	5	0	3	34	17	10	28	1	32	3	2	1	0	0	—	0	.152	.311	.258
1997 Oakland	AL	76	201	58	9	1	3	78	30	22	35	0	46	2	2	1	0	1	.00	2	.289	.397	.388
2000 San Diego	NL	11	16	3	0	0	1	6	2	2	0	0	4	1	0	0	0	0	—	0	.188	.235	.375
11 Min. YEARS		652	2128	611	134	8	65	956	360	351	389	22	404	50	13	16	31	26	.54	53	.287	.407	.449
4 Maj. YEARS		172	428	104	19	2	10	157	62	48	74	3	103	8	4	4	0	1	.00	6	.243	.362	.367

Glenn Williams

Bats: Both **Throws:** Right **Pos:** 3B-98; 2B-22; SS-15; 1B-8; PH-2; DH-1 — **Ht:** 6'2" **Wt:** 195 **Born:** 7/18/77 **Age:** 24

Year Team	Lg Org	G	AB	H	2B	3B	HR	TB	R	RBI	TBB	IBB	SO	HBP	SH	SF	SB	CS	SB%	GDP	Avg	OBP	SLG
1994 Braves	R Atl	24	89	18	2	0	2	26	8	7	9	0	32	0	0	1	4	1	.80	0	.202	.273	.292
Danville	R+ Atl	24	79	20	2	0	1	25	11	9	8	0	20	3	0	0	2	4	.33	4	.253	.344	.316
1995 Macon	A Atl	38	120	21	4	0	0	25	14	16	10	0	42	1	1	3	2	1	.67	3	.175	.271	.208
Eugene	A- Atl	71	268	60	11	4	7	100	39	36	21	1	71	5	0	2	7	4	.64	4	.224	.291	.373
1996 Macon	A Atl	51	181	35	7	3	3	57	14	18	18	2	47	2	1	4	4	2	.67	3	.193	.271	.315
1997 Macon	A Atl	77	297	79	18	2	14	143	52	52	24	1	105	5	1	4	9	6	.60	4	.266	.327	.481
1998 Danville	A+ Atl	134	470	101	26	1	9	156	40	44	37	3	132	6	3	3	1	3	.25	5	.215	.279	.332
1999 Greenville	AA Atl	57	204	46	11	0	4	69	19	15	7	1	58	4	1	1	1	4	.20	2	.225	.264	.338
2000 Dunedin	A+ Tor	107	391	102	26	4	13	175	53	77	33	1	91	6	0	6	4	2	.67	11	.261	.323	.448
2001 Tennessee	AA Tor	130	487	124	28	0	11	185	63	65	45	4	120	5	2	5	1	5	.17	8	.255	.321	.380
8 Min. YEARS		713	2586	606	135	14	64	961	312	337	218	13	718	37	9	27	35	32	.52	44	.234	.300	.372

Jerome Williams

Pitches: Right **Bats:** Right **Pos:** SP-23 — **Ht:** 6'3" **Wt:** 190 **Born:** 12/4/81 **Age:** 20

Year Team	Lg Org	G	GS	CG	GF	IP	BFP	H	R	ER	HR	SH	SF	HB	TBB	IBB	SO	WP	Bk	W	L	Pct.	ShO	Sv	ERA
1999 Salem-Keizr	A- SF	7	7	1	0	37	151	29	13	9	1	0	1	3	11	0	34	1	0	1	1	.500	1	0	2.19
2000 San Jose	A+ SF	23	19	0	2	125.2	512	89	53	41	6	5	6	10	48	3	115	9	2	7	6	.538	0	0	2.94
2001 Shreveport	AA SF	23	23	2	0	130	542	116	69	57	14	2	3	9	34	0	84	6	1	9	7	.563	1	0	3.95
3 Min. YEARS		53	49	3	2	292.2	1205	234	135	107	21	7	10	22	93	3	233	16	3	17	14	.548	2	0	3.29

Matt Williams

Pitches: Left **Bats:** Both **Pos:** RP-51 — **Ht:** 6'0" **Wt:** 190 **Born:** 4/12/71 **Age:** 31

Year Team	Lg Org	G	GS	CG	GF	IP	BFP	H	R	ER	HR	SH	SF	HB	TBB	IBB	SO	WP	Bk	W	L	Pct.	ShO	Sv	ERA
1992 Watertown	A- Cle	6	6	0	0	32.2	130	22	15	8	2	0	4	3	9	0	29	1	2	1	0	1.000	0	0	2.20
1993 Kinston	A+ Cle	27	27	2	0	153.1	672	125	65	54	6	7	5	8	100	0	134	12	6	12	12	.500	1	0	3.17
1994 Canton-Akrn	AA Cle	5	4	0	1	23.2	112	30	22	20	3	1	3	1	14	0	9	1	0	0	3	.000	0	1	7.61
High Desert	A+ Cle	5	5	0	0	18	101	33	29	26	7	2	3	1	13	1	10	2	0	1	4	.200	0	0	13.00
Kinston	A+ Cle	15	15	1	0	81.1	358	86	63	55	17	0	2	2	33	0	67	4	2	4	6	.400	0	0	6.09
1995 Bakersfield	A+ Hou	7	7	0	0	34.1	150	34	9	9	1	3	2	3	14	0	30	1	1	2	0	1.000	0	0	2.36
Kissimmee	A+ Hou	19	18	2	0	101	446	115	60	52	7	5	3	2	44	1	71	5	1	4	6	.400	0	0	4.63
1996 Lynchburg	A+ Pit	23	0	0	5	41.1	189	40	27	24	9	0	1	2	28	1	45	3	1	0	0	—	0	0	5.23
1997 St. Pete	A+ TB	43	0	0	15	63.2	267	57	26	21	4	2	0	2	24	3	50	3	3	9	5	.643	0	1	2.97
1998 Norwich	AA NYY	31	28	2	0	160.1	719	186	93	82	14	3	7	4	66	2	112	8	2	8	11	.421	0	0	4.60
1999 Norwich	AA NYY	22	0	0	5	30	128	22	9	8	3	0	1	1	18	3	44	1	1	1	1	.500	0	0	2.40
Columbus	AAA NYY	13	1	0	3	21	87	15	9	9	1	0	0	0	11	0	22	0	1	0	2	.000	0	0	3.86
2000 Columbus	AAA NYY	27	0	0	14	36	160	37	24	21	4	0	1	0	16	1	35	3	0	4	2	.667	0	2	5.25
2001 Indianapols	AAA Mil	51	0	0	18	72	318	65	33	31	4	2	1	4	42	1	45	3	0	2	2	.500	0	0	3.88
2000 Milwaukee	NL	11	0	0	1	9	46	7	7	7	2	0	0	1	13	0	7	0	0	0	0	—	0	0	7.00
10 Min. YEARS		294	111	7	61	868.2	3837	867	484	420	82	25	33	33	432	13	703	49	19	48	54	.471	1	4	4.35

Peanut Williams

Bats: Right **Throws:** Right **Pos:** 1B-28; DH-18; PH-1 — **Ht:** 6'3" **Wt:** 235 **Born:** 10/3/77 **Age:** 24

Year Team	Lg Org	G	AB	H	2B	3B	HR	TB	R	RBI	TBB	IBB	SO	HBP	SH	SF	SB	CS	SB%	GDP	Avg	OBP	SLG
1996 Mariners	R Sea	38	140	35	4	1	6	59	18	26	12	1	46	5	0	1	1	1	.50	1	.250	.329	.421
1997 Everett	A- Sea	64	255	68	7	0	12	111	38	48	19	0	93	3	0	3	1	0	1.00	4	.267	.321	.435
1998 Wisconsin	A Sea	71	229	55	8	0	11	96	35	36	17	2	78	4	0	3	5	1	.83	5	.240	.300	.419
1999 Wisconsin	A Sea	9	32	8	1	0	2	15	6	7	4	0	12	1	0	0	0	0	—	0	.250	.351	.469
Lancaster	A+ Sea	68	272	88	12	0	26	178	60	59	35	1	89	4	0	1	0	0	—	5	.324	.407	.654
2000 Mariners	R Sea	4	17	6	2	0	0	8	6	3	4	1	6	0	0	0	0	0	—	0	.353	.476	.471
Lancaster	A+ Sea	76	292	74	15	0	8	113	53	55	24	0	109	5	1	1	3	2	.60	6	.253	.320	.387

Year Team	Lg Org	G	AB	H	2B	3B	HR	TB	R	RBI	TBB	IBB	SO	HBP	SH	SF	SB	CS	SB%	GDP	Avg	OBP	SLG
2001 San Antonio	AA Sea	38	125	25	9	0	1	37	11	9	14	1	37	1	0	1	1	1	.50	4	.200	.284	.296
Lincoln	IND —	9	38	5	1	0	1	9	4	2	1	0	18	0	0	0	0	0	—	1	.132	.154	.237
6 Min. YEARS		377	1400	364	59	1	67	626	231	245	130	6	488	23	1	10	11	5	.69	28	.260	.331	.447

Shad Williams

Pitches: Right **Bats:** Right **Pos:** RP-12; SP-7   **Ht:** 6'0" **Wt:** 198 **Born:** 3/10/71 **Age:** 31

		HOW MUCH HE PITCHED						WHAT HE GAVE UP											THE RESULTS				
Year Team	Lg Org	G	GS	CG	GF	IP	BFP	H	R	ER	HR	SH	SF	HB	TBB	IBB	SO	WP	Bk	W	L	Pct.	ShO	Sv	ERA
1992 Quad City	A Ana	27	26	7	0	179.1	748	161	81	65	14	6	6	7	55	0	152	9	1	13	11	.542	0	0	3.26
1993 Midland	AA Ana	27	27	2	0	175.2	758	192	100	92	16	6	6	3	65	1	91	9	1	7	10	.412	0	0	4.71
1994 Midland	AA Ana	5	5	1	0	32.1	112	13	4	4	1	0	0	1	4	0	29	2	0	3	0	1.000	1	0	1.11
Vancouver	AAA Ana	16	16	1	0	86	386	100	61	44	14	3	2	3	30	0	42	6	0	4	6	.400	1	0	4.60
1995 Vancouver	AAA Ana	25	25	3	0	149.2	627	142	65	56	16	3	3	4	48	2	114	7	1	9	7	.563	1	0	3.37
1996 Vancouver	AAA Ana	15	13	1	1	75	321	73	36	33	8	4	0	2	28	0	57	2	0	6	2	.750	1	0	3.96
1997 Vancouver	AAA Ana	40	10	0	7	99	464	98	52	42	13	0	4	5	41	2	52	5	0	6	2	.750	0	0	3.82
1998 Columbus	AAA NYY	5	1	0	0	12	66	24	19	17	1	0	1	1	8	0	10	0	0	0	1	.000	0	0	12.75
Norwich	AA NYY	9	8	0	0	42	188	55	22	20	4	2	0	2	11	0	18	2	0	4	2	.667	0	0	4.29
Vancouver	AAA Ana	14	10	1	1	68	281	65	30	24	9	2	0	1	18	0	29	2	1	1	4	.200	0	0	3.18
1999 Scranton-WB	AAA Phi	2	2	0	0	5	33	17	11	11	0	0	2	1	3	0	2	0	0	0	2	.000	0	0	19.80
Reading	AA Phi	16	2	0	5	31.2	133	30	17	11	3	3	2	0	10	0	19	1	0	2	2	.500	0	2	3.13
Edmonton	AAA Ana	16	11	1	1	75	303	73	36	31	9	1	3	1	19	0	35	2	0	5	3	.625	0	0	3.72
2000 Edmonton	AAA Ana	22	5	0	5	54	247	67	41	33	5	1	1	2	23	0	34	1	0	1	5	.167	0	1	5.50
2001 Arkansas	AA Ana	11	6	0	3	35.1	162	42	26	23	3	1	0	0	13	0	26	2	1	3	4	.429	0	1	5.86
Salt Lake	AAA Ana	8	1	0	1	13.1	69	26	13	13	6	0	0	1	7	0	9	0	0	0	0	—	0	0	8.78
1996 California	AL	13	2	0	3	28.1	150	42	34	28	7	3	1	2	21	4	26	2	0	0	2	.000	0	0	8.89
1997 Anaheim	AL	1	0	0	1	1	5	1	0	0	0	0	0	0	1	0	0	0	0	0	0	—	0	0	0.00
10 Min. YEARS		258	168	17	24	1133.1	4858	1178	614	519	122	32	30	34	383	5	719	50	5	64	61	.512	4	4	4.12
2 Maj. YEARS		14	2	0	4	29.1	155	43	34	28	7	3	1	2	22	4	26	2	0	0	2	.000	0	0	8.59

Craig Wilson

Bats: Right **Throws:** Right **Pos:** 3B-73; 1B-21; DH-13; SS-12; 2B-6; P-2; PH-1   **Ht:** 6'0" **Wt:** 185 **Born:** 9/3/70 **Age:** 31

		BATTING															BASERUNNING				PERCENTAGES		
Year Team	Lg Org	G	AB	H	2B	3B	HR	TB	R	RBI	TBB	IBB	SO	HBP	SH	SF	SB	CS	SB%	GDP	Avg	OBP	SLG
1993 South Bend	A CWS	132	455	118	27	2	5	164	56	59	49	2	50	8	7	6	4	4	.50	16	.259	.338	.360
1994 Pr William	A+ CWS	131	496	131	36	4	4	187	70	66	58	2	44	6	5	6	1	2	.33	16	.264	.345	.377
1995 Birmingham	AA CWS	132	471	136	19	1	4	169	56	46	43	0	44	5	10	2	2	2	.50	21	.289	.353	.359
1996 Nashville	AAA CWS	44	123	22	4	1	1	31	13	6	10	0	15	0	5	1	0	0	—	6	.179	.239	.252
Birmingham	AA CWS	58	202	57	9	0	3	75	36	26	40	1	28	1	6	4	1	1	.50	7	.282	.397	.371
1997 Nashville	AAA CWS	137	453	123	20	2	6	165	71	42	48	1	31	1	12	0	4	4	.50	19	.272	.343	.364
1998 Calgary	AAA CWS	120	432	132	21	1	14	197	67	69	37	1	41	3	9	5	4	2	.67	13	.306	.361	.456
2000 Charlotte	AAA CWS	62	230	85	14	2	3	112	43	34	32	0	26	4	0	4	0	1	.00	7	.370	.448	.487
2001 Omaha	AAA KC	125	473	140	27	3	11	206	78	69	45	0	58	4	3	9	6	4	.60	21	.296	.356	.436
1998 Chicago	AL	13	47	22	5	0	3	36	14	10	3	0	6	0	2	1	1	0	1.00	4	.468	.490	.766
1999 Chicago	AL	98	252	60	8	1	4	82	28	26	23	0	22	0	6	1	1	1	.50	5	.238	.301	.325
2000 Chicago	AL	28	73	19	3	0	0	22	12	4	5	0	11	1	4	0	1	0	1.00	5	.260	.316	.301
8 Min. YEARS		941	3335	944	177	16	51	1306	490	417	362	7	337	32	57	37	22	20	.52	126	.283	.355	.392
3 Maj. YEARS		139	372	101	16	1	7	140	54	40	31	0	39	1	12	2	3	1	.75	10	.272	.328	.376

Desi Wilson

Bats: Left **Throws:** Left **Pos:** 1B-58; OF-15; PH-8; DH-4   **Ht:** 6'7" **Wt:** 230 **Born:** 5/9/69 **Age:** 33

		BATTING															BASERUNNING				PERCENTAGES		
Year Team	Lg Org	G	AB	H	2B	3B	HR	TB	R	RBI	TBB	IBB	SO	HBP	SH	SF	SB	CS	SB%	GDP	Avg	OBP	SLG
1991 Rangers	R Tex	8	25	4	2	0	0	6	1	7	3	0	2	0	0	1	0	0	—	0	.160	.241	.240
1992 Butte	R+ Tex	72	253	81	9	4	5	113	45	42	31	1	45	1	0	0	13	11	.54	1	.320	.396	.447
1993 Charlotte	A+ Tex	131	511	156	21	7	3	200	83	70	50	4	90	7	0	2	29	11	.73	18	.305	.374	.391
1994 Tulsa	AA Tex	129	493	142	27	0	6	187	69	55	40	5	115	2	0	1	16	14	.53	14	.288	.343	.379
1995 Shreveport	AA SF	122	482	138	27	3	5	186	77	72	40	2	68	1	0	7	11	9	.55	18	.286	.338	.386
1996 Phoenix	AAA SF	113	407	138	26	7	5	193	56	59	18	3	80	3	0	3	15	4	.79	9	.339	.369	.474
1997 Phoenix	AAA SF	121	451	155	27	6	7	215	76	53	44	5	73	4	0	3	16	3	.84	11	.344	.404	.477
1999 Tucson	AAA Ari	130	452	146	27	7	6	205	65	62	34	2	76	2	0	3	2	3	.40	18	.323	.371	.454
2000 Charlotte	AAA CWS	124	439	118	23	1	3	152	58	55	51	2	79	4	0	2	17	4	.81	11	.269	.349	.346
2001 Tucson	AAA Ari	83	320	105	20	1	3	136	45	38	14	0	48	2	0	1	4	2	.67	8	.328	.359	.425
1996 San Francisco	NL	41	118	32	2	0	2	40	10	12	12	2	27	0	0	0	0	2	.00	2	.271	.338	.339
10 Min. YEARS		1033	3833	1183	209	36	43	1593	575	513	325	24	676	26	0	23	123	61	.67	108	.309	.365	.416

Jeff Wilson

Pitches: Left **Bats:** Right **Pos:** SP-17; RP-16   **Ht:** 6'2" **Wt:** 180 **Born:** 5/30/76 **Age:** 26

		HOW MUCH HE PITCHED						WHAT HE GAVE UP											THE RESULTS				
Year Team	Lg Org	G	GS	CG	GF	IP	BFP	H	R	ER	HR	SH	SF	HB	TBB	IBB	SO	WP	Bk	W	L	Pct.	ShO	Sv	ERA
1997 Lethbridge	R+ Ari	22	0	0	0	36.1	157	35	22	18	4	2	1	0	12	0	49	5	0	1	1	.500	0	0	4.46
1998 High Desert	A+ Ari	12	0	0	4	20.2	96	28	14	12	1	1	0	0	8	0	18	0	0	2	0	1.000	0	0	5.23
South Bend	A Ari	12	4	0	6	38.2	163	34	17	11	0	2	1	1	13	2	30	6	1	1	5	.167	0	0	2.56
1999 High Desert	A+ Ari	32	17	0	2	110.2	494	106	66	53	12	2	4	3	67	2	122	8	2	7	4	.636	0	1	4.31
2000 Bowie	AA Bal	19	18	2	0	111	462	101	51	41	6	2	3	3	38	0	79	3	0	6	7	.462	0	0	3.32
Rochester	AAA Bal	11	3	0	1	35	157	26	16	15	1	0	0	3	29	0	25	1	1	2	2	.500	0	0	3.86
2001 Rochester	AAA Bal	28	12	1	5	99.2	457	118	73	67	17	4	2	1	42	4	56	9	1	2	11	.154	0	0	6.05
Bowie	AA Bal	5	5	0	0	34	146	32	19	15	3	0	2	2	9	0	31	1	0	1	1	.500	0	0	3.97
5 Min. YEARS		141	59	3	27	486	2134	480	278	232	44	13	16	12	218	8	410	33	5	22	31	.415	0	1	4.30

318

Phil Wilson

Pitches: Right **Bats:** Right **Pos:** SP-28   **Ht:** 6'8" **Wt:** 210 **Born:** 4/1/81 **Age:** 21

Year Team	Lg Org	G	GS	CG	GF	IP	BFP	H	R	ER	HR	SH	SF	HB	TBB	IBB	SO	WP	Bk	W	L	Pct.	ShO	Sv	ERA
2000 Cedar Rapds	A Ana	21	21	1	0	129.1	544	114	61	49	9	4	4	7	49	0	82	9	1	8	5	.615	0	0	3.41
Lk Elsinore	A+ Ana	6	6	0	0	41.1	165	32	9	9	1	0	2	2	10	0	33	2	0	3	0	1.000	0	0	1.96
2001 Rancho Cuca	A+ Ana	26	26	1	0	160	704	173	102	93	15	2	8	13	55	0	134	19	0	8	10	.444	0	0	5.23
Arkansas	AA Ana	2	2	0	0	6.1	38	10	12	8	1	0	0	2	6	0	5	0	1	1	1	.500	0	0	11.37
2 Min. YEARS		55	55	2	0	337	1451	329	184	159	26	6	14	24	120	0	254	30	2	20	16	.556	0	0	4.25

Travis Wilson

Bats: Right **Throws:** Right **Pos:** 2B-62; OF-62; 3B-11; 1B-9; DH-3; PH-2; PR-1   **Ht:** 6'2" **Wt:** 185 **Born:** 7/10/77 **Age:** 24

Year Team	Lg Org	G	AB	H	2B	3B	HR	TB	R	RBI	TBB	IBB	SO	HBP	SH	SF	SB	CS	SB%	GDP	Avg	OBP	SLG
1997 Danville	R+ Atl	61	233	50	14	6	0	76	29	27	14	0	60	8	1	0	4	1	.80	5	.215	.282	.326
1998 Danville	R+ Atl	65	269	87	25	5	9	149	48	48	17	1	54	4	0	1	16	5	.76	5	.323	.371	.554
Macon	A Atl	3	13	6	0	0	1	9	2	4	0	0	3	0	0	0	0	0	—	0	.462	.462	.692
1999 Macon	A Atl	90	363	112	20	4	11	173	65	63	9	1	66	15	0	3	14	8	.64	8	.309	.349	.477
2000 Myrtle Bch	A+ Atl	125	484	133	33	5	12	212	62	63	16	0	111	9	3	4	7	8	.47	9	.275	.308	.438
2001 Greenville	AA Atl	31	123	40	8	1	2	56	13	21	3	1	24	1	0	1	2	5	.29	4	.325	.344	.455
Richmond	AAA Atl	103	383	93	22	3	3	130	34	38	7	3	81	4	1	1	4	2	.67	10	.243	.263	.339
5 Min. YEARS		478	1868	521	122	24	38	805	253	264	66	6	399	41	5	10	47	29	.62	41	.279	.316	.431

Larry Wimberly

Pitches: Left **Bats:** Left **Pos:** RP-18; SP-10   **Ht:** 6'0" **Wt:** 190 **Born:** 8/22/75 **Age:** 26

Year Team	Lg Org	G	GS	CG	GF	IP	BFP	H	R	ER	HR	SH	SF	HB	TBB	IBB	SO	WP	Bk	W	L	Pct.	ShO	Sv	ERA
1994 Martinsvlle	R+ Phi	13	13	0	0	69.2	281	55	24	20	6	2	2	3	25	0	67	5	1	3	2	.600	0	0	2.58
1995 Piedmont	A Phi	24	24	0	0	135	542	99	48	40	9	1	3	9	44	0	139	8	4	10	3	.769	0	0	2.67
1996 Sarasota	A+ Bos	6	6	0	0	30	142	38	26	23	2	1	2	2	16	1	16	1	0	2	4	.333	0	0	6.90
Michigan	A Bos	14	14	2	0	66.1	272	58	27	21	5	1	3	4	24	1	41	1	2	3	4	.429	1	0	2.85
1997 Red Sox	R Bos	1	0	0	0	3	10	2	1	1	0	0	0	1	0	0	1	0	0	1	0	1.000	0	0	3.00
Michigan	A Bos	13	4	0	4	31.1	138	34	25	24	4	0	0	2	9	0	27	3	0	1	3	.250	0	1	6.89
1998 Clearwater	A+ Phi	14	10	0	1	72	293	77	30	29	4	0	4	3	12	0	66	0	0	7	2	.778	0	0	3.63
1999 Hickory	A Pit	17	5	0	3	47.2	182	32	8	8	2	2	1	1	11	3	57	3	0	3	1	.750	0	0	1.51
Lynchburg	A+ Pit	11	10	0	0	55.1	257	77	40	31	5	2	0	5	13	0	41	2	1	5	3	.625	0	0	5.04
2000 Altoona	AA Pit	10	2	0	4	21	104	29	22	16	4	0	1	2	11	0	25	2	0	4	1	.800	0	0	6.86
Lynchburg	A+ Pit	24	10	0	4	96	370	82	23	20	9	4	1	3	16	0	90	3	0	12	2	.857	0	1	1.88
2001 Altoona	AA Pit	24	7	0	3	69	293	75	36	32	7	2	3	2	18	0	43	2	0	3	2	.600	0	0	4.17
Nashville	AAA Pit	4	3	0	0	13.2	58	16	8	8	5	1	0	0	4	0	3	0	0	2	1	.667	0	0	5.27
8 Min. YEARS		175	108	2	21	710	2942	674	318	273	62	16	20	37	203	5	616	30	8	56	28	.667	1	1	3.46

Joe Winkelsas

Pitches: Right **Bats:** Right **Pos:** RP-24   **Ht:** 6'3" **Wt:** 188 **Born:** 9/14/73 **Age:** 28

Year Team	Lg Org	G	GS	CG	GF	IP	BFP	H	R	ER	HR	SH	SF	HB	TBB	IBB	SO	WP	Bk	W	L	Pct.	ShO	Sv	ERA
1996 Danville	R+ Atl	8	0	0	6	11.1	54	11	10	9	0	0	0	4	4	0	9	2	0	1	1	.500	0	2	7.15
1997 Macon	A Atl	38	0	0	15	62.2	242	44	17	14	1	3	0	4	13	0	45	4	2	3	2	.600	0	5	2.01
Durham	A+ Atl	13	0	0	8	19	93	24	18	15	0	5	2	4	11	1	17	1	0	1	4	.200	0	1	7.11
1998 Danville	A+ Atl	50	0	0	36	69	298	66	26	17	3	7	0	3	24	8	53	0	0	6	9	.400	0	22	2.22
Greenville	AA Atl	4	0	0	0	4.1	20	3	2	2	0	0	0	0	4	0	3	0	0	0	0	—	0	0	4.15
1999 Greenville	AA Atl	55	0	0	40	62.1	280	71	32	26	5	2	0	2	30	6	38	3	1	4	4	.500	0	12	3.75
2000 Richmond	AAA Atl	4	0	0	1	5	33	12	9	8	1	2	0	1	5	2	1	0	0	0	1	.000	0	0	14.40
2001 Myrtle Bch	A+ Atl	4	0	0	4	5.2	20	2	0	0	0	0	0	0	1	0	5	0	0	1	0	1.000	0	3	0.00
Greenville	AA Atl	20	0	0	11	33	133	24	12	12	0	2	0	0	14	2	14	3	2	4	2	.667	0	3	3.27
1999 Atlanta	NL	1	0	0	0	0.1	6	4	2	2	0	1	0	0	1	1	0	0	0	0	0	—	0	0	54.00
6 Min. YEARS		196	0	0	121	272.1	1173	257	126	103	10	21	2	18	106	19	185	13	5	20	23	.465	0	48	3.40

Dewayne Wise

Bats: Left **Throws:** Left **Pos:** OF-112; DH-3; PH-1   **Ht:** 6'1" **Wt:** 180 **Born:** 2/24/78 **Age:** 24

Year Team	Lg Org	G	AB	H	2B	3B	HR	TB	R	RBI	TBB	IBB	SO	HBP	SH	SF	SB	CS	SB%	GDP	Avg	OBP	SLG
1997 Billings	R+ Cin	62	268	84	13	9	7	136	53	41	9	0	47	2	1	3	18	8	.69	2	.313	.337	.507
1998 Burlington	A Cin	127	496	111	15	9	2	150	61	44	41	1	111	1	7	9	27	17	.61	4	.224	.280	.302
1999 Rockford	A Cin	131	502	127	20	13	11	206	70	81	42	2	81	7	5	14	35	13	.73	6	.253	.312	.410
2000 Tennessee	AA Tor	15	56	14	5	2	2	29	10	8	7	0	13	0	0	0	3	2	.60	2	.250	.333	.518
2001 Syracuse	AAA Tor	3	13	3	0	0	0	3	1	0	0	0	8	0	0	0	0	1	.00	0	.231	.231	.231
Dunedin	A+ Tor	25	103	23	3	1	2	34	9	16	5	0	13	0	0	3	5	0	1.00	1	.223	.252	.330
Tennessee	AA Tor	87	351	84	13	6	8	133	44	44	21	1	58	1	4	2	13	5	.72	6	.239	.283	.379
2000 Toronto	AL	28	22	3	0	0	0	3	3	0	1	0	5	1	0	0	1	0	1.00	0	.136	.208	.136
5 Min. YEARS		450	1789	446	69	40	32	691	248	234	125	4	331	11	17	31	101	46	.69	21	.249	.298	.386

Steve Wojciechowski

Pitches: Left **Bats:** Left **Pos:** RP-7; SP-1   **Ht:** 6'2" **Wt:** 195 **Born:** 7/29/70 **Age:** 31

Year Team	Lg Org	G	GS	CG	GF	IP	BFP	H	R	ER	HR	SH	SF	HB	TBB	IBB	SO	WP	Bk	W	L	Pct.	ShO	Sv	ERA
1991 Sou Oregon	A- Oak	16	11	0	1	67	311	74	45	28	4	4	2	1	29	2	50	6	1	2	5	.286	0	0	3.76
1992 Modesto	A+ Oak	14	14	0	0	66.1	282	60	32	26	2	2	3	1	27	0	53	5	2	6	3	.667	0	0	3.53
1993 Modesto	A+ Oak	14	14	1	0	84.2	341	64	29	24	3	3	2	0	36	0	52	1	1	8	2	.800	1	0	2.55
Huntsville	AA Oak	13	13	1	0	67.2	310	91	50	40	6	1	5	2	30	1	52	5	1	4	6	.400	1	0	5.32

Year Team	Lg Org	G	GS	CG	GF	IP	BFP	H	R	ER	HR	SH	SF	HB	TBB	IBB	SO	WP	Bk	W	L	Pct.	ShO	Sv	ERA
1994 Huntsville	AA Oak	27	26	1	1	177	716	148	72	61	7	7	3	0	62	1	114	10	2	10	5	.667	0	0	3.10
1995 Edmonton	AAA Oak	14	12	2	1	78	320	75	37	32	5	1	4	1	21	0	39	4	2	6	3	.667	1	0	3.69
1996 Edmonton	AAA Oak	11	11	1	0	60.1	257	56	32	25	3	2	2	2	21	1	46	4	0	4	3	.571	1	0	3.73
1997 Edmonton	AAA Oak	26	7	0	3	65.2	286	68	33	28	6	1	1	2	23	1	49	2	1	8	2	.800	0	1	3.84
1998 Twins	R Min	2	0	0	0	3.2	13	2	0	0	0	0	0	0	0	0	7	0	0	0	0	—	0	0	0.00
Salt Lake	AAA Min	9	1	0	1	11	52	13	10	8	0	0	1	0	7	0	6	1	0	0	2	.000	0	0	6.55
1999 Sonoma Cty	IND —	10	10	0	0	63.1	271	61	42	31	6	4	1	2	25	0	55	3	0	6	3	.667	0	0	4.41
2000 Fresno	AAA SF	13	8	0	4	44	213	66	38	33	5	2	1	0	23	0	37	3	0	0	4	.000	0	0	6.75
Calgary	AAA Fla	20	6	0	3	47.1	219	64	36	30	10	1	2	0	16	1	27	2	0	2	2	.500	0	1	5.70
2001 Calgary	AAA Fla	8	1	0	4	10.1	50	16	8	8	0	0	1	0	3	1	7	2	0	0	1	.000	0	0	6.97
1995 Oakland	AL	14	7	0	3	48.2	219	51	28	28	7	1	2	1	28	1	13	0	0	2	3	.400	0	0	5.18
1996 Oakland	AL	16	15	0	0	79.2	356	97	57	50	10	1	2	2	28	0	30	3	1	5	5	.500	0	0	5.65
1997 Oakland	AL	2	2	0	0	10.1	46	17	9	9	2	1	0	0	1	0	5	0	0	0	2	.000	0	0	7.84
11 Min. YEARS		197	134	6	18	846.1	3641	858	464	374	57	28	28	11	323	8	594	48	10	56	41	.577	4	2	3.98
3 Maj. YEARS		32	24	0	3	138.2	621	165	94	87	19	3	4	3	57	1	48	3	1	7	10	.412	0	0	5.65

Bryan Wolff

Pitches: Right **Bats:** Right **Pos:** SP-21; RP-2 **Ht:** 6'2" **Wt:** 189 **Born:** 3/16/72 **Age:** 30

Year Team	Lg Org	G	GS	CG	GF	IP	BFP	H	R	ER	HR	SH	SF	HB	TBB	IBB	SO	WP	Bk	W	L	Pct.	ShO	Sv	ERA
1993 Spokane	A- SD	25	8	0	7	57	269	52	50	35	4	4	1	5	44	0	48	10	2	3	9	.250	0	1	5.53
1994 Springfield	A SD	60	0	0	47	63.2	298	46	43	38	3	7	1	0	58	4	99	11	4	3	8	.273	0	24	5.37
1995 Rancho Cuca	A+ SD	54	0	0	43	57	262	39	23	21	4	4	3	3	54	0	77	15	0	2	7	.222	0	18	3.32
1996 Wilmington	A+ KC	42	0	0	28	62.1	280	49	35	25	2	3	1	3	38	1	56	6	0	1	2	.333	0	4	3.61
1997 Wichita	AA KC	12	0	0	8	9.2	50	18	7	7	2	1	1	1	5	1	8	1	0	1	1	.500	0	1	6.52
Rancho Cuca	A+ SD	9	2	0	3	33.1	125	19	6	6	2	0	0	3	6	0	39	2	1	3	0	1.000	0	1	1.62
Mobile	AA SD	20	0	0	5	30	141	34	18	16	6	0	1	0	19	1	37	4	1	1	2	.333	0	0	4.80
1998 Las Vegas	AAA SD	9	0	0	5	10.2	50	14	8	8	5	2	0	0	5	0	8	0	0	0	0	—	0	1	6.75
Mobile	AA SD	33	14	3	7	133.2	527	90	40	34	7	5	2	4	43	2	134	4	1	9	3	.750	2	0	2.29
1999 Las Vegas	AAA SD	28	27	2	0	177.2	770	199	99	92	22	10	6	8	57	0	151	8	1	8	12	.400	0	0	4.66
2000 New Orleans	AAA Hou	11	11	1	0	62	268	63	38	34	6	3	1	3	26	0	46	4	1	2	3	.400	1	0	4.94
Salt Lake	AAA Min	9	7	0	1	51.2	227	53	33	32	8	1	3	1	19	0	43	4	0	4	1	.800	0	0	5.57
2001 Edmonton	AAA Min	15	13	0	0	74	328	96	51	50	14	2	2	3	22	0	52	0	0	2	4	.333	0	0	6.08
Akron	AA Cle	8	8	1	0	53.1	222	52	24	24	8	2	2	2	15	1	47	1	0	2	3	.400	1	0	4.05
9 Min. YEARS		335	90	7	154	876	3817	824	475	422	93	44	24	36	411	10	845	70	11	41	55	.427	4	50	4.34

Jason Wood

Bats: Right **Throws:** Right **Pos:** 3B-78; SS-33; PH-3; 2B-2; 1B-1 **Ht:** 6'1" **Wt:** 200 **Born:** 12/16/69 **Age:** 32

Year Team	Lg Org	G	AB	H	2B	3B	HR	TB	R	RBI	TBB	IBB	SO	HBP	SH	SF	SB	CS	SB%	GDP	Avg	OBP	SLG
1991 Sou Oregon	A- Oak	44	142	44	3	4	3	64	30	23	28	0	30	2	2	3	5	2	.71	0	.310	.423	.451
1992 Modesto	A+ Oak	128	454	105	28	3	6	157	66	49	40	1	106	4	3	5	5	4	.56	15	.231	.296	.346
1993 Huntsville	AA Oak	103	370	85	21	2	3	119	44	36	33	0	97	2	9	3	2	4	.33	7	.230	.294	.322
1994 Huntsville	AA Oak	134	468	128	29	2	6	179	54	84	46	1	83	6	5	15	3	6	.33	9	.274	.336	.382
1995 Edmonton	AAA Oak	127	421	99	20	5	2	135	49	50	29	3	72	3	6	12	1	4	.20	13	.235	.282	.321
1996 Huntsville	AA Oak	133	491	128	21	1	20	211	77	84	72	2	87	5	2	11	2	5	.29	14	.261	.354	.430
Edmonton	AAA Oak	3	12	0	0	0	0	0	0	0	5	0	6	0	0	0	0	1	.00	0	.000	.294	.000
1997 Edmonton	AAA Oak	130	505	162	35	7	19	268	83	87	45	0	74	8	2	4	2	4	.33	21	.321	.383	.531
1998 Edmonton	AAA Oak	80	307	86	20	0	18	160	52	73	37	1	71	2	0	6	1	1	.50	5	.280	.355	.521
Toledo	AAA Det	46	169	47	9	0	7	77	24	29	16	1	30	1	0	1	0	0	—	5	.278	.342	.456
1999 Lakeland	A+ Det	5	17	4	0	0	0	4	0	1	4	1	2	1	0	0	0	1	.00	0	.235	.409	.235
Toledo	AAA Det	48	185	53	11	0	6	82	34	24	22	0	43	1	0	2	0	2	.00	6	.286	.362	.443
2000 Nashville	AAA Pit	88	316	75	18	0	7	114	40	45	28	0	84	1	2	4	2	5	.50	7	.237	.298	.361
2001 Nashville	AAA Pit	113	379	92	19	1	8	137	46	38	27	3	73	6	4	1	0	0	—	12	.243	.303	.361
1998 Oakland	AL	3	3	0	0	0	0	0	1	0	0	0	1	0	0	0	0	0	—	0	.000	.000	.000
Detroit	AL	10	23	8	2	0	1	13	5	1	3	0	4	0	0	0	0	1	.00	0	.348	.423	.565
1999 Detroit	AL	27	44	7	1	0	1	11	5	8	2	0	13	0	1	0	0	0	—	0	.159	.196	.250
11 Min. YEARS		1182	4236	1108	234	25	105	1707	599	623	432	13	858	42	35	67	23	36	.39	114	.262	.331	.403
2 Maj. YEARS		40	68	15	3	0	2	24	11	9	5	0	18	0	1	0	0	0	.00	0	.221	.274	.353

Orlando Woodards

Pitches: Right **Bats:** Right **Pos:** RP-41 **Ht:** 6'2" **Wt:** 200 **Born:** 1/2/78 **Age:** 24

Year Team	Lg Org	G	GS	CG	GF	IP	BFP	H	R	ER	HR	SH	SF	HB	TBB	IBB	SO	WP	Bk	W	L	Pct.	ShO	Sv	ERA
1997 St.Cathrnes	A- Tor	21	0	0	6	36.2	174	41	23	21	2	0	3	1	24	0	32	5	2	2	2	.500	0	2	5.15
1998 Medcine Hat	R+ Tor	26	1	0	8	50.1	215	48	27	20	4	3	1	2	11	0	58	5	2	1	3	.250	0	3	3.58
1999 Hagerstown	A Tor	44	3	0	12	80.1	352	66	45	37	5	6	1	7	43	3	79	7	1	7	4	.636	0	2	4.15
2000 Dunedin	A+ Tor	41	1	0	16	87.1	353	65	26	22	4	1	3	3	32	1	69	2	0	8	1	.889	0	7	2.27
2001 Tennessee	AA Tor	15	0	0	5	18	89	19	15	14	1	1	1	1	15	0	14	2	0	1	2	.333	0	0	7.00
Dunedin	A+ Tor	17	0	0	9	26.2	132	37	21	17	2	0	1	3	15	1	15	2	0	2	1	.667	0	0	5.74
Brevard Cty	A+ Fla	9	0	0	2	14.1	63	15	5	3	1	1	1	2	2	0	13	0	0	0	0	—	0	0	1.88
5 Min. YEARS		173	5	0	58	313.2	1378	291	162	134	19	12	11	19	142	5	280	23	5	21	13	.618	0	14	3.84

Ken Woods

Bats: Right **Throws:** Right **Pos:** OF-50; PH-8; PR-4; DH-1 **Ht:** 5'10" **Wt:** 175 **Born:** 8/2/70 **Age:** 31

Year Team	Lg Org	G	AB	H	2B	3B	HR	TB	R	RBI	TBB	IBB	SO	HBP	SH	SF	SB	CS	SB%	GDP	Avg	OBP	SLG
1992 Everett	A- SF	64	257	65	9	1	0	76	50	31	35	1	46	7	1	0	20	17	.54	2	.253	.358	.296
1993 Clinton	A SF	108	320	90	10	1	4	114	56	44	41	1	55	4	7	2	30	5	.86	13	.281	.368	.356
1994 San Jose	A+ SF	90	336	100	18	3	6	142	58	49	45	0	43	4	3	3	15	7	.68	9	.298	.384	.423

Year Team	Lg Org	G	AB	H	2B	3B	HR	TB	R	RBI	TBB	IBB	SO	HBP	SH	SF	SB	CS	SB%	GDP	Avg	OBP	SLG
1995 Shreveport	AA SF	89	209	53	11	0	3	73	30	23	23	2	29	1	2	1	4	5	.44	4	.254	.329	.349
1996 Shreveport	AA SF	83	287	80	17	1	1	102	36	29	29	0	35	4	4	6	14	10	.58	11	.279	.347	.355
Phoenix	AAA SF	56	208	58	12	1	2	78	32	13	19	0	29	1	0	3	3	4	.43	6	.279	.338	.375
1997 Phoenix	AAA SF	1	1	1	0	0	0	1	0	1	0	0	0	0	0	0	0	0	—	0	1.000	1.000	1.000
Shreveport	AA SF	104	293	88	14	2	2	112	41	32	28	0	40	3	4	3	6	4	.60	6	.300	.364	.382
1998 Shreveport	AA SF	94	335	103	20	2	4	139	44	33	28	1	31	2	0	3	8	9	.47	8	.307	.361	.415
Fresno	AAA SF	23	44	16	5	0	0	21	9	5	2	1	8	1	1	0	0	0	—	1	.364	.404	.477
1999 Fresno	AAA SF	124	469	152	23	4	6	201	77	73	33	0	45	3	2	9	19	4	.83	8	.324	.366	.429
2000 Scranton-WB	AAA Phi	133	512	155	28	6	2	201	89	35	39	0	47	5	8	1	20	7	.74	7	.303	.357	.393
2001 Rochester	AAA Bal	26	75	18	3	1	0	23	6	8	13	0	7	0	1	0	4	2	.67	2	.240	.352	.307
Iowa	AAA ChC	11	36	9	1	0	0	10	3	2	0	0	9	1	0	0	0	0	—	2	.250	.270	.278
Richmond	AAA Atl	23	70	19	4	0	0	23	8	3	2	0	7	1	0	0	1	1	.50	0	.271	.301	.329
Scranton-WB	AAA Phi	1	4	0	0	0	0	0	2	0	1	0	0	0	0	0	1	0	1.00	0	.000	.200	.000
10 Min. YEARS		1030	3456	1007	175	22	30	1316	541	381	338	6	431	37	33	31	145	75	.66	81	.291	.358	.381

Jay Woolf

Bats: Right **Throws:** Right **Pos:** OF-3; SS-1; PR-1 — **Ht:** 6'1" **Wt:** 170 **Born:** 6/6/77 **Age:** 25

Year Team	Lg Org	G	AB	H	2B	3B	HR	TB	R	RBI	TBB	IBB	SO	HBP	SH	SF	SB	CS	SB%	GDP	Avg	OBP	SLG
1995 Johnson Cty	R+ StL	31	111	31	7	1	0	40	16	14	8	0	21	1	1	3	6	3	.67	0	.279	.325	.360
1996 Peoria	A StL	108	362	93	12	8	1	124	68	27	57	1	87	2	3	1	28	12	.70	3	.257	.360	.343
1997 Pr William	A+ StL	70	251	62	11	3	6	97	59	18	55	1	75	5	1	1	26	5	.84	0	.247	.391	.386
1998 Arkansas	AA StL	76	294	78	22	5	4	122	63	16	34	0	84	9	2	1	28	5	.85	2	.265	.358	.415
1999 Arkansas	AA StL	86	320	87	18	4	8	137	46	15	28	0	86	8	6	1	11	3	.79	3	.272	.345	.428
2000 Memphis	AAA StL	32	103	25	5	1	0	32	21	6	19	0	23	2	0	0	5	3	.63	1	.243	.371	.311
Arkansas	AA StL	45	165	39	8	2	3	60	22	13	16	3	40	4	1	0	7	8	.47	2	.236	.319	.364
2001 Memphis	AAA StL	5	16	3	0	0	1	6	3	4	2	0	2	0	0	1	2	0	1.00	0	.188	.263	.375
7 Min. YEARS		453	1622	418	83	24	23	618	298	113	219	5	418	31	14	8	113	39	.74	11	.258	.355	.381

Greg Wooten

Pitches: Right **Bats:** Right **Pos:** SP-26; RP-1 — **Ht:** 6'7" **Wt:** 210 **Born:** 3/30/74 **Age:** 28

		HOW MUCH HE PITCHED						WHAT HE GAVE UP												THE RESULTS					
Year Team	Lg Org	G	GS	CG	GF	IP	BFP	H	R	ER	HR	SH	SF	HB	TBB	IBB	SO	WP	Bk	W	L	Pct.	ShO	Sv	ERA
1996 Wisconsin	A Sea	13	13	3	0	83.2	336	58	27	23	3	1	2	5	29	0	68	4	1	7	1	.875	1	0	2.47
Lancaster	A+ Sea	14	14	1	0	97	408	101	47	41	7	1	2	3	25	1	71	9	0	8	4	.667	0	0	3.80
1997 Memphis	AA Sea	26	26	0	0	155	681	166	91	77	14	5	5	6	59	1	98	12	0	11	10	.524	0	0	4.47
1998 Lancaster	A+ Sea	6	6	0	0	31.1	144	43	26	25	5	0	2	1	12	0	22	2	0	2	2	.500	0	0	7.18
1999 Lancaster	A+ Sea	17	17	3	0	114.1	489	123	62	55	13	2	3	6	30	1	72	5	0	10	4	.714	0	0	4.33
2000 New Haven	AA Sea	26	26	6	0	179.1	702	166	50	46	9	2	3	7	15	1	115	5	0	17	3	.850	4	0	2.31
2001 Tacoma	AAA Sea	27	26	5	0	169.1	728	201	91	75	18	5	9	7	32	1	116	6	0	11	8	.579	1	0	3.99
6 Min. YEARS		129	128	18	0	830	3488	858	394	342	69	16	26	35	202	5	562	43	1	66	32	.673	6	0	3.71

Corey Wright

Bats: Left **Throws:** Left **Pos:** OF-110; PH-6; DH-4; PR-1 — **Ht:** 5'11" **Wt:** 165 **Born:** 11/26/79 **Age:** 22

Year Team	Lg Org	G	AB	H	2B	3B	HR	TB	R	RBI	TBB	IBB	SO	HBP	SH	SF	SB	CS	SB%	GDP	Avg	OBP	SLG
1997 Rangers	R Tex	43	145	36	2	3	0	44	19	11	22	0	25	1	3	0	14	11	.56	1	.248	.351	.303
1998 Rangers	R Tex	11	44	12	2	1	0	16	6	3	7	0	11	0	0	0	3	2	.60	0	.273	.373	.364
Pulaski	R+ Tex	39	133	37	4	3	3	56	41	26	45	0	23	1	0	2	14	4	.78	2	.278	.459	.421
1999 Savannah	A Tex	95	316	83	15	5	1	111	61	23	64	1	73	5	1	1	13	13	.50	2	.263	.394	.351
2000 Tulsa	AA Tex	17	69	13	0	0	0	13	6	3	5	0	20	1	1	0	1	1	.50	1	.188	.253	.188
Charlotte	A+ Tex	99	370	94	17	5	0	121	76	24	79	4	81	10	3	2	31	11	.74	6	.254	.397	.327
2001 Tulsa	AA Tex	117	418	106	19	3	0	131	62	26	58	2	103	12	7	1	23	15	.61	4	.254	.360	.313
5 Min. YEARS		421	1495	381	59	20	4	492	271	116	280	7	336	30	15	6	99	57	.63	16	.255	.382	.329

Mike Wright

Bats: Right **Throws:** Right **Pos:** C-61; PH-3 — **Ht:** 6'2" **Wt:** 210 **Born:** 3/13/76 **Age:** 26

Year Team	Lg Org	G	AB	H	2B	3B	HR	TB	R	RBI	TBB	IBB	SO	HBP	SH	SF	SB	CS	SB%	GDP	Avg	OBP	SLG
1999 Salem-Keizr	A- SF	24	63	17	4	0	1	24	14	7	17	0	12	2	0	1	0	0	—	2	.270	.434	.381
2000 San Jose	A+ SF	97	299	57	10	1	6	87	29	33	31	0	102	6	10	0	1	0	1.00	6	.191	.280	.291
2001 Shreveport	AA SF	62	182	44	10	0	3	63	13	19	12	1	62	1	4	2	0	2	.00	0	.242	.289	.346
Fresno	AAA SF	2	8	3	0	0	1	6	2	3	0	0	2	0	0	0	0	0	—	0	.375	.375	.750
3 Min. YEARS		185	552	121	24	1	11	180	58	62	60	1	178	9	14	3	1	2	.33	9	.219	.304	.326

Nate Wright

Bats: Right **Throws:** Right **Pos:** OF-4; 2B-1; 3B-1; DH-1 — **Ht:** 5'10" **Wt:** 170 **Born:** 1/22/78 **Age:** 24

Year Team	Lg Org	G	AB	H	2B	3B	HR	TB	R	RBI	TBB	IBB	SO	HBP	SH	SF	SB	CS	SB%	GDP	Avg	OBP	SLG
2000 Yakima	A- LA	4	9	2	0	0	0	2	1	2	1	0	4	0	0	0	0	0	—	0	.222	.300	.222
Great Falls	R+ LA	4	4	0	0	0	0	0	2	0	3	0	1	0	0	0	0	0	—	0	.000	.429	.000
2001 Jacksnville	A+ LA	1	1	0	0	0	0	0	0	0	0	0	0	0	0	0	0	0	—	0	.000	.000	.000
Vero Beach	A+ LA	2	2	0	0	0	0	0	0	0	1	0	1	0	0	1	0	0	—	1	.000	.333	.000
Dodgers	R LA	4	10	2	0	0	0	2	3	1	1	0	1	0	0	0	0	0	—	0	.200	.273	.200
2 Min. YEARS		15	26	4	0	0	0	4	6	3	6	0	6	0	0	0	0	0	—	1	.154	.313	.154

Ron Wright

Bats: Right **Throws:** Right **Pos:** 1B-118; DH-3; PH-1 **Ht:** 6'1" **Wt:** 230 **Born:** 1/21/76 **Age:** 26

		BATTING														BASERUNNING				PERCENTAGES		
Year Team	Lg Org	G	AB	H	2B	3B	HR	TB	R	RBI	TBB	IBB	SO	HBP	SH	SF	SB	CS	SB%	GDP	Avg	OBP	SLG
1994 Braves	R Atl	45	169	29	9	0	1	41	10	16	10	0	21	0	0	0	1	0	1.00	3	.172	.218	.243
1995 Macon	A Atl	135	527	143	23	1	32	264	93	104	62	1	118	2	0	3	2	0	1.00	11	.271	.348	.501
1996 Durham	A+ Atl	66	240	66	15	2	20	145	47	62	37	2	71	0	0	7	1	0	1.00	5	.275	.363	.604
Greenville	AA Atl	63	232	59	11	1	16	120	39	52	38	5	73	2	0	3	1	0	1.00	2	.254	.360	.517
Carolina	AA Pit	4	14	2	0	0	0	2	1	0	2	0	7	0	0	0	0	1	.00	0	.143	.250	.143
1997 Calgary	AAA Pit	91	336	102	31	0	16	181	50	63	24	2	81	2	0	6	0	2	.00	4	.304	.348	.539
1998 Nashville	AAA Pit	17	56	12	3	0	0	15	6	9	9	0	18	1	0	1	0	0	—	2	.214	.328	.268
Pirates	R Pit	3	10	6	0	0	2	12	4	5	2	0	0	0	0	1	0	0	—	0	.600	.615	1.200
1999 Altoona	AA Pit	24	80	17	6	0	0	23	2	4	9	0	27	1	0	0	0	0	—	1	.213	.300	.288
2000 Louisville	AAA Cin	18	60	12	5	0	2	23	10	13	8	0	18	0	0	0	0	0	—	1	.200	.294	.383
Chattanooga	AA Cin	79	237	63	18	0	12	117	36	50	37	0	70	2	0	2	2	2	.50	3	.266	.367	.494
2001 Durham	AAA TB	121	439	115	27	0	20	202	63	75	51	3	103	3	0	4	2	2	.50	11	.262	.340	.460
8 Min. YEARS		666	2400	626	148	4	121	1145	361	453	289	13	607	13	0	27	9	7	.56	43	.261	.340	.477

Jase Wrigley

Pitches: Right **Bats:** Right **Pos:** RP-47 **Ht:** 6'4" **Wt:** 220 **Born:** 11/6/75 **Age:** 26

		HOW MUCH HE PITCHED						WHAT HE GAVE UP										THE RESULTS				
Year Team	Lg Org	G	GS	CG	GF	IP	BFP	H	R	ER	HR	SH	SF	HB	TBB	IBB	SO	WP	Bk	W	L	Pct.	ShO	Sv	ERA
1998 Asheville	A Col	13	0	0	5	15.2	70	18	11	10	3	0	0	1	4	0	12	1	1	1	1	.500	0	0	5.74
1999 Asheville	A Col	28	0	0	18	58.1	259	63	32	20	2	2	2	2	16	0	58	6	2	3	2	.600	0	6	3.09
Salem	A+ Col	8	0	0	5	9.1	36	9	1	1	0	0	0	0	0	0	6	1	0	2	0	1.000	0	0	0.96
2000 Salem	A+ Col	47	0	0	36	61	250	52	26	18	3	5	2	1	22	1	38	4	0	3	2	.600	0	16	2.66
2001 Carolina	AA Col	47	0	0	16	64.1	310	93	53	45	4	6	2	2	28	4	33	2	0	6	6	.500	0	2	6.30
4 Min. YEARS		143	0	0	80	208.2	925	235	123	94	12	13	6	6	70	5	147	14	3	15	11	.577	0	24	4.05

Mike Wuertz

Pitches: Right **Bats:** Right **Pos:** SP-27 **Ht:** 6'3" **Wt:** 190 **Born:** 12/15/78 **Age:** 23

		HOW MUCH HE PITCHED						WHAT HE GAVE UP										THE RESULTS				
Year Team	Lg Org	G	GS	CG	GF	IP	BFP	H	R	ER	HR	SH	SF	HB	TBB	IBB	SO	WP	Bk	W	L	Pct.	ShO	Sv	ERA
1998 Williamsprt	A- ChC	14	14	1	0	86.1	359	79	36	33	4	3	2	0	19	0	59	1	2	7	5	.583	0	0	3.44
1999 Lansing	A ChC	28	28	1	0	161.1	716	191	104	86	11	2	10	1	44	0	127	11	0	11	12	.478	0	0	4.80
2000 Daytona	A+ ChC	28	28	3	0	171.1	732	166	79	72	15	6	4	3	64	1	142	7	1	12	7	.632	2	0	3.78
2001 West Tenn	AA ChC	27	27	1	0	160	694	160	80	71	20	9	6	6	58	2	135	10	0	4	9	.308	1	0	3.99
4 Min. YEARS		97	97	6	0	579	2501	596	299	262	50	20	22	10	185	3	463	29	3	34	33	.507	3	0	4.07

Mitch Wylie

Pitches: Right **Bats:** Right **Pos:** SP-25 **Ht:** 6'3" **Wt:** 190 **Born:** 1/14/77 **Age:** 25

		HOW MUCH HE PITCHED						WHAT HE GAVE UP										THE RESULTS				
Year Team	Lg Org	G	GS	CG	GF	IP	BFP	H	R	ER	HR	SH	SF	HB	TBB	IBB	SO	WP	Bk	W	L	Pct.	ShO	Sv	ERA
1998 Bristol	R+ CWS	20	0	0	14	30	133	34	12	11	1	0	2	0	11	2	32	7	0	0	2	.000	0	6	3.30
1999 Burlington	A CWS	6	6	0	0	32	134	28	11	7	0	0	3	2	11	0	27	0	0	1	0	1.000	0	0	1.97
2000 Winston-Sal	A+ CWS	17	17	0	0	95.1	422	112	59	46	8	4	4	3	34	0	57	1	2	3	7	.300	0	0	4.34
2001 Winston-Sal	A+ CWS	1	1	0	0	5	23	7	2	2	0	0	0	0	1	0	4	0	0	1	0	1.000	0	0	3.60
Birmingham	AA CWS	24	24	0	0	141	612	138	70	66	13	2	6	12	46	1	123	4	3	15	4	.789	0	0	4.21
4 Min. YEARS		68	48	0	14	303.1	1324	319	154	132	22	6	15	17	103	3	243	12	5	19	14	.576	0	6	3.92

Tyler Yates

Pitches: Right **Bats:** Right **Pos:** RP-60 **Ht:** 6'4" **Wt:** 220 **Born:** 8/7/77 **Age:** 24

		HOW MUCH HE PITCHED						WHAT HE GAVE UP										THE RESULTS				
Year Team	Lg Org	G	GS	CG	GF	IP	BFP	H	R	ER	HR	SH	SF	HB	TBB	IBB	SO	WP	Bk	W	L	Pct.	ShO	Sv	ERA
1998 Athletics	R Oak	15	0	0	8	23	107	28	12	10	0	0	0	1	14	0	20	1	2	0	0	—	0	2	3.91
Sou Oregon	A- Oak	2	0	0	1	2.1	9	2	0	0	0	0	0	0	0	0	1	0	0	0	0	—	0	0	0.00
1999 Visalia	A+ Oak	47	1	0	19	82.1	382	98	64	50	12	3	2	4	35	3	74	12	0	2	5	.286	0	4	5.47
2000 Modesto	A+ Oak	30	0	0	5	56.2	237	50	23	18	2	1	1	1	23	4	61	8	0	4	2	.667	0	1	2.86
Midland	AA Oak	22	0	0	8	26.1	121	28	20	18	2	2	2	0	15	3	24	2	0	1	1	.500	0	0	6.15
2001 Midland	AA Oak	56	0	0	35	62.2	282	66	39	30	4	1	0	1	27	8	61	7	0	4	6	.400	0	17	4.31
Sacramento	AAA Oak	4	0	0	2	5.1	20	3	0	0	0	0	0	1	1	0	3	0	0	1	0	1.000	0	0	0.00
4 Min. YEARS		176	1	0	78	258.2	1158	275	158	126	20	7	5	8	115	18	244	30	2	12	14	.462	0	26	4.38

Ernie Young

Bats: Right **Throws:** Right **Pos:** OF-89; DH-21; PH-8 **Ht:** 6'1" **Wt:** 234 **Born:** 7/8/69 **Age:** 32

		BATTING														BASERUNNING				PERCENTAGES		
Year Team	Lg Org	G	AB	H	2B	3B	HR	TB	R	RBI	TBB	IBB	SO	HBP	SH	SF	SB	CS	SB%	GDP	Avg	OBP	SLG
1990 Sou Oregon	A- Oak	50	168	47	8	2	6	75	34	23	28	2	53	3	0	2	4	4	.50	2	.280	.388	.446
1991 Madison	A Oak	114	362	92	19	2	15	160	75	71	58	0	115	9	9	6	20	9	.69	4	.254	.366	.442
1992 Modesto	A+ Oak	74	253	63	12	4	11	116	55	33	47	1	74	6	2	1	11	3	.79	5	.249	.378	.458
1993 Modesto	A+ Oak	85	301	92	18	6	23	191	83	71	72	0	92	4	0	3	23	7	.77	2	.306	.442	.635
Huntsville	AA Oak	45	120	25	5	0	5	45	26	15	24	0	36	2	2	1	8	5	.62	1	.208	.345	.375
1994 Tacoma	AAA Oak	29	102	29	4	0	6	51	19	16	13	0	27	2	0	2	0	5	.00	3	.284	.370	.500
Huntsville	AA Oak	72	257	89	19	4	14	158	45	55	37	2	45	2	4	4	5	6	.45	6	.346	.427	.615
1995 Edmonton	AAA Oak	95	347	96	21	4	15	170	70	72	49	1	73	3	1	7	2	2	.50	5	.277	.365	.490
1997 Edmonton	AAA Oak	54	195	63	10	0	9	100	39	45	37	1	46	6	1	2	5	2	.71	4	.323	.442	.513
1998 Omaha	AAA KC	79	297	97	13	2	22	178	58	55	29	2	68	5	0	1	6	4	.60	8	.327	.395	.599
1999 Tucson	AAA Ari	126	453	133	25	1	30	250	78	95	57	1	129	5	0	6	4	1	.80	9	.294	.374	.552
2000 Memphis	AAA StL	124	453	119	16	0	35	240	76	98	66	6	117	4	0	4	11	1	.92	17	.263	.359	.530

Year Team	Lg Org	G	AB	H	2B	3B	HR	TB	R	RBI	TBB	IBB	SO	HBP	SH	SF	SB	CS	SB%	GDP	Avg	OBP	SLG
2001 Portland	AAA SD	116	409	112	21	2	20	197	66	67	38	1	115	14	0	1	0	3	.00	13	.274	.355	.482
1994 Oakland	AL	11	30	2	1	0	0	3	2	3	1	0	8	0	0	0	0	0	—	1	.067	.097	.100
1995 Oakland	AL	26	50	10	3	0	2	19	9	5	8	0	12	0	0	0	0	0	—	1	.200	.310	.380
1996 Oakland	AL	141	462	112	19	4	19	196	72	64	52	1	118	7	3	4	7	5	.58	13	.242	.326	.424
1997 Oakland	AL	71	175	39	7	0	5	61	22	15	19	0	57	2	2	2	1	3	.25	6	.223	.303	.349
1998 Kansas City	AL	25	53	10	3	0	1	16	2	3	2	0	9	1	0	0	2	1	.67	1	.189	.232	.302
1999 Arizona	NL	6	11	2	0	0	0	2	1	0	3	0	2	1	0	0	0	0	—	0	.182	.400	.182
11 Min. YEARS		1063	3717	1057	189	26	211	1931	724	716	555	17	990	65	17	41	99	52	.66	82	.284	.383	.520
6 Maj. YEARS		280	781	175	33	4	27	297	108	90	85	1	206	11	5	6	10	9	.53	24	.224	.307	.380

Travis Young

Bats: Right **Throws:** Right **Pos:** 2B-4; PH-3; SS-2; 3B-2   **Ht:** 6'1" **Wt:** 185 **Born:** 9/8/74 **Age:** 27

Year Team	Lg Org	G	AB	H	2B	3B	HR	TB	R	RBI	TBB	IBB	SO	HBP	SH	SF	SB	CS	SB%	GDP	Avg	OBP	SLG
1997 Salem-Keizr	A- SF	76	320	107	11	6	1	133	80	34	30	0	50	5	1	3	40	8	.83	3	.334	.397	.416
1998 San Jose	A+ SF	133	517	126	21	2	4	163	79	63	61	2	101	8	11	6	27	12	.69	14	.244	.329	.315
1999 Fresno	AAA SF	26	92	23	1	1	2	32	15	11	9	1	23	3	1	1	3	2	.60	1	.250	.333	.348
Shreveport	AA SF	108	416	110	28	2	5	157	68	38	33	0	75	8	7	2	16	11	.59	11	.264	.329	.377
2000 Fresno	AAA SF	13	32	5	0	0	0	5	2	0	3	0	8	0	2	0	0	0	—	1	.156	.229	.156
Shreveport	AA SF	97	334	83	14	4	6	123	41	31	25	0	65	7	2	4	14	7	.67	8	.249	.311	.368
2001 Shreveport	AA SF	6	14	5	1	0	0	6	2	1	0	0	3	0	0	0	0	0	—	0	.357	.357	.429
Fresno	AAA SF	4	3	0	0	0	0	0	0	0	0	0	2	0	1	0	0	0	—	0	.000	.000	.000
5 Min. YEARS		463	1728	459	76	15	18	619	287	178	161	3	327	31	25	16	100	40	.71	38	.266	.336	.358

Junior Zamora

Bats: Right **Throws:** Right **Pos:** 3B-36; 1B-13; DH-8; 2B-4; PH-2; PR-1   **Ht:** 6'2" **Wt:** 193 **Born:** 5/3/76 **Age:** 26

Year Team	Lg Org	G	AB	H	2B	3B	HR	TB	R	RBI	TBB	IBB	SO	HBP	SH	SF	SB	CS	SB%	GDP	Avg	OBP	SLG
1995 Mets	R NYM	20	56	13	2	2	0	19	9	4	5	0	10	1	1	1	0	0	—	2	.232	.302	.339
1996 Kingsport	R+ NYM	60	227	55	13	0	7	89	37	41	11	0	59	7	0	3	2	1	.67	3	.242	.294	.392
Capital Cty	A NYM	1	4	0	0	0	0	0	0	0	0	0	3	0	0	0	0	0	—	0	.000	.000	.000
1997 Capital Cty	A NYM	36	124	31	5	0	8	60	16	19	10	0	29	0	0	0	0	0	.00	1	.250	.306	.484
1998 Mets	R NYM	2	5	1	0	1	0	3	1	2	1	0	0	0	0	0	0	0	—	1	.200	.333	.600
St. Lucie	A+ NYM	99	368	105	17	4	10	160	58	53	25	1	60	5	0	0	4	3	.57	9	.285	.339	.435
1999 Binghamton	AA NYM	67	255	61	17	0	10	108	28	33	12	1	62	3	0	2	2	1	.67	13	.239	.279	.424
2000 Binghamton	AA NYM	40	130	21	3	0	4	36	14	11	9	0	29	2	0	0	3	1	.75	4	.162	.227	.277
2001 Rancho Cuca	A+ Ana	12	52	15	2	1	3	28	9	8	1	0	14	0	0	0	3	0	1.00	2	.288	.302	.538
Arkansas	AA Ana	42	144	30	5	1	4	49	15	18	9	0	32	1	1	2	1	1	.50	5	.208	.256	.340
Salt Lake	AAA Ana	6	20	6	1	1	2	15	3	4	2	0	3	0	0	0	1	0	.00	0	.300	.364	.750
7 Min. YEARS		385	1385	338	65	10	48	567	190	193	85	2	301	19	2	8	15	8	.65	41	.244	.295	.409

Pete Zamora

Pitches: Left **Bats:** Left **Pos:** RP-39; SP-6   **Ht:** 6'3" **Wt:** 185 **Born:** 8/13/75 **Age:** 26

Year Team	Lg Org	G	GS	CG	GF	IP	BFP	H	R	ER	HR	SH	SF	HB	TBB	IBB	SO	WP	Bk	W	L	Pct.	ShO	Sv	ERA
1997 Great Falls	R+ LA	13	10	1	2	69.2	289	59	27	20	3	1	1	3	30	0	73	3	1	2	5	.286	0	2	2.58
1998 San Berndno	A+ LA	25	5	0	15	81.2	321	43	21	19	1	5	1	4	33	0	77	3	2	4	1	.800	0	6	2.09
San Antonio	AA LA	12	12	0	0	66.2	299	71	52	33	6	4	3	1	27	0	47	1	1	3	8	.273	0	0	4.46
1999 San Antonio	AA LA	35	0	0	8	63.2	292	79	48	43	5	3	5	4	30	2	41	1	1	2	1	.667	0	3	6.08
2000 Reading	AA Phi	43	7	1	13	101.1	455	105	50	46	6	3	1	7	45	3	94	5	0	2	3	.400	1	6	4.09
2001 Scranton-WB	AAA Phi	45	6	0	22	89	369	64	29	29	7	6	2	3	41	6	79	5	2	8	4	.667	0	3	2.93
5 Min. YEARS		173	40	2	60	472	2025	421	227	190	28	22	13	22	206	11	411	21	7	21	22	.488	1	20	3.62

Dave Zancanaro

Pitches: Left **Bats:** Left **Pos:** SP-25; RP-3   **Ht:** 6'1" **Wt:** 190 **Born:** 1/8/69 **Age:** 33

Year Team	Lg Org	G	GS	CG	GF	IP	BFP	H	R	ER	HR	SH	SF	HB	TBB	IBB	SO	WP	Bk	W	L	Pct.	ShO	Sv	ERA
1990 Sou Oregon	A- Oak	10	8	0	0	44.1	188	44	22	19	2	1	0	1	13	0	42	3	4	3	0	1.000	0	0	3.86
Modesto	A+ Oak	4	2	0	0	13	64	13	9	9	1	0	0	0	14	0	7	0	0	1	2	.333	0	0	6.23
1991 Huntsville	AA Oak	29	28	0	1	165	727	151	87	62	7	3	4	6	92	0	104	8	4	5	10	.333	0	0	3.38
1992 Tacoma	AAA Oak	23	19	0	0	105.2	486	108	61	50	3	5	7	2	75	0	47	7	2	2	11	.154	0	0	4.26
1995 W Michigan	A Oak	16	16	0	0	32.2	132	19	8	8	1	2	0	3	15	0	42	1	0	2	0	.000	0	0	2.20
1996 Modesto	A+ Oak	20	3	0	6	77.1	331	61	38	29	9	4	2	3	37	0	66	5	1	7	3	.700	0	3	3.38
Huntsville	AA Oak	10	10	0	0	43.1	206	54	32	27	4	0	1	2	26	1	36	3	0	3	3	.500	0	0	5.61
1997 Las Vegas	AAA SD	3	3	0	0	13.1	77	27	24	23	3	0	0	2	8	0	9	0	0	0	3	.000	0	0	15.53
Mobile	AA SD	27	19	3	3	133.2	581	140	69	66	15	5	3	4	57	0	66	10	1	10	8	.556	0	1	4.44
1998 Norwich	AA NYY	16	13	0	2	69	300	80	42	36	9	2	1	3	23	0	49	3	0	3	4	.429	0	0	4.70
1999 Norwich	AA NYY	15	11	1	0	79	327	64	25	20	4	5	1	2	32	1	61	2	0	6	1	.857	0	0	2.28
Columbus	AAA NYY	13	13	1	0	77.2	336	85	40	36	11	0	1	0	28	0	45	1	2	7	2	.778	0	0	4.17
2000 Iowa	AAA ChC	25	20	0	2	115.1	517	131	80	67	19	3	0	6	54	2	67	5	2	4	10	.286	0	0	5.23
2001 New Haven	AA StL	1	1	0	0	5	22	4	1	1	0	0	0	0	4	0	0	0	0	0	0	—	0	0	1.80
Memphis	AAA StL	27	24	1	1	142.2	640	171	103	95	28	8	4	6	48	0	107	3	0	6	14	.300	1	1	5.99
10 Min. YEARS		239	190	6	16	1117	4934	1152	641	548	116	38	24	40	526	5	753	52	18	57	73	.438	1	5	4.42

A.J. Zapp

Bats: Left **Throws:** Right **Pos:** 1B-74; PH-2 **Ht:** 6'3" **Wt:** 190 **Born:** 4/24/78 **Age:** 24

Year Team	Lg Org	G	AB	H	2B	3B	HR	TB	R	RBI	TBB	IBB	SO	HBP	SH	SF	SB	CS	SB%	GDP	Avg	OBP	SLG
1996 Braves	R Atl	47	161	24	9	0	0	33	9	5	15	0	58	1	1	1	0	0	—	0	.149	.225	.205
1997 Danville	R+ Atl	65	234	79	23	2	7	127	34	56	35	0	78	7	0	1	0	1	.00	3	.338	.437	.543
1998 Macon	A Atl	20	73	19	6	1	3	36	9	12	8	0	18	2	0	0	1	0	1.00	1	.260	.349	.493
1999 Macon	A Atl	119	428	98	24	1	22	190	60	65	40	0	163	7	0	4	4	1	.80	4	.229	.303	.444
2000 Myrtle Bch	A+ Atl	107	385	103	28	1	8	157	59	49	57	3	106	10	0	0	3	2	.60	4	.268	.376	.408
2001 Greenville	AA Atl	75	292	68	17	0	8	109	36	34	21	0	87	5	0	0	5	1	.83	11	.233	.296	.373
6 Min. YEARS		433	1573	391	107	5	48	652	207	221	176	3	510	32	1	6	13	5	.72	23	.249	.335	.414

Scott Zech

Bats: Right **Throws:** Right **Pos:** 3B-54; 2B-11; PH-10; SS-9; DH-2 **Ht:** 5'10" **Wt:** 175 **Born:** 6/6/74 **Age:** 28

Year Team	Lg Org	G	AB	H	2B	3B	HR	TB	R	RBI	TBB	IBB	SO	HBP	SH	SF	SB	CS	SB%	GDP	Avg	OBP	SLG
1997 Vermont	A- Mon	63	204	54	11	0	1	68	31	20	27	1	36	7	5	6	17	7	.71	4	.265	.361	.333
1998 Cape Fear	A Mon	102	304	87	20	2	3	120	53	45	43	0	48	13	9	4	13	8	.62	3	.286	.393	.395
1999 Cape Fear	A Mon	3	10	3	0	0	0	3	1	1	3	0	1	0	0	0	1	0	1.00	0	.300	.462	.300
Harrisburg	AA Mon	22	72	20	4	1	1	29	8	10	4	0	13	0	2	2	3	2	.60	0	.278	.308	.403
Jupiter	A+ Mon	68	203	57	13	0	1	73	28	18	29	0	30	5	10	3	15	5	.75	1	.281	.379	.360
2000 Jupiter	A+ Mon	2	3	0	0	0	0	0	1	0	2	0	0	0	0	0	0	0	—	0	.000	.400	.000
Harrisburg	AA Mon	87	178	35	5	1	0	42	28	18	37	1	31	3	6	1	6	3	.67	5	.197	.342	.236
2001 Ottawa	AAA Mon	13	36	6	2	0	0	8	2	2	5	1	8	1	0	0	1	1	.50	1	.167	.286	.222
Harrisburg	AA Mon	34	85	22	3	0	0	25	14	8	13	0	14	1	3	1	2	5	.29	5	.259	.360	.294
Jupiter	A+ Mon	32	99	22	1	0	0	23	10	7	14	0	17	1	2	0	2	0	1.00	4	.222	.325	.232
5 Min. YEARS		426	1194	306	59	4	6	391	176	129	177	3	198	31	37	17	60	31	.66	23	.256	.362	.327

Jordan Zimmerman

Pitches: Left **Bats:** Right **Pos:** RP-37; SP-4 **Ht:** 6'0" **Wt:** 200 **Born:** 4/28/75 **Age:** 27

Year Team	Lg Org	HOW MUCH HE PITCHED						WHAT HE GAVE UP												THE RESULTS					
		G	GS	CG	GF	IP	BFP	H	R	ER	HR	SH	SF	HB	TBB	IBB	SO	WP	Bk	W	L	Pct.	ShO	Sv	ERA
1997 Everett	A- Sea	11	9	0	1	39	177	37	27	18	2	0	3	3	23	0	54	1	2	2	3	.400	0	0	4.15
Wisconsin	A Sea	3	3	0	0	17	75	18	11	11	0	0	1	0	10	0	18	2	0	0	1	.000	0	0	5.82
1998 Mariners	R Sea	5	3	0	1	12	55	14	6	4	1	0	0	2	7	0	11	0	0	0	1	.000	0	0	3.00
Lancaster	A+ Sea	3	3	0	0	16.2	74	21	9	9	2	0	0	0	8	0	8	1	0	0	1	.000	0	0	4.86
1999 Everett	A- Sea	1	0	0	0	0.2	5	3	2	2	0	0	0	0	0	0	1	0	0	0	0	—	0	0	27.00
Tacoma	AAA Sea	9	0	0	2	7	35	13	4	4	1	0	0	0	4	1	4	0	0	0	0	—	0	0	5.14
New Haven	AA Sea	22	0	0	8	33.1	141	26	8	4	0	0	1	2	19	0	33	1	1	1	4	.200	0	2	1.08
2000 Mariners	R Sea	10	10	0	0	12	46	7	3	0	0	0	0	0	3	0	14	0	0	0	0	—	0	0	0.00
Lancaster	A+ Sea	3	0	0	1	3.1	13	0	0	0	0	0	0	1	2	0	2	0	0	0	0	—	0	0	0.00
Tacoma	AAA Sea	15	0	0	2	23	108	27	20	17	3	0	0	1	11	1	23	1	0	0	1	.000	0	0	6.65
2001 Tacoma	AAA Sea	41	4	0	25	58.1	279	83	52	45	8	5	5	4	23	0	45	5	0	4	3	.571	0	4	6.94
1999 Seattle	AL	12	0	0	2	8	41	14	8	7	0	0	0	1	4	0	3	1	0	0	0	—	0	0	7.88
5 Min. YEARS		123	32	0	40	222.1	1016	249	142	114	17	5	10	13	110	2	213	13	3	7	14	.333	0	6	4.61

Alan Zinter

Bats: Both **Throws:** Right **Pos:** 1B-57; C-21; DH-21; PH-13; OF-1 **Ht:** 6'2" **Wt:** 200 **Born:** 5/19/68 **Age:** 34

Year Team	Lg Org	G	AB	H	2B	3B	HR	TB	R	RBI	TBB	IBB	SO	HBP	SH	SF	SB	CS	SB%	GDP	Avg	OBP	SLG
1989 Pittsfield	A- NYM	12	41	15	2	1	2	25	11	12	12	0	4	0	0	1	0	1	.00	0	.366	.500	.610
St. Lucie	A+ NYM	48	264	63	10	0	3	82	17	32	18	2	31	1	0	5	0	1	.00	5	.239	.311	.358
1990 St. Lucie	A+ NYM	98	333	97	19	6	7	149	63	63	54	1	70	1	0	6	8	1	.89	10	.291	.386	.447
Jackson	AA NYM	6	20	4	1	0	0	5	2	1	3	0	11	0	0	0	1	0	1.00	1	.200	.304	.250
1991 Williamsprt	AA NYM	124	422	93	13	6	9	145	44	54	59	1	106	3	2	2	3	3	.50	10	.220	.319	.344
1992 Binghamton	AA NYM	128	431	96	13	5	16	167	63	50	70	5	117	4	0	0	0	0	—	5	.223	.337	.387
1993 Binghamton	AA NYM	134	432	113	24	4	24	217	68	87	90	7	105	1	0	5	1	0	1.00	4	.262	.386	.502
1994 Toledo	AAA Det	134	471	112	29	5	21	214	66	58	69	4	185	7	0	0	13	5	.72	3	.238	.344	.454
1995 Toledo	AAA Det	101	334	74	15	4	13	136	42	48	36	1	102	2	2	5	4	1	.80	5	.222	.297	.407
1996 Pawtucket	AAA Bos	108	357	96	19	5	26	203	78	69	58	2	123	4	0	5	5	1	.83	3	.269	.373	.569
1997 Tacoma	AAA Sea	110	404	116	19	4	20	203	69	70	64	9	113	3	1	1	3	1	.75	7	.287	.388	.502
1998 Iowa	AAA ChC	129	419	130	23	1	23	224	82	81	75	1	116	3	0	3	3	5	.38	10	.310	.416	.535
1999 Iowa	AAA ChC	14	51	13	2	0	3	24	7	8	5	0	13	0	0	0	0	0	—	0	.255	.321	.471
2000 Iowa	AAA ChC	90	233	53	12	2	14	111	27	35	39	2	78	2	0	3	0	0	—	3	.227	.339	.476
Tucson	AAA Ari	11	36	13	5	1	1	23	9	5	8	1	8	0	0	0	0	0	—	0	.361	.477	.639
2001 New Orleans	AAA Hou	104	332	88	16	0	19	161	58	65	33	1	85	3	0	3	1	1	.50	13	.265	.334	.485
13 Min. YEARS		1351	4475	1151	222	44	201	2064	706	738	693	37	1267	34	6	39	42	20	.68	82	.257	.358	.461

Tony Zuniga

Bats: Right **Throws:** Right **Pos:** 3B-117; PH-5; 1B-2; DH-1 **Ht:** 6'0" **Wt:** 185 **Born:** 1/13/75 **Age:** 27

Year Team	Lg Org	G	AB	H	2B	3B	HR	TB	R	RBI	TBB	IBB	SO	HBP	SH	SF	SB	CS	SB%	GDP	Avg	OBP	SLG
1996 Bellingham	A- SF	69	264	79	11	1	2	98	36	35	34	2	47	0	4	2	0	5	.00	4	.299	.377	.371
1997 San Jose	A+ SF	97	289	53	10	0	1	66	24	32	33	0	48	11	6	2	3	3	.50	11	.183	.290	.228
1998 San Jose	A+ SF	113	397	97	20	4	8	149	52	59	39	0	64	5	0	3	1	2	.33	7	.244	.318	.375
1999 San Jose	A+ SF	136	533	144	33	3	10	213	82	66	65	0	89	13	3	4	4	9	.69	8	.270	.361	.400
2000 Shreveport	AA SF	125	407	106	24	0	17	181	54	62	49	2	50	3	3	4	3	4	.43	12	.260	.341	.445
2001 Fresno	AAA SF	123	413	112	16	1	26	208	77	74	55	2	83	6	0	3	6	1	.86	7	.271	.363	.504
6 Min. YEARS		663	2303	591	114	9	64	915	325	328	275	6	381	38	16	18	22	19	.54	47	.257	.343	.397

Mike Zywica

Bats: Right **Throws:** Right **Pos:** OF-88; DH-25; PH-4; PR-1 **Ht:** 6'4" **Wt:** 190 **Born:** 9/14/74 **Age:** 27

Year Team	Lg Org	G	AB	H	2B	3B	HR	TB	R	RBI	TBB	IBB	SO	HBP	SH	SF	SB	CS	SB%	GDP	Avg	OBP	SLG
1996 Rangers	R Tex	33	110	30	7	1	3	48	18	22	14	1	24	8	0	0	3	0	1.00	1	.273	.394	.436
Chston-SC	A Tex	20	67	9	1	1	2	18	5	4	7	0	13	1	0	0	3	1	.75	2	.134	.227	.269
1997 Charlotte	A+ Tex	126	462	119	25	5	12	190	75	64	50	0	116	12	0	6	19	19	.50	10	.258	.342	.411
1998 Charlotte	A+ Tex	68	252	96	21	3	11	156	67	49	34	2	40	6	0	4	16	5	.76	4	.381	.459	.619
Tulsa	AA Tex	58	214	60	15	4	5	98	40	45	19	0	56	5	0	4	7	3	.70	3	.280	.347	.458
1999 Oklahoma	AAA Tex	135	495	131	31	3	9	195	80	79	33	0	119	7	1	7	4	1	.80	13	.265	.315	.394
2000 Tulsa	AA Tex	5	19	8	1	0	1	12	7	8	2	0	2	1	0	0	0	0	—	0	.421	.500	.632
Oklahoma	AAA Tex	126	420	110	25	4	9	170	57	58	46	0	123	5	3	4	8	7	.53	6	.262	.339	.405
2001 Tulsa	AA Tex	47	163	39	9	0	5	63	23	22	6	0	60	5	0	1	0	1	.00	0	.239	.286	.387
Lincoln	IND —	32	123	22	3	1	5	42	14	12	7	0	31	2	1	1	3	2	.60	1	.179	.233	.341
Adirondack	IND —	38	133	38	8	1	7	69	25	22	15	0	44	1	0	2	6	2	.75	2	.286	.358	.519
6 Min. YEARS		688	2458	662	146	23	69	1061	411	385	233	3	628	53	5	29	69	41	.63	42	.269	.342	.432

2001 Class-A and Rookie Statistics

Any player who appeared in Class-A or Rookie ball without reaching Double-A or Triple-A has his 2001 statistics in this section. Class-A (A+, A, A-) and Rookie (R+, R) have subclassifications to distinguish the level of competition. Ages are as of June 30, 2002. A complete list of statistical abbreviations can be found in the introduction to the Career Register section on page 2.

The handedness and position of each player is provided. An asterisk (*) identifies a lefthanded-hitting player or lefthanded pitcher. A player who switch-hits is noted with a pound sign (#).

A number of players in this section will be well-known prospects a year from now. That is the case with Cincinnati outfielder Adam Dunn, a star in the making who appeared in this section of last year's *Handbook*. Also in these pages a year ago were several young starters who were impressive in major league rotations in 2001: Pittsburgh's Dave Williams, Toronto's Brandon Lyon, Juan Cruz of the Cubs, Ryan Drese of Cleveland, Houston's Carlos Hernandez and Jose Acevedo of the Reds. A few relievers—including Detroit's Luis Pineda, Brad Voyles of the Royals, and two promising Padres prospects, Jeremy Fikac and Jose Nunez—held their own in big-league bullpens after appearing here last year.

Very few players reach Double-A or higher in their first pro season, so nearly all future major leaguers will be found in this section before reaching the majors. There are plenty of gems hidden away in these pages. Among those who may emerge in 2002 are Seattle's Jamal Strong, Adrian Gonzalez of the Marlins, Atlanta's Brett Evert, Jimmy Gobble of the Royals, San Francisco's Boof Bonser and Boston's Seung Song.

2001 Batting — Class-A and Rookie Leagues

BATTING																					BASERUNNING				PERCENTAGES		
Player	Pos	Team	Org	Lg	A	G	AB	H	2B	3B	HR	TB	R	RBI	TBB	IBB	SO	HBP	SH	SF	SB	CS	SB%	GDP	Avg	OBP	SLG
Abad, Noel	of	Angels	Ana	R	19	19	58	17	1	1	1	23	9	7	3	0	14	2	1	1	6	1	.86	1	.293	.344	.397
Abercrombie, R.	of	Wilmington	LA	A	20	125	486	110	17	3	10	163	63	41	19	1	154	12	12	2	44	11	.80	3	.226	.272	.335
Abram, Matt	3b	Elizabethtn	Min	R+	22	55	190	46	11	0	5	72	26	24	16	0	38	4	2	2	3	3	.50	3	.242	.311	.379
Abreu, Dave#	2b	Capital Cty	NYM	A	23	16	59	10	3	0	1	16	10	4	9	0	15	1	1	0	5	1	.83	0	.169	.290	.271
		Brooklyn	NYM	A-	23	4	11	2	0	0	1	5	1	1	0	0	2	0	0	0	0	0	.00	1	.182	.182	.455
		St. Lucie	NYM	A+	23	20	40	10	0	0	1	13	6	2	4	0	5	0	1	0	2	4	.33	1	.250	.318	.325
Abreu, Lazaro	dh	Mariners	Sea	R	20	4	8	3	0	0	0	3	3	2	2	0	3	0	0	0	0	0	.00	0	.375	.500	.375
Abreu, Nielsen	2b	Phillies	Phi	R	21	35	131	36	3	0	1	42	14	10	6	0	19	0	0	1	3	5	.38	4	.275	.304	.321
Abruzzo, Jared#	c	Cedar Rapds	Ana	A	20	87	323	78	20	0	10	128	41	53	44	2	104	5	0	1	1	1	.50	3	.241	.340	.396
		Rancho Cuca	Ana	A+	20	28	101	21	1	0	2	28	13	13	9	0	30	0	0	1	1	0	1.00	1	.208	.270	.277
Acevedo, Anthony*	of	Michigan	Hou	A	24	120	429	111	35	4	12	190	74	70	69	3	130	7	0	3	21	5	.81	3	.259	.368	.443
Acevedo, Carlos	of	Lakewood	Phi	A	21	109	409	103	18	3	2	133	33	47	28	1	74	3	3	4	10	10	.50	8	.252	.302	.325
Acevedo, Freddy	of	Martinsvlle	Hou	R+	20	56	173	30	3	2	2	43	16	10	4	0	66	8	2	0	7	1	.88	2	.173	.227	.249
Acevedo, Inocencio	2b	Savannah	Tex	A	23	109	392	91	14	6	2	123	52	26	23	1	79	6	11	2	34	11	.76	3	.232	.284	.314
Acevedo, Juan#	of	Reds	Cin	R	20	37	100	14	6	0	0	20	10	3	8	0	50	1	0	0	2	1	.67	0	.140	.211	.200
Ackerman, Scott	c	Jupiter	Mon	A+	23	90	324	81	12	1	3	104	31	44	25	1	52	0	4	3	1	4	.20	7	.250	.301	.321
Acosta, Johe	of	Pirates	Pit	R	20	20	66	14	2	2	0	20	7	10	8	0	17	4	0	0	2	0	1.00	1	.212	.333	.303
Acuna, Ron	of	St. Lucie	NYM	A+	23	33	119	29	9	0	2	44	13	13	6	0	22	1	2	1	7	1	.88	3	.244	.283	.370
		Capital Cty	NYM	A	23	96	376	107	17	3	6	148	63	62	19	1	67	9	2	3	23	8	.74	10	.285	.332	.394
Adames, Epidaro	3b	Provo	Ana	R+	22	1	4	0	0	0	0	0	0	0	0	0	1	0	0	0	0	0	.00	0	.000	.000	.000
		Cedar Rapds	Ana	A	22	53	202	48	11	1	0	61	16	17	9	0	46	7	4	1	2	3	.40	5	.238	.292	.302
Agar, Cory	dh-c	Elizabethtn	Min	R+	21	57	193	53	15	1	8	94	26	33	17	1	62	4	1	1	0	0	.00	5	.275	.344	.487
Agramonte, M.#	2b	Charlotte	Tex	A+	21	10	37	12	3	3	0	21	2	3	0	0	7	0	0	0	1	2	.33	0	.324	.324	.568
		Savannah	Tex	A	21	72	252	46	8	2	3	67	20	19	3	0	62	1	3	2	8	8	.50	5	.183	.194	.266
Alayon, Jean#	ss	Mahoning Vy	Cle	A-	18	3	8	1	0	0	0	1	1	0	0	0	3	0	0	0	0	0	.00	0	.125	.125	.125
Albert, Luke#	c	Braves	Atl	R	23	38	114	24	3	0	1	30	5	12	10	0	30	1	0	0	0	1	.00	1	.211	.280	.263
Alcala, Juan	c	San Berndno	Sea	A+	24	72	233	59	9	1	0	70	23	24	9	2	55	6	4	3	1	1	.50	8	.253	.295	.300
Alexander, Alexis	of	Royals	KC	R	19	36	108	20	5	0	0	25	11	5	8	0	29	5	2	2	9	3	.75	3	.185	.268	.231
Alexander, Kevin	3b	Hagerstown	SF	A	21	83	266	61	14	1	2	83	25	30	25	0	58	2	10	1	5	1	.83	10	.229	.299	.312
Alexander, L.	of	Phillies	Phi	R	21	39	127	35	3	0	0	38	21	10	16	0	26	2	1	0	3	4	.43	0	.276	.366	.299
Alfonzo, Eliezer	c-dh	Beloit	Mil	A	23	106	397	110	28	2	14	184	52	48	13	3	65	8	3	3	0	1	.00	10	.277	.311	.463
Aliendo, Humberto	of-dh	Hickory	Pit	A	21	19	69	9	1	0	0	10	3	5	2	0	21	2	0	1	1	0	1.00	1	.130	.176	.145
		Williamsprt	Pit	A-	21	45	152	32	9	1	2	49	17	15	11	0	45	1	0	0	1	0	1.00	2	.211	.268	.322
Allegra, Matt	of	Modesto	Oak	A+	20	51	153	32	3	2	2	45	19	17	21	0	61	4	2	3	3	1	.75	3	.209	.315	.294
		Vancouver	Oak	A-	20	71	273	60	16	2	11	113	36	39	30	1	104	5	1	1	5	6	.45	2	.220	.307	.414
Alleva, J.D.*	c-dh	Spokane	KC	A-	23	67	247	70	23	1	2	101	25	38	18	4	26	2	1	1	0	1	.00	3	.283	.336	.409
Alvarado, Damien*	c	San Berndno	Sea	A+	24	3	9	0	0	0	0	0	0	0	0	0	2	0	0	0	0	0	.00	1	.000	.000	.000
Alvarado, Joel	c	Ogden	Mil	R+	22	18	52	10	0	0	0	10	5	3	3	0	5	1	1	0	0	1	.00	1	.192	.250	.192
		High Desert	Mil	A+	22	22	64	9	1	0	1	13	9	5	8	0	12	1	1	2	2	2	.50	2	.141	.240	.203
Alvarado, Oscar	c	Martinsvlle	Hou	R+	22	5	21	4	2	0	0	6	1	2	1	0	5	0	0	0	0	0	.00	0	.190	.227	.286
		Pittsfield	Hou	A-	22	26	71	11	2	0	1	16	9	4	8	0	28	1	0	0	0	0	.00	1	.155	.250	.225
Alvarez, Aaron	c	Utica	Fla	A-	22	20	48	10	1	0	1	14	7	2	6	0	13	0	0	1	0	0	.00	0	.208	.291	.292
Alvarez, Henrry	c	Burlington	KC	A	22	45	161	33	7	1	4	54	21	23	3	0	44	5	3	1	1	0	1.00	4	.205	.241	.335
Alvarez, Nick	1b-of	Vero Beach	LA	A+	25	118	420	120	15	2	21	202	63	71	29	1	80	17	2	4	14	7	.67	11	.286	.353	.481
Amado, Jose	3b	Mudville	Cin	A+	27	52	174	42	7	0	2	55	17	17	19	0	15	4	1	1	2	0	1.00	9	.241	.328	.316
Amador, Chris	2b	Kannapolis	CWS	A	19	102	322	63	8	6	3	92	42	28	15	2	127	8	8	2	29	12	.71	1	.196	.248	.286
Amador, Jerry	of	W Michigan	Det	A	22	81	289	64	7	1	4	85	24	31	15	0	47	5	1	1	4	3	.57	8	.221	.271	.294
Amaya, Pilar#	of	Johnson Cty	StL	R+	22	54	169	36	11	0	3	56	24	16	22	0	40	4	3	1	2	2	.50	5	.213	.316	.331
Ambres, Chip	of	Kane County	Fla	A	22	96	377	100	26	8	5	157	79	41	53	0	81	11	5	3	19	15	.56	7	.265	.369	.416
Ambrosini, Anthony	c-dh	Expos	Mon	R	23	25	85	19	1	0	0	20	5	5	5	0	24	3	2	0	1	1	.50	3	.224	.290	.235
		Clinton	Mon	A	23	3	8	2	0	0	0	2	1	1	0	0	2	1	0	0	0	0	.00	0	.250	.333	.250
Ambrosini, D.*	1b	Clinton	Mon	A	21	67	252	49	8	1	0	59	19	21	17	1	58	1	0	2	3	4	.43	7	.194	.246	.234
		Vermont	Mon	A-	21	44	159	36	7	1	2	51	19	19	14	0	37	0	0	0	1	3	.25	3	.226	.289	.321
Anderson, Dennis#	c	Kane County	Fla	A	24	78	242	57	14	2	6	93	43	35	37	0	45	14	2	3	2	3	.40	6	.236	.365	.384
Anderson, Jon#	2b	Sarasota	Bos	A+	25	4	7	0	0	0	0	0	0	1	1	0	1	0	0	0	0	1	.00	0	.000	.125	.000
		Augusta	Bos	A	25	47	128	27	2	0	0	29	12	6	8	0	30	1	1	1	5	4	.56	0	.211	.261	.227
Anderson, Keith	c	Salem-Keizr	SF	A-	23	57	155	32	9	0	4	53	18	21	18	1	34	3	3	1	1	0	1.00	4	.206	.299	.342
Anderson, Keto*	of-dh	Lansing	ChC	A	23	18	62	10	1	0	0	11	4	3	2	0	9	0	5	0	5	3	.63	1	.161	.188	.177
		Boise	ChC	A-	23	70	290	109	13	6	6	152	70	41	12	2	34	3	0	2	24	7	.77	1	.376	.404	.524
Anderson, Melvin	of	Lakewood	Phi	A	22	21	39	4	1	0	0	5	8	1	4	0	17	2	2	1	1	1	.50	0	.103	.217	.128
Anderson, Sam	c	Tigers	Det	R	23	33	82	22	1	0	0	23	9	5	10	0	16	2	0	0	0	1	.00	5	.268	.362	.280
Anderson, Travis	c	Jamestown	Atl	A-	22	37	130	32	11	0	1	46	16	17	11	0	19	7	2	0	1	0	1.00	4	.246	.338	.354
Andrianoff, Jon	3b-ss	Michigan	Hou	A	21	14	38	7	1	0	0	8	5	1	8	0	12	1	0	0	3	1	.75	1	.184	.340	.211
		Pittsfield	Hou	A-	21	23	55	8	3	0	0	11	5	6	6	0	19	2	0	0	4	1	.80	0	.145	.254	.200
Andujar, Elvin	of	Reds	Cin	R	21	58	197	58	9	9	3	94	32	34	16	1	43	5	0	2	21	4	.84	6	.294	.359	.477
		Dayton	Cin	A	21	5	16	3	0	0	0	3	2	1	1	0	6	0	0	0	1	0	1.00	1	.188	.235	.188
Angel, Tony	1b	Michigan	Hou	A	23	65	219	57	16	0	5	88	35	26	8	1	30	6	0	3	3	3	.50	5	.260	.301	.402
Angell, Rick	of	Rangers	Tex	R	25	3	11	4	0	1	0	6	1	0	0	0	2	0	0	0	0	0	.00	0	.364	.364	.545
		Charlotte	Tex	A+	25	46	161	35	5	0	0	40	12	10	10	0	30	3	4	1	4	5	.44	5	.217	.274	.248
Ansman, Craig	c	South Bend	Ari	A	24	97	345	114	30	4	21	215	73	82	29	2	85	16	0	6	4	1	.80	5	.330	.402	.623
Aquino, Jack#	ss	Idaho Falls	SD	R+	19	56	196	49	5	5	2	70	30	23	23	0	35	0	2	3	6	5	.55	2	.250	.324	.357
Aracena, Sandy	c	Vero Beach	LA	A+	21	2	6	2	0	0	0	2	0	0	1	0	1	0	0	0	0	0	.00	0	.333	.429	.333
		Great Falls	LA	R+	21	44	164	42	9	1	4	65	26	25	12	0	20	2	1	1	2	0	1.00	4	.256	.313	.396
Arias, Leandro	2b	St. Lucie	NYM	A+	21	5	15	3	1	0	0	4	1	1	0	0	5	0	0	0	1	0	1.00	0	.200	.200	.267
		Capital Cty	NYM	A	21	15	62	11	3	0	0	14	7	2	1	0	16	0	2	0	3	2	.60	2	.177	.190	.226
		Brooklyn	NYM	A-	21	36	112	27	7	1	3	45	12	11	10	0	31	0	2	0	2	2	.50	0	.241	.303	.402
Aristigueta, Darwin#	3b-2b	Braves	Atl	R	19	37	117	19	4	0	1	26	11	8	8	0	31	3	1	1	3	0	1.00	1	.162	.233	.222
Arko, Tommy	c	Bluefield	Bal	R+	19	36	124	24	4	1	5	45	16	16	13	0	47	1	1	2	0	1	.00	5	.194	.271	.363
Arnerich, Tony	c	Burlington	KC	A	22	11	37	6	2	0	0	8	0	3	3	0	9	0	0	1	0	0	.00	1	.162	.220	.216
Arrieche, Gabriel	2b	Auburn	Tor	A-	23	41	121	32	4	3	0	42	11	12	11	0	15	7	3	1	8	4	.67	4	.264	.357	.347
Arroyo, William#	ss	Marlins	Fla	R	20	42	144	37	1	1	0	40	15	14	12	1	28	2	2	1	5	1	.83	2	.257	.321	.278
		Brevard Cty	Fla	A+	20	6	13	3	0	0	0	3	3	0	2	0	2	0	0	0	0	0	.00	0	.231	.333	.231
Arroyo-Cruz, Abner*	of	Fort Wayne	SD	A	22	68	266	90	19	0	8	133	41	38	28	0	62	1	1	1	1	4	.20	6	.338	.402	.500
Arteaga, Joshua	ss	Boise	ChC	A-	22	40	157	50	13	0	3	72	31	27	10	0	28	1	1	2	3	4	.43	2	.318	.359	.459
Asadoorian, Rick	of	Augusta	Bos	A	21	116	406	86	13	6	6	129	50	40	47	2	139	4	2	1	13	4	.76	6	.212	.299	.318

2001 Batting — Class-A and Rookie Leagues

BATTING																					BASERUNNING				PERCENTAGES		
Player	Pos	Team	Org	Lg	A	G	AB	H	2B	3B	HR	TB	R	RBI	TBB	IBB	SO	HBP	SH	SF	SB	CS	SB%	GDP	Avg	OBP	SLG
Asahina, Jon#	dh-p	Utica	Fla	A-	21	30	60	13	1	0	0	14	5	4	6	0	14	1	0	0	0	0	.00	0	.217	.299	.233
Ascencion, Quincy	of	Frederick	Bal	A+	19	18	55	10	2	0	2	18	7	9	3	0	13	2	0	0	1	0	1.00	3	.182	.250	.327
		Delmarva	Bal	A	19	48	152	32	3	2	1	42	11	13	12	0	38	4	2	1	5	1	.83	1	.211	.284	.276
Aspito, Jason*	of	Winston-Sal	CWS	A+	23	127	402	102	30	3	6	156	46	35	21	4	113	10	10	2	7	10	.41	8	.254	.306	.388
Asprilla, Avelino	ss	Williamsprt	Pit	A-	20	56	183	47	9	2	1	63	28	20	7	0	36	1	6	2	9	3	.75	0	.257	.285	.344
Athas, Jamie*	ss	Hagerstown	SF	A	22	65	234	64	10	3	2	86	44	28	31	0	55	5	6	0	17	5	.77	3	.274	.370	.368
Atkins, Garrett	1b	Salem	Col	A+	22	135	465	151	43	5	5	219	70	67	74	10	98	8	2	6	6	4	.60	8	.325	.421	.471
Auterson, Jeff	of	Asheville	Col	A	24	28	97	20	4	1	2	32	9	9	7	0	32	2	0	0	4	1	.80	1	.206	.274	.330
Avila, Esteban*	3b	Martinsvlle	Hou	R+	20	44	155	32	4	1	2	44	12	14	4	1	29	2	2	0	1	1	.50	0	.206	.236	.284
Avila, Rob	c-dh	Lakewood	Phi	A	23	91	305	83	21	1	0	106	31	32	24	1	50	8	2	1	1	3	.25	9	.272	.340	.348
Ayala, Abraham	c	Pittsfield	Hou	A-	21	8	21	5	1	0	0	6	2	2	4	0	0	0	2	0	0	0	.00	2	.238	.360	.286
		Martinsvlle	Hou	R+	21	33	111	15	2	0	1	20	5	8	6	0	13	3	1	2	1	2	.33	1	.135	.197	.180
Ayala, Elio	2b	Beloit	Mil	A	23	101	400	106	19	2	0	129	65	25	34	2	61	7	9	3	11	2	.85	7	.265	.331	.323
Ayala, Odannys	of	Burlington	KC	A	21	53	180	38	6	5	2	60	16	16	17	0	25	0	2	1	2	1	.67	7	.211	.278	.333
Aybar, Francisco	of	White Sox	CWS	R	20	46	162	43	11	2	0	58	23	17	12	2	41	2	1	2	7	2	.78	3	.265	.320	.358
Aybar, Willy#	3b	Wilmington	LA	A	19	120	431	102	25	2	4	143	45	48	43	3	64	3	3	5	7	9	.44	4	.237	.307	.332
		Vero Beach	LA	A+	19	2	7	2	0	0	0	2	0	0	1	0	2	0	0	0	0	0	.00	0	.286	.375	.286
Bacani, David	2b	Kingsport	NYM	R+	22	19	71	25	8	1	2	41	19	13	13	0	12	1	0	0	5	2	.71	0	.352	.459	.577
		Brooklyn	NYM	A-	22	23	95	28	6	0	0	34	13	9	5	0	12	2	2	1	5	4	.56	2	.295	.340	.358
Bacon, Dwaine#	of	Boise	ChC	A-	23	57	150	29	5	0	0	34	22	3	17	0	51	3	2	0	8	5	.62	1	.193	.288	.227
Baez, Carlos	3b	Idaho Falls	SD	R+	19	55	180	41	5	2	1	53	18	21	8	0	50	3	1	0	1	2	.33	4	.228	.272	.294
Baez, Federico	ss-2b	Orioles	Bal	R	20	28	81	21	3	0	0	24	9	6	14	0	29	0	0	0	2	3	.40	0	.259	.368	.296
Bailie, Stefan	1b	Lowell	Bos	A-	22	23	90	21	4	0	2	31	9	15	6	0	21	3	0	0	0	0	.00	0	.233	.303	.344
Baker, Casey	2b	Greensboro	NYY	A	21	8	14	1	0	0	0	1	1	1	2	0	6	0	1	0	1	1	.50	0	.071	.188	.071
		Staten Ilnd	NYY	A-	21	6	14	1	0	0	0	1	0	0	1	0	3	0	0	0	0	0	.00	0	.071	.133	.071
		Columbus	Cle	A	21	4	12	1	0	0	0	1	1	0	0	0	2	2	0	0	2	1	.67	0	.083	.214	.083
Baldelli, Rocco	of	Chston-SC	TB	A	20	113	406	101	23	6	8	160	58	55	23	0	89	11	5	6	25	9	.74	7	.249	.303	.394
Ball, Jarred#	of	Missoula	Ari	R+	19	19	57	14	2	1	0	18	13	3	7	0	14	2	1	0	1	1	.50	1	.246	.348	.316
Banks, Almonzo	of	Orioles	Bal	R	21	38	100	15	4	1	1	24	8	8	12	0	39	2	1	1	3	0	1.00	4	.150	.252	.240
Banks, Gary	of	Cubs	ChC	R	20	53	200	34	3	1	1	42	30	14	20	0	80	11	3	1	11	3	.79	2	.170	.280	.210
		Boise	ChC	A-	20	2	4	1	0	0	0	1	0	1	0	0	1	0	0	0	0	0	.00	1	.250	.250	.250
Bannon, Jeff	ss	Billings	Cin	R+	23	60	235	61	11	3	1	81	37	31	16	0	33	3	0	3	5	2	.71	4	.260	.311	.345
Barbier, Blair	1b-3b	Lansing	ChC	A	24	131	488	153	38	1	16	241	77	77	52	6	63	14	2	4	3	6	.33	13	.314	.392	.494
Barfield, Josh	2b	Idaho Falls	SD	R+	19	66	277	86	15	4	4	121	51	53	16	1	54	3	0	4	12	4	.75	7	.310	.350	.437
Barmes, Clint	ss	Asheville	Col	A	23	74	285	74	14	1	5	105	40	24	17	0	37	7	3	3	21	7	.75	6	.260	.314	.368
		Salem	Col	A+	23	38	121	30	3	3	0	39	17	9	15	0	20	4	2	0	4	1	.80	5	.248	.350	.322
Barnette, Jason*	of	Lakewood	Phi	A	25	126	449	106	18	5	0	134	54	25	24	0	130	6	7	0	30	10	.75	4	.236	.284	.298
Barningham, Steve*	of	Charlotte	Tex	A+	27	70	219	61	15	4	1	87	50	24	42	2	38	5	2	3	17	8	.68	6	.279	.401	.397
Barnowski, Bryan	c-dh	Augusta	Bos	A	21	42	143	27	6	0	3	42	17	15	13	0	50	6	0	1	0	1	.00	2	.189	.282	.294
		Lowell	Bos	A-	21	14	51	8	5	0	1	16	7	2	6	0	22	2	0	0	0	0	.00	0	.157	.271	.314
Barnwell, Chris	ss-3b	Ogden	Mil	R+	23	69	261	80	19	5	0	109	49	37	7	2	28	7	3	4	17	2	.89	2	.307	.337	.418
Baron, Brian*	of	Fort Myers	Min	A+	23	69	265	81	10	3	1	100	38	37	18	1	40	1	2	3	0	0	.00	8	.306	.348	.377
Barrera, Reinaldo#	ss	Yakima	Ari	A-	19	45	140	29	4	0	0	33	12	5	10	0	22	0	2	0	1	2	.33	5	.207	.260	.236
Barrett, Rich	of	Yakima	Ari	A-	22	73	227	51	8	0	2	65	29	19	12	0	68	9	5	2	14	3	.82	6	.225	.288	.286
Barski, Chris*	dh	Rancho Cuca	Ana	A+	24	30	89	19	3	2	1	29	9	10	9	1	23	1	1	0	0	1	.00	4	.213	.293	.326
Barthel, Cole	3b	Braves	Atl	R	19	45	152	33	1	0	0	34	14	12	14	0	27	5	2	1	8	3	.73	2	.217	.302	.224
Bartlett, Jason	ss	Eugene	SD	A-	22	68	267	80	12	4	3	109	49	37	28	0	47	4	2	3	12	4	.75	6	.300	.371	.408
Basabe, Jesus	of	Modesto	Oak	A+	25	119	426	110	21	7	21	208	74	93	47	1	130	27	1	4	12	5	.71	6	.258	.365	.488
Basil, Jason	of	Vancouver	Oak	A-	23	50	177	46	8	1	5	71	23	30	23	2	42	3	0	2	1	0	1.00	6	.260	.351	.401
Bass, Brian#	ss	Orioles	Bal	R	20	21	74	22	3	6	0	37	12	7	5	0	25	0	0	2	4	0	1.00	1	.297	.333	.500
		Bluefield	Bal	R+	20	19	71	23	6	1	5	46	17	20	10	0	17	0	0	0	0	0	.00	2	.324	.407	.648
Bass, Chris	dh	Lynchburg	Pit	A+	20	7	20	3	1	0	0	4	4	3	5	0	8	0	0	0	1	1	.50	1	.150	.320	.200
		Hickory	Pit	A	20	106	352	87	18	1	3	116	34	34	22	0	80	6	3	5	6	3	.67	10	.247	.299	.330
Bass, Kevin#	of-dh	Daytona	ChC	A+	23	87	276	52	11	0	7	84	32	20	28	0	106	0	0	0	4	2	.67	9	.188	.263	.304
Bastardo, Angel	c	Mahoning Vy	Cle	A-	23	36	130	34	8	0	3	51	12	13	6	0	19	2	0	0	1	1	.50	4	.262	.304	.392
Bastardo, Frederick	2b	Marlins	Fla	R	20	44	147	35	12	0	2	53	18	14	9	0	32	3	2	1	7	4	.64	1	.238	.294	.361
Batista, Christian	3b	Angels	Ana	R	20	35	127	34	7	0	2	47	26	17	18	0	33	3	0	2	4	5	.44	5	.268	.367	.370
		Provo	Ana	R+	20	17	54	16	1	1	2	25	10	8	10	0	13	1	0	0	0	1	.00	1	.296	.415	.463
Batista, Jose	dh	Royals	KC	R	20	49	167	44	7	0	1	54	18	22	11	0	22	5	1	1	4	3	.57	6	.263	.326	.323
Batista, Juan#	ss-2b	Angels	Ana	R	17	36	72	9	2	2	0	15	8	7	9	0	34	1	0	1	6	0	1.00	0	.125	.229	.208
Bautista, Augusto	2b	Reds	Cin	R	20	20	42	8	0	0	1	11	7	7	1	0	16	2	1	1	0	3	.00	2	.190	.239	.262
		Billings	Cin	R+	20	6	12	1	0	0	0	1	1	0	1	0	5	1	0	0	1	0	1.00	0	.083	.214	.083
Bautista, Jose	3b	Williamsprt	Pit	A-	21	62	220	63	10	3	5	94	43	30	21	0	41	6	0	0	8	1	.89	5	.286	.364	.427
Bautista, Rayner	ss	Lakeland	Det	A+	22	101	354	92	18	4	8	142	43	43	20	0	89	2	6	7	8	4	.67	3	.260	.298	.401
Baxter, Andy*	1b	Burlington	Cle	R+	23	63	209	51	16	4	11	108	41	46	35	2	60	8	1	2	3	1	.75	1	.244	.370	.517
Bay, Jason	of	Jupiter	Mon	A+	23	38	123	24	4	1	1	33	12	10	18	1	26	2	1	1	10	3	.77	4	.195	.306	.268
		Clinton	Mon	A	23	87	318	115	20	4	13	182	67	61	48	0	62	4	1	2	15	2	.88	4	.362	.449	.572
Becker, Jeff	1b	Columbus	Cle	A	25	65	206	53	10	1	1	68	33	19	34	0	38	16	2	3	2	2	.50	2	.257	.398	.330
		Kinston	Cle	A+	25	24	69	17	5	0	1	25	7	11	9	0	16	3	0	0	0	0	.00	2	.246	.358	.362
Belcher, Jason*	dh-c	Beloit	Mil	A	20	38	144	47	6	0	2	59	23	23	15	1	16	1	1	0	0	1	.00	6	.326	.394	.410
Bell, Derek#	3b	Hagerstown	SF	A	25	111	381	96	30	2	2	136	50	49	62	2	76	2	3	6	1	3	.25	8	.252	.355	.357
Bell, Paul	dh	Brewers	Mil	R	22	18	65	19	2	0	0	21	13	9	3	1	12	3	0	0	1	0	1.00	2	.292	.352	.323
Bello, Vladimir	of	Casper	Col	R+	20	49	161	49	5	5	1	67	27	27	7	0	36	2	2	1	16	3	.84	1	.304	.339	.416
Bellorin, Edwin	c	Dodgers	LA	R	20	28	80	14	1	0	0	15	11	6	8	0	6	4	2	0	1	0	1.00	0	.175	.283	.188
Benavidez, Julian	3b	Salem-Keizr	SF	A-	20	50	188	60	12	1	9	101	36	39	24	0	54	1	0	2	2	1	.67	2	.319	.395	.537
Benick, Jon#	1b-dh	Eugene	SD	A-	22	64	237	62	12	1	10	106	31	45	19	0	53	0	0	1	2	2	.50	4	.262	.315	.447
Bennett, Kris	2b-3b	Batavia	Phi	A-	22	44	157	38	4	1	0	44	13	14	14	0	22	5	1	0	5	5	.50	4	.242	.324	.280
Berger, Matt	1b	Winston-Sal	CWS	A+	27	70	239	62	18	1	5	97	20	24	20	1	74	5	2	3	0	3	.00	5	.259	.326	.406
Bergolla, William	2b	Billings	Cin	R+	19	57	232	75	5	3	4	98	47	24	24	0	21	2	1	3	22	7	.76	1	.323	.387	.422
Bernard, Dagoberto	ss	Asheville	Col	A	22	38	109	30	7	0	0	37	9	11	1	0	24	1	1	0	3	7	.30	4	.275	.288	.339
Bernard, Miguel	c	Macon	Atl	A	21	47	159	30	1	0	3	40	19	17	8	1	41	2	1	3	5	2	.71	6	.189	.233	.252
		Danville	Atl	R+	21	39	128	31	8	1	1	44	13	16	8	0	29	2	1	0	1	1	.50	6	.242	.297	.344
Bernhardt, Joe	1b	Dunedin	Tor	A+	21	120	420	107	25	1	7	155	50	52	28	0	100	4	1	3	2	3	.40	9	.255	.305	.369
Berry, Sean	dh	Dunedin	Tor	A+	36	12	42	8	2	0	2	16	9	7	8	1	10	2	0	1	0	0	.00	2	.190	.340	.381
Bessa, Laumin	of	Danville	Atl	R+	19	55	173	42	10	3	3	67	24	17	11	1	49	2	1	0	3	2	.60	3	.243	.296	.387

2001 Batting — Class-A and Rookie Leagues

BATTING																					BASERUNNING				PERCENTAGES		
Player	Pos	Team	Org	Lg	A	G	AB	H	2B	3B	HR	TB	R	RBI	TBB	IBB	SO	HBP	SH	SF	SB	CS	SB%	GDP	Avg	OBP	SLG
Beuerlein, Tyler#	c	Brooklyn	NYM	A-	23	21	75	19	5	0	0	24	10	6	8	0	26	2	0	0	0	1	.00	1	.253	.341	.320
Bikowski, Scott*	of	Rancho Cuca	Ana	A+	25	128	482	143	28	5	10	211	81	53	63	2	94	5	3	2	24	9	.73	8	.297	.382	.438
Bird, T.J.*	1b	Tri-City	Col	A-	23	52	164	40	10	1	4	64	20	22	13	1	37	3	1	2	0	0	.00	4	.244	.308	.390
Birkett, Matthew	of	Tigers	Det	R	20	35	90	17	1	1	0	20	14	3	6	0	16	1	4	0	2	3	.40	1	.189	.247	.222
Bitter, Jarrod	c	Fort Wayne	SD	A	23	26	83	17	3	0	2	26	6	8	8	1	26	8	0	0	1	0	1.00	2	.205	.333	.313
		Lk Elsinore	SD	A+	23	35	119	26	9	0	2	41	13	16	5	0	37	1	0	1	0	0	.00	3	.218	.254	.345
Blackburn, Franco*	of	Utica	Fla	A-	23	37	107	24	4	0	2	34	14	11	21	1	37	0	0	0	0	0	.00	0	.224	.352	.318
Blackburn, John	c	Medcine Hat	Tor	R+	19	42	139	35	6	0	2	47	19	14	15	0	41	1	2	0	1	1	.50	1	.252	.329	.338
Blanco, Luis	1b	Expos	Mon	R	20	45	151	30	6	0	2	42	11	13	6	0	54	4	0	2	1	0	1.00	5	.199	.245	.278
Blanco, Tony	3b-dh	Augusta	Bos	A	20	96	370	98	23	2	17	176	44	69	17	2	78	7	0	2	1	0	1.00	17	.265	.308	.476
Blasi, Blake#	2b	Lansing	ChC	A	23	61	228	62	7	0	1	72	34	19	33	0	29	0	1	0	7	4	.64	4	.272	.364	.316
		Daytona	ChC	A+	23	46	144	35	1	1	0	38	17	14	25	0	14	1	2	2	3	4	.43	2	.243	.355	.264
Bledsoe, Hunter	1b	Dodgers	LA	R	26	4	13	5	1	0	0	6	2	1	1	0	1	0	0	0	1	0	1.00	0	.385	.429	.462
		Vero Beach	LA	A+	26	65	232	75	8	0	4	95	28	25	24	0	27	2	0	1	5	2	.71	15	.323	.390	.409
Blount, Pierre	of	Princeton	TB	R+	21	41	127	33	2	3	8	65	33	18	29	0	58	5	1	0	8	1	.89	1	.260	.416	.512
Blue, Vincent*	of	Tigers	Det	R	19	42	113	28	2	2	0	34	16	4	24	0	24	0	3	0	8	4	.67	0	.248	.380	.301
Blum, Greg	c	Jupiter	Mon	A+	23	64	201	39	13	0	3	61	22	22	21	0	53	15	1	1	2	2	.50	5	.194	.315	.303
Boitel, Rafael#	of	Quad City	Min	A	21	116	462	110	15	5	1	138	65	32	43	0	87	5	7	8	36	15	.71	6	.238	.305	.299
Boll, Javier	of	Yakima	Ari	A-	20	17	62	20	7	0	2	33	10	8	4	0	13	0	1	1	2	1	.67	2	.323	.358	.532
		Missoula	Ari	R+	20	35	119	32	7	1	3	50	17	21	11	0	19	5	0	1	2	2	.50	2	.269	.353	.420
Bone, Blake*	3b-dh	Wisconsin	Sea	A	23	78	257	56	19	1	7	98	40	36	37	0	50	2	3	3	6	2	.75	7	.218	.318	.381
Bonifay, Josh	of	Hickory	Pit	A	23	17	65	21	4	0	2	31	10	10	5	0	15	1	0	0	2	3	.40	2	.323	.380	.477
		Lynchburg	Pit	A+	23	85	323	96	14	1	13	151	42	41	26	0	87	4	0	2	5	4	.56	6	.297	.355	.467
Bonner, Adam*	of	Chston-SC	TB	A	21	116	364	79	27	1	3	117	48	29	63	6	115	10	5	0	21	6	.78	2	.217	.348	.321
Bonvechio, Brett*	3b	Red Sox	Bos	R	19	19	69	15	5	1	1	25	4	5	9	0	12	0	0	1	0	2	.00	3	.217	.304	.362
Boone, Matt	3b	Lakeland	Det	A+	22	104	375	96	16	5	4	134	47	33	29	0	95	1	3	3	8	3	.73	11	.256	.309	.357
Boscan, Jean	c	Myrtle Bch	Atl	A+	22	18	54	9	2	0	0	11	3	6	3	0	25	1	1	1	0	1	.00	1	.167	.220	.204
		Braves	Atl	R	22	8	30	10	4	0	0	14	5	6	0	0	3	0	0	1	0	1	.00	1	.333	.323	.467
		Macon	Atl	A	22	35	124	35	7	0	4	54	16	22	14	0	27	1	2	1	2	0	1.00	1	.282	.357	.435
Botts, Jason#	1b-of	Savannah	Tex	A	21	114	392	121	24	2	9	176	63	50	53	4	88	20	0	1	13	7	.65	10	.309	.416	.449
		Charlotte	Tex	A+	21	4	12	2	1	0	0	3	1	0	4	0	4	0	0	0	0	0	.00	0	.167	.375	.250
Bounds, Brandon*	1b	White Sox	CWS	R	20	37	113	27	4	2	1	38	13	4	10	0	33	0	1	0	2	1	.67	1	.239	.301	.336
Bouras, Brad	1b	Boise	ChC	A-	22	62	238	83	25	0	6	126	44	60	27	1	39	3	0	2	1	1	.50	5	.349	.419	.529
Bourgeois, Jason#	2b	Pulaski	Tex	R+	20	62	251	78	12	2	7	115	60	34	26	0	47	6	0	1	21	7	.75	3	.311	.387	.458
Bowen, Rob#	c	Quad City	Min	A	21	106	385	98	18	2	18	174	47	70	37	2	112	2	2	3	4	0	1.00	11	.255	.321	.452
Bowser, Matt*	of	Visalia	Oak	A+	23	131	479	131	32	7	21	240	92	83	70	3	92	9	0	8	10	5	.67	6	.273	.371	.501
Boyd, Dan	of	Ogden	Mil	R+	23	5	14	5	1	0	0	6	1	1	1	0	1	0	0	0	0	0	.00	0	.357	.400	.429
Boyd, Shaun	2b	Peoria	StL	A	20	81	277	78	12	2	5	109	42	27	33	0	42	1	2	3	20	3	.87	7	.282	.357	.394
Boyer, Bret#	2b	Clinton	Mon	A	21	107	420	105	21	1	3	137	58	23	22	0	90	3	2	1	29	5	.85	7	.250	.291	.326
Bozanich, Sam	2b	Tampa	NYY	A+	23	14	44	8	0	0	0	8	6	0	8	0	10	1	0	0	1	3	.25	1	.182	.321	.182
		Greensboro	NYY	A	23	65	204	55	12	2	3	80	30	17	18	1	51	1	3	3	5	5	.50	1	.270	.327	.392
Brack, Josh	2b-3b	Vancouver	Oak	A-	25	42	136	30	7	1	0	39	16	12	25	1	41	1	0	0	2	1	.67	4	.221	.346	.287
Brackley, Carlos	of	Red Sox	Bos	R	22	49	152	50	8	1	6	78	24	21	9	0	27	3	0	1	3	3	.50	4	.329	.376	.513
		Lowell	Bos	A-	22	6	25	9	3	1	1	17	6	6	1	0	8	1	0	0	0	1	.00	0	.360	.407	.680
Brand, Kevin#	ss	Missoula	Ari	R+	22	18	59	13	0	0	0	13	6	2	3	0	8	1	1	0	1	1	.50	0	.220	.270	.220
		South Bend	Ari	A	22	14	37	9	1	1	0	12	3	3	2	0	5	1	2	0	2	0	1.00	1	.243	.300	.324
Brandes, Landon	dh-3b	Peoria	StL	A	23	47	161	33	10	1	3	54	20	12	11	0	38	0	2	1	2	3	.40	3	.205	.254	.335
		Potomac	StL	A+	23	27	82	18	4	0	3	31	6	13	3	0	23	0	2	1	1	2	.33	0	.220	.244	.378
Brazell, Craig*	1b	Capital Cty	NYM	A	22	83	331	102	25	5	19	194	51	72	15	3	74	5	0	5	0	3	.00	3	.308	.343	.586
Brewer, Anthony	of	Marlins	Fla	R	19	58	211	53	7	3	0	66	35	16	28	0	55	8	3	1	27	10	.73	1	.251	.359	.313
Brewer, Jace	ss	Chston-SC	TB	A	23	108	414	90	12	4	3	119	50	35	18	1	74	3	5	5	6	6	.50	7	.217	.252	.287
Brisson, Dustin*	1b	Augusta	Bos	A	24	90	319	94	13	1	10	139	49	53	40	7	76	4	1	4	3	0	1.00	3	.295	.376	.436
Brito, Anyelo	ss	Phillies	Phi	R	18	27	86	16	5	0	1	24	9	15	7	0	27	1	1	1	2	0	1.00	2	.186	.253	.279
Brito, Obispo	c	Beloit	Mil	A	24	21	76	17	5	0	0	22	5	5	1	0	16	2	1	1	1	0	1.00	2	.224	.250	.289
Brooks, Doc	dh-of	Eugene	SD	A-	22	39	127	30	5	2	7	60	21	22	13	1	57	7	0	1	4	2	.67	1	.236	.338	.472
Brooks, Jeff	3b	South Bend	Ari	A	22	18	65	11	2	1	0	15	2	8	3	0	24	2	0	0	0	0	.00	0	.169	.229	.231
		Yakima	Ari	A-	22	72	268	65	14	2	5	98	30	35	13	0	83	5	1	1	2	1	.67	6	.243	.289	.366
Brosseau, Rick*	2b	Auburn	Tor	A-	23	51	174	34	7	2	2	51	12	20	20	0	24	0	3	2	4	2	.67	4	.195	.276	.293
Brostrom, Jeremy*	of-dh	Oneonta	Det	A-	24	2	3	1	1	0	0	2	2	0	4	0	0	0	0	0	0	0	.00	0	.333	.714	.667
Brown, Andy*	dh	Tampa	NYY	A+	22	93	306	59	13	3	11	111	45	45	52	3	129	3	0	1	7	5	.58	2	.193	.315	.363
Brown, Dustin	c	Red Sox	Bos	R	20	36	126	32	5	4	0	45	15	14	7	0	24	0	0	2	1	2	.33	3	.254	.289	.357
Brown, Kevin	1b	Jamestown	Atl	A-	23	49	158	25	8	0	6	51	17	20	33	0	70	6	0	2	0	1	.00	6	.158	.322	.323
Brown, Larry*	of	Mariners	Sea	R	21	34	111	31	3	1	3	45	23	13	13	1	19	1	0	1	3	0	1.00	2	.279	.357	.405
Brown, Matt*	2b-3b	Angels	Ana	R	19	46	141	23	7	1	1	35	14	21	18	1	30	5	1	3	1	3	.25	1	.163	.275	.248
Brown, Matthew#	1b	Vermont	Mon	A-	21	53	197	43	14	1	4	71	22	22	15	0	61	1	0	0	4	3	.57	5	.218	.277	.360
Brown, Tim*	1b	Pirates	Pit	R	19	46	142	30	4	1	2	42	11	18	29	1	32	4	0	2	1	0	1.00	2	.211	.356	.296
Brown, Trevor	c	Eugene	SD	A-	23	31	75	21	5	0	2	32	11	17	15	1	17	5	0	2	0	0	.00	6	.280	.423	.427
Brunner, Ryan*	1b	Lowell	Bos	A-	23	69	261	63	16	1	1	84	35	34	41	0	57	3	0	1	1	0	1.00	4	.241	.350	.322
Bryan, Jason	of	Savannah	Tex	A	20	26	72	9	1	0	0	10	5	8	13	0	28	1	0	1	1	1	.50	3	.125	.264	.139
		Pulaski	Tex	R+	20	55	176	35	7	0	8	66	26	23	25	0	75	5	1	1	3	1	.75	3	.199	.314	.375
Bubela, Jaime*	of	Wisconsin	Sea	A	24	132	530	161	27	12	6	230	96	68	44	4	116	1	1	2	34	13	.72	5	.304	.357	.434
Buck, John	c	Lexington	Hou	A	21	122	443	122	24	1	22	214	72	73	37	0	84	12	2	4	4	9	.31	8	.275	.345	.483
Buckley, Brandon	c	Michigan	Hou	A	25	67	197	40	7	0	1	50	17	14	19	0	31	1	0	1	0	1	.00	6	.203	.275	.254
Bunch, J.C.	1b	Rangers	Tex	R	23	35	102	34	7	3	2	53	16	19	13	0	12	1	1	0	7	2	.78	0	.333	.414	.520
Burke, Chris	ss	Michigan	Hou	A	22	56	233	70	11	6	3	102	47	17	26	2	31	3	2	1	21	8	.72	3	.300	.376	.438
Burkholder, David*	1b	Tri-City	Col	A-	24	13	41	11	3	0	2	20	5	9	3	0	10	1	0	1	1	0	1.00	2	.268	.326	.488
Burnett, Mark*	2b-of	Mudville	Cin	A+	25	123	434	97	16	5	5	138	67	43	84	4	88	1	3	7	11	4	.73	3	.224	.346	.318
Burns, Kevan*	of	Lancaster	Ari	A+	25	74	255	92	21	7	11	160	48	45	23	2	42	1	0	1	11	4	.73	1	.361	.414	.627
Burns, Pat#	1b	St. Lucie	NYM	A+	24	131	466	111	22	1	8	159	54	66	48	5	131	3	1	4	1	4	.20	9	.238	.311	.341
Burress, Andy	of	Mudville	Cin	A+	24	33	122	33	6	1	3	50	13	16	10	0	40	0	0	0	8	2	.80	2	.270	.326	.410
Burrows, Angelo*	of	Macon	Atl	A	21	117	426	109	15	2	4	140	52	36	28	0	61	2	4	2	31	15	.67	2	.256	.303	.329
Burrus, Josh	ss	Braves	Atl	R	18	52	197	38	8	2	3	59	24	19	14	0	40	8	2	2	10	2	.83	0	.193	.271	.299
Buscher, Greg	3b	Rangers	Tex	R	19	40	121	29	9	2	1	45	14	10	11	3	35	2	0	0	1	0	1.00	1	.240	.313	.372
Bush, Brian	of	Clearwater	Phi	A+	25	4	10	1	0	0	0	1	0	2	1	0	2	0	0	1	1	0	1.00	0	.100	.167	.100
		Lakewood	Phi	A	25	20	83	15	2	1	1	22	10	3	3	0	15	1	2	0	2	2	.50	2	.181	.218	.265

2001 Batting — Class-A and Rookie Leagues

BATTING																					BASERUNNING				PERCENTAGES		
Player	Pos	Team	Org	Lg	A	G	AB	H	2B	3B	HR	TB	R	RBI	TBB	IBB	SO	HBP	SH	SF	SB	CS	SB%	GDP	Avg	OBP	SLG
Bush, Darren*	dh-of	Clearwater	Phi	A+	28	46	137	24	5	1	2	37	15	18	18	0	33	4	1	2	1	1	.50	2	.175	.286	.270
Buttler, Vic*	of	Hickory	Pit	A	21	92	299	73	10	2	2	93	38	23	15	1	49	3	7	0	11	3	.79	3	.244	.287	.311
Bynum, Freddie*	ss-2b	Modesto	Oak	A+	22	120	440	115	19	7	2	154	59	46	41	0	95	1	4	1	28	11	.72	8	.261	.325	.350
Cabrera, Andres	of	Giants	SF	R	18	7	7	1	0	0	0	1	0	1	0	0	4	0	0	0	0	0	.00	0	.143	.143	.143
Cabrera, Jose	ss	Kane County	Fla	A	19	110	422	113	19	4	7	161	61	66	37	2	76	2	1	3	3	0	1.00	10	.268	.328	.382
Cabrera, Leonel	2b	Giants	SF	R	21	46	205	66	14	2	1	87	45	31	6	0	22	2	1	2	12	1	.92	3	.322	.344	.424
		Hagerstown	SF	A	21	10	30	9	1	0	0	10	8	1	1	0	7	0	1	0	3	3	.50	0	.300	.323	.333
Cabrera, Ray	of	Frederick	Bal	A+	23	123	460	126	21	4	14	197	62	65	23	1	73	12	1	1	16	7	.70	15	.274	.325	.428
Cabrera, Yoelmis	of	Williamsprt	Pit	A-	20	42	127	23	5	1	1	33	12	12	7	0	27	1	2	1	5	5	.50	3	.181	.228	.260
Cabrerra, Ulises	ss	Rangers	Tex	R	24	42	126	36	9	1	0	47	26	8	23	1	32	11	2	0	15	2	.88	3	.286	.438	.373
Cadena, Alejandro	dh-1b	Mariners	Sea	R	22	55	217	71	21	1	7	115	39	55	14	0	23	9	1	4	0	1	.00	5	.327	.385	.530
		Everett	Sea	A-	22	3	10	1	1	0	0	2	0	1	0	0	4	0	0	0	0	0	.00	0	.100	.100	.200
Cahill, Jonathan	ss	Provo	Ana	R+	24	8	31	13	3	0	0	16	7	5	2	0	2	1	0	0	4	1	.80	0	.419	.471	.516
		Cedar Rapds	Ana	A	24	44	172	47	7	0	1	57	21	13	8	0	28	0	5	0	2	2	.50	1	.273	.306	.331
Calabrese, Tony	ss	Greensboro	NYY	A	23	43	134	39	8	1	5	64	25	20	22	0	29	0	1	2	1	1	.50	3	.291	.386	.478
		Tampa	NYY	A+	23	20	60	14	2	0	0	16	8	3	8	0	9	2	1	0	3	1	.75	1	.233	.343	.267
Calahan, Scott*	3b	Kannapolis	CWS	A	24	6	13	2	0	0	0	2	1	2	1	0	2	0	0	0	0	0	.00	1	.154	.214	.154
		Bristol	CWS	R+	24	18	51	13	2	2	1	22	10	7	11	0	9	1	0	1	1	1	.50	3	.255	.391	.431
		Winston-Sal	CWS	A+	24	13	44	11	2	0	1	16	5	11	4	0	8	1	2	1	0	2	.00	0	.250	.320	.364
Caligiuri, Jay	1b	Brooklyn	NYM	A-	22	66	238	78	14	3	5	113	38	34	26	1	31	6	0	3	4	2	.67	5	.328	.403	.475
Calitri, Mike	3b	Mudville	Cin	A+	24	22	74	13	2	0	2	21	8	10	11	0	28	1	0	0	0	0	.00	2	.176	.291	.284
		Dayton	Cin	A	24	97	317	79	18	0	16	145	57	44	57	2	98	3	1	2	1	3	.25	4	.249	.367	.457
Callahan, Dave*	1b	Brevard Cty	Fla	A+	22	123	476	121	14	2	9	166	68	68	54	2	89	3	3	3	10	7	.59	13	.254	.332	.349
Calzado, Napolean	3b	Frederick	Bal	A+	22	121	464	133	20	2	5	172	50	41	16	2	52	6	5	4	34	14	.71	9	.287	.316	.371
Camacaro, A.	c	Burlington	Cle	R+	21	40	122	25	3	0	1	31	11	8	12	0	27	7	4	0	3	4	.43	3	.205	.312	.254
Camacho, Juan#	3b	Staten Ilnd	NYY	A-	21	72	274	76	14	3	10	126	42	51	20	2	36	6	0	2	0	1	.00	10	.277	.338	.460
Cameron, Antoine*	of	Lansing	ChC	A	22	94	343	91	20	2	9	142	47	47	37	3	87	3	2	3	2	2	.50	4	.265	.339	.414
Cameron, Troy#	3b	Myrtle Bch	Atl	A+	23	65	223	56	13	1	7	92	27	38	23	0	62	6	0	2	2	6	.25	7	.251	.335	.413
		Kinston	Cle	A+	23	61	224	56	14	1	8	96	39	38	36	2	53	3	1	0	0	0	.00	6	.250	.361	.429
Campana, Wandel	2b	Mudville	Cin	A+	22	44	167	38	9	0	1	50	14	15	7	0	34	3	3	0	2	2	.50	4	.228	.271	.299
		Dayton	Cin	A	22	79	295	78	19	3	0	103	46	23	10	0	41	4	10	2	8	5	.62	4	.264	.296	.349
Campo, Mike*	of	Cedar Rapds	Ana	A	25	101	358	112	20	3	7	159	69	46	43	0	65	26	3	5	21	11	.66	1	.313	.419	.444
Campos, Julio	3b	Phillies	Phi	R	24	13	40	6	2	0	0	8	2	1	1	0	9	1	0	1	0	1	.00	1	.150	.186	.200
		Clearwater	Phi	A+	24	9	24	5	1	0	0	6	1	1	0	0	4	0	1	0	1	0	1.00	0	.208	.208	.250
Campos, Mario	of	Lowell	Bos	A-	23	60	225	52	16	0	5	83	22	31	11	0	80	2	1	3	2	3	.40	5	.231	.270	.369
Canales, Josh	ss	Great Falls	LA	R+	23	9	30	15	2	0	0	17	4	6	2	1	3	2	0	0	0	0	.00	0	.500	.559	.567
		Wilmington	LA	A	23	52	163	37	2	1	1	44	14	12	14	0	28	2	10	1	10	5	.67	2	.227	.294	.270
Cancio, Antonio	1b-dh	Phillies	Phi	R	20	49	171	50	13	0	2	69	22	29	16	0	51	3	0	0	0	0	.00	6	.292	.363	.404
Candelaria, Scott	2b	Beloit	Mil	A	23	69	256	64	11	0	2	81	35	27	12	1	50	2	7	2	3	4	.43	3	.250	.287	.316
Candelario, Luis	of	Hudson Val	TB	A-	20	56	225	58	16	0	6	92	26	28	7	0	62	3	0	2	9	1	.90	7	.258	.287	.409
Cannizaro, Andy	2b-ss	Staten Ilnd	NYY	A-	23	67	254	72	9	2	0	85	38	20	22	1	21	6	3	3	5	3	.63	15	.283	.351	.335
Cano, Robinson*	2b	Yankees	NYY	R	19	57	200	46	14	2	3	73	37	34	28	0	27	3	0	2	11	2	.85	4	.230	.330	.365
		Staten Ilnd	NYY	A-	19	2	8	2	0	0	0	2	0	2	0	0	2	0	0	0	0	0	.00	0	.250	.250	.250
Caperton, Freddy	c	Pulaski	Tex	R+	22	17	47	11	1	0	0	12	5	5	7	0	15	1	0	0	0	0	.00	1	.234	.345	.255
Caraballo, Carlos	of	Red Sox	Bos	R	22	47	137	29	3	3	1	41	16	14	8	0	39	3	2	0	8	3	.73	6	.212	.270	.299
Caracciolo, Tony	ss	Vermont	Mon	A-	22	52	171	36	5	0	1	44	18	8	19	0	38	4	1	0	13	1	.93	3	.211	.304	.257
Cardona, David	of	Dodgers	LA	R	19	47	168	39	5	1	0	46	20	21	10	0	42	2	5	0	2	1	.67	3	.232	.283	.274
Carolfiles, Bladimir	of	Marlins	Fla	R	20	43	147	38	9	1	1	52	13	20	4	0	20	4	3	1	13	4	.76	2	.259	.295	.354
Carroll, Mark	c	Wisconsin	Sea	A	23	84	257	59	10	0	1	72	34	27	45	0	63	10	2	3	2	4	.33	5	.230	.362	.280
Carroll, Rich	1b	Rangers	Tex	R	22	48	158	41	15	1	1	61	22	18	13	0	37	1	0	2	2	0	1.00	3	.259	.316	.386
Carroll, Wes	2b	Clearwater	Phi	A+	23	7	15	3	0	0	0	3	2	1	3	0	2	1	0	0	0	0	.00	0	.200	.368	.200
		Batavia	Phi	A-	23	12	42	12	2	0	0	14	7	3	4	0	2	0	1	0	2	1	.67	0	.286	.348	.333
		Lakewood	Phi	A	23	36	130	45	8	0	1	56	17	11	10	1	24	2	1	1	3	3	.50	1	.346	.399	.431
Carrow, Thomas	of	Ogden	Mil	R+	21	45	157	52	7	0	5	74	37	20	33	1	34	3	0	1	7	3	.70	1	.331	.454	.471
Carter, Bryan*	of	Hagerstown	SF	A	24	56	197	36	7	2	2	53	18	14	15	1	63	4	3	3	11	3	.79	3	.183	.251	.269
		Salem-Keizr	SF	A-	24	67	238	53	12	1	6	85	36	31	22	1	46	6	2	1	13	5	.72	4	.223	.303	.357
Carter, Josh	of	Eugene	SD	A-	21	23	86	16	3	1	1	24	6	9	3	0	14	1	0	1	2	0	1.00	0	.186	.220	.279
Carter, Ryan	dh-of	Dodgers	LA	R	19	30	92	25	3	1	1	33	16	10	10	0	29	9	2	1	4	0	1.00	1	.272	.393	.359
Carvajal, Jhonny	ss	San Jose	SF	A+	27	113	448	117	20	1	4	151	57	50	31	0	70	3	8	8	14	7	.67	11	.261	.308	.337
Carvajal, Ramon#	ss	Potomac	StL	A+	21	125	456	99	16	4	8	147	59	39	22	0	115	5	10	2	17	4	.81	5	.217	.260	.322
Cash, Condor	of	Boise	ChC	A-	22	66	245	85	18	4	10	141	33	49	26	4	37	1	0	4	6	3	.67	4	.347	.406	.576
Cash, Kevin	c	Dunedin	Tor	A+	24	105	371	105	27	0	12	168	55	66	43	2	80	8	4	1	4	3	.57	11	.283	.369	.453
Castaneda, Jose	c	Capital Cty	NYM	A	24	38	116	19	2	0	1	24	8	8	14	0	39	3	0	1	0	0	.00	2	.164	.269	.207
Castellano, John	c	Wisconsin	Sea	A	24	99	377	126	34	0	14	202	59	81	19	2	35	6	3	6	13	5	.72	7	.334	.370	.536
Castellanos, Jose	of	Danville	Atl	R+	21	42	129	40	10	1	3	61	14	21	10	0	21	1	0	0	0	0	.00	8	.310	.364	.473
Castillo, Alberto*	1b	Bakersfield	TB	A+	26	94	347	95	12	2	11	144	45	54	28	4	120	1	1	1	1	3	.25	4	.274	.329	.415
Castillo, Carlos#	2b	Capital Cty	NYM	A	21	83	310	75	8	6	2	101	42	30	21	2	63	1	10	2	9	4	.69	4	.242	.290	.326
Castillo, David#	of	Eugene	SD	A-	21	36	82	16	0	1	1	21	8	5	14	0	26	2	0	1	4	1	.80	1	.195	.323	.256
Castillo, Jose	ss	Lynchburg	Pit	A+	21	125	485	119	20	7	7	174	57	49	21	2	94	9	4	2	23	10	.70	9	.245	.288	.359
Castillo, Oscar	c	Athletics	Oak	R	20	35	120	22	5	0	1	30	8	19	11	0	31	0	1	2	2	0	1.00	4	.183	.248	.250
Castro, Bernabel#	2b	Greensboro	NYY	A	20	101	389	101	15	7	1	133	71	36	54	1	67	1	5	2	67	20	.77	5	.260	.350	.342
		Staten Ilnd	NYY	A-	20	15	57	20	1	0	0	21	6	7	11	0	12	1	0	0	8	3	.73	0	.351	.464	.368
Castro, Vince	of	Hickory	Pit	A	22	55	172	37	6	2	1	50	16	20	7	1	47	2	1	0	6	2	.75	4	.215	.254	.291
Catalanotte, Greg#	of	Salem	Col	A+	25	119	401	87	24	0	11	144	45	40	44	1	125	5	5	2	8	5	.62	6	.217	.301	.359
Cates, Gary	2b	Frederick	Bal	A+	20	28	91	22	4	0	0	26	8	4	4	0	16	0	3	0	0	1	.00	0	.242	.274	.286
		Delmarva	Bal	A	20	101	342	100	14	3	2	126	44	33	17	1	30	10	17	3	16	8	.67	8	.292	.341	.368
Cavin, Jonathan*	of	Bristol	CWS	R+	22	53	179	57	7	1	3	75	24	19	17	1	45	4	0	1	2	1	.67	2	.318	.388	.419
Cedeno, Ronny	ss	Cubs	ChC	R	19	52	206	72	13	4	1	96	36	17	13	0	32	5	3	2	17	10	.63	3	.350	.398	.466
		Lansing	ChC	A	19	17	56	11	4	1	1	20	9	2	2	0	18	1	0	0	0	2	.00	1	.196	.237	.357
Ceminaro, Michael	2b	Boise	ChC	A-	23	41	131	31	4	1	0	37	23	7	5	0	23	0	1	1	2	1	.67	0	.237	.263	.282
Centeno, Irwin	2b	Chston-SC	TB	A	21	102	372	86	8	3	1	103	61	22	41	1	91	12	6	1	48	12	.80	5	.231	.326	.277
Cerda, Jose	c	Hagerstown	SF	A	25	13	33	8	0	0	0	8	4	2	6	0	7	2	0	1	0	0	.00	0	.242	.381	.242
		San Jose	SF	A+	25	30	87	19	4	2	0	27	10	3	4	0	25	3	2	0	0	0	.00	0	.218	.277	.310
Ceriani, Matt	c	Beloit	Mil	A	25	22	79	21	3	0	1	27	8	6	8	1	16	1	1	1	2	0	1.00	1	.266	.337	.342
		High Desert	Mil	A+	25	25	84	16	3	0	1	22	5	8	4	0	22	0	0	0	0	0	.00	2	.190	.227	.262

2001 Batting — Class-A and Rookie Leagues

BATTING																					BASERUNNING				PERCENTAGES		
Player	Pos	Team	Org	Lg	A	G	AB	H	2B	3B	HR	TB	R	RBI	TBB	IBB	SO	HBP	SH	SF	SB	CS	SB%	GDP	Avg	OBP	SLG
Chandler, Marcus#	of	Spokane	KC	A-	22	41	119	29	4	2	0	37	15	10	8	0	29	0	1	2	4	2	.67	1	.244	.287	.311
Chapman, Travis	c	Williamsprt	Pit	A-	21	17	55	16	3	1	0	21	6	4	1	0	9	2	0	1	0	1	.00	0	.291	.322	.382
Charles, Julin	of	Rangers	Tex	R	19	52	187	45	15	4	1	71	23	22	12	1	41	1	2	2	17	2	.89	6	.241	.287	.380
Chauncey, Clinton	c	Yankees	NYY	R	21	10	18	2	0	0	0	2	1	0	1	0	8	1	0	0	0	0	.00	0	.111	.200	.111
Chaves, Brandon#	ss	Hickory	Pit	A	22	110	356	71	12	4	2	97	29	32	28	0	89	10	4	5	8	4	.67	11	.199	.273	.272
Chavez, Angel	3b	Hagerstown	SF	A	20	13	37	7	2	0	2	15	5	3	1	0	12	1	0	0	1	0	1.00	0	.189	.231	.405
		San Jose	SF	A+	20	84	316	77	22	2	3	112	37	28	16	0	60	1	5	3	10	4	.71	9	.244	.280	.354
Chavez, Ender*	of	Casper	Col	R+	21	64	228	78	9	1	0	89	49	22	38	0	31	1	3	0	24	7	.77	3	.342	.438	.390
Chavez, Ozzie#	ss	Brewers	Mil	R	18	52	210	64	12	6	0	88	38	27	13	0	36	2	0	3	9	8	.53	8	.305	.346	.419
Checksfield, Steven	1b	Pittsfield	Hou	A-	23	60	200	38	7	4	7	74	32	23	18	1	49	3	2	3	5	3	.63	3	.190	.263	.370
Chilsom, Marques	of	Missoula	Ari	R+	20	21	36	7	1	0	0	8	6	2	7	0	14	0	1	0	0	1	.00	0	.194	.326	.222
Chirinos, Germain	of	Visalia	Oak	A+	23	94	251	67	11	0	5	93	47	27	38	0	78	3	3	0	12	7	.63	7	.267	.370	.371
Chirinos, Robinson	3b	Cubs	ChC	R	18	47	154	36	12	0	2	54	15	15	10	0	42	4	6	3	4	3	.57	0	.234	.292	.351
Choo, Shin-Soo*	of	Mariners	Sea	R	19	51	199	60	10	10	4	102	51	35	34	2	49	9	0	3	12	4	.75	1	.302	.420	.513
		Wisconsin	Sea	A	19	3	13	6	0	0	0	6	1	3	1	0	3	1	0	0	2	0	1.00	0	.462	.533	.462
Chourio, Jorjanis	of	Billings	Cin	R+	21	45	133	31	6	3	1	46	24	12	10	0	37	2	2	0	5	5	.50	0	.233	.297	.346
Choy Foo, B.#	2b	Columbus	Cle	A	20	12	40	10	0	0	0	10	2	5	4	0	9	0	0	1	1	0	1.00	2	.250	.311	.250
		Burlington	Cle	R+	20	7	24	8	2	0	1	13	2	3	1	0	5	0	0	0	0	2	.00	0	.333	.360	.542
Christensen, Jeff*	of	Staten Ilnd	NYY	A-	23	19	58	13	4	2	2	27	13	9	5	0	14	5	0	0	7	1	.88	0	.224	.338	.466
Christianson, Ryan	c	San Berndno	Sea	A+	21	134	527	131	42	5	12	219	65	85	53	6	112	5	0	4	3	2	.60	17	.249	.321	.416
Christy, Jeff*	c	Vancouver	Oak	A-	22	3	0	0	0	0	0	0	1	0	0	0	0	0	0	0	0	1	.00	0	.000	.000	.000
Church, Ryan*	of	Columbus	Cle	A	23	101	363	104	23	3	17	184	64	76	54	0	79	6	0	3	4	6	.40	6	.287	.385	.507
		Kinston	Cle	A+	23	24	83	20	7	0	5	42	16	15	18	2	23	1	0	1	1	0	1.00	1	.241	.379	.506
Ciarrachi, Kevin	c	Hickory	Pit	A	24	2	7	0	0	0	0	0	1	0	1	0	3	0	0	0	0	0	.00	1	.000	.125	.000
Ciesluk, Chris	3b	Giants	SF	R	19	51	170	43	3	3	0	52	22	17	17	0	31	3	2	2	4	1	.80	1	.253	.328	.306
Ciofrone, Paul*	of	Lakewood	Phi	A	24	7	12	0	0	0	0	0	0	0	2	0	5	0	0	0	0	0	.00	0	.000	.143	.000
		Phillies	Phi	R	24	42	134	36	7	1	4	57	23	21	33	0	42	1	0	1	2	0	1.00	3	.269	.414	.425
		Batavia	Phi	A-	24	3	9	1	1	0	0	2	0	0	1	0	5	0	0	0	0	0	.00	0	.111	.200	.222
Ciraco, Darren	of	Kannapolis	CWS	A	21	111	388	98	15	7	5	142	43	52	25	1	92	3	1	6	14	11	.56	11	.253	.299	.366
Cirone, Joe	of	Vancouver	Oak	A-	24	37	133	30	5	0	0	35	13	10	7	1	43	0	0	1	3	2	.60	6	.226	.262	.263
Cisneros, Josh	c	Phillies	Phi	R	22	24	73	21	3	0	0	24	8	7	6	1	9	5	0	0	1	0	1.00	5	.288	.381	.329
Clark, Aaron*	of	Hudson Val	TB	A-	23	66	254	51	16	2	6	89	31	35	22	1	66	4	0	6	4	2	.67	3	.201	.269	.350
Clark, Daryl*	3b	Beloit	Mil	A	22	133	501	142	24	2	21	233	76	92	61	3	135	7	2	8	4	5	.44	8	.283	.364	.465
Clark, Greg	c	Potomac	StL	A+	25	8	15	3	2	0	0	5	0	2	0	0	4	0	0	0	0	1	.00	0	.200	.200	.333
Cleto, Ambioris	3b	Lynchburg	Pit	A+	22	71	193	32	12	0	1	47	22	14	9	0	53	3	5	1	7	1	.88	3	.166	.214	.244
Cleto, Carlos*	of	Giants	SF	R	19	54	214	56	10	4	1	77	38	35	18	0	55	2	0	2	6	1	.86	5	.262	.322	.360
Cleveland, Matt	2b	Spokane	KC	A-	23	37	134	32	5	2	1	44	12	17	11	0	33	3	1	3	1	5	.17	2	.239	.305	.328
Cleveland, Russ	c	W Michigan	Det	A	22	61	205	50	9	0	2	65	18	13	13	0	51	3	0	0	0	3	.00	3	.244	.299	.317
Cliffords, Woody*	of	Bluefield	Bal	R+	21	62	198	55	13	2	6	90	36	29	32	1	40	1	1	0	8	1	.89	6	.278	.381	.455
Closser, J.D.#	c	Lancaster	Ari	A+	22	128	468	136	26	6	21	237	85	87	65	4	106	2	1	4	6	7	.46	9	.291	.377	.506
Clute, Kris	2b	Utica	Fla	A-	23	29	94	18	2	1	0	22	11	12	13	0	25	1	1	0	1	1	.50	1	.191	.296	.234
Coates, Brad	ss	Myrtle Bch	Atl	A+	23	18	53	6	1	0	0	7	4	3	5	0	20	1	0	1	0	0	.00	1	.113	.200	.132
Coats, Buck*	of	Cubs	ChC	R	20	33	123	32	3	3	1	44	11	18	4	0	19	2	1	1	3	4	.43	1	.260	.292	.358
Cochrane, Mark	c	Bristol	CWS	R+	22	6	17	5	2	0	0	7	3	2	1	0	3	0	0	0	0	0	.00	0	.294	.333	.412
		White Sox	CWS	R	22	21	51	14	2	0	0	16	6	7	11	0	11	0	0	0	0	1	.00	2	.275	.403	.314
Cockrell, Mike	2b	Pirates	Pit	R	20	48	168	47	7	1	0	56	32	11	19	0	17	1	1	1	31	5	.86	7	.280	.354	.333
Coffey, Josh	dh	Marlins	Fla	R	18	9	30	1	0	0	0	1	1	0	0	0	10	0	0	0	1	0	1.00	2	.033	.033	.033
Coffey, Kris	of	Lowell	Bos	A-	23	69	274	75	5	0	0	80	27	13	28	1	50	1	3	1	22	9	.71	3	.274	.342	.292
Cole, John	2b	Everett	Sea	A-	22	13	55	16	4	0	0	20	8	6	3	0	14	0	0	0	2	1	.67	0	.291	.328	.364
Coleman, Alph	of	Macon	Atl	A	23	120	476	143	18	7	7	196	84	57	24	3	73	8	3	3	38	13	.75	9	.300	.342	.412
Coleman, Andy	c	Greensboro	NYY	A	24	3	8	1	0	0	0	1	0	0	0	0	4	0	0	0	0	0	.00	0	.125	.125	.125
		Tampa	NYY	A+	24	7	17	1	1	0	0	2	3	1	3	0	7	2	1	0	0	0	.00	0	.059	.273	.118
Colina, Alvin	c	Tri-City	Col	A-	20	47	164	35	10	0	5	60	12	17	12	0	50	4	2	0	0	2	.00	2	.213	.283	.366
Collazo, Julio	2b	Lakewood	Phi	A	21	44	128	26	4	0	0	30	12	5	10	1	33	2	2	1	2	3	.40	3	.203	.270	.234
Collins, Chris	3b	Mariners	Sea	R	20	42	161	55	14	0	2	75	25	29	20	0	26	1	1	1	0	1	.00	2	.342	.415	.466
		Everett	Sea	A-	20	4	12	1	0	0	0	1	0	2	1	0	8	0	0	0	0	0	.00	1	.083	.154	.083
Collins, Kevin*	1b	Cubs	ChC	R	21	39	132	37	6	6	3	64	25	16	22	1	55	1	0	1	2	2	.50	1	.280	.385	.485
Collum, Mike	ss	Pirates	Pit	R	20	35	114	33	9	2	5	61	17	21	15	0	40	3	0	1	2	1	.67	2	.289	.383	.535
Colmenter, Jesus#	ss	Columbus	Cle	A	20	39	136	38	1	1	0	41	12	8	4	0	26	2	0	2	1	2	.33	4	.279	.306	.301
		Mahoning Vy	Cle	A-	20	17	65	12	0	2	0	16	6	6	3	0	15	1	1	1	2	0	1.00	2	.185	.229	.246
Combs, Chris*	1b	Lynchburg	Pit	A+	27	133	463	105	18	4	12	167	68	53	66	4	153	5	0	2	2	1	.67	11	.227	.328	.361
Conrad, Brooks#	2b	Pittsfield	Hou	A-	22	65	232	65	16	5	4	103	41	39	26	3	52	13	4	6	14	2	.88	1	.280	.375	.444
Conroy, Mike*	of	Burlington	Cle	R+	19	43	156	38	7	1	2	53	19	23	13	1	49	0	3	0	5	5	.50	3	.244	.302	.340
Contreras, Sergio*	1b-of	Rancho Cuca	Ana	A+	22	104	351	95	15	5	3	129	47	37	29	2	68	5	3	2	15	9	.63	4	.271	.333	.368
Conway, Dan	c	Asheville	Col	A	22	86	273	62	12	1	5	91	31	27	38	1	82	3	2	1	2	1	.67	4	.227	.327	.333
Cook, Josh	3b	San Jose	SF	A+	24	8	19	8	3	0	0	11	2	5	2	1	2	0	0	0	0	0	.00	1	.421	.476	.579
Cooper, Matt	1b	Augusta	Bos	A	21	37	124	22	4	0	3	35	9	12	14	0	46	7	0	2	1	1	.50	3	.177	.293	.282
		Red Sox	Bos	R	21	56	187	50	14	1	7	87	33	34	32	1	57	9	0	1	2	0	1.00	2	.267	.397	.465
Cooper, Sam#	ss-2b	Lansing	ChC	A	24	3	11	3	0	0	0	3	0	1	0	0	1	0	0	0	0	1	.00	0	.273	.273	.273
		Daytona	ChC	A+	24	13	37	4	1	0	0	5	6	0	4	0	8	3	1	0	1	0	1.00	4	.108	.250	.135
Copeland, Nate*	of	Danville	Atl	R+	23	43	81	22	3	0	0	25	13	8	13	0	24	1	1	1	2	1	.67	1	.272	.375	.309
Corbeil, Alfred*	c-1b	Provo	Ana	R+	23	60	217	78	18	0	6	114	48	49	40	4	41	6	0	5	0	1	.00	5	.359	.463	.525
Cordell, Brent#	c	Princeton	TB	R+	22	48	163	50	13	0	7	84	23	26	12	0	32	5	0	3	0	3	.00	0	.307	.366	.515
		Chston-SC	TB	A	22	2	7	1	0	0	0	1	2	1	2	0	2	0	0	0	0	0	.00	0	.143	.333	.143
Cordova, Ben*	of	Burlington	KC	A	22	108	384	113	30	0	6	161	58	44	38	0	55	2	0	2	7	2	.78	8	.294	.359	.419
Cordova, Ricardo#	3b	Great Falls	LA	R+	20	34	116	23	3	1	0	28	17	11	12	0	22	0	1	3	0	1	.00	3	.198	.267	.241
Cordova, Roman#	2b	Mariners	Sea	R	17	42	145	51	8	3	1	68	27	19	9	0	23	8	3	0	4	4	.50	8	.352	.420	.469
Corporan, Elvis#	3b	Greensboro	NYY	A	22	135	484	109	25	6	15	191	65	53	35	2	124	3	1	4	15	8	.65	8	.225	.279	.395
Corporan, Roberto#	ss	Missoula	Ari	R+	19	3	5	0	0	0	0	0	1	0	2	0	3	0	0	0	0	0	.00	0	.000	.286	.000
Corr, Frank	of	Brooklyn	NYM	A-	23	61	212	64	21	1	13	126	38	46	14	2	32	7	1	0	6	6	.50	3	.302	.365	.594
Corrente, David	c	Medcine Hat	Tor	R+	18	35	99	19	5	0	1	27	7	6	8	0	32	7	2	0	1	0	1.00	2	.192	.298	.273
Cortes, Jorge*	of	Williamsprt	Pit	A-	21	51	189	48	17	1	2	73	23	31	20	2	25	1	0	0	2	2	.50	5	.254	.329	.386
Cortez, Fernando*	3b	Hudson Val	TB	A-	20	55	234	65	14	3	1	88	36	25	15	1	26	3	3	2	6	3	.67	5	.278	.327	.376
Cosby, Quan*	of	Angels	Ana	R	19	41	148	36	4	1	0	42	21	8	9	1	40	1	3	1	8	7	.53	1	.243	.289	.284
Cosby, Rob	3b	Chston-WV	Tor	A	21	120	412	94	22	1	5	133	48	43	32	2	60	2	3	2	6	4	.60	5	.228	.286	.323

2001 Batting — Class-A and Rookie Leagues

BATTING																					BASERUNNING				PERCENTAGES		
Player	Pos	Team	Org	Lg	A	G	AB	H	2B	3B	HR	TB	R	RBI	TBB	IBB	SO	HBP	SH	SF	SB	CS	SB%	GDP	Avg	OBP	SLG
Cota, Jesus*	1b	Missoula	Ari	R+	20	75	272	100	22	0	16	170	74	71	56	6	52	2	0	2	2	0	1.00	5	.368	.476	.625
Cotten, Jeremy	1b	Hickory	Pit	A	21	125	443	112	20	2	25	211	58	78	42	1	132	15	0	2	12	5	.71	9	.253	.337	.476
Cotto, Luis	ss	Burlington	KC	A	20	46	143	21	0	0	0	21	14	9	17	0	41	5	2	0	2	2	.50	4	.147	.261	.147
		Spokane	KC	A-	20	72	236	51	5	0	2	62	28	20	31	0	60	3	3	3	7	5	.58	2	.216	.311	.263
Coulie, Jason	of	Cedar Rapds	Ana	A	24	117	434	105	22	3	9	160	49	50	23	0	105	10	4	2	9	7	.56	7	.242	.294	.369
Cowan, Justin	dh	Burlington	KC	A	24	88	319	70	20	1	7	113	34	38	23	0	63	6	1	4	0	1	.00	4	.219	.281	.354
Coyne, Anthony	dh	Brooklyn	NYM	A-	23	1	2	0	0	0	0	0	0	0	0	0	1	0	0	0	0	0	.00	0	.000	.000	.000
Craig, Beau#	c	Visalia	Oak	A+	23	96	344	67	16	1	1	88	34	32	23	0	77	2	4	2	1	1	.50	9	.195	.248	.256
Crespo, Manny	dh	San Berndno	Sea	A+	23	2	6	3	0	0	0	3	0	0	0	0	0	0	0	0	0	0	.00	0	.500	.500	.500
		Chston-WV	Tor	A	23	61	186	41	9	0	3	59	21	12	27	2	45	3	7	1	0	2	.00	2	.220	.327	.317
Crisp, Covelli#	of	Potomac	StL	A+	22	139	530	162	23	3	11	224	80	47	52	6	64	1	7	1	39	21	.65	8	.306	.368	.423
Crocker, Nick*	of	Myrtle Bch	Atl	A+	24	81	246	53	10	1	6	83	27	27	20	1	91	4	1	0	6	5	.55	2	.215	.285	.337
Cronin, Shane	c	Greensboro	NYY	A	26	58	191	48	6	0	4	66	23	25	7	0	32	3	1	5	1	0	1.00	2	.251	.282	.346
Crosby, Bobby	ss	Modesto	Oak	A+	22	11	38	15	5	0	1	23	7	3	3	0	8	0	0	0	0	0	.00	1	.395	.439	.605
Crosby, Kelly	of	Yankees	NYY	R	23	22	62	18	3	0	0	21	9	5	4	0	8	2	0	0	1	1	.50	2	.290	.353	.339
Crozier, Eric*	of	Columbus	Cle	A	23	67	221	52	9	2	4	77	41	19	37	1	84	1	2	1	5	3	.63	3	.235	.346	.348
Cruz, Alex	2b-ss	Pirates	Pit	R	21	19	65	19	3	2	1	29	12	7	13	0	8	0	1	0	3	0	1.00	2	.292	.410	.446
		Williamsprt	Pit	A-	21	26	83	15	1	1	0	18	9	11	4	0	14	0	2	2	1	0	1.00	1	.181	.213	.217
Cruz, Edgar	c	Kinston	Cle	A+	23	15	47	6	1	0	0	7	5	3	3	0	10	0	0	0	0	0	.00	1	.128	.180	.149
		Columbus	Cle	A	23	33	112	23	6	0	4	41	11	10	10	0	28	3	0	0	2	2	.50	3	.205	.288	.366
Cruz, Enrique	3b	Capital Cty	NYM	A	20	124	438	110	20	2	9	161	60	59	59	0	106	6	3	3	33	7	.83	7	.251	.346	.368
Cruz, Israel	2b	San Berndno	Sea	A+	22	31	67	12	2	0	0	14	6	3	2	0	22	1	2	0	3	1	.75	2	.179	.214	.209
Cruz, Luis	ss	Red Sox	Bos	R	18	53	197	51	9	0	3	69	18	18	7	0	17	1	0	2	1	4	.20	8	.259	.285	.350
Cruz, Nelson	of	Athletics	Oak	R	20	23	88	22	3	1	3	36	11	16	4	0	29	0	1	0	6	3	.67	1	.250	.283	.409
Cruz, Orlando	of	Savannah	Tex	A	20	34	114	21	0	0	1	24	3	6	3	0	31	2	2	1	1	4	.20	0	.184	.217	.211
		Pulaski	Tex	R+	20	47	178	44	9	3	1	62	25	18	12	0	59	1	6	2	9	2	.82	3	.247	.295	.348
Cuello, Domingo	2b	Hickory	Pit	A	19	18	59	13	0	1	0	15	6	2	2	0	11	0	4	1	6	1	.86	1	.220	.242	.254
		Williamsprt	Pit	A-	19	62	230	64	9	2	6	95	35	30	16	1	40	1	9	0	28	6	.82	3	.278	.328	.413
Cuevas, Aneudi	ss	Martinsvlle	Hou	R+	20	57	173	49	9	1	1	63	23	16	12	0	57	6	1	0	8	7	.53	3	.283	.351	.364
Cummings, Frank	3b	Jamestown	Atl	A-	25	3	1	0	0	0	0	0	0	0	0	0	1	0	0	0	0	0	.00	0	.000	.000	.000
Cunningham, Marco	of	Wilmington	KC	A+	24	138	497	141	22	4	4	183	82	61	95	7	119	19	9	1	17	8	.68	14	.284	.417	.368
Cust, Kevin	1b-dh	Danville	Atl	R+	20	24	62	8	0	0	1	11	2	4	1	0	32	2	0	1	0	1	.00	1	.129	.167	.177
		Braves	Atl	R	20	17	52	14	2	0	2	22	6	5	6	0	14	1	0	0	1	0	1.00	0	.269	.356	.423
Dacey, Ryan	1b	Wilmington	LA	A	24	66	198	50	8	0	1	61	22	24	32	0	45	5	2	2	10	7	.59	1	.253	.367	.308
Daeley, Scott	of	San Jose	SF	A+	25	114	411	93	14	1	3	118	77	29	64	0	76	6	9	2	30	5	.86	4	.226	.337	.287
Daigle, Leo	1b	Lakeland	Det	A+	22	95	313	79	19	1	11	133	42	58	24	3	77	5	0	5	4	1	.80	5	.252	.311	.425
Dancy, Cliff	of	Lakewood	Phi	A	22	7	18	2	0	0	0	2	0	0	1	0	7	0	0	0	0	0	.00	1	.111	.158	.111
		Batavia	Phi	A-	22	47	141	27	6	0	1	36	13	10	17	0	61	1	2	0	8	3	.73	4	.191	.283	.255
Daniel, Stevie	ss	Kannapolis	CWS	A	22	57	180	35	5	3	1	49	25	13	23	0	39	5	0	1	4	3	.57	3	.194	.301	.272
Daubert, Jake*	3b	Wisconsin	Sea	A	23	97	351	90	19	0	4	121	43	52	33	0	74	5	3	3	4	3	.57	3	.256	.327	.345
Davenport, Ron*	of	Chston-WV	Tor	A	20	79	298	86	18	2	4	120	37	54	20	1	53	1	0	7	11	5	.69	3	.289	.328	.403
Davidson, Seth#	ss-2b	New Jersey	StL	A-	23	63	217	60	7	1	0	69	18	15	23	1	13	4	5	3	5	13	.28	3	.276	.352	.318
Davie, Andrew*	dh	Johnson Cty	StL	R+	19	39	113	25	6	0	2	37	8	22	20	1	43	2	0	0	2	1	.67	1	.221	.348	.327
Davis, Daniel*	of	Tigers	Det	R	21	9	31	5	1	0	0	6	2	1	1	0	15	0	0	0	1	0	1.00	1	.161	.188	.194
Davis, J.P.	1b	Princeton	TB	R+	23	49	166	37	10	0	4	59	20	13	11	0	37	8	1	1	0	2	.00	3	.223	.301	.355
Davis, Justin*	of	Billings	Cin	R+	23	25	88	26	7	1	0	35	18	18	13	1	11	1	0	0	3	0	1.00	1	.295	.392	.398
Davis, Michael	dh	Fort Wayne	SD	A	25	80	294	80	16	2	4	112	40	45	28	1	57	10	0	2	10	4	.71	12	.272	.353	.381
Davis, Morrin	of	Auburn	Tor	A-	19	65	217	31	8	2	4	55	17	20	14	0	88	1	0	1	2	2	.50	5	.143	.197	.253
Davis, Rajai#	of	Williamsprt	Pit	A-	21	6	12	1	0	0	0	1	1	0	2	0	4	0	0	0	0	1	.00	0	.083	.214	.083
		Pirates	Pit	R	21	26	84	22	1	0	0	23	19	4	13	0	26	1	3	1	11	3	.79	0	.262	.364	.274
Davis, Ryan*	1b	Giants	SF	R	23	54	193	55	11	2	0	70	23	20	19	0	34	4	0	3	6	2	.75	3	.285	.356	.363
Davis, Tyrel	of	White Sox	CWS	R	21	43	140	34	4	1	0	40	11	11	10	0	37	2	2	1	1	3	.25	5	.243	.301	.286
Day, Nick	of	Fort Wayne	SD	A	24	5	12	0	0	0	0	0	0	0	0	0	3	0	1	0	0	0	.00	0	.000	.000	.000
Dean, Herman	of	Oneonta	Det	A-	21	7	24	5	1	1	0	8	3	0	1	0	10	0	0	0	1	0	1.00	0	.208	.240	.333
		Tigers	Det	R	21	28	82	21	4	0	3	34	18	10	4	0	24	3	2	0	13	0	1.00	1	.256	.315	.415
de Aza, Modesto	of	Pittsfield	Hou	A-	23	58	168	47	6	1	1	58	30	20	14	0	50	7	2	2	27	11	.71	2	.280	.356	.345
DeCaster, Yurendell	3b	Lynchburg	Pit	A+	22	13	48	5	2	0	0	7	1	4	3	0	16	0	0	0	0	0	.00	3	.104	.157	.146
		Hickory	Pit	A	22	97	341	99	17	4	19	181	56	74	35	2	83	8	0	5	4	4	.50	8	.290	.365	.531
DeCola, Dan	dh-c	Quad City	Min	A	22	34	101	22	4	0	1	29	6	13	6	1	23	8	2	1	0	0	.00	1	.218	.310	.287
Dees, Charlie	of	Savannah	Tex	A	24	41	140	35	6	2	5	60	16	19	13	0	52	0	0	2	1	3	.25	1	.250	.310	.429
DeGroote, Casey*	3b	Staten Ilnd	NYY	A-	22	14	22	4	3	0	0	7	0	4	4	0	10	0	0	0	0	0	.00	0	.182	.308	.318
Deitrick, Jeremy	c-dh	Clearwater	Phi	A+	25	55	195	40	11	2	5	70	12	28	8	0	62	3	1	0	3	3	.50	1	.205	.248	.359
de la Cruz, Eric	of	High Desert	Mil	A+	23	9	23	7	0	0	0	7	4	1	0	0	4	1	0	0	1	1	.50	0	.304	.333	.304
		Beloit	Mil	A	23	67	224	45	8	0	1	56	20	14	4	0	41	2	5	2	3	1	.75	6	.201	.220	.250
de la Cruz, Miguel	3b-1b	Hickory	Pit	A	22	12	36	8	1	0	0	9	3	1	4	0	12	3	0	0	0	1	.00	1	.222	.349	.250
		Williamsprt	Pit	A-	22	42	131	27	9	2	0	40	19	15	18	0	33	1	1	2	1	2	.33	2	.206	.303	.305
Del Chiaro, Brenton	c	Angels	Ana	R	23	20	58	15	1	1	1	21	9	4	7	0	18	3	0	0	0	0	.00	0	.259	.368	.362
		Provo	Ana	R+	23	22	57	9	1	0	0	10	2	5	7	0	20	0	1	2	1	0	1.00	0	.158	.242	.175
DeLeon, Carlos	c	Angels	Ana	R	19	28	101	31	4	1	0	37	12	13	5	0	10	4	0	1	2	2	.50	2	.307	.360	.366
		Angels	Ana	R	19	27	58	10	5	1	0	17	9	3	3	0	28	3	1	0	3	1	.75	0	.172	.250	.293
DeLeon, Virgilio	of	Tigers	Det	R	22	9	37	9	2	0	1	14	2	5	1	0	5	1	0	0	1	1	.50	2	.243	.282	.378
Delfino, Lee	ss	Auburn	Tor	A-	22	13	50	11	2	0	0	13	5	5	7	0	5	3	1	0	3	0	1.00	1	.220	.350	.260
		Chston-WV	Tor	A	22	41	146	39	10	2	0	53	16	13	12	1	29	4	0	0	2	1	.67	5	.267	.340	.363
Delgado, Dario	1b	Lakewood	Phi	A	22	84	281	54	11	1	3	76	19	27	11	1	53	8	2	1	0	0	.00	8	.192	.243	.270
Delgado, Jorge	dh	South Bend	Ari	A	21	101	348	105	26	2	4	147	53	50	46	0	43	12	1	2	0	2	.00	15	.302	.400	.422
Delgado, Mario*	1b	Phillies	Phi	R	22	2	8	4	0	0	1	7	1	4	0	0	1	0	0	0	0	0	.00	0	.500	.500	.875
		Lakewood	Phi	A	22	60	224	60	11	2	9	102	27	36	12	3	58	3	0	3	3	2	.60	4	.268	.310	.455
de los San, Pedro#	2b	Idaho Falls	SD	R+	18	12	46	16	4	1	0	22	11	5	2	0	10	1	1	0	5	0	1.00	1	.348	.388	.478
de los Santos, E.#	3b	Phillies	Phi	R	19	38	123	24	6	4	2	44	18	13	8	1	27	2	1	1	3	5	.38	1	.195	.254	.358
de los Santos, H.	2b	Quad City	Min	A	22	99	336	76	4	4	0	88	35	29	14	0	58	7	8	4	25	11	.69	11	.226	.269	.262
de los Santos, N.#	of	Brewers	Mil	R	23	26	95	24	6	3	1	39	15	15	11	0	15	1	0	3	1	0	1.00	1	.253	.327	.411
		Beloit	Mil	A	23	28	107	21	3	0	1	27	9	10	2	0	22	0	3	1	0	2	.00	0	.196	.209	.252
de los Santos, O.	3b	Dodgers	LA	R	20	9	33	10	4	0	0	14	7	3	3	0	4	0	1	1	1	1	.50	0	.303	.351	.424
		Great Falls	LA	R+	20	37	102	19	1	0	1	23	13	7	5	0	32	1	2	1	2	1	.67	5	.186	.229	.225
de los Santos, Rene	ss-2b	New Jersey	StL	A-	21	66	252	57	9	1	0	68	34	17	29	0	57	2	6	2	18	4	.82	1	.226	.309	.270

2001 Batting — Class-A and Rookie Leagues

BATTING																					BASERUNNING				PERCENTAGES		
Player	Pos	Team	Org	Lg	A	G	AB	H	2B	3B	HR	TB	R	RBI	TBB	IBB	SO	HBP	SH	SF	SB	CS	SB%	GDP	Avg	OBP	SLG
DeMarco, Matt*	3b-2b	Kane County	Fla	A	22	77	222	56	6	2	0	66	25	22	20	0	31	4	4	6	9	2	.82	5	.252	.317	.297
Dement, Dan	2b	Chston-SC	TB	A	24	108	394	106	24	11	8	176	52	54	31	2	108	3	5	2	6	14	.30	7	.269	.326	.447
		Bakersfield	TB	A+	24	5	17	1	0	0	0	1	0	1	1	0	3	0	1	0	0	0	.00	0	.059	.111	.059
Dempsey, Nick	1b-dh	Vermont	Mon	A-	23	15	60	18	3	0	2	27	4	10	3	1	10	0	1	0	0	0	.00	0	.300	.333	.450
		Clinton	Mon	A	23	34	115	35	6	0	1	44	16	18	8	0	29	3	0	0	0	0	.00	6	.304	.365	.383
DePaula, Luis	ss	Hudson Val	TB	A-	19	70	303	71	12	6	7	116	42	26	19	0	54	1	5	0	6	3	.67	6	.234	.282	.383
Deschaine, Jim	ss-3b	Daytona	ChC	A+	24	134	485	140	26	2	21	233	68	82	62	2	103	4	1	3	6	10	.38	10	.289	.372	.480
Deschenes, Pat*	3b-1b	St. Lucie	NYM	A+	24	65	213	55	8	1	1	68	26	24	27	5	32	2	0	2	1	1	.50	7	.258	.344	.319
		Capital Cty	NYM	A	24	53	195	53	10	1	0	65	26	36	24	0	33	0	0	2	2	2	.50	3	.272	.348	.333
Detienne, Dave	2b	Wilmington	LA	A	22	83	280	74	10	3	1	93	36	13	14	2	63	4	4	0	25	4	.86	5	.264	.309	.332
Devarez, Noel	of	Capital Cty	NYM	A	20	9	32	5	2	0	1	10	4	3	3	0	12	1	0	0	0	0	.00	0	.156	.250	.313
		Brooklyn	NYM	A-	20	54	188	47	10	0	10	87	30	33	10	0	63	3	0	2	3	3	.50	3	.250	.296	.463
Devinney, Rick	c	Cubs	ChC	R	18	6	18	6	1	0	0	7	1	1	2	0	3	0	0	0	0	2	.00	0	.333	.400	.389
DeVries, Jonathan	c	Red Sox	Bos	R	19	21	57	18	5	0	0	23	8	6	6	1	19	4	0	0	0	0	.00	0	.316	.418	.404
Diaz, Aneuris	3b	Peoria	StL	A	21	120	418	100	22	5	3	141	43	43	16	0	122	2	3	3	10	8	.56	4	.239	.269	.337
Diaz, Eduardo	2b	Casper	Col	R+	21	71	269	75	17	6	7	125	44	51	31	0	63	0	1	4	13	10	.57	3	.279	.349	.465
Diaz, Frank	of	Expos	Mon	R	18	38	128	28	5	1	0	35	10	8	12	1	27	3	1	2	10	3	.77	6	.219	.297	.273
Diaz, Jose	c	Wilmington	LA	A	22	23	80	14	4	0	2	24	7	5	4	0	31	0	2	0	1	0	1.00	1	.175	.214	.300
		Great Falls	LA	R+	22	48	159	30	8	0	3	47	18	17	15	0	38	7	0	2	2	1	.67	3	.189	.284	.296
Diaz, Maikell	2b-ss	Frederick	Bal	A+	23	95	310	77	14	1	2	99	34	18	11	0	75	4	7	1	9	9	.50	4	.248	.282	.319
Diaz, Matt	of	Bakersfield	TB	A+	24	131	524	172	40	2	17	267	79	81	24	3	73	14	4	5	11	5	.69	11	.328	.370	.510
Diaz, Randor	1b	Giants	SF	R	19	16	21	6	1	0	0	7	3	2	3	0	6	0	1	0	1	0	1.00	0	.286	.375	.333
Diaz, Victor	2b	Dodgers	LA	R	20	53	195	69	22	2	3	104	36	31	16	1	23	6	1	3	6	3	.67	3	.354	.414	.533
Dibetta, John	2b	Eugene	SD	A-	21	67	231	53	10	0	3	72	27	27	33	0	52	5	0	5	4	3	.57	2	.229	.332	.312
Dill, Jason*	of-1b	Savannah	Tex	A	23	43	132	16	4	0	1	23	8	7	22	0	35	0	0	0	1	0	1.00	3	.121	.247	.174
Dion, Nathanael	of	Hudson Val	TB	A-	20	52	172	38	5	3	1	52	18	9	9	0	54	3	2	0	0	2	.00	0	.221	.272	.302
Diredo, Curtis	of	Missoula	Ari	R+	23	19	61	15	2	0	0	17	8	5	4	0	15	1	0	0	3	2	.60	3	.246	.303	.279
Dirosa, Michael	c	Yakima	Ari	A-	22	45	127	39	9	0	4	60	20	25	23	0	35	4	2	0	0	0	.00	2	.307	.429	.472
D'Jesus, Francisco	c	Giants	SF	R	21	45	160	40	4	1	3	55	16	20	4	0	32	3	0	2	0	2	.00	3	.250	.278	.344
Dobbs, Greg*	1b	Everett	Sea	A-	23	65	249	80	17	2	6	119	37	41	30	3	39	2	1	2	5	3	.63	2	.321	.396	.478
		San Berndno	Sea	A+	23	3	13	5	1	0	1	9	2	3	0	0	4	0	0	1	0	0	.00	0	.385	.357	.692
Docen, Jose#	2b	Clinton	Mon	A	22	87	301	74	12	0	0	86	28	32	25	0	54	2	5	4	11	14	.44	6	.246	.304	.286
Dogero, Matt	c	New Jersey	StL	A-	21	4	5	0	0	0	0	0	0	0	0	0	1	0	0	0	0	0	.00	0	.000	.000	.000
		Peoria	StL	A	21	17	34	8	1	0	1	12	3	3	3	0	6	0	0	0	2	1	.67	0	.235	.297	.353
Donato, Greg	dh	Macon	Atl	A	21	3	12	3	0	0	0	3	1	1	2	1	1	0	0	0	0	0	.00	0	.250	.357	.250
Donovan, Todd	of	Lk Elsinore	SD	A+	23	41	168	51	7	0	1	61	37	12	19	0	25	1	2	0	23	2	.92	5	.304	.378	.363
Dorner, David*	c	Princeton	TB	R+	24	27	84	17	2	0	1	22	13	4	8	0	18	0	2	0	0	0	.00	5	.202	.272	.262
Dorsey, Ryan	2b	Pulaski	Tex	R+	20	16	38	5	2	1	0	9	1	2	5	0	20	1	0	0	2	0	1.00	0	.132	.250	.237
Dorta, Melvin	2b	Red Sox	Bos	R	20	21	76	31	6	0	2	43	19	8	11	0	5	1	0	0	7	3	.70	0	.408	.489	.566
		Augusta	Bos	A	20	36	135	36	4	1	0	42	19	18	8	0	16	3	1	1	6	5	.55	2	.267	.320	.311
Doudt, Tony	1b-c	Cedar Rapds	Ana	A	25	39	129	24	7	0	3	40	13	15	2	0	32	3	6	0	1	1	.50	3	.186	.216	.310
Downing, Brad*	of-dh	W Michigan	Det	A	26	49	154	41	4	2	5	64	19	23	15	3	18	1	1	0	0	3	.00	2	.266	.335	.416
		Lakeland	Det	A+	26	34	94	24	7	0	5	46	15	27	16	0	19	1	2	4	0	0	.00	2	.255	.357	.489
Downing, Phil*	of	Clinton	Mon	A	23	37	123	31	4	6	4	59	18	20	22	1	35	0	1	1	2	0	1.00	2	.252	.363	.480
		Jupiter	Mon	A+	23	67	227	54	15	3	3	84	28	30	29	0	69	1	0	2	8	4	.67	2	.238	.324	.370
Draper, John	c	Spokane	KC	A-	21	58	222	58	7	0	6	83	34	31	22	1	37	10	3	1	7	2	.78	4	.261	.353	.374
Duarte, Justin	c	Clearwater	Phi	A+	25	48	157	37	10	0	1	50	17	22	8	0	42	4	0	2	0	0	.00	5	.236	.287	.318
Dubois, Jason	of	Lansing	ChC	A	23	118	443	131	28	9	24	249	76	92	46	2	120	14	2	3	1	2	.33	8	.296	.377	.562
Duffy, Chris#	of	Williamsprt	Pit	A-	22	64	221	70	12	4	1	93	50	24	33	1	33	17	4	2	30	5	.86	0	.317	.440	.421
Duncan, Chris*	1b	Potomac	StL	A+	21	49	168	30	6	0	3	45	12	16	10	0	47	1	1	0	4	4	.50	5	.179	.229	.268
		Peoria	StL	A	21	80	297	91	23	2	13	157	44	59	36	2	55	3	0	1	13	3	.81	10	.306	.386	.529
Duncan, Jeff*	of	Capital Cty	NYM	A	23	88	318	69	16	8	3	110	49	23	46	0	97	3	4	2	41	3	.93	2	.217	.320	.346
Duncan, Shelly	dh	Staten Ilnd	NYY	A-	22	70	273	67	17	2	8	112	43	39	21	1	62	6	0	2	5	3	.63	5	.245	.311	.410
Duran, Carlos*	of	Braves	Atl	R	19	54	204	62	10	3	2	84	35	17	12	0	30	2	0	0	16	4	.80	0	.304	.349	.412
Duran, Deudis#	2b	Phillies	Phi	R	20	35	117	30	8	2	2	48	17	14	8	0	21	2	2	0	0	0	.00	1	.256	.315	.410
		Clearwater	Phi	A+	20	5	21	4	1	0	0	5	1	2	0	0	7	0	0	0	0	0	.00	1	.190	.190	.238
Duran, Frank	2b	Cedar Rapds	Ana	A	23	50	170	29	4	0	2	39	26	16	30	1	40	6	4	2	12	3	.80	1	.171	.313	.229
Durand, Jose	c	Spokane	KC	A-	21	16	46	6	2	1	0	10	4	0	3	0	19	2	0	0	0	0	.00	0	.130	.216	.217
Durango, Ariel#	ss	San Berndno	Sea	A+	23	27	87	16	1	0	0	17	8	6	10	0	18	1	3	0	7	4	.64	2	.184	.276	.195
		Wisconsin	Sea	A	23	87	307	88	10	4	4	118	48	31	25	1	71	4	4	0	32	11	.74	6	.287	.348	.384
Durazo, Ernie*	1b	Auburn	Tor	A-	23	64	238	65	22	0	1	90	26	36	21	0	54	2	0	4	1	1	.50	3	.273	.332	.378
Durham, Chad	of	Winston-Sal	CWS	A+	24	133	528	134	16	4	2	164	56	38	43	1	92	3	9	6	50	22	.69	9	.254	.310	.311
Durham, Miles*	of	W Michigan	Det	A	23	68	257	56	6	3	0	68	29	20	25	0	74	1	6	1	33	7	.83	4	.218	.289	.265
Dusan, Joe*	1b	Wisconsin	Sea	A	24	119	378	88	19	1	7	130	49	52	41	0	100	2	1	8	4	3	.57	6	.233	.305	.344
Dzurilla, Mike	1b	Daytona	ChC	A+	24	123	434	125	21	2	8	174	60	45	38	0	77	5	4	5	9	6	.60	8	.288	.349	.401
Eddlemon, Kelly	3b-2b	Bakersfield	TB	A+	23	104	367	84	25	4	7	138	46	49	36	3	85	3	1	5	7	4	.64	8	.229	.299	.376
Edge, Dwight	of	Lancaster	Ari	A+	23	20	62	12	1	0	0	13	5	6	6	0	23	0	0	1	3	3	.50	0	.194	.261	.210
		Yakima	Ari	A-	23	8	26	3	0	0	0	3	0	2	2	0	14	0	0	0	1	0	1.00	1	.115	.179	.115
		South Bend	Ari	A	23	46	164	38	5	1	2	51	15	18	16	0	42	2	1	1	5	2	.71	0	.232	.306	.311
Edwards, Dytarious*	2b	Fort Wayne	SD	A	25	69	220	47	4	0	0	51	35	6	24	0	50	0	5	1	23	5	.82	2	.214	.290	.232
Edwards, John	c	Fort Myers	Min	A+	24	87	278	58	14	2	4	88	24	33	22	0	77	4	0	2	4	2	.67	12	.209	.275	.317
Elder, Rick*	1b-of	Delmarva	Bal	A	22	112	382	96	20	5	16	174	66	64	63	10	130	2	0	2	7	1	.88	4	.251	.359	.455
Eldridge, Rashad#	of	Burlington	Cle	R+	20	61	229	59	8	6	5	94	39	27	27	0	65	3	1	2	3	2	.60	1	.258	.341	.410
Ellis, Alvyn	1b	Vancouver	Oak	A-	22	31	89	19	4	2	1	30	8	11	11	0	38	3	1	0	0	1	.00	0	.213	.320	.337
Ellis, Ryan	2b	Vermont	Mon	A-	23	42	137	32	3	3	1	44	15	13	13	0	24	2	5	1	4	2	.67	3	.234	.307	.321
Ellison, Jason	of	Hagerstown	SF	A	24	130	494	144	38	3	8	212	95	55	71	3	68	10	13	5	19	15	.56	6	.291	.388	.429
Ellison, Josh	of	Mariners	Sea	R	18	33	84	18	3	1	0	23	21	10	15	0	24	2	1	0	2	1	.67	0	.214	.347	.274
Elwood, Brad	c	Tampa	NYY	A+	26	45	118	25	6	0	0	31	11	10	8	0	21	2	1	0	1	1	.50	3	.212	.273	.263
Emmerick, Josh	c	Vermont	Mon	A-	21	43	144	26	5	0	0	31	11	10	11	0	32	2	0	0	0	0	.00	4	.181	.248	.215
Encarnacion, Edwin	3b	Savannah	Tex	A	19	45	170	52	9	2	4	77	23	25	12	0	34	2	1	2	3	3	.50	5	.306	.355	.453
		Dayton	Cin	A	19	9	37	6	2	0	1	11	2	6	1	0	5	0	0	0	0	1	.00	1	.162	.184	.297
		Billings	Cin	R+	19	52	211	55	8	2	5	82	27	26	15	0	29	0	0	2	8	1	.89	6	.261	.307	.389
Encarnacion, H.#	ss-3b	Expos	Mon	R	20	50	166	34	4	1	0	40	23	10	26	0	38	1	1	1	10	0	1.00	3	.205	.314	.241
Encarnacion, Julio	of	Bristol	CWS	R+	20	26	76	16	3	0	2	25	11	12	0	0	31	1	1	0	2	0	1.00	2	.211	.221	.329
Encarnacion, S.	of	Eugene	SD	A-	22	33	102	19	3	1	0	24	11	3	5	0	35	1	1	0	4	0	1.00	4	.186	.231	.235

2001 Batting — Class-A and Rookie Leagues

BATTING																					BASERUNNING				PERCENTAGES		
Player	Pos	Team	Org	Lg	A	G	AB	H	2B	3B	HR	TB	R	RBI	TBB	IBB	SO	HBP	SH	SF	SB	CS	SB%	GDP	Avg	OBP	SLG
Escalera, Jose	of	Wilmington	LA	A	21	8	34	5	0	0	0	5	4	5	0	0	7	0	0	1	0	0	.00	1	.147	.143	.147
		Great Falls	LA	R+	21	9	42	7	0	0	0	7	4	2	3	1	5	0	0	1	0	0	.00	1	.167	.217	.167
Escalona, Felix	2b	Lexington	Hou	A	23	130	536	155	42	2	16	249	92	64	30	2	85	16	5	5	46	12	.79	8	.289	.342	.465
Escobar, Gustavo	ss-2b	Potomac	StL	A+	22	4	8	3	0	0	0	3	0	0	0	0	1	1	0	0	0	0	.00	0	.375	.444	.375
Escobar, Luis*	c	Royals	KC	R	19	34	94	26	3	0	2	35	8	10	12	1	18	4	2	1	0	0	.00	3	.277	.378	.372
Esparragoz, Pedro	c	Brewers	Mil	R	20	48	153	37	5	1	2	50	25	22	16	1	39	7	1	1	4	1	.80	4	.242	.339	.327
		Ogden	Mil	R+	20	1	1	0	0	0	0	0	0	0	0	0	1	0	0	0	0	0	.00	0	.000	.000	.000
Espino, Damaso#	3b	Reds	Cin	R	19	39	104	26	2	0	1	31	8	11	5	0	26	2	1	2	6	2	.75	4	.250	.292	.298
Espino, Jose	of-dh	New Jersey	StL	A-	22	20	53	15	5	1	1	25	10	11	5	0	13	0	0	1	0	2	.00	1	.283	.339	.472
Espinosa, David#	ss	Dayton	Cin	A	20	122	493	129	29	8	7	195	88	37	55	1	120	4	2	1	15	10	.60	3	.262	.340	.396
Espinoza, Efren	2b	Hickory	Pit	A	21	50	162	36	9	0	5	60	18	21	5	0	49	5	2	1	2	0	1.00	1	.222	.266	.370
		Lynchburg	Pit	A+	21	19	62	9	2	0	0	11	4	4	2	0	19	1	0	0	1	1	.50	0	.145	.185	.177
Esposito, Brian	c	Augusta	Bos	A	23	90	311	59	13	0	3	81	21	30	13	0	81	2	2	5	0	0	.00	5	.190	.224	.260
Esprit, Jermaine#	of	Burlington	Cle	R+	22	35	112	27	1	0	0	28	13	2	4	0	29	2	1	0	8	4	.67	1	.241	.280	.250
Espy, Nate	1b	Clearwater	Phi	A+	24	133	470	134	31	2	11	202	75	68	88	3	90	6	0	7	6	2	.75	10	.285	.399	.430
Esquivel, Lale	1b-dh	Pulaski	Tex	R+	24	7	27	7	2	0	2	15	2	8	2	0	5	0	1	0	0	0	.00	0	.259	.310	.556
		Savannah	Tex	A	24	51	177	42	10	0	5	67	13	20	11	0	43	2	0	3	0	1	.00	5	.237	.285	.379
Essery, Fred	c	Casper	Col	R+	24	24	60	9	0	0	0	9	4	9	1	0	12	0	1	1	0	0	.00	2	.150	.161	.150
Esterlin, Ivan*	of	Cubs	ChC	R	21	24	77	17	4	2	1	28	11	10	7	0	19	1	1	2	4	0	1.00	1	.221	.287	.364
Estilow, Chris	c	Marlins	Fla	R	21	18	40	5	0	0	0	5	3	3	7	0	20	0	0	0	0	0	.00	0	.125	.255	.125
Eum, Jong	c	Myrtle Bch	Atl	A+	28	24	72	11	1	0	1	15	5	7	7	0	33	2	1	0	0	0	.00	1	.153	.247	.208
Eure, Jeff	of	Ogden	Mil	R+	21	50	144	31	7	0	3	47	16	24	7	0	41	6	1	1	6	2	.75	3	.215	.278	.326
Evans, Austin*	of	Savannah	Tex	A	24	51	147	29	5	0	0	34	18	5	12	0	27	1	2	0	5	2	.71	0	.197	.263	.231
Evans, Mitch	c	Staten Ilnd	NYY	A-	21	26	49	6	2	0	0	8	1	3	8	0	16	1	0	0	0	0	.00	3	.122	.259	.163
Ewing, Byron	1b	Kinston	Cle	A+	25	90	301	73	14	1	7	110	41	38	35	0	67	8	0	0	7	7	.50	6	.243	.337	.365
Eylward, Mike	1b	Provo	Ana	R+	22	7	20	6	3	0	0	9	7	5	2	0	5	3	0	0	0	0	.00	0	.300	.440	.450
		Cedar Rapds	Ana	A	22	23	90	21	6	1	2	35	12	12	5	0	21	2	1	1	0	0	.00	2	.233	.286	.389
Ezi, Travis	of	Dodgers	LA	R	20	58	238	55	10	4	2	79	33	24	17	1	90	4	6	0	15	1	.94	2	.231	.293	.332
Fagan, John	1b	Martinsvlle	Hou	R+	22	59	201	42	12	0	5	69	20	22	19	3	50	6	0	2	1	0	1.00	4	.209	.294	.343
Fagan, Shawn	3b	Dunedin	Tor	A+	24	132	475	143	18	5	10	201	68	71	86	1	114	2	0	4	7	2	.78	11	.301	.407	.423
Fahey, Patrick	c	Dodgers	LA	R	22	8	17	3	0	0	0	3	3	2	3	0	4	1	0	0	0	0	.00	0	.176	.333	.176
Faison, Vince*	of	Fort Wayne	SD	A	21	41	140	28	5	0	1	36	14	8	18	1	35	3	1	1	10	3	.77	4	.200	.302	.257
		Lk Elsinore	SD	A+	21	73	275	64	11	3	7	102	27	36	24	1	94	2	1	2	12	7	.63	2	.233	.297	.371
Falcon, Omar	c	Idaho Falls	SD	R+	19	37	107	20	5	0	5	40	24	9	33	0	50	4	0	0	0	1	.00	0	.187	.396	.374
Fallon, Chris*	1b	Spokane	KC	A-	23	64	198	50	8	0	2	64	28	26	32	5	57	0	2	4	2	0	1.00	1	.253	.350	.323
Farmer, John	2b	Braves	Atl	R	23	2	6	0	0	0	0	0	0	0	0	0	2	0	0	0	0	0	.00	0	.000	.000	.000
		Danville	Atl	R+	23	12	16	4	1	0	0	5	1	1	1	0	4	2	0	0	0	0	.00	1	.250	.368	.313
Fatur, Brian	of	Peoria	StL	A	23	56	193	40	7	0	5	62	27	24	25	0	35	3	4	2	9	10	.47	1	.207	.305	.321
		Potomac	StL	A+	23	60	226	53	13	0	2	72	20	20	6	1	38	6	4	2	3	1	.75	5	.235	.271	.319
Faulkner, Todd	1b	Yankees	NYY	R	24	7	19	2	1	0	0	3	2	0	2	0	6	0	0	0	0	0	.00	0	.105	.190	.158
		Staten Ilnd	NYY	A-	24	24	55	12	1	1	0	15	4	3	4	0	13	1	0	1	1	0	1.00	0	.218	.279	.273
Fears, Chris#	of	Fort Wayne	SD	A	24	86	263	66	5	1	1	76	30	19	30	1	53	5	7	2	20	7	.74	4	.251	.337	.289
Feliciano, Jesus*	of	Vero Beach	LA	A+	23	116	401	105	11	3	3	131	48	29	31	2	35	4	4	2	22	10	.69	15	.262	.320	.327
Feliz, Henry*	1b	Yankees	NYY	R	21	25	64	13	2	1	1	20	7	9	2	0	22	1	2	1	0	1	.00	2	.203	.235	.313
Fennell, Jason#	1b	Kannapolis	CWS	A	24	10	22	3	0	0	0	3	1	0	3	0	2	0	0	0	0	0	.00	1	.136	.240	.136
		Winston-Sal	CWS	A+	24	63	175	33	5	0	0	38	17	14	18	1	33	3	0	0	1	1	.50	3	.189	.276	.217
Fenster, Darren	2b	Burlington	KC	A	23	97	356	102	19	0	2	127	47	45	33	0	63	6	5	5	1	3	.25	4	.287	.353	.357
Fera, Aaron	of	Peoria	StL	A	24	16	59	10	4	0	2	20	5	9	4	0	32	0	0	0	1	1	.50	0	.169	.222	.339
Fermin, Angelo#	2b	Twins	Min	R	18	13	43	12	0	0	0	12	5	5	6	0	10	1	1	2	2	2	.50	1	.279	.365	.279
Fernandez, A.	c	Staten Ilnd	NYY	A-	21	29	84	16	2	0	1	21	7	5	8	0	26	3	3	0	0	0	.00	1	.190	.284	.250
Fernandez, Alex*	of-dh	San Berndno	Sea	A+	21	111	417	119	21	6	8	176	51	52	35	3	67	2	5	1	17	6	.74	9	.285	.343	.422
Ferrand, Frank*	of	Brevard Cty	Fla	A+	22	31	113	22	0	1	3	33	14	13	4	0	28	0	0	0	0	0	.00	2	.195	.222	.292
		Kane County	Fla	A	22	85	297	86	20	2	6	128	43	45	17	2	49	3	2	3	3	1	.75	1	.290	.331	.431
Figuereo, Anibal	1b	Royals	KC	R	20	51	176	40	7	2	2	57	18	18	18	0	47	3	2	0	8	2	.80	3	.227	.310	.324
Figueroa, Carlos*	2b	Asheville	Col	A	21	12	40	10	2	0	0	12	6	5	4	0	8	0	1	0	4	1	.80	0	.250	.318	.300
		Tri-City	Col	A-	21	42	128	20	1	0	0	21	10	11	13	0	23	1	1	2	1	3	.25	1	.156	.236	.164
Figueroa, Daniel*	of-dh	Red Sox	Bos	R	20	27	86	22	4	1	6	46	16	24	21	1	28	1	0	5	3	0	1.00	0	.256	.389	.535
Figueroa, Eduardo	of	Everett	Sea	A-	20	49	187	58	10	2	3	81	35	24	17	0	45	6	1	3	7	5	.58	2	.310	.380	.433
		Wisconsin	Sea	A	20	15	49	10	1	1	0	13	6	5	5	0	11	2	0	0	2	1	.67	1	.204	.304	.265
Finnerty, Francis#	3b	Mahoning Vy	Cle	A-	21	45	153	25	3	0	1	31	7	10	6	0	26	1	0	0	2	0	1.00	6	.163	.200	.203
Firlit, Dan	ss	Peoria	StL	A	23	41	105	22	6	0	1	31	12	7	9	1	33	3	1	1	2	1	.67	0	.210	.288	.295
Fisher, Tim	c	Missoula	Ari	R+	22	16	28	2	0	0	0	2	5	0	2	0	12	4	0	0	0	0	.00	0	.071	.235	.071
Fitzpatrick, Reggie*	of	Expos	Mon	R	19	31	118	33	1	0	0	34	17	7	9	1	28	0	0	0	5	4	.56	2	.280	.331	.288
		Vermont	Mon	A-	19	4	16	2	0	0	0	2	2	1	0	0	2	0	0	0	1	1	.50	1	.125	.125	.125
Flaherty, Tim	1b	San Jose	SF	A+	25	135	466	119	26	5	26	233	69	83	66	2	162	8	0	4	2	5	.29	12	.255	.355	.500
Flannigan, Tim	3b	Capital Cty	NYM	A	23	15	53	11	1	0	0	12	3	3	3	0	10	2	1	0	2	1	.67	2	.208	.276	.226
Florence, Branden	dh	Salem-Keizr	SF	A-	24	32	124	34	6	1	1	45	20	15	12	1	8	4	0	2	2	0	1.00	3	.274	.352	.363
Flores, Ralphs	ss	Winston-Sal	CWS	A+	22	25	80	16	0	0	0	16	5	6	4	0	14	0	0	0	1	1	.50	2	.200	.238	.200
		Kannapolis	CWS	A	22	61	186	53	7	0	1	63	18	19	13	0	39	3	2	3	3	3	.50	6	.285	.337	.339
Floyd, Dan	of-3b	Wisconsin	Sea	A	19	90	338	88	19	1	5	124	47	38	20	1	61	10	5	5	6	6	.50	6	.260	.316	.367
Floyd, Mike	of	Peoria	StL	A	24	83	246	53	9	0	2	68	26	23	17	0	62	2	6	5	18	9	.67	3	.215	.267	.276
Folsom, Mark	of	Burlington	Cle	R+	21	29	100	21	7	1	2	36	15	23	17	0	41	0	0	0	0	1	.00	2	.210	.325	.360
Forbes, Mike*	1b	Macon	Atl	A	22	117	378	97	23	0	10	150	53	64	72	2	106	3	2	3	10	8	.56	4	.257	.377	.397
Foreman, Julius*	of	South Bend	Ari	A	23	61	212	66	6	5	0	82	47	16	42	3	25	0	2	0	23	7	.77	1	.311	.425	.387
Foster, Brian	c	High Desert	Mil	A+	20	9	28	7	3	1	2	18	6	5	5	0	14	0	1	0	1	0	1.00	1	.250	.364	.643
		Beloit	Mil	A	20	36	123	18	8	0	4	38	14	9	10	0	55	1	5	0	0	0	.00	2	.146	.216	.309
Foster, Gregg	of	Batavia	Phi	A-	23	8	17	3	2	0	0	5	5	1	2	0	6	0	0	1	1	0	1.00	0	.176	.250	.294
		Lakewood	Phi	A	23	87	281	63	11	2	6	96	37	23	21	0	74	9	0	2	17	5	.77	3	.224	.297	.342
Fowler, David	of	Greensboro	NYY	A	22	110	291	58	15	3	5	94	30	26	27	0	125	5	4	2	8	12	.40	6	.199	.277	.323
Fox, Matt	3b-2b	Spokane	KC	A-	23	58	226	62	6	2	1	75	25	29	6	0	39	5	4	3	5	2	.71	3	.274	.304	.332
Fox, Mike	2b	New Jersey	StL	A-	22	27	90	20	7	0	2	33	13	5	13	0	29	1	3	1	1	1	.50	0	.222	.324	.367
Francia, Juan#	2b	Oneonta	Det	A-	20	47	191	65	5	2	0	74	30	8	11	0	32	2	3	1	17	14	.55	2	.340	.380	.387
Francisco, Ruben*	of	Delmarva	Bal	A	21	39	103	22	4	4	0	34	14	13	6	0	17	0	2	0	1	3	.25	2	.214	.257	.330
		Bluefield	Bal	R+	21	57	199	65	16	0	3	90	35	21	17	0	32	7	1	0	18	5	.78	10	.327	.399	.452
Franco, Esterlin	3b	Pittsfield	Hou	A-	21	42	134	33	5	1	0	40	20	10	15	0	22	0	4	2	5	1	.83	6	.246	.318	.299

2001 Batting — Class-A and Rookie Leagues

						BATTING															BASERUNNING				PERCENTAGES		
Player	Pos	Team	Org	Lg	A	G	AB	H	2B	3B	HR	TB	R	RBI	TBB	IBB	SO	HBP	SH	SF	SB	CS	SB%	GDP	Avg	OBP	SLG
Franco, Iker	c	Chston-SC	TB	A	21	87	265	53	10	2	3	76	15	21	19	0	81	1	4	3	1	2	.33	7	.200	.253	.287
Francois, Francisco	ss	Athletics	Oak	R	19	46	155	26	5	2	0	35	22	7	15	0	37	8	4	0	10	8	.56	1	.168	.275	.226
Franke, Michael#	3b	Brewers	Mil	R	20	25	81	13	4	0	0	17	8	5	5	0	31	2	1	1	4	0	1.00	2	.160	.225	.210
Frazier, Charlie	of	Utica	Fla	A-	21	67	243	59	15	3	2	86	35	18	27	0	72	2	0	1	11	4	.73	3	.243	.322	.354
Freeman, Ashley	3b-1b	Tri-City	Col	A-	23	66	236	48	13	3	1	70	39	28	18	0	52	13	1	4	6	1	.86	2	.203	.292	.297
Freeman, Choo	of	Salem	Col	A+	22	132	517	124	16	5	8	174	63	42	31	1	108	9	8	5	19	7	.73	8	.240	.292	.337
Freeman, Miguel	of	Vermont	Mon	A-	22	54	180	31	3	2	6	56	21	26	19	0	73	1	1	1	3	0	1.00	5	.172	.254	.311
Friar, Roddy	c	Peoria	StL	A	26	36	85	14	5	0	0	19	10	5	18	0	38	2	1	0	0	1	.00	2	.165	.324	.224
		Potomac	StL	A+	26	18	41	9	2	0	0	11	4	2	6	0	20	1	0	0	1	1	.50	0	.220	.333	.268
Frick, Matt	c	Brevard Cty	Fla	A+	26	42	133	30	12	0	2	48	19	12	10	0	30	4	0	1	1	0	1.00	2	.226	.297	.361
Frome, Jason*	of	Tri-City	Col	A-	22	58	219	49	12	4	1	72	28	21	23	2	64	3	1	2	6	3	.67	1	.224	.304	.329
Fry, Ryan	3b	Reds	Cin	R	22	56	181	50	9	3	4	77	30	22	25	1	61	5	0	2	9	2	.82	3	.276	.376	.425
		Billings	Cin	R+	22	3	9	2	0	0	0	2	1	2	0	0	4	0	0	0	0	0	.00	1	.222	.222	.222
Fuentes, Omar	c	Greensboro	NYY	A	22	100	342	91	24	1	8	141	59	62	45	2	57	9	2	7	0	2	.00	9	.266	.360	.412
		Tampa	NYY	A+	22	2	6	5	1	0	1	9	4	3	2	0	0	0	0	0	0	0	.00	0	.833	.875	1.500
Fulse, Sheldon#	of	San Berndno	Sea	A+	20	34	122	20	2	1	2	30	14	11	14	0	43	3	1	1	7	6	.54	3	.164	.264	.246
		Wisconsin	Sea	A	20	80	255	56	16	5	2	88	38	17	31	0	73	7	2	2	21	3	.88	3	.220	.319	.345
Furbush, Mark	of	Kingsport	NYM	R+	24	39	140	38	12	1	3	61	18	19	10	0	34	0	0	0	8	4	.67	2	.271	.320	.436
Furmaniak, J.J.	ss	Fort Wayne	SD	A	22	123	436	96	24	3	5	141	57	35	55	0	117	4	3	7	11	6	.65	10	.220	.309	.323
Gajewski, Matt#	c	Charlotte	Tex	A+	24	26	79	11	4	1	1	20	4	4	12	1	26	0	0	0	0	0	.00	0	.139	.253	.253
		Savannah	Tex	A	24	30	84	20	2	0	2	28	7	8	10	0	30	1	0	1	0	2	.00	0	.238	.323	.333
Galante, Matt	2b	Potomac	StL	A+	23	4	6	1	0	0	0	1	0	0	0	0	2	1	0	0	0	0	.00	0	.167	.286	.167
Gall, John	1b	Peoria	StL	A	24	57	205	62	23	0	4	97	27	44	16	1	18	4	0	7	0	3	.00	3	.302	.353	.473
		Potomac	StL	A+	24	84	319	101	25	0	4	138	44	33	24	4	40	3	0	1	5	6	.45	9	.317	.369	.433
Gallo, Ismael*	2b	Dodgers	LA	R	25	4	6	1	0	0	0	1	2	0	1	0	1	1	0	0	1	0	1.00	0	.167	.375	.167
		Vero Beach	LA	A+	25	64	237	60	9	3	2	81	26	22	24	0	15	0	7	3	2	1	.67	5	.253	.318	.342
Gambino, Mike	2b	Augusta	Bos	A	24	7	26	2	1	0	0	3	2	0	2	0	4	0	0	0	0	1	.00	0	.077	.143	.115
		Lowell	Bos	A-	24	45	169	41	10	2	0	55	20	25	18	0	25	2	4	5	0	1	.00	4	.243	.314	.325
Gandolfo, Rob*	2b	San Berndno	Sea	A+	24	94	312	64	6	3	0	76	33	26	23	1	47	3	3	2	4	6	.40	3	.205	.265	.244
Gann, Bryan	2b	Hagerstown	SF	A	24	111	397	94	16	0	0	110	49	26	28	0	50	7	20	6	2	3	.40	10	.237	.295	.277
Garabito, Vianney	dh	Billings	Cin	R+	22	10	39	7	4	0	0	11	9	4	3	0	5	0	0	1	0	0	.00	0	.179	.233	.282
		Dayton	Cin	A	22	10	23	2	1	0	1	6	4	2	1	0	4	1	0	0	0	0	.00	1	.087	.160	.261
Garbe, B.J.	of	Fort Myers	Min	A+	21	127	463	112	14	4	6	152	55	61	51	2	86	12	0	3	13	7	.65	8	.242	.331	.328
Garcia, Danny	2b	Brooklyn	NYM	A-	22	15	56	18	2	0	1	23	10	6	4	0	10	2	0	0	3	2	.60	0	.321	.387	.411
		Capital Cty	NYM	A	22	30	103	31	12	1	2	51	25	16	15	0	18	6	4	3	7	3	.70	0	.301	.409	.495
Garcia, Douglas*	of	Charlotte	Tex	A+	23	127	473	115	17	7	4	158	40	51	27	4	78	5	4	3	11	4	.73	7	.243	.289	.334
Garcia, Hector	of	Beloit	Mil	A	22	109	404	107	14	2	6	143	43	37	9	0	71	2	4	2	20	6	.77	7	.265	.283	.354
Garcia, Isaac	2b-ss	Modesto	Oak	A+	21	53	168	42	7	1	2	57	11	16	8	0	40	1	0	3	5	1	.83	3	.250	.283	.339
Garcia, Jose	of	Great Falls	LA	R+	21	74	306	89	23	4	8	144	46	50	13	1	49	5	0	0	15	9	.63	9	.291	.330	.471
Garcia, J.-Carlos#	3b-1b	Marlins	Fla	R	20	40	108	20	4	0	1	27	8	10	14	0	44	0	1	1	2	3	.40	1	.185	.276	.250
Garcia, Kenji	1b	Kingsport	NYM	R+	21	17	48	1	1	0	0	2	1	1	6	0	25	1	0	0	0	1	.00	0	.021	.145	.042
Garcia, Kevys	ss	Pittsfield	Hou	A-	21	20	44	8	0	1	1	13	3	9	6	0	13	0	3	2	1	0	1.00	0	.182	.269	.295
Garcia, Lino	of	Missoula	Ari	R+	18	46	140	34	6	2	4	56	34	22	14	0	32	5	2	0	8	2	.80	1	.243	.333	.400
Garcia, Nick	ss	Delmarva	Bal	A	22	130	442	116	14	1	2	138	42	42	20	0	59	9	15	5	2	3	.40	10	.262	.305	.312
Garcia, Oscar	2b	Columbus	Cle	A	21	16	47	5	1	0	0	6	3	0	5	0	15	2	0	0	0	2	.00	0	.106	.222	.128
Garcia, Rafaelito#	ss-2b	Burlington	Cle	R+	20	51	195	50	6	1	1	61	28	12	20	0	37	1	5	0	12	5	.71	5	.256	.329	.313
Garcia, Sandy	of	Yankees	NYY	R	22	35	112	28	8	2	3	49	18	18	10	1	37	2	0	2	3	1	.75	0	.250	.317	.438
Garland, Ross	c	Lakeland	Det	A+	22	1	4	1	0	0	0	1	0	0	0	0	2	0	0	0	0	0	.00	0	.250	.250	.250
		Oneonta	Det	A-	22	32	106	16	3	1	1	24	8	10	5	0	31	3	0	0	0	1	.00	2	.151	.211	.226
Garrett, Shawn#	of	Lk Elsinore	SD	A+	23	77	275	86	16	8	7	139	41	44	24	1	57	5	2	4	16	7	.70	5	.313	.373	.505
		Lynchburg	Pit	A+	23	52	194	57	13	0	9	97	28	28	17	0	64	3	0	0	6	4	.60	3	.294	.360	.500
Garrido, Tomas	ss	Hagerstown	SF	A	20	45	142	31	3	0	0	34	13	7	2	0	34	1	5	0	2	1	.67	3	.218	.234	.239
		Giants	SF	R	20	40	131	33	3	0	0	36	17	8	2	0	19	5	0	0	3	0	1.00	6	.252	.290	.275
Gastelum, Carlos	2b	Rancho Cuca	Ana	A+	20	118	363	74	11	6	0	97	39	28	15	0	57	4	23	3	20	6	.77	11	.204	.242	.267
Gates, James	of	Provo	Ana	R+	21	48	170	50	13	0	3	72	31	33	29	0	43	6	0	0	4	3	.57	6	.294	.415	.424
Gatti, William	of	Dodgers	LA	R	24	11	31	5	0	0	0	5	5	1	3	0	8	2	0	0	0	0	.00	1	.161	.278	.161
		Wilmington	LA	A	24	6	23	5	1	0	1	9	3	3	1	0	10	1	0	1	1	0	1.00	2	.217	.269	.391
Gay, Curt*	1b	Mahoning Vy	Cle	A-	24	29	92	13	3	0	1	19	8	5	11	0	31	0	0	0	0	3	.00	4	.141	.233	.207
Gearlds, Aaron	of	Tri-City	Col	A-	22	58	197	47	9	5	0	66	30	19	17	0	61	8	1	0	21	1	.95	3	.239	.324	.335
Gelotti, Matt	of	Brewers	Mil	R	25	4	18	3	0	1	0	5	0	4	1	0	4	0	0	0	0	0	.00	0	.167	.211	.278
Gemoll, Brandon*	1b	Brewers	Mil	R	21	8	31	10	2	1	0	14	8	9	3	0	7	0	0	2	0	0	.00	0	.323	.361	.452
		Ogden	Mil	R+	21	6	13	4	0	0	0	4	1	0	1	0	2	0	0	0	0	1	.00	0	.308	.357	.308
Gemoll, Justin	3b	Burlington	KC	A	24	128	482	131	27	3	10	194	78	70	50	0	90	13	3	4	5	1	.83	14	.272	.353	.402
Gentry, Garett*	c	Michigan	Hou	A	21	98	358	107	18	3	24	203	62	103	39	8	45	8	0	5	5	0	1.00	9	.299	.376	.567
Gerlits, Gooby	c	Marlins	Fla	R	19	16	43	7	1	0	0	8	1	2	1	0	12	1	0	0	0	0	.00	0	.163	.200	.186
German, Amado#	of	Princeton	TB	R+	21	52	184	52	10	5	5	87	33	31	19	0	50	0	0	1	16	4	.80	1	.283	.348	.473
German, Franklin	of	Daytona	ChC	A+	22	71	196	36	6	2	0	46	29	12	25	0	63	3	6	0	13	7	.65	4	.184	.286	.235
German, Ramon#	3b	Lexington	Hou	A	22	129	461	122	37	3	13	204	72	93	55	1	107	9	0	4	21	9	.70	8	.265	.352	.443
Gettis, Byron	of	Burlington	KC	A	22	37	140	44	9	2	5	72	26	26	14	1	25	4	1	3	4	3	.57	3	.314	.385	.514
		Wilmington	KC	A+	22	82	303	76	21	2	6	119	34	51	20	0	70	12	3	1	4	5	.44	7	.251	.321	.393
Ghutzman, Phillip	c	Reds	Cin	R	23	27	68	14	6	0	0	20	6	7	10	0	11	0	1	1	0	0	.00	5	.206	.304	.294
Gil, Jerry	ss	South Bend	Ari	A	19	105	363	78	14	5	2	108	40	31	8	0	103	4	8	0	19	7	.73	12	.215	.240	.298
Gillikin, Joe	of	Kannapolis	CWS	A	25	77	221	53	11	2	8	92	27	35	18	0	74	6	1	4	3	7	.30	3	.240	.309	.416
Gillitzer, Scott	2b	Great Falls	LA	R+	23	66	253	66	11	0	1	80	34	41	21	2	23	4	3	3	10	1	.91	5	.261	.324	.316
Giorgis, David#	of	Idaho Falls	SD	R+	20	65	242	70	16	0	7	107	28	41	24	2	69	4	0	3	2	4	.33	6	.289	.359	.442
Giron, Alejandro	of	Clearwater	Phi	A+	23	113	418	109	26	3	6	159	59	41	19	1	84	4	2	2	9	9	.50	10	.261	.298	.380
Godwin, Tyrell*	of-dh	Auburn	Tor	A-	22	33	117	43	8	2	2	61	26	15	19	0	27	2	0	0	9	5	.64	1	.368	.464	.521
Golden, Bryan	c	Cubs	ChC	R	21	22	57	8	1	0	2	15	11	4	11	0	15	1	0	0	0	3	.00	3	.140	.290	.263
Goldfield, Josh*	c	Lancaster	Ari	A+	22	5	17	3	0	0	0	3	2	1	1	0	2	0	0	0	0	0	.00	2	.176	.222	.176
Gomersall, Richard	2b	Oneonta	Det	A-	23	43	120	20	2	0	1	25	18	8	11	0	45	2	3	1	3	2	.60	2	.167	.246	.208
Gomes, Jonny	of	Princeton	TB	R+	21	62	206	60	11	2	16	123	58	44	33	0	73	26	1	4	15	4	.79	1	.291	.442	.597
Gomez, Andre	c-of	Eugene	SD	A-	23	6	14	2	0	0	1	5	1	3	0	0	4	1	0	0	1	0	1.00	0	.143	.200	.357
		Lk Elsinore	SD	A+	23	21	70	16	3	0	1	22	7	11	3	0	24	0	0	1	0	0	.00	2	.229	.257	.314
Gomez, Frank	ss	Visalia	Oak	A+	20	120	384	90	15	2	5	124	43	45	28	0	100	4	7	3	9	7	.56	9	.234	.291	.323
Gomez, Jose	of	Johnson Cty	StL	R+	21	16	35	5	1	1	0	8	4	0	6	0	13	0	2	0	1	0	1.00	1	.143	.268	.229

2001 Batting — Class-A and Rookie Leagues

						BATTING															BASERUNNING				PERCENTAGES		
Player	Pos	Team	Org	Lg	A	G	AB	H	2B	3B	HR	TB	R	RBI	TBB	IBB	SO	HBP	SH	SF	SB	CS	SB%	GDP	Avg	OBP	SLG
Gomez, Raul#	1b	White Sox	CWS	R	22	39	131	30	7	2	0	41	8	16	19	0	42	0	0	1	1	2	.33	3	.229	.325	.313
Gomon, Dusty	1b	Twins	Min	R	19	19	74	24	6	0	2	36	13	10	5	0	15	0	0	0	1	0	1.00	0	.324	.367	.486
		Fort Myers	Min	A+	19	6	18	5	0	0	1	8	2	3	0	0	6	0	0	0	0	0	.00	0	.278	.278	.444
Gonzalez, Adrian*	1b	Kane County	Fla	A	20	127	516	161	37	1	17	251	86	103	57	6	83	5	0	6	5	5	.50	17	.312	.382	.486
Gonzalez, Andy	ss	White Sox	CWS	R	20	48	189	61	18	1	5	96	33	30	15	0	36	3	0	0	13	2	.87	5	.323	.382	.508
Gonzalez, Carlos	c	Lowell	Bos	A-	20	3	9	2	0	0	0	2	1	0	1	0	3	0	0	0	0	0	.00	0	.222	.300	.222
		Red Sox	Bos	R	20	8	14	3	0	0	0	3	0	1	2	0	3	0	0	0	0	0	.00	1	.214	.313	.214
Gonzalez, Daniel#	ss	Batavia	Phi	A-	20	73	281	67	9	4	0	84	33	20	18	2	52	3	5	2	1	3	.25	7	.238	.289	.299
Gonzalez, Edgar	3b	Hudson Val	TB	A-	24	73	277	92	19	4	9	146	49	34	37	6	56	3	2	4	6	3	.67	5	.332	.411	.527
Gonzalez, Jose#	2b	Rangers	Tex	R	21	52	180	43	4	2	0	51	23	14	22	0	40	5	2	2	21	7	.75	1	.239	.335	.283
Gonzalez, Jose	c	Giants	SF	R	20	6	15	3	0	0	0	3	1	2	2	0	7	0	0	1	0	0	.00	0	.200	.278	.200
Gonzalez, Juan	ss	Dodgers	LA	R	19	26	67	18	0	0	0	18	9	7	3	0	8	0	3	2	3	0	1.00	1	.269	.292	.269
Gonzalez, Juan#	3b	Tigers	Det	R	20	54	192	64	6	0	3	79	30	33	19	0	30	3	1	3	19	6	.76	3	.333	.396	.411
		Oneonta	Det	A-	20	10	32	11	2	1	0	15	5	8	3	0	5	1	0	1	2	2	.50	1	.344	.405	.469
Gonzalez, Reggie	2b-dh	Quad City	Min	A	22	51	173	39	11	1	6	70	23	23	5	0	30	1	1	3	2	0	1.00	3	.225	.247	.405
Goodman, Scott*	of	Brevard Cty	Fla	A+	24	34	99	24	12	0	1	39	12	13	12	1	23	1	3	0	0	0	.00	0	.242	.330	.394
Gordon, Alex*	of	Orioles	Bal	R	22	9	24	8	2	0	3	19	7	10	4	1	14	1	0	0	1	0	1.00	0	.333	.448	.792
		Frederick	Bal	A+	22	27	80	22	3	1	1	30	4	15	4	0	31	2	0	1	2	0	1.00	3	.275	.322	.375
Gordon, Brian*	of	Lancaster	Ari	A+	23	103	392	119	21	10	16	208	74	70	26	1	100	1	4	4	13	7	.65	3	.304	.345	.531
Gorneault, Nick	of	Provo	Ana	R+	23	54	168	53	12	4	6	91	38	30	11	1	65	5	2	1	5	2	.71	0	.315	.373	.542
Gotay, Ruben#	2b	Royals	KC	R	19	52	184	58	15	1	3	84	29	19	26	1	22	0	2	1	5	6	.45	2	.315	.398	.457
Graham, Tyson	of	Marlins	Fla	R	19	35	93	16	1	1	1	22	12	6	8	0	32	2	1	0	1	0	1.00	1	.172	.252	.237
Gray, Josh	dh	Provo	Ana	R+	21	57	200	48	6	0	6	72	32	31	22	0	58	5	1	2	2	1	.67	8	.240	.328	.360
Gredvig, Doug	1b	Frederick	Bal	A+	22	129	484	123	35	2	20	222	71	62	37	1	125	5	0	2	2	3	.40	8	.254	.313	.459
Green, Andy	2b	South Bend	Ari	A	24	128	477	143	18	6	5	188	76	59	59	1	50	7	11	8	51	15	.77	7	.300	.379	.394
Green, Kevin	dh	Jamestown	Atl	A-	23	11	33	3	0	0	1	6	2	2	2	0	20	2	1	0	0	0	.00	0	.091	.189	.182
		Macon	Atl	A	23	17	34	5	2	0	1	10	5	3	3	0	18	2	0	1	0	0	.00	1	.147	.250	.294
Green, Steve*	of	Johnson Cty	StL	R+	23	44	125	37	4	2	2	51	21	9	10	0	28	7	0	0	4	1	.80	1	.296	.380	.408
		Potomac	StL	A+	23	2	5	0	0	0	0	0	0	0	1	0	3	0	0	0	0	0	.00	0	.000	.167	.000
Greene, Jason*	2b	Expos	Mon	R	19	31	104	29	7	3	0	42	14	13	18	0	30	1	0	0	2	2	.50	2	.279	.390	.404
Gregg, Mitch*	of	Visalia	Oak	A+	25	121	401	99	22	1	17	174	66	68	58	3	154	9	0	3	10	2	.83	8	.247	.352	.434
Gretz, Nick*	1b	Tri-City	Col	A-	24	29	92	32	6	2	0	42	5	21	11	4	18	1	0	1	0	1	.00	3	.348	.419	.457
		Asheville	Col	A	24	3	9	5	0	0	0	5	1	3	0	0	1	0	0	0	0	0	.00	0	.556	.556	.556
Griffin, Daniel	of	Vermont	Mon	A-	21	38	118	23	4	2	1	34	12	6	9	0	60	1	2	0	2	1	.67	2	.195	.258	.288
Griffin, John-Ford*	of	Staten Ilnd	NYY	A-	22	66	238	74	17	1	5	108	46	43	40	0	41	3	1	2	10	4	.71	5	.311	.413	.454
Griggs, Reggie*	1b-dh	Lakewood	Phi	A	24	13	49	12	3	0	1	18	3	4	1	0	22	1	0	1	0	0	.00	0	.245	.269	.367
Groff, Matt	of	Athletics	Oak	R	24	24	72	24	4	2	0	32	14	9	12	0	9	4	1	1	6	6	.50	2	.333	.449	.444
Grove, Jason*	of	Greensboro	NYY	A	23	115	446	132	21	8	15	214	68	68	36	2	108	6	1	5	0	2	.00	10	.296	.353	.480
		Tampa	NYY	A+	23	1	5	2	2	0	0	4	1	2	0	0	2	0	0	0	0	0	.00	0	.400	.400	.800
Guance, Walkill	2b	Tri-City	Col	A-	20	59	218	43	7	2	3	63	31	17	15	0	57	4	1	1	15	6	.71	4	.197	.261	.289
Guante, Domingo	of	Elizabethtn	Min	R+	21	40	84	11	1	0	0	12	16	5	16	0	27	1	0	0	4	1	.80	2	.131	.277	.143
Guerrero, Aneudis	of	Medcine Hat	Tor	R+	19	72	263	64	10	1	8	100	35	36	10	0	61	2	3	2	10	10	.50	2	.243	.274	.380
Guerrero, Cristian	of	High Desert	Mil	A+	21	85	327	102	18	2	7	145	50	41	18	1	79	1	0	1	22	11	.67	9	.312	.349	.443
Guerrero, Hector*	of	Vero Beach	LA	A+	20	39	148	38	11	1	0	51	16	10	4	0	35	1	1	0	2	3	.40	2	.257	.281	.345
		Great Falls	LA	R+	20	31	124	26	5	2	3	44	18	12	6	1	15	2	1	0	6	2	.75	1	.210	.258	.355
Guerrero, Jorge	3b	Marlins	Fla	R	21	46	140	41	9	1	2	58	18	13	18	0	27	2	2	1	11	6	.65	4	.293	.379	.414
Guerrero, Julio	of	Augusta	Bos	A	21	94	314	62	9	1	1	76	27	25	21	0	56	1	3	2	14	6	.70	7	.197	.249	.242
Guglielmelli, Brad	c	Mahoning Vy	Cle	A-	22	20	64	9	3	0	2	18	4	5	5	0	15	2	0	0	0	2	.00	2	.141	.225	.281
Guilliams, Earl	c	Danville	Atl	R+	21	18	48	8	0	0	0	8	3	2	1	0	12	1	0	0	0	0	.00	2	.167	.200	.167
Gulledge, Kelley	c	Quad City	Min	A	23	39	131	36	9	0	3	54	15	16	8	0	37	3	0	3	0	2	.00	4	.275	.324	.412
		Fort Myers	Min	A+	23	58	213	57	16	0	10	103	33	45	20	1	60	7	0	1	1	1	.50	5	.268	.349	.484
Gunn, Cody*	c	Johnson Cty	StL	R+	20	25	71	14	5	0	0	19	4	5	6	0	30	3	1	0	1	1	.50	1	.197	.288	.268
Gunny, Peter	of	Spokane	KC	A-	22	29	77	14	1	0	1	18	7	7	4	0	26	1	1	1	3	1	.75	0	.182	.229	.234
Gustafson, Troy	of	Giants	SF	R	22	56	222	62	10	3	0	78	28	22	8	0	28	5	0	2	10	6	.63	7	.279	.316	.351
Gutierrez, Derrick	2b-ss	Everett	Sea	A-	23	10	27	7	0	0	1	10	5	3	2	0	10	0	2	0	3	0	1.00	0	.259	.310	.370
		Wisconsin	Sea	A	23	10	34	9	2	0	1	14	5	6	4	0	8	2	0	0	1	1	.50	0	.265	.375	.412
Gutierrez, Franklin	of	Dodgers	LA	R	19	56	234	63	16	0	4	91	38	30	16	0	39	4	2	2	9	3	.75	1	.269	.324	.389
Gutierrez, Jesse	1b	Billings	Cin	R+	24	72	269	79	21	0	16	148	45	61	29	2	43	7	0	7	1	0	1.00	7	.294	.369	.550
Gutierrez, Said	c	Chston-WV	Tor	A	22	11	28	2	0	0	0	2	0	0	2	0	5	0	0	0	0	0	.00	1	.071	.133	.071
		Auburn	Tor	A-	22	41	131	28	6	0	3	43	10	13	7	0	28	4	1	1	1	1	.50	3	.214	.273	.328
Guy, Jason*	of	Rangers	Tex	R	20	47	140	29	7	4	0	44	17	15	11	1	45	1	4	1	5	3	.63	1	.207	.268	.314
Guyton, Eric	3b	St. Lucie	NYM	A+	25	5	11	2	1	0	0	3	0	0	2	0	6	0	0	0	0	0	.00	0	.182	.308	.273
Guzman, Carlos#	of	Braves	Atl	R	20	40	139	37	7	0	3	53	20	23	15	0	44	4	0	1	3	2	.60	1	.266	.352	.381
Guzman, Carlos	of	Jamestown	Atl	A-	18	6	6	0	0	0	0	0	2	0	0	0	3	0	0	0	0	0	.00	0	.000	.000	.000
Guzman, Garrett*	of	Twins	Min	R	19	39	138	49	14	5	2	79	22	22	9	1	16	3	0	2	4	2	.67	1	.355	.401	.572
Guzman, Jacob	c	Royals	KC	R	19	29	76	14	2	0	0	16	4	4	10	0	19	1	1	0	0	1	.00	2	.184	.287	.211
Guzman, Jon	of	Burlington	KC	A	21	121	411	97	12	12	13	172	58	46	36	0	155	4	5	2	34	11	.76	7	.236	.302	.418
Guzman, Juan#	ss	Burlington	KC	A	22	54	171	41	9	1	1	55	20	13	13	0	64	1	4	0	4	4	.50	1	.240	.297	.322
Guzman, Junior	c	Provo	Ana	R+	19	11	35	12	0	0	5	27	11	13	4	0	5	0	0	1	0	0	.00	1	.343	.400	.771
Guzman, Robert*	of	Elizabethtn	Min	R+	22	25	78	26	4	2	1	37	10	8	5	0	17	3	2	0	1	1	.50	1	.333	.395	.474
		Quad City	Min	A	22	21	77	18	1	1	0	21	12	5	4	1	14	3	4	0	4	0	1.00	1	.234	.298	.273
Guzman, Wander#	ss-2b	Marlins	Fla	R	19	51	199	45	7	0	0	52	16	13	3	0	34	4	1	0	14	2	.88	1	.226	.252	.261
Haase, Jeff	c	Columbus	Cle	A	24	41	135	32	9	0	1	44	15	12	13	0	26	6	1	2	2	5	.29	3	.237	.327	.326
		Kinston	Cle	A+	24	19	60	12	2	1	2	22	4	9	4	0	20	2	0	0	0	0	.00	1	.200	.273	.367
Habel, Jason	of	Princeton	TB	R+	21	37	127	32	3	0	1	38	11	14	8	0	36	2	1	1	3	3	.50	1	.252	.304	.299
Hadad, Jorge	dh	Orioles	Bal	R	20	15	47	11	4	0	0	15	4	5	3	0	11	1	0	0	0	0	.00	1	.234	.294	.319
Haggard, Chris	c	Ogden	Mil	R+	23	34	83	16	0	0	2	22	14	12	19	0	28	6	2	2	1	0	1.00	0	.193	.373	.265
Hairr, Kevin*	of	Boise	ChC	A-	23	28	109	31	7	0	4	50	29	13	8	0	24	3	0	0	5	4	.56	1	.284	.350	.459
Hairston, Scott	2b	Missoula	Ari	R+	22	74	291	101	16	6	14	171	81	65	38	2	50	7	0	2	2	2	.50	5	.347	.432	.588
Hake, Travis	2b	Beloit	Mil	A	25	6	15	3	3	0	0	6	2	0	3	0	3	0	1	0	0	0	.00	1	.200	.333	.400
Hall, Victor*	of	South Bend	Ari	A	21	113	415	114	13	12	0	151	82	39	52	0	71	7	3	4	60	15	.80	4	.275	.362	.364
Hambrick, Marcus*	of	Jamestown	Atl	A-	23	36	97	14	7	1	0	23	8	1	8	0	32	1	1	0	1	3	.25	1	.144	.217	.237
Hamill, Ryan	c	Peoria	StL	A	23	110	371	98	23	0	10	151	44	45	33	0	62	4	2	3	2	2	.50	8	.264	.328	.407
Hamilton, Mark*	of	Michigan	Hou	A	24	107	371	93	23	4	13	163	59	50	37	2	98	5	0	0	15	7	.68	9	.251	.327	.439
Hammond, Derry	of	Beloit	Mil	A	22	96	360	97	23	0	19	177	57	73	32	3	109	3	1	5	2	1	.67	7	.269	.330	.492

2001 Batting — Class-A and Rookie Leagues

BATTING																					BASERUNNING				PERCENTAGES		
Player	Pos	Team	Org	Lg	A	G	AB	H	2B	3B	HR	TB	R	RBI	TBB	IBB	SO	HBP	SH	SF	SB	CS	SB%	GDP	Avg	OBP	SLG
Hankins, Ryan	3b-dh	Winston-Sal	CWS	A+	26	108	389	104	26	0	15	175	54	58	57	5	76	7	0	1	4	5	.44	6	.267	.370	.450
Hanna, Warren	c	Boise	ChC	A-	22	39	133	31	3	0	0	34	13	11	13	0	28	3	2	1	4	3	.57	5	.233	.313	.256
Hannahan, Buzz	3b	Clearwater	Phi	A+	26	82	268	70	10	1	1	85	43	27	39	2	44	6	3	3	17	7	.71	6	.261	.364	.317
Hannahan, John*	3b	Oneonta	Det	A-	22	14	55	16	4	1	0	22	11	8	5	0	7	0	0	3	2	1	.67	2	.291	.333	.400
		W Michigan	Det	A	22	46	170	54	11	0	1	68	24	27	26	0	39	1	0	1	4	2	.67	5	.318	.409	.400
Hansen, Bryan*	1b-dh	Phillies	Phi	R	19	30	111	27	2	0	1	32	9	11	10	0	21	0	2	1	1	0	1.00	1	.243	.303	.288
Hardy, J.J.	ss	Brewers	Mil	R	19	5	20	5	2	1	0	9	6	1	1	0	2	0	1	0	0	0	.00	0	.250	.286	.450
		Ogden	Mil	R+	19	35	125	31	5	0	2	42	20	15	15	0	12	0	3	1	1	2	.33	2	.248	.326	.336
Hargreaves, Brad	c	Dayton	Cin	A	24	7	18	4	1	0	0	5	4	2	3	0	4	0	0	1	0	0	.00	0	.222	.318	.278
Harper, Brett*	1b	Kingsport	NYM	R+	20	38	146	49	9	1	0	60	24	19	8	0	30	4	0	0	3	2	.60	2	.336	.386	.411
		Capital Cty	NYM	A	20	10	33	6	1	0	0	7	1	4	3	0	14	0	0	0	0	0	.00	0	.182	.250	.212
Harris, Brendan	2b	Lansing	ChC	A	21	32	113	31	5	1	4	50	25	22	17	0	26	2	1	3	5	1	.83	4	.274	.370	.442
Harris, Cory	of	Capital Cty	NYM	A	22	102	357	92	23	1	8	141	52	49	43	0	57	15	3	6	13	9	.59	8	.258	.356	.395
Harris, Josh	2b	Cubs	ChC	R	23	2	8	2	0	0	0	2	3	2	0	0	2	0	0	0	1	0	1.00	0	.250	.250	.250
		Lansing	ChC	A	23	22	76	23	5	1	0	30	10	9	2	0	6	3	1	2	0	1	.00	4	.303	.337	.395
Harrison, Vince	2b	Hudson Val	TB	A-	22	57	197	60	10	1	1	75	21	30	16	1	34	2	0	1	4	4	.50	6	.305	.361	.381
Hart, Bo	2b	Potomac	StL	A+	25	81	279	85	23	3	5	129	48	34	17	1	69	15	4	1	16	7	.70	3	.305	.375	.462
Hart, Jon	1b	Ogden	Mil	R+	20	69	262	89	18	1	11	142	53	62	26	1	47	2	0	6	14	1	.93	4	.340	.395	.542
Hartig, Philip	1b	Utica	Fla	A-	24	46	170	44	4	4	3	65	12	17	8	1	37	0	0	0	0	3	.00	8	.259	.292	.382
Harts, Jeremy#	of	Lynchburg	Pit	A+	22	125	410	86	17	1	3	114	50	34	46	0	151	6	5	2	10	11	.48	10	.210	.297	.278
Hastings, Joseph*	1b	Idaho Falls	SD	R+	24	34	124	42	16	0	5	73	24	34	15	1	32	0	0	1	1	1	.50	0	.339	.407	.589
Hattenburg, Ray#	dh	Wilmington	KC	A+	25	83	244	51	9	0	0	60	28	25	39	0	67	6	5	0	4	4	.50	7	.209	.332	.246
Hattig, John#	1b	Lowell	Bos	A-	22	11	45	5	0	1	1	10	4	5	3	0	7	1	0	0	1	0	1.00	6	.111	.184	.222
		Augusta	Bos	A	22	50	179	51	9	1	1	65	25	23	22	1	42	3	0	1	4	1	.80	3	.285	.371	.363
Hawes, B.J.	of	Dayton	Cin	A	23	25	69	13	2	2	0	19	8	6	4	0	14	2	2	0	1	2	.33	2	.188	.253	.275
		Billings	Cin	R+	23	47	182	49	5	0	0	54	30	19	11	0	26	3	1	1	5	4	.56	2	.269	.320	.297
Hawpe, Brad*	of-1b	Asheville	Col	A	23	111	393	105	22	3	22	199	78	72	59	3	113	6	0	10	7	4	.64	8	.267	.363	.506
Hawthorne, Kyle	3b	Fort Myers	Min	A+	24	47	165	36	5	0	4	53	16	21	7	0	29	5	0	4	3	2	.60	4	.218	.265	.321
Haynes, Dee	of	Potomac	StL	A+	24	114	417	121	24	3	13	190	45	72	14	1	82	11	4	2	5	1	.83	12	.290	.329	.456
Headley, Justin*	of	Sarasota	Bos	A+	26	114	409	104	28	1	6	152	54	53	54	2	60	4	4	5	13	6	.68	3	.254	.343	.372
Heard, Scott*	c	Pulaski	Tex	R+	20	32	114	34	6	1	5	57	24	20	12	0	31	0	0	2	3	1	.75	4	.298	.359	.500
		Savannah	Tex	A	20	77	268	61	13	1	5	91	25	36	30	0	71	2	2	2	1	2	.33	4	.228	.308	.340
Heath, Demetrius	2b	Tigers	Det	R	21	50	175	53	5	6	0	70	34	19	18	1	16	0	4	2	21	4	.84	3	.303	.364	.400
		Oneonta	Det	A-	21	6	16	5	0	0	0	5	0	1	1	0	2	0	1	0	0	1	.00	0	.313	.353	.313
Helps, Jason#	ss	Utica	Fla	A-	23	24	65	9	3	0	0	12	6	4	12	0	17	5	1	0	0	1	.00	0	.138	.317	.185
Helquist, Jon	2b-ss	Michigan	Hou	A	21	112	415	100	17	5	14	169	55	47	37	0	107	8	0	1	10	3	.77	11	.241	.315	.407
Hensler, Brad	dh	Kingsport	NYM	R+	24	4	9	3	1	0	1	7	4	2	2	0	1	3	0	0	0	0	.00	1	.333	.571	.778
		Capital Cty	NYM	A	24	23	72	14	3	0	1	20	11	3	4	0	24	4	0	0	1	0	1.00	2	.194	.275	.278
Hensley, Anthony#	of	Clearwater	Phi	A+	24	12	38	6	3	1	0	11	4	3	3	0	9	0	1	2	2	0	1.00	1	.158	.209	.289
		Lakewood	Phi	A	24	64	214	47	10	4	2	71	38	13	46	1	57	2	1	1	19	12	.61	3	.220	.361	.332
Hernandez, A.#	ss	Tigers	Det	R	19	55	216	57	5	11	0	84	37	18	13	0	38	0	3	2	34	8	.81	0	.264	.303	.389
		Lakeland	Det	A+	19	7	21	4	0	1	0	6	2	1	0	0	8	0	2	0	0	0	.00	0	.190	.190	.286
Hernandez, J.#	of	Potomac	StL	A+	22	131	464	107	20	4	1	138	42	28	32	2	108	2	1	3	7	12	.37	9	.231	.281	.297
Hernandez, Jose	c	Hickory	Pit	A	21	53	161	26	4	0	1	33	19	13	12	0	35	5	2	2	3	0	1.00	7	.161	.239	.205
		Lynchburg	Pit	A+	21	24	80	13	3	0	0	16	7	6	4	1	13	2	3	0	1	0	1.00	2	.163	.221	.200
Hernandez, Orlando	of	San Berndno	Sea	A+	23	18	48	8	0	0	0	8	4	3	3	0	15	0	1	0	0	0	.00	1	.167	.216	.167
		Everett	Sea	A-	23	32	115	35	5	1	1	45	16	17	10	0	21	2	0	2	3	4	.43	2	.304	.364	.391
Hernandez, Vladimir	2b	Brooklyn	NYM	A-	25	15	49	12	1	1	0	15	2	4	2	0	7	0	0	1	2	2	.50	2	.245	.269	.306
		Capital Cty	NYM	A	25	5	21	3	1	0	0	4	2	1	1	0	2	0	1	0	1	0	1.00	0	.143	.182	.190
Herr, Aaron	2b	Danville	Atl	R+	21	64	239	58	12	1	2	78	31	21	24	0	64	6	3	1	6	4	.60	7	.243	.326	.326
Herrera, Christian	ss	Dodgers	LA	R	20	46	153	49	3	0	0	52	24	20	12	0	23	4	6	3	9	2	.82	3	.320	.378	.340
Hetherington, Luke	of	Medcine Hat	Tor	R+	19	51	174	36	3	4	2	53	22	14	18	0	54	5	1	0	6	1	.86	4	.207	.299	.305
Hewes, Robert	3b	Savannah	Tex	A	27	27	92	26	4	2	0	34	14	8	10	0	18	5	0	1	0	2	.00	3	.283	.380	.370
Hickman, Brian	c	White Sox	CWS	R	24	23	55	7	2	0	0	9	8	2	8	0	17	5	0	0	0	0	.00	1	.127	.294	.164
		Kannapolis	CWS	A	24	7	19	5	0	0	0	5	1	2	4	0	4	1	1	0	0	0	.00	0	.263	.417	.263
Hicks, Brian*	of	Ogden	Mil	R+	20	28	103	24	10	2	1	41	17	12	9	0	24	0	2	0	1	1	.50	0	.233	.295	.398
		Brewers	Mil	R	20	15	54	12	3	0	0	15	5	2	6	0	18	1	0	0	0	0	.00	1	.222	.311	.278
Hicks, Scott*	of-1b	Brevard Cty	Fla	A+	22	2	7	2	0	0	0	2	0	0	0	0	0	0	0	0	0	0	.00	0	.286	.286	.286
		Utica	Fla	A-	22	56	211	65	15	1	4	94	25	36	24	2	52	2	0	3	7	2	.78	2	.308	.379	.445
		Kane County	Fla	A	22	1	3	2	1	0	0	3	1	0	0	0	0	0	0	0	0	1	.00	0	.667	.667	1.000
Hilario, Enderson	dh-c	White Sox	CWS	R	20	3	12	2	1	0	0	3	1	0	1	0	1	0	0	0	0	0	.00	0	.167	.231	.250
		Bristol	CWS	R+	20	25	84	25	11	0	0	36	8	11	2	0	14	2	0	0	0	0	.00	4	.298	.330	.429
Hileman, Jutt	ss	Johnson Cty	StL	R+	20	61	220	56	8	2	9	95	36	35	25	0	81	2	1	3	4	4	.50	4	.255	.332	.432
Hilinski, Scott	ss	Yakima	Ari	A-	22	6	12	3	2	0	0	5	1	5	3	0	4	0	0	0	0	0	.00	0	.250	.400	.417
		Missoula	Ari	R+	22	42	138	34	5	2	2	49	34	18	25	2	45	1	0	2	4	1	.80	2	.246	.361	.355
Hill, Bobby*	3b	St. Lucie	NYM	A+	23	63	173	43	6	2	2	59	22	18	15	0	34	1	4	1	6	9	.40	3	.249	.311	.341
Hill, Koyie#	c	Wilmington	LA	A	23	134	498	150	20	2	8	198	65	79	49	14	82	7	2	6	21	12	.64	7	.301	.368	.398
Hill, Mike	of	Lexington	Hou	A	25	119	465	142	31	6	12	221	82	65	48	3	102	11	0	4	27	9	.75	12	.305	.381	.475
Hill, Willy*	of	Kane County	Fla	A	25	6	21	7	1	0	0	8	3	1	0	0	2	0	0	0	0	1	.00	1	.333	.333	.381
		Brevard Cty	Fla	A+	25	10	37	11	0	0	0	11	6	2	2	0	7	1	4	0	1	2	.33	0	.297	.350	.297
Hinton, Travis*	of	Ogden	Mil	R+	21	69	235	65	17	0	8	106	44	41	29	1	58	0	0	5	3	4	.43	3	.277	.349	.451
Hiraldo, Inocencio#	ss	Twins	Min	R	20	49	163	46	12	4	2	72	26	18	13	1	31	2	2	2	12	3	.80	2	.282	.339	.442
Hodges, Jarrod*	of	Mariners	Sea	R	19	45	143	39	8	2	5	66	30	26	16	1	26	7	1	1	2	3	.40	0	.273	.371	.462
Hoffpauir, Josh*	2b	Vancouver	Oak	A-	24	28	93	29	3	0	0	32	18	5	11	1	7	1	2	1	15	4	.79	1	.312	.387	.344
		Modesto	Oak	A+	24	71	228	54	13	3	0	73	27	21	19	0	26	3	2	4	10	2	.83	5	.237	.299	.320
Holliday, Matt	dh-of	Salem	Col	A+	22	72	255	70	16	1	11	121	36	52	33	3	42	3	0	5	11	3	.79	10	.275	.358	.475
Holm, Stephen	3b	Salem-Keizr	SF	A-	22	33	72	15	3	1	0	20	8	2	10	0	16	1	1	1	1	0	1.00	4	.208	.310	.278
Holst, Micah	of	Salem-Keizr	SF	A-	25	60	217	59	15	1	4	88	41	36	18	0	38	8	2	3	10	4	.71	1	.272	.346	.406
Holt, Daylan	of	Modesto	Oak	A+	23	101	341	61	15	1	2	84	31	39	40	0	90	2	3	4	5	2	.71	2	.179	.266	.246
Honeycutt, S.*	of	Expos	Mon	R	21	38	131	26	3	0	0	29	9	8	5	0	38	1	1	2	4	3	.57	1	.198	.230	.221
Hooper, Clay	ss	Tampa	NYY	A+	25	93	268	58	10	2	1	75	43	20	35	0	44	6	3	3	3	9	.25	5	.216	.317	.280
Hoover, Clint	1b	Pittsfield	Hou	A-	23	27	84	24	8	0	0	32	7	16	8	0	29	5	2	0	1	0	1.00	0	.286	.381	.381
Hopper, Norris	of	Wilmington	KC	A+	23	110	389	96	6	2	1	109	38	38	32	2	60	5	11	0	16	4	.80	15	.247	.312	.280
Horsman, Stephen*	of-dh	Orioles	Bal	R	24	5	14	1	0	0	0	1	0	1	3	0	5	0	0	0	0	1	.00	0	.071	.235	.071
Housel, David#	2b	Kingsport	NYM	R+	20	23	66	12	1	0	0	13	6	5	5	0	21	1	0	1	2	3	.40	2	.182	.247	.197

2001 Batting — Class-A and Rookie Leagues

						BATTING															BASERUNNING				PERCENTAGES		
Player	Pos	Team	Org	Lg	A	G	AB	H	2B	3B	HR	TB	R	RBI	TBB	IBB	SO	HBP	SH	SF	SB	CS	SB%	GDP	Avg	OBP	SLG
Howard, Ryan*	1b	Batavia	Phi	A-	22	48	169	46	7	3	6	77	26	35	30	5	55	2	0	2	0	0	.00	1	.272	.384	.456
Howe, Matt	3b	Modesto	Oak	A+	25	134	507	129	28	4	22	231	81	73	67	0	123	8	4	6	13	3	.81	8	.254	.347	.456
Hrynio, Mike	3b	Mariners	Sea	R	19	20	56	9	2	0	0	11	4	5	2	0	21	1	0	0	0	1	.00	0	.161	.203	.196
Huber, Justin	c	St. Lucie	NYM	A+	19	2	6	0	0	0	0	0	0	0	0	0	2	0	0	0	0	0	.00	0	.000	.000	.000
		Kingsport	NYM	R+	19	47	159	50	11	1	7	84	24	31	17	0	42	13	1	4	4	2	.67	4	.314	.415	.528
		Brooklyn	NYM	A-	19	3	9	0	0	0	0	0	0	0	0	0	4	0	0	0	0	0	.00	1	.000	.000	.000
Hudnall, Josh	of	Williamsprt	Pit	A-	22	40	124	35	4	3	0	45	17	16	7	0	31	4	1	1	17	2	.89	3	.282	.338	.363
Hudson, Ben	c	Mariners	Sea	R	22	5	18	3	1	0	0	4	3	1	1	0	1	2	0	0	0	0	.00	1	.167	.286	.222
		Wisconsin	Sea	A	22	14	43	15	1	0	0	16	4	6	3	0	12	1	1	1	0	0	.00	0	.349	.396	.372
Huff, Ken*	1b-of	Elizabethtn	Min	R+	22	43	126	33	6	1	0	41	11	14	9	0	23	0	1	1	0	1	.00	5	.262	.309	.325
Huguet, J.C.	c	Mudville	Cin	A+	24	3	5	2	0	0	1	5	2	1	0	0	2	1	0	0	0	0	.00	0	.400	.500	1.000
		Dayton	Cin	A	24	38	107	24	2	0	1	29	10	5	23	0	31	2	0	1	2	3	.40	1	.224	.368	.271
Humphries, Justin	dh	Martinsvlle	Hou	R+	19	19	40	9	2	0	0	11	3	5	3	0	20	0	0	0	0	0	.00	0	.225	.279	.275
Huntingford, Matt*	of	Salem-Keizr	SF	A-	23	62	220	50	5	5	3	74	35	37	13	1	37	11	2	2	8	3	.73	4	.227	.301	.336
Hurtado, Omar	of	Mudville	Cin	A+	23	17	48	5	2	0	0	7	8	1	10	0	16	0	0	1	3	0	1.00	3	.104	.254	.146
		Dayton	Cin	A	23	63	205	48	7	2	5	74	23	20	19	0	59	2	1	1	3	3	.50	4	.234	.304	.361
Huson, Tim*	3b-1b	Bristol	CWS	R+	22	49	148	27	5	0	2	38	23	9	24	0	67	3	2	0	2	4	.33	0	.182	.309	.257
Hyde, Nathan	of	Medcine Hat	Tor	R+	23	57	190	44	7	3	3	66	27	18	12	0	47	4	1	1	5	0	1.00	4	.232	.290	.347
Imperiali, Francesco	2b	Mariners	Sea	R	18	40	116	33	7	0	0	40	17	12	13	0	26	2	1	0	2	3	.40	2	.284	.366	.345
Infante, Franklin	2b	Braves	Atl	R	19	43	128	31	7	2	0	42	10	16	1	0	38	2	3	2	3	0	1.00	1	.242	.256	.328
Inglett, Joe*	2b	Columbus	Cle	A	24	62	237	71	9	2	2	90	34	33	24	0	22	0	0	2	5	3	.63	7	.300	.361	.380
Ingram, Bryan	c-dh	Casper	Col	R+	23	22	76	18	3	2	1	28	7	10	6	0	25	4	0	1	0	2	.00	1	.237	.322	.368
Iorg, Isaac	dh	Medcine Hat	Tor	R+	23	24	80	20	3	0	2	29	8	10	1	0	16	1	0	0	0	1	.00	2	.250	.268	.363
Ison, Jeremy	2b-3b	Bristol	CWS	R+	23	29	96	25	9	0	2	40	12	12	9	0	32	1	1	0	0	1	.00	2	.260	.330	.417
		Kannapolis	CWS	A	23	20	52	8	1	0	1	12	7	2	6	0	21	0	1	0	0	0	.00	2	.154	.241	.231
Ivy, Bo	of	Bristol	CWS	R+	20	56	156	31	4	2	0	39	30	11	25	0	47	3	3	0	18	3	.86	1	.199	.321	.250
Izturis, Maicer#	2b	Kinston	Cle	A+	21	114	433	104	16	6	1	135	47	39	31	1	81	8	10	4	32	9	.78	8	.240	.300	.312
Jackson, Nick*	of	Daytona	ChC	A+	22	131	503	149	30	6	19	248	87	85	39	5	96	10	0	5	24	10	.71	7	.296	.355	.493
Jackson, Steve	1b	Visalia	Oak	A+	24	121	435	110	27	3	16	191	72	64	46	1	123	6	1	1	5	5	.50	5	.253	.332	.439
Jacobo, Kervin#	ss	South Bend	Ari	A	19	9	30	8	2	1	1	15	5	6	4	0	10	0	0	0	4	0	1.00	2	.267	.353	.500
		Missoula	Ari	R+	19	59	219	59	10	3	5	90	36	36	22	2	72	1	1	2	4	3	.57	1	.269	.336	.411
Jacobs, John	of	Chston-SC	TB	A	22	79	198	37	5	2	1	49	18	11	15	0	69	4	5	3	6	2	.75	1	.187	.255	.247
Jacobs, Mike*	c	Brooklyn	NYM	A-	21	19	66	19	5	0	1	27	12	15	6	0	11	3	0	2	1	1	.50	1	.288	.364	.409
		Capital Cty	NYM	A	21	46	180	50	13	0	2	69	18	26	13	0	46	1	1	1	0	1	.00	4	.278	.328	.383
Jacobson, Russ	c	Clearwater	Phi	A+	24	102	351	73	21	2	4	110	35	40	27	0	99	10	2	5	1	0	1.00	11	.208	.280	.313
Jaile, Chris	c	Charlotte	Tex	A+	21	42	151	33	5	0	2	44	17	10	12	1	31	1	2	2	0	0	.00	3	.219	.277	.291
		Pulaski	Tex	R+	21	29	100	25	5	0	0	30	15	12	13	0	20	1	0	1	0	0	.00	2	.250	.339	.300
Janowicz, Nate*	of	Kinston	Cle	A+	24	46	154	39	7	1	0	48	21	23	18	0	30	2	1	3	4	1	.80	3	.253	.333	.312
		Columbus	Cle	A	24	51	201	59	10	5	2	85	29	26	9	0	38	1	2	2	4	1	.80	5	.294	.324	.423
Jansen, Ardley	of	Danville	Atl	R+	19	64	211	47	3	0	6	68	25	23	15	1	64	4	0	0	9	7	.56	2	.223	.287	.322
January, Javerro	of	Brewers	Mil	R	21	38	134	38	6	1	0	46	27	10	13	0	42	6	3	1	5	5	.50	0	.284	.370	.343
		Ogden	Mil	R+	21	11	19	5	1	1	0	8	6	3	2	0	6	1	0	0	0	0	.00	0	.263	.364	.421
Janz, Jeramy*	of	Missoula	Ari	R+	22	67	259	76	14	8	5	121	40	62	16	0	46	2	1	3	2	2	.50	5	.293	.336	.467
Jaramillo, Milko#	ss	Dodgers	LA	R	22	3	8	2	0	1	0	4	2	1	1	0	0	1	0	0	0	0	.00	0	.250	.400	.500
		Vero Beach	LA	A+	22	50	153	28	2	2	1	37	15	5	4	0	25	1	5	0	1	0	1.00	5	.183	.209	.242
Jeffcoat, Bryon	3b-2b	Jamestown	Atl	A-	23	36	122	29	3	3	2	44	15	16	12	0	24	4	0	1	1	1	.50	2	.238	.324	.361
		Macon	Atl	A	23	26	90	20	5	1	2	33	11	7	10	0	28	2	0	1	3	2	.60	1	.222	.311	.367
Jenkins, Kevin*	1b-of	Angels	Ana	R	20	42	115	20	3	1	1	28	15	11	12	0	39	5	0	0	5	5	.50	0	.174	.280	.243
Jenkins, Neil	of	Lakeland	Det	A+	21	23	86	26	8	1	1	39	14	6	2	0	25	0	0	1	0	1	.00	5	.302	.315	.453
Jiannetti, Joe	3b	Kingsport	NYM	R+	20	23	85	23	5	2	2	38	13	17	9	0	11	0	1	3	4	2	.67	1	.271	.330	.447
		Brooklyn	NYM	A-	20	41	158	55	13	0	3	77	24	29	18	0	29	3	0	2	8	5	.62	1	.348	.420	.487
Jimenez, Carlos	2b	Lakeland	Det	A+	22	54	135	26	7	1	0	35	17	11	17	0	47	1	2	0	6	2	.75	3	.193	.288	.259
Jimenez, Luis*	dh	Athletics	Oak	R	20	23	69	15	1	1	0	18	8	12	8	0	22	0	0	4	2	0	1.00	0	.217	.284	.261
Jimenez, Luis#	dh-of	Yankees	NYY	R	18	10	30	6	1	0	0	7	2	2	1	0	10	1	0	0	0	0	.00	1	.200	.250	.233
Jimenez, Rich#	of	Chston-WV	Tor	A	20	26	76	14	1	0	0	15	14	4	8	0	18	1	0	1	11	2	.85	0	.184	.267	.197
		Auburn	Tor	A-	20	35	114	32	3	1	0	37	12	6	7	1	25	3	1	1	14	2	.88	3	.281	.336	.325
Jimerson, Charlton	of	Pittsfield	Hou	A-	22	51	197	46	12	1	9	87	35	31	18	1	79	2	1	0	15	4	.79	4	.234	.304	.442
Johnson, Ben	of	Lk Elsinore	SD	A+	21	136	503	139	35	6	12	222	79	63	54	1	141	11	1	2	22	7	.76	15	.276	.358	.441
Johnson, Dale	2b	Provo	Ana	R+	23	27	83	23	3	0	0	26	12	12	4	0	17	3	4	1	0	1	.00	0	.277	.330	.313
Johnson, Dan*	1b	Vancouver	Oak	A-	22	69	247	70	15	2	11	122	36	41	27	2	63	2	0	4	0	0	.00	6	.283	.354	.494
Johnson, Eric	of	Kinston	Cle	A+	24	127	482	111	17	5	7	159	77	45	57	0	124	10	4	3	22	14	.61	8	.230	.322	.330
Johnson, Forrest	dh	W Michigan	Det	A	23	114	420	109	19	1	15	175	64	61	36	1	89	11	0	10	3	0	1.00	10	.260	.327	.417
Johnson, Gabe	3b	Potomac	StL	A+	22	86	281	53	14	0	4	79	24	22	21	0	113	3	1	3	2	3	.40	8	.189	.250	.281
		Peoria	StL	A	22	36	134	30	10	4	2	54	17	17	16	0	49	2	0	2	1	1	.50	2	.224	.312	.403
Johnson, J.J.	of	Boise	ChC	A-	20	70	287	91	15	5	7	137	55	61	20	0	50	4	0	7	18	4	.82	9	.317	.362	.477
Johnson, Josh	c	Twins	Min	R	19	24	64	9	1	1	0	12	5	2	7	0	14	2	2	1	1	0	1.00	2	.141	.243	.188
Johnson, Kade	c	High Desert	Mil	A+	23	101	370	94	21	1	21	180	57	67	35	1	118	14	0	6	9	2	.82	12	.254	.336	.486
Johnson, Kelly*	ss	Macon	Atl	A	20	124	415	120	22	1	23	213	75	66	71	7	111	10	1	1	25	6	.81	0	.289	.404	.513
Johnson, Michael*	of-dh	Great Falls	LA	R+	23	45	154	38	3	3	0	47	32	13	31	2	32	2	1	0	14	4	.78	2	.247	.380	.305
Johnson, Patrick*	of	Lowell	Bos	A-	23	6	21	3	0	0	0	3	1	2	4	0	6	0	0	0	0	1	.00	2	.143	.280	.143
Johnson, Seth	1b	Vermont	Mon	A-	20	57	208	37	7	0	1	47	15	19	13	0	37	2	3	4	2	2	.50	2	.178	.229	.226
Johnson, Tripper	dh	Bluefield	Bal	R+	20	43	157	41	6	1	2	55	24	26	11	0	37	2	0	3	4	0	1.00	3	.261	.312	.350
Johnson, Tristan	1b	Pirates	Pit	R	20	25	77	11	1	0	0	12	5	4	6	0	32	0	0	1	1	0	1.00	4	.143	.202	.156
Johnston, Gabrial	c	Lakewood	Phi	A	23	4	6	1	1	0	0	2	1	0	1	0	2	0	0	0	0	0	.00	0	.167	.286	.333
		Batavia	Phi	A-	23	13	40	8	1	0	0	9	3	1	3	0	10	2	1	0	0	0	.00	0	.200	.289	.225
Johnstone, Ben	of	Daytona	ChC	A+	24	82	308	82	6	0	1	91	39	30	10	0	32	10	7	3	20	13	.61	1	.266	.308	.295
Jones, Brian*	c-dh	Dayton	Cin	A	24	63	191	44	10	0	5	69	17	19	11	0	47	1	0	2	4	1	.80	6	.230	.273	.361
Jones, Damien*	of	Myrtle Bch	Atl	A+	22	129	460	122	20	3	1	151	57	41	38	3	114	3	4	4	9	12	.43	10	.265	.323	.328
Jones, Garrett*	1b	Danville	Atl	R+	21	40	149	43	11	0	3	63	13	23	9	0	58	1	0	0	0	1	.00	0	.289	.333	.423
Jones, Jack	2b	Daytona	ChC	A+	27	9	21	5	1	0	0	6	3	2	0	0	4	1	0	0	0	0	.00	0	.238	.273	.286
Jones, Jared	of-dh	Mariners	Sea	R	22	9	33	8	1	0	0	9	1	3	3	0	8	0	0	0	0	0	.00	2	.242	.306	.273
Jones, Jeff	of	New Jersey	StL	A-	23	37	90	26	6	1	1	37	20	12	8	0	17	9	1	1	11	1	.92	2	.289	.398	.411
Jones, Kendall	c	Pittsfield	Hou	A-	21	36	113	20	6	0	1	29	11	14	19	0	20	0	1	0	1	0	1.00	4	.177	.295	.257
Jones, Mitch	of	Tampa	NYY	A+	24	137	487	109	36	3	21	214	85	71	81	3	135	7	1	5	9	2	.82	12	.224	.340	.439
Jones, Ryan	1b	Lancaster	Ari	A+	27	125	447	121	25	3	22	218	74	77	44	0	100	8	2	5	2	3	.40	13	.271	.343	.488

2001 Batting — Class-A and Rookie Leagues

						BATTING															BASERUNNING				PERCENTAGES		
Player	Pos	Team	Org	Lg	A	G	AB	H	2B	3B	HR	TB	R	RBI	TBB	IBB	SO	HBP	SH	SF	SB	CS	SB%	GDP	Avg	OBP	SLG
Jones, Terry	3b	Phillies	Phi	R	19	9	36	7	0	0	0	7	3	4	2	0	5	0	0	0	0	0	.00	0	.194	.237	.194
Jordan, Ed	of	Orioles	Bal	R	23	50	156	43	9	1	6	72	32	22	17	1	35	4	5	1	16	2	.89	2	.276	.360	.462
Jova, Maikel	of	Chston-WV	Tor	A	21	46	162	28	6	0	3	43	12	14	1	0	33	0	1	1	1	1	.50	4	.173	.177	.265
		Auburn	Tor	A-	21	67	261	70	12	0	9	109	44	39	7	0	37	5	1	1	6	2	.75	6	.268	.299	.418
Joyce, Jesse	dh	Lexington	Hou	A	26	18	53	6	1	0	2	13	12	4	15	0	16	2	0	0	3	1	.75	1	.113	.329	.245
Joyce, Thomas*	of	Orioles	Bal	R	20	49	152	33	8	1	0	43	18	12	20	1	45	0	3	2	2	4	.33	1	.217	.305	.283
Jung, Young-Jin	1b	Idaho Falls	SD	R+	24	23	57	9	2	0	0	11	9	3	7	0	23	2	0	0	0	0	.00	0	.158	.273	.193
Kahr, Danny#	c-dh	Expos	Mon	R	19	16	59	10	2	1	1	17	5	6	4	0	24	1	0	0	0	0	.00	0	.169	.234	.288
Kantrovitz, Dan	dh	Johnson Cty	StL	R+	23	1	3	1	0	0	0	1	0	0	0	0	0	0	0	0	0	0	.00	0	.333	.333	.333
Katz, Damon	ss	Columbus	Cle	A	24	14	42	5	0	0	1	8	3	3	1	0	9	3	0	0	1	0	1.00	4	.119	.196	.190
		Kinston	Cle	A+	24	13	31	5	1	0	0	6	0	0	3	0	9	3	0	0	0	0	.00	3	.161	.297	.194
Kaup, Nathan	of	Chston-SC	TB	A	24	4	15	4	2	0	0	6	0	2	0	0	3	0	0	1	0	0	.00	2	.267	.250	.400
		Bakersfield	TB	A+	24	113	427	138	34	3	13	217	65	68	35	2	81	5	0	7	3	2	.60	9	.323	.376	.508
Kavourias, Jim	of	Kane County	Fla	A	22	120	460	120	30	4	23	227	77	88	48	1	126	10	0	6	11	3	.79	10	.261	.340	.493
Kay, Brett	c	Brooklyn	NYM	A-	22	49	180	56	13	0	5	84	28	18	16	0	28	4	1	0	2	1	.67	9	.311	.380	.467
Keating, Matt*	1b	Giants	SF	R	24	16	63	17	1	2	1	25	9	16	6	1	9	0	0	1	0	2	.00	0	.270	.329	.397
		Salem-Keizr	SF	A-	24	26	49	11	3	0	1	17	7	2	4	0	9	0	0	0	0	0	.00	1	.224	.283	.347
Keene, Kurt	2b	Chston-WV	Tor	A	24	16	58	10	2	0	1	15	7	4	0	0	10	0	0	0	0	0	.00	2	.172	.172	.259
		Dunedin	Tor	A+	24	53	132	24	4	0	0	28	16	8	9	0	23	3	4	2	0	2	.00	5	.182	.247	.212
Keller, G.W.	dh-of	Visalia	Oak	A+	25	11	32	3	0	0	0	3	3	3	2	0	9	2	1	0	0	0	.00	2	.094	.194	.094
Kelly, Donald*	ss	Oneonta	Det	A-	22	67	262	75	8	3	0	89	41	25	25	1	16	0	2	3	8	5	.62	6	.286	.345	.340
Kelly, Otis	1b	Athletics	Oak	R	23	45	164	51	13	2	5	83	34	26	32	0	36	4	0	1	5	2	.71	2	.311	.433	.506
Kennedy, Bryan*	c	Elizabethtn	Min	R+	23	10	28	7	1	0	0	8	2	1	4	0	6	0	0	0	0	0	.00	0	.250	.344	.286
		Quad City	Min	A	23	14	40	8	3	0	0	11	8	5	9	0	3	3	0	0	0	0	.00	1	.200	.385	.275
Kenney, Jeff	2b	Beloit	Mil	A	24	41	151	32	6	0	3	47	21	19	26	0	33	8	2	1	6	3	.67	2	.212	.355	.311
		High Desert	Mil	A+	24	49	169	49	12	1	3	72	32	21	25	0	46	6	5	1	8	2	.80	6	.290	.398	.426
Kent, Bryan	ss	Lowell	Bos	A-	24	40	117	27	6	0	0	33	16	13	15	1	26	7	0	4	7	2	.78	5	.231	.343	.282
Kent, Mailon	of	Jamestown	Atl	A-	23	50	187	58	9	3	2	79	26	27	21	0	20	1	2	0	5	3	.63	6	.310	.383	.422
Keppinger, Billy*	of	Burlington	KC	A	23	76	279	68	13	1	2	89	42	26	43	1	45	5	1	5	9	3	.75	5	.244	.349	.319
Kerner, Craig*	of	Jupiter	Mon	A+	23	8	15	3	0	0	0	3	2	1	3	0	6	2	0	0	0	0	.00	0	.200	.400	.200
		Clinton	Mon	A	23	53	190	36	7	0	3	52	21	17	21	0	49	3	0	3	10	4	.71	4	.189	.276	.274
Kerrigan Jr., Joe*	2b-dh	Sarasota	Bos	A+	24	103	367	91	14	2	5	124	43	31	49	3	51	5	4	3	5	3	.63	7	.248	.342	.338
Kessick, Jon	c	Delmarva	Bal	A	24	34	115	32	9	0	5	56	14	21	15	1	40	2	1	2	0	2	.00	0	.278	.366	.487
Khairy, Masjid#	of	Rangers	Tex	R	21	40	141	36	2	3	0	44	15	16	9	0	34	3	4	2	26	3	.90	0	.255	.310	.312
Kimberley, Glynn	of	Medcine Hat	Tor	R+	20	52	190	44	8	1	9	81	21	26	18	0	64	5	0	2	0	0	.00	3	.232	.312	.426
Kimpton, Nick*	of	Angels	Ana	R	18	49	186	50	4	2	0	58	30	23	21	0	39	4	0	1	9	5	.64	3	.269	.354	.312
Kinchen, Jason*	dh	Greensboro	NYY	A	26	134	489	151	24	1	30	267	81	82	50	6	102	9	0	5	2	0	1.00	5	.309	.380	.546
King, Brennan	3b	Dodgers	LA	R	21	3	9	5	2	0	1	10	3	4	0	0	0	1	0	1	0	0	.00	0	.556	.545	1.111
		Vero Beach	LA	A+	21	73	255	62	10	0	1	75	24	28	13	0	48	3	1	2	0	0	.00	6	.243	.286	.294
Kirby, Brian*	of	Burlington	Cle	R+	22	25	84	16	3	1	4	33	14	14	15	1	31	4	0	0	1	1	.50	2	.190	.340	.393
		Mahoning Vy	Cle	A-	22	37	124	25	11	1	2	44	12	14	19	0	45	0	1	0	1	1	.50	1	.202	.308	.355
Kison, Robbie	3b	Mudville	Cin	A+	25	67	204	51	11	0	2	68	31	23	24	0	38	2	3	3	4	4	.50	8	.250	.330	.333
Klatt, Joel	1b	Idaho Falls	SD	R+	20	45	125	26	7	0	2	39	13	10	14	0	47	1	0	0	3	0	1.00	4	.208	.293	.312
Knight, Marcus#	of	Cedar Rapds	Ana	A	23	27	92	23	4	0	5	42	13	17	5	0	14	1	1	3	0	1	.00	2	.250	.287	.457
Knoedler, Jason#	of	Oneonta	Det	A-	21	59	208	47	3	4	4	70	30	20	28	1	61	1	0	1	11	4	.73	1	.226	.319	.337
Knox, Matt	3b	Burlington	Cle	R+	22	62	222	46	11	1	2	65	26	33	20	0	46	3	0	5	1	1	.50	3	.207	.276	.293
Kochen, Ryan	3b	Martinsvlle	Hou	R+	23	56	180	54	12	3	5	87	29	23	10	1	37	1	6	2	5	1	.83	3	.300	.337	.483
		Pittsfield	Hou	A-	23	4	17	7	4	0	0	11	4	5	0	0	3	0	0	0	0	0	.00	0	.412	.412	.647
Kolodzey, Chris	of	Oneonta	Det	A-	22	65	237	59	13	5	2	88	29	25	20	0	37	4	2	3	4	5	.44	5	.249	.314	.371
Koone, Chuck#	of	Charlotte	Tex	A+	26	7	18	6	0	0	0	6	1	0	1	0	4	0	1	0	0	2	.00	0	.333	.368	.333
		Savannah	Tex	A	26	71	247	53	5	1	2	66	31	11	23	0	66	0	5	2	8	4	.67	2	.215	.279	.267
Koslowski, Kasey	c	White Sox	CWS	R	23	43	147	35	4	0	0	39	17	9	13	0	22	1	2	0	3	2	.60	1	.238	.304	.265
Kotchman, Casey*	1b	Angels	Ana	R	19	4	15	9	1	0	1	13	5	5	3	1	2	0	0	1	0	0	.00	0	.600	.632	.867
		Provo	Ana	R+	19	7	22	11	3	0	0	14	6	7	2	0	0	0	0	0	0	0	.00	0	.500	.542	.636
Krga, Mike	2b	Princeton	TB	R+	19	38	130	27	1	1	0	30	11	8	11	0	33	1	0	1	0	0	.00	2	.208	.273	.231
Kroeger, Josh*	of	South Bend	Ari	A	19	79	292	80	15	1	3	106	36	37	18	0	49	4	0	1	4	4	.50	10	.274	.324	.363
Krynzel, Dave*	of	Beloit	Mil	A	20	35	141	43	1	1	1	49	22	19	9	2	28	4	0	0	11	5	.69	1	.305	.364	.348
		High Desert	Mil	A+	20	89	383	106	19	5	5	150	65	33	27	1	122	4	3	2	34	17	.67	0	.277	.329	.392
Kubel, Jason*	of	Twins	Min	R	20	37	124	41	10	4	1	62	14	30	19	3	14	2	0	2	3	2	.60	3	.331	.422	.500
Kuhaulua, Kaulana	ss	Elizabethtn	Min	R+	22	20	69	17	4	1	0	23	8	6	1	0	19	1	2	0	4	1	.80	1	.246	.268	.333
Kulbe, Eric*	of	Idaho Falls	SD	R+	24	15	16	2	1	0	0	3	4	0	4	0	5	1	0	0	0	0	.00	1	.125	.333	.188
Kweon, Yoon-Min	c	Lansing	ChC	A	23	88	326	88	15	1	6	123	33	51	15	0	44	5	1	9	0	0	.00	10	.270	.304	.377
Lababera, Michael	2b	Expos	Mon	R	22	34	104	24	2	0	0	26	9	4	3	0	11	2	0	0	3	2	.60	3	.231	.266	.250
Labandeira, John	ss	Vermont	Mon	A-	23	1	3	1	0	0	0	1	2	0	0	0	0	0	0	0	0	0	.00	0	.333	.333	.333
Lachapel, Juan	of	Athletics	Oak	R	21	10	43	11	1	1	0	14	7	3	1	0	11	2	0	0	3	0	1.00	0	.256	.304	.326
Lackaff, John	3b	Kannapolis	CWS	A	23	127	451	111	21	3	11	171	68	65	33	0	75	15	1	9	24	11	.69	7	.246	.313	.379
Lagana, Shawn	2b	South Bend	Ari	A	21	43	134	32	7	0	1	42	13	16	2	0	25	0	2	2	5	2	.71	3	.239	.246	.313
		Provo	Ana	R+	21	38	143	38	6	1	1	49	27	17	10	0	22	2	3	1	5	2	.71	4	.266	.321	.343
Laidlaw, Jake	of	Utica	Fla	A-	20	65	223	51	12	2	5	82	27	25	29	1	59	5	1	4	2	1	.67	10	.229	.326	.368
Laird, Gerald	c	Modesto	Oak	A+	22	119	443	113	13	5	5	151	71	46	48	1	101	10	4	6	10	9	.53	9	.255	.337	.341
Lambert, Casey	3b-ss	Tri-City	Col	A-	22	55	172	39	5	1	1	49	20	16	28	1	31	5	0	2	3	4	.43	3	.227	.348	.285
Lambert, Shawn	1b	Tigers	Det	R	20	36	107	14	3	0	1	20	5	5	9	0	49	1	0	2	0	0	.00	0	.131	.202	.187
Lane, Rich*	1b	Jupiter	Mon	A+	22	125	447	105	20	3	4	143	41	49	33	1	118	5	0	0	2	5	.29	10	.235	.295	.320
Langerhans, Ryan*	of	Myrtle Bch	Atl	A+	22	125	450	129	30	3	7	186	66	48	55	3	104	8	2	0	22	13	.63	6	.287	.374	.413
Langill, Eric	c	Clinton	Mon	A	23	47	134	27	8	0	1	38	14	9	16	0	31	3	1	0	1	2	.33	5	.201	.301	.284
Langs, Ronte	of	Vero Beach	LA	A+	23	5	11	3	0	0	0	3	1	1	2	0	1	0	0	0	1	1	.50	0	.273	.385	.273
		Wilmington	LA	A	23	105	376	101	14	8	1	134	49	29	43	2	88	7	9	2	18	7	.72	5	.269	.353	.356
Lanoix, Gilbert*	dh	Great Falls	LA	R+	23	1	4	1	0	0	0	1	0	0	0	0	0	0	0	0	0	0	.00	0	.250	.250	.250
		Dodgers	LA	R	23	2	8	2	1	0	0	3	1	0	0	0	1	0	0	0	0	0	.00	0	.250	.250	.375
Lara, David	of	Lakeland	Det	A+	24	16	42	10	5	1	0	17	4	4	2	0	11	1	0	0	2	0	1.00	3	.238	.289	.405
Larned, Drew	c	Sarasota	Bos	A+	26	69	192	35	10	0	1	48	23	18	32	0	53	2	2	3	3	5	.38	5	.182	.301	.250
LaRoche, Adam*	1b	Myrtle Bch	Atl	A+	22	126	471	118	31	0	7	170	49	47	30	3	108	9	0	4	10	8	.56	13	.251	.305	.361
Laureano, Wilfredo	dh	Spokane	KC	A-	21	6	19	3	0	0	0	3	1	1	0	0	7	0	0	0	0	0	.00	1	.158	.158	.158
Lawler, Daniel*	1b	Boise	ChC	A-	23	40	104	28	8	0	2	42	17	11	16	1	23	2	0	1	1	3	.25	3	.269	.374	.404
Lawson, Forrest	of	Capital Cty	NYM	A	21	23	70	11	1	0	0	12	4	6	6	0	25	1	3	0	2	1	.67	2	.157	.234	.171

2001 Batting — Class-A and Rookie Leagues

						BATTING															BASERUNNING				PERCENTAGES		
Player	Pos	Team	Org	Lg	A	G	AB	H	2B	3B	HR	TB	R	RBI	TBB	IBB	SO	HBP	SH	SF	SB	CS	SB%	GDP	Avg	OBP	SLG
		Brooklyn	NYM	A-	21	49	164	46	6	2	1	59	18	15	6	1	23	3	0	2	7	4	.64	10	.280	.314	.360
Leal, Jaeme	dh	Myrtle Bch	Atl	A+	23	63	215	46	7	1	15	100	32	39	20	1	88	14	0	3	0	0	.00	6	.214	.317	.465
Leaumont, Jeff*	1b	Tampa	NYY	A+	25	76	249	60	11	3	6	95	28	22	21	4	50	2	0	3	1	1	.50	5	.241	.302	.382
		Greensboro	NYY	A	25	27	94	23	5	0	0	28	9	5	8	0	25	0	0	2	0	1	.00	2	.245	.298	.298
Lebron, Edgardo#	ss	Elizabethtn	Min	R+	19	38	115	24	3	0	2	33	15	10	8	1	42	2	0	0	1	2	.33	4	.209	.272	.287
Lebron, Francisco	1b	Kannapolis	CWS	A	27	35	112	32	8	0	5	55	13	14	16	0	31	0	0	2	0	1	.00	1	.286	.369	.491
Lebron, Freddie#	2b	White Sox	CWS	R	20	39	120	28	8	0	0	36	22	13	11	0	29	4	0	1	7	1	.88	1	.233	.316	.300
Lee, Carlos	3b	White Sox	CWS	R	20	23	90	25	3	0	2	34	14	18	3	0	4	3	0	0	2	0	1.00	3	.278	.323	.378
Lee, Eric	of	Michigan	Hou	A	24	69	210	55	8	2	1	70	27	26	21	1	58	3	1	1	6	5	.55	4	.262	.336	.333
Leer, David	of	Lakeland	Det	A+	25	50	129	27	6	3	0	39	17	5	3	0	36	5	2	0	8	1	.89	2	.209	.255	.302
Legendre, Curtis	dh-3b	Royals	KC	R	20	48	168	54	15	2	0	73	23	29	16	1	25	2	1	2	7	1	.88	2	.321	.383	.435
Lehmann, Thomas*	of	Tigers	Det	R	18	34	90	16	3	0	0	19	8	12	9	0	21	0	2	1	1	0	1.00	2	.178	.250	.211
Lehr, Ryan	3b	Cedar Rapds	Ana	A	23	22	81	21	8	0	3	38	12	16	7	0	7	1	0	2	0	0	.00	2	.259	.319	.469
		Rancho Cuca	Ana	A+	23	54	197	53	14	3	4	85	28	25	13	0	40	4	0	2	1	1	.50	9	.269	.324	.431
Lemon, Tim	of	Peoria	StL	A	21	130	482	107	32	3	15	190	60	61	27	1	165	6	2	4	31	7	.82	12	.222	.270	.394
Lentini, Fehlandt	of	Martinsvlle	Hou	R+	24	12	46	13	1	1	1	19	8	4	5	0	5	0	0	1	11	1	.92	1	.283	.346	.413
		Pittsfield	Hou	A-	24	15	52	18	3	1	0	23	13	8	4	0	6	0	0	0	8	1	.89	0	.346	.393	.442
		Lexington	Hou	A	24	29	122	36	11	2	1	54	27	21	10	0	16	1	0	1	10	4	.71	2	.295	.351	.443
Leon, Alfredo	3b	Frederick	Bal	A+	22	10	32	6	1	0	0	7	2	0	2	0	7	1	0	0	0	1	.00	1	.188	.257	.219
		Delmarva	Bal	A	22	90	318	76	12	0	0	88	26	41	14	2	48	8	2	0	3	0	1.00	18	.239	.288	.277
Leone, Justin	3b	San Berndno	Sea	A+	25	130	485	113	27	4	22	214	70	69	57	2	158	5	6	3	4	3	.57	8	.233	.318	.441
Levy, Mike	dh	Johnson Cty	StL	R+	23	19	43	11	1	1	2	20	7	8	6	0	18	0	0	0	0	0	.00	1	.256	.347	.465
Lewis, Domonique	2b	Billings	Cin	R+	22	41	148	38	3	1	2	49	33	15	18	0	27	3	6	0	15	1	.94	2	.257	.349	.331
Lewis, Richard	2b	Frederick	Bal	A+	22	1	0	0	0	0	0	0	0	0	0	0	0	0	0	0	0	0	.00	0	.000	.000	.000
		Jamestown	Atl	A-	22	71	285	69	7	1	4	90	37	27	20	2	50	4	3	3	16	4	.80	7	.242	.298	.316
Lewis, Russell*	2b	Lowell	Bos	A-	24	47	168	49	14	3	2	75	26	27	22	0	34	3	3	3	0	1	.00	2	.292	.378	.446
Likely, Cameron	of	Pittsfield	Hou	A-	24	40	79	23	1	1	1	29	20	11	8	0	10	2	0	0	6	3	.67	0	.291	.371	.367
Lillash, Keith	2b	Mahoning Vy	Cle	A-	23	33	94	24	5	2	1	36	17	2	14	0	19	3	1	0	2	1	.67	0	.255	.369	.383
Lincoln, Justin	3b	Salem	Col	A+	23	50	156	26	6	0	3	41	15	10	9	0	63	4	2	1	1	0	1.00	0	.167	.229	.263
		Asheville	Col	A	23	62	226	62	12	4	10	112	37	41	17	0	84	1	1	2	2	2	.50	4	.274	.325	.496
Lindberg, Russell	1b	Marlins	Fla	R	22	20	55	7	2	0	0	9	2	5	3	0	8	2	0	0	0	3	.00	1	.127	.200	.164
Lindsey, Cordell	1b-3b	Cedar Rapds	Ana	A	24	65	248	62	14	1	7	99	31	32	14	0	46	2	0	3	4	4	.50	11	.250	.292	.399
		Spokane	KC	A-	24	6	21	2	0	0	1	5	2	4	1	0	4	0	0	0	1	0	1.00	1	.095	.136	.238
Lindsey, John	dh	Salem	Col	A+	25	51	168	47	13	0	7	81	19	32	13	2	51	5	0	0	1	1	.50	2	.280	.349	.482
Liriano, Pedro	2b	Wisconsin	Sea	A	20	113	442	144	28	3	4	190	76	47	30	2	50	7	2	6	65	20	.76	5	.326	.373	.430
Lisk, Charlie	c	Bristol	CWS	R+	19	12	35	10	1	0	0	11	7	6	5	0	12	1	0	1	3	0	1.00	1	.286	.381	.314
Littleton, Brandon#	of	Delmarva	Bal	A	22	133	508	128	11	18	3	184	84	45	61	2	108	10	9	5	17	9	.65	4	.252	.341	.362
Llamas, Juan	3b	Burlington	KC	A	22	42	152	36	7	0	4	55	17	25	15	0	37	5	2	3	0	0	.00	5	.237	.320	.362
		Spokane	KC	A-	22	57	204	53	13	1	5	83	31	25	15	1	46	3	4	1	2	2	.50	9	.260	.318	.407
Lockhart, Paul#	of-dh	Lexington	Hou	A	24	99	320	79	17	4	6	122	48	40	29	0	73	5	3	3	3	2	.60	5	.247	.317	.381
Loeb, Bryan	c	South Bend	Ari	A	24	16	48	10	3	0	0	13	7	4	5	0	8	1	1	1	0	0	.00	1	.208	.291	.271
		Yakima	Ari	A-	24	40	115	28	8	1	1	41	12	12	8	0	29	4	1	0	1	0	1.00	0	.243	.315	.357
Logan, Nook#	of	W Michigan	Det	A	22	128	522	137	19	8	1	175	82	27	53	2	129	2	3	4	67	19	.78	3	.262	.330	.335
Lopez, Chuck*	of	Wisconsin	Sea	A	25	49	194	58	7	7	4	91	24	29	10	0	19	4	3	4	9	5	.64	2	.299	.340	.469
		San Berndno	Sea	A+	25	24	102	30	1	3	4	49	14	24	6	1	23	1	0	1	2	1	.67	2	.294	.336	.480
Lopez, Jose	ss	Everett	Sea	A-	18	70	289	74	15	0	2	95	42	20	13	0	44	10	1	2	13	6	.68	3	.256	.309	.329
Lopez, Mike	3b	Missoula	Ari	R+	24	73	284	89	21	4	8	142	70	37	36	0	52	16	2	1	6	2	.75	2	.313	.418	.500
Lopez, Pedro	2b-ss	White Sox	CWS	R	18	50	199	62	11	3	1	82	26	19	16	0	24	0	3	2	12	6	.67	4	.312	.359	.412
Lopez, Raul*	1b	Macon	Atl	A	23	45	150	31	9	1	4	54	14	25	8	1	26	0	2	1	0	1	.00	2	.207	.245	.360
Lora, Tom#	2b	Burlington	KC	A	23	112	442	110	11	7	2	141	80	28	45	0	84	5	9	0	27	15	.64	4	.249	.325	.319
Louisa, Lorvin	of	Expos	Mon	R	19	46	156	27	1	1	2	36	9	16	11	0	54	3	2	0	1	3	.25	2	.173	.241	.231
Louwsma, Chris	3b	Utica	Fla	A-	23	44	140	32	6	2	2	48	20	17	10	0	34	0	0	2	0	0	.00	3	.229	.276	.343
Lovelady, Greg	c	Utica	Fla	A-	23	20	65	10	1	0	0	11	4	5	3	0	21	0	0	0	0	1	.00	2	.154	.191	.169
Lucas, Matt	c	Lexington	Hou	A	23	29	67	18	8	0	3	35	9	8	0	0	18	1	0	0	0	1	.00	1	.269	.279	.522
Lugo, Felix#	3b	Jupiter	Mon	A+	21	77	269	66	12	6	5	105	31	36	14	1	89	6	0	4	7	3	.70	4	.245	.294	.390
Luna, Hector	ss	Columbus	Cle	A	20	66	241	64	8	3	3	87	36	23	23	0	48	5	3	2	15	4	.79	2	.266	.339	.361
Luna, Leonardo	3b-2b	White Sox	CWS	R	20	28	103	25	4	2	0	33	12	14	5	0	14	0	4	0	1	4	.20	5	.243	.278	.320
		Bristol	CWS	R+	20	16	41	7	0	0	0	7	4	1	0	0	15	1	3	1	3	2	.60	0	.171	.186	.171
Lundquist, Ryan	3b-of	Mudville	Cin	A+	25	122	436	119	31	0	14	192	66	72	54	2	117	6	3	6	9	2	.82	12	.273	.357	.440
Lunsford, James	c	Hagerstown	SF	A	23	114	396	94	19	0	5	128	53	50	45	1	89	5	4	4	10	5	.67	12	.237	.320	.323
Lush, Zach	c	Marlins	Fla	R	25	7	26	3	0	0	0	3	4	1	5	1	5	2	0	0	5	0	1.00	1	.115	.303	.115
		Brevard Cty	Fla	A+	25	10	20	3	1	0	0	4	2	0	2	0	7	1	0	0	0	0	.00	0	.150	.261	.200
Lutz, David*	c-dh	Clinton	Mon	A	20	7	25	6	1	0	0	7	4	2	2	0	2	0	0	0	1	0	1.00	0	.240	.296	.280
		Vermont	Mon	A-	20	46	167	38	7	1	0	47	19	16	16	0	30	0	1	2	2	1	.67	4	.228	.292	.281
Luuloa, Miles#	2b	W Michigan	Det	A	21	84	250	46	9	2	2	65	30	17	35	0	76	0	4	1	5	4	.56	8	.184	.283	.260
Lydic, Joe	3b	Michigan	Hou	A	23	94	330	81	22	1	5	120	38	38	8	0	95	4	1	3	2	4	.33	6	.245	.270	.364
Lydon, Wayne	of	Kingsport	NYM	R+	21	26	98	18	7	0	0	25	14	8	11	0	35	0	1	0	15	1	.94	1	.184	.266	.255
		Brooklyn	NYM	A-	21	21	57	14	1	1	0	17	12	1	7	0	18	2	0	0	10	1	.91	1	.246	.348	.298
Lynam, Guy	c	Utica	Fla	A-	21	22	57	20	5	0	1	28	10	10	4	0	10	2	0	1	1	0	1.00	2	.351	.406	.491
Macchi, Brandon#	of	Martinsvlle	Hou	R+	22	42	113	12	4	0	0	16	12	5	9	0	30	0	0	1	5	2	.71	3	.106	.171	.142
Mace, Clark*	of	Yakima	Ari	A-	23	53	165	36	9	2	1	52	22	9	11	0	45	5	0	0	0	4	.00	1	.218	.287	.315
Macha, Erick	ss	Yakima	Ari	A-	22	52	196	48	3	2	1	58	24	16	12	0	40	1	1	2	1	4	.20	4	.245	.289	.296
Machado, Alejandro	2b-ss	Macon	Atl	A	20	82	306	83	6	3	1	98	43	24	34	1	56	13	5	0	20	13	.61	1	.271	.368	.320
		Burlington	KC	A	20	28	109	26	5	0	0	31	17	11	10	0	16	2	1	1	5	2	.71	2	.239	.311	.284
Mack, Tony	of	Frederick	Bal	A+	23	110	332	66	12	0	5	93	33	33	18	0	102	2	6	2	9	8	.53	9	.199	.243	.280
Maddox, Jeremy	3b	Princeton	TB	R+	23	53	188	51	11	0	5	77	20	27	12	0	47	4	0	1	1	1	.50	6	.271	.327	.410
Made, Maximo*	2b	Mahoning Vy	Cle	A-	20	50	157	32	8	0	1	43	14	7	11	0	31	5	1	0	6	2	.75	3	.204	.277	.274
Madera, Sandy	c	Vancouver	Oak	A-	21	35	77	18	3	1	1	26	8	12	15	0	24	3	1	1	0	1	.00	0	.234	.375	.338
Maduro, Jorge	c	Hudson Val	TB	A-	21	32	120	22	6	0	1	31	19	13	6	1	31	1	0	0	0	0	.00	3	.183	.228	.258
Maestrales, Pete#	3b	Salem-Keizr	SF	A-	22	19	66	17	5	1	1	27	6	11	3	0	19	1	1	0	0	0	.00	0	.258	.300	.409
		Giants	SF	R	22	26	94	24	5	2	0	33	12	6	8	1	17	1	1	1	5	2	.71	0	.255	.317	.351
Magness, Pat*	dh	Kane County	Fla	A	24	68	227	58	14	0	6	90	25	39	53	1	41	3	0	2	2	1	.67	6	.256	.400	.396
		Brevard Cty	Fla	A+	24	35	117	32	7	0	1	42	11	16	16	1	28	1	0	1	0	0	.00	0	.274	.363	.359
Maldonado, Ed	2b	Salem-Keizr	SF	A-	23	1	2	1	0	0	1	4	1	1	0	0	0	0	0	0	0	0	.00	0	.500	.500	2.000
		San Jose	SF	A+	23	44	160	52	9	1	7	84	23	24	3	0	34	3	3	3	0	2	.00	4	.325	.343	.525

2001 Batting — Class-A and Rookie Leagues

						BATTING															BASERUNNING				PERCENTAGES		
Player	Pos	Team	Org	Lg	A	G	AB	H	2B	3B	HR	TB	R	RBI	TBB	IBB	SO	HBP	SH	SF	SB	CS	SB%	GDP	Avg	OBP	SLG
Mallory, Mike	of	Lansing	ChC	A	21	127	434	99	17	3	12	158	51	47	28	0	132	12	1	3	17	3	.85	8	.228	.291	.364
Malone, Billy	3b	Great Falls	LA	R+	24	55	176	37	5	1	0	44	23	18	25	1	49	5	0	3	15	6	.71	6	.210	.321	.250
Malpica, Martin	1b	Chston-WV	Tor	A	22	15	60	11	1	0	0	12	4	6	1	0	14	0	1	0	0	0	.00	0	.183	.197	.200
		Auburn	Tor	A-	22	40	136	32	3	0	1	38	17	7	9	0	24	2	2	2	3	0	1.00	7	.235	.289	.279
Mancebo, Deni#	ss	Expos	Mon	R	18	46	166	32	2	1	0	36	21	7	17	0	44	8	4	2	6	3	.67	0	.193	.295	.217
Manley, Adam*	of-1b	Orioles	Bal	R	23	9	34	6	1	1	1	12	3	5	0	0	9	1	0	0	0	0	.00	1	.176	.200	.353
		Bluefield	Bal	R+	23	27	84	16	3	1	3	30	13	17	4	0	30	3	0	0	1	0	1.00	0	.190	.253	.357
		Delmarva	Bal	A	23	23	66	10	3	1	1	18	1	9	7	0	26	1	0	0	1	1	.50	0	.152	.243	.273
Manning, Pat	2b	Macon	Atl	A	22	62	211	60	13	1	13	114	40	29	37	0	46	6	5	4	6	2	.75	5	.284	.399	.540
		Myrtle Bch	Atl	A+	22	62	220	49	12	0	10	91	23	30	28	0	41	5	2	1	2	3	.40	4	.223	.323	.414
Manning, Ricky*	of	Elizabethtn	Min	R+	21	22	75	19	4	1	0	25	15	4	9	0	15	4	0	0	4	3	.57	1	.253	.364	.333
Manriquez, S.	c	Expos	Mon	R	19	34	120	26	9	0	0	35	8	8	7	1	30	3	0	0	0	0	.00	4	.217	.277	.292
Mapes, Jake	c-dh	Hagerstown	SF	A	23	2	6	0	0	0	0	0	0	0	0	0	2	0	0	0	0	0	.00	0	.000	.000	.000
Margalski, Ben*	c	Batavia	Phi	A-	22	40	130	29	6	3	1	44	16	18	12	0	41	0	2	1	0	0	.00	2	.223	.287	.338
Marin, Daniel	c	Twins	Min	R	19	31	95	26	5	0	0	31	16	11	10	0	10	1	2	0	5	1	.83	2	.274	.349	.326
Mariot, Lino	ss	Pirates	Pit	R	19	31	85	14	0	0	0	14	6	2	4	0	22	2	0	0	4	1	.80	3	.165	.220	.165
Marmol, Carlos	of	Cubs	ChC	R	19	40	129	38	11	0	0	49	15	12	9	0	30	3	1	0	4	3	.57	0	.295	.355	.380
Marsh, Jason	c	Chston-SC	TB	A	24	66	216	53	9	0	4	74	24	24	4	1	41	4	2	1	3	2	.60	4	.245	.271	.343
Marshall, Andre#	of	Phillies	Phi	R	21	36	115	33	9	0	1	45	22	13	11	0	32	3	0	0	5	1	.83	1	.287	.364	.391
Marte, Andy	3b	Danville	Atl	R+	18	37	125	25	6	0	1	34	12	12	20	0	45	0	1	2	3	0	1.00	3	.200	.306	.272
Martel, Normand*	of	Kannapolis	CWS	A	23	71	135	38	2	2	1	47	15	7	18	1	29	2	0	0	7	3	.70	2	.281	.374	.348
Martin, Brian	of	Chston-SC	TB	A	22	131	456	106	22	3	8	158	42	44	35	2	150	10	0	3	7	15	.32	8	.232	.300	.346
Martin, Cesar	3b	Medcine Hat	Tor	R+	21	67	254	56	16	0	8	96	34	43	27	0	54	13	4	1	4	3	.57	7	.220	.325	.378
Martin, Chris	2b	Yankees	NYY	R	23	2	5	0	0	0	0	0	1	1	1	0	1	0	0	0	0	0	.00	0	.000	.167	.000
		Staten Ilnd	NYY	A-	23	27	75	15	2	0	1	20	8	5	4	0	18	1	0	0	0	0	.00	1	.200	.250	.267
Martin, Craig	2b	Brewers	Mil	R	23	21	76	17	5	0	0	22	6	7	9	0	21	1	0	0	0	0	.00	2	.224	.314	.289
Martin, Kyle	c-dh	Bluefield	Bal	R+	22	44	130	40	11	0	1	54	16	13	13	0	39	0	1	1	1	2	.33	1	.308	.368	.415
Martin, Tyler#	3b	Savannah	Tex	A	24	35	107	16	1	1	0	19	7	4	13	1	28	2	0	0	1	2	.33	3	.150	.254	.178
		Charlotte	Tex	A+	24	47	147	32	6	2	4	54	24	15	20	1	30	0	1	3	0	1	.00	2	.218	.306	.367
Martinez, Candido	of-dh	Wilmington	LA	A	21	120	443	115	27	4	7	171	69	66	29	0	138	6	1	6	54	18	.75	3	.260	.310	.386
Martinez, Dionnar#	ss	Lansing	ChC	A	21	17	56	18	2	1	0	22	8	6	3	0	8	1	2	0	0	1	.00	0	.321	.367	.393
		Daytona	ChC	A+	21	26	60	16	3	0	0	19	10	0	7	0	11	1	3	0	1	0	1.00	1	.267	.353	.317
Martinez, Edgar	c	Lowell	Bos	A-	20	49	175	56	12	2	3	81	21	25	10	1	23	5	0	2	1	0	1.00	2	.320	.370	.463
Martinez, G.#	ss	Wisconsin	Sea	A	22	56	181	44	6	2	1	57	24	23	4	0	45	1	1	1	2	2	.50	6	.243	.262	.315
		San Berndno	Sea	A+	22	44	166	42	8	1	1	55	26	16	13	1	43	2	7	1	1	2	.33	4	.253	.313	.331
Martinez, Luis	ss	Kingsport	NYM	R+	21	28	78	10	3	0	1	16	14	4	7	0	26	2	0	0	2	1	.67	0	.128	.218	.205
Martinez, Octavio	c	Frederick	Bal	A+	22	98	336	73	14	0	1	90	23	29	10	0	47	11	4	1	3	2	.60	15	.217	.263	.268
Martinez, Peter#	2b	Elizabethtn	Min	R+	20	35	98	22	11	0	0	33	11	12	13	0	26	5	0	1	5	2	.71	2	.224	.342	.337
Martinez, Ramon#	2b	Charlotte	Tex	A+	22	128	515	124	20	1	2	152	69	32	28	0	65	5	8	1	28	18	.61	7	.241	.286	.295
Martinez, Raul	c	Orioles	Bal	R	—	35	101	25	4	1	1	34	13	17	15	3	23	1	0	3	2	0	1.00	1	.248	.342	.337
Martinez, Thomas	c	Idaho Falls	SD	R+	19	36	117	32	7	0	2	45	15	16	1	0	26	2	0	0	0	0	.00	6	.274	.292	.385
Martinez, Victor#	c	Kinston	Cle	A+	23	114	420	138	33	2	10	205	59	57	39	1	60	8	0	3	3	3	.50	12	.329	.394	.488
Masino, Adam	1b	Twins	Min	R	20	39	123	27	7	0	1	37	10	10	10	1	41	1	0	0	3	0	1.00	1	.220	.284	.301
Massiatte, Danny	c	Bakersfield	TB	A+	23	96	330	70	20	2	4	106	37	29	26	0	84	6	6	4	1	2	.33	9	.212	.279	.321
Mateo, Alejandro	of	Rangers	Tex	R	20	32	72	11	1	1	0	14	6	7	16	0	30	1	1	0	6	3	.67	2	.153	.315	.194
Mateo, Daniel#	ss	Reds	Cin	R	19	53	180	44	6	0	1	53	29	14	15	0	48	6	1	0	27	6	.82	2	.244	.323	.294
		Billings	Cin	R+	19	4	9	5	0	0	0	5	1	2	0	0	3	0	0	0	0	1	.00	0	.556	.556	.556
Materano, Oscar	3b	Casper	Col	R+	20	69	271	68	11	0	6	97	34	38	9	0	59	7	0	2	5	5	.50	5	.251	.291	.358
Mather, Joe	3b	Johnson Cty	StL	R+	19	45	165	41	3	0	5	59	25	21	7	0	60	3	1	2	2	2	.50	5	.248	.288	.358
Mathis, Jeff	c	Angels	Ana	R	19	7	23	7	1	0	0	8	1	3	2	0	4	0	0	1	0	0	.00	1	.304	.346	.348
		Provo	Ana	R+	19	22	77	23	6	3	0	35	14	18	11	0	13	2	0	3	1	0	1.00	1	.299	.387	.455
Matos, Angel	dh-c	Savannah	Tex	A	22	26	65	13	2	0	0	15	6	4	4	0	27	1	1	0	0	0	.00	0	.200	.257	.231
Matos, Bernie	c	Elizabethtn	Min	R+	20	14	44	10	3	0	0	13	5	4	1	0	9	0	0	0	0	1	.00	1	.227	.244	.295
Mattle, David*	of	Oneonta	Det	A-	22	40	142	29	8	1	1	42	14	22	17	1	33	2	2	3	2	0	1.00	3	.204	.293	.296
Mauer, Jake	3b	Elizabethtn	Min	R+	23	27	58	9	1	0	0	10	8	6	8	0	5	5	0	0	3	1	.75	4	.155	.310	.172
Mauer, Joe*	c-dh	Elizabethtn	Min	R+	19	32	110	44	6	2	0	54	14	14	19	0	10	1	0	0	4	0	1.00	5	.400	.492	.491
Maule, Jason*	3b-2b	Michigan	Hou	A	24	124	412	143	23	5	1	179	101	63	74	1	62	7	4	7	56	6	.90	3	.347	.448	.434
Mayo, Terry	of	Ogden	Mil	R+	20	8	17	4	2	0	0	6	3	1	3	0	8	0	0	1	0	1	.00	0	.235	.333	.353
		Brewers	Mil	R	20	18	61	13	1	2	1	21	4	6	3	0	31	3	1	2	0	1	.00	0	.213	.275	.344
Mayorson, Manuel	ss	Chston-WV	Tor	A	19	1	2	0	0	0	0	0	0	0	0	0	1	0	0	0	0	0	.00	0	.000	.000	.000
		Auburn	Tor	A-	19	62	247	65	5	0	0	70	28	18	21	0	19	4	5	5	25	13	.66	3	.263	.325	.283
		Dunedin	Tor	A+	19	18	37	7	0	0	0	7	6	2	2	0	2	0	0	0	0	0	.00	0	.189	.231	.189
Maza, Luis	ss	Quad City	Min	A	22	116	429	120	24	1	9	173	74	46	30	0	66	23	2	2	12	4	.75	9	.280	.357	.403
McAffee, Josh	c	St. Lucie	NYM	A+	24	5	15	1	0	0	0	1	0	0	2	0	6	0	0	0	0	0	.00	0	.067	.176	.067
McArthur, Kennon#	c	Lakewood	Phi	A	22	22	71	10	2	0	0	12	3	5	3	0	29	1	1	0	0	0	.00	0	.141	.187	.169
		Batavia	Phi	A-	22	1	3	0	0	0	0	0	0	0	0	0	1	0	0	0	0	0	.00	0	.000	.000	.000
McAuley, Jim	c	Wilmington	KC	A+	24	54	163	34	5	0	0	39	17	15	19	1	46	2	5	1	1	0	1.00	4	.209	.297	.239
McAuliff, James	of	Giants	SF	R	23	43	173	58	14	3	1	81	41	18	23	0	35	2	0	0	6	3	.67	0	.335	.419	.468
		Salem-Keizr	SF	A-	23	20	66	16	2	0	1	21	10	4	10	0	18	2	1	0	3	1	.75	1	.242	.359	.318
McCallum, Geoff	ss	San Berndno	Sea	A+	24	32	98	24	6	0	0	30	13	12	18	1	34	0	1	0	2	1	.67	1	.245	.362	.306
McCarthy, Billy	of	Jamestown	Atl	A-	22	74	285	84	17	2	2	111	38	39	20	0	47	7	0	4	7	4	.64	8	.295	.351	.389
McClanahan, Jonah	of	Ogden	Mil	R+	21	26	98	29	5	3	0	40	17	8	2	0	13	1	5	0	2	0	1.00	0	.296	.317	.408
McCool, Lee	2b	Fort Wayne	SD	A	23	102	392	93	17	3	1	119	35	36	20	0	77	4	2	4	8	5	.62	2	.237	.279	.304
McCorkle, Shawn*	1b	San Berndno	Sea	A+	24	136	520	143	36	4	13	226	81	81	69	2	151	3	5	6	2	2	.50	10	.275	.360	.435
McCormack, Taylor	3b	Brewers	Mil	R	19	36	131	26	4	1	0	32	15	18	13	0	48	2	1	1	1	0	1.00	2	.198	.279	.244
McCuistion, Mike*	c	Pirates	Pit	R	20	27	82	18	3	0	0	21	4	3	9	0	8	1	0	0	0	0	.00	3	.220	.304	.256
McDonald, Chamar	of	Royals	KC	R	19	40	125	26	7	1	1	38	13	11	9	0	43	2	1	0	5	1	.83	1	.208	.272	.304
McDougall, Marshall	3b	Visalia	Oak	A+	23	134	534	137	43	7	12	230	79	84	46	2	110	7	7	4	14	2	.88	9	.257	.321	.431
McDowell, Arturo*	of	San Jose	SF	A+	22	118	425	103	12	11	1	140	57	31	46	3	132	4	3	1	25	14	.64	4	.242	.321	.329
McEachran, Aaron*	1b	Medcine Hat	Tor	R+	23	69	256	86	12	1	5	115	34	41	32	2	55	8	1	0	3	1	.75	7	.336	.426	.449
McIntyre, Robert	ss	Brooklyn	NYM	A-	21	67	233	46	10	1	8	82	35	35	18	1	67	3	1	1	7	5	.58	1	.197	.263	.352
McKee, Mickey	1b	Lexington	Hou	A	24	73	238	64	16	4	5	103	35	35	21	1	61	3	0	2	4	3	.57	5	.269	.333	.433
McKinley, Josh#	2b	Jupiter	Mon	A+	22	128	464	117	19	2	2	146	63	54	70	2	83	3	0	5	28	10	.74	11	.252	.351	.315
McKinney, Tony	of	Dunedin	Tor	A+	24	128	450	120	25	5	3	164	68	48	48	0	106	6	6	3	23	6	.79	8	.267	.343	.364
McKnight, Lukas*	c	Boise	ChC	A-	22	27	69	20	3	1	3	34	8	14	6	1	18	0	0	0	0	0	.00	1	.290	.347	.493

2001 Batting — Class-A and Rookie Leagues

Player	Pos	Team	Org	Lg	A	G	AB	H	2B	3B	HR	TB	R	RBI	TBB	IBB	SO	HBP	SH	SF	SB	CS	SB%	GDP	Avg	OBP	SLG
						BATTING															BASERUNNING				PERCENTAGES		
McLouth, Nate*	of	Hickory	Pit	A	20	96	351	100	17	5	12	163	59	54	43	6	54	7	2	3	21	5	.81	5	.285	.371	.464
McMahon, James	c	Orioles	Bal	R	19	18	46	12	0	0	0	12	1	3	7	0	19	0	1	1	0	1	.00	2	.261	.352	.261
McMains, Derin#	2b	Salem-Keizr	SF	A-	22	69	258	70	18	2	4	104	40	40	32	0	26	1	5	3	6	1	.86	11	.271	.350	.403
McMillan, Drew	c	Clinton	Mon	A	21	94	320	63	12	0	6	93	25	30	12	0	67	15	0	1	1	0	1.00	8	.197	.259	.291
McMillin, Brian	of	Fort Myers	Min	A+	25	93	250	45	10	0	2	61	31	15	29	0	76	1	7	1	15	3	.83	5	.180	.267	.244
McPherson, Dallas*	3b	Provo	Ana	R+	21	31	124	49	11	0	5	75	30	29	12	0	22	0	0	0	1	0	1.00	2	.395	.449	.605
McQueen, Eric	c	Salem	Col	A+	25	2	5	0	0	0	0	0	0	0	1	0	5	0	1	0	0	0	.00	0	.000	.167	.000
McRoberts, Mark	c	Phillies	Phi	R	20	27	80	16	3	1	4	33	14	6	10	0	25	0	0	0	0	0	.00	1	.200	.289	.413
		Batavia	Phi	A-	20	7	20	7	2	0	0	9	2	3	0	0	3	2	0	0	0	0	.00	1	.350	.409	.450
Meath, Matt#	of	Pirates	Pit	R	22	14	34	5	2	0	0	7	7	1	12	1	6	2	0	0	5	1	.83	1	.147	.396	.206
		Williamsprt	Pit	A-	22	32	102	33	5	2	1	45	22	8	21	0	24	4	3	3	13	3	.81	0	.324	.446	.441
Medina, Ricardo	of	Expos	Mon	R	20	38	129	28	5	1	3	44	12	14	8	0	37	1	1	0	0	3	.00	0	.217	.268	.341
Medina, Rodney#	of	Auburn	Tor	A-	20	11	39	7	1	0	0	8	4	3	4	0	5	0	0	0	1	0	1.00	2	.179	.256	.205
		Medcine Hat	Tor	R+	20	50	195	60	7	0	7	88	37	21	19	0	29	2	2	0	6	2	.75	2	.308	.375	.451
Medrano, Jesus	2b	Brevard Cty	Fla	A+	23	124	454	114	15	2	1	136	93	32	51	0	81	5	7	4	61	8	.88	9	.251	.331	.300
Mejia, Andy	c	Lansing	ChC	A	20	12	37	5	2	0	0	7	3	3	1	0	9	0	0	0	0	0	.00	0	.135	.158	.189
		Cubs	ChC	R	20	4	12	3	0	0	0	3	1	1	1	0	2	0	0	0	0	0	.00	1	.250	.308	.250
		Boise	ChC	A-	20	24	80	16	4	1	2	28	9	14	6	0	21	0	0	0	0	0	.00	2	.200	.256	.350
Mejia, Manuel	c	Hickory	Pit	A	22	46	125	27	2	0	2	35	6	13	18	0	37	3	1	1	0	0	.00	3	.216	.327	.280
Melgarejo, Ransel	of	Angels	Ana	R	20	45	138	39	7	2	1	53	25	20	19	0	19	6	2	1	12	5	.71	3	.283	.390	.384
Melo, Hanlet	of	Danville	Atl	R+	20	55	178	40	7	3	1	56	22	12	9	0	47	1	1	1	7	3	.70	1	.225	.265	.315
Menchaca, Eriberto	ss	Mariners	Sea	R	21	49	170	46	7	2	0	57	30	18	8	0	29	2	4	3	1	0	1.00	3	.271	.306	.335
		Everett	Sea	A-	21	3	5	0	0	0	0	0	1	0	1	0	1	1	0	0	1	0	1.00	0	.000	.286	.000
Mendez, Deivi	ss	Greensboro	NYY	A	19	49	172	37	6	0	2	49	25	15	14	0	35	2	5	2	5	2	.71	4	.215	.279	.285
		Staten IInd	NYY	A-	19	53	186	43	10	2	1	60	23	21	9	0	31	3	0	4	2	4	.33	6	.231	.272	.323
Mendoza, Adrian*	1b	Dodgers	LA	R	23	52	172	52	7	1	4	73	34	37	29	0	55	9	0	4	9	4	.69	2	.302	.421	.424
Mercado, Onix	c	Billings	Cin	R+	22	29	86	24	6	1	1	35	15	13	7	0	26	3	2	0	0	1	.00	0	.279	.354	.407
Mercado, Wilkins	3b	Wilmington	KC	A+	23	60	165	24	7	0	1	34	10	13	11	0	43	1	5	0	0	0	.00	3	.145	.203	.206
Mercedes, Ramon	ss	Princeton	TB	R+	20	48	163	41	5	0	1	49	22	19	11	0	26	1	5	0	5	3	.63	3	.252	.303	.301
Merchan, Jesus	ss	Elizabethtn	Min	R+	21	47	133	36	10	1	1	51	19	14	6	0	18	2	0	3	4	2	.67	1	.271	.306	.383
Merriman, Terrell*	of	Winston-Sal	CWS	A+	24	17	48	5	0	0	0	5	4	1	9	0	17	0	0	0	4	0	1.00	0	.104	.246	.104
Merritt, Graig	c	Chston-SC	TB	A	23	5	9	0	0	0	0	0	0	1	2	0	3	0	1	0	1	0	1.00	0	.000	.182	.000
		Hudson Val	TB	A-	23	35	116	30	4	0	1	37	13	12	9	0	14	0	0	3	1	1	.50	1	.259	.305	.319
Merritt, Tim	2b	Everett	Sea	A-	22	51	196	60	13	3	5	94	33	30	9	0	35	0	1	3	11	3	.79	1	.306	.332	.480
		Wisconsin	Sea	A	22	3	13	4	0	0	0	4	1	1	0	0	2	0	0	1	0	1	.00	0	.308	.286	.308
Messner, Jake*	of-dh	San Jose	SF	A+	25	83	279	68	14	1	2	90	36	39	34	1	83	3	0	3	1	2	.33	11	.244	.329	.323
Meyer, Robert	of	Salem-Keizr	SF	A-	23	70	274	80	19	1	5	116	47	35	25	0	53	5	1	2	0	0	.00	11	.292	.359	.423
Michaelis, Derek*	1b	Wilmington	LA	A	23	33	117	23	4	1	0	29	10	17	6	0	36	3	1	3	6	0	1.00	4	.197	.248	.248
		Great Falls	LA	R+	23	37	134	37	9	1	4	60	21	28	17	1	31	1	1	0	2	1	.67	2	.276	.362	.448
Milauskas, Adam	of	Pirates	Pit	R	19	31	92	20	0	0	0	20	8	3	10	0	18	2	0	1	0	0	.00	3	.217	.305	.217
Miliano, Hector	of	Cubs	ChC	R	20	52	196	51	10	3	3	76	22	25	7	0	52	4	1	1	6	6	.50	4	.260	.298	.388
Millan, Carlos	of	Idaho Falls	SD	R+	20	14	42	8	0	0	1	11	7	6	5	0	15	0	0	0	0	1	.00	1	.190	.277	.262
Miller, Eric	ss	Jupiter	Mon	A+	24	19	63	17	3	1	0	22	4	7	3	0	8	1	2	1	2	1	.67	1	.270	.309	.349
		Clinton	Mon	A	24	69	276	79	11	3	2	102	28	35	16	0	42	0	0	1	8	1	.89	8	.286	.324	.370
Miller, Greg	of	Jamestown	Atl	A-	23	61	240	67	10	2	0	81	24	17	20	0	28	5	2	3	9	5	.64	2	.279	.343	.338
Miller, Tony	of	Casper	Col	R+	21	70	268	82	17	3	10	135	68	34	41	0	63	3	0	4	28	10	.74	3	.306	.399	.504
Minges, Tyler	of	Columbus	Cle	A	22	15	59	22	5	0	1	30	9	7	3	0	12	3	0	0	2	0	1.00	2	.373	.431	.508
		Kinston	Cle	A+	22	66	250	63	12	2	5	94	30	35	12	1	48	4	2	3	3	2	.60	6	.252	.294	.376
Minus, Steve	1b	Sarasota	Bos	A+	25	112	387	88	10	4	8	130	41	40	59	0	102	3	1	4	6	2	.75	7	.227	.331	.336
Miranda, Miguel#	ss	Salem-Keizr	SF	A-	23	59	194	54	7	0	0	61	21	22	18	0	20	1	5	3	4	3	.57	0	.278	.338	.314
Mojica, Robinson	of	Johnson Cty	StL	R+	20	36	118	26	5	1	0	33	7	8	3	0	25	1	1	2	0	3	.00	1	.220	.242	.280
Molidor, Dave	dh	Billings	Cin	R+	23	53	191	47	10	0	3	66	28	30	31	2	55	7	1	2	5	1	.83	7	.246	.368	.346
Molina, Angel	c	Marlins	Fla	R	20	36	110	28	7	0	1	38	9	13	10	0	26	0	0	0	0	2	.00	2	.255	.317	.345
Molina, Felix#	3b	Twins	Min	R	19	51	189	54	12	3	2	78	27	21	16	1	25	0	3	1	8	6	.57	0	.286	.340	.413
Molina, Gustavo	c	Bristol	CWS	R+	20	46	166	47	9	0	2	62	18	24	9	1	26	5	1	3	3	1	.75	2	.283	.333	.373
Molina, Yadier	c	Johnson Cty	StL	R+	19	44	158	41	11	0	4	64	18	18	12	1	23	3	0	2	1	1	.50	4	.259	.320	.405
Monegan, Anthony*	of	Bristol	CWS	R+	23	54	188	52	5	1	1	62	35	17	21	1	58	1	1	3	21	8	.72	1	.277	.347	.330
Money, Freddie	of	Augusta	Bos	A	23	21	74	14	2	1	1	21	9	7	10	0	21	0	1	1	5	5	.50	2	.189	.282	.284
		Lowell	Bos	A-	23	57	221	55	13	1	2	76	40	21	29	0	46	2	2	2	27	5	.84	4	.249	.339	.344
Mongeluzzo, A.	3b-of	Savannah	Tex	A	23	72	258	64	14	3	7	105	32	35	21	0	67	7	0	2	9	1	.90	8	.248	.319	.407
Monroy, Sam*	2b	Chston-SC	TB	A	23	19	38	6	0	0	0	6	6	0	6	0	7	0	0	0	3	1	.75	2	.158	.273	.158
		Hudson Val	TB	A-	23	13	50	10	0	0	0	10	3	2	4	0	9	0	0	0	2	0	1.00	2	.200	.259	.200
Montanez, Luis	ss	Lansing	ChC	A	20	124	499	127	33	6	5	187	70	54	34	0	121	12	3	3	20	7	.74	12	.255	.316	.375
Montero, Esteban	ss	Tri-City	Col	A-	19	57	165	32	10	4	2	56	23	16	12	0	63	5	2	2	1	1	.50	2	.194	.266	.339
Montero, Roberto	c	Giants	SF	R	20	11	16	4	2	0	0	6	2	0	0	0	7	0	0	0	0	0	.00	1	.250	.250	.375
Montilla, Samuel	c	Missoula	Ari	R+	20	46	159	42	8	2	0	54	21	20	2	0	20	1	0	1	2	1	.67	1	.264	.276	.340
Mooney, Dan	c	Augusta	Bos	A	25	27	88	21	8	0	3	38	11	14	2	0	23	6	0	1	1	0	1.00	3	.239	.299	.432
Moore, Bryan*	1b	Johnson Cty	StL	R+	22	54	179	41	7	0	3	57	20	26	21	0	37	9	1	2	4	1	.80	6	.229	.336	.318
Moore, Chris*	1b-dh	Asheville	Col	A	25	7	26	4	0	0	0	4	1	3	1	0	9	0	0	1	0	0	.00	1	.154	.179	.154
		Salem	Col	A+	25	19	44	7	2	0	0	9	3	1	9	0	11	0	0	1	0	0	.00	0	.159	.296	.205
Moore, Frank*	of	Bakersfield	TB	A+	23	129	505	155	29	6	7	217	75	60	25	3	106	6	6	2	9	3	.75	9	.307	.346	.430
Moore, Jason#	ss-2b	Lk Elsinore	SD	A+	24	132	509	129	30	2	13	202	79	67	61	0	110	4	5	8	1	3	.25	8	.253	.333	.397
Moore, Mewelde	of	Idaho Falls	SD	R+	19	24	89	21	1	0	1	25	19	5	6	0	29	4	0	0	4	2	.67	1	.236	.313	.281
Mora, Ruben#	of	Idaho Falls	SD	R+	20	54	184	37	6	4	0	51	33	17	18	0	55	3	2	2	12	3	.80	3	.201	.280	.277
Moraga, Omar*	2b	Kinston	Cle	A+	25	13	43	10	1	0	1	14	4	2	1	0	6	0	0	0	0	1	.00	1	.233	.250	.326
Morales, Jose#	2b	Twins	Min	R	19	35	117	29	6	2	0	39	13	18	6	0	26	2	2	0	4	1	.80	1	.248	.296	.333
Morales, Michael	2b	Braves	Atl	R	23	16	49	8	2	0	0	10	8	4	4	0	4	9	0	1	0	1	.00	4	.163	.333	.204
		Macon	Atl	A	23	26	69	13	2	0	1	18	8	6	6	0	15	3	1	0	1	0	1.00	3	.188	.282	.261
Morban, Dany*	of	Reds	Cin	R	20	27	63	9	1	0	0	10	4	3	1	0	22	1	0	0	3	1	.75	1	.143	.169	.159
Morban, Jose	ss	Savannah	Tex	A	22	122	474	119	20	11	8	185	71	47	42	0	119	2	5	3	46	18	.72	11	.251	.313	.390
Morel, Robinson	3b	Casper	Col	R+	20	36	108	27	3	1	5	47	19	16	9	0	32	3	0	0	5	3	.63	3	.250	.325	.435
Morency, Vernand	of	Tri-City	Col	A-	22	54	183	42	12	2	4	70	30	27	20	1	59	9	3	1	16	3	.84	4	.230	.333	.383
Moreno, Chris	3b	Orioles	Bal	R	24	6	20	5	0	0	0	5	1	0	0	0	5	0	1	0	1	0	1.00	1	.250	.250	.250
		Frederick	Bal	A+	24	19	32	2	2	0	0	4	7	2	4	0	15	0	1	0	0	0	.00	0	.063	.167	.125
Moreno, Jorge	of	Kinston	Cle	A+	21	101	368	75	7	1	5	99	31	35	26	2	94	3	8	1	7	8	.47	6	.204	.261	.269

2001 Batting — Class-A and Rookie Leagues

BATTING																					BASERUNNING				PERCENTAGES		
Player	Pos	Team	Org	Lg	A	G	AB	H	2B	3B	HR	TB	R	RBI	TBB	IBB	SO	HBP	SH	SF	SB	CS	SB%	GDP	Avg	OBP	SLG
		Columbus	Cle	A	21	24	93	19	5	2	3	37	13	6	4	0	28	0	2	0	4	0	1.00	0	.204	.237	.398
Morillo, Roberto#	c	Giants	SF	R	17	5	5	1	0	0	0	1	1	0	0	0	3	1	0	0	0	0	.00	0	.200	.333	.200
Morris, Chris#	of	Peoria	StL	A	22	134	480	141	11	9	2	176	89	39	83	0	101	1	18	2	111	24	.82	1	.294	.398	.367
Morrissey, Adam	2b	Lansing	ChC	A	21	122	418	129	26	11	14	219	88	62	80	3	82	8	1	2	10	9	.53	9	.309	.427	.524
Morrow, Alvin	dh-of	Chston-WV	Tor	A	24	54	172	43	8	1	6	71	22	23	36	0	73	1	0	0	0	4	.00	4	.250	.383	.413
		Dunedin	Tor	A+	24	52	174	37	8	1	2	53	20	30	23	0	65	1	2	1	1	1	.50	5	.213	.307	.305
Morse, Mike#	ss	Bristol	CWS	R+	20	56	176	41	7	3	4	66	23	26	17	1	54	9	0	0	6	2	.75	4	.233	.332	.375
Morton, Rickie	1b	Mahoning Vy	Cle	A-	23	69	238	67	15	3	12	124	34	40	37	2	55	0	1	0	3	3	.50	5	.282	.378	.521
Mote, Trevor#	2b	Martinsvlle	Hou	R+	22	47	168	42	8	1	1	55	18	13	14	1	36	0	3	0	9	3	.75	4	.250	.308	.327
Motooka, Rafael	c	Reds	Cin	R	19	26	80	20	2	0	1	25	5	10	6	0	8	0	1	0	1	0	1.00	1	.250	.302	.313
Mounts, J.R.	of	Rancho Cuca	Ana	A+	23	106	378	83	15	4	9	133	45	38	15	2	145	2	3	2	13	6	.68	6	.220	.252	.352
Moye, Alan	of	Reds	Cin	R	19	48	171	49	9	2	2	68	24	18	8	2	34	3	1	0	12	3	.80	5	.287	.330	.398
Moylan, Dan*	c	New Jersey	StL	A-	23	59	192	56	9	1	1	70	23	22	45	0	31	0	1	1	6	7	.46	11	.292	.424	.365
Mujica, Andres	of	Mariners	Sea	R	19	45	159	45	6	3	0	57	27	24	15	0	36	2	1	0	5	3	.63	6	.283	.352	.358
Mujica, Jean	3b	Expos	Mon	R	19	41	128	33	4	1	1	42	16	12	11	0	34	2	2	0	1	0	1.00	5	.258	.326	.328
Mulqueen, Dave#	1b	Casper	Col	R+	21	73	286	80	19	0	12	135	49	49	36	2	89	3	0	0	8	2	.80	7	.280	.366	.472
Murch, Jeremy*	of	Bakersfield	TB	A+	23	72	221	52	12	4	9	99	27	32	18	1	63	1	1	1	1	1	.50	4	.235	.295	.448
Muro, Robert	3b-dh	Winston-Sal	CWS	A+	26	96	354	87	25	0	12	148	39	54	47	2	71	9	0	1	4	4	.50	6	.246	.348	.418
Murphy, Tommy	ss	Cedar Rapds	Ana	A+	22	74	280	57	15	3	4	90	32	31	16	1	94	6	6	3	7	10	.41	5	.204	.259	.321
		Rancho Cuca	Ana	A+	22	50	200	38	8	0	0	46	16	11	5	0	69	1	1	0	7	3	.70	4	.190	.214	.230
Muth, Edmund*	of	Asheville	Col	A	24	117	398	104	21	3	18	185	53	70	44	2	105	10	3	4	13	3	.81	6	.261	.346	.465
Myers, Casey	c	Vancouver	Oak	A-	23	59	198	55	15	0	7	91	24	35	22	3	34	9	2	2	0	0	.00	8	.278	.372	.460
Myers, Corey	3b	South Bend	Ari	A	22	59	211	69	17	2	3	99	28	36	12	0	33	4	1	9	2	0	1.00	9	.327	.360	.469
		Lancaster	Ari	A+	22	53	183	52	13	1	5	82	20	33	15	0	49	0	0	0	0	0	.00	0	.284	.338	.448
Myers, Kenton	c	Mahoning Vy	Cle	A-	22	24	79	17	0	0	0	17	9	6	7	0	19	1	0	0	0	2	.00	2	.215	.287	.215
Myler, Jonathan	c	Williamsprt	Pit	A-	22	23	74	14	5	0	1	22	6	8	10	1	20	0	2	0	0	0	.00	1	.189	.286	.297
Myrow, Brian*	3b	Tampa	NYY	A+	25	48	149	38	11	1	3	60	30	28	32	0	29	5	4	2	5	1	.83	4	.255	.399	.403
Nady, Xavier	1b	Lk Elsinore	SD	A+	23	137	524	158	38	1	26	276	96	100	62	7	109	10	0	8	6	0	1.00	14	.302	.381	.527
Nagle, Austin	of	Athletics	Oak	R	19	50	188	47	7	9	0	72	36	22	26	0	53	2	2	1	7	5	.58	5	.250	.346	.383
Napoli, Mike	c	Rancho Cuca	Ana	A+	20	7	20	4	0	0	1	7	3	4	8	0	11	0	0	0	0	0	.00	0	.200	.429	.350
		Cedar Rapds	Ana	A	20	43	155	36	10	1	5	63	23	18	24	0	54	2	1	1	3	2	.60	1	.232	.341	.406
Nash, Toe#	of	Princeton	TB	R+	20	47	171	41	10	1	8	77	23	29	19	0	69	1	0	1	0	1	.00	1	.240	.318	.450
Nathans, John	c	Red Sox	Bos	R	23	5	5	1	1	0	0	2	1	0	1	0	2	0	0	0	0	0	.00	0	.200	.333	.400
		Lowell	Bos	A-	23	31	75	12	2	0	0	14	16	3	18	0	30	0	0	0	2	0	1.00	2	.160	.323	.187
Navarrete, Ray	of	Pirates	Pit	R	24	3	9	2	1	0	0	3	1	1	2	0	3	0	0	0	0	1	.00	0	.222	.364	.333
		Hickory	Pit	A	24	92	354	95	23	2	10	152	53	49	21	0	70	8	3	5	9	4	.69	4	.268	.320	.429
Navarro, Dioner#	c	Yankees	NYY	R	18	43	143	40	10	1	2	58	27	22	17	0	23	0	1	5	6	0	1.00	4	.280	.345	.406
Navarro, Mandy#	2b	Daytona	ChC	A+	21	3	6	2	0	0	0	2	2	0	2	0	3	0	0	0	0	0	.00	0	.333	.500	.333
		Cubs	ChC	R	21	8	22	7	0	2	0	11	3	1	1	0	4	0	0	0	1	0	1.00	0	.318	.348	.500
		Boise	ChC	A-	21	30	96	22	5	0	2	33	10	11	10	0	17	1	1	2	1	1	.50	1	.229	.303	.344
Negron, Miguel*	of	Chston-WV	Tor	A	19	25	99	19	1	0	0	20	11	2	6	0	21	0	0	0	5	3	.63	2	.192	.238	.202
		Auburn	Tor	A-	19	50	186	47	6	1	1	58	27	13	15	1	22	2	2	1	7	4	.64	1	.253	.314	.312
Neill, Ryan	1b-of	W Michigan	Det	A	24	130	419	100	23	6	7	156	68	61	71	1	122	19	1	2	35	8	.81	4	.239	.372	.372
Nelson, Brad*	1b	Brewers	Mil	R	19	17	63	19	6	1	0	27	10	13	8	0	18	2	1	1	0	0	.00	1	.302	.392	.429
		Ogden	Mil	R+	19	13	42	11	4	0	0	15	5	10	3	0	9	0	0	2	0	0	.00	2	.262	.298	.357
Nelson, Bruce	c	New Jersey	StL	A-	23	16	40	10	1	1	0	13	6	3	2	0	6	0	1	0	2	1	.67	3	.250	.286	.325
Nelson, Chris	of	Billings	Cin	R+	22	8	30	7	1	0	0	8	4	2	1	0	7	0	0	0	0	0	.00	0	.233	.258	.267
Nelson, Eric#	2b	Wilmington	KC	A+	25	113	421	114	27	6	2	159	44	41	30	2	99	7	16	2	6	6	.50	6	.271	.328	.378
Nelson, John	of	New Jersey	StL	A-	23	66	252	60	16	3	8	106	43	26	35	3	76	3	4	5	14	3	.82	3	.238	.332	.421
Nelson, Nate	3b-1b	Lexington	Hou	A	25	19	64	15	1	0	0	16	3	6	1	0	10	0	1	1	2	3	.40	2	.234	.242	.250
		Pittsfield	Hou	A-	25	38	134	31	8	0	1	42	9	14	7	0	22	2	2	0	7	5	.58	7	.231	.280	.313
Nelson, Reggie	2b	Vero Beach	LA	A+	23	102	348	79	12	0	0	91	51	23	46	1	54	12	10	5	22	13	.63	7	.227	.333	.261
Nettles, Marcus*	of	Eugene	SD	A-	22	55	213	64	3	0	0	67	37	10	27	0	54	3	5	1	35	17	.67	2	.300	.385	.315
Nettles, Tim	of	Greensboro	NYY	A	25	3	11	4	0	0	0	4	0	1	0	0	3	0	0	0	0	0	.00	0	.364	.364	.364
		Yankees	NYY	R	25	3	0	0	0	0	0	0	0	0	0	0	0	0	0	0	0	0	.00	0	.000	.000	.000
		Tampa	NYY	A+	25	10	18	1	0	0	0	1	2	1	1	0	5	0	0	0	1	0	1.00	0	.056	.105	.056
Netwall, Chris	c	New Jersey	StL	A-	22	28	81	22	4	1	0	28	13	7	8	0	14	2	1	1	0	0	.00	3	.272	.348	.346
Neubart, Adam	of	Wilmington	KC	A+	24	26	55	10	3	0	0	13	13	5	6	0	13	4	1	1	0	2	.00	0	.182	.303	.236
Neufeld, Andy*	2b	Vancouver	Oak	A-	23	55	157	28	5	1	1	38	15	13	19	0	41	2	2	2	8	3	.73	4	.178	.272	.242
Nevels, Craig	dh	Missoula	Ari	R+	23	48	135	31	8	0	1	42	21	20	10	0	32	9	0	0	1	0	1.00	1	.230	.325	.311
Nevins, Ryan*	3b	Provo	Ana	R+	23	4	7	2	1	0	0	3	0	3	0	0	1	0	0	1	0	0	.00	0	.286	.250	.429
		Angels	Ana	R	23	25	82	27	4	4	0	39	12	17	5	1	15	1	0	0	1	2	.33	0	.329	.375	.476
Nichols, Leslie	1b	Yakima	Ari	A-	24	75	284	79	24	0	12	139	41	51	29	2	69	2	0	2	1	0	1.00	5	.278	.347	.489
Nichols, Tommy	1b	Princeton	TB	R+	18	43	151	31	4	1	1	40	14	18	6	0	51	2	1	0	1	0	1.00	4	.205	.245	.265
Nicholson, Tommy*	2b	Winston-Sal	CWS	A+	22	138	477	117	22	1	2	147	46	40	42	2	97	5	10	3	10	14	.42	7	.245	.311	.308
Nickerson, Brian	1b-3b	Great Falls	LA	R+	24	9	38	6	0	0	0	6	3	3	0	0	5	1	0	0	0	0	.00	1	.158	.179	.158
		Dodgers	LA	R	24	36	103	26	4	0	0	30	9	14	5	0	14	8	1	7	4	1	.80	6	.252	.317	.291
Nicolas, Jose	of	Hickory	Pit	A	23	31	102	21	7	1	3	39	13	10	9	0	41	2	0	1	3	0	1.00	0	.206	.281	.382
Niekro, Lance	3b	San Jose	SF	A+	23	42	163	47	11	0	3	67	18	34	4	0	14	0	0	4	4	2	.67	2	.288	.298	.411
Nieves, Raul#	2b	Augusta	Bos	A	23	114	390	96	13	0	1	112	49	37	26	1	75	6	11	4	12	2	.86	12	.246	.300	.287
Nina, Amuarys	of	Charlotte	Tex	A+	24	99	323	75	9	3	3	99	27	18	25	0	99	4	3	0	8	3	.73	6	.232	.295	.307
Nix, Jayson	ss	Casper	Col	R+	19	42	153	45	10	1	5	72	28	24	21	1	43	3	0	2	1	5	.17	1	.294	.385	.471
Nix, Laynce*	of	Savannah	Tex	A	21	104	407	113	26	8	8	179	50	59	37	2	94	2	1	5	9	6	.60	7	.278	.337	.440
		Charlotte	Tex	A+	21	9	37	11	3	1	0	16	4	2	1	0	13	0	0	0	0	0	.00	2	.297	.316	.432
Nixon, Jason	of	Burlington	Cle	R+	20	9	26	4	1	0	1	8	2	3	2	0	13	1	0	0	0	0	.00	0	.154	.241	.308
Noboa, Joel	of	Lowell	Bos	A-	22	46	155	28	2	0	5	45	16	19	1	0	60	2	0	0	4	2	.67	2	.181	.196	.290
Nolasco, Jose#	3b	Johnson Cty	StL	R+	21	55	191	39	7	0	3	55	25	22	22	0	48	1	5	0	8	3	.73	1	.204	.290	.288
Norris, Shawn*	3b	Vermont	Mon	A-	21	57	197	43	4	0	2	53	18	21	38	0	57	2	0	2	0	4	.00	2	.218	.347	.269
Nova, Willian#	2b	Brewers	Mil	R	20	25	80	17	2	1	1	24	7	8	7	0	22	0	4	2	2	0	1.00	0	.213	.270	.300
Noviskey, Josh#	of	Burlington	Cle	R+	19	38	114	16	2	0	0	18	10	4	23	0	50	1	0	0	1	1	.50	4	.140	.290	.158
Nowlin, Cody*	dh	Rangers	Tex	R	22	6	22	6	3	0	1	12	2	7	1	0	3	1	0	0	0	0	.00	1	.273	.333	.545
		Charlotte	Tex	A+	22	53	188	47	10	3	2	69	16	25	17	2	48	1	0	0	0	0	.00	6	.250	.316	.367
Nulton, Kevin	3b-2b	Idaho Falls	SD	R+	19	53	187	54	7	2	0	65	28	21	21	0	33	1	0	3	5	3	.63	8	.289	.358	.348
Nunez, Alexis*	2b	Twins	Min	R	21	4	11	2	0	0	0	2	1	0	0	0	1	0	0	0	0	0	.00	0	.182	.182	.182
		Elizabethtn	Min	R+	21	21	57	17	3	0	0	20	10	11	11	0	9	0	0	1	3	2	.60	1	.298	.406	.351

2001 Batting — Class-A and Rookie Leagues

BATTING																					BASERUNNING				PERCENTAGES		
Player	Pos	Team	Org	Lg	A	G	AB	H	2B	3B	HR	TB	R	RBI	TBB	IBB	SO	HBP	SH	SF	SB	CS	SB%	GDP	Avg	OBP	SLG
Nunez, Andres	3b	Yankees	NYY	R	19	55	180	41	2	1	1	48	21	15	21	1	28	4	1	4	5	1	.83	2	.228	.316	.267
Nunez, Argelis	of	South Bend	Ari	A	20	82	284	61	13	2	3	87	36	25	16	0	108	7	3	2	11	5	.69	6	.215	.272	.306
Nunez, Felix	1b-dh	Chston-SC	TB	A	19	103	361	67	12	1	7	102	28	32	7	0	141	2	3	2	2	7	.22	9	.186	.204	.283
Nunez, Manuel	ss	Vero Beach	LA	A+	22	16	44	6	1	0	1	10	5	5	3	0	21	0	3	0	0	1	.00	0	.136	.191	.227
		Great Falls	LA	R+	22	69	244	61	8	0	6	87	46	29	38	2	60	0	6	1	32	8	.80	5	.250	.350	.357
Oborn, Spencer	of	Winston-Sal	CWS	A+	24	120	402	110	25	2	3	148	54	37	20	0	64	2	11	3	13	3	.81	11	.274	.309	.368
O'Bradovich, Mark#	c	Pittsfield	Hou	A-	21	42	141	35	10	1	2	53	21	23	21	4	36	1	0	3	7	5	.58	2	.248	.343	.376
		Michigan	Hou	A	21	8	28	6	2	0	0	8	1	3	0	0	7	1	0	0	0	0	.00	0	.214	.241	.286
O'Brien, Kevin*	1b	Hudson Val	TB	A-	21	55	203	56	10	1	0	68	24	17	13	0	44	1	0	4	1	2	.33	4	.276	.317	.335
Ochoa, Ivan	ss	Burlington	Cle	R+	19	51	176	38	2	0	0	40	30	14	24	0	57	11	5	0	14	5	.74	1	.216	.346	.227
Ochoa, Javier	c	Columbus	Cle	A	23	51	173	39	7	0	0	46	21	15	15	0	24	3	3	2	2	1	.67	4	.225	.295	.266
O'Connell, Bradley	3b	Great Falls	LA	R+	24	23	84	26	3	2	2	39	12	11	3	0	16	5	1	0	3	3	.50	3	.310	.370	.464
O'Connor, Brian	c	Michigan	Hou	A	25	24	42	3	0	0	0	3	2	0	5	0	20	1	0	0	0	1	.00	1	.071	.188	.071
O'Donnell, Ryan*	of	Lk Elsinore	SD	A+	23	15	51	13	2	0	0	15	7	1	5	0	10	1	0	0	0	1	.00	0	.255	.333	.294
		Fort Wayne	SD	A	23	29	108	29	4	0	0	33	16	7	9	0	20	0	3	1	4	0	1.00	0	.269	.322	.306
Oetting, Todd	c	Reds	Cin	R	21	23	63	15	2	0	0	17	7	8	4	0	11	3	0	1	1	0	1.00	1	.238	.310	.270
Oh, Chul*	of	Red Sox	Bos	R	21	42	130	25	4	0	1	32	16	9	17	0	41	1	2	2	1	0	1.00	2	.192	.287	.246
O'Keefe, Mike*	of	Rancho Cuca	Ana	A+	24	115	409	135	25	5	15	215	75	91	42	2	81	1	1	6	20	1	.95	9	.330	.389	.526
O'Kelly, Mike	3b-1b	Danville	Atl	R+	23	52	165	33	12	1	3	56	14	22	9	1	60	2	4	1	0	0	.00	3	.200	.249	.339
Oletjen, Trent*	of	Twins	Min	R	19	44	133	43	7	3	0	56	21	18	14	0	15	3	2	4	10	3	.77	2	.323	.390	.421
		Elizabethtn	Min	R+	19	9	30	7	1	0	0	8	4	4	0	0	6	0	1	1	2	0	1.00	0	.233	.226	.267
Olivari, Reinaldo	3b	Rangers	Tex	R	21	54	203	47	14	4	2	75	24	27	12	2	45	3	2	0	8	5	.62	5	.232	.284	.369
Oliveros, Luis	c	Mariners	Sea	R	19	25	91	34	6	1	1	45	21	15	5	0	10	3	0	0	2	2	.50	2	.374	.424	.495
		Everett	Sea	A-	19	26	100	24	3	0	4	39	7	17	1	0	15	2	0	0	0	0	.00	2	.240	.262	.390
Olmedo, Ranier	ss	Mudville	Cin	A+	21	129	536	131	23	4	0	162	57	28	24	0	121	8	13	4	38	17	.69	15	.244	.285	.302
Olson, David	of	Idaho Falls	SD	R+	20	48	98	24	1	0	0	25	21	9	10	0	45	3	0	1	4	5	.44	0	.245	.330	.255
Olszta, Eddie	c	Everett	Sea	A-	23	27	74	12	2	0	0	14	5	4	3	0	34	1	3	0	3	1	.75	1	.162	.205	.189
Oropeza, Asdrubal	3b	Macon	Atl	A	21	109	362	75	18	0	8	117	37	40	38	0	105	4	3	1	4	5	.44	4	.207	.289	.323
Orr, Pete*	ss	Myrtle Bch	Atl	A+	23	92	317	74	10	1	4	98	38	23	19	0	70	11	3	1	17	6	.74	3	.233	.299	.309
Ortega, Felix	c	Phillies	Phi	R	20	20	56	14	4	1	1	23	10	9	12	0	15	2	1	1	0	0	.00	2	.250	.394	.411
Ortega, Sixto	c	Casper	Col	R+	22	10	37	12	1	0	1	16	4	5	2	0	7	1	0	0	0	1	.00	1	.324	.375	.432
		Tri-City	Col	A-	22	18	63	10	1	0	0	11	8	3	0	0	14	1	0	0	1	0	1.00	3	.159	.172	.175
Osborne, Mark*	dh	Fort Myers	Min	A+	24	47	137	30	4	0	3	43	14	8	21	2	36	1	0	1	1	1	.50	3	.219	.325	.314
Osborne, Steve	of	Yankees	NYY	R	23	1	2	0	0	0	0	0	0	0	0	0	0	0	0	0	0	0	.00	0	.000	.000	.000
		Tampa	NYY	A+	23	6	15	3	1	0	0	4	2	1	0	0	5	1	0	0	0	0	.00	2	.200	.250	.267
Pack, Branden#	c	Savannah	Tex	A	23	99	327	72	17	1	5	106	37	34	33	2	111	1	3	1	4	6	.40	6	.220	.293	.324
Padgett, Matt*	of-dh	Brevard Cty	Fla	A+	24	125	440	129	37	2	8	194	68	81	64	4	101	8	0	3	10	1	.91	9	.293	.390	.441
Padilla, Jorge	of	Clearwater	Phi	A+	22	100	358	93	13	2	16	158	62	66	40	4	73	7	0	3	23	6	.79	11	.260	.343	.441
Padilla, Juan	of	Vermont	Mon	A-	21	28	88	14	4	1	0	20	6	7	6	0	43	3	1	0	0	2	.00	0	.159	.237	.227
Pagan, Andres	c	Fort Wayne	SD	A	21	90	319	71	13	0	1	87	24	25	6	0	85	0	1	3	4	1	.80	9	.223	.235	.273
Pagan, Angel#	of	Capital Cty	NYM	A	20	15	57	17	1	1	0	20	4	5	6	0	5	0	1	0	3	2	.60	1	.298	.365	.351
		Brooklyn	NYM	A-	20	62	238	75	10	2	0	89	46	15	22	0	30	7	3	1	30	18	.63	3	.315	.388	.374
Parker, Chris	c	W Michigan	Det	A	22	74	237	60	13	0	1	76	25	22	23	0	46	8	4	2	2	1	.67	7	.253	.337	.321
Parnell, Sean	dh	Mariners	Sea	R	24	8	27	10	2	1	0	14	2	4	1	0	7	3	0	2	0	0	.00	0	.370	.424	.519
Parrish, Dave	c	Tampa	NYY	A+	23	115	367	93	25	0	6	136	43	49	54	1	88	5	4	2	2	1	.67	7	.253	.355	.371
Parrott, Corry	of	Ogden	Mil	R+	22	31	71	14	1	1	0	17	9	3	3	0	17	0	0	0	1	1	.50	1	.197	.230	.239
		Brewers	Mil	R	22	4	12	3	0	0	0	3	1	0	3	0	3	0	0	0	0	0	.00	0	.250	.400	.250
Parrott, Tom	1b	Jamestown	Atl	A-	21	42	117	30	5	1	1	40	17	8	15	0	39	1	1	1	3	1	.75	3	.256	.343	.342
Partridge, D.	of	Braves	Atl	R	18	26	83	17	2	0	2	25	13	9	6	0	26	2	1	1	3	1	.75	1	.205	.272	.301
Patchett, Gary	2b	Dayton	Cin	A	23	85	259	63	8	1	0	73	42	17	27	0	52	16	5	1	6	3	.67	4	.243	.350	.282
Patten, Chris	2b-3b	High Desert	Mil	A+	23	103	345	78	5	1	2	91	42	34	35	0	123	12	2	2	11	5	.69	10	.226	.317	.264
Patty, Jason*	ss	Pulaski	Tex	R+	22	53	177	48	4	3	5	73	26	32	10	0	47	11	1	2	6	3	.67	2	.271	.345	.412
Paula, Manuel	of	Billings	Cin	R+	21	49	170	46	7	4	3	70	24	23	12	0	53	5	1	2	5	3	.63	0	.271	.333	.412
Paulino, Robert	2b	Cubs	ChC	R	20	47	153	50	10	4	2	74	20	28	9	0	26	3	4	0	4	1	.80	0	.327	.376	.484
Paulino, Ron	c	Lynchburg	Pit	A+	21	103	352	102	16	1	6	138	30	51	36	0	76	2	3	7	4	1	.80	11	.290	.353	.392
Paulk, Barry*	of	Kingsport	NYM	R+	23	31	88	22	3	3	1	34	24	4	17	1	17	5	0	2	11	2	.85	0	.250	.393	.386
Pearl, Matt	of	New Jersey	StL	A-	23	22	54	15	3	0	0	18	6	6	6	0	6	2	0	0	4	1	.80	2	.278	.371	.333
Pearson, Shawn	of	Dunedin	Tor	A+	24	30	60	11	1	0	0	12	13	1	10	0	14	0	2	0	3	1	.75	0	.183	.300	.200
Peck, Bryan	of	Asheville	Col	A	24	72	214	58	13	0	5	86	48	26	47	0	51	6	0	4	7	2	.78	6	.271	.410	.402
Peguero, Miguel#	ss	W Michigan	Det	A	21	109	368	83	15	1	1	103	31	30	22	0	73	2	1	5	5	6	.45	10	.226	.270	.280
Peirce, Justin	of	Vancouver	Oak	A-	22	36	97	18	5	0	0	23	11	5	5	0	36	1	2	0	0	3	.00	3	.186	.233	.237
Peless, Sean*	1b	Mariners	Sea	R	21	45	159	50	6	1	1	61	21	18	14	1	47	2	0	0	1	1	.50	4	.314	.377	.384
Pena, Amaury	3b	Winston-Sal	CWS	A+	22	62	127	23	5	1	1	33	9	12	11	0	45	4	1	1	4	6	.40	4	.181	.266	.260
Pena, Brayan#	dh-c	Danville	Atl	R+	20	64	235	87	16	2	1	110	39	33	31	2	30	0	1	2	3	1	.75	5	.370	.440	.468
Pena, Rodolfo	c	Sarasota	Bos	A+	23	64	198	47	4	0	2	57	13	11	8	0	40	6	2	1	0	2	.00	4	.237	.286	.288
Pena, Tony	ss	Jamestown	Atl	A-	21	72	264	65	12	2	0	81	26	18	10	0	48	2	3	1	8	6	.57	7	.246	.278	.307
Pena, Wily Mo	of	Dayton	Cin	A	20	135	511	135	25	5	26	248	87	113	33	1	177	17	0	4	26	10	.72	6	.264	.327	.485
Peralta, John	ss	Kinston	Cle	A+	20	125	441	106	24	2	7	155	57	47	58	0	148	1	2	3	4	8	.33	9	.240	.328	.351
Perea, Jean	1b	Pulaski	Tex	R+	23	68	256	78	15	0	3	102	40	39	24	1	53	5	2	4	13	1	.93	6	.305	.370	.398
Pereyra, Joel	c	Royals	KC	R	19	21	66	12	3	0	0	15	6	0	3	0	21	1	0	0	0	0	.00	1	.182	.229	.227
Perez, Felipe	1b	Bluefield	Bal	R+	22	55	189	40	9	2	7	74	27	32	9	1	66	4	1	2	9	3	.75	1	.212	.260	.392
Perez, Jay#	c-dh	Casper	Col	R+	22	35	127	45	7	1	6	72	22	27	16	1	28	2	0	1	3	0	1.00	4	.354	.432	.567
Perez, Juan	of	Kingsport	NYM	R+	21	42	140	41	4	4	3	62	18	15	8	0	35	3	2	0	14	7	.67	0	.293	.344	.443
Perez, Kenny#	ss	Augusta	Bos	A	20	120	407	101	21	2	6	144	44	37	48	0	62	3	3	2	11	6	.65	9	.248	.330	.354
Perez, Nestor	ss	Bakersfield	TB	A+	25	118	407	98	16	3	0	120	44	37	27	0	57	2	9	3	11	4	.73	8	.241	.289	.295
Perez, Radhame	of-dh	Athletics	Oak	R	22	25	86	17	1	2	0	22	9	8	10	0	29	2	0	0	1	1	.50	1	.198	.296	.256
Perich, Josh	of	Capital Cty	NYM	A	22	89	297	72	11	3	7	110	32	38	23	0	78	2	2	0	6	2	.75	13	.242	.301	.370
Perkins, Kevin	2b	Brevard Cty	Fla	A+	24	56	195	46	3	1	6	69	25	18	15	1	45	8	0	0	0	4	.00	4	.236	.317	.354
Perozo, Hector	3b	Dodgers	LA	R	18	55	184	41	4	3	1	54	32	26	27	0	63	17	0	3	2	2	.50	2	.223	.368	.293
Perry, Rod	of	Batavia	Phi	A-	23	70	278	69	13	2	1	89	35	28	26	1	47	7	5	1	8	8	.50	3	.248	.327	.320
Peshke, Chad	3b	Mahoning Vy	Cle	A-	22	52	168	42	10	1	2	60	23	14	19	0	21	3	2	0	2	5	.29	6	.250	.337	.357
Peters, Samone	1b-dh	Dayton	Cin	A	23	120	452	93	20	0	28	197	61	78	29	2	158	8	0	2	2	2	.50	8	.206	.265	.436
Petersen, Ryan	3b	Red Sox	Bos	R	24	49	143	40	11	0	1	54	26	17	10	0	32	4	0	0	11	3	.79	2	.280	.344	.378
Peterson, Brian	c	Billings	Cin	R+	23	10	40	13	2	1	1	20	5	7	5	0	9	1	0	0	0	0	.00	1	.325	.413	.500
		Dayton	Cin	A	23	35	113	28	5	0	2	39	14	18	14	0	33	0	2	0	0	0	.00	1	.248	.331	.345

2001 Batting — Class-A and Rookie Leagues

						BATTING															BASERUNNING				PERCENTAGES		
Player	Pos	Team	Org	Lg	A	G	AB	H	2B	3B	HR	TB	R	RBI	TBB	IBB	SO	HBP	SH	SF	SB	CS	SB%	GDP	Avg	OBP	SLG
		Lowell	Bos	A-	23	8	27	7	2	0	0	9	5	6	6	0	3	2	0	0	5	0	1.00	0	.259	.429	.333
Phelps, Jeff	1b	Batavia	Phi	A-	23	40	133	30	7	1	2	45	18	16	10	1	35	0	0	1	2	0	1.00	3	.226	.278	.338
Phillips, Dan	of	Salem	Col	A+	23	132	493	129	35	0	16	212	65	68	27	2	106	14	5	6	11	12	.48	9	.262	.315	.430
Pichardo, Henry	2b	Kinston	Cle	A+	23	14	45	13	3	0	1	19	6	7	4	0	11	1	0	0	0	1	.00	3	.289	.360	.422
		Columbus	Cle	A	23	84	299	72	12	1	16	134	49	44	36	0	67	7	2	3	11	6	.65	4	.241	.333	.448
Pichardo, Maximo	2b	Rancho Cuca	Ana	A+	23	3	10	3	0	1	0	5	1	0	0	0	2	0	0	0	0	1	.00	1	.300	.300	.500
		Provo	Ana	R+	23	22	88	32	7	1	2	47	16	16	6	0	8	5	0	1	12	5	.71	2	.364	.430	.534
		Cedar Rapds	Ana	A	23	44	178	37	4	1	1	46	21	12	9	0	30	2	3	0	11	7	.61	3	.208	.254	.258
Pickens, Jordan	of	Idaho Falls	SD	R+	21	52	183	43	13	1	8	82	29	26	19	1	57	9	0	1	0	0	.00	2	.235	.335	.448
Pickering, Kelvin	c	Bluefield	Bal	R+	22	14	22	2	0	0	0	2	3	1	2	0	13	0	0	1	0	0	.00	1	.091	.160	.091
Pieper, William	1b	Spokane	KC	A-	24	37	106	15	1	1	1	21	8	8	14	1	43	2	0	0	0	1	.00	3	.142	.254	.198
Pierce, Sean	of	Great Falls	LA	R+	23	72	273	85	11	7	6	128	59	43	43	1	54	5	0	0	29	6	.83	5	.311	.414	.469
		Wilmington	LA	A	23	3	12	3	0	0	0	3	0	0	0	0	2	0	0	0	1	1	.50	0	.250	.250	.250
Piercy, Mike*	of	St. Lucie	NYM	A+	26	7	14	4	1	0	0	5	4	2	1	0	1	1	1	0	2	0	1.00	0	.286	.375	.357
		Brooklyn	NYM	A-	26	3	1	0	0	0	0	0	0	1	1	0	0	0	0	0	1	0	1.00	0	.000	.500	.000
Pilkington, Ross	of	Casper	Col	R+	20	41	129	29	9	0	1	41	19	9	19	1	34	2	1	1	0	5	.00	2	.225	.331	.318
Pimentel, Hector	3b	Jamestown	Atl	A-	23	53	181	49	8	3	5	78	22	24	7	0	39	3	2	2	6	2	.75	4	.271	.306	.431
Pinango, Ever#	of	Giants	SF	R	20	21	55	9	0	0	0	9	5	3	3	0	11	0	4	1	1	3	.25	2	.164	.203	.164
Pines, Gregory	dh	San Berndno	Sea	A+	23	18	34	7	0	0	0	7	1	4	2	0	8	0	2	0	0	0	.00	1	.206	.250	.206
Pinon, Alex	ss	Salem-Keizr	SF	A-	23	51	121	28	5	0	0	33	20	16	31	1	20	2	2	2	8	1	.89	1	.231	.391	.273
Pitney, Jared*	1b	Staten Ilnd	NYY	A-	23	3	7	0	0	0	0	0	0	0	1	0	6	0	0	0	1	0	1.00	0	.000	.125	.000
		Yankees	NYY	R	23	44	147	40	8	0	2	54	21	24	10	0	36	2	2	3	3	0	1.00	3	.272	.321	.367
Pittman, Richard#	ss-2b	Kingsport	NYM	R+	24	47	181	58	11	3	1	78	24	26	21	0	36	0	3	3	17	7	.71	3	.320	.385	.431
		Brooklyn	NYM	A-	24	5	12	4	0	0	0	4	0	0	1	0	5	0	0	0	0	0	.00	0	.333	.385	.333
Pittman, Thomas	dh	Jupiter	Mon	A+	22	78	281	60	7	3	4	85	31	37	23	1	83	6	0	0	2	2	.50	11	.214	.287	.302
Plasencia, F.*	of	Brewers	Mil	R	18	49	200	54	7	1	0	63	38	19	31	1	46	0	0	0	10	4	.71	2	.270	.368	.315
Pohle, Richard*	dh	Batavia	Phi	A-	23	50	187	45	12	0	5	72	24	30	17	1	22	0	0	3	0	1	.00	6	.241	.300	.385
Pollaro, Dallas	2b	Potomac	StL	A+	22	50	162	41	7	0	0	48	15	15	10	0	26	0	1	0	4	0	1.00	6	.253	.297	.296
Polo, Fernando	of	Braves	Atl	R	19	38	118	24	3	0	3	36	13	13	10	0	33	0	0	0	5	2	.71	1	.203	.266	.305
Porter, Greg	of	Provo	Ana	R+	21	39	127	42	3	1	10	77	34	34	18	1	21	1	0	2	3	1	.75	2	.331	.412	.606
Porzel, Alec	ss	Lowell	Bos	A-	23	44	172	44	10	2	1	61	16	19	13	0	19	1	1	1	2	1	.67	3	.256	.310	.355
Pospishil, Jason#	dh	Twins	Min	R	19	19	57	10	4	0	0	14	5	2	6	0	19	1	0	0	1	0	1.00	1	.175	.266	.246
Postell, Matt*	c	Kane County	Fla	A	25	34	95	27	6	0	3	42	16	6	11	0	36	1	0	0	2	2	.50	1	.284	.364	.442
Pregnalato, Bob	of	Beloit	Mil	A	24	81	259	64	30	1	0	96	43	19	24	0	57	3	8	1	11	1	.92	4	.247	.317	.371
Price, Jared	c	Dodgers	LA	R	20	33	94	9	1	0	0	10	10	5	14	0	41	6	2	1	0	2	.00	0	.096	.252	.106
Pride, Josh	dh-c	Tri-City	Col	A-	24	42	127	33	10	0	3	52	12	22	15	0	43	1	0	2	1	1	.50	2	.260	.338	.409
Prieto, Jon#	2b	Lynchburg	Pit	A+	22	115	395	83	12	2	1	102	41	32	37	1	76	6	2	4	21	7	.75	6	.210	.285	.258
Prince, Bryan	c	Billings	Cin	R+	23	51	157	40	12	1	3	63	26	25	17	1	36	2	1	0	2	1	.67	5	.255	.335	.401
Puccinelli, John	3b	Eugene	SD	A-	21	9	27	5	1	0	0	6	1	5	2	0	8	0	0	0	0	0	.00	0	.185	.241	.222
		Fort Wayne	SD	A	21	64	179	34	8	0	2	48	14	13	25	0	49	0	2	0	1	2	.33	2	.190	.289	.268
Quattlebaum, Hugh	3b	W Michigan	Det	A	24	121	415	99	26	4	3	142	63	55	68	0	68	10	0	6	8	4	.67	10	.239	.355	.342
Queroz, Pedro	3b-c	Cubs	ChC	R	20	49	164	47	9	1	2	64	24	21	13	1	18	3	2	2	8	3	.73	1	.287	.346	.390
Quickstad, Barry*	of	Elizabethtn	Min	R+	21	42	117	32	4	0	9	63	20	23	14	0	45	2	0	2	5	0	1.00	1	.274	.356	.538
Quintana, Miguel*	of	Mahoning Vy	Cle	A-	23	69	279	62	17	4	5	102	29	33	13	0	65	4	0	1	6	3	.67	6	.222	.266	.366
Quintana, Wil	of	San Berndno	Sea	A+	24	48	175	39	7	1	3	57	21	27	10	2	50	5	1	2	1	1	.50	4	.223	.281	.326
		Wisconsin	Sea	A	24	35	131	30	6	2	8	64	21	29	8	0	43	2	2	2	1	1	.50	4	.229	.280	.489
Quintin, Luis	of	Rangers	Tex	R	19	10	24	1	1	0	0	2	0	2	3	0	11	1	0	0	2	1	.67	0	.042	.179	.083
Quiroz, Guillermo	c	Chston-WV	Tor	A	20	82	261	52	12	0	7	85	25	25	29	0	67	6	7	0	5	1	.83	5	.199	.294	.326
Rabe, Josh	of	Quad City	Min	A	23	119	397	112	25	3	6	161	58	44	32	0	64	8	4	3	9	7	.56	9	.282	.345	.406
Rabelo, Mike#	c	Oneonta	Det	A-	22	53	194	63	4	2	0	71	27	32	23	0	45	4	0	1	1	2	.33	4	.325	.405	.366
Raburn, Johnny#	2b	Cedar Rapds	Ana	A	23	68	235	74	2	1	0	78	56	12	63	1	43	5	4	1	37	7	.84	1	.315	.467	.332
Raburn, Ryan	3b	Tigers	Det	R	21	19	58	9	2	0	1	14	4	5	9	1	19	3	0	0	2	1	.67	0	.155	.300	.241
		Oneonta	Det	A-	21	44	171	62	17	8	8	119	25	42	17	1	42	0	0	1	1	3	.25	7	.363	.418	.696
Rachels, Wes	dh	Frederick	Bal	A+	26	108	357	93	12	0	0	105	43	26	58	4	52	6	3	2	4	5	.44	8	.261	.371	.294
Rafael, Alberto	of	White Sox	CWS	R	20	17	29	4	1	0	0	5	2	2	1	0	16	0	0	0	1	0	1.00	0	.138	.167	.172
Raffo, John*	1b	Capital Cty	NYM	A	24	17	60	10	1	0	1	14	6	4	8	0	17	0	0	1	1	1	.50	2	.167	.261	.233
Ragsdale, Corey	ss	Kingsport	NYM	R+	19	22	69	10	3	2	1	20	9	5	9	0	36	1	0	0	4	4	.50	2	.145	.253	.290
Rainey, Jason*	of	San Berndno	Sea	A+	23	15	42	9	3	0	0	12	2	5	0	0	17	3	2	1	0	1	.00	0	.214	.261	.286
		Everett	Sea	A-	23	33	106	24	4	1	1	33	17	9	9	1	31	4	0	0	7	2	.78	2	.226	.311	.311
Ramirez, Alexander	ss-2b	Giants	SF	R	20	32	107	27	2	4	0	37	14	10	10	1	37	3	2	0	1	1	.50	1	.252	.333	.346
Ramirez, Jordy#	dh-p	Reds	Cin	R	22	2	3	0	0	0	0	0	0	0	0	0	2	0	0	0	0	0	.00	0	.000	.000	.000
Ramirez, Manuel	dh-c	Brewers	Mil	R	19	45	177	50	16	4	5	89	27	29	12	0	23	4	0	2	0	1	.00	3	.282	.338	.503
Ramistella, John	of	Yankees	NYY	R	20	53	180	49	11	1	5	77	30	33	21	1	48	6	0	0	5	2	.71	3	.272	.367	.428
		Greensboro	NYY	A	20	2	7	2	0	0	0	2	0	0	0	0	5	0	0	0	0	0	.00	0	.286	.286	.286
Ramos, Victor*	c	Pirates	Pit	R	20	29	80	16	2	0	0	18	5	4	6	0	10	1	1	1	0	1	.00	3	.200	.261	.225
Rapp, Travis	c-dh	Charlotte	Tex	A+	27	5	13	2	0	0	0	2	0	0	1	0	7	0	0	0	0	0	.00	0	.154	.214	.154
Ravelo, Manny	of	Hickory	Pit	A	20	93	365	109	12	7	1	138	57	20	28	0	64	6	3	1	54	17	.76	2	.299	.358	.378
		Lynchburg	Pit	A+	20	20	80	20	0	2	0	24	17	2	9	1	15	4	2	0	16	3	.84	2	.250	.355	.300
Raymundo, G.J.	3b	Rancho Cuca	Ana	A+	25	109	389	114	30	2	9	175	49	58	25	3	75	19	3	3	4	4	.50	15	.293	.362	.450
Recio, Bolivar	3b	Pirates	Pit	R	21	6	22	3	1	0	0	4	4	2	2	0	7	0	2	1	0	1	.00	0	.136	.200	.182
		Twins	Min	R	21	1	1	0	0	0	0	0	0	0	0	0	1	0	0	0	0	0	.00	0	.000	.000	.000
		Orioles	Bal	R	21	29	91	28	8	2	2	46	14	7	4	1	18	3	2	0	1	0	1.00	5	.308	.357	.505
Redman, Prentice	of	St. Lucie	NYM	A+	22	132	495	129	18	1	9	176	70	65	42	0	91	6	4	6	29	8	.78	7	.261	.322	.356
Reece, Eric*	1b-dh	Hudson Val	TB	A-	24	68	271	74	20	1	3	105	35	48	29	2	56	3	0	4	0	1	.00	5	.273	.345	.387
Reed, Robert	c	Lowell	Bos	A-	24	4	15	4	1	0	0	5	2	0	0	0	5	0	1	0	0	0	.00	0	.267	.267	.333
Reese, Kevin*	of	Fort Wayne	SD	A	24	125	459	151	30	6	13	232	84	73	54	3	62	5	2	4	30	10	.75	5	.329	.402	.505
Rengifo, Amado	of	Marlins	Fla	R	20	3	13	4	0	0	0	4	4	0	1	0	2	0	0	0	2	2	.50	0	.308	.357	.308
Renick, Josh	2b	Fort Myers	Min	A+	23	49	142	38	7	0	0	45	17	17	25	0	17	0	1	3	3	1	.75	5	.268	.371	.317
Repko, Jason	ss	Wilmington	LA	A	21	88	337	74	17	4	4	111	36	32	15	0	68	3	6	3	17	8	.68	2	.220	.257	.329
Requena, Alex#	of	Columbus	Cle	A	21	33	137	35	6	0	2	47	22	13	9	0	40	1	3	0	15	7	.68	0	.255	.306	.343
		Kinston	Cle	A+	21	62	259	55	7	4	2	76	30	13	19	1	80	4	3	0	32	10	.76	1	.212	.277	.293
Resop, Chris	of	Marlins	Fla	R	19	26	86	10	2	0	0	12	5	5	7	0	34	1	1	1	0	3	.00	4	.116	.189	.140
		Utica	Fla	A-	19	2	3	1	0	0	0	1	0	0	0	0	2	0	0	0	0	0	.00	0	.333	.333	.333
Rethwisch, Justin*	of	Pirates	Pit	R	21	39	135	26	8	0	0	34	11	11	5	0	41	1	0	1	4	1	.80	1	.193	.225	.252
Reyes, Ambiorix	ss-2b	Lakewood	Phi	A	23	72	267	76	7	1	0	85	30	16	13	1	33	1	6	1	13	8	.62	9	.285	.319	.318

2001 Batting — Class-A and Rookie Leagues

						BATTING															BASERUNNING				PERCENTAGES		
Player	Pos	Team	Org	Lg	A	G	AB	H	2B	3B	HR	TB	R	RBI	TBB	IBB	SO	HBP	SH	SF	SB	CS	SB%	GDP	Avg	OBP	SLG
		Clearwater	Phi	A+	23	27	95	29	2	0	0	31	17	7	5	0	12	1	0	0	7	1	.88	2	.305	.347	.326
Reyes, Christian#	3b	Modesto	Oak	A+	24	31	91	18	4	0	1	25	13	4	15	0	32	1	1	0	1	1	.50	2	.198	.318	.275
		Vancouver	Oak	A-	24	59	195	43	12	1	0	57	30	20	26	1	55	0	3	2	3	0	1.00	1	.221	.309	.292
Reyes, Deurys*	of	Fort Myers	Min	A+	22	95	263	63	10	1	0	75	47	20	41	0	80	1	7	4	12	3	.80	6	.240	.340	.285
Reyes, Eduardo	2b	Johnson Cty	StL	R+	20	19	42	8	2	0	1	13	5	4	2	0	15	1	0	2	0	1	.00	0	.190	.234	.310
Reyes, Guillermo#	ss	Kannapolis	CWS	A	20	71	280	78	8	5	0	96	49	26	27	1	30	2	2	2	29	8	.78	3	.279	.344	.343
		Winston-Sal	CWS	A+	20	59	216	45	4	1	0	51	24	24	14	0	33	5	4	1	16	4	.80	7	.208	.271	.236
Reyes, Henry#	ss	San Jose	SF	A+	19	7	24	8	1	1	1	14	1	5	0	0	7	0	2	0	1	0	1.00	0	.333	.333	.583
Reyes, Ivan	ss	Tampa	NYY	A+	21	3	4	2	0	0	1	5	2	1	3	0	1	0	0	0	0	0	.00	0	.500	.714	1.250
		Greensboro	NYY	A	21	51	170	42	9	1	7	74	17	23	20	0	58	1	1	2	3	2	.60	0	.247	.326	.435
Reyes, Jose#	ss	Capital Cty	NYM	A	19	108	407	125	22	15	5	192	71	48	18	0	71	2	5	3	30	10	.75	4	.307	.337	.472
Reyes, Jose#	3b	Athletics	Oak	R	22	42	158	43	4	2	0	51	25	9	15	0	40	7	2	1	13	9	.59	2	.272	.359	.323
Reyes, Julio*	of-dh	Bristol	CWS	R+	22	56	194	47	10	0	7	78	18	37	6	2	47	4	0	2	1	2	.33	7	.242	.277	.402
Reyes, Milver	c	Pirates	Pit	R	19	13	37	2	1	0	0	3	3	1	2	0	5	1	2	1	0	0	.00	0	.054	.122	.081
		Lynchburg	Pit	A+	19	9	29	3	0	0	0	3	2	1	2	0	7	1	0	0	0	0	.00	1	.103	.188	.103
Reyes, Rene#	of-1b	Asheville	Col	A	24	128	484	156	27	2	11	220	71	61	28	2	80	12	0	4	53	12	.82	9	.322	.371	.455
Reynoso, Danilo	c	Kingsport	NYM	R+	21	11	26	4	1	0	0	5	0	0	0	0	12	0	0	0	0	0	.00	0	.154	.154	.192
Rich, Dominic*	2b	Chston-WV	Tor	A	22	91	327	91	16	1	4	121	67	32	47	1	54	10	4	3	20	8	.71	3	.278	.382	.370
Richardson, Corey#	of	Lakeland	Det	A+	25	131	498	131	23	3	2	166	76	38	71	0	93	8	2	2	31	11	.74	5	.263	.363	.333
Richardson, Juan	3b	Lakewood	Phi	A	21	137	505	121	31	2	22	222	68	83	51	2	147	15	1	5	7	9	.44	13	.240	.325	.440
Richardson, Miguel	of	Everett	Sea	A-	21	23	76	21	4	1	2	33	8	11	5	0	25	1	0	0	2	0	1.00	1	.276	.329	.434
		Wisconsin	Sea	A	21	9	28	9	1	0	2	16	7	5	9	0	10	0	0	0	1	1	.50	0	.321	.486	.571
Rico, Matt	of	Hudson Val	TB	A-	20	46	154	34	5	0	1	42	21	16	12	0	34	2	0	1	1	1	.50	4	.221	.284	.273
Ridley, Shayne#	3b-1b	Delmarva	Bal	A	24	53	153	36	6	0	0	42	13	18	17	1	48	1	1	3	0	0	.00	4	.235	.310	.275
		Burlington	KC	A	24	7	20	1	0	0	0	1	0	1	4	0	8	0	0	1	0	1	.00	0	.050	.200	.050
Riepe, Andy	c	Sarasota	Bos	A+	25	5	11	2	0	0	0	2	2	1	1	0	2	0	0	0	0	0	.00	1	.182	.250	.182
		Augusta	Bos	A	25	33	107	25	2	0	0	27	11	17	13	0	23	1	1	1	0	0	.00	2	.234	.320	.252
Riera, Zack#	c	Hickory	Pit	A	23	34	98	14	4	0	0	18	11	6	9	0	21	11	2	0	0	1	.00	3	.143	.288	.184
		Williamsprt	Pit	A-	23	2	4	2	0	0	0	2	3	0	4	0	0	0	0	0	1	1	.50	0	.500	.750	.500
Rifkin, Aaron*	1b	Staten Ilnd	NYY	A-	23	69	245	78	19	5	10	137	41	49	31	0	47	2	2	5	3	2	.60	6	.318	.392	.559
Riggans, Shawn	c	Princeton	TB	R+	21	15	58	20	4	0	8	48	15	17	9	0	18	0	0	0	1	0	1.00	0	.345	.433	.828
Rigsby, Randy*	of	Brevard Cty	Fla	A+	25	95	320	87	15	3	3	117	41	38	22	1	62	7	1	4	14	5	.74	1	.272	.329	.366
Rijo, Carlos	3b	Orioles	Bal	R	19	53	201	56	10	4	1	77	18	23	6	2	32	2	3	1	8	3	.73	5	.279	.305	.383
Riley, Ryan	3b	Princeton	TB	R+	23	46	140	36	6	3	1	51	25	16	11	0	23	3	3	0	3	5	.38	1	.257	.325	.364
Riordan, Matt	of	Delmarva	Bal	A	24	59	210	47	8	0	2	61	29	21	15	1	38	2	0	5	5	0	1.00	2	.224	.276	.290
Rios, Alexis	of	Chston-WV	Tor	A	21	130	480	126	20	9	2	170	40	58	25	1	59	4	3	14	22	14	.61	16	.263	.296	.354
Rios, Fernando	of	Mudville	Cin	A+	23	114	426	118	16	4	4	154	57	49	34	1	45	3	2	1	6	5	.55	14	.277	.334	.362
Risinger, Ben	3b-c	Lk Elsinore	SD	A+	24	105	351	88	16	0	1	107	32	46	32	0	86	13	2	4	2	5	.29	9	.251	.333	.305
Rittenhous, Marc	2b	Utica	Fla	A-	23	40	128	30	6	0	3	45	21	12	16	1	43	3	1	0	0	1	.00	4	.234	.333	.352
Rivas, Arturo	of-dh	Bluefield	Bal	R+	18	11	34	5	0	0	0	5	4	2	5	0	13	2	0	1	4	0	1.00	0	.147	.286	.147
		Orioles	Bal	R	18	8	26	8	1	0	0	9	6	2	4	0	5	2	0	2	2	1	.67	0	.308	.412	.346
Rivas, Norberto	of	Clinton	Mon	A	20	7	27	4	0	0	1	7	2	2	0	0	9	0	0	0	0	1	.00	0	.148	.148	.259
		Expos	Mon	R	20	19	48	9	1	0	1	13	6	6	8	0	17	1	1	1	3	2	.60	0	.188	.310	.271
Rivera, Carlos	1b-dh	Phillies	Phi	R	20	24	71	10	2	0	0	12	3	5	2	0	30	0	0	0	0	0	.00	0	.141	.164	.169
Rivera, Erick	of	Batavia	Phi	A-	21	68	261	67	11	2	1	85	28	23	10	0	54	3	3	3	4	7	.36	3	.257	.289	.326
Rivera, Rene	c	Everett	Sea	A-	18	15	45	4	1	0	2	11	3	3	1	0	19	0	1	1	0	0	.00	1	.089	.106	.244
		Mariners	Sea	R	18	21	71	24	4	0	2	34	13	12	2	0	11	1	0	1	0	0	.00	0	.338	.360	.479
Rivera, William*	2b	Medcine Hat	Tor	R+	20	48	173	36	4	0	0	40	18	11	9	0	38	1	4	1	3	0	1.00	2	.208	.250	.231
Rivero, Luis	of	Phillies	Phi	R	21	38	128	32	7	1	1	44	17	11	9	0	27	2	2	0	4	1	.80	4	.250	.309	.344
Roat, Kyle	c	Jamestown	Atl	A-	22	33	107	23	5	0	0	28	10	4	10	0	32	1	1	0	2	0	1.00	2	.215	.288	.262
Roberson, Chris	of	Phillies	Phi	R	22	38	133	33	8	1	0	43	17	13	16	0	30	2	5	1	6	2	.75	3	.248	.336	.323
Roberts, Mike	of	Royals	KC	R	26	1	3	0	0	0	0	0	0	0	1	0	1	0	0	0	0	0	.00	0	.000	.250	.000
Robinson, Carlos	1b	Missoula	Ari	R+	20	43	122	30	8	1	3	49	12	28	6	0	25	2	0	1	0	2	.00	2	.246	.290	.402
Robison, Jordan	of	New Jersey	StL	A-	23	66	243	62	17	3	7	106	27	34	15	1	79	2	3	1	7	6	.54	4	.255	.303	.436
Rock, Jamie	of	Asheville	Col	A	24	30	106	21	6	0	1	30	8	17	3	0	25	1	2	2	1	1	.50	3	.198	.223	.283
Rodgers, Albert	1b-of	Peoria	StL	A	23	77	261	56	14	1	9	99	31	33	18	2	83	6	2	1	8	5	.62	4	.215	.280	.379
		Potomac	StL	A+	23	36	129	35	9	0	2	50	19	10	6	0	39	3	1	0	0	2	.00	4	.271	.319	.388
Rodgers, Mackeel#	of	Royals	KC	R	21	21	69	15	5	0	1	23	4	6	4	0	18	1	0	0	1	0	1.00	1	.217	.270	.333
		Burlington	KC	A	21	4	10	2	0	0	0	2	1	1	1	0	1	0	0	0	0	0	.00	0	.200	.273	.200
Rodriguez, Alex#	ss	Royals	KC	R	19	50	166	39	4	0	0	43	24	13	19	0	43	3	2	3	8	2	.80	1	.235	.319	.259
Rodriguez, Andres	1b	Kingsport	NYM	R+	21	26	86	28	8	0	2	42	10	10	5	0	22	0	0	1	2	1	.67	2	.326	.359	.488
Rodriguez, Carlos	of	Sarasota	Bos	A+	25	128	502	107	21	2	12	168	56	54	27	2	144	8	0	4	15	15	.50	21	.213	.262	.335
Rodriguez, Carlos#	ss	Phillies	Phi	R	18	35	128	38	10	1	3	59	22	23	11	1	25	4	0	1	6	4	.60	1	.297	.368	.461
Rodriguez, Elbi	3b	Brooklyn	NYM	A-	18	27	92	22	5	0	5	42	8	13	4	0	23	3	0	2	0	0	.00	3	.239	.287	.457
Rodriguez, Ivan	c	Red Sox	Bos	R	21	19	59	21	3	2	3	37	11	7	8	0	12	1	0	0	8	0	1.00	1	.356	.441	.627
		Lowell	Bos	A-	21	25	88	27	3	0	1	33	11	10	8	0	20	0	0	0	6	4	.60	1	.307	.365	.375
Rodriguez, Jeff	c	Myrtle Bch	Atl	A+	25	76	248	51	10	0	4	73	22	27	24	1	57	5	0	1	0	1	.00	6	.206	.288	.294
Rodriguez, Joe	dh-c	Wisconsin	Sea	A	24	39	109	25	6	0	3	40	9	22	11	0	33	6	2	2	2	2	.50	2	.229	.328	.367
Rodriguez, Jose#	2b	Orioles	Bal	R	22	5	17	3	1	0	0	4	0	0	2	0	4	0	0	0	0	0	.00	1	.176	.263	.235
		Bluefield	Bal	R+	22	22	34	5	0	1	0	7	3	4	5	0	15	0	1	0	2	1	.67	1	.147	.256	.206
Rodriguez, Luis#	ss-2b	Fort Myers	Min	A+	22	125	463	127	21	3	4	166	71	64	82	2	42	6	14	5	11	8	.58	14	.274	.387	.359
Rodriguez, Michael*	2b	Delmarva	Bal	A	23	26	57	11	0	0	0	11	3	2	6	0	16	1	1	1	3	0	1.00	2	.193	.277	.193
Rodriguez, Mike*	of	Pittsfield	Hou	A-	21	47	157	50	14	4	0	72	38	14	33	0	30	2	3	0	13	5	.72	0	.318	.443	.459
Rodriguez, Ricardo	ss	Macon	Atl	A	21	5	16	3	0	0	0	3	2	2	1	0	5	2	1	0	1	0	1.00	0	.188	.316	.188
		Danville	Atl	R+	21	58	231	44	5	2	2	59	30	14	17	0	62	7	3	0	12	5	.71	1	.190	.267	.255
Rodriguez, Ronny	c	Red Sox	Bos	R	21	1	1	0	0	0	0	0	0	0	0	0	0	0	0	0	0	0	.00	0	.000	.000	.000
Rodriguez, Serafin	of	Mudville	Cin	A+	23	58	200	48	9	1	2	65	22	25	8	0	27	2	5	2	0	0	.00	6	.240	.274	.325
Roenicke, Jarett*	of	Eugene	SD	A-	22	9	25	4	0	0	0	4	2	2	1	0	10	0	0	0	0	0	.00	0	.160	.192	.160
		Idaho Falls	SD	R+	22	24	84	24	2	0	0	26	10	6	5	0	25	0	0	0	0	0	.00	0	.286	.326	.310
Rogers, Brandon	c	Cedar Rapds	Ana	A	24	19	70	24	7	0	0	31	13	10	8	0	16	3	0	0	0	1	.00	1	.343	.432	.443
		Rancho Cuca	Ana	A+	24	24	76	16	4	0	1	23	4	11	6	0	20	1	0	1	0	1	.00	1	.211	.274	.303
Rogers, Omar	2b	Bluefield	Bal	R+	19	63	226	73	12	1	2	93	41	32	29	1	41	10	1	2	22	10	.69	4	.323	.419	.412
Rogowski, Casey*	1b	Kannapolis	CWS	A	21	130	439	126	18	3	14	192	66	69	62	3	95	7	0	3	16	8	.67	6	.287	.382	.437
Rojas, Randy	2b	Martinsvlle	Hou	R+	22	62	223	56	10	2	2	76	23	19	12	1	36	9	7	5	17	7	.71	3	.251	.309	.341
Rojas, Tom	c	Tampa	NYY	A+	20	1	0	0	0	0	0	0	0	0	0	0	0	0	0	0	0	0	.00	0	.000	.000	.000

2001 Batting — Class-A and Rookie Leagues

BATTING																					BASERUNNING				PERCENTAGES		
Player	Pos	Team	Org	Lg	A	G	AB	H	2B	3B	HR	TB	R	RBI	TBB	IBB	SO	HBP	SH	SF	SB	CS	SB%	GDP	Avg	OBP	SLG
		Yankees	NYY	R	20	25	66	23	6	0	0	29	12	8	7	1	10	1	0	0	2	1	.67	1	.348	.419	.439
		Greensboro	NYY	A	20	1	3	1	0	0	0	1	0	0	0	0	2	0	0	0	0	0	.00	0	.333	.333	.333
Rollins, Antwon	of	Pulaski	Tex	R+	22	65	240	61	15	2	12	116	43	37	16	0	80	6	1	2	18	1	.95	2	.254	.314	.483
Roman, Jesse*	1b	New Jersey	StL	A-	23	71	255	69	16	3	3	100	39	39	51	2	39	2	0	1	5	5	.50	3	.271	.395	.392
Rombley, Danny	of	Clinton	Mon	A	22	35	136	26	5	1	1	36	14	9	7	0	35	1	1	0	9	1	.90	2	.191	.236	.265
		Vermont	Mon	A-	22	70	267	56	4	2	0	64	42	12	19	0	70	6	3	1	19	12	.61	1	.210	.276	.240
Romero, Nicholas	of	Eugene	SD	A-	22	55	179	39	8	3	1	56	24	19	18	0	75	0	0	0	8	2	.80	0	.218	.289	.313
Rooi, Vince	3b	Clinton	Mon	A	20	120	422	107	22	0	9	156	53	60	61	1	94	4	0	6	5	4	.56	12	.254	.349	.370
Rooke, Brian	of	Vancouver	Oak	A-	22	47	108	16	5	1	0	23	12	8	16	0	43	4	4	2	9	4	.69	1	.148	.277	.213
Roper, Chad	3b	Charlotte	Tex	A+	28	42	143	30	9	0	2	45	13	14	14	0	31	0	0	0	0	0	.00	5	.210	.280	.315
Roper, Zach	dh	Cedar Rapds	Ana	A	24	124	471	146	27	2	15	222	64	87	29	2	82	13	2	4	8	3	.73	18	.310	.364	.471
Rosa, Wally	c	Kannapolis	CWS	A	20	98	305	69	14	0	4	95	27	23	13	0	88	9	4	1	6	6	.50	11	.226	.277	.311
Rosado, Francisco	of	Tigers	Det	R	20	34	98	18	4	0	2	28	9	4	13	0	26	3	0	0	2	0	1.00	2	.184	.298	.286
Rosario, Carlos#	2b	Visalia	Oak	A+	22	116	441	115	15	3	6	154	91	42	73	0	98	2	6	3	54	24	.69	6	.261	.366	.349
Rosario, Melvin*	of	Asheville	Col	A	23	102	276	63	4	0	0	67	44	18	44	0	89	6	2	2	23	13	.64	6	.228	.345	.243
Rosario, Vicente	of	Everett	Sea	A-	24	33	136	34	7	1	0	43	22	6	12	0	29	9	1	0	17	6	.74	3	.250	.350	.316
Rosario, Victor*	of	Spokane	KC	A-	21	69	247	60	5	5	3	84	36	24	28	0	63	0	2	1	18	3	.86	2	.243	.319	.340
Ross, Cody	of	Lakeland	Det	A+	21	127	482	133	34	5	15	222	84	80	44	0	96	5	6	9	28	5	.85	9	.276	.337	.461
Ross, Don*	1b	Wilmington	KC	A+	24	134	459	96	18	1	13	155	60	59	62	4	159	16	5	5	3	0	1.00	10	.209	.321	.338
Rouse, Mike*	2b-ss	Dunedin	Tor	A+	22	48	180	49	17	2	5	85	27	24	13	0	45	2	6	1	3	1	.75	2	.272	.327	.472
Rowan, Chris	3b	High Desert	Mil	A+	23	90	320	71	15	5	13	135	45	44	12	0	124	8	2	0	7	3	.70	2	.222	.268	.422
Royer, Lissandro	3b	Capital Cty	NYM	A	20	35	102	27	3	0	0	30	15	7	10	0	15	1	1	0	4	4	.50	1	.265	.336	.294
Rudecindo, Carlos	2b	Marlins	Fla	R	19	3	9	0	0	0	0	0	0	1	1	0	7	0	0	0	0	0	.00	0	.000	.100	.000
Rueffert, Mark	1b	Oneonta	Det	A-	23	24	68	15	1	0	0	16	6	3	13	0	26	0	0	0	1	1	.50	2	.221	.346	.235
Ruelas, Alonzo	c	Braves	Atl	R	21	47	134	37	10	0	2	53	16	12	12	0	16	3	0	1	6	0	1.00	3	.276	.347	.396
Ruiz, Carlos	c-dh	Lakewood	Phi	A	22	73	249	65	14	3	4	97	21	32	10	0	27	1	1	2	5	4	.56	5	.261	.290	.390
Ruiz, Daniel	ss-dh	Danville	Atl	R+	22	23	78	19	7	0	0	26	9	6	4	1	15	2	2	0	2	0	1.00	0	.244	.298	.333
		Jamestown	Atl	A-	22	9	28	7	1	0	0	8	3	1	1	0	5	0	0	0	0	0	.00	0	.250	.276	.286
Ruiz, Junior*	2b	Reds	Cin	R	22	45	149	43	4	3	0	53	31	12	33	1	17	2	0	0	13	3	.81	2	.289	.424	.356
		Billings	Cin	R+	22	5	9	0	0	0	0	0	1	0	4	0	0	2	0	0	0	0	.00	1	.000	.400	.000
Ruiz, Randy	1b-dh	Dayton	Cin	A	24	123	466	125	34	3	20	225	82	92	48	4	116	14	0	3	21	9	.70	10	.268	.352	.483
Ruiz, Reinaldo	c	Martinsvlle	Hou	R+	22	46	168	44	5	0	4	61	15	18	8	0	27	3	1	2	0	1	.00	1	.262	.304	.363
		Lexington	Hou	A	22	3	5	1	0	0	0	1	0	1	0	0	0	0	0	0	0	0	.00	0	.200	.200	.200
Ruiz, Willy	3b-2b	Wilmington	KC	A+	23	105	337	81	6	0	0	87	45	30	29	0	44	0	7	3	26	13	.67	8	.240	.298	.258
Rundgren, Rex	ss	Utica	Fla	A-	21	55	195	49	5	1	3	65	15	25	5	0	33	2	2	2	3	5	.38	3	.251	.275	.333
Rush, Travis	dh	Pirates	Pit	R	20	33	82	20	5	1	1	30	4	5	12	0	16	3	1	0	5	2	.71	0	.244	.361	.366
Russell, Mike	c	Delmarva	Bal	A	20	17	45	12	2	0	1	17	4	7	3	0	16	0	0	0	0	0	.00	1	.267	.313	.378
		Bluefield	Bal	R+	20	10	32	9	2	0	2	17	7	6	2	0	7	1	0	0	1	0	1.00	2	.281	.343	.531
Ryan, Billy	3b	Oneonta	Det	A-	20	11	33	6	0	0	0	6	2	4	1	0	7	4	3	0	1	0	1.00	0	.182	.289	.182
		Tigers	Det	R	20	20	57	14	1	0	0	15	7	5	10	0	10	4	0	1	0	0	.00	1	.246	.389	.263
Ryan, Kelvin	of	Bakersfield	TB	A+	23	103	363	96	26	1	6	142	46	36	9	0	83	16	3	1	4	2	.67	7	.264	.311	.391
Saba, Cesar#	3b	Fort Wayne	SD	A	20	84	291	65	10	1	6	95	29	31	21	2	61	4	2	3	2	6	.25	6	.223	.282	.326
Sadler, Ray	of	Lansing	ChC	A	21	94	378	129	27	3	10	192	74	50	22	3	58	3	1	4	18	7	.72	3	.341	.378	.508
Sain, Greg	1b	Eugene	SD	A-	22	67	256	75	19	1	16	144	48	40	21	2	68	5	0	2	1	2	.33	2	.293	.356	.563
St. Clair, Jason	2b	Princeton	TB	R+	19	32	116	28	6	1	0	36	16	8	2	0	25	3	1	3	1	4	.20	3	.241	.266	.310
St. Pierre, Maxim	c	Lakeland	Det	A+	22	99	330	82	15	0	4	109	42	43	43	1	50	4	0	5	2	5	.29	11	.248	.338	.330
Salas, Francisco	2b	Cubs	ChC	R	19	15	51	18	2	0	1	23	12	4	2	0	8	3	0	0	3	1	.75	0	.353	.411	.451
Salas, Jose#	c	Macon	Atl	A	20	12	38	6	2	0	0	8	0	3	0	0	11	1	0	1	1	0	1.00	2	.158	.175	.211
		Braves	Atl	R	20	3	4	1	0	0	0	1	0	0	0	0	0	0	0	0	0	0	.00	0	.250	.250	.250
Salas, Juan	3b	Chston-SC	TB	A	20	135	500	114	25	3	7	166	53	62	17	1	93	4	1	8	9	15	.38	11	.228	.255	.332
Salas, Michael#	dh-c	Jamestown	Atl	A-	18	37	129	28	8	0	2	42	8	17	9	0	21	4	1	2	0	1	.00	2	.217	.285	.326
Salazar, Juan#	2b	Red Sox	Bos	R	20	46	161	40	2	0	0	42	23	12	15	1	12	3	1	1	16	7	.70	1	.248	.322	.261
		Lowell	Bos	A-	20	7	26	7	0	0	0	7	1	4	3	0	4	2	0	1	2	2	.50	0	.269	.375	.269
Salvesen, Matt*	1b	Bristol	CWS	R+	22	2	8	0	0	0	0	0	0	0	0	0	4	0	0	0	0	0	.00	0	.000	.000	.000
Salvo, Andrew*	2b	Bristol	CWS	R+	22	62	209	61	11	0	3	81	36	34	27	1	23	6	0	3	14	6	.70	4	.292	.384	.388
Sanchez, Angel	ss-3b	Royals	KC	R	18	30	95	23	4	0	0	27	10	6	6	0	28	0	2	0	3	1	.75	2	.242	.287	.284
Sanchez, Danilo	c	Tigers	Det	R	21	38	108	20	2	0	4	34	15	17	17	0	27	6	0	1	2	0	1.00	4	.185	.326	.315
Sanchez, Tino#	c	Salem	Col	A+	23	91	283	66	9	0	3	84	32	26	32	2	30	3	2	2	4	4	.50	6	.233	.316	.297
Sandberg, Eric*	1b	Fort Myers	Min	A+	22	81	274	64	11	1	2	83	37	33	35	2	50	5	1	0	0	1	.00	9	.234	.331	.303
		Quad City	Min	A	22	42	166	53	8	2	4	77	28	23	16	1	25	4	1	1	1	1	.50	2	.319	.390	.464
Sandoval, Abigail	dh-ss	Rangers	Tex	R	20	36	111	23	3	2	1	33	14	9	3	0	20	1	1	1	3	2	.60	2	.207	.233	.297
Sandoval, Jhensy	dh	South Bend	Ari	A	23	9	35	7	1	0	2	14	6	5	4	0	13	0	0	1	0	0	.00	1	.200	.275	.400
Sandoval, Jjallil#	2b	Pittsfield	Hou	A-	22	23	58	11	2	0	0	13	9	2	9	0	19	1	0	0	3	2	.60	0	.190	.309	.224
Sandoval, Michael	3b	Quad City	Min	A	20	47	153	34	6	0	1	43	18	22	11	0	32	2	1	3	2	0	1.00	7	.222	.278	.281
Santa, Alexander*	of	Yankees	NYY	R	19	52	179	47	1	4	2	62	32	16	23	1	52	3	2	0	10	5	.67	0	.263	.356	.346
		Greensboro	NYY	A	19	3	9	0	0	0	0	0	0	0	0	0	1	0	0	0	0	0	.00	2	.000	.000	.000
Santamarina, Juan*	3b	Bristol	CWS	R+	22	10	27	7	1	1	1	13	4	3	7	0	8	0	0	0	0	1	.00	0	.259	.412	.481
		Kannapolis	CWS	A	22	13	27	7	2	0	3	18	5	6	0	0	9	0	0	0	0	0	.00	1	.259	.259	.667
		Winston-Sal	CWS	A+	22	17	60	12	2	0	2	20	9	8	3	0	16	0	1	0	0	0	.00	0	.200	.238	.333
Santana, E.*	1b	Everett	Sea	A-	21	68	250	67	13	3	6	104	35	49	24	2	47	5	1	1	0	2	.00	2	.268	.343	.416
Santana, Hector	c	Burlington	Cle	R+	19	29	103	20	3	2	2	33	7	8	7	0	45	0	1	0	0	1	.00	1	.194	.245	.320
Santana, Juan#	2b	Tigers	Det	R	21	7	28	10	2	0	0	12	6	1	2	0	6	0	0	0	1	0	1.00	1	.357	.400	.429
Santana, M.	1b	Bristol	CWS	R+	20	41	143	38	5	1	3	54	26	15	8	0	36	1	0	1	2	1	.67	1	.266	.307	.378
Santana, Pedro	of	Tampa	NYY	A+	23	17	54	13	3	0	1	19	4	6	2	0	17	3	0	0	1	1	.50	1	.241	.305	.352
		Yankees	NYY	R	23	15	48	19	3	1	1	27	6	10	1	0	7	0	0	0	3	1	.75	2	.396	.408	.563
		Greensboro	NYY	A	23	6	19	2	1	0	0	3	2	0	0	0	2	2	0	0	0	0	.00	0	.105	.190	.158
Santana, Ralph*	2b	Ogden	Mil	R+	21	68	261	88	6	1	1	99	57	26	37	1	37	3	2	0	30	12	.71	3	.337	.425	.379
Santana, Roberto*	1b	Braves	Atl	R	19	48	138	31	4	0	1	38	15	14	11	0	21	2	2	2	1	0	1.00	2	.225	.288	.275
Santana, Sandy	2b	Peoria	StL	A	21	65	197	40	7	1	1	52	19	17	7	0	36	6	2	3	5	5	.50	5	.203	.249	.264
Santiago, Ramon#	dh	Lakeland	Det	A+	20	120	429	115	15	3	2	142	64	46	54	0	60	11	14	4	34	8	.81	7	.268	.361	.331
Santini, Travis	of	Mahoning Vy	Cle	A-	21	34	117	25	9	0	3	43	9	13	1	0	30	0	0	0	0	1	.00	1	.214	.220	.368
Santor, John#	1b-3b	New Jersey	StL	A-	20	54	185	42	12	2	2	64	17	26	22	0	64	0	0	1	3	2	.60	4	.227	.308	.346
Santoro, Pat	2b	Sarasota	Bos	A+	23	106	335	69	10	1	10	111	44	35	30	1	112	4	5	1	3	4	.43	6	.206	.278	.331
Santos, Chad*	1b	Burlington	KC	A	21	121	444	112	32	0	16	192	58	83	52	4	101	6	1	3	0	1	.00	14	.252	.337	.432
Santos, Deivis*	1b	Hagerstown	SF	A	22	131	520	151	27	3	12	220	64	80	25	6	91	4	0	5	16	10	.62	15	.290	.325	.423

2001 Batting — Class-A and Rookie Leagues

						BATTING															BASERUNNING				PERCENTAGES		
Player	Pos	Team	Org	Lg	A	G	AB	H	2B	3B	HR	TB	R	RBI	TBB	IBB	SO	HBP	SH	SF	SB	CS	SB%	GDP	Avg	OBP	SLG
Santos, Jose	3b	Brevard Cty	Fla	A+	24	121	411	109	22	0	18	185	73	81	78	3	93	11	0	7	10	5	.67	12	.265	.391	.450
Santos, Juan#	c	Lakeland	Det	A+	24	23	62	10	2	1	1	17	7	4	3	1	18	0	0	1	0	0	.00	2	.161	.197	.274
Santos, Luis	3b	Lancaster	Ari	A+	23	14	37	7	0	0	0	7	4	1	1	0	2	0	0	0	0	0	.00	2	.189	.211	.189
Santos, Omir	c	Staten Ilnd	NYY	A-	21	44	117	32	5	1	0	39	11	8	6	0	25	1	1	2	0	1	.00	2	.274	.310	.333
Santos, Sneideer*	of	Yakima	Ari	A-	22	31	81	14	2	2	2	26	11	10	7	0	32	0	0	0	1	1	.50	0	.173	.239	.321
Sardinha, Bronson*	ss	Yankees	NYY	R	19	55	188	57	14	3	4	89	42	27	28	2	51	3	1	2	11	2	.85	6	.303	.398	.473
Sardinha, Dane	c	Mudville	Cin	A+	23	109	422	99	24	2	9	154	45	55	12	2	97	3	4	4	0	1	.00	12	.235	.259	.365
Sassanella, Justin*	of	Kingsport	NYM	R+	19	20	64	11	2	0	0	13	7	5	8	0	29	0	1	1	4	3	.57	1	.172	.260	.203
Sato, G.G.	c	Batavia	Phi	A-	23	37	138	36	10	3	4	64	22	21	6	1	33	1	2	0	2	1	.67	2	.261	.297	.464
Saucke, Casey	2b	Delmarva	Bal	A	24	20	45	9	2	0	0	11	4	5	7	0	20	0	1	0	0	1	.00	1	.200	.308	.244
Scales, Bobby#	2b	Lk Elsinore	SD	A+	24	98	362	98	24	4	5	145	46	42	44	1	78	10	1	0	20	7	.74	7	.271	.365	.401
Scanlon, Matt*	3b	Fort Myers	Min	A+	24	107	348	88	12	2	3	113	39	35	43	4	67	3	3	0	2	1	.67	6	.253	.340	.325
Scarborough, Steve	2b-ss	High Desert	Mil	A+	24	138	546	139	36	4	14	225	101	91	65	1	126	5	9	7	21	6	.78	8	.255	.335	.412
Schader, Troy	3b	Lk Elsinore	SD	A+	25	94	363	88	17	4	14	155	55	55	28	1	111	6	0	1	1	4	.20	6	.242	.307	.427
Schmidt, J.P.*	of-2b	Vancouver	Oak	A-	22	32	122	36	9	2	0	49	18	10	9	1	24	0	0	0	7	4	.64	0	.295	.344	.402
		Visalia	Oak	A+	22	18	63	17	3	0	0	20	5	7	4	0	13	0	0	0	3	2	.60	4	.270	.313	.317
Schmitt, Billy	dh-3b	New Jersey	StL	A-	19	62	238	58	9	3	2	79	14	37	9	2	59	1	0	4	1	2	.33	9	.244	.270	.332
Schmitt, Brian*	1b	Lexington	Hou	A	23	99	376	91	22	3	9	146	51	50	31	2	100	9	0	1	5	8	.38	2	.242	.314	.388
Schnabel, Nick	2b	Vermont	Mon	A-	24	27	83	17	2	0	0	19	11	6	17	0	13	3	3	0	6	2	.75	1	.205	.359	.229
		Clinton	Mon	A	24	16	39	10	2	0	0	12	4	2	4	0	7	1	1	0	0	0	.00	1	.256	.341	.308
Schneidmiller, Gary	3b	Visalia	Oak	A+	22	113	374	104	17	4	3	138	60	34	53	0	83	7	2	3	12	8	.60	9	.278	.375	.369
Schrock, Chris	3b	Bakersfield	TB	A+	26	94	320	78	16	0	0	94	38	24	18	0	51	3	9	1	3	3	.50	10	.244	.289	.294
Schuda, Justin*	1b-dh	Chston-SC	TB	A	21	127	430	103	15	0	25	193	56	71	65	6	166	12	2	4	2	2	.50	4	.240	.352	.449
Schumaker, Skip*	of	New Jersey	StL	A-	22	49	162	41	10	1	0	53	22	14	29	1	33	1	2	1	11	2	.85	4	.253	.368	.327
Scott, Bill	1b	High Desert	Mil	A+	23	132	513	145	42	1	16	237	73	102	50	2	135	8	1	9	9	11	.45	15	.283	.350	.462
Scott, Charlie	c-dh	Mahoning Vy	Cle	A-	24	6	15	2	0	0	0	2	0	1	1	0	3	0	0	1	0	0	.00	0	.133	.176	.133
		Burlington	Cle	R+	24	11	33	7	0	0	3	16	5	6	4	0	12	0	0	0	0	1	.00	1	.212	.297	.485
Scott, Ed	of	Chston-SC	TB	A	22	3	2	0	0	0	0	0	1	0	0	0	1	0	0	0	0	0	.00	0	.000	.000	.000
Scott, Mike*	of	Oneonta	Det	A-	23	2	3	0	0	0	0	0	0	1	0	0	2	0	0	0	0	0	.00	0	.000	.000	.000
Seale, Marvin#	of	St. Lucie	NYM	A+	23	129	479	114	24	4	10	176	72	38	61	0	127	10	5	2	37	18	.67	3	.238	.335	.367
Searage, Ray	of	Marlins	Fla	R	21	12	34	3	0	0	0	3	4	1	3	0	10	0	0	0	0	1	.00	1	.088	.162	.088
Seestedt, Mike	c	Delmarva	Bal	A	24	90	231	51	9	0	1	63	28	18	39	0	37	9	4	1	0	0	.00	7	.221	.354	.273
Seever, Brian	of	Angels	Ana	R	25	5	17	7	0	1	0	9	5	1	0	0	2	0	0	0	1	1	.50	0	.412	.412	.529
		Cedar Rapds	Ana	A	25	45	166	37	6	1	1	48	25	14	31	0	34	2	3	2	14	7	.67	1	.223	.348	.289
Segar, Jeff	of	Staten Ilnd	NYY	A-	23	34	116	31	14	0	1	48	16	21	9	2	18	1	1	3	4	1	.80	3	.267	.318	.414
		Greensboro	NYY	A	23	27	84	14	2	2	0	20	5	9	8	0	19	0	1	2	0	0	.00	3	.167	.234	.238
Segura, Rolando	dh	Fort Wayne	SD	A	23	12	46	9	0	0	0	9	3	2	2	0	9	1	0	1	0	0	.00	2	.196	.240	.196
Seiber, Antron	of	Augusta	Bos	A	22	120	462	103	16	3	5	140	59	27	50	1	113	8	7	2	36	12	.75	5	.223	.308	.303
Self, Todd*	of	Pittsfield	Hou	A-	23	73	261	79	13	4	3	109	52	49	46	3	61	2	1	6	10	6	.63	2	.303	.403	.418
Selmo, Francisco	c	Idaho Falls	SD	R+	20	53	197	54	15	1	3	80	22	26	14	0	42	0	0	1	4	0	1.00	2	.274	.321	.406
Selmo, Wilson#	ss	Angels	Ana	R	19	48	183	55	5	2	0	64	23	21	1	0	24	4	4	3	10	0	1.00	0	.301	.314	.350
Senjem, Guye*	c	Mudville	Cin	A+	27	42	141	50	9	1	10	91	25	32	22	1	31	1	1	1	0	1	.00	0	.355	.442	.645
Sequea, Jorge#	2b	Lakeland	Det	A+	21	104	328	81	16	1	6	117	39	54	32	0	47	5	8	6	9	7	.56	1	.247	.318	.357
Serafini, Matt	c	Ogden	Mil	R+	22	20	62	10	1	0	2	17	6	4	4	0	8	0	0	0	1	0	1.00	2	.161	.212	.274
		Brewers	Mil	R	22	20	74	26	6	0	7	53	16	24	6	0	19	0	0	2	0	0	.00	1	.351	.390	.716
		Beloit	Mil	A	22	4	19	2	0	0	0	2	2	0	0	0	3	0	0	0	0	0	.00	1	.105	.105	.105
Serrano, Eddie	2b-3b	Eugene	SD	A-	20	7	17	5	1	0	1	9	2	1	2	0	5	1	0	0	0	0	.00	0	.294	.400	.529
		Idaho Falls	SD	R+	20	20	68	22	2	0	2	30	9	10	2	0	20	2	0	2	1	0	1.00	1	.324	.351	.441
Serrano, Ray	c	Macon	Atl	A	21	63	215	43	10	0	4	65	20	27	11	0	37	0	2	1	2	0	1.00	2	.200	.238	.302
Serrano, Sammy	c	San Jose	SF	A+	25	39	139	29	12	1	1	46	14	12	7	1	38	1	1	2	0	0	.00	3	.209	.248	.331
Servais, Eric*	3b-dh	Boise	ChC	A-	22	36	106	26	5	2	2	41	9	12	11	1	29	1	1	1	0	1	.00	1	.245	.319	.387
Severino, Wanell	2b	Orioles	Bal	R	19	34	125	38	5	0	0	43	21	16	6	0	17	1	1	1	8	5	.62	1	.304	.338	.344
Shaffer, Josh*	ss	Rancho Cuca	Ana	A+	22	58	193	54	7	2	2	71	17	20	11	2	34	1	4	0	2	4	.33	0	.280	.322	.368
Shanks, James	of	Spokane	KC	A-	23	67	251	74	7	3	0	87	39	13	21	0	50	6	10	2	24	5	.83	2	.295	.361	.347
Shelley, Randall	3b	Pulaski	Tex	R+	22	67	233	58	18	1	9	105	47	43	35	0	81	8	0	2	8	2	.80	1	.249	.363	.451
Shelton, Chris	c	Williamsprt	Pit	A-	22	50	174	53	11	0	2	70	22	33	33	1	31	2	1	3	4	1	.80	1	.305	.415	.402
Sherlock, Jon	c	Missoula	Ari	R+	20	25	53	12	1	0	0	13	11	3	11	0	16	6	2	0	1	1	.50	1	.226	.414	.245
Sherrill, J.J.#	of	Columbus	Cle	A	21	111	407	102	19	11	4	155	62	50	32	0	123	27	10	4	29	9	.76	1	.251	.343	.381
Sherrod, Justin	3b	Augusta	Bos	A	24	87	307	89	24	3	11	152	53	43	34	1	102	21	1	2	16	7	.70	4	.290	.396	.495
		Sarasota	Bos	A+	24	37	141	43	8	3	7	78	20	23	11	0	37	2	0	3	5	1	.83	2	.305	.357	.553
Shier, Pete	ss	Frederick	Bal	A+	21	13	40	8	1	0	0	9	5	3	2	0	7	0	0	0	1	1	.50	0	.200	.238	.225
		Bluefield	Bal	R+	21	65	202	48	10	2	1	65	30	19	36	0	51	3	3	1	17	4	.81	6	.238	.360	.322
Shipp, Brian	2b	St. Lucie	NYM	A+	23	114	372	103	21	6	8	160	47	48	25	0	107	11	14	4	25	6	.81	3	.277	.337	.430
Sickles, Jeremy	c	Lynchburg	Pit	A+	24	29	92	22	6	0	2	34	4	6	6	0	23	2	1	0	1	2	.33	3	.239	.300	.370
Silver, Travis	c	Boise	ChC	A-	24	3	6	1	0	0	1	4	1	2	0	0	2	0	0	0	0	0	.00	0	.167	.167	.667
		Lansing	ChC	A	24	22	57	9	0	0	0	9	7	4	6	0	23	3	1	1	0	1	.00	2	.158	.269	.158
Silvera, Andres	2b	Batavia	Phi	A-	20	58	195	43	10	2	4	69	24	20	18	0	63	2	2	3	13	4	.76	3	.221	.289	.354
Simoneaux, Neil	2b	Johnson Cty	StL	R+	22	49	153	31	6	3	2	49	29	5	20	0	42	2	3	1	5	1	.83	2	.203	.301	.320
Simpson, Bodie	of	Yakima	Ari	A-	24	56	195	46	11	0	1	60	25	19	16	0	39	3	0	2	4	2	.67	4	.236	.301	.308
Sing, Brandon	3b-1b	Lansing	ChC	A	21	121	417	102	27	2	16	181	54	50	46	0	109	8	2	5	3	5	.38	6	.245	.328	.434
Singer, Matt*	of	Yankees	NYY	R	23	41	105	19	1	1	1	25	11	13	9	0	22	1	0	0	4	4	.50	2	.181	.252	.238
Siriveaw, Nom#	3b	Auburn	Tor	A-	21	66	239	40	8	3	6	72	32	25	23	0	88	2	1	1	8	1	.89	5	.167	.245	.301
Sisk, Aaron	of	Chston-WV	Tor	A	23	68	223	40	9	3	4	67	21	28	15	1	78	1	0	3	5	6	.45	2	.179	.231	.300
		Dunedin	Tor	A+	23	15	35	4	1	1	1	10	2	4	2	0	14	1	2	0	1	1	.50	0	.114	.184	.286
Sitzman, Jay*	of	Clearwater	Phi	A+	24	118	465	115	21	6	6	166	63	34	35	2	100	8	7	3	31	17	.65	5	.247	.309	.357
Sizemore, Grady*	of	Clinton	Mon	A	19	123	451	121	16	4	2	151	64	61	81	4	92	4	0	5	32	11	.74	7	.268	.381	.335
Slavik, Corey*	3b	Boise	ChC	A-	22	63	227	65	15	1	10	112	43	31	39	3	47	0	0	2	5	3	.63	5	.286	.388	.493
Sledd, Aaron*	of	Mudville	Cin	A+	26	1	3	0	0	0	0	0	0	0	0	0	2	0	0	0	0	0	.00	1	.000	.000	.000
		Dayton	Cin	A	26	13	37	9	3	0	0	12	6	3	7	0	14	0	0	1	0	0	.00	0	.243	.356	.324
		Daytona	ChC	A+	26	7	17	2	0	0	0	2	1	1	3	0	6	0	0	1	0	0	.00	1	.118	.238	.118
Small, Buster	c	Mahoning Vy	Cle	A-	24	2	2	1	0	0	0	1	0	0	1	0	1	0	0	0	0	0	.00	0	.500	.667	.500
Smiley, Jermaine*	of	Spokane	KC	A-	22	61	182	41	5	2	0	50	22	17	25	1	56	3	2	0	4	4	.50	7	.225	.329	.275
Smith, Brenton*	dh-of	Reds	Cin	R	23	47	138	36	7	0	0	43	16	10	22	0	35	8	2	1	11	6	.65	4	.261	.391	.312
Smith, Corey	3b	Columbus	Cle	A	20	130	500	130	26	5	18	220	59	85	37	1	149	5	0	9	10	7	.59	4	.260	.312	.440
Smith, Dustin	c	Rangers	Tex	R	21	34	103	23	2	0	1	28	16	16	13	0	14	4	1	0	2	2	.50	3	.223	.333	.272

2001 Batting — Class-A and Rookie Leagues

BATTING																					BASERUNNING				PERCENTAGES		
Player	Pos	Team	Org	Lg	A	G	AB	H	2B	3B	HR	TB	R	RBI	TBB	IBB	SO	HBP	SH	SF	SB	CS	SB%	GDP	Avg	OBP	SLG
Smith, Ryan	c	Capital Cty	NYM	A	23	20	53	5	0	0	0	5	5	1	6	0	20	2	0	1	0	1	.00	2	.094	.210	.094
		St. Lucie	NYM	A+	23	31	70	20	3	0	0	23	9	5	11	0	18	4	2	1	2	1	.67	1	.286	.407	.329
Smith, Ryan#	1b	Twins	Min	R	21	44	121	24	4	0	2	34	14	7	25	3	32	5	0	1	6	2	.75	1	.198	.355	.281
Smith, Sam	3b-dh	Asheville	Col	A	23	30	105	16	4	0	0	20	5	7	8	1	37	4	0	0	1	1	.50	0	.152	.239	.190
Smith, Sean	of	Pirates	Pit	R	19	46	148	30	7	1	3	48	14	14	20	0	56	3	0	2	12	1	.92	2	.203	.306	.324
Smith, Steven	ss	Provo	Ana	R+	23	62	249	80	11	1	1	96	60	34	37	1	40	3	9	3	6	4	.60	0	.321	.411	.386
Smith, Will	of	Augusta	Bos	A	25	72	228	65	13	0	0	78	45	13	37	1	44	6	10	4	19	9	.68	2	.285	.393	.342
Smith, Will*	of	Kane County	Fla	A	20	125	535	150	26	2	16	228	92	91	32	2	74	5	0	5	4	5	.44	12	.280	.324	.426
Smitherman, Steve	of	Dayton	Cin	A	23	134	497	139	45	2	20	248	89	73	43	1	113	10	0	2	16	7	.70	9	.280	.348	.499
Snelling, Chris*	of	San Berndno	Sea	A+	20	114	450	151	29	10	7	221	90	73	45	4	63	21	2	3	12	5	.71	7	.336	.418	.491
Snyder, Mike*	1b	Chston-WV	Tor	A	21	119	414	91	18	2	8	137	47	45	40	6	101	2	1	2	12	5	.71	14	.220	.290	.331
Sobet, Renato	of	Fort Wayne	SD	A	22	14	38	6	2	0	0	8	1	2	2	0	8	1	0	0	1	0	1.00	4	.158	.220	.211
		Eugene	SD	A-	22	9	31	6	1	0	0	7	2	3	1	0	9	0	0	1	0	0	.00	0	.194	.212	.226
Soler, Ramon#	2b	Bakersfield	TB	A+	20	103	418	110	14	4	2	138	72	27	46	0	75	3	8	3	25	5	.83	2	.263	.338	.330
Soriano, Carlos	of	Ogden	Mil	R+	22	60	224	69	15	2	7	109	39	43	20	0	77	2	2	4	18	6	.75	1	.308	.364	.487
Soriano, Jairo#	3b	Bluefield	Bal	R+	21	41	102	21	4	3	0	31	14	15	12	0	30	5	2	0	4	4	.50	1	.206	.319	.304
Sosa, Francisco	c	Kingsport	NYM	R+	21	1	4	0	0	0	0	0	0	1	0	0	1	0	0	0	0	0	.00	0	.000	.000	.000
		Brooklyn	NYM	A-	21	24	72	28	3	1	1	36	12	8	2	0	7	2	0	0	2	4	.33	3	.389	.421	.500
Sosa, Jovanny	dh-of	Delmarva	Bal	A	22	36	117	32	5	0	5	52	17	18	16	0	37	2	0	2	1	0	1.00	2	.274	.365	.444
		Frederick	Bal	A+	22	64	207	37	4	0	7	62	27	25	34	2	72	1	0	1	1	1	.50	6	.179	.296	.300
Sosa, Nick	1b	Modesto	Oak	A+	24	125	462	128	31	0	13	198	54	63	65	3	157	3	1	3	1	2	.33	10	.277	.368	.429
Soto, Geovany	c	Cubs	ChC	R	19	41	150	39	16	0	1	58	18	20	15	1	33	3	1	0	1	0	1.00	3	.260	.339	.387
Soto, Jorge	c-dh	Modesto	Oak	A+	24	19	55	11	2	1	3	24	5	12	12	0	31	0	1	0	0	0	.00	0	.200	.343	.436
		Vancouver	Oak	A-	24	44	165	34	12	1	7	69	16	21	8	0	84	5	0	0	0	0	.00	2	.206	.264	.418
Soto, Jose#	of	Brevard Cty	Fla	A+	22	2	5	1	0	0	0	1	1	0	1	0	2	0	0	0	0	0	.00	0	.200	.333	.200
		Utica	Fla	A-	22	48	192	44	7	3	2	63	22	17	13	0	52	0	2	1	15	3	.83	3	.229	.277	.328
Soto, T.J.	1b	Michigan	Hou	A	24	110	404	116	27	5	22	219	73	62	35	1	128	4	1	4	19	5	.79	12	.287	.347	.542
Southward, D.	of	Quad City	Min	A	24	10	21	3	2	0	0	5	3	1	2	0	4	0	1	0	1	0	1.00	0	.143	.217	.238
Spataro, Ryan*	of	Twins	Min	R	19	16	48	10	0	0	0	10	4	2	3	0	16	0	1	1	1	1	.50	1	.208	.250	.208
Spidale, Mike	of	Kannapolis	CWS	A	20	126	431	100	8	0	0	108	51	32	52	0	65	14	5	4	35	15	.70	8	.232	.331	.251
Spoerl, Josh	dh	Mudville	Cin	A+	23	116	420	108	23	6	12	179	56	60	47	6	124	8	0	4	1	2	.33	7	.257	.340	.426
Sprowl, Jon-Mark*	dh	Lansing	ChC	A	21	54	155	34	9	0	3	52	12	28	18	0	24	4	1	3	0	3	.00	6	.219	.311	.335
Stanley, Henry*	of-dh	Michigan	Hou	A	24	114	400	120	24	12	14	210	75	76	73	4	84	1	2	1	30	5	.86	7	.300	.408	.525
Stegall, Ryan	ss	Pittsfield	Hou	A-	22	67	235	54	17	0	3	80	29	26	20	1	47	4	2	1	5	4	.56	5	.230	.300	.340
Stern, Adam*	of	Jamestown	Atl	A-	22	21	75	23	4	2	0	31	20	11	15	0	11	0	0	2	9	4	.69	0	.307	.413	.413
Stocker, Myreon#	2b	Spokane	KC	A-	21	28	73	17	2	2	0	23	10	7	14	0	20	0	1	0	4	2	.67	1	.233	.356	.315
Stockton, Brad*	of	Pulaski	Tex	R+	22	64	232	60	18	4	7	107	43	41	40	2	67	2	1	4	3	3	.50	2	.259	.367	.461
		Savannah	Tex	A	22	6	17	3	0	0	1	6	1	4	4	0	1	0	0	0	0	0	.00	0	.176	.333	.353
Stockton, Jeff	2b	Cedar Rapds	Ana	A	24	7	25	3	1	0	0	4	3	0	0	0	7	0	0	0	0	0	.00	0	.120	.120	.160
Stockton, Rick*	of-1b	Cedar Rapds	Ana	A	22	7	22	6	2	0	0	8	2	3	2	0	5	1	0	1	1	0	1.00	0	.273	.346	.364
		Angels	Ana	R	22	36	118	31	2	2	1	40	17	11	7	0	20	3	1	1	8	2	.80	0	.263	.318	.339
Stokes, Jason	dh	Utica	Fla	A-	20	35	130	30	2	1	6	52	12	19	11	0	48	2	0	1	0	0	.00	0	.231	.299	.400
Stone, Jon#	c	Fort Wayne	SD	A	23	53	169	39	10	0	1	52	15	20	18	0	48	4	0	1	3	0	1.00	4	.231	.318	.308
Storey, Eric	3b	Asheville	Col	A	24	87	300	75	10	3	10	121	45	53	50	2	116	0	0	2	6	4	.60	4	.250	.355	.403
Story-Harden, T.	1b	Wilmington	LA	A	22	22	68	13	2	1	1	20	4	5	4	0	29	0	1	1	0	1	.00	2	.191	.233	.294
		Great Falls	LA	R+	22	24	80	21	4	0	3	34	11	14	12	0	25	6	0	1	2	2	.50	1	.263	.394	.425
Stotts, J.T.	ss	Vancouver	Oak	A-	22	62	241	65	5	2	0	74	35	17	26	1	34	4	3	2	19	4	.83	6	.270	.348	.307
Stringham, Jed	1b	Oneonta	Det	A-	24	44	134	25	5	0	1	33	10	11	8	0	38	1	1	0	1	1	.50	6	.187	.238	.246
Strong, Brian*	dh	Braves	Atl	R	22	37	106	30	3	1	3	44	11	16	6	0	24	3	0	2	1	5	.17	1	.283	.333	.415
Strong, Jamal	of	Wisconsin	Sea	A	23	51	184	65	12	1	0	79	41	19	40	2	27	5	1	1	35	4	.90	2	.353	.478	.429
		San Berndno	Sea	A+	23	81	331	103	11	2	0	118	74	32	51	2	60	5	6	0	47	8	.85	4	.311	.411	.356
Suarez, Marc	c	Dayton	Cin	A	26	47	150	38	9	0	6	65	18	23	13	0	44	4	0	2	4	0	1.00	1	.253	.325	.433
Suarez, Victor#	3b	Royals	KC	R	20	28	78	15	4	1	0	21	6	4	4	0	16	0	0	0	2	1	.67	2	.192	.232	.269
Sulbaran, Orlando	c	Savannah	Tex	A	20	2	6	2	1	0	0	3	0	2	1	0	0	0	0	0	0	0	.00	0	.333	.429	.500
		Rangers	Tex	R	20	36	122	32	7	1	2	47	18	12	9	0	25	1	1	1	8	2	.80	1	.262	.316	.385
Sullivan, Cory*	of	Asheville	Col	A	22	67	258	71	12	1	5	100	36	22	25	0	56	2	0	0	13	9	.59	2	.275	.344	.388
Summerville, K.	of	Staten Ilnd	NYY	A-	23	35	59	11	0	0	0	11	14	4	7	0	18	4	0	0	13	1	.93	0	.186	.314	.186
Suomi, Richard*	c	Athletics	Oak	R	21	52	175	45	14	2	4	75	31	43	27	1	36	8	2	4	7	2	.78	1	.257	.374	.429
Sutter, Tony#	1b	Greensboro	NYY	A	24	16	43	7	0	0	1	10	7	6	8	0	9	1	1	1	0	1	.00	3	.163	.302	.233
Svihlik, D.J.*	2b	Greensboro	NYY	A	24	4	7	1	0	1	0	3	1	0	0	0	1	0	0	0	0	0	.00	0	.143	.143	.429
Swedlow, Sean*	1b	Columbus	Cle	A	20	106	401	80	18	2	4	114	30	35	28	1	146	5	1	3	1	2	.33	5	.200	.259	.284
Sweeney, James	c	Casper	Col	R+	19	26	90	25	4	1	3	40	19	12	8	0	32	4	0	1	1	1	.50	1	.278	.359	.444
Swenson, Leland	2b	Charlotte	Tex	A+	25	47	120	21	3	0	0	24	16	12	21	0	30	1	3	1	0	2	.00	5	.175	.301	.200
Swenson, Sam*	of	Provo	Ana	R+	24	63	225	79	16	4	13	142	61	55	24	0	64	14	0	4	7	1	.88	5	.351	.438	.631
Tablado, Raul	ss	Chston-WV	Tor	A	20	122	388	98	23	2	9	152	49	44	45	1	127	5	4	3	5	10	.33	6	.253	.336	.392
Tamburrino, Brett#	2b	Quad City	Min	A	20	42	141	37	3	5	0	50	23	16	15	1	32	4	1	0	4	2	.67	3	.262	.350	.355
Tapia, Roman	3b	Kannapolis	CWS	A	22	18	30	3	2	0	0	5	2	0	2	0	17	0	2	0	0	0	.00	0	.100	.156	.167
Tarbett, Brent	of	Red Sox	Bos	R	21	47	138	31	8	0	5	54	20	20	19	2	40	9	1	0	2	3	.40	4	.225	.355	.391
Tavarez, Ydel	dh	Burlington	Cle	R+	21	13	36	7	1	0	0	8	5	2	2	0	20	0	0	0	1	0	1.00	0	.194	.237	.222
Taveras, Frank	3b	Marlins	Fla	R	20	28	89	19	2	0	0	21	12	4	12	0	29	2	0	1	6	2	.75	0	.213	.317	.236
Taveras, Willy	of	Columbus	Cle	A	20	97	395	107	15	7	3	145	55	32	22	0	73	6	4	3	29	9	.76	7	.271	.317	.367
Taylor, Mark	3b	Pirates	Pit	R	22	38	130	28	5	1	0	35	9	10	0	0	32	2	0	1	0	3	.00	3	.215	.226	.269
Taylor, Samuel#	2b-ss	Twins	Min	R	19	35	92	24	1	1	1	30	14	8	13	0	10	3	1	0	8	2	.80	3	.261	.370	.326
Taylor, Seth	ss	Salem	Col	A+	24	131	480	126	26	1	8	178	52	45	26	0	66	4	8	2	6	8	.43	7	.263	.305	.371
Teilon, Nilson	of	Kannapolis	CWS	A	21	67	163	31	6	1	3	48	20	8	11	0	47	1	1	1	2	2	.50	4	.190	.244	.294
Tejada, Mike#	c-dh	Asheville	Col	A	23	107	363	74	17	0	15	136	35	49	22	1	102	1	0	3	3	0	1.00	3	.204	.249	.375
Tejeda, Juan	1b	Tigers	Det	R	20	50	173	51	8	1	4	73	17	37	8	2	32	5	0	0	0	0	.00	2	.295	.344	.422
Tejero, Armando*	1b	Braves	Atl	R	19	20	51	5	2	0	0	7	2	0	11	0	19	0	0	0	1	0	1.00	0	.098	.258	.137
Tellis, Antoine	c	Tigers	Det	R	20	1	0	0	0	0	0	0	0	0	0	0	0	0	0	0	0	0	.00	0	.000	.000	.000
Tempesta, Nick*	2b	Medcine Hat	Tor	R+	23	72	263	88	16	1	8	130	49	46	24	2	51	9	1	1	3	1	.75	3	.335	.407	.494
Tena, Hector	ss	Casper	Col	R+	20	35	123	29	6	1	2	43	15	13	6	1	36	4	0	1	3	7	.30	0	.236	.291	.350
		Asheville	Col	A	20	32	103	15	1	0	2	22	5	19	5	0	32	0	0	6	0	0	.00	4	.146	.175	.214
Terrero, Wandy	c	White Sox	CWS	R	20	13	30	12	1	0	0	13	3	3	3	0	3	0	0	0	0	1	.00	0	.400	.455	.433
Terveen, Bryce*	c	Macon	Atl	A	24	61	190	43	5	0	4	60	25	26	32	3	42	9	3	1	1	3	.25	5	.226	.362	.316
		Myrtle Bch	Atl	A+	24	20	61	11	3	0	2	20	7	7	4	0	17	3	0	1	0	0	.00	3	.180	.261	.328

2001 Batting — Class-A and Rookie Leagues

BATTING																					BASERUNNING				PERCENTAGES		
Player	Pos	Team	Org	Lg	A	G	AB	H	2B	3B	HR	TB	R	RBI	TBB	IBB	SO	HBP	SH	SF	SB	CS	SB%	GDP	Avg	OBP	SLG
Testa, Chris*	of	Tri-City	Col	A-	21	54	182	49	12	3	2	73	23	22	21	3	49	5	0	1	5	4	.56	3	.269	.359	.401
Thede, Matthew	1b	Expos	Mon	R	24	34	120	25	4	1	0	31	9	18	9	0	32	3	1	2	1	3	.25	7	.208	.276	.258
Theriot, Ryan	ss	Daytona	ChC	A+	22	30	103	21	5	0	0	26	20	9	21	0	17	1	3	1	2	4	.33	2	.204	.341	.252
Thiessen, Mike	of	Yakima	Ari	A-	23	27	104	32	4	0	0	36	14	11	6	0	17	3	1	3	6	2	.75	1	.308	.353	.346
Thissen, Greg	2b-ss	Vermont	Mon	A-	21	59	221	52	13	0	1	68	27	19	20	0	43	3	1	1	9	4	.69	0	.235	.306	.308
Thomas, Adam*	of	Bluefield	Bal	R+	22	62	227	67	8	3	4	93	45	26	36	0	39	6	2	0	16	5	.76	4	.295	.405	.410
Thomas, C.J.	of	Dodgers	LA	R	22	7	16	4	0	0	0	4	5	2	3	0	0	0	0	0	3	0	1.00	1	.250	.368	.250
		Vero Beach	LA	A+	22	66	253	66	18	0	1	87	28	20	23	2	58	1	1	3	9	6	.60	6	.261	.321	.344
Thomas, Chuck*	of	Myrtle Bch	Atl	A+	23	12	44	7	1	0	0	8	4	6	3	1	8	0	0	1	1	0	1.00	3	.159	.208	.182
		Macon	Atl	A	23	108	408	102	19	5	11	164	59	59	32	3	87	3	0	3	17	7	.71	6	.250	.307	.402
Thomman, John	of	Twins	Min	R	20	36	79	16	5	0	1	24	7	10	6	1	30	4	0	0	0	2	.00	1	.203	.292	.304
Thompson, Alva	dh	Macon	Atl	A	25	17	51	8	1	0	2	15	7	5	1	0	11	2	0	0	1	1	.50	0	.157	.204	.294
Thompson, Craig#	of	Fort Wayne	SD	A	24	87	310	81	27	2	10	142	53	59	41	1	35	2	4	7	8	1	.89	2	.261	.344	.458
Thompson, Eric*	of	Mahoning Vy	Cle	A-	23	26	66	14	0	0	0	14	5	3	3	0	28	0	2	0	2	2	.50	0	.212	.246	.212
Thompson, Kevin	of	Staten Ilnd	NYY	A-	22	68	260	68	11	4	6	105	46	33	36	0	48	5	1	2	11	5	.69	5	.262	.360	.404
Thompson, Zach*	of	Brewers	Mil	R	20	22	67	13	1	0	0	14	7	3	10	0	32	5	1	0	1	1	.50	0	.194	.341	.209
		High Desert	Mil	A+	20	5	13	1	0	0	0	1	2	1	3	0	3	0	1	0	0	0	.00	0	.077	.250	.077
Thorn.-Murray, J.#	ss	Boise	ChC	A-	21	56	205	49	14	5	4	85	24	26	12	0	45	2	2	4	4	1	.80	3	.239	.283	.415
Threinen, Scott	3b	Burlington	Cle	R+	20	37	110	22	2	1	1	29	19	12	25	0	34	3	0	1	6	3	.67	1	.200	.360	.264
Tiesing, Tyler	c	Yakima	Ari	A-	22	30	86	16	6	0	0	22	6	5	7	0	30	2	0	0	0	1	.00	1	.186	.263	.256
Tiffee, Terry#	3b	Quad City	Min	A	23	128	495	153	32	1	11	220	65	86	32	4	48	1	0	8	3	1	.75	13	.309	.347	.444
Timaure, Jesus	of	Marlins	Fla	R	22	44	156	35	12	0	1	50	18	21	10	0	45	8	0	2	3	0	1.00	2	.224	.301	.321
Todd, Jeremy*	1b	Capital Cty	NYM	A	24	19	67	11	2	0	1	16	5	7	7	0	35	0	0	2	0	0	.00	2	.164	.237	.239
		Brooklyn	NYM	A-	24	17	44	8	1	0	0	9	4	3	7	0	13	1	0	3	0	1	.00	0	.182	.291	.205
Todd, Kelvin	of-dh	Athletics	Oak	R	21	5	17	4	1	0	0	5	2	4	1	0	5	0	0	0	0	0	.00	0	.235	.278	.294
Tolli, Barry	of	Cedar Rapds	Ana	A	22	23	71	10	1	0	1	14	5	2	2	0	23	0	0	0	3	4	.43	1	.141	.164	.197
Tolzien, Edward*	1b	Cedar Rapds	Ana	A	22	20	71	13	2	0	0	15	9	8	6	1	20	3	0	0	0	0	.00	2	.183	.275	.211
		Provo	Ana	R+	22	39	132	35	9	1	2	52	27	23	18	1	22	4	0	0	4	1	.80	4	.265	.370	.394
Tomlin, James	of	Elizabethtn	Min	R+	19	63	237	71	14	4	1	96	38	23	21	0	33	8	3	2	15	7	.68	2	.300	.373	.405
Toner, John	of	Brooklyn	NYM	A-	22	38	124	32	8	1	1	45	10	16	8	1	33	5	1	1	3	4	.43	1	.258	.326	.363
Tope, Stephen	1b	Elizabethtn	Min	R+	20	40	130	28	7	1	1	40	13	9	6	0	46	1	0	2	0	0	.00	3	.215	.252	.308
Topolski, Jon*	of	Lexington	Hou	A	25	136	550	158	27	7	24	271	98	96	75	6	128	4	1	3	28	11	.72	3	.287	.375	.493
Torres, Digno*	of	Quad City	Min	A	22	88	264	51	15	2	3	79	31	27	33	0	72	6	1	1	1	2	.33	9	.193	.296	.299
Torres, Erik	2b	Ogden	Mil	R+	23	20	58	10	3	0	0	13	9	4	4	0	16	0	1	0	0	2	.00	0	.172	.226	.224
		Brewers	Mil	R	23	1	3	0	0	0	0	0	0	0	0	0	0	1	0	0	0	0	.00	0	.000	.250	.000
Torres, Frederick	c	Charlotte	Tex	A+	22	111	407	101	18	1	9	148	37	52	20	0	103	3	3	2	1	0	1.00	5	.248	.287	.364
Tosca, Daniel*	c	Lakewood	Phi	A	21	56	183	29	9	0	1	41	16	12	22	1	66	0	0	2	1	1	.50	3	.158	.246	.224
Tousa, Scott*	2b	Oneonta	Det	A-	22	8	24	4	0	0	0	4	6	1	2	0	5	1	0	0	2	0	1.00	0	.167	.259	.167
		Lakeland	Det	A+	22	39	111	24	4	0	0	28	18	8	18	0	21	3	2	0	3	1	.75	1	.216	.341	.252
Toven, John	2b	Lexington	Hou	A	27	56	167	43	5	0	2	54	34	16	8	0	32	4	1	2	12	5	.71	2	.257	.304	.323
Tracy, Chad*	3b	Yakima	Ari	A-	22	10	36	10	1	0	0	11	2	5	3	0	5	1	0	0	1	0	1.00	1	.278	.350	.306
		South Bend	Ari	A	22	54	215	73	11	0	4	96	43	36	19	2	19	2	0	3	3	0	1.00	4	.340	.393	.447
Trezza, Alex*	1b-dh	Oneonta	Det	A-	21	53	183	41	11	2	1	59	23	19	13	0	65	2	1	1	0	1	.00	4	.224	.281	.322
Trinidad, Edgar	2b	Athletics	Oak	R	19	44	163	48	6	4	0	62	29	17	32	0	28	2	3	1	9	10	.47	4	.294	.414	.380
Tritle, Chris	of	Athletics	Oak	R	20	52	214	72	6	8	9	121	47	42	22	1	55	2	0	1	26	1	.96	2	.336	.402	.565
Truitt, Steve	of	Pittsfield	Hou	A-	24	11	39	12	1	1	1	18	8	6	0	0	5	0	0	0	1	2	.33	0	.308	.308	.462
		Lexington	Hou	A	24	28	88	26	7	0	3	42	18	13	9	0	26	1	1	1	7	1	.88	0	.295	.364	.477
Trumble, Dan	dh	Hagerstown	SF	A	22	119	399	94	18	1	26	192	70	75	63	1	157	5	0	1	10	5	.67	10	.236	.346	.481
Trzesniak, Nick	c	Eugene	SD	A-	21	57	193	45	8	1	2	61	24	21	22	0	59	5	0	2	0	1	.00	3	.233	.324	.316
Tucker, Mamon	of	Delmarva	Bal	A	22	59	224	55	7	1	2	70	37	24	28	1	44	2	2	4	10	3	.77	3	.246	.329	.313
		Frederick	Bal	A+	22	69	256	73	9	1	1	87	33	23	25	3	46	0	2	4	7	5	.58	4	.285	.344	.340
Tucker, Michael	3b	Utica	Fla	A-	22	49	159	34	4	0	2	44	29	9	23	1	40	1	0	0	0	2	.00	3	.214	.317	.277
Turay, Alhaji	of	Kingsport	NYM	R+	19	42	159	39	8	3	1	56	20	19	9	0	44	1	1	2	8	3	.73	5	.245	.287	.352
Turco, Anthony*	c	Salem-Keizr	SF	A-	22	42	86	21	1	1	2	30	15	11	12	0	20	0	2	0	0	0	.00	1	.244	.337	.349
Turner, Jason*	1b-of	Greensboro	NYY	A	24	88	303	79	15	2	8	122	43	47	45	1	63	2	1	8	5	2	.71	1	.261	.352	.403
		Staten Ilnd	NYY	A-	24	33	110	37	7	2	1	51	24	19	18	0	31	0	3	0	1	1	.50	1	.336	.430	.464
Turner, Justin*	3b	Provo	Ana	R+	22	52	176	38	3	0	6	59	36	27	28	1	65	1	0	0	9	4	.69	3	.216	.327	.335
Uegawachi, Bryce#	ss	Mahoning Vy	Cle	A-	23	55	162	33	0	1	0	35	14	5	28	0	32	1	3	0	4	5	.44	1	.204	.325	.216
Uggla, Daniel	2b	Yakima	Ari	A-	22	72	278	77	21	0	5	113	39	40	20	0	52	9	1	4	8	4	.67	9	.277	.341	.406
Ugueto, Luis#	ss	Brevard Cty	Fla	A+	23	121	392	103	12	5	3	134	53	43	38	0	96	2	9	1	22	7	.76	7	.263	.330	.342
Umbria, Jose	c	Chston-WV	Tor	A	24	45	128	30	3	0	1	36	12	19	15	0	27	1	0	1	1	2	.33	5	.234	.317	.281
Utley, Chase*	2b	Clearwater	Phi	A+	23	122	467	120	25	2	16	197	65	59	37	4	88	12	1	6	19	8	.70	6	.257	.324	.422
Valdez, Angel	of	Tampa	NYY	A+	24	46	148	35	9	2	1	51	22	7	7	0	43	2	2	2	5	1	.83	1	.236	.277	.345
		Cedar Rapds	Ana	A	24	31	114	28	8	0	3	45	19	11	4	0	29	2	2	0	3	1	.75	0	.246	.283	.395
Valdez, Kelvin	2b	Angels	Ana	R	18	23	46	10	2	1	0	14	4	5	3	0	18	0	0	0	2	0	1.00	0	.217	.265	.304
Valdez, Wilson	ss	Clinton	Mon	A	22	59	214	54	8	1	0	64	31	11	9	0	22	2	5	2	6	7	.46	5	.252	.286	.299
		Jupiter	Mon	A+	22	64	233	58	13	2	2	81	34	19	10	0	33	2	10	0	7	3	.70	4	.249	.286	.348
VanBenschoten, J.	dh-p	Williamsprt	Pit	A-	22	32	75	17	5	0	0	22	9	8	7	0	23	2	0	2	3	2	.60	2	.227	.302	.293
Van Buizen, R.	2b	Wilmington	LA	A	21	90	285	63	16	0	5	94	29	34	23	1	54	8	3	2	12	7	.63	5	.221	.296	.330
Van Every, Jon*	of	Mahoning Vy	Cle	A-	22	41	135	34	4	2	6	60	30	17	28	1	50	7	0	0	1	2	.33	1	.252	.406	.444
Van Meetren, Jason	of	Everett	Sea	A-	22	45	152	35	8	1	5	60	18	22	20	0	47	2	1	2	0	2	.00	1	.230	.324	.395
Vargas, Inakel	c	Lakeland	Det	A+	24	7	22	4	0	0	0	4	1	2	3	0	3	1	0	0	0	0	.00	2	.182	.308	.182
Varitek, Justin	c	Mariners	Sea	R	24	4	6	2	1	0	0	3	2	0	1	0	2	0	0	0	0	0	.00	0	.333	.429	.500
Varner, Gary	of	Billings	Cin	R+	21	72	291	102	20	5	8	156	55	55	29	1	64	3	0	3	7	4	.64	3	.351	.411	.536
Vasquez, Geraldo	ss	Peoria	StL	A	22	4	9	0	0	0	0	0	1	0	2	0	4	0	0	0	1	0	1.00	1	.000	.182	.000
Vasquez, Jose*	dh-of	Casper	Col	R+	19	64	228	53	6	3	14	107	40	39	27	2	96	9	0	4	1	6	.14	1	.232	.332	.469
Vasquez, Wuillians#	2b	Yankees	NYY	R	18	43	140	31	1	1	2	40	16	16	21	2	33	1	0	3	5	1	.83	4	.221	.321	.286
Vavao, Jason	1b	Reds	Cin	R	21	53	175	38	9	2	1	54	13	19	10	0	38	7	0	3	2	2	.50	4	.217	.282	.309
Vaz, Roberto*	dh	Modesto	Oak	A+	27	48	180	53	13	0	1	69	24	25	23	3	35	2	0	2	19	2	.90	8	.294	.377	.383
Vazquez, Rafael	3b	Cubs	ChC	R	20	6	15	7	1	0	0	8	2	3	0	0	2	0	0	1	0	0	.00	0	.467	.438	.533
Vega, Jesus	c	Angels	Ana	R	20	25	54	18	3	0	1	24	3	9	7	0	14	3	0	1	1	1	.50	0	.333	.431	.444
Velasquez, Cesar	c	Angels	Ana	R	18	20	39	7	0	0	0	7	2	1	3	0	11	1	0	0	1	0	1.00	1	.179	.256	.179
Veleber, Troy#	of	Williamsprt	Pit	A-	23	14	26	4	1	0	1	8	8	2	1	0	8	0	2	0	6	0	1.00	0	.154	.185	.308
Vento, Mike	of	Tampa	NYY	A+	24	130	457	137	20	10	20	237	71	87	45	1	88	9	0	3	13	10	.57	9	.300	.372	.519
Victorino, Shane	of	Wilmington	LA	A	21	112	435	123	21	9	4	174	71	32	36	0	61	5	13	1	47	13	.78	3	.283	.344	.400

2001 Batting — Class-A and Rookie Leagues

						BATTING															BASERUNNING				PERCENTAGES		
Player	Pos	Team	Org	Lg	A	G	AB	H	2B	3B	HR	TB	R	RBI	TBB	IBB	SO	HBP	SH	SF	SB	CS	SB%	GDP	Avg	OBP	SLG
		Vero Beach	LA	A+	21	2	6	1	0	0	0	1	2	0	3	0	1	0	0	0	0	0	.00	0	.167	.444	.167
Viera, Orlando*	of	Brewers	Mil	R	18	27	83	22	2	1	0	26	8	4	6	0	27	1	0	1	1	1	.50	2	.265	.319	.313
Villanueva, Froilan	3b	Ogden	Mil	R+	21	68	273	84	21	2	6	127	52	53	18	0	27	5	1	3	5	3	.63	4	.308	.358	.465
Villegas, Ernest	1b	Charlotte	Tex	A+	23	34	126	34	5	0	2	45	7	15	2	0	35	6	2	1	3	0	1.00	2	.270	.311	.357
		Savannah	Tex	A	23	39	130	29	4	0	8	57	22	21	6	0	35	10	0	0	4	1	.80	2	.223	.308	.438
Villilo, Miguel#	3b	Wisconsin	Sea	A	20	14	42	7	1	0	0	8	1	3	3	0	14	1	0	0	0	4	.00	0	.167	.239	.190
		Everett	Sea	A-	20	50	195	48	10	0	5	73	33	22	22	2	69	2	1	0	7	2	.78	0	.246	.329	.374
Vilorio, Miguel	2b	Salem	Col	A+	22	12	45	16	2	0	0	18	6	0	0	0	9	0	0	0	1	0	1.00	0	.356	.356	.400
		Asheville	Col	A	22	113	453	115	15	7	3	153	55	32	22	0	58	11	6	4	20	15	.57	5	.254	.302	.338
Virgen, Constancio	dh	Great Falls	LA	R+	20	31	107	28	4	0	1	35	13	16	15	0	17	0	1	2	3	2	.60	1	.262	.347	.327
Vizcaino, Maximo	ss	South Bend	Ari	A	21	52	165	39	8	1	0	49	18	16	6	0	35	0	1	1	2	5	.29	5	.236	.262	.297
Volquez, Bolivar	ss	Chston-SC	TB	A	20	38	126	21	3	0	0	24	13	7	14	0	39	2	2	1	4	1	.80	1	.167	.259	.190
		Princeton	TB	R+	20	19	0	0	0	0	0	0	0	0	0	0	0	0	0	0	0	0	.00	0	.000	.000	.000
Volquez, Julio#	ss	Pulaski	Tex	R+	21	48	178	39	10	2	0	53	25	15	4	0	37	3	0	0	11	6	.65	3	.219	.249	.298
Voltz, Jude*	1b	Beloit	Mil	A	24	126	462	109	18	1	18	183	68	69	55	6	135	3	0	2	3	2	.60	4	.236	.320	.396
Von Schell, Tyler	1b	Salem-Keizr	SF	A-	22	75	293	80	18	2	10	132	50	45	26	1	63	4	0	3	1	2	.33	2	.273	.337	.451
Voshell, Chase	ss	Peoria	StL	A	23	90	325	84	19	3	5	124	53	23	33	1	80	4	0	1	9	5	.64	7	.258	.333	.382
Voshell, Key	2b	Lakewood	Phi	A	25	36	111	30	8	0	0	38	18	12	6	0	27	2	2	1	2	3	.40	4	.270	.317	.342
Vugteveen, Dustin	of	Missoula	Ari	R+	22	60	232	68	14	1	6	102	40	51	11	0	58	5	0	4	7	3	.70	3	.293	.333	.440
Vukovich, Vince*	of	Batavia	Phi	A-	22	46	149	30	6	0	1	39	19	14	14	0	25	2	2	3	4	2	.67	1	.201	.274	.262
Wagner, Jeff	1b	Rancho Cuca	Ana	A+	25	113	402	117	37	1	8	180	51	56	38	2	82	9	1	2	4	3	.57	2	.291	.364	.448
Waldron, Jeff*	c-dh	Lancaster	Ari	A+	25	54	151	44	12	1	2	64	13	35	13	1	22	2	3	2	0	0	.00	3	.291	.351	.424
Walker, Matt	of	W Michigan	Det	A	24	112	415	108	23	2	10	165	53	65	34	0	80	7	0	7	11	4	.73	14	.260	.322	.398
Wallace, Kellen*	of-dh	Angels	Ana	R	21	27	67	8	0	1	1	13	5	5	6	0	19	0	0	0	1	0	1.00	3	.119	.192	.194
Wallis, Jacob	c	Jupiter	Mon	A+	22	2	7	1	0	0	0	1	0	0	0	0	4	0	0	0	0	0	.00	0	.143	.143	.143
		Clinton	Mon	A	22	26	80	17	1	0	1	21	5	7	4	0	18	1	0	0	2	0	1.00	2	.213	.259	.263
		Vermont	Mon	A-	22	6	16	1	0	0	0	1	0	0	0	0	8	1	0	0	0	0	.00	0	.063	.118	.063
Walsh, Sean	3b	Batavia	Phi	A-	22	63	215	59	20	2	2	89	35	24	27	0	44	11	1	3	8	6	.57	6	.274	.379	.414
Walter, Scott	c	Burlington	KC	A	23	33	124	34	12	1	6	66	24	22	6	0	16	4	1	2	0	0	.00	7	.274	.324	.532
		Wilmington	KC	A+	23	60	201	50	9	0	7	80	19	33	18	1	36	9	2	1	1	0	1.00	6	.249	.336	.398
Ward, Brian	2b-3b	Fort Myers	Min	A+	24	15	47	12	1	0	0	13	5	6	7	0	6	0	0	1	0	1	.00	2	.255	.345	.277
Warner, J.R.*	1b	Cedar Rapds	Ana	A	23	14	53	10	2	1	0	14	9	4	4	0	11	1	0	0	1	0	1.00	1	.189	.259	.264
Warren, Chris#	of	Salem	Col	A+	25	74	132	26	7	1	6	53	20	18	26	0	51	4	1	1	3	4	.43	1	.197	.344	.402
Warren, Chris	of	Sarasota	Bos	A+	25	106	382	101	20	3	10	157	49	51	32	0	112	14	0	2	11	5	.69	4	.264	.342	.411
Washington, Dion	1b	Tampa	NYY	A+	25	29	84	16	4	1	0	22	5	8	10	0	22	1	1	0	0	1	.00	1	.190	.284	.262
Watkins, Cedric	of	Royals	KC	R	19	35	93	13	0	0	0	13	9	5	9	1	38	8	2	0	0	1	.00	1	.140	.273	.140
Watkins, Tommy	ss	Quad City	Min	A	22	73	191	44	9	0	2	59	31	16	28	0	36	2	6	1	4	2	.67	4	.230	.333	.309
Watson, Brandon*	of	Clinton	Mon	A	20	117	489	160	16	9	2	200	74	38	29	0	65	1	3	3	33	20	.62	6	.327	.364	.409
Watson, Matt*	of	Jupiter	Mon	A+	23	124	446	147	33	4	5	203	70	74	63	4	45	6	0	3	17	9	.65	11	.330	.417	.455
Watts, Derran	of	Kingsport	NYM	R+	22	16	50	12	0	0	0	12	9	3	9	0	19	0	0	0	5	0	1.00	0	.240	.356	.240
Wayment, Kory	ss-3b	Athletics	Oak	R	21	51	192	44	9	2	0	57	24	16	16	1	53	1	0	2	7	4	.64	4	.229	.289	.297
Webb, Ryan	of	Provo	Ana	R+	24	7	6	3	0	1	0	5	1	1	2	0	0	1	0	0	0	1	.00	0	.500	.667	.833
		Cedar Rapds	Ana	A	24	44	145	45	5	1	0	52	14	14	7	0	28	1	5	0	7	4	.64	1	.310	.346	.359
Webster, Anthony*	of	White Sox	CWS	R	19	55	225	69	9	7	0	92	38	30	9	0	33	1	5	3	18	7	.72	4	.307	.332	.409
Webster, Robert	c	Orioles	Bal	R	24	17	52	12	2	0	1	17	4	9	0	0	12	2	0	1	0	1	.00	1	.231	.255	.327
		Bluefield	Bal	R+	24	10	21	5	0	0	0	5	2	1	5	0	4	1	0	0	1	0	1.00	0	.238	.407	.238
		Frederick	Bal	A+	24	5	16	7	2	0	0	9	3	2	1	0	2	1	0	0	0	0	.00	0	.438	.500	.563
Weichard, Paul#	of	Lynchburg	Pit	A+	22	19	70	17	1	0	0	18	10	5	3	0	22	0	1	1	1	0	1.00	3	.243	.270	.257
Welch, Ed*	of	Provo	Ana	R+	22	59	216	61	9	5	1	83	47	26	16	0	59	0	2	3	18	4	.82	1	.282	.328	.384
Wendt, Justin*	dh	Kingsport	NYM	R+	20	29	87	23	3	0	1	29	16	17	16	1	21	4	0	1	0	6	.00	4	.264	.398	.333
Wenner, Mike	of	Modesto	Oak	A+	23	114	427	118	14	3	5	153	57	48	18	0	73	6	9	2	33	10	.77	5	.276	.313	.358
West, Eric	ss	Red Sox	Bos	R	19	25	82	21	5	1	4	40	11	11	9	0	22	2	0	0	1	0	1.00	5	.256	.344	.488
West, Kevin	of	Quad City	Min	A	22	126	443	120	33	3	8	183	74	62	62	1	99	28	1	5	6	2	.75	7	.271	.390	.413
West, Todd	ss	Beloit	Mil	A	23	132	408	96	14	0	0	110	62	40	60	0	62	7	26	3	16	4	.80	5	.235	.341	.270
Weston, Aron*	of	Hickory	Pit	A	21	20	74	9	2	1	0	13	8	2	3	0	25	4	0	1	5	1	.83	0	.122	.195	.176
White, Dean	ss	Braves	Atl	R	19	2	7	1	0	0	0	1	1	0	1	0	2	0	0	0	1	0	1.00	1	.143	.250	.143
White, Kenneth#	of	Orioles	Bal	R	23	49	160	47	11	1	1	63	22	12	12	1	42	3	3	0	5	2	.71	1	.294	.354	.394
		Frederick	Bal	A+	23	3	11	2	1	0	0	3	0	0	0	0	4	0	0	0	0	0	.00	0	.182	.182	.273
Whiteside, Dustin	c	Delmarva	Bal	A	22	61	212	53	11	0	7	85	30	28	9	1	45	7	0	2	1	1	.50	11	.250	.300	.401
Whitesides, Jake*	of	Martinsvlle	Hou	R+	21	53	178	41	6	4	1	58	20	8	10	0	55	3	1	1	5	1	.83	2	.230	.281	.326
Whitrock, Scott	of	Twins	Min	R	21	36	105	18	4	0	0	22	11	6	7	0	40	1	3	0	7	2	.78	1	.171	.230	.210
Whittaker, Tim	c	Auburn	Tor	A-	23	42	127	38	7	2	2	55	23	16	13	2	20	4	1	1	1	3	.25	2	.299	.379	.433
Widger, Chris	dh-1b	Everett	Sea	A-	31	5	13	1	0	0	0	1	2	0	6	1	1	0	0	0	0	0	.00	0	.077	.368	.077
Wigginton, Derek*	of	Kannapolis	CWS	A	23	114	373	98	16	4	8	146	42	50	23	3	95	3	2	1	2	6	.25	8	.263	.310	.391
Wilder, Paul*	dh	Bakersfield	TB	A+	24	30	98	26	5	0	2	37	15	13	15	0	45	3	0	0	1	0	1.00	1	.265	.379	.378
Wilfong, Nick*	of	San Jose	SF	A+	23	17	48	10	2	0	1	15	7	7	9	0	23	0	2	1	1	1	.50	1	.208	.328	.313
		Hagerstown	SF	A	23	109	370	88	15	2	15	152	44	58	39	1	138	4	6	5	15	2	.88	4	.238	.313	.411
Wilken, Kris#	1b	Delmarva	Bal	A	23	93	304	64	13	2	3	90	26	30	43	3	81	3	1	2	0	1	.00	8	.211	.313	.296
Williams, Brady	1b	Sarasota	Bos	A+	22	79	251	49	20	3	5	90	37	21	43	1	80	2	0	0	5	3	.63	5	.195	.318	.359
Williams, Clyde*	1b	Clinton	Mon	A	22	88	347	87	12	3	10	135	45	52	11	0	92	2	1	3	7	2	.78	6	.251	.275	.389
Williams, Edwin*	of	Tigers	Det	R	19	28	73	12	1	0	0	13	13	6	5	0	14	1	0	0	2	3	.40	0	.164	.228	.178
Williams, Jason	ss	Lancaster	Ari	A+	23	95	295	62	14	2	3	89	38	29	35	0	78	1	7	1	6	5	.55	9	.210	.295	.302
Williams, Jon*	c-dh	Giants	SF	R	23	39	136	44	7	3	3	66	24	26	16	1	14	5	0	3	1	1	.50	2	.324	.406	.485
		Salem-Keizr	SF	A-	23	6	13	8	1	0	2	15	5	4	1	0	2	0	0	0	0	0	.00	0	.615	.643	1.154
Williams, Matt	3b	New Jersey	StL	A-	23	41	136	40	11	2	2	61	25	17	25	1	43	4	0	1	1	2	.33	6	.294	.416	.449
Williams, Melvin#	of	Potomac	StL	A+	24	42	85	12	1	0	1	16	10	6	16	0	25	1	2	0	1	4	.20	0	.141	.284	.188
Williams, Mervin*	of	Royals	KC	R	18	39	113	21	1	0	0	22	15	9	14	1	35	1	3	0	10	4	.71	1	.186	.281	.195
Williams, P.J.	of	San Berndno	Sea	A+	25	30	108	25	2	0	0	27	13	8	11	0	20	1	2	3	7	4	.64	0	.231	.301	.250
Williamson, Chris*	of	Dayton	Cin	A	23	37	114	24	5	1	5	46	16	18	22	3	39	2	0	1	0	2	.00	1	.211	.345	.404
		Billings	Cin	R+	23	29	96	26	3	0	6	47	21	18	20	2	39	1	0	1	0	0	.00	0	.271	.398	.490
Williamson, John#	of	Everett	Sea	A-	23	53	188	52	16	2	5	87	26	34	22	2	52	4	1	1	2	1	.67	0	.277	.363	.463
Williamson, N.	of-dh	Cubs	ChC	R	21	11	23	4	0	0	0	4	1	2	2	0	10	0	0	0	0	1	.00	1	.174	.240	.174
Willingham, Josh	3b	Kane County	Fla	A	23	97	320	83	20	2	7	128	57	36	53	0	85	13	0	4	24	2	.92	7	.259	.382	.400
Wilson, Brandon	dh	Kingsport	NYM	R+	19	30	93	20	2	0	3	31	9	12	14	0	43	0	0	1	3	0	1.00	2	.215	.315	.333
Wilson, Heath	c	Columbus	Cle	A	23	39	114	20	5	0	3	34	14	16	26	1	41	10	2	1	2	1	.67	0	.175	.371	.298

2001 Batting — Class-A and Rookie Leagues

Player	Pos	Team	Org	Lg	A	G	AB	H	2B	3B	HR	TB	R	RBI	TBB	IBB	SO	HBP	SH	SF	SB	CS	SB%	GDP	Avg	OBP	SLG
Wilson, John	c-dh	Capital Cty	NYM	A	23	88	304	76	10	1	3	97	41	32	47	3	41	9	2	3	7	6	.54	5	.250	.364	.319
Wilson, Josh	2b-ss	Kane County	Fla	A	21	123	506	144	28	5	4	194	65	61	28	0	60	4	4	4	17	11	.61	11	.285	.325	.383
Winchester, Jeff	c	Salem	Col	A+	22	95	304	49	13	0	7	83	29	26	23	0	75	8	4	2	2	2	.50	3	.161	.237	.273
Winrow, Tommy*	of	Greensboro	NYY	A	21	63	222	37	5	0	7	63	21	24	15	0	56	3	0	1	2	1	.67	0	.167	.228	.284
Wise, Brad*	dh	Tigers	Det	R	18	11	25	5	0	0	0	5	2	3	3	0	10	1	0	1	0	0	.00	0	.200	.300	.200
Withey, Ryan	of	Cedar Rapds	Ana	A	24	62	202	50	11	0	6	79	31	28	20	0	53	7	2	1	20	5	.80	1	.248	.335	.391
Wolotka, Brian*	of	Hudson Val	TB	A-	21	39	124	33	6	3	4	57	14	20	12	0	39	3	0	0	1	0	1.00	2	.266	.345	.460
Wood, Stephen	dh-1b	Medcine Hat	Tor	R+	24	2	6	2	1	0	0	3	0	2	0	0	1	1	0	0	0	0	.00	0	.333	.429	.500
		Auburn	Tor	A-	24	33	129	27	5	1	2	40	9	11	7	1	25	0	0	1	0	0	.00	1	.209	.248	.310
Woodrow, Justin*	of	Johnson Cty	StL	R+	20	60	211	66	11	3	2	89	32	21	38	0	27	1	1	1	4	4	.50	4	.313	.418	.422
Woods, Ahmad	of	Braves	Atl	R	20	38	110	19	4	1	1	28	18	8	6	0	42	3	1	0	2	1	.67	0	.173	.233	.255
Woods, Blake	2b-3b	San Berndno	Sea	A+	23	10	22	2	0	0	1	5	3	4	4	0	7	1	0	0	3	0	1.00	5	.091	.259	.227
		Everett	Sea	A-	23	43	146	38	7	1	5	62	20	19	18	0	36	2	1	0	8	4	.67	0	.260	.349	.425
Woods, Michael	2b	Oneonta	Det	A-	21	9	37	10	2	0	0	12	6	3	4	0	5	1	0	0	5	1	.83	0	.270	.357	.324
		W Michigan	Det	A	21	44	163	44	8	4	0	60	30	17	32	1	44	5	1	2	13	7	.65	2	.270	.401	.368
Woodward, J.P.*	1b	Fort Wayne	SD	A	25	116	414	81	23	1	15	151	48	64	49	0	114	6	0	2	7	4	.64	1	.196	.289	.365
Woodward, Steve#	of	Lancaster	Ari	A+	24	47	144	29	6	1	0	37	19	6	17	0	40	1	2	0	5	5	.50	1	.201	.290	.257
Woody, Dominic	c	Kane County	Fla	A	23	66	227	54	11	3	6	89	38	33	21	0	47	7	0	2	6	2	.75	5	.238	.319	.392
Wright, David	3b	Kingsport	NYM	R+	19	35	116	35	7	0	4	54	27	16	16	0	29	2	0	0	9	1	.90	3	.302	.396	.466
Wright, Gavin	of	Michigan	Hou	A	23	100	392	107	17	6	8	160	68	52	28	0	76	5	4	5	26	6	.81	6	.273	.326	.408
Wyant, Hunter	2b-3b	Utica	Fla	A-	23	30	94	26	6	0	0	32	11	6	6	0	14	3	3	0	1	2	.33	1	.277	.340	.340
		Kane County	Fla	A	23	7	13	0	0	0	0	0	0	0	0	0	3	0	1	0	0	0	.00	0	.000	.000	.000
Yakopich, Joe	dh	Lancaster	Ari	A+	21	14	42	8	0	0	0	8	3	2	2	0	9	1	1	0	0	0	.00	0	.190	.244	.190
		Yakima	Ari	A-	21	45	101	23	3	0	0	26	16	6	21	0	23	1	2	1	2	2	.50	1	.228	.363	.257
Yan, Edwin#	2b-ss	Hickory	Pit	A	20	128	446	126	8	4	2	148	58	24	42	0	62	3	16	2	56	21	.73	6	.283	.347	.332
Yepez, Jose	c	Dunedin	Tor	A+	21	4	3	0	0	0	0	0	0	0	0	0	1	1	0	0	0	0	.00	0	.000	.250	.000
		Medcine Hat	Tor	R+	21	5	58	16	5	0	0	21	5	3	4	0	4	3	0	1	3	0	1.00	0	.276	.354	.362
Youkilis, Kevin	3b	Lowell	Bos	A-	23	59	183	58	14	2	3	85	52	28	70	0	28	5	0	2	4	3	.57	0	.317	.512	.464
		Augusta	Bos	A	23	5	12	2	0	0	0	2	0	0	3	0	3	1	0	0	0	0	.00	0	.167	.375	.167
Young, Eddie	of	White Sox	CWS	R	20	43	145	29	5	0	0	34	22	13	11	0	42	6	0	0	6	3	.73	0	.200	.284	.234
Young, Walter*	1b	Williamsprt	Pit	A-	22	66	232	67	10	1	13	118	40	47	19	5	43	5	0	2	1	1	.50	6	.289	.353	.509
Youngbauer, Scott#	ss	Lakewood	Phi	A	23	125	467	102	35	1	5	154	40	40	30	2	97	1	3	4	4	6	.40	6	.218	.265	.330
Yount, Andy	of	Oneonta	Det	A-	25	63	207	56	8	4	6	90	31	31	32	0	83	5	1	0	11	4	.73	5	.271	.381	.435
Yount, Dustin*	1b	Orioles	Bal	R	19	44	145	33	11	1	3	55	15	18	22	1	38	1	0	0	0	2	.00	3	.228	.333	.379
Zapey, Winton	c	Kane County	Fla	A	22	1	1	0	0	0	0	0	0	0	0	0	0	0	0	0	0	0	.00	0	.000	.000	.000
		Utica	Fla	A-	22	32	77	15	3	1	1	23	6	8	7	1	24	2	1	0	0	0	.00	4	.195	.279	.299
Zaragoza, Joel	3b	Brooklyn	NYM	A-	22	28	53	9	2	0	0	11	5	1	3	0	16	1	1	0	1	1	.50	1	.170	.228	.208
Zeber, Ryan	dh-c	Rancho Cuca	Ana	A+	24	31	92	22	4	0	2	32	11	12	10	0	29	1	0	1	0	0	.00	3	.239	.317	.348
Zieour, Neesan	of	Auburn	Tor	A-	21	8	21	8	0	2	0	12	3	2	1	0	1	1	0	0	1	0	1.00	0	.381	.435	.571
		Chston-WV	Tor	A	21	22	75	21	3	0	0	24	8	6	9	0	16	1	3	0	0	2	.00	2	.280	.365	.320
		Dunedin	Tor	A+	21	29	86	22	9	0	2	37	19	11	11	2	16	4	0	1	0	1	1.00	3	.256	.363	.430
Zoccolillo, Pete*	of	Daytona	ChC	A+	25	96	326	86	18	4	2	118	42	35	35	1	57	1	2	6	7	5	.58	4	.264	.332	.362
		Beloit	Mil	A	25	31	123	41	8	0	6	67	16	23	10	0	19	1	0	1	0	2	.00	3	.333	.385	.545
Zumwalt, Sean	of	Macon	Atl	A	21	101	349	73	20	2	6	115	43	38	34	0	101	4	3	1	8	1	.89	7	.209	.286	.330

2001 Pitching — Class-A and Rookie Leagues

HOW MUCH HE PITCHED											WHAT HE GAVE UP												THE RESULTS					
Player	Team	Org	Lg	A	G	GS	CG	GF	IP	BFP	H	R	ER	HR	SH	SF	HB	TBB	IBB	SO	WP	Bk	W	L	Pct.	ShO	Sv	ERA
Abbott, David	Chston-WV	Tor	A	24	8	8	0	0	49	192	39	10	6	0	1	0	1	8	0	35	0	1	2	3	.400	0	0	1.10
	Dunedin	Tor	A+	24	10	10	0	0	51.1	229	61	35	34	9	1	4	3	20	0	35	3	0	5	4	.556	0	0	5.96
Abbott, Jim	Twins	Min	R	22	2	0	0	1	1.2	8	1	1	1	0	0	0	0	2	0	1	0	0	0	0	.000	0	0	5.40
Abell, Joe	Asheville	Col	A	24	16	6	1	2	43	180	40	14	12	2	1	1	4	12	1	38	0	0	2	2	.500	1	0	2.51
Abraham, Paul	Pulaski	Tex	R+	22	15	0	0	9	31	140	26	22	17	2	1	1	5	16	0	28	6	1	3	2	.600	0	2	4.94
Abrams, Grant	Jamestown	Atl	A-	22	22	0	0	10	35.2	166	40	14	12	3	1	0	2	17	1	31	3	0	3	3	.500	0	0	3.03
Abreu, Jonathan*	Giants	SF	R	19	23	0	0	4	35.2	155	40	20	19	1	0	2	2	11	0	32	1	0	2	2	.500	0	1	4.79
Acosta, Domingo	Kingsport	NYM	R+	21	17	5	0	6	39	181	49	31	24	2	2	2	4	11	0	39	3	0	0	5	.000	0	0	5.54
Acosta, Manuel	Tampa	NYY	A+	21	2	2	0	0	7	31	7	7	6	1	0	0	0	6	0	8	4	0	0	1	.000	0	0	7.71
	Greensboro	NYY	A	21	10	10	1	0	65.2	267	37	14	11	2	4	1	2	37	0	67	7	2	5	2	.714	1	0	1.51
Acuna, Jose	Expos	Mon	R	20	14	6	0	3	51.1	201	41	13	11	2	3	0	6	11	0	45	4	0	2	4	.333	0	0	1.93
Adams, Brian*	Augusta	Bos	A	24	34	2	0	7	79.1	345	81	45	31	2	8	3	4	36	2	60	6	0	9	8	.529	0	1	3.52
Adams, Dan	Lakewood	Phi	A	24	50	0	0	26	68.2	287	67	25	16	4	4	1	3	12	6	55	0	0	4	6	.400	0	3	2.10
Adams, Jay	Billings	Cin	R+	23	28	0	0	12	36.2	164	41	20	16	3	1	0	2	5	0	28	1	0	1	1	.500	0	0	3.93
Adams, Jon	Ogden	Mil	R+	23	23	0	0	21	32	129	26	10	10	4	1	1	3	6	1	44	0	0	2	2	.500	0	12	2.81
Adinolfi, Timothy*	Spokane	KC	A-	24	18	4	0	3	47.2	215	48	29	25	7	1	1	4	19	0	39	4	1	2	3	.400	0	0	4.72
Advincola, Jose*	Delmarva	Bal	A	22	11	0	0	3	11.2	64	20	14	12	2	0	0	2	5	0	7	1	0	0	0	.000	0	0	9.26
	Bluefield	Bal	R+	22	22	0	0	5	39.1	177	37	28	23	6	2	3	4	22	0	50	9	2	1	2	.333	0	0	5.26
Aguilar, Edwin	Martinsvlle	Hou	R+	22	1	0	0	0	1.1	5	0	0	0	0	0	0	0	1	0	0	0	0	0	0	.000	0	0	0.00
	Pittsfield	Hou	A-	22	3	0	0	1	8	28	1	0	0	0	0	0	1	2	0	12	0	0	2	0	1.000	0	0	0.00
	Michigan	Hou	A	22	14	0	0	9	28.2	130	25	15	13	1	3	3	5	15	0	30	7	1	2	1	.667	0	3	4.08
Aguilar, Ray*	Braves	Atl	R	22	7	5	0	1	30	115	18	5	5	1	1	0	0	6	0	42	2	0	3	1	.750	0	0	1.50
	Jamestown	Atl	A-	22	2	2	0	0	12	46	7	4	2	1	0	0	0	3	0	16	0	0	1	1	.500	0	0	1.50
Aguilera, Adrian*	Dodgers	LA	R	22	4	0	0	0	4.2	22	2	4	4	1	1	1	0	3	0	6	0	0	0	0	.000	0	0	7.71
	Wilmington	LA	A	22	5	0	0	4	5.1	25	8	5	4	3	0	0	0	2	0	4	1	0	0	1	.000	0	1	6.75
Aiello, Nick*	Hudson Val	TB	A-	22	22	0	0	7	40	163	36	17	11	0	4	2	1	8	1	24	4	0	6	1	.857	0	0	2.47
Akens, Phil	Marlins	Fla	R	19	6	3	0	2	33.2	134	19	11	6	0	2	2	4	9	0	24	2	0	2	0	1.000	0	0	1.60
	Utica	Fla	A-	19	9	9	0	0	50	208	40	24	18	3	2	3	1	22	0	34	1	0	2	5	.286	0	0	3.24
Albaladejo, Jon	Pirates	Pit	R	19	10	2	0	5	19	85	22	13	10	1	2	3	1	2	0	24	2	0	0	3	.000	0	1	4.74
Albertus, Roberto*	Danville	Atl	R+	20	16	5	0	3	60.1	239	46	20	16	3	0	0	1	13	0	56	4	0	3	2	.600	0	2	2.39
Albright, Eric	Lansing	ChC	A	24	34	0	0	23	40.2	186	49	31	28	6	2	2	1	11	3	50	2	0	1	5	.167	0	8	6.20
Alcala, Jason	Hickory	Pit	A	21	34	0	0	18	41	173	35	12	8	0	1	0	2	13	1	56	4	1	3	1	.750	0	7	1.76
	Lynchburg	Pit	A+	21	18	0	0	17	26.2	105	21	7	7	2	1	1	1	5	1	27	2	0	0	2	.000	0	7	2.36
Allen, Blakely*	Provo	Ana	R+	22	28	0	0	18	50.2	193	35	13	12	0	1	0	1	8	4	55	2	0	7	3	.700	0	8	2.13
Allen, Rodney	High Desert	Mil	A+	28	43	0	0	13	78.1	329	72	44	38	9	6	3	2	28	1	95	5	0	4	6	.400	0	1	4.37
Allen, Travis	Mariners	Sea	R	21	17	0	0	12	23.1	96	25	12	11	1	1	2	1	4	0	26	2	0	2	2	.500	0	4	4.24
	Everett	Sea	A-	21	4	0	0	2	5.2	28	7	4	3	0	0	1	0	2	0	6	0	0	0	0	.000	0	0	4.76
Allen, Wyatt	Kannapolis	CWS	A	22	12	11	2	0	62.2	263	60	29	22	4	2	3	5	16	1	45	4	1	4	5	.444	0	0	3.16
Ally, Ben	Batavia	Phi	A-	23	21	0	0	5	43	183	42	15	5	1	1	5	0	14	2	26	5	0	3	2	.600	0	1	1.05
Almeida, Brian	Braves	Atl	R	20	2	0	0	0	4	17	2	1	1	0	1	0	1	2	0	3	0	0	0	1	.000	0	0	2.25
Almond, Casey	Tri-City	Col	A-	23	4	0	0	2	7	31	5	3	2	1	1	0	2	8	0	5	1	0	0	0	.000	0	0	2.57
	Casper	Col	R+	23	19	0	0	2	31.2	149	37	30	26	3	0	3	6	15	1	20	2	0	2	2	.500	0	0	7.39
Almonte, Henry	Pirates	Pit	R	21	2	1	0	0	10	41	11	4	3	1	0	0	1	1	1	10	2	0	1	0	1.000	0	0	2.70
	Hickory	Pit	A	21	20	1	0	3	26	134	39	25	19	1	3	1	2	17	0	17	2	0	2	2	.500	0	0	6.58
Alston, Travis	Clearwater	Phi	A+	25	12	1	0	5	18.1	91	19	13	11	1	0	1	1	16	0	7	0	0	1	2	.333	0	2	5.40
Altman, Gene	High Desert	Mil	A+	23	38	0	0	29	39	207	46	36	34	2	3	2	1	39	0	46	13	0	2	2	.500	0	12	7.85
Altman, Heath	Columbus	Cle	A	31	3	0	0	0	4	25	6	7	7	0	0	0	2	5	0	6	5	0	1	0	1.000	0	0	15.75
Alvarado, Luis*	Burlington	Cle	R+	19	16	0	0	4	31.1	141	34	18	16	1	0	0	4	12	0	31	3	2	1	0	1.000	0	0	4.60
Alvarez, Juan*	Braves	Atl	R	20	11	6	0	1	41.2	177	36	15	8	0	1	0	1	13	0	39	5	0	3	1	.750	0	0	1.73
Alvarez, Larry	Lansing	ChC	A	22	30	0	0	14	44	187	38	13	11	1	4	1	4	14	2	54	2	0	1	2	.333	0	2	2.25
Alvarez, Melvin*	Pirates	Pit	R	20	7	3	0	1	27	118	34	16	12	0	2	4	0	7	0	16	1	0	1	4	.200	0	0	4.00
Alvarez, Oscar*	Columbus	Cle	A	21	17	17	0	0	95	409	94	54	44	11	2	3	8	37	1	69	10	2	5	9	.357	0	0	4.17
Amancio, Jose	Athletics	Oak	R	20	14	8	0	2	53.1	225	51	23	22	3	1	2	8	16	0	33	1	0	7	3	.700	0	0	3.71
Ammons, Cary*	Wilmington	KC	A+	25	12	12	1	0	58	240	50	26	25	5	5	3	4	21	0	64	1	1	2	6	.250	0	0	3.88
	Mudville	Cin	A+	25	14	9	0	2	64.1	277	53	28	21	6	0	1	3	31	0	81	2	1	1	4	.200	0	0	2.94
An, Byeong*	Sarasota	Bos	A+	21	23	21	1	1	119.1	523	122	68	48	10	4	3	11	42	0	84	8	5	2	8	.200	0	0	3.62
Andara, Miguel	Pirates	Pit	R	20	8	3	0	3	32.1	143	28	18	13	0	1	1	4	20	1	20	4	0	0	4	.000	0	0	3.62
Anderegg, Jason	Eugene	SD	A-	23	14	13	0	1	63.2	286	64	46	34	4	3	3	5	27	0	62	5	0	3	7	.300	0	0	4.81
Andersen, Derek*	Chston-SC	TB	A	24	29	0	0	12	39.2	152	27	10	10	3	2	0	4	3	0	49	5	0	2	0	1.000	0	3	2.27
	Bakersfield	TB	A+	24	18	0	0	2	24	93	19	9	9	1	0	1	0	6	0	26	1	1	2	1	.667	0	0	3.38
Anderson, Craig*	San Berndno	Sea	A+	21	28	28	0	0	179	718	142	65	45	16	3	7	7	39	0	178	4	1	11	4	.733	0	0	2.26
Anderson, Jason	Greensboro	NYY	A	23	23	19	1	3	124.1	530	127	68	52	9	3	8	3	40	1	101	8	0	7	9	.438	0	1	3.76
	Staten Ilnd	NYY	A-	23	7	7	0	0	47.2	184	32	9	9	2	0	0	4	12	0	56	1	1	5	1	.833	0	0	1.70
Anderson, Julius	Hudson Val	TB	A-	22	10	0	0	6	15.2	69	17	9	7	1	0	0	1	6	0	4	2	0	0	0	.000	0	0	4.02
Anderson, Luke	San Jose	SF	A+	24	59	0	0	56	66	268	56	22	19	4	0	0	1	13	0	76	4	0	2	2	.500	0	30	2.59
Anderson, Travis	Michigan	Hou	A	24	31	22	1	4	140	634	165	102	89	12	4	4	11	52	0	99	17	1	6	8	.429	0	1	5.72
Anderson, Wes	Brevard Cty	Fla	A+	22	8	8	0	0	32	164	48	26	20	3	1	2	4	21	0	17	1	0	1	6	.143	0	0	5.63
	Marlins	Fla	R	22	1	1	0	0	0.1	6	3	2	1	1	0	0	0	1	0	0	0	0	0	1	.000	0	0	27.00
Andrade, Jancy	Delmarva	Bal	A	24	8	8	0	0	48.1	204	46	22	20	2	0	1	3	16	1	43	1	0	2	4	.333	0	0	3.72
	Frederick	Bal	A+	24	20	13	0	2	75	326	80	47	37	6	4	6	6	28	1	57	6	1	5	5	.500	0	0	4.44
Andrade, Steve	Provo	Ana	R+	24	1	0	0	0	2	9	3	0	0	0	0	0	0	0	0	5	0	0	0	0	.000	0	0	0.00
	Cedar Rapds	Ana	A	24	20	0	0	9	29	129	33	24	21	3	2	1	2	8	0	31	7	0	2	1	.667	0	0	6.52
Andrews, Aron	Dodgers	LA	R	24	6	0	0	6	7.1	25	2	0	0	0	0	0	0	1	0	9	0	0	0	0	.000	0	3	0.00
	Wilmington	LA	A	24	15	1	0	7	44	176	40	14	10	3	1	3	3	7	0	26	2	0	4	3	.571	0	2	2.05
Andujar, Jesse	Angels	Ana	R	22	3	0	0	0	5.1	26	6	3	3	0	0	0	2	4	0	6	1	0	0	0	.000	0	0	5.06
	Cedar Rapds	Ana	A	22	5	0	0	3	5	24	6	4	3	1	0	0	1	2	0	6	1	0	0	0	.000	0	0	5.40
Anez, Omar	Delmarva	Bal	A	21	12	0	0	3	15.2	88	23	16	14	2	1	2	1	18	1	17	8	0	0	0	.000	0	0	8.04
	Bluefield	Bal	R+	21	15	6	0	3	41.1	206	51	46	35	5	0	4	10	17	0	46	8	0	2	7	.222	0	0	7.62
Aquino, Danny	Burlington	Cle	R+	20	6	0	0	2	7.2	36	8	7	7	3	0	0	0	4	0	3	0	0	1	0	1.000	0	0	8.22
Arellano, Salvador	Idaho Falls	SD	R+	19	3	3	0	0	12.1	65	17	13	5	0	0	0	3	5	0	8	2	0	0	1	.000	0	0	3.65
Arias, Daniel	Angels	Ana	R	20	16	3	0	3	47.2	215	64	25	16	0	2	3	8	9	0	42	5	4	1	2	.333	0	1	3.02
Arias, Miguel	Spokane	KC	A-	22	5	0	0	1	7.2	49	12	13	9	2	0	3	3	10	1	6	1	0	0	0	.000	0	0	10.57
Armitage, Barry	Spokane	KC	A-	23	15	14	0	0	72.1	322	79	57	49	8	0	5	4	26	1	70	4	0	1	7	.125	0	0	6.10
Arnold, Jason	Staten Ilnd	NYY	A-	23	10	10	2	0	66	243	35	13	11	2	2	1	3	15	0	74	2	0	7	2	.778	1	0	1.50
Arteaga, Francisco	Braves	Atl	R	20	18	0	0	14	33.2	140	20	13	9	1	0	1	3	13	0	30	0	2	0	1	.000	0	5	2.41

2001 Pitching — Class-A and Rookie Leagues

HOW MUCH HE PITCHED											WHAT HE GAVE UP												THE RESULTS					
Player	Team	Org	Lg	A	G	GS	CG	GF	IP	BFP	H	R	ER	HR	SH	SF	HB	TBB	IBB	SO	WP	Bk	W	L	Pct.	ShO	Sv	ERA
	Jamestown	Atl	A-	20	3	0	0	2	3.2	14	3	1	1	0	0	0	0	2	0	5	0	0	0	0	.000	0	1	2.45
Arteaja, Erick	Phillies	Phi	R	21	10	9	0	0	52	219	58	28	21	0	1	0	2	7	0	28	1	0	4	1	.800	0	0	3.63
Arthur, Tony*	Provo	Ana	R+	23	10	10	1	0	55	222	48	32	23	5	0	3	2	11	0	49	4	0	7	1	.875	1	0	3.76
	Cedar Rapds	Ana	A	23	5	5	0	0	28	127	33	11	8	1	3	2	1	9	0	28	0	0	3	1	.750	0	0	2.57
Artieta, Corey*	Beloit	Mil	A	25	26	4	0	9	63.1	282	62	40	32	7	0	2	4	38	0	36	10	0	2	1	.667	0	0	4.55
Artiles, Carlos*	Tampa	NYY	A+	21	5	0	0	1	9	38	7	5	5	2	1	0	0	5	1	9	0	0	0	1	.000	0	0	5.00
	Yankees	NYY	R	21	10	5	0	1	36.1	159	41	15	15	1	2	2	1	12	0	37	3	1	1	3	.250	0	1	3.72
	Staten Ilnd	NYY	A-	21	1	1	0	0	5	18	1	0	0	0	0	0	0	3	0	4	0	0	0	0	.000	0	0	0.00
Artman, Dane*	Brewers	Mil	R	20	5	5	0	0	12.1	56	15	8	8	0	0	1	0	5	0	14	0	0	0	1	.000	0	0	5.84
	Ogden	Mil	R+	20	6	3	0	0	11.1	62	21	22	20	4	0	0	1	8	0	10	3	0	0	3	.000	0	0	15.88
Asahina, Jon	Utica	Fla	A-	21	15	13	0	1	69.2	283	56	27	20	3	2	2	5	19	0	55	3	0	4	6	.400	0	0	2.58
Ascencio, Miguel	Clearwater	Phi	A+	21	28	21	2	1	155.1	649	124	62	49	7	3	6	2	70	1	123	9	2	12	5	.706	1	0	2.84
Asencio, Dalmiro	Bristol	CWS	R+	18	6	3	0	2	18.1	78	24	10	10	3	2	0	2	4	1	6	2	1	0	1	.000	0	0	4.91
Asencio, Domingo*	White Sox	CWS	R	20	7	7	0	0	48	195	45	23	13	5	1	1	2	8	0	29	0	1	2	1	.667	0	0	2.44
Ashlock, Chad	Salem-Keizr	SF	A-	23	11	10	0	0	46.2	190	46	26	23	4	0	1	0	15	0	39	1	0	4	3	.571	0	0	4.44
Astacio, Andres	Great Falls	LA	R+	21	17	12	0	3	73.2	332	87	52	41	6	3	2	6	13	0	62	2	3	2	6	.250	0	0	5.01
Astacio, Ezequiel	Phillies	Phi	R	21	9	9	0	0	47	196	48	16	12	2	2	1	4	10	0	42	1	0	4	2	.667	0	0	2.30
Astacio, Hector	Angels	Ana	R	18	21	4	0	6	43	182	45	21	15	1	1	2	5	6	0	36	0	1	3	2	.600	0	1	3.14
Atencio, Donald	Athletics	Oak	R	20	15	2	0	3	28	132	33	19	14	0	1	2	3	13	0	29	6	1	0	2	.000	0	0	4.50
Axelson, Josh	Peoria	StL	A	23	18	18	1	0	109.1	467	112	62	56	12	2	6	7	28	0	77	19	0	5	7	.417	1	0	4.61
	Potomac	StL	A+	23	10	10	1	0	56.2	251	61	41	35	10	2	1	7	19	0	38	2	0	2	5	.286	0	0	5.56
Ayala, Luis	Salem	Col	A+	24	13	0	0	12	13.1	61	19	10	6	0	1	0	2	5	0	10	2	1	0	1	.000	0	7	4.05
Ayala, Roberto*	Princeton	TB	R+	21	5	0	0	2	3	19	5	5	4	0	0	0	1	5	0	1	2	0	0	0	.000	0	0	12.00
Backsmeyer, Justin	Charlotte	Tex	A+	22	33	0	0	10	60	276	56	32	25	3	1	5	5	42	2	47	6	1	1	2	.333	0	0	3.75
Baek, Cha	San Berndno	Sea	A+	22	5	4	0	0	21	81	17	10	8	2	0	1	2	2	0	16	0	0	1	0	1.000	0	0	3.43
Baez, Hebel	Athletics	Oak	R	21	12	4	0	3	35.1	166	41	24	14	2	2	2	3	7	0	22	1	2	1	2	.333	0	0	3.57
Bailey, David	Daytona	ChC	A+	25	34	0	0	25	39.2	177	45	25	22	5	1	4	1	15	2	39	2	1	0	2	.000	0	8	4.99
Bailey, Ryan	Provo	Ana	R+	22	15	6	0	1	52.1	239	62	29	23	2	0	1	2	16	0	48	8	1	4	1	.800	0	1	3.96
Baker, Bo	Royals	KC	R	21	1	0	0	1	2	6	2	0	0	0	0	0	0	0	0	1	0	0	0	0	.000	0	0	0.00
Baker, Brad	Sarasota	Bos	A+	21	24	23	0	0	120	563	132	77	63	8	2	3	9	64	0	103	12	0	7	9	.438	0	0	4.72
Baker, Jason	Kinston	Cle	A+	27	13	8	1	1	49.2	212	44	21	19	5	0	1	1	22	0	44	3	0	4	1	.800	1	0	3.44
Baker, Joey	Burlington	KC	A	23	27	23	0	2	140	613	155	97	83	19	4	6	8	45	1	71	9	0	7	10	.412	0	0	5.34
Baker, Ryan	Macon	Atl	A	24	40	0	0	32	47.1	195	40	13	11	2	3	1	1	15	1	56	3	0	2	3	.400	0	18	2.09
Balbuena, Caleb	San Berndno	Sea	A+	25	36	5	0	18	63	321	78	57	48	4	1	2	13	44	0	56	5	0	0	5	.000	0	0	6.86
Balser, Jeffrey	Angels	Ana	R	21	20	0	0	12	22.1	130	50	29	22	1	2	1	4	5	1	12	5	0	2	3	.400	0	3	8.87
Banks, Tyler	Marlins	Fla	R	21	10	2	0	4	31.1	124	24	9	8	2	2	0	0	6	1	26	1	0	0	2	.000	0	1	2.30
Barbarossa, Josh*	Idaho Falls	SD	R+	22	7	3	0	0	27.2	136	33	22	12	2	1	0	2	17	0	25	3	0	2	1	.667	0	0	3.90
Barber, Scott	Yakima	Ari	A-	23	2	2	0	0	12	48	11	3	3	1	0	0	1	3	0	11	0	0	2	0	1.000	0	0	2.25
	Lancaster	Ari	A+	23	29	12	0	8	85	405	121	76	68	16	0	1	5	27	2	83	5	0	7	7	.500	0	2	7.20
Barnes, Pat*	Wisconsin	Sea	A	22	10	0	0	2	11	38	4	2	1	0	0	0	0	4	0	10	1	0	1	0	1.000	0	0	0.82
Barnett, John	Spokane	KC	A-	20	20	0	0	16	34	152	40	20	17	3	1	0	4	10	2	29	2	0	0	3	.000	0	1	4.50
Barr, Adam*	Burlington	Cle	R+	21	8	3	0	0	23	111	17	15	10	2	0	1	2	25	0	29	1	1	2	0	1.000	0	0	3.91
	Columbus	Cle	A	21	6	0	0	1	7.2	44	9	14	11	2	0	1	1	11	0	10	0	0	0	0	.000	0	0	12.91
Barreto, Armando	Expos	Mon	R	20	14	1	0	5	34.2	157	37	21	12	2	2	2	3	15	1	24	3	1	1	3	.250	0	2	3.12
Barrett, Jimmy	Michigan	Hou	A	21	27	25	1	2	130.2	594	122	76	65	12	0	4	24	62	0	98	8	1	10	5	.667	0	0	4.48
Barrios, Angel	Martinsvlle	Hou	R+	20	11	10	0	0	45.2	189	45	17	16	0	0	0	1	16	0	54	2	0	3	5	.375	0	0	3.15
Barrios, Rafael	Tigers	Det	R	20	23	0	0	18	33.2	144	24	12	8	1	4	1	2	17	3	29	2	2	3	3	.500	0	6	2.14
Barry, Kevin	Jamestown	Atl	A-	23	29	0	0	23	31.1	126	14	5	3	0	0	1	0	18	0	54	0	0	1	0	1.000	0	12	0.86
Bartel, Richard	Reds	Cin	R	19	1	0	0	0	1	3	0	0	0	0	0	0	0	0	0	0	0	0	0	0	.000	0	0	0.00
Bartlett, Richard	Delmarva	Bal	A	20	19	18	0	1	95.1	414	109	54	48	6	5	2	5	30	1	60	5	1	5	9	.357	0	0	4.53
Bartsch, John	Orioles	Bal	R	22	10	0	0	5	18	73	19	8	8	4	0	0	2	1	0	10	2	0	2	1	.667	0	0	4.00
Barzilla, Philip*	Pittsfield	Hou	A-	23	16	14	0	0	78.1	352	87	52	41	1	1	2	1	34	0	56	9	0	4	5	.444	0	0	4.71
Basham, Bobby	Billings	Cin	R+	22	6	6	0	0	29.2	140	36	23	16	2	1	0	2	17	0	37	4	2	1	2	.333	0	0	4.85
Basilio, Manuel	Princeton	TB	R+	21	11	9	0	1	48.1	219	49	32	30	4	0	0	9	23	0	57	2	3	2	4	.333	0	0	5.59
Bass, Brian	Burlington	KC	A	20	26	26	1	0	139.1	613	138	82	72	16	3	5	15	53	0	75	14	1	3	10	.231	1	0	4.65
Bastardo, Jose*	Giants	SF	R	21	18	0	0	6	17.1	88	16	14	10	3	0	0	0	20	0	24	1	0	1	3	.250	0	0	5.19
Batista, Cristian	Brewers	Mil	R	21	13	0	0	6	21.1	106	26	24	12	0	0	0	4	10	1	16	5	5	0	1	.000	0	0	5.06
Batista, Gorky	Reds	Cin	R	21	10	8	2	1	52	220	55	18	16	0	1	1	1	10	0	53	1	1	5	3	.625	1	1	2.77
Batista, Roberto	Johnson Cty	StL	R+	20	20	3	0	3	42.2	190	54	23	16	3	1	0	5	9	0	30	6	3	2	3	.400	0	0	3.38
Bausher, Tim	Everett	Sea	A-	23	11	1	0	3	15.2	80	25	15	15	2	1	0	0	8	0	18	2	1	0	3	.000	0	1	8.62
Bautista, Denny	Utica	Fla	A-	19	7	7	0	0	39	156	25	16	9	0	0	2	4	6	0	31	3	0	3	1	.750	0	0	2.08
	Kane County	Fla	A	19	8	7	0	0	39.1	172	43	21	19	2	2	1	2	14	0	20	4	2	3	1	.750	0	0	4.35
Baxter, Allen	Marlins	Fla	R	18	9	7	0	0	34	138	25	13	9	0	1	3	5	8	0	40	4	0	2	3	.400	0	0	2.38
	Utica	Fla	A-	18	1	1	0	0	5	21	3	2	2	0	0	0	1	3	0	5	2	0	0	0	.000	0	0	3.60
Bayrer, Thomas	Martinsvlle	Hou	R+	22	16	0	0	5	26	124	27	19	15	3	1	1	2	22	1	33	4	2	0	3	.000	0	1	5.19
	Pittsfield	Hou	A-	22	5	0	0	2	8	37	5	2	2	0	1	0	0	11	0	5	1	0	0	0	.000	0	1	2.25
Beal, Andy*	Greensboro	NYY	A	23	2	2	0	0	10.1	40	10	1	0	0	0	0	0	3	0	6	2	0	1	0	1.000	0	0	0.00
	Tampa	NYY	A+	23	17	17	0	0	99	431	101	57	33	6	2	4	1	30	1	72	7	0	5	5	.500	0	0	3.00
Beck, David*	Athletics	Oak	R	24	18	0	0	17	18	76	13	3	2	0	1	0	3	7	1	32	0	0	0	0	.000	0	9	1.00
Beckstead, Jentry	Casper	Col	R+	22	23	0	0	21	28	118	23	13	9	1	0	1	3	12	1	28	3	0	1	0	1.000	0	12	2.89
Bedard, Erik*	Orioles	Bal	R	23	2	2	0	0	6	25	4	2	2	0	0	0	2	3	0	7	0	0	0	1	.000	0	0	3.00
	Frederick	Bal	A+	23	17	17	0	0	96.1	382	68	27	23	4	3	1	9	26	0	130	3	0	9	2	.818	0	0	2.15
Beigh, David	Pirates	Pit	R	21	10	7	0	1	30.2	149	30	28	22	0	0	0	5	28	0	24	10	1	0	5	.000	0	0	6.46
Belanger, Brandon	Fort Wayne	SD	A	24	33	0	0	9	47.2	213	57	36	34	3	1	6	3	18	4	39	2	1	1	3	.250	0	2	6.42
Belicic, Adam*	Danville	Atl	R+	23	21	0	0	13	26.1	131	31	18	14	5	0	1	3	16	0	22	4	0	0	2	.000	0	1	4.78
Belizario, Ronald	Marlins	Fla	R	19	13	10	1	0	73	309	62	29	19	4	4	3	11	20	0	54	8	1	4	6	.400	1	0	2.34
Bell, Tom	Utica	Fla	A-	21	18	0	0	4	23.2	111	29	22	21	3	1	1	1	13	0	21	6	0	0	1	.000	0	0	7.99
Belson, Greg	South Bend	Ari	A	23	46	0	0	39	57.2	243	54	24	16	3	3	2	2	17	3	50	2	0	6	4	.600	0	16	2.50
Beltran, Frank	Daytona	ChC	A+	21	21	18	0	0	95.1	424	93	62	53	10	1	4	9	40	1	72	4	0	6	9	.400	0	0	5.00
Beltre, Omar	Pulaski	Tex	R+	19	13	12	0	0	69.1	290	56	28	26	4	3	3	9	23	0	83	12	1	6	3	.667	0	0	3.37
Benedetti, John	Chston-SC	TB	A	24	44	0	0	22	68.2	312	74	35	25	4	5	8	6	21	4	63	4	0	2	4	.333	0	4	3.28
Benik, B.J.	Boise	ChC	A-	23	20	0	0	10	33	153	34	30	14	3	3	2	3	9	4	29	6	1	6	2	.750	0	2	3.82
Benitez, Fabricio	Lowell	Bos	A-	21	9	9	0	0	49.1	203	47	25	23	2	2	5	3	11	0	23	1	0	0	3	.000	0	0	4.20
Benjamin, Petersen	Salem-Keizr	SF	A-	23	15	5	0	1	55.2	224	51	24	20	2	2	2	1	7	1	50	3	0	3	1	.750	0	1	3.23
Bennett, Jamie*	Batavia	Phi	A-	24	18	0	0	4	30	128	26	14	12	0	1	0	1	11	2	31	3	0	1	1	.500	0	1	3.60

2001 Pitching — Class-A and Rookie Leagues

HOW MUCH HE PITCHED											WHAT HE GAVE UP												THE RESULTS					
Player	Team	Org	Lg	A	G	GS	CG	GF	IP	BFP	H	R	ER	HR	SH	SF	HB	TBB	IBB	SO	WP	Bk	W	L	Pct.	ShO	Sv	ERA
Bennett, Steve	Capital Cty	NYM	A	25	12	11	0	0	52	226	37	26	17	5	0	2	4	25	0	77	6	1	0	4	.000	0	0	2.94
	St. Lucie	NYM	A+	25	7	6	0	0	26.1	122	31	26	23	1	0	1	2	12	0	20	1	1	0	1	.000	0	0	7.86
Bent, Andy	Myrtle Bch	Atl	A+	23	29	0	0	9	56	237	44	29	21	5	5	2	3	25	3	53	3	4	1	5	.167	0	1	3.38
Bentz, Chad*	Vermont	Mon	A-	22	8	8	0	0	36.2	163	39	23	20	2	2	2	0	11	0	38	4	0	1	3	.250	0	0	4.91
Bernard, Jason	Batavia	Phi	A-	23	13	12	0	0	64.2	300	79	43	28	6	2	4	7	24	0	30	4	0	2	6	.250	0	0	3.90
Berney, Scott	Asheville	Col	A	24	33	1	0	11	50	225	59	37	28	3	2	0	6	21	1	28	0	0	2	2	.500	0	0	5.04
Berry, Casey	Pulaski	Tex	R+	21	14	1	0	9	41.1	183	40	20	18	6	1	0	3	15	1	38	2	0	4	2	.667	0	2	3.92
Berube, Martin	Bluefield	Bal	R+	20	11	11	0	0	53	247	78	42	36	6	2	4	2	10	0	49	4	0	4	2	.667	0	0	6.11
Biddlestone, Jason	Williamsprt	Pit	A-	23	16	1	0	7	31.1	135	28	11	5	1	1	3	0	17	0	25	2	0	3	1	.750	0	1	1.44
Birdsong, Tim	Mudville	Cin	A+	25	23	0	0	20	28.2	143	39	21	16	3	1	1	2	15	2	31	2	1	3	4	.429	0	5	5.02
Birk, Ben*	Marlins	Fla	R	24	3	0	0	1	6	22	3	0	0	0	0	0	0	1	0	4	0	0	0	0	.000	0	0	0.00
Birkins, Kurt*	Orioles	Bal	R	21	5	4	0	1	22	85	13	5	5	2	0	0	4	3	0	24	1	0	2	1	.667	0	0	2.05
	Bluefield	Bal	R+	21	6	6	0	0	37	144	28	14	12	2	1	0	2	5	0	42	3	0	4	1	.800	0	0	2.92
Birtwell, John	Oneonta	Det	A-	22	23	0	0	18	26.1	114	25	12	11	1	1	0	4	6	0	43	1	0	1	2	.333	0	7	3.76
Bittner, Tim*	Bristol	CWS	R+	22	8	8	1	0	49	197	34	14	6	0	2	0	4	12	0	53	4	2	6	1	.857	1	0	1.10
	Kannapolis	CWS	A	22	4	4	0	0	20.1	93	21	18	10	1	2	0	4	9	0	15	4	1	0	3	.000	0	0	4.43
Blackley, Travis*	Everett	Sea	A-	19	14	14	0	0	78.2	319	60	34	29	7	2	2	1	29	0	90	3	0	6	1	.857	0	0	3.32
Blackwell, Scott	Quad City	Min	A	22	13	0	0	3	19.1	87	17	17	11	1	2	0	2	9	2	19	0	1	1	2	.333	0	0	5.12
Blake, Peter*	Twins	Min	R	23	6	0	0	1	7.2	26	5	3	3	0	0	0	1	1	0	7	0	0	0	1	.000	0	0	3.52
Blaney, Matthew	Dodgers	LA	R	23	11	0	0	8	16	75	21	17	17	2	0	0	8	5	0	8	2	0	1	3	.250	0	1	9.56
Blankenship, John*	Greensboro	NYY	A	23	27	9	0	3	75.2	305	53	21	20	5	3	1	4	28	0	85	5	0	5	5	.500	0	0	2.38
	Staten Ilnd	NYY	A-	23	5	5	0	0	35	143	29	16	12	2	0	1	0	8	0	22	1	0	4	0	1.000	0	0	3.09
Blanton, Jason	Boise	ChC	A-	22	8	0	0	4	15.1	71	16	9	7	2	0	1	2	8	2	9	1	0	0	3	.000	0	0	4.11
	Lansing	ChC	A	22	7	0	0	2	11	49	14	6	5	0	0	0	1	3	0	7	0	0	0	0	.000	0	0	4.09
	Daytona	ChC	A+	22	6	2	0	3	20.2	83	10	3	1	0	0	1	0	15	2	21	1	0	3	0	1.000	0	0	0.44
Blasdell, Jared	New Jersey	StL	A-	23	26	0	0	19	28.2	114	18	6	4	2	1	0	4	7	1	36	2	0	0	1	.000	0	11	1.26
Blethen, Matt*	Burlington	Cle	R+	22	18	0	0	5	49	203	42	17	15	5	3	1	1	15	0	42	3	0	4	1	.800	0	1	2.76
	Columbus	Cle	A	22	1	0	0	0	2	16	7	5	3	1	0	0	0	3	0	1	0	0	0	0	.000	0	0	13.50
Blood, Justin*	Everett	Sea	A-	22	10	0	0	5	11.2	57	15	15	13	1	0	1	0	9	0	14	2	0	1	1	.500	0	0	10.03
Bludau, Frank	Dayton	Cin	A	25	42	0	0	37	53.2	217	42	16	15	0	1	1	1	10	3	39	4	0	6	3	.667	0	21	2.52
Bobbitt, Seth	Pittsfield	Hou	A-	23	8	5	0	0	28	122	27	8	5	2	0	1	2	10	0	23	2	0	0	0	.000	0	0	1.61
Bohannon, Gary	St. Lucie	NYM	A+	26	15	0	0	7	29.2	126	35	15	12	2	3	1	1	10	1	11	2	0	1	0	1.000	0	1	3.64
Bong, Jung*	Myrtle Bch	Atl	A+	21	28	28	0	0	168	677	151	67	56	7	6	3	4	47	0	145	7	1	13	9	.591	0	0	3.00
Bonilla, Vincent	Quad City	Min	A	23	53	0	0	47	58.2	259	61	22	21	3	2	1	2	23	2	55	4	0	5	6	.455	0	25	3.22
Bonser, Boof	Hagerstown	SF	A	20	27	27	0	0	134	548	91	40	37	7	2	3	9	61	2	178	10	1	16	4	.800	0	0	2.49
Borner, Brady*	Williamsprt	Pit	A-	23	3	1	0	1	12.2	41	4	1	1	1	0	0	0	1	0	13	0	0	1	0	1.000	0	0	0.71
	Hickory	Pit	A	23	9	8	3	1	59.1	226	43	18	16	5	1	0	0	12	0	58	0	1	5	1	.833	1	0	2.43
Borrell, Danny*	Tampa	NYY	A+	23	22	20	0	0	111	474	109	58	49	6	4	6	5	38	2	84	8	2	7	9	.438	0	0	3.97
Bostick, Adam*	Marlins	Fla	R	19	7	1	0	0	12.2	57	16	8	6	0	0	1	0	3	0	13	2	0	1	1	.500	0	0	4.26
Bott, Glenn*	Mariners	Sea	R	20	2	0	0	2	3	14	5	2	2	0	0	0	0	0	0	4	0	0	0	0	.000	0	1	6.00
	Everett	Sea	A-	20	19	0	0	11	43	189	32	17	11	4	1	1	1	23	0	57	8	0	2	3	.400	0	4	2.30
Bouknight, Kip	Tri-City	Col	A-	23	15	15	0	0	81	335	69	29	25	3	2	5	8	19	0	86	8	2	3	5	.375	0	0	2.78
Boutwell, Andy	Dayton	Cin	A	22	32	2	0	6	67.2	292	57	41	37	8	1	2	1	34	3	83	5	1	4	4	.500	0	2	4.92
Bowen, Chad	Brooklyn	NYM	A-	20	3	2	0	0	9.1	42	14	5	5	0	0	0	0	3	0	11	0	0	1	2	.333	0	0	4.82
Bowers, Rob	Savannah	Tex	A	24	11	0	0	6	18.2	84	26	13	13	4	0	0	1	5	0	8	0	1	0	0	.000	0	0	6.27
	Pulaski	Tex	R+	24	4	0	0	4	9	46	13	7	4	0	1	0	0	4	3	7	0	0	1	1	.500	0	0	4.00
Bowles, Larry*	Provo	Ana	R+	23	19	1	0	4	27.1	116	32	18	17	4	1	1	0	6	0	25	3	0	4	1	.800	0	0	5.60
Bowyer, Travis	Elizabethtn	Min	R+	20	9	8	0	0	38.1	170	38	30	26	3	1	3	3	20	0	34	7	0	2	5	.286	0	0	6.10
Boyer, Blaine	Danville	Atl	R+	20	13	12	0	0	50	220	48	35	24	4	3	1	5	19	0	57	9	1	4	5	.444	0	0	4.32
Bradley, Bobby	Lynchburg	Pit	A+	21	9	9	0	0	49	209	44	23	17	3	3	0	1	20	0	46	5	0	1	2	.333	0	0	3.12
Bradley, Dave	Mudville	Cin	A+	24	15	1	0	5	31.1	153	36	25	22	2	2	3	3	24	0	31	1	0	1	1	.500	0	1	6.32
	Dayton	Cin	A	24	16	0	0	11	29	124	30	15	12	2	2	0	2	9	0	33	5	0	0	2	.000	0	0	3.72
Bradshaw, Chris	Pulaski	Tex	R+	23	14	3	0	3	47.2	206	42	28	21	2	0	0	7	14	0	52	2	3	2	2	.500	0	1	3.97
Brandon, Keith	Tigers	Det	R	22	19	0	0	5	33.1	162	44	28	21	1	1	0	0	20	0	35	2	2	2	0	1.000	0	0	5.67
Brandt, Jon	Eugene	SD	A-	23	13	6	0	1	45	194	45	25	16	3	1	2	2	13	0	44	4	0	3	2	.600	0	0	3.20
Brannon, Nick*	Reds	Cin	R	24	17	0	0	17	21.1	88	13	4	1	0	1	0	0	9	2	25	0	0	1	2	.333	0	10	0.42
	Dayton	Cin	A	24	2	0	0	0	4.1	22	8	6	6	2	0	0	0	2	0	4	1	0	0	0	.000	0	0	12.46
Bravo, Edgar	Johnson Cty	StL	R+	20	18	0	0	11	21.1	95	17	15	12	1	1	2	3	16	2	15	3	1	0	3	.000	0	1	5.06
Bridenbaugh, C.*	Wilmington	LA	A	22	21	20	1	0	127.1	532	131	58	52	11	4	5	7	30	0	76	5	0	3	6	.333	0	0	3.68
Bright, Nathan	Pulaski	Tex	R+	22	12	0	0	5	20.2	103	31	18	13	3	1	0	0	10	0	16	5	0	1	3	.250	0	0	5.66
Brito, Eude*	Lakewood	Phi	A	20	44	0	0	20	69.1	273	53	28	21	7	5	0	2	14	2	58	3	2	4	3	.571	0	6	2.73
Britton, Chris	Orioles	Bal	R	19	12	3	0	2	32.2	153	35	20	10	3	2	2	5	12	1	20	1	0	2	3	.400	0	0	2.76
Brooks, Conor	Visalia	Oak	A+	24	45	4	0	12	84.1	376	98	55	42	11	3	5	8	22	1	64	2	1	5	5	.500	0	0	4.48
Brooks, Frank*	Clearwater	Phi	A+	23	37	15	0	5	112.2	504	113	70	59	18	1	5	9	58	2	92	9	0	5	10	.333	0	1	4.71
Brous, Dave*	San Jose	SF	A+	22	11	9	0	2	32	160	28	25	22	2	2	1	4	36	0	18	4	0	2	4	.333	0	0	6.19
	Hagerstown	SF	A	22	20	0	0	6	32.2	156	30	18	13	3	1	3	5	29	0	21	6	0	0	1	.000	0	3	3.58
Brown, Andrew	Jamestown	Atl	A-	21	14	12	0	0	64.1	267	50	29	28	5	0	0	3	31	0	59	5	0	3	4	.429	0	0	3.92
Brown, Eric	Cubs	ChC	R	23	11	0	0	8	17.1	77	15	4	2	0	1	1	2	4	0	14	1	0	0	1	.000	0	4	1.04
	Lansing	ChC	A	23	16	0	0	7	20.2	85	18	6	6	0	1	1	0	5	1	23	1	0	3	1	.750	0	1	2.61
Brown, Ira	Royals	KC	R	19	11	10	0	0	39.2	186	40	27	22	2	0	1	2	25	0	42	5	0	2	5	.286	0	0	4.99
Brown, Jeremy	Elizabethtn	Min	R+	23	3	2	0	0	11	46	10	4	4	1	0	0	0	3	0	9	0	0	0	0	.000	0	0	3.27
Brueggemann, D.*	Salem	Col	A+	26	48	0	0	18	64	294	66	40	34	0	1	3	14	37	1	36	2	1	2	0	1.000	0	2	4.78
Bruney, Brian	South Bend	Ari	A	20	26	0	0	20	32.2	142	24	19	15	1	2	1	3	19	2	40	3	2	1	4	.200	0	8	4.13
	Yakima	Ari	A-	20	15	0	0	11	21	102	19	14	12	2	3	2	2	11	0	28	7	0	1	2	.333	0	2	5.14
Buchanan, Brian*	Greensboro	NYY	A	25	37	4	0	4	79.1	348	82	42	36	9	4	3	6	34	0	82	1	2	4	2	.667	0	0	4.08
Buchholz, Taylor	Lakewood	Phi	A	20	28	26	5	0	176.2	741	165	83	66	8	5	7	11	57	0	136	1	0	9	14	.391	3	0	3.36
Bucktrot, Keith	Lakewood	Phi	A	21	24	24	3	0	134.2	604	139	93	79	16	8	7	15	58	0	97	11	0	6	11	.353	0	0	5.28
Buglovsky, Chris	Asheville	Col	A	22	26	26	0	0	143.1	629	158	83	65	14	3	2	14	32	0	119	6	0	8	10	.444	0	0	4.08
Bukowski, Stan	Cedar Rapds	Ana	A	20	8	8	1	0	47.2	214	53	39	35	10	3	1	3	25	0	29	4	1	2	4	.333	0	0	6.61
	Angels	Ana	R	20	4	4	0	0	11	52	11	6	5	0	0	1	0	5	0	8	0	0	0	1	.000	0	0	4.09
	Provo	Ana	R+	20	5	0	0	2	7	30	9	3	1	0	0	0	0	2	0	2	2	0	0	0	.000	0	0	1.29
Bullard, Jim*	Bristol	CWS	R+	22	4	4	1	0	20.2	84	20	12	7	4	0	1	0	1	0	31	3	0	1	2	.333	0	0	3.05
	Kannapolis	CWS	A	22	8	8	1	0	45.1	184	45	18	15	4	4	1	3	6	0	26	1	1	3	2	.600	1	0	2.98
Bullock, Trevor*	Lakewood	Phi	A	25	48	0	0	35	72	280	53	14	9	5	4	3	2	17	3	62	3	0	5	3	.625	0	16	1.13

2001 Pitching — Class-A and Rookie Leagues

HOW MUCH HE PITCHED											WHAT HE GAVE UP												THE RESULTS					
Player	Team	Org	Lg	A	G	GS	CG	GF	IP	BFP	H	R	ER	HR	SH	SF	HB	TBB	IBB	SO	WP	Bk	W	L	Pct.	ShO	Sv	ERA
Bumatay, Mike*	Hickory	Pit	A	22	15	1	0	2	26.1	107	20	10	8	0	1	1	1	8	1	31	2	0	1	0	1.000	0	0	2.73
	Lynchburg	Pit	A+	22	23	1	0	13	43.1	214	55	39	35	4	1	1	4	26	3	40	3	0	1	7	.125	0	2	7.27
Bumstead, Mike	Fort Wayne	SD	A	24	36	0	0	31	39.2	163	26	12	10	2	1	1	3	15	1	52	4	0	4	2	.667	0	17	2.27
	Lk Elsinore	SD	A+	24	19	0	0	6	32.1	148	35	25	24	5	1	1	0	18	5	33	1	0	1	2	.333	0	0	6.68
Burch, Matt	Wilmington	KC	A+	25	28	22	0	1	148.1	639	145	73	61	6	9	7	21	50	2	92	8	0	11	10	.524	0	0	3.70
Buret, Jorge	Casper	Col	R+	20	16	15	1	0	80.2	376	110	66	47	8	2	2	1	23	0	54	6	1	4	6	.400	0	0	5.24
Burgess, Richie	New Jersey	StL	A-	22	16	6	0	4	62.2	282	66	31	28	4	2	2	5	28	1	44	5	0	3	3	.500	0	1	4.02
Burke, Erick*	Savannah	Tex	A	24	34	4	0	16	76.2	340	81	47	34	3	2	3	12	22	0	69	6	2	2	6	.250	0	1	3.99
Burnau, Ryan	Cubs	ChC	R	20	14	9	0	0	49.2	229	58	43	27	0	1	2	3	20	0	46	4	1	3	6	.333	0	0	4.89
Burnett, Sean*	Hickory	Pit	A	19	26	26	1	0	161.1	667	164	63	47	11	6	5	4	33	0	134	7	1	11	8	.579	0	0	2.62
Burnette, Weston	Reds	Cin	R	20	10	0	0	3	11.2	54	13	13	11	0	0	0	1	5	0	17	1	0	2	1	.667	0	0	8.49
Burns, Casey	Fort Wayne	SD	A	24	20	16	0	0	88.2	399	87	60	50	7	2	2	6	43	1	59	5	0	5	8	.385	0	0	5.08
Burns, Mike	Michigan	Hou	A	23	29	21	1	3	132	552	131	67	58	10	4	5	13	27	0	108	0	1	7	7	.500	0	1	3.95
Burres, Brian*	Salem-Keizr	SF	A-	21	14	6	0	2	40.2	174	43	20	14	2	3	2	1	11	0	38	5	0	3	1	.750	0	1	3.10
Burruezo, Joe	Williamsprt	Pit	A-	21	14	2	0	5	20	99	22	16	8	1	3	1	4	10	0	17	2	0	1	2	.333	0	1	3.60
Burton, O.J.	Wisconsin	Sea	A	25	39	0	0	15	59.1	255	54	31	21	4	3	1	4	21	4	39	4	0	4	3	.571	0	1	3.19
Burzynski, Cole	Pirates	Pit	R	20	7	5	0	0	23.2	119	26	19	17	5	1	1	1	23	0	28	3	0	1	2	.333	0	0	6.46
Bustillos, Oscar	Hudson Val	TB	A-	22	26	0	0	24	33.1	145	25	21	10	2	0	0	1	16	1	44	3	0	4	3	.571	0	13	2.70
Butler, John	Wisconsin	Sea	A	24	40	0	0	14	67	286	68	27	15	1	3	0	3	16	1	62	5	0	5	3	.625	0	1	2.01
Butler, Matt	Myrtle Bch	Atl	A+	22	22	22	1	0	114.2	514	127	81	75	12	9	5	5	48	0	78	1	0	7	8	.467	0	0	5.89
Butto, Francisco	Phillies	Phi	R	20	15	0	0	6	26	109	22	10	7	1	0	1	1	12	1	20	1	0	2	3	.400	0	2	2.42
Byard, Dave	Brooklyn	NYM	A-	24	22	0	0	20	37	141	21	7	6	0	0	1	1	11	0	32	1	0	3	1	.750	0	9	1.46
Bye, Chris	Clinton	Mon	A	24	21	0	0	6	29.2	122	18	7	3	1	6	2	0	13	0	34	4	0	1	1	.500	0	3	0.91
	Jupiter	Mon	A+	24	19	0	0	13	23.2	103	24	8	8	3	2	0	1	9	0	15	4	0	1	0	1.000	0	0	3.04
Byron, Terry	Kane County	Fla	A	23	4	2	0	0	13.2	61	12	13	12	0	1	0	1	7	0	11	4	0	1	2	.333	0	0	7.90
	Brevard Cty	Fla	A+	23	4	0	0	1	7	35	7	9	8	1	0	0	2	5	1	7	0	0	0	0	.000	0	0	10.29
Cabell, Shannon*	Hickory	Pit	A	23	42	0	0	13	62.2	281	73	35	24	3	5	3	1	26	2	58	5	1	1	9	.100	0	2	3.45
Cable, Taft	Batavia	Phi	A-	21	14	12	1	0	67.1	285	65	33	25	2	1	0	2	19	0	64	1	1	1	3	.250	0	0	3.34
Cabreja, Eny*	Martinsvlle	Hou	R+	20	12	12	1	0	74	289	54	19	13	6	2	3	4	20	0	67	4	1	4	3	.571	0	0	1.58
Cabrera, Carlos	Phillies	Phi	R	19	10	8	0	0	43.1	194	35	23	14	2	2	3	7	23	0	40	6	3	2	2	.500	0	0	2.91
Cabrera, Daniel	Orioles	Bal	R	21	12	7	0	0	40.2	188	31	29	25	1	0	0	5	39	2	36	2	0	2	3	.400	0	0	5.53
Cabrera, Fernando	Columbus	Cle	A	20	20	20	0	0	94.2	410	89	49	38	7	2	1	2	37	1	96	10	0	5	6	.455	0	0	3.61
Cabrera, Yunior*	Brooklyn	NYM	A-	21	1	0	0	0	3	15	4	1	1	0	0	0	0	2	0	4	1	0	0	0	.000	0	0	3.00
	Kingsport	NYM	R+	21	11	10	0	1	44	191	38	22	19	3	2	1	5	19	0	49	5	1	3	3	.500	0	0	3.89
Cali, Carmen*	Peoria	StL	A	23	39	0	0	15	48	229	53	40	32	4	6	0	1	29	0	47	9	1	7	3	.700	0	1	6.00
	Potomac	StL	A+	23	12	0	0	4	12.1	52	12	4	3	1	2	0	1	6	1	9	3	0	1	0	1.000	0	0	2.19
Calvo, Jose	Pittsfield	Hou	A-	22	1	0	0	0	2	7	1	0	0	0	0	0	0	1	0	3	0	0	0	0	.000	0	0	0.00
Camacho, Jose	Martinsvlle	Hou	R+	21	8	0	0	4	12.1	47	8	2	2	0	0	0	1	0	0	14	2	0	1	0	1.000	0	0	1.46
Cameron, Kevin	Elizabethtn	Min	R+	22	22	0	0	22	23	94	16	4	4	0	0	0	3	5	0	30	3	0	1	1	.500	0	13	1.57
Caminero, C.	Cubs	ChC	R	20	15	0	0	3	23.1	110	27	19	13	1	1	2	3	14	0	18	1	0	1	1	.500	0	0	5.01
Campbell, Andrew*	Rangers	Tex	R	20	14	0	0	13	23.2	105	25	15	12	2	1	0	3	9	1	11	3	0	2	2	.500	0	5	4.56
Campbell, Dayle	W Michigan	Det	A	23	21	13	0	7	69	346	83	67	54	6	1	5	8	57	0	47	14	4	1	7	.125	0	1	7.04
Campbell, Jarrett	Chston-SC	TB	A	22	39	5	0	4	84.1	372	90	51	37	6	4	5	7	18	4	71	10	3	3	6	.333	0	0	3.95
Campos, Juan	Michigan	Hou	A	22	13	13	2	0	78.1	341	90	50	40	8	2	1	8	10	0	69	3	2	5	4	.556	0	0	4.60
Canale, Tom	Columbus	Cle	A	22	8	0	0	4	14.1	64	18	9	5	1	1	2	1	2	1	7	1	0	3	1	.750	0	0	3.14
Capellan, Jose	Danville	Atl	R+	21	3	3	0	0	15.2	66	12	7	3	1	0	0	2	4	0	25	1	1	0	0	.000	0	0	1.72
Caputo, Rob	Vermont	Mon	A-	22	20	1	0	6	30.1	144	32	20	16	5	1	1	5	16	0	28	3	0	0	2	.000	0	3	4.75
	Clinton	Mon	A	22	4	0	0	4	5	27	4	4	0	0	0	1	0	5	0	8	2	1	0	2	.000	0	0	0.00
Carbajal, Alex*	Bakersfield	TB	A+	24	24	0	0	13	31.2	150	43	26	25	7	1	1	1	11	0	34	1	0	2	1	.667	0	0	7.11
Cardwell, Brian	Chston-WV	Tor	A	21	19	19	2	0	92	410	101	70	53	9	2	4	9	33	1	60	10	0	3	10	.231	0	0	5.18
Carlsen, Jeff	Boise	ChC	A-	23	16	0	0	7	36	139	23	7	6	3	0	1	2	5	0	41	1	1	1	0	1.000	0	3	1.50
Carlson, Steve*	Yankees	NYY	R	23	21	0	0	12	31.1	122	19	7	4	0	1	1	0	12	0	41	1	0	2	2	.500	0	3	1.15
	Staten Ilnd	NYY	A-	23	3	0	0	0	2.2	10	1	0	0	0	0	0	0	1	0	2	0	0	1	0	1.000	0	0	0.00
Carney, Jake	Hudson Val	TB	A-	22	8	0	0	2	14	57	8	2	1	0	0	1	0	6	2	16	0	0	1	0	1.000	0	1	0.64
	Chston-SC	TB	A	22	10	0	0	3	28	115	20	5	2	0	0	0	2	8	0	24	1	0	1	0	1.000	0	0	0.64
Carpenter, Calvin	Brewers	Mil	R	19	11	10	0	0	37.2	169	39	24	17	0	2	2	1	22	0	29	3	1	3	3	.500	0	0	4.06
Carrasco, Edelyn	Twins	Min	R	19	14	9	1	1	51.1	215	49	26	20	3	0	0	3	15	0	45	2	1	3	4	.429	1	0	3.51
Carter, Justin*	Reds	Cin	R	25	4	4	1	0	14.2	61	9	3	1	0	0	0	0	6	0	20	3	1	1	0	1.000	0	0	0.61
	Mudville	Cin	A+	25	10	10	1	0	49.2	225	42	32	24	1	2	2	3	38	0	43	7	0	3	5	.375	1	0	4.35
Carter, Mark*	Boise	ChC	A-	21	16	0	0	7	25.1	122	30	15	13	3	0	0	1	17	1	31	3	0	2	1	.667	0	1	4.62
Carter, Ramsey	Royals	KC	R	21	9	0	0	5	16	65	13	5	3	0	2	1	1	5	0	15	0	0	2	0	1.000	0	2	1.69
Carter, Ryan*	Lakewood	Phi	A	22	14	13	0	0	80.1	345	73	39	35	6	4	0	8	34	0	76	5	0	3	7	.300	0	0	3.92
	Clearwater	Phi	A+	22	11	11	1	0	58.1	270	67	39	36	9	1	1	3	36	0	56	3	0	3	4	.429	0	0	5.55
Casadiego, Gerardo	Clinton	Mon	A	21	42	1	0	28	72.1	311	67	37	32	8	5	6	4	28	1	43	8	3	5	5	.500	0	6	3.98
Cash, David	San Jose	SF	A+	22	20	0	0	6	39	157	23	9	9	4	1	1	3	17	0	46	3	0	4	0	1.000	0	1	2.08
Cassel, Jack	Fort Wayne	SD	A	21	25	23	0	1	128.1	591	163	104	79	7	5	4	12	35	0	89	6	5	4	14	.222	0	0	5.54
Castellanos, Jon	South Bend	Ari	A	20	8	8	0	0	37	172	47	24	20	3	2	1	3	15	0	34	1	0	1	3	.250	0	0	4.86
	Yakima	Ari	A-	20	15	15	0	0	86	369	100	43	39	4	0	1	3	26	2	73	1	1	2	3	.400	0	0	4.08
Castillo, Dan	Lancaster	Ari	A+	25	23	7	0	12	52.2	235	56	33	31	6	1	1	3	21	0	64	12	0	1	3	.250	0	4	5.30
Castillo, Geraldo	Ogden	Mil	R+	20	15	10	0	3	68.1	297	77	42	33	7	0	1	5	11	0	49	5	3	6	4	.600	0	0	4.35
Castillo, Ramon	Kane County	Fla	A	23	28	28	0	0	158.2	688	178	79	67	19	1	3	12	31	1	108	11	1	11	2	.846	0	0	3.80
Castro, Julio	Kannapolis	CWS	A	21	40	0	0	20	54	234	46	22	16	3	3	2	2	21	6	68	6	1	3	1	.750	0	4	2.67
Cautaulin, Heath	Utica	Fla	A-	22	25	0	0	11	37.2	179	44	37	31	5	2	5	4	19	1	32	2	0	0	3	.000	0	4	7.41
Cavazos, Andy	Savannah	Tex	A	21	29	19	1	3	122	569	149	87	75	13	1	3	10	63	0	96	10	3	6	10	.375	0	0	5.53
Cave, Kevin	Utica	Fla	A-	22	14	5	0	4	38.2	162	38	16	14	4	1	1	0	14	0	23	1	0	1	2	.333	0	1	3.26
Cedeno, Jovanny	Charlotte	Tex	A+	22	3	3	0	0	9.2	38	3	2	2	0	0	0	1	5	0	12	0	0	0	0	.000	0	0	1.86
Cercy, Rick	Salem	Col	A+	25	39	0	0	12	57	240	47	22	20	5	4	2	3	24	6	51	2	0	4	1	.800	0	5	3.16
Cetani, Bryan*	Jamestown	Atl	A-	20	3	0	0	0	1.2	10	1	5	3	0	0	1	0	4	0	0	2	0	0	0	.000	0	0	16.20
	Danville	Atl	R+	20	15	0	0	7	17.2	103	29	20	12	1	2	1	2	17	0	13	2	0	1	1	.500	0	2	6.11
Chadwick, John	Medcine Hat	Tor	R+	24	23	0	0	8	61	276	65	38	30	4	0	1	8	19	1	42	9	3	1	1	.500	0	2	4.43
Charron, Eric	Jupiter	Mon	A+	23	2	0	0	2	3	13	4	3	2	1	0	0	0	1	0	1	0	0	0	1	.000	0	0	6.00
	Vermont	Mon	A-	23	7	0	0	2	9.2	39	9	4	4	0	0	0	0	2	0	12	0	0	0	0	.000	0	0	3.72
	Clinton	Mon	A	23	14	0	0	7	20.1	89	19	11	4	0	0	0	0	5	0	21	0	0	1	0	1.000	0	0	1.77
Chavez, Wilton	Lansing	ChC	A	21	8	8	2	0	47	207	38	24	21	4	2	2	3	27	0	60	2	1	2	6	.250	1	0	4.02
	Daytona	ChC	A+	21	17	16	0	0	89.2	401	96	46	41	8	4	3	7	30	1	59	3	0	3	4	.429	0	0	4.12

2001 Pitching — Class-A and Rookie Leagues

HOW MUCH HE PITCHED											WHAT HE GAVE UP												THE RESULTS					
Player	Team	Org	Lg	A	G	GS	CG	GF	IP	BFP	H	R	ER	HR	SH	SF	HB	TBB	IBB	SO	WP	Bk	W	L	Pct.	ShO	Sv	ERA
Chenard, Ken	Capital Cty	NYM	A	23	4	4	0	0	16	68	14	8	8	1	1	0	1	8	0	12	2	0	0	1	.000	0	0	4.50
	St. Lucie	NYM	A+	23	2	2	0	0	1.2	12	3	7	7	1	0	0	1	4	0	2	0	0	0	2	.000	0	0	37.80
Childress, Daylan	Billings	Cin	R+	23	14	8	0	4	63.1	263	59	32	25	4	1	1	4	17	0	54	3	0	6	1	.857	0	1	3.55
Chipperfield, Calvin	Lakeland	Det	A+	24	24	24	1	0	124	574	132	73	66	5	4	4	8	81	1	109	5	0	7	8	.467	0	0	4.79
Chirinos, Jesus	Brewers	Mil	R	20	11	7	0	0	53	228	56	31	24	3	1	1	4	11	0	36	3	1	5	3	.625	0	0	4.08
Chisnall, Wes	Clinton	Mon	A	21	24	1	0	6	51	222	67	31	27	4	2	3	4	7	0	18	5	3	2	3	.400	0	0	4.76
	Vermont	Mon	A-	21	18	2	0	4	37.1	158	37	16	11	2	2	1	1	7	0	30	0	0	2	2	.500	0	0	2.65
Chourio, Jorge	Burlington	Cle	R+	19	3	0	0	1	2.2	17	8	7	7	2	0	0	1	1	0	1	1	0	0	1	.000	0	0	23.63
Christ, John	Columbus	Cle	A	24	4	0	0	1	9	44	14	7	5	1	0	0	1	3	0	8	2	0	0	0	.000	0	0	5.00
Cimorelli, Brett	Angels	Ana	R	20	11	2	0	3	20.1	104	25	22	16	2	1	1	0	13	0	14	5	1	2	2	.500	0	0	7.08
Cislak, Chad	Burlington	Cle	R+	23	1	0	0	0	0.1	5	0	4	1	0	0	1	0	4	0	0	5	0	0	1	.000	0	0	27.00
Clark, Claudell*	Williamsprt	Pit	A-	22	18	0	0	7	30.1	130	17	19	13	2	5	1	1	24	2	26	3	0	1	4	.200	0	1	3.86
Clark, Jeff	Hagerstown	SF	A	22	27	27	0	0	148	608	152	72	60	18	2	8	10	15	1	131	4	0	14	9	.609	0	0	3.65
Clark, Josh	Yakima	Ari	A-	23	17	7	0	2	49.2	223	58	38	32	4	0	2	6	17	0	42	5	0	1	4	.200	0	0	5.80
Clark, Ryan*	Staten Ilnd	NYY	A-	22	29	0	0	16	31.1	114	14	5	4	0	2	1	1	7	0	37	2	1	2	0	1.000	0	7	1.15
Clarke, Darren	Casper	Col	R+	21	14	14	0	0	55.1	271	76	47	37	3	1	3	8	33	0	42	5	0	3	6	.333	0	0	6.02
Clelland, James	Vermont	Mon	A-	22	18	0	0	8	32.1	151	40	22	17	2	0	3	5	6	0	24	4	0	3	1	.750	0	0	4.73
Clifton, Derek	Pittsfield	Hou	A-	22	9	0	0	3	11.1	52	11	9	7	0	1	0	3	6	0	6	0	0	2	0	1.000	0	0	5.56
Coa, Jesus	Burlington	KC	A	22	36	0	0	13	63.1	305	82	52	47	9	1	6	8	28	0	38	6	1	2	3	.400	0	1	6.68
Coenen, Matt*	Oneonta	Det	A-	22	10	9	1	1	47.1	206	44	26	16	1	1	1	2	16	0	37	3	0	2	2	.500	0	1	3.04
Coffey, Todd	Reds	Cin	R	21	3	2	0	0	12.2	55	11	11	6	1	1	1	1	5	0	15	0	0	0	1	.000	0	0	4.26
	Billings	Cin	R+	21	14	2	0	6	33.1	151	34	21	13	2	1	1	2	15	0	33	2	0	2	2	.500	0	1	3.51
Cole, Joey	Capital Cty	NYM	A	24	25	25	0	0	137.1	593	125	69	59	7	3	6	11	67	0	123	17	0	7	6	.538	0	0	3.87
	St. Lucie	NYM	A+	24	1	1	0	0	6	26	3	4	4	1	0	0	0	6	0	2	0	0	1	0	1.000	0	0	6.00
Coleman, Jeff	Athletics	Oak	R	21	8	0	0	7	11.2	43	7	2	2	0	2	0	1	3	0	8	0	0	0	0	.000	0	6	1.54
	Visalia	Oak	A+	21	16	4	0	0	37.2	186	57	32	27	3	1	1	3	16	0	38	2	0	0	4	.000	0	0	6.45
Collado, Jerry	Casper	Col	R+	22	21	0	0	3	29	141	36	24	18	1	1	0	4	15	1	18	5	1	0	2	.000	0	1	5.59
Collazo, William*	Jamestown	Atl	A-	22	9	0	0	7	15	55	9	2	1	0	1	0	1	0	0	13	2	0	3	1	.750	0	1	0.60
	Macon	Atl	A	22	12	0	0	6	23.1	88	13	9	7	3	3	3	2	4	0	23	2	0	3	2	.600	0	1	2.70
Collins, Clint	Dayton	Cin	A	23	6	1	0	2	11.2	56	20	7	6	1	0	0	0	3	0	7	3	0	2	1	.667	0	0	4.63
	Billings	Cin	R+	23	10	10	0	0	55.2	220	46	19	17	2	1	2	2	14	0	45	2	1	5	2	.714	0	0	2.75
Collins, Pat	Jupiter	Mon	A+	24	33	12	0	7	110.2	513	101	71	53	6	2	6	12	71	0	90	12	0	9	12	.429	0	1	4.31
Colon, Jose	Columbus	Cle	A	24	44	0	0	42	51.2	210	38	19	11	5	1	1	4	6	0	47	2	0	2	3	.400	0	22	1.92
Colon, Roman	Macon	Atl	A	22	23	21	0	1	128	543	136	69	51	9	5	7	3	26	0	91	16	4	7	7	.500	0	0	3.59
Colson, Jason	Auburn	Tor	A-	23	8	8	0	0	36.1	154	28	14	11	2	1	1	4	13	0	31	0	0	1	2	.333	0	0	2.72
	Dunedin	Tor	A+	23	1	1	0	0	1.1	7	0	1	0	0	0	1	0	3	0	1	0	0	0	0	.000	0	0	0.00
Colton, Kyle	Jamestown	Atl	A-	21	11	8	0	0	38	180	45	32	30	9	1	1	1	23	0	26	4	0	1	4	.200	0	0	7.11
Colvard, Ron	Mahoning Vy	Cle	A-	24	17	0	0	9	21.2	114	26	25	20	2	0	3	3	17	1	16	7	0	0	1	.000	0	0	8.31
Colyer, Steve*	Vero Beach	LA	A+	23	24	24	0	0	120.1	524	101	62	53	16	4	4	7	77	0	118	3	1	4	8	.333	0	0	3.96
Connolly, Jon*	Tigers	Det	R	18	8	6	0	0	35.1	147	30	16	15	0	2	2	1	10	1	23	2	0	1	1	.500	0	0	3.82
	Oneonta	Det	A-	18	1	1	0	0	3	17	8	6	6	1	1	0	0	1	0	1	1	0	0	1	.000	0	0	18.00
Connolly, Mike*	Hickory	Pit	A	20	33	15	2	0	121	509	116	59	53	10	5	3	6	41	1	107	9	0	11	7	.611	0	0	3.94
Contreras, J.C.*	Fort Myers	Min	A+	20	6	0	0	4	8	33	6	3	3	0	0	0	0	6	0	4	0	1	0	0	.000	0	1	3.38
	Quad City	Min	A	20	26	0	0	11	33.2	139	28	14	10	0	2	2	1	11	1	38	3	0	2	0	1.000	0	2	2.67
Cook, Aaron	Salem	Col	A+	23	27	27	0	0	155	649	157	73	53	4	5	1	7	38	0	122	6	1	11	11	.500	0	0	3.08
Cook, Jeremy	Peoria	StL	A	24	52	0	0	34	68	310	78	37	28	7	3	0	5	20	2	61	2	0	3	7	.300	0	14	3.71
Cooksey, Wes	Staten Ilnd	NYY	A-	24	20	0	0	7	28.2	124	27	16	15	3	0	1	2	11	1	13	2	0	1	0	1.000	0	1	4.71
Cooper, Dexter	Braves	Atl	R	19	12	1	0	3	19.1	97	18	19	10	1	0	1	2	18	0	21	5	0	2	1	.667	0	0	4.66
Coose, Austin	Princeton	TB	R+	23	8	0	0	7	9.1	35	4	2	0	0	0	0	0	2	0	16	0	0	0	0	.000	0	2	0.00
	Chston-SC	TB	A	23	10	0	0	7	13.2	61	13	8	7	0	1	0	1	7	0	21	0	0	0	1	.000	0	2	4.61
Coppinger, Joe	Orioles	Bal	R	19	11	8	0	1	40	205	53	37	26	3	2	0	7	17	1	28	5	1	2	4	.333	0	0	5.85
Corbin, John	Lansing	ChC	A	25	14	0	0	4	25	119	37	16	10	1	3	0	1	4	1	23	2	0	3	1	.750	0	1	3.60
	Daytona	ChC	A+	25	10	0	0	9	21.2	94	26	9	9	2	0	1	0	4	2	12	0	0	2	0	1.000	0	2	3.74
Corcoran, Roy	Jupiter	Mon	A+	22	1	0	0	0	2	8	0	0	0	0	0	0	0	2	0	0	0	0	0	0	.000	0	0	0.00
	Expos	Mon	R	22	13	0	0	9	17.1	69	12	4	3	2	0	0	2	2	0	21	0	0	2	0	1.000	0	2	1.56
Cordero, Frangil*	Lansing	ChC	A	21	9	0	0	2	13.2	77	18	16	11	1	1	0	1	15	0	11	5	1	2	0	1.000	0	0	7.24
Cordero, Jesus	Wilmington	LA	A	23	33	1	0	22	69.1	278	49	20	19	1	4	4	6	25	0	56	13	1	8	4	.667	0	9	2.47
	Vero Beach	LA	A+	23	4	1	0	1	8.1	36	7	5	4	0	1	1	0	3	0	10	1	1	0	1	.000	0	0	4.32
Cordero, Victor	Beloit	Mil	A	22	46	0	0	24	81	354	61	45	41	10	3	2	7	45	2	98	9	2	7	5	.583	0	5	4.56
Cordova, Jorge	Mudville	Cin	A+	24	30	25	0	1	154.2	671	157	81	64	11	6	8	3	67	0	132	13	1	9	8	.529	0	0	3.72
Corey, Mike	High Desert	Mil	A+	27	47	0	0	19	76	338	83	45	35	7	3	1	5	35	2	70	6	0	3	3	.500	0	2	4.14
Cornejo, Jesse*	Bakersfield	TB	A+	25	9	0	0	1	13.1	69	17	12	6	3	1	0	1	8	1	16	0	0	0	1	.000	0	0	4.05
Corona, Ronnie	Fort Myers	Min	A+	23	16	7	0	3	49.1	206	45	15	12	3	1	2	1	16	0	47	2	1	3	1	.750	0	0	2.19
Corrado, Matthew	Lakeland	Det	A+	23	16	12	1	0	63.1	280	62	45	40	9	2	1	7	31	0	48	7	1	3	7	.300	0	0	5.68
Correa, Alexander*	Brewers	Mil	R	19	12	3	0	0	32.1	148	42	23	21	1	1	1	5	13	0	29	2	0	1	0	1.000	0	0	5.85
Correa, Cristobal	New Jersey	StL	A-	22	15	1	0	4	40	189	48	34	24	3	0	2	7	17	0	32	2	0	1	3	.250	0	3	5.40
Correa, Dominic	Greensboro	NYY	A	25	16	0	0	12	18.1	77	12	9	9	1	3	0	1	9	1	17	1	0	2	2	.500	0	3	4.42
Cortez, Renee	Mariners	Sea	R	19	11	9	0	0	53	233	60	34	26	4	1	2	4	10	0	52	6	0	2	0	1.000	0	0	4.42
Costello, Ryan*	Medcine Hat	Tor	R+	22	14	8	0	1	51.2	217	38	33	22	5	3	2	1	21	1	56	4	1	1	5	.167	0	1	3.83
Cotton, Nathan	Dayton	Cin	A	22	12	0	0	5	25	111	36	15	9	4	1	1	0	3	0	17	4	1	0	1	.000	0	2	3.24
	Billings	Cin	R+	22	28	0	0	28	29	127	30	10	9	2	0	1	4	3	1	37	1	0	4	1	.800	0	13	2.79
Cotts, Neal*	Vancouver	Oak	A-	22	9	7	0	0	35	145	28	14	12	2	0	1	1	13	0	44	4	1	1	0	1.000	0	0	3.09
	Visalia	Oak	A+	22	7	7	0	0	31	139	27	14	8	0	0	1	3	15	0	34	0	0	3	2	.600	0	0	2.32
Coughenour, Jory	Michigan	Hou	A	24	35	14	0	4	126.1	554	152	68	53	4	4	3	4	22	1	65	5	1	11	5	.688	0	2	3.78
Coward, Tim	Chston-SC	TB	A	23	5	0	0	0	10	43	11	3	1	0	0	0	0	4	2	13	1	0	0	0	.000	0	0	0.90
	Bakersfield	TB	A+	23	32	4	0	10	67.1	279	59	20	15	1	3	0	1	22	2	65	2	0	2	2	.500	0	3	2.00
Cowie, Steve	Kinston	Cle	A+	25	2	0	0	1	6	21	5	1	1	0	1	0	0	1	0	4	0	0	0	0	.000	0	0	1.50
	Salem	Col	A+	25	1	1	0	0	3.1	17	6	4	4	0	0	0	0	2	0	1	0	0	0	1	.000	0	0	10.80
Cox, Mike*	Capital Cty	NYM	A	23	15	0	0	5	32.1	148	27	18	16	1	3	0	6	19	0	40	6	0	2	3	.400	0	1	4.45
	Brooklyn	NYM	A-	23	13	7	0	0	52.2	234	40	25	17	2	1	1	2	41	0	73	6	0	6	1	.857	0	0	2.91
Cozier, Vance	San Jose	SF	A+	24	30	29	1	0	169.2	698	158	71	68	17	5	4	6	45	1	98	9	0	15	7	.682	0	0	3.61
Cram, Josh	Salem-Keizr	SF	A-	21	19	0	0	3	35.2	161	41	16	12	3	3	2	2	10	1	34	4	1	5	2	.714	0	0	3.03
Cramblitt, Joey	South Bend	Ari	A	23	35	8	0	14	104.1	426	104	54	39	9	4	3	4	19	2	91	1	0	5	7	.417	0	2	3.36
Crawford, Chris*	Hudson Val	TB	A-	24	24	0	0	7	39.2	171	26	14	13	0	5	2	4	23	0	46	2	0	1	1	.500	0	2	2.95
Crawford, Tristan	Twins	Min	R	19	13	0	0	6	16.1	74	15	5	4	0	0	0	2	6	0	19	2	0	0	0	.000	0	3	2.20

2001 Pitching — Class-A and Rookie Leagues

HOW MUCH HE PITCHED											WHAT HE GAVE UP												THE RESULTS					
Player	Team	Org	Lg	A	G	GS	CG	GF	IP	BFP	H	R	ER	HR	SH	SF	HB	TBB	IBB	SO	WP	Bk	W	L	Pct.	ShO	Sv	ERA
Crawford, Wes*	Rancho Cuca	Ana	A+	25	21	13	0	1	93.1	418	109	60	54	9	2	2	5	28	0	56	2	0	6	7	.462	0	0	5.21
Crider, George	Vancouver	Oak	A-	22	22	0	0	14	33	145	20	15	12	3	2	0	3	26	0	29	5	1	1	3	.250	0	3	3.27
Cristobal, Luis	Rangers	Tex	R	22	11	4	0	4	34	150	34	20	16	1	1	0	2	20	0	35	1	0	0	1	.000	0	0	4.24
Cromer, Jason*	Princeton	TB	R+	21	5	2	0	0	22.2	85	14	5	4	2	0	1	0	8	0	18	2	0	2	0	1.000	0	0	1.59
Cromer, Nathan*	Hudson Val	TB	A-	21	15	15	0	0	79	344	94	38	35	6	2	3	0	24	0	39	8	0	4	3	.571	0	0	3.99
Crouthers, Dave	Bluefield	Bal	R+	22	10	10	1	0	44.2	194	41	28	22	7	1	2	4	18	0	45	3	0	2	3	.400	0	0	4.43
Crowell, Kyle	Modesto	Oak	A+	23	37	10	0	8	112.1	502	135	70	67	6	8	4	10	33	4	97	3	0	3	10	.231	0	2	5.37
Crowther, Jackson	Clinton	Mon	A	25	8	0	0	1	12.2	57	19	10	9	0	0	1	1	1	0	9	2	0	0	0	.000	0	0	6.39
Crump, Joel*	Orioles	Bal	R	20	7	0	0	3	15.1	70	15	5	4	0	0	0	2	12	0	11	4	0	1	0	1.000	0	0	2.35
	Bluefield	Bal	R+	20	10	0	0	7	12	51	10	4	3	1	0	0	0	6	0	15	3	0	0	0	.000	0	1	2.25
Cruz, Jeffrey*	Tri-City	Col	A-	23	12	0	0	3	11.2	67	21	15	11	3	0	0	0	8	0	6	4	0	0	1	.000	0	0	8.49
Cruz, Ramon	White Sox	CWS	R	21	6	5	0	0	24.1	90	15	6	3	1	1	0	0	3	0	21	0	0	1	2	.333	0	0	1.11
Cuello, Manolin	Tigers	Det	R	21	1	0	0	1	0.2	3	1	0	0	0	1	0	0	0	0	1	0	0	0	0	.000	0	0	0.00
	W Michigan	Det	A	21	23	3	0	9	55	266	47	44	33	7	0	4	5	47	0	61	13	2	2	3	.400	0	0	5.40
Cuen, David*	Dodgers	LA	R	18	13	6	0	0	50.2	198	32	14	8	1	0	0	2	17	0	49	4	1	4	0	1.000	0	0	1.42
Cullen, Phil	Everett	Sea	A-	22	14	14	0	0	56.2	267	52	36	32	6	1	1	8	49	0	64	3	0	1	4	.200	0	0	5.08
Cullen, Ryan*	Modesto	Oak	A+	22	40	3	0	12	83	380	112	58	39	5	3	1	4	24	3	53	2	0	2	4	.333	0	1	4.23
Culp, Brandon	Reds	Cin	R	24	6	4	0	1	28.1	117	23	6	5	0	1	0	1	13	0	33	0	1	1	1	.500	0	0	1.59
	Mudville	Cin	A+	24	9	3	0	1	24.1	110	24	15	11	2	0	2	2	14	0	25	0	0	1	0	1.000	0	0	4.07
Culp, Todd	Mahoning Vy	Cle	A-	23	22	0	0	5	44.2	191	36	21	18	3	0	2	4	21	0	60	3	0	2	2	.500	0	2	3.63
Cummings, Jeremy	Peoria	StL	A	25	18	18	0	0	95	388	93	45	34	5	1	3	3	10	0	75	1	1	4	6	.400	0	0	3.22
	Potomac	StL	A+	25	4	4	0	0	19	87	25	18	18	2	1	2	5	2	1	15	2	0	0	3	.000	0	0	8.53
Cunningham, J.	Hagerstown	SF	A	23	10	0	0	2	18.1	86	23	16	12	3	1	1	2	7	0	17	0	0	1	1	.500	0	0	5.89
Currier, Bryan	Staten Ilnd	NYY	A-	31	7	7	0	0	31	149	37	20	13	2	0	1	3	13	0	27	1	1	2	2	.500	0	0	3.77
Currier, Rik	Greensboro	NYY	A	24	6	6	0	0	31.2	144	32	22	16	1	2	2	2	17	0	25	3	0	0	4	.000	0	0	4.55
Curtin, Brian	Mahoning Vy	Cle	A-	24	21	0	0	7	30.2	145	36	14	13	3	4	2	3	16	7	26	4	0	1	3	.250	0	2	3.82
Curtiss, Tom*	Myrtle Bch	Atl	A+	25	12	0	0	9	12.2	57	11	7	6	3	1	0	0	8	0	10	1	0	0	1	.000	0	0	4.26
Cyr, Eric*	Lk Elsinore	SD	A+	23	21	16	0	0	100.2	399	68	28	18	1	3	0	3	24	0	131	1	0	7	4	.636	0	0	1.61
Daigle, Casey	South Bend	Ari	A	21	28	27	2	0	164	727	180	100	75	11	3	9	14	55	0	85	16	4	10	10	.500	1	0	4.12
D'Amato, Dan*	Williamsprt	Pit	A-	22	20	0	0	14	29	117	21	10	7	1	1	0	0	13	0	32	5	0	4	1	.800	0	2	2.17
D'Amico, Leonardo	Angels	Ana	R	20	14	5	0	5	38.1	176	44	32	22	2	1	3	4	13	1	33	5	0	0	6	.000	0	0	5.17
	Provo	Ana	R+	20	1	0	0	0	2	11	4	2	2	0	0	0	0	1	0	4	1	0	1	0	1.000	0	0	9.00
Danly, Ryan*	Kingsport	NYM	R+	21	14	1	0	6	23.1	102	27	8	8	0	0	0	0	6	0	29	0	4	1	2	.333	0	3	3.09
Dannemiller, Beau	Tri-City	Col	A-	22	23	1	0	14	46	189	33	13	11	2	1	1	2	17	0	53	5	0	3	1	.750	0	6	2.15
David, Toby*	Utica	Fla	A-	24	20	0	0	8	34.2	153	41	25	20	3	0	0	3	11	0	18	2	0	0	3	.000	0	0	5.19
Davies, Kyle	Braves	Atl	R	18	12	9	1	1	56	220	47	17	14	2	1	0	1	8	0	53	2	0	4	2	.667	1	0	2.25
	Macon	Atl	A	18	1	1	0	0	5.2	20	2	0	0	0	0	0	0	1	0	7	0	0	1	0	1.000	0	0	0.00
Davies, Michael*	Casper	Col	R+	21	10	7	0	0	36	161	40	23	18	2	2	2	4	10	1	37	3	1	2	2	.500	0	0	4.50
Davis, Jason	Columbus	Cle	A	22	27	27	1	0	160	677	147	72	48	9	2	2	14	51	1	115	5	2	14	6	.700	1	0	2.70
Davis, Lance	Marlins	Fla	R	19	14	3	0	4	31	131	33	15	11	0	3	2	5	4	0	26	2	0	2	1	.667	0	1	3.19
Davis, Mikael	Missoula	Ari	R+	21	15	4	0	2	39.2	174	44	25	17	7	1	0	1	12	0	33	7	1	4	1	.800	0	0	3.86
Davis, Tim*	Batavia	Phi	A-	23	16	0	0	2	33.1	135	25	16	13	1	1	3	2	13	0	26	1	0	2	0	1.000	0	0	3.51
Daws, Josh	Elizabethtn	Min	R+	23	20	1	0	6	45.1	172	34	8	7	2	1	4	3	5	1	56	2	1	1	1	.500	0	2	1.39
Dawson, Carl	Phillies	Phi	R	22	10	8	0	1	47.2	196	42	20	11	2	0	0	1	5	0	51	4	1	3	3	.500	0	1	2.08
Dean, Aaron	Dunedin	Tor	A+	23	27	27	2	0	160	720	172	113	97	16	4	10	10	75	1	121	14	4	11	12	.478	1	0	5.46
Deaton, Kevin	Kingsport	NYM	R+	20	17	4	0	4	47.1	193	40	17	11	2	0	0	7	10	0	43	0	0	5	2	.714	0	1	2.09
	Capital Cty	NYM	A	20	1	1	0	0	4	19	4	2	2	1	0	0	0	3	0	6	0	0	0	0	.000	0	0	4.50
DeChristofaro, V.*	Phillies	Phi	R	20	9	9	0	0	37.1	156	32	12	9	0	1	0	0	14	0	33	3	0	1	2	.333	0	0	2.17
DeHart, Casey*	Mudville	Cin	A+	24	49	0	0	20	68.2	292	54	20	17	3	5	2	3	36	1	64	7	0	4	3	.571	0	4	2.23
DeJesus, Elvis	Marlins	Fla	R	21	13	7	0	4	41.2	193	49	35	24	2	1	1	7	12	0	33	5	1	0	4	.000	0	2	5.18
DeJesus, Henky	Missoula	Ari	R+	21	3	0	0	1	4.2	25	7	7	6	1	0	0	1	3	1	0	0	0	0	1	.000	0	0	11.57
de la Cruz, Carlos	Burlington	Cle	R+	20	6	4	0	0	28.2	118	17	11	9	2	0	1	3	12	0	33	1	0	1	1	.500	0	0	2.83
	Columbus	Cle	A	20	6	6	0	0	29.1	124	29	17	14	4	2	1	0	13	0	31	0	1	2	1	.667	0	0	4.30
de la Rosa, Felix	Brewers	Mil	R	20	6	0	0	1	15.2	71	20	10	9	0	1	1	3	7	0	5	1	0	0	1	.000	0	0	5.17
Delcarmen, Manny	Red Sox	Bos	R	20	11	8	0	2	46	195	35	16	13	0	2	1	7	19	0	62	2	0	4	2	.667	0	1	2.54
DeLeon, Joey	Martinsvlle	Hou	R+	19	13	7	0	2	42.2	165	27	12	11	1	1	1	3	11	0	44	2	0	1	2	.333	0	0	2.32
Delgado, Danny	San Berndno	Sea	A+	24	36	10	0	7	103.1	464	130	68	62	13	3	7	6	24	1	90	4	0	4	7	.364	0	1	5.40
de los Santos, C.	Hickory	Pit	A	21	13	7	0	3	37.2	184	44	33	28	6	1	3	8	28	0	31	5	0	2	5	.286	0	0	6.69
	Williamsprt	Pit	A-	21	14	13	0	0	81.2	338	73	34	27	7	3	0	7	29	0	80	3	0	5	3	.625	0	0	2.98
Denham, Dan	Burlington	Cle	R+	19	8	8	0	0	30.2	150	30	21	15	5	1	0	6	26	0	31	1	1	0	4	.000	0	0	4.40
Denney, Kyle	Kinston	Cle	A+	24	11	10	0	0	57	219	32	14	13	2	1	1	3	13	1	80	0	0	5	3	.625	0	0	2.05
Dennis, Jason*	Provo	Ana	R+	23	14	13	0	1	74.2	299	53	20	17	3	1	1	2	21	0	79	2	0	5	0	1.000	0	0	2.05
DePaula, Freddy*	Visalia	Oak	A+	21	15	5	0	5	32	141	31	20	20	3	1	0	1	19	0	30	0	1	2	1	.667	0	0	5.63
	Vancouver	Oak	A-	21	7	7	0	0	30.2	141	27	16	12	2	1	4	0	20	0	37	1	0	2	4	.333	0	0	3.52
DePaula, Julio	Asheville	Col	A	22	3	3	0	0	16.2	76	19	13	7	3	0	0	3	2	0	26	1	0	1	1	.500	0	0	3.78
	Greensboro	NYY	A	22	8	8	0	0	55.2	221	35	19	17	2	1	0	4	21	0	67	2	3	6	1	.857	0	0	2.75
	Tampa	NYY	A+	22	16	13	0	1	83	365	65	43	33	3	1	2	3	53	2	77	3	1	9	5	.643	0	0	3.58
DeQuin, Benji*	Clinton	Mon	A	22	26	24	0	0	129	576	125	81	76	18	5	4	7	70	0	129	7	0	6	11	.353	0	0	5.30
Desalme, Gene*	Ogden	Mil	R+	22	8	0	0	3	14.1	73	15	11	8	4	0	0	2	14	0	16	1	1	0	0	.000	0	0	5.02
Detillion, Jamie*	W Michigan	Det	A	24	48	0	0	21	77	323	66	21	18	3	3	4	0	27	4	66	9	0	2	3	.400	0	4	2.10
Devenney, Nick	Rangers	Tex	R	21	17	0	0	11	20.1	114	35	28	21	2	0	2	1	20	0	14	6	0	0	1	.000	0	1	9.30
Devine, Travis	Fort Wayne	SD	A	22	29	1	0	8	49.2	228	66	41	29	6	0	1	2	14	1	42	8	0	3	3	.500	0	1	5.26
Deza, Fredy	Orioles	Bal	R	19	9	7	1	0	48.2	210	49	26	17	3	2	4	2	15	2	42	2	1	1	4	.200	0	0	3.14
	Delmarva	Bal	A	19	3	2	0	0	15	57	10	6	5	3	0	0	1	0	0	12	0	0	0	2	.000	0	0	3.00
D'Frank, Carlos	Burlington	Cle	R+	19	5	0	0	1	7	28	5	3	3	2	0	0	2	1	0	6	1	0	0	0	.000	0	0	3.86
Diaz, Alexander	Visalia	Oak	A+	22	32	0	0	7	48.2	219	62	33	30	10	3	2	3	12	2	33	1	0	3	1	.750	0	0	5.55
	Vancouver	Oak	A-	22	10	0	0	3	17.2	82	20	6	5	1	0	1	2	5	0	12	0	0	0	2	.000	0	1	2.55
Diaz, Eddie	Expos	Mon	R	19	13	6	0	0	31.1	167	33	42	36	0	1	1	15	27	0	30	5	0	1	7	.125	0	0	10.34
Diaz, Eddy	Lansing	ChC	A	21	20	6	0	6	56.2	278	71	55	44	7	2	2	6	34	0	41	20	1	0	2	.000	0	0	6.99
Diaz, Felix	Hagerstown	SF	A	20	15	12	0	0	51.2	222	49	27	21	4	0	2	4	16	0	56	3	0	1	4	.200	0	0	3.66
Diaz, Luis	Tigers	Det	R	21	13	10	0	2	55.1	241	53	30	27	6	0	3	4	27	0	71	6	0	2	4	.333	0	0	4.39
Dickinson, Rodney	Augusta	Bos	A	27	23	0	0	21	29	114	28	7	6	0	1	1	0	0	0	30	1	0	2	0	1.000	0	11	1.86
	Sarasota	Bos	A+	27	29	0	0	25	29.1	149	46	29	22	5	2	1	1	13	2	27	1	0	3	5	.375	0	11	6.75
Digby, Bryan	Danville	Atl	R+	20	12	12	1	0	61.1	273	52	33	23	2	1	1	5	32	0	49	13	0	3	5	.375	0	0	3.38
	Macon	Atl	A	20	3	1	0	0	8	33	3	1	1	0	0	0	1	7	0	6	1	0	1	0	1.000	0	0	1.13

2001 Pitching — Class-A and Rookie Leagues

HOW MUCH HE PITCHED											WHAT HE GAVE UP												THE RESULTS					
Player	Team	Org	Lg	A	G	GS	CG	GF	IP	BFP	H	R	ER	HR	SH	SF	HB	TBB	IBB	SO	WP	Bk	W	L	Pct.	ShO	Sv	ERA
Diggins, Ben	Wilmington	LA	A	23	21	21	0	0	105.2	446	88	49	42	5	2	0	3	48	0	79	10	0	7	6	.538	0	0	3.58
Dinardo, Lenny*	Brooklyn	NYM	A-	22	9	5	0	0	36	148	26	10	8	0	0	0	1	17	0	40	4	0	1	2	.333	0	0	2.00
Dischiavo, John	Hudson Val	TB	A-	20	15	15	1	0	73.1	342	91	58	53	7	1	5	8	31	0	51	13	0	3	8	.273	0	0	6.50
Dittfurth, Ryan	Charlotte	Tex	A+	22	27	24	2	2	147.1	632	123	66	57	9	6	1	17	66	1	134	15	0	9	6	.600	2	0	3.48
Dittler, Jake	Burlington	Cle	R+	19	6	5	0	0	22	101	25	14	9	0	1	0	1	12	0	20	4	0	1	2	.333	0	0	3.68
Doble, Eric	Spokane	KC	A-	23	18	0	0	10	34.1	160	41	22	17	4	4	0	2	11	2	31	4	0	0	3	.000	0	3	4.46
Dobyns, Heath	Bristol	CWS	R+	23	13	0	0	7	17.1	76	21	9	7	1	0	0	1	3	0	15	2	0	2	0	1.000	0	1	3.63
Dohmann, Scott	Asheville	Col	A	24	28	28	3	0	173	717	165	88	83	27	5	3	18	33	5	154	3	0	11	13	.458	1	0	4.32
Dominguez, Jose	Rangers	Tex	R	19	11	9	1	0	58.1	243	56	29	26	4	0	2	5	12	0	55	0	1	4	2	.667	1	0	4.01
	Charlotte	Tex	A+	19	2	0	0	0	5	19	4	2	2	1	0	1	0	1	0	5	0	0	1	0	1.000	0	0	3.60
Dominguez, Raul*	Yankees	NYY	R	20	12	0	0	0	19.1	90	21	13	12	2	1	0	1	13	0	20	3	1	1	0	1.000	0	0	5.59
Donaghey, Steve	Columbus	Cle	A	23	23	0	0	11	49.2	211	58	28	23	8	0	4	0	7	0	23	3	0	2	3	.400	0	4	4.17
Done, Juan	Mariners	Sea	R	21	5	0	0	2	9	40	5	3	1	0	0	0	0	6	0	12	1	0	0	0	.000	0	2	1.00
	Everett	Sea	A-	21	8	1	0	1	18.1	95	24	21	17	3	0	1	4	14	0	13	4	0	0	0	.000	0	0	8.35
Dorman, Rich	Chston-SC	TB	A	23	17	9	0	1	56.2	263	61	47	41	3	3	1	2	41	1	41	6	0	1	5	.167	0	0	6.51
	Hudson Val	TB	A-	23	17	3	0	3	45.1	189	37	14	13	2	3	0	2	20	1	34	6	0	3	0	1.000	0	0	2.58
Dorn, Grant	Clinton	Mon	A	24	31	0	0	19	48.1	215	56	33	30	7	1	3	0	21	0	33	1	0	4	1	.800	0	4	5.59
	Lexington	Hou	A	24	10	0	0	5	22	89	23	6	5	2	2	0	1	2	0	17	2	0	0	0	.000	0	1	2.05
Dossett, William	Royals	KC	R	22	8	0	0	6	16.1	59	11	5	4	0	0	1	1	0	0	11	0	0	2	2	.500	0	0	2.20
	Spokane	KC	A-	22	12	0	0	3	21.1	105	34	20	14	1	2	0	3	7	2	13	1	0	1	2	.333	0	0	5.91
Dotel, Melido	Casper	Col	R+	25	2	0	0	0	0.1	9	3	6	6	0	0	0	0	5	0	0	2	0	0	0	.000	0	0	162.0
Douglas, Rod	Braves	Atl	R	20	4	0	0	2	7	35	8	6	6	0	0	0	0	7	0	9	0	0	0	2	.000	0	0	7.71
Douglass, Ryan	Wilmington	KC	A+	23	1	1	0	0	5.1	18	1	0	0	0	0	0	0	3	0	7	0	0	1	0	1.000	0	0	0.00
	Royals	KC	R	23	2	1	0	0	2	6	0	0	0	0	0	0	0	0	0	2	0	0	0	0	.000	0	0	0.00
	Burlington	KC	A	23	7	1	0	3	15.1	68	18	10	10	1	0	0	0	5	0	7	0	0	1	2	.333	0	0	5.87
Dowdy, Justin*	White Sox	CWS	R	18	18	1	0	5	43.1	189	46	26	18	0	0	3	3	8	0	46	0	0	5	3	.625	0	1	3.74
Doyne, Cory	Martinsvlle	Hou	R+	20	13	13	0	0	61	264	57	31	24	2	2	2	3	30	0	56	5	1	4	3	.571	0	0	3.54
Dukeman, Greg	Lynchburg	Pit	A+	23	27	12	0	5	107.2	462	108	66	48	9	3	2	10	36	1	70	2	0	6	6	.500	0	0	4.01
Dulkowski, Marc	Idaho Falls	SD	R+	20	22	0	0	15	25.1	118	25	17	15	1	3	2	1	16	0	25	3	0	0	1	.000	0	2	5.33
	Eugene	SD	A-	20	7	0	0	4	6.1	28	6	3	3	0	1	0	1	2	0	8	2	0	1	1	.500	0	1	4.26
Dumatrait, Phil*	Red Sox	Bos	R	20	8	8	0	0	32.2	128	27	10	10	0	1	0	0	9	0	33	1	0	3	0	1.000	0	0	2.76
	Lowell	Bos	A-	20	2	2	0	0	10.1	44	9	4	4	0	0	0	0	4	0	15	1	0	1	1	.500	0	0	3.48
Dunn, Gerald	Tigers	Det	R	21	12	8	1	3	54	232	47	26	21	1	0	0	6	20	0	46	4	4	2	4	.333	0	2	3.50
	Lakeland	Det	A+	21	2	1	0	1	6	28	11	3	3	0	0	0	0	1	0	2	0	0	1	1	.500	0	0	4.50
Dunning, Justin	St. Lucie	NYM	A+	25	39	0	0	21	65.2	305	46	31	25	4	5	2	7	62	1	64	8	0	5	4	.556	0	1	3.43
Durbin, J.D.	Elizabethtn	Min	R+	20	8	7	0	0	33.2	145	23	13	7	2	1	1	4	17	0	39	5	1	3	2	.600	0	0	1.87
Durham, Chad	Pittsfield	Hou	A-	23	8	0	0	5	15.2	61	13	4	4	0	1	0	1	2	0	23	0	0	1	2	.333	0	0	2.30
Dutremble, Jeff*	Williamsprt	Pit	A-	23	17	0	0	8	23.2	123	29	20	18	1	1	2	0	27	0	25	7	0	1	0	1.000	0	0	6.85
Earey, Ryan	Fort Wayne	SD	A	23	24	7	0	8	65.1	279	70	38	35	7	1	5	2	17	1	59	1	1	1	4	.200	0	0	4.82
Earley, Andrew	Boise	ChC	A-	22	14	3	0	4	30.1	148	32	16	12	1	1	3	7	20	1	15	1	1	1	1	.500	0	0	3.56
Echols, Justin	Savannah	Tex	A	21	36	13	1	8	123	524	88	58	52	4	5	3	11	67	1	156	21	1	5	9	.357	0	3	3.80
Eckert, Harold	Kingsport	NYM	R+	24	2	2	0	0	12	44	8	3	3	1	0	0	0	1	0	17	0	0	1	0	1.000	0	0	2.25
	Brooklyn	NYM	A-	24	13	11	0	1	70	284	51	31	26	4	1	1	6	21	0	75	9	0	9	1	.900	0	0	3.34
Edwards, Bryan	Dayton	Cin	A	22	29	14	1	6	107.2	496	127	75	56	8	4	0	7	40	0	58	14	1	6	7	.462	0	0	4.68
Edwards, Mike*	Bluefield	Bal	R+	22	16	1	0	3	35.1	159	25	23	22	3	1	2	3	28	0	37	9	0	0	1	.000	0	0	5.60
Elliott, Chad*	Capital Cty	NYM	A	24	35	3	0	19	84	358	78	44	31	4	5	0	3	26	1	91	4	0	4	4	.500	0	5	3.32
Ellis, Steve	Boise	ChC	A-	23	20	0	0	14	25.2	107	18	8	7	1	1	2	3	11	1	31	1	0	2	1	.667	0	6	2.45
Elskamp, Andy	Lakewood	Phi	A	23	23	0	0	10	39.2	168	28	15	10	4	2	1	2	19	1	41	3	0	0	1	.000	0	1	2.27
Engels, Jackson*	Rangers	Tex	R	23	10	0	0	7	28.1	120	21	8	7	1	1	0	6	15	2	11	1	0	2	2	.500	0	0	2.22
Ennis, John	Myrtle Bch	Atl	A+	22	25	25	1	0	138.1	569	111	63	55	12	4	5	7	45	0	144	2	3	6	8	.429	0	0	3.58
Eppeneder, Jim*	Daytona	ChC	A+	23	42	0	0	17	67.1	296	54	37	26	3	0	1	5	34	0	56	3	1	4	2	.667	0	5	3.48
Eriksen, Tanner	Lancaster	Ari	A+	23	19	13	0	1	71	351	95	66	51	3	4	5	2	49	1	52	11	0	3	6	.333	0	0	6.46
	Yakima	Ari	A-	23	3	3	0	0	15.2	67	17	9	6	3	0	0	0	4	0	14	2	1	1	1	.500	0	0	3.45
Esarey, Brad*	Auburn	Tor	A-	23	17	0	0	4	35	152	33	18	15	2	1	1	3	12	0	34	1	0	2	0	1.000	0	0	3.86
Escobedo, Edgar	Dodgers	LA	R	19	17	4	0	0	43.1	175	42	9	8	1	0	0	3	9	0	24	3	0	4	1	.800	0	0	1.66
Espaillat, Ezequiel	Marlins	Fla	R	21	15	0	0	9	32	145	34	22	18	2	1	3	8	10	0	23	1	0	0	0	.000	0	3	5.06
Esquivia, Manuel	Kane County	Fla	A	22	24	18	0	1	105.1	462	92	66	60	7	3	7	5	51	0	82	15	2	8	7	.533	0	1	5.13
Esteves, Jake	San Jose	SF	A+	26	9	9	0	0	14.2	65	13	12	12	3	0	0	1	9	0	19	0	0	0	3	.000	0	0	7.36
Evans, Kyle	Kinston	Cle	A+	23	7	7	0	0	30	123	35	9	9	0	0	1	1	9	0	16	1	0	2	1	.667	0	0	2.70
Evans, Louis*	Marlins	Fla	R	21	14	0	0	8	25	109	18	10	6	0	4	1	4	12	2	26	3	1	3	3	.500	0	0	2.16
Evert, Brett	Macon	Atl	A	21	6	6	0	0	36.1	140	25	5	3	0	0	0	0	3	0	34	0	0	1	0	1.000	0	0	0.74
	Myrtle Bch	Atl	A+	21	13	13	1	0	72.1	300	63	25	18	4	2	0	4	15	0	75	2	0	7	2	.778	1	0	2.24
Ewin, Ryan	Braves	Atl	R	20	1	0	0	0	2	11	4	2	2	0	0	0	0	1	0	4	0	0	0	0	.000	0	0	9.00
	Danville	Atl	R+	20	10	9	0	0	37.2	160	36	20	19	4	0	0	4	13	0	39	3	0	2	2	.500	0	0	4.54
Eyre, Willie	Quad City	Min	A	23	17	0	0	6	22.1	87	19	6	6	1	0	0	1	2	0	21	1	0	3	0	1.000	0	4	2.42
	Fort Myers	Min	A+	23	32	0	0	10	64.1	280	54	27	18	2	2	7	4	33	2	51	5	0	2	5	.286	0	1	2.52
Faigin, Jason	Greensboro	NYY	A	23	60	1	0	33	66	291	63	32	25	0	2	0	2	26	3	67	3	1	4	8	.333	0	8	3.41
Farizo, Brad	Brevard Cty	Fla	A+	23	9	7	0	1	46	179	39	13	11	2	1	2	0	5	0	31	1	0	4	2	.667	0	0	2.15
Farley, Chris	Red Sox	Bos	R	19	3	2	0	0	4.1	28	8	8	8	0	1	0	0	8	0	3	0	0	0	1	.000	0	0	16.62
Farley, Joe*	San Jose	SF	A+	23	18	0	0	4	26.2	126	28	22	21	3	0	2	1	20	0	15	4	1	1	0	1.000	0	0	7.09
Farman, Brian	Mahoning Vy	Cle	A-	23	10	0	0	6	16	67	16	5	5	0	2	0	1	2	1	12	1	0	0	2	.000	0	1	2.81
Farmer, Jason	San Jose	SF	A+	23	14	13	0	0	62.1	281	77	37	32	4	2	0	5	20	0	52	0	0	6	1	.857	0	0	4.62
Farrell, Sean*	Kingsport	NYM	R+	20	18	0	0	5	25	124	30	25	20	4	1	1	3	16	0	26	2	1	1	0	1.000	0	0	7.20
Farren, Dave	Delmarva	Bal	A	21	32	19	0	4	121.1	511	113	66	53	16	4	3	7	30	1	84	1	0	4	7	.364	0	0	3.93
Faust, Wes	Hagerstown	SF	A	24	46	0	0	17	90.2	361	79	28	25	4	4	3	3	18	2	66	2	0	7	5	.583	0	4	2.48
Featherstone, D.	Giants	SF	R	25	15	4	0	3	28.1	136	30	32	31	4	1	1	7	21	0	36	3	1	2	1	.667	0	0	9.85
Febles, Hector	Princeton	TB	R+	19	12	10	2	0	46.1	217	55	40	35	4	1	0	3	25	0	39	7	0	3	3	.500	2	0	6.80
Feliciano, Ruben	Pulaski	Tex	R+	22	4	0	0	2	7.2	27	1	0	0	0	0	0	1	4	0	6	0	1	0	0	.000	0	1	0.00
	Savannah	Tex	A	22	6	0	0	2	14.2	74	16	14	13	3	0	0	7	7	0	6	0	0	0	1	.000	0	0	7.98
Ferguson, Ian	Burlington	KC	A	22	10	10	0	0	58	240	62	39	34	9	3	3	4	10	0	30	2	1	3	2	.600	0	0	5.28
	Wilmington	KC	A+	22	18	18	0	0	96.1	403	85	47	41	5	1	2	11	27	0	72	5	0	10	3	.769	0	0	3.83
Fernley, Nate	Mahoning Vy	Cle	A-	25	13	0	0	6	18.1	96	30	18	9	2	1	1	1	8	3	21	0	0	0	2	.000	0	0	4.42
Ferrand, Dario	Kannapolis	CWS	A	21	27	27	3	0	162	672	156	67	55	9	2	4	11	36	6	111	7	1	9	13	.409	1	0	3.06
Ferrand, Julian	Casper	Col	R+	22	17	0	0	5	28.2	141	40	27	21	3	1	2	3	11	0	26	4	0	0	0	.000	0	0	6.59
Ferrari, Anthony*	Jupiter	Mon	A+	24	51	0	0	40	56.2	226	36	11	5	1	4	1	4	17	0	45	1	0	2	3	.400	0	21	0.79

2001 Pitching — Class-A and Rookie Leagues

HOW MUCH HE PITCHED											WHAT HE GAVE UP												THE RESULTS					
Player	Team	Org	Lg	A	G	GS	CG	GF	IP	BFP	H	R	ER	HR	SH	SF	HB	TBB	IBB	SO	WP	Bk	W	L	Pct.	ShO	Sv	ERA
Ferreira, Emilo	Twins	Min	R	19	12	10	0	0	60	233	52	10	8	2	0	0	2	10	0	47	3	0	8	1	.889	0	0	1.20
Ferreras, Yorkin*	Boise	ChC	A-	21	18	0	0	12	25.2	114	27	12	9	2	1	3	0	13	2	23	1	1	1	0	1.000	0	6	3.16
Fields, Josh	Bristol	CWS	R+	22	17	0	0	10	32.1	135	32	21	13	2	1	1	1	8	1	34	2	0	3	1	.750	0	2	3.62
Figueroa, Juan	Tigers	Det	R	20	17	4	0	2	38.2	182	33	28	20	0	1	1	4	30	2	41	12	5	1	4	.200	0	0	4.66
Figueroa, Williams	Expos	Mon	R	18	12	0	0	3	17.1	79	9	10	9	1	0	2	0	19	0	13	6	2	1	2	.333	0	0	4.67
Fingers, Jason	Burlington	KC	A	23	33	0	0	18	43.2	186	46	21	18	4	3	1	2	10	1	37	4	1	1	6	.143	0	4	3.71
Fischer, Eric*	Winston-Sal	CWS	A+	22	25	22	0	1	123.2	554	144	87	73	9	4	3	10	47	1	84	3	0	3	13	.188	0	0	5.31
Fischer, Rich	Cedar Rapds	Ana	A	21	20	20	2	0	130.2	550	131	73	61	8	5	6	5	33	0	97	6	1	9	7	.563	0	0	4.20
Fischer, Steve	Visalia	Oak	A+	24	34	19	0	6	121	540	140	77	62	12	5	6	7	41	2	88	5	0	7	7	.500	0	1	4.61
Fisher, Marc	Cubs	ChC	R	23	15	1	0	10	30	111	19	5	4	0	1	1	2	3	0	35	1	0	0	1	.000	0	7	1.20
	Daytona	ChC	A+	23	2	1	0	1	4	17	5	1	1	0	0	0	0	1	0	4	0	1	0	0	.000	0	0	2.25
Flading, Cameron	Cedar Rapds	Ana	A	23	15	0	0	12	17	79	12	13	10	2	0	0	0	16	0	29	5	0	0	0	.000	0	1	5.29
Flannery, Mike	Kane County	Fla	A	22	53	0	0	33	56.1	260	58	35	30	5	2	3	3	31	0	47	5	1	3	4	.429	0	16	4.79
Flinn, Chris	Hudson Val	TB	A-	21	15	10	0	4	68.2	284	54	33	18	3	2	0	3	21	0	72	12	1	3	4	.429	0	2	2.36
Flores, Ron*	Modesto	Oak	A+	22	47	0	0	23	66	282	53	24	21	4	6	2	1	29	7	71	3	0	5	2	.714	0	6	2.86
Foley, Travis	Burlington	Cle	R+	19	10	10	0	0	45	175	26	16	14	4	2	3	3	15	0	59	1	0	2	3	.400	0	0	2.80
Foli, Daniel	Cubs	ChC	R	21	11	10	0	0	46.2	195	40	29	25	1	0	5	3	15	0	40	1	0	2	5	.286	0	0	4.82
Fontana, Tony	Augusta	Bos	A	23	24	4	0	11	69.2	289	66	21	15	2	0	0	1	9	0	62	7	0	2	2	.500	0	6	1.94
	Sarasota	Bos	A+	23	9	7	0	2	48.2	208	57	25	19	3	0	3	4	8	0	32	1	0	2	3	.400	0	0	3.51
Foote, Joe	Fort Myers	Min	A+	22	17	14	0	1	86	373	101	45	37	5	3	5	4	25	2	57	6	1	2	8	.200	0	0	3.87
	Quad City	Min	A	22	13	8	0	1	55.2	242	64	37	32	7	2	1	5	10	1	46	3	0	3	2	.600	0	0	5.17
Foppert, Jesse	Salem-Keizr	SF	A-	21	14	14	0	0	70	264	35	18	15	7	0	3	5	23	0	88	4	3	8	1	.889	0	0	1.93
Forbes, Derek	Bluefield	Bal	R+	23	6	0	0	4	8.1	43	12	7	6	1	0	0	0	6	0	11	2	0	1	1	.500	0	0	6.48
Ford, Matt*	Dunedin	Tor	A+	21	13	12	0	0	60	270	67	41	39	8	0	3	2	37	0	48	7	0	2	7	.222	0	0	5.85
	Chston-WV	Tor	A	21	11	11	1	0	70.2	287	62	28	19	2	2	1	0	22	0	69	8	1	4	4	.500	0	0	2.42
Ford, Tom*	Delmarva	Bal	A	25	13	0	0	3	14	64	13	8	7	0	1	1	1	8	0	23	0	0	2	0	1.000	0	0	4.50
	Frederick	Bal	A+	25	33	0	0	18	47.2	203	45	18	17	3	0	1	4	16	0	55	2	0	1	1	.500	0	5	3.21
Fortin, Mike	Williamsprt	Pit	A-	24	4	0	0	0	6	26	5	4	4	2	0	0	0	6	0	5	0	0	1	0	1.000	0	0	6.00
Fortunato, B.	Hudson Val	TB	A-	21	16	9	0	2	59.2	266	70	35	34	3	1	0	2	29	0	53	11	0	2	5	.286	0	0	5.13
Forystek, Brian*	Frederick	Bal	A+	23	41	1	0	6	59.1	264	61	27	19	3	2	1	4	30	1	68	9	0	1	3	.250	0	0	2.88
Fox, Ben*	Idaho Falls	SD	R+	21	13	0	0	9	16	80	22	16	16	0	0	1	3	8	0	17	1	0	1	1	.500	0	5	9.00
	Fort Wayne	SD	A	21	11	5	0	1	27.2	132	43	25	23	2	0	0	0	13	1	22	3	1	1	1	.500	0	0	7.48
Frachiseur, Zach	Daytona	ChC	A+	25	22	0	0	11	30	130	34	19	17	3	3	0	0	10	1	34	2	1	1	3	.250	0	4	5.10
Francisco, Frank	Augusta	Bos	A	22	37	0	0	8	68	280	40	25	22	3	5	1	6	30	0	90	6	1	4	3	.571	0	2	2.91
Franco, Martire	Clearwater	Phi	A+	21	26	24	4	1	161.1	694	178	84	74	12	6	5	8	41	1	97	7	2	11	8	.579	0	0	4.13
Frary, Levi	Tri-City	Col	A-	23	22	0	0	14	21.2	95	27	17	13	0	2	0	3	5	1	11	1	1	1	1	.500	0	9	5.40
Frawley, Patrick	Marlins	Fla	R	25	5	0	0	3	5.2	24	4	3	2	0	1	0	1	2	0	4	3	0	0	1	.000	0	0	3.18
Freed, Mark*	Daytona	ChC	A+	23	23	22	1	0	130	541	120	54	45	7	4	3	2	51	4	90	6	1	6	8	.429	1	0	3.12
Freeman, Eric*	Spokane	KC	A-	22	21	0	0	7	37.1	169	40	23	20	3	1	1	1	18	0	24	2	0	1	3	.250	0	1	4.82
Frendling, Neal	Bakersfield	TB	A+	22	20	20	0	0	112	486	105	62	57	8	5	4	10	38	0	107	12	0	6	8	.429	0	0	4.58
Frey, Jason	Johnson Cty	StL	R+	24	3	3	0	0	13	51	11	6	6	2	1	0	2	4	0	13	1	0	1	0	1.000	0	0	4.15
Frias, Juan	San Jose	SF	A+	23	4	0	0	1	6	37	9	8	7	0	0	1	1	9	0	5	4	0	0	0	.000	0	0	10.50
	Salem-Keizr	SF	A-	23	4	0	0	1	5	25	7	5	5	0	0	0	1	3	0	2	3	0	0	0	.000	0	0	9.00
	Hagerstown	SF	A	23	24	0	0	5	31	139	36	17	11	3	5	4	2	10	2	27	1	1	3	1	.750	0	1	3.19
Frick, Mike	Vancouver	Oak	A-	22	21	1	0	10	40	173	38	15	12	1	1	0	1	15	0	54	2	1	7	2	.778	0	3	2.70
Friedberg, Drew*	Williamsprt	Pit	A-	23	4	0	0	4	4	13	2	0	0	0	0	0	0	0	0	6	0	0	0	0	.000	0	3	0.00
	Hickory	Pit	A	23	17	0	0	7	20.1	96	26	16	14	3	4	0	2	9	2	15	3	1	0	1	.000	0	1	6.20
Fries, Scott*	Lansing	ChC	A	24	43	0	0	19	71.2	291	65	35	26	4	1	2	2	11	1	64	1	1	6	5	.545	0	5	3.27
Fries, Tim	Danville	Atl	R+	22	24	0	0	13	36.2	172	39	22	20	1	1	2	3	20	0	54	7	1	2	3	.400	0	5	4.91
Friske, Parker*	Lowell	Bos	A-	23	19	3	0	6	53.1	252	70	38	31	5	4	0	2	23	1	38	2	0	3	2	.600	0	1	5.23
Frost, Clint	Royals	KC	R	18	4	2	0	1	17	67	14	6	6	0	0	0	0	3	0	15	1	0	0	1	.000	0	0	3.18
Fruto, Emiliano	Mariners	Sea	R	18	12	12	0	0	61.2	282	73	45	40	3	2	4	3	22	0	51	1	2	5	3	.625	0	0	5.84
Fry, Justin	Clearwater	Phi	A+	25	30	0	0	12	54	251	54	34	28	3	4	3	4	34	0	43	3	0	2	2	.500	0	1	4.67
Fryson, Andrew	White Sox	CWS	R	21	8	6	0	1	23.1	100	29	14	8	0	0	1	0	3	0	23	2	0	0	3	.000	0	0	3.09
	Bristol	CWS	R+	21	2	2	0	0	12	49	11	5	4	0	0	0	1	2	0	5	0	0	1	0	1.000	0	0	3.00
Fuell, Jerrod	W Michigan	Det	A	21	14	0	0	6	21.2	93	13	8	7	2	2	2	3	12	3	13	1	0	0	1	.000	0	1	2.91
Fulchino, Jeff	Utica	Fla	A-	22	14	13	0	1	60.2	267	48	34	24	2	1	0	8	31	0	33	3	3	3	8	.273	0	0	3.56
Fuller, Brendan	Medcine Hat	Tor	R+	21	18	0	0	4	25.1	116	21	20	19	1	1	1	10	16	1	38	12	0	0	1	.000	0	0	6.75
Furnald, Donnie	Braves	Atl	R	22	4	0	0	3	8	25	3	1	1	1	0	0	0	1	0	7	1	0	0	0	.000	0	3	1.13
	Jamestown	Atl	A-	22	11	5	0	2	39.1	181	37	30	29	3	1	2	0	34	0	34	8	0	4	1	.800	0	0	6.64
Gaal, Bryan	Fort Wayne	SD	A	25	23	0	0	9	32.1	118	20	7	7	0	0	0	2	4	1	42	2	1	1	1	.500	0	2	1.95
	Lk Elsinore	SD	A+	25	35	0	0	11	47	195	37	23	19	3	1	4	2	17	1	50	4	1	3	3	.500	0	3	3.64
Gabbard, Kason*	Red Sox	Bos	R	20	6	6	0	0	14.1	65	11	11	9	1	0	2	1	9	0	17	3	0	0	1	.000	0	0	5.65
Gage, Matt	Vancouver	Oak	A-	24	17	3	0	5	35	161	46	25	16	1	1	0	3	7	1	18	1	0	1	1	.500	0	0	4.11
Gahan, Matthew	Brooklyn	NYM	A-	26	10	3	0	5	40.2	164	29	16	9	1	1	0	1	7	0	42	2	0	4	1	.800	0	4	1.99
	Capital Cty	NYM	A	26	5	4	0	0	14	67	20	14	9	2	0	0	0	4	0	11	1	0	0	3	.000	0	0	5.79
Gallagher, Shawn*	Tri-City	Col	A-	23	17	0	0	2	17.2	85	22	12	9	0	3	0	4	8	0	19	0	0	0	3	.000	0	1	4.58
Gallo, Mike*	Michigan	Hou	A	24	44	0	0	17	84.1	360	83	38	36	4	1	2	8	19	1	67	3	1	9	2	.818	0	4	3.84
Gamble, Jerome	Sarasota	Bos	A+	22	3	2	0	1	8	37	11	8	7	0	0	0	0	4	0	7	1	0	0	0	.000	0	1	7.88
Garber, Mike*	Yakima	Ari	A-	21	3	0	0	0	2.2	11	3	2	1	0	0	1	0	0	0	2	1	0	0	0	.000	0	0	3.38
	Lancaster	Ari	A+	21	25	0	0	3	24	126	41	22	17	4	1	3	0	14	1	21	4	0	0	2	.000	0	0	6.38
Garcia, Anderson	Staten Ilnd	NYY	A-	18	1	1	0	0	4.2	20	7	3	3	0	0	0	0	1	0	1	1	0	0	1	.000	0	0	5.79
Garcia, Angel	Twins	Min	R	18	9	6	0	1	17.2	84	20	15	11	0	1	1	0	12	0	22	2	1	0	3	.000	0	0	5.60
Garcia, Jairo	Athletics	Oak	R	19	12	7	0	3	47.1	184	37	19	15	2	2	0	2	6	0	50	5	0	4	2	.667	0	0	2.85
Garcia, Rafael	Spokane	KC	A-	24	10	10	0	0	41.2	198	54	41	33	7	0	2	5	17	0	33	4	0	2	5	.286	0	0	7.13
Garcia, Reynaldo	Charlotte	Tex	A+	24	35	16	0	9	116.1	499	107	62	46	7	6	4	8	45	3	111	8	1	5	10	.333	0	4	3.56
Garcia, Ruddy	Giants	SF	R	18	5	0	0	2	5.2	28	7	3	2	0	0	0	0	5	0	3	1	0	0	0	.000	0	0	3.18
Gardner, Hayden	Charlotte	Tex	A+	21	1	1	0	0	5.2	23	5	1	1	0	0	0	1	2	0	3	1	0	1	0	1.000	0	0	1.59
	Pulaski	Tex	R+	21	13	13	2	0	83.1	340	71	32	23	4	1	0	8	15	0	70	6	0	4	4	.500	1	0	2.48
Garris, Antonio	Clinton	Mon	A	24	15	0	0	10	17	84	16	14	10	3	1	1	1	18	0	11	1	0	0	3	.000	0	1	5.29
	Vermont	Mon	A-	24	15	0	0	14	16.2	74	12	7	3	1	0	0	3	9	0	20	1	0	0	0	.000	0	5	1.62
Garza, Alberto	Columbus	Cle	A	25	1	0	0	1	2.1	9	2	0	0	0	0	0	0	1	0	2	0	0	1	0	1.000	0	0	0.00
	Kinston	Cle	A+	25	41	0	0	14	76.2	336	60	29	27	2	3	2	5	48	3	123	2	0	5	3	.625	0	2	3.17
Garza, Rolando	Bristol	CWS	R+	22	5	0	0	3	7.2	40	9	6	6	2	0	0	0	10	0	4	5	0	0	1	.000	0	0	7.04
	Kannapolis	CWS	A	22	9	0	0	7	9.1	50	12	10	10	1	0	2	1	9	0	10	1	1	1	0	1.000	0	0	9.64

2001 Pitching — Class-A and Rookie Leagues

HOW MUCH HE PITCHED											WHAT HE GAVE UP												THE RESULTS					
Player	Team	Org	Lg	A	G	GS	CG	GF	IP	BFP	H	R	ER	HR	SH	SF	HB	TBB	IBB	SO	WP	Bk	W	L	Pct.	ShO	Sv	ERA
Gassner, Dave*	Chston-WV	Tor	A	23	13	11	1	1	74.1	307	72	30	25	3	0	2	2	11	0	51	4	0	4	4	.500	0	0	3.03
Gates, Brian	Quad City	Min	A	22	15	0	0	7	29	121	25	10	7	2	0	0	2	8	1	24	2	0	2	1	.667	0	0	2.17
Gawer, Matt*	Myrtle Bch	Atl	A+	24	42	0	0	37	43	193	41	18	12	1	1	1	4	16	1	46	2	0	2	0	1.000	0	14	2.51
Gehrke, Jay	Wilmington	KC	A+	24	42	0	0	21	71.2	325	82	51	45	3	5	2	5	32	0	65	11	0	5	7	.417	0	3	5.65
Geigel, Rolando	Kane County	Fla	A	22	30	1	0	6	44.1	199	39	22	20	1	1	2	10	28	1	19	7	0	3	3	.500	0	0	4.06
Gelatka, Todd	Brewers	Mil	R	20	1	0	0	0	1.1	6	2	1	1	0	0	0	0	0	0	1	0	0	0	0	.000	0	0	6.75
Generelli, Dan	Lowell	Bos	A-	21	16	14	0	0	70.2	318	69	49	37	4	3	5	4	38	0	51	6	1	1	8	.111	0	0	4.71
George, Brad	Dayton	Cin	A	20	8	8	0	0	34.2	155	44	26	23	3	1	5	4	13	2	13	0	0	2	1	.667	0	0	5.97
	Billings	Cin	R+	20	5	5	0	0	23.1	113	29	31	24	6	0	3	3	8	0	16	4	0	0	2	.000	0	0	9.26
	Reds	Cin	R	20	7	7	0	0	42	174	33	7	6	0	1	2	2	14	0	33	0	2	6	1	.857	0	0	1.29
George, Chris	Lexington	Hou	A	24	40	0	0	27	51	232	43	26	22	7	0	1	2	30	0	65	9	0	5	1	.833	0	2	3.88
George, Todd	Jupiter	Mon	A+	23	1	0	0	0	3	13	4	0	0	0	0	0	0	0	0	2	0	0	1	0	1.000	0	0	0.00
	Expos	Mon	R	23	8	0	0	5	10	44	8	3	3	1	0	0	3	3	0	13	0	0	0	0	.000	0	1	2.70
	Vermont	Mon	A-	23	5	2	0	0	17	70	20	8	8	1	0	0	1	4	0	15	0	0	0	0	.000	0	0	4.24
	Clinton	Mon	A	23	2	2	0	0	11	51	12	9	9	2	0	1	2	4	0	8	1	0	0	2	.000	0	0	7.36
Gerk, Jordan*	Oneonta	Det	A-	22	4	0	0	1	8	37	10	3	2	0	0	0	0	2	1	10	0	0	1	0	1.000	0	0	2.25
German, Franklyn	Visalia	Oak	A+	22	53	0	0	45	63.1	294	67	34	28	7	3	2	2	31	1	93	11	0	2	4	.333	0	19	3.98
German, Yon*	St. Lucie	NYM	A+	24	2	0	0	1	4.2	21	5	2	2	0	1	0	0	4	0	0	0	0	1	0	1.000	0	0	3.86
Germano, Justin	Fort Wayne	SD	A	19	13	13	0	0	65	293	80	47	36	7	2	3	7	16	1	55	6	0	2	6	.250	0	0	4.98
	Eugene	SD	A-	19	13	13	2	0	80	333	77	35	31	5	1	3	5	11	0	74	1	0	6	5	.545	0	0	3.49
Giese, Dan	Augusta	Bos	A	25	46	0	0	39	74	297	65	27	18	2	0	0	1	8	3	95	2	0	6	4	.600	0	9	2.19
Gilbert, Rich*	Savannah	Tex	A	22	21	20	3	0	134	568	120	75	63	13	5	3	11	44	0	155	7	2	6	11	.353	0	0	4.23
Gilchrist, Ronald*	Williamsprt	Pit	A-	24	16	0	0	5	22.2	98	21	8	8	0	0	1	3	8	0	27	0	0	4	0	1.000	0	0	3.18
Gill, Chris	Athletics	Oak	R	21	13	1	0	2	24	105	23	20	16	1	0	2	1	9	0	21	1	0	3	1	.750	0	0	6.00
Gill, Ryan	Staten Ilnd	NYY	A-	25	19	0	0	6	24	114	23	20	15	2	1	0	4	16	2	25	3	1	2	2	.500	0	0	5.63
Gillman, Justin	Reds	Cin	R	19	9	7	0	1	36	136	19	10	7	1	0	1	2	11	0	38	2	0	4	2	.667	0	0	1.75
	Billings	Cin	R+	19	1	1	0	0	6	22	0	1	0	0	0	0	0	5	0	2	0	0	1	0	1.000	0	0	0.00
Gilpatrick, Tyler	Vancouver	Oak	A-	23	19	1	0	7	42.1	179	42	23	18	3	1	3	3	14	0	34	1	0	2	2	.500	0	1	3.83
Girdley, Josh*	Clinton	Mon	A	21	6	6	0	0	29.1	133	28	15	12	2	0	0	1	18	0	21	1	0	0	2	.000	0	0	3.68
Giron, Roberto	High Desert	Mil	A+	26	45	0	0	30	63.1	283	64	35	23	4	4	4	3	20	1	86	6	0	3	2	.600	0	12	3.27
Gittings, Chris	Brewers	Mil	R	19	6	3	0	2	11.2	49	15	10	10	1	0	0	1	1	0	12	1	0	1	1	.500	0	0	7.71
Glascock, J.-Paul	Cubs	ChC	R	22	16	1	0	5	19.2	106	22	23	21	0	0	2	1	24	0	15	8	1	0	1	.000	0	0	9.61
Glaser, Eric	Sarasota	Bos	A+	24	37	5	0	12	88.2	364	74	28	25	6	2	2	5	27	1	82	2	0	4	3	.571	0	1	2.54
Glaser, Nick	Batavia	Phi	A-	23	24	0	0	21	28.2	126	27	13	8	0	1	2	0	7	2	21	6	0	3	4	.429	0	6	2.51
Glen, William	Chston-WV	Tor	A	24	23	0	0	9	45	204	46	27	17	5	0	1	0	26	0	50	4	0	2	1	.667	0	1	3.40
Gobble, Jimmy*	Wilmington	KC	A+	20	27	27	0	0	162.1	649	134	58	46	8	9	4	9	33	3	154	7	0	10	6	.625	0	0	2.55
Gold, J.M.	Brewers	Mil	R	22	4	4	0	0	8.1	41	17	7	7	0	0	1	0	2	0	7	0	0	0	1	.000	0	0	7.56
	Ogden	Mil	R+	22	7	7	0	0	29	116	20	12	7	1	0	1	1	9	0	42	2	0	1	1	.500	0	0	2.17
Gomer, Jeramy*	Lansing	ChC	A	23	10	1	0	4	22	96	22	8	6	1	1	1	0	12	2	22	3	0	0	0	.000	0	0	2.45
	Daytona	ChC	A+	23	24	2	0	7	49	223	51	36	34	4	1	2	5	29	0	44	3	0	3	1	.750	0	1	6.24
Gomez, Benito*	Chston-SC	TB	A	23	39	0	0	22	58.1	257	59	32	25	9	2	2	1	19	4	46	7	0	1	1	.500	0	0	3.86
Gomez, Deibis	Johnson Cty	StL	R+	22	4	0	0	1	3	17	6	2	1	0	0	0	0	2	0	2	2	0	0	1	.000	0	1	3.00
Gomez, Diogenes	Asheville	Col	A	23	50	1	0	21	84	352	82	34	21	3	10	3	2	21	6	55	4	1	12	4	.750	0	3	2.25
Gomez, Jose	Kingsport	NYM	R+	21	3	2	0	0	9	35	3	2	1	0	0	0	0	4	0	14	1	1	0	0	.000	0	0	1.00
Gomez, Jose	Reds	Cin	R	20	14	0	0	6	31.2	127	24	7	5	0	0	2	4	6	0	27	1	0	0	1	.000	0	1	1.42
Gomez, Mariano*	Burlington	Cle	R+	19	13	12	0	0	59.1	265	69	47	40	4	2	3	0	21	0	57	5	1	2	8	.200	0	0	6.07
	Mahoning Vy	Cle	A-	19	1	1	0	0	5	22	5	3	3	1	1	0	0	2	0	6	1	0	1	0	1.000	0	0	5.40
Gomez, Ricardo	Greensboro	NYY	A	24	9	2	0	1	15.1	79	20	19	15	0	3	0	2	12	0	10	1	0	2	2	.500	0	1	8.80
	Staten Ilnd	NYY	A-	24	8	0	0	0	18.1	77	13	7	3	2	1	0	2	10	1	11	1	2	1	1	.500	0	0	1.47
Gomez, Warmar	Expos	Mon	R	19	18	0	0	7	21.2	103	32	22	19	5	0	1	1	5	0	14	2	0	0	1	.000	0	1	7.89
Gonzales, Jim	Oneonta	Det	A-	22	16	0	0	11	24.2	105	24	10	7	1	0	1	1	8	2	20	6	0	3	3	.500	0	2	2.55
Gonzales, Jose	Greensboro	NYY	A	24	35	0	0	11	49	210	52	30	28	5	2	4	1	19	3	36	2	1	2	6	.250	0	0	5.14
Gonzalez, Alfredo	Great Falls	LA	R+	22	11	8	0	1	48	203	43	26	19	1	1	1	5	12	0	56	4	0	3	4	.429	0	0	3.56
	Wilmington	LA	A	22	2	1	0	1	9	42	10	4	3	0	1	1	0	3	0	12	1	0	1	0	1.000	0	0	3.00
Gonzalez, Carlos	Missoula	Ari	R+	22	10	0	0	4	13.2	69	19	13	8	0	0	1	2	6	0	15	5	0	0	2	.000	0	0	5.27
	Yakima	Ari	A-	22	13	0	0	5	24	105	19	12	9	1	1	0	1	15	1	21	5	0	0	1	.000	0	3	3.38
Gonzalez, Cesar	South Bend	Ari	A	19	26	26	1	0	146	630	142	81	65	9	3	11	10	53	0	92	10	0	4	12	.250	0	0	4.01
Gonzalez, Christian	Vancouver	Oak	A-	23	16	16	0	0	87.2	368	90	36	26	4	1	3	5	15	1	59	5	2	2	7	.222	0	0	2.67
Gonzalez, Gilberto*	St. Lucie	NYM	A+	25	7	0	0	3	12	57	11	9	7	1	0	0	1	7	0	6	0	0	0	1	.000	0	0	5.25
	Capital Cty	NYM	A	25	5	4	0	1	19	80	15	6	5	1	1	0	2	5	0	24	2	1	1	2	.333	0	0	2.37
Gonzalez, Giovanni	Spokane	KC	A-	22	4	3	0	0	11.1	61	21	18	18	4	0	0	4	3	0	8	0	0	0	3	.000	0	0	14.29
Gonzalez, Jose	Red Sox	Bos	R	22	1	0	0	0	2	7	0	0	0	0	1	0	0	2	0	0	0	0	0	0	.000	0	0	0.00
Gonzalez, Kiwi	Princeton	TB	R+	19	14	8	0	2	50.2	223	52	31	25	2	1	0	3	18	0	38	4	2	3	2	.600	0	0	4.44
Gonzalez, Luis*	Dodgers	LA	R	19	13	2	0	0	25.1	117	25	15	10	0	0	1	1	14	0	25	2	0	4	2	.667	0	0	3.55
Gonzalez, Miguel	Casper	Col	R+	22	24	0	0	2	40.1	179	40	21	15	0	3	3	4	12	1	41	4	2	2	2	.500	0	0	3.35
Good, Eric*	Jupiter	Mon	A+	22	21	20	1	0	108.1	456	104	42	34	4	3	4	4	26	0	70	4	1	5	5	.500	0	0	2.82
Gooding, Jason*	Royals	KC	R	27	1	1	0	0	1	6	3	2	2	0	0	0	0	0	0	0	0	0	0	1	.000	0	0	18.00
Goodrum, Kevin*	Staten Ilnd	NYY	A-	23	7	3	0	2	16.2	75	18	9	7	0	1	0	0	6	0	14	0	0	1	1	.500	0	0	3.78
	Greensboro	NYY	A	23	7	7	0	0	38.2	169	45	21	18	4	2	0	3	12	0	25	0	0	2	2	.500	0	0	4.19
Goodwin, Ron	Utica	Fla	A-	22	20	0	0	7	45	191	51	22	18	1	2	3	1	10	1	25	5	0	3	3	.500	0	3	3.60
Gordon, Justin*	Beloit	Mil	A	23	27	24	0	1	124.1	563	112	83	61	13	2	4	14	84	0	103	16	2	3	4	.429	0	0	4.42
Grace, Bryan	Tampa	NYY	A+	26	3	0	0	0	2	13	5	4	3	0	0	1	0	1	0	5	0	0	0	0	.000	0	0	13.50
Gracesqui, Frank*	Chston-WV	Tor	A	22	35	2	0	11	65.1	286	60	40	23	1	2	2	2	34	0	66	9	1	2	8	.200	0	1	3.17
	Dunedin	Tor	A+	22	4	0	0	0	5.2	24	2	0	0	0	0	0	0	8	0	6	0	0	1	0	1.000	0	0	0.00
Graham, Elgin	Hagerstown	SF	A	24	32	9	0	6	67	317	75	56	44	9	3	8	4	43	3	37	12	0	3	4	.429	0	1	5.91
Graham, Frank	Sarasota	Bos	A+	23	39	1	0	18	82	396	119	68	53	7	5	5	8	27	3	52	8	0	2	10	.167	0	0	5.82
Graham, Tom	Savannah	Tex	A	24	40	0	0	32	54	217	46	19	15	0	3	2	5	10	0	71	2	1	1	4	.200	0	17	2.50
	Charlotte	Tex	A+	24	9	0	0	4	23.2	87	13	7	7	1	1	0	0	9	2	20	1	0	2	2	.500	0	1	2.66
Granados, Bernie	Casper	Col	R+	23	21	0	0	1	25	126	33	24	19	5	0	1	5	13	1	23	6	1	0	0	.000	0	0	6.84
Grant, Michael	Lowell	Bos	A-	22	5	1	0	2	10.1	51	14	7	7	0	0	0	1	6	0	7	0	0	0	2	.000	0	1	6.10
Grassing, Bryan	Potomac	StL	A+	24	48	0	0	14	62.1	289	80	51	34	8	5	2	7	22	1	25	7	0	5	1	.833	0	1	4.91
Graves, Don	Peoria	StL	A	21	34	15	0	1	104	463	99	67	58	7	3	5	2	53	1	71	9	0	2	6	.250	0	0	5.02
Graves, Robert*	Tigers	Det	R	22	9	1	0	2	21.2	81	13	5	2	1	0	0	2	6	0	31	0	0	2	0	1.000	0	0	0.83
	Lakeland	Det	A+	22	15	0	0	2	26.1	114	21	12	8	1	1	2	2	14	0	14	1	0	0	1	.000	0	0	2.73
Gray, Brett	Mudville	Cin	A+	25	29	18	0	2	141.1	585	133	48	38	6	2	2	4	37	0	110	8	1	10	4	.714	0	0	2.42

2001 Pitching — Class-A and Rookie Leagues

HOW MUCH HE PITCHED											WHAT HE GAVE UP												THE RESULTS					
Player	Team	Org	Lg	A	G	GS	CG	GF	IP	BFP	H	R	ER	HR	SH	SF	HB	TBB	IBB	SO	WP	Bk	W	L	Pct.	ShO	Sv	ERA
Gray, Rusty	Beloit	Mil	A	24	7	0	0	3	17.1	75	26	13	13	2	0	1	1	4	0	7	1	3	1	0	1.000	0	0	6.75
Greco, Sam	New Jersey	StL	A-	23	21	0	0	1	30	134	30	19	15	1	1	3	5	11	0	29	3	0	1	4	.200	0	0	4.50
Green, Sean	Asheville	Col	A	23	43	0	0	9	58	271	66	43	38	4	4	1	4	28	1	37	8	2	3	4	.429	0	0	5.90
Greenbush, Peter	Casper	Col	R+	23	14	6	0	2	42.1	193	55	32	24	1	0	1	3	15	2	26	6	3	4	2	.667	0	1	5.10
Grezlovski, Ben	Rancho Cuca	Ana	A+	25	48	0	0	21	64.1	285	60	37	30	6	3	3	7	29	1	74	8	1	2	4	.333	0	8	4.20
Griffin, Colt	Spokane	KC	A-	19	2	1	0	0	1.2	12	2	3	3	0	0	0	0	5	0	0	1	0	0	0	.000	0	0	16.20
Grimes, Sean*	Medcine Hat	Tor	R+	19	12	7	0	0	38	182	48	26	21	3	2	1	3	20	1	21	11	1	1	4	.200	0	0	4.97
Grippo, Mike*	Potomac	StL	A+	26	6	0	0	1	4	29	9	8	8	2	0	0	2	5	0	2	0	0	0	0	.000	0	0	18.00
Griswold, Jordan*	Expos	Mon	R	20	16	0	0	3	29	133	31	13	8	0	2	4	3	16	0	22	0	0	1	0	1.000	0	0	2.48
Gross, Kyle	Hagerstown	SF	A	23	22	12	0	1	53	262	43	45	38	2	2	3	18	51	1	46	12	0	2	6	.250	0	0	6.45
Gruban, Jarret	Provo	Ana	R+	23	1	0	0	0	1	5	2	1	0	0	0	0	0	0	0	0	0	0	0	0	.000	0	0	0.00
	Cedar Rapds	Ana	A	23	13	2	0	2	34	165	44	30	20	4	0	6	2	14	0	22	3	0	0	2	.000	0	0	5.29
Grunwald, Erik	Wisconsin	Sea	A	25	29	21	1	1	157.1	661	138	66	59	10	4	7	14	48	0	128	5	1	8	6	.571	1	0	3.38
Guerrero, Julio	Hickory	Pit	A	21	11	9	0	1	54.2	251	65	37	27	4	4	2	4	17	1	24	0	1	1	4	.200	0	0	4.45
	Pirates	Pit	R	21	3	2	0	0	6.1	23	5	2	2	0	0	0	0	1	0	6	2	0	0	0	.000	0	0	2.84
	Williamsprt	Pit	A-	21	7	0	0	1	16	69	18	14	8	1	1	0	1	4	1	13	0	0	2	2	.500	0	0	4.50
Guerrero, Thomas	Expos	Mon	R	20	19	0	0	14	28	126	31	21	17	1	1	0	2	7	0	37	4	0	3	2	.600	0	3	5.46
	Vermont	Mon	A-	20	2	0	0	1	3.2	17	4	2	2	0	0	0	0	2	0	3	1	0	0	0	.000	0	0	4.91
Guillory, Dan	Kinston	Cle	A+	26	23	0	0	19	29	113	19	5	4	0	0	1	1	6	1	36	3	0	2	1	.667	0	7	1.24
Gutierrez, Fernando	Delmarva	Bal	A	21	22	0	0	10	28.2	128	18	16	11	0	2	2	1	21	1	28	7	0	1	1	.500	0	0	3.45
Gutierrez, Jannio	Twins	Min	R	20	23	0	0	21	28.2	110	11	2	1	0	1	1	0	13	2	48	0	0	0	0	.000	0	16	0.31
Gutierrez, Lazaro*	Fort Wayne	SD	A	26	16	0	0	4	18.1	83	18	10	10	2	1	1	0	10	3	16	3	0	1	1	.500	0	0	4.91
Guzman, Alex	Chston-WV	Tor	A	22	52	0	0	21	78	316	82	38	31	2	3	3	3	10	1	45	3	1	2	7	.222	0	2	3.58
Guzman, Angel	Boise	ChC	A-	20	14	14	0	0	76.2	318	68	27	19	2	2	5	0	19	0	63	2	1	9	1	.900	0	0	2.23
Gwyn, Mark	Modesto	Oak	A+	24	28	25	0	1	140	617	137	85	72	9	6	4	9	59	3	101	6	0	3	13	.188	0	0	4.63
Haase, Frank*	Tri-City	Col	A-	22	19	0	0	0	31	133	22	11	5	2	2	1	1	19	0	25	5	0	2	1	.667	0	0	1.45
Hadden, Randy	Vero Beach	LA	A+	24	34	1	0	12	67	305	75	44	38	9	3	1	7	29	1	58	4	0	4	4	.500	0	2	5.10
Haeger, Charles	White Sox	CWS	R	18	13	4	0	1	31	153	44	29	22	2	1	3	1	17	0	17	4	1	0	3	.000	0	0	6.39
Halamicek, Kevin	Utica	Fla	A-	24	7	0	0	2	15.1	72	12	12	6	2	3	0	0	10	0	12	3	0	4	0	1.000	0	0	3.52
	Kane County	Fla	A	24	20	0	0	9	30.2	137	31	17	16	3	3	1	4	13	0	17	5	0	0	3	.000	0	0	4.70
Hall, Chris*	New Jersey	StL	A-	23	18	0	0	7	22	103	26	11	9	1	0	1	4	11	0	13	0	0	0	0	.000	0	0	3.68
Hall, Dan	Beloit	Mil	A	23	38	0	0	30	52.2	235	47	30	24	5	1	1	3	27	0	53	7	0	4	3	.571	0	13	4.10
Hall, Josh	Dayton	Cin	A	21	22	22	2	0	132.1	549	117	52	39	4	2	1	2	39	1	122	18	2	11	5	.688	0	0	2.65
Hall, Shane	Red Sox	Bos	R	22	4	0	0	1	9.1	48	6	3	3	0	2	0	3	10	2	10	3	1	1	1	.500	0	1	2.89
	Lowell	Bos	A-	22	14	0	0	8	27	130	36	19	14	1	2	1	5	9	2	21	2	1	0	3	.000	0	2	4.67
Halvorson, Greg	St. Lucie	NYM	A+	25	22	13	2	4	100	430	109	55	48	7	5	3	3	24	1	47	3	0	5	6	.455	0	2	4.32
Hamann, Rob	Dunedin	Tor	A+	25	39	0	0	20	65.1	279	69	40	32	9	1	1	6	17	0	44	6	0	4	0	1.000	0	5	4.41
Hamilton, Ryan	Martinsvlle	Hou	R+	24	2	1	0	0	3	12	0	0	0	0	0	0	0	3	0	3	0	0	0	0	.000	0	0	0.00
	Pittsfield	Hou	A-	24	9	1	0	1	15	76	15	13	8	0	0	0	6	14	0	9	8	0	1	0	1.000	0	0	4.80
Hammons, Matt	Daytona	ChC	A+	25	7	6	0	0	24.1	114	25	16	10	0	1	0	3	13	0	27	2	0	1	1	.500	0	0	3.70
Hampson, Justin*	Tri-City	Col	A-	22	15	15	0	0	81.2	354	84	55	41	5	1	5	9	23	0	63	4	0	4	6	.400	0	0	4.52
Hampton, Royce*	Rangers	Tex	R	19	12	4	0	3	43	182	38	23	20	3	2	3	0	15	1	29	2	0	2	2	.500	0	1	4.19
Hamulack, Tim*	Brevard Cty	Fla	A+	25	40	0	0	13	71.1	319	83	42	25	3	3	3	3	21	1	39	1	0	2	4	.333	0	1	3.15
Hannaman, Ryan*	Giants	SF	R	20	11	11	0	0	54	227	34	14	12	1	2	2	5	31	0	67	2	5	4	1	.800	0	0	2.00
	Salem-Keizr	SF	A-	20	3	3	0	0	13	55	8	5	3	1	0	0	0	8	0	19	0	1	1	1	.500	0	0	2.08
Hannaway, Patrick	Giants	SF	R	23	12	0	0	2	13.1	61	13	5	4	0	2	1	1	9	0	7	2	0	1	1	.500	0	0	2.70
Hanrahan, Joel	Wilmington	LA	A	20	27	26	0	1	144	615	136	71	54	13	5	1	11	55	0	116	8	1	9	11	.450	0	0	3.38
Harber, Ryan*	Brevard Cty	Fla	A+	25	29	5	0	8	90.1	393	94	44	35	8	3	1	1	30	1	48	1	0	6	4	.600	0	1	3.49
Harden, James	Vancouver	Oak	A-	20	18	14	0	3	74.1	309	47	29	28	3	3	1	4	38	0	100	8	1	2	4	.333	0	0	3.39
Haren, Danny	New Jersey	StL	A-	21	12	8	0	1	52.1	210	47	22	18	6	0	0	5	8	0	57	1	0	3	3	.500	0	1	3.10
Haring, Brett*	Charlotte	Tex	A+	27	17	2	0	7	45.2	187	41	17	12	3	1	0	3	13	1	22	2	0	1	1	.500	0	1	2.36
Harper, Jesse	Auburn	Tor	A-	21	14	14	0	0	67.2	304	79	40	36	3	1	2	8	20	0	58	0	0	3	4	.429	0	0	4.79
Harris, Julian*	Cedar Rapds	Ana	A	24	18	3	0	4	25.2	118	28	18	16	0	1	1	0	14	1	20	4	0	2	2	.500	0	0	5.61
	Rancho Cuca	Ana	A+	24	25	0	0	10	35.2	160	36	22	13	3	1	2	0	17	1	31	3	0	0	1	.000	0	0	3.28
Harvey, Ian	Fort Wayne	SD	A	25	8	0	0	6	12.2	49	6	4	4	0	1	0	0	5	1	15	0	0	0	0	.000	0	3	2.84
Hashimoto, Kei	Vermont	Mon	A-	22	10	0	0	1	15.1	77	17	15	11	1	0	2	2	9	1	10	4	0	0	1	.000	0	0	6.46
Hawk, David*	Williamsprt	Pit	A-	23	2	0	0	0	4	15	2	2	2	0	1	0	0	2	0	4	1	0	0	0	.000	0	0	4.50
	Hickory	Pit	A	23	17	3	0	3	24.2	117	25	15	11	0	1	1	1	17	0	18	4	0	2	1	.667	0	0	4.01
Hawkins, Chad	Savannah	Tex	A	23	4	4	0	0	28	104	13	2	1	0	0	1	1	5	0	25	0	0	1	0	1.000	0	0	0.32
	Charlotte	Tex	A+	23	4	4	0	0	17	71	18	7	7	0	1	1	2	3	0	8	2	1	2	1	.667	0	0	3.71
Haworth, Brent	Rancho Cuca	Ana	A+	25	5	0	0	2	8	43	15	13	12	2	0	0	4	2	0	4	0	0	0	0	.000	0	0	13.50
Haynes, Brad	Kane County	Fla	A	20	17	17	0	0	89.2	402	86	50	38	4	5	4	11	39	0	73	6	1	7	3	.700	0	0	3.81
Hays, Sam*	Mariners	Sea	R	20	7	7	0	0	29	137	36	25	22	0	1	1	6	14	0	22	2	2	1	2	.333	0	0	6.83
Heal, Darren	Medcine Hat	Tor	R+	22	9	0	0	2	9.1	69	21	29	20	5	0	1	4	13	1	7	8	0	0	1	.000	0	0	19.29
Hecker, Steven	Auburn	Tor	A-	23	17	1	0	12	35.1	160	34	18	12	1	3	1	3	19	0	37	4	0	1	5	.167	0	0	3.06
Hee, Aaron*	St. Lucie	NYM	A+	23	2	0	0	2	3	16	4	2	2	0	0	0	0	3	0	3	1	0	0	0	.000	0	1	6.00
	Capital Cty	NYM	A	23	35	0	0	16	77.2	331	62	28	22	3	4	1	1	43	0	95	3	3	6	4	.600	0	2	2.55
Heflin, Theo*	Mariners	Sea	R	21	18	0	0	9	23.1	118	34	21	17	1	3	1	2	13	0	21	2	0	2	1	.667	0	1	6.56
Heiberger, Heath*	Missoula	Ari	R+	22	7	0	0	1	10.2	42	5	4	2	0	0	0	1	3	0	13	2	0	0	0	.000	0	0	1.69
	South Bend	Ari	A	22	12	0	0	6	18.2	77	15	10	8	0	1	0	0	7	0	21	1	0	1	1	.500	0	1	3.86
Heilman, Aaron	St. Lucie	NYM	A+	23	7	7	0	0	38.1	153	26	11	10	0	1	1	1	13	0	39	1	0	0	1	.000	0	0	2.35
Hemus, Jared*	Elizabethtn	Min	R+	21	16	6	0	4	48.2	193	33	9	8	3	2	0	6	16	0	49	1	0	6	1	.857	0	3	1.48
Henderson, Kenny*	Hickory	Pit	A	24	27	0	0	10	34	152	29	22	20	2	0	2	5	16	2	35	4	1	0	3	.000	0	1	5.29
Hendrickson, Ben	Beloit	Mil	A	21	25	25	1	0	133.1	576	122	58	42	3	1	1	6	72	0	133	9	1	8	9	.471	0	0	2.84
Henkel, Robert*	Marlins	Fla	R	23	9	8	0	0	29.2	121	17	9	5	0	0	0	1	11	0	38	4	0	1	3	.250	0	0	1.52
	Utica	Fla	A-	23	3	3	0	0	8.1	39	7	4	4	0	0	0	0	6	0	11	2	0	0	0	.000	0	0	4.32
	Kane County	Fla	A	23	1	1	0	0	4	20	6	3	2	0	0	0	0	1	0	2	1	1	0	0	.000	0	0	4.50
Henn, Sean*	Staten Ilnd	NYY	A-	21	9	8	0	1	42	163	26	15	14	3	0	1	1	15	0	49	4	0	3	1	.750	0	1	3.00
Hennessey, Brad	Salem-Keizr	SF	A-	22	9	9	0	0	34	140	28	9	9	1	0	0	4	11	0	22	2	0	1	0	1.000	0	0	2.38
Henriquez, Hector*	Brevard Cty	Fla	A+	23	25	0	0	10	39.1	186	36	28	27	2	0	3	5	33	1	28	4	2	0	1	.000	0	0	6.18
Hensley, Matt	Cedar Rapds	Ana	A	23	11	11	1	0	71.2	321	80	42	29	10	0	2	4	19	0	63	6	3	5	3	.625	0	0	3.64
	Rancho Cuca	Ana	A+	23	14	12	0	0	68.1	319	85	57	45	4	2	7	8	24	0	58	4	1	2	7	.222	0	0	5.93
Herauf, Jeremy	Oneonta	Det	A-	23	5	0	0	0	11.2	49	10	5	3	0	1	0	1	3	0	13	3	0	0	1	.000	0	0	2.31
	Lakeland	Det	A+	23	6	0	0	0	6.2	38	13	8	8	0	0	0	1	5	0	3	0	0	0	0	.000	0	0	10.80
Herbison, Brett	Brooklyn	NYM	A-	25	6	5	0	0	12	59	15	11	9	0	0	1	1	6	0	9	1	0	0	2	.000	0	0	6.75

2001 Pitching — Class-A and Rookie Leagues

HOW MUCH HE PITCHED											WHAT HE GAVE UP												THE RESULTS					
Player	Team	Org	Lg	A	G	GS	CG	GF	IP	BFP	H	R	ER	HR	SH	SF	HB	TBB	IBB	SO	WP	Bk	W	L	Pct.	ShO	Sv	ERA
	Capital Cty	NYM	A	25	5	0	0	0	9	37	11	4	4	1	0	0	0	4	0	4	0	0	1	0	1.000	0	0	4.00
Hernandez, Buddy	Macon	Atl	A	23	7	0	0	3	14	58	13	8	5	1	0	1	0	1	0	29	0	0	0	0	.000	0	0	3.21
	Myrtle Bch	Atl	A+	23	34	0	0	22	53.2	211	28	7	7	1	1	0	1	18	2	77	5	0	1	1	.500	0	6	1.17
Hernandez, Fausto	W Michigan	Det	A	22	9	0	0	4	16.2	75	21	11	10	3	0	0	0	6	0	16	3	1	1	1	.500	0	0	5.40
Hernandez, R.	Burlington	KC	A	21	17	17	0	0	100.2	426	94	46	38	5	2	2	3	29	0	100	6	3	7	5	.583	0	0	3.40
Hernandez, Yoel	Lakewood	Phi	A	20	25	25	1	0	160.2	700	153	94	62	7	4	7	18	42	1	111	6	2	6	9	.400	0	0	3.47
Herndon, Eric	Macon	Atl	A	25	10	0	0	5	18.2	73	13	5	4	0	1	1	1	6	1	15	1	1	0	2	.000	0	2	1.93
	Myrtle Bch	Atl	A+	25	24	2	0	6	44.2	179	39	13	12	5	4	1	2	11	0	38	4	0	2	2	.500	0	2	2.42
Herrera, Jose	Wisconsin	Sea	A	22	4	1	0	0	14.2	63	10	7	5	2	0	1	3	3	0	20	2	2	1	0	1.000	0	0	3.07
Herrera, Junior	Tigers	Det	R	22	18	3	0	13	28.2	149	44	30	24	3	2	0	3	13	2	19	5	0	0	2	.000	0	7	7.53
Hickman, Ben	Marlins	Fla	R	25	6	0	0	3	7.1	31	7	2	2	0	2	1	0	1	0	8	0	0	0	0	.000	0	0	2.45
Hickman, Jason*	Great Falls	LA	R+	23	17	2	0	9	40.1	197	45	29	22	3	2	2	5	29	2	31	8	0	1	2	.333	0	2	4.91
Higgins, Josh	Hickory	Pit	A	23	55	0	0	49	61	239	40	15	14	3	3	2	4	11	1	71	2	0	2	2	.500	0	23	2.07
Hill, Jeremy	Burlington	KC	A	24	40	0	0	31	47.2	190	22	11	8	2	2	0	3	25	0	66	6	0	0	2	.000	0	12	1.51
	Wilmington	KC	A+	24	9	0	0	7	12.1	52	10	2	1	0	1	0	0	8	1	13	2	0	4	0	1.000	0	2	0.73
Hill, Joshua	Twins	Min	R	19	12	0	0	0	17.1	74	15	8	7	2	0	0	3	8	0	17	6	0	2	2	.500	0	0	3.63
Hill, Shawn	Vermont	Mon	A-	21	7	7	0	0	35.2	144	22	12	9	0	1	0	7	8	0	23	2	0	2	2	.500	0	0	2.27
Hills, Mark*	Hagerstown	SF	A	23	10	1	0	4	19	99	34	26	20	4	1	2	1	6	0	16	1	1	0	3	.000	0	0	9.47
	Salem-Keizr	SF	A-	23	10	0	0	1	13.2	78	20	17	14	4	0	2	4	12	0	11	1	0	0	0	.000	0	0	9.22
Hinckley, Mike*	Expos	Mon	R	19	8	5	0	0	34.1	158	46	23	20	1	1	2	3	12	0	28	6	1	2	2	.500	0	0	5.24
Hines, Carlos	Princeton	TB	R+	21	13	7	0	2	48.2	220	51	33	24	3	1	2	3	17	0	56	6	1	2	3	.400	0	0	4.44
Hintz, Beau*	Everett	Sea	A-	22	15	11	0	2	56.1	250	63	50	40	5	0	3	2	15	1	43	1	2	3	4	.429	0	1	6.39
Hixson, David	Salem-Keizr	SF	A-	23	22	0	0	7	47.2	205	46	14	12	0	4	1	4	16	4	49	3	0	3	1	.750	0	0	2.27
Hodges, Trey	Myrtle Bch	Atl	A+	24	26	26	1	0	173	686	156	64	53	13	4	2	5	18	0	139	7	0	15	8	.652	0	0	2.76
Hoerman, Jared	San Berndno	Sea	A+	25	11	0	0	5	18.2	84	16	11	8	1	1	0	4	7	0	18	0	0	0	0	.000	0	0	3.86
	Wisconsin	Sea	A	25	21	13	0	0	90.2	374	60	32	15	2	3	2	14	29	0	101	4	1	9	2	.818	0	0	1.49
Holdzkom, Lincoln	Marlins	Fla	R	20	12	7	0	3	43.1	188	26	18	12	0	3	2	8	27	0	43	4	1	1	3	.250	0	2	2.49
Hollifield, Alec	Winston-Sal	CWS	A+	21	9	9	0	0	41.2	196	53	29	23	3	1	1	3	21	1	28	0	1	0	8	.000	0	0	4.97
	Kannapolis	CWS	A	21	5	3	0	1	10.2	65	22	20	13	2	0	2	1	7	1	6	3	0	0	2	.000	0	0	10.97
	Bristol	CWS	R+	21	4	2	0	0	13.1	62	19	7	7	0	0	1	0	4	0	15	0	0	2	1	.667	0	0	4.72
Hollis, Barton	Red Sox	Bos	R	21	7	0	0	3	9.2	52	17	10	9	0	0	1	0	8	0	5	0	0	2	0	1.000	0	2	8.38
Holsten, Ryan	Missoula	Ari	R+	23	17	12	0	1	89	361	84	33	25	5	0	2	1	12	0	60	4	0	9	3	.750	0	0	2.53
Holubec, Ken*	Quad City	Min	A	23	27	22	1	3	134	568	107	57	48	7	4	3	9	63	0	129	9	1	4	8	.333	0	1	3.22
Honel, Kris	White Sox	CWS	R	19	3	1	0	1	10	39	9	3	2	0	0	0	1	3	0	8	0	0	2	0	1.000	0	0	1.80
	Bristol	CWS	R+	19	8	8	0	0	46	184	41	19	16	4	1	2	1	9	0	45	3	0	2	3	.400	0	0	3.13
Hooker, Jon	Bristol	CWS	R+	23	16	0	0	6	28.2	128	27	24	18	3	1	1	1	14	2	34	7	1	2	2	.500	0	2	5.65
Hopper, Kevin	Jamestown	Atl	A-	24	7	0	0	4	9	41	15	6	5	0	0	0	1	0	0	8	0	0	1	0	1.000	0	2	5.00
Horne, Travis*	Ogden	Mil	R+	21	4	0	0	2	10.2	48	11	9	8	1	0	0	1	8	0	11	4	0	0	0	.000	0	0	6.75
Hosford, Clinton	Great Falls	LA	R+	21	15	12	0	3	79.1	322	72	28	22	3	2	1	4	16	0	69	3	1	6	3	.667	0	0	2.50
Houlton, D.J.	Martinsvlle	Hou	R+	22	13	13	1	0	72	292	67	24	20	7	1	2	3	7	0	71	2	0	5	4	.556	0	0	2.50
	Michigan	Hou	A	22	1	1	0	0	5	24	7	5	3	0	0	0	0	1	0	4	0	0	0	1	.000	0	0	5.40
Houston, Ryan	Dunedin	Tor	A+	22	26	23	0	3	133.1	583	147	77	62	10	4	7	12	46	0	85	5	0	7	5	.583	0	1	4.18
Howell, Jason*	Lowell	Bos	A-	23	20	0	0	6	52.2	227	55	38	33	6	1	1	0	16	1	38	3	0	4	2	.667	0	2	5.64
Howell, Michael	Oneonta	Det	A-	22	6	6	0	0	34.2	141	27	12	7	0	2	3	3	6	0	26	3	1	5	0	1.000	0	0	1.82
	W Michigan	Det	A	22	8	8	0	0	51	198	41	12	10	2	0	4	0	7	0	42	1	1	3	0	1.000	0	0	1.76
Howton, Jared*	Billings	Cin	R+	24	18	1	0	3	36.1	156	39	25	19	1	0	0	1	7	0	35	1	0	1	1	.500	0	0	4.71
Hoyt, Mike	Eugene	SD	A-	24	28	0	0	2	40.1	182	39	19	16	2	2	3	7	23	0	38	4	0	1	1	.500	0	0	3.57
Huang, Jun-Chung	Red Sox	Bos	R	20	10	0	0	10	12.1	60	14	5	5	0	2	0	0	10	4	15	2	0	0	2	.000	0	3	3.65
	Lowell	Bos	A-	20	10	8	0	0	48	189	41	16	12	2	1	1	0	12	0	55	2	0	5	2	.714	0	0	2.25
Huber, Jon	Idaho Falls	SD	R+	20	15	15	0	0	73	344	77	61	49	7	4	4	7	48	0	75	10	0	5	9	.357	0	0	6.04
Huffaker, Mike	Charlotte	Tex	A+	26	43	0	0	23	76.2	322	60	25	16	0	5	6	2	39	0	67	8	0	4	3	.571	0	1	1.88
Huggins, Dave	High Desert	Mil	A+	26	14	9	0	2	53.1	259	68	51	41	10	1	0	5	24	0	35	3	0	2	1	.667	0	0	6.92
Huggins, Rusty*	Ogden	Mil	R+	22	10	0	0	3	12.2	54	18	6	5	2	0	0	0	2	0	6	3	0	0	0	.000	0	0	3.55
Hughes, Nial*	Dodgers	LA	R	24	2	2	0	0	10	38	5	2	2	0	0	0	1	4	0	10	1	0	1	0	1.000	0	0	1.80
	Wilmington	LA	A	24	25	1	0	9	40.1	192	25	27	19	3	2	3	5	45	2	57	9	0	1	4	.200	0	2	4.24
Hughes, Rocky*	Kannapolis	CWS	A	23	19	0	0	8	28.1	129	30	16	16	2	1	2	0	19	1	21	4	0	0	1	.000	0	1	5.08
	Winston-Sal	CWS	A+	23	16	0	0	7	28	119	20	8	6	1	2	0	0	16	3	19	0	0	1	0	1.000	0	1	1.93
Huisman, Justin	Asheville	Col	A	23	55	0	0	51	58.1	230	35	20	11	1	1	2	3	14	2	53	4	0	0	3	.000	0	30	1.70
Humrich, Cris	Clinton	Mon	A	24	33	0	0	11	47	218	44	22	19	4	2	2	3	33	0	45	4	1	2	3	.400	0	0	3.64
Hurley, Derek*	Hickory	Pit	A	24	17	14	0	2	82.1	367	97	59	40	14	5	0	3	32	0	42	4	0	4	7	.364	0	0	4.37
	Lynchburg	Pit	A+	24	17	1	0	13	38.1	171	39	23	15	0	8	5	2	19	2	20	2	0	0	3	.000	0	1	3.52
Hutchison, Ryan	Batavia	Phi	A-	23	26	0	0	23	33	132	21	3	2	0	3	0	3	10	5	31	1	0	3	1	.750	0	9	0.55
Hutchison, Wesley	Salem-Keizr	SF	A-	23	25	0	0	25	33	132	21	8	6	2	1	1	3	14	3	45	2	0	6	2	.750	0	10	1.64
Imotichey, Tory*	Expos	Mon	R	19	10	8	0	0	40.1	184	39	23	14	0	1	4	7	16	0	32	4	0	1	5	.167	0	0	3.12
Jackson, Brian	Kinston	Cle	A+	24	53	0	0	47	68	296	66	25	20	2	4	1	6	28	6	53	1	0	2	6	.250	0	25	2.65
Jackson, Dan	Provo	Ana	R+	23	7	0	0	4	9	43	11	6	6	0	1	0	0	5	0	13	0	0	0	0	.000	0	3	6.00
	Cedar Rapds	Ana	A	23	8	5	0	0	30	127	24	9	8	1	0	0	3	14	0	28	4	1	1	1	.500	0	0	2.40
Jackson, Edwin	Dodgers	LA	R	18	12	2	0	1	22	106	14	12	6	1	3	0	3	19	0	23	2	0	2	1	.667	0	0	2.45
Jacob, Russell	Red Sox	Bos	R	27	5	0	0	2	13	56	14	7	7	1	0	2	1	4	0	7	0	0	1	1	.500	0	0	4.85
	Sarasota	Bos	A+	27	3	0	0	1	4	19	4	4	3	0	0	0	2	2	0	0	2	1	0	0	.000	0	0	6.75
Jacobs, Greg*	Rancho Cuca	Ana	A+	25	31	0	0	5	44	219	59	47	37	8	3	1	7	22	1	49	3	0	2	4	.333	0	0	7.57
	Lancaster	Ari	A+	25	20	0	0	4	20.2	89	20	12	12	2	1	0	1	8	0	22	0	1	1	1	.500	0	0	5.23
Jacobsen, Landon	Hickory	Pit	A	23	9	9	0	0	53.1	213	45	24	20	3	2	1	3	9	0	50	0	0	1	4	.200	0	0	3.38
	Lynchburg	Pit	A+	23	17	17	1	0	105	450	101	50	39	7	3	2	11	38	1	83	4	0	5	7	.417	1	0	3.34
Jacobson, Billy	Martinsvlle	Hou	R+	23	18	0	0	7	34	135	20	7	4	0	2	0	9	8	0	25	4	1	0	1	.000	0	3	1.06
Javier, Tony	Mariners	Sea	R	22	12	2	0	6	27.2	110	27	10	7	1	0	1	1	11	0	23	0	0	3	1	.750	0	2	2.28
	Everett	Sea	A-	22	5	0	0	0	6.2	36	8	9	9	0	2	0	4	4	0	9	4	0	1	0	1.000	0	0	12.15
Jimenez, Kelvin	Pulaski	Tex	R+	19	4	4	0	0	14.1	73	24	14	10	2	0	0	1	4	0	10	1	0	0	3	.000	0	0	6.28
	Rangers	Tex	R	19	9	6	1	1	45.2	183	36	19	13	2	1	3	2	9	0	51	2	0	3	3	.500	1	1	2.56
Jobe, John*	Mariners	Sea	R	23	16	0	0	5	29.2	143	38	26	14	2	0	1	3	12	0	26	4	0	1	1	.500	0	0	4.25
Johansen, Ryan	Dodgers	LA	R	22	21	0	0	16	37	140	26	10	10	2	2	2	2	6	0	39	2	1	6	2	.750	0	2	2.43
Johnson, James	Orioles	Bal	R	19	7	4	0	0	18.2	81	17	10	8	3	1	0	2	7	1	19	1	0	0	1	.000	0	0	3.86
Johnson, Jeremy	Lakeland	Det	A+	19	4	2	0	1	12	55	15	8	7	2	0	0	2	6	1	6	0	0	1	1	.500	0	0	5.25
	Oneonta	Det	A-	19	12	12	1	0	76.1	311	76	39	29	3	4	2	5	13	0	48	3	1	7	1	.875	1	0	3.42
	W Michigan	Det	A	19	3	3	0	0	17.1	76	18	10	9	2	1	0	1	6	0	7	2	0	1	1	.500	0	0	4.67

2001 Pitching — Class-A and Rookie Leagues

HOW MUCH HE PITCHED											WHAT HE GAVE UP												THE RESULTS					
Player	Team	Org	Lg	A	G	GS	CG	GF	IP	BFP	H	R	ER	HR	SH	SF	HB	TBB	IBB	SO	WP	Bk	W	L	Pct.	ShO	Sv	ERA
Johnson, Kelly	New Jersey	StL	A-	22	13	0	0	4	15.1	66	15	8	4	1	0	0	0	6	0	17	4	0	0	0	.000	0	0	2.35
	Peoria	StL	A	22	13	0	0	4	19.2	83	20	13	11	3	1	2	1	5	0	11	3	0	1	0	1.000	0	0	5.03
Johnson, Rett	Wisconsin	Sea	A	22	16	16	2	0	99.1	407	92	33	25	4	3	1	2	30	0	96	3	0	5	5	.500	2	0	2.27
	San Berndno	Sea	A+	22	12	12	0	0	66	283	56	36	30	5	1	2	4	33	0	70	5	2	6	2	.750	0	0	4.09
Johnson, Thad	Athletics	Oak	R	23	13	8	0	1	46	194	45	25	19	4	4	0	2	10	0	44	3	1	2	1	.667	0	0	3.72
Johnson, Tyler*	Johnson Cty	StL	R+	21	9	9	0	0	40.2	168	26	17	12	1	0	0	3	21	0	58	9	5	1	1	.500	0	0	2.66
	Peoria	StL	A	21	3	3	0	0	13.2	65	14	9	6	1	0	0	0	10	0	15	2	1	0	1	.000	0	0	3.95
Johnston, Clint*	Pirates	Pit	R	24	2	2	0	0	3	10	1	0	0	0	0	0	0	1	0	4	0	0	0	0	.000	0	0	0.00
	Lynchburg	Pit	A+	24	11	0	0	4	17	82	15	11	10	1	2	4	2	14	1	23	1	0	1	1	.500	0	0	5.29
Johnston, Mike*	Hickory	Pit	A	23	16	16	0	0	93.1	404	88	47	35	5	0	4	5	42	1	80	7	1	4	5	.444	0	0	3.38
	Lynchburg	Pit	A+	23	11	10	1	0	62	276	66	27	23	2	4	2	3	24	0	44	4	2	4	4	.500	0	0	3.34
Johnston, Rikki*	W Michigan	Det	A	21	13	13	0	0	74	318	72	43	36	7	1	2	5	28	1	59	4	2	2	8	.200	0	0	4.38
Jones, Alvin	White Sox	CWS	R	20	11	2	0	1	20.2	118	25	34	29	0	0	0	5	26	0	19	13	0	0	3	.000	0	0	12.63
Jones, Chris*	Hagerstown	SF	A	22	39	4	0	9	73.2	330	77	42	37	3	3	7	7	40	3	60	9	1	6	3	.667	0	1	4.52
Jones, D.J.*	Bluefield	Bal	R+	24	4	1	0	0	12	44	8	2	1	0	0	1	0	2	0	8	0	1	1	0	1.000	0	0	0.75
	Delmarva	Bal	A	24	17	6	0	6	40.2	178	52	23	18	0	5	1	3	7	0	30	0	2	1	4	.200	0	0	3.98
Jones, Geoffrey*	Eugene	SD	A-	22	15	15	1	0	82.2	366	90	57	46	8	1	5	2	27	1	73	4	1	3	7	.300	0	0	5.01
Jones, Greg	Rancho Cuca	Ana	A+	25	6	6	0	0	27.2	118	25	15	13	2	1	1	0	11	0	27	3	0	1	3	.250	0	0	4.23
	Angels	Ana	R	25	2	2	0	0	2	10	3	0	0	0	0	0	0	2	0	2	0	0	0	0	.000	0	0	0.00
Jones, Kiki	Charlotte	Tex	A+	32	3	0	0	0	4.1	26	9	9	9	0	0	1	0	4	0	2	0	0	0	1	.000	0	0	18.69
Jones, Mike	Ogden	Mil	R+	19	9	7	0	0	33.2	137	29	17	14	1	0	1	3	10	0	32	6	0	4	1	.800	0	0	3.74
Jones, Quentin	Macon	Atl	A	23	35	0	0	25	37	172	32	26	23	3	1	3	4	33	1	51	6	1	1	2	.333	0	9	5.59
Jones, Sean	Frederick	Bal	A+	24	39	0	0	15	83.1	358	86	35	30	3	5	2	7	21	3	57	10	0	5	4	.556	0	1	3.24
Jongejan, Feranc*	Lansing	ChC	A	23	48	0	0	41	58.2	257	64	21	13	4	3	1	2	31	4	52	2	1	2	5	.286	0	16	1.99
Joseph, Jake	St. Lucie	NYM	A+	24	25	24	0	1	128	586	162	93	76	6	5	6	9	52	0	69	9	3	4	12	.250	0	0	5.34
Julianel, Ben*	New Jersey	StL	A-	22	15	15	0	0	85.1	359	88	38	33	1	1	2	4	26	0	86	7	0	6	6	.500	0	0	3.48
Kaanoi, Jason	Royals	KC	R	19	14	3	0	3	38.1	172	40	29	25	3	1	3	6	8	0	24	2	1	2	5	.286	0	1	5.87
	Spokane	KC	A-	19	2	2	0	0	6	31	9	7	6	1	1	0	0	4	0	4	0	0	0	1	.000	0	0	9.00
Kauffman, Matt*	Great Falls	LA	R+	23	10	0	0	4	14.2	80	21	20	14	3	0	0	0	14	1	13	4	0	0	0	.000	0	0	8.59
Keefer, Ryan	Bluefield	Bal	R+	20	29	0	0	27	30.2	125	20	4	2	1	2	0	3	8	2	46	1	0	1	0	1.000	0	15	0.59
Keelin, Chris	Clearwater	Phi	A+	25	46	0	0	36	72	294	44	22	16	3	2	1	7	40	6	87	10	0	2	4	.333	0	14	2.00
Kegley, Chuck	Dunedin	Tor	A+	22	26	20	0	2	112	533	120	94	75	13	5	4	12	76	0	76	9	0	6	9	.400	0	0	6.03
Keirstead, Michael	Great Falls	LA	R+	21	25	3	0	19	34.2	154	35	14	9	1	0	0	2	12	0	52	5	1	1	1	.500	0	5	2.34
	Wilmington	LA	A	21	7	1	0	5	9.1	42	9	7	5	0	0	0	0	5	0	12	1	0	0	1	.000	0	0	4.82
Keiter, Ben	Pulaski	Tex	R+	22	10	10	0	0	43.2	186	30	23	21	4	1	2	4	20	0	42	2	2	4	2	.667	0	0	4.33
Kelly, Dan*	Myrtle Bch	Atl	A+	24	18	1	0	5	40	154	31	10	9	4	3	0	0	7	2	22	1	0	2	1	.667	0	1	2.03
Kelly, Scott*	Eugene	SD	A-	24	14	14	0	0	64	294	73	42	36	5	1	3	3	26	0	66	5	2	2	4	.333	0	0	5.06
Kelly, Steve	Billings	Cin	R+	22	12	7	0	0	54.2	227	50	16	14	3	2	1	1	11	1	54	2	0	4	2	.667	0	0	2.30
Kemp, Beau	Quad City	Min	A	21	31	0	0	15	43	175	29	17	12	4	3	3	2	15	2	46	1	0	0	1	.000	0	4	2.51
Kennard, Jeff	Yankees	NYY	R	20	19	0	0	16	23.2	100	17	4	4	0	0	1	3	10	1	30	3	0	0	0	.000	0	9	1.52
Kennedy, Jodie*	Red Sox	Bos	R	22	3	0	0	3	5	17	3	2	1	0	0	0	0	0	0	6	0	0	0	0	.000	0	2	1.80
	Lowell	Bos	A-	22	9	0	0	7	17.2	74	17	6	6	1	1	0	0	6	0	6	0	0	0	1	.000	0	1	3.06
Kent, Steve*	San Berndno	Sea	A+	23	51	0	0	12	65.1	285	50	21	16	2	3	2	2	34	0	73	4	1	0	3	.000	0	1	2.20
Kentner, Brandon	Kingsport	NYM	R+	20	21	0	0	11	29.1	152	26	18	14	1	0	2	1	36	0	37	5	1	1	0	1.000	0	1	4.30
Keppel, Bob	Capital Cty	NYM	A	20	26	20	1	3	124.1	516	118	58	43	6	2	2	14	25	1	87	7	0	6	7	.462	0	0	3.11
Kesten, Michael*	Everett	Sea	A-	20	5	0	0	2	6.2	35	9	8	8	0	1	0	1	8	1	5	2	0	0	2	.000	0	0	10.80
Ketchner, Ryan*	Everett	Sea	A-	20	20	5	0	6	52.1	215	38	19	17	3	2	0	3	18	0	58	4	0	3	3	.500	0	2	2.92
Key, Chris*	Kane County	Fla	A	24	54	1	0	13	92	369	89	30	24	6	6	2	2	10	1	71	7	0	7	0	1.000	0	3	2.35
Khoury, Josh	Utica	Fla	A-	24	29	0	0	17	37.2	175	34	28	20	0	2	2	4	26	4	33	5	0	2	4	.333	0	1	4.78
Kiley, Jason	Pirates	Pit	R	19	8	1	0	3	16.2	86	29	20	17	2	1	0	4	10	0	9	3	0	1	2	.333	0	0	9.18
Killalea, John*	Johnson Cty	StL	R+	19	7	7	0	0	25.1	120	32	19	18	1	2	0	2	16	0	29	4	1	0	3	.000	0	0	6.39
Kim, Il	Batavia	Phi	A-	22	13	13	2	0	76	306	72	28	26	5	2	1	1	9	0	48	3	2	6	4	.600	2	0	3.08
King, Jay*	Wilmington	KC	A+	24	11	9	1	0	52.1	202	41	20	17	5	1	1	2	11	0	46	2	0	4	3	.571	0	0	2.92
King, Jeremy	Yankees	NYY	R	20	11	9	0	1	48.2	214	50	26	24	0	1	0	4	26	0	40	4	0	5	2	.714	0	0	4.44
	Greensboro	NYY	A	20	1	1	0	0	5	25	8	7	7	2	0	0	1	3	0	5	0	0	0	1	.000	0	0	12.60
King, Robert	Giants	SF	R	21	12	1	0	2	17	78	21	11	10	1	0	0	2	7	0	19	4	0	2	0	1.000	0	0	5.29
King, Seth	Eugene	SD	A-	24	1	0	0	0	1	4	1	0	0	0	0	0	0	1	0	1	0	0	0	0	.000	0	0	0.00
King, Timothy*	Princeton	TB	R+	18	11	7	0	3	35.2	163	40	20	18	1	2	1	2	15	0	26	1	0	1	3	.250	0	0	4.54
Kinney, Josh	New Jersey	StL	A-	23	3	0	0	0	5.2	18	2	0	0	0	0	0	0	0	0	5	0	0	2	0	1.000	0	0	0.00
	Peoria	StL	A	23	27	0	0	5	41	192	47	24	20	1	4	2	7	15	0	35	4	1	1	4	.200	0	0	4.39
Kirkland, Aaron	White Sox	CWS	R	23	29	0	0	29	45.1	169	25	5	2	1	2	2	3	4	4	62	1	0	0	2	.000	0	13	0.40
Kirkman, Tyler*	Expos	Mon	R	19	2	0	0	0	2.1	13	6	3	3	0	0	0	0	1	0	1	0	0	0	0	.000	0	0	11.57
Kleine, Victor*	Mahoning Vy	Cle	A-	22	14	14	0	0	70.1	320	88	42	41	5	1	3	5	25	1	50	7	0	1	8	.111	0	0	5.25
	Columbus	Cle	A	22	1	1	0	0	7	29	5	5	3	0	0	1	0	0	0	9	0	0	0	0	.000	0	0	3.86
Klepacki, Ed	Jupiter	Mon	A+	24	26	26	1	0	136.1	582	135	69	53	10	9	6	5	49	0	74	3	0	9	9	.500	0	0	3.50
Knoedler, Justin	Salem-Keizr	SF	A-	21	13	0	0	2	28.2	116	22	4	4	0	2	1	0	9	1	38	1	0	1	1	.500	0	1	1.26
Knowles, Mike	Tampa	NYY	A+	22	8	0	0	5	8	45	15	10	9	0	0	2	0	8	0	9	1	1	0	0	.000	0	2	10.13
	Greensboro	NYY	A	22	38	7	0	29	64.1	287	63	26	23	4	2	3	2	35	3	62	5	2	3	4	.429	0	21	3.22
Kobow, Mike	Oneonta	Det	A-	23	7	0	0	2	11	49	16	8	8	3	1	0	0	1	0	13	0	0	1	0	1.000	0	0	6.55
Koenig, Ross	Oneonta	Det	A-	22	16	8	0	1	54	244	43	31	22	3	4	2	5	30	1	58	11	1	4	2	.667	0	0	3.67
Kohl, Doug	Potomac	StL	A+	22	51	0	0	30	56.1	236	40	21	13	2	3	0	3	21	8	44	2	1	3	5	.375	0	6	2.08
Kolb, Dan	Ogden	Mil	R+	22	16	2	0	2	43	191	53	35	34	8	1	2	3	13	0	33	4	0	4	0	1.000	0	0	7.12
Korneev, Oleg	Mariners	Sea	R	20	1	0	0	0	1	3	0	0	0	0	0	0	0	0	0	1	0	0	0	0	.000	0	0	0.00
Kosderka, Matt	Charlotte	Tex	A+	26	7	0	0	1	12	56	16	11	9	1	0	0	0	6	0	10	1	0	1	1	.500	0	0	6.75
Koziara, Matt	Dayton	Cin	A	25	14	0	0	9	18.2	86	27	10	9	1	0	0	2	4	2	14	2	0	0	0	.000	0	2	4.34
Kozlowski, Ben*	Macon	Atl	A	21	26	23	1	1	145.1	588	134	60	40	8	8	2	10	27	0	147	7	1	10	7	.588	1	0	2.48
	Myrtle Bch	Atl	A+	21	2	2	0	0	14.1	61	15	7	6	1	1	2	1	3	1	13	2	0	0	2	.000	0	0	3.77
Krawiec, Aaron*	Lansing	ChC	A	23	27	26	1	1	153.1	695	183	108	78	15	6	8	13	51	0	170	7	3	7	11	.389	0	0	4.58
Kremer, John	Greensboro	NYY	A	25	40	0	0	9	50.2	220	40	26	14	4	2	0	2	26	1	39	4	1	4	1	.800	0	1	2.49
	Tampa	NYY	A+	25	6	0	0	2	9	47	15	7	6	0	0	1	1	3	0	8	3	0	0	0	.000	0	0	6.00
Krysa, John	Lexington	Hou	A	23	16	0	0	4	29.1	120	24	13	12	3	1	2	3	8	1	25	5	0	1	3	.250	0	1	3.68
Kuo, Hong-Chih*	Dodgers	LA	R	20	7	6	0	0	19.1	76	13	5	5	0	0	0	2	4	0	21	0	0	0	0	.000	0	0	2.33
Kupper, Dustin	Utica	Fla	A-	21	8	3	0	1	13.2	67	10	13	8	0	0	0	4	7	0	14	6	0	0	1	.000	0	0	5.27
Labitzke, Jesse*	Tri-City	Col	A-	24	17	0	0	2	22.1	104	16	12	8	0	0	0	3	15	0	15	5	1	0	0	.000	0	0	3.22
LaCorte, Vince	Cedar Rapds	Ana	A	23	36	10	0	11	105	461	119	61	51	9	5	3	3	19	0	87	6	1	3	10	.231	0	2	4.37

2001 Pitching — Class-A and Rookie Leagues

HOW MUCH HE PITCHED											WHAT HE GAVE UP												THE RESULTS					
Player	Team	Org	Lg	A	G	GS	CG	GF	IP	BFP	H	R	ER	HR	SH	SF	HB	TBB	IBB	SO	WP	Bk	W	L	Pct.	ShO	Sv	ERA
Laesch, Mike	Dayton	Cin	A	24	29	0	0	14	50.2	221	41	25	22	3	3	2	3	25	2	62	7	1	2	3	.400	0	3	3.91
Lajara, Eudy*	Kane County	Fla	A	22	36	0	0	10	48.2	210	44	29	24	5	3	3	5	21	0	48	6	0	5	2	.714	0	0	4.44
Lammers, Kris*	Phillies	Phi	R	23	12	1	0	2	22.1	97	23	12	9	1	2	0	2	8	0	25	3	1	0	1	.000	0	0	3.63
Landaeta, Argeni	Yankees	NYY	R	20	10	7	0	3	45	186	35	17	12	2	0	1	4	15	0	42	1	0	6	1	.857	0	0	2.40
	Staten Ilnd	NYY	A-	20	1	1	0	0	6	27	8	4	4	0	0	0	1	2	0	6	2	0	0	1	.000	0	0	6.00
Landeros, Leonard*	Athletics	Oak	R	21	11	4	0	1	38.1	164	35	16	12	1	1	1	2	13	0	31	2	0	2	1	.667	0	1	2.82
Landestoy, Gilbert	Cedar Rapds	Ana	A	25	36	0	0	14	65	286	51	40	30	5	0	3	10	33	0	54	2	0	3	2	.600	0	2	4.15
Lane, Brian	Lowell	Bos	A-	21	6	6	0	0	27	125	29	19	16	2	0	1	1	12	0	22	5	1	2	1	.667	0	0	5.33
Langen, Brian*	Potomac	StL	A+	24	43	0	0	8	48.2	220	48	28	15	4	1	2	2	27	2	32	9	0	2	2	.500	0	0	2.77
Lansford, Dustin	Beloit	Mil	A	22	3	1	0	1	8.1	35	3	2	2	0	1	1	0	10	0	12	2	0	1	1	.500	0	0	2.16
LaPlante, Reggie	Greensboro	NYY	A	22	7	0	0	4	6.2	34	9	7	6	0	2	0	1	4	0	5	0	0	0	2	.000	0	2	8.10
	Staten Ilnd	NYY	A-	22	19	0	0	8	25.2	128	28	15	15	0	1	0	5	17	0	32	4	1	0	1	.000	0	0	5.26
Lara, Mauricio*	Augusta	Bos	A	23	20	19	1	0	107.1	443	114	45	36	5	0	4	7	24	0	96	6	0	7	6	.538	0	0	3.02
Lara, Nelson	Sarasota	Bos	A+	23	27	0	0	16	30	165	40	40	35	2	4	3	8	28	2	29	6	3	1	3	.250	0	1	10.50
	Reds	Cin	R	23	4	1	0	0	8.1	32	2	2	2	0	0	0	1	4	0	9	0	0	0	0	.000	0	0	2.16
	Mudville	Cin	A+	23	2	0	0	0	2.2	20	4	5	5	0	0	0	1	7	0	0	0	0	0	0	.000	0	0	16.88
LaRoche, Jeff*	Asheville	Col	A	24	26	0	0	8	37.1	183	45	37	20	6	2	3	3	24	1	21	3	0	1	2	.333	0	0	4.82
Larrison, Preston	Oneonta	Det	A-	21	10	8	0	1	47.1	205	37	22	13	1	0	4	2	21	0	50	4	1	1	3	.250	0	0	2.47
Larson, Ryan	Columbus	Cle	A	23	31	0	0	18	52.2	194	30	5	3	3	2	0	2	7	0	60	2	0	5	1	.833	0	4	0.51
	Kinston	Cle	A+	23	12	0	0	6	29	115	20	7	5	0	1	0	1	6	0	30	3	0	3	1	.750	0	2	1.55
Lavery, Tim*	Lansing	ChC	A	23	30	1	0	4	85.1	342	74	25	23	4	1	4	2	13	0	55	2	1	2	1	.667	0	2	2.43
Lavigne, Tim	Capital Cty	NYM	A	23	33	0	0	29	63	267	51	24	16	1	5	1	4	21	2	44	10	1	5	3	.625	0	12	2.29
	St. Lucie	NYM	A+	23	4	0	0	3	5.1	22	4	2	0	0	1	0	0	2	0	2	1	0	1	0	1.000	0	0	0.00
Lawson, Brett	Elizabethtn	Min	R+	23	10	1	0	6	12.1	73	14	19	13	0	0	1	2	16	2	14	7	1	1	0	1.000	0	0	9.49
Lawson, Jarrod	Lakewood	Phi	A	23	23	11	0	3	72.1	318	76	42	35	7	6	0	8	22	0	62	0	0	2	5	.286	0	0	4.35
Lawton, Charles	Idaho Falls	SD	R+	20	23	7	0	5	61.1	314	99	69	58	12	1	2	5	32	0	34	3	1	1	4	.200	0	0	8.51
Layfield, Scotty	Potomac	StL	A+	25	47	0	0	44	53.2	214	36	13	11	1	0	2	2	18	3	66	1	0	1	2	.333	0	31	1.84
League, Brandon	Medcine Hat	Tor	R+	19	9	9	0	0	38.2	165	36	23	20	3	1	2	4	11	1	38	2	0	2	2	.500	0	0	4.66
Lebron, Obispo	Cubs	ChC	R	20	12	0	0	12	12.1	67	16	7	7	1	0	1	2	5	0	14	0	1	1	1	.500	0	3	5.11
LeClair, Aric*	South Bend	Ari	A	24	37	2	0	10	52.2	243	48	28	20	0	0	1	4	34	2	53	7	2	3	1	.750	0	1	3.42
Ledbetter, Aaron	Johnson Cty	StL	R+	21	11	11	0	0	47	226	72	40	32	5	0	2	4	12	0	54	4	0	1	7	.125	0	0	6.13
Ledden, Ryan	Lynchburg	Pit	A+	24	27	25	3	0	152.2	695	184	112	92	18	3	6	16	53	2	73	6	1	9	13	.409	0	0	5.42
Lee, Clifton*	Jupiter	Mon	A+	23	21	20	0	1	109.2	451	78	43	34	13	5	5	4	46	0	129	2	3	6	7	.462	0	0	2.79
Lee, Kevin	Pirates	Pit	R	20	9	0	0	6	21.2	89	16	6	5	1	0	0	3	7	0	23	1	0	2	2	.500	0	0	2.08
Lee, Seung	Phillies	Phi	R	23	3	3	0	0	9	42	12	7	3	0	1	1	1	0	0	4	0	0	1	0	1.000	0	0	3.00
	Batavia	Phi	A-	23	4	4	0	0	20	98	31	24	17	3	0	1	2	4	0	14	1	0	0	3	.000	0	0	7.65
Leicester, Jon	Lansing	ChC	A	23	28	27	1	1	153	693	182	117	90	16	2	4	16	58	0	109	12	1	9	10	.474	0	0	5.29
Leon, Brigmer	Athletics	Oak	R	21	14	7	0	3	46.2	196	46	26	17	2	3	1	3	7	0	40	4	4	4	3	.571	0	0	3.28
Lerew, Anthony	Braves	Atl	R	19	12	7	0	1	49.1	205	43	25	16	3	0	1	0	14	0	40	4	2	1	2	.333	0	0	2.92
Leu, Trevor*	Oneonta	Det	A-	23	8	0	0	2	17.2	73	13	5	2	0	1	1	3	7	1	18	3	0	3	0	1.000	0	0	1.02
	W Michigan	Det	A	23	13	0	0	4	21	105	23	18	13	0	0	1	1	16	0	28	4	1	1	3	.250	0	0	5.57
Leuenberger, Jeff	W Michigan	Det	A	23	30	0	0	11	49.1	211	46	19	17	2	5	3	4	19	4	40	3	0	3	2	.600	0	0	3.10
Levesque, Ben	Hickory	Pit	A	22	16	0	0	9	18.1	97	23	20	19	1	2	2	9	15	3	8	5	0	1	2	.333	0	0	9.33
Levinsky, Donald	Expos	Mon	R	19	3	3	0	0	13	58	15	5	5	1	1	0	0	7	0	15	1	0	0	0	.000	0	0	3.46
Lewis, Craig	Vermont	Mon	A-	25	6	0	0	2	15	61	17	5	3	0	0	0	1	0	0	5	1	0	1	1	.500	0	0	1.80
	Jupiter	Mon	A+	25	17	0	0	2	25.2	107	20	10	3	1	1	0	2	5	2	9	2	0	2	1	.667	0	0	1.05
Lewis, Jeremy*	Oneonta	Det	A-	21	15	7	1	2	48.2	253	83	56	43	8	2	4	6	19	1	29	5	0	2	5	.286	0	1	7.95
	W Michigan	Det	A	21	9	9	1	0	49.2	209	41	20	16	1	2	3	3	21	0	35	2	0	3	4	.429	1	0	2.90
Lewis, Rommie*	Orioles	Bal	R	19	10	7	0	1	33.2	144	37	16	8	3	1	1	2	6	0	27	2	1	1	1	.500	0	0	2.14
Leyva, Julian	Modesto	Oak	A+	24	5	0	0	0	14	67	21	16	12	4	0	0	1	2	0	7	0	0	0	0	.000	0	0	7.71
Light, Scott	Reds	Cin	R	22	8	7	0	0	29	128	23	12	11	0	2	1	3	15	0	30	3	1	1	1	.500	0	0	3.41
Lima, Juan	Jupiter	Mon	A+	20	1	0	0	1	2	6	0	0	0	0	0	0	0	0	0	1	0	0	0	0	.000	0	0	0.00
	Vermont	Mon	A-	20	12	9	0	1	50	217	55	34	26	4	1	1	4	17	0	34	2	2	2	6	.250	0	0	4.68
Lincoln, Jeff	Quad City	Min	A	24	31	12	0	8	96.2	435	83	47	39	7	3	0	3	67	0	101	9	2	7	4	.636	0	1	3.63
Linderbaum, M.*	Idaho Falls	SD	R+	23	23	0	0	6	30	160	45	28	26	3	0	0	5	20	0	27	3	2	1	0	1.000	0	0	7.80
Liriano, Francisco*	Giants	SF	R	18	13	12	0	0	62	246	51	26	25	3	1	0	1	24	0	67	6	3	5	4	.556	0	0	3.63
	Salem-Keizr	SF	A-	18	2	2	0	0	9	35	7	5	5	2	0	0	0	1	0	12	0	0	0	0	.000	0	0	5.00
Liriano, Pedro	Provo	Ana	R+	21	15	14	0	1	77.2	342	80	39	24	3	1	3	5	31	0	76	4	3	11	2	.846	0	0	2.78
Lissir, Alexander	Pirates	Pit	R	19	6	0	0	3	13.2	63	13	5	1	1	0	0	0	6	0	18	1	0	2	0	1.000	0	1	0.66
	Williamsprt	Pit	A-	19	2	0	0	0	5	19	4	1	1	0	0	0	0	2	0	6	0	0	0	0	.000	0	0	1.80
Little, Carmen	Martinsvlle	Hou	R+	20	20	0	0	12	38	186	51	31	23	1	3	3	3	16	0	43	6	1	2	6	.250	0	0	5.45
Lizarraga, Edgar	Great Falls	LA	R+	21	14	4	0	7	48.1	203	43	25	19	4	3	0	4	11	0	56	4	1	4	2	.667	0	2	3.54
	Wilmington	LA	A	21	3	0	0	2	5.2	21	2	0	0	0	0	0	1	1	1	10	0	0	0	0	.000	0	0	0.00
Lizarraga, Sergio	Missoula	Ari	R+	20	15	15	0	0	81.1	372	104	57	46	10	1	1	8	23	0	57	7	3	6	2	.750	0	0	5.09
Lockwood, Brian	Hudson Val	TB	A-	21	12	10	0	1	58.1	237	50	28	21	5	1	3	2	20	0	48	5	0	4	5	.444	0	0	3.24
Lockwood, Luke*	Clinton	Mon	A	20	26	26	3	0	163.1	688	152	78	49	8	6	6	14	49	0	114	8	1	5	10	.333	1	0	2.70
Lohse, Eric	Twins	Min	R	22	10	10	1	0	49.1	185	42	16	14	2	0	2	2	4	0	34	1	0	4	3	.571	0	0	2.55
	Elizabethtn	Min	R+	22	3	2	0	1	8.2	40	12	7	4	1	0	0	1	1	0	5	1	0	1	1	.500	0	0	4.15
Long, Nick	Expos	Mon	R	19	4	3	0	0	19	83	24	8	7	0	2	0	3	4	0	12	2	0	1	1	.500	0	0	3.32
Looper, Aaron	San Berndno	Sea	A+	25	56	0	0	24	71	295	59	34	22	1	5	2	3	22	5	77	7	0	6	11	.353	0	5	2.79
Lopez, Arturo	Dodgers	LA	R	22	14	7	0	3	61.2	230	46	20	14	2	0	2	0	12	0	45	2	0	5	1	.833	0	1	2.04
Lopez, Gonzalo	Braves	Atl	R	18	12	11	0	0	58.2	230	44	17	16	2	3	2	3	10	0	69	3	2	5	4	.556	0	0	2.45
Lopez, Gustavo	Kane County	Fla	A	23	17	17	0	0	93	392	89	42	37	2	1	2	2	27	0	63	11	0	6	4	.600	0	0	3.58
	Brevard Cty	Fla	A+	23	6	6	2	0	33.2	139	32	18	12	4	1	1	0	6	0	19	0	0	3	1	.750	0	0	3.21
Lopez, Juan*	Winston-Sal	CWS	A+	22	26	0	0	9	36.2	166	34	23	16	3	0	1	7	21	1	37	6	0	0	1	.000	0	0	3.93
Lopez, Rafael	Capital Cty	NYM	A	21	25	24	0	0	122	522	127	66	56	10	4	8	7	36	0	87	7	0	6	7	.462	0	0	4.13
Lopez, Samuel	Royals	KC	R	20	3	0	0	1	5	28	6	4	3	0	0	0	1	5	0	5	0	0	0	0	.000	0	0	5.40
Lord, Justin	Spokane	KC	A-	22	2	2	0	0	3	15	5	3	1	0	0	1	0	0	0	4	0	0	0	0	.000	0	0	3.00
Lorenzen, Jonathan	Dodgers	LA	R	20	7	1	0	2	20.1	84	18	5	4	0	0	1	3	5	0	19	1	0	2	1	.667	0	0	1.77
	Great Falls	LA	R+	20	5	0	0	1	10	54	15	14	12	4	0	0	0	8	0	11	1	0	0	0	.000	0	0	10.80
Lorenzo, Javier	Asheville	Col	A	23	38	0	0	15	47	227	42	35	27	4	4	2	7	35	1	55	14	0	0	0	.000	0	1	5.17
Lowery, Devon	Royals	KC	R	19	11	6	0	4	41	178	38	25	19	2	0	3	2	12	0	19	3	0	2	3	.400	0	1	4.17
Lowry, Noah*	Salem-Keizr	SF	A-	21	8	7	0	0	25	109	26	15	10	2	0	2	1	8	0	28	2	0	1	1	.500	0	0	3.60
Lubisich, Nik*	Bristol	CWS	R+	23	11	11	2	0	70	274	65	26	22	2	2	3	2	12	0	49	0	2	5	2	.714	1	0	2.83
Lugo, Ruddy	Beloit	Mil	A	22	10	0	0	8	15	60	10	1	1	0	1	0	1	6	0	20	0	0	1	0	1.000	0	5	0.60

2001 Pitching — Class-A and Rookie Leagues

HOW MUCH HE PITCHED											WHAT HE GAVE UP												THE RESULTS					
Player	Team	Org	Lg	A	G	GS	CG	GF	IP	BFP	H	R	ER	HR	SH	SF	HB	TBB	IBB	SO	WP	Bk	W	L	Pct.	ShO	Sv	ERA
	Wilmington	LA	A	22	16	0	0	7	31	133	29	14	13	2	2	4	2	13	0	23	2	0	0	2	.000	0	2	3.77
Luna, Brandon	Savannah	Tex	A	23	11	0	0	10	13.2	57	8	3	0	0	1	0	1	8	1	16	2	0	2	1	.667	0	2	0.00
Lundgren, Wayne	Red Sox	Bos	R	20	13	1	0	7	42.1	184	48	26	25	3	3	0	1	15	2	20	2	0	4	2	.667	0	2	5.31
Luque, Roger*	Lk Elsinore	SD	A+	22	1	0	0	0	1	7	3	3	3	1	0	0	0	1	0	1	0	0	0	0	.000	0	0	27.00
	Fort Wayne	SD	A	22	42	0	0	14	60	243	47	24	16	6	2	0	2	17	0	61	2	3	5	2	.714	0	0	2.40
Luther, Heath*	Provo	Ana	R+	23	3	0	0	0	3.1	15	4	0	0	0	0	0	0	1	0	2	0	0	0	0	.000	0	0	0.00
	Angels	Ana	R	23	13	6	0	3	38.2	185	52	26	20	2	3	2	3	15	1	34	2	0	1	3	.250	0	0	4.66
Lutz, Kenneth	Reds	Cin	R	20	6	3	0	0	16.1	82	20	10	9	0	0	0	3	13	0	10	1	0	1	1	.500	0	0	4.96
Lynch, Jim	High Desert	Mil	A+	26	37	8	0	8	85.1	401	98	71	63	15	0	0	7	40	1	114	10	0	2	5	.286	0	0	6.64
Lynch, Pat	Tri-City	Col	A-	24	4	0	0	2	9	31	4	2	2	1	0	0	0	0	0	10	1	0	1	0	1.000	0	1	2.00
Lyons, Tom	Tigers	Det	R	19	5	3	0	0	14	67	17	11	10	0	0	0	1	5	0	22	0	0	1	0	1.000	0	0	6.43
Maberry, Mark	Kingsport	NYM	R+	27	2	0	0	1	3	10	1	0	0	0	0	0	0	0	0	1	0	0	0	0	.000	0	1	0.00
	St. Lucie	NYM	A+	27	3	0	0	1	5.2	20	2	0	0	0	0	0	0	2	1	2	1	0	1	0	1.000	0	0	0.00
Mabeus, Chris	Vancouver	Oak	A-	23	20	8	0	6	62	273	75	34	31	3	1	4	0	18	0	28	3	1	2	5	.286	0	2	4.50
Mabry, Barry	Danville	Atl	R+	20	20	2	0	3	56.1	245	60	26	20	3	2	1	1	18	2	55	2	1	3	3	.500	0	0	3.20
MacHen, Mike	Braves	Atl	R	20	13	0	0	4	26	124	25	17	14	2	1	2	8	10	0	30	2	0	2	2	.500	0	0	4.85
Mackintosh, Jason*	Mahoning Vy	Cle	A-	21	6	1	0	4	13.1	64	20	13	11	0	1	1	0	2	1	14	4	0	1	1	.500	0	0	7.43
Made, Luis*	Princeton	TB	R+	19	8	0	0	3	16.2	80	18	16	15	2	0	0	2	13	0	14	6	0	0	0	.000	0	0	8.10
Madere, Ronnie	Princeton	TB	R+	23	19	0	0	7	21	113	32	31	25	2	0	0	4	14	0	22	4	1	1	2	.333	0	0	10.71
Madril, Steve*	Kannapolis	CWS	A	24	42	2	0	7	65.1	285	68	28	21	3	4	4	3	21	3	59	7	1	2	2	.500	0	2	2.89
Madson, Ryan	Clearwater	Phi	A+	21	22	21	1	0	117.2	530	137	68	51	4	0	5	5	49	1	101	5	1	9	9	.500	0	0	3.90
Majewski, Gary	Vero Beach	LA	A+	22	23	13	0	5	75	351	103	57	52	9	3	4	5	36	0	41	3	1	4	5	.444	0	1	6.24
	Winston-Sal	CWS	A+	22	9	6	1	3	43	176	42	15	14	3	2	0	6	10	0	31	1	0	4	2	.667	0	0	2.93
Malaska, Mark*	Chston-SC	TB	A	24	25	25	1	0	157	659	153	71	51	11	5	2	2	35	0	152	13	1	7	12	.368	0	0	2.92
	Bakersfield	TB	A+	24	3	3	0	0	17.2	70	14	8	8	1	1	0	0	5	0	13	1	0	2	1	.667	0	0	4.08
Malerich, Will*	Hagerstown	SF	A	26	5	0	0	1	7	40	13	9	9	2	0	1	3	4	1	7	0	0	0	0	.000	0	0	11.57
Mangrum, Micah	Burlington	KC	A	24	23	0	0	9	37	149	33	10	8	3	3	1	1	6	1	34	3	0	7	2	.778	0	2	1.95
	Wilmington	KC	A+	24	29	0	0	19	58.2	245	52	27	20	3	3	2	5	11	2	55	5	0	4	2	.667	0	3	3.07
Manning, Charlie*	Staten Ilnd	NYY	A-	23	14	14	0	0	80	326	73	33	31	4	0	2	5	21	0	87	5	0	8	4	.667	0	0	3.49
Mansfield, Monte	Michigan	Hou	A	21	40	3	0	15	72.1	340	72	52	45	12	2	2	11	42	1	81	3	0	5	4	.556	0	2	5.60
Marcano, Luis	Rangers	Tex	R	21	3	2	0	0	10	50	16	10	10	1	0	1	2	5	0	10	2	0	0	1	.000	0	0	9.00
	Pulaski	Tex	R+	21	11	0	0	9	26.2	116	27	15	11	1	2	2	2	8	2	27	1	0	3	2	.600	0	5	3.71
Marceau, P.-Luc*	Vermont	Mon	A-	21	15	15	0	0	74	328	86	54	46	8	1	3	6	30	0	64	13	2	1	7	.125	0	0	5.59
Marchetti, Dan	Delmarva	Bal	A	23	10	0	0	2	18.1	76	10	5	5	0	0	3	1	8	0	17	4	0	1	1	.500	0	1	2.45
Marietta, Ron*	Yankees	NYY	R	24	2	0	0	1	3.1	12	1	1	1	0	1	0	0	1	0	5	2	0	0	0	.000	0	0	2.70
	Greensboro	NYY	A	24	4	1	0	1	3	18	4	6	6	2	0	0	1	4	0	1	1	0	1	0	1.000	0	0	18.00
Markert, Jackson	Hagerstown	SF	A	23	58	0	0	55	60.2	259	57	26	19	4	1	2	4	18	2	45	4	0	3	3	.500	0	39	2.82
Markray, Thad	Dayton	Cin	A	22	32	0	0	14	65	289	70	32	26	3	5	0	2	30	3	54	4	1	2	3	.400	0	3	3.60
Markwell, D.*	Chston-WV	Tor	A	21	22	21	3	0	123.1	511	121	58	53	10	3	3	8	32	0	99	6	0	5	7	.417	0	0	3.87
	Dunedin	Tor	A+	21	5	5	0	0	33.2	136	27	12	12	4	1	1	1	13	0	26	1	0	3	1	.750	0	0	3.21
Marquez, Jose	Missoula	Ari	R+	21	15	0	0	5	19.1	104	22	23	14	3	0	1	3	19	1	10	4	0	1	0	1.000	0	0	6.52
Marrero, Darwin	Vermont	Mon	A-	21	1	1	0	0	6	27	7	4	2	0	0	0	0	3	0	5	0	0	1	0	1.000	0	0	3.00
	Jupiter	Mon	A+	21	21	17	1	0	103	426	103	47	42	10	3	1	1	25	0	62	1	0	5	8	.385	0	0	3.67
Marsonek, Sam	Tampa	NYY	A+	23	24	23	5	0	138.1	590	128	67	54	6	5	2	21	39	2	120	12	1	8	8	.500	2	0	3.51
Martin, Chandler	Tri-City	Col	A-	28	4	4	0	0	18	72	14	6	6	3	0	0	3	1	0	11	2	0	1	0	1.000	0	0	3.00
	Asheville	Col	A	28	2	2	0	0	13.2	54	10	2	2	1	0	1	2	5	0	8	2	0	2	0	1.000	0	0	1.32
	Salem	Col	A+	28	9	9	0	0	57	250	68	35	30	5	0	0	5	14	0	32	2	1	3	5	.375	0	0	4.74
Martin, J.D.	Burlington	Cle	R+	19	10	10	0	0	45.2	174	26	9	7	3	0	0	4	11	0	72	3	1	5	1	.833	0	0	1.38
Martin, Kevin	Mahoning Vy	Cle	A-	23	19	1	0	9	38.2	179	39	27	23	4	1	3	3	18	2	25	3	0	0	2	.000	0	1	5.35
Martin, Larry*	Greensboro	NYY	A	25	13	0	0	5	15.2	80	15	11	7	1	0	1	2	19	0	20	3	0	1	0	1.000	0	0	4.02
Martin, Lucas*	Quad City	Min	A	23	33	19	1	5	137.2	580	146	74	61	12	2	6	1	32	0	117	6	3	8	6	.571	1	1	3.99
Martin, Nick*	Cubs	ChC	R	22	10	0	0	3	21.2	93	26	9	8	0	1	1	2	5	0	18	1	1	3	0	1.000	0	0	3.32
	Lansing	ChC	A	22	1	1	0	0	2	15	6	5	4	1	0	0	0	3	0	0	0	0	0	1	.000	0	0	18.00
Martinez, Anastacio	Sarasota	Bos	A+	21	25	24	1	0	145	606	130	69	54	12	4	1	9	39	0	123	6	0	9	12	.429	0	0	3.35
Martinez, Angel	Casper	Col	R+	20	18	8	0	1	57.2	251	56	34	28	5	1	6	5	18	1	44	7	0	4	3	.571	0	0	4.37
Martinez, Antonio	Dayton	Cin	A	19	8	0	0	7	8	36	6	4	3	1	1	1	1	4	0	13	0	0	1	0	1.000	0	4	3.38
	Idaho Falls	SD	R+	19	10	8	0	0	42	195	42	35	30	6	2	2	4	26	0	38	4	0	1	4	.200	0	0	6.43
Martinez, Dan*	Bristol	CWS	R+	23	18	0	0	14	26	107	21	8	4	0	2	1	2	11	0	24	4	0	3	1	.750	0	6	1.38
Martinez, Dave*	Greensboro	NYY	A	22	11	11	3	0	79.1	312	54	17	10	1	0	0	4	28	0	67	6	0	6	0	1.000	2	0	1.13
	Tampa	NYY	A+	22	4	3	1	1	19.1	85	20	15	13	3	0	1	0	9	0	19	1	0	0	3	.000	0	0	6.05
Martinez, Hancer	Idaho Falls	SD	R+	19	11	1	0	0	21.2	97	25	11	10	2	0	2	0	10	1	21	2	0	1	0	1.000	0	0	4.15
Martinez, Miguel	Peoria	StL	A	20	18	18	1	0	97.1	443	114	72	48	7	5	5	5	27	1	52	7	0	5	8	.385	0	0	4.44
Martinez, Oscar	Tampa	NYY	A+	23	29	0	0	23	29.1	129	26	12	10	2	0	1	3	10	0	40	1	0	2	3	.400	0	14	3.07
Martinez, Paul*	Burlington	Cle	R+	20	19	0	0	5	35	171	39	29	25	4	3	0	3	26	0	40	3	5	2	2	.500	0	0	6.43
	Mahoning Vy	Cle	A-	20	2	0	0	0	4	20	5	2	2	0	0	0	0	4	0	6	1	0	0	0	.000	0	0	4.50
Martinez, Pedro*	Athletics	Oak	R	19	16	3	0	3	22	98	24	13	10	2	1	1	3	6	0	22	1	1	1	1	.500	0	0	4.09
Martinez, Renan*	Rancho Cuca	Ana	A+	20	43	1	0	16	54	261	65	34	26	5	3	2	7	28	0	49	3	1	4	3	.571	0	0	4.33
Martinez, Wilmer	Johnson Cty	StL	R+	21	23	0	0	11	34.1	150	32	18	8	0	2	1	5	11	1	25	6	1	6	3	.667	0	0	2.10
Marx, Tom*	Lakeland	Det	A+	22	28	27	1	0	150.1	674	160	92	82	14	4	8	8	78	0	97	11	3	8	11	.421	0	0	4.91
Mason, Robert*	Braves	Atl	R	18	14	0	0	4	33.2	146	28	16	9	2	3	1	4	10	1	34	2	0	3	3	.500	0	1	2.41
Masset, Nick	Rangers	Tex	R	20	15	14	0	0	31	131	34	21	15	2	0	1	2	7	0	32	1	0	0	6	.000	0	0	4.35
Mata, Gustavo	Expos	Mon	R	19	10	9	0	0	48.1	212	44	27	11	0	2	1	4	13	0	38	5	0	3	4	.429	0	0	2.05
	Vermont	Mon	A-	19	4	4	0	0	19.2	86	22	16	15	2	0	0	0	5	0	14	1	0	0	3	.000	0	0	6.86
Matcuk, Steve	Salem	Col	A+	26	24	0	0	9	42.1	189	47	19	14	0	2	1	9	13	2	33	4	0	4	1	.800	0	3	2.98
Mateo, Aneudis	Red Sox	Bos	R	19	3	2	0	0	7.2	30	6	4	0	0	0	0	0	0	0	6	1	1	0	1	.000	0	0	0.00
Mateo, Julio	San Berndno	Sea	A+	22	56	0	0	47	66	273	58	28	21	5	2	1	2	16	5	79	1	1	5	4	.556	0	26	2.86
Matheny, Brandon*	Columbus	Cle	A	23	24	22	1	1	115	474	90	45	38	6	1	2	7	45	1	97	9	2	7	8	.467	0	0	2.97
Mathews, Dan	High Desert	Mil	A+	26	36	0	0	15	51.1	238	61	38	35	6	1	0	4	25	0	59	3	1	4	3	.571	0	1	6.14
Mathiesen, Ryan	Braves	Atl	R	21	22	0	0	19	27	114	25	9	9	1	0	0	4	5	0	38	4	0	0	2	.000	0	10	3.00
	Macon	Atl	A	21	1	0	0	0	2	12	5	2	2	0	0	0	0	2	0	1	0	0	0	0	.000	0	0	9.00
Matos, Jesus	Tri-City	Col	A-	22	6	0	0	3	9.2	41	8	3	3	1	1	0	0	3	2	11	0	0	2	1	.667	0	0	2.79
	Asheville	Col	A	22	21	0	0	3	32	139	36	19	18	6	1	0	2	8	3	25	2	0	1	1	.500	0	0	5.06
Matos, Raymond*	Giants	SF	R	19	14	12	0	0	61.2	284	64	35	16	0	2	1	6	29	0	66	12	0	4	3	.571	0	0	2.34
Matsko, Rick	Kinston	Cle	A+	25	10	0	0	6	16	72	14	15	10	2	1	1	3	9	1	19	2	0	0	0	.000	0	0	5.63
	Columbus	Cle	A	25	24	0	0	14	45.2	202	53	25	19	4	3	3	2	10	1	41	5	0	3	2	.600	0	4	3.74

2001 Pitching — Class-A and Rookie Leagues

HOW MUCH HE PITCHED											WHAT HE GAVE UP												THE RESULTS					
Player	Team	Org	Lg	A	G	GS	CG	GF	IP	BFP	H	R	ER	HR	SH	SF	HB	TBB	IBB	SO	WP	Bk	W	L	Pct.	ShO	Sv	ERA
Matthews, Barry*	Lakeland	Det	A+	24	22	7	1	3	62.1	278	70	31	28	6	2	1	2	23	1	42	8	1	2	2	.500	1	0	4.04
Mattioni, Nick	Capital Cty	NYM	A	23	37	0	0	24	79.1	347	77	35	26	6	3	2	6	23	2	98	7	1	8	4	.667	0	6	2.95
Mattison, Corey	New Jersey	StL	A-	24	15	15	0	0	79.1	331	70	44	34	8	4	0	2	26	0	59	5	0	5	7	.417	0	0	3.86
Mattox, David	Kingsport	NYM	R+	22	14	8	1	5	56.1	241	48	22	15	3	1	0	8	19	0	58	10	0	5	1	.833	0	0	2.40
	Brooklyn	NYM	A-	22	2	2	0	0	10	38	5	2	1	0	0	1	0	3	0	12	0	0	1	0	1.000	0	0	0.90
Mau, Ryan	Marlins	Fla	R	23	4	0	0	3	10	38	6	1	1	0	0	0	1	3	0	6	1	0	1	0	1.000	0	0	0.90
Maust, David*	Vermont	Mon	A-	23	18	3	1	7	49.2	188	30	10	4	0	2	3	4	6	0	45	1	0	4	2	.667	0	1	0.72
	Jupiter	Mon	A+	23	1	1	0	0	3	15	7	5	5	2	0	0	0	1	0	0	0	0	0	1	.000	0	0	15.00
Mayfield, James	Batavia	Phi	A-	23	15	14	0	0	85	367	88	47	40	6	4	5	7	27	0	42	5	0	5	5	.500	0	0	4.24
Maysonet, Roberto	Beloit	Mil	A	22	28	17	0	4	111	495	99	64	52	8	5	3	11	61	0	109	12	1	5	10	.333	0	0	4.22
McAdoo, Duncan	Fort Wayne	SD	A	24	28	28	0	0	157.2	683	173	87	62	15	1	6	11	36	0	121	4	3	6	16	.273	0	0	3.54
McAvoy, Jeff	Jupiter	Mon	A+	25	46	1	0	12	76.2	321	70	31	23	8	6	2	2	20	1	52	1	3	2	2	.500	0	3	2.70
McBride, Macay*	Braves	Atl	R	19	13	11	0	0	55	237	51	30	23	0	2	2	4	23	1	67	8	0	4	4	.500	0	0	3.76
McCall, Dan*	Phillies	Phi	R	23	16	0	0	7	33.1	135	23	13	9	2	1	1	0	11	1	34	3	0	5	3	.625	0	2	2.43
McCall, Derell	Modesto	Oak	A+	20	39	4	0	23	86.2	378	105	50	40	8	6	1	1	20	2	55	10	1	1	6	.143	0	3	4.15
McCasland, Ralph*	Jupiter	Mon	A+	23	17	0	0	3	28	119	32	15	14	3	1	0	0	6	0	10	2	0	0	1	.000	0	0	4.50
	Clinton	Mon	A	23	26	0	0	19	41	164	31	15	14	2	2	0	0	13	0	22	1	1	1	2	.333	0	4	3.07
McClain, Kevin	Cedar Rapds	Ana	A	24	24	0	0	7	31.2	131	22	9	8	3	2	2	2	9	0	36	2	0	2	1	.667	0	0	2.27
	Rancho Cuca	Ana	A+	24	23	0	0	2	36	155	33	17	17	3	2	3	4	12	0	40	2	1	2	0	1.000	0	0	4.25
McClellan, Zach	Burlington	KC	A	23	24	22	0	0	127	554	142	79	64	5	2	3	6	36	0	87	7	0	5	10	.333	0	0	4.54
McClung, Mike	Chston-SC	TB	A	21	28	28	2	0	164.1	683	142	72	51	6	4	1	11	53	1	165	3	2	10	11	.476	1	0	2.79
McCormick, Terry*	Chston-SC	TB	A	23	14	0	0	12	19.1	80	14	3	3	0	4	2	1	8	3	22	4	0	3	0	1.000	0	2	1.40
McCracken, Vance	Great Falls	LA	R+	23	14	9	0	2	63.1	263	63	31	27	4	2	1	9	11	0	46	3	0	4	5	.444	0	1	3.84
McCrotty, Wes*	Utica	Fla	A-	23	17	9	0	3	63.1	266	50	34	29	3	2	1	2	24	0	39	3	0	1	7	.125	0	0	4.12
McCrotty, Will	Wilmington	LA	A	23	21	0	0	12	36.2	146	24	9	8	2	1	0	4	10	0	46	4	0	2	1	.667	0	4	1.96
	Vero Beach	LA	A+	23	20	0	0	14	22.2	105	22	11	11	3	1	1	2	14	1	17	2	0	0	2	.000	0	5	4.37
McCulloch, Andy	Chston-WV	Tor	A	24	55	0	0	50	62.1	254	53	25	15	0	5	1	1	12	3	54	2	0	5	2	.714	0	17	2.17
McCutcheon, Mike*	Lancaster	Ari	A+	24	12	0	0	4	8.2	41	9	10	10	1	1	1	0	7	2	8	1	0	1	2	.333	0	1	10.38
McDowell, Kevin*	Oneonta	Det	A-	23	14	7	0	1	46	204	40	25	14	3	1	3	4	27	0	35	4	1	2	4	.333	0	0	2.74
McGee, Chris	Beloit	Mil	A	24	37	2	0	10	68.2	310	69	40	32	6	4	5	6	34	2	51	3	2	4	2	.667	0	1	4.19
McGerry, Kevin	Modesto	Oak	A+	22	15	9	0	4	35	194	39	45	33	4	0	2	5	45	0	30	3	0	1	7	.125	0	0	8.49
	Vancouver	Oak	A-	22	8	0	0	1	6	43	4	15	13	0	0	1	4	17	0	7	6	0	0	1	.000	0	0	19.50
McGill, Trae	Burlington	KC	A	24	5	5	1	0	25.1	106	29	17	13	3	1	0	0	5	0	27	1	1	0	2	.000	0	0	4.62
McGinley, Blake*	Brooklyn	NYM	A-	23	18	0	0	14	46.1	179	30	12	10	3	0	1	3	11	0	59	3	1	5	0	1.000	0	4	1.94
McGlinchy, Kevin	Braves	Atl	R	25	2	2	0	0	2	7	1	0	0	0	0	0	1	0	0	2	0	0	0	0	.000	0	0	0.00
McGowan, Dustin	Auburn	Tor	A-	20	15	14	0	0	67	300	57	33	28	1	1	2	4	49	0	80	16	0	3	6	.333	0	0	3.76
McMachen, Clifford*	Yakima	Ari	A-	21	20	6	0	2	56.2	251	54	24	18	1	1	0	4	28	0	62	0	1	2	3	.400	0	0	2.86
McMillan, Josh*	Chston-WV	Tor	A	23	9	1	0	2	18.1	87	21	13	11	2	3	1	2	13	0	18	7	0	1	1	.500	0	0	5.40
	Medcine Hat	Tor	R+	23	15	0	0	5	25.2	144	41	35	30	7	0	2	1	27	1	15	8	0	0	2	.000	0	1	10.52
McMurray, Heath	Ogden	Mil	R+	23	10	0	0	3	24.2	101	24	14	9	0	1	0	2	7	1	24	2	1	2	3	.400	0	1	3.28
	Beloit	Mil	A	23	9	0	0	3	15.1	68	13	9	8	3	0	0	3	8	0	20	1	0	3	0	1.000	0	0	4.70
McNair, James	Martinsvlle	Hou	R+	23	18	0	0	7	33.2	144	35	20	19	1	1	2	6	11	0	26	7	0	1	2	.333	0	0	5.08
McNutt, Mike	Kane County	Fla	A	22	28	25	1	1	146.1	602	152	72	64	14	2	5	6	20	0	107	13	3	9	5	.643	0	1	3.94
McWhirter, Kris	Kannapolis	CWS	A	23	14	14	2	0	90.1	362	79	37	31	7	1	3	4	23	3	91	3	0	7	6	.538	0	0	3.09
	Winston-Sal	CWS	A+	23	13	10	0	1	57.1	254	60	39	34	7	5	1	5	25	1	49	1	0	2	3	.400	0	0	5.34
McWilliams, Matt	Billings	Cin	R+	29	14	0	0	3	21.2	92	17	10	8	0	1	0	0	12	1	26	2	0	2	2	.500	0	0	3.32
Mead, David	Savannah	Tex	A	21	19	19	0	0	96.1	450	91	63	59	13	6	5	19	64	0	79	10	2	2	10	.167	0	0	5.51
Mears, Chris	San Berndno	Sea	A+	24	38	12	0	4	107	470	104	59	53	10	7	3	11	49	1	74	6	1	7	6	.538	0	0	4.46
Meaux, Ryan*	Salem-Keizr	SF	A-	23	17	3	0	6	29	137	39	20	18	4	0	2	4	11	0	27	4	3	2	2	.500	0	0	5.59
Medders, Brandon	Lancaster	Ari	A+	22	31	0	0	15	41	163	26	8	6	1	2	1	2	15	3	53	2	1	1	2	.333	0	3	1.32
Medina, Franklin	Missoula	Ari	R+	20	15	14	1	0	87.2	381	89	42	33	5	3	2	4	28	0	55	12	1	8	2	.800	0	0	3.39
Medina, Frewing	Medcine Hat	Tor	R+	21	19	3	0	4	44.1	216	67	51	37	7	2	2	2	16	1	26	6	4	3	5	.375	0	0	7.51
Medina, Roberto*	Missoula	Ari	R+	21	21	0	0	9	34.1	151	32	18	14	1	2	1	2	17	1	29	2	0	3	2	.600	0	0	3.67
Medlin, Corbey	Missoula	Ari	R+	20	21	0	0	14	41.2	165	27	12	11	1	0	1	2	16	0	46	4	1	2	1	.667	0	6	2.38
Medlock, Chet	Peoria	StL	A	23	30	0	0	7	43.2	188	45	23	18	4	3	1	4	15	0	27	6	0	2	2	.500	0	0	3.71
	Potomac	StL	A+	23	12	0	0	4	16.1	70	17	5	1	0	1	1	1	5	0	14	0	0	1	1	.500	0	0	0.55
Meisenheimer, Matt	Savannah	Tex	A	20	3	3	0	0	6.2	38	11	11	10	0	0	0	2	7	0	4	2	0	0	1	.000	0	0	13.50
	Rangers	Tex	R	20	15	0	0	6	34	161	49	22	21	1	1	0	4	18	2	30	5	1	3	3	.500	0	1	5.56
Mejia, Juan	Eugene	SD	A-	22	22	0	0	16	23	92	9	7	7	1	0	0	0	12	0	11	1	0	0	1	.000	0	6	2.74
	Fort Wayne	SD	A	22	9	0	0	3	14	65	18	8	8	1	1	1	0	7	0	6	2	0	0	2	.000	0	0	5.14
Meldahl, Todd*	Batavia	Phi	A-	24	2	0	0	0	4	15	3	1	1	0	0	0	0	1	0	3	0	0	0	0	.000	0	0	2.25
	Lakewood	Phi	A	24	11	0	0	3	20.1	90	16	12	6	2	1	0	1	11	0	14	0	0	1	2	.333	0	0	2.66
	Clearwater	Phi	A+	24	7	0	0	3	11.1	46	8	2	2	1	0	0	1	5	0	10	2	0	0	0	.000	0	0	1.59
Melnyk, Brian*	Spokane	KC	A-	21	4	1	0	1	8.2	35	4	1	0	0	0	0	1	2	0	11	1	0	0	0	.000	0	1	0.00
Mendez, Dave*	Macon	Atl	A	22	35	1	0	12	68.1	291	55	34	31	7	3	1	4	29	1	55	12	1	5	4	.556	0	2	4.08
Mendoza, Cristian	Yankees	NYY	R	20	3	0	0	2	5.1	25	5	3	3	2	0	0	2	2	0	8	0	0	0	0	.000	0	0	5.06
Mendoza, Edgardo*	Mariners	Sea	R	21	13	4	0	1	42	187	38	25	20	0	1	1	3	21	0	34	6	2	3	3	.500	0	0	4.29
Mendoza, Jorge	Rangers	Tex	R	20	11	6	1	0	52	220	51	29	26	5	1	1	2	17	0	51	1	0	5	5	.500	0	0	4.50
Mendoza, Marcos*	Mahoning Vy	Cle	A-	21	11	11	0	0	48.2	205	40	23	19	1	0	1	3	28	0	39	6	0	4	3	.571	0	0	3.51
Mendoza, Mario	Rancho Cuca	Ana	A+	23	8	8	0	0	43	200	56	37	26	5	2	0	4	12	0	22	4	1	2	4	.333	0	0	5.44
Mercedes, Gabriel	Missoula	Ari	R+	19	15	14	0	0	80	357	81	47	33	1	1	3	5	30	0	66	10	2	8	3	.727	0	0	3.71
Merricks, Charles*	Tri-City	Col	A-	23	13	13	0	0	55.1	258	71	48	35	9	5	3	6	24	0	35	6	2	3	2	.600	0	0	5.69
Merricks, Matt*	Danville	Atl	R+	19	12	11	0	0	58	225	42	19	18	5	0	4	2	18	0	78	2	4	4	5	.444	0	0	2.79
Merrigan, Josh*	New Jersey	StL	A-	24	29	0	0	9	33.2	136	33	13	8	2	2	1	0	8	2	30	4	0	4	2	.667	0	0	2.14
Messenger, Randy	Kane County	Fla	A	20	14	0	0	7	18.1	85	22	13	8	0	3	2	2	5	0	14	0	0	2	1	.667	0	0	3.93
	Brevard Cty	Fla	A+	20	18	18	0	0	92.2	401	99	55	42	3	1	3	5	35	0	42	3	0	7	4	.636	0	0	4.08
Messer, Brian	Hickory	Pit	A	25	17	0	0	8	24.2	115	27	19	16	1	3	3	4	9	2	13	1	0	1	0	1.000	0	0	5.84
Metzger, Jon*	Royals	KC	R	23	6	5	0	0	9	41	9	5	4	0	0	0	0	4	0	11	0	1	0	0	.000	0	0	4.00
Meyer, Dave	Vero Beach	LA	A+	26	12	0	0	8	14.1	70	20	11	10	0	3	1	3	6	1	13	1	2	0	1	.000	0	3	6.28
Meyer, Mike	New Jersey	StL	A-	24	10	0	0	9	12	55	16	8	6	2	0	0	0	4	1	12	0	0	1	2	.333	0	5	4.50
	Peoria	StL	A	24	17	0	0	5	24	112	29	19	8	0	1	2	1	5	0	17	3	0	2	3	.400	0	1	3.00
Meyer, Scott*	Reds	Cin	R	23	14	0	0	8	30.1	129	24	7	6	0	3	0	1	13	2	34	0	0	5	2	.714	0	3	1.78
Michaels, Carl	Brewers	Mil	R	21	9	0	0	8	17.2	74	23	7	7	0	1	1	0	3	0	10	1	0	2	1	.667	0	2	3.57
Middleton, Brian	Martinsvlle	Hou	R+	23	10	0	0	4	20.1	90	13	9	7	2	2	0	0	16	0	22	2	1	1	3	.250	0	0	3.10
	Lexington	Hou	A	23	11	1	0	3	18.2	85	18	13	11	2	2	0	0	11	1	19	1	0	1	1	.500	0	0	5.30

2001 Pitching — Class-A and Rookie Leagues

HOW MUCH HE PITCHED											WHAT HE GAVE UP												THE RESULTS					
Player	Team	Org	Lg	A	G	GS	CG	GF	IP	BFP	H	R	ER	HR	SH	SF	HB	TBB	IBB	SO	WP	Bk	W	L	Pct.	ShO	Sv	ERA
Middleton, Kyle	Spokane	KC	A-	22	16	14	0	0	79.1	345	92	48	41	5	0	0	15	23	0	68	10	1	3	6	.333	0	0	4.65
Mikels, Jason	Macon	Atl	A	22	23	1	0	11	36	167	43	28	20	4	1	0	1	16	1	27	2	0	1	4	.200	0	0	5.00
	Jamestown	Atl	A-	22	7	3	0	1	20.2	82	18	8	8	1	0	1	0	5	0	13	0	0	1	1	.500	0	0	3.48
Miller, Colby	Elizabethtn	Min	R+	20	15	6	0	2	48	198	39	15	13	4	2	0	4	12	0	61	7	0	5	1	.833	0	0	2.44
Miller, Corey	Modesto	Oak	A+	25	43	0	0	17	70.1	297	70	29	27	9	3	2	0	25	7	65	1	0	5	4	.556	0	2	3.45
Miller, Eric*	Princeton	TB	R+	19	16	1	0	3	35.2	164	32	23	20	5	4	0	3	18	0	40	8	0	4	2	.667	0	0	5.05
Miller, Jason*	Elizabethtn	Min	R+	19	12	11	1	0	53.1	228	46	26	24	4	1	3	4	19	0	66	3	1	4	3	.571	0	0	4.05
Miller, Jeff	Williamsprt	Pit	A-	22	21	0	0	19	24	93	17	3	3	1	1	0	1	5	0	28	0	0	0	0	.000	0	15	1.13
Miller, Josh	Batavia	Phi	A-	23	17	0	0	4	31.1	137	36	11	9	2	1	2	3	4	2	21	0	0	2	1	.667	0	0	2.59
Miller, Matt*	Jamestown	Atl	A-	24	28	0	0	10	40	173	40	14	14	0	2	1	3	12	2	36	2	0	2	4	.333	0	1	3.15
Miller, Ryan	Beloit	Mil	A	24	22	22	0	0	105.1	462	100	70	62	17	0	3	14	47	0	112	9	0	10	6	.625	0	0	5.30
Milner, Robert	Vermont	Mon	A-	23	19	0	0	8	33.1	157	42	23	20	2	1	2	3	14	0	37	1	0	0	1	.000	0	0	5.40
Mims, Brandon*	Red Sox	Bos	R	20	11	6	0	3	50.2	215	56	25	23	3	2	4	0	14	0	34	3	0	1	2	.333	0	1	4.09
Minaya, Edwin	Visalia	Oak	A+	22	13	3	0	2	28.2	145	41	33	17	1	0	5	0	16	0	22	9	1	0	3	.000	0	2	5.34
	Vancouver	Oak	A-	22	13	0	0	10	20.2	83	13	7	4	3	1	0	0	7	0	19	2	0	1	0	1.000	0	5	1.74
Mincey, T.W.*	Bluefield	Bal	R+	22	15	1	0	4	30.2	155	38	31	23	2	2	1	4	21	3	29	2	0	1	1	.500	0	1	6.75
Miner, Zach	Jamestown	Atl	A-	20	15	15	0	0	90.2	358	76	26	19	6	2	0	4	16	0	68	4	1	3	4	.429	0	0	1.89
Miniel, Rene	Augusta	Bos	A	21	27	23	0	0	122	492	93	49	37	1	4	6	3	38	0	114	9	2	8	4	.667	0	0	2.73
Miniel, Roberto	Beloit	Mil	A	22	25	16	1	4	103.2	444	104	57	47	6	3	2	5	27	0	117	5	1	4	6	.400	1	0	4.08
	Lansing	ChC	A	22	8	5	0	0	32	133	26	18	17	4	1	1	3	11	0	23	1	0	2	1	.667	0	0	4.78
Minix, Travis	Bakersfield	TB	A+	24	44	0	0	25	67.1	287	67	27	25	3	2	0	1	19	3	70	4	1	5	1	.833	0	10	3.34
Mitchell, Andy	Orioles	Bal	R	23	12	0	0	11	24.2	103	18	10	7	1	2	0	3	10	3	21	1	1	4	2	.667	0	2	2.55
Mitchell, Jay	Casper	Col	R+	19	14	14	0	0	55.1	261	54	47	39	4	0	3	5	38	0	35	15	0	4	5	.444	0	0	6.34
Mitchell, Tom	Clinton	Mon	A	21	5	5	0	0	22.1	105	29	20	16	5	0	1	0	9	0	5	4	1	0	4	.000	0	0	6.45
	Vermont	Mon	A-	21	14	14	0	0	61	303	84	55	47	3	2	6	6	39	0	33	8	1	2	7	.222	0	0	6.93
Mitre, Sergio	Boise	ChC	A-	21	15	15	1	0	91	371	85	37	31	2	0	0	3	18	1	71	3	3	8	4	.667	1	0	3.07
Miyamoto, Eiji	Vermont	Mon	A-	22	1	0	0	0	1	3	0	0	0	0	0	0	0	0	0	1	0	0	0	0	.000	0	0	0.00
	Clinton	Mon	A	22	20	0	0	6	28.2	130	22	21	13	3	2	2	3	19	1	23	5	2	2	4	.333	0	1	4.08
Moak, Curtus*	Billings	Cin	R+	23	20	0	0	4	36.1	157	34	18	15	2	0	2	8	11	3	24	4	0	3	1	.750	0	0	3.72
Moates, Jason	Oneonta	Det	A-	23	1	0	0	0	2	7	1	0	0	0	0	0	0	0	0	4	0	0	0	0	.000	0	0	0.00
Modica, Greg	Eugene	SD	A-	22	17	1	0	5	24.2	114	37	21	17	1	2	1	0	8	2	15	2	0	2	4	.333	0	0	6.20
Montani, Jeff	Bluefield	Bal	R+	21	7	0	0	1	8	34	5	2	2	1	0	0	0	4	0	9	0	0	0	0	.000	0	0	2.25
Montano, Ignacio*	Columbus	Cle	A	22	11	0	0	3	17.2	75	16	8	6	0	1	1	1	6	0	17	2	0	1	1	.500	0	1	3.06
Montero, Agustin	Wilmington	LA	A	24	18	0	0	9	27.1	113	13	11	10	1	0	1	5	19	1	30	5	1	2	1	.667	0	1	3.29
	Vero Beach	LA	A+	24	16	0	0	7	31.1	134	29	14	12	7	1	1	3	13	0	23	1	0	1	0	1.000	0	1	3.45
Montero, Jose	Charlotte	Tex	A+	23	6	0	0	2	7.2	41	9	10	9	2	1	0	3	7	0	5	1	1	0	4	.000	0	0	10.57
	Rangers	Tex	R	23	5	1	0	4	7	29	4	1	1	1	1	0	1	1	0	6	0	0	0	0	.000	0	0	1.29
Montero, Oscar	Daytona	ChC	A+	24	11	1	0	0	16	68	7	6	6	1	0	0	0	14	0	13	3	0	2	0	1.000	0	0	3.38
Montes, Albert	Salem-Keizr	SF	A-	22	17	0	0	13	22.2	96	21	10	9	1	1	0	2	6	2	19	3	1	2	1	.667	0	7	3.57
Montgomery, Steve	Lk Elsinore	SD	A+	31	2	1	0	0	1.2	9	4	4	4	2	0	1	0	0	0	2	1	0	0	0	.000	0	0	21.60
Montilla, Elvis	Bluefield	Bal	R+	20	5	4	1	1	25	109	28	13	13	1	1	1	1	8	0	18	2	0	2	2	.500	0	0	4.68
	Delmarva	Bal	A	20	26	18	0	3	107.1	444	104	53	50	10	0	4	8	28	2	53	6	0	7	6	.538	0	0	4.19
Montilla, Felix	Lynchburg	Pit	A+	22	7	0	0	5	7	34	11	7	7	2	0	0	1	2	0	3	1	0	0	1	.000	0	1	9.00
Montoya, Saul	South Bend	Ari	A	21	7	1	0	1	13.2	60	17	6	6	1	0	2	1	5	0	11	1	0	0	0	.000	0	0	3.95
	Yakima	Ari	A-	21	4	4	0	0	17.2	85	22	13	9	1	0	0	2	8	0	12	2	1	1	2	.333	0	0	4.58
	Lancaster	Ari	A+	21	9	0	0	4	14.1	68	20	11	9	3	0	0	2	7	0	8	1	1	0	1	.000	0	0	5.65
Moore, Darin	Visalia	Oak	A+	25	38	3	0	8	58.2	307	66	69	57	7	0	5	12	51	3	56	15	1	1	4	.200	0	0	8.74
Moore, Greg	Tri-City	Col	A-	23	22	3	0	1	50.1	235	65	27	24	1	2	2	6	11	0	50	9	0	4	2	.667	0	0	4.29
Mora, Ramon	Auburn	Tor	A-	21	16	1	0	5	59	235	40	19	13	4	1	1	3	19	0	61	5	0	2	2	.500	0	0	1.98
Morales, Juan	Johnson Cty	StL	R+	19	4	3	0	0	13.1	60	17	12	8	1	0	1	4	2	0	10	2	0	0	0	.000	0	0	5.40
Morales, Leo	Pirates	Pit	R	18	10	7	1	0	53.1	236	62	28	26	4	3	3	3	9	0	34	4	0	2	2	.500	1	0	4.39
Morales, Ruddy	White Sox	CWS	R	20	6	5	0	0	29	126	31	15	8	2	0	1	1	6	0	26	0	2	3	2	.600	0	0	2.48
Moran, Nick	Mahoning Vy	Cle	A-	22	15	15	0	0	79.1	340	82	36	30	6	1	5	6	13	0	66	4	0	5	2	.714	0	0	3.40
Moravek, Rob	Pulaski	Tex	R+	22	13	11	0	0	63	269	70	34	25	3	0	3	2	17	1	54	7	0	4	2	.667	0	0	3.57
Morban, Carlos	Angels	Ana	R	19	11	1	0	5	12.1	69	17	22	18	0	1	1	1	12	0	10	8	1	0	1	.000	0	0	13.14
Morban, Domingo*	Kingsport	NYM	R+	20	16	0	0	9	22	118	29	20	19	2	2	0	8	16	1	26	6	0	1	4	.200	0	1	7.77
Mordan, Pedro	Idaho Falls	SD	R+	22	21	8	0	3	58	294	86	63	53	3	0	6	4	37	2	43	7	2	1	7	.125	0	0	8.22
Moreira, Greg	Brewers	Mil	R	19	4	4	0	0	14.2	65	17	10	8	0	0	1	2	1	0	11	1	0	1	1	.500	0	0	4.91
Morel, Eudy	Idaho Falls	SD	R+	19	14	0	0	6	20	92	24	15	11	3	1	1	1	6	0	25	3	0	0	2	.000	0	0	4.95
Morel, Jhosandy*	Pirates	Pit	R	20	6	0	0	4	9.1	41	7	2	2	1	0	0	1	5	0	12	1	0	0	0	.000	0	0	1.93
Moreno, Edwin	Charlotte	Tex	A+	21	28	28	1	0	152	645	142	83	68	10	2	5	11	51	0	92	4	0	8	9	.471	1	0	4.03
Moreno, Victor	Phillies	Phi	R	22	15	0	0	14	26.2	109	21	9	5	3	0	0	1	6	0	25	1	0	4	2	.667	0	0	1.69
Morgan, Russ*	Wisconsin	Sea	A	24	17	0	0	8	28	125	22	10	7	0	1	0	2	18	0	38	3	0	2	1	.667	0	1	2.25
	Everett	Sea	A-	24	22	2	0	8	51.2	227	60	38	30	2	2	2	1	17	0	56	2	1	2	5	.286	0	1	5.23
Morris, Cory	Bluefield	Bal	R+	23	1	0	0	0	3	12	1	0	0	0	0	0	0	2	0	4	0	0	1	0	1.000	0	0	0.00
	Frederick	Bal	A+	23	13	12	0	0	69.1	282	50	30	26	7	1	3	6	24	1	81	2	0	3	5	.375	0	0	3.37
Morris, Will	Cedar Rapds	Ana	A	24	40	0	0	12	81	373	99	51	40	11	6	3	4	23	0	88	4	1	6	6	.500	0	2	4.44
Morrison, Robbie	Royals	KC	R	25	2	2	0	0	2	7	1	0	0	0	0	0	0	0	0	2	0	0	0	0	.000	0	0	0.00
Morse, Bryan*	Brevard Cty	Fla	A+	24	37	0	0	12	62	270	57	32	28	2	6	2	1	36	3	33	4	0	3	2	.600	0	3	4.06
Moseley, Dustin	Dayton	Cin	A	20	25	25	0	0	148	638	158	83	69	10	4	1	8	42	0	108	3	2	10	8	.556	0	0	4.20
Moseley, Marcus	Quad City	Min	A	21	20	8	0	5	57.1	278	52	44	40	4	3	4	14	46	2	35	13	1	3	5	.375	0	0	6.28
Moser, Todd*	Marlins	Fla	R	25	1	1	0	0	2	8	2	2	2	2	0	0	0	0	0	3	0	0	0	0	.000	0	0	9.00
	Brevard Cty	Fla	A+	25	2	2	0	0	5.1	22	3	3	1	0	2	1	0	1	0	2	0	0	0	0	.000	0	0	1.69
Mosley, Eric	Tampa	NYY	A+	21	1	1	1	0	6	25	6	3	3	0	0	0	0	3	0	0	3	0	0	1	.000	0	0	4.50
	Greensboro	NYY	A	21	11	10	0	0	45.2	214	48	31	25	5	3	3	6	22	1	32	2	0	1	4	.200	0	0	4.93
	Yankees	NYY	R	21	6	6	0	0	33.1	134	28	8	6	2	1	0	0	9	0	21	2	0	4	1	.800	0	0	1.62
Mottl, Ryan	Dayton	Cin	A	24	26	26	2	0	152.2	653	155	74	61	15	3	6	10	42	2	119	7	0	15	6	.714	0	0	3.60
Mowday, Chris	Chston-WV	Tor	A	20	13	1	0	3	22.1	103	22	16	14	2	1	1	4	9	0	27	3	0	0	1	.000	0	0	5.64
	Auburn	Tor	A-	20	17	2	0	4	37	156	28	17	16	2	2	0	5	21	1	50	5	1	4	3	.571	0	0	3.89
Mozingo, Dan*	Kannapolis	CWS	A	22	37	9	1	5	94	378	59	30	25	6	5	3	4	43	1	114	8	0	8	4	.667	0	1	2.39
	Winston-Sal	CWS	A+	22	3	3	0	0	11.1	63	21	19	15	3	0	0	2	6	0	17	2	0	0	3	.000	0	0	11.91
Muessig, Jeff	Athletics	Oak	R	20	14	0	0	2	18.2	77	14	5	5	0	0	1	2	7	0	18	2	0	5	0	1.000	0	0	2.41
Munoz, Arnaldo*	Kannapolis	CWS	A	20	60	0	0	30	79.2	310	41	24	22	2	2	4	7	42	2	115	8	4	6	3	.667	0	12	2.49
Munter, Scott	Salem-Keizr	SF	A-	22	15	0	0	1	35	156	42	26	23	3	0	1	1	12	0	28	3	0	1	2	.333	0	0	5.91
	Hagerstown	SF	A	22	1	1	0	0	5.1	21	5	3	2	0	1	1	0	1	0	2	0	0	1	0	1.000	0	0	3.38

2001 Pitching — Class-A and Rookie Leagues

HOW MUCH HE PITCHED											WHAT HE GAVE UP												THE RESULTS					
Player	Team	Org	Lg	A	G	GS	CG	GF	IP	BFP	H	R	ER	HR	SH	SF	HB	TBB	IBB	SO	WP	Bk	W	L	Pct.	ShO	Sv	ERA
Murphy, Matt*	Daytona	ChC	A+	23	53	0	0	18	75	332	82	44	33	0	7	1	5	25	4	77	4	1	4	6	.400	0	3	3.96
Murray, Arlington*	Rangers	Tex	R	20	12	8	0	2	53.1	207	48	15	11	1	1	1	1	10	2	45	4	1	3	3	.500	0	0	1.86
Murray, Brad*	Kannapolis	CWS	A	23	9	0	0	6	13.2	64	16	12	10	0	1	0	1	7	1	12	3	0	0	0	.000	0	0	6.59
	Winston-Sal	CWS	A+	23	32	0	0	9	50	218	42	13	11	1	2	0	3	30	5	30	2	0	3	2	.600	0	0	1.98
Musser, Neal*	Capital Cty	NYM	A	21	17	17	1	0	95	387	86	38	30	3	4	3	3	18	0	98	8	1	7	4	.636	0	0	2.84
	St. Lucie	NYM	A+	21	9	9	0	0	45.2	201	45	24	18	2	0	2	5	19	0	40	2	0	3	4	.429	0	0	3.55
Mutch, Paul	Twins	Min	R	19	17	1	0	5	24.2	125	35	28	23	0	0	1	3	15	0	14	7	0	1	0	1.000	0	0	8.39
Nacar, Leslie	Giants	SF	R	18	23	0	0	17	31.2	135	31	10	9	3	1	1	1	11	1	36	4	0	0	3	.000	0	5	2.56
Nacar, Yimmy	Giants	SF	R	19	16	5	0	3	38.2	178	36	24	23	0	0	3	11	20	0	37	4	2	1	0	1.000	0	0	5.35
Nageotte, Clint	Wisconsin	Sea	A	21	28	26	0	0	152.1	648	141	65	53	10	10	1	11	50	1	187	6	4	11	8	.579	0	0	3.13
Nall, Mike	Batavia	Phi	A-	23	16	0	0	7	27	132	34	27	26	1	1	0	0	20	1	26	11	0	1	1	.500	0	0	8.67
Nall, T.J.	Dodgers	LA	R	21	4	4	0	0	12	53	14	6	6	0	0	1	0	5	0	10	0	0	0	0	.000	0	0	4.50
	Great Falls	LA	R+	21	7	2	0	0	23.1	108	26	18	13	2	0	0	5	6	1	25	2	0	2	2	.500	0	0	5.01
Nannini, Mike	Lexington	Hou	A	21	28	27	4	0	190.1	771	176	70	57	17	10	5	6	36	0	151	7	0	15	5	.750	1	0	2.70
Narveson, Chris*	Peoria	StL	A	20	8	8	0	0	50	190	32	14	11	3	2	1	3	11	0	53	0	0	3	3	.500	0	0	1.98
	Potomac	StL	A+	20	11	11	1	0	66.2	263	52	22	19	4	2	3	0	13	1	53	3	0	4	3	.571	0	0	2.57
Natale, Mike	Wilmington	KC	A+	22	28	27	0	0	159.1	662	152	75	58	8	2	6	13	33	0	134	13	1	9	8	.529	0	0	3.28
Navarro, Scott*	Visalia	Oak	A+	27	14	0	0	5	21.1	91	20	12	12	2	1	0	2	7	0	22	0	0	0	1	.000	0	1	5.06
Negrette, Richard	Daytona	ChC	A+	26	4	0	0	1	3	29	11	12	11	1	0	0	1	7	1	1	2	0	0	1	.000	0	0	33.00
Neil, Dan*	Columbus	Cle	A	23	24	0	0	13	48	189	33	14	9	3	5	1	1	8	1	35	2	0	3	4	.429	0	2	1.69
	Kinston	Cle	A+	23	16	0	0	2	33	130	26	6	3	1	3	1	1	3	0	27	3	0	3	0	1.000	0	0	0.82
Nelson, Justin*	Royals	KC	R	19	12	10	0	0	39.1	189	49	33	19	1	0	0	0	21	0	31	6	1	1	6	.143	0	0	4.35
Nelson, Kenny	Macon	Atl	A	20	25	24	2	1	151	649	144	76	66	16	5	9	6	57	1	154	9	1	12	8	.600	0	0	3.93
Nelson, Steve	Dodgers	LA	R	19	10	6	0	0	29	112	19	9	7	0	1	1	1	4	0	26	1	0	1	2	.333	0	0	2.17
Neu, Mike	Mudville	Cin	A+	24	53	0	0	44	64.2	277	50	21	17	3	4	1	3	30	4	102	5	1	3	2	.600	0	21	2.37
Neuage, Leigh	Dodgers	LA	R	18	3	2	0	0	5.2	21	2	1	1	0	0	0	0	3	0	3	0	0	0	0	.000	0	0	1.59
Newell, Mark	Wilmington	KC	A+	25	18	0	0	6	25.2	132	34	22	17	1	2	4	7	15	0	7	2	0	2	0	1.000	0	0	5.96
	Royals	KC	R	25	5	0	0	1	7.1	52	12	18	10	0	0	1	5	13	0	4	5	0	0	1	.000	0	0	12.27
Newton, Stan	Yankees	NYY	R	23	19	0	0	8	33.1	154	38	14	12	0	4	0	0	13	1	34	5	0	2	2	.500	0	1	3.24
Neylan, Chris*	Medcine Hat	Tor	R+	19	10	5	0	0	34	159	49	29	25	5	0	2	3	10	0	22	4	0	0	2	.000	0	0	6.62
Nicholson, Scott*	Tri-City	Col	A-	22	14	14	1	0	76.2	307	69	29	25	3	2	4	4	12	0	50	4	0	4	3	.571	1	0	2.93
Nicolas, Mike	Fort Wayne	SD	A	20	54	0	0	29	62.2	265	44	30	24	4	5	4	8	34	4	70	4	3	1	5	.167	0	7	3.45
	Lk Elsinore	SD	A+	20	8	0	0	2	12	51	11	7	7	2	1	0	1	5	0	15	1	0	0	1	.000	0	0	5.25
Niedbalski, Nick*	Twins	Min	R	21	14	8	0	1	46.2	196	44	25	22	1	1	0	1	16	0	41	5	0	2	2	.500	0	0	4.24
Nielsen, Brian*	Brewers	Mil	R	20	7	6	0	0	24.1	101	21	12	10	0	0	1	1	5	0	21	1	0	0	1	.000	0	0	3.70
Nieve, Fernando	Martinsvlle	Hou	R+	19	12	8	1	0	38	161	27	20	16	2	0	0	3	21	0	49	3	1	4	2	.667	0	0	3.79
Nolasco, David	Ogden	Mil	R+	23	20	2	0	7	42.2	184	38	27	21	3	0	3	3	14	3	35	6	0	3	3	.500	0	2	4.43
Nolasco, Ricky	Cubs	ChC	R	19	5	4	0	0	18	69	11	3	3	0	0	0	1	5	0	23	1	0	1	0	1.000	0	0	1.50
Norderum, Jason*	Clinton	Mon	A	20	28	28	2	0	155	706	176	96	84	17	5	3	19	60	0	101	9	1	7	7	.500	0	0	4.88
Nova, W.*	Brewers	Mil	R	19	16	0	0	9	22.1	105	32	15	14	1	1	1	4	9	1	10	2	0	4	1	.800	0	0	5.64
Novinsky, John	Peoria	StL	A	23	25	25	1	0	138.2	615	165	95	85	17	1	4	10	43	0	115	13	1	9	11	.450	0	0	5.52
Novoa, Roberto	Williamsprt	Pit	A-	20	14	13	1	1	79.2	331	76	40	30	4	5	1	7	20	0	55	4	1	5	5	.500	0	0	3.39
Nunez, Kelvin	Royals	KC	R	19	19	0	0	9	48	217	49	33	24	3	1	1	2	24	2	25	5	3	3	1	.750	0	2	4.50
Nunez, Mike	Staten Ilnd	NYY	A-	23	4	0	0	1	6	26	6	2	1	1	0	0	0	3	0	5	0	0	0	0	.000	0	0	1.50
Nunez, Renny	Reds	Cin	R	20	8	0	0	4	17.1	79	18	11	9	2	0	1	1	6	0	12	3	0	0	0	.000	0	0	4.67
Nunez, Severino*	Brewers	Mil	R	21	9	0	0	1	15.1	65	11	8	8	1	0	0	0	4	0	19	1	0	0	0	.000	0	0	4.70
	Ogden	Mil	R+	21	7	0	0	2	9	34	3	3	2	1	1	1	1	3	0	12	1	0	0	0	.000	0	0	2.00
Nunley, Derrek	Chston-WV	Tor	A	21	14	0	0	6	18.1	90	22	12	8	1	2	0	2	8	0	23	2	0	1	2	.333	0	0	3.93
Oakes, Gerard	Brewers	Mil	R	20	12	7	0	1	53.2	233	50	24	17	2	2	2	5	25	0	44	10	1	2	4	.333	0	0	2.85
Obermueller, Wes	Wilmington	KC	A+	25	20	6	0	1	38	163	38	15	13	3	2	1	1	16	1	28	2	0	0	2	.000	0	0	3.08
O'Brien, Matt*	Visalia	Oak	A+	25	27	24	0	2	145.2	637	161	86	76	12	4	4	6	39	0	148	12	0	9	9	.500	0	0	4.70
O'Brien, Pat	Hickory	Pit	A	21	11	11	0	0	74	303	73	30	26	5	2	1	3	14	0	67	4	0	6	5	.545	0	0	3.16
O'Brien, Weston	Cubs	ChC	R	19	13	3	0	3	41.1	175	49	18	15	0	1	2	5	8	0	34	0	3	3	3	.500	0	0	3.27
Ockerman, Justin	Mariners	Sea	R	19	10	10	0	0	40.1	186	49	30	22	1	0	0	5	16	0	27	4	1	1	4	.200	0	0	4.91
Ogiltree, John	Medcine Hat	Tor	R+	24	28	0	0	23	32	138	33	17	12	1	4	1	4	10	2	25	3	0	2	4	.333	0	6	3.38
Ogle, Rylie*	Kingsport	NYM	R+	24	6	5	0	0	23.2	108	31	15	9	2	0	0	0	7	0	18	1	0	2	2	.500	0	0	3.42
	Brooklyn	NYM	A-	24	6	0	0	4	14.1	61	15	3	2	0	1	1	0	5	1	14	0	0	0	1	.000	0	0	1.26
Olivero, Pedro	Cubs	ChC	R	20	17	0	0	4	30	135	38	24	22	2	1	1	0	10	0	27	2	0	2	0	1.000	0	3	6.60
Olivo, Rigal	Bristol	CWS	R+	20	11	6	0	2	41	185	41	22	18	4	1	1	7	11	0	40	1	1	1	4	.200	0	0	3.95
	Winston-Sal	CWS	A+	20	8	0	0	3	13.1	57	16	9	7	2	0	0	0	3	0	9	3	0	0	0	.000	0	1	4.72
Olore, Kevin	Wisconsin	Sea	A	23	27	27	0	0	154.2	641	134	70	57	14	4	3	14	40	0	158	6	1	13	4	.765	0	0	3.32
Olson, Jason	Great Falls	LA	R+	24	5	0	0	5	7.2	30	2	1	1	0	0	0	1	1	0	13	0	0	2	0	1.000	0	1	1.17
	Wilmington	LA	A	24	15	0	0	11	29.1	125	23	12	12	2	1	1	2	15	3	28	4	1	2	4	.333	0	1	3.68
Olson, Ryan*	Capital Cty	NYM	A	22	1	0	0	0	3.2	16	5	1	1	0	1	0	0	1	0	4	1	0	0	0	.000	0	0	2.45
	Kingsport	NYM	R+	22	2	1	0	0	7.1	33	9	4	2	1	1	0	1	1	0	6	0	0	0	0	.000	0	0	2.45
	Brooklyn	NYM	A-	22	7	1	0	4	25	99	15	6	6	0	1	0	0	9	0	22	3	0	0	1	.000	0	2	2.16
O'Neal, Brandon	Rancho Cuca	Ana	A+	23	10	6	0	0	32	157	37	24	20	1	2	1	5	25	0	20	7	0	0	3	.000	0	0	5.63
	Cedar Rapds	Ana	A	23	16	15	0	0	82.2	385	95	67	54	6	1	3	11	40	0	51	9	2	2	8	.200	0	0	5.88
Oquendo, Ian	Pirates	Pit	R	20	3	3	0	0	19	71	12	2	1	0	1	0	0	5	0	13	0	0	3	0	1.000	0	0	0.47
	Williamsprt	Pit	A-	20	10	9	1	0	64.2	255	55	16	10	2	3	2	1	10	0	56	2	0	7	0	1.000	0	0	1.39
Orloski, Joe	Dunedin	Tor	A+	23	46	0	0	28	66.2	283	55	28	21	4	0	3	3	29	2	52	2	0	4	2	.667	0	10	2.84
Orr, Benjamin*	Boise	ChC	A-	24	12	1	0	6	24.1	124	37	27	27	3	0	0	4	11	0	21	5	0	0	3	.000	0	4	9.99
	Daytona	ChC	A+	24	5	0	0	4	5	27	6	4	3	0	2	2	0	6	2	6	2	0	0	1	.000	0	1	5.40
Ortega, Carlos*	White Sox	CWS	R	23	4	0	0	0	11	44	10	3	3	0	0	1	0	0	0	13	0	0	2	0	1.000	0	0	2.45
	Winston-Sal	CWS	A+	23	10	6	0	3	40	173	43	23	21	5	0	4	7	10	0	33	2	0	0	3	.000	0	0	4.72
Ortega, Jose*	Spokane	KC	A-	23	21	0	0	14	35	153	25	11	11	2	2	0	4	20	3	33	1	0	2	2	.500	0	1	2.83
Ortiz, Javier	Yankees	NYY	R	22	2	0	0	1	4	13	1	0	0	0	0	0	0	1	0	2	0	0	0	0	.000	0	0	0.00
	Staten Ilnd	NYY	A-	22	3	3	0	0	13.2	55	11	4	3	1	0	0	0	4	0	12	1	0	1	1	.500	0	0	1.98
Ortiz, Jose	Bakersfield	TB	A+	24	35	0	0	16	71.1	321	77	34	30	5	4	3	8	29	3	57	7	2	3	3	.500	0	0	3.79
Ortiz, Omar	Brevard Cty	Fla	A+	24	28	21	0	2	112	509	120	78	67	12	4	3	8	65	0	78	9	0	4	10	.286	0	0	5.38
Osberg, Tanner	Kingsport	NYM	R+	19	12	12	0	0	63.1	269	64	30	28	4	0	5	9	21	0	33	6	1	2	1	.667	0	0	3.98
Ostlund, Ian*	Oneonta	Det	A-	23	14	10	0	2	65.2	276	63	29	23	1	1	4	0	20	1	44	0	0	2	5	.286	0	0	3.15
O'Sullivan, Mark	Provo	Ana	R+	23	22	0	0	11	34	157	35	23	15	5	3	1	3	16	2	36	1	0	1	2	.333	0	2	3.97
Ott, Thom	Great Falls	LA	R+	22	14	0	0	7	22.1	108	29	19	12	0	0	0	2	7	0	24	3	0	2	1	.667	0	2	4.84
Ough, Wayne	Brooklyn	NYM	A-	23	7	3	0	0	16.2	80	11	12	12	1	1	0	1	17	1	19	2	0	0	1	.000	0	0	6.48

2001 Pitching — Class-A and Rookie Leagues

HOW MUCH HE PITCHED											WHAT HE GAVE UP												THE RESULTS					
Player	Team	Org	Lg	A	G	GS	CG	GF	IP	BFP	H	R	ER	HR	SH	SF	HB	TBB	IBB	SO	WP	Bk	W	L	Pct.	ShO	Sv	ERA
Ovalles, Juan	Yakima	Ari	A-	20	16	6	0	3	43.1	195	48	21	19	4	0	0	3	19	0	28	1	0	2	5	.286	0	0	3.95
Owens, Henry	Pirates	Pit	R	23	6	0	0	5	7	28	5	1	1	0	0	0	0	2	0	8	0	0	1	0	1.000	0	1	1.29
Oxspring, Chris	Fort Wayne	SD	A	25	41	2	0	8	56.1	256	66	29	26	5	3	3	3	25	5	54	2	2	4	1	.800	0	0	4.15
	Lk Elsinore	SD	A+	25	7	0	0	2	14	56	10	2	1	1	0	0	0	6	2	17	0	0	0	0	.000	0	0	0.64
Pace, Adam*	Cedar Rapds	Ana	A	22	17	12	1	2	87.1	377	84	52	38	3	4	5	3	24	0	68	11	0	5	6	.455	0	0	3.92
	Rancho Cuca	Ana	A+	22	3	3	1	0	21.2	98	30	11	10	2	0	0	0	6	2	13	0	0	1	1	.500	0	0	4.15
Pacheco, E.	Salem	Col	A+	23	27	3	0	14	42.1	198	55	27	22	4	2	2	0	18	0	29	1	0	4	2	.667	0	1	4.68
	Asheville	Col	A	23	7	7	0	0	36.1	157	38	23	17	0	0	0	4	9	1	34	0	0	1	2	.333	0	0	4.21
Padgett, Dan*	Salem-Keizr	SF	A-	24	4	0	0	1	3.1	22	11	8	8	1	0	0	1	2	0	1	1	0	0	0	.000	0	0	21.60
	Hagerstown	SF	A	24	19	0	0	6	24.1	110	24	18	18	3	0	3	1	18	1	16	0	0	0	1	.000	0	0	6.66
Padilla, Juan	Fort Myers	Min	A+	25	56	0	0	49	69.1	306	72	35	23	2	1	1	3	25	6	77	1	0	6	4	.600	0	23	2.99
Padilla, Roy*	Marlins	Fla	R	26	4	0	0	1	6	20	1	1	0	0	0	1	0	1	0	6	0	1	0	0	.000	0	1	0.00
	Brevard Cty	Fla	A+	26	6	0	0	3	6.1	33	6	4	4	1	0	0	0	12	0	3	0	0	0	0	.000	0	0	5.68
Palmer, Travis	Johnson Cty	StL	R+	22	10	7	0	0	38.2	172	45	22	18	3	1	0	4	14	0	29	1	0	1	2	.333	0	0	4.19
Pannone, Anthony	Salem-Keizr	SF	A-	20	14	14	0	0	76.2	323	82	41	35	9	0	0	8	13	0	61	7	1	7	1	.875	0	0	4.11
Pape, Stace	Dayton	Cin	A	24	7	0	0	3	11	57	20	13	10	3	0	0	0	2	0	13	1	1	0	0	.000	0	0	8.18
Parker, Brandon	Mariners	Sea	R	26	9	0	0	2	11	52	15	5	5	2	0	0	1	5	0	13	0	0	2	0	1.000	0	0	4.09
	San Berndno	Sea	A+	26	15	0	0	5	23	102	18	13	11	5	1	0	1	18	0	28	0	0	4	0	1.000	0	0	4.30
Parker, Josh	Princeton	TB	R+	21	22	0	0	17	30.2	126	29	12	8	0	0	1	3	6	0	34	3	1	2	1	.667	0	5	2.35
	Chston-SC	TB	A	21	3	0	0	1	6.2	32	7	3	2	0	0	2	0	4	1	4	2	0	2	1	.667	0	0	2.70
Parker, Matt	High Desert	Mil	A+	23	28	28	1	0	161	704	167	88	77	17	2	6	8	67	1	134	9	0	13	6	.684	0	0	4.30
Parker, Zach*	Casper	Col	R+	20	8	8	0	0	26.1	122	42	26	22	2	0	1	1	12	0	19	3	1	1	2	.333	0	0	7.52
Parrott, Rhett	New Jersey	StL	A-	22	11	11	0	0	45.2	202	45	27	25	3	1	0	1	28	0	58	4	0	1	3	.250	0	0	4.93
Patten, Lanny	Auburn	Tor	A-	23	3	0	0	1	2.2	21	7	9	8	1	0	0	0	5	0	2	3	0	0	1	.000	0	0	27.00
	Medcine Hat	Tor	R+	23	25	0	0	8	38.1	170	30	30	23	2	0	1	8	22	1	31	2	1	1	4	.200	0	1	5.40
Patten, Scott	Winston-Sal	CWS	A+	21	2	1	0	0	1	9	2	3	3	0	0	0	2	3	0	0	0	0	0	1	.000	0	0	27.00
	Bristol	CWS	R+	21	12	12	1	0	61	266	67	42	37	12	0	1	7	21	1	43	7	0	3	4	.429	0	0	5.46
Patterson, Quenten	Capital Cty	NYM	A	24	33	1	0	20	63.1	282	62	46	43	11	4	1	9	29	2	43	8	1	3	4	.429	0	6	6.11
Pauley, David	Idaho Falls	SD	R+	19	15	15	0	0	68.2	315	88	57	46	8	1	3	1	24	0	53	6	0	4	9	.308	0	0	6.03
Paustian, Mike	Pulaski	Tex	R+	21	14	2	0	9	29.1	130	25	16	11	2	3	1	1	16	0	27	5	0	2	1	.667	0	5	3.38
Pavon, Julio	San Jose	SF	A+	26	6	0	0	3	11.1	50	14	12	11	2	0	1	2	2	1	14	0	0	1	0	1.000	0	0	8.74
	Hagerstown	SF	A	26	29	15	1	4	112.2	455	109	45	39	6	1	2	3	21	0	107	4	3	6	4	.600	1	2	3.12
Paz, Jackson*	Braves	Atl	R	19	12	0	0	4	32.2	148	40	19	13	1	2	1	1	7	1	31	1	0	2	1	.667	0	0	3.58
Pearson, Brent	Pirates	Pit	R	22	11	0	0	11	13.1	61	8	4	2	0	1	0	2	8	1	15	1	0	0	2	.000	0	7	1.35
	Hickory	Pit	A	22	3	0	0	0	4.2	17	3	0	0	0	0	0	0	2	0	4	1	0	2	0	1.000	0	0	0.00
Peeples, Jim*	Staten Ilnd	NYY	A-	21	11	0	0	5	14.2	81	18	15	15	1	1	1	1	19	0	14	3	0	1	0	1.000	0	0	9.20
	Greensboro	NYY	A	21	1	0	0	0	1	3	0	0	0	0	0	0	0	0	0	0	0	0	0	0	.000	0	0	0.00
Peeples, Ross*	Brooklyn	NYM	A-	22	16	15	1	0	80.1	330	63	19	12	1	2	3	1	29	0	67	4	0	9	3	.750	1	0	1.34
Peguero, Darwin*	Lexington	Hou	A	23	34	15	0	9	124.1	509	112	67	56	14	4	3	6	37	0	134	8	2	8	10	.444	0	2	4.05
Peguero, Radhame	Hudson Val	TB	A-	24	17	1	0	6	39.2	190	30	29	21	3	0	1	6	40	0	22	5	0	2	0	1.000	0	0	4.76
Pember, Dave	Beloit	Mil	A	24	8	8	0	0	44	185	49	20	16	3	0	2	1	10	0	39	5	0	3	4	.429	0	0	3.27
	High Desert	Mil	A+	24	20	20	0	0	121.1	533	135	73	65	12	2	7	7	35	1	96	14	0	9	6	.600	0	0	4.82
Pena, Alex	Lynchburg	Pit	A+	24	25	3	0	13	53	257	61	39	36	3	3	2	9	35	2	31	3	0	2	4	.333	0	3	6.11
Pena, Ed*	Winston-Sal	CWS	A+	22	31	5	0	7	47.1	225	52	30	22	6	7	2	7	24	3	35	4	1	1	6	.143	0	0	4.18
Pena, Geronimo	Royals	KC	R	19	17	0	0	8	36.2	157	42	22	16	2	3	1	3	8	0	29	1	1	1	3	.250	0	0	3.93
Pena, Juan	Sarasota	Bos	A+	25	8	8	0	0	26	118	29	15	15	3	0	0	1	11	0	31	1	1	0	3	.000	0	0	5.19
Pena, Luismar	Brewers	Mil	R	19	11	2	0	1	35	164	42	23	18	2	2	1	8	13	1	20	1	2	3	4	.429	0	0	4.63
Pennington, Todd	Mahoning Vy	Cle	A-	22	13	0	0	1	30.2	135	27	12	12	0	1	2	1	18	1	32	3	0	0	2	.000	0	0	3.52
Percell, Brody*	Columbus	Cle	A	26	26	0	0	6	54.1	235	55	34	23	5	3	4	2	22	2	41	11	0	1	2	.333	0	2	3.81
Percosky, Mark	Fort Wayne	SD	A	24	8	6	0	1	28.2	130	33	20	18	5	0	0	2	12	0	30	2	1	0	2	.000	0	0	5.65
Perez, Armando*	White Sox	CWS	R	21	15	5	1	1	63.1	265	56	27	21	1	2	0	2	23	2	44	6	1	3	3	.500	1	0	2.98
Perez, Beltran	South Bend	Ari	A	20	27	27	2	0	160	651	142	59	50	10	5	3	6	35	0	157	5	3	12	4	.750	0	0	2.81
Perez, Carlos*	Orioles	Bal	R	20	14	0	0	6	29.2	139	29	22	18	1	2	0	2	17	1	29	7	3	1	1	.500	0	0	5.46
Perez, Elvis	Macon	Atl	A	22	27	0	0	8	51.1	215	35	22	17	3	2	2	3	19	2	48	1	1	5	5	.500	0	0	2.98
Perez, Frank	Clearwater	Phi	A+	19	31	0	0	17	64	272	58	29	25	2	1	1	7	26	2	45	8	2	4	2	.667	0	3	3.52
Perez, Frank	W Michigan	Det	A	22	36	1	0	12	78	317	63	27	23	2	0	3	3	29	1	81	6	3	7	2	.778	0	2	2.65
Perez, George	Dunedin	Tor	A+	23	41	0	0	23	86.2	380	81	39	30	3	1	7	6	42	1	48	7	1	4	3	.571	0	8	3.12
Perez, Henry	Idaho Falls	SD	R+	19	15	15	0	0	71.2	328	79	60	50	10	2	2	5	39	0	82	4	1	4	8	.333	0	0	6.28
Perez, Julio	Jupiter	Mon	A+	23	34	0	0	20	47.1	218	58	26	19	1	1	3	4	16	1	46	1	0	6	3	.667	0	4	3.61
Perez, Luis*	Augusta	Bos	A	21	26	25	0	1	125.2	525	118	69	50	14	2	7	3	42	0	113	9	0	8	8	.500	0	0	3.58
Perez, Oliver*	Fort Wayne	SD	A	20	19	19	0	0	101.1	415	84	46	39	9	0	5	1	43	0	98	1	2	8	5	.615	0	0	3.46
	Lk Elsinore	SD	A+	20	9	9	0	0	53	231	45	22	16	4	3	2	1	25	0	62	6	0	2	4	.333	0	0	2.72
Perez, Randy*	Frederick	Bal	A+	22	20	20	3	0	122.2	520	145	56	54	8	6	3	5	23	0	101	3	0	8	7	.533	0	0	3.96
Perkin, Gregory	Missoula	Ari	R+	21	12	5	0	5	32.2	157	43	29	18	1	1	2	5	9	0	34	4	2	1	2	.333	0	0	4.96
Perkins, Vince	Auburn	Tor	A-	20	14	14	0	0	52.1	223	41	23	19	1	0	0	0	37	0	67	4	0	1	4	.200	0	0	3.27
Perry, Andrew	Pittsfield	Hou	A-	23	23	1	0	7	42	205	50	37	27	2	3	3	0	23	1	39	7	1	1	6	.143	0	0	5.79
Persby, Andy	Quad City	Min	A	24	20	0	0	5	27	108	18	6	3	1	1	1	2	13	0	17	3	0	3	0	1.000	0	1	1.00
	Fort Myers	Min	A+	24	18	0	0	6	26	128	25	22	20	0	2	0	4	23	1	14	3	0	1	3	.250	0	0	6.92
Peterson, Matt	Brooklyn	NYM	A-	20	6	6	0	0	33.1	139	26	7	6	0	1	1	3	14	0	19	2	0	2	2	.500	0	0	1.62
	Capital Cty	NYM	A	20	18	14	0	1	79.1	357	87	46	44	9	3	5	4	29	0	72	9	0	2	6	.250	0	0	4.99
Petty, Chad*	Tigers	Det	R	20	12	10	2	1	57	222	35	11	7	2	1	2	1	13	0	52	3	0	6	0	1.000	1	0	1.11
	Oneonta	Det	A-	20	1	1	0	0	6.1	28	6	5	2	0	0	2	0	2	0	0	0	0	0	1	.000	0	0	2.84
Phillips, Chase	Bluefield	Bal	R+	21	25	2	0	8	40.1	190	52	32	23	5	2	1	1	18	2	27	2	1	3	5	.375	0	0	5.13
Phillips, Mark*	Eugene	SD	A-	20	4	4	0	0	21.2	87	16	10	9	1	0	0	1	9	0	19	1	0	3	1	.750	0	0	3.74
	Fort Wayne	SD	A	20	5	5	0	0	30.2	127	19	11	9	1	1	0	3	14	0	27	1	0	4	1	.800	0	0	2.64
	Lk Elsinore	SD	A+	20	5	5	0	0	28	116	19	8	8	0	1	1	0	14	0	34	2	0	2	1	.667	0	0	2.57
Phillips, Mike*	Kannapolis	CWS	A	20	14	12	1	1	71.2	304	74	36	29	1	5	6	7	18	1	54	1	1	2	7	.222	0	0	3.64
Pichardo, Carlos	Wilmington	KC	A+	24	31	2	0	7	65.2	275	67	36	33	3	0	2	4	19	1	38	6	0	1	2	.333	0	2	4.52
Pierce, Tony	Macon	Atl	A	26	2	0	0	2	4	22	7	6	6	2	0	0	0	3	0	4	3	0	0	0	.000	0	0	13.50
Pignatiello, C.*	Boise	ChC	A-	19	16	12	0	3	78	337	70	37	26	2	4	1	6	22	0	83	6	0	7	3	.700	0	1	3.00
Pike, Matt	Billings	Cin	R+	23	13	8	0	2	55.1	242	60	39	32	5	0	1	6	15	0	57	3	1	3	4	.429	0	0	5.20
	Dayton	Cin	A	23	2	1	0	0	6.2	30	7	4	4	3	0	0	1	3	0	8	0	0	0	1	.000	0	0	5.40
Pilkington, Brian	Great Falls	LA	R+	19	5	2	0	0	16	69	19	11	10	2	1	1	1	2	0	17	2	0	0	1	.000	0	0	5.63
Pinango, Miguel	Kingsport	NYM	R+	19	14	13	0	1	59	255	63	35	29	6	3	2	5	13	0	49	2	5	3	8	.273	0	0	4.42
Pinkerton, Brad*	Provo	Ana	R+	22	17	1	0	6	35.1	157	37	24	22	3	0	1	2	13	0	35	5	0	0	2	.000	0	0	5.60

2001 Pitching — Class-A and Rookie Leagues

HOW MUCH HE PITCHED											WHAT HE GAVE UP												THE RESULTS					
Player	Team	Org	Lg	A	G	GS	CG	GF	IP	BFP	H	R	ER	HR	SH	SF	HB	TBB	IBB	SO	WP	Bk	W	L	Pct.	ShO	Sv	ERA
Pinto, Renyel*	Lansing	ChC	A	19	20	20	1	0	88	393	94	64	51	9	4	4	3	44	1	69	5	3	4	8	.333	0	0	5.22
Pitney, Jim	W Michigan	Det	A	24	15	0	0	7	26.1	115	23	12	10	1	0	0	4	12	0	27	2	0	1	0	1.000	0	1	3.42
Plancich, Nick	Johnson Cty	StL	R+	23	9	9	0	0	38	154	32	12	5	0	0	1	1	10	0	19	3	0	2	2	.500	0	0	1.18
Plank, Terry	Frederick	Bal	A+	24	38	4	0	12	71	328	71	51	42	8	2	1	9	43	2	58	5	1	2	8	.200	0	1	5.32
Pluta, Tony	Lexington	Hou	A	19	26	26	0	0	132.1	570	107	52	47	7	3	6	12	86	0	138	11	0	12	4	.750	0	0	3.20
Polanco, Elvis	High Desert	Mil	A+	24	42	0	0	13	84	371	98	47	42	16	0	2	8	19	1	77	4	1	3	3	.500	0	2	4.50
Polk, Scott	St. Lucie	NYM	A+	25	6	0	0	4	7.2	39	9	6	6	1	1	0	1	10	0	4	1	0	1	0	1.000	0	0	7.04
Polo, Bienvenido	Peoria	StL	A	23	18	1	0	2	28	134	25	22	14	4	1	4	4	19	0	19	10	1	0	0	.000	0	0	4.50
Ponce de Leon, D.	Peoria	StL	A	24	19	0	0	12	21.2	90	17	13	11	3	0	0	1	8	0	15	0	1	1	1	.500	0	2	4.57
	Potomac	StL	A+	24	23	3	0	5	41	171	30	19	13	6	0	1	5	12	2	30	3	1	1	4	.200	0	0	2.85
Pope, Justin	New Jersey	StL	A-	22	15	15	0	0	69.1	286	64	32	20	6	0	0	5	14	0	66	0	0	2	4	.333	0	0	2.60
Porter, Scott	Dunedin	Tor	A+	25	3	0	0	0	3	19	8	7	7	1	0	1	1	2	0	2	2	0	0	1	.000	0	0	21.00
Portobanco, Luz	Capital Cty	NYM	A	22	1	1	0	0	6	26	7	3	3	0	1	0	0	1	0	5	0	0	0	1	.000	0	0	4.50
	Brooklyn	NYM	A-	22	13	12	0	0	70.2	293	51	20	16	1	4	4	13	29	0	52	3	2	5	3	.625	0	0	2.04
Powell, Greg	Pittsfield	Hou	A-	23	8	1	0	3	18.2	74	13	7	1	1	0	2	1	2	0	9	0	0	1	1	.500	0	0	0.48
Powers, Joe	Billings	Cin	R+	23	27	0	0	11	30	131	25	17	9	0	0	1	1	13	0	30	2	0	3	1	.750	0	3	2.70
Prahm, Ryan	Burlington	Cle	R+	23	1	1	0	0	4.1	22	8	5	5	0	0	0	0	1	0	4	1	0	0	0	.000	0	0	10.38
	Columbus	Cle	A	23	11	11	0	0	59.2	237	53	18	16	4	1	0	0	12	0	47	5	0	7	2	.778	0	0	2.41
Prater, Andy	Fort Wayne	SD	A	24	1	0	0	0	0.2	6	3	4	4	0	0	0	0	1	0	0	0	0	0	0	.000	0	0	54.00
Prendes, Alex*	Lowell	Bos	A-	23	15	0	0	13	19.2	88	13	7	3	2	0	3	1	15	0	20	1	0	1	2	.333	0	2	1.37
	Augusta	Bos	A	23	8	0	0	4	21	88	22	7	6	3	2	0	1	5	1	14	2	0	1	0	1.000	0	2	2.57
Price, Brett*	Vancouver	Oak	A-	22	20	4	0	3	50	211	32	18	13	2	4	0	3	31	0	59	3	0	7	2	.778	0	0	2.34
Price, Matt	Brewers	Mil	R	23	2	0	0	0	3	14	4	4	4	0	0	0	0	1	0	0	1	0	0	0	.000	0	0	12.00
Price, Ryan	Salem	Col	A+	24	28	21	0	2	103	497	101	93	84	12	4	1	12	85	0	79	45	1	4	11	.267	0	0	7.34
Pridie, Jon	Quad City	Min	A	22	12	11	1	0	55.2	229	40	26	21	5	0	0	8	24	0	48	2	0	6	3	.667	0	0	3.40
	Fort Myers	Min	A+	22	14	9	0	2	57	257	54	31	29	3	2	0	3	37	2	42	6	1	1	3	.250	0	0	4.58
Pruitt, Jason*	Delmarva	Bal	A	21	12	0	0	1	17	76	14	10	10	2	0	1	2	9	0	13	4	0	0	0	.000	0	1	5.29
Puello, Ignacio	Expos	Mon	R	21	8	8	0	0	35	148	28	11	8	0	0	0	7	10	0	37	3	1	1	3	.250	0	0	2.06
	Clinton	Mon	A	21	7	7	0	0	32.1	155	29	21	20	4	1	3	6	26	0	21	4	1	3	3	.500	0	0	5.57
Pugmire, Rob	Mudville	Cin	A+	23	4	4	0	0	17.1	85	25	16	15	4	1	0	0	10	0	19	1	0	0	2	.000	0	0	7.79
Purcell, Brian*	Pirates	Pit	R	21	9	0	0	3	16.1	74	17	10	8	1	0	1	1	6	0	15	2	0	2	0	1.000	0	1	4.41
Pylate, Chad	Twins	Min	R	21	10	3	0	3	18.1	86	18	9	7	0	0	1	2	14	0	12	5	0	1	1	.500	0	0	3.44
Qualls, Chad	Michigan	Hou	A	23	26	26	3	0	162	673	149	77	67	8	2	6	11	31	0	125	10	2	15	6	.714	2	0	3.72
Queen, Mike*	St. Lucie	NYM	A+	24	31	0	0	13	62.1	276	60	32	24	3	5	4	9	23	1	39	1	1	4	3	.571	0	1	3.47
Quick, Ben	Chston-WV	Tor	A	23	17	5	0	0	51	214	51	23	21	6	1	2	4	9	0	39	4	0	3	1	.750	0	0	3.71
Rada, Gerald	Yankees	NYY	R	20	8	1	0	2	16.1	71	20	16	15	4	0	0	0	5	0	21	0	0	0	1	.000	0	0	8.27
Rahrer, Josh	Rangers	Tex	R	21	5	0	0	4	6	29	9	4	2	0	0	2	0	1	0	8	0	0	0	1	.000	0	0	3.00
Ramirez, Carlos*	Brewers	Mil	R	17	11	2	0	0	36.2	158	43	22	19	2	1	0	3	9	0	25	0	1	2	2	.500	0	0	4.66
Ramirez, Enrique	Delmarva	Bal	A	22	45	0	0	17	66	308	76	47	38	4	5	4	1	33	4	66	10	0	6	4	.600	0	1	5.18
	Frederick	Bal	A+	22	7	0	0	6	11.2	43	5	2	2	1	0	0	1	4	0	9	2	0	2	1	.667	0	1	1.54
Ramirez, Hector	Giants	SF	R	22	25	1	0	11	40.1	163	33	13	13	0	3	2	1	12	1	21	2	1	3	2	.600	0	3	2.90
Ramirez, Ismael	Medcine Hat	Tor	R+	21	14	14	0	0	74	319	77	48	44	12	2	2	6	21	0	35	2	1	5	6	.455	0	0	5.35
Ramirez, Jordy	Reds	Cin	R	22	1	0	0	1	0.2	4	2	0	0	0	0	0	0	0	0	0	0	0	0	0	.000	0	0	0.00
Ramirez, Rafael	Giants	SF	R	19	8	8	0	0	33	139	30	15	13	1	3	0	0	15	0	29	2	0	1	0	1.000	0	0	3.55
Ramirez, Santiago	Lexington	Hou	A	21	45	0	0	23	79.1	328	69	35	32	2	4	2	3	28	1	85	8	1	8	2	.800	0	4	3.63
Ramirez, Victor	Charlotte	Tex	A+	21	3	3	0	0	9	51	11	16	11	1	0	1	0	13	0	11	2	0	0	3	.000	0	0	11.00
	Savannah	Tex	A	21	19	16	0	2	88.2	418	93	60	50	12	0	6	15	57	0	94	12	2	5	8	.385	0	0	5.08
Ramos, Eddy	Pulaski	Tex	R+	23	17	0	0	15	31.2	140	39	20	17	4	0	2	0	8	0	30	5	1	2	1	.667	0	3	4.83
Ramos, Juan	San Berndno	Sea	A+	26	39	0	0	10	65	275	45	23	19	1	3	0	6	30	1	57	7	2	4	3	.571	0	2	2.63
Ramos, Luis	Ogden	Mil	R+	24	15	0	0	5	23.1	114	31	26	23	4	0	2	4	7	0	25	1	0	2	3	.400	0	0	8.87
	Beloit	Mil	A	24	2	0	0	2	4	18	4	2	2	0	0	0	0	2	0	8	1	0	0	0	.000	0	1	4.50
Randazzo, Jeff*	Quad City	Min	A	20	20	18	0	0	103.1	440	116	58	53	7	5	4	6	31	1	69	10	1	9	3	.750	0	0	4.62
Ransom, Troy	Salem-Keizr	SF	A-	23	17	0	0	11	19.2	101	31	15	14	4	1	2	3	11	2	13	0	1	0	2	.000	0	0	6.41
Rawson, Anthony*	Johnson Cty	StL	R+	21	23	0	0	20	30	115	19	3	2	0	3	0	2	7	0	45	2	0	3	1	.750	0	10	0.60
	New Jersey	StL	A-	21	3	0	0	3	3	14	3	1	1	0	0	0	0	2	0	3	0	0	0	0	.000	0	0	3.00
Reames, Jay	Expos	Mon	R	27	3	0	0	0	3.2	18	4	2	2	0	0	0	1	2	0	7	2	1	0	0	.000	0	0	4.91
	Jupiter	Mon	A+	27	12	0	0	2	12.1	56	11	5	2	0	2	1	0	8	1	4	1	0	0	0	.000	0	0	1.46
Reed, Rylan	White Sox	CWS	R	20	13	13	0	0	58	277	56	46	20	2	1	6	10	34	0	53	6	3	4	4	.500	0	0	3.10
Reina, Dimas	Dodgers	LA	R	20	25	0	0	20	41.2	167	34	6	6	0	2	0	5	6	0	35	1	0	3	1	.750	0	8	1.30
Rengifo, Nohemar	Expos	Mon	R	19	14	0	0	4	30.2	148	38	30	20	0	3	1	3	13	0	28	4	0	0	2	.000	0	0	5.87
Renteria, Juan	Chston-SC	TB	A	22	39	4	0	14	75.2	311	60	28	19	3	5	2	4	24	4	90	7	0	4	4	.500	0	1	2.26
	Bakersfield	TB	A+	22	1	0	0	1	1.1	4	0	0	0	0	0	0	0	0	0	1	0	0	0	0	.000	0	0	0.00
Reyes, Hipolito	Spokane	KC	A-	21	19	0	0	7	43.1	190	31	26	25	5	1	2	4	27	0	49	2	0	3	5	.375	0	0	5.19
Reyes, Junior*	Boise	ChC	A-	20	13	0	0	6	24.1	110	22	10	9	2	1	3	0	15	1	17	1	1	1	0	1.000	0	1	3.33
Reyes, Luis	Cubs	ChC	R	21	15	0	0	6	26	130	38	21	18	0	2	2	4	15	1	12	3	2	4	1	.800	0	0	6.23
Reyes, Maximo	Phillies	Phi	R	20	17	0	0	13	26	105	16	9	7	2	0	0	2	7	0	33	2	2	1	2	.333	0	2	2.42
Reynolds, Eric*	Staten Ilnd	NYY	A-	22	2	0	0	1	2.2	13	3	2	2	0	0	0	0	2	0	3	0	0	0	0	.000	0	0	6.75
	Yankees	NYY	R	22	11	2	0	4	27.1	126	35	23	21	2	0	2	1	13	0	21	3	0	1	3	.250	0	2	6.91
	Greensboro	NYY	A	22	1	0	0	1	1	4	1	0	0	0	0	0	0	1	0	1	0	0	0	0	.000	0	0	0.00
Reynolds, Josh	St. Lucie	NYM	A+	22	17	11	0	1	60	279	83	39	33	1	4	2	4	20	0	48	0	1	3	6	.333	0	0	4.95
Reynoso, Paulino*	White Sox	CWS	R	21	15	3	0	2	39.1	175	41	27	16	1	0	2	4	13	1	31	5	1	0	2	.000	0	1	3.66
Reynoso, Roberto	Angels	Ana	R	20	14	6	0	2	51.2	244	70	46	31	1	2	2	1	9	0	34	12	2	1	4	.200	0	0	5.40
Rheinecker, John*	Vancouver	Oak	A-	23	6	5	0	0	22.2	86	13	5	4	0	1	0	0	4	0	17	1	0	0	1	.000	0	0	1.59
	Modesto	Oak	A+	23	2	2	0	0	10	45	10	7	7	1	1	0	0	5	1	5	1	0	0	1	.000	0	0	6.30
Rhodes, Shane*	Lowell	Bos	A-	22	15	14	1	0	71.2	302	62	28	23	2	2	2	6	25	0	58	2	0	4	4	.500	0	0	2.89
Ribaudo, Mike	Michigan	Hou	A	27	30	0	0	19	47.2	223	50	26	19	5	2	1	5	30	1	37	5	1	2	2	.500	0	0	3.59
Ricciardi, Joe	Yakima	Ari	A-	22	19	2	0	7	36.1	154	34	21	20	3	0	1	2	9	0	48	1	0	1	3	.250	0	3	4.95
	South Bend	Ari	A	22	20	0	0	7	33	164	43	25	23	3	3	0	7	19	1	28	1	0	5	4	.556	0	0	6.27
Riccobono, Rick	Sarasota	Bos	A+	22	35	6	0	14	79	382	100	62	51	9	3	5	5	38	4	50	2	0	1	3	.250	0	0	5.81
Rice, Scott*	Bluefield	Bal	R+	20	12	12	0	0	63.1	281	58	44	29	4	3	1	7	28	0	53	7	3	4	3	.571	0	0	4.12
Richards, John*	Idaho Falls	SD	R+	23	13	0	0	4	14.2	71	15	9	7	0	0	2	0	13	0	13	3	3	0	0	.000	0	0	4.30
Richardson, Jason	Twins	Min	R	22	4	1	0	0	6.2	29	4	1	1	0	0	0	1	5	0	7	0	0	0	1	.000	0	0	1.35
	Fort Myers	Min	A+	22	8	1	0	3	12.1	53	10	5	3	0	0	3	1	7	0	6	3	0	1	0	1.000	0	0	2.19
Richardson, Judd	Ogden	Mil	R+	22	5	5	0	0	18	76	23	12	10	1	2	1	1	2	0	18	1	1	0	1	.000	0	0	5.00
Ridgway, Jeff*	Chston-SC	TB	A	21	22	22	0	0	104	458	110	55	47	4	2	2	9	42	0	71	11	0	7	8	.467	0	0	4.07

2001 Pitching — Class-A and Rookie Leagues

HOW MUCH HE PITCHED											WHAT HE GAVE UP												THE RESULTS					
Player	Team	Org	Lg	A	G	GS	CG	GF	IP	BFP	H	R	ER	HR	SH	SF	HB	TBB	IBB	SO	WP	Bk	W	L	Pct.	ShO	Sv	ERA
Riethmaier, Matt	Lakewood	Phi	A	23	19	11	2	3	77.2	358	90	53	49	5	1	4	8	38	2	48	4	2	4	4	.500	1	0	5.68
Rigueiro, Rafael	Hagerstown	SF	A	25	26	14	0	4	96	404	77	37	34	8	2	1	12	35	0	104	8	1	5	3	.625	0	0	3.19
Rijo, Fernando	Wilmington	LA	A	24	26	26	0	0	139	562	107	64	46	12	4	5	8	54	0	128	11	1	11	7	.611	0	0	2.98
	Vero Beach	LA	A+	24	2	2	0	0	11	49	7	7	7	2	2	0	0	10	0	11	1	0	0	1	.000	0	0	5.73
Rivard, Reggie	Savannah	Tex	A	24	44	1	0	23	77.1	337	84	35	28	7	1	2	5	21	0	52	8	0	5	4	.556	0	1	3.26
Rivas, Gabriel	Tigers	Det	R	20	18	4	0	3	36.1	172	46	25	24	2	1	1	6	21	0	33	2	2	5	3	.625	0	0	5.94
	Lakeland	Det	A+	20	1	0	0	0	2	6	0	0	0	0	0	0	0	1	0	2	0	0	0	0	.000	0	0	0.00
Rivera, Jimmy	Mariners	Sea	R	22	16	0	0	6	37.1	167	44	21	17	2	2	1	1	17	0	18	3	1	3	1	.750	0	2	4.10
Rleal, Sendy	Delmarva	Bal	A	22	20	20	1	0	103.1	420	79	50	41	9	0	5	7	27	0	83	6	2	3	6	.333	0	0	3.57
Roberson, Brandon	Pittsfield	Hou	A-	24	14	14	0	0	87	354	81	41	36	4	3	2	2	12	0	70	2	1	5	4	.556	0	0	3.72
Roberts, Ralph	Danville	Atl	R+	22	17	0	0	14	20	80	18	6	4	2	1	1	0	4	0	31	2	1	0	1	.000	0	6	1.80
Roberts, Rick*	Wilmington	LA	A	23	7	2	0	1	19.2	78	12	7	6	2	0	0	2	7	0	26	1	0	3	1	.750	0	0	2.75
	Vero Beach	LA	A+	23	29	14	0	8	86	379	70	42	26	6	2	3	7	47	0	92	7	2	4	5	.444	0	4	2.72
Robertson, Nate*	Brevard Cty	Fla	A+	24	19	19	2	0	106.1	445	95	44	34	3	6	2	5	43	1	67	5	1	11	4	.733	0	0	2.88
Robinson, Jeff	High Desert	Mil	A+	25	5	5	0	0	22.2	105	20	16	14	2	0	0	5	15	0	24	0	0	2	1	.667	0	0	5.56
Robinson, Jeremy*	Bakersfield	TB	A+	24	5	0	0	2	7.1	43	12	11	9	0	0	1	0	12	0	3	1	0	0	1	.000	0	0	11.05
Rodarmel, Rich	Visalia	Oak	A+	25	2	0	0	2	2.1	13	3	3	3	0	0	0	0	3	0	3	1	0	0	0	.000	0	1	11.57
Rodaway, Brian*	Pittsfield	Hou	A-	23	17	13	1	2	88.1	346	76	28	23	6	2	0	1	11	0	56	1	1	7	3	.700	0	1	2.34
Rodney, Lee	W Michigan	Det	A	24	27	27	0	0	158	684	149	85	68	14	3	4	7	70	4	149	9	1	8	8	.500	0	0	3.87
Rodriguez, C.	Jupiter	Mon	A+	23	14	0	0	12	13.2	59	11	5	5	0	2	0	0	7	0	19	1	0	1	0	1.000	0	7	3.29
Rodriguez, Enoc*	Reds	Cin	R	21	2	0	0	1	4	17	5	2	2	0	0	0	0	1	0	2	0	0	0	0	.000	0	0	4.50
Rodriguez, F.	Rancho Cuca	Ana	A+	20	20	20	1	0	113.2	523	127	72	68	13	2	1	6	55	1	147	17	4	5	7	.417	1	0	5.38
Rodriguez, George	Clearwater	Phi	A+	22	8	0	0	2	12.1	61	14	14	14	1	0	1	0	13	0	7	3	0	0	2	.000	0	0	10.22
	Lakewood	Phi	A	22	31	2	0	12	56	215	39	12	5	2	2	2	1	16	2	45	1	0	4	3	.571	0	3	0.80
Rodriguez, Jose	Jamestown	Atl	A-	20	12	12	1	0	64	263	55	27	25	4	0	2	6	20	0	30	3	0	5	5	.500	1	0	3.52
Rodriguez, Jose	Eugene	SD	A-	21	9	0	0	5	8.1	49	11	9	8	2	1	0	0	13	0	9	2	2	0	1	.000	0	0	8.64
	Idaho Falls	SD	R+	21	18	0	0	2	21	112	27	23	17	5	0	0	2	21	0	28	4	0	0	1	.000	0	0	7.29
Rodriguez, Juan	Williamsprt	Pit	A-	21	13	13	0	0	81	317	61	23	17	2	1	4	3	15	0	58	3	0	8	2	.800	0	0	1.89
Rodriguez, Kenneth	Brewers	Mil	R	20	8	0	0	4	15.2	67	16	3	2	0	1	0	0	8	1	12	1	0	0	1	.000	0	1	1.15
Rodriguez, Luis	Charlotte	Tex	A+	20	5	5	0	0	19	94	20	17	16	1	0	3	1	20	0	15	4	0	0	3	.000	0	0	7.58
	Savannah	Tex	A	20	16	16	1	0	77.2	327	60	38	32	9	1	3	9	30	0	88	1	0	5	5	.500	0	0	3.71
Rodriguez, Manuel	Athletics	Oak	R	21	17	0	0	5	19.2	92	25	14	9	1	1	0	0	9	0	21	4	0	2	2	.500	0	0	4.12
Rodriguez, Miguel	Red Sox	Bos	R	20	11	7	0	4	55.2	228	52	18	16	2	2	0	1	12	1	53	2	1	3	2	.600	0	0	2.59
Rodriguez, O.*	Great Falls	LA	R+	21	15	10	0	2	60.2	273	58	41	28	11	1	0	4	26	0	79	7	0	3	3	.500	0	1	4.15
Rodriguez, Ricardo	Vero Beach	LA	A+	23	26	26	2	0	154.1	645	133	67	55	13	7	2	3	60	0	154	18	1	14	6	.700	0	0	3.21
Rogers, Brad	Delmarva	Bal	A	20	34	14	0	6	92.1	410	106	63	47	8	2	2	5	36	2	79	5	0	3	7	.300	0	1	4.58
Rogers, Devin	Mahoning Vy	Cle	A-	23	3	3	0	0	10.2	53	10	8	7	1	0	1	4	10	0	7	3	0	0	1	.000	0	0	5.91
	Columbus	Cle	A	23	7	7	0	0	28	135	32	20	16	5	0	0	2	21	0	22	5	1	2	3	.400	0	0	5.14
Rogers, Jed	Lowell	Bos	A-	23	23	0	0	15	40	184	43	21	17	3	1	3	0	26	1	35	1	0	2	2	.500	0	4	3.83
Rogers, Joe*	Johnson Cty	StL	R+	20	15	0	0	2	28	117	22	15	10	3	1	0	4	8	1	46	2	1	1	1	.500	0	1	3.21
Rogers, Jon	Danville	Atl	R+	20	6	0	0	4	8.1	37	5	7	2	1	1	1	1	2	0	11	0	0	0	1	.000	0	1	2.16
Rohlicek, Russel*	Pittsfield	Hou	A-	22	12	9	0	2	42.2	199	32	28	13	0	2	3	3	37	1	33	4	0	4	1	.800	0	1	2.74
Rohling, Stuart	Kannapolis	CWS	A	24	5	0	0	2	4.2	25	6	5	5	1	0	1	0	6	0	5	0	0	0	0	.000	0	0	9.64
Rojas, Chris	Lk Elsinore	SD	A+	25	28	28	0	0	160	681	135	72	61	14	3	2	12	71	0	149	16	2	10	5	.667	0	0	3.43
Rojas, Jose	Wilmington	LA	A	20	24	23	1	0	135.2	540	107	42	32	7	7	2	7	42	0	116	9	0	10	3	.769	0	0	2.12
	Vero Beach	LA	A+	20	1	0	0	1	3	14	3	2	2	0	0	0	1	1	0	3	0	0	0	0	.000	0	0	6.00
Rojas, Ramon	Giants	SF	R	21	27	0	0	6	47	209	45	22	18	3	3	1	6	15	0	28	1	1	3	5	.375	0	0	3.45
Rojas, Yorlan	Johnson Cty	StL	R+	22	19	0	0	5	25	110	23	15	11	3	1	2	2	12	0	25	4	0	2	0	1.000	0	0	3.96
Rollandini, David	Phillies	Phi	R	23	9	8	0	0	39.1	173	37	23	15	0	2	1	5	14	0	38	3	0	0	4	.000	0	0	3.43
Roman, Orlando	Capital Cty	NYM	A	23	4	1	0	2	15.2	77	17	11	10	2	3	0	3	8	0	20	5	0	1	2	.333	0	0	5.74
	Kingsport	NYM	R+	23	4	1	0	2	9	34	4	2	1	0	0	0	1	2	0	13	0	0	1	0	1.000	0	1	1.00
	Brooklyn	NYM	A-	23	9	0	0	3	19.2	83	14	13	11	1	0	0	2	8	0	18	0	0	1	1	.500	0	2	5.03
Romero, Felix	Auburn	Tor	A-	22	26	0	0	20	26	116	27	14	14	2	1	0	2	9	0	35	0	0	2	2	.500	0	12	4.85
Romero, Josmir	Quad City	Min	A	21	30	14	2	5	121.2	531	134	72	60	11	3	7	9	40	1	61	9	4	7	7	.500	0	1	4.44
Romero, Luis	Burlington	Cle	R+	21	16	0	0	11	33	152	37	25	14	3	1	1	6	16	0	24	6	0	2	3	.400	0	3	3.82
Roney, Matt	Asheville	Col	A	22	23	23	1	0	121	540	131	74	67	16	2	5	13	43	0	115	6	1	8	10	.444	0	0	4.98
Rosado, Hector*	Royals	KC	R	21	14	6	1	7	52	222	44	19	10	1	1	1	1	15	2	48	3	0	3	5	.375	0	2	1.73
Rosario, Francisco	Medcine Hat	Tor	R+	21	16	15	0	0	75.2	344	79	61	47	8	1	4	9	38	0	55	6	6	3	7	.300	0	0	5.59
Rosario, Rodrigo	Lexington	Hou	A	22	30	21	1	5	147	584	105	46	35	8	7	2	10	36	1	131	3	0	13	4	.765	0	2	2.14
Rose, Mike	Expos	Mon	R	25	3	3	0	0	7.2	34	9	3	2	0	0	2	1	1	0	5	2	0	0	0	.000	0	0	2.35
Ross, Brian*	Reds	Cin	R	24	2	2	0	0	1.1	14	10	9	9	1	0	0	0	1	0	2	0	0	0	0	.000	0	0	60.75
Rouwenhorst, Jon*	Angels	Ana	R	22	7	0	0	2	8.2	35	2	1	0	0	0	0	1	5	1	14	0	0	1	0	1.000	0	0	0.00
Rowland-Smith, R.*	Mariners	Sea	R	19	17	0	0	10	33.1	128	25	11	11	1	1	0	2	9	1	39	0	0	1	1	.500	0	5	2.97
Royal, Shannon*	Red Sox	Bos	R	24	10	0	0	9	10.2	41	7	4	4	0	1	0	1	3	1	5	1	0	0	1	.000	0	2	3.38
Royce, Ramon	Everett	Sea	A-	22	20	3	0	10	38.1	172	42	27	25	4	1	2	4	15	2	29	4	0	3	5	.375	0	0	5.87
Rudrude, Brett	Lowell	Bos	A-	23	17	7	0	5	73.1	302	65	30	24	1	2	3	4	21	0	44	5	0	5	3	.625	0	1	2.95
Rundles, Rich*	Augusta	Bos	A	21	19	19	0	0	115	468	109	46	31	5	5	5	7	10	0	94	4	0	7	6	.538	0	0	2.43
	Clinton	Mon	A	21	4	4	0	0	27	112	26	10	7	0	0	1	3	3	1	20	1	0	1	1	.500	0	0	2.33
Runser, Greg	Charlotte	Tex	A+	23	50	0	0	47	67.2	289	66	26	22	3	5	3	0	28	4	66	2	0	3	4	.429	0	30	2.93
Rupp, Mike	Winston-Sal	CWS	A+	24	27	3	0	11	53.1	227	56	29	20	3	2	2	2	17	0	45	3	2	2	3	.400	0	0	3.38
Russ, Chris*	Charlotte	Tex	A+	22	13	12	0	0	70	293	67	36	27	5	1	2	4	19	0	56	0	4	5	2	.714	0	0	3.47
Russ, Chris	Staten Ilnd	NYY	A-	23	20	0	0	18	24	91	15	7	5	1	1	0	0	4	0	21	0	0	1	2	.333	0	12	1.88
Russelburg, Aaron	New Jersey	StL	A-	22	5	5	0	0	25.2	101	19	6	4	0	1	1	1	10	0	17	4	0	3	0	1.000	0	0	1.40
	Peoria	StL	A	22	10	10	0	0	51.1	227	53	31	26	3	1	2	2	27	0	31	6	1	4	3	.571	0	0	4.56
Russo, Scott*	Jupiter	Mon	A+	24	5	0	0	1	6	22	3	0	0	0	0	0	0	1	0	8	1	0	0	0	.000	0	0	0.00
	Clinton	Mon	A	24	15	0	0	9	20	88	13	9	4	1	0	2	0	12	0	21	1	0	1	1	.500	0	1	1.80
Rust, Evan	Chston-SC	TB	A	24	35	11	0	20	97	411	88	47	33	3	6	2	6	27	2	88	5	0	7	6	.538	0	12	3.06
Ryan, Jeremy	Pittsfield	Hou	A-	24	2	2	0	0	10	43	8	4	4	1	0	0	1	6	0	12	2	0	1	0	1.000	0	0	3.60
	Michigan	Hou	A	24	15	7	0	1	43	197	47	33	28	9	3	1	7	13	0	39	4	0	0	3	.000	0	0	5.86
Ryu, Jae-kuk	Cubs	ChC	R	19	4	3	0	0	14.2	61	11	2	1	0	0	0	0	5	0	20	2	0	1	0	1.000	0	0	0.61
Saarloos, Kirk	Lexington	Hou	A	23	22	0	0	19	30.2	119	18	5	4	1	2	0	1	7	0	40	2	0	1	1	.500	0	11	1.17
Sabens, Mike	Hickory	Pit	A	25	10	0	0	3	12.1	70	22	16	15	1	0	1	1	10	0	10	2	0	0	1	.000	0	0	10.95
Sabourin, Brian	Mariners	Sea	R	18	1	1	0	0	2	10	5	4	4	0	0	1	0	1	0	1	3	0	0	1	.000	0	0	18.00
Sadowski, Chad	Lakewood	Phi	A	24	35	1	0	15	59	233	48	17	14	4	2	2	2	11	1	41	0	1	4	2	.667	0	2	2.14
Saenz, Chris	Ogden	Mil	R+	20	21	4	0	5	46.2	195	43	25	22	5	4	3	2	14	2	48	1	0	3	1	.750	0	0	4.24

2001 Pitching — Class-A and Rookie Leagues

HOW MUCH HE PITCHED											WHAT HE GAVE UP												THE RESULTS					
Player	Team	Org	Lg	A	G	GS	CG	GF	IP	BFP	H	R	ER	HR	SH	SF	HB	TBB	IBB	SO	WP	Bk	W	L	Pct.	ShO	Sv	ERA
Sala, Marino	Orioles	Bal	R	21	15	0	0	13	18.2	89	21	12	10	0	1	1	1	13	4	10	0	1	1	5	.167	0	6	4.82
Saladin, Miguel	Michigan	Hou	A	24	46	0	0	26	73.2	323	72	27	24	2	2	2	10	24	1	66	3	1	7	3	.700	0	11	2.93
Salazar, Richard*	Orioles	Bal	R	21	1	0	0	0	2	8	2	0	0	0	0	0	0	1	0	2	0	0	0	0	.000	0	0	0.00
	Bluefield	Bal	R+	21	2	0	0	1	4.2	21	5	2	2	0	0	0	2	0	0	7	1	0	1	0	1.000	0	0	3.86
Salmon, Brad	Mudville	Cin	A+	22	33	18	1	8	135.1	587	132	75	61	10	5	3	6	51	0	110	11	0	5	8	.385	0	0	4.06
Samora, Santo	Peoria	StL	A	22	52	0	0	38	62	295	62	50	29	4	0	2	9	27	0	38	6	1	1	7	.125	0	12	4.21
Sampson, Benj*	Fort Myers	Min	A+	27	15	15	0	0	70.1	293	61	30	25	4	0	4	2	31	0	36	2	0	2	3	.400	0	0	3.20
Sams, Aaron*	Lowell	Bos	A-	26	4	0	0	1	10.2	49	14	7	7	1	0	0	0	6	0	7	1	0	2	1	.667	0	0	5.91
	Augusta	Bos	A	26	17	0	0	10	28.2	129	25	10	9	0	0	1	2	18	0	31	5	0	1	1	.500	0	1	2.83
	Sarasota	Bos	A+	26	2	0	0	2	3	13	1	2	0	0	0	0	0	2	0	2	0	0	0	0	.000	0	1	0.00
Sanchez, Cade	Modesto	Oak	A+	25	39	0	0	21	55	260	57	30	24	1	6	3	9	34	9	54	8	0	3	6	.333	0	3	3.93
Sanchez, Elby	Royals	KC	R	19	18	0	0	7	41.2	182	39	26	15	2	2	0	2	17	2	25	4	0	2	3	.400	0	0	3.24
Sanchez, Felix*	Cubs	ChC	R	19	12	9	0	0	60.2	254	57	38	27	2	1	1	2	22	0	55	6	2	2	5	.286	0	0	4.01
	Boise	ChC	A-	19	3	3	0	0	17.1	71	11	4	3	0	0	0	0	10	0	16	0	0	2	0	1.000	0	0	1.56
Sanchez, Jesus	Cubs	ChC	R	—	3	0	0	0	4.2	26	7	3	2	0	0	1	1	3	0	5	1	1	1	0	1.000	0	0	3.86
Sanchez, Juan	Princeton	TB	R+	19	12	12	0	0	45.1	208	50	43	39	6	1	6	4	23	0	47	3	1	2	6	.250	0	0	7.74
Sanchez, Rafael	Red Sox	Bos	R	20	10	8	0	0	50.2	195	36	12	10	3	0	3	5	7	0	45	2	1	5	1	.833	0	0	1.78
Sanchez, Roberto	Royals	KC	R	19	12	9	0	1	30	133	30	18	15	2	0	2	3	12	0	18	0	1	0	1	.000	0	1	4.50
Sander, Richard	Lowell	Bos	A-	21	4	0	0	2	9.2	41	9	3	3	2	0	0	0	3	0	20	3	0	1	0	1.000	0	1	2.79
Sandoval, Marcos	Dunedin	Tor	A+	21	5	1	0	0	7	41	6	10	9	0	1	0	1	12	0	2	3	0	1	0	1.000	0	0	11.57
	Chston-WV	Tor	A	21	21	8	1	6	55.1	252	47	44	42	7	2	2	15	33	0	28	8	0	1	6	.143	0	0	6.83
Santana, Eddy	Yankees	NYY	R	21	7	2	0	1	18.1	73	11	7	7	1	0	0	0	11	0	12	1	0	2	0	1.000	0	0	3.44
Santana, Johan	Angels	Ana	R	18	10	9	1	0	58.2	256	40	27	21	0	2	0	2	35	0	69	8	1	3	2	.600	1	0	3.22
	Provo	Ana	R+	18	4	4	0	0	18.2	93	19	17	16	1	0	2	2	12	1	22	3	1	2	1	.667	0	0	7.71
Santana, Leonardo*	Martinsvlle	Hou	R+	20	19	0	0	16	35	142	23	9	7	0	3	2	3	14	0	44	5	1	3	0	1.000	0	10	1.80
Santillan, Manny	Lexington	Hou	A	22	38	7	0	8	96.2	408	83	43	38	4	5	3	6	43	1	90	7	0	6	5	.545	0	1	3.54
Santos, Alex	Bakersfield	TB	A+	24	24	24	0	0	134.1	603	149	75	62	10	2	5	6	49	0	150	4	1	11	9	.550	0	0	4.15
Santos, Bernaldo	Pittsfield	Hou	A-	23	24	0	0	14	36	158	39	25	14	0	2	1	3	15	1	19	5	1	2	2	.500	0	5	3.50
Sarfate, Dennis	Ogden	Mil	R+	21	9	4	0	1	23.1	100	20	13	12	4	1	0	2	10	0	32	2	0	1	2	.333	0	1	4.63
Sauer, Marc	Kane County	Fla	A	22	9	5	0	0	30	123	30	15	14	2	0	0	5	1	0	13	1	0	2	2	.500	0	0	4.20
Sawyer, Steve	Kane County	Fla	A	23	55	0	0	25	70.2	316	78	39	33	5	3	4	4	27	0	37	10	2	10	2	.833	0	7	4.20
Scarcella, Chris	Vancouver	Oak	A-	23	8	4	0	1	20	104	29	25	19	2	0	1	3	11	0	11	1	0	1	1	.500	0	0	8.55
Schaub, Greg	Beloit	Mil	A	25	25	0	0	6	41.1	190	37	24	17	1	3	2	3	24	2	47	5	1	0	2	.000	0	1	3.70
Schmitt, Eric	Greensboro	NYY	A	23	7	7	0	0	37.1	152	32	15	14	4	0	1	3	9	0	35	1	0	2	1	.667	0	0	3.38
Schneider, Scott	Rancho Cuca	Ana	A+	24	53	0	0	17	78.2	358	81	37	37	4	5	0	5	42	5	79	12	2	4	6	.400	0	3	4.23
Schriner, Brian	Phillies	Phi	R	23	16	0	0	9	25	125	36	21	15	0	3	4	4	10	0	14	3	1	2	0	1.000	0	2	5.40
Schroder, Chris	Vermont	Mon	A-	23	11	0	0	7	12	48	8	2	2	1	0	0	0	5	0	18	0	0	0	0	.000	0	2	1.50
	Jupiter	Mon	A+	23	10	0	0	2	15.2	64	12	5	4	1	0	0	0	4	0	20	4	0	1	0	1.000	0	0	2.30
Schultz, Jeff	Visalia	Oak	A+	26	56	0	0	20	73	328	75	34	28	4	4	1	6	33	5	60	6	2	3	6	.333	0	2	3.45
Schwager, Matt	Frederick	Bal	A+	24	7	3	0	2	27.1	114	28	13	11	2	0	2	2	3	0	30	0	0	0	1	.000	0	1	3.62
	Delmarva	Bal	A	24	27	14	4	8	103.1	411	85	41	26	7	2	3	6	14	1	80	2	0	10	8	.556	1	1	2.26
Sclafani, Anthony	Jamestown	Atl	A-	20	8	0	0	3	21	87	17	7	7	3	2	2	1	7	1	15	2	0	1	2	.333	0	1	3.00
	Macon	Atl	A	20	5	0	0	4	14	55	11	4	3	0	0	0	0	4	0	12	1	0	1	0	1.000	0	1	1.93
	Augusta	Bos	A	20	8	0	0	7	16	73	20	10	10	3	2	0	0	6	0	10	2	0	1	3	.250	0	0	5.63
Scobie, Jason	Brooklyn	NYM	A-	23	18	0	0	16	40.1	149	22	4	4	2	1	1	2	8	0	32	0	0	3	0	1.000	0	7	0.89
Scott, J.K.	Idaho Falls	SD	R+	20	20	0	0	3	16.2	115	29	38	28	6	0	2	2	36	0	10	11	2	0	1	.000	0	0	15.12
Scott, Josh*	Batavia	Phi	A-	22	14	0	0	5	22	92	17	10	8	1	0	1	0	11	0	12	2	0	1	2	.333	0	0	3.27
Scuglik, Mike*	Savannah	Tex	A	25	27	0	0	12	40.1	203	54	45	38	3	2	4	4	27	1	29	8	3	0	1	.000	0	0	8.48
Seabury, Jaron	High Desert	Mil	A+	26	3	0	0	1	6.1	45	18	17	14	2	0	0	0	6	0	5	4	0	0	1	.000	0	0	19.89
Searles, Jon	Williamsprt	Pit	A-	21	14	11	0	0	73	299	63	38	31	8	0	0	1	23	0	65	4	2	5	4	.556	0	0	3.82
Seddon, Chris*	Princeton	TB	R+	18	4	2	0	1	12.1	56	15	7	7	2	0	0	0	6	0	18	0	0	1	2	.333	0	0	5.11
Seibel, Phil*	Jupiter	Mon	A+	23	29	21	0	1	134.1	572	144	70	59	12	5	6	6	28	0	88	5	1	10	7	.588	0	0	3.95
Selmo, Santo	Marlins	Fla	R	19	17	0	0	13	36.1	148	28	16	12	2	1	0	5	7	0	22	6	0	5	2	.714	0	4	2.97
Sequea, Jacobo	Frederick	Bal	A+	20	18	18	0	0	102	426	85	54	45	16	2	2	7	37	1	80	4	1	6	9	.400	0	0	3.97
Serafini, Vince*	Elizabethtn	Min	R+	22	14	9	0	1	52	217	54	24	22	4	5	2	3	8	0	40	2	1	3	3	.500	0	0	3.81
Sergent, Joe*	Brevard Cty	Fla	A+	23	27	25	0	0	143.1	607	154	70	53	11	1	4	5	32	1	89	1	1	12	6	.667	0	0	3.33
Serrano, Alex	Casper	Col	R+	21	12	0	0	10	18	66	10	0	0	0	2	0	1	1	0	23	1	0	2	0	1.000	0	6	0.00
	Asheville	Col	A	21	14	0	0	9	13.2	61	13	4	1	0	0	0	2	5	1	13	0	1	0	0	.000	0	0	0.66
Serrano, Willy	Lakeland	Det	A+	21	50	0	0	14	82.1	366	91	41	29	7	3	5	4	28	4	56	10	0	3	8	.273	0	4	3.17
Severino, Cleris*	Billings	Cin	R+	20	15	13	1	0	67	293	66	37	32	9	4	0	4	30	0	54	3	1	3	3	.500	1	0	4.30
Sexton, Joey	Braves	Atl	R	20	2	0	0	1	2	13	2	0	0	0	1	0	0	2	0	5	0	0	0	0	.000	0	0	0.00
Shabansky, Rob*	Lancaster	Ari	A+	25	29	0	0	9	30.1	150	41	31	25	3	2	0	3	17	0	35	6	0	0	2	.000	0	0	7.42
	Yakima	Ari	A-	25	19	2	0	3	38.2	175	45	24	22	1	3	1	0	18	2	32	3	0	4	1	.800	0	0	5.12
Shafer, Kurt	Pirates	Pit	R	20	12	6	1	3	54	216	54	24	21	2	1	1	5	9	0	41	4	1	3	4	.429	0	1	3.50
	Hickory	Pit	A	20	1	1	0	0	6.1	25	5	1	1	0	0	0	0	3	0	5	1	0	0	0	.000	0	0	1.42
Shaffar, Ben	Daytona	ChC	A+	24	19	19	2	0	106.2	448	83	42	37	3	1	2	6	45	3	118	4	1	6	4	.600	2	0	3.12
	Mudville	Cin	A+	24	6	6	0	0	30.2	130	29	15	12	3	0	1	3	12	0	24	3	0	3	2	.600	0	0	3.52
Sharber, Jeffery	Pirates	Pit	R	20	3	3	0	0	18	61	5	1	1	1	1	0	1	4	0	19	0	0	1	0	1.000	0	0	0.50
	Hickory	Pit	A	20	7	7	0	0	45.1	185	34	13	10	2	1	0	1	19	0	57	4	0	2	2	.500	0	0	1.99
Shaw, Elliott	Princeton	TB	R+	22	6	0	0	0	13.2	63	15	10	9	0	1	0	0	11	0	17	3	0	0	0	.000	0	0	5.93
Sheefel, Adam*	Dayton	Cin	A	24	40	2	0	12	69	313	80	37	31	5	5	3	3	25	4	59	5	1	3	4	.429	0	1	4.04
Sheffield, Aaron	Brewers	Mil	R	20	8	0	0	4	12.2	59	14	12	11	0	1	0	6	7	0	11	2	0	1	1	.500	0	0	7.82
Sheffield, Chris	Dunedin	Tor	A+	22	6	0	0	4	4.1	33	9	11	11	1	0	1	1	11	1	2	4	0	1	0	1.000	0	0	22.85
	Chston-WV	Tor	A	22	6	3	0	0	11.1	60	7	13	13	0	0	1	2	20	0	12	4	0	1	3	.250	0	0	10.32
Shell, Steven	Angels	Ana	R	19	3	0	0	1	4	15	1	0	0	0	0	0	0	2	0	3	0	0	1	0	1.000	0	0	0.00
	Provo	Ana	R+	19	14	4	0	3	37.2	182	52	31	30	3	0	1	9	15	0	33	3	0	0	3	.000	0	1	7.17
Sherman, Chris	Kingsport	NYM	R+	22	14	0	0	5	24.2	116	25	15	9	3	2	0	4	9	1	19	2	0	3	3	.500	0	2	3.28
	Capital Cty	NYM	A	22	2	0	0	0	8.2	36	10	2	2	1	0	0	0	2	0	5	0	0	0	0	.000	0	0	2.08
	Brooklyn	NYM	A-	22	3	0	0	2	9.2	40	10	4	4	1	0	0	0	5	0	6	1	0	0	0	.000	0	1	3.72
Shibilo, Andy	Lk Elsinore	SD	A+	25	60	0	0	30	82.2	343	66	24	18	4	2	2	6	27	1	105	8	2	10	2	.833	0	15	1.96
Shields, Jamie	Hudson Val	TB	A-	20	5	5	0	0	27.1	113	27	8	7	1	1	0	1	5	0	25	1	1	2	1	.667	0	0	2.30
	Chston-SC	TB	A	20	10	10	2	0	71.1	284	63	24	21	7	3	2	2	10	0	60	2	1	4	5	.444	1	0	2.65
Shiyuk, Todd*	Lk Elsinore	SD	A+	25	50	0	0	18	72.1	305	66	35	32	4	4	3	1	28	4	75	5	0	6	3	.667	0	2	3.98
Shorey, Jeremy	Ogden	Mil	R+	21	22	1	0	8	40.2	180	47	32	25	7	1	1	1	16	0	30	7	1	3	2	.600	0	1	5.53
Shortslef, Josh*	Pirates	Pit	R	20	10	4	1	2	34.2	148	39	23	14	1	4	1	1	9	0	14	0	2	2	3	.400	0	0	3.63

2001 Pitching — Class-A and Rookie Leagues

HOW MUCH HE PITCHED											WHAT HE GAVE UP												THE RESULTS					
Player	Team	Org	Lg	A	G	GS	CG	GF	IP	BFP	H	R	ER	HR	SH	SF	HB	TBB	IBB	SO	WP	Bk	W	L	Pct.	ShO	Sv	ERA
Shouse, Dan*	Johnson Cty	StL	R+	23	12	0	0	1	16.1	77	23	15	9	1	1	0	1	5	0	12	0	0	2	2	.500	0	0	4.96
	Peoria	StL	A	23	11	0	0	3	14	61	17	9	8	0	0	0	0	4	0	11	3	0	1	0	1.000	0	0	5.14
Shrout, Kevin	Beloit	Mil	A	24	6	0	0	3	13	63	22	13	12	1	0	0	1	4	0	11	1	0	1	1	.500	0	0	8.31
Shroyer, Dustin*	Pirates	Pit	R	22	5	0	0	2	4.2	32	3	11	9	0	0	1	4	11	0	4	3	0	0	0	.000	0	0	17.36
Shull, Johnathan	Angels	Ana	R	20	17	8	0	2	53.1	244	61	42	29	1	1	1	1	24	0	40	7	0	2	3	.400	0	0	4.89
Shwam, Mike	Beloit	Mil	A	24	47	0	0	24	93.1	382	75	36	27	3	8	0	2	31	3	97	5	1	9	3	.750	0	9	2.60
Sierra, Auvin*	W Michigan	Det	A	24	17	1	0	3	23	105	24	15	13	2	0	1	3	16	0	20	2	0	2	2	.500	0	0	5.09
	Oneonta	Det	A-	24	18	0	0	12	29.2	124	30	10	7	0	0	1	3	8	0	31	2	0	1	2	.333	0	1	2.12
Sierra, Edwardo	Athletics	Oak	R	20	12	6	0	1	44.2	185	45	19	15	1	0	1	3	9	0	41	4	4	2	1	.667	0	1	3.02
Silva, Jesus	Missoula	Ari	R+	19	26	2	0	24	38.1	161	33	12	10	1	0	0	1	8	0	43	1	0	3	0	1.000	0	14	2.35
Silverio, Carlos	Batavia	Phi	A-	23	9	7	0	1	33.2	149	31	19	17	3	0	0	9	12	0	25	5	0	3	2	.600	0	0	4.54
Simmering, Bryan	Athletics	Oak	R	21	13	6	0	3	48.2	186	41	16	13	1	0	1	3	5	0	57	0	0	2	2	.500	0	0	2.40
Simon, Billy	Red Sox	Bos	R	19	3	3	0	0	9	32	6	2	1	0	0	0	2	1	0	7	1	0	0	0	.000	0	0	1.00
Simon, Janewrys	Twins	Min	R	20	13	7	0	0	43.2	200	51	29	23	2	2	2	4	22	1	33	6	1	2	5	.286	0	0	4.74
Simpson, Andre	Wilmington	LA	A	21	24	9	0	6	97.2	386	75	27	25	8	4	1	3	20	0	96	2	0	9	3	.750	0	1	2.30
	Vero Beach	LA	A+	21	5	5	0	0	19.2	99	23	24	19	1	0	2	1	20	1	17	0	0	1	3	.250	0	0	8.69
Simpson, Gerrit	Tri-City	Col	A-	22	8	3	1	1	24.1	93	14	5	3	0	1	0	0	3	0	40	0	0	2	1	.667	0	1	1.11
Simpson, Joe	Casper	Col	R+	23	19	0	0	14	19.2	100	30	19	18	2	0	0	1	12	0	17	5	0	0	1	.000	0	0	8.24
Sinclair, Ernnie	Pittsfield	Hou	A-	22	16	15	0	0	80.1	346	86	46	37	3	0	3	1	29	0	70	7	2	5	4	.556	0	0	4.15
Sisco, Andy*	Cubs	ChC	R	19	10	7	0	0	34.1	152	36	28	20	1	1	0	6	10	0	31	2	1	1	0	1.000	0	0	5.24
Skaggs, Jon	Staten Ilnd	NYY	A-	24	1	1	0	0	4.2	19	4	1	1	1	0	0	0	1	0	4	1	1	0	0	.000	0	0	1.93
Skinner, John	Utica	Fla	A-	25	4	0	0	3	4.2	22	5	3	2	0	0	0	0	1	0	6	1	0	0	0	.000	0	2	3.86
	Kane County	Fla	A	25	25	0	0	5	36	151	36	16	12	1	1	1	1	8	1	26	3	0	1	4	.200	0	0	3.00
Skyles, Matt*	Burlington	Cle	R+	24	6	3	0	0	27	117	35	17	12	4	1	0	1	4	0	15	3	0	0	2	.000	0	0	4.00
	Columbus	Cle	A	24	11	1	0	6	31	135	30	13	10	2	1	1	1	8	1	23	3	1	0	0	.000	0	2	2.90
Slaten, Doug*	Lancaster	Ari	A+	22	28	27	1	0	157.2	723	207	105	84	16	5	5	4	45	3	110	6	5	9	8	.529	0	0	4.79
Sloan, Brandon	Kane County	Fla	A	24	41	13	0	22	107	435	108	48	40	4	4	5	6	26	0	65	2	0	3	4	.429	0	9	3.36
Smalley, Mike*	Myrtle Bch	Atl	A+	23	9	5	0	0	29.2	139	42	25	22	5	2	2	1	10	0	25	0	0	0	6	.000	0	0	6.67
	Macon	Atl	A	23	5	0	0	4	4.1	29	12	10	6	0	1	2	0	2	1	3	0	0	0	0	.000	0	0	12.46
Smart, Pete*	Ogden	Mil	R+	24	4	2	0	1	16.2	70	18	9	7	1	0	1	0	2	0	11	1	0	1	0	1.000	0	0	3.78
	Beloit	Mil	A	24	11	11	0	0	70.1	294	64	30	24	2	4	2	4	24	0	47	5	0	0	8	.000	0	0	3.07
Smart, Richard*	Elizabethtn	Min	R+	22	17	0	0	6	32.2	158	32	22	12	3	1	1	1	25	1	31	1	0	3	0	1.000	0	0	3.31
Smiley, Gerald	Rangers	Tex	R	19	3	0	0	0	5.2	25	4	1	1	0	0	0	1	4	0	2	0	0	0	0	.000	0	0	1.59
Smith, Chris*	Orioles	Bal	R	22	2	0	0	1	2	10	2	2	0	0	0	0	0	1	0	0	0	0	0	0	.000	0	0	0.00
Smith, Cliff	Provo	Ana	R+	22	21	0	0	7	35	151	29	20	13	5	2	0	2	15	1	47	7	0	2	1	.667	0	1	3.34
Smith, Clint	Lakeland	Det	A+	25	20	0	0	2	29.1	140	25	18	15	2	0	1	2	24	0	37	6	0	0	2	.000	0	0	4.60
Smith, Dan	Oneonta	Det	A-	23	20	0	0	6	36	162	27	24	16	0	1	2	5	22	1	27	5	2	1	2	.333	0	0	4.00
Smith, Hans*	Bakersfield	TB	A+	23	31	0	0	23	37.1	165	36	10	6	2	1	2	0	15	1	42	1	0	1	0	1.000	0	17	1.45
Smith, Jared	Pittsfield	Hou	A-	23	8	0	0	2	12	52	4	2	2	0	0	0	2	12	0	22	0	1	1	0	1.000	0	1	1.50
Smith, Jason	Tampa	NYY	A+	20	1	0	0	0	3	12	1	0	0	0	0	0	0	2	1	1	0	0	1	0	1.000	0	0	0.00
	Yankees	NYY	R	20	11	11	2	0	60.2	248	52	25	13	1	2	1	4	11	0	41	2	0	5	2	.714	2	0	1.93
	Greensboro	NYY	A	20	5	4	0	0	22	105	34	19	14	3	3	0	3	7	0	13	0	0	1	2	.333	0	0	5.73
	Staten Ilnd	NYY	A-	20	1	1	0	0	6	25	8	4	3	0	0	1	0	0	0	6	0	0	0	1	.000	0	0	4.50
Smith, Joe	Hagerstown	SF	A	24	24	2	0	9	70	288	64	21	20	1	0	4	3	21	4	45	0	1	7	2	.778	0	0	2.57
	Greensboro	NYY	A	24	11	10	1	0	51.2	237	68	35	30	1	4	3	1	12	0	25	0	0	3	6	.333	1	0	5.23
Smith, Matt	Bristol	CWS	R+	23	4	0	0	3	8	35	4	4	4	0	0	0	2	5	1	6	2	0	1	0	1.000	0	2	4.50
	Kannapolis	CWS	A	23	20	0	0	5	27	133	26	15	15	0	3	1	3	26	3	14	5	0	2	3	.400	0	1	5.00
Smith, Matt*	Greensboro	NYY	A	23	16	16	1	0	97.1	389	69	37	28	1	3	1	3	32	0	116	8	0	5	3	.625	1	0	2.59
	Tampa	NYY	A+	23	11	11	0	0	68.1	276	54	21	17	2	1	1	1	22	0	71	4	4	6	2	.750	0	0	2.24
Smith, Toebius	Jamestown	Atl	A-	22	14	0	0	3	27.2	112	27	13	12	1	0	0	0	6	1	24	2	0	4	0	1.000	0	0	3.90
Snare, Ryan*	Dayton	Cin	A	23	21	20	0	0	115	472	101	45	39	7	1	1	9	37	1	118	9	2	9	5	.643	0	0	3.05
Sneed, John	Fort Myers	Min	A+	26	25	19	0	3	114	480	95	51	41	5	1	1	4	49	0	88	5	0	8	3	.727	0	0	3.24
Sobscuk, Justin	Vancouver	Oak	A-	21	17	2	0	5	27.1	132	35	25	21	3	2	0	2	15	1	30	5	0	2	2	.500	0	0	6.91
Sokoll, Adam	Danville	Atl	R+	22	22	0	0	8	29	131	21	28	20	2	0	0	5	19	0	19	5	0	2	3	.400	0	0	6.21
Solano, Alex	Sarasota	Bos	A+	22	39	2	0	11	90.1	413	113	71	48	5	2	5	2	32	1	61	1	0	2	9	.182	0	1	4.78
Song, Seung	Augusta	Bos	A	22	14	14	0	0	75	290	56	24	17	3	0	1	2	18	0	79	4	0	3	2	.600	0	0	2.04
	Sarasota	Bos	A+	22	8	8	0	0	48.1	190	28	11	9	1	0	0	0	18	0	56	1	1	5	2	.714	0	0	1.68
Songster, Judson	Tri-City	Col	A-	22	17	0	0	6	22.2	88	15	6	5	0	0	1	0	5	0	32	2	1	2	1	.667	0	1	1.99
Sosa, Jorge	Everett	Sea	A-	24	21	7	0	11	58.2	247	45	22	11	2	2	3	2	19	0	57	8	1	3	1	.750	0	7	1.69
	Wisconsin	Sea	A	24	2	0	0	0	2	9	3	2	2	1	0	0	0	0	0	4	0	0	0	0	.000	0	0	9.00
Soto, Darwin	Eugene	SD	A-	20	30	1	0	7	42.2	179	35	23	18	1	2	1	1	15	0	39	3	0	4	5	.444	0	0	3.80
Spaulding, Richard*	Burlington	Cle	R+	21	14	0	0	9	16.2	87	19	16	13	1	0	3	3	15	0	9	2	0	0	0	.000	0	0	7.02
Spear, Russ	Lakeland	Det	A+	24	8	0	0	1	12.1	58	5	8	7	2	0	1	5	13	0	18	4	0	1	1	.500	0	0	5.11
Speier, Ryan	Casper	Col	R+	22	17	0	0	8	25.2	109	19	12	9	2	1	0	2	9	4	24	2	0	1	2	.333	0	1	3.16
Sperring, Jayme	Delmarva	Bal	A	23	53	0	0	46	63.2	268	50	25	21	6	3	0	3	30	3	75	5	1	2	4	.333	0	26	2.97
Spillers, Larry*	Orioles	Bal	R	20	10	10	0	0	51.2	226	53	25	23	3	4	2	5	19	1	13	3	2	3	3	.500	0	0	4.01
Spillman, Jeromie*	Medcine Hat	Tor	R+	23	28	0	0	10	39.1	183	41	23	18	5	0	1	1	18	0	42	6	0	0	3	.000	0	1	4.12
	Chston-WV	Tor	A	23	20	0	0	10	27.1	141	49	29	23	4	3	2	4	6	0	22	3	0	1	2	.333	0	0	7.57
Squires, Matt*	Phillies	Phi	R	23	17	0	0	5	29.2	117	16	5	4	0	5	1	3	11	0	33	2	0	0	2	.000	0	0	1.21
	Clearwater	Phi	A+	23	4	0	0	3	5.1	28	5	4	4	1	0	0	0	7	0	8	1	0	0	1	.000	0	0	6.75
Stafford, Mike*	Tampa	NYY	A+	27	4	0	0	2	2.1	15	8	2	2	0	0	0	0	1	0	4	0	0	0	1	.000	0	0	7.71
	High Desert	Mil	A+	27	24	0	0	6	20.2	88	20	10	10	2	0	0	0	6	0	17	0	0	1	1	.500	0	0	4.35
Stahl, Rich*	Delmarva	Bal	A	21	6	6	0	0	33.2	135	24	15	10	3	1	0	2	15	0	31	3	0	2	3	.400	0	0	2.67
	Frederick	Bal	A+	21	6	6	1	0	32.1	134	26	13	7	1	3	2	2	15	0	24	3	1	1	1	.500	1	0	1.95
	Orioles	Bal	R	21	1	1	0	0	2	7	1	0	0	0	0	0	0	1	0	1	0	0	0	0	.000	0	0	0.00
Stamler, Keith	Savannah	Tex	A	22	7	1	0	1	16.2	70	13	7	4	0	0	1	2	3	0	16	0	0	2	1	.667	0	0	2.16
	Charlotte	Tex	A+	22	23	11	1	2	87	351	64	35	24	3	3	2	7	28	2	61	4	0	8	4	.667	0	0	2.48
Stanford, Derek	Michigan	Hou	A	23	5	5	0	0	23	108	24	11	7	2	0	1	4	17	0	14	3	0	1	2	.333	0	0	2.74
	Lexington	Hou	A	23	3	3	0	0	11.2	48	9	9	9	2	1	0	1	7	0	5	0	0	0	2	.000	0	0	6.94
Stanton, Tim*	Tampa	NYY	A+	25	26	0	0	11	47.2	192	46	15	10	2	0	1	0	13	2	39	1	1	1	0	1.000	0	1	1.89
Staveland, Toby	Jamestown	Atl	A-	22	15	11	0	0	54.1	240	62	33	25	2	1	1	3	21	0	42	7	0	3	2	.600	0	0	4.14
Stavros, Tony	Brewers	Mil	R	21	5	0	0	3	14.2	57	13	2	1	0	2	0	0	3	1	11	0	0	0	1	.000	0	0	0.61
Steele, Mike	W Michigan	Det	A	23	38	0	0	36	46.2	194	23	13	6	2	0	0	4	26	4	78	2	0	4	3	.571	0	19	1.16
	Lakeland	Det	A+	23	15	0	0	13	18.2	83	17	12	8	0	2	1	4	7	1	10	0	0	0	1	.000	0	4	3.86
Stefani, Jason*	Great Falls	LA	R+	23	19	2	0	2	39.1	187	48	30	22	2	1	3	2	19	2	35	7	1	3	1	.750	0	1	5.03

2001 Pitching — Class-A and Rookie Leagues

HOW MUCH HE PITCHED											WHAT HE GAVE UP												THE RESULTS					
Player	Team	Org	Lg	A	G	GS	CG	GF	IP	BFP	H	R	ER	HR	SH	SF	HB	TBB	IBB	SO	WP	Bk	W	L	Pct.	ShO	Sv	ERA
Steffek, Brian	Great Falls	LA	R+	24	8	3	0	2	21	103	28	18	18	2	0	2	4	11	1	19	1	1	0	2	.000	0	1	7.71
	Wilmington	LA	A	24	9	1	0	5	23.1	87	12	5	5	2	3	0	0	8	4	22	1	0	0	1	.000	0	2	1.93
Steitz, Jon	Ogden	Mil	R+	21	11	10	0	0	33.2	169	44	32	25	1	0	0	4	25	0	28	13	6	2	4	.333	0	0	6.68
Stephenson, Eric*	Auburn	Tor	A-	19	15	14	0	0	78	344	80	45	35	7	2	1	3	44	0	62	5	1	3	6	.333	0	0	4.04
Stepka, Tom	Asheville	Col	A	26	2	0	0	0	5.2	24	5	4	2	0	0	0	0	1	0	4	0	0	0	0	.000	0	0	3.18
	Salem	Col	A+	26	32	2	0	13	67.2	299	72	36	28	5	4	2	1	25	1	42	2	0	2	2	.500	0	2	3.72
Sterrett, Adam	Marlins	Fla	R	19	1	0	0	0	1	7	1	1	1	0	0	1	0	3	0	0	0	0	0	0	.000	0	0	9.00
Stevens, Josh	Greensboro	NYY	A	23	19	2	0	3	36.2	145	29	12	12	3	0	0	2	9	0	42	0	0	1	0	1.000	0	0	2.95
Stevens, Kris*	Expos	Mon	R	24	4	4	0	0	11.1	45	7	0	0	0	0	0	0	5	0	7	2	0	1	0	1.000	0	0	0.00
Stevenson, Jason*	Vermont	Mon	A-	20	25	1	0	10	41.2	184	49	31	27	3	2	2	1	17	1	33	1	1	6	3	.667	0	0	5.83
Steward, Edward	Angels	Ana	R	23	19	4	1	5	49	205	47	19	11	1	1	0	2	11	1	40	1	0	5	3	.625	1	1	2.02
	Provo	Ana	R+	23	1	0	0	0	6.2	29	7	4	4	1	0	0	1	1	0	9	0	0	1	0	1.000	0	0	5.40
Stewart, James	Dodgers	LA	R	20	11	1	0	2	23.1	93	19	9	8	2	0	0	1	4	0	14	0	0	1	1	.500	0	0	3.09
Stewart, Paul	High Desert	Mil	A+	23	28	27	0	1	151.2	693	169	106	87	23	3	8	15	64	1	127	12	0	9	8	.529	0	0	5.16
Stiehl, Rob	Lexington	Hou	A	21	14	12	0	0	50	207	28	17	11	2	0	0	2	34	0	59	5	2	2	3	.400	0	0	1.98
Stiles, Brad*	Burlington	KC	A	21	30	6	0	7	60.2	290	81	45	34	3	2	6	1	33	1	49	5	3	5	5	.500	0	0	5.04
	Wilmington	KC	A+	21	1	0	0	0	0.2	5	1	0	0	0	0	0	1	1	0	2	1	0	0	0	.000	0	0	0.00
Stockman, Landon	Oneonta	Det	A-	22	11	0	0	11	10.2	44	9	4	3	0	0	0	1	1	0	7	0	0	0	1	.000	0	6	2.53
	W Michigan	Det	A	22	18	0	0	15	26	112	21	7	7	0	1	0	2	13	3	23	3	0	2	2	.500	0	6	2.42
Stockman, Phil	Lancaster	Ari	A+	22	8	0	0	1	17.2	70	11	11	10	2	1	4	1	9	0	18	1	0	0	0	.000	0	0	5.09
	Yakima	Ari	A-	22	15	14	0	0	76	329	81	39	36	5	3	1	5	22	0	48	5	0	3	4	.429	0	0	4.26
Stodolka, Mike*	Burlington	KC	A	20	20	20	0	0	94.1	420	105	67	49	9	5	5	7	30	0	49	6	0	3	8	.273	0	0	4.67
Stokes, Brian	Bakersfield	TB	A+	22	32	20	1	5	128.2	565	118	65	56	11	4	5	8	64	0	92	9	0	8	6	.571	0	1	3.92
Stokes, Shaun	Peoria	StL	A	23	13	13	0	0	58	278	87	57	46	8	1	4	2	22	0	42	1	0	2	7	.222	0	0	7.14
Stokley, Billy	Cedar Rapds	Ana	A	25	22	0	0	7	41	173	31	14	9	1	0	0	3	18	2	45	6	1	5	3	.625	0	1	1.98
	Rancho Cuca	Ana	A+	25	27	0	0	24	28	126	27	15	13	2	0	0	1	18	3	24	2	0	0	2	.000	0	10	4.18
Story, Aaron*	Williamsprt	Pit	A-	21	3	0	0	0	4	21	7	4	4	0	1	0	0	3	0	5	0	0	0	0	.000	0	0	9.00
Strayhorn, Kole	Great Falls	LA	R+	19	2	0	0	0	2.1	13	4	4	4	1	0	0	1	1	0	1	0	1	0	0	.000	0	0	15.43
	Dodgers	LA	R	19	12	6	0	2	53.1	214	41	15	13	1	2	0	5	17	0	47	1	1	5	3	.625	0	0	2.19
Strelitz, Brian	Staten Ilnd	NYY	A-	22	24	0	0	7	37.2	171	37	23	14	3	3	3	6	14	0	21	3	0	3	3	.500	0	1	3.35
Stumm, Jason	White Sox	CWS	R	21	4	4	0	0	12	45	6	4	3	0	0	0	1	5	0	12	0	1	0	2	.000	0	0	2.25
Sturkie, Scott	Mahoning Vy	Cle	A-	23	18	4	0	4	39	177	53	27	26	4	0	0	3	12	0	28	2	1	2	1	.667	0	1	6.00
Suarez, Pedro	Red Sox	Bos	R	18	8	0	0	2	14.1	74	17	9	9	1	0	2	1	13	1	14	1	0	0	0	.000	0	1	5.65
Sundbeck, Cody	Yakima	Ari	A-	24	4	0	0	1	6	29	7	2	2	0	1	0	0	4	0	3	0	0	0	0	.000	0	0	3.00
	South Bend	Ari	A	24	11	0	0	3	14.1	62	8	6	6	1	0	0	2	10	2	16	2	0	0	1	.000	0	0	3.77
Surkont, Keith	Modesto	Oak	A+	25	24	24	0	0	123.2	564	152	90	73	7	3	7	1	42	0	93	8	0	8	9	.471	0	0	5.31
Suttles, Donnie	Columbus	Cle	A	25	21	0	0	5	43.2	180	36	19	17	2	2	1	6	15	0	29	4	0	4	0	1.000	0	4	3.50
Sutton, Kris	Provo	Ana	R+	23	23	0	0	15	25	130	43	20	11	0	1	1	1	8	2	20	4	0	2	1	.667	0	4	3.96
Swanson, Erick*	Everett	Sea	A-	23	14	0	0	3	19.1	90	21	10	10	0	0	1	2	9	0	15	2	0	1	0	1.000	0	1	4.66
Sweeney, James*	Kannapolis	CWS	A	22	21	16	0	1	102	406	83	35	30	4	4	4	4	37	3	110	2	0	8	4	.667	0	0	2.65
Sweeney, Matt	Phillies	Phi	R	19	9	5	0	3	29.1	127	28	12	11	3	1	2	3	16	0	16	2	1	2	2	.500	0	0	3.38
Swindell, Jeremy*	W Michigan	Det	A	24	4	0	0	0	1.2	12	1	3	3	0	0	0	0	6	0	1	0	0	0	0	.000	0	0	16.20
Switzer, Jon*	Hudson Val	TB	A-	22	5	0	0	2	14.1	57	9	3	1	0	1	0	2	2	0	20	2	0	2	0	1.000	0	0	0.63
Szado, Craig*	Bristol	CWS	R+	23	15	8	0	6	56	230	52	23	19	3	2	3	1	12	0	56	1	0	2	3	.400	0	1	3.05
Szuminski, Jason	Lansing	ChC	A	23	14	4	0	2	36.1	177	56	27	26	2	1	1	2	17	0	22	2	0	4	3	.571	0	0	6.44
Tacker, Trevor	Staten Ilnd	NYY	A-	21	3	0	0	0	10	46	8	7	7	1	0	0	3	4	0	8	2	0	0	0	.000	0	0	6.30
	Yankees	NYY	R	21	9	4	1	0	30.1	136	35	19	16	3	1	1	1	11	1	16	1	0	1	3	.250	0	0	4.75
Talanoa, Charles	Medcine Hat	Tor	R+	21	15	15	0	0	55	268	65	53	35	3	2	1	6	33	1	30	8	4	1	8	.111	0	0	5.73
Tallet, Brian*	Kinston	Cle	A+	24	27	27	2	0	160	644	134	62	54	12	3	2	4	38	0	164	2	0	9	7	.563	0	0	3.04
Tamayo, Ignacio	Spokane	KC	A-	23	14	14	1	0	67.1	276	60	39	34	7	1	1	2	16	0	64	3	0	3	3	.500	0	0	4.54
Tarkington, Shawn	Twins	Min	R	22	13	0	0	5	21	88	25	8	7	0	0	0	2	1	0	25	2	0	1	0	1.000	0	1	3.00
	Elizabethtn	Min	R+	22	6	0	0	3	8	41	17	10	10	1	0	0	0	3	0	7	0	0	0	0	.000	0	0	11.25
Taschner, Jack*	San Jose	SF	A+	24	14	14	0	0	65.2	292	62	33	30	7	1	3	5	29	0	72	8	2	4	4	.500	0	0	4.11
Tate, Matt	Delmarva	Bal	A	21	13	3	0	3	36.2	166	33	29	25	4	2	2	3	21	1	25	1	0	2	3	.400	0	0	6.14
	Bluefield	Bal	R+	21	12	12	0	0	62	284	80	37	34	7	2	1	9	18	0	64	4	3	5	5	.500	0	0	4.94
Taulli, Sam*	Missoula	Ari	R+	22	15	0	0	2	18.2	93	26	16	13	0	1	1	0	12	0	18	1	0	1	1	.500	0	0	6.27
Taylor, Aaron	Wisconsin	Sea	A	24	28	0	0	26	29.1	119	19	9	8	1	2	1	2	11	2	50	4	2	3	1	.750	0	9	2.45
Taylor, David	Dodgers	LA	R	19	3	3	0	0	6	24	5	3	2	0	0	1	1	0	0	6	4	0	0	1	.000	0	0	3.00
Taylor, John	Medcine Hat	Tor	R+	24	6	0	0	5	11.1	55	15	11	6	1	0	0	1	4	0	8	0	0	0	0	.000	0	0	4.76
	Auburn	Tor	A-	24	12	0	0	5	29.2	132	32	16	14	0	2	1	4	9	0	23	2	0	1	2	.333	0	0	4.25
Teekel, Josh	New Jersey	StL	A-	21	15	0	0	6	36	143	23	7	7	1	0	0	5	15	0	31	1	1	1	0	1.000	0	3	1.75
Tejada, Frailyn*	Marlins	Fla	R	19	10	8	0	0	52.1	210	47	19	15	2	0	1	4	7	0	54	0	0	6	1	.857	0	0	2.58
	Brevard Cty	Fla	A+	19	2	1	0	0	5.2	30	13	8	4	0	2	0	0	1	0	4	0	0	0	2	.000	0	0	6.35
Tejada, Sandy	Quad City	Min	A	20	4	2	0	0	10	47	7	8	5	1	1	0	1	9	0	13	1	0	0	1	.000	0	0	4.50
	Elizabethtn	Min	R+	20	11	10	0	0	56.1	233	43	26	20	6	1	2	4	20	0	87	4	1	5	3	.625	0	0	3.20
Tejeda, Frank	Potomac	StL	A+	22	25	25	2	0	136	574	152	76	67	14	3	3	7	19	0	70	2	2	6	14	.300	0	0	4.43
Tejeda, Rob	Lakewood	Phi	A	20	26	24	1	0	150.2	639	128	74	57	10	6	5	8	58	1	152	11	2	8	9	.471	1	0	3.40
Templet, Eric	Kingsport	NYM	R+	23	12	2	0	2	20.2	96	30	14	12	0	0	0	0	4	0	27	1	0	1	2	.333	0	0	5.23
	Capital Cty	NYM	A	23	2	0	0	1	6	26	8	7	6	2	0	1	0	1	0	9	0	0	0	2	.000	0	0	9.00
Tetz, Kris	Jupiter	Mon	A+	23	2	0	0	1	3	12	1	1	1	0	0	0	1	1	0	3	0	0	0	0	.000	0	0	3.00
	Columbus	Cle	A	23	1	0	0	0	2	6	0	0	0	0	0	0	0	1	0	3	0	0	0	0	.000	0	0	0.00
Thames, Charlie	Rancho Cuca	Ana	A+	23	29	0	0	26	29.2	118	21	9	5	1	1	0	0	9	1	26	2	0	4	2	.667	0	13	1.52
Therneau, Dave	Reds	Cin	R	26	5	5	0	0	30	113	26	12	8	0	1	0	0	0	0	35	0	0	2	2	.500	0	0	2.40
	Mudville	Cin	A+	26	10	9	0	0	46	213	64	39	31	5	1	1	0	11	0	41	0	0	1	5	.167	0	0	6.07
Thigpen, Josh	Red Sox	Bos	R	20	10	6	0	2	39.1	150	20	15	11	1	0	4	1	14	0	44	4	0	4	2	.667	0	1	2.52
Thomas, Adam	Cedar Rapds	Ana	A	23	19	16	2	0	96.1	409	109	63	55	13	1	1	6	23	0	61	4	0	4	7	.364	1	0	5.14
Thomas, Jeb	Spokane	KC	A-	23	15	2	0	6	39.1	172	36	18	13	3	0	1	3	15	0	33	7	0	2	0	1.000	0	3	2.97
Thomas, John*	Hagerstown	SF	A	20	15	15	0	0	71.1	302	70	40	33	5	1	3	6	22	0	65	3	2	3	3	.500	0	0	4.16
Thomas, Matt	Johnson Cty	StL	R+	23	20	0	0	8	25	107	23	17	13	4	3	0	0	7	0	22	1	0	4	2	.667	0	0	4.68
Thomas, Scott	Burlington	Cle	R+	22	9	0	0	3	9.2	52	7	8	7	2	2	0	1	12	1	10	2	0	0	0	.000	0	0	6.52
Thomas, Stephen	Utica	Fla	A-	24	24	0	0	12	40.2	175	48	23	18	3	3	3	2	9	0	26	1	0	1	2	.333	0	3	3.98
Thompson, Derek*	Columbus	Cle	A	21	2	2	0	0	12	54	16	13	13	2	0	1	0	3	0	5	1	0	0	2	.000	0	0	9.75
Thompson, Matt	Augusta	Bos	A	20	25	24	0	1	134.1	535	115	58	48	9	1	5	6	19	0	97	6	0	9	10	.474	0	0	3.22
Thompson, Mike	Fort Wayne	SD	A	21	1	1	0	0	6	28	8	4	4	0	0	0	0	2	0	1	0	0	0	1	.000	0	0	6.00
	Lk Elsinore	SD	A+	21	19	12	0	1	74	318	82	46	44	7	5	2	3	25	0	39	5	2	5	4	.556	0	0	5.35

2001 Pitching — Class-A and Rookie Leagues

HOW MUCH HE PITCHED											WHAT HE GAVE UP												THE RESULTS					
Player	Team	Org	Lg	A	G	GS	CG	GF	IP	BFP	H	R	ER	HR	SH	SF	HB	TBB	IBB	SO	WP	Bk	W	L	Pct.	ShO	Sv	ERA
Thompson, Tyson	Princeton	TB	R+	22	3	1	0	0	5.2	29	9	7	2	0	0	0	0	2	0	6	1	0	0	1	.000	0	0	3.18
	Hudson Val	TB	A-	22	12	0	0	7	20	108	21	18	15	1	0	0	4	21	0	15	12	0	0	1	.000	0	1	6.75
Thoms, Hank	Columbus	Cle	A	26	19	1	0	8	45.1	194	40	20	15	3	5	0	1	15	1	51	2	0	3	1	.750	0	1	2.98
	Kinston	Cle	A+	26	14	14	1	0	79.2	321	70	26	20	2	1	1	3	20	0	74	3	0	7	2	.778	0	0	2.26
Thornton, Matt*	San Berndno	Sea	A+	25	27	27	0	0	157	650	126	56	44	9	2	5	11	60	0	192	12	0	14	7	.667	0	0	2.52
Thorpe, Tracy	Chston-WV	Tor	A	21	24	23	0	0	102.2	472	108	77	58	8	6	6	10	51	0	81	11	1	4	13	.235	0	0	5.08
Threets, Erick*	San Jose	SF	A+	20	14	14	0	0	59.1	270	49	34	28	2	1	3	7	40	0	60	14	3	0	10	.000	0	0	4.25
	Hagerstown	SF	A	20	12	0	0	3	24	94	13	3	2	1	0	0	1	9	0	32	2	1	2	0	1.000	0	1	0.75
Tibbs, Jeff	Great Falls	LA	R+	20	15	7	0	0	41.1	217	62	57	46	2	2	3	3	30	0	25	10	0	2	5	.286	0	0	10.02
Tierney, Chris*	Royals	KC	R	18	8	3	0	1	21.2	109	31	19	16	1	0	1	4	8	1	21	0	0	0	2	.000	0	0	6.65
Tiller, James	Orioles	Bal	R	19	16	1	0	6	36.2	160	30	18	15	3	1	2	5	15	1	44	4	0	0	3	.000	0	0	3.68
Tillery, Josh	Jamestown	Atl	A-	23	21	1	0	5	38.2	162	43	14	10	2	1	1	0	12	1	39	2	1	2	0	1.000	0	2	2.33
Tingley, Pat*	Twins	Min	R	21	15	0	0	7	21.1	101	35	22	21	5	0	0	0	8	0	18	2	1	4	1	.800	0	1	8.86
Tisdale, Marlyn	Billings	Cin	R+	24	14	14	1	0	82.2	336	88	31	28	1	2	2	6	13	0	76	8	0	7	4	.636	1	0	3.05
Tomaszewski, Eliot	Delmarva	Bal	A	22	18	4	0	4	40.2	187	59	25	20	3	1	3	1	7	0	32	3	0	1	3	.250	0	2	4.43
Torres, Carlos	Reds	Cin	R	21	11	4	0	4	39.1	164	27	13	13	0	2	2	5	18	0	29	1	0	5	1	.833	0	0	2.97
Torres, Joe*	Cedar Rapds	Ana	A	19	4	4	0	0	17	80	16	12	11	0	1	1	2	14	0	14	4	0	0	3	.000	0	0	5.82
	Provo	Ana	R+	19	9	8	0	0	31.1	145	32	20	14	2	1	1	5	15	0	39	5	0	2	2	.500	0	0	4.02
Torres, Luis	Pirates	Pit	R	22	3	1	0	0	3	14	3	3	1	0	0	0	0	1	0	2	2	0	0	0	.000	0	0	3.00
	Lynchburg	Pit	A+	22	4	0	0	0	3.1	19	6	7	5	1	0	0	0	3	0	4	4	0	0	0	.000	0	0	13.50
Torres, Luis	Clinton	Mon	A	21	18	18	0	0	104.1	461	116	76	60	10	1	7	5	42	0	56	9	0	6	8	.429	0	0	5.18
Torres, Melqui	San Berndno	Sea	A+	25	26	26	0	0	154	666	159	79	71	4	10	4	23	56	0	113	8	1	7	7	.500	0	0	4.15
Totten, Heath	Dodgers	LA	R	23	2	2	0	0	11	37	5	1	1	0	0	0	0	0	0	8	0	0	1	0	1.000	0	0	0.82
	Vero Beach	LA	A+	23	9	9	2	0	49.2	218	64	40	39	9	1	3	1	10	0	25	1	1	0	8	.000	0	0	7.07
Tranchina, Scott	Daytona	ChC	A+	25	42	8	0	17	92.2	404	91	50	37	8	2	3	4	42	1	89	6	0	11	8	.579	0	1	3.59
Trejo, Francisco*	Lancaster	Ari	A+	22	5	0	0	1	9	43	14	4	4	0	0	1	0	4	0	7	0	0	0	0	.000	0	0	4.00
	Yakima	Ari	A-	22	13	6	0	5	39.2	193	61	38	26	4	1	2	0	17	0	23	8	0	2	2	.500	0	1	5.90
Tremblay, Max*	Lexington	Hou	A	26	48	0	0	27	67.1	308	74	37	31	9	4	3	3	29	2	84	7	0	6	4	.600	0	4	4.14
Trevino, Chris*	Jamestown	Atl	A-	21	15	6	0	3	43	186	44	27	18	3	2	2	0	11	0	43	0	0	1	4	.200	0	0	3.77
Tricoglou, Jamie	Tri-City	Col	A-	22	24	0	0	14	28.2	130	19	11	9	1	2	2	5	20	4	29	3	0	1	1	.500	0	2	2.83
Troilo, Joe	Augusta	Bos	A	24	30	2	0	18	58.1	252	49	33	23	5	1	5	4	21	1	40	6	0	4	3	.571	0	1	3.55
Trosper, Tanner	Vancouver	Oak	A-	24	18	2	0	6	44.1	185	26	16	15	2	2	0	3	18	0	47	8	0	4	2	.667	0	2	3.05
	Modesto	Oak	A+	24	2	0	0	1	2	12	5	6	4	1	0	0	0	1	0	3	0	0	0	0	.000	0	0	18.00
Truitt, Derrick	Myrtle Bch	Atl	A+	24	16	0	0	3	24.2	117	37	24	23	3	1	0	2	10	0	25	1	0	2	2	.500	0	0	8.39
Truselo, Randy	Rangers	Tex	R	21	7	5	0	0	34	147	30	10	2	0	1	2	4	15	0	21	1	0	0	3	.000	0	0	0.53
	Pulaski	Tex	R+	21	4	4	0	0	18	91	27	24	16	3	0	0	1	7	0	16	1	0	1	2	.333	0	0	8.00
Trytten, Ryan	Brewers	Mil	R	21	18	0	0	16	25	113	23	12	11	1	1	1	2	11	2	21	1	0	2	0	1.000	0	6	3.96
Tsao, Chin-Hui	Salem	Col	A+	21	4	4	0	0	17.1	78	23	11	9	1	2	1	1	5	0	18	1	1	0	4	.000	0	0	4.67
Tucker, Rusty*	Idaho Falls	SD	R+	21	30	0	0	7	35.1	195	41	41	28	4	3	1	3	50	1	43	14	0	0	2	.000	0	0	7.13
Turner, Brad	Johnson Cty	StL	R+	24	15	0	0	3	25.2	111	18	14	8	2	1	1	1	15	0	37	3	0	0	1	.000	0	0	2.81
Turuda, Miyoki	Great Falls	LA	R+	23	17	0	0	8	28.2	135	25	16	10	2	1	0	3	18	0	32	9	0	2	1	.667	0	2	3.14
Tyler, Scott	Twins	Min	R	19	5	3	0	0	10.2	46	11	8	8	0	0	0	1	2	0	14	2	0	0	1	.000	0	0	6.75
Ungs, Nick	Utica	Fla	A-	22	12	11	0	0	61	236	57	14	11	3	1	2	0	0	0	40	1	1	3	1	.750	0	0	1.62
Urdaneta, Lino	Wilmington	LA	A	22	10	4	0	3	23.2	110	31	23	20	7	0	2	3	11	0	16	2	0	1	2	.333	0	0	7.61
Uzzell, Todd	Salem-Keizr	SF	A-	24	6	2	0	1	14.1	70	19	13	13	1	0	0	3	9	0	6	0	0	2	2	.500	0	0	8.16
	San Jose	SF	A+	24	15	0	0	7	33	148	30	18	16	1	2	1	4	18	0	25	2	0	1	1	.500	0	0	4.36
	Hagerstown	SF	A	24	1	1	0	0	5	20	5	2	2	0	1	0	0	3	0	3	0	0	0	0	.000	0	0	3.60
Valdez, Domingo	Savannah	Tex	A	22	15	15	1	0	86	346	50	33	31	7	1	3	8	38	1	107	7	1	6	4	.600	0	0	3.24
	Charlotte	Tex	A+	22	9	9	0	0	42.1	189	36	26	23	3	0	1	8	19	0	40	4	4	3	4	.429	0	0	4.89
Valdez, Fernando	Burlington	Cle	R+	22	7	0	0	3	15	62	12	6	3	1	0	0	0	2	0	20	3	0	1	0	1.000	0	1	1.80
Valdez, Henry*	Red Sox	Bos	R	21	16	0	0	6	39.1	177	42	22	19	2	0	1	3	17	0	29	0	1	5	2	.714	0	3	4.35
Valdez, Richard	Cubs	ChC	R	20	12	4	0	1	35	175	50	39	32	4	1	0	10	15	0	25	3	2	1	4	.200	0	0	8.23
Valentin, Emmanuel	Tigers	Det	R	19	21	0	0	6	35	161	32	16	16	2	2	1	3	21	0	34	3	3	7	1	.875	0	0	4.11
Valentine, Joe	Kannapolis	CWS	A	22	30	0	0	29	30.2	123	21	10	10	0	2	0	3	10	1	33	1	1	2	2	.500	0	14	2.93
	Winston-Sal	CWS	A+	22	27	0	0	18	44.2	179	18	7	5	0	3	0	1	27	3	50	2	0	5	1	.833	0	8	1.01
Valera, Greg	Lancaster	Ari	A+	23	25	4	0	6	42	208	59	40	38	7	3	1	2	24	0	39	6	0	2	5	.286	0	0	8.14
	Yakima	Ari	A-	23	8	8	0	0	46.1	187	39	18	17	2	1	0	2	14	1	39	10	0	4	2	.667	0	0	3.30
Valera, Luis	Reds	Cin	R	20	10	0	0	6	15	58	7	4	4	0	0	0	0	6	0	16	2	0	1	0	1.000	0	3	2.40
Valles, Rolando*	Pittsfield	Hou	A-	22	22	0	0	7	34.1	169	48	29	21	1	2	0	4	20	1	35	9	2	2	2	.500	0	0	5.50
VanBenschoten, J.	Williamsprt	Pit	A-	22	9	9	0	0	25.2	104	23	11	10	0	0	0	1	10	0	19	5	0	0	2	.000	0	0	3.51
Van Buren, J.	Casper	Col	R+	21	6	3	1	0	23.2	103	25	15	14	2	1	1	0	10	0	25	1	0	3	0	1.000	0	0	5.32
	Tri-City	Col	A-	21	1	1	0	0	5	26	7	4	4	0	0	0	0	3	0	2	0	0	1	0	1.000	0	0	7.20
Vance, Cory*	Salem	Col	A+	23	26	26	1	0	154	641	129	65	53	9	3	2	14	65	0	142	4	4	10	8	.556	0	0	3.10
Vandermeer, Scott	Hudson Val	TB	A-	21	12	8	1	3	55.1	261	74	44	37	4	3	1	7	23	0	31	2	1	2	5	.286	0	1	6.02
Van Dusen, D.*	San Berndno	Sea	A+	21	1	1	0	0	3.1	14	3	2	2	0	0	0	0	1	0	3	0	0	0	1	.000	0	0	5.40
	Wisconsin	Sea	A	21	18	18	1	0	96	395	82	40	34	6	1	3	1	24	0	103	8	0	5	4	.556	1	0	3.19
Vargas, Javier	Tigers	Det	R	20	9	7	1	0	38	156	31	19	15	5	1	0	0	11	0	25	3	1	2	4	.333	0	0	3.55
	Oneonta	Det	A-	20	2	1	0	0	5.1	35	14	12	8	0	0	0	0	6	0	4	0	0	0	1	.000	0	0	13.50
Vargas, Jose	Kinston	Cle	A+	25	8	0	0	2	13.1	54	6	2	2	0	1	0	2	7	1	22	0	0	0	1	.000	0	1	1.35
Vargas, Reynardo	Casper	Col	R+	19	21	0	0	5	28	135	43	25	19	2	0	0	3	14	1	21	4	1	3	4	.429	0	0	6.11
Vasquez, Jorge	Royals	KC	R	20	4	2	0	1	16	63	10	2	2	0	0	0	2	1	0	19	0	0	0	1	.000	0	0	1.13
	Spokane	KC	A-	20	10	8	0	0	50.1	214	50	33	28	3	1	2	5	13	0	67	3	10	1	6	.143	0	0	5.01
Vaughn, Josh*	Expos	Mon	R	21	11	2	0	6	23	114	38	27	21	0	2	1	1	6	0	17	4	0	0	3	.000	0	0	8.22
Vazquez, Will	Asheville	Col	A	22	16	14	0	1	85.2	383	92	62	54	9	3	2	5	35	2	64	4	2	4	7	.364	0	0	5.67
	Tri-City	Col	A-	22	8	4	0	1	21.2	117	30	25	19	1	0	2	2	17	1	15	0	0	0	5	.000	0	0	7.89
Velazquez, Ernesto	Eugene	SD	A-	20	1	0	0	1	0.2	5	1	0	0	0	0	0	0	2	0	0	1	0	0	0	.000	0	0	0.00
Vent, Kevin	San Jose	SF	A+	25	41	10	0	7	103.2	456	105	70	54	14	0	4	8	34	2	74	7	0	5	6	.455	0	0	4.69
Veras, Enger	Bakersfield	TB	A+	20	27	27	0	0	153	678	163	104	77	13	5	4	20	55	0	138	14	2	9	8	.529	0	0	4.53
Victorino, Pedro	Princeton	TB	R+	20	13	8	0	0	43.2	204	49	35	30	5	2	3	4	23	1	39	5	2	2	3	.400	0	0	6.18
Viera, Rolando*	Sarasota	Bos	A+	28	6	0	0	0	12	55	12	8	8	2	0	0	1	6	0	12	1	1	0	2	.000	0	0	6.00
Vigeland, Will	Savannah	Tex	A	25	39	0	0	12	72.2	302	55	27	20	3	2	2	2	34	0	67	5	0	5	4	.556	0	2	2.48
Vigue, John	Princeton	TB	R+	23	20	0	0	14	33.1	139	34	13	12	1	1	2	1	6	0	35	4	0	1	5	.167	0	4	3.24
Villacis, Eduardo	Tri-City	Col	A-	22	11	0	0	6	19	81	14	9	9	2	1	1	1	8	1	20	1	0	4	1	.800	0	0	4.26
	Casper	Col	R+	22	1	1	0	0	6	25	5	1	0	0	0	0	0	2	0	3	0	0	1	0	1.000	0	0	0.00
Villalon, Julio	Bakersfield	TB	A+	24	25	24	0	0	133	582	148	83	72	12	2	3	8	45	0	146	8	0	4	9	.308	0	0	4.87

2001 Pitching — Class-A and Rookie Leagues

HOW MUCH HE PITCHED											WHAT HE GAVE UP												THE RESULTS					
Player	Team	Org	Lg	A	G	GS	CG	GF	IP	BFP	H	R	ER	HR	SH	SF	HB	TBB	IBB	SO	WP	Bk	W	L	Pct.	ShO	Sv	ERA
Villatoro, Wilmer	Idaho Falls	SD	R+	19	30	0	0	15	37.2	170	39	24	22	7	1	1	1	21	2	35	5	0	0	3	.000	0	3	5.26
Villegas, Felix	Augusta	Bos	A	23	34	7	0	11	90.1	409	100	63	36	9	5	2	6	30	2	62	10	0	2	5	.286	0	6	3.59
Vincent, Matt*	Peoria	StL	A	25	14	0	0	3	16.2	72	18	7	6	1	0	1	2	4	0	10	0	0	0	1	.000	0	0	3.24
Viole, Paul	St. Lucie	NYM	A+	24	46	0	0	37	59.2	278	47	32	23	1	2	0	7	50	0	55	11	0	1	5	.167	0	11	3.47
Vitek, Josh	Eugene	SD	A-	22	11	0	0	8	11	45	7	4	3	0	0	1	0	4	0	11	2	0	0	0	.000	0	3	2.45
Vorwald, Matt	Elizabethtn	Min	R+	22	23	0	0	11	46.2	200	31	12	6	0	1	0	5	22	0	60	4	0	6	1	.857	0	4	1.16
Vriesenga, Matt	Peoria	StL	A	24	35	9	0	6	92	391	103	50	41	4	1	2	5	11	0	48	10	0	4	1	.800	0	0	4.01
Waddell, Jason*	Giants	SF	R	21	1	1	0	0	6	26	8	3	2	0	0	0	1	0	0	3	0	0	0	1	.000	0	0	3.00
	Salem-Keizr	SF	A-	21	15	1	0	1	28	125	30	19	17	2	1	1	1	11	1	30	3	0	1	1	.500	0	0	5.46
Wade, Matt	Columbus	Cle	A	22	10	10	0	0	59	249	61	23	22	4	2	0	5	16	0	33	4	0	4	2	.667	0	0	3.36
Waechter, Doug	Chston-SC	TB	A	21	26	26	1	0	153.1	684	179	97	74	14	7	6	5	38	1	107	12	3	8	11	.421	0	0	4.34
Wagner, Denny	Modesto	Oak	A+	25	30	30	1	0	169	744	181	101	75	14	6	6	12	59	3	127	8	0	7	9	.438	0	0	3.99
Wagner, Frank*	Beloit	Mil	A	24	8	0	0	2	8.1	59	18	20	20	1	0	0	4	13	0	8	2	1	0	1	.000	0	0	21.60
Wagnon, Dwayne	Reds	Cin	R	20	10	0	0	2	20.2	94	14	9	7	0	0	1	5	14	0	23	4	0	1	1	.500	0	0	3.05
Wainwright, Adam	Macon	Atl	A	20	28	28	1	0	164.2	691	144	89	69	9	7	2	8	48	1	184	9	2	10	10	.500	0	0	3.77
Walk, Mitch*	San Jose	SF	A+	24	27	19	0	0	117	499	115	57	46	13	4	6	7	39	0	59	3	0	9	6	.600	0	0	3.54
Walker, Brian*	Brooklyn	NYM	A-	22	13	1	0	6	28	125	26	11	8	2	0	1	1	12	1	24	1	0	1	2	.333	0	2	2.57
Walker, Jason*	Vermont	Mon	A-	22	18	8	0	3	52.2	236	48	31	29	3	1	1	5	26	0	35	3	0	3	6	.333	0	1	4.96
Wallace, Ben*	Beloit	Mil	A	21	8	6	0	1	27.1	135	44	32	29	3	0	1	3	14	0	15	5	0	1	4	.200	0	0	9.55
	Ogden	Mil	R+	21	13	8	0	3	45.2	222	64	43	37	7	1	1	3	23	1	33	6	1	0	3	.000	0	0	7.29
Wallace, Shane*	Kinston	Cle	A+	21	13	13	1	0	84	328	65	22	15	3	0	1	5	16	0	60	1	0	10	2	.833	1	0	1.61
Walton, Sam*	Wisconsin	Sea	A	23	3	2	0	0	5.2	30	7	3	3	0	0	1	0	6	0	8	1	0	0	1	.000	0	0	4.76
Warden, Jim Ed	Burlington	Cle	R+	23	12	12	0	0	52.2	232	56	32	25	6	1	1	6	13	0	52	6	1	4	5	.444	0	0	4.27
Waroff, Shane	Missoula	Ari	R+	21	26	0	0	6	40	169	38	16	11	4	1	3	1	9	0	24	1	0	4	1	.800	0	1	2.47
Warren, Andy	W Michigan	Det	A	24	3	3	0	0	15.2	69	17	7	6	0	0	0	2	3	0	12	0	2	1	1	.500	0	0	3.45
Washburn, Ben	Clinton	Mon	A	23	30	15	1	4	129.2	560	141	84	69	19	3	6	7	30	0	89	6	3	4	12	.250	1	0	4.79
Wassong, Michael*	Medcine Hat	Tor	R+	22	11	0	0	6	8.2	49	14	10	8	4	0	3	0	6	0	13	2	0	0	1	.000	0	0	8.31
Waters, Chris*	Macon	Atl	A	21	25	24	3	0	147.2	616	131	71	55	14	4	4	7	52	0	78	8	2	8	6	.571	1	0	3.35
Watkins, Dave	Macon	Atl	A	20	24	0	0	7	49	202	33	17	15	0	3	1	1	27	1	59	4	1	3	1	.750	0	2	2.76
Watson, Greg	Lakeland	Det	A+	25	57	0	0	32	66	298	55	35	23	5	5	3	12	35	2	53	9	0	3	6	.333	0	9	3.14
Watson, Tanner	Mariners	Sea	R	20	11	11	1	0	59.1	268	70	40	29	3	4	0	9	15	0	57	6	0	8	2	.800	0	0	4.40
	Everett	Sea	A-	20	1	0	0	1	2	8	1	0	0	0	0	0	0	1	0	2	1	0	0	0	.000	0	0	0.00
Wawrzyniak, Alan	Cedar Rapds	Ana	A	24	5	5	0	0	22.2	113	25	16	9	3	0	2	0	22	0	21	8	0	2	2	.500	0	0	3.57
Wayne, Hawkeye	Wisconsin	Sea	A	24	30	5	0	6	59	276	55	38	30	1	2	3	6	45	0	48	12	1	4	2	.667	0	1	4.58
Weatherby, Charles	Lowell	Bos	A-	23	13	10	0	0	50.2	208	45	21	17	0	1	2	2	15	0	41	1	0	2	3	.400	0	0	3.02
Webb, Brandon	Lancaster	Ari	A+	23	29	28	0	0	162.1	711	174	90	72	9	3	5	27	44	0	158	11	1	6	10	.375	0	0	3.99
Webb, John	Daytona	ChC	A+	23	5	4	0	0	20	91	23	13	12	0	0	0	2	7	1	20	2	1	1	1	.500	0	0	5.40
Webb, Nick*	Asheville	Col	A	22	19	18	1	1	116.1	475	111	52	43	10	2	1	7	27	0	92	5	3	9	5	.643	0	1	3.33
Webster, Jeremy*	Eugene	SD	A-	23	6	0	0	0	8.1	29	2	1	1	0	0	1	0	2	0	9	1	0	0	0	.000	0	0	1.08
	Fort Wayne	SD	A	23	16	0	0	2	27.1	119	19	15	9	3	4	1	0	22	0	31	4	0	0	1	.000	0	0	2.96
Wechsler, Justin	Missoula	Ari	R+	22	10	10	0	0	37.1	169	35	21	12	3	3	1	6	15	1	29	0	0	2	3	.400	0	0	2.89
Weintraub, Jason	Kingsport	NYM	R+	19	11	0	0	4	23.2	106	27	15	15	4	0	0	2	11	0	25	1	0	1	2	.333	0	1	5.70
Weir, Jayson*	Kingsport	NYM	R+	19	9	0	0	3	14	69	21	13	10	0	2	0	0	6	0	16	2	0	0	0	.000	0	0	6.43
Wellemeyer, Todd	Lansing	ChC	A	23	27	27	1	0	147	667	165	85	68	14	4	5	11	74	0	167	10	1	13	9	.591	0	0	4.16
Wells, Carl*	South Bend	Ari	A	22	40	0	0	15	71.2	303	74	31	23	2	4	4	2	13	0	52	7	2	4	4	.500	0	2	2.89
Wells, Matt	Giants	SF	R	27	1	0	0	0	1	8	3	2	2	0	0	0	2	1	0	1	1	0	0	1	.000	0	0	18.00
Wells, Roy	Wisconsin	Sea	A	23	39	6	0	15	92	389	82	37	33	4	2	2	3	27	3	97	3	0	7	6	.538	0	3	3.23
Weslowski, Rob	St. Lucie	NYM	A+	23	9	0	0	2	16.2	83	25	16	11	0	0	0	0	6	1	10	1	0	1	3	.250	0	0	5.94
	Capital Cty	NYM	A	23	23	5	0	11	61	264	68	32	29	7	2	6	3	16	0	59	2	0	3	6	.333	0	1	4.28
West, Brian	Winston-Sal	CWS	A+	21	28	28	3	0	169	735	179	75	65	11	8	10	9	70	2	130	8	0	7	12	.368	1	0	3.46
Wheatland, Matt	W Michigan	Det	A	20	3	3	0	0	14	71	21	18	17	1	0	2	2	4	0	17	4	1	0	2	.000	0	0	10.93
	Tigers	Det	R	20	3	3	0	0	9	33	3	0	0	0	0	0	0	3	0	5	0	0	0	0	.000	0	0	0.00
Wheeler, Adam	Yankees	NYY	R	19	10	5	0	2	30	131	24	16	13	0	1	0	5	15	0	28	5	0	3	2	.600	0	0	3.90
Wheldon, Rhys	Twins	Min	R	18	13	0	0	2	15.1	70	11	5	2	0	1	0	1	13	1	12	5	0	2	0	1.000	0	0	1.17
Wiemeyer, Jason*	Eugene	SD	A-	23	8	6	0	0	34	135	28	14	12	2	1	0	1	10	0	30	0	1	1	3	.250	0	0	3.18
	Fort Wayne	SD	A	23	6	6	1	0	34	154	38	14	7	5	0	1	1	13	0	29	3	1	1	1	.500	1	0	1.85
Wiles, Chad	Wisconsin	Sea	A	24	39	0	0	36	45.1	191	49	19	11	2	0	2	0	8	4	45	2	0	3	4	.429	0	17	2.18
Wiley, Skip	Everett	Sea	A-	20	7	0	0	2	10	51	19	7	7	1	0	1	0	3	0	11	2	1	1	0	1.000	0	1	6.30
Wilkerson, Wes	Burlington	KC	A	25	43	0	0	23	61.1	277	67	39	33	2	6	2	4	26	0	46	9	0	1	4	.200	0	8	4.84
Wilkinson, Matthew	Yakima	Ari	A-	24	9	0	0	2	15.2	69	14	8	3	0	0	2	1	8	0	23	2	0	2	0	1.000	0	1	1.72
	South Bend	Ari	A	24	14	0	0	5	18.2	92	27	17	15	1	2	1	0	10	2	23	0	0	1	2	.333	0	0	7.23
Williams, Adam*	Wilmington	LA	A	23	25	1	0	9	54.1	233	41	21	16	2	2	0	9	21	0	47	2	2	1	1	.500	0	2	2.65
	Vero Beach	LA	A+	23	10	0	0	2	14	76	16	13	10	1	1	2	5	12	0	13	5	4	0	1	.000	0	0	6.43
Williams, Blake	Potomac	StL	A+	23	17	17	2	0	107.1	434	82	43	29	12	5	2	8	30	1	92	10	1	4	10	.286	1	0	2.43
Williams, Ruddy	Martinsvlle	Hou	R+	21	15	4	0	8	36	160	40	23	18	4	0	1	1	16	1	24	2	0	2	3	.400	0	0	4.50
Willis, Dontrelle*	Boise	ChC	A-	20	15	15	0	0	93.2	374	76	36	31	1	0	1	3	19	0	77	5	1	8	2	.800	0	0	2.98
Wilson, C.J.*	Pulaski	Tex	R+	21	8	8	0	0	37.2	149	24	6	4	2	0	0	4	9	0	49	0	0	1	0	1.000	0	0	0.96
	Savannah	Tex	A	21	5	5	2	0	34	132	30	13	12	2	2	1	1	9	0	26	3	2	1	2	.333	0	0	3.18
Wilson, Mike	Batavia	Phi	A-	22	14	14	1	0	80.1	351	89	37	23	6	2	0	5	23	1	51	2	0	4	4	.500	0	0	2.58
Wing, Ryan*	Bristol	CWS	R+	20	1	0	0	1	1	5	1	1	1	0	0	0	0	0	0	2	2	0	1	0	1.000	0	0	9.00
Withelder, Greg*	Dodgers	LA	R	23	6	6	0	0	17.1	72	15	8	8	1	0	1	0	11	0	15	0	1	1	0	1.000	0	0	4.15
Withers, Darvin	Visalia	Oak	A+	22	28	17	0	2	117	513	128	75	65	17	3	6	3	43	1	85	10	1	4	7	.364	0	0	5.00
Witte, Lou	Tampa	NYY	A+	25	29	0	0	11	33.2	134	39	13	10	0	0	2	0	5	0	29	0	1	3	1	.750	0	0	2.67
Wolcott, Bob	Modesto	Oak	A+	28	3	3	0	0	15	69	22	13	12	2	0	1	1	1	0	10	0	0	0	3	.000	0	0	7.20
Wolensky, Dave	Rancho Cuca	Ana	A+	22	8	7	0	1	32.1	132	24	13	12	2	2	1	2	14	0	26	5	0	2	0	1.000	0	0	3.34
Wolfe, Brian	Quad City	Min	A	21	28	23	2	2	160	641	128	64	50	11	2	4	5	32	2	128	8	0	13	8	.619	2	0	2.81
Wombacher, Mike*	Greensboro	NYY	A	24	38	0	0	14	49.2	214	54	26	20	4	2	3	0	13	0	41	6	0	1	2	.333	0	0	3.62
Wood, Bobby	Staten Ilnd	NYY	A-	22	12	12	2	0	69.1	303	69	33	31	3	1	1	5	28	0	59	2	0	3	4	.429	0	0	4.02
Wood, Brandon	Pittsfield	Hou	A-	23	29	0	0	23	51.1	211	44	13	13	2	2	2	2	12	2	61	3	0	6	0	1.000	0	9	2.28
Wood, Mike	Vancouver	Oak	A-	22	5	2	0	2	21.2	86	17	4	3	0	0	1	0	4	0	24	2	0	2	0	1.000	0	0	1.25
	Modesto	Oak	A+	22	10	9	0	0	58.1	233	46	22	20	6	3	0	2	10	3	52	2	0	4	3	.571	0	0	3.09
Woodnicki, Mike	New Jersey	StL	A-	22	22	0	0	9	29.2	118	17	10	8	3	3	1	1	13	1	26	2	0	2	3	.400	0	0	2.43
Woods, Jake	Provo	Ana	R+	20	15	14	1	1	64.2	291	70	41	38	6	2	3	2	29	0	84	2	2	4	3	.571	1	0	5.29
Woodyard, Mark	W Michigan	Det	A	23	25	25	2	0	143.2	636	147	81	72	5	1	6	9	69	2	84	13	0	7	12	.368	1	0	4.51
Wray, Fred	Danville	Atl	R+	22	17	0	0	1	33	145	30	26	22	6	0	2	3	17	0	25	6	0	3	0	1.000	0	0	6.00

2001 Pitching — Class-A and Rookie Leagues

Player	Team	Org	Lg	A	G	GS	CG	GF	IP	BFP	H	R	ER	HR	SH	SF	HB	TBB	IBB	SO	WP	Bk	W	L	Pct.	ShO	Sv	ERA
Wright, Chase*	Yankees	NYY	R	19	10	7	0	1	25	131	33	28	22	0	2	3	1	21	1	33	7	1	2	3	.400	0	0	7.92
Wright, Chris	Bakersfield	TB	A+	25	49	0	0	24	87.2	369	83	42	34	6	2	3	4	32	4	79	5	0	7	7	.500	0	5	3.49
Wright, Matt	Danville	Atl	R+	20	14	14	1	0	72.2	301	60	40	30	4	2	0	2	26	0	89	13	2	3	5	.375	0	0	3.72
Wright, Shayne	Provo	Ana	R+	21	1	1	0	0	6	22	3	2	2	0	0	0	1	0	0	5	1	0	0	0	.000	0	0	3.00
	Angels	Ana	R	21	9	2	0	3	12.2	61	20	9	4	0	0	0	2	1	0	11	0	0	0	1	.000	0	2	2.84
Wrightsman, Dusty	Burlington	KC	A	22	34	4	0	8	79.2	348	90	43	38	6	1	5	3	22	2	54	5	2	5	6	.455	0	0	4.29
Wykoff, Zach	Eugene	SD	A-	22	25	0	0	6	30.2	161	48	37	33	4	2	4	4	19	1	24	3	0	0	1	.000	0	0	9.68
Wynegar, Adam*	Boise	ChC	A-	21	14	12	0	1	71	306	77	34	23	7	1	3	3	19	0	63	2	0	4	2	.667	0	0	2.92
Yacco, Anthony	Hagerstown	SF	A	21	24	0	0	6	38	169	27	15	11	2	2	0	8	23	1	37	5	0	3	0	1.000	0	0	2.61
	San Jose	SF	A+	21	7	0	0	1	13.1	61	10	7	5	2	1	0	1	12	0	15	1	0	1	0	1.000	0	0	3.38
Yankosky, L.J.	Braves	Atl	R	27	4	3	0	0	14	54	10	3	3	0	1	1	2	1	0	11	0	0	1	1	.500	0	0	1.93
	Macon	Atl	A	27	1	1	0	0	4	16	2	1	0	0	1	0	0	0	0	2	0	0	0	0	.000	0	0	0.00
	Myrtle Bch	Atl	A+	27	9	8	0	0	55.1	216	50	20	16	4	0	0	2	4	0	50	0	0	2	3	.400	0	0	2.60
Yeatman, Matt	Ogden	Mil	R+	19	13	8	0	3	60	272	72	40	33	6	0	1	5	27	0	61	6	0	2	4	.333	0	1	4.95
Yoshida, Nobuaki*	Fort Wayne	SD	A	20	5	5	1	0	23.1	99	23	13	10	2	0	1	0	13	0	12	2	1	1	2	.333	0	0	3.86
	Eugene	SD	A-	20	8	3	0	0	22.2	93	23	7	3	1	1	1	2	4	0	17	0	0	0	0	.000	0	0	1.19
Young, Chris	Hickory	Pit	A	23	12	12	2	0	74.1	320	79	39	34	6	2	1	3	20	0	72	0	0	5	3	.625	0	0	4.12
Young, Colin*	Salem	Col	A+	24	47	0	0	35	57	215	35	11	9	5	0	0	0	12	0	72	1	0	4	3	.571	0	21	1.42
Young, Curtis	Kannapolis	CWS	A	22	6	0	0	5	6.2	37	9	12	2	3	0	0	2	4	0	7	0	0	0	0	.000	0	0	2.70
	Bristol	CWS	R	22	10	0	0	5	13.1	66	17	12	10	1	0	3	1	9	1	14	1	0	3	0	1.000	0	1	6.75
Young, Doug	Lk Elsinore	SD	A+	26	20	0	0	5	29.2	136	26	17	10	2	1	0	1	12	1	23	1	0	4	0	1.000	0	0	3.03
Young, Jason	Salem	Col	A+	22	17	17	2	0	104.2	439	104	47	40	8	0	0	10	28	0	91	5	0	6	7	.462	1	0	3.44
Young, Simon*	Columbus	Cle	A	24	8	7	0	0	39.1	168	48	18	17	3	1	3	1	13	0	35	2	1	0	2	.000	0	0	3.89
	Kinston	Cle	A+	24	15	13	0	0	60	290	85	54	45	9	4	1	1	21	0	48	1	0	3	5	.375	0	0	6.75
Zary, Rick	Spokane	KC	A-	24	15	0	0	7	28	133	30	18	13	1	1	1	5	11	1	12	2	0	1	1	.500	0	0	4.18
Zervas, Paul	Lowell	Bos	A-	22	17	0	0	10	29.1	129	27	18	15	3	4	0	1	11	3	16	5	0	0	3	.000	0	1	4.60
Ziegler, Mike	Visalia	Oak	A+	22	29	27	0	0	152	665	181	87	73	13	8	2	8	39	1	142	8	0	9	11	.450	0	0	4.32
Zirelli, Mike	San Jose	SF	A+	22	38	1	0	7	83	377	119	62	53	8	2	7	3	13	2	62	4	1	3	3	.500	0	0	5.75
Zorrilla, Reinaldo	White Sox	CWS	R	20	25	0	0	14	32.1	141	35	20	15	2	2	1	3	9	0	25	4	1	1	3	.250	0	0	4.18
Zurita, Tom	Burlington	KC	A	22	35	0	0	17	56.2	263	71	34	30	5	2	2	2	22	1	39	1	0	5	2	.714	0	2	4.76

2001 Team Statistics

How do the different leagues at a classification compare? This section answers that question, as team statistics for all 16 minor leagues follow. (A complete list of abbreviations can be found in the back of this book.)

For instance, a quick look at these numbers reveals that Triple-A hitters fare significantly better in the Pacific Coast League than in the International League.

The team stats also can help identify the most extreme parks in the minors. Check out the Texas League numbers, and you'll know why pitchers hate working in El Paso and Midland.

International League Batting - AAA

Team	Org	G	AB	H	2B	3B	HR	TB	R	RBI	TBB	IBB	SO	HBP	SH	SF	SB	CS	SB%	GDP	Avg	OBP	SLG
Louisville	Cin	144	4978	1380	296	29	127	2115	728	673	432	25	957	72	39	42	75	49	.60	125	.277	.341	.425
Buffalo	Cle	142	4730	1225	238	30	149	1970	697	650	471	27	979	61	50	47	92	47	.66	105	.259	.331	.416
Syracuse	Tor	144	4905	1311	270	51	128	2067	690	633	458	24	938	52	39	53	148	83	.64	93	.267	.333	.421
Toledo	Det	144	4967	1332	277	39	152	2143	686	632	449	20	996	52	62	41	95	48	.66	112	.268	.333	.431
Durham	TB	144	4861	1329	256	28	133	2040	677	616	406	13	896	61	44	34	110	52	.68	113	.273	.335	.420
Indianapolis	Mil	144	4941	1294	264	31	124	1992	666	629	462	25	1065	74	51	43	72	39	.65	107	.262	.332	.403
Columbus	NYY	143	4775	1234	239	35	148	1987	663	607	478	20	982	60	27	41	101	64	.61	114	.258	.331	.416
Scranton-WB	Phi	143	4947	1281	276	32	100	1921	642	594	495	32	989	62	42	29	131	49	.73	113	.259	.332	.388
Pawtucket	Bos	142	4814	1235	237	15	171	2015	612	578	412	17	1098	63	35	22	59	28	.68	113	.257	.322	.419
Charlotte	CWS	144	4882	1251	253	19	155	2007	611	567	388	12	922	52	48	32	72	32	.69	95	.256	.316	.411
Norfolk	NYM	142	4727	1232	244	20	103	1825	602	562	439	30	913	58	60	51	110	48	.70	109	.261	.328	.386
Rochester	Bal	144	4903	1230	243	27	95	1812	576	544	398	14	1018	52	48	33	139	50	.74	109	.251	.312	.370
Ottawa	Mon	144	4919	1222	242	37	106	1866	573	533	451	34	1081	64	60	26	171	64	.73	87	.248	.318	.377
Richmond	Atl	144	4861	1296	261	31	68	1823	559	516	311	26	866	46	62	41	87	71	.55	124	.267	.314	.375
Total		1004	68210	17852	3596	424	1759	27573	8982	8334	6050	321	13700	829	667	535	1462	724	.67	1519	.262	.327	.404

International League Pitching - AAA

Team	Org	G	GS	CG	GF	IP	BFP	H	R	ER	HR	SH	SF	HB	TBB	IBB	SO	WP	Bk	W	L	Pct.	ShO	Sv	ERA
Scranton-WB	Phi	143	143	8	135	1300.1	5365	1164	507	461	116	52	26	47	395	34	1095	43	9	78	65	.545	7	33	3.19
Norfolk	NYM	142	142	4	138	1256	5319	1246	565	495	108	47	37	64	411	25	919	42	9	81	57	.599	10	52	3.55
Buffalo	Cle	142	142	8	134	1253.2	5315	1212	569	500	114	30	23	83	395	14	988	38	13	91	51	.641	11	53	3.59
Durham	TB	144	144	4	140	1260	5352	1228	611	527	142	48	52	60	418	7	925	75	6	74	70	.514	10	37	3.76
Charlotte	CWS	144	144	8	136	1268	5406	1221	623	557	133	47	41	51	464	40	1029	64	8	67	77	.465	7	35	3.95
Louisville	Cin	144	144	8	136	1287	5479	1326	632	556	136	52	27	60	382	18	912	66	2	84	60	.583	10	46	3.89
Richmond	Atl	144	144	3	141	1275	5443	1212	634	587	113	57	40	45	506	52	1046	54	4	68	76	.472	7	36	4.14
Ottawa	Mon	144	144	5	139	1290.1	5462	1241	639	557	119	59	41	66	432	9	996	68	9	68	76	.472	11	40	3.89
Syracuse	Tor	144	144	5	139	1282	5526	1293	655	581	124	38	35	83	433	17	935	80	7	71	73	.493	9	37	4.08
Columbus	NYY	143	143	8	135	1240	5417	1298	690	583	121	44	39	50	456	17	1039	62	10	67	76	.469	5	34	4.23
Rochester	Bal	144	144	7	137	1287.2	5643	1304	709	589	131	53	42	50	474	29	1100	81	9	60	84	.417	10	32	4.12
Pawtucket	Bos	142	142	8	134	1237	5349	1352	710	616	137	45	45	49	357	25	908	43	17	60	82	.423	6	35	4.48
Indianapolis	Mil	144	144	3	141	1279.1	5600	1353	716	616	147	54	43	60	465	20	898	49	9	66	78	.458	7	27	4.33
Toledo	Det	144	144	5	139	1279.2	5626	1402	722	620	138	41	44	61	462	14	910	71	9	65	79	.451	3	32	4.36
Total		1004	1004	84	920	17796	76302	17852	8982	7845	1759	667	535	829	6050	321	13700	836	121	1004	1004	.500	113	529	3.97

Pacific Coast League Batting - AAA

Team	Org	G	AB	H	2B	3B	HR	TB	R	RBI	TBB	IBB	SO	HBP	SH	SF	SB	CS	SB%	GDP	Avg	OBP	SLG
Salt Lake	Ana	143	5017	1444	311	57	160	2349	820	762	397	20	1016	59	34	33	114	55	.67	90	.288	.345	.468
Calgary	Fla	143	4887	1425	315	21	187	2343	810	758	408	17	1048	55	43	33	65	42	.61	125	.292	.351	.479
Col. Springs	Col	141	4894	1424	293	35	146	2225	774	734	424	20	1017	53	35	50	81	58	.58	121	.291	.350	.453
Sacramento	Oak	144	4892	1300	269	20	173	2128	750	695	561	22	1048	70	28	49	129	44	.75	109	.266	.347	.435
Tacoma	Sea	144	4910	1399	316	39	118	2147	749	699	445	18	968	50	31	38	83	51	.62	104	.285	.348	.437
Las Vegas	LA	144	4932	1362	291	36	184	2277	740	684	458	23	1047	58	61	34	101	53	.66	110	.276	.343	.462
Edmonton	Min	143	4887	1395	291	38	142	2188	719	677	484	16	987	62	28	37	52	49	.51	134	.285	.355	.448
Fresno	SF	139	4887	1297	250	33	170	2123	698	656	358	20	1041	44	43	31	86	37	.70	93	.277	.332	.453
Iowa	ChC	143	4830	1331	302	36	139	2122	698	659	395	19	1000	64	57	39	114	62	.65	101	.276	.336	.439
Oklahoma	Tex	143	4843	1291	255	36	143	2047	690	647	511	14	973	42	52	39	69	57	.55	109	.267	.339	.423
Omaha	KC	144	4795	1272	243	22	152	2015	687	637	440	10	975	71	41	52	95	57	.63	116	.265	.335	.420
New Orleans	Hou	139	4573	1217	256	32	130	1927	683	635	461	15	1018	87	57	38	95	49	.66	103	.266	.342	.421
Tucson	Ari	142	4910	1361	269	37	118	2058	682	630	428	26	968	50	57	38	74	47	.60	115	.277	.339	.419
Nashville	Pit	141	4811	1326	244	32	132	2024	669	616	372	22	987	55	52	38	85	50	.63	89	.276	.332	.421
Memphis	StL	143	4868	1277	254	29	114	1931	643	601	384	20	1017	59	34	30	55	41	.57	114	.262	.322	.397
Portland	SD	144	4840	1241	255	31	154	2020	623	585	397	17	1138	52	43	36	96	47	.67	103	.256	.317	.417
Total		1140	77590	21362	4414	534	2360	33924	11435	10675	6923	299	16248	931	696	615	1394	801	.64	1736	.275	.339	.437

Pacific Coast League Pitching - AAA

Team	Org	G	GS	CG	GF	IP	BFP	H	R	ER	HR	SH	SF	HB	TBB	IBB	SO	WP	Bk	W	L	Pct.	ShO	Sv	ERA
New Orleans	Hou	139	139	8	131	1203.2	5229	1211	591	501	121	28	26	56	331	24	959	47	4	82	57	.590	8	41	3.75
Iowa	ChC	143	143	4	139	1263.1	5399	1204	599	540	133	58	39	55	475	36	1228	56	4	83	60	.580	12	46	3.85
Tacoma	Sea	144	144	11	133	1250	5312	1210	610	519	131	48	49	58	414	7	1079	41	4	85	59	.590	11	38	3.74
Portland	SD	144	144	0	144	1266.1	5406	1300	653	588	134	49	45	52	390	14	998	40	3	71	73	.493	11	36	4.18
Oklahoma	Tex	143	143	10	133	1266.1	5470	1259	677	602	133	41	32	61	495	6	1107	34	2	74	69	.517	7	33	4.28
Nashville	Pit	141	141	7	134	1222	5304	1276	702	613	147	46	37	45	426	25	840	57	4	64	77	.454	7	30	4.51
Salt Lake	Ana	143	143	9	134	1261.1	5406	1320	716	638	142	27	31	59	392	4	1036	59	9	79	64	.552	4	34	4.55
Omaha	KC	144	144	2	142	1249.1	5431	1359	731	666	181	33	29	56	442	12	967	53	9	70	74	.486	2	34	4.80
Sacramento	Oak	144	144	7	137	1266.1	5547	1359	741	660	159	36	35	60	465	23	1075	52	2	75	69	.521	4	27	4.70
Fresno	SF	139	139	1	138	1198	5315	1297	745	669	176	49	42	66	497	11	983	58	5	68	71	.489	4	40	5.03
Memphis	StL	143	143	2	141	1252.1	5574	1358	751	668	156	55	47	66	505	15	962	52	4	62	81	.434	8	28	4.80
Edmonton	Min	143	143	7	136	1229	5441	1441	755	664	149	32	42	58	439	10	968	60	2	60	83	.420	7	29	4.86
Tucson	Ari	142	142	4	138	1243	5501	1405	757	632	112	49	49	51	402	33	937	53	0	65	77	.458	6	33	4.58
Las Vegas	LA	144	144	5	139	1264	5602	1412	780	700	156	51	50	74	474	34	1090	55	9	68	76	.472	10	33	4.98
Calgary	Fla	143	143	3	140	1222.1	5462	1492	801	725	163	45	44	39	402	30	977	71	5	72	71	.503	5	34	5.34
Col. Springs	Col	141	141	4	136	1231	5525	1459	826	718	163	40	26	81	400	19	1042	69	7	62	79	.440	6	21	5.25
Total		1140	1140	85	1055	19886	86772	21362	11435	10103	2360	696	615	931	6923	299	16248	857	80	1140	1140	.500	112	537	4.57

Eastern League Batting - AA

Team	Org	G	AB	H	2B	3B	HR	TB	R	RBI	TBB	IBB	SO	HBP	SH	SF	SB	CS	SB%	GDP	Avg	OBP	SLG
Erie	Det	142	4789	1320	259	24	143	2056	741	671	453	13	1014	88	20	43	120	58	.67	97	.276	.346	.429
Norwich	NYY	142	4862	1309	287	22	141	2063	703	646	413	27	1029	77	25	40	64	45	.59	97	.269	.334	.424
Reading	Phi	142	4782	1243	237	34	134	1950	691	634	421	26	872	80	48	45	123	52	.70	99	.260	.327	.408
Trenton	Bos	142	4784	1250	292	26	128	1978	625	578	398	14	1029	54	23	37	87	55	.61	93	.261	.323	.413
New Britain	Min	142	4823	1259	250	34	126	1955	620	575	379	22	892	60	54	34	60	49	.55	98	.261	.321	.405
Binghamton	NYM	141	4688	1196	252	20	143	1917	618	572	427	23	1193	57	40	24	106	72	.60	96	.255	.323	.409
Akron	Cle	142	4749	1210	260	30	135	1935	606	560	351	16	996	48	40	46	108	73	.60	70	.255	.310	.407
Bowie	Bal	141	4678	1219	238	24	91	1778	597	529	426	14	1021	55	34	34	148	82	.64	114	.261	.327	.380
Portland	Fla	142	4688	1142	213	37	96	1717	590	540	530	21	1097	77	43	28	131	89	.60	105	.244	.329	.366
Harrisburg	Mon	142	4635	1169	203	39	98	1744	587	527	398	23	950	56	63	34	161	77	.68	86	.252	.317	.376
Altoona	Pit	142	4760	1226	267	38	91	1842	557	514	376	21	1027	58	45	29	120	78	.61	94	.258	.318	.387
New Haven	StL	142	4639	1079	211	24	81	1581	491	449	335	23	1028	71	58	27	151	89	.63	94	.233	.293	.341
Total		851	56877	14622	2969	352	1407	22516	7426	6795	4907	243	12148	781	493	421	1379	819	.63	1143	.257	.322	.396

Eastern League Pitching - AA

Team	Org	G	GS	CG	GF	IP	BFP	H	R	ER	HR	SH	SF	HB	TBB	IBB	SO	WP	Bk	W	L	Pct.	ShO	Sv	ERA
New Britain	Min	142	142	5	137	1268.1	5282	1136	499	426	79	34	22	66	389	31	1148	56	3	87	55	.613	11	44	3.02
Portland	Fla	142	142	4	138	1257	5118	1067	517	452	143	55	19	55	356	15	1141	38	3	77	65	.542	12	38	3.24
Norwich	NYY	142	142	7	135	1253.1	5328	1129	578	455	95	37	39	49	463	11	1207	60	8	83	59	.585	13	40	3.27
Akron	Cle	142	142	8	134	1235.2	5224	1203	607	539	101	43	32	54	423	13	931	73	13	68	74	.479	12	31	3.93
Erie	Det	142	142	16	126	1235.2	5274	1216	612	529	129	36	42	80	395	16	1003	55	2	84	58	.592	11	42	3.85
Altoona	Pit	142	142	4	138	1245.2	5345	1257	613	516	83	43	31	59	430	19	872	50	10	63	79	.444	8	30	3.73
Reading	Phi	142	142	8	134	1247.2	5258	1233	622	557	137	43	33	65	351	22	958	53	6	77	65	.542	12	35	4.02
Harrisburg	Mon	142	142	10	132	1224	5303	1244	666	563	148	43	43	75	440	23	958	58	5	66	76	.465	6	30	4.14
Binghamton	NYM	141	141	4	137	1231.2	5399	1328	667	579	114	43	51	63	451	28	959	70	8	73	68	.518	9	40	4.23
Bowie	Bal	141	141	13	128	1228	5254	1263	672	568	138	38	47	52	351	19	906	60	7	59	82	.418	11	28	4.16
Trenton	Bos	142	142	1	141	1232.2	5326	1298	683	577	114	34	24	90	380	23	1121	71	7	67	75	.472	9	34	4.21
New Haven	StL	142	142	4	138	1229.2	5382	1248	690	580	126	44	38	73	478	23	944	69	4	47	95	.331	9	24	4.25
Total		851	851	84	767	14889.1	63493	14622	7426	6341	1407	493	421	781	4907	243	12148	713	76	851	851	.500	123	416	3.83

Southern League Batting - AA

Team	Org	G	AB	H	2B	3B	HR	TB	R	RBI	TBB	IBB	SO	HBP	SH	SF	SB	CS	SB%	GDP	Avg	OBP	SLG
Tennessee	Tor	140	4732	1282	257	37	136	2018	717	664	504	24	1031	76	43	42	133	59	.69	94	.271	.348	.426
Birmingham	CWS	140	4701	1262	261	27	129	1964	717	673	547	17	978	55	45	61	82	49	.63	113	.268	.348	.418
Chattanooga	Cin	139	4598	1187	265	17	155	1951	708	661	513	24	1013	80	50	35	122	63	.66	99	.258	.341	.424
Jacksonville	LA	139	4638	1206	248	37	103	1837	623	556	479	20	993	58	84	42	165	72	.70	77	.260	.334	.396
Huntsville	Mil	138	4604	1174	227	16	121	1796	596	545	420	28	946	45	67	31	90	59	.60	82	.255	.321	.390
West Tenn	ChC	139	4620	1128	200	30	106	1706	590	553	501	16	1104	82	46	40	100	56	.64	82	.244	.326	.369
Carolina	Col	138	4569	1152	239	29	76	1677	555	507	472	25	957	70	79	38	131	61	.68	84	.252	.329	.367
Greenville	Atl	139	4596	1136	224	18	120	1756	541	495	427	11	1095	67	48	28	75	48	.61	100	.247	.318	.382
Mobile	SD	138	4651	1159	234	30	87	1714	528	500	459	17	1039	41	45	47	96	50	.66	92	.249	.319	.369
Orlando	TB	140	4657	1194	223	29	58	1649	514	469	336	12	886	73	54	35	98	62	.61	103	.256	.314	.354
Total		695	46366	11880	2378	270	1090	18068	6089	5623	4658	194	10042	647	561	399	1092	579	.65	926	.256	.330	.390

Southern League Pitching - AA

Team	Org	G	GS	CG	GF	IP	BFP	H	R	ER	HR	SH	SF	HB	TBB	IBB	SO	WP	Bk	W	L	Pct.	ShO	Sv	ERA
Jacksonville	LA	139	139	2	137	1232.1	5164	1109	530	451	119	58	28	70	417	11	1031	43	8	83	56	.597	8	42	3.29
Huntsville	Mil	138	138	2	136	1215.2	5191	1149	540	467	103	50	37	57	429	25	1085	63	3	75	63	.543	12	39	3.46
Tennessee	Tor	140	140	4	137	1229	5199	1155	576	512	134	48	33	82	386	14	874	51	1	80	60	.571	14	38	3.75
Mobile	SD	138	138	1	137	1225.2	5252	1171	613	536	110	59	49	63	473	26	975	45	2	65	73	.471	8	39	3.94
Greenville	Atl	139	139	4	135	1212.2	5237	1181	614	534	106	76	41	47	484	32	1012	69	13	60	79	.432	7	33	3.96
Chattanooga	Cin	139	139	4	133	1216.2	5293	1206	625	546	92	67	36	45	497	16	1084	45	4	72	67	.518	14	30	4.04
Orlando	TB	140	140	3	137	1220.1	5298	1242	640	548	116	50	44	66	457	11	956	73	9	59	81	.421	13	30	4.04
Birmingham	CWS	140	140	3	137	1230.1	5311	1215	642	548	86	40	44	72	488	19	935	78	9	80	60	.571	12	43	4.01
West Tenn	ChC	139	139	5	134	1216.1	5330	1196	654	576	119	59	44	72	519	26	1114	73	5	59	80	.424	9	28	4.26
Carolina	Col	138	138	6	132	1210	5367	1256	655	562	105	54	43	73	508	14	976	67	6	62	76	.449	11	28	4.18
Total		695	695	46	649	12209	52642	11880	6089	5280	1090	561	399	647	4658	194	10042	607	60	695	695	.500	108	350	3.89

Texas League Batting - AA

Team	Org	G	AB	H	2B	3B	HR	TB	R	RBI	TBB	IBB	SO	HBP	SH	SF	SB	CS	SB%	GDP	Avg	OBP	SLG
Wichita	KC	137	4678	1308	252	39	146	2076	776	733	420	19	842	6	44	47	116	76	.60	108	.280	.337	.444
Midland	Oak	140	4764	1241	280	36	139	2010	742	677	548	12	1031	96	38	40	123	54	.69	92	.260	.346	.422
Round Rock	Hou	140	4812	1317	273	33	139	2073	713	645	442	30	962	84	45	37	117	57	.67	85	.274	.343	.431
Arkansas	Ana	136	4578	1217	255	43	110	1888	654	596	418	23	948	53	20	43	146	86	.63	68	.266	.332	.412
El Paso	Ari	140	4862	1368	311	33	78	1979	650	608	429	25	1054	69	39	40	95	61	.61	100	.281	.346	.407
Tulsa	Tex	139	4747	1218	260	35	116	1896	650	606	473	17	965	61	69	39	87	55	.61	85	.257	.329	.399
San Antonio	Sea	137	4729	1205	227	28	81	1731	615	567	459	12	925	43	36	43	109	52	.68	98	.255	.324	.366
Shreveport	SF	135	4589	1192	224	28	62	1658	564	513	397	15	982	65	56	44	141	66	.68	90	.260	.325	.361
Total		552	37759	10066	2082	275	871	15311	5364	4945	3586	153	7709	477	347	333	934	507	.65	726	.267	.335	.405

Texas League Pitching - AA

Team	Org	G	GS	CG	GF	IP	BFP	H	R	ER	HR	SH	SF	HB	TBB	IBB	SO	WP	Bk	W	L	Pct.	ShO	Sv	ERA
Round Rock	Hou	140	140	3	137	1241.1	5265	1136	569	499	105	43	45	56	461	5	1138	56	4	86	54	.614	17	39	3.62
Wichita	KC	137	137	3	134	1200	5211	1181	619	541	116	34	34	73	472	24	965	68	9	79	58	.577	13	39	4.06
San Antonio	Sea	137	137	7	130	1236	5348	1277	622	529	92	54	35	78	387	25	1062	66	6	70	67	.511	16	36	3.85
Shreveport	SF	135	135	5	130	1193.1	5182	1232	647	540	116	60	46	71	378	24	774	56	6	54	81	.400	7	33	4.07
Tulsa	Tex	139	139	8	131	1237.1	5355	1222	666	588	115	44	43	74	474	12	1063	73	6	69	70	.496	8	28	4.28
Midland	Oak	140	140	1	139	1237.2	5494	1379	709	605	117	37	26	60	433	37	926	44	8	71	69	.507	8	41	4.40
Arkansas	Ana	136	136	9	127	1170	5191	1246	722	621	113	35	46	91	434	4	757	80	9	66	70	.485	3	27	4.78
El Paso	Ari	140	140	3	137	1220	5563	1393	810	664	97	40	58	74	547	22	1024	81	19	57	83	.407	5	35	4.90
Total		552	552	39	513	9735.2	42609	10066	5364	4587	871	347	333	577	3586	153	7709	524	67	552	552	.500	77	278	4.24

California League Batting - A+

Team	Org	G	AB	H	2B	3B	HR	TB	R	RBI	TBB	IBB	SO	HBP	SH	SF	SB	CS	SB%	GDP	Avg	OBP	SLG
High Desert	Mil	140	4888	1364	291	43	158	2215	837	753	506	15	1267	95	33	45	211	96	.69	90	.279	.355	.453
Lancaster	Ari	140	4928	1385	269	51	145	2191	801	737	511	16	1127	52	36	33	132	81	.62	74	.281	.353	.445
Visalia	Oak	140	4813	1242	262	32	130	1958	763	677	576	18	1215	80	31	42	160	74	.68	92	.258	.344	.407
San Bernardino	Sea	140	4895	1257	245	45	76	1810	689	619	467	27	1112	80	63	38	137	56	.71	98	.257	.329	.370
Lake Elsinore	SD	140	4806	1268	270	35	109	1935	683	634	496	16	1167	79	22	41	124	56	.69	111	.264	.340	.403
Bakersfield	TB	140	4932	1344	292	31	96	1986	677	603	348	17	1048	76	51	34	82	39	.68	95	.273	.328	.403
San Jose	SF	140	4744	1245	258	38	89	1846	667	598	462	15	1165	76	51	45	147	69	.68	92	.262	.335	.389
Modesto	Oak	140	4818	1225	233	38	90	1804	665	594	554	15	1200	87	45	41	177	61	.74	87	.254	.339	.374
Rancho Cuca.	Ana	140	4767	1226	256	47	88	1840	629	562	379	20	1157	64	54	28	167	62	.73	94	.257	.319	.386
Mudville	Cin	140	4755	1195	238	25	100	1783	623	572	456	25	1066	63	42	44	102	46	.69	116	.251	.322	.375
Total		700	48346	12751	2604	385	1081	19368	7034	6349	4755	184	11524	752	428	391	1439	640	.69	949	.264	.337	.401

California League Pitching - A+

Team	Org	G	GS	CG	GF	IP	BFP	H	R	ER	HR	SH	SF	HB	TBB	IBB	SO	WP	Bk	W	L	Pct.	ShO	Sv	ERA
Lake Elsinore	SD	140	140	1	139	1255.2	5248	1069	534	423	76	42	26	43	427	25	1343	72	11	91	49	.650	13	44	3.03
San Bernardino	Sea	140	140	2	138	1283	5457	1133	598	492	83	45	39	100	487	15	1262	67	9	76	64	.543	12	36	3.45
Mudville	Cin	140	140	3	137	1248.2	5448	1204	618	500	93	40	34	58	548	7	1209	80	9	71	66	.529	9	38	3.60
Bakersfield	TB	140	140	1	139	1244.1	5448	1268	668	559	101	39	36	72	471	16	1206	77	9	71	69	.507	9	41	4.04
San Jose	SF	140	140	1	139	1225.2	5349	1233	686	588	110	34	48	81	460	6	954	92	10	77	63	.550	7	40	4.32
Modesto	Oak	140	140	1	139	1239.1	5453	1313	721	584	93	57	37	65	447	49	1006	64	4	55	85	.393	5	23	4.24
Rancho Cuca.	Ana	140	140	5	135	1238.2	5511	1318	742	635	116	44	39	88	484	20	1110	109	11	63	77	.450	7	36	4.61
Visalia	Oak	140	140	1	139	1232.2	5545	1398	796	657	125	47	44	76	451	18	1133	97	8	61	79	.436	2	31	4.80
Lancaster	Ari	140	140	3	137	1233	5573	1423	827	678	128	50	46	88	463	19	1118	100	18	61	79	.436	6	26	4.95
High Desert	Mil	140	140	1	139	1249.1	5644	1392	844	731	156	30	42	81	517	9	1183	103	3	71	69	.507	4	30	5.27
Total		700	700	19	681	12450.1	54676	12751	7034	5847	1081	428	391	752	4755	184	11524	861	92	700	700	.500	74	345	4.23

Carolina League Batting - A+

Team	Org	G	AB	H	2B	3B	HR	TB	R	RBI	TBB	IBB	SO	HBP	SH	SF	SB	CS	SB%	GDP	Avg	OBP	SLG
Kinston	Cle	140	4694	1182	233	34	92	1759	629	564	460	14	1066	88	34	34	131	79	.62	91	.252	.328	.375
Wilmington	KC	140	4583	1149	204	25	64	1595	610	534	521	28	1091	18	85	22	110	62	.64	117	.251	.328	.348
Salem	Col	138	4540	1124	257	24	96	1717	558	509	405	24	961	83	53	45	88	58	.60	77	.248	.318	.378
Myrtle Beach	Atl	138	4499	1083	221	14	95	1617	553	512	422	16	1147	6	23	36	97	72	.57	102	.241	.304	.359
Frederick	Bal	139	4597	1146	209	16	84	1639	538	480	382	16	964	69	41	23	134	79	.63	110	.249	.310	.357
Lynchburg	Pit	137	4542	1110	208	25	67	1569	538	478	382	12	1144	66	30	29	123	67	.65	96	.244	.310	.345
Potomac	StL	140	4619	1160	229	22	74	1655	532	469	326	19	1003	74	43	24	127	84	.60	92	.251	.309	.358
Winston-Salem	CWS	140	4658	1122	226	19	61	1569	507	459	389	20	987	76	66	36	147	91	.62	97	.241	.308	.337
Total		556	36732	9076	1787	179	633	13120	4465	4005	3253	149	8363	480	375	249	957	592	.62	782	.247	.315	.357

Carolina League Pitching - A+

Team	Org	G	GS	CG	GF	IP	BFP	H	R	ER	HR	SH	SF	HB	TBB	IBB	SO	WP	Bk	W	L	Pct.	ShO	Sv	ERA
Kinston	Cle	140	140	6	134	1251.1	5186	1073	461	380	65	34	24	65	390	19	1260	39	5	89	51	.636	17	46	2.73
Frederick	Bal	139	139	8	131	1220	5112	1127	526	435	82	47	35	85	372	16	1137	63	6	70	69	.504	10	40	3.21
Myrtle Beach	Atl	138	138	4	134	1205.2	5018	1086	526	450	88	51	27	53	347	14	1102	54	8	71	67	.514	16	39	3.36
Wilmington	KC	140	140	2	138	1235.1	5171	1115	537	449	62	48	39	108	379	15	1052	81	5	78	62	.557	13	35	3.27
Potomac	StL	140	140	8	132	1207	5093	1128	566	437	92	43	33	90	348	26	909	67	7	66	74	.471	12	38	3.26
Salem	Col	138	138	3	135	1198	5178	1165	607	502	73	38	21	103	468	13	985	98	13	70	68	.507	12	44	3.77
Winston-Salem	CWS	140	140	10	130	1243.2	5382	1191	611	506	83	63	35	89	532	30	1022	61	5	54	86	.386	7	27	3.66
Lynchburg	Pit	137	137	8	129	1192	5164	1191	631	513	88	51	35	87	427	16	896	55	8	58	79	.423	9	37	3.87
Total		556	556	49	507	9753	41304	9076	4465	3672	633	375	249	680	3253	149	8363	518	57	556	556	.500	96	306	3.39

Florida State League Batting - A+

Team	Org	G	AB	H	2B	3B	HR	TB	R	RBI	TBB	IBB	SO	HBP	SH	SF	SB	CS	SB%	GDP	Avg	OBP	SLG
Dunedin	Tor	135	4613	1224	232	33	71	1735	701	625	494	12	1030	69	42	39	136	54	.72	91	.265	.343	.376
Brevard County	Fla	135	4469	1186	213	25	86	1707	677	595	520	19	899	76	34	42	158	52	.75	90	.265	.349	.382
Tampa	NYY	139	4439	1083	233	40	112	1732	634	574	555	17	1038	85	26	50	95	73	.57	88	.244	.336	.390
Lakeland	Det	136	4506	1150	233	36	70	1665	625	567	499	15	935	62	50	54	154	53	.74	86	.255	.334	.370
Clearwater	Phi	137	4506	1152	230	33	81	1691	618	563	447	21	923	85	37	50	189	73	.72	92	.256	.331	.375
Fort Myers	Min	137	4602	1151	193	24	57	1563	614	546	529	19	890	81	45	44	111	49	.69	110	.250	.335	.340
Daytona	ChC	136	4455	1134	211	21	97	1678	604	553	471	13	1016	71	36	40	191	90	.68	77	.255	.333	.377
St. Lucie	NYM	139	4473	1116	222	28	83	1643	590	528	443	13	1016	59	46	47	162	83	.66	93	.249	.322	.367
Jupiter	Mon	139	4535	1129	201	40	43	1539	578	498	472	16	952	74	45	24	162	90	.64	97	.249	.321	.339
Sarasota	Bos	137	4576	1121	222	26	91	1668	550	499	463	16	1039	68	28	37	101	67	.60	97	.245	.321	.365
Charlotte	Tex	137	4544	1123	219	38	62	1604	529	476	401	27	910	44	44	27	97	67	.59	87	.247	.313	.353
Vero Beach	LA	133	4336	1101	192	21	63	1524	517	461	450	14	804	77	50	34	94	55	.63	113	.254	.332	.351
Total		820	54054	13670	2601	365	916	19749	7237	6485	5744	202	11351	851	483	488	1600	796	.67	1110	.253	.331	.365

Florida State League Pitching - A+

Team	Org	G	GS	CG	GF	IP	BFP	H	R	ER	HR	SH	SF	HB	TBB	IBB	SO	WP	Bk	W	L	Pct.	ShO	Sv	ERA
Tampa	NYY	139	139	7	132	1193.2	5095	1097	539	421	52	32	36	66	431	23	1132	82	15	77	62	.554	11	44	3.17
Jupiter	Mon	139	139	4	135	1206.2	5155	1131	551	431	79	54	41	60	406	7	875	55	10	70	69	.504	13	37	3.21
Vero Beach	LA	133	133	5	128	1160.1	4992	1070	557	476	111	39	32	72	504	9	1060	80	15	67	66	.504	9	42	3.69
Charlotte	Tex	137	137	5	132	1203.1	5104	1050	566	451	64	48	46	77	491	21	986	74	15	67	70	.489	9	41	3.37
Brevard County	Fla	135	135	4	131	1163	4989	1119	579	443	64	45	36	55	438	15	828	37	5	80	55	.593	14	38	3.43
St. Lucie	NYM	139	139	5	134	1182.2	5127	1132	594	493	52	55	34	76	468	9	895	68	10	63	76	.453	5	27	3.75
Clearwater	Phi	137	137	9	128	1184.2	5139	1160	601	502	77	30	37	63	513	17	931	69	9	68	69	.496	6	38	3.81
Daytona	ChC	136	136	4	132	1167	5070	1120	601	495	67	35	38	64	471	30	1020	60	9	68	68	.500	10	33	3.82
Fort Myers	Min	137	137	1	136	1211.2	5224	1151	605	484	58	35	52	58	521	26	951	86	11	67	69	.493	9	41	3.60
Lakeland	Det	136	136	6	130	1178.1	5161	1158	607	514	88	41	41	85	521	16	847	81	8	67	69	.493	9	41	3.93
Sarasota	Bos	137	137	2	135	1201	5313	1242	701	551	95	40	38	80	443	16	990	59	15	54	83	.394	5	26	4.13
Dunedin	Tor	135	135	5	130	1177.1	5269	1240	736	610	109	29	57	95	529	13	836	95	8	71	64	.526	4	35	4.66
Total		820	820	57	763	14229.2	61638	13670	7237	5871	916	483	488	851	5744	202	11351	846	130	820	820	.500	101	433	3.71

Midwest League Batting - A

Team	Org	G	AB	H	2B	3B	HR	TB	R	RBI	TBB	IBB	SO	HBP	SH	SF	SB	CS	SB%	GDP	Avg	OBP	SLG
Kane County	Fla	138	4779	1295	268	37	108	1961	767	690	515	14	899	86	20	51	120	59	.67	106	.271	.349	.410
Michigan	Hou	137	4628	1264	259	54	125	2006	764	674	498	23	1033	71	17	37	222	67	.77	91	.273	.350	.433
Dayton	Cin	139	4640	1145	259	31	144	1898	709	626	434	14	1241	93	27	27	119	63	.65	73	.247	.322	.409
Lansing	ChC	140	4692	1266	270	42	121	1983	690	635	453	17	990	95	28	48	91	58	.61	100	.270	.343	.423
Wisconsin	Sea	136	4622	1254	248	40	74	1804	688	610	431	12	946	84	40	52	245	98	.71	72	.271	.341	.390
South Bend	Ari	136	4563	1232	221	49	74	1773	678	606	399	14	946	81	37	44	211	72	.75	101	.270	.337	.389
Quad City	Min	137	4641	1218	239	32	85	1776	666	589	413	12	880	13	42	50	114	49	.70	105	.262	.321	.383
Beloit	Mil	138	4680	1191	234	12	100	1749	647	561	389	22	1012	62	79	36	93	40	.70	80	.254	.318	.374
Cedar Rapids	Ana	137	4608	1157	227	20	87	1685	639	552	422	8	1057	14	56	34	167	84	.67	75	.251	.314	.366
Burlington	KC	134	4478	1109	225	34	81	1645	620	538	435	6	965	73	42	38	101	50	.67	97	.248	.322	.367
West Michigan	Det	138	4610	1152	204	37	60	1610	616	524	506	10	1009	83	24	48	205	78	.72	95	.250	.332	.349
Peoria	StL	138	4566	1126	253	32	83	1692	599	514	427	8	1092	51	46	42	249	95	.72	79	.247	.315	.371
Clinton	Mon	137	4688	1208	192	33	59	1643	591	511	415	7	955	51	21	34	175	78	.69	98	.258	.323	.350
Fort Wayne	SD	137	4556	1111	224	19	70	1583	560	496	454	10	1000	59	36	40	156	61	.72	79	.244	.318	.347
Total		961	64751	16728	3323	472	1271	24808	9234	8126	6191	177	14025	916	515	581	2268	952	.70	1251	.258	.329	.383

Midwest League Pitching - A

Team	Org	G	GS	CG	GF	IP	BFP	H	R	ER	HR	SH	SF	HB	TBB	IBB	SO	WP	Bk	W	L	Pct.	ShO	Sv	ERA
Wisconsin	Sea	136	136	4	132	1202	5077	1049	513	395	65	38	29	86	398	17	1225	71	13	84	52	.618	16	34	2.96
Quad City	Min	137	137	7	130	1204.1	5148	1112	593	481	84	36	37	75	454	17	1010	88	13	80	57	.584	14	42	3.59
South Bend	Ari	136	136	5	131	1176.2	5074	1158	609	488	75	43	47	68	420	14	960	75	16	70	66	.515	9	31	3.73
West Michigan	Det	138	138	3	135	1214.2	5275	1121	609	502	69	21	46	76	545	30	1054	109	22	65	72	.474	15	34	3.72
Dayton	Cin	139	139	6	133	1219	5242	1226	613	498	86	35	26	59	396	23	1049	94	13	82	57	.590	13	40	3.68
Kane County	Fla	138	138	1	137	1232.2	5270	1223	619	528	81	42	45	84	373	4	865	112	15	88	50	.638	4	39	3.86
Michigan	Hou	137	137	8	129	1189	5228	1222	661	558	93	34	36	124	380	7	948	75	13	82	55	.599	7	36	4.22
Burlington	KC	134	134	2	132	1151	5052	1236	692	579	101	40	47	67	385	7	809	84	13	55	79	.410	5	29	4.53
Fort Wayne	SD	137	137	2	135	1184.2	5172	1218	695	558	100	31	45	68	433	24	1035	68	25	54	83	.394	9	32	4.24
Beloit	Mil	138	138	2	136	1213.1	5339	1156	696	570	95	36	32	65	586	9	1153	113	11	67	71	.486	5	35	4.23
Clinton	Mon	137	137	6	131	1197.1	5277	1210	704	567	118	42	55	80	487	3	853	84	18	51	85	.375	6	20	4.26
Lansing	ChC	140	140	8	132	1205	5355	1293	731	579	98	42	42	79	483	15	1132	88	17	65	75	.464	8	35	4.32
Cedar Rapids	Ana	137	137	7	130	1207	5325	1218	738	587	108	39	47	81	456	3	1054	111	12	60	77	.438	3	33	4.38
Peoria	StL	138	138	3	135	1207.1	5336	1286	761	588	98	36	47	74	395	4	878	115	9	57	81	.413	4	30	4.38
Total		961	961	64	897	16804	73170	16728	9234	7478	1271	515	581	1116	6191	177	14025	1287	214	960	960	.500	118	470	4.01

South Atlantic League Batting - A

Team	Org	G	AB	H	2B	3B	HR	TB	R	RBI	TBB	IBB	SO	HBP	SH	SF	SB	CS	SB%	GDP	Avg	OBP	SLG
Lexington	Hou	140	4799	1321	297	43	153	2163	781	706	447	19	1089	90	18	35	221	104	.68	71	.275	.346	.451
Greensboro	NYY	140	4625	1168	216	38	117	1811	637	574	435	20	1087	57	30	59	123	63	.66	76	.253	.321	.392
Hagerstown	SF	140	4586	1143	239	21	83	1673	630	544	504	15	1091	64	81	39	137	67	.67	104	.249	.329	.365
Asheville	Col	139	4590	1157	206	26	116	1763	628	575	444	12	1152	73	21	48	183	83	.69	78	.252	.325	.384
Columbus	Cle	136	4571	1143	204	45	89	1704	618	537	430	4	1127	14	37	43	149	73	.67	68	.250	.314	.373
Capital City	NYM	135	4473	1122	211	47	72	1643	615	549	424	9	1000	74	46	38	193	71	.73	81	.251	.323	.367
Macon	Atl	133	4479	1102	198	23	108	1670	614	557	466	22	1008	77	38	28	176	79	.69	61	.246	.326	.373
Hickory	Pit	140	4585	1133	183	36	92	1664	570	505	363	11	1032	8	50	36	211	76	.74	84	.247	.301	.363
Delmarva	Bal	140	4539	1096	175	39	57	1520	565	496	454	24	982	85	69	40	92	37	.71	94	.241	.319	.335
Wilmington	LA	138	4523	1130	205	39	56	1581	561	480	366	23	994	75	70	38	278	107	.72	57	.250	.314	.350
Kannapolis	CWS	139	4352	1067	159	37	69	1507	556	473	375	12	1003	86	39	39	181	99	.65	84	.245	.315	.346
Augusta	Bos	139	4530	1080	196	21	71	1531	556	486	428	16	1084	90	44	37	147	64	.70	84	.238	.314	.338
Charleston-SC	TB	140	4584	1031	198	36	79	1538	530	473	364	20	1276	78	46	40	144	94	.61	77	.225	.291	.336
Savannah	Tex	136	4470	1053	190	42	76	1555	524	458	390	10	1146	68	37	31	149	84	.64	81	.236	.306	.348
Charleston-WV	Tor	138	4423	1028	199	28	60	1463	519	461	405	16	1052	43	40	38	131	77	.63	83	.232	.301	.331
Lakewood	Phi	139	4669	1101	240	26	61	1576	508	449	371	16	1099	72	36	33	123	83	.60	88	.236	.300	.338
Total		1106	72798	17875	3316	547	1359	26362	9412	8323	6675	249	17222	1054	702	622	2638	1261	.68	1271	.246	.316	.362

South Atlantic League Pitching - A

Team	Org	G	GS	CG	GF	IP	BFP	H	R	ER	HR	SH	SF	HB	TBB	IBB	SO	WP	Bk	W	L	Pct.	ShO	Sv	ERA
Wilmington	LA	138	138	2	136	1208	4997	994	496	407	89	44	34	81	449	11	1058	94	7	75	63	.543	12	44	3.03
Kannapolis	CWS	139	139	12	127	1179.2	4925	1025	499	406	61	44	45	70	441	18	1128	73	14	76	63	.547	15	35	3.10
Lexington	Hou	140	140	8	132	1245.1	5141	1049	505	429	93	49	33	66	424	7	1235	84	5	92	48	.657	5	28	3.10
Augusta	Bos	139	139	1	138	1213.2	5029	1101	539	395	66	36	41	53	314	9	1087	85	3	74	65	.532	10	39	2.93
Columbus	Cle	136	136	2	134	1207	5105	1132	568	439	96	37	33	65	381	11	979	97	10	77	59	.566	9	46	3.27
Macon	Atl	133	133	7	126	1180.2	4962	1051	568	445	82	48	40	53	387	11	1104	87	15	72	61	.541	8	35	3.39
Greensboro	NYY	140	140	7	133	1215.2	5193	1116	581	471	73	50	34	61	485	13	1106	71	12	70	70	.500	11	37	3.49
Capital City	NYM	135	135	2	133	1173.2	5059	1120	592	486	84	49	38	81	416	8	1115	105	9	62	73	.459	6	33	3.73
Charleston-SC	TB	140	140	6	134	1233.2	5279	1188	599	457	75	55	37	68	369	28	1107	96	10	64	76	.457	13	31	3.33
Lakewood	Phi	139	139	12	127	1241	5264	1130	602	465	87	54	39	89	412	19	1001	48	9	60	79	.432	11	31	3.37
Hagerstown	SF	140	140	1	139	1234.1	5295	1154	606	506	92	33	61	106	472	24	1120	87	12	83	57	.593	12	52	3.69
Hickory	Pit	140	140	8	132	1219	5252	1215	628	505	86	52	76	72	423	17	1063	76	8	67	73	.479	4	34	3.73
Charleston-WV	Tor	138	138	10	128	1178	5045	1137	645	503	98	41	38	88	391	6	963	104	6	51	87	.370	6	23	3.84
Savannah	Tex	136	136	9	127	1181	5160	1088	650	550	96	32	42	126	521	4	1164	104	20	54	82	.397	8	26	4.19
Delmarva	Bal	140	140	5	135	1199.1	5168	1175	660	536	98	36	41	69	405	10	991	80	7	61	79	.436	8	34	4.02
Asheville	Col	139	139	7	132	1199.2	5199	1200	674	536	112	42	30	106	385	25	1001	69	10	68	71	.489	13	35	4.02
Total		1106	1106	99	1007	19309.2	82073	17875	9412	7536	1359	702	622	1254	6675	249	17222	1360	157	1106	1106	.500	161	563	3.51

New York-Penn League Batting - A-

Team	Org	G	AB	H	2B	3B	HR	TB	R	RBI	TBB	IBB	SO	HBP	SH	SF	SB	CS	SB%	GDP	Avg	OBP	SLG
Pittsfield	Hou	75	2492	625	139	25	35	919	398	332	290	13	600	47	29	25	133	55	.71	39	.251	.337	.369
Staten Island	NYY	76	2561	678	138	25	46	1004	383	346	265	6	498	49	15	26	71	30	.70	63	.265	.342	.392
Williamsport	Pit	74	2432	637	125	25	36	920	374	318	243	11	489	48	33	21	132	36	.79	34	.262	.338	.378
Brooklyn	NYM	76	2548	711	143	14	58	1056	368	321	199	6	524	59	12	21	97	67	.59	53	.279	.343	.414
Lowell	Bos	76	2594	653	138	15	28	905	354	308	315	3	578	44	15	25	86	35	.71	45	.252	.340	.349
Hudson Valley	TB	76	2700	694	143	24	41	1008	352	315	210	12	579	29	12	27	41	23	.64	53	.257	.315	.373
New Jersey	StL	76	2545	653	142	24	29	930	330	291	325	11	580	33	27	24	89	52	.63	59	.257	.345	.365
Oneonta	Det	74	2450	631	98	35	25	874	327	282	244	4	597	33	19	19	73	48	.60	52	.258	.331	.357
Batavia	Phi	76	2565	617	129	23	28	876	323	281	229	11	581	41	27	23	58	41	.59	46	.241	.310	.342
Auburn	Tor	74	2547	610	107	19	33	854	306	261	206	5	507	42	21	22	94	40	.70	52	.239	.305	.335
Utica	Fla	74	2479	588	103	19	38	854	297	260	244	8	649	31	12	16	41	26	.61	50	.237	.312	.340
Jamestown	Atl	75	2452	606	115	20	26	839	292	250	217	2	511	48	19	22	68	35	.66	54	.247	.318	.342
Mahoning Vlly	Cle	75	2487	561	111	19	48	854	292	253	257	3	554	35	14	8	38	43	.47	52	.226	.306	.343
Vermont	Mon	75	2432	506	85	13	21	680	264	215	232	1	638	31	22	12	66	38	.63	36	.208	.284	.280
Total		526	35284	8770	1716	300	492	12562	4660	4033	3476	96	7885	570	277	291	1087	569	.66	688	.249	.323	.356

New York-Penn League Pitching - A-

Team	Org	G	GS	CG	GF	IP	BFP	H	R	ER	HR	SH	SF	HB	TBB	IBB	SO	WP	Bk	W	L	Pct.	ShO	Sv	ERA
Brooklyn	NYM	76	76	1	75	671	2769	505	223	177	20	14	17	38	261	3	644	43	3	52	24	.684	6	31	2.37
Williamsport	Pit	74	74	2	72	640.1	2651	550	275	207	34	27	15	30	229	3	567	41	3	48	26	.649	5	23	2.91
Staten Island	NYY	76	76	4	72	664.1	2787	556	284	238	34	14	14	46	240	6	633	42	3	48	28	.632	3	22	3.22
Jamestown	Atl	75	75	1	74	651	2752	603	297	252	43	14	15	25	242	6	556	46	2	39	36	.520	3	20	3.48
New Jersey	StL	76	76	0	76	676.1	2861	630	317	246	44	16	13	49	234	6	621	44	1	35	41	.461	5	24	3.27
Batavia	Phi	76	76	4	72	679.1	2936	686	341	260	37	20	24	42	209	15	471	50	3	37	39	.487	3	17	3.44
Pittsfield	Hou	75	75	1	74	670	2899	644	349	258	23	20	19	34	260	6	564	60	9	45	30	.600	4	18	3.47
Auburn	Tor	74	74	0	74	675	2940	631	349	297	39	21	17	45	306	2	685	61	2	32	42	.432	2	16	3.96
Lowell	Bos	76	76	1	75	673.1	2923	666	356	292	37	24	27	30	259	8	518	41	3	33	43	.434	3	14	3.90
Utica	Fla	74	74	0	74	648.2	2783	598	356	275	35	22	25	40	231	6	458	50	4	27	47	.365	3	14	3.82
Oneonta	Det	74	74	3	71	634.1	2779	630	357	249	27	21	31	45	223	8	529	54	9	37	37	.500	4	18	3.53
Hudson Valley	TB	76	76	2	74	683.2	2996	669	371	297	38	24	18	44	295	5	544	88	3	39	37	.513	1	20	3.91
Mahoning Vlly	Cle	75	75	0	75	660.2	2961	722	391	312	41	24	29	48	250	22	568	62	2	26	49	.347	4	18	4.25
Vermont	Mon	75	75	1	74	650.2	2876	680	394	322	40	16	27	54	237	2	527	50	6	28	47	.373	1	12	4.45
Total		526	526	20	506	9278.2	39913	8770	4660	3682	492	277	291	570	3476	96	7885	732	58	526	526	.500	53	267	3.57

Northwest League Batting - A-

Team	Org	G	AB	H	2B	3B	HR	TB	R	RBI	TBB	IBB	SO	HBP	SH	SF	SB	CS	SB%	GDP	Avg	OBP	SLG
Boise	ChC	75	2637	768	157	26	62	1163	441	394	238	13	517	27	10	29	82	41	.67	45	.291	.352	.441
Salem-Keizer	SF	76	2636	689	141	17	54	1026	416	372	279	6	483	50	27	25	59	21	.74	50	.261	.340	.389
Everett	Sea	75	2636	698	141	18	55	1040	376	343	230	11	628	53	17	17	91	42	.68	24	.265	.334	.395
Eugene	SD	76	2540	641	116	16	57	960	361	320	270	4	681	45	8	27	80	37	.68	38	.252	.332	.378
Spokane	KC	76	2608	637	94	22	25	850	327	277	253	13	615	40	35	22	82	35	.70	42	.244	.318	.326
Yakima	Ari	75	2456	633	138	10	36	899	323	287	210	2	631	49	17	19	45	30	.60	49	.248	.315	.352
Tri-City	Col	75	2513	563	126	30	28	833	322	279	236	12	669	69	15	21	84	34	.71	41	.224	.306	.331
Vancouver	Oak	76	2508	597	129	17	44	892	320	289	280	14	713	43	21	20	72	34	.68	50	.238	.323	.356
Total		302	20634	5226	1042	156	361	7663	2886	2561	1996	75	4937	376	150	180	595	274	.68	339	.253	.328	.371

Northwest League Pitching - A-

Team	Org	G	GS	CG	GF	IP	BFP	H	R	ER	HR	SH	SF	HB	TBB	IBB	SO	WP	Bk	W	L	Pct.	ShO	Sv	ERA
Boise	ChC	75	75	1	74	667.2	2865	626	309	237	34	14	25	37	216	13	590	52	10	52	23	.693	8	24	3.19
Vancouver	Oak	76	76	0	76	670.1	2906	602	328	264	35	21	20	37	278	3	629	58	7	37	39	.487	4	17	3.54
Salem-Keizer	SF	76	76	0	76	686.1	2938	676	338	289	55	18	23	49	223	15	660	52	11	51	25	.671	7	20	3.79
Tri-City	Col	75	75	2	73	676	2927	638	345	271	38	26	27	59	234	9	595	61	7	39	36	.520	4	20	3.61
Yakima	Ari	75	75	0	75	663.1	2923	706	363	302	42	15	13	33	255	11	580	66	5	33	42	.440	4	22	4.10
Eugene	SD	76	76	3	73	648.2	2831	638	373	304	42	21	29	37	240	4	593	44	9	32	44	.421	3	14	4.22
Everett	Sea	75	75	0	75	668	2939	625	376	313	49	19	23	55	291	8	692	63	6	36	39	.480	2	20	4.22
Spokane	KC	76	76	1	75	670.1	3013	715	454	381	66	16	20	69	259	12	598	53	13	22	54	.289	1	10	5.12
Total		302	302	7	295	5350.2	23342	5226	2886	2361	361	150	180	376	1996	75	4937	435	68	302	302	.500	37	147	3.97

Appalachian League Batting - R+

Team	Org	G	AB	H	2B	3B	HR	TB	R	RBI	TBB	IBB	SO	HBP	SH	SF	SB	CS	SB%	GDP	Avg	OBP	SLG
Pulaski	Tex	68	2247	583	124	19	59	922	382	329	231	3	637	50	13	21	97	27	.78	32	.259	.339	.410
Bluefield	Bal	66	2162	570	109	19	47	858	357	304	261	3	557	50	14	15	109	40	.73	47	.264	.354	.397
Princeton	TB	67	2175	557	99	17	66	888	338	292	201	0	596	61	16	16	54	31	.64	32	.256	.334	.408
Kingsport	NYM	66	2090	537	111	21	33	789	313	253	226	2	592	42	10	19	120	52	.70	35	.257	.339	.378
Burlington	Cle	68	2177	485	81	18	42	728	308	263	268	4	660	46	21	12	61	37	.62	34	.223	.319	.334
Bristol	CWS	64	1994	509	92	11	31	716	292	246	189	7	531	43	12	16	78	33	.70	34	.255	.331	.359
Johnson City	StL	66	2105	508	95	13	48	773	286	255	232	3	558	41	19	16	38	25	.60	38	.241	.326	.367
Elizabethton	Min	63	1972	512	109	14	28	733	271	225	184	2	456	43	12	16	58	27	.68	42	.260	.334	.372
Danville	Atl	68	2250	551	111	14	27	771	265	236	184	6	617	34	19	9	48	26	.65	44	.245	.310	.343
Martinsville	Hou	68	2153	498	96	15	26	702	230	185	126	7	515	51	27	18	75	32	.70	30	.231	.287	.326
Total		332	21325	5310	1027	161	407	7880	3042	2588	2102	37	5719	461	163	158	738	330	.69	368	.249	.327	.370

Appalachian League Pitching - R+

Team	Org	G	GS	CG	GF	IP	BFP	H	R	ER	HR	SH	SF	HB	TBB	IBB	SO	WP	Bk	W	L	Pct.	ShO	Sv	ERA
Elizabethton	Min	63	63	1	62	518	2208	442	229	180	34	16	17	43	192	4	588	47	6	41	22	.651	6	22	3.13
Martinsville	Hou	68	68	3	65	573	2405	494	243	194	29	18	17	42	212	2	575	50	9	41	22	.456	6	14	3.05
Bristol	CWS	64	64	5	59	521.2	2201	506	265	209	41	14	18	33	148	7	476	46	7	38	26	.594	4	15	3.61
Johnson City	StL	66	66	1	65	555	2367	514	285	201	31	19	10	49	189	4	629	61	12	31	35	.470	6	13	3.26
Pulaski	Tex	68	68	2	66	575	2493	546	307	237	42	14	14	48	191	7	555	55	9	38	30	.559	4	19	3.71
Kingsport	NYM	66	66	1	65	555.2	2477	573	311	249	38	16	13	58	212	2	545	47	14	31	35	.470	1	11	4.03
Danville	Atl	68	68	2	66	583	2528	529	327	246	44	13	15	39	238	2	623	73	11	30	38	.441	4	17	3.80
Burlington	Cle	68	68	0	68	581.1	2562	546	341	268	55	18	16	49	256	1	606	58	12	31	37	.456	1	15	4.15
Bluefield	Bal	66	66	2	64	552.1	2486	579	360	289	52	19	21	54	222	7	562	61	10	33	33	.500	1	17	4.71
Princeton	TB	67	67	2	65	552.1	2489	581	374	315	41	16	17	46	242	1	560	62	11	28	39	.418	3	11	5.13
Total		332	332	19	313	5567.1	24216	5310	3042	2388	407	163	158	461	2102	37	5719	560	101	332	332	.500	36	154	3.86

Pioneer League Batting - R+

Team	Org	G	AB	H	2B	3B	HR	TB	R	RBI	TBB	IBB	SO	HBP	SH	SF	SB	CS	SB%	GDP	Avg	OBP	SLG
Provo	Ana	76	2631	801	145	23	69	1199	557	481	315	9	607	63	22	30	82	33	.71	45	.304	.388	.456
Missoula	Ari	76	2701	768	146	31	69	1183	535	472	290	12	596	70	11	19	47	26	.64	36	.284	.366	.438
Ogden	Mil	74	2575	731	143	18	48	1054	460	382	246	6	499	37	23	30	107	42	.72	29	.284	.351	.409
Billings	Cin	75	2637	734	131	25	54	1077	452	387	266	9	533	46	15	25	84	31	.73	41	.278	.352	.408
Casper	Col	76	2614	724	127	25	74	1123	448	385	277	8	686	48	8	23	108	67	.62	38	.277	.354	.430
Idaho Falls	SD	75	2619	680	130	20	43	979	405	341	247	5	722	43	6	21	60	31	.66	49	.260	.331	.374
Great Falls	LA	76	2590	657	109	22	42	936	400	346	273	13	496	48	18	18	137	47	.74	57	.254	.334	.361
Medicine Hat	Tor	76	2640	675	111	14	55	979	361	304	223	5	594	62	23	10	63	28	.69	42	.256	.327	.371
Total		302	21007	5770	1042	178	454	8530	3618	3098	2137	67	4733	417	126	176	688	305	.69	337	.275	.351	.406

Pioneer League Pitching - R+

Team	Org	G	GS	CG	GF	IP	BFP	H	R	ER	HR	SH	SF	HB	TBB	IBB	SO	WP	Bk	W	L	Pct.	ShO	Sv	ERA
Billings	Cin	75	75	2	73	661	2834	654	350	277	42	14	15	46	196	6	608	42	5	46	29	.613	4	18	3.77
Provo	Ana	76	76	2	74	656.1	2881	670	365	290	43	14	19	40	226	10	688	57	7	53	23	.697	6	20	3.98
Missoula	Ari	76	76	1	75	669.2	2952	689	375	270	43	14	19	43	222	4	532	64	10	52	24	.684	4	21	3.63
Ogden	Mil	74	74	0	76	643.1	2841	702	443	368	72	13	20	47	232	8	605	75	14	36	38	.486	1	18	5.15
Great Falls	LA	76	76	0	76	676	3055	725	454	349	53	19	16	62	247	7	668	75	10	37	39	.487	5	18	4.65
Casper	Col	76	76	2	74	657.2	3036	777	492	389	46	15	29	59	280	14	526	84	11	37	39	.487	1	21	5.32
Medicine Hat	Tor	76	76	0	76	662.1	3070	740	537	417	76	18	27	71	305	12	504	93	21	20	56	.263	3	12	5.67
Idaho Falls	SD	75	75	0	75	653	3201	813	602	483	79	19	31	49	429	6	602	88	11	21	54	.280	2	10	6.66
Total		302	302	7	295	5279.1	23870	5770	3618	2843	454	126	176	417	2137	67	4733	578	89	302	302	.500	26	138	4.85

Arizona League Batting - R

Team	Org	G	AB	H	2B	3B	HR	TB	R	RBI	TBB	IBB	SO	HBP	SH	SF	SB	CS	SB%	GDP	Avg	OBP	SLG
Mariners	Sea	56	1974	592	110	26	26	832	360	301	188	5	391	55	13	16	34	24	.59	38	.300	.374	.421
Athletics	Oak	56	1926	495	80	38	22	717	311	256	235	3	479	43	17	18	104	51	.67	30	.257	.348	.372
Giants	SF	56	1987	549	87	29	10	724	301	237	145	4	371	36	11	20	56	25	.69	34	.276	.334	.364
Brewers	Mil	56	1894	489	93	25	17	683	284	236	180	3	496	41	14	23	39	23	.63	31	.258	.332	.361
Cubs	ChC	56	1901	510	102	26	20	724	262	215	150	3	456	44	23	14	70	42	.63	21	.268	.334	.381
White Sox	CWS	56	1941	507	95	20	9	669	259	208	158	2	405	27	18	10	76	35	.68	38	.261	.324	.345
Angels	Ana	56	1869	467	63	25	11	613	258	215	168	4	435	50	13	19	81	40	.67	21	.250	.325	.328
Total		196	13492	3609	630	189	115	4962	2035	1668	1224	24	3033	296	109	120	460	240	.66	213	.267	.339	.368

Arizona League Pitching - R

Team	Org	G	GS	CG	GF	IP	BFP	H	R	ER	HR	SH	SF	HB	TBB	IBB	SO	WP	Bk	W	L	Pct.	ShO	Sv	ERA
Athletics	Oak	56	56	0	56	502.1	2123	480	244	184	20	19	14	39	127	1	469	34	13	35	21	.625	7	17	3.31
Giants	SF	56	56	0	56	496.2	2174	463	249	209	20	18	15	46	232	2	478	46	13	29	27	.518	6	9	3.79
White Sox	CWS	56	56	1	55	491	2126	473	282	183	17	10	21	36	162	7	429	41	11	23	33	.411	4	16	3.35
Brewers	Mil	56	56	0	56	493	2184	546	293	239	14	17	15	49	171	7	373	38	11	27	29	.482	0	15	4.36
Mariners	Sea	56	56	1	55	486	2174	549	314	248	21	16	15	41	176	1	427	40	8	34	22	.607	1	17	4.59
Cubs	ChC	56	56	0	56	497.1	2217	532	319	249	12	12	23	48	185	1	445	37	15	26	30	.464	2	17	4.51
Angels	Ana	56	56	2	54	488	2246	566	334	236	11	17	17	37	171	5	412	60	10	22	34	.393	5	8	4.35
Total		196	196	4	192	3454.1	15244	3609	2035	1549	115	109	120	296	1224	24	3033	296	81	196	196	.500	19	93	4.04

Gulf Coast League Batting - R

Team	Org	G	AB	H	2B	3B	HR	TB	R	RBI	TBB	IBB	SO	HBP	SH	SF	SB	CS	SB%	GDP	Avg	OBP	SLG
Dodgers	LA	60	1983	516	84	13	20	686	315	252	188	2	461	79	31	28	70	20	.78	27	.260	.344	.346
Yankees	NYY	60	1905	487	87	18	27	691	298	257	209	9	434	32	9	22	69	22	.76	37	.256	.336	.363
Red Sox	Bos	59	1892	496	97	14	43	750	278	225	207	8	400	43	6	16	66	30	.69	43	.262	.346	.396
Phillies	Phi	60	1911	480	98	13	24	676	261	222	189	3	449	30	15	9	39	24	.62	38	.251	.327	.354
Tigers	Det	60	1872	454	54	21	20	610	253	200	185	4	405	34	19	13	110	31	.78	28	.243	.326	.326
Rangers	Tex	59	1845	443	99	29	12	636	239	202	172	8	434	37	21	11	124	34	.78	29	.240	.316	.345
Twins	Min	58	1819	477	100	24	14	667	237	201	182	12	376	32	19	16	77	30	.72	24	.262	.337	.367
Braves	Atl	60	1939	441	76	9	24	607	227	194	147	0	446	48	12	16	63	23	.74	20	.227	.296	.313
Reds	Cin	58	1743	447	75	19	15	591	226	186	169	5	431	45	8	16	108	33	.77	40	.248	.328	.339
Orioles	Bal	56	1739	447	92	19	21	640	214	189	161	11	445	24	20	15	55	26	.68	31	.257	.326	.368
Royals	KC	60	1884	444	86	7	11	577	210	173	178	5	446	36	22	10	63	27	.70	33	.236	.312	.306
Marlins	Fla	60	1923	425	80	7	10	549	209	168	166	2	490	41	16	10	100	43	.70	27	.221	.295	.285
Pirates	Pit	56	1686	372	65	11	14	501	185	141	190	3	398	31	11	14	81	21	.79	38	.221	.309	.297
Expos	Mon	60	1913	413	57	11	10	522	184	155	159	3	522	37	16	12	48	29	.62	43	.216	.287	.273
Total		413	26054	6328	1150	215	265	8703	3336	2765	2502	75	6137	549	225	208	1074	393	.73	458	.243	.320	.334

Gulf Coast League Pitching - R

Team	Org	G	GS	CG	GF	IP	BFP	H	R	ER	HR	SH	SF	HB	TBB	IBB	SO	WP	Bk	W	L	Pct.	ShO	Sv	ERA
Dodgers	LA	60	60	0	60	517	2079	400	171	140	14	11	11	38	149	0	442	26	4	41	19	.683	7	15	2.44
Reds	Cin	58	58	3	55	474.2	2010	397	185	147	6	14	13	33	176	4	477	22	6	36	22	.621	6	18	2.79
Red Sox	Bos	59	59	0	59	491.2	2067	440	217	191	18	17	20	28	176	11	440	30	5	37	22	.627	3	21	3.50
Phillies	Phi	60	60	0	60	494	2100	449	220	152	18	21	15	36	154	2	436	35	9	31	29	.517	6	9	2.77
Braves	Atl	60	60	1	59	517.2	2185	433	221	161	17	18	12	35	163	3	562	43	7	30	30	.500	9	19	2.80
Twins	Min	58	58	2	56	477.1	2029	457	224	160	17	6	8	28	176	4	434	51	4	32	26	.552	7	23	3.49
Marlins	Fla	60	60	1	59	519.1	2181	427	226	160	17	25	22	66	148	3	460	46	5	29	31	.483	5	14	2.77
Yankees	NYY	60	60	3	57	497	2153	473	245	202	20	17	12	28	203	4	459	43	4	35	25	.583	7	16	3.66
Pirates	Pit	56	56	3	53	449.2	1964	444	247	194	22	18	16	38	179	7	368	48	4	22	34	.393	5	12	3.88
Orioles	Bal	56	56	1	55	454	2022	440	251	188	30	19	13	49	196	17	354	36	10	22	34	.393	0	8	3.73
Rangers	Tex	59	59	3	56	487.1	2099	490	255	204	26	11	18	36	178	8	411	29	3	24	35	.407	6	9	3.77
Tigers	Det	60	60	4	58	491.2	2155	453	257	210	24	16	11	33	218	8	468	44	19	34	26	.567	5	5	3.84
Royals	KC	60	60	1	59	490	2181	490	300	217	20	11	16	35	186	7	371	35	8	20	40	.333	1	10	3.99
Expos	Mon	60	60	0	60	515.1	2322	535	317	236	16	21	21	66	200	1	455	62	6	20	40	.333	2	9	4.12
Total		413	413	22	391	6876.2	29547	6328	3336	2587	265	225	208	549	2502	75	6137	550	94	413	413	.500	69	196	3.39

2001 Leader Boards

It's hard to find leader boards like these. We offer plenty of categories and break them down five different ways. In addition to leader lists for Triple-A, Double-A, full-season Class-A and short-season leagues, you'll find a leader board for all full-season leagues regardless of classification.

The leader board for all full-season leagues demonstrates how dominant Florida pitching prospect Josh Beckett was during the 2001 season. Splitting the season between high Class-A Brevard County and Double-A Portland, he led all full-season starters in ERA (1.54), strikeouts/9 IP (13.05) and fewest hits/9 IP (5.27). With numbers like those, it's no surprise that he enjoyed major league success during his September debut.

For short-season ball, three players ranked at the top of several key hitting categories. Cubs prospect Syketo Anderson (Boise-NWL) led all short-season leagues in batting (.376) and hits (109). Arizona's Scott Hairston (Missoula-PIO) placed first in total bases (171) and runs (81), and teammate Jesus Cota (Missoula-PIO) finished first in RBI (71) and tied three others at the top in homers (16). The most patient hitter in short-season ball may have been its leader in walks (70) and on-base percentage (.512): Boston's Kevin Youkilis (Lowell-NYP).

If a player appeared with more than one team in a given breakdown, we list him with his last team in that category. To qualify for leadership, full-season players had to have 383 plate appearances (350 PA for catchers), 112 innings pitched, 18 starts (starting pitchers) or 40 games with fewer than 18 starts (relief pitchers). Short-season players required 150 plate appearances, 55 innings pitched, nine starts (starting pitchers) or 20 games with fewer than nine starts (relief pitchers).

League abbreviations are as follows:

INT—International League (AAA)
PCL—Pacific Coast League (AAA)
EL—Eastern League (AA)
SL—Southern League (AA)
TL—Texas League (AA)
CAL—California League (A+)
CAR—Carolina League (A+)
FSL—Florida State League (A+)
MWL—Midwest League (A)
SAL—South Atlantic League (A)
NYP—New York-Penn League (A-)
NWL—Northwest League (A-)
APP—Appalachian League (R+)
PIO—Pioneer League (R+)
AZL—Arizona League (R)
GCL—Gulf Coast League (R)

Full-Season Batting Leaders

Batting Average

Player, Team	Lg	Org	Avg
Jim Rushford, Huntsville	**SL**	**Mil**	**.354**
Hank Blalock, Tulsa	TL	Tex	.352
Lyle Overbay, El Paso	TL	Ari	.352
Ken Harvey, Wichita	TL	KC	.350
Jason Maule, Michigan	MWL	Hou	.347
Roosevelt Brown, Iowa	PCL	ChC	.346
Ray Sadler, Lansing	MWL	ChC	.341
Jose Fernandez, Salt Lake	PCL	Ana	.338
Quinton McCracken, Edmonton	PCL	Min	.338
Dustan Mohr, New Britain	EL	Min	.336

Catchers Batting Average

Player, Team	Lg	Org	Avg
Ramon Castro, Calgary	**PCL**	**Fla**	**.336**
Toby Hall, Durham	INT	TB	.335
John Castellano, Wisconsin	MWL	Sea	.334
Craig Ansman, South Bend	MWL	Ari	.330
Victor Martinez, Kinston	CAR	Cle	.329
Corky Miller, Louisville	INT	Cin	.309
Ken Huckaby, Tucson	PCL	Ari	.306
Koyie Hill, Wilmington	SAL	LA	.301
Wil Nieves, Mobile	SL	SD	.300
Garett Gentry, Michigan	MWL	Hou	.299

First Basemen Batting Average

Player, Team	Lg	Org	Avg
Lyle Overbay, El Paso	**TL**	**Ari**	**.352**
Ken Harvey, Wichita	TL	KC	.350
Garrett Atkins, Salem	CAR	Col	.325
Luis Lopez, Syracuse	INT	Tor	.324
Butch Huskey, Colo Sprngs	PCL	Col	.323
Gary Burnham, Reading	EL	Phi	.318
Justin Morneau, New Britain	EL	Min	.314
Blair Barbier, Lansing	MWL	ChC	.314
Adrian Gonzalez, Kane County	MWL	Fla	.312
Todd Sears, Edmonton	PCL	Min	.311

Second Basemen Batting Average

Player, Team	Lg	Org	Avg
Pedro Liriano, Wisconsin	**MWL**	**Sea**	**.326**
Marco Pernalete, San Jose	CAL	SF	.321
Juan Melo, Fresno	PCL	SF	.312
Luis Gonzalez, Akron	EL	Cle	.312
Esteban German, Sacramento	PCL	Oak	.311
Matt Erickson, Calgary	PCL	Fla	.310
Adam Morrissey, Lansing	MWL	ChC	.309
Orlando Hudson, Syracuse	INT	Tor	.306
Kevin Hooper, Portland	EL	Fla	.306
P.J. Forbes, Scranton-WB	INT	Phi	.305

Third Basemen Batting Average

Player, Team	Lg	Org	Avg
Hank Blalock, Tulsa	**TL**	**Tex**	**.352**
Jason Maule, Michigan	MWL	Hou	.347
Jose Fernandez, Salt Lake	PCL	Ana	.338
Phil Hiatt, Las Vegas	PCL	LA	.330
Brian Dallimore, El Paso	TL	Ari	.327
Brian Rios, Toledo	INT	Det	.325
Mike Gulan, Calgary	PCL	Fla	.324
Sean Burroughs, Portland	PCL	SD	.322
J.P. Roberge, Scranton-WB	INT	Phi	.310
Casey Blake, Edmonton	PCL	Min	.309

Shortstops Batting Average

Player, Team	Lg	Org	Avg
Freddy Sanchez, Trenton	**EL**	**Bos**	**.334**
Tom Whiteman, Round Rock	TL	Hou	.316
Ronnie Merrill, Erie	EL	Det	.309
Jose Reyes, Capital Cty	SAL	NYM	.307
Wilson Betemit, Greenville	SL	Atl	.305
Angel Berroa, Wichita	TL	KC	.304
Omar Infante, Erie	EL	Det	.302
Tim Olson, El Paso	TL	Ari	.300
Ramon Vazquez, Tacoma	PCL	Sea	.300
Luis Figueroa, Norfolk	INT	NYM	.294

Outfielders Batting Average

Player, Team	Lg	Org	Avg
Jim Rushford, Huntsville	**SL**	**Mil**	**.354**
Roosevelt Brown, Iowa	PCL	ChC	.346
Ray Sadler, Lansing	MWL	ChC	.341
Quinton McCracken, Edmonton	PCL	Min	.338
Dustan Mohr, New Britain	EL	Min	.336
Chris Snelling, San Berndno	CAL	Sea	.336
Adam Dunn, Louisville	INT	Cin	.334
Mike O'Keefe, Rancho Cuca	CAL	Ana	.330
Matt Watson, Jupiter	FSL	Mon	.330
Kevin Reese, Fort Wayne	MWL	SD	.329

Switch-Hitters Batting Average

Player, Team	Lg	Org	Avg
Quinton McCracken, Edmonton	**PCL**	**Min**	**.338**
Victor Martinez, Kinston	CAR	Cle	.329
Rene Reyes, Asheville	SAL	Col	.322
Marco Pernalete, San Jose	CAL	SF	.321
Juan Melo, Fresno	PCL	SF	.312
Ronnie Merrill, Erie	EL	Det	.309
Terry Tiffee, Quad City	MWL	Min	.309
Jose Reyes, Capital Cty	SAL	NYM	.307
Orlando Hudson, Syracuse	INT	Tor	.306
Covelli Crisp, Potomac	CAR	StL	.306

Full-Season Batting Leaders

Hits

Player, Team	Lg	Org	H
Lyle Overbay, El Paso	**TL**	**Ari**	**187**
Hank Blalock, Tulsa	TL	Tex	179
Tony Torcato, Fresno	PCL	SF	179
Reed Johnson, Tennessee	SL	Tor	174
Dustan Mohr, New Britain	EL	Min	174
Matt Diaz, Bakersfield	CAL	TB	172
Brian Dallimore, El Paso	TL	Ari	169
Jason Conti, Durham	INT	TB	168
Jamal Strong, San Berndno	CAL	Sea	168
Marcus Thames, Norwich	EL	NYY	167

Doubles

Player, Team	Lg	Org	2B
Lyle Overbay, El Paso	**TL**	**Ari**	**49**
John Gall, Potomac	CAR	StL	48
Chad Alexander, Tacoma	PCL	Sea	45
Steve Smitherman, Dayton	MWL	Cin	45
Mike Gulan, Calgary	PCL	Fla	44
Garrett Atkins, Salem	CAR	Col	43
Marshall McDougall, Visalia	CAL	Oak	43
Marcus Thames, Norwich	EL	NYY	43
3 tied with			42

Triples

Player, Team	Lg	Org	3B
Brandon Littleton, Delmarva	**SAL**	**Bal**	**18**
Jose Reyes, Capital Cty	SAL	NYM	15
Jaime Bubela, Wisconsin	MWL	Sea	12
Jon Guzman, Burlington	MWL	KC	12
Victor Hall, South Bend	MWL	Ari	12
Henry Mateo, Ottawa	INT	Mon	12
Henry Stanley, Michigan	MWL	Hou	12
7 tied with			11

Home Runs

Player, Team	Lg	Org	HR
Phil Hiatt, Las Vegas	**PCL**	**LA**	**44**
Brandon Berger, Wichita	TL	KC	40
Jason Lane, Round Rock	TL	Hou	38
Israel Alcantara, Pawtucket	INT	Bos	36
Jacques Landry, Midland	TL	Oak	36
Mike Rivera, Erie	EL	Det	33
Lance Burkhart, Huntsville	SL	Mil	32
Adam Dunn, Louisville	INT	Cin	32
3 tied with			31

Extra-Base Hits

Player, Team	Lg	Org	XBH
Phil Hiatt, Las Vegas	**PCL**	**LA**	**78**
Marcus Thames, Norwich	**EL**	**NYY**	**78**
Jason Lane, Round Rock	TL	Hou	76
Brandon Berger, Wichita	TL	KC	71
Scott Morgan, Salt Lake	PCL	Ana	70
Mike Cuddyer, New Britain	EL	Min	69
Jose Fernandez, Salt Lake	PCL	Ana	68
Mike Gulan, Calgary	PCL	Fla	68
Dustan Mohr, New Britain	EL	Min	68
Josh Phelps, Tennessee	SL	Tor	68

Total Bases

Player, Team	Lg	Org	TB
Jason Lane, Round Rock	**TL**	**Hou**	**320**
Phil Hiatt, Las Vegas	PCL	LA	315
Marcus Thames, Norwich	EL	NYY	311
Brandon Berger, Wichita	TL	KC	294
Dustan Mohr, New Britain	EL	Min	293
Juan Rivera, Columbus	INT	NYY	287
Mike Cuddyer, New Britain	EL	Min	285
Marlon Byrd, Reading	EL	Phi	283
Jose Fernandez, Salt Lake	PCL	Ana	282
Lyle Overbay, El Paso	TL	Ari	281

Runs

Player, Team	Lg	Org	R
Esteban German, Sacramento	**PCL**	**Oak**	**119**
Jamal Strong, San Berndno	CAL	Sea	115
Marcus Thames, Norwich	EL	NYY	114
Marlon Byrd, Reading	EL	Phi	108
Phil Hiatt, Las Vegas	PCL	LA	107
Angel Berroa, Wichita	TL	KC	106
Reed Johnson, Tennessee	SL	Tor	104
Jason Lane, Round Rock	TL	Hou	103
Jim Rushford, Huntsville	SL	Mil	103
Jacques Landry, Midland	TL	Oak	102

Runs Batted In

Player, Team	Lg	Org	RBI
Jason Lane, Round Rock	**TL**	**Hou**	**124**
Brandon Berger, Wichita	TL	KC	118
Jose Fernandez, Salt Lake	PCL	Ana	114
Wily Mo Pena, Dayton	MWL	Cin	113
Hank Blalock, Tulsa	TL	Tex	108
Billy Martin, El Paso	TL	Ari	107
Garett Gentry, Michigan	MWL	Hou	103
Adrian Gonzalez, Kane County	MWL	Fla	103
Ryan Ludwick, Sacramento	PCL	Oak	103
2 tied with			102

Full-Season Batting Leaders

Walks

Player, Team	Lg	Org	BB
Lamont Matthews, Vero Beach	**FSL**	**LA**	**107**
Jack Cust, Tucson	PCL	Ari	102
Billy Martin, El Paso	TL	Ari	96
Marco Cunningham, Wilmington	CAR	KC	95
Gray Koonce, Portland	PCL	SD	94
Jamal Strong, San Berndno	CAL	Sea	91
Nate Espy, Clearwater	FSL	Phi	88
Shawn Fagan, Dunedin	FSL	Tor	86
Mark Burnett, Mudville	CAL	Cin	84
Eric Munson, Erie	EL	Det	84

Strikeouts

Player, Team	Lg	Org	K
Rob Stratton, Norfolk	**INT**	**NYM**	**203**
Darron Ingram, Birmingham	SL	CWS	188
Jeremy Owens, Lk Elsinore	CAL	SD	188
Jacques Landry, Midland	TL	Oak	184
Wily Mo Pena, Dayton	MWL	Cin	177
Justin Schuda, Chston-SC	SAL	TB	166
Tim Lemon, Peoria	MWL	StL	165
Tommy Murphy, Rancho Cuca	CAL	Ana	163
Tim Flaherty, San Jose	CAL	SF	162
Gabe Johnson, Peoria	MWL	StL	162

Plate Appearances/Strikeout

Player, Team	Lg	Org	PA/K
Mike Caruso, Durham	**INT**	**TB**	**19.41**
Toby Hall, Durham	INT	TB	18.55
Kary Bridges, Columbus	INT	NYY	15.66
Bryant Nelson, Nashville	PCL	Pit	15.31
Luis Figueroa, Norfolk	INT	NYM	14.09
Luis Rodriguez, Fort Myers	FSL	Min	13.60
Tony Medrano, Buffalo	INT	Cle	13.53
Shawn Schumacher, New Haven	EL	StL	13.43
Jason Phillips, Norfolk	INT	NYM	13.06
Victor Rodriguez, Norwich	EL	NYY	12.76

Hit By Pitch

Player, Team	Lg	Org	HBP
Angel Berroa, Wichita	**TL**	**KC**	**36**
Corky Miller, Louisville	INT	Cin	31
Kevin West, Quad City	MWL	Min	28
Jesus Basabe, Modesto	CAL	Oak	27
J.J. Sherrill, Columbus	SAL	Cle	27
Mike Campo, Cedar Rapds	MWL	Ana	26
Chad Meyers, Iowa	PCL	ChC	26
Jay Pecci, Midland	TL	Oak	26
4 tied with			23

Stolen Bases

Player, Team	Lg	Org	SB
Chris Morris, Peoria	**MWL**	**StL**	**111**
Jamal Strong, San Berndno	CAL	Sea	82
Manny Ravelo, Lynchburg	CAR	Pit	70
Bernabel Castro, Greensboro	SAL	NYY	67
Nook Logan, W Michigan	MWL	Det	67
Pedro Liriano, Wisconsin	MWL	Sea	65
Esix Snead, New Haven	EL	StL	64
Jesus Medrano, Brevard Cty	FSL	Fla	61
Victor Hall, South Bend	MWL	Ari	60
2 tied with			56

On-Base Percentage

Player, Team	Lg	Org	OBP
Jason Maule, Michigan	**MWL**	**Hou**	**.448**
Adam Dunn, Louisville	INT	Cin	.444
Jim Rushford, Huntsville	SL	Mil	.438
Lamont Matthews, Vero Beach	FSL	LA	.436
Jamal Strong, San Berndno	CAL	Sea	.436
Gray Koonce, Portland	PCL	SD	.429
Esteban German, Sacramento	PCL	Oak	.427
Adam Morrissey, Lansing	MWL	ChC	.427
Hank Blalock, Tulsa	TL	Tex	.424
Lyle Overbay, El Paso	TL	Ari	.423

Slugging Percentage

Player, Team	Lg	Org	SLG
Phil Hiatt, Las Vegas	**PCL**	**LA**	**.722**
Adam Dunn, Louisville	INT	Cin	.671
Brandon Berger, Wichita	TL	KC	.648
Ramon Castro, Calgary	PCL	Fla	.628
Roosevelt Brown, Iowa	PCL	ChC	.626
Jose Fernandez, Salt Lake	PCL	Ana	.624
Craig Ansman, South Bend	MWL	Ari	.623
Jason Lane, Round Rock	TL	Hou	.608
Lance Burkhart, Huntsville	SL	Mil	.604
Israel Alcantara, Pawtucket	INT	Bos	.599

Errors

Player, Team	Lg	Org	E
Ramon Carvajal, Potomac	**CAR**	**StL**	**48**
David Espinosa, Dayton	**MWL**	**Cin**	**48**
Daryl Clark, Beloit	MWL	Mil	47
Bill Hall, Huntsville	SL	Mil	45
Kelly Johnson, Macon	SAL	Atl	45
Corey Smith, Columbus	SAL	Cle	45
Tim Olson, El Paso	TL	Ari	44
Scott Youngbauer, Lakewood	SAL	Phi	43
5 tied with			42

Full-Season Pitching Leaders

Earned Run Average

Player, Team	Lg	Org	ERA
Josh Beckett, Portland	**EL**	**Fla**	**1.54**
Seung Song, Sarasota	FSL	Bos	1.90
Brad Thomas, New Britain	EL	Min	1.96
Corwin Malone, Birmingham	SL	CWS	1.98
Dennis Tankersley, Portland	PCL	SD	1.98
Rodrigo Rosario, Lexington	SAL	Hou	2.14
Ryan Kibler, Carolina	SL	Col	2.15
Jose Rojas, Vero Beach	FSL	LA	2.21
Mike Smith, Tennessee	SL	Tor	2.26
Craig Anderson, San Berndno	CAL	Sea	2.26
Denny Stark, Tacoma	PCL	Sea	2.28
Ty Howington, Chattanooga	SL	Cin	2.30
Brandon Claussen, Norwich	EL	NYY	2.31
Chris Narveson, Potomac	CAR	StL	2.31
Chris Elmore, Trenton	EL	Bos	2.34

Wins

Player, Team	Lg	Org	W
Matt Guerrier, Charlotte	**INT**	**CWS**	**18**
Boof Bonser, Hagerstown	SAL	SF	16
Nate Cornejo, Toledo	INT	Det	16
Julio DePaula, Tampa	FSL	NYY	16
Hansel Izquierdo, Portland	EL	Fla	16
Mario Ramos, Sacramento	PCL	Oak	16
14 tied with			15

Losses

Player, Team	Lg	Org	L
Rick Guttormson, Mobile	**SL**	**SD**	**17**
Duncan McAdoo, Fort Wayne	MWL	SD	16
Jason Saenz, Binghamton	EL	NYM	15
Brent Schoening, Fort Myers	FSL	Min	15
Rob Averette, Colo Sprngs	PCL	Col	14
Taylor Buchholz, Lakewood	SAL	Phi	14
Jack Cassel, Fort Wayne	MWL	SD	14
Frank Tejeda, Potomac	CAR	StL	14
Dave Zancanaro, Memphis	PCL	StL	14
14 tied with			13

Saves

Player, Team	Lg	Org	S
Jackson Markert, Hagerstown	**SAL**	**SF**	**39**
Edwin Almonte, Birmingham	SL	CWS	36
Scott Chiasson, Iowa	PCL	ChC	34
Scotty Layfield, Potomac	CAR	StL	31
Luke Anderson, San Jose	CAL	SF	30
Justin Huisman, Asheville	SAL	Col	30
Greg Runser, Charlotte	FSL	Tex	30
Mark Corey, Norfolk	INT	NYM	27
Matt DeWitt, Syracuse	INT	Tor	27
Jarrod Kingrey, Tennessee	SL	Tor	27
Jim Mann, New Orleans	PCL	Hou	27
Bart Miadich, Salt Lake	PCL	Ana	27
Johnny Ruffin, Louisville	INT	Cin	27
3 tied with			26

Games

Player, Team	Lg	Org	G
Brian Bowles, Syracuse	**INT**	**Tor**	**66**
Clay Condrey, Portland	**PCL**	**SD**	**66**
J.J. Trujillo, Mobile	**SL**	**SD**	**66**
Ray Beasley, Richmond	INT	Atl	65
Leslie Brea, Rochester	INT	Bal	63
Scott Chiasson, Iowa	PCL	ChC	63
Robbie Crabtree, Fresno	PCL	SF	63
Jason Martines, El Paso	TL	Ari	63
Tim McClaskey, Portland	EL	Fla	63
Mike Crudale, New Haven	EL	StL	62
Scott Eyre, Syracuse	INT	Tor	62
Mike Nicolas, Lk Elsinore	CAL	SD	62
Billy Sylvester, Richmond	INT	Atl	62
Chris Booker, Chattanooga	SL	Cin	61
7 tied with			60

Innings Pitched

Player, Team	Lg	Org	IP
Tim Kalita, Erie	**EL**	**Det**	**200.0**
Jared Fernandez, Louisville	INT	Cin	196.1
Mike Nannini, Lexington	SAL	Hou	190.1
John Stephens, Rochester	INT	Bal	190.0
Mike Smith, Tennessee	SL	Tor	187.1
Brandon Claussen, Norwich	EL	NYY	187.0
Randy Leek, Erie	EL	Det	186.1
John Lackey, Salt Lake	PCL	Ana	185.0
Josh Pearce, Memphis	PCL	StL	185.0
Ryan Kibler, Carolina	SL	Col	184.0
Nick Roberts, Round Rock	TL	Hou	182.2
Jim Magrane, Orlando	SL	TB	182.0
Ryan Baerlocher, Wichita	TL	KC	180.2
Dennis Ulacia, Birmingham	SL	CWS	180.1
2 tied with			180.0

Full-Season Pitching Leaders

Walks

Player, Team	Lg	Org	BB
Chad Hutchinson, Memphis	**PCL**	**StL**	**104**
Scott Dunn, Chattanooga	SL	Cin	102
Carlos Chantres, Indianapols	INT	Mil	93
Steve Sparks, Altoona	EL	Pit	89
Dave Elder, Oklahoma	PCL	Tex	86
Tony Pluta, Lexington	SAL	Hou	86
Ryan Price, Salem	CAR	Col	85
Justin Gordon, Beloit	MWL	Mil	84
Calvin Chipperfield, Lakeland	FSL	Det	81
Jason Saenz, Binghamton	EL	NYM	80
Joaquin Benoit, Oklahoma	PCL	Tex	79
Elvin Nina, Salt Lake	PCL	Ana	79
Tom Marx, Lakeland	FSL	Det	78
Steve Colyer, Vero Beach	FSL	LA	77
5 tied with			76

Strikeouts

Player, Team	Lg	Org	K
Brandon Claussen, Norwich	**EL**	**NYY**	**220**
Josh Beckett, Portland	EL	Fla	203
Matt Thornton, San Berndno	CAL	Sea	192
John Stephens, Rochester	INT	Bal	191
Jake Peavy, Mobile	SL	SD	188
Clint Nageotte, Wisconsin	MWL	Sea	187
Matt Smith, Tampa	FSL	NYY	187
Adam Wainwright, Macon	SAL	Atl	184
Wayne Nix, Midland	TL	Oak	179
Craig Anderson, San Berndno	CAL	Sea	178
Boof Bonser, Hagerstown	SAL	SF	178
Corwin Malone, Birmingham	SL	CWS	177
Justin Duchscherer, Oklahoma	PCL	Tex	176
Nick Neugebauer, Indianapols	INT	Mil	175
Mark Kiefer, Las Vegas	PCL	LA	174

Strikeouts/9 Innings—Starters

Player, Team	Lg	Org	K/9
Josh Beckett, Portland	**EL**	**Fla**	**13.05**
Jake Peavy, Mobile	SL	SD	12.69
Nick Neugebauer, Indianapols	INT	Mil	12.05
Boof Bonser, Hagerstown	SAL	SF	11.96
Francisco Rodriguez, Rancho Cuca	CAL	Ana	11.64
Dennis Tankersley, Portland	PCL	SD	11.42
Clint Nageotte, Wisconsin	MWL	Sea	11.05
Matt Thornton, San Berndno	CAL	Sea	11.01
Tim Redding, New Orleans	PCL	Hou	10.87
Carlos Hernandez, Round Rock	TL	Hou	10.81
Cary Ammons, Mudville	CAL	Cin	10.67
Brandon Claussen, Norwich	EL	NYY	10.59
Clifton Lee, Jupiter	FSL	Mon	10.59
Rich Gilbert, Savannah	SAL	Tex	10.41
Domingo Valdez, Charlotte	FSL	Tex	10.31

Strikeouts/9 Innings—Relievers

Player, Team	Lg	Org	K/9
Alberto Garza, Kinston	**CAR**	**Cle**	**14.24**
Mike Neu, Mudville	CAL	Cin	14.20
Buddy Hernandez, Myrtle Bch	CAR	Atl	14.10
Chris Booker, Chattanooga	SL	Cin	13.37
Franklyn German, Visalia	CAL	Oak	13.22
Arnaldo Munoz, Kannapolis	SAL	CWS	12.99
Johnny Ruffin, Louisville	INT	Cin	12.63
Chris Piersoll, Chattanooga	SL	Cin	12.54
Justin Kaye, Tacoma	PCL	Sea	12.51
Jim Serrano, Ottawa	INT	Mon	12.26
Jeremy Lambert, Memphis	PCL	StL	12.23
Roberto Giron, High Desert	CAL	Mil	12.22
Ryan Bukvich, Wichita	TL	KC	12.14
Mike Steele, Lakeland	FSL	Det	12.12
Doug Bochtler, Edmonton	PCL	Min	12.09

Hits/9 Innings—Starters

Player, Team	Lg	Org	H/9
Josh Beckett, Portland	**EL**	**Fla**	**5.27**
Rafael Soriano, San Antonio	TL	Sea	5.44
Dennis Tankersley, Portland	PCL	SD	5.88
Tim Redding, New Orleans	PCL	Hou	6.03
Domingo Valdez, Charlotte	FSL	Tex	6.03
Boof Bonser, Hagerstown	SAL	SF	6.11
Seung Song, Sarasota	FSL	Bos	6.13
Corwin Malone, Birmingham	SL	CWS	6.20
Joey Dawley, Greenville	SL	Atl	6.39
Clifton Lee, Jupiter	FSL	Mon	6.40
Jake Peavy, Mobile	SL	SD	6.41
Rodrigo Rosario, Lexington	SAL	Hou	6.43
Ty Howington, Chattanooga	SL	Cin	6.44
Adrian Burnside, Altoona	EL	Pit	6.48
Chris Narveson, Potomac	CAR	StL	6.48

Hits/9 Innings—Relievers

Player, Team	Lg	Org	H/9
Alex Pacheco, Norwich	**EL**	**NYY**	**4.50**
Arnaldo Munoz, Kannapolis	SAL	CWS	4.63
Joe Valentine, Winston-Sal	CAR	CWS	4.66
Jeremy Hill, Wilmington	CAR	KC	4.80
Kyle Kane, Birmingham	SL	CWS	5.22
Shane Heams, Toledo	INT	Det	5.23
Justin Huisman, Asheville	SAL	Col	5.40
Buddy Hernandez, Myrtle Bch	CAR	Atl	5.45
Chris Keelin, Clearwater	FSL	Phi	5.50
Ryan Larson, Kinston	CAR	Cle	5.51
Mike Steele, Lakeland	FSL	Det	5.51
Colin Young, Salem	CAR	Col	5.53
Brandon Puffer, Round Rock	TL	Hou	5.66
Shane Nance, Jacksnville	SL	LA	5.69
Pat Flury, Columbus	INT	NYY	5.71

396

Triple-A Batting Leaders

Batting Average

Player, Team	Lg	Org	Avg
Roosevelt Brown, Iowa	**PCL**	**ChC**	**.346**
Jose Fernandez, Salt Lake	PCL	Ana	.338
Quinton McCracken, Edmonton	PCL	Min	.338
Ramon Castro, Calgary	PCL	Fla	.336
Toby Hall, Durham	INT	TB	.335
Phil Hiatt, Las Vegas	PCL	LA	.330
Matt LeCroy, Edmonton	PCL	Min	.328
Brian Rios, Toledo	INT	Det	.325
Luis Lopez, Syracuse	INT	Tor	.324
Mike Gulan, Calgary	PCL	Fla	.324

Catchers Batting Average

Player, Team	Lg	Org	Avg
Ramon Castro, Calgary	**PCL**	**Fla**	**.336**
Toby Hall, Durham	INT	TB	.335
Humberto Cota, Nashville	PCL	Pit	.297
Geronimo Gil, Rochester	INT	Bal	.289
Javier Valentin, Edmonton	PCL	Min	.281
Brian Schneider, Ottawa	INT	Mon	.275
Yorvit Torrealba, Fresno	PCL	SF	.274
Cody McKay, Sacramento	PCL	Oak	.263
Keith McDonald, Memphis	PCL	StL	.261
Matt Walbeck, Scranton-WB	INT	Phi	.257

First Basemen Batting Average

Player, Team	Lg	Org	Avg
Luis Lopez, Syracuse	**INT**	**Tor**	**.324**
Butch Huskey, Colo Sprngs	PCL	Col	.323
Todd Sears, Edmonton	PCL	Min	.311
Todd Betts, Tacoma	PCL	Sea	.308
Damon Minor, Fresno	PCL	SF	.308
Kit Pellow, Omaha	PCL	KC	.291
Larry Barnes, Salt Lake	PCL	Ana	.290
Kevin Witt, Portland	PCL	SD	.289
Carlos Pena, Oklahoma	PCL	Tex	.288
Calvin Pickering, Louisville	INT	Cin	.282

Second Basemen Batting Average

Player, Team	Lg	Org	Avg
Juan Melo, Fresno	**PCL**	**SF**	**.312**
Matt Erickson, Calgary	PCL	Fla	.310
P.J. Forbes, Scranton-WB	INT	Phi	.305
Marty Malloy, Louisville	INT	Cin	.303
Chad Meyers, Iowa	PCL	ChC	.300
Kary Bridges, Columbus	INT	NYY	.297
Marcos Scutaro, Indianapols	INT	Mil	.295
Mike Caruso, Durham	INT	TB	.292
Liu Rodriguez, Charlotte	INT	CWS	.291
Tony Medrano, Buffalo	INT	Cle	.290

Third Basemen Batting Average

Player, Team	Lg	Org	Avg
Jose Fernandez, Salt Lake	**PCL**	**Ana**	**.338**
Phil Hiatt, Las Vegas	PCL	LA	.330
Brian Rios, Toledo	INT	Det	.325
Mike Gulan, Calgary	PCL	Fla	.324
Sean Burroughs, Portland	PCL	SD	.322
Casey Blake, Edmonton	PCL	Min	.309
Bryant Nelson, Nashville	PCL	Pit	.305
Reed Secrist, Nashville	PCL	Pit	.305
Jason Grabowski, Tacoma	PCL	Sea	.297
Craig Wilson, Omaha	PCL	KC	.296

Shortstops Batting Average

Player, Team	Lg	Org	Avg
Ramon Vazquez, Tacoma	**PCL**	**Sea**	**.300**
Luis Figueroa, Norfolk	INT	NYM	.294
Alex Cintron, Tucson	PCL	Ari	.292
Erick Almonte, Columbus	INT	NYY	.287
Julius Matos, Portland	PCL	SD	.279
Felipe Lopez, Syracuse	INT	Tor	.279
Chris Sexton, Louisville	INT	Cin	.279
Chris Snopek, Iowa	PCL	ChC	.277
Mark Ellis, Sacramento	PCL	Oak	.273
Jesse Garcia, Richmond	INT	Atl	.267

Outfielders Batting Average

Player, Team	Lg	Org	Avg
Roosevelt Brown, Iowa	**PCL**	**ChC**	**.346**
Quinton McCracken, Edmonton	PCL	Min	.338
Jason Conti, Durham	INT	TB	.324
Cliff Brumbaugh, Colo Sprngs	PCL	Col	.320
Chris Magruder, Oklahoma	PCL	Tex	.311
Tike Redman, Nashville	PCL	Pit	.304
Andy Abad, Sacramento	PCL	Oak	.301
Trenidad Hubbard, Iowa	PCL	ChC	.301
Bobby Smith, Durham	INT	TB	.301
Mike Peeples, Colo Sprngs	PCL	Col	.300

Switch-Hitters Batting Average

Player, Team	Lg	Org	Avg
Quinton McCracken, Edmonton	**PCL**	**Min**	**.338**
Juan Melo, Fresno	PCL	SF	.312
Chris Magruder, Oklahoma	PCL	Tex	.311
Bryant Nelson, Nashville	PCL	Pit	.305
Tony Mota, Las Vegas	PCL	LA	.296
Luis Figueroa, Norfolk	INT	NYM	.294
Alex Cintron, Tucson	PCL	Ari	.292
Liu Rodriguez, Charlotte	INT	CWS	.291
Ryan Balfe, Memphis	PCL	StL	.289
Bobby Kielty, Edmonton	PCL	Min	.287

Triple-A Batting Leaders

Hits

Player, Team	Lg	Org	H
Jason Conti, Durham	**INT**	**TB**	**168**
Raul Gonzalez, Louisville	INT	Cin	161
P.J. Forbes, Scranton-WB	INT	Phi	157
Mike Gulan, Calgary	PCL	Fla	157
Todd Betts, Tacoma	PCL	Sea	156
Bryant Nelson, Nashville	PCL	Pit	156
Chris Wakeland, Toledo	INT	Det	155
Chad Alexander, Tacoma	PCL	Sea	153
Jose Fernandez, Salt Lake	PCL	Ana	153
Mike Ryan, Edmonton	PCL	Min	152

Doubles

Player, Team	Lg	Org	2B
Chad Alexander, Tacoma	**PCL**	**Sea**	**45**
Mike Gulan, Calgary	PCL	Fla	44
Todd Betts, Tacoma	PCL	Sea	40
Raul Gonzalez, Louisville	INT	Cin	39
Scott Morgan, Salt Lake	PCL	Ana	39
Juan Thomas, Tacoma	PCL	Sea	39
Mark Ellis, Sacramento	PCL	Oak	38
Carlos Pena, Oklahoma	PCL	Tex	38
Jose Fernandez, Salt Lake	PCL	Ana	37
3 tied with			36

Triples

Player, Team	Lg	Org	3B
Henry Mateo, Ottawa	**INT**	**Mon**	**12**
Ross Gload, Iowa	PCL	ChC	10
Tike Redman, Nashville	PCL	Pit	10
Mike Caruso, Durham	INT	TB	9
Midre Cummings, Tucson	PCL	Ari	9
Chris Latham, Syracuse	INT	Tor	9
Donzell McDonald, Columbus	INT	NYY	9
Reggie Taylor, Scranton-WB	INT	Phi	9
6 tied with			8

Home Runs

Player, Team	Lg	Org	HR
Phil Hiatt, Las Vegas	**PCL**	**LA**	**44**
Israel Alcantara, Pawtucket	INT	Bos	36
Karim Garcia, Buffalo	INT	Cle	31
Jose Fernandez, Salt Lake	PCL	Ana	30
Scott Morgan, Salt Lake	PCL	Ana	28
Ramon Castro, Calgary	PCL	Fla	27
Jack Cust, Tucson	PCL	Ari	27
Kevin Witt, Portland	PCL	SD	27
Tony Zuniga, Fresno	PCL	SF	26
2 tied with			25

Extra-Base Hits

Player, Team	Lg	Org	XBH
Phil Hiatt, Las Vegas	**PCL**	**LA**	**78**
Scott Morgan, Salt Lake	PCL	Ana	70
Jose Fernandez, Salt Lake	PCL	Ana	68
Mike Gulan, Calgary	PCL	Fla	68
Carlos Pena, Oklahoma	PCL	Tex	64
Juan Thomas, Tacoma	PCL	Sea	64
Israel Alcantara, Pawtucket	INT	Bos	63
Mike Ryan, Edmonton	PCL	Min	61
Ramon Castro, Calgary	PCL	Fla	60
Kevin Witt, Portland	PCL	SD	60

Total Bases

Player, Team	Lg	Org	TB
Phil Hiatt, Las Vegas	**PCL**	**LA**	**315**
Jose Fernandez, Salt Lake	PCL	Ana	282
Mike Gulan, Calgary	PCL	Fla	271
Israel Alcantara, Pawtucket	INT	Bos	270
Juan Thomas, Tacoma	PCL	Sea	263
Chris Wakeland, Toledo	INT	Det	263
Scott Morgan, Salt Lake	PCL	Ana	262
Jason Conti, Durham	INT	TB	257
Mike Ryan, Edmonton	PCL	Min	256
Kevin Witt, Portland	PCL	SD	251

Runs

Player, Team	Lg	Org	R
Phil Hiatt, Las Vegas	**PCL**	**LA**	**107**
Jose Fernandez, Salt Lake	PCL	Ana	99
Chris Prieto, Las Vegas	PCL	LA	98
Scott Morgan, Salt Lake	PCL	Ana	93
Jason Conti, Durham	INT	TB	92
Chad Meyers, Iowa	PCL	ChC	92
Raul Gonzalez, Louisville	INT	Cin	90
Mike Ryan, Edmonton	PCL	Min	89
Todd Betts, Tacoma	PCL	Sea	87
Marcos Scutaro, Indianapolis	INT	Mil	87

Runs Batted In

Player, Team	Lg	Org	RBI
Jose Fernandez, Salt Lake	**PCL**	**Ana**	**114**
Phil Hiatt, Las Vegas	PCL	LA	99
Calvin Pickering, Louisville	INT	Cin	99
Juan Thomas, Tacoma	PCL	Sea	95
Ross Gload, Iowa	PCL	ChC	93
Mike Gulan, Calgary	PCL	Fla	92
Israel Alcantara, Pawtucket	INT	Bos	90
Ramon Castro, Calgary	PCL	Fla	90
Butch Huskey, Colo Sprngs	PCL	Col	87
Kevin Witt, Portland	PCL	SD	87

Triple-A Batting Leaders

Walks

Player, Team	Lg	Org	BB
Jack Cust, Tucson	**PCL**	**Ari**	**102**
Nick Johnson, Columbus	INT	NYY	81
Carlos Pena, Oklahoma	PCL	Tex	80
Kevin Orie, Scranton-WB	INT	Phi	77
Rich Becker, Toledo	INT	Det	76
Ramon Vazquez, Tacoma	PCL	Sea	76
Ryan Radmanovich, Nashville	PCL	Pit	70
Morgan Burkhart, Pawtucket	INT	Bos	68
Nick Punto, Scranton-WB	INT	Phi	68
Rob Ryan, Sacramento	PCL	Oak	68

Strikeouts

Player, Team	Lg	Org	K
Jack Cust, Tucson	**PCL**	**Ari**	**160**
Chad Hermansen, Nashville	PCL	Pit	154
Calvin Pickering, Louisville	INT	Cin	151
Sean McNally, Tucson	PCL	Ari	148
Keith Ginter, New Orleans	PCL	Hou	147
Alex Escobar, Norfolk	INT	NYM	146
Mike Gulan, Calgary	PCL	Fla	145
Juan Thomas, Tacoma	PCL	Sea	141
Cody Ransom, Fresno	PCL	SF	137
Danny Peoples, Buffalo	INT	Cle	133

Plate Appearances/Strikeout

Player, Team	Lg	Org	PA/K
Mike Caruso, Durham	**INT**	**TB**	**19.41**
Toby Hall, Durham	INT	TB	18.55
Kary Bridges, Columbus	INT	NYY	15.66
Bryant Nelson, Nashville	PCL	Pit	15.31
Luis Figueroa, Norfolk	INT	NYM	14.09
Tony Medrano, Buffalo	INT	Cle	13.53
Luis Lopez, Syracuse	INT	Tor	12.45
Tike Redman, Nashville	PCL	Pit	11.68
Kevin Sefcik, Buffalo	INT	Cle	10.63
Todd Betts, Tacoma	PCL	Sea	10.27

Hit By Pitch

Player, Team	Lg	Org	HBP
Chad Meyers, Iowa	**PCL**	**ChC**	**26**
Keith Ginter, New Orleans	PCL	Hou	23
Adam Everett, New Orleans	PCL	Hou	16
Nick Johnson, Columbus	INT	NYY	14
Ernie Young, Portland	PCL	SD	14
Jason Conti, Durham	INT	TB	13
Aaron Guiel, Omaha	PCL	KC	13
Mike Moriarty, Edmonton	PCL	Min	13
Kit Pellow, Omaha	PCL	KC	13
Chris Prieto, Las Vegas	PCL	LA	13

Stolen Bases

Player, Team	Lg	Org	SB
Henry Mateo, Ottawa	**INT**	**Mon**	**47**
Pedro Santana, Toledo	INT	Det	36
Nick Punto, Scranton-WB	INT	Phi	33
Reggie Taylor, Scranton-WB	INT	Phi	31
Gene Kingsale, Tacoma	PCL	Sea	28
Chad Meyers, Iowa	PCL	ChC	27
Alex Sanchez, Indianapols	INT	Mil	27
4 tied with			25

On-Base Percentage

Player, Team	Lg	Org	OBP
Jose Fernandez, Salt Lake	**PCL**	**Ana**	**.421**
Trenidad Hubbard, Iowa	PCL	ChC	.416
Jack Cust, Tucson	PCL	Ari	.415
Cliff Brumbaugh, Colo Sprngs	PCL	Col	.412
Carlos Pena, Oklahoma	PCL	Tex	.408
Chad Meyers, Iowa	PCL	ChC	.407
Nick Johnson, Columbus	INT	NYY	.407
Phil Hiatt, Las Vegas	PCL	LA	.406
Chris Prieto, Las Vegas	PCL	LA	.398
Reed Secrist, Nashville	PCL	Pit	.398

Slugging Percentage

Player, Team	Lg	Org	SLG
Phil Hiatt, Las Vegas	**PCL**	**LA**	**.722**
Ramon Castro, Calgary	PCL	Fla	.628
Roosevelt Brown, Iowa	PCL	ChC	.626
Jose Fernandez, Salt Lake	PCL	Ana	.624
Israel Alcantara, Pawtucket	INT	Bos	.599
Toby Hall, Durham	INT	TB	.568
Reed Secrist, Nashville	PCL	Pit	.565
Mike Gulan, Calgary	PCL	Fla	.559
Brian Banks, Calgary	PCL	Fla	.556
Damon Minor, Fresno	PCL	SF	.554

Errors

Player, Team	Lg	Org	E
Alex Cintron, Tucson	**PCL**	**Ari**	**32**
Elvis Pena, Indianapols	INT	Mil	31
Pedro Santana, Toledo	INT	Det	31
Eddy Garabito, Rochester	INT	Bal	28
Erick Almonte, Columbus	INT	NYY	27
Wilton Veras, Pawtucket	INT	Bos	26
Giomar Guevara, Toledo	INT	Det	25
Kelly Dransfeldt, Oklahoma	PCL	Tex	24
Adam Everett, New Orleans	PCL	Hou	24
Eddy Martinez, Rochester	INT	Bal	24

Triple-A Pitching Leaders

Earned Run Average

Player, Team	Lg	Org	ERA
Denny Stark, Tacoma	**PCL**	**Sea**	**2.37**
Brandon Duckworth, Scranton-WB	INT	Phi	2.63
Rigo Beltran, Scranton-WB	INT	Phi	2.96
Ruben Quevedo, Iowa	PCL	ChC	2.99
Pete Walker, Norfolk	INT	NYM	2.99
J.D. Arteaga, New Orleans	PCL	Hou	3.07
Mickey Callaway, Durham	INT	TB	3.07
Willie Banks, Pawtucket	INT	Bos	3.11
Brian Powell, New Orleans	PCL	Hou	3.17
Mike Meyers, Iowa	PCL	ChC	3.23
Mike Bacsik, Buffalo	INT	Cle	3.26
Trey Moore, Richmond	INT	Atl	3.31
Brett Jodie, Portland	PCL	SD	3.36
Carlos Castillo, Pawtucket	INT	Bos	3.41
Eric Moody, Nashville	PCL	Pit	3.45

Wins

Player, Team	Lg	Org	W
Denny Stark, Tacoma	**PCL**	**Sea**	**14**
Brandon Duckworth, Scranton-WB	INT	Phi	13
Nate Teut, Iowa	PCL	ChC	13
Pete Walker, Norfolk	INT	NYM	13
Mike Bacsik, Buffalo	INT	Cle	12
Brian Cooper, Salt Lake	PCL	Ana	12
Travis Harper, Durham	INT	TB	12
Brett Jodie, Portland	PCL	SD	12
Brandon Knight, Columbus	INT	NYY	12
9 tied with			11

Losses

Player, Team	Lg	Org	L
Rob Averette, Colo Sprngs	**PCL**	**Col**	**14**
Dave Zancanaro, Memphis	**PCL**	**StL**	**14**
Jason Simontacchi, Edmonton	PCL	Min	13
Evan Thomas, Scranton-WB	INT	Phi	13
14 tied with			11

Saves

Player, Team	Lg	Org	S
Matt DeWitt, Syracuse	**INT**	**Tor**	**27**
Jim Mann, New Orleans	**PCL**	**Hou**	**27**
Bart Miadich, Salt Lake	**PCL**	**Ana**	**27**
Johnny Ruffin, Louisville	**INT**	**Cin**	**27**
Bob Scanlan, Ottawa	INT	Mon	23
Kevin Gryboski, Tacoma	PCL	Sea	22
Oscar Henriquez, Norfolk	INT	NYM	19
Carlos Almanzar, Columbus	INT	NYY	18
Kris Foster, Rochester	INT	Bal	18
Roy Smith, Buffalo	INT	Cle	18
Matt Miller, Portland	PCL	SD	17
Chris Nichting, Louisville	INT	Cin	17
Rusty Meacham, Durham	INT	TB	15
David Riske, Buffalo	INT	Cle	15
5 tied with			14

Games

Player, Team	Lg	Org	G
Brian Bowles, Syracuse	**INT**	**Tor**	**66**
Ray Beasley, Richmond	INT	Atl	65
Leslie Brea, Rochester	INT	Bal	63
Robbie Crabtree, Fresno	PCL	SF	63
Scott Eyre, Syracuse	INT	Tor	62
Jim Dougherty, Las Vegas	PCL	LA	59
Derek Hasselhoff, Fresno	PCL	SF	59
Corey Brittan, Norfolk	INT	NYM	58
Archie Corbin, Charlotte	INT	CWS	58
Kevin Gryboski, Tacoma	PCL	Sea	58
Eric Gunderson, Columbus	INT	NYY	58
Jake Robbins, Richmond	INT	Atl	57
Lee Gardner, Durham	INT	TB	56
Justin Kaye, Tacoma	PCL	Sea	56
Brian Shouse, New Orleans	PCL	Hou	56

Innings Pitched

Player, Team	Lg	Org	IP
Jared Fernandez, Louisville	**INT**	**Cin**	**196.1**
Travis Driskill, New Orleans	PCL	Hou	178.2
Brian Cooper, Salt Lake	PCL	Ana	173.0
Tim Harikkala, Indianapols	INT	Mil	172.0
Kennie Steenstra, Tucson	PCL	Ari	170.0
Greg Wooten, Tacoma	PCL	Sea	169.1
Eric Ireland, Sacramento	PCL	Oak	168.1
Pete Walker, Norfolk	INT	NYM	168.1
Carlos Chantres, Indianapols	INT	Mil	167.1
Nate Teut, Iowa	PCL	ChC	167.0
Rob Averette, Colo Sprngs	PCL	Col	166.1
Justin Miller, Sacramento	PCL	Oak	165.0
Carlos Castillo, Pawtucket	INT	Bos	163.2
R.A. Dickey, Oklahoma	PCL	Tex	163.0
Trey Moore, Richmond	INT	Atl	163.0

Triple-A Pitching Leaders

Walks

Player, Team	Lg	Org	BB
Chad Hutchinson, Memphis	**PCL**	**StL**	**104**
Carlos Chantres, Indianapols	INT	Mil	93
Elvin Nina, Salt Lake	PCL	Ana	79
Mike MacDougal, Omaha	PCL	KC	76
Matt Kinney, Edmonton	PCL	Min	74
Joaquin Benoit, Oklahoma	PCL	Tex	73
Shane Loux, Toledo	INT	Det	73
Nate Teut, Iowa	PCL	ChC	69
Carlos Zambrano, Iowa	PCL	ChC	68
Mike Meyers, Iowa	PCL	ChC	64
Justin Miller, Sacramento	PCL	Oak	64
Steve Sparks, Nashville	PCL	Pit	64
Sean Douglass, Rochester	INT	Bal	61
3 tied with			60

Strikeouts

Player, Team	Lg	Org	K
Mark Kiefer, Las Vegas	**PCL**	**LA**	**174**
Brandon Knight, Columbus	INT	NYY	173
Kurt Ainsworth, Fresno	PCL	SF	157
Sean Douglass, Rochester	INT	Bal	156
Carlos Zambrano, Iowa	PCL	ChC	155
Brandon Duckworth, Scranton-WB	INT	Phi	150
Ruben Quevedo, Iowa	PCL	ChC	150
Matt Kinney, Edmonton	PCL	Min	146
Travis Driskill, New Orleans	PCL	Hou	145
Joaquin Benoit, Oklahoma	PCL	Tex	142
Justin Miller, Sacramento	PCL	Oak	134
Willie Banks, Pawtucket	INT	Bos	133
Joe Borowski, Iowa	PCL	ChC	131
Denny Stark, Tacoma	PCL	Sea	130
John Parrish, Rochester	INT	Bal	126

Strikeouts/9 Innings—Starters

Player, Team	Lg	Org	K/9
Chad Hutchinson, Memphis	**PCL**	**StL**	**10.23**
Joaquin Benoit, Oklahoma	PCL	Tex	9.76
Brandon Knight, Columbus	INT	NYY	9.59
Ruben Quevedo, Iowa	PCL	ChC	9.53
Kurt Ainsworth, Fresno	PCL	SF	9.48
Carlos Zambrano, Iowa	PCL	ChC	9.26
Brandon Duckworth, Scranton-WB	INT	Phi	9.18
Sean Douglass, Rochester	INT	Bal	8.65
John Parrish, Rochester	INT	Bal	8.53
Julio Santana, Fresno	PCL	SF	8.48
Brett Tomko, Tacoma	PCL	Sea	8.29
Randy Keisler, Columbus	INT	NYY	8.14
Matt Kinney, Edmonton	PCL	Min	8.13
Matt Wise, Salt Lake	PCL	Ana	8.10
Gary Knotts, Calgary	PCL	Fla	7.89

Strikeouts/9 Innings—Relievers

Player, Team	Lg	Org	K/9
Johnny Ruffin, Louisville	**INT**	**Cin**	**12.63**
Justin Kaye, Tacoma	PCL	Sea	12.51
Kevin Tolar, Toledo	INT	Det	11.73
Sean Lawrence, Tucson	PCL	Ari	11.73
Will Ohman, Iowa	PCL	ChC	11.65
Pat Flury, Columbus	INT	NYY	11.44
Toby Borland, Salt Lake	PCL	Ana	11.14
Bart Miadich, Salt Lake	PCL	Ana	11.14
Dave Maurer, Sacramento	PCL	Oak	10.97
Scott Eyre, Syracuse	INT	Tor	10.89
Chad Ricketts, Las Vegas	PCL	LA	10.74
Jim Mann, New Orleans	PCL	Hou	10.72
Leslie Brea, Rochester	INT	Bal	10.71
Roy Smith, Buffalo	INT	Cle	10.46
Craig Dingman, Colo Sprngs	PCL	Col	10.31

Hits/9 Innings—Starters

Player, Team	Lg	Org	H/9
Denny Stark, Tacoma	**PCL**	**Sea**	**7.36**
Carlos Zambrano, Iowa	PCL	ChC	7.41
Brandon Duckworth, Scranton-WB	INT	Phi	7.47
Richie Lewis, Norfolk	INT	NYM	7.55
Trey Moore, Richmond	INT	Atl	7.73
Pete Walker, Norfolk	INT	NYM	7.75
Joaquin Benoit, Oklahoma	PCL	Tex	7.76
John Parrish, Rochester	INT	Bal	7.78
Mike Meyers, Iowa	PCL	ChC	7.86
Ruben Quevedo, Iowa	PCL	ChC	7.88
Chris George, Omaha	PCL	KC	7.90
Bobby Munoz, Ottawa	INT	Mon	8.02
Travis Harper, Durham	INT	TB	8.09
Kurt Ainsworth, Fresno	PCL	SF	8.40
Mike Bacsik, Buffalo	INT	Cle	8.53

Hits/9 Innings—Relievers

Player, Team	Lg	Org	H/9
Tim Spooneybarger, Richmond	**INT**	**Atl**	**5.86**
Pat Flury, Columbus	INT	NYY	5.95
Justin Kaye, Tacoma	PCL	Sea	5.96
Ron Mahay, Iowa	PCL	ChC	5.97
Bart Miadich, Salt Lake	PCL	Ana	6.10
Toby Borland, Salt Lake	PCL	Ana	6.42
Pete Zamora, Scranton-WB	INT	Phi	6.47
Scott Linebrink, New Orleans	PCL	Hou	6.50
Doug Nickle, Scranton-WB	INT	Phi	6.51
Brian Bowles, Syracuse	INT	Tor	6.52
Derek Hasselhoff, Fresno	PCL	SF	6.59
Jason Boyd, Scranton-WB	INT	Phi	6.67
Archie Corbin, Charlotte	INT	CWS	6.75
Matt Skrmetta, Louisville	INT	Cin	6.79
Ken Vining, Charlotte	INT	CWS	6.85

Double-A Batting Leaders

Batting Average

Player, Team	Lg	Org	Avg
Lyle Overbay, El Paso	**TL**	**Ari**	**.352**
Dustan Mohr, New Britain	EL	Min	.336
Brian Dallimore, El Paso	TL	Ari	.327
Marcus Thames, Norwich	EL	NYY	.321
Ben Broussard, Chattanooga	SL	Cin	.320
Gary Burnham, Reading	EL	Phi	.318
Marlon Byrd, Reading	EL	Phi	.316
Jason Lane, Round Rock	TL	Hou	.316
Reed Johnson, Tennessee	SL	Tor	.314
Royce Huffman, Round Rock	TL	Hou	.309

Catchers Batting Average

Player, Team	Lg	Org	Avg
Wil Nieves, Mobile	**SL**	**SD**	**.300**
Jason Phillips, Binghamton	EL	NYM	.293
Josh Phelps, Tennessee	SL	Tor	.292
Mike Rivera, Erie	EL	Det	.289
Brad Cresse, El Paso	TL	Ari	.289
Jeff Smith, New Britain	EL	Min	.285
Jayson Werth, Tennessee	SL	Tor	.285
Josh Bard, Akron	EL	Cle	.270
Miguel Olivo, Birmingham	SL	CWS	.259
J.R. House, Altoona	EL	Pit	.258

First Basemen Batting Average

Player, Team	Lg	Org	Avg
Lyle Overbay, El Paso	**TL**	**Ari**	**.352**
Ben Broussard, Chattanooga	SL	Cin	.320
Gary Burnham, Reading	EL	Phi	.318
Franky Figueroa, Bowie	EL	Bal	.300
Robb Quinlan, Arkansas	TL	Ana	.295
Kevin Burford, Carolina	SL	Col	.289
Joe Dillon, Wichita	TL	KC	.287
Todd Mensik, Midland	TL	Oak	.283
Travis Hafner, Tulsa	TL	Tex	.282
Earl Snyder, Binghamton	EL	NYM	.281

Second Basemen Batting Average

Player, Team	Lg	Org	Avg
Kevin Hooper, Portland	**EL**	**Fla**	**.308**
Willie Harris, Bowie	EL	Bal	.305
Dave Matranga, Round Rock	TL	Hou	.302
Ruben Salazar, New Britain	EL	Min	.298
Tim Hummel, Birmingham	SL	CWS	.290
Mike Metcalfe, Chattanooga	SL	Cin	.289
Jeff Pickler, Huntsville	SL	Mil	.287
Esteban German, Midland	TL	Oak	.284
Rod Metzler, Wichita	TL	KC	.283
Craig Kuzmic, San Antonio	TL	Sea	.282

Third Basemen Batting Average

Player, Team	Lg	Org	Avg
Brian Dallimore, El Paso	**TL**	**Ari**	**.327**
Royce Huffman, Round Rock	TL	Hou	.309
Mike Cuddyer, New Britain	EL	Min	.301
Chris Saunders, Birmingham	SL	CWS	.294
Bo Robinson, San Antonio	TL	Sea	.293
Jerry Salzano, Trenton	EL	Bos	.283
Alex Pelaez, Mobile	SL	SD	.281
Mike Cervenak, Norwich	EL	NYY	.274
Andrew Beinbrink, Orlando	SL	TB	.273
Rodney Nye, Binghamton	EL	NYM	.270

Shortstops Batting Average

Player, Team	Lg	Org	Avg
Omar Infante, Erie	**EL**	**Det**	**.302**
Nelson Castro, Shreveport	TL	SF	.296
Jerson Perez, Tennessee	SL	Tor	.282
Joey Hammond, Bowie	EL	Bal	.278
Shaun Skrehot, Altoona	EL	Pit	.267
Oscar Salazar, Midland	TL	Oak	.267
Eric Bruntlett, Round Rock	TL	Hou	.266
Jorge Nunez, Jacksnville	SL	LA	.260
Jorge Cantu, Orlando	SL	TB	.256
Willie Bloomquist, San Antonio	TL	Sea	.255

Outfielders Batting Average

Player, Team	Lg	Org	Avg
Dustan Mohr, New Britain	**EL**	**Min**	**.336**
Marcus Thames, Norwich	EL	NYY	.321
Marlon Byrd, Reading	EL	Phi	.316
Jason Lane, Round Rock	TL	Hou	.316
Reed Johnson, Tennessee	SL	Tor	.314
Brandon Berger, Wichita	TL	KC	.308
Bubba Crosby, Jacksnville	SL	LA	.302
Joe Borchard, Birmingham	SL	CWS	.295
Doug Devore, El Paso	TL	Ari	.294
Jake Weber, San Antonio	TL	Sea	.293

Switch-Hitters Batting Average

Player, Team	Lg	Org	Avg
Joe Borchard, Birmingham	**SL**	**CWS**	**.295**
Mike Metcalfe, Chattanooga	SL	Cin	.289
Rod Metzler, Wichita	TL	KC	.283
Craig Kuzmic, San Antonio	TL	Sea	.282
Jeremy Luster, Shreveport	TL	SF	.273
Mickey Lopez, Reading	EL	Phi	.272
Jake Thrower, Mobile	SL	SD	.272
Angel Santos, Trenton	EL	Bos	.271
Albenis Machado, Harrisburg	EL	Mon	.261
Jay Pecci, Midland	TL	Oak	.260

Double-A Batting Leaders

Hits

Player, Team	Lg	Org	H
Lyle Overbay, El Paso	**TL**	**Ari**	**187**
Reed Johnson, Tennessee	SL	Tor	174
Dustan Mohr, New Britain	EL	Min	174
Brian Dallimore, El Paso	TL	Ari	169
Marcus Thames, Norwich	EL	NYY	167
Jason Lane, Round Rock	TL	Hou	166
Omar Infante, Erie	EL	Det	163
Marlon Byrd, Reading	EL	Phi	161
Franky Figueroa, Bowie	EL	Bal	160
Willie Harris, Bowie	EL	Bal	160

Extra-Base Hits

Player, Team	Lg	Org	XBH
Marcus Thames, Norwich	**EL**	**NYY**	**78**
Jason Lane, Round Rock	TL	Hou	76
Brandon Berger, Wichita	TL	KC	71
Mike Cuddyer, New Britain	EL	Min	69
Dustan Mohr, New Britain	EL	Min	68
Josh Phelps, Tennessee	SL	Tor	68
Lyle Overbay, El Paso	TL	Ari	65
Kevin Mench, Tulsa	TL	Tex	62
Eric Munson, Erie	EL	Det	62
3 tied with			60

Doubles

Player, Team	Lg	Org	2B
Lyle Overbay, El Paso	**TL**	**Ari**	**49**
Marcus Thames, Norwich	EL	NYY	43
Dustan Mohr, New Britain	EL	Min	41
Brad Cresse, El Paso	TL	Ari	39
Brian Dallimore, El Paso	TL	Ari	38
Mike Cervenak, Norwich	EL	NYY	37
Mike Cuddyer, New Britain	EL	Min	36
Jason Lane, Round Rock	TL	Hou	36
Mike Lockwood, Midland	TL	Oak	36
Josh Phelps, Tennessee	SL	Tor	36

Total Bases

Player, Team	Lg	Org	TB
Jason Lane, Round Rock	**TL**	**Hou**	**320**
Marcus Thames, Norwich	EL	NYY	311
Brandon Berger, Wichita	TL	KC	294
Dustan Mohr, New Britain	EL	Min	293
Mike Cuddyer, New Britain	EL	Min	285
Marlon Byrd, Reading	EL	Phi	283
Lyle Overbay, El Paso	TL	Ari	281
Josh Phelps, Tennessee	SL	Tor	273
Joe Borchard, Birmingham	SL	CWS	262
Jacques Landry, Midland	TL	Oak	252

Triples

Player, Team	Lg	Org	3B
Doug Devore, El Paso	**TL**	**Ari**	**11**
Abraham Nunez, Portland	EL	Fla	9
9 tied with			8

Runs

Player, Team	Lg	Org	R
Marcus Thames, Norwich	**EL**	**NYY**	**114**
Marlon Byrd, Reading	EL	Phi	108
Reed Johnson, Tennessee	SL	Tor	104
Jason Lane, Round Rock	TL	Hou	103
Jacques Landry, Midland	TL	Oak	102
Brandon Berger, Wichita	TL	KC	98
Joe Borchard, Birmingham	SL	CWS	95
Mike Cuddyer, New Britain	EL	Min	95
Josh Phelps, Tennessee	SL	Tor	95
Dustan Mohr, New Britain	EL	Min	90

Home Runs

Player, Team	Lg	Org	HR
Brandon Berger, Wichita	**TL**	**KC**	**40**
Jason Lane, Round Rock	TL	Hou	38
Jacques Landry, Midland	TL	Oak	36
Mike Rivera, Erie	EL	Det	33
Josh Phelps, Tennessee	SL	Tor	31
Marcus Thames, Norwich	EL	NYY	31
Mike Cuddyer, New Britain	EL	Min	30
Rob Stratton, Binghamton	EL	NYM	29
Marlon Byrd, Reading	EL	Phi	28
Joe Borchard, Birmingham	SL	CWS	27

Runs Batted In

Player, Team	Lg	Org	RBI
Jason Lane, Round Rock	**TL**	**Hou**	**124**
Brandon Berger, Wichita	TL	KC	118
Eric Munson, Erie	EL	Det	102
Mike Rivera, Erie	EL	Det	101
Lyle Overbay, El Paso	TL	Ari	100
Joe Borchard, Birmingham	SL	CWS	98
Charley Carter, Round Rock	TL	Hou	97
Josh Phelps, Tennessee	SL	Tor	97
Marcus Thames, Norwich	EL	NYY	97
Ryan Ludwick, Midland	TL	Oak	96

Double-A Batting Leaders

Walks

Player, Team	Lg	Org	BB
Gray Koonce, Mobile	**SL**	**SD**	**89**
Eric Munson, Erie	EL	Det	84
Abraham Nunez, Portland	EL	Fla	83
Bo Robinson, San Antonio	TL	Sea	81
Eric Battersby, Birmingham	SL	CWS	80
Josh Phelps, Tennessee	SL	Tor	80
Mike Cuddyer, New Britain	EL	Min	75
Marcus Thames, Norwich	EL	NYY	73
Ryan Owens, Carolina	SL	Col	68
4 tied with			67

Strikeouts

Player, Team	Lg	Org	K
Rob Stratton, Binghamton	**EL**	**NYM**	**201**
Darron Ingram, Birmingham	SL	CWS	188
Jacques Landry, Midland	TL	Oak	184
Joe Borchard, Birmingham	SL	CWS	158
Abraham Nunez, Portland	EL	Fla	155
Chris Haas, West Tenn	SL	ChC	151
Jeremy Owens, Mobile	SL	SD	149
Mark Fischer, Trenton	EL	Bos	148
Glenn Davis, Jacksnville	SL	LA	142
Eric Munson, Erie	EL	Det	141

Plate Appearances/Strikeout

Player, Team	Lg	Org	PA/K
Jeff Pickler, Huntsville	**SL**	**Mil**	**11.61**
Brooks Badeaux, Orlando	SL	TB	10.42
Brian Dallimore, El Paso	TL	Ari	10.23
Bo Robinson, San Antonio	TL	Sea	10.11
Juan Munoz, New Haven	EL	StL	10.08
Gary Burnham, Reading	EL	Phi	9.91
Jay Pecci, Midland	TL	Oak	9.79
Willie Bloomquist, San Antonio	TL	Sea	9.65
Jake Weber, San Antonio	TL	Sea	9.55
Joe Thurston, Jacksnville	SL	LA	9.48

Hit By Pitch

Player, Team	Lg	Org	HBP
Jay Pecci, Midland	**TL**	**Oak**	**26**
Joe Caruso, Wichita	TL	KC	23
Angel Berroa, Wichita	TL	KC	22
Jason Lane, Round Rock	TL	Hou	21
Corky Miller, Chattanooga	SL	Cin	19
Brad Cresse, El Paso	TL	Ari	18
Reed Johnson, Tennessee	SL	Tor	18
Josh Phelps, Tennessee	SL	Tor	17
Dusty Wathan, Portland	EL	Fla	17
Rich Gomez, Erie	EL	Det	16

Stolen Bases

Player, Team	Lg	Org	SB
Esix Snead, New Haven	**EL**	**StL**	**64**
Willie Harris, Bowie	EL	Bal	54
Jorge Nunez, Jacksnville	SL	LA	44
Reed Johnson, Tennessee	SL	Tor	42
Nelson Castro, Shreveport	TL	SF	38
Jacques Landry, Midland	TL	Oak	37
Carl Crawford, Orlando	SL	TB	36
Willie Bloomquist, San Antonio	TL	Sea	34
Chone Figgins, Arkansas	TL	Ana	34
Jeff Pickler, Huntsville	SL	Mil	34

On-Base Percentage

Player, Team	Lg	Org	OBP
Gray Koonce, Mobile	**SL**	**SD**	**.429**
Ben Broussard, Chattanooga	SL	Cin	.428
Lyle Overbay, El Paso	TL	Ari	.423
Esteban German, Midland	TL	Oak	.415
Marcus Thames, Norwich	EL	NYY	.410
Jason Lane, Round Rock	TL	Hou	.407
Josh Phelps, Tennessee	SL	Tor	.406
Travis Hafner, Tulsa	TL	Tex	.396
Dustan Mohr, New Britain	EL	Min	.395
Bo Robinson, San Antonio	TL	Sea	.395

Slugging Percentage

Player, Team	Lg	Org	SLG
Brandon Berger, Wichita	**TL**	**KC**	**.648**
Jason Lane, Round Rock	TL	Hou	.608
Marcus Thames, Norwich	EL	NYY	.598
Ben Broussard, Chattanooga	SL	Cin	.592
Mike Rivera, Erie	EL	Det	.578
Dustan Mohr, New Britain	EL	Min	.566
Josh Phelps, Tennessee	SL	Tor	.562
Mike Cuddyer, New Britain	EL	Min	.560
Marlon Byrd, Reading	EL	Phi	.555
Travis Hafner, Tulsa	TL	Tex	.545

Errors

Player, Team	Lg	Org	E
Jason Bowers, New Haven	**EL**	**StL**	**42**
Teuris Olivares, Norwich	EL	NYY	37
Oscar Salazar, Midland	TL	Oak	37
Nelson Castro, Shreveport	TL	SF	32
Jerson Perez, Tennessee	SL	Tor	31
Gabe Alvarez, Chattanooga	SL	Cin	30
Jorge Nunez, Jacksnville	SL	LA	30
Cleatus Davidson, Mobile	SL	SD	29
4 tied with			28

Double-A Pitching Leaders

Earned Run Average

Player, Team	Lg	Org	ERA
John Stephens, Bowie	**EL**	**Bal**	**1.84**
Brad Thomas, New Britain	EL	Min	1.96
Brandon Claussen, Norwich	EL	NYY	2.13
Justin Duchscherer, Tulsa	TL	Tex	2.31
Steve Smyth, West Tenn	SL	ChC	2.54
Lindsay Gulin, Jacksnville	SL	LA	2.64
Kevin Olsen, Portland	EL	Fla	2.68
Nate Cornejo, Erie	EL	Det	2.68
Randy Flores, Norwich	EL	NYY	2.78
Dan Wright, Birmingham	SL	CWS	2.82
Casey Fossum, Trenton	EL	Bos	2.83
Juan Rincon, New Britain	EL	Min	2.88
Jim Magrane, Orlando	SL	TB	2.97
Joey Dawley, Greenville	SL	Atl	3.04
Travis Smith, Round Rock	TL	Hou	3.09

Wins

Player, Team	Lg	Org	W
Chris Baker, Tennessee	**SL**	**Tor**	**15**
Tim Kalita, Erie	**EL**	**Det**	**15**
Carlos Silva, Reading	**EL**	**Phi**	**15**
Travis Smith, Round Rock	**TL**	**Hou**	**15**
Mitch Wylie, Birmingham	**SL**	**CWS**	**15**
Kiko Calero, Wichita	TL	KC	14
Randy Flores, Norwich	EL	NYY	14
Rick Kirsten, Erie	EL	Det	14
Juan Rincon, New Britain	EL	Min	14
Ryan Baerlocher, Wichita	TL	KC	13
Brett Myers, Reading	EL	Phi	13
Corey Thurman, Wichita	TL	KC	13
4 tied with			12

Losses

Player, Team	Lg	Org	L
Rick Guttormson, Mobile	**SL**	**SD**	**16**
Jason Saenz, Binghamton	EL	NYM	15
Dusty Bergman, Arkansas	TL	Ana	13
Mike Paradis, Bowie	EL	Bal	13
Luke Hudson, Carolina	SL	Col	12
Corey Lee, Tulsa	TL	Tex	12
Chuck Lehr, Midland	TL	Oak	12
Jim Magrane, Orlando	SL	TB	12
Nick Maness, Binghamton	EL	NYM	12
Nick Stocks, New Haven	EL	StL	12
7 tied with			11

Saves

Player, Team	Lg	Org	S
Edwin Almonte, Birmingham	**SL**	**CWS**	**36**
Jarrod Kingrey, Tennessee	SL	Tor	27
Alex Pacheco, Norwich	EL	NYY	26
Scott Chiasson, West Tenn	SL	ChC	24
Terry Pearson, Erie	EL	Det	23
Travis Wade, Round Rock	TL	Hou	23
Jeff Verplancke, Shreveport	TL	SF	22
Blaine Neal, Portland	EL	Fla	21
Jim Serrano, Harrisburg	EL	Mon	20
Corey Spencer, Trenton	EL	Bos	20
Nathan Field, Wichita	TL	KC	19
Chris Piersoll, Chattanooga	SL	Cin	19
Jeremy Fikac, Mobile	SL	SD	18
4 tied with			17

Games

Player, Team	Lg	Org	G
Mike Crudale, New Haven	**EL**	**StL**	**62**
Chris Booker, Chattanooga	SL	Cin	61
Travis Wade, Round Rock	TL	Hou	60
Terry Pearson, Erie	EL	Det	59
Talley Haines, Orlando	SL	TB	58
Rick Palma, West Tenn	SL	ChC	57
Jeriome Robertson, Round Rock	TL	Hou	57
Brandon Puffer, Round Rock	TL	Hou	56
Tyler Yates, Midland	TL	Oak	56
Claudio Galva, Midland	TL	Oak	55
Corey Spencer, Trenton	EL	Bos	55
5 tied with			54

Innings Pitched

Player, Team	Lg	Org	IP
Tim Kalita, Erie	**EL**	**Det**	**200.0**
Jim Magrane, Orlando	SL	TB	182.0
Ryan Baerlocher, Wichita	TL	KC	180.2
Carlos Silva, Reading	EL	Phi	180.0
Randy Leek, Erie	EL	Det	179.1
Chris Baker, Tennessee	SL	Tor	179.0
Jeff Heaverlo, San Antonio	TL	Sea	178.2
Brian Rogers, Norwich	EL	NYY	177.1
Andy Pratt, Tulsa	TL	Tex	168.0
Travis Thompson, Chattanooga	SL	Cin	167.0
Alex Graman, Norwich	EL	NYY	166.1
Luke Hudson, Carolina	SL	Col	165.0
Eric Junge, Jacksnville	SL	LA	164.0
Derek Lee, Huntsville	SL	Mil	162.1
Rick Kirsten, Erie	EL	Det	161.2

Double-A Pitching Leaders

Walks

Player, Team	Lg	Org	BB
Jason Saenz, Binghamton	**EL**	**NYM**	**80**
Ron Chiavacci, Harrisburg	EL	Mon	76
Chris Capuano, El Paso	TL	Ari	75
Scott Dunn, Chattanooga	SL	Cin	71
Rob Purvis, Birmingham	SL	CWS	70
Carlos Hernandez, Round Rock	TL	Hou	69
Luke Hudson, Carolina	SL	Col	68
Claudio Vargas, Portland	EL	Fla	67
Josh Kalinowski, Carolina	SL	Col	65
Nick Maness, Binghamton	EL	NYM	65
Corey Thurman, Wichita	TL	KC	65
5 tied with			63

Strikeouts

Player, Team	Lg	Org	K
Jeff Heaverlo, San Antonio	**TL**	**Sea**	**173**
Chris Capuano, El Paso	TL	Ari	167
Carlos Hernandez, Round Rock	TL	Hou	167
Colby Lewis, Tulsa	TL	Tex	162
Ron Chiavacci, Harrisburg	EL	Mon	161
Brandon Claussen, Norwich	EL	NYY	151
Claudio Vargas, Portland	EL	Fla	151
Brian Rogers, Norwich	EL	NYY	150
Nick Neugebauer, Huntsville	SL	Mil	149
Corey Thurman, Wichita	TL	KC	148
Tim Kalita, Erie	EL	Det	147
Luke Hudson, Carolina	SL	Col	145
Kevin Olsen, Portland	EL	Fla	144
Rick Kirsten, Erie	EL	Det	143
Alex Graman, Norwich	EL	NYY	138

Strikeouts/9 Innings—Starters

Player, Team	Lg	Org	K/9
Nick Neugebauer, Huntsville	**SL**	**Mil**	**12.57**
Carlos Hernandez, Round Rock	TL	Hou	10.81
Brandon Claussen, Norwich	EL	NYY	10.37
Juan Cruz, West Tenn	SL	ChC	10.16
Casey Fossum, Trenton	EL	Bos	9.94
Ron Chiavacci, Harrisburg	EL	Mon	9.83
Justin Duchscherer, Tulsa	TL	Tex	9.54
Chris Capuano, El Paso	TL	Ari	9.43
Colby Lewis, Tulsa	TL	Tex	9.35
Joey Dawley, Greenville	SL	Atl	9.19
Adrian Burnside, Altoona	EL	Pit	8.91
Adam Johnson, New Britain	EL	Min	8.76
Jeff Heaverlo, San Antonio	TL	Sea	8.71
Dan Wright, Birmingham	SL	CWS	8.60
Corey Thurman, Wichita	TL	KC	8.59

Strikeouts/9 Innings—Relievers

Player, Team	Lg	Org	K/9
Chris Booker, Chattanooga	**SL**	**Cin**	**13.37**
Chris Piersoll, Chattanooga	SL	Cin	12.54
Jim Serrano, Harrisburg	EL	Mon	12.24
Kevin Frederick, New Britain	EL	Min	11.87
Alex Pacheco, Norwich	EL	NYY	11.70
Brian Mallette, Huntsville	SL	Mil	11.62
Mike Nakamura, New Britain	EL	Min	11.36
Aquilino Lopez, San Antonio	TL	Sea	11.35
Tom Shearn, Round Rock	TL	Hou	11.13
Aaron Rakers, Bowie	EL	Bal	11.04
Cam Esslinger, Carolina	SL	Col	10.93
Eric Eckenstahler, Erie	EL	Det	10.16
Brandon Puffer, Round Rock	TL	Hou	9.91
Jeremy Fikac, Mobile	SL	SD	9.83
Mike Crudale, New Haven	EL	StL	9.52

Hits/9 Innings—Starters

Player, Team	Lg	Org	H/9
Adrian Burnside, Altoona	**EL**	**Pit**	**6.48**
Joey Dawley, Greenville	SL	Atl	6.71
Justin Duchscherer, Tulsa	TL	Tex	6.77
Corey Thurman, Wichita	TL	KC	6.79
Brad Thomas, New Britain	EL	Min	6.86
Claudio Vargas, Portland	EL	Fla	6.91
Brandon Claussen, Norwich	EL	NYY	6.94
Kevin Olsen, Portland	EL	Fla	7.16
Carlos Hernandez, Round Rock	TL	Hou	7.45
John Lackey, Arkansas	TL	Ana	7.49
Dan Wright, Birmingham	SL	CWS	7.52
Juan Rincon, New Britain	EL	Min	7.63
Jimmy Osting, Mobile	SL	SD	7.71
Nate Cornejo, Erie	EL	Det	7.75
Casey Fossum, Trenton	EL	Bos	7.80

Hits/9 Innings—Relievers

Player, Team	Lg	Org	H/9
Alex Pacheco, Norwich	**EL**	**NYY**	**4.50**
Jim Serrano, Harrisburg	EL	Mon	5.03
Kevin Lovingier, Norwich	EL	NYY	5.62
Brandon Puffer, Round Rock	TL	Hou	5.66
Kevin Frederick, New Britain	EL	Min	6.10
Pedro Feliciano, Jacksnville	SL	LA	6.12
Scott Chiasson, West Tenn	SL	ChC	6.31
Kevin Sheredy, New Haven	EL	StL	6.47
Jeremy Blevins, Norwich	EL	NYY	6.54
Cary Hiles, Reading	EL	Phi	6.61
Jarrod Kingrey, Tennessee	SL	Tor	6.75
Cam Esslinger, Carolina	SL	Col	6.86
Chris Booker, Chattanooga	SL	Cin	6.88
Aquilino Lopez, San Antonio	TL	Sea	6.89
Joe Cotton, Midland	TL	Oak	6.92

Class-A Batting Leaders

Batting Average

Player, Team	Lg	Org	Avg
Jason Maule, Michigan	**MWL**	**Hou**	**.347**
Ray Sadler, Lansing	MWL	ChC	.341
Chris Snelling, San Berndno	CAL	Sea	.336
John Castellano, Wisconsin	MWL	Sea	.334
Craig Ansman, South Bend	MWL	Ari	.330
Mike O'Keefe, Rancho Cuca	CAL	Ana	.330
Matt Watson, Jupiter	FSL	Mon	.330
Kevin Reese, Fort Wayne	MWL	SD	.329
Victor Martinez, Kinston	CAR	Cle	.329
Matt Diaz, Bakersfield	CAL	TB	.328

Catchers Batting Average

Player, Team	Lg	Org	Avg
John Castellano, Wisconsin	**MWL**	**Sea**	**.334**
Craig Ansman, South Bend	MWL	Ari	.330
Victor Martinez, Kinston	CAR	Cle	.329
Koyie Hill, Wilmington	SAL	LA	.301
Garett Gentry, Michigan	MWL	Hou	.299
J.D. Closser, Lancaster	CAL	Ari	.291
Ron Paulino, Lynchburg	CAR	Pit	.290
Kevin Cash, Dunedin	FSL	Tor	.283
Eliezer Alfonzo, Beloit	MWL	Mil	.277
Omar Fuentes, Tampa	FSL	NYY	.276

First Basemen Batting Average

Player, Team	Lg	Org	Avg
Justin Morneau, Fort Myers	**FSL**	**Min**	**.328**
Garrett Atkins, Salem	CAR	Col	.325
Blair Barbier, Lansing	MWL	ChC	.314
Adrian Gonzalez, Kane County	MWL	Fla	.312
John Gall, Potomac	CAR	StL	.311
Jason Botts, Charlotte	FSL	Tex	.304
Xavier Nady, Lk Elsinore	CAL	SD	.302
Billy Martin, Lancaster	CAL	Ari	.299
Jeff Wagner, Rancho Cuca	CAL	Ana	.291
Deivis Santos, Hagerstown	SAL	SF	.290

Second Basemen Batting Average

Player, Team	Lg	Org	Avg
Pedro Liriano, Wisconsin	**MWL**	**Sea**	**.326**
Adam Morrissey, Lansing	MWL	ChC	.309
Andy Green, South Bend	MWL	Ari	.300
Matt Kata, Lancaster	CAL	Ari	.296
Felix Escalona, Lexington	SAL	Hou	.289
Darren Fenster, Burlington	MWL	KC	.287
Javier Colina, Salem	CAR	Col	.285
Josh Wilson, Kane County	MWL	Fla	.285
Edwin Yan, Hickory	SAL	Pit	.283
Gary Cates, Delmarva	SAL	Bal	.282

Third Basemen Batting Average

Player, Team	Lg	Org	Avg
Jason Maule, Michigan	**MWL**	**Hou**	**.347**
Terry Tiffee, Quad City	MWL	Min	.309
Corey Myers, Lancaster	CAL	Ari	.307
Travis Chapman, Clearwater	FSL	Phi	.307
Shawn Fagan, Dunedin	FSL	Tor	.301
Justin Sherrod, Sarasota	FSL	Bos	.295
G.J. Raymundo, Rancho Cuca	CAL	Ana	.293
Napolean Calzado, Frederick	CAR	Bal	.287
Daryl Clark, Beloit	MWL	Mil	.283
Curt Fiore, Myrtle Bch	CAR	Atl	.283

Shortstops Batting Average

Player, Team	Lg	Org	Avg
Tom Whiteman, Lexington	**SAL**	**Hou**	**.319**
Jose Reyes, Capital Cty	SAL	NYM	.307
Ambiorix Reyes, Clearwater	FSL	Phi	.290
Kelly Johnson, Macon	SAL	Atl	.289
Jim Deschaine, Daytona	FSL	ChC	.289
Jimmy Alvarez, Dunedin	FSL	Tor	.283
Luis Maza, Quad City	MWL	Min	.280
Luis Rodriguez, Fort Myers	FSL	Min	.274
Jose Cabrera, Kane County	MWL	Fla	.268
Ariel Durango, Wisconsin	MWL	Sea	.264

Outfielders Batting Average

Player, Team	Lg	Org	Avg
Ray Sadler, Lansing	**MWL**	**ChC**	**.341**
Chris Snelling, San Berndno	CAL	Sea	.336
Mike O'Keefe, Rancho Cuca	CAL	Ana	.330
Matt Watson, Jupiter	FSL	Mon	.330
Kevin Reese, Fort Wayne	MWL	SD	.329
Matt Diaz, Bakersfield	CAL	TB	.328
Brandon Watson, Clinton	MWL	Mon	.327
Jamal Strong, San Berndno	CAL	Sea	.326
Rene Reyes, Asheville	SAL	Col	.322
Nathan Kaup, Bakersfield	CAL	TB	.321

Switch-Hitters Batting Average

Player, Team	Lg	Org	Avg
Victor Martinez, Kinston	**CAR**	**Cle**	**.329**
Rene Reyes, Asheville	SAL	Col	.322
Terry Tiffee, Quad City	MWL	Min	.309
Jose Reyes, Capital Cty	SAL	NYM	.307
Covelli Crisp, Potomac	CAR	StL	.306
Shawn Garrett, Lynchburg	CAR	Pit	.305
Jason Botts, Charlotte	FSL	Tex	.304
Koyie Hill, Wilmington	SAL	LA	.301
Matt Kata, Lancaster	CAL	Ari	.296
Chris Morris, Peoria	MWL	StL	.294

Class-A Batting Leaders

Hits

Player, Team	Lg	Org	H
Matt Diaz, Bakersfield	**CAL**	**TB**	**172**
Jamal Strong, San Berndno	CAL	Sea	168
John Gall, Potomac	CAR	StL	163
Covelli Crisp, Potomac	CAR	StL	162
Jaime Bubela, Wisconsin	MWL	Sea	161
Adrian Gonzalez, Kane County	MWL	Fla	161
Brandon Watson, Clinton	MWL	Mon	160
Xavier Nady, Lk Elsinore	CAL	SD	158
Jon Topolski, Lexington	SAL	Hou	158
Rene Reyes, Asheville	SAL	Col	156

Doubles

Player, Team	Lg	Org	2B
John Gall, Potomac	**CAR**	**StL**	**48**
Steve Smitherman, Dayton	MWL	Cin	45
Garrett Atkins, Salem	CAR	Col	43
Marshall McDougall, Visalia	CAL	Oak	43
Ryan Christianson, San Berndno	CAL	Sea	42
Felix Escalona, Lexington	SAL	Hou	42
Bill Scott, High Desert	CAL	Mil	42
Matt Diaz, Bakersfield	CAL	TB	40
3 tied with			38

Triples

Player, Team	Lg	Org	3B
Brandon Littleton, Delmarva	**SAL**	**Bal**	**18**
Jose Reyes, Capital Cty	SAL	NYM	15
Jaime Bubela, Wisconsin	MWL	Sea	12
Jon Guzman, Burlington	MWL	KC	12
Victor Hall, South Bend	MWL	Ari	12
Henry Stanley, Michigan	MWL	Hou	12
5 tied with			11

Home Runs

Player, Team	Lg	Org	HR
Jason Kinchen, Greensboro	**SAL**	**NYY**	**30**
Samone Peters, Dayton	MWL	Cin	28
Tim Flaherty, San Jose	CAL	SF	26
Billy Martin, Lancaster	CAL	Ari	26
Xavier Nady, Lk Elsinore	CAL	SD	26
Wily Mo Pena, Dayton	MWL	Cin	26
Dan Trumble, Hagerstown	SAL	SF	26
Jeremy Cotten, Hickory	SAL	Pit	25
Justin Schuda, Chston-SC	SAL	TB	25
3 tied with			24

Extra-Base Hits

Player, Team	Lg	Org	XBH
Steve Smitherman, Dayton	**MWL**	**Cin**	**67**
Xavier Nady, Lk Elsinore	CAL	SD	65
Billy Martin, Lancaster	CAL	Ari	63
Marshall McDougall, Visalia	CAL	Oak	62
Jason Dubois, Lansing	MWL	ChC	61
Matt Bowser, Visalia	CAL	Oak	60
Felix Escalona, Lexington	SAL	Hou	60
Mitch Jones, Tampa	FSL	NYY	60
3 tied with			59

Total Bases

Player, Team	Lg	Org	TB
Xavier Nady, Lk Elsinore	**CAL**	**SD**	**276**
Jon Topolski, Lexington	SAL	Hou	271
Matt Diaz, Bakersfield	CAL	TB	267
Jason Kinchen, Greensboro	SAL	NYY	267
Billy Martin, Lancaster	CAL	Ari	260
Adrian Gonzalez, Kane County	MWL	Fla	251
Jason Dubois, Lansing	MWL	ChC	249
Felix Escalona, Lexington	SAL	Hou	249
3 tied with			248

Runs

Player, Team	Lg	Org	R
Jamal Strong, San Berndno	**CAL**	**Sea**	**115**
Jason Maule, Michigan	MWL	Hou	101
Steve Scarborough, High Desert	CAL	Mil	101
Billy Martin, Lancaster	CAL	Ari	98
Jon Topolski, Lexington	SAL	Hou	98
Jaime Bubela, Wisconsin	MWL	Sea	96
Xavier Nady, Lk Elsinore	CAL	SD	96
Jason Ellison, Hagerstown	SAL	SF	95
Jesus Medrano, Brevard Cty	FSL	Fla	93
3 tied with			92

Runs Batted In

Player, Team	Lg	Org	RBI
Wily Mo Pena, Dayton	**MWL**	**Cin**	**113**
Billy Martin, Lancaster	CAL	Ari	106
Garett Gentry, Michigan	MWL	Hou	103
Adrian Gonzalez, Kane County	MWL	Fla	103
Bill Scott, High Desert	CAL	Mil	102
Xavier Nady, Lk Elsinore	CAL	SD	100
Jon Topolski, Lexington	SAL	Hou	96
Jesus Basabe, Modesto	CAL	Oak	93
Ramon German, Lexington	SAL	Hou	93
Justin Morneau, Fort Myers	FSL	Min	93

Class-A Batting Leaders

Walks

Player, Team	Lg	Org	BB
Marco Cunningham, Wilmington	**CAR**	**KC**	**95**
Billy Martin, Lancaster	**CAL**	**Ari**	**95**
Lamont Matthews, Vero Beach	**FSL**	**LA**	**95**
Jamal Strong, San Berndno	CAL	Sea	91
Nate Espy, Clearwater	FSL	Phi	88
Shawn Fagan, Dunedin	FSL	Tor	86
Mark Burnett, Mudville	CAL	Cin	84
Chris Morris, Peoria	MWL	StL	83
Luis Rodriguez, Fort Myers	FSL	Min	82
2 tied with			81

Strikeouts

Player, Team	Lg	Org	K
Wily Mo Pena, Dayton	**MWL**	**Cin**	**177**
Justin Schuda, Chston-SC	SAL	TB	166
Tim Lemon, Peoria	MWL	StL	165
Tommy Murphy, Rancho Cuca	CAL	Ana	163
Tim Flaherty, San Jose	CAL	SF	162
Gabe Johnson, Peoria	MWL	StL	162
Nick Wilfong, Hagerstown	SAL	SF	161
Don Ross, Wilmington	CAR	KC	159
Justin Leone, San Berndno	CAL	Sea	158
Samone Peters, Dayton	MWL	Cin	158

Plate Appearances/Strikeout

Player, Team	Lg	Org	PA/K
Luis Rodriguez, Fort Myers	**FSL**	**Min**	**13.60**
Jesus Feliciano, Vero Beach	FSL	LA	12.63
John Castellano, Wisconsin	MWL	Sea	11.74
Matt Watson, Jupiter	FSL	Mon	11.51
Andy Green, South Bend	MWL	Ari	11.24
Terry Tiffee, Quad City	MWL	Min	11.17
Gary Cates, Delmarva	SAL	Bal	10.59
Fernando Rios, Mudville	CAL	Cin	10.36
Blake Blasi, Daytona	FSL	ChC	10.14
Travis Chapman, Clearwater	FSL	Phi	10.05

Hit By Pitch

Player, Team	Lg	Org	HBP
Kevin West, Quad City	**MWL**	**Min**	**28**
Jesus Basabe, Modesto	CAL	Oak	27
J.J. Sherrill, Columbus	SAL	Cle	27
Mike Campo, Cedar Rapds	MWL	Ana	26
Luis Maza, Quad City	MWL	Min	23
Justin Sherrod, Sarasota	FSL	Bos	23
Chris Snelling, San Berndno	CAL	Sea	21
Jason Botts, Charlotte	FSL	Tex	20
5 tied with			19

Stolen Bases

Player, Team	Lg	Org	SB
Chris Morris, Peoria	**MWL**	**StL**	**111**
Jamal Strong, San Berndno	CAL	Sea	82
Manny Ravelo, Lynchburg	CAR	Pit	70
Bernabel Castro, Greensboro	SAL	NYY	67
Nook Logan, W Michigan	MWL	Det	67
Pedro Liriano, Wisconsin	MWL	Sea	65
Jesus Medrano, Brevard Cty	FSL	Fla	61
Victor Hall, South Bend	MWL	Ari	60
Jason Maule, Michigan	MWL	Hou	56
Edwin Yan, Hickory	SAL	Pit	56

On-Base Percentage

Player, Team	Lg	Org	OBP
Lamont Matthews, Vero Beach	**FSL**	**LA**	**.458**
Jason Maule, Michigan	MWL	Hou	.448
Jamal Strong, San Berndno	CAL	Sea	.436
Adam Morrissey, Lansing	MWL	ChC	.427
Garrett Atkins, Salem	CAR	Col	.421
Billy Martin, Lancaster	CAL	Ari	.420
Mike Campo, Cedar Rapids	MWL	Ana	.419
Chris Snelling, San Berndno	CAL	Sea	.418
Matt Watson, Jupiter	FSL	Mon	.417
Marco Cunningham, Wilmington	CAR	KC	.417

Slugging Percentage

Player, Team	Lg	Org	SLG
Craig Ansman, South Bend	**MWL**	**Ari**	**.623**
Garett Gentry, Michigan	MWL	Hou	.567
Tom Whiteman, Lexington	SAL	Hou	.566
Jason Dubois, Lansing	MWL	ChC	.562
Billy Martin, Lancaster	CAL	Ari	.551
Jason Kinchen, Greensboro	SAL	NYY	.546
T.J. Soto, Michigan	MWL	Hou	.542
John Castellano, Wisconsin	MWL	Sea	.536
Brian Gordon, Lancaster	CAL	Ari	.531
Xavier Nady, Lk Elsinore	CAL	SD	.527

Errors

Player, Team	Lg	Org	E
Ramon Carvajal, Potomac	**CAR**	**StL**	**48**
David Espinosa, Dayton	**MWL**	**Cin**	**48**
Daryl Clark, Beloit	MWL	Mil	47
Kelly Johnson, Macon	SAL	Atl	45
Corey Smith, Columbus	SAL	Cle	45
Scott Youngbauer, Lakewood	SAL	Phi	43
Gabe Johnson, Peoria	MWL	StL	42
Tommy Murphy, Rancho Cuca	CAL	Ana	42
Vince Rooi, Clinton	MWL	Mon	42
Juan Salas, Chston-SC	SAL	TB	42

Class-A Pitching Leaders

Earned Run Average

Player, Team	Lg	Org	ERA
Seung Song, Sarasota	**FSL**	**Bos**	**1.90**
Corwin Malone, Winston-Sal	CAR	CWS	1.93
Rodrigo Rosario, Lexington	SAL	Hou	2.14
Ryan Kibler, Salem	CAR	Col	2.17
Jose Rojas, Vero Beach	FSL	LA	2.21
Craig Anderson, San Berndno	CAL	Sea	2.26
Chris Narveson, Potomac	CAR	StL	2.31
Rich Rundles, Clinton	MWL	Mon	2.41
Brett Gray, Mudville	CAL	Cin	2.42
Matt Smith, Tampa	FSL	NYY	2.44
Boof Bonser, Hagerstown	SAL	SF	2.49
Jimmy Journell, Potomac	CAR	StL	2.50
Hank Thoms, Kinston	CAR	Cle	2.52
Matt Thornton, San Berndno	CAL	Sea	2.52
Matt Schwager, Delmarva	SAL	Bal	2.55

Saves

Player, Team	Lg	Org	S
Jackson Markert, Hagerstown	**SAL**	**SF**	**39**
Scotty Layfield, Potomac	CAR	StL	31
Luke Anderson, San Jose	CAL	SF	30
Justin Huisman, Asheville	SAL	Col	30
Greg Runser, Charlotte	FSL	Tex	30
Julio Mateo, San Berndno	CAL	Sea	26
Jayme Sperring, Delmarva	SAL	Bal	26
Vincent Bonilla, Quad City	MWL	Min	25
Brian Jackson, Kinston	CAR	Cle	25
7 tied with			23

Wins

Player, Team	Lg	Org	W
Boof Bonser, Hagerstown	**SAL**	**SF**	**16**
Julio DePaula, Tampa	**FSL**	**NYY**	**16**
Vance Cozier, San Jose	CAL	SF	15
Trey Hodges, Myrtle Bch	CAR	Atl	15
Ryan Mottl, Dayton	MWL	Cin	15
Mike Nannini, Lexington	SAL	Hou	15
Chad Qualls, Michigan	MWL	Hou	15
Jeff Clark, Hagerstown	SAL	SF	14
Jason Davis, Columbus	SAL	Cle	14
Jimmy Journell, Potomac	CAR	StL	14
Ricardo Rodriguez, Vero Beach	FSL	LA	14
Matt Thornton, San Berndno	CAL	Sea	14
8 tied with			13

Games

Player, Team	Lg	Org	G
Mike Nicolas, Lk Elsinore	**CAL**	**SD**	**62**
Jason Faigin, Greensboro	SAL	NYY	60
Arnaldo Munoz, Kannapolis	SAL	CWS	60
Andy Shibilo, Lk Elsinore	CAL	SD	60
Luke Anderson, San Jose	CAL	SF	59
Bryan Gaal, Lk Elsinore	CAL	SD	58
Jackson Markert, Hagerstown	SAL	SF	58
Joe Valentine, Winston-Sal	CAR	CWS	57
Greg Watson, Lakeland	FSL	Det	57
Aaron Looper, San Berndno	CAL	Sea	56
Julio Mateo, San Berndno	CAL	Sea	56
Juan Padilla, Fort Myers	FSL	Min	56
Jeff Schultz, Visalia	CAL	Oak	56
5 tied with			55

Losses

Player, Team	Lg	Org	L
Duncan McAdoo, Fort Wayne	**MWL**	**SD**	**16**
Taylor Buchholz, Lakewood	SAL	Phi	14
Jack Cassel, Fort Wayne	MWL	SD	14
Frank Tejeda, Potomac	CAR	StL	14
Scott Dohmann, Asheville	SAL	Col	13
Dario Ferrand, Kannapolis	SAL	CWS	13
Eric Fischer, Winston-Sal	CAR	CWS	13
Mark Gwyn, Modesto	CAL	Oak	13
Ryan Ledden, Lynchburg	CAR	Pit	13
Mark Malaska, Bakersfield	CAL	TB	13
Tracy Thorpe, Chstn-WV	SAL	Tor	13
9 tied with			12

Innings Pitched

Player, Team	Lg	Org	IP
Mike Nannini, Lexington	**SAL**	**Hou**	**190.1**
Craig Anderson, San Berndno	CAL	Sea	179.0
Taylor Buchholz, Lakewood	SAL	Phi	176.2
Mark Malaska, Bakersfield	CAL	TB	174.2
Scott Dohmann, Asheville	SAL	Col	173.0
Trey Hodges, Myrtle Bch	CAR	Atl	173.0
Vance Cozier, San Jose	CAL	SF	169.2
Denny Wagner, Modesto	CAL	Oak	169.0
Brian West, Winston-Sal	CAR	CWS	169.0
Jung Bong, Myrtle Bch	CAR	Atl	168.0
Josh Axelson, Potomac	CAR	StL	166.0
Jeff Bennett, Lynchburg	CAR	Pit	166.0
Matt Smith, Tampa	FSL	NYY	165.2
Rett Johnson, San Berndno	CAL	Sea	165.1
Dave Pember, High Desert	CAL	Mil	165.1

Class-A Pitching Leaders

Walks

Player, Team	Lg	Org	BB
Tony Pluta, Lexington	**SAL**	**Hou**	**86**
Ryan Price, Salem	CAR	Col	85
Justin Gordon, Beloit	MWL	Mil	84
Calvin Chipperfield, Lakeland	FSL	Det	81
Tom Marx, Lakeland	FSL	Det	78
Steve Colyer, Vero Beach	FSL	LA	77
Julio DePaula, Tampa	FSL	NYY	76
Chuck Kegley, Dunedin	FSL	Tor	76
Aaron Dean, Dunedin	FSL	Tor	75
Todd Wellemeyer, Lansing	MWL	ChC	74
Joey Cole, St. Lucie	FSL	NYM	73
Ben Hendrickson, Beloit	MWL	Mil	72
Pat Collins, Jupiter	FSL	Mon	71
Chris Rojas, Lk Elsinore	CAL	SD	71
6 tied with			70

Strikeouts

Player, Team	Lg	Org	K
Matt Thornton, San Berndno	**CAL**	**Sea**	**192**
Clint Nageotte, Wisconsin	MWL	Sea	187
Matt Smith, Tampa	FSL	NYY	187
Adam Wainwright, Macon	SAL	Atl	184
Craig Anderson, San Berndno	CAL	Sea	178
Boof Bonser, Hagerstown	SAL	SF	178
Julio DePaula, Tampa	FSL	NYY	170
Aaron Krawiec, Lansing	MWL	ChC	170
Wayne Nix, Visalia	CAL	Oak	167
Todd Wellemeyer, Lansing	MWL	ChC	167
Rett Johnson, San Berndno	CAL	Sea	166
Mark Malaska, Bakersfield	CAL	TB	165
Mike McClung, Chston-SC	SAL	TB	165
Brian Tallet, Kinston	CAR	Cle	164
2 tied with			160

Strikeouts/9 Innings—Starters

Player, Team	Lg	Org	K/9
Jake Peavy, Lk Elsinore	**CAL**	**SD**	**12.30**
Boof Bonser, Hagerstown	SAL	SF	11.96
Francisco Rodriguez, Rancho Cuca	CAL	Ana	11.64
Clint Nageotte, Wisconsin	MWL	Sea	11.05
Matt Thornton, San Berndno	CAL	Sea	11.01
Cary Ammons, Mudville	CAL	Cin	10.67
Clifton Lee, Jupiter	FSL	Mon	10.59
Rich Gilbert, Savannah	SAL	Tex	10.41
Domingo Valdez, Charlotte	FSL	Tex	10.31
Todd Wellemeyer, Lansing	MWL	ChC	10.22
Matt Smith, Tampa	FSL	NYY	10.16
Wayne Nix, Visalia	CAL	Oak	10.16
Adam Wainwright, Macon	SAL	Atl	10.06
Alex Santos, Bakersfield	CAL	TB	10.05
Aaron Krawiec, Lansing	MWL	ChC	9.98

Strikeouts/9 Innings—Relievers

Player, Team	Lg	Org	K/9
Alberto Garza, Kinston	**CAR**	**Cle**	**14.24**
Mike Neu, Mudville	CAL	Cin	14.20
Buddy Hernandez, Myrtle Bch	CAR	Atl	14.10
Franklyn German, Visalia	CAL	Oak	13.22
Arnaldo Munoz, Kannapolis	SAL	CWS	12.99
Roberto Giron, High Desert	CAL	Mil	12.22
Mike Steele, Lakeland	FSL	Det	12.12
Jeremy Hill, Wilmington	CAR	KC	11.85
Dan Giese, Augusta	SAL	Bos	11.55
Chris George, Lexington	SAL	Hou	11.47
Andy Shibilo, Lk Elsinore	CAL	SD	11.43
Tom Ford, Frederick	CAR	Bal	11.38
Colin Young, Salem	CAR	Col	11.37
Julio Castro, Kannapolis	SAL	CWS	11.33
Joel Peralta, Cedar Rapds	MWL	Ana	11.27

Hits/9 Innings—Starters

Player, Team	Lg	Org	H/9
Domingo Valdez, Charlotte	**FSL**	**Tex**	**6.03**
Boof Bonser, Hagerstown	SAL	SF	6.11
Seung Song, Sarasota	FSL	Bos	6.13
Clifton Lee, Jupiter	FSL	Mon	6.40
Rodrigo Rosario, Lexington	SAL	Hou	6.43
Chris Narveson, Potomac	CAR	StL	6.48
Jake Peavy, Lk Elsinore	CAL	SD	6.49
Corwin Malone, Winston-Sal	CAR	CWS	6.52
Matt Smith, Tampa	FSL	NYY	6.68
Ryan Kibler, Salem	CAR	Col	6.77
Fernando Rijo, Vero Beach	FSL	LA	6.84
Rene Miniel, Augusta	SAL	Bos	6.86
Eduardo Lantigua, Winston-Sal	CAR	CWS	6.86
Jose Cueto, Daytona	FSL	ChC	6.87
Sendy Rleal, Delmarva	SAL	Bal	6.88

Hits/9 Innings—Relievers

Player, Team	Lg	Org	H/9
Arnaldo Munoz, Kannapolis	**SAL**	**CWS**	**4.63**
Joe Valentine, Winston-Sal	CAR	CWS	4.66
Jeremy Hill, Wilmington	CAR	KC	4.80
Justin Huisman, Asheville	SAL	Col	5.40
Buddy Hernandez, Myrtle Bch	CAR	Atl	5.45
Chris Keelin, Clearwater	FSL	Phi	5.50
Ryan Larson, Kinston	CAR	Cle	5.51
Mike Steele, Lakeland	FSL	Det	5.51
Colin Young, Salem	CAR	Col	5.53
Adam Roller, Tampa	FSL	NYY	5.59
Anthony Ferrari, Jupiter	FSL	Mon	5.72
Joel Peralta, Cedar Rapds	MWL	Ana	5.74
Josh Higgins, Hickory	SAL	Pit	5.90
Scotty Layfield, Potomac	CAR	StL	6.04
Doug Kohl, Potomac	CAR	StL	6.39

Short-Season Batting Leaders

Batting Average

Player, Team	Lg	Org	Avg
Syketo Anderson, Boise	**NWL**	**ChC**	**.376**
Brayan Pena, Danville	APP	Atl	.370
Jesus Cota, Missoula	PIO	Ari	.368
Alfred Corbeil, Provo	PIO	Ana	.359
Garrett Guzman, Twins	GCL	Min	.355
Victor Diaz, Dodgers	GCL	LA	.354
Roman Cordova, Mariners	AZL	Sea	.352
Sam Swenson, Provo	PIO	Ana	.351
Gary Varner, Billings	PIO	Cin	.351
Ronny Cedeno, Cubs	AZL	ChC	.350

Third Basemen Batting Average

Player, Team	Lg	Org	Avg
Juan Gonzalez, Oneonta	**NYP**	**Det**	**.335**
Edgar Gonzalez, Hudson Val	NYP	TB	.332
Chris Collins, Everett	NWL	Sea	.324
Joe Jiannetti, Brooklyn	NYP	NYM	.321
Julian Benavidez, Salem-Keizr	NWL	SF	.319
Kevin Youkilis, Lowell	NYP	Bos	.317
Mike Lopez, Missoula	PIO	Ari	.313
Ryan Raburn, Oneonta	NYP	Det	.310
Ryan Kochen, Pittsfield	NYP	Hou	.310
Jake Gautreau, Eugene	NWL	SD	.309

Catchers Batting Average

Player, Team	Lg	Org	Avg
Alfred Corbeil, Provo	**PIO**	**Ana**	**.359**
Jon Williams, Salem-Keizr	NWL	SF	.349
Ivan Rodriguez, Lowell	NYP	Bos	.327
Mike Rabelo, Oneonta	NYP	Det	.325
Edgar Martinez, Lowell	NYP	Bos	.320
Brett Kay, Brooklyn	NYP	NYM	.311
Michael Dirosa, Yakima	NWL	Ari	.307
Brent Cordell, Princeton	APP	TB	.307
Chris Shelton, Williamsprt	NYP	Pit	.305
Luis Oliveros, Everett	NWL	Sea	.304

Shortstops Batting Average

Player, Team	Lg	Org	Avg
Ronny Cedeno, Cubs	**AZL**	**ChC**	**.350**
Andy Gonzalez, White Sox	AZL	CWS	.323
Steven Smith, Provo	PIO	Ana	.321
Richard Pittman, Brooklyn	NYP	NYM	.321
Christian Herrera, Dodgers	GCL	LA	.320
Joshua Arteaga, Boise	NWL	ChC	.318
Brian Bass, Bluefield	APP	Bal	.310
Chris Barnwell, Ogden	PIO	Mil	.307
Ozzie Chavez, Brewers	AZL	Mil	.305
Bronson Sardinha, Yankees	GCL	NYY	.303

First Basemen Batting Average

Player, Team	Lg	Org	Avg
Jesus Cota, Missoula	**PIO**	**Ari**	**.368**
Brad Bouras, Boise	NWL	ChC	.349
Jon Hart, Ogden	PIO	Mil	.340
Aaron McEachran, Medcine Hat	PIO	Tor	.336
Brett Harper, Kingsport	APP	NYM	.336
Jay Caligiuri, Brooklyn	NYP	NYM	.328
Greg Dobbs, Everett	NWL	Sea	.321
Aaron Rifkin, Staten Ilnd	NYP	NYY	.318
Sean Peless, Mariners	AZL	Sea	.314
Otis Kelly, Athletics	AZL	Oak	.311

Outfielders Batting Average

Player, Team	Lg	Org	Avg
Garrett Guzman, Twins	**GCL**	**Min**	**.355**
Sam Swenson, Provo	PIO	Ana	.351
Gary Varner, Billings	PIO	Cin	.351
Condor Cash, Boise	NWL	ChC	.347
Ender Chavez, Casper	PIO	Col	.342
Chris Tritle, Athletics	AZL	Oak	.336
Carlos Brackley, Lowell	NYP	Bos	.333
Thomas Carrow, Ogden	PIO	Mil	.331
Ruben Francisco, Bluefield	APP	Bal	.327
Mike Rodriguez, Pittsfield	NYP	Hou	.318

Second Basemen Batting Average

Player, Team	Lg	Org	Avg
Victor Diaz, Dodgers	**GCL**	**LA**	**.354**
Roman Cordova, Mariners	AZL	Sea	.352
Scott Hairston, Missoula	PIO	Ari	.347
Juan Francia, Oneonta	NYP	Det	.340
Ralph Santana, Ogden	PIO	Mil	.337
Nick Tempesta, Medcine Hat	PIO	Tor	.335
Robert Paulino, Cubs	AZL	ChC	.327
William Bergolla, Billings	PIO	Cin	.323
Omar Rogers, Bluefield	APP	Bal	.323
Leonel Cabrera, Giants	AZL	SF	.322

Switch-Hitters Batting Average

Player, Team	Lg	Org	Avg
Brayan Pena, Danville	**APP**	**Atl**	**.370**
Roman Cordova, Mariners	AZL	Sea	.352
Juan Francia, Oneonta	NYP	Det	.340
Juan Gonzalez, Oneonta	NYP	Det	.335
Mike Rabelo, Oneonta	NYP	Det	.325
Richard Pittman, Brooklyn	NYP	NYM	.321
Chris Duffy, Williamsprt	NYP	Pit	.317
Ruben Gotay, Royals	GCL	KC	.315
Angel Pagan, Brooklyn	NYP	NYM	.315
Jason Bourgeois, Pulaski	APP	Tex	.311

Short-Season Batting Leaders

Hits

Player, Team	Lg	Org	H
Syketo Anderson, Boise	**NWL**	**ChC**	**109**
Gary Varner, Billings	PIO	Cin	102
Scott Hairston, Missoula	PIO	Ari	101
Jesus Cota, Missoula	PIO	Ari	100
Edgar Gonzalez, Hudson Val	NYP	TB	92
J.J. Johnson, Boise	NWL	ChC	91
Jose Garcia, Great Falls	PIO	LA	89
Jon Hart, Ogden	PIO	Mil	89
Mike Lopez, Missoula	PIO	Ari	89
2 tied with			88

Extra-Base Hits

Player, Team	Lg	Org	XBH
Jesus Cota, Missoula	**PIO**	**Ari**	**38**
Jesse Gutierrez, Billings	PIO	Cin	37
Scott Hairston, Missoula	PIO	Ari	36
Leslie Nichols, Yakima	NWL	Ari	36
Ryan Raburn, Oneonta	NYP	Det	36
Greg Sain, Eugene	NWL	SD	36
Frank Corr, Brooklyn	NYP	NYM	35
Jose Garcia, Great Falls	PIO	LA	35
Aaron Rifkin, Staten Ilnd	NYP	NYY	34
3 tied with			33

Doubles

Player, Team	Lg	Org	2B
Brad Bouras, Boise	**NWL**	**ChC**	**25**
Leslie Nichols, Yakima	NWL	Ari	24
Joseph Alleva, Spokane	NWL	KC	23
Jose Garcia, Great Falls	PIO	LA	23
Alejandro Cadena, Everett	NWL	Sea	22
Jesus Cota, Missoula	PIO	Ari	22
Victor Diaz, Dodgers	GCL	LA	22
Ernie Durazo, Auburn	NYP	Tor	22
5 tied with			21

Total Bases

Player, Team	Lg	Org	TB
Scott Hairston, Missoula	**PIO**	**Ari**	**171**
Jesus Cota, Missoula	PIO	Ari	170
Gary Varner, Billings	PIO	Cin	156
Syketo Anderson, Boise	NWL	ChC	152
Jesse Gutierrez, Billings	PIO	Cin	148
Edgar Gonzalez, Hudson Val	NYP	TB	146
Jose Garcia, Great Falls	PIO	LA	144
Greg Sain, Eugene	NWL	SD	144
3 tied with			142

Triples

Player, Team	Lg	Org	3B
Anderson Hernandez, Tigers	**GCL**	**Det**	**11**
Shin-Soo Choo, Mariners	AZL	Sea	10
Elvin Andujar, Reds	GCL	Cin	9
Austin Nagle, Athletics	AZL	Oak	9
Jeramy Janz, Missoula	PIO	Ari	8
Ryan Raburn, Oneonta	NYP	Det	8
Chris Tritle, Athletics	AZL	Oak	8
Brian Bass, Bluefield	APP	Bal	7
Sean Pierce, Great Falls	PIO	LA	7
Anthony Webster, White Sox	AZL	CWS	7

Runs

Player, Team	Lg	Org	R
Scott Hairston, Missoula	**PIO**	**Ari**	**81**
Jesus Cota, Missoula	PIO	Ari	74
Syketo Anderson, Boise	NWL	ChC	70
Mike Lopez, Missoula	PIO	Ari	70
Tony Miller, Casper	PIO	Col	68
Sam Swenson, Provo	PIO	Ana	61
Jason Bourgeois, Pulaski	APP	Tex	60
Steven Smith, Provo	PIO	Ana	60
Sean Pierce, Great Falls	PIO	LA	59
Jonny Gomes, Princeton	APP	TB	58

Home Runs

Player, Team	Lg	Org	HR
Jesus Cota, Missoula	**PIO**	**Ari**	**16**
Jonny Gomes, Princeton	**APP**	**TB**	**16**
Jesse Gutierrez, Billings	**PIO**	**Cin**	**16**
Greg Sain, Eugene	**NWL**	**SD**	**16**
Scott Hairston, Missoula	PIO	Ari	14
Jose Vasquez, Casper	PIO	Col	14
Frank Corr, Brooklyn	NYP	NYM	13
Sam Swenson, Provo	PIO	Ana	13
Walter Young, Williamsprt	NYP	Pit	13
4 tied with			12

Runs Batted In

Player, Team	Lg	Org	RBI
Jesus Cota, Missoula	**PIO**	**Ari**	**71**
Scott Hairston, Missoula	PIO	Ari	65
Jon Hart, Ogden	PIO	Mil	62
Jeramy Janz, Missoula	PIO	Ari	62
Jesse Gutierrez, Billings	PIO	Cin	61
J.J. Johnson, Boise	NWL	ChC	61
Brad Bouras, Boise	NWL	ChC	60
Alejandro Cadena, Everett	NWL	Sea	56
Sam Swenson, Provo	PIO	Ana	55
Gary Varner, Billings	PIO	Cin	55

Short-Season Batting Leaders

Walks

Player, Team	Lg	Org	BB
Kevin Youkilis, Lowell	**NYP**	**Bos**	**70**
Jesus Cota, Missoula	PIO	Ari	56
Jesse Roman, New Jersey	NYP	StL	51
Todd Self, Pittsfield	NYP	Hou	46
Dan Moylan, New Jersey	NYP	StL	45
Sean Pierce, Great Falls	PIO	LA	43
Ryan Brunner, Lowell	NYP	Bos	41
Tony Miller, Casper	PIO	Col	41
3 tied with			40

Strikeouts

Player, Team	Lg	Org	K
Matt Allegra, Vancouver	**NWL**	**Oak**	**104**
Jose Vasquez, Casper	PIO	Col	96
Travis Ezi, Dodgers	GCL	LA	90
Dave Mulqueen, Casper	PIO	Col	89
Morrin Davis, Auburn	NYP	Tor	88
Nom Siriveaw, Auburn	NYP	Tor	88
Jorge Soto, Vancouver	NWL	Oak	84
Jeff Brooks, Yakima	NWL	Ari	83
Andy Yount, Oneonta	NYP	Det	83
3 tied with			81

Plate Appearances/Strikeout

Player, Team	Lg	Org	PA/K
Seth Davidson, New Jersey	**NYP**	**StL**	**19.38**
Donald Kelly, Oneonta	NYP	Det	18.25
Manuel Mayorson, Auburn	NYP	Tor	14.84
Andy Cannizaro, Staten Ilnd	NYP	NYY	13.71
Juan Salazar, Lowell	NYP	Bos	13.31
William Bergolla, Billings	PIO	Cin	12.48
Scott Gillitzer, Great Falls	PIO	LA	12.35
Luis Cruz, Red Sox	GCL	Bos	12.18
Demetrius Heath, Oneonta	NYP	Det	12.06
J.J. Hardy, Ogden	PIO	Mil	11.86

Hit By Pitch

Player, Team	Lg	Org	HBP
Jonny Gomes, Princeton	**APP**	**TB**	**26**
Chris Duffy, Williamsprt	NYP	Pit	17
Hector Perozo, Dodgers	GCL	LA	17
Mike Lopez, Missoula	PIO	Ari	16
Sam Swenson, Provo	PIO	Ana	14
Brooks Conrad, Pittsfield	NYP	Hou	13
Ashley Freeman, Tri-City	NWL	Col	13
Justin Huber, Brooklyn	NYP	NYM	13
Cesar Martin, Medcine Hat	PIO	Tor	13
6 tied with			11

Stolen Bases

Player, Team	Lg	Org	SB
Marcus Nettles, Eugene	**NWL**	**SD**	**35**
Anderson Hernandez, Tigers	GCL	Det	34
Manuel Nunez, Great Falls	PIO	LA	32
Mike Cockrell, Pirates	GCL	Pit	31
Chris Duffy, Williamsprt	NYP	Pit	30
Angel Pagan, Brooklyn	NYP	NYM	30
Ralph Santana, Ogden	PIO	Mil	30
Sean Pierce, Great Falls	PIO	LA	29
Domingo Cuello, Williamsprt	NYP	Pit	28
Tony Miller, Casper	PIO	Col	28

On-Base Percentage

Player, Team	Lg	Org	OBP
Kevin Youkilis, Lowell	**NYP**	**Bos**	**.512**
Jesus Cota, Missoula	PIO	Ari	.476
Alfred Corbeil, Provo	PIO	Ana	.463
Thomas Carrow, Ogden	PIO	Mil	.454
Mike Rodriguez, Pittsfield	NYP	Hou	.443
Jonny Gomes, Princeton	APP	TB	.442
Brayan Pena, Danville	APP	Atl	.440
Chris Duffy, Williamsprt	NYP	Pit	.440
Ender Chavez, Casper	PIO	Col	.438
Sam Swenson, Provo	PIO	Ana	.438

Slugging Percentage

Player, Team	Lg	Org	SLG
Sam Swenson, Provo	**PIO**	**Ana**	**.631**
Jesus Cota, Missoula	PIO	Ari	.625
Jonny Gomes, Princeton	APP	TB	.597
Frank Corr, Brooklyn	NYP	NYM	.594
Scott Hairston, Missoula	PIO	Ari	.588
Ryan Raburn, Oneonta	NYP	Det	.581
Condor Cash, Boise	NWL	ChC	.576
Garrett Guzman, Twins	GCL	Min	.572
Brian Bass, Bluefield	APP	Bal	.572
Chris Tritle, Athletics	AZL	Oak	.565

Errors

Player, Team	Lg	Org	E
Juan Peralta, Medcine Hat	**PIO**	**Tor**	**35**
Kervin Jacobo, Missoula	PIO	Ari	33
Jutt Hileman, Johnson Cty	APP	StL	32
Luis Cotto, Spokane	NWL	KC	30
Henry Encarnacion, Expos	GCL	Mon	27
Manuel Nunez, Great Falls	PIO	LA	27
Tony Caracciolo, Vermont	NYP	Mon	26
Cesar Martin, Medcine Hat	PIO	Tor	26
Daniel Gonzalez, Batavia	NYP	Phi	25
4 tied with			24

Short-Season Pitching Leaders

Earned Run Average

Player, Team	Lg	Org	ERA
Ian Oquendo, Williamsprt	**NYP**	**Pit**	**1.18**
Emilo Ferreira, Twins	GCL	Min	1.20
Chad Petty, Oneonta	NYP	Det	1.28
Rick Ankiel, Johnson Cty	APP	StL	1.33
Ross Peeples, Brooklyn	NYP	NYM	1.34
Jason Arnold, Staten Ilnd	NYP	NYY	1.50
Eny Cabreja, Martinsvlle	APP	Hou	1.58
Nick Ungs, Utica	NYP	Fla	1.62
Jorge Sosa, Everett	NWL	Sea	1.69
Zach Miner, Jamestown	NYP	Atl	1.89
Juan Rodriguez, Williamsprt	NYP	Pit	1.89
Jesse Foppert, Salem-Keizr	NWL	SF	1.93
Ramon Mora, Auburn	NYP	Tor	1.98
Ryan Hannaman, Salem-Keizr	NWL	SF	2.01
Luz Portobanco, Brooklyn	NYP	NYM	2.04

Wins

Player, Team	Lg	Org	W
Pedro Liriano, Provo	**PIO**	**Ana**	**11**
Harold Eckert, Brooklyn	NYP	NYM	10
Ian Oquendo, Williamsprt	NYP	Pit	10
Angel Guzman, Boise	NWL	ChC	9
Ryan Holsten, Missoula	PIO	Ari	9
Ross Peeples, Brooklyn	NYP	NYM	9
Emilo Ferreira, Twins	GCL	Min	8
Jesse Foppert, Salem-Keizr	NWL	SF	8
Charlie Manning, Staten Ilnd	NYP	NYY	8
Franklin Medina, Missoula	PIO	Ari	8
Gabriel Mercedes, Missoula	PIO	Ari	8
Sergio Mitre, Boise	NWL	ChC	8
Juan Rodriguez, Williamsprt	NYP	Pit	8
Tanner Watson, Everett	NWL	Sea	8
Dontrelle Willis, Boise	NWL	ChC	8

Losses

Player, Team	Lg	Org	L
Jon Huber, Idaho Falls	**PIO**	**SD**	**9**
David Pauley, Idaho Falls	**PIO**	**SD**	**9**
John Dischiavo, Hudson Val	NYP	TB	8
Jeff Fulchino, Utica	NYP	Fla	8
Dan Generelli, Lowell	NYP	Bos	8
Mariano Gomez, Mahoning Vy	NYP	Cle	8
Victor Kleine, Mahoning Vy	NYP	Cle	8
Henry Perez, Idaho Falls	PIO	SD	8
Miguel Pinango, Kingsport	APP	NYM	8
Charles Talanoa, Medcine Hat	PIO	Tor	8
15 tied with			7

Saves

Player, Team	Lg	Org	S
Jannio Gutierrez, Twins	**GCL**	**Min**	**16**
Ryan Keefer, Bluefield	APP	Bal	15
Jeff Miller, Williamsprt	NYP	Pit	15
Jesus Silva, Missoula	PIO	Ari	14
Oscar Bustillos, Hudson Val	NYP	TB	13
Kevin Cameron, Elizabethtn	APP	Min	13
Nathan Cotton, Billings	PIO	Cin	13
Aaron Kirkland, White Sox	AZL	CWS	13
Mike Adams, Ogden	PIO	Mil	12
Kevin Barry, Jamestown	NYP	Atl	12
Jentry Beckstead, Casper	PIO	Col	12
Felix Romero, Auburn	NYP	Tor	12
Chris Russ, Staten Ilnd	NYP	NYY	12
Jared Blasdell, New Jersey	NYP	StL	11
Chris Cooper, Mahoning Vy	NYP	Cle	11

Games

Player, Team	Lg	Org	G
Darwin Soto, Eugene	**NWL**	**SD**	**30**
Rusty Tucker, Idaho Falls	**PIO**	**SD**	**30**
Wilmer Villatoro, Idaho Falls	**PIO**	**SD**	**30**
Kevin Barry, Jamestown	NYP	Atl	29
Ryan Clark, Staten Ilnd	NYP	NYY	29
Marc Dulkowski, Eugene	NWL	SD	29
Ryan Keefer, Bluefield	APP	Bal	29
Josh Khoury, Utica	NYP	Fla	29
Aaron Kirkland, White Sox	AZL	CWS	29
Josh Merrigan, New Jersey	NYP	StL	29
Brandon Wood, Pittsfield	NYP	Hou	29
9 tied with			28

Innings Pitched

Player, Team	Lg	Org	IP
Dontrelle Willis, Boise	**NWL**	**ChC**	**93.2**
Sergio Mitre, Boise	NWL	ChC	91.0
Zach Miner, Jamestown	NYP	Atl	90.2
Ryan Holsten, Missoula	PIO	Ari	89.0
Brian Rodaway, Pittsfield	NYP	Hou	88.1
Rick Ankiel, Johnson Cty	APP	StL	87.2
Christian Gonzalez, Vancouver	NWL	Oak	87.2
Franklin Medina, Missoula	PIO	Ari	87.2
Brandon Roberson, Pittsfield	NYP	Hou	87.0
Jonathan Castellanos, Yakima	NWL	Ari	86.0
Ben Julianel, New Jersey	NYP	StL	85.1
James Mayfield, Batavia	NYP	Phi	85.0
Gustavo Martinez, Everett	NWL	Sea	84.1
Phil Akens, Utica	NYP	Fla	83.2
Ian Oquendo, Williamsprt	NYP	Pit	83.2

Short-Season Pitching Leaders

Walks

Player, Team	Lg	Org	BB
Rusty Tucker, Idaho Falls	**PIO**	**SD**	**50**
Phil Cullen, Everett	NWL	Sea	49
Dustin McGowan, Auburn	NYP	Tor	49
Jon Huber, Idaho Falls	PIO	SD	48
Johan Santana, Provo	PIO	Ana	47
Eric Stephenson, Auburn	NYP	Tor	44
Mike Cox, Brooklyn	NYP	NYM	41
Radhame Peguero, Hudson Val	NYP	TB	40
Daniel Cabrera, Orioles	GCL	Bal	39
Ryan Hannaman, Salem-Keizr	NWL	SF	39
Tom Mitchell, Vermont	NYP	Mon	39
Henry Perez, Idaho Falls	PIO	SD	39
4 tied with			38

Strikeouts

Player, Team	Lg	Org	K
Rick Ankiel, Johnson Cty	**APP**	**StL**	**158**
James Harden, Vancouver	NWL	Oak	100
Gustavo Martinez, Everett	NWL	Sea	100
Harold Eckert, Brooklyn	NYP	NYM	92
Johan Santana, Provo	PIO	Ana	91
Travis Blackley, Everett	NWL	Sea	90
Matt Wright, Danville	APP	Atl	89
Jesse Foppert, Salem-Keizr	NWL	SF	88
Charlie Manning, Staten Ilnd	NYP	NYY	87
Sandy Tejada, Elizabethtn	APP	Min	87
Kip Bouknight, Tri-City	NWL	Col	86
Ryan Hannaman, Salem-Keizr	NWL	SF	86
Ben Julianel, New Jersey	NYP	StL	86
Jorge Vasquez, Spokane	NWL	KC	86
Jake Woods, Provo	PIO	Ana	84

Strikeouts/9 Innings—Starters

Player, Team	Lg	Org	K/9
Rick Ankiel, Johnson Cty	**APP**	**StL**	**16.22**
J.D. Martin, Burlington	APP	Cle	14.19
Sandy Tejada, Elizabethtn	APP	Min	13.90
Tyler Johnson, Johnson Cty	APP	StL	12.84
James Harden, Vancouver	NWL	Oak	12.11
Matt Merricks, Danville	APP	Atl	12.10
J.M. Gold, Ogden	PIO	Mil	11.81
Travis Foley, Burlington	APP	Cle	11.80
Orlando Rodriguez, Great Falls	PIO	LA	11.72
Jake Woods, Provo	PIO	Ana	11.69
Jorge Vasquez, Spokane	NWL	KC	11.67
Robert Henkel, Utica	NYP	Fla	11.61
Ryan Hannaman, Salem-Keizr	NWL	SF	11.55
Luis Diaz, Tigers	GCL	Det	11.55
Vince Perkins, Auburn	NYP	Tor	11.52

Strikeouts/9 Innings—Relievers

Player, Team	Lg	Org	K/9
Kevin Barry, Jamestown	**NYP**	**Atl**	**15.51**
Jannio Gutierrez, Twins	GCL	Min	15.07
John Birtwell, Oneonta	NYP	Det	14.70
Ryan Keefer, Bluefield	APP	Bal	13.50
Michael Keirstead, Great Falls	PIO	LA	13.50
Lee Gronkiewicz, Burlington	APP	Cle	13.36
Tim Fries, Danville	APP	Atl	13.25
Anthony Rawson, New Jersey	NYP	StL	13.09
Ryan Mathiesen, Braves	GCL	Atl	12.67
Mike Adams, Ogden	PIO	Mil	12.38
Aaron Kirkland, White Sox	AZL	CWS	12.31
Wesley Hutchison, Salem-Keizr	NWL	SF	12.27
Mike Frick, Vancouver	NWL	Oak	12.15
Felix Romero, Auburn	NYP	Tor	12.12
Todd Culp, Mahoning Vy	NYP	Cle	12.09

Hits/9 Innings—Starters

Player, Team	Lg	Org	H/9
Rick Ankiel, Johnson Cty	**APP**	**StL**	**4.31**
Jesse Foppert, Salem-Keizr	NWL	SF	4.50
Jason Arnold, Staten Ilnd	NYP	NYY	4.77
J.D. Martin, Burlington	APP	Cle	5.12
Travis Foley, Burlington	APP	Cle	5.20
Ryan Hannaman, Salem-Keizr	NWL	SF	5.64
Robert Henkel, Utica	NYP	Fla	5.68
James Harden, Vancouver	NWL	Oak	5.69
Tyler Johnson, Johnson Cty	APP	StL	5.75
Chad Petty, Oneonta	NYP	Det	5.83
Ben Keiter, Pulaski	APP	Tex	6.18
Kurt Birkins, Bluefield	APP	Bal	6.25
Phil Akens, Utica	NYP	Fla	6.35
Jason Dennis, Provo	PIO	Ana	6.39
Harold Eckert, Brooklyn	NYP	NYM	6.48

Hits/9 Innings—Relievers

Player, Team	Lg	Org	H/9
Jannio Gutierrez, Twins	**GCL**	**Min**	**3.45**
Juan Mejia, Eugene	NWL	SD	3.52
Kevin Barry, Jamestown	NYP	Atl	4.02
Ryan Clark, Staten Ilnd	NYP	NYY	4.02
Aaron Kirkland, White Sox	AZL	CWS	4.96
Dave Byard, Brooklyn	NYP	NYM	5.11
Lee Gronkiewicz, Burlington	APP	Cle	5.12
Mike Woodnicki, New Jersey	NYP	StL	5.16
Steve Carlson, Staten Ilnd	NYP	NYY	5.29
George Crider, Vancouver	NWL	Oak	5.45
Francisco Arteaga, Jamestown	NYP	Atl	5.54
Chris Russ, Staten Ilnd	NYP	NYY	5.63
Jared Blasdell, New Jersey	NYP	StL	5.65
Ryan Hutchison, Batavia	NYP	Phi	5.73
Wesley Hutchison, Salem-Keizr	NWL	SF	5.73

2001 Triple-A and Double-A Splits

This section features lefty/righty and home/road splits for Triple-A and Double-A players. To be listed in this section, a hitter required 200 at-bats for a single team at a classification, while a pitcher needed either 200 at-bats against (lefty/righty) or 80 innings pitched (home/road).

These statistics will help you identify which hitters can handle all types of pitching, and vice versa. Other hitters might have to be platooned while certain pitchers may be best suited for specialized relief work. You'll also see which players had legitimate big seasons, and which were assisted by their ballparks.

Triple-A Batting vs. Lefthanded and Righthanded Pitchers

Player	Team	Org	vs Left AB	H	HR	RBI	Avg	vs Right AB	H	HR	RBI	Avg
Andy Abad	Sacramento	Oak	102	34	7	28	.333	360	105	12	54	.292
Brent Abernathy	Durham	TB	62	16	2	6	.258	190	60	2	17	.316
Chad Akers	Tacoma	Sea	60	17	0	2	.283	256	77	3	30	.301
Israel Alcantara	Pawtucket	Bos	119	34	11	19	.286	332	100	25	71	.301
Chad Alexander	Tacoma	Sea	83	25	3	16	.301	444	128	11	61	.288
Manny Alexander	Tacoma	Sea	74	23	2	11	.311	270	74	6	40	.274
J.Allensworth	Toledo	Det	102	30	2	13	.294	383	102	8	39	.266
Erick Almonte	Columbus	NYY	74	26	3	17	.351	271	73	9	38	.269
Wady Almonte	Rochester	Bal	76	17	1	10	.224	240	51	2	21	.213
Jerome Alviso	Col. Springs	Col	46	9	0	2	.196	220	55	1	16	.250
Alfredo Amezaga	Salt Lake	Ana	44	6	0	2	.136	156	44	1	14	.282
Danny Ardoin	Edmonton	Min	92	27	3	15	.293	210	50	2	22	.238
Bruce Aven	Las Vegas	LA	72	26	3	9	.361	220	50	5	23	.227
Kevin Baez	Norfolk	NYM	90	19	1	5	.211	221	49	3	23	.222
Ryan Balfe	Memphis	StL	32	12	1	6	.375	200	62	7	31	.310
Brian Banks	Calgary	Fla	61	18	4	10	.295	296	86	19	53	.291
Andy Barkett	Nashville	Pit	49	12	1	10	.245	227	54	5	33	.238
John Barnes	Edmonton	Min	60	22	2	7	.367	251	69	6	35	.275
Larry Barnes	Salt Lake	Ana	99	25	3	15	.253	305	92	15	58	.302
Jeff Barry	Las Vegas	LA	82	25	3	12	.305	232	66	9	30	.284
Blake Barthol	Tacoma	Sea	56	14	0	6	.250	222	63	9	31	.284
Jayson Bass	Iowa	ChC	55	14	2	9	.255	171	60	6	33	.351
Howard Battle	Richmond	Atl	109	33	3	15	.303	382	102	7	61	.267
Justin Baughman	Salt Lake	Ana	57	19	2	9	.333	231	68	1	23	.294
Rich Becker	Toledo	Det	40	11	0	2	.275	194	46	5	15	.237
Mike Bell	Col. Springs	Col	66	27	5	21	.409	254	63	8	32	.248
Jeff Berblinger	Omaha	KC	56	19	2	6	.339	214	39	3	17	.182
Peter Bergeron	Ottawa	Mon	41	11	0	1	.268	165	38	0	7	.230
Harry Berrios	Oklahoma	Tex	86	25	4	12	.291	145	34	3	21	.234
Todd Betts	Tacoma	Sea	86	25	1	14	.291	420	131	13	51	.312
Kurt Bierek	Toledo	Det	81	19	4	15	.235	313	88	12	38	.281
Casey Blake	Edmonton	Min	95	29	2	13	.305	280	87	8	36	.311
Pat Borders	Durham	TB	73	21	1	3	.288	240	53	1	25	.221
Jeff Branson	Las Vegas	LA	39	13	1	2	.333	250	66	3	18	.264
Kary Bridges	Columbus	NYY	104	31	0	9	.298	304	90	5	30	.296
Kevin Brown	Indianapolis	Mil	68	15	1	10	.221	222	52	8	24	.234
Roosevelt Brown	Iowa	ChC	92	27	6	16	.293	272	99	16	61	.364
Cliff Brumbaugh	Oklahoma	Tex	51	14	0	4	.275	151	48	8	38	.318
Cliff Brumbaugh	Col. Springs	Col	42	16	0	10	.381	166	53	3	29	.319
Mark Budzinski	Buffalo	Cle	106	20	0	3	.189	330	92	2	36	.279
Jamie Burke	Salt Lake	Ana	58	16	0	8	.276	157	31	0	19	.197
Morgan Burkhart	Pawtucket	Bos	126	33	6	18	.262	286	78	19	44	.273
Sean Burroughs	Portland	SD	83	29	1	10	.349	314	98	8	45	.312
Brent Butler	Col. Springs	Col	60	21	0	7	.350	212	70	7	31	.330
Eric Byrnes	Sacramento	Oak	97	30	3	14	.309	318	90	17	37	.283
Wilmy Caceres	Salt Lake	Ana	68	23	0	7	.338	257	58	0	14	.226
Ron Calloway	Ottawa	Mon	61	13	2	5	.213	174	49	7	28	.282
Dustin Carr	Durham	TB	59	16	0	4	.271	168	39	4	22	.232
Jamey Carroll	Ottawa	Mon	82	21	0	5	.256	183	43	0	11	.235
Mike Carter	Richmond	Atl	90	24	1	6	.267	298	90	1	14	.302
Mike Caruso	Durham	TB	86	23	0	6	.267	301	90	0	29	.299
Ramon Castro	Calgary	Fla	70	19	1	8	.271	320	112	26	82	.350
Jim Chamblee	Pawtucket	Bos	106	33	4	12	.311	272	58	6	20	.213
Frank Charles	Rochester	Bal	50	14	1	5	.280	190	44	0	19	.232
Raul Chavez	New Orleans	Hou	66	22	2	13	.333	212	62	6	27	.292
Hee Seop Choi	Iowa	ChC	70	20	5	19	.286	196	41	8	26	.209
McKay Christensen	Charlotte	CWS	61	14	1	6	.230	212	61	6	19	.288
Ryan Christenson	Tucson	Ari	59	17	1	5	.288	156	45	5	22	.288
Alex Cintron	Tucson	Ari	110	32	0	6	.291	315	92	3	29	.292
Stubby Clapp	Memphis	StL	43	10	1	5	.233	256	81	4	28	.316
Jermaine Clark	Tacoma	Sea	30	4	0	2	.133	186	50	1	24	.269
Edgard Clemente	Pawtucket	Bos	76	17	3	13	.224	224	57	9	22	.254
Ivanon Coffie	Rochester	Bal	40	11	2	5	.275	166	44	6	30	.265
Eric Cole	New Orleans	Hou	101	33	0	6	.327	296	72	3	35	.243
Lou Collier	Indianapolis	Mil	102	24	4	11	.235	210	66	10	25	.314
Jason Conti	Tucson	Ari	77	31	1	15	.403	285	89	8	37	.312
Mike Coolbaugh	Indianapolis	Mil	88	24	3	14	.273	259	69	7	36	.266
Chris Coste	Buffalo	Cle	62	18	3	21	.290	209	60	4	29	.287
Humberto Cota	Nashville	Pit	88	27	4	17	.307	293	86	10	55	.294
Darron Cox	Col. Springs	Col	40	8	1	6	.200	169	50	2	19	.296
Joe Crede	Charlotte	CWS	112	33	1	10	.295	351	95	16	55	.271
Cesar Crespo	Portland	SD	62	10	1	3	.161	215	61	7	26	.284
D.T. Cromer	Louisville	Cin	69	15	3	14	.217	173	54	8	35	.312
Midre Cummings	Tucson	Ari	58	18	1	7	.310	205	69	4	31	.337
Jack Cust	Tucson	Ari	119	29	6	23	.244	323	94	21	56	.291
Mark Dalesandro	Charlotte	CWS	78	16	1	7	.205	184	52	3	16	.283
Jeff Davanon	Salt Lake	Ana	73	27	2	12	.370	183	53	8	36	.290
Tommy Davis	Louisville	Cin	117	31	0	15	.265	279	76	6	32	.272
Kory DeHaan	Portland	SD	62	17	1	8	.274	246	60	6	20	.244
Tomas de la Rosa	Ottawa	Mon	91	23	2	10	.253	326	77	5	20	.236
Wilson Delgado	Omaha	KC	47	11	0	1	.234	208	52	4	29	.250
Jason Dellaero	Charlotte	CWS	101	18	3	6	.178	276	49	8	22	.178
Chris Demetral	Oklahoma	Tex	64	16	0	8	.250	258	60	2	19	.233
Edwin Diaz	Edmonton	Min	90	29	3	18	.322	291	75	8	38	.258
Juan Diaz	Pawtucket	Bos	59	11	2	5	.186	220	64	18	46	.291
Kelly Dransfeldt	Oklahoma	Tex	144	43	4	22	.299	407	95	5	41	.233
Adam Dunn	Louisville	Cin	68	20	5	14	.294	142	49	15	39	.345
Todd Dunwoody	Iowa	ChC	50	9	0	2	.180	201	62	8	30	.308
Mark Ellis	Sacramento	Oak	93	25	3	13	.269	379	104	7	40	.274
Morgan Ensberg	New Orleans	Hou	70	23	5	12	.329	246	75	18	49	.305

Player	Team	Org	vs Left AB	H	HR	RBI	Avg	vs Right AB	H	HR	RBI	Avg
Matt Erickson	Calgary	Fla	70	21	0	5	.300	343	107	2	24	.312
Alex Escobar	Norfolk	NYM	119	32	6	24	.269	278	74	6	28	.266
Josue Espada	Calgary	Fla	61	20	0	5	.328	229	67	3	25	.293
Adam Everett	New Orleans	Hou	98	19	1	8	.194	343	91	4	32	.265
Jose Fernandez	Salt Lake	Ana	78	23	4	21	.295	374	130	26	93	.348
Luis Figueroa	Nashville	Pit	81	20	3	9	.247	266	84	1	20	.316
Jose Flores	Col. Springs	Col	64	16	0	5	.250	252	77	2	31	.306
P.J. Forbes	Scranton-WB	Phi	123	42	2	13	.341	391	115	3	48	.294
Dave Francia	Scranton-WB	Phi	81	18	1	11	.222	266	61	2	26	.229
Matt Franco	Norfolk	NYM	122	23	1	13	.189	311	83	7	34	.267
Mike Frank	Columbus	NYY	91	22	0	7	.242	265	68	10	46	.257
Micah Franklin	Indianapolis	Mil	107	21	9	20	.196	224	55	14	43	.246
Ryan Freel	Syracuse	Tor	64	20	2	8	.313	255	63	3	25	.247
Hanley Frias	Memphis	StL	42	11	0	3	.262	198	47	2	16	.237
Eddy Garabito	Rochester	Bal	134	31	1	9	.231	383	107	2	25	.279
Carlos Garcia	Columbus	NYY	63	19	1	7	.302	152	35	2	12	.230
Jesse Garcia	Richmond	Atl	75	23	0	6	.307	300	77	2	16	.257
Karim Garcia	Buffalo	Cle	118	30	4	15	.254	340	90	27	70	.265
Luis Garcia	Memphis	StL	93	23	4	10	.247	329	85	3	34	.258
Geronimo Gil	Las Vegas	LA	68	18	1	10	.265	213	65	8	30	.305
Shawn Gilbert	Las Vegas	LA	48	13	1	3	.271	176	61	7	33	.347
Marcus Giles	Richmond	Atl	63	18	1	11	.286	189	66	5	33	.349
Keith Ginter	New Orleans	Hou	109	36	3	18	.330	348	87	13	52	.250
Ross Gload	Iowa	ChC	98	25	0	12	.255	377	116	15	81	.308
Jimmy Gonzalez	Ottawa	Mon	58	8	1	2	.138	157	30	5	17	.191
Raul Gonzalez	Louisville	Cin	145	46	5	19	.317	394	115	6	47	.292
Curtis Goodwin	Oklahoma	Tex	59	16	0	6	.271	177	38	2	13	.215
Jason Grabowski	Tacoma	Sea	82	24	2	10	.293	312	93	7	48	.298
Charlie Greene	Portland	SD	43	3	0	2	.070	180	29	2	9	.161
Wilton Guerrero	Louisville	Cin	56	16	0	7	.286	171	53	0	21	.310
Giomar Guevara	Toledo	Det	79	22	0	6	.278	321	72	6	30	.224
Aaron Guiel	Omaha	KC	88	25	5	17	.284	354	93	16	56	.263
Jeff Guiel	Salt Lake	Ana	37	10	0	5	.270	187	62	10	30	.332
Mike Gulan	Calgary	Fla	98	27	2	9	.276	387	130	20	83	.336
Toby Hall	Durham	TB	79	25	4	16	.316	294	100	15	56	.340
Jed Hansen	Omaha	KC	63	20	2	4	.317	225	53	8	18	.236
Jason Hardtke	Charlotte	CWS	55	12	1	2	.218	153	42	9	23	.275
Jason Hart	Sacramento	Oak	105	25	7	18	.238	389	97	12	57	.249
Chris Hatcher	Durham	TB	59	14	3	6	.237	192	53	8	32	.276
Drew Henson	Columbus	NYY	63	15	1	7	.238	207	45	10	31	.217
Chad Hermansen	Nashville	Pit	99	22	3	16	.222	348	88	14	47	.253
Alex Hernandez	Nashville	Pit	78	24	0	5	.308	264	77	8	31	.292
Phil Hiatt	Las Vegas	LA	102	37	12	18	.363	334	107	32	81	.320
Eric Hinske	Sacramento	Oak	93	26	3	17	.280	343	97	22	62	.283
Aaron Holbert	Syracuse	Tor	58	13	1	6	.224	154	39	1	13	.253
Damon Hollins	Edmonton	Min	60	20	0	10	.333	172	44	6	20	.256
Dave Hollins	Buffalo	Cle	82	24	10	22	.293	233	62	6	45	.266
Paul Hoover	Durham	TB	62	16	1	7	.258	231	47	2	14	.203
Jim Horner	Tacoma	Sea	39	14	1	8	.359	197	53	5	21	.269
Ken Huckaby	Tucson	Ari	74	27	0	8	.365	188	49	2	26	.261
Scott Hunter	Norfolk	NYM	70	16	0	2	.229	169	51	2	29	.302
Butch Huskey	Col. Springs	Col	91	31	5	18	.341	367	117	14	69	.319
Norm Hutchins	Durham	TB	62	12	1	8	.194	199	48	6	20	.241
Adam Hyzdu	Nashville	Pit	61	17	3	9	.279	204	60	9	31	.294
Jeff Inglin	Charlotte	CWS	125	30	10	22	.240	356	101	14	53	.284
Cesar Izturis	Syracuse	Tor	75	15	0	2	.200	267	85	2	33	.318
Bucky Jacobsen	Indianapolis	Mil	73	22	4	15	.301	227	52	8	38	.229
D'Angelo Jimenez	Columbus	NYY	56	17	2	6	.304	158	39	3	13	.247
Keith Johnson	Las Vegas	LA	111	31	2	8	.279	324	78	10	42	.241
Nick Johnson	Columbus	NYY	100	24	4	14	.240	259	68	14	35	.263
Roberto Kelly	Col. Springs	Col	44	11	2	10	.250	168	50	10	38	.298
Bobby Kielty	Edmonton	Min	97	32	3	19	.330	244	66	9	31	.270
Brooks Kieschnick	Col. Springs	Col	47	13	1	5	.277	205	61	12	40	.298
Eugene Kingsale	Rochester	Bal	55	9	0	1	.164	189	40	0	14	.212
Eugene Kingsale	Tacoma	Sea	42	14	2	8	.333	173	49	1	16	.283
Jason Knupfer	Scranton-WB	Phi	85	19	1	4	.224	191	47	0	21	.246
Tim Laker	Buffalo	Cle	77	16	5	13	.208	239	62	15	44	.259
Mike Lamb	Oklahoma	Tex	81	25	2	13	.309	192	56	6	27	.292
Selwyn Langaigne	Syracuse	Tor	35	5	0	3	.143	166	43	3	20	.259
Greg Larocca	Buffalo	Cle	64	21	4	10	.328	148	45	8	25	.304
Brandon Larson	Louisville	Cin	114	28	5	13	.246	310	80	9	42	.258
Chris Latham	Syracuse	Tor	64	17	5	13	.266	224	63	8	39	.281
Joe Lawrence	Syracuse	Tor	82	20	1	10	.244	236	50	0	16	.212
Jalal Leach	Fresno	SF	99	29	2	18	.293	368	104	14	52	.283
Matthew Lecroy	Edmonton	Min	94	31	3	15	.330	302	99	17	65	.328
Jose Leon	Rochester	Bal	96	24	0	8	.250	320	92	12	45	.287
Brian Lesher	Indianapolis	Mil	90	30	2	20	.333	256	68	5	43	.266
Dave Lindstrom	Toledo	Det	36	9	0	4	.250	167	43	1	18	.257
Cole Liniak	Syracuse	Tor	98	32	4	14	.327	246	51	6	35	.207
Felipe Lopez	Syracuse	Tor	70	20	1	8	.286	288	80	15	36	.278
Luis Lopez	Syracuse	Tor	80	27	4	19	.338	259	83	6	54	.320
Mendy Lopez	New Orleans	Hou	52	15	6	13	.288	156	43	8	23	.276
Terrell Lowery	Durham	TB	55	12	1	4	.218	198	54	0	14	.273
Lou Lucca	Memphis	StL	91	23	0	12	.253	388	104	9	52	.268
Keith Luuloa	Portland	SD	44	10	1	2	.227	173	49	3	14	.283
Scott Lydy	New Orleans	Hou	77	23	2	14	.299	206	52	5	29	.252
Chris Magruder	Fresno	SF	41	12	0	4	.293	173	48	10	26	.277
Mike Mahoney	Iowa	ChC	69	12	1	7	.174	220	53	2	20	.241
Marty Malloy	Louisville	Cin	100	25	0	8	.250	368	117	6	41	.318
Paco Martin	Calgary	Fla	70	24	1	9	.343	263	78	4	29	.297

Triple-A Batting vs. Lefthanded and Righthanded Pitchers

			vs Left					vs Right				
Player	Team	Org	AB	H	HR	RBI	Avg	AB	H	HR	RBI	Avg
Eddy Martinez	Rochester	Bal	75	15	0	8	.200	239	70	7	25	.293
Greg Martinez	Durham	TB	77	25	0	9	.325	165	46	1	12	.279
Damon Mashore	Memphis	StL	64	17	1	12	.266	225	69	6	25	.307
Henry Mateo	Ottawa	Mon	126	42	3	16	.333	370	90	2	27	.243
Ruben Mateo	Louisville	Cin	70	15	0	5	.214	181	48	2	20	.265
Julius Matos	Portland	SD	70	16	1	6	.229	313	91	6	28	.291
Pascual Matos	Columbus	NYY	70	13	1	3	.186	186	43	3	23	.231
Quinton McCracken	Edmonton	Min	106	40	1	16	.377	255	82	3	29	.322
Darnell McDonald	Rochester	Bal	94	21	1	7	.223	297	72	1	28	.242
Donzell McDonald	Columbus	NYY	93	22	2	6	.237	281	74	6	30	.263
John McDonald	Buffalo	Cle	110	24	1	4	.218	298	75	1	29	.252
Keith McDonald	Memphis	StL	66	22	3	9	.333	267	65	8	33	.243
Sean McGowan	Fresno	SF	73	20	1	11	.274	318	92	13	54	.289
Ryan McGuire	Calgary	Fla	39	10	1	9	.256	200	62	7	33	.310
Cody McKay	Sacramento	Oak	61	11	0	5	.180	289	81	6	36	.280
Dan McKinley	Ottawa	Mon	94	32	1	8	.340	263	69	4	31	.262
Sean McNally	Tucson	Ari	53	13	4	8	.245	196	47	2	20	.240
Tony Medrano	Buffalo	Cle	116	35	2	13	.302	346	100	5	38	.289
Juan Melo	Fresno	SF	94	34	2	21	.362	281	83	7	34	.295
Carlos Mendez	Toledo	Det	96	23	7	22	.240	302	75	11	54	.248
Chad Meyers	Iowa	ChC	103	31	4	16	.301	343	103	5	38	.300
Jason Michaels	Scranton-WB	Phi	96	30	6	23	.313	322	79	11	46	.245
Damon Minor	Fresno	SF	107	31	4	13	.290	299	94	20	58	.314
Chad Moeller	Tucson	Ari	62	18	3	10	.290	212	57	5	26	.269
Izzy Molina	Syracuse	Tor	47	19	4	9	.404	209	59	12	29	.282
Jose Molina	Salt Lake	Ana	41	15	1	8	.366	172	49	4	23	.285
Craig Monroe	Oklahoma	Tex	110	38	4	19	.345	297	76	16	56	.256
Scott Morgan	Salt Lake	Ana	112	34	9	19	.304	389	99	19	64	.254
Mike Moriarty	Edmonton	Min	95	23	4	18	.242	309	75	9	32	.243
Warren Morris	Nashville	Pit	51	15	1	10	.294	176	53	4	30	.301
Tony Mota	Las Vegas	LA	93	27	1	14	.290	349	104	7	43	.298
Chad Mottola	Calgary	Fla	93	25	4	12	.269	364	110	11	54	.302
Lyle Mouton	Toledo	Det	61	25	7	16	.410	201	58	11	33	.289
Adrian Myers	Tacoma	Sea	38	10	0	5	.263	220	56	0	28	.255
Mike Neill	Pawtucket	Bos	49	13	2	8	.265	159	38	3	14	.239
Bryant Nelson	Tucson	Ari	80	22	2	12	.275	246	76	4	29	.309
Jose Nieves	Salt Lake	Ana	55	11	3	7	.200	203	74	8	30	.365
Dax Norris	Richmond	Atl	82	24	1	14	.293	235	65	2	24	.277
Jon Nunnally	Omaha	KC	61	14	5	13	.230	255	52	13	40	.204
Talmadge Nunnari	Ottawa	Mon	74	11	0	3	.149	269	64	4	32	.238
Kevin Orie	Scranton-WB	Phi	119	39	4	13	.328	390	110	9	32	.282
Bill Ortega	Memphis	StL	110	35	0	8	.318	385	107	6	54	.278
Jose Ortiz	Sacramento	Oak	43	14	4	9	.326	213	56	3	30	.263
Nick Ortiz	Omaha	KC	67	17	1	7	.254	249	62	5	33	.249
Corey Patterson	Iowa	ChC	89	20	0	5	.225	278	73	7	27	.263
Jarrod Patterson	Toledo	Det	39	11	1	5	.282	174	52	6	20	.299
Mike Peeples	Col. Springs	Col	94	27	6	15	.287	330	100	13	54	.303
Kit Pellow	Omaha	KC	98	26	7	18	.265	386	115	13	63	.298
Carlos Pena	Oklahoma	Tex	129	37	7	26	.287	302	87	16	48	.288
Elvis Pena	Indianapolis	Mil	128	34	0	8	.266	309	71	1	20	.230
Danny Peoples	Buffalo	Cle	82	12	2	7	.146	288	70	15	41	.243
Chan Perry	Richmond	Atl	86	24	1	6	.279	264	72	7	33	.273
Calvin Pickering	Rochester	Bal	108	25	4	18	.231	353	105	17	80	.297
Scott Podsednik	Tacoma	Sea	62	21	0	10	.339	207	57	3	20	.275
Bo Porter	Oklahoma	Tex	62	13	3	14	.210	162	42	10	26	.259
Colin Porter	New Orleans	Hou	46	8	1	4	.174	266	66	6	29	.248
Dante Powell	Fresno	SF	100	30	4	12	.300	326	90	18	50	.276
Alejandro Prieto	Omaha	KC	70	24	2	13	.343	306	82	6	31	.268
Chris Prieto	Las Vegas	LA	96	28	1	16	.292	350	102	18	42	.291
Chris Pritchett	Salt Lake	Ana	99	20	2	14	.202	377	124	15	61	.329
Nick Punto	Scranton-WB	Phi	120	24	1	9	.200	343	82	0	30	.239
Ryan Radmanovich	Portland	SD	52	7	2	8	.135	247	71	12	44	.287
Julio Ramirez	Charlotte	CWS	84	13	2	6	.155	235	56	6	19	.238
Omar Ramirez	New Orleans	Hou	103	27	0	12	.262	260	64	2	27	.246
Cody Ransom	Fresno	SF	104	29	3	12	.279	365	84	20	66	.230
Tike Redman	Nashville	Pit	100	20	0	5	.200	302	102	3	37	.338
Adam Riggs	Portland	SD	84	25	4	18	.298	314	78	17	47	.248
Brian Rios	Toledo	Det	93	33	5	22	.355	279	88	9	40	.315
Dave Roberts	Buffalo	Cle	70	22	0	5	.314	168	50	0	17	.298
Mike Robertson	Richmond	Atl	73	19	1	6	.260	361	99	5	34	.274
Liu Rodriguez	Charlotte	CWS	127	39	0	14	.307	317	90	0	23	.284
Aaron Rowand	Charlotte	CWS	91	18	4	13	.198	238	79	12	35	.332
Toby Rumfield	Charlotte	CWS	119	35	6	16	.294	344	91	14	53	.265
Mike Ryan	Edmonton	Min	126	35	8	19	.278	401	117	10	54	.292
Rob Ryan	Tucson	Ari	61	15	3	12	.246	155	56	9	38	.361
Rob Ryan	Sacramento	Oak	47	6	1	5	.128	171	43	6	27	.251
Marc Sagmoen	Oklahoma	Tex	49	12	1	5	.245	186	44	3	11	.237
Alex Sanchez	Indianapolis	Mil	93	31	1	11	.333	242	74	0	15	.306
Jared Sandberg	Durham	TB	74	19	3	8	.257	248	58	13	42	.234
Pedro Santana	Toledo	Det	91	21	0	3	.231	341	77	5	27	.226
Luis Saturria	Memphis	StL	75	14	3	6	.187	338	79	10	43	.234
Gene Schall	Scranton-WB	Phi	68	16	4	11	.235	195	58	10	43	.297
Brian Schneider	Ottawa	Mon	81	24	2	13	.296	253	68	4	30	.269
Marcos Scutaro	Indianapolis	Mil	137	39	4	17	.285	358	107	7	33	.299
Scott Seabol	Columbus	NYY	70	19	3	11	.271	212	56	7	31	.264
Todd Sears	Edmonton	Min	84	26	4	7	.310	324	101	9	43	.312
Reed Secrist	Nashville	Pit	67	20	7	17	.299	275	85	16	46	.309
Kevin Sefcik	Buffalo	Cle	56	13	1	8	.232	177	33	4	16	.186
Fernando Seguignol	Ottawa	Mon	62	21	4	15	.339	176	54	10	30	.307
Bill Selby	Louisville	Cin	88	19	3	8	.216	242	66	11	48	.273

			vs Left					vs Right				
Player	Team	Org	AB	H	HR	RBI	Avg	AB	H	HR	RBI	Avg
Chip Sell	Tucson	Ari	35	4	0	1	.114	213	61	6	27	.286
Chris Sexton	Louisville	Cin	109	28	1	15	.257	300	86	1	32	.287
Jon Shave	Pawtucket	Bos	85	26	3	11	.306	223	53	3	16	.238
Andy Sheets	Durham	TB	41	10	0	3	.244	184	53	4	19	.288
Chris Sheff	Louisville	Cin	101	31	5	14	.307	211	55	4	37	.261
Rick Short	Iowa	ChC	86	22	1	10	.256	227	64	4	24	.282
Brian Simmons	Syracuse	Tor	59	16	1	5	.271	142	37	1	15	.261
Randall Simon	Toledo	Det	43	12	1	6	.279	179	63	9	25	.352
Steve Sisco	Rochester	Bal	81	20	1	4	.247	257	60	5	25	.233
Bobby Smith	Durham	TB	96	26	5	12	.271	300	93	17	58	.310
Jason Smith	Iowa	ChC	48	10	0	2	.208	192	46	4	13	.240
Chris Snopek	Iowa	ChC	108	34	5	15	.315	362	96	9	42	.265
Andy Stankiewicz	Las Vegas	LA	48	17	0	6	.354	154	36	0	7	.234
Dave Steed	Oklahoma	Tex	52	11	1	4	.212	175	42	6	25	.240
Dernell Stenson	Pawtucket	Bos	145	36	6	31	.248	319	74	10	38	.232
Pedro Swann	Richmond	Atl	101	37	1	14	.366	387	105	7	58	.271
Mark Sweeney	Indianapolis	Mil	128	46	1	30	.359	276	70	5	39	.254
Tony Tarasco	Norfolk	NYM	93	22	0	12	.237	273	85	7	45	.311
Reggie Taylor	Scranton-WB	Phi	131	37	1	17	.282	333	85	6	33	.255
Juan Thomas	Tacoma	Sea	93	21	1	12	.226	410	130	22	83	.317
Ryan Thompson	Calgary	Fla	66	17	5	19	.258	234	76	14	50	.325
Jorge Toca	Norfolk	NYM	113	35	6	15	.310	294	74	5	36	.252
Juan Tolentino	Salt Lake	Ana	97	29	6	21	.299	355	96	5	45	.270
Yorvit Torrealba	Fresno	SF	87	31	2	10	.356	307	77	6	26	.251
Chris Truby	New Orleans	Hou	82	26	3	17	.317	239	74	9	54	.310
Josh Tyler	Fresno	SF	60	19	1	6	.317	170	47	2	20	.276
Juan Uribe	Col. Springs	Col	58	18	1	8	.310	223	69	6	40	.309
Eric Valent	Scranton-WB	Phi	128	40	4	23	.313	320	82	17	55	.256
Javier Valentin	Edmonton	Min	110	39	5	23	.355	321	82	12	48	.255
Ramon Vazquez	Tacoma	Sea	79	21	1	16	.266	387	119	9	63	.307
Jorge Velandia	Norfolk	NYM	65	17	1	8	.262	195	48	4	29	.246
Wilton Veras	Pawtucket	Bos	132	28	3	13	.212	389	92	5	39	.237
Chris Wakeland	Toledo	Det	123	32	2	14	.260	424	123	21	70	.290
Turner Ward	Scranton-WB	Phi	67	17	0	11	.254	155	44	4	16	.284
B.J. Waszgis	Calgary	Fla	75	19	6	18	.253	236	59	17	47	.250
Pat Watkins	Omaha	KC	58	15	1	5	.259	187	47	6	24	.251
Vernon Wells	Syracuse	Tor	88	33	4	17	.375	325	83	8	35	.255
Darrell Whitmore	Memphis	StL	33	11	2	12	.333	295	80	9	40	.271
Ty Wigginton	Norfolk	NYM	70	22	3	7	.314	190	43	4	17	.226
Brad Wilkerson	Ottawa	Mon	55	10	2	13	.182	176	53	10	35	.301
Rick Wilkins	Portland	SD	43	8	1	3	.186	179	39	5	30	.218
Craig Wilson	Omaha	KC	98	29	4	16	.296	370	108	6	50	.292
Desi Wilson	Tucson	Ari	86	29	0	13	.337	234	76	3	25	.325
Tom Wilson	Sacramento	Oak	61	21	1	15	.344	198	52	7	33	.263
Travis Wilson	Richmond	Atl	93	21	0	12	.226	290	72	3	26	.248
Vance Wilson	Norfolk	NYM	65	16	2	8	.246	163	40	4	23	.245
Kevin Witt	Portland	SD	78	24	3	15	.308	378	108	24	72	.286
Jason Wood	Nashville	Pit	93	24	3	10	.258	289	68	5	28	.235
Ron Wright	Durham	TB	99	31	6	20	.313	340	84	14	55	.247
Ernie Young	Portland	SD	84	31	5	17	.369	329	82	16	51	.249
Alan Zinter	New Orleans	Hou	50	10	0	6	.200	282	78	19	59	.277
Tony Zuniga	Fresno	SF	87	27	7	18	.310	326	85	19	56	.261

Triple-A Batting at Home and on the Road

			Home					Road				
Player	Team	Org	AB	H	HR	RBI	Avg	AB	H	HR	RBI	Avg
Andy Abad	Sacramento	Oak	216	65	11	44	.301	246	74	8	38	.301
Brent Abernathy	Durham	TB	131	34	2	13	.260	121	42	2	10	.347
Chad Akers	Tacoma	Sea	148	48	2	19	.324	168	46	1	13	.274
Israel Alcantara	Pawtucket	Bos	232	78	19	57	.336	219	56	17	33	.256
Chad Alexander	Tacoma	Sea	237	71	5	19	.300	290	82	9	58	.283
Manny Alexander	Tacoma	Sea	153	39	6	24	.255	191	58	2	27	.304
Jermain Allensworth	Toledo	Det	226	70	5	28	.310	259	62	5	24	.239
Erick Almonte	Columbus	NYY	166	44	6	30	.265	179	55	6	25	.307
Wady Almonte	Rochester	Bal	167	33	2	16	.198	149	35	1	15	.235
Alfredo Amezaga	Salt Lake	Ana	88	26	1	13	.295	112	24	0	3	.214
Danny Ardoin	Col. Springs	Col	151	34	1	14	.225	151	43	4	23	.285
Bruce Aven	Edmonton	Min	176	45	4	20	.256	116	31	4	12	.267
Kevin Baez	Norfolk	NYM	161	37	2	14	.230	150	31	2	14	.207
Ryan Balfe	Las Vegas	LA	135	43	6	25	.319	97	31	2	12	.320
Ryan Balfe	Memphis	StL	135	43	6	25	.319	97	31	2	12	.320
Brian Banks	Calgary	Fla	176	55	17	41	.313	181	49	6	22	.271
Andy Barkett	Nashville	Pit	132	26	3	19	.197	141	40	3	23	.284
John Barnes	Col. Springs	Col	148	44	6	26	.297	163	47	2	16	.288
Larry Barnes	Salt Lake	Ana	186	64	10	38	.344	218	53	8	35	.243
Jeff Barry	Edmonton	Min	169	49	8	24	.290	145	42	4	18	.290
Blake Barthol	Tacoma	Sea	122	26	0	7	.213	156	51	9	30	.327
Jayson Bass	Iowa	ChC	110	30	5	20	.273	116	44	3	22	.379
Howard Battle	Richmond	Atl	236	62	4	39	.263	255	73	6	37	.286
Justin Baughman	Salt Lake	Ana	152	47	1	18	.309	136	40	2	14	.294
Rich Becker	Toledo	Det	127	30	2	10	.236	107	27	3	7	.252
Jeff Berblinger	Omaha	KC	117	20	2	15	.171	153	38	3	8	.248
Peter Bergeron	Ottawa	Mon	95	22	0	5	.232	111	27	0	3	.243
Harry Berrios	Oklahoma	Tex	99	27	4	22	.273	132	32	3	11	.242
Todd Betts	Tacoma	Sea	225	67	6	26	.298	281	89	8	39	.317
Kurt Bierek	Toledo	Det	197	47	6	25	.239	197	60	10	28	.305
Casey Blake	Col. Springs	Col	158	56	4	25	.354	217	60	6	24	.276
Pat Borders	Durham	TB	164	39	1	14	.238	149	35	1	14	.235
Jeff Branson	Edmonton	Min	145	37	4	13	.255	144	42	0	7	.292
Kary Bridges	Columbus	NYY	206	61	3	24	.296	202	60	2	15	.297
Kevin Brown	Indianapolis	Mil	144	34	3	17	.236	146	33	6	17	.226
Roosevelt Brown	Iowa	ChC	189	57	15	45	.302	175	69	7	32	.394
Cliff Brumbaugh	Oklahoma	Tex	113	41	4	23	.363	89	21	4	19	.236
Mark Budzinski	Buffalo	Cle	218	54	1	16	.248	220	58	1	23	.264
Jamie Burke	Salt Lake	Ana	103	29	0	16	.282	112	18	0	11	.161
Morgan Burkhart	Pawtucket	Bos	192	52	14	37	.271	220	59	11	25	.268
Sean Burroughs	Portland	SD	193	58	7	32	.301	201	69	2	23	.343
Eric Byrnes	Sacramento	Oak	215	60	9	27	.279	200	60	11	24	.300
Wilmy Caceres	Salt Lake	Ana	148	41	0	11	.277	177	40	0	10	.226
Ron Calloway	Ottawa	Mon	119	31	5	15	.261	120	32	5	20	.267
Dustin Carr	Durham	TB	94	20	3	10	.213	133	35	1	16	.263
Jamey Carroll	Ottawa	Mon	145	33	0	5	.228	122	31	0	11	.254
Mike Carter	Richmond	Atl	162	48	0	7	.296	226	66	2	13	.292
Mike Caruso	Durham	TB	182	53	0	14	.291	205	60	0	21	.293
Ramon Castro	Calgary	Fla	188	70	15	45	.372	202	61	12	45	.302
Jim Chamblee	Pawtucket	Bos	189	39	5	14	.206	189	52	5	18	.275
Frank Charles	Rochester	Bal	132	29	0	12	.220	108	29	1	12	.269
Raul Chavez	New Orleans	Hou	119	28	2	10	.235	159	56	6	30	.352
Hee Seop Choi	Iowa	ChC	123	30	5	18	.244	143	31	8	27	.217
McKay Christensen	Charlotte	CWS	126	31	4	11	.246	147	44	3	14	.299
Ryan Christenson	Tucson	Ari	130	45	2	14	.346	85	17	4	13	.200
Alex Cintron	Tucson	Ari	195	54	0	18	.277	230	70	3	17	.304
Stubby Clapp	Las Vegas	LA	152	47	2	12	.309	147	44	3	21	.299
Stubby Clapp	Memphis	StL	152	47	2	12	.309	147	44	3	21	.299
Jermaine Clark	Tacoma	Sea	86	21	1	11	.244	130	33	0	15	.254
Edgard Clemente	Pawtucket	Bos	153	38	6	16	.248	147	36	6	19	.245
Ivanon Coffie	Rochester	Bal	88	24	2	11	.273	118	31	6	24	.263
Eric Cole	New Orleans	Hou	190	45	1	18	.237	207	60	2	23	.290
Lou Collier	Indianapolis	Mil	154	51	6	18	.331	158	39	8	18	.247
Jason Conti	Tucson	Ari	167	52	2	21	.311	195	68	7	31	.349
Mike Coolbaugh	Indianapolis	Mil	179	54	8	31	.302	168	39	2	19	.232
Chris Coste	Buffalo	Cle	126	33	4	27	.262	145	45	3	23	.310
Humberto Cota	Nashville	Pit	182	53	5	34	.291	195	59	9	38	.303
Joe Crede	Charlotte	CWS	221	63	12	32	.285	242	65	5	33	.269
Cesar Crespo	Portland	SD	157	44	3	13	.280	116	27	5	16	.233
D.T. Cromer	Louisville	Cin	111	30	6	23	.270	131	39	5	26	.298
Midre Cummings	Tucson	Ari	135	47	1	16	.348	128	40	4	22	.313
Jack Cust	Tucson	Ari	215	60	12	39	.279	227	63	15	40	.278
Mark Dalesandro	Charlotte	CWS	110	27	2	9	.245	152	41	2	14	.270
Jeff Davanon	Salt Lake	Ana	134	44	7	31	.328	122	36	3	17	.295
Tommy Davis	Louisville	Cin	186	51	4	22	.274	210	56	2	25	.267
Kory DeHaan	Portland	SD	147	40	5	16	.272	157	37	2	12	.236
Tomas de la Rosa	Ottawa	Mon	198	43	1	13	.217	222	57	6	17	.257
Wilson Delgado	Omaha	KC	152	44	2	20	.289	103	19	2	10	.184
Jason Dellaero	Charlotte	CWS	182	26	6	16	.143	195	41	5	12	.210
Chris Demetral	Oklahoma	Tex	129	31	0	11	.240	193	45	2	16	.233
Edwin Diaz	Col. Springs	Col	199	61	3	29	.307	182	43	8	27	.236
Juan Diaz	Pawtucket	Bos	136	32	9	20	.235	143	43	11	31	.301
Kelly Dransfeldt	Oklahoma	Tex	269	68	1	25	.253	282	70	8	38	.248
Adam Dunn	Louisville	Cin	82	33	11	28	.402	128	36	9	25	.281
Todd Dunwoody	Iowa	ChC	111	34	5	19	.306	140	37	3	13	.264
Mark Ellis	Sacramento	Oak	230	55	8	30	.239	242	74	2	23	.306
Morgan Ensberg	New Orleans	Hou	139	41	7	19	.295	177	57	16	42	.322
Matt Erickson	Calgary	Fla	193	62	0	16	.321	220	66	2	13	.300
Alex Escobar	Norfolk	NYM	207	57	7	29	.275	190	49	5	23	.258
Josue Espada	Calgary	Fla	146	44	1	15	.301	144	43	2	15	.299

			Home					Road				
Player	Team	Org	AB	H	HR	RBI	Avg	AB	H	HR	RBI	Avg
Adam Everett	New Orleans	Hou	216	49	1	9	.227	225	61	4	31	.271
Jose Fernandez	Salt Lake	Ana	228	76	16	54	.333	224	77	14	60	.344
Luis Figueroa	Nashville	Pit	183	57	3	20	.311	164	47	1	9	.287
P.J. Forbes	Scranton-WB	Phi	248	73	3	23	.294	266	84	2	38	.316
Dave Francia	Scranton-WB	Phi	149	29	1	20	.195	198	50	2	17	.253
Matt Franco	Norfolk	NYM	215	55	3	26	.256	218	51	5	21	.234
Mike Frank	Columbus	NYY	175	46	8	22	.263	181	44	2	31	.243
Micah Franklin	Indianapolis	Mil	163	42	14	35	.258	168	34	9	28	.202
Ryan Freel	Syracuse	Tor	148	37	3	13	.250	171	46	2	20	.269
Hanley Frias	Las Vegas	LA	134	36	2	10	.269	106	22	0	9	.208
Hanley Frias	Memphis	StL	134	36	2	10	.269	106	22	0	9	.208
Eddy Garabito	Rochester	Bal	245	62	0	17	.253	272	76	3	17	.279
Carlos Garcia	Columbus	NYY	113	21	0	9	.186	102	33	3	10	.324
Jesse Garcia	Richmond	Atl	183	51	2	11	.279	192	49	0	11	.255
Karim Garcia	Buffalo	Cle	238	67	15	51	.282	224	55	16	34	.246
Luis Garcia	Las Vegas	LA	206	55	3	18	.267	216	53	4	26	.245
Luis Garcia	Memphis	StL	206	55	3	18	.267	216	53	4	26	.245
Geronimo Gil	Edmonton	Min	147	47	7	29	.320	134	36	2	11	.269
Shawn Gilbert	Edmonton	Min	122	44	4	20	.361	102	30	4	16	.294
Marcus Giles	Richmond	Atl	115	35	2	14	.304	137	49	4	20	.358
Keith Ginter	New Orleans	Hou	204	51	5	26	.250	253	72	11	44	.285
Ross Gload	Iowa	ChC	218	64	9	43	.294	257	77	6	50	.300
Jimmy Gonzalez	Ottawa	Mon	120	21	3	14	.175	95	17	3	5	.179
Raul Gonzalez	Louisville	Cin	264	70	5	24	.265	275	91	6	42	.331
Curtis Goodwin	Oklahoma	Tex	121	30	0	8	.248	115	24	2	11	.209
Jason Grabowski	Tacoma	Sea	208	64	4	35	.308	186	53	5	23	.285
Charlie Greene	Portland	SD	95	14	0	3	.147	116	15	1	7	.129
Wilton Guerrero	Louisville	Cin	112	40	0	16	.357	115	29	0	12	.252
Giomar Guevara	Toledo	Det	194	48	6	24	.247	206	46	0	12	.223
Aaron Guiel	Omaha	KC	208	62	11	41	.298	234	56	10	32	.239
Jeff Guiel	Salt Lake	Ana	106	35	3	15	.330	118	37	7	20	.314
Mike Gulan	Calgary	Fla	239	90	13	60	.377	246	67	9	32	.272
Toby Hall	Durham	TB	188	63	15	38	.335	185	62	4	34	.335
Jed Hansen	Omaha	KC	169	40	5	13	.237	119	33	5	9	.277
Jason Hardtke	Charlotte	CWS	103	27	6	11	.262	105	27	4	14	.257
Jason Hart	Sacramento	Oak	245	57	11	41	.233	249	65	8	34	.261
Chris Hatcher	Durham	TB	122	34	5	18	.279	129	33	6	20	.256
Drew Henson	Columbus	NYY	156	38	6	22	.244	114	22	5	16	.193
Chad Hermansen	Nashville	Pit	230	63	9	28	.274	217	47	8	35	.217
Alex Hernandez	Nashville	Pit	173	51	4	19	.295	169	50	4	17	.296
Phil Hiatt	Edmonton	Min	221	74	27	63	.335	215	70	17	36	.326
Eric Hinske	Sacramento	Oak	204	53	10	28	.260	232	70	15	51	.302
Aaron Holbert	Syracuse	Tor	103	26	1	9	.252	109	26	1	10	.239
Damon Hollins	Col. Springs	Col	136	42	5	21	.309	96	22	1	9	.229
Dave Hollins	Buffalo	Cle	169	47	13	43	.278	147	39	3	24	.265
Paul Hoover	Durham	TB	124	25	3	12	.202	169	38	0	9	.225
Jim Horner	Tacoma	Sea	123	30	3	13	.244	113	37	3	16	.327
Ken Huckaby	Tucson	Ari	120	33	1	11	.275	142	43	1	23	.303
Scott Hunter	Norfolk	NYM	114	33	0	19	.289	125	34	2	12	.272
Norm Hutchins	Durham	TB	130	34	4	14	.262	131	26	3	14	.198
Adam Hyzdu	Nashville	Pit	103	32	3	14	.311	158	44	8	25	.278
Jeff Inglin	Charlotte	CWS	231	69	17	46	.299	250	62	7	29	.248
Cesar Izturis	Syracuse	Tor	197	56	2	20	.284	145	44	0	15	.303
Bucky Jacobsen	Indianapolis	Mil	160	41	8	37	.256	140	33	4	16	.236
D'Angelo Jimenez	Columbus	NYY	108	24	3	8	.222	106	32	2	11	.302
Keith Johnson	Edmonton	Min	208	46	7	28	.221	227	63	5	22	.278
Nick Johnson	Columbus	NYY	182	52	10	25	.286	177	40	8	24	.226
Bobby Kielty	Col. Springs	Col	168	49	4	23	.292	173	49	8	27	.283
Eugene Kingsale	Rochester	Bal	139	29	0	10	.209	105	20	0	5	.190
Eugene Kingsale	Tacoma	Sea	112	28	1	8	.250	103	35	2	16	.340
Jason Knupfer	Scranton-WB	Phi	129	31	0	10	.240	147	35	1	15	.238
Tim Laker	Buffalo	Cle	138	34	12	30	.246	182	45	8	27	.247
Mike Lamb	Oklahoma	Tex	148	41	3	27	.277	125	40	5	13	.320
Selwyn Langaigne	Syracuse	Tor	93	24	2	14	.258	108	24	1	9	.222
Greg Larocca	Buffalo	Cle	101	35	3	17	.347	115	32	9	20	.278
Brandon Larson	Louisville	Cin	205	49	3	22	.239	219	59	11	33	.269
Chris Latham	Syracuse	Tor	134	38	7	29	.284	154	42	6	25	.273
Joe Lawrence	Syracuse	Tor	160	35	0	13	.219	158	35	1	13	.222
Jalal Leach	Fresno	SF	241	70	10	39	.290	226	63	6	31	.279
Matthew Lecroy	Col. Springs	Col	175	57	7	32	.326	221	73	13	48	.330
Jose Leon	Rochester	Bal	203	55	8	29	.271	213	61	4	24	.286
Brian Lesher	Indianapolis	Mil	160	43	3	30	.269	186	55	4	33	.296
Dave Lindstrom	Toledo	Det	128	38	1	16	.297	75	14	0	6	.187
Cole Liniak	Syracuse	Tor	149	31	6	23	.208	195	52	4	26	.267
Felipe Lopez	Syracuse	Tor	183	53	7	24	.290	175	47	9	20	.269
Luis Lopez	Syracuse	Tor	177	56	4	38	.316	162	54	6	35	.333
Mendy Lopez	New Orleans	Hou	89	28	5	16	.315	119	30	9	20	.252
Terrell Lowery	Durham	TB	117	35	1	9	.299	136	31	0	9	.228
Lou Lucca	Las Vegas	LA	235	59	4	31	.251	244	68	5	33	.279
Lou Lucca	Memphis	StL	235	59	4	31	.251	244	68	5	33	.279
Keith Luuloa	Portland	SD	93	25	3	7	.269	124	34	1	9	.274
Scott Lydy	New Orleans	Hou	148	38	4	24	.257	135	37	3	19	.274
Chris Magruder	Fresno	SF	109	34	8	22	.312	105	26	2	8	.248
Mike Mahoney	Iowa	ChC	137	28	1	10	.204	152	37	2	17	.243
Marty Malloy	Louisville	Cin	216	75	2	20	.347	252	67	4	29	.266
Paco Martin	Calgary	Fla	183	67	4	27	.366	150	35	1	11	.233
Eddy Martinez	Rochester	Bal	145	43	3	18	.297	169	42	4	15	.249
Greg Martinez	Durham	TB	114	33	0	13	.289	128	38	1	8	.297
Damon Mashore	Las Vegas	LA	142	50	4	22	.352	147	36	3	15	.245
Damon Mashore	Memphis	StL	142	50	4	22	.352	147	36	3	15	.245

Triple-A Batting at Home and on the Road

			Home					Road				
Player	Team	Org	AB	H	HR	RBI	Avg	AB	H	HR	RBI	Avg
Henry Mateo	Ottawa	Mon	244	83	2	21	.340	256	51	3	22	.199
Ruben Mateo	Louisville	Cin	109	29	1	10	.266	142	34	1	15	.239
Julius Matos	Portland	SD	177	52	5	22	.294	206	55	2	12	.267
Pascual Matos	Columbus	NYY	102	22	1	7	.216	154	34	3	19	.221
Quinton McCracken	Col. Springs	Col	172	61	3	27	.355	189	61	1	18	.323
Darnell McDonald	Rochester	Bal	193	46	2	16	.238	198	47	0	19	.237
Donzell McDonald	Columbus	NYY	187	52	4	19	.278	187	44	4	17	.235
John McDonald	Buffalo	Cle	189	42	2	14	.222	221	58	0	19	.262
Keith McDonald	Las Vegas	LA	157	36	5	12	.229	176	51	6	30	.290
Keith McDonald	Memphis	StL	157	36	5	12	.229	176	51	6	30	.290
Sean McGowan	Fresno	SF	204	65	9	37	.319	187	47	5	28	.251
Ryan McGuire	Calgary	Fla	103	30	3	22	.291	136	42	5	20	.309
Cody McKay	Sacramento	Oak	178	45	3	22	.253	172	47	3	19	.273
Dan McKinley	Ottawa	Mon	183	44	0	14	.240	177	57	5	25	.322
Sean McNally	Tucson	Ari	114	31	2	16	.272	135	29	4	12	.215
Tony Medrano	Buffalo	Cle	223	71	4	26	.318	243	64	3	26	.263
Juan Melo	Fresno	SF	181	57	7	28	.315	194	60	2	27	.309
Carlos Mendez	Toledo	Det	212	51	11	48	.241	186	47	7	28	.253
Chad Meyers	Iowa	ChC	200	63	5	28	.315	246	71	4	26	.289
Jason Michaels	Scranton-WB	Phi	192	57	12	38	.297	226	52	5	31	.230
Damon Minor	Fresno	SF	203	61	13	36	.300	203	64	11	35	.315
Chad Moeller	Tucson	Ari	139	43	6	22	.309	135	32	2	14	.237
Izzy Molina	Syracuse	Tor	120	34	7	15	.283	136	44	9	23	.324
Jose Molina	Salt Lake	Ana	99	30	4	14	.303	114	34	1	17	.298
Craig Monroe	Oklahoma	Tex	225	51	9	34	.227	185	64	11	41	.346
Scott Morgan	Salt Lake	Ana	238	65	15	42	.273	263	68	13	41	.259
Mike Moriarty	Col. Springs	Col	199	52	9	33	.261	205	46	4	17	.224
Warren Morris	Nashville	Pit	105	29	3	21	.276	118	39	2	19	.331
Tony Mota	Edmonton	Min	188	56	2	23	.298	254	75	6	34	.295
Chad Mottola	Calgary	Fla	197	59	7	31	.299	260	76	8	35	.292
Lyle Mouton	Toledo	Det	137	43	7	24	.314	125	40	11	25	.320
Adrian Myers	Tacoma	Sea	101	30	0	15	.297	159	36	0	18	.226
Mike Neill	Pawtucket	Bos	97	26	4	10	.268	111	25	1	12	.225
Bryant Nelson	Tucson	Ari	163	51	2	26	.313	163	47	4	15	.288
Jose Nieves	Salt Lake	Ana	142	51	5	21	.359	116	34	6	16	.293
Dax Norris	Richmond	Atl	166	43	1	16	.259	151	46	2	22	.305
Jon Nunnally	Omaha	KC	167	38	12	33	.228	149	28	6	20	.188
Talmadge Nunnari	Ottawa	Mon	183	52	1	22	.284	160	23	3	13	.144
Kevin Orie	Scranton-WB	Phi	244	75	10	26	.307	265	74	3	19	.279
Bill Ortega	Las Vegas	LA	242	68	4	32	.281	253	74	2	30	.292
Bill Ortega	Memphis	StL	242	68	4	32	.281	253	74	2	30	.292
Jose Ortiz	Sacramento	Oak	111	36	2	12	.324	145	34	5	27	.234
Nick Ortiz	Omaha	KC	146	38	3	17	.260	170	41	3	23	.241
Corey Patterson	Iowa	ChC	175	50	4	15	.286	192	43	3	17	.224
Jarrod Patterson	Toledo	Det	90	32	4	16	.356	123	31	3	9	.252
Kit Pellow	Omaha	KC	226	68	10	36	.301	258	73	10	45	.283
Carlos Pena	Oklahoma	Tex	196	56	11	36	.286	235	68	12	38	.289
Elvis Pena	Indianapolis	Mil	225	56	0	14	.249	212	49	1	14	.231
Danny Peoples	Buffalo	Cle	171	40	8	21	.234	199	42	9	27	.211
Chan Perry	Richmond	Atl	158	39	4	16	.247	192	57	4	23	.297
Calvin Pickering	Rochester	Bal	228	65	9	46	.285	233	65	12	52	.279
Scott Podsednik	Tacoma	Sea	124	28	0	7	.226	145	50	3	23	.345
Bo Porter	Oklahoma	Tex	116	28	5	15	.241	108	27	8	25	.250
Colin Porter	New Orleans	Hou	146	36	4	17	.247	166	38	3	16	.229
Dante Powell	Fresno	SF	221	56	14	36	.253	205	64	8	26	.312
Alejandro Prieto	Omaha	KC	190	62	6	29	.326	186	44	2	15	.237
Chris Prieto	Edmonton	Min	228	75	13	38	.329	218	55	6	20	.252
Chris Pritchett	Salt Lake	Ana	254	82	12	50	.323	222	62	5	25	.279
Nick Punto	Scranton-WB	Phi	226	59	0	23	.261	237	47	1	16	.198
Ryan Radmanovich	Portland	SD	120	27	7	17	.225	176	51	7	35	.290
Julio Ramirez	Charlotte	CWS	162	35	6	14	.216	157	34	2	11	.217
Omar Ramirez	New Orleans	Hou	168	44	1	20	.262	195	47	1	19	.241
Cody Ransom	Fresno	SF	245	61	15	45	.249	224	52	8	33	.232
Tike Redman	Nashville	Pit	181	51	2	23	.282	217	70	1	19	.323
Adam Riggs	Portland	SD	186	39	8	26	.210	208	64	13	39	.308
Brian Rios	Toledo	Det	192	66	9	36	.344	180	55	5	26	.306
Dave Roberts	Buffalo	Cle	118	41	0	11	.347	123	32	0	11	.260
Mike Robertson	Richmond	Atl	216	66	2	20	.306	218	52	4	20	.239
Liu Rodriguez	Charlotte	CWS	227	64	0	14	.282	217	65	0	23	.300
Aaron Rowand	Charlotte	CWS	144	36	6	15	.250	185	61	10	33	.330
Toby Rumfield	Charlotte	CWS	218	53	11	31	.243	245	73	9	38	.298
Mike Ryan	Col. Springs	Col	260	80	9	34	.308	267	72	9	39	.270
Rob Ryan	Tucson	Ari	100	34	7	26	.340	116	37	5	24	.319
Rob Ryan	Sacramento	Oak	96	21	1	16	.219	122	28	6	16	.230
Marc Sagmoen	Oklahoma	Tex	109	32	1	7	.294	126	24	3	9	.190
Alex Sanchez	Indianapolis	Mil	166	54	1	11	.325	169	51	0	15	.302
Jared Sandberg	Durham	TB	162	40	10	31	.247	160	37	6	19	.231
Pedro Santana	Toledo	Det	205	41	2	16	.200	227	57	3	14	.251
Luis Saturria	Las Vegas	LA	205	46	8	22	.224	208	47	5	27	.226
Luis Saturria	Memphis	StL	205	46	8	22	.224	208	47	5	27	.226
Gene Schall	Scranton-WB	Phi	141	39	5	27	.277	122	35	9	27	.287
Brian Schneider	Ottawa	Mon	154	36	4	20	.234	184	57	2	23	.310
Marcos Scutaro	Indianapolis	Mil	260	90	7	35	.346	235	56	4	15	.238
Scott Seabol	Columbus	NYY	129	42	3	20	.326	153	33	7	22	.216
Todd Sears	Col. Springs	Col	200	60	4	20	.300	208	67	9	30	.322
Reed Secrist	Nashville	Pit	166	54	6	23	.325	172	49	16	38	.285
Kevin Sefcik	Buffalo	Cle	107	20	1	9	.187	126	26	4	15	.206
Fernando Seguignol	Ottawa	Mon	120	40	3	18	.333	122	35	11	27	.287
Bill Selby	Louisville	Cin	173	43	6	24	.249	157	42	8	32	.268
Chip Sell	Tucson	Ari	116	36	4	16	.310	132	29	2	12	.220
Chris Sexton	Louisville	Cin	207	61	1	27	.295	202	53	1	20	.262
Jon Shave	Pawtucket	Bos	150	38	4	13	.253	158	41	2	14	.259
Andy Sheets	Durham	TB	126	39	2	12	.310	99	24	2	10	.242
Chris Sheff	Louisville	Cin	140	42	6	25	.300	172	44	3	26	.256
Rick Short	Iowa	ChC	151	42	4	22	.278	162	44	1	12	.272
Brian Simmons	Syracuse	Tor	99	28	1	12	.283	102	25	1	8	.245
Randall Simon	Toledo	Det	95	28	3	8	.295	127	47	7	23	.370
Steve Sisco	Rochester	Bal	193	48	2	12	.249	145	32	4	17	.221
Bobby Smith	Durham	TB	170	53	11	34	.312	226	66	11	36	.292
Jason Smith	Iowa	ChC	98	23	2	5	.235	142	33	2	10	.232
Chris Snopek	Iowa	ChC	222	63	4	20	.284	248	67	10	37	.270
Andy Stankiewicz	Edmonton	Min	102	26	0	2	.255	100	27	0	11	.270
Dave Steed	Oklahoma	Tex	111	24	4	14	.216	116	29	3	15	.250
Dernell Stenson	Pawtucket	Bos	227	57	7	33	.251	237	53	9	36	.224
Pedro Swann	Richmond	Atl	238	78	5	36	.328	250	64	3	36	.256
Mark Sweeney	Indianapolis	Mil	209	64	3	42	.306	195	52	3	27	.267
Tony Tarasco	Norfolk	NYM	172	48	1	22	.279	194	59	6	35	.304
Reggie Taylor	Scranton-WB	Phi	223	53	1	18	.238	241	69	6	32	.286
Juan Thomas	Tacoma	Sea	235	67	11	50	.285	268	84	12	45	.313
Ryan Thompson	Calgary	Fla	154	55	16	52	.357	146	38	3	17	.260
Jorge Toca	Norfolk	NYM	203	56	5	28	.276	204	53	6	23	.260
Juan Tolentino	Salt Lake	Ana	224	70	7	38	.313	228	55	4	28	.241
Yorvit Torrealba	Fresno	SF	203	58	6	26	.286	191	50	2	10	.262
Chris Truby	New Orleans	Hou	154	43	2	26	.279	167	57	10	45	.341
Josh Tyler	Fresno	SF	109	38	3	15	.349	121	28	0	11	.231
Eric Valent	Scranton-WB	Phi	228	67	6	40	.294	220	55	15	38	.250
Javier Valentin	Col. Springs	Col	227	60	10	40	.264	204	61	7	31	.299
Ramon Vazquez	Tacoma	Sea	243	81	5	40	.333	223	59	5	39	.265
Jorge Velandia	Norfolk	NYM	131	31	3	19	.237	129	34	2	18	.264
Wilton Veras	Pawtucket	Bos	248	59	8	35	.238	273	61	0	17	.223
Chris Wakeland	Toledo	Det	268	79	10	39	.295	279	76	13	45	.272
Turner Ward	Scranton-WB	Phi	120	35	1	10	.292	102	26	3	17	.255
B.J. Waszgis	Calgary	Fla	147	38	11	41	.259	164	40	12	24	.244
Pat Watkins	Omaha	KC	84	24	3	8	.286	161	38	4	21	.236
Vernon Wells	Syracuse	Tor	192	58	9	27	.302	221	58	3	25	.262
Darrell Whitmore	Las Vegas	LA	153	49	6	22	.320	175	42	5	30	.240
Darrell Whitmore	Memphis	StL	153	49	6	22	.320	175	42	5	30	.240
Ty Wigginton	Norfolk	NYM	133	33	4	9	.248	127	32	3	15	.252
Brad Wilkerson	Ottawa	Mon	112	28	5	25	.250	121	35	7	23	.289
Rick Wilkins	Portland	SD	98	19	1	14	.194	124	28	5	19	.226
Craig Wilson	Omaha	KC	232	69	6	37	.297	241	71	5	32	.295
Desi Wilson	Tucson	Ari	159	54	2	22	.340	161	51	1	16	.317
Tom Wilson	Sacramento	Oak	137	43	6	28	.314	122	30	2	20	.246
Travis Wilson	Richmond	Atl	181	44	0	18	.243	202	49	3	20	.243
Vance Wilson	Norfolk	NYM	100	27	3	16	.270	128	29	3	15	.227
Kevin Witt	Portland	SD	222	62	13	34	.279	234	70	14	53	.299
Jason Wood	Nashville	Pit	189	44	5	22	.233	190	48	3	16	.253
Ron Wright	Durham	TB	222	54	10	31	.243	217	61	10	44	.281
Ernie Young	Portland	SD	201	56	8	29	.279	208	56	12	38	.269
Alan Zinter	New Orleans	Hou	165	43	9	30	.261	167	45	10	35	.269
Tony Zuniga	Fresno	SF	215	63	20	48	.293	198	49	6	26	.247

Triple-A Pitching vs. Lefthanded and Righthanded Batters

			vs Left					vs Right				
Player	Team	Org	AB	H	HR	SO	Avg	AB	H	HR	SO	Avg
Pat Ahearne	Calgary	Fla	215	77	4	22	.358	397	135	10	58	.340
Kurt Ainsworth	Fresno	SF	202	56	9	55	.277	361	83	13	102	.230
Juan Alvarez	Salt Lake	Ana	80	19	4	22	.237	177	49	9	22	.277
Victor Alvarez	Las Vegas	LA	122	28	2	28	.230	327	87	10	66	.266
Jamie Arnold	Fresno	SF	112	37	6	22	.330	197	59	7	34	.299
Bronson Arroyo	Nashville	Pit	121	30	2	22	.248	134	33	4	27	.246
J.D. Arteaga	New Orleans	Hou	138	30	1	27	.217	398	113	10	63	.284
Jeff Austin	Omaha	KC	135	44	6	26	.326	148	45	8	29	.304
Rob Averette	Col. Springs	Col	253	73	9	48	.289	429	131	20	77	.305
Mike Bacsik	Buffalo	Cle	75	18	1	22	.240	396	97	12	59	.245
Benito Baez	Calgary	Fla	68	14	0	27	.206	153	39	5	29	.255
Willie Banks	Syracuse	Tor	260	66	2	59	.254	309	85	10	62	.275
Travis Baptist	Charlotte	CWS	69	21	1	13	.304	187	53	7	30	.283
Rick Bauer	Rochester	Bal	212	53	7	45	.250	240	66	3	44	.275
Ray Beasley	Richmond	Atl	80	21	2	21	.262	133	37	2	16	.278
Matt Beech	Oklahoma	Tex	60	19	3	13	.317	193	64	7	31	.332
Todd Belitz	Sacramento	Oak	68	15	2	21	.221	133	37	4	33	.278
Rigo Beltran	Scranton-WB	Phi	68	13	0	25	.191	345	74	10	88	.214
Alan Benes	Memphis	StL	247	76	4	37	.308	323	88	9	59	.272
Joaquin Benoit	Oklahoma	Tex	215	55	9	65	.256	268	58	5	77	.216
Adam Bernero	Toledo	Det	224	65	6	44	.290	343	107	7	55	.312
Jason Beverlin	Salt Lake	Ana	116	27	3	34	.233	199	55	6	40	.276
Willie Blair	Buffalo	Cle	110	29	1	18	.264	176	43	2	32	.244
Matt Blank	Ottawa	Mon	66	19	3	8	.288	255	70	10	50	.275
Toby Borland	Salt Lake	Ana	89	23	2	30	.258	179	30	0	62	.168
Joe Borowski	Iowa	ChC	145	32	5	41	.221	258	55	5	90	.213
Shawn Boskie	Tucson	Ari	107	34	1	10	.318	166	61	7	21	.367
Heath Bost	Col. Springs	Col	108	31	6	22	.287	190	51	7	42	.268
Cedrick Bowers	Durham	TB	97	25	2	17	.258	248	58	8	50	.234
Micah Bowie	Sacramento	Oak	109	26	3	23	.239	344	97	10	79	.282
Brian Bowles	Syracuse	Tor	97	22	1	32	.227	184	34	2	49	.185
Jason Boyd	Scranton-WB	Phi	54	10	1	14	.185	161	34	3	52	.211
Lesli Brea	Rochester	Bal	103	26	1	28	.252	219	54	5	70	.247
Jamie Brewington	Edmonton	Min	111	36	4	22	.324	163	51	7	31	.313
Donnie Bridges	Ottawa	Mon	76	24	2	16	.316	137	36	9	33	.263
Corey Brittan	Norfolk	NYM	118	30	1	14	.254	198	56	3	31	.283
Chris Brock	Scranton-WB	Phi	97	32	2	4	.330	198	43	7	42	.217
Will Brunson	Salt Lake	Ana	78	15	0	24	.192	191	58	9	28	.304
Jim Bruske	Salt Lake	Ana	86	25	1	27	.291	151	45	8	31	.298
Jim Bullinger	Memphis	StL	87	25	4	15	.287	128	43	7	21	.336
Mickey Callaway	Durham	TB	181	48	3	37	.265	314	83	6	44	.264
Scott Cassidy	Syracuse	Tor	106	30	6	21	.283	137	30	0	27	.219
Carlos Castillo	Pawtucket	Bos	270	78	5	39	.289	375	101	7	75	.269
Blas Cedeno	Scranton-WB	Phi	62	11	2	12	.177	160	45	7	40	.281
Juan Cerros	Norfolk	NYM	69	23	1	8	.333	154	42	4	24	.273
Carlos Chantres	Indianapolis	Mil	229	70	9	34	.306	414	106	6	53	.256
Anthony Chavez	Tucson	Ari	122	33	2	25	.270	232	76	3	51	.328
Jin Ho Cho	Pawtucket	Bos	190	50	5	33	.263	272	83	9	44	.305
Pasqual Coco	Syracuse	Tor	218	57	5	36	.261	245	71	6	46	.290
Dave Coggin	Scranton-WB	Phi	119	31	2	15	.261	248	62	4	38	.250
Clay Condrey	Portland	SD	73	23	4	17	.315	134	40	3	28	.299
Steve Connelly	Fresno	SF	69	19	0	12	.275	141	28	2	28	.199
Brian Cooper	Salt Lake	Ana	227	56	9	43	.247	437	125	17	66	.286
Archie Corbin	Charlotte	CWS	86	22	1	12	.256	185	36	2	52	.195
Bryan Corey	Portland	SD	156	42	5	21	.269	257	82	7	45	.319
Brad Cornett	Durham	TB	89	18	2	20	.202	148	38	1	35	.257
Robbie Crabtree	Fresno	SF	138	44	4	21	.319	291	71	7	78	.244
Jeff D'Amico	Omaha	KC	234	75	8	34	.321	305	76	11	58	.249
Pat Daneker	Syracuse	Tor	90	29	2	5	.322	122	46	7	9	.377
Lance Davis	Louisville	Cin	42	13	0	8	.310	267	68	7	39	.255
Matt DeWitt	Syracuse	Tor	91	18	2	10	.198	127	27	2	34	.213
R.A. Dickey	Oklahoma	Tex	262	70	6	59	.267	363	94	8	61	.259
Jason Dickson	Syracuse	Tor	80	31	4	12	.387	154	44	7	28	.286
John Dillinger	Syracuse	Tor	264	70	5	50	.265	323	80	5	58	.248
Jim Dougherty	Las Vegas	LA	109	35	3	30	.321	197	47	5	55	.239
Sean Douglass	Rochester	Bal	267	63	7	68	.236	368	97	6	88	.264
Ryan Drese	Buffalo	Cle	105	23	4	31	.219	124	37	3	21	.298
Tim Drew	Buffalo	Cle	157	41	2	36	.261	248	70	10	36	.282
Travis Driskill	New Orleans	Hou	304	75	8	63	.247	381	100	13	82	.262
Brandon Duckworth	Scranton-WB	Phi	204	41	8	57	.201	330	81	6	93	.245
Mike Duvall	Edmonton	Min	93	25	0	29	.269	158	48	7	34	.304
Dave Elder	Oklahoma	Tex	89	19	1	27	.213	128	35	3	29	.273
Todd Erdos	Pawtucket	Bos	95	20	2	25	.211	155	39	1	29	.252
Horacio Estrada	Col. Springs	Col	75	17	1	16	.227	285	85	10	61	.298
Leo Estrella	Louisville	Cin	81	24	1	7	.296	161	43	7	30	.267
Luis Estrella	Fresno	SF	168	51	9	32	.304	275	72	10	41	.262
Keith Evans	Ottawa	Mon	116	34	4	32	.293	220	60	3	40	.273
Scott Eyre	Syracuse	Tor	87	26	2	24	.299	212	41	6	72	.193
Jared Fernandez	Louisville	Cin	286	75	5	46	.262	490	143	19	72	.292
Ozzie Fernandez	Louisville	Cin	100	27	5	19	.270	105	27	1	12	.257
Nelson Figueroa	Scranton-WB	Phi	117	26	1	22	.222	214	48	5	52	.224
Tony Fiore	Edmonton	Min	117	35	0	23	.299	195	50	4	35	.256
Josh Fogg	Charlotte	CWS	157	48	4	32	.306	299	81	15	57	.271
Gus Gandarillas	Indianapolis	Mil	83	23	3	16	.277	167	39	1	36	.234
Lee Gardner	Durham	TB	120	39	4	14	.325	174	37	6	41	.213
Chris George	Omaha	KC	89	23	4	16	.258	345	80	10	68	.232
Matt Ginter	Charlotte	CWS	115	23	2	23	.200	168	39	1	44	.232
Isabel Giron	Portland	SD	88	22	3	24	.250	172	52	11	45	.302
Ryan Glynn	Oklahoma	Tex	132	39	5	20	.295	176	48	5	32	.273
Dicky Gonzalez	Norfolk	NYM	128	31	3	29	.242	230	65	7	41	.283

			vs Left					vs Right				
Player	Team	Org	AB	H	HR	SO	Avg	AB	H	HR	SO	Avg
Arnie Gooch	Louisville	Cin	246	77	5	35	.313	350	98	11	60	.280
Steve Green	Salt Lake	Ana	79	21	0	11	.266	151	38	3	29	.252
Kip Gross	Col. Springs	Col	133	53	2	20	.398	209	59	8	28	.282
Kevin Gryboski	Tacoma	Sea	90	30	2	12	.333	141	34	6	38	.241
Mark Guerra	New Orleans	Hou	192	60	2	21	.313	247	69	7	35	.279
Matt Guerrier	Charlotte	CWS	126	30	2	21	.238	174	45	5	22	.259
Eric Gunderson	Columbus	NYY	79	15	2	23	.190	195	55	4	37	.282
Geraldo Guzman	Tucson	Ari	143	50	6	20	.350	218	42	3	65	.193
Juan Guzman	Durham	TB	81	19	1	17	.235	134	31	6	25	.231
Jimmy Hamilton	Rochester	Bal	67	23	1	23	.343	144	35	3	26	.243
Chris Hammond	Buffalo	Cle	54	17	5	14	.315	149	36	0	40	.242
Tim Harikkala	Indianapolis	Mil	250	65	6	38	.260	440	145	9	58	.330
Travis Harper	Durham	TB	226	54	11	57	.239	354	86	14	58	.243
Mark Hendrickson	Syracuse	Tor	85	28	4	10	.329	207	52	9	23	.251
Butch Henry	Syracuse	Tor	73	21	0	20	.288	234	70	5	29	.299
Adrian Hernandez	Columbus	NYY	207	65	5	29	.314	230	51	8	68	.222
Junior Herndon	Portland	SD	175	52	5	20	.297	285	80	13	27	.281
Erik Hiljus	Sacramento	Oak	153	36	7	43	.235	219	43	11	65	.196
Brett Hinchliffe	Norfolk	NYM	97	20	0	16	.206	143	47	7	30	.329
Kevin Hodges	Tacoma	Sea	135	38	3	12	.281	206	59	5	43	.286
Craig House	Col. Springs	Col	74	23	2	14	.311	142	27	2	48	.190
Chad Hutchinson	Memphis	StL	157	41	3	45	.261	213	58	5	66	.272
Eric Ireland	Sacramento	Oak	276	94	10	45	.341	420	121	14	57	.288
Jason Jacome	Tucson	Ari	116	42	2	22	.362	367	107	9	50	.292
Tom Jacquez	Scranton-WB	Phi	69	16	1	20	.232	337	84	7	66	.249
Delvin James	Durham	TB	141	43	3	24	.305	194	56	5	27	.289
Jason Jennings	Col. Springs	Col	210	70	4	32	.333	306	75	5	78	.245
Ryan Jensen	Fresno	SF	122	35	2	22	.287	279	62	9	73	.222
Brett Jodie	Columbus	NYY	194	50	3	27	.258	270	73	6	32	.270
Barry Johnson	Columbus	NYY	87	20	3	17	.230	154	44	4	20	.286
Jonathan Johnson	Tucson	Ari	107	25	1	16	.234	168	38	6	35	.226
Mark Johnson	Toledo	Det	212	66	7	34	.311	360	104	14	45	.289
Mike Johnson	Oklahoma	Tex	157	45	4	30	.287	195	56	8	37	.287
Marcus Jones	Sacramento	Oak	120	33	0	13	.275	168	48	4	38	.286
Jeff Juden	Charlotte	CWS	103	20	4	27	.194	130	24	1	36	.185
Scott Karl	Nashville	Pit	69	19	2	10	.275	252	60	7	44	.238
Jason Karnuth	Memphis	StL	110	27	2	19	.245	179	55	5	23	.307
Justin Kaye	Tacoma	Sea	110	17	1	46	.155	163	34	4	61	.209
Randy Keisler	Columbus	NYY	82	24	3	18	.293	314	87	7	70	.277
Kris Keller	Toledo	Det	68	12	2	17	.176	189	52	8	43	.275
Mark Kiefer	Las Vegas	LA	225	56	11	63	.249	333	70	10	111	.210
Sun-Woo Kim	Pawtucket	Bos	136	38	3	28	.279	206	55	7	51	.267
Matt Kinney	Edmonton	Min	277	75	10	55	.271	359	103	15	91	.287
Brandon Knight	Columbus	NYY	264	76	6	58	.288	365	98	10	115	.268
Brian Knoll	Fresno	SF	88	26	8	16	.295	174	62	4	31	.356
Eric Knott	Tucson	Ari	76	21	0	10	.276	212	61	6	33	.288
Gary Knotts	Calgary	Fla	194	57	8	42	.294	283	79	8	62	.279
Brandon Kolb	Indianapolis	Mil	72	18	3	16	.250	140	31	4	41	.221
Rick Krivda	Memphis	StL	88	29	2	16	.330	224	58	7	30	.259
John Lackey	Salt Lake	Ana	99	32	3	17	.323	134	43	2	25	.321
Denny Lail	Columbus	NYY	192	52	6	39	.271	335	92	5	66	.275
Frank Lankford	Sacramento	Oak	90	24	2	16	.267	189	63	6	21	.333
Andy Larkin	Col. Springs	Col	165	45	10	36	.273	310	89	7	63	.287
Brett Laxton	Omaha	KC	157	36	2	33	.229	207	56	5	42	.271
Sang Lee	Pawtucket	Bos	52	11	2	17	.212	154	41	9	27	.266
Derrick Lewis	Richmond	Atl	91	16	0	21	.176	125	34	2	29	.272
Richie Lewis	Norfolk	NYM	116	25	7	18	.216	228	58	1	48	.254
Mike Lincoln	Nashville	Pit	129	31	3	27	.240	229	59	7	44	.258
Scott Linebrink	New Orleans	Hou	97	20	1	28	.206	158	32	3	44	.203
Doug Linton	Norfolk	NYM	112	29	3	30	.259	171	45	5	37	.263
Felipe Lira	Ottawa	Mon	74	18	0	13	.243	152	38	4	34	.250
Carlton Loewer	Portland	SD	136	41	4	23	.301	183	56	3	41	.306
Andrew Lorraine	Calgary	Fla	131	34	3	25	.260	501	175	16	76	.349
Shane Loux	Toledo	Det	238	83	9	25	.349	387	120	13	47	.310
Larry Luebbers	Louisville	Cin	200	60	6	28	.300	257	69	2	32	.268
Spike Lundberg	Oklahoma	Tex	103	35	4	14	.340	131	37	4	17	.282
Dave Lundquist	Portland	SD	93	18	1	22	.194	147	41	5	45	.279
Brandon Lyon	Syracuse	Tor	97	24	1	15	.247	168	44	6	38	.262
Mike MacDougal	Omaha	KC	253	69	7	50	.273	303	75	6	60	.248
Calvin Maduro	Rochester	Bal	102	22	1	23	.216	154	39	8	25	.253
Jim Mann	New Orleans	Hou	102	22	4	33	.216	144	30	3	48	.208
Julio Manon	Ottawa	Mon	102	26	4	25	.255	201	45	7	42	.224
Mike Maroth	Toledo	Det	111	30	0	13	.270	412	128	11	50	.311
Rob Marquez	Ottawa	Mon	69	30	3	6	.435	157	27	2	21	.172
Lee Marshall	Edmonton	Min	73	22	2	11	.301	132	28	0	26	.212
Willie Martinez	Edmonton	Min	189	60	10	40	.317	274	87	8	46	.318
Onan Masaoka	Las Vegas	LA	86	27	2	21	.314	205	60	7	40	.293
Troy Mattes	Ottawa	Mon	110	25	1	26	.227	199	50	2	44	.251
Matt McClellan	Syracuse	Tor	71	20	1	15	.282	131	29	3	29	.221
Sam McConnell	Nashville	Pit	104	31	6	22	.298	442	128	14	76	.290
Allen McDill	Pawtucket	Bos	59	7	1	21	.119	204	55	6	51	.270
Tony McKnight	New Orleans	Hou	153	39	3	26	.255	210	65	7	35	.310
Brian Meadows	Omaha	KC	200	79	11	33	.395	231	64	10	41	.277
Geronimo Mendoza	Charlotte	CWS	130	45	5	20	.346	238	58	11	48	.244
Mike Meyers	Iowa	ChC	239	60	3	48	.251	317	69	6	76	.218
Bart Miadich	Salt Lake	Ana	83	13	2	31	.157	128	27	2	42	.211
Jason Middlebrook	Portland	SD	123	32	2	21	.260	231	57	3	47	.247
Justin Miller	Sacramento	Oak	270	74	13	54	.274	360	100	13	80	.278
Matt Miller	Toledo	Det	65	17	1	10	.262	167	43	2	39	.257
Trever Miller	Pawtucket	Bos	117	29	2	36	.248	346	113	14	57	.327

Triple-A Pitching vs. Lefthanded and Righthanded Batters

Player	Team	Org	vs Left AB	H	HR	SO	Avg	vs Right AB	H	HR	SO	Avg
Gabe Molina	Calgary	Fla	137	48	5	31	.350	299	78	9	74	.261
Eric Moody	Nashville	Pit	170	42	9	19	.247	262	70	6	31	.267
Trey Moore	Richmond	Atl	107	19	0	18	.178	496	121	9	104	.244
Damian Moss	Richmond	Atl	48	15	3	14	.313	276	60	7	80	.217
Scott Mullen	Omaha	KC	76	23	3	15	.303	133	43	5	23	.323
Bobby Munoz	Ottawa	Mon	137	34	4	22	.248	263	64	1	44	.243
Pete Munro	Oklahoma	Tex	140	31	4	33	.221	197	58	8	40	.294
Dan Murray	Omaha	KC	166	38	4	30	.229	214	67	6	40	.313
Aaron Myette	Oklahoma	Tex	117	33	1	31	.282	149	31	4	45	.208
Doug Nickle	Scranton-WB	Phi	91	21	0	21	.231	210	41	2	39	.195
Elvin Nina	Salt Lake	Ana	220	71	3	34	.323	416	124	16	67	.298
Phil Norton	Iowa	ChC	93	22	2	27	.237	166	43	1	48	.259
Pablo Ochoa	Norfolk	NYM	103	28	1	19	.272	179	43	6	30	.240
Brian O'Connor	Nashville	Pit	102	26	4	26	.255	342	98	11	48	.287
Steve Ontiveros	Sacramento	Oak	118	36	3	27	.305	217	58	8	37	.267
Mike Oquist	Edmonton	Min	184	61	3	30	.332	264	71	9	46	.269
Delvis Pacheco	Richmond	Atl	80	28	2	14	.350	160	50	2	37	.313
Vicente Padilla	Scranton-WB	Phi	101	23	3	28	.228	194	41	5	47	.211
John Parrish	Rochester	Bal	103	20	2	35	.194	394	95	9	91	.241
John Patterson	Tucson	Ari	115	35	3	22	.304	157	47	6	18	.299
Josh Pearce	Memphis	StL	121	34	6	15	.281	150	38	5	21	.253
Jesus Pena	Pawtucket	Bos	60	20	2	6	.333	231	72	8	36	.312
Chris Peters	Columbus	NYY	36	11	0	2	.306	176	45	7	27	.256
Kyle Peterson	Indianapolis	Mil	151	43	6	27	.285	315	100	11	46	.317
Adam Pettyjohn	Toledo	Det	82	13	1	16	.159	328	94	8	62	.287
Tommy Phelps	Toledo	Det	50	17	0	10	.340	198	57	4	43	.288
Joel Pineiro	Tacoma	Sea	122	26	4	37	.213	159	42	4	27	.264
Mike Porzio	Charlotte	CWS	110	37	3	17	.336	407	101	11	90	.248
Brian Powell	New Orleans	Hou	229	58	6	47	.253	318	84	7	49	.264
Jeremy Powell	Portland	SD	122	23	0	23	.189	152	24	3	46	.158
Eddie Priest	Las Vegas	LA	91	30	4	19	.330	296	102	10	48	.345
Ruben Quevedo	Iowa	ChC	238	56	6	66	.235	285	68	7	84	.239
Jason Rakers	Omaha	KC	162	40	9	44	.247	216	60	7	55	.278
Mario Ramos	Sacramento	Oak	45	13	1	12	.289	262	61	4	70	.233
Rob Ramsay	Tacoma	Sea	133	44	7	28	.331	458	116	19	85	.253
Scott Randall	Col. Springs	Col	111	29	6	22	.261	170	45	5	25	.265
Fred Rath	Memphis	StL	145	52	9	22	.359	182	51	3	35	.280
Jon Ratliff	Sacramento	Oak	114	42	4	20	.368	149	42	5	21	.282
Todd Revenig	Tucson	Ari	101	29	3	12	.287	171	53	6	30	.310
Chad Ricketts	Las Vegas	LA	78	22	2	16	.282	139	27	3	54	.194
Mike Riley	Fresno	SF	63	16	1	17	.254	154	43	8	35	.279
Joe Roa	Calgary	Fla	169	47	8	29	.278	317	87	8	52	.274
Jake Robbins	Richmond	Atl	96	21	0	15	.219	194	52	1	38	.268
Grant Roberts	Norfolk	NYM	102	31	1	16	.304	167	49	3	38	.293
Frank Rodriguez	Louisville	Cin	108	22	2	18	.204	186	45	3	38	.242
Jose Rodriguez	Memphis	StL	73	13	1	22	.178	152	39	6	32	.257
J.C. Romero	Edmonton	Min	63	16	0	14	.254	180	51	4	41	.283
Rafael Roque	Pawtucket	Bos	96	24	1	15	.250	290	77	14	53	.266
Brian Rose	Durham	TB	135	37	4	28	.274	230	51	7	60	.222
Ted Rose	Ottawa	Mon	162	46	2	40	.284	297	79	7	55	.266
Jason Ryan	Nashville	Pit	76	19	2	12	.250	129	33	5	13	.256
Jesus Sanchez	Calgary	Fla	52	7	1	12	.135	231	54	3	46	.234
Julio Santana	Fresno	SF	197	62	10	43	.315	339	98	18	82	.289
Brian Schmack	Oklahoma	Tex	85	23	4	11	.271	129	33	1	23	.256
Jason Secoda	Charlotte	CWS	232	90	9	36	.388	323	78	8	69	.241
Shawn Sedlacek	Omaha	KC	141	50	6	12	.355	176	48	7	32	.273
Chris Seelbach	Richmond	Atl	121	28	4	26	.231	211	57	5	56	.270
Wascar Serrano	Portland	SD	157	54	5	24	.344	196	44	5	49	.224
Scot Shields	Salt Lake	Ana	213	52	6	41	.244	316	89	18	63	.282
Brian Shouse	New Orleans	Hou	87	22	1	33	.253	118	29	3	23	.246
Tony Shumaker	Rochester	Bal	95	27	1	19	.284	179	43	6	34	.240
Brian Sikorski	Oklahoma	Tex	133	36	4	30	.271	190	53	4	43	.279
Ben Simon	Las Vegas	LA	82	26	4	19	.317	121	35	4	24	.289
Jason Simontacchi	Edmonton	Min	237	71	7	38	.300	351	121	14	45	.345
Steve Sinclair	Charlotte	CWS	93	21	2	22	.226	151	45	3	35	.298
Aaron Small	Richmond	Atl	120	32	6	21	.267	258	65	8	40	.252
Bud Smith	Memphis	StL	105	31	2	20	.295	314	83	4	58	.264
Dan Smith	Buffalo	Cle	169	52	8	25	.308	233	58	9	43	.249
Roy Smith	Buffalo	Cle	93	21	1	24	.226	170	38	1	62	.224
John Snyder	Indianapolis	Mil	241	88	6	26	.365	385	114	9	58	.296
Shawn Sonnier	Omaha	KC	111	27	7	31	.243	166	42	8	32	.253
Steve Sparks	Nashville	Pit	101	28	1	24	.277	188	49	9	40	.261
Sean Spencer	Ottawa	Mon	64	14	1	17	.219	171	39	3	41	.228
Stan Spencer	Portland	SD	154	43	1	38	.279	236	67	10	43	.284
Dennis Springer	Las Vegas	LA	173	47	8	16	.272	286	95	8	35	.332
Jay Spurgeon	Rochester	Bal	154	43	4	23	.279	181	42	8	38	.232
Jason Standridge	Durham	TB	161	60	6	20	.373	252	70	7	28	.278
Rob Stanifer	Iowa	ChC	99	35	3	17	.354	188	50	6	62	.266
Dennis Stark	Tacoma	Sea	229	64	1	36	.279	323	60	11	94	.186
Kennie Steenstra	Tucson	Ari	271	74	5	48	.273	404	113	9	66	.280
John Stephens	Rochester	Bal	102	19	2	35	.186	118	33	3	26	.280
Dave Stevens	Richmond	Atl	86	24	4	24	.279	141	43	10	23	.305
Ricky Stone	New Orleans	Hou	139	38	5	27	.273	225	60	3	51	.267
Joe Strong	Calgary	Fla	75	16	4	17	.213	170	64	5	31	.376
Anthony Telford	Ottawa	Mon	93	25	2	24	.269	194	54	5	38	.278
Jay Tessmer	Indianapolis	Mil	78	21	2	12	.269	146	35	1	27	.240
Nate Teut	Iowa	ChC	141	36	4	33	.255	528	148	24	92	.280
Evan Thomas	Scranton-WB	Phi	149	48	4	20	.322	272	75	10	54	.276
John Thomson	Col. Springs	Col	107	26	1	24	.243	163	48	5	28	.294
Kevin Tolar	Toledo	Det	56	10	0	22	.179	151	39	3	51	.258

Player	Team	Org	vs Left AB	H	HR	SO	Avg	vs Right AB	H	HR	SO	Avg
Brett Tomko	Tacoma	Sea	210	63	4	49	.300	278	61	8	68	.219
T.J. Tucker	Ottawa	Mon	98	21	5	23	.214	190	42	5	38	.221
Jason Turman	Tacoma	Sea	118	25	1	39	.212	153	29	5	46	.190
Marc Valdes	Richmond	Atl	172	47	4	42	.273	304	86	9	55	.283
Dario Veras	Buffalo	Cle	95	30	5	26	.316	165	39	5	43	.236
Brandon Villafuerte	Oklahoma	Tex	106	27	2	31	.255	130	36	2	34	.277
Ismael Villegas	Richmond	Atl	193	57	6	25	.295	313	71	15	75	.227
Ryan Vogelsong	Fresno	SF	98	17	2	28	.173	108	18	4	25	.167
Dave Wainhouse	Iowa	ChC	117	35	5	20	.299	177	51	4	41	.288
Jamie Walker	Buffalo	Cle	78	18	5	15	.231	291	86	7	36	.296
Pete Walker	Norfolk	NYM	234	62	6	39	.265	386	83	6	67	.215
Don Wengert	Nashville	Pit	171	43	9	27	.251	305	96	8	42	.315
Jake Westbrook	Buffalo	Cle	90	27	1	16	.300	151	33	1	29	.219
Dan Wheeler	Durham	TB	103	30	6	20	.291	163	42	5	19	.258
Matt Whisenant	Las Vegas	LA	68	16	2	12	.235	176	43	2	44	.244
Brian Williams	Columbus	NYY	71	29	2	9	.408	163	43	3	24	.264
Jeff Williams	Las Vegas	LA	102	29	4	26	.284	253	73	8	35	.289
Jeff Wilson	Rochester	Bal	90	23	3	14	.256	317	95	14	42	.300
Scott Winchester	Louisville	Cin	81	17	1	15	.210	123	33	4	22	.268
Matt Wise	Salt Lake	Ana	191	52	6	44	.272	303	82	13	67	.271
Bryan Wolff	Edmonton	Min	129	43	3	16	.333	170	53	11	36	.312
Greg Wooten	Tacoma	Sea	277	85	9	52	.307	397	116	9	64	.292
Carlos Zambrano	Iowa	ChC	232	65	5	65	.280	317	59	4	90	.186
Pete Zamora	Scranton-WB	Phi	75	18	2	25	.240	242	46	5	54	.190
Dave Zancanaro	Memphis	StL	143	39	10	25	.273	430	132	18	82	.307
Jordan Zimmerman	Tacoma	Sea	66	28	5	11	.424	176	55	3	34	.313

Triple-A Pitching at Home and on the Road

			Home					Road				
Player	Team	Org	G	IP	W	L	ERA	G	IP	W	L	ERA
Pat Ahearne	Calgary	Fla	13	68.0	5	4	6.09	15	76.1	1	6	6.48
Kurt Ainsworth	Fresno	SF	16	92.1	9	3	3.61	11	56.2	1	6	7.46
Victor Alvarez	Edmonton	Min	8	50.2	4	2	3.73	12	67.0	3	2	4.70
J.D. Arteaga	New Orleans	Hou	15	68.0	2	4	2.51	17	69.1	6	2	3.63
Mike Bacsik	Buffalo	Cle	10	56.2	6	1	3.49	11	64.1	6	4	3.08
Willie Banks	Syracuse	Tor	9	52.0	4	3	4.50	15	94.1	4	2	2.58
Rick Bauer	Rochester	Bal	9	54.0	5	2	4.33	10	59.0	5	2	3.51
Rigo Beltran	Scranton-WB	Phi	16	52.0	1	3	3.12	21	63.0	1	2	2.86
Alan Benes	Las Vegas	LA	15	86.1	4	2	2.81	10	55.2	3	4	4.69
Alan Benes	Memphis	StL	15	86.1	4	2	2.81	10	55.2	3	4	4.69
Joaquin Benoit	Oklahoma	Tex	13	81.1	7	2	3.87	11	49.0	2	3	4.78
Adam Bernero	Toledo	Det	14	72.0	2	8	5.75	12	68.0	4	3	4.50
Jason Beverlin	Salt Lake	Ana	11	51.1	1	1	4.91	11	50.0	5	1	3.78
Matt Blank	Ottawa	Mon	5	27.2	2	2	6.18	9	54.0	4	5	4.67
Joe Borowski	Iowa	ChC	18	61.0	6	1	1.48	21	48.2	2	6	4.07
Cedrick Bowers	Durham	TB	23	49.2	3	3	2.72	19	44.0	3	2	3.48
Micah Bowie	Sacramento	Oak	22	49.2	3	2	4.17	16	66.0	3	6	5.73
Lesli Brea	Rochester	Bal	38	46.0	1	3	3.52	25	36.0	1	3	4.25
Corey Brittan	Norfolk	NYM	30	42.0	3	0	1.29	28	39.0	1	2	2.77
Carlos Castillo	Pawtucket	Bos	14	81.0	6	4	3.00	14	82.1	3	7	3.83
Carlos Chantres	Indianapolis	Mil	14	87.0	6	2	3.93	14	80.0	1	9	4.95
Anthony Chavez	Tucson	Ari	29	51.0	6	2	4.59	22	35.0	1	4	4.63
Jin Ho Cho	Pawtucket	Bos	20	64.1	0	5	4.48	17	53.0	3	5	4.58
Pasqual Coco	Syracuse	Tor	11	64.0	5	3	4.36	11	57.2	3	3	4.99
Dave Coggin	Scranton-WB	Phi	8	51.0	3	2	1.41	7	46.0	2	3	4.89
Brian Cooper	Salt Lake	Ana	15	91.0	5	3	5.04	13	82.0	7	5	4.17
Robbie Crabtree	Fresno	SF	34	63.0	3	1	2.86	29	51.0	5	9	4.76
Jeff D'Amico	Omaha	KC	15	66.0	4	3	3.00	17	73.1	1	4	4.05
R.A. Dickey	Oklahoma	Tex	12	78.0	6	3	3.69	12	85.0	5	4	3.81
John Dillinger	Syracuse	Tor	14	87.1	7	3	3.81	12	68.0	4	4	4.24
Jim Dougherty	Edmonton	Min	31	40.0	1	1	6.08	28	41.0	3	4	2.41
Sean Douglass	Rochester	Bal	15	85.1	3	6	4.96	12	76.1	5	3	1.89
Tim Drew	Buffalo	Cle	8	50.0	5	2	2.16	10	57.2	3	4	5.46
Travis Driskill	New Orleans	Hou	15	105.1	6	2	2.99	13	73.0	5	3	4.93
Brandon Duckworth	Scranton-WB	Phi	13	91.0	8	2	2.47	9	56.0	5	0	2.89
Luis Estrella	Fresno	SF	14	64.1	5	2	3.92	16	51.0	3	1	5.29
Keith Evans	Ottawa	Mon	27	42.2	3	1	2.95	18	41.0	4	2	5.05
Jared Fernandez	Louisville	Cin	16	82.1	4	4	4.48	17	113.1	6	5	3.89
Nelson Figueroa	Scranton-WB	Phi	8	50.0	2	1	2.88	5	37.0	2	1	1.95
Tony Fiore	Col. Springs	Col	17	42.0	3	0	2.79	15	38.0	2	0	4.74
Josh Fogg	Charlotte	CWS	20	60.2	1	3	4.01	20	54.0	3	4	5.67
Chris George	Omaha	KC	10	58.0	3	2	4.34	10	59.0	8	1	2.75
Dicky Gonzalez	Norfolk	NYM	11	62.2	3	3	2.87	6	33.0	3	2	3.55
Arnie Gooch	Louisville	Cin	17	86.0	3	5	6.28	11	62.2	4	5	4.74
Mark Guerra	New Orleans	Hou	15	59.0	4	5	3.51	13	49.0	3	3	4.41
Matt Guerrier	Charlotte	CWS	7	48.2	5	0	2.77	5	32.2	2	1	4.68
Geraldo Guzman	Tucson	Ari	12	54.0	0	3	5.50	8	40.0	3	3	4.05
Tim Harikkala	Indianapolis	Mil	18	94.0	5	8	5.46	13	78.0	6	2	3.92
Travis Harper	Durham	TB	13	78.0	6	2	4.04	12	77.0	6	4	3.39
Adrian Hernandez	Columbus	NYY	9	57.0	4	4	4.11	12	60.0	4	3	6.90
Junior Herndon	Portland	SD	8	46.0	2	2	4.70	13	70.0	7	3	4.50
Erik Hiljus	Sacramento	Oak	10	69.0	5	4	3.78	5	32.2	3	1	3.31
Kevin Hodges	Tacoma	Sea	7	41.2	1	3	3.67	7	45.0	4	2	4.60
Chad Hutchinson	Las Vegas	LA	12	41.2	2	2	7.78	15	56.0	2	7	8.04
Chad Hutchinson	Memphis	StL	12	41.2	2	2	7.78	15	56.0	2	7	8.04
Eric Ireland	Sacramento	Oak	16	95.1	5	5	4.44	13	72.1	3	6	6.35
Jason Jacome	Tucson	Ari	16	46.0	0	3	4.50	19	74.0	1	5	5.84
Tom Jacquez	Scranton-WB	Phi	17	56.0	5	2	2.41	16	53.0	5	4	3.91
Delvin James	Durham	TB	14	35.0	1	4	5.40	17	49.0	2	3	4.41
Ryan Jensen	Fresno	SF	11	60.0	8	0	3.00	9	46.0	3	2	4.11
Brett Jodie	Columbus	NYY	12	81.0	5	3	2.56	7	38.2	5	1	3.96
Mark Johnson	Toledo	Det	14	86.1	4	6	3.75	10	54.0	3	5	6.50
Mike Johnson	Oklahoma	Tex	14	60.2	2	4	4.90	9	27.2	1	1	3.90
Scott Karl	Nashville	Pit	6	39.0	2	1	2.77	8	45.0	2	2	4.80
Randy Keisler	Columbus	NYY	8	47.2	3	4	4.15	10	49.2	2	3	6.16
Mark Kiefer	Edmonton	Min	17	84.0	6	4	3.86	15	61.0	5	3	4.72
Sun-Woo Kim	Pawtucket	Bos	10	48.0	4	4	4.88	9	41.0	2	3	5.93
Matt Kinney	Col. Springs	Col	14	77.1	2	5	5.70	15	84.0	4	6	4.50
Brandon Knight	Columbus	NYY	11	73.1	5	2	2.82	14	88.1	7	5	4.38
Gary Knotts	Calgary	Fla	12	67.1	5	3	6.95	9	51.0	1	4	3.53
Rick Krivda	Las Vegas	LA	5	34.0	1	2	1.59	9	46.0	3	4	6.46
Rick Krivda	Memphis	StL	5	34.0	1	2	1.59	9	46.0	3	4	6.46
Denny Lail	Columbus	NYY	15	67.0	1	5	4.84	18	69.0	5	1	4.43
Brett Laxton	Omaha	KC	24	57.2	3	3	2.65	21	38.2	0	4	6.05
Richie Lewis	Norfolk	NYM	8	46.0	4	1	2.93	9	45.2	3	3	5.12
Mike Lincoln	Nashville	Pit	10	49.0	4	2	2.76	8	42.2	1	2	4.22
Carlton Loewer	Portland	SD	8	47.2	4	2	3.97	6	33.2	1	2	3.74
Andrew Lorraine	Calgary	Fla	15	77.0	4	3	5.26	15	72.1	5	2	5.60
Shane Loux	Toledo	Det	13	67.0	5	6	6.58	15	84.0	5	5	5.14
Larry Luebbers	Louisville	Cin	12	65.0	4	2	3.32	9	56.0	3	4	3.86
Mike MacDougal	Omaha	KC	14	73.1	3	4	3.93	14	70.1	5	4	5.50
Julio Manon	Ottawa	Mon	10	62.0	0	3	2.61	5	22.0	1	1	4.50
Mike Maroth	Toledo	Det	12	63.0	2	5	5.86	12	68.1	5	5	3.56
Willie Martinez	Col. Springs	Col	11	62.0	3	4	4.79	10	50.0	4	4	6.66
Troy Mattes	Ottawa	Mon	7	38.0	2	3	3.55	8	44.0	3	2	3.68
Sam McConnell	Nashville	Pit	11	61.0	5	4	5.46	15	73.0	2	6	6.53
Tony McKnight	New Orleans	Hou	11	54.0	6	3	4.17	7	38.2	3	2	5.59
Brian Meadows	Omaha	KC	10	60.0	5	3	5.40	8	44.2	1	2	7.25
Geronimo Mendoza	Charlotte	CWS	9	50.0	3	4	5.58	8	46.0	2	4	4.30
Mike Meyers	Iowa	ChC	14	84.0	5	3	2.57	11	63.0	2	1	4.14
Jason Middlebrook	Portland	SD	9	58.2	4	2	2.15	6	31.2	3	2	5.40
Justin Miller	Sacramento	Oak	15	83.1	4	5	4.75	14	81.0	3	5	4.78
Trever Miller	Pawtucket	Bos	16	63.0	1	6	5.86	17	52.2	2	5	4.44
Gabe Molina	Calgary	Fla	20	52.0	3	1	6.23	20	54.2	2	8	5.60
Eric Moody	Nashville	Pit	23	63.2	2	2	2.40	19	48.2	3	4	4.81
Trey Moore	Richmond	Atl	14	91.0	3	4	2.97	12	72.0	6	4	3.75
Damian Moss	Richmond	Atl	7	35.0	2	1	1.80	10	53.2	3	3	4.02
Bobby Munoz	Ottawa	Mon	9	51.0	0	3	3.53	10	59.0	4	3	3.36
Pete Munro	Oklahoma	Tex	16	44.2	5	1	4.03	17	44.0	3	5	5.32
Dan Murray	Omaha	KC	26	56.2	2	1	3.49	22	41.0	1	2	4.61
Doug Nickle	Scranton-WB	Phi	25	40.2	4	1	1.55	22	45.0	5	2	1.80
Elvin Nina	Salt Lake	Ana	13	71.1	5	4	4.92	16	86.1	5	7	5.94
Brian O'Connor	Nashville	Pit	17	56.2	3	3	6.35	20	55.0	3	6	6.05
Steve Ontiveros	Sacramento	Oak	8	45.2	5	1	3.35	8	39.0	2	5	6.00
Mike Oquist	Col. Springs	Col	10	56.0	4	3	4.02	11	54.0	1	5	4.33
Vicente Padilla	Scranton-WB	Phi	8	34.0	3	0	1.85	8	47.0	4	0	2.87
John Parrish	Rochester	Bal	13	71.0	3	5	4.06	13	62.0	4	2	2.90
Kyle Peterson	Indianapolis	Mil	11	59.0	1	4	6.71	10	56.0	1	6	4.66
Adam Pettyjohn	Toledo	Det	7	46.0	2	4	3.13	10	61.0	3	4	3.69
Mike Porzio	Charlotte	CWS	13	53.2	4	1	3.86	18	80.1	2	5	4.71
Brian Powell	New Orleans	Hou	10	62.0	3	3	2.76	14	82.1	6	5	3.50
Eddie Priest	Edmonton	Min	13	51.0	2	5	6.88	10	42.0	2	3	5.36
Ruben Quevedo	Iowa	ChC	9	57.0	4	2	2.84	13	84.0	5	3	3.11
Jason Rakers	Omaha	KC	20	46.0	3	3	5.09	24	51.0	3	1	3.88
Mario Ramos	Sacramento	Oak	5	33.0	3	2	3.27	8	47.0	5	1	3.06
Rob Ramsay	Tacoma	Sea	13	75.0	5	6	4.20	13	74.0	5	5	5.47
Joe Roa	Calgary	Fla	8	51.0	3	3	4.94	11	72.1	3	3	3.24
Frank Rodriguez	Louisville	Cin	21	43.2	5	1	2.27	22	36.2	3	5	2.70
Rafael Roque	Pawtucket	Bos	11	51.2	4	2	4.18	9	47.0	4	3	4.21
Brian Rose	Durham	TB	12	64.1	6	1	2.24	7	34.0	3	1	4.76
Ted Rose	Ottawa	Mon	20	75.0	5	3	3.24	17	45.0	2	6	5.40
Julio Santana	Fresno	SF	13	71.1	5	6	5.55	12	61.0	3	2	6.20
Jason Secoda	Charlotte	CWS	18	73.0	2	4	4.81	16	66.0	1	5	5.59
Shawn Sedlacek	Omaha	KC	6	39.0	3	0	3.92	8	42.0	2	4	6.00
Chris Seelbach	Richmond	Atl	12	55.0	5	4	4.58	10	33.0	2	3	6.00
Wascar Serrano	Portland	SD	13	50.0	4	3	4.14	14	43.0	2	2	5.02
Scot Shields	Salt Lake	Ana	9	58.0	3	3	5.59	12	79.1	3	8	4.54
Brian Sikorski	Oklahoma	Tex	7	47.2	4	2	2.45	7	39.2	2	2	4.99
Jason Simontacchi	Col. Springs	Col	15	67.0	5	6	5.10	17	76.0	2	7	5.57
Aaron Small	Richmond	Atl	24	59.0	5	5	4.42	17	37.0	5	2	2.92
Bud Smith	Las Vegas	LA	8	53.0	2	4	2.21	9	54.2	6	1	3.29
Bud Smith	Memphis	StL	8	53.0	2	4	2.21	9	54.2	6	1	3.29
Dan Smith	Buffalo	Cle	9	50.0	2	1	3.78	12	55.2	4	3	5.17
John Snyder	Indianapolis	Mil	15	76.0	3	2	4.03	17	71.0	0	9	7.23
Stan Spencer	Portland	SD	10	42.2	2	2	3.80	10	56.0	3	4	6.11
Dennis Springer	Edmonton	Min	9	59.0	4	1	5.03	10	55.0	3	6	5.56
Jay Spurgeon	Rochester	Bal	7	41.0	1	3	4.83	8	46.0	2	2	4.30
Jason Standridge	Durham	TB	10	50.0	2	6	6.48	10	52.0	3	4	4.15
Dennis Stark	Tacoma	Sea	11	71.1	5	1	2.40	13	80.0	9	1	2.36
Kennie Steenstra	Tucson	Ari	13	77.0	2	2	3.97	15	92.1	7	4	4.39
Ricky Stone	New Orleans	Hou	27	46.2	3	3	2.51	24	48.2	3	0	4.62
Nate Teut	Iowa	ChC	17	97.1	7	5	5.83	12	69.0	6	3	4.17
Evan Thomas	Scranton-WB	Phi	9	46.2	2	5	5.98	10	57.0	1	8	4.74
Brett Tomko	Tacoma	Sea	8	58.2	6	1	2.30	11	68.0	4	5	5.56
T.J. Tucker	Ottawa	Mon	9	56.0	0	4	3.70	5	28.0	3	1	1.93
Marc Valdes	Richmond	Atl	15	63.0	3	6	4.14	14	60.0	6	5	4.95
Ismael Villegas	Richmond	Atl	17	67.0	2	4	4.16	17	67.0	2	3	4.16
Jamie Walker	Buffalo	Cle	18	49.2	5	1	3.44	20	43.0	2	1	4.40
Pete Walker	Norfolk	NYM	11	73.0	6	2	3.21	15	95.1	7	2	2.83
Don Wengert	Nashville	Pit	10	63.0	4	3	2.43	8	48.2	3	4	6.29
Jeff Williams	Edmonton	Min	9	50.2	4	3	4.09	7	40.0	3	2	3.83
Jeff Wilson	Rochester	Bal	16	45.2	1	4	6.90	12	54.0	1	7	5.33
Matt Wise	Salt Lake	Ana	9	56.0	4	3	4.66	12	67.0	5	6	5.37
Greg Wooten	Tacoma	Sea	15	100.1	8	4	3.05	12	69.0	3	4	5.35
Carlos Zambrano	Iowa	ChC	12	69.0	4	1	3.00	14	81.1	6	4	4.65
Pete Zamora	Scranton-WB	Phi	27	49.0	5	3	2.39	18	40.0	3	1	3.60
Dave Zancanaro	Las Vegas	LA	15	79.0	4	8	6.49	12	63.2	2	6	5.37
Dave Zancanaro	Memphis	StL	15	79.0	4	8	6.49	12	63.2	2	6	5.37

Double-A Batting vs. Lefthanded and Righthanded Pitchers

			vs Left					vs Right				
Player	Team	Org	AB	H	HR	RBI	Avg	AB	H	HR	RBI	Avg
Dennis Abreu	West Tenn	ChC	68	19	0	3	.279	263	65	4	27	.247
Chris Aguila	Portland	Fla	82	20	1	12	.244	159	42	3	17	.264
Kurt Airoso	Erie	Det	90	24	4	16	.267	186	41	10	28	.220
Cory Aldridge	Greenville	Atl	139	38	6	16	.273	313	73	13	40	.233
Jason Alfaro	Round Rock	Hou	69	20	1	10	.290	215	49	1	19	.228
Luke Allen	Jacksonville	LA	131	29	3	14	.221	355	112	13	59	.315
Gabe Alvarez	Chattanooga	Cin	101	21	2	9	.208	235	64	14	41	.272
Tony Alvarez	Altoona	Pit	68	25	1	6	.368	186	56	5	19	.301
Alfredo Amezaga	Arkansas	Ana	78	22	3	5	.282	207	67	1	16	.324
Mike Amrhein	West Tenn	ChC	93	30	0	9	.323	218	45	4	24	.206
Brooks Badeaux	Orlando	TB	129	29	0	7	.225	341	88	1	20	.258
Jeff Bailey	Portland	Fla	159	37	8	30	.233	273	67	5	36	.245
Rod Bair	Carolina	Col	80	18	3	10	.225	193	51	4	21	.264
Kevin Barker	Huntsville	Mil	72	24	2	16	.333	160	51	6	22	.319
Eric Battersby	Birmingham	CWS	103	33	4	17	.320	335	78	10	50	.233
Trey Beamon	San Antonio	Sea	62	13	0	7	.210	176	48	1	12	.273
Brian Becker	Orlando	TB	129	29	2	10	.225	282	64	5	32	.227
Andy Beinbrink	Orlando	TB	129	40	2	17	.310	314	81	3	32	.258
Al Benjamin	Mobile	SD	83	28	3	11	.337	291	74	9	39	.254
Brandon Berger	Wichita	KC	149	52	14	35	.349	305	88	26	83	.289
Angel Berroa	Wichita	KC	98	28	1	10	.286	206	62	7	32	.301
Andy Bevins	New Haven	StL	127	24	5	16	.189	221	45	8	24	.204
Larry Bigbie	Bowie	Bal	90	22	2	10	.244	172	55	6	23	.320
Hank Blalock	Tulsa	Tex	88	27	4	18	.307	184	62	7	43	.337
Willie Bloomquist	San Antonio	Sea	167	39	0	8	.234	324	86	0	20	.265
Joe Borchard	Birmingham	CWS	131	36	6	19	.275	384	116	21	79	.302
Jason Bowers	New Haven	StL	159	35	1	13	.220	301	76	3	21	.252
Junior Brignac	Greenville	Atl	61	14	0	1	.230	142	27	1	11	.190
Juan Brito	Wichita	KC	75	28	3	10	.373	161	35	1	18	.217
Ben Broussard	Chattanooga	Cin	119	39	9	29	.328	234	74	14	40	.316
Tonayne Brown	Trenton	Bos	109	41	3	14	.376	287	74	1	17	.258
Eric Bruntlett	Round Rock	Hou	137	46	2	17	.336	366	88	1	23	.240
Kevin Burford	Carolina	Col	95	22	2	10	.232	268	83	4	25	.310
Gary Burnham	Reading	Phi	106	39	4	28	.368	265	79	11	49	.298
Kevin Burns	Round Rock	Hou	53	8	3	6	.151	252	75	17	50	.298
Darren Burton	Altoona	Pit	94	29	3	5	.309	205	57	4	27	.278
Mike Byas	Shreveport	SF	101	31	0	9	.307	215	53	0	16	.247
Marlon Byrd	Reading	Phi	158	53	10	24	.335	352	108	18	65	.307
Brett Cadiente	Tulsa	Tex	76	25	2	6	.329	186	48	1	18	.258
Henry Calderon	Wichita	KC	103	28	1	17	.272	224	58	4	32	.259
Ron Calloway	Harrisburg	Mon	73	27	5	18	.370	206	65	4	29	.316
Jorge Cantu	Orlando	TB	157	37	1	19	.236	355	94	3	26	.265
Aaron Capista	Trenton	Bos	90	22	0	5	.244	314	64	2	35	.204
Charley Carter	Round Rock	Hou	136	43	2	23	.316	389	95	23	74	.244
Joe Caruso	Wichita	KC	133	41	3	20	.308	291	71	5	39	.244
Uriel Casillas	Reading	Phi	130	34	2	15	.262	254	58	3	25	.228
Carlos Casimiro	Bowie	Bal	97	21	2	7	.216	205	46	2	17	.224
Nelson Castro	Shreveport	SF	133	48	6	22	.361	346	94	5	38	.272
Ramon Castro	Greenville	Atl	72	21	2	9	.292	189	59	4	22	.312
Matt Cepicky	Harrisburg	Mon	135	31	3	15	.230	324	90	16	62	.278
Mike Cervenak	Norwich	NYY	123	37	4	16	.301	340	90	7	44	.265
Dionys Cesar	Huntsville	Mil	70	17	2	5	.243	157	47	6	26	.299
Chin-Feng Chen	Jacksonville	LA	71	22	4	12	.310	153	48	13	38	.314
Virgil Chevalier	Trenton	Bos	119	34	4	18	.286	337	85	12	49	.252
Mike Christensen	Arkansas	Ana	90	23	4	15	.256	208	47	2	18	.226
Doug Clark	Shreveport	SF	104	28	3	18	.269	310	86	3	33	.277
Greg Connors	San Antonio	Sea	163	38	5	28	.233	292	71	6	41	.243
Julio Cordido	Shreveport	SF	113	18	1	12	.159	320	76	0	35	.237
Carl Crawford	Orlando	TB	150	39	0	6	.260	387	108	4	45	.279
Brad Cresse	El Paso	Ari	125	43	4	23	.344	304	81	10	58	.266
Mark Cridland	Huntsville	Mil	45	6	0	2	.133	189	48	7	29	.254
Bubba Crosby	Jacksonville	LA	96	31	0	4	.323	288	85	6	33	.295
Michael Cuddyer	New Britain	Min	149	53	13	28	.356	348	98	17	59	.282
Mike Curry	Binghamton	NYM	132	32	1	8	.242	268	84	4	20	.313
Brian Dallimore	El Paso	Ari	135	47	2	21	.348	382	122	6	46	.319
Cleatus Davidson	Mobile	SD	125	21	1	11	.168	342	81	1	23	.237
Glenn Davis	Jacksonville	LA	130	29	6	26	.223	348	87	14	63	.250
J.J. Davis	Altoona	Pit	57	14	1	6	.246	171	43	3	20	.251
Travis Dawkins	Chattanooga	Cin	118	38	3	15	.322	276	51	5	25	.185
Jeff Deardorff	Huntsville	Mil	66	21	4	12	.318	135	35	10	31	.259
Eddy de los Santos	Orlando	TB	122	28	1	8	.230	293	79	1	30	.270
Darrell Dent	Jacksonville	LA	91	20	0	5	.220	285	85	4	27	.298
Jeff DePippo	Akron	Cle	53	13	1	6	.245	187	50	5	22	.267
Keoni DeRenne	Greenville	Atl	162	40	1	11	.247	291	68	2	31	.234
Tony DeRosso	Huntsville	Mil	61	16	2	6	.262	157	35	4	19	.223
Doug Devore	El Paso	Ari	106	31	2	14	.292	370	109	13	60	.295
Jason Dewey	Carolina	Col	63	12	2	8	.190	180	46	3	19	.256
Joe Dillon	Wichita	KC	104	31	4	15	.298	265	75	11	44	.283
Allen Dina	Binghamton	NYM	96	27	1	10	.281	162	41	1	22	.253
Andy Dominique	Reading	Phi	68	26	2	11	.382	193	47	10	38	.244
Alex Eckelman	New Haven	StL	152	34	2	20	.224	259	53	3	18	.205
Corey Erickson	Akron	Cle	110	33	7	18	.300	373	77	15	47	.206
Lee Evans	Altoona	Pit	158	36	3	10	.228	270	70	8	38	.259
Troy Farnsworth	New Haven	StL	148	33	3	20	.223	274	65	15	50	.237
Chone Figgins	Carolina	Col	85	16	0	2	.188	247	57	2	23	.231
Franky Figueroa	Bowie	Bal	157	50	4	21	.318	377	110	10	51	.292
Mark Fischer	Trenton	Bos	121	22	5	22	.182	342	81	6	33	.237
Jason Fitzgerald	Akron	Cle	49	8	0	2	.163	190	57	4	17	.300
Ryan Fleming	Tennessee	Tor	73	20	1	8	.274	276	77	9	27	.279
Lew Ford	New Britain	Min	68	18	4	10	.265	172	35	2	13	.203

			vs Left					vs Right				
Player	Team	Org	AB	H	HR	RBI	Avg	AB	H	HR	RBI	Avg
Quincy Foster	Portland	Fla	62	16	1	5	.258	138	27	1	9	.196
Jason Fox	Huntsville	Mil	73	21	0	8	.288	216	50	3	20	.231
Alejandro Freire	Erie	Det	136	39	4	18	.287	365	109	13	64	.299
Nate Frese	West Tenn	ChC	42	4	0	1	.095	191	38	4	18	.199
Shawn Gallagher	Wichita	KC	111	27	1	11	.243	234	64	11	37	.274
Luis Garcia	Trenton	Bos	52	17	4	13	.327	177	54	10	32	.305
Osmani Garcia	Tulsa	Tex	78	17	1	9	.218	182	50	5	26	.275
Esteban German	Midland	Oak	83	21	2	10	.253	252	74	4	20	.294
David Gibralter	Huntsville	Mil	87	25	4	8	.287	267	71	9	40	.266
Steve Gibralter	Chattanooga	Cin	94	27	4	18	.287	212	57	12	35	.269
Eric Gillespie	Portland	Fla	56	13	2	11	.232	184	41	2	24	.223
Mike Glendenning	Shreveport	SF	38	9	2	2	.237	169	29	5	16	.172
Jim Goelz	Akron	Cle	76	18	0	5	.237	207	56	1	23	.271
Alexis Gomez	Wichita	KC	119	32	1	19	.269	223	64	3	15	.287
Rich Gomez	Erie	Det	102	33	5	14	.324	244	60	9	30	.246
Manuel Gonzalez	Reading	Phi	105	34	1	10	.324	133	36	2	14	.271
Nate Grindell	Akron	Cle	58	23	2	21	.397	171	42	8	24	.246
Ryan Gripp	West Tenn	ChC	63	17	2	15	.270	192	41	6	30	.214
Dan Grummitt	Orlando	TB	69	11	2	8	.159	175	47	9	33	.269
Elpidio Guzman	Arkansas	Ana	123	26	1	9	.211	336	86	6	37	.256
Chris Haas	West Tenn	ChC	78	17	4	14	.218	339	85	21	58	.251
Travis Hafner	Tulsa	Tex	105	36	7	34	.343	218	55	13	40	.252
Jon Hamilton	Akron	Cle	105	30	6	18	.286	366	102	11	47	.279
Joey Hammond	Bowie	Bal	117	27	0	6	.231	225	68	1	20	.302
Brandon Harper	Portland	Fla	91	16	0	6	.176	156	43	3	18	.276
Brian Harris	Reading	Phi	179	50	4	28	.279	332	75	9	30	.226
Willie Harris	Bowie	Bal	181	53	4	18	.293	344	107	5	31	.311
Ken Harvey	Wichita	KC	111	40	4	20	.360	203	66	5	43	.325
Nathan Haynes	Arkansas	Ana	82	24	2	9	.293	234	74	3	14	.316
Carlos Hernandez	Binghamton	NYM	98	29	3	14	.296	168	55	2	18	.327
Mike Hessman	Greenville	Atl	172	39	9	27	.227	306	71	17	53	.232
Bobby Hill	West Tenn	ChC	52	17	2	4	.327	157	46	1	17	.293
Jason Hill	Arkansas	Ana	96	24	3	7	.250	202	53	8	38	.262
Josh Hochgesang	Midland	Oak	80	13	1	5	.162	223	57	5	28	.256
Scott Hodges	Harrisburg	Mon	88	20	0	6	.227	217	64	5	26	.295
Heath Honeycutt	Portland	Fla	166	51	4	19	.307	309	64	5	40	.207
Kevin Hooper	Portland	Fla	165	51	0	10	.309	303	93	2	29	.307
J.R. House	Altoona	Pit	144	39	4	16	.271	282	71	7	40	.252
Orlando Hudson	Tennessee	Tor	84	31	0	14	.369	222	63	4	38	.284
Royce Huffman	Round Rock	Hou	131	43	2	14	.328	380	115	2	35	.303
Jason Huisman	Arkansas	Ana	126	33	2	14	.262	245	70	8	37	.286
Tim Hummel	Birmingham	CWS	134	40	1	15	.299	390	112	6	48	.287
Scott Hunter	Binghamton	NYM	76	22	6	18	.289	177	46	9	23	.260
Omar Infante	Erie	Det	150	49	0	13	.327	390	114	2	49	.292
Darron Ingram	Birmingham	CWS	140	42	12	35	.300	374	93	10	56	.249
Gary Johnson	West Tenn	ChC	118	34	0	15	.288	345	87	8	49	.252
Gary Johnson	Arkansas	Ana	141	31	4	21	.220	325	83	7	51	.255
Reed Johnson	Tennessee	Tor	151	51	2	23	.338	403	123	11	51	.305
Rontrez Johnson	Trenton	Bos	56	16	2	7	.286	199	56	8	24	.281
Jeremy Jones	Tulsa	Tex	82	18	2	13	.220	221	50	2	16	.226
Austin Kearns	Chattanooga	Cin	56	15	1	9	.268	149	40	5	27	.268
Brian Keck	Carolina	Col	103	27	3	14	.262	224	59	1	27	.263
Rusty Keith	Midland	Oak	105	31	3	14	.295	186	45	0	17	.242
Kenny Kelly	San Antonio	Sea	172	46	4	19	.267	306	79	7	27	.258
Dave Kelton	West Tenn	ChC	49	20	2	12	.408	175	50	10	33	.286
Brad King	San Antonio	Sea	92	31	4	23	.337	170	51	6	33	.300
Josh Klimek	Huntsville	Mil	57	15	3	12	.263	253	73	15	39	.289
Graham Koonce	Mobile	SD	62	16	1	7	.258	258	69	12	41	.267
Scott Krause	Akron	Cle	78	18	1	8	.231	225	59	14	44	.262
Craig Kuzmic	San Antonio	Sea	168	52	6	33	.310	311	83	9	58	.267
Dave Lamb	Carolina	Col	82	21	0	5	.256	205	57	5	27	.278
Luis Landaeta	Carolina	Col	48	14	0	4	.292	193	54	1	19	.280
Jacques Landry	Midland	Oak	158	35	7	23	.222	348	87	29	72	.250
Jason Lane	Round Rock	Hou	124	47	11	44	.379	402	119	27	80	.296
Juan Lebron	Binghamton	NYM	115	35	9	18	.304	240	53	9	33	.221
Chris Lemonis	El Paso	Ari	77	21	2	10	.273	256	82	0	42	.320
Donny Leon	Norwich	NYY	114	36	8	30	.316	322	75	7	44	.233
Rodney Lindsey	Erie	Det	97	28	0	7	.289	288	69	2	27	.240
Mike Lockwood	Midland	Oak	136	28	1	18	.206	357	100	5	51	.280
Kyle Logan	Round Rock	Hou	62	14	0	9	.226	196	67	6	23	.342
Matt Logan	Tennessee	Tor	64	10	2	8	.156	213	47	7	26	.221
Steve Lomasney	Trenton	Bos	39	6	1	3	.154	170	46	9	26	.271
Mickey Lopez	Reading	Phi	136	35	5	16	.257	246	69	6	31	.280
Juan Lorenzo	New Britain	Min	102	26	1	7	.255	217	49	2	17	.226
Brian Luderer	Midland	Oak	100	26	1	12	.260	207	53	4	22	.256
Ryan Ludwick	Midland	Oak	116	29	9	24	.250	327	90	16	72	.275
Jeremy Luster	Shreveport	SF	145	46	3	28	.317	361	92	1	48	.255
Ryan Luther	Shreveport	SF	110	35	2	13	.318	343	92	2	29	.268
Albenis Machado	Harrisburg	Mon	113	26	1	14	.230	228	63	2	19	.276
Garry Maddox Jr.	Trenton	Bos	58	13	1	9	.224	229	73	10	39	.319
T.J. Maier	New Haven	StL	86	27	2	14	.314	169	45	2	21	.266
Carlos Maldonado	Round Rock	Hou	62	17	0	6	.274	200	58	4	27	.290
Brandon Marsters	New Britain	Min	105	24	5	15	.229	236	50	4	21	.212
Belvani Martinez	Carolina	Col	113	29	1	6	.257	317	83	4	31	.262
Jared Mathis	Huntsville	Mil	68	21	0	3	.309	136	29	2	14	.213
Dave Matranga	Round Rock	Hou	90	34	5	22	.378	297	83	5	38	.279
Scott Maynard	San Antonio	Sea	95	15	0	8	.158	134	27	0	11	.201
Brian McClure	Erie	Det	84	22	0	10	.262	168	41	1	12	.244
Troy McNaughton	New Haven	StL	108	25	1	6	.231	279	66	7	33	.237
Aaron McNeal	Binghamton	NYM	86	20	5	11	.233	168	31	6	14	.185

Double-A Batting vs. Lefthanded and Righthanded Pitchers

Player	Team	Org	AB	H	HR	RBI	Avg	AB	H	HR	RBI	Avg
			vs Left					**vs Right**				
Aaron McNeal	Mobile	SD	64	17	0	3	.266	156	47	6	26	.301
Dan Meier	Altoona	Pit	97	22	4	12	.227	215	58	9	26	.270
Dave Meliah	Tulsa	Tex	71	21	1	13	.296	236	68	11	34	.288
Jackson Melian	Chattanooga	Cin	144	38	6	15	.264	282	63	10	37	.223
Kevin Mench	Tulsa	Tex	128	45	10	30	.352	347	81	16	53	.233
Todd Mensik	Midland	Oak	161	44	5	24	.273	341	98	16	55	.287
Mike Metcalfe	Chattanooga	Cin	169	56	0	16	.331	305	81	3	31	.266
Rod Metzler	Wichita	KC	117	28	2	18	.239	264	80	2	44	.303
Aaron Miles	Birmingham	CWS	84	23	2	14	.274	259	66	6	28	.255
Derek Mitchell	Birmingham	CWS	57	12	0	8	.211	180	38	2	13	.211
Dustan Mohr	New Britain	Min	146	50	5	29	.342	365	121	18	58	.332
Brian Moon	Huntsville	Mil	98	8	0	3	.143	231	37	0	13	.160
Bobby Morris	Chattanooga	Cin	54	16	0	8	.296	170	47	9	36	.276
Julio Mosquera	Norwich	NYY	78	19	2	9	.244	190	53	7	24	.279
Juan Munoz	New Haven	StL	142	36	2	16	.254	314	90	7	40	.287
Eric Munson	Erie	Det	167	42	6	35	.251	352	93	20	67	.264
Mike Murphy	Carolina	Col	99	25	2	6	.253	311	83	5	37	.267
Tootie Myers	Harrisburg	Mon	124	39	5	17	.315	272	65	5	32	.239
Papy Ndungidi	Bowie	Bal	87	15	1	13	.172	252	57	2	22	.226
Scott Neuberger	Orlando	TB	108	25	2	13	.231	311	86	2	30	.277
Tom Nevers	Chattanooga	Cin	126	29	8	27	.230	276	72	9	40	.261
Wil Nieves	Mobile	SD	100	41	1	14	.410	230	58	2	27	.252
Abraham Nunez	Portland	Fla	113	33	6	24	.292	322	76	14	40	.236
Jorge Nunez	Jacksonville	LA	112	40	0	8	.357	361	83	4	20	.230
Rodney Nye	Binghamton	NYM	115	33	1	14	.287	251	66	6	31	.263
Teuris Olivares	Norwich	NYY	130	28	1	8	.215	309	65	3	22	.210
Miguel Olivo	Birmingham	CWS	67	21	4	13	.313	249	61	10	42	.245
Willis Otanez	Greenville	Atl	113	33	6	24	.292	195	49	6	19	.251
Paul Ottavinia	Norwich	NYY	70	22	1	7	.314	232	56	5	27	.241
Lyle Overbay	El Paso	Ari	141	41	1	20	.291	391	146	12	80	.373
Jeremy Owens	Mobile	SD	97	24	3	8	.247	298	61	4	18	.205
Ryan Owens	Carolina	Col	99	35	1	13	.354	293	70	7	34	.239
Val Pascucci	Harrisburg	Mon	156	43	8	26	.276	320	73	13	41	.228
Rich Paz	Altoona	Pit	60	9	2	6	.150	188	50	2	24	.266
Jay Pecci	Midland	Oak	137	32	1	11	.234	332	90	2	38	.271
Alex Pelaez	Mobile	SD	120	38	5	19	.317	296	79	5	34	.267
Jerson Perez	Tennessee	Tor	120	41	1	14	.342	302	78	3	35	.258
Jhonny Perez	Erie	Det	71	16	1	5	.225	222	62	4	25	.279
Tommy Peterman	New Britain	Min	71	13	0	10	.183	226	57	3	23	.252
Tony Peters	Tennessee	Tor	103	24	9	20	.233	153	39	2	13	.255
Josh Phelps	Tennessee	Tor	135	44	8	30	.326	351	98	23	67	.279
Brandon Phillips	Harrisburg	Mon	85	28	2	7	.329	180	51	5	29	.283
Jason Phillips	Binghamton	NYM	106	31	5	22	.292	211	62	6	33	.294
Wynter Phoenix	Bowie	Bal	86	19	1	3	.221	181	41	3	17	.227
Jeff Pickler	Huntsville	Mil	145	33	0	9	.228	378	117	0	23	.310
Jorge Piedra	West Tenn	ChC	88	18	1	12	.205	353	90	7	42	.255
Tony Pigott	Orlando	TB	76	18	0	11	.237	174	42	2	17	.241
Juan Piniella	Tulsa	Tex	133	43	0	13	.323	240	54	3	21	.225
Simon Pond	Akron	Cle	78	19	0	5	.244	310	85	11	41	.274
John Powers	Mobile	SD	69	16	1	4	.232	246	71	3	31	.289
Scott Pratt	Akron	Cle	45	16	1	7	.356	219	58	3	17	.265
Rick Prieto	Birmingham	CWS	74	14	0	5	.189	239	61	4	29	.255
Matt Quatraro	Orlando	TB	69	22	3	13	.319	202	66	3	22	.327
Robb Quinlan	Arkansas	Ana	139	39	4	18	.281	353	106	10	61	.300
Tim Raines Jr.	Bowie	Bal	79	29	1	9	.367	175	45	3	21	.257
Jaisen Randolph	West Tenn	ChC	84	20	0	4	.238	281	64	0	13	.228
Josh Reding	Harrisburg	Mon	105	26	1	8	.248	267	49	2	26	.184
Michael Restovich	New Britain	Min	145	34	7	23	.234	343	98	16	60	.286
Eric Riggs	Jacksonville	LA	92	15	0	1	.163	302	86	6	35	.285
Carlos Rivera	Altoona	Pit	106	20	1	9	.189	283	71	9	41	.251
Juan Rivera	Norwich	NYY	77	31	5	19	.403	239	70	9	39	.293
Mike Rivera	Erie	Det	111	29	3	19	.261	304	91	30	82	.299
Roberto Rivera	Greenville	Atl	149	35	1	6	.235	243	58	5	21	.239
J.P. Roberge	Reading	Phi	115	35	9	26	.304	228	75	10	45	.329
Bo Robinson	San Antonio	Sea	163	45	4	22	.276	311	94	9	52	.302
Guillermo Rodriguez	Shreveport	SF	57	16	1	5	.281	159	28	4	20	.176
John Rodriguez	Norwich	NYY	96	23	1	16	.240	304	91	19	52	.299
Victor Rodriguez	Norwich	NYY	45	10	0	1	.222	166	52	3	14	.313
Mike Rose	El Paso	Ari	52	12	2	7	.231	153	41	1	16	.268
Dave Ross	Jacksonville	LA	67	20	4	13	.299	179	45	7	32	.251
Oscar Salazar	Midland	Oak	149	48	9	28	.322	372	91	9	67	.245
Ruben Salazar	New Britain	Min	152	55	3	25	.362	368	100	7	40	.272
Jerry Salzano	Trenton	Bos	119	24	3	8	.202	334	104	4	46	.311
Wellington Sanchez	Huntsville	Mil	59	14	0	3	.237	153	34	1	11	.222
Danny Sandoval	Birmingham	CWS	47	14	0	6	.298	156	43	0	23	.276
Scott Sandusky	Harrisburg	Mon	124	33	1	8	.266	263	63	1	15	.240
Jack Santora	El Paso	Ari	59	14	0	3	.237	206	48	0	10	.233
Angel Santos	Trenton	Bos	133	38	1	12	.286	377	100	13	40	.265
Chris Saunders	Birmingham	CWS	116	34	2	18	.293	326	96	8	50	.294
Brian Shackelford	Wichita	KC	49	3	1	3	.061	317	92	19	69	.290
Juan Silvestre	San Antonio	Sea	163	39	5	23	.239	209	46	3	16	.220
Shaun Skrehot	Altoona	Pit	133	30	2	11	.226	335	95	4	34	.284
Terrmel Sledge	Harrisburg	Mon	154	45	3	14	.292	294	79	6	34	.269
Jeff Smith	New Britain	Min	74	13	0	5	.176	273	86	7	37	.315
Nestor Smith	New Britain	Min	71	18	1	6	.254	224	56	2	11	.250
Esix Snead	New Haven	StL	186	44	0	13	.237	334	77	1	20	.231
Earl Snyder	Binghamton	NYM	133	35	7	28	.263	268	78	13	47	.291
Danny Solano	Tulsa	Tex	112	33	3	20	.295	311	71	3	25	.228
Tony Stevens	New Britain	Min	81	17	0	9	.210	152	24	1	11	.158
Robert Stratton	Binghamton	NYM	147	40	8	25	.272	324	77	20	54	.238

Player	Team	Org	AB	H	HR	RBI	Avg	AB	H	HR	RBI	Avg
			vs Left					**vs Right**				
Jamie Sykes	El Paso	Ari	63	13	1	3	.206	153	41	2	13	.268
Marcus Thames	Norwich	NYY	143	48	6	22	.336	377	119	25	75	.316
Jake Thrower	Mobile	SD	89	29	1	7	.326	297	76	3	24	.256
Joe Thurston	Jacksonville	LA	142	31	0	10	.218	402	114	7	36	.284
Mike Tonis	Wichita	KC	63	21	2	14	.333	163	40	7	29	.245
Steve Torrealba	Greenville	Atl	105	33	2	9	.314	190	47	6	25	.247
Andres Torres	Erie	Det	68	25	1	10	.368	184	49	0	13	.266
Chris Tremie	Round Rock	Hou	59	16	2	5	.271	161	34	3	23	.211
Torre Tyson	Norwich	NYY	60	18	0	4	.300	164	37	0	10	.226
Derick Urquhart	Arkansas	Ana	30	7	0	3	.233	220	59	5	42	.268
Brant Ust	Erie	Det	82	18	1	9	.220	241	59	5	22	.245
Jerry Valdez	Reading	Phi	95	21	3	11	.221	147	39	6	28	.265
Vic Valencia	Chattanooga	Cin	60	18	2	9	.300	170	35	4	24	.206
Mario Valenzuela	Birmingham	CWS	86	25	4	15	.291	255	74	8	38	.290
Yohanny Valera	Orlando	TB	66	23	1	9	.348	184	41	5	23	.223
Bobby Van Iten	Reading	Phi	104	17	0	8	.163	300	75	7	44	.250
Gil Velazquez	Binghamton	NYM	112	25	0	6	.223	239	48	3	13	.201
Rico Washington	Altoona	Pit	96	26	1	9	.289	201	62	3	20	.308
Derek Wathan	Portland	Fla	139	33	0	11	.237	305	76	4	24	.249
Jake Weber	San Antonio	Sea	137	38	2	23	.277	314	94	2	35	.299
Jayson Werth	Tennessee	Tor	86	26	5	15	.302	283	79	13	54	.279
Barry Wesson	Round Rock	Hou	130	38	6	17	.292	342	81	10	37	.237
Luke Wilcox	Portland	Fla	72	18	3	18	.250	148	35	6	23	.236
Glenn Williams	Tennessee	Tor	132	34	5	20	.258	355	90	6	45	.254
Dewayne Wise	Tennessee	Tor	92	16	0	3	.174	259	68	8	41	.263
Corey Wright	Tulsa	Tex	80	16	0	5	.200	338	90	0	21	.266
A.J. Zapp	Greenville	Atl	97	22	2	10	.227	195	46	6	24	.236

Double-A Batting at Home and on the Road

Player	Team	Org	Home AB	Home H	Home HR	Home RBI	Home Avg	Road AB	Road H	Road HR	Road RBI	Road Avg
Dennis Abreu	West Tenn	ChC	155	40	1	11	.258	176	44	3	19	.250
Chris Aguila	Portland	Fla	119	33	2	17	.277	122	29	2	12	.238
Kurt Airoso	Erie	Det	130	33	9	22	.254	146	32	5	22	.219
Cory Aldridge	Greenville	Atl	230	59	11	32	.257	222	52	8	24	.234
Jason Alfaro	Round Rock	Hou	125	30	1	13	.240	159	39	1	16	.245
Luke Allen	Jacksonville	LA	222	66	9	36	.297	264	75	7	37	.284
Gabe Alvarez	Chattanooga	Cin	155	38	6	19	.245	181	47	10	31	.260
Tony Alvarez	Altoona	Pit	115	42	3	15	.365	139	39	3	10	.281
Alfredo Amezaga	Arkansas	Ana	139	42	2	8	.302	146	47	2	13	.322
Mike Amrhein	West Tenn	ChC	144	31	3	18	.215	167	44	1	15	.263
Brooks Badeaux	Orlando	TB	224	56	1	10	.250	246	61	0	17	.248
Jeff Bailey	Portland	Fla	199	46	4	27	.231	233	58	9	39	.249
Rod Bair	Carolina	Col	138	39	4	18	.283	135	30	3	13	.222
Kevin Barker	Huntsville	Mil	115	40	6	20	.348	117	35	2	18	.299
Eric Battersby	Birmingham	CWS	201	42	5	21	.209	237	69	9	46	.291
Trey Beamon	San Antonio	Sea	127	36	0	8	.283	111	25	1	11	.225
Brian Becker	Orlando	TB	190	44	3	18	.232	221	49	4	24	.222
Andy Beinbrink	Orlando	TB	198	42	1	17	.212	245	79	4	32	.322
Al Benjamin	Mobile	SD	211	62	8	33	.294	163	40	4	17	.245
Brandon Berger	Wichita	KC	209	68	24	56	.325	245	72	16	62	.294
Angel Berroa	Wichita	KC	148	36	1	18	.243	156	54	7	24	.346
Andy Bevins	New Haven	StL	157	31	4	20	.197	191	38	9	20	.199
Larry Bigbie	Bowie	Bal	133	38	5	16	.286	129	39	3	17	.302
Hank Blalock	Tulsa	Tex	136	54	6	35	.397	136	35	5	26	.257
Willie Bloomquist	San Antonio	Sea	238	69	0	14	.290	253	56	0	14	.221
Joe Borchard	Birmingham	CWS	258	70	9	37	.271	257	82	18	61	.319
Jason Bowers	New Haven	StL	214	50	2	14	.234	246	61	2	20	.248
Junior Brignac	Greenville	Atl	96	17	0	3	.177	107	24	1	9	.224
Juan Brito	Wichita	KC	104	21	2	11	.202	132	42	2	17	.318
Ben Broussard	Chattanooga	Cin	177	54	8	33	.305	176	59	15	36	.335
Tonayne Brown	Trenton	Bos	209	62	2	13	.297	187	53	2	18	.283
Eric Bruntlett	Round Rock	Hou	229	61	2	13	.266	274	73	1	27	.266
Kevin Burford	Carolina	Col	179	58	3	20	.324	184	47	3	15	.255
Gary Burnham	Reading	Phi	177	61	11	40	.345	194	57	4	37	.294
Kevin Burns	Round Rock	Hou	140	32	7	16	.229	165	51	13	40	.309
Darren Burton	Altoona	Pit	141	38	0	8	.270	158	48	7	24	.304
Mike Byas	Shreveport	SF	148	47	0	9	.318	168	37	0	16	.220
Marlon Byrd	Reading	Phi	258	88	13	43	.341	252	73	15	46	.290
Brett Cadiente	Tulsa	Tex	140	37	0	13	.264	122	36	3	11	.295
Henry Calderon	Wichita	KC	169	41	2	17	.243	158	45	3	32	.285
Ron Calloway	Harrisburg	Mon	143	61	5	29	.427	136	31	4	18	.228
Jorge Cantu	Orlando	TB	231	53	2	18	.229	281	78	2	27	.278
Aaron Capista	Trenton	Bos	183	35	0	15	.191	221	51	2	25	.231
Charley Carter	Round Rock	Hou	252	67	14	44	.266	273	71	11	53	.260
Joe Caruso	Wichita	KC	199	49	2	25	.246	225	63	6	34	.280
Uriel Casillas	Reading	Phi	170	37	2	18	.218	214	55	3	22	.257
Carlos Casimiro	Bowie	Bal	156	31	2	11	.199	146	36	2	13	.247
Nelson Castro	Shreveport	SF	221	67	3	34	.303	258	75	8	26	.291
Ramon Castro	Greenville	Atl	127	38	2	12	.299	134	42	4	19	.313
Matt Cepicky	Harrisburg	Mon	240	68	13	53	.283	219	53	6	24	.242
Mike Cervenak	Norwich	NYY	232	59	3	25	.254	231	68	8	35	.294
Dionys Cesar	Huntsville	Mil	116	32	6	19	.276	111	32	2	12	.288
Chin-Feng Chen	Jacksonville	LA	103	32	6	20	.311	121	38	11	30	.314
Virgil Chevalier	Trenton	Bos	242	67	8	37	.277	214	52	8	30	.243
Mike Christensen	Arkansas	Ana	165	36	2	12	.218	133	34	4	21	.256
Doug Clark	Shreveport	SF	192	56	2	23	.292	222	58	4	28	.261
Greg Connors	San Antonio	Sea	223	55	6	40	.247	232	54	5	29	.233
Julio Cordido	Shreveport	SF	210	47	0	25	.224	223	47	1	22	.211
Carl Crawford	Orlando	TB	270	78	1	25	.289	267	69	3	26	.258
Brad Cresse	El Paso	Ari	225	71	8	53	.316	204	53	6	28	.260
Mark Cridland	Huntsville	Mil	122	31	4	15	.254	112	23	3	16	.205
Bubba Crosby	Jacksonville	LA	192	59	3	21	.307	192	57	3	26	.297
Michael Cuddyer	New Britain	Min	242	79	15	48	.326	267	74	15	39	.277
Mike Curry	Binghamton	NYM	214	67	3	17	.313	186	49	2	11	.263
Brian Dallimore	El Paso	Ari	265	102	5	43	.385	252	67	3	24	.266
Cleatus Davidson	Mobile	SD	254	51	1	17	.201	213	51	1	17	.239
Glenn Davis	Jacksonville	LA	224	56	7	46	.250	254	60	13	43	.236
J.J. Davis	Altoona	Pit	116	31	3	19	.267	112	26	1	7	.232
Travis Dawkins	Chattanooga	Cin	177	41	3	19	.232	217	48	5	21	.221
Jeff Deardorff	Huntsville	Mil	80	30	5	19	.375	121	26	9	24	.215
Eddy de los Santos	Orlando	TB	192	53	0	18	.276	223	54	2	20	.242
Darrell Dent	Jacksonville	LA	181	49	2	17	.271	195	56	2	15	.287
Jeff DePippo	Akron	Cle	119	30	2	9	.252	121	33	4	19	.273
Keoni DeRenne	Greenville	Atl	228	60	1	26	.263	225	48	2	16	.213
Tony DeRosso	Huntsville	Mil	99	20	1	9	.202	119	31	5	16	.261
Doug Devore	El Paso	Ari	253	84	11	50	.332	223	56	4	24	.251
Jason Dewey	Carolina	Col	114	27	1	10	.237	129	31	4	17	.240
Joe Dillon	Wichita	KC	144	45	9	29	.313	225	61	6	30	.271
Allen Dina	Binghamton	NYM	127	46	2	25	.362	142	28	1	10	.197
Andy Dominique	Reading	Phi	115	26	7	22	.226	146	47	5	27	.322
Alex Eckelman	New Haven	StL	206	47	3	25	.228	205	40	2	13	.195
Corey Erickson	Akron	Cle	245	58	9	28	.237	238	52	13	37	.218
Lee Evans	Altoona	Pit	219	53	6	31	.242	209	53	5	17	.254
Troy Farnsworth	New Haven	StL	202	50	11	35	.248	220	48	7	35	.218
Chone Figgins	Carolina	Col	163	31	2	17	.190	169	42	0	8	.249
Franky Figueroa	Bowie	Bal	274	85	7	38	.310	260	75	7	34	.288
Mark Fischer	Trenton	Bos	228	50	8	31	.219	235	53	3	24	.226
Jason Fitzgerald	Akron	Cle	105	37	3	9	.352	134	28	1	10	.209
Ryan Fleming	Tennessee	Tor	148	45	7	17	.304	201	52	3	18	.259
Lew Ford	New Britain	Min	131	22	0	10	.168	121	33	7	15	.273

Player	Team	Org	Home AB	Home H	Home HR	Home RBI	Home Avg	Road AB	Road H	Road HR	Road RBI	Road Avg
Quincy Foster	Portland	Fla	105	21	2	6	.200	95	22	0	8	.232
Jason Fox	Huntsville	Mil	138	31	2	15	.225	151	40	1	13	.265
Alejandro Freire	Erie	Det	260	83	9	50	.319	241	65	8	32	.270
Nate Frese	West Tenn	ChC	112	23	0	6	.205	121	19	4	13	.157
Shawn Gallagher	Wichita	KC	141	31	2	12	.220	204	60	10	36	.294
Luis Garcia	Trenton	Bos	106	30	9	24	.283	123	41	5	21	.333
Osmani Garcia	Tulsa	Tex	135	37	1	10	.274	125	30	5	25	.240
Esteban German	Midland	Oak	175	54	1	15	.309	160	41	5	15	.256
David Gibralter	Huntsville	Mil	185	50	9	27	.270	169	46	4	21	.272
Steve Gibralter	Chattanooga	Cin	152	45	8	20	.296	154	39	8	33	.253
Eric Gillespie	Portland	Fla	109	23	0	13	.211	131	31	4	22	.237
Mike Glendenning	Shreveport	SF	105	15	0	4	.143	102	23	7	14	.225
Jim Goelz	Akron	Cle	141	39	1	14	.277	142	35	0	14	.246
Alexis Gomez	Wichita	KC	162	37	2	14	.228	180	59	2	20	.328
Rich Gomez	Erie	Det	185	46	8	25	.249	161	47	6	19	.292
Manuel Gonzalez	Reading	Phi	103	34	2	12	.330	135	36	1	12	.267
Nate Grindell	Akron	Cle	120	37	4	22	.308	109	28	6	23	.257
Ryan Gripp	West Tenn	ChC	118	30	5	27	.254	137	28	3	18	.204
Dan Grummitt	Orlando	TB	118	22	3	14	.186	126	36	8	27	.286
Elpidio Guzman	Arkansas	Ana	229	51	1	14	.223	230	61	6	32	.265
Chris Haas	West Tenn	ChC	196	48	14	40	.245	221	54	11	32	.244
Travis Hafner	Tulsa	Tex	162	44	9	38	.272	161	47	11	36	.292
Jon Hamilton	Akron	Cle	236	58	5	26	.246	235	74	12	39	.315
Joey Hammond	Bowie	Bal	177	53	1	15	.299	165	42	0	11	.255
Brandon Harper	Portland	Fla	112	23	2	8	.205	135	36	1	16	.267
Brian Harris	Reading	Phi	239	50	5	26	.209	272	75	8	32	.276
Willie Harris	Bowie	Bal	252	83	6	22	.329	273	77	3	27	.282
Ken Harvey	Wichita	KC	137	41	3	17	.299	177	65	6	46	.367
Nathan Haynes	Arkansas	Ana	163	48	3	14	.294	153	50	2	9	.327
Carlos Hernandez	Binghamton	NYM	124	43	1	17	.347	142	41	4	15	.289
Mike Hessman	Greenville	Atl	257	66	18	50	.257	221	44	8	30	.199
Bobby Hill	West Tenn	ChC	89	28	3	12	.315	120	35	0	9	.292
Jason Hill	Arkansas	Ana	145	34	4	18	.234	153	43	7	27	.281
Josh Hochgesang	Midland	Oak	143	36	3	15	.252	160	34	3	18	.213
Scott Hodges	Harrisburg	Mon	140	46	4	21	.329	165	38	1	11	.230
Heath Honeycutt	Portland	Fla	242	63	4	34	.260	233	52	5	25	.223
Kevin Hooper	Portland	Fla	228	67	1	20	.294	240	77	1	19	.321
J.R. House	Altoona	Pit	215	61	5	25	.284	211	49	6	31	.232
Orlando Hudson	Tennessee	Tor	149	46	2	27	.309	157	48	2	25	.306
Royce Huffman	Round Rock	Hou	246	76	3	17	.309	265	82	1	32	.309
Jason Huisman	Arkansas	Ana	185	54	4	24	.292	186	49	6	27	.263
Tim Hummel	Birmingham	CWS	256	79	1	34	.309	268	73	6	29	.272
Scott Hunter	Binghamton	NYM	127	39	10	27	.307	126	29	5	14	.230
Omar Infante	Erie	Det	262	76	0	27	.290	278	87	2	35	.313
Darron Ingram	Birmingham	CWS	245	70	12	49	.286	269	65	10	42	.242
Gary Johnson	West Tenn	ChC	216	60	3	30	.278	247	61	5	34	.247
Gary Johnson	Arkansas	Ana	239	59	6	42	.247	227	55	5	30	.242
Reed Johnson	Tennessee	Tor	274	86	6	36	.314	280	88	7	38	.314
Rontrez Johnson	Trenton	Bos	133	39	3	12	.293	122	33	7	19	.270
Jeremy Jones	Tulsa	Tex	161	43	1	17	.267	150	29	3	12	.193
Austin Kearns	Chattanooga	Cin	118	34	4	24	.288	87	21	2	12	.241
Brian Keck	Carolina	Col	165	45	1	19	.273	162	41	3	22	.253
Rusty Keith	Midland	Oak	162	44	1	13	.272	129	32	2	18	.248
Kenny Kelly	San Antonio	Sea	234	56	4	16	.239	244	69	7	30	.283
Dave Kelton	West Tenn	ChC	101	33	6	21	.327	123	37	6	24	.301
Brad King	San Antonio	Sea	144	41	6	28	.285	118	41	4	28	.347
Josh Klimek	Huntsville	Mil	167	52	13	38	.311	143	36	5	13	.252
Graham Koonce	Mobile	SD	170	47	7	29	.276	150	38	6	19	.253
Scott Krause	Akron	Cle	130	33	5	26	.254	173	44	10	26	.254
Craig Kuzmic	San Antonio	Sea	233	61	3	29	.262	246	74	12	62	.301
Dave Lamb	Carolina	Col	166	44	4	23	.265	121	34	1	9	.281
Luis Landaeta	Carolina	Col	98	30	0	6	.306	143	38	1	17	.266
Jacques Landry	Midland	Oak	251	72	23	64	.287	255	50	13	31	.196
Jason Lane	Round Rock	Hou	249	79	24	57	.317	277	87	14	67	.314
Juan Lebron	Binghamton	NYM	172	39	9	26	.227	191	50	9	26	.262
Chris Lemonis	El Paso	Ari	160	53	1	33	.331	173	50	1	19	.289
Donny Leon	Norwich	NYY	208	61	7	39	.293	228	50	8	35	.219
Rodney Lindsey	Erie	Det	182	49	1	16	.269	203	48	1	18	.236
Mike Lockwood	Midland	Oak	242	67	5	41	.277	251	61	1	28	.243
Kyle Logan	Round Rock	Hou	116	35	3	11	.302	142	46	3	21	.324
Matt Logan	Tennessee	Tor	134	34	5	20	.254	143	23	4	14	.161
Steve Lomasney	Trenton	Bos	106	28	4	13	.264	103	24	6	16	.233
Mickey Lopez	Reading	Phi	183	50	5	26	.273	199	54	6	21	.271
Juan Lorenzo	New Britain	Min	172	40	0	12	.233	147	35	3	12	.238
Brian Luderer	Midland	Oak	157	45	4	18	.287	150	34	1	16	.227
Ryan Ludwick	Midland	Oak	222	72	15	58	.324	221	47	10	38	.213
Jeremy Luster	Shreveport	SF	240	57	2	37	.237	266	81	2	39	.305
Ryan Luther	Shreveport	SF	204	56	0	10	.275	249	71	4	32	.285
Albenis Machado	Harrisburg	Mon	161	45	3	18	.280	180	44	0	15	.244
Garry Maddox Jr.	Trenton	Bos	144	46	7	26	.319	143	40	4	22	.280
T.J. Maier	New Haven	StL	127	35	2	14	.276	128	37	2	21	.289
Carlos Maldonado	Round Rock	Hou	118	35	2	15	.297	144	40	2	18	.278
Brandon Marsters	New Britain	Min	170	33	5	19	.194	179	44	4	17	.246
Belvani Martinez	Carolina	Col	207	52	1	16	.251	223	60	4	21	.269
Jared Mathis	Huntsville	Mil	91	21	0	6	.231	113	29	2	11	.257
Dave Matranga	Round Rock	Hou	190	51	5	25	.268	197	66	5	35	.335
Scott Maynard	San Antonio	Sea	104	17	0	6	.163	125	25	0	13	.200
Brian McClure	Erie	Det	129	33	1	10	.256	126	31	0	12	.246
Troy McNaughton	New Haven	StL	172	46	4	22	.267	215	45	4	17	.209
Aaron McNeal	Binghamton	NYM	127	28	7	12	.220	137	25	4	13	.182

Double-A Batting at Home and on the Road

Player	Team	Org	Home AB	H	HR	RBI	Avg	Road AB	H	HR	RBI	Avg
Aaron McNeal	Mobile	SD	114	31	3	16	.272	106	33	3	13	.311
Dan Meier	Altoona	Pit	142	33	2	11	.232	170	47	11	27	.276
Dave Meliah	Tulsa	Tex	132	36	4	15	.273	175	53	8	32	.303
Jackson Melian	Chattanooga	Cin	207	54	9	24	.261	219	47	7	28	.215
Kevin Mench	Tulsa	Tex	237	63	15	47	.266	238	63	11	36	.265
Todd Mensik	Midland	Oak	241	86	14	48	.357	261	56	7	31	.215
Mike Metcalfe	Chattanooga	Cin	248	72	3	25	.290	226	65	0	22	.288
Rod Metzler	Wichita	KC	179	50	1	23	.279	202	58	3	39	.287
Aaron Miles	Birmingham	CWS	198	43	4	19	.217	145	46	4	23	.317
Derek Mitchell	Birmingham	CWS	93	18	2	10	.194	144	32	0	11	.222
Dustan Mohr	New Britain	Min	254	90	10	41	.354	264	84	14	50	.318
Brian Moon	Huntsville	Mil	127	24	0	9	.189	160	21	0	7	.131
Bobby Morris	Chattanooga	Cin	99	27	3	26	.273	125	36	6	18	.288
Julio Mosquera	Norwich	NYY	126	29	1	11	.230	142	43	8	22	.303
Juan Munoz	New Haven	StL	216	60	5	30	.278	240	66	4	26	.275
Eric Munson	Erie	Det	252	65	11	51	.258	267	70	15	51	.262
Mike Murphy	Carolina	Col	211	60	2	22	.284	199	48	5	21	.241
Tootie Myers	Harrisburg	Mon	197	41	4	23	.208	199	63	6	26	.317
Papy Ndungidi	Bowie	Bal	171	33	2	11	.193	168	39	1	14	.232
Scott Neuberger	Orlando	TB	206	51	3	17	.248	213	60	1	26	.282
Tom Nevers	Chattanooga	Cin	201	53	9	30	.264	201	48	8	37	.239
Wil Nieves	Mobile	SD	170	48	1	22	.282	160	51	2	19	.319
Abraham Nunez	Portland	Fla	229	60	6	27	.262	238	52	11	26	.218
Jorge Nunez	Jacksonville	LA	220	62	3	16	.282	253	61	1	12	.241
Rodney Nye	Binghamton	NYM	172	55	6	29	.320	194	44	1	16	.227
Teuris Olivares	Norwich	NYY	199	47	1	14	.236	240	46	3	16	.192
Miguel Olivo	Birmingham	CWS	165	40	5	23	.242	151	42	9	32	.278
Willis Otanez	Greenville	Atl	170	46	8	31	.271	138	36	4	12	.261
Paul Ottavinia	Norwich	NYY	133	37	2	14	.278	169	41	4	20	.243
Lyle Overbay	El Paso	Ari	270	107	5	65	.396	262	80	8	35	.305
Jeremy Owens	Mobile	SD	194	43	4	16	.222	201	42	3	10	.209
Ryan Owens	Carolina	Col	197	54	4	27	.274	195	51	4	20	.262
Val Pascucci	Harrisburg	Mon	242	60	10	41	.248	234	56	11	26	.239
Rich Paz	Altoona	Pit	110	24	2	14	.218	138	35	2	16	.254
Jay Pecci	Midland	Oak	236	63	1	27	.267	233	59	2	22	.253
Alex Pelaez	Mobile	SD	204	57	4	30	.279	212	60	6	23	.283
Jerson Perez	Tennessee	Tor	222	64	2	23	.288	200	55	2	26	.275
Jhonny Perez	Erie	Det	154	42	3	16	.273	139	36	2	14	.259
Tommy Peterman	New Britain	Min	141	35	2	22	.248	161	37	1	12	.230
Tony Peters	Tennessee	Tor	140	37	7	24	.264	116	26	4	9	.224
Josh Phelps	Tennessee	Tor	244	70	16	50	.287	242	72	15	47	.298
Brandon Phillips	Harrisburg	Mon	144	35	3	15	.243	121	44	4	21	.364
Jason Phillips	Binghamton	NYM	169	49	7	31	.290	148	44	4	24	.297
Wynter Phoenix	Bowie	Bal	116	24	1	6	.207	151	36	3	14	.238
Jeff Pickler	Huntsville	Mil	245	74	0	10	.302	278	76	0	22	.273
Jorge Piedra	West Tenn	ChC	196	48	4	28	.245	245	60	4	26	.245
Tony Pigott	Orlando	TB	109	28	1	11	.257	141	32	1	17	.227
Juan Piniella	Tulsa	Tex	212	52	2	19	.245	161	45	1	15	.280
Simon Pond	Akron	Cle	197	49	5	19	.249	191	55	6	27	.288
John Powers	Mobile	SD	143	43	2	16	.301	172	44	2	19	.256
Scott Pratt	Akron	Cle	139	30	1	8	.216	125	44	3	16	.352
Rick Prieto	Birmingham	CWS	177	51	4	24	.288	136	24	0	10	.176
Matt Quatraro	Orlando	TB	122	43	2	11	.352	149	45	4	24	.302
Robb Quinlan	Arkansas	Ana	235	78	5	43	.332	257	67	9	36	.261
Tim Raines Jr.	Bowie	Bal	136	46	3	18	.338	118	28	1	12	.237
Jaisen Randolph	West Tenn	ChC	183	43	0	11	.235	182	41	0	6	.225
Josh Reding	Harrisburg	Mon	194	31	2	14	.160	178	44	1	20	.247
Michael Restovich	New Britain	Min	247	67	10	43	.271	254	68	13	41	.268
Eric Riggs	Jacksonville	LA	170	43	2	14	.253	224	58	4	22	.259
Carlos Rivera	Altoona	Pit	177	47	4	28	.266	212	44	6	22	.208
Juan Rivera	Norwich	NYY	147	52	5	27	.354	169	49	9	31	.290
Mike Rivera	Erie	Det	206	63	23	59	.306	209	57	10	42	.273
Roberto Rivera	Greenville	Atl	191	50	3	15	.262	201	43	3	12	.214
J.P. Roberge	Reading	Phi	163	54	8	32	.331	180	56	11	39	.311
Bo Robinson	San Antonio	Sea	229	65	3	35	.284	245	74	10	39	.302
Guillermo Rodriguez	Shreveport	SF	106	23	2	16	.217	110	21	3	9	.191
John Rodriguez	Norwich	NYY	200	55	10	28	.275	193	57	12	38	.295
Victor Rodriguez	Norwich	NYY	91	23	1	9	.253	127	41	2	8	.323
Mike Rose	El Paso	Ari	99	32	3	14	.323	106	21	0	9	.198
Dave Ross	Jacksonville	LA	130	36	6	27	.277	116	29	5	18	.250
Oscar Salazar	Midland	Oak	241	62	7	40	.257	280	77	11	55	.275
Ruben Salazar	New Britain	Min	259	80	3	34	.309	271	78	7	32	.288
Jerry Salzano	Trenton	Bos	215	66	2	26	.307	238	62	5	28	.261
Wellington Sanchez	Huntsville	Mil	99	28	1	12	.283	113	20	0	2	.177
Danny Sandoval	Birmingham	CWS	106	30	0	20	.283	97	27	0	9	.278
Scott Sandusky	Harrisburg	Mon	198	52	2	12	.263	189	44	0	11	.233
Jack Santora	El Paso	Ari	126	30	0	10	.238	134	32	0	3	.230
Angel Santos	Trenton	Bos	260	72	8	28	.277	250	66	6	24	.264
Chris Saunders	Birmingham	CWS	232	69	5	33	.297	210	61	5	35	.290
Brian Shackelford	Wichita	KC	159	43	8	35	.270	207	52	12	37	.251
Juan Silvestre	San Antonio	Sea	195	46	4	24	.236	177	39	4	15	.220
Shaun Skrehot	Altoona	Pit	220	64	3	26	.291	248	61	3	19	.246
Termmel Sledge	Harrisburg	Mon	238	68	6	26	.286	210	56	3	22	.267
Jeff Smith	New Britain	Min	175	55	4	23	.314	176	45	3	19	.256
Nestor Smith	New Britain	Min	139	37	2	9	.266	155	36	1	8	.232
Esix Snead	New Haven	StL	263	65	0	17	.247	257	56	1	16	.218
Earl Snyder	Binghamton	NYM	204	59	11	43	.289	201	55	9	32	.274
Danny Solano	Tulsa	Tex	205	44	4	21	.215	218	60	2	24	.275
Tony Stevens	New Britain	Min	112	18	0	9	.161	133	24	1	12	.180
Robert Stratton	Binghamton	NYM	235	66	15	41	.281	248	54	14	42	.218

Player	Team	Org	Home AB	H	HR	RBI	Avg	Road AB	H	HR	RBI	Avg
Jamie Sykes	El Paso	Ari	109	27	1	12	.248	107	27	2	4	.252
Marcus Thames	Norwich	NYY	232	72	13	38	.310	288	95	18	59	.330
Jake Thrower	Mobile	SD	199	63	4	24	.317	187	42	0	7	.225
Joe Thurston	Jacksonville	LA	252	58	4	19	.230	292	87	3	27	.298
Mike Tonis	Wichita	KC	106	28	4	22	.264	120	33	5	21	.275
Steve Torrealba	Greenville	Atl	162	49	5	24	.302	133	31	3	10	.233
Andres Torres	Erie	Det	117	35	1	16	.299	135	39	0	7	.289
Chris Tremie	Round Rock	Hou	99	23	4	17	.232	121	27	1	11	.223
Torre Tyson	Norwich	NYY	98	20	0	11	.204	126	35	0	3	.278
Derick Urquhart	Arkansas	Ana	116	29	2	20	.250	134	37	3	25	.276
Brant Ust	Erie	Det	156	34	3	16	.218	167	43	3	15	.257
Jerry Valdez	Reading	Phi	105	20	1	15	.190	137	40	8	24	.292
Vic Valencia	Chattanooga	Cin	111	24	4	21	.216	119	29	2	12	.244
Mario Valenzuela	Birmingham	CWS	168	42	4	18	.250	173	57	8	35	.329
Yohanny Valera	Orlando	TB	126	32	3	15	.254	124	32	3	17	.258
Bobby Van Iten	Reading	Phi	188	43	4	22	.229	216	49	3	30	.227
Gil Velazquez	Binghamton	NYM	184	40	2	10	.217	174	34	1	9	.195
Rico Washington	Altoona	Pit	173	53	2	17	.306	118	35	2	12	.297
Derek Wathan	Portland	Fla	234	65	3	20	.278	235	53	1	15	.226
Jake Weber	San Antonio	Sea	215	59	0	21	.274	236	73	4	37	.309
Jayson Werth	Tennessee	Tor	186	55	11	39	.296	183	50	7	33	.273
Barry Wesson	Round Rock	Hou	222	56	7	23	.252	250	63	9	31	.252
Luke Wilcox	Portland	Fla	83	22	4	21	.265	137	31	5	20	.226
Glenn Williams	Tennessee	Tor	252	65	5	35	.258	235	59	6	30	.251
Dewayne Wise	Tennessee	Tor	188	43	3	20	.238	183	44	5	24	.240
Corey Wright	Tulsa	Tex	204	50	0	12	.245	214	56	0	14	.262
A.J. Zapp	Greenville	Atl	148	38	6	24	.257	144	30	2	10	.208

Double-A Pitching vs. Lefthanded and Righthanded Batters

			vs Left					vs Right				
Player	Team	Org	AB	H	HR	SO	Avg	AB	H	HR	SO	Avg
Winston Abreu	Greenville	Atl	117	29	2	35	.248	145	27	7	58	.186
Jose Acevedo	Chattanooga	Cin	143	32	3	43	.224	142	36	3	39	.254
Jon Adkins	Midland	Oak	176	52	5	16	.295	362	95	4	58	.262
Tim Adkins	Norwich	NYY	67	16	2	15	.239	239	54	5	68	.226
Jeremy Affeldt	Wichita	KC	113	27	0	32	.239	441	126	9	96	.286
B. Agamennone	Harrisburg	Mon	76	20	6	16	.263	155	39	4	35	.252
Stevenson Agosto	Orlando	TB	98	14	1	33	.143	372	100	11	80	.269
Ed Almonte	Birmingham	CWS	123	28	1	31	.228	131	30	3	31	.229
Carlos Alvarado	Altoona	Pit	139	38	2	25	.273	178	36	4	48	.202
Jeff Andra	Shreveport	SF	71	12	1	17	.169	326	104	10	40	.319
Scott Atchison	San Antonio	Sea	202	67	4	28	.332	341	104	7	55	.305
Ryan Baerlocher	Wichita	KC	246	70	7	43	.285	456	110	19	81	.241
Matt Bailie	Reading	Phi	99	25	5	29	.253	162	51	8	43	.315
Brad Baisley	Reading	Phi	103	32	7	13	.311	158	50	7	24	.316
Chris Baker	Tennessee	Tor	286	62	10	59	.217	378	100	12	62	.265
Pete Bauer	Tennessee	Tor	215	65	4	18	.302	304	82	8	53	.270
Rick Bauer	Bowie	Bal	99	31	2	11	.313	130	21	6	23	.162
Steve Bechler	Bowie	Bal	98	24	3	17	.245	192	39	11	41	.203
Josh Beckett	Portland	Fla	88	14	1	33	.159	174	36	7	69	.207
Heath Bell	Binghamton	NYM	98	31	2	26	.316	148	47	11	26	.318
Dusty Bergman	Arkansas	Ana	119	32	1	16	.269	506	164	9	67	.324
Brent Billingsley	Harrisburg	Mon	84	19	4	26	.226	365	109	16	71	.299
Jeremy Blevins	Norwich	NYY	59	11	1	18	.186	173	35	1	45	.202
Brad Bohannan	Birmingham	CWS	78	24	2	7	.308	123	37	7	18	.301
Ryan Bradley	Norwich	NYY	76	22	4	15	.289	136	25	3	38	.184
Derek Brown	Bowie	Bal	114	25	2	24	.219	148	44	4	20	.297
Elliot Brown	Shreveport	SF	108	38	3	7	.352	146	39	3	21	.267
Mark Brownson	Huntsville	Mil	200	47	7	41	.235	323	96	11	74	.297
Sean Brummett	Arkansas	Ana	54	8	1	18	.148	202	57	7	27	.282
Nate Bump	Portland	Fla	92	19	3	21	.207	120	36	7	20	.300
Adrian Burnside	Jacksonville	LA	28	3	1	8	.107	215	41	5	59	.191
Mike Bynum	Mobile	SD	63	11	1	13	.175	260	79	13	56	.304
Kiko Calero	Wichita	KC	182	49	5	37	.269	282	61	5	57	.216
Ryan Cameron	Carolina	Col	164	50	5	34	.305	207	62	5	40	.300
Chris Capuano	El Paso	Ari	98	22	0	37	.224	537	162	13	130	.302
Angel Caraballo	Tennessee	Tor	84	25	2	14	.298	118	26	5	22	.220
Lance Caraccioli	Jacksonville	LA	76	16	0	14	.211	419	123	7	73	.294
Matt Carnes	New Britain	Min	97	25	1	20	.258	148	35	3	42	.236
Joe Casey	Tennessee	Tor	101	35	3	14	.347	145	39	5	28	.269
Scott Cassidy	Tennessee	Tor	184	45	4	39	.245	173	33	6	42	.191
Hugo Castellanos	Tennessee	Tor	87	28	3	15	.322	149	25	1	32	.168
Chris Cervantes	El Paso	Ari	84	22	1	25	.262	302	88	13	62	.291
Gustavo Chacin	Tennessee	Tor	103	19	5	16	.184	434	119	12	70	.274
Jake Chapman	Harrisburg	Mon	88	17	0	39	.193	164	38	5	30	.232
Scott Chiasson	West Tenn	ChC	92	20	0	22	.217	126	23	2	40	.183
Ron Chiavacci	Harrisburg	Mon	237	56	6	77	.236	316	81	6	84	.256
Jason Childers	Huntsville	Mil	120	20	1	37	.167	208	56	6	48	.269
Chris Clark	Arkansas	Ana	82	24	1	7	.293	174	50	7	27	.287
Brandon Claussen	Norwich	NYY	102	21	1	34	.206	379	80	5	117	.211
Patrick Coogan	New Haven	StL	213	57	6	34	.268	375	111	13	81	.296
B.R. Cook	New Haven	StL	170	33	1	32	.194	295	82	10	52	.278
Nate Cornejo	Erie	Det	186	48	4	33	.258	282	59	8	72	.209
Joe Cotton	Midland	Oak	80	19	2	21	.237	157	31	2	42	.197
Ryan Cox	Shreveport	SF	228	62	7	24	.272	308	83	1	37	.269
Chuck Crowder	Carolina	Col	89	20	0	23	.225	318	106	7	48	.333
Mike Crudale	New Haven	StL	112	30	3	28	.268	200	46	4	57	.230
Chuck Crumpton	Harrisburg	Mon	106	26	2	16	.245	149	47	4	28	.315
Juan Cruz	West Tenn	ChC	209	53	3	64	.254	241	54	3	73	.224
Chris Cumberland	Greenville	Atl	93	20	1	17	.215	380	106	4	68	.279
Ryan Cummings	Arkansas	Ana	84	28	1	7	.333	171	33	2	35	.193
Dave Darwin	Akron	Cle	35	5	0	7	.143	185	57	6	36	.308
Allen Davis	Harrisburg	Mon	34	11	2	4	.324	166	37	2	32	.223
Joey Dawley	Greenville	Atl	191	49	7	42	.257	267	46	8	88	.172
Zach Day	Akron	Cle	184	46	3	29	.250	335	77	5	65	.230
Phil Devey	Jacksonville	LA	59	20	2	6	.339	386	101	10	70	.262
Scott DeWitt	Carolina	Col	68	17	3	23	.250	175	49	2	29	.280
Mark DiFelice	Carolina	Col	170	39	2	27	.229	294	69	11	71	.235
Ryan Drese	Akron	Cle	98	16	1	24	.163	199	48	3	49	.241
Mike Drumright	Portland	Fla	143	30	1	33	.210	244	70	12	52	.287
Justin Duchscherer	Trenton	Bos	79	11	2	22	.139	195	38	4	47	.195
Scott Dunn	Chattanooga	Cin	139	34	4	28	.245	228	62	6	59	.272
Radhames Dykhoff	Arkansas	Ana	60	19	1	7	.317	251	66	3	30	.263
Derrin Ebert	Trenton	Bos	95	25	2	17	.263	366	109	10	72	.298
Eric Eckenstahler	Erie	Det	79	18	0	20	.228	174	47	7	53	.270
Scott Eibey	Bowie	Bal	76	19	2	20	.250	209	65	7	28	.311
Dave Elder	Tulsa	Tex	91	31	0	27	.341	169	33	1	51	.195
Jason Ellison	San Antonio	Sea	91	29	0	23	.319	165	47	3	34	.285
Chris Elmore	Trenton	Bos	38	5	0	12	.132	260	71	4	44	.273
Jamie Emiliano	Carolina	Col	98	25	3	13	.255	142	31	1	25	.218
Chris Enochs	Midland	Oak	153	45	4	20	.294	239	57	5	47	.238
Brian Falkenborg	San Antonio	Sea	115	39	4	24	.339	147	41	5	32	.279
Jeff Farnsworth	San Antonio	Sea	248	75	6	51	.302	378	107	4	62	.283
Pedro Feliciano	Jacksonville	LA	46	5	1	15	.109	165	36	2	40	.218
Miguel Felix	Bowie	Bal	121	30	0	19	.248	175	43	7	39	.246
Nathan Field	Wichita	KC	96	31	2	14	.323	179	30	1	53	.168
Juan Figueroa	Bowie	Bal	152	49	3	27	.322	250	77	11	25	.308
Jeremy Fikac	Mobile	SD	99	26	1	30	.263	148	28	2	45	.189
Adam Flohr	New Britain	Min	60	15	1	16	.250	239	79	7	32	.331
Randy Flores	Norwich	NYY	113	24	2	18	.212	492	132	11	97	.268
Casey Fossum	Trenton	Bos	95	17	1	29	.179	347	85	4	101	.245

			vs Left					vs Right				
Player	Team	Org	AB	H	HR	SO	Avg	AB	H	HR	SO	Avg
John Foster	Greenville	Atl	74	23	2	18	.311	180	48	4	45	.267
Lance Franks	New Haven	StL	124	30	2	26	.242	222	56	9	46	.252
Kevin Frederick	New Britain	Min	99	21	2	38	.212	185	35	3	70	.189
Kai Freeman	Birmingham	CWS	156	59	0	15	.378	172	41	4	23	.238
Claudio Galva	Midland	Oak	81	15	1	14	.185	152	41	4	30	.270
Randy Galvez	Altoona	Pit	154	33	2	17	.214	177	60	1	28	.339
Jose Garcia	Huntsville	Mil	188	42	3	44	.223	225	57	3	40	.253
Cecilio Garibaldi	Orlando	TB	179	57	7	28	.318	222	54	9	38	.243
Josh Garrett	Trenton	Bos	93	26	3	25	.280	222	58	7	43	.261
Geoff Geary	Reading	Phi	155	42	3	28	.271	258	59	11	60	.229
Dave Gil	Chattanooga	Cin	107	28	1	26	.262	127	37	3	29	.291
Chris Gissell	West Tenn	ChC	276	81	7	65	.293	334	78	6	71	.234
Mike Gonzalez	Altoona	Pit	63	19	2	13	.302	260	62	3	53	.238
Andrew Good	El Paso	Ari	101	28	1	14	.277	143	51	1	32	.357
Alex Graman	Norwich	NYY	93	21	3	17	.226	558	153	7	121	.274
Kevin Gregg	Midland	Oak	97	27	1	26	.278	224	61	4	46	.272
Matt Guerrier	Birmingham	CWS	170	45	4	27	.265	189	40	4	48	.212
Lindsay Gulin	Jacksonville	LA	98	30	1	13	.306	382	98	9	98	.257
Rick Guttormson	Mobile	SD	224	67	9	28	.299	328	79	9	50	.241
Brad Guy	Altoona	Pit	81	28	1	13	.346	121	31	2	17	.256
Talley Haines	Orlando	TB	112	38	4	22	.339	164	35	3	51	.213
Beau Hale	Bowie	Bal	109	33	5	23	.303	133	41	3	17	.308
Josh Hancock	Trenton	Bos	154	44	1	43	.286	352	94	7	76	.267
Aaron Harang	Midland	Oak	212	71	2	33	.335	396	102	7	79	.258
Tim Harrell	Jacksonville	LA	109	26	7	21	.239	193	44	4	50	.228
Jeff Heaverlo	San Antonio	Sea	260	78	6	56	.300	425	86	6	117	.202
Bryan Hebson	Harrisburg	Mon	118	32	8	22	.271	169	46	4	32	.272
Scott Henderson	Portland	Fla	77	19	3	22	.247	131	33	6	33	.252
Carlos Hernandez	Round Rock	Hou	86	21	2	33	.244	418	94	9	134	.225
Cary Hiles	Reading	Phi	102	24	2	15	.235	190	36	4	47	.189
Joe Horgan	Shreveport	SF	88	18	3	15	.205	306	79	7	46	.258
Luke Hudson	Carolina	Col	269	70	10	66	.260	368	89	9	79	.242
Travis Hughes	Tulsa	Tex	103	26	1	30	.252	234	65	7	56	.278
Jeff Hundley	Arkansas	Ana	40	8	2	4	.200	177	55	5	27	.311
Johnny Hunter	Mobile	SD	147	41	3	22	.279	231	64	4	39	.277
Hansel Izquierdo	Portland	Fla	75	13	3	14	.173	134	34	7	31	.254
Adam Johnson	New Britain	Min	170	44	5	40	.259	254	61	5	70	.240
Eric Junge	Jacksonville	LA	236	58	5	32	.246	367	85	14	84	.232
Josh Kalinowski	Carolina	Col	97	26	2	24	.268	436	125	13	92	.287
Tim Kalita	Erie	Det	176	42	6	42	.239	580	148	19	105	.255
Nathan Kent	Greenville	Atl	307	88	5	51	.287	322	98	7	60	.304
Jason Kershner	Reading	Phi	110	30	2	15	.273	376	117	16	55	.311
Kyle Kessel	Round Rock	Hou	49	14	0	8	.286	187	61	7	31	.326
Andrew Kimball	Huntsville	Mil	87	30	3	13	.345	187	43	4	26	.230
Rick Kirsten	Erie	Det	275	77	10	45	.280	352	84	12	98	.239
Ed Kofler	Orlando	TB	142	39	3	25	.275	112	42	4	14	.375
John Koronka	Chattanooga	Cin	42	13	1	8	.310	175	49	6	36	.280
Jack Krawczyk	Huntsville	Mil	110	26	8	27	.236	188	41	1	39	.218
Mike Kusiewicz	Trenton	Bos	44	12	2	11	.273	287	71	4	81	.247
John Lackey	Arkansas	Ana	152	34	2	27	.224	314	72	9	67	.229
Corey Lee	Tulsa	Tex	85	19	0	17	.224	382	98	14	86	.257
Derek Lee	Huntsville	Mil	88	20	0	20	.227	553	153	10	89	.277
Garrett Lee	Greenville	Atl	166	42	3	32	.253	197	61	9	31	.310
Randy Leek	Erie	Det	159	55	6	26	.346	537	135	18	97	.251
Chuck Lehr	Midland	Oak	238	79	10	25	.332	409	127	10	78	.311
Colby Lewis	Tulsa	Tex	212	56	3	62	.264	382	94	12	100	.246
Alejandro Lontayo	Greenville	Atl	47	14	1	11	.298	155	45	2	32	.290
Aquilino Lopez	San Antonio	Sea	79	22	1	14	.278	151	26	3	65	.172
Kevin Lovingier	Norwich	NYY	72	11	0	25	.153	238	45	0	69	.189
Larry Luebbers	Chattanooga	Cin	104	29	2	19	.279	101	19	0	29	.188
Spike Lundberg	Tulsa	Tex	83	25	1	13	.301	179	50	3	28	.279
Brandon Lyon	Tennessee	Tor	97	27	3	21	.278	129	30	4	24	.233
Scott MacRae	Chattanooga	Cin	105	29	1	19	.276	125	31	3	23	.248
Jim Magrane	Orlando	TB	333	84	7	55	.252	348	82	8	71	.236
Brian Mallette	Huntsville	Mil	73	18	2	16	.247	128	25	2	55	.195
Nick Maness	Binghamton	NYM	248	73	8	50	.294	323	95	5	57	.294
Mark Mangum	Harrisburg	Mon	213	62	2	29	.291	339	99	12	30	.292
Jason Marr	New Haven	StL	85	22	0	12	.259	158	46	5	15	.291
Jason Martines	El Paso	Ari	59	24	2	8	.407	194	38	1	41	.196
Jose Martinez	Tulsa	Tex	122	30	4	15	.246	247	68	8	43	.275
Brian Matz	Harrisburg	Mon	98	25	7	21	.255	296	91	15	41	.307
Neal McDade	Altoona	Pit	112	32	1	23	.286	182	53	2	32	.291
Jon McDonald	New Britain	Min	146	33	6	32	.226	218	55	1	36	.252
Marty McLeary	Trenton	Bos	56	17	0	17	.304	156	41	2	25	.263
Geronimo Mendoza	Birmingham	CWS	119	35	2	12	.294	158	49	5	26	.310
Benji Miller	Shreveport	SF	86	18	1	14	.209	167	45	6	25	.269
Kevin Mobley	Tulsa	Tex	96	26	0	17	.271	181	45	6	41	.249
David Moraga	West Tenn	ChC	58	17	0	9	.293	263	65	11	49	.247
Ryan Moskau	Portland	Fla	76	20	1	17	.263	308	83	11	61	.269
Aaron Myers	Huntsville	Mil	103	19	0	29	.184	155	34	4	39	.219
Brett Myers	Reading	Phi	246	63	7	51	.256	358	93	14	79	.260
Mike Nakamura	New Britain	Min	112	34	2	31	.304	205	38	1	74	.185
Joe Nathan	Shreveport	SF	85	20	2	9	.235	159	53	9	24	.333
Jason Navarro	New Haven	StL	59	10	1	18	.169	181	54	10	30	.298
Nick Neugebauer	Huntsville	Mil	162	45	2	63	.278	229	49	4	86	.214
Ben Norris	El Paso	Ari	35	12	0	7	.343	223	92	1	18	.413
Dave Noyce	West Tenn	ChC	79	21	1	24	.266	293	77	8	63	.263
Franklin Nunez	Reading	Phi	155	40	4	36	.258	269	67	5	76	.249
Kevin Olsen	Portland	Fla	226	42	3	61	.186	349	81	8	83	.232
Jimmy Osting	Mobile	SD	83	14	0	14	.169	277	71	6	55	.256

Double-A Pitching vs. Lefthanded and Righthanded Batters

Player	Team	Org	vs Left					vs Right				
			AB	H	HR	SO	Avg	AB	H	HR	SO	Avg
Mark Outlaw	Reading	Phi	89	20	2	27	.225	167	54	3	32	.323
Todd Ozias	Shreveport	SF	63	16	1	8	.254	146	31	5	24	.212
Jeromy Palki	New Britain	Min	72	18	1	20	.250	135	30	0	34	.222
Rick Palma	West Tenn	ChC	76	27	1	18	.355	183	34	5	52	.186
Mike Paradis	Bowie	Bal	241	66	5	48	.274	321	91	8	60	.283
Christian Parra	Greenville	Atl	140	45	3	31	.321	198	42	6	51	.212
Josh Pearce	New Haven	StL	167	44	3	31	.263	271	67	8	65	.247
J.J. Pearsall	Tulsa	Tex	52	11	3	18	.212	170	43	4	40	.253
Jason Pearson	Mobile	SD	64	18	2	15	.281	264	70	3	52	.265
Terry Pearson	Erie	Det	96	30	1	14	.313	153	35	0	48	.229
Juan Pena	Midland	Oak	127	34	5	22	.268	461	130	8	84	.282
Chris Piersoll	Chattanooga	Cin	88	22	0	30	.250	125	26	2	48	.208
Luis Pineda	Erie	Det	121	25	2	26	.207	181	43	6	66	.238
Andy Pratt	Tulsa	Tex	130	39	6	20	.300	524	136	12	112	.260
Jason Pruett	Orlando	TB	57	11	1	12	.193	150	48	4	17	.320
Brandon Puffer	Round Rock	Hou	90	17	0	43	.189	197	35	4	48	.178
Ken Pumphrey	New Britain	Min	128	31	1	16	.242	222	53	3	32	.239
Rob Purvis	Birmingham	CWS	271	89	4	22	.328	276	76	5	31	.275
Joe Putz	San Antonio	Sea	215	52	5	54	.242	344	93	6	81	.270
Aaron Rakers	Bowie	Bal	96	22	4	31	.229	137	31	4	43	.226
Mario Ramos	Midland	Oak	57	13	1	15	.228	291	58	6	53	.199
Steve Randolph	El Paso	Ari	59	16	4	13	.271	224	53	7	53	.237
Tim Redding	Round Rock	Hou	116	27	1	34	.233	217	37	4	79	.171
Nick Regilio	Tulsa	Tex	82	32	0	10	.390	127	30	2	30	.236
Justin Reid	Altoona	Pit	171	44	2	27	.257	254	60	3	43	.236
Chris Reinike	Akron	Cle	70	22	2	10	.314	136	33	3	30	.243
Brian Reith	Chattanooga	Cin	161	40	4	33	.248	237	63	6	56	.266
Juan Rincon	New Britain	Min	219	54	3	43	.247	352	76	6	89	.216
Jason Roach	Binghamton	NYM	157	42	0	26	.268	301	87	7	44	.289
Jeriome Robertson	Round Rock	Hou	89	20	2	34	.225	212	69	8	38	.325
Nerio Rodriguez	Akron	Cle	84	23	4	12	.274	179	41	6	37	.229
Wil Rodriguez	Round Rock	Hou	74	22	3	22	.297	277	72	7	72	.260
Brian Rogers	Norwich	NYY	281	72	3	56	.256	411	115	18	94	.280
Juan Rosario	Orlando	TB	117	36	1	26	.308	142	33	2	29	.232
Jason Saenz	Binghamton	NYM	80	28	3	13	.350	476	137	13	81	.288
Brian Sanches	Wichita	KC	181	61	3	30	.337	345	91	9	65	.264
Duaner Sanchez	El Paso	Ari	96	29	1	8	.302	188	63	4	33	.335
Bobby Seay	Orlando	TB	61	14	0	6	.230	200	67	9	43	.335
Shawn Sedlacek	Wichita	KC	116	32	2	21	.276	219	53	5	45	.242
Ryan Seifert	Carolina	Col	172	42	6	42	.244	222	61	4	46	.275
Jason Sekany	Trenton	Bos	75	23	1	17	.307	147	48	9	24	.327
Jae Seo	Binghamton	NYM	100	19	1	17	.190	114	25	2	30	.219
Doug Sessions	Round Rock	Hou	134	38	4	23	.284	254	60	9	55	.236
Ronis Severino	Orlando	TB	86	32	5	18	.372	278	84	7	45	.302
Tom Shearn	Round Rock	Hou	151	38	1	40	.252	251	56	6	96	.223
Kevin Sheredy	New Haven	StL	72	18	2	12	.250	152	28	4	46	.184
Jason Shiell	Mobile	SD	116	32	1	20	.276	192	59	4	40	.307
Carlos Silva	Reading	Phi	296	84	10	33	.284	398	113	10	67	.284
Ben Simon	Jacksonville	LA	126	24	3	34	.190	167	40	9	42	.240
Ken Sims	Bowie	Bal	192	55	8	20	.286	242	68	1	31	.281
Cam Smith	Chattanooga	Cin	82	23	1	21	.280	123	26	4	28	.211
Mike Smith	Tennessee	Tor	154	43	2	25	.279	200	37	5	52	.185
Travis Smith	Round Rock	Hou	230	63	4	27	.274	383	91	3	58	.238
Steve Smyth	West Tenn	ChC	73	18	2	11	.247	374	92	7	82	.246
Scott Sobkowiak	Greenville	Atl	105	30	5	15	.286	149	41	5	33	.275
Corey Spencer	Trenton	Bos	65	21	1	16	.323	242	64	8	66	.264
Chris Spurling	Altoona	Pit	205	66	6	25	.322	271	67	3	38	.247
Jason Stanford	Akron	Cle	82	19	3	24	.232	468	133	8	84	.284
Steve Stemle	New Haven	StL	199	56	5	32	.281	344	103	7	43	.299
Jason Stephens	Arkansas	Ana	149	43	6	23	.289	312	74	6	52	.237
John Stephens	Bowie	Bal	208	36	4	62	.173	264	59	6	68	.223
Josh Stewart	Birmingham	CWS	70	24	1	5	.343	263	86	6	42	.327
Nick Stocks	New Haven	StL	113	30	5	13	.265	209	59	5	50	.282
Pat Strange	Binghamton	NYM	245	69	9	44	.282	324	97	9	55	.299
Felipe Suarez	Arkansas	Ana	81	18	3	15	.222	185	59	9	31	.319
Brian Sweeney	San Antonio	Sea	163	37	2	40	.227	251	80	6	56	.319
Jeff Taglienti	Chattanooga	Cin	99	28	0	23	.283	117	36	3	22	.308
Kazuhiro Takeoka	Greenville	Atl	116	39	2	7	.336	168	37	0	39	.220
Dennis Tankersley	Mobile	SD	108	23	4	31	.213	145	21	2	58	.145
Mike Tejera	Portland	Fla	94	28	3	20	.298	444	115	14	111	.259
Brad Thomas	New Britain	Min	92	16	1	16	.174	349	75	3	81	.215
Eric Thompson	Midland	Oak	84	16	1	18	.190	175	58	8	51	.331
Travis Thompson	Chattanooga	Cin	296	81	6	54	.274	347	89	4	64	.256
Corey Thurman	Wichita	KC	213	44	3	62	.207	353	73	13	86	.207
Brian Tokarse	Birmingham	CWS	97	19	1	28	.196	147	37	3	53	.252
T.J. Tucker	Harrisburg	Mon	121	28	1	20	.231	181	49	9	37	.271
Enmanuel Ulloa	San Antonio	Sea	105	25	1	23	.238	209	56	2	41	.268
Jeff Urban	Shreveport	SF	121	36	1	23	.298	496	142	15	94	.286
Claudio Vargas	Portland	Fla	231	45	8	57	.195	347	77	17	94	.222
Rene Vega	Binghamton	NYM	65	18	1	15	.277	335	97	11	53	.290
Mike Villano	Wichita	KC	87	36	3	12	.414	183	43	5	28	.235
Oscar Villarreal	El Paso	Ari	182	53	1	31	.291	380	101	9	57	.266
Travis Wade	Round Rock	Hou	71	15	0	15	.211	184	52	7	41	.283
Adam Walker	Reading	Phi	47	9	0	9	.191	269	41	2	72	.152
Les Walrond	New Haven	StL	34	7	1	8	.206	266	61	4	59	.229
Steve Watkins	Mobile	SD	169	41	5	27	.243	212	67	9	28	.316
Justin Wayne	Harrisburg	Mon	137	33	1	26	.241	214	54	3	44	.252
Jeremy Wedel	Reading	Phi	88	24	1	11	.273	165	43	3	32	.261
Matt White	Akron	Cle	84	21	4	14	.250	462	130	14	58	.281
Dave Williams	Altoona	Pit	46	10	0	9	.217	167	35	8	30	.210

Player	Team	Org	vs Left					vs Right				
			AB	H	HR	SO	Avg	AB	H	HR	SO	Avg
Jerome Williams	Shreveport	SF	202	48	5	31	.238	292	68	9	53	.233
Larry Wimberly	Altoona	Pit	48	10	0	10	.208	220	65	7	33	.295
Bryan Wolff	Akron	Cle	56	17	2	10	.304	145	35	6	37	.241
Danny Wright	Birmingham	CWS	209	41	3	58	.196	281	71	3	70	.253
Jase Wrigley	Carolina	Col	106	35	0	13	.330	166	58	4	20	.349
Mike Wuertz	West Tenn	ChC	284	79	11	53	.278	331	81	9	82	.245
Mitch Wylie	Birmingham	CWS	229	61	7	56	.266	317	77	6	67	.243
Tyler Yates	Midland	Oak	69	24	3	17	.348	184	42	1	44	.228

Double-A Pitching at Home and on the Road

			Home					Road				
Player	Team	Org	G	IP	W	L	ERA	G	IP	W	L	ERA
Jon Adkins	Midland	Oak	12	66.0	4	5	4.64	12	71.0	4	3	4.31
Tim Adkins	Norwich	NYY	18	22.0	0	0	2.86	22	58.0	3	1	3.57
Jeremy Affeldt	Wichita	KC	12	68.1	4	3	3.95	13	76.1	6	3	3.89
Stevenson Agosto	Orlando	TB	17	59.0	2	7	5.03	13	70.0	6	3	2.96
Carlos Alvarado	Altoona	Pit	13	48.0	3	3	2.63	13	35.0	2	4	4.37
Jeff Andra	Shreveport	SF	9	48.2	1	5	5.18	9	49.0	2	4	4.22
Scott Atchison	San Antonio	Sea	13	79.0	4	6	3.19	11	57.0	5	4	5.68
Ryan Baerlocher	Wichita	KC	12	78.0	6	3	3.23	16	102.1	7	5	4.57
Chris Baker	Tennessee	Tor	15	97.1	6	4	3.98	13	81.1	9	2	2.66
Dusty Bergman	Arkansas	Ana	15	90.1	2	8	5.08	12	62.2	5	5	5.17
Brent Billingsley	Harrisburg	Mon	11	57.0	2	7	7.26	8	55.0	5	2	3.44
Mark Brownson	Huntsville	Mil	12	63.2	5	2	4.52	12	67.0	5	3	4.43
Mike Bynum	Mobile	SD	9	48.0	2	3	4.88	7	36.0	0	4	5.25
Kiko Calero	Wichita	KC	12	62.0	7	1	1.89	15	62.0	7	4	4.79
Ryan Cameron	Carolina	Col	7	39.2	2	3	6.13	11	50.0	5	3	4.50
Chris Capuano	El Paso	Ari	13	79.0	5	5	5.47	15	80.0	5	6	5.18
Lance Caracciolo	Jacksonville	LA	10	42.0	3	2	4.29	18	88.0	5	2	4.81
Scott Cassidy	Tennessee	Tor	10	66.0	4	4	3.14	6	30.2	2	2	4.11
Chris Cervantes	El Paso	Ari	24	45.0	1	2	6.80	21	51.0	2	5	4.24
Gustavo Chacin	Tennessee	Tor	12	64.1	5	6	5.04	13	75.1	6	2	3.11
Ron Chiavacci	Harrisburg	Mon	16	95.1	2	5	3.59	9	51.2	1	6	4.70
Jason Childers	Huntsville	Mil	18	44.2	4	3	2.22	22	43.0	3	3	3.56
Brandon Claussen	Norwich	NYY	11	68.0	4	1	2.65	10	63.0	5	1	1.57
Patrick Coogan	New Haven	StL	18	87.1	6	3	3.92	15	61.0	2	5	6.79
B.R. Cook	New Haven	StL	12	71.1	1	5	4.29	8	50.0	4	3	3.60
Nate Cornejo	Erie	Det	12	74.0	7	2	3.65	7	50.0	5	1	1.26
Ryan Cox	Shreveport	SF	12	72.0	5	3	2.75	12	64.1	3	5	4.76
Chuck Crowder	Carolina	Col	18	61.2	5	3	3.65	14	39.0	1	3	8.08
Mike Crudale	New Haven	StL	33	45.0	2	6	3.20	29	35.0	2	3	3.34
Juan Cruz	West Tenn	ChC	11	56.2	4	3	4.45	12	64.1	5	3	3.64
Chris Cumberland	Greenville	Atl	12	76.0	2	4	3.20	8	49.0	1	3	3.86
Joey Dawley	Greenville	Atl	11	66.1	5	1	1.90	11	60.2	2	4	4.30
Zach Day	Akron	Cle	12	74.0	4	5	3.41	10	62.0	5	5	2.76
Phil Devey	Jacksonville	LA	13	61.0	5	1	5.31	11	51.0	3	1	1.94
Mark DiFelice	Carolina	Col	9	57.0	3	2	3.63	10	66.0	3	2	2.73
Ryan Drese	Akron	Cle	7	41.0	1	4	4.39	7	45.0	4	3	2.40
Mike Drumright	Portland	Fla	10	58.0	4	4	3.88	8	44.0	1	4	4.30
Scott Dunn	Chattanooga	Cin	9	52.0	4	2	4.50	8	46.0	3	0	3.72
Radhames Dykhoff	Arkansas	Ana	13	44.2	1	2	3.43	14	36.0	1	1	6.00
Derrin Ebert	Trenton	Bos	9	56.0	3	5	3.70	11	60.0	4	4	5.55
Chris Enochs	Midland	Oak	19	53.0	4	0	4.08	20	46.0	1	4	4.70
Jeff Farnsworth	San Antonio	Sea	12	73.0	6	1	2.59	15	82.0	5	9	5.93
Juan Figueroa	Bowie	Bal	8	47.0	2	5	4.98	10	52.0	1	5	4.85
Randy Flores	Norwich	NYY	12	80.0	5	4	2.59	13	78.0	9	2	3.00
Casey Fossum	Trenton	Bos	13	75.0	2	4	3.36	7	42.0	1	3	1.93
Lance Franks	New Haven	StL	14	51.0	0	7	4.24	14	39.0	2	1	3.92
Kevin Frederick	New Britain	Min	20	37.0	2	2	3.16	24	45.2	4	0	0.39
Kai Freeman	Birmingham	CWS	16	44.2	2	2	5.64	12	38.2	3	1	4.42
Randy Galvez	Altoona	Pit	10	54.0	3	4	3.33	5	32.0	2	2	3.66
Jose Garcia	Huntsville	Mil	9	46.0	2	2	4.30	12	65.0	4	3	3.32
Cecilio Garibaldi	Orlando	TB	20	61.0	4	3	4.87	15	43.0	1	3	3.98
Josh Garrett	Trenton	Bos	26	38.2	2	3	6.05	20	42.2	1	3	5.27
Geoff Geary	Reading	Phi	16	59.2	4	5	3.77	13	52.2	5	2	3.42
Chris Gissell	West Tenn	ChC	14	75.1	2	6	4.06	14	84.0	3	5	4.93
Mike Gonzalez	Altoona	Pit	7	45.0	3	1	3.20	7	42.0	2	3	4.29
Alex Graman	Norwich	NYY	15	95.1	7	4	2.74	13	70.1	5	5	4.61
Kevin Gregg	Midland	Oak	23	43.0	3	1	5.02	21	38.0	2	4	4.03
Matt Guerrier	Birmingham	CWS	6	45.0	5	1	1.60	9	53.2	6	2	4.36
Lindsay Gulin	Jacksonville	LA	15	70.0	4	3	3.34	11	56.0	3	2	1.77
Rick Guttormson	Mobile	SD	14	75.0	4	7	4.20	13	68.0	1	9	5.29
Josh Hancock	Trenton	Bos	17	93.0	6	4	3.39	7	37.2	2	2	4.30
Aaron Harang	Midland	Oak	14	80.0	6	3	4.05	13	70.0	4	5	4.24
Tim Harrell	Jacksonville	LA	25	43.0	2	2	3.56	22	38.0	3	2	2.37
Jeff Heaverlo	San Antonio	Sea	12	80.0	5	2	2.59	15	98.1	6	4	3.57
Carlos Hernandez	Round Rock	Hou	11	63.0	5	2	3.86	13	76.0	7	1	3.55
Cary Hiles	Reading	Phi	25	40.2	0	1	2.88	26	41.0	2	2	1.98
Joe Horgan	Shreveport	SF	14	50.2	2	2	2.31	17	53.0	1	3	4.92
Luke Hudson	Carolina	Col	15	85.0	4	7	4.34	14	79.1	3	5	4.08
Travis Hughes	Tulsa	Tex	26	48.0	2	5	4.69	21	39.0	3	2	4.62
Johnny Hunter	Mobile	SD	8	42.0	1	1	4.07	11	56.0	2	5	5.46
Adam Johnson	New Britain	Min	8	50.0	4	3	4.68	10	62.2	1	3	3.16
Eric Junge	Jacksonville	LA	13	74.0	4	6	3.41	14	90.0	6	5	3.50
Josh Kalinowski	Carolina	Col	13	71.1	5	4	4.67	12	65.1	2	4	3.44
Tim Kalita	Erie	Det	15	102.1	7	4	3.96	15	97.1	8	5	3.70
Nathan Kent	Greenville	Atl	13	85.1	4	5	2.95	13	69.0	4	5	5.48
Jason Kershner	Reading	Phi	10	49.0	1	6	5.51	16	74.1	4	3	4.36
Jack Krawczyk	Huntsville	Mil	23	47.2	5	1	3.21	24	33.2	1	1	3.74
Mike Kusiewicz	Trenton	Bos	8	42.0	1	1	2.36	10	47.0	3	4	4.40
John Lackey	Arkansas	Ana	9	61.2	3	4	3.21	9	65.1	6	3	3.72
Corey Lee	Tulsa	Tex	14	70.0	3	7	5.91	11	55.0	2	5	4.58
Derek Lee	Huntsville	Mil	16	96.1	5	7	3.46	12	65.1	2	4	3.31
Garrett Lee	Greenville	Atl	16	50.2	3	4	4.26	16	41.0	1	5	5.05
Randy Leek	Erie	Det	13	84.0	7	2	2.79	16	95.1	4	5	4.81
Chuck Lehr	Midland	Oak	15	78.0	5	6	7.27	14	77.0	6	6	3.62
Colby Lewis	Tulsa	Tex	12	71.1	2	7	5.68	13	84.0	8	3	3.54
Kevin Lovingier	Norwich	NYY	24	40.2	2	2	2.43	29	49.0	1	3	1.47
Jim Magrane	Orlando	TB	14	82.1	4	6	1.97	15	99.1	4	6	3.81
Nick Maness	Binghamton	NYM	11	55.0	3	6	5.24	17	87.1	3	6	4.84
Mark Mangum	Harrisburg	Mon	10	65.0	4	2	4.15	16	75.0	3	6	5.04
Jose Martinez	Tulsa	Tex	14	51.0	4	2	5.12	10	42.0	2	4	4.29
Brian Matz	Harrisburg	Mon	18	46.0	0	5	7.24	19	50.2	1	3	3.91
Jon McDonald	New Britain	Min	11	61.2	4	2	3.36	6	35.0	4	1	3.60
David Moraga	West Tenn	ChC	12	38.0	2	0	3.55	11	45.0	2	5	4.60
Ryan Moskau	Portland	Fla	20	55.0	1	1	2.78	19	48.0	2	1	4.31
Brett Myers	Reading	Phi	14	84.1	8	3	3.09	12	71.0	5	1	4.82
Mike Nakamura	New Britain	Min	27	48.2	3	0	1.29	21	37.2	2	1	2.39
Nick Neugebauer	Huntsville	Mil	11	56.0	2	4	3.38	10	50.2	3	2	3.55
Dave Noyce	West Tenn	ChC	27	47.2	1	3	3.21	23	48.0	2	5	4.88
Franklin Nunez	Reading	Phi	21	62.2	5	2	5.31	18	47.0	3	5	3.26
Kevin Olsen	Portland	Fla	13	74.0	5	1	1.70	13	80.0	5	2	3.60
Jimmy Osting	Mobile	SD	9	50.0	4	2	4.14	9	47.2	5	2	3.02
Mike Paradis	Bowie	Bal	12	65.0	5	6	3.60	15	72.0	3	7	5.75
Christian Parra	Greenville	Atl	9	50.0	3	3	3.78	9	39.0	0	5	7.62
Josh Pearce	New Haven	StL	9	60.2	4	3	2.23	9	54.2	2	5	5.43
Jason Pearson	Mobile	SD	27	42.0	3	2	3.86	27	44.0	2	3	4.50
Juan Pena	Midland	Oak	13	74.0	6	5	4.38	14	74.0	5	4	3.77
Luis Pineda	Erie	Det	11	60.0	5	2	2.85	5	25.1	1	0	3.55
Andy Pratt	Tulsa	Tex	11	68.1	1	5	5.40	16	99.1	7	5	4.08
Brandon Puffer	Round Rock	Hou	25	36.0	2	1	2.50	31	46.2	4	0	1.74
Ken Pumphrey	New Britain	Min	12	55.2	4	2	2.26	10	47.0	4	0	3.64
Rob Purvis	Birmingham	CWS	10	59.2	3	5	4.68	14	80.0	2	4	5.74
Joe Putz	San Antonio	Sea	16	87.1	4	5	3.92	11	60.2	3	4	3.71
Mario Ramos	Midland	Oak	7	45.0	4	1	3.40	8	48.2	4	0	2.77
Justin Reid	Altoona	Pit	11	75.0	3	2	1.44	6	35.0	2	3	4.89
Brian Reith	Chattanooga	Cin	11	69.0	4	1	2.74	7	35.0	2	3	6.43
Juan Rincon	New Britain	Min	15	73.1	7	3	2.58	14	79.1	7	3	3.18
Jason Roach	Binghamton	NYM	7	37.0	2	3	4.62	15	79.0	6	4	2.62
Wil Rodriguez	Round Rock	Hou	24	48.2	1	3	4.44	18	43.2	4	6	5.15
Brian Rogers	Norwich	NYY	13	83.0	5	5	4.23	16	94.1	5	4	3.72
Jason Saenz	Binghamton	NYM	18	92.1	5	1	5.95	10	50.0	3	5	5.22
Brian Sanches	Wichita	KC	16	80.0	5	5	5.18	13	53.2	2	4	7.21
Shawn Sedlacek	Wichita	KC	6	38.0	2	3	2.61	8	48.2	4	4	4.44
Ryan Seifert	Carolina	Col	19	59.2	2	2	2.87	14	43.2	2	4	3.50
Doug Sessions	Round Rock	Hou	22	64.0	4	2	3.80	19	39.0	2	2	5.31
Ronis Severino	Orlando	TB	19	48.0	1	5	3.75	19	41.2	2	3	6.48
Tom Shearn	Round Rock	Hou	21	52.2	1	4	4.10	22	57.0	4	2	3.63
Jason Shiell	Mobile	SD	24	39.2	2	0	3.18	21	41.0	0	3	5.71
Carlos Silva	Reading	Phi	14	86.1	6	5	4.80	14	93.1	9	3	3.09
Ben Simon	Jacksonville	LA	8	37.0	3	3	4.14	7	44.0	4	3	2.66
Ken Sims	Bowie	Bal	14	64.0	5	2	4.36	10	47.2	3	2	3.78
Travis Smith	Round Rock	Hou	15	91.1	7	5	2.86	14	68.1	8	3	3.42
Steve Smyth	West Tenn	ChC	10	69.0	7	0	1.96	8	51.0	2	3	3.35
Chris Spurling	Altoona	Pit	15	38.2	3	2	3.03	19	42.0	5	5	3.14
Jason Stanford	Akron	Cle	12	70.0	1	7	4.63	12	71.1	5	4	3.53
Steve Stemle	New Haven	StL	8	40.0	2	2	4.28	18	94.0	5	8	4.98
Jason Stephens	Arkansas	Ana	9	61.0	4	1	2.07	10	58.0	2	6	5.90
John Stephens	Bowie	Bal	7	49.0	3	3	2.76	11	83.0	8	1	1.30
Josh Stewart	Birmingham	CWS	7	36.0	2	2	7.00	9	46.0	1	2	6.46
Nick Stocks	New Haven	StL	5	22.2	0	4	6.35	11	59.0	2	8	4.73
Pat Strange	Binghamton	NYM	15	86.1	6	3	5.53	11	66.1	5	3	4.07
Brian Sweeney	San Antonio	Sea	21	55.2	4	1	2.43	16	48.2	3	3	5.36
Mike Tejera	Portland	Fla	11	61.0	3	4	3.98	14	80.0	6	4	3.26
Brad Thomas	New Britain	Min	11	73.1	4	2	1.72	8	45.2	6	1	2.36
Travis Thompson	Chattanooga	Cin	12	82.1	7	2	2.62	16	84.0	5	8	5.14
Corey Thurman	Wichita	KC	11	70.0	7	3	3.21	14	84.1	6	2	3.52
T.J. Tucker	Harrisburg	Mon	6	36.0	3	2	3.50	7	46.0	2	3	3.91
Jeff Urban	Shreveport	SF	11	63.0	1	5	4.00	16	93.1	6	6	3.86
Claudio Vargas	Portland	Fla	11	66.0	4	3	3.00	16	92.1	4	6	5.07
Rene Vega	Binghamton	NYM	20	58.2	1	4	4.45	21	47.2	2	2	2.64
Oscar Villarreal	El Paso	Ari	16	85.1	6	5	4.32	11	55.0	0	4	4.58
Adam Walker	Reading	Phi	6	37.0	3	1	1.46	9	54.0	4	3	2.17
Les Walrond	New Haven	StL	9	48.0	1	5	3.75	7	33.0	1	3	4.09
Steve Watkins	Mobile	SD	11	51.0	2	4	5.82	12	46.0	2	4	5.67
Justin Wayne	Harrisburg	Mon	6	39.0	4	1	3.23	8	53.0	5	1	2.21
Matt White	Akron	Cle	14	80.1	5	4	4.59	11	63.0	3	6	5.14
Jerome Williams	Shreveport	SF	12	67.1	6	3	4.14	11	62.0	3	4	3.77
Danny Wright	Birmingham	CWS	15	104.0	5	6	2.68	5	30.0	2	1	3.30
Mike Wuertz	West Tenn	ChC	15	90.0	3	4	3.70	12	70.0	1	5	4.37
Mitch Wylie	Birmingham	CWS	9	53.0	5	1	3.23	15	87.1	10	3	4.84

2001 Major League Equivalencies

When Bill James first devised Major League Equivalencies 16 years ago, he said it was easily the most important research he ever had done. That's quite a statement, considering how much he has contributed to the study of baseball.

An MLE translates a Double-A or Triple-A hitter's statistics into big league numbers. It does this by making a series of adjustments for a player's minor league home ballpark, his minor league and his future major league home park. If he plays in a pitcher's league, his MLE will get a boost. If he's a Rockies prospect, then his numbers will be inflated, just like they are for all hitters at Coors Field. The MLE also recognizes that it's significantly tougher to hit in the majors than in the upper minors, and makes a further adjustment.

The end result is an estimation of what the hitter would have done had he gotten similar playing time in the major leagues with his parent club in 2001. Please understand that an MLE is not a projection for the future. If a player's MLE gives him 30 homers, that doesn't mean he'll hit 30 homers in the majors if given a chance to play in 2002. Treat an MLE as a single season in the major league career of a player. It's quite possible that a player with a banner MLE had the misfortune of spending his career year in Triple-A or Double-A.

The MLE can't tell you if a player is going to get a chance to play in the majors. But it can show you, with a high degree of accuracy, what he would have done with that opportunity in 2001. Ages are as of June 30, 2001.

Major League Equivalencies for 2001 AAA/AA Batters

ANAHEIM ANGELS		Age	Avg	G	AB	R	H	2B	3B	HR	RBI	BB	SO	SB	CS	OBP	SLG
Amezaga,Alfredo	SS	23	.251	119	462	57	116	12	4	3	26	23	101	21	12	.287	.314
Barnes,Larry	1B	26	.249	100	382	53	95	17	4	12	49	19	92	3	1	.284	.408
Baughman,Justin	2B	26	.258	77	271	35	70	12	3	2	21	13	55	13	5	.292	.347
Burke,Jamie	C	29	.180	61	205	17	37	8	1	0	18	12	28	0	0	.226	.229
Caceres,Wilmy	SS	22	.210	87	309	26	65	4	2	0	14	8	45	7	6	.230	.236
Christensen,Mike	3B	25	.208	86	288	24	60	20	1	4	25	12	79	2	2	.240	.326
DaVanon,Jeff	OF	27	.267	69	240	31	64	15	4	7	32	21	57	5	3	.326	.450
Durrington,Trent	2B	25	.255	112	341	48	87	22	2	10	42	29	92	19	10	.314	.419
Fernandez,Jose	3B	26	.293	122	423	67	124	30	0	21	78	37	93	5	7	.350	.513
Figgins,Chone	2B	23	.241	125	474	60	114	26	7	3	35	45	95	26	10	.306	.344
Guiel,Jeff	OF	27	.280	116	379	50	106	21	1	16	51	24	94	3	2	.323	.467
Guzman,Elpidio	OF	22	.218	117	444	45	97	18	5	5	35	11	93	12	14	.237	.315
Haynes,Nathan	OF	21	.281	79	303	38	85	9	3	3	17	20	68	22	8	.325	.360
Hill,Jason	C	24	.237	93	312	34	74	15	0	8	37	12	64	0	1	.265	.362
Huisman,Jason	2B	25	.249	109	357	42	89	19	0	8	39	25	66	2	9	.298	.370
Johnson,Gary	OF	25	.220	128	451	49	99	20	1	8	56	39	97	5	7	.282	.322
Molina,Jose	C	26	.255	61	200	19	51	9	0	3	21	9	50	0	2	.287	.345
Morgan,Scott	OF	27	.227	128	476	63	108	31	1	20	56	27	120	1	0	.268	.422
Nieves,Jose	2B	26	.282	61	241	34	68	12	2	7	25	5	37	5	7	.297	.436
Pritchett,Chris	DH-1B	31	.261	125	449	45	117	29	1	11	51	30	104	1	2	.307	.403
Quinlan,Robb	1B	24	.263	129	471	63	124	28	4	11	61	34	88	0	4	.313	.410
Tolentino,Juan	OF	25	.236	114	428	47	101	28	1	7	45	16	89	11	4	.264	.355
Urquhart,Derick	OF	25	.237	81	241	32	57	9	1	3	35	21	38	2	1	.298	.320
ARIZ. DIAMONDBACKS		Age	Avg	G	AB	R	H	2B	3B	HR	RBI	BB	SO	SB	CS	OBP	SLG
Christenson,Ryan	OF	27	.227	76	273	29	62	17	0	4	22	20	58	4	2	.280	.333
Cintron,Alex	SS	22	.259	107	406	40	105	20	2	2	26	11	50	6	6	.278	.333
Cresse,Brad	C	22	.254	118	409	40	104	33	0	10	59	27	124	0	1	.300	.408
Cummings,Midre	OF	29	.296	77	250	28	74	20	6	3	28	18	51	1	3	.343	.460
Cust,Jack	OF	22	.246	135	423	61	104	20	1	20	59	77	168	4	3	.362	.440
Dallimore,Brian	3B	27	.290	127	490	54	142	32	4	5	49	18	59	7	13	.315	.402
Devore,Doug	OF	23	.258	128	453	49	117	27	8	11	54	28	126	7	3	.301	.426
Glendenning,M.	DH-OF	24	.183	100	338	30	62	9	0	8	29	27	124	0	0	.244	.281
Huckaby,Ken	C-1B	30	.270	108	348	33	94	16	0	2	35	6	82	0	3	.282	.333
Lemonis,Chris	2B	27	.257	105	362	36	93	17	1	1	38	15	64	5	3	.286	.318
McNally,Sean	3B	28	.214	125	416	40	89	13	1	11	48	40	154	2	2	.283	.329
Moeller,Chad	C	26	.240	78	262	31	63	17	0	6	27	18	56	0	4	.289	.374
Murphy,Nate	OF	26	.218	91	285	35	62	12	2	5	27	21	85	3	4	.271	.326
Overbay,Lyle	1B	24	.313	138	502	60	157	42	2	9	73	41	98	3	4	.365	.458
Petersen,Chris	2B-SS	30	.219	102	269	25	59	10	0	2	29	20	53	1	4	.273	.279
Santora,Jack	SS	24	.204	86	255	25	52	12	0	0	9	21	51	2	5	.264	.251
Sosa,Juan	SS	25	.191	107	324	23	62	9	0	0	15	14	50	6	4	.225	.219
Sykes,Jamie	OF	26	.217	64	207	16	45	6	0	2	11	8	80	6	2	.247	.275
Wilson,Desi	1B	32	.293	83	304	34	89	17	0	2	28	10	50	2	2	.315	.368
ATLANTA BRAVES		Age	Avg	G	AB	R	H	2B	3B	HR	RBI	BB	SO	SB	CS	OBP	SLG
Aldridge,Cory	OF	22	.229	131	442	49	101	17	1	16	48	35	147	8	6	.285	.380
Battle,Howard	3B	29	.249	131	474	42	118	18	0	7	61	19	80	1	5	.278	.331
Carter,Mike	OF	32	.265	104	373	44	99	14	2	1	16	7	46	7	10	.279	.322
Castro,Ramon	SS	21	.255	112	384	41	98	24	4	5	38	23	90	3	10	.297	.378
DeRenne,Keoni	2B	22	.221	130	443	36	98	13	1	2	36	32	60	2	2	.274	.269
Garcia,Jesse	SS	27	.240	105	362	40	87	19	2	1	17	17	56	13	6	.274	.312

434

Major League Equivalencies for 2001 AAA/AA Batters

ATLANTA BRAVES		Age	Avg	G	AB	R	H	2B	3B	HR	RBI	BB	SO	SB	CS	OBP	SLG
Giles,Marcus	2B	23	.303	67	241	38	73	16	0	4	35	17	49	9	5	.349	.419
Greene,Charlie	C	30	.129	90	272	12	35	1	0	0	12	9	67	0	0	.157	.132
Hessman,Mike	3B	23	.212	129	467	57	99	21	1	21	69	28	131	1	4	.257	.396
Hollins,Damon	OF	27	.241	112	377	43	91	15	2	7	42	27	82	3	5	.292	.347
Norris,Dax	C	28	.252	95	305	20	77	22	0	2	30	12	45	1	2	.281	.344
Otanez,Willis	1B	28	.247	93	300	33	74	12	1	10	37	30	63	1	2	.315	.393
Perry,Chan	1B	28	.246	98	337	30	83	13	2	6	31	15	62	0	6	.278	.350
Rivera,Roberto	OF	24	.219	121	383	42	84	17	0	5	23	21	82	6	4	.260	.303
Robertson,Mike	1B	30	.246	127	419	33	103	16	3	4	32	23	58	2	12	.285	.327
Ross,Jason	OF	27	.215	112	303	35	65	10	0	12	31	29	104	12	8	.283	.366
Sisco,Steve	2B	31	.219	95	343	34	75	14	0	5	26	25	73	4	5	.272	.303
Swann,Pedro	OF	30	.264	139	470	54	124	29	3	6	57	41	98	8	6	.323	.377
Tebbs,Nate	SS	28	.167	74	215	13	36	7	0	0	5	10	61	3	2	.204	.200
Torrealba,Steve	C	23	.251	90	287	32	72	19	0	6	29	24	57	0	0	.309	.380
Urquiola,Carlos	OF	21	.263	81	274	34	72	10	0	0	14	16	32	8	7	.303	.299
Wilson,Travis	2B-OF	23	.239	134	490	38	117	26	2	3	48	7	109	3	7	.249	.318
Zapp,A.J.	1B	23	.217	75	286	31	62	15	0	6	29	15	92	3	1	.256	.332
BALTIMORE ORIOLES		Age	Avg	G	AB	R	H	2B	3B	HR	RBI	BB	SO	SB	CS	OBP	SLG
Almonte,Wady	OF	26	.200	87	310	22	62	7	2	2	28	14	57	5	3	.235	.255
Bigbie,Larry	OF	23	.267	81	292	40	78	14	2	6	29	31	66	7	8	.337	.390
Blake,Casey	3B	27	.279	94	359	49	100	22	4	7	37	26	70	10	3	.327	.421
Casimiro,Carlos	3B-OF	24	.208	128	457	38	95	19	0	6	33	19	130	4	6	.239	.289
Coffie,Ivanon	DH	24	.245	56	200	30	49	8	0	7	31	13	49	2	0	.291	.390
Figueroa,Franky	1B	24	.278	137	518	53	144	27	0	12	63	15	149	0	4	.298	.400
Garabito,Eddy	2B	22	.248	127	504	59	125	24	4	2	31	27	81	18	7	.286	.323
Gil,Geronimo	C	25	.248	105	343	34	85	16	0	7	40	11	82	0	1	.271	.356
Hammond,Joey	SS	23	.258	102	333	43	86	11	1	0	22	31	63	1	3	.321	.297
Harris,Willie	2B	23	.279	133	506	72	141	23	2	7	43	33	76	39	15	.323	.374
Leon,Jose	3B	24	.275	135	498	64	137	24	2	14	65	27	123	5	4	.312	.416
Martinez,Eddy	SS	23	.258	122	426	56	110	12	0	6	38	29	102	8	3	.305	.329
McDonald,Darnell	OF	22	.230	134	496	47	114	22	1	3	49	32	109	12	12	.277	.296
Ndungidi,Papy	OF-DH	22	.191	104	330	29	63	14	0	2	30	27	97	2	5	.252	.252
Phoenix,Wynter	OF	26	.205	105	317	35	65	15	2	4	22	21	83	8	6	.254	.303
Raines Jr.,Tim	OF	21	.258	105	376	57	97	15	0	4	36	33	97	28	11	.318	.330
Roberts,Brian	SS	23	.255	66	235	24	60	8	0	0	16	31	36	24	7	.342	.289
Rust,Brian	1B	26	.225	93	307	35	69	15	0	12	42	23	88	3	5	.279	.391
BOSTON RED SOX		Age	Avg	G	AB	R	H	2B	3B	HR	RBI	BB	SO	SB	CS	OBP	SLG
Alcantara,Israel	OF-DH	28	.276	119	438	66	121	25	0	28	74	47	113	6	2	.346	.525
Brown,Tonayne	OF	23	.268	111	384	33	103	20	0	3	25	10	82	2	12	.287	.344
Burkhart,Morgan	1B	29	.249	120	401	52	100	19	0	18	51	56	120	0	0	.341	.431
Capista,Aaron	SS	22	.197	117	396	38	78	25	3	1	32	13	52	1	1	.222	.283
Chevalier,Virgil	1B	27	.239	128	469	48	112	25	0	12	57	29	65	2	3	.283	.369
Clemente,Edgard	OF	25	.241	97	336	31	81	15	0	11	33	21	95	1	1	.286	.384
Diaz,Juan	DH-1B	25	.247	74	271	37	67	16	0	16	42	14	90	0	0	.284	.483
Fischer,Mark	OF	25	.204	127	452	38	92	21	1	8	44	17	160	2	1	.232	.308
Garcia,Luis	1B	22	.285	63	221	28	63	19	0	10	36	19	73	0	1	.342	.507
Johnson,Rontrez	OF	24	.268	117	429	64	115	29	2	10	43	23	80	16	11	.305	.415
Lofton,James	SS	27	.292	71	253	32	74	15	0	7	18	14	55	3	4	.330	.435
Lomasney,Steve	C	23	.235	75	264	27	62	16	1	8	30	18	104	1	1	.284	.394
Maddox Jr.,G.	OF-DH	26	.262	92	305	37	80	24	3	8	38	27	90	2	5	.322	.439

Major League Equivalencies for 2001 AAA/AA Batters

BOSTON RED SOX		Age	Avg	G	AB	R	H	2B	3B	HR	RBI	BB	SO	SB	CS	OBP	SLG
Pickering,Calvin	1B-DH	24	.259	132	451	56	117	21	0	18	89	57	160	0	1	.343	.426
Rodriguez,Luis	C	27	.208	84	255	30	53	9	1	6	21	8	66	1	1	.232	.322
Rose,Mike	C	24	.202	91	272	28	55	11	1	2	23	36	68	2	5	.295	.272
Salzano,Jerry	3B-DH	26	.261	125	440	52	115	30	0	5	43	34	97	10	6	.314	.364
Santos,Angel	2B	21	.247	133	510	60	126	33	0	10	42	37	119	17	7	.298	.371
Shave,Jon	SS-2B	33	.237	84	300	28	71	9	0	4	22	18	51	2	3	.280	.307
Stenson,Dernell	OF	23	.220	122	454	43	100	17	0	12	57	35	123	0	0	.276	.337
Veras,Wilton	3B	23	.212	136	509	36	108	15	1	6	43	11	66	3	6	.229	.281
CHICAGO CUBS		**Age**	**Avg**	**G**	**AB**	**R**	**H**	**2B**	**3B**	**HR**	**RBI**	**BB**	**SO**	**SB**	**CS**	**OBP**	**SLG**
Abreu,Dennis	2B-SS	23	.249	106	337	34	84	6	0	3	27	15	81	11	4	.281	.294
Amrhein,Mike	C-1B	26	.229	96	306	27	70	13	0	3	30	18	48	0	1	.272	.301
Bass,Jayson	OF	27	.296	118	375	42	111	18	0	11	55	32	112	9	9	.351	.432
Brown,Roosevelt	OF	25	.314	88	347	54	109	29	0	17	61	11	70	2	5	.335	.545
Choi,Hee Seop	1B	22	.205	77	258	30	53	9	0	10	36	27	70	3	1	.281	.357
Dunwoody,Todd	OF	26	.253	75	241	24	61	15	2	6	25	13	78	4	4	.291	.407
Frese,Nate	SS	23	.170	72	230	23	39	4	0	3	17	30	66	0	1	.265	.226
Gripp,Ryan	3B	23	.215	68	251	28	54	17	0	7	41	19	64	1	0	.270	.367
Haas,Chris	1B	24	.232	126	410	59	95	14	3	22	66	51	161	1	2	.317	.441
Hill,Bobby	2B	23	.288	57	205	27	59	7	0	2	19	25	41	15	6	.365	.351
Hubbard,Trenidad	OF	35	.278	98	335	60	93	17	2	13	48	54	62	18	9	.378	.457
Johnson,Gary	OF	24	.248	135	455	80	113	26	3	7	59	46	112	11	5	.317	.365
Kelton,Dave	3B	21	.300	58	220	30	66	8	3	11	41	19	58	0	3	.356	.514
Mahoney,Mike	C	28	.200	95	280	17	56	12	0	2	21	17	66	0	3	.246	.264
Meyers,Chad	2B	25	.271	132	428	73	116	26	3	7	43	46	75	19	7	.342	.395
Patterson,Corey	OF	21	.228	89	355	50	81	19	2	5	25	23	68	14	8	.275	.335
Piedra,Jorge	OF	22	.233	124	434	51	101	24	4	7	50	29	85	9	5	.281	.355
Short,Rick	3B	28	.247	113	320	34	79	16	0	4	27	20	45	1	2	.291	.334
Snopek,Chris	SS	30	.249	130	453	52	113	28	0	11	45	25	70	4	5	.289	.384
CHICAGO WHITE SOX		**Age**	**Avg**	**G**	**AB**	**R**	**H**	**2B**	**3B**	**HR**	**RBI**	**BB**	**SO**	**SB**	**CS**	**OBP**	**SLG**
Barry,Jeff	OF	32	.225	102	334	39	75	14	0	8	30	27	76	7	5	.283	.338
Battersby,Eric	1B	25	.243	133	432	65	105	18	0	13	63	64	93	4	4	.341	.375
Borchard,Joe	OF	22	.284	133	507	89	144	25	0	26	92	54	169	3	4	.353	.487
Bravo,Danny	SS	24	.238	81	290	30	69	12	1	4	32	20	34	2	3	.287	.328
Crede,Joe	3B	23	.272	124	460	66	125	33	0	17	64	46	92	1	1	.338	.454
Dalesandro,Mark	C	33	.254	75	260	15	66	17	0	4	22	6	25	0	1	.271	.365
Dellaero,Jason	SS	24	.173	115	375	31	65	9	0	11	27	17	118	3	4	.209	.285
Hardtke,Jason	2B	29	.250	96	332	50	83	19	2	10	37	33	44	1	2	.318	.410
Hummel,Tim	2B	22	.279	134	516	78	144	31	4	6	59	50	73	10	3	.343	.390
Inglin,Jeff	DH-OF	25	.268	128	478	65	128	24	5	25	74	43	108	2	4	.328	.496
Ingram,Darron	OF-DH	25	.252	136	507	72	128	32	3	21	85	42	201	4	6	.310	.452
Miles,Aaron	DH	24	.249	84	338	49	84	15	2	7	39	21	37	2	5	.292	.367
Mitchell,Derek	SS	26	.201	82	234	34	47	7	0	1	19	27	72	3	4	.284	.244
Olivo,Miguel	C	22	.250	93	312	42	78	21	0	13	51	29	66	4	3	.314	.442
Prieto,Rick	OF	28	.228	103	334	51	76	11	3	3	32	48	56	6	6	.325	.305
Ramirez,Julio	OF	23	.211	88	317	35	67	10	0	8	24	20	84	12	6	.258	.319
Rodriguez,Liu	2B	24	.284	118	440	52	125	24	0	0	36	41	62	5	4	.345	.339
Rowand,Aaron	OF	23	.291	82	327	53	95	27	0	16	47	21	49	6	2	.333	.520
Rumfield,Toby	1B	28	.267	121	460	48	123	27	0	20	68	28	67	0	0	.309	.457
Sandoval,Danny	SS	22	.270	58	200	22	54	6	0	0	27	13	27	13	4	.315	.300
Saunders,Chris	3B	30	.275	130	473	71	130	31	0	11	66	53	98	3	1	.348	.410

Major League Equivalencies for 2001 AAA/AA Batters

CHICAGO WHITE SOX		Age	Avg	G	AB	R	H	2B	3B	HR	RBI	BB	SO	SB	CS	OBP	SLG
Valenzuela,Mario	OF	24	.272	137	511	65	139	22	2	21	74	24	100	4	5	.305	.446
Wilson,Craig	3B	30	.279	125	462	67	129	24	2	9	59	38	58	4	3	.334	.398
CINCINNATI REDS		Age	Avg	G	AB	R	H	2B	3B	HR	RBI	BB	SO	SB	CS	OBP	SLG
Broussard,Ben	1B	24	.300	100	343	68	103	26	0	19	58	44	73	7	2	.380	.542
Cromer,D.T.	1B	30	.261	62	234	28	61	11	1	9	40	12	49	3	1	.297	.432
Davis,Tommy	1B	28	.249	112	385	39	96	23	1	5	38	22	100	0	0	.290	.353
Dawkins,Gookie	SS	22	.210	104	386	50	81	15	2	7	34	23	93	10	3	.254	.313
Dunn,Adam	OF	21	.311	94	338	61	105	20	0	26	69	49	85	7	2	.398	.601
Gibralter,Steve	OF	28	.258	82	299	43	77	20	0	14	45	18	69	7	1	.300	.465
Gonzalez,Raul	OF	27	.277	142	523	74	145	37	0	9	54	54	72	4	7	.345	.400
Guerrero,Wilton	2B	26	.282	54	220	19	62	13	1	0	23	10	30	9	4	.313	.350
Jennings,Robin	OF	29	.271	77	284	40	77	14	2	10	36	14	58	4	3	.305	.440
Kearns,Austin	OF	21	.250	59	200	25	50	10	1	5	30	19	45	5	4	.315	.385
Larson,Brandon	3B	25	.235	115	413	50	97	21	1	12	45	20	127	3	5	.270	.378
Malloy,Marty	2B	28	.282	126	454	57	128	34	2	5	40	22	53	6	6	.315	.399
Mateo,Ruben	OF	23	.224	79	294	30	66	17	2	1	27	11	54	1	1	.252	.306
Melian,Jackson	OF	21	.221	120	417	54	92	21	0	14	44	26	100	7	6	.266	.372
Metcalfe,Mike	2B	28	.263	129	480	57	126	25	2	2	39	31	67	26	8	.307	.335
Miller,Corky	C	25	.289	103	305	45	88	21	0	14	58	26	52	1	1	.344	.495
Morris,Bobby	2B	28	.261	85	218	29	57	17	0	7	37	30	43	2	3	.351	.436
Nevers,Tom	3B	29	.228	125	412	53	94	31	0	15	58	31	112	3	4	.282	.413
Selby,Bill	2B	31	.237	88	321	38	76	18	0	11	46	21	48	0	0	.284	.396
Sexton,Chris	SS	29	.257	105	397	48	102	23	2	1	38	33	59	3	4	.314	.332
Sheff,Chris	OF	30	.254	94	303	44	77	18	0	7	42	33	75	3	2	.327	.383
Valencia,Vic	C	24	.213	76	225	20	48	7	1	5	28	19	62	1	0	.275	.320
CLEVELAND INDIANS		Age	Avg	G	AB	R	H	2B	3B	HR	RBI	BB	SO	SB	CS	OBP	SLG
Bard,Josh	C	23	.274	87	325	40	89	26	0	5	49	30	50	0	1	.335	.400
Bradley,Milton	OF	23	.249	65	245	35	61	9	1	5	25	37	63	17	2	.348	.355
Budzinski,Mark	OF	27	.249	122	434	66	108	25	3	1	37	26	131	10	4	.291	.327
Coste,Chris	C	28	.265	81	291	29	77	15	1	6	47	14	55	0	2	.298	.385
DePippo,Jeff	C	25	.259	82	239	31	62	10	1	5	27	11	54	4	8	.292	.372
Erickson,Corey	3B	24	.222	136	487	66	108	28	1	21	64	27	144	5	4	.263	.413
Fitzgerald,Jason	OF	25	.269	61	238	22	64	12	0	4	18	8	40	8	2	.293	.370
Garcia,Karim	OF	25	.258	125	458	69	118	15	3	30	81	42	111	3	4	.320	.500
Goelz,Jim	SS	25	.256	105	285	29	73	20	1	0	27	11	48	4	3	.284	.333
Green,Chad	OF	26	.225	100	325	44	73	17	3	4	29	24	105	11	5	.278	.332
Grindell,Nate	3B	24	.281	63	228	33	64	17	0	9	44	8	48	4	4	.305	.474
Hamilton,Jon	OF	23	.275	136	473	59	130	24	3	17	64	35	127	7	12	.325	.446
Hollins,Dave	DH	35	.265	89	313	47	83	24	1	15	64	43	82	0	0	.354	.492
Krause,Scott	DH-OF	27	.249	87	301	46	75	16	0	14	51	22	89	0	3	.300	.442
Laker,Tim	C	31	.240	86	317	43	76	12	0	18	54	26	55	1	1	.297	.448
LaRocca,Greg	3B-SS	28	.304	92	316	52	96	20	0	13	53	26	47	1	3	.357	.491
McDonald,John	SS	26	.236	116	406	49	96	16	0	1	31	31	75	14	10	.291	.283
Medrano,Tony	2B	26	.282	121	461	65	130	27	0	6	49	51	42	17	6	.354	.380
Peoples,Danny	1B	26	.215	106	367	59	79	19	0	16	45	53	139	0	3	.314	.398
Pond,Simon	1B	24	.264	114	386	45	102	29	2	11	45	25	74	1	3	.309	.435
Pratt,Scott	2B	24	.278	68	263	32	73	13	3	4	23	22	51	13	11	.333	.395
Roberts,Dave	OF	29	.272	79	301	40	82	16	3	0	22	24	54	17	6	.326	.346
Sefcik,Kevin	OF-2B	30	.247	119	430	58	106	22	1	6	40	36	46	6	9	.305	.344

437

Major League Equivalencies for 2001 AAA/AA Batters

COLORADO ROCKIES		Age	Avg	G	AB	R	H	2B	3B	HR	RBI	BB	SO	SB	CS	OBP	SLG
Alviso,Jerome	2B	25	.238	111	265	24	63	12	0	1	14	11	40	2	1	.268	.294
Bair,Rod	OF	26	.282	72	284	26	80	14	0	9	33	9	48	4	6	.304	.426
Barnes,John	OF	25	.264	81	299	32	79	19	1	5	32	20	29	2	2	.310	.385
Bartee,Kimera	OF	28	.220	64	236	26	52	12	1	7	30	16	54	5	1	.270	.369
Bell,Mike	3B	26	.283	84	321	35	91	20	0	13	43	13	78	0	4	.311	.467
Brumbaugh,Cliff	OF	27	.314	107	407	60	128	27	2	10	70	57	92	5	5	.399	.464
Burford,Kevin	1B	23	.312	101	375	54	117	23	4	7	37	41	78	3	1	.380	.451
Butler,Brent	2B	23	.337	65	273	41	92	19	2	7	31	12	25	2	2	.365	.498
Carpenter,Bubba	OF	32	.243	109	305	40	74	22	0	2	31	38	58	5	6	.327	.334
Cox,Darron	C	33	.278	76	209	27	58	9	0	3	20	19	41	2	1	.338	.364
Dewey,Jason	C	24	.263	71	251	25	66	23	0	7	28	20	77	0	0	.317	.438
Encarnacion,Mario	OF	23	.278	67	223	29	62	10	1	11	34	16	70	2	4	.326	.480
Espada,Josue	SS	25	.249	86	297	46	74	16	1	2	20	30	57	10	9	.318	.330
Flores,Jose	SS	28	.294	100	316	49	93	20	4	2	29	39	55	5	2	.372	.402
Gload,Ross	OF-1B	25	.268	133	456	56	122	27	7	11	74	28	92	6	7	.310	.430
Huskey,Butch	1B	29	.328	122	461	62	151	28	0	20	71	34	92	1	2	.374	.518
Keck,Brian	SS	27	.291	100	340	37	99	16	1	5	44	20	45	10	5	.331	.388
Kelly,Roberto	OF	36	.291	63	213	26	62	9	0	12	39	14	46	0	2	.335	.502
Kieschnick,Brooks	OF	29	.291	71	251	36	73	8	2	12	36	19	70	2	2	.341	.482
Landaeta,Luis	OF	24	.305	66	249	28	76	12	4	1	24	14	26	6	6	.342	.398
Martinez,Belvani	OF	22	.290	115	448	49	130	23	7	7	39	6	58	24	9	.300	.420
Morales,Willie	C	28	.203	69	212	19	43	6	0	1	11	4	40	2	1	.218	.245
Murphy,Mike	OF	29	.293	114	427	61	125	21	1	9	46	56	113	17	6	.375	.410
Ortiz,Jose	2B	24	.241	65	245	32	59	13	2	5	30	19	51	5	4	.295	.371
Owens,Ryan	3B	23	.286	127	462	72	132	23	2	11	50	60	125	9	5	.368	.416
Peeples,Mike	OF	24	.304	115	427	58	130	22	3	20	56	22	61	6	9	.339	.511
Uribe,Juan	SS	21	.308	77	295	33	91	27	6	7	40	9	44	8	8	.329	.512
DETROIT TIGERS		Age	Avg	G	AB	R	H	2B	3B	HR	RBI	BB	SO	SB	CS	OBP	SLG
Airoso,Kurt	OF	26	.206	92	296	39	61	14	1	10	37	26	71	0	1	.270	.361
Allensworth,J.	OF	29	.244	133	467	46	114	19	5	6	42	40	75	9	9	.304	.345
Becker,Rich	OF	29	.220	117	381	53	84	14	2	7	31	57	106	6	4	.322	.323
Bierek,Kurt	OF	28	.247	105	381	52	94	24	0	12	43	26	77	1	2	.295	.404
Coquillette,Trace	OF	27	.190	83	258	35	49	9	2	7	29	28	68	0	2	.269	.322
Freire,Alejandro	DH	26	.269	133	483	62	130	30	0	12	70	33	117	1	3	.316	.406
Gomez,Rich	OF	23	.243	93	334	51	81	19	1	10	37	18	77	19	7	.281	.395
Guevara,Giomar	SS	28	.209	109	387	40	81	13	2	4	29	27	98	5	2	.261	.284
Infante,Omar	SS	19	.279	132	523	73	146	19	3	1	52	33	90	19	7	.322	.333
Lindsey,Rod	OF	25	.230	111	374	43	86	12	0	1	29	16	79	21	8	.262	.270
McClure,Brian	3B-2B	27	.233	75	249	24	58	12	1	0	18	16	46	0	0	.279	.289
Mendez,Carlos	1B-C	27	.217	102	383	36	83	24	0	12	61	7	53	0	0	.231	.373
Munson,Eric	1B	23	.241	142	506	75	122	32	0	21	87	61	146	0	3	.323	.429
Patterson,Jarrod	3B	27	.297	89	273	47	81	17	1	10	35	32	58	1	1	.370	.476
Perez,Jhonny	2B	24	.238	115	400	50	95	17	3	3	36	21	71	12	6	.276	.318
Rios,Brian	3B	26	.293	104	355	38	104	25	4	9	50	18	67	1	4	.327	.462
Rivera,Mike	C	24	.259	112	398	64	103	17	0	23	86	32	99	1	2	.314	.475
Santana,Pedro	2B	24	.203	115	419	36	85	8	2	3	24	22	98	26	10	.243	.253
Simon,Randall	1B	26	.310	59	213	22	66	11	0	7	25	17	21	0	3	.361	.460
Torres,Andres	OF	23	.270	64	244	46	66	14	2	0	19	26	50	13	11	.341	.344
Ust,Brant	3B	22	.217	87	314	30	68	14	0	4	26	11	84	0	1	.243	.299
Wakeland,Chris	OF	27	.259	140	529	69	137	29	2	17	68	32	128	5	8	.301	.418

Major League Equivalencies for 2001 AAA/AA Batters

FLORIDA MARLINS		Age	Avg	G	AB	R	H	2B	3B	HR	RBI	BB	SO	SB	CS	OBP	SLG
Aguila,Chris	OF	22	.232	64	233	20	54	14	0	3	24	13	54	3	7	.272	.330
Bailey,Jeff	1B	22	.215	129	418	46	90	24	1	10	55	46	148	4	2	.293	.349
Banks,Brian	1B	30	.232	118	371	47	86	21	3	13	44	24	116	3	4	.278	.410
Candelaria,Ben	OF	26	.269	90	242	24	65	18	0	3	31	15	34	0	1	.311	.380
Castro,Ramon	C	25	.281	108	360	53	101	25	0	16	59	25	79	0	1	.327	.483
Clapinski,Chris	2B-SS	29	.201	63	204	25	41	7	0	4	14	13	48	0	2	.249	.294
Erickson,Matt	SS-2B	25	.258	115	384	43	99	16	0	1	19	26	73	7	4	.305	.307
Gillespie,Eric	OF	26	.202	82	233	23	47	14	1	3	29	21	49	2	1	.268	.309
Gulan,Mike	3B	30	.269	124	449	51	121	34	1	13	60	23	155	1	6	.305	.437
Harper,Brandon	C	25	.213	76	239	17	51	11	0	2	20	19	56	0	0	.271	.285
Honeycutt,Heath	3B	24	.217	132	460	46	100	21	1	7	49	29	140	7	8	.264	.313
Hooper,Kevin	2B	24	.282	117	451	58	127	16	5	1	32	42	85	17	6	.343	.346
Lamb,David	SS-2B	26	.285	110	368	43	105	23	0	7	37	40	51	1	3	.355	.405
Martin,Paco	2B	34	.255	93	310	29	79	15	3	3	25	9	43	5	3	.276	.352
McGuire,Ryan	OF-1B	29	.248	62	222	29	55	11	1	4	27	17	52	0	1	.301	.360
Mottola,Chad	OF	29	.246	119	427	43	105	18	1	9	43	20	91	7	5	.280	.356
Nunez,Abraham	OF	21	.216	136	453	62	98	12	8	12	44	60	171	18	7	.308	.358
Waszgis,B.J.	C	30	.205	96	293	32	60	14	0	14	42	20	96	0	1	.256	.396
Wathan,Derek	SS	24	.229	127	455	54	104	10	7	2	29	33	91	18	7	.281	.295
HOUSTON ASTROS		**Age**	**Avg**	**G**	**AB**	**R**	**H**	**2B**	**3B**	**HR**	**RBI**	**BB**	**SO**	**SB**	**CS**	**OBP**	**SLG**
Alfaro,Jason	2B	23	.232	87	280	23	65	15	1	1	26	5	43	1	1	.246	.304
Bruntlett,Eric	SS	23	.250	128	511	78	128	22	2	2	36	39	83	17	6	.304	.313
Burns,Kevin	1B-DH	25	.266	123	402	69	107	24	3	21	60	48	104	1	1	.344	.498
Carter,Charley	1B	25	.253	133	518	58	131	25	0	23	87	26	114	0	1	.289	.434
Chamblee,Jim	2B	26	.225	114	404	35	91	23	0	9	29	28	123	5	5	.275	.349
Charles,Frank	C	32	.224	71	237	13	53	10	0	0	21	9	59	0	1	.252	.266
Chavez,Raul	C	27	.297	85	276	36	82	17	0	8	38	18	36	0	1	.340	.446
Cole,Eric	OF	25	.259	121	394	44	102	25	1	3	39	36	99	0	4	.321	.350
Ensberg,Morgan	3B	25	.306	87	314	62	96	20	0	23	58	43	63	4	3	.389	.589
Everett,Adam	SS	24	.246	114	439	66	108	20	7	5	38	37	78	19	7	.305	.358
Ginter,Keith	2B	25	.266	132	455	72	121	31	4	16	66	58	155	6	6	.349	.457
Huffman,Royce	3B	24	.298	137	503	67	150	34	0	3	44	39	97	9	8	.349	.384
Lane,Jason	OF	24	.306	137	519	93	159	35	1	36	112	46	106	10	2	.363	.586
Logan,Kyle	OF	25	.306	73	255	32	78	21	2	6	28	14	47	9	3	.342	.475
Luuloa,Keith	2B	26	.234	100	303	40	71	18	1	5	24	23	43	0	1	.288	.350
Lydy,Scott	OF	32	.260	95	281	35	73	20	0	7	41	44	65	6	5	.360	.406
Maldonado,Carlos	C	22	.275	76	258	26	71	13	0	3	29	20	59	0	2	.327	.360
Matranga,Dave	2B	24	.290	107	396	72	115	34	1	10	56	34	103	12	7	.347	.457
Mouton,Lyle	OF	32	.280	69	257	48	72	17	1	13	39	23	70	2	1	.339	.506
Porter,Colin	OF	25	.254	126	410	57	104	18	4	9	41	35	138	8	9	.312	.383
Ramirez,Omar	OF	30	.244	118	360	38	88	20	0	2	37	27	44	7	4	.297	.317
Tremie,Chris	C	31	.206	74	233	25	48	7	0	4	26	19	37	0	4	.266	.288
Truby,Chris	3B-1B	27	.307	81	319	50	98	25	5	12	67	22	69	8	5	.352	.530
Wesson,Barry	OF	24	.244	133	467	60	114	22	6	15	48	31	146	15	6	.291	.413
Zinter,Alan	1B	33	.263	104	331	55	87	16	0	21	62	31	90	0	1	.326	.502
KANSAS CITY ROYALS		**Age**	**Avg**	**G**	**AB**	**R**	**H**	**2B**	**3B**	**HR**	**RBI**	**BB**	**SO**	**SB**	**CS**	**OBP**	**SLG**
Berger,Brandon	OF	26	.288	120	441	82	127	25	2	34	98	30	93	10	5	.333	.585
Berroa,Angel	SS	21	.277	80	296	52	82	17	3	6	35	11	56	10	5	.303	.416
Brito,Juan	C	21	.248	70	230	18	57	8	0	3	23	11	29	2	2	.282	.322
Calderon,Henry	3B	23	.245	97	319	41	78	18	4	4	41	12	52	2	7	.272	.364

Major League Equivalencies for 2001 AAA/AA Batters

KANSAS CITY ROYALS		Age	Avg	G	AB	R	H	2B	3B	HR	RBI	BB	SO	SB	CS	OBP	SLG
Caruso,Joe	OF	26	.245	120	413	62	101	23	0	6	49	34	66	8	5	.302	.344
Chavez,Endy	OF	23	.294	66	265	37	78	10	0	0	13	11	26	10	7	.322	.332
Delgado,Wilson	2B	25	.232	76	250	20	58	9	2	3	26	13	42	6	2	.270	.320
Dillon,Joe	1B	25	.267	101	359	51	96	17	2	12	49	25	61	2	2	.315	.426
Gallagher,Shawn	DH-1B	24	.246	96	337	36	83	17	3	10	40	17	63	3	6	.282	.404
Gomez,Alexis	OF	20	.263	83	334	46	88	13	5	3	28	18	71	11	9	.301	.359
Guiel,Aaron	OF	28	.252	121	433	67	109	24	2	18	63	43	92	4	3	.319	.441
Hansen,Jed	OF	28	.253	97	336	46	85	19	0	10	24	34	96	10	6	.322	.399
Harvey,Ken	1B	23	.316	79	304	45	96	17	2	7	52	12	61	2	0	.342	.454
Metzler,Rod	2B	26	.264	110	371	51	98	17	3	3	51	31	81	9	10	.321	.350
Nunnally,Jon	OF	29	.196	97	311	43	61	8	0	15	46	45	109	8	2	.298	.367
Ortiz,Nicky	SS	27	.235	99	310	33	73	18	0	5	34	28	65	1	5	.299	.342
Pellow,Kit	1B	27	.275	129	473	70	130	13	0	17	70	31	101	3	2	.319	.410
Prieto,Alejandro	3B-2B	25	.266	105	368	39	98	19	2	7	38	30	59	6	1	.322	.386
Shackelford,Brian	OF	24	.241	110	357	51	86	16	2	16	60	23	81	2	3	.287	.431
Tonis,Mike	C	22	.250	63	220	30	55	9	0	7	36	15	42	0	0	.298	.386
Watkins,Pat	OF	28	.238	67	240	25	57	10	0	6	25	11	41	1	6	.271	.354
LA DODGERS		Age	Avg	G	AB	R	H	2B	3B	HR	RBI	BB	SO	SB	CS	OBP	SLG
Allen,Luke	OF	22	.261	127	476	65	124	27	3	14	64	31	118	9	3	.306	.418
Aven,Bruce	OF	29	.217	86	276	30	60	13	0	5	22	16	61	3	1	.260	.319
Branson,Jeff	2B-SS	34	.228	96	272	19	62	13	0	2	14	18	74	2	2	.276	.298
Chen,Chin-Feng	OF-DH	23	.284	66	215	41	61	13	1	14	44	30	69	3	4	.371	.549
Christensen,M.	OF	25	.254	85	323	57	82	15	5	7	26	33	65	16	4	.323	.396
Crosby,Bubba	OF	24	.262	120	408	63	107	20	3	5	44	27	72	16	7	.308	.363
Davis,Glenn	1B	25	.218	134	463	54	101	23	4	17	78	49	152	10	5	.293	.395
Dent,Darrell	OF	24	.253	117	363	44	92	12	1	3	28	31	97	22	9	.312	.317
Gilbert,Shawn	2B-SS	36	.279	59	208	17	58	10	1	5	25	13	45	7	4	.321	.409
Hiatt,Phil	3B	32	.279	113	405	75	113	22	2	30	69	36	114	4	4	.338	.565
Johnson,Keith	SS	30	.207	125	411	38	85	24	2	8	35	11	91	2	5	.227	.333
Mota,Tony	OF	23	.247	120	413	43	102	21	3	5	40	27	82	10	7	.293	.349
Nunez,Jorge	SS	23	.236	123	458	55	108	12	1	3	24	24	94	33	13	.274	.286
Prieto,Chris	OF	28	.244	118	418	69	102	20	3	13	40	46	82	16	6	.319	.400
Riggs,Eric	3B	24	.231	118	381	45	88	22	0	5	31	31	52	5	4	.289	.328
Rosario,Mel	C	28	.224	84	255	22	57	12	2	7	33	6	68	0	5	.241	.369
Ross,Dave	C	24	.239	74	238	30	57	11	0	9	39	25	77	0	1	.312	.399
Thurston,Joe	2B	21	.241	134	526	70	127	21	4	6	40	35	69	14	5	.289	.331
MILWAUKEE BREWERS		Age	Avg	G	AB	R	H	2B	3B	HR	RBI	BB	SO	SB	CS	OBP	SLG
Barker,Kevin	1B	25	.253	117	383	46	97	18	0	10	50	42	95	0	1	.327	.379
Brown,Kevin	C	28	.209	82	282	15	59	14	0	7	28	14	114	0	0	.247	.333
Cancel,Robinson	C	25	.179	80	251	20	45	5	0	0	18	11	57	0	4	.214	.199
Cesar,Dionys	SS	24	.272	95	346	43	94	20	0	7	41	27	75	2	2	.324	.390
Collier,Lou	OF	27	.262	86	301	39	79	15	1	11	29	19	66	6	2	.306	.429
Coolbaugh,Mike	3B	29	.244	94	336	40	82	21	2	8	41	32	95	2	1	.310	.390
Cridland,Mark	OF	26	.217	70	230	22	50	7	0	6	27	9	59	2	3	.247	.326
Fox,Jason	OF	24	.230	90	283	28	65	9	1	2	25	13	77	14	6	.264	.290
Franklin,Micah	OF	29	.208	110	322	44	67	10	2	20	52	38	75	0	2	.292	.438
Gibralter,Dave	OF-1B	26	.264	122	440	56	116	25	0	13	57	31	60	0	1	.312	.409
Jacobsen,Bucky	1B	25	.268	113	380	52	102	24	0	17	68	32	95	0	1	.325	.466
Jones,Chris	OF	35	.228	100	307	36	70	6	1	7	33	26	88	5	5	.288	.322
Klimek,Josh	3B	27	.262	126	405	53	106	16	1	17	48	42	95	1	0	.331	.432

Major League Equivalencies for 2001 AAA/AA Batters

MILWAUKEE BREWERS		Age	Avg	G	AB	R	H	2B	3B	HR	RBI	BB	SO	SB	CS	OBP	SLG
Lesher,Brian	OF	30	.257	93	334	42	86	15	2	5	52	33	81	0	0	.324	.359
Levis,Jesse	C	33	.246	79	224	17	55	5	0	1	26	20	21	1	0	.307	.281
Mathis,Jared	OF	25	.230	87	200	13	46	10	0	1	15	4	26	0	0	.245	.295
Moon,Brian	C	23	.145	97	283	15	41	10	1	0	14	15	52	0	1	.188	.187
Pena,Elvis	SS	24	.219	127	425	46	93	13	2	0	23	24	78	8	4	.261	.259
Perez,Robert	OF	32	.295	56	220	26	65	14	2	7	35	6	35	4	5	.314	.473
Pickler,Jeff	2B	25	.273	134	513	66	140	15	1	0	28	45	54	25	9	.332	.306
Sanchez,Alex	OF	24	.288	83	323	42	93	12	3	0	21	18	45	19	7	.326	.344
Sanchez,W.	SS	24	.212	89	208	25	44	9	0	0	12	16	59	2	2	.268	.255
Scutaro,Marcos	2B	25	.270	132	478	71	129	25	2	9	41	51	86	8	10	.340	.387
Sell,Chip	OF	30	.230	128	352	33	81	15	1	4	33	13	81	4	2	.258	.313
Sweeney,Mark	OF-DH	31	.263	109	391	53	103	30	0	5	57	46	73	2	0	.341	.379
MINNESOTA TWINS		Age	Avg	G	AB	R	H	2B	3B	HR	RBI	BB	SO	SB	CS	OBP	SLG
Ardoin,Danny	C	26	.227	88	291	28	66	16	0	3	28	16	86	1	6	.267	.313
Cuddyer,Mike	3B-1B	22	.284	141	497	83	141	35	2	25	76	56	115	3	9	.356	.513
Diaz,Edwin	2B	26	.245	113	367	45	90	23	2	8	43	19	69	2	6	.282	.384
Ford,Lew	OF	24	.202	62	247	26	50	8	2	5	22	14	38	3	5	.245	.312
Kielty,Bobby	OF	24	.259	94	328	44	85	23	1	9	38	40	82	3	0	.340	.418
LeCroy,Matt	DH	25	.294	101	377	40	111	15	0	14	61	27	101	0	2	.342	.446
Lorenzo,Juan	SS-3B	23	.220	101	313	28	69	9	2	2	21	3	35	1	2	.228	.281
Marsters,Brandon	C	26	.207	100	343	30	71	15	0	7	31	21	81	1	1	.253	.312
McCracken,Q.	OF	31	.307	81	345	40	106	25	3	3	34	16	58	5	10	.338	.423
Mohr,Dustan	OF	25	.319	135	505	79	161	40	2	20	80	36	121	6	9	.364	.525
Moriarty,Mike	SS	27	.215	131	390	50	84	15	1	9	38	44	100	3	4	.295	.328
Peterman,Tommy	1B	26	.226	88	297	30	67	15	0	2	29	15	43	0	1	.263	.296
Restovich,Mike	OF	22	.255	140	491	60	125	32	3	19	74	40	136	11	7	.311	.448
Ryan,Mike	OF	23	.262	135	508	68	133	33	5	14	56	40	129	0	6	.316	.429
Salazar,Ruben	2B	23	.282	137	518	61	146	28	1	8	58	27	84	4	1	.317	.386
Sears,Todd	1B	25	.281	118	391	47	110	23	1	9	38	31	76	1	1	.334	.414
Smith,Jeff	C	27	.270	102	344	33	93	14	0	6	37	11	62	0	0	.293	.363
Smith,Nestor	OF	23	.235	95	289	25	68	5	7	2	14	5	81	3	6	.248	.322
Stevens,Tony	SS	22	.161	72	242	16	39	7	0	0	18	7	32	2	3	.185	.190
Sutton,Larry	1B-OF	31	.228	74	237	26	54	10	2	3	28	34	50	0	2	.325	.325
Valentin,Javier	C	25	.253	121	415	40	105	27	1	13	54	36	117	0	1	.313	.417
MONTREAL EXPOS		Age	Avg	G	AB	R	H	2B	3B	HR	RBI	BB	SO	SB	CS	OBP	SLG
Bergeron,Peter	OF	23	.223	52	202	25	45	4	2	0	6	17	44	11	6	.283	.262
Calloway,Ron	OF	24	.281	135	505	65	142	32	3	15	71	30	116	26	7	.321	.446
Carroll,Jamey	2B	27	.222	83	261	22	58	7	1	0	13	15	43	3	4	.264	.257
Cepicky,Matt	OF	23	.247	122	449	51	111	22	6	15	67	15	103	3	11	.272	.423
Cotton,John	3B	30	.200	101	305	28	61	11	0	11	39	16	99	1	2	.240	.344
de la Rosa,Tomas	SS	23	.221	121	411	48	91	23	0	5	26	34	66	9	8	.281	.314
Gonzalez,Jimmy	C	28	.161	58	211	15	34	7	0	5	16	6	51	0	0	.184	.265
Hodges,Scott	3B	22	.258	85	298	26	77	10	1	4	28	18	59	2	1	.301	.339
Machado,Albenis	2B	22	.246	99	334	50	82	13	2	2	28	32	59	7	6	.311	.314
Mateo,Henry	2B	24	.250	118	488	61	122	14	9	3	37	28	93	36	13	.291	.334
McKinley,Dan	OF	25	.264	105	352	26	93	17	4	4	33	17	89	9	5	.298	.369
Myers,Tootie	OF	22	.245	123	387	43	95	14	6	8	43	25	126	12	6	.291	.375
Nunnari,Talmadge	1B	26	.198	119	368	33	73	15	0	3	33	32	91	10	1	.263	.264
Pascucci,Val	OF	22	.227	138	466	69	106	16	0	18	58	48	122	5	7	.300	.378
Phillips,Brandon	SS	20	.279	67	258	30	72	18	0	6	31	8	44	9	5	.301	.419

Major League Equivalencies for 2001 AAA/AA Batters

MONTREAL EXPOS		Age	Avg	G	AB	R	H	2B	3B	HR	RBI	BB	SO	SB	CS	OBP	SLG
Reding,Josh	SS	24	.181	123	382	21	69	8	3	2	30	13	106	7	4	.208	.233
Sandusky,Scott	C	25	.232	114	379	31	88	19	0	1	20	25	81	5	1	.280	.290
Schneider,Brian	C	24	.260	97	331	28	86	26	0	4	37	23	57	1	0	.308	.375
Seguignol,F.	1B	26	.289	60	235	31	68	12	0	11	39	12	51	0	0	.324	.481
Sledge,Terrmel	1B	24	.262	129	439	57	115	21	4	7	42	37	77	22	8	.319	.376
Thompson,Ryan	OF	33	.230	99	361	39	83	23	0	12	52	11	92	2	4	.253	.393
Ware,Jeremy	OF	25	.254	80	228	21	58	17	0	3	25	10	39	1	0	.286	.368
Wilkerson,Brad	OF	24	.251	69	227	37	57	9	0	9	41	51	71	9	4	.388	.410
NEW YORK METS		Age	Avg	G	AB	R	H	2B	3B	HR	RBI	BB	SO	SB	CS	OBP	SLG
Baez,Kevin	SS	34	.195	100	302	29	59	14	0	3	23	27	65	0	3	.261	.272
Curry,Mike	OF	24	.249	119	417	54	104	13	3	3	22	35	126	17	7	.308	.317
Dina,Allen	OF	27	.233	92	270	26	63	14	0	2	29	11	59	6	6	.263	.307
Escobar,Alex	OF	22	.242	111	384	46	93	18	3	9	44	29	154	13	3	.295	.375
Figueroa,Luis	SS	27	.267	109	390	41	104	12	0	3	27	29	32	5	5	.317	.321
Franco,Matt	3B	31	.223	124	421	41	94	22	0	6	40	43	76	3	2	.295	.318
Hernandez,Carlos	2B	25	.247	126	441	57	109	19	0	3	33	26	77	15	6	.289	.311
Hunter,Scott	OF	25	.245	130	473	54	116	17	3	12	58	10	92	13	9	.261	.370
LeBron,Juan	OF	24	.215	113	349	34	75	13	3	13	41	26	130	1	4	.269	.381
Martinez,Gabby	2B	27	.233	73	227	23	53	10	1	0	13	12	35	11	7	.272	.286
McNeal,Aaron	1B	23	.219	129	470	44	103	17	0	13	46	20	140	0	4	.251	.338
Nye,Rodney	3B	24	.239	109	351	36	84	19	0	5	36	33	88	3	5	.305	.336
Phillips,Jason	C	24	.262	112	366	39	96	19	0	9	55	25	35	0	1	.309	.388
Randolph,Jaisen	OF	22	.214	113	398	44	85	10	0	0	15	44	70	17	11	.292	.239
Snyder,Earl	1B	25	.255	120	404	59	103	32	1	14	62	41	121	2	3	.324	.443
Stratton,Rob	OF	23	.215	135	470	56	101	25	0	21	68	35	219	6	5	.269	.402
Tamargo,John	2B	26	.238	89	252	19	60	8	0	0	17	18	37	2	3	.289	.270
Tarasco,Tony	OF	30	.268	105	354	45	95	27	3	5	48	40	45	10	8	.343	.404
Toca,Jorge	1B-OF	26	.244	111	394	45	96	11	0	8	43	19	66	8	2	.278	.332
Velandia,Jorge	SS	26	.226	67	252	21	57	18	0	3	31	13	49	6	4	.264	.333
Velazquez,Gil	SS	21	.182	106	347	26	63	9	1	2	15	17	90	0	1	.220	.231
Wigginton,Ty	3B-2B	23	.227	86	278	28	63	12	0	5	20	25	74	2	3	.290	.324
Wilson,Vance	C	28	.222	65	221	20	49	12	0	4	26	10	36	0	1	.255	.330
NEW YORK YANKEES		Age	Avg	G	AB	R	H	2B	3B	HR	RBI	BB	SO	SB	CS	OBP	SLG
Almonte,Erick	SS	23	.259	100	344	47	89	17	2	10	46	37	100	3	5	.331	.407
Bragg,Darren	OF-DH	31	.279	85	287	43	80	12	1	9	22	41	76	5	4	.369	.422
Bridges,Kary	2B	28	.273	109	395	49	108	15	0	4	32	30	30	3	8	.325	.342
Cervenak,Mike	3B	24	.257	128	452	56	116	34	0	9	54	33	80	1	4	.307	.392
Frank,Mike	OF	26	.231	106	346	37	80	18	1	8	44	34	54	8	3	.300	.358
Garcia,Carlos	3B	33	.230	61	209	18	48	10	0	2	16	11	40	6	1	.268	.306
Henson,Drew	3B	21	.210	76	281	25	59	5	0	9	33	8	93	1	2	.232	.324
Johnson,Nick	1B	22	.235	110	349	57	82	18	0	15	41	68	110	6	2	.360	.415
Leon,Donny	3B-DH	25	.230	128	469	43	108	23	1	13	68	16	137	0	2	.256	.367
Loggins,Josh	OF	24	.224	86	259	30	58	13	0	2	29	16	84	1	2	.269	.297
Matos,Pascual	C	26	.197	77	249	19	49	10	0	3	21	10	62	0	3	.228	.273
McDonald,Donzell	OF	26	.234	105	363	49	85	9	5	6	30	35	82	15	5	.302	.336
Mosquera,Julio	C	29	.246	104	301	32	74	17	0	8	30	10	78	1	1	.270	.382
Olivares,Teuris	SS	22	.197	128	431	49	85	13	2	3	27	16	99	3	4	.226	.258
Ottavinia,Paul	1B-OF	28	.244	118	438	62	107	26	3	6	41	33	64	10	5	.297	.358
Rivera,Juan	OF	22	.299	132	498	77	149	25	2	23	85	23	85	6	12	.330	.496
Rodriquez,John	OF	23	.268	103	384	57	103	28	0	20	59	19	125	1	3	.303	.497

Major League Equivalencies for 2001 AAA/AA Batters

NEW YORK YANKEES		Age	Avg	G	AB	R	H	2B	3B	HR	RBI	BB	SO	SB	CS	OBP	SLG
Rodriguez,Victor	2B	24	.274	57	212	29	58	8	0	2	15	11	19	1	3	.309	.340
Seabol,Scott	3B	26	.239	109	398	40	95	23	0	11	52	14	90	2	5	.265	.379
Thames,Marcus	OF	24	.301	139	505	102	152	39	2	27	87	55	108	7	4	.370	.547
Tyson,Torre	OF	25	.228	71	219	38	50	7	0	0	12	26	52	6	3	.310	.260
Wilcox,Luke	OF	27	.199	80	251	22	50	12	0	7	39	17	52	0	2	.250	.331
OAKLAND ATHLETICS		Age	Avg	G	AB	R	H	2B	3B	HR	RBI	BB	SO	SB	CS	OBP	SLG
Abad,Andy	OF	28	.268	124	441	57	118	16	1	14	65	45	69	2	2	.335	.404
Byrnes,Eric	OF	25	.257	100	397	64	102	19	1	15	40	25	68	18	7	.301	.423
Ellis,Mark	SS	24	.243	132	453	56	110	32	0	7	42	42	81	15	6	.307	.360
German,Esteban	2B	22	.274	130	460	91	126	23	2	7	34	54	89	32	10	.350	.378
Hart,Jason	1B	23	.218	134	476	56	104	22	0	14	59	44	106	2	3	.285	.353
Hinske,Eric	3B	23	.249	121	417	56	104	23	0	18	62	42	117	14	5	.318	.434
Hochgesang,Josh	3B	24	.199	83	291	36	58	15	2	4	25	19	89	5	3	.248	.306
Keith,Rusty	OF	23	.227	89	278	29	63	17	0	2	23	29	45	0	4	.300	.309
Landry,Jacques	OF	27	.210	134	486	78	102	11	2	27	72	40	195	24	10	.270	.407
Lockwood,Mike	OF	24	.227	131	472	54	107	30	2	4	53	31	84	6	4	.274	.324
Luderer,Brian	C	22	.224	86	294	23	66	17	0	3	26	14	51	0	1	.260	.313
Ludwick,Ryan	OF	22	.230	136	478	70	110	21	2	18	78	36	135	7	10	.284	.395
McKay,Cody	C	27	.232	99	336	28	78	16	0	4	32	21	66	0	0	.277	.315
Mensik,Todd	1B	26	.247	132	478	53	118	29	0	15	60	38	110	0	1	.302	.402
Pecci,Jay	2B-SS	24	.227	125	449	55	102	25	4	2	37	26	58	10	7	.269	.314
Ryan,Rob	OF	28	.243	125	415	61	101	20	5	14	62	51	88	0	6	.326	.417
Salazar,Oscar	SS	23	.226	135	513	57	116	26	2	13	72	31	111	6	3	.270	.361
Wilson,Tom	C	30	.250	77	248	34	62	12	0	6	38	38	64	0	1	.350	.371
PHIL. PHILLIES		Age	Avg	G	AB	R	H	2B	3B	HR	RBI	BB	SO	SB	CS	OBP	SLG
Burnham,Gary	1B	26	.293	109	358	47	105	24	1	12	62	24	46	0	1	.338	.466
Byrd,Marlon	OF	23	.289	137	491	87	142	21	6	22	72	36	101	22	8	.338	.491
Casillas,Uriel	3B	25	.217	113	373	37	81	16	1	3	32	18	51	2	4	.253	.290
Dominique,Andy	C-1B	25	.223	116	386	48	86	21	0	11	55	37	85	2	0	.291	.363
Forbes,P.J.	2B	33	.292	133	504	71	147	29	1	4	55	44	77	3	0	.349	.377
Francia,Dave	OF	26	.216	110	342	30	74	13	1	2	33	42	62	14	6	.266	.278
Gonzalez,Manny	OF	25	.259	73	255	27	66	19	0	2	19	9	44	1	3	.284	.357
Harris,Brian	2B-SS	26	.223	135	497	57	111	27	4	10	47	32	68	14	5	.270	.354
Knupfer,Jason	2B	26	.228	90	272	37	62	12	1	0	22	27	63	7	4	.298	.279
Lopez,Mickey	2B	27	.249	107	370	57	92	18	5	9	38	44	64	14	5	.329	.397
Michaels,Jason	OF	25	.248	109	411	52	102	19	2	15	62	34	134	8	2	.306	.414
Orie,Kevin	3B	28	.280	134	500	69	140	34	1	11	40	70	67	8	5	.368	.418
Punto,Nick	SS	23	.217	123	456	51	99	20	4	0	35	63	123	25	9	.312	.279
Roberge,J.P.	3B	28	.285	113	424	58	121	20	0	15	66	25	62	8	3	.325	.439
Schall,Gene	1B	31	.267	73	258	36	69	20	0	12	48	28	61	0	0	.339	.484
Taylor,Reggie	OF	24	.252	111	457	50	115	20	7	6	45	22	100	24	9	.286	.365
Valdez,Jerry	C	27	.227	79	247	25	56	13	1	7	32	7	54	0	1	.248	.372
Valent,Eric	OF	24	.262	117	442	58	116	30	1	19	70	45	112	0	0	.331	.464
Van Iten,Bobby	C-1B	23	.208	113	394	37	82	22	0	5	42	25	131	0	0	.255	.302
Walbeck,Matt	C	31	.239	107	330	32	79	17	0	3	38	29	47	0	1	.301	.318
Ward,Turner	DH	36	.265	70	219	25	58	23	3	3	24	28	33	7	0	.348	.438
PITTSBURGH PIRATES		Age	Avg	G	AB	R	H	2B	3B	HR	RBI	BB	SO	SB	CS	OBP	SLG
Alvarez,Tony	OF	22	.300	67	247	30	74	15	0	5	22	6	31	13	11	.316	.421
Barkett,Andy	1B	26	.219	91	265	30	58	15	0	4	34	30	47	1	2	.298	.321
Berblinger,Jeff	2B	30	.208	79	283	33	59	10	2	4	19	18	58	6	4	.256	.300

Major League Equivalencies for 2001 AAA/AA Batters

PITTSBURGH PIRATES		Age	Avg	G	AB	R	H	2B	3B	HR	RBI	BB	SO	SB	CS	OBP	SLG
Burton,Darren	OF	28	.271	85	292	32	79	14	1	6	28	17	64	3	1	.311	.387
Cota,Humberto	C	22	.270	111	363	49	98	20	1	10	58	20	76	5	2	.308	.413
Davis,J.J.	OF	22	.233	67	223	18	52	12	2	3	23	15	82	1	5	.282	.345
Evans,Lee	C	23	.232	118	419	47	97	20	5	9	42	28	120	9	5	.280	.368
Haverbusch,Kevin	2B	25	.272	93	290	34	79	15	2	6	40	6	58	2	3	.287	.400
Hermansen,Chad	OF	23	.222	123	433	61	96	20	4	13	51	33	158	16	6	.277	.376
Hernandez,Alex	1B-OF	24	.267	88	329	36	88	14	0	6	29	10	66	2	4	.289	.365
House,J.R.	C	21	.242	112	417	45	101	23	0	9	50	28	108	0	1	.290	.362
Hyzdu,Adam	OF	29	.263	69	251	31	66	15	1	8	31	13	69	0	3	.299	.426
Lopez,Mendy	2B	26	.275	63	207	35	57	11	0	14	34	17	51	1	2	.330	.531
Meier,Dan	OF	23	.239	97	305	38	73	13	2	11	33	34	83	0	1	.316	.403
Morris,Warren	2B	27	.276	57	214	21	59	14	1	4	32	9	21	2	4	.305	.407
Nelson,Bryant	3B-2B	27	.274	134	489	45	134	19	0	7	43	20	37	8	8	.303	.356
Paz,Rich	2B-3B	23	.222	85	243	26	54	14	0	3	26	39	57	5	6	.330	.317
Radmanovich,R.	OF	29	.244	123	377	52	92	21	0	15	57	60	113	1	4	.348	.419
Redman,Tike	OF	24	.275	95	382	43	105	16	7	2	34	19	38	15	6	.309	.369
Rivera,Carlos	1B	23	.220	111	382	39	84	28	0	8	44	9	74	0	2	.238	.356
Secrist,Reed	3B	31	.266	108	338	49	90	18	0	17	49	39	89	2	0	.342	.470
Skrehot,Shaun	SS	25	.245	135	514	60	126	30	4	5	45	28	78	18	9	.284	.348
Stoner,Mike	OF	28	.266	87	293	39	78	13	3	4	46	13	40	0	3	.297	.372
Washington,Rico	3B	23	.285	75	284	27	81	16	0	3	25	15	51	3	5	.321	.373
Wood,Jason	3B	31	.220	113	368	37	81	17	0	6	31	22	75	0	0	.264	.315
ST. LOUIS CARDINALS		Age	Avg	G	AB	R	H	2B	3B	HR	RBI	BB	SO	SB	CS	OBP	SLG
Balfe,Ryan	OF	25	.268	118	410	48	110	27	1	10	51	34	117	0	3	.324	.412
Bevins,Andy	OF	25	.200	142	485	59	97	20	0	17	53	38	118	3	9	.258	.346
Bowers,Jason	SS	23	.231	137	454	33	105	18	3	3	31	20	118	7	10	.264	.304
Brown,Brant	1B	30	.218	102	331	42	72	10	0	7	25	26	110	1	2	.275	.311
Clapp,Stubby	2B	28	.278	86	288	38	80	12	5	4	26	35	48	5	4	.356	.396
Eckelman,Alex	2B	26	.202	130	406	30	82	16	0	4	35	16	72	11	5	.232	.271
Farnsworth,Troy	3B	25	.223	115	417	44	93	20	0	17	65	22	111	3	7	.262	.393
Frias,Hanley	SS-2B	27	.197	107	371	32	73	12	1	1	20	20	76	5	7	.238	.243
Garcia,Luis	SS	26	.232	118	409	33	95	17	0	5	35	6	74	1	1	.243	.311
Green,S.	OF	27	.215	107	302	27	65	7	0	0	17	27	75	17	5	.280	.238
Lucca,Lou	3B	30	.240	135	463	46	111	28	0	7	51	22	70	1	3	.274	.346
Maier,T.J.	2B	26	.266	80	267	46	71	19	1	3	32	31	65	6	4	.342	.378
Mashore,Damon	OF	31	.270	79	278	28	75	15	0	5	29	14	65	2	4	.305	.378
McDonald,Keith	C	28	.236	94	322	33	76	19	0	8	33	19	62	0	0	.279	.370
McNaughton,Troy	OF	26	.218	121	404	57	88	28	2	7	36	30	120	4	10	.272	.349
Munoz,Juan	1B	27	.265	126	449	36	119	18	1	8	52	19	51	7	7	.295	.363
Ortega,Bill	OF	24	.260	134	477	44	124	23	2	4	50	32	77	4	6	.306	.342
Saturria,Luis	OF	24	.205	127	429	54	88	16	3	10	42	27	127	4	8	.252	.326
Snead,Esix	OF	25	.222	133	513	66	114	20	4	1	30	35	123	50	19	.272	.283
Whitmore,Darrell	OF	32	.252	112	317	38	80	19	0	9	42	17	64	1	3	.290	.397
SAN DIEGO PADRES		Age	Avg	G	AB	R	H	2B	3B	HR	RBI	BB	SO	SB	CS	OBP	SLG
Alvarez,Gabe	3B	27	.237	99	329	50	78	22	0	14	42	44	86	2	3	.327	.432
Benjamin,Al	OF	23	.255	110	365	46	93	20	1	10	46	13	79	6	3	.280	.397
Burroughs,Sean	3B	20	.297	104	380	54	113	24	0	7	49	32	57	6	2	.352	.416
Colangelo,Mike	OF	24	.240	70	208	28	50	9	0	2	22	30	55	3	3	.336	.313
Crespo,Cesar	2B	22	.238	78	265	41	63	14	1	6	26	33	71	17	7	.322	.366
Davidson,Cleatus	SS	24	.203	125	458	35	93	15	2	1	31	17	111	9	8	.232	.251

444

Major League Equivalencies for 2001 AAA/AA Batters

SAN DIEGO PADRES		Age	Avg	G	AB	R	H	2B	3B	HR	RBI	BB	SO	SB	CS	OBP	SLG
DeHaan,Kory	OF	24	.247	129	450	57	111	14	4	8	46	33	105	17	13	.298	.349
DeRosso,Tony	3B	25	.219	93	306	25	67	19	0	7	38	20	59	0	0	.267	.350
Jimenez,D'Angelo	2B	23	.237	56	207	27	49	9	0	4	16	20	32	3	6	.304	.338
Koonce,Gray	1B	26	.243	115	325	51	79	15	0	11	45	72	96	0	0	.380	.391
Matos,Julius	SS	26	.267	125	438	47	117	15	1	6	31	13	56	4	10	.288	.347
Nieves,Wil	C	23	.280	95	321	25	90	21	0	2	37	13	43	0	0	.308	.364
Owens,Jeremy	OF	24	.199	107	387	42	77	17	4	6	23	42	162	24	9	.277	.310
Pelaez,Alex	3B	25	.264	114	406	40	107	19	0	9	48	24	56	1	0	.305	.377
Powers,John	2B-3B	27	.255	96	306	37	78	13	4	3	32	28	63	5	5	.317	.353
Riggs,Adam	2B	28	.242	110	384	37	93	15	1	18	58	10	83	6	3	.261	.427
Roskos,John	1B	26	.221	80	217	21	48	11	0	3	29	18	54	0	0	.281	.313
Thrower,Jake	2B	25	.245	118	429	44	105	20	0	3	28	35	81	2	3	.302	.312
Wilkins,Rick	C	34	.190	68	216	16	41	13	1	5	29	13	82	0	1	.236	.329
Witt,Kevin	1B	25	.265	129	441	59	117	24	3	23	78	19	136	0	1	.296	.490
Young,Ernie	OF	31	.254	116	398	59	101	18	1	17	60	33	123	0	3	.311	.432
SF GIANTS		Age	Avg	G	AB	R	H	2B	3B	HR	RBI	BB	SO	SB	CS	OBP	SLG
Byas,Mike	OF	25	.243	100	329	53	80	12	1	0	22	42	65	15	6	.329	.286
Castro,Nelson	SS	25	.271	128	490	71	133	25	4	9	54	32	134	28	11	.316	.394
Clark,Doug	OF	25	.256	123	403	48	103	15	3	4	46	34	88	15	5	.314	.337
Cordido,Julio	3B	20	.204	121	426	40	87	13	1	0	42	23	72	8	3	.245	.239
Leach,Jalal	OF	32	.246	130	443	51	109	26	2	10	52	23	97	9	6	.283	.381
Lowery,Terrell	OF	30	.240	71	246	23	59	13	2	0	14	23	73	4	2	.305	.309
Luster,Jeremy	1B	24	.257	130	495	49	127	31	1	3	69	25	99	4	3	.292	.341
Luther,Ryan	2B	24	.264	127	443	49	117	24	1	3	38	24	82	4	8	.302	.343
McGowan,Sean	OF	24	.261	135	495	54	129	31	1	12	63	20	118	0	1	.289	.400
Melo,Juan	2B	25	.273	100	355	34	97	19	2	5	41	14	66	6	9	.301	.380
Minor,Damon	1B	27	.266	112	383	55	102	19	2	16	53	32	86	0	1	.323	.452
Powell,Dante	OF	27	.246	114	406	55	100	19	2	16	46	25	126	17	6	.290	.421
Ransom,Cody	SS	25	.211	134	451	57	95	18	4	16	58	32	142	11	2	.263	.375
Rodriguez,G.	C	23	.189	65	212	19	40	6	0	4	22	6	42	2	0	.211	.274
Torcato,Tony	OF-DH	21	.275	71	284	26	78	14	0	1	26	7	35	0	2	.292	.335
Torrealba,Yorvit	C	22	.241	115	377	42	91	19	2	5	27	14	67	1	3	.269	.342
Tyler,Josh	OF	27	.252	94	262	17	66	15	0	2	21	14	49	5	5	.290	.332
Zuniga,Tony	3B	26	.238	123	395	57	94	13	0	19	55	40	86	4	1	.308	.415
SEATTLE MARINERS		Age	Avg	G	AB	R	H	2B	3B	HR	RBI	BB	SO	SB	CS	OBP	SLG
Akers,Chad	OF	29	.270	86	304	38	82	14	2	2	27	11	38	4	4	.295	.349
Alexander,Chad	OF	27	.264	137	508	65	134	40	0	11	66	46	97	0	0	.325	.407
Alexander,Manny	2B	30	.256	97	332	39	85	23	1	6	44	12	58	3	8	.282	.386
Barthol,Blake	C	28	.250	79	268	31	67	13	0	7	31	20	71	3	0	.302	.377
Beamon,Trey	OF	27	.230	64	230	29	53	12	1	0	16	13	34	5	2	.272	.291
Betts,Todd	1B	28	.280	135	486	75	136	35	3	12	56	44	58	2	3	.340	.438
Bloomquist,Willie	SS-2B	23	.233	123	477	51	111	20	1	0	24	21	59	25	9	.265	.279
Borders,Pat	C-DH	38	.218	90	316	22	69	14	0	1	24	13	65	2	1	.249	.272
Clark,Jermaine	2B	24	.225	74	209	30	47	6	2	0	22	23	41	9	1	.302	.273
Connors,Greg	1B	26	.217	121	442	59	96	12	4	9	60	24	101	3	4	.258	.324
Grabowski,Jason	3B	25	.269	114	379	51	102	28	2	7	50	53	99	5	3	.359	.409
Horner,Jim	C	27	.256	65	227	38	58	14	0	4	25	8	43	0	0	.281	.370
Kelly,Kenny	OF	22	.238	121	463	63	110	18	3	9	40	34	120	13	11	.290	.348
King,Brad	C	26	.286	80	252	29	72	14	0	8	49	24	35	2	3	.348	.437
Kingsale,Gene	OF	24	.222	115	446	53	99	21	3	2	33	30	72	21	5	.271	.296

445

Major League Equivalencies for 2001 AAA/AA Batters

SEATTLE MARINERS		Age	Avg	G	AB	R	H	2B	3B	HR	RBI	BB	SO	SB	CS	OBP	SLG
Kuzmic,Craig	2B-3B	24	.257	131	463	69	119	27	3	12	80	51	144	5	3	.331	.406
Maynard,Scott	C	23	.165	70	224	14	37	9	0	0	16	15	63	2	0	.218	.205
Myers,Adrian	OF	26	.221	104	376	37	83	11	6	0	41	27	94	7	6	.273	.282
Neill,Mike	OF	31	.227	67	203	22	46	9	1	3	18	25	74	1	1	.311	.325
Podsednik,Scott	OF	25	.263	66	259	39	68	13	2	2	25	11	48	9	4	.293	.351
Robinson,Bo	3B	25	.269	133	458	66	123	20	0	10	65	61	60	2	0	.355	.378
Silvestre,Juan	OF	23	.207	101	362	25	75	11	0	6	34	15	122	0	1	.239	.287
Thomas,Juan	DH	29	.273	129	484	64	132	34	1	18	82	34	149	1	1	.320	.459
Vazquez,Ramon	SS	24	.272	127	448	73	122	24	0	8	68	66	89	6	6	.366	.379
Weber,Jake	OF	25	.267	126	435	58	116	25	2	3	51	30	57	8	5	.314	.354
TAMPA BAY DEVIL RAYS		Age	Avg	G	AB	R	H	2B	3B	HR	RBI	BB	SO	SB	CS	OBP	SLG
Abernathy,Brent	2B	23	.279	61	244	37	68	18	0	3	19	13	24	8	3	.315	.389
Badeaux,Brooks	2B-OF	24	.244	127	467	47	114	11	5	1	26	27	54	10	6	.285	.296
Becker,Brian	DH-1B	26	.222	115	409	37	91	22	0	6	41	35	103	0	0	.284	.320
Beinbrink,Andrew	3B	24	.270	126	441	50	119	22	5	4	48	45	74	3	1	.337	.370
Cantu,Jorge	SS	19	.253	130	510	56	129	26	2	3	44	14	100	3	8	.273	.329
Carr,Dustin	3B	26	.222	73	221	20	49	5	0	3	21	20	49	3	1	.286	.285
Caruso,Mike	2B-SS	24	.269	110	375	51	101	9	7	0	29	18	23	8	8	.303	.331
Conti,Jason	OF	26	.292	130	496	70	145	31	4	10	53	31	88	3	5	.334	.431
Crawford,Carl	OF	19	.268	132	533	62	143	24	2	4	50	29	97	28	11	.306	.343
de los Santos,E.	2B	23	.254	114	413	32	105	13	0	1	37	18	64	11	10	.285	.293
Grummitt,Dan	1B	25	.235	71	243	36	57	11	0	10	40	19	80	1	1	.290	.403
Hall,Toby	C	25	.313	94	361	49	113	26	0	15	59	23	23	0	2	.354	.510
Hatcher,Chris	DH-OF	32	.246	69	244	25	60	11	0	9	31	15	66	2	1	.290	.402
Hoover,Paul	C	25	.199	89	287	30	57	16	3	2	17	9	69	3	2	.223	.296
Hutchins,Norm	OF	25	.212	108	359	39	76	10	0	7	31	11	100	13	2	.235	.298
Martinez,Greg	OF	29	.272	62	235	29	64	5	1	0	17	23	49	10	6	.337	.302
Neuberger,Scott	OF	23	.261	120	417	48	109	25	0	3	42	29	89	3	2	.309	.343
Pigott,Anthony	OF	25	.237	82	249	28	59	10	0	1	27	5	42	6	2	.252	.289
Quatraro,Matt	C	27	.320	81	269	37	86	24	1	5	34	14	64	3	0	.353	.472
Sandberg,Jared	3B	23	.223	101	341	35	76	17	0	13	44	35	95	0	0	.295	.387
Sheets,Andy	SS	29	.260	66	219	23	57	13	1	3	18	20	47	5	2	.322	.370
Smith,Bobby	OF	27	.279	107	384	55	107	23	1	18	58	37	96	7	1	.342	.484
Smith,Jason	SS	23	.202	78	262	25	53	6	4	3	14	9	85	4	3	.229	.290
Valera,Yohanny	C	24	.253	75	249	25	63	20	2	5	31	10	72	0	1	.282	.410
Wright,Ron	1B	25	.243	121	428	52	104	25	0	16	62	42	109	1	1	.311	.414
TEXAS RANGERS		Age	Avg	G	AB	R	H	2B	3B	HR	RBI	BB	SO	SB	CS	OBP	SLG
Ashby,Chris	OF	26	.222	95	315	30	70	13	0	3	25	27	64	1	3	.284	.292
Berrios,Harry	OF-DH	29	.248	98	375	47	93	16	3	12	50	20	82	4	0	.286	.403
Blalock,Hank	3B	20	.312	68	266	44	83	16	3	10	53	29	39	2	2	.380	.508
Cadiente,Brett	OF	24	.264	69	261	28	69	15	4	2	21	11	71	6	4	.294	.375
Camilli,Jason	2B	25	.237	68	207	23	49	7	0	2	23	25	45	2	2	.319	.300
Demetral,Chris	2B	31	.226	92	318	30	72	10	0	1	25	31	32	0	0	.295	.267
Dransfeldt,Kelly	SS	26	.244	143	546	71	133	28	4	8	58	46	119	9	8	.302	.353
Garcia,Osmani	3B	26	.239	118	427	39	102	23	3	5	49	9	47	0	2	.255	.342
Hafner,Travis	1B	24	.268	88	317	52	85	23	0	18	65	44	86	2	0	.357	.511
Jensen,Marcus	C	28	.263	80	285	48	75	16	2	9	32	47	74	0	0	.367	.428
Jones,Jeremy	C	23	.219	93	306	30	67	12	0	3	25	22	64	0	2	.271	.288
Lamb,Mike	3B	25	.289	69	270	32	78	18	2	7	37	12	31	0	1	.319	.448
Magruder,Chris	OF	24	.270	127	474	73	128	24	6	11	51	43	93	5	5	.331	.416

Major League Equivalencies for 2001 AAA/AA Batters

TEXAS RANGERS		Age	Avg	G	AB	R	H	2B	3B	HR	RBI	BB	SO	SB	CS	OBP	SLG
Meliah,Dave	2B	24	.270	110	363	43	98	19	3	11	47	26	62	3	4	.319	.430
Mench,Kevin	OF	23	.251	120	466	68	117	31	1	22	73	25	79	2	5	.289	.464
Monroe,Craig	OF	24	.272	114	405	56	110	24	4	18	70	43	87	7	7	.342	.484
Pena,Carlos	1B	23	.279	119	426	66	119	36	2	22	69	74	130	8	2	.386	.528
Piniella,Juan	OF	23	.246	110	366	45	90	22	1	2	30	28	102	9	2	.299	.328
Porter,Bo	OF	28	.235	58	221	37	52	8	1	12	37	24	61	7	3	.310	.443
Romano,Jason	2B	22	.264	87	330	45	87	13	0	3	28	30	60	7	5	.325	.330
Sagmoen,Marc	OF	30	.208	80	318	26	66	12	0	3	21	11	77	2	1	.234	.274
Solano,Danny	SS	22	.233	120	416	51	97	15	4	5	39	34	80	2	3	.291	.325
Steed,Dave	C	28	.223	67	224	26	50	9	0	6	27	23	62	0	0	.296	.344
Taveras,Luis	C	23	.187	67	209	29	39	3	1	4	21	15	48	3	0	.241	.268
Wright,Corey	OF	21	.239	117	410	54	98	17	2	0	22	43	108	16	6	.311	.290
TORONTO BLUE JAYS		Age	Avg	G	AB	R	H	2B	3B	HR	RBI	BB	SO	SB	CS	OBP	SLG
Fleming,Ryan	OF	25	.261	106	341	51	89	18	3	8	31	28	51	4	6	.317	.402
Freel,Ryan	OF	25	.251	85	315	55	79	21	2	4	30	38	43	17	6	.331	.368
Haltiwanger,G.	OF	26	.238	69	202	27	48	9	0	3	24	23	55	7	6	.316	.327
Holbert,Aaron	2B	28	.234	55	209	23	49	10	1	1	17	7	34	7	0	.259	.306
Hudson,Orlando	2B	23	.292	139	490	73	143	36	8	6	71	49	79	15	6	.356	.435
Izturis,Cesar	SS	21	.280	87	336	29	94	16	2	1	32	9	22	19	7	.299	.348
Johnson,Reed	OF	24	.299	136	542	93	162	28	3	11	66	34	83	32	12	.340	.423
Langaigne,S.	OF-1B	25	.233	81	258	33	60	10	0	2	27	17	66	3	4	.280	.295
Latham,Chris	OF	28	.268	79	284	52	76	20	7	11	50	47	92	11	11	.372	.504
Lawrence,Joe	C	24	.210	93	314	25	66	11	3	0	24	33	64	4	9	.285	.264
Liniak,Cole	3B	24	.232	103	340	37	79	21	0	9	45	29	57	0	2	.293	.374
Logan,Matt	1B	21	.191	96	272	28	52	11	0	7	30	21	86	2	1	.249	.309
Lopez,Felipe	SS	21	.256	108	422	70	108	21	5	15	43	33	121	13	9	.310	.436
Lopez,Luis	1B	27	.312	87	333	52	104	26	1	9	67	36	32	0	1	.379	.477
Molina,Izzy	C	30	.294	73	252	31	74	20	0	14	35	16	54	0	0	.336	.540
Perez,Jerson	SS	25	.261	121	429	53	112	23	3	3	43	22	108	10	3	.297	.350
Peters,Tony	OF	26	.231	91	251	41	58	8	0	9	29	19	88	6	1	.285	.371
Phelps,Josh	C-DH	23	.277	136	476	85	132	35	0	27	86	60	134	2	3	.358	.521
Wells,Vernon	OF	22	.270	107	407	52	110	27	3	10	48	26	70	12	11	.314	.425
Werth,Jayson	C	22	.271	104	362	45	98	22	0	15	61	47	98	8	3	.355	.456
Williams,Glenn	3B	23	.241	130	478	56	115	28	0	9	58	34	126	0	5	.291	.356
Wise,DeWayne	OF	23	.222	90	356	39	79	12	4	6	39	15	69	10	6	.253	.329

Appendix

Minor League Team	Organization	League	Level
Akron Aeros	Indians	EL	AA
Altoona Curve	Pirates	EL	AA
Angels (Mesa)	Angels	AZL	R
Arkansas Travelers	Angels	TL	AA
Asheville Tourists	Rockies	SAL	A
Athletics (Phoenix)	Athletics	AZL	R
Auburn Doubledays	Blue Jays	NYP	A-
Augusta GreenJackets	Red Sox	SAL	A
Bakersfield Blaze	Devil Rays	CAL	A+
Batavia Muckdogs	Phillies	NYP	A-
Beloit Snappers	Brewers	MWL	A
Billings Mustangs	Reds	PIO	R+
Binghamton Mets	Mets	EL	AA
Birmingham Barons	White Sox	SL	AA
Bluefield Orioles	Orioles	APP	R+
Boise Hawks	Cubs	NWL	A-
Bowie Baysox	Orioles	EL	AA
Braves (Orlando)	Braves	GCL	R
Brevard County Manatees	Marlins	FSL	A+
Brewers (Phoenix)	Brewers	AZL	R
Bristol Sox	White Sox	APP	R+
Brooklyn Cyclones	Mets	NYP	A-
Buffalo Bisons	Indians	IL	AAA
Burlington Bees	Royals	MWL	A
Burlington Indians	Indians	APP	R+
Calgary Cannons	Marlins	PCL	AAA
Capital City Bombers	Mets	SAL	A
Carolina Mudcats	Rockies	SL	AA
Cedar Rapids Kernels	Angels	MWL	A
Charleston (S.C.) RiverDogs	Devil Rays	SAL	A
Charleston (W.Va.) Alley Cats	Blue Jays	SAL	A
Charlotte Knights	White Sox	IL	AAA
Charlotte Rangers	Rangers	FSL	A+
Chattanooga Lookouts	Reds	SL	AA
Clearwater Phillies	Phillies	FSL	A+
Clinton LumberKings	Expos	MWL	A
Colorado Springs Sky Sox	Rockies	PCL	AAA
Columbus Clippers	Yankees	IL	AAA
Columbus RedStixx	Indians	SAL	A
Cubs (Mesa)	Cubs	AZL	R
Danville Braves	Braves	APP	R+
Dayton Dragons	Reds	MWL	A
Daytona Cubs	Cubs	FSL	A+
Delmarva Shorebirds	Orioles	SAL	A
Diamondbacks (Tucson)	Diamondbacks	AZL	R
Dodgers (Vero Beach)	Dodgers	GCL	R
Dunedin Blue Jays	Blue Jays	FSL	A+
Durham Bulls	Devil Rays	IL	AAA
Edmonton Trappers	Twins	PCL	AAA
El Paso Diablos	Diamondbacks	TL	AA
Elizabethton Twins	Twins	APP	R+
Erie SeaWolves	Tigers	EL	AA
Eugene Emeralds	Padres	NWL	A-
Everett AquaSox	Mariners	NWL	A-

Minor League Team	Organization	League	Level
Expos (Jupiter)	Expos	GCL	R
Frederick Keys	Orioles	CAR	A+
Fresno Grizzlies	Giants	PCL	AAA
Fort Myers Miracle	Twins	FSL	A+
Fort Wayne Wizards	Padres	MWL	A
Giants (Scottsdale)	Giants	AZL	R
Great Falls Dodgers	Dodgers	PIO	R+
Greensboro Bats	Yankees	SAL	A
Greenville Braves	Braves	SL	AA
Hagerstown Suns	Giants	SAL	A
Harrisburg Senators	Expos	EL	AA
Hickory Crawdads	Pirates	SAL	A
High Desert Mavericks	Brewers	CAL	A+
Hudson Valley Renegades	Devil Rays	NYP	A-
Huntsville Stars	Brewers	SL	AA
Idaho Falls Padres	Padres	PIO	R+
Indianapolis Indians	Brewers	IL	AAA
Iowa Cubs	Cubs	PCL	AAA
Jacksonville Suns	Dodgers	SL	AA
Jamestown Jammers	Braves	NYP	A-
Johnson City Cardinals	Cardinals	APP	R+
Jupiter Hammerheads	Expos	FSL	A+
Kane County Cougars	Marlins	MWL	A
Kannapolis Intimdators	White Sox	SAL	A
Kingsport Mets	Mets	APP	R+
Kinston Indians	Indians	CAR	A+
Lake Elsinore Storm	Padres	CAL	A+
Lakeland Tigers	Tigers	FSL	A+
Lakewood BlueClaws	Phillies	SAL	A
Lancaster JetHawks	Diamondbacks	CAL	A+
Lansing Lugnuts	Cubs	MWL	A
Las Vegas 51s	Dodgers	PCL	AAA
Lexington Legends	Astros	SAL	A
Louisville RiverBats	Reds	IL	AAA
Lowell Spinners	Red Sox	NYP	A-
Lynchburg Hillcats	Pirates	CAR	A+
Macon Braves	Braves	SAL	A
Mahoning Valley Scrappers	Indians	NYP	A-
Mariners (Peoria)	Mariners	AZL	R
Marlins (Melbourne)	Marlins	GCL	R
Martinsville Astros	Astros	APP	R+
Medicine Hat Blue Jays	Blue Jays	PIO	R+
Memphis Redbirds	Cardinals	PCL	AAA
Michigan Battle Cats	Astros	MWL	A
Midland RockHounds	Athletics	TL	AA
Missoula Osprey	Diamondbacks	PIO	R+
Mobile BayBears	Padres	SL	AA
Modesto A's	Athletics	CAL	A+
Mudville Nine	Reds	CAL	A+
Myrtle Beach Pelicans	Braves	CAR	A+
Nashville Sounds	Pirates	PCL	AAA
New Britain Rock Cats	Twins	EL	AA
New Haven Ravens	Cardinals	EL	AA
New Jersey Cardinals	Cardinals	NYP	A-

449

Minor League Team	Organization	League	Level	Minor League Team	Organization	League	Level
New Orleans Zephyrs	Astros	PCL	AAA	San Antonio Missions	Mariners	TL	AA
Norfolk Tides	Mets	IL	AAA	San Bernardino Stampede	Mariners	CAL	A+
Norwich Navigators	Yankees	EL	AA	San Jose Giants	Giants	CAL	A+
Ogden Raptors	Brewers	PIO	R+	Sarasota Red Sox	Red Sox	FSL	A+
Oklahoma RedHawks	Rangers	PCL	AAA	Savannah Sand Gnats	Rangers	SAL	A
Omaha Golden Spikes	Royals	PCL	AAA	Scranton/Wilkes-Barre Red Barons	Phillies	IL	AAA
Oneonta Tigers	Tigers	NYP	A-	Shreveport Swamp Dragons	Giants	TL	AA
Orioles (Sarasota)	Orioles	GCL	R	South Bend Silver Hawks	Diamondbacks	MWL	A
Orlando Rays	Devil Rays	SL	AA	Spokane Indians	Royals	NWL	A-
Ottawa Lynx	Expos	IL	AAA	Staten Island Yankees	Yankees	NYP	A-
Pawtucket Red Sox	Red Sox	IL	AAA	Syracuse SkyChiefs	Blue Jays	IL	AAA
Peoria Chiefs	Cardinals	MWL	A	Tacoma Rainiers	Mariners	PCL	AAA
Phillies (Clearwater)	Phillies	GCL	R	Tampa Yankees	Yankees	FSL	A+
Pirates (Bradenton)	Pirates	GCL	R	Tennessee Smokies	Blue Jays	SL	AA
Pittsfield Astros	Astros	NYP	A-	Tigers (Lakeland)	Tigers	GCL	R
Portland Beavers	Padres	PCL	AAA	Toledo Mud Hens	Tigers	IL	AAA
Portland Sea Dogs	Marlins	EL	AA	Tucson Sidewinders	Diamondbacks	PCL	AAA
Potomac Cannons	Cardinals	CAR	A+	Trenton Thunder	Red Sox	EL	AA
Princeton Devil Rays	Devil Rays	APP	R+	Tri-City Dust Devils	Rockies	NWL	A-
Provo Angels	Angels	PIO	R+	Tulsa Drillers	Rangers	TL	AA
Pulaski Rangers	Rangers	APP	R+	Twins (Fort Myers)	Twins	GCL	R
Quad City River Bandits	Twins	MWL	A	Utica Blue Sox	Marlins	NYP	A-
Rancho Cucamonga Quakes	Angels	CAL	A+	Vancouver Canadians	Athletics	NWL	A-
Rangers (Port Charlotte)	Rangers	GCL	R	Vermont Expos	Expos	NYP	A-
Reading Phillies	Phillies	EL	AA	Vero Beach Dodgers	Dodgers	FSL	A+
Red Sox (Fort Myers)	Red Sox	GCL	R	Visalia Oaks	Athletics	CAL	A+
Reds (Sarasota)	Reds	GCL	R	West Michigan Whitecaps	Tigers	MWL	A
Richmond Braves	Braves	IL	AAA	West Tenn Diamond Jaxx	Cubs	SL	AA
Rochester Red Wings	Orioles	IL	AAA	White Sox (Tucson)	White Sox	AZL	R
Round Rock Express	Astros	TL	AA	Wichita Wranglers	Royals	TL	AA
Royals (Baseball City)	Royals	GCL	R	Williamsport Crosscutters	Pirates	NYP	A-
St. Lucie Mets	Mets	FSL	A+	Wilmington Blue Rocks	Royals	CAR	A+
Sacramento RiverCats	Athletics	PCL	AAA	Winston-Salem Warthogs	White Sox	CAR	A+
Salem Avalanche	Rockies	CAR	A+	Wisconsin Timber Rattlers	Mariners	MWL	A
Salem-Keizer Volcanoes	Giants	NWL	A-	Yakima Bears	Diamondbacks	NWL	A-
Salt Lake Stingers	Angels	PCL	AAA	Yankees (Tampa)	Yankees	GCL	R

About STATS, Inc.

STATS, Inc., a News Corporation company, is affiliated with, and the official statistics provider to FOX Sports. STATS collects and disseminates most, if not all, of the information found within these pages, in addition to the statistics you might find on your favorite web site. STATS, Inc. is the nation's leading sports information and statistical analysis company, providing detailed sports services for a wide array of consumer and commercial clients.

As one of the elite companies in sports, STATS provides the most detailed, up-to-the-minute sports information to professional teams, print and broadcast media, software developers and interactive service providers around the country. STATS' network of trained sports reporters records the details of more than 3,800 sporting events across the four major sports annually. Some of our major clients include FOX Sports, the Associated Press, Lycos, *The Sporting News*, ESPN.com, Yahoo!, Electronic Arts, MSNBC, SONY and Topps.

STATS Publishing, a division of STATS, Inc., produces 10 pro sports annuals, including the *Major League Handbook*, *The Scouting Notebook*, the *Pro Football Handbook*, the *Pro Basketball Handbook* and the *Hockey Handbook*. In 1998, we introduced two baseball encyclopedias, the *All-Time Major League Handbook* (second edition updated through 1999) and the *All-Time Baseball Sourcebook*. Together they combine for more than 5,000 pages of baseball history. We added the *Pro Football Sourcebook* as an annual in 2000. Also, original articles by STATS authors appear three times per week in the Insider section of ESPN.com. All of our publications and additional editorial content deliver STATS' expertise to fans, scouts, general managers and media across the country.

In addition, STATS Fantasy Sports is at the forefront of the fantasy sports industry. We develop fantasy baseball, football, basketball, hockey, golf and auto racing games for a host of sites. We also feature the first historical baseball simulation game created specifically for the Internet—Diamond Legends. No matter what time of year, STATS Fantasy Sports has a fantasy game to keep even the most passionate sports fan satisfied.

Information technology has grown by leaps and bounds in the last decade. STATS will continue to be at the forefront as a supplier of the most up-to-date, in-depth sports information available.

For more information on our products, or on joining our reporter network, contact us via:

Internet — www.stats.com
        http://biz.stats.com

Toll Free in the USA at 1-800-63-STATS (1-800-637-8287)

Outside the USA at 1-847-470-8798

Or write to:

STATS, Inc.
8130 Lehigh Ave.
Morton Grove, IL 60053

About Howe Sportsdata

Howe Sportsdata has been compiling statistics on professional baseball since 1910. Currently, Howe is the official statistician for all 16 U.S.-based National Association professional baseball leagues. Howe also compiles statistics for the Arizona Fall League, the Hawaiian Winter League and winter leagues located in Mexico, Puerto Rico, the Dominican Republic, Venezuela and Australia. In addition, Howe keeps the official statistics of the Continental Basketball Association, all professional minor hockey leagues and the National Professional Soccer League.

Originally based in Chicago, Howe Sportsdata is now located in Boston, MA and is under the ownership of SportsTicker Enterprises, L.P., the instant sports news and information service of ESPN, Inc. All told, Howe is responsible for maintaining statistics for more than 300 teams who collectively play more than 14,000 games per year.

Howe also provides statistical information to all 30 major league teams and to major media outlets such as *USA Today*, *The Sporting News*, *Baseball America*, the Associated Press and *Sports Illustrated*. Howe also counts as its customers many leading newspapers, of which the following are a small representative sample: the *Los Angeles Times*, the *Detroit Free Press*, the *Miami Herald* and both the *Chicago Sun-Times* and *Chicago Tribune*. For more information about Howe, write to:

Howe Sportsdata
Boston Fish Pier, West Building #1, Suite 302
Boston, Massachusetts 02110

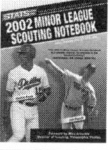

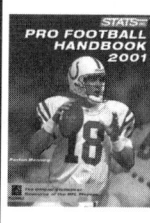